ALTITUDE CORRECTION TABLES 0°-10°—SUN, STARS, PLANETS

App. Alt.	OCT.—MAR. SUN APR.—SEPT.				STARS PLANETS
	Lower Limb	Upper Limb	Lower Limb	Upper Limb	
° ′	′	′	′	′	′
0 00	− 18·2	− 50·5	− 18·4	− 50·2	− 34·5
03	17·5	49·8	17·8	49·6	33·8
06	16·9	49·2	17·1	48·9	33·2
09	16·3	48·6	16·5	48·3	32·6
12	15·7	48·0	15·9	47·7	32·0
15	15·1	47·4	15·3	47·1	31·4
0 18	− 14·5	− 46·8	− 14·8	− 46·6	− 30·8
21	14·0	46·3	14·2	46·0	30·3
24	13·5	45·8	13·7	45·5	29·8
27	12·9	45·2	13·2	45·0	29·2
30	12·4	44·7	12·7	44·5	28·7
33	11·9	44·2	12·2	44·0	28·2
0 36	− 11·5	− 43·8	− 11·7	− 43·5	− 27·8
39	11·0	43·3	11·2	43·0	27·3
42	10·5	42·8	10·8	42·6	26·8
45	10·1	42·4	10·3	42·1	26·4
48	9·6	41·9	9·9	41·7	25·9
51	9·2	41·5	9·5	41·3	25·5
0 54	− 8·8	− 41·1	− 9·1	− 40·9	− 25·1
0 57	8·4	40·7	8·7	40·5	24·7
1 00	8·0	40·3	8·3	40·1	24·3
03	7·7	40·0	7·9	39·7	24·0
06	7·3	39·6	7·5	39·3	23·6
09	6·9	39·2	7·2	39·0	23·2
1 12	− 6·6	− 38·9	− 6·8	− 38·6	− 22·9
15	6·2	38·5	6·5	38·3	22·5
18	5·9	38·2	6·2	38·0	22·2
21	5·6	37·9	5·8	37·6	21·9
24	5·3	37·6	5·5	37·3	21·6
27	4·9	37·2	5·2	37·0	21·2
1 30	− 4·6	− 36·9	− 4·9	− 36·7	− 20·9
35	4·2	36·5	4·4	36·2	20·5
40	3·7	36·0	4·0	35·8	20·0
45	3·2	35·5	3·5	35·3	19·5
50	2·8	35·1	3·1	34·9	19·1
1 55	2·4	34·7	2·6	34·4	18·7
2 00	− 2·0	− 34·3	− 2·2	− 34·0	− 18·3
05	1·6	33·9	1·8	33·6	17·9
10	1·2	33·5	1·5	33·3	17·5
15	0·9	33·2	1·1	32·9	17·2
20	0·5	32·8	0·8	32·6	16·8
25	− 0·2	32·5	0·4	32·2	16·5
2 30	+ 0·2	− 32·1	− 0·1	− 31·9	− 16·1
35	0·5	31·8	+ 0·2	31·6	15·8
40	0·8	31·5	0·5	31·3	15·5
45	1·1	31·2	0·8	31·0	15·2
50	1·4	30·9	1·1	30·7	14·9
2 55	1·6	30·7	1·4	30·4	14·7
3 00	+ 1·9	− 30·4	+ 1·7	− 30·1	− 14·4
05	2·2	30·1	1·9	29·9	14·1
10	2·4	29·9	2·1	29·7	13·9
15	2·6	29·7	2·4	29·4	13·7
20	2·9	29·4	2·6	29·2	13·4
25	3·1	29·2	2·9	28·9	13·2
3 30	+ 3·3	− 29·0	+ 3·1	− 28·7	− 13·0

App. Alt.	OCT.—MAR. SUN APR.—SEPT.				STARS PLANETS
	Lower Limb	Upper Limb	Lower Limb	Upper Limb	
° ′	′	′	′	′	′
3 30	+ 3·3	− 29·0	+ 3·1	− 28·7	− 13·0
35	3·6	28·7	3·3	28·5	12·7
40	3·8	28·5	3·5	28·3	12·5
45	4·0	28·3	3·7	28·1	12·3
50	4·2	28·1	3·9	27·9	12·1
3 55	4·4	27·9	4·1	27·7	11·9
4 00	+ 4·5	− 27·8	+ 4·3	− 27·5	− 11·8
05	4·7	27·6	4·5	27·3	11·6
10	4·9	27·4	4·6	27·2	11·4
15	5·1	27·2	4·8	27·0	11·2
20	5·2	27·1	5·0	26·8	11·1
25	5·4	26·9	5·1	26·7	10·9
4 30	+ 5·6	− 26·7	+ 5·3	− 26·5	− 10·7
35	5·7	26·6	5·5	26·3	10·6
40	5·9	26·4	5·6	26·2	10·4
45	6·0	26·3	5·8	26·0	10·3
50	6·2	26·1	5·9	25·9	10·1
4 55	6·3	26·0	6·0	25·8	10·0
5 00	+ 6·4	− 25·9	+ 6·2	− 25·6	− 9·9
05	6·6	25·7	6·3	25·5	9·7
10	6·7	25·6	6·4	25·4	9·6
15	6·8	25·5	6·6	25·3	9·5
20	6·9	25·4	6·7	25·1	9·4
25	7·1	25·2	6·8	25·0	9·2
5 30	+ 7·2	− 25·1	+ 6·9	− 24·9	− 9·1
35	7·3	25·0	7·0	24·8	9·0
40	7·4	24·9	7·2	24·6	8·9
45	7·5	24·8	7·3	24·5	8·8
50	7·6	24·7	7·4	24·4	8·7
5 55	7·7	24·6	7·5	24·3	8·6
6 00	+ 7·8	− 24·5	+ 7·6	− 24·2	− 8·5
10	8·0	24·3	7·8	24·0	8·3
20	8·2	24·1	8·0	23·8	8·1
30	8·4	23·9	8·1	23·7	7·9
40	8·6	23·7	8·3	23·5	7·7
50	8·7	23·6	8·5	23·3	7·6
7 00	+ 8·9	− 23·4	+ 8·6	− 23·2	− 7·4
10	9·1	23·2	8·8	23·0	7·2
20	9·2	23·1	9·0	22·8	7·1
30	9·3	23·0	9·1	22·7	7·0
40	9·5	22·8	9·2	22·6	6·8
7 50	9·6	22·7	9·4	22·4	6·7
8 00	+ 9·7	− 22·6	+ 9·5	− 22·3	− 6·6
10	9·9	22·4	9·6	22·2	6·4
20	10·0	22·3	9·7	22·1	6·3
30	10·1	22·2	9·8	22·0	6·2
40	10·2	22·1	10·0	21·8	6·1
8 50	10·3	22·0	10·1	21·7	6·0
9 00	+ 10·4	− 21·9	+ 10·2	− 21·6	− 5·9
10	10·5	21·8	10·3	21·5	5·8
20	10·6	21·7	10·4	21·4	5·7
30	10·7	21·6	10·5	21·3	5·6
40	10·8	21·5	10·6	21·2	5·5
9 50	10·9	21·4	10·6	21·2	5·4
10 00	+ 11·0	− 21·3	+ 10·7	− 21·1	− 5·3

Additional corrections for temperature and pressure are given on the following page.

For bubble sextant observations ignore dip and use the star corrections for Sun, planets and stars.

ADDITIONAL REFRACTION CORRECTIONS FOR NON-STANDARD CONDITIONS

App. Alt.	A	B	C	D	E	F	G	H	J	K	L	M	N	App. Alt.
0° 00′	−6·9	−5·7	−4·6	−3·4	−2·3	−1·1	0·0	+1·1	+2·3	+3·4	+4·6	+5·7	+6·9	0° 00′
0 30	5·2	4·4	3·5	2·6	1·7	0·9	0·0	0·9	1·7	2·6	3·5	4·4	5·2	0 30
1 00	4·3	3·5	2·8	2·1	1·4	0·7	0·0	0·7	1·4	2·1	2·8	3·5	4·3	0 30
1 30	3·5	2·9	2·4	1·8	1·2	0·6	0·0	0·6	1·2	1·8	2·4	2·9	3·5	1 00
2 00	3·0	2·5	2·0	1·5	1·0	0·5	0·0	0·5	1·0	1·5	2·0	2·5	3·0	1 30
2 30	−2·5	−2·1	−1·6	−1·2	−0·8	−0·4	0·0	+0·4	+0·8	+1·2	+1·6	+2·1	+2·5	2 00
3 00	2·2	1·8	1·5	1·1	0·7	0·4	0·0	0·4	0·7	1·1	1·5	1·8	2·2	2 30
3 30	2·0	1·6	1·3	1·0	0·7	0·3	0·0	0·3	0·7	1·0	1·3	1·6	2·0	3 00
4 00	1·8	1·5	1·2	0·9	0·6	0·3	0·0	0·3	0·6	0·9	1·2	1·5	1·8	3 30
4 30	1·6	1·4	1·1	0·8	0·5	0·3	0·0	0·3	0·5	0·8	1·1	1·4	1·6	4 00
5 00	−1·5	−1·3	−1·0	−0·8	−0·5	−0·2	0·0	+0·2	+0·5	+0·8	+1·0	+1·3	+1·5	4 30
6	1·3	1·1	0·9	0·6	0·4	0·2	0·0	0·2	0·4	0·6	0·9	1·1	1·3	5 00
7	1·1	0·9	0·7	0·6	0·4	0·2	0·0	0·2	0·4	0·6	0·7	0·9	1·1	6
8	1·0	0·8	0·7	0·5	0·3	0·2	0·0	0·2	0·3	0·5	0·7	0·8	1·0	7
9	0·9	0·7	0·6	0·4	0·3	0·1	0·0	0·1	0·3	0·4	0·6	0·7	0·9	8
10 00	−0·8	−0·7	−0·5	−0·4	−0·3	−0·1	0·0	+0·1	+0·3	+0·4	+0·5	+0·7	+0·8	9
12	0·7	0·6	0·5	0·3	0·2	0·1	0·0	0·1	0·2	0·3	0·5	0·6	0·7	10 00
14	0·6	0·5	0·4	0·3	0·2	0·1	0·0	0·1	0·2	0·3	0·4	0·5	0·6	12
16	0·5	0·4	0·3	0·3	0·2	0·1	0·0	0·1	0·2	0·3	0·3	0·4	0·5	14
18	0·4	0·4	0·3	0·2	0·2	0·1	0·0	0·1	0·2	0·2	0·3	0·4	0·4	16
20 00	−0·4	−0·3	−0·3	−0·2	−0·1	−0·1	0·0	+0·1	+0·1	+0·2	+0·3	+0·3	+0·4	18
25	0·3	0·3	0·2	0·2	0·1	−0·1	0·0	+0·1	0·1	0·2	0·2	0·3	0·3	20 00
30	0·3	0·2	0·2	0·1	0·1	0·0	0·0	0·0	0·1	0·1	0·2	0·2	0·3	25
35	0·2	0·2	0·1	0·1	0·1	0·0	0·0	0·0	0·1	0·1	0·1	0·2	0·2	30
40	0·2	0·1	0·1	0·1	−0·1	0·0	0·0	0·0	+0·1	0·1	0·1	0·1	0·2	35
50 00	−0·1	−0·1	−0·1	−0·1	0·0	0·0	0·0	0·0	0·0	+0·1	+0·1	+0·1	+0·1	40
														50 00

The graph is entered with arguments temperature and pressure to find a zone letter; using as arguments this zone letter and apparent altitude (sextant altitude corrected for dip), a correction is taken from the table. This correction is to be applied to the sextant altitude in addition to the corrections for standard conditions (for the Sun, stars and planets from page A2 and for the Moon from pages xxxiv and xxxv).

THE

NAUTICAL ALMANAC

FOR THE YEAR

1999

WASHINGTON:	LONDON:
Issued by the	Issued by
Nautical Almanac Office	Her Majesty's
United States	Nautical Almanac Office
Naval Observatory	by order
under the	of the
authority of the	Secretary of State
Secretary of the Navy	for Defence

U.S. GOVERNMENT PRINTING OFFICE

WASHINGTON : 1998

For sale by the U.S. Government Printing Office
Superintendent of Documents, Mail Stop: SSOP, Washington, DC 20402-9328
ISBN 0-16-049486-9

PREFACE

The British and American editions of *The Nautical Almanac*, which are identical in content, are produced jointly by H. M. Nautical Almanac Office, Royal Greenwich Observatory, under the supervision of A. T. Sinclair and C. Y. Hohenkerk, and by the Nautical Almanac Office, United States Naval Observatory, under the supervision of A. D. Fiala and R. J. Miller to the general requirements of the Royal Navy and of the United States Navy. The almanac is printed separately in the United Kingdom and in the United States of America.

The data in this almanac can be made available, in a form suitable for direct photographic reproduction, to the appropriate almanac-producing agency in any country; language changes in the headings of the ephemeral pages can be introduced, if desired, during reproduction. Under this arrangement, this almanac, with minor modifications and changes in language, has been adopted for the Brazilian, Chilean, Danish, Greek, Indian, Indonesian, Italian, Korean, Mexican and Norwegian almanacs.

J. V. WALL
Director,
Royal Greenwich Observatory,
Madingley Road,
Cambridge, CB3 0EZ, England

DENNIS G. LARSEN
Captain, U.S. Navy,
Superintendent, U.S. Naval Observatory,
Washington, D.C. 20392,
U.S.A.

November 1997

RELIGIOUS CALENDARS

Epiphany	Jan. 6	Low Sunday	Apr. 11
Septuagesima Sunday	Jan. 31	Rogation Sunday	May 9
Quinquagesima Sunday	Feb. 14	Ascension Day—Holy Thursday	May 13
Ash Wednesday	Feb. 17	Whit Sunday—Pentecost	May 23
Quadragesima Sunday	Feb. 21	Trinity Sunday	May 30
Palm Sunday	Mar. 28	Corpus Christi	June 3
Good Friday	Apr. 2	First Sunday in Advent	Nov. 28
Easter Day	Apr. 4	Christmas Day (Saturday)	Dec. 25
First Day of Passover (Pesach)	Apr. 1	Day of Atonement (Yom Kippur)	Sept. 20
Feast of Weeks (Shavuot)	May 21	First day of Tabernacles (Succoth)	Sept. 25
Jewish New Year 5760 (Rosh Hashanah)	Sept. 11		
Islamic New Year (1420)	Apr. 17	Ramadân, First day of (tabular)	Dec. 9

The Jewish and Islamic dates above are tabular dates, which begin at sunset on the previous evening and end at sunset on the date tabulated. In practice, the dates of Islamic fasts and festivals are determined by an actual sighting of the appropriate new moon.

CIVIL CALENDAR—UNITED KINGDOM

Accession of Queen Elizabeth II	Feb. 6	Birthday of Prince Philip, Duke of	
St David (Wales)	Mar. 1	Edinburgh	June 10
Commonwealth Day	Mar. 8	The Queen's Official Birthday†	June 12
St Patrick (Ireland)	Mar. 17	Remembrance Sunday	Nov. 14
Birthday of Queen Elizabeth II	Apr. 21	Birthday of the Prince of Wales	Nov. 14
St George (England)	Apr. 23	St Andrew (Scotland)	Nov. 30
Coronation Day	June 2		

PUBLIC HOLIDAYS

England and Wales—Jan. 1†, Apr. 2, Apr. 5, May 3†, May 31, Aug. 30, Dec. 27–28†, Dec. 31†
Northern Ireland—Jan. 1†, Mar. 17, Apr. 2, Apr. 5, May 3†, May 31, July 12†, Aug. 30, Dec. 27–28†, Dec. 31†
Scotland—Jan. 1, Jan. 4†, Apr. 2, May 3, May 31†, Aug. 2, Dec. 27†–28†, Dec. 31†

CIVIL CALENDAR—UNITED STATES OF AMERICA

New Year's Day	Jan. 1	Labor Day	Sept. 6
Martin Luther King's Birthday	Jan. 18	Columbus Day	Oct. 11
Washington's Birthday	Feb. 15	Election Day (in certain States)	Nov. 2
Memorial Day	May 31	Veterans Day	Nov. 11
Independence Day	July 4	Thanksgiving Day	Nov. 25

†Dates subject to confirmation

PHASES OF THE MOON

New Moon			First Quarter			Full Moon			Last Quarter		
d	h	m	d	h	m	d	h	m	d	h	m
						Jan. 2	02	49	Jan. 9	14	22
Jan. 17	15	46	Jan. 24	19	15	Jan. 31	16	06	Feb. 8	11	58
Feb. 16	06	39	Feb. 23	02	43	Mar. 2	06	58	Mar. 10	08	40
Mar. 17	18	48	Mar. 24	10	18	Mar. 31	22	49	Apr. 9	02	51
Apr. 16	04	22	Apr. 22	19	01	Apr. 30	14	55	May 8	17	28
May 15	12	05	May 22	05	34	May 30	06	40	June 7	04	20
June 13	19	03	June 20	18	13	June 28	21	37	July 6	11	57
July 13	02	24	July 20	09	00	July 28	11	25	Aug. 4	17	27
Aug. 11	11	08	Aug. 19	01	47	Aug. 26	23	48	Sept. 2	22	17
Sept. 9	22	02	Sept. 17	20	06	Sept. 25	10	51	Oct. 2	04	02
Oct. 9	11	34	Oct. 17	15	00	Oct. 24	21	02	Oct. 31	12	04
Nov. 8	03	53	Nov. 16	09	03	Nov. 23	07	04	Nov. 29	23	18
Dec. 7	22	32	Dec. 16	00	50	Dec. 22	17	31	Dec. 29	14	04

DAYS OF THE WEEK AND DAYS OF THE YEAR

Day	JAN.		FEB.		MAR.		APR.		MAY		JUNE		JULY		AUG.		SEPT.		OCT.		NOV.		DEC.	
	Wk	Yr	Wk	Yr	Wk	Yr	Wk	Yr	Wk	Yr	Wk	Yr	Wk	Yr	Wk	Yr	Wk	Yr	Wk	Yr	Wk	Yr	Wk	Yr
1	F.	1	M.	32	M.	60	Th.	91	Sa.	121	Tu.	152	Th.	182	Su.	213	W.	244	F.	274	M.	305	W.	335
2	Sa.	2	Tu.	33	Tu.	61	F.	92	Su.	122	W.	153	F.	183	M.	214	Th.	245	Sa.	275	Tu.	306	Th.	336
3	Su.	3	W.	34	W.	62	Sa.	93	M.	123	Th.	154	Sa.	184	Tu.	215	F.	246	Su.	276	W.	307	F.	337
4	M.	4	Th.	35	Th.	63	Su.	94	Tu.	124	F.	155	Su.	185	W.	216	Sa.	247	M.	277	Th.	308	Sa.	338
5	Tu.	5	F.	36	F.	64	M.	95	W.	125	Sa.	156	M.	186	Th.	217	Su.	248	Tu.	278	F.	309	Su.	339
6	W.	6	Sa.	37	Sa.	65	Tu.	96	Th.	126	Su.	157	Tu.	187	F.	218	M.	249	W.	279	Sa.	310	M.	340
7	Th.	7	Su.	38	Su.	66	W.	97	F.	127	M.	158	W.	188	Sa.	219	Tu.	250	Th.	280	Su.	311	Tu.	341
8	F.	8	M.	39	M.	67	Th.	98	Sa.	128	Tu.	159	Th.	189	Su.	220	W.	251	F.	281	M.	312	W.	342
9	Sa.	9	Tu.	40	Tu.	68	F.	99	Su.	129	W.	160	F.	190	M.	221	Th.	252	Sa.	282	Tu.	313	Th.	343
10	Su.	10	W.	41	W.	69	Sa.	100	M.	130	Th.	161	Sa.	191	Tu.	222	F.	253	Su.	283	W.	314	F.	344
11	M.	11	Th.	42	Th.	70	Su.	101	Tu.	131	F.	162	Su.	192	W.	223	Sa.	254	M.	284	Th.	315	Sa.	345
12	Tu.	12	F.	43	F.	71	M.	102	W.	132	Sa.	163	M.	193	Th.	224	Su.	255	Tu.	285	F.	316	Su.	346
13	W.	13	Sa.	44	Sa.	72	Tu.	103	Th.	133	Su.	164	Tu.	194	F.	225	M.	256	W.	286	Sa.	317	M.	347
14	Th.	14	Su.	45	Su.	73	W.	104	F.	134	M.	165	W.	195	Sa.	226	Tu.	257	Th.	287	Su.	318	Tu.	348
15	F.	15	M.	46	M.	74	Th.	105	Sa.	135	Tu.	166	Th.	196	Su.	227	W.	258	F.	288	M.	319	W.	349
16	Sa.	16	Tu.	47	Tu.	75	F.	106	Su.	136	W.	167	F.	197	M.	228	Th.	259	Sa.	289	Tu.	320	Th.	350
17	Su.	17	W.	48	W.	76	Sa.	107	M.	137	Th.	168	Sa.	198	Tu.	229	F.	260	Su.	290	W.	321	F.	351
18	M.	18	Th.	49	Th.	77	Su.	108	Tu.	138	F.	169	Su.	199	W.	230	Sa.	261	M.	291	Th.	322	Sa.	352
19	Tu.	19	F.	50	F.	78	M.	109	W.	139	Sa.	170	M.	200	Th.	231	Su.	262	Tu.	292	F.	323	Su.	353
20	W.	20	Sa.	51	Sa.	79	Tu.	110	Th.	140	Su.	171	Tu.	201	F.	232	M.	263	W.	293	Sa.	324	M.	354
21	Th.	21	Su.	52	Su.	80	W.	111	F.	141	M.	172	W.	202	Sa.	233	Tu.	264	Th.	294	Su.	325	Tu.	355
22	F.	22	M.	53	M.	81	Th.	112	Sa.	142	Tu.	173	Th.	203	Su.	234	W.	265	F.	295	M.	326	W.	356
23	Sa.	23	Tu.	54	Tu.	82	F.	113	Su.	143	W.	174	F.	204	M.	235	Th.	266	Sa.	296	Tu.	327	Th.	357
24	Su.	24	W.	55	W.	83	Sa.	114	M.	144	Th.	175	Sa.	205	Tu.	236	F.	267	Su.	297	W.	328	F.	358
25	M.	25	Th.	56	Th.	84	Su.	115	Tu.	145	F.	176	Su.	206	W.	237	Sa.	268	M.	298	Th.	329	Sa.	359
26	Tu.	26	F.	57	F.	85	M.	116	W.	146	Sa.	177	M.	207	Th.	238	Su.	269	Tu.	299	F.	330	Su.	360
27	W.	27	Sa.	58	Sa.	86	Tu.	117	Th.	147	Su.	178	Tu.	208	F.	239	M.	270	W.	300	Sa.	331	M.	361
28	Th.	28	Su.	59	Su.	87	W.	118	F.	148	M.	179	W.	209	Sa.	240	Tu.	271	Th.	301	Su.	332	Tu.	362
29	F.	29			M.	88	Th.	119	Sa.	149	Tu.	180	Th.	210	Su.	241	W.	272	F.	302	M.	333	W.	363
30	Sa.	30			Tu.	89	F.	120	Su.	150	W.	181	F.	211	M.	242	Th.	273	Sa.	303	Tu.	334	Th.	364
31	Su.	31			W.	90			M.	151			Sa.	212	Tu.	243			Su.	304			F.	365

ECLIPSES

1. An annular eclipse of the Sun, February 16. See map on page 6. The eclipse begins at 3^h 52^m and ends at 09^h 15^m; the annular phase begins at 04^h 57^m and ends at 08^h 10^m. The maximum duration of the annular phase is 1^m 16^s.

2. A partial eclipse of the Moon, July 28. The eclipse begins at 10^h 22^m and ends at 12^h 46^m. The time of maximum eclipse is 11^h 34^m, when 0·40 of the Moon's diameter is obscured. It is visible from part of Antarctica, southern and western parts of South America, Central America, western parts of North America except northern Alaska, the Pacific Ocean, Australasia and the eastern part of Asia.

3. A total eclipse of the Sun, August 11. See map on page 7. The eclipse begins at 08^h 26^m and ends at 13^h 40^m; the total phase begins at 09^h 30^m and ends at 12^h 36^m. The maximum duration of totality is 2^m 27^s.

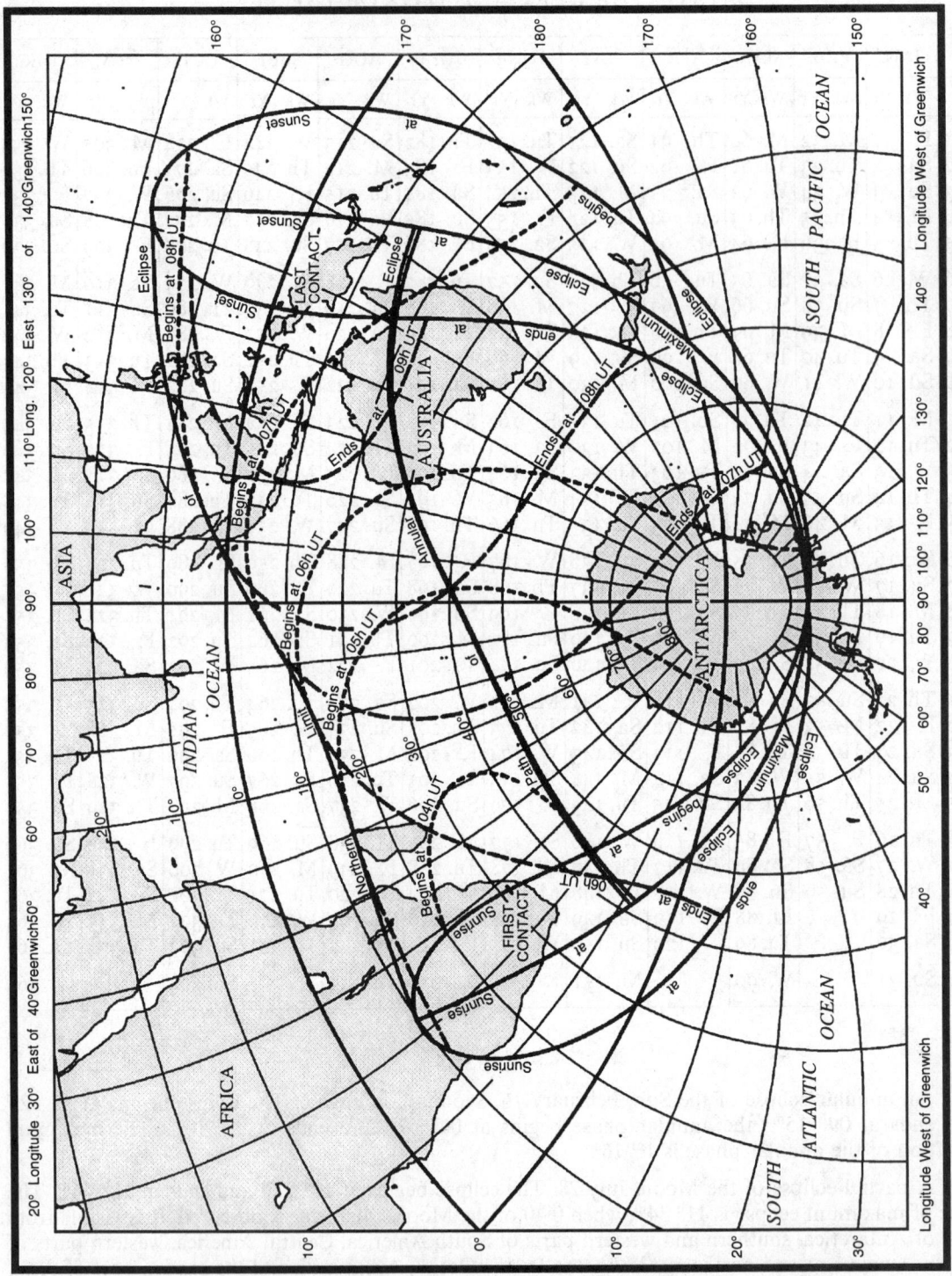

SOLAR ECLIPSE DIAGRAMS

The principal features shown on the above diagrams are: the paths of total and annular eclipses; the northern and southern limits of partial eclipse; the sunrise and sunset curves; dashed lines which show the times of beginning and end of partial eclipse at hourly intervals.

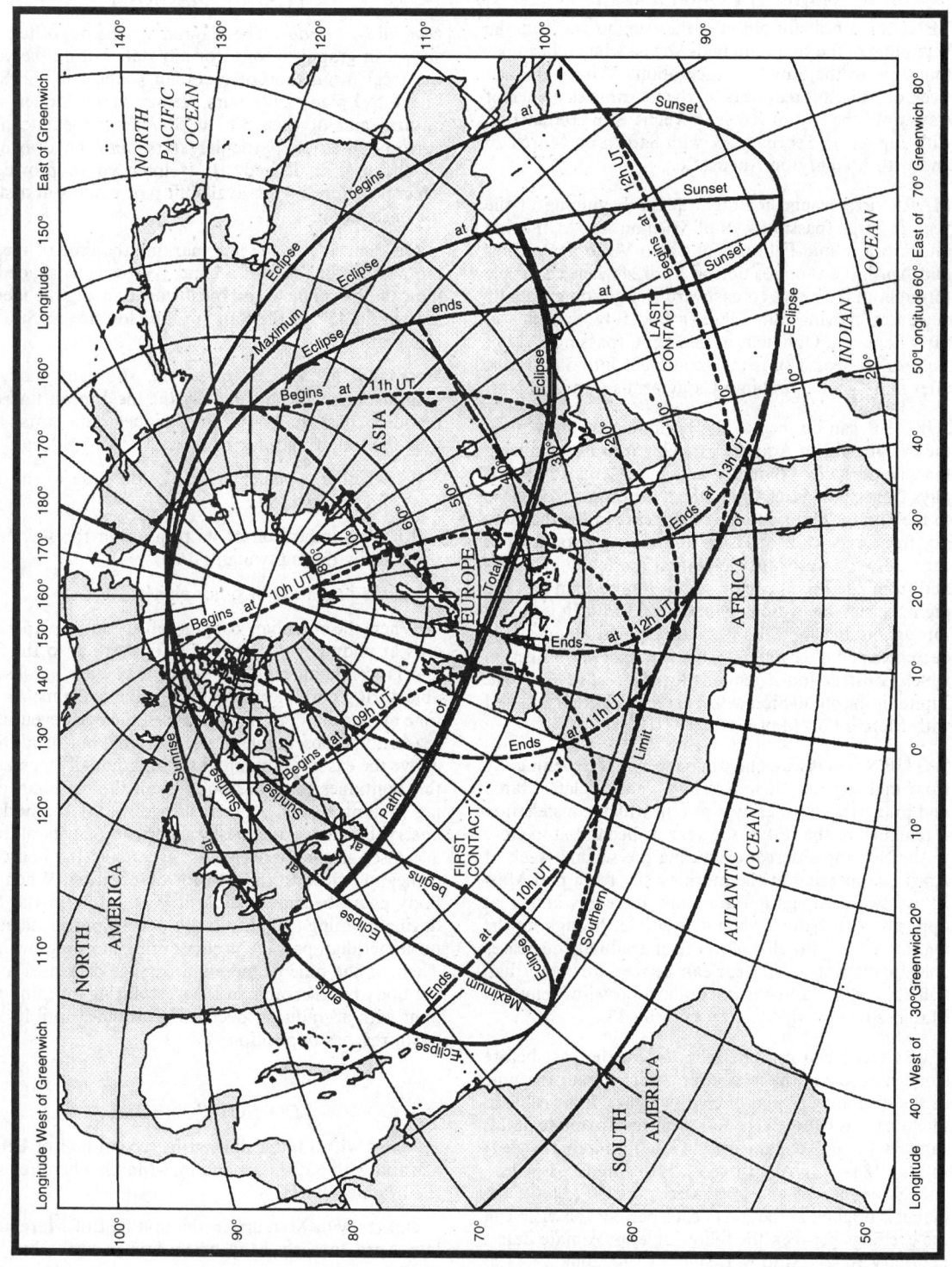

SOLAR ECLIPSE DIAGRAMS

Further details of the paths and times of central eclipse are given in *The Astronomical Almanac.*

VISIBILITY OF PLANETS

VENUS is a brilliant object in the evening sky from the beginning of the year until mid-August when it becomes too close to the Sun for observation. During the last week of August it reappears in the morning sky where it stays until the end of the year. Venus is in conjunction with Jupiter on February 23, with Saturn on March 20 and with Mercury on August 26.

MARS rises around midnight at the beginning of the year, in Virgo (passing 4° N of *Spica* on Jan. 8), moving into Libra in mid-February and into Virgo again after mid-April. It is at opposition on April 24 when it is visible throughout the night. Its eastward elongation gradually decreases, moving into Libra in late July, Scorpius in early Sept. and Ophiucus in mid-Sept. (passing 3° N of *Antares* on Sept. 17). It then continues into Sagittarius after mid-October and into Capricornus from late Nov.

JUPITER can be seen at the beginning of the year in the evening sky in Aquarius, moving into Pisces during the second half of January and into Cetus for a few days from mid-March after which it becomes too close to the Sun for observation. It reappears in the morning sky from mid-April in Pisces and moves into Aries in early July. Its westward elongation gradually increases and from late July it can be seen for more than half the night. It is at opposition on October 23 when it is visible throughout the night. Its eastward elongation gradually decreases and after mid-October it passes into Pisces, in which constellation it remains for the rest of the year. Jupiter is in conjunction with Venus on February 23 and with Mercury on May 1.

SATURN is in Pisces, and can be seen in the evening sky from mid-January. It moves into Cetus in late March and into Aries from early April, in which constellation it remains for the rest of the year. It becomes too close to the Sun for observation during the second week of April, reappearing in the morning sky from mid-May. Its westward elongation gradually increases and is at opposition on Nov. 6 when it is visible throughout the night. Its eastward elongation then gradually decreases and for the rest of the year can be seen for more than half the night. Saturn is in conjunction with Venus on March 20 and with Mercury on May 13.

MERCURY can only be seen low in the east before sunrise, or low in the west after sunset (about the time of the beginning or end of civil twilight). It is visible in the mornings between the following approximate dates: January 1 (−0·4) to January 21 (−0·7), March 27 (+2·7) to May 18 (−1·3), August 4 (+2·5) to August 31 (−1·4), and November 22 (+1·5) to December 30 (−0·6); the planet is brighter at the end of each period. It is visible in the evenings between the following approximate dates: February 16 (−1·3) to March 12 (+1·8), June 2 (−1·5) to July 18 (+2·8) and September 20 (−0·8) to November 10 (+1·8); the planet is brighter at the beginning of each period. The figures in parentheses are the magnitudes.

PLANET DIAGRAM

General Description. The diagram on the opposite page shows, in graphical form for any date during the year, the local mean time of meridian passage of the Sun, of the five planets Mercury, Venus, Mars, Jupiter, and Saturn, and of each 30° of SHA; intermediate lines corresponding to particular stars, may be drawn in by the user if desired. It is intended to provide a general picture of the availability of planets and stars for observation.

On each side of the line marking the time of meridian passage of the Sun a band, 45^m wide, is shaded to indicate that planets and most stars crossing the meridian within 45^m of the Sun are too close to the Sun for observation.

Method of use and interpretation. For any date the diagram provides immediately the local mean times of meridian passage of the Sun, planets and stars, and thus the following information:

(a) whether a planet or star is too close to the Sun for observation;

(b) some indication of its position in the sky, especially during twilight;

(c) the proximity of other planets.

When the meridian passage of an outer planet occurs at midnight the body is in opposition to the Sun and is visible all night; a planet may then be observable during both morning and evening twilights. As the time of meridian passage decreases, the body eventually ceases to be observable in the morning, but its altitude above the eastern horizon at sunset gradually increases; this continues until the body is on the meridian during evening twilight. From then onwards the body is observable above the western horizon and its altitude at sunset gradually decreases; eventually the body becomes too close to the Sun for observation. When the body again becomes visible it is seen low in the east during morning twilight; its altitude at sunrise increases until meridian passage occurs during morning twilight. Then, as the time of meridian passage decreases to 0^h, the body is observable in the west during morning twilight with a gradually decreasing altitude, until it once again reaches opposition.

DO NOT CONFUSE

Venus with Jupiter during the second half of February and with Saturn around mid-March when Venus is the brighter object

Jupiter with Mercury in the first half of March and late April to early May when Jupiter is the brighter object.

Saturn with Mercury in mid-May when Mercury is the brighter object.

LOCAL MEAN TIME OF MERIDIAN PASSAGE

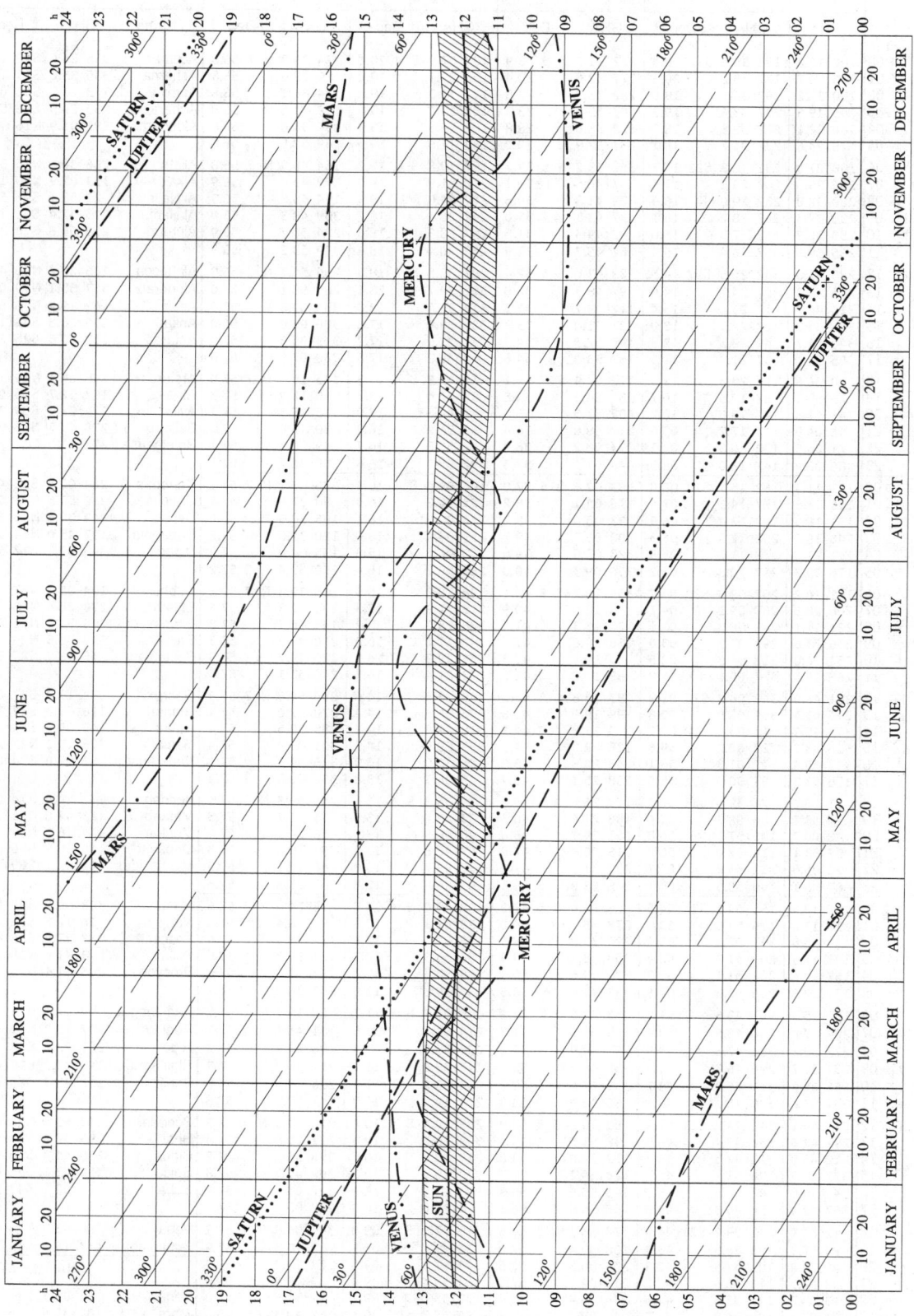

1999 JANUARY 1, 2, 3 (FRI., SAT., SUN.)

UT	ARIES GHA	VENUS −3.9 GHA	Dec	MARS +1.0 GHA	Dec	JUPITER −2.3 GHA	Dec	SATURN +0.4 GHA	Dec	STARS Name	SHA	Dec
1 00	100 12.2	162 36.0	S22 20.8	262 31.3	S 5 26.9	107 07.0	S 4 20.1	74 26.2	N 7 56.8	Acamar	315 26.6	S40 18.9
01	115 14.7	177 35.2	20.3	277 32.6	27.4	122 09.1	19.9	89 28.6	56.8	Achernar	335 35.0	S57 14.9
02	130 17.2	192 34.3	19.8	292 33.9	27.8	137 11.2	19.8	104 31.1	56.8	Acrux	173 21.7	S63 05.2
03	145 19.6	207 33.4 ..	19.3	307 35.2 ..	28.3	152 13.4 ..	19.6	119 33.5 ..	56.8	Adhara	255 20.9	S28 58.4
04	160 22.1	222 32.5	18.7	322 36.6	28.8	167 15.5	19.5	134 36.0	56.8	Aldebaran	291 01.9	N16 30.3
05	175 24.6	237 31.7	18.2	337 37.9	29.2	182 17.6	19.3	149 38.5	56.8			
06	190 27.0	252 30.8	S22 17.7	352 39.2	S 5 29.7	197 19.8	S 4 19.2	164 40.9	N 7 56.8	Alioth	166 30.6	N55 57.7
07	205 29.5	267 29.9	17.1	7 40.5	30.1	212 21.9	19.0	179 43.4	56.9	Alkaid	153 07.9	N49 18.9
F 08	220 32.0	282 29.0	16.6	22 41.8	30.6	227 24.0	18.9	194 45.8	56.9	Al Na'ir	27 58.1	S46 58.2
R 09	235 34.4	297 28.2 ..	16.1	37 43.1 ..	31.0	242 26.1 ..	18.7	209 48.3 ..	56.9	Alnilam	275 57.4	S 1 12.3
I 10	250 36.9	312 27.3	15.6	52 44.4	31.5	257 28.3	18.6	224 50.7	56.9	Alphard	218 06.8	S 8 39.3
D 11	265 39.3	327 26.4	15.0	67 45.7	31.9	272 30.4	18.4	239 53.2	56.9			
A 12	280 41.8	342 25.5	S22 14.5	82 47.0	S 5 32.4	287 32.5	S 4 18.3	254 55.7	N 7 56.9	Alphecca	126 20.7	N26 43.1
Y 13	295 44.3	357 24.7	14.0	97 48.3	32.8	302 34.7	18.1	269 58.1	57.0	Alpheratz	357 55.1	N29 05.2
14	310 46.7	12 23.8	13.4	112 49.7	33.3	317 36.8	18.0	285 00.6	57.0	Altair	62 19.4	N 8 52.0
15	325 49.2	27 22.9 ..	12.9	127 51.0 ..	33.7	332 38.9 ..	17.8	300 03.0 ..	57.0	Ankaa	353 26.8	S42 19.0
16	340 51.7	42 22.1	12.3	142 52.3	34.2	347 41.0	17.7	315 05.5	57.0	Antares	112 40.3	S26 25.6
17	355 54.1	57 21.2	11.8	157 53.6	34.6	2 43.2	17.5	330 07.9	57.0			
18	10 56.6	72 20.3	S22 11.3	172 54.9	S 5 35.1	17 45.3	S 4 17.3	345 10.4	N 7 57.0	Arcturus	146 06.1	N19 11.3
19	25 59.1	87 19.5	10.7	187 56.2	35.5	32 47.4	17.2	0 12.9	57.1	Atria	107 52.7	S69 01.3
20	41 01.5	102 18.6	10.2	202 57.5	36.0	47 49.5	17.0	15 15.3	57.1	Avior	234 21.9	S59 30.3
21	56 04.0	117 17.7 ..	09.6	217 58.8 ..	36.4	62 51.7 ..	16.9	30 17.8 ..	57.1	Bellatrix	278 43.7	N 6 20.8
22	71 06.5	132 16.8	09.1	233 00.2	36.9	77 53.8	16.7	45 20.2	57.1	Betelgeuse	271 13.0	N 7 24.3
23	86 08.9	147 16.0	08.5	248 01.5	37.3	92 55.9	16.6	60 22.7	57.1			
2 00	101 11.4	162 15.1	S22 08.0	263 02.8	S 5 37.8	107 58.0	S 4 16.4	75 25.1	N 7 57.1	Canopus	264 00.5	S52 41.9
01	116 13.8	177 14.3	07.4	278 04.1	38.2	123 00.2	16.3	90 27.6	57.2	Capella	280 50.5	N45 59.8
02	131 16.3	192 13.4	06.9	293 05.4	38.7	138 02.3	16.1	105 30.0	57.2	Deneb	49 39.5	N45 16.8
03	146 18.8	207 12.5 ..	06.3	308 06.7 ..	39.1	153 04.4 ..	16.0	120 32.5 ..	57.2	Denebola	182 45.0	N14 34.6
04	161 21.2	222 11.7	05.8	323 08.0	39.6	168 06.5	15.8	135 34.9	57.2	Diphda	349 07.1	S17 59.7
05	176 23.7	237 10.8	05.2	338 09.3	40.0	183 08.7	15.6	150 37.4	57.2			
06	191 26.2	252 09.9	S22 04.7	353 10.7	S 5 40.5	198 10.8	S 4 15.5	165 39.8	N 7 57.2	Dubhe	194 05.1	N61 45.1
07	206 28.6	267 09.1	04.1	8 12.0	40.9	213 12.9	15.3	180 42.3	57.3	Elnath	278 26.4	N28 36.3
S 08	221 31.1	282 08.2	03.6	23 13.3	41.4	228 15.0	15.2	195 44.7	57.3	Eltanin	90 51.9	N51 29.4
A 09	236 33.6	297 07.3 ..	03.0	38 14.6 ..	41.8	243 17.2 ..	15.0	210 47.2 ..	57.3	Enif	33 58.3	N 9 52.3
T 10	251 36.0	312 06.5	02.5	53 15.9	42.3	258 19.3	14.9	225 49.7	57.3	Fomalhaut	15 36.5	S29 37.9
U 11	266 38.5	327 05.6	01.9	68 17.2	42.7	273 21.4	14.7	240 52.1	57.3			
R 12	281 41.0	342 04.8	S22 01.3	83 18.6	S 5 43.2	288 23.5	S 4 14.6	255 54.6	N 7 57.3	Gacrux	172 13.3	S57 06.1
D 13	296 43.4	357 03.9	00.8	98 19.9	43.6	303 25.6	14.4	270 57.0	57.4	Gienah	176 03.7	S17 32.0
A 14	311 45.9	12 03.0	22 00.2	113 21.2	44.1	318 27.8	14.2	285 59.5	57.4	Hadar	149 04.0	S60 21.7
Y 15	326 48.3	27 02.2	21 59.6	128 22.5 ..	44.5	333 29.9 ..	14.1	301 01.9 ..	57.4	Hamal	328 13.2	N23 27.4
16	341 50.8	42 01.3	59.1	143 23.8	45.0	348 32.0	13.9	316 04.4	57.4	Kaus Aust.	83 59.0	S34 23.0
17	356 53.3	57 00.5	58.5	158 25.1	45.4	3 34.1	13.8	331 06.8	57.4			
18	11 55.7	71 59.6	S21 57.9	173 26.5	S 5 45.9	18 36.3	S 4 13.6	346 09.3	N 7 57.5	Kochab	137 20.4	N74 09.4
19	26 58.2	86 58.7	57.4	188 27.8	46.3	33 38.4	13.5	1 11.7	57.5	Markab	13 49.6	N15 12.0
20	42 00.7	101 57.9	56.8	203 29.1	46.8	48 40.5	13.3	16 14.2	57.5	Menkar	314 26.5	N 4 05.0
21	57 03.1	116 57.0 ..	56.2	218 30.4 ..	47.2	63 42.6 ..	13.2	31 16.6 ..	57.5	Menkent	148 20.9	S36 21.6
22	72 05.6	131 56.2	55.7	233 31.7	47.7	78 44.7	13.0	46 19.1	57.5	Miaplacidus	221 41.1	S69 42.6
23	87 08.1	146 55.3	55.1	248 33.0	48.1	93 46.9	12.8	61 21.5	57.5			
3 00	102 10.5	161 54.5	S21 54.5	263 34.4	S 5 48.6	108 49.0	S 4 12.7	76 24.0	N 7 57.6	Mirfak	308 56.0	N49 51.5
01	117 13.0	176 53.6	53.9	278 35.7	49.0	123 51.1	12.5	91 26.4	57.6	Nunki	76 12.5	S26 17.8
02	132 15.5	191 52.8	53.3	293 37.0	49.5	138 53.2	12.4	106 28.9	57.6	Peacock	53 37.4	S56 44.4
03	147 17.9	206 51.9 ..	52.8	308 38.3 ..	49.9	153 55.3 ..	12.2	121 31.3 ..	57.6	Pollux	243 41.0	N28 01.6
04	162 20.4	221 51.1	52.2	323 39.6	50.4	168 57.5	12.1	136 33.8	57.6	Procyon	245 11.1	N 5 13.5
05	177 22.8	236 50.2	51.6	338 41.0	50.8	183 59.6	11.9	151 36.2	57.7			
06	192 25.3	251 49.3	S21 51.0	353 42.3	S 5 51.2	199 01.7	S 4 11.7	166 38.7	N 7 57.7	Rasalhague	96 17.1	N12 33.7
07	207 27.8	266 48.5	50.4	8 43.6	51.7	214 03.8	11.6	181 41.1	57.7	Regulus	207 55.2	N11 58.2
S 08	222 30.2	281 47.6	49.9	23 44.9	52.1	229 05.9	11.4	196 43.6	57.7	Rigel	281 22.5	S 8 12.4
U 09	237 32.7	296 46.8 ..	49.3	38 46.2 ..	52.6	244 08.0 ..	11.3	211 46.0 ..	57.7	Rigil Kent.	140 07.3	S60 49.5
N 10	252 35.2	311 45.9	48.7	53 47.6	53.0	259 10.2	11.1	226 48.5	57.8	Sabik	102 25.7	S15 43.3
D 11	267 37.6	326 45.1	48.1	68 48.9	53.5	274 12.3	11.0	241 50.9	57.8			
A 12	282 40.1	341 44.2	S21 47.5	83 50.2	S 5 53.9	289 14.4	S 4 10.8	256 53.3	N 7 57.8	Schedar	349 53.2	N56 32.1
Y 13	297 42.6	356 43.4	46.9	98 51.5	54.4	304 16.5	10.6	271 55.8	57.8	Shaula	96 37.5	S37 06.0
14	312 45.0	11 42.5	46.3	113 52.8	54.8	319 18.6	10.5	286 58.2	57.8	Sirius	258 43.2	S16 43.0
15	327 47.5	26 41.7 ..	45.7	128 54.2 ..	55.3	334 20.8 ..	10.3	302 00.7 ..	57.8	Spica	158 43.1	S11 09.2
16	342 49.9	41 40.8	45.1	143 55.5	55.7	349 22.9	10.2	317 03.1	57.9	Suhail	223 00.2	S43 25.6
17	357 52.4	56 40.0	44.6	158 56.8	56.1	4 25.0	10.0	332 05.6	57.9			
18	12 54.9	71 39.2	S21 44.0	173 58.1	S 5 56.6	19 27.1	S 4 09.8	347 08.0	N 7 57.9	Vega	80 46.9	N38 47.1
19	27 57.3	86 38.3	43.4	188 59.4	57.0	34 29.2	09.7	2 10.5	57.9	Zuben'ubi	137 18.0	S16 02.1
20	42 59.8	101 37.5	42.8	204 00.8	57.5	49 31.3	09.5	17 12.9	57.9			
21	58 02.3	116 36.6 ..	42.2	219 02.1 ..	57.9	64 33.4 ..	09.4	32 15.4 ..	58.0		SHA	Mer. Pass.
22	73 04.7	131 35.8	41.6	234 03.4	58.4	79 35.6	09.2	47 17.8	58.0	Venus	61 03.7	13 12
23	88 07.2	146 34.9	41.0	249 04.7	58.8	94 37.7	09.1	62 20.3	58.0	Mars	161 51.4	6 27
Mer. Pass. 17 12.4		v −0.9	d 0.6	v 1.3	d 0.4	v 2.1	d 0.2	v 2.5	d 0.0	Jupiter	6 46.7	16 46
										Saturn	334 13.7	18 55

UT	SUN		MOON				
	GHA	Dec	GHA	v	Dec	d	HP
d h	° ′	° ′	° ′	′	° ′	′	′
1 00	179 12.5	S23 03.2	15 30.6	4.9	N18 59.1	3.0	60.1
01	194 12.2	03.0	29 54.5	4.9	19 02.1	2.9	60.1
02	209 11.9	02.8	44 18.4	4.8	19 05.0	2.7	60.1
03	224 11.6	.. 02.6	58 42.2	4.9	19 07.7	2.7	60.1
04	239 11.3	02.4	73 06.1	4.8	19 10.4	2.5	60.0
05	254 11.0	02.2	87 29.9	4.8	19 12.9	2.3	60.0
06	269 10.7	S23 02.0	101 53.7	4.9	N19 15.2	2.2	60.0
07	284 10.4	01.8	116 17.6	4.8	19 17.4	2.1	60.0
F 08	299 10.1	01.6	130 41.4	4.9	19 19.5	1.9	60.0
R 09	314 09.8	.. 01.4	145 05.3	4.8	19 21.4	1.9	60.0
I 10	329 09.5	01.2	159 29.1	4.9	19 23.3	1.6	59.9
D 11	344 09.3	01.0	173 53.0	4.8	19 24.9	1.6	59.9
A 12	359 09.0	S23 00.8	188 16.8	4.9	N19 26.5	1.4	59.9
Y 13	14 08.7	00.6	202 40.7	4.9	19 27.9	1.2	59.9
14	29 08.4	00.4	217 04.6	4.9	19 29.1	1.1	59.9
15	44 08.1	.. 00.2	231 28.5	4.9	19 30.2	1.0	59.9
16	59 07.8	23 00.0	245 52.4	4.9	19 31.2	0.9	59.8
17	74 07.5	22 59.8	260 16.3	5.0	19 32.1	0.7	59.8
18	89 07.2	S22 59.5	274 40.3	4.9	N19 32.8	0.6	59.8
19	104 06.9	59.3	289 04.2	5.0	19 33.4	0.4	59.8
20	119 06.6	59.1	303 28.2	5.0	19 33.8	0.3	59.8
21	134 06.3	.. 58.9	317 52.2	5.1	19 34.1	0.2	59.7
22	149 06.0	58.7	332 16.3	5.0	19 34.3	0.0	59.7
23	164 05.7	58.5	346 40.3	5.1	19 34.3	0.1	59.7
2 00	179 05.4	S22 58.3	1 04.4	5.1	N19 34.2	0.2	59.7
01	194 05.1	58.1	15 28.5	5.2	19 34.0	0.4	59.7
02	209 04.9	57.9	29 52.7	5.1	19 33.6	0.5	59.6
03	224 04.6	.. 57.6	44 16.8	5.2	19 33.1	0.6	59.6
04	239 04.3	57.4	58 41.0	5.3	19 32.5	0.8	59.6
05	254 04.0	57.2	73 05.3	5.3	19 31.7	0.9	59.6
06	269 03.7	S22 57.0	87 29.6	5.3	N19 30.8	1.0	59.5
S 07	284 03.4	56.8	101 53.9	5.3	19 29.8	1.2	59.5
A 08	299 03.1	56.6	116 18.2	5.4	19 28.6	1.3	59.5
T 09	314 02.8	.. 56.3	130 42.6	5.5	19 27.3	1.4	59.5
U 10	329 02.5	56.1	145 07.1	5.5	19 25.9	1.5	59.5
R 11	344 02.2	55.9	159 31.6	5.5	19 24.4	1.7	59.4
D 12	359 01.9	S22 55.7	173 56.1	5.6	N19 22.7	1.8	59.4
A 13	14 01.6	55.5	188 20.7	5.6	19 20.9	2.0	59.4
Y 14	29 01.4	55.2	202 45.3	5.7	19 18.9	2.1	59.4
15	44 01.1	.. 55.0	217 10.0	5.7	19 16.8	2.2	59.3
16	59 00.8	54.8	231 34.7	5.8	19 14.6	2.3	59.3
17	74 00.5	54.6	245 59.5	5.8	19 12.3	2.4	59.3
18	89 00.2	S22 54.3	260 24.3	5.9	N19 09.9	2.6	59.2
19	103 59.9	54.1	274 49.2	5.9	19 07.3	2.7	59.2
20	118 59.6	53.9	289 14.1	6.0	19 04.6	2.8	59.2
21	133 59.3	.. 53.7	303 39.1	6.1	19 01.8	3.0	59.2
22	148 59.0	53.4	318 04.2	6.1	18 58.8	3.0	59.1
23	163 58.7	53.2	332 29.3	6.1	18 55.8	3.2	59.1
3 00	178 58.5	S22 53.0	346 54.4	6.3	N18 52.6	3.3	59.1
01	193 58.2	52.7	1 19.7	6.3	18 49.3	3.5	59.0
02	208 57.9	52.5	15 45.0	6.3	18 45.8	3.5	59.0
03	223 57.6	.. 52.3	30 10.3	6.5	18 42.3	3.7	59.0
04	238 57.3	52.0	44 35.8	6.5	18 38.6	3.7	59.0
05	253 57.0	51.8	59 01.3	6.5	18 34.9	3.9	58.9
06	268 56.7	S22 51.6	73 26.8	6.7	N18 31.0	4.1	58.9
07	283 56.4	51.3	87 52.5	6.6	18 26.9	4.1	58.9
08	298 56.1	51.1	102 18.1	6.8	18 22.8	4.2	58.8
S 09	313 55.9	.. 50.8	116 43.9	6.9	18 18.6	4.4	58.8
U 10	328 55.6	50.6	131 09.8	6.9	18 14.2	4.4	58.8
N 11	343 55.3	50.4	145 35.7	6.9	18 09.8	4.6	58.7
D 12	358 55.0	S22 50.1	160 01.6	7.1	N18 05.2	4.7	58.7
A 13	13 54.7	49.9	174 27.7	7.1	18 00.5	4.7	58.7
Y 14	28 54.4	49.6	188 53.8	7.2	17 55.8	4.9	58.6
15	43 54.1	.. 49.4	203 20.0	7.3	17 50.9	5.0	58.6
16	58 53.9	49.2	217 46.3	7.3	17 45.9	5.1	58.6
17	73 53.6	48.9	232 12.6	7.5	17 40.8	5.2	58.6
18	88 53.3	S22 48.7	246 39.1	7.5	N17 35.6	5.3	58.5
19	103 53.0	48.4	261 05.6	7.6	17 30.3	5.4	58.5
20	118 52.7	48.2	275 32.2	7.6	17 24.9	5.5	58.5
21	133 52.4	.. 47.9	289 58.8	7.8	17 19.4	5.7	58.4
22	148 52.1	47.7	304 25.6	7.8	17 13.7	5.7	58.4
23	163 51.8	47.4	318 52.4	7.9	N17 08.0	5.8	58.4
	SD 16.3	d 0.2	SD 16.3		16.2		16.0

Lat.	Twilight Naut.	Twilight Civil	Sunrise	Moonrise 1	2	3	4
°	h m	h m	h m	h m	h m	h m	h m
N 72	08 23	10 41	■	□	□	14 01	16 39
N 70	08 05	09 49	■	12 32	13 37	15 23	17 14
68	07 49	09 16	■	13 30	14 33	16 02	17 39
66	07 37	08 53	10 27	14 04	15 07	16 29	17 59
64	07 26	08 34	09 49	14 29	15 32	16 49	18 14
62	07 17	08 18	09 22	14 49	15 51	17 06	18 27
60	07 09	08 05	09 02	15 05	16 07	17 20	18 38
N 58	07 02	07 54	08 45	15 18	16 20	17 31	18 47
56	06 56	07 44	08 31	15 30	16 32	17 42	18 55
54	06 50	07 35	08 19	15 40	16 42	17 51	19 03
52	06 44	07 28	08 08	15 49	16 51	17 59	19 09
50	06 39	07 20	07 58	15 58	16 59	18 06	19 15
45	06 28	07 05	07 38	16 15	17 16	18 21	19 28
N 40	06 18	06 52	07 22	16 29	17 30	18 34	19 38
35	06 09	06 40	07 08	16 41	17 42	18 45	19 47
30	06 00	06 30	06 56	16 52	17 53	18 54	19 55
20	05 44	06 11	06 35	17 10	18 10	19 10	20 09
N 10	05 28	05 54	06 17	17 26	18 26	19 24	20 20
0	05 12	05 38	06 00	17 41	18 41	19 38	20 31
S 10	04 53	05 20	05 43	17 56	18 55	19 51	20 42
20	04 31	05 00	05 24	18 12	19 11	20 05	20 54
30	04 02	04 35	05 03	18 31	19 29	20 21	21 07
35	03 44	04 21	04 50	18 41	19 39	20 30	21 15
40	03 21	04 03	04 35	18 54	19 51	20 41	21 24
45	02 52	03 41	04 18	19 08	20 05	20 53	21 34
S 50	02 08	03 12	03 56	19 26	20 22	21 09	21 46
52	01 42	02 57	03 45	19 35	20 30	21 16	21 52
54	01 02	02 40	03 33	19 44	20 39	21 24	21 59
56	////	02 19	03 20	19 54	20 49	21 32	22 06
58	////	01 51	03 03	20 07	21 01	21 42	22 13
S 60	////	01 08	02 44	20 21	21 14	21 54	22 22

Lat.	Sunset	Twilight Civil	Twilight Naut.	Moonset 1	2	3	4
°	h m	h m	h m	h m	h m	h m	h m
N 72	■	13 27	15 45	□	□	12 54	12 10
N 70	■	14 20	16 04	10 17	11 17	11 31	11 34
68	■	14 52	16 19	09 19	10 20	10 52	11 08
66	13 41	15 16	16 31	08 45	09 46	10 25	10 47
64	14 19	15 34	16 42	08 20	09 21	10 04	10 31
62	14 46	15 50	16 51	08 00	09 02	09 47	10 18
60	15 06	16 03	16 59	07 44	08 46	09 32	10 06
N 58	15 23	16 14	17 06	07 31	08 32	09 20	09 56
56	15 37	16 24	17 12	07 19	08 21	09 10	09 48
54	15 49	16 32	17 18	07 09	08 10	09 00	09 40
52	16 00	16 40	17 24	07 00	08 01	08 52	09 33
50	16 09	16 48	17 29	06 52	07 53	08 44	09 27
45	16 30	17 03	17 40	06 35	07 36	08 28	09 13
N 40	16 46	17 16	17 50	06 21	07 21	08 15	09 02
35	17 00	17 28	17 59	06 09	07 09	08 04	08 52
30	17 12	17 38	18 08	05 58	06 59	07 54	08 44
20	17 32	17 56	18 24	05 40	06 41	07 37	08 29
N 10	17 51	18 13	18 40	05 23	06 25	07 22	08 16
0	18 08	18 30	18 56	05 10	06 10	07 08	08 04
S 10	18 25	18 48	19 15	04 55	05 55	06 54	07 52
20	18 43	19 08	19 37	04 39	05 39	06 39	07 38
30	19 05	19 32	20 05	04 21	05 20	06 22	07 23
35	19 17	19 47	20 23	04 11	05 10	06 12	07 15
40	19 32	20 05	20 46	03 59	04 57	06 00	07 05
45	19 50	20 27	21 15	03 45	04 43	05 46	06 53
S 50	20 11	20 55	21 59	03 27	04 25	05 30	06 38
52	20 22	21 10	22 24	03 19	04 17	05 22	06 32
54	20 34	21 27	23 03	03 10	04 07	05 13	06 24
56	20 48	21 48	////	03 00	03 57	05 03	06 16
58	21 04	22 15	////	02 48	03 45	04 52	06 06
S 60	21 23	22 57	////	02 35	03 31	04 39	05 55

	SUN			MOON		
Day	Eqn. of Time 00ʰ	12ʰ	Mer. Pass.	Mer. Pass. Upper	Lower	Age Phase
d	m s	m s	h m	h m	h m	d %
1	03 09	03 24	12 03	23 56	11 25	14 99
2	03 38	03 52	12 04	24 54	12 25	15 100
3	04 06	04 19	12 04	00 54	13 23	16 97

1999 JANUARY 4, 5, 6 (MON., TUES., WED.)

UT	ARIES	VENUS −3.9		MARS +1.0		JUPITER −2.3		SATURN +0.4		STARS		
	GHA	GHA	Dec	GHA	Dec	GHA	Dec	GHA	Dec	Name	SHA	Dec
d h	° ′	° ′	° ′	° ′	° ′	° ′	° ′	° ′	° ′		° ′	° ′
4 00	103 09.7	161 34.1	S21 40.4	264 06.1	S 5 59.3	109 39.8	S 4 08.9	77 22.7	N 7 58.0	Acamar	315 26.6	S40 18.9
01	118 12.1	176 33.2	39.8	279 07.4	5 59.7	124 41.9	08.7	92 25.1	58.0	Achernar	335 35.0	S57 14.9
02	133 14.6	191 32.4	39.2	294 08.7	6 00.1	139 44.0	08.6	107 27.6	58.1	Acrux	173 21.6	S63 05.3
03	148 17.1	206 31.6	.. 38.5	309 10.0	.. 00.6	154 46.1	.. 08.4	122 30.0	.. 58.1	Adhara	255 20.9	S28 58.4
04	163 19.5	221 30.7	37.9	324 11.4	01.0	169 48.2	08.3	137 32.5	58.1	Aldebaran	291 01.9	N16 30.3
05	178 22.0	236 29.9	37.3	339 12.7	01.5	184 50.4	08.1	152 34.9	58.1			
06	193 24.4	251 29.0	S21 36.7	354 14.0	S 6 01.9	199 52.5	S 4 07.9	167 37.4	N 7 58.2	Alioth	166 30.5	N55 57.7
07	208 26.9	266 28.2	36.1	9 15.3	02.4	214 54.6	07.8	182 39.8	58.2	Alkaid	153 07.8	N49 18.9
08	223 29.4	281 27.4	35.5	24 16.7	02.8	229 56.7	07.6	197 42.3	58.2	Al Na'ir	27 58.1	S46 58.2
M 09	238 31.8	296 26.5	.. 34.9	39 18.0	.. 03.2	244 58.8	.. 07.5	212 44.7	.. 58.2	Alnilam	275 54.4	S 1 12.3
O 10	253 34.3	311 25.7	34.3	54 19.3	03.7	260 00.9	07.3	227 47.1	58.2	Alphard	218 06.8	S 8 39.3
N 11	268 36.8	326 24.8	33.7	69 20.6	04.1	275 03.0	07.1	242 49.6	58.3			
D 12	283 39.2	341 24.0	S21 33.0	84 22.0	S 6 04.6	290 05.2	S 4 07.0	257 52.0	N 7 58.3	Alphecca	126 20.7	N26 43.1
A 13	298 41.7	356 23.2	32.4	99 23.3	05.0	305 07.3	06.8	272 54.5	58.3	Alpheratz	357 55.1	N29 05.2
Y 14	313 44.2	11 22.3	31.8	114 24.6	05.4	320 09.4	06.7	287 56.9	58.3	Altair	62 19.4	N 8 52.0
15	328 46.6	26 21.5	.. 31.2	129 25.9	.. 05.9	335 11.5	.. 06.5	302 59.4	.. 58.3	Ankaa	353 26.8	S42 19.0
16	343 49.1	41 20.7	30.6	144 27.3	06.3	350 13.6	06.3	318 01.8	58.4	Antares	112 40.3	S26 25.6
17	358 51.6	56 19.8	30.0	159 28.6	06.8	5 15.7	06.2	333 04.2	58.4			
18	13 54.0	71 19.0	S21 29.3	174 29.9	S 6 07.2	20 17.8	S 4 06.0	348 06.7	N 7 58.4	Arcturus	146 06.1	N19 11.2
19	28 56.5	86 18.2	28.7	189 31.3	07.6	35 19.9	05.9	3 09.1	58.4	Atria	107 52.6	S69 01.3
20	43 58.9	101 17.3	28.1	204 32.6	08.1	50 22.0	05.7	18 11.6	58.4	Avior	234 21.9	S59 30.4
21	59 01.4	116 16.5	.. 27.5	219 33.9	.. 08.5	65 24.2	.. 05.5	33 14.0	.. 58.5	Bellatrix	278 43.7	N 6 20.8
22	74 03.9	131 15.7	26.8	234 35.2	09.0	80 26.3	05.4	48 16.5	58.5	Betelgeuse	271 13.0	N 7 24.3
23	89 06.3	146 14.8	26.2	249 36.6	09.4	95 28.4	05.2	63 18.9	58.5			
5 00	104 08.8	161 14.0	S21 25.6	264 37.9	S 6 09.8	110 30.5	S 4 05.1	78 21.3	N 7 58.5	Canopus	264 00.5	S52 41.9
01	119 11.3	176 13.2	24.9	279 39.2	10.3	125 32.6	04.9	93 23.8	58.6	Capella	280 50.5	N45 59.8
02	134 13.7	191 12.3	24.3	294 40.6	10.7	140 34.7	04.7	108 26.2	58.6	Deneb	49 39.5	N45 16.8
03	149 16.2	206 11.5	.. 23.7	309 41.9	.. 11.2	155 36.8	.. 04.6	123 28.7	.. 58.6	Denebola	182 44.9	N14 34.6
04	164 18.7	221 10.7	23.0	324 43.2	11.6	170 38.9	04.4	138 31.1	58.6	Diphda	349 07.1	S17 59.7
05	179 21.1	236 09.8	22.4	339 44.6	12.0	185 41.0	04.2	153 33.5	58.6			
06	194 23.6	251 09.0	S21 21.8	354 45.9	S 6 12.5	200 43.1	S 4 04.1	168 36.0	N 7 58.7	Dubhe	194 05.1	N61 45.1
07	209 26.1	266 08.2	21.1	9 47.2	12.9	215 45.2	03.9	183 38.4	58.7	Elnath	278 26.4	N28 36.3
T 08	224 28.5	281 07.4	20.5	24 48.5	13.4	230 47.3	03.8	198 40.9	58.7	Eltanin	90 51.9	N51 29.4
U 09	239 31.0	296 06.5	.. 19.9	39 49.9	.. 13.8	245 49.5	.. 03.6	213 43.3	.. 58.7	Enif	33 58.3	N 9 52.3
E 10	254 33.4	311 05.7	19.2	54 51.2	14.2	260 51.6	03.4	228 45.7	58.8	Fomalhaut	15 36.5	S29 37.9
S 11	269 35.9	326 04.9	18.6	69 52.5	14.7	275 53.7	03.3	243 48.2	58.8			
D 12	284 38.4	341 04.1	S21 17.9	84 53.9	S 6 15.1	290 55.8	S 4 03.1	258 50.6	N 7 58.8	Gacrux	172 13.2	S57 06.1
A 13	299 40.8	356 03.2	17.3	99 55.2	15.5	305 57.9	03.0	273 53.1	58.8	Gienah	176 03.7	S17 32.0
Y 14	314 43.3	11 02.4	16.7	114 56.5	16.0	321 00.0	02.8	288 55.5	58.8	Hadar	149 03.9	S60 21.7
15	329 45.8	26 01.6	.. 16.0	129 57.9	.. 16.4	336 02.1	.. 02.6	303 57.9	.. 58.9	Hamal	328 13.2	N23 27.4
16	344 48.2	41 00.8	15.4	144 59.2	16.9	351 04.2	02.5	319 00.4	58.9	Kaus Aust.	83 59.0	S34 23.0
17	359 50.7	55 59.9	14.7	160 00.5	17.3	6 06.3	02.3	334 02.8	58.9			
18	14 53.2	70 59.1	S21 14.1	175 01.9	S 6 17.7	21 08.4	S 4 02.1	349 05.2	N 7 58.9	Kochab	137 20.3	N74 09.4
19	29 55.6	85 58.3	13.4	190 03.2	18.2	36 10.5	02.0	4 07.7	59.0	Markab	13 49.6	N15 12.0
20	44 58.1	100 57.5	12.8	205 04.5	18.6	51 12.6	01.8	19 10.1	59.0	Menkar	314 26.5	N 4 05.0
21	60 00.5	115 56.6	.. 12.1	220 05.9	.. 19.0	66 14.7	.. 01.7	34 12.6	.. 59.0	Menkent	148 20.9	S36 21.6
22	75 03.0	130 55.8	11.5	235 07.2	19.5	81 16.8	01.5	49 15.0	59.0	Miaplacidus	221 41.1	S69 42.7
23	90 05.5	145 55.0	10.8	250 08.5	19.9	96 18.9	01.3	64 17.4	59.1			
6 00	105 07.9	160 54.2	S21 10.1	265 09.9	S 6 20.3	111 21.0	S 4 01.2	79 19.9	N 7 59.1	Mirfak	308 56.0	N49 51.5
01	120 10.4	175 53.4	09.5	280 11.2	20.8	126 23.2	01.0	94 22.3	59.1	Nunki	76 12.5	S26 17.8
02	135 12.9	190 52.5	08.8	295 12.5	21.2	141 25.3	00.8	109 24.7	59.1	Peacock	53 37.4	S56 44.4
03	150 15.3	205 51.7	.. 08.2	310 13.9	.. 21.6	156 27.4	.. 00.7	124 27.2	.. 59.2	Pollux	243 41.0	N28 01.6
04	165 17.8	220 50.9	07.5	325 15.2	22.1	171 29.5	00.5	139 29.6	59.2	Procyon	245 11.1	N 5 13.5
05	180 20.3	235 50.1	06.9	340 16.6	22.5	186 31.6	00.3	154 32.0	59.2			
06	195 22.7	250 49.3	S21 06.2	355 17.9	S 6 23.0	201 33.7	S 4 00.2	169 34.5	N 7 59.2	Rasalhague	96 17.1	N12 33.7
W 07	210 25.2	265 48.5	05.5	10 19.2	23.4	216 35.8	4 00.0	184 36.9	59.2	Regulus	207 55.1	N11 58.2
E 08	225 27.7	280 47.6	04.9	25 20.6	23.8	231 37.9	3 59.9	199 39.4	59.3	Rigel	281 22.5	S 8 12.4
D 09	240 30.1	295 46.8	.. 04.2	40 21.9	.. 24.3	246 40.0	.. 59.7	214 41.8	.. 59.3	Rigil Kent.	140 07.3	S60 49.5
N 10	255 32.6	310 46.0	03.5	55 23.2	24.7	261 42.1	59.5	229 44.2	59.3	Sabik	102 25.7	S15 43.3
E 11	270 35.0	325 45.2	02.9	70 24.6	25.1	276 44.2	59.4	244 46.7	59.3			
S 12	285 37.5	340 44.4	S21 02.2	85 25.9	S 6 25.6	291 46.3	S 3 59.2	259 49.1	N 7 59.4	Schedar	349 53.2	N56 32.1
D 13	300 40.0	355 43.6	01.5	100 27.2	26.0	306 48.4	59.0	274 51.5	59.4	Shaula	96 37.5	S37 06.0
A 14	315 42.4	10 42.8	00.9	115 28.6	26.4	321 50.5	58.9	289 54.0	59.4	Sirius	258 43.2	S16 43.0
Y 15	330 44.9	25 42.0	21 00.2	130 29.9	.. 26.9	336 52.6	.. 58.7	304 56.4	.. 59.4	Spica	158 43.1	S11 09.2
16	345 47.4	40 41.1	20 59.5	145 31.3	27.3	351 54.7	58.5	319 58.8	59.5	Suhail	223 00.2	S43 25.7
17	0 49.8	55 40.3	58.8	160 32.6	27.7	6 56.8	58.4	335 01.3	59.5			
18	15 52.3	70 39.5	S20 58.2	175 33.9	S 6 28.2	21 58.9	S 3 58.2	350 03.7	N 7 59.5	Vega	80 46.9	N38 47.0
19	30 54.8	85 38.7	57.5	190 35.3	28.6	37 01.0	58.0	5 06.1	59.5	Zuben'ubi	137 17.9	S16 02.1
20	45 57.2	100 37.9	56.8	205 36.6	29.0	52 03.1	57.9	20 08.6	59.6		SHA	Mer. Pass.
21	60 59.7	115 37.1	.. 56.1	220 38.0	.. 29.5	67 05.2	.. 57.7	35 11.0	.. 59.6		° ′	h m
22	76 02.2	130 36.3	55.5	235 39.3	29.9	82 07.3	57.6	50 13.4	59.6	Venus	57 05.2	13 16
23	91 04.6	145 35.5	54.8	250 40.6	30.3	97 09.4	57.4	65 15.9	59.6	Mars	160 29.1	6 21
	h m									Jupiter	6 21.7	16 36
Mer. Pass. 17 00.6		v −0.8	d 0.6	v 1.3	d 0.4	v 2.1	d 0.2	v 2.4	d 0.0	Saturn	334 12.5	18 44

UT	SUN		MOON				
	GHA	Dec	GHA	v	Dec	d	HP
d h	° ′	° ′	° ′	′	° ′	′	′
4 00	178 51.6	S22 47.2	333 19.3	8.0	N17 02.2	5.8	58.3
01	193 51.3	46.9	347 46.3	8.0	16 56.4	6.0	58.3
02	208 51.0	46.7	2 13.3	8.2	16 50.4	6.1	58.3
03	223 50.7	.. 46.4	16 40.5	8.2	16 44.3	6.2	58.2
04	238 50.4	46.2	31 07.7	8.3	16 38.1	6.3	58.2
05	253 50.1	45.9	45 35.0	8.4	16 31.8	6.3	58.2
06	268 49.9	S22 45.7	60 02.4	8.4	N16 25.5	6.5	58.1
07	283 49.6	45.4	74 29.8	8.6	16 19.0	6.5	58.1
08	298 49.3	45.2	88 57.4	8.6	16 12.5	6.6	58.0
M 09	313 49.0	.. 44.9	103 25.0	8.7	16 05.9	6.7	58.0
O 10	328 48.7	44.6	117 52.7	8.8	15 59.2	6.8	58.0
N 11	343 48.4	44.4	132 20.5	8.9	15 52.4	6.9	57.9
D 12	358 48.2	S22 44.1	146 48.4	9.0	N15 45.5	6.9	57.9
A 13	13 47.9	43.9	161 16.4	9.0	15 38.6	7.0	57.9
Y 14	28 47.6	43.6	175 44.4	9.1	15 31.6	7.2	57.8
15	43 47.3	.. 43.3	190 12.5	9.2	15 24.4	7.1	57.8
16	58 47.0	43.1	204 40.7	9.3	15 17.3	7.3	57.8
17	73 46.7	42.8	219 09.0	9.4	15 10.0	7.4	57.7
18	88 46.5	S22 42.5	233 37.4	9.5	N15 02.6	7.4	57.7
19	103 46.2	42.3	248 05.9	9.5	14 55.2	7.5	57.7
20	118 45.9	42.0	262 34.4	9.6	14 47.7	7.5	57.6
21	133 45.6	.. 41.8	277 03.0	9.8	14 40.2	7.7	57.6
22	148 45.3	41.5	291 31.8	9.7	14 32.5	7.7	57.6
23	163 45.0	41.2	306 00.5	9.9	14 24.8	7.7	57.5
5 00	178 44.8	S22 40.9	320 29.4	10.0	N14 17.1	7.9	57.5
01	193 44.5	40.7	334 58.4	10.0	14 09.2	7.9	57.5
02	208 44.2	40.4	349 27.4	10.1	14 01.3	8.0	57.4
03	223 43.9	.. 40.1	3 56.5	10.2	13 53.3	8.0	57.4
04	238 43.6	39.9	18 25.7	10.3	13 45.3	8.1	57.3
05	253 43.4	39.6	32 55.0	10.4	13 37.2	8.2	57.3
06	268 43.1	S22 39.3	47 24.4	10.5	N13 29.0	8.2	57.3
07	283 42.8	39.0	61 53.9	10.5	13 20.8	8.3	57.2
08	298 42.5	38.8	76 23.4	10.6	13 12.5	8.3	57.2
T 09	313 42.2	.. 38.5	90 53.0	10.7	13 04.2	8.4	57.2
U 10	328 42.0	38.2	105 22.7	10.8	12 55.8	8.5	57.1
E 11	343 41.7	37.9	119 52.5	10.8	12 47.3	8.5	57.1
S 12	358 41.4	S22 37.7	134 22.3	10.9	N12 38.8	8.5	57.1
D 13	13 41.1	37.4	148 52.2	11.0	12 30.3	8.7	57.0
A 14	28 40.8	37.1	163 22.2	11.1	12 21.6	8.6	57.0
Y 15	43 40.6	.. 36.8	177 52.3	11.2	12 13.0	8.7	56.9
16	58 40.3	36.5	192 23.5	11.2	12 04.2	8.7	56.9
17	73 40.0	36.3	206 52.7	11.3	11 55.5	8.9	56.9
18	88 39.7	S22 36.0	221 23.0	11.4	N11 46.6	8.8	56.9
19	103 39.5	35.7	235 53.4	11.5	11 37.8	9.0	56.8
20	118 39.2	35.4	250 23.9	11.5	11 28.8	9.0	56.8
21	133 38.9	.. 35.1	264 54.4	11.6	11 19.9	9.0	56.8
22	148 38.6	34.8	279 25.0	11.7	11 10.9	9.1	56.7
23	163 38.3	34.6	293 55.7	11.8	11 01.8	9.1	56.7
6 00	178 38.1	S22 34.3	308 26.5	11.8	N10 52.7	9.1	56.7
01	193 37.8	34.0	322 57.3	11.9	10 43.6	9.2	56.6
02	208 37.5	33.7	337 28.2	12.0	10 34.4	9.2	56.6
03	223 37.2	.. 33.4	351 59.2	12.1	10 25.2	9.3	56.6
04	238 37.0	33.1	6 30.3	12.1	10 15.9	9.3	56.5
05	253 36.7	32.8	21 01.4	12.2	10 06.6	9.3	56.5
06	268 36.4	S22 32.5	35 32.6	12.3	N 9 57.3	9.4	56.5
W 07	283 36.1	32.2	50 03.9	12.3	9 47.9	9.4	56.4
E 08	298 35.9	31.9	64 35.2	12.4	9 38.5	9.5	56.4
D 09	313 35.6	.. 31.6	79 06.6	12.4	9 29.0	9.4	56.4
N 10	328 35.3	31.3	93 38.0	12.6	9 19.6	9.6	56.3
E 11	343 35.0	31.1	108 09.6	12.6	9 10.0	9.5	56.3
S 12	358 34.8	S22 30.8	122 41.2	12.6	N 9 00.5	9.6	56.3
D 13	13 34.5	30.5	137 12.8	12.8	8 50.9	9.6	56.2
A 14	28 34.2	30.2	151 44.6	12.7	8 41.3	9.6	56.2
Y 15	43 33.9	.. 29.9	166 16.3	12.9	8 31.7	9.7	56.2
16	58 33.6	29.6	180 48.2	12.9	8 22.0	9.6	56.1
17	73 33.4	29.3	195 20.1	13.0	8 12.4	9.8	56.1
18	88 33.1	S22 29.0	209 52.1	13.0	N 8 02.6	9.7	56.1
19	103 32.8	28.7	224 24.1	13.1	7 52.9	9.8	56.0
20	118 32.6	28.4	238 56.2	13.2	7 43.1	9.7	56.0
21	133 32.3	.. 28.1	253 28.4	13.2	7 33.4	9.9	56.0
22	148 32.0	27.7	268 00.6	13.3	7 23.5	9.8	55.9
23	163 31.8	27.4	282 32.9	13.3	N 7 13.7	9.8	55.9
	SD 16.3	d 0.3	SD 15.8		15.5		15.3

Lat.	Twilight		Sunrise	Moonrise			
	Naut.	Civil		4	5	6	7
°	h m	h m	h m	h m	h m	h m	h m
N 72	08 20	10 31	■	16 39	18 40	20 29	22 12
N 70	08 02	09 43	■	17 14	19 00	20 41	22 16
68	07 47	09 13	11 32	17 39	19 17	20 50	22 20
66	07 35	08 50	10 21	17 59	19 29	20 58	22 23
64	07 25	08 32	09 45	18 14	19 40	21 04	22 26
62	07 16	08 17	09 20	18 27	19 49	21 10	22 28
60	07 08	08 04	09 00	18 38	19 57	21 15	22 30
N 58	07 01	07 53	08 44	18 47	20 04	21 19	22 32
56	06 55	07 43	08 30	18 55	20 10	21 23	22 34
54	06 49	07 35	08 18	19 03	20 15	21 26	22 35
52	06 44	07 27	08 07	19 09	20 20	21 29	22 36
50	06 39	07 20	07 58	19 15	20 24	21 32	22 37
45	06 28	07 05	07 38	19 28	20 34	21 38	22 40
N 40	06 18	06 52	07 22	19 38	20 42	21 43	22 42
35	06 09	06 41	07 08	19 47	20 48	21 47	22 44
30	06 01	06 30	06 57	19 55	20 54	21 51	22 46
20	05 45	06 12	06 36	20 09	21 04	21 58	22 49
N 10	05 29	05 56	06 18	20 20	21 13	22 03	22 51
0	05 13	05 39	06 02	20 31	21 22	22 09	22 53
S 10	04 55	05 22	05 45	20 42	21 30	22 14	22 56
20	04 33	05 02	05 26	20 54	21 39	22 20	22 58
30	04 05	04 38	05 05	21 07	21 49	22 26	23 01
35	03 47	04 23	04 52	21 15	21 55	22 30	23 03
40	03 25	04 06	04 38	21 24	22 01	22 34	23 05
45	02 55	03 44	04 21	21 34	22 09	22 39	23 07
S 50	02 13	03 16	03 59	21 46	22 18	22 45	23 09
52	01 48	03 01	03 49	21 52	22 22	22 48	23 10
54	01 11	02 44	03 37	21 59	22 27	22 51	23 12
56	////	02 24	03 24	22 06	22 32	22 54	23 13
58	////	01 57	03 08	22 13	22 38	22 57	23 15
S 60	////	01 18	02 49	22 22	22 44	23 02	23 17

Lat.	Sunset	Twilight		Moonset			
		Civil	Naut.	4	5	6	7
°	h m	h m	h m	h m	h m	h m	h m
N 72	■	13 40	15 51	12 10	11 55	11 44	11 36
N 70	■	14 28	16 09	11 34	11 33	11 31	11 29
68	12 39	14 58	16 24	11 08	11 16	11 20	11 23
66	13 50	15 21	16 36	10 47	11 02	11 11	11 18
64	14 26	15 39	16 46	10 31	10 50	11 04	11 14
62	14 51	15 54	16 55	10 18	10 40	10 57	11 11
60	15 11	16 07	17 02	10 06	10 32	10 51	11 07
N 58	15 27	16 18	17 09	09 56	10 24	10 46	11 05
56	15 41	16 27	17 16	09 48	10 17	10 42	11 02
54	15 53	16 36	17 22	09 40	10 11	10 38	11 00
52	16 03	16 44	17 27	09 33	10 06	10 34	10 58
50	16 13	16 51	17 32	09 27	10 01	10 30	10 56
45	16 32	17 06	17 43	09 13	09 51	10 23	10 52
N 40	16 49	17 19	17 53	09 02	09 42	10 17	10 49
35	17 02	17 30	18 02	08 52	09 34	10 12	10 46
30	17 14	17 40	18 10	08 44	09 27	10 07	10 43
20	17 34	17 58	18 26	08 29	09 16	09 59	10 38
N 10	17 52	18 15	18 41	08 16	09 05	09 51	10 34
0	18 09	18 31	18 57	08 04	08 56	09 44	10 30
S 10	18 26	18 49	19 16	07 52	08 46	09 38	10 26
20	18 44	19 08	19 37	07 38	08 36	09 30	10 22
30	19 05	19 32	20 05	07 23	08 24	09 22	10 18
35	19 18	19 47	20 23	07 15	08 17	09 17	10 15
40	19 32	20 05	20 45	07 05	08 09	09 11	10 12
45	19 49	20 26	21 14	06 53	07 59	09 05	10 08
S 50	20 11	20 54	21 56	06 38	07 48	08 57	10 03
52	20 21	21 08	22 21	06 32	07 43	08 53	10 01
54	20 33	21 25	22 57	06 24	07 37	08 49	09 59
56	20 46	21 45	////	06 16	07 31	08 45	09 57
58	21 02	22 12	////	06 06	07 23	08 40	09 54
S 60	21 20	22 50	////	05 55	07 15	08 34	09 51

Day	SUN		MOON			
	Eqn. of Time		Mer.	Mer. Pass.		Age	Phase
	00h	12h	Pass.	Upper	Lower	
d	m s	m s	h m	h m	h m	d %
4	04 33	04 47	12 05	01 51	14 18	17 93
5	05 00	05 14	12 05	02 44	15 09	18 86
6	05 27	05 40	12 06	03 33	15 57	19 79

1999 JANUARY 7, 8, 9 (THURS., FRI., SAT.)

UT	ARIES	VENUS −3.9		MARS +0.9		JUPITER −2.3		SATURN +0.4		STARS		
	GHA	GHA	Dec	GHA	Dec	GHA	Dec	GHA	Dec	Name	SHA	Dec
d h	° ′	° ′	° ′	° ′	° ′	° ′	° ′	° ′	° ′		° ′	° ′
7 00	106 07.1	160 34.7	S20 54.1	265 42.0	S 6 30.7	112 11.5	S 3 57.2	80 18.3	N 7 59.7	Acamar	315 26.6	S40 18.9
01	121 09.5	175 33.9	53.4	280 43.3	31.2	127 13.6	57.1	95 20.7	59.7	Achernar	335 35.0	S57 14.9
02	136 12.0	190 33.1	52.7	295 44.7	31.6	142 15.7	56.9	110 23.2	59.7	Acrux	173 21.6	S63 05.3
03	151 14.5	205 32.3 ..	52.1	310 46.0 ..	32.0	157 17.8 ..	56.7	125 25.6 ..	59.7	Adhara	255 20.9	S28 58.4
04	166 16.9	220 31.4	51.4	325 47.3	32.5	172 19.9	56.6	140 28.0	59.8	Aldebaran	291 01.9	N16 30.3
05	181 19.4	235 30.6	50.7	340 48.7	32.9	187 22.0	56.4	155 30.5	59.8			
06	196 21.9	250 29.8	S20 50.0	355 50.0	S 6 33.3	202 24.1	S 3 56.2	170 32.9	N 7 59.8	Alioth	166 30.5	N55 57.7
07	211 24.3	265 29.0	49.3	10 51.4	33.8	217 26.2	56.1	185 35.3	59.8	Alkaid	153 07.8	N49 18.9
T 08	226 26.8	280 28.2	48.6	25 52.7	34.2	232 28.3	55.9	200 37.7	59.9	Al Na'ir	27 58.1	S46 58.1
H 09	241 29.3	295 27.4 ..	47.9	40 54.1 ..	34.6	247 30.4 ..	55.7	215 40.2 ..	59.9	Alnilam	275 57.4	S 1 12.3
U 10	256 31.7	310 26.6	47.2	55 55.4	35.1	262 32.5	55.6	230 42.6	59.9	Alphard	218 06.8	S 8 39.3
R 11	271 34.2	325 25.8	46.5	70 56.7	35.5	277 34.6	55.4	245 45.0	7 59.9			
S 12	286 36.6	340 25.0	S20 45.8	85 58.1	S 6 35.9	292 36.7	S 3 55.2	260 47.5	N 8 00.0	Alphecca	126 20.7	N26 43.1
D 13	301 39.1	355 24.2	45.2	100 59.4	36.3	307 38.8	55.1	275 49.9	00.0	Alpheratz	357 55.1	N29 05.2
A 14	316 41.6	10 23.4	44.5	116 00.8	36.8	322 40.9	54.9	290 52.3	00.0	Altair	62 19.4	N 8 52.0
Y 15	331 44.0	25 22.6 ..	43.8	131 02.1 ..	37.2	337 43.0 ..	54.7	305 54.8 ..	00.0	Ankaa	353 26.8	S42 19.0
16	346 46.5	40 21.8	43.1	146 03.5	37.6	352 45.1	54.6	320 57.2	00.1	Antares	112 40.2	S26 25.6
17	1 49.0	55 21.0	42.4	161 04.8	38.1	7 47.2	54.4	335 59.6	00.1			
18	16 51.4	70 20.2	S20 41.7	176 06.2	S 6 38.5	22 49.3	S 3 54.2	351 02.0	N 8 00.1	Arcturus	146 06.0	N19 11.2
19	31 53.9	85 19.4	41.0	191 07.5	38.9	37 51.3	54.1	6 04.5	00.2	Atria	107 52.6	S69 01.3
20	46 56.4	100 18.6	40.3	206 08.8	39.3	52 53.4	53.9	21 06.9	00.2	Avior	234 21.9	S59 30.4
21	61 58.8	115 17.8 ..	39.6	221 10.2 ..	39.8	67 55.5 ..	53.7	36 09.3 ..	00.2	Bellatrix	278 43.7	N 6 20.8
22	77 01.3	130 17.0	38.9	236 11.5	40.2	82 57.6	53.6	51 11.8	00.2	Betelgeuse	271 13.0	N 7 24.3
23	92 03.8	145 16.3	38.1	251 12.9	40.6	97 59.7	53.4	66 14.2	00.3			
8 00	107 06.2	160 15.5	S20 37.4	266 14.2	S 6 41.1	113 01.8	S 3 53.2	81 16.6	N 8 00.3	Canopus	264 00.5	S52 41.9
01	122 08.7	175 14.7	36.7	281 15.6	41.5	128 03.9	53.1	96 19.0	00.3	Capella	280 50.5	N45 59.8
02	137 11.1	190 13.9	36.0	296 16.9	41.9	143 06.0	52.9	111 21.5	00.3	Deneb	49 39.5	N45 16.7
03	152 13.6	205 13.1 ..	35.3	311 18.3 ..	42.3	158 08.1 ..	52.7	126 23.9 ..	00.4	Denebola	182 44.9	N14 34.6
04	167 16.1	220 12.3	34.6	326 19.6	42.8	173 10.2	52.6	141 26.3	00.4	Diphda	349 07.1	S17 59.8
05	182 18.5	235 11.5	33.9	341 21.0	43.2	188 12.3	52.4	156 28.8	00.4			
06	197 21.0	250 10.7	S20 33.2	356 22.3	S 6 43.6	203 14.4	S 3 52.2	171 31.2	N 8 00.5	Dubhe	194 05.0	N61 45.1
07	212 23.5	265 09.9	32.5	11 23.7	44.0	218 16.5	52.1	186 33.6	00.5	Elnath	278 26.4	N28 36.3
08	227 25.9	280 09.1	31.8	26 25.0	44.5	233 18.6	51.9	201 36.0	00.5	Eltanin	90 51.8	N51 29.4
F 09	242 28.4	295 08.3 ..	31.0	41 26.4 ..	44.9	248 20.7 ..	51.7	216 38.5 ..	00.5	Enif	33 58.3	N 9 52.2
R 10	257 30.9	310 07.5	30.3	56 27.7	45.3	263 22.8	51.6	231 40.9	00.6	Fomalhaut	15 36.5	S29 37.9
I 11	272 33.3	325 06.8	29.6	71 29.1	45.8	278 24.9	51.4	246 43.3	00.6			
D 12	287 35.8	340 06.0	S20 28.9	86 30.4	S 6 46.2	293 26.9	S 3 51.2	261 45.7	N 8 00.6	Gacrux	172 13.2	S57 06.1
A 13	302 38.3	355 05.2	28.2	101 31.8	46.6	308 29.0	51.1	276 48.2	00.6	Gienah	176 03.7	S17 32.1
Y 14	317 40.7	10 04.4	27.4	116 33.1	47.0	323 31.1	50.9	291 50.6	00.7	Hadar	149 03.9	S60 21.7
15	332 43.2	25 03.6 ..	26.7	131 34.5 ..	47.5	338 33.2 ..	50.7	306 53.0 ..	00.7	Hamal	328 13.2	N23 27.4
16	347 45.6	40 02.8	26.0	146 35.8	47.9	353 35.3	50.5	321 55.4	00.7	Kaus Aust.	83 59.0	S34 23.0
17	2 48.1	55 02.0	25.3	161 37.2	48.3	8 37.4	50.4	336 57.9	00.8			
18	17 50.6	70 01.3	S20 24.6	176 38.5	S 6 48.7	23 39.5	S 3 50.2	352 00.3	N 8 00.8	Kochab	137 20.3	N74 09.4
19	32 53.0	85 00.5	23.8	191 39.9	49.2	38 41.6	50.0	7 02.7	00.8	Markab	13 49.6	N15 12.0
20	47 55.5	99 59.7	23.1	206 41.2	49.6	53 43.7	49.9	22 05.1	00.8	Menkar	314 26.5	N 4 05.0
21	62 58.0	114 58.9 ..	22.4	221 42.6 ..	50.0	68 45.8 ..	49.7	37 07.6 ..	00.9	Menkent	148 20.8	S36 21.6
22	78 00.4	129 58.1	21.6	236 43.9	50.4	83 47.9	49.5	52 10.0	00.9	Miaplacidus	221 41.1	S69 42.7
23	93 02.9	144 57.3	20.9	251 45.3	50.8	98 49.9	49.4	67 12.4	00.9			
9 00	108 05.4	159 56.6	S20 20.2	266 46.6	S 6 51.3	113 52.0	S 3 49.2	82 14.8	N 8 01.0	Mirfak	308 56.0	N49 51.5
01	123 07.8	174 55.8	19.4	281 48.0	51.7	128 54.1	49.0	97 17.3	01.0	Nunki	76 12.5	S26 17.8
02	138 10.3	189 55.0	18.7	296 49.3	52.1	143 56.2	48.9	112 19.7	01.0	Peacock	53 37.4	S56 44.4
03	153 12.7	204 54.2 ..	18.0	311 50.7 ..	52.5	158 58.3 ..	48.7	127 22.1 ..	01.0	Pollux	243 41.0	N28 01.6
04	168 15.2	219 53.4	17.2	326 52.0	53.0	174 00.4	48.5	142 24.5	01.1	Procyon	245 11.1	N 5 13.5
05	183 17.7	234 52.7	16.5	341 53.4	53.4	189 02.5	48.3	157 26.9	01.1			
06	198 20.1	249 51.9	S20 15.8	356 54.7	S 6 53.8	204 04.6	S 3 48.2	172 29.4	N 8 01.1	Rasalhague	96 17.1	N12 33.7
07	213 22.6	264 51.1	15.0	11 56.1	54.2	219 06.7	48.0	187 31.8	01.2	Regulus	207 55.1	N11 58.2
S 08	228 25.1	279 50.3	14.3	26 57.5	54.7	234 08.7	47.8	202 34.2	01.2	Rigel	281 22.5	S 8 12.4
A 09	243 27.5	294 49.5 ..	13.6	41 58.8 ..	55.1	249 10.8 ..	47.7	217 36.6 ..	01.2	Rigil Kent.	140 07.3	S60 49.5
T 10	258 30.0	309 48.8	12.8	57 00.2	55.5	264 12.9	47.5	232 39.1	01.2	Sabik	102 25.6	S15 43.3
U 11	273 32.5	324 48.0	12.1	72 01.5	55.9	279 15.0	47.3	247 41.5	01.3			
R 12	288 34.9	339 47.2	S20 11.3	87 02.9	S 6 56.3	294 17.1	S 3 47.2	262 43.9	N 8 01.3	Schedar	349 53.3	N56 32.1
D 13	303 37.4	354 46.4	10.6	102 04.2	56.8	309 19.2	47.0	277 46.3	01.3	Shaula	96 37.4	S37 06.0
A 14	318 39.9	9 45.7	09.8	117 05.6	57.2	324 21.3	46.8	292 48.7	01.4	Sirius	258 43.2	S16 43.0
Y 15	333 42.3	24 44.9 ..	09.1	132 06.9 ..	57.6	339 23.4 ..	46.6	307 51.2 ..	01.4	Spica	158 43.0	S11 09.2
16	348 44.8	39 44.1	08.3	147 08.3	58.0	354 25.4	46.5	322 53.6	01.4	Suhail	223 00.2	S43 25.7
17	3 47.2	54 43.4	07.6	162 09.7	58.4	9 27.5	46.3	337 56.0	01.4			
18	18 49.7	69 42.6	S20 06.8	177 11.0	S 6 58.9	24 29.6	S 3 46.1	352 58.4	N 8 01.5	Vega	80 46.9	N38 47.0
19	33 52.2	84 41.8	06.1	192 12.4	59.3	39 31.7	46.0	8 00.8	01.5	Zuben'ubi	137 17.9	S16 02.1
20	48 54.6	99 41.0	05.3	207 13.7	6 59.7	54 33.8	45.8	23 03.3	01.5		SHA	Mer. Pass.
21	63 57.1	114 40.3 ..	04.6	222 15.1	7 00.1	69 35.9 ..	45.6	38 05.7 ..	01.6		° ′	h m
22	78 59.6	129 39.5	03.8	237 16.4	00.5	84 38.0	45.4	53 08.1	01.6	Venus	53 09.2	13 20
23	94 02.0	144 38.7	03.1	252 17.8	01.0	99 40.0	45.3	68 10.5	01.6	Mars	159 08.0	6 14
	h m									Jupiter	5 55.6	16 26
Mer. Pass. 16 48.8		v −0.8	d 0.7	v 1.3	d 0.4	v 2.1	d 0.2	v 2.4	d 0.0	Saturn	334 10.4	18 32

UT	SUN GHA	SUN Dec	MOON GHA	v	Dec	d	HP
d h	° ′	° ′	° ′	′	° ′	′	′
7 00	178 31.5	S22 27.1	297 05.2	13.4	N 7 03.9	9.9	55.9
01	193 31.2	26.8	311 37.6	13.4	6 54.0	9.9	55.8
02	208 30.9	26.5	326 10.0	13.5	6 44.1	9.9	55.8
03	223 30.7	.. 26.2	340 42.5	13.6	6 34.2	10.0	55.8
04	238 30.4	25.9	355 15.1	13.6	6 24.2	9.9	55.8
05	253 30.1	25.6	9 47.7	13.6	6 14.3	10.0	55.7
06	268 29.9	S22 25.3	24 20.3	13.7	N 6 04.3	10.0	55.7
07	283 29.6	25.0	38 53.0	13.8	5 54.3	10.0	55.7
T 08	298 29.3	24.7	53 25.8	13.8	5 44.3	10.0	55.6
H 09	313 29.0	.. 24.3	67 58.6	13.9	5 34.3	10.0	55.6
U 10	328 28.8	24.0	82 31.5	13.9	5 24.3	10.0	55.6
R 11	343 28.5	23.7	97 04.4	13.9	5 14.3	10.1	55.6
S 12	358 28.2	S22 23.4	111 37.3	14.0	N 5 04.2	10.0	55.5
D 13	13 28.0	23.1	126 10.3	14.1	4 54.2	10.1	55.5
A 14	28 27.7	22.8	140 43.4	14.0	4 44.1	10.1	55.5
Y 15	43 27.4	.. 22.5	155 16.4	14.2	4 34.0	10.1	55.4
16	58 27.2	22.1	169 49.6	14.2	4 23.9	10.1	55.4
17	73 26.9	21.8	184 22.8	14.2	4 13.8	10.1	55.4
18	88 26.6	S22 21.5	198 56.0	14.2	N 4 03.7	10.1	55.4
19	103 26.3	21.2	213 29.2	14.3	3 53.6	10.1	55.3
20	118 26.1	20.9	228 02.5	14.4	3 43.5	10.2	55.3
21	133 25.8	.. 20.5	242 35.9	14.4	3 33.3	10.1	55.3
22	148 25.5	20.2	257 09.3	14.4	3 23.2	10.1	55.3
23	163 25.3	19.9	271 42.7	14.4	3 13.1	10.2	55.2
8 00	178 25.0	S22 19.6	286 16.1	14.5	N 3 02.9	10.1	55.2
01	193 24.7	19.2	300 49.6	14.6	2 52.8	10.2	55.2
02	208 24.5	18.9	315 23.2	14.5	2 42.6	10.1	55.2
03	223 24.2	.. 18.6	329 56.7	14.6	2 32.5	10.1	55.1
04	238 23.9	18.3	344 30.3	14.6	2 22.3	10.1	55.1
05	253 23.7	17.9	359 03.9	14.7	2 12.2	10.1	55.1
06	268 23.4	S22 17.6	13 37.6	14.7	N 2 02.0	10.1	55.1
07	283 23.1	17.3	28 11.3	14.7	1 51.9	10.2	55.1
F 08	298 22.9	16.9	42 45.0	14.8	1 41.7	10.1	55.0
R 09	313 22.6	.. 16.6	57 18.8	14.8	1 31.6	10.2	55.0
I 10	328 22.3	16.3	71 52.6	14.8	1 21.4	10.1	55.0
D 11	343 22.1	15.9	86 26.4	14.8	1 11.3	10.2	55.0
A 12	358 21.8	S22 15.6	101 00.2	14.9	N 1 01.1	10.1	54.9
Y 13	13 21.6	15.3	115 34.1	14.9	0 51.0	10.1	54.9
14	28 21.3	14.9	130 08.0	14.9	0 40.9	10.2	54.9
15	43 21.0	.. 14.6	144 41.9	14.9	0 30.7	10.1	54.9
16	58 20.8	14.3	159 15.8	15.0	0 20.6	10.1	54.9
17	73 20.5	13.9	173 49.8	15.0	0 10.5	10.1	54.8
18	88 20.2	S22 13.6	188 23.8	15.0	N 0 00.4	10.1	54.8
19	103 20.0	13.3	202 57.8	15.0	S 0 09.7	10.1	54.8
20	118 19.7	12.9	217 31.8	15.0	0 19.8	10.1	54.8
21	133 19.4	.. 12.6	232 05.8	15.1	0 29.9	10.1	54.8
22	148 19.2	12.2	246 39.9	15.1	0 40.0	10.0	54.7
23	163 18.9	11.9	261 14.0	15.1	0 50.0	10.1	54.7
9 00	178 18.7	S22 11.6	275 48.1	15.1	S 1 00.1	10.0	54.7
01	193 18.4	11.2	290 22.2	15.1	1 10.1	10.1	54.7
02	208 18.1	10.9	304 56.3	15.2	1 20.1	10.1	54.7
03	223 17.9	.. 10.5	319 30.5	15.2	1 30.2	10.0	54.6
04	238 17.6	10.2	334 04.7	15.1	1 40.2	10.0	54.6
05	253 17.3	09.8	348 38.8	15.2	1 50.2	9.9	54.6
06	268 17.1	S22 09.5	3 13.0	15.2	S 2 00.1	10.0	54.6
07	283 16.8	09.1	17 47.2	15.2	2 10.1	9.9	54.6
S 08	298 16.6	08.8	32 21.4	15.2	2 20.0	10.0	54.6
A 09	313 16.3	.. 08.4	46 55.6	15.3	2 30.0	9.9	54.6
T 10	328 16.0	08.1	61 29.9	15.2	2 39.9	9.9	54.5
U 11	343 15.8	07.7	76 04.1	15.2	2 49.8	9.9	54.5
R 12	358 15.5	S22 07.4	90 38.3	15.3	S 2 59.7	9.9	54.5
D 13	13 15.3	07.0	105 12.6	15.2	3 09.6	9.8	54.5
A 14	28 15.0	06.7	119 46.8	15.3	3 19.4	9.8	54.5
Y 15	43 14.7	.. 06.3	134 21.1	15.3	3 29.2	9.9	54.5
16	58 14.5	06.0	148 55.4	15.2	3 39.1	9.7	54.5
17	73 14.2	05.6	163 29.6	15.3	3 48.8	9.8	54.4
18	88 14.0	S22 05.3	178 03.9	15.3	S 3 58.6	9.8	54.4
19	103 13.7	04.9	192 38.2	15.3	4 08.4	9.7	54.4
20	118 13.5	04.5	207 12.5	15.2	4 18.1	9.7	54.4
21	133 13.2	.. 04.2	221 46.7	15.3	4 27.8	9.7	54.4
22	148 12.9	03.8	236 21.0	15.2	4 37.5	9.7	54.4
23	163 12.7	03.5	250 55.3	15.2	S 4 47.2	9.6	54.4
	SD 16.3	d 0.3	SD 15.1		15.0		14.9

Lat.	Twilight Naut.	Twilight Civil	Sunrise	Moonrise 7	8	9	10
°	h m	h m	h m	h m	h m	h m	h m
N 72	08 16	10 20	■	22 12	23 50	25 27	01 27
N 70	07 58	09 37	■	22 16	23 48	25 19	01 19
68	07 44	09 08	11 12	22 20	23 47	25 13	01 13
66	07 33	08 46	10 14	22 23	23 46	25 07	01 07
64	07 23	08 29	09 41	22 26	23 45	25 03	01 03
62	07 14	08 14	09 16	22 28	23 44	24 59	00 59
60	07 07	08 02	08 57	22 30	23 44	24 56	00 56
N 58	07 00	07 52	08 41	22 32	23 43	24 53	00 53
56	06 54	07 42	08 28	22 34	23 43	24 50	00 50
54	06 48	07 34	08 16	22 35	23 42	24 48	00 48
52	06 43	07 26	08 06	22 36	23 42	24 46	00 46
50	06 38	07 19	07 57	22 37	23 41	24 44	00 44
45	06 28	07 04	07 38	22 40	23 41	24 40	00 40
N 40	06 18	06 52	07 22	22 42	23 40	24 37	00 37
35	06 09	06 41	07 09	22 44	23 39	24 34	00 34
30	06 01	06 31	06 57	22 46	23 39	24 31	00 31
20	05 46	06 13	06 37	22 49	23 38	24 27	00 27
N 10	05 31	05 57	06 19	22 51	23 37	24 23	00 23
0	05 14	05 40	06 03	22 53	23 37	24 19	00 19
S 10	04 56	05 23	05 46	22 56	23 36	24 15	00 15
20	04 35	05 04	05 28	22 58	23 35	24 11	00 11
30	04 07	04 40	05 07	23 01	23 34	24 07	00 07
35	03 50	04 26	04 55	23 03	23 34	24 05	00 05
40	03 28	04 09	04 41	23 05	23 33	24 02	00 02
45	02 59	03 47	04 24	23 07	23 33	23 59	24 25
S 50	02 18	03 20	04 03	23 09	23 32	23 55	24 18
52	01 55	03 06	03 53	23 10	23 32	23 53	24 15
54	01 21	02 50	03 41	23 12	23 32	23 51	24 12
56	////	02 30	03 28	23 13	23 31	23 49	24 08
58	////	02 05	03 13	23 15	23 31	23 47	24 04
S 60	////	01 28	02 55	23 17	23 30	23 44	23 59

Lat.	Sunset	Twilight Civil	Twilight Naut.	Moonset 7	8	9	10
°	h m	h m	h m	h m	h m	h m	h m
N 72	■	13 53	15 58	11 36	11 27	11 19	11 11
N 70	■	14 36	16 15	11 29	11 26	11 23	11 21
68	13 02	15 05	16 29	11 23	11 25	11 27	11 28
66	14 00	15 27	16 41	11 18	11 24	11 29	11 35
64	14 33	15 45	16 51	11 14	11 23	11 32	11 41
62	14 57	15 59	16 59	11 11	11 23	11 34	11 46
60	15 16	16 11	17 07	11 07	11 22	11 36	11 50
N 58	15 32	16 22	17 13	11 05	11 21	11 37	11 54
56	15 45	16 31	17 19	11 02	11 21	11 39	11 57
54	15 57	16 40	17 25	11 00	11 20	11 40	12 00
52	16 07	16 47	17 30	10 58	11 20	11 41	12 03
50	16 16	16 54	17 35	10 56	11 20	11 42	12 05
45	16 36	17 09	17 46	10 52	11 19	11 45	12 11
N 40	16 51	17 22	17 55	10 49	11 18	11 47	12 15
35	17 05	17 33	18 04	10 46	11 18	11 48	12 19
30	17 16	17 42	18 12	10 43	11 17	11 50	12 23
20	17 36	18 00	18 27	10 38	11 16	11 52	12 29
N 10	17 54	18 16	18 43	10 34	11 15	11 55	12 34
0	18 10	18 33	18 59	10 30	11 14	11 57	12 39
S 10	18 27	18 50	19 17	10 26	11 13	11 59	12 44
20	18 45	19 09	19 38	10 22	11 13	12 01	12 50
30	19 06	19 33	20 05	10 18	11 11	12 04	12 56
35	19 18	19 47	20 23	10 15	11 11	12 06	13 00
40	19 32	20 04	20 45	10 12	11 10	12 07	13 04
45	19 49	20 25	21 13	10 08	11 09	12 09	13 08
S 50	20 10	20 53	21 54	10 03	11 08	12 12	13 14
52	20 20	21 06	22 17	10 01	11 08	12 13	13 17
54	20 31	21 22	22 49	09 59	11 07	12 14	13 19
56	20 44	21 42	////	09 57	11 07	12 15	13 23
58	20 59	22 07	////	09 54	11 06	12 17	13 26
S 60	21 17	22 42	////	09 51	11 05	12 18	13 30

	SUN Eqn. of Time 00ʰ	12ʰ	Mer. Pass.	MOON Mer. Pass. Upper	Lower	Age	Phase
Day							
d	m s	m s	h m	h m	h m	d	%
7	05 54	06 07	12 06	04 20	16 42	20	70
8	06 19	06 32	12 07	05 04	17 25	21	61
9	06 45	06 57	12 07	05 47	18 08	22	51

UT	ARIES GHA	VENUS −3.9 GHA	Dec	MARS +0.9 GHA	Dec	JUPITER −2.2 GHA	Dec	SATURN +0.4 GHA	Dec	STARS Name	SHA	Dec
d h	° ′	° ′	° ′	° ′	° ′	° ′	° ′	° ′	° ′		° ′	° ′
10 00	109 04.5	159 38.0	S20 02.3	267 19.2	S 7 01.4	114 42.1	S 3 45.1	83 12.9	N 8 01.7	Acamar	315 26.6	S40 18.9
01	124 07.0	174 37.2	01.6	282 20.5	01.8	129 44.2	44.9	98 15.4	01.7	Achernar	335 35.1	S57 14.9
02	139 09.4	189 36.4	00.8	297 21.9	02.2	144 46.3	44.8	113 17.8	01.7	Acrux	173 21.5	S63 05.3
03	154 11.9	204 35.7	20 00.1	312 23.2 ..	02.6	159 48.4 ..	44.6	128 20.2 ..	01.7	Adhara	255 20.9	S28 58.4
04	169 14.4	219 34.9	19 59.3	327 24.6	03.1	174 50.5	44.4	143 22.6	01.8	Aldebaran	291 01.9	N16 30.3
05	184 16.8	234 34.1	58.5	342 26.0	03.5	189 52.6	44.2	158 25.0	01.8			
06	199 19.3	249 33.4	S19 57.8	357 27.3	S 7 03.9	204 54.6	S 3 44.1	173 27.5	N 8 01.8	Alioth	166 30.5	N55 57.7
07	214 21.7	264 32.6	57.0	12 28.7	04.3	219 56.7	43.9	188 29.9	01.9	Alkaid	153 07.8	N49 18.9
08	229 24.2	279 31.8	56.2	27 30.0	04.7	234 58.8	43.7	203 32.3	01.9	Al Na'ir	27 58.1	S46 58.1
S 09	244 26.7	294 31.1 ..	55.5	42 31.4 ..	05.2	250 00.9 ..	43.6	218 34.7 ..	01.9	Alnilam	275 57.4	S 1 12.3
U 10	259 29.1	309 30.3	54.7	57 32.8	05.6	265 03.0	43.4	233 37.1	02.0	Alphard	218 06.7	S 8 39.3
N 11	274 31.6	324 29.5	53.9	72 34.1	06.0	280 05.1	43.2	248 39.5	02.0			
D 12	289 34.1	339 28.8	S19 53.2	87 35.5	S 7 06.4	295 07.1	S 3 43.0	263 42.0	N 8 02.0	Alphecca	126 20.7	N26 43.0
A 13	304 36.5	354 28.0	52.4	102 36.9	06.8	310 09.2	42.9	278 44.4	02.0	Alpheratz	357 55.1	N29 05.2
Y 14	319 39.0	9 27.3	51.6	117 38.2	07.2	325 11.3	42.7	293 46.8	02.1	Altair	62 19.4	N 8 52.0
15	334 41.5	24 26.5 ..	50.9	132 39.6 ..	07.7	340 13.4 ..	42.5	308 49.2 ..	02.1	Ankaa	353 26.8	S42 19.0
16	349 43.9	39 25.7	50.1	147 40.9	08.1	355 15.5	42.4	323 51.6	02.1	Antares	112 40.2	S26 25.6
17	4 46.4	54 25.0	49.3	162 42.3	08.5	10 17.5	42.2	338 54.0	02.2			
18	19 48.8	69 24.2	S19 48.6	177 43.7	S 7 08.9	25 19.6	S 3 42.0	353 56.5	N 8 02.2	Arcturus	146 06.0	N19 11.2
19	34 51.3	84 23.5	47.8	192 45.0	09.3	40 21.7	41.8	8 58.9	02.2	Atria	107 52.6	S69 01.2
20	49 53.8	99 22.7	47.0	207 46.4	09.7	55 23.8	41.7	24 01.3	02.3	Avior	234 21.9	S59 30.4
21	64 56.2	114 21.9 ..	46.2	222 47.8 ..	10.2	70 25.9 ..	41.5	39 03.7 ..	02.3	Bellatrix	278 43.7	N 6 20.8
22	79 58.7	129 21.2	45.4	237 49.1	10.6	85 28.0	41.3	54 06.1	02.3	Betelgeuse	271 13.0	N 7 24.2
23	95 01.2	144 20.4	44.7	252 50.5	11.0	100 30.0	41.1	69 08.5	02.4			
11 00	110 03.6	159 19.7	S19 43.9	267 51.9	S 7 11.4	115 32.1	S 3 41.0	84 11.0	N 8 02.4	Canopus	264 00.5	S52 41.9
01	125 06.1	174 18.9	43.1	282 53.2	11.8	130 34.2	40.8	99 13.4	02.4	Capella	280 50.5	N45 59.8
02	140 08.6	189 18.2	42.3	297 54.6	12.2	145 36.3	40.6	114 15.8	02.5	Deneb	49 39.5	N45 16.7
03	155 11.0	204 17.4 ..	41.5	312 56.0 ..	12.6	160 38.4 ..	40.4	129 18.2 ..	02.5	Denebola	182 44.9	N14 34.6
04	170 13.5	219 16.7	40.8	327 57.3	13.1	175 40.4	40.3	144 20.6	02.5	Diphda	349 07.1	S17 59.8
05	185 16.0	234 15.9	40.0	342 58.7	13.5	190 42.5	40.1	159 23.0	02.6			
06	200 18.4	249 15.2	S19 39.2	358 00.1	S 7 13.9	205 44.6	S 3 39.9	174 25.4	N 8 02.6	Dubhe	194 05.0	N61 45.1
07	215 20.9	264 14.4	38.4	13 01.4	14.3	220 46.7	39.8	189 27.9	02.6	Elnath	278 26.4	N28 36.3
08	230 23.3	279 13.7	37.6	28 02.8	14.7	235 48.8	39.6	204 30.3	02.6	Eltanin	90 51.8	N51 29.4
M 09	245 25.8	294 12.9 ..	36.8	43 04.2 ..	15.1	250 50.8 ..	39.4	219 32.7 ..	02.7	Enif	33 58.3	N 9 52.2
O 10	260 28.3	309 12.2	36.0	58 05.5	15.5	265 52.9	39.2	234 35.1	02.7	Fomalhaut	15 36.5	S29 37.9
N 11	275 30.7	324 11.4	35.3	73 06.9	16.0	280 55.0	39.1	249 37.5	02.7			
D 12	290 33.2	339 10.7	S19 34.5	88 08.3	S 7 16.4	295 57.1	S 3 38.9	264 39.9	N 8 02.8	Gacrux	172 13.2	S57 06.1
A 13	305 35.7	354 09.9	33.7	103 09.6	16.8	310 59.1	38.7	279 42.3	02.8	Gienah	176 03.7	S17 32.1
Y 14	320 38.1	9 09.2	32.9	118 11.0	17.2	326 01.2	38.5	294 44.7	02.8	Hadar	149 03.8	S60 21.7
15	335 40.6	24 08.4 ..	32.1	133 12.4 ..	17.6	341 03.3 ..	38.4	309 47.2 ..	02.9	Hamal	328 13.3	N23 27.4
16	350 43.1	39 07.7	31.3	148 13.7	18.0	356 05.4	38.2	324 49.6	02.9	Kaus Aust.	83 59.0	S34 23.0
17	5 45.5	54 06.9	30.5	163 15.1	18.4	11 07.5	38.0	339 52.0	02.9			
18	20 48.0	69 06.2	S19 29.7	178 16.5	S 7 18.8	26 09.5	S 3 37.8	354 54.4	N 8 03.0	Kochab	137 20.2	N74 09.4
19	35 50.5	84 05.4	28.9	193 17.9	19.3	41 11.6	37.7	9 56.8	03.0	Markab	13 49.6	N15 12.0
20	50 52.9	99 04.7	28.1	208 19.2	19.7	56 13.7	37.5	24 59.2	03.0	Menkar	314 26.6	N 4 05.0
21	65 55.4	114 04.0 ..	27.3	223 20.6 ..	20.1	71 15.8 ..	37.3	40 01.6 ..	03.1	Menkent	148 20.8	S36 21.6
22	80 57.8	129 03.2	26.5	238 22.0	20.5	86 17.8	37.1	55 04.0	03.1	Miaplacidus	221 41.1	S69 42.7
23	96 00.3	144 02.5	25.7	253 23.3	20.9	101 19.9	37.0	70 06.4	03.1			
12 00	111 02.8	159 01.7	S19 24.9	268 24.7	S 7 21.3	116 22.0	S 3 36.8	85 08.9	N 8 03.2	Mirfak	308 56.0	N49 51.5
01	126 05.2	174 01.0	24.1	283 26.1	21.7	131 24.1	36.6	100 11.3	03.2	Nunki	76 12.5	S26 17.8
02	141 07.7	189 00.2	23.3	298 27.5	22.1	146 26.1	36.4	115 13.7	03.2	Peacock	53 37.4	S56 44.3
03	156 10.2	203 59.5 ..	22.5	313 28.8 ..	22.5	161 28.2 ..	36.3	130 16.1 ..	03.3	Pollux	243 41.0	N28 01.6
04	171 12.6	218 58.8	21.7	328 30.2	23.0	176 30.3	36.1	145 18.5	03.3	Procyon	245 11.0	N 5 13.5
05	186 15.1	233 58.0	20.9	343 31.6	23.4	191 32.4	35.9	160 20.9	03.3			
06	201 17.6	248 57.3	S19 20.0	358 33.0	S 7 23.8	206 34.4	S 3 35.7	175 23.3	N 8 03.4	Rasalhague	96 17.1	N12 33.7
07	216 20.0	263 56.5	19.2	13 34.3	24.2	221 36.5	35.6	190 25.7	03.4	Regulus	207 55.1	N11 58.2
08	231 22.5	278 55.8	18.4	28 35.7	24.6	236 38.6	35.4	205 28.1	03.4	Rigel	281 22.5	S 8 12.4
T 09	246 24.9	293 55.1 ..	17.6	43 37.1 ..	25.0	251 40.7 ..	35.2	220 30.5 ..	03.5	Rigil Kent.	140 07.2	S60 49.5
U 10	261 27.4	308 54.3	16.8	58 38.4	25.4	266 42.7	35.0	235 33.0	03.5	Sabik	102 25.6	S15 43.3
E 11	276 29.9	323 53.6	16.0	73 39.8	25.8	281 44.8	34.8	250 35.4	03.5			
S 12	291 32.3	338 52.9	S19 15.2	88 41.2	S 7 26.2	296 46.9	S 3 34.7	265 37.8	N 8 03.6	Schedar	349 53.3	N56 32.1
D 13	306 34.8	353 52.1	14.4	103 42.6	26.6	311 49.0	34.5	280 40.2	03.6	Shaula	96 37.4	S37 06.0
A 14	321 37.3	8 51.4	13.5	118 44.0	27.1	326 51.0	34.3	295 42.6	03.6	Sirius	258 43.2	S16 43.0
Y 15	336 39.7	23 50.7 ..	12.7	133 45.3 ..	27.5	341 53.1 ..	34.1	310 45.0 ..	03.7	Spica	158 43.0	S11 09.3
16	351 42.2	38 49.9	11.9	148 46.7	27.9	356 55.2	34.0	325 47.4	03.7	Suhail	223 00.2	S43 25.7
17	6 44.7	53 49.2	11.1	163 48.1	28.3	11 57.2	33.8	340 49.8	03.8			
18	21 47.1	68 48.5	S19 10.3	178 49.5	S 7 28.7	26 59.3	S 3 33.6	355 52.2	N 8 03.8	Vega	80 46.9	N38 47.0
19	36 49.6	83 47.7	09.4	193 50.8	29.1	42 01.4	33.4	10 54.6	03.8	Zuben'ubi	137 17.9	S16 02.1
20	51 52.1	98 47.0	08.6	208 52.2	29.5	57 03.5	33.3	25 57.0	03.9			
21	66 54.5	113 46.3 ..	07.8	223 53.6 ..	29.9	72 05.5 ..	33.1	40 59.4 ..	03.9		SHA	Mer. Pass.
22	81 57.0	128 45.5	07.0	238 55.0	30.3	87 07.6	32.9	56 01.8	03.9	Venus	49 16.0	13 23
23	96 59.4	143 44.8	06.2	253 56.3	30.7	102 09.7	32.7	71 04.3	04.0	Mars	157 48.2	6 08
Mer. Pass. 16 37.0		v −0.7	d 0.8	v 1.4	d 0.4	v 2.1	d 0.2	v 2.4	d 0.0	Jupiter	5 28.5	16 16
										Saturn	334 07.3	18 20

UT	SUN GHA	SUN Dec	MOON GHA	v	MOON Dec	d	HP
d h	° ′	° ′	° ′	′	° ′	′	′
10 00	178 12.4	S22 03.1	265 29.5	15.3	S 4 56.8	9.6	54.4
01	193 12.2	02.7	280 03.8	15.3	5 06.4	9.6	54.3
02	208 11.9	02.4	294 38.1	15.2	5 16.0	9.6	54.3
03	223 11.7 ..	02.0	309 12.3	15.3	5 25.6	9.5	54.3
04	238 11.4	01.7	323 46.6	15.2	5 35.1	9.6	54.3
05	253 11.1	01.3	338 20.8	15.3	5 44.7	9.5	54.3
06	268 10.9	S22 00.9	352 55.1	15.2	S 5 54.2	9.4	54.3
07	283 10.6	00.6	7 29.3	15.2	6 03.6	9.5	54.3
S 08	298 10.4	22 00.2	22 03.5	15.3	6 13.1	9.4	54.3
U 09	313 10.1	21 59.8	36 37.8	15.2	6 22.5	9.4	54.3
N 10	328 09.9	59.5	51 12.0	15.2	6 31.9	9.3	54.3
D 11	343 09.6	59.1	65 46.2	15.1	6 41.2	9.4	54.3
A 12	358 09.4	S21 58.7	80 20.3	15.2	S 6 50.6	9.3	54.2
Y 13	13 09.1	58.4	94 54.5	15.2	6 59.9	9.2	54.2
14	28 08.9	58.0	109 28.7	15.1	7 09.1	9.3	54.2
15	43 08.6 ..	57.6	124 02.8	15.2	7 18.4	9.2	54.2
16	58 08.3	57.2	138 37.0	15.1	7 27.6	9.1	54.2
17	73 08.1	56.9	153 11.1	15.1	7 36.7	9.2	54.2
18	88 07.8	S21 56.5	167 45.2	15.1	S 7 45.9	9.1	54.2
19	103 07.6	56.1	182 19.3	15.0	7 55.0	9.1	54.2
20	118 07.3	55.7	196 53.3	15.1	8 04.1	9.0	54.2
21	133 07.1 ..	55.4	211 27.4	15.0	8 13.1	9.0	54.2
22	148 06.8	55.0	226 01.4	15.0	8 22.1	9.0	54.2
23	163 06.6	54.6	240 35.4	15.0	8 31.1	8.9	54.2
11 00	178 06.3	S21 54.2	255 09.4	15.0	S 8 40.0	8.9	54.2
01	193 06.1	53.8	269 43.4	15.0	8 48.9	8.9	54.2
02	208 05.8	53.5	284 17.4	14.9	8 57.8	8.8	54.2
03	223 05.6 ..	53.1	298 51.3	14.9	9 06.6	8.8	54.2
04	238 05.3	52.7	313 25.2	14.9	9 15.4	8.8	54.2
05	253 05.1	52.3	327 59.1	14.9	9 24.2	8.7	54.2
06	268 04.8	S21 51.9	342 33.0	14.8	S 9 32.9	8.7	54.2
07	283 04.6	51.6	357 06.8	14.8	9 41.6	8.6	54.2
M 08	298 04.3	51.2	11 40.6	14.8	9 50.2	8.6	54.2
O 09	313 04.1 ..	50.8	26 14.4	14.8	9 58.8	8.5	54.2
N 10	328 03.8	50.4	40 48.2	14.7	10 07.3	8.6	54.2
D 11	343 03.6	50.0	55 21.9	14.7	10 15.9	8.4	54.2
A 12	358 03.3	S21 49.6	69 55.6	14.7	S10 24.3	8.5	54.2
Y 13	13 03.1	49.2	84 29.3	14.7	10 32.8	8.4	54.2
14	28 02.8	48.9	99 03.0	14.6	10 41.2	8.3	54.2
15	43 02.6 ..	48.5	113 36.6	14.6	10 49.5	8.3	54.2
16	58 02.3	48.1	128 10.2	14.6	10 57.8	8.3	54.2
17	73 02.1	47.7	142 43.8	14.5	11 06.1	8.2	54.2
18	88 01.8	S21 47.3	157 17.3	14.5	S11 14.3	8.1	54.2
19	103 01.6	46.9	171 50.8	14.5	11 22.4	8.2	54.2
20	118 01.4	46.5	186 24.3	14.4	11 30.6	8.0	54.2
21	133 01.1 ..	46.1	200 57.7	14.4	11 38.6	8.1	54.2
22	148 00.9	45.7	215 31.1	14.4	11 46.7	7.9	54.2
23	163 00.6	45.3	230 04.5	14.3	11 54.6	8.0	54.2
12 00	178 00.4	S21 44.9	244 37.8	14.3	S12 02.6	7.9	54.2
01	193 00.1	44.5	259 11.1	14.3	12 10.5	7.8	54.2
02	207 59.9	44.1	273 44.4	14.2	12 18.3	7.8	54.2
03	222 59.6 ..	43.7	288 17.6	14.2	12 26.1	7.7	54.2
04	237 59.4	43.3	302 50.8	14.2	12 33.8	7.7	54.2
05	252 59.2	42.9	317 24.0	14.1	12 41.5	7.6	54.2
06	267 58.9	S21 42.5	331 57.1	14.1	S12 49.1	7.6	54.2
07	282 58.7	42.1	346 30.2	14.1	12 56.7	7.5	54.2
T 08	297 58.4	41.7	1 03.3	14.0	13 04.2	7.5	54.2
U 09	312 58.2 ..	41.3	15 36.3	14.0	13 11.7	7.4	54.2
E 10	327 57.9	40.9	30 09.3	13.9	13 19.1	7.4	54.2
S 11	342 57.7	40.5	44 42.2	13.9	13 26.5	7.3	54.2
D 12	357 57.4	S21 40.1	59 15.1	13.8	S13 33.8	7.3	54.2
A 13	12 57.2	39.7	73 47.9	13.8	13 41.1	7.2	54.3
Y 14	27 57.0	39.3	88 20.7	13.8	13 48.3	7.1	54.3
15	42 56.7 ..	38.9	102 53.5	13.7	13 55.4	7.1	54.3
16	57 56.5	38.5	117 26.2	13.7	14 02.5	7.0	54.3
17	72 56.2	38.1	131 58.9	13.7	14 09.5	7.0	54.3
18	87 56.0	S21 37.7	146 31.6	13.6	S14 16.5	6.9	54.3
19	102 55.8	37.3	161 04.2	13.6	14 23.4	6.8	54.3
20	117 55.5	36.8	175 36.8	13.5	14 30.2	6.8	54.3
21	132 55.3 ..	36.4	190 09.3	13.4	14 37.0	6.8	54.3
22	147 55.0	36.0	204 41.7	13.5	14 43.8	6.6	54.3
23	162 54.8	35.6	219 14.2	13.4	S14 50.4	6.6	54.3
	SD 16.3	d 0.4	SD 14.8		14.8		14.8

Lat.	Twilight Naut.	Twilight Civil	Sunrise	Moonrise 10	Moonrise 11	Moonrise 12	Moonrise 13
°	h m	h m	h m	h m	h m	h m	h m
N 72	08 10	10 09	■		01 27	03 05	04 47
							06 38
N 70	07 54	09 30	■	01 19	02 50	04 22	05 58
68	07 41	09 03	10 55	01 13	02 38	04 04	05 30
66	07 30	08 42	10 06	01 07	02 28	03 49	05 10
64	07 20	08 25	09 35	01 03	02 20	03 37	04 53
62	07 12	08 12	09 12	00 59	02 13	03 27	04 40
60	07 05	08 00	08 54	00 56	02 07	03 18	04 28
N 58	06 58	07 49	08 39	00 53	02 02	03 11	04 18
56	06 52	07 40	08 26	00 50	01 57	03 04	04 10
54	06 47	07 32	08 14	00 48	01 53	02 58	04 02
52	06 42	07 25	08 05	00 46	01 50	02 53	03 55
50	06 37	07 18	07 56	00 44	01 46	02 48	03 49
45	06 27	07 04	07 37	00 40	01 39	02 37	03 36
N 40	06 18	06 51	07 21	00 37	01 33	02 29	03 25
35	06 09	06 41	07 08	00 34	01 27	02 21	03 16
30	06 01	06 31	06 57	00 31	01 23	02 15	03 07
20	05 46	06 14	06 37	00 27	01 15	02 04	02 53
N 10	05 32	05 58	06 20	00 23	01 08	01 54	02 41
0	05 16	05 42	06 04	00 19	01 02	01 45	02 30
S 10	04 58	05 25	05 48	00 15	00 55	01 36	02 19
20	04 37	05 06	05 30	00 11	00 48	01 26	02 07
30	04 10	04 43	05 10	00 07	00 41	01 15	01 53
35	03 53	04 29	04 58	00 05	00 36	01 09	01 45
40	03 32	04 12	04 44	00 02	00 31	01 02	01 36
45	03 04	03 51	04 27	24 25	00 25	00 54	01 25
S 50	02 24	03 24	04 07	24 18	00 18	00 44	01 13
52	02 02	03 11	03 57	24 15	00 15	00 39	01 07
54	01 31	02 55	03 46	24 12	00 12	00 34	01 01
56	00 26	02 36	03 33	24 08	00 08	00 29	00 53
58	////	02 12	03 19	24 04	00 04	00 23	00 45
S 60	////	01 39	03 01	23 59	24 16	00 16	00 36

Lat.	Sunset	Twilight Civil	Twilight Naut.	Moonset 10	Moonset 11	Moonset 12	Moonset 13
°	h m	h m	h m	h m	h m	h m	h m
N 72	■	14 07	16 06	11 11	11 02	10 50	10 33
N 70	■	14 46	16 22	11 21	11 18	11 16	11 14
68	13 21	15 13	16 36	11 28	11 31	11 35	11 42
66	14 10	15 34	16 46	11 35	11 42	11 51	12 03
64	14 41	15 51	16 56	11 41	11 51	12 03	12 20
62	15 04	16 05	17 04	11 46	11 59	12 14	12 34
60	15 22	16 16	17 11	11 50	12 05	12 24	12 46
N 58	15 37	16 27	17 18	11 54	12 11	12 32	12 57
56	15 50	16 36	17 24	11 57	12 17	12 39	13 06
54	16 01	16 44	17 29	12 00	12 21	12 46	13 14
52	16 11	16 51	17 34	12 03	12 26	12 51	13 21
50	16 20	16 58	17 39	12 05	12 30	12 57	13 28
45	16 39	17 12	17 49	12 11	12 38	13 08	13 42
N 40	16 54	17 24	17 58	12 15	12 45	13 18	13 53
35	17 07	17 35	18 06	12 19	12 51	13 26	14 03
30	17 19	17 45	18 14	12 23	12 57	13 33	14 12
20	17 38	18 02	18 29	12 29	13 06	13 45	14 27
N 10	17 55	18 18	18 44	12 34	13 15	13 56	14 40
0	18 11	18 34	19 00	12 39	13 22	14 06	14 52
S 10	18 28	18 50	19 17	12 44	13 30	14 17	15 05
20	18 45	19 09	19 38	12 50	13 38	14 28	15 18
30	19 06	19 32	20 05	12 56	13 48	14 40	15 33
35	19 17	19 47	20 22	13 00	13 53	14 47	15 42
40	19 31	20 03	20 43	13 04	14 00	14 56	15 52
45	19 48	20 24	21 11	13 08	14 07	15 06	16 04
S 50	20 08	20 50	21 50	13 14	14 16	15 17	16 18
52	20 18	21 04	22 12	13 17	14 20	15 23	16 25
54	20 29	21 19	22 42	13 19	14 24	15 29	16 32
56	20 41	21 38	23 39	13 23	14 29	15 36	16 40
58	20 56	22 01	////	13 26	14 35	15 43	16 50
S 60	21 13	22 34	////	13 30	14 41	15 52	17 01

	SUN			MOON			
Day	Eqn. of Time 00ʰ	Eqn. of Time 12ʰ	Mer. Pass.	Mer. Pass. Upper	Mer. Pass. Lower	Age	Phase
d	m s	m s	h m	h m	h m	d	%
10	07 10	07 22	12 07	06 29	18 50	23	42
11	07 34	07 46	12 08	07 12	19 34	24	33
12	07 58	08 10	12 08	07 56	20 18	25	24

UT	ARIES GHA	VENUS −3.9 GHA	VENUS Dec	MARS +0.8 GHA	MARS Dec	JUPITER −2.2 GHA	JUPITER Dec	SATURN +0.5 GHA	SATURN Dec	STARS Name	SHA	Dec
13 00	112 01.9	158 44.1	S19 05.3	268 57.7	S 7 31.1	117 11.7	S 3 32.6	86 06.7	N 8 04.0	Acamar	315 26.6	S40 18.9
01	127 04.4	173 43.4	04.5	283 59.1	31.5	132 13.8	32.4	101 09.1	04.0	Achernar	335 35.1	S57 14.9
02	142 06.8	188 42.6	03.7	299 00.5	31.9	147 15.9	32.2	116 11.5	04.1	Acrux	173 21.5	S63 05.3
03	157 09.3	203 41.9	.. 02.8	314 01.9	.. 32.3	162 18.0	.. 32.0	131 13.9	.. 04.1	Adhara	255 20.9	S28 58.4
04	172 11.8	218 41.2	02.0	329 03.2	32.8	177 20.0	31.8	146 16.3	04.1	Aldebaran	291 01.9	N16 30.3
05	187 14.2	233 40.5	01.2	344 04.6	33.2	192 22.1	31.7	161 18.7	04.2			
06	202 16.7	248 39.7	S19 00.4	359 06.0	S 7 33.6	207 24.2	S 3 31.5	176 21.1	N 8 04.2	Alioth	166 30.4	N55 57.7
W 07	217 19.2	263 39.0	18 59.5	14 07.4	34.0	222 26.2	31.3	191 23.5	04.2	Alkaid	153 07.8	N49 18.9
E 08	232 21.6	278 38.3	58.7	29 08.8	34.4	237 28.3	31.1	206 25.9	04.3	Al Na'ir	27 58.1	S46 58.1
D 09	247 24.1	293 37.6	.. 57.9	44 10.2	.. 34.8	252 30.4	.. 31.0	221 28.3	.. 04.3	Alnilam	275 57.4	S 1 12.3
N 10	262 26.6	308 36.8	57.0	59 11.5	35.2	267 32.4	30.8	236 30.7	04.3	Alphard	218 06.7	S 8 39.3
E 11	277 29.0	323 36.1	56.2	74 12.9	35.6	282 34.5	30.6	251 33.1	04.4			
S 12	292 31.5	338 35.4	S18 55.3	89 14.3	S 7 36.0	297 36.6	S 3 30.4	266 35.5	N 8 04.4	Alphecca	126 20.7	N26 43.0
D 13	307 33.9	353 34.7	54.5	104 15.7	36.4	312 38.7	30.2	281 37.9	04.5	Alpheratz	357 55.1	N29 05.1
A 14	322 36.4	8 33.9	53.7	119 17.1	36.8	327 40.7	30.1	296 40.3	04.5	Altair	62 19.4	N 8 52.0
Y 15	337 38.9	23 33.2	.. 52.8	134 18.4	.. 37.2	342 42.8	.. 29.9	311 42.7	.. 04.5	Ankaa	353 26.8	S42 19.0
16	352 41.3	38 32.5	52.0	149 19.8	37.6	357 44.9	29.7	326 45.1	04.6	Antares	112 40.2	S26 25.6
17	7 43.8	53 31.8	51.1	164 21.2	38.0	12 46.9	29.5	341 47.5	04.6			
18	22 46.3	68 31.1	S18 50.3	179 22.6	S 7 38.4	27 49.0	S 3 29.3	356 49.9	N 8 04.6	Arcturus	146 06.0	N19 11.2
19	37 48.7	83 30.4	49.5	194 24.0	38.8	42 51.1	29.2	11 52.3	04.7	Atria	107 52.5	S69 01.2
20	52 51.2	98 29.6	48.6	209 25.4	39.2	57 53.1	29.0	26 54.7	04.7	Avior	234 21.9	S59 30.4
21	67 53.7	113 28.9	.. 47.8	224 26.8	.. 39.6	72 55.2	.. 28.8	41 57.1	.. 04.7	Bellatrix	278 43.7	N 6 20.8
22	82 56.1	128 28.2	46.9	239 28.1	40.0	87 57.3	28.6	56 59.6	04.8	Betelgeuse	271 13.0	N 7 24.2
23	97 58.6	143 27.5	46.1	254 29.5	40.4	102 59.3	28.5	72 02.0	04.8			
14 00	113 01.0	158 26.8	S18 45.2	269 30.9	S 7 40.8	118 01.4	S 3 28.3	87 04.4	N 8 04.9	Canopus	264 00.5	S52 41.9
01	128 03.5	173 26.1	44.4	284 32.3	41.2	133 03.5	28.1	102 06.8	04.9	Capella	280 50.5	N45 59.8
02	143 06.0	188 25.3	43.5	299 33.7	41.6	148 05.5	27.9	117 09.2	04.9	Deneb	49 39.5	N45 16.7
03	158 08.4	203 24.6	.. 42.7	314 35.1	.. 42.0	163 07.6	.. 27.7	132 11.6	.. 05.0	Denebola	182 44.9	N14 34.6
04	173 10.9	218 23.9	41.8	329 36.5	42.4	178 09.7	27.6	147 14.0	05.0	Diphda	349 07.1	S17 59.8
05	188 13.4	233 23.2	41.0	344 37.8	42.8	193 11.7	27.4	162 16.4	05.0			
06	203 15.8	248 22.5	S18 40.1	359 39.2	S 7 43.2	208 13.8	S 3 27.2	177 18.8	N 8 05.1	Dubhe	194 05.0	N61 45.1
07	218 18.3	263 21.8	39.3	14 40.6	43.6	223 15.9	27.0	192 21.2	05.1	Elnath	278 26.4	N28 36.3
T 08	233 20.8	278 21.1	38.4	29 42.0	44.0	238 17.9	26.8	207 23.6	05.2	Eltanin	90 51.8	N51 29.3
H 09	248 23.2	293 20.4	.. 37.5	44 43.4	.. 44.4	253 20.0	.. 26.7	222 26.0	.. 05.2	Enif	33 58.3	N 9 52.2
U 10	263 25.7	308 19.7	36.7	59 44.8	44.8	268 22.1	26.5	237 28.4	05.2	Fomalhaut	15 36.5	S29 37.9
R 11	278 28.2	323 19.0	35.8	74 46.2	45.2	283 24.1	26.3	252 30.8	05.3			
S 12	293 30.6	338 18.2	S18 35.0	89 47.6	S 7 45.6	298 26.2	S 3 26.1	267 33.2	N 8 05.3	Gacrux	172 13.1	S57 06.1
D 13	308 33.1	353 17.5	34.1	104 49.0	46.0	313 28.2	25.9	282 35.6	05.3	Gienah	176 03.6	S17 32.1
A 14	323 35.5	8 16.8	33.2	119 50.3	46.4	328 30.3	25.8	297 38.0	05.4	Hadar	149 03.8	S60 21.7
Y 15	338 38.0	23 16.1	.. 32.4	134 51.7	.. 46.8	343 32.4	.. 25.6	312 40.4	.. 05.4	Hamal	328 13.3	N23 27.4
16	353 40.5	38 15.4	31.5	149 53.1	47.2	358 34.4	25.4	327 42.8	05.4	Kaus Aust.	83 59.0	S34 23.0
17	8 42.9	53 14.7	30.7	164 54.5	47.6	13 36.5	25.2	342 45.2	05.5			
18	23 45.4	68 14.0	S18 29.8	179 55.9	S 7 48.0	28 38.6	S 3 25.0	357 47.6	N 8 05.5	Kochab	137 20.2	N74 09.4
19	38 47.9	83 13.3	28.9	194 57.3	48.4	43 40.6	24.9	12 50.0	05.6	Markab	13 49.6	N15 12.0
20	53 50.3	98 12.6	28.1	209 58.7	48.8	58 42.7	24.7	27 52.4	05.6	Menkar	314 26.6	N 4 05.0
21	68 52.8	113 11.9	.. 27.2	225 00.1	.. 49.2	73 44.8	.. 24.5	42 54.8	.. 05.6	Menkent	148 20.8	S36 21.6
22	83 55.3	128 11.2	26.3	240 01.5	49.6	88 46.8	24.3	57 57.2	05.7	Miaplacidus	221 41.0	S69 42.7
23	98 57.7	143 10.5	25.5	255 02.9	50.0	103 48.9	24.1	72 59.6	05.7			
15 00	114 00.2	158 09.8	S18 24.6	270 04.3	S 7 50.4	118 50.9	S 3 23.9	88 02.0	N 8 05.7	Mirfak	308 56.0	N49 51.5
01	129 02.7	173 09.1	23.7	285 05.7	50.8	133 53.0	23.8	103 04.3	05.8	Nunki	76 12.5	S26 17.8
02	144 05.1	188 08.4	22.8	300 07.1	51.2	148 55.1	23.6	118 06.7	05.8	Peacock	53 37.4	S56 44.3
03	159 07.6	203 07.7	.. 22.0	315 08.4	.. 51.6	163 57.1	.. 23.4	133 09.1	.. 05.9	Pollux	243 41.0	N28 01.6
04	174 10.0	218 07.0	21.1	330 09.8	52.0	178 59.2	23.2	148 11.5	05.9	Procyon	245 11.0	N 5 13.5
05	189 12.5	233 06.3	20.2	345 11.2	52.4	194 01.2	23.0	163 13.9	05.9			
06	204 15.0	248 05.6	S18 19.3	0 12.6	S 7 52.8	209 03.3	S 3 22.9	178 16.3	N 8 06.0	Rasalhague	96 17.1	N12 33.7
07	219 17.4	263 04.9	18.5	15 14.0	53.2	224 05.4	22.7	193 18.7	06.0	Regulus	207 55.1	N11 58.2
08	234 19.9	278 04.2	17.6	30 15.4	53.6	239 07.4	22.5	208 21.1	06.1	Rigel	281 22.5	S 8 12.4
F 09	249 22.4	293 03.5	.. 16.7	45 16.8	.. 54.0	254 09.5	.. 22.3	223 23.5	.. 06.1	Rigil Kent.	140 07.2	S60 49.5
R 10	264 24.8	308 02.8	15.8	60 18.2	54.4	269 11.6	22.1	238 25.9	06.1	Sabik	102 25.6	S15 43.3
I 11	279 27.3	323 02.1	14.9	75 19.6	54.8	284 13.6	22.0	253 28.3	06.2			
D 12	294 29.8	338 01.4	S18 14.1	90 21.0	S 7 55.2	299 15.7	S 3 21.8	268 30.7	N 8 06.2	Schedar	349 53.3	N56 32.1
A 13	309 32.2	353 00.7	13.2	105 22.4	55.6	314 17.7	21.6	283 33.1	06.2	Shaula	96 37.4	S37 06.0
Y 14	324 34.7	8 00.0	12.3	120 23.8	56.0	329 19.8	21.4	298 35.5	06.3	Sirius	258 43.2	S16 43.1
15	339 37.2	22 59.3	.. 11.4	135 25.2	.. 56.4	344 21.9	.. 21.2	313 37.9	.. 06.3	Spica	158 43.0	S11 09.3
16	354 39.6	37 58.7	10.5	150 26.6	56.8	359 23.9	21.0	328 40.3	06.4	Suhail	223 00.2	S43 25.7
17	9 42.1	52 58.0	09.6	165 28.0	57.2	14 26.0	20.9	343 42.7	06.4			
18	24 44.5	67 57.3	S18 08.8	180 29.4	S 7 57.6	29 28.0	S 3 20.7	358 45.1	N 8 06.4	Vega	80 46.9	N38 47.0
19	39 47.0	82 56.6	07.9	195 30.8	58.0	44 30.1	20.5	13 47.5	06.5	Zuben'ubi	137 17.9	S16 02.1
20	54 49.5	97 55.9	07.0	210 32.2	58.4	59 32.1	20.3	28 49.9	06.5		SHA	Mer. Pass.
21	69 51.9	112 55.2	.. 06.1	225 33.6	.. 58.7	74 34.2	.. 20.1	43 52.3	.. 06.6			h m
22	84 54.4	127 54.5	05.2	240 35.0	59.1	89 36.3	19.9	58 54.7	06.6	Venus	45 25.7	13 27
23	99 56.9	142 53.8	04.3	255 36.4	59.5	104 38.3	19.8	73 57.1	06.6	Mars	156 29.9	6 01
Mer. Pass. 16 25.2		v −0.7	d 0.9	v 1.4	d 0.4	v 2.1	d 0.2	v 2.4	d 0.0	Jupiter	5 00.3	16 06
										Saturn	334 03.3	18 09

SUN and MOON

UT	SUN GHA	SUN Dec	MOON GHA	v	MOON Dec	d	HP
d h	° ′	° ′	° ′	′	° ′	′	′
13 00	177 54.6	S21 35.2	233 46.6	13.3	S14 57.0	6.6	54.3
01	192 54.3	34.8	248 18.9	13.3	15 03.6	6.5	54.4
02	207 54.1	34.4	262 51.2	13.3	15 10.1	6.4	54.4
03	222 53.8	.. 33.9	277 23.5	13.2	15 16.5	6.3	54.4
04	237 53.6	33.5	291 55.7	13.1	15 22.8	6.3	54.4
05	252 53.4	33.1	306 27.8	13.2	15 29.1	6.2	54.4
06	267 53.1	S21 32.7	321 00.0	13.0	S15 35.3	6.2	54.4
W 07	282 52.9	32.3	335 32.0	13.1	15 41.5	6.1	54.4
E 08	297 52.7	31.9	350 04.1	12.9	15 47.6	6.0	54.4
D 09	312 52.4	.. 31.4	4 36.0	13.0	15 53.6	6.0	54.4
N 10	327 52.2	31.0	19 08.0	12.9	15 59.6	5.8	54.5
E 11	342 51.9	30.6	33 39.9	12.8	16 05.4	5.9	54.5
S 12	357 51.7	S21 30.2	48 11.7	12.8	S16 11.3	5.7	54.5
D 13	12 51.5	29.8	62 43.5	12.8	16 17.0	5.7	54.5
A 14	27 51.2	29.3	77 15.3	12.7	16 22.7	5.6	54.5
Y 15	42 51.0	.. 28.9	91 47.0	12.6	16 28.3	5.5	54.5
16	57 50.8	28.5	106 18.6	12.6	16 33.8	5.5	54.5
17	72 50.5	28.1	120 50.2	12.6	16 39.3	5.4	54.5
18	87 50.3	S21 27.6	135 21.8	12.5	S16 44.7	5.3	54.6
19	102 50.1	27.2	149 53.3	12.5	16 50.0	5.2	54.6
20	117 49.8	26.8	164 24.8	12.4	16 55.2	5.2	54.6
21	132 49.6	.. 26.3	178 56.2	12.3	17 00.4	5.1	54.6
22	147 49.4	25.9	193 27.5	12.4	17 05.5	5.0	54.6
23	162 49.1	25.5	207 58.9	12.2	17 10.5	4.9	54.6
14 00	177 48.9	S21 25.0	222 30.1	12.3	S17 15.4	4.9	54.6
01	192 48.7	24.6	237 01.4	12.1	17 20.3	4.8	54.7
02	207 48.4	24.2	251 32.5	12.2	17 25.1	4.7	54.7
03	222 48.2	.. 23.8	266 03.7	12.1	17 29.8	4.6	54.7
04	237 48.0	23.3	280 34.8	12.0	17 34.4	4.6	54.7
05	252 47.7	22.9	295 05.8	12.0	17 39.0	4.4	54.7
06	267 47.5	S21 22.4	309 36.8	11.9	S17 43.4	4.4	54.7
T 07	282 47.3	22.0	324 07.7	11.9	17 47.8	4.3	54.8
H 08	297 47.0	21.6	338 38.6	11.9	17 52.1	4.2	54.8
U 09	312 46.8	.. 21.1	353 09.5	11.8	17 56.3	4.2	54.8
R 10	327 46.6	20.7	7 40.3	11.7	18 00.5	4.0	54.8
S 11	342 46.4	20.3	22 11.0	11.7	18 04.5	4.0	54.8
D 12	357 46.1	S21 19.8	36 41.7	11.7	S18 08.5	3.9	54.8
A 13	12 45.9	19.4	51 12.4	11.6	18 12.4	3.8	54.9
Y 14	27 45.7	18.9	65 43.0	11.6	18 16.2	3.7	54.9
15	42 45.4	.. 18.5	80 13.6	11.5	18 19.9	3.7	54.9
16	57 45.2	18.1	94 44.1	11.5	18 23.6	3.5	54.9
17	72 45.0	17.6	109 14.6	11.4	18 27.1	3.5	54.9
18	87 44.8	S21 17.2	123 45.0	11.4	S18 30.6	3.4	54.9
19	102 44.5	16.7	138 15.4	11.3	18 34.0	3.3	55.0
20	117 44.3	16.3	152 45.7	11.3	18 37.3	3.2	55.0
21	132 44.1	.. 15.8	167 16.0	11.3	18 40.5	3.1	55.0
22	147 43.8	15.4	181 46.3	11.2	18 43.6	3.0	55.0
23	162 43.6	14.9	196 16.5	11.1	18 46.6	2.9	55.0
15 00	177 43.4	S21 14.5	210 46.6	11.2	S18 49.5	2.9	55.1
01	192 43.2	14.0	225 16.8	11.0	18 52.4	2.7	55.1
02	207 42.9	13.6	239 46.8	11.1	18 55.1	2.7	55.1
03	222 42.7	.. 13.1	254 16.9	11.0	18 57.8	2.6	55.1
04	237 42.5	12.7	268 46.9	10.9	19 00.4	2.4	55.1
05	252 42.3	12.2	283 16.8	10.9	19 02.8	2.4	55.2
06	267 42.0	S21 11.8	297 46.7	10.9	S19 05.2	2.3	55.2
07	282 41.8	11.3	312 16.6	10.8	19 07.5	2.2	55.2
08	297 41.6	10.9	326 46.4	10.8	19 09.7	2.1	55.2
F 09	312 41.4	.. 10.4	341 16.2	10.8	19 11.8	2.0	55.2
R 10	327 41.2	10.0	355 46.0	10.7	19 13.8	1.9	55.3
I 11	342 40.9	09.5	10 15.7	10.6	19 15.7	1.8	55.3
D 12	357 40.7	S21 09.1	24 45.3	10.7	S19 17.5	1.8	55.3
A 13	12 40.5	08.6	39 15.0	10.6	19 19.3	1.6	55.3
Y 14	27 40.3	08.1	53 44.6	10.5	19 20.9	1.5	55.3
15	42 40.0	.. 07.7	68 14.1	10.5	19 22.4	1.4	55.4
16	57 39.8	07.2	82 43.6	10.5	19 23.8	1.4	55.4
17	72 39.6	06.8	97 13.1	10.5	19 25.2	1.2	55.4
18	87 39.4	S21 06.3	111 42.6	10.4	S19 26.4	1.1	55.4
19	102 39.2	05.8	126 12.0	10.4	19 27.5	1.1	55.4
20	117 38.9	05.4	140 41.4	10.3	19 28.6	0.9	55.5
21	132 38.7	.. 04.9	155 10.7	10.3	19 29.5	0.9	55.5
22	147 38.5	04.5	169 40.0	10.3	19 30.4	0.7	55.5
23	162 38.3	04.0	184 09.3	10.2	S19 31.1	0.6	55.5
SD	16.3	d 0.4	SD 14.8		14.9		15.1

Twilight, Sunrise, Moonrise

Lat.	Naut.	Civil	Sunrise	Moonrise 13	14	15	16
°	h m	h m	h m	h m	h m	h m	h m
N 72	08 04	09 57	■	06 38	■	■	■
N 70	07 49	09 22	■	05 58	07 36	09 12	10 22
68	07 36	08 57	10 40	05 30	06 56	08 13	09 13
66	07 26	08 37	09 57	05 10	06 28	07 39	08 37
64	07 17	08 21	09 29	04 53	06 07	07 14	08 11
62	07 09	08 08	09 07	04 40	05 50	06 55	07 51
60	07 02	07 57	08 50	04 28	05 36	06 39	07 34
N 58	06 56	07 47	08 35	04 18	05 24	06 25	07 20
56	06 51	07 38	08 23	04 10	05 14	06 14	07 08
54	06 45	07 30	08 12	04 02	05 04	06 04	06 58
52	06 41	07 23	08 02	03 55	04 56	05 55	06 48
50	06 36	07 17	07 54	03 49	04 49	05 47	06 40
45	06 26	07 03	07 35	03 36	04 33	05 29	06 22
N 40	06 17	06 51	07 21	03 25	04 21	05 15	06 08
35	06 09	06 40	07 08	03 16	04 10	05 04	05 56
30	06 02	06 31	06 57	03 07	04 00	04 53	05 45
20	05 47	06 14	06 38	02 53	03 44	04 35	05 27
N 10	05 33	05 59	06 21	02 41	03 30	04 20	05 11
0	05 17	05 43	06 05	02 30	03 17	04 05	04 56
S 10	05 00	05 27	05 49	02 19	03 04	03 51	04 41
20	04 39	05 08	05 32	02 07	02 50	03 36	04 25
30	04 13	04 45	05 12	01 53	02 34	03 18	04 07
35	03 56	04 32	05 01	01 45	02 24	03 08	03 57
40	03 35	04 15	04 47	01 36	02 14	02 56	03 44
45	03 09	03 55	04 31	01 25	02 01	02 43	03 30
S 50	02 31	03 29	04 11	01 13	01 46	02 26	03 13
52	02 10	03 16	04 02	01 07	01 39	02 18	03 04
54	01 41	03 01	03 51	01 01	01 32	02 09	02 55
56	00 54	02 43	03 39	00 53	01 23	02 00	02 45
58	////	02 21	03 25	00 45	01 13	01 48	02 33
S 60	////	01 50	03 08	00 36	01 02	01 36	02 20

Sunset, Twilight, Moonset

Lat.	Sunset	Civil	Naut.	Moonset 13	14	15	16
°	h m	h m	h m	h m	h m	h m	h m
N 72	■	14 21	16 15	10 33	■	■	■
N 70	■	14 57	16 30	11 14	11 14	11 19	11 56
68	13 39	15 22	16 42	11 42	11 54	12 19	13 05
66	14 21	15 41	16 53	12 03	12 23	12 53	13 41
64	14 50	15 57	17 02	12 20	12 44	13 18	14 07
62	15 11	16 10	17 09	12 34	13 01	13 38	14 27
60	15 29	16 22	17 16	12 46	13 16	13 54	14 43
N 58	15 43	16 32	17 22	12 57	13 28	14 07	14 57
56	15 55	16 40	17 28	13 06	13 39	14 19	15 09
54	16 06	16 48	17 33	13 14	13 48	14 29	15 20
52	16 16	16 55	17 38	13 21	13 56	14 39	15 29
50	16 24	17 02	17 42	13 28	14 04	14 47	15 37
45	16 43	17 16	17 52	13 42	14 20	15 04	15 55
N 40	16 58	17 27	18 01	13 53	14 33	15 18	16 09
35	17 10	17 38	18 09	14 03	14 44	15 30	16 21
30	17 21	17 47	18 17	14 12	14 54	15 41	16 32
20	17 40	18 04	18 31	14 27	15 11	15 59	16 50
N 10	17 57	18 19	18 45	14 40	15 26	16 15	17 06
0	18 13	18 35	19 01	14 52	15 40	16 30	17 21
S 10	18 28	18 51	19 19	15 05	15 54	16 44	17 36
20	18 45	19 10	19 38	15 18	16 09	17 00	17 51
30	19 05	19 32	20 04	15 33	16 26	17 18	18 09
35	19 17	19 46	20 21	15 42	16 36	17 29	18 20
40	19 30	20 02	20 42	15 52	16 47	17 41	18 32
45	19 46	20 22	21 08	16 04	17 00	17 55	18 46
S 50	20 06	20 48	21 46	16 18	17 17	18 12	19 03
52	20 15	21 01	22 06	16 25	17 24	18 21	19 11
54	20 26	21 15	22 34	16 32	17 33	18 30	19 20
56	20 38	21 33	23 18	16 40	17 42	18 40	19 31
58	20 52	21 55	////	16 50	17 53	18 52	19 42
S 60	21 08	22 25	////	17 01	18 06	19 05	19 56

SUN and MOON

Day	Eqn. of Time 00h	12h	Mer. Pass.	Mer. Pass. Upper	Lower	Age	Phase
d	m s	m s	h m	h m	h m	d	%
13	08 21	08 33	12 09	08 41	21 04	26	16
14	08 44	08 55	12 09	09 28	21 53	27	10
15	09 06	09 17	12 09	10 18	22 43	28	5

UT (d h)	ARIES GHA	VENUS −3.9 GHA	Dec	MARS +0.8 GHA	Dec	JUPITER −2.2 GHA	Dec	SATURN +0.5 GHA	Dec	STARS Name	SHA	Dec
16 00	114 59.3	157 53.1	S18 03.4	270 37.8	S 7 59.9	119 40.4	S 3 19.6	88 59.4	N 8 06.7	Acamar	315 26.7	S40 18.9
01	130 01.8	172 52.5	02.5	285 39.2	8 00.3	134 42.4	19.4	104 01.8	06.7	Achernar	335 35.1	S57 14.9
02	145 04.3	187 51.8	01.6	300 40.6	00.7	149 44.5	19.2	119 04.2	06.8	Acrux	173 21.5	S63 05.3
03	160 06.7	202 51.1	18 00.7	315 42.0	.. 01.1	164 46.6	.. 19.0	134 06.6	.. 06.8	Adhara	255 20.9	S28 58.4
04	175 09.2	217 50.4	17 59.8	330 43.4	01.5	179 48.6	18.9	149 09.0	06.8	Aldebaran	291 01.9	N16 30.3
05	190 11.7	232 49.7	59.0	345 44.8	01.9	194 50.7	18.7	164 11.4	06.9			
06	205 14.1	247 49.0	S17 58.1	0 46.2	S 8 02.3	209 52.7	S 3 18.5	179 13.8	N 8 06.9	Alioth	166 30.4	N55 57.7
07	220 16.6	262 48.3	57.2	15 47.6	02.7	224 54.8	18.3	194 16.2	07.0	Alkaid	153 07.7	N49 18.9
08	235 19.0	277 47.7	56.3	30 49.0	03.1	239 56.8	18.1	209 18.6	07.0	Al Na'ir	27 58.1	S46 58.1
09	250 21.5	292 47.0	.. 55.4	45 50.4	.. 03.5	254 58.9	.. 17.9	224 21.0	.. 07.0	Alnilam	275 57.4	S 1 12.4
10	265 24.0	307 46.3	54.5	60 51.8	03.9	270 00.9	17.7	239 23.4	07.1	Alphard	218 06.7	S 8 39.3
11	280 26.4	322 45.6	53.6	75 53.2	04.2	285 03.0	17.6	254 25.8	07.1			
12	295 28.9	337 44.9	S17 52.7	90 54.6	S 8 04.6	300 05.1	S 3 17.4	269 28.2	N 8 07.2	Alphecca	126 20.6	N26 43.0
13	310 31.4	352 44.3	51.8	105 56.0	05.0	315 07.1	17.2	284 30.5	07.2	Alpheratz	357 55.1	N29 05.1
14	325 33.8	7 43.6	50.8	120 57.4	05.4	330 09.2	17.0	299 32.9	07.2	Altair	62 19.4	N 8 52.0
15	340 36.3	22 42.9	.. 49.9	135 58.8	.. 05.8	345 11.2	.. 16.8	314 35.3	.. 07.3	Ankaa	353 26.8	S42 19.0
16	355 38.8	37 42.2	49.0	151 00.2	06.2	0 13.3	16.6	329 37.7	07.3	Antares	112 40.2	S26 25.6
17	10 41.2	52 41.5	48.1	166 01.7	06.6	15 15.3	16.5	344 40.1	07.4			
18	25 43.7	67 40.9	S17 47.2	181 03.1	S 8 07.0	30 17.4	S 3 16.3	359 42.5	N 8 07.4	Arcturus	146 06.0	N19 11.2
19	40 46.1	82 40.2	46.3	196 04.5	07.4	45 19.4	16.1	14 44.9	07.4	Atria	107 52.4	S69 01.2
20	55 48.6	97 39.5	45.4	211 05.9	07.8	60 21.5	15.9	29 47.3	07.5	Avior	234 21.9	S59 30.4
21	70 51.1	112 38.8	.. 44.5	226 07.3	.. 08.1	75 23.6	.. 15.7	44 49.7	.. 07.5	Bellatrix	278 43.7	N 6 20.8
22	85 53.5	127 38.2	43.6	241 08.7	08.5	90 25.6	15.5	59 52.1	07.6	Betelgeuse	271 13.0	N 7 24.2
23	100 56.0	142 37.5	42.7	256 10.1	08.9	105 27.7	15.4	74 54.4	07.6			
17 00	115 58.5	157 36.8	S17 41.8	271 11.5	S 8 09.3	120 29.7	S 3 15.2	89 56.8	N 8 07.7	Canopus	264 00.5	S52 42.0
01	131 00.9	172 36.1	40.8	286 12.9	09.7	135 31.8	15.0	104 59.2	07.7	Capella	280 50.5	N45 59.8
02	146 03.4	187 35.5	39.9	301 14.3	10.1	150 33.8	14.8	120 01.6	07.7	Deneb	49 39.5	N45 16.7
03	161 05.9	202 34.8	.. 39.0	316 15.7	.. 10.5	165 35.9	.. 14.6	135 04.0	.. 07.8	Denebola	182 44.8	N14 34.6
04	176 08.3	217 34.1	38.1	331 17.1	10.9	180 37.9	14.4	150 06.4	07.8	Diphda	349 07.1	S17 59.8
05	191 10.8	232 33.5	37.2	346 18.5	11.3	195 40.0	14.2	165 08.8	07.9			
06	206 13.3	247 32.8	S17 36.3	1 20.0	S 8 11.6	210 42.0	S 3 14.1	180 11.2	N 8 07.9	Dubhe	194 04.9	N61 45.1
07	221 15.7	262 32.1	35.3	16 21.4	12.0	225 44.1	13.9	195 13.6	07.9	Elnath	278 26.4	N28 36.3
08	236 18.2	277 31.4	34.4	31 22.8	12.4	240 46.1	13.7	210 15.9	08.0	Eltanin	90 51.8	N51 29.3
09	251 20.6	292 30.8	.. 33.5	46 24.2	.. 12.8	255 48.2	.. 13.5	225 18.3	.. 08.0	Enif	33 58.3	N 9 52.2
10	266 23.1	307 30.1	32.6	61 25.6	13.2	270 50.2	13.3	240 20.7	08.1	Fomalhaut	15 36.5	S29 37.8
11	281 25.6	322 29.4	31.7	76 27.0	13.6	285 52.3	13.1	255 23.1	08.1			
12	296 28.0	337 28.8	S17 30.7	91 28.4	S 8 14.0	300 54.3	S 3 12.9	270 25.5	N 8 08.2	Gacrux	172 13.1	S57 06.2
13	311 30.5	352 28.1	29.8	106 29.8	14.4	315 56.4	12.8	285 27.9	08.2	Gienah	176 03.6	S17 32.1
14	326 33.0	7 27.4	28.9	121 31.3	14.7	330 58.4	12.6	300 30.3	08.2	Hadar	149 03.7	S60 21.7
15	341 35.4	22 26.8	.. 28.0	136 32.7	.. 15.1	346 00.5	.. 12.4	315 32.7	.. 08.3	Hamal	328 13.3	N23 27.4
16	356 37.9	37 26.1	27.0	151 34.1	15.5	1 02.5	12.2	330 35.0	08.3	Kaus Aust.	83 59.0	S34 23.0
17	11 40.4	52 25.4	26.1	166 35.5	15.9	16 04.6	12.0	345 37.4	08.4			
18	26 42.8	67 24.8	S17 25.2	181 36.9	S 8 16.3	31 06.7	S 3 11.8	0 39.8	N 8 08.4	Kochab	137 20.1	N74 09.4
19	41 45.3	82 24.1	24.3	196 38.3	16.7	46 08.7	11.6	15 42.2	08.4	Markab	13 49.6	N15 12.0
20	56 47.8	97 23.5	23.3	211 39.7	17.0	61 10.8	11.5	30 44.6	08.5	Menkar	314 26.6	N 4 05.0
21	71 50.2	112 22.8	.. 22.4	226 41.2	.. 17.4	76 12.8	.. 11.3	45 47.0	.. 08.5	Menkent	148 20.7	S36 21.6
22	86 52.7	127 22.1	21.5	241 42.6	17.8	91 14.9	11.1	60 49.4	08.6	Miaplacidus	221 41.0	S69 42.7
23	101 55.1	142 21.5	20.5	256 44.0	18.2	106 16.9	10.9	75 51.7	08.6			
18 00	116 57.6	157 20.8	S17 19.6	271 45.4	S 8 18.6	121 18.9	S 3 10.7	90 54.1	N 8 08.7	Mirfak	308 56.1	N49 51.5
01	132 00.1	172 20.2	18.7	286 46.8	19.0	136 21.0	10.5	105 56.5	08.7	Nunki	76 12.5	S26 17.8
02	147 02.5	187 19.5	17.7	301 48.2	19.4	151 23.0	10.3	120 58.9	08.7	Peacock	53 37.4	S56 44.3
03	162 05.0	202 18.8	.. 16.8	316 49.6	.. 19.7	166 25.1	.. 10.2	136 01.3	.. 08.8	Pollux	243 41.0	N28 01.6
04	177 07.5	217 18.2	15.9	331 51.1	20.1	181 27.1	10.0	151 03.7	08.8	Procyon	245 11.0	N 5 13.5
05	192 09.9	232 17.5	14.9	346 52.5	20.5	196 29.2	09.8	166 06.0	08.9			
06	207 12.4	247 16.9	S17 14.0	1 53.9	S 8 20.9	211 31.2	S 3 09.6	181 08.4	N 8 08.9	Rasalhague	96 17.1	N12 33.7
07	222 14.9	262 16.2	13.0	16 55.3	21.3	226 33.3	09.4	196 10.8	09.0	Regulus	207 55.1	N11 58.2
08	237 17.3	277 15.6	12.1	31 56.7	21.7	241 35.3	09.2	211 13.2	09.0	Rigel	281 22.5	S 8 12.4
09	252 19.8	292 14.9	.. 11.2	46 58.2	.. 22.0	256 37.4	.. 09.0	226 15.6	.. 09.0	Rigil Kent.	140 07.1	S60 49.5
10	267 22.3	307 14.2	10.2	61 59.6	22.4	271 39.4	08.8	241 18.0	09.1	Sabik	102 25.6	S15 43.3
11	282 24.7	322 13.6	09.3	77 01.0	22.8	286 41.5	08.7	256 20.3	09.1			
12	297 27.2	337 12.9	S17 08.3	92 02.4	S 8 23.2	301 43.5	S 3 08.5	271 22.7	N 8 09.2	Schedar	349 53.3	N56 32.1
13	312 29.6	352 12.3	07.4	107 03.8	23.6	316 45.6	08.3	286 25.1	09.2	Shaula	96 37.4	S37 06.0
14	327 32.1	7 11.6	06.4	122 05.3	23.9	331 47.6	08.1	301 27.5	09.3	Sirius	258 43.2	S16 43.1
15	342 34.6	22 11.0	.. 05.5	137 06.7	.. 24.3	346 49.7	.. 07.9	316 29.9	.. 09.3	Spica	158 43.0	S11 09.3
16	357 37.0	37 10.3	04.6	152 08.1	24.7	1 51.7	07.7	331 32.3	09.4	Suhail	223 00.2	S43 25.7
17	12 39.5	52 09.7	03.6	167 09.5	25.1	16 53.8	07.5	346 34.6	09.4			
18	27 42.0	67 09.0	S17 02.7	182 10.9	S 8 25.5	31 55.8	S 3 07.3	1 37.0	N 8 09.4	Vega	80 46.9	N38 47.0
19	42 44.4	82 08.4	01.7	197 12.4	25.8	46 57.9	07.2	16 39.4	09.5	Zuben'ubi	137 17.9	S16 02.1
20	57 46.9	97 07.7	17 00.8	212 13.8	26.2	61 59.9	07.0	31 41.8	09.5			
21	72 49.4	112 07.1	16 59.8	227 15.2	.. 26.6	77 01.9	.. 06.8	46 44.2	.. 09.6			
22	87 51.8	127 06.4	58.9	242 16.6	27.0	92 04.0	06.6	61 46.5	09.6			
23	102 54.3	142 05.8	57.9	257 18.1	27.4	107 06.0	06.4	76 48.9	09.7			

	SHA	Mer. Pass.
	° ′	h m
Venus	41 38.3	13 30
Mars	155 13.0	5 55
Jupiter	4 31.2	15 56
Saturn	333 58.4	17 57

Mer. Pass. 16 13.4 | v −0.7　d 0.9 | v 1.4　d 0.4 | v 2.1　d 0.2 | v 2.4　d 0.0

SUN and MOON

UT (d h)	SUN GHA	SUN Dec	MOON GHA	v	MOON Dec	d	HP
16 00	177 38.1	S21 03.5	198 38.5	10.2	S19 31.7	0.6	55.5
01	192 37.8	03.1	213 07.7	10.2	19 32.3	0.4	55.6
02	207 37.6	02.6	227 36.9	10.2	19 32.7	0.3	55.6
03	222 37.4	.. 02.1	242 06.1	10.1	19 33.0	0.3	55.6
04	237 37.2	01.7	256 35.2	10.1	19 33.3	0.1	55.6
05	252 37.0	01.2	271 04.3	10.1	19 33.4	0.0	55.7
06	267 36.7	S21 00.7	285 33.4	10.0	S19 33.4	0.0	55.7
S 07	282 36.5	21 00.2	300 02.4	10.0	19 33.4	0.2	55.7
A 08	297 36.3	20 59.8	314 31.4	10.0	19 33.2	0.3	55.7
T 09	312 36.1	.. 59.3	329 00.4	10.0	19 32.9	0.4	55.7
U 10	327 35.9	58.8	343 29.4	9.9	19 32.5	0.5	55.8
R 11	342 35.7	58.4	357 58.3	9.9	19 32.0	0.5	55.8
D 12	357 35.4	S20 57.9	12 27.2	9.9	S19 31.5	0.7	55.8
A 13	12 35.2	57.4	26 56.1	9.8	19 30.8	0.8	55.8
Y 14	27 35.0	56.9	41 24.9	9.9	19 30.0	0.9	55.9
15	42 34.8	.. 56.5	55 53.8	9.8	19 29.1	1.0	55.9
16	57 34.6	56.0	70 22.6	9.8	19 28.1	1.1	55.9
17	72 34.4	55.5	84 51.4	9.8	19 27.0	1.2	55.9
18	87 34.2	S20 55.0	99 20.2	9.7	S19 25.8	1.4	55.9
19	102 33.9	54.6	113 48.9	9.8	19 24.4	1.4	56.0
20	117 33.7	54.1	128 17.7	9.7	19 23.0	1.5	56.0
21	132 33.5	.. 53.6	142 46.4	9.7	19 21.5	1.6	56.0
22	147 33.3	53.1	157 15.1	9.7	19 19.9	1.8	56.0
23	162 33.1	52.6	171 43.8	9.6	19 18.1	1.8	56.1
17 00	177 32.9	S20 52.2	186 12.4	9.7	S19 16.3	1.9	56.1
01	192 32.7	51.7	200 41.1	9.6	19 14.4	2.1	56.1
02	207 32.5	51.2	215 09.7	9.7	19 12.3	2.1	56.1
03	222 32.2	.. 50.7	229 38.4	9.6	19 10.2	2.3	56.1
04	237 32.0	50.2	244 07.0	9.6	19 07.9	2.4	56.2
05	252 31.8	49.7	258 35.6	9.6	19 05.5	2.4	56.2
06	267 31.6	S20 49.2	273 04.2	9.6	S19 03.1	2.6	56.2
S 07	282 31.4	48.8	287 32.8	9.5	19 00.5	2.7	56.2
U 08	297 31.2	48.3	302 01.3	9.5	18 57.8	2.8	56.3
N 09	312 31.0	.. 47.8	316 29.9	9.5	18 55.0	2.9	56.3
D 10	327 30.8	47.3	330 58.4	9.4	18 52.1	2.9	56.3
A 11	342 30.6	46.8	345 27.0	9.5	18 49.2	3.1	56.3
Y 12	357 30.4	S20 46.3	359 55.5	9.6	S18 46.1	3.2	56.4
13	12 30.1	45.8	14 24.1	9.5	18 42.9	3.3	56.4
14	27 29.9	45.3	28 52.6	9.5	18 39.6	3.5	56.4
15	42 29.7	.. 44.8	43 21.1	9.5	18 36.1	3.5	56.4
16	57 29.5	44.4	57 49.6	9.5	18 32.6	3.6	56.4
17	72 29.3	43.9	72 18.1	9.5	18 29.0	3.7	56.5
18	87 29.1	S20 43.4	86 46.6	9.5	S18 25.3	3.8	56.5
19	102 28.9	42.9	101 15.1	9.5	18 21.5	4.0	56.5
20	117 28.7	42.4	115 43.6	9.5	18 17.5	4.0	56.5
21	132 28.5	.. 41.9	130 12.2	9.5	18 13.5	4.1	56.6
22	147 28.3	41.4	144 40.7	9.5	18 09.4	4.3	56.6
23	162 28.1	40.9	159 09.2	9.5	18 05.1	4.3	56.6
18 00	177 27.9	S20 40.4	173 37.7	9.5	S18 00.8	4.4	56.6
01	192 27.7	39.9	188 06.2	9.5	17 56.4	4.6	56.6
02	207 27.5	39.4	202 34.7	9.5	17 51.8	4.6	56.7
03	222 27.3	.. 38.9	217 03.2	9.5	17 47.2	4.8	56.7
04	237 27.1	38.4	231 31.7	9.5	17 42.4	4.8	56.7
05	252 26.9	37.9	246 00.2	9.6	17 37.6	4.9	56.7
06	267 26.7	S20 37.4	260 28.8	9.5	S17 32.7	5.1	56.8
M 07	282 26.5	36.9	274 57.3	9.6	17 27.6	5.1	56.8
O 08	297 26.2	36.4	289 25.8	9.6	17 22.5	5.3	56.8
N 09	312 26.0	.. 35.9	303 54.4	9.5	17 17.2	5.3	56.8
D 10	327 25.8	35.4	318 22.9	9.6	17 11.9	5.4	56.8
A 11	342 25.6	34.9	332 51.5	9.5	17 06.5	5.6	56.9
Y 12	357 25.4	S20 34.3	347 20.0	9.6	S17 00.9	5.6	56.9
13	12 25.2	33.8	1 48.6	9.6	16 55.3	5.7	56.9
14	27 25.0	33.3	16 17.2	9.6	16 49.6	5.9	56.9
15	42 24.8	.. 32.8	30 45.8	9.6	16 43.7	5.9	57.0
16	57 24.6	32.3	45 14.4	9.6	16 37.8	6.0	57.0
17	72 24.4	31.8	59 43.0	9.6	16 31.8	6.1	57.0
18	87 24.2	S20 31.3	74 11.6	9.7	S16 25.7	6.2	57.0
19	102 24.0	30.8	88 40.3	9.6	16 19.5	6.3	57.0
20	117 23.8	30.3	103 08.9	9.7	16 13.2	6.4	57.1
21	132 23.6	.. 29.8	117 37.6	9.6	16 06.8	6.5	57.1
22	147 23.4	29.3	132 06.3	9.6	16 00.3	6.6	57.1
23	162 23.3	28.7	146 34.9	9.7	S15 53.7	6.7	57.1
	SD 16.3	d 0.5	SD 15.2		15.4		15.5

Twilight, Sunrise, Moonrise

Lat.	Twilight Naut.	Twilight Civil	Sunrise	Moonrise 16	17	18	19
N 72	07 57	09 45	■	■	■	11 38	11 12
N 70	07 43	09 13	11 51	10 22	10 40	10 42	10 41
68	07 31	08 50	10 25	09 13	09 49	10 09	10 19
66	07 21	08 31	09 48	08 37	09 18	09 44	10 01
64	07 13	08 16	09 22	08 11	08 54	09 25	09 47
62	07 06	08 04	09 02	07 51	08 35	09 09	09 35
60	06 59	07 53	08 45	07 34	08 20	08 56	09 24
N 58	06 53	07 44	08 31	07 20	08 07	08 45	09 15
56	06 48	07 35	08 19	07 08	07 55	08 35	09 07
54	06 43	07 28	08 09	06 58	07 45	08 26	09 00
52	06 39	07 21	08 00	06 48	07 36	08 18	08 54
50	06 35	07 15	07 51	06 40	07 28	08 11	08 48
45	06 25	07 01	07 34	06 22	07 12	07 56	08 36
N 40	06 16	06 50	07 19	06 08	06 58	07 43	08 25
35	06 09	06 40	07 07	05 56	06 46	07 33	08 16
30	06 01	06 31	06 56	05 45	06 35	07 23	08 08
20	05 47	06 14	06 38	05 27	06 18	07 07	07 55
N 10	05 33	05 59	06 22	05 11	06 02	06 53	07 43
0	05 18	05 44	06 06	04 56	05 48	06 40	07 32
S 10	05 02	05 28	05 51	04 41	05 33	06 27	07 21
20	04 42	05 10	05 34	04 25	05 18	06 13	07 09
30	04 16	04 48	05 15	04 07	05 00	05 56	06 55
35	04 00	04 35	05 04	03 57	04 50	05 47	06 47
40	03 41	04 19	04 50	03 44	04 38	05 36	06 38
45	03 14	03 59	04 35	03 30	04 24	05 24	06 28
S 50	02 37	03 34	04 17	03 13	04 07	05 08	06 15
52	02 17	03 22	04 07	03 04	03 59	05 01	06 09
54	01 52	03 07	03 56	02 55	03 50	04 53	06 02
56	01 13	02 50	03 45	02 45	03 40	04 44	05 55
58	////	02 29	03 31	02 33	03 28	04 34	05 46
S 60	////	02 02	03 15	02 20	03 15	04 22	05 37

Sunset, Twilight, Moonset

Lat.	Sunset	Twilight Civil	Twilight Naut.	Moonset 16	17	18	19
N 72	■	14 36	16 24	■	■	14 18	16 32
N 70	12 29	15 08	16 38	11 56	13 26	15 12	17 01
68	13 55	15 31	16 50	13 05	14 16	15 45	17 23
66	14 33	15 49	16 59	13 41	14 48	16 09	17 39
64	14 59	16 04	17 08	14 07	15 11	16 28	17 53
62	15 19	16 17	17 15	14 27	15 29	16 43	18 04
60	15 35	16 28	17 21	14 43	15 45	16 56	18 14
N 58	15 49	16 37	17 27	14 57	15 58	17 07	18 23
56	16 01	16 45	17 32	15 09	16 09	17 16	18 30
54	16 11	16 53	17 37	15 20	16 19	17 25	18 37
52	16 21	17 00	17 42	15 29	16 27	17 32	18 42
50	16 29	17 06	17 46	15 37	16 35	17 39	18 48
45	16 46	17 19	17 55	15 55	16 52	17 54	18 59
N 40	17 01	17 31	18 04	16 09	17 05	18 05	19 09
35	17 13	17 41	18 12	16 21	17 17	18 16	19 17
30	17 24	17 50	18 19	16 32	17 27	18 24	19 24
20	17 42	18 06	18 33	16 50	17 44	18 40	19 36
N 10	17 58	18 21	18 47	17 06	17 59	18 53	19 47
0	18 14	18 36	19 01	17 21	18 13	19 05	19 57
S 10	18 29	18 52	19 18	17 36	18 27	19 17	20 06
20	18 46	19 10	19 38	17 51	18 42	19 30	20 17
30	19 05	19 31	20 03	18 09	18 59	19 45	20 29
35	19 16	19 45	20 20	18 20	19 08	19 54	20 36
40	19 29	20 00	20 40	18 32	19 20	20 03	20 43
45	19 44	20 20	21 05	18 46	19 33	20 15	20 52
S 50	20 03	20 45	21 41	19 03	19 49	20 28	21 03
52	20 12	20 57	22 01	19 11	19 56	20 35	21 08
54	20 23	21 11	22 26	19 20	20 05	20 42	21 13
56	20 34	21 28	23 03	19 31	20 14	20 50	21 19
58	20 47	21 49	////	19 42	20 24	20 58	21 26
S 60	21 03	22 15	////	19 56	20 36	21 09	21 34

SUN and MOON

Day	Eqn. of Time 00h	Eqn. of Time 12h	Mer. Pass.	Mer. Pass. Upper	Mer. Pass. Lower	Age	Phase
	m s	m s	h m	h m	h m	d	%
16	09 27	09 38	12 10	11 08	23 34	29	1
17	09 48	09 58	12 10	12 00	24 26	30	0
18	10 08	10 18	12 10	12 52	00 26	01	1

1999 JANUARY 19, 20, 21 (TUES., WED., THURS.)

UT	ARIES GHA	VENUS −3.9 GHA	Dec	MARS +0.7 GHA	Dec	JUPITER −2.2 GHA	Dec	SATURN +0.5 GHA	Dec	STARS Name	SHA	Dec
19 00	117 56.8	157 05.1 S16	57.0	272 19.5 S 8	27.7	122 08.1 S 3	06.2	91 51.3 N 8	09.7	Acamar	315 26.7	S40 18.9
01	132 59.2	172 04.5	56.0	287 20.9	28.1	137 10.1	06.0	106 53.7	09.8	Achernar	335 35.1	S57 14.9
02	148 01.7	187 03.9	55.0	302 22.3	28.5	152 12.2	05.8	121 56.1	09.8	Acrux	173 21.4	S63 05.3
03	163 04.1	202 03.2 ..	54.1	317 23.8 ..	28.9	167 14.2 ..	05.7	136 58.5 ..	09.8	Adhara	255 20.9	S28 58.5
04	178 06.6	217 02.6	53.1	332 25.2	29.3	182 16.3	05.5	152 00.8	09.9	Aldebaran	291 01.9	N16 30.3
05	193 09.1	232 01.9	52.2	347 26.6	29.6	197 18.3	05.3	167 03.2	09.9			
06	208 11.5	247 01.3 S16	51.2	2 28.0 S 8	30.0	212 20.4 S 3	05.1	182 05.6 N 8	10.0	Alioth	166 30.3	N55 57.7
07	223 14.0	262 00.6	50.3	17 29.5	30.4	227 22.4	04.9	197 08.0	10.0	Alkaid	153 07.7	N49 18.9
T 08	238 16.5	277 00.0	49.3	32 30.9	30.8	242 24.4	04.7	212 10.4	10.1	Al Na'ir	27 58.1	S46 58.1
U 09	253 18.9	291 59.4 ..	48.3	47 32.3 ..	31.2	257 26.5 ..	04.5	227 12.7 ..	10.1	Alnilam	275 57.4	S 1 12.4
E 10	268 21.4	306 58.7	47.4	62 33.7	31.5	272 28.5	04.3	242 15.1	10.2	Alphard	218 06.7	S 8 39.3
S 11	283 23.9	321 58.1	46.4	77 35.2	31.9	287 30.6	04.1	257 17.5	10.2			
D 12	298 26.3	336 57.4 S16	45.5	92 36.6 S 8	32.3	302 32.6 S 3	04.0	272 19.9 N 8	10.2	Alphecca	126 20.6	N26 43.0
A 13	313 28.8	351 56.8	44.5	107 38.0	32.7	317 34.7	03.8	287 22.2	10.3	Alpheratz	357 55.2	N29 05.1
Y 14	328 31.2	6 56.2	43.5	122 39.5	33.0	332 36.7	03.6	302 24.6	10.3	Altair	62 19.4	N 8 52.0
15	343 33.7	21 55.5 ..	42.6	137 40.9 ..	33.4	347 38.7 ..	03.4	317 27.0 ..	10.4	Ankaa	353 26.9	S42 19.0
16	358 36.2	36 54.9	41.6	152 42.3	33.8	2 40.8	03.2	332 29.4	10.4	Antares	112 40.1	S26 25.6
17	13 38.6	51 54.2	40.6	167 43.7	34.2	17 42.8	03.0	347 31.8	10.5			
18	28 41.1	66 53.6 S16	39.7	182 45.2 S 8	34.5	32 44.9 S 3	02.8	2 34.1 N 8	10.5	Arcturus	146 05.9	N19 11.2
19	43 43.6	81 53.0	38.7	197 46.6	34.9	47 46.9	02.6	17 36.5	10.6	Atria	107 52.4	S69 01.2
20	58 46.0	96 52.3	37.7	212 48.0	35.3	62 49.0	02.4	32 38.9	10.6	Avior	234 21.8	S59 30.5
21	73 48.5	111 51.7 ..	36.8	227 49.5 ..	35.7	77 51.0 ..	02.3	47 41.3 ..	10.7	Bellatrix	278 43.7	N 6 20.7
22	88 51.0	126 51.1	35.8	242 50.9	36.0	92 53.0	02.1	62 43.6	10.7	Betelgeuse	271 13.0	N 7 24.2
23	103 53.4	141 50.4	34.8	257 52.3	36.4	107 55.1	01.9	77 46.0	10.7			
20 00	118 55.9	156 49.8 S16	33.8	272 53.8 S 8	36.8	122 57.1 S 3	01.7	92 48.4 N 8	10.8	Canopus	264 00.6	S52 42.0
01	133 58.4	171 49.2	32.9	287 55.2	37.2	137 59.2	01.5	107 50.8	10.8	Capella	280 50.5	N45 59.8
02	149 00.8	186 48.5	31.9	302 56.6	37.5	153 01.2	01.3	122 53.1	10.9	Deneb	49 39.5	N45 16.7
03	164 03.3	201 47.9 ..	30.9	317 58.1 ..	37.9	168 03.2 ..	01.1	137 55.5 ..	10.9	Denebola	182 44.8	N14 34.6
04	179 05.7	216 47.3	29.9	332 59.5	38.3	183 05.3	00.9	152 57.9	11.0	Diphda	349 07.2	S17 59.8
05	194 08.2	231 46.7	29.0	348 00.9	38.7	198 07.3	00.7	168 00.3	11.0			
06	209 10.7	246 46.0 S16	28.0	3 02.4 S 8	39.0	213 09.4 S 3	00.5	183 02.7 N 8	11.1	Dubhe	194 04.9	N61 45.1
W 07	224 13.1	261 45.4	27.0	18 03.8	39.4	228 11.4	00.4	198 05.0	11.1	Elnath	278 26.4	N28 36.3
E 08	239 15.6	276 44.8	26.0	33 05.2	39.8	243 13.4	00.2	213 07.4	11.2	Eltanin	90 51.8	N51 29.3
D 09	254 18.1	291 44.1 ..	25.1	48 06.7 ..	40.2	258 15.5 3	00.0	228 09.8 ..	11.2	Enif	33 58.3	N 9 52.2
N 10	269 20.5	306 43.5	24.1	63 08.1	40.5	273 17.5 2	59.8	243 12.2	11.3	Fomalhaut	15 36.5	S29 37.8
E 11	284 23.0	321 42.9	23.1	78 09.5	40.9	288 19.6	59.6	258 14.5	11.3			
S 12	299 25.5	336 42.3 S16	22.1	93 11.0 S 8	41.3	303 21.6 S 2	59.4	273 16.9 N 8	11.3	Gacrux	172 13.1	S57 06.2
D 13	314 27.9	351 41.6	21.1	108 12.4	41.7	318 23.6	59.2	288 19.3	11.4	Gienah	176 03.6	S17 32.1
A 14	329 30.4	6 41.0	20.1	123 13.9	42.0	333 25.7	59.0	303 21.7	11.4	Hadar	149 03.7	S60 21.7
Y 15	344 32.9	21 40.4 ..	19.2	138 15.3 ..	42.4	348 27.7 ..	58.8	318 24.0 ..	11.5	Hamal	328 13.3	N23 27.4
16	359 35.3	36 39.8	18.2	153 16.7	42.8	3 29.8	58.6	333 26.4	11.5	Kaus Aust.	83 58.9	S34 23.0
17	14 37.8	51 39.1	17.2	168 18.2	43.1	18 31.8	58.4	348 28.8	11.6			
18	29 40.2	66 38.5 S16	16.2	183 19.6 S 8	43.5	33 33.8 S 2	58.3	3 31.1 N 8	11.6	Kochab	137 20.0	N74 09.4
19	44 42.7	81 37.9	15.2	198 21.0	43.9	48 35.9	58.1	18 33.5	11.7	Markab	13 49.6	N15 12.0
20	59 45.2	96 37.3	14.2	213 22.5	44.2	63 37.9	57.9	33 35.9	11.7	Menkar	314 26.6	N 4 05.0
21	74 47.6	111 36.7 ..	13.2	228 23.9 ..	44.6	78 39.9 ..	57.7	48 38.3 ..	11.8	Menkent	148 20.7	S36 21.7
22	89 50.1	126 36.0	12.3	243 25.4	45.0	93 42.0	57.5	63 40.6	11.8	Miaplacidus	221 41.0	S69 42.7
23	104 52.6	141 35.4	11.3	258 26.8	45.4	108 44.0	57.3	78 43.0	11.9			
21 00	119 55.0	156 34.8 S16	10.3	273 28.2 S 8	45.7	123 46.1 S 2	57.1	93 45.4 N 8	11.9	Mirfak	308 56.1	N49 51.5
01	134 57.5	171 34.2	09.3	288 29.7	46.1	138 48.1	56.9	108 47.8	12.0	Nunki	76 12.5	S26 17.8
02	150 00.0	186 33.6	08.3	303 31.1	46.5	153 50.1	56.7	123 50.1	12.0	Peacock	53 37.3	S56 44.3
03	165 02.4	201 32.9 ..	07.3	318 32.6 ..	46.8	168 52.2 ..	56.5	138 52.5 ..	12.0	Pollux	243 40.9	N28 01.6
04	180 04.9	216 32.3	06.3	333 34.0	47.2	183 54.2	56.3	153 54.9	12.1	Procyon	245 11.0	N 5 13.5
05	195 07.3	231 31.7	05.3	348 35.5	47.6	198 56.2	56.1	168 57.2	12.1			
06	210 09.8	246 31.1 S16	04.3	3 36.9 S 8	47.9	213 58.3 S 2	56.0	183 59.6 N 8	12.2	Rasalhague	96 17.1	N12 33.7
07	225 12.3	261 30.5	03.3	18 38.3	48.3	229 00.3	55.8	199 02.0	12.2	Regulus	207 55.1	N11 58.2
T 08	240 14.7	276 29.9	02.3	33 39.8	48.7	244 02.3	55.6	214 04.4	12.3	Rigel	281 22.5	S 8 12.4
H 09	255 17.2	291 29.2 ..	01.3	48 41.2 ..	49.1	259 04.4 ..	55.4	229 06.7 ..	12.3	Rigil Kent.	140 07.1	S60 49.5
U 10	270 19.7	306 28.6 16	00.3	63 42.7	49.4	274 06.4	55.2	244 09.1	12.4	Sabik	102 25.6	S15 43.3
R 11	285 22.1	321 28.0 15	59.3	78 44.1	49.8	289 08.5	55.0	259 11.5	12.4			
S 12	300 24.6	336 27.4 S15	58.3	93 45.6 S 8	50.2	304 10.5 S 2	54.8	274 13.8 N 8	12.5	Schedar	349 53.4	N56 32.1
D 13	315 27.1	351 26.8	57.3	108 47.0	50.5	319 12.5	54.6	289 16.2	12.5	Shaula	96 37.4	S37 06.0
A 14	330 29.5	6 26.2	56.3	123 48.5	50.9	334 14.6	54.4	304 18.6	12.6	Sirius	258 43.2	S16 43.1
Y 15	345 32.0	21 25.6 ..	55.3	138 49.9 ..	51.3	349 16.6 ..	54.2	319 20.9 ..	12.6	Spica	158 42.9	S11 09.3
16	0 34.5	36 25.0	54.3	153 51.3	51.6	4 18.6	54.0	334 23.3	12.7	Suhail	223 00.1	S43 25.7
17	15 36.9	51 24.4	53.3	168 52.8	52.0	19 20.7	53.8	349 25.7	12.7			
18	30 39.4	66 23.8 S15	52.3	183 54.2 S 8	52.4	34 22.7 S 2	53.6	4 28.1 N 8	12.8	Vega	80 46.9	N38 47.0
19	45 41.8	81 23.1	51.3	198 55.7	52.7	49 24.7	53.5	19 30.4	12.8	Zuben'ubi	137 17.8	S16 02.1
20	60 44.3	96 22.5	50.3	213 57.1	53.1	64 26.8	53.3	34 32.8	12.9			
21	75 46.8	111 21.9 ..	49.3	228 58.6 ..	53.5	79 28.8 ..	53.1	49 35.2 ..	12.9			
22	90 49.2	126 21.3	48.3	244 00.0	53.8	94 30.8	52.9	64 37.5	13.0			
23	105 51.7	141 20.7	47.3	259 01.5	54.2	109 32.9	52.7	79 39.9	13.0			

	SHA	Mer. Pass.
Venus	37 53.9	13 33
Mars	153 57.9	5 48
Jupiter	4 01.2	15 46
Saturn	333 52.5	17 46

Mer. Pass. 16 01.6 | *v* −0.6 *d* 1.0 | *v* 1.4 *d* 0.4 | *v* 2.0 *d* 0.2 | *v* 2.4 *d* 0.0

UT	SUN GHA	SUN Dec	MOON GHA	v	Dec	d	HP
d h	° ′	° ′	° ′	′	° ′	′	′
19 00	177 23.1	S20 28.2	161 03.6	9.8	S15 47.0	6.7	57.1
01	192 22.9	27.7	175 32.4	9.7	15 40.3	6.9	57.2
02	207 22.7	27.2	190 01.1	9.7	15 33.4	6.9	57.2
03	222 22.5	.. 26.7	204 29.8	9.8	15 26.5	7.1	57.2
04	237 22.3	26.2	218 58.6	9.8	15 19.4	7.1	57.2
05	252 22.1	25.6	233 27.4	9.7	15 12.3	7.2	57.2
06	267 21.9	S20 25.1	247 56.1	9.8	S15 05.1	7.3	57.3
07	282 21.7	24.6	262 24.9	9.9	14 57.8	7.4	57.3
T 08	297 21.5	24.1	276 53.8	9.8	14 50.4	7.5	57.3
U 09	312 21.3	.. 23.6	291 22.6	9.8	14 42.9	7.5	57.3
E 10	327 21.1	23.0	305 51.4	9.9	14 35.4	7.7	57.4
S 11	342 20.9	22.5	320 20.3	9.9	14 27.7	7.7	57.4
D 12	357 20.7	S20 22.0	334 49.2	9.9	S14 20.0	7.8	57.4
A 13	12 20.5	21.5	349 18.1	9.9	14 12.2	7.9	57.4
Y 14	27 20.3	21.0	3 47.0	10.0	14 04.3	8.0	57.4
15	42 20.1	.. 20.4	18 16.0	9.9	13 56.3	8.0	57.5
16	57 19.9	19.9	32 44.9	10.0	13 48.3	8.2	57.5
17	72 19.7	19.4	47 13.9	10.0	13 40.1	8.2	57.5
18	87 19.6	S20 18.8	61 42.9	10.0	S13 31.9	8.3	57.5
19	102 19.4	18.3	76 11.9	10.0	13 23.6	8.4	57.5
20	117 19.2	17.8	90 40.9	10.0	13 15.2	8.4	57.6
21	132 19.0	.. 17.2	105 09.9	10.1	13 06.8	8.5	57.6
22	147 18.8	16.7	119 39.0	10.1	12 58.3	8.6	57.6
23	162 18.6	16.2	134 08.1	10.1	12 49.7	8.7	57.6
20 00	177 18.4	S20 15.7	148 37.2	10.1	S12 41.0	8.8	57.6
01	192 18.2	15.1	163 06.3	10.1	12 32.2	8.8	57.6
02	207 18.0	14.6	177 35.4	10.2	12 23.4	8.9	57.7
03	222 17.8	.. 14.1	192 04.6	10.2	12 14.5	9.0	57.7
04	237 17.7	13.5	206 33.8	10.2	12 05.5	9.0	57.7
05	252 17.5	13.0	221 03.0	10.2	11 56.5	9.1	57.7
06	267 17.3	S20 12.5	235 32.2	10.2	S11 47.4	9.2	57.7
W 07	282 17.1	11.9	250 01.4	10.2	11 38.2	9.3	57.8
E 08	297 16.9	11.4	264 30.6	10.3	11 28.9	9.3	57.8
D 09	312 16.7	.. 10.9	278 59.9	10.3	11 19.6	9.4	57.8
N 10	327 16.5	10.3	293 29.2	10.3	11 10.2	9.4	57.8
E 11	342 16.3	09.8	307 58.5	10.3	11 00.8	9.5	57.8
S 12	357 16.2	S20 09.3	322 27.8	10.3	S10 51.3	9.6	57.9
D 13	12 16.0	08.7	336 57.1	10.3	10 41.7	9.7	57.9
A 14	27 15.8	08.2	351 26.4	10.4	10 32.0	9.7	57.9
Y 15	42 15.6	.. 07.6	5 55.8	10.4	10 22.3	9.7	57.9
16	57 15.4	07.1	20 25.2	10.4	10 12.6	9.9	57.9
17	72 15.2	06.6	34 54.6	10.4	10 02.7	9.9	57.9
18	87 15.1	S20 06.0	49 24.0	10.4	S 9 52.8	9.9	58.0
19	102 14.9	05.5	63 53.4	10.5	9 42.9	10.0	58.0
20	117 14.7	04.9	78 22.9	10.4	9 32.9	10.1	58.0
21	132 14.5	.. 04.4	92 52.3	10.5	9 22.8	10.1	58.0
22	147 14.3	03.8	107 21.8	10.5	9 12.7	10.2	58.0
23	162 14.1	03.3	121 51.3	10.5	9 02.5	10.2	58.0
21 00	177 14.0	S20 02.8	136 20.8	10.5	S 8 52.3	10.3	58.1
01	192 13.8	02.2	150 50.3	10.6	8 42.0	10.3	58.1
02	207 13.6	01.7	165 19.9	10.5	8 31.7	10.4	58.1
03	222 13.4	.. 01.1	179 49.4	10.6	8 21.3	10.4	58.1
04	237 13.2	00.6	194 19.0	10.5	8 10.9	10.5	58.1
05	252 13.1	20 00.0	208 48.5	10.6	8 00.4	10.5	58.1
06	267 12.9	S19 59.5	223 18.1	10.6	S 7 49.9	10.6	58.2
07	282 12.7	58.9	237 47.7	10.6	7 39.3	10.6	58.2
T 08	297 12.5	58.4	252 17.3	10.6	7 28.7	10.7	58.2
H 09	312 12.3	.. 57.8	266 46.9	10.7	7 18.0	10.7	58.2
U 10	327 12.2	57.3	281 16.6	10.6	7 07.3	10.8	58.2
R 11	342 12.0	56.7	295 46.2	10.7	6 56.5	10.8	58.2
S 12	357 11.8	S19 56.1	310 15.9	10.6	S 6 45.7	10.8	58.3
D 13	12 11.6	55.6	324 45.5	10.7	6 34.9	10.9	58.3
A 14	27 11.4	55.0	339 15.2	10.7	6 24.0	10.9	58.3
Y 15	42 11.3	.. 54.5	353 44.9	10.7	6 13.1	11.0	58.3
16	57 11.1	53.9	8 14.6	10.6	6 02.1	11.0	58.3
17	72 10.9	53.4	22 44.2	10.7	5 51.1	11.0	58.3
18	87 10.7	S19 52.8	37 13.9	10.8	S 5 40.1	11.1	58.3
19	102 10.6	52.3	51 43.7	10.7	5 29.0	11.1	58.4
20	117 10.4	51.7	66 13.4	10.7	5 17.9	11.1	58.4
21	132 10.2	.. 51.1	80 43.1	10.7	5 06.8	11.2	58.4
22	147 10.0	50.6	95 12.8	10.7	4 55.6	11.2	58.4
23	162 09.9	50.0	109 42.5	10.8	S 4 44.4	11.2	58.4
SD 16.3	d 0.5		SD 15.6	15.8			15.9

Lat.	Twilight Naut.	Civil	Sunrise	Moonrise 19	20	21	22
°	h m	h m	h m	h m	h m	h m	h m
N 72	07 49	09 32	■	11 12	10 58	10 47	10 38
N 70	07 36	09 04	11 09	10 41	10 39	10 37	10 34
68	07 25	08 42	10 12	10 19	10 25	10 29	10 31
66	07 16	08 25	09 39	10 01	10 13	10 22	10 29
64	07 09	08 11	09 14	09 47	10 03	10 16	10 27
62	07 02	07 59	08 56	09 35	09 54	10 11	10 25
60	06 56	07 49	08 40	09 24	09 47	10 06	10 23
N 58	06 50	07 40	08 27	09 15	09 41	10 02	10 22
56	06 45	07 32	08 16	09 07	09 35	09 59	10 20
54	06 41	07 25	08 06	09 00	09 30	09 55	10 19
52	06 36	07 18	07 57	08 54	09 25	09 52	10 18
50	06 32	07 12	07 49	08 48	09 21	09 50	10 17
45	06 23	06 59	07 32	08 36	09 11	09 44	10 15
N 40	06 15	06 48	07 18	08 25	09 04	09 39	10 13
35	06 08	06 39	07 06	08 16	08 57	09 35	10 12
30	06 01	06 30	06 56	08 08	08 51	09 31	10 10
20	05 47	06 14	06 38	07 55	08 41	09 25	10 08
N 10	05 34	06 00	06 22	07 43	08 32	09 19	10 06
0	05 20	05 45	06 07	07 32	08 23	09 14	10 04
S 10	05 03	05 30	05 52	07 21	08 15	09 09	10 02
20	04 44	05 12	05 36	07 09	08 06	09 03	10 00
30	04 19	04 51	05 18	06 55	07 55	08 56	09 58
35	04 03	04 38	05 07	06 47	07 49	08 53	09 56
40	03 44	04 23	04 54	06 38	07 43	08 48	09 55
45	03 19	04 04	04 39	06 28	07 35	08 43	09 53
S 50	02 44	03 40	04 20	06 15	07 25	08 38	09 51
52	02 26	03 28	04 12	06 09	07 21	08 35	09 50
54	02 02	03 14	04 02	06 02	07 16	08 32	09 49
56	01 28	02 58	03 51	05 55	07 10	08 28	09 48
58	////	02 38	03 38	05 46	07 04	08 25	09 47
S 60	////	02 13	03 23	05 37	06 57	08 21	09 45

Lat.	Sunset	Twilight Civil	Naut.	Moonset 19	20	21	22
°	h m	h m	h m	h m	h m	h m	h m
N 72	■	14 50	16 34	16 32	18 33	20 29	22 23
N 70	13 14	15 19	16 47	17 01	18 50	20 37	22 24
68	14 11	15 41	16 57	17 23	19 03	20 43	22 24
66	14 44	15 58	17 06	17 39	19 13	20 49	22 25
64	15 08	16 12	17 14	17 53	19 22	20 53	22 25
62	15 27	16 24	17 21	18 04	19 30	20 57	22 25
60	15 42	16 34	17 27	18 14	19 36	21 00	22 25
N 58	15 56	16 43	17 32	18 23	19 42	21 03	22 26
56	16 07	16 51	17 37	18 30	19 47	21 06	22 26
54	16 17	16 58	17 42	18 37	19 52	21 08	22 26
52	16 26	17 04	17 46	18 42	19 56	21 10	22 26
50	16 34	17 10	17 50	18 48	19 59	21 12	22 26
45	16 50	17 23	17 59	18 59	20 07	21 17	22 27
N 40	17 04	17 34	18 07	19 09	20 14	21 20	22 27
35	17 16	17 43	18 14	19 17	20 20	21 23	22 27
30	17 26	17 52	18 21	19 24	20 25	21 26	22 27
20	17 44	18 08	18 35	19 36	20 33	21 30	22 28
N 10	18 00	18 22	18 48	19 47	20 41	21 34	22 28
0	18 15	18 37	19 02	19 57	20 48	21 38	22 28
S 10	18 29	18 52	19 18	20 06	20 54	21 41	22 28
20	18 45	19 09	19 38	20 17	21 02	21 45	22 28
30	19 04	19 30	20 02	20 29	21 10	21 50	22 28
35	19 15	19 43	20 18	20 36	21 15	21 52	22 28
40	19 27	19 59	20 37	20 43	21 20	21 55	22 29
45	19 42	20 17	21 02	20 52	21 26	21 58	22 29
S 50	20 01	20 41	21 36	21 03	21 34	22 02	22 29
52	20 09	20 53	21 54	21 08	21 37	22 04	22 29
54	20 19	21 06	22 17	21 13	21 41	22 06	22 29
56	20 30	21 22	22 49	21 19	21 45	22 08	22 29
58	20 43	21 42	////	21 26	21 49	22 11	22 29
S 60	20 57	22 06	////	21 34	21 55	22 13	22 29

	SUN Eqn. of Time 00ʰ	12ʰ	Mer. Pass.	MOON Mer. Pass. Upper	Lower	Age	Phase
Day	m s	m s	h m	h m	h m	d	%
19	10 27	10 37	12 11	13 44	01 18	02	4
20	10 46	10 55	12 11	14 35	02 10	03	9
21	11 04	11 12	12 11	15 26	03 01	04	16

UT	ARIES GHA	VENUS −3.9 GHA	Dec	MARS +0.7 GHA	Dec	JUPITER −2.2 GHA	Dec	SATURN +0.5 GHA	Dec	Name	SHA	Dec
d h	° ′	° ′	° ′	° ′	° ′	° ′	° ′	° ′	° ′		° ′	° ′
22 00	120 54.2	156 20.1	S15 46.3	274 02.9	S 8 54.5	124 34.9	S 2 52.5	94 42.3	N 8 13.1	Acamar	315 26.7	S40 18.9
01	135 56.6	171 19.5	45.3	289 04.4	54.9	139 36.9	52.3	109 44.6	13.1	Achernar	335 35.2	S57 14.9
02	150 59.1	186 18.9	44.2	304 05.8	55.3	154 39.0	52.1	124 47.0	13.2	Acrux	173 21.4	S63 05.3
03	166 01.6	201 18.3 ..	43.2	319 07.3 ..	55.6	169 41.0 ..	51.9	139 49.4 ..	13.2	Adhara	255 20.9	S28 58.5
04	181 04.0	216 17.7	42.2	334 08.7	56.0	184 43.0	51.7	154 51.7	13.3	Aldebaran	291 01.9	N16 30.3
05	196 06.5	231 17.1	41.2	349 10.2	56.4	199 45.1	51.5	169 54.1	13.3			
06	211 08.9	246 16.5	S15 40.2	4 11.6	S 8 56.7	214 47.1	S 2 51.3	184 56.5	N 8 13.4	Alioth	166 30.3	N55 57.7
07	226 11.4	261 15.9	39.2	19 13.1	57.1	229 49.1	51.1	199 58.8	13.4	Alkaid	153 07.7	N49 18.9
08	241 13.9	276 15.3	38.2	34 14.5	57.5	244 51.2	50.9	215 01.2	13.5	Al Na'ir	27 58.1	S46 58.1
F 09	256 16.3	291 14.7 ..	37.1	49 16.0 ..	57.8	259 53.2 ..	50.8	230 03.6 ..	13.5	Alnilam	275 57.4	S 1 12.4
R 10	271 18.8	306 14.1	36.1	64 17.4	58.2	274 55.2	50.6	245 05.9	13.6	Alphard	218 06.7	S 8 39.4
I 11	286 21.3	321 13.5	35.1	79 18.9	58.6	289 57.3	50.4	260 08.3	13.6			
D 12	301 23.7	336 12.9	S15 34.1	94 20.4	S 8 58.9	304 59.3	S 2 50.2	275 10.7	N 8 13.7	Alphecca	126 20.6	N26 43.0
A 13	316 26.2	351 12.3	33.1	109 21.8	59.3	320 01.3	50.0	290 13.0	13.7	Alpheratz	357 55.2	N29 05.1
Y 14	331 28.7	6 11.7	32.1	124 23.3	8 59.6	335 03.4	49.8	305 15.4	13.8	Altair	62 19.4	N 8 52.0
15	346 31.1	21 11.1 ..	31.0	139 24.7	9 00.0	350 05.4 ..	49.6	320 17.8 ..	13.8	Ankaa	353 26.9	S42 19.0
16	1 33.6	36 10.5	30.0	154 26.2	00.4	5 07.4	49.4	335 20.1	13.9	Antares	112 40.1	S26 25.6
17	16 36.1	51 09.9	29.0	169 27.6	00.7	20 09.4	49.2	350 22.5	13.9			
18	31 38.5	66 09.3	S15 28.0	184 29.1	S 9 01.1	35 11.5	S 2 49.0	5 24.9	N 8 14.0	Arcturus	146 05.9	N19 11.2
19	46 41.0	81 08.7	26.9	199 30.5	01.4	50 13.5	48.8	20 27.2	14.0	Atria	107 52.4	S69 01.2
20	61 43.4	96 08.1	25.9	214 32.0	01.8	65 15.5	48.6	35 29.6	14.1	Avior	234 21.8	S59 30.5
21	76 45.9	111 07.5 ..	24.9	229 33.5 ..	02.2	80 17.6 ..	48.4	50 32.0 ..	14.1	Bellatrix	278 43.7	N 6 20.7
22	91 48.4	126 06.9	23.9	244 34.9	02.5	95 19.6	48.2	65 34.3	14.2	Betelgeuse	271 13.0	N 7 24.2
23	106 50.8	141 06.3	22.8	259 36.4	02.9	110 21.6	48.0	80 36.7	14.2			
23 00	121 53.3	156 05.7	S15 21.8	274 37.8	S 9 03.2	125 23.7	S 2 47.8	95 39.1	N 8 14.3	Canopus	264 00.6	S52 42.0
01	136 55.8	171 05.2	20.8	289 39.3	03.6	140 25.7	47.6	110 41.4	14.3	Capella	280 50.5	N45 59.8
02	151 58.2	186 04.6	19.8	304 40.7	04.0	155 27.7	47.4	125 43.8	14.4	Deneb	49 39.5	N45 16.7
03	167 00.7	201 04.0 ..	18.7	319 42.2 ..	04.3	170 29.7 ..	47.3	140 46.2 ..	14.4	Denebola	182 44.8	N14 34.5
04	182 03.2	216 03.4	17.7	334 43.7	04.7	185 31.8	47.1	155 48.5	14.5	Diphda	349 07.2	S17 59.8
05	197 05.6	231 02.8	16.7	349 45.1	05.0	200 33.8	46.9	170 50.9	14.5			
06	212 08.1	246 02.2	S15 15.6	4 46.6	S 9 05.4	215 35.8	S 2 46.7	185 53.2	N 8 14.6	Dubhe	194 04.8	N61 45.1
07	227 10.6	261 01.6	14.6	19 48.0	05.8	230 37.9	46.5	200 55.6	14.6	Elnath	278 26.4	N28 36.3
S 08	242 13.0	276 01.0	13.6	34 49.5	06.1	245 39.9	46.3	215 58.0	14.7	Eltanin	90 51.8	N51 29.3
A 09	257 15.5	291 00.4 ..	12.5	49 51.0 ..	06.5	260 41.9 ..	46.1	231 00.3 ..	14.7	Enif	33 58.3	N 9 52.2
T 10	272 17.9	305 59.9	11.5	64 52.4	06.8	275 43.9	45.9	246 02.7	14.8	Fomalhaut	15 36.5	S29 37.8
U 11	287 20.4	320 59.3	10.5	79 53.9	07.2	290 46.0	45.7	261 05.1	14.8			
R 12	302 22.9	335 58.7	S15 09.4	94 55.4	S 9 07.6	305 48.0	S 2 45.5	276 07.4	N 8 14.9	Gacrux	172 13.0	S57 06.2
D 13	317 25.3	350 58.1	08.4	109 56.8	07.9	320 50.0	45.3	291 09.8	14.9	Gienah	176 03.6	S17 32.1
A 14	332 27.8	5 57.5	07.4	124 58.3	08.3	335 52.0	45.1	306 12.1	15.0	Hadar	149 03.7	S60 21.7
Y 15	347 30.3	20 56.9 ..	06.3	139 59.7 ..	08.6	350 54.1 ..	44.9	321 14.5 ..	15.0	Hamal	328 13.3	N23 27.4
16	2 32.7	35 56.3	05.3	155 01.2	09.0	5 56.1	44.7	336 16.9	15.1	Kaus Aust.	83 58.9	S34 23.0
17	17 35.2	50 55.8	04.3	170 02.7	09.3	20 58.1	44.5	351 19.2	15.1			
18	32 37.7	65 55.2	S15 03.2	185 04.1	S 9 09.7	36 00.2	S 2 44.3	6 21.6	N 8 15.2	Kochab	137 20.0	N74 09.4
19	47 40.1	80 54.6	02.2	200 05.6	10.1	51 02.2	44.1	21 23.9	15.2	Markab	13 49.6	N15 12.0
20	62 42.6	95 54.0	01.1	215 07.1	10.4	66 04.2	43.9	36 26.3	15.3	Menkar	314 26.6	N 4 05.0
21	77 45.0	110 53.4	15 00.1	230 08.5 ..	10.8	81 06.2 ..	43.7	51 28.7 ..	15.3	Menkent	148 20.7	S36 21.7
22	92 47.5	125 52.9	14 59.1	245 10.0	11.1	96 08.3	43.5	66 31.0	15.4	Miaplacidus	221 41.0	S69 42.8
23	107 50.0	140 52.3	58.0	260 11.5	11.5	111 10.3	43.3	81 33.4	15.4			
24 00	122 52.4	155 51.7	S14 57.0	275 12.9	S 9 11.8	126 12.3	S 2 43.1	96 35.7	N 8 15.5	Mirfak	308 56.1	N49 51.5
01	137 54.9	170 51.1	55.9	290 14.4	12.2	141 14.3	42.9	111 38.1	15.5	Nunki	76 12.4	S26 17.8
02	152 57.4	185 50.5	54.9	305 15.9	12.5	156 16.4	42.8	126 40.5	15.6	Peacock	53 37.3	S56 44.3
03	167 59.8	200 50.0 ..	53.8	320 17.3 ..	12.9	171 18.4 ..	42.6	141 42.8 ..	15.6	Pollux	243 40.9	N28 01.6
04	183 02.3	215 49.4	52.8	335 18.8	13.2	186 20.4	42.4	156 45.2	15.7	Procyon	245 11.0	N 5 13.5
05	198 04.8	230 48.8	51.7	350 20.3	13.6	201 22.4	42.2	171 47.5	15.7			
06	213 07.2	245 48.2	S14 50.7	5 21.7	S 9 14.0	216 24.5	S 2 42.0	186 49.9	N 8 15.8	Rasalhague	96 17.0	N12 33.7
07	228 09.7	260 47.7	49.6	20 23.2	14.3	231 26.5	41.8	201 52.3	15.8	Regulus	207 55.0	N11 58.2
08	243 12.2	275 47.1	48.6	35 24.7	14.7	246 28.5	41.6	216 54.6	15.9	Rigel	281 22.5	S 8 12.4
S 09	258 14.6	290 46.5 ..	47.5	50 26.2 ..	15.0	261 30.5 ..	41.4	231 57.0 ..	15.9	Rigil Kent.	140 07.0	S60 49.5
U 10	273 17.1	305 45.9	46.5	65 27.6	15.4	276 32.6	41.2	246 59.3	16.0	Sabik	102 25.5	S15 43.3
N 11	288 19.5	320 45.4	45.4	80 29.1	15.7	291 34.6	41.0	262 01.7	16.0			
D 12	303 22.0	335 44.8	S14 44.4	95 30.6	S 9 16.1	306 36.6	S 2 40.8	277 04.1	N 8 16.1	Schedar	349 53.4	N56 32.1
A 13	318 24.5	350 44.2	43.3	110 32.0	16.4	321 38.6	40.6	292 06.4	16.2	Shaula	96 37.3	S37 06.0
Y 14	333 26.9	5 43.7	42.3	125 33.5	16.8	336 40.7	40.4	307 08.8	16.2	Sirius	258 43.2	S16 43.1
15	348 29.4	20 43.1 ..	41.2	140 35.0 ..	17.1	351 42.7 ..	40.2	322 11.1 ..	16.3	Spica	158 42.9	S11 09.3
16	3 31.9	35 42.5	40.2	155 36.5	17.5	6 44.7	40.0	337 13.5	16.3	Suhail	223 00.1	S43 25.8
17	18 34.3	50 41.9	39.1	170 37.9	17.8	21 46.7	39.8	352 15.8	16.4			
18	33 36.8	65 41.4	S14 38.1	185 39.4	S 9 18.2	36 48.8	S 2 39.6	7 18.2	N 8 16.4	Vega	80 46.9	N38 46.9
19	48 39.3	80 40.8	37.0	200 40.9	18.5	51 50.8	39.4	22 20.6	16.5	Zuben'ubi	137 17.8	S16 02.1
20	63 41.7	95 40.2	35.9	215 42.4	18.9	66 52.8	39.2	37 22.9	16.5		SHA	Mer. Pass.
21	78 44.2	110 39.7 ..	34.9	230 43.8 ..	19.2	81 54.8 ..	39.0	52 25.3 ..	16.6		° ′	h m
22	93 46.7	125 39.1	33.8	245 45.3	19.6	96 56.8	38.8	67 27.6	16.6	Venus	34 12.4	13 36
23	108 49.1	140 38.5	32.8	260 46.8	19.9	111 58.9	38.6	82 30.0	16.7	Mars	152 44.5	5 41
	h m									Jupiter	3 30.4	15 36
Mer. Pass. 15 49.8		v −0.6	d 1.0	v 1.5	d 0.4	v 2.0	d 0.2	v 2.4	d 0.1	Saturn	333 45.8	17 35

UT	SUN GHA	SUN Dec	MOON GHA	v	MOON Dec	d	HP
d h	° '	° '	° '	'	° '	'	'
22 00	177 09.7	S19 49.4	124 12.3	10.7	S 4 33.2	11.3	58.4
01	192 09.5	48.9	138 42.0	10.7	4 21.9	11.3	58.5
02	207 09.3	48.3	153 11.7	10.8	4 10.6	11.3	58.5
03	222 09.2 ..	47.8	167 41.5	10.7	3 59.3	11.3	58.5
04	237 09.0	47.2	182 11.2	10.8	3 48.0	11.4	58.5
05	252 08.8	46.6	196 41.0	10.7	3 36.6	11.4	58.5
06	267 08.7	S19 46.1	211 10.7	10.8	S 3 25.2	11.4	58.5
07	282 08.5	45.5	225 40.5	10.7	3 13.8	11.4	58.5
08	297 08.3	44.9	240 10.2	10.7	3 02.4	11.5	58.5
F 09	312 08.1 ..	44.4	254 39.9	10.8	2 50.9	11.4	58.6
R 10	327 08.0	43.8	269 09.7	10.7	2 39.5	11.5	58.6
I 11	342 07.8	43.2	283 39.4	10.8	2 28.0	11.6	58.6
D 12	357 07.6	S19 42.7	298 09.2	10.7	S 2 16.4	11.5	58.6
A 13	12 07.5	42.1	312 38.9	10.7	2 04.9	11.5	58.6
Y 14	27 07.3	41.5	327 08.6	10.7	1 53.4	11.6	58.6
15	42 07.1 ..	40.9	341 38.3	10.8	1 41.8	11.6	58.6
16	57 07.0	40.4	356 08.1	10.7	1 30.2	11.5	58.7
17	72 06.8	39.8	10 37.8	10.7	1 18.7	11.6	58.7
18	87 06.6	S19 39.2	25 07.5	10.7	S 1 07.1	11.6	58.7
19	102 06.5	38.7	39 37.2	10.6	0 55.5	11.7	58.7
20	117 06.3	38.1	54 06.8	10.7	0 43.8	11.6	58.7
21	132 06.1 ..	37.5	68 36.5	10.7	0 32.2	11.6	58.7
22	147 06.0	36.9	83 06.2	10.6	0 20.6	11.7	58.7
23	162 05.8	36.4	97 35.8	10.7	S 0 08.9	11.6	58.7
23 00	177 05.6	S19 35.8	112 05.5	10.6	N 0 02.7	11.6	58.8
01	192 05.5	35.2	126 35.1	10.6	0 14.3	11.7	58.8
02	207 05.3	34.6	141 04.7	10.6	0 26.0	11.6	58.8
03	222 05.1 ..	34.0	155 34.3	10.6	0 37.6	11.7	58.8
04	237 05.0	33.5	170 03.9	10.6	0 49.3	11.6	58.8
05	252 04.8	32.9	184 33.5	10.6	1 00.9	11.7	58.8
06	267 04.6	S19 32.3	199 03.1	10.5	N 1 12.6	11.6	58.8
S 07	282 04.5	31.7	213 32.6	10.6	1 24.2	11.7	58.8
A 08	297 04.3	31.1	228 02.2	10.5	1 35.9	11.6	58.8
T 09	312 04.2 ..	30.6	242 31.7	10.5	1 47.5	11.6	58.9
U 10	327 04.0	30.0	257 01.2	10.5	1 59.1	11.7	58.9
R 11	342 03.8	29.4	271 30.7	10.4	2 10.8	11.6	58.9
D 12	357 03.7	S19 28.8	286 00.1	10.5	N 2 22.4	11.6	58.9
A 13	12 03.5	28.2	300 29.6	10.4	2 34.0	11.6	58.9
Y 14	27 03.3	27.6	314 59.0	10.4	2 45.6	11.6	58.9
15	42 03.2 ..	27.0	329 28.4	10.3	2 57.2	11.5	58.9
16	57 03.0	26.5	343 57.7	10.4	3 08.7	11.6	58.9
17	72 02.9	25.9	358 27.1	10.3	3 20.3	11.5	58.9
18	87 02.7	S19 25.3	12 56.4	10.3	N 3 31.8	11.6	59.0
19	102 02.5	24.7	27 25.7	10.3	3 43.4	11.5	59.0
20	117 02.4	24.1	41 55.0	10.3	3 54.9	11.5	59.0
21	132 02.2 ..	23.5	56 24.3	10.2	4 06.4	11.4	59.0
22	147 02.1	22.9	70 53.5	10.2	4 17.8	11.5	59.0
23	162 01.9	22.3	85 22.7	10.2	4 29.3	11.4	59.0
24 00	177 01.8	S19 21.7	99 51.9	10.1	N 4 40.7	11.4	59.0
01	192 01.6	21.2	114 21.0	10.1	4 52.1	11.3	59.0
02	207 01.4	20.6	128 50.1	10.1	5 03.5	11.4	59.0
03	222 01.3 ..	20.0	143 19.2	10.1	5 14.9	11.3	59.0
04	237 01.1	19.4	157 48.3	10.0	5 26.2	11.3	59.1
05	252 01.0	18.8	172 17.3	10.0	5 37.5	11.3	59.1
06	267 00.8	S19 18.2	186 46.3	10.0	N 5 48.8	11.2	59.1
07	282 00.7	17.6	201 15.3	9.9	6 00.0	11.2	59.1
08	297 00.5	17.0	215 44.2	9.9	6 11.2	11.2	59.1
S 09	312 00.4 ..	16.4	230 13.1	9.9	6 22.4	11.2	59.1
U 10	327 00.2	15.8	244 42.0	9.8	6 33.6	11.1	59.1
N 11	342 00.1	15.2	259 10.8	9.8	6 44.7	11.1	59.1
D 12	356 59.9	S19 14.6	273 39.6	9.8	N 6 55.8	11.0	59.1
A 13	11 59.7	14.0	288 08.4	9.7	7 06.8	11.0	59.1
Y 14	26 59.6	13.4	302 37.1	9.7	7 17.8	11.0	59.1
15	41 59.4 ..	12.8	317 05.8	9.6	7 28.8	10.9	59.1
16	56 59.3	12.2	331 34.4	9.6	7 39.7	10.9	59.2
17	71 59.1	11.6	346 03.0	9.6	7 50.6	10.8	59.2
18	86 59.0	S19 11.0	0 31.6	9.5	N 8 01.4	10.8	59.2
19	101 58.8	10.4	15 00.1	9.5	8 12.2	10.8	59.2
20	116 58.7	09.8	29 28.6	9.5	8 23.0	10.7	59.2
21	131 58.5 ..	09.2	43 57.1	9.4	8 33.7	10.6	59.2
22	146 58.4	08.6	58 25.5	9.4	8 44.3	10.7	59.2
23	161 58.2	08.0	72 53.9	9.3	N 8 55.0	10.5	59.2
	SD 16.3	d 0.6	SD 16.0		16.0		16.1

Lat.	Twilight Naut.	Twilight Civil	Sunrise	Moonrise 22	23	24	25
°	h m	h m	h m	h m	h m	h m	h m
N 72	07 40	09 20	■■■	10 38	10 29	10 20	10 10
N 70	07 29	08 54	10 44	10 34	10 32	10 29	10 27
68	07 19	08 34	09 58	10 31	10 34	10 37	10 41
66	07 11	08 18	09 29	10 29	10 36	10 43	10 52
64	07 03	08 05	09 07	10 27	10 37	10 48	11 02
62	06 57	07 54	08 49	10 25	10 39	10 53	11 10
60	06 52	07 44	08 34	10 23	10 40	10 57	11 17
N 58	06 47	07 36	08 22	10 22	10 41	11 01	11 23
56	06 42	07 28	08 11	10 20	10 42	11 04	11 29
54	06 38	07 21	08 02	10 19	10 43	11 07	11 34
52	06 34	07 15	07 53	10 18	10 43	11 10	11 38
50	06 30	07 10	07 46	10 17	10 44	11 12	11 42
45	06 22	06 57	07 29	10 15	10 46	11 17	11 51
N 40	06 14	06 47	07 16	10 13	10 47	11 22	11 59
35	06 07	06 38	07 05	10 12	10 48	11 26	12 05
30	06 00	06 29	06 55	10 10	10 49	11 29	12 11
20	05 47	06 14	06 38	10 08	10 51	11 35	12 21
N 10	05 35	06 00	06 22	10 06	10 53	11 40	12 30
0	05 21	05 46	06 08	10 04	10 54	11 45	12 38
S 10	05 05	05 31	05 54	10 02	10 56	11 51	12 46
20	04 46	05 14	05 38	10 00	10 58	11 56	12 55
30	04 22	04 54	05 20	09 58	11 00	12 02	13 06
35	04 07	04 41	05 10	09 56	11 01	12 06	13 12
40	03 48	04 27	04 57	09 55	11 02	12 10	13 18
45	03 24	04 08	04 43	09 53	11 04	12 15	13 26
S 50	02 51	03 45	04 25	09 51	11 06	12 21	13 36
52	02 34	03 34	04 17	09 50	11 06	12 23	13 41
54	02 12	03 21	04 08	09 49	11 07	12 26	13 46
56	01 43	03 06	03 57	09 48	11 08	12 30	13 51
58	00 50	02 47	03 45	09 47	11 10	12 33	13 57
S 60	////	02 24	03 31	09 45	11 11	12 37	14 04

Lat.	Sunset	Twilight Civil	Twilight Naut.	Moonset 22	23	24	25
°	h m	h m	h m	h m	h m	h m	h m
N 72	■■■	15 05	16 44	22 23	24 18	00 18	02 17
N 70	13 41	15 31	16 56	22 24	24 12	00 12	02 02
68	14 26	15 51	17 06	22 24	24 06	00 06	01 49
66	14 56	16 06	17 14	22 25	24 02	00 02	01 40
64	15 18	16 19	17 21	22 25	23 58	25 31	01 31
62	15 35	16 31	17 27	22 25	23 54	25 24	01 24
60	15 50	16 40	17 33	22 25	23 51	25 18	01 18
N 58	16 02	16 49	17 38	22 26	23 49	25 13	01 13
56	16 13	16 56	17 42	22 26	23 47	25 08	01 08
54	16 22	17 03	17 46	22 26	23 45	25 04	01 04
52	16 31	17 09	17 50	22 26	23 43	25 00	01 00
50	16 38	17 14	17 54	22 26	23 41	24 56	00 56
45	16 54	17 27	18 02	22 27	23 37	24 49	00 49
N 40	17 08	17 37	18 10	22 27	23 34	24 43	00 43
35	17 19	17 46	18 17	22 27	23 32	24 37	00 37
30	17 29	17 54	18 24	22 27	23 29	24 32	00 32
20	17 46	18 09	18 36	22 28	23 25	24 24	00 24
N 10	18 01	18 23	18 49	22 28	23 22	24 17	00 17
0	18 15	18 37	19 03	22 28	23 19	24 10	00 10
S 10	18 30	18 52	19 18	22 28	23 15	24 04	00 04
20	18 45	19 09	19 37	22 28	23 12	23 56	24 44
30	19 03	19 29	20 01	22 28	23 08	23 48	24 32
35	19 13	19 42	20 16	22 29	23 05	23 44	24 25
40	19 25	19 56	20 35	22 29	23 03	23 38	24 17
45	19 40	20 14	20 58	22 29	23 00	23 32	24 08
S 50	19 57	20 37	21 31	22 29	22 56	23 25	23 57
52	20 05	20 48	21 48	22 29	22 54	23 21	23 52
54	20 15	21 01	22 09	22 29	22 53	23 18	23 46
56	20 25	21 16	22 37	22 29	22 51	23 14	23 40
58	20 37	21 34	23 24	22 29	22 48	23 09	23 33
S 60	20 51	21 57	////	22 29	22 46	23 04	23 26

	SUN Eqn. of Time 00h	SUN Eqn. of Time 12h	SUN Mer. Pass.	MOON Mer. Pass. Upper	MOON Mer. Pass. Lower	Age	Phase
Day	m s	m s	h m	h m	h m	d	%
22	11 21	11 29	12 11	16 16	03 51	05	25
23	11 37	11 45	12 12	17 06	04 41	06	36
24	11 53	12 00	12 12	17 58	05 32	07	47

1999 JANUARY 25, 26, 27 (MON., TUES., WED.)

UT (d h)	ARIES GHA	VENUS −3.9 GHA	VENUS Dec	MARS +0.6 GHA	MARS Dec	JUPITER −2.2 GHA	JUPITER Dec	SATURN +0.5 GHA	SATURN Dec	Star Name	SHA	Dec
25 00	123 51.6	155 38.0	S14 31.7	275 48.3	S 9 20.3	127 00.9	S 2 38.4	97 32.3	N 8 16.7	Acamar	315 26.7	S40 18.9
01	138 54.0	170 37.4	30.6	290 49.7	20.6	142 02.9	38.2	112 34.7	16.8	Achernar	335 35.2	S57 14.9
02	153 56.5	185 36.8	29.6	305 51.2	21.0	157 04.9	38.0	127 37.1	16.8	Acrux	173 21.3	S63 05.3
03	168 59.0	200 36.3 ..	28.5	320 52.7 ..	21.3	172 07.0 ..	37.8	142 39.4 ..	16.9	Adhara	255 20.9	S28 58.5
04	184 01.4	215 35.7	27.5	335 54.2	21.7	187 09.0	37.6	157 41.8	16.9	Aldebaran	291 01.9	N16 30.3
05	199 03.9	230 35.2	26.4	350 55.7	22.0	202 11.0	37.4	172 44.1	17.0			
06	214 06.4	245 34.6	S14 25.3	5 57.1	S 9 22.4	217 13.0	S 2 37.2	187 46.5	N 8 17.1	Alioth	166 30.3	N55 57.7
07	229 08.8	260 34.0	24.3	20 58.6	22.7	232 15.0	37.0	202 48.8	17.1	Alkaid	153 07.6	N49 18.9
08	244 11.3	275 33.5	23.2	36 00.1	23.1	247 17.1	36.8	217 51.2	17.2	Al Na'ir	27 58.1	S46 58.1
M 09	259 13.8	290 32.9 ..	22.1	51 01.6 ..	23.4	262 19.1 ..	36.6	232 53.5 ..	17.2	Alnilam	275 57.4	S 1 12.4
O 10	274 16.2	305 32.3	21.1	66 03.0	23.8	277 21.1	36.4	247 55.9	17.3	Alphard	218 06.7	S 8 39.4
N 11	289 18.7	320 31.8	20.0	81 04.5	24.1	292 23.1	36.2	262 58.2	17.3			
D 12	304 21.1	335 31.2	S14 18.9	96 06.0	S 9 24.5	307 25.1	S 2 36.0	278 00.6	N 8 17.4	Alphecca	126 20.6	N26 43.0
A 13	319 23.6	350 30.7	17.9	111 07.5	24.8	322 27.2	35.8	293 03.0	17.4	Alpheratz	357 55.2	N29 05.1
Y 14	334 26.1	5 30.1	16.8	126 09.0	25.2	337 29.2	35.6	308 05.3	17.5	Altair	62 19.4	N 8 51.9
15	349 28.5	20 29.6 ..	15.7	141 10.5 ..	25.5	352 31.2 ..	35.4	323 07.7 ..	17.5	Ankaa	353 26.9	S42 19.0
16	4 31.0	35 29.0	14.6	156 11.9	25.9	7 33.2	35.2	338 10.0	17.6	Antares	112 40.1	S26 25.6
17	19 33.5	50 28.4	13.6	171 13.4	26.2	22 35.2	35.0	353 12.4	17.6			
18	34 35.9	65 27.9	S14 12.5	186 14.9	S 9 26.6	37 37.3	S 2 34.8	8 14.7	N 8 17.7	Arcturus	146 05.9	N19 11.2
19	49 38.4	80 27.3	11.4	201 16.4	26.9	52 39.3	34.6	23 17.1	17.8	Atria	107 52.3	S69 01.2
20	64 40.9	95 26.8	10.4	216 17.9	27.3	67 41.3	34.4	38 19.4	17.8	Avior	234 21.8	S59 30.5
21	79 43.3	110 26.2 ..	09.3	231 19.4 ..	27.6	82 43.3 ..	34.2	53 21.8 ..	17.9	Bellatrix	278 43.7	N 6 20.7
22	94 45.8	125 25.7	08.2	246 20.8	27.9	97 45.3	34.0	68 24.1	17.9	Betelgeuse	271 13.1	N 7 24.2
23	109 48.3	140 25.1	07.1	261 22.3	28.3	112 47.4	33.8	83 26.5	18.0			
26 00	124 50.7	155 24.6	S14 06.1	276 23.8	S 9 28.6	127 49.4	S 2 33.6	98 28.8	N 8 18.0	Canopus	264 00.6	S52 42.0
01	139 53.2	170 24.0	05.0	291 25.3	29.0	142 51.4	33.4	113 31.2	18.1	Capella	280 50.5	N45 59.8
02	154 55.6	185 23.5	03.9	306 26.8	29.3	157 53.4	33.2	128 33.5	18.1	Deneb	49 39.5	N45 16.6
03	169 58.1	200 22.9 ..	02.8	321 28.3 ..	29.7	172 55.4 ..	33.0	143 35.9 ..	18.2	Denebola	182 44.8	N14 34.5
04	185 00.6	215 22.4	01.7	336 29.8	30.0	187 57.4	32.8	158 38.2	18.2	Diphda	349 07.2	S17 59.8
05	200 03.0	230 21.8	14 00.7	351 31.2	30.4	202 59.5	32.6	173 40.6	18.3			
06	215 05.5	245 21.3	S13 59.6	6 32.7	S 9 30.7	218 01.5	S 2 32.4	188 42.9	N 8 18.4	Dubhe	194 04.8	N61 45.1
07	230 08.0	260 20.7	58.5	21 34.2	31.0	233 03.5	32.2	203 45.3	18.4	Elnath	278 26.4	N28 36.3
08	245 10.4	275 20.2	57.4	36 35.7	31.4	248 05.5	32.0	218 47.6	18.5	Eltanin	90 51.7	N51 29.3
T 09	260 12.9	290 19.6 ..	56.3	51 37.2 ..	31.7	263 07.5 ..	31.8	233 50.0 ..	18.5	Enif	33 58.3	N 9 52.2
U 10	275 15.4	305 19.1	55.3	66 38.7	32.1	278 09.5	31.6	248 52.3	18.6	Fomalhaut	15 36.5	S29 37.8
E 11	290 17.8	320 18.5	54.2	81 40.2	32.4	293 11.6	31.4	263 54.7	18.6			
S 12	305 20.3	335 18.0	S13 53.1	96 41.7	S 9 32.8	308 13.6	S 2 31.2	278 57.0	N 8 18.7	Gacrux	172 13.0	S57 06.2
D 13	320 22.8	350 17.4	52.0	111 43.2	33.1	323 15.6	31.0	293 59.4	18.7	Gienah	176 03.6	S17 32.1
A 14	335 25.2	5 16.9	50.9	126 44.7	33.5	338 17.6	30.8	309 01.7	18.8	Hadar	149 03.6	S60 21.7
Y 15	350 27.7	20 16.3 ..	49.8	141 46.1 ..	33.8	353 19.6 ..	30.6	324 04.1 ..	18.9	Hamal	328 13.3	N23 27.4
16	5 30.1	35 15.8	48.7	156 47.6	34.1	8 21.6	30.4	339 06.4	18.9	Kaus Aust.	83 58.9	S34 23.0
17	20 32.6	50 15.2	47.7	171 49.1	34.5	23 23.7	30.2	354 08.8	19.0			
18	35 35.1	65 14.7	S13 46.6	186 50.6	S 9 34.8	38 25.7	S 2 30.0	9 11.1	N 8 19.0	Kochab	137 19.9	N74 09.3
19	50 37.5	80 14.2	45.5	201 52.1	35.2	53 27.7	29.8	24 13.5	19.1	Markab	13 49.6	N15 12.0
20	65 40.0	95 13.6	44.4	216 53.6	35.5	68 29.7	29.6	39 15.8	19.1	Menkar	314 26.6	N 4 05.0
21	80 42.5	110 13.1 ..	43.3	231 55.1 ..	35.8	83 31.7	29.4	54 18.2 ..	19.2	Menkent	148 20.7	S36 21.7
22	95 44.9	125 12.5	42.2	246 56.6	36.2	98 33.7	29.2	69 20.5	19.2	Miaplacidus	221 41.0	S69 42.8
23	110 47.4	140 12.0	41.1	261 58.1	36.5	113 35.8	29.0	84 22.9	19.3			
27 00	125 49.9	155 11.5	S13 40.0	276 59.6	S 9 36.9	128 37.8	S 2 28.8	99 25.2	N 8 19.4	Mirfak	308 56.1	N49 51.5
01	140 52.3	170 10.9	38.9	292 01.1	37.2	143 39.8	28.6	114 27.6	19.4	Nunki	76 12.4	S26 17.8
02	155 54.8	185 10.4	37.8	307 02.6	37.5	158 41.8	28.4	129 29.9	19.5	Peacock	53 37.3	S56 44.3
03	170 57.2	200 09.8 ..	36.7	322 04.1 ..	37.9	173 43.8 ..	28.2	144 32.3 ..	19.5	Pollux	243 40.9	N28 01.6
04	185 59.7	215 09.3	35.6	337 05.6	38.2	188 45.8	28.0	159 34.6	19.6	Procyon	245 11.0	N 5 13.5
05	201 02.2	230 08.8	34.6	352 07.1	38.6	203 47.8	27.8	174 37.0	19.6			
06	216 04.6	245 08.2	S13 33.5	7 08.6	S 9 38.9	218 49.9	S 2 27.6	189 39.3	N 8 19.7	Rasalhague	96 17.0	N12 33.6
W 07	231 07.1	260 07.7	32.4	22 10.1	39.2	233 51.9	27.4	204 41.7	19.8	Regulus	207 55.0	N11 58.2
E 08	246 09.6	275 07.2	31.3	37 11.6	39.6	248 53.9	27.2	219 44.0	19.8	Rigel	281 22.5	S 8 12.4
D 09	261 12.0	290 06.6 ..	30.2	52 13.1 ..	39.9	263 55.9 ..	27.0	234 46.4 ..	19.9	Rigil Kent.	140 07.0	S60 49.5
N 10	276 14.5	305 06.1	29.1	67 14.6	40.3	278 57.9	26.8	249 48.7	19.9	Sabik	102 25.5	S15 43.3
E 11	291 17.0	320 05.6	28.0	82 16.1	40.6	293 59.9	26.6	264 51.1	20.0			
S 12	306 19.4	335 05.0	S13 26.9	97 17.6	S 9 40.9	309 01.9	S 2 26.4	279 53.4	N 8 20.0	Schedar	349 53.4	N56 32.1
D 13	321 21.9	350 04.5	25.8	112 19.1	41.3	324 04.0	26.2	294 55.7	20.1	Shaula	96 37.3	S37 06.0
A 14	336 24.4	5 04.0	24.7	127 20.6	41.6	339 06.0	26.0	309 58.1	20.2	Sirius	258 43.2	S16 43.1
Y 15	351 26.8	20 03.4 ..	23.6	142 22.1 ..	41.9	354 08.0 ..	25.8	325 00.4 ..	20.2	Spica	158 42.9	S11 09.3
16	6 29.3	35 02.9	22.5	157 23.6	42.3	9 10.0	25.6	340 02.8	20.3	Suhail	223 00.1	S43 25.8
17	21 31.7	50 02.4	21.4	172 25.1	42.6	24 12.0	25.4	355 05.1	20.3			
18	36 34.2	65 01.8	S13 20.3	187 26.6	S 9 43.0	39 14.0	S 2 25.2	10 07.5	N 8 20.4	Vega	80 46.9	N38 46.9
19	51 36.7	80 01.3	19.2	202 28.1	43.3	54 16.0	25.0	25 09.8	20.4	Zuben'ubi	137 17.8	S16 02.1
20	66 39.1	95 00.8	18.1	217 29.6	43.6	69 18.0	24.8	40 12.2	20.5		SHA	Mer. Pass.
21	81 41.6	110 00.2 ..	16.9	232 31.1 ..	44.0	84 20.1 ..	24.6	55 14.5 ..	20.5	Venus	30 33.8	13 39
22	96 44.1	124 59.7	15.8	247 32.6	44.3	99 22.1	24.4	70 16.9	20.6	Mars	151 33.1	5 34
23	111 46.5	139 59.2	14.7	262 34.1	44.6	114 24.1	24.2	85 19.2	20.7	Jupiter	2 58.7	15 27
Mer. Pass. 15 38.1		v −0.5	d 1.1	v 1.5	d 0.3	v 2.0	d 0.2	v 2.4	d 0.1	Saturn	333 38.1	17 23

UT	SUN GHA	SUN Dec	MOON GHA	v	MOON Dec	d	HP
d h	° ′	° ′	° ′	′	° ′	′	′
25 00	176 58.1	S19 07.4	87 22.2	9.3	N 9 05.5	10.5	59.2
01	191 57.9	06.7	101 50.5	9.3	9 16.0	10.5	59.2
02	206 57.8	06.1	116 18.8	9.2	9 26.5	10.4	59.2
03	221 57.6	.. 05.5	130 47.0	9.1	9 36.9	10.4	59.2
04	236 57.5	04.9	145 15.1	9.2	9 47.3	10.3	59.2
05	251 57.4	04.3	159 43.3	9.0	9 57.6	10.2	59.2
06	266 57.2	S19 03.7	174 11.3	9.1	N10 07.8	10.2	59.3
07	281 57.1	03.1	188 39.4	9.0	10 18.0	10.1	59.3
08	296 56.9	02.5	203 07.4	8.9	10 28.1	10.1	59.3
M 09	311 56.8	.. 01.9	217 35.3	8.9	10 38.2	10.0	59.3
O 10	326 56.6	01.3	232 03.2	8.9	10 48.2	10.0	59.3
N 11	341 56.5	00.6	246 31.1	8.8	10 58.2	9.8	59.3
D 12	356 56.3	S19 00.0	260 58.9	8.7	N11 08.0	9.9	59.3
A 13	11 56.2	18 59.4	275 26.6	8.7	11 17.9	9.7	59.3
Y 14	26 56.0	58.8	289 54.3	8.7	11 27.6	9.7	59.3
15	41 55.9	.. 58.2	304 22.0	8.6	11 37.3	9.6	59.3
16	56 55.8	57.6	318 49.6	8.6	11 46.9	9.6	59.3
17	71 55.6	56.9	333 17.2	8.5	11 56.5	9.5	59.3
18	86 55.5	S18 56.3	347 44.7	8.5	N12 06.0	9.4	59.3
19	101 55.3	55.7	2 12.2	8.4	12 15.4	9.3	59.3
20	116 55.2	55.1	16 39.6	8.4	12 24.7	9.3	59.3
21	131 55.0	.. 54.5	31 07.0	8.3	12 34.0	9.2	59.3
22	146 54.9	53.9	45 34.3	8.3	12 43.2	9.1	59.3
23	161 54.8	53.2	60 01.6	8.3	12 52.3	9.0	59.3
26 00	176 54.6	S18 52.6	74 28.9	8.2	N13 01.3	9.0	59.3
01	191 54.5	52.0	88 56.1	8.1	13 10.3	8.9	59.3
02	206 54.3	51.4	103 23.2	8.1	13 19.2	8.8	59.3
03	221 54.2	.. 50.7	117 50.3	8.0	13 28.0	8.7	59.4
04	236 54.1	50.1	132 17.3	8.0	13 36.7	8.6	59.4
05	251 53.9	49.5	146 44.3	8.0	13 45.3	8.6	59.4
06	266 53.8	S18 48.9	161 11.3	7.9	N13 53.9	8.4	59.4
07	281 53.7	48.2	175 38.2	7.8	14 02.3	8.4	59.4
08	296 53.5	47.6	190 05.0	7.8	14 10.7	8.3	59.4
T 09	311 53.4	.. 47.0	204 31.8	7.8	14 19.0	8.2	59.4
U 10	326 53.2	46.4	218 58.6	7.7	14 27.2	8.2	59.4
E 11	341 53.1	45.7	233 25.3	7.6	14 35.4	8.0	59.4
S 12	356 53.0	S18 45.1	247 51.9	7.6	N14 43.4	7.9	59.4
D 13	11 52.8	44.5	262 18.5	7.6	14 51.3	7.9	59.4
A 14	26 52.7	43.9	276 45.1	7.5	14 59.2	7.7	59.4
Y 15	41 52.6	.. 43.2	291 11.6	7.5	15 06.9	7.7	59.4
16	56 52.4	42.6	305 38.1	7.4	15 14.6	7.6	59.4
17	71 52.3	42.0	320 04.5	7.4	15 22.2	7.4	59.4
18	86 52.2	S18 41.3	334 30.9	7.3	N15 29.6	7.4	59.4
19	101 52.0	40.7	348 57.2	7.3	15 37.0	7.3	59.4
20	116 51.9	40.1	3 23.5	7.2	15 44.3	7.2	59.4
21	131 51.8	.. 39.4	17 49.7	7.2	15 51.5	7.0	59.4
22	146 51.6	38.8	32 15.9	7.1	15 58.5	7.0	59.4
23	161 51.5	38.2	46 42.0	7.2	16 05.5	6.9	59.4
27 00	176 51.4	S18 37.5	61 08.2	7.0	N16 12.4	6.8	59.4
01	191 51.2	36.9	75 34.2	7.0	16 19.2	6.6	59.4
02	206 51.1	36.3	90 00.2	7.0	16 25.8	6.6	59.4
03	221 51.0	.. 35.6	104 26.2	6.9	16 32.4	6.4	59.4
04	236 50.8	35.0	118 52.1	6.9	16 38.8	6.4	59.4
05	251 50.7	34.3	133 18.0	6.9	16 45.2	6.2	59.4
06	266 50.6	S18 33.7	147 43.9	6.8	N16 51.4	6.2	59.4
W 07	281 50.5	33.1	162 09.7	6.7	16 57.6	6.0	59.4
E 08	296 50.3	32.4	176 35.4	6.8	17 03.6	5.9	59.4
D 09	311 50.2	.. 31.8	191 01.2	6.7	17 09.5	5.8	59.4
N 10	326 50.1	31.1	205 26.9	6.6	17 15.3	5.7	59.4
E 11	341 49.9	30.5	219 52.5	6.6	17 21.0	5.6	59.4
S 12	356 49.8	S18 29.9	234 18.1	6.6	N17 26.6	5.5	59.4
D 13	11 49.7	29.2	248 43.7	6.5	17 32.1	5.3	59.4
A 14	26 49.6	28.6	263 09.2	6.5	17 37.4	5.3	59.4
Y 15	41 49.4	.. 27.9	277 34.7	6.5	17 42.7	5.1	59.4
16	56 49.3	27.3	292 00.2	6.5	17 47.8	5.0	59.3
17	71 49.2	26.6	306 25.7	6.4	17 52.8	4.9	59.3
18	86 49.1	S18 26.0	320 51.1	6.3	N17 57.7	4.8	59.3
19	101 48.9	25.3	335 16.4	6.4	18 02.5	4.6	59.3
20	116 48.8	24.7	349 41.8	6.3	18 07.1	4.6	59.3
21	131 48.7	.. 24.0	4 07.1	6.3	18 11.7	4.4	59.3
22	146 48.6	23.4	18 32.4	6.3	18 16.1	4.3	59.3
23	161 48.4	22.8	32 57.7	6.2	N18 20.4	4.2	59.3
	SD 16.3	d 0.6	SD 16.2		16.2		16.2

Twilight / Sunrise / Moonrise

Lat.	Twilight Naut.	Twilight Civil	Sunrise	Moonrise 25	26	27	28
°	h m	h m	h m	h m	h m	h m	h m
N 72	07 31	09 07	11 50	10 10	09 57	09 34	☐
N 70	07 21	08 43	10 23	10 27	10 26	10 27	10 36
68	07 12	08 25	09 45	10 41	10 48	11 01	11 25
66	07 04	08 11	09 19	10 52	11 05	11 25	11 57
64	06 58	07 58	08 58	11 02	11 19	11 44	12 20
62	06 52	07 48	08 42	11 10	11 31	12 00	12 39
60	06 47	07 39	08 28	11 17	11 41	12 13	12 54
N 58	06 42	07 31	08 17	11 23	11 50	12 24	13 08
56	06 38	07 24	08 06	11 29	11 58	12 34	13 19
54	06 34	07 18	07 57	11 34	12 05	12 43	13 29
52	06 31	07 12	07 49	11 38	12 11	12 51	13 38
50	06 27	07 07	07 42	11 42	12 17	12 58	13 46
45	06 19	06 55	07 27	11 51	12 29	13 13	14 03
N 40	06 12	06 45	07 14	11 59	12 40	13 25	14 17
35	06 06	06 36	07 03	12 05	12 48	13 36	14 29
30	05 59	06 28	06 54	12 11	12 56	13 45	14 39
20	05 47	06 14	06 37	12 21	13 10	14 02	14 57
N 10	05 35	06 00	06 23	12 30	13 21	14 16	15 12
0	05 22	05 47	06 09	12 38	13 33	14 29	15 27
S 10	05 07	05 33	05 55	12 46	13 44	14 43	15 42
20	04 49	05 16	05 40	12 55	13 56	14 57	15 58
30	04 25	04 57	05 23	13 06	14 10	15 13	16 16
35	04 11	04 45	05 13	13 12	14 18	15 23	16 26
40	03 53	04 30	05 01	13 18	14 27	15 34	16 38
45	03 30	04 13	04 47	13 26	14 38	15 47	16 53
S 50	02 59	03 51	04 30	13 36	14 51	16 03	17 10
52	02 42	03 40	04 22	13 41	14 57	16 11	17 18
54	02 16	03 28	04 14	13 46	15 04	16 19	17 28
56	01 56	03 14	04 04	13 51	15 11	16 28	17 38
58	01 16	02 56	03 52	13 57	15 20	16 39	17 50
S 60	////	02 35	03 39	14 04	15 30	16 51	18 04

Sunset / Twilight / Moonset

Lat.	Sunset	Twilight Civil	Twilight Naut.	Moonset 25	26	27	28
°	h m	h m	h m	h m	h m	h m	h m
N 72	12 36	15 19	16 55	02 17	04 22	06 43	☐
N 70	14 03	15 43	17 06	02 02	03 55	05 50	07 43
68	14 41	16 01	17 14	01 49	03 34	05 18	06 54
66	15 07	16 15	17 22	01 40	03 18	04 55	06 22
64	15 27	16 27	17 28	01 31	03 05	04 36	05 59
62	15 44	16 38	17 34	01 24	02 54	04 21	05 41
60	15 57	16 47	17 39	01 18	02 44	04 08	05 26
N 58	16 09	16 55	17 43	01 13	02 36	03 57	05 13
56	16 19	17 02	17 47	01 08	02 29	03 48	05 02
54	16 28	17 08	17 51	01 04	02 23	03 40	04 52
52	16 36	17 14	17 55	01 00	02 17	03 32	04 43
50	16 43	17 19	17 58	00 56	02 12	03 25	04 35
45	16 59	17 30	18 06	00 49	02 00	03 11	04 19
N 40	17 11	17 40	18 13	00 43	01 51	02 59	04 05
35	17 22	17 49	18 20	00 37	01 43	02 49	03 53
30	17 32	17 57	18 26	00 32	01 36	02 40	03 43
20	17 48	18 11	18 38	00 24	01 24	02 25	03 26
N 10	18 02	18 25	18 50	00 17	01 14	02 12	03 11
0	18 16	18 38	19 03	00 10	01 04	01 59	02 57
S 10	18 30	18 52	19 18	00 04	00 54	01 47	02 43
20	18 45	19 08	19 36	24 44	00 44	01 34	02 27
30	19 02	19 28	19 59	24 32	00 32	01 19	02 10
35	19 12	19 40	20 14	24 25	00 25	01 10	02 00
40	19 23	19 54	20 32	24 17	00 17	01 00	01 48
45	19 37	20 11	20 54	24 08	00 08	00 48	01 35
S 50	19 54	20 33	21 25	23 57	24 34	00 34	01 18
52	20 01	20 43	21 41	23 52	24 28	00 28	01 11
54	20 10	20 55	22 00	23 46	24 20	00 20	01 02
56	20 20	21 10	22 25	23 40	24 12	00 12	00 52
58	20 31	21 26	23 03	23 33	24 03	00 03	00 42
S 60	20 45	21 47	////	23 26	23 53	24 29	00 29

	SUN			MOON			
Day	Eqn. of Time 00ʰ	12ʰ	Mer. Pass.	Mer. Pass. Upper	Lower	Age	Phase
d	m s	m s	h m	h m	h m	d	%
25	12 07	12 14	12 12	18 51	06 24	08	58
26	12 21	12 28	12 12	19 46	07 18	09	69
27	12 34	12 40	12 13	20 43	08 14	10	79

UT	ARIES GHA	VENUS −3.9 GHA	Dec	MARS +0.6 GHA	Dec	JUPITER −2.2 GHA	Dec	SATURN +0.5 GHA	Dec	STARS Name	SHA	Dec
28 00	126 49.0	154 58.7	S13 13.6	277 35.6	S 9 45.0	129 26.1	S 2 24.0	100 21.5	N 8 20.7	Acamar	315 26.7	S40 18.9
01	141 51.5	169 58.1	12.5	292 37.1	45.3	144 28.1	23.8	115 23.9	20.8	Achernar	335 35.2	S57 14.9
02	156 53.9	184 57.6	11.4	307 38.6	45.6	159 30.1	23.6	130 26.2	20.8	Acrux	173 21.3	S63 05.4
03	171 56.4	199 57.1	.. 10.3	322 40.1	.. 46.0	174 32.1	.. 23.4	145 28.6	.. 20.9	Adhara	255 20.9	S28 58.5
04	186 58.9	214 56.5	09.2	337 41.6	46.3	189 34.1	23.2	160 30.9	21.0	Aldebaran	291 01.9	N16 30.3
05	202 01.3	229 56.0	08.1	352 43.1	46.6	204 36.1	23.0	175 33.3	21.0			
06	217 03.8	244 55.5	S13 07.0	7 44.6	S 9 47.0	219 38.2	S 2 22.8	190 35.6	N 8 21.1	Alioth	166 30.2	N55 57.7
T 07	232 06.2	259 55.0	05.9	22 46.1	47.3	234 40.2	22.6	205 37.9	21.1	Alkaid	153 07.6	N49 18.9
H 08	247 08.7	274 54.5	04.8	37 47.7	47.6	249 42.2	22.4	220 40.3	21.2	Al Na'ir	27 58.1	S46 58.1
U 09	262 11.2	289 53.9	.. 03.6	52 49.2	.. 48.0	264 44.2	.. 22.2	235 42.6	.. 21.2	Alnilam	275 57.4	S 1 12.4
R 10	277 13.6	304 53.4	02.5	67 50.7	48.3	279 46.2	22.0	250 45.0	21.3	Alphard	218 06.7	S 8 39.4
S 11	292 16.1	319 52.9	01.4	82 52.2	48.6	294 48.2	21.8	265 47.3	21.4			
D 12	307 18.6	334 52.4	S13 00.3	97 53.7	S 9 49.0	309 50.2	S 2 21.6	280 49.7	N 8 21.4	Alphecca	126 20.5	N26 43.0
A 13	322 21.0	349 51.8	12 59.2	112 55.2	49.3	324 52.2	21.4	295 52.0	21.5	Alpheratz	357 55.2	N29 05.1
Y 14	337 23.5	4 51.3	58.1	127 56.7	49.6	339 54.2	21.2	310 54.3	21.5	Altair	62 19.4	N 8 51.9
15	352 26.0	19 50.8	.. 57.0	142 58.2	.. 50.0	354 56.2	.. 21.0	325 56.7	.. 21.6	Ankaa	353 26.9	S42 19.0
16	7 28.4	34 50.3	55.8	157 59.7	50.3	9 58.3	20.8	340 59.0	21.6	Antares	112 40.1	S26 25.6
17	22 30.9	49 49.8	54.7	173 01.3	50.6	25 00.3	20.6	356 01.4	21.7			
18	37 33.4	64 49.2	S12 53.6	188 02.8	S 9 51.0	40 02.3	S 2 20.4	11 03.7	N 8 21.8	Arcturus	146 05.9	N19 11.2
19	52 35.8	79 48.7	52.5	203 04.3	51.3	55 04.3	20.1	26 06.1	21.8	Atria	107 52.2	S69 01.2
20	67 38.3	94 48.2	51.4	218 05.8	51.6	70 06.3	19.9	41 08.4	21.9	Avior	234 21.8	S59 30.5
21	82 40.7	109 47.7	.. 50.2	233 07.3	.. 52.0	85 08.3	.. 19.7	56 10.7	.. 21.9	Bellatrix	278 43.7	N 6 20.7
22	97 43.2	124 47.2	49.1	248 08.8	52.3	100 10.3	19.5	71 13.1	22.0	Betelgeuse	271 13.1	N 7 24.2
23	112 45.7	139 46.7	48.0	263 10.3	52.6	115 12.3	19.3	86 15.4	22.1			
29 00	127 48.1	154 46.1	S12 46.9	278 11.9	S 9 52.9	130 14.3	S 2 19.1	101 17.8	N 8 22.1	Canopus	264 00.6	S52 42.0
01	142 50.6	169 45.6	45.8	293 13.4	53.3	145 16.3	18.9	116 20.1	22.2	Capella	280 50.5	N45 59.8
02	157 53.1	184 45.1	44.6	308 14.9	53.6	160 18.3	18.7	131 22.4	22.2	Deneb	49 39.5	N45 16.6
03	172 55.5	199 44.6	.. 43.5	323 16.4	.. 53.9	175 20.3	.. 18.5	146 24.8	.. 22.3	Denebola	182 44.8	N14 34.5
04	187 58.0	214 44.1	42.4	338 17.9	54.3	190 22.4	18.3	161 27.1	22.4	Diphda	349 07.2	S17 59.8
05	203 00.5	229 43.6	41.3	353 19.4	54.6	205 24.4	18.1	176 29.5	22.4			
06	218 02.9	244 43.1	S12 40.1	8 21.0	S 9 54.9	220 26.4	S 2 17.9	191 31.8	N 8 22.5	Dubhe	194 04.8	N61 45.2
07	233 05.4	259 42.6	39.0	23 22.5	55.2	235 28.4	17.7	206 34.1	22.5	Elnath	278 26.4	N28 36.3
08	248 07.9	274 42.0	37.9	38 24.0	55.6	250 30.4	17.5	221 36.5	22.6	Eltanin	90 51.7	N51 29.3
F 09	263 10.3	289 41.5	.. 36.8	53 25.5	.. 55.9	265 32.4	.. 17.3	236 38.8	.. 22.7	Enif	33 58.3	N 9 52.2
R 10	278 12.8	304 41.0	35.6	68 27.0	56.2	280 34.4	17.1	251 41.1	22.7	Fomalhaut	15 36.5	S29 37.8
I 11	293 15.2	319 40.5	34.5	83 28.5	56.6	295 36.4	16.9	266 43.5	22.8			
D 12	308 17.7	334 40.0	S12 33.4	98 30.1	S 9 56.9	310 38.4	S 2 16.7	281 45.8	N 8 22.8	Gacrux	172 13.0	S57 06.2
A 13	323 20.2	349 39.5	32.3	113 31.6	57.2	325 40.4	16.5	296 48.2	22.9	Gienah	176 03.5	S17 32.1
Y 14	338 22.6	4 39.0	31.1	128 33.1	57.5	340 42.4	16.3	311 50.5	22.9	Hadar	149 03.6	S60 21.8
15	353 25.1	19 38.5	.. 30.0	143 34.6	.. 57.9	355 44.4	.. 16.1	326 52.8	.. 23.0	Hamal	328 13.3	N23 27.4
16	8 27.6	34 38.0	28.9	158 36.2	58.2	10 46.4	15.9	341 55.2	23.1	Kaus Aust.	83 58.9	S34 23.0
17	23 30.0	49 37.5	27.7	173 37.7	58.5	25 48.4	15.7	356 57.5	23.1			
18	38 32.5	64 37.0	S12 26.6	188 39.2	S 9 58.8	40 50.4	S 2 15.5	11 59.9	N 8 23.2	Kochab	137 19.8	N74 09.3
19	53 35.0	79 36.4	25.5	203 40.7	59.2	55 52.5	15.2	27 02.2	23.2	Markab	13 49.6	N15 12.0
20	68 37.4	94 35.9	24.3	218 42.2	59.5	70 54.5	15.0	42 04.5	23.3	Menkar	314 26.6	N 4 05.0
21	83 39.9	109 35.4	.. 23.2	233 43.8	9 59.8	85 56.5	.. 14.8	57 06.9	.. 23.4	Menkent	148 20.6	S36 21.7
22	98 42.3	124 34.9	22.1	248 45.3	10 00.2	100 58.5	14.6	72 09.2	23.4	Miaplacidus	221 41.0	S69 42.8
23	113 44.8	139 34.4	20.9	263 46.8	00.5	116 00.5	14.4	87 11.5	23.5			
30 00	128 47.3	154 33.9	S12 19.8	278 48.3	S10 00.8	131 02.5	S 2 14.2	102 13.9	N 8 23.5	Mirfak	308 56.1	N49 51.5
01	143 49.7	169 33.4	18.7	293 49.9	01.1	146 04.5	14.0	117 16.2	23.6	Nunki	76 12.4	S26 17.8
02	158 52.2	184 32.9	17.5	308 51.4	01.5	161 06.5	13.8	132 18.5	23.7	Peacock	53 37.3	S56 44.3
03	173 54.7	199 32.4	.. 16.4	323 52.9	.. 01.8	176 08.5	.. 13.6	147 20.9	.. 23.7	Pollux	243 40.9	N28 01.6
04	188 57.1	214 31.9	15.3	338 54.4	02.1	191 10.5	13.4	162 23.2	23.8	Procyon	245 11.0	N 5 13.5
05	203 59.6	229 31.4	14.1	353 56.0	02.4	206 12.5	13.2	177 25.6	23.8			
06	219 02.1	244 30.9	S12 13.0	8 57.5	S10 02.7	221 14.5	S 2 13.0	192 27.9	N 8 23.9	Rasalhague	96 17.0	N12 33.6
07	234 04.5	259 30.4	11.8	23 59.0	03.1	236 16.5	12.8	207 30.2	24.0	Regulus	207 55.0	N11 58.2
S 08	249 07.0	274 29.9	10.7	39 00.6	03.4	251 18.5	12.6	222 32.6	24.0	Rigel	281 22.5	S 8 12.4
A 09	264 09.5	289 29.4	.. 09.6	54 02.1	.. 03.7	266 20.5	.. 12.4	237 34.9	.. 24.1	Rigil Kent.	140 07.0	S60 49.5
T 10	279 11.9	304 28.9	08.4	69 03.6	04.0	281 22.5	12.2	252 37.2	24.2	Sabik	102 25.5	S15 43.3
U 11	294 14.4	319 28.4	07.3	84 05.2	04.4	296 24.5	12.0	267 39.6	24.2			
R 12	309 16.8	334 27.9	S12 06.1	99 06.7	S10 04.7	311 26.5	S 2 11.8	282 41.9	N 8 24.3	Schedar	349 53.4	N56 32.1
D 13	324 19.3	349 27.4	05.0	114 08.2	05.0	326 28.5	11.6	297 44.2	24.3	Shaula	96 37.3	S37 06.0
A 14	339 21.8	4 26.9	03.9	129 09.7	05.3	341 30.5	11.3	312 46.6	24.4	Sirius	258 43.2	S16 43.1
Y 15	354 24.2	19 26.4	.. 02.7	144 11.3	.. 05.6	356 32.5	.. 11.1	327 48.9	.. 24.5	Spica	158 42.9	S11 09.3
16	9 26.7	34 25.9	01.6	159 12.8	06.0	11 34.5	10.9	342 51.2	24.5	Suhail	223 00.1	S43 25.8
17	24 29.2	49 25.4	12 00.4	174 14.3	06.3	26 36.5	10.7	357 53.6	24.6			
18	39 31.6	64 24.9	S11 59.3	189 15.9	S10 06.6	41 38.5	S 2 10.5	12 55.9	N 8 24.6	Vega	80 46.8	N38 46.9
19	54 34.1	79 24.5	58.1	204 17.4	06.9	56 40.5	10.3	27 58.2	24.7	Zuben'ubi	137 17.8	S16 02.1
20	69 36.6	94 24.0	57.0	219 18.9	07.3	71 42.5	10.1	43 00.6	24.8			
21	84 39.0	109 23.5	.. 55.8	234 20.5	.. 07.6	86 44.5	.. 09.9	58 02.9	.. 24.8			
22	99 41.5	124 23.0	54.7	249 22.0	07.9	101 46.5	09.7	73 05.2	24.9	Venus	26 58.0	13 41
23	114 44.0	139 22.5	53.5	264 23.5	08.2	116 48.6	09.5	88 07.6	24.9	Mars	150 23.7	5 27
Mer. Pass. 15 26.3		v −0.5 d 1.1		v 1.5 d 0.3		v 2.0 d 0.2		v 2.3 d 0.1		Jupiter	2 26.2	15 17
										Saturn	333 29.6	17 12

SHA Mer. Pass.

UT	SUN GHA	SUN Dec	MOON GHA	v	Dec	d	HP
d h	° ′	° ′	° ′	′	° ′	′	′
28 00	176 48.3	S18 22.1	47 22.9	6.2	N18 24.6	4.0	59.3
01	191 48.2	21.5	61 48.1	6.2	18 28.6	3.9	59.3
02	206 48.1	20.8	76 13.3	6.1	18 32.5	3.9	59.3
03	221 47.9 ..	20.2	90 38.4	6.2	18 36.4	3.6	59.3
04	236 47.8	19.5	105 03.6	6.1	18 40.0	3.6	59.3
05	251 47.7	18.8	119 28.7	6.1	18 43.6	3.5	59.3
06	266 47.6	S18 18.2	133 53.8	6.1	N18 47.1	3.3	59.3
07	281 47.5	17.5	148 18.9	6.0	18 50.4	3.2	59.3
T 08	296 47.3	16.9	162 43.9	6.1	18 53.6	3.0	59.3
H 09	311 47.2 ..	16.2	177 09.0	6.0	18 56.6	3.0	59.3
U 10	326 47.1	15.6	191 34.0	6.0	18 59.6	2.8	59.2
R 11	341 47.0	14.9	205 59.0	6.0	19 02.4	2.7	59.2
S 12	356 46.9	S18 14.3	220 24.0	6.0	N19 05.1	2.5	59.2
D 13	11 46.7	13.6	234 49.0	5.9	19 07.6	2.5	59.2
A 14	26 46.6	13.0	249 13.9	6.0	19 10.1	2.3	59.2
Y 15	41 46.5 ..	12.3	263 38.9	6.0	19 12.4	2.2	59.2
16	56 46.4	11.6	278 03.9	5.9	19 14.6	2.0	59.2
17	71 46.3	11.0	292 28.8	6.0	19 16.6	1.9	59.2
18	86 46.2	S18 10.3	306 53.8	5.9	N19 18.5	1.8	59.2
19	101 46.0	09.7	321 18.7	5.9	19 20.3	1.7	59.2
20	116 45.9	09.0	335 43.6	6.0	19 22.0	1.6	59.2
21	131 45.8 ..	08.3	350 08.6	5.9	19 23.6	1.4	59.1
22	146 45.7	07.7	4 33.5	5.9	19 25.0	1.2	59.1
23	161 45.6	07.0	18 58.4	6.0	19 26.2	1.2	59.1
29 00	176 45.5	S18 06.3	33 23.4	5.9	N19 27.4	1.0	59.1
01	191 45.3	05.7	47 48.3	5.9	19 28.4	0.9	59.1
02	206 45.2	05.0	62 13.2	6.0	19 29.3	0.8	59.1
03	221 45.1 ..	04.4	76 38.2	5.9	19 30.1	0.6	59.1
04	236 45.0	03.7	91 03.1	6.0	19 30.7	0.5	59.1
05	251 44.9	03.0	105 28.1	6.0	19 31.2	0.4	59.1
06	266 44.8	S18 02.4	119 53.1	5.9	N19 31.6	0.3	59.0
07	281 44.7	01.7	134 18.0	6.0	19 31.9	0.1	59.0
F 08	296 44.6	01.0	148 43.0	6.0	19 32.0	0.0	59.0
R 09	311 44.4	18 00.4	163 08.0	6.1	19 32.0	0.2	59.0
I 10	326 44.3	17 59.7	177 33.1	6.0	19 31.8	0.2	59.0
D 11	341 44.2	59.0	191 58.1	6.0	19 31.6	0.4	59.0
A 12	356 44.1	S17 58.3	206 23.1	6.1	N19 31.2	0.5	59.0
Y 13	11 44.0	57.7	220 48.2	6.1	19 30.7	0.7	58.9
14	26 43.9	57.0	235 13.3	6.1	19 30.0	0.7	58.9
15	41 43.8 ..	56.3	249 38.4	6.2	19 29.3	0.9	58.9
16	56 43.7	55.7	264 03.6	6.1	19 28.4	1.1	58.9
17	71 43.6	55.0	278 28.7	6.2	19 27.3	1.1	58.9
18	86 43.5	S17 54.3	292 53.9	6.2	N19 26.2	1.3	58.9
19	101 43.4	53.6	307 19.1	6.3	19 24.9	1.4	58.9
20	116 43.2	53.0	321 44.4	6.2	19 23.5	1.5	58.8
21	131 43.1 ..	52.3	336 09.6	6.4	19 22.0	1.7	58.8
22	146 43.0	51.6	350 35.0	6.3	19 20.3	1.8	58.8
23	161 42.9	50.9	5 00.3	6.4	19 18.5	1.9	58.8
30 00	176 42.8	S17 50.3	19 25.7	6.4	N19 16.6	2.0	58.8
01	191 42.7	49.6	33 51.1	6.4	19 14.6	2.2	58.8
02	206 42.6	48.9	48 16.5	6.5	19 12.4	2.2	58.7
03	221 42.5 ..	48.2	62 42.0	6.5	19 10.2	2.4	58.7
04	236 42.4	47.6	77 07.5	6.5	19 07.8	2.5	58.7
05	251 42.3	46.9	91 33.0	6.6	19 05.3	2.7	58.7
06	266 42.2	S17 46.2	105 58.6	6.6	N19 02.6	2.7	58.7
07	281 42.1	45.5	120 24.2	6.7	18 59.9	2.9	58.7
S 08	296 42.0	44.8	134 49.9	6.7	18 57.0	3.0	58.6
A 09	311 41.9 ..	44.2	149 15.6	6.8	18 54.0	3.1	58.6
T 10	326 41.8	43.5	163 41.4	6.8	18 50.9	3.3	58.6
U 11	341 41.7	42.8	178 07.2	6.8	18 47.6	3.3	58.6
R 12	356 41.6	S17 42.1	192 33.0	6.9	N18 44.3	3.5	58.5
D 13	11 41.5	41.4	206 58.9	7.0	18 40.8	3.5	58.5
A 14	26 41.4	40.7	221 24.9	7.0	18 37.3	3.7	58.5
Y 15	41 41.3 ..	40.1	235 50.9	7.0	18 33.6	3.9	58.5
16	56 41.2	39.4	250 16.9	7.1	18 29.7	3.9	58.5
17	71 41.1	38.7	264 43.0	7.2	18 25.8	4.0	58.5
18	86 41.0	S17 38.0	279 09.2	7.2	N18 21.8	4.2	58.4
19	101 40.9	37.3	293 35.4	7.3	18 17.6	4.2	58.4
20	116 40.8	36.6	308 01.7	7.3	18 13.4	4.4	58.4
21	131 40.7 ..	35.9	322 28.0	7.3	18 09.0	4.5	58.4
22	146 40.6	35.3	336 54.3	7.5	18 04.5	4.5	58.4
23	161 40.5	34.6	351 20.8	7.5	N18 00.0	4.7	58.3
	SD 16.3	d 0.7	SD 16.1		16.1		16.0

Twilight / Sunrise / Moonrise

Lat.	Twilight Naut.	Twilight Civil	Sunrise	Moonrise 28	29	30	31
°	h m	h m	h m	h m	h m	h m	h m
N 72	07 21	08 54	11 00	□	□	□	13 43
N 70	07 12	08 33	10 05	10 36	11 12	12 42	14 32
68	07 04	08 16	09 32	11 25	12 13	13 29	15 03
66	06 58	08 03	09 08	11 57	12 48	14 00	15 26
64	06 52	07 51	08 50	12 20	13 13	14 23	15 44
62	06 47	07 42	08 35	12 39	13 33	14 41	15 59
60	06 42	07 33	08 22	12 54	13 49	14 56	16 11
N 58	06 38	07 26	08 11	13 08	14 03	15 08	16 22
56	06 34	07 19	08 01	13 19	14 14	15 19	16 31
54	06 30	07 14	07 53	13 29	14 25	15 29	16 39
52	06 27	07 08	07 45	13 38	14 34	15 38	16 46
50	06 24	07 03	07 38	13 46	14 42	15 45	16 53
45	06 17	06 52	07 24	14 03	14 59	16 02	17 07
N 40	06 10	06 43	07 12	14 17	15 14	16 15	17 19
35	06 04	06 35	07 01	14 29	15 26	16 27	17 29
30	05 58	06 27	06 52	14 39	15 36	16 37	17 37
20	05 47	06 13	06 36	14 57	15 55	16 54	17 52
N 10	05 35	06 01	06 23	15 12	16 11	17 09	18 05
0	05 22	05 48	06 10	15 27	16 25	17 23	18 18
S 10	05 08	05 34	05 56	15 42	16 40	17 37	18 30
20	04 51	05 19	05 42	15 58	16 56	17 51	18 43
30	04 28	05 00	05 26	16 16	17 14	18 09	18 58
35	04 14	04 48	05 16	16 26	17 25	18 19	19 06
40	03 57	04 34	05 05	16 38	17 37	18 30	19 16
45	03 35	04 18	04 52	16 53	17 52	18 43	19 27
S 50	03 06	03 57	04 36	17 10	18 09	18 59	19 41
52	02 51	03 47	04 28	17 18	18 18	19 07	19 47
54	02 32	03 35	04 20	17 28	18 27	19 16	19 55
56	02 09	03 22	04 10	17 38	18 37	19 25	20 03
58	01 36	03 06	03 59	17 50	18 49	19 36	20 11
S 60	////	02 46	03 47	18 04	19 03	19 48	20 22

Sunset / Twilight / Moonset

Lat.	Sunset	Twilight Civil	Twilight Naut.	Moonset 28	29	30	31
°	h m	h m	h m	h m	h m	h m	h m
N 72	13 27	15 34	17 06	□	□	□	10 35
N 70	14 22	15 55	17 15	07 43	09 08	09 39	09 45
68	14 55	16 11	17 23	06 54	08 08	08 51	09 14
66	15 19	16 24	17 30	06 22	07 33	08 21	08 50
64	15 37	16 36	17 35	05 59	07 08	07 58	08 31
62	15 52	16 45	17 40	05 41	06 48	07 39	08 16
60	16 05	16 54	17 45	05 26	06 32	07 24	08 03
N 58	16 16	17 01	17 49	05 13	06 18	07 11	07 52
56	16 26	17 07	17 53	05 02	06 06	07 00	07 42
54	16 34	17 13	17 56	04 52	05 56	06 50	07 34
52	16 42	17 19	18 00	04 43	05 47	06 41	07 26
50	16 48	17 24	18 03	04 35	05 39	06 33	07 19
45	17 03	17 34	18 12	04 19	05 21	06 17	07 04
N 40	17 15	17 44	18 16	04 05	05 07	06 03	06 52
35	17 25	17 52	18 22	03 53	04 55	05 51	06 42
30	17 34	17 59	18 28	03 43	04 44	05 41	06 32
20	17 50	18 13	18 40	03 26	04 26	05 23	06 16
N 10	18 04	18 26	18 51	03 11	04 10	05 07	06 02
0	18 17	18 38	19 04	02 57	03 55	04 53	05 49
S 10	18 30	18 52	19 18	02 43	03 40	04 38	05 36
20	18 44	19 07	19 35	02 27	03 24	04 23	05 22
30	19 00	19 26	19 57	02 10	03 06	04 05	05 06
35	19 10	19 38	20 11	02 00	02 55	03 54	04 56
40	19 21	19 51	20 28	01 48	02 43	03 42	04 45
45	19 34	20 07	20 50	01 35	02 28	03 28	04 32
S 50	19 50	20 28	21 19	01 18	02 11	03 11	04 17
52	19 57	20 38	21 34	01 11	02 02	03 03	04 09
54	20 05	20 50	21 52	01 02	01 53	02 53	04 01
56	20 15	21 03	22 14	00 52	01 43	02 43	03 52
58	20 25	21 21	22 45	00 42	01 31	02 33	03 42
S 60	20 38	21 37	23 49	00 29	01 17	02 18	03 30

SUN / MOON

Day	Eqn. of Time 00h	Eqn. of Time 12h	Mer. Pass.	Mer. Pass. Upper	Mer. Pass. Lower	Age	Phase
d	m s	m s	h m	h m	h m	d	%
28	12 47	12 52	12 13	21 41	09 12	11	88
29	12 58	13 03	12 13	22 39	10 10	12	94
30	13 09	13 13	12 13	23 36	11 08	13	98

UT	ARIES GHA	VENUS −3.9 GHA	Dec	MARS +0.5 GHA	Dec	JUPITER −2.1 GHA	Dec	SATURN +0.5 GHA	Dec	STARS Name	SHA	Dec
31 00	129 46.4	154 22.0	S11 52.4	279 25.1	S10 08.5	131 50.6	S 2 09.3	103 09.9	N 8 25.0	Acamar	315 26.7	S40 18.9
01	144 48.9	169 21.5	51.3	294 26.6	08.9	146 52.6	09.1	118 12.2	25.1	Achernar	335 35.2	S57 14.9
02	159 51.3	184 21.0	50.1	309 28.2	09.2	161 54.6	08.9	133 14.6	25.1	Acrux	173 21.3	S63 05.4
03	174 53.8	199 20.5	.. 49.0	324 29.7	.. 09.5	176 56.6	.. 08.7	148 16.9	.. 25.2	Adhara	255 20.9	S28 58.5
04	189 56.3	214 20.0	47.8	339 31.2	09.8	191 58.6	08.5	163 19.2	25.3	Aldebaran	291 01.9	N16 30.3
05	204 58.7	229 19.5	46.7	354 32.8	10.1	207 00.6	08.3	178 21.6	25.3			
06	220 01.2	244 19.1	S11 45.5	9 34.3	S10 10.4	222 02.6	S 2 08.0	193 23.9	N 8 25.4	Alioth	166 30.2	N55 57.7
07	235 03.7	259 18.6	44.3	24 35.9	10.8	237 04.6	07.8	208 26.2	25.4	Alkaid	153 07.6	N49 18.9
08	250 06.1	274 18.1	43.2	39 37.4	11.1	252 06.6	07.6	223 28.6	25.5	Al Na'ir	27 58.1	S46 58.1
S 09	265 08.6	289 17.6	.. 42.0	54 38.9	.. 11.4	267 08.6	.. 07.4	238 30.9	.. 25.6	Alnilam	275 57.4	S 1 12.4
U 10	280 11.1	304 17.1	40.9	69 40.5	11.7	282 10.6	07.2	253 33.2	25.6	Alphard	218 06.6	S 8 39.4
N 11	295 13.5	319 16.6	39.7	84 42.0	12.0	297 12.6	07.0	268 35.5	25.7			
D **12**	310 16.0	334 16.1	S11 38.6	99 43.6	S10 12.4	312 14.6	S 2 06.8	283 37.9	N 8 25.8	Alphecca	126 20.5	N26 43.0
A 13	325 18.5	349 15.6	37.4	114 45.1	12.7	327 16.6	06.6	298 40.2	25.8	Alpheratz	357 55.2	N29 05.1
Y 14	340 20.9	4 15.2	36.3	129 46.6	13.0	342 18.6	06.4	313 42.5	25.9	Altair	62 19.4	N 8 51.9
15	355 23.4	19 14.7	.. 35.1	144 48.2	.. 13.3	357 20.6	.. 06.2	328 44.9	.. 25.9	Ankaa	353 26.9	S42 19.0
16	10 25.8	34 14.2	34.0	159 49.7	13.6	12 22.6	06.0	343 47.2	26.0	Antares	112 40.0	S26 25.6
17	25 28.3	49 13.7	32.8	174 51.3	13.9	27 24.6	05.8	358 49.5	26.1			
18	40 30.8	64 13.2	S11 31.6	189 52.8	S10 14.3	42 26.6	S 2 05.6	13 51.9	N 8 26.1	Arcturus	146 05.8	N19 11.2
19	55 33.2	79 12.7	30.5	204 54.4	14.6	57 28.6	05.4	28 54.2	26.2	Atria	107 52.2	S69 01.2
20	70 35.7	94 12.3	29.3	219 55.9	14.9	72 30.6	05.1	43 56.5	26.2	Avior	234 21.8	S59 30.5
21	85 38.2	109 11.8	.. 28.2	234 57.4	.. 15.2	87 32.6	.. 04.9	58 58.8	.. 26.3	Bellatrix	278 43.7	N 6 20.7
22	100 40.6	124 11.3	27.0	249 59.0	15.5	102 34.6	04.7	74 01.2	26.4	Betelgeuse	271 13.1	N 7 24.2
23	115 43.1	139 10.8	25.8	265 00.5	15.8	117 36.6	04.5	89 03.5	26.4			
1 00	130 45.6	154 10.3	S11 24.7	280 02.1	S10 16.1	132 38.5	S 2 04.3	104 05.8	N 8 26.5	Canopus	264 00.6	S52 42.0
01	145 48.0	169 09.9	23.5	295 03.6	16.5	147 40.5	04.1	119 08.2	26.6	Capella	280 50.5	N45 59.8
02	160 50.5	184 09.4	22.4	310 05.2	16.8	162 42.5	03.9	134 10.5	26.6	Deneb	49 39.5	N45 16.6
03	175 53.0	199 08.9	.. 21.2	325 06.7	.. 17.1	177 44.5	.. 03.7	149 12.8	.. 26.7	Denebola	182 44.7	N14 34.5
04	190 55.4	214 08.4	20.0	340 08.3	17.4	192 46.5	03.5	164 15.1	26.8	Diphda	349 07.2	S17 59.8
05	205 57.9	229 07.9	18.9	355 09.8	17.7	207 48.5	03.3	179 17.5	26.8			
06	221 00.3	244 07.5	S11 17.7	10 11.4	S10 18.0	222 50.5	S 2 03.1	194 19.8	N 8 26.9	Dubhe	194 04.7	N61 45.2
07	236 02.8	259 07.0	16.5	25 12.9	18.3	237 52.5	02.9	209 22.1	26.9	Elnath	278 26.4	N28 36.3
08	251 05.3	274 06.5	15.4	40 14.5	18.6	252 54.5	02.6	224 24.5	27.0	Eltanin	90 51.7	N51 29.2
M 09	266 07.7	289 06.0	.. 14.2	55 16.0	.. 19.0	267 56.5	.. 02.4	239 26.8	.. 27.1	Enif	33 58.3	N 9 52.2
O 10	281 10.2	304 05.6	13.0	70 17.6	19.3	282 58.5	02.2	254 29.1	27.1	Fomalhaut	15 36.5	S29 37.8
N 11	296 12.7	319 05.1	11.9	85 19.1	19.6	298 00.5	02.0	269 31.4	27.2			
D **12**	311 15.1	334 04.6	S11 10.7	100 20.7	S10 19.9	313 02.5	S 2 01.8	284 33.8	N 8 27.3	Gacrux	172 12.9	S57 06.2
A 13	326 17.6	349 04.1	09.5	115 22.2	20.2	328 04.5	01.6	299 36.1	27.3	Gienah	176 03.5	S17 32.1
Y 14	341 20.1	4 03.7	08.4	130 23.8	20.5	343 06.5	01.4	314 38.4	27.4	Hadar	149 03.5	S60 21.8
15	356 22.5	19 03.2	.. 07.2	145 25.3	.. 20.8	358 08.5	.. 01.2	329 40.7	.. 27.4	Hamal	328 13.3	N23 27.4
16	11 25.0	34 02.7	06.0	160 26.9	21.1	13 10.5	01.0	344 43.1	27.5	Kaus Aust.	83 58.9	S34 23.0
17	26 27.4	49 02.2	04.9	175 28.5	21.5	28 12.5	00.8	359 45.4	27.6			
18	41 29.9	64 01.8	S11 03.7	190 30.0	S10 21.8	43 14.5	S 2 00.6	14 47.7	N 8 27.6	Kochab	137 19.8	N74 09.3
19	56 32.4	79 01.3	02.5	205 31.6	22.1	58 16.5	00.4	29 50.1	27.7	Markab	13 49.6	N15 12.0
20	71 34.8	94 00.8	01.4	220 33.1	22.4	73 18.5	2 00.1	44 52.4	27.8	Menkar	314 26.6	N 4 05.0
21	86 37.3	109 00.4	11 00.2	235 34.7	.. 22.7	88 20.5	1 59.9	59 54.7	.. 27.8	Menkent	148 20.6	S36 21.7
22	101 39.8	123 59.9	10 59.0	250 36.2	23.0	103 22.5	59.7	74 57.0	27.9	Miaplacidus	221 41.0	S69 42.8
23	116 42.2	138 59.4	57.8	265 37.8	23.3	118 24.5	59.5	89 59.4	28.0			
2 00	131 44.7	153 58.9	S10 56.7	280 39.3	S10 23.6	133 26.5	S 1 59.3	105 01.7	N 8 28.0	Mirfak	308 56.1	N49 51.5
01	146 47.2	168 58.5	55.5	295 40.9	23.9	148 28.5	59.1	120 04.0	28.1	Nunki	76 12.4	S26 17.8
02	161 49.6	183 58.0	54.3	310 42.5	24.2	163 30.5	58.9	135 06.3	28.2	Peacock	53 37.3	S56 44.3
03	176 52.1	198 57.5	.. 53.2	325 44.0	.. 24.5	178 32.5	.. 58.7	150 08.7	.. 28.2	Pollux	243 40.9	N28 01.6
04	191 54.6	213 57.1	52.0	340 45.6	24.9	193 34.5	58.5	165 11.0	28.3	Procyon	245 11.0	N 5 13.5
05	206 57.0	228 56.6	50.8	355 47.1	25.2	208 36.4	58.3	180 13.3	28.3			
06	221 59.5	243 56.1	S10 49.6	10 48.7	S10 25.5	223 38.4	S 1 58.1	195 15.6	N 8 28.4	Rasalhague	96 17.0	N12 33.6
07	237 01.9	258 55.7	48.4	25 50.3	25.8	238 40.4	57.8	210 18.0	28.5	Regulus	207 55.0	N11 58.2
08	252 04.4	273 55.2	47.3	40 51.8	26.1	253 42.4	57.6	225 20.3	28.5	Rigel	281 22.5	S 8 12.4
T 09	267 06.9	288 54.7	.. 46.1	55 53.4	.. 26.4	268 44.4	.. 57.4	240 22.6	.. 28.6	Rigil Kent.	140 06.9	S60 49.5
U 10	282 09.3	303 54.3	44.9	70 55.0	26.7	283 46.4	57.2	255 24.9	28.7	Sabik	102 25.5	S15 43.3
E 11	297 11.8	318 53.8	43.7	85 56.5	27.0	298 48.4	57.0	270 27.2	28.7			
S **12**	312 14.3	333 53.3	S10 42.6	100 58.1	S10 27.3	313 50.4	S 1 56.8	285 29.6	N 8 28.8	Schedar	349 53.4	N56 32.1
D 13	327 16.7	348 52.9	41.4	115 59.6	27.6	328 52.4	56.6	300 31.9	28.9	Shaula	96 37.3	S37 06.0
A 14	342 19.2	3 52.4	40.2	131 01.2	27.9	343 54.4	56.4	315 34.2	28.9	Sirius	258 43.2	S16 43.1
Y 15	357 21.7	18 52.0	.. 39.0	146 02.8	.. 28.2	358 56.4	.. 56.2	330 36.5	.. 29.0	Spica	158 42.8	S11 09.3
16	12 24.1	33 51.5	37.8	161 04.3	28.5	13 58.4	56.0	345 38.9	29.1	Suhail	223 00.1	S43 25.8
17	27 26.6	48 51.0	36.7	176 05.9	28.8	29 00.4	55.7	0 41.2	29.1			
18	42 29.0	63 50.6	S10 35.5	191 07.5	S10 29.1	44 02.4	S 1 55.5	15 43.5	N 8 29.2	Vega	80 46.8	N38 46.9
19	57 31.5	78 50.1	34.3	206 09.0	29.4	59 04.4	55.3	30 45.8	29.3	Zuben'ubi	137 17.7	S16 02.2
20	72 34.0	93 49.6	33.1	221 10.6	29.8	74 06.3	55.1	45 48.1	29.3			
21	87 36.4	108 49.2	.. 31.9	236 12.2	.. 30.1	89 08.3	.. 54.9	60 50.5	.. 29.4		SHA	Mer. Pass.
22	102 38.9	123 48.7	30.7	251 13.7	30.4	104 10.3	54.7	75 52.8	29.4	Venus	° ′ 23 24.8	h m 13 44
23	117 41.4	138 48.3	29.6	266 15.3	30.7	119 12.3	54.5	90 55.1	29.5	Mars	149 16.5	5 19
	h m									Jupiter	1 53.0	15 07
Mer. Pass. 15 14.5	v −0.5 d 1.2	v 1.6	d 0.3	v 2.0	d 0.2	v 2.3	d 0.1			Saturn	333 20.3	17 01

UT	SUN GHA	SUN Dec	MOON GHA	v	MOON Dec	d	HP
d h	° ′	° ′	° ′	′	° ′	′	′
31 00	176 40.4	S17 33.9	5 47.3	7.5	N17 55.3	4.8	58.3
01	191 40.3	33.2	20 13.8	7.6	17 50.5	4.9	58.3
02	206 40.2	32.5	34 40.4	7.7	17 45.6	5.0	58.3
03	221 40.1	.. 31.8	49 07.1	7.7	17 40.6	5.2	58.2
04	236 40.0	31.1	63 33.8	7.8	17 35.4	5.2	58.2
05	251 39.9	30.4	78 00.6	7.8	17 30.2	5.3	58.2
06	266 39.8	S17 29.7	92 27.4	7.9	N17 24.9	5.4	58.2
07	281 39.7	29.0	106 54.3	8.0	17 19.5	5.5	58.1
08	296 39.6	28.3	121 21.3	8.0	17 14.0	5.6	58.1
S 09	311 39.5	.. 27.6	135 48.3	8.1	17 08.4	5.8	58.1
U 10	326 39.4	26.9	150 15.4	8.2	17 02.6	5.8	58.1
N 11	341 39.3	26.3	164 42.6	8.2	16 56.8	5.9	58.1
D 12	356 39.2	S17 25.6	179 09.8	8.3	N16 50.9	6.0	58.0
A 13	11 39.2	24.9	193 37.1	8.4	16 44.9	6.1	58.0
Y 14	26 39.1	24.2	208 04.5	8.4	16 38.8	6.2	58.0
15	41 39.0	.. 23.5	222 31.9	8.5	16 32.6	6.2	58.0
16	56 38.9	22.8	236 59.4	8.6	16 26.4	6.4	57.9
17	71 38.8	22.1	251 27.0	8.6	16 20.0	6.5	57.9
18	86 38.7	S17 21.4	265 54.6	8.7	N16 13.5	6.5	57.9
19	101 38.6	20.7	280 22.3	8.8	16 07.0	6.7	57.9
20	116 38.5	20.0	294 50.1	8.9	16 00.3	6.7	57.8
21	131 38.4	.. 19.3	309 18.0	8.9	15 53.6	6.8	57.8
22	146 38.3	18.6	323 45.9	8.9	15 46.8	6.9	57.8
23	161 38.2	17.9	338 13.8	9.1	15 39.9	7.0	57.8
1 00	176 38.2	S17 17.2	352 41.9	9.1	N15 32.9	7.0	57.7
01	191 38.1	16.5	7 10.0	9.2	15 25.9	7.2	57.7
02	206 38.0	15.8	21 38.2	9.3	15 18.7	7.2	57.7
03	221 37.9	.. 15.1	36 06.5	9.3	15 11.5	7.3	57.7
04	236 37.8	14.4	50 34.8	9.4	15 04.2	7.4	57.6
05	251 37.7	13.6	65 03.2	9.5	14 56.8	7.4	57.6
06	266 37.6	S17 12.9	79 31.7	9.5	N14 49.4	7.6	57.6
07	281 37.5	12.2	94 00.2	9.7	14 41.8	7.6	57.5
M 08	296 37.5	11.5	108 28.9	9.6	14 34.2	7.7	57.5
O 09	311 37.4	.. 10.8	122 57.5	9.8	14 26.5	7.7	57.5
N 10	326 37.3	10.1	137 26.3	9.8	14 18.8	7.8	57.5
D 11	341 37.2	09.4	151 55.1	9.9	14 11.0	7.9	57.4
A 12	356 37.1	S17 08.7	166 24.0	10.1	N14 03.1	8.0	57.4
Y 13	11 37.0	08.0	180 53.0	10.1	13 55.1	8.0	57.4
14	26 36.9	07.3	195 22.1	10.1	13 47.1	8.1	57.4
15	41 36.9	.. 06.6	209 51.2	10.2	13 39.0	8.2	57.3
16	56 36.8	05.9	224 20.4	10.2	13 30.8	8.2	57.3
17	71 36.7	05.1	238 49.6	10.4	13 22.6	8.3	57.3
18	86 36.6	S17 04.4	253 19.0	10.4	N13 14.3	8.4	57.2
19	101 36.5	03.7	267 48.4	10.4	13 05.9	8.4	57.2
20	116 36.4	03.0	282 17.8	10.6	12 57.5	8.5	57.2
21	131 36.4	.. 02.3	296 47.4	10.6	12 49.0	8.5	57.2
22	146 36.3	01.6	311 17.0	10.7	12 40.5	8.6	57.1
23	161 36.2	00.9	325 46.7	10.7	12 31.9	8.6	57.1
2 00	176 36.1	S17 00.2	340 16.4	10.9	N12 23.3	8.7	57.1
01	191 36.0	16 59.4	354 46.3	10.9	12 14.6	8.8	57.1
02	206 36.0	58.7	9 16.2	10.9	12 05.8	8.8	57.0
03	221 35.9	.. 58.0	23 46.1	11.1	11 57.0	8.9	57.0
04	236 35.8	57.3	38 16.2	11.1	11 48.1	8.9	57.0
05	251 35.7	56.6	52 46.3	11.1	11 39.2	9.0	56.9
06	266 35.6	S16 55.9	67 16.4	11.3	N11 30.2	9.0	56.9
07	281 35.6	55.1	81 46.7	11.3	11 21.2	9.1	56.9
T 08	296 35.5	54.4	96 17.0	11.4	11 12.1	9.1	56.9
U 09	311 35.4	.. 53.7	110 47.4	11.4	11 03.0	9.2	56.8
E 10	326 35.3	53.0	125 17.8	11.5	10 53.8	9.2	56.8
S 11	341 35.3	52.3	139 48.3	11.6	10 44.6	9.2	56.8
D 12	356 35.2	S16 51.5	154 18.9	11.6	N10 35.4	9.3	56.7
A 13	11 35.1	50.8	168 49.5	11.7	10 26.1	9.4	56.7
Y 14	26 35.0	50.1	183 20.2	11.8	10 16.7	9.4	56.7
15	41 35.0	.. 49.4	197 51.0	11.8	10 07.3	9.4	56.7
16	56 34.9	48.6	212 21.8	11.9	9 57.9	9.4	56.6
17	71 34.8	47.9	226 52.7	12.0	9 48.5	9.5	56.6
18	86 34.7	S16 47.2	241 23.7	12.0	N 9 39.0	9.6	56.6
19	101 34.7	46.5	255 54.7	12.1	9 29.4	9.5	56.5
20	116 34.6	45.7	270 25.8	12.1	9 19.9	9.7	56.5
21	131 34.5	.. 45.0	284 56.9	12.2	9 10.2	9.6	56.5
22	146 34.4	44.3	299 28.1	12.3	9 00.6	9.7	56.5
23	161 34.4	43.6	313 59.4	12.3	N 8 50.9	9.7	56.4
	SD 16.3	d 0.7	SD 15.8		15.6		15.5

Lat.	Twilight Naut.	Twilight Civil	Sunrise	Moonrise 31	1	2	3
°	h m	h m	h m	h m	h m	h m	h m
N 72	07 11	08 40	10 31	13 43	15 54	17 49	19 36
N 70	07 03	08 22	09 48	14 32	16 21	18 05	19 44
68	06 56	08 07	09 19	15 03	16 41	18 17	19 50
66	06 50	07 54	08 58	15 26	16 57	18 28	19 56
64	06 45	07 44	08 41	15 44	17 10	18 36	20 00
62	06 41	07 35	08 27	15 59	17 21	18 43	20 04
60	06 37	07 27	08 15	16 11	17 30	18 49	20 07
N 58	06 33	07 21	08 05	16 22	17 38	18 55	20 10
56	06 30	07 15	07 56	16 31	17 45	19 00	20 13
54	06 26	07 09	07 48	16 39	17 52	19 04	20 15
52	06 23	07 04	07 41	16 46	17 57	19 08	20 17
50	06 20	06 59	07 34	16 53	18 03	19 12	20 19
45	06 14	06 49	07 20	17 07	18 14	19 19	20 23
N 40	06 08	06 40	07 09	17 19	18 23	19 26	20 27
35	06 02	06 33	06 59	17 29	18 31	19 31	20 30
30	05 57	06 26	06 51	17 37	18 38	19 36	20 33
20	05 46	06 13	06 36	17 52	18 50	19 45	20 37
N 10	05 35	06 01	06 22	18 05	19 00	19 52	20 41
0	05 23	05 48	06 10	18 18	19 10	19 59	20 45
S 10	05 09	05 35	05 57	18 30	19 19	20 06	20 49
20	04 53	05 20	05 44	18 43	19 30	20 13	20 53
30	04 31	05 02	05 28	18 58	19 41	20 21	20 58
35	04 18	04 51	05 19	19 06	19 48	20 26	21 00
40	04 02	04 38	05 08	19 16	19 56	20 31	21 03
45	03 41	04 23	04 56	19 27	20 05	20 38	21 07
S 50	03 13	04 03	04 41	19 41	20 16	20 45	21 11
52	02 59	03 53	04 34	19 47	20 21	20 49	21 13
54	02 42	03 42	04 26	19 55	20 26	20 52	21 15
56	02 21	03 30	04 17	20 03	20 32	20 56	21 17
58	01 52	03 15	04 07	20 11	20 39	21 01	21 20
S 60	01 06	02 57	03 55	20 22	20 47	21 06	21 23

Lat.	Sunset	Twilight Civil	Twilight Naut.	Moonset 31	1	2	3
°	h m	h m	h m	h m	h m	h m	h m
N 72	13 58	15 48	17 18	10 35	10 14	10 02	09 53
N 70	14 40	16 07	17 25	09 45	09 46	09 45	09 43
68	15 09	16 22	17 32	09 14	09 25	09 31	09 35
66	15 30	16 34	17 38	08 50	09 08	09 20	09 28
64	15 47	16 44	17 43	08 31	08 54	09 10	09 22
62	16 01	16 53	17 47	08 16	08 42	09 02	09 17
60	16 13	17 00	17 51	08 03	08 32	08 55	09 13
N 58	16 23	17 07	17 55	07 52	08 24	08 49	09 09
56	16 32	17 13	17 58	07 42	08 16	08 43	09 05
54	16 40	17 19	18 01	07 34	08 09	08 38	09 02
52	16 47	17 24	18 04	07 26	08 03	08 33	08 59
50	16 53	17 28	18 07	07 19	07 57	08 29	08 57
45	17 07	17 38	18 14	07 04	07 45	08 20	08 51
N 40	17 18	17 47	18 20	06 52	07 35	08 13	08 46
35	17 28	17 55	18 25	06 42	07 26	08 06	08 42
30	17 37	18 02	18 31	06 32	07 19	08 01	08 39
20	17 52	18 15	18 41	06 16	07 05	07 51	08 32
N 10	18 05	18 27	18 52	06 02	06 54	07 42	08 27
0	18 17	18 39	19 04	05 49	06 43	07 33	08 21
S 10	18 30	18 52	19 17	05 36	06 32	07 25	08 16
20	18 43	19 06	19 34	05 22	06 20	07 16	08 10
30	18 58	19 24	19 55	05 06	06 06	07 06	08 04
35	19 08	19 35	20 08	04 56	05 58	07 00	08 00
40	19 18	19 48	20 25	04 45	05 49	06 53	07 55
45	19 30	20 03	20 45	04 32	05 39	06 45	07 50
S 50	19 45	20 23	21 12	04 17	05 26	06 36	07 44
52	19 52	20 33	21 26	04 09	05 20	06 31	07 41
54	20 00	20 43	21 43	04 01	05 13	06 26	07 38
56	20 09	20 56	22 03	03 52	05 06	06 21	07 35
58	20 19	21 10	22 30	03 42	04 57	06 15	07 31
S 60	20 30	21 28	23 13	03 30	04 48	06 08	07 27

	SUN Eqn. of Time 00h	SUN Eqn. of Time 12h	SUN Mer. Pass.	MOON Mer. Pass. Upper	MOON Mer. Pass. Lower	MOON Age	MOON Phase
Day	m s	m s	h m	h m	h m	d	%
31	13 18	13 23	12 13	24 30	12 03	14	100
1	13 27	13 31	12 14	00 30	12 56	15	99
2	13 35	13 39	12 14	01 22	13 46	16	96

UT	ARIES GHA	VENUS −3.9 GHA	Dec	MARS +0.4 GHA	Dec	JUPITER −2.1 GHA	Dec	SATURN +0.5 GHA	Dec	STARS Name	SHA	Dec
d h	° ′	° ′	° ′	° ′	° ′	° ′	° ′	° ′	° ′		° ′	° ′
3 00	132 43.8	153 47.8	S10 28.4	281 16.9	S10 31.0	134 14.3	S 1 54.3	105 57.4	N 8 29.6	Acamar	315 26.8	S40 18.9
01	147 46.3	168 47.4	27.2	296 18.5	31.3	149 16.3	54.1	120 59.8	29.6	Achernar	335 35.3	S57 14.9
02	162 48.8	183 46.9	26.0	311 20.0	31.6	164 18.3	53.9	136 02.1	29.7	Acrux	173 21.2	S63 05.4
03	177 51.2	198 46.4 ..	24.8	326 21.6 ..	31.9	179 20.3 ..	53.6	151 04.4 ..	29.8	Adhara	255 20.9	S28 58.5
04	192 53.7	213 46.0	23.6	341 23.2	32.2	194 22.3	53.4	166 06.7	29.8	Aldebaran	291 02.0	N16 30.3
05	207 56.2	228 45.5	22.4	356 24.7	32.5	209 24.3	53.2	181 09.0	29.9			
06	222 58.6	243 45.1	S10 21.3	11 26.3	S10 32.8	224 26.3	S 1 53.0	196 11.4	N 8 30.0	Alioth	166 30.2	N55 57.7
W 07	238 01.1	258 44.6	20.1	26 27.9	33.1	239 28.3	52.8	211 13.7	30.0	Alkaid	153 07.5	N49 18.9
E 08	253 03.5	273 44.2	18.9	41 29.5	33.4	254 30.3	52.6	226 16.0	30.1	Al Na'ir	27 58.1	S46 58.1
D 09	268 06.0	288 43.7 ..	17.7	56 31.0 ..	33.7	269 32.2 ..	52.4	241 18.3 ..	30.2	Alnilam	275 57.4	S 1 12.4
N 10	283 08.5	303 43.2	16.5	71 32.6	34.0	284 34.2	52.2	256 20.6	30.2	Alphard	218 06.6	S 8 39.4
E 11	298 10.9	318 42.8	15.3	86 34.2	34.3	299 36.2	52.0	271 23.0	30.3			
S 12	313 13.4	333 42.3	S10 14.1	101 35.8	S10 34.6	314 38.2	S 1 51.8	286 25.3	N 8 30.4	Alphecca	126 20.5	N26 43.0
D 13	328 15.9	348 41.9	12.9	116 37.3	34.9	329 40.2	51.5	301 27.6	30.4	Alpheratz	357 55.2	N29 05.1
A 14	343 18.3	3 41.4	11.7	131 38.9	35.2	344 42.2	51.3	316 29.9	30.5	Altair	62 19.4	N 8 51.9
Y 15	358 20.8	18 41.0 ..	10.5	146 40.5 ..	35.5	359 44.2 ..	51.1	331 32.2 ..	30.6	Ankaa	353 26.9	S42 19.0
16	13 23.3	33 40.5	09.4	161 42.1	35.8	14 46.2	50.9	346 34.6	30.6	Antares	112 40.0	S26 25.6
17	28 25.7	48 40.1	08.2	176 43.6	36.1	29 48.2	50.7	1 36.9	30.7			
18	43 28.2	63 39.6	S10 07.0	191 45.2	S10 36.4	44 50.2	S 1 50.5	16 39.2	N 8 30.8	Arcturus	146 05.8	N19 11.1
19	58 30.7	78 39.2	05.8	206 46.8	36.7	59 52.1	50.3	31 41.5	30.8	Atria	107 52.1	S69 01.2
20	73 33.1	93 38.7	04.6	221 48.4	37.0	74 54.1	50.1	46 43.8	30.9	Avior	234 21.9	S59 30.5
21	88 35.6	108 38.3 ..	03.4	236 50.0 ..	37.3	89 56.1 ..	49.9	61 46.1 ..	31.0	Bellatrix	278 43.7	N 6 20.7
22	103 38.0	123 37.8	02.2	251 51.5	37.6	104 58.1	49.6	76 48.5	31.0	Betelgeuse	271 13.1	N 7 24.2
23	118 40.5	138 37.4	10 01.0	266 53.1	37.9	120 00.1	49.4	91 50.8	31.1			
4 00	133 43.0	153 36.9	S 9 59.8	281 54.7	S10 38.2	135 02.1	S 1 49.2	106 53.1	N 8 31.2	Canopus	264 00.6	S52 42.0
01	148 45.4	168 36.5	58.6	296 56.3	38.5	150 04.1	49.0	121 55.4	31.2	Capella	280 50.6	N45 59.8
02	163 47.9	183 36.0	57.4	311 57.9	38.8	165 06.1	48.8	136 57.7	31.3	Deneb	49 39.5	N45 16.6
03	178 50.4	198 35.6 ..	56.2	326 59.4 ..	39.1	180 08.1 ..	48.6	152 00.1 ..	31.4	Denebola	182 44.7	N14 34.5
04	193 52.8	213 35.1	55.0	342 01.0	39.4	195 10.0	48.4	167 02.4	31.4	Diphda	349 07.2	S17 59.8
05	208 55.3	228 34.7	53.8	357 02.6	39.7	210 12.0	48.2	182 04.7	31.5			
06	223 57.8	243 34.2	S 9 52.6	12 04.2	S10 40.0	225 14.0	S 1 47.9	197 07.0	N 8 31.6	Dubhe	194 04.7	N61 45.2
07	239 00.2	258 33.8	51.4	27 05.8	40.3	240 16.0	47.7	212 09.3	31.6	Elnath	278 26.4	N28 36.3
T 08	254 02.7	273 33.4	50.2	42 07.4	40.6	255 18.0	47.5	227 11.6	31.7	Eltanin	90 51.7	N51 29.2
H 09	269 05.1	288 32.9 ..	49.0	57 08.9 ..	40.9	270 20.0 ..	47.3	242 14.0 ..	31.8	Enif	33 58.3	N 9 52.2
U 10	284 07.6	303 32.5	47.8	72 10.5	41.2	285 22.0	47.1	257 16.3	31.8	Fomalhaut	15 36.5	S29 37.8
R 11	299 10.1	318 32.0	46.6	87 12.1	41.5	300 24.0	46.9	272 18.6	31.9			
S 12	314 12.5	333 31.6	S 9 45.4	102 13.7	S10 41.8	315 26.0	S 1 46.7	287 20.9	N 8 32.0	Gacrux	172 12.9	S57 06.2
D 13	329 15.0	348 31.1	44.2	117 15.3	42.0	330 27.9	46.5	302 23.2	32.0	Gienah	176 03.5	S17 32.2
A 14	344 17.5	3 30.7	43.0	132 16.9	42.3	345 29.9	46.3	317 25.5	32.1	Hadar	149 03.5	S60 21.8
Y 15	359 19.9	18 30.3 ..	41.8	147 18.5 ..	42.6	0 31.9 ..	46.0	332 27.8 ..	32.2	Hamal	328 13.3	N23 27.4
16	14 22.4	33 29.8	40.6	162 20.1	42.9	15 33.9	45.8	347 30.2	32.2	Kaus Aust.	83 58.8	S34 23.0
17	29 24.9	48 29.4	39.4	177 21.6	43.2	30 35.9	45.6	2 32.5	32.3			
18	44 27.3	63 28.9	S 9 38.2	192 23.2	S10 43.5	45 37.9	S 1 45.4	17 34.8	N 8 32.4	Kochab	137 19.7	N74 09.3
19	59 29.8	78 28.5	37.0	207 24.8	43.8	60 39.9	45.2	32 37.1	32.4	Markab	13 49.7	N15 11.9
20	74 32.3	93 28.0	35.8	222 26.4	44.1	75 41.8	45.0	47 39.4	32.5	Menkar	314 26.6	N 4 05.0
21	89 34.7	108 27.6 ..	34.6	237 28.0 ..	44.4	90 43.8 ..	44.8	62 41.7 ..	32.6	Menkent	148 20.6	S36 21.7
22	104 37.2	123 27.2	33.4	252 29.6	44.7	105 45.8	44.6	77 44.0	32.6	Miaplacidus	221 41.0	S69 42.8
23	119 39.6	138 26.7	32.2	267 31.2	45.0	120 47.8	44.3	92 46.4	32.7			
5 00	134 42.1	153 26.3	S 9 31.0	282 32.8	S10 45.3	135 49.8	S 1 44.1	107 48.7	N 8 32.8	Mirfak	308 56.2	N49 51.5
01	149 44.6	168 25.9	29.8	297 34.4	45.6	150 51.8	43.9	122 51.0	32.8	Nunki	76 12.4	S26 17.8
02	164 47.0	183 25.4	28.6	312 36.0	45.9	165 53.8	43.7	137 53.3	32.9	Peacock	53 37.3	S56 44.2
03	179 49.5	198 25.0 ..	27.3	327 37.6 ..	46.2	180 55.8 ..	43.5	152 55.6 ..	33.0	Pollux	243 40.9	N28 01.6
04	194 52.0	213 24.5	26.1	342 39.2	46.5	195 57.7	43.3	167 57.9	33.1	Procyon	245 11.0	N 5 13.5
05	209 54.4	228 24.1	24.9	357 40.8	46.7	210 59.7	43.1	183 00.2	33.1			
06	224 56.9	243 23.7	S 9 23.7	12 42.4	S10 47.0	226 01.7	S 1 42.8	198 02.6	N 8 33.2	Rasalhague	96 17.0	N12 33.6
07	239 59.4	258 23.2	22.5	27 44.0	47.3	241 03.7	42.6	213 04.9	33.3	Regulus	207 55.0	N11 58.2
08	255 01.8	273 22.8	21.3	42 45.6	47.6	256 05.7	42.4	228 07.2	33.3	Rigel	281 22.5	S 8 12.4
F 09	270 04.3	288 22.4 ..	20.1	57 47.2 ..	47.9	271 07.7 ..	42.2	243 09.5 ..	33.4	Rigil Kent.	140 06.9	S60 49.5
R 10	285 06.7	303 21.9	18.9	72 48.8	48.2	286 09.6	42.0	258 11.8	33.5	Sabik	102 25.5	S15 43.3
I 11	300 09.2	318 21.5	17.7	87 50.4	48.5	301 11.6	41.8	273 14.1	33.5			
D 12	315 11.7	333 21.1	S 9 16.5	102 52.0	S10 48.8	316 13.6	S 1 41.6	288 16.4	N 8 33.6	Schedar	349 53.5	N56 32.0
A 13	330 14.1	348 20.6	15.3	117 53.6	49.1	331 15.6	41.4	303 18.7	33.7	Shaula	96 37.2	S37 06.0
Y 14	345 16.6	3 20.2	14.0	132 55.2	49.4	346 17.6	41.1	318 21.1	33.7	Sirius	258 43.2	S16 43.1
15	0 19.1	18 19.8 ..	12.8	147 56.8 ..	49.6	1 19.6 ..	40.9	333 23.4 ..	33.8	Spica	158 42.8	S11 09.3
16	15 21.5	33 19.3	11.6	162 58.4	49.9	16 21.6	40.7	348 25.7	33.9	Suhail	223 00.1	S43 25.8
17	30 24.0	48 18.9	10.4	178 00.0	50.2	31 23.5	40.5	3 28.0	33.9			
18	45 26.5	63 18.5	S 9 09.2	193 01.6	S10 50.5	46 25.5	S 1 40.3	18 30.3	N 8 34.0	Vega	80 46.8	N38 46.9
19	60 28.9	78 18.0	08.0	208 03.2	50.8	61 27.5	40.1	33 32.6	34.1	Zuben'ubi	137 17.7	S16 02.2
20	75 31.4	93 17.6	06.8	223 04.8	51.1	76 29.5	39.9	48 34.9	34.1		SHA	Mer. Pass.
21	90 33.9	108 17.2 ..	05.5	238 06.4 ..	51.4	91 31.5 ..	39.6	63 37.2 ..	34.2		° ′	h m
22	105 36.3	123 16.7	04.3	253 08.0	51.7	106 33.5	39.4	78 39.5	34.3	Venus	19 54.0	13 46
23	120 38.8	138 16.3	03.1	268 09.6	52.0	121 35.4	39.2	93 41.9	34.4	Mars	148 11.7	5 12
Mer. Pass. 15 02.7		v −0.4	d 1.2	v 1.6	d 0.3	v 2.0	d 0.2	v 2.3	d 0.1	Jupiter	1 19.1	14 58
										Saturn	333 10.1	16 50

UT	SUN GHA	SUN Dec	MOON GHA	MOON v	MOON Dec	MOON d	MOON HP	Lat.	Twilight Naut.	Twilight Civil	Sunrise	Moonrise 3	Moonrise 4	Moonrise 5	Moonrise 6
d h	° ′	° ′	° ′	′	° ′	′	′	°	h m	h m	h m	h m	h m	h m	h m
								N 72	07 00	08 27	10 07	19 36	21 18	22 56	24 34
3 00	176 34.3	S16 42.8	328 30.7	12.4	N 8 41.2	9.7	56.4	N 70	06 53	08 10	09 31	19 44	21 19	22 51	24 23
01	191 34.2	42.1	343 02.1	12.5	8 31.5	9.8	56.4	68	06 48	07 57	09 06	19 50	21 20	22 47	24 13
02	206 34.2	41.4	357 33.6	12.5	8 21.7	9.8	56.3	66	06 43	07 46	08 47	19 56	21 21	22 44	24 06
03	221 34.1	.. 40.7	12 05.1	12.6	8 11.9	9.8	56.3	64	06 38	07 36	08 32	20 00	21 22	22 41	23 59
04	236 34.0	39.9	26 36.7	12.6	8 02.1	9.9	56.3	62	06 34	07 28	08 19	20 04	21 22	22 39	23 54
05	251 33.9	39.2	41 08.3	12.7	7 52.2	9.9	56.3	60	06 31	07 21	08 08	20 07	21 23	22 37	23 49
06	266 33.9	S16 38.5	55 40.0	12.7	N 7 42.3	9.9	56.2	N 58	06 28	07 15	07 58	20 10	21 23	22 35	23 45
W 07	281 33.8	37.7	70 11.7	12.8	7 32.4	9.9	56.2	56	06 25	07 09	07 50	20 13	21 24	22 33	23 41
E 08	296 33.7	37.0	84 43.5	12.9	7 22.5	10.0	56.2	54	06 22	07 04	07 43	20 15	21 24	22 32	23 38
D 09	311 33.7	.. 36.3	99 15.4	12.9	7 12.5	10.0	56.2	52	06 19	07 00	07 36	20 17	21 25	22 30	23 35
N 10	326 33.6	35.5	113 47.3	12.9	7 02.5	10.0	56.1	50	06 17	06 55	07 30	20 19	21 25	22 29	23 32
E 11	341 33.5	34.8	128 19.2	13.0	6 52.5	10.0	56.1	45	06 11	06 46	07 17	20 23	21 26	22 27	23 26
S 12	356 33.5	S16 34.1	142 51.2	13.1	N 6 42.5	10.1	56.1	N 40	06 05	06 38	07 06	20 27	21 26	22 24	23 21
D 13	11 33.4	33.3	157 23.3	13.1	6 32.4	10.0	56.0	35	06 00	06 30	06 57	20 30	21 27	22 22	23 17
A 14	26 33.3	32.6	171 55.4	13.2	6 22.4	10.1	56.0	30	05 55	06 24	06 49	20 33	21 27	22 21	23 13
Y 15	41 33.3	.. 31.9	186 27.6	13.2	6 12.3	10.1	56.0	20	05 45	06 12	06 35	20 37	21 28	22 18	23 07
16	56 33.2	31.1	200 59.8	13.3	6 02.2	10.1	56.0	N 10	05 35	06 00	06 22	20 41	21 29	22 15	23 01
17	71 33.1	30.4	215 32.1	13.3	5 52.1	10.2	55.9	0	05 24	05 49	06 10	20 45	21 30	22 13	22 56
18	86 33.1	S16 29.7	230 04.4	13.4	N 5 41.9	10.1	55.9	S 10	05 11	05 36	05 58	20 49	21 30	22 11	22 51
19	101 33.0	28.9	244 36.8	13.4	5 31.8	10.2	55.9	·20	04 55	05 22	05 46	20 53	21 31	22 08	22 45
20	116 32.9	28.2	259 09.2	13.5	5 21.6	10.2	55.9	30	04 35	05 05	05 31	20 58	21 32	22 06	22 39
21	131 32.9	.. 27.5	273 41.7	13.5	5 11.4	10.2	55.8	35	04 22	04 55	05 22	21 00	21 33	22 04	22 35
22	146 32.8	26.7	288 14.2	13.5	5 01.2	10.2	55.8	40	04 06	04 42	05 12	21 03	21 33	22 02	22 31
23	161 32.7	26.0	302 46.7	13.7	4 51.0	10.2	55.8	45	03 46	04 27	05 00	21 07	21 34	22 00	22 27
4 00	176 32.7	S16 25.2	317 19.4	13.6	N 4 40.8	10.2	55.7	S 50	03 20	04 09	04 46	21 11	21 35	21 58	22 21
01	191 32.6	24.5	331 52.0	13.7	4 30.6	10.3	55.7	52	03 07	04 00	04 39	21 13	21 35	21 57	22 19
02	206 32.5	23.8	346 24.7	13.7	4 20.3	10.3	55.7	54	02 51	03 49	04 32	21 15	21 36	21 56	22 16
03	221 32.5	.. 23.0	0 57.4	13.8	4 10.1	10.3	55.7	56	02 32	03 37	04 24	21 17	21 36	21 54	22 13
04	236 32.4	22.3	15 30.2	13.8	3 59.8	10.3	55.6	58	02 07	03 24	04 14	21 20	21 37	21 53	22 09
05	251 32.4	21.5	30 03.0	13.9	3 49.6	10.3	55.6	S 60	01 31	03 07	04 03	21 23	21 37	21 51	22 05

UT	SUN GHA	SUN Dec	MOON GHA	MOON v	MOON Dec	MOON d	MOON HP	Lat.	Sunset	Twilight Civil	Twilight Naut.	Moonset 3	Moonset 4	Moonset 5	Moonset 6
06	266 32.3	S16 20.8	44 35.9	13.9	N 3 39.3	10.3	55.6	°	h m	h m	h m	h m	h m	h m	h m
07	281 32.2	20.0	59 08.8	14.0	3 29.0	10.3	55.6	N 72	14 22	16 02	17 29	09 53	09 44	09 36	09 28
T 08	296 32.2	19.3	73 41.8	13.9	3 18.7	10.3	55.5	N 70	14 58	16 19	17 36	09 43	09 40	09 38	09 35
H 09	311 32.1	.. 18.6	88 14.7	14.1	3 08.4	10.3	55.5	68	15 22	16 32	17 41	09 35	09 37	09 39	09 41
U 10	326 32.1	17.8	102 47.8	14.0	2 58.1	10.2	55.5	66	15 42	16 43	17 46	09 28	09 34	09 40	09 46
R 11	341 32.0	17.1	117 20.8	14.1	2 47.9	10.3	55.5	64	15 57	16 52	17 51	09 22	09 32	09 41	09 50
S 12	356 31.9	S16 16.3	131 53.9	14.1	N 2 37.6	10.3	55.4	62	16 10	17 00	17 54	09 17	09 30	09 42	09 53
D 13	11 31.9	15.6	146 27.0	14.2	2 27.3	10.3	55.4	60	16 21	17 07	17 58	09 13	09 28	09 42	09 57
A 14	26 31.8	14.8	161 00.2	14.2	2 17.0	10.3	55.4	N 58	16 30	17 14	18 01	09 09	09 27	09 43	09 59
Y 15	41 31.8	.. 14.1	175 33.4	14.3	2 06.7	10.3	55.4	56	16 39	17 19	18 04	09 05	09 25	09 44	10 02
16	56 31.7	13.3	190 06.7	14.2	1 56.4	10.3	55.4	54	16 46	17 24	18 07	09 02	09 24	09 44	10 04
17	71 31.6	12.6	204 39.9	14.3	1 46.1	10.3	55.3	52	16 53	17 29	18 09	08 59	09 23	09 45	10 06
18	86 31.6	S16 11.8	219 13.2	14.4	N 1 35.8	10.3	55.3	50	16 59	17 33	18 12	08 57	09 22	09 45	10 08
19	101 31.5	11.1	233 46.6	14.3	1 25.5	10.3	55.3	45	17 11	17 42	18 18	08 51	09 19	09 46	10 12
20	116 31.5	10.3	248 19.9	14.4	1 15.2	10.3	55.3	N 40	17 22	17 51	18 23	08 46	09 17	09 47	10 16
21	131 31.4	.. 09.6	262 53.3	14.4	1 04.9	10.3	55.2	35	17 31	17 58	18 28	08 42	09 16	09 47	10 19
22	146 31.4	08.8	277 26.7	14.5	0 54.6	10.3	55.2	30	17 39	18 04	18 33	08 39	09 14	09 48	10 21
23	161 31.3	08.1	292 00.2	14.5	0 44.4	10.3	55.2	20	17 53	18 16	18 43	08 32	09 11	09 49	10 26
5 00	176 31.3	S16 07.3	306 33.7	14.5	N 0 34.1	10.3	55.2	N 10	18 06	18 27	18 53	08 27	09 09	09 50	10 30
01	191 31.2	06.6	321 07.2	14.5	0 23.8	10.2	55.1	0	18 17	18 39	19 04	08 21	09 07	09 51	10 34
02	206 31.1	05.8	335 40.7	14.6	0 13.6	10.3	55.1	S 10	18 29	18 51	19 17	08 16	09 05	09 51	10 37
03	221 31.1	.. 05.1	350 14.3	14.6	N 0 03.3	10.2	55.1	20	18 42	19 05	19 32	08 10	09 02	09 52	10 42
04	236 31.0	04.3	4 47.9	14.6	S 0 06.9	10.2	55.1	30	18 57	19 22	19 53	08 04	08 59	09 53	10 46
05	251 31.0	03.6	19 21.5	14.6	0 17.1	10.3	55.1	35	19 05	19 32	20 05	08 00	08 58	09 54	10 49
06	266 30.9	S16 02.8	33 55.1	14.7	S 0 27.4	10.2	55.0	40	19 15	19 45	20 21	07 55	08 56	09 54	10 52
07	281 30.9	02.1	48 28.8	14.7	0 37.6	10.2	55.0	45	19 27	19 59	20 40	07 50	08 54	09 55	10 55
08	296 30.8	01.3	63 02.5	14.7	0 47.8	10.2	55.0	S 50	19 41	20 18	21 06	07 44	08 51	09 56	11 00
F 09	311 30.8	16 00.6	77 36.2	14.7	0 58.0	10.1	55.0	52	19 47	20 27	21 19	07 41	08 50	09 56	11 01
R 10	326 30.7	15 59.8	92 09.9	14.7	1 08.1	10.1	55.0	54	19 54	20 37	21 34	07 38	08 48	09 57	11 04
I 11	341 30.7	59.1	106 43.6	14.8	1 18.3	10.1	54.9	56	20 03	20 48	21 53	07 35	08 47	09 57	11 06
D 12	356 30.6	S15 58.3	121 17.4	14.8	S 1 28.4	10.2	54.9	58	20 12	21 02	22 17	07 31	08 45	09 58	11 09
A 13	11 30.6	57.5	135 51.2	14.8	1 38.6	10.1	54.9	S 60	20 23	21 18	22 50	07 27	08 44	09 58	11 11
Y 14	26 30.5	56.8	150 25.0	14.8	1 48.7	10.1	54.9								
15	41 30.5	.. 56.0	164 58.8	14.8	1 58.8	10.1	54.9								
16	56 30.4	55.3	179 32.6	14.8	2 08.9	10.0	54.8			SUN			MOON		
17	71 30.4	54.5	194 06.4	14.9	2 18.9	10.1	54.8								
18	86 30.3	S15 53.7	208 40.3	14.9	S 2 29.0	10.0	54.8	Day	Eqn. of Time 00ʰ	Eqn. of Time 12ʰ	Mer. Pass.	Mer. Pass. Upper	Mer. Pass. Lower	Age	Phase
19	101 30.3	53.0	223 14.2	14.9	2 39.0	10.0	54.8								
20	116 30.2	52.2	237 48.1	14.8	2 49.0	10.0	54.8	d	m s	m s	h m	h m	h m	d %	
21	131 30.2	.. 51.5	252 21.9	15.0	2 59.0	10.0	54.7	3	13 43	13 46	12 14	02 10	14 33	17 91	
22	146 30.1	50.7	266 55.9	14.9	3 09.0	10.0	54.7	4	13 49	13 52	12 14	02 56	15 18	18 85	
23	161 30.1	49.9	281 29.8	14.9	S 3 19.0	9.9	54.7	5	13 55	13 57	12 14	03 40	16 02	19 77	
	SD 16.3	d 0.7	SD 15.3		15.1		15.0									

UT	ARIES GHA	VENUS −3.9 GHA	VENUS Dec	MARS +0.4 GHA	MARS Dec	JUPITER −2.1 GHA	JUPITER Dec	SATURN +0.5 GHA	SATURN Dec	STARS Name	SHA	Dec
d h	° ′	° ′	° ′	° ′	° ′	° ′	° ′	° ′	° ′		° ′	° ′
6 00	135 41.2	153 15.9	S 9 01.9	283 11.2	S10 52.2	136 37.4	S 1 39.0	108 44.2	N 8 34.4	Acamar	315 26.8	S40 18.9
01	150 43.7	168 15.5	9 00.7	298 12.8	52.5	151 39.4	38.8	123 46.5	34.5	Achernar	335 35.3	S57 14.9
02	165 46.2	183 15.0	8 59.5	313 14.4	52.8	166 41.4	38.6	138 48.8	34.6	Acrux	173 21.2	S63 05.4
03	180 48.6	198 14.6	.. 58.2	328 16.0	.. 53.1	181 43.4	.. 38.4	153 51.1	.. 34.6	Adhara	255 20.9	S28 58.5
04	195 51.1	213 14.2	57.0	343 17.6	53.4	196 45.4	38.1	168 53.4	34.7	Aldebaran	291 02.0	N16 30.3
05	210 53.6	228 13.7	55.8	358 19.2	53.7	211 47.3	37.9	183 55.7	34.8			
06	225 56.0	243 13.3	S 8 54.6	13 20.8	S10 54.0	226 49.3	S 1 37.7	198 58.0	N 8 34.8	Alioth	166 30.1	N55 57.7
07	240 58.5	258 12.9	53.4	28 22.4	54.2	241 51.3	37.5	214 00.3	34.9	Alkaid	153 07.5	N49 18.9
S 08	256 01.0	273 12.5	52.1	43 24.0	54.5	256 53.3	37.3	229 02.6	35.0	Al Na'ir	27 58.1	S46 58.1
A 09	271 03.4	288 12.0	.. 50.9	58 25.7	.. 54.8	271 55.3	.. 37.1	244 04.9	.. 35.0	Alnilam	275 57.4	S 1 12.4
T 10	286 05.9	303 11.6	49.7	73 27.3	55.1	286 57.3	36.9	259 07.3	35.1	Alphard	218 06.6	S 8 39.4
U 11	301 08.4	318 11.2	48.5	88 28.9	55.4	301 59.2	36.6	274 09.6	35.2			
R 12	316 10.8	333 10.8	S 8 47.3	103 30.5	S10 55.7	317 01.2	S 1 36.4	289 11.9	N 8 35.3	Alphecca	126 20.5	N26 43.0
D 13	331 13.3	348 10.3	46.0	118 32.1	56.0	332 03.2	36.2	304 14.2	35.3	Alpheratz	357 55.2	N29 05.1
A 14	346 15.7	3 09.9	44.8	133 33.7	56.2	347 05.2	36.0	319 16.5	35.4	Altair	62 19.4	N 8 51.9
Y 15	1 18.2	18 09.5	.. 43.6	148 35.3	.. 56.5	2 07.2	.. 35.8	334 18.8	.. 35.5	Ankaa	353 26.9	S42 19.0
16	16 20.7	33 09.1	42.4	163 36.9	56.8	17 09.1	35.6	349 21.1	35.5	Antares	112 40.0	S26 25.6
17	31 23.1	48 08.7	41.2	178 38.6	57.1	32 11.1	35.4	4 23.4	35.6			
18	46 25.6	63 08.2	S 8 39.9	193 40.2	S10 57.4	47 13.1	S 1 35.1	19 25.7	N 8 35.7	Arcturus	146 05.8	N19 11.1
19	61 28.1	78 07.8	38.7	208 41.8	57.7	62 15.1	34.9	34 28.0	35.7	Atria	107 52.1	S69 01.2
20	76 30.5	93 07.4	37.5	223 43.4	57.9	77 17.1	34.7	49 30.3	35.8	Avior	234 21.9	S59 30.6
21	91 33.0	108 07.0	.. 36.3	238 45.0	.. 58.2	92 19.0	.. 34.5	64 32.6	.. 35.9	Bellatrix	278 43.7	N 6 20.7
22	106 35.5	123 06.5	35.0	253 46.6	58.5	107 21.0	34.3	79 35.0	36.0	Betelgeuse	271 13.1	N 7 24.2
23	121 37.9	138 06.1	33.8	268 48.3	58.8	122 23.0	34.1	94 37.3	36.0			
7 00	136 40.4	153 05.7	S 8 32.6	283 49.9	S10 59.1	137 25.0	S 1 33.9	109 39.6	N 8 36.1	Canopus	264 00.6	S52 42.1
01	151 42.8	168 05.3	31.4	298 51.5	59.3	152 27.0	33.6	124 41.9	36.2	Capella	280 50.6	N45 59.8
02	166 45.3	183 04.9	30.1	313 53.1	59.6	167 28.9	33.4	139 44.2	36.2	Deneb	49 39.5	N45 16.6
03	181 47.8	198 04.4	.. 28.9	328 54.7	10 59.9	182 30.9	.. 33.2	154 46.5	.. 36.3	Denebola	182 44.7	N14 34.5
04	196 50.2	213 04.0	27.7	343 56.4	11 00.2	197 32.9	33.0	169 48.8	36.4	Diphda	349 07.2	S17 59.8
05	211 52.7	228 03.6	26.4	358 58.0	00.5	212 34.9	32.8	184 51.1	36.5			
06	226 55.2	243 03.2	S 8 25.2	13 59.6	S11 00.7	227 36.9	S 1 32.6	199 53.4	N 8 36.5	Dubhe	194 04.7	N61 45.2
07	241 57.6	258 02.8	24.0	29 01.2	01.0	242 38.8	32.4	214 55.7	36.6	Elnath	278 26.4	N28 36.3
08	257 00.1	273 02.4	22.8	44 02.8	01.3	257 40.8	32.1	229 58.0	36.7	Eltanin	90 51.7	N51 29.2
S 09	272 02.6	288 01.9	.. 21.5	59 04.5	.. 01.6	272 42.8	.. 31.9	245 00.3	.. 36.7	Enif	33 58.3	N 9 52.2
U 10	287 05.0	303 01.5	20.3	74 06.1	01.9	287 44.8	31.7	260 02.6	36.8	Fomalhaut	15 36.5	S29 37.8
N 11	302 07.5	318 01.1	19.1	89 07.7	02.1	302 46.8	31.5	275 04.9	36.9			
D 12	317 10.0	333 00.7	S 8 17.8	104 09.3	S11 02.4	317 48.7	S 1 31.3	290 07.2	N 8 36.9	Gacrux	172 12.9	S57 06.2
A 13	332 12.4	348 00.3	16.6	119 11.0	02.7	332 50.7	31.1	305 09.5	37.0	Gienah	176 03.5	S17 32.2
Y 14	347 14.9	2 59.9	15.4	134 12.6	03.0	347 52.7	30.8	320 11.8	37.1	Hadar	149 03.5	S60 21.8
15	2 17.3	17 59.5	.. 14.1	149 14.2	.. 03.3	2 54.7	.. 30.6	335 14.1	.. 37.2	Hamal	328 13.4	N23 27.4
16	17 19.8	32 59.0	12.9	164 15.9	03.5	17 56.7	30.4	350 16.5	37.2	Kaus Aust.	83 58.8	S34 23.0
17	32 22.3	47 58.6	11.7	179 17.5	03.8	32 58.6	30.2	5 18.8	37.3			
18	47 24.7	62 58.2	S 8 10.5	194 19.1	S11 04.1	48 00.6	S 1 30.0	20 21.1	N 8 37.4	Kochab	137 19.6	N74 09.3
19	62 27.2	77 57.8	09.2	209 20.7	04.4	63 02.6	29.8	35 23.4	37.4	Markab	13 49.7	N15 11.9
20	77 29.7	92 57.4	08.0	224 22.4	04.6	78 04.6	29.5	50 25.7	37.5	Menkar	314 26.7	N 4 05.0
21	92 32.1	107 57.0	.. 06.8	239 24.0	.. 04.9	93 06.5	.. 29.3	65 28.0	.. 37.6	Menkent	148 20.6	S36 21.7
22	107 34.6	122 56.6	05.5	254 25.6	05.2	108 08.5	29.1	80 30.3	37.7	Miaplacidus	221 41.0	S69 42.9
23	122 37.1	137 56.2	04.3	269 27.3	05.5	123 10.5	28.9	95 32.6	37.7			
8 00	137 39.5	152 55.7	S 8 03.0	284 28.9	S11 05.8	138 12.5	S 1 28.7	110 34.9	N 8 37.8	Mirfak	308 56.2	N49 51.5
01	152 42.0	167 55.3	01.8	299 30.5	06.0	153 14.5	28.5	125 37.2	37.9	Nunki	76 12.4	S26 17.8
02	167 44.5	182 54.9	8 00.6	314 32.2	06.3	168 16.4	28.2	140 39.5	37.9	Peacock	53 37.3	S56 44.2
03	182 46.9	197 54.5	7 59.3	329 33.8	.. 06.6	183 18.4	.. 28.0	155 41.8	.. 38.0	Pollux	243 40.9	N28 01.6
04	197 49.4	212 54.1	58.1	344 35.4	06.9	198 20.4	27.8	170 44.1	38.1	Procyon	245 11.0	N 5 13.5
05	212 51.8	227 53.7	56.9	359 37.1	07.1	213 22.4	27.6	185 46.4	38.2			
06	227 54.3	242 53.3	S 7 55.6	14 38.7	S11 07.4	228 24.3	S 1 27.4	200 48.7	N 8 38.2	Rasalhague	96 17.0	N12 33.6
07	242 56.8	257 52.9	54.4	29 40.3	07.7	243 26.3	27.2	215 51.0	38.3	Regulus	207 55.0	N11 58.2
08	257 59.2	272 52.5	53.2	44 42.0	08.0	258 28.3	27.0	230 53.3	38.4	Rigel	281 22.5	S 8 12.4
M 09	273 01.7	287 52.1	.. 51.9	59 43.6	.. 08.2	273 30.3	.. 26.7	245 55.6	.. 38.4	Rigil Kent.	140 06.8	S60 49.5
O 10	288 04.2	302 51.7	50.7	74 45.2	08.5	288 32.3	26.5	260 57.9	38.5	Sabik	102 25.4	S15 43.3
N 11	303 06.6	317 51.2	49.4	89 46.9	08.8	303 34.2	26.3	276 00.2	38.6			
D 12	318 09.1	332 50.8	S 7 48.2	104 48.5	S11 09.0	318 36.2	S 1 26.1	291 02.5	N 8 38.7	Schedar	349 53.5	N56 32.0
A 13	333 11.6	347 50.4	47.0	119 50.2	09.3	333 38.2	25.9	306 04.8	38.7	Shaula	96 37.2	S37 06.0
Y 14	348 14.0	2 50.0	45.7	134 51.8	09.6	348 40.2	25.6	321 07.1	38.8	Sirius	258 43.2	S16 43.1
15	3 16.5	17 49.6	.. 44.5	149 53.4	.. 09.9	3 42.1	.. 25.4	336 09.4	.. 38.9	Spica	158 42.8	S11 09.3
16	18 18.9	32 49.2	43.2	164 55.1	10.1	18 44.1	25.2	351 11.7	39.0	Suhail	223 00.1	S43 25.8
17	33 21.4	47 48.8	42.0	179 56.7	10.4	33 46.1	25.0	6 14.0	39.0			
18	48 23.9	62 48.4	S 7 40.8	194 58.4	S11 10.7	48 48.1	S 1 24.8	21 16.3	N 8 39.1	Vega	80 46.8	N38 46.9
19	63 26.3	77 48.0	39.5	210 00.0	10.9	63 50.0	24.6	36 18.6	39.2	Zuben'ubi	137 17.7	S16 02.2
20	78 28.8	92 47.6	38.3	225 01.6	11.2	78 52.0	24.3	51 20.9	39.2			
21	93 31.3	107 47.2	.. 37.0	240 03.3	.. 11.5	93 54.0	.. 24.1	66 23.2	.. 39.3		SHA	Mer. Pass.
22	108 33.7	122 46.8	35.8	255 04.9	11.8	108 56.0	23.9	81 25.5	39.4	Venus	16 25.3	13 48
23	123 36.2	137 46.4	34.5	270 06.6	12.0	123 57.9	23.7	96 27.8	39.5	Mars	147 09.5	5 04
Mer. Pass. 14 50.9		v −0.4	d 1.2	v 1.6	d 0.3	v 2.0	d 0.2	v 2.3	d 0.1	Jupiter	0 44.6	14 48
										Saturn	332 59.2	16 39

UT	SUN GHA	SUN Dec	MOON GHA	v	Dec	d	HP
d h	° ′	° ′	° ′	′	° ′	′	′
6 00	176 30.0	S15 49.2	296 03.7	14.9	S 3 28.9	9.9	54.7
01	191 30.0	48.4	310 37.6	15.0	3 38.8	9.9	54.7
02	206 29.9	47.7	325 11.6	14.9	3 48.7	9.9	54.7
03	221 29.9	.. 46.9	339 45.5	15.0	3 58.6	9.8	54.7
04	236 29.8	46.1	354 19.5	15.0	4 08.4	9.9	54.6
05	251 29.8	45.4	8 53.5	15.0	4 18.3	9.8	54.6
S 06	266 29.7	S15 44.6	23 27.5	14.9	S 4 28.1	9.8	54.6
A 07	281 29.7	43.8	38 01.4	15.0	4 37.9	9.7	54.6
T 08	296 29.7	43.1	52 35.4	15.0	4 47.6	9.7	54.6
U 09	311 29.6	.. 42.3	67 09.4	15.0	4 57.3	9.7	54.6
R 10	326 29.6	41.5	81 43.4	15.0	5 07.0	9.7	54.6
D 11	341 29.5	40.8	96 17.4	15.0	5 16.7	9.7	54.5
A 12	356 29.5	S15 40.0	110 51.4	15.0	S 5 26.4	9.6	54.5
Y 13	11 29.4	39.2	125 25.4	15.0	5 36.0	9.6	54.5
14	26 29.4	38.5	139 59.4	15.0	5 45.6	9.5	54.5
15	41 29.4	.. 37.7	154 33.4	14.9	5 55.1	9.6	54.5
16	56 29.3	36.9	169 07.3	15.0	6 04.7	9.5	54.5
17	71 29.3	36.1	183 41.3	15.0	6 14.2	9.5	54.5
18	86 29.2	S15 35.4	198 15.3	15.0	S 6 23.7	9.4	54.5
19	101 29.2	34.6	212 49.3	15.0	6 33.1	9.4	54.4
20	116 29.2	33.8	227 23.3	14.9	6 42.5	9.4	54.4
21	131 29.1	.. 33.1	241 57.2	15.0	6 51.9	9.3	54.4
22	146 29.1	32.3	256 31.2	15.0	7 01.2	9.4	54.4
23	161 29.0	31.5	271 05.2	14.9	7 10.6	9.2	54.4
7 00	176 29.0	S15 30.7	285 39.1	15.0	S 7 19.8	9.3	54.4
01	191 29.0	30.0	300 13.1	14.9	7 29.1	9.2	54.4
02	206 28.9	29.2	314 47.0	14.9	7 38.3	9.2	54.4
03	221 28.9	.. 28.4	329 20.9	14.9	7 47.5	9.1	54.4
04	236 28.8	27.6	343 54.8	15.0	7 56.6	9.1	54.4
05	251 28.8	26.9	358 28.8	14.8	8 05.7	9.1	54.3
S 06	266 28.8	S15 26.1	13 02.6	14.9	S 8 14.8	9.1	54.3
U 07	281 28.7	25.3	27 36.5	14.9	8 23.9	8.9	54.3
N 08	296 28.7	24.5	42 10.4	14.9	8 32.8	9.0	54.3
D 09	311 28.7	.. 23.8	56 44.3	14.8	8 41.8	8.9	54.3
A 10	326 28.6	23.0	71 18.1	14.8	8 50.7	8.9	54.3
Y 11	341 28.6	22.2	85 51.9	14.8	8 59.6	8.9	54.3
12	356 28.6	S15 21.4	100 25.7	14.8	S 9 08.5	8.8	54.3
13	11 28.5	20.6	114 59.5	14.8	9 17.3	8.7	54.3
14	26 28.5	19.9	129 33.3	14.8	9 26.0	8.8	54.3
15	41 28.5	.. 19.1	144 07.1	14.7	9 34.8	8.6	54.3
16	56 28.4	18.3	158 40.8	14.7	9 43.4	8.7	54.3
17	71 28.4	17.5	173 14.5	14.8	9 52.1	8.6	54.3
18	86 28.4	S15 16.7	187 48.3	14.6	S10 00.7	8.5	54.3
19	101 28.3	16.0	202 21.9	14.7	10 09.2	8.5	54.3
20	116 28.3	15.2	216 55.6	14.7	10 17.7	8.5	54.2
21	131 28.3	.. 14.4	231 29.3	14.6	10 26.2	8.4	54.2
22	146 28.2	13.6	246 02.9	14.6	10 34.6	8.4	54.2
23	161 28.2	12.8	260 36.5	14.6	10 43.0	8.3	54.2
8 00	176 28.2	S15 12.0	275 10.1	14.5	S10 51.3	8.3	54.2
01	191 28.1	11.2	289 43.6	14.5	10 59.6	8.3	54.2
02	206 28.1	10.5	304 17.1	14.6	11 07.9	8.2	54.2
03	221 28.1	.. 09.7	318 50.7	14.4	11 16.1	8.1	54.2
04	236 28.0	08.9	333 24.1	14.5	11 24.2	8.1	54.2
05	251 28.0	08.1	347 57.6	14.4	11 32.3	8.0	54.2
M 06	266 28.0	S15 07.3	2 31.0	14.4	S11 40.3	8.0	54.2
O 07	281 28.0	06.5	17 04.4	14.4	11 48.3	8.0	54.2
N 08	296 27.9	05.7	31 37.8	14.4	11 56.3	7.9	54.2
D 09	311 27.9	.. 05.0	46 11.2	14.3	12 04.2	7.9	54.2
A 10	326 27.9	04.2	60 44.5	14.3	12 12.1	7.8	54.2
Y 11	341 27.8	03.4	75 17.8	14.2	12 19.9	7.7	54.2
12	356 27.8	S15 02.6	89 51.0	14.3	S12 27.6	7.7	54.2
13	11 27.8	01.8	104 24.3	14.2	12 35.3	7.6	54.2
14	26 27.8	01.0	118 57.5	14.1	12 42.9	7.6	54.2
15	41 27.7	15 00.2	133 30.6	14.2	12 50.5	7.6	54.2
16	56 27.7	14 59.4	148 03.8	14.1	12 58.1	7.4	54.2
17	71 27.7	58.6	162 36.9	14.0	13 05.5	7.5	54.2
18	86 27.7	S14 57.8	177 09.9	14.1	S13 13.0	7.3	54.2
19	101 27.6	57.0	191 43.0	14.0	13 20.3	7.4	54.2
20	116 27.6	56.2	206 16.0	14.0	13 27.7	7.2	54.2
21	131 27.6	.. 55.5	220 49.0	13.9	13 34.9	7.2	54.2
22	146 27.6	54.7	235 21.9	13.9	13 42.1	7.2	54.3
23	161 27.5	53.9	249 54.8	13.9	S13 49.3	7.1	54.3
	SD 16.2	d 0.8	SD 14.9		14.8		14.8

Lat.	Twilight Naut.	Twilight Civil	Sunrise	Moonrise 6	7	8	9
°	h m	h m	h m	h m	h m	h m	h m
N 72	06 49	08 13	09 46	24 34	00 34	02 14	04 00
N 70	06 43	07 59	09 16	24 23	00 23	01 55	03 29
68	06 39	07 47	08 54	24 13	00 13	01 39	03 06
66	06 35	07 37	08 36	24 06	00 06	01 27	02 48
64	06 31	07 28	08 22	23 59	25 17	01 17	02 33
62	06 28	07 21	08 10	23 54	25 08	01 08	02 21
60	06 25	07 15	08 00	23 49	25 01	01 01	02 11
N 58	06 22	07 09	07 52	23 45	24 54	00 54	02 02
56	06 19	07 04	07 44	23 41	24 48	00 48	01 54
54	06 17	06 59	07 37	23 38	24 43	00 43	01 47
52	06 15	06 55	07 31	23 35	24 38	00 38	01 41
50	06 13	06 51	07 25	23 32	24 34	00 34	01 35
45	06 07	06 42	07 13	23 26	24 25	00 25	01 23
N 40	06 03	06 35	07 03	23 21	24 18	00 18	01 13
35	05 58	06 28	06 54	23 17	24 11	00 11	01 05
30	05 54	06 22	06 47	23 13	24 05	00 05	00 58
20	05 44	06 11	06 33	23 07	23 56	24 45	00 45
N 10	05 35	06 00	06 22	23 01	23 47	24 34	00 34
0	05 24	05 49	06 11	22 56	23 39	24 23	00 23
S 10	05 12	05 38	05 59	22 51	23 31	24 13	00 13
20	04 57	05 24	05 47	22 45	23 23	24 02	00 02
30	04 38	05 08	05 33	22 39	23 13	23 49	24 28
35	04 25	04 58	05 25	22 35	23 08	23 42	24 20
40	04 10	04 46	05 16	22 31	23 02	23 34	24 10
45	03 52	04 32	05 05	22 27	22 54	23 24	23 58
S 50	03 27	04 15	04 51	22 21	22 46	23 13	23 44
52	03 15	04 06	04 45	22 19	22 42	23 08	23 38
54	03 00	03 56	04 38	22 16	22 37	23 02	23 30
56	02 43	03 45	04 30	22 13	22 33	22 55	23 22
58	02 21	03 33	04 22	22 09	22 27	22 48	23 13
S 60	01 51	03 18	04 12	22 05	22 21	22 40	23 03

Lat.	Sunset	Twilight Civil	Twilight Naut.	Moonset 6	7	8	9
°	h m	h m	h m	h m	h m	h m	h m
N 72	14 44	16 16	17 41	09 28	09 19	09 09	08 55
N 70	15 14	16 31	17 46	09 35	09 32	09 30	09 28
68	15 36	16 43	17 51	09 41	09 43	09 46	09 52
66	15 53	16 53	17 55	09 46	09 52	10 00	10 10
64	16 07	17 01	17 58	09 50	09 59	10 11	10 26
62	16 19	17 08	18 02	09 53	10 06	10 20	10 38
60	16 29	17 15	18 04	09 57	10 12	10 29	10 49
N 58	16 37	17 20	18 07	09 59	10 17	10 36	10 58
56	16 45	17 25	18 10	10 02	10 21	10 42	11 07
54	16 52	17 30	18 12	10 04	10 25	10 48	11 14
52	16 58	17 34	18 14	10 06	10 29	10 53	11 21
50	17 04	17 38	18 16	10 08	10 32	10 58	11 27
45	17 16	17 47	18 21	10 12	10 39	11 08	11 40
N 40	17 26	17 54	18 26	10 16	10 45	11 16	11 50
35	17 34	18 01	18 31	10 19	10 50	11 24	11 59
30	17 42	18 07	18 35	10 21	10 55	11 30	12 08
20	17 55	18 18	18 44	10 26	11 03	11 41	12 21
N 10	18 07	18 28	18 53	10 30	11 10	11 51	12 34
0	18 18	18 39	19 04	10 34	11 17	12 00	12 45
S 10	18 29	18 51	19 16	10 37	11 23	12 09	12 57
20	18 41	19 04	19 31	10 42	11 30	12 19	13 09
30	18 54	19 20	19 50	10 46	11 38	12 31	13 23
35	19 02	19 30	20 02	10 49	11 43	12 37	13 31
40	19 12	19 41	20 17	10 52	11 48	12 45	13 40
45	19 23	19 55	20 35	10 55	11 53	12 53	13 51
S 50	19 36	20 12	20 59	11 00	12 02	13 04	14 04
52	19 42	20 21	21 11	11 01	12 05	13 09	14 11
54	19 49	20 30	21 26	11 04	12 09	13 14	14 17
56	19 56	20 41	21 42	11 06	12 13	13 20	14 25
58	20 05	20 53	22 04	11 09	12 18	13 27	14 34
S 60	20 15	21 08	22 32	11 11	12 23	13 34	14 44

	SUN			MOON			
Day	Eqn. of Time 00ʰ	12ʰ	Mer. Pass.	Mer. Pass. Upper	Lower	Age	Phase
d	m s	m s	h m	h m	h m	d	%
6	14 00	14 02	12 14	04 23	16 45	20	69
7	14 04	14 06	12 14	05 06	17 28	21	60
8	14 07	14 09	12 14	05 50	18 12	22	50

UT	ARIES GHA	VENUS −3.9 GHA	Dec	MARS +0.3 GHA	Dec	JUPITER −2.1 GHA	Dec	SATURN +0.5 GHA	Dec
9 00	138 38.7	152 46.0	S 7 33.3	285 08.2	S11 12.3	138 59.9	S 1 23.5	111 30.1	N 8 39.5
01	153 41.1	167 45.6	32.1	300 09.9	12.6	154 01.9	23.3	126 32.4	39.6
02	168 43.6	182 45.2	30.8	315 11.5	12.8	169 03.9	23.0	141 34.7	39.7
03	183 46.1	197 44.8 ..	29.6	330 13.2 ..	13.1	184 05.8 ..	22.8	156 37.0 ..	39.8
04	198 48.5	212 44.4	28.3	345 14.8	13.4	199 07.8	22.6	171 39.3	39.8
05	213 51.0	227 44.0	27.1	0 16.5	13.7	214 09.8	22.4	186 41.6	39.9
T 06	228 53.4	242 43.6	S 7 25.8	15 18.1	S11 13.9	229 11.8	S 1 22.2	201 43.9	N 8 40.0
U 07	243 55.9	257 43.2	24.6	30 19.8	14.2	244 13.7	22.0	216 46.2	40.0
E 08	258 58.4	272 42.8	23.3	45 21.4	14.5	259 15.7	21.7	231 48.5	40.1
S 09	274 00.8	287 42.4 ..	22.1	60 23.1 ..	14.7	274 17.7 ..	21.5	246 50.8 ..	40.2
D 10	289 03.3	302 42.0	20.9	75 24.7	15.0	289 19.7	21.3	261 53.1	40.3
A 11	304 05.8	317 41.6	19.6	90 26.4	15.3	304 21.6	21.1	276 55.4	40.3
Y 12	319 08.2	332 41.2	S 7 18.4	105 28.0	S11 15.6	319 23.6	S 1 20.9	291 57.7	N 8 40.4
13	334 10.7	347 40.8	17.1	120 29.7	15.8	334 25.6	20.6	307 00.0	40.5
14	349 13.2	2 40.4	15.9	135 31.3	16.1	349 27.5	20.4	322 02.3	40.6
15	4 15.6	17 40.0 ..	14.6	150 33.0 ..	16.3	4 29.5 ..	20.2	337 04.6 ..	40.6
16	19 18.1	32 39.6	13.4	165 34.6	16.6	19 31.5	20.0	352 06.9	40.7
17	34 20.6	47 39.2	12.1	180 36.3	16.9	34 33.5	19.8	7 09.2	40.8
18	49 23.0	62 38.8	S 7 10.9	195 37.9	S11 17.1	49 35.4	S 1 19.6	22 11.5	N 8 40.9
19	64 25.5	77 38.4	09.6	210 39.6	17.4	64 37.4	19.3	37 13.8	40.9
20	79 27.9	92 38.0	08.4	225 41.2	17.7	79 39.4	19.1	52 16.1	41.0
21	94 30.4	107 37.6 ..	07.1	240 42.9 ..	17.9	94 41.4 ..	18.9	67 18.4 ..	41.1
22	109 32.9	122 37.2	05.9	255 44.6	18.2	109 43.3	18.7	82 20.7	41.1
23	124 35.3	137 36.8	04.6	270 46.2	18.5	124 45.3	18.5	97 23.0	41.2
10 00	139 37.8	152 36.4	S 7 03.4	285 47.9	S11 18.7	139 47.3	S 1 18.2	112 25.3	N 8 41.3
01	154 40.3	167 36.0	02.1	300 49.5	19.0	154 49.2	18.0	127 27.6	41.4
02	169 42.7	182 35.6	7 00.9	315 51.2	19.2	169 51.2	17.8	142 29.8	41.4
03	184 45.2	197 35.2	6 59.6	330 52.9 ..	19.5	184 53.2 ..	17.6	157 32.1 ..	41.5
04	199 47.7	212 34.9	58.4	345 54.5	19.8	199 55.2	17.4	172 34.4	41.6
05	214 50.1	227 34.5	57.1	0 56.2	20.0	214 57.1	17.2	187 36.7	41.7
W 06	229 52.6	242 34.1	S 6 55.9	15 57.9	S11 20.3	229 59.1	S 1 16.9	202 39.0	N 8 41.7
E 07	244 55.0	257 33.7	54.6	30 59.5	20.6	245 01.1	16.7	217 41.3	41.8
D 08	259 57.5	272 33.3	53.3	46 01.2	20.8	260 03.0	16.5	232 43.6	41.9
N 09	275 00.0	287 32.9 ..	52.1	61 02.8 ..	21.1	275 05.0 ..	16.3	247 45.9 ..	42.0
E 10	290 02.4	302 32.5	50.8	76 04.5	21.3	290 07.0	16.1	262 48.2	42.0
S 11	305 04.9	317 32.1	49.6	91 06.2	21.6	305 09.0	15.8	277 50.5	42.1
D 12	320 07.4	332 31.7	S 6 48.3	106 07.8	S11 21.9	320 10.9	S 1 15.6	292 52.8	N 8 42.2
A 13	335 09.8	347 31.3	47.1	121 09.5	22.1	335 12.9	15.4	307 55.1	42.3
Y 14	350 12.3	2 30.9	45.8	136 11.2	22.4	350 14.9	15.2	322 57.4	42.3
15	5 14.8	17 30.5 ..	44.6	151 12.8 ..	22.7	5 16.8 ..	15.0	337 59.7 ..	42.4
16	20 17.2	32 30.2	43.3	166 14.5	22.9	20 18.8	14.7	353 02.0	42.5
17	35 19.7	47 29.8	42.1	181 16.2	23.2	35 20.8	14.5	8 04.3	42.6
18	50 22.2	62 29.4	S 6 40.8	196 17.9	S11 23.4	50 22.7	S 1 14.3	23 06.6	N 8 42.6
19	65 24.6	77 29.0	39.5	211 19.5	23.7	65 24.7	14.1	38 08.9	42.7
20	80 27.1	92 28.6	38.3	226 21.2	24.0	80 26.7	13.9	53 11.1	42.8
21	95 29.5	107 28.2 ..	37.0	241 22.9 ..	24.2	95 28.7 ..	13.7	68 13.4 ..	42.9
22	110 32.0	122 27.8	35.8	256 24.5	24.5	110 30.6	13.4	83 15.7	42.9
23	125 34.5	137 27.4	34.5	271 26.2	24.7	125 32.6	13.2	98 18.0	43.0
11 00	140 36.9	152 27.1	S 6 33.2	286 27.9	S11 25.0	140 34.6	S 1 13.0	113 20.3	N 8 43.1
01	155 39.4	167 26.7	32.0	301 29.6	25.3	155 36.5	12.8	128 22.6	43.2
02	170 41.9	182 26.3	30.7	316 31.2	25.5	170 38.5	12.6	143 24.9	43.2
03	185 44.3	197 25.9 ..	29.5	331 32.9 ..	25.8	185 40.5 ..	12.3	158 27.2 ..	43.3
04	200 46.8	212 25.5	28.2	346 34.6	26.0	200 42.4	12.1	173 29.5	43.4
05	215 49.3	227 25.1	26.9	1 36.3	26.3	215 44.4	11.9	188 31.8	43.5
T 06	230 51.7	242 24.7	S 6 25.7	16 37.9	S11 26.5	230 46.4	S 1 11.7	203 34.1	N 8 43.5
H 07	245 54.2	257 24.4	24.4	31 39.6	26.8	245 48.4	11.5	218 36.4	43.6
U 08	260 56.7	272 24.0	23.2	46 41.3	27.1	260 50.3	11.2	233 38.7	43.7
R 09	275 59.1	287 23.6 ..	21.9	61 43.0 ..	27.3	275 52.3 ..	11.0	248 40.9 ..	43.8
S 10	291 01.6	302 23.2	20.6	76 44.7	27.6	290 54.3	10.8	263 43.2	43.8
D 11	306 04.0	317 22.8	19.4	91 46.3	27.8	305 56.2	10.6	278 45.5	43.9
A 12	321 06.5	332 22.4	S 6 18.1	106 48.0	S11 28.1	320 58.2	S 1 10.4	293 47.8	N 8 44.0
Y 13	336 09.0	347 22.1	16.9	121 49.7	28.3	336 00.2	10.1	308 50.1	44.1
14	351 11.4	2 21.7	15.6	136 51.4	28.6	351 02.1	09.9	323 52.4	44.1
15	6 13.9	17 21.3 ..	14.3	151 53.1 ..	28.8	6 04.1 ..	09.7	338 54.7 ..	44.2
16	21 16.4	32 20.9	13.1	166 54.7	29.1	21 06.1	09.5	353 57.0	44.3
17	36 18.8	47 20.5	11.8	181 56.4	29.4	36 08.0	09.3	8 59.3	44.4
18	51 21.3	62 20.1	S 6 10.5	196 58.1	S11 29.6	51 10.0	S 1 09.0	24 01.6	N 8 44.4
19	66 23.8	77 19.8	09.3	211 59.8	29.9	66 12.0	08.8	39 03.8	44.5
20	81 26.2	92 19.4	08.0	227 01.5	30.1	81 13.9	08.6	54 06.1	44.6
21	96 28.7	107 19.0 ..	06.8	242 03.2 ..	30.4	96 15.9 ..	08.4	69 08.4 ..	44.7
22	111 31.1	122 18.6	05.5	257 04.9	30.6	111 17.9	08.2	84 10.7	44.7
23	126 33.6	137 18.2	04.2	272 06.5	30.9	126 19.8	07.9	99 13.0	44.8
Mer. Pass. 14 39.1		v −0.4	d 1.3	v 1.7	d 0.3	v 2.0	d 0.2	v 2.3	d 0.1

STARS

Name	SHA	Dec
Acamar	315 26.8	S40 18.9
Achernar	335 35.3	S57 14.9
Acrux	173 21.2	S63 05.4
Adhara	255 20.9	S28 58.5
Aldebaran	291 02.0	N16 30.3
Alioth	166 30.1	N55 57.7
Alkaid	153 07.5	N49 18.9
Al Na'ir	27 58.1	S46 58.0
Alnilam	275 57.4	S 1 12.4
Alphard	218 06.6	S 8 39.4
Alphecca	126 20.4	N26 43.0
Alpheratz	357 55.2	N29 05.1
Altair	62 19.3	N 8 51.9
Ankaa	353 26.9	S42 19.0
Antares	112 40.0	S26 25.6
Arcturus	146 05.8	N19 11.1
Atria	107 52.0	S69 01.2
Avior	234 21.9	S59 30.6
Bellatrix	278 43.7	N 6 20.7
Betelgeuse	271 13.1	N 7 24.2
Canopus	264 00.7	S52 42.1
Capella	280 56.6	N45 59.8
Deneb	49 39.5	N45 16.6
Denebola	182 44.7	N14 34.5
Diphda	349 07.2	S17 59.8
Dubhe	194 04.7	N61 45.2
Elnath	278 26.4	N28 36.3
Eltanin	90 51.6	N51 29.2
Enif	33 58.3	N 9 52.2
Fomalhaut	15 36.5	S29 37.8
Gacrux	172 12.8	S57 06.3
Gienah	176 03.5	S17 32.2
Hadar	149 03.4	S60 21.8
Hamal	328 13.4	N23 27.4
Kaus Aust.	83 58.8	S34 23.0
Kochab	137 19.6	N74 09.3
Markab	13 49.7	N15 11.9
Menkar	314 26.7	N 4 05.0
Menkent	148 20.5	S36 21.7
Miaplacidus	221 41.0	S69 42.9
Mirfak	308 56.2	N49 51.5
Nunki	76 12.3	S26 17.8
Peacock	53 37.3	S56 44.2
Pollux	243 40.9	N28 01.6
Procyon	245 11.0	N 5 13.5
Rasalhague	96 16.9	N12 33.6
Regulus	207 55.0	N11 58.2
Rigel	281 22.5	S 8 12.4
Rigil Kent.	140 06.8	S60 49.5
Sabik	102 25.4	S15 43.3
Schedar	349 53.5	N56 32.0
Shaula	96 37.2	S37 06.0
Sirius	258 43.2	S16 43.1
Spica	158 42.8	S11 09.3
Suhail	223 00.1	S43 25.9
Vega	80 46.8	N38 46.9
Zuben'ubi	137 17.7	S16 02.2

	SHA	Mer. Pass.
Venus	12 58.6	13 50
Mars	146 10.1	4 56
Jupiter	0 09.5	14 39
Saturn	332 47.5	16 28

UT	SUN		MOON				Lat.	Twilight		Sunrise	Moonrise			
								Naut.	Civil		9	10	11	12
	GHA	Dec	GHA	v	Dec	d	HP							
d h	° ′	° ′	° ′	′	° ′	′	′	N 72	h m 06 37	h m 08 00	h m 09 26	h m 04 00	h m 06 02	h m ▬▬	h m ▬▬
9 00	176 27.5	S14 53.1	264 27.7 13.8		S13 56.4	7.0	54.3	N 70	06 33	07 47	09 01	03 29	05 05	06 42	08 08
01	191 27.5	52.3	279 00.5 13.8		14 03.4	7.0	54.3	68	06 29	07 36	08 41	03 06	04 31	05 52	07 01
02	206 27.5	51.5	293 33.3 13.8		14 10.4	6.9	54.3	66	06 26	07 27	08 25	02 48	04 07	05 21	06 25
03	221 27.5 . .	50.7	308 06.1 13.7		14 17.3	6.8	54.3	64	06 23	07 20	08 13	02 33	03 48	04 58	05 59
04	236 27.4	49.9	322 38.8 13.7		14 24.1	6.8	54.3	62	06 21	07 13	08 02	02 21	03 32	04 39	05 39
05	251 27.4	49.1	337 11.5 13.6		14 30.9	6.8	54.3	60	06 18	07 08	07 53	02 11	03 19	04 24	05 23
06	266 27.4	S14 48.3	351 44.1 13.6		S14 37.7	6.6	54.3	N 58	06 16	07 03	07 45	02 02	03 08	04 11	05 09
07	281 27.4	47.5	6 16.7 13.6		14 44.3	6.6	54.3	56	06 14	06 58	07 37	01 54	02 59	04 00	04 57
08	296 27.4	46.7	20 49.3 13.5		14 50.9	6.6	54.3	54	06 12	06 54	07 31	01 47	02 50	03 50	04 47
T 09	311 27.3 . .	45.9	35 21.8 13.5		14 57.5	6.5	54.3	52	06 10	06 50	07 25	01 41	02 42	03 42	04 37
U 10	326 27.3	45.1	49 54.3 13.5		15 04.0	6.4	54.3	50	06 08	06 46	07 20	01 35	02 36	03 34	04 29
E 11	341 27.3	44.3	64 26.8 13.4		15 10.4	6.3	54.3	45	06 04	06 38	07 09	01 23	02 21	03 17	04 12
S 12	356 27.3	S14 43.5	78 59.2 13.4		S15 16.7	6.3	54.3	N 40	06 00	06 32	07 00	01 13	02 09	03 04	03 57
D 13	11 27.3	42.7	93 31.6 13.3		15 23.0	6.3	54.3	35	05 56	06 25	06 52	01 05	01 59	02 52	03 45
A 14	26 27.2	41.9	108 03.9 13.3		15 29.3	6.1	54.4	30	05 52	06 20	06 44	00 58	01 50	02 42	03 34
Y 15	41 27.2 . .	41.1	122 36.2 13.2		15 35.4	6.1	54.4	20	05 43	06 09	06 32	00 45	01 35	02 25	03 16
16	56 27.2	40.3	137 08.4 13.2		15 41.5	6.0	54.4	N 10	05 34	06 00	06 21	00 34	01 21	02 10	03 01
17	71 27.2	39.5	151 40.6 13.2		15 47.5	6.0	54.4	0	05 25	05 49	06 11	00 23	01 09	01 56	02 46
18	86 27.2	S14 38.7	166 12.8 13.1		S15 53.5	5.9	54.4	S 10	05 13	05 38	06 00	00 13	00 56	01 42	02 31
19	101 27.2	37.9	180 44.9 13.1		15 59.4	5.8	54.4	20	04 59	05 26	05 49	00 02	00 43	01 28	02 15
20	116 27.1	37.1	195 17.0 13.0		16 05.2	5.7	54.4	30	04 41	05 11	05 36	24 28	00 28	01 11	01 57
21	131 27.1 . .	36.3	209 49.0 13.0		16 10.9	5.7	54.4	35	04 29	05 01	05 28	24 20	00 20	01 01	01 47
22	146 27.1	35.5	224 21.0 13.0		16 16.6	5.6	54.4	40	04 15	04 50	05 19	24 10	00 10	00 50	01 35
23	161 27.1	34.7	238 53.0 12.9		16 22.2	5.6	54.4	45	03 57	04 37	05 09	23 58	24 37	00 37	01 21
10 00	176 27.1	S14 33.9	253 24.9 12.8		S16 27.8	5.5	54.5	S 50	03 34	04 20	04 57	23 44	24 21	00 21	01 04
01	191 27.1	33.0	267 56.7 12.9		16 33.3	5.4	54.5	52	03 23	04 12	04 51	23 38	24 13	00 13	00 56
02	206 27.0	32.2	282 28.6 12.7		16 38.7	5.3	54.5	54	03 09	04 03	04 44	23 30	24 05	00 05	00 47
03	221 27.0 . .	31.4	297 00.3 12.8		16 44.0	5.2	54.5	56	02 53	03 53	04 37	23 22	23 55	24 36	00 36
04	236 27.0	30.6	311 32.1 12.7		16 49.2	5.2	54.5	58	02 34	03 41	04 29	23 13	23 45	24 25	00 25
05	251 27.0	29.8	326 03.8 12.6		16 54.4	5.1	54.5	S 60	02 08	03 28	04 20	23 03	23 33	24 12	00 12
06	266 27.0	S14 29.0	340 35.4 12.6		S16 59.5	5.1	54.5	Lat.	Sunset	Twilight		Moonset			
W 07	281 27.0	28.2	355 07.0 12.5		17 04.6	4.9	54.6			Civil	Naut.	9	10	11	12
E 08	296 27.0	27.4	9 38.5 12.5		17 09.5	4.9	54.6								
D 09	311 27.0 . .	26.6	24 10.0 12.5		17 14.4	4.8	54.6	°	h m	h m	h m	h m	h m	h m	h m
N 10	326 27.0	25.8	38 41.5 12.4		17 19.2	4.7	54.6	N 72	15 03	16 30	17 53	08 55	08 29	▬▬	▬▬
E 11	341 26.9	25.0	53 12.9 12.4		17 23.9	4.7	54.6	N 70	15 29	16 43	17 57	09 28	09 27	09 30	09 47
S 12	356 26.9	S14 24.2	67 44.3 12.3		S17 28.6	4.5	54.6	68	15 49	16 54	18 01	09 52	10 01	10 20	10 54
D 13	11 26.9	23.3	82 15.6 12.3		17 33.1	4.5	54.6	66	16 04	17 02	18 04	10 10	10 26	10 51	11 30
A 14	26 26.9	22.5	96 46.9 12.2		17 37.6	4.5	54.7	64	16 17	17 10	18 06	10 26	10 46	11 15	11 56
Y 15	41 26.9 . .	21.7	111 18.1 12.2		17 42.1	4.3	54.7	62	16 28	17 16	18 09	10 38	11 02	11 33	12 16
16	56 26.9	20.9	125 49.3 12.2		17 46.4	4.2	54.7	60	16 37	17 22	18 11	10 49	11 15	11 49	12 33
17	71 26.9	20.1	140 20.5 12.1		17 50.6	4.2	54.7								
18	86 26.9	S14 19.3	154 51.6 12.0		S17 54.8	4.1	54.7	N 58	16 45	17 27	18 13	10 58	11 26	12 02	12 46
19	101 26.9	18.5	169 22.6 12.0		17 58.9	4.0	54.7	56	16 52	17 31	18 15	11 07	11 36	12 13	12 58
20	116 26.9	17.6	183 53.6 12.0		18 02.9	4.0	54.8	54	16 58	17 36	18 17	11 14	11 45	12 23	13 09
21	131 26.8 . .	16.8	198 24.6 11.9		18 06.9	3.8	54.8	52	17 04	17 39	18 19	11 21	11 53	12 32	13 18
22	146 26.8	16.0	212 55.5 11.8		18 10.7	3.8	54.8	50	17 09	17 43	18 21	11 27	12 00	12 40	13 26
23	161 26.8	15.2	227 26.3 11.9		18 14.5	3.7	54.8	45	17 20	17 51	18 25	11 40	12 15	12 57	13 44
11 00	176 26.8	S14 14.4	241 57.2 11.7		S18 18.2	3.6	54.8	N 40	17 29	17 57	18 29	11 50	12 28	13 10	13 58
01	191 26.8	13.6	256 27.9 11.8		18 21.8	3.5	54.8	35	17 37	18 03	18 33	11 59	12 39	13 22	14 11
02	206 26.8	12.8	270 58.7 11.7		18 25.3	3.4	54.9	30	17 44	18 09	18 37	12 08	12 48	13 32	14 21
03	221 26.8 . .	11.9	285 29.4 11.6		18 28.7	3.3	54.9	20	17 57	18 19	18 45	12 21	13 04	13 50	14 39
04	236 26.8	11.1	300 00.0 11.6		18 32.0	3.3	54.9	N 10	18 07	18 29	18 54	12 34	13 18	14 06	14 55
05	251 26.8	10.3	314 30.6 11.5		18 35.3	3.2	54.9	0	18 18	18 39	19 04	12 45	13 32	14 20	15 10
06	266 26.8	S14 09.5	329 01.1 11.5		S18 38.5	3.0	54.9	S 10	18 28	18 50	19 15	12 57	13 45	14 34	15 25
07	281 26.8	08.7	343 31.6 11.5		18 41.5	3.0	55.0	20	18 39	19 02	19 29	13 09	13 59	14 50	15 41
T 08	296 26.8	07.8	358 02.1 11.4		18 44.5	2.9	55.0	30	18 52	19 17	19 47	13 23	14 15	15 07	15 59
H 09	311 26.8 . .	07.0	12 32.5 11.4		18 47.4	2.9	55.0	35	19 00	19 26	19 59	13 31	14 25	15 18	16 10
U 10	326 26.8	06.2	27 02.9 11.3		18 50.3	2.7	55.0	40	19 08	19 37	20 13	13 40	14 35	15 30	16 22
R 11	341 26.8	05.4	41 33.2 11.3		18 53.0	2.6	55.0	45	19 18	19 50	20 30	13 51	14 48	15 43	16 36
S 12	356 26.8	S14 04.6	56 03.5 11.2		S18 55.6	2.6	55.1	S 50	19 31	20 07	20 53	14 04	15 04	16 00	16 53
D 13	11 26.8	03.7	70 33.7 11.2		18 58.2	2.4	55.1	52	19 36	20 15	21 04	14 11	15 11	16 08	17 02
A 14	26 26.8	02.9	85 03.9 11.2		19 00.6	2.4	55.1	54	19 43	20 23	21 17	14 17	15 19	16 17	17 11
Y 15	41 26.8 . .	02.1	99 34.1 11.1		19 03.0	2.2	55.1	56	19 50	20 33	21 32	14 25	15 28	16 27	17 21
16	56 26.8	01.3	114 04.2 11.0		19 05.2	2.2	55.1	58	19 58	20 45	21 51	14 34	15 38	16 39	17 33
17	71 26.8	14 00.5	128 34.2 11.0		19 07.4	2.1	55.2	S 60	20 07	20 58	22 16	14 44	15 50	16 52	17 46
18	86 26.8	S13 59.6	143 04.2 11.0		S19 09.5	2.0	55.2		SUN			MOON			
19	101 26.8	58.8	157 34.2 11.0		19 11.5	1.9	55.2	Day	Eqn. of Time		Mer.	Mer. Pass.		Age	Phase
20	116 26.8	58.0	172 04.2 10.8		19 13.4	1.8	55.2		00ʰ	12ʰ	Pass.	Upper	Lower		
21	131 26.8 . .	57.2	186 34.0 10.9		19 15.2	1.7	55.3	d	m s	m s	h m	h m	h m	d	%
22	146 26.8	56.3	201 03.9 10.8		19 16.9	1.6	55.3	9	14 10	14 11	12 14	06 34	18 57	23	41
23	161 26.8	55.5	215 33.7 10.8		S19 18.5	1.6	55.3	10	14 12	14 12	12 14	07 20	19 44	24	32
	SD 16.2	d 0.8	SD 14.8		14.9		15.0	11	14 13	14 13	12 14	08 08	20 33	25	23

UT	ARIES GHA	VENUS −3.9 GHA	Dec	MARS +0.2 GHA	Dec	JUPITER −2.1 GHA	Dec	SATURN +0.5 GHA	Dec
12 00	141 36.1	152 17.9	S 6 03.0	287 08.2	S11 31.1	141 21.8	S 1 07.7	114 15.3	N 8 44.9
01	156 38.5	167 17.5	01.7	302 09.9	31.4	156 23.8	07.5	129 17.6	45.0
02	171 41.0	182 17.1	6 00.4	317 11.6	31.6	171 25.7	07.3	144 19.9	45.1
03	186 43.5	197 16.7	5 59.2	332 13.3 ..	31.9	186 27.7 ..	07.1	159 22.2 ..	45.1
04	201 45.9	212 16.3	57.9	347 15.0	32.1	201 29.7	06.8	174 24.4	45.2
05	216 48.4	227 16.0	56.6	2 16.7	32.4	216 31.6	06.6	189 26.7	45.3
06	231 50.9	242 15.6	S 5 55.4	17 18.4	S11 32.6	231 33.6	S 1 06.4	204 29.0	N 8 45.4
07	246 53.3	257 15.2	54.1	32 20.1	32.9	246 35.6	06.2	219 31.3	45.4
08	261 55.8	272 14.8	52.8	47 21.8	33.1	261 37.5	05.9	234 33.6	45.5
F 09	276 58.3	287 14.5 ..	51.6	62 23.5 ..	33.4	276 39.5 ..	05.7	249 35.9 ..	45.6
R 10	292 00.7	302 14.1	50.3	77 25.2	33.6	291 41.5	05.5	264 38.2	45.7
I 11	307 03.2	317 13.7	49.0	92 26.9	33.9	306 43.4	05.3	279 40.5	45.7
D 12	322 05.6	332 13.3	S 5 47.7	107 28.5	S11 34.1	321 45.4	S 1 05.1	294 42.8	N 8 45.8
A 13	337 08.1	347 12.9	46.5	122 30.2	34.6	336 47.4	04.8	309 45.0	45.9
Y 14	352 10.6	2 12.6	45.2	137 31.9	34.6	351 49.3	04.6	324 47.3	46.0
15	7 13.0	17 12.2 ..	43.9	152 33.6 ..	34.9	6 51.3 ..	04.4	339 49.6 ..	46.0
16	22 15.5	32 11.8	42.7	167 35.3	35.1	21 53.3	04.2	354 51.9	46.1
17	37 18.0	47 11.4	41.4	182 37.0	35.4	36 55.2	04.0	9 54.2	46.2
18	52 20.4	62 11.1	S 5 40.1	197 38.7	S11 35.6	51 57.2	S 1 03.7	24 56.5	N 8 46.3
19	67 22.9	77 10.7	38.9	212 40.4	35.9	66 59.2	03.5	39 58.8	46.4
20	82 25.4	92 10.3	37.6	227 42.1	36.1	82 01.1	03.3	55 01.0	46.4
21	97 27.8	107 10.0 ..	36.3	242 43.8 ..	36.4	97 03.1 ..	03.1	70 03.3 ..	46.5
22	112 30.3	122 09.6	35.0	257 45.5	36.6	112 05.0	02.9	85 05.6	46.6
23	127 32.8	137 09.2	33.8	272 47.2	36.9	127 07.0	02.6	100 07.9	46.7
13 00	142 35.2	152 08.8	S 5 32.5	287 48.9	S11 37.1	142 09.0	S 1 02.4	115 10.2	N 8 46.7
01	157 37.7	167 08.5	31.2	302 50.7	37.4	157 10.9	02.2	130 12.5	46.8
02	172 40.1	182 08.1	30.0	317 52.4	37.6	172 12.9	02.0	145 14.8	46.9
03	187 42.6	197 07.7 ..	28.7	332 54.1 ..	37.9	187 14.9 ..	01.7	160 17.0 ..	47.0
04	202 45.1	212 07.3	27.4	347 55.8	38.1	202 16.8	01.5	175 19.3	47.1
05	217 47.5	227 07.0	26.1	2 57.5	38.3	217 18.8	01.3	190 21.6	47.1
06	232 50.0	242 06.6	S 5 24.9	17 59.2	S11 38.6	232 20.8	S 1 01.1	205 23.9	N 8 47.2
07	247 52.5	257 06.2	23.6	33 00.9	38.8	247 22.7	00.9	220 26.2	47.3
S 08	262 54.9	272 05.9	22.3	48 02.6	39.1	262 24.7	00.6	235 28.5	47.4
A 09	277 57.4	287 05.5 ..	21.0	63 04.3 ..	39.3	277 26.7 ..	00.4	250 30.8 ..	47.4
T 10	292 59.9	302 05.1	19.8	78 06.0	39.6	292 28.6	00.2	265 33.0	47.5
U 11	308 02.3	317 04.8	18.5	93 07.7	39.8	307 30.6	1 00.0	280 35.3	47.6
R 12	323 04.8	332 04.4	S 5 17.2	108 09.4	S11 40.1	322 32.5	S 0 59.8	295 37.6	N 8 47.7
D 13	338 07.3	347 04.0	16.0	123 11.2	40.3	337 34.5	59.5	310 39.9	47.7
A 14	353 09.7	2 03.6	14.7	138 12.9	40.5	352 36.5	59.3	325 42.2	47.8
Y 15	8 12.2	17 03.3 ..	13.4	153 14.6 ..	40.8	7 38.4 ..	59.1	340 44.5 ..	47.9
16	23 14.6	32 02.9	12.1	168 16.3	41.0	22 40.4	58.9	355 46.7	48.0
17	38 17.1	47 02.5	10.8	183 18.0	41.3	37 42.4	58.6	10 49.0	48.1
18	53 19.6	62 02.2	S 5 09.6	198 19.7	S11 41.6	52 44.3	S 0 58.4	25 51.3	N 8 48.1
19	68 22.0	77 01.8	08.3	213 21.4	41.8	67 46.3	58.2	40 53.6	48.2
20	83 24.5	92 01.4	07.0	228 23.2	42.0	82 48.2	58.0	55 55.9	48.3
21	98 27.0	107 01.1 ..	05.7	243 24.9 ..	42.2	97 50.2 ..	57.8	70 58.2 ..	48.4
22	113 29.4	122 00.7	04.5	258 26.6	42.5	112 52.2	57.5	86 00.4	48.5
23	128 31.9	137 00.3	03.2	273 28.3	42.7	127 54.1	57.3	101 02.7	48.5
14 00	143 34.4	152 00.0	S 5 01.9	288 30.0	S11 43.0	142 56.1	S 0 57.1	116 05.0	N 8 48.6
01	158 36.8	166 59.6	5 00.6	303 31.7	43.2	157 58.1	56.9	131 07.3	48.7
02	173 39.3	181 59.2	4 59.4	318 33.5	43.4	173 00.0	56.6	146 09.6	48.8
03	188 41.7	196 58.9 ..	58.1	333 35.2 ..	43.7	188 02.0 ..	56.4	161 11.8 ..	48.8
04	203 44.2	211 58.5	56.8	348 36.9	43.9	203 03.9	56.2	176 14.1	48.9
05	218 46.7	226 58.1	55.5	3 38.6	44.2	218 05.9	56.0	191 16.4	49.0
06	233 49.1	241 57.8	S 4 54.2	18 40.4	S11 44.4	233 07.9	S 0 55.7	206 18.7	N 8 49.1
07	248 51.6	256 57.4	53.0	33 42.1	44.6	248 09.8	55.5	221 21.0	49.2
08	263 54.1	271 57.0	51.7	48 43.8	44.9	263 11.8	55.3	236 23.3	49.2
S 09	278 56.5	286 56.7 ..	50.4	63 45.5 ..	45.1	278 13.7 ..	55.1	251 25.5 ..	49.3
U 10	293 59.0	301 56.3	49.1	78 47.3	45.4	293 15.7	54.9	266 27.8	49.4
N 11	309 01.5	316 56.0	47.8	93 49.0	45.6	308 17.7	54.6	281 30.1	49.5
D 12	324 03.9	331 55.6	S 4 46.6	108 50.7	S11 45.8	323 19.6	S 0 54.4	296 32.4	N 8 49.6
A 13	339 06.4	346 55.2	45.3	123 52.4	46.1	338 21.6	54.2	311 34.7	49.6
Y 14	354 08.9	1 54.9	44.0	138 54.2	46.3	353 23.5	54.0	326 36.9	49.7
15	9 11.3	16 54.5 ..	42.7	153 55.9 ..	46.5	8 25.5 ..	53.7	341 39.2 ..	49.8
16	24 13.8	31 54.1	41.4	168 57.6	46.8	23 27.5	53.5	356 41.5	49.9
17	39 16.2	46 53.8	40.2	183 59.4	47.0	38 29.4	53.3	11 43.8	49.9
18	54 18.7	61 53.4	S 4 38.9	199 01.1	S11 47.3	53 31.4	S 0 53.1	26 46.1	N 8 50.0
19	69 21.2	76 53.1	37.6	214 02.8	47.5	68 33.3	52.9	41 48.3	50.1
20	84 23.6	91 52.7	36.3	229 04.5	47.7	83 35.3	52.6	56 50.6	50.2
21	99 26.1	106 52.3 ..	35.0	244 06.3 ..	48.0	98 37.3 ..	52.4	71 52.9 ..	50.3
22	114 28.6	121 52.0	33.8	259 08.0	48.2	113 39.2	52.2	86 55.2	50.3
23	129 31.0	136 51.6	32.5	274 09.8	48.4	128 41.2	52.0	101 57.5	50.4
Mer. Pass.	h m 14 27.3	v −0.4	d 1.3	v 1.7	d 0.2	v 2.0	d 0.2	v 2.3	d 0.1

STARS

Name	SHA	Dec
Acamar	315 26.8	S40 18.9
Achernar	335 35.3	S57 14.9
Acrux	173 21.1	S63 05.4
Adhara	255 20.9	S28 58.5
Aldebaran	291 02.0	N16 30.3
Alioth	166 30.1	N55 57.7
Alkaid	153 07.4	N49 18.9
Al Na'ir	27 58.1	S46 58.0
Alnilam	275 57.4	S 1 12.4
Alphard	218 06.6	S 8 39.4
Alphecca	126 20.4	N26 42.9
Alpheratz	357 55.2	N29 05.1
Altair	62 19.3	N 8 51.9
Ankaa	353 27.0	S42 19.0
Antares	112 40.0	S26 25.6
Arcturus	146 05.7	N19 11.1
Atria	107 52.0	S69 01.2
Avior	234 21.9	S59 30.6
Bellatrix	278 43.7	N 6 20.7
Betelgeuse	271 13.1	N 7 24.2
Canopus	264 00.7	S52 42.1
Capella	280 50.6	N45 59.8
Deneb	49 39.4	N45 16.6
Denebola	182 44.7	N14 34.5
Diphda	349 07.2	S17 59.8
Dubhe	194 04.6	N61 45.2
Elnath	278 26.4	N28 36.3
Eltanin	90 51.6	N51 29.2
Enif	33 58.3	N 9 52.2
Fomalhaut	15 36.5	S29 37.8
Gacrux	172 12.8	S57 06.3
Gienah	176 03.4	S17 32.2
Hadar	149 03.4	S60 21.8
Hamal	328 13.4	N23 27.4
Kaus Aust.	83 58.8	S34 23.0
Kochab	137 19.5	N74 09.3
Markab	13 49.7	N15 11.9
Menkar	314 26.7	N 4 05.0
Menkent	148 20.5	S36 21.7
Miaplacidus	221 41.0	S69 42.9
Mirfak	308 56.2	N49 51.5
Nunki	76 12.3	S26 17.8
Peacock	53 37.2	S56 44.2
Pollux	243 40.9	N28 01.6
Procyon	245 11.0	N 5 13.5
Rasalhague	96 16.9	N12 33.6
Regulus	207 55.0	N11 58.2
Rigel	281 22.6	S 8 12.4
Rigil Kent.	140 06.8	S60 49.5
Sabik	102 25.4	S15 43.3
Schedar	349 53.5	N56 32.0
Shaula	96 37.2	S37 06.0
Sirius	258 43.2	S16 43.1
Spica	158 42.8	S11 09.4
Suhail	223 00.1	S43 25.9
Vega	80 46.8	N38 46.9
Zuben'ubi	137 17.6	S16 02.2

	SHA	Mer. Pass.
	° ′	h m
Venus	9 33.6	13 52
Mars	145 13.7	4 48
Jupiter	359 33.8	14 30
Saturn	332 35.0	16 17

SUN and MOON

UT	SUN GHA	SUN Dec	MOON GHA	v	MOON Dec	d	HP
d h	° ′	° ′	° ′	′	° ′	′	′
12 00	176 26.8	S13 54.7	230 03.5	10.7	S19 20.1	1.4	55.3
01	191 26.8	53.9	244 33.2	10.7	19 21.5	1.3	55.4
02	206 26.8	53.0	259 02.9	10.6	19 22.8	1.2	55.4
03	221 26.8	.. 52.2	273 32.5	10.6	19 24.0	1.2	55.4
04	236 26.8	51.4	288 02.1	10.6	19 25.2	1.0	55.4
05	251 26.8	50.6	302 31.7	10.5	19 26.2	1.0	55.4
06	266 26.8	S13 49.7	317 01.2	10.5	S19 27.2	0.8	55.5
07	281 26.8	48.9	331 30.7	10.5	19 28.0	0.7	55.5
08	296 26.8	48.1	346 00.2	10.4	19 28.7	0.7	55.5
F 09	311 26.8	.. 47.2	0 29.6	10.4	19 29.4	0.5	55.5
R 10	326 26.8	46.4	14 59.0	10.3	19 29.9	0.5	55.6
I 11	341 26.8	45.6	29 28.3	10.3	19 30.4	0.3	55.6
D 12	356 26.8	S13 44.8	43 57.6	10.3	S19 30.7	0.3	55.6
A 13	11 26.8	43.9	58 26.9	10.2	19 31.0	0.1	55.7
Y 14	26 26.8	43.1	72 56.1	10.2	19 31.1	0.0	55.7
15	41 26.8	.. 42.3	87 25.3	10.2	19 31.1	0.0	55.7
16	56 26.8	41.4	101 54.5	10.1	19 31.1	0.2	55.7
17	71 26.8	40.6	116 23.6	10.1	19 30.9	0.3	55.8
18	86 26.8	S13 39.8	130 52.7	10.1	S19 30.6	0.3	55.8
19	101 26.8	38.9	145 21.8	10.0	19 30.3	0.5	55.8
20	116 26.8	38.1	159 50.8	10.0	19 29.8	0.6	55.8
21	131 26.9	.. 37.3	174 19.8	10.0	19 29.2	0.6	55.9
22	146 26.9	36.4	188 48.8	10.0	19 28.6	0.8	55.9
23	161 26.9	35.6	203 17.8	9.9	19 27.8	0.9	55.9
13 00	176 26.9	S13 34.8	217 46.7	9.8	S19 26.9	1.0	55.9
01	191 26.9	33.9	232 15.5	9.9	19 25.9	1.1	56.0
02	206 26.9	33.1	246 44.4	9.8	19 24.8	1.2	56.0
03	221 26.9	.. 32.3	261 13.2	9.8	19 23.6	1.3	56.0
04	236 26.9	31.4	275 42.0	9.8	19 22.3	1.4	56.1
05	251 26.9	30.6	290 10.8	9.7	19 20.9	1.5	56.1
06	266 26.9	S13 29.7	304 39.5	9.8	S19 19.4	1.6	56.1
07	281 26.9	28.9	319 08.3	9.7	19 17.8	1.7	56.1
S 08	296 27.0	28.1	333 37.0	9.6	19 16.1	1.8	56.2
A 09	311 27.0	.. 27.2	348 05.6	9.7	19 14.3	2.0	56.2
T 10	326 27.0	26.4	2 34.3	9.6	19 12.3	2.0	56.2
U 11	341 27.0	25.6	17 02.9	9.6	19 10.3	2.1	56.3
R 12	356 27.0	S13 24.7	31 31.5	9.6	S19 08.2	2.3	56.3
D 13	11 27.0	23.9	46 00.1	9.5	19 05.9	2.3	56.3
A 14	26 27.0	23.0	60 28.6	9.6	19 03.6	2.5	56.3
Y 15	41 27.0	.. 22.2	74 57.2	9.5	19 01.1	2.6	56.4
16	56 27.1	21.4	89 25.7	9.5	18 58.5	2.6	56.4
17	71 27.1	20.5	103 54.2	9.5	18 55.9	2.8	56.4
18	86 27.1	S13 19.7	118 22.7	9.4	S18 53.1	2.9	56.5
19	101 27.1	18.8	132 51.1	9.5	18 50.2	3.0	56.5
20	116 27.1	18.0	147 19.6	9.4	18 47.2	3.1	56.5
21	131 27.1	.. 17.1	161 48.0	9.4	18 44.1	3.2	56.5
22	146 27.2	16.3	176 16.4	9.4	18 40.9	3.3	56.6
23	161 27.2	15.5	190 44.8	9.4	18 37.6	3.4	56.6
14 00	176 27.2	S13 14.6	205 13.2	9.3	S18 34.2	3.5	56.6
01	191 27.2	13.8	219 41.5	9.4	18 30.7	3.7	56.7
02	206 27.2	12.9	234 09.9	9.3	18 27.0	3.7	56.7
03	221 27.2	.. 12.1	248 38.2	9.3	18 23.3	3.8	56.7
04	236 27.3	11.2	263 06.5	9.3	18 19.5	4.0	56.7
05	251 27.3	10.4	277 34.8	9.3	18 15.5	4.0	56.8
06	266 27.3	S13 09.5	292 03.1	9.3	S18 11.5	4.2	56.8
07	281 27.3	08.7	306 31.4	9.3	18 07.3	4.2	56.8
08	296 27.3	07.8	320 59.7	9.3	18 03.1	4.4	56.9
S 09	311 27.3	.. 07.0	335 28.0	9.2	17 58.7	4.5	56.9
U 10	326 27.4	06.1	349 56.2	9.3	17 54.2	4.5	56.9
N 11	341 27.4	05.3	4 24.5	9.2	17 49.7	4.7	56.9
D 12	356 27.4	S13 04.5	18 52.7	9.3	S17 45.0	4.8	57.0
A 13	11 27.4	03.6	33 21.0	9.2	17 40.2	4.9	57.0
Y 14	26 27.4	02.8	47 49.2	9.2	17 35.3	5.0	57.0
15	41 27.5	.. 01.9	62 17.4	9.3	17 30.3	5.0	57.1
16	56 27.5	01.1	76 45.7	9.2	17 25.3	5.2	57.1
17	71 27.5	13 00.2	91 13.9	9.2	17 20.1	5.3	57.1
18	86 27.5	S12 59.4	105 42.1	9.2	S17 14.8	5.4	57.2
19	101 27.6	58.5	120 10.3	9.2	17 09.4	5.5	57.2
20	116 27.6	57.6	134 38.5	9.2	17 03.9	5.6	57.2
21	131 27.6	.. 56.8	149 06.7	9.2	16 58.3	5.7	57.2
22	146 27.6	55.9	163 34.9	9.2	16 52.6	5.9	57.3
23	161 27.6	55.1	178 03.1	9.2	S16 46.7	5.9	57.3
	SD 16.2	d 0.8	SD 15.2		15.3		15.5

Twilight, Sunrise and Moonrise

Lat.	Naut.	Civil	Sunrise	Moonrise 12	13	14	15
°	h m	h m	h m	h m	h m	h m	h m
N 72	06 25	07 46	09 08	▬	▬	10 32	09 32
N 70	06 22	07 35	08 46	08 08	08 47	08 54	08 54
68	06 19	07 26	08 28	07 01	07 47	08 14	08 27
66	06 17	07 18	08 14	06 25	07 13	07 46	08 07
64	06 15	07 11	08 03	05 59	06 48	07 25	07 50
62	06 13	07 05	07 53	05 39	06 29	07 07	07 37
60	06 11	07 00	07 45	05 23	06 13	06 53	07 25
N 58	06 10	06 56	07 37	05 09	05 59	06 41	07 15
56	06 08	06 52	07 31	04 57	05 47	06 30	07 06
54	06 07	06 48	07 25	04 47	05 37	06 21	06 58
52	06 05	06 45	07 20	04 37	05 28	06 13	06 51
50	06 04	06 41	07 15	04 29	05 20	06 05	06 45
45	06 00	06 34	07 05	04 12	05 02	05 49	06 31
N 40	05 56	06 28	06 56	03 57	04 48	05 36	06 20
35	05 53	06 23	06 49	03 45	04 36	05 25	06 10
30	05 49	06 18	06 42	03 34	04 25	05 15	06 02
20	05 42	06 08	06 31	03 16	04 07	04 58	05 47
N 10	05 34	05 59	06 20	03 01	03 52	04 43	05 34
0	05 25	05 50	06 11	02 46	03 37	04 29	05 22
S 10	05 14	05 39	06 01	02 31	03 22	04 15	05 10
20	05 01	05 28	05 50	02 15	03 06	04 00	04 57
30	04 43	05 13	05 38	01 57	02 48	03 43	04 42
35	04 32	05 05	05 31	01 47	02 38	03 34	04 33
40	04 19	04 54	05 23	01 35	02 26	03 22	04 23
45	04 03	04 42	05 14	01 21	02 12	03 09	04 12
S 50	03 41	04 26	05 02	01 04	01 54	02 53	03 58
52	03 30	04 19	04 57	00 56	01 46	02 45	03 51
54	03 18	04 11	04 51	00 47	01 37	02 37	03 44
56	03 03	04 01	04 44	00 36	01 27	02 27	03 36
58	02 46	03 50	04 37	00 25	01 15	02 16	03 27
S 60	02 24	03 37	04 28	00 12	01 02	02 04	03 16

Sunset, Twilight and Moonset

Lat.	Sunset	Civil	Naut.	Moonset 12	13	14	15
°	h m	h m	h m	h m	h m	h m	h m
N 72	15 22	16 44	18 06	▬	▬	11 00	13 50
N 70	15 44	16 55	18 08	09 47	10 55	12 38	14 27
68	16 01	17 04	18 11	10 54	11 54	13 17	14 53
66	16 15	17 12	18 13	11 30	12 28	13 44	15 13
64	16 27	17 18	18 15	11 56	12 53	14 05	15 28
62	16 36	17 24	18 16	12 16	13 13	14 22	15 41
60	16 45	17 29	18 18	12 33	13 29	14 36	15 53
N 58	16 52	17 34	18 20	12 46	13 42	14 48	16 02
56	16 58	17 38	18 21	12 58	13 54	14 58	16 10
54	17 04	17 41	18 23	13 09	14 04	15 07	16 18
52	17 09	17 45	18 24	13 18	14 13	15 15	16 24
50	17 14	17 48	18 26	13 26	14 21	15 23	16 30
45	17 24	17 55	18 29	13 44	14 38	15 38	16 43
N 40	17 33	18 01	18 33	13 58	14 52	15 51	16 54
35	17 40	18 06	18 36	14 11	15 04	16 02	17 03
30	17 47	18 11	18 39	14 21	15 14	16 11	17 11
20	17 58	18 21	18 47	14 39	15 32	16 27	17 24
N 10	18 08	18 30	18 55	14 55	15 47	16 41	17 36
0	18 18	18 39	19 04	15 10	16 02	16 54	17 47
S 10	18 27	18 49	19 14	15 25	16 16	17 07	17 58
20	18 38	19 00	19 27	15 41	16 32	17 21	18 10
30	18 50	19 15	19 44	15 59	16 49	17 37	18 23
35	18 57	19 23	19 55	16 10	16 59	17 46	18 30
40	19 05	19 33	20 08	16 22	17 11	17 57	18 39
45	19 14	19 46	20 24	16 36	17 25	18 09	18 49
S 50	19 25	20 01	20 46	16 53	17 41	18 24	19 01
52	19 31	20 08	20 56	17 02	17 49	18 31	19 07
54	19 36	20 16	21 08	17 11	17 58	18 38	19 13
56	19 43	20 26	21 22	17 21	18 08	18 47	19 20
58	19 50	20 36	21 39	17 33	18 19	18 57	19 27
S 60	19 58	20 49	22 01	17 46	18 31	19 08	19 36

SUN and MOON

Day	SUN Eqn. of Time 00h	12h	Mer. Pass.	MOON Mer. Pass. Upper	Lower	Age	Phase
d	m s	m s	h m	h m	h m	d	%
12	14 13	14 13	12 14	08 58	21 23	26	15
13	14 13	14 12	12 14	09 49	22 15	27	9
14	14 11	14 10	12 14	10 42	23 08	28	4

UT	ARIES GHA	VENUS −3.9 GHA	VENUS Dec	MARS +0.2 GHA	MARS Dec	JUPITER −2.1 GHA	JUPITER Dec	SATURN +0.5 GHA	SATURN Dec
15 00	144 33.5	151 51.3	S 4 31.2	289 11.5	S11 48.7	143 43.1	S 0 51.7	116 59.7	N 8 50.5
01	159 36.0	166 50.9	29.9	304 13.2	48.9	158 45.1	51.5	132 02.0	50.6
02	174 38.4	181 50.5	28.6	319 15.0	49.1	173 47.1	51.3	147 04.3	50.7
03	189 40.9	196 50.2	.. 27.3	334 16.7	.. 49.4	188 49.0	.. 51.1	162 06.6	.. 50.7
04	204 43.4	211 49.8	26.1	349 18.4	49.6	203 51.0	50.8	177 08.9	50.8
05	219 45.8	226 49.5	24.8	4 20.2	49.8	218 52.9	50.6	192 11.1	50.9
M 06	234 48.3	241 49.1	S 4 23.5	19 21.9	S11 50.1	233 54.9	S 0 50.4	207 13.4	N 8 51.0
O 07	249 50.7	256 48.7	22.2	34 23.7	50.3	248 56.9	50.2	222 15.7	51.1
N 08	264 53.2	271 48.4	20.9	49 25.4	50.5	263 58.8	49.9	237 18.0	51.1
D 09	279 55.7	286 48.0	.. 19.6	64 27.1	.. 50.8	279 00.8	.. 49.7	252 20.2	.. 51.2
A 10	294 58.1	301 47.7	18.3	79 28.9	51.0	294 02.7	49.5	267 22.5	51.3
Y 11	310 00.6	316 47.3	17.1	94 30.6	51.2	309 04.7	49.3	282 24.8	51.4
12	325 03.1	331 46.9	S 4 15.8	109 32.4	S11 51.5	324 06.7	S 0 49.1	297 27.1	N 8 51.5
13	340 05.5	346 46.6	14.5	124 34.1	51.7	339 08.6	48.8	312 29.4	51.5
14	355 08.0	1 46.2	13.2	139 35.8	51.9	354 10.6	48.6	327 31.6	51.6
15	10 10.5	16 45.9	.. 11.9	154 37.6	.. 52.2	9 12.5	.. 48.4	342 33.9	.. 51.7
16	25 12.9	31 45.5	10.6	169 39.3	52.4	24 14.5	48.2	357 36.2	51.8
17	40 15.4	46 45.2	09.3	184 41.1	52.6	39 16.4	47.9	12 38.5	51.9
18	55 17.9	61 44.8	S 4 08.1	199 42.8	S11 52.8	54 18.4	S 0 47.7	27 40.7	N 8 51.9
19	70 20.3	76 44.4	06.8	214 44.6	53.1	69 20.4	47.5	42 43.0	52.0
20	85 22.8	91 44.1	05.5	229 46.3	53.3	84 22.3	47.3	57 45.3	52.1
21	100 25.2	106 43.7	.. 04.2	244 48.1	.. 53.5	99 24.3	.. 47.0	72 47.6	.. 52.2
22	115 27.7	121 43.4	02.9	259 49.8	53.8	114 26.2	46.8	87 49.8	52.3
23	130 30.2	136 43.0	01.6	274 51.6	54.0	129 28.2	46.6	102 52.1	52.3
16 00	145 32.6	151 42.7	S 4 00.3	289 53.3	S11 54.2	144 30.1	S 0 46.4	117 54.4	N 8 52.4
01	160 35.1	166 42.3	3 59.1	304 55.1	54.5	159 32.1	46.1	132 56.7	52.5
02	175 37.6	181 42.0	57.8	319 56.8	54.7	174 34.1	45.9	147 58.9	52.6
03	190 40.0	196 41.6	.. 56.5	334 58.6	.. 54.9	189 36.0	.. 45.7	163 01.2	.. 52.7
04	205 42.5	211 41.3	55.2	350 00.3	55.1	204 38.0	45.5	178 03.5	52.7
05	220 45.0	226 40.9	53.9	5 02.1	55.4	219 39.9	45.2	193 05.8	52.8
T 06	235 47.4	241 40.5	S 3 52.6	20 03.9	S11 55.6	234 41.9	S 0 45.0	208 08.0	N 8 52.9
U 07	250 49.9	256 40.2	51.3	35 05.6	55.8	249 43.8	44.8	223 10.3	53.0
E 08	265 52.3	271 39.8	50.0	50 07.4	56.0	264 45.8	44.6	238 12.6	53.1
S 09	280 54.8	286 39.5	.. 48.7	65 09.1	.. 56.3	279 47.8	.. 44.3	253 14.9	.. 53.2
D 10	295 57.3	301 39.1	47.5	80 10.9	56.5	294 49.7	44.1	268 17.1	53.2
A 11	310 59.7	316 38.8	46.2	95 12.6	56.7	309 51.7	43.9	283 19.4	53.3
Y 12	326 02.2	331 38.4	S 3 44.9	110 14.4	S11 56.9	324 53.6	S 0 43.7	298 21.7	N 8 53.4
13	341 04.7	346 38.1	43.6	125 16.2	57.2	339 55.6	43.4	313 24.0	53.5
14	356 07.1	1 37.7	42.3	140 17.9	57.4	354 57.5	43.2	328 26.2	53.6
15	11 09.6	16 37.4	.. 41.0	155 19.7	.. 57.6	9 59.5	.. 43.0	343 28.5	.. 53.6
16	26 12.1	31 37.0	39.7	170 21.5	57.8	25 01.4	42.8	358 30.8	53.7
17	41 14.5	46 36.7	38.4	185 23.2	58.1	40 03.4	42.5	13 33.1	53.8
18	56 17.0	61 36.3	S 3 37.1	200 25.0	S11 58.3	55 05.4	S 0 42.3	28 35.3	N 8 53.9
19	71 19.5	76 36.0	35.8	215 26.7	58.5	70 07.3	42.1	43 37.6	54.0
20	86 21.9	91 35.6	34.6	230 28.5	58.7	85 09.3	41.9	58 39.9	54.0
21	101 24.4	106 35.3	.. 33.3	245 30.3	.. 59.0	100 11.2	.. 41.6	73 42.2	.. 54.1
22	116 26.8	121 34.9	32.0	260 32.0	59.2	115 13.2	41.4	88 44.4	54.2
23	131 29.3	136 34.6	30.7	275 33.8	59.4	130 15.1	41.2	103 46.7	54.3
17 00	146 31.8	151 34.2	S 3 29.4	290 35.6	S11 59.6	145 17.1	S 0 41.0	118 49.0	N 8 54.4
01	161 34.2	166 33.9	28.1	305 37.3	11 59.9	160 19.0	40.7	133 51.2	54.5
02	176 36.7	181 33.5	26.8	320 39.1	12 00.1	175 21.0	40.5	148 53.5	54.5
03	191 39.2	196 33.2	.. 25.5	335 40.9	.. 00.3	190 23.0	.. 40.3	163 55.8	.. 54.6
04	206 41.6	211 32.8	24.2	350 42.7	00.5	205 24.9	40.1	178 58.1	54.7
05	221 44.1	226 32.5	22.9	5 44.4	00.7	220 26.9	39.8	194 00.3	54.8
W 06	236 46.6	241 32.1	S 3 21.6	20 46.2	S12 01.0	235 28.8	S 0 39.6	209 02.6	N 8 54.9
E 07	251 49.0	256 31.8	20.3	35 48.0	01.2	250 30.8	39.4	224 04.9	54.9
D 08	266 51.5	271 31.4	19.0	50 49.8	01.4	265 32.7	39.2	239 07.1	55.0
N 09	281 53.9	286 31.1	.. 17.8	65 51.5	.. 01.6	280 34.7	.. 38.9	254 09.4	.. 55.1
E 10	296 56.4	301 30.7	16.5	80 53.3	01.8	295 36.6	38.7	269 11.7	55.2
S 11	311 58.9	316 30.4	15.2	95 55.1	02.1	310 38.6	38.5	284 14.0	55.3
D 12	327 01.3	331 30.0	S 3 13.9	110 56.9	S12 02.3	325 40.5	S 0 38.3	299 16.2	N 8 55.4
A 13	342 03.8	346 29.7	12.6	125 58.6	02.5	340 42.5	38.0	314 18.5	55.4
Y 14	357 06.3	1 29.4	11.3	141 00.4	02.7	355 44.4	37.8	329 20.8	55.5
15	12 08.7	16 29.0	.. 10.0	156 02.2	.. 02.9	10 46.4	.. 37.6	344 23.0	.. 55.6
16	27 11.2	31 28.7	08.7	171 04.0	03.1	25 48.4	37.4	359 25.3	55.7
17	42 13.7	46 28.3	07.4	186 05.8	03.4	40 50.3	37.1	14 27.6	55.8
18	57 16.1	61 28.0	S 3 06.1	201 07.5	S12 03.6	55 52.3	S 0 36.9	29 29.9	N 8 55.8
19	72 18.6	76 27.6	04.8	216 09.3	03.8	70 54.2	36.7	44 32.1	55.9
20	87 21.1	91 27.3	03.5	231 11.1	04.0	85 56.2	36.5	59 34.4	56.0
21	102 23.5	106 26.9	.. 02.2	246 12.9	.. 04.2	100 58.1	.. 36.2	74 36.7	.. 56.1
22	117 26.0	121 26.6	3 00.9	261 14.7	04.5	116 00.1	36.0	89 38.9	56.2
23	132 28.4	136 26.2	S 2 59.6	276 16.4	04.7	131 02.0	35.8	104 41.2	56.3
Mer. Pass.	14 15.5	v −0.4	d 1.3	v 1.8	d 0.2	v 2.0	d 0.2	v 2.3	d 0.1

STARS

Name	SHA	Dec
Acamar	315 26.8	S40 18.9
Achernar	335 35.3	S57 14.9
Acrux	173 21.1	S63 05.4
Adhara	255 20.9	S28 58.6
Aldebaran	291 02.0	N16 30.3
Alioth	166 30.0	N55 57.7
Alkaid	153 07.4	N49 18.9
Al Na'ir	27 58.1	S46 58.0
Alnilam	275 57.4	S 1 12.4
Alphard	218 06.6	S 8 39.4
Alphecca	126 20.4	N26 42.9
Alpheratz	357 55.2	N29 05.1
Altair	62 19.3	N 8 51.9
Ankaa	353 27.0	S42 19.0
Antares	112 39.9	S26 25.6
Arcturus	146 05.7	N19 11.1
Atria	107 51.9	S69 01.2
Avior	234 21.9	S59 30.6
Bellatrix	278 43.7	N 6 20.7
Betelgeuse	271 13.1	N 7 24.2
Canopus	264 00.7	S52 42.1
Capella	280 50.6	N45 59.8
Deneb	49 39.4	N45 16.5
Denebola	182 44.7	N14 34.5
Diphda	349 07.2	S17 59.7
Dubhe	194 04.6	N61 45.2
Elnath	278 26.4	N28 36.3
Eltanin	90 51.6	N51 29.2
Enif	33 58.3	N 9 52.2
Fomalhaut	15 36.5	S29 37.8
Gacrux	172 12.8	S57 06.3
Gienah	176 03.4	S17 32.2
Hadar	149 03.3	S60 21.8
Hamal	328 13.4	N23 27.4
Kaus Aust.	83 58.7	S34 23.0
Kochab	137 19.4	N74 09.3
Markab	13 49.7	N15 11.9
Menkar	314 26.7	N 4 05.0
Menkent	148 20.5	S36 21.7
Miaplacidus	221 41.0	S69 42.9
Mirfak	308 56.2	N49 51.5
Nunki	76 12.3	S26 17.8
Peacock	53 37.2	S56 44.2
Pollux	243 40.9	N28 01.6
Procyon	245 11.0	N 5 13.5
Rasalhague	96 16.9	N12 33.6
Regulus	207 55.0	N11 58.2
Rigel	281 22.6	S 8 12.4
Rigil Kent.	140 06.7	S60 49.5
Sabik	102 25.4	S15 43.3
Schedar	349 53.5	N56 32.0
Shaula	96 37.1	S37 06.0
Sirius	258 43.2	S16 43.2
Spica	158 42.7	S11 09.4
Suhail	223 00.1	S43 25.9
Vega	80 46.7	N38 46.8
Zuben'ubi	137 17.6	S16 02.2

	SHA	Mer. Pass.
Venus	6 10.0	13 53
Mars	144 20.7	4 40
Jupiter	358 57.5	14 20
Saturn	332 21.8	16 06

UT	SUN GHA	SUN Dec	MOON GHA	v	MOON Dec	d	HP
d h	° ′	° ′	° ′	′	° ′	′	′
15 00	176 27.7	S12 54.2	192 31.3	9.2	S16 40.8	6.0	57.3
01	191 27.7	53.4	206 59.5	9.2	16 34.8	6.1	57.4
02	206 27.7	52.5	221 27.7	9.2	16 28.7	6.2	57.4
03	221 27.7	.. 51.7	235 55.9	9.2	16 22.5	6.3	57.4
04	236 27.8	50.8	250 24.1	9.2	16 16.2	6.4	57.4
05	251 27.8	50.0	264 52.3	9.2	16 09.8	6.5	57.5
06	266 27.8	S12 49.1	279 20.5	9.3	S16 03.3	6.6	57.5
07	281 27.8	48.3	293 48.8	9.2	15 56.7	6.7	57.5
M 08	296 27.9	47.4	308 17.0	9.2	15 50.0	6.8	57.6
O 09	311 27.9	.. 46.5	322 45.2	9.2	15 43.2	6.8	57.6
N 10	326 27.9	45.7	337 13.4	9.2	15 36.4	7.0	57.6
D 11	341 28.0	44.8	351 41.6	9.3	15 29.4	7.1	57.6
A 12	356 28.0	S12 44.0	6 09.9	9.2	S15 22.3	7.2	57.7
Y 13	11 28.0	43.1	20 38.1	9.2	15 15.1	7.2	57.7
14	26 28.0	42.3	35 06.3	9.3	15 07.9	7.4	57.7
15	41 28.1	.. 41.4	49 34.6	9.2	15 00.5	7.4	57.7
16	56 28.1	40.5	64 02.8	9.3	14 53.1	7.6	57.8
17	71 28.1	39.7	78 31.1	9.3	14 45.5	7.6	57.8
18	86 28.2	S12 38.8	92 59.4	9.2	S14 37.9	7.7	57.8
19	101 28.2	38.0	107 27.6	9.3	14 30.2	7.9	57.9
20	116 28.2	37.1	121 55.9	9.3	14 22.3	7.9	57.9
21	131 28.2	.. 36.2	136 24.2	9.3	14 14.4	7.9	57.9
22	146 28.3	35.4	150 52.5	9.3	14 06.5	8.1	57.9
23	161 28.3	34.5	165 20.8	9.3	13 58.4	8.2	58.0
16 00	176 28.3	S12 33.7	179 49.1	9.4	S13 50.2	8.2	58.0
01	191 28.4	32.8	194 17.5	9.3	13 42.0	8.4	58.0
02	206 28.4	31.9	208 45.8	9.4	13 33.6	8.4	58.0
03	221 28.4	.. 31.1	223 14.2	9.3	13 25.2	8.5	58.1
04	236 28.5	30.2	237 42.5	9.4	13 16.7	8.6	58.1
05	251 28.5	29.3	252 10.9	9.3	S13 08.1	8.7	58.1
06	266 28.5	S12 28.5					
07	281 28.6	27.6					
T 08	296 28.6	26.8					
U 09	311 28.6	.. 25.9					
E 10	326 28.7	25.0					
S 11	341 28.7	24.2					
D 12	356 28.7	S12 23.3	353 29.7	9.5	S12 05.7	9.2	58.3
A 13	11 28.8	22.4	7 58.2	9.4	11 56.5	9.3	58.3
Y 14	26 28.8	21.6	22 26.6	9.5	11 47.2	9.4	58.3
15	41 28.9	.. 20.7	36 55.1	9.5	11 37.8	9.4	58.4
16	56 28.9	19.8	51 23.6	9.5	11 28.4	9.5	58.4
17	71 28.9	19.0	65 52.1	9.5	11 18.9	9.6	58.4
18	86 29.0	S12 18.1	80 20.6	9.5	S11 09.3	9.7	58.4
19	101 29.0	17.2	94 49.1	9.6	10 59.6	9.7	58.4
20	116 29.0	16.4	109 17.7	9.5	10 49.9	9.8	58.5
21	131 29.1	.. 15.5	123 46.2	9.6	10 40.1	9.9	58.5
22	146 29.1	14.6	138 14.8	9.5	10 30.2	9.9	58.5
23	161 29.2	13.7	152 43.3	9.6	10 20.3	10.0	58.5
17 00	176 29.2	S12 12.9	167 11.9	9.6	S10 10.3	10.1	58.6
01	191 29.2	12.0	181 40.5	9.6	10 00.2	10.1	58.6
02	206 29.3	11.1	196 09.1	9.6	9 50.1	10.2	58.6
03	221 29.3	.. 10.3	210 37.7	9.7	9 39.9	10.3	58.6
04	236 29.4	09.4	225 06.4	9.6	9 29.6	10.3	58.6
05	251 29.4	08.5	239 35.0	9.6	9 19.3	10.4	58.7
06	266 29.4	S12 07.7	254 03.6	9.7	S 9 08.9	10.4	58.7
W 07	281 29.5	06.8	268 32.3	9.7	8 58.5	10.5	58.7
E 08	296 29.5	05.9	283 01.0	9.7	8 48.0	10.6	58.7
D 09	311 29.6	.. 05.0	297 29.7	9.6	8 37.4	10.6	58.7
N 10	326 29.6	04.2	311 58.3	9.7	8 26.8	10.7	58.8
E 11	341 29.6	03.3	326 27.0	9.8	8 16.1	10.7	58.8
S 12	356 29.7	S12 02.4	340 55.8	9.7	S 8 05.4	10.8	58.8
D 13	11 29.7	01.5	355 24.5	9.7	7 54.6	10.8	58.8
A 14	26 29.8	12 00.7	9 53.2	9.8	7 43.8	10.8,	58.8
Y 15	41 29.8	11 59.8	24 22.0	9.7	7 33.0	11.0	58.9
16	56 29.9	58.9	38 50.7	9.8	7 22.0	10.9	58.9
17	71 29.9	58.0	53 19.5	9.7	7 11.1	11.1	58.9
18	86 29.9	S11 57.2	67 48.2	9.8	S 7 00.0	11.0	58.9
19	101 30.0	56.3	82 17.0	9.8	6 49.0	11.1	58.9
20	116 30.0	55.4	96 45.8	9.8	6 37.9	11.2	58.9
21	131 30.1	.. 54.5	111 14.6	9.8	6 26.7	11.2	59.0
22	146 30.1	53.7	125 43.4	9.8	6 15.5	11.2	59.0
23	161 30.2	52.8	140 12.2	9.8	S 6 04.3	11.3	59.0
	SD 16.2	d 0.9	SD 15.7		15.9		16.0

An annular eclipse of the Sun occurs on this date. See page 5.

Lat.	Twilight Naut.	Civil	Sunrise	Moonrise 15	16	17	18
°	h m	h m	h m	h m	h m	h m	h m
N 72	06 12	07 32	08 50	09 32	09 15	09 03	08 54
N 70	06 11	07 22	08 31	08 54	08 53	08 50	08 48
68	06 09	07 15	08 16	08 27	08 35	08 40	08 43
66	06 08	07 08	08 03	08 07	08 21	08 31	08 39
64	06 07	07 02	07 53	07 50	08 09	08 24	08 35
62	06 05	06 57	07 44	07 37	07 59	08 17	08 32
60	06 04	06 53	07 37	07 25	07 51	08 12	08 30
N 58	06 03	06 49	07 30	07 15	07 43	08 07	08 27
56	06 02	06 45	07 24	07 06	07 36	08 02	08 25
54	06 01	06 42	07 19	06 58	07 30	07 58	08 23
52	06 00	06 39	07 14	06 51	07 25	07 55	08 22
50	05 59	06 36	07 10	06 45	07 20	07 51	08 20
45	05 56	06 30	07 00	06 31	07 09	07 44	08 17
N 40	05 53	06 25	06 52	06 20	07 00	07 38	08 14
35	05 50	06 20	06 45	06 10	06 53	07 33	08 11
30	05 47	06 15	06 39	06 02	06 46	07 28	08 09
20	05 41	06 06	06 29	05 47	06 34	07 20	08 05
N 10	05 33	05 58	06 20	05 34	06 24	07 13	08 02
0	05 25	05 50	06 11	05 22	06 14	07 07	07 58
S 10	05 15	05 40	06 02	05 10	06 05	07 00	07 55
20	05 03	05 29	05 52	04 57	05 55	06 53	07 52
30	04 46	05 16	05 41	04 42	05 43	06 45	07 48
35	04 36	05 08	05 34	04 33	05 36	06 40	07 46
40	04 23	04 58	05 27	04 23	05 28	06 35	07 43
45	04 08	04 47	05 18	04 12	05 19	06 29	07 40
S 50	03 48	04 32	05 07	03 58	05 08	06 21	07 37
52	03 38	04 25	05 02	03 51	05 03	06 18	07 35
54	03 27	04 17	04 57	03 44	04 57	06 14	07 33
56	03 13	04 09	04 51	03 36	04 51	06 10	07 31
58	02 57	03 59	04 44	03 27	04 44	06 05	07 29
S 60	02 37	03 47	04 36	03 16	04 36	06 00	07 27

Lat.	Sunset	Twilight Civil	Naut.	Moonset 15	16	17	18
°	h m	h m	h m	h m	h m	h m	h m
N 72	15 39	16 58	18 18	13 50	15 57	17 58	19 56
N 70	15 59	17 07	18 19	14 27	16 18	18 09	19 59
68	16 14	17 15	18 21	14 53	16 34	18 17	20 01
66	16 26	17 22	18 22	15 13	16 47	18 25	20 03
64	16 36	17 27	18 23	15 28	16 58	18 31	20 05
62	16 45	17 32	18 24	15 41	17 07	18 36	20 07
60	16 53	17 36	18 25	15 53	17 15	18 41	20 08
N 58	16 59	17 40	18 26	16 02	17 22	18 45	20 09
56	17 05	17 44	18 27	16 10	17 28	18 48	20 10
54	17 10	17 47	18 28	16 18	17 33	18 52	20 11
52	17 15	17 50	18 29	16 24	17 38	18 54	20 12
50	17 19	17 53	18 30	16 30	17 42	18 57	20 13
45	17 29	17 59	18 33	16 43	17 52	19 03	20 15
N 40	17 36	18 04	18 36	16 54	18 00	19 07	20 16
35	17 43	18 09	18 39	17 03	18 06	19 11	20 17
30	17 49	18 14	18 42	17 11	18 12	19 15	20 18
20	18 00	18 22	18 48	17 24	18 22	19 21	20 20
N 10	18 09	18 30	18 55	17 36	18 31	19 26	20 22
0	18 17	18 39	19 03	17 47	18 39	19 31	20 23
S 10	18 26	18 48	19 13	17 58	18 48	19 36	20 24
20	18 36	18 59	19 25	18 10	18 56	19 41	20 26
30	18 47	19 12	19 41	18 23	19 06	19 47	20 27
35	18 53	19 20	19 51	18 30	19 12	19 51	20 28
40	19 01	19 29	20 04	18 39	19 18	19 54	20 29
45	19 09	19 41	20 19	18 49	19 25	19 59	20 31
S 50	19 20	19 55	20 39	19 01	19 34	20 04	20 32
52	19 25	20 02	20 48	19 07	19 38	20 06	20 33
54	19 30	20 09	21 00	19 13	19 43	20 09	20 33
56	19 36	20 18	21 13	19 20	19 47	20 12	20 34
58	19 42	20 27	21 28	19 27	19 53	20 15	20 35
S 60	19 50	20 39	21 47	19 36	19 59	20 18	20 36

Day	SUN Eqn. of Time 00h	12h	Mer. Pass.	MOON Mer. Pass. Upper	Lower	Age	Phase
d	m s	m s	h m	h m	h m	d	%
15	14 09	14 08	12 14	11 34	24 01	29	1
16	14 07	14 05	12 14	12 27	00 01	00	0
17	14 03	14 01	12 14	13 19	00 53	01	2

UT	ARIES GHA	VENUS GHA	VENUS Dec	MARS GHA	MARS Dec	JUPITER GHA	JUPITER Dec	SATURN GHA	SATURN Dec	Star Name	SHA	Dec
18 00	147 30.9	151 25.9	S 2 58.3	291 18.2	S12 04.9	146 04.0	S 0 35.6	119 43.5	N 8 56.3	Acamar	315 26.8	S40 18.9
01	162 33.4	166 25.6	57.0	306 20.0	05.1	161 05.9	35.3	134 45.7	56.4	Achernar	335 35.4	S57 14.9
02	177 35.8	181 25.2	55.7	321 21.8	05.3	176 07.9	35.1	149 48.0	56.5	Acrux	173 21.1	S63 05.5
03	192 38.3	196 24.9	.. 54.5	336 23.6	.. 05.5	191 09.8	.. 34.9	164 50.3	.. 56.6	Adhara	255 20.9	S28 58.6
04	207 40.8	211 24.5	53.2	351 25.4	05.7	206 11.8	34.7	179 52.5	56.7	Aldebaran	291 02.0	N16 30.3
05	222 43.2	226 24.2	51.9	6 27.2	06.0	221 13.7	34.4	194 54.8	56.8			
T 06	237 45.7	241 23.8	S 2 50.6	21 29.0	S12 06.2	236 15.7	S 0 34.2	209 57.1	N 8 56.8	Alioth	166 30.0	N55 57.7
H 07	252 48.2	256 23.5	49.3	36 30.8	06.4	251 17.6	34.0	224 59.4	56.9	Alkaid	153 07.4	N49 18.9
U 08	267 50.6	271 23.2	48.0	51 32.5	06.6	266 19.6	33.7	240 01.6	57.0	Al Na'ir	27 58.1	S46 58.0
R 09	282 53.1	286 22.8	.. 46.7	66 34.3	.. 06.8	281 21.5	.. 33.5	255 03.9	.. 57.1	Alnilam	275 57.5	S 1 12.4
10	297 55.6	301 22.5	45.4	81 36.1	07.0	296 23.5	33.3	270 06.2	57.2	Alphard	218 06.6	S 8 39.4
S 11	312 58.0	316 22.1	44.1	96 37.9	07.2	311 25.4	33.1	285 08.4	57.3			
D 12	328 00.5	331 21.8	S 2 42.8	111 39.7	S12 07.5	326 27.4	S 0 32.8	300 10.7	N 8 57.3	Alphecca	126 20.4	N26 42.9
A 13	343 02.9	346 21.4	41.5	126 41.5	07.7	341 29.4	32.6	315 13.0	57.4	Alpheratz	357 55.2	N29 05.1
Y 14	358 05.4	1 21.1	40.2	141 43.3	07.9	356 31.3	32.4	330 15.2	57.5	Altair	62 19.3	N 8 51.9
15	13 07.9	16 20.8	.. 38.9	156 45.1	.. 08.1	11 33.3	.. 32.2	345 17.5	.. 57.6	Ankaa	353 27.0	S42 18.9
16	28 10.3	31 20.4	37.6	171 46.9	08.3	26 35.2	31.9	0 19.8	57.7	Antares	112 39.9	S26 25.6
17	43 12.8	46 20.1	36.3	186 48.7	08.5	41 37.2	31.7	15 22.0	57.7			
18	58 15.3	61 19.7	S 2 35.0	201 50.5	S12 08.7	56 39.1	S 0 31.5	30 24.3	N 8 57.8	Arcturus	146 05.7	N19 11.1
19	73 17.7	76 19.4	33.7	216 52.3	08.9	71 41.1	31.3	45 26.6	57.9	Atria	107 51.9	S69 01.2
20	88 20.2	91 19.0	32.4	231 54.1	09.2	86 43.0	31.0	60 28.8	58.0	Avior	234 21.9	S59 30.6
21	103 22.7	106 18.7	.. 31.1	246 55.9	.. 09.4	101 45.0	.. 30.8	75 31.1	.. 58.1	Bellatrix	278 43.8	N 6 20.7
22	118 25.1	121 18.4	29.8	261 57.7	09.6	116 46.9	30.6	90 33.4	58.2	Betelgeuse	271 13.1	N 7 24.2
23	133 27.6	136 18.0	28.5	276 59.5	09.8	131 48.9	30.4	105 35.6	58.2			
19 00	148 30.0	151 17.7	S 2 27.2	292 01.3	S12 10.0	146 50.8	S 0 30.1	120 37.9	N 8 58.3	Canopus	264 00.7	S52 42.1
01	163 32.5	166 17.3	25.9	307 03.1	10.2	161 52.8	29.9	135 40.2	58.4	Capella	280 50.6	N45 59.8
02	178 35.0	181 17.0	24.6	322 04.9	10.4	176 54.7	29.7	150 42.4	58.5	Deneb	49 39.4	N45 16.5
03	193 37.4	196 16.7	.. 23.3	337 06.7	.. 10.6	191 56.7	.. 29.4	165 44.7	.. 58.6	Denebola	182 44.7	N14 34.5
04	208 39.9	211 16.3	22.0	352 08.5	10.8	206 58.6	29.2	180 47.0	58.7	Diphda	349 07.2	S17 59.7
05	223 42.4	226 16.0	20.7	7 10.3	11.0	222 00.6	29.0	195 49.2	58.8			
06	238 44.8	241 15.6	S 2 19.4	22 12.1	S12 11.2	237 02.5	S 0 28.8	210 51.5	N 8 58.8	Dubhe	194 04.6	N61 45.2
07	253 47.3	256 15.3	18.1	37 14.0	11.5	252 04.5	28.5	225 53.8	58.9	Elnath	278 26.5	N28 36.3
08	268 49.8	271 15.0	16.8	52 15.8	11.7	267 06.4	28.3	240 56.0	59.0	Eltanin	90 51.6	N51 29.2
F 09	283 52.2	286 14.6	.. 15.5	67 17.6	.. 11.9	282 08.4	.. 28.1	255 58.3	.. 59.1	Enif	33 58.3	N 9 52.2
R 10	298 54.7	301 14.3	14.2	82 19.4	12.1	297 10.3	27.9	271 00.5	59.2	Fomalhaut	15 36.5	S29 37.8
I 11	313 57.2	316 14.0	12.9	97 21.2	12.3	312 12.3	27.6	286 02.8	59.3			
D 12	328 59.6	331 13.6	S 2 11.6	112 23.0	S12 12.5	327 14.2	S 0 27.4	301 05.1	N 8 59.3	Gacrux	172 12.8	S57 06.3
A 13	344 02.1	346 13.3	10.3	127 24.8	12.7	342 16.2	27.2	316 07.3	59.4	Gienah	176 03.4	S17 32.2
Y 14	359 04.5	1 12.9	09.0	142 26.6	12.9	357 18.1	26.9	331 09.6	59.5	Hadar	149 03.3	S60 21.8
15	14 07.0	16 12.6	.. 07.7	157 28.4	.. 13.1	12 20.1	.. 26.7	346 11.9	.. 59.6	Hamal	328 13.4	N23 27.4
16	29 09.5	31 12.3	06.4	172 30.3	13.3	27 22.0	26.5	1 14.1	59.7	Kaus Aust.	83 58.7	S34 23.0
17	44 11.9	46 11.9	05.1	187 32.1	13.5	42 24.0	26.3	16 16.4	59.8			
18	59 14.4	61 11.6	S 2 03.8	202 33.9	S12 13.7	57 25.9	S 0 26.0	31 18.7	N 8 59.8	Kochab	137 19.4	N74 09.3
19	74 16.9	76 11.3	02.5	217 35.7	13.9	72 27.9	25.8	46 20.9	8 59.9	Markab	13 49.4	N15 11.9
20	89 19.3	91 10.9	2 01.2	232 37.5	14.1	87 29.8	25.6	61 23.2	9 00.0	Menkar	314 26.7	N 4 05.0
21	104 21.8	106 10.6	1 59.9	247 39.3	.. 14.3	102 31.8	.. 25.4	76 25.5	.. 00.1	Menkent	148 20.5	S36 21.8
22	119 24.3	121 10.2	58.6	262 41.2	14.5	117 33.7	25.1	91 27.7	00.2	Miaplacidus	221 41.0	S69 42.9
23	134 26.7	136 09.9	57.3	277 43.0	14.7	132 35.7	24.9	106 30.0	00.3			
20 00	149 29.2	151 09.6	S 1 56.0	292 44.8	S12 14.9	147 37.6	S 0 24.7	121 32.2	N 9 00.3	Mirfak	308 56.3	N49 51.5
01	164 31.6	166 09.2	54.7	307 46.6	15.1	162 39.5	24.4	136 34.5	00.4	Nunki	76 12.3	S26 17.8
02	179 34.1	181 08.9	53.4	322 48.5	15.4	177 41.5	24.2	151 36.8	00.5	Peacock	53 37.2	S56 44.2
03	194 36.6	196 08.6	.. 52.1	337 50.3	.. 15.6	192 43.4	.. 24.0	166 39.0	.. 00.6	Pollux	243 40.9	N28 01.6
04	209 39.0	211 08.2	50.8	352 52.1	15.8	207 45.4	23.8	181 41.3	00.7	Procyon	245 11.0	N 5 13.5
05	224 41.5	226 07.9	49.5	7 53.9	16.0	222 47.3	23.5	196 43.6	00.8			
06	239 44.0	241 07.6	S 1 48.2	22 55.8	S12 16.2	237 49.3	S 0 23.3	211 45.8	N 9 00.9	Rasalhague	96 16.9	N12 33.6
07	254 46.4	256 07.2	46.9	37 57.6	16.4	252 51.2	23.1	226 48.1	00.9	Regulus	207 55.0	N11 58.2
S 08	269 48.9	271 06.9	45.6	52 59.4	16.6	267 53.2	22.9	241 50.3	01.0	Rigel	281 22.6	S 8 12.4
A 09	284 51.4	286 06.6	.. 44.3	68 01.2	.. 16.8	282 55.1	.. 22.6	256 52.6	.. 01.1	Rigil Kent.	140 06.7	S60 49.5
T 10	299 53.8	301 06.2	43.0	83 03.1	17.0	297 57.1	22.4	271 54.9	01.2	Sabik	102 25.3	S15 43.3
U 11	314 56.3	316 05.9	41.7	98 04.9	17.2	312 59.0	22.2	286 57.1	01.3			
R 12	329 58.8	331 05.6	S 1 40.4	113 06.7	S12 17.4	328 01.0	S 0 21.9	301 59.4	N 9 01.4	Schedar	349 53.6	N56 32.0
D 13	345 01.2	346 05.2	39.1	128 08.6	17.6	343 02.9	21.7	317 01.6	01.5	Shaula	96 37.1	S37 06.0
A 14	0 03.7	1 04.9	37.8	143 10.4	17.8	358 04.9	21.5	332 03.9	01.5	Sirius	258 43.3	S16 43.2
Y 15	15 06.1	16 04.6	.. 36.5	158 12.2	.. 18.0	13 06.8	.. 21.3	347 06.2	.. 01.6	Spica	158 42.7	S11 09.4
16	30 08.6	31 04.2	35.2	173 14.1	18.2	28 08.8	21.0	2 08.4	01.7	Suhail	223 00.1	S43 25.9
17	45 11.1	46 03.9	33.9	188 15.9	18.4	43 10.7	20.8	17 10.7	01.8			
18	60 13.5	61 03.5	S 1 32.6	203 17.7	S12 18.6	58 12.7	S 0 20.6	32 13.0	N 9 01.9	Vega	80 46.7	N38 46.8
19	75 16.0	76 03.2	31.3	218 19.6	18.8	73 14.6	20.3	47 15.2	02.0	Zuben'ubi	137 17.6	S16 02.2
20	90 18.5	91 02.9	30.0	233 21.4	19.0	88 16.5	20.1	62 17.5	02.0			
21	105 20.9	106 02.6	.. 28.7	248 23.2	.. 19.2	103 18.5	.. 19.9	77 19.7	.. 02.1		SHA	Mer. Pass.
22	120 23.4	121 02.2	27.4	263 25.1	19.4	118 20.4	19.7	92 22.0	02.2	Venus	2 47.6	13 55
23	135 25.9	136 01.9	26.1	278 26.9	19.6	133 22.4	19.4	107 24.3	02.3	Mars	143 31.3	4 31
Mer. Pass. 14 03.7		v −0.3 d 1.3		v 1.8 d 0.2		v 1.9 d 0.2		v 2.3 d 0.1		Jupiter	358 20.8	14 11
										Saturn	332 07.8	15 55

UT	SUN		MOON					Lat.	Twilight		Sunrise	Moonrise			
									Naut.	Civil		18	19	20	21
	GHA	Dec	GHA	v	Dec	d	HP	°	h m	h m	h m	h m	h m	h m	h m
d h	° ′	° ′	° ′	′	° ′	′	′	N 72	05 59	07 18	08 33	08 54	08 45	08 36	08 26
18 00	176 30.2	S11 51.9	154 41.0	9.8	S 5 53.0	11.3	59.0	N 70	05 59	07 10	08 17	08 48	08 45	08 43	08 41
01	191 30.3	51.0	169 09.8	9.9	5 41.7	11.4	59.0	68	05 59	07 03	08 03	08 43	08 46	08 49	08 52
02	206 30.3	50.1	183 38.7	9.8	5 30.3	11.5	59.0	66	05 58	06 58	07 52	08 39	08 46	08 53	09 02
03	221 30.4	. . 49.3	198 07.5	9.8	5 19.0	11.5	59.1	64	05 58	06 53	07 43	08 35	08 46	08 58	09 10
04	236 30.4	48.4	212 36.3	9.9	5 07.5	11.4	59.1	62	05 57	06 49	07 35	08 32	08 47	09 01	09 17
05	251 30.5	47.5	227 05.2	9.8	4 56.1	11.5	59.1	60	05 57	06 45	07 28	08 30	08 47	09 04	09 24
06	266 30.5	S11 46.6	241 34.0	9.9	S 4 44.6	11.5	59.1	N 58	05 56	06 42	07 22	08 27	08 47	09 07	09 29
07	281 30.6	45.8	256 02.9	9.9	4 33.1	11.6	59.1	56	05 56	06 39	07 17	08 25	08 47	09 10	09 34
T 08	296 30.6	44.9	270 31.8	9.8	4 21.5	11.6	59.1	54	05 55	06 36	07 12	08 23	08 47	09 12	09 38
H 09	311 30.6	. . 44.0	285 00.6	9.9	4 09.9	11.6	59.1	52	05 54	06 33	07 08	08 22	08 48	09 14	09 42
U 10	326 30.7	43.1	299 29.5	9.9	3 58.3	11.6	59.1	50	05 53	06 31	07 04	08 20	08 48	09 16	09 46
R 11	341 30.7	42.2	313 58.4	9.8	3 46.7	11.7	59.2	45	05 51	06 26	06 56	08 17	08 48	09 20	09 54
S 12	356 30.8	S11 41.3	328 27.2	9.9	S 3 35.0	11.7	59.2	N 40	05 49	06 21	06 48	08 14	08 48	09 23	10 00
D 13	11 30.8	40.5	342 56.1	9.9	3 23.3	11.7	59.2	35	05 47	06 16	06 42	08 11	08 49	09 26	10 06
A 14	26 30.9	39.6	357 25.0	9.9	3 11.6	11.7	59.2	30	05 44	06 12	06 37	08 09	08 49	09 29	10 11
Y 15	41 31.0	. . 38.7	11 53.9	9.8	2 59.9	11.8	59.2	20	05 39	06 05	06 27	08 05	08 49	09 34	10 20
16	56 31.0	37.8	26 22.7	9.9	2 48.1	11.8	59.2	N 10	05 32	05 57	06 19	08 02	08 50	09 38	10 27
17	71 31.1	36.9	40 51.6	9.9	2 36.3	11.8	59.2	0	05 25	05 49	06 10	07 58	08 50	09 42	10 35
18	86 31.1	S11 36.0	55 20.5	9.9	S 2 24.5	11.8	59.2	S 10	05 16	05 41	06 02	07 55	08 50	09 46	10 42
19	101 31.2	35.2	69 49.4	9.9	2 12.7	11.8	59.3	20	05 04	05 31	05 53	07 52	08 51	09 50	10 50
20	116 31.2	34.3	84 18.3	9.8	2 00.9	11.9	59.3	30	04 49	05 18	05 43	07 48	08 51	09 55	10 59
21	131 31.3	. . 33.4	98 47.1	9.9	1 49.0	11.9	59.3	35	04 39	05 11	05 37	07 46	08 52	09 58	11 05
22	146 31.3	32.5	113 16.0	9.9	1 37.2	11.9	59.3	40	04 28	05 02	05 30	07 43	08 52	10 01	11 11
23	161 31.4	31.6	127 44.9	9.9	1 25.3	11.9	59.3	45	04 13	04 51	05 22	07 40	08 53	10 05	11 18
19 00	176 31.4	S11 30.7	142 13.8	9.8	S 1 13.4	11.9	59.3	S 50	03 54	04 38	05 13	07 37	08 53	10 10	11 26
01	191 31.5	29.9	156 42.6	9.9	1 01.5	11.8	59.3	52	03 45	04 31	05 08	07 35	08 53	10 12	11 30
02	206 31.5	29.0	171 11.5	9.9	0 49.7	12.0	59.3	54	03 35	04 24	05 03	07 33	08 54	10 14	11 34
03	221 31.6	. . 28.1	185 40.4	9.8	0 37.7	11.9	59.3	56	03 23	04 16	04 58	07 31	08 54	10 17	11 39
04	236 31.6	27.2	200 09.2	9.9	0 25.8	11.9	59.4	58	03 08	04 07	04 51	07 29	08 54	10 20	11 45
05	251 31.7	26.3	214 38.1	9.8	0 13.9	11.9	59.3	S 60	02 50	03 56	04 44	07 27	08 55	10 23	11 51

UT	SUN		MOON					Lat.	Sunset	Twilight		Moonset			
										Civil	Naut.	18	19	20	21
d h	° ′	° ′	° ′	′	° ′	′	′	°	h m	h m	h m	h m	h m	h m	h m
06	266 31.8	S11 25.4	229 06.9	9.9	S 0 02.0	11.9	59.4	N 72	15 56	17 12	18 31	19 56	21 53	23 53	25 56
07	281 31.8	24.5	243 35.8	9.8	N 0 09.9	12.0	59.4	N 70	16 13	17 19	18 31	19 59	21 49	23 40	25 33
F 08	296 31.9	23.6	258 04.6	9.8	0 21.9	11.9	59.4	68	16 26	17 26	18 31	20 01	21 45	23 30	25 16
R 09	311 31.9	. . 22.8	272 33.4	9.8	0 33.8	11.9	59.4	66	16 37	17 31	18 31	20 03	21 42	23 22	25 01
I 10	326 32.0	21.9	287 02.2	9.8	0 45.7	11.9	59.4	64	16 46	17 36	18 31	20 05	21 40	23 15	24 50
D 11	341 32.0	21.0	301 31.0	9.8	0 57.6	11.9	59.4	62	16 54	17 40	18 32	20 07	21 38	23 09	24 40
A 12	356 32.1	S11 20.1	315 59.8	9.8	N 1 09.5	12.0	59.4	60	17 00	17 44	18 32	20 08	21 36	23 04	24 31
Y 13	11 32.1	19.2	330 28.6	9.8	1 21.5	11.9	59.4	N 58	17 06	17 47	18 33	20 09	21 34	23 00	24 24
14	26 32.2	18.3	344 57.4	9.8	1 33.4	11.9	59.4	56	17 12	17 50	18 33	20 10	21 33	22 56	24 18
15	41 32.3	. . 17.4	359 26.2	9.8	1 45.3	11.9	59.4	54	17 16	17 53	18 34	20 11	21 32	22 52	24 12
16	56 32.3	16.5	13 55.0	9.7	1 57.2	11.8	59.4	52	17 21	17 55	18 34	20 12	21 30	22 49	24 07
17	71 32.4	15.6	28 23.7	9.7	2 09.0	11.9	59.4	50	17 24	17 58	18 35	20 13	21 29	22 46	24 02
18	86 32.4	S11 14.7	42 52.4	9.8	N 2 20.9	11.9	59.4	45	17 33	18 03	18 37	20 15	21 27	22 40	23 52
19	101 32.5	13.9	57 21.2	9.7	2 32.8	11.8	59.4	N 40	17 40	18 07	18 39	20 16	21 25	22 34	23 43
20	116 32.6	13.0	71 49.9	9.7	2 44.6	11.8	59.4	35	17 46	18 12	18 41	20 17	21 23	22 30	23 36
21	131 32.6	. . 12.1	86 18.6	9.7	2 56.4	11.8	59.4	30	17 51	18 16	18 44	20 18	21 22	22 26	23 30
22	146 32.7	11.2	100 47.3	9.6	3 08.2	11.8	59.4	20	18 01	18 23	18 49	20 20	21 19	22 19	23 19
23	161 32.7	10.3	115 15.9	9.7	3 20.0	11.8	59.5	N 10	18 09	18 31	18 55	20 22	21 17	22 13	23 09
20 00	176 32.8	S11 09.4	129 44.6	9.6	N 3 31.8	11.8	59.5	0	18 17	18 38	19 03	20 23	21 15	22 07	23 00
01	191 32.9	08.5	144 13.2	9.7	3 43.6	11.7	59.5	S 10	18 25	18 47	19 12	20 24	21 12	22 01	22 51
02	206 32.9	07.6	158 41.9	9.6	3 55.3	11.7	59.5	20	18 34	18 57	19 23	20 26	21 10	21 55	22 42
03	221 33.0	. . 06.7	173 10.5	9.6	4 07.0	11.7	59.5	30	18 44	19 09	19 38	20 27	21 07	21 48	22 31
04	236 33.0	05.8	187 39.1	9.5	4 18.7	11.7	59.5	35	18 50	19 16	19 48	20 28	21 06	21 44	22 25
05	251 33.1	04.9	202 07.6	9.6	4 30.4	11.6	59.5	40	18 57	19 25	19 59	20 29	21 04	21 40	22 18
06	266 33.2	S11 04.0	216 36.2	9.5	N 4 42.0	11.6	59.5	45	19 05	19 36	20 13	20 31	21 02	21 35	22 10
S 07	281 33.2	03.1	231 04.7	9.6	4 53.6	11.6	59.5	S 50	19 14	19 49	20 32	20 32	21 00	21 28	22 00
A 08	296 33.3	02.2	245 33.3	9.5	5 05.2	11.5	59.5	52	19 18	19 55	20 41	20 33	20 59	21 26	21 55
T 09	311 33.4	. . 01.3	260 01.8	9.4	5 16.7	11.6	59.5	54	19 23	20 02	20 51	20 33	20 57	21 23	21 50
U 10	326 33.4	11 00.5	274 30.2	9.5	5 28.3	11.5	59.5	56	19 29	20 10	21 03	20 34	20 56	21 19	21 45
R 11	341 33.5	10 59.6	288 58.7	9.4	5 39.8	11.4	59.5	58	19 35	20 19	21 17	20 35	20 55	21 15	21 39
D 12	356 33.6	S10 58.7	303 27.1	9.4	N 5 51.2	11.4	59.5	S 60	19 41	20 29	21 34	20 36	20 53	21 11	21 32
A 13	11 33.6	57.8	317 55.5	9.4	6 02.6	11.4	59.5								
Y 14	26 33.7	56.9	332 23.9	9.4	6 14.0	11.4	59.5			SUN			MOON		
15	41 33.7	. . 56.0	346 52.3	9.4	6 25.4	11.3	59.5	Day	Eqn. of Time		Mer.	Mer. Pass.		Age	Phase
16	56 33.8	55.1	1 20.7	9.3	6 36.7	11.2	59.5		00ʰ	12ʰ	Pass.	Upper	Lower		
17	71 33.9	54.2	15 49.0	9.3	6 47.9	11.3	59.5	d	m s	m s	h m	h m	h m	d %	
18	86 33.9	S10 53.3	30 17.3	9.3	N 6 59.2	11.1	59.5	18	13 59	13 57	12 14	14 11	01 45	02 6	
19	101 34.0	52.4	44 45.6	9.2	7 10.3	11.2	59.5	19	13 54	13 52	12 14	15 02	02 36	03 13	
20	116 34.1	51.5	59 13.8	9.3	7 21.5	11.1	59.5	20	13 49	13 46	12 14	15 54	03 28	04 22	
21	131 34.1	. . 50.6	73 42.1	9.2	7 32.6	11.0	59.5								
22	146 34.2	49.7	88 10.3	9.1	7 43.6	11.0	59.5								
23	161 34.3	48.8	102 38.4	9.2	N 7 54.6	11.0	59.5								
	SD 16.2	d 0.9	SD 16.1		16.2		16.2									

UT	ARIES GHA	VENUS −4.0 GHA	Dec	MARS +0.0 GHA	Dec	JUPITER −2.1 GHA	Dec	SATURN +0.5 GHA	Dec	STARS Name	SHA	Dec
d h	° ′	° ′	° ′	° ′	° ′	° ′	° ′	° ′	° ′		° ′	° ′
21 00	150 28.3	151 01.6	S 1 24.8	293 28.7	S12 19.7	148 24.3	S 0 19.2	122 26.5	N 9 02.4	Acamar	315 26.9	S40 18.9
01	165 30.8	166 01.2	23.5	308 30.6	19.9	163 26.3	19.0	137 28.8	02.5	Achernar	335 35.4	S57 14.9
02	180 33.2	181 00.9	22.2	323 32.4	20.1	178 28.2	18.7	152 31.0	02.6	Acrux	173 21.1	S63 05.5
03	195 35.7	196 00.6	.. 20.8	338 34.3	.. 20.3	193 30.2	.. 18.5	167 33.3	.. 02.6	Adhara	255 21.0	S28 58.6
04	210 38.2	211 00.2	19.5	353 36.1	20.5	208 32.1	18.3	182 35.6	02.7	Aldebaran	291 02.0	N16 30.3
05	225 40.6	225 59.9	18.2	8 38.0	20.7	223 34.1	18.1	197 37.8	02.8			
06	240 43.1	240 59.6	S 1 16.9	23 39.8	S12 20.9	238 36.0	S 0 17.8	212 40.1	N 9 02.9	Alioth	166 30.0	N55 57.7
07	255 45.6	255 59.2	15.6	38 41.6	21.1	253 38.0	17.6	227 42.3	03.0	Alkaid	153 07.4	N49 18.9
08	270 48.0	270 58.9	14.3	53 43.5	21.3	268 39.9	17.4	242 44.6	03.1	Al Na'ir	27 58.1	S46 58.0
S 09	285 50.5	285 58.6	.. 13.0	68 45.3	.. 21.5	283 41.8	.. 17.1	257 46.8	.. 03.2	Alnilam	275 57.5	S 1 12.4
U 10	300 53.0	300 58.2	11.7	83 47.2	21.7	298 43.8	16.9	272 49.1	03.2	Alphard	218 06.6	S 8 39.4
N 11	315 55.4	315 57.9	10.4	98 49.0	21.9	313 45.7	16.7	287 51.4	03.3			
D 12	330 57.9	330 57.6	S 1 09.1	113 50.9	S12 22.1	328 47.7	S 0 16.5	302 53.6	N 9 03.4	Alphecca	126 20.3	N26 42.9
A 13	346 00.4	345 57.2	07.8	128 52.7	22.3	343 49.6	16.2	317 55.9	03.5	Alpheratz	357 55.3	N29 05.0
Y 14	1 02.8	0 56.9	06.5	143 54.6	22.5	358 51.6	16.0	332 58.1	03.6	Altair	62 19.3	N 8 51.9
15	16 05.3	15 56.6	.. 05.2	158 56.4	.. 22.7	13 53.5	.. 15.8	348 00.4	.. 03.7	Ankaa	353 27.0	S42 18.9
16	31 07.7	30 56.3	03.9	173 58.3	22.9	28 55.5	15.5	3 02.7	03.8	Antares	112 39.9	S26 25.6
17	46 10.2	45 55.9	02.6	189 00.1	23.1	43 57.4	15.3	18 04.9	03.8			
18	61 12.7	60 55.6	S 1 01.3	204 02.0	S12 23.2	58 59.4	S 0 15.1	33 07.2	N 9 03.9	Arcturus	146 05.7	N19 11.1
19	76 15.1	75 55.3	1 00.0	219 03.8	23.4	74 01.3	14.9	48 09.4	04.0	Atria	107 51.8	S69 01.2
20	91 17.6	90 54.9	0 58.7	234 05.7	23.6	89 03.2	14.6	63 11.7	04.1	Avior	234 21.9	S59 30.6
21	106 20.1	105 54.6	.. 57.4	249 07.6	.. 23.8	104 05.2	.. 14.4	78 13.9	.. 04.2	Bellatrix	278 43.8	N 6 20.7
22	121 22.5	120 54.3	56.1	264 09.4	24.0	119 07.1	14.2	93 16.2	04.3	Betelgeuse	271 13.1	N 7 24.2
23	136 25.0	135 53.9	54.8	279 11.3	24.2	134 09.1	13.9	108 18.5	04.4			
22 00	151 27.5	150 53.6	S 0 53.5	294 13.1	S12 24.4	149 11.0	S 0 13.7	123 20.7	N 9 04.5	Canopus	264 00.7	S52 42.1
01	166 29.9	165 53.3	52.2	309 15.0	24.6	164 13.0	13.5	138 23.0	04.5	Capella	280 50.7	N45 59.8
02	181 32.4	180 53.0	50.9	324 16.8	24.8	179 14.9	13.3	153 25.2	04.6	Deneb	49 39.4	N45 16.5
03	196 34.9	195 52.6	.. 49.5	339 18.7	.. 25.0	194 16.9	.. 13.0	168 27.5	.. 04.7	Denebola	182 44.6	N14 34.5
04	211 37.3	210 52.3	48.2	354 20.6	25.2	209 18.8	12.8	183 29.7	04.8	Diphda	349 07.2	S17 59.7
05	226 39.8	225 52.0	46.9	9 22.4	25.3	224 20.7	12.6	198 32.0	04.9			
06	241 42.2	240 51.6	S 0 45.6	24 24.3	S12 25.5	239 22.7	S 0 12.3	213 34.3	N 9 05.0	Dubhe	194 04.6	N61 45.2
07	256 44.7	255 51.3	44.3	39 26.2	25.7	254 24.6	12.1	228 36.5	05.1	Elnath	278 26.5	N28 36.3
08	271 47.2	270 51.0	43.0	54 28.0	25.9	269 26.6	11.9	243 38.8	05.1	Eltanin	90 51.5	N51 29.2
M 09	286 49.6	285 50.7	.. 41.7	69 29.9	.. 26.1	284 28.5	.. 11.7	258 41.0	.. 05.2	Enif	33 58.3	N 9 52.1
O 10	301 52.1	300 50.3	40.4	84 31.8	26.3	299 30.5	11.4	273 43.3	05.3	Fomalhaut	15 36.5	S29 37.8
N 11	316 54.6	315 50.0	39.1	99 33.6	26.5	314 32.4	11.2	288 45.5	05.4			
D 12	331 57.0	330 49.7	S 0 37.8	114 35.5	S12 26.7	329 34.4	S 0 11.0	303 47.8	N 9 05.5	Gacrux	172 12.8	S57 06.3
A 13	346 59.5	345 49.3	36.5	129 37.4	26.9	344 36.3	10.7	318 50.0	05.6	Gienah	176 03.4	S17 32.2
Y 14	2 02.0	0 49.0	35.2	144 39.2	27.0	359 38.2	10.5	333 52.3	05.7	Hadar	149 03.3	S60 21.8
15	17 04.4	15 48.7	.. 33.9	159 41.1	.. 27.2	14 40.2	.. 10.3	348 54.6	.. 05.8	Hamal	328 13.4	N23 27.4
16	32 06.9	30 48.4	32.6	174 43.0	27.4	29 42.1	10.0	3 56.8	05.8	Kaus Aust.	83 58.7	S34 23.0
17	47 09.3	45 48.0	31.3	189 44.8	27.6	44 44.1	09.8	18 59.1	05.9			
18	62 11.8	60 47.7	S 0 30.0	204 46.7	S12 27.8	59 46.0	S 0 09.6	34 01.3	N 9 06.0	Kochab	137 19.3	N74 09.3
19	77 14.3	75 47.4	28.7	219 48.6	28.0	74 48.0	09.4	49 03.6	06.1	Markab	13 49.7	N15 11.9
20	92 16.7	90 47.1	27.4	234 50.5	28.2	89 49.9	09.1	64 05.8	06.2	Menkar	314 26.7	N 4 05.0
21	107 19.2	105 46.7	.. 26.0	249 52.3	.. 28.3	104 51.8	.. 08.9	79 08.1	.. 06.3	Menkent	148 20.4	S36 21.8
22	122 21.7	120 46.4	24.7	264 54.2	28.5	119 53.8	08.7	94 10.3	06.4	Miaplacidus	221 41.0	S69 43.0
23	137 24.1	135 46.1	23.4	279 56.1	28.7	134 55.7	08.4	109 12.6	06.4			
23 00	152 26.6	150 45.8	S 0 22.1	294 58.0	S12 28.9	149 57.7	S 0 08.2	124 14.8	N 9 06.5	Mirfak	308 56.3	N49 51.5
01	167 29.1	165 45.4	20.8	309 59.8	29.1	164 59.6	08.0	139 17.1	06.6	Nunki	76 12.3	S26 17.8
02	182 31.5	180 45.1	19.5	325 01.7	29.3	180 01.6	07.8	154 19.4	06.7	Peacock	53 37.2	S56 44.2
03	197 34.0	195 44.8	.. 18.2	340 03.6	.. 29.4	195 03.5	.. 07.5	169 21.6	.. 06.8	Pollux	243 41.0	N28 01.6
04	212 36.5	210 44.4	16.9	355 05.5	29.6	210 05.4	07.3	184 23.9	06.9	Procyon	245 11.0	N 5 13.5
05	227 38.9	225 44.1	15.6	10 07.4	29.8	225 07.4	07.1	199 26.1	07.0			
06	242 41.4	240 43.8	S 0 14.3	25 09.2	S12 30.0	240 09.3	S 0 06.8	214 28.4	N 9 07.1	Rasalhague	96 16.8	N12 33.6
07	257 43.8	255 43.5	13.0	40 11.1	30.2	255 11.3	06.6	229 30.6	07.1	Regulus	207 55.0	N11 58.2
T 08	272 46.3	270 43.1	11.7	55 13.0	30.4	270 13.2	06.4	244 32.9	07.2	Rigel	281 22.6	S 8 12.4
U 09	287 48.8	285 42.8	.. 10.4	70 14.9	.. 30.5	285 15.1	.. 06.1	259 35.1	.. 07.3	Rigil Kent.	140 06.6	S60 49.6
E 10	302 51.2	300 42.5	09.1	85 16.8	30.7	300 17.1	05.9	274 37.4	07.4	Sabik	102 25.3	S15 43.3
S 11	317 53.7	315 42.2	07.8	100 18.7	30.9	315 19.0	05.7	289 39.6	07.5			
D 12	332 56.2	330 41.8	S 0 06.5	115 20.6	S12 31.1	330 21.0	S 0 05.5	304 41.9	N 9 07.6	Schedar	349 53.6	N56 32.0
A 13	347 58.6	345 41.5	05.2	130 22.4	31.3	345 22.9	05.2	319 44.1	07.7	Shaula	96 37.1	S37 06.0
Y 14	3 01.1	0 41.2	03.8	145 24.3	31.4	0 24.9	05.0	334 46.4	07.8	Sirius	258 43.3	S16 43.2
15	18 03.6	15 40.9	.. 02.5	160 26.2	.. 31.6	15 26.8	.. 04.8	349 48.6	.. 07.8	Spica	158 42.7	S11 09.4
16	33 06.0	30 40.5	01.2	175 28.1	31.8	30 28.7	04.5	4 50.9	07.9	Suhail	223 00.1	S43 25.9
17	48 08.5	45 40.2	N 00.1	190 30.0	32.0	45 30.7	04.3	19 53.1	08.0			
18	63 11.0	60 39.9	N 0 01.4	205 31.9	S12 32.2	60 32.6	S 0 04.1	34 55.4	N 9 08.1	Vega	80 46.7	N38 46.8
19	78 13.4	75 39.6	02.7	220 33.8	32.3	75 34.6	03.8	49 57.6	08.2	Zuben'ubi	137 17.6	S16 02.2
20	93 15.9	90 39.2	04.0	235 35.7	32.5	90 36.5	03.6	64 59.9	08.3			
21	108 18.3	105 38.9	.. 05.3	250 37.6	.. 32.7	105 38.4	.. 03.4	80 02.2	.. 08.4		SHA	Mer. Pass.
22	123 20.8	120 38.6	06.6	265 39.5	32.9	120 40.4	03.2	95 04.4	08.5	Venus	359 26.2	h m 13 57
23	138 23.3	135 38.3	07.9	280 41.4	33.1	135 42.3	02.9	110 06.7	08.6	Mars	142 45.7	4 23
	h m									Jupiter	357 43.6	14 01
Mer. Pass. 13 51.9	v −0.3 d 1.3			v 1.9 d 0.2		v 1.9 d 0.2		v 2.3 d 0.1		Saturn	331 53.3	15 44

UT	SUN GHA	SUN Dec	MOON GHA	v	MOON Dec	d	HP
d h	° ′	° ′	° ′	′	° ′	′	′
21 00	176 34.3	S10 47.9	117 06.6	9.1	N 8 05.6	10.9	59.5
01	191 34.4	47.0	131 34.7	9.1	8 16.5	10.9	59.5
02	206 34.5	46.1	146 02.8	9.1	8 27.4	10.8	59.5
03	221 34.6	.. 45.2	160 30.9	9.0	8 38.2	10.7	59.5
04	236 34.6	44.3	174 58.9	9.0	8 48.9	10.7	59.5
05	251 34.7	43.4	189 26.9	9.0	8 59.6	10.7	59.5
06	266 34.8	S10 42.5	203 54.9	9.0	N 9 10.3	10.6	59.5
07	281 34.8	41.6	218 22.9	8.9	9 20.9	10.5	59.5
08	296 34.9	40.7	232 50.8	8.9	9 31.4	10.5	59.4
S 09	311 35.0	.. 39.8	247 18.7	8.9	9 41.9	10.4	59.4
U 10	326 35.0	38.9	261 46.6	8.8	9 52.3	10.3	59.4
N 11	341 35.1	38.0	276 14.4	8.8	10 02.6	10.3	59.4
D 12	356 35.2	S10 37.1	290 42.2	8.8	N10 12.9	10.2	59.4
A 13	11 35.3	36.2	305 10.0	8.8	10 23.1	10.2	59.4
Y 14	26 35.3	35.2	319 37.8	8.7	10 33.3	10.1	59.4
15	41 35.4	.. 34.3	334 05.5	8.7	10 43.4	10.0	59.4
16	56 35.5	33.4	348 33.2	8.6	10 53.4	10.0	59.4
17	71 35.5	32.5	3 00.8	8.6	11 03.4	9.9	59.4
18	86 35.6	S10 31.6	17 28.4	8.6	N11 13.3	9.8	59.4
19	101 35.7	30.7	31 56.0	8.6	11 23.1	9.8	59.4
20	116 35.8	29.8	46 23.6	8.5	11 32.9	9.7	59.4
21	131 35.8	.. 28.9	60 51.1	8.5	11 42.6	9.6	59.4
22	146 35.9	28.0	75 18.6	8.5	11 52.2	9.5	59.4
23	161 36.0	27.1	89 46.1	8.4	12 01.7	9.5	59.4
22 00	176 36.1	S10 26.2	104 13.5	8.4	N12 11.2	9.4	59.4
01	191 36.1	25.3	118 40.9	8.3	12 20.6	9.3	59.4
02	206 36.2	24.4	133 08.2	8.4	12 29.9	9.2	59.4
03	221 36.3	.. 23.5	147 35.6	8.3	12 39.1	9.2	59.4
04	236 36.4	22.6	162 02.9	8.2	12 48.3	9.0	59.3
05	251 36.4	21.7	176 30.1	8.3	12 57.3	9.0	59.3
06	266 36.5	S10 20.7	190 57.4	8.1	N13 06.3	8.9	59.3
07	281 36.6	19.8	205 24.5	8.2	13 15.2	8.9	59.3
08	296 36.7	18.9	219 51.7	8.1	13 24.1	8.7	59.3
M 09	311 36.7	.. 18.0	234 18.8	8.1	13 32.8	8.7	59.3
O 10	326 36.8	17.1	248 45.9	8.1	13 41.5	8.5	59.3
N 11	341 36.9	16.2	263 13.0	8.0	13 50.0	8.5	59.3
D 12	356 37.0	S10 15.3	277 40.0	8.0	N13 58.5	8.4	59.3
A 13	11 37.1	14.4	292 07.0	8.0	14 06.9	8.3	59.3
Y 14	26 37.1	13.5	306 34.0	7.9	14 15.2	8.2	59.3
15	41 37.2	.. 12.6	321 00.9	7.9	14 23.4	8.1	59.3
16	56 37.3	11.6	335 27.8	7.9	14 31.5	8.1	59.3
17	71 37.4	10.7	349 54.7	7.8	14 39.6	7.9	59.2
18	86 37.5	S10 09.8	4 21.5	7.8	N14 47.5	7.9	59.2
19	101 37.5	08.9	18 48.3	7.8	14 55.4	7.7	59.2
20	116 37.6	08.0	33 15.1	7.7	15 03.1	7.7	59.2
21	131 37.7	.. 07.1	47 41.8	7.7	15 10.8	7.5	59.2
22	146 37.8	06.2	62 08.5	7.7	15 18.3	7.5	59.2
23	161 37.9	05.3	76 35.2	7.6	15 25.8	7.4	59.2
23 00	176 37.9	S10 04.3	91 01.8	7.6	N15 33.2	7.2	59.2
01	191 38.0	03.4	105 28.4	7.6	15 40.4	7.2	59.2
02	206 38.1	02.5	119 55.0	7.6	15 47.6	7.1	59.2
03	221 38.2	.. 01.6	134 21.6	7.5	15 54.7	6.9	59.2
04	236 38.3	10 00.7	148 48.1	7.5	16 01.6	6.9	59.1
05	251 38.4	9 59.8	163 14.6	7.4	16 08.5	6.7	59.1
06	266 38.5	S 9 58.9	177 41.0	7.5	N16 15.2	6.7	59.1
07	281 38.5	57.9	192 07.5	7.4	16 21.9	6.6	59.1
08	296 38.6	57.0	206 33.9	7.4	16 28.5	6.4	59.1
T 09	311 38.7	.. 56.1	221 00.2	7.4	16 34.9	6.3	59.1
U 10	326 38.8	55.2	235 26.6	7.3	16 41.2	6.3	59.1
E 11	341 38.9	54.3	249 52.9	7.3	16 47.5	6.1	59.1
S 12	356 38.9	S 9 53.4	264 19.2	7.3	N16 53.6	6.0	59.1
D 13	11 39.0	52.5	278 45.5	7.2	16 59.6	5.9	59.1
A 14	26 39.1	51.5	293 11.7	7.2	17 05.5	5.8	59.0
Y 15	41 39.2	.. 50.6	307 37.9	7.2	17 11.3	5.7	59.0
16	56 39.3	49.7	322 04.1	7.2	17 17.0	5.6	59.0
17	71 39.4	48.8	336 30.3	7.1	17 22.6	5.5	59.0
18	86 39.5	S 9 47.9	350 56.4	7.2	N17 28.1	5.3	59.0
19	101 39.6	46.9	5 22.6	7.1	17 33.4	5.3	59.0
20	116 39.6	46.0	19 48.7	7.0	17 38.7	5.1	59.0
21	131 39.7	.. 45.1	34 14.7	7.1	17 43.8	5.0	59.0
22	146 39.8	44.2	48 40.8	7.0	17 48.8	4.9	58.9
23	161 39.9	43.3	63 06.8	7.1	N17 53.7	4.8	58.9
	SD 16.2	d 0.9	SD 16.2		16.2		16.1

Twilight / Sunrise / Moonrise

Lat.	Twilight Naut.	Twilight Civil	Sunrise	Moonrise 21	22	23	24
°	h m	h m	h m	h m	h m	h m	h m
N 72	05 46	07 04	08 17	08 26	08 15	07 56	☐
N 70	05 47	06 57	08 02	08 41	08 39	08 40	08 44
68	05 48	06 52	07 51	08 52	08 58	09 09	09 28
66	05 48	06 48	07 41	09 02	09 14	09 31	09 57
64	05 49	06 44	07 33	09 10	09 26	09 48	10 20
62	05 49	06 40	07 26	09 17	09 37	10 03	10 37
60	05 49	06 37	07 20	09 24	09 46	10 15	10 52
N 58	05 49	06 35	07 15	09 29	09 54	10 25	11 05
56	05 49	06 32	07 10	09 34	10 01	10 35	11 16
54	05 49	06 30	07 06	09 38	10 08	10 43	11 26
52	05 48	06 28	07 02	09 42	10 14	10 50	11 34
50	05 48	06 26	06 58	09 46	10 19	10 57	11 42
45	05 47	06 21	06 51	09 54	10 30	11 11	11 58
N 40	05 45	06 17	06 44	10 00	10 40	11 23	12 12
35	05 44	06 13	06 39	10 06	10 48	11 34	12 24
30	05 42	06 10	06 34	10 11	10 55	11 42	12 34
20	05 37	06 03	06 25	10 20	11 07	11 58	12 51
N 10	05 32	05 56	06 18	10 27	11 18	12 11	13 06
0	05 25	05 49	06 10	10 35	11 29	12 24	13 21
S 10	05 16	05 41	06 03	10 42	11 39	12 37	13 35
20	05 06	05 32	05 55	10 50	11 50	12 51	13 51
30	04 52	05 21	05 45	10 59	12 03	13 07	14 08
35	04 43	05 14	05 40	11 05	12 11	13 16	14 19
40	04 32	05 06	05 34	11 11	12 19	13 26	14 30
45	04 18	04 56	05 27	11 18	12 29	13 39	14 44
S 50	04 01	04 43	05 18	11 26	12 41	13 54	15 02
52	03 52	04 38	05 14	11 30	12 47	14 01	15 10
54	03 43	04 31	05 09	11 34	12 53	14 09	15 19
56	03 32	04 24	05 04	11 39	13 00	14 18	15 29
58	03 18	04 15	04 59	11 45	13 08	14 28	15 40
S 60	03 03	04 06	04 53	11 51	13 17	14 39	15 54

Sunset / Twilight / Moonset

Lat.	Sunset	Twilight Civil	Twilight Naut.	Moonset 21	22	23	24
°	h m	h m	h m	h m	h m	h m	h m
N 72	16 12	17 25	18 44	25 56	01 56	04 10	☐
N 70	16 26	17 31	18 42	25 33	01 33	03 28	05 21
68	16 38	17 37	18 41	25 16	01 16	03 00	04 38
66	16 47	17 41	18 40	25 01	01 01	02 39	04 09
64	16 55	17 45	18 40	24 50	00 50	02 22	03 47
62	17 02	17 48	18 39	24 40	00 40	02 08	03 29
60	17 08	17 51	18 39	24 31	00 31	01 56	03 15
N 58	17 13	17 54	18 39	24 24	00 24	01 46	03 02
56	17 18	17 56	18 39	24 18	00 18	01 37	02 52
54	17 22	17 58	18 39	24 12	00 12	01 29	02 42
52	17 26	18 00	18 40	24 07	00 07	01 22	02 34
50	17 30	18 02	18 40	24 02	00 02	01 16	02 26
45	17 37	18 07	18 41	23 52	25 02	01 02	02 10
N 40	17 43	18 11	18 42	23 43	24 51	00 51	01 57
35	17 49	18 14	18 44	23 36	24 42	00 42	01 46
30	17 54	18 18	18 46	23 30	24 34	00 34	01 36
20	18 02	18 24	18 50	23 19	24 19	00 19	01 19
N 10	18 10	18 31	18 56	23 09	24 07	00 07	01 05
0	18 17	18 38	19 02	23 00	23 55	24 51	00 51
S 10	18 24	18 46	19 10	22 51	23 43	24 37	00 37
20	18 32	18 55	19 21	22 42	23 31	24 23	00 23
30	18 41	19 06	19 35	22 31	23 17	24 06	00 06
35	18 46	19 13	19 44	22 25	23 09	23 56	24 49
40	18 53	19 21	19 54	22 18	22 59	23 45	24 37
45	19 00	19 30	20 08	22 10	22 48	23 32	24 22
S 50	19 08	19 42	20 25	22 00	22 35	23 16	24 05
52	19 12	19 48	20 33	21 55	22 29	23 09	23 57
54	19 16	19 55	20 42	21 50	22 22	23 01	23 48
56	19 21	20 02	20 53	21 45	22 15	22 52	23 37
58	19 27	20 10	21 06	21 39	22 06	22 41	23 26
S 60	19 33	20 19	21 21	21 32	21 57	22 29	23 12

SUN / MOON

Day	Eqn. of Time 00h	12h	Mer. Pass.	Mer. Pass. Upper	Lower	Age	Phase
d	m s	m s	h m	h m	h m	d	%
21	13 43	13 39	12 14	16 47	04 21	05	32
22	13 36	13 32	12 14	17 42	05 15	06	43
23	13 28	13 24	12 13	18 38	06 10	07	55

UT	ARIES GHA	VENUS −4.0 GHA	Dec	MARS −0.1 GHA	Dec	JUPITER −2.1 GHA	Dec	SATURN +0.5 GHA	Dec	STARS Name	SHA	Dec
24 00	153 25.7	150 37.9	N 0 09.2	295 43.3	S12 33.2	150 44.3	S 0 02.7	125 08.9	N 9 08.6	Acamar	315 26.9	S40 18.9
01	168 28.2	165 37.6	10.5	310 45.2	33.4	165 46.2	02.5	140 11.2	08.7	Achernar	335 35.4	S57 14.8
02	183 30.7	180 37.3	11.8	325 47.1	33.6	180 48.1	02.2	155 13.4	08.8	Acrux	173 21.0	S63 05.5
03	198 33.1	195 37.0	.. 13.1	340 49.0	.. 33.8	195 50.1	.. 02.0	170 15.7	.. 08.9	Adhara	255 21.0	S28 58.6
04	213 35.6	210 36.7	14.4	355 50.9	33.9	210 52.0	01.8	185 17.9	09.0	Aldebaran	291 02.0	N16 30.3
05	228 38.1	225 36.3	15.8	10 52.8	34.1	225 54.0	01.5	200 20.2	09.1			
W 06	243 40.5	240 36.0	N 0 17.1	25 54.7	S12 34.3	240 55.9	S 0 01.3	215 22.4	N 9 09.2	Alioth	166 30.0	N55 57.7
E 07	258 43.0	255 35.7	18.4	40 56.6	34.5	255 57.8	01.1	230 24.7	09.3	Alkaid	153 07.3	N49 18.9
D 08	273 45.5	270 35.4	19.7	55 58.5	34.6	270 59.8	00.8	245 26.9	09.3	Al Na'ir	27 58.1	S46 58.0
N 09	288 47.9	285 35.0	.. 21.0	71 00.4	.. 34.8	286 01.7	.. 00.6	260 29.2	.. 09.4	Alnilam	275 57.5	S 1 12.4
E 10	303 50.4	300 34.7	22.3	86 02.3	35.0	301 03.7	00.4	275 31.4	09.5	Alphard	218 06.6	S 8 39.5
S 11	318 52.8	315 34.4	23.6	101 04.2	35.2	316 05.6	S 00.2	290 33.7	09.6			
D 12	333 55.3	330 34.1	N 0 24.9	116 06.1	S12 35.3	331 07.5	N 0 00.1	305 35.9	N 9 09.7	Alphecca	126 20.3	N26 42.9
A 13	348 57.8	345 33.7	26.2	131 08.0	35.5	346 09.5	00.3	320 38.2	09.8	Alpheratz	357 55.3	N29 05.0
Y 14	4 00.2	0 33.4	27.5	146 09.9	35.7	1 11.4	00.5	335 40.4	09.9	Altair	62 19.3	N 8 51.9
15	19 02.7	15 33.1	.. 28.8	161 11.8	.. 35.9	16 13.4	.. 00.8	350 42.7	.. 10.0	Ankaa	353 27.0	S42 18.9
16	34 05.2	30 32.8	30.1	176 13.7	36.0	31 15.3	01.0	5 44.9	10.1	Antares	112 39.9	S26 25.6
17	49 07.6	45 32.5	31.4	191 15.6	36.2	46 17.2	01.2	20 47.2	10.1			
18	64 10.1	60 32.1	N 0 32.7	206 17.6	S12 36.4	61 19.2	N 0 01.5	35 49.4	N 9 10.2	Arcturus	146 05.7	N19 11.1
19	79 12.6	75 31.8	34.0	221 19.5	36.6	76 21.1	01.7	50 51.7	10.3	Atria	107 51.7	S69 01.2
20	94 15.0	90 31.5	35.3	236 21.4	36.7	91 23.1	01.9	65 53.9	10.4	Avior	234 21.9	S59 30.7
21	109 17.5	105 31.2	.. 36.7	251 23.3	.. 36.9	106 25.0	.. 02.2	80 56.2	.. 10.5	Bellatrix	278 43.8	N 6 20.7
22	124 19.9	120 30.8	38.0	266 25.2	37.1	121 26.9	02.4	95 58.4	10.6	Betelgeuse	271 13.1	N 7 24.2
23	139 22.4	135 30.5	39.3	281 27.1	37.2	136 28.9	02.6	111 00.6	10.7			
25 00	154 24.9	150 30.2	N 0 40.6	296 29.0	S12 37.4	151 30.8	N 0 02.8	126 02.9	N 9 10.8	Canopus	264 00.8	S52 42.1
01	169 27.3	165 29.9	41.9	311 31.0	37.6	166 32.8	03.1	141 05.1	10.9	Capella	280 50.7	N45 59.8
02	184 29.8	180 29.6	43.2	326 32.9	37.8	181 34.7	03.3	156 07.4	10.9	Deneb	49 39.4	N45 16.5
03	199 32.3	195 29.2	.. 44.5	341 34.8	.. 37.9	196 36.6	.. 03.5	171 09.6	.. 11.0	Denebola	182 44.6	N14 34.5
04	214 34.7	210 28.9	45.8	356 36.7	38.1	211 38.6	03.8	186 11.9	11.1	Diphda	349 07.2	S17 59.7
05	229 37.2	225 28.6	47.1	11 38.6	38.3	226 40.5	04.0	201 14.1	11.2			
T 06	244 39.7	240 28.3	N 0 48.4	26 40.6	S12 38.4	241 42.5	N 0 04.2	216 16.4	N 9 11.3	Dubhe	194 04.6	N61 45.2
H 07	259 42.1	255 27.9	49.7	41 42.5	38.6	256 44.4	04.5	231 18.6	11.4	Elnath	278 26.5	N28 36.3
U 08	274 44.6	270 27.6	51.0	56 44.4	38.8	271 46.3	04.7	246 20.9	11.5	Eltanin	90 51.5	N51 29.2
R 09	289 47.1	285 27.3	.. 52.3	71 46.3	.. 38.9	286 48.3	.. 04.9	261 23.1	.. 11.6	Enif	33 58.3	N 9 52.1
S 10	304 49.5	300 27.0	53.6	86 48.3	39.1	301 50.2	05.2	276 25.4	11.7	Fomalhaut	15 36.5	S29 37.8
11	319 52.0	315 26.7	54.9	101 50.2	39.3	316 52.1	05.4	291 27.6	11.7			
D 12	334 54.4	330 26.3	N 0 56.3	116 52.1	S12 39.4	331 54.1	N 0 05.6	306 29.9	N 9 11.8	Gacrux	172 12.7	S57 06.3
A 13	349 56.9	345 26.0	57.6	131 54.0	39.6	346 56.0	05.9	321 32.1	11.9	Gienah	176 03.4	S17 32.2
Y 14	4 59.4	0 25.7	0 58.9	146 56.0	39.8	1 58.0	06.1	336 34.4	12.0	Hadar	149 03.2	S60 21.8
15	20 01.8	15 25.4	1 00.2	161 57.9	.. 40.0	16 59.9	.. 06.3	351 36.6	.. 12.1	Hamal	328 13.4	N23 27.4
16	35 04.3	30 25.1	01.5	176 59.8	40.1	32 01.8	06.5	6 38.9	12.2	Kaus Aust.	83 58.7	S34 22.9
17	50 06.8	45 24.7	02.8	192 01.8	40.3	47 03.8	06.8	21 41.1	12.3			
18	65 09.2	60 24.4	N 1 04.1	207 03.7	S12 40.5	62 05.7	N 0 07.0	36 43.3	N 9 12.4	Kochab	137 19.3	N74 09.3
19	80 11.7	75 24.1	05.4	222 05.6	40.6	77 07.6	07.2	51 45.6	12.5	Markab	13 49.7	N15 11.9
20	95 14.2	90 23.8	06.7	237 07.6	40.8	92 09.6	07.5	66 47.8	12.6	Menkar	314 26.7	N 4 05.0
21	110 16.6	105 23.5	.. 08.0	252 09.5	.. 40.9	107 11.5	.. 07.7	81 50.1	.. 12.6	Menkent	148 20.4	S36 21.8
22	125 19.1	120 23.1	09.3	267 11.4	41.1	122 13.5	07.9	96 52.3	12.7	Miaplacidus	221 41.1	S69 43.0
23	140 21.6	135 22.8	10.6	282 13.4	41.3	137 15.4	08.2	111 54.6	12.8			
26 00	155 24.0	150 22.5	N 1 11.9	297 15.3	S12 41.4	152 17.3	N 0 08.4	126 56.8	N 9 12.9	Mirfak	308 56.3	N49 51.5
01	170 26.5	165 22.2	13.2	312 17.2	41.6	167 19.3	08.6	141 59.1	13.0	Nunki	76 12.2	S26 17.8
02	185 28.9	180 21.9	14.5	327 19.2	41.8	182 21.2	08.9	157 01.3	13.1	Peacock	53 37.1	S56 44.2
03	200 31.4	195 21.5	.. 15.8	342 21.1	.. 41.9	197 23.1	.. 09.1	172 03.6	.. 13.2	Pollux	243 41.0	N28 01.6
04	215 33.9	210 21.2	17.1	357 23.1	42.1	212 25.1	09.3	187 05.8	13.3	Procyon	245 11.0	N 5 13.5
05	230 36.3	225 20.9	18.5	12 25.0	42.3	227 27.0	09.6	202 08.0	13.4			
F 06	245 38.8	240 20.6	N 1 19.8	27 26.9	S12 42.4	242 29.0	N 0 09.8	217 10.3	N 9 13.5	Rasalhague	96 16.8	N12 33.6
R 07	260 41.3	255 20.3	21.1	42 28.9	42.6	257 30.9	10.0	232 12.5	13.5	Regulus	207 54.9	N11 58.2
I 08	275 43.7	270 19.9	22.4	57 30.8	42.8	272 32.8	10.3	247 14.8	13.6	Rigel	281 22.6	S 8 12.4
D 09	290 46.2	285 19.6	.. 23.7	72 32.8	.. 42.9	287 34.8	.. 10.5	262 17.0	.. 13.7	Rigil Kent.	140 06.6	S60 49.6
A 10	305 48.7	300 19.3	25.0	87 34.7	43.1	302 36.7	10.7	277 19.3	13.8	Sabik	102 25.3	S15 43.3
Y 11	320 51.1	315 19.0	26.3	102 36.7	43.2	317 38.6	10.9	292 21.5	13.9			
12	335 53.6	330 18.7	N 1 27.6	117 38.6	S12 43.4	332 40.6	N 0 11.2	307 23.8	N 9 14.0	Schedar	349 53.6	N56 32.0
13	350 56.1	345 18.3	28.9	132 40.6	43.6	347 42.5	11.4	322 26.0	14.1	Shaula	96 37.1	S37 06.0
14	5 58.5	0 18.0	30.2	147 42.5	43.7	2 44.4	11.6	337 28.2	14.2	Sirius	258 43.3	S16 43.2
15	21 01.0	15 17.7	.. 31.5	162 44.5	.. 43.9	17 46.4	.. 11.9	352 30.5	.. 14.3	Spica	158 42.7	S11 09.4
16	36 03.4	30 17.4	32.8	177 46.4	44.0	32 48.3	12.1	7 32.7	14.4	Suhail	223 00.1	S43 25.9
17	51 05.9	45 17.1	34.1	192 48.4	44.2	47 50.3	12.3	22 35.0	14.4			
18	66 08.4	60 16.7	N 1 35.4	207 50.3	S12 44.4	62 52.2	N 0 12.6	37 37.2	N 9 14.5	Vega	80 46.7	N38 46.8
19	81 10.8	75 16.4	36.7	222 52.3	44.5	77 54.1	12.8	52 39.5	14.6	Zuben'ubi	137 17.5	S16 02.2
20	96 13.3	90 16.1	38.0	237 54.2	44.7	92 56.1	13.0	67 41.7	14.7			
21	111 15.8	105 15.8	.. 39.3	252 56.2	.. 44.8	107 58.0	.. 13.3	82 43.9	.. 14.8		SHA	Mer. Pass.
22	126 18.2	120 15.5	40.6	267 58.1	45.0	122 59.9	13.5	97 46.2	14.9	Venus	356 05.3	13 58
23	141 20.7	135 15.1	42.0	283 00.1	45.2	138 01.9	13.7	112 48.4	15.0	Mars	142 04.2	4 14
Mer. Pass.	13 40.1	v −0.3	d 1.3	v 1.9	d 0.2	v 1.9	d 0.2	v 2.2	d 0.1	Jupiter	357 05.9	13 52
										Saturn	331 38.0	15 33

UT	SUN GHA	SUN Dec	MOON GHA	v	MOON Dec	d	HP
d h	° ′	° ′	° ′	′	° ′	′	′
24 00	176 40.0	S 9 42.4	77 32.9	7.0	N17 58.5	4.7	58.9
01	191 40.1	41.4	91 58.9	6.9	18 03.2	4.5	58.9
02	206 40.2	40.5	106 24.8	7.0	18 07.7	4.5	58.9
03	221 40.2	.. 39.6	120 50.8	6.9	18 12.2	4.3	58.9
04	236 40.3	38.7	135 16.7	7.0	18 16.5	4.2	58.9
05	251 40.4	37.8	149 42.7	6.9	18 20.7	4.1	58.9
06	266 40.5	S 9 36.8	164 08.6	6.9	N18 24.8	4.0	58.8
W 07	281 40.6	35.9	178 34.5	6.9	18 28.8	3.8	58.8
E 08	296 40.7	35.0	193 00.4	6.9	18 32.6	3.8	58.8
D 09	311 40.8	.. 34.1	207 26.3	6.8	18 36.4	3.6	58.8
N 10	326 40.9	33.1	221 52.1	6.9	18 40.0	3.5	58.8
E 11	341 41.0	32.2	236 18.0	6.8	18 43.5	3.3	58.8
S 12	356 41.1	S 9 31.3	250 43.8	6.8	N18 46.8	3.3	58.8
D 13	11 41.1	30.4	265 09.6	6.9	18 50.1	3.1	58.8
A 14	26 41.2	29.5	279 35.5	6.8	18 53.2	3.0	58.7
Y 15	41 41.3	.. 28.5	294 01.3	6.8	18 56.2	2.9	58.7
16	56 41.4	27.6	308 27.1	6.8	18 59.1	2.8	58.7
17	71 41.5	26.7	322 52.9	6.8	19 01.9	2.7	58.7
18	86 41.6	S 9 25.8	337 18.7	6.8	N19 04.6	2.5	58.7
19	101 41.7	24.8	351 44.5	6.8	19 07.1	2.4	58.7
20	116 41.8	23.9	6 10.3	6.8	19 09.5	2.3	58.7
21	131 41.9	.. 23.0	20 36.1	6.7	19 11.8	2.1	58.7
22	146 42.0	22.1	35 01.8	6.8	19 13.9	2.1	58.6
23	161 42.1	21.1	49 27.6	6.8	19 16.0	1.9	58.6
25 00	176 42.2	S 9 20.2	63 53.4	6.8	N19 17.9	1.8	58.6
01	191 42.3	19.3	78 19.2	6.8	19 19.7	1.6	58.6
02	206 42.4	18.4	92 45.0	6.8	19 21.3	1.6	58.6
03	221 42.5	.. 17.4	107 10.8	6.8	19 22.9	1.4	58.6
04	236 42.6	16.5	121 36.6	6.8	19 24.3	1.3	58.6
05	251 42.6	15.6	136 02.4	6.8	19 25.6	1.2	58.5
06	266 42.7	S 9 14.7	150 28.2	6.8	N19 26.8	1.0	58.5
T 07	281 42.8	13.7	164 54.0	6.8	19 27.8	1.0	58.5
H 08	296 42.9	12.8	179 19.8	6.9	19 28.8	0.8	58.5
U 09	311 43.0	.. 11.9	193 45.7	6.8	19 29.6	0.7	58.5
R 10	326 43.1	10.9	208 11.5	6.9	19 30.3	0.5	58.5
S 11	341 43.2	10.0	222 37.4	6.9	19 30.8	0.5	58.5
D 12	356 43.3	S 9 09.1	237 03.3	6.8	N19 31.3	0.3	58.4
A 13	11 43.4	08.2	251 29.1	6.9	19 31.6	0.2	58.4
Y 14	26 43.5	07.2	265 55.0	7.0	19 31.8	0.0	58.4
15	41 43.6	.. 06.3	280 21.0	6.9	19 31.8	0.0	58.4
16	56 43.7	05.4	294 46.9	6.9	19 31.8	0.2	58.4
17	71 43.8	04.4	309 12.8	7.0	19 31.6	0.3	58.4
18	86 43.9	S 9 03.5	323 38.8	7.0	N19 31.3	0.4	58.3
19	101 44.0	02.6	338 04.8	7.0	19 30.9	0.6	58.3
20	116 44.1	01.7	352 30.8	7.0	19 30.3	0.6	58.3
21	131 44.2	9 00.7	6 56.8	7.1	19 29.7	0.8	58.3
22	146 44.3	8 59.8	21 22.9	7.0	19 28.9	0.9	58.3
23	161 44.4	58.9	35 48.9	7.1	19 28.0	1.0	58.3
26 00	176 44.5	S 8 57.9	50 15.0	7.2	N19 27.0	1.2	58.3
01	191 44.6	57.0	64 41.2	7.1	19 25.8	1.2	58.2
02	206 44.7	56.1	79 07.3	7.2	19 24.6	1.4	58.2
03	221 44.8	.. 55.1	93 33.5	7.2	19 23.2	1.5	58.2
04	236 44.9	54.2	107 59.7	7.2	19 21.7	1.7	58.2
05	251 45.0	53.3	122 25.9	7.3	19 20.0	1.7	58.2
06	266 45.1	S 8 52.3	136 52.2	7.3	N19 18.3	1.9	58.2
07	281 45.2	51.4	151 18.5	7.3	19 16.4	1.9	58.1
08	296 45.3	50.5	165 44.8	7.4	19 14.5	2.1	58.1
F 09	311 45.4	.. 49.5	180 11.2	7.4	19 12.4	2.2	58.1
R 10	326 45.5	48.6	194 37.6	7.4	19 10.2	2.4	58.1
I 11	341 45.6	47.7	209 04.0	7.5	19 07.8	2.4	58.1
D 12	356 45.7	S 8 46.7	223 30.5	7.5	N19 05.4	2.6	58.1
A 13	11 45.9	45.8	237 57.0	7.5	19 02.8	2.6	58.0
Y 14	26 46.0	44.9	252 23.5	7.6	19 00.2	2.8	58.0
15	41 46.1	.. 43.9	266 50.1	7.6	18 57.4	2.9	58.0
16	56 46.2	43.0	281 16.7	7.6	18 54.5	3.0	58.0
17	71 46.3	42.1	295 43.3	7.7	18 51.5	3.2	58.0
18	86 46.4	S 8 41.1	310 10.0	7.8	N18 48.3	3.2	57.9
19	101 46.5	40.2	324 36.8	7.8	18 45.1	3.4	57.9
20	116 46.6	39.3	339 03.6	7.8	18 41.7	3.4	57.9
21	131 46.7	.. 38.3	353 30.4	7.8	18 38.3	3.6	57.9
22	146 46.8	37.4	7 57.2	8.0	18 34.7	3.7	57.9
23	161 46.9	36.4	22 24.2	7.9	N18 31.0	3.8	57.9
	SD 16.2	d 0.9	SD 16.0		15.9		15.8

Moonrise

Lat.	Naut.	Civil	Sunrise	24	25	26	27
°	h m	h m	h m	h m	h m	h m	h m
N 72	05 32	06 49	08 01	▭	▭	▭	10 51
N 70	05 34	06 45	07 48	08 44	09 06	10 17	12 00
68	05 37	06 41	07 38	09 28	10 06	11 11	12 37
66	05 38	06 37	07 30	09 57	10 40	11 43	13 03
64	05 39	06 34	07 23	10 20	11 05	12 07	13 23
62	05 40	06 32	07 17	10 37	11 25	12 26	13 39
60	05 41	06 29	07 11	10 52	11 41	12 42	13 53
N 58	05 42	06 27	07 07	11 05	11 55	12 55	14 04
56	05 42	06 25	07 03	11 16	12 06	13 07	14 14
54	05 42	06 23	06 59	11 26	12 17	13 17	14 23
52	05 42	06 21	06 56	11 34	12 26	13 25	14 31
50	05 42	06 19	06 52	11 42	12 34	13 33	14 38
45	05 42	06 16	06 46	11 58	12 52	13 50	14 53
N 40	05 41	06 13	06 40	12 12	13 06	14 04	15 06
35	05 40	06 10	06 35	12 24	13 18	14 16	15 16
30	05 39	06 07	06 31	12 34	13 29	14 26	15 25
20	05 35	06 01	06 23	12 51	13 47	14 44	15 41
N 10	05 30	05 55	06 16	13 06	14 03	14 59	15 55
0	05 25	05 49	06 10	13 21	14 18	15 14	16 08
S 10	05 17	05 42	06 03	13 35	14 33	15 28	16 21
20	05 07	05 34	05 56	13 51	14 48	15 44	16 35
30	04 54	05 23	05 48	14 08	15 07	16 01	16 51
35	04 46	05 17	05 43	14 19	15 18	16 12	17 00
40	04 36	05 09	05 37	14 30	15 30	16 23	17 10
45	04 23	05 00	05 31	14 44	15 44	16 37	17 23
S 50	04 07	04 49	05 23	15 02	16 02	16 54	17 38
52	03 59	04 44	05 19	15 10	16 10	17 02	17 45
54	03 50	04 38	05 15	15 19	16 20	17 11	17 52
56	03 40	04 31	05 11	15 29	16 30	17 21	18 01
58	03 28	04 23	05 06	15 40	16 42	17 32	18 10
S 60	03 14	04 15	05 00	15 54	16 56	17 45	18 22

Moonset

Lat.	Sunset	Civil	Naut.	24	25	26	27
°	h m	h m	h m	h m	h m	h m	h m
N 72	16 28	17 39	18 57	▭	▭	▭	09 07
N 70	16 40	17 43	18 54	05 21	06 58	07 45	07 56
68	16 50	17 47	18 52	04 38	05 58	06 51	07 19
66	16 58	17 51	18 50	04 09	05 24	06 18	06 53
64	17 05	17 53	18 48	03 47	04 59	05 54	06 32
62	17 11	17 56	18 47	03 29	04 39	05 35	06 16
60	17 16	17 58	18 46	03 15	04 23	05 19	06 02
N 58	17 20	18 00	18 46	03 02	04 10	05 06	05 50
56	17 25	18 02	18 45	02 52	03 58	04 54	05 40
54	17 28	18 04	18 45	02 42	03 48	04 44	05 30
52	17 32	18 06	18 45	02 34	03 39	04 35	05 22
50	17 35	18 07	18 45	02 26	03 31	04 27	05 15
45	17 41	18 11	18 45	02 10	03 13	04 10	04 59
N 40	17 47	18 15	18 46	01 57	02 59	03 56	04 46
35	17 52	18 17	18 47	01 46	02 47	03 44	04 35
30	17 56	18 20	18 48	01 36	02 37	03 33	04 25
20	18 03	18 26	18 51	01 19	02 18	03 15	04 09
N 10	18 10	18 31	18 56	01 05	02 03	02 59	03 54
0	18 16	18 37	19 02	00 51	01 48	02 45	03 40
S 10	18 23	18 44	19 09	00 37	01 33	02 30	03 26
20	18 30	18 52	19 19	00 23	01 17	02 14	03 11
30	18 38	19 03	19 31	00 06	00 59	01 56	02 54
35	18 43	19 09	19 40	24 49	00 49	01 45	02 44
40	18 48	19 16	19 49	24 37	00 37	01 33	02 33
45	18 55	19 25	20 02	24 22	00 22	01 18	02 20
S 50	19 02	19 36	20 18	24 05	00 05	01 01	02 03
52	19 06	19 41	20 25	23 57	24 53	00 53	01 55
54	19 10	19 47	20 34	23 48	24 43	00 43	01 47
56	19 14	19 54	20 44	23 37	24 33	00 33	01 37
58	19 19	20 01	20 56	23 26	24 21	00 21	01 26
S 60	19 24	20 10	21 09	23 12	24 07	00 07	01 13

SUN / MOON

Day	Eqn. of Time 00ʰ	Eqn. of Time 12ʰ	Mer. Pass.	Mer. Pass. Upper	Mer. Pass. Lower	Age	Phase
d	m s	m s	h m	h m	h m	d	%
24	13 20	13 16	12 13	19 34	07 06	08	66
25	13 11	13 07	12 13	20 31	08 03	09	76
26	13 02	12 57	12 13	21 27	08 59	10	85

UT	ARIES GHA	VENUS −4.0 GHA	Dec	MARS −0.1 GHA	Dec	JUPITER −2.1 GHA	Dec	SATURN +0.5 GHA	Dec	STARS Name	SHA	Dec
27 00	156 23.2	150 14.8	N 1 43.3	298 02.1	S12 45.3	153 03.8	N 0 14.0	127 50.7	N 9 15.1	Acamar	315 26.9	S40 18.9
01	171 25.6	165 14.5	44.6	313 04.0	45.5	168 05.7	14.2	142 52.9	15.2	Achernar	335 35.4	S57 14.8
02	186 28.1	180 14.2	45.9	328 06.0	45.6	183 07.7	14.4	157 55.2	15.3	Acrux	173 21.0	S63 05.5
03	201 30.5	195 13.9	.. 47.2	343 07.9	.. 45.8	198 09.6	.. 14.7	172 57.4	.. 15.4	Adhara	255 21.0	S28 58.6
04	216 33.0	210 13.5	48.5	358 09.9	45.9	213 11.5	14.9	187 59.6	15.4	Aldebaran	291 02.1	N16 30.3
05	231 35.5	225 13.2	49.8	13 11.9	46.1	228 13.5	15.1	203 01.9	15.5			
S 06	246 37.9	240 12.9	N 1 51.1	28 13.8	S12 46.3	243 15.4	N 0 15.4	218 04.1	N 9 15.6	Alioth	166 29.9	N55 57.7
A 07	261 40.4	255 12.6	52.4	43 15.8	46.4	258 17.4	15.6	233 06.4	15.7	Alkaid	153 07.3	N49 18.9
T 08	276 42.9	270 12.3	53.7	58 17.8	46.6	273 19.3	15.8	248 08.6	15.8	Al Na'ir	27 58.0	S46 58.0
U 09	291 45.3	285 12.0	.. 55.0	73 19.7	.. 46.7	288 21.2	.. 16.1	263 10.9	.. 15.9	Alnilam	275 57.5	S 1 12.4
R 10	306 47.8	300 11.6	56.3	88 21.7	46.9	303 23.2	16.3	278 13.1	16.0	Alphard	218 06.6	S 8 39.5
D 11	321 50.3	315 11.3	57.6	103 23.7	47.0	318 25.1	16.5	293 15.3	16.1			
A 12	336 52.7	330 11.0	N 1 58.9	118 25.6	S12 47.2	333 27.0	N 0 16.7	308 17.6	N 9 16.2	Alphecca	126 20.3	N26 42.9
Y 13	351 55.2	345 10.7	2 00.2	133 27.6	47.3	348 29.0	17.0	323 19.8	16.3	Alpheratz	357 55.3	N29 05.0
14	6 57.7	0 10.4	01.5	148 29.6	47.5	3 30.9	17.2	338 22.1	16.4	Altair	62 19.2	N 8 51.9
15	22 00.1	15 10.0	.. 02.8	163 31.5	.. 47.7	18 32.8	.. 17.4	353 24.3	.. 16.4	Ankaa	353 27.0	S42 18.9
16	37 02.6	30 09.7	04.1	178 33.5	47.8	33 34.8	17.7	8 26.5	16.5	Antares	112 39.8	S26 25.7
17	52 05.0	45 09.4	05.4	193 35.5	48.0	48 36.7	17.9	23 28.8	16.6			
18	67 07.5	60 09.1	N 2 06.7	208 37.5	S12 48.1	63 38.6	N 0 18.1	38 31.0	N 9 16.7	Arcturus	146 05.6	N19 11.1
19	82 10.0	75 08.8	08.0	223 39.4	48.3	78 40.6	18.4	53 33.3	16.8	Atria	107 51.7	S69 01.2
20	97 12.4	90 08.4	09.3	238 41.4	48.4	93 42.5	18.6	68 35.5	16.9	Avior	234 22.0	S59 30.7
21	112 14.9	105 08.1	.. 10.6	253 43.4	.. 48.6	108 44.4	.. 18.8	83 37.7	.. 17.0	Bellatrix	278 43.8	N 6 20.7
22	127 17.4	120 07.8	12.0	268 45.4	48.7	123 46.4	19.1	98 40.0	17.1	Betelgeuse	271 13.1	N 7 24.2
23	142 19.8	135 07.5	13.3	283 47.3	48.9	138 48.3	19.3	113 42.2	17.2			
28 00	157 22.3	150 07.2	N 2 14.6	298 49.3	S12 49.0	153 50.2	N 0 19.5	128 44.5	N 9 17.3	Canopus	264 00.8	S52 42.1
01	172 24.8	165 06.9	15.9	313 51.3	49.2	168 52.2	19.8	143 46.7	17.4	Capella	280 50.7	N45 59.8
02	187 27.2	180 06.5	17.2	328 53.3	49.3	183 54.1	20.0	158 48.9	17.5	Deneb	49 39.4	N45 16.5
03	202 29.7	195 06.2	.. 18.5	343 55.3	.. 49.5	198 56.0	.. 20.2	173 51.2	.. 17.5	Denebola	182 44.6	N14 34.5
04	217 32.2	210 05.9	19.8	358 57.3	49.6	213 58.0	20.5	188 53.4	17.6	Diphda	349 07.2	S17 59.7
05	232 34.6	225 05.6	21.1	13 59.2	49.8	228 59.9	20.7	203 55.7	17.7			
S 06	247 37.1	240 05.3	N 2 22.4	29 01.2	S12 49.9	244 01.8	N 0 20.9	218 57.9	N 9 17.8	Dubhe	194 04.6	N61 45.3
U 07	262 39.5	255 04.9	23.7	44 03.2	50.1	259 03.8	21.2	234 00.1	17.9	Elnath	278 26.5	N28 36.3
N 08	277 42.0	270 04.6	25.0	59 05.2	50.2	274 05.7	21.4	249 02.4	18.0	Eltanin	90 51.5	N51 29.1
D 09	292 44.5	285 04.3	.. 26.3	74 07.2	.. 50.4	289 07.6	.. 21.6	264 04.6	.. 18.1	Enif	33 58.3	N 9 52.1
A 10	307 46.9	300 04.0	27.6	89 09.2	50.5	304 09.6	21.9	279 06.9	18.2	Fomalhaut	15 36.5	S29 37.8
Y 11	322 49.4	315 03.7	28.9	104 11.2	50.7	319 11.5	22.1	294 09.1	18.3			
12	337 51.9	330 03.4	N 2 30.2	119 13.1	S12 50.8	334 13.4	N 0 22.3	309 11.3	N 9 18.4	Gacrux	172 12.7	S57 06.4
13	352 54.3	345 03.0	31.5	134 15.1	51.0	349 15.4	22.6	324 13.6	18.5	Gienah	176 03.4	S17 32.2
14	7 56.8	0 02.7	32.8	149 17.1	51.1	4 17.3	22.8	339 15.8	18.6	Hadar	149 03.2	S60 21.9
15	22 59.3	15 02.4	.. 34.1	164 19.1	.. 51.3	19 19.2	.. 23.0	354 18.0	.. 18.6	Hamal	328 13.4	N23 27.4
16	38 01.7	30 02.1	35.4	179 21.1	51.4	34 21.2	23.3	9 20.3	18.7	Kaus Aust.	83 58.6	S34 22.9
17	53 04.2	45 01.8	36.7	194 23.1	51.6	49 23.1	23.5	24 22.5	18.8			
18	68 06.6	60 01.4	N 2 38.0	209 25.1	S12 51.7	64 25.0	N 0 23.7	39 24.8	N 9 18.9	Kochab	137 19.2	N74 09.3
19	83 09.1	75 01.1	39.3	224 27.1	51.8	79 27.0	24.0	54 27.0	19.0	Markab	13 49.7	N15 11.9
20	98 11.6	90 00.8	40.6	239 29.1	52.0	94 28.9	24.2	69 29.2	19.1	Menkar	314 26.7	N 4 05.0
21	113 14.0	105 00.5	.. 41.9	254 31.1	.. 52.1	109 30.8	.. 24.4	84 31.5	.. 19.2	Menkent	148 20.4	S36 21.8
22	128 16.5	120 00.2	43.2	269 33.1	52.3	124 32.8	24.7	99 33.7	19.3	Miaplacidus	221 41.1	S69 43.0
23	143 19.0	134 59.9	44.5	284 35.1	52.4	139 34.7	24.9	114 35.9	19.4			
1 00	158 21.4	149 59.5	N 2 45.8	299 37.1	S12 52.6	154 36.6	N 0 25.1	129 38.2	N 9 19.5	Mirfak	308 56.3	N49 51.5
01	173 23.9	164 59.2	47.1	314 39.1	52.7	169 38.6	25.4	144 40.4	19.6	Nunki	76 12.2	S26 17.8
02	188 26.4	179 58.9	48.4	329 41.1	52.9	184 40.5	25.6	159 42.7	19.7	Peacock	53 37.1	S56 44.2
03	203 28.8	194 58.6	.. 49.7	344 43.1	.. 53.0	199 42.4	.. 25.8	174 44.9	.. 19.8	Pollux	243 41.0	N28 01.6
04	218 31.3	209 58.3	51.0	359 45.1	53.1	214 44.4	26.1	189 47.1	19.8	Procyon	245 11.1	N 5 13.4
05	233 33.8	224 57.9	52.3	14 47.1	53.3	229 46.3	26.3	204 49.4	19.9			
M 06	248 36.2	239 57.6	N 2 53.6	29 49.1	S12 53.4	244 48.2	N 0 26.5	219 51.6	N 9 20.0	Rasalhague	96 16.8	N12 33.6
O 07	263 38.7	254 57.3	54.9	44 51.1	53.6	259 50.2	26.8	234 53.8	20.1	Regulus	207 54.9	N11 58.2
N 08	278 41.1	269 57.0	56.2	59 53.1	53.7	274 52.1	27.0	249 56.1	20.2	Rigel	281 22.6	S 8 12.4
D 09	293 43.6	284 56.7	.. 57.5	74 55.2	.. 53.9	289 54.0	.. 27.2	264 58.3	.. 20.3	Rigil Kent.	140 06.6	S60 49.6
A 10	308 46.1	299 56.4	2 58.8	89 57.2	54.0	304 56.0	27.5	280 00.6	20.4	Sabik	102 25.3	S15 43.3
Y 11	323 48.5	314 56.0	3 00.1	104 59.2	54.1	319 57.9	27.7	295 02.8	20.5			
12	338 51.0	329 55.7	N 3 01.4	120 01.2	S12 54.3	334 59.8	N 0 27.9	310 05.0	N 9 20.6	Schedar	349 53.6	N56 32.0
13	353 53.5	344 55.4	02.7	135 03.2	54.4	350 01.7	28.2	325 07.3	20.7	Shaula	96 37.0	S37 06.0
14	8 55.9	359 55.1	04.0	150 05.2	54.6	5 03.7	28.4	340 09.5	20.8	Sirius	258 43.3	S16 43.2
15	23 58.4	14 54.8	.. 05.3	165 07.2	.. 54.7	20 05.6	.. 28.6	355 11.7	.. 20.9	Spica	158 42.7	S11 09.4
16	39 00.9	29 54.4	06.6	180 09.3	54.8	35 07.5	28.9	10 14.0	21.0	Suhail	223 00.1	S43 25.9
17	54 03.3	44 54.1	07.9	195 11.3	55.0	50 09.5	29.1	25 16.2	21.0			
18	69 05.8	59 53.8	N 3 09.2	210 13.3	S12 55.1	65 11.4	N 0 29.3	40 18.4	N 9 21.1	Vega	80 46.6	N38 46.8
19	84 08.3	74 53.5	10.5	225 15.3	55.3	80 13.3	29.6	55 20.7	21.2	Zuben'ubi	137 17.5	S16 02.2
20	99 10.7	89 53.2	11.8	240 17.3	55.4	95 15.3	29.8	70 22.9	21.3		SHA	Mer. Pass.
21	114 13.2	104 52.8	.. 13.1	255 19.3	.. 55.5	110 17.2	.. 30.0	85 25.1	.. 21.4			
22	129 15.6	119 52.5	14.4	270 21.4	55.7	125 19.1	30.3	100 27.4	21.5	Venus	352 44.9	14 00
23	144 18.1	134 52.2	15.7	285 23.4	55.8	140 21.1	30.5	115 29.6	21.6	Mars	141 27.0	4 04
Mer. Pass. 13 28.3		v −0.3	d 1.3	v 2.0	d 0.1	v 1.9	d 0.2	v 2.2	d 0.1	Jupiter	356 27.9	13 43
										Saturn	331 22.2	15 23

UT	SUN GHA	Dec	MOON GHA	v	Dec	d	HP
d h	° ′	° ′	° ′	′	° ′	′	′
27 00	176 47.0	S 8 35.5	36 51.1	8.0	N18 27.2	3.8	57.8
01	191 47.1	34.6	51 18.1	8.1	18 23.4	4.1	57.8
02	206 47.2	33.6	65 45.2	8.0	18 19.3	4.1	57.8
03	221 47.3	.. 32.7	80 12.2	8.2	18 15.2	4.2	57.8
04	236 47.4	31.8	94 39.4	8.2	18 11.0	4.3	57.8
05	251 47.6	30.8	109 06.6	8.2	18 06.7	4.4	57.8
06	266 47.7	S 8 29.9	123 33.8	8.3	N18 02.3	4.6	57.7
07	281 47.8	29.0	138 01.1	8.3	17 57.7	4.6	57.7
S 08	296 47.9	28.0	152 28.4	8.4	17 53.1	4.7	57.7
A 09	311 48.0	.. 27.1	166 55.8	8.5	17 48.4	4.9	57.7
T 10	326 48.1	26.1	181 23.3	8.5	17 43.5	4.9	57.7
U 11	341 48.2	25.2	195 50.8	8.5	17 38.6	5.0	57.6
R 12	356 48.3	S 8 24.3	210 18.3	8.6	N17 33.6	5.2	57.6
D 13	11 48.4	23.3	224 45.9	8.7	17 28.4	5.2	57.6
A 14	26 48.5	22.4	239 13.6	8.7	17 23.2	5.3	57.6
Y 15	41 48.6	.. 21.4	253 41.3	8.7	17 17.9	5.5	57.6
16	56 48.8	20.5	268 09.0	8.8	17 12.4	5.5	57.5
17	71 48.9	19.6	282 36.8	8.9	17 06.9	5.6	57.5
18	86 49.0	S 8 18.6	297 04.7	8.9	N17 01.3	5.7	57.5
19	101 49.1	17.7	311 32.6	9.0	16 55.6	5.8	57.5
20	116 49.2	16.7	326 00.6	9.0	16 49.8	5.9	57.5
21	131 49.3	.. 15.8	340 28.6	9.1	16 43.9	6.0	57.4
22	146 49.4	14.9	354 56.7	9.2	16 37.9	6.1	57.4
23	161 49.5	13.9	9 24.9	9.2	16 31.8	6.1	57.4
28 00	176 49.6	S 8 13.0	23 53.1	9.3	N16 25.7	6.3	57.4
01	191 49.8	12.0	38 21.4	9.3	16 19.4	6.4	57.4
02	206 49.9	11.1	52 49.7	9.4	16 13.0	6.4	57.3
03	221 50.0	.. 10.1	67 18.1	9.4	16 06.6	6.5	57.3
04	236 50.1	09.2	81 46.5	9.5	16 00.1	6.6	57.3
05	251 50.2	08.3	96 15.0	9.6	15 53.5	6.7	57.3
06	266 50.3	S 8 07.3	110 43.6	9.6	N15 46.8	6.8	57.3
07	281 50.4	06.4	125 12.2	9.7	15 40.0	6.8	57.2
S 08	296 50.6	05.4	139 40.9	9.7	15 33.2	7.0	57.2
U 09	311 50.7	.. 04.5	154 09.6	9.8	15 26.2	7.0	57.2
N 10	326 50.8	03.5	168 38.4	9.9	15 19.2	7.1	57.2
D 11	341 50.9	02.6	183 07.3	9.9	15 12.1	7.1	57.2
A 12	356 51.0	S 8 01.7	197 36.2	10.0	N15 05.0	7.3	57.1
Y 13	11 51.1	8 00.7	212 05.2	10.0	14 57.7	7.3	57.1
14	26 51.2	7 59.8	226 34.2	10.1	14 50.4	7.4	57.1
15	41 51.4	.. 58.8	241 03.3	10.2	14 43.0	7.5	57.1
16	56 51.5	57.9	255 32.5	10.2	14 35.5	7.5	57.1
17	71 51.6	56.9	270 01.7	10.3	14 28.0	7.7	57.0
18	86 51.7	S 7 56.0	284 31.0	10.3	N14 20.3	7.7	57.0
19	101 51.8	55.0	299 00.3	10.4	14 12.6	7.7	57.0
20	116 51.9	54.1	313 29.7	10.4	14 04.9	7.8	57.0
21	131 52.1	.. 53.2	327 59.1	10.6	13 57.1	8.0	57.0
22	146 52.2	52.2	342 28.7	10.6	13 49.1	7.9	56.9
23	161 52.3	51.3	356 58.3	10.6	13 41.2	8.1	56.9
1 00	176 52.4	S 7 50.3	11 27.9	10.7	N13 33.1	8.1	56.9
01	191 52.5	49.4	25 57.6	10.8	13 25.0	8.1	56.9
02	206 52.7	48.4	40 27.4	10.8	13 16.9	8.3	56.9
03	221 52.8	.. 47.5	54 57.2	10.9	13 08.6	8.3	56.8
04	236 52.9	46.5	69 27.1	10.9	13 00.3	8.3	56.8
05	251 53.0	45.6	83 57.0	11.0	12 52.0	8.4	56.8
06	266 53.1	S 7 44.6	98 27.0	11.1	N12 43.6	8.5	56.8
07	281 53.3	43.7	112 57.1	11.1	12 35.1	8.5	56.7
M 08	296 53.4	42.7	127 27.2	11.2	12 26.6	8.6	56.7
O 09	311 53.5	.. 41.8	141 57.4	11.2	12 18.0	8.7	56.7
N 10	326 53.6	40.8	156 27.6	11.3	12 09.3	8.7	56.7
D 11	341 53.7	39.9	170 57.9	11.3	12 00.6	8.8	56.7
A 12	356 53.8	S 7 38.9	185 28.2	11.4	N11 51.8	8.8	56.6
Y 13	11 54.0	38.0	199 58.6	11.5	11 43.0	8.8	56.6
14	26 54.1	37.0	214 29.1	11.5	11 34.2	9.0	56.6
15	41 54.2	.. 36.1	228 59.6	11.6	11 25.2	8.9	56.6
16	56 54.3	35.1	243 30.2	11.7	11 16.3	9.1	56.6
17	71 54.5	34.2	258 00.9	11.7	11 07.2	9.0	56.5
18	86 54.6	S 7 33.2	272 31.6	11.7	N10 58.2	9.1	56.5
19	101 54.7	32.3	287 02.3	11.8	10 49.1	9.2	56.5
20	116 54.8	31.3	301 33.1	11.9	10 39.9	9.2	56.5
21	131 55.0	.. 30.4	316 04.0	11.9	10 30.7	9.3	56.4
22	146 55.1	29.4	330 34.9	12.0	10 21.4	9.3	56.4
23	161 55.2	28.5	345 05.9	12.0	N10 12.1	9.3	56.4
	SD 16.2	d 0.9	SD 15.7		15.6		15.4

Lat.	Twilight Naut.	Civil	Sunrise	Moonrise 27	28	1	2
°	h m	h m	h m	h m	h m	h m	h m
N 72	05 17	06 35	07 44	10 51	13 14	15 13	17 03
N 70	05 21	06 32	07 34	12 00	13 48	15 33	17 14
68	05 25	06 29	07 26	12 37	14 12	15 49	17 22
66	05 28	06 27	07 19	13 03	14 31	16 01	17 30
64	05 30	06 24	07 13	13 23	14 46	16 11	17 36
62	05 31	06 23	07 07	13 39	14 59	16 20	17 41
60	05 33	06 21	07 03	13 53	15 09	16 28	17 46
N 58	05 34	06 19	06 59	14 04	15 18	16 34	17 50
56	05 35	06 18	06 55	14 14	15 26	16 40	17 53
54	05 36	06 16	06 52	14 23	15 34	16 45	17 57
52	05 36	06 15	06 49	14 31	15 40	16 50	18 00
50	05 37	06 14	06 46	14 38	15 46	16 54	18 02
45	05 37	06 11	06 41	14 53	15 58	17 03	18 08
N 40	05 37	06 08	06 36	15 06	16 08	17 11	18 13
35	05 37	06 06	06 31	15 16	16 17	17 18	18 17
30	05 36	06 04	06 28	15 25	16 25	17 23	18 20
20	05 33	05 59	06 21	15 41	16 38	17 33	18 27
N 10	05 29	05 54	06 15	15 55	16 50	17 42	18 32
0	05 24	05 48	06 09	16 08	17 00	17 50	18 37
S 10	05 17	05 42	06 03	16 21	17 11	17 58	18 42
20	05 09	05 35	05 57	16 35	17 23	18 07	18 48
30	04 57	05 25	05 50	16 51	17 36	18 17	18 54
35	04 49	05 20	05 46	17 00	17 43	18 22	18 58
40	04 40	05 13	05 41	17 10	17 52	18 29	19 02
45	04 28	05 05	05 35	17 23	18 02	18 36	19 06
S 50	04 13	04 54	05 28	17 38	18 14	18 45	19 12
52	04 06	04 50	05 25	17 45	18 20	18 49	19 15
54	03 58	04 44	05 21	17 52	18 26	18 54	19 17
56	03 49	04 38	05 18	18 01	18 33	18 59	19 20
58	03 38	04 31	05 13	18 10	18 40	19 04	19 24
S 60	03 25	04 23	05 08	18 22	18 49	19 10	19 28

Lat.	Sunset	Twilight Civil	Naut.	Moonset 27	28	1	2
°	h m	h m	h m	h m	h m	h m	h m
N 72	16 43	17 52	19 11	09 07	08 33	08 19	08 09
N 70	16 53	17 56	19 06	07 56	07 58	07 58	07 56
68	17 01	17 58	19 02	07 19	07 33	07 41	07 45
66	17 08	18 00	19 00	06 53	07 14	07 27	07 37
64	17 14	18 02	18 57	06 32	06 58	07 16	07 29
62	17 19	18 04	18 55	06 16	06 45	07 06	07 23
60	17 24	18 06	18 54	06 02	06 34	06 58	07 17
N 58	17 27	18 07	18 53	05 50	06 24	06 51	07 13
56	17 31	18 08	18 52	05 40	06 15	06 44	07 08
54	17 34	18 10	18 51	05 30	06 08	06 38	07 04
52	17 37	18 11	18 50	05 22	06 01	06 33	07 01
50	17 40	18 12	18 50	05 15	05 55	06 28	06 57
45	17 45	18 15	18 49	04 59	05 41	06 18	06 50
N 40	17 50	18 17	18 49	04 46	05 30	06 09	06 44
35	17 54	18 20	18 49	04 35	05 21	06 02	06 39
30	17 58	18 22	18 50	04 25	05 13	05 55	06 35
20	18 05	18 27	18 52	04 09	04 58	05 44	06 27
N 10	18 10	18 32	18 56	03 54	04 45	05 34	06 20
0	18 16	18 37	19 01	03 40	04 34	05 25	06 13
S 10	18 22	18 43	19 08	03 26	04 22	05 15	06 06
20	18 28	18 50	19 16	03 11	04 09	05 05	05 59
30	18 35	18 59	19 28	02 54	03 54	04 53	05 51
35	18 39	19 05	19 35	02 44	03 45	04 46	05 46
40	18 44	19 12	19 44	02 33	03 35	04 38	05 41
45	18 49	19 20	19 56	02 20	03 24	04 29	05 34
S 50	18 56	19 30	20 10	02 03	03 10	04 18	05 27
52	18 59	19 34	20 17	01 55	03 03	04 13	05 23
54	19 03	19 40	20 25	01 47	02 56	04 08	05 19
56	19 06	19 46	20 35	01 37	02 48	04 01	05 15
58	19 11	19 52	20 45	01 26	02 38	03 54	05 10
S 60	19 15	20 00	20 58	01 13	02 28	03 46	05 05

Day	SUN Eqn. of Time 00h	12h	Mer. Pass.	MOON Mer. Pass. Upper	Lower	Age	Phase
d	m s	m s	h m	h m	h m	d	%
27	12 52	12 47	12 13	22 21	09 54	11	92
28	12 42	12 36	12 13	23 13	10 47	12	97
1	12 31	12 25	12 12	24 02	11 37	13	99

UT	ARIES GHA	VENUS −4.0 GHA	Dec	MARS −0.2 GHA	Dec	JUPITER −2.1 GHA	Dec	SATURN +0.5 GHA	Dec	STARS Name	SHA	Dec
2 00	159 20.6	149 51.9	N 3 17.0	300 25.4	S12 56.0	155 23.0	N 0 30.7	130 31.8	N 9 21.7	Acamar	315 26.9	S40 18.9
01	174 23.0	164 51.6	18.3	315 27.4	56.1	170 24.9	31.0	145 34.1	21.8	Achernar	335 35.4	S57 14.8
02	189 25.5	179 51.3	19.6	330 29.5	56.2	185 26.9	31.2	160 36.3	21.9	Acrux	173 21.0	S63 05.5
03	204 28.0	194 50.9	.. 20.9	345 31.5	.. 56.4	200 28.8	.. 31.4	175 38.6	.. 22.0	Adhara	255 21.0	S28 58.6
04	219 30.4	209 50.6	22.2	0 33.5	56.5	215 30.7	31.7	190 40.8	22.1	Aldebaran	291 02.1	N16 30.3
05	234 32.9	224 50.3	23.5	15 35.5	56.6	230 32.6	31.9	205 43.0	22.2			
06	249 35.4	239 50.0	N 3 24.8	30 37.6	S12 56.8	245 34.6	N 0 32.1	220 45.3	N 9 22.3	Alioth	166 29.9	N55 57.7
07	264 37.8	254 49.7	26.1	45 39.6	56.9	260 36.5	32.4	235 47.5	22.3	Alkaid	153 07.3	N49 18.9
T 08	279 40.3	269 49.3	27.4	60 41.6	57.1	275 38.4	32.6	250 49.7	22.4	Al Na'ir	27 58.0	S46 58.0
U 09	294 42.7	284 49.0	.. 28.7	75 43.7	.. 57.2	290 40.4	.. 32.8	265 52.0	.. 22.5	Alnilam	275 57.5	S 1 12.4
E 10	309 45.2	299 48.7	30.0	90 45.7	57.3	305 42.3	33.1	280 54.2	22.6	Alphard	218 06.6	S 8 39.5
S 11	324 47.7	314 48.4	31.3	105 47.7	57.5	320 44.2	33.3	295 56.4	22.7			
D 12	339 50.1	329 48.1	N 3 32.6	120 49.8	S12 57.6	335 46.2	N 0 33.5	310 58.7	N 9 22.8	Alphecca	126 20.3	N26 42.9
A 13	354 52.6	344 47.8	33.9	135 51.8	57.7	350 48.1	33.8	326 00.9	22.9	Alpheratz	357 55.3	N29 05.0
Y 14	9 55.1	359 47.4	35.2	150 53.8	57.9	5 50.0	34.0	341 03.1	23.0	Altair	62 19.2	N 8 51.9
15	24 57.5	14 47.1	.. 36.5	165 55.9	.. 58.0	20 51.9	.. 34.2	356 05.4	.. 23.1	Ankaa	353 27.0	S42 18.9
16	40 00.0	29 46.8	37.8	180 57.9	58.1	35 53.9	34.5	11 07.6	23.2	Antares	112 39.8	S26 25.7
17	55 02.5	44 46.5	39.1	196 00.0	58.3	50 55.8	34.7	26 09.8	23.3			
18	70 04.9	59 46.2	N 3 40.4	211 02.0	S12 58.4	65 57.7	N 0 34.9	41 12.1	N 9 23.4	Arcturus	146 05.6	N19 11.1
19	85 07.4	74 45.8	41.7	226 04.0	58.5	80 59.7	35.2	56 14.3	23.5	Atria	107 51.6	S69 01.2
20	100 09.9	89 45.5	43.0	241 06.1	58.7	96 01.6	35.4	71 16.5	23.6	Avior	234 22.0	S59 30.7
21	115 12.3	104 45.2	.. 44.3	256 08.1	.. 58.8	111 03.5	.. 35.6	86 18.7	.. 23.7	Bellatrix	278 43.8	N 6 20.7
22	130 14.8	119 44.9	45.6	271 10.2	58.9	126 05.5	35.9	101 21.0	23.7	Betelgeuse	271 13.2	N 7 24.2
23	145 17.2	134 44.6	46.9	286 12.2	59.1	141 07.4	36.1	116 23.2	23.8			
3 00	160 19.7	149 44.2	N 3 48.2	301 14.3	S12 59.2	156 09.3	N 0 36.3	131 25.4	N 9 23.9	Canopus	264 00.8	S52 42.1
01	175 22.2	164 43.9	49.5	316 16.3	59.3	171 11.2	36.6	146 27.7	24.0	Capella	280 50.7	N45 59.9
02	190 24.6	179 43.6	50.8	331 18.4	59.4	186 13.2	36.8	161 29.9	24.1	Deneb	49 39.4	N45 16.5
03	205 27.1	194 43.3	.. 52.0	346 20.4	.. 59.6	201 15.1	.. 37.1	176 32.1	.. 24.2	Denebola	182 44.6	N14 34.5
04	220 29.6	209 43.0	53.3	1 22.5	59.7	216 17.0	37.3	191 34.4	24.3	Diphda	349 07.3	S17 59.7
05	235 32.0	224 42.7	54.6	16 24.5	12 59.8	231 19.0	37.5	206 36.6	24.4			
06	250 34.5	239 42.3	N 3 55.9	31 26.6	S13 00.0	246 20.9	N 0 37.8	221 38.8	N 9 24.5	Dubhe	194 04.6	N61 45.3
W 07	265 37.0	254 42.0	57.2	46 28.6	00.1	261 22.8	38.0	236 41.1	24.6	Elnath	278 26.5	N28 36.3
E 08	280 39.4	269 41.7	58.5	61 30.7	00.2	276 24.7	38.2	251 43.3	24.7	Eltanin	90 51.4	N51 29.1
D 09	295 41.9	284 41.4	3 59.8	76 32.7	.. 00.4	291 26.7	.. 38.5	266 45.5	.. 24.8	Enif	33 58.3	N 9 52.1
N 10	310 44.3	299 41.1	4 01.1	91 34.8	00.5	306 28.6	38.7	281 47.8	24.9	Fomalhaut	15 36.5	S29 37.8
E 11	325 46.8	314 40.7	02.4	106 36.8	00.6	321 30.5	38.9	296 50.0	25.0			
S 12	340 49.3	329 40.4	N 4 03.7	121 38.9	S13 00.7	336 32.5	N 0 39.2	311 52.2	N 9 25.1	Gacrux	172 12.7	S57 06.4
D 13	355 51.7	344 40.1	05.0	136 41.0	00.9	351 34.4	39.4	326 54.4	25.2	Gienah	176 03.4	S17 32.3
A 14	10 54.2	359 39.8	06.3	151 43.0	01.0	6 36.3	39.6	341 56.7	25.3	Hadar	149 03.2	S60 21.9
Y 15	25 56.7	14 39.5	.. 07.6	166 45.1	.. 01.1	21 38.2	.. 39.9	356 58.9	.. 25.3	Hamal	328 13.4	N23 27.4
16	40 59.1	29 39.1	08.9	181 47.1	01.2	36 40.2	40.1	12 01.1	25.4	Kaus Aust.	83 58.6	S34 22.9
17	56 01.6	44 38.8	10.2	196 49.2	01.4	51 42.1	40.3	27 03.4	25.5			
18	71 04.1	59 38.5	N 4 11.5	211 51.3	S13 01.5	66 44.0	N 0 40.6	42 05.6	N 9 25.6	Kochab	137 19.1	N74 09.3
19	86 06.5	74 38.2	12.8	226 53.3	01.6	81 46.0	40.8	57 07.8	25.7	Markab	13 49.7	N15 11.9
20	101 09.0	89 37.9	14.1	241 55.4	01.7	96 47.9	41.0	72 10.1	25.8	Menkar	314 26.7	N 4 05.0
21	116 11.5	104 37.5	.. 15.3	256 57.5	.. 01.9	111 49.8	.. 41.3	87 12.3	.. 25.9	Menkent	148 20.4	S36 21.8
22	131 13.9	119 37.2	16.6	271 59.5	02.0	126 51.7	41.5	102 14.5	26.0	Miaplacidus	221 41.1	S69 43.0
23	146 16.4	134 36.9	17.9	287 01.6	02.1	141 53.7	41.7	117 16.7	26.1			
4 00	161 18.8	149 36.6	N 4 19.2	302 03.7	S13 02.2	156 55.6	N 0 42.0	132 19.0	N 9 26.2	Mirfak	308 56.3	N49 51.5
01	176 21.3	164 36.3	20.5	317 05.7	02.4	171 57.5	42.2	147 21.2	26.3	Nunki	76 12.2	S26 17.8
02	191 23.8	179 35.9	21.8	332 07.8	02.5	186 59.5	42.4	162 23.4	26.4	Peacock	53 37.1	S56 44.1
03	206 26.2	194 35.6	.. 23.1	347 09.9	.. 02.6	202 01.4	.. 42.7	177 25.7	.. 26.5	Pollux	243 41.0	N28 01.6
04	221 28.7	209 35.3	24.4	2 12.0	02.7	217 03.3	42.9	192 27.9	26.6	Procyon	245 11.1	N 5 13.5
05	236 31.2	224 35.0	25.7	17 14.0	02.9	232 05.2	43.1	207 30.1	26.7			
06	251 33.6	239 34.7	N 4 27.0	32 16.1	S13 03.0	247 07.2	N 0 43.4	222 32.4	N 9 26.8	Rasalhague	96 16.8	N12 33.6
07	266 36.1	254 34.3	28.3	47 18.2	03.1	262 09.1	43.6	237 34.6	26.9	Regulus	207 54.9	N11 58.2
T 08	281 38.6	269 34.0	29.6	62 20.3	03.2	277 11.0	43.9	252 36.8	27.0	Rigel	281 22.6	S 8 12.4
H 09	296 41.0	284 33.7	.. 30.8	77 22.3	.. 03.4	292 12.9	.. 44.1	267 39.0	.. 27.0	Rigil Kent.	140 06.5	S60 49.6
U 10	311 43.5	299 33.4	32.1	92 24.4	03.5	307 14.9	44.3	282 41.3	27.1	Sabik	102 25.3	S15 43.4
R 11	326 45.9	314 33.1	33.4	107 26.5	03.6	322 16.8	44.6	297 43.5	27.2			
S 12	341 48.4	329 32.7	N 4 34.7	122 28.6	S13 03.7	337 18.7	N 0 44.8	312 45.7	N 9 27.3	Schedar	349 53.6	N56 31.9
D 13	356 50.9	344 32.4	36.0	137 30.7	03.8	352 20.7	45.0	327 48.0	27.4	Shaula	96 37.0	S37 06.0
A 14	11 53.3	359 32.1	37.3	152 32.8	04.0	7 22.6	45.3	342 50.2	27.5	Sirius	258 43.3	S16 43.2
Y 15	26 55.8	14 31.8	.. 38.6	167 34.8	.. 04.1	22 24.5	.. 45.5	357 52.4	.. 27.6	Spica	158 42.7	S11 09.4
16	41 58.3	29 31.5	39.9	182 36.9	04.2	37 26.4	45.7	12 54.6	27.7	Suhail	223 00.1	S43 26.0
17	57 00.7	44 31.1	41.2	197 39.0	04.3	52 28.4	46.0	27 56.9	27.8			
18	72 03.2	59 30.8	N 4 42.5	212 41.1	S13 04.4	67 30.3	N 0 46.2	42 59.1	N 9 27.9	Vega	80 46.6	N38 46.8
19	87 05.7	74 30.5	43.7	227 43.2	04.6	82 32.2	46.4	58 01.3	28.0	Zuben'ubi	137 17.5	S16 02.2
20	102 08.1	89 30.2	45.0	242 45.3	04.7	97 34.1	46.7	73 03.5	28.1		SHA	Mer. Pass.
21	117 10.6	104 29.8	.. 46.3	257 47.4	.. 04.8	112 36.1	.. 46.9	88 05.8	.. 28.2	Venus	349 24.5	14 01
22	132 13.1	119 29.5	47.6	272 49.5	04.9	127 38.0	47.1	103 08.0	28.3	Mars	140 54.6	3 55
23	147 15.5	134 29.2	48.9	287 51.6	05.0	142 39.9	47.4	118 10.2	28.4	Jupiter	355 49.6	13 34
Mer. Pass. 13 16.5		v −0.3	d 1.3	v 2.1	d 0.1	v 1.9	d 0.2	v 2.2	d 0.1	Saturn	331 05.7	15 12

SUN and MOON

UT	SUN GHA	SUN Dec	MOON GHA	v	MOON Dec	d	HP
d h	° '	° '	° '	'	° '	'	'
2 00	176 55.3	S 7 27.5	359 36.9	12.1	N10 02.8	9.4	56.4
01	191 55.4	26.6	14 08.0	12.2	9 53.4	9.4	56.4
02	206 55.6	25.6	28 39.2	12.2	9 44.0	9.5	56.3
03	221 55.7	.. 24.7	43 10.4	12.2	9 34.5	9.5	56.3
04	236 55.8	23.7	57 41.6	12.3	9 25.0	9.6	56.3
05	251 55.9	22.8	72 12.9	12.4	9 15.4	9.5	56.3
06	266 56.1	S 7 21.8	86 44.3	12.4	N 9 05.9	9.7	56.2
07	281 56.2	20.9	101 15.7	12.4	8 56.2	9.6	56.2
T 08	296 56.3	19.9	115 47.1	12.5	8 46.6	9.7	56.2
U 09	311 56.4	.. 19.0	130 18.6	12.6	8 36.9	9.7	56.2
E 10	326 56.6	18.0	144 50.2	12.6	8 27.2	9.8	56.2
S 11	341 56.7	17.1	159 21.8	12.6	8 17.4	9.8	56.1
D 12	356 56.8	S 7 16.1	173 53.4	12.7	N 8 07.6	9.8	56.1
A 13	11 56.9	15.2	188 25.1	12.8	7 57.8	9.8	56.1
Y 14	26 57.1	14.2	202 56.9	12.8	7 48.0	9.9	56.1
15	41 57.2	.. 13.3	217 28.7	12.9	7 38.1	9.9	56.1
16	56 57.3	12.3	232 00.6	12.9	7 28.2	10.0	56.0
17	71 57.5	11.3	246 32.5	12.9	7 18.2	9.9	56.0
18	86 57.6	S 7 10.4	261 04.4	13.0	N 7 08.3	10.0	56.0
19	101 57.7	09.4	275 36.4	13.0	6 58.3	10.0	56.0
20	116 57.8	08.5	290 08.4	13.1	6 48.3	10.1	55.9
21	131 58.0	.. 07.5	304 40.5	13.2	6 38.2	10.0	55.9
22	146 58.1	06.6	319 12.7	13.1	6 28.2	10.1	55.9
23	161 58.2	05.6	333 44.8	13.2	6 18.1	10.1	55.9
3 00	176 58.4	S 7 04.7	348 17.0	13.3	N 6 08.0	10.1	55.9
01	191 58.5	03.7	2 49.3	13.3	5 57.9	10.2	55.8
02	206 58.6	02.8	17 21.6	13.4	5 47.7	10.1	55.8
03	221 58.7	.. 01.8	31 54.0	13.3	5 37.6	10.2	55.8
04	236 58.9	7 00.8	46 26.3	13.5	5 27.4	10.2	55.8
05	251 59.0	6 59.9	60 58.8	13.4	5 17.2	10.2	55.8
06	266 59.1	S 6 58.9	75 31.2	13.5	N 5 07.0	10.2	55.7
W 07	281 59.3	58.0	90 03.7	13.6	4 56.8	10.3	55.7
E 08	296 59.4	57.0	104 36.3	13.6	4 46.5	10.2	55.7
D 09	311 59.5	.. 56.1	119 08.9	13.6	4 36.3	10.3	55.7
N 10	326 59.6	55.1	133 41.5	13.7	4 26.0	10.3	55.6
E 11	341 59.8	54.1	148 14.2	13.7	4 15.7	10.3	55.6
S 12	356 59.9	S 6 53.2	162 46.9	13.7	N 4 05.4	10.3	55.6
D 13	12 00.0	52.2	177 19.6	13.8	3 55.1	10.3	55.6
A 14	27 00.2	51.3	191 52.4	13.8	3 44.8	10.3	55.6
Y 15	42 00.3	.. 50.3	206 25.2	13.8	3 34.5	10.3	55.5
16	57 00.4	49.4	220 58.0	13.9	3 24.2	10.4	55.5
17	72 00.6	48.4	235 30.9	13.9	3 13.8	10.3	55.5
18	87 00.7	S 6 47.4	250 03.8	13.9	N 3 03.5	10.3	55.5
19	102 00.8	46.5	264 36.7	14.0	2 53.2	10.4	55.5
20	117 01.0	45.5	279 09.7	14.0	2 42.8	10.3	55.4
21	132 01.1	.. 44.6	293 42.7	14.1	2 32.5	10.4	55.4
22	147 01.2	43.6	308 15.8	14.0	2 22.1	10.4	55.4
23	162 01.4	42.6	322 48.8	14.1	2 11.7	10.3	55.4
4 00	177 01.5	S 6 41.7	337 21.9	14.1	N 2 01.4	10.4	55.4
01	192 01.6	40.7	351 55.0	14.2	1 51.0	10.4	55.3
02	207 01.8	39.8	6 28.2	14.2	1 40.7	10.4	55.3
03	222 01.9	.. 38.8	21 01.4	14.2	1 30.3	10.4	55.3
04	237 02.0	37.8	35 34.6	14.2	1 19.9	10.3	55.3
05	252 02.2	36.9	50 07.8	14.3	1 09.6	10.4	55.3
06	267 02.3	S 6 35.9	64 41.1	14.3	N 0 59.2	10.3	55.2
07	282 02.4	35.0	79 14.4	14.3	0 48.9	10.4	55.2
T 08	297 02.6	34.0	93 47.7	14.3	0 38.5	10.3	55.2
H 09	312 02.7	.. 33.0	108 21.0	14.4	0 28.2	10.4	55.2
U 10	327 02.8	32.1	122 54.4	14.4	0 17.8	10.3	55.2
R 11	342 03.0	31.1	137 27.8	14.4	N 0 07.5	10.3	55.1
S 12	357 03.1	S 6 30.2	152 01.2	14.4	S 0 02.8	10.3	55.1
D 13	12 03.3	29.2	166 34.6	14.5	0 13.1	10.3	55.1
A 14	27 03.4	28.2	181 08.1	14.4	0 23.4	10.3	55.1
Y 15	42 03.5	.. 27.3	195 41.5	14.5	0 33.7	10.3	55.1
16	57 03.7	26.3	210 15.0	14.5	0 44.0	10.3	55.0
17	72 03.8	25.4	224 48.5	14.5	0 54.3	10.3	55.0
18	87 03.9	S 6 24.4	239 22.0	14.6	S 1 04.6	10.2	55.0
19	102 04.1	23.4	253 55.6	14.6	1 14.8	10.3	55.0
20	117 04.2	22.5	268 29.2	14.6	1 25.1	10.2	55.0
21	132 04.3	.. 21.5	283 02.7	14.6	1 35.3	10.2	55.0
22	147 04.5	20.5	297 36.3	14.6	1 45.5	10.2	54.9
23	162 04.6	19.6	312 09.9	14.7	S 1 55.7	10.2	54.9
	SD 16.2	d 1.0	SD 15.3		15.1		15.0

Twilight / Moonrise

Lat.	Naut.	Civil	Sunrise	Moonrise 2	3	4	5
°	h m	h m	h m	h m	h m	h m	h m
N 72	05 02	06 20	07 29	17 03	18 46	20 27	22 05
N 70	05 08	06 19	07 20	17 14	18 50	20 24	21 57
68	05 13	06 17	07 13	17 22	18 54	20 22	21 50
66	05 17	06 16	07 07	17 30	18 56	20 21	21 44
64	05 20	06 15	07 02	17 36	18 59	20 20	21 39
62	05 22	06 13	06 58	17 41	19 01	20 19	21 35
60	05 24	06 12	06 54	17 46	19 02	20 18	21 31
N 58	05 26	06 11	06 51	17 50	19 04	20 17	21 28
56	05 28	06 10	06 48	17 53	19 05	20 16	21 25
54	05 29	06 10	06 45	17 57	19 07	20 15	21 22
52	05 30	06 09	06 43	18 00	19 08	20 15	21 18
50	05 31	06 08	06 40	18 02	19 09	20 14	21 18
45	05 32	06 06	06 35	18 08	19 11	20 13	21 13
N 40	05 33	06 04	06 31	18 13	19 13	20 12	21 10
35	05 33	06 02	06 28	18 17	19 15	20 11	21 06
30	05 33	06 00	06 24	18 20	19 16	20 10	21 03
20	05 31	05 57	06 19	18 27	19 18	20 09	20 58
N 10	05 28	05 52	06 14	18 32	19 21	20 08	20 54
0	05 24	05 48	06 09	18 37	19 23	20 07	20 50
S 10	05 18	05 43	06 04	18 42	19 25	20 06	20 46
20	05 10	05 36	05 58	18 48	19 27	20 05	20 42
30	04 59	05 28	05 52	18 54	19 29	20 03	20 37
35	04 52	05 23	05 48	18 58	19 31	20 03	20 34
40	04 44	05 16	05 44	19 02	19 32	20 02	20 31
45	04 33	05 09	05 39	19 06	19 34	20 01	20 27
S 50	04 19	05 00	05 33	19 12	19 37	20 00	20 23
52	04 13	04 55	05 30	19 15	19 38	19 59	20 21
54	04 05	04 51	05 27	19 17	19 39	19 59	20 19
56	03 57	04 45	05 24	19 20	19 40	19 58	20 17
58	03 47	04 39	05 20	19 24	19 41	19 58	20 14
S 60	03 35	04 32	05 16	19 28	19 43	19 57	20 11

Sunset / Twilight / Moonset

Lat.	Sunset	Civil	Naut.	Moonset 2	3	4	5
°	h m	h m	h m	h m	h m	h m	h m
N 72	16 57	18 06	19 25	08 09	08 00	07 51	07 43
N 70	17 06	18 08	19 18	07 56	07 53	07 51	07 48
68	17 13	18 09	19 13	07 45	07 48	07 50	07 52
66	17 18	18 10	19 09	07 37	07 44	07 50	07 55
64	17 23	18 11	19 06	07 29	07 40	07 49	07 58
62	17 27	18 12	19 03	07 23	07 37	07 49	08 00
60	17 31	18 13	19 01	07 17	07 34	07 48	08 02
N 58	17 34	18 14	18 59	07 13	07 31	07 48	08 04
56	17 37	18 15	18 58	07 08	07 29	07 48	08 06
54	17 40	18 15	18 56	07 04	07 27	07 47	08 08
52	17 42	18 16	18 55	07 01	07 25	07 47	08 09
50	17 45	18 17	18 54	06 57	07 23	07 47	08 10
45	17 49	18 19	18 53	06 50	07 19	07 47	08 13
N 40	17 53	18 21	18 52	06 44	07 16	07 46	08 15
35	17 57	18 22	18 52	06 39	07 13	07 46	08 17
30	18 00	18 24	18 52	06 35	07 11	07 45	08 19
20	18 06	18 28	18 53	06 27	07 07	07 45	08 22
N 10	18 11	18 32	18 56	06 20	07 03	07 44	08 25
0	18 15	18 36	19 00	06 13	06 59	07 44	08 28
S 10	18 20	18 41	19 06	06 06	06 56	07 43	08 30
20	18 25	18 48	19 14	05 59	06 52	07 43	08 33
30	18 32	18 56	19 24	05 51	06 47	07 42	08 36
35	18 35	19 01	19 31	05 46	06 45	07 42	08 38
40	18 39	19 07	19 40	05 41	06 42	07 41	08 40
45	18 44	19 14	19 50	05 34	06 38	07 41	08 42
S 50	18 50	19 23	20 03	05 27	06 34	07 40	08 45
52	18 52	19 27	20 10	05 23	06 32	07 40	08 46
54	18 55	19 32	20 17	05 19	06 30	07 40	08 48
56	18 59	19 37	20 25	05 15	06 28	07 39	08 49
58	19 02	19 43	20 35	05 10	06 25	07 39	08 51
S 60	19 06	19 50	20 46	05 05	06 22	07 38	08 53

SUN / MOON

Day	Eqn. of Time 00h	12h	Mer. Pass.	Mer. Pass. Upper	Lower	Age	Phase
d	m s	m s	h m	h m	h m	d %	
2	12 19	12 13	12 12	00 02	12 25	14 100	◯
3	12 07	12 01	12 12	00 48	13 11	15 98	
4	11 54	11 48	12 12	01 33	13 55	16 95	

UT	ARIES GHA	VENUS −4.0 GHA	Dec	MARS −0.3 GHA	Dec	JUPITER −2.1 GHA	Dec	SATURN +0.5 GHA	Dec	STARS Name	SHA	Dec
5 00	162 18.0	149 28.9	N 4 50.2	302 53.6	S13 05.1	157 41.8	N 0 47.6	133 12.5	N 9 28.5	Acamar	315 26.9	S40 18.9
01	177 20.4	164 28.6	51.5	317 55.7	05.3	172 43.8	47.8	148 14.7	28.6	Achernar	335 35.5	S57 14.8
02	192 22.9	179 28.2	52.8	332 57.8	05.4	187 45.7	48.1	163 16.9	28.7	Acrux	173 21.0	S63 05.5
03	207 25.4	194 27.9	.. 54.1	347 59.9	.. 05.5	202 47.6	.. 48.3	178 19.1	.. 28.8	Adhara	255 21.0	S28 58.6
04	222 27.8	209 27.6	55.3	3 02.0	05.6	217 49.6	48.5	193 21.4	28.8	Aldebaran	291 02.1	N16 30.3
05	237 30.3	224 27.3	56.6	18 04.1	05.7	232 51.5	48.8	208 23.6	28.9			
06	252 32.8	239 26.9	N 4 57.9	33 06.2	S13 05.8	247 53.4	N 0 49.0	223 25.8	N 9 29.0	Alioth	166 29.9	N55 57.7
07	267 35.2	254 26.6	4 59.2	48 08.3	06.0	262 55.3	49.3	238 28.0	29.1	Alkaid	153 07.3	N49 18.9
F 08	282 37.7	269 26.3	5 00.5	63 10.4	06.1	277 57.3	49.5	253 30.3	29.2	Al Na'ir	27 58.0	S46 58.0
R 09	297 40.2	284 26.0	.. 01.8	78 12.5	.. 06.2	292 59.2	.. 49.7	268 32.5	.. 29.3	Alnilam	275 57.5	S 1 12.4
I 10	312 42.6	299 25.7	03.1	93 14.6	06.3	308 01.1	50.0	283 34.7	29.4	Alphard	218 06.6	S 8 39.5
D 11	327 45.1	314 25.3	04.4	108 16.7	06.4	323 03.0	50.2	298 36.9	29.5			
A 12	342 47.5	329 25.0	N 5 05.6	123 18.8	S13 06.5	338 05.0	N 0 50.4	313 39.2	N 9 29.6	Alphecca	126 20.2	N26 42.9
Y 13	357 50.0	344 24.7	06.9	138 21.0	06.6	353 06.9	50.7	328 41.4	29.7	Alpheratz	357 55.3	N29 05.0
14	12 52.5	359 24.4	08.2	153 23.1	06.7	8 08.8	50.9	343 43.6	29.8	Altair	62 19.2	N 8 51.9
15	27 54.9	14 24.0	.. 09.5	168 25.2	.. 06.9	23 10.7	.. 51.1	358 45.8	.. 29.9	Ankaa	353 27.0	S42 18.9
16	42 57.4	29 23.7	10.8	183 27.3	07.0	38 12.7	51.4	13 48.1	30.0	Antares	112 39.8	S26 25.7
17	57 59.9	44 23.4	12.1	198 29.4	07.1	53 14.6	51.6	28 50.3	30.1			
18	73 02.3	59 23.1	N 5 13.4	213 31.5	S13 07.2	68 16.5	N 0 51.8	43 52.5	N 9 30.2	Arcturus	146 05.6	N19 11.1
19	88 04.8	74 22.8	14.6	228 33.6	07.3	83 18.4	52.1	58 54.7	30.3	Atria	107 51.6	S69 01.2
20	103 07.3	89 22.4	15.9	243 35.7	07.4	98 20.4	52.3	73 57.0	30.4	Avior	234 22.0	S59 30.7
21	118 09.7	104 22.1	.. 17.2	258 37.8	.. 07.5	113 22.3	.. 52.5	88 59.2	.. 30.5	Bellatrix	278 43.8	N 6 20.7
22	133 12.2	119 21.8	18.5	273 40.0	07.6	128 24.2	52.8	104 01.4	30.6	Betelgeuse	271 13.2	N 7 24.2
23	148 14.7	134 21.5	19.8	288 42.1	07.8	143 26.1	53.0	119 03.6	30.7			
6 00	163 17.1	149 21.1	N 5 21.1	303 44.2	S13 07.9	158 28.1	N 0 53.3	134 05.9	N 9 30.8	Canopus	264 00.8	S52 42.1
01	178 19.6	164 20.8	22.3	318 46.3	08.0	173 30.0	53.5	149 08.1	30.9	Capella	280 50.7	N45 59.9
02	193 22.0	179 20.5	23.6	333 48.4	08.1	188 31.9	53.7	164 10.3	31.0	Deneb	49 39.4	N45 16.5
03	208 24.5	194 20.2	.. 24.9	348 50.6	.. 08.2	203 33.8	.. 54.0	179 12.5	.. 31.0	Denebola	182 44.6	N14 34.5
04	223 27.0	209 19.8	26.2	3 52.7	08.3	218 35.8	54.2	194 14.8	31.1	Diphda	349 07.3	S17 59.7
05	238 29.4	224 19.5	27.5	18 54.8	08.4	233 37.7	54.4	209 17.0	31.2			
06	253 31.9	239 19.2	N 5 28.8	33 56.9	S13 08.5	248 39.6	N 0 54.7	224 19.2	N 9 31.3	Dubhe	194 04.6	N61 45.3
S 07	268 34.4	254 18.9	30.0	48 59.1	08.6	263 41.5	54.9	239 21.4	31.4	Elnath	278 26.5	N28 36.3
A 08	283 36.8	269 18.5	31.3	64 01.2	08.7	278 43.5	55.1	254 23.7	31.5	Eltanin	90 51.4	N51 29.1
T 09	298 39.3	284 18.2	.. 32.6	79 03.3	.. 08.8	293 45.4	.. 55.4	269 25.9	.. 31.6	Enif	33 58.3	N 9 52.1
U 10	313 41.8	299 17.9	33.9	94 05.4	09.0	308 47.3	55.6	284 28.1	31.7	Fomalhaut	15 36.5	S29 37.8
R 11	328 44.2	314 17.6	35.2	109 07.6	09.1	323 49.2	55.8	299 30.3	31.8			
D 12	343 46.7	329 17.3	N 5 36.4	124 09.7	S13 09.2	338 51.2	N 0 56.1	314 32.6	N 9 31.9	Gacrux	172 12.7	S57 06.4
A 13	358 49.2	344 16.9	37.7	139 11.8	09.3	353 53.1	56.3	329 34.8	32.0	Gienah	176 03.4	S17 32.3
Y 14	13 51.6	359 16.6	39.0	154 14.0	09.4	8 55.0	56.6	344 37.0	32.1	Hadar	149 03.2	S60 21.9
15	28 54.1	14 16.3	.. 40.3	169 16.1	.. 09.5	23 56.9	.. 56.8	359 39.2	.. 32.2	Hamal	328 13.5	N23 27.4
16	43 56.5	29 16.0	41.6	184 18.2	09.6	38 58.9	57.0	14 41.4	32.3	Kaus Aust.	83 58.6	S34 22.9
17	58 59.0	44 15.6	42.9	199 20.4	09.7	54 00.8	57.3	29 43.7	32.4			
18	74 01.5	59 15.3	N 5 44.1	214 22.5	S13 09.8	69 02.7	N 0 57.5	44 45.9	N 9 32.5	Kochab	137 19.1	N74 09.4
19	89 03.9	74 15.0	45.4	229 24.6	09.9	84 04.6	57.7	59 48.1	32.6	Markab	13 49.7	N15 11.9
20	104 06.4	89 14.7	46.7	244 26.8	10.0	99 06.6	58.0	74 50.3	32.7	Menkar	314 26.8	N 4 05.0
21	119 08.9	104 14.3	.. 48.0	259 28.9	.. 10.1	114 08.5	.. 58.2	89 52.6	.. 32.8	Menkent	148 20.3	S36 21.8
22	134 11.3	119 14.0	49.3	274 31.1	10.2	129 10.4	58.4	104 54.8	32.9	Miaplacidus	221 41.1	S69 43.0
23	149 13.8	134 13.7	50.5	289 33.2	10.3	144 12.3	58.7	119 57.0	33.0			
7 00	164 16.3	149 13.4	N 5 51.8	304 35.3	S13 10.4	159 14.2	N 0 58.9	134 59.2	N 9 33.1	Mirfak	308 56.4	N49 51.5
01	179 18.7	164 13.0	53.1	319 37.5	10.5	174 16.2	59.1	150 01.4	33.2	Nunki	76 12.2	S26 17.8
02	194 21.2	179 12.7	54.4	334 39.6	10.6	189 18.1	59.4	165 03.7	33.3	Peacock	53 37.1	S56 44.1
03	209 23.6	194 12.4	.. 55.6	349 41.8	.. 10.7	204 20.0	.. 59.6	180 05.9	.. 33.4	Pollux	243 41.0	N28 01.6
04	224 26.1	209 12.0	56.9	4 43.9	10.8	219 21.9	0 59.9	195 08.1	33.5	Procyon	245 11.1	N 5 13.4
05	239 28.6	224 11.7	58.2	19 46.1	10.9	234 23.9	1 00.1	210 10.3	33.5			
06	254 31.0	239 11.4	N 5 59.5	34 48.2	S13 11.0	249 25.8	N 1 00.3	225 12.5	N 9 33.6	Rasalhague	96 16.8	N12 33.6
07	269 33.5	254 11.1	6 00.8	49 50.4	11.1	264 27.7	00.6	240 14.8	33.7	Regulus	207 54.9	N11 58.2
08	284 36.0	269 10.7	02.0	64 52.5	11.2	279 29.6	00.8	255 17.0	33.8	Rigel	281 22.7	S 8 12.5
S 09	299 38.4	284 10.4	.. 03.3	79 54.7	.. 11.3	294 31.6	.. 01.0	270 19.2	.. 33.9	Rigil Kent.	140 06.5	S60 49.6
U 10	314 40.9	299 10.1	04.6	94 56.8	11.4	309 33.5	01.3	285 21.4	34.0	Sabik	102 25.2	S15 43.4
N 11	329 43.4	314 09.8	05.9	109 59.0	11.5	324 35.4	01.5	300 23.7	34.1			
D 12	344 45.8	329 09.4	N 6 07.1	125 01.1	S13 11.6	339 37.3	N 1 01.7	315 25.9	N 9 34.2	Schedar	349 53.6	N56 31.9
A 13	359 48.3	344 09.1	08.4	140 03.3	11.7	354 39.3	02.0	330 28.1	34.3	Shaula	96 37.0	S37 06.0
Y 14	14 50.8	359 08.8	09.7	155 05.5	11.8	9 41.2	02.2	345 30.3	34.4	Sirius	258 43.3	S16 43.2
15	29 53.2	14 08.5	.. 11.0	170 07.6	.. 11.9	24 43.1	.. 02.4	0 32.5	.. 34.5	Spica	158 42.6	S11 09.4
16	44 55.7	29 08.1	12.2	185 09.8	12.0	39 45.0	02.7	15 34.8	34.6	Suhail	223 00.2	S43 26.0
17	59 58.1	44 07.8	13.5	200 11.9	12.1	54 46.9	02.9	30 37.0	34.7			
18	75 00.6	59 07.5	N 6 14.8	215 14.1	S13 12.2	69 48.9	N 1 03.2	45 39.2	N 9 34.8	Vega	80 46.6	N38 46.8
19	90 03.1	74 07.1	16.1	230 16.3	12.3	84 50.8	03.4	60 41.4	34.9	Zuben'ubi	137 17.5	S16 02.2
20	105 05.5	89 06.8	17.3	245 18.4	12.4	99 52.7	03.6	75 43.6	35.0		SHA	Mer. Pass.
21	120 08.0	104 06.5	.. 18.6	260 20.6	.. 12.5	114 54.6	.. 03.9	90 45.9	.. 35.1	Venus	346 04.0	14 03
22	135 10.5	119 06.2	19.9	275 22.8	12.6	129 56.6	04.1	105 48.1	35.2	Mars	140 27.1	3 45
23	150 12.9	134 05.8	21.2	290 24.9	12.7	144 58.5	04.3	120 50.3	35.3	Jupiter	355 10.9	13 24
Mer. Pass.	h m 13 04.7	v −0.3	d 1.3	v 2.1	d 0.1	v 1.9	d 0.2	v 2.2	d 0.1	Saturn	330 48.7	15 01

UT	SUN GHA	SUN Dec	MOON GHA	v	Dec	d	HP
d h	° ′	° ′	° ′	′	° ′	′	′
5 00	177 04.8	S 6 18.6	326 43.6	14.6	S 2 05.9	10.2	54.9
01	192 04.9	17.6	341 17.2	14.7	2 16.1	10.1	54.9
02	207 05.0	16.7	355 50.9	14.6	2 26.2	10.1	54.9
03	222 05.2	.. 15.7	10 24.5	14.7	2 36.4	10.1	54.9
04	237 05.3	14.8	24 58.2	14.7	2 46.5	10.1	54.8
05	252 05.5	13.8	39 31.9	14.7	2 56.6	10.1	54.8
06	267 05.6	S 6 12.8	54 05.6	14.7	S 3 06.7	10.0	54.8
07	282 05.7	11.9	68 39.3	14.7	3 16.7	10.1	54.8
08	297 05.9	10.9	83 13.0	14.7	3 26.8	10.0	54.8
F 09	312 06.0	.. 09.9	97 46.7	14.8	3 36.8	10.0	54.8
R 10	327 06.2	09.0	112 20.5	14.7	3 46.8	9.9	54.7
I 11	342 06.3	08.0	126 54.2	14.8	3 56.7	10.0	54.7
D 12	357 06.4	S 6 07.0	141 28.0	14.7	S 4 06.7	9.9	54.7
A 13	12 06.6	06.1	156 01.7	14.8	4 16.6	9.9	54.7
Y 14	27 06.7	05.1	170 35.5	14.8	4 26.5	9.9	54.7
15	42 06.9	.. 04.1	185 09.3	14.8	4 36.4	9.9	54.7
16	57 07.0	03.2	199 43.1	14.7	4 46.3	9.8	54.7
17	72 07.1	02.2	214 16.8	14.8	4 56.1	9.8	54.6
18	87 07.3	S 6 01.2	228 50.6	14.8	S 5 05.9	9.8	54.6
19	102 07.4	6 00.3	243 24.4	14.8	5 15.7	9.7	54.6
20	117 07.6	5 59.3	257 58.2	14.8	5 25.4	9.7	54.6
21	132 07.7	.. 58.4	272 32.0	14.8	5 35.1	9.7	54.6
22	147 07.8	57.4	287 05.8	14.8	5 44.8	9.7	54.6
23	162 08.0	56.4	301 39.6	14.8	5 54.5	9.6	54.6
6 00	177 08.1	S 5 55.5	316 13.4	14.7	S 6 04.1	9.6	54.5
01	192 08.3	54.5	330 47.1	14.8	6 13.7	9.6	54.5
02	207 08.4	53.5	345 20.9	14.8	6 23.3	9.5	54.5
03	222 08.6	.. 52.6	359 54.7	14.8	6 32.8	9.6	54.5
04	237 08.7	51.6	14 28.5	14.8	6 42.4	9.4	54.5
05	252 08.8	50.6	29 02.3	14.8	6 51.8	9.5	54.5
06	267 09.0	S 5 49.6	43 36.1	14.7	S 7 01.3	9.4	54.5
S 07	282 09.1	48.7	58 09.8	14.8	7 10.7	9.4	54.5
A 08	297 09.3	47.7	72 43.6	14.8	7 20.1	9.3	54.4
T 09	312 09.4	.. 46.7	87 17.4	14.7	7 29.4	9.3	54.4
U 10	327 09.6	45.8	101 51.1	14.8	7 38.7	9.3	54.4
R 11	342 09.7	44.8	116 24.9	14.7	7 48.0	9.2	54.4
D 12	357 09.9	S 5 43.8	130 58.6	14.8	S 7 57.2	9.2	54.4
A 13	12 10.0	42.9	145 32.4	14.7	8 06.4	9.1	54.4
Y 14	27 10.1	41.9	160 06.1	14.7	8 15.5	9.2	54.4
15	42 10.3	.. 40.9	174 39.8	14.7	8 24.7	9.0	54.4
16	57 10.4	40.0	189 13.5	14.7	8 33.7	9.1	54.4
17	72 10.6	39.0	203 47.2	14.7	8 42.8	9.0	54.3
18	87 10.7	S 5 38.0	218 20.9	14.7	S 8 51.8	8.9	54.3
19	102 10.9	37.1	232 54.6	14.6	9 00.7	8.9	54.3
20	117 11.0	36.1	247 28.2	14.7	9 09.6	8.9	54.3
21	132 11.2	.. 35.1	262 01.9	14.6	9 18.5	8.9	54.3
22	147 11.3	34.1	276 35.5	14.7	9 27.4	8.8	54.3
23	162 11.5	33.2	291 09.2	14.6	9 36.2	8.7	54.3
7 00	177 11.6	S 5 32.2	305 42.8	14.6	S 9 44.9	8.7	54.3
01	192 11.8	31.2	320 16.4	14.5	9 53.6	8.7	54.3
02	207 11.9	30.3	334 49.9	14.6	10 02.3	8.6	54.3
03	222 12.0	.. 29.3	349 23.5	14.6	10 10.9	8.6	54.3
04	237 12.2	28.3	3 57.1	14.5	10 19.5	8.5	54.3
05	252 12.3	27.4	18 30.6	14.5	10 28.0	8.5	54.3
06	267 12.5	S 5 26.4	33 04.1	14.5	S10 36.5	8.4	54.2
07	282 12.6	25.4	47 37.6	14.5	10 44.9	8.4	54.2
08	297 12.8	24.4	62 11.1	14.5	10 53.3	8.3	54.2
S 09	312 12.9	.. 23.5	76 44.6	14.4	11 01.6	8.3	54.2
U 10	327 13.1	22.5	91 18.0	14.4	11 09.9	8.2	54.2
N 11	342 13.2	21.5	105 51.4	14.4	11 18.1	8.2	54.2
D 12	357 13.4	S 5 20.6	120 24.8	14.4	S11 26.3	8.2	54.2
A 13	12 13.5	19.6	134 58.2	14.4	11 34.5	8.1	54.2
Y 14	27 13.7	18.6	149 31.6	14.3	11 42.6	8.0	54.2
15	42 13.8	.. 17.6	164 04.9	14.4	11 50.6	8.0	54.2
16	57 14.0	16.7	178 38.3	14.3	11 58.6	7.9	54.2
17	72 14.1	15.7	193 11.6	14.2	12 06.5	7.9	54.2
18	87 14.3	S 5 14.7	207 44.8	14.3	S12 14.4	7.9	54.2
19	102 14.4	13.8	222 18.1	14.2	12 22.3	7.7	54.2
20	117 14.6	12.8	236 51.3	14.2	12 30.0	7.8	54.2
21	132 14.7	.. 11.8	251 24.5	14.2	12 37.8	7.6	54.2
22	147 14.9	10.8	265 57.7	14.1	12 45.4	7.7	54.2
23	162 15.0	09.9	280 30.8	14.2	S12 53.1	7.5	54.2
	SD 16.1	d 1.0	SD 14.9		14.8		14.8

Lat.	Twilight Naut.	Civil	Sunrise	Moonrise 5	6	7	8
°	h m	h m	h m	h m	h m	h m	h m
N 72	04 47	06 05	07 13	22 05	23 45	25 29	01 29
N 70	04 54	06 05	07 06	21 57	23 29	25 03	01 03
68	05 00	06 05	07 01	21 50	23 16	24 43	00 43
66	05 05	06 05	06 56	21 44	23 06	24 27	00 27
64	05 09	06 04	06 52	21 39	22 57	24 15	00 15
62	05 13	06 04	06 48	21 35	22 50	24 04	00 04
60	05 16	06 04	06 45	21 31	22 44	23 55	25 04
N 58	05 18	06 03	06 43	21 28	22 38	23 47	24 54
56	05 20	06 03	06 40	21 25	22 33	23 40	24 45
54	05 22	06 03	06 38	21 22	22 29	23 33	24 37
52	05 23	06 02	06 36	21 20	22 25	23 28	24 30
50	05 24	06 02	06 34	21 18	22 21	23 23	24 23
45	05 27	06 01	06 30	21 13	22 13	23 12	24 10
N 40	05 28	06 00	06 27	21 10	22 07	23 03	23 58
35	05 29	05 58	06 24	21 06	22 01	22 55	23 49
30	05 29	05 57	06 21	21 03	21 56	22 48	23 41
20	05 29	05 54	06 16	20 58	21 48	22 37	23 26
N 10	05 27	05 51	06 12	20 54	21 40	22 27	23 14
0	05 23	05 47	06 08	20 50	21 33	22 17	23 02
S 10	05 18	05 43	06 04	20 46	21 26	22 08	22 50
20	05 11	05 37	05 59	20 42	21 19	21 58	22 38
30	05 01	05 30	05 54	20 37	21 11	21 46	22 24
35	04 55	05 25	05 51	20 34	21 06	21 40	22 16
40	04 47	05 20	05 47	20 31	21 01	21 32	22 06
45	04 38	05 13	05 43	20 27	20 55	21 24	21 56
S 50	04 25	05 05	05 38	20 23	20 47	21 13	21 43
52	04 19	05 01	05 36	20 21	20 44	21 08	21 36
54	04 12	04 57	05 33	20 19	20 40	21 03	21 30
56	04 05	04 52	05 30	20 17	20 36	20 57	21 22
58	03 56	04 46	05 27	20 14	20 31	20 51	21 14
S 60	03 45	04 40	05 24	20 11	20 26	20 44	21 05

Lat.	Sunset	Twilight Civil	Naut.	Moonset 5	6	7	8
°	h m	h m	h m	h m	h m	h m	h m
N 72	17 12	18 20	19 39	07 43	07 35	07 25	07 13
N 70	17 18	18 20	19 31	07 48	07 45	07 42	07 40
68	17 24	18 20	19 25	07 52	07 54	07 56	08 01
66	17 28	18 20	19 19	07 55	08 01	08 08	08 17
64	17 32	18 20	19 15	07 58	08 07	08 18	08 31
62	17 36	18 20	19 12	08 00	08 12	08 26	08 42
60	17 39	18 20	19 09	08 02	08 17	08 33	08 52
N 58	17 41	18 21	19 06	08 04	08 21	08 39	09 00
56	17 44	18 21	19 04	08 06	08 25	08 45	09 08
54	17 46	18 21	19 02	08 08	08 28	08 50	09 15
52	17 48	18 21	19 01	08 09	08 31	08 55	09 21
50	17 50	18 22	18 59	08 10	08 34	08 59	09 26
45	17 53	18 23	18 57	08 13	08 40	09 08	09 38
N 40	17 57	18 24	18 55	08 15	08 45	09 15	09 48
35	18 00	18 25	18 54	08 17	08 49	09 22	09 56
30	18 02	18 26	18 54	08 19	08 53	09 27	10 04
20	18 07	18 29	18 54	08 22	08 59	09 37	10 17
N 10	18 11	18 32	18 56	08 25	09 05	09 46	10 28
0	18 15	18 35	19 00	08 28	09 11	09 54	10 39
S 10	18 19	18 40	19 04	08 30	09 16	10 02	10 49
20	18 23	18 45	19 11	08 33	09 22	10 11	11 01
30	18 28	18 52	19 21	08 36	09 29	10 21	11 14
35	18 31	18 57	19 27	08 38	09 33	10 27	11 21
40	18 35	19 02	19 34	08 40	09 37	10 34	11 30
45	18 39	19 08	19 44	08 42	09 42	10 41	11 40
S 50	18 43	19 16	19 56	08 45	09 48	10 51	11 52
52	18 46	19 20	20 02	08 46	09 51	10 55	11 58
54	18 48	19 24	20 09	08 48	09 54	11 00	12 04
56	18 51	19 29	20 16	08 49	09 58	11 05	12 11
58	18 54	19 35	20 25	08 51	10 02	11 11	12 19
S 60	18 57	19 41	20 35	08 53	10 06	11 18	12 28

Day	SUN Eqn. of Time 00h	12h	Mer. Pass.	MOON Mer. Pass. Upper	Lower	Age	Phase
d	m s	m s	h m	h m	h m	d	%
5	11 41	11 35	12 12	02 17	14 39	17	90
6	11 28	11 21	12 11	03 00	15 22	18	83
7	11 14	11 07	12 11	03 44	16 06	19	76

UT (d h)	ARIES GHA	VENUS −4.0 GHA	VENUS Dec	MARS −0.4 GHA	MARS Dec	JUPITER −2.1 GHA	JUPITER Dec	SATURN +0.5 GHA	SATURN Dec	STAR Name	STAR SHA	STAR Dec
8 MONDAY												
00	165 15.4	149 05.5	N 6 22.4	305 27.1	S13 12.8	160 00.4	N 1 04.6	135 52.5	N 9 35.4	Acamar	315 26.9	S40 18.9
01	180 17.9	164 05.2	23.7	320 29.3	12.9	175 02.3	04.8	150 54.7	35.5	Achernar	335 35.5	S57 14.8
02	195 20.3	179 04.8	25.0	335 31.4	13.0	190 04.2	05.0	165 57.0	35.6	Acrux	173 21.0	S63 05.6
03	210 22.8	194 04.5 ..	26.3	350 33.6 ..	13.1	205 06.2 ..	05.3	180 59.2 ..	35.7	Adhara	255 21.0	S28 58.6
04	225 25.2	209 04.2	27.5	5 35.8	13.2	220 08.1	05.5	196 01.4	35.8	Aldebaran	291 02.1	N16 30.3
05	240 27.7	224 03.9	28.8	20 37.9	13.3	235 10.0	05.8	211 03.6	35.9			
06	255 30.2	239 03.5	N 6 30.1	35 40.1	S13 13.4	250 11.9	N 1 06.0	226 05.8	N 9 36.0	Alioth	166 29.9	N55 57.8
07	270 32.6	254 03.2	31.3	50 42.3	13.5	265 13.9	06.2	241 08.0	36.1	Alkaid	153 07.2	N49 18.9
08	285 35.1	269 02.9	32.6	65 44.5	13.6	280 15.8	06.5	256 10.3	36.2	Al Na'ir	27 58.0	S46 57.9
09	300 37.6	284 02.5 ..	33.9	80 46.7 ..	13.7	295 17.7 ..	06.7	271 12.5 ..	36.3	Alnilam	275 57.5	S 1 12.4
10	315 40.0	299 02.2	35.2	95 48.8	13.7	310 19.6	06.9	286 14.7	36.4	Alphard	218 06.6	S 8 39.5
11	330 42.5	314 01.9	36.4	110 51.0	13.8	325 21.5	07.2	301 16.9	36.5			
12	345 45.0	329 01.5	N 6 37.7	125 53.2	S13 13.9	340 23.5	N 1 07.4	316 19.1	N 9 36.6	Alphecca	126 20.2	N26 42.9
13	0 47.4	344 01.2	39.0	140 55.4	14.0	355 25.4	07.6	331 21.4	36.7	Alpheratz	357 55.3	N29 05.0
14	15 49.9	359 00.9	40.2	155 57.6	14.1	10 27.3	07.9	346 23.6	36.8	Altair	62 19.2	N 8 51.9
15	30 52.4	14 00.6 ..	41.5	170 59.7 ..	14.2	25 29.2 ..	08.1	1 25.8 ..	36.8	Ankaa	353 27.0	S42 18.9
16	45 54.8	29 00.2	42.8	186 01.9	14.3	40 31.2	08.4	16 28.0	36.9	Antares	112 39.8	S26 25.7
17	60 57.3	43 59.9	44.1	201 04.1	14.4	55 33.1	08.6	31 30.2	37.0			
18	75 59.7	58 59.6	N 6 45.3	216 06.3	S13 14.5	70 35.0	N 1 08.8	46 32.5	N 9 37.1	Arcturus	146 05.6	N19 11.1
19	91 02.2	73 59.2	46.6	231 08.5	14.6	85 36.9	09.1	61 34.7	37.2	Atria	107 51.5	S69 01.2
20	106 04.7	88 58.9	47.9	246 10.7	14.7	100 38.8	09.3	76 36.9	37.3	Avior	234 22.0	S59 30.7
21	121 07.1	103 58.6 ..	49.1	261 12.9 ..	14.7	115 40.8 ..	09.5	91 39.1 ..	37.4	Bellatrix	278 43.8	N 6 20.7
22	136 09.6	118 58.2	50.4	276 15.1	14.8	130 42.7	09.8	106 41.3	37.5	Betelgeuse	271 13.2	N 7 24.2
23	151 12.1	133 57.9	51.7	291 17.3	14.9	145 44.6	10.0	121 43.5	37.6			
9 TUESDAY												
00	166 14.5	148 57.6	N 6 52.9	306 19.5	S13 15.0	160 46.5	N 1 10.2	136 45.8	N 9 37.7	Canopus	264 00.9	S52 42.1
01	181 17.0	163 57.2	54.2	321 21.7	15.1	175 48.4	10.5	151 48.0	37.8	Capella	280 50.8	N45 59.8
02	196 19.5	178 56.9	55.5	336 23.9	15.2	190 50.4	10.7	166 50.2	37.9	Deneb	49 39.3	N45 16.5
03	211 21.9	193 56.6 ..	56.7	351 26.0 ..	15.3	205 52.3 ..	11.0	181 52.4 ..	38.0	Denebola	182 44.6	N14 34.5
04	226 24.4	208 56.2	58.0	6 28.2	15.4	220 54.2	11.2	196 54.6	38.1	Diphda	349 07.3	S17 59.7
05	241 26.9	223 55.9	6 59.3	21 30.4	15.5	235 56.1	11.4	211 56.8	38.2			
06	256 29.3	238 55.6	N 7 00.5	36 32.6	S13 15.5	250 58.1	N 1 11.7	226 59.1	N 9 38.3	Dubhe	194 04.6	N61 45.3
07	271 31.8	253 55.3	01.8	51 34.9	15.6	266 00.0	11.9	242 01.3	38.4	Elnath	278 26.6	N28 36.3
08	286 34.2	268 54.9	03.1	66 37.1	15.7	281 01.9	12.1	257 03.5	38.5	Eltanin	90 51.4	N51 29.1
09	301 36.7	283 54.6 ..	04.3	81 39.3 ..	15.8	296 03.8 ..	12.4	272 05.7 ..	38.6	Enif	33 58.3	N 9 52.1
10	316 39.2	298 54.3	05.6	96 41.5	15.9	311 05.7	12.6	287 07.9	38.7	Fomalhaut	15 36.5	S29 37.7
11	331 41.6	313 53.9	06.9	111 43.7	16.0	326 07.7	12.8	302 10.1	38.8			
12	346 44.1	328 53.6	N 7 08.1	126 45.9	S13 16.1	341 09.6	N 1 13.1	317 12.4	N 9 38.9	Gacrux	172 12.7	S57 06.4
13	1 46.6	343 53.3	09.4	141 48.1	16.1	356 11.5	13.3	332 14.6	39.0	Gienah	176 03.4	S17 32.3
14	16 49.0	358 52.9	10.6	156 50.3	16.2	11 13.4	13.6	347 16.8	39.1	Hadar	149 03.1	S60 21.9
15	31 51.5	13 52.6 ..	11.9	171 52.5 ..	16.3	26 15.3 ..	13.8	2 19.0 ..	39.2	Hamal	328 13.5	N23 27.4
16	46 54.0	28 52.3	13.2	186 54.7	16.4	41 17.3	14.0	17 21.2	39.3	Kaus Aust.	83 58.6	S34 22.9
17	61 56.4	43 51.9	14.4	201 56.9	16.5	56 19.2	14.3	32 23.4	39.4			
18	76 58.9	58 51.6	N 7 15.7	216 59.1	S13 16.6	71 21.1	N 1 14.5	47 25.6	N 9 39.5	Kochab	137 19.0	N74 09.4
19	92 01.3	73 51.2	17.0	232 01.4	16.6	86 23.0	14.7	62 27.9	39.6	Markab	13 49.7	N15 11.9
20	107 03.8	88 50.9	18.2	247 03.6	16.7	101 24.9	15.0	77 30.1	39.7	Menkar	314 26.8	N 4 05.0
21	122 06.3	103 50.6 ..	19.5	262 05.8 ..	16.8	116 26.9 ..	15.2	92 32.3 ..	39.8	Menkent	148 20.3	S36 21.8
22	137 08.7	118 50.2	20.7	277 08.0	16.9	131 28.8	15.4	107 34.5	39.9	Miaplacidus	221 41.1	S69 43.0
23	152 11.2	133 49.9	22.0	292 10.2	17.0	146 30.7	15.7	122 36.7	40.0			
10 WEDNESDAY												
00	167 13.7	148 49.6	N 7 23.3	307 12.5	S13 17.1	161 32.6	N 1 15.9	137 38.9	N 9 40.1	Mirfak	308 56.4	N49 51.5
01	182 16.1	163 49.2	24.5	322 14.7	17.1	176 34.5	16.2	152 41.2	40.2	Nunki	76 12.1	S26 17.8
02	197 18.6	178 48.9	25.8	337 16.9	17.2	191 36.5	16.4	167 43.4	40.3	Peacock	53 37.0	S56 44.1
03	212 21.1	193 48.6 ..	27.0	352 19.1 ..	17.3	206 38.4 ..	16.6	182 45.6 ..	40.4	Pollux	243 41.0	N28 01.6
04	227 23.5	208 48.2	28.3	7 21.4	17.4	221 40.3	16.9	197 47.8	40.5	Procyon	245 11.1	N 5 13.4
05	242 26.0	223 47.9	29.6	22 23.6	17.5	236 42.2	17.1	212 50.0	40.6			
06	257 28.5	238 47.6	N 7 30.8	37 25.8	S13 17.5	251 44.1	N 1 17.3	227 52.2	N 9 40.7	Rasalhague	96 16.7	N12 33.6
07	272 30.9	253 47.2	32.1	52 28.0	17.6	266 46.1	17.6	242 54.4	40.8	Regulus	207 54.9	N11 58.2
08	287 33.4	268 46.9	33.3	67 30.3	17.7	281 48.0	17.8	257 56.7	40.9	Rigel	281 22.7	S 8 12.5
09	302 35.8	283 46.5 ..	34.6	82 32.5 ..	17.8	296 49.9 ..	18.1	272 58.9 ..	41.0	Rigil Kent.	140 06.5	S60 49.6
10	317 38.3	298 46.2	35.9	97 34.7	17.8	311 51.8	18.3	288 01.1	41.1	Sabik	102 25.2	S15 43.4
11	332 40.8	313 45.9	37.1	112 37.0	17.9	326 53.7	18.5	303 03.3	41.2			
12	347 43.2	328 45.5	N 7 38.4	127 39.2	S13 18.0	341 55.7	N 1 18.8	318 05.5	N 9 41.3	Schedar	349 53.6	N56 31.9
13	2 45.7	343 45.2	39.6	142 41.4	18.1	356 57.6	19.0	333 07.7	41.4	Shaula	96 37.0	S37 06.0
14	17 48.2	358 44.9	40.9	157 43.7	18.2	11 59.5	19.2	348 09.9	41.5	Sirius	258 43.3	S16 43.2
15	32 50.6	13 44.5 ..	42.1	172 45.9 ..	18.2	27 01.4 ..	19.5	3 12.1 ..	41.6	Spica	158 42.6	S11 09.4
16	47 53.1	28 44.2	43.4	187 48.1	18.3	42 03.3	19.7	18 14.4	41.7	Suhail	223 00.2	S43 26.0
17	62 55.6	43 43.8	44.7	202 50.4	18.4	57 05.3	20.0	33 16.6	41.8			
18	77 58.0	58 43.5	N 7 45.9	217 52.6	S13 18.5	72 07.2	N 1 20.2	48 18.8	N 9 41.9	Vega	80 46.6	N38 46.8
19	93 00.5	73 43.2	47.2	232 54.9	18.5	87 09.1	20.4	63 21.0	42.0	Zuben'ubi	137 17.5	S16 02.2
20	108 03.0	88 42.8	48.4	247 57.1	18.6	102 11.0	20.7	78 23.2	42.1		SHA	Mer. Pass.
21	123 05.4	103 42.5 ..	49.7	262 59.4 ..	18.7	117 12.9 ..	20.9	93 25.4 ..	42.2	Venus	342 43.0	14 04
22	138 07.9	118 42.2	50.9	278 01.6	18.8	132 14.9	21.1	108 27.6	42.2	Mars	140 04.9	3 34
23	153 10.3	133 41.8	52.2	293 03.9	18.8	147 16.8	21.4	123 29.9	42.3	Jupiter	354 32.0	13 15
Mer. Pass. 12 52.9		v −0.3 d 1.3		v 2.2 d 0.1		v 1.9 d 0.2		v 2.2 d 0.1		Saturn	330 31.2	14 51

UT	SUN GHA	Dec	MOON GHA	v	Dec	d	HP
d h	° ′	° ′	° ′	′	° ′	′	′
8 00	177 15.2	S 5 08.9	295 04.0	14.1	S13 00.6	7.5	54.2
01	192 15.3	07.9	309 37.1	14.0	13 08.1	7.5	54.2
02	207 15.5	06.9	324 10.1	14.1	13 15.6	7.4	54.2
03	222 15.6	.. 06.0	338 43.2	14.0	13 23.0	7.3	54.2
04	237 15.8	05.0	353 16.2	14.0	13 30.3	7.3	54.2
05	252 15.9	04.0	7 49.2	14.0	13 37.6	7.2	54.2
06	267 16.1	S 5 03.0	22 22.2	13.9	S13 44.8	7.2	54.2
07	282 16.2	02.1	36 55.1	13.9	13 52.0	7.1	54.2
08	297 16.4	01.1	51 28.0	13.9	13 59.1	7.0	54.2
M 09	312 16.5	5 00.1	66 00.9	13.8	14 06.1	7.0	54.2
O 10	327 16.7	4 59.2	80 33.7	13.9	14 13.1	6.9	54.2
N 11	342 16.8	58.2	95 06.6	13.8	14 20.0	6.9	54.2
D 12	357 17.0	S 4 57.2	109 39.4	13.7	S14 26.9	6.8	54.2
A 13	12 17.2	56.2	124 12.1	13.7	14 33.7	6.7	54.2
Y 14	27 17.3	55.3	138 44.8	13.7	14 40.4	6.7	54.2
15	42 17.5	.. 54.3	153 17.5	13.7	14 47.1	6.6	54.2
16	57 17.6	53.3	167 50.2	13.6	14 53.7	6.5	54.2
17	72 17.8	52.3	182 22.8	13.6	15 00.2	6.5	54.2
18	87 17.9	S 4 51.4	196 55.4	13.6	S15 06.7	6.4	54.2
19	102 18.1	50.4	211 28.0	13.5	15 13.1	6.4	54.2
20	117 18.2	49.4	226 00.5	13.5	15 19.5	6.2	54.2
21	132 18.4	.. 48.4	240 33.0	13.5	15 25.7	6.3	54.2
22	147 18.5	47.5	255 05.5	13.4	15 32.0	6.1	54.2
23	162 18.7	46.5	269 37.9	13.4	15 38.1	6.1	54.2
9 00	177 18.8	S 4 45.5	284 10.3	13.4	S15 44.2	6.0	54.2
01	192 19.0	44.5	298 42.7	13.3	15 50.2	6.0	54.2
02	207 19.2	43.6	313 15.0	13.3	15 56.2	5.8	54.2
03	222 19.3	.. 42.6	327 47.3	13.3	16 02.0	5.9	54.2
04	237 19.5	41.6	342 19.6	13.2	16 07.9	5.7	54.3
05	252 19.6	40.6	356 51.8	13.2	16 13.6	5.7	54.3
06	267 19.8	S 4 39.6	11 24.0	13.1	S16 19.3	5.6	54.3
07	282 19.9	38.7	25 56.1	13.1	16 24.9	5.5	54.3
T 08	297 20.1	37.7	40 28.2	13.1	16 30.4	5.5	54.3
U 09	312 20.2	36.7	55 00.3	13.1	16 35.9	5.3	54.3
E 10	327 20.4	35.7	69 32.4	13.0	16 41.2	5.4	54.3
S 11	342 20.6	34.8	84 04.4	12.9	16 46.6	5.2	54.3
D 12	357 20.7	S 4 33.8	98 36.3	13.0	S16 51.8	5.2	54.3
A 13	12 20.9	32.8	113 08.3	12.8	16 57.0	5.1	54.3
Y 14	27 21.0	31.8	127 40.1	12.9	17 02.1	5.0	54.3
15	42 21.2	.. 30.9	142 12.0	12.8	17 07.1	4.9	54.3
16	57 21.3	29.9	156 43.8	12.8	17 12.0	4.9	54.4
17	72 21.5	28.9	171 15.6	12.7	17 16.9	4.8	54.4
18	87 21.6	S 4 27.9	185 47.3	12.7	S17 21.7	4.7	54.4
19	102 21.8	26.9	200 19.0	12.7	17 26.4	4.6	54.4
20	117 22.0	26.0	214 50.7	12.6	17 31.0	4.6	54.4
21	132 22.1	.. 25.0	229 22.3	12.6	17 35.6	4.5	54.4
22	147 22.3	24.0	243 53.9	12.6	17 40.1	4.4	54.4
23	162 22.4	23.0	258 25.5	12.5	17 44.5	4.3	54.4
10 00	177 22.6	S 4 22.1	272 57.0	12.4	S17 48.8	4.2	54.5
01	192 22.8	21.1	287 28.4	12.5	17 53.0	4.2	54.5
02	207 22.9	20.1	301 59.9	12.4	17 57.2	4.1	54.5
03	222 23.1	.. 19.1	316 31.3	12.3	18 01.3	4.0	54.5
04	237 23.2	18.1	331 02.6	12.3	18 05.3	3.9	54.5
05	252 23.4	17.2	345 33.9	12.3	18 09.2	3.9	54.5
06	267 23.5	S 4 16.2	0 05.2	12.2	S18 13.1	3.7	54.5
W 07	282 23.7	15.2	14 36.4	12.2	18 16.8	3.7	54.5
E 08	297 23.9	14.2	29 07.6	12.2	18 20.5	3.6	54.6
D 09	312 24.0	.. 13.2	43 38.8	12.1	18 24.1	3.5	54.6
N 10	327 24.2	12.3	58 09.9	12.1	18 27.6	3.4	54.6
E 11	342 24.3	11.3	72 41.0	12.0	18 31.0	3.4	54.6
S 12	357 24.5	S 4 10.3	87 12.0	12.0	S18 34.4	3.2	54.6
D 13	12 24.7	09.3	101 43.0	12.0	18 37.6	3.2	54.6
A 14	27 24.8	08.3	116 14.0	11.9	18 40.8	3.1	54.7
Y 15	42 25.0	.. 07.4	130 44.9	11.9	18 43.9	3.0	54.7
16	57 25.1	06.4	145 15.8	11.8	18 46.9	2.9	54.7
17	72 25.3	05.4	159 46.6	11.9	18 49.8	2.8	54.7
18	87 25.5	S 4 04.4	174 17.5	11.7	S18 52.6	2.8	54.7
19	102 25.6	03.4	188 48.2	11.7	18 55.4	2.6	54.7
20	117 25.8	02.5	203 18.9	11.7	18 58.0	2.6	54.8
21	132 25.9	.. 01.5	217 49.6	11.7	19 00.6	2.5	54.8
22	147 26.1	4 00.5	232 20.3	11.6	19 03.1	2.3	54.8
23	162 26.3	S 3 59.5	246 50.9	11.6	S19 05.4	2.3	54.8
SD 16.1	d 1.0		SD 14.8		14.8		14.9

Lat.	Twilight Naut.	Civil	Sunrise	Moonrise 8	9	10	11
°	h m	h m	h m	h m	h m	h m	h m
N 72	04 31	05 50	06 57	01 29	03 22	■	■
N 70	04 40	05 52	06 52	01 03	02 38	04 15	05 49
68	04 48	05 53	06 48	00 43	02 09	03 32	04 46
66	04 54	05 54	06 44	00 27	01 47	03 03	04 12
64	04 59	05 54	06 41	00 15	01 30	02 42	03 46
62	05 03	05 55	06 39	00 04	01 16	02 24	03 27
60	05 07	05 55	06 36	25 04	01 04	02 10	03 11
N 58	05 10	05 55	06 34	24 54	00 54	01 58	02 57
56	05 12	05 55	06 32	24 45	00 45	01 47	02 45
54	05 15	05 56	06 31	24 37	00 37	01 38	02 35
52	05 17	05 56	06 29	24 30	00 30	01 30	02 26
50	05 18	05 56	06 28	24 23	00 23	01 22	02 18
45	05 21	05 55	06 25	24 10	00 10	01 06	02 01
N 40	05 24	05 55	06 22	23 58	24 53	00 53	01 47
35	05 25	05 54	06 20	23 49	24 42	00 42	01 35
30	05 26	05 54	06 18	23 41	24 33	00 33	01 24
20	05 26	05 52	06 14	23 26	24 14	00 16	01 06
N 10	05 25	05 50	06 11	23 14	24 02	00 02	00 51
0	05 23	05 47	06 07	23 02	23 48	24 36	00 36
S 10	05 18	05 43	06 04	22 50	23 35	24 22	00 22
20	05 12	05 38	06 00	22 38	23 21	24 06	00 06
30	05 04	05 32	05 56	22 24	23 04	23 48	24 37
35	04 58	05 28	05 54	22 16	22 55	23 38	24 26
40	04 51	05 23	05 51	22 06	22 44	23 26	24 14
45	04 42	05 17	05 47	21 56	22 32	23 13	24 00
S 50	04 31	05 09	05 43	21 43	22 16	22 56	23 42
52	04 25	05 07	05 41	21 36	22 09	22 48	23 34
54	04 19	05 03	05 39	21 30	22 01	22 39	23 25
56	04 12	04 59	05 37	21 22	21 52	22 29	23 14
58	04 04	04 54	05 34	21 14	21 42	22 18	23 03
S 60	03 55	04 48	05 31	21 05	21 31	22 05	22 49

Lat.	Sunset	Twilight Civil	Naut.	Moonset 8	9	10	11
°	h m	h m	h m	h m	h m	h m	h m
N 72	17 26	18 33	19 54	07 13	06 53	■	■
N 70	17 31	18 32	19 44	07 40	07 38	07 38	07 45
68	17 35	18 31	19 36	08 01	08 08	08 21	08 47
66	17 38	18 30	19 30	08 17	08 30	08 50	09 22
64	17 41	18 29	19 24	08 31	08 48	09 12	09 47
62	17 44	18 28	19 20	08 42	09 03	09 30	10 07
60	17 46	18 28	19 16	08 52	09 15	09 45	10 23
N 58	17 48	18 27	19 13	09 00	09 26	09 57	10 37
56	17 50	18 27	19 10	09 08	09 35	10 08	10 49
54	17 52	18 27	19 08	09 15	09 43	10 18	10 59
52	17 53	18 27	19 06	09 21	09 51	10 26	11 08
50	17 54	18 27	19 04	09 26	09 57	10 34	11 17
45	17 57	18 27	19 01	09 38	10 12	10 50	11 34
N 40	18 00	18 27	18 58	09 48	10 24	11 04	11 48
35	18 02	18 27	18 57	09 56	10 34	11 15	12 00
30	18 04	18 28	18 56	10 04	10 43	11 25	12 11
20	18 08	18 30	18 55	10 17	10 58	11 42	12 29
N 10	18 11	18 32	18 56	10 28	11 11	11 57	12 45
0	18 14	18 35	18 59	10 39	11 24	12 11	13 00
S 10	18 17	18 38	19 03	10 49	11 37	12 25	13 15
20	18 21	18 43	19 09	11 01	11 50	12 40	13 30
30	18 25	18 49	19 17	11 14	12 06	12 57	13 49
35	18 27	18 53	19 23	11 21	12 15	13 07	13 59
40	18 30	18 57	19 29	11 30	12 25	13 19	14 11
45	18 33	19 03	19 38	11 40	12 37	13 32	14 25
S 50	18 37	19 10	19 49	11 52	12 52	13 49	14 43
52	18 39	19 13	19 54	11 58	12 59	13 57	14 51
54	18 41	19 17	20 00	12 04	13 06	14 05	15 00
56	18 43	19 21	20 07	12 11	13 15	14 15	15 11
58	18 46	19 26	20 15	12 19	13 24	14 26	15 22
S 60	18 48	19 31	20 24	12 28	13 36	14 39	15 36

Day	SUN Eqn. of Time 00h	12h	Mer. Pass.	MOON Mer. Pass. Upper	Lower	Age	Phase
d	m s	m s	h m	h m	h m	d	%
8	11 00	10 52	12 11	04 28	16 50	20	67
9	10 45	10 37	12 11	05 13	17 36	21	58
10	10 30	10 22	12 10	06 00	18 24	22	49

UT	ARIES	VENUS −4.0		MARS −0.5		JUPITER −2.1		SATURN +0.5		STARS		
	GHA	GHA	Dec	GHA	Dec	GHA	Dec	GHA	Dec	Name	SHA	Dec
d h	° ′	° ′	° ′	° ′	° ′	° ′	° ′	° ′	° ′		° ′	° ′
11 00	168 12.8	148 41.5 N 7 53.4		308 06.1 S13 18.9		162 18.7 N 1 21.6		138 32.1 N 9 42.4		Acamar	315 27.0	S40 18.9
01	183 15.3	163 41.1	54.7	323 08.4	19.0	177 20.6	21.8	153 34.3	42.5	Achernar	335 35.5	S57 14.8
02	198 17.7	178 40.8	56.0	338 10.6	19.1	192 22.5	22.1	168 36.5	42.6	Acrux	173 21.0	S63 05.6
03	213 20.2	193 40.5 . .	57.2	353 12.9 . .	19.1	207 24.4 . .	22.3	183 38.7 . .	42.7	Adhara	255 21.0	S28 58.6
04	228 22.7	208 40.1	58.5	8 15.1	19.2	222 26.4	22.6	198 40.9	42.8	Aldebaran	291 02.1	N16 30.3
05	243 25.1	223 39.8	7 59.7	23 17.4	19.3	237 28.3	22.8	213 43.1	42.9			
06	258 27.6	238 39.4 N 8 01.0		38 19.6 S13 19.3		252 30.2 N 1 23.0		228 45.3 N 9 43.0		Alioth	166 29.9	N55 57.8
07	273 30.1	253 39.1	02.2	53 21.9	19.4	267 32.1	23.3	243 47.5	43.1	Alkaid	153 07.2	N49 18.9
T 08	288 32.5	268 38.8	03.5	68 24.1	19.5	282 34.0	23.5	258 49.8	43.2	Al Na'ir	27 58.0	S46 57.9
H 09	303 35.0	283 38.4 . .	04.7	83 26.4 . .	19.6	297 36.0 . .	23.7	273 52.0 . .	43.3	Alnilam	275 57.5	S 1 12.4
U 10	318 37.4	298 38.1	06.0	98 28.6	19.6	312 37.9	24.0	288 54.2	43.4	Alphard	218 06.6	S 8 39.5
R 11	333 39.9	313 37.7	07.2	113 30.9	19.7	327 39.8	24.2	303 56.4	43.5			
S 12	348 42.4	328 37.4 N 8 08.5		128 33.2 S13 19.8		342 41.7 N 1 24.5		318 58.6 N 9 43.6		Alphecca	126 20.2	N26 42.9
D 13	3 44.8	343 37.1	09.7	143 35.4	19.8	357 43.6	24.7	334 00.8	43.7	Alpheratz	357 55.3	N29 05.0
A 14	18 47.3	358 36.7	11.0	158 37.7	19.9	12 45.5	24.9	349 03.0	43.8	Altair	62 19.2	N 8 51.9
Y 15	33 49.8	13 36.4 . .	12.2	173 40.0 . .	20.0	27 47.5 . .	25.2	4 05.2 . .	43.9	Ankaa	353 27.0	S42 18.9
16	48 52.2	28 36.0	13.5	188 42.2	20.1	42 49.4	25.4	19 07.5	44.0	Antares	112 39.7	S26 25.7
17	63 54.7	43 35.7	14.7	203 44.5	20.1	57 51.3	25.6	34 09.7	44.1			
18	78 57.2	58 35.3 N 8 16.0		218 46.8 S13 20.2		72 53.2 N 1 25.9		49 11.9 N 9 44.2		Arcturus	146 05.6	N19 11.1
19	93 59.6	73 35.0	17.2	233 49.0	20.3	87 55.1	26.1	64 14.1	44.3	Atria	107 51.5	S69 01.2
20	109 02.1	88 34.7	18.5	248 51.3	20.3	102 57.1	26.4	79 16.3	44.4	Avior	234 22.0	S59 30.7
21	124 04.6	103 34.3 . .	19.7	263 53.6 . .	20.4	117 59.0 . .	26.6	94 18.5 . .	44.5	Bellatrix	278 43.8	N 6 20.7
22	139 07.0	118 34.0	21.0	278 55.9	20.5	133 00.9	26.8	109 20.7	44.6	Betelgeuse	271 13.2	N 7 24.2
23	154 09.5	133 33.6	22.2	293 58.1	20.5	148 02.8	27.1	124 22.9	44.7			
12 00	169 11.9	148 33.3 N 8 23.4		309 00.4 S13 20.6		163 04.7 N 1 27.3		139 25.1 N 9 44.8		Canopus	264 00.9	S52 42.1
01	184 14.4	163 32.9	24.7	324 02.7	20.7	178 06.6	27.5	154 27.3	44.9	Capella	280 50.8	N45 59.8
02	199 16.9	178 32.6	25.9	339 05.0	20.7	193 08.6	27.8	169 29.6	45.0	Deneb	49 39.3	N45 16.4
03	214 19.3	193 32.3 . .	27.2	354 07.2 . .	20.8	208 10.5 . .	28.0	184 31.8 . .	45.1	Denebola	182 44.6	N14 34.5
04	229 21.8	208 31.9	28.4	9 09.5	20.9	223 12.4	28.3	199 34.0	45.2	Diphda	349 07.3	S17 59.7
05	244 24.3	223 31.6	29.7	24 11.8	20.9	238 14.3	28.5	214 36.2	45.3			
06	259 26.7	238 31.2 N 8 30.9		39 14.1 S13 21.0		253 16.2 N 1 28.7		229 38.4 N 9 45.4		Dubhe	194 04.5	N61 45.3
07	274 29.2	253 30.9	32.2	54 16.4	21.0	268 18.2	29.0	244 40.6	45.5	Elnath	278 26.6	N28 36.3
08	289 31.7	268 30.5	33.4	69 18.6	21.1	283 20.1	29.2	259 42.8	45.6	Eltanin	90 51.3	N51 29.1
F 09	304 34.1	283 30.2 . .	34.7	84 20.9 . .	21.2	298 22.0 . .	29.4	274 45.0 . .	45.7	Enif	33 58.2	N 9 52.1
R 10	319 36.6	298 29.8	35.9	99 23.2	21.2	313 23.9	29.7	289 47.2	45.8	Fomalhaut	15 36.5	S29 37.7
I 11	334 39.1	313 29.5	37.1	114 25.5	21.3	328 25.8	29.9	304 49.4	45.9			
D 12	349 41.5	328 29.2 N 8 38.4		129 27.8 S13 21.4		343 27.7 N 1 30.2		319 51.7 N 9 46.0		Gacrux	172 12.6	S57 06.4
A 13	4 44.0	343 28.8	39.6	144 30.1	21.4	358 29.7	30.4	334 53.9	46.1	Gienah	176 03.3	S17 32.3
Y 14	19 46.4	358 28.5	40.9	159 32.4	21.5	13 31.6	30.6	349 56.1	46.2	Hadar	149 03.1	S60 21.9
15	34 48.9	13 28.1 . .	42.1	174 34.7 . .	21.6	28 33.5 . .	30.9	4 58.3 . .	46.3	Hamal	328 13.5	N23 27.4
16	49 51.4	28 27.8	43.3	189 37.0	21.6	43 35.4	31.1	20 00.5	46.4	Kaus Aust.	83 58.5	S34 22.9
17	64 53.8	43 27.4	44.6	204 39.3	21.7	58 37.3	31.3	35 02.7	46.5			
18	79 56.3	58 27.1 N 8 45.8		219 41.6 S13 21.7		73 39.2 N 1 31.6		50 04.9 N 9 46.6		Kochab	137 19.0	N74 09.4
19	94 58.8	73 26.7	47.1	234 43.9	21.8	88 41.2	31.8	65 07.1	46.7	Markab	13 49.6	N15 11.9
20	110 01.2	88 26.4	48.3	249 46.2	21.9	103 43.1	32.1	80 09.3	46.8	Menkar	314 26.8	N 4 05.0
21	125 03.7	103 26.0 . .	49.6	264 48.5 . .	21.9	118 45.0 . .	32.3	95 11.5 . .	46.9	Menkent	148 20.3	S36 21.8
22	140 06.2	118 25.7	50.8	279 50.8	22.0	133 46.9	32.5	110 13.7	47.0	Miaplacidus	221 41.2	S69 43.1
23	155 08.6	133 25.3	52.0	294 53.1	22.0	148 48.8	32.8	125 15.9	47.1			
13 00	170 11.1	148 25.0 N 8 53.3		309 55.4 S13 22.1		163 50.7 N 1 33.0		140 18.2 N 9 47.2		Mirfak	308 56.4	N49 51.5
01	185 13.6	163 24.6	54.5	324 57.7	22.2	178 52.7	33.2	155 20.4	47.3	Nunki	76 12.1	S26 17.8
02	200 16.0	178 24.3	55.7	340 00.0	22.2	193 54.6	33.5	170 22.6	47.4	Peacock	53 37.0	S56 44.1
03	215 18.5	193 23.9 . .	57.0	355 02.3 . .	22.3	208 56.5 . .	33.7	185 24.8 . .	47.5	Pollux	243 41.0	N28 01.6
04	230 20.9	208 23.6	58.2	10 04.6	22.3	223 58.4	34.0	200 27.0	47.6	Procyon	245 11.1	N 5 13.4
05	245 23.4	223 23.2	8 59.5	25 06.9	22.4	239 00.3	34.2	215 29.2	47.7			
06	260 25.9	238 22.9 N 9 00.7		40 09.2 S13 22.4		254 02.2 N 1 34.4		230 31.4 N 9 47.8		Rasalhague	96 16.7	N12 33.6
07	275 28.3	253 22.5	01.9	55 11.5	22.5	269 04.2	34.7	245 33.6	47.9	Regulus	207 54.9	N11 58.2
S 08	290 30.8	268 22.2	03.2	70 13.8	22.6	284 06.1	34.9	260 35.8	48.0	Rigel	281 22.7	S 8 12.5
A 09	305 33.3	283 21.8 . .	04.4	85 16.2 . .	22.6	299 08.0 . .	35.1	275 38.0 . .	48.1	Rigil Kent.	140 06.4	S60 49.6
T 10	320 35.7	298 21.5	05.6	100 18.5	22.7	314 09.9	35.4	290 40.2	48.2	Sabik	102 25.2	S15 43.4
U 11	335 38.2	313 21.1	06.9	115 20.8	22.7	329 11.8	35.6	305 42.4	48.3			
R 12	350 40.7	328 20.8 N 9 08.1		130 23.1 S13 22.8		344 13.7 N 1 35.9		320 44.6 N 9 48.4		Schedar	349 53.6	N56 31.9
D 13	5 43.1	343 20.4	09.3	145 25.4	22.8	359 15.7	36.1	335 46.9	48.5	Shaula	96 36.9	S37 06.0
A 14	20 45.6	358 20.1	10.6	160 27.7	22.9	14 17.6	36.3	350 49.1	48.6	Sirius	258 43.3	S16 43.2
Y 15	35 48.0	13 19.7 . .	11.8	175 30.1 . .	22.9	29 19.5 . .	36.6	5 51.3 . .	48.7	Spica	158 42.6	S11 09.4
16	50 50.5	28 19.4	13.0	190 32.4	23.0	44 21.4	36.8	20 53.5	48.8	Suhail	223 00.2	S43 26.0
17	65 53.0	43 19.0	14.3	205 34.7	23.0	59 23.3	37.0	35 55.7	48.9			
18	80 55.4	58 18.7 N 9 15.5		220 37.0 S13 23.1		74 25.2 N 1 37.3		50 57.9 N 9 49.0		Vega	80 46.6	N38 46.8
19	95 57.9	73 18.3	16.7	235 39.4	23.2	89 27.2	37.5	66 00.1	49.1	Zuben'ubi	137 17.4	S16 02.2
20	111 00.4	88 18.0	18.0	250 41.7	23.2	104 29.1	37.8	81 02.3	49.2		SHA	Mer. Pass.
21	126 02.8	103 17.6 . .	19.2	265 44.0 . .	23.3	119 31.0 . .	38.0	96 04.5 . .	49.3		° ′	h m
22	141 05.3	118 17.3	20.4	280 46.4	23.3	134 32.9	38.2	111 06.7	49.4	Venus	339 21.3	14 06
23	156 07.8	133 16.9	21.7	295 48.7	23.4	149 34.8	38.5	126 08.9	49.5	Mars	139 48.5	3 23
	h m									Jupiter	353 52.8	13 06
Mer. Pass. 12 41.1		v −0.3 d 1.2		v 2.3 d 0.1		v 1.9 d 0.2		v 2.2 d 0.1		Saturn	330 13.2	14 40

UT	SUN GHA	SUN Dec	MOON GHA	v	MOON Dec	d	HP
d h	° ′	° ′	° ′	′	° ′	′	′
11 00	177 26.4	S 3 58.5	261 21.5	11.5	S19 07.7	2.2	54.8
01	192 26.6	57.6	275 52.0	11.5	19 09.9	2.2	54.9
02	207 26.8	56.6	290 22.5	11.5	19 12.1	2.0	54.9
03	222 26.9	.. 55.6	304 53.0	11.4	19 14.1	1.9	54.9
04	237 27.1	54.6	319 23.4	11.4	19 16.0	1.9	54.9
05	252 27.2	53.6	333 53.8	11.3	19 17.9	1.7	54.9
06	267 27.4	S 3 52.7	348 24.1	11.3	S19 19.6	1.7	55.0
07	282 27.6	51.7	2 54.4	11.3	19 21.3	1.5	55.0
08	297 27.7	50.7	17 24.7	11.2	19 22.8	1.5	55.0
T 09	312 27.9	.. 49.7	31 54.9	11.2	19 24.3	1.4	55.0
H 10	327 28.1	48.7	46 25.1	11.2	19 25.7	1.3	55.0
U 11	342 28.2	47.8	60 55.3	11.1	19 27.0	1.1	55.1
R 12	357 28.4	S 3 46.8	75 25.4	11.1	S19 28.1	1.1	55.1
S 13	12 28.5	45.8	89 55.5	11.1	19 29.2	1.0	55.1
D 14	27 28.7	44.8	104 25.6	11.0	19 30.2	0.9	55.1
A 15	42 28.9	.. 43.8	118 55.6	11.0	19 31.1	0.8	55.2
Y 16	57 29.0	42.8	133 25.6	10.9	19 31.9	0.8	55.2
17	72 29.2	41.9	147 55.5	10.9	19 32.7	0.6	55.2
18	87 29.4	S 3 40.9	162 25.4	10.9	S19 33.3	0.5	55.2
19	102 29.5	39.9	176 55.3	10.8	19 33.8	0.4	55.3
20	117 29.7	38.9	191 25.1	10.9	19 34.2	0.3	55.3
21	132 29.8	.. 37.9	205 55.0	10.7	19 34.5	0.3	55.3
22	147 30.0	37.0	220 24.7	10.8	19 34.8	0.1	55.3
23	162 30.2	36.0	234 54.5	10.7	19 34.9	0.0	55.4
12 00	177 30.3	S 3 35.0	249 24.2	10.7	S19 34.9	0.1	55.4
01	192 30.5	34.0	263 53.9	10.6	19 34.8	0.1	55.4
02	207 30.7	33.0	278 23.5	10.6	19 34.7	0.3	55.4
03	222 30.8	.. 32.0	292 53.1	10.6	19 34.4	0.4	55.5
04	237 31.0	31.1	307 22.7	10.6	19 34.0	0.4	55.5
05	252 31.2	30.1	321 52.3	10.5	19 33.6	0.6	55.5
06	267 31.3	S 3 29.1	336 21.8	10.5	S19 33.0	0.7	55.6
07	282 31.5	28.1	350 51.3	10.4	19 32.3	0.7	55.6
08	297 31.7	27.1	5 20.7	10.5	19 31.6	0.9	55.6
F 09	312 31.8	.. 26.1	19 50.2	10.4	19 30.7	1.0	55.6
R 10	327 32.0	25.2	34 19.6	10.3	19 29.7	1.1	55.7
I 11	342 32.2	24.2	48 48.9	10.4	19 28.6	1.1	55.7
D 12	357 32.3	S 3 23.2	63 18.3	10.3	S19 27.5	1.3	55.7
A 13	12 32.5	22.2	77 47.6	10.3	19 26.2	1.4	55.8
Y 14	27 32.7	21.2	92 16.9	10.2	19 24.8	1.5	55.8
15	42 32.8	.. 20.2	106 46.1	10.3	19 23.3	1.5	55.8
16	57 33.0	19.3	121 15.4	10.2	19 21.8	1.7	55.8
17	72 33.2	18.3	135 44.6	10.2	19 20.1	1.8	55.9
18	87 33.4	S 3 17.3	150 13.8	10.1	S19 18.3	1.9	55.9
19	102 33.5	16.3	164 42.9	10.1	19 16.4	2.0	55.9
20	117 33.7	15.3	179 12.0	10.1	19 14.4	2.1	56.0
21	132 33.8	.. 14.3	193 41.1	10.1	19 12.3	2.2	56.0
22	147 34.0	13.4	208 10.2	10.1	19 10.1	2.3	56.0
23	162 34.2	12.4	222 39.3	10.0	19 07.8	2.4	56.1
13 00	177 34.3	S 3 11.4	237 08.3	10.0	S19 05.4	2.5	56.1
01	192 34.5	10.4	251 37.3	10.0	19 02.9	2.6	56.1
02	207 34.7	09.4	266 06.3	10.0	19 00.3	2.8	56.1
03	222 34.8	.. 08.4	280 35.3	9.9	18 57.5	2.8	56.2
04	237 35.0	07.4	295 04.2	9.9	18 54.7	2.9	56.2
05	252 35.2	06.5	309 33.1	9.9	18 51.8	3.0	56.2
06	267 35.3	S 3 05.5	324 02.0	9.9	S18 48.8	3.2	56.3
07	282 35.5	04.5	338 30.9	9.8	18 45.6	3.2	56.3
08	297 35.7	03.5	352 59.7	9.9	18 42.4	3.3	56.3
S 09	312 35.8	.. 02.5	7 28.6	9.8	18 39.1	3.5	56.4
A 10	327 36.0	01.5	21 57.4	9.8	18 35.6	3.5	56.4
T 11	342 36.2	3 00.6	36 26.2	9.8	18 32.1	3.7	56.4
U 12	357 36.3	S 2 59.6	50 55.0	9.7	S18 28.4	3.8	56.5
R 13	12 36.5	58.6	65 23.7	9.8	18 24.6	3.8	56.5
D 14	27 36.7	57.6	79 52.5	9.7	18 20.8	4.0	56.5
A 15	42 36.9	.. 56.6	94 21.2	9.7	18 16.8	4.1	56.6
Y 16	57 37.0	55.6	108 49.9	9.7	18 12.7	4.1	56.6
17	72 37.2	54.6	123 18.6	9.7	18 08.6	4.3	56.6
18	87 37.4	S 2 53.7	137 47.3	9.6	S18 04.3	4.4	56.7
19	102 37.5	52.7	152 15.9	9.7	17 59.9	4.5	56.7
20	117 37.7	51.7	166 44.6	9.6	17 55.4	4.6	56.7
21	132 37.9	.. 50.7	181 13.2	9.6	17 50.8	4.7	56.8
22	147 38.0	49.7	195 41.8	9.6	17 46.1	4.7	56.8
23	162 38.2	48.7	210 10.4	9.6	S17 41.4	4.9	56.8
	SD 16.1	d 1.0	SD 15.0		15.2		15.4

Lat.	Twilight Naut.	Twilight Civil	Sunrise	Moonrise 11	12	13	14
°	h m	h m	h m	h m	h m	h m	h m
N 72	04 14	05 35	06 42	■■■	■■■	■■■	08 00
N 70	04 25	05 38	06 38	05 49	06 51	07 06	07 07
68	04 35	05 40	06 35	04 46	05 43	06 17	06 35
66	04 42	05 42	06 33	04 12	05 06	05 45	06 10
64	04 48	05 44	06 31	03 46	04 40	05 22	05 52
62	04 53	05 45	06 29	03 27	04 20	05 03	05 36
60	04 58	05 46	06 27	03 11	04 04	04 48	05 23
N 58	05 01	05 47	06 26	02 57	03 50	04 35	05 12
56	05 04	05 48	06 25	02 45	03 38	04 24	05 02
54	05 07	05 48	06 23	02 35	03 27	04 14	04 53
52	05 10	05 49	06 22	02 26	03 18	04 05	04 46
50	05 12	05 49	06 21	02 18	03 10	03 57	04 39
45	05 16	05 50	06 19	02 01	02 52	03 40	04 24
N 40	05 19	05 50	06 17	01 47	02 38	03 26	04 11
35	05 21	05 50	06 16	01 35	02 26	03 14	04 01
30	05 23	05 50	06 14	01 24	02 15	03 04	03 51
20	05 24	05 49	06 11	01 06	01 57	02 46	03 36
N 10	05 24	05 48	06 09	00 51	01 41	02 31	03 22
0	05 22	05 46	06 07	00 36	01 26	02 17	03 09
S 10	05 19	05 43	06 04	00 22	01 11	02 02	02 55
20	05 13	05 39	06 01	00 06	00 55	01 47	02 41
30	05 06	05 34	05 58	24 37	00 37	01 29	02 25
35	05 01	05 31	05 56	24 26	00 26	01 19	02 16
40	04 54	05 27	05 54	24 14	00 14	01 07	02 05
45	04 47	05 22	05 51	24 00	00 00	00 53	01 53
S 50	04 36	05 15	05 48	23 42	24 36	00 36	01 38
52	04 31	05 12	05 47	23 34	24 28	00 28	01 30
54	04 26	05 09	05 45	23 25	24 19	00 19	01 22
56	04 19	05 05	05 43	23 14	24 09	00 09	01 14
58	04 12	05 01	05 41	23 03	23 58	25 03	01 03
S 60	04 04	04 56	05 39	22 49	23 45	24 52	00 52

Lat.	Sunset	Twilight Civil	Twilight Naut.	Moonset 11	12	13	14
°	h m	h m	h m	h m	h m	h m	h m
N 72	17 40	18 47	20 09	■■■	■■■	■■■	10 53
N 70	17 43	18 44	19 57	07 45	08 26	09 58	11 45
68	17 46	18 41	19 48	08 47	09 34	10 47	12 17
66	17 48	18 39	19 40	09 22	10 11	11 18	12 40
64	17 50	18 38	19 34	09 47	10 36	11 41	12 59
62	17 52	18 36	19 28	10 07	10 57	11 59	13 14
60	17 54	18 35	19 24	10 23	11 13	12 14	13 26
N 58	17 55	18 34	19 20	10 37	11 27	12 27	13 37
56	17 56	18 33	19 17	10 49	11 39	12 38	13 46
54	17 57	18 33	19 14	10 59	11 49	12 48	13 55
52	17 58	18 32	19 11	11 08	11 58	12 57	14 02
50	17 59	18 31	19 09	11 17	12 07	13 04	14 09
45	18 01	18 31	19 05	11 34	12 24	13 21	14 23
N 40	18 03	18 30	19 02	11 48	12 39	13 34	14 35
35	18 05	18 30	18 59	12 00	12 51	13 46	14 45
30	18 06	18 30	18 58	12 11	13 01	13 56	14 53
20	18 09	18 31	18 56	12 29	13 19	14 13	15 08
N 10	18 11	18 32	18 56	12 45	13 35	14 28	15 21
0	18 13	18 34	18 58	13 00	13 50	14 41	15 34
S 10	18 15	18 37	19 01	13 15	14 05	14 55	15 46
20	18 18	18 40	19 06	13 30	14 21	15 10	15 58
30	18 21	18 45	19 13	13 49	14 39	15 27	16 13
35	18 23	18 48	19 18	13 59	14 49	15 37	16 22
40	18 25	18 52	19 24	14 11	15 01	15 48	16 31
45	18 28	18 57	19 32	14 25	15 15	16 01	16 42
S 50	18 31	19 03	19 42	14 43	15 32	16 17	16 56
52	18 32	19 06	19 47	14 51	15 40	16 24	17 02
54	18 34	19 09	19 52	15 00	15 49	16 32	17 09
56	18 35	19 13	19 58	15 11	16 00	16 42	17 17
58	18 37	19 17	20 06	15 22	16 11	16 52	17 25
S 60	18 39	19 22	20 14	15 36	16 24	17 04	17 35

	SUN Eqn. of Time 00h	12h	Mer. Pass.	MOON Mer. Pass. Upper	Lower	Age	Phase
Day	m s	m s	h m	h m	h m	d	%
11	10 15	10 07	12 10	06 48	19 13	23	39
12	09 59	09 51	12 10	07 38	20 03	24	30
13	09 43	09 35	12 10	08 29	20 55	25	21

UT (d h)	ARIES GHA	VENUS −4.0 GHA	Dec	MARS −0.6 GHA	Dec	JUPITER −2.1 GHA	Dec	SATURN +0.5 GHA	Dec	STARS Name	SHA	Dec
14 00	171 10.2	148 16.6	N 9 22.9	310 51.0	S13 23.4	164 36.7	N 1 38.7	141 11.1	N 9 49.6	Acamar	315 27.0	S40 18.9
01	186 12.7	163 16.2	24.1	325 53.4	23.5	179 38.6	38.9	156 13.3	49.7	Achernar	335 35.5	S57 14.8
02	201 15.2	178 15.9	25.3	340 55.7	23.5	194 40.6	39.2	171 15.5	49.8	Acrux	173 20.9	S63 05.6
03	216 17.6	193 15.5 . .	26.6	355 58.0 . .	23.6	209 42.5 . .	39.4	186 17.7 . .	49.9	Adhara	255 21.1	S28 58.6
04	231 20.1	208 15.2	27.8	11 00.4	23.6	224 44.4	39.7	201 19.9	50.0	Aldebaran	291 02.1	N16 30.3
05	246 22.5	223 14.8	29.0	26 02.7	23.7	239 46.3	39.9	216 22.2	50.1			
S 06	261 25.0	238 14.4	N 9 30.3	41 05.0	S13 23.7	254 48.2	N 1 40.1	231 24.4	N 9 50.2	Alioth	166 29.9	N55 57.8
U 07	276 27.5	253 14.1	31.5	56 07.4	23.8	269 50.1	40.4	246 26.6	50.3	Alkaid	153 07.2	N49 18.9
N 08	291 29.9	268 13.7	32.7	71 09.7	23.8	284 52.1	40.6	261 28.8	50.4	Al Na'ir	27 58.0	S46 57.9
D 09	306 32.4	283 13.4 . .	33.9	86 12.1 . .	23.9	299 54.0 . .	40.8	276 31.0 . .	50.5	Alnilam	275 57.6	S 1 12.4
A 10	321 34.9	298 13.0	35.2	101 14.4	23.9	314 55.9	41.1	291 33.2	50.6	Alphard	218 06.6	S 8 39.5
Y 11	336 37.3	313 12.7	36.4	116 16.8	24.0	329 57.8	41.3	306 35.4	50.7			
12	351 39.8	328 12.3	N 9 37.6	131 19.1	S13 24.0	344 59.7	N 1 41.6	321 37.6	N 9 50.8	Alphecca	126 20.2	N26 42.9
13	6 42.3	343 12.0	38.8	146 21.5	24.1	0 01.6	41.8	336 39.8	50.9	Alpheratz	357 55.3	N29 05.0
14	21 44.7	358 11.6	40.1	161 23.8	24.1	15 03.5	42.0	351 42.0	51.0	Altair	62 19.2	N 8 51.9
15	36 47.2	13 11.2 . .	41.3	176 26.2 . .	24.1	30 05.5 . .	42.3	6 44.2 . .	51.1	Ankaa	353 27.0	S42 18.9
16	51 49.7	28 10.9	42.5	191 28.5	24.2	45 07.4	42.5	21 46.4	51.2	Antares	112 39.7	S26 25.7
17	66 52.1	43 10.5	43.7	206 30.9	24.2	60 09.3	42.7	36 48.6	51.3			
18	81 54.6	58 10.2	N 9 45.0	221 33.2	S13 24.3	75 11.2	N 1 43.0	51 50.8	N 9 51.4	Arcturus	146 05.6	N19 11.1
19	96 57.0	73 09.8	46.2	236 35.6	24.3	90 13.1	43.2	66 53.0	51.5	Atria	107 51.4	S69 01.2
20	111 59.5	88 09.5	47.4	251 37.9	24.4	105 15.0	43.5	81 55.2	51.6	Avior	234 22.1	S59 30.7
21	127 02.0	103 09.1 . .	48.6	266 40.3 . .	24.4	120 17.0 . .	43.7	96 57.4 . .	51.7	Bellatrix	278 43.9	N 6 20.7
22	142 04.4	118 08.7	49.9	281 42.6	24.5	135 18.9	43.9	111 59.6	51.8	Betelgeuse	271 13.2	N 7 24.2
23	157 06.9	133 08.4	51.1	296 45.0	24.5	150 20.8	44.2	127 01.8	51.9			
15 00	172 09.4	148 08.0	N 9 52.3	311 47.4	S13 24.6	165 22.7	N 1 44.4	142 04.0	N 9 52.1	Canopus	264 00.9	S52 42.1
01	187 11.8	163 07.7	53.5	326 49.7	24.6	180 24.6	44.7	157 06.2	52.2	Capella	280 50.8	N45 59.8
02	202 14.3	178 07.3	54.7	341 52.1	24.6	195 26.5	44.9	172 08.4	52.3	Deneb	49 39.3	N45 16.4
03	217 16.8	193 06.9 . .	56.0	356 54.5 . .	24.7	210 28.4 . .	45.1	187 10.7 . .	52.4	Denebola	182 44.6	N14 34.5
04	232 19.2	208 06.6	57.2	11 56.8	24.7	225 30.4	45.4	202 12.9	52.5	Diphda	349 07.3	S17 59.7
05	247 21.7	223 06.2	58.4	26 59.2	24.8	240 32.3	45.6	217 15.1	52.6			
M 06	262 24.1	238 05.9	N 9 59.6	42 01.6	S13 24.8	255 34.2	N 1 45.8	232 17.3	N 9 52.7	Dubhe	194 04.5	N61 45.3
O 07	277 26.6	253 05.5	10 00.8	57 03.9	24.8	270 36.1	46.1	247 19.5	52.8	Elnath	278 26.6	N28 36.3
N 08	292 29.1	268 05.1	02.1	72 06.3	24.9	285 38.0	46.3	262 21.7	52.9	Eltanin	90 51.3	N51 29.1
D 09	307 31.5	283 04.8 . .	03.3	87 08.7 . .	24.9	300 39.9 . .	46.6	277 23.9 . .	53.0	Enif	33 58.2	N 9 52.1
A 10	322 34.0	298 04.4	04.5	102 11.0	25.0	315 41.8	46.8	292 26.1	53.1	Fomalhaut	15 36.5	S29 37.7
Y 11	337 36.5	313 04.1	05.7	117 13.4	25.0	330 43.8	47.0	307 28.3	53.2			
12	352 38.9	328 03.7	N10 06.9	132 15.8	S13 25.0	345 45.7	N 1 47.3	322 30.5	N 9 53.3	Gacrux	172 12.6	S57 06.4
13	7 41.4	343 03.3	08.1	147 18.2	25.1	0 47.6	47.5	337 32.7	53.4	Gienah	176 03.3	S17 32.3
14	22 43.9	358 03.0	09.4	162 20.6	25.1	15 49.5	47.7	352 34.9	53.5	Hadar	149 03.1	S60 21.9
15	37 46.3	13 02.6 . .	10.6	177 22.9 . .	25.2	30 51.4 . .	48.0	7 37.1 . .	53.6	Hamal	328 13.5	N23 27.4
16	52 48.8	28 02.3	11.8	192 25.3	25.2	45 53.3	48.2	22 39.3	53.7	Kaus Aust.	83 58.5	S34 22.9
17	67 51.3	43 01.9	13.0	207 27.7	25.2	60 55.2	48.5	37 41.5	53.8			
18	82 53.7	58 01.5	N10 14.2	222 30.1	S13 25.3	75 57.2	N 1 48.7	52 43.7	N 9 53.9	Kochab	137 18.9	N74 09.4
19	97 56.2	73 01.2	15.4	237 32.5	25.3	90 59.1	48.9	67 45.9	54.0	Markab	13 49.6	N15 11.9
20	112 58.6	88 00.8	16.6	252 34.8	25.4	106 01.0	49.2	82 48.1	54.1	Menkar	314 26.8	N 4 05.0
21	128 01.1	103 00.4 . .	17.8	267 37.2 . .	25.4	121 02.9 . .	49.4	97 50.3 . .	54.2	Menkent	148 20.3	S36 21.8
22	143 03.6	118 00.1	19.1	282 39.6	25.4	136 04.8	49.6	112 52.5	54.3	Miaplacidus	221 41.2	S69 43.1
23	158 06.0	132 59.7	20.3	297 42.0	25.5	151 06.7	49.9	127 54.7	54.4			
16 00	173 08.5	147 59.3	N10 21.5	312 44.4	S13 25.5	166 08.6	N 1 50.1	142 56.9	N 9 54.5	Mirfak	308 56.4	N49 51.5
01	188 11.0	162 59.0	22.7	327 46.8	25.5	181 10.6	50.4	157 59.1	54.6	Nunki	76 12.1	S26 17.8
02	203 13.4	177 58.6	23.9	342 49.2	25.6	196 12.5	50.6	173 01.3	54.7	Peacock	53 37.0	S56 44.1
03	218 15.9	192 58.3 . .	25.1	357 51.6 . .	25.6	211 14.4 . .	50.8	188 03.5 . .	54.8	Pollux	243 41.0	N28 01.6
04	233 18.4	207 57.9	26.3	12 54.0	25.6	226 16.3	51.1	203 05.7	54.9	Procyon	245 11.1	N 5 13.4
05	248 20.8	222 57.5	27.5	27 56.4	25.7	241 18.2	51.3	218 07.9	55.0			
T 06	263 23.3	237 57.2	N10 28.7	42 58.8	S13 25.7	256 20.1	N 1 51.6	233 10.1	N 9 55.1	Rasalhague	96 16.7	N12 33.5
U 07	278 25.8	252 56.8	30.0	58 01.2	25.7	271 22.0	51.8	248 12.3	55.2	Regulus	207 54.9	N11 58.2
E 08	293 28.2	267 56.4	31.2	73 03.6	25.8	286 24.0	52.0	263 14.5	55.3	Rigel	281 22.7	S 8 12.5
S 09	308 30.7	282 56.1 . .	32.4	88 06.0 . .	25.8	301 25.9 . .	52.3	278 16.7 . .	55.4	Rigil Kent.	140 06.4	S60 49.6
D 10	323 33.1	297 55.7	33.6	103 08.4	25.8	316 27.8	52.5	293 18.9	55.5	Sabik	102 25.2	S15 43.4
A 11	338 35.6	312 55.3	34.8	118 10.8	25.9	331 29.7	52.7	308 21.1	55.6			
Y 12	353 38.1	327 55.0	N10 36.0	133 13.2	S13 25.9	346 31.6	N 1 53.0	323 23.3	N 9 55.7	Schedar	349 53.6	N56 31.9
13	8 40.5	342 54.6	37.2	148 15.6	25.9	1 33.5	53.2	338 25.5	55.8	Shaula	96 36.9	S37 06.0
14	23 43.0	357 54.2	38.4	163 18.0	26.0	16 35.4	53.5	353 27.7	55.9	Sirius	258 43.4	S16 43.2
15	38 45.5	12 53.9 . .	39.6	178 20.4 . .	26.0	31 37.3 . .	53.7	8 29.9 . .	56.0	Spica	158 42.6	S11 09.4
16	53 47.9	27 53.5	40.8	193 22.8	26.0	46 39.3	53.9	23 32.1	56.1	Suhail	223 00.2	S43 26.0
17	68 50.4	42 53.1	42.0	208 25.2	26.1	61 41.2	54.2	38 34.3	56.2			
18	83 52.9	57 52.7	N10 43.2	223 27.7	S13 26.1	76 43.1	N 1 54.4	53 36.5	N 9 56.3	Vega	80 46.5	N38 46.8
19	98 55.3	72 52.4	44.4	238 30.1	26.1	91 45.0	54.6	68 38.7	56.4	Zuben'ubi	137 17.4	S16 02.2
20	113 57.8	87 52.0	45.6	253 32.5	26.1	106 46.9	54.9	83 40.9	56.5		SHA	Mer. Pass.
21	129 00.2	102 51.6 . .	46.8	268 34.9 . .	26.2	121 48.8 . .	55.1	98 43.1 . .	56.6	Venus	335 58.7	14 08
22	144 02.7	117 51.3	48.0	283 37.3	26.2	136 50.7	55.4	113 45.3	56.7	Mars	139 38.0	3 12
23	159 05.2	132 50.9	49.2	298 39.7	26.2	151 52.7	55.6	128 47.5	56.8	Jupiter	353 13.3	12 57
Mer. Pass. 12 29.3		v −0.4	d 1.2	v 2.4	d 0.0	v 1.9	d 0.2	v 2.2	d 0.1	Saturn	329 54.7	14 30

UT	SUN GHA	SUN Dec	MOON GHA	v	Dec	d	HP
d h	° ′	° ′	° ′	′	° ′	′	′
14 00	177 38.4	S 2 47.7	224 39.0	9.6	S17 36.5	5.0	56.9
01	192 38.6	46.8	239 07.6	9.5	17 31.5	5.2	56.9
02	207 38.7	45.8	253 36.1	9.6	17 26.3	5.2	57.0
03	222 38.9 ..	44.8	268 04.7	9.5	17 21.1	5.3	57.0
04	237 39.1	43.8	282 33.2	9.5	17 15.8	5.4	57.0
05	252 39.2	42.8	297 01.7	9.6	17 10.4	5.5	57.1
06	267 39.4 S 2	41.8	311 30.3	9.5	S17 04.9	5.6	57.1
07	282 39.6	40.8	325 58.8	9.5	16 59.3	5.7	57.1
08	297 39.7	39.9	340 27.3	9.4	16 53.6	5.8	57.2
S 09	312 39.9 ..	38.9	354 55.7	9.5	16 47.8	6.0	57.2
U 10	327 40.1	37.9	9 24.2	9.5	16 41.8	6.0	57.2
N 11	342 40.3	36.9	23 52.7	9.4	16 35.8	6.1	57.3
D 12	357 40.4 S 2	35.9	38 21.1	9.5	S16 29.7	6.2	57.3
A 13	12 40.6	34.9	52 49.6	9.4	16 23.5	6.3	57.3
Y 14	27 40.8	33.9	67 18.0	9.5	16 17.2	6.5	57.4
15	42 40.9 ..	33.0	81 46.5	9.4	16 10.7	6.5	57.4
16	57 41.1	32.0	96 14.9	9.4	16 04.2	6.6	57.4
17	72 41.3	31.0	110 43.3	9.4	15 57.6	6.7	57.5
18	87 41.5 S 2	30.0	125 11.7	9.4	S15 50.9	6.8	57.5
19	102 41.6	29.0	139 40.1	9.4	15 44.1	6.9	57.6
20	117 41.8	28.0	154 08.5	9.4	15 37.2	7.0	57.6
21	132 42.0 ..	27.0	168 36.9	9.4	15 30.2	7.1	57.6
22	147 42.2	26.0	183 05.3	9.3	15 23.1	7.2	57.7
23	162 42.3	25.1	197 33.6	9.4	15 15.9	7.3	57.7
15 00	177 42.5 S 2	24.1	212 02.0	9.4	S15 08.6	7.4	57.7
01	192 42.7	23.1	226 30.4	9.3	15 01.2	7.5	57.8
02	207 42.8	22.1	240 58.7	9.4	14 53.7	7.6	57.8
03	222 43.0 ..	21.1	255 27.1	9.4	14 46.1	7.6	57.8
04	237 43.2	20.1	269 55.5	9.3	14 38.5	7.8	57.9
05	252 43.4	19.1	284 23.8	9.4	14 30.7	7.9	57.9
06	267 43.5 S 2	18.2	298 52.2	9.3	S14 22.8	7.9	57.9
07	282 43.7	17.2	313 20.5	9.3	14 14.9	8.0	58.0
08	297 43.9	16.2	327 48.8	9.4	14 06.9	8.2	58.0
M 09	312 44.1 ..	15.2	342 17.2	9.3	13 58.7	8.2	58.0
O 10	327 44.2	14.2	356 45.5	9.3	13 50.5	8.3	58.1
N 11	342 44.4	13.2	11 13.8	9.4	13 42.2	8.4	58.1
D 12	357 44.6 S 2	12.2	25 42.2	9.3	S13 33.8	8.5	58.2
A 13	12 44.8	11.2	40 10.5	9.3	13 25.3	8.6	58.2
Y 14	27 44.9	10.3	54 38.8	9.3	13 16.7	8.6	58.2
15	42 45.1 ..	09.3	69 07.1	9.3	13 08.1	8.8	58.3
16	57 45.3	08.3	83 35.4	9.4	12 59.3	8.8	58.3
17	72 45.5	07.3	98 03.8	9.3	12 50.5	8.9	58.3
18	87 45.6 S 2	06.3	112 32.1	9.3	S12 41.6	9.0	58.4
19	102 45.8	05.3	127 00.4	9.3	12 32.6	9.1	58.4
20	117 46.0	04.3	141 28.7	9.3	12 23.5	9.2	58.4
21	132 46.1 ..	03.3	155 57.0	9.3	12 14.3	9.2	58.5
22	147 46.3	02.4	170 25.3	9.3	12 05.1	9.3	58.5
23	162 46.5	01.4	184 53.6	9.3	11 55.8	9.4	58.5
16 00	177 46.7 S 2	00.4	199 21.9	9.3	S11 46.4	9.5	58.6
01	192 46.8	1 59.4	213 50.2	9.3	11 36.9	9.6	58.6
02	207 47.0	58.4	228 18.5	9.3	11 27.3	9.6	58.6
03	222 47.2 ..	57.4	242 46.8	9.3	11 17.7	9.8	58.7
04	237 47.4	56.4	257 15.1	9.3	11 07.9	9.8	58.7
05	252 47.6	55.4	271 43.4	9.3	10 58.1	9.8	58.7
06	267 47.7 S 1	54.5	286 11.7	9.3	S10 48.3	10.0	58.8
07	282 47.9	53.5	300 40.0	9.3	10 38.3	10.0	58.8
08	297 48.1	52.5	315 08.3	9.3	10 28.3	10.1	58.8
T 09	312 48.3 ..	51.5	329 36.6	9.3	10 18.2	10.2	58.9
U 10	327 48.4	50.5	344 04.9	9.3	10 08.0	10.2	58.9
E 11	342 48.6	49.5	358 33.2	9.2	9 57.8	10.3	58.9
S 12	357 48.8 S 1	48.5	13 01.4	9.3	S 9 47.5	10.4	58.9
D 13	12 49.0	47.5	27 29.7	9.3	9 37.1	10.4	59.0
A 14	27 49.1	46.5	41 58.0	9.3	9 26.7	10.5	59.0
Y 15	42 49.3 ..	45.6	56 26.3	9.3	9 16.2	10.6	59.0
16	57 49.5	44.6	70 54.6	9.2	9 05.6	10.6	59.1
17	72 49.7	43.6	85 22.8	9.3	8 55.0	10.7	59.1
18	87 49.8 S 1	42.6	99 51.1	9.3	S 8 44.3	10.8	59.1
19	102 50.0	41.6	114 19.4	9.3	8 33.5	10.8	59.2
20	117 50.2	40.6	128 47.7	9.2	8 22.7	10.9	59.2
21	132 50.4 ..	39.6	143 15.9	9.3	8 11.8	10.9	59.2
22	147 50.5	38.6	157 44.2	9.2	8 00.9	11.0	59.2
23	162 50.7	37.7	172 12.4	9.3	S 7 49.9	11.1	59.3
	SD 16.1	d 1.0	SD 15.6		15.8		16.1

Twilight / Moonrise

Lat.	Naut.	Civil	Sunrise	14	15	16	17
°	h m	h m	h m	h m	h m	h m	h m
N 72	03 56	05 20	06 27	08 00	07 35	07 21	07 10
N 70	04 10	05 24	06 25	07 07	07 06	07 04	07 01
68	04 21	05 28	06 23	06 35	06 44	06 50	06 54
66	04 30	05 31	06 22	06 10	06 27	06 39	06 47
64	04 37	05 33	06 20	05 52	06 13	06 29	06 42
62	04 43	05 35	06 19	05 36	06 01	06 21	06 37
60	04 48	05 37	06 18	05 23	05 51	06 14	06 33
N 58	04 53	05 39	06 18	05 12	05 42	06 08	06 30
56	04 56	05 40	06 17	05 02	05 34	06 02	06 27
54	05 00	05 41	06 16	04 53	05 28	05 57	06 24
52	05 03	05 42	06 15	04 46	05 21	05 53	06 21
50	05 05	05 43	06 15	04 39	05 16	05 48	06 19
45	05 10	05 44	06 14	04 24	05 03	05 40	06 13
N 40	05 14	05 46	06 12	04 11	04 53	05 32	06 09
35	05 17	05 46	06 11	04 01	04 44	05 26	06 05
30	05 19	05 47	06 11	03 51	04 37	05 20	06 02
20	05 21	05 47	06 09	03 36	04 23	05 10	05 56
N 10	05 22	05 46	06 07	03 22	04 12	05 02	05 51
0	05 21	05 45	06 06	03 09	04 01	04 53	05 46
S 10	05 19	05 43	06 04	02 55	03 50	04 45	05 41
20	05 14	05 40	06 02	02 41	03 38	04 37	05 36
30	05 08	05 36	06 00	02 25	03 25	04 27	05 30
35	05 04	05 33	05 59	02 16	03 17	04 21	05 27
40	04 58	05 30	05 57	02 05	03 08	04 14	05 23
45	04 51	05 26	05 55	01 53	02 58	04 07	05 19
S 50	04 42	05 20	05 53	01 38	02 45	03 58	05 13
52	04 37	05 18	05 52	01 30	02 39	03 53	05 11
54	04 32	05 15	05 51	01 22	02 33	03 49	05 08
56	04 27	05 12	05 49	01 14	02 26	03 43	05 05
58	04 20	05 08	05 48	01 03	02 17	03 38	05 02
S 60	04 13	05 04	05 46	00 52	02 08	03 31	04 58

Twilight / Moonset

Lat.	Sunset	Civil	Naut.	14	15	16	17
°	h m	h m	h m	h m	h m	h m	h m
N 72	17 54	19 01	20 26	10 53	13 08	15 12	17 14
N 70	17 56	18 56	20 11	11 45	13 36	15 28	17 20
68	17 57	18 53	20 00	12 17	13 56	15 40	17 26
66	17 58	18 49	19 51	12 40	14 12	15 50	17 30
64	17 59	18 47	19 43	12 59	14 26	15 58	17 34
62	18 00	18 44	19 37	13 14	14 37	16 05	17 37
60	18 01	18 43	19 32	13 26	14 46	16 11	17 40
N 58	18 02	18 41	19 27	13 37	14 54	16 17	17 42
56	18 02	18 39	19 23	13 46	15 02	16 21	17 44
54	18 03	18 38	19 20	13 55	15 08	16 26	17 46
52	18 04	18 37	19 17	14 02	15 14	16 30	17 48
50	18 04	18 36	19 14	14 09	15 19	16 33	17 50
45	18 05	18 35	19 09	14 23	15 30	16 41	17 53
N 40	18 06	18 33	19 05	14 35	15 39	16 47	17 56
35	18 07	18 32	19 02	14 45	15 47	16 52	17 59
30	18 08	18 32	19 00	14 53	15 54	16 57	18 01
20	18 09	18 31	18 57	15 08	16 06	17 05	18 05
N 10	18 11	18 32	18 57	15 21	16 16	17 12	18 08
0	18 12	18 33	18 57	15 34	16 26	17 19	18 11
S 10	18 14	18 35	18 59	15 46	16 36	17 25	18 14
20	18 16	18 38	19 03	15 58	16 46	17 32	18 17
30	18 18	18 42	19 10	16 13	16 57	17 40	18 21
35	18 19	18 44	19 14	16 22	17 04	17 44	18 23
40	18 20	18 47	19 19	16 31	17 11	17 49	18 25
45	18 22	18 51	19 26	16 42	17 20	17 55	18 28
S 50	18 24	18 57	19 35	16 56	17 31	18 02	18 31
52	18 25	18 59	19 39	17 02	17 35	18 05	18 33
54	18 26	19 02	19 44	17 09	17 41	18 09	18 34
56	18 27	19 05	19 50	17 17	17 47	18 12	18 36
58	18 29	19 08	19 56	17 25	17 53	18 15	18 38
S 60	18 30	19 12	20 03	17 35	18 00	18 21	18 40

SUN / MOON

Day	Eqn. of Time 00ʰ	Eqn. of Time 12ʰ	Mer. Pass.	Mer. Pass. Upper	Mer. Pass. Lower	Age	Phase
d	m s	m s	h m	h m	h m	d	%
14	09 27	09 19	12 09	09 21	21 47	26	13
15	09 10	09 02	12 09	10 13	22 40	27	7
16	08 54	08 45	12 09	11 06	23 32	28	2

UT	ARIES GHA	VENUS −4.0 GHA	VENUS Dec	MARS −0.7 GHA	MARS Dec	JUPITER −2.1 GHA	JUPITER Dec	SATURN +0.5 GHA	SATURN Dec
17 00	174 07.6	147 50.5	N10 50.4	313 42.2	S13 26.3	166 54.6	N 1 55.8	143 49.7	N 9 56.9
01	189 10.1	162 50.2	51.6	328 44.6	26.3	181 56.5	56.1	158 51.9	57.0
02	204 12.6	177 49.8	52.8	343 47.0	26.3	196 58.4	56.3	173 54.1	57.1
03	219 15.0	192 49.4	.. 54.0	358 49.4	.. 26.3	212 00.3	.. 56.6	188 56.3	.. 57.2
04	234 17.5	207 49.0	55.2	13 51.9	26.4	227 02.2	56.8	203 58.5	57.3
05	249 20.0	222 48.7	56.4	28 54.3	26.4	242 04.1	57.0	219 00.7	57.4
W 06	264 22.4	237 48.3	N10 57.6	43 56.7	S13 26.4	257 06.0	N 1 57.3	234 02.9	N 9 57.5
E 07	279 24.9	252 47.9	10 58.8	58 59.1	26.4	272 08.0	57.5	249 05.1	57.6
D 08	294 27.4	267 47.6	11 00.0	74 01.6	26.5	287 09.9	57.7	264 07.3	57.7
N 09	309 29.8	282 47.2	.. 01.2	89 04.0	.. 26.5	302 11.8	.. 58.0	279 09.5	.. 57.8
E 10	324 32.3	297 46.8	02.4	104 06.4	26.5	317 13.7	58.2	294 11.7	57.9
S 11	339 34.7	312 46.4	03.6	119 08.9	26.5	332 15.6	58.5	309 13.9	58.0
D 12	354 37.2	327 46.1	N11 04.8	134 11.3	S13 26.6	347 17.5	N 1 58.7	324 16.1	N 9 58.1
A 13	9 39.7	342 45.7	06.0	149 13.7	26.6	2 19.4	58.9	339 18.3	58.3
Y 14	24 42.1	357 45.3	07.2	164 16.2	26.6	17 21.3	59.2	354 20.5	58.4
15	39 44.6	12 44.9	.. 08.4	179 18.6	.. 26.6	32 23.3	.. 59.4	9 22.7	.. 58.5
16	54 47.1	27 44.6	09.6	194 21.1	26.7	47 25.2	59.7	24 24.9	58.6
17	69 49.5	42 44.2	10.8	209 23.5	26.7	62 27.1	1 59.9	39 27.1	58.7
18	84 52.0	57 43.8	N11 12.0	224 26.0	S13 26.7	77 29.0	N 2 00.1	54 29.3	N 9 58.8
19	99 54.5	72 43.4	13.2	239 28.4	26.7	92 30.9	00.4	69 31.5	58.9
20	114 56.9	87 43.1	14.4	254 30.8	26.8	107 32.8	00.6	84 33.7	59.0
21	129 59.4	102 42.7	.. 15.6	269 33.3	.. 26.8	122 34.7	.. 00.8	99 35.9	.. 59.1
22	145 01.8	117 42.3	16.8	284 35.7	26.8	137 36.6	01.1	114 38.1	59.2
23	160 04.3	132 41.9	18.0	299 38.2	26.8	152 38.6	01.3	129 40.3	59.3
18 00	175 06.8	147 41.6	N11 19.1	314 40.6	S13 26.8	167 40.5	N 2 01.6	144 42.5	N 9 59.4
01	190 09.2	162 41.2	20.3	329 43.1	26.9	182 42.4	01.8	159 44.7	59.5
02	205 11.7	177 40.8	21.5	344 45.5	26.9	197 44.3	02.0	174 46.9	59.6
03	220 14.2	192 40.4	.. 22.7	359 48.0	.. 26.9	212 46.2	.. 02.3	189 49.1	.. 59.7
04	235 16.6	207 40.1	23.9	14 50.5	26.9	227 48.1	02.5	204 51.3	59.8
05	250 19.1	222 39.7	25.1	29 52.9	26.9	242 50.0	02.7	219 53.5	9 59.9
T 06	265 21.6	237 39.3	N11 26.3	44 55.4	S13 26.9	257 51.9	N 2 03.0	234 55.7	N10 00.0
H 07	280 24.0	252 38.9	27.5	59 57.8	27.0	272 53.9	03.2	249 57.9	00.1
U 08	295 26.5	267 38.5	28.7	75 00.3	27.0	287 55.8	03.5	265 00.1	00.2
R 09	310 29.0	282 38.2	.. 29.8	90 02.8	.. 27.0	302 57.7	.. 03.7	280 02.3	.. 00.3
S 10	325 31.4	297 37.8	31.0	105 05.2	27.0	317 59.6	03.9	295 04.5	00.4
D 11	340 33.9	312 37.4	32.2	120 07.7	27.0	333 01.5	04.2	310 06.7	00.5
A 12	355 36.3	327 37.0	N11 33.4	135 10.2	S13 27.0	348 03.4	N 2 04.4	325 08.9	N10 00.6
Y 13	10 38.8	342 36.6	34.6	150 12.6	27.1	3 05.3	04.7	340 11.1	00.7
14	25 41.3	357 36.3	35.8	165 15.1	27.1	18 07.2	04.9	355 13.3	00.8
15	40 43.7	12 35.9	.. 37.0	180 17.6	.. 27.1	33 09.1	.. 05.1	10 15.4	.. 00.9
16	55 46.2	27 35.5	38.1	195 20.0	27.1	48 11.1	05.4	25 17.6	01.0
17	70 48.7	42 35.1	39.3	210 22.5	27.1	63 13.0	05.6	40 19.8	01.1
18	85 51.1	57 34.7	N11 40.5	225 25.0	S13 27.1	78 14.9	N 2 05.8	55 22.0	N10 01.2
19	100 53.6	72 34.4	41.7	240 27.5	27.2	93 16.8	06.1	70 24.2	01.3
20	115 56.1	87 34.0	42.9	255 29.9	27.2	108 18.7	06.3	85 26.4	01.4
21	130 58.5	102 33.6	.. 44.0	270 32.4	.. 27.2	123 20.6	.. 06.6	100 28.6	.. 01.5
22	146 01.0	117 33.2	45.2	285 34.9	27.2	138 22.5	06.8	115 30.8	01.6
23	161 03.4	132 32.8	46.4	300 37.4	27.2	153 24.4	07.0	130 33.0	01.7
19 00	176 05.9	147 32.4	N11 47.6	315 39.8	S13 27.2	168 26.4	N 2 07.3	145 35.2	N10 01.8
01	191 08.4	162 32.1	48.8	330 42.3	27.2	183 28.3	07.5	160 37.4	01.9
02	206 10.8	177 31.7	49.9	345 44.8	27.2	198 30.2	07.8	175 39.6	02.0
03	221 13.3	192 31.3	.. 51.1	0 47.3	.. 27.3	213 32.1	.. 08.0	190 41.8	.. 02.1
04	236 15.8	207 30.9	52.3	15 49.8	27.3	228 34.0	08.2	205 44.0	02.3
05	251 18.2	222 30.5	53.5	30 52.3	27.3	243 35.9	08.5	220 46.2	02.4
F 06	266 20.7	237 30.1	N11 54.7	45 54.8	S13 27.3	258 37.8	N 2 08.7	235 48.4	N10 02.5
R 07	281 23.2	252 29.8	55.8	60 57.3	27.3	273 39.7	08.9	250 50.6	02.6
I 08	296 25.6	267 29.4	57.0	75 59.7	27.3	288 41.6	09.2	265 52.8	02.7
D 09	311 28.1	282 29.0	.. 58.2	91 02.2	.. 27.3	303 43.6	.. 09.4	280 55.0	.. 02.8
A 10	326 30.6	297 28.6	11 59.4	106 04.7	27.3	318 45.5	09.7	295 57.2	02.9
Y 11	341 33.0	312 28.2	12 00.5	121 07.2	27.3	333 47.4	09.9	310 59.4	03.0
12	356 35.5	327 27.8	N12 01.7	136 09.7	S13 27.3	348 49.3	N 2 10.1	326 01.6	N10 03.1
13	11 37.9	342 27.4	02.9	151 12.2	27.3	3 51.2	10.4	341 03.8	03.2
14	26 40.4	357 27.1	04.1	166 14.7	27.4	18 53.1	10.6	356 05.9	03.3
15	41 42.9	12 26.7	.. 05.2	181 17.2	.. 27.4	33 55.0	.. 10.9	11 08.1	.. 03.4
16	56 45.3	27 26.3	06.4	196 19.7	27.4	48 56.9	11.1	26 10.3	03.5
17	71 47.8	42 25.9	07.6	211 22.2	27.4	63 58.8	11.3	41 12.5	03.6
18	86 50.3	57 25.5	N12 08.7	226 24.7	S13 27.4	79 00.8	N 2 11.6	56 14.7	N10 03.7
19	101 52.7	72 25.1	09.9	241 27.2	27.4	94 02.7	11.8	71 16.9	03.8
20	116 55.2	87 24.7	11.1	256 29.7	27.4	109 04.6	12.0	86 19.1	03.9
21	131 57.7	102 24.3	.. 12.3	271 32.3	.. 27.4	124 06.5	.. 12.3	101 21.3	.. 04.0
22	147 00.1	117 23.9	13.4	286 34.8	27.4	139 08.4	12.5	116 23.5	04.1
23	162 02.6	132 23.6	14.6	301 37.3	27.4	154 10.3	12.8	131 25.7	04.2
Mer.Pass.	12h 17.5m	v −0.4	d 1.2	v 2.5	d 0.0	v 1.9	d 0.2	v 2.2	d 0.1

STARS

Name	SHA	Dec
Acamar	315 27.0	S40 18.9
Achernar	335 35.5	S57 14.8
Acrux	173 20.9	S63 05.6
Adhara	255 21.1	S28 58.6
Aldebaran	291 02.1	N16 30.3
Alioth	166 29.8	N55 57.8
Alkaid	153 07.2	N49 18.9
Al Na'ir	27 58.0	S46 57.9
Alnilam	275 57.6	S 1 12.4
Alphard	218 06.7	S 8 39.5
Alphecca	126 20.2	N26 42.9
Alpheratz	357 55.3	N29 05.0
Altair	62 19.1	N 8 51.9
Ankaa	353 27.0	S42 18.8
Antares	112 39.7	S26 25.7
Arcturus	146 05.5	N19 11.1
Atria	107 51.3	S69 01.2
Avior	234 22.1	S59 30.7
Bellatrix	278 43.9	N 6 20.7
Betelgeuse	271 13.2	N 7 24.2
Canopus	264 01.0	S52 42.1
Capella	280 50.8	N45 59.8
Deneb	49 39.3	N45 16.4
Denebola	182 44.6	N14 34.5
Diphda	349 07.3	S17 59.7
Dubhe	194 04.5	N61 45.3
Elnath	278 26.6	N28 36.3
Eltanin	90 51.3	N51 29.1
Enif	33 58.2	N 9 52.1
Fomalhaut	15 36.5	S29 37.7
Gacrux	172 12.6	S57 06.5
Gienah	176 03.3	S17 32.3
Hadar	149 03.0	S60 21.9
Hamal	328 13.5	N23 27.4
Kaus Aust.	83 58.5	S34 22.9
Kochab	137 18.9	N74 09.4
Markab	13 49.6	N15 11.9
Menkar	314 26.8	N 4 05.0
Menkent	148 20.3	S36 21.9
Miaplacidus	221 41.2	S69 43.1
Mirfak	308 56.4	N49 51.5
Nunki	76 12.1	S26 17.8
Peacock	53 36.9	S56 44.1
Pollux	243 41.0	N28 01.6
Procyon	245 11.1	N 5 13.4
Rasalhague	96 16.7	N12 33.5
Regulus	207 55.0	N11 58.2
Rigel	281 22.7	S 8 12.5
Rigil Kent.	140 06.4	S60 49.6
Sabik	102 25.1	S15 43.4
Schedar	349 53.6	N56 31.9
Shaula	96 36.9	S37 06.0
Sirius	258 43.4	S16 43.2
Spica	158 42.6	S11 09.4
Suhail	223 00.2	S43 26.0
Vega	80 46.5	N38 46.8
Zuben'ubi	137 17.4	S16 02.3

	SHA	Mer. Pass.
Venus	332 34.8	14 10
Mars	139 33.9	3 01
Jupiter	352 33.7	12 48
Saturn	329 35.7	14 19

SUN / MOON

UT	SUN GHA	Dec	MOON GHA	v	Dec	d	HP
d h	° '	° '	° '	'	° '	'	'
17 00	177 50.9	S 1 36.7	186 40.7	9.3	S 7 38.8	11.1	59.3
01	192 51.1	35.7	201 09.0	9.2	7 27.7	11.2	59.3
02	207 51.3	34.7	215 37.2	9.2	7 16.5	11.2	59.4
03	222 51.4	.. 33.7	230 05.4	9.3	7 05.3	11.3	59.4
04	237 51.6	32.7	244 33.7	9.2	6 54.0	11.3	59.4
05	252 51.8	31.7	259 01.9	9.3	6 42.7	11.4	59.4
06	267 52.0	S 1 30.7	273 30.2	9.2	S 6 31.3	11.4	59.5
W 07	282 52.1	29.7	287 58.4	9.2	6 19.9	11.4	59.5
E 08	297 52.3	28.8	302 26.6	9.2	6 08.5	11.6	59.5
D 09	312 52.5	.. 27.8	316 54.8	9.3	5 56.9	11.5	59.5
N 10	327 52.7	26.8	331 23.1	9.2	5 45.4	11.6	59.6
E 11	342 52.9	25.8	345 51.3	9.2	5 33.8	11.7	59.6
S 12	357 53.0	S 1 24.8	0 19.5	9.2	S 5 22.1	11.7	59.6
D 13	12 53.2	23.8	14 47.7	9.2	5 10.4	11.7	59.6
A 14	27 53.4	22.8	29 15.9	9.1	4 58.7	11.8	59.7
Y 15	42 53.6	.. 21.8	43 44.0	9.2	4 46.9	11.8	59.7
16	57 53.8	20.8	58 12.2	9.2	4 35.1	11.8	59.7
17	72 53.9	19.9	72 40.4	9.1	4 23.3	11.9	59.7
18	87 54.1	S 1 18.9	87 08.5	9.2	S 4 11.4	11.9	59.8
19	102 54.3	17.9	101 36.7	9.1	3 59.5	12.0	59.8
20	117 54.5	16.9	116 04.8	9.2	3 47.5	12.0	59.8
21	132 54.6	.. 15.9	130 33.0	9.1	3 35.5	12.0	59.8
22	147 54.8	14.9	145 01.1	9.1	3 23.5	12.0	59.9
23	162 55.0	13.9	159 29.2	9.1	3 11.5	12.1	59.9
18 00	177 55.2	S 1 12.9	173 57.3	9.1	S 2 59.4	12.1	59.9
01	192 55.4	12.0	188 25.4	9.1	2 47.3	12.1	59.9
02	207 55.5	11.0	202 53.5	9.1	2 35.2	12.1	59.9
03	222 55.7	.. 10.0	217 21.6	9.1	2 23.1	12.2	59.9
04	237 55.9	09.0	231 49.7	9.0	2 10.9	12.2	59.9
05	252 56.1	08.0	246 17.7	9.1	1 58.7	12.2	60.0
06	267 56.3	S 1 07.0	260 45.8	9.0	S 1 46.5	12.2	60.0
T 07	282 56.4	06.0	275 13.8	9.0	1 34.3	12.2	60.0
H 08	297 56.6	05.0	289 41.8	9.1	1 22.1	12.3	60.0
U 09	312 56.8	.. 04.0	304 09.9	8.9	1 09.8	12.2	60.0
R 10	327 57.0	03.1	318 37.8	9.0	0 57.6	12.3	60.1
S 11	342 57.2	02.1	333 05.8	9.0	0 45.3	12.3	60.1
D 12	357 57.3	S 1 01.1	347 33.8	9.0	S 0 33.0	12.3	60.1
A 13	12 57.5	1 00.1	2 01.8	8.9	0 20.7	12.3	60.1
Y 14	27 57.7	0 59.1	16 29.7	8.9	S 0 08.4	12.3	60.1
15	42 57.9	.. 58.1	30 57.6	8.9	N 0 03.9	12.3	60.1
16	57 58.0	57.1	45 25.5	8.9	0 16.2	12.4	60.1
17	72 58.2	56.1	59 53.4	8.9	0 28.6	12.3	60.2
18	87 58.4	S 0 55.1	74 21.3	8.9	N 0 40.9	12.3	60.2
19	102 58.6	54.2	88 49.2	8.8	0 53.2	12.3	60.2
20	117 58.8	53.2	103 17.0	8.9	1 05.5	12.3	60.2
21	132 59.0	.. 52.2	117 44.9	8.8	1 17.8	12.4	60.2
22	147 59.2	51.2	132 12.7	8.8	1 30.2	12.3	60.2
23	162 59.3	50.2	146 40.5	8.7	1 42.5	12.3	60.2
19 00	177 59.5	S 0 49.2	161 08.2	8.8	N 1 54.8	12.3	60.2
01	192 59.7	48.2	175 36.0	8.7	2 07.1	12.3	60.3
02	207 59.9	47.2	190 03.7	8.8	2 19.4	12.3	60.3
03	223 00.1	.. 46.2	204 31.5	8.7	2 31.7	12.3	60.3
04	238 00.2	45.3	218 59.2	8.6	2 43.9	12.3	60.3
05	253 00.4	44.3	233 26.8	8.7	2 56.2	12.2	60.3
06	268 00.6	S 0 43.3	247 54.5	8.6	N 3 08.4	12.2	60.3
07	283 00.8	42.3	262 22.1	8.7	3 20.6	12.2	60.3
08	298 01.0	41.3	276 49.8	8.6	3 32.8	12.2	60.3
F 09	313 01.1	.. 40.3	291 17.4	8.5	3 45.0	12.2	60.3
R 10	328 01.3	39.3	305 44.9	8.6	3 57.2	12.1	60.3
I 11	343 01.5	38.3	320 12.5	8.5	4 09.3	12.1	60.3
D 12	358 01.7	S 0 37.3	334 40.0	8.5	N 4 21.4	12.1	60.3
A 13	13 01.9	36.4	349 07.5	8.5	4 33.5	12.1	60.3
Y 14	28 02.1	35.4	3 35.0	8.5	4 45.6	12.0	60.3
15	43 02.2	.. 34.4	18 02.5	8.4	4 57.6	12.0	60.3
16	58 02.4	33.4	32 29.9	8.4	5 09.6	12.0	60.4
17	73 02.6	32.4	46 57.3	8.4	5 21.6	12.0	60.4
18	88 02.8	S 0 31.4	61 24.7	8.4	N 5 33.6	11.9	60.4
19	103 03.0	30.4	75 52.1	8.3	5 45.5	11.9	60.4
20	118 03.2	29.4	90 19.4	8.3	5 57.4	11.8	60.4
21	133 03.3	.. 28.4	104 46.7	8.3	6 09.2	11.8	60.4
22	148 03.5	27.5	119 14.0	8.3	6 21.0	11.8	60.4
23	163 03.7	26.5	133 41.3	8.2	N 6 32.8	11.7	60.4
	SD 16.1	d 1.0	SD 16.2		16.4		16.4

Twilight / Moonrise

Lat.	Naut.	Civil	Sunrise	17	18	19	20
°	h m	h m	h m	h m	h m	h m	h m
N 72	03 38	05 04	06 11	07 10	07 01	06 51	06 42
N 70	03 54	05 10	06 11	07 01	06 58	06 56	06 53
68	04 07	05 15	06 10	06 54	06 56	06 59	07 02
66	04 17	05 19	06 10	06 47	06 55	07 02	07 10
64	04 26	05 23	06 10	06 42	06 53	07 05	07 17
62	04 33	05 25	06 10	06 37	06 52	07 07	07 22
60	04 39	05 28	06 09	06 33	06 51	07 09	07 28
N 58	04 44	05 30	06 09	06 30	06 50	07 10	07 32
56	04 48	05 32	06 09	06 27	06 49	07 12	07 36
54	04 52	05 34	06 09	06 24	06 49	07 13	07 40
52	04 55	05 35	06 09	06 21	06 48	07 15	07 43
50	04 58	05 36	06 08	06 19	06 47	07 16	07 46
45	05 05	05 39	06 08	06 13	06 46	07 18	07 52
N 40	05 09	05 41	06 08	06 09	06 45	07 21	07 58
35	05 13	05 42	06 07	06 05	06 44	07 23	08 02
30	05 15	05 43	06 07	06 02	06 43	07 24	08 07
20	05 19	05 44	06 06	05 56	06 41	07 27	08 14
N 10	05 20	05 45	06 06	05 51	06 40	07 30	08 20
0	05 20	05 44	06 05	05 46	06 39	07 32	08 27
S 10	05 19	05 43	06 04	05 41	06 38	07 35	08 33
20	05 15	05 41	06 03	05 36	06 37	07 38	08 39
30	05 10	05 38	06 02	05 30	06 35	07 41	08 47
35	05 06	05 36	06 01	05 27	06 34	07 43	08 52
40	05 01	05 33	06 00	05 23	06 33	07 45	08 57
45	04 55	05 30	05 59	05 19	06 32	07 47	09 02
S 50	04 47	05 25	05 58	05 13	06 31	07 50	09 10
52	04 43	05 23	05 57	05 11	06 31	07 52	09 13
54	04 39	05 21	05 56	05 08	06 30	07 53	09 17
56	04 34	05 18	05 56	05 05	06 29	07 55	09 21
58	04 28	05 15	05 55	05 02	06 28	07 57	09 25
S 60	04 21	05 12	05 54	04 58	06 28	07 59	09 30

Sunset / Twilight / Moonset

Lat.	Sunset	Civil	Naut.	17	18	19	20
°	h m	h m	h m	h m	h m	h m	h m
N 72	18 08	19 16	20 43	17 14	19 15	21 17	23 24
N 70	18 08	19 09	20 26	17 20	19 14	21 08	23 05
68	18 08	19 04	20 13	17 26	19 13	21 01	22 50
66	18 08	18 59	20 02	17 30	19 12	20 55	22 38
64	18 08	18 56	19 53	17 34	19 11	20 50	22 28
62	18 08	18 53	19 46	17 37	19 11	20 45	22 20
60	18 08	18 50	19 40	17 40	19 10	20 41	22 13
N 58	18 09	18 48	19 34	17 42	19 10	20 38	22 06
56	18 09	18 46	19 30	17 44	19 09	20 35	22 01
54	18 09	18 44	19 26	17 46	19 09	20 32	21 56
52	18 09	18 43	19 22	17 48	19 08	20 30	21 51
50	18 09	18 41	19 19	17 50	19 08	20 28	21 47
45	18 09	18 38	19 13	17 53	19 08	20 23	21 38
N 40	18 09	18 36	19 08	17 56	19 07	20 19	21 31
35	18 10	18 35	19 04	17 59	19 07	20 15	21 24
30	18 10	18 34	19 02	18 01	19 06	20 12	21 19
20	18 10	18 32	18 58	18 05	19 06	20 07	21 09
N 10	18 11	18 32	18 56	18 08	19 05	20 02	21 01
0	18 11	18 32	18 56	18 11	19 04	19 58	20 53
S 10	18 12	18 33	18 58	18 14	19 04	19 54	20 45
20	18 13	18 35	19 01	18 17	19 03	19 49	20 37
30	18 14	18 38	19 06	18 21	19 02	19 44	20 27
35	18 15	18 40	19 10	18 23	19 01	19 41	20 22
40	18 16	18 43	19 14	18 25	19 01	19 37	20 15
45	18 16	18 46	19 20	18 28	19 00	19 33	20 08
S 50	18 18	18 50	19 28	18 31	18 59	19 28	20 00
52	18 18	18 52	19 32	18 33	18 59	19 26	19 56
54	18 19	18 54	19 36	18 34	18 59	19 24	19 51
56	18 19	18 57	19 41	18 36	18 58	19 21	19 46
58	18 20	19 00	19 47	18 38	18 58	19 19	19 41
S 60	18 21	19 03	19 53	18 40	18 57	19 15	19 35

SUN / MOON

Day	Eqn. of Time 00h	Eqn. of Time 12h	Mer. Pass.	Mer. Pass. Upper	Mer. Pass. Lower	Age	Phase
d	m s	m s	h m	h m	h m	d	%
17	08 37	08 28	12 08	11 59	24 25	29	0
18	08 20	08 11	12 08	12 52	00 25	01	1
19	08 02	07 54	12 08	13 45	01 18	02	4

UT	ARIES GHA	VENUS −4.0 GHA	Dec	MARS −0.7 GHA	Dec	JUPITER −2.1 GHA	Dec	SATURN +0.5 GHA	Dec
20 00	177 05.0	147 23.2	N12 15.8	316 39.8	S13 27.4	169 12.2	N 2 13.0	146 27.9	N10 04.3
01	192 07.5	162 22.8	16.9	331 42.3	27.4	184 14.1	13.2	161 30.1	04.4
02	207 10.0	177 22.4	18.1	346 44.8	27.4	199 16.0	13.5	176 32.3	04.5
03	222 12.4	192 22.0 ..	19.3	1 47.3 ..	27.4	214 18.0 ..	13.7	191 34.5 ..	04.6
04	237 14.9	207 21.6	20.4	16 49.9	27.4	229 19.9	13.9	206 36.7	04.7
05	252 17.4	222 21.2	21.6	31 52.4	27.4	244 21.8	14.2	221 38.9	04.8
S 06	267 19.8	237 20.8	N12 22.8	46 54.9	S13 27.4	259 23.7	N 2 14.4	236 41.1	N10 04.9
A 07	282 22.3	252 20.4	23.9	61 57.4	27.4	274 25.6	14.7	251 43.2	05.0
T 08	297 24.8	267 20.0	25.1	76 59.9	27.4	289 27.5	14.9	266 45.4	05.1
U 09	312 27.2	282 19.6 ..	26.3	92 02.5 ..	27.4	304 29.4 ..	15.1	281 47.6 ..	05.2
R 10	327 29.7	297 19.2	27.4	107 05.0	27.4	319 31.3	15.4	296 49.8	05.3
D 11	342 32.2	312 18.9	28.6	122 07.5	27.4	334 33.2	15.6	311 52.0	05.5
A 12	357 34.6	327 18.5	N12 29.7	137 10.0	S13 27.4	349 35.1	N 2 15.9	326 54.2	N10 05.6
Y 13	12 37.1	342 18.1	30.9	152 12.6	27.4	4 37.1	16.1	341 56.4	05.7
14	27 39.5	357 17.7	32.1	167 15.1	27.4	19 39.0	16.3	356 58.6	05.8
15	42 42.0	12 17.3 ..	33.2	182 17.6 ..	27.4	34 40.9 ..	16.6	12 00.8 ..	05.9
16	57 44.5	27 16.9	34.4	197 20.2	27.4	49 42.8	16.8	27 03.0	06.0
17	72 46.9	42 16.5	35.6	212 22.7	27.4	64 44.7	17.0	42 05.2	06.1
18	87 49.4	57 16.1	N12 36.7	227 25.2	S13 27.4	79 46.6	N 2 17.3	57 07.4	N10 06.2
19	102 51.9	72 15.7	37.9	242 27.8	27.4	94 48.5	17.5	72 09.6	06.3
20	117 54.3	87 15.3	39.0	257 30.3	27.4	109 50.4	17.8	87 11.8	06.4
21	132 56.8	102 14.9 ..	40.2	272 32.8 ..	27.4	124 52.3 ..	18.0	102 13.9 ..	06.5
22	147 59.3	117 14.5	41.3	287 35.4	27.4	139 54.3	18.2	117 16.1	06.6
23	163 01.7	132 14.1	42.5	302 37.9	27.4	154 56.2	18.5	132 18.3	06.7
21 00	178 04.2	147 13.7	N12 43.7	317 40.5	S13 27.4	169 58.1	N 2 18.7	147 20.5	N10 06.8
01	193 06.7	162 13.3	44.8	332 43.0	27.4	185 00.0	19.0	162 22.7	06.9
02	208 09.1	177 12.9	46.0	347 45.6	27.4	200 01.9	19.2	177 24.9	07.0
03	223 11.6	192 12.5 ..	47.1	2 48.1 ..	27.4	215 03.8 ..	19.4	192 27.1 ..	07.1
04	238 14.0	207 12.1	48.3	17 50.7	27.4	230 05.7	19.7	207 29.3	07.2
05	253 16.5	222 11.7	49.4	32 53.2	27.4	245 07.6	19.9	222 31.5	07.3
S 06	268 19.0	237 11.3	N12 50.6	47 55.8	S13 27.4	260 09.5	N 2 20.1	237 33.7	N10 07.4
U 07	283 21.4	252 10.9	51.7	62 58.3	27.4	275 11.4	20.4	252 35.9	07.5
N 08	298 23.9	267 10.5	52.9	78 00.9	27.4	290 13.4	20.6	267 38.1	07.6
D 09	313 26.4	282 10.1 ..	54.0	93 03.4 ..	27.4	305 15.3 ..	20.9	282 40.3 ..	07.7
A 10	328 28.8	297 09.7	55.2	108 06.0	27.4	320 17.2	21.1	297 42.4	07.8
Y 11	343 31.3	312 09.3	56.3	123 08.5	27.4	335 19.1	21.3	312 44.6	07.9
12	358 33.8	327 08.9	N12 57.5	138 11.1	S13 27.3	350 21.0	N 2 21.6	327 46.8	N10 08.0
13	13 36.2	342 08.5	58.6	153 13.7	27.3	5 22.9	21.8	342 49.0	08.1
14	28 38.7	357 08.1	12 59.8	168 16.2	27.3	20 24.8	22.1	357 51.2	08.2
15	43 41.1	12 07.7	13 00.9	183 18.8 ..	27.3	35 26.7 ..	22.3	12 53.4 ..	08.4
16	58 43.6	27 07.3	02.1	198 21.3	27.3	50 28.6	22.5	27 55.6	08.5
17	73 46.1	42 06.9	03.2	213 23.9	27.3	65 30.5	22.8	42 57.8	08.6
18	88 48.5	57 06.5	N13 04.4	228 26.5	S13 27.3	80 32.5	N 2 23.0	58 00.0	N10 08.7
19	103 51.0	72 06.1	05.5	243 29.0	27.3	95 34.4	23.2	73 02.2	08.8
20	118 53.5	87 05.7	06.7	258 31.6	27.3	110 36.3	23.5	88 04.4	08.9
21	133 55.9	102 05.3 ..	07.8	273 34.2 ..	27.3	125 38.2 ..	23.7	103 06.5 ..	09.0
22	148 58.4	117 04.9	09.0	288 36.8	27.2	140 40.1	24.0	118 08.7	09.1
23	164 00.9	132 04.5	10.1	303 39.3	27.2	155 42.0	24.2	133 10.9	09.2
22 00	179 03.3	147 04.1	N13 11.3	318 41.9	S13 27.2	170 43.9	N 2 24.4	148 13.1	N10 09.3
01	194 05.8	162 03.7	12.4	333 44.5	27.2	185 45.8	24.7	163 15.3	09.4
02	209 08.3	177 03.3	13.5	348 47.1	27.2	200 47.7	24.9	178 17.5	09.5
03	224 10.7	192 02.9 ..	14.7	3 49.6 ..	27.2	215 49.6 ..	25.2	193 19.7 ..	09.6
04	239 13.2	207 02.5	15.8	18 52.2	27.2	230 51.5	25.4	208 21.9	09.7
05	254 15.6	222 02.1	17.0	33 54.8	27.2	245 53.5	25.6	223 24.1	09.8
M 06	269 18.1	237 01.7	N13 18.1	48 57.4	S13 27.1	260 55.4	N 2 25.9	238 26.3	N10 09.9
O 07	284 20.6	252 01.3	19.2	64 00.0	27.1	275 57.3	26.1	253 28.4	10.0
N 08	299 23.0	267 00.9	20.4	79 02.5	27.1	290 59.2	26.3	268 30.6	10.1
D 09	314 25.5	282 00.4 ..	21.5	94 05.1 ..	27.1	306 01.1 ..	26.6	283 32.8 ..	10.2
A 10	329 28.0	297 00.0	22.7	109 07.7	27.1	321 03.0	26.8	298 35.0	10.3
Y 11	344 30.4	311 59.6	23.8	124 10.3	27.1	336 04.9	27.1	313 37.2	10.4
12	359 32.9	326 59.2	N13 24.9	139 12.9	S13 27.1	351 06.8	N 2 27.3	328 39.4	N10 10.5
13	14 35.4	341 58.8	26.1	154 15.5	27.0	6 08.7	27.5	343 41.6	10.6
14	29 37.8	356 58.4	27.2	169 18.1	27.0	21 10.6	27.8	358 43.8	10.7
15	44 40.3	11 58.0 ..	28.4	184 20.7 ..	27.0	36 12.6 ..	28.0	13 46.0 ..	10.8
16	59 42.8	26 57.6	29.5	199 23.3	27.0	51 14.5	28.3	28 48.2	11.0
17	74 45.2	41 57.2	30.6	214 25.9	27.0	66 16.4	28.5	43 50.3	11.1
18	89 47.7	56 56.8	N13 31.8	229 28.5	S13 27.0	81 18.3	N 2 28.7	58 52.5	N10 11.2
19	104 50.1	71 56.4	32.9	244 31.1	26.9	96 20.2	29.0	73 54.7	11.3
20	119 52.6	86 55.9	34.0	259 33.7	26.9	111 22.1	29.2	88 56.9	11.4
21	134 55.1	101 55.5 ..	35.2	274 36.3 ..	26.9	126 24.0 ..	29.4	103 59.1 ..	11.5
22	149 57.5	116 55.1	36.3	289 38.9	26.9	141 25.9	29.7	119 01.3	11.6
23	165 00.0	131 54.7	37.4	304 41.5	26.9	156 27.8	29.9	134 03.5	11.7
Mer. Pass. 12 05.7		v −0.4	d 1.1	v 2.6	d 0.0	v 1.9	d 0.2	v 2.2	d 0.1

STARS

Name	SHA	Dec
Acamar	315 27.0	S40 18.8
Achernar	335 35.5	S57 14.7
Acrux	173 20.9	S63 05.6
Adhara	255 21.1	S28 58.6
Aldebaran	291 02.2	N16 30.3
Alioth	166 29.8	N55 57.8
Alkaid	153 07.2	N49 18.9
Al Na'ir	27 58.0	S46 57.9
Alnilam	275 57.6	S 1 12.4
Alphard	218 06.7	S 8 39.5
Alphecca	126 20.1	N26 42.9
Alpheratz	357 55.3	N29 05.0
Altair	62 19.1	N 8 51.9
Ankaa	353 27.0	S42 18.8
Antares	112 39.7	S26 25.7
Arcturus	146 05.5	N19 11.1
Atria	107 51.3	S69 01.2
Avior	234 22.1	S59 30.8
Bellatrix	278 43.9	N 6 20.7
Betelgeuse	271 13.2	N 7 24.2
Canopus	264 01.0	S52 42.1
Capella	280 50.8	N45 59.8
Deneb	49 39.3	N45 16.4
Denebola	182 44.6	N14 34.5
Diphda	349 07.3	S17 59.7
Dubhe	194 04.6	N61 45.4
Elnath	278 26.6	N28 36.3
Eltanin	90 51.3	N51 29.1
Enif	33 58.2	N 9 52.1
Fomalhaut	15 36.5	S29 37.7
Gacrux	172 12.6	S57 06.5
Gienah	176 03.3	S17 32.3
Hadar	149 03.0	S60 22.0
Hamal	328 13.5	N23 27.3
Kaus Aust.	83 58.5	S34 22.9
Kochab	137 18.8	N74 09.4
Markab	13 49.6	N15 11.9
Menkar	314 26.8	N 4 05.0
Menkent	148 20.3	S36 21.9
Miaplacidus	221 41.3	S69 43.1
Mirfak	308 56.5	N49 51.5
Nunki	76 12.1	S26 17.8
Peacock	53 36.9	S56 44.1
Pollux	243 41.1	N28 01.6
Procyon	245 11.1	N 5 13.4
Rasalhague	96 16.7	N12 33.5
Regulus	207 55.0	N11 58.2
Rigel	281 22.7	S 8 12.5
Rigil Kent.	140 06.4	S60 49.7
Sabik	102 25.1	S15 43.4
Schedar	349 53.7	N56 31.9
Shaula	96 36.8	S37 06.0
Sirius	258 43.4	S16 43.2
Spica	158 42.6	S11 09.4
Suhail	223 00.2	S43 26.0
Vega	80 46.5	N38 46.8
Zuben'ubi	137 17.4	S16 02.3

	SHA	Mer. Pass.
	° ′	h m
Venus	329 09.5	14 11
Mars	139 36.3	2 49
Jupiter	351 53.9	12 39
Saturn	329 16.3	14 09

UT	SUN GHA	SUN Dec	MOON GHA	v	Dec	d	HP
d h	° ′	° ′	° ′	′	° ′	′	′
20 00	178 03.9	S 0 25.5	148 08.5	8.2	N 6 44.5	11.6	60.4
01	193 04.1	24.5	162 35.7	8.2	6 56.1	11.7	60.4
02	208 04.2	23.5	177 02.9	8.2	7 07.8	11.6	60.4
03	223 04.4	.. 22.5	191 30.1	8.1	7 19.4	11.5	60.4
04	238 04.6	21.5	205 57.2	8.1	7 30.9	11.5	60.4
05	253 04.8	20.5	220 24.3	8.1	7 42.4	11.4	60.4
06	268 05.0	S 0 19.5	234 51.4	8.1	N 7 53.8	11.4	60.4
07	283 05.2	18.6	249 18.5	8.0	8 05.2	11.4	60.4
S 08	298 05.3	17.6	263 45.5	8.0	8 16.6	11.3	60.3
A 09	313 05.5	.. 16.6	278 12.5	8.0	8 27.9	11.2	60.3
T 10	328 05.7	15.6	292 39.5	7.9	8 39.1	11.2	60.3
U 11	343 05.9	14.6	307 06.4	7.9	8 50.3	11.1	60.3
R 12	358 06.1	S 0 13.6	321 33.3	7.9	N 9 01.4	11.0	60.3
D 13	13 06.3	12.6	336 00.2	7.8	9 12.4	11.0	60.3
A 14	28 06.5	11.6	350 27.0	7.9	9 23.4	11.0	60.3
Y 15	43 06.6	.. 10.6	4 53.9	7.8	9 34.4	10.8	60.3
16	58 06.8	09.7	19 20.7	7.7	9 45.2	10.8	60.3
17	73 07.0	08.7	33 47.4	7.8	9 56.0	10.8	60.3
18	88 07.2	S 0 07.7	48 14.2	7.7	N10 06.8	10.6	60.3
19	103 07.4	06.7	62 40.9	7.7	10 17.4	10.7	60.3
20	118 07.6	05.7	77 07.6	7.6	10 28.1	10.5	60.3
21	133 07.7	.. 04.7	91 34.2	7.6	10 38.6	10.4	60.3
22	148 07.9	03.7	106 00.8	7.6	10 49.0	10.4	60.3
23	163 08.1	02.7	120 27.4	7.6	10 59.4	10.4	60.3
21 00	178 08.3	S 0 01.8	134 54.0	7.5	N11 09.8	10.2	60.3
01	193 08.5	S 00.8	149 20.5	7.6	11 20.0	10.2	60.2
02	208 08.7	N 00.2	163 47.1	7.4	11 30.2	10.1	60.2
03	223 08.8	.. 01.2	178 13.5	7.5	11 40.3	10.0	60.2
04	238 09.0	02.2	192 40.0	7.4	11 50.3	9.9	60.2
05	253 09.2	03.2	207 06.4	7.4	12 00.2	9.8	60.2
06	268 09.4	N 0 04.2	221 32.8	7.4	N12 10.0	9.8	60.2
07	283 09.6	05.2	235 59.2	7.3	12 19.8	9.7	60.2
S 08	298 09.8	06.2	250 25.5	7.3	12 29.5	9.6	60.2
U 09	313 10.0	.. 07.1	264 51.8	7.3	12 39.1	9.5	60.2
N 10	328 10.1	08.1	279 18.1	7.2	12 48.6	9.4	60.1
D 11	343 10.3	09.1	293 44.3	7.3	12 58.0	9.4	60.1
A 12	358 10.5	N 0 10.1	308 10.6	7.2	N13 07.4	9.2	60.1
Y 13	13 10.7	11.1	322 36.8	7.1	13 16.6	9.2	60.1
14	28 10.9	12.1	337 02.9	7.2	13 25.8	9.1	60.1
15	43 11.1	.. 13.1	351 29.1	7.1	13 34.9	8.9	60.1
16	58 11.3	14.1	5 55.2	7.1	13 43.8	8.9	60.1
17	73 11.4	15.0	20 21.3	7.0	13 52.7	8.8	60.1
18	88 11.6	N 0 16.0	34 47.3	7.1	N14 01.5	8.7	60.0
19	103 11.8	17.0	49 13.4	7.0	14 10.2	8.6	60.0
20	118 12.0	18.0	63 39.4	7.0	14 18.8	8.5	60.0
21	133 12.2	.. 19.0	78 05.4	6.9	14 27.3	8.4	60.0
22	148 12.4	20.0	92 31.3	7.0	14 35.7	8.3	60.0
23	163 12.6	21.0	106 57.3	6.9	14 44.0	8.2	60.0
22 00	178 12.7	N 0 22.0	121 23.2	6.9	N14 52.2	8.1	59.9
01	193 12.9	22.9	135 49.1	6.8	15 00.3	8.0	59.9
02	208 13.1	23.9	150 14.9	6.9	15 08.3	7.9	59.9
03	223 13.3	.. 24.9	164 40.8	6.8	15 16.2	7.8	59.9
04	238 13.5	25.9	179 06.6	6.8	15 24.0	7.7	59.9
05	253 13.7	26.9	193 32.4	6.8	15 31.7	7.6	59.9
06	268 13.9	N 0 27.9	207 58.2	6.7	N15 39.3	7.4	59.8
07	283 14.0	28.9	222 23.9	6.8	15 46.7	7.4	59.8
M 08	298 14.2	29.9	236 49.7	6.7	15 54.1	7.3	59.8
O 09	313 14.4	.. 30.8	251 15.4	6.7	16 01.4	7.1	59.8
N 10	328 14.6	31.8	265 41.1	6.7	16 08.5	7.0	59.8
D 11	343 14.8	32.8	280 06.8	6.6	16 15.5	7.0	59.8
A 12	358 15.0	N 0 33.8	294 32.4	6.7	N16 22.5	6.8	59.7
Y 13	13 15.2	34.8	308 58.1	6.6	16 29.3	6.7	59.7
14	28 15.3	35.8	323 23.7	6.6	16 36.0	6.6	59.7
15	43 15.5	.. 36.8	337 49.3	6.6	16 42.6	6.5	59.7
16	58 15.7	37.8	352 14.9	6.5	16 49.1	6.3	59.7
17	73 15.9	38.7	6 40.4	6.6	16 55.4	6.3	59.6
18	88 16.1	N 0 39.7	21 06.0	6.6	N17 01.7	6.1	59.6
19	103 16.3	40.7	35 31.6	6.5	17 07.8	6.0	59.6
20	118 16.5	41.7	49 57.1	6.5	17 13.8	5.9	59.6
21	133 16.7	.. 42.7	64 22.6	6.5	17 19.7	5.8	59.6
22	148 16.8	43.7	78 48.1	6.5	17 25.5	5.7	59.5
23	163 17.0	44.7	93 13.6	6.5	N17 31.2	5.6	59.5
	SD 16.1	d 1.0	SD 16.4		16.4		16.3

Twilight / Sunrise / Moonrise

Lat.	Naut.	Civil	Sunrise	Moonrise 20	21	22	23
°	h m	h m	h m	h m	h m	h m	h m
N 72	03 18	04 48	05 56	06 42	06 30	06 14	05 24
N 70	03 37	04 56	05 57	06 53	06 51	06 50	06 51
68	03 52	05 02	05 58	07 02	07 07	07 15	07 31
66	04 04	05 07	05 59	07 10	07 20	07 35	07 59
64	04 14	05 12	05 59	07 17	07 32	07 51	08 20
62	04 22	05 15	06 00	07 22	07 41	08 05	08 37
60	04 29	05 19	06 00	07 28	07 49	08 16	08 51
N 58	04 35	05 21	06 01	07 32	07 57	08 26	09 03
56	04 40	05 24	06 01	07 36	08 03	08 35	09 14
54	04 44	05 26	06 01	07 40	08 09	08 43	09 23
52	04 48	05 28	06 02	07 43	08 14	08 50	09 32
50	04 52	05 30	06 02	07 46	08 19	08 56	09 39
45	04 59	05 33	06 02	07 52	08 29	09 09	09 55
N 40	05 04	05 36	06 03	07 58	08 37	09 21	10 09
35	05 08	05 38	06 03	08 02	08 45	09 30	10 20
30	05 12	05 40	06 03	08 07	08 51	09 39	10 30
20	05 16	05 42	06 04	08 14	09 03	09 54	10 47
N 10	05 19	05 43	06 04	08 20	09 13	10 06	11 02
0	05 19	05 43	06 04	08 27	09 22	10 19	11 16
S 10	05 19	05 43	06 04	08 33	09 32	10 31	11 30
20	05 16	05 42	06 04	08 39	09 42	10 44	11 45
30	05 12	05 40	06 04	08 47	09 53	10 59	12 03
35	05 09	05 38	06 04	08 52	10 00	11 08	12 13
40	05 05	05 36	06 03	08 57	10 08	11 18	12 24
45	04 59	05 34	06 03	09 02	10 17	11 30	12 38
S 50	04 52	05 30	06 03	09 10	10 28	11 44	12 55
52	04 49	05 29	06 02	09 13	10 33	11 51	13 03
54	04 45	05 27	06 02	09 17	10 39	11 58	13 12
56	04 40	05 25	06 02	09 21	10 45	12 07	13 22
58	04 35	05 22	06 02	09 25	10 52	12 16	13 33
S 60	04 29	05 20	06 01	09 30	11 01	12 27	13 46

Sunset / Twilight / Moonset

Lat.	Sunset	Civil	Naut.	Moonset 20	21	22	23
°	h m	h m	h m	h m	h m	h m	h m
N 72	18 21	19 30	21 02	23 24	25 39	01 39	04 29
N 70	18 20	19 22	20 41	23 05	25 04	01 04	03 02
68	18 19	19 15	20 26	22 50	24 39	00 39	02 23
66	18 18	19 09	20 13	22 38	24 20	00 20	01 56
64	18 17	19 05	20 03	22 28	24 05	00 05	01 35
62	18 16	19 01	19 55	22 20	23 52	25 19	01 19
60	18 16	18 57	19 48	22 13	23 41	25 05	01 05
N 58	18 15	18 55	19 42	22 06	23 32	24 53	00 53
56	18 15	18 52	19 36	22 01	23 24	24 42	00 42
54	18 14	18 50	19 32	21 56	23 17	24 33	00 33
52	18 14	18 48	19 28	21 51	23 10	24 25	00 25
50	18 14	18 46	19 24	21 47	23 04	24 18	00 18
45	18 13	18 42	19 17	21 38	22 52	24 03	00 03
N 40	18 12	18 40	19 11	21 31	22 41	23 50	24 54
35	18 12	18 37	19 07	21 24	22 33	23 39	24 42
30	18 12	18 36	19 03	21 19	22 25	23 30	24 32
20	18 11	18 33	18 59	21 09	22 11	23 13	24 14
N 10	18 11	18 32	18 56	21 01	22 00	22 59	23 58
0	18 11	18 31	18 55	20 53	21 49	22 46	23 43
S 10	18 10	18 31	18 56	20 45	21 38	22 33	23 29
20	18 10	18 32	18 58	20 37	21 26	22 19	23 13
30	18 10	18 34	19 02	20 27	21 13	22 02.	22 55
35	18 11	18 36	19 05	20 22	21 05	21 53	22 45
40	18 11	18 38	19 09	20 15	20 57	21 42	22 33
45	18 11	18 40	19 14	20 08	20 47	21 30	22 19
S 50	18 11	18 43	19 21	20 00	20 34	21 15	22 01
52	18 11	18 45	19 25	19 56	20 29	21 07	21 53
54	18 11	18 47	19 30	19 51	20 22	21 00	21 44
56	18 12	18 49	19 33	19 46	20 16	20 51	21 34
58	18 12	18 51	19 38	19 41	20 08	20 41	21 23
S 60	18 12	18 53	19 43	19 35	19 59	20 29	21 09

SUN / MOON

Day	Eqn. of Time 00ʰ	12ʰ	Mer. Pass.	Mer. Pass. Upper	Lower	Age	Phase
d	m s	m s	h m	h m	h m	d	%
20	07 45	07 36	12 08	14 40	02 12	03	10
21	07 27	07 18	12 07	15 35	03 07	04	19
22	07 09	07 00	12 07	16 32	04 04	05	29

1999 MARCH 23, 24, 25 (TUES., WED., THURS.)

UT	ARIES	VENUS −4.0		MARS −0.8		JUPITER −2.1		SATURN +0.5		STARS		
	GHA	GHA	Dec	GHA	Dec	GHA	Dec	GHA	Dec	Name	SHA	Dec
d h	° ′	° ′	° ′	° ′	° ′	° ′	° ′	° ′	° ′		° ′	° ′
23 00	180 02.5	146 54.3	N13 38.5	319 44.1	S13 26.8	171 29.7	N 2 30.2	149 05.7	N10 11.8	Acamar	315 27.0	S40 18.8
01	195 04.9	161 53.9	39.7	334 46.7	26.8	186 31.6	30.4	164 07.9	11.9	Achernar	335 35.5	S57 14.7
02	210 07.4	176 53.5	40.8	349 49.3	26.8	201 33.6	30.6	179 10.0	12.0	Acrux	173 20.9	S63 05.7
03	225 09.9	191 53.1	.. 41.9	4 51.9	.. 26.8	216 35.5	.. 30.9	194 12.2	.. 12.1	Adhara	255 21.1	S28 58.6
04	240 12.3	206 52.7	43.1	19 54.5	26.8	231 37.4	31.1	209 14.4	12.2	Aldebaran	291 02.2	N16 30.3
05	255 14.8	221 52.2	44.2	34 57.1	26.7	246 39.3	31.4	224 16.6	12.3			
06	270 17.2	236 51.8	N13 45.3	49 59.7	S13 26.7	261 41.2	N 2 31.6	239 18.8	N10 12.4	Alioth	166 29.8	N55 57.8
07	285 19.7	251 51.4	46.4	65 02.4	26.7	276 43.1	31.8	254 21.0	12.5	Alkaid	153 07.2	N49 19.0
T 08	300 22.2	266 51.0	47.6	80 05.0	26.7	291 45.0	32.1	269 23.2	12.6	Al Na'ir	27 57.9	S46 57.9
U 09	315 24.6	281 50.6	.. 48.7	95 07.6	.. 26.7	306 46.9	.. 32.3	284 25.4	.. 12.7	Alnilam	275 57.6	S 1 12.4
E 10	330 27.1	296 50.2	49.8	110 10.2	26.6	321 48.8	32.5	299 27.5	12.8	Alphard	218 06.7	S 8 39.5
S 11	345 29.6	311 49.7	50.9	125 12.8	26.6	336 50.7	32.8	314 29.7	12.9			
D 12	0 32.0	326 49.3	N13 52.1	140 15.5	S13 26.6	351 52.6	N 2 33.0	329 31.9	N10 13.0	Alphecca	126 20.1	N26 42.9
A 13	15 34.5	341 48.9	53.2	155 18.1	26.6	6 54.6	33.3	344 34.1	13.1	Alpheratz	357 55.3	N29 05.0
Y 14	30 37.0	356 48.5	54.3	170 20.7	26.5	21 56.5	33.5	359 36.3	13.3	Altair	62 19.1	N 8 51.9
15	45 39.4	11 48.1	.. 55.4	185 23.3	.. 26.5	36 58.4	.. 33.7	14 38.5	.. 13.4	Ankaa	353 27.0	S42 18.8
16	60 41.9	26 47.7	56.6	200 26.0	26.5	52 00.3	34.0	29 40.7	13.5	Antares	112 39.6	S26 25.7
17	75 44.4	41 47.3	57.7	215 28.6	26.5	67 02.2	34.2	44 42.9	13.6			
18	90 46.8	56 46.8	N13 58.8	230 31.2	S13 26.4	82 04.1	N 2 34.4	59 45.0	N10 13.7	Arcturus	146 05.5	N19 11.1
19	105 49.3	71 46.4	13 59.9	245 33.8	26.4	97 06.0	34.7	74 47.2	13.8	Atria	107 51.2	S69 01.2
20	120 51.7	86 46.0	14 01.0	260 36.5	26.4	112 07.9	34.9	89 49.4	13.9	Avior	234 22.2	S59 30.8
21	135 54.2	101 45.6	.. 02.2	275 39.1	.. 26.4	127 09.8	.. 35.2	104 51.6	.. 14.0	Bellatrix	278 43.9	N 6 20.7
22	150 56.7	116 45.2	03.3	290 41.7	26.3	142 11.7	35.4	119 53.8	14.1	Betelgeuse	271 13.3	N 7 24.2
23	165 59.1	131 44.7	04.4	305 44.4	26.3	157 13.6	35.6	134 56.0	14.2			
24 00	181 01.6	146 44.3	N14 05.5	320 47.0	S13 26.3	172 15.5	N 2 35.9	149 58.2	N10 14.3	Canopus	264 01.0	S52 42.1
01	196 04.1	161 43.9	06.6	335 49.7	26.2	187 17.5	36.1	165 00.4	14.4	Capella	280 50.9	N45 59.8
02	211 06.5	176 43.5	07.7	350 52.3	26.2	202 19.4	36.4	180 02.5	14.5	Deneb	49 39.2	N45 16.4
03	226 09.0	191 43.1	.. 08.9	5 54.9	.. 26.2	217 21.3	.. 36.6	195 04.7	.. 14.6	Denebola	182 44.6	N14 34.5
04	241 11.5	206 42.6	10.0	20 57.6	26.2	232 23.2	36.8	210 06.9	14.7	Diphda	349 07.3	S17 59.7
05	256 13.9	221 42.2	11.1	36 00.2	26.1	247 25.1	37.1	225 09.1	14.8			
06	271 16.4	236 41.8	N14 12.2	51 02.9	S13 26.1	262 27.0	N 2 37.3	240 11.3	N10 14.9	Dubhe	194 04.6	N61 45.4
W 07	286 18.9	251 41.4	13.3	66 05.5	26.1	277 28.9	37.5	255 13.5	15.0	Elnath	278 26.6	N28 36.3
E 08	301 21.3	266 41.0	14.4	81 08.2	26.0	292 30.8	37.8	270 15.7	15.1	Eltanin	90 51.2	N51 29.1
D 09	316 23.8	281 40.5	.. 15.5	96 10.8	.. 26.0	307 32.7	.. 38.0	285 17.8	.. 15.2	Enif	33 58.2	N 9 52.1
N 10	331 26.2	296 40.1	16.7	111 13.5	26.0	322 34.6	38.3	300 20.0	15.3	Fomalhaut	15 36.5	S29 37.7
E 11	346 28.7	311 39.7	17.8	126 16.1	26.0	337 36.5	38.5	315 22.2	15.4			
S 12	1 31.2	326 39.3	N14 18.9	141 18.8	S13 25.9	352 38.5	N 2 38.7	330 24.4	N10 15.6	Gacrux	172 12.6	S57 06.5
D 13	16 33.6	341 38.8	20.0	156 21.4	25.9	7 40.4	39.0	345 26.6	15.7	Gienah	176 03.3	S17 32.3
A 14	31 36.1	356 38.4	21.1	171 24.1	25.9	22 42.3	39.2	0 28.8	15.8	Hadar	149 03.0	S60 22.0
Y 15	46 38.6	11 38.0	.. 22.2	186 26.7	.. 25.8	37 44.2	.. 39.5	15 31.0	.. 15.9	Hamal	328 13.5	N23 27.3
16	61 41.0	26 37.6	23.3	201 29.4	25.8	52 46.1	39.7	30 33.2	16.0	Kaus Aust.	83 58.4	S34 22.9
17	76 43.5	41 37.1	24.4	216 32.1	25.8	67 48.0	39.9	45 35.3	16.1			
18	91 46.0	56 36.7	N14 25.5	231 34.7	S13 25.7	82 49.9	N 2 40.2	60 37.5	N10 16.2	Kochab	137 18.8	N74 09.4
19	106 48.4	71 36.3	26.6	246 37.4	25.7	97 51.8	40.4	75 39.7	16.3	Markab	13 49.6	N15 11.9
20	121 50.9	86 35.9	27.7	261 40.0	25.7	112 53.7	40.6	90 41.9	16.4	Menkar	314 26.8	N 4 05.0
21	136 53.4	101 35.4	.. 28.8	276 42.7	.. 25.6	127 55.6	.. 40.9	105 44.1	.. 16.5	Menkent	148 20.2	S36 21.9
22	151 55.8	116 35.0	29.9	291 45.4	25.6	142 57.5	41.1	120 46.3	16.6	Miaplacidus	221 41.3	S69 43.1
23	166 58.3	131 34.6	31.0	306 48.0	25.5	157 59.4	41.4	135 48.5	16.7			
25 00	182 00.7	146 34.2	N14 32.2	321 50.7	S13 25.5	173 01.4	N 2 41.6	150 50.6	N10 16.8	Mirfak	308 56.5	N49 51.5
01	197 03.2	161 33.7	33.3	336 53.4	25.5	188 03.3	41.8	165 52.8	16.9	Nunki	76 12.0	S26 17.8
02	212 05.7	176 33.3	34.4	351 56.1	25.4	203 05.2	42.1	180 55.0	17.0	Peacock	53 36.9	S56 44.1
03	227 08.1	191 32.9	.. 35.5	6 58.7	.. 25.4	218 07.1	.. 42.3	195 57.2	.. 17.1	Pollux	243 41.1	N28 01.6
04	242 10.6	206 32.4	36.6	22 01.4	25.4	233 09.0	42.5	210 59.4	17.2	Procyon	245 11.1	N 5 13.4
05	257 13.1	221 32.0	37.7	37 04.1	25.3	248 10.9	42.8	226 01.6	17.3			
06	272 15.5	236 31.6	N14 38.8	52 06.8	S13 25.3	263 12.8	N 2 43.0	241 03.7	N10 17.4	Rasalhague	96 16.6	N12 33.6
07	287 18.0	251 31.2	39.9	67 09.4	25.3	278 14.7	43.3	256 05.9	17.5	Regulus	207 55.0	N11 58.2
T 08	302 20.5	266 30.7	41.0	82 12.1	25.2	293 16.6	43.5	271 08.1	17.7	Rigel	281 22.7	S 8 12.5
H 09	317 22.9	281 30.3	.. 42.1	97 14.8	.. 25.2	308 18.5	.. 43.7	286 10.3	.. 17.8	Rigil Kent.	140 06.3	S60 49.7
U 10	332 25.4	296 29.9	43.2	112 17.5	25.1	323 20.4	44.0	301 12.5	17.9	Sabik	102 25.1	S15 43.4
R 11	347 27.8	311 29.4	44.2	127 20.2	25.1	338 22.3	44.2	316 14.7	18.0			
S 12	2 30.3	326 29.0	N14 45.3	142 22.8	S13 25.1	353 24.2	N 2 44.5	331 16.9	N10 18.1	Schedar	349 53.6	N56 31.9
D 13	17 32.8	341 28.6	46.4	157 25.5	25.0	8 26.2	44.7	346 19.0	18.2	Shaula	96 36.8	S37 06.0
A 14	32 35.2	356 28.1	47.5	172 28.2	25.0	23 28.1	44.9	1 21.2	18.3	Sirius	258 43.4	S16 43.2
Y 15	47 37.7	11 27.7	.. 48.6	187 30.9	.. 24.9	38 30.0	.. 45.2	16 23.4	.. 18.4	Spica	158 42.6	S11 09.4
16	62 40.2	26 27.3	49.7	202 33.6	24.9	53 31.9	45.4	31 25.6	18.5	Suhail	223 00.2	S43 26.0
17	77 42.6	41 26.8	50.8	217 36.3	24.9	68 33.8	45.6	46 27.8	18.6			
18	92 45.1	56 26.4	N14 51.9	232 39.0	S13 24.8	83 35.7	N 2 45.9	61 30.0	N10 18.7	Vega	80 46.5	N38 46.8
19	107 47.6	71 26.0	53.0	247 41.7	24.8	98 37.6	46.1	76 32.1	18.8	Zuben'ubi	137 17.4	S16 02.3
20	122 50.0	86 25.5	54.1	262 44.4	24.7	113 39.5	46.4	91 34.3	18.9		SHA	Mer. Pass.
21	137 52.5	101 25.1	.. 55.2	277 47.1	.. 24.7	128 41.4	.. 46.6	106 36.5	.. 19.0		° ′	h m
22	152 55.0	116 24.7	56.3	292 49.8	24.6	143 43.3	46.8	121 38.7	19.1	Venus	325 42.7	14 13
23	167 57.4	131 24.2	57.4	307 52.5	24.6	158 45.2	47.1	136 40.9	19.2	Mars	139 45.4	2 36
	h m									Jupiter	351 13.9	12 29
Mer. Pass. 11 53.9	v −0.4 d 1.1			v 2.7 d 0.0		v 1.9 d 0.2		v 2.2 d 0.1		Saturn	328 56.6	13 58

UT	SUN GHA	SUN Dec	MOON GHA	MOON v	MOON Dec	MOON d	MOON HP
d h	° ′	° ′	° ′	′	° ′	′	′
23 00	178 17.2	N 0 45.6	107 39.1	6.5	N17 36.8	5.4	59.5
01	193 17.4	46.6	122 04.6	6.5	17 42.2	5.3	59.5
02	208 17.6	47.6	136 30.1	6.4	17 47.5	5.2	59.5
03	223 17.8	.. 48.6	150 55.5	6.5	17 52.7	5.1	59.4
04	238 18.0	49.6	165 21.0	6.4	17 57.8	4.9	59.4
05	253 18.1	50.6	179 46.4	6.5	18 02.7	4.8	59.4
06	268 18.3	N 0 51.6	194 11.9	6.4	N18 07.5	4.8	59.4
07	283 18.5	52.6	208 37.3	6.4	18 12.3	4.5	59.3
T 08	298 18.7	53.5	223 02.7	6.5	18 16.8	4.5	59.3
U 09	313 18.9	.. 54.5	237 28.2	6.4	18 21.3	4.3	59.3
E 10	328 19.1	55.5	251 53.6	6.4	18 25.6	4.3	59.3
S 11	343 19.3	56.5	266 19.0	6.4	18 29.9	4.1	59.3
D 12	358 19.5	N 0 57.5	280 44.4	6.5	N18 34.0	3.9	59.2
A 13	13 19.6	58.5	295 09.9	6.4	18 37.9	3.9	59.2
Y 14	28 19.8	0 59.5	309 35.3	6.4	18 41.8	3.7	59.2
15	43 20.0	1 00.4	324 00.7	6.5	18 45.5	3.6	59.2
16	58 20.2	01.4	338 26.2	6.4	18 49.1	3.5	59.1
17	73 20.4	02.4	352 51.6	6.4	18 52.6	3.3	59.1
18	88 20.6	N 1 03.4	7 17.0	6.5	N18 55.9	3.3	59.1
19	103 20.8	04.4	21 42.5	6.4	18 59.2	3.1	59.1
20	118 21.0	05.4	36 07.9	6.5	19 02.3	2.9	59.0
21	133 21.1	.. 06.4	50 33.4	6.5	19 05.2	2.9	59.0
22	148 21.3	07.3	64 58.9	6.5	19 08.1	2.7	59.0
23	163 21.5	08.3	79 24.4	6.4	19 10.8	2.6	59.0
24 00	178 21.7	N 1 09.3	93 49.8	6.5	N19 13.4	2.5	58.9
01	193 21.9	10.3	108 15.3	6.6	19 15.9	2.3	58.9
02	208 22.1	11.3	122 40.9	6.5	19 18.2	2.2	58.9
03	223 22.3	.. 12.3	137 06.4	6.6	19 20.4	2.1	58.9
04	238 22.5	13.3	151 31.9	6.6	19 22.5	2.0	58.9
05	253 22.7	14.2	165 57.5	6.6	19 24.5	1.9	58.8
06	268 22.8	N 1 15.2	180 23.1	6.5	N19 26.4	1.7	58.8
W 07	283 23.0	16.2	194 48.6	6.7	19 28.1	1.6	58.8
E 08	298 23.2	17.2	209 14.3	6.6	19 29.7	1.4	58.8
D 09	313 23.4	.. 18.2	223 39.9	6.6	19 31.1	1.4	58.7
N 10	328 23.6	19.2	238 05.5	6.7	19 32.5	1.2	58.7
E 11	343 23.8	20.1	252 31.2	6.7	19 33.7	1.1	58.7
S 12	358 24.0	N 1 21.1	266 56.9	6.7	N19 34.8	1.0	58.7
D 13	13 24.2	22.1	281 22.6	6.7	19 35.8	0.8	58.6
A 14	28 24.3	23.1	295 48.3	6.8	19 36.6	0.7	58.6
Y 15	43 24.5	.. 24.1	310 14.1	6.8	19 37.3	0.6	58.6
16	58 24.7	25.1	324 39.9	6.8	19 37.9	0.5	58.6
17	73 24.9	26.1	339 05.7	6.8	19 38.4	0.3	58.5
18	88 25.1	N 1 27.0	353 31.5	6.9	N19 38.7	0.2	58.5
19	103 25.3	28.0	7 57.4	6.9	19 38.9	0.1	58.5
20	118 25.5	29.0	22 23.3	6.9	19 39.0	0.0	58.5
21	133 25.7	.. 30.0	36 49.2	7.0	19 39.0	0.1	58.4
22	148 25.9	31.0	51 15.2	7.0	19 38.9	0.3	58.4
23	163 26.0	32.0	65 41.2	7.0	19 38.6	0.4	58.4
25 00	178 26.2	N 1 32.9	80 07.2	7.0	N19 38.2	0.5	58.4
01	193 26.4	33.9	94 33.2	7.1	19 37.7	0.6	58.3
02	208 26.6	34.9	108 59.3	7.2	19 37.1	0.8	58.3
03	223 26.8	.. 35.9	123 25.5	7.1	19 36.3	0.9	58.3
04	238 27.0	36.9	137 51.6	7.2	19 35.4	1.0	58.3
05	253 27.2	37.9	152 17.8	7.3	19 34.4	1.1	58.2
06	268 27.4	N 1 38.8	166 44.1	7.2	N19 33.3	1.2	58.2
07	283 27.6	39.8	181 10.3	7.3	19 32.1	1.4	58.2
T 08	298 27.7	40.8	195 36.6	7.4	19 30.7	1.5	58.2
H 09	313 27.9	.. 41.8	210 03.0	7.4	19 29.2	1.6	58.1
U 10	328 28.1	42.8	224 29.4	7.4	19 27.6	1.7	58.1
R 11	343 28.3	43.8	238 55.8	7.5	19 25.9	1.8	58.1
S 12	358 28.5	N 1 44.7	253 22.3	7.5	N19 24.1	1.9	58.1
D 13	13 28.7	45.7	267 48.8	7.6	19 22.2	2.1	58.0
A 14	28 28.9	46.7	282 15.4	7.6	19 20.1	2.2	58.0
Y 15	43 29.1	.. 47.7	296 42.0	7.7	19 17.9	2.3	58.0
16	58 29.3	48.7	311 08.7	7.7	19 15.6	2.4	58.0
17	73 29.4	49.7	325 35.4	7.7	19 13.2	2.5	57.9
18	88 29.6	N 1 50.6	340 02.1	7.8	N19 10.7	2.6	57.9
19	103 29.8	51.6	354 28.9	7.9	19 08.1	2.8	57.9
20	118 30.0	52.6	8 55.8	7.9	19 05.3	2.8	57.9
21	133 30.2	.. 53.6	23 22.7	7.9	19 02.5	3.0	57.8
22	148 30.4	54.6	37 49.6	8.0	18 59.5	3.1	57.8
23	163 30.6	55.6	52 16.6	8.0	N18 56.4	3.1	57.8
	SD 16.1	d 1.0	SD 16.1	16.0			15.8

Twilight / Sunrise / Moonrise

Lat.	Naut.	Civil	Sunrise	Moonrise 23	24	25	26
°	h m	h m	h m	h m	h m	h m	h m
N 72	02 56	04 31	05 40	05 24	▭	▭	▭
N 70	03 19	04 41	05 43	06 51	07 03	07 57	09 37
68	03 37	04 49	05 45	07 31	08 02	08 58	10 20
66	03 51	04 55	05 47	07 59	08 36	09 33	10 48
64	04 02	05 01	05 49	08 20	09 01	09 58	11 10
62	04 11	05 05	05 50	08 37	09 21	10 18	11 27
60	04 19	05 09	05 51	08 51	09 37	10 34	11 42
N 58	04 25	05 13	05 52	09 03	09 50	10 48	11 54
56	04 31	05 16	05 53	09 14	10 02	10 59	12 04
54	04 36	05 19	05 54	09 23	10 12	11 10	12 14
52	04 41	05 21	05 55	09 32	10 21	11 19	12 22
50	04 45	05 23	05 55	09 39	10 30	11 27	12 30
45	04 53	05 27	05 57	09 55	10 47	11 44	12 46
N 40	04 59	05 31	05 58	10 09	11 01	11 58	12 59
35	05 04	05 34	05 59	10 20	11 14	12 11	13 10
30	05 08	05 36	06 00	10 30	11 24	12 21	13 19
20	05 13	05 39	06 01	10 47	11 42	12 39	13 36
N 10	05 17	05 41	06 02	11 02	11 58	12 55	13 51
0	05 18	05 42	06 03	11 16	12 13	13 10	14 04
S 10	05 19	05 43	06 04	11 30	12 28	13 24	14 18
20	05 17	05 43	06 05	11 45	12 44	13 40	14 32
30	05 14	05 42	06 06	12 03	13 03	13 58	14 49
35	05 11	05 41	06 06	12 13	13 14	14 09	14 58
40	05 08	05 39	06 06	12 24	13 26	14 21	15 09
45	05 03	05 38	06 07	12 38	13 40	14 35	15 22
S 50	04 57	05 35	06 07	12 55	13 58	14 53	15 38
52	04 54	05 34	06 07	13 03	14 07	15 01	15 45
54	04 51	05 32	06 08	13 12	14 16	15 10	15 54
56	04 47	05 31	06 08	13 22	14 27	15 20	16 03
58	04 43	05 29	06 08	13 33	14 39	15 32	16 13
S 60	04 37	05 27	06 09	13 46	14 53	15 45	16 25

Sunset / Twilight / Moonset

Lat.	Sunset	Civil	Naut.	Moonset 23	24	25	26
°	h m	h m	h m	h m	h m	h m	h m
N 72	18 35	19 45	21 22	04 29	▭	▭	▭
N 70	18 32	19 35	20 58	03 02	04 51	05 55	06 10
68	18 30	19 27	20 39	02 23	03 52	04 54	05 27
66	18 28	19 20	20 25	01 56	03 18	04 19	04 58
64	18 26	19 14	20 14	01 35	02 53	03 54	04 36
62	18 24	19 09	20 04	01 19	02 34	03 34	04 18
60	18 23	19 05	19 56	01 05	02 18	03 18	04 04
N 58	18 22	19 01	19 49	00 53	02 04	03 04	03 51
56	18 21	18 58	19 43	00 42	01 53	02 52	03 40
54	18 20	18 56	19 38	00 33	01 43	02 42	03 31
52	18 19	18 53	19 33	00 25	01 34	02 33	03 22
50	18 18	18 51	19 29	00 18	01 25	02 24	03 14
45	18 17	18 46	19 21	00 03	01 08	02 07	02 58
N 40	18 16	18 43	19 14	24 54	00 54	01 53	02 44
35	18 14	18 40	19 09	24 42	00 42	01 40	02 33
30	18 13	18 37	19 05	24 32	00 32	01 30	02 23
20	18 12	18 34	19 00	24 14	00 14	01 11	02 05
N 10	18 11	18 32	18 56	23 58	24 55	00 55	01 50
0	18 10	18 30	18 54	23 43	24 40	00 40	01 36
S 10	18 09	18 30	18 54	23 29	24 25	00 25	01 22
20	18 08	18 30	18 55	23 13	24 09	00 09	01 06
30	18 07	18 31	18 58	22 55	23 51	24 49	00 49
35	18 06	18 32	19 01	22 45	23 40	24 38	00 38
40	18 06	18 33	19 04	22 33	23 28	24 27	00 27
45	18 05	18 34	19 09	22 19	23 13	24 13	00 13
S 50	18 04	18 37	19 14	22 01	22 55	23 56	25 01
52	18 04	18 38	19 17	21 53	22 47	23 48	24 53
54	18 04	18 39	19 21	21 44	22 38	23 39	24 46
56	18 03	18 41	19 24	21 34	22 27	23 29	24 37
58	18 03	18 42	19 29	21 23	22 15	23 17	24 27
S 60	18 03	18 44	19 34	21 09	22 01	23 04	24 15

SUN / MOON

Day	Eqn. of Time 00h	Eqn. of Time 12h	Mer. Pass.	Mer. Pass. Upper	Mer. Pass. Lower	Age	Phase
d	m s	m s	h m	h m	h m	d	%
23	06 52	06 43	12 07	17 30	05 01	06	40
24	06 34	06 24	12 06	18 27	05 58	07	51
25	06 15	06 06	12 06	19 23	06 55	08	62

UT	ARIES GHA	VENUS −4.0 GHA	Dec	MARS −0.9 GHA	Dec	JUPITER −2.1 GHA	Dec	SATURN +0.5 GHA	Dec	STARS Name	SHA	Dec
26 00	182 59.9	146 23.8	N14 58.4	322 55.2	S13 24.6	173 47.1	N 2 47.3	151 43.1	N10 19.3	Acamar	315 27.0	S40 18.8
01	198 02.3	161 23.4	14 59.5	337 57.9	24.5	188 49.1	47.5	166 45.2	19.4	Achernar	335 35.5	S57 14.7
02	213 04.8	176 22.9	15 00.6	353 00.6	24.5	203 51.0	47.8	181 47.4	19.5	Acrux	173 20.9	S63 05.7
03	228 07.3	191 22.5	.. 01.7	8 03.3	.. 24.4	218 52.9	.. 48.0	196 49.6	.. 19.7	Adhara	255 21.1	S28 58.6
04	243 09.7	206 22.1	02.8	23 06.0	24.4	233 54.8	48.3	211 51.8	19.8	Aldebaran	291 02.2	N16 30.3
05	258 12.2	221 21.6	03.9	38 08.7	24.3	248 56.7	48.5	226 54.0	19.9			
06	273 14.7	236 21.2	N15 05.0	53 11.4	S13 24.3	263 58.6	N 2 48.7	241 56.2	N10 20.0	Alioth	166 29.8	N55 57.8
07	288 17.1	251 20.7	06.0	68 14.1	24.2	279 00.5	49.0	256 58.4	20.1	Alkaid	153 07.1	N49 19.0
08	303 19.6	266 20.3	07.1	83 16.8	24.2	294 02.4	49.2	272 00.5	20.2	Al Na'ir	27 57.9	S46 57.9
F 09	318 22.1	281 19.9	.. 08.2	98 19.5	.. 24.2	309 04.3	.. 49.5	287 02.7	.. 20.3	Alnilam	275 57.6	S 1 12.4
R 10	333 24.5	296 19.4	09.3	113 22.2	24.1	324 06.2	49.7	302 04.9	20.4	Alphard	218 06.7	S 8 39.5
I 11	348 27.0	311 19.0	10.4	128 25.0	24.1	339 08.1	49.9	317 07.1	20.5			
D 12	3 29.5	326 18.5	N15 11.5	143 27.7	S13 24.0	354 10.0	N 2 50.2	332 09.3	N10 20.6	Alphecca	126 20.1	N26 42.9
A 13	18 31.9	341 18.1	12.5	158 30.4	24.0	9 11.9	50.4	347 11.4	20.7	Alpheratz	357 55.3	N29 05.0
Y 14	33 34.4	356 17.7	13.6	173 33.1	23.9	24 13.9	50.6	2 13.6	20.8	Altair	62 19.1	N 8 51.9
15	48 36.8	11 17.2	.. 14.7	188 35.8	.. 23.9	39 15.8	.. 50.9	17 15.8	.. 20.9	Ankaa	353 27.0	S42 18.8
16	63 39.3	26 16.8	15.8	203 38.6	23.8	54 17.7	51.1	32 18.0	21.0	Antares	112 39.6	S26 25.7
17	78 41.8	41 16.3	16.9	218 41.3	23.8	69 19.6	51.4	47 20.2	21.1			
18	93 44.2	56 15.9	N15 17.9	233 44.0	S13 23.7	84 21.5	N 2 51.6	62 22.4	N10 21.2	Arcturus	146 05.5	N19 11.1
19	108 46.7	71 15.5	19.0	248 46.7	23.7	99 23.4	51.8	77 24.5	21.3	Atria	107 51.2	S69 01.2
20	123 49.2	86 15.0	20.1	263 49.5	23.6	114 25.3	52.1	92 26.7	21.4	Avior	234 22.2	S59 30.8
21	138 51.6	101 14.6	.. 21.2	278 52.2	.. 23.6	129 27.2	.. 52.3	107 28.9	.. 21.5	Bellatrix	278 43.9	N 6 20.7
22	153 54.1	116 14.1	22.2	293 54.9	23.5	144 29.1	52.5	122 31.1	21.7	Betelgeuse	271 13.3	N 7 24.2
23	168 56.6	131 13.7	23.3	308 57.6	23.5	159 31.0	52.8	137 33.3	21.8			
27 00	183 59.0	146 13.2	N15 24.4	324 00.4	S13 23.4	174 32.9	N 2 53.0	152 35.5	N10 21.9	Canopus	264 01.0	S52 42.1
01	199 01.5	161 12.8	25.5	339 03.1	23.4	189 34.8	53.3	167 37.6	22.0	Capella	280 50.9	N45 59.8
02	214 03.9	176 12.4	26.5	354 05.8	23.3	204 36.7	53.5	182 39.8	22.1	Deneb	49 39.2	N45 16.4
03	229 06.4	191 11.9	.. 27.6	9 08.6	.. 23.3	219 38.7	.. 53.7	197 42.0	.. 22.2	Denebola	182 44.6	N14 34.5
04	244 08.9	206 11.5	28.7	24 11.3	23.2	234 40.6	54.0	212 44.2	22.3	Diphda	349 07.3	S17 59.7
05	259 11.3	221 11.0	29.7	39 14.1	23.2	249 42.5	54.2	227 46.4	22.4			
06	274 13.8	236 10.6	N15 30.8	54 16.8	S13 23.1	264 44.4	N 2 54.4	242 48.6	N10 22.5	Dubhe	194 04.6	N61 45.4
07	289 16.3	251 10.1	31.9	69 19.5	23.0	279 46.3	54.7	257 50.7	22.6	Elnath	278 26.6	N28 36.3
S 08	304 18.7	266 09.7	32.9	84 22.3	23.0	294 48.2	54.9	272 52.9	22.7	Eltanin	90 51.2	N51 29.1
A 09	319 21.2	281 09.2	.. 34.0	99 25.0	.. 22.9	309 50.1	.. 55.2	287 55.1	.. 22.8	Enif	33 58.2	N 9 52.1
T 10	334 23.7	296 08.8	35.1	114 27.8	22.9	324 52.0	55.4	302 57.3	22.9	Fomalhaut	15 36.4	S29 37.7
U 11	349 26.1	311 08.3	36.1	129 30.5	22.8	339 53.9	55.6	317 59.5	23.0			
R 12	4 28.6	326 07.9	N15 37.2	144 33.3	S13 22.8	354 55.8	N 2 55.9	333 01.6	N10 23.1	Gacrux	172 12.6	S57 06.5
D 13	19 31.1	341 07.4	38.3	159 36.0	22.7	9 57.7	56.1	348 03.8	23.2	Gienah	176 03.3	S17 32.3
A 14	34 33.5	356 07.0	39.3	174 38.8	22.7	24 59.6	56.4	3 06.0	23.3	Hadar	149 03.0	S60 22.0
Y 15	49 36.0	11 06.6	.. 40.4	189 41.5	.. 22.6	40 01.5	.. 56.6	18 08.2	.. 23.5	Hamal	328 13.5	N23 27.3
16	64 38.4	26 06.1	41.5	204 44.3	22.5	55 03.4	56.8	33 10.4	23.6	Kaus Aust.	83 58.4	S34 22.9
17	79 40.9	41 05.7	42.5	219 47.0	22.5	70 05.4	57.1	48 12.5	23.7			
18	94 43.4	56 05.2	N15 43.6	234 49.8	S13 22.4	85 07.3	N 2 57.3	63 14.7	N10 23.8	Kochab	137 18.7	N74 09.4
19	109 45.8	71 04.8	44.7	249 52.5	22.4	100 09.2	57.5	78 16.9	23.9	Markab	13 49.6	N15 11.9
20	124 48.3	86 04.3	45.7	264 55.3	22.3	115 11.1	57.8	93 19.1	24.0	Menkar	314 26.8	N 4 05.0
21	139 50.8	101 03.9	.. 46.8	279 58.1	.. 22.3	130 13.0	.. 58.0	108 21.3	.. 24.1	Menkent	148 20.2	S36 21.9
22	154 53.2	116 03.4	47.8	295 00.8	22.2	145 14.9	58.3	123 23.5	24.2	Miaplacidus	221 41.3	S69 43.1
23	169 55.7	131 02.9	48.9	310 03.6	22.1	160 16.8	58.5	138 25.6	24.3			
28 00	184 58.2	146 02.5	N15 49.9	325 06.3	S13 22.1	175 18.7	N 2 58.7	153 27.8	N10 24.4	Mirfak	308 56.5	N49 51.5
01	200 00.6	161 02.0	51.0	340 09.1	22.0	190 20.6	59.0	168 30.0	24.5	Nunki	76 12.0	S26 17.8
02	215 03.1	176 01.6	52.1	355 11.9	22.0	205 22.5	59.2	183 32.2	24.6	Peacock	53 36.8	S56 44.1
03	230 05.6	191 01.1	.. 53.1	10 14.6	.. 21.9	220 24.4	.. 59.4	198 34.4	.. 24.7	Pollux	243 41.1	N28 01.6
04	245 08.0	206 00.7	54.2	25 17.4	21.8	235 26.3	59.7	213 36.5	24.8	Procyon	245 11.2	N 5 13.4
05	260 10.5	221 00.2	55.2	40 20.2	21.8	250 28.2	2 59.9	228 38.7	24.9			
06	275 12.9	235 59.8	N15 56.3	55 23.0	S13 21.7	265 30.1	N 3 00.2	243 40.9	N10 25.0	Rasalhague	96 16.6	N12 33.5
07	290 15.4	250 59.3	57.3	70 25.7	21.7	280 32.1	00.4	258 43.1	25.1	Regulus	207 55.0	N11 58.2
08	305 17.9	265 58.9	58.4	85 28.5	21.6	295 34.0	00.6	273 45.3	25.2	Rigel	281 22.7	S 8 12.4
S 09	320 20.3	280 58.4	15 59.4	100 31.3	.. 21.5	310 35.9	.. 00.9	288 47.4	.. 25.4	Rigil Kent.	140 06.3	S60 49.7
U 10	335 22.8	295 58.0	16 00.5	115 34.1	21.5	325 37.8	01.1	303 49.6	25.5	Sabik	102 25.1	S15 43.4
N 11	350 25.3	310 57.5	01.5	130 36.8	21.4	340 39.7	01.3	318 51.8	25.6			
D 12	5 27.7	325 57.0	N16 02.6	145 39.6	S13 21.3	355 41.6	N 3 01.6	333 54.0	N10 25.7	Schedar	349 53.6	N56 31.8
A 13	20 30.2	340 56.6	03.6	160 42.4	21.3	10 43.5	01.8	348 56.2	25.8	Shaula	96 36.8	S37 06.0
Y 14	35 32.7	355 56.1	04.7	175 45.2	21.2	25 45.4	02.1	3 58.3	25.9	Sirius	258 43.4	S16 43.2
15	50 35.1	10 55.7	.. 05.7	190 48.0	.. 21.1	40 47.3	.. 02.3	19 00.5	.. 26.0	Spica	158 42.6	S11 09.4
16	65 37.6	25 55.2	06.8	205 50.7	21.1	55 49.2	02.5	34 02.7	26.1	Suhail	223 00.2	S43 26.1
17	80 40.0	40 54.8	07.8	220 53.5	21.0	70 51.1	02.8	49 04.9	26.2			
18	95 42.5	55 54.3	N16 08.9	235 56.3	S13 20.9	85 53.0	N 3 03.0	64 07.1	N10 26.3	Vega	80 46.4	N38 46.8
19	110 45.0	70 53.8	09.9	250 59.1	20.9	100 54.9	03.2	79 09.2	26.4	Zuben'ubi	137 17.4	S16 02.3
20	125 47.4	85 53.4	11.0	266 01.9	20.8	115 56.8	03.5	94 11.4	26.5		SHA	Mer. Pass.
21	140 49.9	100 52.9	.. 12.0	281 04.7	.. 20.7	130 58.8	.. 03.7	109 13.6	.. 26.6		° '	h m
22	155 52.4	115 52.5	13.0	296 07.5	20.7	146 00.7	04.0	124 15.8	26.7	Venus	322 14.2	14 16
23	170 54.8	130 52.0	14.1	311 10.3	20.6	161 02.6	04.2	139 18.0	26.8	Mars	140 01.4	2 24
	h m									Jupiter	350 33.9	12 20
Mer. Pass. 11 42.1	v −0.4 d 1.1	v 2.7	d 0.1	v 1.9	d 0.2	v 2.2	d 0.1			Saturn	328 36.4	13 48

UT	SUN GHA	SUN Dec	MOON GHA	v	MOON Dec	d	HP
d h	° ′	° ′	° ′	′	° ′	′	′
26 00	178 30.8	N 1 56.5	66 43.6	8.1	N18 53.3	3.3	57.8
01	193 31.0	57.5	81 10.7	8.2	18 50.0	3.4	57.7
02	208 31.1	58.5	95 37.9	8.2	18 46.6	3.6	57.7
03	223 31.3	1 59.5	110 05.1	8.2	18 43.0	3.6	57.7
04	238 31.5	2 00.5	124 32.3	8.3	18 39.4	3.7	57.7
05	253 31.7	01.4	138 59.6	8.4	18 35.7	3.8	57.7
06	268 31.9	N 2 02.4	153 27.0	8.4	N18 31.9	4.0	57.6
07	283 32.1	03.4	167 54.4	8.4	18 27.9	4.0	57.6
08	298 32.3	04.4	182 21.8	8.6	18 23.9	4.1	57.6
F 09	313 32.5 ..	05.4	196 49.4	8.5	18 19.8	4.3	57.6
R 10	328 32.7	06.4	211 16.9	8.7	18 15.5	4.3	57.5
I 11	343 32.9	07.3	225 44.6	8.7	18 11.2	4.5	57.5
D 12	358 33.0	N 2 08.3	240 12.3	8.7	N18 06.7	4.5	57.5
A 13	13 33.2	09.3	254 40.0	8.8	18 02.2	4.7	57.5
Y 14	28 33.4	10.3	269 07.8	8.9	17 57.5	4.7	57.4
15	43 33.6 ..	11.3	283 35.7	8.9	17 52.8	4.9	57.4
16	58 33.8	12.2	298 03.6	8.9	17 47.9	4.9	57.4
17	73 34.0	13.2	312 31.5	9.1	17 43.0	5.1	57.4
18	88 34.2	N 2 14.2	326 59.6	9.1	N17 37.9	5.1	57.3
19	103 34.4	15.2	341 27.7	9.1	17 32.8	5.2	57.3
20	118 34.6	16.2	355 55.8	9.2	17 27.6	5.4	57.3
21	133 34.7 ..	17.1	10 24.0	9.3	17 22.2	5.4	57.3
22	148 34.9	18.1	24 52.3	9.3	17 16.8	5.5	57.2
23	163 35.1	19.1	39 20.6	9.4	17 11.3	5.6	57.2
27 00	178 35.3	N 2 20.1	53 49.0	9.4	N17 05.7	5.7	57.2
01	193 35.5	21.1	68 17.4	9.5	17 00.0	5.8	57.2
02	208 35.7	22.0	82 45.9	9.6	16 54.2	5.8	57.2
03	223 35.9 ..	23.0	97 14.5	9.6	16 48.4	6.0	57.1
04	238 36.1	24.0	111 43.1	9.7	16 42.4	6.0	57.1
05	253 36.3	25.0	126 11.8	9.8	16 36.4	6.2	57.1
06	268 36.5	N 2 26.0	140 40.6	9.8	N16 30.2	6.2	57.1
07	283 36.6	26.9	155 09.4	9.8	16 24.0	6.3	57.0
S 08	298 36.8	27.9	169 38.2	10.0	16 17.7	6.4	57.0
A 09	313 37.0 ..	28.9	184 07.2	10.0	16 11.3	6.5	57.0
T 10	328 37.2	29.9	198 36.2	10.0	16 04.8	6.5	57.0
U 11	343 37.4	30.9	213 05.2	10.1	15 58.3	6.6	56.9
R 12	358 37.6	N 2 31.8	227 34.3	10.2	N15 51.7	6.8	56.9
D 13	13 37.8	32.8	242 03.5	10.2	15 44.9	6.8	56.9
A 14	28 38.0	33.8	256 32.7	10.3	15 38.1	6.8	56.9
Y 15	43 38.2 ..	34.8	271 02.0	10.4	15 31.3	7.0	56.9
16	58 38.4	35.8	285 31.4	10.4	15 24.3	7.0	56.8
17	73 38.5	36.7	300 00.8	10.5	15 17.3	7.1	56.8
18	88 38.7	N 2 37.7	314 30.3	10.5	N15 10.2	7.2	56.8
19	103 38.9	38.7	328 59.8	10.6	15 03.0	7.2	56.8
20	118 39.1	39.7	343 29.4	10.6	14 55.8	7.4	56.7
21	133 39.3 ..	40.6	357 59.0	10.7	14 48.4	7.4	56.7
22	148 39.5	41.6	12 28.7	10.8	14 41.0	7.4	56.7
23	163 39.7	42.6	26 58.5	10.9	14 33.6	7.6	56.7
28 00	178 39.9	N 2 43.6	41 28.4	10.9	N14 26.0	7.6	56.7
01	193 40.1	44.6	55 58.3	10.9	14 18.4	7.7	56.6
02	208 40.2	45.5	70 28.2	11.0	14 10.7	7.7	56.6
03	223 40.4 ..	46.5	84 58.2	11.1	14 03.0	7.8	56.6
04	238 40.6	47.5	99 28.3	11.1	13 55.2	7.9	56.6
05	253 40.8	48.5	113 58.4	11.2	13 47.3	7.9	56.5
06	268 41.0	N 2 49.4	128 28.6	11.3	N13 39.4	8.0	56.5
07	283 41.2	50.4	142 58.9	11.3	13 31.4	8.1	56.5
08	298 41.4	51.4	157 29.2	11.3	13 23.3	8.1	56.5
S 09	313 41.6 ..	52.4	171 59.5	11.5	13 15.2	8.2	56.5
U 10	328 41.8	53.4	186 30.0	11.4	13 07.0	8.3	56.4
N 11	343 42.0	54.3	201 00.4	11.6	12 58.7	8.3	56.4
D 12	358 42.1	N 2 55.3	215 31.0	11.6	N12 50.4	8.4	56.4
A 13	13 42.3	56.3	230 01.6	11.6	12 42.0	8.4	56.4
Y 14	28 42.5	57.3	244 32.2	11.7	12 33.6	8.5	56.4
15	43 42.7 ..	58.2	259 02.9	11.8	12 25.1	8.5	56.3
16	58 42.9	2 59.2	273 33.7	11.8	12 16.6	8.6	56.3
17	73 43.1	3 00.2	288 04.5	11.9	12 08.0	8.7	56.3
18	88 43.3	N 3 01.2	302 35.4	11.9	N11 59.3	8.7	56.3
19	103 43.5	02.1	317 06.3	12.0	11 50.6	8.8	56.2
20	118 43.7	03.1	331 37.3	12.0	11 41.8	8.8	56.2
21	133 43.8 ..	04.1	346 08.3	12.1	11 33.0	8.8	56.2
22	148 44.0	05.1	0 39.4	12.2	11 24.2	9.0	56.2
23	163 44.2	06.0	15 10.6	12.2	N11 15.2	8.9	56.2
	SD 16.1	d 1.0	SD 15.7		15.5		15.4

Lat.	Twilight Naut.	Twilight Civil	Sunrise	Moonrise 26	27	28	29
°	h m	h m	h m	h m	h m	h m	h m
N 72	02 33	04 14	05 25	▭	10 43	12 45	14 36
N 70	03 00	04 26	05 29	09 37	11 24	13 09	14 50
68	03 21	04 35	05 33	10 20	11 52	13 28	15 01
66	03 37	04 43	05 35	10 48	12 14	13 42	15 10
64	03 49	04 50	05 38	11 10	12 30	13 54	15 18
62	04 00	04 55	05 40	11 27	12 44	14 04	15 24
60	04 09	05 00	05 42	11 42	12 56	14 13	15 30
N 58	04 16	05 04	05 44	11 54	13 06	14 20	15 35
56	04 23	05 08	05 45	12 04	13 15	14 27	15 39
54	04 28	05 11	05 47	12 14	13 22	14 33	15 43
52	04 33	05 14	05 48	12 22	13 29	14 38	15 47
50	04 38	05 16	05 49	12 30	13 36	14 43	15 50
45	04 47	05 22	05 51	12 46	13 49	14 53	15 57
N 40	04 54	05 26	05 53	12 59	14 00	15 02	16 03
35	05 00	05 29	05 55	13 10	14 10	15 09	16 08
30	05 04	05 32	05 56	13 19	14 18	15 16	16 12
20	05 11	05 36	05 58	13 36	14 32	15 27	16 20
N 10	05 15	05 39	06 00	13 51	14 45	15 37	16 27
0	05 18	05 42	06 02	14 04	14 56	15 46	16 33
S 10	05 19	05 43	06 04	14 18	15 08	15 55	16 39
20	05 18	05 44	06 06	14 32	15 20	16 05	16 46
30	05 16	05 43	06 07	14 49	15 34	16 16	16 53
35	05 14	05 43	06 08	14 58	15 43	16 22	16 58
40	05 11	05 42	06 09	15 09	15 52	16 29	17 03
45	05 07	05 41	06 11	15 22	16 03	16 38	17 08
S 50	05 02	05 40	06 12	15 38	16 16	16 48	17 15
52	05 00	05 39	06 13	15 45	16 22	16 52	17 18
54	04 57	05 38	06 13	15 54	16 29	16 57	17 22
56	04 53	05 37	06 14	16 03	16 36	17 03	17 25
58	04 50	05 36	06 15	16 13	16 44	17 09	17 30
S 60	04 45	05 34	06 16	16 25	16 54	17 16	17 34

Lat.	Sunset	Twilight Civil	Twilight Naut.	Moonset 26	27	28	29
°	h m	h m	h m	h m	h m	h m	h m
N 72	18 49	20 01	21 45	▭	06 55	06 37	06 25
N 70	18 44	19 48	21 15	06 10	06 13	06 12	06 09
68	18 41	19 38	20 54	05 27	05 44	05 52	05 57
66	18 37	19 30	20 38	04 58	05 22	05 37	05 47
64	18 35	19 23	20 24	04 36	05 05	05 24	05 38
62	18 32	19 18	20 14	04 18	04 50	05 13	05 30
60	18 30	19 13	20 05	04 04	04 38	05 04	05 24
N 58	18 29	19 08	19 57	03 51	04 27	04 56	05 18
56	18 27	19 05	19 50	03 40	04 18	04 48	05 13
54	18 26	19 01	19 44	03 31	04 10	04 42	05 08
52	18 24	18 58	19 39	03 22	04 03	04 36	05 04
50	18 23	18 56	19 35	03 14	03 56	04 31	05 00
45	18 21	18 50	19 25	02 58	03 42	04 19	04 52
N 40	18 19	18 46	19 18	02 44	03 30	04 10	04 45
35	18 17	18 42	19 12	02 33	03 20	04 02	04 39
30	18 15	18 39	19 07	02 23	03 11	03 54	04 34
20	18 13	18 35	19 01	02 05	02 56	03 42	04 25
N 10	18 11	18 32	18 56	01 50	02 42	03 31	04 16
0	18 09	18 29	18 53	01 36	02 29	03 20	04 09
S 10	18 07	18 28	18 52	01 22	02 17	03 10	04 01
20	18 05	18 27	18 53	01 06	02 03	02 59	03 53
30	18 03	18 27	18 55	00 49	01 47	02 46	03 43
35	18 02	18 27	18 57	00 38	01 38	02 38	03 38
40	18 01	18 28	18 59	00 27	01 28	02 30	03 31
45	18 00	18 29	19 03	00 13	01 16	02 20	03 24
S 50	17 58	18 30	19 08	25 01	01 01	02 08	03 15
52	17 57	18 31	19 10	24 53	00 53	02 02	03 11
54	17 57	18 32	19 13	24 46	00 46	01 56	03 06
56	17 55	18 33	19 16	24 37	00 37	01 49	03 01
58	17 55	18 34	19 20	24 27	00 27	01 41	02 56
S 60	17 54	18 35	19 24	24 15	00 15	01 32	02 49

Day	SUN Eqn. of Time 00h	SUN Eqn. of Time 12h	SUN Mer. Pass.	MOON Mer. Pass. Upper	MOON Mer. Pass. Lower	Age	Phase
d	m s	m s	h m	h m	h m	d	%
26	05 57	05 48	12 06	20 17	07 50	09	72
27	05 39	05 30	12 05	21 08	08 43	10	81
28	05 21	05 12	12 05	21 57	09 33	11	88

UT	ARIES GHA	VENUS −4.0 GHA	Dec	MARS −1.0 GHA	Dec	JUPITER −2.1 GHA	Dec	SATURN +0.4 GHA	Dec	STARS Name	SHA	Dec
29 00	185 57.3	145 51.5	N16 15.1	326 13.1	S13 20.5	176 04.5	N 3 04.4	154 20.1	N10 26.9	Acamar	315 27.0	S40 18.8
01	200 59.8	160 51.1	16.2	341 15.9	20.5	191 06.4	04.7	169 22.3	27.0	Achernar	335 35.5	S57 14.7
02	216 02.2	175 50.6	17.2	356 18.7	20.4	206 08.3	04.9	184 24.5	27.2	Acrux	173 20.9	S63 05.7
03	231 04.7	190 50.2	.. 18.3	11 21.5	.. 20.3	221 10.2	.. 05.1	199 26.7	.. 27.3	Adhara	255 21.1	S28 58.6
04	246 07.2	205 49.7	19.3	26 24.3	20.3	236 12.1	05.4	214 28.9	27.4	Aldebaran	291 02.2	N16 30.3
05	261 09.6	220 49.2	20.3	41 27.1	20.2	251 14.0	05.6	229 31.0	27.5			
06	276 12.1	235 48.8	N16 21.4	56 29.9	S13 20.1	266 15.9	N 3 05.9	244 33.2	N10 27.6	Alioth	166 29.8	N55 57.8
M 07	291 14.5	250 48.3	22.4	71 32.7	20.1	281 17.8	06.1	259 35.4	27.7	Alkaid	153 07.1	N49 19.0
O 08	306 17.0	265 47.8	23.4	86 35.5	20.0	296 19.7	06.3	274 37.6	27.8	Al Na'ir	27 57.9	S46 57.9
N 09	321 19.5	280 47.4	.. 24.5	101 38.3	.. 19.9	311 21.6	.. 06.6	289 39.7	.. 27.9	Alnilam	275 57.6	S 1 12.4
D 10	336 21.9	295 46.9	25.5	116 41.1	19.9	326 23.5	06.8	304 41.9	28.0	Alphard	218 06.7	S 8 39.5
A 11	351 24.4	310 46.5	26.5	131 43.9	19.8	341 25.5	07.0	319 44.1	28.1			
Y 12	6 26.9	325 46.0	N16 27.6	146 46.7	S13 19.7	356 27.4	N 3 07.3	334 46.3	N10 28.2	Alphecca	126 20.1	N26 42.9
13	21 29.3	340 45.5	28.6	161 49.5	19.6	11 29.3	07.5	349 48.5	28.3	Alpheratz	357 55.2	N29 05.0
14	36 31.8	355 45.1	29.6	176 52.4	19.6	26 31.2	07.8	4 50.6	28.4	Altair	62 19.1	N 8 51.9
15	51 34.3	10 44.6	.. 30.7	191 55.2	.. 19.5	41 33.1	.. 08.0	19 52.8	.. 28.5	Ankaa	353 27.0	S42 18.8
16	66 36.7	25 44.1	31.7	206 58.0	19.4	56 35.0	08.2	34 55.0	28.6	Antares	112 39.6	S26 25.7
17	81 39.2	40 43.7	32.7	222 00.8	19.3	71 36.9	08.5	49 57.2	28.7			
18	96 41.6	55 43.2	N16 33.8	237 03.6	S13 19.3	86 38.8	N 3 08.7	64 59.4	N10 28.9	Arcturus	146 05.5	N19 11.1
19	111 44.1	70 42.7	34.8	252 06.4	19.2	101 40.7	08.9	80 01.5	29.0	Atria	107 51.1	S69 01.2
20	126 46.6	85 42.3	35.8	267 09.3	19.1	116 42.6	09.2	95 03.7	29.1	Avior	234 22.2	S59 30.8
21	141 49.0	100 41.8	.. 36.8	282 12.1	.. 19.1	131 44.5	.. 09.4	110 05.9	.. 29.2	Bellatrix	278 43.9	N 6 20.7
22	156 51.5	115 41.3	37.9	297 14.9	19.0	146 46.4	09.7	125 08.1	29.3	Betelgeuse	271 13.3	N 7 24.2
23	171 54.0	130 40.9	38.9	312 17.7	18.9	161 48.3	09.9	140 10.2	29.4			
30 00	186 56.4	145 40.4	N16 39.9	327 20.6	S13 18.8	176 50.2	N 3 10.1	155 12.4	N10 29.5	Canopus	264 01.1	S52 42.1
01	201 58.9	160 39.9	40.9	342 23.4	18.7	191 52.1	10.4	170 14.6	29.6	Capella	280 50.9	N45 59.8
02	217 01.4	175 39.4	42.0	357 26.2	18.7	206 54.1	10.6	185 16.8	29.7	Deneb	49 39.2	N45 16.4
03	232 03.8	190 39.0	.. 43.0	12 29.1	.. 18.6	221 56.0	.. 10.8	200 19.0	.. 29.8	Denebola	182 44.6	N14 34.5
04	247 06.3	205 38.5	44.0	27 31.9	18.5	236 57.9	11.1	215 21.1	29.9	Diphda	349 07.3	S17 59.7
05	262 08.8	220 38.0	45.0	42 34.7	18.4	251 59.8	11.3	230 23.3	30.0			
06	277 11.2	235 37.6	N16 46.1	57 37.6	S13 18.4	267 01.7	N 3 11.6	245 25.5	N10 30.1	Dubhe	194 04.6	N61 45.4
T 07	292 13.7	250 37.1	47.1	72 40.4	18.3	282 03.6	11.8	260 27.7	30.2	Elnath	278 26.7	N28 36.3
U 08	307 16.1	265 36.6	48.1	87 43.2	18.2	297 05.5	12.0	275 29.8	30.3	Eltanin	90 51.2	N51 29.1
E 09	322 18.6	280 36.1	.. 49.1	102 46.1	.. 18.1	312 07.4	.. 12.3	290 32.0	.. 30.4	Enif	33 58.2	N 9 52.1
S 10	337 21.1	295 35.7	50.1	117 48.9	18.1	327 09.3	12.5	305 34.2	30.5	Fomalhaut	15 36.4	S29 37.7
D 11	352 23.5	310 35.2	51.2	132 51.8	18.0	342 11.2	12.7	320 36.4	30.7			
A 12	7 26.0	325 34.7	N16 52.2	147 54.6	S13 17.9	357 13.1	N 3 13.0	335 38.6	N10 30.8	Gacrux	172 12.6	S57 06.5
Y 13	22 28.5	340 34.3	53.2	162 57.4	17.8	12 15.0	13.2	350 40.7	30.9	Gienah	176 03.3	S17 32.3
14	37 30.9	355 33.8	54.2	178 00.3	17.7	27 16.9	13.4	5 42.9	31.0	Hadar	149 03.0	S60 22.0
15	52 33.4	10 33.3	.. 55.2	193 03.1	.. 17.7	42 18.8	.. 13.7	20 45.1	.. 31.1	Hamal	328 13.5	N23 27.3
16	67 35.9	25 32.8	56.2	208 06.0	17.6	57 20.7	13.9	35 47.3	31.2	Kaus Aust.	83 58.4	S34 22.9
17	82 38.3	40 32.4	57.2	223 08.8	17.5	72 22.7	14.2	50 49.4	31.3			
18	97 40.8	55 31.9	N16 58.3	238 11.7	S13 17.4	87 24.6	N 3 14.4	65 51.6	N10 31.4	Kochab	137 18.7	N74 09.4
19	112 43.3	70 31.4	16 59.3	253 14.5	17.3	102 26.5	14.6	80 53.8	31.5	Markab	13 49.6	N15 11.9
20	127 45.7	85 30.9	17 00.3	268 17.4	17.2	117 28.4	14.9	95 56.0	31.6	Menkar	314 26.8	N 4 05.0
21	142 48.2	100 30.4	.. 01.3	283 20.2	.. 17.2	132 30.3	.. 15.1	110 58.1	.. 31.7	Menkent	148 20.2	S36 21.9
22	157 50.6	115 30.0	02.3	298 23.1	17.1	147 32.2	15.3	126 00.3	31.8	Miaplacidus	221 41.4	S69 43.1
23	172 53.1	130 29.5	03.3	313 26.0	17.0	162 34.1	15.6	141 02.5	31.9			
31 00	187 55.6	145 29.0	N17 04.3	328 28.8	S13 16.9	177 36.0	N 3 15.8	156 04.7	N10 32.0	Mirfak	308 56.5	N49 51.5
01	202 58.0	160 28.5	05.3	343 31.7	16.8	192 37.9	16.1	171 06.9	32.1	Nunki	76 12.0	S26 17.8
02	218 00.5	175 28.1	06.3	358 34.5	16.7	207 39.8	16.3	186 09.0	32.3	Peacock	53 36.8	S56 44.1
03	233 03.0	190 27.6	.. 07.3	13 37.4	.. 16.7	222 41.7	.. 16.5	201 11.2	.. 32.4	Pollux	243 41.1	N28 01.6
04	248 05.4	205 27.1	08.3	28 40.3	16.6	237 43.6	16.8	216 13.4	32.5	Procyon	245 11.2	N 5 13.4
05	263 07.9	220 26.6	09.3	43 43.1	16.5	252 45.5	17.0	231 15.6	32.6			
06	278 10.4	235 26.1	N17 10.3	58 46.0	S13 16.4	267 47.4	N 3 17.2	246 17.7	N10 32.7	Rasalhague	96 16.6	N12 33.6
W 07	293 12.8	250 25.7	11.3	73 48.9	16.3	282 49.3	17.5	261 19.9	32.8	Regulus	207 55.0	N11 58.2
E 08	308 15.3	265 25.2	12.4	88 51.7	16.2	297 51.3	17.7	276 22.1	32.9	Rigel	281 22.8	S 8 12.4
D 09	323 17.7	280 24.7	.. 13.4	103 54.6	.. 16.1	312 53.2	.. 17.9	291 24.3	.. 33.0	Rigil Kent.	140 06.3	S60 49.7
N 10	338 20.2	295 24.2	14.4	118 57.5	16.1	327 55.1	18.2	306 26.4	33.1	Sabik	102 25.1	S15 43.4
E 11	353 22.7	310 23.7	15.4	134 00.4	16.0	342 57.0	18.4	321 28.6	33.2			
S 12	8 25.1	325 23.3	N17 16.4	149 03.2	S13 15.9	357 58.9	N 3 18.7	336 30.8	N10 33.3	Schedar	349 53.6	N56 31.8
D 13	23 27.6	340 22.8	17.4	164 06.1	15.8	13 00.8	18.9	351 33.0	33.4	Shaula	96 36.8	S37 06.0
A 14	38 30.1	355 22.3	18.3	179 09.0	15.7	28 02.7	19.1	6 35.1	33.5	Sirius	258 43.4	S16 43.2
Y 15	53 32.5	10 21.8	.. 19.3	194 11.9	.. 15.6	43 04.6	.. 19.4	21 37.3	.. 33.6	Spica	158 42.6	S11 09.5
16	68 35.0	25 21.3	20.3	209 14.7	15.5	58 06.5	19.6	36 39.5	33.7	Suhail	223 00.3	S43 26.1
17	83 37.5	40 20.8	21.3	224 17.6	15.4	73 08.4	19.8	51 41.7	33.8			
18	98 39.9	55 20.4	N17 22.3	239 20.5	S13 15.4	88 10.3	N 3 20.1	66 43.8	N10 34.0	Vega	80 46.4	N38 46.8
19	113 42.4	70 19.9	23.3	254 23.4	15.3	103 12.2	20.3	81 46.0	34.1	Zuben'ubi	137 17.3	S16 02.3
20	128 44.9	85 19.4	24.3	269 26.3	15.2	118 14.1	20.6	96 48.2	34.2		SHA	Mer. Pass.
21	143 47.3	100 18.9	.. 25.3	284 29.2	.. 15.1	133 16.0	.. 20.8	111 50.4	.. 34.3			
22	158 49.8	115 18.4	26.3	299 32.0	15.0	148 17.9	21.0	126 52.5	34.4	Venus	318 44.0	14 18
23	173 52.2	130 17.9	27.3	314 34.9	14.9	163 19.8	21.3	141 54.7	34.5	Mars	140 24.1	2 10
Mer. Pass. 11 30.3		v −0.5	d 1.0	v 2.8	d 0.1	v 1.9	d 0.2	v 2.2	d 0.1	Jupiter	349 53.8	12 11
										Saturn	328 16.0	13 37

UT	SUN GHA	SUN Dec	MOON GHA	v	MOON Dec	d	HP
d h	° ′	° ′	° ′	′	° ′	′	′
29 00	178 44.4	N 3 07.0	29 41.8	12.2	N11 06.3	9.0	56.1
01	193 44.6	08.0	44 13.0	12.3	10 57.3	9.1	56.1
02	208 44.8	09.0	58 44.3	12.4	10 48.2	9.1	56.1
03	223 45.0 . .	09.9	73 15.7	12.4	10 39.1	9.1	56.1
04	238 45.2	10.9	87 47.1	12.4	10 30.0	9.2	56.1
05	253 45.4	11.9	102 18.5	12.5	10 20.8	9.3	56.0
06	268 45.6	N 3 12.9	116 50.0	12.6	N10 11.5	9.2	56.0
07	283 45.7	13.8	131 21.6	12.6	10 02.3	9.4	56.0
08	298 45.9	14.8	145 53.2	12.6	9 52.9	9.3	56.0
M 09	313 46.1 . .	15.8	160 24.8	12.7	9 43.6	9.4	56.0
O 10	328 46.3	16.8	174 56.5	12.8	9 34.2	9.5	55.9
N 11	343 46.5	17.7	189 28.3	12.8	9 24.7	9.4	55.9
D 12	358 46.7	N 3 18.7	204 00.1	12.8	N 9 15.3	9.6	55.9
A 13	13 46.9	19.7	218 31.9	12.9	9 05.7	9.5	55.9
Y 14	28 47.1	20.7	233 03.8	13.0	8 56.2	9.6	55.9
15	43 47.3 . .	21.6	247 35.8	13.0	8 46.6	9.6	55.8
16	58 47.4	22.6	262 07.8	13.0	8 37.0	9.7	55.8
17	73 47.6	23.6	276 39.8	13.1	8 27.3	9.7	55.8
18	88 47.8	N 3 24.6	291 11.9	13.1	N 8 17.6	9.7	55.8
19	103 48.0	25.5	305 44.0	13.1	8 07.9	9.8	55.8
20	118 48.2	26.5	320 16.1	13.2	7 58.1	9.8	55.7
21	133 48.4 . .	27.5	334 48.3	13.3	7 48.3	9.8	55.7
22	148 48.6	28.5	349 20.6	13.3	7 38.5	9.8	55.7
23	163 48.8	29.4	3 52.9	13.3	7 28.7	9.9	55.7
30 00	178 49.0	N 3 30.4	18 25.2	13.4	N 7 18.8	9.9	55.7
01	193 49.1	31.4	32 57.6	13.4	7 08.9	9.9	55.7
02	208 49.3	32.3	47 30.0	13.5	6 59.0	10.0	55.6
03	223 49.5 . .	33.3	62 02.5	13.4	6 49.0	10.0	55.6
04	238 49.7	34.3	76 34.9	13.6	6 39.0	10.0	55.6
05	253 49.9	35.3	91 07.5	13.5	6 29.0	10.0	55.6
06	268 50.1	N 3 36.2	105 40.0	13.7	N 6 19.0	10.0	55.6
07	283 50.3	37.2	120 12.7	13.6	6 09.0	10.1	55.5
T 08	298 50.5	38.2	134 45.3	13.7	5 58.9	10.1	55.5
U 09	313 50.7 . .	39.2	149 18.0	13.7	5 48.8	10.1	55.5
E 10	328 50.8	40.1	163 50.7	13.8	5 38.7	10.2	55.5
S 11	343 51.0	41.1	178 23.5	13.7	5 28.5	10.1	55.5
D 12	358 51.2	N 3 42.1	192 56.2	13.9	N 5 18.4	10.2	55.4
A 13	13 51.4	43.0	207 29.1	13.8	5 08.2	10.2	55.4
Y 14	28 51.6	44.0	222 01.9	13.9	4 58.0	10.2	55.4
15	43 51.8 . .	45.0	236 34.8	13.9	4 47.8	10.2	55.4
16	58 52.0	45.9	251 07.7	14.0	4 37.6	10.2	55.4
17	73 52.2	46.9	265 40.7	14.0	4 27.4	10.3	55.4
18	88 52.4	N 3 47.9	280 13.7	14.0	N 4 17.1	10.2	55.3
19	103 52.5	48.9	294 46.7	14.0	4 06.9	10.3	55.3
20	118 52.7	49.8	309 19.7	14.1	3 56.6	10.3	55.3
21	133 52.9 . .	50.8	323 52.8	14.1	3 46.3	10.3	55.3
22	148 53.1	51.8	338 25.9	14.1	3 36.0	10.3	55.3
23	163 53.3	52.7	352 59.0	14.2	3 25.7	10.3	55.3
31 00	178 53.5	N 3 53.7	7 32.2	14.2	N 3 15.4	10.3	55.2
01	193 53.7	54.7	22 05.4	14.2	3 05.1	10.3	55.2
02	208 53.9	55.7	36 38.6	14.2	2 54.8	10.4	55.2
03	223 54.1 . .	56.6	51 11.8	14.3	2 44.4	10.3	55.2
04	238 54.2	57.6	65 45.1	14.3	2 34.1	10.3	55.2
05	253 54.4	58.6	80 18.4	14.3	2 23.8	10.4	55.2
06	268 54.6	N 3 59.5	94 51.7	14.4	N 2 13.4	10.3	55.1
07	283 54.8	4 00.5	109 25.1	14.3	2 03.1	10.4	55.1
W 08	298 55.0	01.5	123 58.4	14.4	1 52.7	10.4	55.1
E 09	313 55.2 . .	02.4	138 31.8	14.4	1 42.3	10.3	55.1
D 10	328 55.4	03.4	153 05.2	14.4	1 32.0	10.4	55.1
N 11	343 55.6	04.4	167 38.6	14.5	1 21.6	10.4	55.1
E 12	358 55.7	N 4 05.3	182 12.1	14.5	N 1 11.2	10.3	55.0
S 13	13 55.9	06.3	196 45.6	14.5	1 00.9	10.4	55.0
D 14	28 56.1	07.3	211 19.1	14.5	0 50.5	10.3	55.0
A 15	43 56.3 . .	08.2	225 52.6	14.5	0 40.2	10.4	55.0
Y 16	58 56.5	09.2	240 26.1	14.5	0 29.8	10.4	55.0
17	73 56.7	10.2	254 59.6	14.6	0 19.4	10.3	55.0
18	88 56.9	N 4 11.1	269 33.2	14.6	N 0 09.1	10.3	54.9
19	103 57.1	12.1	284 06.8	14.6	S 0 01.2	10.4	54.9
20	118 57.3	13.1	298 40.4	14.6	0 11.6	10.3	54.9
21	133 57.4 . .	14.1	313 14.0	14.6	0 21.9	10.3	54.9
22	148 57.6	15.0	327 47.6	14.7	0 32.2	10.4	54.9
23	163 57.8	16.0	342 21.3	14.6	S 0 42.6	10.3	54.9
	SD 16.0	d 1.0	SD 15.2		15.1		15.0

Lat.	Twilight Naut.	Twilight Civil	Sunrise	Moonrise 29	30	31	1
°	h m	h m	h m	h m	h m	h m	h m
N 72	02 05	03 56	05 09	14 36	16 21	18 01	19 40
N 70	02 40	04 11	05 15	14 50	16 27	18 01	19 34
68	03 04	04 22	05 20	15 01	16 32	18 01	19 29
66	03 22	04 31	05 24	15 10	16 37	18 01	19 25
64	03 36	04 38	05 27	15 18	16 40	18 02	19 21
62	03 48	04 45	05 30	15 24	16 44	18 02	19 18
60	03 58	04 51	05 33	15 30	16 46	18 02	19 16
N 58	04 07	04 55	05 35	15 35	16 49	18 02	19 13
56	04 14	05 00	05 37	15 39	16 51	18 02	19 11
54	04 20	05 03	05 39	15 43	16 53	18 02	19 09
52	04 26	05 07	05 41	15 47	16 55	18 02	19 08
50	04 31	05 10	05 42	15 50	16 56	18 02	19 06
45	04 41	05 16	05 46	15 57	17 00	18 02	19 03
N 40	04 49	05 21	05 48	16 03	17 03	18 02	19 00
35	04 56	05 25	05 50	16 08	17 05	18 02	18 57
30	05 00	05 28	05 52	16 12	17 08	18 02	18 55
20	05 08	05 34	05 56	16 20	17 12	18 02	18 52
N 10	05 13	05 38	05 59	16 27	17 15	18 02	18 49
0	05 17	05 41	06 01	16 33	17 18	18 02	18 46
S 10	05 18	05 43	06 04	16 39	17 21	18 02	18 43
20	05 19	05 44	06 06	16 46	17 25	18 03	18 39
30	05 18	05 45	06 09	16 53	17 29	18 03	18 36
35	05 16	05 45	06 11	16 58	17 31	18 03	18 34
40	05 14	05 45	06 12	17 03	17 34	18 03	18 32
45	05 11	05 45	06 14	17 08	17 36	18 03	18 29
S 50	05 07	05 44	06 17	17 15	17 40	18 03	18 26
52	05 05	05 44	06 18	17 18	17 42	18 03	18 25
54	05 02	05 44	06 19	17 22	17 43	18 03	18 23
56	05 00	05 43	06 20	17 25	17 45	18 03	18 21
58	04 57	05 42	06 22	17 30	17 47	18 04	18 19
S 60	04 53	05 42	06 23	17 34	17 50	18 04	18 17

Lat.	Sunset	Twilight Civil	Twilight Naut.	Moonset 29	30	31	1
°	h m	h m	h m	h m	h m	h m	h m
N 72	19 03	20 17	22 12	06 25	06 15	06 07	05 58
N 70	18 57	20 02	21 35	06 09	06 07	06 04	06 01
68	18 52	19 50	21 10	05 57	06 00	06 01	06 03
66	18 47	19 41	20 51	05 47	05 54	06 00	06 05
64	18 44	19 33	20 36	05 38	05 49	05 58	06 06
62	18 40	19 26	20 23	05 30	05 44	05 56	06 08
60	18 38	19 20	20 13	05 24	05 40	05 55	06 09
N 58	18 35	19 15	20 05	05 18	05 37	05 54	06 10
56	18 33	19 11	19 57	05 13	05 34	05 53	06 11
54	18 31	19 07	19 51	05 08	05 31	05 52	06 12
52	18 30	19 04	19 45	05 04	05 29	05 51	06 13
50	18 28	19 01	19 40	05 00	05 26	05 50	06 13
45	18 25	18 54	19 29	04 52	05 21	05 49	06 15
N 40	18 22	18 49	19 21	04 45	05 17	05 47	06 16
35	18 19	18 45	19 15	04 39	05 14	05 46	06 17
30	18 17	18 41	19 09	04 34	05 10	05 45	06 18
20	18 14	18 36	19 01	04 25	05 05	05 43	06 20
N 10	18 11	18 32	18 56	04 16	05 00	05 41	06 22
0	18 08	18 29	18 53	04 09	04 55	05 40	06 23
S 10	18 05	18 26	18 51	04 01	04 50	05 38	06 25
20	18 03	18 25	18 50	03 53	04 45	05 36	06 26
30	18 00	18 23	18 51	03 43	04 39	05 34	06 28
35	17 58	18 23	18 52	03 38	04 36	05 33	06 29
40	17 56	18 23	18 54	03 31	04 32	05 31	06 30
45	17 54	18 23	18 57	03 24	04 27	05 30	06 31
S 50	17 52	18 24	19 01	03 15	04 22	05 28	06 33
52	17 50	18 24	19 03	03 11	04 20	05 27	06 33
54	17 49	18 24	19 05	03 06	04 17	05 26	06 34
56	17 48	18 25	19 08	03 01	04 14	05 25	06 35
58	17 46	18 25	19 11	02 56	04 10	05 24	06 36
S 60	17 45	18 26	19 15	02 49	04 07	05 22	06 37

	SUN Eqn. of Time 00h	12h	SUN Mer. Pass.	MOON Mer. Pass. Upper	Lower	Age	Phase
Day	m s	m s	h m	h m	h m	d	%
29	05 03	04 54	12 05	22 44	10 21	12	94
30	04 45	04 35	12 05	23 29	11 07	13	98
31	04 26	04 17	12 04	24 13	11 51	14	100

UT	ARIES GHA	VENUS −4.0 GHA	Dec	MARS −1.1 GHA	Dec	JUPITER −2.1 GHA	Dec	SATURN +0.4 GHA	Dec	Name	SHA	Dec
1 THURSDAY												
00	188 54.7	145 17.4	N17 28.3	329 37.8	S13 14.8	178 21.8	N 3 21.5	156 56.9	N10 34.6	Acamar	315 27.1	S40 18.8
01	203 57.2	160 16.9	29.3	344 40.7	14.7	193 23.7	21.7	171 59.1	34.7	Achernar	335 35.6	S57 14.7
02	218 59.6	175 16.5	30.3	359 43.6	14.6	208 25.6	22.0	187 01.2	34.8	Acrux	173 20.9	S63 05.7
03	234 02.1	190 16.0	.. 31.3	14 46.5	.. 14.5	223 27.5	.. 22.2	202 03.4	.. 34.9	Adhara	255 21.2	S28 58.6
04	249 04.6	205 15.5	32.2	29 49.4	14.4	238 29.4	22.4	217 05.6	35.0	Aldebaran	291 02.2	N16 30.3
05	264 07.0	220 15.0	33.2	44 52.3	14.3	253 31.3	22.7	232 07.8	35.1			
06	279 09.5	235 14.5	N17 34.2	59 55.2	S13 14.3	268 33.2	N 3 22.9	247 09.9	N10 35.2	Alioth	166 29.8	N55 57.9
07	294 12.0	250 14.0	35.2	74 58.1	14.2	283 35.1	23.2	262 12.1	35.3	Alkaid	153 07.1	N49 19.0
08	309 14.4	265 13.5	36.2	90 01.0	14.1	298 37.0	23.4	277 14.3	35.4	Al Na'ir	27 57.9	S46 57.8
09	324 16.9	280 13.0	.. 37.2	105 03.9	.. 14.0	313 38.9	.. 23.6	292 16.5	.. 35.6	Alnilam	275 57.6	S 1 12.4
10	339 19.3	295 12.5	38.1	120 06.8	13.9	328 40.8	23.9	307 18.6	35.7	Alphard	218 06.7	S 8 39.5
11	354 21.8	310 12.1	39.1	135 09.7	13.8	343 42.7	24.1	322 20.8	35.8			
12	9 24.3	325 11.6	N17 40.1	150 12.6	S13 13.7	358 44.6	N 3 24.3	337 23.0	N10 35.9	Alphecca	126 20.1	N26 43.0
13	24 26.7	340 11.1	41.1	165 15.5	13.6	13 46.5	24.6	352 25.2	36.0	Alpheratz	357 55.2	N29 05.0
14	39 29.2	355 10.6	42.1	180 18.4	13.5	28 48.4	24.8	7 27.3	36.1	Altair	62 19.0	N 8 51.9
15	54 31.7	10 10.1	.. 43.1	195 21.3	.. 13.4	43 50.4	.. 25.0	22 29.5	.. 36.2	Ankaa	353 27.0	S42 18.8
16	69 34.1	25 09.6	44.0	210 24.3	13.3	58 52.3	25.3	37 31.7	36.3	Antares	112 39.6	S26 25.7
17	84 36.6	40 09.1	45.0	225 27.2	13.2	73 54.2	25.5	52 33.9	36.4			
18	99 39.1	55 08.6	N17 46.0	240 30.1	S13 13.1	88 56.1	N 3 25.8	67 36.0	N10 36.5	Arcturus	146 05.5	N19 11.1
19	114 41.5	70 08.1	47.0	255 33.0	13.0	103 58.0	26.0	82 38.2	36.6	Atria	107 51.1	S69 01.3
20	129 44.0	85 07.6	47.9	270 35.9	12.9	118 59.9	26.2	97 40.4	36.7	Avior	234 22.2	S59 30.8
21	144 46.5	100 07.1	.. 48.9	285 38.8	.. 12.8	134 01.8	.. 26.5	112 42.6	.. 36.8	Bellatrix	278 43.9	N 6 20.7
22	159 48.9	115 06.6	49.9	300 41.7	12.7	149 03.7	26.7	127 44.7	36.9	Betelgeuse	271 13.3	N 7 24.2
23	174 51.4	130 06.1	50.9	315 44.7	12.6	164 05.6	26.9	142 46.9	37.0			
2 FRIDAY												
00	189 53.8	145 05.6	N17 51.8	330 47.6	S13 12.5	179 07.5	N 3 27.2	157 49.1	N10 37.1	Canopus	264 01.1	S52 42.1
01	204 56.3	160 05.1	52.8	345 50.5	12.4	194 09.4	27.4	172 51.3	37.3	Capella	280 50.9	N45 59.8
02	219 58.8	175 04.6	53.8	0 53.4	12.3	209 11.3	27.7	187 53.4	37.4	Deneb	49 39.2	N45 16.4
03	235 01.2	190 04.2	.. 54.7	15 56.4	.. 12.2	224 13.2	.. 27.9	202 55.6	.. 37.5	Denebola	182 44.6	N14 34.5
04	250 03.7	205 03.7	55.7	30 59.3	12.1	239 15.1	28.1	217 57.8	37.6	Diphda	349 07.3	S17 59.7
05	265 06.2	220 03.2	56.7	46 02.2	12.0	254 17.0	28.4	233 00.0	37.7			
06	280 08.6	235 02.7	N17 57.7	61 05.1	S13 11.9	269 18.9	N 3 28.6	248 02.1	N10 37.8	Dubhe	194 04.6	N61 45.4
07	295 11.1	250 02.2	58.6	76 08.1	11.8	284 20.9	28.8	263 04.3	37.9	Elnath	278 26.7	N28 36.3
08	310 13.6	265 01.7	17 59.6	91 11.0	11.7	299 22.8	29.1	278 06.5	38.0	Eltanin	90 51.1	N51 29.1
09	325 16.0	280 01.2	18 00.5	106 13.9	.. 11.6	314 24.7	.. 29.3	293 08.7	.. 38.1	Enif	33 58.1	N 9 52.1
10	340 18.5	295 00.7	01.5	121 16.9	11.5	329 26.6	29.5	308 10.8	38.2	Fomalhaut	15 36.4	S29 37.7
11	355 20.9	310 00.2	02.5	136 19.8	11.4	344 28.5	29.8	323 13.0	38.3			
12	10 23.4	324 59.7	N18 03.4	151 22.7	S13 11.3	359 30.4	N 3 30.0	338 15.2	N10 38.4	Gacrux	172 12.6	S57 06.5
13	25 25.9	339 59.2	04.4	166 25.7	11.2	14 32.3	30.3	353 17.3	38.5	Gienah	176 03.3	S17 32.3
14	40 28.3	354 58.7	05.4	181 28.6	11.1	29 34.2	30.5	8 19.5	38.6	Hadar	149 02.9	S60 22.0
15	55 30.8	9 58.2	.. 06.3	196 31.6	.. 11.0	44 36.1	.. 30.7	23 21.7	.. 38.7	Hamal	328 13.5	N23 27.3
16	70 33.3	24 57.7	07.3	211 34.5	10.9	59 38.0	31.0	38 23.9	38.9	Kaus Aust.	83 58.4	S34 22.9
17	85 35.7	39 57.2	08.2	226 37.4	10.8	74 39.9	31.2	53 26.0	39.0			
18	100 38.2	54 56.7	N18 09.2	241 40.4	S13 10.7	89 41.8	N 3 31.4	68 28.2	N10 39.1	Kochab	137 18.7	N74 09.5
19	115 40.7	69 56.2	10.2	256 43.3	10.6	104 43.7	31.7	83 30.4	39.2	Markab	13 49.6	N15 11.9
20	130 43.1	84 55.6	11.1	271 46.3	10.5	119 45.6	31.9	98 32.6	39.3	Menkar	314 26.8	N 4 05.0
21	145 45.6	99 55.1	.. 12.1	286 49.2	.. 10.4	134 47.5	.. 32.1	113 34.7	.. 39.4	Menkent	148 20.2	S36 21.9
22	160 48.1	114 54.6	13.0	301 52.2	10.3	149 49.5	32.4	128 36.9	39.5	Miaplacidus	221 41.4	S69 43.1
23	175 50.5	129 54.1	14.0	316 55.1	10.1	164 51.4	32.6	143 39.1	39.6			
3 SATURDAY												
00	190 53.0	144 53.6	N18 14.9	331 58.1	S13 10.0	179 53.3	N 3 32.9	158 41.2	N10 39.7	Mirfak	308 56.5	N49 51.4
01	205 55.4	159 53.1	15.9	347 01.0	09.9	194 55.2	33.1	173 43.4	39.8	Nunki	76 12.0	S26 17.8
02	220 57.9	174 52.6	16.8	2 04.0	09.8	209 57.1	33.3	188 45.6	39.9	Peacock	53 36.8	S56 44.0
03	236 00.4	189 52.1	.. 17.8	17 07.0	.. 09.7	224 59.0	.. 33.6	203 47.8	.. 40.0	Pollux	243 41.1	N28 01.6
04	251 02.8	204 51.6	18.7	32 09.9	09.6	240 00.9	33.8	218 49.9	40.1	Procyon	245 11.2	N 5 13.5
05	266 05.3	219 51.1	19.7	47 12.9	09.5	255 02.8	34.0	233 52.1	40.2			
06	281 07.8	234 50.6	N18 20.6	62 15.8	S13 09.3	270 04.7	N 3 34.3	248 54.3	N10 40.4	Rasalhague	96 16.6	N12 33.6
07	296 10.2	249 50.1	21.6	77 18.8	09.3	285 06.6	34.5	263 56.5	40.5	Regulus	207 55.0	N11 58.2
08	311 12.7	264 49.6	22.5	92 21.8	09.2	300 08.5	34.7	278 58.6	40.6	Rigel	281 22.8	S 8 12.4
09	326 15.2	279 49.1	.. 23.5	107 24.7	.. 09.1	315 10.4	.. 35.0	294 00.8	.. 40.7	Rigil Kent.	140 06.3	S60 49.7
10	341 17.6	294 48.6	24.4	122 27.7	08.9	330 12.3	35.2	309 03.0	40.8	Sabik	102 25.0	S15 43.4
11	356 20.1	309 48.1	25.4	137 30.6	08.8	345 14.2	35.5	324 05.1	40.9			
12	11 22.5	324 47.5	N18 26.3	152 33.6	S13 08.7	0 16.1	N 3 35.7	339 07.3	N10 41.0	Schedar	349 53.6	N56 31.8
13	26 25.0	339 47.0	27.3	167 36.6	08.6	15 18.0	35.9	354 09.5	41.1	Shaula	96 36.7	S37 06.0
14	41 27.5	354 46.5	28.2	182 39.6	08.5	30 20.0	36.2	9 11.7	41.2	Sirius	258 43.5	S16 43.2
15	56 29.9	9 46.0	.. 29.2	197 42.5	.. 08.4	45 21.9	.. 36.4	24 13.8	.. 41.3	Spica	158 42.5	S11 09.5
16	71 32.4	24 45.5	30.1	212 45.5	08.3	60 23.8	36.6	39 16.0	41.4	Suhail	223 00.3	S43 26.1
17	86 34.9	39 45.0	31.0	227 48.5	08.2	75 25.7	36.9	54 18.2	41.5			
18	101 37.3	54 44.5	N18 32.0	242 51.4	S13 08.1	90 27.6	N 3 37.1	69 20.3	N10 41.6	Vega	80 46.4	N38 46.8
19	116 39.8	69 44.0	32.9	257 54.4	07.9	105 29.5	37.3	84 22.5	41.7	Zuben'ubi	137 17.3	S16 02.3
20	131 42.3	84 43.5	33.9	272 57.4	07.8	120 31.4	37.6	99 24.7	41.8			
21	146 44.7	99 42.9	.. 34.8	288 00.4	.. 07.7	135 33.3	.. 37.8	114 26.9	.. 42.0			
22	161 47.2	114 42.4	35.7	303 03.4	07.6	150 35.2	38.0	129 29.0	42.1			
23	176 49.7	129 41.9	36.7	318 06.3	07.5	165 37.1	38.3	144 31.2	42.2			
Mer. Pass.	11 18.6	v −0.5	d 1.0	v 2.9	d 0.1	v 1.9	d 0.2	v 2.2	d 0.1			

Stars, lower right:

Name	SHA	Mer. Pass.
Venus	315 11.8	14 20
Mars	140 53.7	1 56
Jupiter	349 13.7	12 02
Saturn	327 55.2	13 27

UT	SUN GHA	SUN Dec	MOON GHA	v	Dec	d	HP
d h	° ′	° ′	° ′	′	° ′	′	′
1 00	178 58.0	N 4 17.0	356 54.9	14.7	S 0 52.9	10.3	54.9
01	193 58.2	17.9	11 28.6	14.7	1 03.2	10.3	54.8
02	208 58.4	18.9	26 02.3	14.7	1 13.5	10.3	54.8
03	223 58.6	.. 19.9	40 36.0	14.7	1 23.8	10.2	54.8
04	238 58.8	20.8	55 09.7	14.7	1 34.0	10.3	54.8
05	253 58.9	21.8	69 43.4	14.7	1 44.3	10.2	54.8
06	268 59.1	N 4 22.7	84 17.1	14.7	S 1 54.5	10.3	54.8
07	283 59.3	23.7	98 50.8	14.8	2 04.8	10.2	54.8
08	298 59.5	24.7	113 24.6	14.7	2 15.0	10.2	54.7
09	313 59.7	.. 25.6	127 58.3	14.8	2 25.2	10.2	54.7
10	328 59.9	26.6	142 32.1	14.8	2 35.4	10.1	54.7
11	344 00.1	27.6	157 05.9	14.7	2 45.5	10.1	54.7
12	359 00.2	N 4 28.5	171 39.6	14.8	S 2 55.7	10.1	54.7
13	14 00.4	29.5	186 13.4	14.8	3 05.8	10.2	54.7
14	29 00.6	30.5	200 47.2	14.8	3 16.0	10.1	54.7
15	44 00.8	.. 31.4	215 21.0	14.8	3 26.1	10.1	54.6
16	59 01.0	32.4	229 54.8	14.8	3 36.2	10.0	54.6
17	74 01.2	33.4	244 28.6	14.8	3 46.2	10.1	54.6
18	89 01.4	N 4 34.3	259 02.4	14.8	S 3 56.3	10.0	54.6
19	104 01.6	35.3	273 36.2	14.8	4 06.3	10.0	54.6
20	119 01.7	36.3	288 10.0	14.8	4 16.3	10.0	54.6
21	134 01.9	.. 37.2	302 43.8	14.8	4 26.3	9.9	54.6
22	149 02.1	38.2	317 17.6	14.9	4 36.2	10.0	54.6
23	164 02.3	39.1	331 51.5	14.8	4 46.2	9.9	54.5
2 00	179 02.5	N 4 40.1	346 25.3	14.8	S 4 56.1	9.8	54.5
01	194 02.7	41.1	0 59.1	14.8	5 05.9	9.9	54.5
02	209 02.9	42.0	15 32.9	14.8	5 15.8	9.8	54.5
03	224 03.0	.. 43.0	30 06.7	14.8	5 25.6	9.8	54.5
04	239 03.2	44.0	44 40.5	14.8	5 35.4	9.8	54.5
05	254 03.4	44.9	59 14.3	14.8	5 45.2	9.8	54.5
06	269 03.6	N 4 45.9	73 48.1	14.8	S 5 55.0	9.7	54.5
07	284 03.8	46.9	88 21.9	14.8	6 04.7	9.7	54.4
08	299 04.0	47.8	102 55.7	14.8	6 14.4	9.6	54.4
09	314 04.2	.. 48.8	117 29.5	14.8	6 24.0	9.7	54.4
10	329 04.4	49.7	132 03.3	14.8	6 33.7	9.6	54.4
11	344 04.5	50.7	146 37.1	14.8	6 43.3	9.5	54.4
12	359 04.7	N 4 51.7	161 10.9	14.7	S 6 52.8	9.6	54.4
13	14 04.9	52.6	175 44.6	14.8	7 02.4	9.5	54.4
14	29 05.1	53.6	190 18.4	14.8	7 11.9	9.5	54.4
15	44 05.3	.. 54.5	204 52.2	14.7	7 21.4	9.4	54.4
16	59 05.5	55.5	219 25.9	14.7	7 30.8	9.4	54.3
17	74 05.7	56.5	233 59.6	14.8	7 40.2	9.4	54.3
18	89 05.8	N 4 57.4	248 33.4	14.7	S 7 49.6	9.3	54.3
19	104 06.0	58.4	263 07.1	14.7	7 58.9	9.3	54.3
20	119 06.2	4 59.3	277 40.8	14.7	8 08.2	9.2	54.3
21	134 06.4	5 00.3	292 14.5	14.7	8 17.4	9.2	54.3
22	149 06.6	01.3	306 48.2	14.7	8 26.6	9.2	54.3
23	164 06.8	02.2	321 21.9	14.6	8 35.8	9.2	54.3
3 00	179 06.9	N 5 03.2	335 55.5	14.7	S 8 45.0	9.1	54.3
01	194 07.1	04.1	350 29.2	14.6	8 54.1	9.0	54.3
02	209 07.3	05.1	5 02.8	14.7	9 03.1	9.1	54.3
03	224 07.5	.. 06.1	19 36.5	14.6	9 12.2	8.9	54.2
04	239 07.7	07.0	34 10.1	14.6	9 21.1	9.0	54.2
05	254 07.9	08.0	48 43.7	14.6	9 30.1	8.9	54.2
06	269 08.1	N 5 08.9	63 17.3	14.5	S 9 39.0	8.8	54.2
07	284 08.2	09.9	77 50.8	14.6	9 47.8	8.8	54.2
08	299 08.4	10.9	92 24.4	14.5	9 56.6	8.8	54.2
09	314 08.6	.. 11.8	106 57.9	14.5	10 05.4	8.7	54.2
10	329 08.8	12.8	121 31.4	14.5	10 14.1	8.7	54.2
11	344 09.0	13.7	136 04.9	14.5	10 22.8	8.6	54.2
12	359 09.2	N 5 14.7	150 38.4	14.5	S 10 31.4	8.6	54.2
13	14 09.3	15.7	165 11.9	14.5	10 40.0	8.5	54.2
14	29 09.5	16.6	179 45.4	14.4	10 48.5	8.5	54.2
15	44 09.7	.. 17.6	194 18.8	14.4	10 57.0	8.5	54.2
16	59 09.9	18.5	208 52.2	14.4	11 05.5	8.3	54.2
17	74 10.1	19.5	223 25.6	14.4	11 13.8	8.4	54.1
18	89 10.3	N 5 20.4	237 59.0	14.4	S 11 22.2	8.3	54.1
19	104 10.5	21.4	252 32.4	14.3	11 30.5	8.2	54.1
20	119 10.6	22.4	267 05.7	14.3	11 38.7	8.2	54.1
21	134 10.8	.. 23.3	281 39.0	14.3	11 46.9	8.2	54.1
22	149 11.0	24.3	296 12.3	14.3	11 55.1	8.0	54.1
23	164 11.2	25.2	310 45.6	14.2	S12 03.1	8.1	54.1
	SD 16.0	d 1.0	SD 14.9		14.8		14.8

(THURSDAY = day 1; FRIDAY = day 2; SATURDAY = day 3)

Lat.	Twilight Naut.	Twilight Civil	Sunrise	Moonrise 1	2	3	4
°	h m	h m	h m	h m	h m	h m	h m
N 72	01 31	03 38	04 53	19 40	21 20	23 03	24 53
N 70	02 17	03 55	05 01	19 34	21 07	22 41	24 16
68	02 46	04 08	05 07	19 29	20 56	22 24	23 51
66	03 07	04 18	05 12	19 25	20 48	22 10	23 31
64	03 23	04 27	05 17	19 21	20 40	21 59	23 15
62	03 36	04 35	05 21	19 18	20 34	21 49	23 02
60	03 47	04 41	05 24	19 16	20 29	21 41	22 51
N 58	03 57	04 47	05 27	19 13	20 24	21 34	22 42
56	04 05	04 51	05 29	19 11	20 21	21 27	22 33
54	04 12	04 56	05 32	19 09	20 16	21 22	22 26
52	04 18	05 00	05 34	19 08	20 13	21 17	22 19
50	04 24	05 03	05 36	19 06	20 10	21 12	22 13
45	04 35	05 10	05 40	19 03	20 03	21 02	22 01
N 40	04 44	05 16	05 43	19 00	19 57	20 54	21 50
35	04 51	05 21	05 46	18 57	19 52	20 47	21 41
30	04 57	05 25	05 49	18 55	19 48	20 41	21 33
20	05 05	05 31	05 53	18 52	19 41	20 30	21 20
N 10	05 11	05 36	05 57	18 49	19 35	20 21	21 08
0	05 16	05 40	06 00	18 46	19 29	20 12	20 57
S 10	05 18	05 43	06 04	18 43	19 23	20 04	20 46
20	05 20	05 45	06 07	18 39	19 17	19 55	20 34
30	05 19	05 47	06 11	18 36	19 10	19 44	20 21
35	05 18	05 48	06 13	18 34	19 06	19 38	20 13
40	05 17	05 48	06 15	18 32	19 01	19 32	20 05
45	05 15	05 49	06 18	18 29	18 56	19 24	19 54
S 50	05 12	05 49	06 21	18 26	18 49	19 15	19 42
52	05 10	05 49	06 23	18 25	18 47	19 10	19 37
54	05 08	05 49	06 24	18 23	18 43	19 05	19 30
56	05 06	05 49	06 26	18 21	18 40	19 00	19 24
58	05 03	05 49	06 28	18 19	18 36	18 54	19 16
S 60	05 00	05 49	06 30	18 17	18 32	18 48	19 07

Lat.	Sunset	Twilight Civil	Twilight Naut.	Moonset 1	2	3	4
°	h m	h m	h m	h m	h m	h m	h m
N 72	19 17	20 34	22 48	05 58	05 49	05 39	05 27
N 70	19 09	20 16	21 57	06 01	05 57	05 54	05 51
68	19 03	20 03	21 27	06 03	06 04	06 06	06 09
66	18 57	19 52	21 04	06 05	06 10	06 16	06 24
64	18 52	19 42	20 47	06 06	06 15	06 25	06 36
62	18 49	19 35	20 34	06 08	06 19	06 32	06 46
60	18 45	19 28	20 22	06 09	06 23	06 38	06 55
N 58	18 42	19 22	20 13	06 10	06 26	06 44	07 03
56	18 39	19 17	20 04	06 11	06 29	06 48	07 10
54	18 37	19 13	19 57	06 12	06 32	06 53	07 16
52	18 35	19 09	19 51	06 13	06 34	06 57	07 22
50	18 33	19 06	19 45	06 13	06 36	07 01	07 27
45	18 29	19 00	19 34	06 15	06 41	07 08	07 38
N 40	18 25	18 52	19 24	06 16	06 45	07 15	07 47
35	18 22	18 47	19 17	06 17	06 49	07 21	07 55
30	18 19	18 43	19 11	06 18	06 52	07 26	08 01
20	18 14	18 37	19 02	06 20	06 57	07 35	08 13
N 10	18 11	18 32	18 56	06 22	07 02	07 42	08 24
0	18 07	18 28	18 52	06 23	07 06	07 50	08 34
S 10	18 04	18 25	18 49	06 25	07 11	07 57	08 44
20	18 00	18 22	18 48	06 26	07 16	08 05	08 54
30	17 56	18 20	18 48	06 28	07 21	08 14	09 06
35	17 54	18 19	18 48	06 29	07 24	08 19	09 13
40	17 51	18 18	18 50	06 30	07 28	08 25	09 21
45	17 48	18 18	18 52	06 31	07 32	08 31	09 30
S 50	17 45	18 17	18 55	06 33	07 37	08 40	09 42
52	17 44	18 17	18 56	06 33	07 39	08 43	09 47
54	17 42	18 17	18 58	06 34	07 41	08 48	09 53
56	17 40	18 17	19 00	06 35	07 44	08 52	09 59
58	17 38	18 17	19 03	06 36	07 47	08 57	10 06
S 60	17 36	18 17	19 05	06 37	07 51	09 03	10 15

	SUN Eqn. of Time 00ʰ	SUN Eqn. of Time 12ʰ	SUN Mer. Pass.	MOON Mer. Pass. Upper	MOON Mer. Pass. Lower	Age	Phase
d	m s	m s	h m	h m	h m	d	%
1	04 08	03 59	12 04	00 13	12 34	15	100
2	03 50	03 41	12 04	00 56	13 18	16	98
3	03 33	03 24	12 03	01 39	14 01	17	94

1999 APRIL 4, 5, 6 (SUN., MON., TUES.)

UT (d h)	ARIES GHA	VENUS GHA	VENUS Dec	MARS GHA	MARS Dec	JUPITER GHA	JUPITER Dec	SATURN GHA	SATURN Dec	Star Name	SHA	Dec
4 00	191 52.1	144 41.4	N18 37.6	333 09.3	S13 07.4	180 39.0	N 3 38.5	159 33.4	N10 42.3	Acamar	315 27.1	S40 18.8
01	206 54.6	159 40.9	38.5	348 12.3	07.3	195 40.9	38.8	174 35.6	42.4	Achernar	335 35.6	S57 14.7
02	221 57.0	174 40.4	39.5	3 15.3	07.1	210 42.8	39.0	189 37.7	42.5	Acrux	173 20.9	S63 05.7
03	236 59.5	189 39.9 ..	40.4	18 18.3 ..	07.0	225 44.7 ..	39.2	204 39.9 ..	42.6	Adhara	255 21.2	S28 58.6
04	252 02.0	204 39.3	41.3	33 21.3	06.9	240 46.6	39.5	219 42.1	42.7	Aldebaran	291 02.2	N16 30.3
05	267 04.4	219 38.8	42.3	48 24.3	06.8	255 48.5	39.7	234 44.2	42.8			
06	282 06.9	234 38.3	N18 43.2	63 27.3	S13 06.7	270 50.4	N 3 39.9	249 46.4	N10 42.9	Alioth	166 29.8	N55 57.9
07	297 09.4	249 37.8	44.1	78 30.2	06.6	285 52.4	40.2	264 48.6	43.0	Alkaid	153 07.1	N49 19.0
08 S	312 11.8	264 37.3	45.0	93 33.2	06.4	300 54.3	40.4	279 50.7	43.1	Al Na'ir	27 57.9	S46 57.8
09 U	327 14.3	279 36.8 ..	46.0	108 36.2 ..	06.3	315 56.2 ..	40.6	294 52.9 ..	43.2	Alnilam	275 57.7	S 1 12.4
10 N	342 16.8	294 36.2	46.9	123 39.2	06.2	330 58.1	40.9	309 55.1	43.3	Alphard	218 06.7	S 8 39.5
11 D	357 19.2	309 35.7	47.8	138 42.2	06.1	346 00.0	41.1	324 57.3	43.5			
12 A	12 21.7	324 35.2	N18 48.8	153 45.2	S13 06.0	1 01.9	N 3 41.4	339 59.4	N10 43.6	Alphecca	126 20.1	N26 43.0
13 Y	27 24.2	339 34.7	49.7	168 48.2	05.8	16 03.8	41.6	355 01.6	43.7	Alpheratz	357 55.2	N29 04.9
14	42 26.6	354 34.2	50.6	183 51.2	05.7	31 05.7	41.8	10 03.8	43.8	Altair	62 19.0	N 8 51.9
15	57 29.1	9 33.7 ..	51.5	198 54.2 ..	05.6	46 07.6 ..	42.1	25 05.9 ..	43.9	Ankaa	353 27.0	S42 18.8
16	72 31.5	24 33.1	52.4	213 57.2	05.5	61 09.5	42.3	40 08.1	44.0	Antares	112 39.6	S26 25.7
17	87 34.0	39 32.6	53.4	229 00.2	05.4	76 11.4	42.5	55 10.3	44.1			
18	102 36.5	54 32.1	N18 54.3	244 03.2	S13 05.2	91 13.3	N 3 42.8	70 12.5	N10 44.2	Arcturus	146 05.5	N19 11.1
19	117 38.9	69 31.6	55.2	259 06.2	05.1	106 15.2	43.0	85 14.6	44.3	Atria	107 51.0	S69 01.3
20	132 41.4	84 31.1	56.1	274 09.3	05.0	121 17.1	43.2	100 16.8	44.4	Avior	234 22.3	S59 30.8
21	147 43.9	99 30.5 ..	57.0	289 12.3 ..	04.9	136 19.0 ..	43.5	115 19.0 ..	44.5	Bellatrix	278 44.0	N 6 20.7
22	162 46.3	114 30.0	58.0	304 15.3	04.8	151 20.9	43.7	130 21.1	44.6	Betelgeuse	271 13.3	N 7 24.2
23	177 48.8	129 29.5	58.9	319 18.3	04.6	166 22.9	43.9	145 23.3	44.7			
5 00	192 51.3	144 29.0	N18 59.8	334 21.3	S13 04.5	181 24.8	N 3 44.2	160 25.5	N10 44.8	Canopus	264 01.1	S52 42.1
01	207 53.7	159 28.4	19 00.7	349 24.3	04.4	196 26.7	44.4	175 27.7	44.9	Capella	280 50.9	N45 59.8
02	222 56.2	174 27.9	01.6	4 27.3	04.3	211 28.6	44.6	190 29.8	45.1	Deneb	49 39.1	N45 16.4
03	237 58.6	189 27.4 ..	02.5	19 30.3 ..	04.1	226 30.5 ..	44.9	205 32.0 ..	45.2	Denebola	182 44.6	N14 34.5
04	253 01.1	204 26.9	03.5	34 33.4	04.0	241 32.4	45.1	220 34.2	45.3	Diphda	349 07.3	S17 59.7
05	268 03.6	219 26.3	04.4	49 36.4	03.9	256 34.3	45.4	235 36.3	45.4			
06	283 06.0	234 25.8	N19 05.3	64 39.4	S13 03.8	271 36.2	N 3 45.6	250 38.5	N10 45.5	Dubhe	194 04.6	N61 45.4
07	298 08.5	249 25.3	06.2	79 42.4	03.6	286 38.1	45.8	265 40.7	45.6	Elnath	278 26.7	N28 36.3
08 M	313 11.0	264 24.8	07.1	94 45.4	03.5	301 40.0	46.1	280 42.8	45.7	Eltanin	90 51.1	N51 29.1
09 O	328 13.4	279 24.2 ..	08.0	109 48.5 ..	03.4	316 41.9 ..	46.3	295 45.0 ..	45.8	Enif	33 58.1	N 9 52.1
10 N	343 15.9	294 23.7	08.9	124 51.5	03.3	331 43.8	46.5	310 47.2	45.9	Fomalhaut	15 36.4	S29 37.7
11 D	358 18.4	309 23.2	09.8	139 54.5	03.1	346 45.7	46.8	325 49.4	46.0			
12 A	13 20.8	324 22.7	N19 10.7	154 57.5	S13 03.0	1 47.6	N 3 47.0	340 51.5	N10 46.1	Gacrux	172 12.6	S57 06.6
13 Y	28 23.3	339 22.1	11.6	170 00.6	02.9	16 49.5	47.2	355 53.7	46.2	Gienah	176 03.3	S17 32.3
14	43 25.8	354 21.6	12.5	185 03.6	02.8	31 51.4	47.5	10 55.9	46.3	Hadar	149 02.9	S60 22.0
15	58 28.2	9 21.1 ..	13.4	200 06.6 ..	02.6	46 53.4 ..	47.7	25 58.0 ..	46.4	Hamal	328 13.5	N23 27.3
16	73 30.7	24 20.5	14.3	215 09.7	02.5	61 55.3	47.9	41 00.2	46.6	Kaus Aust.	83 58.3	S34 22.9
17	88 33.1	39 20.0	15.2	230 12.7	02.4	76 57.2	48.2	56 02.4	46.7			
18	103 35.6	54 19.5	N19 16.1	245 15.7	S13 02.2	91 59.1	N 3 48.4	71 04.5	N10 46.8	Kochab	137 18.6	N74 09.5
19	118 38.1	69 19.0	17.0	260 18.8	02.1	107 01.0	48.7	86 06.7	46.9	Markab	13 49.6	N15 11.9
20	133 40.5	84 18.4	17.9	275 21.8	02.0	122 02.9	48.9	101 08.9	47.0	Menkar	314 26.8	N 4 05.0
21	148 43.0	99 17.9 ..	18.8	290 24.9 ..	01.9	137 04.8 ..	49.1	116 11.0 ..	47.1	Menkent	148 20.2	S36 21.9
22	163 45.5	114 17.4	19.7	305 27.9	01.7	152 06.7	49.4	131 13.2	47.2	Miaplacidus	221 41.5	S69 43.2
23	178 47.9	129 16.8	20.6	320 30.9	01.6	167 08.6	49.6	146 15.4	47.3			
6 00	193 50.4	144 16.3	N19 21.5	335 34.0	S13 01.5	182 10.5	N 3 49.8	161 17.6	N10 47.4	Mirfak	308 56.5	N49 51.4
01	208 52.9	159 15.8	22.4	350 37.0	01.3	197 12.4	50.1	176 19.7	47.5	Nunki	76 11.9	S26 17.8
02	223 55.3	174 15.2	23.3	5 40.1	01.2	212 14.3	50.3	191 21.9	47.6	Peacock	53 36.7	S56 44.0
03	238 57.8	189 14.7 ..	24.2	20 43.1 ..	01.1	227 16.2 ..	50.5	206 24.1 ..	47.7	Pollux	243 41.1	N28 01.6
04	254 00.3	204 14.2	25.1	35 46.2	00.9	242 18.1	50.8	221 26.2	47.8	Procyon	245 11.2	N 5 13.5
05	269 02.7	219 13.6	26.0	50 49.2	00.8	257 20.0	51.0	236 28.4	47.9			
06	284 05.2	234 13.1	N19 26.9	65 52.3	S13 00.7	272 21.9	N 3 51.2	251 30.6	N10 48.1	Rasalhague	96 16.5	N12 33.6
07	299 07.6	249 12.6	27.8	80 55.3	00.6	287 23.9	51.5	266 32.7	48.2	Regulus	207 55.0	N11 58.2
08 T	314 10.1	264 12.0	28.7	95 58.4	00.4	302 25.8	51.7	281 34.9	48.3	Rigel	281 22.8	S 8 12.4
09 U	329 12.6	279 11.5 ..	29.5	111 01.4 ..	00.3	317 27.7 ..	51.9	296 37.1 ..	48.4	Rigil Kent.	140 06.2	S60 49.7
10 E	344 15.0	294 11.0	30.4	126 04.5	00.2	332 29.6	52.2	311 39.2	48.5	Sabik	102 25.0	S15 43.4
11 S	359 17.5	309 10.4	31.3	141 07.5	13 00.0	347 31.5	52.4	326 41.4	48.6			
12 D	14 20.0	324 09.9	N19 32.2	156 10.6	S12 59.9	2 33.4	N 3 52.7	341 43.6	N10 48.7	Schedar	349 53.6	N56 31.8
13 A	29 22.4	339 09.4	33.1	171 13.6	59.8	17 35.3	52.9	356 45.8	48.8	Shaula	96 36.7	S37 06.0
14 Y	44 24.9	354 08.8	34.0	186 16.7	59.6	32 37.2	53.1	11 47.9	48.9	Sirius	258 43.5	S16 43.2
15	59 27.4	9 08.3 ..	34.9	201 19.8 ..	59.5	47 39.1 ..	53.4	26 50.1 ..	49.0	Spica	158 42.5	S11 09.5
16	74 29.8	24 07.7	35.7	216 22.8	59.3	62 41.0	53.6	41 52.3	49.1	Suhail	223 00.3	S43 26.1
17	89 32.3	39 07.2	36.6	231 25.9	59.2	77 42.9	53.8	56 54.4	49.2			
18	104 34.7	54 06.7	N19 37.5	246 29.0	S12 59.1	92 44.8	N 3 54.1	71 56.6	N10 49.3	Vega	80 46.4	N38 46.8
19	119 37.2	69 06.1	38.4	261 32.0	58.9	107 46.7	54.3	86 58.8	49.4	Zuben'ubi	137 17.3	S16 02.3
20	134 39.7	84 05.6	39.3	276 35.1	58.8	122 48.6	54.5	102 00.9	49.6		SHA	Mer. Pass.
21	149 42.1	99 05.0 ..	40.1	291 38.2 ..	58.7	137 50.5 ..	54.8	117 03.1 ..	49.7	Venus	311 37.7	14 23
22	164 44.6	114 04.5	41.0	306 41.2	58.5	152 52.4	55.0	132 05.3	49.8	Mars	141 30.0	1 42
23	179 47.1	129 04.0	41.9	321 44.3	58.4	167 54.4	55.2	147 07.4	49.9	Jupiter	348 33.5	11 53
Mer. Pass. 11 06.8		v −0.5	d 0.9	v 3.0	d 0.1	v 1.9	d 0.2	v 2.2	d 0.1	Saturn	327 34.2	13 16

SUN and MOON

UT (d h)	SUN GHA	SUN Dec	MOON GHA	v	Dec	d	HP
	° ′	° ′	° ′	′	° ′	′	′
4 00	179 11.4	N 5 26.2	325 18.8	14.3	S12 11.2	8.0	54.1
01	194 11.6	27.1	339 52.1	14.2	12 19.2	7.9	54.1
02	209 11.7	28.1	354 25.3	14.2	12 27.1	7.9	54.1
03	224 11.9	.. 29.0	8 58.5	14.1	12 35.0	7.8	54.1
04	239 12.1	30.0	23 31.6	14.2	12 42.8	7.8	54.1
05	254 12.3	31.0	38 04.8	14.1	12 50.6	7.7	54.1
06	269 12.5	N 5 31.9	52 37.9	14.1	S12 58.3	7.6	54.1
07	284 12.7	32.9	67 11.0	14.0	13 05.9	7.6	54.1
08	299 12.8	33.8	81 44.0	14.1	13 13.5	7.6	54.1
S 09	314 13.0	.. 34.8	96 17.1	14.0	13 21.1	7.4	54.1
U 10	329 13.2	35.7	110 50.1	14.0	13 28.5	7.5	54.1
N 11	344 13.4	36.7	125 23.1	14.0	13 36.0	7.3	54.1
D 12	359 13.6	N 5 37.6	139 56.1	13.9	S13 43.3	7.3	54.1
A 13	14 13.7	38.6	154 29.0	13.9	13 50.6	7.3	54.1
Y 14	29 13.9	39.5	169 01.9	13.9	13 57.9	7.2	54.1
15	44 14.1	.. 40.5	183 34.8	13.9	14 05.1	7.1	54.1
16	59 14.3	41.5	198 07.7	13.8	14 12.2	7.1	54.1
17	74 14.5	42.4	212 40.5	13.8	14 19.3	7.0	54.1
18	89 14.7	N 5 43.4	227 13.3	13.8	S14 26.3	6.9	54.1
19	104 14.8	44.3	241 46.1	13.8	14 33.2	6.9	54.1
20	119 15.0	45.3	256 18.9	13.7	14 40.1	6.8	54.1
21	134 15.2	.. 46.2	270 51.6	13.7	14 46.9	6.7	54.1
22	149 15.4	47.2	285 24.3	13.6	14 53.6	6.7	54.1
23	164 15.6	48.1	299 56.9	13.7	15 00.3	6.6	54.1
5 00	179 15.8	N 5 49.1	314 29.6	13.6	S15 06.9	6.6	54.1
01	194 15.9	50.0	329 02.2	13.6	15 13.5	6.5	54.1
02	209 16.1	51.0	343 34.8	13.5	15 20.0	6.4	54.1
03	224 16.3	.. 51.9	358 07.3	13.6	15 26.4	6.4	54.1
04	239 16.5	52.9	12 39.9	13.4	15 32.8	6.3	54.1
05	254 16.6	53.8	27 12.3	13.5	15 39.1	6.2	54.1
06	269 16.8	N 5 54.8	41 44.8	13.4	S15 45.3	6.1	54.1
07	284 17.0	55.7	56 17.2	13.5	15 51.4	6.1	54.1
08	299 17.2	56.7	70 49.7	13.3	15 57.5	6.0	54.1
M 09	314 17.4	.. 57.6	85 22.0	13.4	16 03.5	6.0	54.1
O 10	329 17.6	58.6	99 54.4	13.3	16 09.5	5.8	54.1
N 11	344 17.7	5 59.5	114 26.7	13.3	16 15.3	5.8	54.1
D 12	359 17.9	N 6 00.5	128 59.0	13.2	S16 21.1	5.8	54.1
A 13	14 18.1	01.4	143 31.2	13.2	16 26.9	5.6	54.1
Y 14	29 18.3	02.4	158 03.4	13.2	16 32.5	5.6	54.1
15	44 18.5	.. 03.3	172 35.6	13.2	16 38.1	5.5	54.1
16	59 18.6	04.3	187 07.8	13.1	16 43.6	5.5	54.1
17	74 18.8	05.2	201 39.9	13.1	16 49.1	5.4	54.1
18	89 19.0	N 6 06.2	216 12.0	13.1	S16 54.5	5.2	54.1
19	104 19.2	07.1	230 44.1	13.0	16 59.7	5.3	54.1
20	119 19.4	08.1	245 16.1	13.0	17 05.0	5.1	54.1
21	134 19.5	.. 09.0	259 48.1	13.0	17 10.1	5.1	54.1
22	149 19.7	10.0	274 20.1	12.9	17 15.2	5.0	54.1
23	164 19.9	10.9	288 52.0	12.9	17 20.2	4.9	54.1
6 00	179 20.1	N 6 11.9	303 23.9	12.9	S17 25.1	4.8	54.1
01	194 20.3	12.8	317 55.8	12.8	17 29.9	4.8	54.2
02	209 20.4	13.8	332 27.6	12.8	17 34.7	4.7	54.2
03	224 20.6	.. 14.7	346 59.4	12.8	17 39.4	4.6	54.2
04	239 20.8	15.7	1 31.2	12.8	17 44.0	4.5	54.2
05	254 21.0	16.6	16 03.0	12.7	17 48.5	4.5	54.2
06	269 21.2	N 6 17.5	30 34.7	12.7	S17 53.0	4.4	54.2
07	284 21.3	18.5	45 06.4	12.6	17 57.4	4.2	54.2
T 08	299 21.5	19.4	59 38.0	12.6	18 01.6	4.3	54.2
U 09	314 21.7	.. 20.4	74 09.6	12.6	18 05.9	4.1	54.2
E 10	329 21.9	21.3	88 41.2	12.6	18 10.0	4.0	54.2
S 11	344 22.1	22.3	103 12.8	12.5	18 14.0	4.0	54.2
D 12	359 22.2	N 6 23.2	117 44.3	12.5	S18 18.0	3.9	54.2
A 13	14 22.4	24.2	132 15.8	12.4	18 21.9	3.8	54.3
Y 14	29 22.6	25.1	146 47.2	12.5	18 25.7	3.7	54.3
15	44 22.8	.. 26.1	161 18.7	12.4	18 29.4	3.7	54.3
16	59 23.0	27.0	175 50.1	12.3	18 33.1	3.5	54.3
17	74 23.1	27.9	190 21.4	12.3	18 36.6	3.5	54.3
18	89 23.3	N 6 28.9	204 52.7	12.3	S18 40.1	3.4	54.3
19	104 23.5	29.8	219 24.0	12.3	18 43.5	3.3	54.3
20	119 23.7	30.8	233 55.3	12.2	18 46.8	3.2	54.3
21	134 23.8	.. 31.7	248 26.5	12.3	18 50.0	3.1	54.3
22	149 24.0	32.7	262 57.8	12.1	18 53.1	3.1	54.4
23	164 24.2	33.6	277 28.9	12.2	S18 56.2	2.9	54.4
	SD 16.0	d 0.9	SD 14.7		14.7		14.8

Twilight, Sunrise and Moonrise

Lat.	Twilight Naut.	Twilight Civil	Sunrise	Moonrise 4	5	6	7
°	h m	h m	h m	h m	h m	h m	h m
N 72	00 35	03 19	04 37	24 53	00 53	03 14	■■
N 70	01 50	03 38	04 47	24 16	00 16	01 54	03 33
68	02 26	03 53	04 54	23 51	25 16	01 16	02 35
66	02 50	04 06	05 01	23 31	24 49	00 49	02 01
64	03 09	04 16	05 06	23 15	24 29	00 29	01 37
62	03 24	04 24	05 11	23 02	24 13	00 13	01 18
60	03 37	04 31	05 15	22 51	23 59	25 02	01 02
N 58	03 47	04 38	05 18	22 42	23 47	24 48	00 48
56	03 56	04 43	05 22	22 33	23 37	24 37	00 37
54	04 04	04 48	05 24	22 26	23 28	24 27	00 27
52	04 10	04 52	05 27	22 19	23 20	24 18	00 18
50	04 16	04 56	05 29	22 13	23 13	24 10	00 10
45	04 29	05 05	05 34	22 01	22 58	23 53	24 45
N 40	04 39	05 11	05 39	21 50	22 45	23 39	24 30
35	04 46	05 17	05 42	21 41	22 35	23 27	24 18
30	04 53	05 21	05 45	21 33	22 25	23 17	24 07
20	05 03	05 29	05 51	21 20	22 09	22 59	23 49
N 10	05 10	05 34	05 55	21 08	21 55	22 44	23 33
0	05 15	05 39	06 00	20 57	21 42	22 29	23 18
S 10	05 18	05 43	06 04	20 46	21 30	22 15	23 03
20	05 20	05 46	06 08	20 34	21 16	22 00	22 47
30	05 21	05 49	06 13	20 21	21 00	21 43	22 29
35	05 21	05 50	06 15	20 13	20 51	21 32	22 18
40	05 20	05 51	06 18	20 05	20 41	21 21	22 06
45	05 19	05 53	06 22	19 54	20 29	21 07	21 51
S 50	05 16	05 54	06 26	19 42	20 14	20 51	21 34
52	05 15	05 54	06 28	19 37	20 07	20 43	21 25
54	05 14	05 55	06 30	19 30	20 00	20 34	21 16
56	05 12	05 55	06 32	19 24	19 51	20 25	21 06
58	05 10	05 55	06 35	19 16	19 42	20 14	20 54
S 60	05 08	05 56	06 37	19 07	19 31	20 01	20 40

Sunset, Twilight and Moonset

Lat.	Sunset	Twilight Civil	Twilight Naut.	Moonset 4	5	6	7
°	h m	h m	h m	h m	h m	h m	h m
N 72	19 31	20 52	////	05 27	05 10	04 25	■■
N 70	19 22	20 31	22 24	05 51	05 48	05 46	05 45
68	19 14	20 15	21 45	06 09	06 15	06 24	06 43
66	19 07	20 03	21 19	06 24	06 35	06 51	07 17
64	19 01	19 52	21 00	06 36	06 51	07 12	07 42
62	18 57	19 44	20 44	06 46	07 05	07 29	08 01
60	18 52	19 36	20 32	06 55	07 16	07 43	08 17
N 58	18 49	19 30	20 21	07 03	07 26	07 55	08 31
56	18 45	19 24	20 12	07 10	07 35	08 05	08 42
54	18 42	19 19	20 04	07 16	07 43	08 15	08 53
52	18 40	19 14	19 57	07 22	07 50	08 23	09 02
50	18 37	19 10	19 51	07 27	07 56	08 30	09 10
45	18 32	19 02	19 38	07 38	08 10	08 46	09 27
N 40	18 28	18 55	19 28	07 47	08 21	08 59	09 41
35	18 24	18 50	19 20	07 55	08 31	09 10	09 54
30	18 21	18 45	19 13	08 01	08 39	09 20	10 04
20	18 15	18 37	19 03	08 13	08 54	09 37	10 22
N 10	18 10	18 32	18 56	08 24	09 07	09 51	10 38
0	18 06	18 27	18 51	08 34	09 19	10 05	10 53
S 10	18 02	18 23	18 47	08 44	09 31	10 19	11 07
20	17 57	18 19	18 45	08 54	09 44	10 33	11 23
30	17 52	18 16	18 44	09 06	09 58	10 50	11 41
35	17 50	18 15	18 44	09 13	10 07	11 00	11 52
40	17 47	18 14	18 45	09 21	10 17	11 11	12 04
45	17 43	18 12	18 46	09 30	10 28	11 24	12 18
S 50	17 39	18 11	18 48	09 42	10 42	11 41	12 35
52	17 37	18 10	18 49	09 47	10 49	11 48	12 44
54	17 35	18 10	18 51	09 53	10 56	11 56	12 53
56	17 32	18 09	18 52	09 59	11 04	12 06	13 03
58	17 30	18 09	18 54	10 06	11 13	12 17	13 15
S 60	17 27	18 08	18 57	10 15	11 24	12 29	13 28

SUN and MOON

Day	SUN Eqn. of Time 00h	SUN Eqn. of Time 12h	Mer. Pass.	MOON Mer. Pass. Upper	MOON Mer. Pass. Lower	Age	Phase
d	m s	m s	h m	h m	h m	d	%
4	03 15	03 06	12 03	02 23	14 45	18	89
5	02 57	02 49	12 03	03 08	15 31	19	82
6	02 40	02 31	12 03	03 54	16 17	20	74

UT	ARIES GHA	VENUS −4.0 GHA	Dec	MARS −1.3 GHA	Dec	JUPITER −2.1 GHA	Dec	SATURN +0.4 GHA	Dec	STARS Name	SHA	Dec
d h	° ′	° ′	° ′	° ′	° ′	° ′	° ′	° ′	° ′		° ′	° ′
7 00	194 49.5	144 03.4	N19 42.8	336 47.4	S12 58.3	182 56.3	N 3 55.5	162 09.6	N10 50.0	Acamar	315 27.1	S40 18.8
01	209 52.0	159 02.9	43.6	351 50.4	58.1	197 58.2	55.7	177 11.8	50.1	Achernar	335 35.6	S57 14.6
02	224 54.5	174 02.3	44.5	6 53.5	58.0	213 00.1	55.9	192 13.9	50.2	Acrux	173 20.9	S63 05.7
03	239 56.9	189 01.8 ..	45.4	21 56.6 ..	57.8	228 02.0 ..	56.2	207 16.1 ..	50.3	Adhara	255 21.2	S28 58.6
04	254 59.4	204 01.3	46.3	36 59.7	57.7	243 03.9	56.4	222 18.3	50.4	Aldebaran	291 02.2	N16 30.3
05	270 01.9	219 00.7	47.1	52 02.7	57.6	258 05.8	56.6	237 20.4	50.5			
06	285 04.3	234 00.2	N19 48.0	67 05.8	S12 57.4	273 07.7	N 3 56.9	252 22.6	N10 50.6	Alioth	166 29.8	N55 57.9
W 07	300 06.8	248 59.6	48.9	82 08.9	57.3	288 09.6	57.1	267 24.8	50.7	Alkaid	153 07.1	N49 19.0
E 08	315 09.2	263 59.1	49.7	97 12.0	57.1	303 11.5	57.3	282 26.9	50.8	Al Na'ir	27 57.8	S46 57.8
D 09	330 11.7	278 58.5 ..	50.6	112 15.1 ..	57.0	318 13.4 ..	57.6	297 29.1 ..	50.9	Alnilam	275 57.7	S 1 12.4
N 10	345 14.2	293 58.0	51.5	127 18.2	56.9	333 15.3	57.8	312 31.3	51.1	Alphard	218 06.7	S 8 39.5
E 11	0 16.6	308 57.5	52.3	142 21.2	56.7	348 17.2	58.1	327 33.5	51.2			
S 12	15 19.1	323 56.9	N19 53.2	157 24.3	S12 56.6	3 19.1	N 3 58.3	342 35.6	N10 51.3	Alphecca	126 20.0	N26 43.0
D 13	30 21.6	338 56.4	54.1	172 27.4	56.4	18 21.0	58.5	357 37.8	51.4	Alpheratz	357 55.2	N29 04.9
A 14	45 24.0	353 55.8	54.9	187 30.5	56.3	33 23.0	58.8	12 40.0	51.5	Altair	62 19.0	N 8 51.9
Y 15	60 26.5	8 55.3 ..	55.8	202 33.6 ..	56.2	48 24.9 ..	59.0	27 42.1 ..	51.6	Ankaa	353 27.0	S42 18.7
16	75 29.0	23 54.7	56.7	217 36.7	56.0	63 26.8	59.2	42 44.3	51.7	Antares	112 39.5	S26 25.7
17	90 31.4	38 54.2	57.5	232 39.8	55.9	78 28.7	59.5	57 46.5	51.8			
18	105 33.9	53 53.6	N19 58.4	247 42.9	S12 55.7	93 30.6	N 3 59.7	72 48.6	N10 51.9	Arcturus	146 05.5	N19 11.2
19	120 36.4	68 53.1	19 59.2	262 46.0	55.6	108 32.5	3 59.9	87 50.8	52.0	Atria	107 51.0	S69 01.3
20	135 38.8	83 52.5	20 00.1	277 49.1	55.4	123 34.4	4 00.2	102 53.0	52.1	Avior	234 22.3	S59 30.8
21	150 41.3	98 52.0 ..	01.0	292 52.2 ..	55.3	138 36.3 ..	00.4	117 55.1 ..	52.2	Bellatrix	278 44.0	N 6 20.7
22	165 43.7	113 51.4	01.8	307 55.3	55.1	153 38.2	00.6	132 57.3	52.3	Betelgeuse	271 13.3	N 7 24.2
23	180 46.2	128 50.9	02.7	322 58.4	55.0	168 40.1	00.9	147 59.5	52.4			
8 00	195 48.7	143 50.3	N20 03.5	338 01.5	S12 54.9	183 42.0	N 4 01.1	163 01.6	N10 52.6	Canopus	264 01.1	S52 42.1
01	210 51.1	158 49.8	04.4	353 04.6	54.7	198 43.9	01.3	178 03.8	52.7	Capella	280 50.9	N45 59.8
02	225 53.6	173 49.2	05.2	8 07.7	54.6	213 45.8	01.6	193 06.0	52.8	Deneb	49 39.1	N45 16.4
03	240 56.1	188 48.7 ..	06.1	23 10.8 ..	54.4	228 47.7 ..	01.8	208 08.1 ..	52.9	Denebola	182 44.6	N14 34.5
04	255 58.5	203 48.1	06.9	38 13.9	54.3	243 49.6	02.0	223 10.3	53.0	Diphda	349 07.3	S17 59.6
05	271 01.0	218 47.6	07.8	53 17.0	54.1	258 51.5	02.3	238 12.5	53.1			
06	286 03.5	233 47.0	N20 08.6	68 20.1	S12 54.0	273 53.5	N 4 02.5	253 14.6	N10 53.2	Dubhe	194 04.6	N61 45.4
T 07	301 05.9	248 46.5	09.5	83 23.2	53.8	288 55.4	02.7	268 16.8	53.3	Elnath	278 26.7	N28 36.3
H 08	316 08.4	263 45.9	10.3	98 26.3	53.7	303 57.3	03.0	283 19.0	53.4	Eltanin	90 51.1	N51 29.1
U 09	331 10.9	278 45.4 ..	11.2	113 29.4 ..	53.5	318 59.2 ..	03.2	298 21.1 ..	53.5	Enif	33 58.1	N 9 52.1
R 10	346 13.3	293 44.8	12.0	128 32.5	53.4	334 01.1	03.4	313 23.3	53.6	Fomalhaut	15 36.4	S29 37.6
S 11	1 15.8	308 44.3	12.9	143 35.6	53.2	349 03.0	03.7	328 25.5	53.7			
D 12	16 18.2	323 43.7	N20 13.7	158 38.7	S12 53.1	4 04.9	N 4 03.9	343 27.6	N10 53.8	Gacrux	172 12.6	S57 06.6
A 13	31 20.7	338 43.2	14.6	173 41.9	52.9	19 06.8	04.1	358 29.8	54.0	Gienah	176 03.3	S17 32.3
Y 14	46 23.2	353 42.6	15.4	188 45.0	52.8	34 08.7	04.4	13 32.0	54.1	Hadar	149 02.9	S60 22.1
15	61 25.6	8 42.0 ..	16.2	203 48.1 ..	52.6	49 10.6 ..	04.6	28 34.1 ..	54.2	Hamal	328 13.5	N23 27.3
16	76 28.1	23 41.5	17.1	218 51.2	52.5	64 12.5	04.9	43 36.3	54.3	Kaus Aust.	83 58.3	S34 22.9
17	91 30.6	38 40.9	17.9	233 54.3	52.3	79 14.4	05.1	58 38.5	54.4			
18	106 33.0	53 40.4	N20 18.8	248 57.5	S12 52.2	94 16.3	N 4 05.3	73 40.6	N10 54.5	Kochab	137 18.6	N74 09.5
19	121 35.5	68 39.8	19.6	264 00.6	52.0	109 18.2	05.6	88 42.8	54.6	Markab	13 49.6	N15 11.9
20	136 38.0	83 39.3	20.4	279 03.7	51.9	124 20.1	05.8	103 45.0	54.7	Menkar	314 26.8	N 4 05.0
21	151 40.4	98 38.7 ..	21.3	294 06.8 ..	51.7	139 22.1 ..	06.0	118 47.1 ..	54.8	Menkent	148 20.2	S36 21.9
22	166 42.9	113 38.2	22.1	309 10.0	51.6	154 24.0	06.3	133 49.3	54.9	Miaplacidus	221 41.5	S69 43.2
23	181 45.3	128 37.6	22.9	324 13.1	51.4	169 25.9	06.5	148 51.5	55.0			
9 00	196 47.8	143 37.0	N20 23.8	339 16.2	S12 51.3	184 27.8	N 4 06.7	163 53.6	N10 55.1	Mirfak	308 56.5	N49 51.4
01	211 50.3	158 36.5	24.6	354 19.3	51.1	199 29.7	07.0	178 55.8	55.2	Nunki	76 11.9	S26 17.8
02	226 52.7	173 35.9	25.4	9 22.5	51.0	214 31.6	07.2	193 58.0	55.3	Peacock	53 36.7	S56 44.0
03	241 55.2	188 35.4 ..	26.3	24 25.6 ..	50.8	229 33.5 ..	07.4	209 00.1 ..	55.5	Pollux	243 41.1	N28 01.7
04	256 57.7	203 34.8	27.1	39 28.7	50.7	244 35.4	07.7	224 02.3	55.6	Procyon	245 11.2	N 5 13.5
05	272 00.1	218 34.2	27.9	54 31.9	50.5	259 37.3	07.9	239 04.5	55.7			
06	287 02.6	233 33.7	N20 28.8	69 35.0	S12 50.4	274 39.2	N 4 08.1	254 06.6	N10 55.8	Rasalhague	96 16.5	N12 33.6
07	302 05.1	248 33.1	29.6	84 38.1	50.2	289 41.1	08.4	269 08.8	55.9	Regulus	207 55.0	N11 58.2
08	317 07.5	263 32.6	30.4	99 41.3	50.1	304 43.0	08.6	284 11.0	56.0	Rigel	281 22.8	S 8 12.4
F 09	332 10.0	278 32.0 ..	31.2	114 44.4 ..	49.9	319 44.9 ..	08.8	299 13.1 ..	56.1	Rigil Kent.	140 06.2	S60 49.7
R 10	347 12.5	293 31.4	32.1	129 47.5	49.7	334 46.8	09.1	314 15.3	56.2	Sabik	102 25.0	S15 43.4
I 11	2 14.9	308 30.9	32.9	144 50.7	49.6	349 48.7	09.3	329 17.5	56.3			
D 12	17 17.4	323 30.3	N20 33.7	159 53.8	S12 49.4	4 50.7	N 4 09.5	344 19.6	N10 56.4	Schedar	349 53.6	N56 31.8
A 13	32 19.8	338 29.7	34.5	174 57.0	49.3	19 52.6	09.8	359 21.8	56.5	Shaula	96 36.7	S37 06.0
Y 14	47 22.3	353 29.2	35.3	190 00.1	49.1	34 54.5	10.0	14 24.0	56.6	Sirius	258 43.5	S16 43.2
15	62 24.8	8 28.6 ..	36.2	205 03.3 ..	49.0	49 56.4 ..	10.2	29 26.1 ..	56.7	Spica	158 42.5	S11 09.5
16	77 27.2	23 28.0	37.0	220 06.4	48.8	64 58.3	10.5	44 28.3	56.8	Suhail	223 00.3	S43 26.1
17	92 29.7	38 27.5	37.8	235 09.6	48.7	80 00.2	10.7	59 30.4	57.0			
18	107 32.2	53 26.9	N20 38.6	250 12.7	S12 48.5	95 02.1	N 4 10.9	74 32.6	N10 57.1	Vega	80 46.3	N38 46.8
19	122 34.6	68 26.4	39.4	265 15.9	48.3	110 04.0	11.2	89 34.8	57.2	Zuben'ubi	137 17.3	S16 02.3
20	137 37.1	83 25.8	40.3	280 19.0	48.2	125 05.9	11.4	104 36.9	57.3		SHA	Mer. Pass.
21	152 39.6	98 25.2 ..	41.1	295 22.2 ..	48.0	140 07.8 ..	11.6	119 39.1 ..	57.4	Venus	308 01.7	14 25
22	167 42.0	113 24.7	41.9	310 25.3	47.9	155 09.7	11.9	134 41.3	57.5	Mars	142 12.8	1 28
23	182 44.5	128 24.1	42.7	325 28.5	47.7	170 11.6	12.1	149 43.4	57.6	Jupiter	347 53.3	11 44
Mer. Pass. 10 55.0		v −0.6	d 0.8	v 3.1	d 0.1	v 1.9	d 0.2	v 2.2	d 0.1	Saturn	327 13.0	13 06

UT	SUN GHA	SUN Dec	MOON GHA	v	Dec	d	HP
	o ′	o ′	o ′	′	o ′	′	′
d h							
7 00	179 24.4	N 6 34.6	292 00.1	12.1	S18 59.1	2.9	54.4
01	194 24.6	35.5	306 31.2	12.1	19 02.0	2.8	54.4
02	209 24.7	36.4	321 02.3	12.0	19 04.8	2.7	54.4
03	224 24.9 ..	37.4	335 33.3	12.0	19 07.5	2.6	54.4
04	239 25.1	38.3	350 04.3	12.0	19 10.1	2.5	54.4
05	254 25.3	39.3	4 35.3	12.0	19 12.6	2.5	54.4
06	269 25.4	N 6 40.2	19 06.3	11.9	S19 15.1	2.3	54.5
W 07	284 25.6	41.1	33 37.2	11.9	19 17.4	2.3	54.5
E 08	299 25.8	42.1	48 08.1	11.9	19 19.7	2.2	54.5
D 09	314 26.0 ..	43.0	62 39.0	11.8	19 21.9	2.0	54.5
N 10	329 26.1	44.0	77 09.8	11.8	19 23.9	2.0	54.5
E 11	344 26.3	44.9	91 40.6	11.8	19 25.9	1.9	54.5
S 12	359 26.5	N 6 45.9	106 11.4	11.7	S19 27.8	1.8	54.6
D 13	14 26.7	46.8	120 42.1	11.7	19 29.6	1.8	54.6
A 14	29 26.8	47.7	135 12.8	11.7	19 31.4	1.6	54.6
Y 15	44 27.0 ..	48.7	149 43.5	11.7	19 33.0	1.5	54.6
16	59 27.2	49.6	164 14.2	11.6	19 34.5	1.5	54.6
17	74 27.4	50.6	178 44.8	11.6	19 36.0	1.3	54.6
18	89 27.6	N 6 51.5	193 15.4	11.6	S19 37.3	1.3	54.7
19	104 27.7	52.4	207 46.0	11.6	19 38.6	1.1	54.7
20	119 27.9	53.4	222 16.6	11.5	19 39.7	1.1	54.7
21	134 28.1 ..	54.3	236 47.1	11.5	19 40.8	1.0	54.7
22	149 28.3	55.3	251 17.6	11.4	19 41.8	0.9	54.7
23	164 28.4	56.2	265 48.0	11.5	19 42.7	0.7	54.7
8 00	179 28.6	N 6 57.1	280 18.5	11.4	S19 43.4	0.7	54.8
01	194 28.8	58.1	294 48.9	11.4	19 44.1	0.6	54.8
02	209 29.0	59.0	309 19.3	11.3	19 44.7	0.6	54.8
03	224 29.1	6 59.9	323 49.6	11.4	19 45.3	0.4	54.8
04	239 29.3	7 00.9	338 20.0	11.3	19 45.7	0.3	54.8
05	254 29.5	01.8	352 50.3	11.3	19 46.0	0.2	54.9
06	269 29.7	N 7 02.8	7 20.6	11.2	S19 46.2	0.1	54.9
T 07	284 29.8	03.7	21 50.8	11.2	19 46.3	0.1	54.9
H 08	299 30.0	04.6	36 21.0	11.3	19 46.4	0.1	54.9
U 09	314 30.2 ..	05.6	50 51.3	11.1	19 46.3	0.2	55.0
R 10	329 30.3	06.5	65 21.4	11.2	19 46.1	0.2	55.0
S 11	344 30.5	07.4	79 51.6	11.1	19 45.9	0.4	55.0
D 12	359 30.7	N 7 08.4	94 21.7	11.1	S19 45.5	0.4	55.0
A 13	14 30.9	09.3	108 51.8	11.1	19 45.1	0.6	55.0
Y 14	29 31.0	10.2	123 21.9	11.1	19 44.5	0.6	55.1
15	44 31.2 ..	11.2	137 52.0	11.0	19 43.9	0.8	55.1
16	59 31.4	12.1	152 22.0	11.1	19 43.1	0.8	55.1
17	74 31.6	13.0	166 52.1	11.0	19 42.3	1.0	55.1
18	89 31.7	N 7 14.0	181 22.1	10.9	S19 41.3	1.0	55.2
19	104 31.9	14.9	195 52.0	11.0	19 40.3	1.2	55.2
20	119 32.1	15.9	210 22.0	10.9	19 39.1	1.2	55.2
21	134 32.3 ..	16.8	224 51.9	10.9	19 37.9	1.3	55.2
22	149 32.4	17.7	239 21.8	10.9	19 36.6	1.5	55.3
23	164 32.6	18.7	253 51.7	10.9	19 35.1	1.5	55.3
9 00	179 32.8	N 7 19.6	268 21.6	10.8	S19 33.6	1.6	55.3
01	194 32.9	20.5	282 51.4	10.9	19 32.0	1.8	55.3
02	209 33.1	21.5	297 21.3	10.8	19 30.2	1.8	55.4
03	224 33.3 ..	22.4	311 51.1	10.8	19 28.4	1.9	55.4
04	239 33.5	23.3	326 20.9	10.8	19 26.5	2.1	55.4
05	254 33.6	24.3	340 50.7	10.7	19 24.4	2.1	55.5
06	269 33.8	N 7 25.2	355 20.4	10.7	S19 22.3	2.2	55.5
F 07	284 34.0	26.1	9 50.1	10.8	19 20.1	2.3	55.5
R 08	299 34.1	27.0	24 19.9	10.7	19 17.8	2.5	55.5
I 09	314 34.3 ..	28.0	38 49.6	10.6	19 15.3	2.5	55.6
D 10	329 34.5	28.9	53 19.2	10.7	19 12.8	2.6	55.6
A 11	344 34.7	29.8	67 48.9	10.7	19 10.2	2.8	55.6
Y 12	359 34.8	N 7 30.8	82 18.6	10.6	S19 07.4	2.8	55.7
13	14 35.0	31.7	96 48.2	10.6	19 04.6	2.9	55.7
14	29 35.2	32.6	111 17.8	10.6	19 01.7	3.0	55.7
15	44 35.3 ..	33.6	125 47.4	10.6	18 58.7	3.2	55.7
16	59 35.5	34.5	140 17.0	10.6	18 55.5	3.2	55.8
17	74 35.7	35.4	154 46.6	10.5	18 52.3	3.3	55.8
18	89 35.9	N 7 36.4	169 16.1	10.5	S18 49.0	3.5	55.8
19	104 36.0	37.3	183 45.6	10.6	18 45.5	3.5	55.9
20	119 36.2	38.2	198 15.2	10.5	18 42.0	3.6	55.9
21	134 36.3 ..	39.1	212 44.7	10.5	18 38.4	3.8	55.9
22	149 36.5	40.1	227 14.2	10.4	18 34.6	3.8	56.0
23	164 36.7	41.0	241 43.6	10.5	S18 30.8	3.9	56.0
	SD 16.0	d 0.9	SD 14.9		15.0		15.2

Lat.	Twilight Naut.	Twilight Civil	Sunrise	Moonrise 7	8	9	10
o	h m	h m	h m	h m	h m	h m	h m
N 72	////	02 58	04 21	■	■	■	■
N 70	01 16	03 21	04 32	03 33	05 01	05 24	05 24
68	02 04	03 39	04 42	02 35	03 40	04 21	04 43
66	02 33	03 53	04 49	02 01	03 02	03 46	04 15
64	02 55	04 04	04 56	01 37	02 35	03 20	03 54
62	03 12	04 14	05 01	01 18	02 14	03 01	03 37
60	03 25	04 22	05 06	01 02	01 57	02 44	03 22
N 58	03 37	04 29	05 10	00 48	01 43	02 31	03 10
56	03 47	04 35	05 14	00 37	01 31	02 19	02 59
54	03 55	04 40	05 17	00 27	01 21	02 08	02 50
52	04 03	04 45	05 20	00 18	01 11	01 59	02 41
50	04 09	04 50	05 23	00 10	01 03	01 51	02 34
45	04 23	04 59	05 29	24 45	00 45	01 33	02 18
N 40	04 33	05 06	05 34	24 30	00 30	01 19	02 04
35	04 42	05 12	05 38	24 18	00 18	01 07	01 53
30	04 49	05 18	05 42	24 07	00 07	00 56	01 43
20	05 00	05 26	05 48	23 49	24 38	00 38	01 26
N 10	05 08	05 32	05 54	23 33	24 22	00 22	01 11
0	05 14	05 38	05 59	23 18	24 07	00 07	00 58
S 10	05 18	05 42	06 04	23 03	23 52	24 44	00 44
20	05 21	05 47	06 09	22 47	23 37	24 29	00 29
30	05 23	05 51	06 15	22 29	23 18	24 12	00 12
35	05 23	05 52	06 18	22 18	23 08	24 02	00 02
40	05 23	05 54	06 21	22 06	22 56	23 50	24 50
45	05 22	05 56	06 26	21 51	22 41	23 37	24 38
S 50	05 21	05 58	06 31	21 34	22 24	23 21	24 24
52	05 20	05 59	06 33	21 25	22 15	23 13	24 17
54	05 19	06 00	06 35	21 16	22 06	23 04	24 10
56	05 18	06 01	06 38	21 06	21 56	22 55	24 02
58	05 16	06 02	06 41	20 54	21 44	22 44	23 53
S 60	05 15	06 03	06 45	20 40	21 30	22 31	23 42

Lat.	Sunset	Twilight Civil	Twilight Naut.	Moonset 7	8	9	10
o	h m	h m	h m	h m	h m	h m	h m
N 72	19 46	21 11	////	■	■	■	■
N 70	19 34	20 47	23 01	05 45	05 58	07 18	09 03
68	19 25	20 29	22 07	06 43	07 19	08 21	09 44
66	19 17	20 14	21 35	07 17	07 57	08 56	10 11
64	19 10	20 02	21 13	07 42	08 24	09 21	10 32
62	19 05	19 52	20 55	08 01	08 45	09 41	10 49
60	19 00	19 44	20 41	08 17	09 02	09 57	11 03
N 58	18 55	19 37	20 29	08 31	09 16	10 11	11 15
56	18 51	19 31	20 19	08 42	09 28	10 22	11 25
54	18 48	19 25	20 10	08 53	09 38	10 32	11 34
52	18 45	19 20	20 03	09 02	09 48	10 42	11 43
50	18 42	19 15	19 56	09 10	09 56	10 50	11 50
45	18 36	19 06	19 42	09 27	10 14	11 07	12 05
N 40	18 31	18 58	19 31	09 41	10 29	11 21	12 18
35	18 26	18 52	19 23	09 54	10 41	11 33	12 29
30	18 23	18 47	19 15	10 04	10 52	11 43	12 38
20	18 16	18 38	19 04	10 22	11 10	12 01	12 55
N 10	18 10	18 32	18 56	10 38	11 26	12 17	13 09
0	18 05	18 26	18 50	10 53	11 42	12 31	13 22
S 10	18 00	18 21	18 46	11 07	11 57	12 46	13 35
20	17 55	18 17	18 43	11 23	12 13	13 01	13 49
30	17 49	18 13	18 41	11 41	12 31	13 19	14 05
35	17 46	18 11	18 40	11 52	12 42	13 29	14 14
40	17 42	18 09	18 40	12 04	12 54	13 41	14 25
45	17 38	18 07	18 41	12 18	13 08	13 55	14 37
S 50	17 32	18 05	18 42	12 35	13 26	14 11	14 52
52	17 30	18 04	18 43	12 44	13 34	14 19	14 59
54	17 27	18 03	18 44	12 53	13 44	14 28	15 06
56	17 25	18 02	18 45	13 03	13 54	14 38	15 15
58	17 22	18 01	18 46	13 15	14 06	14 49	15 25
S 60	17 18	18 00	18 48	13 28	14 20	15 02	15 36

Day	SUN Eqn. of Time 00h	12h	Mer. Pass.	MOON Mer. Pass. Upper	Lower	Age	Phase
d	m s	m s	h m	h m	h m	d	%
7	02 23	02 14	12 02	04 41	17 05	21	66
8	02 06	01 58	12 02	05 30	17 54	22	56
9	01 49	01 41	12 02	06 19	18 44	23	46

UT	ARIES GHA	VENUS −4.0 GHA	Dec	MARS −1.4 GHA	Dec	JUPITER −2.0 GHA	Dec	SATURN +0.4 GHA	Dec	STARS Name	SHA	Dec
10 00	197 47.0	143 23.5	N20 43.5	340 31.6	S12 47.5	185 13.5	N 4 12.3	164 45.6	N10 57.7	Acamar	315 27.1	S40 18.8
01	212 49.4	158 23.0	44.3	355 34.8	47.4	200 15.4	12.6	179 47.8	57.8	Achernar	335 35.6	S57 14.6
02	227 51.9	173 22.4	45.1	10 37.9	47.2	215 17.3	12.8	194 49.9	57.9	Acrux	173 20.9	S63 05.8
03	242 54.3	188 21.8 ..	45.9	25 41.1 ..	47.1	230 19.3 ..	13.0	209 52.1 ..	58.0	Adhara	255 21.2	S28 58.6
04	257 56.8	203 21.2	46.7	40 44.2	46.9	245 21.2	13.3	224 54.3	58.1	Aldebaran	291 02.2	N16 30.3
05	272 59.3	218 20.7	47.6	55 47.4	46.7	260 23.1	13.5	239 56.4	58.2			
06	288 01.7	233 20.1	N20 48.4	70 50.6	S12 46.6	275 25.0	N 4 13.7	254 58.6	N10 58.4	Alioth	166 29.8	N55 57.9
07	303 04.2	248 19.5	49.2	85 53.7	46.4	290 26.9	14.0	270 00.8	58.5	Alkaid	153 07.1	N49 19.0
S 08	318 06.7	263 19.0	50.0	100 56.9	46.3	305 28.8	14.2	285 02.9	58.6	Al Na'ir	27 57.8	S46 57.8
A 09	333 09.1	278 18.4 ..	50.8	116 00.1 ..	46.1	320 30.7 ..	14.4	300 05.1 ..	58.7	Alnilam	275 57.7	S 1 12.4
T 10	348 11.6	293 17.8	51.6	131 03.2	45.9	335 32.6	14.7	315 07.3	58.8	Alphard	218 06.7	S 8 39.5
U 11	3 14.1	308 17.3	52.4	146 06.4	45.8	350 34.5	14.9	330 09.4	58.9			
R 12	18 16.5	323 16.7	N20 53.2	161 09.6	S12 45.6	5 36.4	N 4 15.1	345 11.6	N10 59.0	Alphecca	126 20.0	N26 43.0
D 13	33 19.0	338 16.1	54.0	176 12.7	45.4	20 38.3	15.4	0 13.7	59.1	Alpheratz	357 55.2	N29 04.9
A 14	48 21.4	353 15.5	54.8	191 15.9	45.3	35 40.2	15.6	15 15.9	59.2	Altair	62 19.0	N 8 51.9
Y 15	63 23.9	8 15.0 ..	55.6	206 19.1 ..	45.1	50 42.1 ..	15.8	30 18.1 ..	59.3	Ankaa	353 27.0	S42 18.7
16	78 26.4	23 14.4	56.4	221 22.2	45.0	65 44.0	16.1	45 20.2	59.4	Antares	112 39.5	S26 25.7
17	93 28.8	38 13.8	57.2	236 25.4	44.8	80 46.0	16.3	60 22.4	59.5			
18	108 31.3	53 13.2	N20 58.0	251 28.6	S12 44.6	95 47.9	N 4 16.5	75 24.6	N10 59.6	Arcturus	146 05.5	N19 11.2
19	123 33.8	68 12.7	58.8	266 31.8	44.5	110 49.8	16.8	90 26.7	59.7	Atria	107 50.9	S69 01.3
20	138 36.2	83 12.1	20 59.6	281 34.9	44.3	125 51.7	17.0	105 28.9	10 59.9	Avior	234 22.3	S59 30.8
21	153 38.7	98 11.5	21 00.3	296 38.1 ..	44.1	140 53.6 ..	17.2	120 31.1	11 00.0	Bellatrix	278 44.0	N 6 20.7
22	168 41.2	113 10.9	01.1	311 41.3	44.0	155 55.5	17.5	135 33.2	00.1	Betelgeuse	271 13.3	N 7 24.2
23	183 43.6	128 10.4	01.9	326 44.5	43.8	170 57.4	17.7	150 35.4	00.2			
11 00	198 46.1	143 09.8	N21 02.7	341 47.7	S12 43.6	185 59.3	N 4 17.9	165 37.6	N11 00.3	Canopus	264 01.2	S52 42.1
01	213 48.6	158 09.2	03.5	356 50.8	43.5	201 01.2	18.2	180 39.7	00.4	Capella	280 51.0	N45 59.8
02	228 51.0	173 08.6	04.3	11 54.0	43.3	216 03.1	18.4	195 41.9	00.5	Deneb	49 39.1	N45 16.4
03	243 53.5	188 08.1 ..	05.1	26 57.2 ..	43.1	231 05.0 ..	18.6	210 44.1 ..	00.6	Denebola	182 44.6	N14 34.6
04	258 55.9	203 07.5	05.9	42 00.4	43.0	246 06.9	18.9	225 46.2	00.7	Diphda	349 07.2	S17 59.6
05	273 58.4	218 06.9	06.7	57 03.6	42.8	261 08.8	19.1	240 48.4	00.8			
06	289 00.9	233 06.3	N21 07.4	72 06.8	S12 42.6	276 10.7	N 4 19.3	255 50.5	N11 00.9	Dubhe	194 04.6	N61 45.4
07	304 03.3	248 05.8	08.2	87 10.0	42.5	291 12.7	19.6	270 52.7	01.0	Elnath	278 26.7	N28 36.3
S 08	319 05.8	263 05.2	09.0	102 13.1	42.3	306 14.6	19.8	285 54.9	01.1	Eltanin	90 51.1	N51 29.1
U 09	334 08.3	278 04.6 ..	09.8	117 16.3 ..	42.1	321 16.5 ..	20.0	300 57.0 ..	01.2	Enif	33 58.1	N 9 52.1
N 10	349 10.7	293 04.0	10.6	132 19.5	42.0	336 18.4	20.3	315 59.2	01.4	Fomalhaut	15 36.4	S29 37.6
D 11	4 13.2	308 03.4	11.4	147 22.7	41.8	351 20.3	20.5	331 01.4	01.5			
A 12	19 15.7	323 02.9	N21 12.1	162 25.9	S12 41.6	6 22.2	N 4 20.7	346 03.5	N11 01.6	Gacrux	172 12.6	S57 06.6
Y 13	34 18.1	338 02.3	12.9	177 29.1	41.5	21 24.1	21.0	1 05.7	01.7	Gienah	176 03.3	S17 32.3
14	49 20.6	353 01.7	13.7	192 32.3	41.3	36 26.0	21.2	16 07.9	01.8	Hadar	149 02.9	S60 22.1
15	64 23.1	8 01.1 ..	14.5	207 35.5 ..	41.1	51 27.9 ..	21.4	31 10.0 ..	01.9	Hamal	328 13.5	N23 27.3
16	79 25.5	23 00.5	15.2	222 38.7	40.9	66 29.8	21.7	46 12.2	02.0	Kaus Aust.	83 58.3	S34 22.9
17	94 28.0	38 00.0	16.0	237 41.9	40.8	81 31.7	21.9	61 14.3	02.1			
18	109 30.4	52 59.4	N21 16.8	252 45.1	S12 40.6	96 33.6	N 4 22.1	76 16.5	N11 02.2	Kochab	137 18.6	N74 09.5
19	124 32.9	67 58.8	17.6	267 48.3	40.4	111 35.5	22.3	91 18.7	02.3	Markab	13 49.5	N15 11.9
20	139 35.4	82 58.2	18.3	282 51.5	40.3	126 37.4	22.6	106 20.8	02.4	Menkar	314 26.9	N 4 05.0
21	154 37.8	97 57.6 ..	19.1	297 54.7 ..	40.1	141 39.4 ..	22.8	121 23.0 ..	02.5	Menkent	148 20.2	S36 21.9
22	169 40.3	112 57.0	19.9	312 57.9	39.9	156 41.3	23.1	136 25.2	02.6	Miaplacidus	221 41.5	S69 43.2
23	184 42.8	127 56.5	20.6	328 01.1	39.7	171 43.2	23.3	151 27.3	02.8			
12 00	199 45.2	142 55.9	N21 21.4	343 04.3	S12 39.6	186 45.1	N 4 23.5	166 29.5	N11 02.9	Mirfak	308 56.5	N49 51.4
01	214 47.7	157 55.3	22.2	358 07.5	39.4	201 47.0	23.8	181 31.7	03.0	Nunki	76 11.9	S26 17.7
02	229 50.2	172 54.7	22.9	13 10.7	39.2	216 48.9	24.0	196 33.8	03.1	Peacock	53 36.7	S56 44.0
03	244 52.6	187 54.1 ..	23.7	28 13.9 ..	39.1	231 50.8 ..	24.2	211 36.0 ..	03.2	Pollux	243 41.2	N28 01.7
04	259 55.1	202 53.5	24.5	43 17.1	38.9	246 52.7	24.5	226 38.1	03.3	Procyon	245 11.2	N 5 13.5
05	274 57.5	217 52.9	25.2	58 20.4	38.7	261 54.6	24.7	241 40.3	03.4			
06	290 00.0	232 52.4	N21 26.0	73 23.6	S12 38.5	276 56.5	N 4 24.9	256 42.5	N11 03.5	Rasalhague	96 16.5	N12 33.6
07	305 02.5	247 51.8	26.7	88 26.8	38.4	291 58.4	25.2	271 44.6	03.6	Regulus	207 55.0	N11 58.2
08	320 04.9	262 51.2	27.5	103 30.0	38.2	307 00.3	25.4	286 46.8	03.7	Rigel	281 22.8	S 8 12.4
M 09	335 07.4	277 50.6 ..	28.3	118 33.2 ..	38.0	322 02.2 ..	25.6	301 49.0 ..	03.8	Rigil Kent.	140 06.2	S60 49.8
O 10	350 09.9	292 50.0	29.0	133 36.4	37.8	337 04.1	25.8	316 51.1	03.9	Sabik	102 25.0	S15 43.4
N 11	5 12.3	307 49.4	29.8	148 39.6	37.7	352 06.1	26.1	331 53.3	04.0			
D 12	20 14.8	322 48.8	N21 30.5	163 42.9	S12 37.5	7 08.0	N 4 26.3	346 55.4	N11 04.1	Schedar	349 53.6	N56 31.8
A 13	35 17.3	337 48.2	31.3	178 46.1	37.3	22 09.9	26.5	1 57.6	04.3	Shaula	96 36.7	S37 06.0
Y 14	50 19.7	352 47.7	32.0	193 49.3	37.1	37 11.8	26.8	16 59.8	04.4	Sirius	258 43.5	S16 43.2
15	65 22.2	7 47.1 ..	32.8	208 52.5 ..	36.9	52 13.7 ..	27.0	32 01.9 ..	04.5	Spica	158 42.5	S11 09.5
16	80 24.7	22 46.5	33.6	223 55.7	36.8	67 15.6	27.2	47 04.1	04.6	Suhail	223 00.3	S43 26.1
17	95 27.1	37 45.9	34.3	238 59.0	36.6	82 17.5	27.5	62 06.3	04.7			
18	110 29.6	52 45.3	N21 35.1	254 02.2	S12 36.4	97 19.4	N 4 27.7	77 08.4	N11 04.8	Vega	80 46.3	N38 46.8
19	125 32.0	67 44.7	35.8	269 05.4	36.2	112 21.3	27.9	92 10.6	04.9	Zuben'ubi	137 17.3	S16 02.3
20	140 34.5	82 44.1	36.6	284 08.6	36.1	127 23.2	28.2	107 12.8	05.0		SHA	Mer. Pass.
21	155 37.0	97 43.5 ..	37.3	299 11.9 ..	35.9	142 25.1 ..	28.4	122 14.9 ..	05.1		° ′	h m
22	170 39.4	112 42.9	38.0	314 15.1	35.7	157 27.0	28.6	137 17.1	05.2	Venus	304 23.7	14 28
23	185 41.9	127 42.3	38.8	329 18.3	35.5	172 28.9	28.9	152 19.2	05.3	Mars	143 01.6	1 13
Mer. Pass. 10 43.2		v −0.6	d 0.8	v 3.2	d 0.2	v 1.9	d 0.2	v 2.2	d 0.1	Jupiter	347 13.2	11 35
										Saturn	326 51.5	12 56

SUN and MOON

UT (d h)	SUN GHA	SUN Dec	MOON GHA	v	Dec	d	HP
	° ′	° ′	° ′	′	° ′	′	′
10 00	179 36.9	N 7 41.9	256 13.1	10.5	S18 26.9	4.0	56.0
01	194 37.0	42.9	270 42.6	10.4	18 22.9	4.2	56.1
02	209 37.2	43.8	285 12.0	10.4	18 18.7	4.2	56.1
03	224 37.4	.. 44.7	299 41.4	10.4	18 14.5	4.3	56.1
04	239 37.6	45.6	314 10.8	10.4	18 10.2	4.5	56.2
05	254 37.7	46.6	328 40.2	10.4	18 05.7	4.5	56.2
06	269 37.9	N 7 47.5	343 09.6	10.4	S18 01.2	4.6	56.2
07	284 38.1	48.4	357 39.0	10.4	17 56.6	4.7	56.3
S 08	299 38.2	49.3	12 08.4	10.3	17 51.9	4.9	56.3
A 09	314 38.4	.. 50.3	26 37.7	10.4	17 47.0	4.9	56.3
T 10	329 38.6	51.2	41 07.1	10.3	17 42.1	5.0	56.4
U 11	344 38.7	52.1	55 36.4	10.3	17 37.1	5.1	56.4
R 12	359 38.9	N 7 53.0	70 05.7	10.3	S17 32.0	5.2	56.4
D 13	14 39.1	54.0	84 35.0	10.3	17 26.8	5.4	56.5
A 14	29 39.2	54.9	99 04.3	10.3	17 21.4	5.4	56.5
Y 15	44 39.4	.. 55.8	113 33.6	10.3	17 16.0	5.5	56.5
16	59 39.6	56.7	128 02.9	10.3	17 10.5	5.6	56.6
17	74 39.7	57.7	142 32.2	10.2	17 04.9	5.7	56.6
18	89 39.9	N 7 58.6	157 01.4	10.3	S16 59.2	5.8	56.6
19	104 40.1	7 59.5	171 30.7	10.2	16 53.4	5.9	56.7
20	119 40.2	8 00.4	185 59.9	10.3	16 47.5	6.0	56.7
21	134 40.4	.. 01.4	200 29.1	10.3	16 41.5	6.1	56.7
22	149 40.6	02.3	214 58.4	10.2	16 35.4	6.2	56.8
23	164 40.7	03.2	229 27.6	10.2	16 29.2	6.3	56.8
11 00	179 40.9	N 8 04.1	243 56.8	10.2	S16 22.9	6.4	56.9
01	194 41.1	05.1	258 26.0	10.1	16 16.5	6.5	56.9
02	209 41.2	06.0	272 55.1	10.2	16 10.0	6.6	56.9
03	224 41.4	.. 06.9	287 24.3	10.2	16 03.4	6.6	57.0
04	239 41.6	07.8	301 53.5	10.1	15 56.8	6.8	57.0
05	254 41.7	08.7	316 22.6	10.2	15 50.0	6.9	57.0
06	269 41.9	N 8 09.7	330 51.8	10.1	S15 43.1	6.9	57.1
07	284 42.1	10.6	345 20.9	10.2	15 36.2	7.1	57.1
08	299 42.2	11.5	359 50.1	10.1	15 29.1	7.1	57.2
S 09	314 42.4	.. 12.4	14 19.2	10.1	15 22.0	7.2	57.2
U 10	329 42.6	13.3	28 48.3	10.1	15 14.8	7.4	57.2
N 11	344 42.7	14.3	43 17.4	10.1	15 07.4	7.4	57.3
D 12	359 42.9	N 8 15.2	57 46.5	10.1	S15 00.0	7.5	57.3
A 13	14 43.1	16.1	72 15.6	10.1	14 52.5	7.6	57.3
Y 14	29 43.2	17.0	86 44.7	10.1	14 44.9	7.7	57.4
15	44 43.4	.. 17.9	101 13.8	10.0	14 37.2	7.8	57.4
16	59 43.6	18.9	115 42.8	10.1	14 29.4	7.9	57.5
17	74 43.7	19.8	130 11.9	10.0	14 21.5	7.9	57.5
18	89 43.9	N 8 20.7	144 40.9	10.1	S14 13.6	8.1	57.5
19	104 44.1	21.6	159 10.0	10.0	14 05.5	8.1	57.6
20	119 44.2	22.5	173 39.0	10.0	13 57.4	8.2	57.6
21	134 44.4	.. 23.5	188 08.0	10.1	13 49.2	8.4	57.7
22	149 44.5	24.4	202 37.1	10.0	13 40.8	8.4	57.7
23	164 44.7	25.3	217 06.1	10.0	13 32.4	8.4	57.7
12 00	179 44.9	N 8 26.2	231 35.1	10.0	S13 24.0	8.6	57.8
01	194 45.0	27.1	246 04.1	9.9	13 15.4	8.7	57.8
02	209 45.2	28.0	260 33.0	10.0	13 06.7	8.7	57.9
03	224 45.4	.. 29.0	275 02.0	10.0	12 58.0	8.9	57.9
04	239 45.5	29.9	289 31.0	10.0	12 49.1	8.9	57.9
05	254 45.7	30.8	304 00.0	9.9	12 40.2	9.0	58.0
06	269 45.8	N 8 31.7	318 28.9	9.9	S12 31.2	9.0	58.0
07	284 46.0	32.6	332 57.8	10.0	12 22.2	9.2	58.1
08	299 46.2	33.5	347 26.8	9.9	12 13.0	9.3	58.1
M 09	314 46.3	.. 34.4	1 55.7	9.9	12 03.7	9.3	58.1
O 10	329 46.5	35.4	16 24.6	9.9	11 54.4	9.4	58.2
N 11	344 46.7	36.3	30 53.5	9.9	11 45.0	9.5	58.2
D 12	359 46.8	N 8 37.2	45 22.4	9.9	S11 35.5	9.5	58.2
A 13	14 47.0	38.1	59 51.3	9.9	11 26.0	9.7	58.3
Y 14	29 47.1	39.0	74 20.2	9.8	11 16.3	9.7	58.3
15	44 47.3	.. 39.9	88 49.0	9.9	11 06.6	9.8	58.4
16	59 47.5	40.8	103 17.9	9.8	10 56.8	9.8	58.4
17	74 47.6	41.8	117 46.7	9.9	10 47.0	10.0	58.4
18	89 47.8	N 8 42.7	132 15.6	9.8	S10 37.0	10.0	58.5
19	104 48.0	43.6	146 44.4	9.8	10 27.0	10.1	58.5
20	119 48.1	44.5	161 13.2	9.8	10 16.9	10.1	58.6
21	134 48.3	.. 45.4	175 42.0	9.8	10 06.8	10.3	58.6
22	149 48.4	46.3	190 10.8	9.8	9 56.5	10.3	58.6
23	164 48.6	47.2	204 39.6	9.7	S 9 46.2	10.3	58.7
	SD 16.0	d 0.9	SD 15.4		15.6		15.9

Twilight and Moonrise

Lat.	Twilight Naut.	Twilight Civil	Sunrise	Moonrise 10	11	12	13
°	h m	h m	h m	h m	h m	h m	h m
N 72	////	02 36	04 05	■■■	06 00	05 41	05 28
N 70	////	03 03	04 18	05 24	05 22	05 19	05 15
68	01 38	03 24	04 29	04 43	04 55	05 01	05 05
66	02 14	03 39	04 37	04 15	04 34	04 47	04 56
64	02 39	03 52	04 45	03 54	04 18	04 35	04 48
62	02 59	04 03	04 51	03 37	04 04	04 25	04 42
60	03 14	04 12	04 57	03 22	03 52	04 16	04 36
N 58	03 27	04 20	05 02	03 10	03 42	04 09	04 31
56	03 37	04 27	05 06	02 59	03 33	04 02	04 27
54	03 47	04 33	05 10	02 50	03 25	03 56	04 23
52	03 55	04 38	05 13	02 41	03 18	03 50	04 19
50	04 02	04 43	05 17	02 34	03 12	03 45	04 16
45	04 17	04 53	05 23	02 18	02 58	03 35	04 09
N 40	04 28	05 01	05 29	02 04	02 47	03 26	04 03
35	04 38	05 08	05 34	01 53	02 37	03 18	03 58
30	04 45	05 14	05 38	01 43	02 28	03 11	03 53
20	04 57	05 23	05 46	01 26	02 14	03 00	03 45
N 10	05 06	05 31	05 52	01 11	02 01	02 49	03 38
0	05 13	05 37	05 58	00 58	01 48	02 40	03 31
S 10	05 18	05 42	06 04	00 44	01 36	02 30	03 25
20	05 22	05 47	06 10	00 29	01 23	02 19	03 18
30	05 24	05 52	06 16	00 12	01 08	02 08	03 10
35	05 25	05 55	06 20	00 02	01 00	02 01	03 05
40	05 26	05 57	06 24	24 50	00 50	01 53	03 00
45	05 26	06 00	06 29	24 38	00 38	01 44	02 53
S 50	05 25	06 03	06 35	24 24	00 24	01 33	02 46
52	05 25	06 04	06 38	24 17	00 17	01 28	02 43
54	05 24	06 05	06 41	24 10	00 10	01 22	02 39
56	05 24	06 07	06 44	24 02	00 02	01 16	02 35
58	05 23	06 08	06 48	23 53	25 09	01 09	02 30
S 60	05 22	06 10	06 52	23 42	25 01	01 01	02 25

Sunset, Twilight and Moonset

Lat.	Sunset	Twilight Civil	Twilight Naut.	Moonset 10	11	12	13
°	h m	h m	h m	h m	h m	h m	h m
N 72	20 01	21 32	////	■■■	10 15	12 21	14 23
N 70	19 47	21 03	////	09 03	10 52	12 42	14 34
68	19 36	20 42	22 33	09 44	11 18	12 59	14 42
66	19 27	20 26	21 53	10 11	11 38	13 12	14 50
64	19 19	20 13	21 27	10 32	11 54	13 22	14 56
62	19 13	20 02	21 07	10 49	12 07	13 32	15 01
60	19 07	19 52	20 51	11 03	12 18	13 40	15 06
N 58	19 02	19 44	20 38	11 15	12 28	13 46	15 10
56	18 58	19 37	20 27	11 25	12 36	13 52	15 13
54	18 54	19 31	20 17	11 34	12 43	13 58	15 16
52	18 50	19 25	20 09	11 43	12 50	14 03	15 19
50	18 47	19 20	20 02	11 50	12 56	14 07	15 22
45	18 40	19 10	19 47	12 05	13 09	14 17	15 28
N 40	18 34	19 02	19 35	12 18	13 20	14 24	15 32
35	18 29	18 55	19 25	12 29	13 29	14 31	15 36
30	18 24	18 49	19 18	12 38	13 36	14 37	15 40
20	18 17	18 39	19 05	12 55	13 50	14 47	15 46
N 10	18 10	18 32	18 56	13 09	14 02	14 56	15 51
0	18 04	18 25	18 50	13 22	14 13	15 04	15 56
S 10	17 59	18 20	18 44	13 35	14 24	15 12	16 01
20	17 52	18 15	18 40	13 49	14 36	15 21	16 06
30	17 46	18 10	18 37	14 05	14 49	15 31	16 12
35	17 42	18 07	18 36	14 14	14 56	15 37	16 15
40	17 37	18 04	18 36	14 25	15 05	15 43	16 19
45	17 32	18 02	18 36	14 37	15 15	15 50	16 23
S 50	17 26	17 59	18 36	14 52	15 27	15 59	16 29
52	17 23	17 57	18 36	14 59	15 33	16 03	16 31
54	17 20	17 56	18 37	15 06	15 39	16 08	16 34
56	17 17	17 55	18 37	15 15	15 46	16 13	16 36
58	17 13	17 53	18 38	15 25	15 54	16 18	16 40
S 60	17 09	17 51	18 39	15 36	16 02	16 24	16 43

SUN / MOON

Day	SUN Eqn. of Time 00ʰ	SUN Eqn. of Time 12ʰ	SUN Mer. Pass.	MOON Mer. Pass. Upper	MOON Mer. Pass. Lower	Age	Phase
d	m s	m s	h m	h m	h m	d	%
10	01 33	01 25	12 01	07 10	19 35	24	36
11	01 17	01 09	12 01	08 01	20 26	25	27
12	01 01	00 53	12 01	08 52	21 18	26	18

UT	ARIES	VENUS −4.0		MARS −1.4		JUPITER −2.0		SATURN +0.4		STARS		
	GHA	GHA	Dec	GHA	Dec	GHA	Dec	GHA	Dec	Name	SHA	Dec
d h	° ′	° ′	° ′	° ′	° ′	° ′	° ′	° ′	° ′		° ′	° ′
13 00	200 44.4	142 41.7	N21 39.5	344 21.5	S12 35.3	187 30.9	N 4 29.1	167 21.4	N11 05.4	Acamar	315 27.1	S40 18.8
01	215 46.8	157 41.2	40.3	359 24.8	35.2	202 32.8	29.3	182 23.6	05.5	Achernar	335 35.6	S57 14.6
02	230 49.3	172 40.6	41.0	14 28.0	35.0	217 34.7	29.6	197 25.7	05.6	Acrux	173 20.9	S63 05.8
03	245 51.8	187 40.0	.. 41.8	29 31.2	.. 34.8	232 36.6	.. 29.8	212 27.9	.. 05.8	Adhara	255 21.2	S28 58.6
04	260 54.2	202 39.4	42.5	44 34.5	34.6	247 38.5	30.0	227 30.1	05.9	Aldebaran	291 02.2	N16 30.3
05	275 56.7	217 38.8	43.2	59 37.7	34.4	262 40.4	30.3	242 32.2	06.0			
06	290 59.1	232 38.2	N21 44.0	74 40.9	S12 34.3	277 42.3	N 4 30.5	257 34.4	N11 06.1	Alioth	166 29.8	N55 57.9
07	306 01.6	247 37.6	44.7	89 44.2	34.1	292 44.2	30.7	272 36.5	06.2	Alkaid	153 07.1	N49 19.0
T 08	321 04.1	262 37.0	45.5	104 47.4	33.9	307 46.1	31.0	287 38.7	06.3	Al Na'ir	27 57.8	S46 57.8
U 09	336 06.5	277 36.4	.. 46.2	119 50.7	.. 33.7	322 48.0	.. 31.2	302 40.9	.. 06.4	Alnilam	275 57.7	S 1 12.4
E 10	351 09.0	292 35.8	46.9	134 53.9	33.5	337 49.9	31.4	317 43.0	06.5	Alphard	218 06.7	S 8 39.5
S 11	6 11.5	307 35.2	47.7	149 57.1	33.4	352 51.8	31.6	332 45.2	06.6			
D 12	21 13.9	322 34.6	N21 48.4	165 00.4	S12 33.2	7 53.8	N 4 31.9	347 47.4	N11 06.7	Alphecca	126 20.0	N26 43.0
A 13	36 16.4	337 34.0	49.1	180 03.6	33.0	22 55.7	32.1	2 49.5	06.8	Alpheratz	357 55.2	N29 04.9
Y 14	51 18.9	352 33.4	49.9	195 06.9	32.8	37 57.6	32.3	17 51.7	06.9	Altair	62 19.0	N 8 51.9
15	66 21.3	7 32.8	.. 50.6	210 10.1	.. 32.6	52 59.5	.. 32.6	32 53.8	.. 07.0	Ankaa	353 27.0	S42 18.7
16	81 23.8	22 32.2	51.3	225 13.3	32.4	68 01.4	32.8	47 56.0	07.1	Antares	112 39.5	S26 25.7
17	96 26.3	37 31.6	52.1	240 16.6	32.3	83 03.3	33.0	62 58.2	07.3			
18	111 28.7	52 31.0	N21 52.8	255 19.8	S12 32.1	98 05.2	N 4 33.3	78 00.3	N11 07.4	Arcturus	146 05.4	N19 11.2
19	126 31.2	67 30.4	53.5	270 23.1	31.9	113 07.1	33.5	93 02.5	07.5	Atria	107 50.9	S69 01.3
20	141 33.6	82 29.8	54.2	285 26.3	31.7	128 09.0	33.7	108 04.6	07.6	Avior	234 22.4	S59 30.8
21	156 36.1	97 29.2	.. 55.0	300 29.6	.. 31.5	143 10.9	.. 34.0	123 06.8	.. 07.7	Bellatrix	278 44.0	N 6 20.7
22	171 38.6	112 28.6	55.7	315 32.8	31.3	158 12.8	34.2	138 09.0	07.8	Betelgeuse	271 13.3	N 7 24.2
23	186 41.0	127 28.0	56.4	330 36.1	31.2	173 14.7	34.4	153 11.1	07.9			
14 00	201 43.5	142 27.4	N21 57.1	345 39.3	S12 31.0	188 16.6	N 4 34.7	168 13.3	N11 08.0	Canopus	264 01.2	S52 42.1
01	216 46.0	157 26.8	57.8	0 42.6	30.8	203 18.6	34.9	183 15.5	08.1	Capella	280 51.0	N45 59.8
02	231 48.4	172 26.2	58.6	15 45.8	30.6	218 20.5	35.1	198 17.6	08.2	Deneb	49 39.1	N45 16.4
03	246 50.9	187 25.6	21 59.3	30 49.1	.. 30.4	233 22.4	.. 35.4	213 19.8	.. 08.3	Denebola	182 44.6	N14 34.6
04	261 53.4	202 25.0	22 00.0	45 52.4	30.2	248 24.3	35.6	228 21.9	08.4	Diphda	349 07.2	S17 59.6
05	276 55.8	217 24.4	00.7	60 55.6	30.0	263 26.2	35.8	243 24.1	08.5			
06	291 58.3	232 23.8	N22 01.4	75 58.9	S12 29.9	278 28.1	N 4 36.0	258 26.3	N11 08.6	Dubhe	194 04.6	N61 45.5
W 07	307 00.8	247 23.2	02.1	91 02.1	29.7	293 30.0	36.3	273 28.4	08.7	Elnath	278 26.7	N28 36.3
E 08	322 03.2	262 22.6	02.9	106 05.4	29.5	308 31.9	36.5	288 30.6	08.9	Eltanin	90 51.0	N51 29.1
D 09	337 05.7	277 22.0	.. 03.6	121 08.6	.. 29.3	323 33.8	.. 36.7	303 32.8	.. 09.0	Enif	33 58.1	N 9 52.1
N 10	352 08.1	292 21.4	04.3	136 11.9	29.1	338 35.7	37.0	318 34.9	09.1	Fomalhaut	15 36.4	S29 37.6
E 11	7 10.6	307 20.8	05.0	151 15.2	28.9	353 37.6	37.2	333 37.1	09.2			
S 12	22 13.1	322 20.2	N22 05.7	166 18.4	S12 28.7	8 39.5	N 4 37.4	348 39.2	N11 09.3	Gacrux	172 12.6	S57 06.6
D 13	37 15.5	337 19.6	06.4	181 21.7	28.5	23 41.5	37.7	3 41.4	09.4	Gienah	176 03.3	S17 32.3
A 14	52 18.0	352 19.0	07.1	196 25.0	28.4	38 43.4	37.9	18 43.6	09.5	Hadar	149 02.9	S60 22.1
Y 15	67 20.5	7 18.4	.. 07.8	211 28.2	.. 28.2	53 45.3	.. 38.1	33 45.7	.. 09.6	Hamal	328 13.5	N23 27.3
16	82 22.9	22 17.8	.. 08.5	226 31.5	28.0	68 47.2	38.4	48 47.9	09.7	Kaus Aust.	83 58.3	S34 22.9
17	97 25.4	37 17.2	09.2	241 34.8	27.8	83 49.1	38.6	63 50.0	09.8			
18	112 27.9	52 16.6	N22 09.9	256 38.0	S12 27.6	98 51.0	N 4 38.8	78 52.2	N11 09.9	Kochab	137 18.6	N74 09.5
19	127 30.3	67 16.0	10.6	271 41.3	27.4	113 52.9	39.1	93 54.4	10.0	Markab	13 49.5	N15 11.9
20	142 32.8	82 15.4	11.3	286 44.6	27.2	128 54.8	39.3	108 56.5	10.1	Menkar	314 26.9	N 4 05.0
21	157 35.2	97 14.8	.. 12.1	301 47.8	.. 27.0	143 56.7	.. 39.5	123 58.7	.. 10.3	Menkent	148 20.2	S36 21.9
22	172 37.7	112 14.1	12.8	316 51.1	26.8	158 58.6	39.7	139 00.8	10.4	Miaplacidus	221 41.6	S69 43.2
23	187 40.2	127 13.5	13.4	331 54.4	26.7	174 00.5	40.0	154 03.0	10.5			
15 00	202 42.6	142 12.9	N22 14.1	346 57.6	S12 26.5	189 02.4	N 4 40.2	169 05.2	N11 10.6	Mirfak	308 56.6	N49 51.4
01	217 45.1	157 12.3	14.8	2 00.9	26.3	204 04.4	40.4	184 07.3	10.7	Nunki	76 11.9	S26 17.7
02	232 47.6	172 11.7	15.5	17 04.2	26.1	219 06.3	40.7	199 09.5	10.8	Peacock	53 36.6	S56 44.0
03	247 50.0	187 11.1	.. 16.2	32 07.5	.. 25.9	234 08.2	.. 40.9	214 11.7	.. 10.9	Pollux	243 41.2	N28 01.7
04	262 52.5	202 10.5	16.9	47 10.7	25.7	249 10.1	41.1	229 13.8	11.0	Procyon	245 11.2	N 5 13.5
05	277 55.0	217 09.9	17.6	62 14.0	25.5	264 12.0	41.4	244 16.0	11.1			
06	292 57.4	232 09.3	N22 18.3	77 17.3	S12 25.3	279 13.9	N 4 41.6	259 18.1	N11 11.2	Rasalhague	96 16.5	N12 33.6
07	307 59.9	247 08.7	19.0	92 20.6	25.1	294 15.8	41.8	274 20.3	11.3	Regulus	207 55.0	N11 58.2
T 08	323 02.4	262 08.1	19.7	107 23.9	24.9	309 17.7	42.1	289 22.5	11.4	Rigel	281 22.8	S 8 12.4
H 09	338 04.8	277 07.4	.. 20.4	122 27.1	.. 24.7	324 19.6	.. 42.3	304 24.6	.. 11.5	Rigil Kent.	140 06.2	S60 49.8
U 10	353 07.3	292 06.8	21.1	137 30.4	24.5	339 21.5	42.5	319 26.8	11.6	Sabik	102 25.0	S15 43.4
R 11	8 09.7	307 06.2	21.8	152 33.7	24.4	354 23.4	42.7	334 28.9	11.8			
S 12	23 12.2	322 05.6	N22 22.4	167 37.0	S12 24.2	9 25.4	N 4 43.0	349 31.1	N11 11.9	Schedar	349 53.6	N56 31.8
D 13	38 14.7	337 05.0	23.1	182 40.3	24.0	24 27.3	43.2	4 33.3	12.0	Shaula	96 36.6	S37 06.0
A 14	53 17.1	352 04.4	23.8	197 43.6	23.8	39 29.2	43.4	19 35.4	12.1	Sirius	258 43.5	S16 43.2
Y 15	68 19.6	7 03.8	.. 24.5	212 46.8	.. 23.6	54 31.1	.. 43.7	34 37.6	.. 12.2	Spica	158 42.5	S11 09.5
16	83 22.1	22 03.2	25.2	227 50.1	23.4	69 33.0	43.9	49 39.7	12.3	Suhail	223 00.4	S43 26.1
17	98 24.5	37 02.5	25.9	242 53.4	23.2	84 34.9	44.1	64 41.9	12.4			
18	113 27.0	52 01.9	N22 26.5	257 56.7	S12 23.0	99 36.8	N 4 44.4	79 44.1	N11 12.5	Vega	80 46.3	N38 46.8
19	128 29.5	67 01.3	27.2	273 00.0	22.8	114 38.7	44.6	94 46.2	12.6	Zuben'ubi	137 17.3	S16 02.3
20	143 31.9	82 00.7	27.9	288 03.3	22.6	129 40.6	44.8	109 48.4	12.7			
21	158 34.4	97 00.1	.. 28.6	303 06.6	.. 22.4	144 42.5	.. 45.1	124 50.5	.. 12.8		SHA	Mer. Pass.
22	173 36.8	111 59.5	29.2	318 09.9	22.2	159 44.9	45.3	139 52.7	12.9	Venus	300 43.9	14 31
23	188 39.3	126 58.9	29.9	333 13.2	22.0	174 46.4	45.5	154 54.9	13.0	Mars	143 55.8	0 57
	h m	v −0.6	d 0.7	v 3.3	d 0.2	v 1.9	d 0.2	v 2.2	d 0.1	Jupiter	346 33.1	11 25
Mer. Pass. 10 31.4										Saturn	326 29.8	12 45

UT	SUN GHA	Dec	MOON GHA	v	Dec	d	HP
d h	° '	° '	° '	'	° '	'	'
13 00	179 48.8	N 8 48.1	219 08.3	9.8	S 9 35.9	10.5	58.7
01	194 48.9	49.1	233 37.1	9.7	9 25.4	10.5	58.8
02	209 49.1	50.0	248 05.8	9.7	9 14.9	10.6	58.8
03	224 49.2 ..	50.9	262 34.5	9.7	9 04.3	10.6	58.8
04	239 49.4	51.8	277 03.2	9.7	8 53.7	10.7	58.9
05	254 49.6	52.7	291 31.9	9.7	8 43.0	10.8	58.9
06	269 49.7	N 8 53.6	306 00.6	9.7	S 8 32.2	10.8	59.0
07	284 49.9	54.5	320 29.3	9.6	8 21.4	10.9	59.0
T 08	299 50.0	55.4	334 57.9	9.7	8 10.5	11.0	59.0
U 09	314 50.2 ..	56.3	349 26.6	9.6	7 59.5	11.0	59.1
E 10	329 50.3	57.2	3 55.2	9.6	7 48.5	11.1	59.1
S 11	344 50.5	58.1	18 23.8	9.6	7 37.4	11.1	59.1
D 12	359 50.7	N 8 59.1	32 52.4	9.6	S 7 26.3	11.3	59.2
A 13	14 50.8	9 00.0	47 21.0	9.6	7 15.0	11.2	59.2
Y 14	29 51.0	00.9	61 49.6	9.5	7 03.8	11.3	59.3
15	44 51.1 ..	01.8	76 18.1	9.5	6 52.5	11.4	59.3
16	59 51.3	02.7	90 46.6	9.5	6 41.1	11.4	59.3
17	74 51.5	03.6	105 15.1	9.5	6 29.7	11.5	59.4
18	89 51.6	N 9 04.5	119 43.6	9.5	S 6 18.2	11.5	59.4
19	104 51.8	05.4	134 12.1	9.5	6 06.7	11.6	59.4
20	119 51.9	06.3	148 40.6	9.4	5 55.1	11.6	59.5
21	134 52.1 ..	07.2	163 09.0	9.4	5 43.5	11.7	59.5
22	149 52.2	08.1	177 37.4	9.4	5 31.8	11.7	59.5
23	164 52.4	09.0	192 05.8	9.4	5 20.1	11.8	59.6
14 00	179 52.6	N 9 09.9	206 34.2	9.3	S 5 08.3	11.8	59.6
01	194 52.7	10.8	221 02.5	9.4	4 56.5	11.9	59.6
02	209 52.9	11.7	235 30.9	9.3	4 44.6	11.9	59.7
03	224 53.0 ..	12.6	249 59.2	9.3	4 32.7	11.9	59.7
04	239 53.2	13.5	264 27.5	9.3	4 20.8	12.0	59.7
05	254 53.3	14.4	278 55.8	9.2	4 08.8	12.0	59.8
06	269 53.5	N 9 15.4	293 24.0	9.2	S 3 56.8	12.1	59.8
W 07	284 53.6	16.3	307 52.2	9.2	3 44.7	12.1	59.8
E 08	299 53.8	17.2	322 20.4	9.2	3 32.6	12.1	59.9
D 09	314 54.0 ..	18.1	336 48.6	9.2	3 20.5	12.2	59.9
N 10	329 54.1	19.0	351 16.8	9.1	3 08.3	12.2	59.9
E 11	344 54.3	19.9	5 44.9	9.1	2 56.1	12.2	60.0
S 12	359 54.4	N 9 20.8	20 13.0	9.1	S 2 43.9	12.2	60.0
D 13	14 54.6	21.7	34 41.1	9.0	2 31.7	12.3	60.0
A 14	29 54.7	22.6	49 09.1	9.0	2 19.4	12.3	60.1
Y 15	44 54.9 ..	23.5	63 37.1	9.0	2 07.1	12.4	60.1
16	59 55.0	24.4	78 05.1	9.0	1 54.7	12.4	60.1
17	74 55.2	25.3	92 33.1	8.9	1 42.3	12.3	60.2
18	89 55.4	N 9 26.2	107 01.0	9.0	S 1 30.0	12.5	60.2
19	104 55.5	27.1	121 29.0	8.8	1 17.5	12.4	60.2
20	119 55.7	28.0	135 56.8	8.9	1 05.1	12.4	60.2
21	134 55.8 ..	28.9	150 24.7	8.8	0 52.7	12.5	60.3
22	149 56.0	29.8	164 52.5	8.8	0 40.2	12.5	60.3
23	164 56.1	30.7	179 20.3	8.8	0 27.7	12.5	60.3
15 00	179 56.3	N 9 31.6	193 48.1	8.7	S 0 15.2	12.5	60.4
01	194 56.4	32.5	208 15.8	8.7	S 0 02.7	12.5	60.4
02	209 56.6	33.4	222 43.5	8.7	N 0 09.8	12.6	60.4
03	224 56.7 ..	34.3	237 11.2	8.6	0 22.4	12.5	60.4
04	239 56.9	35.2	251 38.8	8.7	0 34.9	12.6	60.5
05	254 57.0	36.1	266 06.5	8.5	0 47.5	12.5	60.5
06	269 57.2	N 9 37.0	280 34.0	8.6	N 1 00.0	12.6	60.5
07	284 57.3	37.8	295 01.6	8.5	1 12.6	12.5	60.5
T 08	299 57.5	38.7	309 29.1	8.5	1 25.1	12.6	60.6
H 09	314 57.6 ..	39.6	323 56.6	8.4	1 37.7	12.6	60.6
U 10	329 57.8	40.5	338 24.0	8.4	1 50.3	12.5	60.6
R 11	344 57.9	41.4	352 51.4	8.4	2 02.8	12.6	60.6
S 12	359 58.1	N 9 42.3	7 18.8	8.3	N 2 15.4	12.6	60.6
D 13	14 58.3	43.2	21 46.1	8.3	2 28.0	12.5	60.7
A 14	29 58.4	44.1	36 13.4	8.3	2 40.5	12.6	60.7
Y 15	44 58.6 ..	45.0	50 40.7	8.2	2 53.1	12.5	60.7
16	59 58.7	45.9	65 07.9	8.2	3 05.6	12.5	60.7
17	74 58.9	46.8	79 35.1	8.1	3 18.1	12.5	60.7
18	89 59.0	N 9 47.7	94 02.2	8.1	N 3 30.6	12.5	60.8
19	104 59.2	48.6	108 29.3	8.1	3 43.1	12.5	60.8
20	119 59.3	49.5	122 56.4	8.0	3 55.6	12.5	60.8
21	134 59.5 ..	50.4	137 23.4	8.0	4 08.1	12.4	60.8
22	149 59.6	51.3	151 50.4	8.0	4 20.5	12.5	60.8
23	164 59.8	52.2	166 17.4	7.9	N 4 33.0	12.4	60.8
	SD 16.0	d 0.9	SD 16.1		16.3		16.5

Lat.	Twilight Naut.	Twilight Civil	Sunrise	Moonrise 13	14	15	16
°	h m	h m	h m	h m	h m	h m	h m
N 72	////	02 11	03 48	05 28	05 18	05 08	04 58
N 70	////	02 44	04 03	05 15	05 12	05 09	05 06
68	01 01	03 08	04 16	05 05	05 07	05 09	05 12
66	01 53	03 26	04 26	04 56	05 03	05 10	05 17
64	02 23	03 40	04 34	04 48	05 00	05 11	05 22
62	02 45	03 52	04 42	04 42	04 57	05 11	05 26
60	03 02	04 02	04 48	04 36	04 54	05 12	05 29
N 58	03 16	04 11	04 53	04 31	04 52	05 12	05 33
56	03 28	04 19	04 58	04 27	04 50	05 12	05 35
54	03 38	04 25	05 03	04 23	04 48	05 13	05 38
52	03 47	04 31	05 07	04 19	04 46	05 13	05 40
50	03 55	04 36	05 10	04 16	04 45	05 13	05 42
45	04 11	04 48	05 18	04 09	04 41	05 14	05 47
N 40	04 23	04 57	05 25	04 03	04 39	05 14	05 51
35	04 33	05 04	05 30	03 58	04 36	05 15	05 54
30	04 42	05 10	05 35	03 53	04 34	05 15	05 57
20	04 55	05 21	05 43	03 45	04 30	05 16	06 02
N 10	05 04	05 29	05 50	03 38	04 27	05 16	06 07
0	05 12	05 36	05 57	03 31	04 24	05 17	06 11
S 10	05 18	05 42	06 04	03 25	04 21	05 17	06 16
20	05 22	05 48	06 10	03 18	04 17	05 18	06 21
30	05 26	05 54	06 18	03 10	04 13	05 19	06 26
35	05 28	05 57	06 23	03 05	04 11	05 19	06 29
40	05 29	06 00	06 27	03 00	04 09	05 20	06 33
45	05 29	06 03	06 33	02 53	04 06	05 21	06 37
S 50	05 30	06 07	06 40	02 46	04 03	05 22	06 42
52	05 30	06 09	06 43	02 43	04 01	05 22	06 45
54	05 30	06 11	06 46	02 39	03 59	05 22	06 47
56	05 29	06 12	06 50	02 35	03 57	05 23	06 50
58	05 29	06 14	06 54	02 30	03 55	05 23	06 54
S 60	05 28	06 17	06 59	02 25	03 53	05 24	06 57

Lat.	Sunset	Twilight Civil	Twilight Naut.	Moonset 13	14	15	16
°	h m	h m	h m	h m	h m	h m	h m
N 72	20 17	21 57	////	14 23	16 24	18 27	20 36
N 70	20 01	21 21	////	14 34	16 27	18 22	20 21
68	19 48	20 57	23 12	14 42	16 29	18 18	20 10
66	19 37	20 38	22 14	14 50	16 31	18 15	20 01
64	19 28	20 23	21 42	14 56	16 33	18 12	19 53
62	19 21	20 11	21 19	15 01	16 34	18 09	19 47
60	19 14	20 00	21 02	15 06	16 35	18 07	19 41
N 58	19 09	19 52	20 47	15 10	16 36	18 05	19 36
56	19 04	19 44	20 35	15 13	16 37	18 04	19 32
54	18 59	19 37	20 24	15 16	16 38	18 02	19 28
52	18 55	19 31	20 15	15 19	16 39	18 01	19 24
50	18 51	19 26	20 07	15 22	16 40	18 00	19 21
45	18 43	19 14	19 51	15 28	16 41	17 57	19 14
N 40	18 37	19 05	19 38	15 32	16 42	17 54	19 08
35	18 31	18 57	19 28	15 36	16 43	17 53	19 03
30	18 26	18 51	19 20	15 40	16 44	17 51	18 59
20	18 18	18 40	19 07	15 46	16 46	17 48	18 51
N 10	18 10	18 32	18 57	15 51	16 47	17 45	18 44
0	18 04	18 25	18 49	15 56	16 49	17 43	18 38
S 10	17 57	18 18	18 43	16 01	16 50	17 40	18 32
20	17 50	18 12	18 38	16 06	16 51	17 37	18 25
30	17 42	18 06	18 34	16 12	16 53	17 34	18 17
35	17 38	18 03	18 33	16 15	16 54	17 32	18 13
40	17 33	18 00	18 31	16 19	16 55	17 30	18 08
45	17 27	17 57	18 31	16 23	16 56	17 28	18 02
S 50	17 20	17 53	18 30	16 29	16 57	17 25	17 56
52	17 17	17 51	18 30	16 31	16 57	17 24	17 52
54	17 13	17 49	18 30	16 34	16 58	17 23	17 49
56	17 09	17 47	18 30	16 36	16 59	17 21	17 45
58	17 05	17 45	18 31	16 40	17 00	17 19	17 41
S 60	17 01	17 43	18 31	16 43	17 00	17 18	17 36

	SUN			MOON			
Day	Eqn. of Time 00h	12h	Mer. Pass.	Mer. Pass. Upper	Lower	Age	Phase
d	m s	m s	h m	h m	h m	d	%
13	00 45	00 38	12 01	09 44	22 10	27	10
14	00 30	00 23	12 00	10 36	23 03	28	4
15	00 15	00 08	12 00	11 30	23 57	29	1

1999 APRIL 16, 17, 18 (FRI., SAT., SUN.)

UT	ARIES GHA	VENUS −4.1 GHA	Dec	MARS −1.5 GHA	Dec	JUPITER −2.1 GHA	Dec	SATURN +0.4 GHA	Dec	STARS Name	SHA	Dec
d h	° ′	° ′	° ′	° ′	° ′	° ′	° ′	° ′	° ′		° ′	° ′
16 00	203 41.8	141 58.2	N22 30.6	348 16.5	S12 21.8	189 48.3	N 4 45.7	169 57.0	N11 13.1	Acamar	315 27.1	S40 18.7
01	218 44.2	156 57.6	31.3	3 19.7	21.6	204 50.2	46.0	184 59.2	13.3	Achernar	335 35.6	S57 14.6
02	233 46.7	171 57.0	31.9	18 23.0	21.4	219 52.1	46.2	200 01.3	13.4	Acrux	173 20.9	S63 05.8
03	248 49.2	186 56.4 . .	32.6	33 26.3 . .	21.2	234 54.0 . .	46.4	215 03.5 . .	13.5	Adhara	255 21.2	S28 58.6
04	263 51.6	201 55.8	33.3	48 29.6	21.0	249 55.9	46.7	230 05.7	13.6	Aldebaran	291 02.3	N16 30.3
05	278 54.1	216 55.2	34.0	63 32.9	20.8	264 57.8	46.9	245 07.8	13.7			
06	293 56.6	231 54.6	N22 34.6	78 36.2	S12 20.6	279 59.7	N 4 47.1	260 10.0	N11 13.8	Alioth	166 29.8	N55 57.9
07	308 59.0	246 53.9	35.3	93 39.5	20.4	295 01.6	47.4	275 12.2	13.9	Alkaid	153 07.1	N49 19.1
08	324 01.5	261 53.3	36.0	108 42.8	20.2	310 03.5	47.6	290 14.3	14.0	Al Na'ir	27 57.8	S46 57.8
F 09	339 04.0	276 52.7 . .	36.6	123 46.1 . .	20.0	325 05.4 . .	47.8	305 16.5 . .	14.1	Alnilam	275 57.7	S 1 12.4
R 10	354 06.4	291 52.1	37.3	138 49.4	19.8	340 07.4	48.0	320 18.6	14.2	Alphard	218 06.8	S 8 39.5
I 11	9 08.9	306 51.5	37.9	153 52.7	19.6	355 09.3	48.3	335 20.8	14.3			
D 12	24 11.3	321 50.8	N22 38.6	168 56.0	S12 19.5	10 11.2	N 4 48.5	350 23.0	N11 14.4	Alphecca	126 20.0	N26 43.0
A 13	39 13.8	336 50.2	39.3	183 59.3	19.3	25 13.1	48.7	5 25.1	14.5	Alpheratz	357 55.2	N29 04.9
Y 14	54 16.3	351 49.6	39.9	199 02.6	19.1	40 15.0	49.0	20 27.3	14.6	Altair	62 18.9	N 8 51.9
15	69 18.7	6 49.0 . .	40.6	214 05.9 . .	18.9	55 16.9 . .	49.2	35 29.4 . .	14.8	Ankaa	353 27.0	S42 18.7
16	84 21.2	21 48.4	41.2	229 09.2	18.7	70 18.8	49.4	50 31.6	14.9	Antares	112 39.5	S26 25.7
17	99 23.7	36 47.7	41.9	244 12.5	18.5	85 20.7	49.7	65 33.8	15.0			
18	114 26.1	51 47.1	N22 42.6	259 15.9	S12 18.3	100 22.6	N 4 49.9	80 35.9	N11 15.1	Arcturus	146 05.4	N19 11.2
19	129 28.6	66 46.5	43.2	274 19.2	18.1	115 24.5	50.1	95 38.1	15.2	Atria	107 50.8	S69 01.3
20	144 31.1	81 45.9	43.9	289 22.5	17.9	130 26.4	50.3	110 40.2	15.3	Avior	234 22.4	S59 30.8
21	159 33.5	96 45.3 . .	44.5	304 25.8 . .	17.7	145 28.4 . .	50.6	125 42.4 . .	15.4	Bellatrix	278 44.0	N 6 20.7
22	174 36.0	111 44.6	45.2	319 29.1	17.5	160 30.3	50.8	140 44.6	15.5	Betelgeuse	271 13.4	N 7 24.2
23	189 38.4	126 44.0	45.8	334 32.4	17.3	175 32.2	51.0	155 46.7	15.6			
17 00	204 40.9	141 43.4	N22 46.5	349 35.7	S12 17.1	190 34.1	N 4 51.3	170 48.9	N11 15.7	Canopus	264 01.2	S52 42.1
01	219 43.4	156 42.8	47.1	4 39.0	16.9	205 36.0	51.5	185 51.0	15.8	Capella	280 51.0	N45 59.8
02	234 45.8	171 42.2	47.8	19 42.3	16.7	220 37.9	51.7	200 53.2	15.9	Deneb	49 39.0	N45 16.4
03	249 48.3	186 41.5 . .	48.4	34 45.6 . .	16.4	235 39.8 . .	52.0	215 55.3 . .	16.0	Denebola	182 44.6	N14 34.6
04	264 50.8	201 40.9	49.1	49 49.0	16.2	250 41.7	52.2	230 57.5	16.1	Diphda	349 07.2	S17 59.6
05	279 53.2	216 40.3	49.7	64 52.3	16.0	265 43.6	52.4	245 59.7	16.2			
06	294 55.7	231 39.7	N22 50.3	79 55.6	S12 15.8	280 45.5	N 4 52.6	261 01.8	N11 16.4	Dubhe	194 04.7	N61 45.5
07	309 58.2	246 39.0	51.0	94 58.9	15.6	295 47.5	52.9	276 04.0	16.5	Elnath	278 26.7	N28 36.3
S 08	325 00.6	261 38.4	51.6	110 02.2	15.4	310 49.4	53.1	291 06.1	16.6	Eltanin	90 51.0	N51 29.2
A 09	340 03.1	276 37.8 . .	52.3	125 05.5 . .	15.2	325 51.3 . .	53.3	306 08.3 . .	16.7	Enif	33 58.1	N 9 52.1
T 10	355 05.6	291 37.2	52.9	140 08.9	15.0	340 53.2	53.6	321 10.5	16.8	Fomalhaut	15 36.4	S29 37.6
U 11	10 08.0	306 36.5	53.6	155 12.2	14.8	355 55.1	53.8	336 12.6	16.9			
R 12	25 10.5	321 35.9	N22 54.2	170 15.5	S12 14.6	10 57.0	N 4 54.0	351 14.8	N11 17.0	Gacrux	172 12.6	S57 06.6
D 13	40 12.9	336 35.3	54.8	185 18.8	14.4	25 58.9	54.3	6 16.9	17.1	Gienah	176 03.3	S17 32.3
A 14	55 15.4	351 34.7	55.5	200 22.1	14.2	41 00.8	54.5	21 19.1	17.2	Hadar	149 02.9	S60 22.1
Y 15	70 17.9	6 34.0 . .	56.1	215 25.5 . .	14.0	56 02.7 . .	54.7	36 21.3 . .	17.3	Hamal	328 13.5	N23 27.3
16	85 20.3	21 33.4	56.7	230 28.8	13.8	71 04.6	54.9	51 23.4	17.4	Kaus Aust.	83 58.2	S34 22.9
17	100 22.8	36 32.8	57.4	245 32.1	13.6	86 06.6	55.2	66 25.6	17.5			
18	115 25.3	51 32.1	N22 58.0	260 35.4	S12 13.4	101 08.5	N 4 55.4	81 27.7	N11 17.6	Kochab	137 18.5	N74 09.5
19	130 27.7	66 31.5	58.6	275 38.8	13.2	116 10.4	55.6	96 29.9	17.7	Markab	13 49.5	N15 11.9
20	145 30.2	81 30.9	59.2	290 42.1	13.0	131 12.3	55.9	111 32.1	17.9	Menkar	314 26.9	N 4 05.0
21	160 32.7	96 30.3	22 59.9	305 45.4 . .	12.8	146 14.2 . .	56.1	126 34.2 . .	18.0	Menkent	148 20.2	S36 22.0
22	175 35.1	111 29.6	23 00.5	320 48.7	12.6	161 16.1	56.3	141 36.4	18.1	Miaplacidus	221 41.6	S69 43.2
23	190 37.6	126 29.0	01.1	335 52.1	12.4	176 18.0	56.5	156 38.5	18.2			
18 00	205 40.1	141 28.4	N23 01.8	350 55.4	S12 12.2	191 19.9	N 4 56.8	171 40.7	N11 18.3	Mirfak	308 56.6	N49 51.4
01	220 42.5	156 27.8	02.4	5 58.7	12.0	206 21.8	57.0	186 42.9	18.4	Nunki	76 11.8	S26 17.7
02	235 45.0	171 27.1	03.0	21 02.0	11.8	221 23.7	57.2	201 45.0	18.5	Peacock	53 36.6	S56 44.0
03	250 47.4	186 26.5 . .	03.6	36 05.4 . .	11.6	236 25.7 . .	57.5	216 47.2 . .	18.6	Pollux	243 41.2	N28 01.7
04	265 49.9	201 25.9	04.2	51 08.7	11.3	251 27.6	57.7	231 49.3	18.7	Procyon	245 11.3	N 5 13.5
05	280 52.4	216 25.2	04.9	66 12.0	11.1	266 29.5	57.9	246 51.5	18.8			
06	295 54.8	231 24.6	N23 05.5	81 15.4	S12 10.9	281 31.4	N 4 58.1	261 53.7	N11 18.9	Rasalhague	96 16.5	N12 33.6
07	310 57.3	246 24.0	06.1	96 18.7	10.7	296 33.3	58.4	276 55.8	19.0	Regulus	207 55.0	N11 58.2
08	325 59.8	261 23.3	06.7	111 22.0	10.5	311 35.2	58.6	291 58.0	19.1	Rigel	281 22.8	S 8 12.4
S 09	341 02.2	276 22.7 . .	07.3	126 25.4 . .	10.3	326 37.1 . .	58.8	307 00.1 . .	19.2	Rigil Kent.	140 06.2	S60 49.8
U 10	356 04.7	291 22.1	07.9	141 28.7	10.1	341 39.0	59.1	322 02.3	19.3	Sabik	102 24.9	S15 43.4
N 11	11 07.2	306 21.4	08.6	156 32.0	09.9	356 40.9	59.3	337 04.4	19.5			
D 12	26 09.6	321 20.8	N23 09.2	171 35.4	S12 09.7	11 42.9	N 4 59.5	352 06.6	N11 19.6	Schedar	349 53.6	N56 31.8
A 13	41 12.1	336 20.2	09.8	186 38.7	09.5	26 44.8	4 59.7	7 08.8	19.7	Shaula	96 36.6	S37 06.0
Y 14	56 14.5	351 19.6	10.4	201 42.0	09.3	41 46.7	5 00.0	22 10.9	19.8	Sirius	258 43.5	S16 43.2
15	71 17.0	6 18.9 . .	11.0	216 45.4 . .	09.1	56 48.6 . .	00.2	37 13.1 . .	19.9	Spica	158 42.5	S11 09.5
16	86 19.5	21 18.3	11.6	231 48.7	08.9	71 50.5	00.4	52 15.2	20.0	Suhail	223 00 4	S43 26.1
17	101 21.9	36 17.7	12.2	246 52.1	08.7	86 52.4	00.7	67 17.4	20.1			
18	116 24.4	51 17.0	N23 12.8	261 55.4	S12 08.4	101 54.3	N 5 00.9	82 19.6	N11 20.2	Vega	80 46.3	N38 46.8
19	131 26.9	66 16.4	13.4	276 58.7	08.2	116 56.2	01.1	97 21.7	20.3	Zuben'ubi	137 17.3	S16 02.3
20	146 29.3	81 15.8	14.0	292 02.1	08.0	131 58.1	01.4	112 23.9	20.4		SHA	Mer. Pass.
21	161 31.8	96 15.1 . .	14.6	307 05.4 . .	07.8	147 00.0 . .	01.6	127 26.0 . .	20.5		° ′	h m
22	176 34.3	111 14.5	15.2	322 08.8	07.6	162 02.0	01.8	142 28.2	20.6	Venus	297 02.5	14 34
23	191 36.7	126 13.9	15.8	337 12.1	07.4	177 03.9	02.0	157 30.4	20.7	Mars	144 54.8	0 41
	h m									Jupiter	345 53.2	11 16
Mer. Pass. 10 19.6		v −0.6	d 0.6	v 3.3	d 0.2	v 1.9	d 0.2	v 2.2	d 0.1	Saturn	326 08.0	12 35

SUN and MOON

UT	SUN GHA	SUN Dec	MOON GHA	v	MOON Dec	d	HP
d h	° ′	° ′	° ′	′	° ′	′	′
16 00	179 59.9	N 9 53.0	180 44.3	7.9	N 4 45.4	12.4	60.9
01	195 00.1	53.9	195 11.2	7.8	4 57.8	12.3	60.9
02	210 00.2	54.8	209 38.0	7.8	5 10.1	12.3	60.9
03	225 00.4	.. 55.7	224 04.8	7.8	5 22.4	12.3	60.9
04	240 00.5	56.6	238 31.6	7.7	5 34.7	12.3	60.9
05	255 00.6	57.5	252 58.3	7.7	5 47.0	12.3	60.9
06	270 00.8	N 9 58.4	267 25.0	7.6	N 5 59.3	12.2	60.9
07	285 00.9	9 59.3	281 51.6	7.6	6 11.5	12.1	61.0
08	300 01.1	10 00.2	296 18.2	7.6	6 23.6	12.2	61.0
F 09	315 01.2	.. 01.1	310 44.8	7.5	6 35.8	12.1	61.0
R 10	330 01.4	01.9	325 11.3	7.4	6 47.9	12.0	61.0
I 11	345 01.5	02.8	339 37.7	7.5	6 59.9	12.0	61.0
D 12	0 01.7	N10 03.7	354 04.2	7.4	N 7 11.9	12.0	61.0
A 13	15 01.8	04.6	8 30.6	7.3	7 23.9	11.9	61.0
Y 14	30 02.0	05.5	22 56.9	7.3	7 35.8	11.9	61.0
15	45 02.1	.. 06.4	37 23.2	7.3	7 47.7	11.8	61.0
16	60 02.3	07.3	51 49.5	7.2	7 59.5	11.8	61.0
17	75 02.4	08.2	66 15.7	7.1	8 11.3	11.8	61.1
18	90 02.6	N10 09.1	80 41.8	7.2	N 8 23.1	11.6	61.1
19	105 02.7	09.9	95 08.0	7.0	8 34.7	11.7	61.1
20	120 02.9	10.8	109 34.0	7.1	8 46.4	11.5	61.1
21	135 03.0	.. 11.7	124 00.1	7.0	8 57.9	11.5	61.1
22	150 03.2	12.6	138 26.1	6.9	9 09.4	11.5	61.1
23	165 03.3	13.5	152 52.0	7.0	9 20.9	11.4	61.1
17 00	180 03.4	N10 14.4	167 18.0	6.8	N 9 32.3	11.3	61.1
01	195 03.6	15.2	181 43.8	6.8	9 43.6	11.3	61.1
02	210 03.7	16.1	196 09.6	6.8	9 54.9	11.2	61.1
03	225 03.9	.. 17.0	210 35.4	6.8	10 06.1	11.1	61.1
04	240 04.0	17.9	225 01.2	6.7	10 17.2	11.1	61.1
05	255 04.2	18.8	239 26.9	6.6	10 28.3	11.0	61.1
06	270 04.3	N10 19.7	253 52.5	6.6	N10 39.3	10.9	61.1
S 07	285 04.5	20.5	268 18.1	6.6	10 50.2	10.8	61.1
A 08	300 04.6	21.4	282 43.7	6.5	11 01.0	10.8	61.1
T 09	315 04.7	.. 22.3	297 09.2	6.5	11 11.8	10.7	61.1
U 10	330 04.9	23.2	311 34.7	6.5	11 22.5	10.6	61.1
R 11	345 05.0	24.1	326 00.2	6.4	11 33.1	10.6	61.1
D 12	0 05.2	N10 25.0	340 25.6	6.3	N11 43.7	10.4	61.1
A 13	15 05.3	25.8	354 50.9	6.4	11 54.1	10.4	61.1
Y 14	30 05.5	26.7	9 16.3	6.2	12 04.5	10.3	61.1
15	45 05.6	.. 27.6	23 41.5	6.3	12 14.8	10.2	61.1
16	60 05.8	28.5	38 06.8	6.2	12 25.0	10.1	61.1
17	75 05.9	29.4	52 32.0	6.1	12 35.1	10.1	61.1
18	90 06.0	N10 30.2	66 57.1	6.2	N12 45.2	9.9	61.1
19	105 06.2	31.1	81 22.3	6.1	12 55.1	9.9	61.0
20	120 06.3	32.0	95 47.4	6.0	13 05.0	9.7	61.0
21	135 06.5	.. 32.9	110 12.4	6.0	13 14.7	9.7	61.0
22	150 06.6	33.8	124 37.4	6.0	13 24.4	9.6	61.0
23	165 06.8	34.6	139 02.4	5.9	13 34.0	9.4	61.0
18 00	180 06.9	N10 35.5	153 27.3	5.9	N13 43.4	9.4	61.0
01	195 07.0	36.4	167 52.2	5.9	13 52.8	9.3	61.0
02	210 07.2	37.3	182 17.1	5.8	14 02.1	9.2	61.0
03	225 07.3	.. 38.1	196 41.9	5.8	14 11.3	9.0	61.0
04	240 07.5	39.0	211 06.7	5.8	14 20.3	9.0	61.0
05	255 07.6	39.9	225 31.5	5.7	14 29.3	8.9	61.0
06	270 07.7	N10 40.8	239 56.2	5.7	N14 38.2	8.8	60.9
07	285 07.9	41.6	254 20.9	5.6	14 47.0	8.6	60.9
08	300 08.0	42.5	268 45.5	5.7	14 55.6	8.6	60.9
S 09	315 08.2	.. 43.4	283 10.2	5.6	15 04.2	8.4	60.9
U 10	330 08.3	44.3	297 34.8	5.5	15 12.6	8.3	60.9
N 11	345 08.4	45.1	311 59.3	5.6	15 20.9	8.3	60.9
D 12	0 08.6	N10 46.0	326 23.9	5.5	N15 29.2	8.1	60.9
A 13	15 08.7	46.9	340 48.4	5.5	15 37.3	8.0	60.8
Y 14	30 08.9	47.8	355 12.9	5.4	15 45.3	7.9	60.8
15	45 09.0	.. 48.6	9 37.3	5.5	15 53.2	7.7	60.8
16	60 09.1	49.5	24 01.8	5.4	16 00.9	7.7	60.8
17	75 09.3	50.4	38 26.2	5.4	16 08.6	7.5	60.8
18	90 09.4	N10 51.3	52 50.6	5.3	N16 16.1	7.4	60.8
19	105 09.6	52.1	67 14.9	5.4	16 23.5	7.3	60.7
20	120 09.7	53.0	81 39.3	5.3	16 30.8	7.2	60.7
21	135 09.8	.. 53.9	96 03.6	5.3	16 38.0	7.0	60.7
22	150 10.0	54.7	110 27.9	5.2	16 45.0	7.0	60.7
23	165 10.1	55.6	124 52.1	5.3	N16 52.0	6.8	60.7
	SD 16.0	d 0.9	SD 16.6		16.6		16.6

Twilight, Sunrise, Moonrise

Lat.	Twilight Naut.	Civil	Sunrise	Moonrise 16	17	18	19
°	h m	h m	h m	h m	h m	h m	h m
N 72	////	01 43	03 30	04 58	04 46	04 31	04 01
N 70	////	02 24	03 48	05 06	05 02	05 00	04 58
68	////	02 51	04 03	05 12	05 15	05 21	05 33
66	01 28	03 12	04 14	05 17	05 26	05 39	05 58
64	02 05	03 28	04 24	05 22	05 35	05 53	06 17
62	02 31	03 41	04 32	05 26	05 43	06 04	06 33
60	02 50	03 52	04 39	05 29	05 50	06 15	06 47
N 58	03 05	04 02	04 45	05 33	05 56	06 23	06 58
56	03 18	04 10	04 51	05 35	06 01	06 31	07 08
54	03 30	04 18	04 56	05 38	06 06	06 38	07 17
52	03 39	04 24	05 00	05 40	06 10	06 44	07 25
50	03 48	04 30	05 04	05 42	06 14	06 50	07 32
45	04 05	04 42	05 13	05 47	06 23	07 03	07 48
N 40	04 18	04 52	05 20	05 51	06 30	07 13	08 00
35	04 29	05 00	05 26	05 54	06 36	07 22	08 11
30	04 38	05 07	05 32	05 57	06 42	07 29	08 21
20	04 52	05 18	05 41	06 02	06 51	07 43	08 37
N 10	05 03	05 28	05 49	06 07	07 00	07 55	08 52
0	05 11	05 35	05 56	06 11	07 08	08 06	09 05
S 10	05 18	05 42	06 04	06 16	07 16	08 17	09 19
20	05 23	05 49	06 11	06 21	07 25	08 29	09 34
30	05 28	05 56	06 20	06 26	07 35	08 43	09 50
35	05 30	05 59	06 25	06 29	07 40	08 51	10 00
40	05 31	06 03	06 30	06 33	07 47	09 01	10 12
45	05 33	06 07	06 37	06 37	07 55	09 11	10 25
S 50	05 34	06 12	06 45	06 42	08 04	09 25	10 41
52	05 34	06 14	06 48	06 45	08 08	09 31	10 49
54	05 35	06 16	06 52	06 47	08 13	09 38	10 57
56	05 35	06 18	06 56	06 50	08 19	09 45	11 07
58	05 35	06 21	07 01	06 54	08 25	09 54	11 18
S 60	05 35	06 23	07 06	06 57	08 31	10 04	11 30

Sunset, Twilight, Moonset

Lat.	Sunset	Twilight Civil	Naut.	Moonset 16	17	18	19
°	h m	h m	h m	h m	h m	h m	h m
N 72	20 33	22 26	////	20 36	22 51	25 26	01 26
N 70	20 14	21 41	////	20 21	22 24	24 30	00 30
68	20 00	21 12	////	20 10	22 04	23 56	25 38
66	19 48	20 51	22 39	20 01	21 48	23 32	25 05
64	19 38	20 34	21 59	19 53	21 35	23 13	24 41
62	19 29	20 20	21 32	19 47	21 24	22 58	24 22
60	19 22	20 09	21 12	19 41	21 15	22 45	24 06
N 58	19 15	19 59	20 56	19 36	21 07	22 34	23 53
56	19 10	19 51	20 43	19 32	20 59	22 24	23 41
54	19 05	19 43	20 32	19 28	20 53	22 16	23 31
52	19 00	19 37	20 22	19 24	20 47	22 08	23 22
50	18 56	19 31	20 13	19 21	20 42	22 01	23 14
45	18 47	19 18	19 56	19 14	20 31	21 46	22 57
N 40	18 40	19 08	19 42	19 08	20 22	21 34	22 43
35	18 34	19 00	19 31	19 03	20 14	21 24	22 32
30	18 28	18 53	19 22	18 59	20 07	21 15	22 21
20	18 19	18 41	19 08	18 51	19 55	21 00	22 04
N 10	18 11	18 32	18 57	18 44	19 45	20 47	21 48
0	18 03	18 24	18 48	18 38	19 35	20 34	21 34
S 10	17 56	18 17	18 42	18 32	19 25	20 21	21 19
20	17 48	18 10	18 36	18 25	19 15	20 08	21 04
30	17 39	18 03	18 31	18 17	19 03	19 53	20 46
35	17 34	18 00	18 29	18 13	18 57	19 44	20 36
40	17 28	17 56	18 27	18 08	18 49	19 34	20 24
45	17 22	17 52	18 26	18 02	18 40	19 22	20 10
S 50	17 14	17 47	18 24	17 56	18 29	19 08	19 54
52	17 10	17 45	18 24	17 52	18 24	19 01	19 46
54	17 06	17 43	18 24	17 49	18 19	18 54	19 37
56	17 02	17 40	18 23	17 45	18 13	18 46	19 27
58	16 57	17 38	18 23	17 41	18 06	18 37	19 16
S 60	16 52	17 35	18 23	17 36	17 58	18 26	19 03

SUN and MOON

Day	Eqn. of Time 00h	Eqn. of Time 12h	Mer. Pass.	Mer. Pass. Upper	Lower	Age	Phase
d	m s	m s	h m	h m	h m	d	%
16	00 01	00 06	12 00	12 25	24 53	00	0
17	00 13	00 20	12 00	13 21	00 53	01	3
18	00 27	00 34	11 59	14 20	01 50	02	8

1999 APRIL 19, 20, 21 (MON., TUES., WED.)

UT	ARIES	VENUS −4.1		MARS −1.6		JUPITER −2.1		SATURN +0.4		STARS		
	GHA	GHA	Dec	GHA	Dec	GHA	Dec	GHA	Dec	Name	SHA	Dec
d h	° ′	° ′	° ′	° ′	° ′	° ′	° ′	° ′	° ′		° ′	° ′
19 00	206 39.2	141 13.2	N23 16.4	352 15.4	S12 07.2	192 05.8	N 5 02.3	172 32.5	N11 20.8	Acamar	315 27.1	S40 18.7
01	221 41.7	156 12.6	17.0	7 18.8	07.0	207 07.7	02.5	187 34.7	20.9	Achernar	335 35.6	S57 14.6
02	236 44.1	171 11.9	17.6	22 22.1	06.8	222 09.6	02.7	202 36.8	21.1	Acrux	173 20.9	S63 05.8
03	251 46.6	186 11.3 ..	18.2	37 25.5 ..	06.6	237 11.5 ..	02.9	217 39.0 ..	21.2	Adhara	255 21.3	S28 58.6
04	266 49.0	201 10.7	18.8	52 28.8	06.4	252 13.4	03.2	232 41.1	21.3	Aldebaran	291 02.3	N16 30.3
05	281 51.5	216 10.0	19.4	67 32.2	06.1	267 15.3	03.4	247 43.3	21.4			
06	296 54.0	231 09.4	N23 20.0	82 35.5	S12 05.9	282 17.2	N 5 03.6	262 45.5	N11 21.5	Alioth	166 29.8	N55 57.9
07	311 56.4	246 08.8	20.6	97 38.8	05.7	297 19.2	03.9	277 47.6	21.6	Alkaid	153 07.1	N49 19.1
08	326 58.9	261 08.1	21.2	112 42.2	05.5	312 21.1	04.1	292 49.8	21.7	Al Na'ir	27 57.7	S46 57.8
M 09	342 01.4	276 07.5 ..	21.8	127 45.5 ..	05.3	327 23.0 ..	04.3	307 51.9 ..	21.8	Alnilam	275 57.7	S 1 12.4
O 10	357 03.8	291 06.9	22.4	142 48.9	05.1	342 24.9	04.5	322 54.1	21.9	Alphard	218 06.8	S 8 39.5
N 11	12 06.3	306 06.2	23.0	157 52.2	04.9	357 26.8	04.8	337 56.3	22.0			
D 12	27 08.8	321 05.6	N23 23.6	172 55.6	S12 04.7	12 28.7	N 5 05.0	352 58.4	N11 22.1	Alphecca	126 20.0	N26 43.0
A 13	42 11.2	336 04.9	24.1	187 58.9	04.5	27 30.6	05.2	8 00.6	22.2	Alpheratz	357 55.2	N29 04.9
Y 14	57 13.7	351 04.3	24.7	203 02.3	04.2	42 32.5	05.5	23 02.7	22.3	Altair	62 18.9	N 8 51.9
15	72 16.2	6 03.7 ..	25.3	218 05.6 ..	04.0	57 34.4 ..	05.7	38 04.9 ..	22.4	Ankaa	353 26.9	S42 18.7
16	87 18.6	21 03.0	25.9	233 09.0	03.8	72 36.4	05.9	53 07.0	22.5	Antares	112 39.5	S26 25.7
17	102 21.1	36 02.4	26.5	248 12.3	03.6	87 38.3	06.1	68 09.2	22.7			
18	117 23.5	51 01.8	N23 27.1	263 15.7	S12 03.4	102 40.2	N 5 06.4	83 11.4	N11 22.8	Arcturus	146 05.4	N19 11.2
19	132 26.0	66 01.1	27.6	278 19.0	03.2	117 42.1	06.6	98 13.5	22.9	Atria	107 50.8	S69 01.3
20	147 28.5	81 00.5	28.2	293 22.4	03.0	132 44.0	06.8	113 15.7	23.0	Avior	234 22.4	S59 30.8
21	162 30.9	95 59.8 ..	28.8	308 25.8 ..	02.8	147 45.9 ..	07.1	128 17.8 ..	23.1	Bellatrix	278 44.0	N 6 20.7
22	177 33.4	110 59.2	29.4	323 29.1	02.5	162 47.8	07.3	143 20.0	23.2	Betelgeuse	271 13.4	N 7 24.2
23	192 35.9	125 58.6	30.0	338 32.5	02.3	177 49.7	07.5	158 22.2	23.3			
20 00	207 38.3	140 57.9	N23 30.5	353 35.8	S12 02.1	192 51.7	N 5 07.7	173 24.3	N11 23.4	Canopus	264 01.2	S52 42.1
01	222 40.8	155 57.3	31.1	8 39.2	01.9	207 53.6	08.0	188 26.5	23.5	Capella	280 51.0	N45 59.8
02	237 43.3	170 56.6	31.7	23 42.5	01.7	222 55.5	08.2	203 28.6	23.6	Deneb	49 39.0	N45 16.4
03	252 45.7	185 56.0 ..	32.2	38 45.9 ..	01.5	237 57.4 ..	08.4	218 30.8 ..	23.7	Denebola	182 44.6	N14 34.6
04	267 48.2	200 55.3	32.8	53 49.2	01.3	252 59.3	08.7	233 32.9	23.8	Diphda	349 07.2	S17 59.6
05	282 50.7	215 54.7	33.4	68 52.6	01.0	268 01.2	08.9	248 35.1	23.9			
06	297 53.1	230 54.1	N23 34.0	83 56.0	S12 00.8	283 03.1	N 5 09.1	263 37.3	N11 24.0	Dubhe	194 04.7	N61 45.5
07	312 55.6	245 53.4	34.5	98 59.3	00.6	298 05.0	09.3	278 39.4	24.1	Elnath	278 26.7	N28 36.3
T 08	327 58.0	260 52.8	35.1	114 02.7	00.4	313 06.9	09.6	293 41.6	24.3	Eltanin	90 51.0	N51 29.2
U 09	343 00.5	275 52.1 ..	35.7	129 06.0 ..	00.2	328 08.9 ..	09.8	308 43.7 ..	24.4	Enif	33 58.0	N 9 52.1
E 10	358 03.0	290 51.5	36.2	144 09.4	12 00.0	343 10.8	10.0	323 45.9	24.5	Fomalhaut	15 36.3	S29 37.6
S 11	13 05.4	305 50.9	36.8	159 12.8	11 59.8	358 12.7	10.2	338 48.1	24.6			
D 12	28 07.9	320 50.2	N23 37.3	174 16.1	S11 59.5	13 14.6	N 5 10.5	353 50.2	N11 24.7	Gacrux	172 12.6	S57 06.6
A 13	43 10.4	335 49.6	37.9	189 19.5	59.3	28 16.5	10.7	8 52.4	24.8	Gienah	176 03.3	S17 32.3
Y 14	58 12.8	350 48.9	38.5	204 22.9	59.1	43 18.4	10.9	23 54.5	24.9	Hadar	149 02.9	S60 22.1
15	73 15.3	5 48.3 ..	39.0	219 26.2 ..	58.9	58 20.3 ..	11.2	38 56.7 ..	25.0	Hamal	328 13.5	N23 27.3
16	88 17.8	20 47.6	39.6	234 29.6	58.7	73 22.2	11.4	53 58.8	25.1	Kaus Aust.	83 58.2	S34 22.9
17	103 20.2	35 47.0	40.1	249 32.9	58.5	88 24.2	11.6	69 01.0	25.2			
18	118 22.7	50 46.3	N23 40.7	264 36.3	S11 58.3	103 26.1	N 5 11.8	84 03.2	N11 25.3	Kochab	137 18.5	N74 09.5
19	133 25.2	65 45.7	41.2	279 39.7	58.0	118 28.0	12.1	99 05.3	25.4	Markab	13 49.5	N15 11.9
20	148 27.6	80 45.1	41.8	294 43.0	57.8	133 29.9	12.3	114 07.5	25.5	Menkar	314 26.9	N 4 05.0
21	163 30.1	95 44.4 ..	42.4	309 46.4 ..	57.6	148 31.8 ..	12.5	129 09.6 ..	25.6	Menkent	148 20.1	S36 22.0
22	178 32.5	110 43.8	42.9	324 49.8	57.4	163 33.7	12.7	144 11.8	25.7	Miaplacidus	221 41.7	S69 43.2
23	193 35.0	125 43.1	43.5	339 53.1	57.2	178 35.6	13.0	159 13.9	25.8			
21 00	208 37.5	140 42.5	N23 44.0	354 56.5	S11 57.0	193 37.5	N 5 13.2	174 16.1	N11 26.0	Mirfak	308 56.6	N49 51.4
01	223 39.9	155 41.8	44.6	9 59.9	56.7	208 39.5	13.4	189 18.3	26.1	Nunki	76 11.8	S26 17.7
02	238 42.4	170 41.2	45.1	25 03.2	56.5	223 41.4	13.7	204 20.4	26.2	Peacock	53 36.6	S56 44.0
03	253 44.9	185 40.5 ..	45.6	40 06.6 ..	56.3	238 43.3 ..	13.9	219 22.6 ..	26.3	Pollux	243 41.2	N28 01.7
04	268 47.3	200 39.9	46.2	55 10.0	56.1	253 45.2	14.1	234 24.7	26.4	Procyon	245 11.3	N 5 13.5
05	283 49.8	215 39.3	46.7	70 13.3	55.9	268 47.1	14.3	249 26.9	26.5			
06	298 52.3	230 38.6	N23 47.3	85 16.7	S11 55.7	283 49.0	N 5 14.6	264 29.1	N11 26.6	Rasalhague	96 16.4	N12 33.6
W 07	313 54.7	245 38.0	47.8	100 20.1	55.4	298 50.9	14.8	279 31.2	26.7	Regulus	207 55.0	N11 58.2
E 08	328 57.2	260 37.3	48.4	115 23.5	55.2	313 52.8	15.0	294 33.4	26.8	Rigel	281 22.8	S 8 12.4
D 09	343 59.6	275 36.7 ..	48.9	130 26.8 ..	55.0	328 54.8 ..	15.2	309 35.5 ..	26.9	Rigil Kent.	140 06.2	S60 49.8
N 10	359 02.1	290 36.0	49.4	145 30.2	54.8	343 56.7	15.5	324 37.7	27.0	Sabik	102 24.9	S15 43.4
E 11	14 04.6	305 35.4	50.0	160 33.6	54.6	358 58.6	15.7	339 39.8	27.1			
S 12	29 07.0	320 34.7	N23 50.5	175 36.9	S11 54.4	14 00.5	N 5 15.9	354 42.0	N11 27.2	Schedar	349 53.6	N56 31.7
D 13	44 09.5	335 34.1	51.0	190 40.3	54.1	29 02.4	16.1	9 44.2	27.3	Shaula	96 36.6	S37 06.0
A 14	59 12.0	350 33.4	51.6	205 43.7	53.9	44 04.3	16.4	24 46.3	27.4	Sirius	258 43.5	S16 43.2
Y 15	74 14.4	5 32.8 ..	52.1	220 47.1 ..	53.7	59 06.2 ..	16.6	39 48.5 ..	27.5	Spica	158 42.5	S11 09.5
16	89 16.9	20 32.1	52.6	235 50.4	53.5	74 08.1	16.8	54 50.6	27.7	Suhail	223 00.4	S43 26.1
17	104 19.4	35 31.5	53.2	250 53.8	53.3	89 10.1	17.1	69 52.8	27.8			
18	119 21.8	50 30.8	N23 53.7	265 57.2	S11 53.1	104 12.0	N 5 17.3	84 54.9	N11 27.9	Vega	80 46.2	N38 46.8
19	134 24.3	65 30.2	54.2	281 00.6	52.8	119 13.9	17.5	99 57.1	28.0	Zuben'ubi	137 17.3	S16 02.3
20	149 26.8	80 29.5	54.8	296 03.9	52.6	134 15.8	17.7	114 59.3	28.1			
21	164 29.2	95 28.9 ..	55.3	311 07.3 ..	52.4	149 17.7 ..	18.0	130 01.4 ..	28.2		SHA	Mer. Pass.
22	179 31.7	110 28.2	55.8	326 10.7	52.2	164 19.6	18.2	145 03.6	28.3	Venus	293 19.6	14 37
23	194 34.1	125 27.6	56.3	341 14.1	52.0	179 21.5	18.4	160 05.7	28.4	Mars	145 57.5	0 26
	h m									Jupiter	345 13.3	11 07
Mer. Pass. 10 07.8		v −0.6	d 0.6	v 3.4	d 0.2	v 1.9	d 0.2	v 2.2	d 0.1	Saturn	325 46.0	12 25

UT	SUN GHA	SUN Dec	MOON GHA	v	Dec	d	HP
d h	° ′	° ′	° ′	′	° ′	′	′
19 00	180 10.2	N10 56.5	139 16.4	5.2	N16 58.8	6.7	60.6
01	195 10.4	57.4	153 40.6	5.3	17 05.5	6.5	60.6
02	210 10.5	58.2	168 04.9	5.2	17 12.0	6.5	60.6
03	225 10.7	10 59.1	182 29.1	5.2	17 18.5	6.3	60.6
04	240 10.8	11 00.0	196 53.3	5.2	17 24.8	6.2	60.6
05	255 10.9	00.8	211 17.5	5.1	17 31.0	6.0	60.5
06	270 11.1	N11 01.7	225 41.6	5.2	N17 37.0	6.0	60.5
07	285 11.2	02.6	240 05.8	5.1	17 43.0	5.8	60.5
M 08	300 11.3	03.4	254 29.9	5.2	17 48.8	5.7	60.5
O 09	315 11.5	04.3	268 54.1	5.1	17 54.5	5.5	60.4
N 10	330 11.6	05.2	283 18.2	5.1	18 00.0	5.4	60.4
D 11	345 11.8	06.0	297 42.3	5.2	18 05.4	5.3	60.4
A 12	0 11.9	N11 06.9	312 06.5	5.1	N18 10.7	5.2	60.4
Y 13	15 12.0	07.8	326 30.6	5.1	18 15.9	5.0	60.3
14	30 12.2	08.6	340 54.7	5.1	18 20.9	4.9	60.3
15	45 12.3	09.5	355 18.8	5.1	18 25.8	4.7	60.3
16	60 12.4	10.4	9 42.9	5.1	18 30.5	4.7	60.3
17	75 12.6	11.2	24 07.0	5.1	18 35.2	4.4	60.2
18	90 12.7	N11 12.1	38 31.1	5.2	N18 39.6	4.4	60.2
19	105 12.8	13.0	52 55.3	5.1	18 44.0	4.2	60.2
20	120 13.0	13.8	67 19.4	5.1	18 48.2	4.1	60.2
21	135 13.1	14.7	81 43.5	5.1	18 52.3	4.0	60.1
22	150 13.2	15.6	96 07.6	5.2	18 56.3	3.8	60.1
23	165 13.4	16.4	110 31.8	5.1	19 00.1	3.7	60.1
20 00	180 13.5	N11 17.3	124 55.9	5.2	N19 03.8	3.5	60.0
01	195 13.6	18.1	139 20.1	5.2	19 07.3	3.5	60.0
02	210 13.8	19.0	153 44.3	5.2	19 10.8	3.2	60.0
03	225 13.9	19.9	168 08.5	5.2	19 14.0	3.2	60.0
04	240 14.0	20.7	182 32.7	5.2	19 17.2	3.0	59.9
05	255 14.2	21.6	196 56.9	5.2	19 20.2	2.9	59.9
06	270 14.3	N11 22.4	211 21.1	5.3	N19 23.1	2.7	59.9
T 07	285 14.4	23.3	225 45.4	5.3	19 25.8	2.6	59.8
U 08	300 14.6	24.2	240 09.7	5.3	19 28.4	2.5	59.8
E 09	315 14.7	25.0	254 34.0	5.3	19 30.9	2.3	59.8
S 10	330 14.8	25.9	268 58.3	5.3	19 33.2	2.2	59.8
D 11	345 15.0	26.7	283 22.6	5.4	19 35.4	2.0	59.7
A 12	0 15.1	N11 27.6	297 47.0	5.4	N19 37.4	2.0	59.7
Y 13	15 15.2	28.5	312 11.4	5.4	19 39.4	1.8	59.7
14	30 15.4	29.3	326 35.8	5.4	19 41.2	1.6	59.6
15	45 15.5	30.2	341 00.2	5.5	19 42.8	1.5	59.6
16	60 15.6	31.0	355 24.7	5.5	19 44.3	1.4	59.6
17	75 15.8	31.9	9 49.2	5.6	19 45.7	1.3	59.5
18	90 15.9	N11 32.7	24 13.8	5.5	N19 47.0	1.1	59.5
19	105 16.0	33.6	38 38.3	5.6	19 48.1	1.0	59.5
20	120 16.1	34.5	53 02.9	5.7	19 49.1	0.8	59.4
21	135 16.3	35.3	67 27.6	5.7	19 49.9	0.7	59.4
22	150 16.4	36.2	81 52.3	5.7	19 50.6	0.6	59.4
23	165 16.5	37.0	96 17.0	5.7	19 51.2	0.4	59.3
21 00	180 16.7	N11 37.9	110 41.7	5.8	N19 51.6	0.4	59.3
01	195 16.8	38.7	125 06.5	5.9	19 52.0	0.1	59.3
02	210 16.9	39.6	139 31.4	5.9	19 52.1	0.1	59.2
03	225 17.1	40.4	153 56.3	5.9	19 52.2	0.1	59.2
04	240 17.2	41.3	168 21.2	6.0	19 52.1	0.2	59.2
05	255 17.3	42.2	182 46.2	6.0	19 51.9	0.3	59.1
06	270 17.4	N11 43.0	197 11.2	6.0	N19 51.6	0.5	59.1
W 07	285 17.6	43.9	211 36.2	6.1	19 51.1	0.6	59.1
E 08	300 17.7	44.7	226 01.3	6.2	19 50.5	0.7	59.1
D 09	315 17.8	45.6	240 26.5	6.2	19 49.8	0.9	59.0
N 10	330 18.0	46.4	254 51.7	6.3	19 48.9	1.0	59.0
E 11	345 18.1	47.3	269 17.0	6.3	19 47.9	1.1	58.9
S 12	0 18.2	N11 48.1	283 42.3	6.4	N19 46.8	1.2	58.9
D 13	15 18.3	49.0	298 07.7	6.4	19 45.6	1.4	58.9
A 14	30 18.5	49.8	312 33.1	6.4	19 44.2	1.5	58.8
Y 15	45 18.6	50.7	326 58.5	6.6	19 42.7	1.6	58.8
16	60 18.7	51.5	341 24.1	6.6	19 41.1	1.7	58.8
17	75 18.8	52.4	355 49.7	6.6	19 39.4	1.9	58.7
18	90 19.0	N11 53.2	10 15.3	6.7	N19 37.5	1.9	58.7
19	105 19.1	54.1	24 41.0	6.8	19 35.6	2.1	58.7
20	120 19.2	54.9	39 06.8	6.8	19 33.5	2.2	58.6
21	135 19.3	55.8	53 32.6	6.9	19 31.3	2.4	58.6
22	150 19.5	56.6	67 58.5	6.9	19 28.9	2.4	58.6
23	165 19.6	57.4	82 24.4	7.0	N19 26.5	2.6	58.5
	SD 15.9	d 0.9	SD 16.4		16.3		16.1

Lat.	Twilight Naut.	Twilight Civil	Sunrise	Moonrise 19	20	21	22
°	h m	h m	h m	h m	h m	h m	h m
N 72	////	01 04	03 12	04 01	☐	☐	☐
N 70	////	02 01	03 33	04 58	05 01	05 31	07 08
68	////	02 34	03 49	05 33	05 56	06 43	08 00
66	00 55	02 57	04 02	05 58	06 29	07 20	08 32
64	01 46	03 16	04 13	06 17	06 54	07 47	08 56
62	02 15	03 30	04 22	06 33	07 13	08 07	09 15
60	02 37	03 43	04 30	06 47	07 29	08 24	09 30
N 58	02 55	03 53	04 37	06 58	07 42	08 38	09 43
56	03 09	04 02	04 43	07 08	07 54	08 50	09 54
54	03 21	04 10	04 49	07 17	08 04	09 00	10 04
52	03 31	04 17	04 54	07 25	08 13	09 10	10 13
50	03 40	04 23	04 58	07 32	08 22	09 18	10 21
45	03 59	04 37	05 08	07 48	08 39	09 36	10 38
N 40	04 13	04 47	05 16	08 00	08 53	09 51	10 51
35	04 25	04 56	05 22	08 11	09 05	10 03	11 03
30	04 36	05 04	05 28	08 21	09 16	10 14	11 13
20	04 50	05 16	05 39	08 37	09 34	10 32	11 31
N 10	05 01	05 26	05 47	08 52	09 50	10 49	11 46
0	05 10	05 35	05 56	09 05	10 05	11 04	12 00
S 10	05 18	05 42	06 04	09 19	10 20	11 19	12 14
20	05 24	05 50	06 12	09 34	10 36	11 35	12 30
30	05 29	05 57	06 22	09 50	10 54	11 54	12 47
35	05 32	06 02	06 27	10 00	11 05	12 04	12 57
40	05 34	06 06	06 33	10 12	11 18	12 17	13 09
45	05 36	06 11	06 41	10 25	11 32	12 32	13 22
S 50	05 38	06 16	06 49	10 41	11 50	12 50	13 39
52	05 39	06 18	06 53	10 49	11 59	12 58	13 47
54	05 40	06 21	06 57	10 57	12 08	13 08	13 55
56	05 40	06 24	07 02	11 07	12 19	13 18	14 05
58	05 41	06 27	07 08	11 18	12 31	13 30	14 16
S 60	05 42	06 30	07 14	11 30	12 45	13 45	14 29

Lat.	Sunset	Twilight Civil	Twilight Naut.	Moonset 19	20	21	22
°	h m	h m	h m	h m	h m	h m	h m
N 72	20 50	23 11	////	01 26	☐	☐	☐
N 70	20 28	22 04	////	00 30	02 33	04 07	04 29
68	20 11	21 29	////	25 38	01 38	02 54	03 36
66	19 58	21 04	23 18	25 05	01 05	02 17	03 04
64	19 47	20 45	22 18	24 41	00 41	01 51	02 40
62	19 37	20 30	21 47	24 22	00 22	01 30	02 21
60	19 29	20 17	21 24	24 06	00 06	01 13	02 05
N 58	19 22	20 07	21 06	23 53	24 59	00 59	01 52
56	19 16	19 57	20 51	23 41	24 47	00 47	01 40
54	19 10	19 49	20 39	23 31	24 37	00 37	01 30
52	19 05	19 42	20 28	23 22	24 27	00 27	01 21
50	19 01	19 36	20 19	23 14	24 19	00 19	01 13
45	18 51	19 22	20 00	22 57	24 01	00 01	00 56
N 40	18 43	19 11	19 46	22 43	23 46	24 42	00 42
35	18 36	19 02	19 34	22 32	23 34	24 30	00 30
30	18 30	18 55	19 24	22 21	23 23	24 20	00 20
20	18 20	18 42	19 09	22 04	23 05	24 01	00 01
N 10	18 11	18 32	18 57	21 48	22 48	23 46	24 39
0	18 02	18 23	18 48	21 34	22 33	23 31	24 26
S 10	17 54	18 16	18 40	21 19	22 18	23 16	24 13
20	17 46	18 08	18 34	21 04	22 02	23 00	23 58
30	17 36	18 00	18 28	20 46	21 43	22 42	23 42
35	17 30	17 56	18 26	20 36	21 32	22 31	23 32
40	17 24	17 52	18 23	20 24	21 20	22 19	23 21
45	17 17	17 47	18 21	20 10	21 05	22 04	23 08
S 50	17 08	17 41	18 19	19 54	20 47	21 47	22 52
52	17 04	17 39	18 18	19 46	20 38	21 38	22 44
54	17 00	17 36	18 17	19 37	20 29	21 29	22 36
56	16 55	17 33	18 16	19 27	20 18	21 18	22 26
58	16 50	17 30	18 16	19 16	20 06	21 06	22 16
S 60	16 43	17 27	18 15	19 03	19 51	20 52	22 03

Day	SUN Eqn. of Time 00h	12h	Mer. Pass.	MOON Mer. Pass. Upper	Lower	Age	Phase
d	m s	m s	h m	h m	h m	d	%
19	00 41	00 47	11 59	15 20	02 50	03	16
20	00 54	01 00	11 59	16 19	03 49	04	25
21	01 06	01 13	11 59	17 17	04 48	05	36

UT (d h)	ARIES GHA	VENUS GHA	VENUS Dec	MARS GHA	MARS Dec	JUPITER −2.1 GHA	JUPITER Dec	SATURN +0.3 GHA	SATURN Dec	STARS Name	SHA	Dec
22 00	209 36.6	140 26.9	N23 56.9	356 17.4	S11 51.7	194 23.5	N 5 18.6	175 07.9	N11 28.5	Acamar	315 27.1	S40 18.7
01	224 39.1	155 26.3	57.4	11 20.8	51.5	209 25.4	18.9	190 10.0	28.6	Achernar	335 35.6	S57 14.6
02	239 41.5	170 25.6	57.9	26 24.2	51.3	224 27.3	19.1	205 12.2	28.7	Acrux	173 20.9	S63 05.8
03	254 44.0	185 25.0 ..	58.4	41 27.6 ..	51.1	239 29.2 ..	19.3	220 14.4 ..	28.8	Adhara	255 21.3	S28 58.6
04	269 46.5	200 24.3	58.9	56 30.9	50.9	254 31.1	19.5	235 16.5	28.9	Aldebaran	291 02.3	N16 30.3
05	284 48.9	215 23.7	23 59.5	71 34.3	50.6	269 33.0	19.8	250 18.7	29.0			
06	299 51.4	230 23.0	N24 00.0	86 37.7	S11 50.4	284 34.9	N 5 20.0	265 20.8	N11 29.1	Alioth	166 29.8	N55 58.0
07	314 53.9	245 22.4	00.5	101 41.1	50.2	299 36.8	20.2	280 23.0	29.2	Alkaid	153 07.1	N49 19.1
T 08	329 56.3	260 21.7	01.0	116 44.5	50.0	314 38.8	20.4	295 25.1	29.4	Al Na'ir	27 57.7	S46 57.8
H 09	344 58.8	275 21.1 ..	01.5	131 47.8 ..	49.8	329 40.7 ..	20.7	310 27.3 ..	29.5	Alnilam	275 57.7	S 1 12.4
U 10	0 01.3	290 20.4	02.0	146 51.2	49.5	344 42.6	20.9	325 29.5	29.6	Alphard	218 06.8	S 8 39.5
R 11	15 03.7	305 19.8	02.5	161 54.6	49.3	359 44.5	21.1	340 31.6	29.7			
S 12	30 06.2	320 19.1	N24 03.1	176 58.0	S11 49.1	14 46.4	N 5 21.4	355 33.8	N11 29.8	Alphecca	126 20.0	N26 43.0
D 13	45 08.6	335 18.5	03.6	192 01.4	48.9	29 48.3	21.6	10 35.9	29.9	Alpheratz	357 55.2	N29 04.9
A 14	60 11.1	350 17.8	04.1	207 04.7	48.7	44 50.2	21.8	25 38.1	30.0	Altair	62 18.9	N 8 51.9
Y 15	75 13.6	5 17.2 ..	04.6	222 08.1 ..	48.4	59 52.2 ..	22.0	40 40.2 ..	30.1	Ankaa	353 26.9	S42 18.7
16	90 16.0	20 16.5	05.1	237 11.5	48.2	74 54.1	22.3	55 42.4	30.2	Antares	112 39.4	S26 25.7
17	105 18.5	35 15.9	05.6	252 14.9	48.0	89 56.0	22.5	70 44.6	30.3			
18	120 21.0	50 15.2	N24 06.1	267 18.3	S11 47.8	104 57.9	N 5 22.7	85 46.7	N11 30.4	Arcturus	146 05.4	N19 11.2
19	135 23.4	65 14.5	06.6	282 21.7	47.6	119 59.8	22.9	100 48.9	30.5	Atria	107 50.7	S69 01.3
20	150 25.9	80 13.9	07.1	297 25.0	47.3	135 01.7	23.2	115 51.0	30.6	Avior	234 22.5	S59 30.8
21	165 28.4	95 13.2 ..	07.6	312 28.4 ..	47.1	150 03.6 ..	23.4	130 53.2 ..	30.7	Bellatrix	278 44.0	N 6 20.7
22	180 30.8	110 12.6	08.1	327 31.8	46.9	165 05.6	23.6	145 55.3	30.8	Betelgeuse	271 13.4	N 7 24.2
23	195 33.3	125 11.9	08.6	342 35.2	46.7	180 07.5	23.8	160 57.5	30.9			
23 00	210 35.8	140 11.3	N24 09.1	357 38.6	S11 46.5	195 09.4	N 5 24.1	175 59.7	N11 31.1	Canopus	264 01.3	S52 42.1
01	225 38.2	155 10.6	09.6	12 42.0	46.2	210 11.3	24.3	191 01.8	31.2	Capella	280 51.0	N45 59.8
02	240 40.7	170 10.0	10.1	27 45.4	46.0	225 13.2	24.5	206 04.0	31.3	Deneb	49 39.0	N45 16.4
03	255 43.1	185 09.3 ..	10.6	42 48.7 ..	45.8	240 15.1 ..	24.7	221 06.1 ..	31.4	Denebola	182 44.6	N14 34.6
04	270 45.6	200 08.7	11.1	57 52.1	45.6	255 17.0	25.0	236 08.3	31.5	Diphda	349 07.2	S17 59.6
05	285 48.1	215 08.0	11.6	72 55.5	45.4	270 19.0	25.2	251 10.4	31.6			
06	300 50.5	230 07.4	N24 12.0	87 58.9	S11 45.1	285 20.9	N 5 25.4	266 12.6	N11 31.7	Dubhe	194 04.7	N61 45.5
07	315 53.0	245 06.7	12.5	103 02.3	44.9	300 22.8	25.6	281 14.8	31.8	Elnath	278 26.8	N28 36.3
F 08	330 55.5	260 06.0	13.0	118 05.7	44.7	315 24.7	25.9	296 16.9	31.9	Eltanin	90 50.9	N51 29.2
R 09	345 57.9	275 05.4 ..	13.5	133 09.1 ..	44.5	330 26.6 ..	26.1	311 19.1 ..	32.0	Enif	33 58.0	N 9 52.1
I 10	1 00.4	290 04.7	14.0	148 12.4	44.2	345 28.5	26.3	326 21.2	32.1	Fomalhaut	15 36.3	S29 37.6
11	16 02.9	305 04.1	14.5	163 15.8	44.0	0 30.4	26.5	341 23.4	32.2			
D 12	31 05.3	320 03.4	N24 15.0	178 19.2	S11 43.8	15 32.4	N 5 26.8	356 25.5	N11 32.3	Gacrux	172 12.6	S57 06.6
A 13	46 07.8	335 02.8	15.4	193 22.6	43.6	30 34.3	27.0	11 27.7	32.4	Gienah	176 03.3	S17 32.4
Y 14	61 10.2	350 02.1	15.9	208 26.0	43.4	45 36.2	27.2	26 29.9	32.5	Hadar	149 02.8	S60 22.1
15	76 12.7	5 01.5 ..	16.4	223 29.4 ..	43.1	60 38.1 ..	27.4	41 32.0 ..	32.6	Hamal	328 13.5	N23 27.3
16	91 15.2	20 00.8	16.9	238 32.8	42.9	75 40.0	27.7	56 34.2	32.7	Kaus Aust.	83 58.2	S34 22.9
17	106 17.6	35 00.1	17.4	253 36.2	42.7	90 41.9	27.9	71 36.3	32.9			
18	121 20.1	49 59.5	N24 17.8	268 39.6	S11 42.5	105 43.8	N 5 28.1	86 38.5	N11 33.0	Kochab	137 18.5	N74 09.6
19	136 22.6	64 58.8	18.3	283 42.9	42.3	120 45.8	28.3	101 40.6	33.1	Markab	13 49.5	N15 11.9
20	151 25.0	79 58.2	18.8	298 46.3	42.0	135 47.7	28.6	116 42.8	33.2	Menkar	314 26.9	N 4 05.0
21	166 27.5	94 57.5 ..	19.3	313 49.7 ..	41.8	150 49.6 ..	28.8	131 45.0 ..	33.3	Menkent	148 20.1	S36 22.0
22	181 30.0	109 56.9	19.7	328 53.1	41.6	165 51.5	29.0	146 47.1	33.4	Miaplacidus	221 41.7	S69 43.2
23	196 32.4	124 56.2	20.2	343 56.5	41.4	180 53.4	29.2	161 49.3	33.5			
24 00	211 34.9	139 55.5	N24 20.7	358 59.9	S11 41.1	195 55.3	N 5 29.5	176 51.4	N11 33.6	Mirfak	308 56.6	N49 51.4
01	226 37.4	154 54.9	21.2	14 03.3	40.9	210 57.2	29.7	191 53.6	33.7	Nunki	76 11.8	S26 17.7
02	241 39.8	169 54.2	21.6	29 06.7	40.7	225 59.2	29.9	206 55.7	33.8	Peacock	53 36.5	S56 44.0
03	256 42.3	184 53.6 ..	22.1	44 10.1 ..	40.5	241 01.1 ..	30.1	221 57.9 ..	33.9	Pollux	243 41.2	N28 01.7
04	271 44.7	199 52.9	22.6	59 13.5	40.2	256 03.0	30.4	237 00.1	34.0	Procyon	245 11.3	N 5 13.5
05	286 47.2	214 52.3	23.0	74 16.8	40.0	271 04.9	30.6	252 02.2	34.1			
06	301 49.7	229 51.6	N24 23.5	89 20.2	S11 39.8	286 06.8	N 5 30.8	267 04.4	N11 34.2	Rasalhague	96 16.4	N12 33.6
07	316 52.1	244 50.9	23.9	104 23.6	39.6	301 08.7	31.0	282 06.5	34.3	Regulus	207 55.0	N11 57.3
S 08	331 54.6	259 50.3	24.4	119 27.0	39.4	316 10.7	31.3	297 08.7	34.4	Rigel	281 22.8	S 8 12.4
A 09	346 57.1	274 49.6 ..	24.9	134 30.4 ..	39.1	331 12.6 ..	31.5	312 10.8 ..	34.5	Rigil Kent.	140 06.1	S60 49.8
T 10	1 59.5	289 49.0	25.3	149 33.8	38.9	346 14.5	31.7	327 13.0	34.6	Sabik	102 24.9	S15 43.4
U 11	17 02.0	304 48.3	25.8	164 37.2	38.7	1 16.4	31.9	342 15.2	34.8			
R 12	32 04.5	319 47.6	N24 26.2	179 40.6	S11 38.5	16 18.3	N 5 32.2	357 17.3	N11 34.9	Schedar	349 53.6	N56 31.7
D 13	47 06.9	334 47.0	26.7	194 44.0	38.2	31 20.2	32.4	12 19.5	35.0	Shaula	96 36.6	S37 06.0
A 14	62 09.4	349 46.3	27.2	209 47.4	38.0	46 22.1	32.6	27 21.6	35.1	Sirius	258 43.5	S16 43.2
Y 15	77 11.9	4 45.7 ..	27.6	224 50.8 ..	37.8	61 24.1 ..	32.8	42 23.8 ..	35.2	Spica	158 42.5	S11 09.5
16	92 14.3	19 45.0	28.1	239 54.2	37.6	76 26.0	33.1	57 25.9	35.3	Suhail	223 00.4	S43 26.1
17	107 16.8	34 44.3	28.5	254 57.6	37.3	91 27.9	33.3	72 28.1	35.4			
18	122 19.2	49 43.7	N24 29.0	270 01.0	S11 37.1	106 29.8	N 5 33.5	87 30.2	N11 35.5	Vega	80 46.2	N38 46.8
19	137 21.7	64 43.0	29.4	285 04.4	36.9	121 31.7	33.7	102 32.4	35.6	Zuben'ubi	137 17.3	S16 02.3
20	152 24.2	79 42.4	29.9	300 07.7	36.7	136 33.6	34.0	117 34.6	35.7		SHA	Mer. Pass.
21	167 26.6	94 41.7 ..	30.3	315 11.1 ..	36.5	151 35.6 ..	34.2	132 36.7 ..	35.8			
22	182 29.1	109 41.0	30.8	330 14.5	36.2	166 37.5	34.4	147 38.9	35.9	Venus	289 35.5	14 40
23	197 31.6	124 40.4	31.2	345 17.9	36.0	181 39.4	34.6	162 41.0	36.0	Mars	147 02.8	0 09
Mer. Pass. 9 56.0		v −0.7	d 0.5	v 3.4	d 0.2	v 1.9	d 0.2	v 2.2	d 0.1	Jupiter	344 33.6	10 58
										Saturn	325 23.9	12 14

UT	SUN GHA	Dec	MOON GHA	v	Dec	d	HP
d h	° ′	° ′	° ′	′	° ′	′	′
22 00	180 19.7	N11 58.3	96 50.4	7.1	N19 23.9	2.7	58.5
01	195 19.8	11 59.1	111 16.5	7.1	19 21.2	2.8	58.5
02	210 20.0	12 00.0	125 42.6	7.2	19 18.4	3.0	58.4
03	225 20.1	.. 00.8	140 08.8	7.3	19 15.4	3.0	58.4
04	240 20.2	01.7	154 35.1	7.3	19 12.4	3.2	58.4
05	255 20.3	02.5	169 01.4	7.4	19 09.2	3.2	58.3
06	270 20.5	N12 03.4	183 27.8	7.5	N19 06.0	3.4	58.3
07	285 20.6	04.2	197 54.3	7.5	19 02.6	3.5	58.3
08	300 20.7	05.1	212 20.8	7.6	18 59.1	3.6	58.2
09	315 20.8	.. 05.9	226 47.4	7.6	18 55.5	3.7	58.2
10	330 21.0	06.7	241 14.0	7.8	18 51.8	3.9	58.2
11	345 21.1	07.6	255 40.8	7.8	18 47.9	3.9	58.1
12	0 21.2	N12 08.4	270 07.6	7.8	N18 44.0	4.1	58.1
13	15 21.3	09.3	284 34.4	8.0	18 39.9	4.1	58.1
14	30 21.5	10.1	299 01.4	8.0	18 35.8	4.3	58.0
15	45 21.6	.. 11.0	313 28.4	8.1	18 31.5	4.3	58.0
16	60 21.7	11.8	327 55.5	8.1	18 27.2	4.5	58.0
17	75 21.8	12.6	342 22.6	8.2	18 22.7	4.6	57.9
18	90 21.9	N12 13.5	356 49.8	8.3	N18 18.1	4.6	57.9
19	105 22.1	14.3	11 17.1	8.4	18 13.5	4.8	57.9
20	120 22.2	15.2	25 44.5	8.4	18 08.7	4.9	57.8
21	135 22.3	.. 16.0	40 11.9	8.5	18 03.8	5.0	57.8
22	150 22.4	16.8	54 39.4	8.6	17 58.8	5.0	57.8
23	165 22.6	17.7	69 07.0	8.7	17 53.8	5.2	57.7
23 00	180 22.7	N12 18.5	83 34.7	8.7	N17 48.6	5.3	57.7
01	195 22.8	19.3	98 02.4	8.8	17 43.3	5.3	57.7
02	210 22.9	20.2	112 30.2	8.9	17 38.0	5.5	57.6
03	225 23.0	.. 21.0	126 58.1	8.9	17 32.5	5.5	57.6
04	240 23.2	21.9	141 26.0	9.1	17 27.0	5.7	57.6
05	255 23.3	22.7	155 54.1	9.1	17 21.3	5.7	57.5
06	270 23.4	N12 23.5	170 22.2	9.1	N17 15.6	5.8	57.5
07	285 23.5	24.4	184 50.3	9.3	17 09.8	5.9	57.5
08	300 23.6	25.2	199 18.6	9.3	17 03.9	6.0	57.4
09	315 23.8	.. 26.0	213 46.9	9.4	16 57.9	6.1	57.4
10	330 23.9	26.9	228 15.3	9.5	16 51.8	6.2	57.4
11	345 24.0	27.7	242 43.8	9.5	16 45.6	6.3	57.4
12	0 24.1	N12 28.5	257 12.3	9.6	N16 39.3	6.3	57.3
13	15 24.2	29.4	271 40.9	9.7	16 33.0	6.4	57.3
14	30 24.3	30.2	286 09.6	9.8	16 26.6	6.6	57.3
15	45 24.5	.. 31.0	300 38.4	9.8	16 20.0	6.6	57.2
16	60 24.6	31.9	315 07.2	9.9	16 13.4	6.6	57.2
17	75 24.7	32.7	329 36.1	10.0	16 06.8	6.8	57.2
18	90 24.8	N12 33.5	344 05.1	10.1	N16 00.0	6.8	57.1
19	105 24.9	34.4	358 34.2	10.1	15 53.2	6.9	57.1
20	120 25.1	35.2	13 03.3	10.2	15 46.3	7.0	57.1
21	135 25.2	.. 36.0	27 32.5	10.3	15 39.3	7.1	57.0
22	150 25.3	36.9	42 01.8	10.3	15 32.2	7.1	57.0
23	165 25.4	37.7	56 31.1	10.4	15 25.1	7.3	57.0
24 00	180 25.5	N12 38.5	71 00.5	10.5	N15 17.8	7.3	56.9
01	195 25.6	39.3	85 30.0	10.6	15 10.5	7.3	56.9
02	210 25.7	40.2	99 59.6	10.6	15 03.2	7.5	56.9
03	225 25.9	.. 41.0	114 29.2	10.7	14 55.7	7.5	56.9
04	240 26.0	41.8	128 58.9	10.8	14 48.2	7.5	56.8
05	255 26.1	42.7	143 28.7	10.8	14 40.7	7.7	56.8
06	270 26.2	N12 43.5	157 58.5	11.0	N14 33.0	7.7	56.8
07	285 26.3	44.3	172 28.5	10.9	14 25.3	7.8	56.7
08	300 26.4	45.1	186 58.4	11.1	14 17.5	7.8	56.7
09	315 26.6	.. 46.0	201 28.5	11.1	14 09.7	7.9	56.7
10	330 26.7	46.8	215 58.6	11.2	14 01.8	8.0	56.7
11	345 26.8	47.6	230 28.8	11.3	13 53.8	8.0	56.6
12	0 26.9	N12 48.4	244 59.1	11.3	N13 45.8	8.1	56.6
13	15 27.0	49.3	259 29.4	11.4	13 37.7	8.2	56.6
14	30 27.1	50.1	273 59.8	11.5	13 29.5	8.2	56.5
15	45 27.2	.. 50.9	288 30.3	11.5	13 21.3	8.3	56.5
16	60 27.3	51.7	303 00.8	11.6	13 13.0	8.3	56.5
17	75 27.5	52.6	317 31.4	11.6	13 04.7	8.4	56.5
18	90 27.6	N12 53.4	332 02.0	11.8	N12 56.3	8.5	56.4
19	105 27.7	54.2	346 32.8	11.7	12 47.8	8.5	56.4
20	120 27.8	55.0	1 03.5	11.9	12 39.3	8.6	56.4
21	135 27.9	.. 55.9	15 34.4	11.9	12 30.7	8.6	56.3
22	150 28.0	56.7	30 05.3	12.0	12 22.1	8.6	56.3
23	165 28.1	57.5	44 36.3	12.0	N12 13.5	8.8	56.3
	SD 15.9	d 0.8	SD 15.8		15.6		15.4

THURSDAY / FRIDAY / SATURDAY

Lat.	Twilight Naut.	Civil	Sunrise	Moonrise 22	23	24	25
°	h m	h m	h m	h m	h m	h m	h m
N 72	////	////	02 54	▭	08 05	10 19	12 13
N 70	////	01 35	03 18	07 08	09 00	10 48	12 30
68	////	02 15	03 36	08 00	09 33	11 09	12 44
66	////	02 42	03 51	08 32	09 57	11 26	12 55
64	01 22	03 03	04 03	08 56	10 16	11 40	13 04
62	01 59	03 19	04 13	09 15	10 31	11 51	13 11
60	02 24	03 33	04 22	09 30	10 44	12 01	13 18
N 58	02 43	03 44	04 29	09 43	10 55	12 09	13 24
56	02 59	03 54	04 36	09 54	11 04	12 17	13 29
54	03 12	04 03	04 42	10 04	11 13	12 23	13 34
52	03 23	04 10	04 47	10 13	11 20	12 29	13 38
50	03 33	04 17	04 52	10 21	11 27	12 35	13 42
45	03 53	04 31	05 01	10 38	11 42	12 46	13 50
N 40	04 08	04 43	05 11	10 51	11 53	12 56	13 57
35	04 21	04 52	05 19	11 03	12 04	13 04	14 03
30	04 31	05 00	05 25	11 13	12 13	13 11	14 08
20	04 47	05 14	05 36	11 31	12 28	13 23	14 17
N 10	04 59	05 25	05 46	11 46	12 41	13 34	14 24
0	05 09	05 34	05 55	12 00	12 54	13 44	14 32
S 10	05 18	05 42	06 04	12 14	13 06	13 54	14 39
20	05 25	05 51	06 13	12 30	13 19	14 05	14 47
30	05 31	05 59	06 24	12 47	13 34	14 17	14 55
35	05 34	06 04	06 30	12 57	13 43	14 24	15 00
40	05 37	06 09	06 36	13 09	13 53	14 32	15 06
45	05 40	06 14	06 44	13 22	14 05	14 41	15 13
S 50	05 43	06 20	06 54	13 39	14 19	14 52	15 21
52	05 44	06 23	06 58	13 47	14 26	14 58	15 24
54	05 45	06 26	07 03	13 55	14 33	15 03	15 28
56	05 46	06 29	07 08	14 05	14 41	15 10	15 33
58	05 47	06 33	07 14	14 16	14 50	15 17	15 38
S 60	05 48	06 37	07 21	14 29	15 01	15 25	15 43

Lat.	Sunset	Twilight Civil	Naut.	Moonset 22	23	24	25
°	h m	h m	h m	h m	h m	h m	h m
N 72	21 08	////	////	▭	05 26	04 58	04 44
N 70	20 43	22 31	////	04 29	04 30	04 28	04 25
68	20 24	21 47	////	03 36	03 56	04 06	04 11
66	20 09	21 18	////	03 04	03 32	03 48	03 59
64	19 56	20 57	22 42	02 40	03 12	03 34	03 48
62	19 46	20 40	22 02	02 21	02 56	03 21	03 40
60	19 37	20 26	21 36	02 05	02 43	03 11	03 32
N 58	19 29	20 14	21 16	01 52	02 32	03 02	03 26
56	19 22	20 04	21 00	01 40	02 22	02 54	03 20
54	19 16	19 56	20 47	01 30	02 13	02 47	03 15
52	19 11	19 48	20 35	01 21	02 05	02 41	03 10
50	19 06	19 41	20 25	01 13	01 58	02 35	03 05
45	18 55	19 26	20 05	00 56	01 43	02 22	02 56
N 40	18 46	19 15	19 49	00 42	01 30	02 12	02 48
35	18 38	19 05	19 37	00 30	01 19	02 03	02 41
30	18 32	18 57	19 26	00 20	01 10	01 55	02 35
20	18 21	18 43	19 10	00 01	00 54	01 41	02 25
N 10	18 11	18 32	18 58	24 39	00 39	01 29	02 16
0	18 02	18 23	18 48	24 26	00 26	01 18	02 07
S 10	17 53	18 14	18 39	24 13	00 13	01 07	01 58
20	17 43	18 06	18 32	23 58	24 55	00 55	01 49
30	17 33	17 57	18 25	23 42	24 41	00 41	01 38
35	17 27	17 53	18 22	23 32	24 32	00 32	01 32
40	17 20	17 48	18 19	23 21	24 23	00 23	01 25
45	17 12	17 42	18 16	23 08	24 12	00 12	01 17
S 50	17 02	17 36	18 13	22 52	23 59	25 07	01 07
52	16 58	17 33	18 12	22 44	23 53	25 02	01 02
54	16 53	17 30	18 11	22 36	23 46	24 57	00 57
56	16 48	17 26	18 10	22 26	23 38	24 51	00 51
58	16 42	17 23	18 09	22 16	23 30	24 45	00 45
S 60	16 35	17 19	18 08	22 03	23 20	24 37	00 37

Day	SUN Eqn. of Time 00h	12h	Mer. Pass.	MOON Mer. Pass. Upper	Lower	Age	Phase
d	m s	m s	h m	h m	h m	d	%
22	01 19	01 25	11 59	18 13	05 46	06	47
23	01 30	01 36	11 58	19 06	06 40	07	58
24	01 42	01 47	11 58	19 56	07 31	08	68

UT	ARIES	VENUS −4.1		MARS −1.6		JUPITER −2.1		SATURN +0.3	
	GHA	GHA	Dec	GHA	Dec	GHA	Dec	GHA	Dec
d h	° ′	° ′	° ′	° ′	° ′	° ′	° ′	° ′	° ′
25 00	212 34.0	139 39.7	N24 31.6	0 21.3	S11 35.8	196 41.3	N 5 34.9	177 43.2	N11 36.1
01	227 36.5	154 39.1	32.1	15 24.7	35.6	211 43.2	35.1	192 45.3	36.2
02	242 39.0	169 38.4	32.5	30 28.1	35.3	226 45.1	35.3	207 47.5	36.3
03	257 41.4	184 37.7 ..	33.0	45 31.5 ..	35.1	241 47.1 ..	35.5	222 49.7 ..	36.4
04	272 43.9	199 37.1	33.4	60 34.9	34.9	256 49.0	35.7	237 51.8	36.5
05	287 46.3	214 36.4	33.8	75 38.3	34.7	271 50.9	36.0	252 54.0	36.7
06	302 48.8	229 35.8	N24 34.3	90 41.7	S11 34.4	286 52.8	N 5 36.2	267 56.1	N11 36.8
07	317 51.3	244 35.1	34.7	105 45.1	34.2	301 54.7	36.4	282 58.3	36.9
08	332 53.7	259 34.4	35.2	120 48.5	34.0	316 56.6	36.6	298 00.4	37.0
S 09	347 56.2	274 33.8 ..	35.6	135 51.9 ..	33.8	331 58.5 ..	36.9	313 02.6 ..	37.1
U 10	2 58.7	289 33.1	36.0	150 55.3	33.5	347 00.5	37.1	328 04.8	37.2
N 11	18 01.1	304 32.5	36.5	165 58.7	33.3	2 02.4	37.3	343 06.9	37.3
D 12	33 03.6	319 31.8	N24 36.9	181 02.1	S11 33.1	17 04.3	N 5 37.5	358 09.1	N11 37.4
A 13	48 06.1	334 31.1	37.3	196 05.5	32.9	32 06.2	37.8	13 11.2	37.5
Y 14	63 08.5	349 30.5	37.7	211 08.9	32.7	47 08.1	38.0	28 13.4	37.6
15	78 11.0	4 29.8 ..	38.2	226 12.3 ..	32.4	62 10.0 ..	38.2	43 15.5 ..	37.7
16	93 13.5	19 29.1	38.6	241 15.7	32.2	77 12.0	38.4	58 17.7	37.8
17	108 15.9	34 28.5	39.0	256 19.1	32.0	92 13.9	38.7	73 19.8	37.9
18	123 18.4	49 27.8	N24 39.4	271 22.5	S11 31.8	107 15.8	N 5 38.9	88 22.0	N11 38.0
19	138 20.8	64 27.2	39.9	286 25.9	31.5	122 17.7	39.1	103 24.2	38.1
20	153 23.3	79 26.5	40.3	301 29.3	31.3	137 19.6	39.3	118 26.3	38.2
21	168 25.8	94 25.8 ..	40.7	316 32.7 ..	31.1	152 21.5 ..	39.5	133 28.5 ..	38.3
22	183 28.2	109 25.2	41.1	331 36.0	30.9	167 23.5	39.8	148 30.6	38.4
23	198 30.7	124 24.5	41.5	346 39.4	30.6	182 25.4	40.0	163 32.8	38.5
26 00	213 33.2	139 23.8	N24 42.0	1 42.8	S11 30.4	197 27.3	N 5 40.2	178 34.9	N11 38.7
01	228 35.6	154 23.2	42.4	16 46.2	30.2	212 29.2	40.4	193 37.1	38.8
02	243 38.1	169 22.5	42.8	31 49.6	30.0	227 31.1	40.7	208 39.3	38.9
03	258 40.6	184 21.9 ..	43.2	46 53.0 ..	29.7	242 33.0 ..	40.9	223 41.4 ..	39.0
04	273 43.0	199 21.2	43.6	61 56.4	29.5	257 35.0	41.1	238 43.6	39.1
05	288 45.5	214 20.5	44.0	76 59.8	29.3	272 36.9	41.3	253 45.7	39.2
06	303 47.9	229 19.9	N24 44.4	92 03.2	S11 29.1	287 38.8	N 5 41.6	268 47.9	N11 39.3
07	318 50.4	244 19.2	44.8	107 06.6	28.8	302 40.7	41.8	283 50.0	39.4
08	333 52.9	259 18.5	45.3	122 10.0	28.6	317 42.6	42.0	298 52.2	39.5
M 09	348 55.3	274 17.9 ..	45.7	137 13.4 ..	28.4	332 44.6 ..	42.2	313 54.3 ..	39.6
O 10	3 57.8	289 17.2	46.1	152 16.8	28.2	347 46.5	42.4	328 56.5	39.7
N 11	19 00.3	304 16.5	46.5	167 20.2	27.9	2 48.4	42.7	343 58.7	39.8
D 12	34 02.7	319 15.9	N24 46.9	182 23.6	S11 27.7	17 50.3	N 5 42.9	359 00.8	N11 39.9
A 13	49 05.2	334 15.2	47.3	197 27.0	27.5	32 52.2	43.1	14 03.0	40.0
Y 14	64 07.7	349 14.6	47.7	212 30.4	27.3	47 54.1	43.3	29 05.1	40.1
15	79 10.1	4 13.9 ..	48.1	227 33.8 ..	27.0	62 56.1 ..	43.6	44 07.3 ..	40.2
16	94 12.6	19 13.2	48.5	242 37.2	26.8	77 58.0	43.8	59 09.4	40.3
17	109 15.1	34 12.6	48.9	257 40.6	26.6	92 59.9	44.0	74 11.6	40.4
18	124 17.5	49 11.9	N24 49.3	272 44.0	S11 26.4	108 01.8	N 5 44.2	89 13.8	N11 40.5
19	139 20.0	64 11.2	49.7	287 47.4	26.2	123 03.7	44.4	104 15.9	40.6
20	154 22.4	79 10.6	50.1	302 50.8	25.9	138 05.6	44.7	119 18.1	40.8
21	169 24.9	94 09.9 ..	50.5	317 54.2 ..	25.7	153 07.6 ..	44.9	134 20.2 ..	40.9
22	184 27.4	109 09.2	50.8	332 57.6	25.5	168 09.5	45.1	149 22.4	41.0
23	199 29.8	124 08.6	51.2	348 01.0	25.3	183 11.4	45.3	164 24.5	41.1
27 00	214 32.3	139 07.9	N24 51.6	3 04.4	S11 25.0	198 13.3	N 5 45.6	179 26.7	N11 41.2
01	229 34.8	154 07.3	52.0	18 07.8	24.8	213 15.2	45.8	194 28.8	41.3
02	244 37.2	169 06.6	52.4	33 11.2	24.6	228 17.2	46.0	209 31.0	41.4
03	259 39.7	184 05.9 ..	52.8	48 14.6 ..	24.4	243 19.1 ..	46.2	224 33.2 ..	41.5
04	274 42.2	199 05.3	53.2	63 18.0	24.1	258 21.0	46.4	239 35.3	41.6
05	289 44.6	214 04.6	53.6	78 21.4	23.9	273 22.9	46.7	254 37.5	41.7
06	304 47.1	229 03.9	N24 53.9	93 24.8	S11 23.7	288 24.8	N 5 46.9	269 39.6	N11 41.8
07	319 49.6	244 03.3	54.3	108 28.2	23.5	303 26.7	47.1	284 41.8	41.9
08	334 52.0	259 02.6	54.7	123 31.6	23.2	318 28.7	47.3	299 43.9	42.0
T 09	349 54.5	274 01.9 ..	55.1	138 35.0 ..	23.0	333 30.6 ..	47.6	314 46.1 ..	42.1
U 10	4 56.9	289 01.3	55.5	153 38.4	22.8	348 32.5	47.8	329 48.3	42.2
E 11	19 59.4	304 00.6	55.8	168 41.8	22.6	3 34.4	48.0	344 50.4	42.3
S 12	35 01.9	318 59.9	N24 56.2	183 45.2	S11 22.3	18 36.3	N 5 48.2	359 52.6	N11 42.4
D 13	50 04.3	333 59.3	56.6	198 48.6	22.1	33 38.3	48.4	14 54.7	42.5
A 14	65 06.8	348 58.6	57.0	213 52.0	21.9	48 40.2	48.7	29 56.9	42.6
Y 15	80 09.3	3 57.9 ..	57.3	228 55.4 ..	21.7	63 42.1 ..	48.9	44 59.0 ..	42.7
16	95 11.7	18 57.3	57.7	243 58.8	21.4	78 44.0	49.1	60 01.2	42.9
17	110 14.2	33 56.6	58.1	259 02.2	21.2	93 45.9	49.3	75 03.3	43.0
18	125 16.7	48 55.9	N24 58.5	274 05.6	S11 21.0	108 47.8	N 5 49.6	90 05.5	N11 43.1
19	140 19.1	63 55.3	58.8	289 09.0	20.8	123 49.8	49.8	105 07.7	43.2
20	155 21.6	78 54.6	59.2	304 12.4	20.6	138 51.7	50.0	120 09.8	43.3
21	170 24.0	93 54.0 ..	59.6	319 15.8 ..	20.3	153 53.6 ..	50.2	135 12.0 ..	43.4
22	185 26.5	108 53.3	24 59.9	334 19.2	20.1	168 55.5	50.4	150 14.1	43.5
23	200 29.0	123 52.6	N25 00.3	349 22.6	19.9	183 57.4	50.7	165 16.3	43.6
Mer. Pass.	h m 9 44.2	v −0.7	d 0.4	v 3.4	d 0.2	v 1.9	d 0.2	v 2.2	d 0.1

STARS

Name	SHA	Dec
	° ′	° ′
Acamar	315 27.1	S40 18.7
Achernar	335 35.5	S57 14.5
Acrux	173 20.9	S63 05.8
Adhara	255 21.3	S28 58.6
Aldebaran	291 02.3	N16 30.3
Alioth	166 29.8	N55 58.0
Alkaid	153 07.1	N49 19.1
Al Na'ir	27 57.7	S46 57.7
Alnilam	275 57.7	S 1 12.4
Alphard	218 06.8	S 8 39.5
Alphecca	126 20.0	N26 43.0
Alpheratz	357 55.1	N29 04.9
Altair	62 18.9	N 8 51.9
Ankaa	353 26.9	S42 18.7
Antares	112 39.4	S26 25.7
Arcturus	146 05.4	N19 11.2
Atria	107 50.7	S69 01.3
Avior	234 22.5	S59 30.8
Bellatrix	278 44.0	N 6 20.7
Betelgeuse	271 13.4	N 7 24.2
Canopus	264 01.3	S52 42.1
Capella	280 51.0	N45 59.8
Deneb	49 39.0	N45 16.4
Denebola	182 44.6	N14 34.6
Diphda	349 07.2	S17 59.6
Dubhe	194 04.7	N61 45.5
Elnath	278 26.8	N28 36.3
Eltanin	90 50.9	N51 29.2
Enif	33 58.0	N 9 52.1
Fomalhaut	15 36.3	S29 37.6
Gacrux	172 12.6	S57 06.7
Gienah	176 03.3	S17 32.4
Hadar	149 02.8	S60 22.1
Hamal	328 13.5	N23 27.3
Kaus Aust.	83 58.2	S34 22.9
Kochab	137 18.5	N74 09.6
Markab	13 49.5	N15 11.9
Menkar	314 26.9	N 4 05.0
Menkent	148 20.1	S36 22.0
Miaplacidus	221 41.8	S69 43.2
Mirfak	308 56.6	N49 51.4
Nunki	76 11.8	S26 17.7
Peacock	53 36.5	S56 44.0
Pollux	243 41.2	N28 01.7
Procyon	245 11.3	N 5 13.5
Rasalhague	96 16.4	N12 33.6
Regulus	207 55.1	N11 58.2
Rigel	281 22.9	S 8 12.4
Rigil Kent.	140 06.1	S60 49.8
Sabik	102 24.9	S15 43.4
Schedar	349 53.5	N56 31.7
Shaula	96 36.5	S37 06.0
Sirius	258 43.6	S16 43.2
Spica	158 42.5	S11 09.5
Suhail	223 00.4	S43 26.1
Vega	80 46.2	N38 46.8
Zuben'ubi	137 17.2	S16 02.3

	SHA	Mer. Pass.
	° ′	h m
Venus	285 50.7	14 43
Mars	148 09.7	23 48
Jupiter	343 54.1	10 49
Saturn	325 01.8	12 04

UT	SUN GHA	SUN Dec	MOON GHA	v	Dec	d	HP
d h	o '	o '	o '	'	o '	'	'
25 00	180 28.2	N12 58.3	59 07.3	12.1	N12 04.7	8.7	56.3
01	195 28.4	12 59.1	73 38.4	12.2	11 56.0	8.8	56.2
02	210 28.5	13 00.0	88 09.6	12.2	11 47.2	8.9	56.2
03	225 28.6	.. 00.8	102 40.8	12.3	11 38.3	8.9	56.2
04	240 28.7	01.6	117 12.1	12.4	11 29.4	9.0	56.2
05	255 28.8	02.4	131 43.5	12.4	11 20.4	9.0	56.1
06	270 28.9	N13 03.2	146 14.9	12.4	N11 11.4	9.1	56.1
07	285 29.0	04.1	160 46.3	12.6	11 02.3	9.1	56.1
08	300 29.1	04.9	175 17.9	12.5	10 53.2	9.1	56.1
S 09	315 29.2	.. 05.7	189 49.4	12.7	10 44.1	9.2	56.0
U 10	330 29.4	06.5	204 21.1	12.7	10 34.9	9.2	56.0
N 11	345 29.5	07.3	218 52.8	12.7	10 25.6	9.2	56.0
D 12	0 29.6	N13 08.1	233 24.5	12.8	N10 16.4	9.4	56.0
A 13	15 29.7	09.0	247 56.3	12.9	10 07.0	9.3	55.9
Y 14	30 29.8	09.8	262 28.2	12.9	9 57.7	9.4	55.9
15	45 29.9	.. 10.6	277 00.1	12.9	9 48.3	9.4	55.9
16	60 30.0	11.4	291 32.0	13.1	9 38.9	9.5	55.9
17	75 30.1	12.2	306 04.1	13.0	9 29.4	9.5	55.8
18	90 30.2	N13 13.0	320 36.1	13.1	N 9 19.9	9.6	55.8
19	105 30.3	13.8	335 08.2	13.2	9 10.3	9.5	55.8
20	120 30.4	14.7	349 40.4	13.2	9 00.8	9.7	55.8
21	135 30.5	.. 15.5	4 12.6	13.3	8 51.1	9.6	55.7
22	150 30.7	16.3	18 44.9	13.3	8 41.5	9.7	55.7
23	165 30.8	17.1	33 17.2	13.4	8 31.8	9.7	55.7
26 00	180 30.9	N13 17.9	47 49.6	13.4	N 8 22.1	9.7	55.7
01	195 31.0	18.7	62 22.0	13.5	8 12.4	9.8	55.6
02	210 31.1	19.5	76 54.5	13.5	8 02.6	9.8	55.6
03	225 31.2	.. 20.3	91 27.0	13.5	7 52.8	9.8	55.6
04	240 31.3	21.1	105 59.5	13.6	7 43.0	9.9	55.6
05	255 31.4	22.0	120 32.1	13.6	7 33.1	9.9	55.6
06	270 31.5	N13 22.8	135 04.7	13.7	N 7 23.2	9.9	55.5
07	285 31.6	23.6	149 37.4	13.8	7 13.3	9.9	55.5
08	300 31.7	24.4	164 10.2	13.7	7 03.4	10.0	55.5
M 09	315 31.8	.. 25.2	178 42.9	13.8	6 53.4	10.0	55.5
O 10	330 31.9	26.0	193 15.7	13.9	6 43.4	10.0	55.5
N 11	345 32.0	26.8	207 48.6	13.9	6 33.4	10.0	55.4
D 12	0 32.1	N13 27.6	222 21.5	13.9	N 6 23.4	10.1	55.4
A 13	15 32.2	28.4	236 54.4	14.0	6 13.3	10.1	55.4
Y 14	30 32.3	29.2	251 27.4	14.0	6 03.2	10.0	55.4
15	45 32.4	.. 30.0	266 00.4	14.0	5 53.2	10.2	55.3
16	60 32.5	30.8	280 33.4	14.1	5 43.0	10.1	55.3
17	75 32.6	31.6	295 06.5	14.1	5 32.9	10.1	55.3
18	90 32.7	N13 32.4	309 39.6	14.1	N 5 22.8	10.2	55.3
19	105 32.9	33.3	324 12.7	14.2	5 12.6	10.2	55.3
20	120 33.0	34.1	338 45.9	14.2	5 02.4	10.2	55.2
21	135 33.1	.. 34.9	353 19.1	14.3	4 52.2	10.2	55.2
22	150 33.2	35.7	7 52.4	14.3	4 42.0	10.2	55.2
23	165 33.3	36.5	22 25.7	14.3	4 31.8	10.3	55.2
27 00	180 33.4	N13 37.3	36 59.0	14.3	N 4 21.5	10.2	55.2
01	195 33.5	38.1	51 32.3	14.4	4 11.3	10.3	55.2
02	210 33.6	38.9	66 05.7	14.4	4 01.0	10.3	55.1
03	225 33.7	.. 39.7	80 39.1	14.4	3 50.7	10.3	55.1
04	240 33.8	40.5	95 12.5	14.5	3 40.4	10.3	55.1
05	255 33.9	41.3	109 46.0	14.5	3 30.1	10.3	55.1
06	270 34.0	N13 42.1	124 19.5	14.5	N 3 19.8	10.3	55.1
07	285 34.1	42.9	138 53.0	14.6	3 09.5	10.3	55.0
T 08	300 34.2	43.7	153 26.6	14.5	2 59.2	10.3	55.0
U 09	315 34.3	.. 44.5	168 00.1	14.6	2 48.8	10.3	55.0
E 10	330 34.4	45.3	182 33.7	14.6	2 38.5	10.3	55.0
S 11	345 34.5	46.1	197 07.3	14.7	2 28.2	10.4	55.0
D 12	0 34.6	N13 46.9	211 41.0	14.6	N 2 17.8	10.3	55.0
A 13	15 34.7	47.7	226 14.6	14.7	2 07.5	10.4	54.9
Y 14	30 34.8	48.5	240 48.3	14.7	1 57.1	10.4	54.9
15	45 34.9	.. 49.3	255 22.0	14.7	1 46.7	10.3	54.9
16	60 35.0	50.1	269 55.7	14.8	1 36.4	10.4	54.9
17	75 35.1	50.8	284 29.5	14.8	1 26.0	10.4	54.9
18	90 35.2	N13 51.6	299 03.3	14.7	N 1 15.6	10.3	54.9
19	105 35.3	52.4	313 37.0	14.8	1 05.3	10.4	54.8
20	120 35.4	53.2	328 10.8	14.9	0 54.9	10.4	54.8
21	135 35.4	.. 54.0	342 44.7	14.8	0 44.5	10.3	54.8
22	150 35.5	54.8	357 18.5	14.9	0 34.2	10.3	54.8
23	165 35.6	55.6	11 52.4	14.8	N 0 23.8	10.3	54.8
	SD 15.9	d 0.8	SD 15.2		15.1		15.0

Lat.	Twilight Naut.	Twilight Civil	Sunrise	Moonrise 25	26	27	28
o	h m	h m	h m	h m	h m	h m	h m
N 72	////	////	02 34	12 13	13 59	15 40	17 20
N 70	////	01 00	03 02	12 30	14 08	15 43	17 15
68	////	01 55	03 23	12 44	14 15	15 45	17 12
66	////	02 27	03 39	12 55	14 21	15 46	17 09
64	00 52	02 50	03 52	13 04	14 26	15 47	17 07
62	01 41	03 08	04 04	13 11	14 31	15 48	17 05
60	02 10	03 23	04 13	13 18	14 34	15 49	17 03
N 58	02 32	03 35	04 22	13 24	14 38	15 50	17 02
56	02 49	03 46	04 29	13 29	14 41	15 51	17 00
54	03 03	03 55	04 35	13 34	14 43	15 52	16 59
52	03 16	04 04	04 41	13 38	14 46	15 52	16 58
50	03 26	04 11	04 47	13 42	14 48	15 53	16 57
45	03 47	04 26	04 58	13 50	14 53	15 54	16 55
N 40	04 04	04 39	05 07	13 57	14 57	15 55	16 53
35	04 17	04 49	05 15	14 03	15 00	15 56	16 51
30	04 28	04 57	05 22	14 08	15 03	15 57	16 50
20	04 45	05 12	05 34	14 17	15 08	15 58	16 48
N 10	04 58	05 23	05 45	14 24	15 13	16 00	16 46
0	05 09	05 33	05 54	14 32	15 17	16 01	16 44
S 10	05 18	05 42	06 04	14 39	15 21	16 02	16 42
20	05 26	05 52	06 14	14 47	15 26	16 03	16 40
30	05 33	06 01	06 25	14 55	15 31	16 05	16 37
35	05 36	06 06	06 32	15 00	15 34	16 05	16 36
40	05 40	06 12	06 39	15 06	15 37	16 06	16 35
45	05 43	06 18	06 48	15 13	15 41	16 07	16 33
S 50	05 47	06 25	06 58	15 21	15 46	16 09	16 31
52	05 48	06 28	07 03	15 24	15 48	16 09	16 30
54	05 50	06 31	07 08	15 28	15 50	16 10	16 29
56	05 51	06 35	07 14	15 33	15 53	16 11	16 28
58	05 53	06 39	07 21	15 38	15 55	16 11	16 27
S 60	05 54	06 43	07 28	15 43	15 59	16 12	16 26

Lat.	Sunset	Twilight Civil	Twilight Naut.	Moonset 25	26	27	28
o	h m	h m	h m	h m	h m	h m	h m
N 72	21 27	////	////	04 44	04 33	04 23	04 14
N 70	20 58	23 11	////	04 25	04 22	04 19	04 15
68	20 36	22 07	////	04 11	04 13	04 15	04 16
66	20 19	21 33	////	03 59	04 06	04 11	04 16
64	20 06	21 09	23 17	03 48	03 59	04 09	04 17
62	19 54	20 50	22 20	03 40	03 54	04 06	04 17
60	19 44	20 35	21 49	03 32	03 49	04 04	04 17
N 58	19 36	20 22	21 27	03 26	03 45	04 02	04 18
56	19 28	20 11	21 09	03 20	03 41	04 00	04 18
54	19 22	20 02	20 54	03 15	03 38	03 59	04 18
52	19 16	19 53	20 42	03 10	03 35	03 57	04 18
50	19 10	19 46	20 31	03 05	03 32	03 56	04 19
45	18 59	19 30	20 10	02 56	03 26	03 53	04 19
N 40	18 49	19 18	19 53	02 48	03 21	03 51	04 20
35	18 41	19 08	19 40	02 41	03 16	03 49	04 20
30	18 34	18 59	19 29	02 35	03 12	03 47	04 20
20	18 22	18 44	19 11	02 25	03 05	03 44	04 21
N 10	18 11	18 33	18 58	02 16	02 59	03 41	04 21
0	18 01	18 23	18 47	02 07	02 54	03 38	04 21
S 10	17 52	18 13	18 38	01 58	02 48	03 35	04 22
20	17 41	18 04	18 30	01 49	02 42	03 32	04 22
30	17 30	17 54	18 23	01 38	02 34	03 29	04 23
35	17 23	17 49	18 19	01 32	02 30	03 27	04 23
40	17 16	17 44	18 15	01 25	02 26	03 25	04 23
45	17 07	17 37	18 12	01 17	02 20	03 22	04 23
S 50	16 57	17 30	18 08	01 07	02 13	03 19	04 24
52	16 52	17 27	18 07	01 02	02 10	03 18	04 24
54	16 47	17 24	18 05	00 57	02 07	03 16	04 24
56	16 41	17 20	18 04	00 51	02 03	03 14	04 24
58	16 34	17 16	18 02	00 45	01 59	03 13	04 25
S 60	16 27	17 11	18 00	00 37	01 55	03 10	04 25

Day	SUN Eqn. of Time 00h	12h	Mer. Pass.	MOON Mer. Pass. Upper	Lower	Age	Phase
d	m s	m s	h m	h m	h m	d	%
25	01 53	01 58	11 58	20 43	08 19	09	77
26	02 03	02 08	11 58	21 28	09 05	10	85
27	02 13	02 18	11 58	22 11	09 49	11	91

UT	ARIES	VENUS −4.1		MARS −1.6		JUPITER −2.1		SATURN +0.3		STARS		
	GHA	GHA	Dec	GHA	Dec	GHA	Dec	GHA	Dec	Name	SHA	Dec
d h	° ′	° ′	° ′	° ′	° ′	° ′	° ′	° ′	° ′		° ′	° ′
28 00	215 31.4	138 52.0	N25 00.6	4 25.9	S11 19.7	198 59.4	N 5 50.9	180 18.4	N11 43.7	Acamar	315 27.1	S40 18.7
01	230 33.9	153 51.3	01.0	19 29.3	19.4	214 01.3	51.1	195 20.6	43.8	Achernar	335 35.5	S57 14.5
02	245 36.4	168 50.6	01.4	34 32.7	19.2	229 03.2	51.3	210 22.7	43.9	Acrux	173 21.0	S63 05.8
03	260 38.8	183 50.0 . .	01.7	49 36.1 . .	19.0	244 05.1 . .	51.5	225 24.9 . .	44.0	Adhara	255 21.3	S28 58.6
04	275 41.3	198 49.3	02.1	64 39.5	18.8	259 07.0	51.8	240 27.1	44.1	Aldebaran	291 02.3	N16 30.3
05	290 43.8	213 48.6	02.4	79 42.9	18.5	274 09.0	52.0	255 29.2	44.2			
06	305 46.2	228 48.0	N25 02.8	94 46.3	S11 18.3	289 10.9	N 5 52.2	270 31.4	N11 44.3	Alioth	166 29.8	N55 58.0
W 07	320 48.7	243 47.3	03.2	109 49.7	18.1	304 12.8	52.4	285 33.5	44.4	Alkaid	153 07.1	N49 19.1
E 08	335 51.2	258 46.6	03.5	124 53.1	17.9	319 14.7	52.7	300 35.7	44.5	Al Na'ir	27 57.7	S46 57.7
D 09	350 53.6	273 46.0 . .	03.9	139 56.5 . .	17.6	334 16.6 . .	52.9	315 37.8 . .	44.6	Alnilam	275 57.7	S 1 12.4
N 10	5 56.1	288 45.3	04.2	154 59.9	17.4	349 18.6	53.1	330 40.0	44.7	Alphard	218 06.8	S 8 39.5
E 11	20 58.5	303 44.6	04.6	170 03.3	17.2	4 20.5	53.3	345 42.2	44.8			
S 12	36 01.0	318 44.0	N25 04.9	185 06.7	S11 17.0	19 22.4	N 5 53.5	0 44.3	N11 44.9	Alphecca	126 20.0	N26 43.0
D 13	51 03.5	333 43.3	05.3	200 10.1	16.8	34 24.3	53.8	15 46.5	45.0	Alpheratz	357 55.1	N29 04.9
A 14	66 05.9	348 42.6	05.6	215 13.5	16.5	49 26.2	54.0	30 48.6	45.2	Altair	62 18.8	N 8 51.9
Y 15	81 08.4	3 42.0 . .	05.9	230 16.9 . .	16.3	64 28.2 . .	54.2	45 50.8 . .	45.3	Ankaa	353 26.9	S42 18.6
16	96 10.9	18 41.3	06.3	245 20.3	16.1	79 30.1	54.4	60 52.9	45.4	Antares	112 39.4	S26 25.7
17	111 13.3	33 40.6	06.6	260 23.7	15.9	94 32.0	54.6	75 55.1	45.5			
18	126 15.8	48 40.0	N25 07.0	275 27.1	S11 15.6	109 33.9	N 5 54.9	90 57.2	N11 45.6	Arcturus	146 05.4	N19 11.2
19	141 18.3	63 39.3	07.3	290 30.5	15.4	124 35.8	55.1	105 59.4	45.7	Atria	107 50.7	S69 01.3
20	156 20.7	78 38.6	07.7	305 33.9	15.2	139 37.8	55.3	121 01.6	45.8	Avior	234 22.5	S59 30.8
21	171 23.2	93 38.0 . .	08.0	320 37.3 . .	15.0	154 39.7 . .	55.5	136 03.7 . .	45.9	Bellatrix	278 44.0	N 6 20.7
22	186 25.6	108 37.3	08.3	335 40.7	14.7	169 41.6	55.7	151 05.9	46.0	Betelgeuse	271 13.4	N 7 24.2
23	201 28.1	123 36.6	08.7	350 44.1	14.5	184 43.5	56.0	166 08.0	46.1			
29 00	216 30.6	138 36.0	N25 09.0	5 47.5	S11 14.3	199 45.4	N 5 56.2	181 10.2	N11 46.2	Canopus	264 01.3	S52 42.1
01	231 33.0	153 35.3	09.3	20 50.8	14.1	214 47.4	56.4	196 12.3	46.3	Capella	280 51.0	N45 59.8
02	246 35.5	168 34.6	09.7	35 54.2	13.9	229 49.3	56.6	211 14.5	46.4	Deneb	49 38.9	N45 16.4
03	261 38.0	183 34.0 . .	10.0	50 57.6 . .	13.6	244 51.2 . .	56.9	226 16.6 . .	46.5	Denebola	182 44.6	N14 34.6
04	276 40.4	198 33.3	10.3	66 01.0	13.4	259 53.1	57.1	241 18.8	46.6	Diphda	349 07.2	S17 59.6
05	291 42.9	213 32.6	10.7	81 04.4	13.2	274 55.0	57.3	256 21.0	46.7			
06	306 45.4	228 32.0	N25 11.0	96 07.8	S11 13.0	289 57.0	N 5 57.5	271 23.1	N11 46.8	Dubhe	194 04.7	N61 45.5
07	321 47.8	243 31.3	11.3	111 11.2	12.7	304 58.9	57.7	286 25.3	46.9	Elnath	278 26.8	N28 36.3
T 08	336 50.3	258 30.6	11.6	126 14.6	12.5	320 00.8	58.0	301 27.4	47.0	Eltanin	90 50.9	N51 29.2
H 09	351 52.8	273 30.0 . .	12.0	141 18.0 . .	12.3	335 02.7 . .	58.2	316 29.6 . .	47.1	Enif	33 58.0	N 9 52.1
U 10	6 55.2	288 29.3	12.3	156 21.4	12.1	350 04.6	58.4	331 31.7	47.2	Fomalhaut	15 36.3	S29 37.6
R 11	21 57.7	303 28.7	12.6	171 24.8	11.9	5 06.6	58.6	346 33.9	47.3			
S 12	37 00.1	318 28.0	N25 12.9	186 28.2	S11 11.6	20 08.5	N 5 58.8	1 36.1	N11 47.4	Gacrux	172 12.6	S57 06.7
D 13	52 02.6	333 27.3	13.3	201 31.6	11.4	35 10.4	59.1	16 38.2	47.6	Gienah	176 03.3	S17 32.4
A 14	67 05.1	348 26.7	13.6	216 35.0	11.2	50 12.3	59.3	31 40.4	47.7	Hadar	149 02.8	S60 22.2
Y 15	82 07.5	3 26.0 . .	13.9	231 38.4 . .	11.0	65 14.2 . .	59.5	46 42.5 . .	47.8	Hamal	328 13.5	N23 27.3
16	97 10.0	18 25.3	14.2	246 41.7	10.7	80 16.2	59.7	61 44.7	47.9	Kaus Aust.	83 58.1	S34 22.9
17	112 12.5	33 24.7	14.5	261 45.1	10.5	95 18.1	5 59.9	76 46.8	48.0			
18	127 14.9	48 24.0	N25 14.8	276 48.5	S11 10.3	110 20.0	N 6 00.2	91 49.0	N11 48.1	Kochab	137 18.5	N74 09.6
19	142 17.4	63 23.3	15.2	291 51.9	10.1	125 21.9	00.4	106 51.1	48.2	Markab	13 49.4	N15 11.9
20	157 19.9	78 22.7	15.5	306 55.3	09.9	140 23.8	00.6	121 53.3	48.3	Menkar	314 26.9	N 4 05.0
21	172 22.3	93 22.0 . .	15.8	321 58.7 . .	09.6	155 25.8 . .	00.8	136 55.5 . .	48.4	Menkent	148 20.1	S36 22.0
22	187 24.8	108 21.3	16.1	337 02.1	09.4	170 27.7	01.0	151 57.6	48.5	Miaplacidus	221 41.8	S69 43.2
23	202 27.2	123 20.7	16.4	352 05.5	09.2	185 29.6	01.3	166 59.8	48.6			
30 00	217 29.7	138 20.0	N25 16.7	7 08.9	S11 09.0	200 31.5	N 6 01.5	182 01.9	N11 48.7	Mirfak	308 56.6	N49 51.4
01	232 32.2	153 19.3	17.0	22 12.3	08.8	215 33.4	01.7	197 04.1	48.8	Nunki	76 11.7	S26 17.7
02	247 34.6	168 18.7	17.3	37 15.6	08.5	230 35.4	01.9	212 06.2	48.9	Peacock	53 36.4	S56 44.0
03	262 37.1	183 18.0 . .	17.6	52 19.0 . .	08.3	245 37.3 . .	02.1	227 08.4 . .	49.0	Pollux	243 41.2	N28 01.7
04	277 39.6	198 17.3	17.9	67 22.4	08.1	260 39.2	02.4	242 10.5	49.1	Procyon	245 11.3	N 5 13.5
05	292 42.0	213 16.7	18.2	82 25.8	07.9	275 41.1	02.6	257 12.7	49.2			
06	307 44.5	228 16.0	N25 18.5	97 29.2	S11 07.7	290 43.1	N 6 02.8	272 14.9	N11 49.3	Rasalhague	96 16.4	N12 33.6
07	322 47.0	243 15.3	18.8	112 32.6	07.4	305 45.0	03.0	287 17.0	49.4	Regulus	207 55.1	N11 58.2
08	337 49.4	258 14.7	19.1	127 36.0	07.2	320 46.9	03.2	302 19.2	49.5	Rigel	281 22.9	S 8 12.4
F 09	352 51.9	273 14.0 . .	19.4	142 39.4 . .	07.0	335 48.8 . .	03.4	317 21.3 . .	49.6	Rigil Kent.	140 06.1	S60 49.8
R 10	7 54.4	288 13.3	19.7	157 42.8	06.8	350 50.7	03.7	332 23.5	49.7	Sabik	102 24.9	S15 43.4
I 11	22 56.8	303 12.7	20.0	172 46.1	06.6	5 52.7	03.9	347 25.6	49.8			
D 12	37 59.3	318 12.0	N25 20.3	187 49.5	S11 06.3	20 54.6	N 6 04.1	2 27.8	N11 49.9	Schedar	349 53.5	N56 31.7
A 13	53 01.7	333 11.3	20.6	202 52.9	06.1	35 56.5	04.3	17 29.9	50.1	Shaula	96 36.5	S37 06.0
Y 14	68 04.2	348 10.7	20.9	217 56.3	05.9	50 58.4	04.5	32 32.1	50.2	Sirius	258 43.6	S16 43.2
15	83 06.7	3 10.0 . .	21.2	232 59.7 . .	05.7	66 00.4 . .	04.8	47 34.3 . .	50.3	Spica	158 42.5	S11 09.5
16	98 09.1	18 09.3	21.5	248 03.1	05.5	81 02.3	05.0	62 36.4	50.4	Suhail	223 00.4	S43 26.1
17	113 11.6	33 08.7	21.8	263 06.5	05.2	96 04.2	05.2	77 38.6	50.5			
18	128 14.1	48 08.0	N25 22.0	278 09.8	S11 05.0	111 06.1	N 6 05.4	92 40.7	N11 50.6	Vega	80 46.2	N38 46.8
19	143 16.5	63 07.3	22.3	293 13.2	04.8	126 08.0	05.6	107 42.9	50.7	Zuben'ubi	137 17.2	S16 02.3
20	158 19.0	78 06.7	22.6	308 16.6	04.6	141 10.0	05.9	122 45.0	50.8		SHA	Mer. Pass.
21	173 21.5	93 06.0 . .	22.9	323 20.0 . .	04.4	156 11.9 . .	06.1	137 47.2 . .	50.9		° ′	h m
22	188 23.9	108 05.4	23.2	338 23.4	04.1	171 13.8	06.3	152 49.3	51.0	Venus	282 05.4	14 46
23	203 26.4	123 04.7	23.5	353 26.8	03.9	186 15.7	06.5	167 51.5	51.1	Mars	149 16.9	23 32
	h m									Jupiter	343 14.9	10 40
Mer. Pass. 9 32.4		v −0.7	d 0.3	v 3.4	d 0.2	v 1.9	d 0.2	v 2.2	d 0.1	Saturn	324 39.6	11 54

UT	SUN GHA	SUN Dec	MOON GHA	v	MOON Dec	d	HP
28 00	180 35.7	N13 56.4	26 26.2	14.9	N 0 13.5	10.4	54.8
01	195 35.8	57.2	41 00.1	14.9	N 0 03.1	10.3	54.7
02	210 35.9	58.0	55 34.0	14.9	S 0 07.2	10.4	54.7
03	225 36.0	.. 58.8	70 07.9	14.9	0 17.6	10.3	54.7
04	240 36.1	13 59.6	84 41.8	15.0	0 27.9	10.4	54.7
05	255 36.2	14 00.4	99 15.8	14.9	0 38.3	10.3	54.7
W 06	270 36.3	N14 01.2	113 49.7	15.0	S 0 48.6	10.3	54.7
E 07	285 36.4	01.9	128 23.7	14.9	0 58.9	10.3	54.7
D 08	300 36.5	02.7	142 57.6	15.0	1 09.2	10.3	54.6
N 09	315 36.6	.. 03.5	157 31.6	15.0	1 19.5	10.3	54.6
E 10	330 36.7	04.3	172 05.6	15.0	1 29.8	10.3	54.6
S 11	345 36.8	05.1	186 39.6	15.0	1 40.1	10.3	54.6
D 12	0 36.9	N14 05.9	201 13.6	15.0	S 1 50.4	10.2	54.6
A 13	15 37.0	06.7	215 47.6	15.0	2 00.6	10.3	54.6
Y 14	30 37.1	07.5	230 21.6	15.0	2 10.9	10.2	54.6
15	45 37.2	.. 08.3	244 55.6	15.0	2 21.1	10.2	54.6
16	60 37.3	09.0	259 29.6	15.1	2 31.3	10.2	54.5
17	75 37.3	09.8	274 03.7	15.0	2 41.5	10.2	54.5
18	90 37.4	N14 10.6	288 37.7	15.0	S 2 51.7	10.2	54.5
19	105 37.5	11.4	303 11.7	15.1	3 01.9	10.1	54.5
20	120 37.6	12.2	317 45.8	15.0	3 12.0	10.2	54.5
21	135 37.7	.. 13.0	332 19.8	15.1	3 22.2	10.1	54.5
22	150 37.8	13.7	346 53.9	15.0	3 32.3	10.1	54.5
23	165 37.9	14.5	1 27.9	15.0	3 42.4	10.1	54.5
29 00	180 38.0	N14 15.3	16 01.9	15.1	S 3 52.5	10.1	54.4
01	195 38.1	16.1	30 36.0	15.0	4 02.6	10.0	54.4
02	210 38.2	16.9	45 10.0	15.1	4 12.6	10.0	54.4
03	225 38.3	.. 17.7	59 44.1	15.0	4 22.6	10.1	54.4
04	240 38.4	18.4	74 18.1	15.0	4 32.7	9.9	54.4
05	255 38.4	19.2	88 52.1	15.1	4 42.6	10.0	54.4
T 06	270 38.5	N14 20.0	103 26.2	15.0	S 4 52.6	9.9	54.4
H 07	285 38.6	20.8	118 00.2	15.0	5 02.5	10.0	54.4
U 08	300 38.7	21.6	132 34.2	15.0	5 12.5	9.8	54.3
R 09	315 38.8	.. 22.3	147 08.2	15.1	5 22.3	9.9	54.3
S 10	330 38.9	23.1	161 42.3	15.0	5 32.2	9.9	54.3
D 11	345 39.0	23.9	176 16.3	15.0	5 42.1	9.8	54.3
A 12	0 39.1	N14 24.7	190 50.3	15.0	S 5 51.9	9.8	54.3
Y 13	15 39.2	25.5	205 24.3	14.9	6 01.7	9.7	54.3
14	30 39.2	26.2	219 58.2	15.0	6 11.4	9.8	54.3
15	45 39.3	.. 27.0	234 32.2	15.0	6 21.2	9.7	54.3
16	60 39.4	27.8	249 06.2	14.9	6 30.9	9.6	54.3
17	75 39.5	28.6	263 40.1	15.0	6 40.5	9.7	54.3
18	90 39.6	N14 29.3	278 14.1	14.9	S 6 50.2	9.6	54.3
19	105 39.7	30.1	292 48.0	15.0	6 59.8	9.6	54.2
20	120 39.8	30.9	307 22.0	14.9	7 09.4	9.5	54.2
21	135 39.9	.. 31.7	321 55.9	14.9	7 18.9	9.6	54.2
22	150 39.9	32.4	336 29.8	14.9	7 28.5	9.4	54.2
23	165 40.0	33.2	351 03.7	14.9	7 37.9	9.5	54.2
30 00	180 40.1	N14 34.0	5 37.6	14.8	S 7 47.4	9.4	54.2
01	195 40.2	34.8	20 11.4	14.9	7 56.8	9.4	54.2
02	210 40.3	35.5	34 45.3	14.8	8 06.2	9.3	54.2
03	225 40.4	.. 36.3	49 19.1	14.9	8 15.5	9.4	54.2
04	240 40.5	37.1	63 53.0	14.8	8 24.9	9.2	54.2
05	255 40.5	37.8	78 26.8	14.8	8 34.1	9.3	54.2
F 06	270 40.6	N14 38.6	93 00.6	14.7	S 8 43.4	9.2	54.2
R 07	285 40.7	39.4	107 34.3	14.8	8 52.6	9.1	54.1
I 08	300 40.8	40.2	122 08.1	14.8	9 01.7	9.2	54.1
D 09	315 40.9	.. 40.9	136 41.9	14.7	9 10.9	9.0	54.1
A 10	330 41.0	41.7	151 15.6	14.7	9 19.9	9.1	54.1
Y 11	345 41.0	42.5	165 49.3	14.7	9 29.0	9.0	54.1
12	0 41.1	N14 43.2	180 23.0	14.7	S 9 38.0	8.9	54.1
13	15 41.2	44.0	194 56.7	14.6	9 46.9	9.0	54.1
14	30 41.3	44.8	209 30.3	14.7	9 55.9	8.8	54.1
15	45 41.4	.. 45.5	224 04.0	14.6	10 04.7	8.9	54.1
16	60 41.5	46.3	238 37.6	14.6	10 13.6	8.8	54.1
17	75 41.5	47.1	253 11.2	14.5	10 22.4	8.7	54.1
18	90 41.6	N14 47.8	267 44.7	14.6	S10 31.1	8.7	54.1
19	105 41.7	48.6	282 18.3	14.5	10 39.8	8.7	54.1
20	120 41.8	49.4	296 51.8	14.5	10 48.5	8.6	54.1
21	135 41.9	.. 50.1	311 25.3	14.5	10 57.1	8.5	54.1
22	150 41.9	50.9	325 58.8	14.5	11 05.6	8.5	54.1
23	165 42.0	51.7	340 32.3	14.4	S11 14.1	8.5	54.0
	SD 15.9 _d_ 0.8		SD 14.9		14.8		14.7

Lat.	Twilight Naut.	Twilight Civil	Sunrise	Moonrise 28	29	30	1
N 72	////	////	02 12	17 20	18 59	20 41	22 29
N 70	////	////	02 45	17 15	18 48	20 22	21 57
68	////	01 31	03 09	17 12	18 39	20 07	21 35
66	////	02 10	03 27	17 09	18 32	19 55	21 17
64	////	02 37	03 42	17 07	18 26	19 45	21 03
62	01 20	02 57	03 54	17 05	18 21	19 36	20 51
60	01 56	03 13	04 05	17 03	18 17	19 29	20 41
N 58	02 20	03 27	04 14	17 02	18 13	19 23	20 32
56	02 39	03 38	04 22	17 00	18 09	19 17	20 24
54	02 55	03 48	04 29	16 59	18 06	19 12	20 17
52	03 08	03 57	04 35	16 58	18 03	19 07	20 11
50	03 19	04 05	04 41	16 57	18 01	19 03	20 05
45	03 42	04 21	04 53	16 55	17 55	18 54	19 53
N 40	03 59	04 34	05 03	16 53	17 50	18 47	19 44
35	04 13	04 45	05 12	16 51	17 46	18 41	19 35
30	04 24	04 54	05 20	16 50	17 43	18 35	19 28
20	04 42	05 09	05 32	16 48	17 37	18 26	19 15
N 10	04 56	05 22	05 44	16 46	17 31	18 17	19 04
0	05 08	05 33	05 54	16 44	17 26	18 10	18 54
S 10	05 18	05 43	06 04	16 42	17 22	18 02	18 43
20	05 26	05 52	06 15	16 40	17 16	17 54	18 33
30	05 34	06 03	06 27	16 37	17 10	17 44	18 20
35	05 38	06 08	06 34	16 36	17 07	17 39	18 13
40	05 42	06 14	06 42	16 35	17 03	17 33	18 05
45	05 46	06 21	06 52	16 33	16 59	17 26	17 55
S 50	05 51	06 29	07 03	16 31	16 54	17 18	17 44
52	05 52	06 32	07 08	16 30	16 51	17 14	17 39
54	05 54	06 36	07 14	16 29	16 49	17 10	17 33
56	05 56	06 40	07 20	16 28	16 46	17 05	17 27
58	05 58	06 45	07 27	16 27	16 43	17 00	17 20
S 60	06 01	06 50	07 35	16 26	16 39	16 54	17 11

Lat.	Sunset	Twilight Civil	Twilight Naut.	Moonset 28	29	30	1
N 72	21 49	////	////	04 14	04 05	03 55	03 43
N 70	21 14	////	////	04 15	04 11	04 07	04 03
68	20 49	22 31	////	04 16	04 16	04 18	04 19
66	20 30	21 49	////	04 16	04 21	04 26	04 33
64	20 15	21 22	////	04 17	04 25	04 33	04 43
62	20 02	21 01	22 41	04 17	04 28	04 39	04 53
60	19 52	20 44	22 03	04 17	04 31	04 45	05 01
N 58	19 42	20 30	21 38	04 18	04 33	04 50	05 08
56	19 34	20 18	21 18	04 18	04 35	04 54	05 14
54	19 27	20 08	21 02	04 18	04 38	04 58	05 20
52	19 21	19 59	20 49	04 18	04 39	05 01	05 25
50	19 15	19 51	20 37	04 19	04 41	05 04	05 29
45	19 02	19 35	20 14	04 19	04 45	05 11	05 39
N 40	18 52	19 21	19 57	04 20	04 48	05 17	05 48
35	18 43	19 10	19 43	04 20	04 51	05 22	05 55
30	18 36	19 01	19 31	04 20	04 53	05 26	06 01
20	18 23	18 46	19 13	04 21	04 57	05 34	06 12
N 10	18 11	18 33	18 59	04 21	05 01	05 41	06 22
0	18 01	18 22	18 47	04 21	05 04	05 47	06 31
S 10	17 50	18 12	18 37	04 22	05 08	05 54	06 40
20	17 39	18 02	18 28	04 22	05 11	06 00	06 50
30	17 27	17 52	18 20	04 23	05 16	06 08	07 01
35	17 20	17 46	18 16	04 23	05 18	06 13	07 07
40	17 12	17 40	18 12	04 23	05 21	06 18	07 14
45	17 03	17 33	18 08	04 23	05 24	06 24	07 23
S 50	16 51	17 25	18 03	04 24	05 28	06 31	07 33
52	16 46	17 22	18 01	04 24	05 29	06 34	07 38
54	16 40	17 18	18 00	04 24	05 31	06 38	07 43
56	16 34	17 14	17 58	04 24	05 33	06 42	07 49
58	16 27	17 09	17 55	04 25	05 36	06 46	07 56
S 60	16 19	17 04	17 53	04 25	05 38	06 51	08 03

Day	SUN Eqn. of Time 00h	12h	Mer. Pass.	MOON Mer. Pass. Upper	Lower	Age	Phase
d	m s	m s	h m	h m	h m	d %	
28	02 23	02 27	11 58	22 54	10 33	12 96	
29	02 32	02 36	11 57	23 37	11 15	13 99	◯
30	02 40	02 44	11 57	24 20	11 58	14 100	

1999 MAY 1, 2, 3 (SAT., SUN., MON.)

UT	ARIES	VENUS −4.1		MARS −1.6		JUPITER −2.1		SATURN +0.3		STARS		
	GHA	GHA	Dec	GHA	Dec	GHA	Dec	GHA	Dec	Name	SHA	Dec
d h	° ′	° ′	° ′	° ′	° ′	° ′	° ′	° ′	° ′		° ′	° ′
1 00	218 28.9	138 04.0 N25 23.7		8 30.2 S11 03.7		201 17.7 N 6 06.7		182 53.7 N11 51.2		Acamar	315 27.1	S40 18.7
01	233 31.3	153 03.4	24.0	23 33.5	03.5	216 19.6	07.0	197 55.8	51.3	Achernar	335 35.5	S57 14.5
02	248 33.8	168 02.7	24.3	38 36.9	03.3	231 21.5	07.2	212 58.0	51.4	Acrux	173 21.0	S63 05.8
03	263 36.2	183 02.0 . .	24.6	53 40.3 . .	03.0	246 23.4 . .	07.4	228 00.1 . .	51.5	Adhara	255 21.3	S28 58.6
04	278 38.7	198 01.4	24.8	68 43.7	02.8	261 25.3	07.6	243 02.3	51.6	Aldebaran	291 02.3	N16 30.3
05	293 41.2	213 00.7	25.1	83 47.1	02.6	276 27.3	07.8	258 04.4	51.7			
06	308 43.6	228 00.0 N25 25.4		98 50.4 S11 02.4		291 29.2 N 6 08.0		273 06.6 N11 51.8		Alioth	166 29.8	N55 58.0
07	323 46.1	242 59.4	25.7	113 53.8	02.2	306 31.1	08.3	288 08.8	51.9	Alkaid	153 07.1	N49 19.1
S 08	338 48.6	257 58.7	25.9	128 57.2	02.0	321 33.0	08.5	303 10.9	52.0	Al Na'ir	27 57.6	S46 57.7
A 09	353 51.0	272 58.0 . .	26.2	144 00.6 . .	01.7	336 35.0 . .	08.7	318 13.1 . .	52.1	Alnilam	275 57.7	S 1 12.4
T 10	8 53.5	287 57.4	26.5	159 04.0	01.5	351 36.9	08.9	333 15.2	52.2	Alphard	218 06.8	S 8 39.5
U 11	23 56.0	302 56.7	26.7	174 07.4	01.3	6 38.8	09.1	348 17.4	52.3			
R 12	38 58.4	317 56.0 N25 27.0		189 10.7 S11 01.1		21 40.7 N 6 09.4		3 19.5 N11 52.4		Alphecca	126 19.9	N26 43.0
D 13	54 00.9	332 55.4	27.3	204 14.1	00.9	36 42.6	09.6	18 21.7	52.5	Alpheratz	357 55.1	N29 04.9
A 14	69 03.3	347 54.7	27.5	219 17.5	00.6	51 44.6	09.8	33 23.8	52.6	Altair	62 18.8	N 8 51.9
Y 15	84 05.8	2 54.1 . .	27.8	234 20.9 . .	00.4	66 46.5 . .	10.0	48 26.0 . .	52.7	Ankaa	353 26.9	S42 18.6
16	99 08.3	17 53.4	28.1	249 24.2	00.2	81 48.4	10.2	63 28.2	52.9	Antares	112 39.4	S26 25.7
17	114 10.7	32 52.7	28.3	264 27.6 11 00.0		96 50.3	10.4	78 30.3	53.0			
18	129 13.2	47 52.1 N25 28.6		279 31.0 S10 59.8		111 52.3 N 6 10.7		93 32.5 N11 53.1		Arcturus	146 05.4	N19 11.2
19	144 15.7	62 51.4	28.8	294 34.4	59.6	126 54.2	10.9	108 34.6	53.2	Atria	107 50.6	S69 01.4
20	159 18.1	77 50.7	29.1	309 37.8	59.3	141 56.1	11.1	123 36.8	53.3	Avior	234 22.5	S59 30.8
21	174 20.6	92 50.1 . .	29.4	324 41.1 . .	59.1	156 58.0 . .	11.3	138 38.9 . .	53.4	Bellatrix	278 44.0	N 6 20.7
22	189 23.1	107 49.4	29.6	339 44.5	58.9	172 00.0	11.5	153 41.1	53.5	Betelgeuse	271 13.4	N 7 24.2
23	204 25.5	122 48.7	29.9	354 47.9	58.7	187 01.9	11.8	168 43.2	53.6			
2 00	219 28.0	137 48.1 N25 30.1		9 51.3 S10 58.5		202 03.8 N 6 12.0		183 45.4 N11 53.7		Canopus	264 01.3	S52 42.1
01	234 30.5	152 47.4	30.4	24 54.6	58.3	217 05.7	12.2	198 47.6	53.8	Capella	280 51.0	N45 59.8
02	249 32.9	167 46.8	30.6	39 58.0	58.1	232 07.6	12.4	213 49.7	53.9	Deneb	49 38.9	N45 16.4
03	264 35.4	182 46.1 . .	30.9	55 01.4 . .	57.8	247 09.6 . .	12.6	228 51.9 . .	54.0	Denebola	182 44.6	N14 34.6
04	279 37.8	197 45.4	31.1	70 04.8	57.6	262 11.5	12.8	243 54.0	54.1	Diphda	349 07.2	S17 59.6
05	294 40.3	212 44.8	31.4	85 08.1	57.4	277 13.4	13.1	258 56.2	54.2			
06	309 42.8	227 44.1 N25 31.6		100 11.5 S10 57.2		292 15.3 N 6 13.3		273 58.3 N11 54.3		Dubhe	194 04.8	N61 45.5
07	324 45.2	242 43.4	31.8	115 14.9	57.0	307 17.3	13.5	289 00.5	54.4	Elnath	278 26.8	N28 36.3
08	339 47.7	257 42.8	32.1	130 18.3	56.8	322 19.2	13.7	304 02.6	54.5	Eltanin	90 50.9	N51 29.2
S 09	354 50.2	272 42.1 . .	32.3	145 21.6 . .	56.5	337 21.1 . .	13.9	319 04.8 . .	54.6	Enif	33 57.9	N 9 52.2
U 10	9 52.6	287 41.5	32.6	160 25.0	56.3	352 23.0	14.1	334 07.0	54.7	Fomalhaut	15 36.3	S29 37.6
N 11	24 55.1	302 40.8	32.8	175 28.4	56.1	7 25.0	14.4	349 09.1	54.8			
D 12	39 57.6	317 40.1 N25 33.0		190 31.7 S10 55.9		22 26.9 N 6 14.6		4 11.3 N11 54.9		Gacrux	172 12.6	S57 06.7
A 13	55 00.0	332 39.5	33.3	205 35.1	55.7	37 28.8	14.8	19 13.4	55.0	Gienah	176 03.3	S17 32.4
Y 14	70 02.5	347 38.8	33.5	220 38.5	55.5	52 30.7	15.0	34 15.6	55.1	Hadar	149 02.8	S60 22.2
15	85 05.0	2 38.1 . .	33.8	235 41.9 . .	55.3	67 32.7 . .	15.2	49 17.7 . .	55.2	Hamal	328 13.5	N23 27.3
16	100 07.4	17 37.5	34.0	250 45.2	55.0	82 34.6	15.5	64 19.9	55.3	Kaus Aust.	83 58.1	S34 22.9
17	115 09.9	32 36.8	34.2	265 48.6	54.8	97 36.5	15.7	79 22.1	55.4			
18	130 12.3	47 36.2 N25 34.5		280 52.0 S10 54.6		112 38.4 N 6 15.9		94 24.2 N11 55.5		Kochab	137 18.5	N74 09.6
19	145 14.8	62 35.5	34.7	295 55.3	54.4	127 40.4	16.1	109 26.4	55.6	Markab	13 49.4	N15 11.9
20	160 17.3	77 34.8	34.9	310 58.7	54.2	142 42.3	16.3	124 28.5	55.7	Menkar	314 26.9	N 4 05.0
21	175 19.7	92 34.2 . .	35.1	326 02.1 . .	54.0	157 44.2 . .	16.5	139 30.7 . .	55.8	Menkent	148 20.1	S36 22.0
22	190 22.2	107 33.5	35.4	341 05.4	53.8	172 46.1	16.8	154 32.8	55.9	Miaplacidus	221 41.9	S69 43.2
23	205 24.7	122 32.8	35.6	356 08.8	53.5	187 48.1	17.0	169 35.0	56.1			
3 00	220 27.1	137 32.2 N25 35.8		11 12.2 S10 53.3		202 50.0 N 6 17.2		184 37.1 N11 56.2		Mirfak	308 56.6	N49 51.4
01	235 29.6	152 31.5	36.0	26 15.5	53.1	217 51.9	17.4	199 39.3	56.3	Nunki	76 11.7	S26 17.7
02	250 32.1	167 30.9	36.3	41 18.9	52.9	232 53.8	17.6	214 41.5	56.4	Peacock	53 36.4	S56 44.0
03	265 34.5	182 30.2 . .	36.5	56 22.3 . .	52.7	247 55.8 . .	17.8	229 43.6 . .	56.5	Pollux	243 41.3	N28 01.7
04	280 37.0	197 29.5	36.7	71 25.6	52.5	262 57.7	18.1	244 45.8	56.6	Procyon	245 11.3	N 5 13.5
05	295 39.4	212 28.9	36.9	86 29.0	52.3	277 59.6	18.3	259 47.9	56.7			
06	310 41.9	227 28.2 N25 37.1		101 32.4 S10 52.1		293 01.5 N 6 18.5		274 50.1 N11 56.8		Rasalhague	96 16.4	N12 33.6
07	325 44.4	242 27.6	37.4	116 35.7	51.9	308 03.5	18.7	289 52.2	56.9	Regulus	207 55.1	N11 58.2
08	340 46.8	257 26.9	37.6	131 39.1	51.6	323 05.4	18.9	304 54.4	57.0	Rigel	281 22.9	S 8 12.4
M 09	355 49.3	272 26.2 . .	37.8	146 42.4 . .	51.4	338 07.3 . .	19.1	319 56.5 . .	57.1	Rigil Kent.	140 06.1	S60 49.9
O 10	10 51.8	287 25.6	38.0	161 45.8	51.2	353 09.2	19.4	334 58.7	57.2	Sabik	102 24.8	S15 43.4
N 11	25 54.2	302 24.9	38.2	176 49.2	51.0	8 11.2	19.6	350 00.9	57.3			
D 12	40 56.7	317 24.3 N25 38.4		191 52.5 S10 50.8		23 13.1 N 6 19.8		5 03.0 N11 57.4		Schedar	349 53.5	N56 31.7
A 13	55 59.2	332 23.6	38.6	206 55.9	50.6	38 15.0	20.0	20 05.2	57.5	Shaula	96 36.5	S37 06.0
Y 14	71 01.6	347 22.9	38.8	221 59.2	50.4	53 16.9	20.2	35 07.3	57.6	Sirius	258 43.6	S16 43.2
15	86 04.1	2 22.3 . .	39.0	237 02.6 . .	50.2	68 18.9 . .	20.4	50 09.5 . .	57.7	Spica	158 42.5	S11 09.5
16	101 06.6	17 21.6	39.2	252 06.0	50.0	83 20.8	20.7	65 11.6	57.8	Suhail	223 00.5	S43 26.1
17	116 09.0	32 21.0	39.5	267 09.3	49.7	98 22.7	20.9	80 13.8	57.9			
18	131 11.5	47 20.3 N25 39.7		282 12.7 S10 49.5		113 24.6 N 6 21.1		95 15.9 N11 58.0		Vega	80 46.1	N38 46.8
19	146 13.9	62 19.6	39.9	297 16.0	49.3	128 26.6	21.3	110 18.1	58.1	Zuben'ubi	137 17.2	S16 02.3
20	161 16.4	77 19.0	40.1	312 19.4	49.1	143 28.5	21.5	125 20.3	58.2		SHA	Mer. Pass.
21	176 18.9	92 18.3 . .	40.3	327 22.7 . .	48.9	158 30.4 . .	21.7	140 22.4 . .	58.3		° ′	h m
22	191 21.3	107 17.7	40.5	342 26.1	48.7	173 32.3	22.0	155 24.6	58.4	Venus	278 20.1	14 49
23	206 23.8	122 17.0	40.7	357 29.5	48.5	188 34.3	22.2	170 26.7	58.5	Mars	150 23.3	23 15
	h m									Jupiter	342 35.8	10 30
Mer. Pass. 9 20.6		v −0.7 d 0.2		v 3.4 d 0.2		v 1.9 d 0.2		v 2.2 d 0.1		Saturn	324 17.4	11 43

UT	SUN GHA	SUN Dec	MOON GHA	v	MOON Dec	d	HP
d h	° '	° '	° '	'	° '	'	'
1 00	180 42.1	N14 52.4	355 05.7	14.5	S11 22.6	8.4	54.0
01	195 42.2	53.2	9 39.2	14.4	11 31.0	8.4	54.0
02	210 42.3	53.9	24 12.6	14.3	11 39.4	8.3	54.0
03	225 42.3	.. 54.7	38 45.9	14.4	11 47.7	8.3	54.0
04	240 42.4	55.5	53 19.3	14.3	11 56.0	8.2	54.0
05	255 42.5	56.2	67 52.6	14.3	12 04.2	8.2	54.0
06	270 42.6	N14 57.0	82 25.9	14.3	S12 12.4	8.1	54.0
07	285 42.7	57.7	96 59.2	14.2	12 20.5	8.0	54.0
08	300 42.7	58.5	111 32.4	14.3	12 28.5	8.0	54.0
S 09	315 42.8	14 59.3	126 05.7	14.2	12 36.5	8.0	54.0
A 10	330 42.9	15 00.0	140 38.9	14.1	12 44.5	7.9	54.0
T 11	345 43.0	00.8	155 12.0	14.2	12 52.4	7.8	54.0
U 12	0 43.1	N15 01.5	169 45.2	14.1	S13 00.2	7.8	54.0
R 13	15 43.1	02.3	184 18.3	14.1	13 08.0	7.8	54.0
D 14	30 43.2	03.1	198 51.4	14.1	13 15.8	7.6	54.0
A 15	45 43.3	.. 03.8	213 24.5	14.0	13 23.4	7.7	54.0
Y 16	60 43.4	04.6	227 57.5	14.0	13 31.1	7.5	54.0
17	75 43.4	05.3	242 30.5	14.0	13 38.6	7.5	54.0
18	90 43.5	N15 06.1	257 03.5	14.0	S13 46.1	7.5	54.0
19	105 43.6	06.8	271 36.5	13.9	13 53.6	7.3	54.0
20	120 43.7	07.6	286 09.4	13.9	14 00.9	7.4	54.0
21	135 43.7	.. 08.3	300 42.3	13.9	14 08.3	7.2	54.0
22	150 43.8	09.1	315 15.2	13.8	14 15.5	7.2	54.0
23	165 43.9	09.9	329 48.0	13.8	14 22.7	7.2	54.0
2 00	180 44.0	N15 10.6	344 20.8	13.8	S14 29.9	7.1	54.0
01	195 44.0	11.4	358 53.6	13.7	14 37.0	7.0	54.0
02	210 44.1	12.1	13 26.3	13.8	14 44.0	6.9	54.0
03	225 44.2	.. 12.9	27 59.1	13.7	14 50.9	6.9	54.0
04	240 44.3	13.6	42 31.8	13.6	14 57.8	6.8	54.0
05	255 44.3	14.4	57 04.4	13.7	15 04.6	6.8	54.0
06	270 44.4	N15 15.1	71 37.1	13.6	S15 11.4	6.7	54.0
07	285 44.5	15.9	86 09.7	13.5	15 18.1	6.6	54.0
08	300 44.6	16.6	100 42.2	13.6	15 24.7	6.6	54.0
S 09	315 44.6	.. 17.4	115 14.8	13.5	15 31.3	6.5	54.0
U 10	330 44.7	18.1	129 47.3	13.5	15 37.8	6.4	54.0
N 11	345 44.8	18.9	144 19.8	13.4	15 44.2	6.4	54.0
D 12	0 44.8	N15 19.6	158 52.2	13.5	S15 50.6	6.2	54.0
A 13	15 44.9	20.4	173 24.7	13.4	15 56.8	6.3	54.0
Y 14	30 45.0	21.1	187 57.1	13.3	16 03.1	6.1	54.0
15	45 45.1	.. 21.8	202 29.4	13.3	16 09.2	6.1	54.0
16	60 45.1	22.6	217 01.7	13.3	16 15.3	6.0	54.0
17	75 45.2	23.3	231 34.0	13.3	16 21.3	6.0	54.0
18	90 45.3	N15 24.1	246 06.3	13.2	S16 27.3	5.8	54.0
19	105 45.3	24.8	260 38.5	13.3	16 33.1	5.8	54.0
20	120 45.4	25.6	275 10.8	13.1	16 38.9	5.7	54.0
21	135 45.5	.. 26.3	289 42.9	13.2	16 44.6	5.7	54.0
22	150 45.6	27.1	304 15.1	13.1	16 50.3	5.6	54.0
23	165 45.6	27.8	318 47.2	13.1	16 55.9	5.5	54.0
3 00	180 45.7	N15 28.5	333 19.3	13.0	S17 01.4	5.4	54.0
01	195 45.8	29.3	347 51.3	13.0	17 06.8	5.3	54.0
02	210 45.9	30.0	2 23.3	13.0	17 12.1	5.3	54.0
03	225 45.9	.. 30.8	16 55.3	13.0	17 17.4	5.2	54.0
04	240 46.0	31.5	31 27.3	12.9	17 22.6	5.1	54.0
05	255 46.0	32.2	45 59.2	12.9	17 27.7	5.1	54.0
06	270 46.1	N15 33.0	60 31.1	12.9	S17 32.8	5.0	54.0
07	285 46.2	33.7	75 03.0	12.8	17 37.8	4.9	54.0
08	300 46.2	34.5	89 34.8	12.8	17 42.7	4.8	54.0
M 09	315 46.3	.. 35.2	104 06.6	12.8	17 47.5	4.7	54.0
O 10	330 46.4	35.9	118 38.4	12.7	17 52.2	4.7	54.0
N 11	345 46.4	36.7	133 10.1	12.8	17 56.9	4.5	54.0
D 12	0 46.5	N15 37.4	147 41.9	12.6	S18 01.4	4.5	54.0
A 13	15 46.6	38.1	162 13.5	12.7	18 05.9	4.5	54.1
Y 14	30 46.6	38.9	176 45.2	12.6	18 10.4	4.3	54.1
15	45 46.7	.. 39.6	191 16.8	12.6	18 14.7	4.2	54.1
16	60 46.8	40.4	205 48.4	12.6	18 18.9	4.2	54.1
17	75 46.8	41.1	220 20.0	12.5	18 23.1	4.1	54.1
18	90 46.9	N15 41.8	234 51.5	12.5	S18 27.2	4.0	54.1
19	105 47.0	42.6	249 23.0	12.5	18 31.2	3.9	54.1
20	120 47.0	43.3	263 54.5	12.4	18 35.1	3.9	54.1
21	135 47.1	.. 44.0	278 25.9	12.5	18 39.0	3.7	54.1
22	150 47.2	44.8	292 57.4	12.4	18 42.7	3.7	54.1
23	165 47.2	45.5	307 28.8	12.3	S18 46.4	3.6	54.1
	SD 15.9	d 0.7	SD 14.7		14.7		14.7

Lat.	Twilight Naut.	Twilight Civil	Sunrise	Moonrise 1	2	3	4
°	h m	h m	h m	h m	h m	h m	h m
N 72	////	////	01 48	22 29	24 36	00 36	▬▬
N 70	////	////	02 28	21 57	23 36	25 19	01 19
68	////	01 01	02 55	21 35	23 02	24 26	00 26
66	////	01 52	03 15	21 17	22 37	23 53	24 59
64	////	02 23	03 32	21 03	22 18	23 29	24 32
62	00 54	02 45	03 45	20 51	22 03	23 11	24 11
60	01 40	03 03	03 57	20 41	21 50	22 55	23 54
N 58	02 08	03 18	04 06	20 32	21 39	22 42	23 40
56	02 29	03 30	04 15	20 24	21 29	22 31	23 27
54	02 46	03 41	04 23	20 17	21 21	22 21	23 17
52	03 00	03 51	04 29	20 11	21 13	22 12	23 07
50	03 12	03 59	04 36	20 05	21 06	22 04	22 59
45	03 36	04 16	04 49	19 53	20 51	21 47	22 41
N 40	03 54	04 30	05 00	19 44	20 39	21 34	22 26
35	04 09	04 42	05 09	19 35	20 29	21 22	22 14
30	04 21	04 51	05 17	19 28	20 21	21 12	22 03
20	04 40	05 08	05 31	19 15	20 05	20 55	21 44
N 10	04 55	05 21	05 43	19 04	19 51	20 40	21 28
0	05 07	05 32	05 54	18 54	19 39	20 26	21 13
S 10	05 18	05 43	06 05	18 43	19 27	20 12	20 58
20	05 27	05 53	06 16	18 33	19 13	19 57	20 42
30	05 36	06 04	06 29	18 20	18 58	19 39	20 24
35	05 40	06 10	06 37	18 13	18 50	19 30	20 13
40	05 45	06 17	06 45	18 05	18 40	19 18	20 01
45	05 50	06 25	06 55	17 55	18 28	19 05	19 47
S 50	05 55	06 33	07 07	17 44	18 14	18 49	19 29
52	05 57	06 37	07 13	17 39	18 08	18 41	19 21
54	05 59	06 41	07 19	17 33	18 00	18 33	19 12
56	06 01	06 46	07 26	17 27	17 52	18 23	19 01
58	06 04	06 51	07 33	17 20	17 43	18 13	18 49
S 60	06 07	06 56	07 42	17 11	17 33	18 00	18 36

Lat.	Sunset	Twilight Civil	Twilight Naut.	Moonset 1	2	3	4
°	h m	h m	h m	h m	h m	h m	h m
N 72	22 13	////	////	03 43	03 27	02 55	▬▬
N 70	21 31	////	////	04 03	03 59	03 55	03 49
68	21 02	23 05	////	04 19	04 23	04 30	04 43
66	20 41	22 07	////	04 33	04 41	04 55	05 16
64	20 25	21 35	////	04 43	04 57	05 14	05 40
62	20 11	21 11	23 11	04 53	05 09	05 30	05 59
60	19 59	20 53	22 19	05 01	05 20	05 44	06 15
N 58	19 49	20 38	21 50	05 08	05 29	05 55	06 28
56	19 40	20 25	21 28	05 14	05 37	06 05	06 40
54	19 33	20 14	21 10	05 20	05 45	06 14	06 50
52	19 26	20 05	20 56	05 25	05 51	06 22	06 59
50	19 19	19 56	20 44	05 29	05 57	06 29	07 07
45	19 06	19 39	20 19	05 39	06 10	06 45	07 24
N 40	18 55	19 25	20 00	05 48	06 21	06 57	07 38
35	18 46	19 13	19 46	05 55	06 30	07 08	07 50
30	18 38	19 03	19 33	06 01	06 38	07 18	08 00
20	18 24	18 47	19 14	06 12	06 52	07 34	08 18
N 10	18 12	18 34	18 59	06 22	07 04	07 48	08 34
0	18 00	18 22	18 47	06 31	07 15	08 01	08 49
S 10	17 49	18 11	18 36	06 40	07 27	08 15	09 03
20	17 38	18 00	18 27	06 50	07 39	08 29	09 19
30	17 24	17 49	18 18	07 01	07 53	08 45	09 37
35	17 17	17 43	18 13	07 07	08 01	08 55	09 47
40	17 08	17 36	18 08	07 14	08 11	09 06	09 59
45	16 58	17 29	18 04	07 23	08 21	09 19	10 13
S 50	16 46	17 20	17 59	07 33	08 35	09 34	10 31
52	16 40	17 16	17 56	07 38	08 41	09 42	10 39
54	16 34	17 12	17 54	07 43	08 48	09 50	10 48
56	16 27	17 08	17 52	07 49	08 55	09 59	10 58
58	16 20	17 02	17 49	07 56	09 04	10 09	11 10
S 60	16 11	16 57	17 47	08 03	09 14	10 21	11 23

	SUN			MOON			
Day	Eqn. of Time 00h	Eqn. of Time 12h	Mer. Pass.	Mer. Pass. Upper	Mer. Pass. Lower	Age	Phase
d	m s	m s	h m	h m	h m	d	%
1	02 48	02 52	11 57	00 20	12 42	15	99
2	02 56	02 59	11 57	01 05	13 27	16	97
3	03 03	03 06	11 57	01 50	14 13	17	93 ○

UT	ARIES GHA	VENUS −4.1 GHA	Dec	MARS −1.6 GHA	Dec	JUPITER −2.1 GHA	Dec	SATURN +0.3 GHA	Dec	Star Name	SHA	Dec
d h	° ′	° ′	° ′	° ′	° ′	° ′	° ′	° ′	° ′		° ′	° ′
4 00	221 26.3	137 16.4	N25 40.9	12 32.8	S10 48.3	203 36.2	N 6 22.4	185 28.9	N11 58.6	Acamar	315 27.1	S40 18.7
01	236 28.7	152 15.7	41.0	27 36.2	48.1	218 38.1	22.6	200 31.0	58.7	Achernar	335 35.5	S57 14.5
02	251 31.2	167 15.0	41.2	42 39.5	47.9	233 40.0	22.8	215 33.2	58.8	Acrux	173 21.0	S63 05.9
03	266 33.7	182 14.4	.. 41.4	57 42.9	.. 47.6	248 42.0	.. 23.0	230 35.4	.. 58.9	Adhara	255 21.3	S28 58.6
04	281 36.1	197 13.7	41.6	72 46.2	47.4	263 43.9	23.2	245 37.5	59.0	Aldebaran	291 02.3	N16 30.3
05	296 38.6	212 13.1	41.8	87 49.6	47.2	278 45.8	23.5	260 39.7	59.1			
06	311 41.1	227 12.4	N25 42.0	102 52.9	S10 47.0	293 47.8	N 6 23.7	275 41.8	N11 59.2	Alioth	166 29.8	N55 58.0
07	326 43.5	242 11.7	42.2	117 56.3	46.8	308 49.7	23.9	290 44.0	59.3	Alkaid	153 07.1	N49 19.1
08	341 46.0	257 11.1	42.4	132 59.6	46.6	323 51.6	24.1	305 46.1	59.4	Al Na'ir	27 57.6	S46 57.7
T 09	356 48.4	272 10.4	.. 42.6	148 03.0	.. 46.4	338 53.5	.. 24.3	320 48.3	.. 59.5	Alnilam	275 57.8	S 1 12.4
U 10	11 50.9	287 09.8	42.8	163 06.3	46.2	353 55.5	24.5	335 50.4	59.7	Alphard	218 06.8	S 8 39.5
E 11	26 53.4	302 09.1	42.9	178 09.7	46.0	8 57.4	24.8	350 52.6	59.8			
S 12	41 55.8	317 08.5	N25 43.1	193 13.0	S10 45.8	23 59.3	N 6 25.0	5 54.8	N11 59.9	Alphecca	126 19.9	N26 43.1
D 13	56 58.3	332 07.8	43.3	208 16.4	45.6	39 01.2	25.2	20 56.9	12 00.0	Alpheratz	357 55.1	N29 04.9
A 14	72 00.8	347 07.2	43.5	223 19.7	45.4	54 03.2	25.4	35 59.1	00.1	Altair	62 18.8	N 8 51.9
Y 15	87 03.2	2 06.5	.. 43.7	238 23.1	.. 45.2	69 05.1	.. 25.6	51 01.2	.. 00.2	Ankaa	353 26.9	S42 18.6
16	102 05.7	17 05.8	43.8	253 26.4	45.0	84 07.0	25.8	66 03.4	00.3	Antares	112 39.4	S26 25.7
17	117 08.2	32 05.2	44.0	268 29.8	44.7	99 08.9	26.1	81 05.5	00.4			
18	132 10.6	47 04.5	N25 44.2	283 33.1	S10 44.5	114 10.9	N 6 26.3	96 07.7	N12 00.5	Arcturus	146 05.4	N19 11.2
19	147 13.1	62 03.9	44.4	298 36.4	44.3	129 12.8	26.5	111 09.8	00.6	Atria	107 50.6	S69 01.4
20	162 15.6	77 03.2	44.5	313 39.8	44.1	144 14.7	26.7	126 12.0	00.7	Avior	234 22.6	S59 30.8
21	177 18.0	92 02.6	.. 44.7	328 43.1	.. 43.9	159 16.7	.. 26.9	141 14.2	.. 00.8	Bellatrix	278 44.0	N 6 20.7
22	192 20.5	107 01.9	44.9	343 46.5	43.7	174 18.6	27.1	156 16.3	00.9	Betelgeuse	271 13.4	N 7 24.2
23	207 22.9	122 01.3	45.1	358 49.8	43.5	189 20.5	27.3	171 18.5	01.0			
5 00	222 25.4	137 00.6	N25 45.2	13 53.2	S10 43.3	204 22.4	N 6 27.6	186 20.6	N12 01.1	Canopus	264 01.4	S52 42.1
01	237 27.9	151 59.9	45.4	28 56.5	43.1	219 24.4	27.8	201 22.8	01.2	Capella	280 51.1	N45 59.8
02	252 30.3	166 59.3	45.6	43 59.8	42.9	234 26.3	28.0	216 24.9	01.3	Deneb	49 38.9	N45 16.4
03	267 32.8	181 58.6	.. 45.7	59 03.2	.. 42.7	249 28.2	.. 28.2	231 27.1	.. 01.4	Denebola	182 44.6	N14 34.6
04	282 35.3	196 58.0	45.9	74 06.5	42.5	264 30.2	28.4	246 29.3	01.5	Diphda	349 07.2	S17 59.6
05	297 37.7	211 57.3	46.0	89 09.9	42.3	279 32.1	28.6	261 31.4	01.6			
06	312 40.2	226 56.7	N25 46.2	104 13.2	S10 42.1	294 34.0	N 6 28.8	276 33.6	N12 01.7	Dubhe	194 04.8	N61 45.5
W 07	327 42.7	241 56.0	46.4	119 16.5	41.9	309 35.9	29.1	291 35.7	01.8	Elnath	278 26.8	N28 36.3
E 08	342 45.1	256 55.4	46.5	134 19.9	41.7	324 37.9	29.3	306 37.9	01.9	Eltanin	90 50.8	N51 29.2
D 09	357 47.6	271 54.7	.. 46.6	149 23.2	.. 41.5	339 39.8	.. 29.5	321 40.0	.. 02.0	Enif	33 57.9	N 9 52.2
N 10	12 50.0	286 54.1	46.8	164 26.5	41.3	354 41.7	29.7	336 42.2	02.1	Fomalhaut	15 36.2	S29 37.5
E 11	27 52.5	301 53.4	47.0	179 29.9	41.1	9 43.6	29.9	351 44.3	02.2			
S 12	42 55.0	316 52.8	N25 47.2	194 33.2	S10 40.9	24 45.6	N 6 30.1	6 46.5	N12 02.3	Gacrux	172 12.6	S57 06.7
D 13	57 57.4	331 52.1	47.3	209 36.6	40.7	39 47.5	30.3	21 48.7	02.4	Gienah	176 03.3	S17 32.4
A 14	72 59.9	346 51.4	47.5	224 39.9	40.5	54 49.4	30.6	36 50.8	02.5	Hadar	149 02.8	S60 22.2
Y 15	88 02.4	1 50.8	.. 47.6	239 43.2	.. 40.3	69 51.4	.. 30.8	51 53.0	.. 02.6	Hamal	328 13.5	N23 27.3
16	103 04.8	16 50.1	47.8	254 46.6	40.1	84 53.3	31.0	66 55.1	02.7	Kaus Aust.	83 58.1	S34 22.9
17	118 07.3	31 49.5	47.9	269 49.9	39.9	99 55.2	31.2	81 57.3	02.8			
18	133 09.8	46 48.8	N25 48.1	284 53.2	S10 39.7	114 57.1	N 6 31.4	96 59.4	N12 02.9	Kochab	137 18.5	N74 09.6
19	148 12.2	61 48.2	48.2	299 56.5	39.5	129 59.1	31.6	112 01.6	03.0	Markab	13 49.4	N15 11.9
20	163 14.7	76 47.5	48.3	314 59.9	39.3	145 01.0	31.8	127 03.8	03.1	Menkar	314 26.8	N 4 05.0
21	178 17.2	91 46.9	.. 48.5	330 03.2	.. 39.1	160 02.9	.. 32.1	142 05.9	.. 03.2	Menkent	148 20.1	S36 22.0
22	193 19.6	106 46.2	48.6	345 06.5	38.9	175 04.9	32.3	157 08.1	03.3	Miaplacidus	221 41.9	S69 43.2
23	208 22.1	121 45.6	48.8	0 09.9	38.7	190 06.8	32.5	172 10.2	03.4			
6 00	223 24.5	136 44.9	N25 48.9	15 13.2	S10 38.5	205 08.7	N 6 32.7	187 12.4	N12 03.5	Mirfak	308 56.6	N49 51.3
01	238 27.0	151 44.3	49.1	30 16.5	38.3	220 10.6	32.9	202 14.5	03.6	Nunki	76 11.7	S26 17.7
02	253 29.5	166 43.6	49.2	45 19.8	38.1	235 12.6	33.1	217 16.7	03.7	Peacock	53 36.4	S56 44.0
03	268 31.9	181 43.0	.. 49.3	60 23.2	.. 37.9	250 14.5	.. 33.3	232 18.8	.. 03.8	Pollux	243 41.3	N28 01.7
04	283 34.4	196 42.3	49.5	75 26.5	37.7	265 16.4	33.6	247 21.0	03.9	Procyon	245 11.3	N 5 13.5
05	298 36.9	211 41.7	49.6	90 29.8	37.5	280 18.4	33.8	262 23.2	04.0			
06	313 39.3	226 41.0	N25 49.7	105 33.1	S10 37.3	295 20.3	N 6 34.0	277 25.3	N12 04.1	Rasalhague	96 16.4	N12 33.6
07	328 41.8	241 40.4	49.9	120 36.5	37.1	310 22.2	34.2	292 27.5	04.3	Regulus	207 55.1	N11 58.2
T 08	343 44.3	256 39.7	50.0	135 39.8	36.9	325 24.1	34.4	307 29.6	04.4	Rigel	281 22.9	S 8 12.4
H 09	358 46.7	271 39.1	.. 50.1	150 43.1	.. 36.7	340 26.1	.. 34.6	322 31.8	.. 04.5	Rigil Kent.	140 06.1	S60 49.9
U 10	13 49.2	286 38.4	50.3	165 46.4	36.5	355 28.0	34.8	337 33.9	04.6	Sabik	102 24.8	S15 43.4
R 11	28 51.7	301 37.8	50.4	180 49.7	36.3	10 29.9	35.1	352 36.1	04.7			
S 12	43 54.1	316 37.1	N25 50.5	195 53.1	S10 36.1	25 31.9	N 6 35.3	7 38.3	N12 04.8	Schedar	349 53.5	N56 31.7
D 13	58 56.6	331 36.5	50.6	210 56.4	35.9	40 33.8	35.5	22 40.4	04.9	Shaula	96 36.5	S37 06.0
A 14	73 59.0	346 35.9	50.8	225 59.7	35.7	55 35.7	35.7	37 42.6	05.0	Sirius	258 43.6	S16 43.2
Y 15	89 01.5	1 35.2	.. 50.9	241 03.0	.. 35.5	70 37.7	.. 35.9	52 44.7	.. 05.1	Spica	158 42.5	S11 09.5
16	104 04.0	16 34.6	51.0	256 06.3	35.3	85 39.6	36.1	67 46.9	05.2	Suhail	223 00.5	S43 26.1
17	119 06.4	31 33.9	51.1	271 09.6	35.1	100 41.5	36.3	82 49.0	05.3			
18	134 08.9	46 33.3	N25 51.2	286 13.0	S10 34.9	115 43.4	N 6 36.5	97 51.2	N12 05.4	Vega	80 46.1	N38 46.8
19	149 11.4	61 32.6	51.4	301 16.3	34.7	130 45.4	36.8	112 53.4	05.5	Zuben'ubi	137 17.2	S16 02.3
20	164 13.8	76 32.0	51.5	316 19.6	34.5	145 47.3	37.0	127 55.5	05.6			
21	179 16.3	91 31.3	.. 51.6	331 22.9	.. 34.3	160 49.2	.. 37.2	142 57.7	.. 05.7		SHA	Mer. Pass.
22	194 18.8	106 30.7	51.7	346 26.2	34.1	175 51.2	37.4	157 59.8	05.8	Venus	274 35.2	14 53
23	209 21.2	121 30.0	51.8	1 29.5	33.9	190 53.1	37.6	173 02.0	05.9	Mars	151 27.8	22 59
Mer. Pass. 9 08.8		v −0.7	d 0.2	v 3.3	d 0.2	v 1.9	d 0.2	v 2.2	d 0.1	Jupiter	341 57.0	10 21
										Saturn	323 55.2	11 33

UT	SUN GHA	SUN Dec	MOON GHA	v	MOON Dec	d	HP
	° ′	° ′	° ′	′	° ′	′	′
4 00	180 47.3	N15 46.2	322 00.1	12.4	S18 50.0	3.5	54.1
01	195 47.3	47.0	336 31.5	12.3	18 53.5	3.4	54.1
02	210 47.4	47.7	351 02.8	12.2	18 56.9	3.3	54.1
03	225 47.5 ..	48.4	5 34.0	12.3	19 00.2	3.3	54.2
04	240 47.5	49.1	20 05.3	12.2	19 03.5	3.1	54.2
05	255 47.6	49.9	34 36.5	12.2	19 06.6	3.1	54.2
06	270 47.7	N15 50.6	49 07.7	12.2	S19 09.7	3.0	54.2
07	285 47.7	51.3	63 38.9	12.1	19 12.7	2.9	54.2
08	300 47.8	52.1	78 10.0	12.1	19 15.6	2.8	54.2
09	315 47.8 ..	52.8	92 41.1	12.1	19 18.4	2.7	54.2
10	330 47.9	53.5	107 12.2	12.1	19 21.1	2.7	54.2
11	345 48.0	54.2	121 43.3	12.0	19 23.8	2.5	54.2
12	0 48.0	N15 55.0	136 14.3	12.0	S19 26.3	2.5	54.2
13	15 48.1	55.7	150 45.3	12.0	19 28.8	2.3	54.2
14	30 48.1	56.4	165 16.3	12.0	19 31.1	2.3	54.3
15	45 48.2 ..	57.1	179 47.3	11.9	19 33.4	2.2	54.3
16	60 48.3	57.9	194 18.2	11.9	19 35.6	2.1	54.3
17	75 48.3	58.6	208 49.1	11.9	19 37.7	2.0	54.3
18	90 48.4	N15 59.3	223 20.0	11.9	S19 39.7	1.9	54.3
19	105 48.4	16 00.0	237 50.9	11.8	19 41.6	1.8	54.3
20	120 48.5	00.8	252 21.7	11.9	19 43.4	1.8	54.3
21	135 48.6 ..	01.5	266 52.6	11.8	19 45.2	1.6	54.3
22	150 48.6	02.2	281 23.4	11.7	19 46.8	1.6	54.4
23	165 48.7	02.9	295 54.1	11.8	19 48.4	1.4	54.4
5 00	180 48.7	N16 03.6	310 24.9	11.7	S19 49.8	1.4	54.4
01	195 48.8	04.4	324 55.6	11.7	19 51.2	1.2	54.4
02	210 48.8	05.1	339 26.3	11.7	19 52.4	1.2	54.4
03	225 48.9 ..	05.8	353 57.0	11.7	19 53.6	1.1	54.4
04	240 49.0	06.5	8 27.7	11.6	19 54.7	1.0	54.4
05	255 49.0	07.2	22 58.3	11.7	19 55.7	0.9	54.4
06	270 49.1	N16 08.0	37 29.0	11.6	S19 56.6	0.8	54.5
07	285 49.1	08.7	51 59.6	11.6	19 57.4	0.7	54.5
08	300 49.2	09.4	66 30.2	11.5	19 58.1	0.6	54.5
09	315 49.2 ..	10.1	81 00.7	11.6	19 58.7	0.5	54.5
10	330 49.3	10.8	95 31.3	11.5	19 59.2	0.5	54.5
11	345 49.3	11.5	110 01.8	11.5	19 59.7	0.3	54.5
12	0 49.4	N16 12.2	124 32.3	11.5	S20 00.0	0.2	54.5
13	15 49.4	13.0	139 02.8	11.5	20 00.2	0.2	54.6
14	30 49.5	13.7	153 33.3	11.5	20 00.4	0.0	54.6
15	45 49.6 ..	14.4	168 03.8	11.4	20 00.4	0.0	54.6
16	60 49.6	15.1	182 34.2	11.4	20 00.4	0.2	54.6
17	75 49.7	15.8	197 04.6	11.4	20 00.2	0.2	54.6
18	90 49.7	N16 16.5	211 35.0	11.4	S20 00.0	0.4	54.6
19	105 49.8	17.2	226 05.4	11.4	19 59.6	0.4	54.7
20	120 49.8	18.0	240 35.8	11.4	19 59.2	0.5	54.7
21	135 49.9 ..	18.7	255 06.2	11.3	19 58.7	0.7	54.7
22	150 49.9	19.4	269 36.5	11.3	19 58.0	0.7	54.7
23	165 50.0	20.1	284 06.9	11.3	19 57.3	0.8	54.7
6 00	180 50.0	N16 20.8	298 37.2	11.3	S19 56.5	0.9	54.8
01	195 50.1	21.5	313 07.5	11.3	19 55.6	1.0	54.8
02	210 50.1	22.2	327 37.8	11.3	19 54.6	1.2	54.8
03	225 50.2 ..	22.9	342 08.1	11.3	19 53.4	1.2	54.8
04	240 50.2	23.6	356 38.4	11.2	19 52.2	1.3	54.8
05	255 50.3	24.3	11 08.6	11.3	19 50.9	1.4	54.9
06	270 50.3	N16 25.0	25 38.9	11.2	S19 49.5	1.5	54.9
07	285 50.4	25.7	40 09.1	11.2	19 48.0	1.6	54.9
08	300 50.4	26.5	54 39.3	11.3	19 46.4	1.7	54.9
09	315 50.5 ..	27.2	69 09.6	11.2	19 44.7	1.8	54.9
10	330 50.5	27.9	83 39.8	11.1	19 42.9	1.8	55.0
11	345 50.6	28.6	98 09.9	11.2	19 41.1	2.0	55.0
12	0 50.6	N16 29.3	112 40.1	11.2	S19 39.1	2.1	55.0
13	15 50.7	30.0	127 10.3	11.2	19 37.0	2.2	55.0
14	30 50.7	30.7	141 40.5	11.1	19 34.8	2.3	55.0
15	45 50.8 ..	31.4	156 10.6	11.2	19 32.5	2.3	55.1
16	60 50.8	32.1	170 40.8	11.1	19 30.2	2.5	55.1
17	75 50.9	32.8	185 10.9	11.1	19 27.7	2.6	55.1
18	90 50.9	N16 33.5	199 41.0	11.2	S19 25.1	2.7	55.1
19	105 51.0	34.2	214 11.2	11.1	19 22.4	2.7	55.2
20	120 51.0	34.9	228 41.3	11.1	19 19.7	2.9	55.2
21	135 51.1 ..	35.6	243 11.4	11.1	19 16.8	2.9	55.2
22	150 51.1	36.3	257 41.5	11.1	19 13.9	3.1	55.2
23	165 51.1	37.0	272 11.6	11.1	S19 10.8	3.1	55.2
SD 15.9	d 0.7		SD 14.8	14.9			15.0

Day side labels: TUESDAY (4), WEDNESDAY (5), THURSDAY (6)

Twilight / Sunrise / Moonrise

Lat.	Naut.	Civil	Sunrise	Moonrise 4	5	6	7
°	h m	h m	h m	h m	h m	h m	h m
N 72	////	////	01 19	■	■	■	■
N 70	////	////	02 10	01 19	03 19	04 00	03 46
68	////	////	02 41	00 26	01 38	02 27	02 54
66	////	01 32	03 04	24 59	00 59	01 49	02 22
64	////	02 08	03 22	24 32	00 32	01 22	01 58
62	////	02 34	03 36	24 11	00 11	01 01	01 40
60	01 22	02 53	03 49	23 54	24 44	00 44	01 24
N 58	01 55	03 09	03 59	23 40	24 29	00 29	01 11
56	02 19	03 23	04 08	23 27	24 17	00 17	00 59
54	02 37	03 34	04 17	23 17	24 06	00 06	00 49
52	02 52	03 44	04 24	23 07	23 57	24 41	00 41
50	03 05	03 53	04 30	22 59	23 48	24 33	00 33
45	03 31	04 12	04 44	22 41	23 30	24 16	00 16
N 40	03 50	04 26	04 56	22 26	23 16	24 02	00 02
35	04 06	04 38	05 06	22 14	23 03	23 50	24 33
30	04 18	04 49	05 14	22 03	22 52	23 39	24 24
20	04 38	05 06	05 29	21 44	22 33	23 21	24 08
N 10	04 54	05 20	05 42	21 28	22 17	23 06	23 54
0	05 07	05 32	05 53	21 13	22 02	22 51	23 41
S 10	05 18	05 43	06 05	20 58	21 47	22 37	23 28
20	05 28	05 54	06 17	20 42	21 31	22 21	23 14
30	05 38	06 06	06 31	20 24	21 12	22 03	22 58
35	05 43	06 13	06 39	20 13	21 01	21 53	22 48
40	05 48	06 20	06 48	20 01	20 49	21 41	22 38
45	05 53	06 28	06 59	19 47	20 34	21 27	22 25
S 50	05 59	06 37	07 12	19 29	20 16	21 10	22 10
52	06 01	06 41	07 18	19 21	20 08	21 02	22 02
54	06 04	06 46	07 24	19 12	19 58	20 53	21 54
56	06 06	06 51	07 32	19 01	19 48	20 42	21 45
58	06 09	06 57	07 40	18 49	19 35	20 31	21 35
S 60	06 12	07 03	07 49	18 36	19 21	20 17	21 24

Sunset / Twilight / Moonset

Lat.	Sunset	Civil	Naut.	Moonset 4	5	6	7
°	h m	h m	h m	h m	h m	h m	h m
N 72	22 45	////	////	■	■	■	■
N 70	21 49	////	////	03 49	03 30	04 30	06 27
68	21 16	////	////	04 43	05 11	06 02	07 18
66	20 53	22 28	////	05 16	05 50	06 41	07 50
64	20 34	21 49	////	05 40	06 17	07 08	08 13
62	20 19	21 23	////	05 59	06 38	07 29	08 32
60	20 07	21 02	22 37	06 15	06 55	07 46	08 47
N 58	19 56	20 46	22 02	06 28	07 09	08 00	09 00
56	19 46	20 32	21 38	06 40	07 22	08 12	09 11
54	19 38	20 21	21 19	06 50	07 32	08 23	09 21
52	19 31	20 10	21 03	06 59	07 42	08 32	09 30
50	19 24	20 01	20 50	07 07	07 50	08 41	09 37
45	19 10	19 43	20 22	07 24	08 08	08 59	09 54
N 40	18 58	19 28	20 04	07 38	08 23	09 13	10 08
35	18 48	19 16	19 49	07 50	08 36	09 25	10 19
30	18 40	19 05	19 36	08 00	08 47	09 36	10 29
20	18 25	18 48	19 15	08 18	09 05	09 54	10 46
N 10	18 12	18 34	19 00	08 34	09 22	10 11	11 01
0	18 00	18 22	18 47	08 49	09 37	10 26	11 15
S 10	17 48	18 10	18 35	09 03	09 52	10 41	11 29
20	17 36	17 59	18 25	09 19	10 08	10 57	11 44
30	17 22	17 47	18 15	09 37	10 27	11 15	12 01
35	17 14	17 40	18 10	09 47	10 38	11 26	12 11
40	17 05	17 33	18 05	09 59	10 50	11 38	12 22
45	16 54	17 25	18 01	10 13	11 05	11 52	12 35
S 50	16 41	17 16	17 54	10 31	11 23	12 10	12 51
52	16 35	17 11	17 52	10 39	11 31	12 18	12 58
54	16 28	17 07	17 49	10 48	11 41	12 27	13 07
56	16 21	17 02	17 46	10 58	11 51	12 37	13 16
58	16 13	16 56	17 43	11 10	12 04	12 49	13 27
S 60	16 03	16 50	17 40	11 23	12 18	13 03	13 39

SUN / MOON

Day	Eqn. of Time 00h	12h	Mer. Pass.	Mer. Pass. Upper	Lower	Age	Phase
d	m s	m s	h m	h m	h m	d	%
4	03 09	03 12	11 57	02 37	15 01	18	87
5	03 15	03 17	11 57	03 25	15 49	19	80
6	03 20	03 22	11 57	04 14	16 39	20	72

UT	ARIES GHA	VENUS −4.1 GHA	Dec	MARS −1.5 GHA	Dec	JUPITER −2.1 GHA	Dec	SATURN +0.3 GHA	Dec	STARS Name	SHA	Dec
7 00	224 23.7	136 29.4	N25 51.9	16 32.8	S10 33.7	205 55.0	N 6 37.8	188 04.1	N12 06.0	Acamar	315 27.1	S40 18.6
01	239 26.2	151 28.7	52.1	31 36.2	33.5	220 57.0	38.0	203 06.3	06.1	Achernar	335 35.5	S57 14.5
02	254 28.6	166 28.1	52.2	46 39.5	33.3	235 58.9	38.3	218 08.4	06.2	Acrux	173 21.0	S63 05.9
03	269 31.1	181 27.5 ..	52.3	61 42.8 ..	33.1	251 00.8 ..	38.5	233 10.6 ..	06.3	Adhara	255 21.3	S28 58.6
04	284 33.5	196 26.8	52.4	76 46.1	32.9	266 02.7	38.7	248 12.8	06.4	Aldebaran	291 02.3	N16 30.3
05	299 36.0	211 26.2	52.5	91 49.4	32.7	281 04.7	38.9	263 14.9	06.5			
06	314 38.5	226 25.5	N25 52.6	106 52.7	S10 32.6	296 06.6	N 6 39.1	278 17.1	N12 06.6	Alioth	166 29.8	N55 58.0
07	329 40.9	241 24.9	52.7	121 56.0	32.4	311 08.5	39.3	293 19.2	06.7	Alkaid	153 07.1	N49 19.2
08	344 43.4	256 24.2	52.8	136 59.3	32.2	326 10.5	39.5	308 21.4	06.8	Al Na'ir	27 57.6	S46 57.7
F 09	359 45.9	271 23.6 ..	52.9	152 02.6 ..	32.0	341 12.4 ..	39.7	323 23.5 ..	06.9	Alnilam	275 57.8	S 1 12.4
R 10	14 48.3	286 22.9	53.0	167 05.9	31.8	356 14.3	40.0	338 25.7	07.0	Alphard	218 06.8	S 8 39.5
I 11	29 50.8	301 22.3	53.1	182 09.2	31.6	11 16.3	40.2	353 27.9	07.1			
D 12	44 53.3	316 21.7	N25 53.2	197 12.5	S10 31.4	26 18.2	N 6 40.4	8 30.0	N12 07.2	Alphecca	126 19.9	N26 43.1
A 13	59 55.7	331 21.0	53.3	212 15.8	31.2	41 20.1	40.6	23 32.2	07.3	Alpheratz	357 55.1	N29 04.9
Y 14	74 58.2	346 20.4	53.4	227 19.1	31.0	56 22.1	40.8	38 34.3	07.4	Altair	62 18.8	N 8 51.9
15	90 00.6	1 19.7 ..	53.5	242 22.4 ..	30.8	71 24.0 ..	41.0	53 36.5 ..	07.5	Ankaa	353 26.8	S42 18.6
16	105 03.1	16 19.1	53.6	257 25.7	30.6	86 25.9	41.2	68 38.6	07.6	Antares	112 39.4	S26 25.7
17	120 05.6	31 18.5	53.7	272 29.0	30.4	101 27.9	41.4	83 40.8	07.7			
18	135 08.0	46 17.8	N25 53.8	287 32.3	S10 30.3	116 29.8	N 6 41.7	98 43.0	N12 07.8	Arcturus	146 05.4	N19 11.2
19	150 10.5	61 17.2	53.9	302 35.6	30.1	131 31.7	41.9	113 45.1	07.9	Atria	107 50.6	S69 01.4
20	165 13.0	76 16.5	54.0	317 38.9	29.9	146 33.6	42.1	128 47.3	08.0	Avior	234 22.6	S59 30.8
21	180 15.4	91 15.9 ..	54.0	332 42.2 ..	29.7	161 35.6 ..	42.3	143 49.4 ..	08.1	Bellatrix	278 44.0	N 6 20.7
22	195 17.9	106 15.2	54.1	347 45.5	29.5	176 37.5	42.5	158 51.6	08.2	Betelgeuse	271 13.4	N 7 24.2
23	210 20.4	121 14.6	54.2	2 48.8	29.3	191 39.4	42.7	173 53.7	08.3			
8 00	225 22.8	136 14.0	N25 54.3	17 52.1	S10 29.1	206 41.4	N 6 42.9	188 55.9	N12 08.4	Canopus	264 01.4	S52 42.1
01	240 25.3	151 13.3	54.4	32 55.4	28.9	221 43.3	43.1	203 58.1	08.5	Capella	280 51.1	N45 59.8
02	255 27.8	166 12.7	54.5	47 58.7	28.7	236 45.2	43.3	219 00.2	08.6	Deneb	49 38.8	N45 16.4
03	270 30.2	181 12.1 ..	54.6	63 02.0 ..	28.5	251 47.2 ..	43.6	234 02.4 ..	08.7	Denebola	182 44.6	N14 34.6
04	285 32.7	196 11.4	54.6	78 05.3	28.4	266 49.1	43.8	249 04.5	08.8	Diphda	349 07.1	S17 59.5
05	300 35.1	211 10.8	54.7	93 08.5	28.2	281 51.0	44.0	264 06.7	08.9			
06	315 37.6	226 10.1	N25 54.8	108 11.8	S10 28.0	296 53.0	N 6 44.2	279 08.8	N12 09.0	Dubhe	194 04.8	N61 45.5
07	330 40.1	241 09.5	54.9	123 15.1	27.8	311 54.9	44.4	294 11.0	09.1	Elnath	278 26.8	N28 36.3
S 08	345 42.5	256 08.9	54.9	138 18.4	27.6	326 56.8	44.6	309 13.2	09.2	Eltanin	90 50.8	N51 29.2
A 09	0 45.0	271 08.2 ..	55.0	153 21.7 ..	27.4	341 58.8 ..	44.8	324 15.3 ..	09.3	Enif	33 57.9	N 9 52.2
T 10	15 47.5	286 07.6	55.1	168 25.0	27.2	357 00.7	45.0	339 17.5	09.4	Fomalhaut	15 36.2	S29 37.5
U 11	30 49.9	301 07.0	55.2	183 28.3	27.1	12 02.6	45.3	354 19.6	09.5			
R 12	45 52.4	316 06.3	N25 55.2	198 31.6	S10 26.9	27 04.6	N 6 45.5	9 21.8	N12 09.6	Gacrux	172 12.7	S57 06.7
D 13	60 54.9	331 05.7	55.3	213 34.8	26.7	42 06.5	45.7	24 23.9	09.7	Gienah	176 03.3	S17 32.4
A 14	75 57.3	346 05.0	55.4	228 38.1	26.5	57 08.4	45.9	39 26.1	09.8	Hadar	149 02.8	S60 22.2
Y 15	90 59.8	1 04.4 ..	55.4	243 41.4 ..	26.3	72 10.4 ..	46.1	54 28.2 ..	09.9	Hamal	328 13.5	N23 27.3
16	106 02.3	16 03.8	55.5	258 44.7	26.1	87 12.3	46.3	69 30.4	10.0	Kaus Aust.	83 58.1	S34 22.9
17	121 04.7	31 03.1	55.6	273 48.0	25.9	102 14.2	46.5	84 32.6	10.1			
18	136 07.2	46 02.5	N25 55.6	288 51.2	S10 25.8	117 16.2	N 6 46.7	99 34.7	N12 10.2	Kochab	137 18.5	N74 09.6
19	151 09.6	61 01.9	55.7	303 54.5	25.6	132 18.1	46.9	114 36.9	10.3	Markab	13 49.4	N15 11.9
20	166 12.1	76 01.2	55.8	318 57.8	25.4	147 20.0	47.2	129 39.0	10.4	Menkar	314 26.8	N 4 05.0
21	181 14.6	91 00.6 ..	55.8	334 01.1 ..	25.2	162 22.0 ..	47.4	144 41.2 ..	10.5	Menkent	148 20.1	S36 22.0
22	196 17.0	106 00.0	55.9	349 04.3	25.0	177 23.9	47.6	159 43.3	10.6	Miaplacidus	221 41.9	S69 43.2
23	211 19.5	120 59.3	55.9	4 07.6	24.8	192 25.8	47.8	174 45.5	10.7			
9 00	226 22.0	135 58.7	N25 56.0	19 10.9	S10 24.7	207 27.8	N 6 48.0	189 47.7	N12 10.8	Mirfak	308 56.6	N49 51.3
01	241 24.4	150 58.1	56.0	34 14.2	24.5	222 29.7	48.2	204 49.8	10.9	Nunki	76 11.7	S26 17.7
02	256 26.9	165 57.4	56.1	49 17.4	24.3	237 31.6	48.4	219 52.0	11.0	Peacock	53 36.3	S56 44.0
03	271 29.4	180 56.8 ..	56.2	64 20.7 ..	24.1	252 33.6 ..	48.6	234 54.1 ..	11.1	Pollux	243 41.3	N28 01.7
04	286 31.8	195 56.2	56.2	79 24.0	23.9	267 35.5	48.8	249 56.3	11.2	Procyon	245 11.3	N 5 13.5
05	301 34.3	210 55.5	56.3	94 27.3	23.7	282 37.4	49.1	264 58.4	11.3			
06	316 36.8	225 54.9	N25 56.3	109 30.5	S10 23.6	297 39.4	N 6 49.3	280 00.6	N12 11.4	Rasalhague	96 16.3	N12 33.6
07	331 39.2	240 54.3	56.4	124 33.8	23.4	312 41.3	49.5	295 02.8	11.5	Regulus	207 55.1	N11 58.2
08	346 41.7	255 53.6	56.4	139 37.1	23.2	327 43.2	49.7	310 04.9	11.6	Rigel	281 22.9	S 8 12.4
S 09	1 44.1	270 53.0 ..	56.5	154 40.3 ..	23.0	342 45.2 ..	49.9	325 07.1 ..	11.7	Rigil Kent.	140 06.1	S60 49.9
U 10	16 46.6	285 52.4	56.5	169 43.6	22.8	357 47.1	50.1	340 09.2	11.8	Sabik	102 24.8	S15 43.4
N 11	31 49.1	300 51.8	56.5	184 46.9	22.7	12 49.0	50.3	355 11.4	11.9			
D 12	46 51.5	315 51.1	N25 56.6	199 50.1	S10 22.5	27 51.0	N 6 50.5	10 13.5	N12 12.0	Schedar	349 53.5	N56 31.7
A 13	61 54.0	330 50.5	56.6	214 53.4	22.3	42 52.9	50.7	25 15.7	12.1	Shaula	96 36.4	S37 06.0
Y 14	76 56.5	345 49.9	56.7	229 56.7	22.1	57 54.8	50.9	40 17.9	12.2	Sirius	258 43.6	S16 43.1
15	91 58.9	0 49.2 ..	56.7	244 59.9 ..	22.0	72 56.8 ..	51.2	55 20.0 ..	12.3	Spica	158 42.5	S11 09.5
16	107 01.4	15 48.6	56.8	260 03.2	21.8	87 58.7	51.4	70 22.2	12.4	Suhail	223 00.5	S43 26.1
17	122 03.9	30 48.0	56.8	275 06.4	21.6	103 00.6	51.6	85 24.3	12.5			
18	137 06.3	45 47.4	N25 56.8	290 09.7	S10 21.4	118 02.6	N 6 51.8	100 26.5	N12 12.6	Vega	80 46.1	N38 46.9
19	152 08.8	60 46.7	56.9	305 13.0	21.2	133 04.5	52.0	115 28.7	12.7	Zuben'ubi	137 17.2	S16 02.3
20	167 11.2	75 46.1	56.9	320 16.2	21.1	148 06.4	52.2	130 30.8	12.8		SHA	Mer. Pass.
21	182 13.7	90 45.5 ..	56.9	335 19.5 ..	20.9	163 08.4 ..	52.4	145 33.0 ..	12.9	Venus	270 51.1	14 56
22	197 16.2	105 44.8	57.0	350 22.7	20.7	178 10.3	52.6	160 35.1	13.0	Mars	152 29.3	22 44
23	212 18.6	120 44.2	57.0	5 26.0	20.5	193 12.2	52.8	175 37.3	13.1	Jupiter	341 18.5	10 12
Mer. Pass. 8 57.0		v −0.6 d 0.1		v 3.3 d 0.2		v 1.9 d 0.2		v 2.2 d 0.1		Saturn	323 33.1	11 23

UT	SUN GHA	SUN Dec	MOON GHA	MOON v	MOON Dec	MOON d	MOON HP
7 d h	° ′	° ′	° ′	′	° ′	′	′
00	180 51.2	N16 37.7	286 41.7	11.1	S19 07.7	3.3	55.3
01	195 51.2	38.4	301 11.8	11.0	19 04.4	3.3	55.3
02	210 51.3	39.1	315 41.8	11.0	19 01.1	3.5	55.3
03	225 51.3	.. 39.8	330 11.9	11.1	18 57.6	3.5	55.3
04	240 51.4	40.5	344 42.0	11.0	18 54.1	3.7	55.4
05	255 51.4	41.2	359 12.0	11.1	18 50.4	3.7	55.4
06	270 51.5	N16 41.9	13 42.1	11.0	S18 46.7	3.8	55.4
07	285 51.5	42.5	28 12.1	11.1	18 42.9	3.9	55.4
08	300 51.5	43.2	42 42.2	11.0	18 39.0	4.1	55.5
09	315 51.6	.. 43.9	57 12.2	11.1	18 34.9	4.1	55.5
10	330 51.6	44.6	71 42.3	11.0	18 30.8	4.2	55.5
11	345 51.7	45.3	86 12.3	11.0	18 26.6	4.3	55.6
12	0 51.7	N16 46.0	100 42.3	11.1	S18 22.3	4.4	55.6
13	15 51.8	46.7	115 12.4	11.0	18 17.9	4.5	55.6
14	30 51.8	47.4	129 42.4	11.0	18 13.4	4.6	55.6
15	45 51.8	.. 48.1	144 12.4	11.0	18 08.8	4.7	55.7
16	60 51.9	48.8	158 42.4	11.1	18 04.1	4.8	55.7
17	75 51.9	49.5	173 12.5	11.0	17 59.3	4.8	55.7
18	90 52.0	N16 50.2	187 42.5	11.0	S17 54.5	5.0	55.8
19	105 52.0	50.8	202 12.5	11.0	17 49.5	5.1	55.8
20	120 52.0	51.5	216 42.5	11.0	17 44.4	5.1	55.8
21	135 52.1	.. 52.2	231 12.5	11.0	17 39.3	5.3	55.8
22	150 52.1	52.9	245 42.5	11.0	17 34.0	5.4	55.9
23	165 52.2	53.6	260 12.5	11.0	17 28.6	5.4	55.9
8 00	180 52.2	N16 54.3	274 42.5	11.0	S17 23.2	5.5	55.9
01	195 52.2	55.0	289 12.5	11.0	17 17.7	5.7	56.0
02	210 52.3	55.7	303 42.5	11.0	17 12.0	5.7	56.0
03	225 52.3	.. 56.3	318 12.5	11.0	17 06.3	5.8	56.0
04	240 52.4	57.0	332 42.5	11.0	17 00.5	5.9	56.1
05	255 52.4	57.7	347 12.5	11.0	16 54.6	6.0	56.1
06	270 52.4	N16 58.4	1 42.5	11.0	S16 48.6	6.1	56.1
07	285 52.5	59.1	16 12.5	11.0	16 42.5	6.2	56.1
08	300 52.5	16 59.8	30 42.5	10.9	16 36.3	6.2	56.2
09	315 52.5	17 00.4	45 12.4	11.0	16 30.1	6.4	56.2
10	330 52.6	01.1	59 42.4	11.0	16 23.7	6.5	56.2
11	345 52.6	01.8	74 12.4	11.0	16 17.2	6.5	56.3
12	0 52.7	N17 02.5	88 42.4	11.0	S16 10.7	6.6	56.3
13	15 52.7	03.2	103 12.4	11.0	16 04.1	6.8	56.3
14	30 52.7	03.8	117 42.4	10.9	15 57.3	6.8	56.4
15	45 52.8	.. 04.5	132 12.3	11.0	15 50.5	6.9	56.4
16	60 52.8	05.2	146 42.3	11.0	15 43.6	6.9	56.4
17	75 52.8	05.9	161 12.3	11.0	15 36.7	7.1	56.5
18	90 52.9	N17 06.6	175 42.3	10.9	S15 29.6	7.2	56.5
19	105 52.9	07.2	190 12.2	11.0	15 22.4	7.2	56.5
20	120 52.9	07.9	204 42.2	11.0	15 15.2	7.4	56.6
21	135 53.0	.. 08.6	219 12.2	10.9	15 07.8	7.4	56.6
22	150 53.0	09.3	233 42.1	11.0	15 00.4	7.5	56.6
23	165 53.0	09.9	248 12.1	11.0	14 52.9	7.6	56.7
9 00	180 53.1	N17 10.6	262 42.1	10.9	S14 45.3	7.7	56.7
01	195 53.1	11.3	277 12.0	11.0	14 37.6	7.8	56.7
02	210 53.1	12.0	291 42.0	10.9	14 29.8	7.8	56.8
03	225 53.2	.. 12.6	306 11.9	11.0	14 22.0	7.9	56.8
04	240 53.2	13.3	320 41.9	10.9	14 14.1	8.1	56.9
05	255 53.2	14.0	335 11.8	11.0	14 06.0	8.1	56.9
06	270 53.3	N17 14.6	349 41.8	10.9	S13 57.9	8.1	56.9
07	285 53.3	15.3	4 11.7	10.9	13 49.8	8.3	57.0
08	300 53.3	16.0	18 41.6	11.0	13 41.5	8.4	57.0
09	315 53.4	.. 16.7	33 11.6	10.9	13 33.1	8.4	57.0
10	330 53.4	17.3	47 41.5	10.9	13 24.7	8.5	57.1
11	345 53.4	18.0	62 11.4	10.9	13 16.2	8.6	57.1
12	0 53.5	N17 18.7	76 41.3	10.9	S13 07.6	8.7	57.1
13	15 53.5	19.3	91 11.2	11.0	12 58.9	8.7	57.2
14	30 53.5	20.0	105 41.2	10.9	12 50.2	8.8	57.2
15	45 53.5	.. 20.7	120 11.1	10.8	12 41.4	8.9	57.3
16	60 53.6	21.3	134 40.9	10.9	12 32.5	9.0	57.3
17	75 53.6	22.0	149 10.8	10.9	12 23.5	9.1	57.3
18	90 53.6	N17 22.7	163 40.7	10.9	S12 14.4	9.1	57.4
19	105 53.7	23.3	178 10.6	10.9	12 05.3	9.2	57.4
20	120 53.7	24.0	192 40.5	10.8	11 56.1	9.3	57.5
21	135 53.7	.. 24.7	207 10.3	10.9	11 46.8	9.4	57.5
22	150 53.7	25.3	221 40.2	10.9	11 37.4	9.4	57.5
23	165 53.8	26.0	236 10.0	10.9	S11 28.0	9.5	57.6
	SD 15.9	d 0.7	SD 15.1		15.3		15.6

Left-margin labels: **F R I D A Y** (May 7), **S A T U R D A Y** (May 8), **S U N D A Y** (May 9).

Lat.	Twilight Naut.	Twilight Civil	Sunrise	Moonrise 7	Moonrise 8	Moonrise 9	Moonrise 10
°	h m	h m	h m	h m	h m	h m	h m
N 72	////	////	00 36	■■■	04 34	04 05	03 49
N 70	////	////	01 50	03 46	03 41	03 36	03 32
68	////	////	02 26	02 54	03 08	03 14	03 18
66	////	01 08	02 52	02 22	02 43	02 57	03 07
64	////	01 53	03 12	01 58	02 25	02 43	02 57
62	////	02 22	03 27	01 40	02 09	02 31	02 49
60	01 00	02 44	03 41	01 24	01 56	02 21	02 42
N 58	01 41	03 01	03 52	01 11	01 45	02 12	02 35
56	02 08	03 15	04 02	00 59	01 35	02 04	02 30
54	02 28	03 28	04 11	00 49	01 26	01 57	02 25
52	02 45	03 38	04 18	00 41	01 18	01 51	02 20
50	02 58	03 48	04 25	00 33	01 11	01 45	02 16
45	03 26	04 07	04 40	00 16	00 56	01 33	02 07
N 40	03 46	04 23	04 52	00 02	00 44	01 23	02 00
35	04 02	04 35	05 03	24 33	00 33	01 14	01 53
30	04 15	04 46	05 12	24 24	00 24	01 07	01 47
20	04 36	05 04	05 27	24 08	00 08	00 53	01 37
N 10	04 53	05 19	05 41	23 54	24 42	00 42	01 29
0	05 06	05 31	05 53	23 41	24 31	00 31	01 21
S 10	05 18	05 43	06 05	23 28	24 20	00 20	01 12
20	05 29	05 55	06 18	23 14	24 08	00 08	01 04
30	05 39	06 08	06 33	22 58	23 55	24 54	00 54
35	05 45	06 15	06 42	22 48	23 47	24 48	00 48
40	05 50	06 23	06 51	22 38	23 38	24 41	00 41
45	05 56	06 31	07 02	22 25	23 27	24 33	00 33
S 50	06 02	06 41	07 16	22 10	23 15	24 24	00 24
52	06 05	06 46	07 22	22 02	23 09	24 20	00 20
54	06 08	06 51	07 29	21 54	23 02	24 15	00 15
56	06 11	06 56	07 37	21 45	22 55	24 10	00 10
58	06 14	07 02	07 46	21 35	22 47	24 04	00 04
S 60	06 18	07 09	07 56	21 24	22 38	23 57	25 21

Lat.	Sunset	Twilight Civil	Twilight Naut.	Moonset 7	Moonset 8	Moonset 9	Moonset 10
°	h m	h m	h m	h m	h m	h m	h m
N 72	□	////	////	■■■	07 23	09 36	11 36
N 70	22 09	////	////	06 27	08 16	10 04	11 52
68	21 31	////	////	07 18	08 48	10 24	12 04
66	21 04	22 54	////	07 50	09 11	10 41	12 14
64	20 44	22 04	////	08 13	09 30	10 54	12 23
62	20 28	21 34	////	08 32	09 45	11 05	12 30
60	20 14	21 12	23 00	08 47	09 57	11 14	12 36
N 58	20 02	20 54	22 16	09 00	10 08	11 23	12 42
56	19 52	20 39	21 48	09 11	10 18	11 30	12 47
54	19 43	20 27	21 27	09 21	10 26	11 36	12 51
52	19 36	20 16	21 10	09 30	10 33	11 42	12 55
50	19 29	20 07	20 56	09 37	10 40	11 47	12 58
45	19 13	19 47	20 29	09 54	10 54	11 58	13 06
N 40	19 01	19 31	20 08	10 08	11 06	12 08	13 12
35	18 51	19 18	19 52	10 19	11 16	12 16	13 18
30	18 42	19 07	19 38	10 29	11 25	12 23	13 22
20	18 26	18 49	19 17	10 46	11 40	12 34	13 31
N 10	18 12	18 35	19 00	11 01	11 53	12 45	13 38
0	18 00	18 22	18 47	11 15	12 05	12 55	13 44
S 10	17 48	18 09	18 35	11 29	12 17	13 04	13 51
20	17 34	17 57	18 24	11 44	12 30	13 14	13 58
30	17 20	17 45	18 13	12 01	12 44	13 26	14 06
35	17 11	17 38	18 08	12 11	12 53	13 33	14 11
40	17 01	17 30	18 02	12 22	13 03	13 40	14 16
45	16 50	17 21	17 56	12 35	13 14	13 49	14 22
S 50	16 36	17 11	17 50	12 51	13 27	13 59	14 29
52	16 30	17 07	17 47	12 58	13 34	14 04	14 32
54	16 23	17 02	17 44	13 07	13 41	14 10	14 35
56	16 15	16 56	17 41	13 16	13 48	14 16	14 39
58	16 06	16 50	17 38	13 27	13 57	14 22	14 44
S 60	15 56	16 43	17 34	13 39	14 07	14 30	14 48

Day	SUN Eqn. of Time 00ʰ	SUN Eqn. of Time 12ʰ	SUN Mer. Pass.	MOON Mer. Pass. Upper	MOON Mer. Pass. Lower	Age	Phase
d	m s	m s	h m	h m	h m	d	%
7	03 25	03 27	11 57	05 03	17 28	21	62
8	03 29	03 31	11 56	05 53	18 18	22	52
9	03 32	03 34	11 56	06 43	19 08	23	42

UT	ARIES GHA	VENUS −4.1 GHA	Dec	MARS −1.5 GHA	Dec	JUPITER −2.1 GHA	Dec	SATURN +0.3 GHA	Dec	STARS Name	SHA	Dec
d h 10 00	227 21.1	135 43.6	N25 57.0	20 29.2	S10 20.4	208 14.2	N 6 53.0	190 39.4	N12 13.2	Acamar	315 27.1	S40 18.6
01	242 23.6	150 43.0	57.0	35 32.5	20.2	223 16.1	53.3	205 41.6	13.3	Achernar	335 35.5	S57 14.4
02	257 26.0	165 42.3	57.1	50 35.7	20.0	238 18.0	53.5	220 43.8	13.4	Acrux	173 21.0	S63 05.9
03	272 28.5	180 41.7 ..	57.1	65 39.0 ..	19.8	253 20.0 ..	53.7	235 45.9 ..	13.5	Adhara	255 21.4	S28 58.6
04	287 31.0	195 41.1	57.1	80 42.2	19.7	268 21.9	53.9	250 48.1	13.6	Aldebaran	291 02.3	N16 30.3
05	302 33.4	210 40.5	57.1	95 45.5	19.5	283 23.8	54.1	265 50.2	13.7			
06	317 35.9	225 39.9	N25 57.2	110 48.7	S10 19.3	298 25.8	N 6 54.3	280 52.4	N12 13.8	Alioth	166 29.9	N55 58.0
07	332 38.4	240 39.2	57.2	125 52.0	19.1	313 27.7	54.5	295 54.5	13.9	Alkaid	153 07.1	N49 19.2
08	347 40.8	255 38.6	57.2	140 55.2	19.0	328 29.7	54.7	310 56.7	14.0	Al Na'ir	27 57.5	S46 57.7
M 09	2 43.3	270 38.0 ..	57.2	155 58.5 ..	18.8	343 31.6 ..	54.9	325 58.9 ..	14.1	Alnilam	275 57.8	S 1 12.4
O 10	17 45.7	285 37.4	57.3	171 01.7	18.6	358 33.5	55.1	341 01.0	14.2	Alphard	218 06.8	S 8 39.5
N 11	32 48.2	300 36.7	57.3	186 05.0	18.4	13 35.5	55.4	356 03.2	14.3			
D 12	47 50.7	315 36.1	N25 57.3	201 08.2	S10 18.3	28 37.4	N 6 55.6	11 05.3	N12 14.4	Alphecca	126 19.9	N26 43.1
A 13	62 53.1	330 35.5	57.3	216 11.5	18.1	43 39.3	55.8	26 07.5	14.5	Alpheratz	357 55.1	N29 04.9
Y 14	77 55.6	345 34.9	57.3	231 14.7	17.9	58 41.3	56.0	41 09.6	14.6	Altair	62 18.8	N 8 51.9
15	92 58.1	0 34.3 ..	57.3	246 17.9 ..	17.8	73 43.2 ..	56.2	56 11.8 ..	14.7	Ankaa	353 26.8	S42 18.6
16	108 00.5	15 33.6	57.3	261 21.2	17.6	88 45.1	56.4	71 14.0	14.8	Antares	112 39.3	S26 25.7
17	123 03.0	30 33.0	57.3	276 24.4	17.4	103 47.1	56.6	86 16.1	14.9			
18	138 05.5	45 32.4	N25 57.4	291 27.7	S10 17.2	118 49.0	N 6 56.8	101 18.3	N12 15.0	Arcturus	146 05.4	N19 11.2
19	153 07.9	60 31.8	57.4	306 30.9	17.1	133 50.9	57.0	116 20.4	15.1	Atria	107 50.5	S69 01.4
20	168 10.4	75 31.2	57.4	321 34.1	16.9	148 52.9	57.2	131 22.6	15.2	Avior	234 22.6	S59 30.8
21	183 12.8	90 30.5 ..	57.4	336 37.4 ..	16.7	163 54.8 ..	57.4	146 24.7 ..	15.3	Bellatrix	278 44.0	N 6 20.8
22	198 15.3	105 29.9	57.4	351 40.6	16.6	178 56.8	57.6	161 26.9	15.4	Betelgeuse	271 13.4	N 7 24.2
23	213 17.8	120 29.3	57.4	6 43.8	16.4	193 58.7	57.9	176 29.1	15.5			
11 00	228 20.2	135 28.7	N25 57.4	21 47.1	S10 16.2	209 00.6	N 6 58.1	191 31.2	N12 15.6	Canopus	264 01.4	S52 42.1
01	243 22.7	150 28.1	57.4	36 50.3	16.1	224 02.6	58.3	206 33.4	15.7	Capella	280 51.1	N45 59.8
02	258 25.2	165 27.4	57.4	51 53.5	15.9	239 04.5	58.5	221 35.5	15.8	Deneb	49 38.8	N45 16.4
03	273 27.6	180 26.8 ..	57.4	66 56.8 ..	15.7	254 06.4 ..	58.7	236 37.7 ..	15.9	Denebola	182 44.6	N14 34.6
04	288 30.1	195 26.2	57.4	82 00.0	15.6	269 08.4	58.9	251 39.9	16.0	Diphda	349 07.1	S17 59.5
05	303 32.6	210 25.6	57.4	97 03.2	15.4	284 10.3	59.1	266 42.0	16.1			
06	318 35.0	225 25.0	N25 57.4	112 06.4	S10 15.2	299 12.2	N 6 59.3	281 44.2	N12 16.2	Dubhe	194 04.8	N61 45.5
07	333 37.5	240 24.4	57.4	127 09.7	15.1	314 14.2	59.5	296 46.3	16.3	Elnath	278 26.8	N28 36.3
T 08	348 40.0	255 23.7	57.4	142 12.9	14.9	329 16.1	59.7	311 48.5	16.4	Eltanin	90 50.8	N51 29.2
U 09	3 42.4	270 23.1 ..	57.3	157 16.1 ..	14.7	344 18.1	6 59.9	326 50.6 ..	16.5	Enif	33 57.9	N 9 52.2
E 10	18 44.9	285 22.5	57.3	172 19.3	14.6	359 20.0	7 00.2	341 52.8	16.6	Fomalhaut	15 36.2	S29 37.5
S 11	33 47.3	300 21.9	57.3	187 22.6	14.4	14 21.9	00.4	356 55.0	16.7			
D 12	48 49.8	315 21.3	N25 57.3	202 25.8	S10 14.2	29 23.9	N 7 00.6	11 57.1	N12 16.8	Gacrux	172 12.7	S57 06.7
A 13	63 52.3	330 20.7	57.3	217 29.0	14.1	44 25.8	00.8	26 59.3	16.9	Gienah	176 03.3	S17 32.4
Y 14	78 54.7	345 20.1	57.3	232 32.2	13.9	59 27.7	01.0	42 01.4	17.0	Hadar	149 02.8	S60 22.2
15	93 57.2	0 19.5 ..	57.3	247 35.4 ..	13.7	74 29.7 ..	01.2	57 03.6 ..	17.1	Hamal	328 13.5	N23 27.3
16	108 59.7	15 18.8	57.3	262 38.6	13.6	89 31.6	01.4	72 05.8	17.2	Kaus Aust.	83 58.0	S34 22.9
17	124 02.1	30 18.2	57.2	277 41.9	13.4	104 33.6	01.6	87 07.9	17.3			
18	139 04.6	45 17.6	N25 57.2	292 45.1	S10 13.2	119 35.5	N 7 01.8	102 10.1	N12 17.4	Kochab	137 18.5	N74 09.7
19	154 07.1	60 17.0	57.2	307 48.3	13.1	134 37.4	02.0	117 12.2	17.5	Markab	13 49.4	N15 11.9
20	169 09.5	75 16.4	57.2	322 51.5	12.9	149 39.4	02.2	132 14.4	17.6	Menkar	314 26.8	N 4 05.0
21	184 12.0	90 15.8 ..	57.2	337 54.7 ..	12.8	164 41.3 ..	02.4	147 16.5 ..	17.7	Menkent	148 20.1	S36 22.0
22	199 14.5	105 15.2	57.1	352 57.9	12.6	179 43.2	02.6	162 18.7	17.8	Miaplacidus	221 42.0	S69 43.2
23	214 16.9	120 14.6	57.1	8 01.1	12.4	194 45.2	02.9	177 20.9	17.9			
12 00	229 19.4	135 14.0	N25 57.1	23 04.4	S10 12.3	209 47.1	N 7 03.1	192 23.0	N12 18.0	Mirfak	308 56.6	N49 51.3
01	244 21.8	150 13.4	57.1	38 07.6	12.1	224 49.1	03.3	207 25.2	18.1	Nunki	76 11.6	S26 17.7
02	259 24.3	165 12.7	57.0	53 10.8	12.0	239 51.0	03.5	222 27.3	18.2	Peacock	53 36.3	S56 44.0
03	274 26.8	180 12.1 ..	57.0	68 14.0 ..	11.8	254 52.9 ..	03.7	237 29.5 ..	18.3	Pollux	243 41.3	N28 01.7
04	289 29.2	195 11.5	57.0	83 17.2	11.6	269 54.9	03.9	252 31.7	18.4	Procyon	245 11.3	N 5 13.5
05	304 31.7	210 10.9	56.9	98 20.4	11.5	284 56.8	04.1	267 33.8	18.5			
06	319 34.2	225 10.3	N25 56.9	113 23.6	S10 11.3	299 58.8	N 7 04.3	282 36.0	N12 18.6	Rasalhague	96 16.3	N12 33.6
W 07	334 36.6	240 09.7	56.9	128 26.8	11.2	315 00.7	04.5	297 38.1	18.7	Regulus	207 55.1	N11 58.2
E 08	349 39.1	255 09.1	56.8	143 30.0	11.0	330 02.6	04.7	312 40.3	18.8	Rigel	281 22.9	S 8 12.4
D 09	4 41.6	270 08.5 ..	56.8	158 33.2 ..	10.8	345 04.6 ..	04.9	327 42.4 ..	18.9	Rigil Kent.	140 06.1	S60 49.9
N 10	19 44.0	285 07.9	56.8	173 36.4	10.7	0 06.5	05.1	342 44.6	19.0	Sabik	102 24.8	S15 43.4
E 11	34 46.5	300 07.3	56.7	188 39.6	10.5	15 08.4	05.3	357 46.8	19.1			
S 12	49 48.9	315 06.7	N25 56.7	203 42.8	S10 10.4	30 10.4	N 7 05.5	12 48.9	N12 19.2	Schedar	349 53.4	N56 31.7
D 13	64 51.4	330 06.1	56.6	218 46.0	10.2	45 12.3	05.8	27 51.1	19.3	Shaula	96 36.4	S37 06.0
A 14	79 53.9	345 05.5	56.6	233 49.2	10.1	60 14.3	06.0	42 53.2	19.4	Sirius	258 43.6	S16 43.1
Y 15	94 56.3	0 04.9 ..	56.6	248 52.4 ..	09.9	75 16.2 ..	06.2	57 55.4 ..	19.5	Spica	158 42.5	S11 09.5
16	109 58.8	15 04.3	56.5	263 55.6	09.7	90 18.1	06.4	72 57.6	19.6	Suhail	223 00.5	S43 26.1
17	125 01.3	30 03.7	56.5	278 58.8	09.6	105 20.1	06.6	87 59.7	19.7			
18	140 03.7	45 03.1	N25 56.4	294 01.9	S10 09.4	120 22.0	N 7 06.8	103 01.9	N12 19.8	Vega	80 46.1	N38 46.9
19	155 06.2	60 02.5	56.4	309 05.1	09.3	135 24.0	07.0	118 04.0	19.9	Zuben'ubi	137 17.2	S16 02.3
20	170 08.7	75 01.9	56.3	324 08.3	09.1	150 25.9	07.2	133 06.2	20.0		SHA	Mer. Pass.
21	185 11.1	90 01.3 ..	56.3	339 11.5 ..	09.0	165 27.8 ..	07.4	148 08.3 ..	20.1			
22	200 13.6	105 00.7	56.2	354 14.7	08.8	180 29.8	07.6	163 10.5	20.2	Venus	267 08.4	14 59
23	215 16.1	120 00.1	56.2	9 17.9	08.7	195 31.7	07.8	178 12.7	20.3	Mars	153 26.8	22 28
Mer. Pass. 8 45.2		v −0.6 d 0.0		v 3.2 d 0.2		v 1.9 d 0.2		v 2.2 d 0.1		Jupiter	340 40.4	10 03
										Saturn	323 11.0	11 12

SUN / MOON

UT (d h)	SUN GHA	SUN Dec	MOON GHA	v	Dec	d	HP
10 00	180 53.8	N17 26.7	250 39.9	10.8	S11 18.5	9.6	57.6
01	195 53.8	27.3	265 09.7	10.8	11 08.9	9.6	57.6
02	210 53.8	28.0	279 39.5	10.8	10 59.3	9.8	57.7
03	225 53.9	.. 28.6	294 09.3	10.8	10 49.5	9.8	57.7
04	240 53.9	29.3	308 39.1	10.8	10 39.7	9.8	57.8
05	255 53.9	30.0	323 08.9	10.8	10 29.9	10.0	57.8
06	270 53.9	N17 30.6	337 38.7	10.8	S10 19.9	10.0	57.8
07	285 54.0	31.3	352 08.5	10.7	10 09.9	10.0	57.9
08	300 54.0	31.9	6 38.2	10.8	9 59.9	10.2	57.9
09	315 54.0	.. 32.6	21 08.0	10.7	9 49.7	10.2	58.0
10	330 54.0	33.2	35 37.7	10.7	9 39.5	10.3	58.0
11	345 54.1	33.9	50 07.4	10.7	9 29.2	10.3	58.0
12	0 54.1	N17 34.6	64 37.1	10.7	S 9 18.9	10.4	58.1
13	15 54.1	35.2	79 06.8	10.7	9 08.5	10.5	58.1
14	30 54.1	35.9	93 36.5	10.7	8 58.0	10.5	58.2
15	45 54.2	.. 36.5	108 06.2	10.6	8 47.5	10.6	58.2
16	60 54.2	37.2	122 35.8	10.7	8 36.9	10.7	58.2
17	75 54.2	37.8	137 05.5	10.6	8 26.2	10.7	58.3
18	90 54.2	N17 38.5	151 35.1	10.6	S 8 15.5	10.8	58.3
19	105 54.3	39.1	166 04.7	10.6	8 04.7	10.8	58.4
20	120 54.3	39.8	180 34.3	10.5	7 53.9	10.9	58.4
21	135 54.3	.. 40.4	195 03.8	10.6	7 43.0	10.9	58.4
22	150 54.3	41.1	209 33.4	10.5	7 32.1	11.0	58.5
23	165 54.3	41.8	224 02.9	10.5	7 21.1	11.1	58.5
11 00	180 54.4	N17 42.4	238 32.4	10.5	S 7 10.0	11.1	58.6
01	195 54.4	43.1	253 01.9	10.5	6 58.9	11.2	58.6
02	210 54.4	43.7	267 31.4	10.4	6 47.7	11.2	58.6
03	225 54.4	.. 44.3	282 00.8	10.4	6 36.5	11.3	58.7
04	240 54.4	45.0	296 30.2	10.4	6 25.2	11.3	58.7
05	255 54.5	45.6	310 59.6	10.4	6 13.9	11.4	58.7
06	270 54.5	N17 46.3	325 29.0	10.4	S 6 02.5	11.5	58.8
07	285 54.5	46.9	339 58.4	10.3	5 51.0	11.4	58.8
08	300 54.5	47.6	354 27.7	10.3	5 39.6	11.6	58.9
09	315 54.5	.. 48.2	8 57.0	10.3	5 28.0	11.5	58.9
10	330 54.6	48.9	23 26.3	10.3	5 16.5	11.7	58.9
11	345 54.6	49.5	37 55.6	10.2	5 04.8	11.6	59.0
12	0 54.6	N17 50.2	52 24.8	10.2	S 4 53.2	11.7	59.0
13	15 54.6	50.8	66 54.0	10.2	4 41.5	11.8	59.1
14	30 54.6	51.5	81 23.2	10.1	4 29.7	11.8	59.1
15	45 54.6	.. 52.1	95 52.3	10.1	4 17.9	11.8	59.1
16	60 54.7	52.7	110 21.4	10.1	4 06.1	11.9	59.2
17	75 54.7	53.4	124 50.5	10.1	3 54.2	11.9	59.2
18	90 54.7	N17 54.0	139 19.6	10.0	S 3 42.3	11.9	59.3
19	105 54.7	54.7	153 48.6	10.0	3 30.4	12.0	59.3
20	120 54.7	55.3	168 17.6	10.0	3 18.4	12.1	59.3
21	135 54.7	.. 55.9	182 46.6	9.9	3 06.3	12.0	59.4
22	150 54.8	56.6	197 15.5	9.9	2 54.3	12.1	59.4
23	165 54.8	57.2	211 44.4	9.9	2 42.2	12.1	59.4
12 00	180 54.8	N17 57.9	226 13.3	9.8	S 2 30.1	12.2	59.5
01	195 54.8	58.5	240 42.1	9.8	2 17.9	12.1	59.5
02	210 54.8	59.1	255 10.9	9.8	2 05.8	12.3	59.6
03	225 54.8	17 59.8	269 39.7	9.7	1 53.5	12.2	59.6
04	240 54.8	18 00.4	284 08.4	9.7	1 41.3	12.3	59.6
05	255 54.9	01.0	298 37.1	9.7	1 29.0	12.2	59.7
06	270 54.9	N18 01.7	313 05.8	9.6	S 1 16.8	12.4	59.7
07	285 54.9	02.3	327 34.4	9.5	1 04.4	12.3	59.7
08	300 54.9	02.9	342 02.9	9.6	0 52.1	12.3	59.7
09	315 54.9	.. 03.6	356 31.5	9.5	0 39.8	12.4	59.8
10	330 54.9	04.2	11 00.0	9.4	0 27.4	12.4	59.9
11	345 54.9	04.8	25 28.4	9.4	0 15.0	12.4	59.9
12	0 54.9	N18 05.5	39 56.8	9.4	S 0 02.6	12.5	59.9
13	15 55.0	06.1	54 25.2	9.3	N 0 09.9	12.4	60.0
14	30 55.0	06.7	68 53.5	9.3	0 22.3	12.4	60.0
15	45 55.0	.. 07.4	83 21.8	9.3	0 34.7	12.6	60.0
16	60 55.0	08.0	97 50.1	9.2	0 47.2	12.5	60.1
17	75 55.0	08.6	112 18.3	9.1	0 59.7	12.5	60.1
18	90 55.0	N18 09.2	126 46.4	9.1	N 1 12.2	12.5	60.1
19	105 55.0	09.9	141 14.5	9.1	1 24.7	12.5	60.2
20	120 55.0	10.5	155 42.6	9.0	1 37.2	12.5	60.2
21	135 55.0	.. 11.1	170 10.6	9.0	1 49.7	12.5	60.2
22	150 55.0	11.8	184 38.6	8.9	2 02.2	12.5	60.3
23	165 55.1	12.4	199 06.5	8.9	N 2 14.7	12.5	60.3
	SD 15.9	d 0.6	SD 15.8		16.1		16.3

Days: 10 = MONDAY, 11 = TUESDAY, 12 = WEDNESDAY

Twilight / Sunrise / Moonrise

Lat.	Naut.	Civil	Sunrise	Moonrise 10	11	12	13
N 72	☐	☐	☐	03 49	03 37	03 27	03 16
N 70	////	////	01 27	03 32	03 28	03 24	03 20
68	////	////	02 11	03 18	03 20	03 22	03 23
66	////	00 33	02 40	03 07	03 14	03 20	03 26
64	////	01 37	03 02	02 57	03 08	03 18	03 29
62	////	02 10	03 19	02 49	03 04	03 17	03 31
60	00 29	02 34	03 33	02 42	02 59	03 16	03 32
N 58	01 27	02 52	03 45	02 35	02 56	03 15	03 34
56	01 57	03 08	03 56	02 30	02 52	03 14	03 36
54	02 19	03 21	04 05	02 25	02 49	03 13	03 37
52	02 37	03 32	04 13	02 20	02 47	03 12	03 38
50	02 52	03 42	04 21	02 16	02 44	03 12	03 39
45	03 21	04 03	04 36	02 07	02 39	03 10	03 42
N 40	03 42	04 19	04 49	02 00	02 34	03 09	03 44
35	03 59	04 32	05 00	01 53	02 31	03 08	03 46
30	04 13	04 44	05 10	01 47	02 27	03 07	03 47
20	04 35	05 02	05 26	01 37	02 21	03 05	03 50
N 10	04 52	05 18	05 40	01 29	02 16	03 03	03 52
0	05 06	05 31	05 53	01 21	02 11	03 02	03 55
S 10	05 18	05 44	06 06	01 12	02 06	03 01	03 57
20	05 30	05 56	06 19	01 04	02 01	02 59	04 00
30	05 41	06 10	06 35	00 54	01 55	02 58	04 03
35	05 47	06 17	06 44	00 48	01 51	02 57	04 05
40	05 53	06 25	06 54	00 41	01 47	02 56	04 07
45	05 59	06 34	07 06	00 33	01 43	02 54	04 09
S 50	06 06	06 45	07 20	00 24	01 37	02 53	04 12
52	06 09	06 50	07 27	00 20	01 34	02 52	04 13
54	06 12	06 55	07 35	00 15	01 32	02 52	04 14
56	06 16	07 01	07 43	00 10	01 29	02 51	04 16
58	06 20	07 08	07 52	00 04	01 25	02 50	04 18
S 60	06 24	07 15	08 03	25 21	01 21	02 49	04 20

Sunset / Twilight / Moonset

Lat.	Sunset	Civil	Naut.	Moonset 10	11	12	13
N 72	☐	☐	☐	11 36	13 34	15 34	17 39
N 70	22 33	////	////	11 52	13 41	15 33	17 30
68	21 46	////	////	12 04	13 47	15 33	17 22
66	21 16	23 43	////	12 14	13 52	15 32	17 16
64	20 54	22 21	////	12 23	13 56	15 32	17 11
62	20 36	21 46	////	12 30	13 59	15 31	17 07
60	20 21	21 22	23 44	12 36	14 02	15 31	17 03
N 58	20 09	21 02	22 31	12 42	14 05	15 31	17 00
56	19 58	20 47	21 59	12 47	14 07	15 31	16 57
54	19 49	20 33	21 36	12 51	14 09	15 30	16 54
52	19 40	20 22	21 17	12 55	14 11	15 30	16 52
50	19 33	20 12	21 02	12 58	14 13	15 30	16 50
45	19 17	19 51	20 33	13 06	14 16	15 29	16 45
N 40	19 04	19 34	20 12	13 12	14 19	15 29	16 41
35	18 53	19 21	19 55	13 18	14 22	15 29	16 38
30	18 43	19 09	19 41	13 22	14 24	15 28	16 35
20	18 27	18 51	19 18	13 31	14 28	15 28	16 29
N 10	18 13	18 35	19 01	13 38	14 32	15 27	16 25
0	18 00	18 22	18 47	13 44	14 35	15 27	16 21
S 10	17 47	18 09	18 34	13 51	14 38	15 26	16 16
20	17 33	17 56	18 23	13 58	14 42	15 26	16 12
30	17 17	17 43	18 11	14 06	14 45	15 25	16 06
35	17 08	17 35	18 06	14 11	14 48	15 25	16 03
40	16 58	17 27	18 00	14 16	14 50	15 24	16 00
45	16 46	17 18	17 53	14 22	14 53	15 24	15 56
S 50	16 32	17 07	17 46	14 29	14 56	15 23	15 52
52	16 25	17 02	17 43	14 32	14 58	15 23	15 49
54	16 18	16 57	17 40	14 35	14 59	15 23	15 47
56	16 09	16 51	17 36	14 39	15 01	15 22	15 45
58	16 00	16 44	17 32	14 44	15 03	15 22	15 42
S 60	15 49	16 37	17 28	14 48	15 05	15 21	15 38

SUN / MOON

Day	Eqn. of Time 00h	Eqn. of Time 12h	Mer. Pass.	Mer. Pass. Upper	Mer. Pass. Lower	Age	Phase
	m s	m s	h m	h m	h m	d	%
10	03 35	03 36	11 56	07 33	19 58	24	32
11	03 37	03 38	11 56	08 23	20 49	25	22
12	03 39	03 40	11 56	09 14	21 41	26	13

UT	ARIES GHA	VENUS −4.2 GHA	Dec	MARS −1.4 GHA	Dec	JUPITER −2.1 GHA	Dec	SATURN +0.3 GHA	Dec	STARS Name	SHA	Dec
13 00	230 18.5	134 59.5	N25 56.1	24 21.1	S10 08.5	210 33.7	N 7 08.0	193 14.8	N12 20.4	Acamar	315 27.1	S40 18.6
01	245 21.0	149 58.9	56.1	39 24.3	08.4	225 35.6	08.2	208 17.0	20.5	Achernar	335 35.5	S57 14.4
02	260 23.4	164 58.3	56.0	54 27.4	08.2	240 37.5	08.4	223 19.1	20.6	Acrux	173 21.0	S63 05.9
03	275 25.9	179 57.7 ..	56.0	69 30.6 ..	08.1	255 39.5 ..	08.6	238 21.3 ..	20.7	Adhara	255 21.4	S28 58.6
04	290 28.4	194 57.1	55.9	84 33.8	07.9	270 41.4	08.9	253 23.5	20.8	Aldebaran	291 02.3	N16 30.3
05	305 30.8	209 56.5	55.8	99 37.0	07.8	285 43.4	09.1	268 25.6	20.9			
06	320 33.3	224 55.9	N25 55.8	114 40.2	S10 07.6	300 45.3	N 7 09.3	283 27.8	N12 21.0	Alioth	166 29.9	N55 58.0
07	335 35.8	239 55.3	55.7	129 43.3	07.5	315 47.2	09.5	298 29.9	21.1	Alkaid	153 07.1	N49 19.2
T 08	350 38.2	254 54.7	55.7	144 46.5	07.3	330 49.2	09.7	313 32.1	21.2	Al Na'ir	27 57.5	S46 57.7
H 09	5 40.7	269 54.1 ..	55.6	159 49.7 ..	07.2	345 51.1 ..	09.9	328 34.3 ..	21.3	Alnilam	275 57.8	S 1 12.3
U 10	20 43.2	284 53.5	55.5	174 52.9	07.0	0 53.1	10.1	343 36.4	21.4	Alphard	218 06.9	S 8 39.5
R 11	35 45.6	299 52.9	55.5	189 56.0	06.9	15 55.0	10.3	358 38.6	21.5			
S 12	50 48.1	314 52.3	N25 55.3	204 59.2	S10 06.7	30 56.9	N 7 10.5	13 40.7	N12 21.6	Alphecca	126 19.9	N26 43.1
D 13	65 50.5	329 51.7	55.3	220 02.4	06.6	45 58.9	10.7	28 42.9	21.7	Alpheratz	357 55.0	N29 04.9
A 14	80 53.0	344 51.1	55.3	235 05.5	06.4	61 00.8	10.9	43 45.0	21.8	Altair	62 18.7	N 8 51.9
Y 15	95 55.5	359 50.5 ..	55.2	250 08.7 ..	06.3	76 02.8 ..	11.1	58 47.2 ..	21.9	Ankaa	353 26.8	S42 18.6
16	110 57.9	14 49.9	55.1	265 11.9	06.1	91 04.7	11.3	73 49.4	22.0	Antares	112 39.3	S26 25.7
17	126 00.4	29 49.3	55.1	280 15.1	06.0	106 06.7	11.5	88 51.5	22.1			
18	141 02.9	44 48.7	N25 55.0	295 18.2	S10 05.8	121 08.6	N 7 11.7	103 53.7	N12 22.2	Arcturus	146 05.4	N19 11.2
19	156 05.3	59 48.2	54.9	310 21.4	05.7	136 10.5	11.9	118 55.8	22.3	Atria	107 50.5	S69 01.4
20	171 07.8	74 47.6	54.8	325 24.5	05.5	151 12.5	12.1	133 58.0	22.4	Avior	234 22.7	S59 30.8
21	186 10.3	89 47.0 ..	54.8	340 27.7 ..	05.4	166 14.4 ..	12.3	149 00.2 ..	22.5	Bellatrix	278 44.1	N 6 20.8
22	201 12.7	104 46.4	54.7	355 30.9	05.2	181 16.4	12.6	164 02.3	22.6	Betelgeuse	271 13.4	N 7 24.2
23	216 15.2	119 45.8	54.6	10 34.0	05.1	196 18.3	12.8	179 04.5	22.7			
14 00	231 17.7	134 45.2	N25 54.5	25 37.2	S10 04.9	211 20.2	N 7 13.0	194 06.6	N12 22.8	Canopus	264 01.4	S52 42.0
01	246 20.1	149 44.6	54.4	40 40.3	04.8	226 22.2	13.2	209 08.8	22.9	Capella	280 51.1	N45 59.8
02	261 22.6	164 44.0	54.4	55 43.5	04.7	241 24.1	13.4	224 11.0	23.0	Deneb	49 38.8	N45 16.4
03	276 25.0	179 43.4 ..	54.3	70 46.7 ..	04.5	256 26.1 ..	13.6	239 13.1 ..	23.1	Denebola	182 44.6	N14 34.6
04	291 27.5	194 42.9	54.2	85 49.8	04.4	271 28.0	13.8	254 15.3	23.2	Diphda	349 07.1	S17 59.5
05	306 30.0	209 42.3	54.1	100 53.0	04.2	286 30.0	14.0	269 17.4	23.3			
06	321 32.4	224 41.7	N25 54.0	115 56.1	S10 04.1	301 31.9	N 7 14.2	284 19.6	N12 23.4	Dubhe	194 04.9	N61 45.5
07	336 34.9	239 41.1	53.9	130 59.3	03.9	316 33.8	14.4	299 21.8	23.5	Elnath	278 26.8	N28 36.3
08	351 37.4	254 40.5	53.8	146 02.4	03.8	331 35.8	14.6	314 23.9	23.6	Eltanin	90 50.8	N51 29.3
F 09	6 39.8	269 39.9 ..	53.7	161 05.6 ..	03.7	346 37.7 ..	14.8	329 26.1 ..	23.7	Enif	33 57.9	N 9 52.2
R 10	21 42.3	284 39.3	53.7	176 08.7	03.5	1 39.7	15.0	344 28.2	23.8	Fomalhaut	15 36.2	S29 37.5
I 11	36 44.8	299 38.8	53.6	191 11.9	03.4	16 41.6	15.2	359 30.4	23.9			
D 12	51 47.2	314 38.2	N25 53.5	206 15.0	S10 03.2	31 43.6	N 7 15.4	14 32.6	N12 24.0	Gacrux	172 12.7	S57 06.7
A 13	66 49.7	329 37.6	53.4	221 18.2	03.1	46 45.5	15.6	29 34.7	24.1	Gienah	176 03.4	S17 32.4
Y 14	81 52.2	344 37.0	53.3	236 21.3	03.0	61 47.4	15.8	44 36.9	24.1	Hadar	149 02.8	S60 22.2
15	96 54.6	359 36.4 ..	53.2	251 24.4 ..	02.8	76 49.4 ..	16.0	59 39.0 ..	24.2	Hamal	328 13.4	N23 27.3
16	111 57.1	14 35.8	53.1	266 27.6	02.7	91 51.3	16.2	74 41.2	24.3	Kaus Aust.	83 58.0	S34 22.9
17	126 59.5	29 35.3	53.0	281 30.7	02.5	106 53.3	16.4	89 43.4	24.4			
18	142 02.0	44 34.7	N25 52.9	296 33.9	S10 02.4	121 55.2	N 7 16.7	104 45.5	N12 24.5	Kochab	137 18.5	N74 09.7
19	157 04.5	59 34.1	52.8	311 37.0	02.3	136 57.2	16.9	119 47.7	24.6	Markab	13 49.4	N15 11.9
20	172 06.9	74 33.5	52.7	326 40.1	02.1	151 59.1	17.1	134 49.8	24.7	Menkar	314 26.8	N 4 05.0
21	187 09.4	89 32.9 ..	52.6	341 43.3 ..	02.0	167 01.0 ..	17.3	149 52.0 ..	24.8	Menkent	148 20.1	S36 22.0
22	202 11.9	104 32.4	52.5	356 46.4	01.9	182 03.0	17.5	164 54.2	24.9	Miaplacidus	221 42.0	S69 43.2
23	217 14.3	119 31.8	52.4	11 49.6	01.7	197 04.9	17.7	179 56.3	25.0			
15 00	232 16.8	134 31.2	N25 52.3	26 52.7	S10 01.6	212 06.9	N 7 17.9	194 58.5	N12 25.1	Mirfak	308 56.5	N49 51.3
01	247 19.3	149 30.6	52.1	41 55.8	01.5	227 08.8	18.1	210 00.6	25.2	Nunki	76 11.6	S26 17.7
02	262 21.7	164 30.1	52.0	56 58.9	01.3	242 10.8	18.3	225 02.8	25.3	Peacock	53 36.3	S56 44.0
03	277 24.2	179 29.5 ..	51.9	72 02.1 ..	01.2	257 12.7 ..	18.5	240 05.0 ..	25.4	Pollux	243 41.3	N28 01.7
04	292 26.6	194 28.9	51.8	87 05.2	01.1	272 14.6	18.7	255 07.1	25.5	Procyon	245 11.4	N 5 13.5
05	307 29.1	209 28.3	51.7	102 08.3	00.9	287 16.6	18.9	270 09.3	25.6			
06	322 31.6	224 27.7	N25 51.6	117 11.5	S10 00.8	302 18.5	N 7 19.1	285 11.4	N12 25.7	Rasalhague	96 16.3	N12 33.6
07	337 34.0	239 27.2	51.5	132 14.6	00.7	317 20.5	19.3	300 13.6	25.8	Regulus	207 55.1	N11 58.2
S 08	352 36.5	254 26.6	51.4	147 17.7	00.5	332 22.4	19.5	315 15.8	25.9	Rigel	281 22.9	S 8 12.4
A 09	7 39.0	269 26.0 ..	51.2	162 20.8 ..	00.4	347 24.4 ..	19.7	330 17.9 ..	26.0	Rigil Kent.	140 06.1	S60 49.9
T 10	22 41.4	284 25.5	51.1	177 23.9	00.3	2 26.3	19.9	345 20.1	26.1	Sabik	102 24.8	S15 43.4
U 11	37 43.9	299 24.9	51.0	192 27.1	00.1	17 28.3	20.1	0 22.2	26.2			
R 12	52 46.4	314 24.3	N25 50.9	207 30.2	S10 00.0	32 30.2	N 7 20.3	15 24.4	N12 26.3	Schedar	349 53.4	N56 31.7
D 13	67 48.8	329 23.7	50.8	222 33.3	9 59.9	47 32.1	20.5	30 26.6	26.4	Shaula	96 36.4	S37 06.1
A 14	82 51.3	344 23.2	50.6	237 36.4	59.7	62 34.1	20.7	45 28.7	26.5	Sirius	258 43.6	S16 43.1
Y 15	97 53.8	359 22.6 ..	50.5	252 39.5 ..	59.6	77 36.0 ..	20.9	60 30.9 ..	26.6	Spica	158 42.5	S11 09.5
16	112 56.2	14 22.0	50.4	267 42.7	59.5	92 38.0	21.1	75 33.0	26.7	Suhail	223 00.5	S43 26.1
17	127 58.7	29 21.5	50.3	282 45.8	59.3	107 39.9	21.3	90 35.2	26.8			
18	143 01.1	44 20.9	N25 50.1	297 48.9	S 9 59.2	122 41.9	N 7 21.5	105 37.4	N12 26.9	Vega	80 46.1	N38 46.9
19	158 03.6	59 20.3	50.0	312 52.0	59.1	137 43.8	21.7	120 39.5	27.0	Zuben'ubi	137 17.2	S16 02.3
20	173 06.1	74 19.7	49.9	327 55.1	59.0	152 45.8	21.9	135 41.7	27.1		SHA	Mer. Pass.
21	188 08.5	89 19.2 ..	49.7	342 58.2 ..	58.8	167 47.7 ..	22.1	150 43.8 ..	27.2	Venus	263 27.6	15 02
22	203 11.0	104 18.6	49.6	358 01.3	58.7	182 49.6	22.4	165 46.0	27.3	Mars	154 19.5	22 13
23	218 13.5	119 18.0	49.5	13 04.4	58.6	197 51.6	22.6	180 48.2	27.4	Jupiter	340 02.6	9 53
Mer. Pass. 8 33.4		v −0.6 d 0.1		v 3.1 d 0.1		v 1.9 d 0.2		v 2.2 d 0.1		Saturn	322 49.0	11 02

SUN and MOON

UT	SUN GHA	SUN Dec	MOON GHA	v	Dec	d	HP
d h	° ′	° ′	° ′	′	° ′	′	′
13 00	180 55.1	N18 13.0	213 34.4	8.8	N 2 27.2	12.5	60.3
01	195 55.1	13.6	228 02.2	8.8	2 39.7	12.5	60.4
02	210 55.1	14.3	242 30.0	8.7	2 52.2	12.5	60.4
03	225 55.1	.. 14.9	256 57.7	8.6	3 04.7	12.5	60.4
04	240 55.1	15.5	271 25.3	8.7	3 17.2	12.5	60.4
05	255 55.1	16.1	285 53.0	8.5	3 29.7	12.5	60.5
06	270 55.1	N18 16.8	300 20.5	8.5	N 3 42.2	12.5	60.5
07	285 55.1	17.4	314 48.0	8.5	3 54.7	12.5	60.5
08	300 55.1	18.0	329 15.5	8.4	4 07.2	12.4	60.6
09	315 55.1	.. 18.6	343 42.9	8.4	4 19.6	12.5	60.6
10	330 55.1	19.2	358 10.3	8.3	4 32.1	12.4	60.6
11	345 55.1	19.9	12 37.6	8.2	4 44.5	12.4	60.6
12	0 55.2	N18 20.5	27 04.8	8.2	N 4 56.9	12.4	60.7
13	15 55.2	21.1	41 32.0	8.1	5 09.3	12.3	60.7
14	30 55.2	21.7	55 59.1	8.1	5 21.6	12.4	60.7
15	45 55.2	.. 22.3	70 26.2	8.0	5 34.0	12.3	60.8
16	60 55.2	22.9	84 53.2	8.0	5 46.3	12.3	60.8
17	75 55.2	23.6	99 20.2	7.9	5 58.6	12.3	60.8
18	90 55.2	N18 24.2	113 47.1	7.9	N 6 10.9	12.2	60.8
19	105 55.2	24.8	128 14.0	7.7	6 23.1	12.2	60.9
20	120 55.2	25.4	142 40.7	7.8	6 35.3	12.2	60.9
21	135 55.2	.. 26.0	157 07.5	7.6	6 47.5	12.1	60.9
22	150 55.2	26.6	171 34.1	7.7	6 59.6	12.1	60.9
23	165 55.2	27.2	186 00.8	7.5	7 11.7	12.1	60.9
14 00	180 55.2	N18 27.9	200 27.3	7.5	N 7 23.8	12.0	61.0
01	195 55.2	28.5	214 53.8	7.4	7 35.8	12.0	61.0
02	210 55.2	29.1	229 20.2	7.4	7 47.8	12.0	61.0
03	225 55.2	.. 29.7	243 46.6	7.3	7 59.8	11.9	61.0
04	240 55.2	30.3	258 12.9	7.3	8 11.7	11.9	61.1
05	255 55.2	30.9	272 39.2	7.2	8 23.6	11.8	61.1
06	270 55.2	N18 31.5	287 05.4	7.1	N 8 35.4	11.7	61.1
07	285 55.2	32.1	301 31.5	7.1	8 47.1	11.8	61.1
08	300 55.2	32.7	315 57.6	7.0	8 58.9	11.6	61.1
09	315 55.2	.. 33.3	330 23.6	6.9	9 10.5	11.6	61.1
10	330 55.2	34.0	344 49.5	6.9	9 22.1	11.6	61.2
11	345 55.2	34.6	359 15.4	6.8	9 33.7	11.5	61.2
12	0 55.2	N18 35.2	13 41.2	6.8	N 9 45.2	11.4	61.2
13	15 55.2	35.8	28 07.0	6.7	9 56.6	11.4	61.2
14	30 55.2	36.4	42 32.7	6.6	10 08.0	11.3	61.2
15	45 55.2	.. 37.0	56 58.3	6.6	10 19.3	11.3	61.2
16	60 55.2	37.6	71 23.9	6.5	10 30.6	11.2	61.2
17	75 55.2	38.2	85 49.4	6.5	10 41.8	11.1	61.3
18	90 55.2	N18 38.8	100 14.9	6.4	N10 52.9	11.1	61.3
19	105 55.2	39.4	114 40.3	6.3	11 04.0	10.9	61.3
20	120 55.2	40.0	129 05.6	6.3	11 14.9	11.0	61.3
21	135 55.2	.. 40.6	143 30.9	6.2	11 25.9	10.8	61.3
22	150 55.2	41.2	157 56.1	6.1	11 36.7	10.7	61.3
23	165 55.2	41.8	172 21.2	6.1	11 47.4	10.7	61.3
15 00	180 55.2	N18 42.4	186 46.3	6.0	N11 58.1	10.6	61.3
01	195 55.2	43.0	201 11.3	6.0	12 08.7	10.6	61.3
02	210 55.2	43.6	215 36.3	5.9	12 19.3	10.4	61.4
03	225 55.2	.. 44.2	230 01.2	5.9	12 29.7	10.4	61.4
04	240 55.2	44.8	244 26.1	5.7	12 40.1	10.2	61.4
05	255 55.2	45.4	258 50.8	5.8	12 50.3	10.2	61.4
06	270 55.2	N18 46.0	273 15.6	5.6	N13 00.5	10.1	61.4
07	285 55.2	46.6	287 40.2	5.7	13 10.6	10.0	61.4
08	300 55.1	47.2	302 04.9	5.5	13 20.6	9.9	61.4
09	315 55.1	.. 47.8	316 29.4	5.5	13 30.5	9.9	61.4
10	330 55.1	48.4	330 53.9	5.4	13 40.4	9.7	61.4
11	345 55.1	49.0	345 18.3	5.4	13 50.1	9.6	61.4
12	0 55.1	N18 49.5	359 42.7	5.4	N13 59.7	9.6	61.4
13	15 55.1	50.1	14 07.1	5.2	14 09.2	9.5	61.4
14	30 55.1	50.7	28 31.3	5.3	14 18.7	9.3	61.4
15	45 55.1	.. 51.3	42 55.6	5.1	14 28.0	9.2	61.4
16	60 55.1	51.9	57 19.7	5.2	14 37.2	9.2	61.4
17	75 55.1	52.5	71 43.9	5.0	14 46.4	9.0	61.4
18	90 55.1	N18 53.1	86 07.9	5.0	N14 55.4	8.9	61.4
19	105 55.1	53.7	100 31.9	5.0	15 04.3	8.8	61.4
20	120 55.1	54.3	114 55.9	4.9	15 13.1	8.7	61.4
21	135 55.1	.. 54.9	129 19.8	4.9	15 21.8	8.6	61.4
22	150 55.0	55.4	143 43.7	4.8	15 30.4	8.6	61.4
23	165 55.0	56.0	158 07.5	4.8	N15 38.8	8.4	61.4
	SD 15.9	d 0.6	SD 16.5		16.7		16.7

(Thursday = 13, Friday = 14, Saturday = 15)

Twilight — Sunrise — Moonrise

Lat.	Naut.	Civil	Sunrise	13	14	15	16
°	h m	h m	h m	h m	h m	h m	h m
N 72	◻	◻	◻	03 16	03 05	02 51	02 30
N 70	////	////	00 59	03 20	03 16	03 12	03 09
68	////	////	01 55	03 23	03 26	03 29	03 36
66	////	////	02 28	03 26	03 33	03 43	03 57
64	////	01 18	02 52	03 29	03 40	03 54	04 14
62	////	01 57	03 11	03 31	03 46	04 04	04 28
60	////	02 24	03 26	03 32	03 51	04 12	04 40
N 58	01 10	02 44	03 39	03 34	03 55	04 20	04 51
56	01 46	03 01	03 50	03 36	03 59	04 26	05 00
54	02 11	03 15	04 00	03 37	04 03	04 32	05 08
52	02 30	03 27	04 08	03 38	04 06	04 37	05 15
50	02 46	03 37	04 16	03 39	04 09	04 42	05 21
45	03 16	03 59	04 33	03 42	04 15	04 53	05 36
N 40	03 38	04 16	04 46	03 44	04 21	05 02	05 47
35	03 56	04 30	04 58	03 46	04 26	05 09	05 57
30	04 10	04 42	05 08	03 47	04 30	05 16	06 06
20	04 33	05 01	05 25	03 50	04 37	05 27	06 21
N 10	04 51	05 17	05 39	03 52	04 44	05 38	06 35
0	05 06	05 31	05 53	03 55	04 50	05 47	06 47
S 10	05 19	05 44	06 06	03 57	04 56	05 57	07 00
20	05 31	05 57	06 21	04 00	05 03	06 07	07 13
30	05 43	06 11	06 37	04 03	05 10	06 19	07 29
35	05 49	06 19	06 46	04 05	05 15	06 26	07 38
40	05 55	06 28	06 57	04 07	05 20	06 34	07 49
45	06 02	06 38	07 09	04 09	05 26	06 44	08 01
S 50	06 10	06 49	07 25	04 12	05 33	06 55	08 16
52	06 13	06 54	07 32	04 13	05 36	07 00	08 23
54	06 17	07 00	07 40	04 14	05 40	07 06	08 31
56	06 20	07 06	07 48	04 16	05 44	07 13	08 40
58	06 24	07 13	07 58	04 18	05 48	07 20	08 50
S 60	06 29	07 21	08 10	04 20	05 53	07 28	09 01

Sunset — Twilight — Moonset

Lat.	Sunset	Civil	Naut.	13	14	15	16
°	h m	h m	h m	h m	h m	h m	h m
N 72	◻	◻	◻	17 39	19 51	22 17	◻
N 70	23 05	////	////	17 30	19 31	21 39	23 50
68	22 02	////	////	17 22	19 16	21 12	23 05
66	21 28	////	////	17 16	19 04	20 52	22 36
64	21 03	22 40	////	17 11	18 54	20 36	22 13
62	20 44	21 59	////	17 07	18 45	20 23	21 56
60	20 28	21 31	////	17 03	18 38	20 12	21 41
N 58	20 15	21 10	22 48	17 00	18 31	20 02	21 28
56	20 04	20 54	22 10	16 57	18 25	19 54	21 18
54	19 54	20 39	21 44	16 54	18 20	19 46	21 08
52	19 45	20 27	21 25	16 52	18 16	19 39	21 00
50	19 37	20 17	21 09	16 50	18 11	19 33	20 52
45	19 21	19 55	20 38	16 45	18 02	19 20	20 36
N 40	19 07	19 38	20 15	16 41	17 55	19 10	20 23
35	18 55	19 23	19 57	16 38	17 49	19 00	20 11
30	18 45	19 12	19 43	16 35	17 43	18 52	20 02
20	18 28	18 52	19 20	16 29	17 33	18 39	19 45
N 10	18 14	18 36	19 02	16 25	17 25	18 27	19 30
0	18 00	18 22	18 47	16 21	17 17	18 15	19 16
S 10	17 46	18 08	18 34	16 16	17 09	18 04	19 02
20	17 32	17 55	18 22	16 12	17 00	17 52	18 48
30	17 16	17 41	18 11	16 06	16 51	17 38	18 31
35	17 06	17 33	18 04	16 03	16 45	17 31	18 21
40	16 55	17 24	17 57	16 00	16 39	17 22	18 10
45	16 43	17 15	17 50	15 56	16 31	17 11	17 57
S 50	16 28	17 03	17 42	15 52	16 23	16 59	17 41
52	16 20	16 58	17 39	15 49	16 19	16 53	17 34
54	16 12	16 52	17 35	15 47	16 14	16 46	17 26
56	16 04	16 46	17 32	15 45	16 09	16 39	17 16
58	15 54	16 39	17 27	15 42	16 04	16 31	17 06
S 60	15 42	16 31	17 23	15 38	15 58	16 22	16 54

SUN and MOON

Day	Eqn. of Time 00h	Eqn. of Time 12h	Mer. Pass.	Mer. Pass. Upper	Mer. Pass. Lower	Age	Phase
d	m s	m s	h m	h m	h m	d	%
13	03 40	03 41	11 56	10 08	22 35	27	6	●
14	03 41	03 41	11 56	11 03	23 32	28	2	
15	03 41	03 41	11 56	12 01	24 31	29	0	

UT	ARIES	VENUS −4.2		MARS −1.4		JUPITER −2.1		SATURN +0.4		STARS		
d h	GHA	GHA	Dec	GHA	Dec	GHA	Dec	GHA	Dec	Name	SHA	Dec
16 00	233 15.9	134 17.5	N25 49.3	28 07.5	S 9 58.5	212 53.5	N 7 22.8	195 50.3	N12 27.5	Acamar	315 27.1	S40 18.6
01	248 18.4	149 16.9	49.2	43 10.6	58.3	227 55.5	23.0	210 52.5	27.6	Achernar	335 35.5	S57 14.4
02	263 20.9	164 16.4	49.1	58 13.7	58.2	242 57.4	23.2	225 54.6	27.7	Acrux	173 21.0	S63 05.9
03	278 23.3	179 15.8 ..	48.9	73 16.8 ..	58.1	257 59.4 ..	23.4	240 56.8 ..	27.8	Adhara	255 21.4	S28 58.5
04	293 25.8	194 15.2	48.8	88 19.9	58.0	273 01.3	23.6	255 59.0	27.9	Aldebaran	291 02.3	N16 30.3
05	308 28.3	209 14.7	48.7	103 23.0	57.8	288 03.3	23.8	271 01.1	28.0			
06	323 30.7	224 14.1	N25 48.5	118 26.1	S 9 57.7	303 05.2	N 7 24.0	286 03.3	N12 28.1	Alioth	166 29.9	N55 58.1
07	338 33.2	239 13.5	48.4	133 29.2	57.6	318 07.2	24.2	301 05.4	28.1	Alkaid	153 07.1	N49 19.2
08	353 35.6	254 13.0	48.2	148 32.3	57.5	333 09.1	24.4	316 07.6	28.2	Al Na'ir	27 57.5	S46 57.7
S 09	8 38.1	269 12.4 ..	48.1	163 35.4 ..	57.3	348 11.1 ..	24.6	331 09.8 ..	28.3	Alnilam	275 57.8	S 1 12.3
U 10	23 40.6	284 11.8	47.9	178 38.5	57.2	3 13.0	24.8	346 11.9	28.4	Alphard	218 06.9	S 8 39.5
N 11	38 43.0	299 11.3	47.8	193 41.6	57.1	18 14.9	25.0	1 14.1	28.5			
D 12	53 45.5	314 10.7	N25 47.7	208 44.7	S 9 57.0	33 16.9	N 7 25.2	16 16.2	N12 28.6	Alphecca	126 19.9	N26 43.1
A 13	68 48.0	329 10.2	47.5	223 47.8	56.9	48 18.8	25.4	31 18.4	28.7	Alpheratz	357 55.0	N29 04.9
Y 14	83 50.4	344 09.6	47.4	238 50.9	56.7	63 20.8	25.6	46 20.6	28.8	Altair	62 18.7	N 8 51.9
15	98 52.9	359 09.1 ..	47.2	253 54.0 ..	56.6	78 22.7 ..	25.8	61 22.7 ..	28.9	Ankaa	353 26.8	S42 18.6
16	113 55.4	14 08.5	47.1	268 57.0	56.5	93 24.7	26.0	76 24.9	29.0	Antares	112 39.3	S26 25.7
17	128 57.8	29 07.9	46.9	284 00.1	56.4	108 26.6	26.2	91 27.1	29.1			
18	144 00.3	44 07.4	N25 46.7	299 03.2	S 9 56.3	123 28.6	N 7 26.4	106 29.2	N12 29.2	Arcturus	146 05.4	N19 11.2
19	159 02.8	59 06.8	46.6	314 06.3	56.1	138 30.5	26.6	121 31.4	29.3	Atria	107 50.5	S69 01.4
20	174 05.2	74 06.3	46.4	329 09.4	56.0	153 32.5	26.8	136 33.5	29.4	Avior	234 22.7	S59 30.8
21	189 07.7	89 05.7 ..	46.3	344 12.5 ..	55.9	168 34.4 ..	27.0	151 35.7 ..	29.5	Bellatrix	278 44.1	N 6 20.8
22	204 10.1	104 05.2	46.1	359 15.5	55.8	183 36.4	27.2	166 37.9	29.6	Betelgeuse	271 13.4	N 7 24.2
23	219 12.6	119 04.6	46.0	14 18.6	55.7	198 38.3	27.4	181 40.0	29.7			
17 00	234 15.1	134 04.1	N25 45.8	29 21.7	S 9 55.5	213 40.3	N 7 27.6	196 42.2	N12 29.8	Canopus	264 01.4	S52 42.0
01	249 17.5	149 03.5	45.6	44 24.8	55.4	228 42.2	27.8	211 44.3	29.9	Capella	280 51.1	N45 59.7
02	264 20.0	164 02.9	45.5	59 27.8	55.3	243 44.2	28.0	226 46.5	30.0	Deneb	49 38.8	N45 16.4
03	279 22.5	179 02.4 ..	45.3	74 30.9 ..	55.2	258 46.1 ..	28.2	241 48.7 ..	30.1	Denebola	182 44.6	N14 34.6
04	294 24.9	194 01.8	45.2	89 34.0	55.1	273 48.0	28.4	256 50.8	30.2	Diphda	349 07.1	S17 59.5
05	309 27.4	209 01.3	45.0	104 37.1	55.0	288 50.0	28.6	271 53.0	30.3			
06	324 29.9	224 00.7	N25 44.8	119 40.1	S 9 54.9	303 51.9	N 7 28.8	286 55.2	N12 30.4	Dubhe	194 04.9	N61 45.6
07	339 32.3	239 00.2	44.7	134 43.2	54.7	318 53.9	29.0	301 57.3	30.5	Elnath	278 26.8	N28 36.3
08	354 34.8	253 59.6	44.5	149 46.3	54.6	333 55.8	29.2	316 59.5	30.6	Eltanin	90 50.8	N51 29.3
M 09	9 37.3	268 59.1 ..	44.3	164 49.3 ..	54.5	348 57.8 ..	29.4	332 01.6 ..	30.7	Enif	33 57.8	N 9 52.2
O 10	24 39.7	283 58.6	44.1	179 52.4	54.4	3 59.7	29.6	347 03.8	30.8	Fomalhaut	15 36.1	S29 37.5
N 11	39 42.2	298 58.0	44.0	194 55.5	54.3	19 01.7	29.8	2 06.0	30.9			
D 12	54 44.6	313 57.5	N25 43.8	209 58.5	S 9 54.2	34 03.6	N 7 30.0	17 08.1	N12 31.0	Gacrux	172 12.7	S57 06.7
A 13	69 47.1	328 56.9	43.6	225 01.6	54.1	49 05.6	30.2	32 10.3	31.1	Gienah	176 03.4	S17 32.4
Y 14	84 49.6	343 56.4	43.4	240 04.6	54.0	64 07.5	30.4	47 12.4	31.2	Hadar	149 02.8	S60 22.2
15	99 52.0	358 55.8 ..	43.3	255 07.7 ..	53.8	79 09.5 ..	30.6	62 14.6 ..	31.2	Hamal	328 13.4	N23 27.3
16	114 54.5	13 55.3	43.1	270 10.8	53.7	94 11.4	30.8	77 16.8	31.3	Kaus Aust.	83 58.0	S34 22.9
17	129 57.0	28 54.7	42.9	285 13.8	53.6	109 13.4	31.0	92 18.9	31.4			
18	144 59.4	43 54.2	N25 42.7	300 16.9	S 9 53.5	124 15.3	N 7 31.2	107 21.1	N12 31.5	Kochab	137 18.5	N74 09.7
19	160 01.9	58 53.6	42.5	315 19.9	53.4	139 17.3	31.4	122 23.3	31.6	Markab	13 49.3	N15 11.9
20	175 04.4	73 53.1	42.4	330 23.0	53.3	154 19.2	31.6	137 25.4	31.7	Menkar	314 26.8	N 4 05.0
21	190 06.8	88 52.6 ..	42.2	345 26.0 ..	53.2	169 21.2 ..	31.8	152 27.6 ..	31.8	Menkent	148 20.1	S36 22.0
22	205 09.3	103 52.0	42.0	0 29.1	53.1	184 23.1	32.0	167 29.7	31.9	Miaplacidus	221 42.1	S69 43.2
23	220 11.7	118 51.5	41.8	15 32.1	53.0	199 25.1	32.2	182 31.9	32.0			
18 00	235 14.2	133 50.9	N25 41.6	30 35.2	S 9 52.9	214 27.0	N 7 32.4	197 34.1	N12 32.1	Mirfak	308 56.5	N49 51.3
01	250 16.7	148 50.4	41.4	45 38.2	52.8	229 29.0	32.6	212 36.2	32.2	Nunki	76 11.6	S26 17.7
02	265 19.1	163 49.9	41.3	60 41.3	52.7	244 30.9	32.8	227 38.4	32.3	Peacock	53 36.2	S56 44.0
03	280 21.6	178 49.3 ..	41.1	75 44.3 ..	52.6	259 32.9 ..	33.0	242 40.5 ..	32.4	Pollux	243 41.3	N28 01.7
04	295 24.1	193 48.8	40.9	90 47.3	52.5	274 34.8	33.2	257 42.7	32.5	Procyon	245 11.4	N 5 13.5
05	310 26.5	208 48.3	40.7	105 50.4	52.3	289 36.8	33.4	272 44.9	32.6			
06	325 29.0	223 47.7	N25 40.5	120 53.4	S 9 52.2	304 38.7	N 7 33.6	287 47.0	N12 32.7	Rasalhague	96 16.3	N12 33.6
07	340 31.5	238 47.2	40.3	135 56.5	52.1	319 40.7	33.8	302 49.2	32.8	Regulus	207 55.1	N11 58.2
08	355 33.9	253 46.6	40.1	150 59.5	52.0	334 42.6	34.0	317 51.4	32.9	Rigel	281 22.9	S 8 12.4
T 09	10 36.4	268 46.1 ..	39.9	166 02.5 ..	51.9	349 44.6 ..	34.2	332 53.5 ..	33.0	Rigil Kent.	140 06.1	S60 49.9
U 10	25 38.9	283 45.6	39.7	181 05.6	51.8	4 46.5	34.4	347 55.7	33.1	Sabik	102 24.8	S15 43.4
E 11	40 41.3	298 45.0	39.5	196 08.6	51.7	19 48.5	34.6	2 57.8	33.2			
S 12	55 43.8	313 44.5	N25 39.3	211 11.6	S 9 51.6	34 50.4	N 7 34.8	18 00.0	N12 33.3	Schedar	349 53.4	N56 31.7
D 13	70 46.2	328 44.0	39.1	226 14.7	51.5	49 52.4	35.0	33 02.2	33.4	Shaula	96 36.4	S37 06.1
A 14	85 48.7	343 43.5	38.9	241 17.7	51.4	64 54.3	35.2	48 04.3	33.5	Sirius	258 43.6	S16 43.1
Y 15	100 51.2	358 42.9 ..	38.7	256 20.7 ..	51.3	79 56.3 ..	35.4	63 06.5 ..	33.6	Spica	158 42.5	S11 09.5
16	115 53.6	13 42.4	38.5	271 23.8	51.2	94 58.2	35.6	78 08.7	33.6	Suhail	223 00.5	S43 26.1
17	130 56.1	28 41.9	38.3	286 26.8	51.1	110 00.2	35.8	93 10.8	33.7			
18	145 58.6	43 41.3	N25 38.1	301 29.8	S 9 51.0	125 02.1	N 7 36.0	108 13.0	N12 33.8	Vega	80 46.0	N38 46.9
19	161 01.0	58 40.8	37.9	316 32.8	50.9	140 04.1	36.2	123 15.1	33.9	Zuben'ubi	137 17.2	S16 02.3
20	176 03.5	73 40.3	37.7	331 35.9	50.8	155 06.0	36.4	138 17.3	34.0		SHA	Mer. Pass.
21	191 06.0	88 39.7 ..	37.5	346 38.9 ..	50.7	170 08.0 ..	36.6	153 19.5 ..	34.1		° ′	h m
22	206 08.4	103 39.2	37.2	1 41.9	50.6	185 09.9	36.8	168 21.6	34.2	Venus	259 49.0	15 04
23	221 10.9	118 38.7	37.0	16 44.9	50.5	200 11.9	37.0	183 23.8	34.3	Mars	155 06.6	21 58
	h m									Jupiter	339 25.2	9 44
Mer. Pass. 8 21.6		v −0.5	d 0.2	v 3.1	d 0.1	v 1.9	d 0.2	v 2.2	d 0.1	Saturn	322 27.1	10 52

UT	SUN GHA	SUN Dec	MOON GHA	v	Dec	d	HP
d h	° ′	° ′	° ′	′	° ′	′	′
16 00	180 55.0	N18 56.6	172 31.3	4.7	N15 47.2	8.2	61.4
01	195 55.0	57.2	186 55.0	4.7	15 55.4	8.2	61.4
02	210 55.0	57.8	201 18.7	4.6	16 03.6	8.0	61.4
03	225 55.0 ..	58.4	215 42.3	4.6	16 11.6	7.8	61.4
04	240 55.0	59.0	230 05.9	4.6	16 19.4	7.8	61.4
05	255 55.0	18 59.5	244 29.5	4.5	16 27.2	7.7	61.3
06	270 55.0	N19 00.1	258 53.0	4.5	N16 34.9	7.5	61.3
07	285 55.0	00.7	273 16.5	4.4	16 42.4	7.4	61.3
08	300 54.9	01.3	287 39.9	4.4	16 49.8	7.3	61.3
S 09	315 54.9 ..	01.9	302 03.3	4.4	16 57.1	7.1	61.3
U 10	330 54.9	02.5	316 26.7	4.3	17 04.2	7.0	61.3
N 11	345 54.9	03.0	330 50.0	4.3	17 11.2	6.9	61.3
D 12	0 54.9	N19 03.6	345 13.3	4.3	N17 18.1	6.8	61.3
A 13	15 54.9	04.2	359 36.6	4.2	17 24.9	6.6	61.3
Y 14	30 54.9	04.8	13 59.8	4.2	17 31.5	6.5	61.3
15	45 54.9 ..	05.3	28 23.0	4.2	17 38.0	6.4	61.2
16	60 54.8	05.9	42 46.2	4.1	17 44.4	6.2	61.2
17	75 54.8	06.5	57 09.3	4.2	17 50.6	6.1	61.2
18	90 54.8	N19 07.1	71 32.5	4.1	N17 56.7	6.0	61.2
19	105 54.8	07.7	85 55.6	4.1	18 02.7	5.8	61.2
20	120 54.8	08.2	100 18.7	4.0	18 08.5	5.7	61.2
21	135 54.8 ..	08.8	114 41.7	4.1	18 14.2	5.6	61.1
22	150 54.8	09.4	129 04.8	4.0	18 19.8	5.4	61.1
23	165 54.7	09.9	143 27.8	4.0	18 25.2	5.3	61.1
17 00	180 54.7	N19 10.5	157 50.8	4.0	N18 30.5	5.1	61.1
01	195 54.7	11.1	172 13.8	4.0	18 35.6	5.0	61.1
02	210 54.7	11.7	186 36.8	4.0	18 40.6	4.9	61.1
03	225 54.7 ..	12.2	200 59.8	3.9	18 45.5	4.7	61.0
04	240 54.7	12.8	215 22.7	4.0	18 50.2	4.6	61.0
05	255 54.7	13.4	229 45.7	3.9	18 54.8	4.4	61.0
06	270 54.6	N19 13.9	244 08.6	4.0	N18 59.2	4.3	61.0
07	285 54.6	14.5	258 31.6	3.9	19 03.5	4.1	61.0
08	300 54.6	15.1	272 54.5	3.9	19 07.6	4.1	60.9
M 09	315 54.6 ..	15.7	287 17.4	4.0	19 11.7	3.8	60.9
O 10	330 54.6	16.2	301 40.4	3.9	19 15.5	3.7	60.9
N 11	345 54.5	16.8	316 03.3	4.0	19 19.2	3.6	60.9
D 12	0 54.5	N19 17.4	330 26.3	3.9	N19 22.8	3.4	60.8
A 13	15 54.5	17.9	344 49.2	4.0	19 26.2	3.3	60.8
Y 14	30 54.5	18.5	359 12.2	3.9	19 29.5	3.2	60.8
15	45 54.5 ..	19.0	13 35.1	4.0	19 32.7	3.0	60.8
16	60 54.5	19.6	27 58.1	4.0	19 35.7	2.8	60.7
17	75 54.4	20.2	42 21.1	4.0	19 38.5	2.7	60.7
18	90 54.4	N19 20.7	56 44.1	4.0	N19 41.2	2.6	60.7
19	105 54.4	21.3	71 07.1	4.1	19 43.8	2.4	60.7
20	120 54.4	21.9	85 30.2	4.0	19 46.2	2.2	60.6
21	135 54.4 ..	22.4	99 53.2	4.1	19 48.4	2.2	60.6
22	150 54.3	23.0	114 16.3	4.1	19 50.6	1.9	60.6
23	165 54.3	23.5	128 39.4	4.1	19 52.5	1.9	60.5
18 00	180 54.3	N19 24.1	143 02.5	4.2	N19 54.4	1.6	60.5
01	195 54.3	24.7	157 25.7	4.1	19 56.0	1.6	60.5
02	210 54.3	25.2	171 48.8	4.2	19 57.6	1.4	60.5
03	225 54.2 ..	25.8	186 12.0	4.3	19 59.0	1.2	60.4
04	240 54.2	26.3	200 35.3	4.2	20 00.2	1.1	60.4
05	255 54.2	26.9	214 58.5	4.3	20 01.3	1.0	60.4
06	270 54.2	N19 27.4	229 21.8	4.4	N20 02.3	0.8	60.3
07	285 54.1	28.0	243 45.2	4.3	20 03.1	0.7	60.3
08	300 54.1	28.6	258 08.5	4.5	20 03.8	0.5	60.3
T 09	315 54.1 ..	29.1	272 32.0	4.4	20 04.3	0.4	60.2
U 10	330 54.1	29.7	286 55.4	4.5	20 04.7	0.2	60.2
E 11	345 54.1	30.2	301 18.9	4.5	20 04.9	0.1	60.2
S 12	0 54.0	N19 30.8	315 42.4	4.6	N20 05.0	0.0	60.1
D 13	15 54.0	31.3	330 06.0	4.7	20 05.0	0.0	60.1
A 14	30 54.0	31.9	344 29.7	4.6	20 04.8	0.3	60.1
Y 15	45 54.0 ..	32.4	358 53.3	4.8	20 04.5	0.5	60.0
16	60 54.0	33.0	13 17.1	4.7	20 04.0	0.6	60.0
17	75 53.9	33.5	27 40.8	4.9	20 03.4	0.7	60.0
18	90 53.9	N19 34.1	42 04.7	4.9	N20 02.7	0.9	59.9
19	105 53.9	34.6	56 28.6	4.9	20 01.8	1.0	59.9
20	120 53.8	35.2	70 52.5	5.0	20 00.8	1.2	59.9
21	135 53.8 ..	35.7	85 16.5	5.0	19 59.6	1.3	59.8
22	150 53.8	36.3	99 40.5	5.2	19 58.3	1.4	59.8
23	165 53.8	36.8	114 04.7	5.1	N19 56.9	1.6	59.8
	SD 15.8	d 0.6	SD 16.7		16.6		16.4

Lat.	Twilight Naut.	Twilight Civil	Sunrise	Moonrise 16	Moonrise 17	Moonrise 18	Moonrise 19
°	h m	h m	h m	h m	h m	h m	h m
N 72	▭	▭	▭	02 30	▭	▭	▭
N 70	▭	▭	▭	03 09	03 06	03 08	04 23
68	////	////	01 38	03 36	03 52	04 26	05 33
66	////	////	02 16	03 57	04 22	05 04	06 09
64	////	00 56	02 42	04 14	04 44	05 30	06 35
62	////	01 45	03 02	04 28	05 03	05 51	06 55
60	////	02 14	03 19	04 40	05 18	06 08	07 12
N 58	00 51	02 36	03 33	04 51	05 31	06 22	07 26
56	01 35	02 54	03 44	05 00	05 42	06 34	07 38
54	02 02	03 09	03 55	05 08	05 51	06 45	07 48
52	02 23	03 21	04 04	05 15	06 00	06 55	07 57
50	02 39	03 32	04 12	05 21	06 08	07 03	08 06
45	03 11	03 55	04 29	05 36	06 25	07 21	08 23
N 40	03 35	04 13	04 43	05 47	06 39	07 36	08 38
35	03 53	04 27	04 55	05 57	06 50	07 49	08 50
30	04 08	04 39	05 06	06 06	07 01	08 00	09 01
20	04 32	05 00	05 23	06 21	07 19	08 18	09 19
N 10	04 50	05 16	05 39	06 35	07 34	08 35	09 35
0	05 05	05 31	05 53	06 47	07 49	08 50	09 50
S 10	05 19	05 45	06 07	07 00	08 03	09 06	10 05
20	05 32	05 58	06 22	07 13	08 19	09 22	10 21
30	05 44	06 13	06 39	07 29	08 37	09 41	10 39
35	05 51	06 21	06 49	07 38	08 48	09 52	10 50
40	05 58	06 30	07 00	07 49	09 00	10 05	11 02
45	06 05	06 41	07 13	08 01	09 14	10 20	11 17
S 50	06 13	06 53	07 29	08 16	09 32	10 38	11 34
52	06 17	06 58	07 36	08 23	09 40	10 47	11 42
54	06 21	07 04	07 44	08 31	09 49	10 57	11 52
56	06 25	07 11	07 54	08 40	10 00	11 08	12 02
58	06 29	07 18	08 04	08 50	10 12	11 20	12 14
S 60	06 34	07 27	08 17	09 01	10 25	11 35	12 28

Lat.	Sunset	Twilight Civil	Twilight Naut.	Moonset 16	Moonset 17	Moonset 18	Moonset 19
°	h m	h m	h m	h m	h m	h m	h m
N 72	▭	▭	▭	23 50	25 58	01 58	02 50
N 70	▭	▭	▭	23 05	24 40	00 40	01 40
68	22 20	////	////	22 36	24 03	00 03	01 03
66	21 40	////	////	22 13	23 36	24 37	00 37
64	21 13	23 05	////	21 56	23 15	24 17	00 17
62	20 52	22 12	////	21 41	22 59	24 00	00 00
60	20 35	21 41	////	21 28	22 44	23 46	24 32
N 58	20 21	21 18	23 10	21 18	22 32	23 34	24 22
56	20 09	21 00	22 22	21 08	22 22	23 23	24 12
54	19 59	20 45	21 53	21 00	22 12	23 14	24 03
52	19 50	20 33	21 32	20 52	22 04	23 05	23 56
50	19 41	20 21	21 15	20 36	21 46	22 47	23 39
45	19 24	19 59	20 43	20 23	21 31	22 33	23 26
N 40	19 10	19 41	20 00	20 11	21 19	22 20	23 14
35	18 58	19 26	19 45	20 02	21 08	22 09	23 04
30	18 47	19 14	19 21	19 45	20 49	21 51	22 47
20	18 30	18 53	19 03	19 30	20 33	21 34	22 32
N 10	18 14	18 37	18 47	19 16	20 18	21 19	22 17
0	18 00	18 22	18 34	19 02	20 03	21 04	22 03
S 10	17 46	18 08	18 21	18 48	19 47	20 47	21 48
20	17 31	17 54	18 02	18 31	19 28	20 28	21 30
30	17 14	17 39	17 47	18 21	19 17	20 17	21 20
35	17 04	17 31	17 55	18 10	19 05	20 05	21 08
40	16 53	17 22	17 47	17 57	18 50	19 50	20 54
45	16 40	17 12	17 39	17 41	18 32	19 31	20 37
S 50	16 24	16 59	17 35	17 34	18 24	19 23	20 29
52	16 16	16 54	17 32	17 26	18 14	19 13	20 20
54	16 08	16 48	17 27	17 16	18 04	19 02	20 10
56	15 58	16 41	17 23	17 06	17 51	18 49	19 58
58	15 48	16 34	17 18	16 54	17 37	18 35	19 45
S 60	15 36	16 26					

Day	SUN Eqn. of Time 00h	SUN Eqn. of Time 12h	SUN Mer. Pass.	MOON Mer. Pass. Upper	MOON Mer. Pass. Lower	Age	Phase
d	m s	m s	h m	h m	h m	d	%
16	03 40	03 40	11 56	13 02	00 31	01	2
17	03 39	03 38	11 56	14 03	01 32	02	6
18	03 37	03 36	11 56	15 05	02 34	03	13

UT	ARIES	VENUS −4.2		MARS −1.3		JUPITER −2.1		SATURN +0.4		STARS		
	GHA	GHA	Dec	GHA	Dec	GHA	Dec	GHA	Dec	Name	SHA	Dec
d h	° ′	° ′	° ′	° ′	° ′	° ′	° ′	° ′	° ′		° ′	° ′
19 00	236 13.4	133 38.2	N25 36.8	31 47.9	S 9 50.4	215 13.8	N 7 37.2	198 26.0	N12 34.4	Acamar	315 27.1	S40 18.6
01	251 15.8	148 37.6	36.6	46 50.9	50.3	230 15.8	37.4	213 28.1	34.5	Achernar	335 35.4	S57 14.4
02	266 18.3	163 37.1	36.4	61 54.0	50.2	245 17.7	37.6	228 30.3	34.6	Acrux	173 21.1	S63 05.9
03	281 20.7	178 36.6	.. 36.2	76 57.0	.. 50.2	260 19.7	.. 37.8	243 32.4	.. 34.7	Adhara	255 21.4	S28 58.5
04	296 23.2	193 36.1	36.0	92 00.0	50.1	275 21.6	38.0	258 34.6	34.8	Aldebaran	291 02.3	N16 30.3
05	311 25.7	208 35.6	35.7	107 03.0	50.0	290 23.6	38.2	273 36.8	34.9			
06	326 28.1	223 35.0	N25 35.5	122 06.0	S 9 49.9	305 25.5	N 7 38.4	288 38.9	N12 35.0	Alioth	166 29.9	N55 58.1
W 07	341 30.6	238 34.5	35.3	137 09.0	49.8	320 27.5	38.6	303 41.1	35.1	Alkaid	153 07.1	N49 19.2
E 08	356 33.1	253 34.0	35.1	152 12.0	49.7	335 29.5	38.8	318 43.3	35.2	Al Na'ir	27 57.4	S46 57.7
D 09	11 35.5	268 33.5	.. 34.9	167 15.0	.. 49.6	350 31.4	.. 39.0	333 45.4	.. 35.3	Alnilam	275 57.8	S 1 12.3
N 10	26 38.0	283 33.0	34.6	182 18.0	49.5	5 33.4	39.2	348 47.6	35.4	Alphard	218 06.9	S 8 39.5
E 11	41 40.5	298 32.4	34.4	197 21.0	49.4	20 35.3	39.4	3 49.8	35.5			
S 12	56 42.9	313 31.9	N25 34.2	212 24.0	S 9 49.3	35 37.3	N 7 39.6	18 51.9	N12 35.6	Alphecca	126 19.9	N26 43.1
D 13	71 45.4	328 31.4	34.0	227 27.0	49.2	50 39.2	39.8	33 54.1	35.7	Alpheratz	357 55.0	N29 04.9
A 14	86 47.9	343 30.9	33.7	242 30.0	49.1	65 41.2	40.0	48 56.2	35.8	Altair	62 18.7	N 8 52.0
Y 15	101 50.3	358 30.4	.. 33.5	257 33.0	.. 49.0	80 43.1	.. 40.2	63 58.4	.. 35.8	Ankaa	353 26.8	S42 18.5
16	116 52.8	13 29.9	33.3	272 36.0	49.0	95 45.1	40.4	79 00.6	35.9	Antares	112 39.3	S26 25.7
17	131 55.2	28 29.3	33.0	287 39.0	48.9	110 47.0	40.6	94 02.7	36.0			
18	146 57.7	43 28.8	N25 32.8	302 42.0	S 9 48.8	125 49.0	N 7 40.8	109 04.9	N12 36.1	Arcturus	146 05.4	N19 11.3
19	162 00.2	58 28.3	32.6	317 45.0	48.7	140 50.9	41.0	124 07.1	36.2	Atria	107 50.4	S69 01.4
20	177 02.6	73 27.8	32.3	332 48.0	48.6	155 52.9	41.2	139 09.2	36.3	Avior	234 22.7	S59 30.8
21	192 05.1	88 27.3	.. 32.1	347 51.0	.. 48.5	170 54.8	.. 41.4	154 11.4	.. 36.4	Bellatrix	278 44.0	N 6 20.8
22	207 07.6	103 26.8	31.9	2 54.0	48.4	185 56.8	41.6	169 13.5	36.5	Betelgeuse	271 13.4	N 7 24.2
23	222 10.0	118 26.3	31.6	17 57.0	48.3	200 58.7	41.8	184 15.7	36.6			
20 00	237 12.5	133 25.8	N25 31.4	33 00.0	S 9 48.3	216 00.7	N 7 42.0	199 17.9	N12 36.7	Canopus	264 01.4	S52 42.0
01	252 15.0	148 25.2	31.2	48 02.9	48.2	231 02.7	42.2	214 20.0	36.8	Capella	280 51.1	N45 59.7
02	267 17.4	163 24.7	30.9	63 05.9	48.1	246 04.6	42.4	229 22.2	36.9	Deneb	49 38.7	N45 16.5
03	282 19.9	178 24.2	.. 30.7	78 08.9	.. 48.0	261 06.6	.. 42.6	244 24.4	.. 37.0	Denebola	182 44.7	N14 34.6
04	297 22.4	193 23.7	30.4	93 11.9	47.9	276 08.5	42.8	259 26.5	37.1	Diphda	349 07.1	S17 59.5
05	312 24.8	208 23.2	30.2	108 14.9	47.8	291 10.5	43.0	274 28.7	37.2			
06	327 27.3	223 22.7	N25 29.9	123 17.9	S 9 47.7	306 12.4	N 7 43.2	289 30.9	N12 37.3	Dubhe	194 04.9	N61 45.6
T 07	342 29.7	238 22.2	29.7	138 20.8	47.7	321 14.4	43.4	304 33.0	37.4	Elnath	278 26.8	N28 36.3
H 08	357 32.2	253 21.7	29.5	153 23.8	47.6	336 16.3	43.6	319 35.2	37.5	Eltanin	90 50.7	N51 29.3
U 09	12 34.7	268 21.2	.. 29.2	168 26.8	.. 47.5	351 18.3	.. 43.8	334 37.4	.. 37.6	Enif	33 57.8	N 9 52.2
R 10	27 37.1	283 20.7	29.0	183 29.8	47.4	6 20.2	44.0	349 39.5	37.7	Fomalhaut	15 36.1	S29 37.5
11	42 39.6	298 20.2	28.7	198 32.7	47.3	21 22.2	44.2	4 41.7	37.7			
S 12	57 42.1	313 19.7	N25 28.5	213 35.7	S 9 47.3	36 24.2	N 7 44.4	19 43.8	N12 37.8	Gacrux	172 12.7	S57 06.7
D 13	72 44.5	328 19.2	28.2	228 38.7	47.2	51 26.1	44.6	34 46.0	37.9	Gienah	176 03.4	S17 32.4
A 14	87 47.0	343 18.7	28.0	243 41.6	47.1	66 28.1	44.8	49 48.2	38.0	Hadar	149 02.8	S60 22.2
Y 15	102 49.5	358 18.2	.. 27.7	258 44.6	.. 47.0	81 30.0	.. 44.9	64 50.3	.. 38.1	Hamal	328 13.4	N23 27.3
16	117 51.9	13 17.7	27.4	273 47.6	46.9	96 32.0	45.1	79 52.5	38.2	Kaus Aust.	83 58.0	S34 22.9
17	132 54.4	28 17.2	27.2	288 50.5	46.9	111 33.9	45.3	94 54.7	38.3			
18	147 56.8	43 16.7	N25 26.9	303 53.5	S 9 46.8	126 35.9	N 7 45.5	109 56.8	N12 38.4	Kochab	137 18.5	N74 09.7
19	162 59.3	58 16.2	26.7	318 56.5	46.7	141 37.8	45.7	124 59.0	38.5	Markab	13 49.3	N15 11.9
20	178 01.8	73 15.7	26.4	333 59.4	46.6	156 39.8	45.9	140 01.2	38.6	Menkar	314 26.8	N 4 05.0
21	193 04.2	88 15.2	.. 26.2	349 02.4	.. 46.6	171 41.8	.. 46.1	155 03.3	.. 38.7	Menkent	148 20.1	S36 22.0
22	208 06.7	103 14.7	25.9	4 05.3	46.5	186 43.7	46.3	170 05.5	38.8	Miaplacidus	221 42.1	S69 43.2
23	223 09.2	118 14.2	25.6	19 08.3	46.4	201 45.7	46.5	185 07.6	38.8			
21 00	238 11.6	133 13.7	N25 25.4	34 11.2	S 9 46.3	216 47.6	N 7 46.7	200 09.8	N12 39.0	Mirfak	308 56.5	N49 51.3
01	253 14.1	148 13.2	25.1	49 14.2	46.2	231 49.6	46.9	215 12.0	39.1	Nunki	76 11.6	S26 17.7
02	268 16.6	163 12.7	24.8	64 17.2	46.2	246 51.5	47.1	230 14.1	39.2	Peacock	53 36.2	S56 44.0
03	283 19.0	178 12.2	.. 24.6	79 20.1	.. 46.1	261 53.5	.. 47.3	245 16.3	.. 39.3	Pollux	243 41.3	N28 01.7
04	298 21.5	193 11.7	24.3	94 23.1	46.0	276 55.4	47.5	260 18.5	39.4	Procyon	245 11.4	N 5 13.5
05	313 24.0	208 11.3	24.0	109 26.0	46.0	291 57.4	47.7	275 20.6	39.4			
06	328 26.4	223 10.8	N25 23.8	124 29.0	S 9 45.9	306 59.4	N 7 47.9	290 22.8	N12 39.5	Rasalhague	96 16.3	N12 33.7
07	343 28.9	238 10.3	23.5	139 31.9	45.8	322 01.3	48.1	305 25.0	39.6	Regulus	207 55.1	N11 58.2
F 08	358 31.3	253 09.8	23.2	154 34.8	45.7	337 03.3	48.3	320 27.1	39.7	Rigel	281 22.9	S 8 12.4
R 09	13 33.8	268 09.3	.. 22.9	169 37.8	.. 45.7	352 05.2	.. 48.5	335 29.3	.. 39.8	Rigil Kent.	140 06.1	S60 49.9
I 10	28 36.3	283 08.8	22.7	184 40.7	45.6	7 07.2	48.7	350 31.5	39.9	Sabik	102 24.7	S15 43.4
11	43 38.7	298 08.3	22.4	199 43.7	45.5	22 09.1	48.9	5 33.6	40.0			
D 12	58 41.2	313 07.8	N25 22.1	214 46.6	S 9 45.5	37 11.1	N 7 49.1	20 35.8	N12 40.1	Schedar	349 53.3	N56 31.7
A 13	73 43.7	328 07.4	21.8	229 49.5	45.4	52 13.1	49.3	35 38.0	40.2	Shaula	96 36.4	S37 06.1
Y 14	88 46.1	343 06.9	21.6	244 52.5	45.3	67 15.0	49.5	50 40.1	40.3	Sirius	258 43.6	S16 43.1
15	103 48.6	358 06.4	.. 21.3	259 55.4	.. 45.2	82 17.0	.. 49.7	65 42.3	.. 40.4	Spica	158 42.5	S11 09.5
16	118 51.1	13 05.9	21.0	274 58.4	45.2	97 18.9	49.9	80 44.5	40.5	Suhail	223 00.6	S43 26.1
17	133 53.6	28 05.4	20.7	290 01.3	45.1	112 20.9	50.1	95 46.6	40.6			
18	148 56.0	43 04.9	N25 20.4	305 04.2	S 9 45.0	127 22.8	N 7 50.2	110 48.8	N12 40.7	Vega	80 46.0	N38 46.9
19	163 58.5	58 04.5	20.2	320 07.2	45.0	142 24.8	50.4	125 50.9	40.8	Zuben'ubi	137 17.2	S16 02.3
20	179 00.9	73 04.0	19.9	335 10.1	44.9	157 26.8	50.6	140 53.1	40.9		SHA	Mer. Pass.
21	194 03.4	88 03.5	.. 19.6	350 13.0	.. 44.8	172 28.7	.. 50.8	155 55.3	.. 41.0		° ′	h m
22	209 05.8	103 03.0	19.3	5 15.9	44.8	187 30.7	51.0	170 57.4	41.0	Venus	256 13.3	15 07
23	224 08.3	118 02.5	19.0	20 18.9	44.7	202 32.6	51.2	185 59.6	41.1	Mars	155 47.5	21 44
	h m									Jupiter	338 48.2	9 35
Mer. Pass.	8 09.8	v −0.5	d 0.3	v 3.0	d 0.1	v 2.0	d 0.2	v 2.2	d 0.1	Saturn	322 05.4	10 41

UT	SUN GHA	SUN Dec	MOON GHA	v	Dec	d	HP
d h	° ′	° ′	° ′	′	° ′	′	′
19 00	180 53.7	N19 37.3	128 28.8	5.3	N19 55.3	1.7	59.7
01	195 53.7	37.9	142 53.1	5.3	19 53.6	1.8	59.7
02	210 53.7	38.4	157 17.4	5.3	19 51.8	2.0	59.7
03	225 53.6 ..	39.0	171 41.7	5.5	19 49.8	2.1	59.6
04	240 53.6	39.5	186 06.2	5.5	19 47.7	2.2	59.6
05	255 53.6	40.1	200 30.7	5.5	19 45.5	2.4	59.6
06	270 53.6	N19 40.6	214 55.2	5.6	N19 43.1	2.4	59.5
W 07	285 53.5	41.1	229 19.8	5.7	19 40.7	2.6	59.5
E 08	300 53.5	41.7	243 44.5	5.8	19 38.1	2.8	59.4
D 09	315 53.5 ..	42.2	258 09.3	5.9	19 35.3	2.9	59.4
N 10	330 53.4	42.8	272 34.2	5.9	19 32.4	2.9	59.4
E 11	345 53.4	43.3	286 59.1	6.0	19 29.5	3.2	59.3
S 12	0 53.4	N19 43.8	301 24.1	6.0	N19 26.3	3.2	59.3
D 13	15 53.4	44.4	315 49.1	6.2	19 23.1	3.4	59.3
A 14	30 53.3	44.9	330 14.3	6.2	19 19.7	3.4	59.2
Y 15	45 53.3 ..	45.5	344 39.5	6.3	19 16.3	3.6	59.2
16	60 53.3	46.0	359 04.8	6.4	19 12.7	3.8	59.1
17	75 53.2	46.5	13 30.2	6.4	19 08.9	3.8	59.1
18	90 53.2	N19 47.1	27 55.6	6.5	N19 05.1	4.0	59.1
19	105 53.2	47.6	42 21.1	6.6	19 01.1	4.0	59.0
20	120 53.1	48.1	56 46.7	6.7	18 57.1	4.2	59.0
21	135 53.1 ..	48.7	71 12.4	6.8	18 52.9	4.3	58.9
22	150 53.1	49.2	85 38.2	6.9	18 48.6	4.4	58.9
23	165 53.1	49.7	100 04.1	6.9	18 44.2	4.6	58.9
20 00	180 53.0	N19 50.3	114 30.0	7.0	N18 39.6	4.6	58.8
01	195 53.0	50.8	128 56.0	7.1	18 35.0	4.8	58.8
02	210 53.0	51.3	143 22.1	7.2	18 30.2	4.8	58.8
03	225 52.9 ..	51.9	157 48.3	7.3	18 25.4	5.0	58.7
04	240 52.9	52.4	172 14.6	7.4	18 20.4	5.1	58.7
05	255 52.9	52.9	186 41.0	7.4	18 15.3	5.1	58.6
06	270 52.8	N19 53.4	201 07.4	7.5	N18 10.2	5.3	58.6
T 07	285 52.8	54.0	215 33.9	7.6	18 04.9	5.4	58.6
H 08	300 52.8	54.5	230 00.5	7.7	17 59.5	5.5	58.5
U 09	315 52.7 ..	55.0	244 27.2	7.8	17 54.0	5.6	58.5
R 10	330 52.7	55.5	258 54.0	7.9	17 48.4	5.7	58.4
S 11	345 52.7	56.1	273 20.9	8.0	17 42.7	5.7	58.4
D 12	0 52.6	N19 56.6	287 47.9	8.0	N17 37.0	5.9	58.4
A 13	15 52.6	57.1	302 14.9	8.2	17 31.1	6.0	58.3
Y 14	30 52.6	57.6	316 42.1	8.2	17 25.1	6.1	58.3
15	45 52.5 ..	58.2	331 09.3	8.3	17 19.0	6.1	58.2
16	60 52.5	58.7	345 36.6	8.4	17 12.9	6.3	58.2
17	75 52.4	59.2	0 04.0	8.5	17 06.6	6.4	58.2
18	90 52.4	N19 59.7	14 31.5	8.6	N17 00.2	6.4	58.1
19	105 52.4	N20 00.2	28 59.1	8.6	16 53.8	6.5	58.1
20	120 52.3	00.8	43 26.7	8.8	16 47.3	6.6	58.0
21	135 52.3 ..	01.3	57 54.5	8.8	16 40.7	6.7	58.0
22	150 52.3	01.8	72 22.3	9.0	16 34.0	6.8	58.0
23	165 52.2	02.3	86 50.3	9.0	16 27.2	6.9	57.9
21 00	180 52.2	N20 02.8	101 18.3	9.1	N16 20.3	7.0	57.9
01	195 52.1	03.4	115 46.4	9.2	16 13.3	7.0	57.9
02	210 52.1	03.9	130 14.6	9.3	16 06.3	7.1	57.8
03	225 52.1 ..	04.4	144 42.9	9.3	15 59.2	7.2	57.8
04	240 52.0	04.9	159 11.2	9.5	15 52.0	7.3	57.7
05	255 52.0	05.4	173 39.7	9.5	15 44.7	7.4	57.7
06	270 52.0	N20 05.9	188 08.2	9.7	N15 37.3	7.4	57.7
07	285 51.9	06.4	202 36.9	9.7	15 29.9	7.5	57.6
08	300 51.9	07.0	217 05.6	9.8	15 22.4	7.6	57.6
F 09	315 51.8 ..	07.5	231 34.4	9.9	15 14.8	7.7	57.6
R 10	330 51.8	08.0	246 03.3	9.9	15 07.1	7.7	57.5
I 11	345 51.8	08.5	260 32.2	10.1	14 59.4	7.8	57.5
D 12	0 51.7	N20 09.0	275 01.3	10.1	N14 51.6	7.9	57.4
A 13	15 51.7	09.5	289 30.4	10.2	14 43.7	7.9	57.4
Y 14	30 51.6	10.0	303 59.6	10.4	14 35.8	8.0	57.4
15	45 51.6 ..	10.5	318 29.0	10.3	14 27.8	8.1	57.3
16	60 51.6	11.0	332 58.3	10.5	14 19.7	8.1	57.3
17	75 51.5	11.5	347 27.8	10.6	14 11.6	8.2	57.3
18	90 51.5	N20 12.0	1 57.4	10.6	N14 03.4	8.3	57.2
19	105 51.4	12.5	16 27.0	10.7	13 55.1	8.3	57.2
20	120 51.4	13.1	30 56.7	10.8	13 46.8	8.4	57.1
21	135 51.3 ..	13.6	45 26.5	10.9	13 38.4	8.4	57.1
22	150 51.3	14.1	59 56.4	11.0	13 30.0	8.6	57.1
23	165 51.3	14.6	74 26.4	11.0	N13 21.4	8.5	57.0
	SD 15.8	d 0.5	SD 16.2		15.9		15.7

Lat.	Twilight Naut.	Twilight Civil	Sunrise	Moonrise 19	Moonrise 20	Moonrise 21	Moonrise 22
°	h m	h m	h m	h m	h m	h m	h m
N 72	▭	▭	▭	▭	▭	07 42	09 46
N 70	▭	▭	▭	04 23	06 24	08 19	10 07
68	////	////	01 20	05 33	07 05	08 45	10 23
66	////	////	02 04	06 09	07 33	09 05	10 36
64	////	00 23	02 33	06 35	07 55	09 20	10 47
62	////	01 31	02 55	06 55	08 12	09 34	10 56
60	////	02 05	03 12	07 12	08 26	09 45	11 04
N 58	00 20	02 29	03 27	07 26	08 38	09 54	11 11
56	01 22	02 47	03 39	07 38	08 48	10 03	11 17
54	01 53	03 03	03 50	07 48	08 58	10 10	11 22
52	02 16	03 16	04 00	07 57	09 06	10 17	11 27
50	02 33	03 28	04 08	08 06	09 13	10 23	11 32
45	03 07	03 52	04 26	08 23	09 29	10 35	11 41
N 40	03 31	04 10	04 41	08 38	09 42	10 46	11 49
35	03 50	04 25	04 53	08 50	09 53	10 55	11 56
30	04 06	04 38	05 04	09 01	10 02	11 03	12 02
20	04 30	04 59	05 22	09 19	10 19	11 17	12 12
N 10	04 49	05 16	05 38	09 35	10 33	11 29	12 21
0	05 05	05 31	05 53	09 50	10 47	11 40	12 29
S 10	05 19	05 45	06 08	10 05	11 00	11 51	12 38
20	05 33	06 00	06 23	10 21	11 14	12 03	12 47
30	05 46	06 15	06 41	10 39	11 31	12 16	12 57
35	05 53	06 24	06 51	10 50	11 40	12 24	13 03
40	06 01	06 33	07 02	11 02	11 51	12 33	13 09
45	06 08	06 44	07 16	11 17	12 04	12 43	13 17
S 50	06 17	06 56	07 33	11 34	12 19	12 56	13 26
52	06 20	07 02	07 40	11 42	12 26	13 02	13 30
54	06 24	07 09	07 49	11 52	12 34	13 08	13 35
56	06 29	07 15	07 59	12 02	12 43	13 15	13 40
58	06 34	07 23	08 10	12 14	12 54	13 23	13 46
S 60	06 39	07 32	08 23	12 28	13 05	13 32	13 52

Lat.	Sunset	Twilight Civil	Twilight Naut.	Moonset 19	Moonset 20	Moonset 21	Moonset 22
°	h m	h m	h m	h m	h m	h m	h m
N 72	▭	▭	▭	▭	▭	03 24	03 05
N 70	▭	▭	▭	02 50	02 49	02 46	02 43
68	22 39	////	////	01 40	02 07	02 19	02 25
66	21 52	////	////	01 03	01 39	01 59	02 11
64	21 22	////	////	00 37	01 17	01 42	01 59
62	21 00	22 26	////	00 17	00 59	01 29	01 49
60	20 42	21 51	////	00 00	00 45	01 17	01 41
N 58	20 28	21 26	////	24 32	00 32	01 07	01 33
56	20 15	21 07	22 34	24 22	00 22	00 58	01 26
54	20 04	20 51	22 02	24 12	00 12	00 50	01 20
52	19 54	20 38	21 39	24 03	00 03	00 43	01 15
50	19 46	20 26	21 21	23 56	24 37	00 37	01 10
45	19 27	20 02	20 47	23 39	24 23	00 23	00 59
N 40	19 13	19 44	20 22	23 26	24 11	00 11	00 50
35	19 00	19 29	20 03	23 14	24 02	00 02	00 43
30	18 49	19 16	19 48	23 04	23 53	24 36	00 36
20	18 31	18 55	19 23	22 47	23 38	24 24	00 24
N 10	18 15	18 37	19 04	22 32	23 25	24 14	00 14
0	18 00	18 22	18 48	22 17	23 13	24 04	00 04
S 10	17 45	18 08	18 33	22 03	23 00	23 54	24 45
20	17 30	17 53	18 20	21 48	22 47	23 43	24 37
30	17 12	17 38	18 07	21 30	22 32	23 31	24 29
35	17 02	17 29	18 00	21 20	22 23	23 24	24 24
40	16 50	17 20	17 53	21 08	22 12	23 16	24 18
45	16 37	17 09	17 45	20 54	22 00	23 07	24 12
S 50	16 20	16 56	17 36	20 37	21 46	22 55	24 04
52	16 12	16 50	17 32	20 29	21 39	22 50	24 00
54	16 03	16 44	17 28	20 20	21 31	22 44	23 56
56	15 54	16 37	17 23	20 10	21 23	22 38	23 52
58	15 42	16 29	17 19	19 58	21 13	22 30	23 47
S 60	15 29	16 20	17 13	19 45	21 02	22 22	23 41

Day	SUN Eqn. of Time 00ʰ	SUN Eqn. of Time 12ʰ	SUN Mer. Pass.	MOON Mer. Pass. Upper	MOON Mer. Pass. Lower	Age	Phase
d	m s	m s	h m	h m	h m	d	%
19	03 35	03 34	11 56	16 04	03 35	04	22
20	03 32	03 31	11 56	17 00	04 32	05	32
21	03 29	03 27	11 57	17 52	05 26	06	42

UT	ARIES GHA	VENUS −4.2 GHA	Dec	MARS −1.2 GHA	Dec	JUPITER −2.1 GHA	Dec	SATURN +0.4 GHA	Dec	STARS Name	SHA	Dec
22 00	239 10.8	133 02.1	N25 18.7	35 21.8	S 9 44.6	217 34.6	N 7 51.4	201 01.8	N12 41.2	Acamar	315 27.0	S40 18.6
01	254 13.2	148 01.6	18.4	50 24.7	44.6	232 36.6	51.6	216 03.9	41.3	Achernar	335 35.4	S57 14.4
02	269 15.7	163 01.1	18.1	65 27.6	44.5	247 38.5	51.8	231 06.1	41.4	Acrux	173 21.1	S63 05.9
03	284 18.2	178 00.6	.. 17.8	80 30.5	.. 44.5	262 40.5	.. 52.0	246 08.3	.. 41.5	Adhara	255 21.4	S28 58.5
04	299 20.6	193 00.2	17.6	95 33.5	44.4	277 42.4	52.2	261 10.4	41.6	Aldebaran	291 02.3	N16 30.3
05	314 23.1	207 59.7	17.3	110 36.4	44.3	292 44.4	52.4	276 12.6	41.7			
S 06	329 25.6	222 59.2	N25 17.0	125 39.3	S 9 44.3	307 46.3	N 7 52.6	291 14.8	N12 41.8	Alioth	166 29.9	N55 58.1
A 07	344 28.0	237 58.7	16.7	140 42.2	44.2	322 48.3	52.8	306 16.9	41.9	Alkaid	153 07.1	N49 19.2
T 08	359 30.5	252 58.3	16.4	155 45.1	44.1	337 50.3	53.0	321 19.1	42.0	Al Na'ir	27 57.4	S46 57.7
U 09	14 32.9	267 57.8	.. 16.1	170 48.0	.. 44.1	352 52.2	.. 53.2	336 21.3	.. 42.1	Alnilam	275 57.8	S 1 12.3
R 10	29 35.4	282 57.3	15.8	185 50.9	44.0	7 54.2	53.4	351 23.4	42.2	Alphard	218 06.9	S 8 39.5
D 11	44 37.9	297 56.9	15.5	200 53.9	44.0	22 56.1	53.6	6 25.6	42.3			
A 12	59 40.3	312 56.4	N25 15.2	215 56.8	S 9 43.9	37 58.1	N 7 53.8	21 27.8	N12 42.4	Alphecca	126 19.9	N26 43.1
Y 13	74 42.8	327 55.9	14.9	230 59.7	43.8	53 00.1	53.9	36 29.9	42.5	Alpheratz	357 55.0	N29 04.9
14	89 45.3	342 55.5	14.6	246 02.6	43.8	68 02.0	54.1	51 32.1	42.5	Altair	62 18.7	N 8 52.0
15	104 47.7	357 55.0	.. 14.3	261 05.5	.. 43.7	83 04.0	.. 54.3	66 34.3	.. 42.6	Ankaa	353 26.7	S42 18.5
16	119 50.2	12 54.5	14.0	276 08.4	43.7	98 05.9	54.5	81 36.4	42.7	Antares	112 39.3	S26 25.7
17	134 52.7	27 54.1	13.7	291 11.3	43.6	113 07.9	54.7	96 38.6	42.8			
18	149 55.1	42 53.6	N25 13.3	306 14.2	S 9 43.6	128 09.9	N 7 54.9	111 40.8	N12 42.9	Arcturus	146 05.4	N19 11.3
19	164 57.6	57 53.1	13.0	321 17.1	43.5	143 11.8	55.1	126 42.9	43.0	Atria	107 50.4	S69 01.4
20	180 00.1	72 52.7	12.7	336 20.0	43.5	158 13.8	55.3	141 45.1	43.1	Avior	234 22.7	S59 30.8
21	195 02.5	87 52.2	.. 12.4	351 22.9	.. 43.4	173 15.7	.. 55.5	156 47.3	.. 43.2	Bellatrix	278 44.0	N 6 20.8
22	210 05.0	102 51.8	12.1	6 25.8	43.3	188 17.7	55.7	171 49.4	43.3	Betelgeuse	271 13.4	N 7 24.3
23	225 07.4	117 51.3	11.8	21 28.7	43.3	203 19.7	55.9	186 51.6	43.4			
23 00	240 09.9	132 50.8	N25 11.5	36 31.6	S 9 43.2	218 21.6	N 7 56.1	201 53.8	N12 43.5	Canopus	264 01.5	S52 42.0
01	255 12.4	147 50.4	11.2	51 34.4	43.2	233 23.6	56.3	216 55.9	43.6	Capella	280 51.1	N45 59.7
02	270 14.8	162 49.9	10.9	66 37.3	43.1	248 25.5	56.5	231 58.1	43.7	Deneb	49 38.7	N45 16.5
03	285 17.3	177 49.5	.. 10.5	81 40.2	.. 43.1	263 27.5	.. 56.7	247 00.3	.. 43.8	Denebola	182 44.7	N14 34.6
04	300 19.8	192 49.0	10.2	96 43.1	43.0	278 29.5	56.9	262 02.4	43.9	Diphda	349 07.1	S17 59.5
05	315 22.2	207 48.5	09.9	111 46.0	43.0	293 31.4	57.0	277 04.6	43.9			
S 06	330 24.7	222 48.1	N25 09.6	126 48.9	S 9 42.9	308 33.4	N 7 57.2	292 06.8	N12 44.0	Dubhe	194 04.9	N61 45.6
U 07	345 27.2	237 47.6	09.3	141 51.8	42.9	323 35.3	57.4	307 08.9	44.1	Elnath	278 26.8	N28 36.3
N 08	0 29.6	252 47.2	08.9	156 54.6	42.8	338 37.3	57.6	322 11.1	44.2	Eltanin	90 50.7	N51 29.3
D 09	15 32.1	267 46.7	.. 08.6	171 57.5	.. 42.8	353 39.3	.. 57.8	337 13.3	.. 44.3	Enif	33 57.8	N 9 52.2
A 10	30 34.6	282 46.3	08.3	187 00.4	42.7	8 41.2	58.0	352 15.4	44.4	Fomalhaut	15 36.1	S29 37.5
Y 11	45 37.0	297 45.8	08.0	202 03.3	42.7	23 43.2	58.2	7 17.6	44.5			
12	60 39.5	312 45.4	N25 07.6	217 06.2	S 9 42.6	38 45.2	N 7 58.4	22 19.8	N12 44.6	Gacrux	172 12.7	S57 06.8
13	75 41.9	327 44.9	07.3	232 09.0	42.6	53 47.1	58.6	37 21.9	44.7	Gienah	176 03.4	S17 32.4
14	90 44.4	342 44.5	07.0	247 11.9	42.5	68 49.1	58.8	52 24.1	44.8	Hadar	149 02.8	S60 22.3
15	105 46.9	357 44.0	.. 06.7	262 14.8	.. 42.5	83 51.0	.. 59.0	67 26.3	.. 44.9	Hamal	328 13.4	N23 27.3
16	120 49.3	12 43.6	06.3	277 17.6	42.4	98 53.0	59.2	82 28.4	45.0	Kaus Aust.	83 57.9	S34 22.9
17	135 51.8	27 43.1	06.0	292 20.5	42.4	113 55.0	59.4	97 30.6	45.1			
18	150 54.3	42 42.7	N25 05.7	307 23.4	S 9 42.3	128 56.9	N 7 59.6	112 32.8	N12 45.2	Kochab	137 18.6	N74 09.7
19	165 56.7	57 42.2	05.3	322 26.3	42.3	143 58.9	59.8	127 34.9	45.2	Markab	13 49.3	N15 11.9
20	180 59.2	72 41.8	05.0	337 29.1	42.3	159 00.8	7 59.9	142 37.1	45.3	Menkar	314 26.8	N 4 05.0
21	196 01.7	87 41.4	.. 04.7	352 32.0	.. 42.2	174 02.8	8 00.1	157 39.3	.. 45.4	Menkent	148 20.1	S36 22.0
22	211 04.1	102 40.9	04.3	7 34.8	42.2	189 04.8	00.3	172 41.4	45.5	Miaplacidus	221 42.2	S69 43.2
23	226 06.6	117 40.5	04.0	22 37.7	42.1	204 06.7	00.5	187 43.6	45.6			
24 00	241 09.0	132 40.0	N25 03.7	37 40.6	S 9 42.1	219 08.7	N 8 00.7	202 45.8	N12 45.7	Mirfak	308 56.5	N49 51.3
01	256 11.5	147 39.6	03.3	52 43.4	42.0	234 10.7	00.9	217 47.9	45.8	Nunki	76 11.6	S26 17.7
02	271 14.0	162 39.2	03.0	67 46.3	42.0	249 12.6	01.1	232 50.1	45.9	Peacock	53 36.1	S56 44.0
03	286 16.4	177 38.7	.. 02.6	82 49.1	.. 42.0	264 14.6	.. 01.3	247 52.3	.. 46.0	Pollux	243 41.3	N28 01.7
04	301 18.9	192 38.3	02.3	97 52.0	41.9	279 16.6	01.5	262 54.4	46.1	Procyon	245 11.4	N 5 13.5
05	316 21.4	207 37.8	01.9	112 54.8	41.9	294 18.5	01.7	277 56.6	46.2			
M 06	331 23.8	222 37.4	N25 01.6	127 57.7	S 9 41.8	309 20.5	N 8 01.9	292 58.8	N12 46.3	Rasalhague	96 16.3	N12 33.7
O 07	346 26.3	237 37.0	01.3	143 00.5	41.8	324 22.4	02.1	308 00.9	46.4	Regulus	207 55.1	N11 58.2
N 08	1 28.8	252 36.5	00.9	158 03.4	41.8	339 24.4	02.3	323 03.1	46.4	Rigel	281 22.9	S 8 12.3
D 09	16 31.2	267 36.1	.. 00.6	173 06.2	.. 41.7	354 26.4	.. 02.4	338 05.3	.. 46.5	Rigil Kent.	140 06.1	S60 49.9
A 10	31 33.7	282 35.7	25 00.2	188 09.1	41.7	9 28.3	02.6	353 07.4	46.6	Sabik	102 24.7	S15 43.4
Y 11	46 36.2	297 35.2	24 59.9	203 11.9	41.6	24 30.3	02.8	8 09.6	46.7			
12	61 38.6	312 34.8	N24 59.5	218 14.8	S 9 41.6	39 32.3	N 8 03.0	23 11.8	N12 46.8	Schedar	349 53.3	N56 31.7
13	76 41.1	327 34.4	59.2	233 17.6	41.6	54 34.2	03.2	38 13.9	46.9	Shaula	96 36.3	S37 06.1
14	91 43.5	342 33.9	58.8	248 20.5	41.5	69 36.2	03.4	53 16.1	47.0	Sirius	258 43.6	S16 43.1
15	106 46.0	357 33.5	.. 58.5	263 23.3	.. 41.5	84 38.2	.. 03.6	68 18.3	.. 47.1	Spica	158 42.5	S11 09.5
16	121 48.5	12 33.1	58.1	278 26.1	41.5	99 40.1	03.8	83 20.4	47.2	Suhail	223 00.6	S43 26.1
17	136 50.9	27 32.7	57.8	293 29.0	41.4	114 42.1	04.0	98 22.6	47.3			
18	151 53.4	42 32.2	N24 57.4	308 31.8	S 9 41.4	129 44.0	N 8 04.2	113 24.8	N12 47.4	Vega	80 46.0	N38 46.9
19	166 55.9	57 31.8	57.0	323 34.6	41.4	144 46.0	04.4	128 26.9	47.5	Zuben'ubi	137 17.2	S16 02.3
20	181 58.3	72 31.4	56.7	338 37.5	41.3	159 48.0	04.5	143 29.1	47.6			
21	197 00.8	87 30.9	.. 56.3	353 40.3	.. 41.3	174 49.9	.. 04.7	158 31.3	.. 47.6			
22	212 03.3	102 30.5	56.0	8 43.1	41.3	189 51.9	04.9	173 33.5	47.7			
23	227 05.7	117 30.1	55.6	23 46.0	41.2	204 53.9	05.1	188 35.6	47.8			

		SHA	Mer. Pass.
Venus		252 40.9	15 09
Mars		156 21.6	21 30
Jupiter		338 11.7	9 25
Saturn		321 43.8	10 31

	ARIES	VENUS	MARS	JUPITER	SATURN
Mer. Pass.	7 58.0	v −0.5 d 0.3	v 2.9 d 0.0	v 2.0 d 0.2	v 2.2 d 0.1

UT	SUN GHA	SUN Dec	MOON GHA	v	Dec	d	HP
d h	° ′	° ′	° ′	′	° ′	′	′
22 00	180 51.2	N20 15.1	88 56.4	11.1	N13 12.9	8.6	57.0
01	195 51.2	15.6	103 26.5	11.2	13 04.3	8.7	57.0
02	210 51.1	16.1	117 56.7	11.3	12 55.6	8.8	56.9
03	225 51.1	.. 16.6	132 27.0	11.4	12 46.8	8.8	56.9
04	240 51.0	17.1	146 57.4	11.4	12 38.0	8.8	56.9
05	255 51.0	17.6	161 27.8	11.5	12 29.2	8.9	56.9
06	270 51.0	N20 18.1	175 58.3	11.6	N12 20.3	8.9	56.8
07	285 50.9	18.6	190 28.9	11.6	12 11.4	9.0	56.8
S 08	300 50.9	19.1	204 59.5	11.7	12 02.4	9.1	56.7
A 09	315 50.8	.. 19.6	219 30.2	11.8	11 53.3	9.1	56.7
T 10	330 50.8	20.1	234 01.0	11.9	11 44.2	9.1	56.7
U 11	345 50.7	20.6	248 31.9	12.0	11 35.1	9.2	56.6
R 12	0 50.7	N20 21.1	263 02.9	12.0	N11 25.9	9.2	56.6
D 13	15 50.6	21.5	277 33.9	12.1	11 16.7	9.3	56.5
A 14	30 50.6	22.0	292 05.0	12.1	11 07.4	9.3	56.5
Y 15	45 50.6	.. 22.5	306 36.1	12.3	10 58.1	9.4	56.5
16	60 50.5	23.0	321 07.4	12.2	10 48.7	9.4	56.5
17	75 50.5	23.5	335 38.6	12.4	10 39.3	9.4	56.4
18	90 50.4	N20 24.0	350 10.0	12.4	N10 29.9	9.5	56.4
19	105 50.4	24.5	4 41.4	12.5	10 20.4	9.5	56.4
20	120 50.3	25.0	19 12.9	12.6	10 10.9	9.6	56.3
21	135 50.3	.. 25.5	33 44.5	12.6	10 01.3	9.6	56.3
22	150 50.2	26.0	48 16.1	12.7	9 51.7	9.6	56.3
23	165 50.2	26.5	62 47.8	12.8	9 42.1	9.7	56.2
23 00	180 50.1	N20 26.9	77 19.6	12.8	N 9 32.4	9.7	56.2
01	195 50.1	27.4	91 51.4	12.9	9 22.7	9.7	56.2
02	210 50.0	27.9	106 23.3	12.9	9 13.0	9.8	56.1
03	225 50.0	28.4	120 55.2	13.0	9 03.2	9.8	56.1
04	240 49.9	28.9	135 27.2	13.0	8 53.4	9.8	56.1
05	255 49.9	29.4	149 59.2	13.2	8 43.6	9.9	56.0
06	270 49.8	N20 29.9	164 31.4	13.1	N 8 33.7	9.9	56.0
07	285 49.8	30.3	179 03.5	13.3	8 23.8	9.9	56.0
S 08	300 49.7	30.8	193 35.8	13.3	8 13.9	9.9	56.0
U 09	315 49.7	.. 31.3	208 08.1	13.3	8 04.0	10.0	55.9
N 10	330 49.6	31.8	222 40.4	13.4	7 54.0	10.0	55.9
D 11	345 49.6	32.3	237 12.8	13.4	7 44.0	10.0	55.9
A 12	0 49.5	N20 32.8	251 45.2	13.5	N 7 34.0	10.1	55.8
Y 13	15 49.5	33.2	266 17.7	13.6	7 23.9	10.0	55.8
14	30 49.4	33.7	280 50.3	13.6	7 13.9	10.1	55.8
15	45 49.4	.. 34.2	295 22.9	13.7	7 03.8	10.1	55.7
16	60 49.3	34.7	309 55.6	13.7	6 53.7	10.2	55.7
17	75 49.3	35.2	324 28.3	13.7	6 43.5	10.1	55.7
18	90 49.2	N20 35.6	339 01.0	13.8	N 6 33.4	10.2	55.7
19	105 49.2	36.1	353 33.8	13.9	6 23.2	10.2	55.6
20	120 49.1	36.6	8 06.7	13.9	6 13.0	10.2	55.6
21	135 49.1	.. 37.1	22 39.6	13.9	6 02.8	10.2	55.6
22	150 49.0	37.6	37 12.5	14.0	5 52.6	10.3	55.6
23	165 49.0	38.0	51 45.5	14.0	5 42.3	10.3	55.5
24 00	180 48.9	N20 38.5	66 18.5	14.1	N 5 32.0	10.2	55.5
01	195 48.9	39.0	80 51.6	14.1	5 21.8	10.3	55.5
02	210 48.8	39.4	95 24.7	14.2	5 11.5	10.3	55.5
03	225 48.8	.. 39.9	109 57.9	14.2	5 01.2	10.4	55.4
04	240 48.7	40.4	124 31.1	14.2	4 50.8	10.3	55.4
05	255 48.6	40.8	139 04.3	14.3	4 40.5	10.3	55.4
06	270 48.6	N20 41.3	153 37.6	14.3	N 4 30.2	10.4	55.4
07	285 48.5	41.8	168 10.9	14.4	4 19.8	10.4	55.3
M 08	300 48.5	42.2	182 44.2	14.4	4 09.4	10.3	55.3
O 09	315 48.4	.. 42.7	197 17.6	14.4	3 59.1	10.4	55.3
N 10	330 48.4	43.2	211 51.0	14.5	3 48.7	10.4	55.3
D 11	345 48.3	43.6	226 24.5	14.5	3 38.3	10.4	55.2
A 12	0 48.3	N20 44.1	240 58.0	14.5	N 3 27.9	10.4	55.2
Y 13	15 48.2	44.6	255 31.5	14.6	3 17.5	10.4	55.2
14	30 48.1	45.0	270 05.1	14.5	3 07.1	10.5	55.2
15	45 48.1	.. 45.5	284 38.6	14.7	2 56.6	10.4	55.1
16	60 48.0	46.0	299 12.3	14.6	2 46.2	10.4	55.1
17	75 48.0	46.4	313 45.9	14.7	2 35.8	10.4	55.1
18	90 47.9	N20 46.9	328 19.6	14.7	N 2 25.4	10.5	55.1
19	105 47.9	47.4	342 53.3	14.7	2 14.9	10.4	55.1
20	120 47.8	47.8	357 27.0	14.8	2 04.5	10.5	55.0
21	135 47.7	.. 48.3	12 00.8	14.8	1 54.0	10.5	55.0
22	150 47.7	48.7	26 34.6	14.8	1 43.6	10.4	55.0
23	165 47.6	49.2	41 08.4	14.8	N 1 33.2	10.5	55.0
	SD 15.8	d 0.5	SD 15.4		15.2		15.0

Lat.	Twilight Naut.	Twilight Civil	Sunrise	Moonrise 22	23	24	25
°	h m	h m	h m	h m	h m	h m	h m
N 72	☐	☐	☐	09 46	11 36	13 20	14 59
N 70	☐	☐	☐	10 07	11 48	13 24	14 58
68	////	////	00 58	10 23	11 57	13 28	14 56
66	////	////	01 52	10 36	12 05	13 31	14 55
64	////	////	02 24	10 47	12 11	13 34	14 54
62	////	01 17	02 47	10 56	12 17	13 36	14 53
60	////	01 55	03 06	11 04	12 22	13 38	14 52
N 58	////	02 21	03 21	11 11	12 26	13 39	14 51
56	01 09	02 41	03 34	11 17	12 30	13 41	14 51
54	01 45	02 58	03 46	11 22	12 33	13 42	14 50
52	02 09	03 12	03 56	11 27	12 36	13 44	14 50
50	02 28	03 24	04 05	11 32	12 39	13 45	14 49
45	03 03	03 48	04 23	11 41	12 45	13 47	14 48
N 40	03 28	04 07	04 39	11 49	12 50	13 49	14 47
35	03 48	04 23	04 51	11 56	12 54	13 51	14 47
30	04 04	04 36	05 03	12 02	12 58	13 53	14 46
20	04 29	04 58	05 22	12 12	13 05	13 55	14 45
N 10	04 49	05 15	05 38	12 21	13 10	13 58	14 44
0	05 05	05 31	05 53	12 29	13 16	14 00	14 43
S 10	05 20	05 46	06 08	12 38	13 21	14 02	14 42
20	05 34	06 01	06 24	12 47	13 27	14 05	14 41
30	05 47	06 17	06 42	12 57	13 33	14 08	14 40
35	05 55	06 26	06 53	13 03	13 37	14 09	14 40
40	06 02	06 35	07 05	13 10	13 41	14 11	14 39
45	06 10	06 47	07 19	13 17	13 46	14 13	14 38
S 50	06 20	07 00	07 36	13 26	13 52	14 15	14 38
52	06 24	07 06	07 45	13 30	13 55	14 17	14 37
54	06 28	07 13	07 54	13 35	13 58	14 18	14 37
56	06 33	07 20	08 04	13 40	14 01	14 19	14 36
58	06 38	07 28	08 16	13 46	14 04	14 21	14 36
S 60	06 44	07 37	08 29	13 52	14 08	14 22	14 35

Lat.	Sunset	Twilight Civil	Twilight Naut.	Moonset 22	23	24	25
°	h m	h m	h m	h m	h m	h m	h m
N 72	☐	☐	☐	03 05	02 52	02 42	02 32
N 70	☐	☐	☐	02 43	02 39	02 35	02 31
68	23 04	////	////	02 25	02 28	02 29	02 30
66	22 05	////	////	02 11	02 19	02 24	02 29
64	21 32	////	////	01 59	02 11	02 20	02 28
62	21 08	22 41	////	01 49	02 05	02 17	02 28
60	20 49	22 01	////	01 41	01 59	02 14	02 27
N 58	20 33	21 34	////	01 33	01 54	02 11	02 27
56	20 20	21 14	22 48	01 26	01 49	02 09	02 26
54	20 09	20 57	22 11	01 20	01 45	02 06	02 26
52	19 58	20 43	21 46	01 15	01 41	02 04	02 26
50	19 49	20 31	21 27	01 10	01 38	02 03	02 25
45	19 31	20 06	20 51	00 59	01 31	01 59	02 25
N 40	19 15	19 47	20 26	00 50	01 24	01 55	02 24
35	19 02	19 31	20 06	00 43	01 19	01 52	02 24
30	18 51	19 18	19 50	00 36	01 14	01 50	02 23
20	18 32	18 56	19 24	00 24	01 06	01 45	02 22
N 10	18 16	18 38	19 05	00 14	00 59	01 41	02 22
0	18 00	18 22	18 48	00 04	00 52	01 37	02 21
S 10	17 45	18 08	18 33	24 45	00 45	01 33	02 20
20	17 29	17 53	18 20	24 37	00 37	01 29	02 19
30	17 11	17 37	18 06	24 29	00 29	01 25	02 18
35	17 00	17 28	17 59	24 24	00 24	01 22	02 18
40	16 48	17 18	17 51	24 18	00 18	01 19	02 17
45	16 34	17 06	17 43	24 12	00 12	01 15	02 17
S 50	16 17	16 53	17 33	24 04	00 04	01 11	02 16
52	16 08	16 47	17 29	24 00	00 00	01 09	02 15
54	15 59	16 40	17 25	23 56	25 06	01 06	02 15
56	15 49	16 33	17 20	23 52	25 04	01 04	02 15
58	15 37	16 25	17 15	23 47	25 01	01 01	02 14
S 60	15 24	16 16	17 09	23 41	24 58	00 58	02 13

	SUN Eqn. of Time 00h	12h	Mer. Pass.	MOON Mer. Pass. Upper	Lower	Age	Phase
Day							
d	m s	m s	h m	h m	h m	d	%
22	03 25	03 23	11 57	18 41	06 17	07	53
23	03 21	03 18	11 57	19 27	07 04	08	63
24	03 16	03 13	11 57	20 11	07 49	09	72

UT	ARIES	VENUS −4.2		MARS −1.2		JUPITER −2.1		SATURN +0.4		STARS		
	GHA	GHA	Dec	GHA	Dec	GHA	Dec	GHA	Dec	Name	SHA	Dec
d h	° ′	° ′	° ′	° ′	° ′	° ′	° ′	° ′	° ′		° ′	° ′
25 00	242 08.2	132 29.7	N24 55.2	38 48.8	S 9 41.2	219 55.8	N 8 05.3	203 37.8	N12 47.9	Acamar	315 27.0	S40 18.5
01	257 10.7	147 29.3	54.9	53 51.6	41.2	234 57.8	05.5	218 40.0	48.0	Achernar	335 35.4	S57 14.4
02	272 13.1	162 28.8	54.5	68 54.5	41.1	249 59.8	05.7	233 42.1	48.1	Acrux	173 21.1	S63 05.9
03	287 15.6	177 28.4 ..	54.2	83 57.3 ..	41.1	265 01.7 ..	05.9	248 44.3 ..	48.2	Adhara	255 21.4	S28 58.5
04	302 18.0	192 28.0	53.8	99 00.1	41.1	280 03.7	06.1	263 46.5	48.3	Aldebaran	291 02.3	N16 30.3
05	317 20.5	207 27.6	53.4	114 02.9	41.0	295 05.7	06.3	278 48.6	48.4			
06	332 23.0	222 27.2	N24 53.1	129 05.7	S 9 41.0	310 07.6	N 8 06.5	293 50.8	N12 48.5	Alioth	166 29.9	N55 58.1
07	347 25.4	237 26.7	52.7	144 08.6	41.0	325 09.6	06.6	308 53.0	48.6	Alkaid	153 07.1	N49 19.2
T 08	2 27.9	252 26.3	52.3	159 11.4	41.0	340 11.6	06.8	323 55.1	48.7	Al Na'ir	27 57.4	S46 57.7
U 09	17 30.4	267 25.9 ..	51.9	174 14.2 ..	40.9	355 13.5 ..	07.0	338 57.3 ..	48.7	Alnilam	275 57.8	S 1 12.3
E 10	32 32.8	282 25.5	51.6	189 17.0	40.9	10 15.5	07.2	353 59.5	48.8	Alphard	218 06.9	S 8 39.5
S 11	47 35.3	297 25.1	51.2	204 19.8	40.9	25 17.5	07.4	9 01.6	48.9			
D 12	62 37.8	312 24.7	N24 50.8	219 22.6	S 9 40.8	40 19.4	N 8 07.6	24 03.8	N12 49.0	Alphecca	126 19.9	N26 43.1
A 13	77 40.2	327 24.3	50.5	234 25.4	40.8	55 21.4	07.8	39 06.0	49.1	Alpheratz	357 55.0	N29 04.9
Y 14	92 42.7	342 23.9	50.1	249 28.2	40.8	70 23.4	08.0	54 08.2	49.2	Altair	62 18.7	N 8 52.0
15	107 45.1	357 23.4 ..	49.7	264 31.1 ..	40.8	85 25.3 ..	08.2	69 10.3 ..	49.3	Ankaa	353 26.7	S42 18.5
16	122 47.6	12 23.0	49.3	279 33.9	40.7	100 27.3	08.4	84 12.5	49.4	Antares	112 39.3	S26 25.7
17	137 50.1	27 22.6	48.9	294 36.7	40.7	115 29.3	08.6	99 14.7	49.5			
18	152 52.5	42 22.2	N24 48.6	309 39.5	S 9 40.7	130 31.2	N 8 08.7	114 16.8	N12 49.6	Arcturus	146 05.4	N19 11.3
19	167 55.0	57 21.8	48.2	324 42.3	40.7	145 33.2	08.9	129 19.0	49.7	Atria	107 50.4	S69 01.5
20	182 57.5	72 21.4	47.8	339 45.1	40.7	160 35.2	09.1	144 21.2	49.8	Avior	234 22.8	S59 30.8
21	197 59.9	87 21.0 ..	47.4	354 47.9 ..	40.6	175 37.1 ..	09.3	159 23.3 ..	49.8	Bellatrix	278 44.0	N 6 20.8
22	213 02.4	102 20.6	47.0	9 50.7	40.6	190 39.1	09.5	174 25.5	49.9	Betelgeuse	271 13.4	N 7 24.3
23	228 04.9	117 20.2	46.7	24 53.5	40.6	205 41.1	09.7	189 27.7	50.0			
26 00	243 07.3	132 19.8	N24 46.3	39 56.3	S 9 40.6	220 43.0	N 8 09.9	204 29.8	N12 50.1	Canopus	264 01.5	S52 42.0
01	258 09.8	147 19.4	45.9	54 59.1	40.6	235 45.0	10.1	219 32.0	50.2	Capella	280 51.1	N45 59.7
02	273 12.3	162 19.0	45.5	70 01.8	40.5	250 47.0	10.3	234 34.2	50.3	Deneb	49 38.7	N45 16.5
03	288 14.7	177 18.6 ..	45.1	85 04.6 ..	40.5	265 48.9 ..	10.4	249 36.4 ..	50.4	Denebola	182 44.7	N14 34.6
04	303 17.2	192 18.2	44.7	100 07.4	40.5	280 50.9	10.6	264 38.5	50.5	Diphda	349 07.0	S17 59.5
05	318 19.6	207 17.8	44.3	115 10.2	40.5	295 52.9	10.8	279 40.7	50.6			
06	333 22.1	222 17.4	N24 43.9	130 13.0	S 9 40.5	310 54.8	N 8 11.0	294 42.9	N12 50.7	Dubhe	194 05.0	N61 45.6
W 07	348 24.6	237 17.0	43.5	145 15.8	40.4	325 56.8	11.2	309 45.0	50.8	Elnath	278 26.8	N28 36.3
E 08	3 27.0	252 16.6	43.1	160 18.6	40.4	340 58.8	11.4	324 47.2	50.8	Eltanin	90 50.7	N51 29.3
D 09	18 29.5	267 16.2 ..	42.8	175 21.4 ..	40.4	356 00.7 ..	11.6	339 49.4 ..	50.9	Enif	33 57.8	N 9 52.2
N 10	33 32.0	282 15.8	42.4	190 24.1	40.4	11 02.7	11.8	354 51.5	51.0	Fomalhaut	15 36.1	S29 37.5
E 11	48 34.4	297 15.4	42.0	205 26.9	40.4	26 04.7	12.0	9 53.7	51.1			
S 12	63 36.9	312 15.0	N24 41.6	220 29.7	S 9 40.4	41 06.7	N 8 12.1	24 55.9	N12 51.2	Gacrux	172 12.7	S57 06.8
D 13	78 39.4	327 14.6	41.2	235 32.5	40.3	56 08.6	12.3	39 58.1	51.3	Gienah	176 03.4	S17 32.4
A 14	93 41.8	342 14.2	40.8	250 35.2	40.3	71 10.6	12.5	55 00.2	51.4	Hadar	149 02.8	S60 22.3
Y 15	108 44.3	357 13.9 ..	40.4	265 38.0 ..	40.3	86 12.6 ..	12.7	70 02.4 ..	51.5	Hamal	328 13.4	N23 27.3
16	123 46.7	12 13.5	40.0	280 40.8	40.3	101 14.5	12.9	85 04.6	51.6	Kaus Aust.	83 57.9	S34 22.9
17	138 49.2	27 13.1	39.6	295 43.6	40.3	116 16.5	13.1	100 06.7	51.7			
18	153 51.7	42 12.7	N24 39.2	310 46.3	S 9 40.3	131 18.5	N 8 13.3	115 08.9	N12 51.8	Kochab	137 18.6	N74 09.7
19	168 54.1	57 12.3	38.8	325 49.1	40.3	146 20.4	13.5	130 11.1	51.8	Markab	13 49.3	N15 11.9
20	183 56.6	72 11.9	38.4	340 51.9	40.3	161 22.4	13.7	145 13.2	51.9	Menkar	314 26.8	N 4 05.0
21	198 59.1	87 11.5 ..	37.9	355 54.6 ..	40.2	176 24.4 ..	13.8	160 15.4 ..	52.0	Menkent	148 20.1	S36 22.0
22	214 01.5	102 11.2	37.5	10 57.4	40.2	191 26.4	14.0	175 17.6	52.1	Miaplacidus	221 42.2	S69 43.2
23	229 04.0	117 10.8	37.1	26 00.2	40.2	206 28.3	14.2	190 19.8	52.2			
27 00	244 06.5	132 10.4	N24 36.7	41 02.9	S 9 40.2	221 30.3	N 8 14.4	205 21.9	N12 52.3	Mirfak	308 56.5	N49 51.3
01	259 08.9	147 10.0	36.3	56 05.7	40.2	236 32.3	14.6	220 24.1	52.4	Nunki	76 11.5	S26 17.7
02	274 11.4	162 09.6	35.9	71 08.5	40.2	251 34.2	14.8	235 26.3	52.5	Peacock	53 36.1	S56 44.0
03	289 13.9	177 09.2 ..	35.5	86 11.2 ..	40.2	266 36.2 ..	15.0	250 28.4 ..	52.6	Pollux	243 41.3	N28 01.7
04	304 16.3	192 08.9	35.1	101 14.0	40.2	281 38.2	15.2	265 30.6	52.7	Procyon	245 11.4	N 5 13.5
05	319 18.8	207 08.5	34.7	116 16.7	40.2	296 40.1	15.3	280 32.8	52.8			
06	334 21.2	222 08.1	N24 34.3	131 19.5	S 9 40.2	311 42.1	N 8 15.5	295 34.9	N12 52.8	Rasalhague	96 16.3	N12 33.7
07	349 23.7	237 07.7	33.8	146 22.2	40.2	326 44.1	15.7	310 37.1	52.9	Regulus	207 55.2	N11 58.2
T 08	4 26.2	252 07.4	33.4	161 25.0	40.2	341 46.1	15.9	325 39.3	53.0	Rigel	281 22.9	S 8 12.3
H 09	19 28.6	267 07.0 ..	33.0	176 27.7 ..	40.2	356 48.0 ..	16.1	340 41.5 ..	53.1	Rigil Kent.	140 06.1	S60 50.0
U 10	34 31.1	282 06.6	32.6	191 30.5	40.1	11 50.0	16.3	355 43.6	53.2	Sabik	102 24.7	S15 43.4
R 11	49 33.6	297 06.2	32.2	206 33.2	40.1	26 52.0	16.5	10 45.8	53.3			
S 12	64 36.0	312 05.9	N24 31.8	221 36.0	S 9 40.1	41 53.9	N 8 16.7	25 48.0	N12 53.4	Schedar	349 53.3	N56 31.7
D 13	79 38.5	327 05.5	31.3	236 38.7	40.1	56 55.9	16.8	40 50.1	53.5	Shaula	96 36.3	S37 06.1
A 14	94 41.0	342 05.1	30.9	251 41.5	40.1	71 57.9	17.0	55 52.3	53.6	Sirius	258 43.6	S16 43.1
Y 15	109 43.4	357 04.8 ..	30.5	266 44.2 ..	40.1	86 59.9 ..	17.2	70 54.5 ..	53.7	Spica	158 42.5	S11 09.5
16	124 45.9	12 04.4	30.1	281 47.0	40.1	102 01.8	17.4	85 56.7	53.7	Suhail	223 00.6	S43 26.1
17	139 48.4	27 04.0	29.6	296 49.7	40.1	117 03.8	17.6	100 58.8	53.8			
18	154 50.8	42 03.7	N24 29.2	311 52.4	S 9 40.1	132 05.8	N 8 17.8	116 01.0	N12 53.9	Vega	80 46.0	N38 46.9
19	169 53.3	57 03.3	28.8	326 55.2	40.1	147 07.7	18.0	131 03.2	54.0	Zuben'ubi	137 17.2	S16 02.3
20	184 55.7	72 02.9	28.4	341 57.9	40.1	162 09.7	18.2	146 05.3	54.1		SHA	Mer. Pass.
21	199 58.2	87 02.6 ..	27.9	357 00.6 ..	40.1	177 11.7 ..	18.3	161 07.5 ..	54.2		° ′	h m
22	215 00.7	102 02.2	27.5	12 03.4	40.1	192 13.7	18.5	176 09.7	54.3	Venus	249 12.5	15 11
23	230 03.1	117 01.8	27.1	27 06.1	40.1	207 15.6	18.7	191 11.9	54.4	Mars	156 48.9	21 16
	h m									Jupiter	337 35.7	9 16
Mer. Pass. 7 46.2		v −0.4	d 0.4	v 2.8	d 0.0	v 2.0	d 0.2	v 2.2	d 0.1	Saturn	321 22.5	10 21

UT	SUN GHA	SUN Dec	MOON GHA	v	Dec	d	HP
d h	° ′	° ′	° ′	′	° ′	′	′
25 00	180 47.6	N20 49.7	55 42.2	14.9	N 1 22.7	10.4	55.0
01	195 47.5	50.1	70 16.1	14.9	1 12.3	10.4	54.9
02	210 47.5	50.6	84 50.0	14.9	1 01.9	10.5	54.9
03	225 47.4	.. 51.0	99 23.9	14.9	0 51.4	10.4	54.9
04	240 47.3	51.5	113 57.8	14.9	0 41.0	10.4	54.9
05	255 47.3	51.9	128 31.7	15.0	0 30.6	10.5	54.9
06	270 47.2	N20 52.4	143 05.7	15.0	N 0 20.1	10.4	54.8
07	285 47.2	52.8	157 39.7	15.0	N 0 09.7	10.4	54.8
08	300 47.1	53.3	172 13.7	15.0	S 0 00.7	10.4	54.8
09	315 47.0	.. 53.8	186 47.7	15.0	0 11.1	10.4	54.8
10	330 47.0	54.2	201 21.7	15.1	0 21.5	10.4	54.8
11	345 46.9	54.7	215 55.8	15.0	0 31.9	10.4	54.7
12	0 46.9	N20 55.1	230 29.8	15.1	S 0 42.3	10.4	54.7
13	15 46.8	55.6	245 03.9	15.1	0 52.7	10.3	54.7
14	30 46.7	56.0	259 38.0	15.1	1 03.0	10.4	54.7
15	45 46.7	.. 56.5	274 12.1	15.1	1 13.4	10.3	54.7
16	60 46.6	56.9	288 46.2	15.1	1 23.7	10.4	54.7
17	75 46.5	57.4	303 20.3	15.2	1 34.1	10.3	54.6
18	90 46.5	N20 57.8	317 54.5	15.1	S 1 44.4	10.3	54.6
19	105 46.4	58.2	332 28.6	15.2	1 54.7	10.3	54.6
20	120 46.4	58.7	347 02.8	15.1	2 05.0	10.3	54.6
21	135 46.3	.. 59.1	1 36.9	15.2	2 15.3	10.3	54.6
22	150 46.2	20 59.6	16 11.1	15.2	2 25.6	10.2	54.6
23	165 46.2	21 00.0	30 45.3	15.1	2 35.8	10.3	54.5
26 00	180 46.1	N21 00.5	45 19.4	15.2	S 2 46.1	10.2	54.5
01	195 46.0	00.9	59 53.6	15.2	2 56.3	10.2	54.5
02	210 46.0	01.4	74 27.8	15.2	3 06.5	10.2	54.5
03	225 45.9	.. 01.8	89 02.0	15.2	3 16.7	10.2	54.5
04	240 45.9	02.2	103 36.2	15.2	3 26.9	10.1	54.5
05	255 45.8	02.7	118 10.4	15.2	3 37.0	10.2	54.5
06	270 45.7	N21 03.1	132 44.6	15.2	S 3 47.2	10.1	54.4
07	285 45.7	03.6	147 18.8	15.2	3 57.3	10.1	54.4
08	300 45.6	04.0	161 53.0	15.2	4 07.4	10.1	54.4
09	315 45.5	.. 04.4	176 27.2	15.2	4 17.5	10.0	54.4
10	330 45.5	04.9	191 01.4	15.2	4 27.5	10.1	54.4
11	345 45.4	05.3	205 35.6	15.2	4 37.6	10.0	54.4
12	0 45.3	N21 05.7	220 09.8	15.2	S 4 47.6	10.0	54.4
13	15 45.3	06.2	234 44.0	15.2	4 57.6	9.9	54.3
14	30 45.2	06.6	249 18.2	15.2	5 07.5	10.0	54.3
15	45 45.1	.. 07.0	263 52.4	15.2	5 17.5	9.9	54.3
16	60 45.1	07.5	278 26.6	15.2	5 27.4	9.9	54.3
17	75 45.0	07.9	293 00.8	15.1	5 37.3	9.9	54.3
18	90 44.9	N21 08.3	307 34.9	15.2	S 5 47.2	9.8	54.3
19	105 44.9	08.8	322 09.1	15.1	5 57.0	9.8	54.3
20	120 44.8	09.2	336 43.2	15.2	6 06.8	9.8	54.3
21	135 44.7	.. 09.6	351 17.4	15.1	6 16.6	9.8	54.3
22	150 44.7	10.1	5 51.5	15.2	6 26.4	9.7	54.2
23	165 44.6	10.5	20 25.7	15.1	6 36.1	9.7	54.2
27 00	180 44.5	N21 10.9	34 59.8	15.1	S 6 45.8	9.7	54.2
01	195 44.5	11.3	49 33.9	15.1	6 55.5	9.6	54.2
02	210 44.4	11.8	64 08.0	15.1	7 05.1	9.6	54.2
03	225 44.3	.. 12.2	78 42.1	15.0	7 14.7	9.6	54.2
04	240 44.3	12.6	93 16.1	15.1	7 24.3	9.6	54.2
05	255 44.2	13.1	107 50.2	15.0	7 33.9	9.5	54.2
06	270 44.1	N21 13.5	122 24.2	15.1	S 7 43.4	9.5	54.2
07	285 44.0	13.9	136 58.3	15.0	7 52.9	9.4	54.2
08	300 44.0	14.3	151 32.3	15.0	8 02.3	9.4	54.2
09	315 43.9	.. 14.7	166 06.3	15.0	8 11.7	9.4	54.1
10	330 43.8	15.2	180 40.3	14.9	8 21.1	9.4	54.1
11	345 43.8	15.6	195 14.2	15.0	8 30.5	9.3	54.1
12	0 43.7	N21 16.0	209 48.2	14.9	S 8 39.8	9.2	54.1
13	15 43.6	16.4	224 22.1	14.9	8 49.0	9.3	54.1
14	30 43.5	16.9	238 56.0	14.9	8 58.3	9.2	54.1
15	45 43.5	.. 17.3	253 29.9	14.9	9 07.5	9.1	54.1
16	60 43.4	17.7	268 03.8	14.9	9 16.6	9.1	54.1
17	75 43.3	18.1	282 37.7	14.8	9 25.7	9.1	54.1
18	90 43.3	N21 18.5	297 11.5	14.8	S 9 34.8	9.0	54.1
19	105 43.2	18.9	311 45.3	14.8	9 43.8	9.0	54.1
20	120 43.1	19.4	326 19.1	14.8	9 52.8	9.0	54.1
21	135 43.0	.. 19.8	340 52.9	14.8	10 01.8	8.9	54.1
22	150 43.0	20.2	355 26.7	14.7	10 10.7	8.9	54.1
23	165 42.9	20.6	10 00.4	14.7	S10 19.6	8.8	54.0
	SD 15.8	d 0.4	SD 14.9		14.8		14.7

Lat.	Twilight Naut.	Twilight Civil	Sunrise	Moonrise 25	26	27	28
°	h m	h m	h m	h m	h m	h m	h m
N 72	□	□	□	14 59	16 38	18 19	20 05
N 70	□	□	□	14 58	16 30	18 03	19 38
68	////	////	00 26	14 56	16 23	17 51	19 18
66	////	////	01 40	14 55	16 18	17 40	19 03
64	////	////	02 15	14 54	16 13	17 32	18 50
62	////	01 01	02 40	14 53	16 09	17 24	18 39
60	////	01 46	03 00	14 52	16 05	17 18	18 30
N 58	////	02 14	03 16	14 51	16 02	17 12	18 22
56	00 55	02 35	03 30	14 51	15 59	17 08	18 15
54	01 36	02 53	03 42	14 50	15 57	17 03	18 09
52	02 02	03 07	03 52	14 50	15 55	16 59	18 03
50	02 23	03 20	04 02	14 49	15 53	16 56	17 58
45	02 59	03 45	04 21	14 48	15 48	16 48	17 47
N 40	03 26	04 05	04 37	14 47	15 45	16 41	17 38
35	03 46	04 21	04 50	14 47	15 41	16 36	17 30
30	04 02	04 35	05 01	14 46	15 39	16 31	17 23
20	04 28	04 57	05 21	14 45	15 34	16 23	17 12
N 10	04 49	05 15	05 38	14 44	15 30	16 15	17 01
0	05 05	05 31	05 53	14 43	15 26	16 08	16 52
S 10	05 21	05 46	06 09	14 42	15 22	16 02	16 42
20	05 35	06 02	06 25	14 41	15 18	15 54	16 32
30	05 49	06 18	06 44	14 40	15 13	15 46	16 21
35	05 56	06 27	06 55	14 40	15 10	15 42	16 14
40	06 04	06 38	07 07	14 39	15 07	15 36	16 07
45	06 13	06 49	07 22	14 38	15 04	15 30	15 58
S 50	06 23	07 03	07 40	14 38	15 00	15 23	15 48
52	06 27	07 09	07 48	14 37	14 58	15 19	15 43
54	06 32	07 16	07 58	14 37	14 56	15 16	15 38
56	06 37	07 24	08 09	14 36	14 54	15 12	15 32
58	06 42	07 33	08 21	14 36	14 51	15 07	15 26
S 60	06 48	07 42	08 35	14 35	14 48	15 02	15 18

Lat.	Sunset	Twilight Civil	Twilight Naut.	Moonset 25	26	27	28
°	h m	h m	h m	h m	h m	h m	h m
N 72	□	□	□	02 32	02 22	02 12	02 01
N 70	□	□	□	02 31	02 27	02 22	02 18
68	□	□	□	02 30	02 30	02 31	02 32
66	22 18	////	////	02 29	02 33	02 38	02 43
64	21 41	////	////	02 28	02 36	02 44	02 53
62	21 15	22 58	////	02 28	02 38	02 49	03 01
60	20 55	22 11	////	02 27	02 40	02 53	03 08
N 58	20 39	21 42	////	02 27	02 42	02 57	03 15
56	20 25	21 20	23 04	02 26	02 43	03 01	03 20
54	20 13	21 02	22 20	02 26	02 45	03 04	03 25
52	20 03	20 48	21 53	02 26	02 46	03 07	03 30
50	19 53	20 35	21 33	02 25	02 47	03 10	03 34
45	19 34	20 09	20 55	02 25	02 50	03 16	03 43
N 40	19 18	19 49	20 29	02 24	02 52	03 21	03 50
35	19 04	19 33	20 09	02 24	02 54	03 25	03 57
30	18 53	19 20	19 52	02 23	02 56	03 29	04 02
20	18 33	18 57	19 26	02 22	02 59	03 35	04 12
N 10	18 16	18 39	19 06	02 22	03 01	03 41	04 21
0	18 01	18 23	18 49	02 21	03 04	03 46	04 29
S 10	17 45	18 07	18 33	02 20	03 06	03 52	04 37
20	17 28	17 52	18 19	02 19	03 09	03 57	04 46
30	17 10	17 35	18 05	02 18	03 11	04 04	04 56
35	16 59	17 26	17 57	02 18	03 13	04 08	05 02
40	16 46	17 16	17 49	02 17	03 15	04 12	05 09
45	16 32	17 04	17 41	02 17	03 17	04 17	05 16
S 50	16 14	16 50	17 31	02 16	03 20	04 23	05 26
52	16 05	16 44	17 26	02 15	03 21	04 26	05 30
54	15 54	16 37	17 22	02 15	03 22	04 29	05 35
56	15 45	16 30	17 17	02 15	03 24	04 32	05 40
58	15 33	16 21	17 11	02 14	03 25	04 36	05 46
S 60	15 18	16 11	17 05	02 13	03 27	04 40	05 52

	SUN			MOON			
Day	Eqn. of Time 00h	Eqn. of Time 12h	Mer. Pass.	Mer. Pass. Upper	Mer. Pass. Lower	Age	Phase
d	m s	m s	h m	h m	h m	d	%
25	03 10	03 08	11 57	20 53	08 32	10	80
26	03 05	03 01	11 57	21 36	09 15	11	87
27	02 58	02 55	11 57	22 19	09 57	12	93

TUESDAY / WEDNESDAY / THURSDAY

1999 MAY 28, 29, 30 (FRI., SAT., SUN.)

UT	ARIES	VENUS −4.2		MARS −1.1		JUPITER −2.1		SATURN +0.4		STARS		
	GHA	GHA	Dec	GHA	Dec	GHA	Dec	GHA	Dec	Name	SHA	Dec
d h	° ′	° ′	° ′	° ′	° ′	° ′	° ′	° ′	° ′		° ′	° ′
28 00	245 05.6	132 01.5	N24 26.6	42 08.8	S 9 40.1	222 17.6	N 8 18.9	206 14.0	N12 54.5	Acamar	315 27.0	S40 18.5
01	260 08.1	147 01.1	26.2	57 11.6	40.1	237 19.6	19.1	221 16.2	54.6	Achernar	335 35.4	S57 14.3
02	275 10.5	162 00.8	25.8	72 14.3	40.1	252 21.6	19.3	236 18.4	54.6	Acrux	173 21.1	S63 05.9
03	290 13.0	177 00.4 ..	25.3	87 17.0 ..	40.1	267 23.5 ..	19.5	251 20.5 ..	54.7	Adhara	255 21.4	S28 58.5
04	305 15.5	192 00.0	24.9	102 19.7	40.1	282 25.5	19.7	266 22.7	54.8	Aldebaran	291 02.3	N16 30.3
05	320 17.9	206 59.7	24.5	117 22.5	40.1	297 27.5	19.8	281 24.9	54.9			
06	335 20.4	221 59.3	N24 24.0	132 25.2	S 9 40.2	312 29.4	N 8 20.0	296 27.1	N12 55.0	Alioth	166 30.0	N55 58.1
07	350 22.8	236 59.0	23.6	147 27.9	40.2	327 31.4	20.2	311 29.2	55.1	Alkaid	153 07.1	N49 19.2
08	5 25.3	251 58.6	23.2	162 30.6	40.2	342 33.4	20.4	326 31.4	55.2	Al Na'ir	27 57.4	S46 57.6
F 09	20 27.8	266 58.3 ..	22.7	177 33.3 ..	40.2	357 35.4 ..	20.6	341 33.6 ..	55.3	Alnilam	275 57.8	S 1 12.3
R 10	35 30.2	281 57.9	22.3	192 36.1	40.2	12 37.3	20.8	356 35.8	55.4	Alphard	218 06.9	S 8 39.5
I 11	50 32.7	296 57.6	21.8	207 38.8	40.2	27 39.3	21.0	11 37.9	55.5			
D 12	65 35.2	311 57.2	N24 21.4	222 41.5	S 9 40.2	42 41.3	N 8 21.1	26 40.1	N12 55.5	Alphecca	126 19.9	N26 43.1
A 13	80 37.6	326 56.9	20.9	237 44.2	40.2	57 43.3	21.3	41 42.3	55.6	Alpheratz	357 54.9	N29 04.9
Y 14	95 40.1	341 56.5	20.5	252 46.9	40.2	72 45.2	21.5	56 44.4	55.7	Altair	62 18.6	N 8 52.0
15	110 42.6	356 56.2 ..	20.1	267 49.6 .:	40.2	87 47.2 ..	21.7	71 46.6 ..	55.8	Ankaa	353 26.7	S42 18.5
16	125 45.0	11 55.8	19.6	282 52.3	40.2	102 49.2	21.9	86 48.8	55.9	Antares	112 39.3	S26 25.8
17	140 47.5	26 55.5	19.2	297 55.0	40.2	117 51.2	22.1	101 51.0	56.0			
18	155 50.0	41 55.1	N24 18.7	312 57.7	S 9 40.2	132 53.1	N 8 22.3	116 53.1	N12 56.1	Arcturus	146 05.4	N19 11.3
19	170 52.4	56 54.8	18.3	328 00.5	40.3	147 55.1	22.4	131 55.3	56.2	Atria	107 50.4	S69 01.5
20	185 54.9	71 54.4	17.8	343 03.2	40.3	162 57.1	22.6	146 57.5	56.3	Avior	234 22.8	S59 30.8
21	200 57.3	86 54.1 ..	17.4	358 05.9 ..	40.3	177 59.1 ..	22.8	161 59.7 ..	56.3	Bellatrix	278 44.0	N 6 20.8
22	215 59.8	101 53.8	16.9	13 08.6	40.3	193 01.0	23.0	177 01.8	56.4	Betelgeuse	271 13.4	N 7 24.3
23	231 02.3	116 53.4	16.5	28 11.3	40.3	208 03.0	23.2	192 04.0	56.5			
29 00	246 04.7	131 53.1	N24 16.0	43 14.0	S 9 40.3	223 05.0	N 8 23.4	207 06.2	N12 56.6	Canopus	264 01.5	S52 42.0
01	261 07.2	146 52.7	15.6	58 16.7	40.3	238 07.0	23.6	222 08.3	56.7	Capella	280 51.1	N45 59.7
02	276 09.7	161 52.4	15.1	73 19.3	40.3	253 08.9	23.7	237 10.5	56.8	Deneb	49 38.7	N45 16.5
03	291 12.1	176 52.1 ..	14.6	88 22.0 ..	40.4	268 10.9 ..	23.9	252 12.7 ..	56.9	Denebola	182 44.7	N14 34.6
04	306 14.6	191 51.7	14.2	103 24.7	40.4	283 12.9	24.1	267 14.9	57.0	Diphda	349 07.0	S17 59.5
05	321 17.1	206 51.4	13.7	118 27.4	40.4	298 14.9	24.3	282 17.0	57.1			
06	336 19.5	221 51.1	N24 13.3	133 30.1	S 9 40.4	313 16.8	N 8 24.5	297 19.2	N12 57.1	Dubhe	194 05.0	N61 45.6
07	351 22.0	236 50.7	12.8	148 32.8	40.4	328 18.8	24.7	312 21.4	57.2	Elnath	278 26.8	N28 36.3
S 08	6 24.5	251 50.4	12.3	163 35.5	40.4	343 20.8	24.8	327 23.6	57.3	Eltanin	90 50.7	N51 29.3
A 09	21 26.9	266 50.1 ..	11.9	178 38.2 ..	40.5	358 22.8 ..	25.0	342 25.7 ..	57.4	Enif	33 57.7	N 9 52.2
T 10	36 29.4	281 49.7	11.4	193 40.9	40.5	13 24.7	25.2	357 27.9	57.5	Fomalhaut	15 36.0	S29 37.5
U 11	51 31.8	296 49.4	11.0	208 43.5	40.5	28 26.7	25.4	12 30.1	57.6			
R 12	66 34.3	311 49.1	N24 10.5	223 46.2	S 9 40.5	43 28.7	N 8 25.6	27 32.2	N12 57.7	Gacrux	172 12.8	S57 06.8
D 13	81 36.8	326 48.8	10.0	238 48.9	40.5	58 30.7	25.8	42 34.4	57.8	Gienah	176 03.4	S17 32.4
A 14	96 39.2	341 48.4	09.6	253 51.6	40.5	73 32.6	26.0	57 36.6	57.9	Hadar	149 02.9	S60 22.3
Y 15	111 41.7	356 48.1 ..	09.1	268 54.3 ..	40.6	88 34.6 ..	26.1	72 38.8 ..	57.9	Hamal	328 13.4	N23 27.3
16	126 44.2	11 47.8	08.6	283 56.9	40.6	103 36.6	26.3	87 40.9	58.0	Kaus Aust.	83 57.9	S34 22.9
17	141 46.6	26 47.5	08.2	298 59.6	40.6	118 38.6	26.5	102 43.1	58.1			
18	156 49.1	41 47.1	N24 07.7	314 02.3	S 9 40.6	133 40.6	N 8 26.7	117 45.3	N12 58.2	Kochab	137 18.6	N74 09.7
19	171 51.6	56 46.8	07.2	329 05.0	40.6	148 42.5	26.9	132 47.5	58.3	Markab	13 49.2	N15 11.9
20	186 54.0	71 46.5	06.7	344 07.6	40.7	163 44.5	27.1	147 49.6	58.4	Menkar	314 26.8	N 4 05.0
21	201 56.5	86 46.2 ..	06.3	359 10.3 ..	40.7	178 46.5 ..	27.2	162 51.8 ..	58.5	Menkent	148 20.1	S36 22.1
22	216 59.0	101 45.9	05.8	14 13.0	40.7	193 48.5	27.4	177 54.0	58.6	Miaplacidus	221 42.2	S69 43.2
23	232 01.4	116 45.5	05.3	29 15.6	40.7	208 50.4	27.6	192 56.2	58.7			
30 00	247 03.9	131 45.2	N24 04.8	44 18.3	S 9 40.8	223 52.4	N 8 27.8	207 58.3	N12 58.7	Mirfak	308 56.5	N49 51.3
01	262 06.3	146 44.9	04.4	59 21.0	40.8	238 54.4	28.0	223 00.5	58.8	Nunki	76 11.5	S26 17.7
02	277 08.8	161 44.6	03.9	74 23.6	40.8	253 56.4	28.2	238 02.7	58.9	Peacock	53 36.1	S56 44.0
03	292 11.3	176 44.3 ..	03.4	89 26.3 ..	40.8	268 58.4 ..	28.3	253 04.9 ..	59.0	Pollux	243 41.3	N28 01.7
04	307 13.7	191 44.0	02.9	104 28.9	40.9	284 00.3	28.5	268 07.0	59.1	Procyon	245 11.4	N 5 13.5
05	322 16.2	206 43.7	02.5	119 31.6	40.9	299 02.3	28.7	283 09.2	59.2			
06	337 18.7	221 43.3	N24 02.0	134 34.3	S 9 40.9	314 04.3	N 8 28.9	298 11.4	N12 59.3	Rasalhague	96 16.2	N12 33.7
07	352 21.1	236 43.0	01.5	149 36.9	40.9	329 06.3	29.1	313 13.6	59.4	Regulus	207 55.2	N11 58.2
08	7 23.6	251 42.7	01.0	164 39.6	41.0	344 08.3	29.3	328 15.7	59.5	Rigel	281 22.9	S 8 12.3
S 09	22 26.1	266 42.4 ..	00.5	179 42.2 ..	41.0	359 10.2 ..	29.4	343 17.9 ..	59.5	Rigil Kent.	140 06.1	S60 50.0
U 10	37 28.5	281 42.1	24 00.0	194 44.9	41.0	14 12.2	29.6	358 20.1	59.6	Sabik	102 24.7	S15 43.4
N 11	52 31.0	296 41.8	23 59.6	209 47.5	41.1	29 14.2	29.8	13 22.3	59.7			
D 12	67 33.4	311 41.5	N23 59.1	224 50.2	S 9 41.1	44 16.2	N 8 30.0	28 24.4	N12 59.8	Schedar	349 53.3	N56 31.7
A 13	82 35.9	326 41.2	58.6	239 52.8	41.1	59 18.1	30.2	43 26.6	12 59.9	Shaula	96 36.3	S37 06.1
Y 14	97 38.4	341 40.9	58.1	254 55.5	41.1	74 20.1	30.4	58 28.8	13 00.0	Sirius	258 43.6	S16 43.1
15	112 40.8	356 40.6 ..	57.6	269 58.1 ..	41.2	89 22.1 ..	30.5	73 31.0 ..	00.1	Spica	158 42.5	S11 09.5
16	127 43.3	11 40.3	57.1	285 00.8	41.2	104 24.1	30.7	88 33.1	00.2	Suhail	223 00.6	S43 26.1
17	142 45.8	26 40.0	56.6	300 03.4	41.2	119 26.1	30.9	103 35.3	00.2			
18	157 48.2	41 39.7	N23 56.1	315 06.0	S 9 41.3	134 28.0	N 8 31.1	118 37.5	N13 00.3	Vega	80 46.0	N38 46.9
19	172 50.7	56 39.4	55.6	330 08.7	41.3	149 30.0	31.3	133 39.7	00.4	Zuben'ubi	137 17.2	S16 02.3
20	187 53.2	71 39.1	55.1	345 11.3	41.3	164 32.0	31.5	148 41.8	00.5		SHA	Mer. Pass.
21	202 55.6	86 38.8 ..	54.7	0 14.0 ..	41.4	179 34.0 ..	31.6	163 44.0 ..	00.6		° ′	h m
22	217 58.1	101 38.5	54.2	15 16.6	41.4	194 36.0	31.8	178 46.2	00.7	Venus	245 48.3	15 13
23	233 00.6	116 38.2	53.7	30 19.2	41.4	209 37.9	32.0	193 48.4	00.8	Mars	157 09.2	21 03
	h m									Jupiter	337 00.2	9 06
Mer. Pass. 7 34.4		v −0.3	d 0.5	v 2.7	d 0.0	v 2.0	d 0.2	v 2.2	d 0.1	Saturn	321 01.4	10 10

SUN and MOON

UT (d h)	SUN GHA	SUN Dec	MOON GHA	v	Dec	d	HP
28 00	180 42.8	N21 21.0	24 34.1	14.7	S10 28.4	8.8	54.0
01	195 42.8	21.4	39 07.8	14.7	10 37.2	8.7	54.0
02	210 42.7	21.8	53 41.5	14.6	10 45.9	8.7	54.0
03	225 42.6 ..	22.2	68 15.1	14.6	10 54.6	8.7	54.0
04	240 42.5	22.7	82 48.7	14.6	11 03.3	8.6	54.0
05	255 42.5	23.1	97 22.3	14.6	11 11.9	8.5	54.0
06	270 42.4	N21 23.5	111 55.9	14.5	S11 20.4	8.5	54.0
07	285 42.3	23.9	126 29.4	14.5	11 28.9	8.5	54.0
08	300 42.2	24.3	141 02.9	14.5	11 37.4	8.4	54.0
09	315 42.2 ..	24.7	155 36.4	14.5	11 45.8	8.3	54.0
10	330 42.1	25.1	170 09.9	14.4	11 54.1	8.4	54.0
11	345 42.0	25.5	184 43.3	14.4	12 02.5	8.2	54.0
12	0 41.9	N21 25.9	199 16.7	14.4	S12 10.7	8.2	54.0
13	15 41.9	26.3	213 50.1	14.4	12 18.9	8.2	54.0
14	30 41.8	26.7	228 23.5	14.3	12 27.1	8.1	54.0
15	45 41.7 ..	27.1	242 56.8	14.3	12 35.2	8.0	54.0
16	60 41.6	27.5	257 30.1	14.2	12 43.2	8.0	54.0
17	75 41.6	27.9	272 03.3	14.3	12 51.2	8.0	54.0
18	90 41.5	N21 28.3	286 36.6	14.2	S12 59.2	7.9	54.0
19	105 41.4	28.7	301 09.8	14.1	13 07.1	7.8	54.0
20	120 41.3	29.1	315 42.9	14.2	13 14.9	7.8	54.0
21	135 41.2 ..	29.5	330 16.1	14.1	13 22.7	7.7	54.0
22	150 41.2	29.9	344 49.2	14.1	13 30.4	7.7	54.0
23	165 41.1	30.3	359 22.3	14.0	13 38.1	7.6	54.0
29 00	180 41.0	N21 30.7	13 55.3	14.1	S13 45.7	7.6	54.0
01	195 40.9	31.1	28 28.4	13.9	13 53.3	7.5	54.0
02	210 40.9	31.5	43 01.3	14.0	14 00.8	7.4	54.0
03	225 40.8 ..	31.9	57 34.3	13.9	14 08.2	7.4	54.0
04	240 40.7	32.3	72 07.2	13.9	14 15.6	7.3	54.0
05	255 40.6	32.7	86 40.1	13.9	14 22.9	7.2	54.0
06	270 40.5	N21 33.1	101 13.0	13.8	S14 30.1	7.2	54.0
07	285 40.5	33.5	115 45.8	13.8	14 37.3	7.2	54.0
08	300 40.4	33.9	130 18.6	13.7	14 44.5	7.0	54.0
09	315 40.3 ..	34.3	144 51.3	13.8	14 51.5	7.0	54.0
10	330 40.2	34.7	159 24.1	13.7	14 58.5	7.0	54.0
11	345 40.1	35.1	173 56.8	13.6	15 05.5	6.9	54.0
12	0 40.1	N21 35.4	188 29.4	13.7	S15 12.4	6.8	54.0
13	15 40.0	35.8	203 02.1	13.5	15 19.2	6.7	54.0
14	30 39.9	36.2	217 34.6	13.6	15 25.9	6.7	54.0
15	45 39.8 ..	36.6	232 07.2	13.5	15 32.6	6.6	54.0
16	60 39.7	37.0	246 39.7	13.5	15 39.2	6.6	54.0
17	75 39.7	37.4	261 12.2	13.5	15 45.8	6.5	54.0
18	90 39.6	N21 37.8	275 44.7	13.4	S15 52.3	6.4	54.0
19	105 39.5	38.2	290 17.1	13.4	15 58.7	6.3	54.0
20	120 39.4	38.5	304 49.5	13.3	16 05.0	6.3	54.0
21	135 39.3 ..	38.9	319 21.8	13.4	16 11.3	6.2	54.0
22	150 39.3	39.3	333 54.2	13.3	16 17.5	6.1	54.0
23	165 39.2	39.7	348 26.5	13.2	16 23.6	6.1	54.0
30 00	180 39.1	N21 40.1	2 58.7	13.2	S16 29.7	6.0	54.0
01	195 39.0	40.4	17 30.9	13.2	16 35.7	5.9	54.0
02	210 38.9	40.8	32 03.1	13.2	16 41.6	5.9	54.0
03	225 38.8 ..	41.2	46 35.3	13.1	16 47.5	5.7	54.0
04	240 38.8	41.6	61 07.4	13.0	16 53.2	5.7	54.0
05	255 38.7	42.0	75 39.4	13.1	16 58.9	5.5	54.0
06	270 38.6	N21 42.3	90 11.5	13.0	S17 04.6	5.5	54.0
07	285 38.5	42.7	104 43.5	13.0	17 10.1	5.5	54.0
08	300 38.4	43.1	119 15.5	12.9	17 15.6	5.4	54.0
09	315 38.3 ..	43.5	133 47.4	12.9	17 21.0	5.3	54.0
10	330 38.3	43.8	148 19.3	12.9	17 26.3	5.3	54.0
11	345 38.2	44.2	162 51.2	12.8	17 31.6	5.2	54.0
12	0 38.1	N21 44.6	177 23.0	12.9	S17 36.8	5.1	54.0
13	15 38.0	45.0	191 54.9	12.7	17 41.9	5.0	54.0
14	30 37.9	45.3	206 26.6	12.8	17 46.9	4.9	54.0
15	45 37.8 ..	45.7	220 58.4	12.7	17 51.8	4.9	54.0
16	60 37.7	46.1	235 30.1	12.6	17 56.7	4.7	54.0
17	75 37.7	46.5	250 01.7	12.7	18 01.4	4.8	54.0
18	90 37.6	N21 46.8	264 33.4	12.6	S18 06.2	4.6	54.0
19	105 37.5	47.2	279 05.0	12.6	18 10.8	4.5	54.0
20	120 37.4	47.6	293 36.6	12.5	18 15.3	4.5	54.0
21	135 37.3 ..	47.9	308 08.1	12.5	18 19.8	4.3	54.1
22	150 37.2	48.3	322 39.6	12.5	18 24.1	4.3	54.1
23	165 37.1	48.7	337 11.1	12.5	S18 28.4	4.3	54.1
SD	15.8	d 0.4	SD 14.7		14.7		14.7

(Left margin day labels: FRIDAY, SATURDAY, SUNDAY)

Twilight / Sunrise / Moonrise

Lat.	Twilight Naut.	Twilight Civil	Sunrise	Moonrise 28	29	30	31
N 72	□	□	□	20 05	22 04	▬	▬
N 70	□	□	□	19 38	21 17	23 01	25 00
68	□	□	□	19 18	20 47	22 14	23 32
66	////	////	01 27	19 03	20 25	21 43	22 54
64	////	////	02 07	18 50	20 07	21 21	22 27
62	////	00 42	02 34	18 39	19 53	21 03	22 07
60	////	01 36	02 55	18 30	19 40	20 48	21 50
N 58	////	02 07	03 12	18 22	19 30	20 35	21 36
56	00 38	02 30	03 26	18 15	19 21	20 24	21 23
54	01 28	02 48	03 38	18 09	19 13	20 15	21 13
52	01 56	03 04	03 49	18 03	19 06	20 06	21 03
50	02 18	03 17	03 59	17 58	18 59	19 59	20 55
45	02 56	03 43	04 19	17 47	18 45	19 43	20 37
N 40	03 23	04 03	04 35	17 38	18 34	19 29	20 23
35	03 44	04 20	04 49	17 30	18 24	19 18	20 10
30	04 01	04 33	05 00	17 23	18 16	19 08	20 00
20	04 28	04 56	05 20	17 12	18 01	18 51	19 41
N 10	04 48	05 15	05 38	17 01	17 49	18 37	19 25
0	05 06	05 31	05 54	16 52	17 37	18 23	19 10
S 10	05 21	05 47	06 10	16 42	17 25	18 09	18 56
20	05 36	06 03	06 27	16 32	17 12	17 55	18 40
30	05 50	06 20	06 46	16 21	16 58	17 38	18 22
35	05 58	06 29	06 57	16 14	16 50	17 28	18 11
40	06 06	06 40	07 10	16 07	16 40	17 17	17 59
45	06 15	06 52	07 25	15 58	16 29	17 05	17 45
S 50	06 26	07 06	07 43	15 48	16 16	16 49	17 27
52	06 30	07 13	07 52	15 43	16 10	16 42	17 19
54	06 35	07 20	08 02	15 38	16 03	16 34	17 10
56	06 40	07 28	08 13	15 32	15 56	16 25	17 00
58	06 46	07 37	08 26	15 26	15 47	16 14	16 48
S 60	06 52	07 47	08 41	15 18	15 38	16 02	16 35

Sunset / Twilight / Moonset

Lat.	Sunset	Twilight Civil	Twilight Naut.	Moonset 28	29	30	31
N 72	□	□	□	02 01	01 46	01 20	▬
N 70	□	□	□	02 18	02 13	02 08	02 01
68	□	□	□	02 32	02 34	02 39	02 48
66	22 31	////	////	02 43	02 51	03 02	03 19
64	21 50	////	////	02 53	03 04	03 20	03 42
62	21 22	23 20	////	03 01	03 16	03 35	04 00
60	21 01	22 21	////	03 08	03 26	03 48	04 16
N 58	20 44	21 49	////	03 15	03 34	03 58	04 28
56	20 30	21 26	23 23	03 20	03 42	04 08	04 40
54	20 17	21 08	22 29	03 25	03 49	04 16	04 49
52	20 06	20 52	22 02	03 30	03 55	04 24	04 58
50	19 57	20 39	21 38	03 34	04 00	04 31	05 06
45	19 36	20 12	20 59	03 43	04 12	04 45	05 23
N 40	19 20	19 52	20 32	03 50	04 22	04 57	05 37
35	19 06	19 35	20 11	03 57	04 31	05 08	05 48
30	18 55	19 21	19 54	04 02	04 38	05 17	05 58
20	18 34	18 59	19 27	04 12	04 51	05 32	06 16
N 10	18 17	18 40	19 06	04 21	05 03	05 46	06 31
0	18 01	18 23	18 49	04 29	05 13	05 59	06 46
S 10	17 45	18 08	18 34	04 37	05 24	06 12	07 00
20	17 28	17 52	18 19	04 46	05 36	06 25	07 15
30	17 09	17 35	18 04	04 56	05 49	06 41	07 33
35	16 57	17 25	17 57	05 02	05 56	06 50	07 43
40	16 45	17 15	17 48	05 08	06 05	07 01	07 55
45	16 29	17 02	17 39	05 16	06 15	07 13	08 09
S 50	16 11	16 48	17 29	05 26	06 27	07 28	08 26
52	16 02	16 42	17 24	05 30	06 33	07 35	08 34
54	15 52	16 34	17 19	05 35	06 40	07 43	08 43
56	15 41	16 26	17 14	05 40	06 47	07 52	08 53
58	15 29	16 17	17 08	05 46	06 55	08 02	09 04
S 60	15 14	16 07	17 02	05 52	07 04	08 13	09 18

SUN and MOON

Day	Eqn. of Time 00h	12h	Mer. Pass.	Mer. Pass. Upper	Mer. Pass. Lower	Age	Phase
	m s	m s	h m	h m	h m	d	%
28	02 51	02 48	11 57	23 03	10 41	13	97
29	02 44	02 40	11 57	23 48	11 25	14	99
30	02 37	02 33	11 57	24 34	12 11	15	100

(Phase: open circle — full moon)

UT	ARIES	VENUS −4.2		MARS −1.0		JUPITER −2.1		SATURN +0.4		STARS		
	GHA	GHA	Dec	GHA	Dec	GHA	Dec	GHA	Dec	Name	SHA	Dec
d h	° ′	° ′	° ′	° ′	° ′	° ′	° ′	° ′	° ′		° ′	° ′
31 00	248 03.0	131 37.9	N23 53.2	45 21.9	S 9 41.5	224 39.9	N 8 32.2	208 50.5	N13 00.9	Acamar	315 27.0	S40 18.5
01	263 05.5	146 37.6	52.7	60 24.5	41.5	239 41.9	32.4	223 52.7	00.9	Achernar	335 35.3	S57 14.3
02	278 07.9	161 37.3	52.2	75 27.1	41.6	254 43.9	32.6	238 54.9	01.0	Acrux	173 21.1	S63 05.9
03	293 10.4	176 37.0	. . 51.7	90 29.8	41.6	269 45.9	. . 32.7	253 57.1	. . 01.1	Adhara	255 21.4	S28 58.5
04	308 12.9	191 36.7	51.2	105 32.4	41.6	284 47.9	32.9	268 59.2	01.2	Aldebaran	291 02.3	N16 30.3
05	323 15.3	206 36.4	50.7	120 35.0	41.7	299 49.8	33.1	284 01.4	01.3			
06	338 17.8	221 36.2	N23 50.2	135 37.6	S 9 41.7	314 51.8	N 8 33.3	299 03.6	N13 01.4	Alioth	166 30.0	N55 58.1
07	353 20.3	236 35.9	49.7	150 40.3	41.7	329 53.8	33.5	314 05.8	01.5	Alkaid	153 07.1	N49 19.3
08	8 22.7	251 35.6	49.2	165 42.9	41.8	344 55.8	33.6	329 07.9	01.6	Al Na'ir	27 57.3	S46 57.6
M 09	23 25.2	266 35.3	. . 48.7	180 45.5	. . 41.8	359 57.8	. . 33.8	344 10.1	. . 01.6	Alnilam	275 57.8	S 1 12.3
O 10	38 27.7	281 35.0	48.1	195 48.1	41.9	14 59.7	34.0	359 12.3	01.7	Alphard	218 06.9	S 8 39.5
N 11	53 30.1	296 34.7	47.6	210 50.7	41.9	30 01.7	34.2	14 14.5	01.8			
D 12	68 32.6	311 34.5	N23 47.1	225 53.4	S 9 41.9	45 03.7	N 8 34.4	29 16.6	N13 01.9	Alphecca	126 19.9	N26 43.2
A 13	83 35.1	326 34.2	46.6	240 56.0	42.0	60 05.7	34.6	44 18.8	02.0	Alpheratz	357 54.9	N29 05.0
Y 14	98 37.5	341 33.9	46.1	255 58.6	42.0	75 07.7	34.7	59 21.0	02.1	Altair	62 18.6	N 8 52.0
15	113 40.0	356 33.6	. . 45.6	271 01.2	. . 42.1	90 09.7	. . 34.9	74 23.2	. . 02.2	Ankaa	353 26.7	S42 18.5
16	128 42.4	11 33.3	45.1	286 03.8	42.1	105 11.6	35.1	89 25.3	02.3	Antares	112 39.3	S26 25.8
17	143 44.9	26 33.1	44.6	301 06.4	42.1	120 13.6	35.3	104 27.5	02.3			
18	158 47.4	41 32.8	N23 44.1	316 09.0	S 9 42.2	135 15.6	N 8 35.5	119 29.7	N13 02.4	Arcturus	146 05.4	N19 11.3
19	173 49.8	56 32.5	43.6	331 11.6	42.2	150 17.6	35.6	134 31.9	02.5	Atria	107 50.3	S69 01.5
20	188 52.3	71 32.2	43.0	346 14.2	42.3	165 19.6	35.8	149 34.1	02.6	Avior	234 22.8	S59 30.8
21	203 54.8	86 32.0	. . 42.5	1 16.8	. . 42.3	180 21.5	. . 36.0	164 36.2	. . 02.7	Bellatrix	278 44.0	N 6 20.8
22	218 57.2	101 31.7	42.0	16 19.5	42.4	195 23.5	36.2	179 38.4	02.8	Betelgeuse	271 13.4	N 7 24.3
23	233 59.7	116 31.4	41.5	31 22.1	42.4	210 25.5	36.4	194 40.6	02.9			
1 00	249 02.2	131 31.1	N23 41.0	46 24.7	S 9 42.5	225 27.5	N 8 36.5	209 42.8	N13 03.0	Canopus	264 01.5	S52 42.0
01	264 04.6	146 30.9	40.5	61 27.3	42.5	240 29.5	36.7	224 44.9	03.0	Capella	280 51.0	N45 59.7
02	279 07.1	161 30.6	39.9	76 29.9	42.6	255 31.5	36.9	239 47.1	03.1	Deneb	49 38.6	N45 16.5
03	294 09.6	176 30.3	. . 39.4	91 32.5	. . 42.6	270 33.4	. . 37.1	254 49.3	. . 03.2	Denebola	182 44.7	N14 34.6
04	309 12.0	191 30.1	38.9	106 35.0	42.7	285 35.4	37.3	269 51.5	03.3	Diphda	349 07.0	S17 59.4
05	324 14.5	206 29.8	38.4	121 37.6	42.7	300 37.4	37.4	284 53.6	03.4			
06	339 16.9	221 29.5	N23 37.9	136 40.2	S 9 42.7	315 39.4	N 8 37.6	299 55.8	N13 03.5	Dubhe	194 05.0	N61 45.6
07	354 19.4	236 29.3	37.3	151 42.8	42.8	330 41.4	37.8	314 58.0	03.6	Elnath	278 26.8	N28 36.3
T 08	9 21.9	251 29.0	36.8	166 45.4	42.8	345 43.4	38.0	330 00.2	03.7	Eltanin	90 50.7	N51 29.4
U 09	24 24.3	266 28.8	. . 36.3	181 48.0	. . 42.9	0 45.4	. . 38.2	345 02.4	. . 03.7	Enif	33 57.7	N 9 52.2
E 10	39 26.8	281 28.5	35.8	196 50.6	42.9	15 47.3	38.4	0 04.5	03.8	Fomalhaut	15 36.0	S29 37.4
S 11	54 29.3	296 28.2	35.2	211 53.2	43.0	30 49.3	38.5	15 06.7	03.9			
D 12	69 31.7	311 28.0	N23 34.7	226 55.8	S 9 43.1	45 51.3	N 8 38.7	30 08.9	N13 04.0	Gacrux	172 12.8	S57 06.8
A 13	84 34.2	326 27.7	34.2	241 58.3	43.1	60 53.3	38.9	45 11.1	04.1	Gienah	176 03.4	S17 32.4
Y 14	99 36.7	341 27.5	33.6	257 00.9	43.2	75 55.3	39.1	60 13.2	04.2	Hadar	149 02.9	S60 22.3
15	114 39.1	356 27.2	. . 33.1	272 03.5	. . 43.2	90 57.3	. . 39.3	75 15.4	. . 04.3	Hamal	328 13.3	N23 27.3
16	129 41.6	11 26.9	32.6	287 06.1	43.3	105 59.2	39.4	90 17.6	04.3	Kaus Aust.	83 57.9	S34 22.9
17	144 44.0	26 26.7	32.0	302 08.7	43.3	121 01.2	39.6	105 19.8	04.4			
18	159 46.5	41 26.4	N23 31.5	317 11.2	S 9 43.4	136 03.2	N 8 39.8	120 21.9	N13 04.5	Kochab	137 18.6	N74 09.8
19	174 49.0	56 26.2	31.0	332 13.8	43.4	151 05.2	40.0	135 24.1	04.6	Markab	13 49.2	N15 11.9
20	189 51.4	71 25.9	30.4	347 16.4	43.5	166 07.2	40.1	150 26.3	04.7	Menkar	314 26.8	N 4 05.0
21	204 53.9	86 25.7	. . 29.9	2 19.0	. . 43.5	181 09.2	. . 40.3	165 28.5	. . 04.8	Menkent	148 20.1	S36 22.1
22	219 56.4	101 25.4	29.4	17 21.5	43.6	196 11.2	40.5	180 30.7	04.9	Miaplacidus	221 42.3	S69 43.2
23	234 58.8	116 25.2	28.8	32 24.1	43.7	211 13.1	40.7	195 32.8	05.0			
2 00	250 01.3	131 25.0	N23 28.3	47 26.7	S 9 43.7	226 15.1	N 8 40.9	210 35.0	N13 05.0	Mirfak	308 56.5	N49 51.3
01	265 03.8	146 24.7	27.8	62 29.2	43.8	241 17.1	41.0	225 37.2	05.1	Nunki	76 11.5	S26 17.7
02	280 06.2	161 24.5	27.2	77 31.8	43.8	256 19.1	41.2	240 39.4	05.2	Peacock	53 36.0	S56 44.0
03	295 08.7	176 24.2	. . 26.7	92 34.4	. . 43.9	271 21.1	. . 41.4	255 41.6	. . 05.3	Pollux	243 41.3	N28 01.7
04	310 11.2	191 24.0	26.1	107 36.9	43.9	286 23.1	41.6	270 43.7	05.4	Procyon	245 11.4	N 5 13.5
05	325 13.6	206 23.7	25.6	122 39.5	44.0	301 25.1	41.8	285 45.9	05.5			
06	340 16.1	221 23.5	N23 25.0	137 42.1	S 9 44.1	316 27.1	N 8 41.9	300 48.1	N13 05.6	Rasalhague	96 16.2	N12 33.7
W 07	355 18.5	236 23.3	24.5	152 44.6	44.1	331 29.0	42.1	315 50.3	05.6	Regulus	207 55.2	N11 58.2
E 08	10 21.0	251 23.0	24.0	167 47.2	44.2	346 31.0	42.3	330 52.4	05.7	Rigel	281 22.9	S 8 12.3
D 09	25 23.5	266 22.8	. . 23.4	182 49.7	. . 44.2	1 33.0	. . 42.5	345 54.6	. . 05.8	Rigil Kent.	140 06.1	S60 50.0
N 10	40 25.9	281 22.5	22.9	197 52.3	44.3	16 35.0	42.7	0 56.8	05.9	Sabik	102 24.7	S15 43.4
E 11	55 28.4	296 22.3	22.3	212 54.9	44.4	31 37.0	42.8	15 59.0	06.0			
S 12	70 30.9	311 22.1	N23 21.8	227 57.4	S 9 44.4	46 39.0	N 8 43.0	31 01.2	N13 06.1	Schedar	349 53.2	N56 31.7
D 13	85 33.3	326 21.8	21.2	243 00.0	44.5	61 41.0	43.2	46 03.3	06.2	Shaula	96 36.3	S37 06.1
A 14	100 35.8	341 21.6	20.7	258 02.5	44.6	76 42.9	43.4	61 05.5	06.2	Sirius	258 43.6	S16 43.1
Y 15	115 38.3	356 21.4	. . 20.1	273 05.1	. . 44.6	91 44.9	. . 43.5	76 07.7	. . 06.3	Spica	158 42.5	S11 09.5
16	130 40.7	11 21.1	19.6	288 07.6	44.7	106 46.9	43.7	91 09.9	06.4	Suhail	223 00.6	S43 26.1
17	145 43.2	26 20.9	19.0	303 10.2	44.7	121 48.9	43.9	106 12.1	06.5			
18	160 45.7	41 20.7	N23 18.5	318 12.7	S 9 44.8	136 50.9	N 8 44.1	121 14.2	N13 06.6	Vega	80 45.9	N38 47.0
19	175 48.1	56 20.5	17.9	333 15.2	44.9	151 52.9	44.3	136 16.4	06.7	Zuben'ubi	137 17.2	S16 02.3
20	190 50.6	71 20.2	17.4	348 17.8	44.9	166 54.9	44.4	151 18.6	06.8		SHA	Mer. Pass.
21	205 53.0	86 20.0	. . 16.8	3 20.3	. . 45.0	181 56.9	. . 44.6	166 20.8	. . 06.8		° ′	h m
22	220 55.5	101 19.8	16.2	18 22.9	45.1	196 58.9	44.8	181 22.9	06.9	Venus	242 29.0	15 14
23	235 58.0	116 19.6	15.7	33 25.4	45.1	212 00.8	45.0	196 25.1	07.0	Mars	157 22.5	20 51
	h m									Jupiter	336 25.3	8 57
Mer. Pass. 7 22.6		v −0.3	d 0.5	v 2.6	d 0.1	v 2.0	d 0.2	v 2.2	d 0.1	Saturn	320 40.6	10 00

UT	SUN GHA	Dec	MOON GHA	v	Dec	d	HP
	° ′	° ′	° ′	′	° ′	′	′
d h							
31 00	180 37.1	N21 49.0	351 42.6	12.4	S18 32.7	4.1	54.1
01	195 37.0	49.4	6 14.0	12.4	18 36.8	4.0	54.1
02	210 36.9	49.8	20 45.4	12.3	18 40.8	4.0	54.1
03	225 36.8 ..	50.1	35 16.7	12.3	18 44.8	3.9	54.1
04	240 36.7	50.5	49 48.0	12.3	18 48.7	3.8	54.1
05	255 36.6	50.9	64 19.3	12.3	18 52.5	3.7	54.1
06	270 36.5	N21 51.2	78 50.6	12.2	S18 56.2	3.6	54.1
07	285 36.4	51.6	93 21.8	12.2	18 59.8	3.5	54.1
M 08	300 36.4	51.9	107 53.0	12.2	19 03.3	3.5	54.1
O 09	315 36.3 ..	52.3	122 24.2	12.1	19 06.8	3.3	54.1
N 10	330 36.2	52.7	136 55.3	12.2	19 10.1	3.3	54.1
D 11	345 36.1	53.0	151 26.5	12.0	19 13.4	3.2	54.2
A 12	0 36.0	N21 53.4	165 57.5	12.1	S19 16.6	3.1	54.2
Y 13	15 35.9	53.7	180 28.6	12.0	19 19.7	3.0	54.2
14	30 35.8	54.1	194 59.6	12.0	19 22.7	2.9	54.2
15	45 35.7 ..	54.4	209 30.6	12.0	19 25.6	2.8	54.2
16	60 35.6	54.8	224 01.6	12.0	19 28.4	2.8	54.2
17	75 35.5	55.2	238 32.6	11.9	19 31.2	2.6	54.2
18	90 35.5	N21 55.5	253 03.5	11.9	S19 33.8	2.6	54.2
19	105 35.4	55.9	267 34.4	11.9	19 36.4	2.5	54.2
20	120 35.3	56.2	282 05.3	11.8	19 38.9	2.3	54.2
21	135 35.2 ..	56.6	296 36.1	11.8	19 41.2	2.3	54.2
22	150 35.1	56.9	311 06.9	11.8	19 43.5	2.2	54.3
23	165 35.0	57.3	325 37.7	11.8	19 45.7	2.1	54.3
1 00	180 34.9	N21 57.6	340 08.5	11.7	S19 47.8	2.0	54.3
01	195 34.8	58.0	354 39.2	11.8	19 49.8	1.9	54.3
02	210 34.7	58.3	9 10.0	11.7	19 51.7	1.9	54.3
03	225 34.6 ..	58.7	23 40.7	11.7	19 53.6	1.7	54.3
04	240 34.5	59.0	38 11.4	11.6	19 55.3	1.7	54.3
05	255 34.5	59.4	52 42.0	11.7	19 57.0	1.5	54.3
06	270 34.4	N21 59.7	67 12.7	11.6	S19 58.5	1.5	54.3
T 07	285 34.3	22 00.1	81 43.3	11.6	20 00.0	1.3	54.3
U 08	300 34.2	00.4	96 13.9	11.6	20 01.3	1.3	54.4
E 09	315 34.1 ..	00.7	110 44.5	11.5	20 02.6	1.1	54.4
S 10	330 34.0	01.1	125 15.0	11.6	20 03.7	1.1	54.4
D 11	345 33.9	01.4	139 45.6	11.5	20 04.8	1.0	54.4
A 12	0 33.8	N22 01.8	154 16.1	11.5	S20 05.8	0.9	54.4
Y 13	15 33.7	02.1	168 46.6	11.5	20 06.7	0.8	54.4
14	30 33.6	02.5	183 17.1	11.4	20 07.5	0.7	54.4
15	45 33.5 ..	02.8	197 47.5	11.5	20 08.2	0.6	54.4
16	60 33.4	03.1	212 18.0	11.4	20 08.8	0.5	54.4
17	75 33.3	03.5	226 48.4	11.4	20 09.3	0.4	54.5
18	90 33.2	N22 03.8	241 18.8	11.4	S20 09.7	0.3	54.5
19	105 33.1	04.2	255 49.2	11.4	20 10.0	0.2	54.5
20	120 33.0	04.5	270 19.6	11.4	20 10.2	0.1	54.5
21	135 33.0 ..	04.8	284 50.0	11.4	20 10.3	0.1	54.5
22	150 32.9	05.2	299 20.4	11.3	20 10.4	0.1	54.5
23	165 32.8	05.5	313 50.7	11.4	20 10.3	0.2	54.5
2 00	180 32.7	N22 05.8	328 21.1	11.3	S20 10.1	0.3	54.6
01	195 32.6	06.2	342 51.4	11.3	20 09.8	0.3	54.6
02	210 32.5	06.5	357 21.7	11.3	20 09.5	0.5	54.6
03	225 32.4 ..	06.8	11 52.0	11.3	20 09.0	0.5	54.6
04	240 32.3	07.2	26 22.3	11.3	20 08.5	0.7	54.6
05	255 32.2	07.5	40 52.6	11.2	20 07.8	0.8	54.6
06	270 32.1	N22 07.8	55 22.8	11.3	S20 07.0	0.8	54.6
W 07	285 32.0	08.1	69 53.1	11.2	20 06.2	1.0	54.7
E 08	300 31.9	08.5	84 23.3	11.3	20 05.2	1.0	54.7
D 09	315 31.8 ..	08.8	98 53.6	11.2	20 04.2	1.2	54.7
N 10	330 31.7	09.1	113 23.8	11.2	20 03.0	1.2	54.7
E 11	345 31.6	09.5	127 54.0	11.3	20 01.8	1.3	54.7
S 12	0 31.5	N22 09.8	142 24.3	11.2	S20 00.5	1.5	54.7
D 13	15 31.4	10.1	156 54.5	11.2	19 59.0	1.5	54.7
A 14	30 31.3	10.4	171 24.7	11.2	19 57.5	1.6	54.8
Y 15	45 31.2 ..	10.8	185 54.9	11.2	19 55.9	1.8	54.8
16	60 31.1	11.1	200 25.1	11.2	19 54.1	1.8	54.8
17	75 31.0	11.4	214 55.3	11.2	19 52.3	1.9	54.8
18	90 30.9	N22 11.7	229 25.5	11.1	S19 50.4	2.0	54.8
19	105 30.8	12.1	243 55.6	11.2	19 48.4	2.2	54.8
20	120 30.7	12.4	258 25.8	11.2	19 46.2	2.2	54.9
21	135 30.6 ..	12.7	272 56.0	11.2	19 44.0	2.3	54.9
22	150 30.5	13.0	287 26.2	11.1	19 41.7	2.4	54.9
23	165 30.4	13.3	301 56.3	11.2	S19 39.3	2.5	54.9
	SD 15.8	d 0.3	SD 14.8		14.8		14.9

Twilight / Sunrise / Moonrise

Lat.	Naut.	Civil	Sunrise	Moonrise 31	1	2	3
°	h m	h m	h m	h m	h m	h m	h m
N 72	□	□	□	■■	■■	■■	■■
N 70	□	□	□	25 00	01 00	■■	02 12
68	□	□	□	23 32	24 32	00 32	01 05
66	////	////	01 14	22 54	23 50	24 29	00 29
64	////	////	01 59	22 27	23 22	24 03	00 03
62	////	00 10	02 28	22 07	23 01	23 43	24 15
60	////	01 28	02 50	21 50	22 43	23 27	24 01
N 58	////	02 01	03 08	21 36	22 29	23 13	23 49
56	00 09	02 25	03 23	21 23	22 16	23 01	23 38
54	01 20	02 44	03 35	21 13	22 05	22 51	23 29
52	01 51	03 00	03 46	21 03	21 55	22 41	23 21
50	02 13	03 14	03 56	20 55	21 47	22 33	23 13
45	02 53	03 41	04 17	20 37	21 28	22 15	22 57
N 40	03 21	04 01	04 33	20 23	21 13	22 01	22 44
35	03 42	04 18	04 47	20 10	21 01	21 48	22 33
30	04 00	04 32	04 59	20 00	20 50	21 38	22 23
20	04 27	04 56	05 20	19 41	20 31	21 19	22 06
N 10	04 48	05 15	05 38	19 25	20 14	21 03	21 51
0	05 06	05 32	05 54	19 10	19 59	20 48	21 38
S 10	05 22	05 48	06 10	18 56	19 44	20 33	21 24
20	05 37	06 04	06 28	18 40	19 27	20 17	21 09
30	05 52	06 21	06 47	18 22	19 08	19 59	20 52
35	06 00	06 31	06 59	18 11	18 58	19 48	20 42
40	06 08	06 42	07 12	17 59	18 45	19 36	20 31
45	06 18	06 54	07 28	17 45	18 30	19 21	20 17
S 50	06 28	07 09	07 47	17 27	18 12	19 03	20 01
52	06 33	07 16	07 56	17 19	18 03	18 55	19 53
54	06 38	07 23	08 06	17 10	17 54	18 46	19 45
56	06 43	07 31	08 17	17 00	17 43	18 35	19 35
58	06 49	07 41	08 30	16 48	17 31	18 23	19 24
S 60	06 56	07 51	08 46	16 35	17 16	18 09	19 12

Sunset / Twilight / Moonset

Lat.	Sunset	Civil	Naut.	Moonset 31	1	2	3
°	h m	h m	h m	h m	h m	h m	h m
N 72	□	□	□	■■	■■	■■	■■
N 70	□	□	□	02 01	01 41	■■	03 54
68	□	□	□	02 48	03 09	03 51	05 00
66	22 45	////	////	03 19	03 47	04 32	05 35
64	21 59	////	////	03 42	04 14	05 00	06 01
62	21 29	////	////	04 00	04 35	05 22	06 21
60	21 07	22 31	////	04 16	04 52	05 39	06 37
N 58	20 49	21 56	////	04 28	05 06	05 54	06 51
56	20 34	21 32	////	04 40	05 19	06 06	07 02
54	20 21	21 12	22 38	04 49	05 29	06 17	07 13
52	20 10	20 56	22 06	04 58	05 39	06 27	07 22
50	20 01	20 43	21 43	05 06	05 47	06 35	07 30
45	19 39	20 15	21 03	05 23	06 05	06 54	07 47
N 40	19 22	19 55	20 35	05 37	06 20	07 09	08 02
35	19 08	19 38	20 13	05 48	06 33	07 21	08 14
30	18 56	19 23	19 56	05 58	06 44	07 32	08 24
20	18 36	19 00	19 29	06 16	07 02	07 51	08 42
N 10	18 18	18 41	19 07	06 31	07 19	08 07	08 58
0	18 01	18 24	18 50	06 46	07 34	08 23	09 12
S 10	17 45	18 08	18 34	07 00	07 49	08 38	09 27
20	17 28	17 51	18 19	07 15	08 05	08 54	09 42
30	17 08	17 34	18 04	07 33	08 24	09 13	10 00
35	16 56	17 24	17 56	07 43	08 35	09 24	10 10
40	16 43	17 13	17 47	07 55	08 47	09 36	10 22
45	16 27	17 01	17 38	08 09	09 02	09 51	10 36
S 50	16 09	16 46	17 27	08 26	09 20	10 09	10 52
52	16 00	16 39	17 22	08 34	09 29	10 18	11 00
54	15 50	16 32	17 17	08 43	09 38	10 27	11 09
56	15 39	16 24	17 12	08 53	09 49	10 38	11 19
58	15 25	16 15	17 06	09 04	10 01	10 50	11 30
S 60	15 09	16 04	16 59	09 18	10 15	11 04	11 43

	SUN			MOON			
Day	Eqn. of Time 00h	12h	Mer. Pass.	Mer. Pass. Upper	Lower	Age	Phase
d	m s	m s	h m	h m	h m	d	%
31	02 28	02 24	11 58	00 34	12 58	16	99
1	02 20	02 15	11 58	01 22	13 46	17	95
2	02 11	02 06	11 58	02 11	14 36	18	91

UT	ARIES GHA	VENUS −4.3 GHA	VENUS Dec	MARS −1.0 GHA	MARS Dec	JUPITER −2.2 GHA	JUPITER Dec	SATURN +0.4 GHA	SATURN Dec	STARS Name	SHA	Dec
d h	° ′	° ′	° ′	° ′	° ′	° ′	° ′	° ′	° ′		° ′	° ′
3 00	251 00.4	131 19.3	N23 15.1	48 27.9	S 9 45.2	227 02.8	N 8 45.2	211 27.3	N13 07.1	Acamar	315 27.0	S40 18.5
01	266 02.9	146 19.1	14.6	63 30.5	45.3	242 04.8	45.3	226 29.5	07.2	Achernar	335 35.3	S57 14.3
02	281 05.4	161 18.9	14.0	78 33.0	45.4	257 06.8	45.5	241 31.7	07.3	Acrux	173 21.2	S63 06.0
03	296 07.8	176 18.7	.. 13.4	93 35.5	.. 45.4	272 08.8	.. 45.7	256 33.8	.. 07.4	Adhara	255 21.4	S28 58.5
04	311 10.3	191 18.5	12.9	108 38.1	45.5	287 10.8	45.9	271 36.0	07.4	Aldebaran	291 02.2	N16 30.3
05	326 12.8	206 18.3	12.3	123 40.6	45.6	302 12.8	46.0	286 38.2	07.5			
06	341 15.2	221 18.0	N23 11.8	138 43.1	S 9 45.6	317 14.8	N 8 46.2	301 40.4	N13 07.6	Alioth	166 30.0	N55 58.1
T 07	356 17.7	236 17.8	11.2	153 45.7	45.7	332 16.8	46.4	316 42.6	07.7	Alkaid	153 07.2	N49 19.3
H 08	11 20.2	251 17.6	10.6	168 48.2	45.8	347 18.8	46.6	331 44.7	07.8	Al Na'ir	27 57.3	S46 57.6
U 09	26 22.6	266 17.4	.. 10.1	183 50.7	.. 45.8	2 20.7	.. 46.7	346 46.9	.. 07.9	Alnilam	275 57.8	S 1 12.3
R 10	41 25.1	281 17.2	09.5	198 53.2	45.9	17 22.7	46.9	1 49.1	08.0	Alphard	218 06.9	S 8 39.5
S 11	56 27.5	296 17.0	08.9	213 55.8	46.0	32 24.7	47.1	16 51.3	08.0			
D 12	71 30.0	311 16.8	N23 08.4	228 58.3	S 9 46.1	47 26.7	N 8 47.3	31 53.5	N13 08.1	Alphecca	126 19.9	N26 43.2
A 13	86 32.5	326 16.6	07.8	244 00.8	46.1	62 28.7	47.5	46 55.6	08.2	Alpheratz	357 54.9	N29 05.0
Y 14	101 34.9	341 16.4	07.2	259 03.3	46.2	77 30.7	47.6	61 57.8	08.3	Altair	62 18.6	N 8 52.0
15	116 37.4	356 16.1	.. 06.7	274 05.8	.. 46.3	92 32.7	.. 47.8	77 00.0	.. 08.4	Ankaa	353 26.6	S42 18.5
16	131 39.9	11 15.9	06.1	289 08.4	46.4	107 34.7	48.0	92 02.2	08.5	Antares	112 39.3	S26 25.8
17	146 42.3	26 15.7	05.5	304 10.9	46.4	122 36.7	48.2	107 04.4	08.6			
18	161 44.8	41 15.5	N23 04.9	319 13.4	S 9 46.5	137 38.7	N 8 48.3	122 06.5	N13 08.6	Arcturus	146 05.4	N19 11.3
19	176 47.3	56 15.3	04.4	334 15.9	46.6	152 40.6	48.5	137 08.7	08.7	Atria	107 50.3	S69 01.5
20	191 49.7	71 15.1	03.8	349 18.4	46.7	167 42.6	48.7	152 10.9	08.8	Avior	234 22.8	S59 30.8
21	206 52.2	86 14.9	.. 03.2	4 20.9	.. 46.7	182 44.6	.. 48.9	167 13.1	.. 08.9	Bellatrix	278 44.0	N 6 20.8
22	221 54.7	101 14.7	02.6	19 23.4	46.8	197 46.6	49.0	182 15.3	09.0	Betelgeuse	271 13.4	N 7 24.3
23	236 57.1	116 14.5	02.1	34 25.9	46.9	212 48.6	49.2	197 17.5	09.1			
4 00	251 59.6	131 14.3	N23 01.5	49 28.4	S 9 47.0	227 50.6	N 8 49.4	212 19.6	N13 09.2	Canopus	264 01.5	S52 42.0
01	267 02.0	146 14.1	00.9	64 30.9	47.1	242 52.6	49.6	227 21.8	09.2	Capella	280 51.0	N45 59.7
02	282 04.5	161 14.0	23 00.3	79 33.4	47.1	257 54.6	49.7	242 24.0	09.3	Deneb	49 38.6	N45 16.5
03	297 07.0	176 13.8	22 59.8	94 35.9	.. 47.2	272 56.6	.. 49.9	257 26.2	.. 09.4	Denebola	182 44.7	N14 34.6
04	312 09.4	191 13.6	59.2	109 38.4	47.3	287 58.6	50.1	272 28.4	09.5	Diphda	349 07.0	S17 59.4
05	327 11.9	206 13.4	58.6	124 40.9	47.4	303 00.6	50.3	287 30.5	09.6			
06	342 14.4	221 13.2	N22 57.9	139 43.4	S 9 47.5	318 02.6	N 8 50.5	302 32.7	N13 09.7	Dubhe	194 05.0	N61 45.6
07	357 16.8	236 13.0	57.4	154 45.9	47.5	333 04.6	50.6	317 34.9	09.7	Elnath	278 26.8	N28 36.3
F 08	12 19.3	251 12.8	56.8	169 48.4	47.6	348 06.5	50.8	332 37.1	09.8	Eltanin	90 50.7	N51 29.4
R 09	27 21.8	266 12.6	.. 56.3	184 50.9	.. 47.7	3 08.5	.. 51.0	347 39.3	.. 09.9	Enif	33 57.7	N 9 52.2
I 10	42 24.2	281 12.4	55.7	199 53.4	47.8	18 10.5	51.2	2 41.4	10.0	Fomalhaut	15 36.0	S29 37.4
D 11	57 26.7	296 12.3	55.1	214 55.9	47.9	33 12.5	51.3	17 43.6	10.1			
A 12	72 29.1	311 12.1	N22 54.5	229 58.4	S 9 48.0	48 14.5	N 8 51.5	32 45.8	N13 10.2	Gacrux	172 12.8	S57 06.8
Y 13	87 31.6	326 11.9	53.9	245 00.9	48.0	63 16.5	51.7	47 48.0	10.3	Gienah	176 03.4	S17 32.4
14	102 34.1	341 11.7	53.3	260 03.4	48.1	78 18.5	51.9	62 50.2	10.3	Hadar	149 02.9	S60 22.3
15	117 36.5	356 11.5	.. 52.7	275 05.9	.. 48.2	93 20.5	.. 52.0	77 52.4	.. 10.4	Hamal	328 13.3	N23 27.3
16	132 39.0	11 11.3	52.1	290 08.4	48.3	108 22.5	52.2	92 54.5	10.5	Kaus Aust.	83 57.9	S34 23.0
17	147 41.5	26 11.2	51.6	305 10.8	48.4	123 24.5	52.4	107 56.7	10.6			
18	162 43.9	41 11.0	N22 51.0	320 13.3	S 9 48.5	138 26.5	N 8 52.6	122 58.9	N13 10.7	Kochab	137 18.7	N74 09.8
19	177 46.4	56 10.8	50.4	335 15.8	48.6	153 28.5	52.7	138 01.1	10.8	Markab	13 49.2	N15 11.9
20	192 48.9	71 10.6	49.8	350 18.3	48.7	168 30.5	52.9	153 03.3	10.8	Menkar	314 26.7	N 4 05.1
21	207 51.3	86 10.5	.. 49.2	5 20.8	.. 48.7	183 32.5	.. 53.1	168 05.4	.. 10.9	Menkent	148 20.1	S36 22.1
22	222 53.8	101 10.3	48.6	20 23.2	48.8	198 34.5	53.3	183 07.6	11.0	Miaplacidus	221 42.3	S69 43.2
23	237 56.3	116 10.1	48.0	35 25.7	48.9	213 36.5	53.4	198 09.8	11.1			
5 00	252 58.7	131 09.9	N22 47.4	50 28.2	S 9 49.0	228 38.4	N 8 53.6	213 12.0	N13 11.2	Mirfak	308 56.4	N49 51.3
01	268 01.2	146 09.8	46.8	65 30.7	49.1	243 40.4	53.8	228 14.2	11.3	Nunki	76 11.5	S26 17.7
02	283 03.6	161 09.6	46.2	80 33.1	49.2	258 42.4	54.0	243 16.4	11.3	Peacock	53 36.0	S56 44.0
03	298 06.1	176 09.4	.. 45.6	95 35.6	.. 49.3	273 44.4	.. 54.1	258 18.5	.. 11.4	Pollux	243 41.3	N28 01.7
04	313 08.6	191 09.3	45.0	110 38.1	49.4	288 46.4	54.3	273 20.7	11.5	Procyon	245 11.4	N 5 13.5
05	328 11.0	206 09.1	44.4	125 40.5	49.5	303 48.4	54.5	288 22.9	11.6			
06	343 13.5	221 08.9	N22 43.8	140 43.0	S 9 49.6	318 50.4	N 8 54.7	303 25.1	N13 11.7	Rasalhague	96 16.2	N12 33.7
07	358 16.0	236 08.8	43.2	155 45.5	49.6	333 52.4	54.8	318 27.3	11.8	Regulus	207 55.2	N11 58.2
S 08	13 18.4	251 08.6	42.6	170 47.9	49.7	348 54.4	55.0	333 29.5	11.9	Rigel	281 22.9	S 8 12.3
A 09	28 20.9	266 08.5	.. 42.0	185 50.4	.. 49.8	3 56.4	.. 55.2	348 31.6	.. 11.9	Rigil Kent.	140 06.1	S60 50.0
T 10	43 23.4	281 08.3	41.4	200 52.9	49.9	18 58.4	55.3	3 33.8	12.0	Sabik	102 24.7	S15 43.3
U 11	58 25.8	296 08.1	40.8	215 55.3	50.0	34 00.4	55.5	18 36.0	12.1			
R 12	73 28.3	311 08.0	N22 40.2	230 57.8	S 9 50.1	49 02.4	N 8 55.7	33 38.2	N13 12.2	Schedar	349 53.2	N56 31.7
D 13	88 30.8	326 07.8	39.6	246 00.2	50.2	64 04.4	55.9	48 40.4	12.3	Shaula	96 36.3	S37 06.1
A 14	103 33.2	341 07.7	39.0	261 02.7	50.3	79 06.4	56.0	63 42.6	12.4	Sirius	258 43.6	S16 43.1
Y 15	118 35.7	356 07.5	.. 38.4	276 05.1	.. 50.4	94 08.4	.. 56.2	78 44.7	.. 12.4	Spica	158 42.5	S11 09.5
16	133 38.1	11 07.4	37.7	291 07.6	50.5	109 10.4	56.4	93 46.9	12.5	Suhail	223 00.6	S43 26.1
17	148 40.6	26 07.2	37.1	306 10.0	50.6	124 12.4	56.6	108 49.1	12.6			
18	163 43.1	41 07.1	N22 36.5	321 12.5	S 9 50.7	139 14.4	N 8 56.7	123 51.3	N13 12.7	Vega	80 45.9	N38 47.0
19	178 45.5	56 06.9	35.9	336 14.9	50.8	154 16.4	56.9	138 53.5	12.8	Zuben'ubi	137 17.2	S16 02.3
20	193 48.0	71 06.8	35.3	351 17.4	50.9	169 18.4	57.1	153 55.7	12.9			
21	208 50.5	86 06.6	.. 34.7	6 19.8	.. 51.0	184 20.4	.. 57.3	168 57.8	.. 12.9		SHA	Mer. Pass.
22	223 52.9	101 06.5	34.1	21 22.3	51.1	199 22.4	57.4	184 00.0	13.0	Venus	239 14.8	h m 15 15
23	238 55.4	116 06.3	33.5	36 24.7	51.2	214 24.4	57.6	199 02.2	13.1	Mars	157 28.9	20 39
	h m									Jupiter	335 51.0	8 47
Mer. Pass. 7 10.8	v −0.2 d 0.6			v 2.5 d 0.1		v 2.0 d 0.2		v 2.2 d 0.1		Saturn	320 20.1	9 49

SUN and MOON

UT	SUN GHA	SUN Dec	MOON GHA	v	Dec	d	HP
d h	° ′	° ′	° ′	′	° ′	′	′
3 00	180 30.3	N22 13.6	316 26.5	11.2	S19 36.8	2.6	54.9
01	195 30.2	14.0	330 56.7	11.2	19 34.2	2.7	54.9
02	210 30.1	14.3	345 26.9	11.1	19 31.5	2.8	55.0
03	225 30.0	.. 14.6	359 57.0	11.2	19 28.7	2.9	55.0
04	240 29.9	14.9	14 27.2	11.2	19 25.8	3.0	55.0
05	255 29.8	15.2	28 57.4	11.1	19 22.8	3.1	55.0
06	270 29.7	N22 15.5	43 27.5	11.2	S19 19.7	3.2	55.0
07	285 29.6	15.9	57 57.7	11.2	19 16.5	3.3	55.1
T 08	300 29.5	16.2	72 27.9	11.2	19 13.2	3.4	55.1
H 09	315 29.4	.. 16.5	86 58.1	11.1	19 09.8	3.4	55.1
U 10	330 29.3	16.8	101 28.2	11.2	19 06.4	3.6	55.1
R 11	345 29.2	17.1	115 58.4	11.2	19 02.8	3.7	55.1
S 12	0 29.1	N22 17.4	130 28.6	11.2	S18 59.1	3.7	55.2
D 13	15 29.0	17.7	144 58.8	11.2	18 55.4	3.9	55.2
A 14	30 28.9	18.0	159 29.0	11.2	18 51.5	3.9	55.2
Y 15	45 28.8	.. 18.3	173 59.2	11.2	18 47.6	4.1	55.2
16	60 28.7	18.6	188 29.4	11.2	18 43.5	4.1	55.2
17	75 28.6	19.0	202 59.6	11.2	18 39.4	4.3	55.3
18	90 28.5	N22 19.3	217 29.8	11.2	S18 35.1	4.3	55.3
19	105 28.4	19.6	232 00.0	11.2	18 30.8	4.4	55.3
20	120 28.3	19.9	246 30.2	11.2	18 26.4	4.5	55.3
21	135 28.2	.. 20.2	261 00.4	11.2	18 21.9	4.6	55.3
22	150 28.1	20.5	275 30.6	11.3	18 17.3	4.7	55.4
23	165 28.0	20.8	290 00.9	11.2	18 12.6	4.8	55.4
4 00	180 27.9	N22 21.1	304 31.1	11.3	S18 07.8	4.9	55.4
01	195 27.8	21.4	319 01.4	11.2	18 02.9	5.0	55.4
02	210 27.7	21.7	333 31.6	11.3	17 57.9	5.1	55.5
03	225 27.6	.. 22.0	348 01.9	11.3	17 52.8	5.1	55.5
04	240 27.5	22.3	2 32.2	11.2	17 47.7	5.3	55.5
05	255 27.4	22.6	17 02.4	11.3	17 42.4	5.4	55.5
06	270 27.3	N22 22.9	31 32.7	11.3	S17 37.0	5.4	55.5
07	285 27.2	23.2	46 03.0	11.3	17 31.6	5.5	55.6
F 08	300 27.0	23.5	60 33.3	11.3	17 26.1	5.6	55.6
R 09	315 26.9	.. 23.8	75 03.6	11.3	17 20.5	5.7	55.6
I 10	330 26.8	24.1	89 33.9	11.3	17 14.8	5.8	55.6
11	345 26.7	24.4	104 04.2	11.4	17 09.0	5.9	55.7
D 12	0 26.6	N22 24.7	118 34.6	11.3	S17 03.1	6.0	55.7
A 13	15 26.5	24.9	133 04.9	11.4	16 57.1	6.1	55.7
Y 14	30 26.4	25.2	147 35.3	11.3	16 51.0	6.1	55.7
15	45 26.3	.. 25.5	162 05.6	11.4	16 44.9	6.3	55.8
16	60 26.2	25.8	176 36.0	11.3	16 38.6	6.3	55.8
17	75 26.1	26.1	191 06.3	11.4	16 32.3	6.4	55.8
18	90 26.0	N22 26.4	205 36.7	11.4	S16 25.9	6.5	55.8
19	105 25.9	26.7	220 07.1	11.4	16 19.4	6.6	55.9
20	120 25.8	27.0	234 37.5	11.4	16 12.8	6.7	55.9
21	135 25.7	.. 27.3	249 07.9	11.4	16 06.1	6.7	55.9
22	150 25.6	27.6	263 38.3	11.5	15 59.4	6.9	55.9
23	165 25.5	27.8	278 08.8	11.4	15 52.5	6.9	56.0
5 00	180 25.3	N22 28.1	292 39.2	11.4	S15 45.6	7.0	56.0
01	195 25.2	28.4	307 09.6	11.5	15 38.6	7.1	56.0
02	210 25.1	28.7	321 40.1	11.4	15 31.5	7.2	56.0
03	225 25.0	.. 29.0	336 10.5	11.5	15 24.3	7.2	56.1
04	240 24.9	29.3	350 41.0	11.4	15 17.1	7.4	56.1
05	255 24.8	29.5	5 11.5	11.4	15 09.7	7.4	56.1
06	270 24.7	N22 29.8	19 41.9	11.5	S15 02.3	7.5	56.2
07	285 24.6	30.1	34 12.4	11.5	14 54.8	7.6	56.2
S 08	300 24.5	30.4	48 42.9	11.5	14 47.2	7.8	56.2
A 09	315 24.4	.. 30.7	63 13.4	11.5	14 39.6	7.8	56.2
T 10	330 24.3	30.9	77 43.9	11.5	14 31.8	7.9	56.3
U 11	345 24.2	31.2	92 14.4	11.6	14 24.0	7.9	56.3
R 12	0 24.0	N22 31.5	106 45.0	11.5	S14 16.1	8.0	56.3
D 13	15 23.9	31.8	121 15.5	11.5	14 08.1	8.1	56.4
A 14	30 23.8	32.1	135 46.0	11.6	14 00.0	8.1	56.4
Y 15	45 23.7	.. 32.3	150 16.6	11.5	13 51.9	8.2	56.4
16	60 23.6	32.6	164 47.1	11.6	13 43.7	8.3	56.4
17	75 23.5	32.9	179 17.7	11.5	13 35.4	8.4	56.5
18	90 23.4	N22 33.2	193 48.2	11.6	S13 27.0	8.4	56.5
19	105 23.3	33.4	208 18.8	11.6	13 18.6	8.5	56.5
20	120 23.2	33.7	222 49.4	11.5	13 10.1	8.6	56.6
21	135 23.1	.. 34.0	237 19.9	11.6	13 01.5	8.7	56.6
22	150 22.9	34.2	251 50.5	11.6	12 52.8	8.7	56.6
23	165 22.8	34.5	266 21.1	11.6	S12 44.1	8.8	56.6
SD	15.8	d 0.3	SD 15.0		15.2		15.3

Twilight, Sunrise and Moonrise

Lat.	Naut.	Civil	Sunrise	Moonrise 3	4	5	6
°	h m	h m	h m	h m	h m	h m	h m
N 72	□	□	□	■	03 30	02 31	02 11
N 70	□	□	□	02 12	02 01	01 54	01 49
68	□	□	□	01 05	01 21	01 29	01 33
66	////	////	01 01	00 29	00 54	01 09	01 19
64	////	////	01 52	00 03	00 32	00 53	01 07
62	////	////	02 23	24 15	00 15	00 39	00 58
60	////	01 19	02 46	24 01	00 01	00 28	00 49
N 58	////	01 56	03 04	23 49	24 18	00 18	00 42
56	////	02 21	03 20	23 38	24 09	00 09	00 35
54	01 12	02 41	03 33	23 29	24 02	00 02	00 30
52	01 46	02 57	03 44	23 21	23 55	24 24	00 24
50	02 10	03 11	03 54	23 13	23 49	24 19	00 19
45	02 51	03 39	04 15	22 57	23 35	24 09	00 09
N 40	03 19	04 00	04 32	22 44	23 24	24 00	00 00
35	03 41	04 17	04 47	22 33	23 14	23 53	24 30
30	03 59	04 32	04 59	22 23	23 06	23 46	24 25
20	04 27	04 55	05 20	22 06	22 51	23 35	24 17
N 10	04 48	05 15	05 38	21 51	22 39	23 25	24 11
0	05 06	05 32	05 55	21 38	22 27	23 16	24 04
S 10	05 22	05 49	06 11	21 24	22 15	23 06	23 58
20	05 38	06 05	06 29	21 09	22 02	22 56	23 51
30	05 53	06 23	06 49	20 52	21 47	22 45	23 43
35	06 01	06 33	07 01	20 42	21 39	22 38	23 39
40	06 10	06 44	07 14	20 31	21 29	22 30	23 34
45	06 20	06 57	07 30	20 17	21 18	22 21	23 28
S 50	06 31	07 12	07 49	20 01	21 04	22 11	23 20
52	06 35	07 19	07 59	19 53	20 57	22 06	23 17
54	06 41	07 26	08 09	19 45	20 50	22 00	23 13
56	06 46	07 35	08 21	19 35	20 42	21 54	23 09
58	06 53	07 44	08 34	19 24	20 33	21 47	23 05
S 60	06 59	07 55	08 50	19 12	20 23	21 39	23 00

Sunset, Twilight and Moonset

Lat.	Sunset	Civil	Naut.	Moonset 3	4	5	6
°	h m	h m	h m	h m	h m	h m	h m
N 72	□	□	□	■	04 19	07 00	09 02
N 70	□	□	□	03 54	05 47	07 35	09 22
68	□	□	□	05 00	06 26	08 00	09 37
66	23 00	////	////	05 35	06 53	08 19	09 50
64	22 07	////	////	06 01	07 14	08 35	10 00
62	21 35	////	////	06 21	07 30	08 47	10 09
60	21 12	22 40	////	06 37	07 44	08 58	10 17
N 58	20 53	22 02	////	06 51	07 56	09 07	10 23
56	20 38	21 37	////	07 02	08 06	09 16	10 29
54	20 24	21 17	22 47	07 13	08 15	09 23	10 35
52	20 13	21 00	22 12	07 22	08 23	09 29	10 39
50	20 03	20 46	21 48	07 30	08 30	09 35	10 43
45	19 42	20 18	21 06	07 47	08 46	09 48	10 53
N 40	19 24	19 57	20 38	08 02	08 58	09 58	11 00
35	19 10	19 39	20 16	08 14	09 09	10 07	11 07
30	18 58	19 25	19 58	08 24	09 18	10 15	11 12
20	18 37	19 01	19 30	08 42	09 34	10 28	11 22
N 10	18 19	18 42	19 08	08 58	09 48	10 39	11 31
0	18 02	18 24	18 50	09 12	10 01	10 50	11 39
S 10	17 45	18 08	18 34	09 27	10 14	11 01	11 47
20	17 28	17 51	18 19	09 42	10 28	11 12	11 55
30	17 07	17 34	18 03	10 00	10 44	11 25	12 05
35	16 56	17 24	17 55	10 10	10 53	11 33	12 10
40	16 42	17 12	17 46	10 22	11 03	11 41	12 16
45	16 26	17 00	17 36	10 36	11 15	11 51	12 24
S 50	16 07	16 45	17 26	10 52	11 30	12 03	12 32
52	15 58	16 38	17 21	11 00	11 37	12 08	12 36
54	15 47	16 30	17 15	11 09	11 44	12 14	12 40
56	15 35	16 21	17 10	11 19	11 53	12 21	12 45
58	15 22	16 12	17 04	11 30	12 02	12 29	12 50
S 60	15 06	16 01	16 57	11 43	12 13	12 37	12 56

SUN and MOON

Day	Eqn. of Time 00h	12h	Mer. Pass.	Mer. Pass. Upper	Lower	Age	Phase
d	m s	m s	h m	h m	h m	d	%
3	02 01	01 57	11 58	03 00	15 25	19	84
4	01 52	01 47	11 58	03 50	16 14	20	77
5	01 42	01 36	11 58	04 39	17 03	21	67

UT (d h)	ARIES GHA	VENUS GHA	VENUS Dec	MARS GHA	MARS Dec	JUPITER GHA	JUPITER Dec	SATURN GHA	SATURN Dec	Star Name	SHA	Dec
		VENUS −4.3		MARS −0.9		JUPITER −2.2		SATURN +0.4		STARS		
6 00	253 57.9	131 06.2	N22 32.9	51 27.2	S 9 51.3	229 26.4	N 8 57.8	214 04.4	N13 13.2	Acamar	315 27.0	S40 18.5
01	269 00.3	146 06.0	32.2	66 29.6	51.4	244 28.4	57.9	229 06.6	13.3	Achernar	335 35.3	S57 14.3
02	284 02.8	161 05.9	31.6	81 32.1	51.5	259 30.4	58.1	244 08.8	13.4	Acrux	173 21.2	S63 06.0
03	299 05.2	176 05.8 ..	31.0	96 34.5 ..	51.6	274 32.4 ..	58.3	259 10.9 ..	13.4	Adhara	255 21.4	S28 58.5
04	314 07.7	191 05.6	30.4	111 36.9	51.7	289 34.4	58.5	274 13.1	13.5	Aldebaran	291 02.2	N16 30.3
05	329 10.2	206 05.5	29.8	126 39.4	51.8	304 36.4	58.6	289 15.3	13.6			
06	344 12.6	221 05.3	N22 29.1	141 41.8	S 9 51.9	319 38.4	N 8 58.8	304 17.5	N13 13.7	Alioth	166 30.0	N55 58.1
07	359 15.1	236 05.2	28.5	156 44.2	52.0	334 40.4	59.0	319 19.7	13.8	Alkaid	153 07.2	N49 19.3
S 08	14 17.6	251 05.1	27.9	171 46.7	52.1	349 42.3	59.2	334 21.9	13.9	Al Na'ir	27 57.3	S46 57.6
U 09	29 20.0	266 04.9 ..	27.3	186 49.1 ..	52.2	4 44.3 ..	59.3	349 24.0 ..	13.9	Alnilam	275 57.8	S 1 12.3
N 10	44 22.5	281 04.8	26.7	201 51.5	52.3	19 46.3	59.5	4 26.2	14.0	Alphard	218 06.9	S 8 39.5
D 11	59 25.0	296 04.7	26.0	216 54.0	52.4	34 48.3	59.7	19 28.4	14.1			
A 12	74 27.4	311 04.5	N22 25.4	231 56.4	S 9 52.5	49 50.3	N 8 59.8	34 30.6	N13 14.2	Alphecca	126 19.9	N26 43.2
Y 13	89 29.9	326 04.4	24.8	246 58.8	52.6	64 52.3	9 00.0	49 32.8	14.3	Alpheratz	357 54.9	N29 05.0
14	104 32.4	341 04.3	24.2	262 01.2	52.7	79 54.3	00.2	64 35.0	14.4	Altair	62 18.6	N 8 52.0
15	119 34.8	356 04.1 ..	23.5	277 03.7 ..	52.8	94 56.3 ..	00.4	79 37.2 ..	14.4	Ankaa	353 26.6	S42 18.5
16	134 37.3	11 04.0	22.9	292 06.1	52.9	109 58.3	00.5	94 39.3	14.5	Antares	112 39.3	S26 25.8
17	149 39.7	26 03.9	22.3	307 08.5	53.1	125 00.3	00.7	109 41.5	14.6			
18	164 42.2	41 03.8	N22 21.7	322 10.9	S 9 53.2	140 02.3	N 9 00.9	124 43.7	N13 14.7	Arcturus	146 05.4	N19 11.3
19	179 44.7	56 03.6	21.0	337 13.4	53.3	155 04.3	01.1	139 45.9	14.8	Atria	107 50.3	S69 01.5
20	194 47.1	71 03.5	20.4	352 15.8	53.4	170 06.3	01.2	154 48.1	14.9	Avior	234 22.9	S59 30.7
21	209 49.6	86 03.4 ..	19.8	7 18.2 ..	53.5	185 08.3 ..	01.4	169 50.3 ..	14.9	Bellatrix	278 44.0	N 6 20.8
22	224 52.1	101 03.3	19.1	22 20.6	53.6	200 10.3	01.6	184 52.5	15.0	Betelgeuse	271 13.4	N 7 24.3
23	239 54.5	116 03.2	18.5	37 23.0	53.7	215 12.3	01.7	199 54.6	15.1			
7 00	254 57.0	131 03.0	N22 17.9	52 25.4	S 9 53.8	230 14.3	N 9 01.9	214 56.8	N13 15.2	Canopus	264 01.5	S52 41.9
01	269 59.5	146 02.9	17.2	67 27.8	53.9	245 16.3	02.1	229 59.0	15.3	Capella	280 51.0	N45 59.7
02	285 01.9	161 02.8	16.6	82 30.2	54.0	260 18.4	02.3	245 01.2	15.3	Deneb	49 38.6	N45 16.5
03	300 04.4	176 02.7 ..	16.0	97 32.7 ..	54.2	275 20.4 ..	02.4	260 03.4 ..	15.4	Denebola	182 44.7	N14 34.6
04	315 06.9	191 02.6	15.3	112 35.1	54.3	290 22.4	02.6	275 05.6	15.5	Diphda	349 07.0	S17 59.4
05	330 09.3	206 02.5	14.7	127 37.5	54.4	305 24.4	02.8	290 07.8	15.6			
06	345 11.8	221 02.4	N22 14.1	142 39.9	S 9 54.5	320 26.4	N 9 02.9	305 09.9	N13 15.7	Dubhe	194 05.1	N61 45.6
07	0 14.2	236 02.3	13.4	157 42.3	54.6	335 28.4	03.1	320 12.1	15.8	Elnath	278 26.8	N28 36.3
M 08	15 16.7	251 02.1	12.8	172 44.7	54.7	350 30.4	03.3	335 14.3	15.8	Eltanin	90 50.7	N51 29.4
O 09	30 19.2	266 02.0 ..	12.1	187 47.1 ..	54.8	5 32.4 ..	03.4	350 16.5 ..	15.9	Enif	33 57.7	N 9 52.3
N 10	45 21.6	281 01.9	11.5	202 49.5	55.0	20 34.4	03.6	5 18.7	16.0	Fomalhaut	15 36.0	S29 37.4
D 11	60 24.1	296 01.8	10.9	217 51.9	55.1	35 36.4	03.8	20 20.9	16.1			
A 12	75 26.6	311 01.7	N22 10.2	232 54.3	S 9 55.2	50 38.4	N 9 04.0	35 23.1	N13 16.2	Gacrux	172 12.8	S57 06.8
Y 13	90 29.0	326 01.6	09.6	247 56.7	55.3	65 40.4	04.1	50 25.2	16.3	Gienah	176 03.4	S17 32.4
14	105 31.5	341 01.5	08.9	262 59.1	55.4	80 42.4	04.3	65 27.4	16.3	Hadar	149 02.9	S60 22.3
15	120 34.0	356 01.4 ..	08.3	278 01.5 ..	55.5	95 44.4 ..	04.5	80 29.6 ..	16.4	Hamal	328 13.3	N23 27.3
16	135 36.4	11 01.3	07.7	293 03.9	55.6	110 46.4	04.6	95 31.8	16.5	Kaus Aust.	83 57.9	S34 23.0
17	150 38.9	26 01.2	07.0	308 06.2	55.8	125 48.4	04.8	110 34.0	16.6			
18	165 41.3	41 01.1	N22 06.4	323 08.6	S 9 55.9	140 50.4	N 9 05.0	125 36.2	N13 16.7	Kochab	137 18.7	N74 09.8
19	180 43.8	56 01.0	05.7	338 11.0	56.0	155 52.4	05.2	140 38.4	16.7	Markab	13 49.2	N15 12.0
20	195 46.3	71 00.9	05.1	353 13.4	56.1	170 54.4	05.3	155 40.5	16.8	Menkar	314 26.7	N 4 05.1
21	210 48.7	86 00.8 ..	04.4	8 15.8 ..	56.2	185 56.4 ..	05.5	170 42.7 ..	16.9	Menkent	148 20.1	S36 22.1
22	225 51.2	101 00.7	03.8	23 18.2	56.4	200 58.4	05.7	185 44.9	17.0	Miaplacidus	221 42.4	S69 43.2
23	240 53.7	116 00.7	03.1	38 20.6	56.5	216 00.4	05.8	200 47.1	17.1			
8 00	255 56.1	131 00.6	N22 02.5	53 22.9	S 9 56.6	231 02.4	N 9 06.0	215 49.3	N13 17.2	Mirfak	308 56.4	N49 51.3
01	270 58.6	146 00.5	01.8	68 25.3	56.7	246 04.4	06.2	230 51.5	17.2	Nunki	76 11.5	S26 17.7
02	286 01.1	161 00.4	01.2	83 27.7	56.8	261 06.4	06.3	245 53.7	17.3	Peacock	53 36.0	S56 44.0
03	301 03.5	176 00.3	22 00.5	98 30.1 ..	57.0	276 08.4 ..	06.5	260 55.9 ..	17.4	Pollux	243 41.3	N28 01.7
04	316 06.0	191 00.2	21 59.9	113 32.5	57.1	291 10.4	06.7	275 58.0	17.5	Procyon	245 11.4	N 5 13.5
05	331 08.5	206 00.1	59.2	128 34.8	57.2	306 12.4	06.8	291 00.2	17.6			
06	346 10.9	221 00.0	N21 58.6	143 37.2	S 9 57.3	321 14.4	N 9 07.0	306 02.4	N13 17.6	Rasalhague	96 16.2	N12 33.7
07	1 13.4	236 00.0	57.9	158 39.6	57.5	336 16.4	07.2	321 04.6	17.7	Regulus	207 55.2	N11 58.3
T 08	16 15.8	250 59.9	57.2	173 41.9	57.6	351 18.4	07.4	336 06.8	17.8	Rigel	281 22.9	S 8 12.3
U 09	31 18.3	265 59.8 ..	56.6	188 44.3 ..	57.7	6 20.5 ..	07.5	351 09.0 ..	17.9	Rigil Kent.	140 06.1	S60 50.0
E 10	46 20.8	280 59.7	55.9	203 46.7	57.8	21 22.5	07.7	6 11.2	18.0	Sabik	102 24.7	S15 43.3
S 11	61 23.2	295 59.6	55.3	218 49.1	58.0	36 24.5	07.9	21 13.4	18.0			
D 12	76 25.7	310 59.6	N21 54.6	233 51.4	S 9 58.1	51 26.5	N 9 08.0	36 15.5	N13 18.1	Schedar	349 53.2	N56 31.7
A 13	91 28.2	325 59.5	54.0	248 53.8	58.2	66 28.5	08.2	51 17.7	18.2	Shaula	96 36.3	S37 06.1
Y 14	106 30.6	340 59.4	53.3	263 56.1	58.3	81 30.5	08.4	66 19.9	18.3	Sirius	258 43.7	S16 43.1
15	121 33.1	355 59.3 ..	52.6	278 58.5 ..	58.5	96 32.5 ..	08.5	81 22.1 ..	18.4	Spica	158 42.5	S11 09.5
16	136 35.6	10 59.3	52.0	294 00.9	58.6	111 34.5	08.7	96 24.3	18.5	Suhail	223 00.7	S43 26.1
17	151 38.0	25 59.2	51.3	309 03.2	58.7	126 36.5	08.9	111 26.5	18.5			
18	166 40.5	40 59.1	N21 50.7	324 05.6	S 9 58.9	141 38.5	N 9 09.0	126 28.7	N13 18.6	Vega	80 45.9	N38 47.0
19	181 43.0	55 59.1	50.0	339 07.9	59.0	156 40.5	09.2	141 30.9	18.7	Zuben'ubi	137 17.2	S16 02.3
20	196 45.4	70 59.0	49.3	354 10.3	59.1	171 42.5	09.4	156 33.1	18.8			
21	211 47.9	85 58.9 ..	48.7	9 12.7 ..	59.2	186 44.5 ..	09.6	171 35.2 ..	18.9		SHA	Mer. Pass.
22	226 50.3	100 58.9	48.0	24 15.0	59.4	201 46.5	09.7	186 37.4	18.9	Venus	236 06.1	15 16
23	241 52.8	115 58.8	47.3	39 17.4	59.5	216 48.5	09.9	201 39.6	19.0	Mars	157 28.4	20 27
Mer. Pass.	6 59.1	v −0.1	d 0.6	v 2.4	d 0.1	v 2.0	d 0.2	v 2.2	d 0.1	Jupiter	335 17.4	8 38
										Saturn	319 59.8	9 39

SUN and MOON

UT (d h)	SUN GHA	SUN Dec	MOON GHA	v	MOON Dec	d	HP
6 00	180 22.7	N22 34.8	280 51.7	11.6	S12 35.3	8.9	56.7
01	195 22.6	... 35.0	295 22.3	11.6	12 26.4	9.0	56.7
02	210 22.5	35.3	309 52.9	11.6	12 17.4	9.0	56.7
03	225 22.4	.. 35.6	324 23.5	11.6	12 08.4	9.1	56.8
04	240 22.3	35.9	338 54.1	11.6	11 59.3	9.2	56.8
05	255 22.2	36.1	353 24.7	11.6	11 50.1	9.2	56.8
06	270 22.1	N22 36.4	7 55.3	11.6	S11 40.9	9.3	56.9
07	285 21.9	36.6	22 25.9	11.6	11 31.6	9.4	56.9
S 08	300 21.8	36.9	36 56.5	11.6	11 22.2	9.4	56.9
U 09	315 21.7	.. 37.2	51 27.1	11.6	11 12.8	9.5	57.0
N 10	330 21.6	37.4	65 57.7	11.6	11 03.3	9.6	57.0
D 11	345 21.5	37.7	80 28.3	11.6	10 53.7	9.6	57.0
A 12	0 21.4	N22 38.0	94 58.9	11.6	S10 44.1	9.7	57.1
Y 13	15 21.3	38.2	109 29.5	11.6	10 34.4	9.8	57.1
14	30 21.2	38.5	124 00.1	11.6	10 24.6	9.8	57.1
15	45 21.0	.. 38.7	138 30.7	11.6	10 14.8	9.9	57.2
16	60 20.9	39.0	153 01.3	11.6	10 04.9	9.9	57.2
17	75 20.8	39.2	167 31.9	11.5	9 55.0	10.1	57.2
18	90 20.7	N22 39.5	182 02.4	11.6	S 9 44.9	10.0	57.3
19	105 20.6	39.8	196 33.0	11.6	9 34.9	10.2	57.3
20	120 20.5	40.0	211 03.6	11.6	9 24.7	10.2	57.3
21	135 20.4	.. 40.3	225 34.2	11.5	9 14.5	10.2	57.4
22	150 20.2	40.5	240 04.7	11.6	9 04.3	10.3	57.4
23	165 20.1	40.8	254 35.3	11.5	8 54.0	10.4	57.4
7 00	180 20.0	N22 41.0	269 05.8	11.6	S 8 43.6	10.4	57.5
01	195 19.9	41.3	283 36.4	11.5	8 33.2	10.5	57.5
02	210 19.8	41.5	298 06.9	11.6	8 22.7	10.5	57.5
03	225 19.7	.. 41.8	312 37.4	11.6	8 12.2	10.6	57.6
04	240 19.6	42.0	327 08.0	11.5	8 01.6	10.7	57.6
05	255 19.4	42.3	341 38.5	11.5	7 50.9	10.7	57.6
06	270 19.3	N22 42.5	356 09.0	11.4	S 7 40.2	10.7	57.7
07	285 19.2	42.8	10 39.4	11.5	7 29.5	10.8	57.7
M 08	300 19.1	43.0	25 09.9	11.5	7 18.7	10.9	57.7
O 09	315 19.0	.. 43.3	39 40.4	11.4	7 07.8	10.9	57.8
N 10	330 18.9	43.5	54 10.8	11.5	6 56.9	10.9	57.8
D 11	345 18.8	43.8	68 41.3	11.4	6 46.0	11.0	57.8
A 12	0 18.6	N22 44.0	83 11.7	11.4	S 6 35.0	11.1	57.9
Y 13	15 18.5	44.3	97 42.1	11.4	6 23.9	11.1	57.9
14	30 18.4	44.5	112 12.5	11.3	6 12.8	11.1	57.9
15	45 18.3	.. 44.7	126 42.8	11.4	6 01.7	11.2	58.0
16	60 18.2	45.0	141 13.2	11.3	5 50.5	11.2	58.0
17	75 18.1	45.2	155 43.5	11.3	5 39.3	11.3	58.0
18	90 17.9	N22 45.5	170 13.8	11.3	S 5 28.0	11.3	58.1
19	105 17.8	45.7	184 44.1	11.3	5 16.7	11.4	58.1
20	120 17.7	45.9	199 14.4	11.2	5 05.3	11.3	58.1
21	135 17.6	.. 46.2	213 44.6	11.3	4 54.0	11.5	58.2
22	150 17.5	46.4	228 14.9	11.2	4 42.5	11.5	58.2
23	165 17.3	46.7	242 45.1	11.2	4 31.0	11.5	58.3
8 00	180 17.2	N22 46.9	257 15.3	11.1	S 4 19.5	11.5	58.3
01	195 17.1	47.1	271 45.4	11.2	4 08.0	11.6	58.3
02	210 17.0	47.4	286 15.6	11.1	3 56.4	11.6	58.4
03	225 16.9	.. 47.6	300 45.7	11.1	3 44.8	11.7	58.4
04	240 16.8	47.8	315 15.8	11.0	3 33.1	11.7	58.4
05	255 16.6	48.1	329 45.8	11.1	3 21.4	11.7	58.5
06	270 16.5	N22 48.3	344 15.9	11.0	S 3 09.7	11.8	58.5
07	285 16.4	48.5	358 45.9	10.9	2 57.9	11.7	58.5
T 08	300 16.3	48.8	13 15.8	11.0	2 46.2	11.9	58.6
U 09	315 16.2	.. 49.0	27 45.8	10.9	2 34.3	11.8	58.6
E 10	330 16.0	49.2	42 15.7	10.9	2 22.5	11.9	58.6
S 11	345 15.9	49.4	56 45.6	10.8	2 10.6	11.9	58.7
D 12	0 15.8	N22 49.7	71 15.4	10.9	S 1 58.7	11.9	58.7
A 13	15 15.7	49.9	85 45.3	10.7	1 46.8	11.9	58.8
Y 14	30 15.6	50.1	100 15.0	10.8	1 34.9	12.0	58.8
15	45 15.5	.. 50.4	114 44.8	10.7	1 22.9	12.0	58.8
16	60 15.3	50.6	129 14.5	10.7	1 10.9	12.0	58.9
17	75 15.2	50.8	143 44.2	10.6	0 58.9	12.1	58.9
18	90 15.1	N22 51.0	158 13.8	10.6	S 0 46.8	12.0	58.9
19	105 15.0	51.2	172 43.4	10.6	0 34.8	12.1	59.0
20	120 14.9	51.5	187 13.0	10.5	0 22.7	12.1	59.0
21	135 14.7	.. 51.7	201 42.5	10.5	S 0 10.6	12.1	59.0
22	150 14.6	51.9	216 12.0	10.5	N 0 01.5	12.1	59.1
23	165 14.5	52.1	230 41.5	10.4	N 0 13.6	12.2	59.1
	SD 15.8	d 0.2	SD 15.5		15.8		16.0

Twilight, Sunrise, Moonrise

Lat.	Twilight Naut.	Civil	Sunrise	Moonrise 6	7	8	9
N 72	□	□	□	02 11	01 57	01 46	01 35
N 70	□	□	□	01 49	01 45	01 40	01 36
68	□	□	□	01 33	01 35	01 36	01 37
66	////	////	00 47	01 19	01 26	01 32	01 37
64	////	////	01 46	01 07	01 19	01 29	01 38
62	////	////	02 18	00 58	01 13	01 26	01 38
60	////	01 11	02 42	00 49	01 07	01 23	01 39
N 58	////	01 51	03 01	00 42	01 02	01 21	01 39
56	////	02 17	03 17	00 35	00 58	01 19	01 39
54	01 05	02 38	03 30	00 30	00 54	01 17	01 39
52	01 41	02 55	03 42	00 24	00 51	01 15	01 40
50	02 06	03 09	03 53	00 19	00 47	01 14	01 40
45	02 49	03 37	04 14	00 09	00 41	01 11	01 40
N 40	03 18	03 59	04 31	00 00	00 35	01 08	01 41
35	03 40	04 17	04 46	24 30	00 30	01 05	01 41
30	03 58	04 31	04 58	24 25	00 25	01 03	01 42
20	04 26	04 55	05 20	24 17	00 17	01 00	01 42
N 10	04 48	05 15	05 38	24 11	00 11	00 56	01 43
0	05 07	05 33	05 55	24 04	00 04	00 53	01 43
S 10	05 23	05 49	06 12	23 58	24 50	00 50	01 44
20	05 39	06 06	06 30	23 51	24 47	00 47	01 45
30	05 54	06 24	06 50	23 43	24 43	00 43	01 45
35	06 03	06 34	07 02	23 39	24 41	00 41	01 46
40	06 12	06 46	07 16	23 34	24 39	00 39	01 46
45	06 22	06 59	07 32	23 28	24 36	00 36	01 47
S 50	06 33	07 14	07 52	23 20	24 33	00 33	01 48
52	06 38	07 21	08 01	23 17	24 31	00 31	01 48
54	06 43	07 29	08 12	23 13	24 30	00 30	01 48
56	06 49	07 38	08 24	23 09	24 28	00 28	01 49
58	06 55	07 47	08 38	23 05	24 26	00 26	01 49
S 60	07 02	07 58	08 54	23 00	24 23	00 23	01 50

Sunset, Twilight, Moonset

Lat.	Sunset	Twilight Civil	Naut.	Moonset 6	7	8	9
N 72	□	□	□	09 02	10 58	12 53	14 51
N 70	□	□	□	09 22	11 08	12 55	14 46
68	□	□	□	09 37	11 16	12 58	14 42
66	23 15	////	////	09 50	11 23	13 00	14 39
64	22 14	////	////	10 00	11 29	13 01	14 36
62	21 40	////	////	10 09	11 34	13 02	14 34
60	21 16	22 49	////	10 17	11 39	13 04	14 31
N 58	20 57	22 08	////	10 23	11 43	13 05	14 30
56	20 41	21 41	////	10 29	11 46	13 06	14 28
54	20 28	21 20	22 55	10 35	11 49	13 07	14 27
52	20 16	21 03	22 17	10 39	11 52	13 07	14 25
50	20 05	20 49	21 52	10 43	11 54	13 08	14 24
45	19 44	20 21	21 09	10 53	12 00	13 09	14 21
N 40	19 26	19 59	20 40	11 00	12 04	13 11	14 19
35	19 12	19 41	20 18	11 07	12 08	13 12	14 17
30	18 59	19 26	20 00	11 12	12 12	13 13	14 16
20	18 38	19 02	19 31	11 22	12 18	13 14	14 13
N 10	18 19	18 42	19 09	11 31	12 23	13 16	14 10
0	18 02	18 25	18 51	11 39	12 28	13 17	14 08
S 10	17 46	18 08	18 34	11 47	12 32	13 18	14 05
20	17 28	17 51	18 19	11 55	12 37	13 20	14 03
30	17 07	17 33	18 03	12 05	12 43	13 21	14 00
35	16 55	17 23	17 55	12 10	12 46	13 22	13 58
40	16 41	17 12	17 46	12 16	12 50	13 23	13 56
45	16 25	16 59	17 36	12 24	12 54	13 24	13 54
S 50	16 05	16 43	17 24	12 32	12 59	13 25	13 51
52	15 56	16 36	17 19	12 36	13 01	13 26	13 50
54	15 45	16 28	17 14	12 40	13 04	13 26	13 49
56	15 33	16 20	17 08	12 45	13 07	13 27	13 47
58	15 19	16 10	17 02	12 50	13 10	13 28	13 46
S 60	15 03	15 59	16 55	12 56	13 13	13 28	13 44

SUN and MOON (daily)

Day	Eqn. of Time 00h	12h	Mer. Pass.	Mer. Pass. Upper	Lower	Age	Phase
	m s	m s	h m	h m	h m	d	%
6	01 31	01 26	11 59	05 27	17 52	22	57
7	01 20	01 15	11 59	06 16	18 40	23	47
8	01 09	01 03	11 59	07 05	19 30	24	36

UT	ARIES	VENUS −4.3		MARS −0.8		JUPITER −2.2		SATURN +0.4		STARS		
	GHA	GHA	Dec	GHA	Dec	GHA	Dec	GHA	Dec	Name	SHA	Dec
d h	° ′	° ′	° ′	° ′	° ′	° ′	° ′	° ′	° ′		° ′	° ′
9 00	256 55.3	130 58.7	N21 46.7	54 19.7	S 9 59.6	231 50.5	N 9 10.1	216 41.8	N13 19.1	Acamar	315 27.0	S40 18.5
01	271 57.7	145 58.7	46.0	69 22.1	59.8	246 52.6	10.2	231 44.0	19.2	Achernar	335 35.3	S57 14.3
02	287 00.2	160 58.6	45.3	84 24.4	9 59.9	261 54.6	10.4	246 46.2	19.3	Acrux	173 21.2	S63 06.0
03	302 02.7	175 58.6 . .	44.7	99 26.8	10 00.0	276 56.6 . .	10.6	261 48.4 . .	19.3	Adhara	255 21.4	S28 58.5
04	317 05.1	190 58.5	44.0	114 29.1	00.2	291 58.6	10.7	276 50.6	19.4	Aldebaran	291 02.2	N16 30.3
05	332 07.6	205 58.5	43.3	129 31.5	00.3	307 00.6	10.9	291 52.8	19.5			
06	347 10.1	220 58.4	N21 42.7	144 33.8	S10 00.4	322 02.6	N 9 11.1	306 54.9	N13 19.6	Alioth	166 30.0	N55 58.1
W 07	2 12.5	235 58.3	42.0	159 36.1	00.6	337 04.6	11.2	321 57.1	19.7	Alkaid	153 07.2	N49 19.3
E 08	17 15.0	250 58.3	41.3	174 38.5	00.7	352 06.6	11.4	336 59.3	19.8	Al Na'ir	27 57.2	S46 57.6
D 09	32 17.4	265 58.2 . .	40.6	189 40.8 . .	00.8	7 08.6 . .	11.6	352 01.5 . .	19.8	Alnilam	275 57.8	S 1 12.3
N 10	47 19.9	280 58.2	40.0	204 43.2	01.0	22 10.6	11.7	7 03.7	19.9	Alphard	218 06.9	S 8 39.4
E 11	62 22.4	295 58.1	39.3	219 45.5	01.1	37 12.6	11.9	22 05.9	20.0			
S 12	77 24.8	310 58.1	N21 38.6	234 47.8	S10 01.2	52 14.6	N 9 12.1	37 08.1	N13 20.1	Alphecca	126 19.9	N26 43.2
D 13	92 27.3	325 58.0	37.9	249 50.2	01.4	67 16.7	12.2	52 10.3	20.2	Alpheratz	357 54.8	N29 05.0
A 14	107 29.8	340 58.0	37.3	264 52.5	01.5	82 18.7	12.4	67 12.5	20.2	Altair	62 18.6	N 8 52.0
Y 15	122 32.2	355 57.9 . .	36.6	279 54.8 . .	01.7	97 20.7 . .	12.6	82 14.6 . .	20.3	Ankaa	353 26.6	S42 18.4
16	137 34.7	10 57.9	35.9	294 57.2	01.8	112 22.7	12.7	97 16.8	20.4	Antares	112 39.3	S26 25.8
17	152 37.2	25 57.9	35.2	309 59.5	01.9	127 24.7	12.9	112 19.0	20.5			
18	167 39.6	40 57.8	N21 34.5	325 01.8	S10 02.1	142 26.7	N 9 13.1	127 21.2	N13 20.6	Arcturus	146 05.4	N19 11.3
19	182 42.1	55 57.8	33.9	340 04.2	02.2	157 28.7	13.2	142 23.4	20.6	Atria	107 50.3	S69 01.5
20	197 44.6	70 57.7	33.2	355 06.5	02.3	172 30.7	13.4	157 25.6	20.7	Avior	234 22.9	S59 30.7
21	212 47.0	85 57.7 . .	32.5	10 08.8 . .	02.5	187 32.7 . .	13.6	172 27.8 . .	20.8	Bellatrix	278 44.0	N 6 20.8
22	227 49.5	100 57.7	31.8	25 11.1	02.6	202 34.7	13.7	187 30.0	20.9	Betelgeuse	271 13.4	N 7 24.3
23	242 51.9	115 57.6	31.1	40 13.5	02.8	217 36.8	13.9	202 32.2	21.0			
10 00	257 54.4	130 57.6	N21 30.5	55 15.8	S10 02.9	232 38.8	N 9 14.1	217 34.4	N13 21.0	Canopus	264 01.5	S52 41.9
01	272 56.9	145 57.6	29.8	70 18.1	03.0	247 40.8	14.2	232 36.6	21.1	Capella	280 51.0	N45 59.7
02	287 59.3	160 57.5	29.1	85 20.4	03.2	262 42.8	14.4	247 38.7	21.2	Deneb	49 38.6	N45 16.5
03	303 01.8	175 57.5 . .	28.4	100 22.7 . .	03.3	277 44.8 . .	14.6	262 40.9 . .	21.3	Denebola	182 44.7	N14 34.6
04	318 04.3	190 57.5	27.7	115 25.0	03.5	292 46.8	14.7	277 43.1	21.4	Diphda	349 06.9	S17 59.4
05	333 06.7	205 57.4	27.0	130 27.4	03.6	307 48.8	14.9	292 45.3	21.4			
06	348 09.2	220 57.4	N21 26.4	145 29.7	S10 03.8	322 50.8	N 9 15.1	307 47.5	N13 21.5	Dubhe	194 05.1	N61 45.6
T 07	3 11.7	235 57.4	25.7	160 32.0	03.9	337 52.8	15.2	322 49.7	21.6	Elnath	278 26.8	N28 36.3
H 08	18 14.1	250 57.4	25.0	175 34.3	04.1	352 54.9	15.4	337 51.9	21.7	Eltanin	90 50.7	N51 29.4
U 09	33 16.6	265 57.3 . .	24.3	190 36.6 . .	04.2	7 56.9 . .	15.6	352 54.1 . .	21.8	Enif	33 57.7	N 9 52.3
R 10	48 19.1	280 57.3	23.6	205 38.9	04.3	22 58.9	15.7	7 56.3	21.8	Fomalhaut	15 35.9	S29 37.4
S 11	63 21.5	295 57.3	22.9	220 41.2	04.5	38 00.9	15.9	22 58.5	21.9			
D 12	78 24.0	310 57.3	N21 22.2	235 43.5	S10 04.6	53 02.9	N 9 16.1	38 00.7	N13 22.0	Gacrux	172 12.8	S57 06.8
A 13	93 26.4	325 57.3	21.5	250 45.8	04.8	68 04.9	16.2	53 02.8	22.1	Gienah	176 03.4	S17 32.4
Y 14	108 28.9	340 57.2	20.8	265 48.1	04.9	83 06.9	16.4	68 05.0	22.2	Hadar	149 02.9	S60 22.3
15	123 31.4	355 57.2 . .	20.1	280 50.4 . .	05.1	98 08.9 . .	16.6	83 07.2 . .	22.2	Hamal	328 13.3	N23 27.3
16	138 33.8	10 57.2	19.4	295 52.7	05.2	113 11.0	16.7	98 09.4	22.3	Kaus Aust.	83 57.8	S34 23.0
17	153 36.3	25 57.2	18.8	310 55.0	05.4	128 13.0	16.9	113 11.6	22.4			
18	168 38.8	40 57.2	N21 18.1	325 57.3	S10 05.5	143 15.0	N 9 17.1	128 13.8	N13 22.5	Kochab	137 18.7	N74 09.8
19	183 41.2	55 57.2	17.4	340 59.6	05.7	158 17.0	17.2	143 16.0	22.6	Markab	13 49.1	N15 12.0
20	198 43.7	70 57.2	16.7	356 01.9	05.8	173 19.0	17.4	158 18.2	22.6	Menkar	314 26.7	N 4 05.1
21	213 46.2	85 57.2 . .	16.0	11 04.2 . .	06.0	188 21.0 . .	17.5	173 20.4 . .	22.7	Menkent	148 20.1	S36 22.1
22	228 48.6	100 57.2	15.3	26 06.5	06.1	203 23.0	17.7	188 22.6	22.8	Miaplacidus	221 42.4	S69 43.2
23	243 51.1	115 57.1	14.6	41 08.8	06.3	218 25.0	17.9	203 24.8	22.9			
11 00	258 53.5	130 57.1	N21 13.9	56 11.1	S10 06.4	233 27.1	N 9 18.0	218 27.0	N13 23.0	Mirfak	308 56.4	N49 51.3
01	273 56.0	145 57.1	13.2	71 13.4	06.6	248 29.1	18.2	233 29.1	23.0	Nunki	76 11.4	S26 17.7
02	288 58.5	160 57.1	12.5	86 15.7	06.7	263 31.1	18.4	248 31.3	23.1	Peacock	53 35.9	S56 44.0
03	304 00.9	175 57.1 . .	11.8	101 18.0 . .	06.9	278 33.1 . .	18.5	263 33.5 . .	23.2	Pollux	243 41.3	N28 01.7
04	319 03.4	190 57.1	11.1	116 20.3	07.0	293 35.1	18.7	278 35.7	23.3	Procyon	245 11.4	N 5 13.5
05	334 05.9	205 57.1	10.4	131 22.5	07.2	308 37.1	18.9	293 37.9	23.3			
06	349 08.3	220 57.1	N21 09.7	146 24.8	S10 07.3	323 39.1	N 9 19.0	308 40.1	N13 23.4	Rasalhague	96 16.2	N12 33.7
07	4 10.8	235 57.1	09.0	161 27.1	07.5	338 41.2	19.2	323 42.3	23.5	Regulus	207 55.2	N11 58.3
08	19 13.3	250 57.1	08.3	176 29.4	07.6	353 43.2	19.4	338 44.5	23.6	Rigel	281 22.9	S 8 12.3
F 09	34 15.7	265 57.1 . .	07.6	191 31.7 . .	07.8	8 45.2 . .	19.5	353 46.7 . .	23.7	Rigil Kent.	140 06.1	S60 50.0
R 10	49 18.2	280 57.2	06.9	206 33.9	08.0	23 47.2	19.7	8 48.9	23.7	Sabik	102 24.7	S15 43.3
I 11	64 20.7	295 57.2	06.2	221 36.2	08.1	38 49.2	19.9	23 51.1	23.8			
D 12	79 23.1	310 57.2	N21 05.4	236 38.5	S10 08.3	53 51.2	N 9 20.0	38 53.3	N13 23.9	Schedar	349 53.1	N56 31.7
A 13	94 25.6	325 57.2	04.7	251 40.8	08.4	68 53.3	20.2	53 55.5	24.0	Shaula	96 36.3	S37 06.1
Y 14	109 28.0	340 57.2	04.0	266 43.1	08.6	83 55.3	20.3	68 57.7	24.1	Sirius	258 43.7	S16 43.1
15	124 30.5	355 57.2 . .	03.3	281 45.3 . .	08.7	98 57.3 . .	20.5	83 59.8 . .	24.1	Spica	158 42.5	S11 09.5
16	139 33.0	10 57.2	02.6	296 47.6	08.9	113 59.3	20.7	99 02.0	24.2	Suhail	223 00.7	S43 26.1
17	154 35.4	25 57.2	01.9	311 49.9	09.1	129 01.3	20.8	114 04.2	24.3			
18	169 37.9	40 57.3	N21 01.2	326 52.1	S10 09.2	144 03.3	N 9 21.0	129 06.4	N13 24.4	Vega	80 45.9	N38 47.0
19	184 40.4	55 57.3	21 00.4	341 54.4	09.4	159 05.4	21.2	144 08.6	24.5	Zuben'ubi	137 17.2	S16 02.3
20	199 42.8	70 57.3	20 59.8	356 56.7	09.5	174 07.4	21.3	159 10.8	24.5		SHA	Mer. Pass.
21	214 45.3	85 57.3 . .	59.1	11 58.9 . .	09.7	189 09.4 . .	21.5	174 13.0 . .	24.6		° ′	h m
22	229 47.8	100 57.3	58.4	27 01.2	09.9	204 11.4	21.6	189 15.2	24.7	Venus	233 03.2	15 16
23	244 50.2	115 57.4	57.6	42 03.5	10.0	219 13.4	21.8	204 17.4	24.8	Mars	157 21.4	20 16
	h m									Jupiter	334 44.4	8 28
Mer. Pass. 6 47.3		v 0.0	d 0.7	v 2.3	d 0.1	v 2.0	d 0.2	v 2.2	d 0.1	Saturn	319 40.0	9 28

UT	SUN GHA	SUN Dec	MOON GHA	v	Dec	d	HP
d h	° ′	° ′	° ′	′	° ′	′	′
9 00	180 14.4	N22 52.4	245 10.9	10.3	N 0 25.8	12.1	59.1
01	195 14.2	52.6	259 40.2	10.3	0 37.9	12.2	59.1
02	210 14.1	52.8	274 09.5	10.3	0 50.1	12.1	59.2
03	225 14.0	.. 53.0	288 38.8	10.2	1 02.2	12.2	59.2
04	240 13.9	53.2	303 08.0	10.2	1 14.4	12.2	59.3
05	255 13.8	53.4	317 37.2	10.2	1 26.6	12.2	59.3
06	270 13.6	N22 53.7	332 06.4	10.1	N 1 38.8	12.2	59.3
W 07	285 13.5	53.9	346 35.5	10.0	1 51.0	12.2	59.4
E 08	300 13.4	54.1	1 04.5	10.0	2 03.2	12.2	59.4
D 09	315 13.3	.. 54.3	15 33.5	9.9	2 15.4	12.2	59.5
N 10	330 13.2	54.5	30 02.4	9.9	2 27.6	12.2	59.5
E 11	345 13.0	54.7	44 31.3	9.9	2 39.8	12.3	59.5
S 12	0 12.9	N22 54.9	59 00.2	9.8	N 2 52.1	12.2	59.6
D 13	15 12.8	55.1	73 29.0	9.7	3 04.3	12.2	59.6
A 14	30 12.7	55.3	87 57.7	9.7	3 16.5	12.2	59.6
Y 15	45 12.5	.. 55.6	102 26.4	9.6	3 28.7	12.2	59.7
16	60 12.4	55.8	116 55.0	9.6	3 40.9	12.2	59.7
17	75 12.3	56.0	131 23.6	9.5	3 53.1	12.1	59.7
18	90 12.2	N22 56.2	145 52.1	9.5	N 4 05.2	12.2	59.7
19	105 12.1	56.4	160 20.6	9.4	4 17.4	12.2	59.8
20	120 11.9	56.6	174 49.0	9.3	4 29.6	12.1	59.8
21	135 11.8	.. 56.8	189 17.3	9.3	4 41.7	12.1	59.8
22	150 11.7	57.0	203 45.6	9.3	4 53.8	12.2	59.9
23	165 11.6	57.2	218 13.9	9.1	5 06.0	12.1	59.9
10 00	180 11.4	N22 57.4	232 42.0	9.2	N 5 18.1	12.0	59.9
01	195 11.3	57.6	247 10.2	9.0	5 30.1	12.0	60.0
02	210 11.2	57.8	261 38.2	9.0	5 42.2	12.0	60.0
03	225 11.1	.. 58.0	276 06.2	8.9	5 54.2	12.1	60.0
04	240 10.9	58.2	290 34.1	8.9	6 06.3	12.0	60.1
05	255 10.8	58.4	305 02.0	8.8	6 18.3	11.9	60.1
06	270 10.7	N22 58.6	319 29.8	8.7	N 6 30.2	12.0	60.1
T 07	285 10.6	58.8	333 57.5	8.7	6 42.2	11.9	60.2
H 08	300 10.4	59.0	348 25.2	8.6	6 54.1	11.9	60.2
U 09	315 10.3	.. 59.2	2 52.8	8.6	7 06.0	11.8	60.2
R 10	330 10.2	59.4	17 20.4	8.5	7 17.8	11.8	60.2
S 11	345 10.1	59.6	31 47.9	8.4	7 29.7	11.8	60.3
D 12	0 09.9	N22 59.8	46 15.3	8.3	N 7 41.5	11.7	60.3
A 13	15 09.8	23 00.0	60 42.6	8.3	7 53.2	11.7	60.3
Y 14	30 09.7	00.2	75 09.9	8.2	8 04.9	11.7	60.3
15	45 09.6	.. 00.4	89 37.1	8.1	8 16.6	11.7	60.4
16	60 09.4	00.6	104 04.2	8.1	8 28.3	11.5	60.4
17	75 09.3	00.7	118 31.3	8.0	8 39.8	11.6	60.4
18	90 09.2	N23 00.9	132 58.3	7.9	N 8 51.4	11.5	60.5
19	105 09.1	01.1	147 25.2	7.9	9 02.9	11.5	60.5
20	120 08.9	01.3	161 52.1	7.8	9 14.4	11.4	60.5
21	135 08.8	.. 01.5	176 18.9	7.7	9 25.8	11.4	60.5
22	150 08.7	01.7	190 45.6	7.7	9 37.2	11.3	60.6
23	165 08.6	01.9	205 12.3	7.6	9 48.5	11.2	60.6
11 00	180 08.4	N23 02.1	219 38.9	7.5	N 9 59.7	11.2	60.6
01	195 08.3	02.2	234 05.4	7.4	10 10.9	11.2	60.6
02	210 08.2	02.4	248 31.8	7.4	10 22.1	11.1	60.7
03	225 08.1	.. 02.6	262 58.2	7.2	10 33.2	11.0	60.7
04	240 07.9	02.8	277 24.4	7.3	10 44.2	11.0	60.7
05	255 07.8	03.0	291 50.7	7.1	10 55.2	10.9	60.7
06	270 07.7	N23 03.2	306 16.8	7.1	N11 06.1	10.8	60.7
F 07	285 07.6	03.3	320 42.9	7.0	11 16.9	10.8	60.8
R 08	300 07.4	03.5	335 08.9	6.9	11 27.7	10.7	60.8
I 09	315 07.3	.. 03.7	349 34.8	6.8	11 38.4	10.7	60.8
D 10	330 07.2	03.9	4 00.6	6.8	11 49.1	10.6	60.8
A 11	345 07.0	04.1	18 26.4	6.7	11 59.7	10.6	60.8
Y 12	0 06.9	N23 04.2	32 52.1	6.7	N12 10.2	10.4	60.9
13	15 06.8	04.4	47 17.8	6.5	12 20.6	10.3	60.9
14	30 06.7	04.6	61 43.3	6.5	12 30.9	10.3	60.9
15	45 06.5	.. 04.8	76 08.8	6.4	12 41.2	10.2	60.9
16	60 06.4	04.9	90 34.2	6.4	12 51.4	10.1	60.9
17	75 06.3	05.1	104 59.6	6.2	13 01.5	10.1	60.9
18	90 06.2	N23 05.3	119 24.8	6.2	N13 11.6	9.9	61.0
19	105 06.0	05.5	133 50.0	6.1	13 21.5	9.9	61.0
20	120 05.9	05.6	148 15.1	6.1	13 31.4	9.8	61.0
21	135 05.8	.. 05.8	162 40.2	6.0	13 41.2	9.7	61.0
22	150 05.6	06.0	177 05.2	5.9	13 50.9	9.6	61.0
23	165 05.5	06.1	191 30.1	5.8	N14 00.5	9.5	61.0
	SD 15.8	d 0.2	SD 16.2		16.4		16.6

Lat.	Twilight Naut.	Twilight Civil	Sunrise	Moonrise 9	10	11	12
°	h m	h m	h m	h m	h m	h m	h m
N 72	▭	▭	▭	01 35	01 24	01 12	00 55
N 70	▭	▭	▭	01 36	01 32	01 28	01 23
68	▭	▭	▭	01 37	01 38	01 40	01 45
66	////	////	00 31	01 37	01 43	01 51	02 01
64	////	////	01 40	01 38	01 48	01 59	02 15
62	////	////	02 15	01 38	01 51	02 07	02 27
60	////	01 04	02 39	01 39	01 55	02 14	02 37
N 58	////	01 47	02 59	01 39	01 58	02 19	02 46
56	////	02 14	03 15	01 39	02 01	02 25	02 54
54	00 58	02 36	03 29	01 39	02 03	02 29	03 00
52	01 38	02 53	03 41	01 40	02 05	02 34	03 07
50	02 04	03 07	03 51	01 40	02 07	02 37	03 12
45	02 47	03 36	04 13	01 40	02 12	02 46	03 25
N 40	03 17	03 58	04 31	01 41	02 15	02 53	03 35
35	03 40	04 16	04 46	01 41	02 19	02 59	03 44
30	03 58	04 31	04 58	01 42	02 22	03 04	03 51
20	04 26	04 55	05 20	01 42	02 27	03 14	04 05
N 10	04 48	05 15	05 38	01 43	02 31	03 22	04 16
0	05 07	05 33	05 56	01 43	02 35	03 30	04 28
S 10	05 24	05 50	06 13	01 44	02 40	03 38	04 39
20	05 40	06 07	06 31	01 45	02 44	03 46	04 51
30	05 56	06 25	06 52	01 45	02 50	03 56	05 05
35	06 04	06 36	07 04	01 46	02 53	04 02	05 13
40	06 13	06 47	07 18	01 46	02 56	04 08	05 22
45	06 23	07 00	07 34	01 47	03 00	04 16	05 33
S 50	06 35	07 16	07 54	01 48	03 05	04 25	05 46
52	06 40	07 23	08 04	01 48	03 07	04 29	05 52
54	06 45	07 31	08 15	01 48	03 10	04 34	05 59
56	06 51	07 40	08 27	01 49	03 13	04 39	06 07
58	06 58	07 50	08 41	01 49	03 16	04 45	06 15
S 60	07 05	08 01	08 58	01 50	03 19	04 52	06 25

Lat.	Sunset	Twilight Civil	Twilight Naut.	Moonset 9	10	11	12
°	h m	h m	h m	h m	h m	h m	h m
N 72	▭	▭	▭	14 51	16 55	19 10	21 50
N 70	▭	▭	▭	14 46	16 41	18 43	20 53
68	▭	▭	▭	14 42	16 30	18 24	20 19
66	23 34	////	////	14 39	16 22	18 08	19 54
64	22 20	////	////	14 36	16 14	17 55	19 35
62	21 45	////	////	14 34	16 08	17 44	19 20
60	21 20	22 57	////	14 31	16 02	17 35	19 07
N 58	21 00	22 13	////	14 30	15 57	17 27	18 56
56	20 44	21 45	////	14 28	15 53	17 20	18 46
54	20 30	21 24	23 03	14 27	15 49	17 14	18 38
52	20 18	21 06	22 22	14 25	15 46	17 08	18 30
50	20 08	20 52	21 51	14 24	15 43	17 03	18 23
45	19 46	20 23	21 12	14 21	15 36	16 52	18 09
N 40	19 28	20 01	20 42	14 19	15 30	16 43	17 57
35	19 13	19 43	20 19	14 17	15 25	16 35	17 46
30	19 01	19 28	20 01	14 16	15 21	16 28	17 37
20	18 39	19 03	19 32	14 13	15 14	16 17	17 22
N 10	18 20	18 43	19 10	14 10	15 07	16 06	17 09
0	18 03	18 25	18 52	14 08	15 01	15 57	16 56
S 10	17 46	18 09	18 35	14 05	14 55	15 47	16 43
20	17 28	17 52	18 19	14 03	14 48	15 37	16 30
30	17 07	17 33	18 03	14 00	14 41	15 26	16 15
35	16 55	17 23	17 54	13 58	14 37	15 19	16 06
40	16 41	17 11	17 45	13 56	14 32	15 11	15 56
45	16 24	16 58	17 35	13 54	14 26	15 02	15 44
S 50	16 04	16 42	17 24	13 51	14 20	14 52	15 30
52	15 55	16 35	17 19	13 50	14 17	14 47	15 23
54	15 44	16 27	17 13	13 49	14 13	14 42	15 16
56	15 32	16 18	17 07	13 47	14 10	14 36	15 08
58	15 17	16 08	17 01	13 46	14 06	14 29	14 59
S 60	15 00	15 57	16 53	13 44	14 01	14 21	14 48

	SUN Eqn. of Time 00h	SUN Eqn. of Time 12h	SUN Mer. Pass.	MOON Mer. Pass. Upper	MOON Mer. Pass. Lower	Age	Phase
Day	m s	m s	h m	h m	h m	d	%
9	00 58	00 52	11 59	07 56	20 21	25	25
10	00 46	00 40	11 59	08 48	21 15	26	16
11	00 34	00 28	12 00	09 43	22 12	27	8

UT	ARIES GHA	VENUS −4.3 GHA	Dec	MARS −0.8 GHA	Dec	JUPITER −2.2 GHA	Dec	SATURN +0.4 GHA	Dec	STARS Name	SHA	Dec
12 00	259 52.7	130 57.4	N20 56.9	57 05.7	S10 10.2	234 15.4	N 9 22.0	219 19.6	N13 24.8	Acamar	315 27.0	S40 18.4
01	274 55.2	145 57.4	56.2	72 08.0	10.3	249 17.5	22.1	234 21.8	24.9	Achernar	335 35.2	S57 14.3
02	289 57.6	160 57.4	55.5	87 10.2	10.5	264 19.5	22.3	249 24.0	25.0	Acrux	173 21.2	S63 06.0
03	305 00.1	175 57.5	.. 54.8	102 12.5	.. 10.7	279 21.5	.. 22.5	264 26.2	.. 25.1	Adhara	255 21.4	S28 58.5
04	320 02.5	190 57.5	54.1	117 14.8	10.8	294 23.5	22.6	279 28.4	25.2	Aldebaran	291 02.2	N16 30.3
05	335 05.0	205 57.5	53.3	132 17.0	11.0	309 25.5	22.8	294 30.6	25.2			
S 06	350 07.5	220 57.6	N20 52.6	147 19.3	S10 11.2	324 27.5	N 9 23.0	309 32.8	N13 25.3	Alioth	166 30.0	N55 58.1
A 07	5 09.9	235 57.6	51.9	162 21.5	11.3	339 29.6	23.1	324 34.9	25.4	Alkaid	153 07.2	N49 19.3
T 08	20 12.4	250 57.6	51.2	177 23.8	11.5	354 31.6	23.3	339 37.1	25.5	Al Na'ir	27 57.2	S46 57.6
U 09	35 14.9	265 57.7	.. 50.5	192 26.0	.. 11.6	9 33.6	.. 23.4	354 39.3	.. 25.6	Alnilam	275 57.7	S 1 12.3
R 10	50 17.3	280 57.7	49.8	207 28.3	11.8	24 35.6	23.6	9 41.5	25.6	Alphard	218 06.9	S 8 39.4
D 11	65 19.8	295 57.7	49.0	222 30.5	12.0	39 37.6	23.8	24 43.7	25.7			
A 12	80 22.3	310 57.8	N20 48.3	237 32.8	S10 12.1	54 39.7	N 9 23.9	39 45.9	N13 25.8	Alphecca	126 19.9	N26 43.2
Y 13	95 24.7	325 57.8	47.6	252 35.0	12.3	69 41.7	24.1	54 48.1	25.9	Alpheratz	357 54.8	N29 05.0
14	110 27.2	340 57.8	46.9	267 37.3	12.5	84 43.7	24.3	69 50.3	25.9	Altair	62 18.5	N 8 52.0
15	125 29.6	355 57.9	.. 46.2	282 39.5	.. 12.6	99 45.7	.. 24.4	84 52.5	.. 26.0	Ankaa	353 26.6	S42 18.4
16	140 32.1	10 57.9	45.4	297 41.7	12.8	114 47.7	24.6	99 54.7	26.1	Antares	112 39.2	S26 25.8
17	155 34.6	25 58.0	44.7	312 44.0	13.0	129 49.8	24.7	114 56.9	26.2			
18	170 37.0	40 58.0	N20 44.0	327 46.2	S10 13.1	144 51.8	N 9 24.9	129 59.1	N13 26.3	Arcturus	146 05.4	N19 11.3
19	185 39.5	55 58.1	43.3	342 48.5	13.3	159 53.8	25.1	145 01.3	26.3	Atria	107 50.3	S69 01.5
20	200 42.0	70 58.1	42.5	357 50.7	13.5	174 55.8	25.2	160 03.5	26.4	Avior	234 22.9	S59 30.7
21	215 44.4	85 58.2	.. 41.8	12 52.9	.. 13.7	189 57.8	.. 25.4	175 05.7	.. 26.5	Bellatrix	278 44.0	N 6 20.8
22	230 46.9	100 58.2	41.1	27 55.2	13.8	204 59.9	25.5	190 07.9	26.6	Betelgeuse	271 13.4	N 7 24.3
23	245 49.4	115 58.3	40.3	42 57.4	14.0	220 01.9	25.7	205 10.1	26.6			
13 00	260 51.8	130 58.3	N20 39.6	57 59.6	S10 14.2	235 03.9	N 9 25.9	220 12.3	N13 26.7	Canopus	264 01.5	S52 41.9
01	275 54.3	145 58.4	38.9	73 01.9	14.3	250 05.9	26.0	235 14.5	26.8	Capella	280 51.0	N45 59.7
02	290 56.8	160 58.4	38.2	88 04.1	14.5	265 07.9	26.2	250 16.7	26.9	Deneb	49 38.5	N45 16.5
03	305 59.2	175 58.5	.. 37.4	103 06.3	.. 14.7	280 10.0	.. 26.4	265 18.9	.. 27.0	Denebola	182 44.7	N14 34.7
04	321 01.7	190 58.6	36.7	118 08.6	14.9	295 12.0	26.5	280 21.1	27.0	Diphda	349 06.9	S17 59.4
05	336 04.1	205 58.6	36.0	133 10.8	15.0	310 14.0	26.7	295 23.2	27.1			
S 06	351 06.6	220 58.7	N20 35.2	148 13.0	S10 15.2	325 16.0	N 9 26.8	310 25.4	N13 27.2	Dubhe	194 05.1	N61 45.6
U 07	6 09.1	235 58.7	34.5	163 15.2	15.4	340 18.1	27.0	325 27.6	27.3	Elnath	278 26.8	N28 36.3
N 08	21 11.5	250 58.8	33.8	178 17.5	15.5	355 20.1	27.2	340 29.8	27.3	Eltanin	90 50.7	N51 29.4
D 09	36 14.0	265 58.9	.. 33.0	193 19.7	.. 15.7	10 22.1	.. 27.3	355 32.0	.. 27.4	Enif	33 57.6	N 9 52.3
A 10	51 16.5	280 58.9	32.3	208 21.9	15.9	25 24.1	27.5	10 34.2	27.5	Fomalhaut	15 35.9	S29 37.4
Y 11	66 18.9	295 59.0	31.6	223 24.1	16.1	40 26.1	27.6	25 36.4	27.6			
12	81 21.4	310 59.1	N20 30.8	238 26.3	S10 16.2	55 28.2	N 9 27.8	40 38.6	N13 27.6	Gacrux	172 12.8	S57 06.8
13	96 23.9	325 59.2	30.1	253 28.5	16.4	70 30.2	28.0	55 40.8	27.7	Gienah	176 03.4	S17 32.4
14	111 26.3	340 59.2	29.4	268 30.8	16.6	85 32.2	28.1	70 43.0	27.8	Hadar	149 02.9	S60 22.3
15	126 28.8	355 59.3	.. 28.6	283 33.0	.. 16.8	100 34.2	.. 28.3	85 45.2	.. 27.9	Hamal	328 13.3	N23 27.3
16	141 31.3	10 59.4	27.9	298 35.2	17.0	115 36.3	28.4	100 47.4	28.0	Kaus Aust.	83 57.8	S34 23.0
17	156 33.7	25 59.5	27.2	313 37.4	17.1	130 38.3	28.6	115 49.6	28.0			
18	171 36.2	40 59.5	N20 26.4	328 39.6	S10 17.3	145 40.3	N 9 28.8	130 51.8	N13 28.1	Kochab	137 18.8	N74 09.8
19	186 38.6	55 59.6	25.7	343 41.8	17.5	160 42.3	28.9	145 54.0	28.2	Markab	13 49.1	N15 12.0
20	201 41.1	70 59.7	24.9	358 44.0	17.7	175 44.4	29.1	160 56.2	28.3	Menkar	314 26.7	N 4 05.1
21	216 43.6	85 59.8	.. 24.2	13 46.2	.. 17.8	190 46.4	.. 29.2	175 58.4	.. 28.3	Menkent	148 20.1	S36 22.1
22	231 46.0	100 59.8	23.5	28 48.4	18.0	205 48.4	29.4	191 00.6	28.4	Miaplacidus	221 42.4	S69 43.2
23	246 48.5	115 59.9	22.7	43 50.6	18.2	220 50.4	29.6	206 02.8	28.5			
14 00	261 51.0	131 00.0	N20 22.0	58 52.8	S10 18.4	235 52.4	N 9 29.7	221 05.0	N13 28.6	Mirfak	308 56.4	N49 51.3
01	276 53.4	146 00.1	21.2	73 55.1	18.6	250 54.5	29.9	236 07.2	28.6	Nunki	76 11.4	S26 17.7
02	291 55.9	161 00.2	20.5	88 57.3	18.7	265 56.5	30.0	251 09.4	28.7	Peacock	53 35.9	S56 44.0
03	306 58.4	176 00.3	.. 19.7	103 59.5	.. 18.9	280 58.5	.. 30.2	266 11.6	.. 28.8	Pollux	243 41.3	N28 01.7
04	322 00.8	191 00.4	19.0	119 01.7	19.1	296 00.5	30.4	281 13.8	28.9	Procyon	245 11.4	N 5 13.5
05	337 03.3	206 00.5	18.3	134 03.8	19.3	311 02.6	30.5	296 16.0	29.0			
06	352 05.8	221 00.6	N20 17.5	149 06.0	S10 19.5	326 04.6	N 9 30.7	311 18.2	N13 29.0	Rasalhague	96 16.2	N12 33.7
07	7 08.2	236 00.6	16.8	164 08.2	19.7	341 06.6	30.8	326 20.4	29.1	Regulus	207 55.2	N11 58.3
08	22 10.7	251 00.7	16.0	179 10.4	19.8	356 08.7	31.0	341 22.6	29.2	Rigel	281 22.9	S 8 12.3
M 09	37 13.1	266 00.8	.. 15.3	194 12.6	.. 20.0	11 10.7	.. 31.1	356 24.8	.. 29.3	Rigil Kent.	140 06.2	S60 50.0
O 10	52 15.6	281 00.9	14.5	209 14.8	20.2	26 12.7	31.3	11 27.0	29.3	Sabik	102 24.7	S15 43.3
N 11	67 18.1	296 01.0	13.8	224 17.0	20.4	41 14.7	31.5	26 29.2	29.4			
D 12	82 20.5	311 01.1	N20 13.0	239 19.2	S10 20.6	56 16.8	N 9 31.6	41 31.4	N13 29.5	Schedar	349 53.1	N56 31.7
A 13	97 23.0	326 01.2	12.3	254 21.4	20.8	71 18.8	31.8	56 33.6	29.6	Shaula	96 36.3	S37 06.1
Y 14	112 25.5	341 01.3	11.5	269 23.6	21.0	86 20.8	31.9	71 35.8	29.6	Sirius	258 43.7	S16 43.0
15	127 27.9	356 01.4	.. 10.8	284 25.8	.. 21.1	101 22.8	.. 32.1	86 38.0	.. 29.7	Spica	158 42.6	S11 09.5
16	142 30.4	11 01.6	10.0	299 27.9	21.3	116 24.9	32.3	101 40.2	29.8	Suhail	223 00.7	S43 26.0
17	157 32.9	26 01.7	09.3	314 30.1	21.5	131 26.9	32.4	116 42.4	29.9			
18	172 35.3	41 01.8	N20 08.5	329 32.3	S10 21.7	146 28.9	N 9 32.6	131 44.6	N13 29.9	Vega	80 45.9	N38 47.0
19	187 37.8	56 01.9	07.8	344 34.5	21.9	161 30.9	32.7	146 46.8	30.0	Zuben'ubi	137 17.2	S16 02.3
20	202 40.3	71 02.0	07.0	359 36.7	22.1	176 33.0	32.9	161 49.0	30.1		SHA	Mer. Pass.
21	217 42.7	86 02.1	.. 06.3	14 38.8	.. 22.3	191 35.0	.. 33.1	176 51.2	.. 30.2		° ′	h m
22	232 45.2	101 02.2	05.5	29 41.0	22.5	206 37.0	33.2	191 53.4	30.3	Venus	230 06.5	15 16
23	247 47.6	116 02.3	04.8	44 43.2	22.6	221 39.1	33.4	206 55.6	30.3	Mars	157 07.8	20 05
Mer. Pass.	6 35.5	v 0.1	d 0.7	v 2.2	d 0.2	v 2.0	d 0.2	v 2.2	d 0.1	Jupiter	334 12.1	8 19
										Saturn	319 20.4	9 18

SUN / MOON

UT	SUN GHA	SUN Dec	MOON GHA	v	MOON Dec	d	HP
d h	° ′	° ′	° ′	′	° ′	′	′
12 00	180 05.4	N23 06.3	205 54.9	5.8	N14 10.0	9.4	61.1
01	195 05.3	06.5	220 19.7	5.7	14 19.4	9.3	61.1
02	210 05.1	06.6	234 44.4	5.6	14 28.7	9.3	61.1
03	225 05.0 ..	06.8	249 09.0	5.6	14 37.9	9.2	61.1
04	240 04.9	07.0	263 33.6	5.5	14 47.1	9.0	61.1
05	255 04.7	07.1	277 58.1	5.4	14 56.1	8.9	61.1
06	270 04.6	N23 07.3	292 22.5	5.3	N15 05.0	8.9	61.1
S 07	285 04.5	07.5	306 46.8	5.3	15 13.9	8.7	61.1
A 08	300 04.4	07.6	321 11.1	5.2	15 22.6	8.6	61.1
T 09	315 04.2 ..	07.8	335 35.3	5.2	15 31.2	8.5	61.2
U 10	330 04.1	08.0	349 59.5	5.1	15 39.7	8.4	61.2
R 11	345 04.0	08.1	4 23.6	5.0	15 48.1	8.3	61.2
D 12	0 03.8	N23 08.3	18 47.6	5.0	N15 56.4	8.2	61.2
A 13	15 03.7	08.4	33 11.6	4.9	16 04.6	8.1	61.2
Y 14	30 03.6	08.6	47 35.5	4.8	16 12.7	7.9	61.2
15	45 03.4 ..	08.8	61 59.3	4.8	16 20.6	7.9	61.2
16	60 03.3	08.9	76 23.1	4.7	16 28.5	7.7	61.2
17	75 03.2	09.1	90 46.8	4.7	16 36.2	7.6	61.2
18	90 03.1	N23 09.2	105 10.5	4.6	N16 43.8	7.5	61.2
19	105 02.9	09.4	119 34.1	4.6	16 51.3	7.3	61.2
20	120 02.8	09.5	133 57.7	4.5	16 58.6	7.3	61.2
21	135 02.7 ..	09.7	148 21.2	4.4	17 05.9	7.1	61.2
22	150 02.5	09.8	162 44.6	4.4	17 13.0	7.0	61.2
23	165 02.4	10.0	177 08.0	4.3	17 20.0	6.9	61.2
13 00	180 02.3	N23 10.2	191 31.3	4.3	N17 26.9	6.7	61.2
01	195 02.1	10.3	205 54.6	4.3	17 33.6	6.6	61.2
02	210 02.0	10.5	220 17.9	4.2	17 40.2	6.5	61.2
03	225 01.9 ..	10.6	234 41.1	4.1	17 46.7	6.4	61.2
04	240 01.8	10.8	249 04.2	4.1	17 53.1	6.2	61.2
05	255 01.6	10.9	263 27.3	4.1	17 59.3	6.1	61.2
06	270 01.5	N23 11.0	277 50.4	4.0	N18 05.4	5.9	61.2
07	285 01.4	11.2	292 13.4	4.0	18 11.3	5.9	61.2
S 08	300 01.2	11.3	306 36.4	3.9	18 17.2	5.6	61.2
U 09	315 01.1 ..	11.5	320 59.3	3.9	18 22.8	5.6	61.2
N 10	330 01.0	11.6	335 22.2	3.9	18 28.4	5.4	61.2
D 11	345 00.8	11.8	349 45.1	3.8	18 33.8	5.3	61.2
A 12	0 00.7	N23 11.9	4 07.9	3.8	N18 39.1	5.1	61.2
Y 13	15 00.6	12.1	18 30.7	3.8	18 44.2	5.0	61.2
14	30 00.4	12.2	32 53.5	3.7	18 49.2	4.9	61.2
15	45 00.3 ..	12.3	47 16.2	3.7	18 54.1	4.7	61.2
16	60 00.2	12.5	61 38.9	3.7	18 58.8	4.6	61.2
17	75 00.0	12.6	76 01.6	3.6	19 03.4	4.4	61.1
18	89 59.9	N23 12.8	90 24.2	3.7	N19 07.8	4.3	61.1
19	104 59.8	12.9	104 46.9	3.6	19 12.1	4.1	61.1
20	119 59.7	13.0	119 09.5	3.6	19 16.2	4.0	61.1
21	134 59.5 ..	13.2	133 32.1	3.6	19 20.2	3.8	61.1
22	149 59.4	13.3	147 54.7	3.5	19 24.0	3.7	61.1
23	164 59.3	13.5	162 17.2	3.6	19 27.7	3.6	61.1
14 00	179 59.1	N23 13.6	176 39.8	3.5	N19 31.3	3.4	61.1
01	194 59.0	13.7	191 02.3	3.6	19 34.7	3.3	61.1
02	209 58.9	13.9	205 24.9	3.4	19 38.0	3.1	61.0
03	224 58.7 ..	14.0	219 47.4	3.5	19 41.1	3.0	61.0
04	239 58.6	14.1	234 09.9	3.5	19 44.1	2.8	61.0
05	254 58.5	14.3	248 32.4	3.5	19 46.9	2.6	61.0
06	269 58.3	N23 14.4	262 54.9	3.5	N19 49.5	2.6	61.0
07	284 58.2	14.5	277 17.4	3.5	19 52.1	2.3	61.0
08	299 58.1	14.6	291 39.9	3.4	19 54.4	2.2	60.9
M 09	314 57.9 ..	14.8	306 02.5	3.5	19 56.6	2.1	60.9
O 10	329 57.8	14.9	320 25.0	3.5	19 58.7	1.9	60.9
N 11	344 57.7	15.0	334 47.5	3.5	20 00.6	1.8	60.9
D 12	359 57.5	N23 15.2	349 10.0	3.6	N20 02.4	1.6	60.9
A 13	14 57.4	15.3	3 32.6	3.6	20 04.0	1.5	60.9
Y 14	29 57.3	15.4	17 55.2	3.5	20 05.5	1.3	60.8
15	44 57.1 ..	15.5	32 17.7	3.6	20 06.8	1.2	60.8
16	59 57.0	15.6	46 40.3	3.7	20 08.0	1.0	60.8
17	74 56.9	15.8	61 03.0	3.6	20 09.0	0.9	60.8
18	89 56.7	N23 15.9	75 25.6	3.7	N20 09.9	0.7	60.8
19	104 56.6	16.0	89 48.3	3.6	20 10.6	0.6	60.7
20	119 56.5	16.1	104 10.9	3.8	20 11.2	0.4	60.7
21	134 56.3 ..	16.3	118 33.7	3.7	20 11.6	0.3	60.7
22	149 56.2	16.4	132 56.4	3.8	20 11.9	0.1	60.7
23	164 56.1	16.5	147 19.2	3.8	N20 12.0	0.0	60.6
	SD 15.8	d 0.1	SD 16.7		16.7		16.6

Twilight / Sunrise / Moonrise

Lat.	Twilight Naut.	Twilight Civil	Sunrise	Moonrise 12	Moonrise 13	Moonrise 14	Moonrise 15
°	h m	h m	h m	h m	h m	h m	h m
N 72	▭	▭	▭	00 55	00 20	▭	▭
N 70	▭	▭	▭	01 23	01 19	01 14	▭
68	▭	▭	▭	01 45	01 54	02 15	03 03
66	▭	▭	▭	02 01	02 19	02 50	03 43
64	////	////	01 36	02 15	02 39	03 15	04 11
62	////	////	02 12	02 27	02 55	03 35	04 32
60	////	00 57	02 37	02 37	03 08	03 51	04 49
N 58	////	01 43	02 57	02 46	03 20	04 05	05 03
56	////	02 12	03 14	02 54	03 30	04 17	05 16
54	00 52	02 34	03 28	03 00	03 39	04 27	05 27
52	01 35	02 51	03 40	03 07	03 47	04 37	05 36
50	02 02	03 06	03 51	03 12	03 54	04 45	05 45
45	02 46	03 36	04 13	03 25	04 10	05 03	06 03
N 40	03 16	03 58	04 31	03 35	04 23	05 17	06 18
35	03 39	04 16	04 45	03 44	04 34	05 30	06 31
30	03 58	04 31	04 58	03 51	04 43	05 40	06 42
20	04 26	04 56	05 20	04 05	05 00	05 59	07 01
N 10	04 49	05 16	05 39	04 16	05 14	06 15	07 17
0	05 08	05 34	05 56	04 28	05 28	06 30	07 33
S 10	05 24	05 51	06 14	04 39	05 42	06 46	07 48
20	05 40	06 08	06 32	04 51	05 57	07 02	08 05
30	05 57	06 27	06 53	05 05	06 14	07 21	08 24
35	06 05	06 37	07 05	05 13	06 24	07 32	08 35
40	06 15	06 49	07 19	05 22	06 35	07 44	08 47
45	06 25	07 02	07 36	05 33	06 48	07 59	09 02
S 50	06 36	07 18	07 56	05 46	07 05	08 18	09 21
52	06 42	07 25	08 06	05 52	07 13	08 26	09 29
54	06 47	07 33	08 17	05 59	07 21	08 36	09 39
56	06 53	07 42	08 29	06 07	07 31	08 47	09 50
58	07 00	07 52	08 44	06 15	07 42	09 00	10 03
S 60	07 07	08 04	09 01	06 25	07 55	09 14	10 17

Sunset / Twilight / Moonset

Lat.	Sunset	Twilight Civil	Twilight Naut.	Moonset 12	Moonset 13	Moonset 14	Moonset 15
°	h m	h m	h m	h m	h m	h m	h m
N 72	▭	▭	▭	21 50	▭	▭	▭
N 70	▭	▭	▭	20 53	23 08	▭	▭
68	▭	▭	▭	20 19	22 07	23 30	24 13
66	▭	▭	▭	19 54	21 33	22 50	23 39
64	22 25	////	////	19 35	21 08	22 23	23 14
62	21 49	////	////	19 20	20 48	22 01	22 55
60	21 23	23 04	////	19 07	20 32	21 44	22 39
N 58	21 03	22 17	////	18 56	20 19	21 30	22 25
56	20 47	21 48	////	18 46	20 07	21 17	22 13
54	20 33	21 27	23 09	18 38	19 57	21 06	22 03
52	20 20	21 09	22 26	18 30	19 48	20 57	21 54
50	20 10	20 54	21 59	18 23	19 40	20 48	21 46
45	19 47	20 25	21 14	18 09	19 22	20 30	21 28
N 40	19 29	20 02	20 44	17 57	19 08	20 15	21 14
35	19 15	19 44	20 21	17 46	18 56	20 02	21 02
30	19 02	19 29	20 02	17 37	18 46	19 51	20 51
20	18 40	19 04	19 34	17 22	18 28	19 32	20 33
N 10	18 21	18 44	19 11	17 09	18 12	19 16	20 17
0	18 04	18 26	18 52	16 56	17 58	19 00	20 02
S 10	17 46	18 09	18 35	16 43	17 43	18 45	19 46
20	17 28	17 52	18 19	16 30	17 27	18 28	19 30
30	17 07	17 33	18 03	16 15	17 09	18 09	19 12
35	16 55	17 23	17 54	16 06	16 59	17 58	19 01
40	16 41	17 11	17 45	15 56	16 47	17 45	18 48
45	16 24	16 58	17 35	15 44	16 33	17 30	18 33
S 50	16 04	16 42	17 23	15 30	16 16	17 11	18 15
52	15 54	16 35	17 18	15 23	16 08	17 03	18 07
54	15 43	16 27	17 13	15 16	15 59	16 53	17 57
56	15 30	16 18	17 07	15 08	15 49	16 42	17 46
58	15 16	16 07	17 00	14 59	15 37	16 29	17 34
S 60	14 59	15 56	16 52	14 48	15 24	16 14	17 19

SUN / MOON

Day	SUN Eqn. of Time 00h	SUN Eqn. of Time 12h	SUN Mer. Pass.	MOON Mer. Pass. Upper	MOON Mer. Pass. Lower	Age	Phase
d	m s	m s	h m	h m	h m	d	%
12	00 22	00 16	12 00	10 42	23 12	28	3
13	00 09	00 03	12 00	11 43	24 14	29	0
14	00 03	00 10	12 00	12 45	00 14	01	1

120   1999 JUNE 15, 16, 17 (TUES., WED., THURS.)

UT	ARIES GHA	VENUS −4.3 GHA	Dec	MARS −0.7 GHA	Dec	JUPITER −2.2 GHA	Dec	SATURN +0.4 GHA	Dec	STARS Name	SHA	Dec
d h	° ′	° ′	° ′	° ′	° ′	° ′	° ′	° ′	° ′		° ′	° ′
15 00	262 50.1	131 02.4	N20 04.0	59 45.4	S10 22.8	236 41.1	N 9 33.5	221 57.8	N13 30.4	Acamar	315 26.9	S40 18.4
01	277 52.6	146 02.6	03.3	74 47.5	23.0	251 43.1	33.7	237 00.0	30.5	Achernar	335 35.2	S57 14.3
02	292 55.0	161 02.7	02.5	89 49.7	23.2	266 45.1	33.8	252 02.2	30.6	Acrux	173 21.3	S63 06.0
03	307 57.5	176 02.8 ..	01.7	104 51.9 ..	23.4	281 47.2 ..	34.0	267 04.4 ..	30.6	Adhara	255 21.4	S28 58.4
04	323 00.0	191 02.9	01.0	119 54.1	23.6	296 49.2	34.2	282 06.6	30.7	Aldebaran	291 02.2	N16 30.3
05	338 02.4	206 03.0	20 00.2	134 56.2	23.8	311 51.2	34.3	297 08.8	30.8			
06	353 04.9	221 03.2	N19 59.5	149 58.4	S10 24.0	326 53.3	N 9 34.5	312 11.0	N13 30.9	Alioth	166 30.1	N55 58.1
07	8 07.4	236 03.3	58.7	165 00.6	24.2	341 55.3	34.6	327 13.2	30.9	Alkaid	153 07.2	N49 19.3
T 08	23 09.8	251 03.4	57.9	180 02.7	24.4	356 57.3	34.8	342 15.4	31.0	Al Na'ir	27 57.2	S46 57.6
U 09	38 12.3	266 03.5 ..	57.2	195 04.9 ..	24.6	11 59.3 ..	34.9	357 17.6 ..	31.1	Alnilam	275 57.7	S 1 12.3
E 10	53 14.8	281 03.7	56.4	210 07.1	24.8	27 01.4	35.1	12 19.8	31.2	Alphard	218 06.9	S 8 39.4
S 11	68 17.2	296 03.8	55.7	225 09.2	25.0	42 03.4	35.3	27 22.0	31.2			
D 12	83 19.7	311 03.9	N19 54.9	240 11.4	S10 25.1	57 05.4	N 9 35.4	42 24.2	N13 31.3	Alphecca	126 19.9	N26 43.2
A 13	98 22.1	326 04.1	54.1	255 13.5	25.3	72 07.5	35.6	57 26.4	31.4	Alpheratz	357 54.8	N29 05.0
Y 14	113 24.6	341 04.2	53.4	270 15.7	25.5	87 09.5	35.7	72 28.6	31.5	Altair	62 18.5	N 8 52.0
15	128 27.1	356 04.3 ..	52.6	285 17.9 ..	25.7	102 11.5 ..	35.9	87 30.8 ..	31.5	Ankaa	353 26.5	S42 18.4
16	143 29.5	11 04.5	51.9	300 20.0	25.9	117 13.6	36.0	102 33.0	31.6	Antares	112 39.2	S26 25.8
17	158 32.0	26 04.6	51.1	315 22.2	26.1	132 15.6	36.2	117 35.2	31.7			
18	173 34.5	41 04.8	N19 50.3	330 24.3	S10 26.3	147 17.6	N 9 36.4	132 37.4	N13 31.8	Arcturus	146 05.4	N19 11.3
19	188 36.9	56 04.9	49.6	345 26.5	26.5	162 19.6	36.5	147 39.6	31.8	Atria	107 50.3	S69 01.5
20	203 39.4	71 05.0	48.8	0 28.6	26.7	177 21.7	36.7	162 41.8	31.9	Avior	234 22.9	S59 30.7
21	218 41.9	86 05.2 ..	48.0	15 30.8 ..	26.9	192 23.7 ..	36.8	177 44.0 ..	32.0	Bellatrix	278 44.0	N 6 20.8
22	233 44.3	101 05.3	47.3	30 32.9	27.1	207 25.7	37.0	192 46.2	32.1	Betelgeuse	271 13.4	N 7 24.3
23	248 46.8	116 05.5	46.5	45 35.1	27.3	222 27.8	37.1	207 48.4	32.1			
16 00	263 49.3	131 05.6	N19 45.7	60 37.2	S10 27.5	237 29.8	N 9 37.3	222 50.6	N13 32.2	Canopus	264 01.5	S52 41.9
01	278 51.7	146 05.8	45.0	75 39.4	27.7	252 31.8	37.4	237 52.8	32.3	Capella	280 51.0	N45 59.7
02	293 54.2	161 05.9	44.2	90 41.5	27.9	267 33.9	37.6	252 55.0	32.4	Deneb	49 38.5	N45 16.6
03	308 56.6	176 06.1 ..	43.4	105 43.6 ..	28.1	282 35.9 ..	37.8	267 57.2 ..	32.4	Denebola	182 44.7	N14 34.7
04	323 59.1	191 06.2	42.7	120 45.8	28.3	297 37.9	37.9	282 59.4	32.5	Diphda	349 06.9	S17 59.4
05	339 01.6	206 06.4	41.9	135 47.9	28.5	312 40.0	38.1	298 01.6	32.6			
06	354 04.0	221 06.5	N19 41.1	150 50.1	S10 28.7	327 42.0	N 9 38.2	313 03.8	N13 32.7	Dubhe	194 05.1	N61 45.6
W 07	9 06.5	236 06.7	40.3	165 52.2	28.9	342 44.0	38.4	328 06.0	32.7	Elnath	278 26.7	N28 36.3
E 08	24 09.0	251 06.9	39.6	180 54.3	29.1	357 46.1	38.5	343 08.2	32.8	Eltanin	90 50.6	N51 29.4
D 09	39 11.4	266 07.0 ..	38.8	195 56.5 ..	29.3	12 48.1 ..	38.7	358 10.4 ..	32.9	Enif	33 57.6	N 9 52.3
N 10	54 13.9	281 07.2	38.0	210 58.6	29.5	27 50.1	38.8	13 12.6	33.0	Fomalhaut	15 35.9	S29 37.4
E 11	69 16.4	296 07.3	37.3	226 00.7	29.7	42 52.2	39.0	28 14.8	33.0			
S 12	84 18.8	311 07.5	N19 36.5	241 02.9	S10 29.9	57 54.2	N 9 39.2	43 17.0	N13 33.1	Gacrux	172 12.9	S57 06.8
D 13	99 21.3	326 07.7	35.7	256 05.0	30.1	72 56.2	39.3	58 19.2	33.2	Gienah	176 03.4	S17 32.4
A 14	114 23.7	341 07.8	34.9	271 07.1	30.3	87 58.3	39.5	73 21.4	33.3	Hadar	149 02.9	S60 22.3
Y 15	129 26.2	356 08.0 ..	34.2	286 09.3 ..	30.5	103 00.3 ..	39.6	88 23.6 ..	33.3	Hamal	328 13.2	N23 27.3
16	144 28.7	11 08.2	33.4	301 11.4	30.8	118 02.3	39.8	103 25.8	33.4	Kaus Aust.	83 57.8	S34 23.0
17	159 31.1	26 08.4	32.6	316 13.5	31.0	133 04.4	39.9	118 28.0	33.5			
18	174 33.6	41 08.5	N19 31.8	331 15.7	S10 31.2	148 06.4	N 9 40.1	133 30.2	N13 33.6	Kochab	137 18.8	N74 09.8
19	189 36.1	56 08.7	31.1	346 17.8	31.4	163 08.4	40.2	148 32.4	33.6	Markab	13 49.1	N15 12.0
20	204 38.5	71 08.9	30.3	1 19.9	31.6	178 10.5	40.4	163 34.6	33.7	Menkar	314 26.7	N 4 05.1
21	219 41.0	86 09.1 ..	29.5	16 22.0 ..	31.8	193 12.5 ..	40.5	178 36.8 ..	33.8	Menkent	148 20.1	S36 22.1
22	234 43.5	101 09.2	28.7	31 24.1	32.0	208 14.5	40.7	193 39.0	33.9	Miaplacidus	221 42.5	S69 43.2
23	249 45.9	116 09.4	27.9	46 26.3	32.2	223 16.6	40.9	208 41.2	33.9			
17 00	264 48.4	131 09.6	N19 27.2	61 28.4	S10 32.4	238 18.6	N 9 41.0	223 43.5	N13 34.0	Mirfak	308 56.3	N49 51.3
01	279 50.9	146 09.8	26.4	76 30.5	32.6	253 20.7	41.2	238 45.7	34.1	Nunki	76 11.4	S26 17.7
02	294 53.3	161 10.0	25.6	91 32.6	32.8	268 22.7	41.3	253 47.9	34.2	Peacock	53 35.9	S56 44.0
03	309 55.8	176 10.1 ..	24.8	106 34.7 ..	33.0	283 24.7 ..	41.5	268 50.1 ..	34.2	Pollux	243 41.3	N28 01.7
04	324 58.2	191 10.3	24.0	121 36.8	33.2	298 26.8	41.6	283 52.3	34.3	Procyon	245 11.4	N 5 13.5
05	340 00.7	206 10.5	23.3	136 39.0	33.5	313 28.8	41.8	298 54.5	34.4			
06	355 03.2	221 10.7	N19 22.5	151 41.1	S10 33.7	328 30.8	N 9 41.9	313 56.7	N13 34.5	Rasalhague	96 16.2	N12 33.7
07	10 05.6	236 10.9	21.7	166 43.2	33.9	343 32.9	42.1	328 58.9	34.5	Regulus	207 55.2	N11 58.3
T 08	25 08.1	251 11.1	20.9	181 45.3	34.1	358 34.9	42.2	344 01.1	34.6	Rigel	281 22.8	S 8 12.3
H 09	40 10.6	266 11.3 ..	20.1	196 47.4 ..	34.3	13 36.9 ..	42.4	359 03.3 ..	34.7	Rigil Kent.	140 06.2	S60 50.0
U 10	55 13.0	281 11.5	19.3	211 49.5	34.5	28 39.0	42.5	14 05.5	34.7	Sabik	102 24.7	S15 43.3
R 11	70 15.5	296 11.7	18.6	226 51.6	34.7	43 41.0	42.7	29 07.7	34.8			
S 12	85 18.0	311 11.9	N19 17.8	241 53.7	S10 34.9	58 43.1	N 9 42.9	44 09.9	N13 34.9	Schedar	349 53.0	N56 31.7
D 13	100 20.4	326 12.1	17.0	256 55.8	35.2	73 45.1	43.0	59 12.1	35.0	Shaula	96 36.2	S37 06.1
A 14	115 22.9	341 12.3	16.2	271 57.9	35.4	88 47.1	43.2	74 14.3	35.0	Sirius	258 43.6	S16 43.0
Y 15	130 25.4	356 12.5 ..	15.4	287 00.0 ..	35.6	103 49.2 ..	43.3	89 16.5 ..	35.1	Spica	158 42.6	S11 09.5
16	145 27.8	11 12.7	14.6	302 02.1	35.8	118 51.2	43.5	104 18.7	35.2	Suhail	223 00.7	S43 26.0
17	160 30.3	26 12.9	13.8	317 04.2	36.0	133 53.2	43.6	119 20.9	35.3			
18	175 32.7	41 13.1	N19 13.0	332 06.3	S10 36.2	148 55.3	N 9 43.8	134 23.1	N13 35.3	Vega	80 45.9	N38 47.0
19	190 35.2	56 13.3	12.3	347 08.4	36.4	163 57.3	43.9	149 25.3	35.4	Zuben'ubi	137 17.2	S16 02.3
20	205 37.7	71 13.5	11.5	2 10.5	36.7	178 59.4	44.1	164 27.5	35.5		SHA	Mer. Pass.
21	220 40.1	86 13.7 ..	10.7	17 12.6 ..	36.9	194 01.4 ..	44.2	179 29.8 ..	35.6		° ′	h m
22	235 42.6	101 13.9	09.9	32 14.7	37.1	209 03.4	44.4	194 32.0	35.6	Venus	227 16.4	15 15
23	250 45.1	116 14.1	09.1	47 16.8	37.3	224 05.5	44.5	209 34.2	35.7	Mars	156 48.0	19 55
	h m									Jupiter	333 40.6	8 09
Mer. Pass. 6 23.7		v 0.2	d 0.8	v 2.1	d 0.2	v 2.0	d 0.2	v 2.2	d 0.1	Saturn	319 01.3	9 07

UT	SUN GHA	SUN Dec	MOON GHA	v	MOON Dec	d	HP
d h	° ′	° ′	° ′	′	° ′	′	′
15 00	179 55.9	N23 16.6	161 42.0	3.8	N20 12.0	0.2	60.6
01	194 55.8	16.7	176 04.8	3.9	20 11.8	0.3	60.6
02	209 55.7	16.8	190 27.7	3.9	20 11.5	0.5	60.5
03	224 55.5	.. 17.0	204 50.6	4.0	20 11.0	0.6	60.5
04	239 55.4	17.1	219 13.6	4.0	20 10.4	0.8	60.5
05	254 55.3	17.2	233 36.6	4.0	20 09.6	0.9	60.5
06	269 55.1	N23 17.3	247 59.6	4.1	N20 08.7	1.0	60.5
T 07	284 55.0	17.4	262 22.7	4.1	20 07.7	1.2	60.4
U 08	299 54.9	17.5	276 45.8	4.2	20 06.5	1.3	60.4
E 09	314 54.7	.. 17.6	291 09.0	4.2	20 05.2	1.5	60.4
S 10	329 54.6	17.8	305 32.2	4.3	20 03.7	1.6	60.3
D 11	344 54.5	17.9	319 55.5	4.4	20 02.1	1.8	60.3
A 12	359 54.3	N23 18.0	334 18.9	4.3	N20 00.3	1.9	60.3
Y 13	14 54.2	18.1	348 42.2	4.5	19 58.4	2.0	60.3
14	29 54.1	18.2	3 05.7	4.5	19 56.4	2.2	60.2
15	44 53.9	.. 18.3	17 29.2	4.6	19 54.2	2.3	60.2
16	59 53.8	18.4	31 52.8	4.6	19 51.9	2.5	60.2
17	74 53.7	18.5	46 16.4	4.7	19 49.4	2.6	60.1
18	89 53.5	N23 18.6	60 40.1	4.8	N19 46.8	2.7	60.1
19	104 53.4	18.7	75 03.9	4.8	19 44.1	2.9	60.1
20	119 53.3	18.8	89 27.7	4.9	19 41.2	3.0	60.0
21	134 53.1	.. 18.9	103 51.6	4.9	19 38.2	3.1	60.0
22	149 53.0	19.0	118 15.5	5.1	19 35.1	3.3	60.0
23	164 52.9	19.1	132 39.6	5.1	19 31.8	3.4	59.9
16 00	179 52.7	N23 19.2	147 03.7	5.1	N19 28.4	3.5	59.9
01	194 52.6	19.3	161 27.8	5.3	19 24.9	3.7	59.9
02	209 52.4	19.4	175 52.1	5.3	19 21.2	3.7	59.8
03	224 52.3	.. 19.5	190 16.4	5.4	19 17.5	3.9	59.8
04	239 52.2	19.6	204 40.8	5.5	19 13.6	4.1	59.8
05	254 52.0	19.7	219 05.3	5.5	19 09.5	4.1	59.7
06	269 51.9	N23 19.8	233 29.8	5.7	N19 05.4	4.3	59.7
W 07	284 51.8	19.9	247 54.5	5.7	19 01.1	4.4	59.7
E 08	299 51.6	20.0	262 19.2	5.8	18 56.7	4.5	59.6
D 09	314 51.5	.. 20.1	276 44.0	5.8	18 52.2	4.7	59.6
N 10	329 51.4	20.2	291 08.8	6.0	18 47.5	4.8	59.6
E 11	344 51.2	20.3	305 33.8	6.0	18 42.7	4.8	59.5
S 12	359 51.1	N23 20.4	319 58.8	6.2	N18 37.9	5.0	59.5
D 13	14 51.0	20.5	334 24.0	6.2	18 32.9	5.1	59.4
A 14	29 50.8	20.6	348 49.2	6.3	18 27.8	5.3	59.4
Y 15	44 50.7	.. 20.7	3 14.5	6.4	18 22.5	5.3	59.4
16	59 50.6	20.7	17 39.9	6.4	18 17.2	5.5	59.3
17	74 50.4	20.8	32 05.3	6.6	18 11.7	5.5	59.3
18	89 50.3	N23 20.9	46 30.9	6.6	N18 06.2	5.7	59.3
19	104 50.2	21.0	60 56.5	6.8	18 00.5	5.8	59.2
20	119 50.0	21.1	75 22.3	6.8	17 54.7	5.9	59.2
21	134 49.9	.. 21.2	89 48.1	6.9	17 48.8	5.9	59.1
22	149 49.7	21.3	104 14.0	7.0	17 42.9	6.1	59.1
23	164 49.6	21.3	118 40.0	7.1	17 36.8	6.2	59.1
17 00	179 49.5	N23 21.4	133 06.1	7.2	N17 30.6	6.3	59.0
01	194 49.3	21.5	147 32.3	7.3	17 24.3	6.4	59.0
02	209 49.2	21.6	161 58.6	7.4	17 17.9	6.5	59.0
03	224 49.1	.. 21.7	176 25.0	7.4	17 11.4	6.6	58.9
04	239 48.9	21.8	190 51.4	7.6	17 04.8	6.7	58.9
05	254 48.8	21.8	205 18.0	7.7	16 58.1	6.8	58.8
06	269 48.7	N23 21.9	219 44.7	7.7	N16 51.3	6.9	58.8
T 07	284 48.5	22.0	234 11.4	7.8	16 44.4	6.9	58.8
H 08	299 48.4	22.1	248 38.2	8.0	16 37.5	7.1	58.7
U 09	314 48.3	.. 22.2	263 05.2	8.0	16 30.4	7.1	58.7
R 10	329 48.1	22.2	277 32.2	8.1	16 23.3	7.3	58.6
S 11	344 48.0	22.3	291 59.3	8.2	16 16.0	7.3	58.6
D 12	359 47.8	N23 22.4	306 26.5	8.3	N16 08.7	7.4	58.5
A 13	14 47.7	22.5	320 53.8	8.4	16 01.3	7.5	58.5
Y 14	29 47.6	22.5	335 21.2	8.5	15 53.8	7.6	58.5
15	44 47.4	.. 22.6	349 48.7	8.6	15 46.2	7.6	58.4
16	59 47.3	22.7	4 16.3	8.7	15 38.6	7.8	58.4
17	74 47.2	22.7	18 44.0	8.8	15 30.8	7.8	58.4
18	89 47.0	N23 22.8	33 11.8	8.8	N15 23.0	7.9	58.3
19	104 46.9	22.9	47 39.6	9.0	15 15.1	8.0	58.3
20	119 46.8	23.0	62 07.6	9.1	15 07.1	8.0	58.2
21	134 46.6	.. 23.0	76 35.7	9.1	14 59.1	8.1	58.2
22	149 46.5	23.1	91 03.8	9.2	14 51.0	8.2	58.2
23	164 46.4	23.2	105 32.0	9.4	N14 42.8	8.3	58.1
	SD 15.8	d 0.1	SD 16.4		16.2		16.0

Lat.	Naut. (Twilight)	Civil (Twilight)	Sunrise	Moonrise 15	16	17	18
°	h m	h m	h m	h m	h m	h m	h m
N 72	□	□	□	□	□	04 43	07 06
N 70	□	□	□	□	03 32	05 37	07 33
68	□	□	□	03 03	04 28	06 10	07 53
66	□	□	□	03 43	05 01	06 34	08 09
64	////	////	01 33	04 11	05 26	06 52	08 22
62	////	////	02 10	04 32	05 45	07 07	08 33
60	////	00 52	02 36	04 49	06 00	07 20	08 42
N 58	////	01 41	02 56	05 03	06 14	07 31	08 51
56	////	02 11	03 13	05 16	06 25	07 41	08 58
54	00 48	02 33	03 27	05 27	06 35	07 49	09 04
52	01 33	02 51	03 39	05 36	06 44	07 56	09 10
50	02 00	03 06	03 50	05 45	06 52	08 03	09 15
45	02 46	03 35	04 13	06 03	07 09	08 18	09 26
N 40	03 16	03 58	04 31	06 18	07 23	08 30	09 35
35	03 39	04 16	04 46	06 31	07 35	08 40	09 43
30	03 58	04 31	04 59	06 42	07 45	08 48	09 50
20	04 27	04 56	05 20	07 01	08 03	09 04	10 02
N 10	04 49	05 16	05 39	07 17	08 18	09 17	10 12
0	05 08	05 34	05 57	07 33	08 33	09 29	10 22
S 10	05 25	05 51	06 14	07 48	08 47	09 42	10 32
20	05 41	06 09	06 33	08 05	09 02	09 55	10 42
30	05 58	06 28	06 54	08 24	09 20	10 10	10 54
35	06 06	06 38	07 06	08 35	09 30	10 19	11 01
40	06 16	06 50	07 20	08 47	09 42	10 29	11 08
45	06 26	07 03	07 37	09 02	09 56	10 40	11 17
S 50	06 38	07 19	07 58	09 21	10 13	10 54	11 28
52	06 43	07 27	08 08	09 29	10 20	11 01	11 33
54	06 49	07 35	08 19	09 39	10 29	11 08	11 39
56	06 55	07 44	08 31	09 50	10 39	11 16	11 45
58	07 02	07 54	08 46	10 03	10 50	11 25	11 51
S 60	07 09	08 06	09 03	10 17	11 03	11 36	11 59

Lat.	Sunset	Civil (Twilight)	Naut. (Twilight)	Moonset 15	16	17	18
°	h m	h m	h m	h m	h m	h m	h m
N 72	□	□	□	□	□	01 59	01 28
N 70	□	□	□	□	01 09	01 04	01 00
68	□	□	□	24 13	00 13	00 31	00 38
66	□	□	□	23 39	24 06	00 06	00 21
64	22 29	////	////	23 14	23 47	24 07	00 07
62	21 52	////	////	22 55	23 31	23 56	24 13
60	21 26	23 10	////	22 39	23 18	23 46	24 06
N 58	21 05	22 20	////	22 25	23 06	23 37	24 00
56	20 48	21 51	////	22 13	22 56	23 29	23 55
54	20 34	21 29	23 14	22 03	22 47	23 22	23 50
52	20 22	21 11	22 29	21 54	22 40	23 16	23 45
50	20 11	20 56	22 01	21 46	22 32	23 10	23 41
45	19 49	20 26	21 16	21 28	22 17	22 58	23 32
N 40	19 31	20 04	20 45	21 14	22 05	22 48	23 25
35	19 16	19 45	20 22	21 02	21 54	22 39	23 18
30	19 03	19 30	20 04	20 51	21 44	22 31	23 13
20	18 41	19 05	19 35	20 33	21 28	22 18	23 03
N 10	18 22	18 45	19 12	20 17	21 14	22 06	22 54
0	18 04	18 27	18 53	20 02	21 00	21 55	22 46
S 10	17 47	18 10	18 36	19 46	20 47	21 44	22 38
20	17 28	17 52	18 20	19 30	20 32	21 32	22 29
30	17 07	17 34	18 03	19 12	20 15	21 18	22 19
35	16 55	17 23	17 55	19 01	20 06	21 10	22 13
40	16 41	17 11	17 45	18 48	19 54	21 01	22 06
45	16 24	16 58	17 35	18 33	19 41	20 50	21 58
S 50	16 03	16 42	17 23	18 15	19 25	20 37	21 49
52	15 53	16 34	17 18	18 07	19 18	20 31	21 44
54	15 42	16 26	17 12	17 57	19 09	20 24	21 39
56	15 30	16 17	17 06	17 46	19 00	20 17	21 34
58	15 15	16 07	17 00	17 34	18 49	20 08	21 28
S 60	14 58	15 55	16 52	17 19	18 36	19 58	21 21

	SUN Eqn. of Time 00h	SUN Eqn. of Time 12h	Mer. Pass.	MOON Mer. Pass. Upper	Lower	Age	Phase
Day	m s	m s	h m	h m	h m	d	%
15	00 16	00 22	12 00	13 47	01 16	02	4
16	00 29	00 35	12 01	14 47	02 17	03	10
17	00 42	00 48	12 01	15 42	03 15	04	18

UT	ARIES	VENUS −4.4		MARS −0.7		JUPITER −2.2		SATURN +0.4		STARS		
	GHA	GHA	Dec	GHA	Dec	GHA	Dec	GHA	Dec	Name	SHA	Dec
d h	° ′	° ′	° ′	° ′	° ′	° ′	° ′	° ′	° ′		° ′	° ′
18 00	265 47.5	131 14.3	N19 08.3	62 18.9	S10 37.5	239 07.5	N 9 44.7	224 36.4	N13 35.8	Acamar	315 26.9	S40 18.4
01	280 50.0	146 14.6	07.5	77 21.0	37.7	254 09.6	44.8	239 38.6	35.9	Achernar	335 35.2	S57 14.2
02	295 52.5	161 14.8	06.7	92 23.1	38.0	269 11.6	45.0	254 40.8	35.9	Acrux	173 21.3	S63 06.0
03	310 54.9	176 15.0 ..	05.9	107 25.2 ..	38.2	284 13.6 ..	45.1	269 43.0 ..	36.0	Adhara	255 21.4	S28 58.4
04	325 57.4	191 15.2	05.1	122 27.2	38.4	299 15.7	45.3	284 45.2	36.1	Aldebaran	291 02.2	N16 30.3
05	340 59.9	206 15.4	04.3	137 29.3	38.6	314 17.7	45.4	299 47.4	36.1			
06	356 02.3	221 15.7	N19 03.6	152 31.4	S10 38.8	329 19.8	N 9 45.6	314 49.6	N13 36.2	Alioth	166 30.1	N55 58.1
07	11 04.8	236 15.9	02.8	167 33.5	39.1	344 21.8	45.8	329 51.8	36.3	Alkaid	153 07.2	N49 19.3
08	26 07.2	251 16.1	02.0	182 35.6	39.3	359 23.8	45.9	344 54.0	36.4	Al Na'ir	27 57.1	S46 57.6
F 09	41 09.7	266 16.3 ..	01.2	197 37.7 ..	39.5	14 25.9 ..	46.1	359 56.2 ..	36.4	Alnilam	275 57.7	S 1 12.3
R 10	56 12.2	281 16.6	19 00.4	212 39.7	39.7	29 27.9	46.2	14 58.4	36.5	Alphard	218 06.9	S 8 39.4
I 11	71 14.6	296 16.8	18 59.6	227 41.8	39.9	44 30.0	46.4	30 00.6	36.6			
D 12	86 17.1	311 17.0	N18 58.8	242 43.9	S10 40.2	59 32.0	N 9 46.5	45 02.8	N13 36.7	Alphecca	126 19.9	N26 43.2
A 13	101 19.6	326 17.3	58.0	257 46.0	40.4	74 34.1	46.7	60 05.1	36.7	Alpheratz	357 54.8	N29 05.0
Y 14	116 22.0	341 17.5	57.2	272 48.1	40.6	89 36.1	46.8	75 07.3	36.8	Altair	62 18.5	N 8 52.1
15	131 24.5	356 17.7 ..	56.4	287 50.1 ..	40.8	104 38.1 ..	47.0	90 09.5 ..	36.9	Ankaa	353 26.5	S42 18.4
16	146 27.0	11 18.0	55.6	302 52.2	41.0	119 40.2	47.1	105 11.7	36.9	Antares	112 39.2	S26 25.8
17	161 29.4	26 18.2	54.8	317 54.3	41.3	134 42.2	47.3	120 13.9	37.0			
18	176 31.9	41 18.4	N18 54.0	332 56.3	S10 41.5	149 44.3	N 9 47.4	135 16.1	N13 37.1	Arcturus	146 05.4	N19 11.3
19	191 34.3	56 18.7	53.2	347 58.4	41.7	164 46.3	47.6	150 18.3	37.2	Atria	107 50.3	S69 01.6
20	206 36.8	71 18.9	52.4	3 00.5	41.9	179 48.3	47.7	165 20.5	37.2	Avior	234 22.9	S59 30.7
21	221 39.3	86 19.2 ..	51.6	18 02.6 ..	42.2	194 50.4 ..	47.9	180 22.7 ..	37.3	Bellatrix	278 44.0	N 6 20.8
22	236 41.7	101 19.4	50.8	33 04.6	42.4	209 52.4	48.0	195 24.9	37.4	Betelgeuse	271 13.4	N 7 24.3
23	251 44.2	116 19.7	50.0	48 06.7	42.6	224 54.5	48.2	210 27.1	37.5			
19 00	266 46.7	131 19.9	N18 49.2	63 08.7	S10 42.8	239 56.5	N 9 48.3	225 29.3	N13 37.5	Canopus	264 01.5	S52 41.9
01	281 49.1	146 20.2	48.4	78 10.8	43.1	254 58.6	48.5	240 31.5	37.6	Capella	280 51.0	N45 59.7
02	296 51.6	161 20.4	47.6	93 12.9	43.3	270 00.6	48.6	255 33.8	37.7	Deneb	49 38.5	N45 16.6
03	311 54.1	176 20.7 ..	46.8	108 14.9 ..	43.5	285 02.7 ..	48.8	270 36.0 ..	37.7	Denebola	182 44.7	N14 34.7
04	326 56.5	191 20.9	46.0	123 17.0	43.8	300 04.7	48.9	285 38.2	37.8	Diphda	349 06.9	S17 59.4
05	341 59.0	206 21.2	45.2	138 19.1	44.0	315 06.7	49.1	300 40.4	37.9			
06	357 01.5	221 21.4	N18 44.4	153 21.1	S10 44.2	330 08.8	N 9 49.2	315 42.6	N13 38.0	Dubhe	194 05.2	N61 45.6
07	12 03.9	236 21.7	43.6	168 23.2	44.4	345 10.8	49.4	330 44.8	38.0	Elnath	278 26.7	N28 36.3
S 08	27 06.4	251 21.9	42.8	183 25.2	44.7	0 12.9	49.5	345 47.0	38.1	Eltanin	90 50.6	N51 29.4
A 09	42 08.8	266 22.2 ..	42.0	198 27.3 ..	44.9	15 14.9 ..	49.7	0 49.2 ..	38.2	Enif	33 57.6	N 9 52.3
T 10	57 11.3	281 22.5	41.2	213 29.3	45.1	30 17.0	49.8	15 51.4	38.2	Fomalhaut	15 35.8	S29 37.4
U 11	72 13.8	296 22.7	40.3	228 31.4	45.4	45 19.0	50.0	30 53.6	38.3			
R 12	87 16.2	311 23.0	N18 39.5	243 33.4	S10 45.6	60 21.1	N 9 50.1	45 55.8	N13 38.4	Gacrux	172 12.9	S57 06.8
D 13	102 18.7	326 23.3	38.7	258 35.5	45.8	75 23.1	50.3	60 58.1	38.5	Gienah	176 03.4	S17 32.4
A 14	117 21.2	341 23.5	37.9	273 37.5	46.0	90 25.1	50.4	76 00.3	38.5	Hadar	149 02.9	S60 22.3
Y 15	132 23.6	356 23.8 ..	37.1	288 39.6 ..	46.3	105 27.2 ..	50.6	91 02.5 ..	38.6	Hamal	328 13.2	N23 27.3
16	147 26.1	11 24.1	36.3	303 41.6	46.5	120 29.2	50.7	106 04.7	38.7	Kaus Aust.	83 57.8	S34 23.0
17	162 28.6	26 24.4	35.5	318 43.7	46.7	135 31.3	50.9	121 06.9	38.8			
18	177 31.0	41 24.6	N18 34.7	333 45.7	S10 47.0	150 33.3	N 9 51.0	136 09.1	N13 38.8	Kochab	137 18.8	N74 09.8
19	192 33.5	56 24.9	33.9	348 47.8	47.2	165 35.4	51.2	151 11.3	38.9	Markab	13 49.1	N15 12.0
20	207 36.0	71 25.2	33.1	3 49.8	47.4	180 37.4	51.3	166 13.5	39.0	Menkar	314 26.7	N 4 05.1
21	222 38.4	86 25.5 ..	32.3	18 51.8 ..	47.7	195 39.5 ..	51.5	181 15.7 ..	39.0	Menkent	148 20.1	S36 22.1
22	237 40.9	101 25.7	31.5	33 53.9	47.9	210 41.5	51.6	196 17.9	39.1	Miaplacidus	221 42.5	S69 43.2
23	252 43.3	116 26.0	30.6	48 55.9	48.1	225 43.6	51.8	211 20.1	39.2			
20 00	267 45.8	131 26.3	N18 29.8	63 58.0	S10 48.4	240 45.6	N 9 51.9	226 22.4	N13 39.3	Mirfak	308 56.3	N49 51.3
01	282 48.3	146 26.6	29.0	79 00.0	48.6	255 47.7	52.1	241 24.6	39.3	Nunki	76 11.4	S26 17.7
02	297 50.7	161 26.9	28.2	94 02.0	48.8	270 49.7	52.2	256 26.8	39.4	Peacock	53 35.8	S56 44.0
03	312 53.2	176 27.2 ..	27.4	109 04.1 ..	49.1	285 51.8 ..	52.4	271 29.0 ..	39.5	Pollux	243 41.3	N28 01.7
04	327 55.7	191 27.5	26.6	124 06.1	49.3	300 53.8	52.5	286 31.2	39.5	Procyon	245 11.4	N 5 13.5
05	342 58.1	206 27.7	25.8	139 08.1	49.6	315 55.9	52.7	301 33.4	39.6			
06	358 00.6	221 28.0	N18 25.0	154 10.2	S10 49.8	330 57.9	N 9 52.8	316 35.6	N13 39.7	Rasalhague	96 16.2	N12 33.7
07	13 03.1	236 28.3	24.1	169 12.2	50.0	345 59.9	52.9	331 37.8	39.8	Regulus	207 55.2	N11 58.3
08	28 05.5	251 28.6	23.3	184 14.2	50.3	1 02.0	53.1	346 40.0	39.8	Rigel	281 22.8	S 8 12.3
S 09	43 08.0	266 28.9 ..	22.5	199 16.3 ..	50.5	16 04.0 ..	53.2	1 42.3 ..	39.9	Rigil Kent.	140 06.2	S60 50.0
U 10	58 10.4	281 29.2	21.7	214 18.3	50.7	31 06.1	53.4	16 44.5	40.0	Sabik	102 24.6	S15 43.3
N 11	73 12.9	296 29.5	20.9	229 20.3	51.0	46 08.1	53.5	31 46.7	40.0			
D 12	88 15.4	311 29.8	N18 20.1	244 22.3	S10 51.2	61 10.2	N 9 53.7	46 48.9	N13 40.1	Schedar	349 53.0	N56 31.7
A 13	103 17.8	326 30.1	19.2	259 24.4	51.5	76 12.2	53.8	61 51.1	40.2	Shaula	96 36.2	S37 06.1
Y 14	118 20.3	341 30.4	18.4	274 26.4	51.7	91 14.3	54.0	76 53.3	40.2	Sirius	258 43.6	S16 43.0
15	133 22.8	356 30.7 ..	17.6	289 28.4 ..	51.9	106 16.3 ..	54.1	91 55.5 ..	40.3	Spica	158 42.6	S11 09.5
16	148 25.2	11 31.0	16.8	304 30.4	52.2	121 18.4	54.3	106 57.7	40.4	Suhail	223 00.7	S43 26.0
17	163 27.7	26 31.3	16.0	319 32.4	52.4	136 20.4	54.4	121 59.9	40.5			
18	178 30.2	41 31.7	N18 15.2	334 34.5	S10 52.7	151 22.5	N 9 54.6	137 02.2	N13 40.5	Vega	80 45.9	N38 47.0
19	193 32.6	56 32.0	14.3	349 36.5	52.9	166 24.5	54.7	152 04.4	40.6	Zuben'ubi	137 17.2	S16 02.3
20	208 35.1	71 32.3	13.5	4 38.5	53.1	181 26.6	54.9	167 06.6	40.7		SHA	Mer. Pass.
21	223 37.6	86 32.6 ..	12.7	19 40.5 ..	53.4	196 28.6 ..	55.0	182 08.8 ..	40.7		° ′	h m
22	238 40.0	101 32.9	11.9	34 42.5	53.6	211 30.7	55.2	197 11.0	40.8	Venus	224 33.2	15 14
23	253 42.5	116 33.2	11.1	49 44.5	53.9	226 32.7	55.3	212 13.2	40.9	Mars	156 22.1	19 45
	h m									Jupiter	333 09.8	7 59
Mer. Pass. 6 11.9		v 0.3	d 0.8	v 2.1	d 0.2	v 2.0	d 0.1	v 2.2	d 0.1	Saturn	318 42.7	8 57

UT	SUN GHA	SUN Dec	MOON GHA	MOON v	MOON Dec	MOON d	MOON HP
d h	° ′	° ′	° ′	′	° ′	′	′
18 00	179 46.2	N23 23.2	120 00.4	9.4	N14 34.5	8.3	58.1
01	194 46.1	23.3	134 28.8	9.5	14 26.2	8.4	58.0
02	209 45.9	23.4	148 57.3	9.6	14 17.8	8.5	58.0
03	224 45.8 ..	23.4	163 25.9	9.7	14 09.3	8.6	58.0
04	239 45.7	23.5	177 54.6	9.8	14 00.7	8.6	57.9
05	254 45.5	23.5	192 23.4	9.9	13 52.1	8.6	57.9
06	269 45.4	N23 23.6	206 52.3	9.9	N13 43.5	8.8	57.9
07	284 45.3	23.7	221 21.2	10.1	13 34.7	8.8	57.8
08	299 45.1	23.7	235 50.3	10.1	13 25.9	8.8	57.8
F 09	314 45.0 ..	23.8	250 19.4	10.3	13 17.1	8.9	57.7
R 10	329 44.9	23.8	264 48.7	10.3	13 08.2	9.0	57.7
I 11	344 44.7	23.9	279 18.0	10.4	12 59.2	9.0	57.7
D 12	359 44.6	N23 24.0	293 47.4	10.5	N12 50.2	9.1	57.6
A 13	14 44.4	24.0	308 16.9	10.6	12 41.1	9.1	57.6
Y 14	29 44.3	24.1	322 46.5	10.6	12 32.0	9.2	57.5
15	44 44.2 ..	24.1	337 16.1	10.8	12 22.8	9.3	57.5
16	59 44.0	24.2	351 45.9	10.8	12 13.5	9.3	57.5
17	74 43.9	24.2	6 15.7	10.9	12 04.2	9.3	57.4
18	89 43.8	N23 24.3	20 45.6	11.0	N11 54.9	9.4	57.4
19	104 43.6	24.3	35 15.6	11.1	11 45.5	9.5	57.3
20	119 43.5	24.4	49 45.7	11.2	11 36.0	9.4	57.3
21	134 43.4 ..	24.5	64 15.9	11.2	11 26.6	9.6	57.3
22	149 43.2	24.5	78 46.1	11.4	11 17.0	9.6	57.2
23	164 43.1	24.6	93 16.5	11.4	11 07.4	9.6	57.2
19 00	179 42.9	N23 24.6	107 46.9	11.4	N10 57.8	9.6	57.2
01	194 42.8	24.6	122 17.3	11.6	10 48.2	9.7	57.1
02	209 42.7	24.7	136 47.9	11.6	10 38.5	9.8	57.1
03	224 42.5 ..	24.7	151 18.5	11.8	10 28.7	9.8	57.0
04	239 42.4	24.8	165 49.3	11.8	10 18.9	9.8	57.0
05	254 42.3	24.8	180 20.1	11.8	10 09.1	9.9	57.0
06	269 42.1	N23 24.9	194 50.9	12.0	N 9 59.2	9.9	56.9
07	284 42.0	24.9	209 21.9	12.0	9 49.3	9.9	56.9
S 08	299 41.9	25.0	223 52.9	12.1	9 39.4	9.9	56.9
A 09	314 41.7 ..	25.0	238 24.0	12.1	9 29.5	10.0	56.8
T 10	329 41.6	25.1	252 55.1	12.3	9 19.5	10.1	56.8
U 11	344 41.4	25.1	267 26.4	12.3	9 09.4	10.0	56.7
R 12	359 41.3	N23 25.1	281 57.7	12.3	N 8 59.4	10.1	56.7
D 13	14 41.2	25.2	296 29.0	12.5	8 49.3	10.1	56.7
A 14	29 41.0	25.2	311 00.5	12.5	8 39.2	10.2	56.6
Y 15	44 40.9 ..	25.3	325 32.0	12.5	8 29.0	10.2	56.6
16	59 40.8	25.3	340 03.5	12.7	8 18.8	10.2	56.6
17	74 40.6	25.3	354 35.2	12.7	8 08.6	10.2	56.5
18	89 40.5	N23 25.4	9 06.9	12.8	N 7 58.4	10.3	56.5
19	104 40.4	25.4	23 38.7	12.8	7 48.1	10.2	56.5
20	119 40.2	25.4	38 10.5	12.9	7 37.9	10.3	56.4
21	134 40.1 ..	25.5	52 42.4	13.0	7 27.6	10.4	56.4
22	149 39.9	25.5	67 14.4	13.0	7 17.2	10.3	56.4
23	164 39.8	25.5	81 46.4	13.1	7 06.9	10.4	56.3
20 00	179 39.7	N23 25.6	96 18.5	13.1	N 6 56.5	10.3	56.3
01	194 39.5	25.6	110 50.6	13.2	6 46.2	10.4	56.3
02	209 39.4	25.6	125 22.8	13.3	6 35.8	10.5	56.2
03	224 39.3 ..	25.7	139 55.1	13.3	6 25.3	10.4	56.2
04	239 39.1	25.7	154 27.4	13.4	6 14.9	10.4	56.2
05	254 39.0	25.7	168 59.8	13.4	6 04.5	10.5	56.1
06	269 38.9	N23 25.7	183 32.2	13.5	N 5 54.0	10.5	56.1
07	284 38.7	25.8	198 04.7	13.5	5 43.5	10.5	56.1
08	299 38.6	25.8	212 37.2	13.6	5 33.0	10.5	56.0
S 09	314 38.4 ..	25.8	227 09.8	13.6	5 22.5	10.5	56.0
U 10	329 38.3	25.8	241 42.4	13.7	5 12.0	10.5	56.0
N 11	344 38.2	25.9	256 15.1	13.7	5 01.5	10.6	55.9
D 12	359 38.0	N23 25.9	270 47.8	13.8	N 4 50.9	10.5	55.9
A 13	14 37.9	25.9	285 20.6	13.9	4 40.4	10.6	55.9
Y 14	29 37.8	25.9	299 53.5	13.8	4 29.8	10.6	55.8
15	44 37.6 ..	26.0	314 26.3	14.0	4 19.2	10.5	55.8
16	59 37.5	26.0	328 59.3	13.9	4 08.7	10.6	55.7
17	74 37.4	26.0	343 32.2	14.0	3 58.1	10.6	55.7
18	89 37.2	N23 26.0	358 05.2	14.1	N 3 47.5	10.6	55.7
19	104 37.1	26.0	12 38.3	14.1	3 36.9	10.6	55.7
20	119 37.0	26.1	27 11.4	14.1	3 26.3	10.6	55.7
21	134 36.8 ..	26.1	41 44.5	14.2	3 15.7	10.6	55.6
22	149 36.7	26.1	56 17.7	14.3	3 05.1	10.6	55.6
23	164 36.5	26.1	70 51.0	14.2	N 2 54.5	10.6	55.5
	SD 15.8	d 0.0	SD 15.7		15.5		15.2

Lat.	Twilight Naut.	Twilight Civil	Sunrise	Moonrise 18	Moonrise 19	Moonrise 20	Moonrise 21
°	h m	h m	h m	h m	h m	h m	h m
N 72	▭	▭	▭	07 06	09 05	10 53	12 36
N 70	▭	▭	▭	07 33	09 20	11 00	12 36
68	▭	▭	▭	07 53	09 32	11 06	12 37
66	▭	▭	▭	08 09	09 42	11 11	12 37
64	////	////	01 31	08 22	09 50	11 15	12 38
62	////	////	02 09	08 33	09 57	11 19	12 38
60	////	00 50	02 36	08 42	10 03	11 22	12 38
N 58	////	01 40	02 56	08 51	10 09	11 25	12 38
56	////	02 10	03 13	08 58	10 14	11 27	12 39
54	00 45	02 33	03 27	09 04	10 18	11 29	12 39
52	01 32	02 50	03 39	09 10	10 22	11 31	12 39
50	02 00	03 06	03 50	09 15	10 25	11 33	12 39
45	02 46	03 35	04 13	09 26	10 33	11 37	12 39
N 40	03 16	03 58	04 31	09 35	10 39	11 40	12 40
35	03 39	04 16	04 46	09 43	10 44	11 43	12 40
30	03 58	04 31	04 59	09 50	10 48	11 46	12 40
20	04 27	04 56	05 21	10 02	10 57	11 50	12 41
N 10	04 50	05 17	05 40	10 12	11 04	11 54	12 41
0	05 09	05 35	05 58	10 22	11 11	11 57	12 41
S 10	05 26	05 52	06 15	10 32	11 18	12 01	12 42
20	05 42	06 10	06 34	10 42	11 25	12 04	12 42
30	05 59	06 28	06 55	10 54	11 33	12 09	12 42
35	06 07	06 39	07 07	11 01	11 38	12 11	12 43
40	06 17	06 51	07 21	11 08	11 43	12 14	12 43
45	06 27	07 04	07 38	11 17	11 49	12 17	12 43
S 50	06 39	07 20	07 59	11 28	11 56	12 21	12 44
52	06 44	07 28	08 09	11 33	12 00	12 23	12 44
54	06 50	07 36	08 20	11 39	12 03	12 25	12 44
56	06 56	07 45	08 33	11 45	12 07	12 27	12 44
58	07 03	07 55	08 47	11 51	12 12	12 29	12 45
S 60	07 10	08 07	09 05	11 59	12 17	12 32	12 45

Lat.	Sunset	Twilight Civil	Twilight Naut.	Moonset 18	Moonset 19	Moonset 20	Moonset 21
°	h m	h m	h m	h m	h m	h m	h m
N 72	▭	▭	▭	01 28	01 13	01 01	00 50
N 70	▭	▭	▭	01 00	00 56	00 51	00 47
68	▭	▭	▭	00 38	00 42	00 44	00 44
66	▭	▭	▭	00 21	00 31	00 37	00 42
64	22 32	////	////	00 07	00 21	00 32	00 40
62	21 54	////	////	24 13	00 13	00 27	00 38
60	21 27	23 13	////	24 06	00 06	00 23	00 37
N 58	21 07	22 22	////	24 00	00 00	00 19	00 35
56	20 50	21 52	////	23 55	24 16	00 16	00 34
54	20 36	21 30	23 18	23 50	24 13	00 13	00 33
52	20 23	21 12	22 31	23 45	24 10	00 10	00 32
50	20 12	20 57	22 03	23 41	24 08	00 08	00 31
45	19 50	20 27	21 17	23 32	24 02	00 02	00 29
N 40	19 32	20 05	20 46	23 25	23 58	24 28	00 28
35	19 17	19 46	20 23	23 18	23 54	24 26	00 26
30	19 04	19 31	20 04	23 13	23 50	24 25	00 25
20	18 42	19 06	19 35	23 03	23 44	24 22	00 22
N 10	18 23	18 46	19 14	22 54	23 39	24 20	00 20
0	18 05	18 27	18 54	22 46	23 33	24 19	00 19
S 10	17 47	18 10	18 37	22 38	23 28	24 17	00 17
20	17 29	17 53	18 20	22 29	23 23	24 14	00 14
30	17 08	17 34	18 04	22 19	23 16	24 12	00 12
35	16 55	17 23	17 55	22 13	23 13	24 11	00 11
40	16 41	17 12	17 46	22 06	23 09	24 09	00 09
45	16 24	16 58	17 35	21 58	23 04	24 07	00 07
S 50	16 03	16 42	17 24	21 49	22 58	24 05	00 05
52	15 54	16 35	17 18	21 44	22 55	24 04	00 04
54	15 42	16 26	17 13	21 39	22 52	24 03	00 03
56	15 30	16 17	17 06	21 34	22 49	24 01	00 01
58	15 15	16 07	17 00	21 28	22 45	24 00	00 00
S 60	14 58	15 55	16 52	21 21	22 41	23 58	25 14

	SUN Eqn. of Time 00ʰ	SUN Eqn. of Time 12ʰ	SUN Mer. Pass.	MOON Mer. Pass. Upper	MOON Mer. Pass. Lower	MOON Age	MOON Phase
Day	m s	m s	h m	h m	h m	d	%
18	00 55	01 01	12 01	16 34	04 09	05	27
19	01 08	01 14	12 01	17 22	04 59	06	37
20	01 21	01 28	12 01	18 08	05 45	07	48

UT	ARIES GHA	VENUS −4.4 GHA	Dec	MARS −0.6 GHA	Dec	JUPITER −2.2 GHA	Dec	SATURN +0.4 GHA	Dec	STARS Name	SHA	Dec
21 00	268 44.9	131 33.5	N18 10.2	64 46.6	S10 54.1	241 34.8	N 9 55.5	227 15.4	N13 41.0	Acamar	315 26.9	S40 18.4
01	283 47.4	146 33.9	09.4	79 48.6	54.3	256 36.9	55.6	242 17.6	41.0	Achernar	335 35.1	S57 14.2
02	298 49.9	161 34.2	08.6	94 50.6	54.6	271 38.9	55.7	257 19.9	41.1	Acrux	173 21.3	S63 06.0
03	313 52.3	176 34.5	.. 07.8	109 52.6	.. 54.8	286 41.0	.. 55.9	272 22.1	.. 41.2	Adhara	255 21.4	S28 58.4
04	328 54.8	191 34.8	06.9	124 54.6	55.1	301 43.0	56.0	287 24.3	41.2	Aldebaran	291 02.2	N16 30.3
05	343 57.3	206 35.2	06.1	139 56.6	55.3	316 45.1	56.2	302 26.5	41.3			
06	358 59.7	221 35.5	N18 05.3	154 58.6	S10 55.6	331 47.1	N 9 56.3	317 28.7	N13 41.4	Alioth	166 30.1	N55 58.1
07	14 02.2	236 35.8	04.5	170 00.6	55.8	346 49.2	56.5	332 30.9	41.4	Alkaid	153 07.2	N49 19.3
08	29 04.7	251 36.1	03.7	185 02.6	56.1	1 51.2	56.6	347 33.1	41.5	Al Na'ir	27 57.1	S46 57.6
M 09	44 07.1	266 36.5	.. 02.8	200 04.6	.. 56.3	16 53.3	.. 56.8	2 35.3	.. 41.6	Alnilam	275 57.7	S 1 12.3
O 10	59 09.6	281 36.8	02.0	215 06.6	56.6	31 55.3	56.9	17 37.6	41.7	Alphard	218 07.0	S 8 39.4
N 11	74 12.1	296 37.1	01.2	230 08.6	56.8	46 57.4	57.1	32 39.8	41.7			
D 12	89 14.5	311 37.5	N18 00.4	245 10.6	S10 57.0	61 59.4	N 9 57.2	47 42.0	N13 41.8	Alphecca	126 19.9	N26 43.2
A 13	104 17.0	326 37.8	17 59.5	260 12.6	57.3	77 01.5	57.4	62 44.2	41.9	Alpheratz	357 54.7	N29 05.0
Y 14	119 19.4	341 38.2	58.7	275 14.6	57.5	92 03.5	57.5	77 46.4	41.9	Altair	62 18.5	N 8 52.1
15	134 21.9	356 38.5	.. 57.9	290 16.6	.. 57.8	107 05.6	.. 57.6	92 48.6	.. 42.0	Ankaa	353 26.5	S42 18.4
16	149 24.4	11 38.8	57.1	305 18.6	58.0	122 07.6	57.8	107 50.8	42.1	Antares	112 39.2	S26 25.8
17	164 26.8	26 39.2	56.2	320 20.6	58.3	137 09.7	57.9	122 53.1	42.1			
18	179 29.3	41 39.5	N17 55.4	335 22.6	S10 58.5	152 11.8	N 9 58.1	137 55.3	N13 42.2	Arcturus	146 05.5	N19 11.3
19	194 31.8	56 39.9	54.6	350 24.6	58.8	167 13.8	58.2	152 57.5	42.3	Atria	107 50.3	S69 01.6
20	209 34.2	71 40.2	53.7	5 26.6	59.0	182 15.9	58.4	167 59.7	42.4	Avior	234 23.0	S59 30.7
21	224 36.7	86 40.6	.. 52.9	20 28.6	.. 59.3	197 17.9	.. 58.5	183 01.9	.. 42.4	Bellatrix	278 44.0	N 6 20.8
22	239 39.2	101 40.9	52.1	35 30.5	59.5	212 20.0	58.7	198 04.1	42.5	Betelgeuse	271 13.4	N 7 24.3
23	254 41.6	116 41.3	51.3	50 32.5	10 59.8	227 22.0	58.8	213 06.3	42.6			
22 00	269 44.1	131 41.6	N17 50.4	65 34.5	S11 00.0	242 24.1	N 9 58.9	228 08.6	N13 42.6	Canopus	264 01.5	S52 41.9
01	284 46.5	146 42.0	49.6	80 36.5	00.3	257 26.1	59.1	243 10.8	42.7	Capella	280 51.0	N45 59.7
02	299 49.0	161 42.4	48.8	95 38.5	00.5	272 28.2	59.2	258 13.0	42.8	Deneb	49 38.5	N45 16.6
03	314 51.5	176 42.7	.. 47.9	110 40.5	.. 00.8	287 30.3	.. 59.4	273 15.2	.. 42.8	Denebola	182 44.7	N14 34.7
04	329 53.9	191 43.1	47.1	125 42.5	01.0	302 32.3	59.5	288 17.4	42.9	Diphda	349 06.8	S17 59.4
05	344 56.4	206 43.4	46.3	140 44.4	01.3	317 34.4	59.7	303 19.6	43.0			
06	359 58.9	221 43.8	N17 45.4	155 46.4	S11 01.5	332 36.4	N 9 59.8	318 21.9	N13 43.1	Dubhe	194 05.2	N61 45.6
07	15 01.3	236 44.2	44.6	170 48.4	01.8	347 38.5	10 00.0	333 24.1	43.1	Elnath	278 26.7	N28 36.3
T 08	30 03.8	251 44.5	43.8	185 50.4	02.1	2 40.5	00.1	348 26.3	43.2	Eltanin	90 50.6	N51 29.5
U 09	45 06.3	266 44.9	.. 42.9	200 52.4	.. 02.3	17 42.6	.. 00.2	3 28.5	.. 43.3	Enif	33 57.6	N 9 52.3
E 10	60 08.7	281 45.3	42.1	215 54.3	02.6	32 44.6	00.4	18 30.7	43.3	Fomalhaut	15 35.8	S29 37.4
S 11	75 11.2	296 45.6	41.3	230 56.3	02.8	47 46.7	00.5	33 32.9	43.4			
D 12	90 13.7	311 46.0	N17 40.4	245 58.3	S11 03.1	62 48.8	N10 00.7	48 35.1	N13 43.5	Gacrux	172 12.9	S57 06.8
A 13	105 16.1	326 46.4	39.6	261 00.3	03.3	77 50.8	00.8	63 37.4	43.5	Gienah	176 03.4	S17 32.4
Y 14	120 18.6	341 46.8	38.8	276 02.2	03.6	92 52.9	01.0	78 39.6	43.6	Hadar	149 03.0	S60 22.3
15	135 21.0	356 47.1	.. 37.9	291 04.2	.. 03.8	107 54.9	.. 01.1	93 41.8	.. 43.7	Hamal	328 13.2	N23 27.4
16	150 23.5	11 47.5	37.1	306 06.2	04.1	122 57.0	01.3	108 44.0	43.7	Kaus Aust.	83 57.8	S34 23.0
17	165 26.0	26 47.9	36.3	321 08.1	04.3	137 59.1	01.4	123 46.2	43.8			
18	180 28.4	41 48.3	N17 35.4	336 10.1	S11 04.6	153 01.1	N10 01.5	138 48.4	N13 43.9	Kochab	137 18.9	N74 09.8
19	195 30.9	56 48.7	34.6	351 12.1	04.9	168 03.2	01.7	153 50.7	43.9	Markab	13 49.0	N15 12.0
20	210 33.4	71 49.1	33.8	6 14.0	05.1	183 05.2	01.8	168 52.9	44.0	Menkar	314 26.6	N 4 05.1
21	225 35.8	86 49.4	.. 32.9	21 16.0	.. 05.4	198 07.3	.. 02.0	183 55.1	.. 44.1	Menkent	148 20.2	S36 22.1
22	240 38.3	101 49.8	32.1	36 18.0	05.6	213 09.3	02.1	198 57.3	44.2	Miaplacidus	221 42.6	S69 43.2
23	255 40.8	116 50.2	31.2	51 19.9	05.9	228 11.4	02.3	213 59.5	44.2			
23 00	270 43.2	131 50.6	N17 30.4	66 21.9	S11 06.2	243 13.5	N10 02.4	229 01.7	N13 44.3	Mirfak	308 56.3	N49 51.3
01	285 45.7	146 51.0	29.6	81 23.8	06.4	258 15.5	02.5	244 04.0	44.4	Nunki	76 11.4	S26 17.7
02	300 48.2	161 51.4	28.7	96 25.8	06.7	273 17.6	02.7	259 06.2	44.4	Peacock	53 35.8	S56 44.0
03	315 50.6	176 51.8	.. 27.9	111 27.8	.. 06.9	288 19.6	.. 02.8	274 08.4	.. 44.5	Pollux	243 41.3	N28 01.7
04	330 53.1	191 52.2	27.1	126 29.7	07.2	303 21.7	03.0	289 10.6	44.6	Procyon	245 11.4	N 5 13.5
05	345 55.5	206 52.6	26.2	141 31.7	07.4	318 23.8	03.1	304 12.8	44.6			
06	0 58.0	221 53.0	N17 25.4	156 33.6	S11 07.7	333 25.8	N10 03.3	319 15.0	N13 44.7	Rasalhague	96 16.2	N12 33.8
W 07	16 00.5	236 53.4	24.5	171 35.6	08.0	348 27.9	03.4	334 17.3	44.8	Regulus	207 55.2	N11 58.3
E 08	31 02.9	251 53.8	23.7	186 37.5	08.2	3 30.0	03.5	349 19.5	44.8	Rigel	281 22.8	S 8 12.3
D 09	46 05.4	266 54.2	.. 22.9	201 39.5	.. 08.5	18 32.0	.. 03.7	4 21.7	.. 44.9	Rigil Kent.	140 06.2	S60 50.0
N 10	61 07.9	281 54.6	22.0	216 41.4	08.8	33 34.1	03.8	19 23.9	45.0	Sabik	102 24.6	S15 43.3
E 11	76 10.3	296 55.0	21.2	231 43.4	09.0	48 36.1	04.0	34 26.1	45.0			
S 12	91 12.8	311 55.4	N17 20.3	246 45.3	S11 09.3	63 38.2	N10 04.1	49 28.4	N13 45.1	Schedar	349 53.0	N56 31.7
D 13	106 15.3	326 55.9	19.5	261 47.3	09.5	78 40.3	04.3	64 30.6	45.2	Shaula	96 36.2	S37 06.1
A 14	121 17.7	341 56.3	18.7	276 49.2	09.8	93 42.3	04.4	79 32.8	45.2	Sirius	258 43.6	S16 43.0
Y 15	136 20.2	356 56.7	.. 17.8	291 51.2	.. 10.1	108 44.4	.. 04.5	94 35.0	.. 45.3	Spica	158 42.6	S11 09.5
16	151 22.6	11 57.1	17.0	306 53.1	10.3	123 46.4	04.7	109 37.2	45.4	Suhail	223 00.7	S43 26.0
17	166 25.1	26 57.5	16.1	321 55.1	10.6	138 48.5	04.8	124 39.4	45.5			
18	181 27.6	41 57.9	N17 15.3	336 57.0	S11 10.9	153 50.6	N10 05.0	139 41.7	N13 45.5	Vega	80 45.9	N38 47.1
19	196 30.0	56 58.4	14.4	351 59.0	11.1	168 52.6	05.1	154 43.9	45.6	Zuben'ubi	137 17.2	S16 02.3
20	211 32.5	71 58.8	13.6	7 00.9	11.4	183 54.7	05.2	169 46.1	45.7			
21	226 35.0	86 59.2	.. 12.7	22 02.8	.. 11.7	198 56.8	.. 05.4	184 48.3	.. 45.7		SHA	Mer. Pass.
22	241 37.4	101 59.6	11.9	37 04.8	11.9	213 58.8	05.5	199 50.5	45.8	Venus	221 57.6	15 13
23	256 39.9	117 00.1	11.1	52 06.7	12.2	229 00.9	05.7	214 52.8	45.9	Mars	155 50.4	19 35
Mer. Pass. 6 00.1		v 0.4	d 0.8	v 2.0	d 0.3	v 2.1	d 0.1	v 2.2	d 0.1	Jupiter	332 40.0	7 49
										Saturn	318 24.5	8 46

SUN / MOON

UT	SUN GHA	SUN Dec	MOON GHA	v	MOON Dec	d	HP
d h	° ′	° ′	° ′	′	° ′	′	′
21 00	179 36.4	N23 26.1	85 24.2	14.3	N 2 43.9	10.6	55.5
01	194 36.3	26.1	99 57.5	14.4	2 33.3	10.7	55.5
02	209 36.1	26.1	114 30.9	14.3	2 22.6	10.6	55.5
03	224 36.0	.. 26.2	129 04.2	14.4	2 12.0	10.6	55.5
04	239 35.9	26.2	143 37.6	14.5	2 01.4	10.6	55.4
05	254 35.7	26.2	158 11.1	14.5	1 50.8	10.6	55.4
06	269 35.6	N23 26.2	172 44.6	14.5	N 1 40.2	10.6	55.4
07	284 35.5	26.2	187 18.1	14.5	1 29.6	10.6	55.3
08	299 35.3	26.2	201 51.6	14.6	1 19.0	10.6	55.3
M 09	314 35.2	.. 26.2	216 25.2	14.6	1 08.4	10.6	55.3
O 10	329 35.0	26.2	230 58.8	14.6	0 57.8	10.6	55.3
N 11	344 34.9	26.2	245 32.4	14.7	0 47.2	10.6	55.2
D 12	359 34.8	N23 26.2	260 06.1	14.7	N 0 36.6	10.5	55.2
A 13	14 34.6	26.2	274 39.8	14.7	0 26.1	10.6	55.2
Y 14	29 34.5	26.2	289 13.5	14.7	0 15.5	10.6	55.2
15	44 34.4	.. 26.2	303 47.2	14.8	N 0 04.9	10.5	55.1
16	59 34.2	26.3	318 21.0	14.8	S 0 05.6	10.5	55.1
17	74 34.1	26.3	332 54.8	14.8	0 16.1	10.6	55.1
18	89 34.0	N23 26.3	347 28.6	14.8	S 0 26.7	10.5	55.1
19	104 33.8	26.3	2 02.4	14.9	0 37.2	10.5	55.1
20	119 33.7	26.3	16 36.3	14.8	0 47.7	10.5	55.0
21	134 33.6	.. 26.3	31 10.1	14.9	0 58.2	10.5	55.0
22	149 33.4	26.3	45 44.0	14.9	1 08.7	10.5	55.0
23	164 33.3	26.3	60 17.9	14.9	1 19.2	10.4	55.0
22 00	179 33.1	N23 26.3	74 51.9	14.9	S 1 29.6	10.5	54.9
01	194 33.0	26.2	89 25.8	15.0	1 40.1	10.4	54.9
02	209 32.9	26.2	103 59.8	15.0	1 50.5	10.4	54.9
03	224 32.7	.. 26.2	118 33.8	15.0	2 00.9	10.4	54.9
04	239 32.6	26.2	133 07.8	15.0	2 11.3	10.4	54.9
05	254 32.5	26.2	147 41.8	15.0	2 21.7	10.4	54.8
06	269 32.3	N23 26.2	162 15.8	15.0	S 2 32.1	10.3	54.8
07	284 32.2	26.2	176 49.8	15.1	2 42.4	10.3	54.8
T 08	299 32.1	26.2	191 23.9	15.0	2 52.7	10.3	54.8
U 09	314 31.9	.. 26.2	205 57.9	15.1	3 03.0	10.3	54.8
E 10	329 31.8	26.2	220 32.0	15.1	3 13.3	10.3	54.7
S 11	344 31.7	26.2	235 06.1	15.0	3 23.6	10.3	54.7
D 12	359 31.5	N23 26.2	249 40.1	15.1	S 3 33.9	10.2	54.7
A 13	14 31.4	26.2	264 14.2	15.1	3 44.1	10.2	54.7
Y 14	29 31.2	26.1	278 48.3	15.1	3 54.3	10.2	54.7
15	44 31.1	.. 26.1	293 22.4	15.1	4 04.5	10.2	54.6
16	59 31.0	26.1	307 56.5	15.1	4 14.7	10.1	54.6
17	74 30.8	26.1	322 30.6	15.1	4 24.8	10.1	54.6
18	89 30.7	N23 26.1	337 04.7	15.2	S 4 34.9	10.1	54.6
19	104 30.6	26.1	351 38.9	15.1	4 45.0	10.1	54.6
20	119 30.4	26.0	6 13.0	15.1	4 55.1	10.0	54.6
21	134 30.3	.. 26.0	20 47.1	15.1	5 05.1	10.0	54.5
22	149 30.2	26.0	35 21.2	15.1	5 15.2	10.0	54.5
23	164 30.0	26.0	49 55.3	15.2	5 25.2	9.9	54.5
23 00	179 29.9	N23 26.0	64 29.5	15.1	S 5 35.1	10.0	54.5
01	194 29.8	26.0	79 03.6	15.1	5 45.1	9.9	54.5
02	209 29.6	25.9	93 37.7	15.1	5 55.0	9.8	54.5
03	224 29.5	.. 25.9	108 11.8	15.1	6 04.8	9.9	54.4
04	239 29.4	25.9	122 45.9	15.1	6 14.7	9.8	54.4
05	254 29.2	25.9	137 20.0	15.1	6 24.5	9.8	54.4
06	269 29.1	N23 25.8	151 54.1	15.1	S 6 34.3	9.8	54.4
W 07	284 29.0	25.8	166 28.2	15.1	6 44.1	9.7	54.4
E 08	299 28.8	25.8	181 02.3	15.0	6 53.8	9.7	54.4
D 09	314 28.7	.. 25.8	195 36.3	15.1	7 03.5	9.7	54.4
N 10	329 28.5	25.7	210 10.4	15.1	7 13.2	9.6	54.4
E 11	344 28.4	25.7	224 44.5	15.0	7 22.8	9.6	54.3
S 12	359 28.3	N23 25.7	239 18.5	15.0	S 7 32.4	9.6	54.3
D 13	14 28.1	25.7	253 52.5	15.1	7 42.0	9.5	54.3
A 14	29 28.0	25.6	268 26.6	15.0	7 51.5	9.5	54.3
Y 15	44 27.9	.. 25.6	283 00.6	15.0	8 01.0	9.5	54.3
16	59 27.7	25.6	297 34.6	15.0	8 10.5	9.4	54.3
17	74 27.6	25.5	312 08.6	15.0	8 19.9	9.4	54.3
18	89 27.5	N23 25.5	326 42.6	14.9	S 8 29.3	9.3	54.3
19	104 27.3	25.5	341 16.5	15.0	8 38.6	9.3	54.2
20	119 27.2	25.4	355 50.5	14.9	8 47.9	9.3	54.2
21	134 27.1	.. 25.4	10 24.4	14.9	8 57.2	9.3	54.2
22	149 26.9	25.4	24 58.3	14.9	9 06.5	9.1	54.2
23	164 26.8	25.3	39 32.2	14.9	S 9 15.6	9.2	54.2
	SD 15.8	d 0.0	SD 15.0		14.9		14.8

Twilight / Sunrise / Moonrise

Lat.	Naut.	Civil	Sunrise	21	22	23	24
°	h m	h m	h m	h m	h m	h m	h m
N 72	☐	☐	☐	12 36	14 16	15 56	17 39
N 70	☐	. ☐	☐	12 36	14 10	15 43	17 17
68	☐	☐	☐	12 37	14 05	15 32	17 00
66	☐	☐	☐	12 37	14 01	15 24	16 47
64	////	////	01 31	12 38	13 58	15 17	16 35
62	////	////	02 09	12 38	13 55	15 11	16 26
60	////	00 49	02 36	12 38	13 52	15 05	16 18
N 58	////	01 40	02 56	12 38	13 50	15 01	16 11
56	////	02 10	03 13	12 39	13 48	14 57	16 04
54	00 45	02 33	03 27	12 39	13 46	14 53	15 59
52	01 32	02 51	03 40	12 39	13 45	14 50	15 54
50	02 00	03 06	03 51	12 39	13 43	14 47	15 49
45	02 46	03 36	04 13	12 39	13 40	14 40	15 39
N 40	03 17	03 59	04 31	12 40	13 38	14 35	15 31
35	03 40	04 17	04 46	12 40	13 35	14 30	15 24
30	03 59	04 32	05 00	12 40	13 33	14 26	15 18
20	04 28	04 57	05 22	12 41	13 30	14 19	15 08
N 10	04 50	05 18	05 41	12 41	13 27	14 13	14 59
0	05 09	05 36	05 58	12 41	13 24	14 07	14 50
S 10	05 26	05 53	06 16	12 42	13 21	14 01	14 41
20	05 43	06 10	06 34	12 42	13 18	13 55	14 32
30	05 59	06 29	06 56	12 42	13 15	13 48	14 22
35	06 08	06 40	07 08	12 43	13 13	13 44	14 16
40	06 17	06 52	07 22	12 43	13 11	13 40	14 10
45	06 28	07 05	07 39	12 43	13 09	13 35	14 02
S 50	06 40	07 21	08 00	12 44	13 06	13 28	13 53
52	06 45	07 29	08 10	12 44	13 05	13 26	13 48
54	06 51	07 37	08 21	12 44	13 03	13 23	13 44
56	06 57	07 46	08 33	12 45	13 02	13 19	13 38
58	07 04	07 56	08 48	12 45	13 00	13 15	13 33
S 60	07 11	08 08	09 06	12 45	12 58	13 11	13 26

Sunset / Twilight / Moonset

Lat.	Sunset	Civil	Naut.	21	22	23	24
°	h m	h m	h m	h m	h m	h m	h m
N 72	☐	☐	☐	00 50	00 41	00 30	00 19
N 70	☐	☐	☐	00 47	00 43	00 38	00 34
68	☐	☐	☐	00 44	00 45	00 45	00 46
66	☐	☐	////	00 42	00 46	00 50	00 55
64	22 33	////	////	00 40	00 48	00 55	01 04
62	21 54	////	////	00 38	00 49	00 59	01 11
60	21 28	23 14	////	00 37	00 50	01 03	01 17
N 58	21 07	22 23	////	00 35	00 51	01 06	01 22
56	20 51	21 53	////	00 34	00 52	01 09	01 27
54	20 36	21 31	23 19	00 33	00 52	01 11	01 31
52	20 24	21 13	22 31	00 32	00 53	01 14	01 35
50	20 13	20 58	22 03	00 31	00 54	01 16	01 39
45	19 50	20 28	21 18	00 29	00 55	01 20	01 47
N 40	19 32	20 05	20 47	00 28	00 56	01 24	01 53
35	19 17	19 47	20 24	00 26	00 57	01 28	01 59
30	19 04	19 32	20 05	00 25	00 58	01 31	02 04
20	18 42	19 07	19 36	00 22	00 59	01 36	02 13
N 10	18 23	18 46	19 13	00 20	01 01	01 40	02 20
0	18 06	18 28	18 54	00 19	01 02	01 45	02 28
S 10	17 48	18 11	18 37	00 17	01 03	01 49	02 35
20	17 30	17 54	18 21	00 14	01 04	01 54	02 42
30	17 08	17 35	18 05	00 12	01 06	01 59	02 51
35	16 56	17 24	17 56	00 11	01 07	02 02	02 56
40	16 42	17 12	17 46	00 09	01 08	02 05	03 02
45	16 25	16 59	17 36	00 07	01 09	02 09	03 09
S 50	16 04	16 43	17 24	00 05	01 10	02 14	03 17
52	15 54	16 35	17 19	00 04	01 11	02 16	03 21
54	15 43	16 27	17 13	00 03	01 11	02 18	03 25
56	15 30	16 18	17 07	00 01	01 12	02 21	03 29
58	15 16	16 08	17 00	00 00	01 13	02 24	03 34
S 60	14 58	15 56	16 53	25 14	01 14	02 27	03 40

SUN / MOON

Day	Eqn. of Time 00h	Eqn. of Time 12h	Mer. Pass.	Mer. Pass. Upper	Mer. Pass. Lower	Age	Phase
d	m s	m s	h m	h m	h m	d	%
21	01 34	01 41	12 02	18 52	06 30	08	57
22	01 47	01 54	12 02	19 34	07 13	09	67
23	02 00	02 07	12 02	20 17	07 56	10	76

UT	ARIES GHA	VENUS −4.4 GHA	Dec	MARS −0.5 GHA	Dec	JUPITER −2.2 GHA	Dec	SATURN +0.4 GHA	Dec	STARS Name	SHA	Dec
24 00	271 42.4	132 00.5	N17 10.2	67 08.7	S11 12.5	244 03.0	N10 05.8	229 55.0	N13 45.9	Acamar	315 26.9	S40 18.4
01	286 44.8	147 00.9	09.4	82 10.6	12.7	259 05.0	05.9	244 57.2	46.0	Achernar	335 35.1	S57 14.2
02	301 47.3	162 01.4	08.5	97 12.5	13.0	274 07.1	06.1	259 59.4	46.1	Acrux	173 21.3	S63 06.0
03	316 49.8	177 01.8	.. 07.7	112 14.5	.. 13.3	289 09.1	.. 06.2	275 01.6	.. 46.1	Adhara	255 21.4	S28 58.4
04	331 52.2	192 02.2	06.8	127 16.4	13.5	304 11.2	06.4	290 03.9	46.2	Aldebaran	291 02.2	N16 30.3
05	346 54.7	207 02.7	06.0	142 18.3	13.8	319 13.3	06.5	305 06.1	46.3			
06	1 57.1	222 03.1	N17 05.1	157 20.3	S11 14.1	334 15.3	N10 06.6	320 08.3	N13 46.3	Alioth	166 30.1	N55 58.1
07	16 59.6	237 03.5	04.3	172 22.2	14.3	349 17.4	06.8	335 10.5	46.4	Alkaid	153 07.3	N49 19.3
T 08	32 02.1	252 04.0	03.4	187 24.1	14.6	4 19.5	06.9	350 12.7	46.5	Al Na'ir	27 57.1	S46 57.6
H 09	47 04.5	267 04.4	.. 02.6	202 26.0	.. 14.9	19 21.5	.. 07.1	5 15.0	.. 46.5	Alnilam	275 57.7	S 1 12.3
U 10	62 07.0	282 04.9	01.7	217 28.0	15.1	34 23.6	07.2	20 17.2	46.6	Alphard	218 07.0	S 8 39.4
R 11	77 09.5	297 05.3	00.9	232 29.9	15.4	49 25.7	07.4	35 19.4	46.7			
S 12	92 11.9	312 05.8	N17 00.1	247 31.8	S11 15.7	64 27.7	N10 07.5	50 21.6	N13 46.7	Alphecca	126 19.9	N26 43.2
D 13	107 14.4	327 06.2	16 59.2	262 33.7	15.9	79 29.8	07.6	65 23.8	46.8	Alpheratz	357 54.7	N29 05.0
A 14	122 16.9	342 06.7	58.4	277 35.7	16.2	94 31.9	07.8	80 26.1	46.9	Altair	62 18.5	N 8 52.1
Y 15	137 19.3	357 07.1	.. 57.5	292 37.6	.. 16.5	109 33.9	.. 07.9	95 28.3	.. 46.9	Ankaa	353 26.4	S42 18.4
16	152 21.8	12 07.6	56.7	307 39.5	16.8	124 36.0	08.0	110 30.5	47.0	Antares	112 39.2	S26 25.8
17	167 24.3	27 08.0	55.9	322 41.4	17.0	139 38.1	08.2	125 32.7	47.1			
18	182 26.7	42 08.5	N16 55.0	337 43.3	S11 17.3	154 40.1	N10 08.3	140 34.9	N13 47.1	Arcturus	146 05.5	N19 11.3
19	197 29.2	57 09.0	54.1	352 45.3	17.6	169 42.2	08.5	155 37.2	47.2	Atria	107 50.3	S69 01.6
20	212 31.6	72 09.4	53.3	7 47.2	17.8	184 44.3	08.6	170 39.4	47.3	Avior	234 23.0	S59 30.7
21	227 34.1	87 09.9	.. 52.4	22 49.1	.. 18.1	199 46.3	.. 08.7	185 41.6	.. 47.3	Bellatrix	278 44.0	N 6 20.8
22	242 36.6	102 10.4	51.6	37 51.0	18.4	214 48.4	08.9	200 43.8	47.4	Betelgeuse	271 13.4	N 7 24.3
23	257 39.0	117 10.8	50.7	52 52.9	18.7	229 50.5	09.0	215 46.0	47.5			
25 00	272 41.5	132 11.3	N16 49.8	67 54.8	S11 18.9	244 52.5	N10 09.2	230 48.3	N13 47.5	Canopus	264 01.5	S52 41.8
01	287 44.0	147 11.8	49.0	82 56.7	19.2	259 54.6	09.3	245 50.5	47.6	Capella	280 51.0	N45 59.7
02	302 46.4	162 12.2	48.1	97 58.7	19.5	274 56.7	09.4	260 52.7	47.7	Deneb	49 38.5	N45 16.6
03	317 48.9	177 12.7	.. 47.3	113 00.6	.. 19.8	289 58.7	.. 09.6	275 54.9	.. 47.7	Denebola	182 44.8	N14 34.7
04	332 51.4	192 13.2	46.4	128 02.5	20.0	305 00.8	09.7	290 57.2	47.8	Diphda	349 06.8	S17 59.4
05	347 53.8	207 13.7	45.6	143 04.4	20.3	320 02.9	09.9	305 59.4	47.9			
06	2 56.3	222 14.1	N16 44.7	158 06.3	S11 20.6	335 05.0	N10 10.0	321 01.6	N13 47.9	Dubhe	194 05.2	N61 45.6
07	17 58.7	237 14.6	43.9	173 08.2	20.9	350 07.0	10.1	336 03.8	48.0	Elnath	278 26.7	N28 36.3
08	33 01.2	252 15.1	43.0	188 10.1	21.1	5 09.1	10.3	351 06.0	48.1	Eltanin	90 50.6	N51 29.5
F 09	48 03.7	267 15.6	.. 42.2	203 12.0	.. 21.4	20 11.2	.. 10.4	6 08.3	.. 48.1	Enif	33 57.6	N 9 52.3
R 10	63 06.1	282 16.1	41.3	218 13.9	21.7	35 13.2	10.5	21 10.5	48.2	Fomalhaut	15 35.8	S29 37.4
I 11	78 08.6	297 16.6	40.5	233 15.8	22.0	50 15.3	10.7	36 12.7	48.3			
D 12	93 11.1	312 17.0	N16 39.6	248 17.7	S11 22.3	65 17.4	N10 10.8	51 14.9	N13 48.3	Gacrux	172 12.9	S57 06.8
A 13	108 13.5	327 17.5	38.8	263 19.6	22.5	80 19.4	11.0	66 17.2	48.4	Gienah	176 03.5	S17 32.3
Y 14	123 16.0	342 18.0	37.9	278 21.5	22.8	95 21.5	11.1	81 19.4	48.5	Hadar	149 03.0	S60 22.4
15	138 18.5	357 18.5	.. 37.0	293 23.4	.. 23.1	110 23.6	.. 11.2	96 21.6	.. 48.5	Hamal	328 13.2	N23 27.4
16	153 20.9	12 19.0	36.2	308 25.3	23.4	125 25.7	11.4	111 23.8	48.6	Kaus Aust.	83 57.8	S34 23.0
17	168 23.4	27 19.5	35.3	323 27.2	23.6	140 27.7	11.5	126 26.1	48.7			
18	183 25.9	42 20.0	N16 34.5	338 29.1	S11 23.9	155 29.8	N10 11.7	141 28.3	N13 48.7	Kochab	137 18.9	N74 09.8
19	198 28.3	57 20.5	33.6	353 31.0	24.2	170 31.9	11.8	156 30.5	48.8	Markab	13 49.0	N15 12.0
20	213 30.8	72 21.0	32.8	8 32.9	24.5	185 33.9	11.9	171 32.7	48.9	Menkar	314 26.6	N 4 05.1
21	228 33.2	87 21.5	.. 31.9	23 34.8	.. 24.8	200 36.0	.. 12.1	186 34.9	.. 48.9	Menkent	148 20.2	S36 22.1
22	243 35.7	102 22.0	31.0	38 36.7	25.0	215 38.1	12.2	201 37.2	49.0	Miaplacidus	221 42.6	S69 43.1
23	258 38.2	117 22.5	30.2	53 38.6	25.3	230 40.2	12.3	216 39.4	49.1			
26 00	273 40.6	132 23.0	N16 29.3	68 40.4	S11 25.6	245 42.2	N10 12.5	231 41.6	N13 49.1	Mirfak	308 56.3	N49 51.3
01	288 43.1	147 23.5	28.5	83 42.3	25.9	260 44.3	12.6	246 43.8	49.2	Nunki	76 11.4	S26 17.7
02	303 45.6	162 24.0	27.6	98 44.2	26.2	275 46.4	12.8	261 46.1	49.3	Peacock	53 35.8	S56 44.0
03	318 48.0	177 24.6	.. 26.8	113 46.1	.. 26.4	290 48.4	.. 12.9	276 48.3	.. 49.3	Pollux	243 41.3	N28 01.6
04	333 50.5	192 25.1	25.9	128 48.0	26.7	305 50.5	13.0	291 50.5	49.4	Procyon	245 11.4	N 5 13.5
05	348 53.0	207 25.6	25.0	143 49.9	27.0	320 52.6	13.2	306 52.7	49.5			
06	3 55.4	222 26.1	N16 24.2	158 51.8	S11 27.3	335 54.7	N10 13.3	321 55.0	N13 49.5	Rasalhague	96 16.2	N12 33.8
07	18 57.9	237 26.6	23.3	173 53.6	27.6	350 56.7	13.4	336 57.2	49.6	Regulus	207 55.2	N11 58.3
S 08	34 00.4	252 27.1	22.5	188 55.5	27.9	5 58.8	13.6	351 59.4	49.7	Rigel	281 22.8	S 8 12.2
A 09	49 02.8	267 27.7	.. 21.6	203 57.4	.. 28.1	21 00.9	.. 13.7	7 01.6	.. 49.7	Rigil Kent.	140 06.2	S60 50.1
T 10	64 05.3	282 28.2	20.7	218 59.3	28.4	36 03.0	13.8	22 03.9	49.8	Sabik	102 24.6	S15 43.3
U 11	79 07.7	297 28.7	19.9	234 01.2	28.7	51 05.0	14.0	37 06.1	49.8			
R 12	94 10.2	312 29.2	N16 19.0	249 03.0	S11 29.0	66 07.1	N10 14.1	52 08.3	N13 49.9	Schedar	349 52.9	N56 31.7
D 13	109 12.7	327 29.8	18.2	264 04.9	29.3	81 09.2	14.3	67 10.5	50.0	Shaula	96 36.2	S37 06.1
A 14	124 15.1	342 30.3	17.3	279 06.8	29.6	96 11.3	14.4	82 12.8	50.0	Sirius	258 43.6	S16 43.0
Y 15	139 17.6	357 30.8	.. 16.4	294 08.7	.. 29.9	111 13.3	.. 14.5	97 15.0	.. 50.1	Spica	158 42.6	S11 09.5
16	154 20.1	12 31.4	15.6	309 10.5	30.1	126 15.4	14.7	112 17.2	50.2	Suhail	223 00.7	S43 26.0
17	169 22.5	27 31.9	14.7	324 12.4	30.4	141 17.5	14.8	127 19.4	50.2			
18	184 25.0	42 32.5	N16 13.9	339 14.3	S11 30.7	156 19.6	N10 14.9	142 21.7	N13 50.3	Vega	80 45.9	N38 47.1
19	199 27.5	57 33.0	13.0	354 16.1	31.0	171 21.6	15.1	157 23.9	50.4	Zuben'ubi	137 17.2	S16 02.3
20	214 29.9	72 33.5	12.1	9 18.0	31.3	186 23.7	15.2	172 26.1	50.4			
21	229 32.4	87 34.1	.. 11.3	24 19.9	.. 31.6	201 25.8	.. 15.3	187 28.4	.. 50.5			
22	244 34.9	102 34.6	10.4	39 21.8	31.9	216 27.9	15.5	202 30.6	50.6			
23	259 37.3	117 35.2	09.5	54 23.6	32.1	231 29.9	15.6	217 32.8	50.6			

	SHA	Mer. Pass.
	° ′	h m
Venus	219 29.8	15 11
Mars	155 13.3	19 26
Jupiter	332 11.0	7 39
Saturn	318 06.8	8 36

	h m							
Mer. Pass.	5 48.3	v 0.5	d 0.9	v 1.9	d 0.3	v 2.1	d 0.1	v 2.2 d 0.1

UT	SUN GHA	SUN Dec	MOON GHA	v	MOON Dec	d	HP
d h	° ′	° ′	° ′	′	° ′	′	′
24 00	179 26.7	N23 25.3	54 06.1	14.9	S 9 24.8	9.1	54.2
01	194 26.5	25.2	68 40.0	14.8	9 33.9	9.1	54.2
02	209 26.4	25.2	83 13.8	14.8	9 43.0	9.0	54.2
03	224 26.3	.. 25.2	97 47.6	14.8	9 52.0	9.0	54.2
04	239 26.1	25.1	112 21.4	14.8	10 01.0	9.0	54.2
05	254 26.0	25.1	126 55.2	14.8	10 10.0	8.9	54.2
06	269 25.9	N23 25.0	141 29.0	14.7	S10 18.9	8.8	54.2
07	284 25.7	25.0	156 02.7	14.8	10 27.7	8.9	54.1
T 08	299 25.6	25.0	170 36.5	14.7	10 36.6	8.7	54.1
H 09	314 25.5	.. 24.9	185 10.2	14.6	10 45.3	8.7	54.1
U 10	329 25.3	24.9	199 43.8	14.7	10 54.0	8.7	54.1
R 11	344 25.2	24.8	214 17.5	14.6	11 02.7	8.7	54.1
S 12	359 25.1	N23 24.8	228 51.1	14.6	S11 11.4	8.5	54.1
D 13	14 24.9	24.7	243 24.7	14.6	11 19.9	8.6	54.1
A 14	29 24.8	24.7	257 58.3	14.6	11 28.5	8.5	54.1
Y 15	44 24.7	.. 24.6	272 31.9	14.5	11 37.0	8.4	54.1
16	59 24.5	24.6	287 05.4	14.5	11 45.4	8.4	54.1
17	74 24.4	24.5	301 38.9	14.5	11 53.8	8.4	54.1
18	89 24.3	N23 24.5	316 12.4	14.4	S12 02.2	8.2	54.1
19	104 24.1	24.4	330 45.8	14.4	12 10.4	8.3	54.1
20	119 24.0	24.4	345 19.2	14.4	12 18.7	8.2	54.1
21	134 23.9	.. 24.3	359 52.6	14.4	12 26.9	8.1	54.1
22	149 23.7	24.3	14 26.0	14.3	12 35.0	8.1	54.1
23	164 23.6	24.2	28 59.3	14.4	12 43.1	8.0	54.1
25 00	179 23.5	N23 24.2	43 32.7	14.2	S12 51.1	8.0	54.0
01	194 23.3	24.1	58 05.9	14.3	12 59.1	7.9	54.0
02	209 23.2	24.1	72 39.2	14.2	13 07.0	7.9	54.0
03	224 23.1	.. 24.0	87 12.4	14.2	13 14.9	7.8	54.0
04	239 22.9	24.0	101 45.6	14.1	13 22.7	7.8	54.0
05	254 22.8	23.9	116 18.7	14.2	13 30.5	7.7	54.0
06	269 22.7	N23 23.8	130 51.9	14.0	S13 38.2	7.6	54.0
F 07	284 22.5	23.8	145 24.9	14.1	13 45.8	7.6	54.0
R 08	299 22.4	23.7	159 58.0	14.0	13 53.4	7.5	54.0
I 09	314 22.3	.. 23.7	174 31.0	14.0	14 00.9	7.5	54.0
D 10	329 22.1	23.6	189 04.0	14.0	14 08.4	7.4	54.0
A 11	344 22.0	23.5	203 37.0	13.9	14 15.8	7.4	54.0
Y 12	359 21.9	N23 23.5	218 09.9	13.9	S14 23.2	7.2	54.0
13	14 21.7	23.4	232 42.8	13.9	14 30.4	7.3	54.0
14	29 21.6	23.3	247 15.7	13.8	14 37.7	7.1	54.0
15	44 21.5	.. 23.3	261 48.5	13.8	14 44.8	7.1	54.0
16	59 21.3	23.2	276 21.3	13.7	14 51.9	7.1	54.0
17	74 21.2	23.1	290 54.0	13.7	14 59.0	7.0	54.0
18	89 21.1	N23 23.1	305 26.7	13.7	S15 06.0	6.9	54.0
19	104 20.9	23.0	319 59.4	13.7	15 12.9	6.8	54.0
20	119 20.8	22.9	334 32.1	13.6	15 19.7	6.8	54.0
21	134 20.7	.. 22.9	349 04.7	13.6	15 26.5	6.7	54.0
22	149 20.6	22.8	3 37.3	13.5	15 33.2	6.7	54.0
23	164 20.4	22.7	18 09.8	13.5	15 39.9	6.6	54.0
26 00	179 20.3	N23 22.7	32 42.3	13.5	S15 46.5	6.5	54.0
01	194 20.2	22.6	47 14.8	13.4	15 53.0	6.4	54.0
02	209 20.0	22.5	61 47.2	13.4	15 59.4	6.4	54.0
03	224 19.9	.. 22.4	76 19.6	13.4	16 05.8	6.3	54.0
04	239 19.8	22.4	90 52.0	13.3	16 12.1	6.3	54.0
05	254 19.6	22.3	105 24.3	13.3	16 18.4	6.2	54.0
06	269 19.5	N23 22.2	119 56.6	13.2	S16 24.6	6.1	54.0
S 07	284 19.4	22.1	134 28.8	13.2	16 30.7	6.0	54.1
A 08	299 19.2	22.1	149 01.0	13.2	16 36.7	6.0	54.1
T 09	314 19.1	.. 22.0	163 33.2	13.1	16 42.7	5.8	54.1
U 10	329 19.0	21.9	178 05.3	13.1	16 48.5	5.9	54.1
R 11	344 18.8	21.8	192 37.4	13.1	16 54.4	5.7	54.1
D 12	359 18.7	N23 21.7	207 09.5	13.0	S17 00.1	5.7	54.1
A 13	14 18.6	21.7	221 41.5	13.0	17 05.8	5.6	54.1
Y 14	29 18.5	21.6	236 13.5	12.9	17 11.4	5.5	54.1
15	44 18.3	.. 21.5	250 45.4	13.0	17 16.9	5.4	54.1
16	59 18.2	21.4	265 17.4	12.8	17 22.3	5.4	54.1
17	74 18.1	21.3	279 49.2	12.9	17 27.7	5.3	54.1
18	89 17.9	N23 21.3	294 21.1	12.8	S17 33.0	5.2	54.1
19	104 17.8	21.2	308 52.9	12.7	17 38.2	5.1	54.1
20	119 17.7	21.1	323 24.6	12.8	17 43.3	5.1	54.1
21	134 17.5	.. 21.0	337 56.4	12.6	17 48.4	5.0	54.1
22	149 17.4	20.9	352 28.0	12.7	17 53.4	4.9	54.1
23	164 17.3	20.8	6 59.7	12.6	S17 58.3	4.8	54.1
	SD 15.8	d 0.1	SD 14.7		14.7		14.7

Moonrise

Lat.	Twilight Naut.	Twilight Civil	Sunrise	24	25	26	27
°	h m	h m	h m	h m	h m	h m	h m
N 72	☐	☐	☐	17 39	19 32	■	■
N 70	☐	☐	☐	17 17	18 55	20 37	22 28
68	☐	☐	☐	17 00	18 29	19 57	21 20
66	☐	☐	☐	16 47	18 09	19 30	20 44
64	////	////	01 33	16 35	17 53	19 09	20 19
62	////	////	02 11	16 26	17 40	18 52	19 59
60	////	00 51	02 37	16 18	17 29	18 38	19 43
N 58	////	01 42	02 57	16 11	17 19	18 26	19 29
56	////	02 12	03 14	16 04	17 11	18 16	19 17
54	00 47	02 34	03 28	15 59	17 04	18 07	19 07
52	01 34	02 52	03 41	15 54	16 57	17 59	18 58
50	02 01	03 07	03 52	15 49	16 51	17 51	18 49
45	02 47	03 37	04 14	15 39	16 38	17 36	18 32
N 40	03 18	03 59	04 32	15 31	16 28	17 23	18 18
35	03 41	04 18	04 47	15 24	16 19	17 13	18 06
30	03 59	04 33	05 00	15 18	16 11	17 03	17 55
20	04 29	04 58	05 22	15 08	15 57	16 47	17 37
N 10	04 51	05 18	05 41	14 59	15 45	16 33	17 22
0	05 10	05 36	05 59	14 50	15 34	16 20	17 07
S 10	05 27	05 53	06 17	14 41	15 23	16 07	16 53
20	05 43	06 11	06 35	14 32	15 11	15 53	16 37
30	06 00	06 30	06 56	14 22	14 58	15 37	16 19
35	06 09	06 40	07 08	14 16	14 51	15 28	16 09
40	06 18	06 52	07 23	14 10	14 42	15 17	15 57
45	06 28	07 06	07 39	14 02	14 32	15 05	15 43
S 50	06 40	07 22	08 00	13 53	14 19	14 50	15 26
52	06 45	07 29	08 10	13 48	14 14	14 43	15 19
54	06 51	07 37	08 21	13 44	14 08	14 36	15 10
56	06 57	07 46	08 34	13 38	14 01	14 27	15 00
58	07 04	07 57	08 48	13 33	13 53	14 18	14 49
S 60	07 11	08 08	09 06	13 26	13 44	14 07	14 36

Moonset

Lat.	Sunset	Twilight Civil	Twilight Naut.	24	25	26	27
°	h m	h m	h m	h m	h m	h m	h m
N 72	☐	☐	☐	00 19	(00 06 / 23 45)	■	■
N 70	☐	☐	☐	00 34	00 29	00 24	00 17
68	☐	☐	☐	00 46	00 47	00 51	00 57
66	☐	☐	☐	00 55	01 02	01 11	01 25
64	22 32	////	////	01 04	01 14	01 28	01 47
62	21 54	////	////	01 11	01 24	01 41	02 04
60	21 28	23 13	////	01 17	01 33	01 53	02 18
N 58	21 07	22 23	////	01 22	01 41	02 03	02 30
56	20 51	21 53	////	01 27	01 48	02 12	02 41
54	20 36	21 31	23 17	01 31	01 54	02 20	02 50
52	20 24	21 13	22 31	01 35	01 59	02 27	02 59
50	20 13	20 58	22 03	01 39	02 04	02 33	03 06
45	19 51	20 29	21 18	01 47	02 15	02 47	03 22
N 40	19 33	20 06	20 47	01 53	02 24	02 58	03 36
35	19 18	19 47	20 24	01 59	02 32	03 08	03 47
30	19 05	19 32	20 06	02 04	02 39	03 16	03 57
20	18 43	19 07	19 37	02 13	02 51	03 31	04 14
N 10	18 24	18 47	19 14	02 20	03 01	03 44	04 29
0	18 06	18 29	18 55	02 28	03 11	03 56	04 42
S 10	17 49	18 12	18 38	02 35	03 21	04 08	04 56
20	17 30	17 54	18 22	02 42	03 31	04 21	05 11
30	17 09	17 35	18 05	02 51	03 44	04 36	05 28
35	16 57	17 25	17 57	02 56	03 51	04 45	05 38
40	16 43	17 13	17 47	03 02	03 58	04 55	05 50
45	16 26	17 00	17 37	03 09	04 08	05 06	06 03
S 50	16 05	16 44	17 25	03 17	04 19	05 20	06 19
52	15 55	16 36	17 20	03 21	04 24	05 27	06 27
54	15 44	16 28	17 14	03 25	04 30	05 34	06 36
56	15 31	16 19	17 08	03 29	04 36	05 42	06 45
58	15 17	16 09	17 01	03 34	04 44	05 52	06 56
S 60	14 59	15 57	16 54	03 40	04 52	06 02	07 09

Day	SUN Eqn. of Time 00h	SUN Eqn. of Time 12h	SUN Mer. Pass.	MOON Mer. Pass. Upper	MOON Mer. Pass. Lower	Age	Phase
d	m s	m s	h m	h m	h m	d	%
24	02 13	02 19	12 02	21 01	08 39	11	83
25	02 26	02 32	12 03	21 45	09 23	12	90
26	02 39	02 45	12 03	22 31	10 08	13	95

UT	ARIES	VENUS −4.4		MARS −0.5		JUPITER −2.3		SATURN +0.4		STARS		
	GHA	GHA	Dec	GHA	Dec	GHA	Dec	GHA	Dec	Name	SHA	Dec
d h	° ′	° ′	° ′	° ′	° ′	° ′	° ′	° ′	° ′		° ′	° ′
27 00	274 39.8	132 35.7	N16 08.7	69 25.5	S11 32.4	246 32.0	N10 15.7	232 35.0	N13 50.7	Acamar	315 26.9	S40 18.4
01	289 42.2	147 36.3	07.8	84 27.3	32.7	261 34.1	15.9	247 37.3	50.8	Achernar	335 35.1	S57 14.2
02	304 44.7	162 36.8	07.0	99 29.2	33.0	276 36.2	16.0	262 39.5	50.8	Acrux	173 21.4	S63 06.0
03	319 47.2	177 37.4	.. 06.1	114 31.1	.. 33.3	291 38.3	.. 16.1	277 41.7	.. 50.9	Adhara	255 21.4	S28 58.4
04	334 49.6	192 37.9	05.2	129 32.9	33.6	306 40.3	16.3	292 43.9	51.0	Aldebaran	291 02.1	N16 30.3
05	349 52.1	207 38.5	04.4	144 34.8	33.9	321 42.4	16.4	307 46.2	51.0			
06	4 54.6	222 39.0	N16 03.5	159 36.7	S11 34.2	336 44.5	N10 16.6	322 48.4	N13 51.1	Alioth	166 30.1	N55 58.1
07	19 57.0	237 39.6	02.6	174 38.5	34.5	351 46.6	16.7	337 50.6	51.1	Alkaid	153 07.3	N49 19.3
08	34 59.5	252 40.2	01.8	189 40.4	34.8	6 48.6	16.8	352 52.8	51.2	Al Na'ir	27 57.0	S46 57.6
S 09	50 02.0	267 40.7	.. 00.9	204 42.2	.. 35.0	21 50.7	.. 17.0	7 55.1	.. 51.3	Alnilam	275 57.7	S 1 12.2
U 10	65 04.4	282 41.3	16 00.0	219 44.1	35.3	36 52.8	17.1	22 57.3	51.3	Alphard	218 07.0	S 8 39.4
N 11	80 06.9	297 41.9	15 59.2	234 45.9	35.6	51 54.9	17.2	37 59.5	51.4			
D 12	95 09.3	312 42.4	N15 58.3	249 47.8	S11 35.9	66 57.0	N10 17.4	53 01.8	N13 51.5	Alphecca	126 19.9	N26 43.2
A 13	110 11.8	327 43.0	57.4	264 49.7	36.2	81 59.0	17.5	68 04.0	51.5	Alpheratz	357 54.7	N29 05.0
Y 14	125 14.3	342 43.6	56.6	279 51.5	36.5	97 01.1	17.6	83 06.2	51.6	Altair	62 18.5	N 8 52.1
15	140 16.7	357 44.1	.. 55.7	294 53.4	.. 36.8	112 03.2	.. 17.8	98 08.4	.. 51.7	Ankaa	353 26.4	S42 18.4
16	155 19.2	12 44.7	54.8	309 55.2	37.1	127 05.3	17.9	113 10.7	51.7	Antares	112 39.2	S26 25.8
17	170 21.7	27 45.3	54.0	324 57.1	37.4	142 07.4	18.0	128 12.9	51.8			
18	185 24.1	42 45.9	N15 53.1	339 58.9	S11 37.7	157 09.4	N10 18.2	143 15.1	N13 51.9	Arcturus	146 05.5	N19 11.3
19	200 26.6	57 46.5	52.2	355 00.7	38.0	172 11.5	18.3	158 17.4	51.9	Atria	107 50.3	S69 01.6
20	215 29.1	72 47.0	51.4	10 02.6	38.3	187 13.6	18.4	173 19.6	52.0	Avior	234 23.0	S59 30.7
21	230 31.5	87 47.6	.. 50.5	25 04.4	.. 38.6	202 15.7	.. 18.6	188 21.8	.. 52.0	Bellatrix	278 44.0	N 6 20.8
22	245 34.0	102 48.2	49.6	40 06.3	38.8	217 17.8	18.7	203 24.0	52.1	Betelgeuse	271 13.4	N 7 24.3
23	260 36.5	117 48.8	48.8	55 08.1	39.1	232 19.8	18.8	218 26.3	52.2			
28 00	275 38.9	132 49.4	N15 47.9	70 10.0	S11 39.4	247 21.9	N10 19.0	233 28.5	N13 52.2	Canopus	264 01.5	S52 41.8
01	290 41.4	147 50.0	47.0	85 11.8	39.7	262 24.0	19.1	248 30.7	52.3	Capella	280 50.9	N45 59.7
02	305 43.8	162 50.6	46.2	100 13.7	40.0	277 26.1	19.2	263 33.0	52.4	Deneb	49 38.4	N45 16.6
03	320 46.3	177 51.2	.. 45.3	115 15.5	.. 40.3	292 28.2	.. 19.4	278 35.2	.. 52.4	Denebola	182 44.8	N14 34.7
04	335 48.8	192 51.8	44.4	130 17.3	40.6	307 30.3	19.5	293 37.4	52.5	Diphda	349 06.8	S17 59.3
05	350 51.2	207 52.4	43.6	145 19.2	40.9	322 32.3	19.6	308 39.6	52.6			
06	5 53.7	222 53.0	N15 42.7	160 21.0	S11 41.2	337 34.4	N10 19.8	323 41.9	N13 52.6	Dubhe	194 05.2	N61 45.6
07	20 56.2	237 53.6	41.8	175 22.8	41.5	352 36.5	19.9	338 44.1	52.7	Elnath	278 26.7	N28 36.3
08	35 58.6	252 54.2	41.0	190 24.7	41.8	7 38.6	20.0	353 46.3	52.7	Eltanin	90 50.6	N51 29.5
M 09	51 01.1	267 54.8	.. 40.1	205 26.5	.. 42.1	22 40.7	.. 20.2	8 48.6	.. 52.8	Enif	33 57.5	N 9 52.3
O 10	66 03.6	282 55.4	39.2	220 28.3	42.4	37 42.7	20.3	23 50.8	52.9	Fomalhaut	15 35.8	S29 37.4
N 11	81 06.0	297 56.0	38.4	235 30.2	42.7	52 44.8	20.4	38 53.0	52.9			
D 12	96 08.5	312 56.6	N15 37.5	250 32.0	S11 43.0	67 46.9	N10 20.6	53 55.3	N13 53.0	Gacrux	172 12.9	S57 06.8
A 13	111 11.0	327 57.2	36.6	265 33.8	43.3	82 49.0	20.7	68 57.5	53.1	Gienah	176 03.5	S17 32.3
Y 14	126 13.4	342 57.8	35.8	280 35.7	43.6	97 51.1	20.8	83 59.7	53.1	Hadar	149 03.0	S60 22.4
15	141 15.9	357 58.4	.. 34.9	295 37.5	.. 43.9	112 53.2	.. 20.9	99 01.9	.. 53.2	Hamal	328 13.2	N23 27.4
16	156 18.3	12 59.1	34.0	310 39.3	44.2	127 55.3	21.1	114 04.2	53.3	Kaus Aust.	83 57.8	S34 23.0
17	171 20.8	27 59.7	33.1	325 41.2	44.5	142 57.3	21.2	129 06.4	53.3			
18	186 23.3	43 00.3	N15 32.3	340 43.0	S11 44.8	157 59.4	N10 21.3	144 08.6	N13 53.4	Kochab	137 19.0	N74 09.9
19	201 25.7	58 00.9	31.4	355 44.8	45.1	173 01.5	21.5	159 10.9	53.4	Markab	13 49.0	N15 12.0
20	216 28.2	73 01.5	30.5	10 46.6	45.4	188 03.6	21.6	174 13.1	53.5	Menkar	314 26.6	N 4 05.1
21	231 30.7	88 02.2	.. 29.7	25 48.5	.. 45.7	203 05.7	.. 21.7	189 15.3	.. 53.6	Menkent	148 20.2	S36 22.1
22	246 33.1	103 02.8	28.8	40 50.3	46.0	218 07.8	21.9	204 17.6	53.6	Miaplacidus	221 42.6	S69 43.1
23	261 35.6	118 03.4	27.9	55 52.1	46.3	233 09.8	22.0	219 19.8	53.7			
29 00	276 38.1	133 04.1	N15 27.0	70 53.9	S11 46.6	248 11.9	N10 22.1	234 22.0	N13 53.8	Mirfak	308 56.3	N49 51.3
01	291 40.5	148 04.7	26.2	85 55.7	46.9	263 14.0	22.3	249 24.3	53.8	Nunki	76 11.4	S26 17.7
02	306 43.0	163 05.3	25.3	100 57.6	47.2	278 16.1	22.4	264 26.5	53.9	Peacock	53 35.8	S56 44.0
03	321 45.5	178 06.0	.. 24.4	115 59.4	.. 47.5	293 18.2	.. 22.5	279 28.7	.. 53.9	Pollux	243 41.3	N28 01.6
04	336 47.9	193 06.6	23.6	131 01.2	47.8	308 20.3	22.7	294 31.0	54.0	Procyon	245 11.4	N 5 13.5
05	351 50.4	208 07.2	22.7	146 03.0	48.1	323 22.4	22.8	309 33.2	54.1			
06	6 52.8	223 07.9	N15 21.8	161 04.8	S11 48.4	338 24.5	N10 22.9	324 35.4	N13 54.1	Rasalhague	96 16.2	N12 33.8
07	21 55.3	238 08.5	20.9	176 06.6	48.7	353 26.5	23.0	339 37.7	54.2	Regulus	207 55.2	N11 58.3
T 08	36 57.8	253 09.2	20.1	191 08.4	49.0	8 28.6	23.2	354 39.9	54.3	Rigel	281 22.8	S 8 12.2
U 09	52 00.2	268 09.8	.. 19.2	206 10.3	.. 49.3	23 30.7	.. 23.3	9 42.1	.. 54.3	Rigil Kent.	140 06.2	S60 50.1
E 10	67 02.7	283 10.5	18.3	221 12.1	49.6	38 32.8	23.4	24 44.3	54.4	Sabik	102 24.6	S15 43.3
S 11	82 05.2	298 11.1	17.5	236 13.9	49.9	53 34.9	23.6	39 46.6	54.4			
D 12	97 07.6	313 11.8	N15 16.6	251 15.7	S11 50.2	68 37.0	N10 23.7	54 48.8	N13 54.5	Schedar	349 52.9	N56 31.7
A 13	112 10.1	328 12.4	15.7	266 17.5	50.5	83 39.1	23.8	69 51.0	54.6	Shaula	96 36.2	S37 06.1
Y 14	127 12.6	343 13.1	14.8	281 19.3	50.8	98 41.2	24.0	84 53.3	54.6	Sirius	258 43.6	S16 43.0
15	142 15.0	358 13.7	.. 14.0	296 21.1	.. 51.1	113 43.2	.. 24.1	99 55.5	.. 54.7	Spica	158 42.6	S11 09.4
16	157 17.5	13 14.4	13.1	311 22.9	51.5	128 45.3	24.2	114 57.7	54.8	Suhail	223 00.7	S43 26.0
17	172 19.9	28 15.1	12.2	326 24.7	51.8	143 47.4	24.3	130 00.0	54.8			
18	187 22.4	43 15.7	N15 11.3	341 26.5	S11 52.1	158 49.5	N10 24.5	145 02.2	N13 54.9	Vega	80 45.9	N38 47.1
19	202 24.9	58 16.4	10.5	356 28.3	52.4	173 51.6	24.6	160 04.4	54.9	Zuben'ubi	137 17.2	S16 02.3
20	217 27.3	73 17.1	09.6	11 30.1	52.7	188 53.7	24.7	175 06.7	55.0		SHA	Mer. Pass.
21	232 29.8	88 17.7	.. 08.7	26 31.9	.. 53.0	203 55.8	.. 24.9	190 08.9	.. 55.1		° ′	h m
22	247 32.3	103 18.4	07.8	41 33.7	53.3	218 57.9	25.0	205 11.1	55.1	Venus	217 10.5	15 08
23	262 34.7	118 19.1	07.0	56 35.5	53.6	234 00.0	25.1	220 13.4	55.2	Mars	154 31.1	19 17
	h m									Jupiter	331 43.0	7 29
Mer. Pass. 5 36.5		v 0.6	d 0.9	v 1.8	d 0.3	v 2.1	d 0.1	v 2.2	d 0.1	Saturn	317 49.6	8 25

UT	SUN		MOON					Lat.	Twilight		Sunrise	Moonrise			
									Naut.	Civil		27	28	29	30
	GHA	Dec	GHA	v	Dec	d	HP	°	h m	h m	h m	h m	h m	h m	h m
d h	° ′	° ′	° ′	′	° ′	′	′	N 72	☐	☐	☐	■	■	■	■
27 00	179 17.2	N23 20.7	21 31.3	12.6	S18 03.1	4.7	54.1	N 70	☐	☐	☐	22 28	■	■	00 48
01	194 17.0	20.6	36 02.9	12.5	18 07.8	4.7	54.1	68	☐	☐	☐	21 20	22 29	23 12	23 32
02	209 16.9	20.6	50 34.4	12.5	18 12.5	4.6	54.1	66	☐	☐	☐	20 44	21 47	22 33	23 02
03	224 16.8 . .	20.5	65 05.9	12.5	18 17.1	4.5	54.1	64	////	////	01 36	20 19	21 19	22 06	22 39
04	239 16.6	20.4	79 37.4	12.4	18 21.6	4.4	54.2	62	////	////	02 13	19 59	20 57	21 45	22 20
05	254 16.5	20.3	94 08.8	12.4	18 26.0	4.3	54.2	60	////	00 56	02 39	19 43	20 40	21 27	22 05
06	269 16.4	N23 20.2	108 40.2	12.4	S18 30.3	4.3	54.2	N 58	////	01 44	02 59	19 29	20 25	21 13	21 52
07	284 16.2	20.1	123 11.6	12.3	18 34.6	4.2	54.2	56	////	02 14	03 16	19 17	20 13	21 01	21 41
08	299 16.1	20.0	137 42.9	12.3	18 38.8	4.0	54.2	54	00 51	02 36	03 30	19 07	20 02	20 50	21 31
S 09	314 16.0 . .	19.9	152 14.2	12.3	18 42.8	4.0	54.2	52	01 36	02 53	03 42	18 58	19 52	20 40	21 23
U 10	329 15.9	19.8	166 45.5	12.2	18 46.8	4.0	54.2	50	02 03	03 08	03 53	18 49	19 43	20 32	21 15
N 11	344 15.7	19.7	181 16.7	12.2	18 50.8	3.8	54.2	45	02 48	03 38	04 15	18 32	19 25	20 14	20 58.
D 12	359 15.6	N23 19.6	195 47.9	12.1	S18 54.6	3.7	54.2	N 40	03 19	04 00	04 33	18 18	19 10	19 59	20 44
A 13	14 15.5	19.5	210 19.0	12.1	18 58.3	3.7	54.2	35	03 42	04 19	04 48	18 06	18 57	19 46	20 33
Y 14	29 15.3	19.4	224 50.1	12.1	19 02.0	3.6	54.2	30	04 00	04 34	05 01	17 55	18 46	19 36	20 22
15	44 15.2 . .	19.3	239 21.2	12.1	19 05.6	3.4	54.2	20	04 29	04 59	05 23	17 37	18 27	19 17	20 05
16	59 15.1	19.2	253 52.3	12.0	19 09.0	3.4	54.3	N 10	04 52	05 19	05 42	17 22	18 11	19 00	19 49
17	74 15.0	19.1	268 23.3	12.0	19 12.4	3.3	54.3	0	05 11	05 37	05 59	17 07	17 56	18 45	19 35
18	89 14.8	N23 19.0	282 54.3	11.9	S19 15.7	3.3	54.3	S 10	05 28	05 54	06 17	16 53	17 40	18 30	19 21
19	104 14.7	18.9	297 25.2	11.9	19 19.0	3.1	54.3	20	05 44	06 11	06 35	16 37	17 24	18 14	19 05
20	119 14.6	18.8	311 56.1	11.9	19 22.1	3.0	54.3	30	06 00	06 30	06 56	16 19	17 05	17 55	18 48
21	134 14.4 . .	18.7	326 27.0	11.9	19 25.1	3.0	54.3	35	06 09	06 41	07 09	16 09	16 54	17 44	18 37
22	149 14.3	18.6	340 57.9	11.8	19 28.1	2.9	54.3	40	06 18	06 52	07 23	15 57	16 42	17 31	18 25
23	164 14.2	18.5	355 28.7	11.8	19 31.0	2.7	54.3	45	06 28	07 06	07 39	15 43	16 27	17 17	18 12
28 00	179 14.1	N23 18.4	9 59.5	11.8	S19 33.7	2.7	54.3	S 50	06 40	07 22	08 00	15 26	16 09	16 58	17 55
01	194 13.9	18.3	24 30.3	11.7	19 36.4	2.6	54.3	52	06 45	07 29	08 10	15 19	16 01	16 50	17 47
02	209 13.8	18.2	39 01.0	11.7	19 39.0	2.5	54.3	54	06 51	07 37	08 21	15 10	15 51	16 40	17 38
03	224 13.7 . .	18.1	53 31.7	11.7	19 41.5	2.4	54.4	56	06 57	07 46	08 33	15 00	15 40	16 30	17 28
04	239 13.5	18.0	68 02.4	11.7	19 43.9	2.3	54.4	58	07 04	07 56	08 48	14 49	15 28	16 17	17 16
05	254 13.4	17.9	82 33.1	11.6	19 46.2	2.2	54.4	S 60	07 11	08 08	09 05	14 36	15 14	16 03	17 03
06	269 13.3	N23 17.7	97 03.7	11.6	S19 48.4	2.2	54.4								
07	284 13.2	17.6	111 34.3	11.5	19 50.6	2.0	54.4	Lat.	Sunset	Twilight		Moonset			
08	299 13.0	17.5	126 04.8	11.6	19 52.6	1.9	54.4			Civil	Naut.	27	28	29	30
M 09	314 12.9 . .	17.4	140 35.4	11.5	19 54.5	1.9	54.4								
O 10	329 12.8	17.3	155 05.9	11.5	19 56.4	1.7	54.4	°	h m	h m	h m	h m	h m	h m	h m
N 11	344 12.6	17.2	169 36.4	11.4	19 58.1	1.7	54.4	N 72	☐	☐	☐	■	■	■	01 10
D 12	359 12.5	N23 17.1	184 06.8	11.5	S19 59.8	1.6	54.4	N 70	☐	☐	☐	00 17	00 04	■	01 10
A 13	14 12.4	17.0	198 37.3	11.4	20 01.4	1.4	54.5	68	☐	☐	☐	00 57	01 13	01 45	02 46
Y 14	29 12.3	16.8	213 07.7	11.4	20 02.8	1.4	54.5	66	☐	☐	☐	01 25	01 49	02 27	03 25
15	44 12.1 . .	16.7	227 38.1	11.4	20 04.2	1.3	54.5	64	22 30	////	////	01 47	02 15	02 56	03 52
16	59 12.0	16.6	242 08.5	11.3	20 05.5	1.2	54.5	62	21 53	////	////	02 04	02 35	03 17	04 12
17	74 11.9	16.5	256 38.8	11.3	20 06.7	1.0	54.5	60	21 27	23 09	////	02 18	02 51	03 35	04 29
18	89 11.8	N23 16.4	271 09.1	11.3	S20 07.7	1.0	54.5	N 58	21 07	22 21	////	02 30	03 05	03 49	04 44
19	104 11.6	16.3	285 39.4	11.3	20 08.7	0.9	54.5	56	20 50	21 52	////	02 41	03 17	04 02	04 56
20	119 11.5	16.1	300 09.7	11.3	20 09.6	0.8	54.5	54	20 36	21 30	23 14	02 50	03 28	04 13	05 06
21	134 11.4 . .	16.0	314 40.0	11.2	20 10.4	0.7	54.6	52	20 24	21 13	22 30	02 59	03 37	04 23	05 16
22	149 11.3	15.9	329 10.2	11.2	20 11.1	0.6	54.6	50	20 13	20 58	22 03	03 06	03 46	04 31	05 24
23	164 11.1	15.8	343 40.4	11.2	20 11.7	0.5	54.6	45	19 51	20 28	21 18	03 22	04 03	04 50	05 42
29 00	179 11.0	N23 15.6	358 10.6	11.2	S20 12.2	0.4	54.6	N 40	19 33	20 06	20 47	03 36	04 18	05 05	05 57
01	194 10.9	15.5	12 40.8	11.2	20 12.6	0.3	54.6	35	19 18	19 48	20 24	03 47	04 30	05 18	06 09
02	209 10.7	15.4	27 11.0	11.1	20 12.9	0.3	54.6	30	19 05	19 32	20 06	03 57	04 41	05 29	06 20
03	224 10.6 . .	15.3	41 41.1	11.2	20 13.2	0.1	54.6	20	18 43	19 08	19 37	04 14	04 59	05 48	06 38
04	239 10.5	15.2	56 11.3	11.1	20 13.3	0.0	54.6	N 10	18 24	18 47	19 14	04 29	05 15	06 04	06 54
05	254 10.4	15.0	70 41.4	11.1	20 13.3	0.1	54.7	0	18 07	18 29	18 56	04 42	05 30	06 20	07 09
06	269 10.2	N23 14.9	85 11.5	11.1	S20 13.2	0.2	54.7	S 10	17 50	18 12	18 39	04 56	05 45	06 35	07 24
07	284 10.1	14.8	99 41.6	11.0	20 13.0	0.3	54.7	20	17 31	17 55	18 23	05 11	06 02	06 51	07 40
T 08	299 10.0	14.6	114 11.6	11.1	20 12.7	0.4	54.7	30	17 10	17 36	18 06	05 28	06 20	07 10	07 58
U 09	314 09.9 . .	14.5	128 41.7	11.0	20 12.3	0.4	54.7	35	16 58	17 26	17 58	05 38	06 31	07 21	08 09
E 10	329 09.7	14.4	143 11.7	11.1	20 11.9	0.6	54.7	40	16 44	17 14	17 48	05 50	06 43	07 34	08 21
S 11	344 09.6	14.3	157 41.8	11.0	20 11.3	0.7	54.7	45	16 27	17 01	17 38	06 03	06 58	07 49	08 35
D 12	359 09.5	N23 14.1	172 11.8	11.0	S20 10.6	0.8	54.8	S 50	16 06	16 45	17 26	06 19	07 15	08 07	08 53
A 13	14 09.4	14.0	186 41.8	11.0	20 09.8	0.8	54.8	52	15 57	16 37	17 21	06 27	07 24	08 15	09 01
Y 14	29 09.2	13.9	201 11.8	11.0	20 09.0	1.0	54.8	54	15 46	16 29	17 15	06 36	07 33	08 25	09 10
15	44 09.1 . .	13.7	215 41.8	10.9	20 08.0	1.1	54.8	56	15 33	16 20	17 09	06 45	07 44	08 36	09 20
16	59 09.0	13.6	230 11.7	11.0	20 06.9	1.2	54.8	58	15 18	16 10	17 03	06 56	07 56	08 48	09 32
17	74 08.9	13.5	244 41.7	11.0	20 05.7	1.3	54.8	S 60	15 01	15 59	16 55	07 09	08 10	09 03	09 45
18	89 08.7	N23 13.3	259 11.7	10.9	S20 04.4	1.3	54.8			SUN			MOON		
19	104 08.6	13.2	273 41.6	11.0	20 03.1	1.5	54.9	Day	Eqn. of Time		Mer.	Mer. Pass.		Age	Phase
20	119 08.5	13.0	288 11.6	10.9	20 01.6	1.6	54.9		00ʰ	12ʰ	Pass.	Upper	Lower		
21	134 08.4 . .	12.9	302 41.5	10.9	20 00.0	1.6	54.9	d	m s	m s	h m	h m	h m	d	%
22	149 08.2	12.8	317 11.4	11.0	19 58.4	1.8	54.9	27	02 51	02 57	12 03	23 19	10 55	14	98
23	164 08.1	12.6	331 41.4	10.9	S19 56.6	1.9	54.9	28	03 04	03 10	12 03	24 08	11 43	15	100
	SD 15.8	d 0.1	SD 14.8		14.8		14.9	29	03 16	03 22	12 03	00 08	12 32	16	100

UT	ARIES GHA	VENUS −4.4 GHA	Dec	MARS −0.4 GHA	Dec	JUPITER −2.3 GHA	Dec	SATURN +0.4 GHA	Dec	STARS Name	SHA	Dec
30 00	277 37.2	133 19.7	N15 06.1	71 37.3	S11 53.9	249 02.1	N10 25.3	235 15.6	N13 55.3	Acamar	315 26.8	S40 18.3
01	292 39.7	148 20.4	05.2	86 39.1	54.2	264 04.1	25.4	250 17.9	55.3	Achernar	335 35.0	S57 14.2
02	307 42.1	163 21.1	04.3	101 40.9	54.5	279 06.2	25.5	265 20.1	55.4	Acrux	173 21.4	S63 06.0
03	322 44.6	178 21.8 ..	03.5	116 42.7 ..	54.8	294 08.3 ..	25.6	280 22.3 ..	55.4	Adhara	255 21.4	S28 58.4
04	337 47.1	193 22.5	02.6	131 44.5	55.1	309 10.4	25.8	295 24.6	55.5	Aldebaran	291 02.1	N16 30.3
05	352 49.5	208 23.1	01.7	146 46.3	55.5	324 12.5	25.9	310 26.8	55.6			
W 06	7 52.0	223 23.8	N15 00.8	161 48.1	S11 55.8	339 14.6	N10 26.0	325 29.0	N13 55.6	Alioth	166 30.2	N55 58.1
E 07	22 54.4	238 24.5	15 00.0	176 49.9	56.1	354 16.7	26.2	340 31.3	55.7	Alkaid	153 07.3	N49 19.3
D 08	37 56.9	253 25.2	14 59.1	191 51.7	56.4	9 18.8	26.3	355 33.5	55.7	Al Na'ir	27 57.0	S46 57.6
N 09	52 59.4	268 25.9 ..	58.2	206 53.5 ..	56.7	24 20.9 ..	26.4	10 35.7 ..	55.8	Alnilam	275 57.7	S 1 12.2
E 10	68 01.8	283 26.6	57.3	221 55.3	57.0	39 23.0	26.5	25 38.0	55.9	Alphard	218 07.0	S 8 39.4
S 11	83 04.3	298 27.3	56.5	236 57.0	57.3	54 25.1	26.7	40 40.2	55.9			
D 12	98 06.8	313 28.0	N14 55.6	251 58.8	S11 57.6	69 27.2	N10 26.8	55 42.4	N13 56.0	Alphecca	126 19.9	N26 43.2
A 13	113 09.2	328 28.7	54.7	267 00.6	57.9	84 29.2	26.9	70 44.7	56.1	Alpheratz	357 54.7	N29 05.0
Y 14	128 11.7	343 29.4	53.8	282 02.4	58.2	99 31.3	27.1	85 46.9	56.1	Altair	62 18.5	N 8 52.1
15	143 14.2	358 30.1 ..	53.0	297 04.2 ..	58.6	114 33.4 ..	27.2	100 49.1 ..	56.2	Ankaa	353 26.4	S42 18.4
16	158 16.6	13 30.8	52.1	312 06.0	58.9	129 35.5	27.3	115 51.4	56.2	Antares	112 39.2	S26 25.8
17	173 19.1	28 31.5	51.2	327 07.7	59.2	144 37.6	27.4	130 53.6	56.3			
18	188 21.6	43 32.2	N14 50.3	342 09.5	S11 59.5	159 39.7	N10 27.6	145 55.9	N13 56.4	Arcturus	146 05.5	N19 11.4
19	203 24.0	58 32.9	49.5	357 11.3	11 59.8	174 41.8	27.7	160 58.1	56.4	Atria	107 50.3	S69 01.6
20	218 26.5	73 33.6	48.6	12 13.1	12 00.1	189 43.9	27.8	176 00.3	56.5	Avior	234 23.0	S59 30.6
21	233 28.9	88 34.3 ..	47.7	27 14.9 ..	00.4	204 46.0 ..	27.9	191 02.6 ..	56.5	Bellatrix	278 44.0	N 6 20.8
22	248 31.4	103 35.0	46.8	42 16.6	00.7	219 48.1	28.1	206 04.8	56.6	Betelgeuse	271 13.4	N 7 24.3
23	263 33.9	118 35.8	46.0	57 18.4	01.1	234 50.2	28.2	221 07.0	56.7			
1 00	278 36.3	133 36.5	N14 45.1	72 20.2	S12 01.4	249 52.3	N10 28.3	236 09.3	N13 56.7	Canopus	264 01.5	S52 41.8
01	293 38.8	148 37.2	44.2	87 22.0	01.7	264 54.4	28.5	251 11.5	56.8	Capella	280 50.9	N45 59.7
02	308 41.3	163 37.9	43.3	102 23.8	02.0	279 56.5	28.6	266 13.7	56.8	Deneb	49 38.4	N45 16.6
03	323 43.7	178 38.7 ..	42.4	117 25.5 ..	02.3	294 58.6 ..	28.7	281 16.0 ..	56.9	Denebola	182 44.8	N14 34.7
04	338 46.2	193 39.4	41.6	132 27.3	02.6	310 00.7	28.8	296 18.2	57.0	Diphda	349 06.8	S17 59.3
05	353 48.7	208 40.1	40.7	147 29.1	03.0	325 02.8	29.0	311 20.5	57.0			
T 06	8 51.1	223 40.8	N14 39.8	162 30.8	S12 03.3	340 04.9	N10 29.1	326 22.7	N13 57.1	Dubhe	194 05.2	N61 45.5
H 07	23 53.6	238 41.6	38.9	177 32.6	03.6	355 07.0	29.2	341 24.9	57.1	Elnath	278 26.7	N28 36.3
U 08	38 56.1	253 42.3	38.1	192 34.4	03.9	10 09.0	29.3	356 27.2	57.2	Eltanin	90 50.6	N51 29.5
R 09	53 58.5	268 43.0 ..	37.2	207 36.1 ..	04.2	25 11.1 ..	29.5	11 29.4 ..	57.3	Enif	33 57.5	N 9 52.3
S 10	69 01.0	283 43.8	36.3	222 37.9	04.5	40 13.2	29.6	26 31.6	57.3	Fomalhaut	15 35.8	S29 37.4
11	84 03.4	298 44.5	35.4	237 39.7	04.8	55 15.3	29.7	41 33.9	57.4			
D 12	99 05.9	313 45.3	N14 34.6	252 41.4	S12 05.2	70 17.4	N10 29.8	56 36.1	N13 57.5	Gacrux	172 13.0	S57 06.8
A 13	114 08.4	328 46.0	33.7	267 43.2	05.5	85 19.5	30.0	71 38.4	57.5	Gienah	176 03.5	S17 32.3
Y 14	129 10.8	343 46.7	32.8	282 45.0	05.8	100 21.6	30.1	86 40.6	57.6	Hadar	149 03.0	S60 22.4
15	144 13.3	358 47.5 ..	31.9	297 46.7 ..	06.1	115 23.7 ..	30.2	101 42.8 ..	57.6	Hamal	328 13.1	N23 27.4
16	159 15.8	13 48.2	31.0	312 48.5	06.4	130 25.8	30.3	116 45.1	57.7	Kaus Aust.	83 57.8	S34 23.0
17	174 18.2	28 49.0	30.2	327 50.3	06.8	145 27.9	30.5	131 47.3	57.8			
18	189 20.7	43 49.7	N14 29.3	342 52.0	S12 07.1	160 30.0	N10 30.6	146 49.6	N13 57.8	Kochab	137 19.0	N74 09.9
19	204 23.2	58 50.5	28.4	357 53.8	07.4	175 32.1	30.7	161 51.8	57.9	Markab	13 49.0	N15 12.0
20	219 25.6	73 51.2	27.5	12 55.5	07.7	190 34.2	30.8	176 54.0	57.9	Menkar	314 26.6	N 4 05.1
21	234 28.1	88 52.0 ..	26.7	27 57.3 ..	08.0	205 36.3 ..	31.0	191 56.3 ..	58.0	Menkent	148 20.2	S36 22.1
22	249 30.6	103 52.8	25.8	42 59.1	08.3	220 38.4	31.1	206 58.5	58.1	Miaplacidus	221 42.6	S69 43.1
23	264 33.0	118 53.5	24.9	58 00.8	08.7	235 40.5	31.2	222 00.7	58.1			
2 00	279 35.5	133 54.3	N14 24.0	73 02.6	S12 09.0	250 42.6	N10 31.3	237 03.0	N13 58.2	Mirfak	308 56.2	N49 51.3
01	294 37.9	148 55.1	23.1	88 04.3	09.3	265 44.7	31.5	252 05.2	58.2	Nunki	76 11.3	S26 17.7
02	309 40.4	163 55.8	22.3	103 06.1	09.6	280 46.8	31.6	267 07.5	58.3	Peacock	53 35.7	S56 44.0
03	324 42.9	178 56.6 ..	21.4	118 07.8 ..	10.0	295 48.9 ..	31.7	282 09.7 ..	58.4	Pollux	243 41.3	N28 01.6
04	339 45.3	193 57.4	20.5	133 09.6	10.3	310 51.0	31.8	297 11.9	58.4	Procyon	245 11.4	N 5 13.5
05	354 47.8	208 58.1	19.6	148 11.3	10.6	325 53.1	32.0	312 14.2	58.5			
06	9 50.3	223 58.9	N14 18.7	163 13.1	S12 10.9	340 55.2	N10 32.1	327 16.4	N13 58.5	Rasalhague	96 16.2	N12 33.8
07	24 52.7	238 59.7	17.9	178 14.8	11.2	355 57.3	32.2	342 18.7	58.6	Regulus	207 55.2	N11 58.3
08	39 55.2	254 00.5	17.0	193 16.6	11.6	10 59.4	32.3	357 20.9	58.6	Rigel	281 22.8	S 8 12.2
F 09	54 57.7	269 01.2 ..	16.1	208 18.3 ..	11.9	26 01.5 ..	32.5	12 23.1 ..	58.7	Rigil Kent.	140 06.2	S60 50.1
R 10	70 00.1	284 02.0	15.2	223 20.1	12.2	41 03.6	32.6	27 25.4	58.8	Sabik	102 24.6	S15 43.3
I 11	85 02.6	299 02.8	14.4	238 21.8	12.5	56 05.7	32.7	42 27.6	58.8			
D 12	100 05.0	314 03.6	N14 13.5	253 23.6	S12 12.8	71 07.8	N10 32.8	57 29.9	N13 58.9	Schedar	349 52.9	N56 31.7
A 13	115 07.5	329 04.4	12.6	268 25.3	13.2	86 09.9	33.0	72 32.1	58.9	Shaula	96 36.2	S37 06.1
Y 14	130 10.0	344 05.2	11.7	283 27.0	13.5	101 12.0	33.1	87 34.3	59.0	Sirius	258 43.6	S16 43.0
15	145 12.4	359 06.0 ..	10.8	298 28.8 ..	13.8	116 14.1 ..	33.2	102 36.6 ..	59.1	Spica	158 42.6	S11 09.4
16	160 14.9	14 06.8	10.0	313 30.5	14.1	131 16.2	33.3	117 38.8	59.1	Suhail	223 00.7	S43 26.0
17	175 17.4	29 07.6	09.1	328 32.3	14.5	146 18.3	33.5	132 41.1	59.2			
18	190 19.8	44 08.4	N14 08.2	343 34.0	S12 14.8	161 20.5	N10 33.6	147 43.3	N13 59.2	Vega	80 45.8	N38 47.1
19	205 22.3	59 09.2	07.3	358 35.7	15.1	176 22.6	33.7	162 45.6	59.3	Zuben'ubi	137 17.2	S16 02.3
20	220 24.8	74 10.0	06.4	13 37.5	15.4	191 24.7	33.8	177 47.8	59.4		SHA	Mer. Pass.
21	235 27.2	89 10.8 ..	05.6	28 39.2 ..	15.8	206 26.8 ..	34.0	192 50.0 ..	59.4		° ′	h m
22	250 29.7	104 11.6	04.7	43 40.9	16.1	221 28.9	34.1	207 52.3	59.5	Venus	215 00.1	15 05
23	265 32.2	119 12.4	03.8	58 42.7	16.4	236 31.0	34.2	222 54.5	59.5	Mars	153 43.9	19 08
	h m									Jupiter	331 15.9	7 19
Mer. Pass.	5 24.7	v 0.7	d 0.9	v 1.8	d 0.3	v 2.1	d 0.1	v 2.2	d 0.1	Saturn	317 32.9	8 14

SUN / MOON

UT	SUN GHA	SUN Dec	MOON GHA	v	Dec	d	HP
d h	° ′	° ′	° ′	′	° ′	′	′
30 00	179 08.0	N23 12.5	346 11.3	10.9	S19 54.7	2.0	54.9
01	194 07.9	12.4	0 41.2	10.9	19 52.7	2.0	55.0
02	209 07.7	12.2	15 11.1	10.9	19 50.7	2.2	55.0
03	224 07.6	. . 12.1	29 41.0	10.9	19 48.5	2.3	55.0
04	239 07.5	11.9	44 10.9	10.9	19 46.2	2.3	55.0
05	254 07.4	11.8	58 40.8	10.9	19 43.9	2.5	55.0
06	269 07.3	N23 11.6	73 10.7	10.9	S19 41.4	2.6	55.0
W 07	284 07.1	11.5	87 40.6	11.0	19 38.8	2.6	55.0
E 08	299 07.0	11.4	102 10.6	10.9	19 36.2	2.8	55.1
D 09	314 06.9	. . 11.2	116 40.5	10.9	19 33.4	2.9	55.1
N 10	329 06.8	11.1	131 10.4	10.9	19 30.5	2.9	55.1
E 11	344 06.6	10.9	145 40.3	10.9	19 27.6	3.1	55.1
S 12	359 06.5	N23 10.8	160 10.2	10.9	S19 24.5	3.2	55.1
D 13	14 06.4	10.6	174 40.1	10.9	19 21.3	3.2	55.2
A 14	29 06.3	10.5	189 10.0	10.9	19 18.1	3.4	55.2
Y 15	44 06.1	. . 10.3	203 39.9	10.9	19 14.7	3.4	55.2
16	59 06.0	10.2	218 09.8	11.0	19 11.3	3.6	55.2
17	74 05.9	10.0	232 39.8	10.9	19 07.7	3.6	55.2
18	89 05.8	N23 09.9	247 09.7	10.9	S19 04.1	3.8	55.2
19	104 05.7	09.7	261 39.6	11.0	19 00.3	3.8	55.3
20	119 05.5	09.6	276 09.6	10.9	18 56.5	3.9	55.3
21	134 05.4	. . 09.4	290 39.5	11.0	18 52.6	4.1	55.3
22	149 05.3	09.2	305 09.5	10.9	18 48.5	4.1	55.3
23	164 05.2	09.1	319 39.4	11.0	18 44.4	4.2	55.3
1 00	179 05.0	N23 08.9	334 09.4	11.0	S18 40.2	4.3	55.3
01	194 04.9	08.8	348 39.4	10.9	18 35.9	4.4	55.4
02	209 04.8	08.6	3 09.3	11.0	18 31.5	4.6	55.4
03	224 04.7	. . 08.5	17 39.3	11.0	18 26.9	4.6	55.4
04	239 04.6	08.3	32 09.3	11.0	18 22.3	4.7	55.4
05	254 04.4	08.1	46 39.3	11.1	18 17.6	4.8	55.4
06	269 04.3	N23 08.0	61 09.4	11.0	S18 12.8	4.8	55.5
07	284 04.2	07.8	75 39.4	11.0	18 08.0	5.0	55.5
T 08	299 04.1	07.7	90 09.4	11.1	18 03.0	5.1	55.5
H 09	314 04.0	. . 07.5	104 39.5	11.0	17 57.9	5.2	55.5
U 10	329 03.8	07.3	119 09.5	11.1	17 52.7	5.2	55.5
R 11	344 03.7	07.2	133 39.6	11.1	17 47.5	5.4	55.5
S 12	359 03.6	N23 07.0	148 09.7	11.1	S17 42.1	5.4	55.6
D 13	14 03.5	06.8	162 39.8	11.1	17 36.7	5.5	55.6
A 14	29 03.4	06.7	177 09.9	11.1	17 31.2	5.7	55.6
Y 15	44 03.2	. . 06.5	191 40.0	11.2	17 25.5	5.7	55.6
16	59 03.1	06.3	206 10.2	11.1	17 19.8	5.8	55.6
17	74 03.0	06.2	220 40.3	11.2	17 14.0	5.9	55.7
18	89 02.9	N23 05.8	235 10.5	11.1	S17 08.1	5.9	55.7
19	104 02.8	05.8	249 40.6	11.2	17 02.2	6.1	55.7
20	119 02.6	05.7	264 10.8	11.2	16 56.1	6.2	55.7
21	134 02.5	. . 05.5	278 41.0	11.3	16 49.9	6.2	55.7
22	149 02.4	05.3	293 11.3	11.2	16 43.7	6.3	55.8
23	164 02.3	05.1	307 41.5	11.2	16 37.4	6.5	55.8
2 00	179 02.2	N23 05.0	322 11.7	11.3	S16 30.9	6.5	55.8
01	194 02.0	04.8	336 42.0	11.3	16 24.4	6.6	55.8
02	209 01.9	04.6	351 12.3	11.3	16 17.8	6.6	55.9
03	224 01.8	. . 04.4	5 42.6	11.3	16 11.2	6.8	55.9
04	239 01.7	04.3	20 12.9	11.3	16 04.4	6.8	55.9
05	254 01.6	04.1	34 43.2	11.3	15 57.6	7.0	55.9
06	269 01.4	N23 03.9	49 13.5	11.4	S15 50.6	6.9	55.9
07	284 01.3	03.7	63 43.9	11.3	15 43.6	7.1	56.0
F 08	299 01.2	03.6	78 14.2	11.4	15 36.5	7.2	56.0
R 09	314 01.1	. . 03.4	92 44.6	11.4	15 29.3	7.2	56.0
I 10	329 01.0	03.2	107 15.0	11.4	15 22.1	7.4	56.0
11	344 00.9	03.0	121 45.4	11.4	15 14.7	7.4	56.0
D 12	359 00.7	N23 02.8	136 15.8	11.5	S15 07.3	7.5	56.1
A 13	14 00.6	02.6	150 46.3	11.4	14 59.8	7.6	56.1
Y 14	29 00.5	02.5	165 16.7	11.5	14 52.2	7.6	56.1
15	44 00.4	. . 02.3	179 47.2	11.5	14 44.6	7.8	56.1
16	59 00.3	02.1	194 17.7	11.5	14 36.8	7.8	56.1
17	74 00.1	01.9	208 48.2	11.5	14 29.0	7.9	56.2
18	89 00.0	N23 01.7	223 18.7	11.6	S14 21.1	8.0	56.2
19	103 59.9	01.5	237 49.3	11.5	14 13.1	8.0	56.2
20	118 59.8	01.4	252 19.8	11.6	14 05.1	8.1	56.2
21	133 59.7	. . 01.2	266 50.4	11.5	13 57.0	8.2	56.3
22	148 59.6	01.0	281 20.9	11.6	13 48.8	8.3	56.3
23	163 59.4	00.8	295 51.5	11.6	S13 40.5	8.4	56.3
	SD 15.8	d 0.2	SD 15.0		15.1		15.3

Twilight / Sunrise / Moonrise

Lat.	Twilight Naut.	Twilight Civil	Sunrise	Moonrise 30	1	2	3
°	h m	h m	h m	h m	h m	h m	h m
N 72	▭	▭	▭	■■■■	■■■■	00 57	00 32
N 70	▭	▭	▭	00 48	00 19	00 12	00 06
68	▭	▭	▭	23 32	23 42	23 46	23 49
66	////	////	00 13	23 02	23 19	23 31	23 38
64	////	////	01 40	22 39	23 02	23 18	23 30
62	////	////	02 16	22 20	22 47	23 07	23 22
60	////	01 02	02 42	22 05	22 34	22 57	23 16
N 58	////	01 48	03 02	21 52	22 24	22 49	23 10
56	////	02 16	03 18	21 41	22 14	22 42	23 05
54	00 57	02 38	03 32	21 31	22 06	22 35	23 01
52	01 39	02 56	03 44	21 23	21 59	22 29	22 56
50	02 06	03 10	03 55	21 15	21 52	22 24	22 53
45	02 50	03 40	04 17	20 58	21 37	22 13	22 44
N 40	03 20	04 02	04 35	20 44	21 25	22 03	22 38
35	03 43	04 20	04 49	20 33	21 15	21 55	22 32
30	04 02	04 35	05 02	20 22	21 06	21 47	22 27
20	04 30	04 59	05 24	20 05	20 51	21 35	22 17
N 10	04 53	05 20	05 43	19 49	20 37	21 24	22 09
0	05 11	05 38	06 00	19 35	20 25	21 14	22 02
S 10	05 28	05 55	06 17	19 21	20 12	21 03	21 54
20	05 44	06 12	06 36	19 05	19 58	20 52	21 46
30	06 00	06 30	06 57	18 48	19 43	20 39	21 37
35	06 09	06 41	07 09	18 37	19 34	20 32	21 32
40	06 18	06 52	07 23	18 25	19 23	20 24	21 26
45	06 28	07 06	07 39	18 12	19 11	20 14	21 19
S 50	06 40	07 21	08 00	17 55	18 56	20 02	21 10
52	06 45	07 29	08 09	17 47	18 49	19 56	21 07
54	06 51	07 37	08 20	17 38	18 42	19 50	21 02
56	06 57	07 46	08 33	17 28	18 33	19 43	20 57
58	07 03	07 56	08 47	17 16	18 23	19 36	20 52
S 60	07 11	08 07	09 04	17 03	18 12	19 27	20 46

Sunset / Twilight / Moonset

Lat.	Sunset	Twilight Civil	Twilight Naut.	Moonset 30	1	2	3
°	h m	h m	h m	h m	h m	h m	h m
N 72	▭	▭	▭	■■■■	■■■■	04 29	06 36
N 70	▭	▭	▭	01 10	03 22	05 13	07 00
68	▭	▭	▭	02 46	04 09	05 42	07 18
66	23 44	////	////	03 25	04 39	06 03	07 33
64	22 26	////	////	03 52	05 01	06 21	07 45
62	21 50	////	////	04 12	05 19	06 35	07 55
60	21 25	23 03	////	04 29	05 34	06 47	08 04
N 58	21 05	22 19	////	04 44	05 47	06 57	08 12
56	20 49	21 50	////	04 56	05 58	07 06	08 18
54	20 35	21 29	23 09	05 06	06 07	07 14	08 24
52	20 23	21 11	22 27	05 16	06 16	07 21	08 29
50	20 13	20 57	22 01	05 24	06 23	07 27	08 34
45	19 50	20 28	21 17	05 42	06 39	07 41	08 45
N 40	19 33	20 05	20 47	05 57	06 53	07 52	08 53
35	19 18	19 48	20 24	06 09	07 04	08 01	09 01
30	19 05	19 33	20 06	06 20	07 14	08 10	09 07
20	18 43	19 08	19 37	06 38	07 31	08 24	09 18
N 10	18 25	18 48	19 15	06 54	07 45	08 37	09 28
0	18 07	18 30	18 56	07 09	07 59	08 48	09 37
S 10	17 50	18 13	18 39	07 24	08 12	09 00	09 46
20	17 32	17 56	18 23	07 40	08 27	09 12	09 55
30	17 11	17 37	18 07	07 58	08 44	09 26	10 06
35	16 59	17 27	17 59	08 09	08 53	09 34	10 12
40	16 45	17 15	17 49	08 21	09 04	09 43	10 19
45	16 28	17 02	17 39	08 35	09 17	09 54	10 27
S 50	16 08	16 46	17 28	08 53	09 32	10 07	10 37
52	15 58	16 39	17 23	09 01	09 40	10 13	10 42
54	15 47	16 31	17 17	09 10	09 48	10 19	10 47
56	15 35	16 22	17 11	09 20	09 57	10 27	10 52
58	15 21	16 12	17 04	09 32	10 07	10 35	10 58
S 60	15 04	16 01	16 57	09 45	10 19	10 44	11 05

SUN / MOON

Day	Eqn. of Time 00h	Eqn. of Time 12h	Mer. Pass.	Mer. Pass. Upper	Mer. Pass. Lower	Age	Phase
d	m s	m s	h m	h m	h m	d	%
30	03 28	03 34	12 04	00 57	13 22	17	98
1	03 40	03 45	12 04	01 47	14 12	18	94
2	03 51	03 57	12 04	02 36	15 01	19	88

(○)

UT	ARIES GHA	VENUS −4.4 GHA	Dec	MARS −0.4 GHA	Dec	JUPITER −2.3 GHA	Dec	SATURN +0.4 GHA	Dec
3 00	280 34.6	134 13.2	N14 02.9	73 44.4	S12 16.7	251 33.1	N10 34.3	237 56.8	N13 59.6
01	295 37.1	149 14.0	02.0	88 46.1	17.1	266 35.2	34.4	252 59.0	59.7
02	310 39.5	164 14.8	01.2	103 47.9	17.4	281 37.3	34.6	268 01.2	59.7
03	325 42.0	179 15.6	14 00.3	118 49.6 ..	17.7	296 39.4 ..	34.7	283 03.5 ..	59.8
04	340 44.5	194 16.4	13 59.4	133 51.3	18.0	311 41.5	34.8	298 05.7	59.8
05	355 46.9	209 17.3	58.5	148 53.1	18.4	326 43.6	34.9	313 08.0	59.9
06	10 49.4	224 18.1	N13 57.7	163 54.8	S12 18.7	341 45.7	N10 35.1	328 10.2	N13 59.9
S 07	25 51.9	239 18.9	56.8	178 56.5	19.0	356 47.8	35.2	343 12.5	14 00.0
A 08	40 54.3	254 19.7	55.9	193 58.3	19.4	11 49.9	35.3	358 14.7	00.1
T 09	55 56.8	269 20.6 ..	55.0	209 00.0 ..	19.7	26 52.0 ..	35.4	13 16.9 ..	00.1
U 10	70 59.3	284 21.4	54.1	224 01.7	20.0	41 54.1	35.5	28 19.2	00.2
R 11	86 01.7	299 22.2	53.3	239 03.4	20.3	56 56.2	35.7	43 21.4	00.2
D 12	101 04.2	314 23.1	N13 52.4	254 05.2	S12 20.7	71 58.3	N10 35.8	58 23.7	N14 00.3
A 13	116 06.7	329 23.9	51.5	269 06.9	21.0	87 00.5	35.9	73 25.9	00.4
Y 14	131 09.1	344 24.7	50.6	284 08.6	21.3	102 02.6	36.0	88 28.2	00.4
15	146 11.6	359 25.6 ..	49.7	299 10.3 ..	21.7	117 04.7 ..	36.2	103 30.4 ..	00.5
16	161 14.0	14 26.4	48.9	314 12.0	22.0	132 06.8	36.3	118 32.7	00.5
17	176 16.5	29 27.3	48.0	329 13.8	22.3	147 08.9	36.4	133 34.9	00.6
18	191 19.0	44 28.1	N13 47.1	344 15.5	S12 22.6	162 11.0	N10 36.5	148 37.1	N14 00.6
19	206 21.4	59 28.9	46.2	359 17.2	23.0	177 13.1	36.6	163 39.4	00.7
20	221 23.9	74 29.8	45.3	14 18.9	23.3	192 15.2	36.8	178 41.6	00.8
21	236 26.4	89 30.6 ..	44.5	29 20.6 ..	23.6	207 17.3 ..	36.9	193 43.9 ..	00.8
22	251 28.8	104 31.5	43.6	44 22.3	24.0	222 19.4	37.0	208 46.1	00.9
23	266 31.3	119 32.4	42.7	59 24.0	24.3	237 21.5	37.1	223 48.4	00.9
4 00	281 33.8	134 33.2	N13 41.8	74 25.8	S12 24.6	252 23.7	N10 37.2	238 50.6	N14 01.0
01	296 36.2	149 34.1	40.9	89 27.5	25.0	267 25.8	37.4	253 52.9	01.1
02	311 38.7	164 34.9	40.1	104 29.2	25.3	282 27.9	37.5	268 55.1	01.1
03	326 41.1	179 35.8 ..	39.2	119 30.9 ..	25.6	297 30.0 ..	37.6	283 57.3 ..	01.2
04	341 43.6	194 36.7	38.3	134 32.6	26.0	312 32.1	37.7	298 59.6	01.2
05	356 46.1	209 37.5	37.4	149 34.3	26.3	327 34.2	37.9	314 01.8	01.3
06	11 48.5	224 38.4	N13 36.6	164 36.0	S12 26.6	342 36.3	N10 38.0	329 04.1	N14 01.3
07	26 51.0	239 39.3	35.7	179 37.7	27.0	357 38.4	38.1	344 06.3	01.4
S 08	41 53.5	254 40.1	34.8	194 39.4	27.3	12 40.5	38.2	359 08.6	01.5
U 09	56 55.9	269 41.0 ..	33.9	209 41.1 ..	27.6	27 42.6 ..	38.3	14 10.8 ..	01.5
N 10	71 58.4	284 41.9	33.0	224 42.8	28.0	42 44.8	38.5	29 13.1	01.6
11	87 00.9	299 42.8	32.2	239 44.5	28.3	57 46.9	38.6	44 15.3	01.6
D 12	102 03.3	314 43.6	N13 31.3	254 46.3	S12 28.6	72 49.0	N10 38.7	59 17.6	N14 01.7
A 13	117 05.8	329 44.5	30.4	269 48.0	29.0	87 51.1	38.8	74 19.8	01.7
Y 14	132 08.3	344 45.4	29.5	284 49.7	29.3	102 53.2	38.9	89 22.1	01.8
15	147 10.7	359 46.3 ..	28.6	299 51.4 ..	29.6	117 55.3 ..	39.1	104 24.3 ..	01.9
16	162 13.2	14 47.2	27.8	314 53.1	30.0	132 57.4	39.2	119 26.5	01.9
17	177 15.6	29 48.1	26.9	329 54.8	30.3	147 59.5	39.3	134 28.8	02.0
18	192 18.1	44 49.0	N13 26.0	344 56.4	S12 30.6	163 01.7	N10 39.4	149 31.0	N14 02.0
19	207 20.6	59 49.9	25.1	359 58.1	31.0	178 03.8	39.5	164 33.3	02.1
20	222 23.0	74 50.8	24.2	14 59.8	31.3	193 05.9	39.6	179 35.5	02.1
21	237 25.5	89 51.7 ..	23.4	30 01.5 ..	31.6	208 08.0 ..	39.8	194 37.8 ..	02.2
22	252 28.0	104 52.6	22.5	45 03.2	32.0	223 10.1	39.9	209 40.0	02.3
23	267 30.4	119 53.5	21.6	60 04.9	32.3	238 12.2	40.0	224 42.3	02.3
5 00	282 32.9	134 54.4	N13 20.7	75 06.6	S12 32.7	253 14.3	N10 40.1	239 44.5	N14 02.4
01	297 35.4	149 55.3	19.9	90 08.3	33.0	268 16.5	40.2	254 46.8	02.4
02	312 37.8	164 56.2	19.0	105 10.0	33.3	283 18.6	40.4	269 49.0	02.5
03	327 40.3	179 57.1 ..	18.1	120 11.7 ..	33.7	298 20.7 ..	40.5	284 51.3 ..	02.5
04	342 42.8	194 58.0	17.2	135 13.4	34.0	313 22.8	40.6	299 53.5	02.6
05	357 45.2	209 58.9	16.3	150 15.1	34.3	328 24.9	40.7	314 55.8	02.7
06	12 47.7	224 59.8	N13 15.5	165 16.8	S12 34.7	343 27.0	N10 40.8	329 58.0	N14 02.7
07	27 50.1	240 00.8	14.6	180 18.4	35.0	358 29.1	41.0	345 00.3	02.8
08	42 52.6	255 01.7	13.7	195 20.1	35.4	13 31.3	41.1	0 02.5	02.8
M 09	57 55.1	270 02.6 ..	12.8	210 21.8 ..	35.7	28 33.4 ..	41.2	15 04.8 ..	02.9
O 10	72 57.5	285 03.5	12.0	225 23.5	36.0	43 35.5	41.3	30 07.0	02.9
N 11	88 00.0	300 04.5	11.1	240 25.2	36.4	58 37.6	41.4	45 09.3	03.0
D 12	103 02.5	315 05.4	N13 10.2	255 26.9	S12 36.7	73 39.7	N10 41.5	60 11.5	N14 03.0
A 13	118 04.9	330 06.3	09.3	270 28.5	37.1	88 41.8	41.7	75 13.8	03.1
Y 14	133 07.4	345 07.3	08.4	285 30.2	37.4	103 44.0	41.8	90 16.0	03.2
15	148 09.9	0 08.2 ..	07.6	300 31.9 ..	37.7	118 46.1 ..	41.9	105 18.3 ..	03.2
16	163 12.3	15 09.1	06.7	315 33.6	38.1	133 48.2	42.0	120 20.5	03.3
17	178 14.8	30 10.1	05.8	330 35.3	38.4	148 50.3	42.1	135 22.7	03.3
18	193 17.2	45 11.0	N13 04.9	345 36.9	S12 38.8	163 52.4	N10 42.2	150 25.0	N14 03.4
19	208 19.7	60 12.0	04.1	0 38.6	39.1	178 54.6	42.4	165 27.2	03.4
20	223 22.2	75 12.9	03.2	15 40.3	39.4	193 56.7	42.5	180 29.5	03.5
21	238 24.6	90 13.9 ..	02.3	30 42.0 ..	39.8	208 58.8 ..	42.6	195 31.7 ..	03.6
22	253 27.1	105 14.8	01.4	45 43.6	40.1	224 00.9	42.7	210 34.0	03.6
23	268 29.6	120 15.8	00.5	60 45.3	40.5	239 03.0	42.8	225 36.3	03.7
Mer. Pass.	h m 5 12.9	v 0.9	d 0.9	v 1.7	d 0.3	v 2.1	d 0.1	v 2.2	d 0.1

STARS

Name	SHA	Dec
Acamar	315 26.8	S40 18.3
Achernar	335 35.0	S57 14.2
Acrux	173 21.4	S63 06.0
Adhara	255 21.4	S28 58.4
Aldebaran	291 02.1	N16 30.3
Alioth	166 30.2	N55 58.1
Alkaid	153 07.3	N49 19.3
Al Na'ir	27 57.0	S46 57.6
Alnilam	275 57.7	S 1 12.2
Alphard	218 07.0	S 8 39.4
Alphecca	126 19.9	N26 43.3
Alpheratz	357 54.6	N29 05.0
Altair	62 18.4	N 8 52.1
Ankaa	353 26.3	S42 18.4
Antares	112 39.2	S26 25.8
Arcturus	146 05.5	N19 11.4
Atria	107 50.3	S69 01.6
Avior	234 23.0	S59 30.6
Bellatrix	278 43.9	N 6 20.8
Betelgeuse	271 13.3	N 7 24.3
Canopus	264 01.5	S52 41.8
Capella	280 50.9	N45 59.7
Deneb	49 38.4	N45 16.7
Denebola	182 44.8	N14 34.7
Diphda	349 06.7	S17 59.3
Dubhe	194 05.3	N61 45.5
Elnath	278 26.7	N28 36.3
Eltanin	90 50.6	N51 29.5
Enif	33 57.5	N 9 52.3
Fomalhaut	15 35.7	S29 37.4
Gacrux	172 13.0	S57 06.8
Gienah	176 03.5	S17 32.3
Hadar	149 03.0	S60 22.4
Hamal	328 13.1	N23 27.4
Kaus Aust.	83 57.8	S34 23.0
Kochab	137 19.0	N74 09.9
Markab	13 49.0	N15 12.1
Menkar	314 26.6	N 4 05.1
Menkent	148 20.2	S36 22.1
Miaplacidus	221 42.7	S69 43.1
Mirfak	308 56.2	N49 51.3
Nunki	76 11.3	S26 17.7
Peacock	53 35.7	S56 44.0
Pollux	243 41.3	N28 01.6
Procyon	245 11.4	N 5 13.5
Rasalhague	96 16.2	N12 33.8
Regulus	207 55.2	N11 58.3
Rigel	281 22.8	S 8 12.2
Rigil Kent.	140 06.3	S60 50.1
Sabik	102 24.6	S15 43.3
Schedar	349 52.8	N56 31.7
Shaula	96 36.2	S37 06.1
Sirius	258 43.6	S16 43.0
Spica	158 42.6	S11 09.4
Suhail	223 00.8	S43 26.0
Vega	80 45.8	N38 47.1
Zuben'ubi	137 17.2	S16 02.3

	SHA	Mer. Pass.
	° ′	h m
Venus	212 59.5	15 01
Mars	152 52.0	19 00
Jupiter	330 49.9	7 09
Saturn	317 16.9	8 03

UT	SUN GHA	Dec	MOON GHA	v	Dec	d	HP
d h	° '	° '	° '	'	° '	'	'
3 00	178 59.3	N23 00.6	310 22.1	11.6	S13 32.1	8.4	56.3
01	193 59.2	00.4	324 52.7	11.7	13 23.7	8.5	56.4
02	208 59.1	00.2	339 23.4	11.6	13 15.2	8.5	56.4
03	223 59.0	23 00.0	353 54.0	11.7	13 06.7	8.7	56.4
04	238 58.9	22 59.8	8 24.7	11.7	12 58.0	8.7	56.4
05	253 58.7	59.6	22 55.4	11.6	12 49.3	8.7	56.4
S 06	268 58.6	N22 59.4	37 26.0	11.7	S12 40.6	8.9	56.5
A 07	283 58.5	59.2	51 56.7	11.7	12 31.7	8.9	56.5
T 08	298 58.4	59.1	66 27.4	11.8	12 22.8	9.0	56.5
U 09	313 58.3	.. 58.9	80 58.2	11.7	12 13.8	9.0	56.5
R 10	328 58.2	58.7	95 28.9	11.7	12 04.8	9.2	56.6
D 11	343 58.1	58.5	109 59.6	11.8	11 55.6	9.1	56.6
A 12	358 57.9	N22 58.3	124 30.4	11.8	S11 46.5	9.3	56.6
Y 13	13 57.8	58.1	139 01.2	11.7	11 37.2	9.3	56.6
14	28 57.7	57.9	153 31.9	11.8	11 27.9	9.4	56.7
15	43 57.6	.. 57.7	168 02.7	11.8	11 18.5	9.4	56.7
16	58 57.5	57.5	182 33.5	11.8	11 09.1	9.5	56.7
17	73 57.4	57.3	197 04.3	11.9	10 59.6	9.6	56.7
18	88 57.3	N22 57.1	211 35.2	11.8	S10 50.0	9.6	56.8
19	103 57.1	56.9	226 06.0	11.8	10 40.4	9.7	56.8
20	118 57.0	56.6	240 36.8	11.9	10 30.7	9.7	56.8
21	133 56.9	.. 56.4	255 07.7	11.8	10 21.0	9.8	56.8
22	148 56.8	56.2	269 38.5	11.9	10 11.2	9.9	56.9
23	163 56.7	56.0	284 09.4	11.8	10 01.3	9.9	56.9
4 00	178 56.6	N22 55.8	298 40.2	11.9	S 9 51.4	10.0	56.9
01	193 56.5	55.6	313 11.1	11.9	9 41.4	10.0	56.9
02	208 56.3	55.4	327 42.0	11.8	9 31.4	10.1	57.0
03	223 56.2	.. 55.2	342 12.8	11.9	9 21.3	10.2	57.0
04	238 56.1	55.0	356 43.7	11.9	9 11.1	10.2	57.0
05	253 56.0	54.8	11 14.6	11.9	9 00.9	10.2	57.0
S 06	268 55.9	N22 54.6	25 45.5	11.9	S 8 50.7	10.3	57.1
U 07	283 55.8	54.4	40 16.4	11.9	8 40.4	10.4	57.1
N 08	298 55.7	54.1	54 47.3	11.9	8 30.0	10.4	57.1
D 09	313 55.6	.. 53.9	69 18.2	11.9	8 19.6	10.5	57.1
A 10	328 55.4	53.7	83 49.1	11.9	8 09.1	10.5	57.2
Y 11	343 55.3	53.5	98 20.0	11.9	7 58.6	10.5	57.2
12	358 55.2	N22 53.3	112 50.9	11.9	S 7 48.1	10.6	57.2
13	13 55.1	53.1	127 21.8	11.9	7 37.5	10.7	57.2
14	28 55.0	52.9	141 52.7	11.9	7 26.8	10.7	57.3
15	43 54.9	.. 52.6	156 23.6	11.9	7 16.1	10.7	57.3
16	58 54.8	52.4	170 54.5	11.9	7 05.4	10.8	57.3
17	73 54.7	52.2	185 25.4	11.9	6 54.6	10.8	57.3
18	88 54.5	N22 52.0	199 56.3	11.9	S 6 43.8	10.9	57.4
19	103 54.4	51.8	214 27.2	11.8	6 32.9	10.9	57.4
20	118 54.3	51.5	228 58.0	11.9	6 22.0	11.0	57.4
21	133 54.2	.. 51.3	243 28.9	11.9	6 11.0	11.0	57.4
22	148 54.1	51.1	257 59.8	11.9	6 00.0	11.0	57.5
23	163 54.0	50.9	272 30.7	11.8	5 49.0	11.1	57.5
5 00	178 53.9	N22 50.7	287 01.5	11.9	S 5 37.9	11.1	57.5
01	193 53.8	50.4	301 32.4	11.8	5 26.8	11.2	57.6
02	208 53.7	50.2	316 03.2	11.8	5 15.6	11.1	57.6
03	223 53.6	.. 50.0	330 34.0	11.9	5 04.5	11.3	57.6
04	238 53.4	49.8	345 04.9	11.8	4 53.2	11.2	57.6
05	253 53.3	49.5	359 35.7	11.8	4 42.0	11.3	57.7
M 06	268 53.2	N22 49.3	14 06.5	11.8	S 4 30.7	11.3	57.7
O 07	283 53.1	49.1	28 37.3	11.7	4 19.4	11.4	57.7
N 08	298 53.0	48.8	43 08.0	11.8	4 08.0	11.4	57.7
D 09	313 52.9	.. 48.6	57 38.8	11.7	3 56.6	11.4	57.8
A 10	328 52.8	48.4	72 09.5	11.8	3 45.2	11.5	57.8
Y 11	343 52.7	48.2	86 40.3	11.7	3 33.7	11.4	57.8
12	358 52.6	N22 47.9	101 11.0	11.7	S 3 22.3	11.5	57.9
13	13 52.5	47.7	115 41.7	11.7	3 10.8	11.6	57.9
14	28 52.4	47.5	130 12.4	11.6	2 59.2	11.5	57.9
15	43 52.2	.. 47.2	144 43.0	11.7	2 47.7	11.6	57.9
16	58 52.1	47.0	159 13.7	11.6	2 36.1	11.6	58.0
17	73 52.0	46.8	173 44.3	11.6	2 24.5	11.7	58.0
18	88 51.9	N22 46.5	188 14.9	11.6	S 2 12.8	11.6	58.0
19	103 51.8	46.3	202 45.5	11.6	2 01.2	11.7	58.0
20	118 51.7	46.0	217 16.1	11.5	1 49.5	11.7	58.1
21	133 51.6	.. 45.8	231 46.6	11.5	1 37.8	11.7	58.1
22	148 51.5	45.6	246 17.1	11.5	1 26.1	11.7	58.1
23	163 51.4	45.3	260 47.6	11.5	S 1 14.4	11.8	58.2
	SD 15.8	d 0.2	SD 15.4		15.6		15.8

Lat.	Twilight Naut.	Civil	Sunrise	Moonrise 3	4	5	6
°	h m	h m	h m	h m	h m	h m	h m
N 72	▨	▨	▨	00 32	00 16	(00 04 / 23 54)	23 43
N 70	▨	▨	▨	00 06	(23 56 / 00 01)	23 52	23 48
68	▨	▨	▨	23 49	23 50	23 51	23 51
66	////	////	00 38	23 38	23 44	23 50	23 55
64	////	////	01 46	23 30	23 40	23 49	23 58
62	////	////	02 20	23 22	23 36	23 48	24 00
60	////	01 10	02 45	23 16	23 32	23 47	24 02
N 58	////	01 52	03 04	23 10	23 29	23 46	24 04
56	////	02 20	03 21	23 05	23 26	23 46	24 06
54	01 04	02 41	03 34	23 01	23 23	23 45	24 07
52	01 43	02 58	03 46	22 56	23 21	23 45	24 09
50	02 09	03 13	03 57	22 53	23 19	23 44	24 10
45	02 53	03 42	04 19	22 44	23 14	23 43	24 13
N 40	03 22	04 03	04 36	22 38	23 10	23 43	24 15
35	03 45	04 21	04 51	22 32	23 07	23 42	24 17
30	04 03	04 36	05 03	22 27	23 04	23 41	24 19
20	04 31	05 01	05 25	22 17	22 59	23 40	24 23
N 10	04 54	05 21	05 43	22 09	22 54	23 39	24 25
0	05 12	05 38	06 01	22 02	22 50	23 39	24 28
S 10	05 29	05 55	06 18	21 54	22 46	23 38	24 31
20	05 44	06 12	06 36	21 46	22 41	23 37	24 34
30	06 00	06 30	06 56	21 37	22 36	23 36	24 37
35	06 09	06 40	07 09	21 32	22 33	23 36	24 39
40	06 18	06 52	07 22	21 26	22 30	23 35	24 42
45	06 28	07 05	07 39	21 19	22 26	23 34	24 44
S 50	06 39	07 21	07 59	21 10	22 21	23 33	24 48
52	06 44	07 28	08 08	21 07	22 19	23 33	24 49
54	06 50	07 36	08 19	21 02	22 16	23 33	24 51
56	06 56	07 44	08 31	20 57	22 14	23 32	24 53
58	07 02	07 54	08 45	20 52	22 11	23 32	24 55
S 60	07 09	08 06	09 02	20 46	22 08	23 31	24 57

Lat.	Sunset	Twilight Civil	Naut.	Moonset 3	4	5	6
°	h m	h m	h m	h m	h m	h m	h m
N 72	▨	▨	▨	06 36	08 32	10 25	12 18
N 70	▨	▨	▨	07 00	08 45	10 30	12 17
68	▨	▨	▨	07 18	08 56	10 35	12 15
66	23 25	////	////	07 33	09 05	10 39	12 14
64	22 21	////	////	07 45	09 12	10 42	12 13
62	21 47	////	////	07 55	09 19	10 44	12 12
60	21 23	22 57	////	08 04	09 24	10 47	12 11
N 58	21 03	22 15	////	08 12	09 29	10 49	12 11
56	20 47	21 48	////	08 18	09 33	10 51	12 10
54	20 34	21 27	23 03	08 24	09 37	10 52	12 09
52	20 22	21 10	22 24	08 29	09 41	10 54	12 09
50	20 12	20 55	21 59	08 34	09 44	10 55	12 08
45	19 50	20 27	21 16	08 45	09 51	10 58	12 07
N 40	19 32	20 05	20 46	08 53	09 56	11 01	12 07
35	19 18	19 47	20 24	09 01	10 01	11 03	12 06
30	19 05	19 32	20 05	09 07	10 05	11 05	12 05
20	18 44	19 08	19 37	09 18	10 13	11 08	12 04
N 10	18 25	18 48	19 15	09 28	10 19	11 11	12 03
0	18 08	18 30	18 57	09 37	10 25	11 13	12 02
S 10	17 51	18 14	18 40	09 46	10 31	11 16	12 01
20	17 33	17 57	18 24	09 55	10 37	11 18	12 00
30	17 12	17 39	18 08	10 06	10 44	11 21	11 59
35	17 00	17 28	18 00	10 12	10 48	11 23	11 58
40	16 46	17 17	17 51	10 19	10 53	11 25	11 57
45	16 30	17 04	17 41	10 27	10 58	11 27	11 56
S 50	16 10	16 48	17 29	10 37	11 04	11 30	11 55
52	16 01	16 41	17 24	10 42	11 07	11 31	11 55
54	15 50	16 33	17 19	10 47	11 10	11 33	11 54
56	15 38	16 24	17 13	10 52	11 14	11 34	11 54
58	15 24	16 15	17 07	10 58	11 18	11 36	11 53
S 60	15 07	16 03	16 59	11 05	11 22	11 37	11 52

Day	SUN Eqn. of Time 00ʰ	12ʰ	Mer. Pass.	MOON Mer. Pass. Upper	Lower	Age	Phase
d	m s	m s	h m	h m	h m	d	%
3	04 02	04 08	12 04	03 25	15 49	20	80
4	04 13	04 19	12 04	04 14	16 38	21	71
5	04 24	04 30	12 04	05 02	17 26	22	61

UT	ARIES	VENUS −4.5		MARS −0.3		JUPITER −2.3		SATURN +0.4		STARS		
	GHA	GHA	Dec	GHA	Dec	GHA	Dec	GHA	Dec	Name	SHA	Dec
d h	° ′	° ′	° ′	° ′	° ′	° ′	° ′	° ′	° ′		° ′	° ′
6 00	283 32.0	135 16.7	N12 59.7	75 47.0	S12 40.8	254 05.2	N10 42.9	240 38.5	N14 03.7	Acamar	315 26.8	S40 18.3
01	298 34.5	150 17.7	58.8	90 48.7	41.1	269 07.3	43.1	255 40.8	03.8	Achernar	335 35.0	S57 14.2
02	313 37.0	165 18.6	57.9	105 50.3	41.5	284 09.4	43.2	270 43.0	03.8	Acrux	173 21.5	S63 06.0
03	328 39.4	180 19.6 ..	57.0	120 52.0 ..	41.8	299 11.5 ..	43.3	285 45.3 ..	03.9	Adhara	255 21.4	S28 58.3
04	343 41.9	195 20.6	56.2	135 53.7	42.2	314 13.6	43.4	300 47.5	03.9	Aldebaran	291 02.1	N16 30.3
05	358 44.4	210 21.5	55.3	150 55.3	42.5	329 15.8	43.5	315 49.8	04.0			
06	13 46.8	225 22.5	N12 54.4	165 57.0	S12 42.9	344 17.9	N10 43.6	330 52.0	N14 04.1	Alioth	166 30.2	N55 58.2
07	28 49.3	240 23.5	53.5	180 58.7	43.2	359 20.0	43.8	345 54.3	04.1	Alkaid	153 07.3	N49 19.3
T 08	43 51.7	255 24.4	52.7	196 00.3	43.5	14 22.1	43.9	0 56.5	04.2	Al Na'ir	27 57.0	S46 57.6
U 09	58 54.2	270 25.4 ..	51.8	211 02.0 ..	43.9	29 24.2 ..	44.0	15 58.8 ..	04.2	Alnilam	275 57.7	S 1 12.2
E 10	73 56.7	285 26.4	50.9	226 03.7	44.2	44 26.4	44.1	31 01.0	04.3	Alphard	218 07.0	S 8 39.4
S 11	88 59.1	300 27.4	50.0	241 05.3	44.6	59 28.5	44.2	46 03.3	04.3			
D 12	104 01.6	315 28.3	N12 49.2	256 07.0	S12 44.9	74 30.6	N10 44.3	61 05.5	N14 04.4	Alphecca	126 19.9	N26 43.3
A 13	119 04.1	330 29.3	48.3	271 08.6	45.3	89 32.7	44.5	76 07.8	04.4	Alpheratz	357 54.6	N29 05.1
Y 14	134 06.5	345 30.3	47.4	286 10.3	45.6	104 34.8	44.6	91 10.0	04.5	Altair	62 18.4	N 8 52.1
15	149 09.0	0 31.3 ..	46.5	301 12.0 ..	46.0	119 37.0 ..	44.7	106 12.3 ..	04.5	Ankaa	353 26.3	S42 18.4
16	164 11.5	15 32.3	45.7	316 13.6	46.3	134 39.1	44.8	121 14.5	04.6	Antares	112 39.2	S26 25.8
17	179 13.9	30 33.3	44.8	331 15.3	46.7	149 41.2	44.9	136 16.8	04.7			
18	194 16.4	45 34.3	N12 43.9	346 16.9	S12 47.0	164 43.3	N10 45.0	151 19.0	N14 04.7	Arcturus	146 05.5	N19 11.4
19	209 18.8	60 35.3	43.0	1 18.6	47.3	179 45.5	45.1	166 21.3	04.8	Atria	107 50.3	S69 01.6
20	224 21.3	75 36.2	42.2	16 20.2	47.7	194 47.6	45.3	181 23.5	04.8	Avior	234 23.0	S59 30.6
21	239 23.8	90 37.2 ..	41.3	31 21.9 ..	48.0	209 49.7 ..	45.4	196 25.8 ..	04.9	Bellatrix	278 43.9	N 6 20.8
22	254 26.2	105 38.2	40.4	46 23.6	48.4	224 51.8	45.5	211 28.0	04.9	Betelgeuse	271 13.3	N 7 24.3
23	269 28.7	120 39.3	39.5	61 25.2	48.7	239 54.0	45.6	226 30.3	05.0			
7 00	284 31.2	135 40.3	N12 38.7	76 26.9	S12 49.1	254 56.1	N10 45.7	241 32.5	N14 05.0	Canopus	264 01.5	S52 41.8
01	299 33.6	150 41.3	37.8	91 28.5	49.4	269 58.2	45.8	256 34.8	05.1	Capella	280 50.9	N45 59.7
02	314 36.1	165 42.3	36.9	106 30.2	49.8	285 00.3	45.9	271 37.1	05.2	Deneb	49 38.4	N45 16.7
03	329 38.6	180 43.3 ..	36.0	121 31.8 ..	50.1	300 02.5 ..	46.1	286 39.3 ..	05.2	Denebola	182 44.8	N14 34.7
04	344 41.0	195 44.3	35.2	136 33.5	50.5	315 04.6	46.2	301 41.6	05.3	Diphda	349 06.7	S17 59.3
05	359 43.5	210 45.3	34.3	151 35.1	50.8	330 06.7	46.3	316 43.8	05.3			
06	14 46.0	225 46.3	N12 33.4	166 36.8	S12 51.2	345 08.8	N10 46.4	331 46.1	N14 05.4	Dubhe	194 05.3	N61 45.5
W 07	29 48.4	240 47.4	32.5	181 38.4	51.5	0 11.0	46.5	346 48.3	05.4	Elnath	278 26.7	N28 36.3
E 08	44 50.9	255 48.4	31.7	196 40.0	51.9	15 13.1	46.6	1 50.6	05.5	Eltanin	90 50.6	N51 29.5
D 09	59 53.3	270 49.4 ..	30.8	211 41.7 ..	52.2	30 15.2 ..	46.7	16 52.8 ..	05.5	Enif	33 57.5	N 9 52.4
N 10	74 55.8	285 50.4	29.9	226 43.3	52.6	45 17.3	46.9	31 55.1	05.6	Fomalhaut	15 35.7	S29 37.4
E 11	89 58.3	300 51.5	29.0	241 45.0	52.9	60 19.5	47.0	46 57.3	05.6			
S 12	105 00.7	315 52.5	N12 28.2	256 46.6	S12 53.3	75 21.6	N10 47.1	61 59.6	N14 05.7	Gacrux	172 13.0	S57 06.8
D 13	120 03.2	330 53.5	27.3	271 48.3	53.6	90 23.7	47.2	77 01.9	05.7	Gienah	176 03.5	S17 32.3
A 14	135 05.7	345 54.6	26.4	286 49.9	54.0	105 25.9	47.3	92 04.1	05.8	Hadar	149 03.1	S60 22.4
Y 15	150 08.1	0 55.6 ..	25.6	301 51.5 ..	54.3	120 28.0 ..	47.4	107 06.4 ..	05.9	Hamal	328 13.1	N23 27.4
16	165 10.6	15 56.6	24.7	316 53.2	54.7	135 30.1	47.5	122 08.6	05.9	Kaus Aust.	83 57.7	S34 23.0
17	180 13.1	30 57.7	23.8	331 54.8	55.0	150 32.2	47.7	137 10.9	06.0			
18	195 15.5	45 58.7	N12 22.9	346 56.5	S12 55.4	165 34.4	N10 47.8	152 13.1	N14 06.0	Kochab	137 19.1	N74 09.9
19	210 18.0	60 59.8	22.1	1 58.1	55.7	180 36.5	47.9	167 15.4	06.1	Markab	13 48.9	N15 12.1
20	225 20.5	76 00.8	21.2	16 59.7	56.1	195 38.6	48.0	182 17.6	06.1	Menkar	314 26.5	N 4 05.1
21	240 22.9	91 01.9 ..	20.3	32 01.4 ..	56.4	210 40.8 ..	48.1	197 19.9 ..	06.2	Menkent	148 20.2	S36 22.1
22	255 25.4	106 02.9	19.5	47 03.0	56.8	225 42.9	48.2	212 22.2	06.2	Miaplacidus	221 42.7	S69 43.1
23	270 27.8	121 04.0	18.6	62 04.6	57.1	240 45.0	48.3	227 24.4	06.3			
8 00	285 30.3	136 05.0	N12 17.7	77 06.3	S12 57.5	255 47.1	N10 48.4	242 26.7	N14 06.3	Mirfak	308 56.2	N49 51.2
01	300 32.8	151 06.1	16.8	92 07.9	57.8	270 49.3	48.6	257 28.9	06.4	Nunki	76 11.3	S26 17.7
02	315 35.2	166 07.2	16.0	107 09.5	58.2	285 51.4	48.7	272 31.2	06.4	Peacock	53 35.7	S56 44.0
03	330 37.7	181 08.2 ..	15.1	122 11.2 ..	58.5	300 53.5 ..	48.8	287 33.4 ..	06.5	Pollux	243 41.3	N28 01.6
04	345 40.2	196 09.3	14.2	137 12.8	58.9	315 55.7	48.9	302 35.7	06.6	Procyon	245 11.4	N 5 13.5
05	0 42.6	211 10.4	13.4	152 14.4	59.2	330 57.8	49.0	317 37.9	06.6			
06	15 45.1	226 11.4	N12 12.5	167 16.0	S12 59.6	345 59.9	N10 49.1	332 40.2	N14 06.7	Rasalhague	96 16.2	N12 33.8
07	30 47.6	241 12.5	11.6	182 17.7	12 59.9	1 02.1	49.2	347 42.5	06.7	Regulus	207 55.3	N11 58.3
T 08	45 50.0	256 13.6	10.7	197 19.3	13 00.3	16 04.2	49.3	2 44.7	06.8	Rigel	281 22.8	S 8 12.2
H 09	60 52.5	271 14.7 ..	09.9	212 20.9 ..	00.6	31 06.3 ..	49.4	17 47.0 ..	06.8	Rigil Kent.	140 06.3	S60 50.1
U 10	75 54.9	286 15.7	09.0	227 22.5	01.0	46 08.5	49.6	32 49.2	06.9	Sabik	102 24.6	S15 43.3
R 11	90 57.4	301 16.8	08.1	242 24.2	01.4	61 10.6	49.7	47 51.5	06.9			
S 12	105 59.9	316 17.9	N12 07.3	257 25.8	S13 01.7	76 12.7	N10 49.8	62 53.7	N14 07.0	Schedar	349 52.8	N56 31.7
D 13	121 02.3	331 19.0	06.4	272 27.4	02.1	91 14.9	49.9	77 56.0	07.0	Shaula	96 36.2	S37 06.1
A 14	136 04.8	346 20.1	05.5	287 29.0	02.4	106 17.0	50.0	92 58.3	07.1	Sirius	258 43.6	S16 43.0
Y 15	151 07.3	1 21.2 ..	04.7	302 30.7 ..	02.8	121 19.1 ..	50.1	108 00.5 ..	07.1	Spica	158 42.6	S11 09.4
16	166 09.7	16 22.3	03.8	317 32.3	03.1	136 21.2	50.2	123 02.8	07.2	Suhail	223 00.8	S43 26.0
17	181 12.2	31 23.3	02.9	332 33.9	03.5	151 23.4	50.3	138 05.0	07.2			
18	196 14.7	46 24.4	N12 02.1	347 35.5	S13 03.8	166 25.5	N10 50.4	153 07.3	N14 07.3	Vega	80 45.8	N38 47.1
19	211 17.1	61 25.5	01.2	2 37.1	04.2	181 27.7	50.6	168 09.6	07.3	Zuben'ubi	137 17.2	S16 02.3
20	226 19.6	76 26.6	12 00.3	17 38.7	04.6	196 29.8	50.7	183 11.8	07.4		SHA	Mer. Pass.
21	241 22.1	91 27.8	11 59.4	32 40.4 ..	04.9	211 31.9 ..	50.8	198 14.1 ..	07.5		° ′	h m
22	256 24.5	106 28.9	58.6	47 42.0	05.3	226 34.1	50.9	213 16.3	07.5	Venus	211 09.1	14 56
23	271 27.0	121 30.0	57.7	62 43.6	05.6	241 36.2	51.0	228 18.6	07.6	Mars	151 55.7	18 52
	h m									Jupiter	330 24.9	6 59
Mer. Pass. 5 01.1		v 1.0	d 0.9	v 1.6	d 0.3	v 2.1	d 0.1	v 2.3	d 0.1	Saturn	317 01.4	7 53

SUN and MOON

UT (d h)	SUN GHA	SUN Dec	MOON GHA	v	Dec	d	HP
6 00	178 51.3	N22 45.1	275 18.1	11.4	S 1 02.6	11.7	58.2
01	193 51.2	44.8	289 48.5	11.4	0 50.9	11.8	58.2
02	208 51.1	44.6	304 18.9	11.4	0 39.1	11.8	58.2
03	223 51.0	.. 44.4	318 49.3	11.4	0 27.3	11.8	58.3
04	238 50.8	44.1	333 19.7	11.3	0 15.5	11.9	58.3
05	253 50.7	43.9	347 50.0	11.3	S 0 03.6	11.8	58.3
06	268 50.6	N22 43.6	2 20.3	11.2	N 0 08.2	11.8	58.4
07	283 50.5	43.4	16 50.5	11.3	0 20.0	11.9	58.4
08	298 50.4	43.1	31 20.8	11.2	0 31.9	11.8	58.4
09	313 50.3	.. 42.9	45 51.0	11.1	0 43.7	11.9	58.4
10	328 50.2	42.7	60 21.1	11.2	0 55.6	11.9	58.5
11	343 50.1	42.4	74 51.3	11.1	1 07.5	11.9	58.5
12	358 50.0	N22 42.2	89 21.4	11.0	N 1 19.4	11.9	58.5
13	13 49.9	41.9	103 51.4	11.1	1 31.3	11.8	58.5
14	28 49.8	41.7	118 21.5	11.0	1 43.1	11.9	58.6
15	43 49.7	.. 41.4	132 51.5	10.9	1 55.0	11.9	58.6
16	58 49.6	41.2	147 21.4	10.9	2 06.9	11.9	58.6
17	73 49.5	40.9	161 51.3	10.9	2 18.8	11.9	58.7
18	88 49.4	N22 40.7	176 21.2	10.8	N 2 30.7	11.9	58.7
19	103 49.3	40.4	190 51.0	10.8	2 42.6	11.9	58.7
20	118 49.2	40.1	205 20.8	10.8	2 54.5	11.9	58.7
21	133 49.1	.. 39.9	219 50.6	10.7	3 06.4	11.8	58.8
22	148 49.0	39.6	234 20.3	10.6	3 18.2	11.9	58.8
23	163 48.8	39.4	248 49.9	10.6	3 30.1	11.9	58.8
7 00	178 48.7	N22 39.1	263 19.5	10.6	N 3 42.0	11.8	58.8
01	193 48.6	38.9	277 49.1	10.5	3 53.8	11.8	58.9
02	208 48.5	38.6	292 18.6	10.5	4 05.6	11.9	58.9
03	223 48.4	.. 38.4	306 48.1	10.4	4 17.5	11.8	58.9
04	238 48.3	38.1	321 17.5	10.4	4 29.3	11.8	59.0
05	253 48.2	37.8	335 46.9	10.3	4 41.1	11.8	59.0
06	268 48.1	N22 37.6	350 16.2	10.3	N 4 52.9	11.8	59.0
07	283 48.0	37.3	4 45.5	10.2	5 04.7	11.7	59.0
08	298 47.9	37.0	19 14.7	10.2	5 16.4	11.7	59.1
09	313 47.8	.. 36.8	33 43.9	10.1	5 28.1	11.8	59.1
10	328 47.7	36.5	48 13.0	10.1	5 39.9	11.7	59.1
11	343 47.6	36.3	62 42.1	10.0	5 51.6	11.6	59.1
12	358 47.5	N22 36.0	77 11.1	10.0	N 6 03.2	11.7	59.2
13	13 47.4	35.7	91 40.1	9.9	6 14.9	11.6	59.2
14	28 47.3	35.5	106 09.0	9.8	6 26.5	11.6	59.2
15	43 47.2	.. 35.2	120 37.8	9.8	6 38.1	11.6	59.3
16	58 47.1	34.9	135 06.6	9.7	6 49.7	11.5	59.3
17	73 47.0	34.7	149 35.3	9.7	7 01.2	11.5	59.3
18	88 46.9	N22 34.4	164 04.0	9.6	N 7 12.7	11.5	59.3
19	103 46.8	34.1	178 32.6	9.6	7 24.2	11.5	59.4
20	118 46.7	33.9	193 01.2	9.5	7 35.7	11.4	59.4
21	133 46.6	.. 33.6	207 29.7	9.4	7 47.1	11.4	59.4
22	148 46.5	33.3	221 58.1	9.4	7 58.5	11.3	59.4
23	163 46.4	33.0	236 26.5	9.3	8 09.8	11.3	59.5
8 00	178 46.3	N22 32.8	250 54.8	9.2	N 8 21.1	11.3	59.5
01	193 46.2	32.5	265 23.0	9.2	8 32.4	11.2	59.5
02	208 46.1	32.2	279 51.2	9.1	8 43.6	11.2	59.5
03	223 46.0	.. 31.9	294 19.3	9.1	8 54.8	11.2	59.6
04	238 45.9	31.7	308 47.4	9.0	9 06.0	11.1	59.6
05	253 45.8	31.4	323 15.4	8.9	9 17.1	11.0	59.6
06	268 45.7	N22 31.1	337 43.3	8.8	N 9 28.1	11.0	59.6
07	283 45.6	30.8	352 11.1	8.8	9 39.1	11.0	59.7
08	298 45.5	30.6	6 38.9	8.7	9 50.1	10.9	59.7
09	313 45.4	.. 30.3	21 06.6	8.7	10 01.0	10.9	59.7
10	328 45.3	30.0	35 34.3	8.6	10 11.9	10.8	59.7
11	343 45.2	29.7	50 01.9	8.5	10 22.7	10.7	59.7
12	358 45.1	N22 29.4	64 29.4	8.4	N10 33.4	10.7	59.8
13	13 45.0	29.2	78 56.8	8.4	10 44.1	10.7	59.8
14	28 44.9	28.9	93 24.2	8.3	10 54.8	10.5	59.8
15	43 44.8	.. 28.6	107 51.5	8.3	11 05.3	10.6	59.8
16	58 44.7	28.3	122 18.8	8.1	11 15.9	10.4	59.9
17	73 44.6	28.0	136 45.9	8.1	11 26.3	10.4	59.9
18	88 44.5	N22 27.7	151 13.0	8.0	N11 36.7	10.4	59.9
19	103 44.4	27.5	165 40.0	8.0	11 47.1	10.2	59.9
20	118 44.3	27.2	180 07.0	7.9	11 57.3	10.2	59.9
21	133 44.2	.. 26.9	194 33.9	7.8	12 07.5	10.2	60.0
22	148 44.1	26.6	209 00.7	7.7	12 17.7	10.0	60.0
23	163 44.0	26.3	223 27.4	7.7	N12 27.7	10.0	60.0
	SD 15.8	d 0.3	SD 15.9		16.1		16.3

Twilight / Sunrise / Moonrise

Lat.	Naut.	Civil	Sunrise	Moonrise 6	7	8	9
N 72	□	□	□	23 43	23 31	23 17	22 56
N 70	□	□	□	23 48	23 43	23 39	23 35
68	□	□	□	23 51	23 53	23 56	24 02
66	////	////	00 55	23 55	24 01	00 01	00 09
64	////	////	01 53	23 58	24 08	00 08	00 21
62	////	////	02 25	24 00	00 00	00 14	00 31
60	////	01 18	02 49	24 02	00 02	00 19	00 39
N 58	////	01 58	03 08	24 04	00 04	00 24	00 46
56	////	02 24	03 24	24 06	00 06	00 28	00 53
54	01 12	02 45	03 37	24 07	00 07	00 31	00 59
52	01 48	03 01	03 49	24 09	00 09	00 35	01 04
50	02 13	03 16	03 59	24 10	00 10	00 38	01 09
45	02 55	03 44	04 21	24 13	00 13	00 44	01 20
N 40	03 24	04 05	04 38	24 15	00 15	00 50	01 28
35	03 47	04 23	04 52	24 17	00 17	00 55	01 36
30	04 05	04 38	05 05	24 19	00 19	00 59	01 43
20	04 33	05 02	05 26	24 23	00 23	01 07	01 54
N 10	04 54	05 21	05 44	24 25	00 25	01 13	02 04
0	05 13	05 39	06 01	24 28	00 28	01 20	02 14
S 10	05 29	05 55	06 18	24 31	00 31	01 26	02 24
20	05 45	06 12	06 36	24 34	00 34	01 33	02 34
30	06 00	06 30	06 56	24 37	00 37	01 41	02 46
35	06 09	06 40	07 08	24 39	00 39	01 45	02 53
40	06 18	06 51	07 22	24 42	00 42	01 51	03 01
45	06 27	07 04	07 38	24 44	00 44	01 57	03 11
S 50	06 38	07 20	07 57	24 48	00 48	02 04	03 22
52	06 43	07 27	08 07	24 49	00 49	02 07	03 27
54	06 49	07 34	08 17	24 51	00 51	02 11	03 33
56	06 54	07 43	08 29	24 53	00 53	02 15	03 39
58	07 01	07 53	08 43	24 55	00 55	02 20	03 47
S 60	07 08	08 04	08 59	24 57	00 57	02 25	03 55

Sunset / Twilight / Moonset

Lat.	Sunset	Civil	Naut.	Moonset 6	7	8	9
N 72	□	□	□	12 18	14 16	16 21	18 41
N 70	□	□	□	12 17	14 06	16 01	18 03
68	□	□	□	12 15	13 59	15 46	17 37
66	23 10	////	////	12 14	13 52	15 33	17 17
64	22 15	////	////	12 13	13 47	15 23	17 01
62	21 43	////	////	12 12	13 42	15 14	16 48
60	21 20	22 49	////	12 11	13 38	15 07	16 37
N 58	21 01	22 11	////	12 11	13 34	15 00	16 27
56	20 45	21 45	////	12 10	13 31	14 55	16 19
54	20 32	21 24	22 56	12 09	13 28	14 49	16 11
52	20 20	21 08	22 20	12 09	13 26	14 45	16 05
50	20 10	20 54	21 56	12 08	13 24	14 41	15 59
45	19 49	20 25	21 14	12 07	13 18	14 31	15 46
N 40	19 32	20 04	20 45	12 07	13 14	14 24	15 35
35	19 17	19 47	20 23	12 06	13 11	14 17	15 26
30	19 05	19 32	20 05	12 05	13 07	14 12	15 18
20	18 44	19 08	19 37	12 04	13 02	14 02	15 04
N 10	18 25	18 48	19 15	12 03	12 57	13 53	14 52
0	18 08	18 31	18 57	12 02	12 52	13 45	14 41
S 10	17 52	18 14	18 41	12 01	12 48	13 37	14 30
20	17 34	17 58	18 25	12 00	12 43	13 29	14 18
30	17 14	17 40	18 09	11 59	12 38	13 19	14 04
35	17 02	17 30	18 01	11 58	12 34	13 13	13 56
40	16 48	17 18	17 52	11 57	12 31	13 07	13 47
45	16 32	17 06	17 43	11 56	12 27	13 00	13 37
S 50	16 12	16 50	17 31	11 55	12 22	12 51	13 24
52	16 03	16 43	17 27	11 55	12 19	12 47	13 19
54	15 53	16 36	17 21	11 54	12 17	12 42	13 12
56	15 41	16 27	17 15	11 54	12 14	12 37	13 05
58	15 27	16 17	17 09	11 53	12 11	12 32	12 57
S 60	15 11	16 06	17 02	11 52	12 08	12 26	12 48

SUN / MOON

Day	Eqn. of Time 00h	Eqn. of Time 12h	Mer. Pass.	Mer. Pass. Upper	Lower	Age	Phase
	m s	m s	h m	h m	h m	d	%
6	04 35	04 40	12 05	05 50	18 15	23	50
7	04 45	04 50	12 05	06 40	19 06	24	39
8	04 55	04 59	12 05	07 32	20 00	25	28

UT	ARIES GHA	VENUS −4.5 GHA	Dec	MARS −0.3 GHA	Dec	JUPITER −2.3 GHA	Dec	SATURN +0.4 GHA	Dec	STARS Name	SHA	Dec
d h	° ′	° ′	° ′	° ′	° ′	° ′	° ′	° ′	° ′		° ′	° ′
9 00	286 29.4	136 31.1	N11 56.8	77 45.2	S13 06.0	256 38.3	N10 51.1	243 20.9	N14 07.6	Acamar	315 26.8	S40 18.3
01	301 31.9	151 32.2	56.0	92 46.8	06.3	271 40.5	51.2	258 23.1	07.7	Achernar	335 34.9	S57 14.2
02	316 34.4	166 33.3	55.1	107 48.4	06.7	286 42.6	51.3	273 25.4	07.7	Acrux	173 21.5	S63 06.0
03	331 36.8	181 34.4 ..	54.2	122 50.0 ..	07.0	301 44.7 ..	51.4	288 27.6 ..	07.8	Adhara	255 21.4	S28 58.3
04	346 39.3	196 35.5	53.4	137 51.6	07.4	316 46.9	51.5	303 29.9	07.8	Aldebaran	291 02.1	N16 30.3
05	1 41.8	211 36.7	52.5	152 53.3	07.8	331 49.0	51.7	318 32.1	07.9			
06	16 44.2	226 37.8	N11 51.6	167 54.9	S13 08.1	346 51.1	N10 51.8	333 34.4	N14 07.9	Alioth	166 30.2	N55 58.1
07	31 46.7	241 38.9	50.8	182 56.5	08.5	1 53.3	51.9	348 36.7	08.0	Alkaid	153 07.3	N49 19.3
08	46 49.2	256 40.0	49.9	197 58.1	08.8	16 55.4	52.0	3 38.9	08.0	Al Na'ir	27 56.9	S46 57.6
F 09	61 51.6	271 41.2 ..	49.1	212 59.7 ..	09.2	31 57.6 ..	52.1	18 41.2 ..	08.1	Alnilam	275 57.7	S 1 12.2
R 10	76 54.1	286 42.3	48.2	228 01.3	09.6	46 59.7	52.2	33 43.5	08.1	Alphard	218 07.0	S 8 39.4
I 11	91 56.6	301 43.4	47.3	243 02.9	09.9	62 01.8	52.3	48 45.7	08.2			
D 12	106 59.0	316 44.6	N11 46.5	258 04.5	S13 10.3	77 04.0	N10 52.4	63 48.0	N14 08.2	Alphecca	126 19.9	N26 43.3
A 13	122 01.5	331 45.7	45.6	273 06.1	10.6	92 06.1	52.5	78 50.2	08.3	Alpheratz	357 54.6	N29 05.1
Y 14	137 03.9	346 46.9	44.7	288 07.7	11.0	107 08.2	52.6	93 52.5	08.3	Altair	62 18.4	N 8 52.1
15	152 06.4	1 48.0 ..	43.9	303 09.3 ..	11.4	122 10.4 ..	52.7	108 54.8 ..	08.4	Ankaa	353 26.3	S42 18.4
16	167 08.9	16 49.2	43.0	318 10.9	11.7	137 12.5	52.9	123 57.0	08.4	Antares	112 39.2	S26 25.8
17	182 11.3	31 50.3	42.1	333 12.5	12.1	152 14.7	53.0	138 59.3	08.5			
18	197 13.8	46 51.5	N11 41.3	348 14.1	S13 12.4	167 16.8	N10 53.1	154 01.5	N14 08.6	Arcturus	146 05.5	N19 11.4
19	212 16.3	61 52.6	40.4	3 15.7	12.8	182 18.9	53.2	169 03.8	08.6	Atria	107 50.3	S69 01.6
20	227 18.7	76 53.8	39.5	18 17.3	13.2	197 21.1	53.3	184 06.1	08.7	Avior	234 23.0	S59 30.6
21	242 21.2	91 54.9 ..	38.7	33 18.9 ..	13.5	212 23.2 ..	53.4	199 08.3 ..	08.7	Bellatrix	278 43.9	N 6 20.9
22	257 23.7	106 56.1	37.8	48 20.5	13.9	227 25.4	53.5	214 10.6	08.8	Betelgeuse	271 13.3	N 7 24.3
23	272 26.1	121 57.3	37.0	63 22.1	14.2	242 27.5	53.6	229 12.8	08.8			
10 00	287 28.6	136 58.4	N11 36.1	78 23.7	S13 14.6	257 29.6	N10 53.7	244 15.1	N14 08.9	Canopus	264 01.5	S52 41.8
01	302 31.1	151 59.6	35.2	93 25.3	15.0	272 31.8	53.8	259 17.4	08.9	Capella	280 50.9	N45 59.6
02	317 33.5	167 00.8	34.4	108 26.9	15.3	287 33.9	53.9	274 19.6	09.0	Deneb	49 38.4	N45 16.7
03	332 36.0	182 01.9 ..	33.5	123 28.4 ..	15.7	302 36.1 ..	54.0	289 21.9 ..	09.0	Denebola	182 44.8	N14 34.7
04	347 38.4	197 03.1	32.7	138 30.0	16.0	317 38.2	54.2	304 24.2	09.1	Diphda	349 06.7	S17 59.3
05	2 40.9	212 04.3	31.8	153 31.6	16.4	332 40.3	54.3	319 26.4	09.1			
06	17 43.4	227 05.5	N11 30.9	168 33.2	S13 16.8	347 42.5	N10 54.4	334 28.7	N14 09.2	Dubhe	194 05.3	N61 45.5
07	32 45.8	242 06.6	30.1	183 34.8	17.1	2 44.6	54.5	349 30.9	09.2	Elnath	278 26.6	N28 36.3
S 08	47 48.3	257 07.8	29.2	198 36.4	17.5	17 46.8	54.6	4 33.2	09.3	Eltanin	90 50.6	N51 29.6
A 09	62 50.8	272 09.0 ..	28.3	213 38.0 ..	17.9	32 48.9 ..	54.7	19 35.5 ..	09.3	Enif	33 57.5	N 9 52.4
T 10	77 53.2	287 10.2	27.5	228 39.6	18.2	47 51.1	54.8	34 37.7	09.4	Fomalhaut	15 35.7	S29 37.4
U 11	92 55.7	302 11.4	26.6	243 41.1	18.6	62 53.2	54.9	49 40.0	09.4			
R 12	107 58.2	317 12.6	N11 25.8	258 42.7	S13 18.9	77 55.3	N10 55.0	64 42.3	N14 09.5	Gacrux	172 13.0	S57 06.8
D 13	123 00.6	332 13.8	24.9	273 44.3	19.3	92 57.5	55.1	79 44.5	09.5	Gienah	176 03.5	S17 32.3
A 14	138 03.1	347 15.0	24.1	288 45.9	19.7	107 59.6	55.2	94 46.8	09.6	Hadar	149 03.1	S60 22.4
Y 15	153 05.6	2 16.2 ..	23.2	303 47.5 ..	20.0	123 01.8 ..	55.3	109 49.1 ..	09.6	Hamal	328 13.1	N23 27.4
16	168 08.0	17 17.4	22.3	318 49.1	20.4	138 03.9	55.4	124 51.3	09.7	Kaus Aust.	83 57.7	S34 23.0
17	183 10.5	32 18.6	21.5	333 50.6	20.8	153 06.1	55.5	139 53.6	09.7			
18	198 12.9	47 19.8	N11 20.6	348 52.2	S13 21.1	168 08.2	N10 55.7	154 55.9	N14 09.8	Kochab	137 19.2	N74 09.9
19	213 15.4	62 21.0	19.8	3 53.8	21.5	183 10.3	55.8	169 58.1	09.8	Markab	13 48.9	N15 12.1
20	228 17.9	77 22.2	18.9	18 55.4	21.9	198 12.5	55.9	185 00.4	09.9	Menkar	314 26.5	N 4 05.2
21	243 20.3	92 23.4 ..	18.0	33 57.0 ..	22.2	213 14.6 ..	56.0	200 02.6 ..	09.9	Menkent	148 20.2	S36 22.1
22	258 22.8	107 24.7	17.2	48 58.5	22.6	228 16.8	56.1	215 04.9	10.0	Miaplacidus	221 42.7	S69 43.1
23	273 25.3	122 25.9	16.3	64 00.1	23.0	243 18.9	56.2	230 07.2	10.0			
11 00	288 27.7	137 27.1	N11 15.5	79 01.7	S13 23.3	258 21.1	N10 56.3	245 09.4	N14 10.1	Mirfak	308 56.1	N49 51.2
01	303 30.2	152 28.3	14.6	94 03.3	23.7	273 23.2	56.4	260 11.7	10.1	Nunki	76 11.3	S26 17.7
02	318 32.7	167 29.6	13.8	109 04.8	24.1	288 25.4	56.5	275 14.0	10.2	Peacock	53 35.7	S56 44.0
03	333 35.1	182 30.8 ..	12.9	124 06.4 ..	24.4	303 27.5 ..	56.6	290 16.2 ..	10.2	Pollux	243 41.3	N28 01.6
04	348 37.6	197 32.0	12.1	139 08.0	24.8	318 29.7	56.7	305 18.5	10.3	Procyon	245 11.4	N 5 13.6
05	3 40.0	212 33.3	11.2	154 09.5	25.2	333 31.8	56.8	320 20.8	10.3			
06	18 42.5	227 34.5	N11 10.3	169 11.1	S13 25.5	348 34.0	N10 56.9	335 23.0	N14 10.4	Rasalhague	96 16.2	N12 33.8
07	33 45.0	242 35.7	09.5	184 12.7	25.9	3 36.1	57.0	350 25.3	10.4	Regulus	207 55.3	N11 58.3
08	48 47.4	257 37.0	08.6	199 14.2	26.3	18 38.3	57.1	5 27.6	10.5	Rigel	281 22.8	S 8 12.2
S 09	63 49.9	272 38.2 ..	07.8	214 15.8 ..	26.6	33 40.4 ..	57.2	20 29.8 ..	10.5	Rigil Kent.	140 06.3	S60 50.1
U 10	78 52.4	287 39.5	06.9	229 17.4	27.0	48 42.5	57.3	35 32.1	10.6	Sabik	102 24.6	S15 43.3
N 11	93 54.8	302 40.7	06.1	244 18.9	27.4	63 44.7	57.4	50 34.4	10.6			
D 12	108 57.3	317 42.0	N11 05.2	259 20.5	S13 27.7	78 46.8	N10 57.5	65 36.6	N14 10.7	Schedar	349 52.8	N56 31.7
A 13	123 59.8	332 43.2	04.4	274 22.1	28.1	93 49.0	57.7	80 38.9	10.7	Shaula	96 36.2	S37 06.1
Y 14	139 02.2	347 44.5	03.5	289 23.6	28.5	108 51.1	57.8	95 41.2	10.8	Sirius	258 43.6	S16 43.0
15	154 04.7	2 45.7 ..	02.7	304 25.2 ..	28.8	123 53.3 ..	57.9	110 43.4 ..	10.8	Spica	158 42.6	S11 09.4
16	169 07.2	17 47.0	01.8	319 26.8	29.2	138 55.4	58.0	125 45.7	10.9	Suhail	223 00.8	S43 25.9
17	184 09.6	32 48.3	01.0	334 28.3	29.6	153 57.6	58.1	140 48.0	10.9			
18	199 12.1	47 49.5	N11 00.1	349 29.9	S13 29.9	168 59.7	N10 58.2	155 50.2	N14 11.0	Vega	80 45.8	N38 47.2
19	214 14.5	62 50.8	10 59.3	4 31.4	30.3	184 01.9	58.3	170 52.5	11.0	Zuben'ubi	137 17.2	S16 02.3
20	229 17.0	77 52.1	58.4	19 33.0	30.7	199 04.0	58.4	185 54.8	11.1			
21	244 19.5	92 53.3 ..	57.6	34 34.6 ..	31.0	214 06.2 ..	58.5	200 57.0 ..	11.1		SHA	Mer. Pass.
22	259 21.9	107 54.6	56.7	49 36.1	31.4	229 08.3	58.6	215 59.3	11.2	Venus	209 29.8	14 51
23	274 24.4	122 55.9	55.9	64 37.7	31.8	244 10.5	58.7	231 01.6	11.2	Mars	150 55.1	18 44
Mer. Pass. 4 49.3		v 1.2 d 0.9		v 1.6 d 0.4		v 2.1 d 0.1		v 2.3 d 0.1		Jupiter	330 01.0	6 49
										Saturn	316 46.5	7 42

SUN / MOON

UT	SUN GHA	SUN Dec	MOON GHA	v	MOON Dec	d	HP
d h	° ′	° ′	° ′	′	° ′	′	′
9 00	178 44.0	N22 26.0	237 54.1	7.6	N12 37.7	10.0	60.0
01	193 43.9	25.7	252 20.7	7.5	12 47.7	9.8	60.0
02	208 43.8	25.4	266 47.2	7.4	12 57.5	9.8	60.1
03	223 43.7 ..	25.2	281 13.6	7.4	13 07.3	9.7	60.1
04	238 43.6	24.9	295 40.0	7.3	13 17.0	9.6	60.1
05	253 43.5	24.6	310 06.3	7.2	13 26.6	9.5	60.1
06	268 43.4	N22 24.3	324 32.5	7.2	N13 36.1	9.5	60.1
07	283 43.3	24.0	338 58.7	7.1	13 45.6	9.4	60.2
08	298 43.2	23.7	353 24.8	7.0	13 55.0	9.3	60.2
F 09	313 43.1 ..	23.4	7 50.8	6.9	14 04.3	9.2	60.2
R 10	328 43.0	23.1	22 16.7	6.9	14 13.5	9.1	60.2
I 11	343 42.9	22.8	36 42.6	6.8	14 22.6	9.0	60.2
D 12	358 42.8	N22 22.5	51 08.4	6.7	N14 31.6	9.0	60.2
A 13	13 42.7	22.2	65 34.1	6.6	14 40.6	8.8	60.3
Y 14	28 42.6	21.9	79 59.7	6.6	14 49.4	8.8	60.3
15	43 42.5 ..	21.6	94 25.3	6.5	14 58.2	8.7	60.3
16	58 42.4	21.3	108 50.8	6.4	15 06.9	8.5	60.3
17	73 42.3	21.0	123 16.2	6.4	15 15.4	8.5	60.3
18	88 42.2	N22 20.7	137 41.6	6.3	N15 23.9	8.4	60.3
19	103 42.2	20.4	152 06.9	6.2	15 32.3	8.3	60.4
20	118 42.1	20.1	166 32.1	6.1	15 40.6	8.1	60.4
21	133 42.0 ..	19.8	180 57.2	6.1	15 48.7	8.1	60.4
22	148 41.9	19.5	195 22.3	6.0	15 56.8	8.0	60.4
23	163 41.8	19.2	209 47.3	6.0	16 04.8	7.8	60.4
10 00	178 41.7	N22 18.9	224 12.3	5.8	N16 12.6	7.8	60.4
01	193 41.6	18.6	238 37.1	5.9	16 20.4	7.7	60.4
02	208 41.5	18.3	253 02.0	5.7	16 28.1	7.5	60.4
03	223 41.4 ..	18.0	267 26.7	5.7	16 35.6	7.4	60.5
04	238 41.3	17.7	281 51.4	5.6	16 43.0	7.4	60.5
05	253 41.2	17.4	296 16.0	5.5	16 50.4	7.2	60.5
06	268 41.1	N22 17.0	310 40.5	5.5	N16 57.6	7.1	60.5
S 07	283 41.1	16.7	325 05.0	5.4	17 04.7	7.0	60.5
A 08	298 41.0	16.4	339 29.4	5.4	17 11.7	6.8	60.5
T 09	313 40.9 ..	16.1	353 53.8	5.3	17 18.5	6.8	60.5
U 10	328 40.8	15.8	8 18.1	5.2	17 25.3	6.6	60.5
R 11	343 40.7	15.5	22 42.3	5.2	17 31.9	6.5	60.5
D 12	358 40.6	N22 15.2	37 06.5	5.1	N17 38.4	6.4	60.5
A 13	13 40.5	14.9	51 30.6	5.1	17 44.8	6.3	60.5
Y 14	28 40.4	14.5	65 54.7	5.0	17 51.1	6.1	60.6
15	43 40.3 ..	14.2	80 18.7	5.0	17 57.2	6.0	60.6
16	58 40.2	13.9	94 42.7	4.9	18 03.2	5.9	60.6
17	73 40.2	13.6	109 06.6	4.8	18 09.1	5.8	60.6
18	88 40.1	N22 13.3	123 30.4	4.8	N18 14.9	5.6	60.6
19	103 40.0	13.0	137 54.2	4.7	18 20.5	5.6	60.6
20	118 39.9	12.6	152 17.9	4.7	18 26.0	5.4	60.6
21	133 39.8 ..	12.3	166 41.6	4.7	18 31.4	5.3	60.6
22	148 39.7	12.0	181 05.3	4.6	18 36.7	5.1	60.6
23	163 39.6	11.7	195 28.9	4.5	18 41.8	5.0	60.6
11 00	178 39.5	N22 11.4	209 52.4	4.6	N18 46.8	4.8	60.6
01	193 39.5	11.0	224 16.0	4.4	18 51.6	4.7	60.6
02	208 39.4	10.7	238 39.4	4.5	18 56.3	4.6	60.6
03	223 39.3 ..	10.4	253 02.9	4.4	19 00.9	4.5	60.6
04	238 39.2	10.1	267 26.3	4.3	19 05.4	4.3	60.6
05	253 39.1	09.8	281 49.6	4.3	19 09.7	4.1	60.6
06	268 39.0	N22 09.4	296 12.9	4.3	N19 13.8	4.1	60.6
07	283 38.9	09.1	310 36.2	4.3	19 17.9	3.9	60.6
08	298 38.8	08.8	324 59.5	4.2	19 21.8	3.7	60.6
S 09	313 38.8 ..	08.4	339 22.7	4.2	19 25.5	3.6	60.6
U 10	328 38.7	08.1	353 45.9	4.1	19 29.1	3.5	60.6
N 11	343 38.6	07.8	8 09.0	4.2	19 32.6	3.3	60.6
D 12	358 38.5	N22 07.5	22 32.2	4.1	N19 35.9	3.2	60.5
A 13	13 38.4	07.1	36 55.3	4.1	19 39.1	3.1	60.5
Y 14	28 38.3	06.8	51 18.4	4.0	19 42.2	2.9	60.5
15	43 38.2 ..	06.5	65 41.4	4.1	19 45.1	2.7	60.6
16	58 38.2	06.1	80 04.5	4.0	19 47.8	2.6	60.5
17	73 38.1	05.8	94 27.5	4.0	19 50.4	2.5	60.5
18	88 38.0	N22 05.5	108 50.5	4.0	N19 52.9	2.3	60.6
19	103 37.9	05.1	123 13.5	4.0	19 55.2	2.2	60.5
20	118 37.8	04.8	137 36.5	3.9	19 57.4	2.1	60.6
21	133 37.7 ..	04.5	151 59.4	4.0	19 59.5	1.8	60.5
22	148 37.7	04.1	166 22.4	4.0	20 01.3	1.8	60.5
23	163 37.6	03.8	180 45.4	3.9	N20 03.1	1.6	60.5
	SD 15.8	d 0.3	SD 16.4		16.5		16.5

Twilight / Moonrise

Lat.	Twilight Naut.	Twilight Civil	Sunrise	Moonrise 9	10	11	12
°	h m	h m	h m	h m	h m	h m	h m
N 72	☐	☐	☐	22 56	☐	☐	☐
N 70	☐	☐	☐	23 35	23 30	23 22	24 34
68	☐	☐	☐	24 02	00 02	00 15	00 46
66	////	////	01 10	00 09	00 23	00 45	01 25
64	////	////	02 00	00 21	00 39	01 08	01 52
62	////	////	02 31	00 31	00 53	01 26	02 13
60	////	01 27	02 54	00 39	01 05	01 41	02 30
N 58	////	02 04	03 12	00 46	01 15	01 54	02 44
56	////	02 29	03 27	00 53	01 24	02 05	02 56
54	01 20	02 49	03 40	00 59	01 32	02 14	03 07
52	01 54	03 05	03 52	01 04	01 40	02 23	03 17
50	02 17	03 19	04 02	01 09	01 46	02 31	03 25
45	02 58	03 46	04 23	01 20	02 00	02 48	03 44
N 40	03 27	04 07	04 40	01 28	02 12	03 02	03 58
35	03 49	04 25	04 54	01 36	02 22	03 13	04 11
30	04 06	04 39	05 06	01 43	02 30	03 24	04 22
20	04 34	05 03	05 27	01 54	02 46	03 41	04 41
N 10	04 55	05 22	05 45	02 04	02 59	03 57	04 58
0	05 13	05 39	06 02	02 14	03 11	04 11	05 13
S 10	05 29	05 56	06 18	02 24	03 24	04 26	05 29
20	05 45	06 12	06 36	02 34	03 37	04 42	05 45
30	06 00	06 30	06 56	02 46	03 53	05 00	06 04
35	06 08	06 40	07 07	02 53	04 02	05 10	06 15
40	06 17	06 51	07 21	03 01	04 13	05 23	06 28
45	06 26	07 03	07 36	03 11	04 25	05 37	06 43
S 50	06 37	07 18	07 56	03 22	04 40	05 54	07 02
52	06 42	07 25	08 05	03 27	04 47	06 03	07 11
54	06 47	07 33	08 15	03 33	04 54	06 12	07 21
56	06 53	07 41	08 27	03 39	05 03	06 22	07 32
58	06 59	07 50	08 40	03 47	05 13	06 34	07 45
S 60	07 06	08 01	08 56	03 55	05 24	06 48	07 59

Sunset / Twilight / Moonset

Lat.	Sunset	Twilight Civil	Twilight Naut.	Moonset 9	10	11	12
°	h m	h m	h m	h m	h m	h m	h m
N 72	☐	☐	☐	18 41	☐	☐	☐
N 70	☐	☐	☐	18 03	20 12	22 28	23 27
68	☐	☐	☐	17 37	19 28	21 05	22 08
66	22 56	////	////	17 17	18 58	20 26	21 30
64	22 08	////	////	17 01	18 36	20 00	21 03
62	21 38	////	////	16 48	18 18	19 39	20 42
60	21 16	22 41	////	16 37	18 04	19 22	20 25
N 58	20 58	22 05	////	16 27	17 51	19 08	20 11
56	20 43	21 41	////	16 19	17 41	18 55	19 59
54	20 30	21 21	22 48	16 11	17 31	18 45	19 48
52	20 18	21 05	22 15	16 05	17 23	18 35	19 38
50	20 08	20 51	21 52	15 59	17 15	18 27	19 30
45	19 47	20 24	21 11	15 46	16 59	18 09	19 12
N 40	19 31	20 03	20 43	15 35	16 46	17 54	18 57
35	19 16	19 46	20 22	15 26	16 35	17 42	18 44
30	19 04	19 31	20 04	15 18	16 25	17 31	18 33
20	18 43	19 08	19 37	15 04	16 08	17 12	18 14
N 10	18 26	18 48	19 15	14 52	15 53	16 56	17 58
0	18 09	18 31	18 57	14 41	15 40	16 41	17 42
S 10	17 52	18 15	18 41	14 30	15 26	16 25	17 27
20	17 35	17 59	18 26	14 18	15 11	16 09	17 10
30	17 15	17 41	18 11	14 04	14 55	15 51	16 51
35	17 03	17 31	18 03	13 56	14 45	15 40	16 40
40	16 50	17 20	17 54	13 47	14 34	15 27	16 27
45	16 34	17 08	17 44	13 37	14 21	15 12	16 12
S 50	16 15	16 53	17 34	13 24	14 05	14 54	15 54
52	16 06	16 46	17 29	13 19	13 58	14 46	15 45
54	15 56	16 38	17 24	13 12	13 49	14 37	15 35
56	15 44	16 30	17 18	13 05	13 40	14 26	15 24
58	15 31	16 21	17 12	12 57	13 30	14 14	15 11
S 60	15 15	16 10	17 05	12 48	13 18	14 00	14 56

SUN / MOON

Day	SUN Eqn. of Time 00h	12h	SUN Mer. Pass.	MOON Mer. Pass. Upper	Lower	Age	Phase
d	m s	m s	h m	h m	h m	d	%
9	05 04	05 09	12 05	08 27	20 56	26	18
10	05 13	05 17	12 05	09 25	21 55	27	10
11	05 22	05 26	12 05	10 26	22 57	28	4

UT	ARIES	VENUS −4.5		MARS −0.2		JUPITER −2.4		SATURN +0.3		STARS		
	GHA	GHA	Dec	GHA	Dec	GHA	Dec	GHA	Dec	Name	SHA	Dec
d h	° ′	° ′	° ′	° ′	° ′	° ′	° ′	° ′	° ′		° ′	° ′
12 00	289 26.9	137 57.2	N10 55.0	79 39.2	S13 32.2	259 12.6	N10 58.8	246 03.8	N14 11.3	Acamar	315 26.7	S40 18.5
01	304 29.3	152 58.4	54.2	94 40.8	32.5	274 14.8	58.9	261 06.1	11.3	Achernar	335 34.9	S57 14.2
02	319 31.8	167 59.7	53.3	109 42.3	32.9	289 17.0	59.0	276 08.4	11.4	Acrux	173 21.5	S63 06.0
03	334 34.3	183 01.0 ..	52.5	124 43.9 ..	33.3	304 19.1 ..	59.1	291 10.7 ..	11.4	Adhara	255 21.4	S28 58.3
04	349 36.7	198 02.3	51.6	139 45.4	33.6	319 21.3	59.2	306 12.9	11.5	Aldebaran	291 02.0	N16 30.4
05	4 39.2	213 03.6	50.8	154 47.0	34.0	334 23.4	59.3	321 15.2	11.5			
06	19 41.7	228 04.9	N10 49.9	169 48.6	S13 34.4	349 25.6	N10 59.4	336 17.5	N14 11.6	Alioth	166 30.2	N55 58.1
07	34 44.1	243 06.2	49.1	184 50.1	34.8	4 27.7	59.5	351 19.7	11.6	Alkaid	153 07.4	N49 19.3
08	49 46.6	258 07.5	48.2	199 51.7	35.1	19 29.9	59.6	6 22.0	11.7	Al Na'ir	27 56.9	S46 57.6
M 09	64 49.0	273 08.8 ..	47.4	214 53.2 ..	35.5	34 32.0 ..	59.7	21 24.3 ..	11.7	Alnilam	275 57.6	S 1 12.2
O 10	79 51.5	288 10.1	46.5	229 54.7	35.9	49 34.2	59.8	36 26.5	11.8	Alphard	218 07.0	S 8 39.4
N 11	94 54.0	303 11.4	45.7	244 56.3	36.2	64 36.3	10 59.9	51 28.8	11.8			
D 12	109 56.4	318 12.7	N10 44.9	259 57.8	S13 36.6	79 38.5	N11 00.0	66 31.1	N14 11.9	Alphecca	126 19.9	N26 43.3
A 13	124 58.9	333 14.0	44.0	274 59.4	37.0	94 40.6	00.1	81 33.4	11.9	Alpheratz	357 54.6	N29 05.1
Y 14	140 01.4	348 15.4	43.2	290 00.9	37.4	109 42.8	00.2	96 35.6	12.0	Altair	62 18.4	N 8 52.1
15	155 03.8	3 16.7 ..	42.3	305 02.5 ..	37.7	124 44.9 ..	00.3	111 37.9 ..	12.0	Ankaa	353 26.3	S42 18.4
16	170 06.3	18 18.0	41.5	320 04.0	38.1	139 47.1	00.4	126 40.2	12.1	Antares	112 39.2	S26 25.8
17	185 08.8	33 19.3	40.6	335 05.6	38.5	154 49.3	00.5	141 42.4	12.1			
18	200 11.2	48 20.6	N10 39.8	350 07.1	S13 38.8	169 51.4	N11 00.6	156 44.7	N14 12.2	Arcturus	146 05.5	N19 11.4
19	215 13.7	63 22.0	38.9	5 08.6	39.2	184 53.6	00.7	171 47.0	12.2	Atria	107 50.3	S69 01.7
20	230 16.2	78 23.3	38.1	20 10.2	39.6	199 55.7	00.8	186 49.2	12.3	Avior	234 23.0	S59 30.6
21	245 18.6	93 24.6 ..	37.3	35 11.7 ..	40.0	214 57.9 ..	00.9	201 51.5 ..	12.3	Bellatrix	278 43.9	N 6 20.9
22	260 21.1	108 26.0	36.4	50 13.3	40.3	230 00.0	01.0	216 53.8	12.4	Betelgeuse	271 13.3	N 7 24.3
23	275 23.5	123 27.3	35.6	65 14.8	40.7	245 02.2	01.2	231 56.1	12.4			
13 00	290 26.0	138 28.6	N10 34.7	80 16.3	S13 41.1	260 04.4	N11 01.3	246 58.3	N14 12.4	Canopus	264 01.5	S52 41.7
01	305 28.5	153 30.0	33.9	95 17.9	41.5	275 06.5	01.4	262 00.6	12.5	Capella	280 50.8	N45 59.6
02	320 30.9	168 31.3	33.1	110 19.4	41.8	290 08.7	01.5	277 02.9	12.5	Deneb	49 38.4	N45 16.7
03	335 33.4	183 32.7 ..	32.2	125 20.9 ..	42.2	305 10.8 ..	01.6	292 05.1 ..	12.6	Denebola	182 44.8	N14 34.7
04	350 35.9	198 34.0	31.4	140 22.5	42.6	320 13.0	01.7	307 07.4	12.6	Diphda	349 06.7	S17 59.3
05	5 38.3	213 35.4	30.5	155 24.0	43.0	335 15.1	01.8	322 09.7	12.7			
06	20 40.8	228 36.7	N10 29.7	170 25.5	S13 43.3	350 17.3	N11 01.9	337 12.0	N14 12.7	Dubhe	194 05.3	N61 45.5
07	35 43.3	243 38.1	28.9	185 27.1	43.7	5 19.5	02.0	352 14.2	12.8	Elnath	278 26.6	N28 36.3
T 08	50 45.7	258 39.5	28.0	200 28.6	44.1	20 21.6	02.1	7 16.5	12.8	Eltanin	90 50.7	N51 29.6
U 09	65 48.2	273 40.8 ..	27.2	215 30.1 ..	44.5	35 23.8 ..	02.2	22 18.8 ..	12.9	Enif	33 57.4	N 9 52.4
E 10	80 50.7	288 42.2	26.3	230 31.7	44.8	50 25.9	02.3	37 21.1	12.9	Fomalhaut	15 35.7	S29 37.4
S 11	95 53.1	303 43.6	25.5	245 33.2	45.2	65 28.1	02.4	52 23.3	13.0			
D 12	110 55.6	318 44.9	N10 24.7	260 34.7	S13 45.6	80 30.3	N11 02.5	67 25.6	N14 13.0	Gacrux	172 13.0	S57 06.8
A 13	125 58.0	333 46.3	23.8	275 36.3	46.0	95 32.4	02.6	82 27.9	13.1	Gienah	176 03.5	S17 32.3
Y 14	141 00.5	348 47.7	23.0	290 37.8	46.3	110 34.6	02.7	97 30.1	13.1	Hadar	149 03.1	S60 22.4
15	156 03.0	3 49.1 ..	22.2	305 39.3 ..	46.7	125 36.7 ..	02.8	112 32.4 ..	13.2	Hamal	328 13.0	N23 27.4
16	171 05.4	18 50.4	21.3	320 40.8	47.1	140 38.9	02.9	127 34.7	13.2	Kaus Aust.	83 57.7	S34 23.0
17	186 07.9	33 51.8	20.5	335 42.4	47.5	155 41.1	03.0	142 37.0	13.3			
18	201 10.4	48 53.2	N10 19.7	350 43.9	S13 47.8	170 43.2	N11 03.1	157 39.2	N14 13.3	Kochab	137 19.2	N74 09.9
19	216 12.8	63 54.6	18.8	5 45.4	48.2	185 45.4	03.2	172 41.5	13.4	Markab	13 48.9	N15 12.1
20	231 15.3	78 56.0	18.0	20 46.9	48.6	200 47.5	03.3	187 43.8	13.4	Menkar	314 26.5	N 4 05.2
21	246 17.8	93 57.4 ..	17.2	35 48.4 ..	49.0	215 49.7 ..	03.4	202 46.1 ..	13.5	Menkent	148 20.2	S36 22.1
22	261 20.2	108 58.8	16.3	50 50.0	49.4	230 51.9	03.5	217 48.3	13.5	Miaplacidus	221 42.7	S69 43.1
23	276 22.7	124 00.2	15.5	65 51.5	49.7	245 54.0	03.6	232 50.6	13.5			
14 00	291 25.2	139 01.6	N10 14.7	80 53.0	S13 50.1	260 56.2	N11 03.7	247 52.9	N14 13.6	Mirfak	308 56.1	N49 51.3
01	306 27.6	154 03.0	13.8	95 54.5	50.5	275 58.4	03.8	262 55.2	13.6	Nunki	76 11.3	S26 17.7
02	321 30.1	169 04.4	13.0	110 56.0	50.9	291 00.5	03.9	277 57.4	13.7	Peacock	53 35.6	S56 44.0
03	336 32.5	184 05.8 ..	12.2	125 57.6 ..	51.2	306 02.7 ..	03.9	292 59.7 ..	13.7	Pollux	243 41.3	N28 01.6
04	351 35.0	199 07.2	11.3	140 59.1	51.6	321 04.9	04.0	308 02.0	13.8	Procyon	245 11.4	N 5 13.6
05	6 37.5	214 08.6	10.5	156 00.6	52.0	336 07.0	04.1	323 04.3	13.8			
06	21 39.9	229 10.0	N10 09.7	171 02.1	S13 52.4	351 09.2	N11 04.2	338 06.5	N14 13.9	Rasalhague	96 16.2	N12 33.8
W 07	36 42.4	244 11.5	08.8	186 03.6	52.8	6 11.3	04.3	353 08.8	13.9	Regulus	207 55.3	N11 58.3
E 08	51 44.9	259 12.9	08.0	201 05.1	53.1	21 13.5	04.4	8 11.1	14.0	Rigel	281 22.7	S 8 12.2
D 09	66 47.3	274 14.3 ..	07.2	216 06.6 ..	53.5	36 15.7 ..	04.5	23 13.4 ..	14.0	Rigil Kent.	140 06.3	S60 50.1
N 10	81 49.8	289 15.7	06.4	231 08.2	53.9	51 17.8	04.6	38 15.6	14.1	Sabik	102 24.6	S15 43.3
E 11	96 52.3	304 17.2	05.5	246 09.7	54.3	66 20.0	04.7	53 17.9	14.1			
S 12	111 54.7	319 18.6	N10 04.7	261 11.2	S13 54.7	81 22.2	N11 04.8	68 20.2	N14 14.2	Schedar	349 52.7	N56 31.7
D 13	126 57.2	334 20.0	03.9	276 12.7	55.0	96 24.3	04.9	83 22.5	14.2	Shaula	96 36.2	S37 06.1
A 14	141 59.6	349 21.5	03.0	291 14.2	55.4	111 26.5	05.0	98 24.8	14.2	Sirius	258 43.6	S16 42.9
Y 15	157 02.1	4 22.9 ..	02.2	306 15.7 ..	55.8	126 28.7 ..	05.1	113 27.0 ..	14.3	Spica	158 42.6	S11 09.4
16	172 04.6	19 24.4	01.4	321 17.2	56.2	141 30.8	05.2	128 29.3	14.3	Suhail	223 00.8	S43 25.9
17	187 07.0	34 25.8	10 00.6	336 18.7	56.6	156 33.0	05.3	143 31.6	14.4			
18	202 09.5	49 27.3	N 9 59.7	351 20.2	S13 56.9	171 35.2	N11 05.4	158 33.9	N14 14.4	Vega	80 45.8	N38 47.2
19	217 12.0	64 28.7	58.9	6 21.7	57.3	186 37.3	05.5	173 36.1	14.5	Zuben'ubi	137 17.2	S16 02.3
20	232 14.4	79 30.2	58.1	21 23.2	57.7	201 39.5	05.6	188 38.4	14.5		SHA	Mer. Pass.
21	247 16.9	94 31.6 ..	57.3	36 24.7 ..	58.1	216 41.7 ..	05.7	203 40.7 ..	14.6		° ′	h m
22	262 19.4	109 33.1	56.4	51 26.2	58.5	231 43.8	05.8	218 43.0	14.6	Venus	208 02.6	14 45
23	277 21.8	124 34.6	55.6	66 27.7	58.9	246 46.0	05.9	233 45.2	14.7	Mars	149 50.3	18 37
	h m									Jupiter	329 38.3	6 39
Mer. Pass. 4 37.5		v 1.4	d 0.8	v 1.5	d 0.4	v 2.2	d 0.1	v 2.3	d 0.0	Saturn	316 32.3	7 31

SUN and MOON

UT (d h)	SUN GHA	SUN Dec	MOON GHA	v	MOON Dec	d	HP
12 00	178 37.5	N22 03.5	195 08.3	4.0	N20 04.7	1.4	60.5
01	193 37.4	03.1	209 31.3	3.9	20 06.1	1.3	60.5
02	208 37.3	02.8	223 54.2	3.9	20 07.4	1.2	60.5
03	223 37.2	.. 02.5	238 17.1	4.0	20 08.6	1.0	60.5
04	238 37.2	02.1	252 40.1	3.9	20 09.6	0.9	60.5
05	253 37.1	01.8	267 03.0	4.0	20 10.5	0.7	60.5
06	268 37.0	N22 01.4	281 26.0	4.0	N20 11.2	0.5	60.5
07	283 36.9	01.1	295 49.0	3.9	20 11.7	0.5	60.5
08	298 36.8	00.7	310 11.9	4.0	20 12.2	0.2	60.5
M 09	313 36.7	.. 00.4	324 34.9	4.0	20 12.4	0.2	60.4
O 10	328 36.7	22 00.1	338 57.9	4.0	20 12.6	0.1	60.4
N 11	343 36.6	21 59.7	353 20.9	4.1	20 12.5	0.1	60.4
D 12	358 36.5	N21 59.4	7 44.0	4.0	N20 12.4	0.3	60.4
A 13	13 36.4	59.0	22 07.0	4.1	20 12.1	0.5	60.4
Y 14	28 36.3	58.7	36 30.1	4.1	20 11.6	0.6	60.4
15	43 36.3	.. 58.3	50 53.2	4.1	20 11.0	0.8	60.4
16	58 36.2	58.0	65 16.3	4.1	20 10.2	0.8	60.4
17	73 36.1	57.6	79 39.4	4.2	20 09.4	1.1	60.3
18	88 36.0	N21 57.3	94 02.6	4.2	N20 08.3	1.2	60.3
19	103 35.9	56.9	108 25.8	4.2	20 07.1	1.3	60.3
20	118 35.9	56.6	122 49.0	4.3	20 05.8	1.5	60.3
21	133 35.8	.. 56.2	137 12.3	4.3	20 04.3	1.6	60.3
22	148 35.7	55.9	151 35.6	4.3	20 02.7	1.7	60.3
23	163 35.6	55.5	165 58.9	4.4	20 01.0	1.9	60.2
13 00	178 35.5	N21 55.2	180 22.3	4.4	N19 59.1	2.1	60.2
01	193 35.5	54.8	194 45.7	4.5	19 57.0	2.2	60.2
02	208 35.4	54.5	209 09.2	4.5	19 54.8	2.3	60.2
03	223 35.3	.. 54.1	223 32.7	4.6	19 52.5	2.4	60.2
04	238 35.2	53.8	237 56.3	4.6	19 50.1	2.6	60.1
05	253 35.2	53.4	252 19.9	4.6	19 47.5	2.8	60.1
06	268 35.1	N21 53.1	266 43.5	4.7	N19 44.7	2.9	60.1
07	283 35.0	52.7	281 07.2	4.7	19 41.8	3.0	60.1
T 08	298 34.9	52.3	295 30.9	4.8	19 38.8	3.1	60.1
U 09	313 34.9	.. 52.0	309 54.7	4.9	19 35.7	3.3	60.0
E 10	328 34.8	51.6	324 18.6	4.9	19 32.4	3.4	60.0
S 11	343 34.7	51.3	338 42.5	5.0	19 29.0	3.5	60.0
D 12	358 34.6	N21 50.9	353 06.5	5.0	N19 25.5	3.7	60.0
A 13	13 34.5	50.5	7 30.5	5.1	19 21.8	3.8	59.9
Y 14	28 34.5	50.2	21 54.6	5.1	19 18.0	4.0	59.9
15	43 34.4	.. 49.8	36 18.7	5.3	19 14.0	4.0	59.9
16	58 34.3	49.5	50 43.0	5.2	19 10.0	4.2	59.9
17	73 34.2	49.1	65 07.2	5.4	19 05.8	4.4	59.8
18	88 34.2	N21 48.7	79 31.6	5.4	N19 01.4	4.4	59.8
19	103 34.1	48.4	93 56.0	5.5	18 57.0	4.6	59.8
20	118 34.0	48.0	108 20.5	5.5	18 52.4	4.7	59.8
21	133 33.9	.. 47.6	122 45.0	5.6	18 47.7	4.8	59.7
22	148 33.9	47.3	137 09.6	5.7	18 42.9	4.9	59.7
23	163 33.8	46.9	151 34.3	5.8	18 38.0	5.1	59.7
14 00	178 33.7	N21 46.5	165 59.1	5.8	N18 32.9	5.2	59.7
01	193 33.7	46.2	180 23.9	5.9	18 27.7	5.3	59.6
02	208 33.6	45.8	194 48.8	6.0	18 22.4	5.4	59.6
03	223 33.5	.. 45.4	209 13.8	6.1	18 17.0	5.5	59.6
04	238 33.4	45.1	223 38.9	6.1	18 11.5	5.7	59.5
05	253 33.4	44.7	238 04.0	6.2	18 05.8	5.7	59.5
06	268 33.3	N21 44.3	252 29.2	6.3	N18 00.1	5.9	59.5
W 07	283 33.2	43.9	266 54.5	6.4	17 54.2	6.0	59.5
E 08	298 33.1	43.6	281 19.9	6.5	17 48.2	6.1	59.4
D 09	313 33.1	.. 43.2	295 45.4	6.5	17 42.1	6.2	59.4
N 10	328 33.0	42.8	310 10.9	6.6	17 35.9	6.3	59.4
E 11	343 32.9	42.4	324 36.5	6.7	17 29.6	6.4	59.3
S 12	358 32.9	N21 42.1	339 02.2	6.8	N17 23.2	6.6	59.3
D 13	13 32.8	41.7	353 28.0	6.9	17 16.6	6.6	59.3
A 14	28 32.7	41.3	7 53.9	6.9	17 10.0	6.7	59.2
Y 15	43 32.6	.. 40.9	22 19.8	7.1	17 03.3	6.8	59.2
16	58 32.6	40.6	36 45.9	7.1	16 56.5	7.0	59.2
17	73 32.5	40.2	51 12.0	7.2	16 49.5	7.0	59.1
18	88 32.4	N21 39.8	65 38.2	7.3	N16 42.5	7.1	59.1
19	103 32.4	39.4	80 04.5	7.4	16 35.4	7.2	59.1
20	118 32.3	39.0	94 30.9	7.4	16 28.2	7.3	59.0
21	133 32.2	.. 38.7	108 57.3	7.6	16 20.9	7.4	59.0
22	148 32.2	38.3	123 23.9	7.6	16 13.5	7.5	59.0
23	163 32.1	37.9	137 50.5	7.8	N16 06.0	7.6	58.9
	SD 15.8	d 0.4	SD 16.5		16.3		16.2

Twilight — Sunrise — Moonrise

Lat.	Naut.	Civil	Sunrise	Moonrise 12	13	14	15
N 72	□	□	□	□	□	□	04 11
N 70	□	□	□	24 34	00 34	02 46	04 48
68	□	□	□	00 46	01 52	03 29	05 14
66	////	////	01 24	01 25	02 30	03 57	05 34
64	////	////	02 08	01 52	02 57	04 19	05 50
62	////	00 24	02 37	02 13	03 17	04 37	06 03
60	////	01 37	02 59	02 30	03 34	04 51	06 14
N 58	////	02 10	03 16	02 44	03 48	05 03	06 24
56	00 23	02 34	03 31	02 56	04 00	05 14	06 32
54	01 29	02 53	03 44	03 07	04 11	05 23	06 39
52	02 00	03 09	03 55	03 17	04 20	05 32	06 46
50	02 22	03 22	04 05	03 25	04 29	05 39	06 52
45	02 57	03 49	04 25	03 44	04 47	05 55	07 05
N 40	03 29	04 10	04 42	03 58	05 01	06 08	07 16
35	03 51	04 27	04 56	04 11	05 14	06 19	07 25
30	04 08	04 41	05 08	04 22	05 25	06 29	07 33
20	04 35	05 04	05 28	04 41	05 43	06 45	07 46
N 10	04 56	05 23	05 46	04 58	05 59	07 00	07 58
0	05 14	05 40	06 02	05 13	06 14	07 14	08 09
S 10	05 30	05 56	06 18	05 29	06 29	07 27	08 20
20	05 44	06 12	06 35	05 45	06 46	07 42	08 32
30	06 00	06 29	06 55	06 04	07 04	07 58	08 46
35	06 07	06 39	07 06	06 15	07 15	08 08	08 54
40	06 16	06 49	07 19	06 28	07 27	08 19	09 03
45	06 25	07 02	07 35	06 43	07 42	08 32	09 13
S 50	06 36	07 16	07 54	07 02	08 00	08 47	09 25
52	06 40	07 23	08 03	07 11	08 08	08 54	09 31
54	06 45	07 30	08 13	07 21	08 18	09 02	09 38
56	06 51	07 38	08 24	07 32	08 28	09 12	09 45
58	06 56	07 48	08 37	07 45	08 40	09 22	09 53
S 60	07 03	07 58	08 52	07 59	08 54	09 34	10 02

Sunset — Twilight — Moonset

Lat.	Sunset	Civil	Naut.	Moonset 12	13	14	15
N 72	□	□	□	□	□	23 54	23 33
N 70	□	□	□	23 27	23 20	23 16	23 11
68	□	□	□	22 08	22 37	22 49	22 54
66	22 43	////	////	21 30	22 07	22 28	22 40
64	22 01	////	////	21 03	21 45	22 11	22 29
62	21 33	23 35	////	20 42	21 27	21 58	22 19
60	21 11	22 32	////	20 25	21 12	21 46	22 10
N 58	20 54	22 00	////	20 11	20 59	21 36	22 03
56	20 39	21 36	23 38	19 59	20 49	21 27	21 56
54	20 27	21 17	22 40	19 48	20 39	21 19	21 50
52	20 16	21 02	22 10	19 38	20 30	21 12	21 45
50	20 06	20 48	21 48	19 30	20 22	21 05	21 40
45	19 46	20 22	21 09	19 12	20 06	20 51	21 29
N 40	19 29	20 01	20 41	18 57	19 52	20 40	21 21
35	19 15	19 44	20 20	18 44	19 41	20 30	21 13
30	19 03	19 30	20 03	18 33	19 30	20 21	21 06
20	18 43	19 07	19 36	18 14	19 13	20 06	20 55
N 10	18 26	18 48	19 15	17 58	18 57	19 53	20 44
0	18 09	18 32	18 57	17 42	18 43	19 41	20 35
S 10	17 53	18 16	18 42	17 27	18 28	19 28	20 25
20	17 36	18 00	18 27	17 10	18 13	19 15	20 14
30	17 17	17 43	18 12	16 51	17 55	18 59	20 02
35	17 05	17 33	18 04	16 40	17 44	18 50	19 55
40	16 52	17 22	17 56	16 27	17 32	18 40	19 47
45	16 37	17 10	17 47	16 12	17 18	18 28	19 38
S 50	16 18	16 55	17 36	15 54	17 01	18 13	19 27
52	16 09	16 49	17 32	15 45	16 53	18 06	19 21
54	15 59	16 41	17 27	15 35	16 44	17 59	19 16
56	15 48	16 33	17 21	15 24	16 33	17 50	19 09
58	15 35	16 24	17 15	15 11	16 21	17 40	19 02
S 60	15 20	16 14	17 09	14 56	16 08	17 29	18 53

SUN and MOON

Day	Eqn. of Time 00h	12h	Mer. Pass.	Mer. Pass. Upper	Lower	Age	Phase
	m s	m s	h m	h m	h m	d	%
12	05 30	05 34	12 06	11 28	23 58	29	1
13	05 38	05 41	12 06	12 29	24 58	00	0
14	05 45	05 48	12 06	13 27	00 58	01	3

UT	ARIES	VENUS −4.5		MARS −0.2		JUPITER −2.4		SATURN +0.3		STARS		
	GHA	GHA	Dec	GHA	Dec	GHA	Dec	GHA	Dec	Name	SHA	Dec
d h	° ′	° ′	° ′	° ′	° ′	° ′	° ′	° ′	° ′		° ′	° ′
15 00	292 24.3	139 36.0	N 9 54.8	81 29.2	S13 59.2	261 48.2	N11 06.0	248 47.5	N14 14.7	Acamar	315 26.7	S40 18.3
01	307 26.8	154 37.5	54.0	96 30.7	13 59.6	276 50.3	06.1	263 49.8	14.8	Achernar	335 34.9	S57 14.2
02	322 29.2	169 39.0	53.2	111 32.2	14 00.0	291 52.5	06.2	278 52.1	14.8	Acrux	173 21.5	S63 06.0
03	337 31.7	184 40.4	.. 52.3	126 33.7	.. 00.4	306 54.7	.. 06.3	293 54.4	.. 14.8	Adhara	255 21.4	S28 58.3
04	352 34.1	199 41.9	51.5	141 35.2	00.8	321 56.9	06.4	308 56.6	14.9	Aldebaran	291 02.0	N16 30.4
05	7 36.6	214 43.4	50.7	156 36.7	01.1	336 59.0	06.5	323 58.9	14.9			
06	22 39.1	229 44.9	N 9 49.9	171 38.2	S14 01.5	352 01.2	N11 06.6	339 01.2	N14 15.0	Alioth	166 30.3	N55 58.1
T 07	37 41.5	244 46.4	49.1	186 39.7	01.9	7 03.4	06.7	354 03.5	15.0	Alkaid	153 07.4	N49 19.3
H 08	52 44.0	259 47.8	48.2	201 41.2	02.3	22 05.5	06.8	9 05.8	15.1	Al Na'ir	27 56.9	S46 57.6
U 09	67 46.5	274 49.3	.. 47.4	216 42.7	.. 02.7	37 07.7	.. 06.9	24 08.0	.. 15.1	Alnilam	275 57.6	S 1 12.2
R 10	82 48.9	289 50.8	46.6	231 44.2	03.1	52 09.9	07.0	39 10.3	15.2	Alphard	218 07.0	S 8 39.4
S 11	97 51.4	304 52.3	45.8	246 45.7	03.4	67 12.1	07.1	54 12.6	15.2			
D 12	112 53.9	319 53.8	N 9 45.0	261 47.2	S14 03.8	82 14.2	N11 07.2	69 14.9	N14 15.3	Alphecca	126 20.0	N26 43.3
A 13	127 56.3	334 55.3	44.2	276 48.7	04.2	97 16.4	07.2	84 17.2	15.3	Alpheratz	357 54.5	N29 05.1
Y 14	142 58.8	349 56.8	43.3	291 50.2	04.6	112 18.6	07.3	99 19.4	15.4	Altair	62 18.4	N 8 52.1
15	158 01.3	4 58.3	.. 42.5	306 51.7	.. 05.0	127 20.7	.. 07.4	114 21.7	.. 15.4	Ankaa	353 26.2	S42 18.3
16	173 03.7	19 59.8	41.7	321 53.1	05.4	142 22.9	07.5	129 24.0	15.4	Antares	112 39.2	S26 25.8
17	188 06.2	35 01.4	40.9	336 54.6	05.7	157 25.1	07.6	144 26.3	15.5			
18	203 08.6	50 02.9	N 9 40.1	351 56.1	S14 06.1	172 27.3	N11 07.7	159 28.6	N14 15.5	Arcturus	146 05.5	N19 11.4
19	218 11.1	65 04.4	39.3	6 57.6	06.5	187 29.4	07.8	174 30.8	15.6	Atria	107 50.3	S69 01.7
20	233 13.6	80 05.9	38.5	21 59.1	06.9	202 31.6	07.9	189 33.1	15.6	Avior	234 23.0	S59 30.6
21	248 16.0	95 07.4	.. 37.6	37 00.6	.. 07.3	217 33.8	.. 08.0	204 35.4	.. 15.7	Bellatrix	278 43.9	N 6 20.9
22	263 18.5	110 09.0	36.8	52 02.1	07.7	232 36.0	08.1	219 37.7	15.7	Betelgeuse	271 13.3	N 7 24.3
23	278 21.0	125 10.5	36.0	67 03.5	08.1	247 38.1	08.2	234 40.0	15.8			
16 00	293 23.4	140 12.0	N 9 35.2	82 05.0	S14 08.4	262 40.3	N11 08.3	249 42.2	N14 15.8	Canopus	264 01.5	S52 41.7
01	308 25.9	155 13.6	34.4	97 06.5	08.8	277 42.5	08.4	264 44.5	15.8	Capella	280 50.8	N45 59.6
02	323 28.4	170 15.1	33.6	112 08.0	09.2	292 44.6	08.5	279 46.8	15.9	Deneb	49 38.4	N45 16.7
03	338 30.8	185 16.6	.. 32.8	127 09.5	.. 09.6	307 46.8	.. 08.6	294 49.1	.. 15.9	Denebola	182 44.8	N14 34.7
04	353 33.3	200 18.2	32.0	142 11.0	10.0	322 49.0	08.7	309 51.4	16.0	Diphda	349 06.6	S17 59.3
05	8 35.7	215 19.7	31.2	157 12.4	10.4	337 51.2	08.8	324 53.6	16.0			
06	23 38.2	230 21.3	N 9 30.4	172 13.9	S14 10.8	352 53.4	N11 08.9	339 55.9	N14 16.1	Dubhe	194 05.3	N61 45.5
07	38 40.7	245 22.8	29.5	187 15.4	11.1	7 55.5	08.9	354 58.2	16.1	Elnath	278 26.6	N28 36.3
08	53 43.1	260 24.4	28.7	202 16.9	11.5	22 57.7	09.0	10 00.5	16.2	Eltanin	90 50.7	N51 29.6
F 09	68 45.6	275 25.9	.. 27.9	217 18.3	.. 11.9	37 59.9	.. 09.1	25 02.8	.. 16.2	Enif	33 57.4	N 9 52.4
R 10	83 48.1	290 27.5	27.1	232 19.8	12.3	53 02.1	09.2	40 05.1	16.2	Fomalhaut	15 35.6	S29 37.3
I 11	98 50.5	305 29.0	26.3	247 21.3	12.7	68 04.2	09.3	55 07.3	16.3			
D 12	113 53.0	320 30.6	N 9 25.5	262 22.8	S14 13.1	83 06.4	N11 09.4	70 09.6	N14 16.3	Gacrux	172 13.1	S57 06.8
A 13	128 55.5	335 32.2	24.7	277 24.2	13.5	98 08.6	09.5	85 11.9	16.4	Gienah	176 03.5	S17 32.3
Y 14	143 57.9	350 33.7	23.9	292 25.7	13.8	113 10.8	09.6	100 14.2	16.4	Hadar	149 03.1	S60 22.4
15	159 00.4	5 35.3	.. 23.1	307 27.2	.. 14.2	128 12.9	.. 09.7	115 16.5	.. 16.5	Hamal	328 13.0	N23 27.4
16	174 02.9	20 36.9	22.3	322 28.7	14.6	143 15.1	09.8	130 18.8	16.5	Kaus Aust.	83 57.7	S34 23.0
17	189 05.3	35 38.5	21.5	337 30.1	15.0	158 17.3	09.9	145 21.0	16.6			
18	204 07.8	50 40.1	N 9 20.7	352 31.6	S14 15.4	173 19.5	N11 10.0	160 23.3	N14 16.6	Kochab	137 19.3	N74 09.9
19	219 10.2	65 41.6	19.9	7 33.1	15.8	188 21.7	10.1	175 25.6	16.6	Markab	13 48.9	N15 12.1
20	234 12.7	80 43.2	19.1	22 34.5	16.2	203 23.8	10.2	190 27.9	16.7	Menkar	314 26.5	N 4 05.2
21	249 15.2	95 44.8	.. 18.3	37 36.0	.. 16.6	218 26.0	.. 10.2	205 30.2	.. 16.7	Menkent	148 20.2	S36 22.1
22	264 17.6	110 46.4	17.5	52 37.5	16.9	233 28.2	10.3	220 32.5	16.8	Miaplacidus	221 42.8	S69 43.1
23	279 20.1	125 48.0	16.7	67 38.9	17.3	248 30.4	10.4	235 34.7	16.8			
17 00	294 22.6	140 49.6	N 9 15.9	82 40.4	S14 17.7	263 32.6	N11 10.5	250 37.0	N14 16.9	Mirfak	308 56.1	N49 51.3
01	309 25.0	155 51.2	15.1	97 41.9	18.1	278 34.7	10.6	265 39.3	16.9	Nunki	76 11.3	S26 17.7
02	324 27.5	170 52.8	14.3	112 43.3	18.5	293 36.9	10.7	280 41.6	17.0	Peacock	53 35.6	S56 44.1
03	339 30.0	185 54.4	.. 13.5	127 44.8	.. 18.9	308 39.1	.. 10.8	295 43.9	.. 17.0	Pollux	243 41.3	N28 01.6
04	354 32.4	200 56.0	12.7	142 46.3	19.3	323 41.3	10.9	310 46.2	17.0	Procyon	245 11.4	N 5 13.6
05	9 34.9	215 57.7	11.9	157 47.7	19.7	338 43.5	11.0	325 48.5	17.1			
06	24 37.4	230 59.3	N 9 11.1	172 49.2	S14 20.1	353 45.6	N11 11.1	340 50.7	N14 17.1	Rasalhague	96 16.2	N12 33.8
07	39 39.8	246 00.9	10.3	187 50.6	20.4	8 47.8	11.2	355 53.0	17.2	Regulus	207 55.3	N11 58.3
S 08	54 42.3	261 02.5	09.5	202 52.1	20.8	23 50.0	11.3	10 55.3	17.2	Rigel	281 22.7	S 8 12.2
A 09	69 44.7	276 04.1	.. 08.7	217 53.6	.. 21.2	38 52.2	.. 11.3	25 57.6	.. 17.3	Rigil Kent.	140 06.3	S60 50.1
T 10	84 47.2	291 05.8	07.9	232 55.0	21.6	53 54.4	11.4	40 59.9	17.3	Sabik	102 24.6	S15 43.3
U 11	99 49.7	306 07.4	07.2	247 56.5	22.0	68 56.6	11.5	56 02.2	17.3			
R 12	114 52.1	321 09.0	N 9 06.4	262 57.9	S14 22.4	83 58.7	N11 11.6	71 04.5	N14 17.4	Schedar	349 52.7	N56 31.8
D 13	129 54.6	336 10.7	05.6	277 59.4	22.8	99 00.9	11.7	86 06.7	17.4	Shaula	96 36.2	S37 06.1
A 14	144 57.1	351 12.3	04.8	293 00.9	23.2	114 03.1	11.8	101 09.0	17.5	Sirius	258 43.6	S16 42.9
Y 15	159 59.5	6 13.9	.. 04.0	308 02.3	.. 23.6	129 05.3	.. 11.9	116 11.3	.. 17.5	Spica	158 42.6	S11 09.4
16	175 02.0	21 15.6	03.2	323 03.8	24.0	144 07.5	12.0	131 13.6	17.6	Suhail	223 00.8	S43 25.9
17	190 04.5	36 17.2	02.4	338 05.2	24.3	159 09.7	12.1	146 15.9	17.6			
18	205 06.9	51 18.9	N 9 01.6	353 06.7	S14 24.7	174 11.8	N11 12.2	161 18.2	N14 17.6	Vega	80 45.8	N38 47.2
19	220 09.4	66 20.5	00.8	8 08.1	25.1	189 14.0	12.3	176 20.5	17.7	Zuben'ubi	137 17.3	S16 02.3
20	235 11.8	81 22.2	9 00.0	23 09.6	25.5	204 16.2	12.3	191 22.8	17.7		SHA	Mer. Pass.
21	250 14.3	96 23.9	8 59.3	38 11.0	.. 25.9	219 18.4	.. 12.4	206 25.0	.. 17.8		° ′	h m
22	265 16.8	111 25.5	58.5	53 12.5	26.3	234 20.6	12.5	221 27.3	17.8	Venus	206 48.6	14 38
23	280 19.2	126 27.2	57.7	68 13.9	26.7	249 22.8	12.6	236 29.6	17.9	Mars	148 41.6	18 30
	h m									Jupiter	329 16.9	6 28
Mer. Pass. 4 25.7		v 1.6	d 0.8	v 1.5	d 0.4	v 2.2	d 0.1	v 2.3	d 0.0	Saturn	316 18.8	7 20

UT	SUN GHA	Dec	MOON GHA	v	Dec	d	HP
d h	° ′	° ′	° ′	′	° ′	′	′
15 00	178 32.0	N21 37.5	152 17.3	7.8	N15 58.4	7.7	58.9
01	193 32.0	37.1	166 44.1	7.9	15 50.7	7.7	58.9
02	208 31.9	36.7	181 11.0	8.0	15 43.0	7.9	58.8
03	223 31.8 ..	36.4	195 38.0	8.1	15 35.1	7.9	58.8
04	238 31.8	36.0	210 05.1	8.2	15 27.2	8.0	58.8
05	253 31.7	35.6	224 32.3	8.2	15 19.2	8.1	58.7
06	268 31.6	N21 35.2	238 59.5	8.4	N15 11.1	8.2	58.7
07	283 31.6	34.8	253 26.9	8.4	15 02.9	8.3	58.7
T 08	298 31.5	34.4	267 54.3	8.6	14 54.6	8.3	58.6
H 09	313 31.4 ..	34.0	282 21.9	8.6	14 46.3	8.4	58.6
U 10	328 31.4	33.6	296 49.5	8.7	14 37.9	8.5	58.6
R 11	343 31.3	33.2	311 17.2	8.8	14 29.4	8.6	58.5
S 12	358 31.2	N21 32.9	325 45.0	8.9	N14 20.8	8.6	58.5
D 13	13 31.2	32.5	340 12.9	8.9	14 12.2	8.7	58.5
A 14	28 31.1	32.1	354 40.8	9.1	14 03.5	8.8	58.4
Y 15	43 31.0 ..	31.7	9 08.9	9.1	13 54.7	8.8	58.4
16	58 31.0	31.3	23 37.0	9.3	13 45.9	8.9	58.4
17	73 30.9	30.9	38 05.3	9.3	13 37.0	9.0	58.3
18	88 30.8	N21 30.5	52 33.6	9.4	N13 28.0	9.1	58.3
19	103 30.8	30.1	67 02.0	9.5	13 18.9	9.1	58.2
20	118 30.7	29.7	81 30.5	9.6	13 09.8	9.1	58.2
21	133 30.6 ..	29.3	95 59.1	9.7	13 00.7	9.3	58.2
22	148 30.6	28.9	110 27.8	9.7	12 51.4	9.2	58.1
23	163 30.5	28.5	124 56.5	9.9	12 42.2	9.4	58.1
16 00	178 30.5	N21 28.1	139 25.4	9.9	N12 32.8	9.4	58.1
01	193 30.4	27.7	153 54.3	10.0	12 23.4	9.4	58.0
02	208 30.3	27.3	168 23.3	10.1	12 14.0	9.6	58.0
03	223 30.3 ..	26.9	182 52.4	10.2	12 04.4	9.5	58.0
04	238 30.2	26.5	197 21.6	10.3	11 54.9	9.6	57.9
05	253 30.1	26.1	211 50.9	10.3	11 45.3	9.7	57.9
06	268 30.1	N21 25.7	226 20.2	10.5	N11 35.6	9.7	57.8
07	283 30.0	25.3	240 49.7	10.5	11 25.9	9.8	57.8
F 08	298 30.0	24.9	255 19.2	10.6	11 16.1	9.8	57.8
R 09	313 29.9 ..	24.5	269 48.8	10.7	11 06.3	9.9	57.7
I 10	328 29.8	24.1	284 18.5	10.7	10 56.4	9.9	57.7
D 11	343 29.8	23.7	298 48.2	10.8	10 46.5	9.9	57.7
A 12	358 29.7	N21 23.3	313 18.0	11.0	N10 36.6	10.0	57.6
Y 13	13 29.7	22.9	327 48.0	11.0	10 26.6	10.0	57.6
14	28 29.6	22.5	342 18.0	11.0	10 16.6	10.1	57.6
15	43 29.5 ..	22.1	356 48.0	11.2	10 06.5	10.1	57.5
16	58 29.5	21.6	11 18.2	11.2	9 56.4	10.2	57.5
17	73 29.4	21.2	25 48.4	11.3	9 46.2	10.1	57.4
18	88 29.4	N21 20.8	40 18.7	11.4	N 9 36.1	10.3	57.4
19	103 29.3	20.4	54 49.1	11.5	9 25.8	10.2	57.4
20	118 29.2	20.0	69 19.6	11.5	9 15.6	10.3	57.3
21	133 29.2 ..	19.6	83 50.1	11.6	9 05.3	10.3	57.3
22	148 29.1	19.2	98 20.7	11.7	8 55.0	10.4	57.3
23	163 29.1	18.8	112 51.4	11.7	8 44.6	10.4	57.2
17 00	178 29.0	N21 18.4	127 22.1	11.8	N 8 34.2	10.4	57.2
01	193 29.0	17.9	141 52.9	11.9	8 23.8	10.4	57.1
02	208 28.9	17.5	156 23.8	12.0	8 13.4	10.5	57.1
03	223 28.8 ..	17.1	170 54.8	12.0	8 02.9	10.5	57.1
04	238 28.8	16.7	185 25.8	12.1	7 52.4	10.5	57.0
05	253 28.7	16.3	199 56.9	12.2	7 41.9	10.5	57.0
06	268 28.7	N21 15.9	214 28.1	12.2	N 7 31.4	10.6	57.0
07	283 28.6	15.4	228 59.3	12.3	7 20.8	10.6	56.9
S 08	298 28.6	15.0	243 30.6	12.4	7 10.2	10.6	56.9
A 09	313 28.5 ..	14.6	258 00.0	12.4	6 59.6	10.6	56.9
T 10	328 28.4	14.2	272 33.4	12.5	6 49.0	10.6	56.8
U 11	343 28.4	13.8	287 04.9	12.5	6 38.4	10.7	56.8
R 12	358 28.3	N21 13.3	301 36.4	12.6	N 6 27.7	10.7	56.8
D 13	13 28.3	12.9	316 08.0	12.7	6 17.0	10.7	56.7
A 14	28 28.2	12.5	330 39.7	12.8	6 06.3	10.7	56.7
Y 15	43 28.2 ..	12.1	345 11.5	12.7	5 55.6	10.7	56.7
16	58 28.1	11.6	359 43.2	12.9	5 44.9	10.7	56.6
17	73 28.1	11.2	14 15.1	12.9	5 34.2	10.8	56.6
18	88 28.0	N21 10.8	28 47.0	13.0	N 5 23.4	10.7	56.6
19	103 28.0	10.4	43 19.0	13.0	5 12.7	10.8	56.5
20	118 27.9	09.9	57 51.0	13.1	5 01.9	10.8	56.5
21	133 27.9 ..	09.5	72 23.1	13.1	4 51.1	10.8	56.4
22	148 27.8	09.1	86 55.2	13.2	4 40.3	10.8	56.4
23	163 27.8	08.7	101 27.4	13.3	N 4 29.5	10.8	56.4
SD 15.8	d 0.4		SD 15.9		15.7		15.5

Lat.	Twilight Naut.	Civil	Sunrise	Moonrise 15	16	17	18
°	h m	h m	h m	h m	h m	h m	h m
N 72	□	□	□	04 11	06 22	08 18	10 05
N 70	□	□	□	04 48	06 42	08 29	10 09
68	□	□	□	05 14	06 58	08 37	10 11
66	////	////	01 38	05 34	07 11	08 44	10 14
64	////	////	02 17	05 50	07 21	08 50	10 16
62	////	00 53	02 44	06 03	07 30	08 55	10 17
60	////	01 46	03 04	06 14	07 38	09 00	10 19
N 58	////	02 17	03 21	06 24	07 45	09 04	10 20
56	00 49	02 40	03 36	06 32	07 51	09 07	10 21
54	01 38	02 58	03 48	06 39	07 56	09 10	10 22
52	02 06	03 13	03 58	06 46	08 01	09 13	10 23
50	02 27	03 26	04 08	06 52	08 05	09 16	10 24
45	03 05	03 52	04 28	07 05	08 14	09 21	10 26
N 40	03 32	04 12	04 44	07 16	08 22	09 26	10 28
35	03 53	04 29	04 58	07 25	08 29	09 30	10 29
30	04 10	04 42	05 09	07 33	08 34	09 33	10 30
20	04 36	05 05	05 29	07 46	08 44	09 40	10 32
N 10	04 57	05 24	05 46	07 58	08 53	09 45	10 34
0	05 14	05 40	06 02	08 09	09 01	09 50	10 36
S 10	05 30	05 56	06 18	08 20	09 10	09 55	10 38
20	05 44	06 11	06 35	08 32	09 18	10 00	10 40
30	05 59	06 28	06 54	08 46	09 28	10 06	10 42
35	06 06	06 38	07 05	08 54	09 34	10 10	10 43
40	06 15	06 48	07 18	09 03	09 40	10 14	10 44
45	06 24	07 00	07 33	09 13	09 48	10 18	10 46
S 50	06 34	07 14	07 51	09 25	09 57	10 24	10 48
52	06 38	07 21	08 00	09 31	10 01	10 26	10 49
54	06 43	07 28	08 10	09 38	10 06	10 29	10 50
56	06 48	07 36	08 20	09 45	10 11	10 32	10 51
58	06 54	07 44	08 33	09 53	10 16	10 35	10 52
S 60	07 00	07 54	08 48	10 02	10 22	10 39	10 53

Lat.	Sunset	Twilight Civil	Naut.	Moonset 15	16	17	18
°	h m	h m	h m	h m	h m	h m	h m
N 72	□	□	□	23 33	23 20	23 09	22 58
N 70	□	□	□	23 11	23 07	23 03	22 58
68	□	□	□	22 54	22 57	22 58	22 58
66	22 31	////	////	22 40	22 48	22 54	22 58
64	21 53	////	////	22 29	22 41	22 50	22 58
62	21 27	23 12	////	22 19	22 34	22 47	22 58
60	21 06	22 23	////	22 10	22 29	22 44	22 58
N 58	20 50	21 53	////	22 03	22 24	22 42	22 58
56	20 35	21 31	23 17	21 56	22 20	22 40	22 58
54	20 23	21 13	22 32	21 50	22 16	22 38	22 58
52	20 13	20 58	22 04	21 45	22 12	22 36	22 58
50	20 03	20 45	21 43	21 40	22 09	22 35	22 58
45	19 44	20 19	21 06	21 29	22 02	22 31	22 58
N 40	19 28	19 59	20 39	21 21	21 56	22 28	22 58
35	19 14	19 43	20 18	21 13	21 51	22 25	22 58
30	19 02	19 29	20 02	21 06	21 46	22 23	22 58
20	18 43	19 07	19 35	20 55	21 39	22 19	22 57
N 10	18 25	18 48	19 15	20 44	21 32	22 16	22 57
0	18 10	18 32	18 58	20 35	21 25	22 12	22 57
S 10	17 54	18 16	18 42	20 25	21 18	22 09	22 57
20	17 37	18 01	18 28	20 14	21 11	22 05	22 57
30	17 18	17 44	18 13	20 02	21 03	22 01	22 57
35	17 07	17 35	18 06	19 55	20 58	21 59	22 57
40	16 54	17 24	17 58	19 47	20 53	21 56	22 56
45	16 39	17 12	17 49	19 38	20 46	21 53	22 56
S 50	16 21	16 58	17 39	19 27	20 39	21 49	22 56
52	16 13	16 52	17 34	19 21	20 35	21 47	22 56
54	16 03	16 45	17 30	19 16	20 31	21 45	22 56
56	15 52	16 37	17 24	19 09	20 27	21 43	22 56
58	15 40	16 28	17 19	19 02	20 22	21 40	22 56
S 60	15 25	16 18	17 13	18 53	20 17	21 38	22 56

Day	Eqn. of Time 00h	12h	Mer. Pass.	Mer. Pass. Upper	Lower	Age	Phase
d	m s	m s	h m	h m	h m	d	%
15	05 52	05 55	12 06	14 22	01 55	02	8
16	05 58	06 01	12 06	15 13	02 48	03	14
17	06 04	06 07	12 06	16 01	03 38	04	23

UT	ARIES	VENUS −4.5		MARS −0.1		JUPITER −2.4		SATURN +0.3		STARS		
d h	GHA	GHA	Dec	GHA	Dec	GHA	Dec	GHA	Dec	Name	SHA	Dec
18 00	295 21.7	141 28.9 N 8 56.9		83 15.4 S14 27.1		264 25.0 N11 12.7		251 31.9 N14 17.9		Acamar	315 26.7	S40 18.3
01	310 24.2	156 30.5	56.1	98 16.8	27.5	279 27.2	12.8	266 34.2	17.9	Achernar	335 34.8	S57 14.1
02	325 26.6	171 32.2	55.3	113 18.3	27.9	294 29.3	12.9	281 36.5	18.0	Acrux	173 21.6	S63 06.0
03	340 29.1	186 33.9 ..	54.6	128 19.7 ..	28.3	309 31.5 ..	13.0	296 38.8 ..	18.0	Adhara	255 21.4	S28 58.3
04	355 31.6	201 35.6	53.8	143 21.2	28.7	324 33.7	13.1	311 41.1	18.1	Aldebaran	291 02.0	N16 30.4
05	10 34.0	216 37.2	53.0	158 22.6	29.0	339 35.9	13.1	326 43.3	18.1			
06	25 36.5	231 38.9 N 8 52.2		173 24.0 S14 29.4		354 38.1 N11 13.2		341 45.6 N14 18.2		Alioth	166 30.3	N55 58.1
07	40 39.0	246 40.6	51.4	188 25.5	29.8	9 40.3	13.3	356 47.9	18.2	Alkaid	153 07.4	N49 19.3
08	55 41.4	261 42.3	50.6	203 26.9	30.2	24 42.5	13.4	11 50.2	18.2	Al Na'ir	27 56.9	S46 57.6
S 09	70 43.9	276 44.0 ..	49.9	218 28.4 ..	30.6	39 44.7 ..	13.5	26 52.5 ..	18.3	Alnilam	275 57.6	S 1 12.2
U 10	85 46.3	291 45.7	49.1	233 29.8	31.0	54 46.8	13.6	41 54.8	18.3	Alphard	218 07.0	S 8 39.4
N 11	100 48.8	306 47.4	48.3	248 31.3	31.4	69 49.0	13.7	56 57.1	18.4			
D 12	115 51.3	321 49.1 N 8 47.5		263 32.7 S14 31.8		84 51.2 N11 13.8		71 59.4 N14 18.4		Alphecca	126 20.0	N26 43.3
A 13	130 53.7	336 50.8	46.8	278 34.1	32.2	99 53.4	13.9	87 01.7	18.4	Alpheratz	357 54.5	N29 05.1
Y 14	145 56.2	351 52.5	46.0	293 35.6	32.6	114 55.6	13.9	102 04.0	18.5	Altair	62 18.4	N 8 52.1
15	160 58.7	6 54.2 ..	45.2	308 37.0 ..	33.0	129 57.8 ..	14.0	117 06.2 ..	18.5	Ankaa	353 26.2	S42 18.3
16	176 01.1	21 56.0	44.4	323 38.4	33.4	145 00.0	14.1	132 08.5	18.6	Antares	112 39.3	S26 25.8
17	191 03.6	36 57.7	43.6	338 39.9	33.8	160 02.2	14.2	147 10.8	18.6			
18	206 06.1	51 59.4 N 8 42.9		353 41.3 S14 34.2		175 04.4 N11 14.3		162 13.1 N14 18.7		Arcturus	146 05.5	N19 11.4
19	221 08.5	67 01.1	42.1	8 42.8	34.5	190 06.6	14.4	177 15.4	18.7	Atria	107 50.4	S69 01.7
20	236 11.0	82 02.9	41.3	23 44.2	34.9	205 08.7	14.5	192 17.7	18.7	Avior	234 23.0	S59 30.6
21	251 13.5	97 04.6 ..	40.6	38 45.6 ..	35.3	220 10.9 ..	14.6	207 20.0 ..	18.8	Bellatrix	278 43.9	N 6 20.9
22	266 15.9	112 06.3	39.8	53 47.1	35.7	235 13.1	14.6	222 22.3	18.8	Betelgeuse	271 13.3	N 7 24.3
23	281 18.4	127 08.1	39.0	68 48.5	36.1	250 15.3	14.7	237 24.6	18.9			
19 00	296 20.8	142 09.8 N 8 38.2		83 49.9 S14 36.5		265 17.5 N11 14.8		252 26.9 N14 18.9		Canopus	264 01.5	S52 41.7
01	311 23.3	157 11.5	37.5	98 51.4	36.9	280 19.7	14.9	267 29.2	18.9	Capella	280 50.8	N45 59.6
02	326 25.8	172 13.3	36.7	113 52.8	37.3	295 21.9	15.0	282 31.4	19.0	Deneb	49 38.3	N45 16.7
03	341 28.2	187 15.0 ..	35.9	128 54.2 ..	37.7	310 24.1 ..	15.1	297 33.7 ..	19.0	Denebola	182 44.8	N14 34.7
04	356 30.7	202 16.8	35.2	143 55.6	38.1	325 26.3	15.2	312 36.0	19.1	Diphda	349 06.6	S17 59.3
05	11 33.2	217 18.6	34.4	158 57.1	38.5	340 28.5	15.3	327 38.3	19.1			
06	26 35.6	232 20.3 N 8 33.6		173 58.5 S14 38.9		355 30.7 N11 15.3		342 40.6 N14 19.2		Dubhe	194 05.3	N61 45.5
07	41 38.1	247 22.1	32.9	188 59.9	39.3	10 32.9	15.4	357 42.9	19.2	Elnath	278 26.6	N28 36.3
08	56 40.6	262 23.8	32.1	204 01.3	39.7	25 35.1	15.5	12 45.2	19.2	Eltanin	90 50.7	N51 29.6
M 09	71 43.0	277 25.6 ..	31.3	219 02.8 ..	40.1	40 37.3 ..	15.6	27 47.5 ..	19.3	Enif	33 57.4	N 9 52.4
O 10	86 45.5	292 27.4	30.6	234 04.2	40.5	55 39.5	15.7	42 49.8	19.3	Fomalhaut	15 35.6	S29 37.3
N 11	101 47.9	307 29.2	29.8	249 05.6	40.9	70 41.6	15.8	57 52.1	19.4			
D 12	116 50.4	322 30.9 N 8 29.1		264 07.0 S14 41.3		85 43.8 N11 15.9		72 54.4 N14 19.4		Gacrux	172 13.1	S57 06.8
A 13	131 52.9	337 32.7	28.3	279 08.5	41.7	100 46.0	15.9	87 56.7	19.4	Gienah	176 03.5	S17 32.3
Y 14	146 55.3	352 34.5	27.5	294 09.9	42.1	115 48.2	16.0	102 59.0	19.5	Hadar	149 03.1	S60 22.4
15	161 57.8	7 36.3 ..	26.8	309 11.3 ..	42.5	130 50.4 ..	16.1	118 01.2 ..	19.5	Hamal	328 13.0	N23 27.4
16	177 00.3	22 38.1	26.0	324 12.7	42.8	145 52.6	16.2	133 03.5	19.6	Kaus Aust.	83 57.7	S34 23.0
17	192 02.7	37 39.9	25.3	339 14.1	43.2	160 54.8	16.3	148 05.8	19.6			
18	207 05.2	52 41.7 N 8 24.5		354 15.6 S14 43.6		175 57.0 N11 16.4		163 08.1 N14 19.7		Kochab	137 19.3	N74 09.9
19	222 07.7	67 43.5	23.7	9 17.0	44.0	190 59.2	16.5	178 10.4	19.7	Markab	13 48.9	N15 12.1
20	237 10.1	82 45.3	23.0	24 18.4	44.4	206 01.4	16.5	193 12.7	19.7	Menkar	314 26.5	N 4 05.2
21	252 12.6	97 47.1 ..	22.2	39 19.8 ..	44.8	221 03.6 ..	16.6	208 15.0 ..	19.8	Menkent	148 20.3	S36 22.1
22	267 15.1	112 48.9	21.5	54 21.2	45.2	236 05.8	16.7	223 17.3	19.8	Miaplacidus	221 42.8	S69 43.0
23	282 17.5	127 50.7	20.7	69 22.7	45.6	251 08.0	16.8	238 19.6	19.8			
20 00	297 20.0	142 52.5 N 8 20.0		84 24.1 S14 46.0		266 10.2 N11 16.9		253 21.9 N14 19.9		Mirfak	308 56.0	N49 51.3
01	312 22.4	157 54.3	19.2	99 25.5	46.4	281 12.4	17.0	268 24.2	19.9	Nunki	76 11.3	S26 17.7
02	327 24.9	172 56.1	18.5	114 26.9	46.8	296 14.6	17.1	283 26.5	20.0	Peacock	53 35.6	S56 44.1
03	342 27.4	187 58.0 ..	17.7	129 28.3 ..	47.2	311 16.8 ..	17.1	298 28.8 ..	20.0	Pollux	243 41.3	N28 01.6
04	357 29.8	202 59.8	16.9	144 29.7	47.6	326 19.0	17.2	313 31.1	20.0	Procyon	245 11.3	N 5 13.6
05	12 32.3	218 01.6	16.2	159 31.1	48.0	341 21.2	17.3	328 33.4	20.1			
06	27 34.8	233 03.5 N 8 15.4		174 32.5 S14 48.4		356 23.4 N11 17.4		343 35.7 N14 20.1		Rasalhague	96 16.2	N12 33.8
07	42 37.2	248 05.3	14.7	189 34.0	48.8	11 25.6	17.5	358 38.0	20.2	Regulus	207 55.3	N11 58.3
T 08	57 39.7	263 07.1	13.9	204 35.4	49.2	26 27.8	17.6	13 40.3	20.2	Rigel	281 22.7	S 8 12.2
U 09	72 42.2	278 09.0 ..	13.2	219 36.8 ..	49.6	41 30.0 ..	17.6	28 42.6 ..	20.2	Rigil Kent.	140 06.4	S60 50.1
E 10	87 44.6	293 10.8	12.5	234 38.2	50.0	56 32.2	17.7	43 44.9	20.3	Sabik	102 24.6	S15 43.3
S 11	102 47.1	308 12.7	11.7	249 39.6	50.4	71 34.4	17.8	58 47.2	20.3			
D 12	117 49.5	323 14.5 N 8 11.0		264 41.0 S14 50.8		86 36.6 N11 17.9		73 49.4 N14 20.4		Schedar	349 52.7	N56 31.8
A 13	132 52.0	338 16.4	10.2	279 42.4	51.2	101 38.8	18.0	88 51.7	20.4	Shaula	96 36.2	S37 06.1
Y 14	147 54.5	353 18.2	09.5	294 43.8	51.6	116 41.0	18.1	103 54.0	20.4	Sirius	258 43.6	S16 42.9
15	162 56.9	8 20.1 ..	08.7	309 45.2 ..	52.0	131 43.2 ..	18.1	118 56.3 ..	20.5	Spica	158 42.6	S11 09.4
16	177 59.4	23 22.0	08.0	324 46.6	52.4	146 45.4	18.2	133 58.6	20.5	Suhail	223 00.8	S43 25.9
17	193 01.9	38 23.8	07.2	339 48.0	52.8	161 47.6	18.3	149 00.9	20.6			
18	208 04.3	53 25.7 N 8 06.5		354 49.4 S14 53.2		176 49.8 N11 18.4		164 03.2 N14 20.6		Vega	80 45.8	N38 47.2
19	223 06.8	68 27.6	05.8	9 50.8	53.6	191 52.0	18.5	179 05.5	20.6	Zuben'ubi	137 17.3	S16 02.3
20	238 09.3	83 29.5	05.0	24 52.2	54.0	206 54.2	18.6	194 07.8	20.7		SHA	Mer. Pass.
21	253 11.7	98 31.3 ..	04.3	39 53.6 ..	54.4	221 56.4 ..	18.6	209 10.1 ..	20.7		° '	h m
22	268 14.2	113 33.2	03.5	54 55.0	54.8	236 58.6	18.7	224 12.4	20.8	Venus	205 49.0	14 30
23	283 16.7	128 35.1	02.8	69 56.4	55.2	252 00.8	18.8	239 14.7	20.8	Mars	147 29.1	18 23
Mer. Pass.	h m 4 13.9	v 1.8	d 0.8	v 1.4	d 0.4	v 2.2	d 0.1	v 2.3	d 0.0	Jupiter Saturn	328 56.7 316 06.0	6 18 7 09

SUN / MOON

UT	SUN GHA	SUN Dec	MOON GHA	v	Dec	d	HP
d h	° '	° '	° '	'	° '	'	'
18 00	178 27.7	N21 08.2	115 59.7	13.2	N 4 18.7	10.8	56.3
01	193 27.6	07.8	130 31.9	13.4	4 07.9	10.8	56.3
02	208 27.6	07.4	145 04.3	13.4	3 57.1	10.8	56.3
03	223 27.5 ..	06.9	159 36.7	13.4	3 46.3	10.9	56.2
04	238 27.5	06.5	174 09.1	13.5	3 35.4	10.8	56.2
05	253 27.4	06.1	188 41.6	13.6	3 24.6	10.8	56.2
06	268 27.4	N21 05.6	203 14.2	13.5	N 3 13.8	10.9	56.2
07	283 27.3	05.2	217 46.7	13.7	3 02.9	10.8	56.1
08	298 27.3	04.8	232 19.4	13.7	2 52.1	10.8	56.1
S 09	313 27.2 ..	04.3	246 52.1	13.7	2 41.3	10.9	56.1
U 10	328 27.2	03.9	261 24.8	13.7	2 30.4	10.8	56.0
N 11	343 27.1	03.5	275 57.5	13.8	2 19.6	10.8	56.0
D 12	358 27.1	N21 03.0	290 30.3	13.9	N 2 08.8	10.9	56.0
A 13	13 27.0	02.6	305 03.2	13.9	1 57.9	10.8	55.9
Y 14	28 27.0	02.2	319 36.1	13.9	1 47.1	10.8	55.9
15	43 26.9 ..	01.7	334 09.0	14.0	1 36.3	10.8	55.9
16	58 26.9	01.3	348 42.0	14.0	1 25.5	10.8	55.8
17	73 26.9	00.8	3 15.0	14.0	1 14.7	10.8	55.8
18	88 26.8	N21 00.4	17 48.0	14.1	N 1 03.9	10.8	55.8
19	103 26.8	21 00.0	32 21.1	14.1	0 53.1	10.8	55.8
20	118 26.7	20 59.5	46 54.2	14.1	0 42.3	10.8	55.7
21	133 26.7 ..	59.1	61 27.3	14.2	0 31.5	10.7	55.7
22	148 26.6	58.6	76 00.5	14.2	0 20.8	10.8	55.7
23	163 26.6	58.2	90 33.7	14.3	N 0 10.0	10.7	55.6
19 00	178 26.5	N20 57.8	105 07.0	14.3	S 0 00.7	10.8	55.6
01	193 26.5	57.3	119 40.3	14.3	0 11.5	10.7	55.6
02	208 26.4	56.9	134 13.6	14.3	0 22.2	10.7	55.6
03	223 26.4 ..	56.4	148 46.9	14.4	0 32.9	10.7	55.5
04	238 26.3	56.0	163 20.3	14.3	0 43.6	10.7	55.5
05	253 26.3	55.5	177 53.6	14.5	0 54.3	10.7	55.5
06	268 26.3	N20 55.1	192 27.1	14.4	S 1 05.0	10.6	55.4
07	283 26.2	54.6	207 00.5	14.5	1 15.6	10.6	55.4
08	298 26.2	54.2	221 34.0	14.5	1 26.2	10.7	55.4
M 09	313 26.1 ..	53.7	236 07.5	14.5	1 36.9	10.6	55.4
O 10	328 26.1	53.3	250 41.0	14.5	1 47.5	10.5	55.3
N 11	343 26.0	52.8	265 14.5	14.6	1 58.0	10.6	55.3
D 12	358 26.0	N20 52.4	279 48.1	14.5	S 2 08.6	10.6	55.3
A 13	13 26.0	51.9	294 21.6	14.6	2 19.2	10.5	55.3
Y 14	28 25.9	51.5	308 55.2	14.7	2 29.7	10.5	55.2
15	43 25.9 ..	51.0	323 28.9	14.6	2 40.2	10.5	55.2
16	58 25.8	50.6	338 02.5	14.6	2 50.7	10.4	55.2
17	73 25.8	50.1	352 36.1	14.7	3 01.1	10.5	55.2
18	88 25.7	N20 49.7	7 09.8	14.7	S 3 11.6	10.4	55.1
19	103 25.7	49.2	21 43.5	14.7	3 22.0	10.4	55.1
20	118 25.7	48.7	36 17.2	14.7	3 32.4	10.4	55.1
21	133 25.6 ..	48.3	50 50.9	14.7	3 42.8	10.3	55.1
22	148 25.6	47.8	65 24.6	14.8	3 53.1	10.4	55.0
23	163 25.5	47.3	79 58.4	14.7	4 03.5	10.3	55.0
20 00	178 25.5	N20 46.9	94 32.1	14.8	S 4 13.8	10.2	55.0
01	193 25.5	46.5	109 05.9	14.7	4 24.0	10.3	55.0
02	208 25.4	46.0	123 39.6	14.8	4 34.3	10.2	55.0
03	223 25.4 ..	45.5	138 13.4	14.8	4 44.5	10.2	54.9
04	238 25.3	45.1	152 47.2	14.8	4 54.7	10.1	54.9
05	253 25.3	44.6	167 21.0	14.8	5 04.8	10.2	54.9
06	268 25.3	N20 44.2	181 54.8	14.8	S 5 15.0	10.1	54.9
07	283 25.2	43.7	196 28.6	14.8	5 25.1	10.1	54.9
08	298 25.2	43.2	211 02.4	14.8	5 35.2	10.0	54.8
T 09	313 25.1 ..	42.8	225 36.2	14.9	5 45.2	10.0	54.8
U 10	328 25.1	42.3	240 10.1	14.8	5 55.2	10.0	54.8
E 11	343 25.1	41.8	254 43.9	14.8	6 05.2	9.9	54.8
S 12	358 25.0	N20 41.4	269 17.7	14.8	S 6 15.1	10.0	54.8
D 13	13 25.0	40.9	283 51.5	14.9	6 25.1	9.8	54.7
A 14	28 25.0	40.4	298 25.4	14.8	6 34.9	9.9	54.7
Y 15	43 24.9 ..	40.0	312 59.2	14.8	6 44.8	9.8	54.7
16	58 24.9	39.5	327 33.0	14.8	6 54.6	9.8	54.7
17	73 24.9	39.0	342 06.8	14.9	7 04.4	9.7	54.7
18	88 24.8	N20 38.6	356 40.7	14.8	S 7 14.1	9.8	54.6
19	103 24.8	38.1	11 14.5	14.8	7 23.9	9.6	54.6
20	118 24.7	37.6	25 48.3	14.8	7 33.5	9.7	54.6
21	133 24.7 ..	37.2	40 22.1	14.8	7 43.2	9.6	54.6
22	148 24.7	36.7	54 55.9	14.8	7 52.8	9.5	54.6
23	163 24.6	36.2	69 29.7	14.8	S 8 02.3	9.6	54.6
	SD 15.8	d 0.5	SD 15.2		15.1		14.9

Twilight / Sunrise / Moonrise

Lat.	Naut.	Civil	Sunrise	18	19	20	21
°	h m	h m	h m	h m	h m	h m	h m
N 72	▭	▭	▭	10 05	11 48	13 29	15 11
N 70	▭	▭	▭	10 09	11 45	13 19	14 53
68	////	////	00 39	10 11	11 42	13 11	14 39
66	////	////	01 51	10 14	11 40	13 04	14 28
64	////	////	02 26	10 16	11 38	12 59	14 18
62	////	01 12	02 51	10 17	11 37	12 54	14 10
60	////	01 56	03 10	10 19	11 35	12 50	14 03
N 58	////	02 24	03 27	10 20	11 34	12 46	13 57
56	01 06	02 46	03 40	10 21	11 33	12 43	13 51
54	01 47	03 03	03 52	10 22	11 32	12 40	13 47
52	02 13	03 18	04 02	10 23	11 31	12 37	13 42
50	02 33	03 30	04 11	10 24	11 30	12 35	13 38
45	03 09	03 55	04 31	10 26	11 29	12 30	13 30
N 40	03 35	04 15	04 46	10 28	11 27	12 25	13 23
35	03 56	04 31	05 00	10 29	11 26	12 22	13 17
30	04 12	04 44	05 11	10 30	11 25	12 18	13 11
20	04 38	05 06	05 30	10 32	11 23	12 13	13 02
N 10	04 58	05 25	05 47	10 34	11 22	12 08	12 54
0	05 15	05 41	06 03	10 36	11 20	12 03	12 47
S 10	05 30	05 56	06 18	10 38	11 19	11 59	12 39
20	05 44	06 11	06 34	10 40	11 17	11 54	12 31
30	05 58	06 27	06 53	10 42	11 15	11 49	12 22
35	06 05	06 36	07 04	10 43	11 14	11 45	12 17
40	06 13	06 46	07 16	10 44	11 13	11 42	12 11
45	06 22	06 58	07 31	10 46	11 12	11 38	12 05
S 50	06 31	07 12	07 48	10 48	11 10	11 33	11 57
52	06 36	07 18	07 57	10 49	11 10	11 31	11 53
54	06 40	07 25	08 06	10 50	11 09	11 28	11 49
56	06 45	07 32	08 17	10 51	11 08	11 26	11 44
58	06 50	07 41	08 29	10 52	11 07	11 23	11 39
S 60	06 56	07 50	08 43	10 53	11 06	11 19	11 34

Sunset / Twilight / Moonset

Lat.	Sunset	Civil	Naut.	18	19	20	21
°	h m	h m	h m	h m	h m	h m	h m
N 72	▭	▭	▭	22 58	22 48	22 38	22 25
N 70	▭	▭	▭	22 58	22 54	22 50	22 45
68	23 22	////	////	22 58	22 59	22 59	23 00
66	22 18	////	////	22 58	23 02	23 07	23 13
64	21 44	////	////	22 58	23 06	23 14	23 23
62	21 20	22 55	////	22 58	23 09	23 20	23 32
60	21 01	22 14	////	22 58	23 11	23 25	23 40
N 58	20 45	21 46	////	22 58	23 13	23 29	23 47
56	20 31	21 25	23 02	22 58	23 15	23 33	23 53
54	20 20	21 08	22 23	22 58	23 17	23 37	23 58
52	20 09	20 54	21 58	22 58	23 19	23 40	24 03
50	20 00	20 42	21 38	22 58	23 20	23 43	24 08
45	19 41	20 17	21 02	22 58	23 24	23 50	24 18
N 40	19 26	19 57	20 36	22 58	23 27	23 55	24 26
35	19 13	19 41	20 16	22 58	23 29	24 00	00 00
30	19 01	19 28	20 00	22 58	23 31	24 04	00 04
20	18 42	19 06	19 34	22 57	23 35	24 12	00 12
N 10	18 25	18 48	19 14	22 57	23 38	24 18	00 18
0	18 10	18 32	18 58	22 57	23 41	24 24	00 24
S 10	17 55	18 17	18 43	22 57	23 44	24 30	00 30
20	17 38	18 02	18 29	22 57	23 47	24 37	00 37
30	17 20	17 46	18 15	22 57	23 51	24 44	00 44
35	17 09	17 36	18 07	22 57	23 53	24 48	00 48
40	16 57	17 26	18 00	22 56	23 55	24 53	00 53
45	16 42	17 15	17 51	22 56	23 58	24 59	00 59
S 50	16 25	17 01	17 42	22 56	24 02	00 02	01 05
52	16 16	16 55	17 37	22 56	24 03	00 03	01 09
54	16 07	16 48	17 33	22 56	24 05	00 05	01 12
56	15 56	16 41	17 28	22 56	24 07	00 07	01 16
58	15 44	16 32	17 23	22 56	24 09	00 09	01 20
S 60	15 31	16 23	17 17	22 56	24 11	00 11	01 25

SUN / MOON

	SUN			MOON			
Day	Eqn. of Time 00ʰ	Eqn. of Time 12ʰ	Mer. Pass.	Mer. Pass. Upper	Mer. Pass. Lower	Age	Phase
d	m s	m s	h m	h m	h m	d	%
18	06 09	06 12	12 06	16 47	04 24	05	32
19	06 14	06 16	12 06	17 30	05 09	06	42
20	06 18	06 20	12 06	18 14	05 52	07	51

UT	ARIES	VENUS −4.5		MARS −0.1		JUPITER −2.4		SATURN +0.3		STARS		
	GHA	GHA	Dec	GHA	Dec	GHA	Dec	GHA	Dec	Name	SHA	Dec
d h	° ′	° ′	° ′	° ′	° ′	° ′	° ′	° ′	° ′		° ′	° ′
21 00	298 19.1	143 37.0	N 8 02.1	84 57.8	S14 55.6	267 03.0	N11 18.9	254 17.0	N14 20.8	Acamar	315 26.7	S40 18.3
01	313 21.6	158 38.9	01.3	99 59.2	56.0	282 05.3	19.0	269 19.3	20.9	Achernar	335 34.8	S57 14.1
02	328 24.0	173 40.8	8 00.6	115 00.6	56.4	297 07.5	19.1	284 21.6	20.9	Acrux	173 21.6	S63 06.0
03	343 26.5	188 42.7	7 59.9	130 02.0 ..	56.8	312 09.7 ..	19.1	299 23.9 ..	21.0	Adhara	255 21.4	S28 58.3
04	358 29.0	203 44.6	59.1	145 03.4	57.2	327 11.9	19.2	314 26.2	21.0	Aldebaran	291 02.0	N16 30.4
05	13 31.4	218 46.5	58.4	160 04.8	57.6	342 14.1	19.3	329 28.5	21.0			
W 06	28 33.9	233 48.4	N 7 57.7	175 06.2	S14 58.0	357 16.3	N11 19.4	344 30.8	N14 21.1	Alioth	166 30.3	N55 58.1
E 07	43 36.4	248 50.3	56.9	190 07.6	58.4	12 18.5	19.5	359 33.1	21.1	Alkaid	153 07.4	N49 19.3
D 08	58 38.8	263 52.2	56.2	205 09.0	58.8	27 20.7	19.5	14 35.4	21.2	Al Na'ir	27 56.8	S46 57.6
N 09	73 41.3	278 54.2 ..	55.5	220 10.4 ..	59.2	42 22.9 ..	19.6	29 37.7 ..	21.2	Alnilam	275 57.6	S 1 12.2
E 10	88 43.8	293 56.1	54.7	235 11.8	14 59.6	57 25.1	19.7	44 40.0	21.2	Alphard	218 07.0	S 8 39.4
S 11	103 46.2	308 58.0	54.0	250 13.2	15 00.0	72 27.3	19.8	59 42.3	21.3			
D 12	118 48.7	323 59.9	N 7 53.3	265 14.5	S15 00.4	87 29.5	N11 19.9	74 44.6	N14 21.3	Alphecca	126 20.0	N26 43.3
A 13	133 51.2	339 01.9	52.6	280 15.9	00.8	102 31.7	20.0	89 46.9	21.3	Alpheratz	357 54.5	N29 05.1
Y 14	148 53.6	354 03.8	51.8	295 17.3	01.2	117 33.9	20.0	104 49.2	21.4	Altair	62 18.4	N 8 52.2
15	163 56.1	9 05.7 ..	51.1	310 18.7 ..	01.6	132 36.1 ..	20.1	119 51.5 ..	21.4	Ankaa	353 26.2	S42 18.3
16	178 58.5	24 07.7	50.4	325 20.1	02.0	147 38.4	20.2	134 53.8	21.5	Antares	112 39.3	S26 25.8
17	194 01.0	39 09.6	49.7	340 21.5	02.4	162 40.6	20.3	149 56.1	21.5			
18	209 03.5	54 11.6	N 7 48.9	355 22.9	S15 02.8	177 42.8	N11 20.4	164 58.4	N14 21.5	Arcturus	146 05.5	N19 11.4
19	224 05.9	69 13.5	48.2	10 24.3	03.2	192 45.0	20.4	180 00.7	21.6	Atria	107 50.4	S69 01.7
20	239 08.4	84 15.5	47.5	25 25.6	03.6	207 47.2	20.5	195 03.0	21.6	Avior	234 23.0	S59 30.5
21	254 10.9	99 17.4 ..	46.8	40 27.0 ..	04.0	222 49.4 ..	20.6	210 05.3 ..	21.7	Bellatrix	278 43.8	N 6 20.9
22	269 13.3	114 19.4	46.1	55 28.4	04.4	237 51.6	20.7	225 07.6	21.7	Betelgeuse	271 13.3	N 7 24.4
23	284 15.8	129 21.4	45.3	70 29.8	04.8	252 53.8	20.8	240 09.9	21.7			
22 00	299 18.3	144 23.3	N 7 44.6	85 31.2	S15 05.2	267 56.0	N11 20.8	255 12.2	N14 21.8	Canopus	264 01.4	S52 41.7
01	314 20.7	159 25.3	43.9	100 32.6	05.6	282 58.2	20.9	270 14.5	21.8	Capella	280 50.8	N45 59.6
02	329 23.2	174 27.3	43.2	115 33.9	06.0	298 00.5	21.0	285 16.8	21.8	Deneb	49 38.3	N45 16.8
03	344 25.6	189 29.3 ..	42.5	130 35.3 ..	06.4	313 02.7 ..	21.1	300 19.1 ..	21.9	Denebola	182 44.8	N14 34.7
04	359 28.1	204 31.2	41.8	145 36.7	06.8	328 04.9	21.2	315 21.4	21.9	Diphda	349 06.6	S17 59.3
05	14 30.6	219 33.2	41.0	160 38.1	07.2	343 07.1	21.2	330 23.7	22.0			
T 06	29 33.0	234 35.2	N 7 40.3	175 39.5	S15 07.6	358 09.3	N11 21.3	345 26.0	N14 22.0	Dubhe	194 05.4	N61 45.5
H 07	44 35.5	249 37.2	39.6	190 40.8	08.0	13 11.5	21.4	0 28.3	22.0	Elnath	278 26.6	N28 36.3
U 08	59 38.0	264 39.2	38.9	205 42.2	08.4	28 13.7	21.5	15 30.6	22.1	Eltanin	90 50.7	N51 29.6
R 09	74 40.4	279 41.2 ..	38.2	220 43.6 ..	08.8	43 15.9 ..	21.6	30 32.9 ..	22.1	Enif	33 57.4	N 9 52.4
S 10	89 42.9	294 43.2	37.5	235 45.0	09.2	58 18.2	21.6	45 35.2	22.1	Fomalhaut	15 35.6	S29 37.3
D 11	104 45.4	309 45.2	36.8	250 46.3	09.6	73 20.4	21.7	60 37.5	22.2			
A 12	119 47.8	324 47.2	N 7 36.1	265 47.7	S15 10.1	88 22.6	N11 21.8	75 39.9	N14 22.2	Gacrux	172 13.1	S57 06.8
Y 13	134 50.3	339 49.2	35.4	280 49.1	10.5	103 24.8	21.9	90 42.2	22.3	Gienah	176 03.5	S17 32.3
14	149 52.8	354 51.2	34.7	295 50.5	10.9	118 27.0	22.0	105 44.5	22.3	Hadar	149 03.2	S60 22.4
15	164 55.2	9 53.3 ..	33.9	310 51.8 ..	11.3	133 29.2 ..	22.0	120 46.8 ..	22.3	Hamal	328 13.0	N23 27.4
16	179 57.7	24 55.3	33.2	325 53.2	11.7	148 31.4	22.1	135 49.1	22.4	Kaus Aust.	83 57.7	S34 23.0
17	195 00.1	39 57.3	32.5	340 54.6	12.1	163 33.7	22.2	150 51.4	22.4			
18	210 02.6	54 59.3	N 7 31.8	355 55.9	S15 12.5	178 35.9	N11 22.3	165 53.7	N14 22.4	Kochab	137 19.4	N74 09.9
19	225 05.1	70 01.4	31.1	10 57.3	12.9	193 38.1	22.3	180 56.0	22.5	Markab	13 48.8	N15 12.1
20	240 07.5	85 03.4	30.4	25 58.7	13.3	208 40.3	22.4	195 58.3	22.5	Menkar	314 26.4	N 4 05.2
21	255 10.0	100 05.4 ..	29.7	41 00.1 ..	13.7	223 42.5 ..	22.5	211 00.6 ..	22.6	Menkent	148 20.3	S36 22.1
22	270 12.5	115 07.5	29.0	56 01.4	14.1	238 44.7	22.6	226 02.9	22.6	Miaplacidus	221 42.8	S69 43.0
23	285 14.9	130 09.5	28.3	71 02.8	14.5	253 47.0	22.7	241 05.2	22.6			
23 00	300 17.4	145 11.6	N 7 27.6	86 04.2	S15 14.9	268 49.2	N11 22.7	256 07.5	N14 22.7	Mirfak	308 56.0	N49 51.3
01	315 19.9	160 13.6	26.9	101 05.5	15.3	283 51.4	22.8	271 09.8	22.7	Nunki	76 11.3	S26 17.7
02	330 22.3	175 15.7	26.2	116 06.9	15.7	298 53.6	22.9	286 12.1	22.7	Peacock	53 35.6	S56 44.1
03	345 24.8	190 17.7 ..	25.5	131 08.2 ..	16.1	313 55.8 ..	23.0	301 14.4 ..	22.8	Pollux	243 41.3	N28 01.6
04	0 27.3	205 19.8	24.9	146 09.6	16.5	328 58.0	23.0	316 16.7	22.8	Procyon	245 11.3	N 5 13.6
05	15 29.7	220 21.9	24.2	161 11.0	16.9	344 00.3	23.1	331 19.0	22.9			
F 06	30 32.2	235 23.9	N 7 23.5	176 12.3	S15 17.3	359 02.5	N11 23.2	346 21.3	N14 22.9	Rasalhague	96 16.2	N12 33.8
R 07	45 34.6	250 26.0	22.8	191 13.7	17.7	14 04.7	23.3	1 23.6	22.9	Regulus	207 55.3	N11 58.3
I 08	60 37.1	265 28.1	22.1	206 15.1	18.1	29 06.9	23.4	16 26.0	23.0	Rigel	281 22.7	S 8 12.2
D 09	75 39.6	280 30.2 ..	21.4	221 16.4 ..	18.5	44 09.1 ..	23.4	31 28.3 ..	23.0	Rigil Kent.	140 06.4	S60 50.1
A 10	90 42.0	295 32.2	20.7	236 17.8	18.9	59 11.4	23.5	46 30.6	23.0	Sabik	102 24.6	S15 43.3
Y 11	105 44.5	310 34.3	20.0	251 19.1	19.4	74 13.6	23.6	61 32.9	23.1			
12	120 47.0	325 36.4	N 7 19.3	266 20.5	S15 19.8	89 15.8	N11 23.7	76 35.2	N14 23.1	Schedar	349 52.6	N56 31.8
13	135 49.4	340 38.5	18.6	281 21.9	20.2	104 18.0	23.7	91 37.5	23.1	Shaula	96 36.2	S37 06.2
14	150 51.9	355 40.6	18.0	296 23.2	20.6	119 20.2	23.8	106 39.8	23.2	Sirius	258 43.6	S16 42.9
15	165 54.4	10 42.7 ..	17.3	311 24.6 ..	21.0	134 22.5 ..	23.9	121 42.1 ..	23.2	Spica	158 42.7	S11 09.4
16	180 56.8	25 44.8	16.6	326 25.9	21.4	149 24.7	24.0	136 44.4	23.3	Suhail	223 00.8	S43 25.9
17	195 59.3	40 46.9	15.9	341 27.3	21.8	164 26.9	24.0	151 46.7	23.3			
18	211 01.8	55 49.0	N 7 15.2	356 28.6	S15 22.2	179 29.1	N11 24.1	166 49.0	N14 23.3	Vega	80 45.8	N38 47.2
19	226 04.2	70 51.1	14.5	11 30.0	22.6	194 31.4	24.2	181 51.3	23.4	Zuben'ubi	137 17.3	S16 02.3
20	241 06.7	85 53.3	13.9	26 31.3	23.0	209 33.6	24.3	196 53.6	23.4		SHA	Mer. Pass.
21	256 09.1	100 55.4 ..	13.2	41 32.7 ..	23.4	224 35.8 ..	24.3	211 56.0 ..	23.4		° ′	h m
22	271 11.6	115 57.5	12.5	56 34.0	23.8	239 38.0	24.4	226 58.3	23.5	Venus	205 05.1	14 21
23	286 14.1	130 59.6	11.8	71 35.4	24.2	254 40.2	24.5	242 00.6	23.5	Mars	146 12.9	18 16
	h m									Jupiter	328 37.8	6 07
Mer. Pass. 4 02.1		v 2.0	d 0.7	v 1.4	d 0.4	v 2.2	d 0.1	v 2.3	d 0.0	Saturn	315 54.0	6 58

UT	SUN GHA	SUN Dec	MOON GHA	v	Dec	d	HP
d h	° ′	° ′	° ′	′	° ′	′	′
21 00	178 24.6	N20 35.7	84 03.5	14.8	S 8 11.9	9.4	54.6
01	193 24.6	35.3	98 37.3	14.8	8 21.3	9.5	54.5
02	208 24.5	34.8	113 11.1	14.7	8 30.8	9.4	54.5
03	223 24.5 ..	34.3	127 44.8	14.8	8 40.2	9.4	54.5
04	238 24.5	33.8	142 18.6	14.7	8 49.6	9.3	54.5
05	253 24.4	33.4	156 52.3	14.8	8 58.9	9.3	54.5
06	268 24.4	N20 32.9	171 26.1	14.7	S 9 08.2	9.2	54.5
W 07	283 24.4	32.4	185 59.8	14.7	9 17.4	9.2	54.5
E 08	298 24.3	31.9	200 33.5	14.7	9 26.6	9.2	54.4
D 09	313 24.3 ..	31.5	215 07.2	14.7	9 35.8	9.1	54.4
N 10	328 24.3	31.0	229 40.9	14.7	9 44.9	9.0	54.4
E 11	343 24.2	30.5	244 14.6	14.6	9 53.9	9.1	54.4
S 12	358 24.2	N20 30.0	258 48.2	14.7	S10 03.0	9.0	54.4
D 13	13 24.2	29.5	273 21.9	14.6	10 12.0	8.9	54.4
A 14	28 24.2	29.1	287 55.5	14.6	10 20.9	8.9	54.4
Y 15	43 24.1 ..	28.6	302 29.1	14.6	10 29.8	8.8	54.4
16	58 24.1	28.1	317 02.7	14.6	10 38.6	8.8	54.3
17	73 24.1	27.6	331 36.3	14.5	10 47.4	8.8	54.3
18	88 24.0	N20 27.1	346 09.8	14.6	S10 56.2	8.7	54.3
19	103 24.0	26.6	0 43.4	14.5	11 04.9	8.6	54.3
20	118 24.0	26.2	15 16.9	14.5	11 13.5	8.6	54.3
21	133 23.9 ..	25.7	29 50.4	14.5	11 22.1	8.6	54.3
22	148 23.9	25.2	44 23.9	14.4	11 30.7	8.5	54.3
23	163 23.9	24.7	58 57.3	14.5	11 39.2	8.4	54.3
22 00	178 23.9	N20 24.2	73 30.8	14.4	S11 47.6	8.4	54.3
01	193 23.8	23.7	88 04.2	14.4	11 56.0	8.4	54.3
02	208 23.8	23.2	102 37.6	14.3	12 04.4	8.2	54.3
03	223 23.8 ..	22.7	117 10.9	14.4	12 12.6	8.3	54.2
04	238 23.8	22.3	131 44.3	14.3	12 20.9	8.2	54.2
05	253 23.7	21.8	146 17.6	14.3	12 29.1	8.1	54.2
06	268 23.7	N20 21.3	160 50.9	14.3	S12 37.2	8.1	54.2
T 07	283 23.7	20.8	175 24.1	14.3	12 45.3	8.0	54.2
H 08	298 23.6	20.3	189 57.4	14.2	12 53.3	8.0	54.2
U 09	313 23.6 ..	19.8	204 30.6	14.2	13 01.3	7.9	54.2
R 10	328 23.6	19.3	219 03.8	14.2	13 09.2	7.9	54.2
S 11	343 23.6	18.8	233 37.0	14.1	13 17.1	7.8	54.2
D 12	358 23.5	N20 18.3	248 10.1	14.1	S13 24.9	7.7	54.2
A 13	13 23.5	17.8	262 43.2	14.1	13 32.6	7.7	54.2
Y 14	28 23.5	17.3	277 16.3	14.0	13 40.3	7.6	54.2
15	43 23.5 ..	16.8	291 49.3	14.0	13 47.9	7.6	54.2
16	58 23.4	16.3	306 22.3	14.0	13 55.5	7.5	54.2
17	73 23.4	15.8	320 55.3	14.0	14 03.0	7.5	54.2
18	88 23.4	N20 15.3	335 28.3	13.9	S14 10.5	7.3	54.2
19	103 23.4	14.8	350 01.2	13.9	14 17.8	7.4	54.2
20	118 23.4	14.3	4 34.1	13.9	14 25.2	7.2	54.2
21	133 23.3 ..	13.8	19 07.0	13.8	14 32.4	7.2	54.2
22	148 23.3	13.3	33 39.8	13.8	14 39.6	7.2	54.2
23	163 23.3	12.8	48 12.6	13.8	14 46.8	7.1	54.2
23 00	178 23.3	N20 12.3	62 45.4	13.7	S14 53.9	7.0	54.2
01	193 23.2	11.8	77 18.1	13.7	15 00.9	6.9	54.2
02	208 23.2	11.3	91 50.8	13.7	15 07.8	6.9	54.2
03	223 23.2 ..	10.8	106 23.5	13.6	15 14.7	6.8	54.2
04	238 23.2	10.3	120 56.1	13.6	15 21.5	6.8	54.2
05	253 23.2	09.8	135 28.7	13.6	15 28.3	6.7	54.2
06	268 23.1	N20 09.3	150 01.3	13.5	S15 35.0	6.6	54.2
F 07	283 23.1	08.8	164 33.8	13.5	15 41.6	6.6	54.2
R 08	298 23.1	08.3	179 06.3	13.4	15 48.2	6.5	54.2
I 09	313 23.1 ..	07.8	193 38.7	13.5	15 54.7	6.4	54.2
D 10	328 23.1	07.3	208 11.2	13.4	16 01.1	6.3	54.2
A 11	343 23.0	06.8	222 43.6	13.3	16 07.4	6.3	54.2
Y 12	358 23.0	N20 06.3	237 15.9	13.3	S16 13.7	6.2	54.2
13	13 23.0	05.8	251 48.2	13.3	16 19.9	6.2	54.2
14	28 23.0	05.3	266 20.5	13.3	16 26.1	6.0	54.2
15	43 23.0 ..	04.7	280 52.8	13.2	16 32.1	6.0	54.2
16	58 22.9	04.2	295 25.0	13.1	16 38.1	5.9	54.2
17	73 22.9	03.7	309 57.1	13.2	16 44.0	5.9	54.2
18	88 22.9	N20 03.2	324 29.3	13.1	S16 49.9	5.8	54.2
19	103 22.9	02.7	339 01.4	13.0	16 55.7	5.7	54.2
20	118 22.9	02.2	353 33.4	13.1	17 01.4	5.6	54.2
21	133 22.9 ..	01.7	8 05.5	12.9	17 07.0	5.6	54.2
22	148 22.8	01.2	22 37.4	13.0	17 12.6	5.5	54.2
23	163 22.8	00.6	37 09.4	12.9	S17 18.1	5.4	54.2
	SD 15.8	d 0.5	SD 14.8		14.8		14.8

Twilight / Sunrise / Moonrise

Lat.	Twilight Naut.	Twilight Civil	Sunrise	Moonrise 21	22	23	24
°	h m	h m	h m	h m	h m	h m	h m
N 72	☐	☐	☐	15 11	17 00	19 06	■■■
N 70	☐	☐	☐	14 53	16 30	18 10	19 56
68	////	////	01 10	14 39	16 08	17 36	19 02
66	////	////	02 03	14 28	15 50	17 12	18 30
64	////	////	02 35	14 18	15 37	16 53	18 06
62	////	01 28	02 58	14 10	15 25	16 38	17 47
60	////	02 06	03 17	14 03	15 15	16 25	17 32
N 58	////	02 32	03 32	13 57	15 06	16 14	17 18
56	01 21	02 52	03 45	13 51	14 59	16 04	17 07
54	01 55	03 08	03 56	13 47	14 52	15 56	16 57
52	02 20	03 22	04 06	13 43	14 46	15 48	16 49
50	02 38	03 34	04 15	13 38	14 41	15 42	16 41
45	03 13	03 59	04 34	13 30	14 29	15 27	16 24
N 40	03 39	04 18	04 49	13 23	14 19	15 15	16 10
35	03 58	04 33	05 02	13 17	14 11	15 05	15 59
30	04 14	04 46	05 13	13 11	14 04	14 56	15 49
20	04 39	05 08	05 32	13 02	13 51	14 41	15 31
N 10	04 59	05 25	05 48	12 54	13 41	14 28	15 16
0	05 15	05 41	06 03	12 47	13 30	14 15	15 02
S 10	05 30	05 55	06 18	12 39	13 20	14 03	14 48
20	05 43	06 10	06 34	12 31	13 10	13 50	14 33
30	05 57	06 26	06 52	12 22	12 58	13 35	14 16
35	06 04	06 35	07 02	12 17	12 51	13 27	14 06
40	06 11	06 45	07 14	12 11	12 43	13 17	13 55
45	06 20	06 56	07 28	12 05	12 33	13 05	13 42
S 50	06 29	07 09	07 45	11 57	12 22	12 51	13 25
52	06 33	07 15	07 53	11 53	12 17	12 45	13 18
54	06 37	07 21	08 02	11 49	12 12	12 38	13 09
56	06 42	07 28	08 12	11 44	12 05	12 30	13 00
58	06 47	07 36	08 24	11 39	11 58	12 21	12 49
S 60	06 52	07 46	08 37	11 34	11 50	12 11	12 37

Sunset / Twilight / Moonset

Lat.	Sunset	Twilight Civil	Twilight Naut.	Moonset 21	22	23	24
°	h m	h m	h m	h m	h m	h m	h m
N 72	☐	☐	☐	22 25	22 09	21 37	■■■
N 70	☐	☐	☐	22 45	22 40	22 34	22 25
68	22 56	////	////	23 00	23 03	23 08	23 19
66	22 06	////	////	23 13	23 21	23 33	23 52
64	21 35	////	////	23 23	23 36	23 52	24 16
62	21 13	22 40	////	23 32	23 48	24 08	00 08
60	20 55	22 04	////	23 40	23 58	24 21	00 21
N 58	20 39	21 39	////	23 47	24 08	00 08	00 33
56	20 27	21 19	22 48	23 53	24 16	00 16	00 43
54	20 15	21 03	22 15	23 58	24 23	00 23	00 51
52	20 06	20 49	21 51	24 03	00 03	00 29	00 59
50	19 57	20 38	21 33	24 08	00 08	00 35	01 06
45	19 38	20 13	20 58	24 18	00 18	00 48	01 22
N 40	19 23	19 55	20 34	24 26	00 26	00 58	01 34
35	19 11	19 39	20 14	00 00	00 33	01 07	01 45
30	19 00	19 26	19 58	00 04	00 39	01 15	01 54
20	18 41	19 05	19 33	00 12	00 49	01 29	02 10
N 10	18 25	18 47	19 14	00 18	00 59	01 41	02 25
0	18 10	18 32	18 58	00 24	01 08	01 52	02 38
S 10	17 55	18 17	18 43	00 30	01 16	02 03	02 51
20	17 39	18 03	18 30	00 37	01 26	02 15	03 05
30	17 21	17 47	18 16	00 44	01 37	02 29	03 22
35	17 11	17 38	18 09	00 48	01 43	02 37	03 31
40	16 59	17 29	18 02	00 53	01 50	02 46	03 42
45	16 45	17 18	17 54	00 59	01 58	02 57	03 55
S 50	16 28	17 05	17 45	01 05	02 08	03 10	04 10
52	16 20	16 59	17 41	01 09	02 13	03 16	04 17
54	16 11	16 52	17 36	01 12	02 18	03 23	04 26
56	16 01	16 45	17 32	01 16	02 24	03 30	04 35
58	15 50	16 37	17 27	01 20	02 30	03 39	04 45
S 60	15 36	16 28	17 21	01 25	02 37	03 49	04 57

SUN / MOON

Day	Eqn. of Time 00h	Eqn. of Time 12h	Mer. Pass.	Mer. Pass. Upper	Mer. Pass. Lower	Age	Phase
d	m s	m s	h m	h m	h m	d	%
21	06 22	06 23	12 06	18 57	06 35	08	61
22	06 24	06 26	12 06	19 41	07 19	09	70
23	06 27	06 28	12 06	20 27	08 04	10	78

UT	ARIES	VENUS −4.4		MARS −0.1		JUPITER −2.4		SATURN +0.3		STARS		
	GHA	GHA	Dec	GHA	Dec	GHA	Dec	GHA	Dec	Name	SHA	Dec
d h	° ′	° ′	° ′	° ′	° ′	° ′	° ′	° ′	° ′		° ′	° ′
24 00	301 16.5	146 01.8	N 7 11.1	86 36.7	S15 24.6	269 42.5	N11 24.6	257 02.9	N14 23.5	Acamar	315 26.6	S40 18.3
01	316 19.0	161 03.9	10.5	101 38.1	25.0	284 44.7	24.6	272 05.2	23.6	Achernar	335 34.8	S57 14.1
02	331 21.5	176 06.0	09.8	116 39.4	25.4	299 46.9	24.7	287 07.5	23.6	Acrux	173 21.6	S63 06.0
03	346 23.9	191 08.2 ..	09.1	131 40.8 ..	25.9	314 49.1 ..	24.8	302 09.8 ..	23.6	Adhara	255 21.4	S28 58.3
04	1 26.4	206 10.3	08.5	146 42.1	26.3	329 51.4	24.9	317 12.1	23.7	Aldebaran	291 02.0	N16 30.4
05	16 28.9	221 12.5	07.8	161 43.5	26.7	344 53.6	24.9	332 14.4	23.7			
06	31 31.3	236 14.6	N 7 07.1	176 44.8	S15 27.1	359 55.8	N11 25.0	347 16.7	N14 23.8	Alioth	166 30.3	N55 58.1
07	46 33.8	251 16.8	06.4	191 46.2	27.5	14 58.0	25.1	2 19.0	23.8	Alkaid	153 07.4	N49 19.3
S 08	61 36.2	266 18.9	05.8	206 47.5	27.9	30 00.3	25.2	17 21.4	23.8	Al Na'ir	27 56.8	S46 57.6
A 09	76 38.7	281 21.1 ..	05.1	221 48.9 ..	28.3	45 02.5 ..	25.2	32 23.7 ..	23.9	Alnilam	275 57.6	S 1 12.2
T 10	91 41.2	296 23.3	04.4	236 50.2	28.7	60 04.7	25.3	47 26.0	23.9	Alphard	218 07.0	S 8 39.4
U 11	106 43.6	311 25.4	03.8	251 51.6	29.1	75 06.9	25.4	62 28.3	23.9			
R 12	121 46.1	326 27.6	N 7 03.1	266 52.9	S15 29.5	90 09.2	N11 25.5	77 30.6	N14 24.0	Alphecca	126 20.0	N26 43.3
D 13	136 48.6	341 29.8	02.4	281 54.2	29.9	105 11.4	25.5	92 32.9	24.0	Alpheratz	357 54.5	N29 05.1
A 14	151 51.0	356 32.0	01.8	296 55.6	30.3	120 13.6	25.6	107 35.2	24.0	Altair	62 18.4	N 8 52.2
Y 15	166 53.5	11 34.1 ..	01.1	311 56.9 ..	30.7	135 15.9 ..	25.7	122 37.5 ..	24.1	Ankaa	353 26.2	S42 18.3
16	181 56.0	26 36.3	7 00.5	326 58.3	31.1	150 18.1	25.8	137 39.8	24.1	Antares	112 39.3	S26 25.8
17	196 58.4	41 38.5	6 59.8	341 59.6	31.6	165 20.3	25.8	152 42.2	24.1			
18	212 00.9	56 40.7	N 6 59.1	357 00.9	S15 32.0	180 22.5	N11 25.9	167 44.5	N14 24.2	Arcturus	146 05.6	N19 11.4
19	227 03.4	71 42.9	58.5	12 02.3	32.4	195 24.8	26.0	182 46.8	24.2	Atria	107 50.4	S69 01.7
20	242 05.8	86 45.1	57.8	27 03.6	32.8	210 27.0	26.1	197 49.1	24.2	Avior	234 23.0	S59 30.5
21	257 08.3	101 47.3 ..	57.2	42 05.0 ..	33.2	225 29.2 ..	26.1	212 51.4 ..	24.3	Bellatrix	278 43.8	N 6 20.9
22	272 10.7	116 49.5	56.5	57 06.3	33.6	240 31.5	26.2	227 53.7	24.3	Betelgeuse	271 13.2	N 7 24.4
23	287 13.2	131 51.7	55.9	72 07.6	34.0	255 33.7	26.3	242 56.0	24.3			
25 00	302 15.7	146 53.9	N 6 55.2	87 09.0	S15 34.4	270 35.9	N11 26.3	257 58.3	N14 24.4	Canopus	264 01.4	S52 41.7
01	317 18.1	161 56.2	54.5	102 10.3	34.8	285 38.1	26.4	273 00.6	24.4	Capella	280 50.7	N45 59.6
02	332 20.6	176 58.4	53.9	117 11.6	35.2	300 40.4	26.5	288 03.0	24.4	Deneb	49 38.3	N45 16.8
03	347 23.1	192 00.6 ..	53.2	132 13.0 ..	35.6	315 42.6 ..	26.6	303 05.3 ..	24.5	Denebola	182 44.8	N14 34.7
04	2 25.5	207 02.8	52.6	147 14.3	36.0	330 44.8	26.6	318 07.6	24.5	Diphda	349 06.6	S17 59.3
05	17 28.0	222 05.1	51.9	162 15.6	36.5	345 47.1	26.7	333 09.9	24.6			
06	32 30.5	237 07.3	N 6 51.3	177 17.0	S15 36.9	0 49.3	N11 26.8	348 12.2	N14 24.6	Dubhe	194 05.4	N61 45.5
07	47 32.9	252 09.5	50.7	192 18.3	37.3	15 51.5	26.9	3 14.5	24.6	Elnath	278 26.5	N28 36.3
08	62 35.4	267 11.8	50.0	207 19.6	37.7	30 53.8	26.9	18 16.8	24.7	Eltanin	90 50.7	N51 29.6
S 09	77 37.9	282 14.0 ..	49.4	222 21.0 ..	38.1	45 56.0 ..	27.0	33 19.2 ..	24.7	Enif	33 57.4	N 9 52.4
U 10	92 40.3	297 16.3	48.7	237 22.3	38.5	60 58.2	27.1	48 21.5	24.7	Fomalhaut	15 35.6	S29 37.3
N 11	107 42.8	312 18.5	48.1	252 23.6	38.9	76 00.5	27.1	63 23.8	24.8			
D 12	122 45.2	327 20.8	N 6 47.4	267 24.9	S15 39.3	91 02.7	N11 27.2	78 26.1	N14 24.8	Gacrux	172 13.1	S57 06.8
A 13	137 47.7	342 23.0	46.8	282 26.3	39.7	106 04.9	27.3	93 28.4	24.8	Gienah	176 03.5	S17 32.3
Y 14	152 50.2	357 25.3	46.2	297 27.6	40.1	121 07.2	27.4	108 30.7	24.9	Hadar	149 03.2	S60 22.4
15	167 52.6	12 27.6 ..	45.5	312 28.9 ..	40.5	136 09.4 ..	27.4	123 33.0 ..	24.9	Hamal	328 12.9	N23 27.4
16	182 55.1	27 29.9	44.9	327 30.2	40.9	151 11.6	27.5	138 35.4	24.9	Kaus Aust.	83 57.7	S34 23.0
17	197 57.6	42 32.1	44.2	342 31.6	41.4	166 13.9	27.6	153 37.7	25.0			
18	213 00.0	57 34.4	N 6 43.6	357 32.9	S15 41.8	181 16.1	N11 27.6	168 40.0	N14 25.0	Kochab	137 19.4	N74 09.9
19	228 02.5	72 36.7	43.0	12 34.2	42.2	196 18.3	27.7	183 42.3	25.0	Markab	13 48.8	N15 12.1
20	243 05.0	87 39.0	42.3	27 35.5	42.6	211 20.6	27.8	198 44.6	25.1	Menkar	314 26.4	N 4 05.2
21	258 07.4	102 41.3 ..	41.7	42 36.9 ..	43.0	226 22.8 ..	27.9	213 46.9 ..	25.1	Menkent	148 20.3	S36 22.1
22	273 09.9	117 43.6	41.1	57 38.2	43.4	241 25.0	27.9	228 49.3	25.1	Miaplacidus	221 42.8	S69 43.0
23	288 12.4	132 45.9	40.4	72 39.5	43.8	256 27.3	28.0	243 51.6	25.2			
26 00	303 14.8	147 48.2	N 6 39.8	87 40.8	S15 44.2	271 29.5	N11 28.1	258 53.9	N14 25.2	Mirfak	308 56.0	N49 51.3
01	318 17.3	162 50.5	39.2	102 42.1	44.6	286 31.8	28.1	273 56.2	25.2	Nunki	76 11.3	S26 17.7
02	333 19.7	177 52.8	38.6	117 43.5	45.0	301 34.0	28.2	288 58.5	25.3	Peacock	53 35.6	S56 44.1
03	348 22.2	192 55.1 ..	37.9	132 44.8 ..	45.5	316 36.2 ..	28.3	304 00.8 ..	25.3	Pollux	243 41.3	N28 01.6
04	3 24.7	207 57.4	37.3	147 46.1	45.9	331 38.5	28.3	319 03.1	25.3	Procyon	245 11.3	N 5 13.6
05	18 27.1	222 59.7	36.7	162 47.4	46.3	346 40.7	28.4	334 05.5	25.4			
06	33 29.6	238 02.0	N 6 36.1	177 48.7	S15 46.7	1 42.9	N11 28.5	349 07.8	N14 25.4	Rasalhague	96 16.2	N12 33.9
07	48 32.1	253 04.4	35.4	192 50.0	47.1	16 45.2	28.6	4 10.1	25.4	Regulus	207 55.3	N11 58.3
08	63 34.5	268 06.7	34.8	207 51.4	47.5	31 47.4	28.6	19 12.4	25.5	Rigel	281 22.7	S 8 12.2
M 09	78 37.0	283 09.0 ..	34.2	222 52.7 ..	47.9	46 49.7 ..	28.7	34 14.7 ..	25.5	Rigil Kent.	140 06.4	S60 50.1
O 10	93 39.5	298 11.4	33.6	237 54.0	48.3	61 51.9	28.8	49 17.1	25.5	Sabik	102 24.6	S15 43.3
N 11	108 41.9	313 13.7	33.0	252 55.3	48.7	76 54.1	28.8	64 19.4	25.6			
D 12	123 44.4	328 16.0	N 6 32.3	267 56.6	S15 49.1	91 56.4	N11 28.9	79 21.7	N14 25.6	Schedar	349 52.6	N56 31.8
A 13	138 46.8	343 18.4	31.7	282 57.9	49.6	106 58.6	29.0	94 24.0	25.6	Shaula	96 36.2	S37 06.2
Y 14	153 49.3	358 20.7	31.1	297 59.2	50.0	122 00.9	29.0	109 26.3	25.7	Sirius	258 43.6	S16 42.9
15	168 51.8	13 23.1 ..	30.5	313 00.5 ..	50.4	137 03.1 ..	29.1	124 28.6 ..	25.7	Spica	158 42.7	S11 09.4
16	183 54.2	28 25.4	29.9	328 01.9	50.8	152 05.3	29.2	139 31.0	25.7	Suhail	223 00.8	S43 25.9
17	198 56.7	43 27.8	29.3	343 03.2	51.2	167 07.6	29.2	154 33.3	25.8			
18	213 59.2	58 30.2	N 6 28.7	358 04.5	S15 51.6	182 09.8	N11 29.3	169 35.6	N14 25.8	Vega	80 45.8	N38 47.2
19	229 01.6	73 32.5	28.1	13 05.8	52.0	197 12.1	29.4	184 37.9	25.8	Zuben'ubi	137 17.3	S16 02.3
20	244 04.1	88 34.9	27.5	28 07.1	52.4	212 14.3	29.5	199 40.2	25.9		SHA	Mer. Pass.
21	259 06.6	103 37.3 ..	26.9	43 08.4 ..	52.8	227 16.5 ..	29.5	214 42.6 ..	25.9		° ′	h m
22	274 09.0	118 39.7	26.2	58 09.7	53.3	242 18.8	29.6	229 44.9	25.9	Venus	204 38.3	14 10
23	289 11.5	133 42.1	25.6	73 11.0	53.7	257 21.0	29.7	244 47.2	26.0	Mars	144 53.3	18 10
	h m									Jupiter	328 20.2	5 57
Mer. Pass. 3 50.3		v 2.3	d 0.6	v 1.3	d 0.4	v 2.2	d 0.1	v 2.3	d 0.0	Saturn	315 42.7	6 47

UT	SUN		MOON					Twilight		Sunrise	Moonrise			
	GHA	Dec	GHA	v	Dec	d	HP	Lat.	Naut.	Civil		24	25	26	27

d h	° ′ ° ′	° ′	° ′ ′	° ′ ′	′	′	°	h m	h m	h m	h m	h m	h m	h m
24 00	178 22.8 N20 00.1		51 41.3 12.9	S17 23.5	5.3	54.2	N 72	☐	☐	☐	■	■	■	■
01	193 22.8 19 59.6		66 13.2 12.8	17 28.8	5.3	54.2	N 70	☐	☐	☐	19 56	■	■	22 36
02	208 22.8 59.1		80 45.0 12.8	17 34.1	5.1	54.2	68	////	////	01 32	19 02	20 18	21 12	21 39
03	223 22.8 . . 58.6		95 16.8 12.8	17 39.2	5.1	54.2	66	////	////	02 16	18 30	19 38	20 31	21 06
04	238 22.8 58.1		109 48.6 12.7	17 44.3	5.0	54.2	64	////	00 37	02 44	18 06	19 10	20 03	20 41
05	253 22.7 57.5		124 20.3 12.7	17 49.3	5.0	54.2	62	////	01 43	03 06	17 47	18 49	19 41	20 21
06	268 22.7 N19 57.0		138 52.0 12.6	S17 54.3	4.9	54.2	60	////	02 16	03 23	17 32	18 32	19 24	20 06
07	283 22.7 56.5		153 23.6 12.6	17 59.2	4.7	54.2	N 58	00 34	02 40	03 38	17 18	18 18	19 09	19 52
S 08	298 22.7 56.0		167 55.2 12.6	18 03.9	4.7	54.2	56	01 34	02 58	03 50	17 07	18 05	18 57	19 40
A 09	313 22.7 . . 55.5		182 26.8 12.5	18 08.6	4.7	54.2	54	02 04	03 14	04 01	16 57	17 54	18 46	19 30
T 10	328 22.7 54.9		196 58.3 12.5	18 13.3	4.5	54.3	52	02 27	03 27	04 11	16 49	17 45	18 36	19 21
U 11	343 22.7 54.4		211 29.8 12.5	18 17.8	4.5	54.3	50	02 44	03 39	04 19	16 41	17 36	18 27	19 13
R 12	358 22.6 N19 53.9		226 01.3 12.4	S18 22.3	4.3	54.3	45	03 18	04 02	04 37	16 24	17 18	18 09	18 55
D 13	13 22.6 53.4		240 32.7 12.4	18 26.6	4.3	54.3	N 40	03 42	04 20	04 52	16 10	17 04	17 54	18 41
A 14	28 22.6 52.9		255 04.1 12.3	18 30.9	4.3	54.3	35	04 01	04 35	05 04	15 59	16 51	17 41	18 29
Y 15	43 22.6 . . 52.3		269 35.4 12.3	18 35.2	4.1	54.3	30	04 16	04 48	05 14	15 49	16 40	17 30	18 19
16	58 22.6 51.8		284 06.7 12.3	18 39.3	4.0	54.3	20	04 41	05 09	05 33	15 31	16 22	17 12	18 00
17	73 22.6 51.3		298 38.0 12.3	18 43.3	4.0	54.3	N 10	05 00	05 26	05 48	15 16	16 05	16 55	17 45
18	88 22.6 N19 50.8		313 09.3 12.2	S18 47.3	3.9	54.3	0	05 15	05 41	06 03	15 02	15 50	16 40	17 30
19	103 22.6 50.2		327 40.5 12.1	18 51.2	3.8	54.3	S 10	05 29	05 55	06 17	14 48	15 35	16 24	17 15
20	118 22.6 49.7		342 11.6 12.1	18 55.0	3.7	54.3	20	05 42	06 09	06 33	14 33	15 19	16 08	16 59
21	133 22.5 . . 49.2		356 42.7 12.1	18 58.7	3.6	54.3	30	05 56	06 25	06 50	14 16	15 01	15 49	16 41
22	148 22.5 48.6		11 13.8 12.1	19 02.3	3.5	54.3	35	06 02	06 33	07 00	14 06	14 50	15 38	16 31
23	163 22.5 48.1		25 44.9 12.0	19 05.8	3.5	54.4	40	06 09	06 42	07 12	13 55	14 38	15 25	16 18
25 00	178 22.5 N19 47.6		40 15.9 12.0	S19 09.3	3.3	54.4	45	06 17	06 53	07 25	13 42	14 23	15 11	16 04
01	193 22.5 47.1		54 46.9 11.9	19 12.6	3.3	54.4	S 50	06 26	07 06	07 42	13 25	14 05	14 52	15 47
02	208 22.5 46.5		69 17.8 11.9	19 15.9	3.2	54.4	52	06 30	07 11	07 49	13 18	13 57	14 44	15 38
03	223 22.5 . . 46.0		83 48.7 11.9	19 19.1	3.0	54.4	54	06 34	07 17	07 58	13 09	13 48	14 34	15 29
04	238 22.5 45.5		98 19.6 11.9	19 22.1	3.0	54.4	56	06 39	07 24	08 08	13 00	13 37	14 23	15 19
05	253 22.5 44.9		112 50.5 11.8	19 25.1	3.0	54.4	58	06 43	07 32	08 18	12 49	13 25	14 11	15 07
06	268 22.5 N19 44.4		127 21.3 11.7	S19 28.1	2.8	54.4	S 60	06 48	07 41	08 31	12 37	13 12	13 57	14 53
07	283 22.5 43.9		141 52.0 11.8	19 30.9	2.7	54.4	Lat.	Sunset	Twilight		Moonset			
S 08	298 22.4 43.3		156 22.8 11.7	19 33.6	2.7	54.5			Civil	Naut.	24	25	26	27
U 09	313 22.4 . . 42.8		170 53.5 11.7	19 36.3	2.5	54.5	°	h m	h m	h m	h m	h m	h m	h m
N 10	328 22.4 42.3		185 24.2 11.6	19 38.8	2.5	54.5	N 72	☐	☐	☐	■	■	■	■
D 11	343 22.4 41.7		199 54.8 11.6	19 41.3	2.3	54.5	N 70	☐	☐	☐	22 25	■	■	■
A 12	358 22.4 N19 41.2		214 25.4 11.6	S19 43.6	2.3	54.5	68	22 35	////	////	23 19	23 44	24 34	00 34
Y 13	13 22.4 40.7		228 56.0 11.5	19 45.9	2.2	54.5	66	21 54	////	////	23 52	24 24	00 24	01 14
14	28 22.4 40.1		243 26.5 11.5	19 48.1	2.1	54.5	64	21 26	23 24	////	24 16	00 16	00 52	01 42
15	43 22.4 . . 39.6		257 57.0 11.5	19 50.2	1.9	54.5	62	21 05	22 26	////	00 08	00 35	01 13	02 04
16	58 22.4 39.0		272 27.5 11.5	19 52.1	1.9	54.6	60	20 48	21 54	////	00 21	00 51	01 31	02 21
17	73 22.4 38.5		286 58.0 11.4	19 54.0	1.8	54.6	N 58	20 34	21 31	23 28	00 33	01 05	01 45	02 36
18	88 22.4 N19 38.0		301 28.4 11.4	S19 55.8	1.8	54.6	56	20 22	21 13	22 36	00 43	01 16	01 57	02 48
19	103 22.4 37.4		315 58.8 11.3	19 57.6	1.6	54.6	54	20 11	20 58	22 06	00 51	01 26	02 08	02 59
20	118 22.4 36.9		330 29.1 11.4	19 59.2	1.5	54.6	52	20 02	20 45	21 45	00 59	01 35	02 18	03 08
21	133 22.4 . . 36.3		344 59.5 11.3	20 00.7	1.4	54.6	50	19 53	20 33	21 27	01 06	01 43	02 27	03 17
22	148 22.4 35.8		359 29.8 11.3	20 02.1	1.3	54.6	45	19 35	20 10	20 54	01 22	02 00	02 45	03 35
23	163 22.4 35.3		14 00.1 11.2	20 03.4	1.3	54.6	N 40	19 21	19 52	20 30	01 34	02 14	03 00	03 50
26 00	178 22.4 N19 34.7		28 30.3 11.2	S20 04.7	1.1	54.7	35	19 09	19 37	20 12	01 45	02 26	03 12	04 03
01	193 22.4 34.2		43 00.5 11.2	20 05.8	1.0	54.7	30	18 58	19 25	19 56	01 54	02 37	03 23	04 14
02	208 22.4 33.6		57 30.7 11.2	20 06.8	1.0	54.7	20	18 40	19 04	19 32	02 10	02 55	03 42	04 32
03	223 22.4 . . 33.1		72 00.9 11.2	20 07.8	0.8	54.7	N 10	18 25	18 47	19 13	02 25	03 11	03 59	04 49
04	238 22.4 32.5		86 31.1 11.1	20 08.6	0.8	54.7	0	18 10	18 32	18 58	02 38	03 25	04 14	05 04
05	253 22.4 32.0		101 01.2 11.1	20 09.4	0.6	54.7	S 10	17 56	18 18	18 44	02 51	03 40	04 29	05 19
06	268 22.4 N19 31.5		115 31.3 11.0	S20 10.0	0.5	54.7	20	17 40	18 04	18 31	03 05	03 56	04 46	05 35
07	283 22.4 30.9		130 01.3 11.1	20 10.5	0.5	54.8	30	17 23	17 49	18 18	03 22	04 14	05 05	05 54
08	298 22.3 30.4		144 31.4 11.0	20 11.0	0.3	54.8	35	17 13	17 40	18 11	03 31	04 24	05 16	06 05
M 09	313 22.3 . . 29.8		159 01.4 11.0	20 11.3	0.3	54.8	40	17 02	17 31	18 04	03 42	04 36	05 28	06 17
O 10	328 22.3 29.3		173 31.4 11.0	20 11.6	0.1	54.8	45	16 48	17 20	17 56	03 55	04 50	05 43	06 32
N 11	343 22.3 28.7		188 01.4 11.0	20 11.7	0.1	54.8	S 50	16 32	17 08	17 48	04 10	05 08	06 01	06 49
D 12	358 22.3 N19 28.2		202 31.4 10.9	S20 11.8	0.0	54.8	52	16 24	17 02	17 44	04 17	05 16	06 10	06 58
A 13	13 22.3 27.6		217 01.3 10.9	20 11.8	0.2	54.9	54	16 16	16 56	17 40	04 26	05 25	06 19	07 07
Y 14	28 22.3 27.1		231 31.2 10.9	20 11.6	0.2	54.9	56	16 06	16 49	17 36	04 35	05 35	06 30	07 18
15	43 22.3 . . 26.5		246 01.1 10.9	20 11.4	0.4	54.9	58	15 55	16 42	17 31	04 45	05 47	06 42	07 30
16	58 22.3 26.0		260 31.0 10.9	20 11.0	0.4	54.9	S 60	15 43	16 33	17 26	04 57	06 01	06 57	07 44
17	73 22.4 25.4		275 00.9 10.8	20 10.6	0.6	54.9								
18	88 22.4 N19 24.9		289 30.7 10.8	S20 10.0	0.6	54.9			SUN		MOON			
19	103 22.4 24.3		304 00.5 10.9	20 09.4	0.8	55.0	Day	Eqn. of Time		Mer.	Mer. Pass.		Age	Phase
20	118 22.4 23.7		318 30.4 10.7	20 08.6	0.8	55.0		00ʰ	12ʰ	Pass.	Upper	Lower		
21	133 22.4 . . 23.2		333 00.1 10.8	20 07.8	1.0	55.0	d	m s	m s	h m	h m	h m	d %	
22	148 22.4 22.6		347 29.9 10.8	20 06.8	1.0	55.0	24	06 29	06 29	12 06	21 14	08 50	11 85	◗
23	163 22.4 22.1		1 59.7 10.7	S20 05.8	1.2	55.0	25	06 30	06 30	12 07	22 02	09 38	12 92	
	SD 15.8 d 0.5		SD 14.8	14.8		14.9	26	06 31	06 31	12 07	22 52	10 27	13 96	

UT (d h)	ARIES GHA	VENUS −4.4 GHA	Dec	MARS +0.0 GHA	Dec	JUPITER −2.4 GHA	Dec	SATURN +0.3 GHA	Dec	Star Name	SHA	Dec
27 00	304 14.0	148 44.4 N 6	25.0	88 12.3 S15	54.1	272 23.3 N11	29.7	259 49.5 N14	26.0	Acamar	315 26.6	S40 18.2
01	319 16.4	163 46.8	24.4	103 13.6	54.5	287 25.5	29.8	274 51.8	26.0	Achernar	335 34.7	S57 14.1
02	334 18.9	178 49.2	23.8	118 14.9	54.9	302 27.8	29.9	289 54.2	26.0	Acrux	173 21.6	S63 05.9
03	349 21.3	193 51.6 ..	23.2	133 16.2 ..	55.3	317 30.0 ..	29.9	304 56.5 ..	26.1	Adhara	255 21.3	S28 58.3
04	4 23.8	208 54.0	22.6	148 17.5	55.7	332 32.3	30.0	319 58.8	26.1	Aldebaran	291 01.9	N16 30.4
05	19 26.3	223 56.4	22.0	163 18.8	56.1	347 34.5	30.1	335 01.1	26.1			
06	34 28.7	238 58.8 N 6	21.4	178 20.1 S15	56.6	2 36.7 N11	30.1	350 03.4 N14	26.2	Alioth	166 30.3	N55 58.1
07	49 31.2	254 01.3	20.8	193 21.4	57.0	17 39.0	30.2	5 05.8	26.2	Alkaid	153 07.4	N49 19.3
08	64 33.7	269 03.7	20.3	208 22.7	57.4	32 41.2	30.3	20 08.1	26.2	Al Na'ir	27 56.8	S46 57.6
09	79 36.1	284 06.1 ..	19.7	223 24.0 ..	57.8	47 43.5 ..	30.3	35 10.4 ..	26.3	Alnilam	275 57.6	S 1 12.2
10	94 38.6	299 08.5	19.1	238 25.3	58.2	62 45.7	30.4	50 12.7	26.3	Alphard	218 07.0	S 8 39.4
11	109 41.1	314 10.9	18.5	253 26.6	58.6	77 48.0	30.5	65 15.0	26.3			
12	124 43.5	329 13.4 N 6	17.9	268 27.9 S15	59.0	92 50.2 N11	30.5	80 17.4 N14	26.4	Alphecca	126 20.0	N26 43.3
13	139 46.0	344 15.8	17.3	283 29.2	59.4	107 52.5	30.6	95 19.7	26.4	Alpheratz	357 54.4	N29 05.1
14	154 48.5	359 18.3	16.7	298 30.5 15	59.8	122 54.7	30.7	110 22.0	26.4	Altair	62 18.4	N 8 52.2
15	169 50.9	14 20.7 ..	16.1	313 31.8 16	00.3	137 57.0 ..	30.7	125 24.3 ..	26.5	Ankaa	353 26.1	S42 18.3
16	184 53.4	29 23.1	15.5	328 33.1	00.7	152 59.2	30.8	140 26.7	26.5	Antares	112 39.3	S26 25.8
17	199 55.8	44 25.6	15.0	343 34.4	01.1	168 01.5	30.9	155 29.0	26.5			
18	214 58.3	59 28.0 N 6	14.4	358 35.7 S16	01.5	183 03.7 N11	30.9	170 31.3 N14	26.6	Arcturus	146 05.6	N19 11.4
19	230 00.8	74 30.5	13.8	13 37.0	01.9	198 05.9	31.0	185 33.6	26.6	Atria	107 50.4	S69 01.7
20	245 03.2	89 33.0	13.2	28 38.3	02.3	213 08.2	31.1	200 35.9	26.6	Avior	234 23.0	S59 30.5
21	260 05.7	104 35.4 ..	12.6	43 39.6 ..	02.7	228 10.4 ..	31.1	215 38.3 ..	26.7	Bellatrix	278 43.8	N 6 20.9
22	275 08.2	119 37.9	12.1	58 40.9	03.1	243 12.7	31.2	230 40.6	26.7	Betelgeuse	271 13.2	N 7 24.4
23	290 10.6	134 40.4	11.5	73 42.2	03.6	258 14.9	31.3	245 42.9	26.7			
28 00	305 13.1	149 42.8 N 6	10.9	88 43.4 S16	04.0	273 17.2 N11	31.3	260 45.2 N14	26.7	Canopus	264 01.4	S52 41.7
01	320 15.6	164 45.3	10.3	103 44.7	04.4	288 19.4	31.4	275 47.6	26.8	Capella	280 50.7	N45 59.6
02	335 18.0	179 47.8	09.8	118 46.0	04.8	303 21.7	31.5	290 49.9	26.8	Deneb	49 38.3	N45 16.8
03	350 20.5	194 50.3 ..	09.2	133 47.3 ..	05.2	318 23.9 ..	31.5	305 52.2 ..	26.8	Denebola	182 44.8	N14 34.7
04	5 23.0	209 52.8	08.6	148 48.6	05.6	333 26.2	31.6	320 54.5	26.9	Diphda	349 06.6	S17 59.3
05	20 25.4	224 55.3	08.0	163 49.9	06.0	348 28.4	31.6	335 56.9	26.9			
06	35 27.9	239 57.8 N 6	07.5	178 51.2 S16	06.4	3 30.7 N11	31.7	350 59.2 N14	26.9	Dubhe	194 05.4	N61 45.5
07	50 30.3	255 00.3	06.9	193 52.5	06.9	18 32.9	31.8	6 01.5	27.0	Elnath	278 26.5	N28 36.3
08	65 32.8	270 02.8	06.3	208 53.7	07.3	33 35.2	31.8	21 03.8	27.0	Eltanin	90 50.7	N51 29.6
09	80 35.3	285 05.3 ..	05.8	223 55.0 ..	07.7	48 37.5 ..	31.9	36 06.2 ..	27.0	Enif	33 57.4	N 9 52.4
10	95 37.7	300 07.8	05.2	238 56.3	08.1	63 39.7	32.0	51 08.5	27.1	Fomalhaut	15 35.6	S29 37.3
11	110 40.2	315 10.3	04.6	253 57.6	08.5	78 42.0	32.0	66 10.8	27.1			
12	125 42.7	330 12.8 N 6	04.1	268 58.9 S16	08.9	93 44.2 N11	32.1	81 13.1 N14	27.1	Gacrux	172 13.2	S57 06.8
13	140 45.1	345 15.4	03.5	284 00.2	09.3	108 46.5	32.2	96 15.5	27.1	Gienah	176 03.5	S17 32.3
14	155 47.6	0 17.9	03.0	299 01.4	09.7	123 48.7	32.2	111 17.8	27.2	Hadar	149 03.2	S60 22.4
15	170 50.1	15 20.4 ..	02.4	314 02.7 ..	10.2	138 51.0 ..	32.3	126 20.1 ..	27.2	Hamal	328 12.9	N23 27.4
16	185 52.5	30 23.0	01.9	329 04.0	10.6	153 53.2	32.4	141 22.4	27.2	Kaus Aust.	83 57.7	S34 23.0
17	200 55.0	45 25.5	01.3	344 05.3	11.0	168 55.5	32.4	156 24.8	27.3			
18	215 57.4	60 28.1 N 6	00.7	359 06.6 S16	11.4	183 57.7 N11	32.5	171 27.1 N14	27.3	Kochab	137 19.5	N74 09.9
19	230 59.9	75 30.6 6	00.2	14 07.8	11.8	199 00.0	32.5	186 29.4	27.3	Markab	13 48.8	N15 12.1
20	246 02.4	90 33.1 5	59.6	29 09.1	12.2	214 02.2	32.6	201 31.7	27.4	Menkar	314 26.4	N 4 05.2
21	261 04.8	105 35.7 ..	59.1	44 10.4 ..	12.6	229 04.5 ..	32.7	216 34.1 ..	27.4	Menkent	148 20.3	S36 22.1
22	276 07.3	120 38.3	58.5	59 11.7	13.1	244 06.8	32.7	231 36.4	27.4	Miaplacidus	221 42.8	S69 43.0
23	291 09.8	135 40.8	58.0	74 12.9	13.5	259 09.0	32.8	246 38.7	27.4			
29 00	306 12.2	150 43.4 N 5	57.4	89 14.2 S16	13.9	274 11.3 N11	32.9	261 41.0 N14	27.5	Mirfak	308 55.9	N49 51.3
01	321 14.7	165 46.0	56.9	104 15.5	14.3	289 13.5	32.9	276 43.4	27.5	Nunki	76 11.3	S26 17.7
02	336 17.2	180 48.5	56.4	119 16.8	14.7	304 15.8	33.0	291 45.7	27.5	Peacock	53 35.6	S56 44.1
03	351 19.6	195 51.1 ..	55.8	134 18.0 ..	15.1	319 18.0 ..	33.1	306 48.0 ..	27.6	Pollux	243 41.3	N28 01.6
04	6 22.1	210 53.7	55.3	149 19.3	15.5	334 20.3	33.1	321 50.4	27.6	Procyon	245 11.3	N 5 13.6
05	21 24.6	225 56.3	54.7	164 20.6	16.0	349 22.6	33.2	336 52.7	27.6			
06	36 27.0	240 58.9 N 5	54.2	179 21.9 S16	16.4	4 24.8 N11	33.2	351 55.0 N14	27.7	Rasalhague	96 16.2	N12 33.9
07	51 29.5	256 01.5	53.7	194 23.1	16.8	19 27.1	33.3	6 57.3	27.7	Regulus	207 55.3	N11 58.3
08	66 31.9	271 04.1	53.1	209 24.4	17.2	34 29.3	33.4	21 59.7	27.7	Rigel	281 22.6	S 8 12.1
09	81 34.4	286 06.7 ..	52.6	224 25.7 ..	17.6	49 31.6 ..	33.4	37 02.0 ..	27.7	Rigil Kent.	140 06.5	S60 50.1
10	96 36.9	301 09.3	52.0	239 26.9	18.0	64 33.8	33.5	52 04.3	27.8	Sabik	102 24.6	S15 43.3
11	111 39.3	316 11.9	51.5	254 28.2	18.4	79 36.1	33.5	67 06.7	27.8			
12	126 41.8	331 14.5 N 5	51.0	269 29.5 S16	18.8	94 38.4 N11	33.6	82 09.0 N14	27.8	Schedar	349 52.6	N56 31.8
13	141 44.3	346 17.1	50.4	284 30.7	19.3	109 40.6	33.7	97 11.3	27.9	Shaula	96 36.2	S37 06.2
14	156 46.7	1 19.7	49.9	299 32.0	19.7	124 42.9	33.7	112 13.6	27.9	Sirius	258 43.5	S16 42.9
15	171 49.2	16 22.3 ..	49.4	314 33.3 ..	20.1	139 45.1 ..	33.8	127 16.0 ..	27.9	Spica	158 42.7	S11 09.4
16	186 51.7	31 25.0	48.9	329 34.5	20.5	154 47.4	33.9	142 18.3	27.9	Suhail	223 00.8	S43 25.9
17	201 54.1	46 27.6	48.3	344 35.8	20.9	169 49.7	33.9	157 20.6	28.0			
18	216 56.6	61 30.2 N 5	47.8	359 37.1 S16	21.3	184 51.9 N11	34.0	172 23.0 N14	28.0	Vega	80 45.9	N38 47.2
19	231 59.1	76 32.9	47.3	14 38.3	21.7	199 54.2	34.0	187 25.3	28.0	Zuben'ubi	137 17.3	S16 02.3
20	247 01.5	91 35.5	46.8	29 39.6	22.2	214 56.5	34.1	202 27.6	28.1			
21	262 04.0	106 38.1 ..	46.3	44 40.9 ..	22.6	229 58.7 ..	34.2	217 30.0 ..	28.1			
22	277 06.4	121 40.8	45.7	59 42.1	23.0	245 01.0	34.2	232 32.3	28.1			
23	292 08.9	136 43.5	45.2	74 43.4	23.4	260 03.2	34.3	247 34.6	28.1			
Mer. Pass. h m 3 38.5		v 2.5	d 0.6	v 1.3	d 0.4	v 2.3	d 0.1	v 2.3	d 0.0			

	SHA	Mer. Pass.
Venus	204 29.7	13 59
Mars	143 30.3	18 04
Jupiter	328 04.1	5 46
Saturn	315 32.1	6 36

UT	SUN GHA	Dec	MOON GHA	v	Dec	d	HP
d h	° ′	° ′	° ′	′	° ′	′	′
27 00	178 22.4	N19 21.5	16 29.4	10.8	S20 04.6	1.2	55.0
01	193 22.4	21.0	30 59.2	10.7	20 03.4	1.4	55.1
02	208 22.4	20.4	45 28.9	10.7	20 02.0	1.4	55.1
03	223 22.4 ..	19.9	59 58.6	10.7	20 00.6	1.6	55.1
04	238 22.4	19.3	74 28.3	10.7	19 59.0	1.7	55.1
05	253 22.4	18.7	88 58.0	10.7	19 57.3	1.7	55.1
06	268 22.4	N19 18.2	103 27.7	10.6	S19 55.6	1.9	55.1
07	283 22.4	17.6	117 57.3	10.7	19 53.7	1.9	55.2
08	298 22.4	17.1	132 27.0	10.6	19 51.8	2.1	55.2
09	313 22.4 ..	16.5	146 56.6	10.7	19 49.7	2.2	55.2
10	328 22.4	15.9	161 26.3	10.6	19 47.5	2.2	55.2
11	343 22.4	15.3	175 55.9	10.6	19 45.3	2.4	55.2
12	358 22.4	N19 14.8	190 25.5	10.7	S19 42.9	2.5	55.3
13	13 22.4	14.2	204 55.2	10.6	19 40.4	2.6	55.3
14	28 22.4	13.7	219 24.8	10.6	19 37.8	2.6	55.3
15	43 22.4 ..	13.1	233 54.4	10.6	19 35.2	2.8	55.3
16	58 22.5	12.6	248 24.0	10.6	19 32.4	2.9	55.3
17	73 22.5	12.0	262 53.6	10.6	19 29.5	2.9	55.3
18	88 22.5	N19 11.4	277 23.2	10.6	S19 26.6	3.1	55.4
19	103 22.5	10.9	291 52.8	10.6	19 23.5	3.2	55.4
20	118 22.5	10.3	306 22.4	10.6	19 20.3	3.3	55.4
21	133 22.5 ..	09.7	320 52.0	10.6	19 17.0	3.4	55.4
22	148 22.5	09.2	335 21.6	10.5	19 13.6	3.4	55.4
23	163 22.5	08.6	349 51.1	10.6	19 10.2	3.6	55.5
28 00	178 22.5	N19 07.9	4 20.7	10.6	S19 06.6	3.7	55.5
01	193 22.5	07.4	18 50.3	10.6	19 02.9	3.8	55.5
02	208 22.5	06.9	33 19.9	10.6	18 59.1	3.8	55.5
03	223 22.5 ..	06.3	47 49.5	10.6	18 55.3	4.0	55.5
04	238 22.6	05.7	62 19.1	10.6	18 51.3	4.1	55.6
05	253 22.6	05.2	76 48.7	10.6	18 47.2	4.2	55.6
06	268 22.6	N19 04.6	91 18.3	10.6	S18 43.0	4.2	55.6
07	283 22.6	04.0	105 47.9	10.6	18 38.8	4.4	55.6
08	298 22.6	03.4	120 17.5	10.6	18 34.4	4.5	55.6
09	313 22.6 ..	02.9	134 47.1	10.6	18 29.9	4.5	55.7
10	328 22.6	02.3	149 16.7	10.6	18 25.4	4.7	55.7
11	343 22.6	01.7	163 46.3	10.7	18 20.7	4.7	55.7
12	358 22.6	N19 01.1	178 16.0	10.6	S18 16.0	4.9	55.7
13	13 22.7	00.6	192 45.6	10.7	18 11.1	5.0	55.7
14	28 22.7	19 00.0	207 15.3	10.6	18 06.1	5.0	55.8
15	43 22.7	18 59.4	221 44.9	10.7	18 01.1	5.2	55.8
16	58 22.7	58.8	236 14.6	10.6	17 55.9	5.2	55.8
17	73 22.7	58.3	250 44.2	10.7	17 50.7	5.3	55.8
18	88 22.7	N18 57.7	265 13.9	10.7	S17 45.4	5.5	55.8
19	103 22.7	57.1	279 43.6	10.7	17 39.9	5.5	55.9
20	118 22.8	56.5	294 13.3	10.7	17 34.4	5.6	55.9
21	133 22.8 ..	55.9	308 43.0	10.7	17 28.8	5.7	55.9
22	148 22.8	55.4	323 12.7	10.7	17 23.1	5.8	55.9
23	163 22.8	54.8	337 42.4	10.8	17 17.3	5.9	55.9
29 00	178 22.8	N18 54.2	352 12.2	10.7	S17 11.4	6.0	56.0
01	193 22.8	53.6	6 41.9	10.8	17 05.4	6.1	56.0
02	208 22.9	53.0	21 11.7	10.7	16 59.3	6.1	56.0
03	223 22.9 ..	52.4	35 41.4	10.8	16 53.2	6.3	56.0
04	238 22.9	51.9	50 11.2	10.8	16 46.9	6.4	56.0
05	253 22.9	51.3	64 41.0	10.8	16 40.5	6.4	56.1
06	268 22.9	N18 50.7	79 10.8	10.9	S16 34.1	6.5	56.1
07	283 22.9	50.1	93 40.7	10.8	16 27.6	6.6	56.1
08	298 23.0	49.5	108 10.5	10.9	16 21.0	6.8	56.1
09	313 23.0 ..	48.9	122 40.4	10.8	16 14.2	6.8	56.1
10	328 23.0	48.3	137 10.2	10.9	16 07.4	6.8	56.2
11	343 23.0	47.7	151 40.1	10.9	16 00.6	7.0	56.2
12	358 23.0	N18 47.2	166 10.0	10.9	S15 53.6	7.1	56.2
13	13 23.0	46.6	180 39.9	10.9	15 46.5	7.1	56.2
14	28 23.1	46.0	195 09.8	11.0	15 39.4	7.2	56.3
15	43 23.1 ..	45.4	209 39.8	10.9	15 32.2	7.3	56.3
16	58 23.1	44.8	224 09.7	11.0	15 24.9	7.4	56.3
17	73 23.1	44.2	238 39.7	11.0	15 17.5	7.6	56.3
18	88 23.1	N18 43.6	253 09.7	11.0	S15 10.0	7.6	56.3
19	103 23.2	43.0	267 39.7	11.0	15 02.4	7.6	56.4
20	118 23.2	42.4	282 09.7	11.0	14 54.8	7.7	56.4
21	133 23.2 ..	41.8	296 39.7	11.1	14 47.1	7.9	56.4
22	148 23.2	41.2	311 09.8	11.0	14 39.2	7.8	56.4
23	163 23.3	40.6	325 39.8	11.1	S14 31.4	8.0	56.4
	SD 15.8	d 0.6	SD 15.1		15.2		15.3

Days of week (left margin): 27 TUESDAY, 28 WEDNESDAY, 29 THURSDAY

Twilight / Moonrise

Lat.	Naut.	Civil	Sunrise	Moonrise 27	28	29	30
°	h m	h m	h m	h m	h m	h m	h m
N 72	□	□	□	■	23 27	22 52	22 34
N 70	////	////	00 21	22 36	22 27	22 21	22 16
68	////	////	01 50	21 39	21 52	21 58	22 01
66	////	////	02 28	21 06	21 27	21 41	21 49
64	////	01 09	02 58	20 41	21 08	21 26	21 39
62	////	01 56	03 14	20 21	20 51	21 14	21 31
60	////	02 26	03 30	20 06	20 38	21 03	21 23
N 58	01 03	02 48	03 44	19 52	20 27	20 54	21 17
56	01 46	03 05	03 56	19 40	20 16	20 46	21 11
54	02 13	03 20	04 06	19 30	20 08	20 39	21 06
52	02 34	03 32	04 15	19 21	20 00	20 33	21 01
50	02 50	03 43	04 23	19 13	19 52	20 27	20 57
45	03 22	04 06	04 40	18 55	19 37	20 14	20 48
N 40	03 45	04 23	04 54	18 41	19 24	20 03	20 40
35	04 04	04 38	05 06	18 29	19 14	19 55	20 33
30	04 19	04 50	05 16	18 19	19 04	19 47	20 27
20	04 42	05 10	05 34	18 00	18 48	19 33	20 17
N 10	05 00	05 27	05 49	17 45	18 34	19 21	20 08
0	05 16	05 41	06 03	17 30	18 20	19 10	19 59
S 10	05 29	05 55	06 17	17 15	18 07	18 59	19 51
20	05 42	06 08	06 32	16 59	17 53	18 47	19 42
30	05 54	06 23	06 48	16 41	17 36	18 33	19 32
35	06 00	06 31	06 58	16 31	17 27	18 25	19 26
40	06 07	06 40	07 09	16 18	17 16	18 16	19 19
45	06 14	06 50	07 22	16 04	17 03	18 05	19 11
S 50	06 23	07 02	07 38	15 47	16 47	17 52	19 01
52	06 26	07 07	07 45	15 38	16 40	17 46	18 57
54	06 30	07 13	07 53	15 29	16 31	17 40	18 52
56	06 34	07 20	08 02	15 19	16 22	17 32	18 46
58	06 38	07 27	08 13	15 07	16 12	17 24	18 40
S 60	06 43	07 35	08 25	14 53	16 00	17 14	18 33

Twilight / Moonset

Lat.	Sunset	Civil	Naut.	Moonset 27	28	29	30
°	h m	h m	h m	h m	h m	h m	h m
N 72	□	□	□	■	■	01 49	04 08
N 70	23 28	////	////	■	00 54	02 48	04 38
68	22 18	////	////	00 34	01 50	03 22	04 59
66	21 42	////	////	01 14	02 24	03 46	05 16
64	21 17	22 57	////	01 42	02 48	04 05	05 30
62	20 57	22 13	////	02 04	03 07	04 21	05 41
60	20 41	21 45	////	02 21	03 23	04 34	05 51
N 58	20 28	21 23	23 04	02 36	03 36	04 45	05 59
56	20 16	21 06	22 24	02 48	03 48	04 55	06 07
54	20 06	20 52	21 58	02 59	03 58	05 03	06 13
52	19 57	20 39	21 37	03 08	04 07	05 11	06 19
50	19 49	20 29	21 21	03 17	04 14	05 18	06 25
45	19 32	20 06	20 50	03 35	04 31	05 32	06 36
N 40	19 18	19 49	20 27	03 50	04 45	05 44	06 46
35	19 07	19 35	20 09	04 03	04 57	05 54	06 54
30	18 56	19 23	19 54	04 14	05 07	06 03	07 01
20	18 39	19 03	19 31	04 32	05 25	06 19	07 13
N 10	18 24	18 46	19 12	04 49	05 40	06 32	07 24
0	18 10	18 32	18 57	05 04	05 54	06 44	07 34
S 10	17 56	18 18	18 44	05 19	06 08	06 57	07 44
20	17 42	18 05	18 31	05 35	06 23	07 10	07 54
30	17 25	17 50	18 19	05 54	06 41	07 25	08 06
35	17 15	17 42	18 13	06 05	06 51	07 33	08 13
40	17 04	17 33	18 06	06 17	07 02	07 43	08 21
45	16 51	17 23	17 59	06 32	07 15	07 55	08 30
S 50	16 36	17 11	17 51	06 49	07 32	08 09	08 41
52	16 28	17 06	17 48	06 58	07 39	08 15	08 46
54	16 20	17 00	17 44	07 07	07 48	08 22	08 51
56	16 11	16 54	17 40	07 18	07 57	08 30	08 57
58	16 01	16 47	17 35	07 30	08 08	08 39	09 04
S 60	15 49	16 39	17 31	07 44	08 21	08 49	09 12

SUN / MOON

Day	Eqn. of Time 00h	12h	Mer. Pass.	Mer. Pass. Upper	Lower	Age	Phase
d	m s	m s	h m	h m	h m	d	%
27	06 31	06 30	12 07	23 42	11 17	14	99
28	06 30	06 29	12 06	24 32	12 07	15	100
29	06 29	06 28	12 06	00 32	12 57	16	99

UT	ARIES GHA	VENUS −4.4 GHA	Dec	MARS +0.0 GHA	Dec	JUPITER −2.5 GHA	Dec	SATURN +0.3 GHA	Dec	STARS Name	SHA	Dec
30 00	307 11.4	151 46.1 N 5	44.7	89 44.6 S16	23.8	275 05.5 N11	34.3	262 36.9 N14	28.2	Acamar	315 26.6	S40 18.2
01	322 13.8	166 48.8	44.2	104 45.9	24.2	290 07.8	34.4	277 39.3	28.2	Achernar	335 34.7	S57 14.1
02	337 16.3	181 51.4	43.7	119 47.2	24.6	305 10.0	34.5	292 41.6	28.2	Acrux	173 21.7	S63 05.9
03	352 18.8	196 54.1 ..	43.2	134 48.4 ..	25.1	320 12.3 ..	34.5	307 43.9 ..	28.3	Adhara	255 21.3	S28 58.2
04	7 21.2	211 56.8	42.6	149 49.7	25.5	335 14.6	34.6	322 46.3	28.3	Aldebaran	291 01.9	N16 30.4
05	22 23.7	226 59.4	42.1	164 50.9	25.9	350 16.8	34.6	337 48.6	28.3			
06	37 26.2	242 02.1 N 5	41.6	179 52.2 S16	26.3	5 19.1 N11	34.7	352 50.9 N14	28.3	Alioth	166 30.4	N55 58.1
07	52 28.6	257 04.8	41.1	194 53.4	26.7	20 21.4	34.8	7 53.3	28.4	Alkaid	153 07.5	N49 19.3
08	67 31.1	272 07.5	40.6	209 54.7	27.1	35 23.6	34.8	22 55.6	28.4	Al Na'ir	27 56.8	S46 57.6
F 09	82 33.6	287 10.2 ..	40.1	224 56.0 ..	27.6	50 25.9 ..	34.9	37 57.9 ..	28.4	Alnilam	275 57.5	S 1 12.2
R 10	97 36.0	302 12.9	39.6	239 57.2	28.0	65 28.2	34.9	53 00.3	28.5	Alphard	218 07.0	S 8 39.3
I 11	112 38.5	317 15.6	39.1	254 58.5	28.4	80 30.4	35.0	68 02.6	28.5			
D 12	127 40.9	332 18.3 N 5	38.6	269 59.7 S16	28.8	95 32.7 N11	35.1	83 04.9 N14	28.5	Alphecca	126 20.0	N26 43.3
A 13	142 43.4	347 21.0	38.1	285 01.0	29.2	110 35.0	35.1	98 07.3	28.5	Alpheratz	357 54.4	N29 05.1
Y 14	157 45.9	2 23.7	37.6	300 02.2	29.6	125 37.2	35.2	113 09.6	28.6	Altair	62 18.4	N 8 52.2
15	172 48.3	17 26.4 ..	37.1	315 03.5 ..	30.0	140 39.5 ..	35.2	128 11.9 ..	28.6	Ankaa	353 26.1	S42 18.3
16	187 50.8	32 29.1	36.6	330 04.7	30.5	155 41.8	35.3	143 14.3	28.6	Antares	112 39.3	S26 25.8
17	202 53.3	47 31.9	36.1	345 06.0	30.9	170 44.0	35.4	158 16.6	28.7			
18	217 55.7	62 34.6 N 5	35.6	0 07.2 S16	31.3	185 46.3 N11	35.4	173 18.9 N14	28.7	Arcturus	146 05.6	N19 11.4
19	232 58.2	77 37.3	35.1	15 08.5	31.7	200 48.6	35.5	188 21.3	28.7	Atria	107 50.4	S69 01.7
20	248 00.7	92 40.0	34.6	30 09.7	32.1	215 50.8	35.5	203 23.6	28.7	Avior	234 23.0	S59 30.5
21	263 03.1	107 42.8 ..	34.2	45 11.0 ..	32.5	230 53.1 ..	35.6	218 25.9 ..	28.8	Bellatrix	278 43.8	N 6 20.9
22	278 05.6	122 45.5	33.7	60 12.2	32.9	245 55.4	35.6	233 28.3	28.8	Betelgeuse	271 13.2	N 7 24.4
23	293 08.0	137 48.3	33.2	75 13.5	33.4	260 57.6	35.7	248 30.6	28.8			
31 00	308 10.5	152 51.0 N 5	32.7	90 14.7 S16	33.8	275 59.9 N11	35.8	263 32.9 N14	28.9	Canopus	264 01.4	S52 41.6
01	323 13.0	167 53.8	32.2	105 16.0	34.2	291 02.2	35.8	278 35.3	28.9	Capella	280 50.7	N45 59.6
02	338 15.4	182 56.5	31.7	120 17.2	34.6	306 04.5	35.9	293 37.6	28.9	Deneb	49 38.3	N45 16.8
03	353 17.9	197 59.3 ..	31.3	135 18.5 ..	35.0	321 06.7 ..	35.9	308 39.9 ..	28.9	Denebola	182 44.8	N14 34.7
04	8 20.4	213 02.0	30.8	150 19.7	35.4	336 09.0	36.0	323 42.3	29.0	Diphda	349 06.5	S17 59.3
05	23 22.8	228 04.8	30.3	165 20.9	35.9	351 11.3	36.1	338 44.6	29.0			
06	38 25.3	243 07.6 N 5	29.8	180 22.2 S16	36.3	6 13.5 N11	36.1	353 46.9 N14	29.0	Dubhe	194 05.4	N61 45.5
07	53 27.8	258 10.4	29.3	195 23.4	36.7	21 15.8	36.2	8 49.3	29.0	Elnath	278 26.5	N28 36.3
S 08	68 30.2	273 13.1	28.9	210 24.7	37.1	36 18.1	36.2	23 51.6	29.1	Eltanin	90 50.7	N51 29.7
A 09	83 32.7	288 15.9 ..	28.4	225 25.9 ..	37.5	51 20.4 ..	36.3	38 54.0 ..	29.1	Enif	33 57.4	N 9 52.4
T 10	98 35.2	303 18.7	27.9	240 27.1	37.9	66 22.6	36.3	53 56.3	29.1	Fomalhaut	15 35.5	S29 37.3
U 11	113 37.6	318 21.5	27.5	255 28.4	38.3	81 24.9	36.4	68 58.6	29.2			
R 12	128 40.1	333 24.3 N 5	27.0	270 29.6 S16	38.8	96 27.2 N11	36.5	84 01.0 N14	29.2	Gacrux	172 13.2	S57 06.8
D 13	143 42.5	348 27.1	26.5	285 30.9	39.2	111 29.4	36.5	99 03.3	29.2	Gienah	176 03.6	S17 32.3
A 14	158 45.0	3 29.9	26.1	300 32.1	39.6	126 31.7	36.6	114 05.6	29.2	Hadar	149 03.2	S60 22.4
Y 15	173 47.5	18 32.7 ..	25.6	315 33.3 ..	40.0	141 34.0 ..	36.6	129 08.0 ..	29.3	Hamal	328 12.9	N23 27.5
16	188 49.9	33 35.5	25.1	330 34.6	40.4	156 36.3	36.7	144 10.3	29.3	Kaus Aust.	83 57.7	S34 23.0
17	203 52.4	48 38.3	24.7	345 35.8	40.8	171 38.5	36.7	159 12.7	29.3			
18	218 54.9	63 41.1 N 5	24.2	0 37.0 S16	41.3	186 40.8 N11	36.8	174 15.0 N14	29.3	Kochab	137 19.5	N74 09.9
19	233 57.3	78 44.0	23.8	15 38.3	41.7	201 43.1	36.8	189 17.3	29.4	Markab	13 48.8	N15 12.2
20	248 59.8	93 46.8	23.3	30 39.5	42.1	216 45.4	36.9	204 19.7	29.4	Menkar	314 26.4	N 4 05.2
21	264 02.3	108 49.6 ..	22.8	45 40.8 ..	42.5	231 47.6 ..	37.0	219 22.0 ..	29.4	Menkent	148 20.3	S36 22.1
22	279 04.7	123 52.5	22.4	60 42.0	42.9	246 49.9	37.0	234 24.3	29.4	Miaplacidus	221 42.8	S69 43.0
23	294 07.2	138 55.3	21.9	75 43.2	43.3	261 52.2	37.0	249 26.7	29.5			
1 00	309 09.6	153 58.1 N 5	21.5	90 44.5 S16	43.7	276 54.5 N11	37.1	264 29.0 N14	29.5	Mirfak	308 55.9	N49 51.3
01	324 12.1	169 01.0	21.0	105 45.7	44.2	291 56.8	37.2	279 31.4	29.5	Nunki	76 11.3	S26 17.7
02	339 14.6	184 03.8	20.6	120 46.9	44.6	306 59.0	37.2	294 33.7	29.6	Peacock	53 35.6	S56 44.1
03	354 17.0	199 06.7 ..	20.1	135 48.1 ..	45.0	322 01.3 ..	37.3	309 36.0 ..	29.6	Pollux	243 41.3	N28 01.6
04	9 19.5	214 09.5	19.7	150 49.4	45.4	337 03.6	37.3	324 38.4	29.6	Procyon	245 11.3	N 5 13.6
05	24 22.0	229 12.4	19.3	165 50.6	45.8	352 05.9	37.4	339 40.7	29.6			
06	39 24.4	244 15.3 N 5	18.8	180 51.8 S16	46.2	7 08.1 N11	37.5	354 43.1 N14	29.7	Rasalhague	96 16.2	N12 33.9
07	54 26.9	259 18.1	18.4	195 53.1	46.7	22 10.4	37.5	9 45.4	29.7	Regulus	207 55.3	N11 58.3
08	69 29.4	274 21.0	17.9	210 54.3	47.1	37 12.7	37.6	24 47.7	29.7	Rigel	281 22.6	S 8 12.1
S 09	84 31.8	289 23.9 ..	17.5	225 55.5 ..	47.5	52 15.0 ..	37.6	39 50.1 ..	29.7	Rigil Kent.	140 06.5	S60 50.1
U 10	99 34.3	304 26.7	17.1	240 56.7	47.9	67 17.3	37.7	54 52.4	29.8	Sabik	102 24.7	S15 43.3
N 11	114 36.8	319 29.6	16.6	255 58.0	48.3	82 19.5	37.7	69 54.8	29.8			
D 12	129 39.2	334 32.5 N 5	16.2	270 59.2 S16	48.7	97 21.8 N11	37.8	84 57.1 N14	29.8	Schedar	349 52.5	N56 31.8
A 13	144 41.7	349 35.4	15.8	286 00.4	49.2	112 24.1	37.8	99 59.4	29.8	Shaula	96 36.2	S37 06.2
Y 14	159 44.1	4 38.3	15.3	301 01.6	49.6	127 26.4	37.9	115 01.8	29.9	Sirius	258 43.5	S16 42.9
15	174 46.6	19 41.2 ..	14.9	316 02.9 ..	50.0	142 28.7 ..	37.9	130 04.1 ..	29.9	Spica	158 42.7	S11 09.4
16	189 49.1	34 44.1	14.5	331 04.1	50.4	157 30.9	38.0	145 06.5	29.9	Suhail	223 00.8	S43 25.9
17	204 51.5	49 47.0	14.0	346 05.3	50.8	172 33.2	38.0	160 08.8	29.9			
18	219 54.0	64 49.9 N 5	13.6	1 06.5 S16	51.2	187 35.5 N11	38.1	175 11.1 N14	30.0	Vega	80 45.9	N38 47.2
19	234 56.5	79 52.8	13.2	16 07.7	51.7	202 37.8	38.2	190 13.5	30.0	Zuben'ubi	137 17.3	S16 02.3
20	249 58.9	94 55.7	12.8	31 09.0	52.1	217 40.1	38.2	205 15.8	30.0			
21	265 01.4	109 58.7 ..	12.4	46 10.2 ..	52.5	232 42.4 ..	38.3	220 18.2 ..	30.0		SHA	Mer. Pass.
22	280 03.9	125 01.6	11.9	61 11.4	52.9	247 44.6	38.3	235 20.5	30.1	Venus	204 40.5	13 46
23	295 06.3	140 04.5	11.5	76 12.6	53.3	262 46.9	38.4	250 22.8	30.1	Mars	142 04.2	17 58
	h m									Jupiter	327 49.4	5 35
Mer. Pass. 3 26.7	v 2.8 d 0.5		v 1.2 d 0.4		v 2.3 d 0.1		v 2.3 d 0.0			Saturn	315 22.4	6 25

UT	SUN		MOON					Lat.	Twilight		Sunrise	Moonrise			
									Naut.	Civil		30	31	1	2
	GHA	Dec	GHA	v	Dec	d	HP								
d h	° ′	° ′	° ′	′	° ′	′	′	°	h m	h m	h m	h m	h m	h m	h m
								N 72	▭	▭	▭	22 34	22 21	22 10	22 00
30 00	178 23.3	N18 40.0	340 09.9	11.1	S14 23.4	8.0	56.5	N 70	////	////	01 12	22 16	22 11	22 07	22 02
01	193 23.3	39.5	354 40.0	11.1	14 15.4	8.2	56.5	68	////	////	02 07	22 01	22 03	22 04	22 04
02	208 23.3	38.9	9 10.1	11.1	14 07.2	8.2	56.5	66	////	////	02 40	21 49	21 56	22 01	22 06
03	223 23.3 ..	38.3	23 40.2	11.2	13 59.0	8.3	56.5	64	////	01 30	03 03	21 39	21 50	21 59	22 08
04	238 23.4	37.7	38 10.4	11.1	13 50.7	8.3	56.5	62	////	02 09	03 22	21 31	21 45	21 57	22 09
05	253 23.4	37.1	52 40.5	11.2	13 42.4	8.4	56.6	60	////	02 35	03 37	21 23	21 40	21 56	22 11
06	268 23.4	N18 36.5	67 10.7	11.2	S13 34.0	8.5	56.6	N 58	01 22	02 55	03 50	21 17	21 36	21 54	22 12
07	283 23.4	35.9	81 40.9	11.2	13 25.5	8.6	56.6	56	01 57	03 12	04 01	21 11	21 33	21 53	22 13
08	298 23.5	35.3	96 11.1	11.3	13 16.9	8.7	56.6	54	02 22	03 26	04 11	21 06	21 30	21 52	22 14
F 09	313 23.5 ..	34.7	110 41.4	11.2	13 08.2	8.7	56.6	52	02 41	03 38	04 19	21 01	21 27	21 51	22 14
R 10	328 23.5	34.1	125 11.6	11.2	12 59.5	8.8	56.7	50	02 56	03 48	04 27	20 57	21 24	21 50	22 15
I 11	343 23.5	33.5	139 41.8	11.3	12 50.7	8.9	56.7	45	03 27	04 10	04 43	20 48	21 18	21 48	22 17
D 12	358 23.6	N18 32.9	154 12.1	11.3	S12 41.8	8.9	56.7	N 40	03 49	04 26	04 57	20 40	21 14	21 46	22 18
A 13	13 23.6	32.3	168 42.4	11.3	12 32.9	9.0	56.7	35	04 06	04 40	05 08	20 33	21 09	21 44	22 19
Y 14	28 23.6	31.7	183 12.7	11.3	12 23.9	9.1	56.8	30	04 21	04 52	05 18	20 27	21 06	21 43	22 21
15	43 23.6 ..	31.1	197 43.0	11.4	12 14.8	9.1	56.8	20	04 43	05 11	05 35	20 17	20 59	21 41	22 22
16	58 23.7	30.5	212 13.4	11.3	12 05.7	9.2	56.8	N 10	05 01	05 27	05 49	20 08	20 54	21 39	22 24
17	73 23.7	29.8	226 43.7	11.4	11 56.5	9.3	56.8	0	05 16	05 41	06 03	19 59	20 48	21 37	22 26
18	88 23.7	N18 29.2	241 14.1	11.4	S11 47.2	9.4	56.8	S 10	05 29	05 54	06 16	19 51	20 43	21 35	22 27
19	103 23.7	28.6	255 44.5	11.4	11 37.8	9.4	56.9	20	05 41	06 07	06 30	19 42	20 37	21 33	22 29
20	118 23.8	28.0	270 14.9	11.4	11 28.4	9.5	56.9	30	05 52	06 21	06 46	19 32	20 31	21 31	22 31
21	133 23.8 ..	27.4	284 45.3	11.4	11 18.9	9.5	56.9	35	05 58	06 29	06 56	19 26	20 27	21 29	22 32
22	148 23.8	26.8	299 15.7	11.4	11 09.4	9.6	56.9	40	06 05	06 37	07 06	19 19	20 23	21 28	22 34
23	163 23.8	26.2	313 46.1	11.5	10 59.8	9.7	56.9	45	06 11	06 47	07 19	19 11	20 18	21 26	22 35
31 00	178 23.9	N18 25.6	328 16.6	11.4	S10 50.1	9.7	57.0	S 50	06 19	06 58	07 34	19 01	20 12	21 24	22 37
01	193 23.9	25.0	342 47.0	11.5	10 40.4	9.8	57.0	52	06 22	07 03	07 41	18 57	20 09	21 23	22 38
02	208 23.9	24.4	357 17.5	11.5	10 30.6	9.8	57.0	54	06 26	07 09	07 48	18 52	20 06	21 22	22 39
03	223 24.0 ..	23.8	11 48.0	11.5	10 20.8	9.9	57.0	56	06 29	07 15	07 57	18 46	20 03	21 21	22 40
04	238 24.0	23.2	26 18.5	11.5	10 10.9	10.0	57.0	58	06 33	07 22	08 07	18 40	19 59	21 20	22 41
05	253 24.0	22.6	40 49.0	11.5	10 00.9	10.0	57.1	S 60	06 38	07 29	08 18	18 33	19 55	21 18	22 43
06	268 24.1	N18 21.9	55 19.5	11.6	S 9 50.9	10.1	57.1								

Lat.	Sunset	Twilight		Moonset			
		Civil	Naut.	30	31	1	2
°	h m	h m	h m	h m	h m	h m	h m
N 72	▭	▭	▭	04 08	06 08	08 03	09 56
N 70	22 52	////	////	04 38	06 25	08 11	09 56
68	22 01	////	////	04 59	06 38	08 17	09 57
66	21 30	////	////	05 16	06 49	08 22	09 57
64	21 07	22 37	////	05 30	06 57	08 27	09 57
62	20 49	22 00	////	05 41	07 05	08 31	09 58
60	20 34	21 35	////	05 51	07 11	08 34	09 58
N 58	20 21	21 15	22 46	05 59	07 17	08 37	09 58
56	20 10	20 59	22 12	06 07	07 22	08 40	09 58
54	20 01	20 46	21 49	06 13	07 27	08 42	09 58
52	19 52	20 34	21 30	06 19	07 31	08 44	09 59
50	19 45	20 24	21 15	06 25	07 35	08 46	09 59
45	19 29	20 02	20 45	06 36	07 42	08 50	09 59
N 40	19 15	19 46	20 23	06 46	07 49	08 54	09 59
35	19 04	19 32	20 06	06 54	07 55	08 57	09 59
30	18 54	19 20	19 52	07 01	08 00	08 59	09 59
20	18 38	19 01	19 29	07 13	08 08	09 04	10 00
N 10	18 23	18 45	19 11	07 24	08 16	09 08	10 00
0	18 10	18 32	18 57	07 34	08 23	09 11	10 00
S 10	17 57	18 19	18 44	07 44	08 30	09 15	10 00
20	17 43	18 06	18 32	07 54	08 37	09 19	10 00
30	17 27	17 52	18 21	08 06	08 45	09 23	10 00
35	17 17	17 44	18 15	08 13	08 50	09 26	10 00
40	17 07	17 36	18 08	08 21	08 56	09 28	10 01
45	16 55	17 26	18 02	08 30	09 02	09 32	10 01
S 50	16 40	17 15	17 54	08 41	09 09	09 35	10 01
52	16 33	17 10	17 51	08 46	09 13	09 37	10 01
54	16 25	17 05	17 48	08 51	09 16	09 39	10 01
56	16 16	16 58	17 44	08 57	09 20	09 41	10 01
58	16 07	16 52	17 40	09 04	09 25	09 43	10 01
S 60	15 55	16 44	17 36	09 12	09 30	09 46	10 01

Continuation of main table:

UT	SUN		MOON				
	GHA	Dec	GHA	v	Dec	d	HP
07	283 24.1	21.3	69 50.1	11.5	9 40.8	10.1	57.1
08	298 24.1	20.7	84 20.6	11.6	9 30.7	10.2	57.1
S 09	313 24.1 ..	20.1	98 51.2	11.5	9 20.5	10.3	57.1
A 10	328 24.2	19.5	113 21.7	11.6	9 10.2	10.3	57.2
T 11	343 24.2	18.9	127 52.3	11.6	8 59.9	10.3	57.2
U 12	358 24.2	N18 18.3	142 22.9	11.6	S 8 49.6	10.4	57.2
R 13	13 24.3	17.7	156 53.5	11.6	8 39.2	10.5	57.2
D 14	28 24.3	17.0	171 24.1	11.6	8 28.7	10.5	57.3
A 15	43 24.3 ..	16.4	185 54.7	11.6	8 18.2	10.5	57.3
Y 16	58 24.4	15.8	200 25.3	11.7	8 07.7	10.6	57.3
17	73 24.4	15.2	214 56.0	11.6	7 57.1	10.7	57.3
18	88 24.4	N18 14.6	229 26.6	11.6	S 7 46.4	10.7	57.3
19	103 24.5	14.0	243 57.2	11.7	7 35.7	10.7	57.4
20	118 24.5	13.3	258 27.9	11.6	7 25.0	10.8	57.4
21	133 24.5 ..	12.7	272 58.5	11.7	7 14.2	10.8	57.4
22	148 24.6	12.1	287 29.2	11.7	7 03.4	10.9	57.4
23	163 24.6	11.5	301 59.9	11.6	6 52.5	10.9	57.4
1 00	178 24.6	N18 10.9	316 30.5	11.7	S 6 41.6	10.9	57.5
01	193 24.7	10.2	331 01.2	11.7	6 30.7	11.0	57.5
02	208 24.7	09.6	345 31.9	11.7	6 19.7	11.0	57.5
03	223 24.7 ..	09.0	0 02.6	11.6	6 08.7	11.1	57.5
04	238 24.8	08.4	14 33.2	11.7	5 57.6	11.1	57.5
05	253 24.8	07.7	29 03.9	11.7	5 46.5	11.2	57.6
06	268 24.8	N18 07.1	43 34.6	11.7	S 5 35.3	11.1	57.6
07	283 24.9	06.5	58 05.3	11.7	5 24.2	11.2	57.6
08	298 24.9	05.9	72 36.0	11.6	5 13.0	11.3	57.6
S 09	313 24.9 ..	05.2	87 06.6	11.7	5 01.7	11.3	57.6
U 10	328 25.0	04.6	101 37.3	11.7	4 50.4	11.3	57.7
N 11	343 25.0	04.0	116 08.0	11.7	4 39.1	11.3	57.7
D 12	358 25.1	N18 03.4	130 38.7	11.7	S 4 27.8	11.4	57.7
A 13	13 25.1	02.7	145 09.4	11.6	4 16.4	11.4	57.7
Y 14	28 25.1	02.1	159 40.0	11.7	4 05.0	11.4	57.7
15	43 25.2 ..	01.5	174 10.7	11.6	3 53.6	11.5	57.8
16	58 25.2	00.9	188 41.3	11.7	3 42.1	11.5	57.8
17	73 25.3	18 00.2	203 12.0	11.6	3 30.7	11.5	57.8
18	88 25.3	N17 59.6	217 42.6	11.7	S 3 19.2	11.6	57.8
19	103 25.3	59.0	232 13.3	11.6	3 07.6	11.5	57.8
20	118 25.4	58.3	246 43.9	11.6	2 56.1	11.6	57.9
21	133 25.4 ..	57.7	261 14.5	11.6	2 44.5	11.6	57.9
22	148 25.4	57.1	275 45.1	11.7	2 32.9	11.6	57.9
23	163 25.5	56.4	290 15.8	11.5	S 2 21.3	11.6	57.9
	SD 15.8	d 0.6	SD 15.5		15.6		15.7

Day	SUN			MOON			
	Eqn. of Time		Mer.	Mer. Pass.		Age	Phase
	00ʰ	12ʰ	Pass.	Upper	Lower		
d	m s	m s	h m	h m	h m	d	%
30	06 27	06 26	12 06	01 22	13 47	17	96
31	06 25	06 23	12 06	02 11	14 36	18	90
1	06 22	06 20	12 06	03 00	15 24	19	83

UT	ARIES GHA	VENUS −4.3 GHA	Dec	MARS +0.1 GHA	Dec	JUPITER −2.5 GHA	Dec	SATURN +0.3 GHA	Dec	STARS Name	SHA	Dec
d h	° ′	° ′	° ′	° ′	° ′	° ′	° ′	° ′	° ′		° ′	° ′
2 00	310 08.8	155 07.5	N 5 11.1	91 13.8	S16 53.7	277 49.2	N11 38.4	265 25.2	N14 30.1	Acamar	315 26.6	S40 18.2
01	325 11.3	170 10.4	10.7	106 15.1	54.1	292 51.5	38.5	280 27.5	30.1	Achernar	335 34.6	S57 14.1
02	340 13.7	185 13.3	10.3	121 16.3	54.6	307 53.8	38.5	295 29.9	30.2	Acrux	173 21.7	S63 05.9
03	355 16.2	200 16.3	.. 09.9	136 17.5	.. 55.0	322 56.1	.. 38.6	310 32.2	.. 30.2	Adhara	255 21.3	S28 58.2
04	10 18.6	215 19.2	09.5	151 18.7	55.4	337 58.3	38.6	325 34.6	30.2	Aldebaran	291 01.9	N16 30.4
05	25 21.1	230 22.2	09.0	166 19.9	55.8	353 00.6	38.7	340 36.9	30.2			
06	40 23.6	245 25.1	N 5 08.6	181 21.1	S16 56.2	8 02.9	N11 38.7	355 39.3	N14 30.3	Alioth	166 30.4	N55 58.1
07	55 26.0	260 28.1	08.2	196 22.4	56.6	23 05.2	38.8	10 41.6	30.3	Alkaid	153 07.5	N49 19.3
M 08	70 28.5	275 31.0	07.8	211 23.6	57.1	38 07.5	38.8	25 43.9	30.3	Al Na'ir	27 56.8	S46 57.6
O 09	85 31.0	290 34.0	.. 07.4	226 24.8	.. 57.5	53 09.8	.. 38.9	40 46.3	.. 30.3	Alnilam	275 55.8	S 1 12.2
N 10	100 33.4	305 37.0	07.0	241 26.0	57.9	68 12.1	38.9	55 48.6	30.4	Alphard	218 07.0	S 8 39.3
D 11	115 35.9	320 40.0	06.6	256 27.2	58.3	83 14.4	39.0	70 51.0	30.4			
A 12	130 38.4	335 42.9	N 5 06.2	271 28.4	S16 58.7	98 16.6	N11 39.0	85 53.3	N14 30.4	Alphecca	126 20.0	N26 43.3
Y 13	145 40.8	350 45.9	05.8	286 29.6	59.1	113 18.9	39.1	100 55.7	30.4	Alpheratz	357 54.4	N29 05.2
14	160 43.3	5 48.9	05.4	301 30.8	16 59.6	128 21.2	39.1	115 58.0	30.5	Altair	62 18.4	N 8 52.2
15	175 45.7	20 51.9	.. 05.0	316 32.0	17 00.0	143 23.5	.. 39.2	131 00.3	.. 30.5	Ankaa	353 26.1	S42 18.3
16	190 48.2	35 54.9	04.6	331 33.2	00.4	158 25.8	39.3	146 02.7	30.5	Antares	112 39.3	S26 25.8
17	205 50.7	50 57.9	04.3	346 34.5	00.8	173 28.1	39.3	161 05.0	30.5			
18	220 53.1	66 00.9	N 5 03.9	1 35.7	S17 01.2	188 30.4	N11 39.4	176 07.4	N14 30.6	Arcturus	146 05.6	N19 11.4
19	235 55.6	81 03.9	03.5	16 36.9	01.6	203 32.7	39.4	191 09.7	30.6	Atria	107 50.5	S69 01.7
20	250 58.1	96 06.9	03.1	31 38.1	02.1	218 34.9	39.5	206 12.1	30.6	Avior	234 23.0	S59 30.5
21	266 00.5	111 09.9	.. 02.7	46 39.3	.. 02.5	233 37.2	.. 39.5	221 14.4	.. 30.6	Bellatrix	278 43.8	N 6 20.9
22	281 03.0	126 12.9	02.3	61 40.5	02.9	248 39.5	39.6	236 16.8	30.7	Betelgeuse	271 13.2	N 7 24.4
23	296 05.5	141 16.0	01.9	76 41.7	03.3	263 41.8	39.6	251 19.1	30.7			
3 00	311 07.9	156 19.0	N 5 01.6	91 42.9	S17 03.7	278 44.1	N11 39.7	266 21.5	N14 30.7	Canopus	264 01.4	S52 41.6
01	326 10.4	171 22.0	01.2	106 44.1	04.1	293 46.4	39.7	281 23.8	30.7	Capella	280 50.7	N45 59.6
02	341 12.9	186 25.0	00.8	121 45.3	04.6	308 48.7	39.8	296 26.2	30.8	Deneb	49 38.3	N45 16.8
03	356 15.3	201 28.1	.. 00.4	136 46.5	.. 05.0	323 51.0	.. 39.8	311 28.5	.. 30.8	Denebola	182 44.9	N14 34.7
04	11 17.8	216 31.1	5 00.1	151 47.7	05.4	338 53.3	39.9	326 30.8	30.8	Diphda	349 06.5	S17 59.3
05	26 20.2	231 34.2	4 59.7	166 48.9	05.8	353 55.6	39.9	341 33.2	30.8			
06	41 22.7	246 37.2	N 4 59.3	181 50.1	S17 06.2	8 57.9	N11 40.0	356 35.5	N14 30.8	Dubhe	194 05.4	N61 45.5
07	56 25.2	261 40.2	58.9	196 51.3	06.6	24 00.2	40.0	11 37.9	30.9	Elnath	278 26.5	N28 36.3
T 08	71 27.6	276 43.3	58.6	211 52.5	07.1	39 02.4	40.1	26 40.2	30.9	Eltanin	90 50.7	N51 29.7
U 09	86 30.1	291 46.4	.. 58.2	226 53.7	.. 07.5	54 04.7	.. 40.1	41 42.6	.. 30.9	Enif	33 57.4	N 9 52.4
E 10	101 32.6	306 49.4	57.9	241 54.9	07.9	69 07.0	40.2	56 44.9	30.9	Fomalhaut	15 35.5	S29 37.3
S 11	116 35.0	321 52.5	57.5	256 56.1	08.3	84 09.3	40.2	71 47.3	31.0			
D 12	131 37.5	336 55.6	N 4 57.1	271 57.3	S17 08.7	99 11.6	N11 40.3	86 49.6	N14 31.0	Gacrux	172 13.2	S57 06.7
A 13	146 40.0	351 58.6	56.8	286 58.5	09.1	114 13.9	40.3	101 52.0	31.0	Gienah	176 03.6	S17 32.3
Y 14	161 42.4	7 01.7	56.4	301 59.7	09.5	129 16.2	40.4	116 54.3	31.0	Hadar	149 03.3	S60 22.4
15	176 44.9	22 04.8	.. 56.1	317 00.9	.. 10.0	144 18.5	.. 40.4	131 56.7	.. 31.1	Hamal	328 12.9	N23 27.5
16	191 47.3	37 07.9	55.7	332 02.1	10.4	159 20.8	40.4	146 59.0	31.1	Kaus Aust.	83 57.7	S34 23.0
17	206 49.8	52 11.0	55.3	347 03.3	10.8	174 23.1	40.5	162 01.4	31.1			
18	221 52.3	67 14.1	N 4 55.0	2 04.5	S17 11.2	189 25.4	N11 40.5	177 03.7	N14 31.1	Kochab	137 19.6	N74 09.9
19	236 54.7	82 17.2	54.6	17 05.7	11.6	204 27.7	40.6	192 06.1	31.2	Markab	13 48.8	N15 12.2
20	251 57.2	97 20.3	54.3	32 06.8	12.0	219 30.0	40.6	207 08.4	31.2	Menkar	314 26.3	N 4 05.2
21	266 59.7	112 23.4	.. 53.9	47 08.0	.. 12.5	234 32.3	.. 40.7	222 10.8	.. 31.2	Menkent	148 20.3	S36 22.1
22	282 02.1	127 26.5	53.6	62 09.2	12.9	249 34.6	40.7	237 13.1	31.2	Miaplacidus	221 42.8	S69 43.0
23	297 04.6	142 29.6	53.3	77 10.4	13.3	264 36.9	40.8	252 15.5	31.2			
4 00	312 07.1	157 32.7	N 4 52.9	92 11.6	S17 13.7	279 39.2	N11 40.8	267 17.8	N14 31.3	Mirfak	308 55.9	N49 51.3
01	327 09.5	172 35.8	52.6	107 12.8	14.1	294 41.5	40.9	282 20.2	31.3	Nunki	76 11.3	S26 17.7
02	342 12.0	187 38.9	52.2	122 14.0	14.5	309 43.8	40.9	297 22.5	31.3	Peacock	53 35.6	S56 44.1
03	357 14.5	202 42.1	.. 51.9	137 15.2	.. 15.0	324 46.1	.. 41.0	312 24.9	.. 31.3	Pollux	243 41.2	N28 01.6
04	12 16.9	217 45.2	51.6	152 16.4	15.4	339 48.4	41.0	327 27.2	31.4	Procyon	245 11.3	N 5 13.6
05	27 19.4	232 48.3	51.2	167 17.6	15.8	354 50.7	41.1	342 29.6	31.4			
06	42 21.8	247 51.5	N 4 50.9	182 18.7	S17 16.2	9 53.0	N11 41.1	357 31.9	N14 31.4	Rasalhague	96 16.2	N12 33.9
W 07	57 24.3	262 54.6	50.6	197 19.9	16.6	24 55.3	41.2	12 34.3	31.4	Regulus	207 55.3	N11 58.3
E 08	72 26.8	277 57.7	50.2	212 21.1	17.0	39 57.6	41.2	27 36.6	31.4	Rigel	281 22.6	S 8 12.1
D 09	87 29.2	293 00.9	.. 49.9	227 22.3	.. 17.5	54 59.9	.. 41.3	42 39.0	.. 31.5	Rigil Kent.	140 06.5	S60 50.1
N 10	102 31.7	308 04.0	49.6	242 23.5	17.9	70 02.2	41.3	57 41.3	31.5	Sabik	102 24.7	S15 43.3
E 11	117 34.2	323 07.2	49.3	257 24.7	18.3	85 04.5	41.4	72 43.7	31.5			
S 12	132 36.6	338 10.4	N 4 48.9	272 25.8	S17 18.7	100 06.8	N11 41.4	87 46.0	N14 31.5	Schedar	349 52.5	N56 31.8
D 13	147 39.1	353 13.5	48.6	287 27.0	19.1	115 09.1	41.4	102 48.4	31.6	Shaula	96 36.2	S37 06.2
A 14	162 41.6	8 16.7	48.3	302 28.2	19.5	130 11.4	41.5	117 50.7	31.6	Sirius	258 43.5	S16 42.9
Y 15	177 44.0	23 19.9	.. 48.0	317 29.4	.. 20.0	145 13.7	.. 41.5	132 53.1	.. 31.6	Spica	158 42.7	S11 09.4
16	192 46.5	38 23.0	47.7	332 30.6	20.4	160 16.0	41.6	147 55.4	31.6	Suhail	223 00.8	S43 25.8
17	207 49.0	53 26.2	47.3	347 31.8	20.8	175 18.3	41.6	162 57.8	31.6			
18	222 51.4	68 29.4	N 4 47.0	2 32.9	S17 21.2	190 20.6	N11 41.7	178 00.2	N14 31.7	Vega	80 45.9	N38 47.3
19	237 53.9	83 32.6	46.7	17 34.1	21.6	205 22.9	41.7	193 02.5	31.7	Zuben'ubi	137 17.3	S16 02.3
20	252 56.3	98 35.8	46.4	32 35.3	22.0	220 25.2	41.8	208 04.9	31.7			
21	267 58.8	113 39.0	.. 46.1	47 36.5	.. 22.5	235 27.5	.. 41.8	223 07.2	.. 31.7			
22	283 01.3	128 42.2	45.8	62 37.6	22.9	250 29.8	41.9	238 09.6	31.8			
23	298 03.7	143 45.4	45.5	77 38.8	23.3	265 32.1	41.9	253 11.9	31.8			
	h m										SHA	Mer. Pass.
Mer. Pass. 3 14.9	v 3.1 d 0.4	v 1.2	d 0.4	v 2.3	d 0.0	v 2.3	d 0.0			Venus	205 11.1	h m 13 32
										Mars	140 35.0	17 52
										Jupiter	327 36.2	5 24
										Saturn	315 13.5	6 14

UT	SUN GHA	SUN Dec	MOON GHA	MOON v	MOON Dec	MOON d	MOON HP
d h	° ′	° ′	° ′	′	° ′	′	′
2 00	178 25.5	N17 55.8	304 46.3	11.6	S 2 09.7	11.7	57.9
01	193 25.6	55.2	319 16.9	11.6	1 58.0	11.7	58.0
02	208 25.6	54.5	333 47.5	11.6	1 46.3	11.7	58.0
03	223 25.7	.. 53.9	348 18.1	11.5	1 34.6	11.7	58.0
04	238 25.7	53.3	2 48.6	11.5	1 22.9	11.7	58.0
05	253 25.7	52.6	17 19.1	11.5	1 11.2	11.7	58.0
06	268 25.8	N17 52.0	31 49.6	11.6	S 0 59.5	11.7	58.1
07	283 25.8	51.4	46 20.2	11.4	0 47.8	11.8	58.1
08	298 25.9	50.7	60 50.6	11.5	0 36.0	11.7	58.1
09	313 25.9	.. 50.1	75 21.1	11.5	0 24.3	11.8	58.1
10	328 25.9	49.5	89 51.6	11.4	0 12.5	11.8	58.1
11	343 26.0	48.8	104 22.0	11.4	S 0 00.7	11.8	58.1
12	358 26.0	N17 48.2	118 52.4	11.4	N 0 11.1	11.8	58.2
13	13 26.1	47.5	133 22.8	11.4	0 22.9	11.8	58.2
14	28 26.1	46.9	147 53.2	11.3	0 34.7	11.8	58.2
15	43 26.2	.. 46.3	162 23.5	11.3	0 46.5	11.8	58.2
16	58 26.2	45.6	176 53.8	11.4	0 58.3	11.8	58.2
17	73 26.3	45.0	191 24.2	11.2	1 10.1	11.8	58.3
18	88 26.3	N17 44.3	205 54.4	11.3	N 1 21.9	11.8	58.3
19	103 26.3	43.7	220 24.7	11.2	1 33.7	11.8	58.3
20	118 26.4	43.0	234 54.9	11.2	1 45.5	11.8	58.3
21	133 26.4	.. 42.4	249 25.1	11.2	1 57.3	11.8	58.3
22	148 26.5	41.8	263 55.3	11.2	2 09.1	11.8	58.4
23	163 26.5	41.1	278 25.5	11.1	2 20.9	11.8	58.4
3 00	178 26.6	N17 40.5	292 55.6	11.1	N 2 32.7	11.8	58.4
01	193 26.6	39.8	307 25.7	11.1	2 44.5	11.7	58.4
02	208 26.7	39.2	321 55.8	11.0	2 56.2	11.8	58.4
03	223 26.7	.. 38.5	336 25.8	11.0	3 08.0	11.8	58.4
04	238 26.8	37.9	350 55.8	11.0	3 19.8	11.7	58.5
05	253 26.8	37.2	5 25.8	10.9	3 31.5	11.7	58.5
06	268 26.9	N17 36.6	19 55.7	10.9	N 3 43.2	11.8	58.5
07	283 26.9	35.9	34 25.6	10.9	3 55.0	11.7	58.5
08	298 27.0	35.3	48 55.5	10.9	4 06.7	11.7	58.5
09	313 27.0	.. 34.6	63 25.4	10.8	4 18.4	11.6	58.6
10	328 27.1	34.0	77 55.2	10.7	4 30.0	11.7	58.6
11	343 27.1	33.3	92 24.9	10.8	4 41.7	11.6	58.6
12	358 27.2	N17 32.7	106 54.7	10.7	N 4 53.3	11.6	58.6
13	13 27.2	32.0	121 24.4	10.6	5 04.9	11.6	58.6
14	28 27.3	31.4	135 54.0	10.6	5 16.5	11.6	58.6
15	43 27.3	.. 30.7	150 23.6	10.6	5 28.1	11.6	58.7
16	58 27.4	30.1	164 53.2	10.6	5 39.7	11.5	58.7
17	73 27.4	29.4	179 22.8	10.5	5 51.2	11.5	58.7
18	88 27.5	N17 28.8	193 52.3	10.4	N 6 02.7	11.5	58.7
19	103 27.5	28.1	208 21.7	10.4	6 14.2	11.4	58.7
20	118 27.6	27.5	222 51.1	10.4	6 25.6	11.4	58.8
21	133 27.6	.. 26.8	237 20.5	10.3	6 37.0	11.4	58.8
22	148 27.7	26.2	251 49.8	10.3	6 48.4	11.3	58.8
23	163 27.7	25.5	266 19.1	10.2	6 59.8	11.3	58.8
4 00	178 27.8	N17 24.8	280 48.3	10.2	N 7 11.1	11.3	58.8
01	193 27.8	24.2	295 17.5	10.2	7 22.4	11.2	58.8
02	208 27.9	23.5	309 46.7	10.1	7 33.6	11.2	58.9
03	223 27.9	.. 22.9	324 15.8	10.0	7 44.8	11.2	58.9
04	238 28.0	22.2	338 44.8	10.0	7 56.0	11.2	58.9
05	253 28.0	21.6	353 13.8	10.0	8 07.2	11.1	58.9
06	268 28.1	N17 20.9	7 42.8	9.9	N 8 18.3	11.0	58.9
07	283 28.1	20.2	22 11.7	9.8	8 29.3	11.1	58.9
08	298 28.2	19.6	36 40.5	9.8	8 40.4	10.9	59.0
09	313 28.3	.. 18.9	51 09.3	9.8	8 51.3	11.0	59.0
10	328 28.3	18.3	65 38.1	9.7	9 02.3	10.9	59.0
11	343 28.4	17.6	80 06.8	9.6	9 13.2	10.8	59.0
12	358 28.4	N17 16.9	94 35.4	9.6	N 9 24.0	10.8	59.0
13	13 28.5	16.3	109 04.0	9.5	9 34.8	10.7	59.0
14	28 28.5	15.6	123 32.5	9.5	9 45.5	10.7	59.0
15	43 28.6	.. 14.9	138 01.0	9.4	9 56.2	10.7	59.1
16	58 28.7	14.3	152 29.4	9.4	10 06.9	10.6	59.1
17	73 28.7	13.6	166 57.8	9.3	10 17.5	10.5	59.1
18	88 28.8	N17 12.9	181 26.1	9.3	N10 28.0	10.5	59.1
19	103 28.8	12.3	195 54.4	9.2	10 38.5	10.4	59.1
20	118 28.9	11.6	210 22.6	9.1	10 48.9	10.4	59.1
21	133 28.9	.. 10.9	224 50.7	9.1	10 59.3	10.3	59.2
22	148 29.0	10.3	239 18.8	9.1	11 09.6	10.2	59.2
23	163 29.1	09.6	253 46.9	8.9	N11 19.8	10.2	59.2
	SD 15.8	d 0.7	SD 15.8		16.0		16.1

Left margin days: MONDAY (2), TUESDAY (3), WEDNESDAY (4)

Lat.	Twilight Naut.	Twilight Civil	Sunrise	Moonrise 2	Moonrise 3	Moonrise 4	Moonrise 5
°	h m	h m	h m	h m	h m	h m	h m
N 72	□	□	□	22 00	21 49	21 36	21 19
N 70	////	////	01 39	22 02	21 58	21 54	21 49
68	////	////	02 23	22 04	22 06	22 08	22 12
66	////	00 46	02 51	22 06	22 12	22 19	22 30
64	////	01 48	03 13	22 08	22 18	22 29	22 45
62	////	02 21	03 30	22 09	22 22	22 37	22 57
60	00 42	02 45	03 44	22 11	22 26	22 45	23 08
N 58	01 38	03 03	03 56	22 12	22 30	22 51	23 17
56	02 08	03 19	04 07	22 13	22 33	22 57	23 25
54	02 30	03 32	04 16	22 14	22 36	23 02	23 32
52	02 48	03 43	04 24	22 14	22 39	23 07	23 39
50	03 03	03 53	04 31	22 15	22 42	23 11	23 45
45	03 31	04 13	04 47	22 17	22 47	23 20	23 57
N 40	03 52	04 29	05 00	22 18	22 52	23 28	24 08
35	04 09	04 43	05 10	22 19	22 56	23 34	24 17
30	04 23	04 54	05 20	22 21	22 59	23 40	24 25
20	04 45	05 12	05 36	22 22	23 05	23 50	24 39
N 10	05 02	05 28	05 50	22 24	23 11	23 59	24 51
0	05 16	05 41	06 03	22 26	23 16	24 08	00 08
S 10	05 28	05 54	06 15	22 27	23 21	24 16	00 16
20	05 39	06 06	06 29	22 29	23 27	24 26	00 26
30	05 50	06 19	06 44	22 31	23 33	24 36	00 36
35	05 56	06 26	06 53	22 32	23 37	24 42	00 42
40	06 02	06 34	07 03	22 34	23 41	24 49	00 49
45	06 08	06 44	07 15	22 35	23 46	24 58	00 58
S 50	06 15	06 54	07 29	22 37	23 52	25 08	01 08
52	06 18	06 59	07 36	22 38	23 55	25 12	01 12
54	06 21	07 04	07 43	22 39	23 58	25 17	01 17
56	06 25	07 10	07 51	22 40	24 01	00 01	01 23
58	06 28	07 16	08 01	22 41	24 05	00 05	01 29
S 60	06 32	07 23	08 11	22 43	24 09	00 09	01 36

Lat.	Sunset	Twilight Civil	Twilight Naut.	Moonset 2	Moonset 3	Moonset 4	Moonset 5
°	h m	h m	h m	h m	h m	h m	h m
N 72	□	□	□	09 56	11 51	13 51	16 00
N 70	22 27	////	////	09 56	11 44	13 35	15 31
68	21 46	////	////	09 57	11 38	13 22	15 09
66	21 18	23 14	////	09 57	11 34	13 12	14 52
64	20 57	22 20	////	09 57	11 30	13 03	14 39
62	20 41	21 48	////	09 58	11 26	12 56	14 27
60	20 27	21 25	23 19	09 58	11 23	12 50	14 17
N 58	20 15	21 07	22 30	09 58	11 21	12 44	14 09
56	20 04	20 52	22 01	09 58	11 18	12 39	14 01
54	19 55	20 39	21 40	09 58	11 16	12 35	13 55
52	19 47	20 28	21 23	09 59	11 14	12 31	13 49
50	19 40	20 18	21 08	09 59	11 13	12 28	13 43
45	19 25	19 58	20 40	09 59	11 09	12 20	13 32
N 40	19 12	19 42	20 19	09 59	11 06	12 13	13 22
35	19 01	19 29	20 03	09 59	11 03	12 08	13 14
30	18 52	19 18	19 49	09 59	11 01	12 03	13 07
20	18 36	19 00	19 27	10 00	10 56	11 55	12 54
N 10	18 22	18 45	19 10	10 00	10 53	11 47	12 44
0	18 10	18 31	18 57	10 00	10 49	11 40	12 34
S 10	17 57	18 19	18 44	10 00	10 46	11 33	12 23
20	17 44	18 07	18 33	10 00	10 42	11 26	12 13
30	17 28	17 53	18 22	10 00	10 38	11 18	12 00
35	17 20	17 46	18 17	10 00	10 36	11 13	11 53
40	17 10	17 38	18 11	10 01	10 33	11 08	11 45
45	16 58	17 29	18 05	10 01	10 30	11 01	11 36
S 50	16 44	17 19	17 58	10 01	10 26	10 54	11 25
52	16 37	17 14	17 55	10 01	10 25	10 50	11 20
54	16 30	17 09	17 52	10 01	10 23	10 47	11 14
56	16 22	17 03	17 48	10 01	10 21	10 42	11 08
58	16 13	16 57	17 45	10 01	10 18	10 38	11 01
S 60	16 02	16 50	17 41	10 01	10 16	10 33	10 53

Day	SUN Eqn. of Time 00h	SUN Eqn. of Time 12h	SUN Mer. Pass.	MOON Mer. Pass. Upper	MOON Mer. Pass. Lower	Age	Phase
d	m s	m s	h m	h m	h m	d	%
2	06 18	06 16	12 06	03 48	16 13	20	74
3	06 14	06 11	12 06	04 38	17 03	21	64
4	06 09	06 06	12 06	05 28	17 54	22	53

UT	ARIES GHA	VENUS −4.3 GHA	Dec	MARS +0.1 GHA	Dec	JUPITER −2.5 GHA	Dec	SATURN +0.3 GHA	Dec	STARS Name	SHA	Dec
d h	° ′	° ′	° ′	° ′	° ′	° ′	° ′	° ′	° ′		° ′	° ′
5 00	313 06.2	158 48.6 N 4	45.2	92 40.0	S17 23.7	280 34.4	N11 41.9	268 14.3	N14 31.8	Acamar	315 26.5	S40 18.2
01	328 08.7	173 51.8	44.9	107 41.2	24.1	295 36.7	42.0	283 16.6	31.8	Achernar	335 34.6	S57 14.1
02	343 11.1	188 55.0	44.6	122 42.3	24.5	310 39.0	42.0	298 19.0	31.8	Acrux	173 21.7	S63 05.9
03	358 13.6	203 58.2 ..	44.3	137 43.5 ..	25.0	325 41.3 ..	42.1	313 21.3 ..	31.9	Adhara	255 21.3	S28 58.2
04	13 16.1	219 01.4	44.0	152 44.7	25.4	340 43.6	42.1	328 23.7	31.9	Aldebaran	291 01.9	N16 30.4
05	28 18.5	234 04.6	43.7	167 45.9	25.8	355 46.0	42.2	343 26.1	31.9			
06	43 21.0	249 07.9 N 4	43.4	182 47.0	S17 26.2	10 48.3	N11 42.2	358 28.4	N14 31.9	Alioth	166 30.4	N55 58.1
07	58 23.4	264 11.1	43.1	197 48.2	26.6	25 50.6	42.3	13 30.8	31.9	Alkaid	153 07.5	N49 19.3
T 08	73 25.9	279 14.3	42.8	212 49.4	27.0	40 52.9	42.3	28 33.1	32.0	Al Na'ir	27 56.8	S46 57.7
H 09	88 28.4	294 17.6 ..	42.5	227 50.6 ..	27.5	55 55.2 ..	42.3	43 35.5 ..	32.0	Alnilam	275 57.5	S 1 12.1
U 10	103 30.8	309 20.8	42.2	242 51.7	27.9	70 57.5	42.4	58 37.8	32.0	Alphard	218 07.0	S 8 39.3
R 11	118 33.3	324 24.0	41.9	257 52.9	28.3	85 59.8	42.4	73 40.2	32.0			
S 12	133 35.8	339 27.3 N 4	41.7	272 54.1	S17 28.7	101 02.1	N11 42.5	88 42.5	N14 32.0	Alphecca	126 20.0	N26 43.3
D 13	148 38.2	354 30.5	41.4	287 55.2	29.1	116 04.4	42.5	103 44.9	32.1	Alpheratz	357 54.4	N29 05.2
A 14	163 40.7	9 33.8	41.1	302 56.4	29.5	131 06.7	42.6	118 47.3	32.1	Altair	62 18.4	N 8 52.2
Y 15	178 43.2	24 37.1 ..	40.8	317 57.6 ..	29.9	146 09.0 ..	42.6	133 49.6 ..	32.1	Ankaa	353 26.1	S42 18.3
16	193 45.6	39 40.3	40.5	332 58.7	30.4	161 11.4	42.7	148 52.0	32.1	Antares	112 39.3	S26 25.8
17	208 48.1	54 43.6	40.3	347 59.9	30.8	176 13.7	42.7	163 54.3	32.2			
18	223 50.6	69 46.9 N 4	40.0	3 01.1	S17 31.2	191 16.0	N11 42.8	178 56.7	N14 32.2	Arcturus	146 05.6	N19 11.4
19	238 53.0	84 50.1	39.7	18 02.2	31.6	206 18.3	42.8	193 59.0	32.2	Atria	107 50.5	S69 01.7
20	253 55.5	99 53.4	39.5	33 03.4	32.0	221 20.6	42.8	209 01.4	32.2	Avior	234 23.0	S59 30.5
21	268 57.9	114 56.7 ..	39.2	48 04.6 ..	32.4	236 22.9 ..	42.9	224 03.8 ..	32.2	Bellatrix	278 43.8	N 6 20.9
22	284 00.4	130 00.0	38.9	63 05.7	32.9	251 25.2	42.9	239 06.1	32.3	Betelgeuse	271 13.2	N 7 24.4
23	299 02.9	145 03.3	38.6	78 06.9	33.3	266 27.5	43.0	254 08.5	32.3			
6 00	314 05.3	160 06.6 N 4	38.4	93 08.0	S17 33.7	281 29.8	N11 43.0	269 10.8	N14 32.3	Canopus	264 01.4	S52 41.6
01	329 07.8	175 09.8	38.1	108 09.2	34.1	296 32.2	43.0	284 13.2	32.3	Capella	280 50.6	N45 59.6
02	344 10.3	190 13.1	37.9	123 10.4	34.5	311 34.5	43.1	299 15.5	32.3	Deneb	49 38.3	N45 16.8
03	359 12.7	205 16.4 ..	37.6	138 11.5 ..	34.9	326 36.8 ..	43.1	314 17.9 ..	32.4	Denebola	182 44.9	N14 34.7
04	14 15.2	220 19.8	37.3	153 12.7	35.4	341 39.1	43.2	329 20.3	32.4	Diphda	349 06.5	S17 59.3
05	29 17.7	235 23.1	37.1	168 13.8	35.8	356 41.4	43.2	344 22.6	32.4			
06	44 20.1	250 26.4 N 4	36.8	183 15.0	S17 36.2	11 43.7	N11 43.3	359 25.0	N14 32.4	Dubhe	194 05.4	N61 45.4
07	59 22.6	265 29.7	36.6	198 16.2	36.6	26 46.0	43.3	14 27.3	32.4	Elnath	278 26.5	N28 36.3
08	74 25.1	280 33.0	36.3	213 17.3	37.0	41 48.4	43.3	29 29.7	32.5	Eltanin	90 50.8	N51 29.7
F 09	89 27.5	295 36.3 ..	36.1	228 18.5 ..	37.4	56 50.7 ..	43.4	44 32.1 ..	32.5	Enif	33 57.3	N 9 52.5
R 10	104 30.0	310 39.7	35.8	243 19.6	37.9	71 53.0	43.4	59 34.4	32.5	Fomalhaut	15 35.5	S29 37.3
I 11	119 32.4	325 43.0	35.6	258 20.8	38.3	86 55.3	43.5	74 36.8	32.5			
D 12	134 34.9	340 46.3 N 4	35.4	273 21.9	S17 38.7	101 57.6	N11 43.5	89 39.1	N14 32.5	Gacrux	172 13.2	S57 06.7
A 13	149 37.4	355 49.7	35.1	288 23.1	39.1	116 59.9	43.5	104 41.5	32.6	Gienah	176 03.6	S17 32.3
Y 14	164 39.8	10 53.0	34.9	303 24.3	39.5	132 02.3	43.6	119 43.9	32.6	Hadar	149 03.3	S60 22.4
15	179 42.3	25 56.4 ..	34.6	318 25.4 ..	39.9	147 04.6 ..	43.6	134 46.2 ..	32.6	Hamal	328 12.8	N23 27.5
16	194 44.8	40 59.7	34.4	333 26.6	40.3	162 06.9	43.7	149 48.6	32.6	Kaus Aust.	83 57.7	S34 23.0
17	209 47.2	56 03.1	34.2	348 27.7	40.8	177 09.2	43.7	164 50.9	32.6			
18	224 49.7	71 06.4 N 4	33.9	3 28.9	S17 41.2	192 11.5	N11 43.7	179 53.3	N14 32.7	Kochab	137 19.6	N74 09.9
19	239 52.2	86 09.8	33.7	18 30.0	41.6	207 13.8	43.8	194 55.7	32.7	Markab	13 48.8	N15 12.2
20	254 54.6	101 13.1	33.5	33 31.2	42.0	222 16.2	43.8	209 58.0	32.7	Menkar	314 26.3	N 4 05.2
21	269 57.1	116 16.5 ..	33.2	48 32.3 ..	42.4	237 18.5 ..	43.9	225 00.4 ..	32.7	Menkent	148 20.3	S36 22.1
22	284 59.6	131 19.9	33.0	63 33.5	42.8	252 20.8	43.9	240 02.8	32.7	Miaplacidus	221 42.8	S69 42.9
23	300 02.0	146 23.2	32.8	78 34.6	43.3	267 23.1	43.9	255 05.1	32.8			
7 00	315 04.5	161 26.6 N 4	32.6	93 35.8	S17 43.7	282 25.4	N11 44.0	270 07.5	N14 32.8	Mirfak	308 55.9	N49 51.3
01	330 06.9	176 30.0	32.3	108 36.9	44.1	297 27.8	44.0	285 09.8	32.8	Nunki	76 11.3	S26 17.7
02	345 09.4	191 33.4	32.1	123 38.1	44.5	312 30.1	44.1	300 12.2	32.8	Peacock	53 35.5	S56 44.1
03	0 11.9	206 36.8 ..	31.9	138 39.2 ..	44.9	327 32.4 ..	44.1	315 14.6 ..	32.8	Pollux	243 41.2	N28 01.6
04	15 14.3	221 40.2	31.7	153 40.4	45.3	342 34.7	44.1	330 16.9	32.8	Procyon	245 11.3	N 5 13.6
05	30 16.8	236 43.6	31.5	168 41.5	45.8	357 37.0	44.2	345 19.3	32.9			
06	45 19.3	251 47.0 N 4	31.3	183 42.6	S17 46.2	12 39.4	N11 44.2	0 21.7	N14 32.9	Rasalhague	96 16.2	N12 33.9
07	60 21.7	266 50.4	31.1	198 43.8	46.6	27 41.7	44.3	15 24.0	32.9	Regulus	207 55.3	N11 58.3
S 08	75 24.2	281 53.8	30.8	213 44.9	47.0	42 44.0	44.3	30 26.4	32.9	Rigel	281 22.6	S 8 12.1
A 09	90 26.7	296 57.2 ..	30.6	228 46.1 ..	47.4	57 46.3 ..	44.3	45 28.7 ..	32.9	Rigil Kent.	140 06.5	S60 50.1
T 10	105 29.1	312 00.6	30.4	243 47.2	47.8	72 48.7	44.4	60 31.1	33.0	Sabik	102 24.7	S15 43.3
U 11	120 31.6	327 04.0	30.2	258 48.4	48.2	87 51.0	44.4	75 33.5	33.0			
R 12	135 34.0	342 07.4 N 4	30.0	273 49.5	S17 48.7	102 53.3	N11 44.5	90 35.8	N14 33.0	Schedar	349 52.5	N56 31.8
D 13	150 36.5	357 10.8	29.8	288 50.6	49.1	117 55.6	44.5	105 38.2	33.0	Shaula	96 36.2	S37 06.2
A 14	165 39.0	12 14.3	29.6	303 51.8	49.5	132 57.9	44.5	120 40.6	33.0	Sirius	258 43.5	S16 42.9
Y 15	180 41.4	27 17.7 ..	29.4	318 52.9 ..	49.9	148 00.3 ..	44.6	135 42.9 ..	33.1	Spica	158 42.7	S11 09.4
16	195 43.9	42 21.1	29.2	333 54.1	50.3	163 02.6	44.6	150 45.3	33.1	Suhail	223 00.8	S43 25.8
17	210 46.4	57 24.6	29.0	348 55.2	50.7	178 04.9	44.6	165 47.7	33.1			
18	225 48.8	72 28.0 N 4	28.8	3 56.3	S17 51.2	193 07.2	N11 44.7	180 50.0	N14 33.1	Vega	80 45.9	N38 47.3
19	240 51.3	87 31.4	28.7	18 57.5	51.6	208 09.6	44.7	195 52.4	33.1	Zuben'ubi	137 17.3	S16 02.3
20	255 53.8	102 34.9	28.5	33 58.6	52.0	223 11.9	44.8	210 54.8	33.1		SHA	Mer. Pass.
21	270 56.2	117 38.3 ..	28.3	48 59.8 ..	52.4	238 14.2 ..	44.8	225 57.1 ..	33.2		° ′	h m
22	285 58.7	132 41.8	28.1	64 00.9	52.8	253 16.6	44.8	240 59.5	33.2	Venus	206 01.2	13 17
23	301 01.2	147 45.2	27.9	79 02.0	53.2	268 18.9	44.9	256 01.9	33.2	Mars	139 02.7	17 46
	h m									Jupiter	327 24.5	5 13
Mer. Pass. 3 03.1		v 3.3 d 0.2		v 1.2 d 0.4		v 2.3 d 0.0		v 2.4 d 0.0		Saturn	315 05.5	6 02

UT	SUN GHA	SUN Dec	MOON GHA	MOON v	MOON Dec	MOON d	MOON HP
d h	° ′	° ′	° ′	′	° ′	′	′
5 00	178 29.1	N17 08.9	268 14.8	8.9	N11 30.0	10.1	59.2
01	193 29.2	08.3	282 42.7	8.9	11 40.1	10.1	59.2
02	208 29.2	07.6	297 10.6	8.8	11 50.2	10.0	59.2
03	223 29.3 ..	06.9	311 38.4	8.7	12 00.2	9.9	59.2
04	238 29.4	06.3	326 06.1	8.7	12 10.1	9.9	59.3
05	253 29.4	05.6	340 33.8	8.6	12 20.0	9.7	59.3
06	268 29.5	N17 04.9	355 01.4	8.6	N12 29.7	9.8	59.3
07	283 29.5	04.2	9 29.0	8.4	12 39.5	9.6	59.3
08	298 29.6	03.6	23 56.4	8.5	12 49.1	9.6	59.3
T 09	313 29.7 ..	02.9	38 23.9	8.3	12 58.7	9.5	59.3
H 10	328 29.7	02.2	52 51.2	8.4	13 08.2	9.4	59.3
U 11	343 29.8	01.6	67 18.6	8.2	13 17.6	9.4	59.4
R 12	358 29.8	N17 00.9	81 45.8	8.2	N13 27.0	9.3	59.4
S 13	13 29.9	17 00.2	96 13.0	8.1	13 36.3	9.1	59.4
D 14	28 30.0	16 59.5	110 40.1	8.1	13 45.4	9.2	59.4
A 15	43 30.0 ..	58.9	125 07.2	8.0	13 54.6	9.0	59.4
Y 16	58 30.1	58.2	139 34.2	7.9	14 03.6	9.0	59.4
17	73 30.2	57.5	154 01.1	7.9	14 12.6	8.8	59.4
18	88 30.2	N16 56.8	168 28.0	7.8	N14 21.4	8.8	59.5
19	103 30.3	56.1	182 54.8	7.7	14 30.2	8.7	59.5
20	118 30.3	55.5	197 21.5	7.7	14 38.9	8.6	59.5
21	133 30.4 ..	54.8	211 48.2	7.6	14 47.5	8.5	59.5
22	148 30.5	54.1	226 14.8	7.6	14 56.0	8.5	59.5
23	163 30.5	53.4	240 41.4	7.5	15 04.5	8.3	59.5
6 00	178 30.6	N16 52.7	255 07.9	7.4	N15 12.8	8.3	59.5
01	193 30.7	52.1	269 34.3	7.4	15 21.1	8.1	59.5
02	208 30.7	51.4	284 00.7	7.3	15 29.2	8.1	59.5
03	223 30.8 ..	50.7	298 27.0	7.3	15 37.3	7.9	59.5
04	238 30.9	50.0	312 53.3	7.2	15 45.2	7.9	59.6
05	253 30.9	49.3	327 19.5	7.1	15 53.1	7.8	59.6
06	268 31.0	N16 48.7	341 45.6	7.1	N16 00.9	7.7	59.6
07	283 31.1	48.0	356 11.7	7.0	16 08.6	7.5	59.6
08	298 31.1	47.3	10 37.7	6.9	16 16.1	7.5	59.6
F 09	313 31.2 ..	46.6	25 03.6	6.9	16 23.6	7.4	59.6
R 10	328 31.3	45.9	39 29.5	6.8	16 31.0	7.2	59.6
I 11	343 31.3	45.2	53 55.3	6.8	16 38.2	7.2	59.6
D 12	358 31.4	N16 44.6	68 21.1	6.7	N16 45.4	7.0	59.6
A 13	13 31.5	43.9	82 46.8	6.7	16 52.4	7.0	59.6
Y 14	28 31.5	43.2	97 12.5	6.6	16 59.4	6.8	59.6
15	43 31.6 ..	42.5	111 38.1	6.5	17 06.2	6.8	59.7
16	58 31.7	41.8	126 03.6	6.5	17 13.0	6.6	59.7
17	73 31.7	41.1	140 29.1	6.4	17 19.6	6.5	59.7
18	88 31.8	N16 40.4	154 54.5	6.4	N17 26.1	6.4	59.7
19	103 31.9	39.7	169 19.9	6.3	17 32.5	6.3	59.7
20	118 31.9	39.0	183 45.2	6.3	17 38.8	6.1	59.7
21	133 32.0 ..	38.4	198 10.5	6.2	17 44.9	6.1	59.7
22	148 32.1	37.7	212 35.7	6.1	17 51.0	5.9	59.7
23	163 32.2	37.0	227 00.8	6.1	17 56.9	5.9	59.7
7 00	178 32.2	N16 36.3	241 25.9	6.1	N18 02.8	5.7	59.7
01	193 32.3	35.6	255 51.0	6.0	18 08.5	5.5	59.7
02	208 32.4	34.9	270 16.0	5.9	18 14.0	5.5	59.7
03	223 32.4 ..	34.2	284 40.9	6.0	18 19.5	5.3	59.7
04	238 32.5	33.5	299 05.9	5.8	18 24.8	5.3	59.7
05	253 32.6	32.8	313 30.7	5.8	18 30.1	5.1	59.7
06	268 32.7	N16 32.1	327 55.5	5.8	N18 35.2	4.9	59.8
07	283 32.8	31.4	342 20.3	5.7	18 40.1	4.9	59.8
08	298 32.8	30.7	356 45.0	5.7	18 45.0	4.7	59.8
S 09	313 32.9 ..	30.0	11 09.7	5.6	18 49.7	4.6	59.8
A 10	328 33.0	29.3	25 34.3	5.6	18 54.3	4.5	59.8
T 11	343 33.0	28.7	39 58.9	5.6	18 58.8	4.3	59.8
U 12	358 33.1	N16 28.0	54 23.5	5.5	N19 03.1	4.2	59.8
R 13	13 33.2	27.3	68 48.0	5.5	19 07.3	4.1	59.8
D 14	28 33.2	26.6	83 12.5	5.4	19 11.4	4.0	59.8
A 15	43 33.3 ..	25.9	97 36.9	5.4	19 15.4	3.8	59.8
Y 16	58 33.4	25.2	112 01.3	5.4	19 19.2	3.7	59.8
17	73 33.5	24.5	126 25.7	5.3	19 22.9	3.6	59.8
18	88 33.5	N16 23.8	140 50.0	5.4	N19 26.5	3.4	59.8
19	103 33.6	23.1	155 14.4	5.2	19 29.9	3.3	59.8
20	118 33.7	22.4	169 38.6	5.3	19 33.2	3.2	59.8
21	133 33.8 ..	21.7	184 02.9	5.2	19 36.4	3.0	59.8
22	148 33.8	21.0	198 27.1	5.2	19 39.4	2.9	59.8
23	163 33.9	20.3	212 51.3	5.2	N19 42.3	2.7	59.8
	SD 15.8	d 0.7	SD 16.2		16.2		16.3

Twilight, Sunrise, Moonrise

Lat.	Twilight Naut.	Twilight Civil	Sunrise	Moonrise 5	Moonrise 6	Moonrise 7	Moonrise 8
°	h m	h m	h m	h m	h m	h m	h m
N 72	////	////	00 49	21 19	20 39	▢	▢
N 70	////	////	02 01	21 49	21 45	21 40	▢
68	////	////	02 37	22 12	22 21	22 42	23 30
66	////	01 19	03 03	22 30	22 47	23 18	24 10
64	////	02 04	03 22	22 45	23 08	23 43	24 37
62	////	02 33	03 38	22 57	23 24	24 03	00 03
60	01 11	02 54	03 51	23 08	23 38	24 20	00 20
N 58	01 52	03 11	04 03	23 17	23 50	24 33	00 33
56	02 18	03 26	04 12	23 25	24 00	00 00	00 45
54	02 39	03 38	04 21	23 32	24 09	00 09	00 56
52	02 55	03 48	04 29	23 39	24 17	00 17	01 05
50	03 09	03 58	04 36	23 45	24 25	00 25	01 13
45	03 36	04 17	04 50	23 57	24 40	00 40	01 31
N 40	03 56	04 33	05 02	24 08	00 08	00 53	01 46
35	04 12	04 45	05 13	24 17	00 17	01 05	01 58
30	04 25	04 56	05 22	24 25	00 25	01 14	02 09
20	04 46	05 14	05 37	24 39	00 39	01 31	02 27
N 10	05 02	05 28	05 50	24 51	00 51	01 46	02 44
0	05 16	05 41	06 02	00 08	01 02	02 00	02 59
S 10	05 27	05 53	06 15	00 16	01 14	02 13	03 14
20	05 38	06 05	06 27	00 26	01 26	02 28	03 30
30	05 48	06 17	06 42	00 36	01 41	02 46	03 49
35	05 54	06 24	06 50	00 42	01 49	02 56	04 00
40	05 59	06 31	07 00	00 49	01 59	03 07	04 13
45	06 05	06 40	07 11	00 58	02 10	03 21	04 28
S 50	06 11	06 50	07 24	01 08	02 23	03 37	04 46
52	06 14	06 54	07 31	01 12	02 30	03 45	04 55
54	06 17	06 59	07 38	01 17	02 37	03 54	05 04
56	06 20	07 04	07 45	01 23	02 45	04 03	05 15
58	06 23	07 10	07 54	01 29	02 54	04 15	05 28
S 60	06 26	07 17	08 04	01 36	03 04	04 28	05 42

Sunset, Twilight, Moonset

Lat.	Sunset	Twilight Civil	Twilight Naut.	Moonset 5	Moonset 6	Moonset 7	Moonset 8
°	h m	h m	h m	h m	h m	h m	h m
N 72	23 07	////	////	16 00	18 38	▢	▢
N 70	22 05	////	////	15 31	17 33	19 41	▢
68	21 31	////	////	15 09	16 57	18 39	19 57
66	21 06	22 45	////	14 52	16 32	18 04	19 17
64	20 47	22 04	////	14 39	16 12	17 39	18 50
62	20 32	21 36	////	14 27	15 56	17 19	18 28
60	20 19	21 15	22 54	14 17	15 43	17 03	18 11
N 58	20 08	20 59	22 16	14 09	15 32	16 49	17 57
56	19 58	20 45	21 51	14 01	15 22	16 38	17 44
54	19 50	20 33	21 31	13 55	15 13	16 27	17 33
52	19 42	20 22	21 15	13 49	15 05	16 18	17 24
50	19 35	20 13	21 02	13 43	14 58	16 10	17 15
45	19 21	19 54	20 35	13 32	14 43	15 53	16 57
N 40	19 09	19 39	20 15	13 22	14 31	15 38	16 42
35	18 59	19 26	19 59	13 14	14 21	15 26	16 29
30	18 50	19 15	19 46	13 07	14 12	15 16	16 18
20	18 35	18 58	19 25	12 54	13 56	14 58	15 59
N 10	18 22	18 44	19 09	12 44	13 42	14 42	15 43
0	18 09	18 31	18 56	12 34	13 29	14 28	15 27
S 10	17 57	18 19	18 44	12 23	13 17	14 13	15 12
20	17 45	18 08	18 34	12 13	13 03	13 57	14 55
30	17 30	17 55	18 24	12 00	12 47	13 39	14 36
35	17 22	17 48	18 19	11 53	12 38	13 29	14 25
40	17 01	17 41	18 13	11 45	12 28	13 17	14 12
45	17 01	17 32	18 08	11 36	12 16	13 03	13 57
S 50	16 48	17 23	18 01	11 25	12 01	12 46	13 39
52	16 42	17 18	17 59	11 20	11 55	12 37	13 30
54	16 35	17 13	17 56	11 14	11 47	12 29	13 20
56	16 27	17 08	17 53	11 08	11 39	12 18	13 09
58	16 19	17 02	17 50	11 01	11 29	12 07	12 57
S 60	16 09	16 56	17 46	10 53	11 18	11 54	12 42

SUN / MOON

Day	SUN Eqn. of Time 00h	SUN Eqn. of Time 12h	SUN Mer. Pass.	MOON Mer. Pass. Upper	MOON Mer. Pass. Lower	Age	Phase
d	m s	m s	h m	h m	h m	d	%
5	06 04	06 01	12 06	06 21	18 48	23	41
6	05 58	05 55	12 06	07 16	19 44	24	30
7	05 51	05 48	12 06	08 14	20 43	25	20

UT	ARIES GHA	VENUS −4.2 GHA	Dec	MARS +0.1 GHA	Dec	JUPITER −2.5 GHA	Dec	SATURN +0.3 GHA	Dec	Name	SHA	Dec
8 00	316 03.6	162 48.7	N 4 27.7	94 03.2	S17 53.6	283 21.2	N11 44.9	271 04.2	N14 33.2	Acamar	315 26.5	S40 18.2
01	331 06.1	177 52.2	27.6	109 04.3	54.1	298 23.5	44.9	286 06.6	33.2	Achernar	335 34.6	S57 14.1
02	346 08.5	192 55.6	27.4	124 05.4	54.5	313 25.9	45.0	301 09.0	33.2	Acrux	173 21.7	S63 05.9
03	1 11.0	207 59.1 ..	27.2	139 06.6 ..	54.9	328 28.2 ..	45.0	316 11.3 ..	33.3	Adhara	255 21.3	S28 58.2
04	16 13.5	223 02.6	27.0	154 07.7	55.3	343 30.5	45.1	331 13.7	33.3	Aldebaran	291 01.9	N16 30.4
05	31 15.9	238 06.0	26.9	169 08.8	55.7	358 32.8	45.1	346 16.1	33.3			
06	46 18.4	253 09.5	N 4 26.7	184 10.0	S17 56.1	13 35.2	N11 45.1	1 18.4	N14 33.3	Alioth	166 30.4	N55 58.1
07	61 20.9	268 13.0	26.5	199 11.1	56.6	28 37.5	45.2	16 20.8	33.3	Alkaid	153 07.5	N49 19.3
08	76 23.3	283 16.5	26.3	214 12.2	57.0	43 39.8	45.2	31 23.2	33.4	Al Na'ir	27 56.7	S46 57.7
S 09	91 25.8	298 20.0 ..	26.2	229 13.3 ..	57.4	58 42.2 ..	45.2	46 25.5 ..	33.4	Alnilam	275 57.5	S 1 12.1
U 10	106 28.3	313 23.5	26.0	244 14.5	57.8	73 44.5	45.3	61 27.9	33.4	Alphard	218 07.0	S 8 39.3
N 11	121 30.7	328 27.0	25.9	259 15.6	58.2	88 46.8	45.3	76 30.3	33.4			
D 12	136 33.2	343 30.5	N 4 25.7	274 16.7	S17 58.6	103 49.2	N11 45.4	91 32.6	N14 33.4	Alphecca	126 20.1	N26 43.3
A 13	151 35.7	358 34.0	25.5	289 17.9	59.0	118 51.5	45.4	106 35.0	33.4	Alpheratz	357 54.4	N29 05.2
Y 14	166 38.1	13 37.5	25.4	304 19.0	59.5	133 53.8	45.4	121 37.4	33.5	Altair	62 18.4	N 8 52.2
15	181 40.6	28 41.0 ..	25.2	319 20.1	17 59.9	148 56.2 ..	45.5	136 39.7 ..	33.5	Ankaa	353 26.0	S42 18.3
16	196 43.0	43 44.5	25.1	334 21.2	18 00.3	163 58.5	45.5	151 42.1	33.5	Antares	112 39.3	S26 25.8
17	211 45.5	58 48.0	24.9	349 22.4	00.7	179 00.8	45.5	166 44.5	33.5			
18	226 48.0	73 51.5	N 4 24.8	4 23.5	S18 01.1	194 03.2	N11 45.6	181 46.8	N14 33.5	Arcturus	146 05.6	N19 11.4
19	241 50.4	88 55.0	24.6	19 24.6	01.5	209 05.5	45.6	196 49.2	33.5	Atria	107 50.5	S69 01.7
20	256 52.9	103 58.6	24.5	34 25.7	01.9	224 07.8	45.6	211 51.6	33.6	Avior	234 23.0	S59 30.4
21	271 55.4	119 02.1 ..	24.3	49 26.9 ..	02.4	239 10.2 ..	45.7	226 54.0 ..	33.6	Bellatrix	278 43.7	N 6 20.9
22	286 57.8	134 05.6	24.2	64 28.0	02.8	254 12.5	45.7	241 56.3	33.6	Betelgeuse	271 13.2	N 7 24.4
23	302 00.3	149 09.2	24.1	79 29.1	03.2	269 14.8	45.7	256 58.7	33.6			
9 00	317 02.8	164 12.7	N 4 23.9	94 30.2	S18 03.6	284 17.2	N11 45.8	272 01.1	N14 33.6	Canopus	264 01.3	S52 41.6
01	332 05.2	179 16.2	23.8	109 31.3	04.0	299 19.5	45.8	287 03.4	33.6	Capella	280 50.6	N45 59.6
02	347 07.7	194 19.8	23.6	124 32.5	04.4	314 21.8	45.8	302 05.8	33.7	Deneb	49 38.3	N45 16.9
03	2 10.2	209 23.3 ..	23.5	139 33.6 ..	04.8	329 24.2 ..	45.9	317 08.2 ..	33.7	Denebola	182 44.9	N14 34.7
04	17 12.6	224 26.9	23.4	154 34.7	05.3	344 26.5	45.9	332 10.6	33.7	Diphda	349 06.5	S17 59.2
05	32 15.1	239 30.4	23.2	169 35.8	05.7	359 28.8	45.9	347 12.9	33.7			
06	47 17.5	254 34.0	N 4 23.1	184 36.9	S18 06.1	14 31.2	N11 46.0	2 15.3	N14 33.7	Dubhe	194 05.4	N61 45.4
07	62 20.0	269 37.5	23.0	199 38.1	06.5	29 33.5	46.0	17 17.7	33.7	Elnath	278 26.4	N28 36.3
08	77 22.5	284 41.1	22.9	214 39.2	06.9	44 35.8	46.0	32 20.0	33.8	Eltanin	90 50.8	N51 29.7
M 09	92 24.9	299 44.7 ..	22.7	229 40.3 ..	07.3	59 38.2 ..	46.1	47 22.4 ..	33.8	Enif	33 57.3	N 9 52.5
O 10	107 27.4	314 48.2	22.6	244 41.4	07.7	74 40.5	46.1	62 24.8	33.8	Fomalhaut	15 35.5	S29 37.3
N 11	122 29.9	329 51.8	22.5	259 42.5	08.2	89 42.9	46.1	77 27.2	33.8			
D 12	137 32.3	344 55.4	N 4 22.4	274 43.6	S18 08.6	104 45.2	N11 46.2	92 29.5	N14 33.8	Gacrux	172 13.2	S57 06.7
A 13	152 34.8	359 59.0	22.3	289 44.8	09.0	119 47.5	46.2	107 31.9	33.8	Gienah	176 03.6	S17 32.3
Y 14	167 37.3	15 02.6	22.2	304 45.9	09.4	134 49.9	46.2	122 34.3	33.9	Hadar	149 03.3	S60 22.4
15	182 39.7	30 06.1 ..	22.0	319 47.0 ..	09.8	149 52.2 ..	46.3	137 36.6 ..	33.9	Hamal	328 12.8	N23 27.5
16	197 42.2	45 09.7	21.9	334 48.1	10.2	164 54.6	46.3	152 39.0	33.9	Kaus Aust.	83 57.7	S34 23.0
17	212 44.7	60 13.3	21.8	349 49.2	10.6	179 56.9	46.3	167 41.4	33.9			
18	227 47.1	75 16.9	N 4 21.7	4 50.3	S18 11.1	194 59.2	N11 46.4	182 43.8	N14 33.9	Kochab	137 19.7	N74 09.9
19	242 49.6	90 20.5	21.6	19 51.4	11.5	210 01.6	46.4	197 46.1	33.9	Markab	13 48.7	N15 12.2
20	257 52.0	105 24.1	21.5	34 52.5	11.9	225 03.9	46.4	212 48.5	34.0	Menkar	314 26.3	N 4 05.2
21	272 54.5	120 27.7 ..	21.4	49 53.6 ..	12.3	240 06.3 ..	46.5	227 50.9 ..	34.0	Menkent	148 20.3	S36 22.1
22	287 57.0	135 31.3	21.3	64 54.8	12.7	255 08.6	46.5	242 53.3	34.0	Miaplacidus	221 42.8	S69 42.9
23	302 59.4	150 34.9	21.2	79 55.9	13.1	270 10.9	46.5	257 55.6	34.0			
10 00	318 01.9	165 38.5	N 4 21.1	94 57.0	S18 13.5	285 13.3	N11 46.6	272 58.0	N14 34.0	Mirfak	308 55.8	N49 51.3
01	333 04.4	180 42.1	21.0	109 58.1	14.0	300 15.6	46.6	288 00.4	34.0	Nunki	76 11.3	S26 17.7
02	348 06.8	195 45.8	20.9	124 59.2	14.4	315 18.0	46.6	303 02.8	34.0	Peacock	53 35.5	S56 44.1
03	3 09.3	210 49.4 ..	20.8	140 00.3 ..	14.8	330 20.3 ..	46.7	318 05.1 ..	34.1	Pollux	243 41.2	N28 01.6
04	18 11.8	225 53.0	20.8	155 01.4	15.2	345 22.7	46.7	333 07.5	34.1	Procyon	245 11.3	N 5 13.6
05	33 14.2	240 56.6	20.7	170 02.5	15.6	0 25.0	46.7	348 09.9	34.1			
06	48 16.7	256 00.3	N 4 20.6	185 03.6	S18 16.0	15 27.3	N11 46.8	3 12.3	N14 34.1	Rasalhague	96 16.2	N12 33.9
07	63 19.1	271 03.9	20.5	200 04.7	16.4	30 29.7	46.8	18 14.6	34.1	Regulus	207 55.3	N11 58.3
08	78 21.6	286 07.5	20.4	215 05.8	16.8	45 32.0	46.8	33 17.0	34.1	Rigel	281 22.6	S 8 12.1
T 09	93 24.1	301 11.2 ..	20.3	230 06.9 ..	17.3	60 34.4 ..	46.9	48 19.4 ..	34.2	Rigil Kent.	140 06.6	S60 50.1
U 10	108 26.5	316 14.8	20.3	245 08.0	17.7	75 36.7	46.9	63 21.8	34.2	Sabik	102 24.7	S15 43.3
E 11	123 29.0	331 18.5	20.2	260 09.1	18.1	90 39.1	46.9	78 24.1	34.2			
S 12	138 31.5	346 22.1	N 4 20.1	275 10.2	S18 18.5	105 41.4	N11 46.9	93 26.5	N14 34.2	Schedar	349 52.4	N56 31.8
D 13	153 33.9	1 25.8	20.0	290 11.3	18.9	120 43.8	47.0	108 28.9	34.2	Shaula	96 36.2	S37 06.2
A 14	168 36.4	16 29.4	20.0	305 12.4	19.3	135 46.1	47.0	123 31.3	34.2	Sirius	258 43.5	S16 42.9
Y 15	183 38.9	31 33.1 ..	19.9	320 13.5 ..	19.7	150 48.5 ..	47.0	138 33.7 ..	34.2	Spica	158 42.7	S11 09.4
16	198 41.3	46 36.7	19.8	335 14.6	20.1	165 50.8	47.1	153 36.0	34.3	Suhail	223 00.8	S43 25.8
17	213 43.8	61 40.4	19.8	350 15.7	20.6	180 53.2	47.1	168 38.4	34.3			
18	228 46.3	76 44.1	N 4 19.7	5 16.8	S18 21.0	195 55.5	N11 47.1	183 40.8	N14 34.3	Vega	80 45.9	N38 47.3
19	243 48.7	91 47.7	19.6	20 17.9	21.4	210 57.8	47.2	198 43.2	34.3	Zuben'ubi	137 17.3	S16 02.3
20	258 51.2	106 51.4	19.6	35 19.0	21.8	226 00.2	47.2	213 45.5	34.3			
21	273 53.6	121 55.1 ..	19.5	50 20.1 ..	22.2	241 02.5 ..	47.2	228 47.9 ..	34.3			
22	288 56.1	136 58.7	19.5	65 21.2	22.6	256 04.9	47.2	243 50.3	34.3			
23	303 58.6	152 02.4	19.4	80 22.3	23.0	271 07.2	47.3	258 52.7	34.4			
Mer. Pass. 2ʰ 51.3ᵐ		*v* 3.6	*d* 0.1	*v* 1.1	*d* 0.4	*v* 2.3	*d* 0.0	*v* 2.4	*d* 0.0			

	SHA	Mer. Pass
Venus	207 09.9	13ʰ 00ᵐ
Mars	137 27.5	17 41
Jupiter	327 14.4	5 02
Saturn	314 58.3	5 51

UT	SUN GHA	SUN Dec	MOON GHA	v	MOON Dec	d	HP
d h	° '	° '	° '	'	° '	'	'
8 00	178 34.0	N16 19.6	227 15.5	5.1	N19 45.0	2.7	59.8
01	193 34.1	18.9	241 39.6	5.1	19 47.7	2.5	59.8
02	208 34.2	18.1	256 03.7	5.1	19 50.2	2.3	59.8
03	223 34.2	.. 17.4	270 27.8	5.1	19 52.5	2.2	59.8
04	238 34.3	16.7	284 51.9	5.1	19 54.7	2.1	59.8
05	253 34.4	16.0	299 16.0	5.0	19 56.8	1.9	59.8
06	268 34.5	N16 15.3	313 40.0	5.0	N19 58.7	1.8	59.8
07	283 34.5	14.6	328 04.0	5.0	20 00.5	1.7	59.8
S 08	298 34.6	13.9	342 28.0	5.0	20 02.2	1.5	59.8
U 09	313 34.7	.. 13.2	356 52.0	5.0	20 03.7	1.4	59.8
N 10	328 34.8	12.5	11 16.0	5.0	20 05.1	1.3	59.8
D 11	343 34.9	11.8	25 40.0	5.0	20 06.4	1.1	59.8
A 12	358 34.9	N16 11.1	40 04.0	4.9	N20 07.5	0.9	59.8
Y 13	13 35.0	10.4	54 27.9	5.0	20 08.4	0.9	59.8
14	28 35.1	09.7	68 51.9	5.0	20 09.3	0.7	59.8
15	43 35.2	.. 09.0	83 15.9	4.9	20 10.0	0.5	59.8
16	58 35.3	08.3	97 39.8	5.0	20 10.5	0.4	59.8
17	73 35.3	07.5	112 03.8	4.9	20 10.9	0.3	59.8
18	88 35.4	N16 06.8	126 27.7	5.0	N20 11.2	0.1	59.7
19	103 35.5	06.1	140 51.7	5.0	20 11.3	0.1	59.7
20	118 35.6	05.4	155 15.7	4.9	20 11.3	0.1	59.7
21	133 35.7	.. 04.7	169 39.6	5.0	20 11.2	0.3	59.7
22	148 35.8	04.0	184 03.6	5.0	20 10.9	0.4	59.7
23	163 35.8	03.3	198 27.6	5.0	20 10.5	0.6	59.7
9 00	178 35.9	N16 02.6	212 51.6	5.0	N20 09.9	0.7	59.7
01	193 36.0	01.8	227 15.6	5.0	20 09.2	0.9	59.7
02	208 36.1	01.1	241 39.6	5.1	20 08.3	0.9	59.7
03	223 36.2	16 00.4	256 03.7	5.1	20 07.4	1.2	59.7
04	238 36.3	15 59.7	270 27.7	5.1	20 06.2	1.2	59.7
05	253 36.3	59.0	284 51.8	5.1	20 05.0	1.4	59.7
06	268 36.4	N15 58.3	299 15.9	5.1	N20 03.6	1.6	59.7
07	283 36.5	57.6	313 40.0	5.1	20 02.0	1.6	59.6
M 08	298 36.6	56.8	328 04.1	5.2	20 00.4	1.8	59.6
O 09	313 36.7	.. 56.1	342 28.3	5.2	19 58.6	2.0	59.6
N 10	328 36.8	55.4	356 52.5	5.2	19 56.6	2.1	59.6
D 11	343 36.8	54.7	11 16.7	5.3	19 54.5	2.2	59.6
A 12	358 36.9	N15 54.0	25 41.0	5.2	N19 52.3	2.3	59.6
Y 13	13 37.0	53.2	40 05.2	5.3	19 50.0	2.5	59.6
14	28 37.1	52.5	54 29.5	5.4	19 47.5	2.6	59.6
15	43 37.2	.. 51.8	68 53.9	5.4	19 44.9	2.6	59.6
16	58 37.3	51.1	83 18.3	5.4	19 42.1	2.9	59.5
17	73 37.4	50.4	97 42.7	5.4	19 39.2	3.0	59.5
18	88 37.5	N15 49.6	112 07.1	5.5	N19 36.2	3.2	59.5
19	103 37.5	48.9	126 31.6	5.5	19 33.0	3.2	59.5
20	118 37.6	48.2	140 56.1	5.6	19 29.8	3.5	59.5
21	133 37.7	.. 47.5	155 20.7	5.6	19 26.3	3.5	59.5
22	148 37.8	46.8	169 45.3	5.7	19 22.8	3.7	59.5
23	163 37.9	46.0	184 10.0	5.7	19 19.1	3.8	59.5
10 00	178 38.0	N15 45.3	198 34.7	5.8	N19 15.3	3.9	59.4
01	193 38.1	44.6	212 59.5	5.8	19 11.4	4.0	59.4
02	208 38.2	43.9	227 24.3	5.8	19 07.4	4.2	59.4
03	223 38.2	.. 43.1	241 49.1	5.9	19 03.2	4.3	59.4
04	238 38.3	42.4	256 14.0	6.0	18 58.9	4.4	59.4
05	253 38.4	41.7	270 39.0	6.0	18 54.5	4.6	59.4
06	268 38.5	N15 41.0	285 04.0	6.0	N18 49.9	4.7	59.3
07	283 38.6	40.2	299 29.0	6.1	18 45.2	4.8	59.3
T 08	298 38.7	39.5	313 54.1	6.2	18 40.4	4.9	59.3
U 09	313 38.8	.. 38.8	328 19.3	6.2	18 35.5	5.0	59.3
E 10	328 38.9	38.0	342 44.5	6.3	18 30.5	5.1	59.3
S 11	343 39.0	37.3	357 09.8	6.4	18 25.4	5.3	59.3
D 12	358 39.1	N15 36.6	11 35.2	6.4	N18 20.1	5.4	59.2
A 13	13 39.2	35.9	26 00.6	6.4	18 14.7	5.5	59.2
Y 14	28 39.2	35.1	40 26.0	6.6	18 09.2	5.6	59.2
15	43 39.3	.. 34.4	54 51.6	6.6	18 03.6	5.7	59.2
16	58 39.4	33.7	69 17.2	6.6	17 57.9	5.9	59.2
17	73 39.5	32.9	83 42.8	6.7	17 52.0	5.9	59.1
18	88 39.6	N15 32.2	98 08.5	6.8	N17 46.1	6.1	59.1
19	103 39.7	31.5	112 34.3	6.9	17 40.0	6.2	59.1
20	118 39.8	30.7	127 00.2	6.9	17 33.8	6.2	59.1
21	133 39.9	.. 30.0	141 26.1	7.0	17 27.6	6.4	59.1
22	148 40.0	29.3	155 52.1	7.0	17 21.2	6.5	59.0
23	163 40.1	28.5	170 18.1	7.2	N17 14.7	6.6	59.0
SD	15.8	d 0.7	SD 16.3		16.2		16.1

Lat.	Twilight Naut.	Twilight Civil	Sunrise	Moonrise 8	9	10	11
°	h m	h m	h m	h m	h m	h m	h m
N 72	////	////	01 30	□	□	□	01 08
N 70	////	////	02 20	□	23 57	26 02	02 02
68	////	////	02 51	23 30	24 53	00 53	02 35
66	////	01 42	03 14	24 10	00 10	01 26	02 59
64	////	02 18	03 32	24 37	00 37	01 51	03 18
62	////	02 44	03 46	00 03	00 58	02 10	03 33
60	01 32	03 03	03 58	00 20	01 15	02 26	03 46
N 58	02 05	03 19	04 09	00 33	01 30	02 39	03 57
56	02 28	03 32	04 18	00 45	01 42	02 50	04 06
54	02 47	03 44	04 26	00 56	01 53	03 00	04 15
52	03 02	03 54	04 33	01 05	02 03	03 09	04 22
50	03 15	04 03	04 40	01 13	02 11	03 17	04 29
45	03 40	04 21	04 54	01 31	02 30	03 34	04 43
N 40	03 59	04 36	05 05	01 46	02 44	03 48	04 55
35	04 15	04 48	05 15	01 58	02 57	04 00	05 05
30	04 27	04 58	05 23	02 09	03 08	04 10	05 14
20	04 47	05 15	05 38	02 27	03 27	04 28	05 29
N 10	05 03	05 29	05 50	02 44	03 43	04 44	05 43
0	05 16	05 41	06 02	02 59	03 59	04 58	05 55
S 10	05 27	05 52	06 14	03 14	04 14	05 12	06 07
20	05 37	06 03	06 26	03 30	04 31	05 28	06 21
30	05 46	06 15	06 40	03 49	04 50	05 45	06 36
35	05 51	06 21	06 47	04 00	05 01	05 56	06 44
40	05 56	06 28	06 56	04 13	05 13	06 07	06 54
45	06 01	06 36	07 07	04 28	05 28	06 21	07 06
S 50	06 07	06 45	07 20	04 46	05 47	06 38	07 20
52	06 09	06 49	07 25	04 55	05 55	06 46	07 26
54	06 12	06 54	07 32	05 04	06 05	06 55	07 34
56	06 14	06 59	07 39	05 15	06 16	07 04	07 42
58	06 17	07 04	07 47	05 28	06 29	07 16	07 51
S 60	06 20	07 10	07 56	05 42	06 43	07 28	08 01

Lat.	Sunset	Twilight Civil	Twilight Naut.	Moonset 8	9	10	11
°	h m	h m	h m	h m	h m	h m	h m
N 72	22 32	////	////	□	□	22 25	21 54
N 70	21 46	////	////	□	21 35	21 30	21 25
68	21 16	23 31	////	19 57	20 38	20 56	21 04
66	20 55	22 23	////	19 17	20 04	20 32	20 47
64	20 37	21 49	////	18 50	19 40	20 12	20 33
62	20 23	21 24	23 35	18 28	19 20	19 56	20 21
60	20 11	21 05	22 34	18 11	19 04	19 43	20 11
N 58	20 01	20 50	22 03	17 57	18 51	19 32	20 03
56	19 52	20 37	21 40	17 44	18 39	19 22	19 55
54	19 44	20 26	21 22	17 33	18 29	19 13	19 48
52	19 37	20 16	21 07	17 24	18 19	19 05	19 42
50	19 30	20 07	20 55	17 15	18 11	18 58	19 36
45	19 16	19 49	20 30	16 57	17 54	18 43	19 24
N 40	19 05	19 35	20 11	16 42	17 39	18 30	19 14
35	18 56	19 23	19 56	16 29	17 27	18 19	19 05
30	18 47	19 13	19 43	16 18	17 17	18 10	18 57
20	18 33	18 56	19 23	15 59	16 58	17 53	18 44
N 10	18 20	18 42	19 08	15 43	16 42	17 39	18 32
0	18 09	18 30	18 55	15 27	16 27	17 25	18 21
S 10	17 58	18 19	18 45	15 12	16 12	17 12	18 10
20	17 46	18 08	18 35	14 55	15 56	16 57	17 58
30	17 32	17 57	18 25	14 36	15 37	16 41	17 44
35	17 24	17 50	18 20	14 25	15 26	16 31	17 36
40	17 15	17 43	18 16	14 12	15 14	16 20	17 27
45	17 05	17 36	18 11	13 57	15 00	16 07	17 16
S 50	16 52	17 27	18 05	13 39	14 41	15 50	17 03
52	16 46	17 23	18 03	13 30	14 33	15 43	16 57
54	16 40	17 18	18 00	13 20	14 23	15 34	16 50
56	16 33	17 13	17 58	13 09	14 12	15 25	16 43
58	16 25	17 08	17 55	12 57	14 00	15 14	16 34
S 60	16 16	17 02	17 52	12 42	13 45	15 02	16 25

Day	SUN Eqn. of Time 00h	SUN Eqn. of Time 12h	Mer. Pass.	MOON Mer. Pass. Upper	MOON Mer. Pass. Lower	Age	Phase
d	m s	m s	h m	h m	h m	d	%
8	05 44	05 40	12 06	09 13	21 43	26	11
9	05 36	05 32	12 06	10 13	22 43	27	5
10	05 28	05 24	12 05	11 12	23 40	28	1	●

UT	ARIES GHA	VENUS −4.1 GHA	Dec	MARS +0.2 GHA	Dec	JUPITER −2.6 GHA	Dec	SATURN +0.3 GHA	Dec	STARS Name	SHA	Dec
11 00	319 01.0	167 06.1	N 4 19.4	95 23.4	S18 23.5	286 09.6	N11 47.3	273 55.1	N14 34.4	Acamar	315 26.5	S40 18.2
01	334 03.5	182 09.8	19.3	110 24.5	23.9	301 11.9	47.3	288 57.4	34.4	Achernar	335 34.5	S57 14.1
02	349 06.0	197 13.5	19.3	125 25.6	24.3	316 14.3	47.4	303 59.8	34.4	Acrux	173 21.8	S63 05.9
03	4 08.4	212 17.2 ..	19.2	140 26.7 ..	24.7	331 16.6 ..	47.4	319 02.2 ..	34.4	Adhara	255 21.3	S28 58.2
04	19 10.9	227 20.9	19.2	155 27.8	25.1	346 19.0	47.4	334 04.6	34.4	Aldebaran	291 01.8	N16 30.4
05	34 13.4	242 24.6	19.1	170 28.9	25.5	1 21.4	47.5	349 07.0	34.4			
06	49 15.8	257 28.2	N 4 19.1	185 29.9	S18 25.9	16 23.7	N11 47.5	4 09.3	N14 34.5	Alioth	166 30.4	N55 58.1
W 07	64 18.3	272 31.9	19.0	200 31.0	26.3	31 26.1	47.5	19 11.7	34.5	Alkaid	153 07.5	N49 19.3
E 08	79 20.8	287 35.7	19.0	215 32.1	26.8	46 28.4	47.5	34 14.1	34.5	Al Na'ir	27 56.7	S46 57.7
D 09	94 23.2	302 39.4 ..	19.0	230 33.2 ..	27.2	61 30.8 ..	47.6	49 16.5 ..	34.5	Alnilam	275 57.5	S 1 12.1
N 10	109 25.7	317 43.1	18.9	245 34.3	27.6	76 33.1	47.6	64 18.9	34.5	Alphard	218 07.0	S 8 39.3
E 11	124 28.1	332 46.8	18.9	260 35.4	28.0	91 35.5	47.6	79 21.2	34.5			
S 12	139 30.6	347 50.5	N 4 18.9	275 36.5	S18 28.4	106 37.8	N11 47.7	94 23.6	N14 34.6	Alphecca	126 20.1	N26 43.3
D 13	154 33.1	2 54.2	18.8	290 37.6	28.8	121 40.2	47.7	109 26.0	34.6	Alpheratz	357 54.3	N29 05.2
A 14	169 35.5	17 57.9	18.8	305 38.7	29.2	136 42.5	47.7	124 28.4	34.6	Altair	62 18.4	N 8 52.2
Y 15	184 38.0	33 01.7 ..	18.8	320 39.7 ..	29.6	151 44.9 ..	47.7	139 30.8 ..	34.6	Ankaa	353 26.0	S42 18.3
16	199 40.5	48 05.4	18.7	335 40.8	30.0	166 47.2	47.8	154 33.1	34.6	Antares	112 39.3	S26 25.8
17	214 42.9	63 09.1	18.7	350 41.9	30.5	181 49.6	47.8	169 35.5	34.6			
18	229 45.4	78 12.8	N 4 18.7	5 43.0	S18 30.9	196 51.9	N11 47.8	184 37.9	N14 34.6	Arcturus	146 05.6	N19 11.4
19	244 47.9	93 16.6	18.7	20 44.1	31.3	211 54.3	47.8	199 40.3	34.6	Atria	107 50.6	S69 01.7
20	259 50.3	108 20.3	18.7	35 45.2	31.7	226 56.7	47.9	214 42.7	34.6	Avior	234 23.0	S59 30.4
21	274 52.8	123 24.0 ..	18.7	50 46.2 ..	32.1	241 59.0 ..	47.9	229 45.1 ..	34.7	Bellatrix	278 43.7	N 6 20.9
22	289 55.2	138 27.8	18.7	65 47.3	32.5	257 01.4	47.9	244 47.4	34.7	Betelgeuse	271 13.1	N 7 24.4
23	304 57.7	153 31.5	18.6	80 48.4	32.9	272 03.7	48.0	259 49.8	34.7			
12 00	320 00.2	168 35.3	N 4 18.6	95 49.5	S18 33.3	287 06.1	N11 48.0	274 52.2	N14 34.7	Canopus	264 01.3	S52 41.6
01	335 02.6	183 39.0	18.6	110 50.6	33.7	302 08.4	48.0	289 54.6	34.7	Capella	280 50.6	N45 59.6
02	350 05.1	198 42.8	18.6	125 51.7	34.2	317 10.8	48.0	304 57.0	34.7	Deneb	49 38.3	N45 16.9
03	5 07.6	213 46.5 ..	18.6	140 52.7 ..	34.6	332 13.2 ..	48.1	319 59.4 ..	34.7	Denebola	182 44.9	N14 34.7
04	20 10.0	228 50.3	18.6	155 53.8	35.0	347 15.5	48.1	335 01.7	34.7	Diphda	349 06.5	S17 59.2
05	35 12.5	243 54.0	18.6	170 54.9	35.4	2 17.9	48.1	350 04.1	34.8			
06	50 15.0	258 57.8	N 4 18.6	185 56.0	S18 35.8	17 20.2	N11 48.1	5 06.5	N14 34.8	Dubhe	194 05.4	N61 45.4
T 07	65 17.4	274 01.6	18.6	200 57.0	36.2	32 22.6	48.2	20 08.9	34.8	Elnath	278 26.4	N28 36.3
H 08	80 19.9	289 05.3	18.6	215 58.1	36.6	47 25.0	48.2	35 11.3	34.8	Eltanin	90 50.8	N51 29.7
U 09	95 22.4	304 09.1 ..	18.6	230 59.2 ..	37.0	62 27.3 ..	48.2	50 13.7 ..	34.8	Enif	33 57.3	N 9 52.5
R 10	110 24.8	319 12.9	18.7	246 00.3	37.4	77 29.7	48.2	65 16.0	34.8	Fomalhaut	15 35.5	S29 37.3
11	125 27.3	334 16.6	18.7	261 01.3	37.9	92 32.0	48.3	80 18.4	34.8			
S 12	140 29.7	349 20.4	N 4 18.7	276 02.4	S18 38.3	107 34.4	N11 48.3	95 20.8	N14 34.8	Gacrux	172 13.3	S57 06.7
D 13	155 32.2	4 24.2	18.7	291 03.5	38.7	122 36.8	48.3	110 23.2	34.9	Gienah	176 03.6	S17 32.3
A 14	170 34.7	19 28.0	18.7	306 04.6	39.1	137 39.1	48.3	125 25.6	34.9	Hadar	149 03.3	S60 22.4
Y 15	185 37.1	34 31.8 ..	18.7	321 05.6 ..	39.5	152 41.5 ..	48.4	140 28.0 ..	34.9	Hamal	328 12.8	N23 27.5
16	200 39.6	49 35.5	18.7	336 06.7	39.9	167 43.9	48.4	155 30.4	34.9	Kaus Aust.	83 57.7	S34 23.0
17	215 42.1	64 39.3	18.8	351 07.8	40.3	182 46.2	48.4	170 32.7	34.9			
18	230 44.5	79 43.1	N 4 18.8	6 08.9	S18 40.7	197 48.6	N11 48.4	185 35.1	N14 34.9	Kochab	137 19.8	N74 09.9
19	245 47.0	94 46.9	18.8	21 09.9	41.1	212 50.9	48.5	200 37.5	34.9	Markab	13 48.7	N15 12.2
20	260 49.5	109 50.7	18.8	36 11.0	41.6	227 53.3	48.5	215 39.9	34.9	Menkar	314 26.3	N 4 05.2
21	275 51.9	124 54.5 ..	18.9	51 12.1 ..	42.0	242 55.7 ..	48.5	230 42.3 ..	35.0	Menkent	148 20.4	S36 22.1
22	290 54.4	139 58.3	18.9	66 13.1	42.4	257 58.0	48.5	245 44.7	35.0	Miaplacidus	221 42.8	S69 42.9
23	305 56.9	155 02.1	18.9	81 14.2	42.8	273 00.4	48.6	260 47.1	35.0			
13 00	320 59.3	170 05.9	N 4 19.0	96 15.3	S18 43.2	288 02.8	N11 48.6	275 49.4	N14 35.0	Mirfak	308 55.8	N49 51.3
01	336 01.8	185 09.7	19.0	111 16.3	43.6	303 05.1	48.6	290 51.8	35.0	Nunki	76 11.3	S26 17.7
02	351 04.2	200 13.5	19.0	126 17.4	44.0	318 07.5	48.6	305 54.2	35.0	Peacock	53 35.5	S56 44.1
03	6 06.7	215 17.3 ..	19.1	141 18.5 ..	44.4	333 09.9 ..	48.7	320 56.6 ..	35.0	Pollux	243 41.2	N28 01.6
04	21 09.2	230 21.2	19.1	156 19.5	44.8	348 12.2	48.7	335 59.0	35.0	Procyon	245 11.3	N 5 13.6
05	36 11.6	245 25.0	19.1	171 20.6	45.2	3 14.6	48.7	351 01.4	35.1			
06	51 14.1	260 28.8	N 4 19.2	186 21.7	S18 45.7	18 17.0	N11 48.7	6 03.8	N14 35.1	Rasalhague	96 16.2	N12 33.9
07	66 16.6	275 32.6	19.2	201 22.7	46.1	33 19.3	48.7	21 06.2	35.1	Regulus	207 55.2	N11 58.3
08	81 19.0	290 36.4	19.3	216 23.8	46.5	48 21.7	48.8	36 08.6	35.1	Rigel	281 22.5	S 8 12.1
F 09	96 21.5	305 40.2 ..	19.3	231 24.9 ..	46.9	63 24.1 ..	48.8	51 10.9 ..	35.1	Rigil Kent.	140 06.6	S60 50.1
R 10	111 24.0	320 44.0	19.4	246 25.9	47.3	78 26.4	48.8	66 13.3	35.1	Sabik	102 24.7	S15 43.3
I 11	126 26.4	335 47.9	19.4	261 27.0	47.7	93 28.8	48.8	81 15.7	35.1			
D 12	141 28.9	350 51.7	N 4 19.5	276 28.1	S18 48.1	108 31.2	N11 48.9	96 18.1	N14 35.1	Schedar	349 52.4	N56 31.9
A 13	156 31.3	5 55.6	19.6	291 29.1	48.5	123 33.5	48.9	111 20.5	35.1	Shaula	96 36.2	S37 06.2
Y 14	171 33.8	20 59.4	19.6	306 30.2	48.9	138 35.9	48.9	126 22.9	35.2	Sirius	258 43.5	S16 42.8
15	186 36.3	36 03.2 ..	19.7	321 31.2 ..	49.3	153 38.3 ..	48.9	141 25.3 ..	35.2	Spica	158 42.7	S11 09.4
16	201 38.7	51 07.1	19.7	336 32.3	49.7	168 40.7	48.9	156 27.7	35.2	Suhail	223 00.8	S43 25.8
17	216 41.2	66 10.9	19.8	351 33.4	50.2	183 43.0	49.0	171 30.1	35.2			
18	231 43.7	81 14.8	N 4 19.9	6 34.4	S18 50.6	198 45.4	N11 49.0	186 32.4	N14 35.2	Vega	80 45.9	N38 47.3
19	246 46.1	96 18.6	19.9	21 35.5	51.0	213 47.8	49.0	201 34.8	35.2	Zuben'ubi	137 17.3	S16 02.3
20	261 48.6	111 22.5	20.0	36 36.5	51.4	228 50.1	49.0	216 37.2	35.2			
21	276 51.1	126 26.3 ..	20.1	51 37.6 ..	51.8	243 52.5 ..	49.1	231 39.6 ..	35.2			
22	291 53.5	141 30.2	20.1	66 38.6	52.2	258 54.9	49.1	246 42.0	35.2			
23	306 56.0	156 34.0	20.2	81 39.7	52.6	273 57.3	49.1	261 44.4	35.3			

		SHA	Mer. Pass.
		° ′	h m
Venus		208 35.1	12 42
Mars		135 49.3	17 35
Jupiter		327 05.9	4 51
Saturn		314 52.0	5 40

Mer. Pass. 2 39.6	v 3.8 d 0.0	v 1.1 d 0.4	v 2.4 d 0.0	v 2.4 d 0.0

UT	SUN GHA	SUN Dec	MOON GHA	v	MOON Dec	d	HP
d h	° ′	° ′	° ′	′	° ′	′	′
11 00	178 40.2	N15 27.8	184 44.3	7.1	N17 08.1	6.7	59.0
01	193 40.3	27.1	199 10.4	7.3	17 01.4	6.8	59.0
02	208 40.4	26.3	213 36.7	7.3	16 54.6	6.9	59.0
03	223 40.5	.. 25.6	228 03.0	7.4	16 47.7	7.0	58.9
04	238 40.6	24.9	242 29.4	7.5	16 40.7	7.1	58.9
05	253 40.7	24.1	256 55.9	7.6	N16 33.6	7.2	58.9
06	268 40.8	N15 23.4					
W 07	283 40.9	22.7					
E 08	298 40.9	21.9					
D 09	313 41.0	.. 21.2					
N 10	328 41.1	20.4					
E 11	343 41.2	19.7					
S 12	358 41.3	N15 19.0	358 03.3	8.1	N15 41.3	7.9	58.7
D 13	13 41.4	18.2	12 30.4	8.1	15 33.4	7.9	58.7
A 14	28 41.5	17.5	26 57.5	8.3	15 25.5	8.0	58.7
Y 15	43 41.6	.. 16.7	41 24.8	8.2	15 17.5	8.1	58.6
16	58 41.7	16.0	55 52.0	8.4	15 09.4	8.2	58.6
17	73 41.8	15.3	70 19.4	8.5	15 01.2	8.2	58.6
18	88 41.9	N15 14.5	84 46.9	8.5	N14 53.0	8.4	58.5
19	103 42.0	13.8	99 14.4	8.6	14 44.6	8.4	58.5
20	118 42.1	13.0	113 42.0	8.7	14 36.2	8.5	58.5
21	133 42.2	.. 12.3	128 09.7	8.7	14 27.7	8.6	58.5
22	148 42.3	11.5	142 37.4	8.9	14 19.1	8.6	58.5
23	163 42.4	10.8	157 05.3	8.9	14 10.5	8.8	58.4
12 00	178 42.5	N15 10.1	171 33.2	8.9	N14 01.7	8.8	58.4
01	193 42.6	09.3	186 01.1	9.1	13 52.9	8.9	58.4
02	208 42.7	08.6	200 29.2	9.1	13 44.0	8.9	58.3
03	223 42.8	.. 07.8	214 57.3	9.3	13 35.1	9.0	58.3
04	238 42.9	07.1	229 25.6	9.3	13 26.1	9.1	58.3
05	253 43.0	06.3	243 53.9	9.3	13 17.0	9.1	58.3
06	268 43.1	N15 05.6	258 22.2	9.5	N13 07.9	9.3	58.2
T 07	283 43.2	04.8	272 50.7	9.5	12 58.6	9.2	58.2
H 08	298 43.3	04.1	287 19.2	9.6	12 49.4	9.4	58.2
U 09	313 43.4	.. 03.3	301 47.8	9.7	12 40.0	9.4	58.1
R 10	328 43.5	02.6	316 16.5	9.7	12 30.6	9.5	58.1
S 11	343 43.7	01.8	330 45.2	9.8	12 21.1	9.5	58.1
D 12	358 43.8	N15 01.1	345 14.0	9.9	N12 11.6	9.6	58.1
A 13	13 43.9	15 00.3	359 42.9	10.0	12 02.0	9.6	58.0
Y 14	28 44.0	14 59.6	14 11.9	10.1	11 52.4	9.7	58.0
15	43 44.1	.. 58.8	28 41.0	10.1	11 42.7	9.7	58.0
16	58 44.2	58.1	43 10.1	10.2	11 33.0	9.8	57.9
17	73 44.3	57.3	57 39.3	10.3	11 23.2	9.9	57.9
18	88 44.4	N14 56.6	72 08.6	10.3	N11 13.3	9.9	57.9
19	103 44.5	55.8	86 37.9	10.4	11 03.4	9.9	57.9
20	118 44.6	55.1	101 07.3	10.5	10 53.5	10.0	57.8
21	133 44.7	.. 54.3	115 36.8	10.6	10 43.5	10.1	57.8
22	148 44.8	53.6	130 06.4	10.6	10 33.4	10.1	57.8
23	163 44.9	52.8	144 36.0	10.7	10 23.3	10.1	57.7
13 00	178 45.0	N14 52.1	159 05.7	10.8	N10 13.2	10.2	57.7
01	193 45.1	51.3	173 35.5	10.8	10 03.0	10.2	57.7
02	208 45.2	50.5	188 05.3	11.0	9 52.8	10.3	57.6
03	223 45.3	.. 49.8	202 35.3	10.9	9 42.5	10.3	57.6
04	238 45.4	49.0	217 05.2	11.1	9 32.2	10.3	57.6
05	253 45.6	48.3	231 35.3	11.1	9 21.9	10.4	57.5
06	268 45.7	N14 47.5	246 05.4	11.2	N 9 11.5	10.4	57.5
F 07	283 45.8	46.8	260 35.6	11.3	9 01.1	10.5	57.5
R 08	298 45.9	46.0	275 05.9	11.3	8 50.6	10.5	57.5
I 09	313 46.0	.. 45.3	289 36.2	11.4	8 40.1	10.5	57.4
D 10	328 46.1	44.5	304 06.6	11.5	8 29.6	10.5	57.4
A 11	343 46.2	43.7	318 37.1	11.5	8 19.1	10.6	57.4
Y 12	358 46.3	N14 43.0	333 07.6	11.6	N 8 08.5	10.6	57.3
13	13 46.4	42.2	347 38.2	11.6	7 57.9	10.7	57.3
14	28 46.5	41.5	2 08.8	11.8	7 47.2	10.6	57.3
15	43 46.6	.. 40.7	16 39.6	11.7	7 36.6	10.7	57.2
16	58 46.8	39.9	31 10.3	11.9	7 25.9	10.7	57.2
17	73 46.9	39.2	45 41.2	11.9	7 15.2	10.8	57.2
18	88 47.0	N14 38.4	60 12.1	12.0	N 7 04.4	10.7	57.1
19	103 47.1	37.6	74 43.1	12.0	6 53.7	10.8	57.1
20	118 47.2	36.9	89 14.1	12.1	6 42.9	10.8	57.1
21	133 47.3	.. 36.1	103 45.2	12.1	6 32.1	10.8	57.1
22	148 47.4	35.4	118 16.3	12.2	6 21.3	10.9	57.0
23	163 47.5	34.6	132 47.5	12.3	N 6 10.4	10.8	57.0
	SD 15.8	d 0.7	SD 16.0		15.8		15.6

Note in MOON column for WEDNESDAY 06–11: A total eclipse of the Sun occurs on this date. See page 5.

Twilight / Sunrise / Moonrise

Lat.	Naut.	Civil	Sunrise	11	12	13	14
°	h m	h m	h m	h m	h m	h m	h m
N 72	////	////	01 58	01 08	03 34	05 36	07 29
N 70	////	////	02 37	02 02	04 01	05 51	07 35
68	////	01 11	03 04	02 35	04 21	06 03	07 41
66	////	02 01	03 25	02 59	04 37	06 13	07 45
64	////	02 32	03 41	03 18	04 49	06 21	07 49
62	01 03	02 54	03 54	03 33	05 00	06 28	07 52
60	01 49	03 12	04 06	03 46	05 10	06 33	07 55
N 58	02 17	03 27	04 15	03 57	05 18	06 39	07 58
56	02 38	03 39	04 24	04 06	05 25	06 43	08 00
54	02 55	03 50	04 32	04 15	05 31	06 47	08 02
52	03 09	03 59	04 38	04 22	05 37	06 51	08 04
50	03 21	04 08	04 44	04 29	05 42	06 55	08 05
45	03 45	04 25	04 57	04 43	05 53	07 02	08 09
N 40	04 03	04 39	05 08	04 55	06 02	07 08	08 12
35	04 18	04 50	05 17	05 05	06 10	07 13	08 14
30	04 30	05 00	05 25	05 14	06 17	07 18	08 17
20	04 49	05 16	05 39	05 29	06 29	07 26	08 21
N 10	05 03	05 29	05 51	05 43	06 39	07 33	08 24
0	05 15	05 40	06 02	05 55	06 49	07 39	08 27
S 10	05 26	05 51	06 13	06 07	06 58	07 46	08 31
20	05 35	06 01	06 24	06 21	07 09	07 53	08 34
30	05 44	06 12	06 37	06 36	07 20	08 01	08 38
35	05 48	06 18	06 44	06 44	07 27	08 05	08 40
40	05 53	06 25	06 53	06 54	07 35	08 11	08 43
45	05 57	06 32	07 03	07 06	07 44	08 17	08 46
S 50	06 02	06 40	07 14	07 20	07 54	08 24	08 49
52	06 04	06 44	07 20	07 26	07 59	08 27	08 51
54	06 06	06 48	07 26	07 34	08 05	08 30	08 53
56	06 08	06 53	07 33	07 42	08 11	08 34	08 55
58	06 11	06 58	07 40	07 51	08 18	08 39	08 57
S 60	06 13	07 03	07 49	08 01	08 25	08 44	08 59

Sunset / Twilight / Moonset

Lat.	Sunset	Civil	Naut.	11	12	13	14
°	h m	h m	h m	h m	h m	h m	h m
N 72	22 06	////	////	21 54	21 38	21 26	21 15
N 70	21 28	////	////	21 25	21 17	21 17	21 12
68	21 02	22 50	////	21 04	21 08	21 09	21 10
66	20 43	22 04	////	20 47	20 57	21 03	21 08
64	20 27	21 35	////	20 33	20 48	20 58	21 07
62	20 14	21 13	22 58	20 21	20 40	20 54	21 05
60	20 03	20 56	22 17	20 11	20 33	20 50	21 04
N 58	19 53	20 41	21 50	20 03	20 27	20 46	21 03
56	19 45	20 29	21 30	19 55	20 21	20 43	21 02
54	19 37	20 16	21 13	19 48	20 16	20 40	21 01
52	19 31	20 09	21 00	19 42	20 12	20 38	21 00
50	19 25	20 01	20 48	19 36	20 08	20 35	21 00
45	19 12	19 44	20 24	19 24	19 59	20 30	20 58
N 40	19 01	19 31	20 06	19 14	19 52	20 26	20 57
35	18 52	19 19	19 52	19 05	19 45	20 22	20 56
30	18 45	19 10	19 40	18 57	19 40	20 19	20 54
20	18 31	18 54	19 21	18 44	19 30	20 13	20 53
N 10	18 19	18 41	19 07	18 32	19 22	20 08	20 51
0	18 08	18 30	18 55	18 21	19 13	20 03	20 49
S 10	17 58	18 19	18 45	18 10	19 05	19 58	20 48
20	17 46	18 09	18 35	17 58	18 56	19 52	20 46
30	17 34	17 58	18 27	17 44	18 46	19 46	20 44
35	17 26	17 52	18 22	17 36	18 41	19 43	20 43
40	17 18	17 46	18 18	17 27	18 34	19 39	20 42
45	17 08	17 39	18 14	17 16	18 26	19 34	20 40
S 50	16 56	17 31	18 09	17 03	18 17	19 29	20 38
52	16 51	17 27	18 07	16 57	18 12	19 26	20 37
54	16 45	17 23	18 05	16 50	18 07	19 23	20 36
56	16 38	17 18	18 03	16 43	18 02	19 20	20 35
58	16 31	17 13	18 00	16 34	17 56	19 16	20 34
S 60	16 22	17 08	17 58	16 25	17 49	19 12	20 33

SUN / MOON

Day	Eqn. of Time 00ʰ	Eqn. of Time 12ʰ	Mer. Pass.	Mer. Pass. Upper	Mer. Pass. Lower	Age	Phase
d	m s	m s	h m	h m	h m	d	%
11	05 19	05 15	12 05	12 08	24 35	00	0
12	05 10	05 05	12 05	13 01	00 35	01	1
13	05 00	04 55	12 05	13 51	01 27	02	5

UT	ARIES	VENUS −4.1		MARS +0.2		JUPITER −2.6		SATURN +0.2		STARS		
	GHA	GHA	Dec	GHA	Dec	GHA	Dec	GHA	Dec	Name	SHA	Dec
d h	° ′	° ′	° ′	° ′	° ′	° ′	° ′	° ′	° ′		° ′	° ′
14 00	321 58.5	171 37.9	N 4 20.3	96 40.7	S18 53.0	288 59.6	N11 49.1	276 46.8	N14 35.3	Acamar	315 26.4	S40 18.2
01	337 00.9	186 41.7	20.4	111 41.8	53.4	304 02.0	49.1	291 49.2	35.3	Achernar	335 34.5	S57 14.1
02	352 03.4	201 45.6	20.5	126 42.9	53.8	319 04.4	49.2	306 51.6	35.3	Acrux	173 21.8	S63 05.9
03	7 05.8	216 49.4	.. 20.5	141 43.9	.. 54.2	334 06.8	.. 49.2	321 54.0	.. 35.3	Adhara	255 21.3	S28 58.2
04	22 08.3	231 53.3	20.6	156 45.0	54.7	349 09.1	49.2	336 56.4	35.3	Aldebaran	291 01.8	N16 30.4
05	37 10.8	246 57.2	20.7	171 46.0	55.1	4 11.5	49.2	351 58.8	35.3			
06	52 13.2	262 01.0	N 4 20.8	186 47.1	S18 55.5	19 13.9	N11 49.2	7 01.1	N14 35.3	Alioth	166 30.5	N55 58.1
07	67 15.7	277 04.9	20.9	201 48.1	55.9	34 16.3	49.3	22 03.5	35.3	Alkaid	153 07.6	N49 19.3
08	82 18.2	292 08.8	21.0	216 49.2	56.3	49 18.6	49.3	37 05.9	35.3	Al Na'ir	27 56.7	S46 57.7
S 09	97 20.6	307 12.6	.. 21.1	231 50.2	.. 56.7	64 21.0	.. 49.3	52 08.3	.. 35.4	Alnilam	275 57.4	S 1 12.1
A 10	112 23.1	322 16.5	21.2	246 51.3	57.1	79 23.4	49.3	67 10.7	35.4	Alphard	218 07.0	S 8 39.3
T 11	127 25.6	337 20.4	21.3	261 52.3	57.5	94 25.8	49.3	82 13.1	35.4			
U 12	142 28.0	352 24.3	N 4 21.4	276 53.4	S18 57.9	109 28.1	N11 49.4	97 15.5	N14 35.4	Alphecca	126 20.1	N26 43.3
R 13	157 30.5	7 28.2	21.5	291 54.4	58.3	124 30.5	49.4	112 17.9	35.4	Alpheratz	357 54.3	N29 05.2
D 14	172 32.9	22 32.0	21.6	306 55.5	58.7	139 32.9	49.4	127 20.3	35.4	Altair	62 18.4	N 8 52.2
A 15	187 35.4	37 35.9	.. 21.7	321 56.5	.. 59.1	154 35.3	.. 49.4	142 22.7	.. 35.4	Ankaa	353 26.0	S42 18.3
Y 16	202 37.9	52 39.8	21.8	336 57.6	18 59.5	169 37.6	49.4	157 25.1	35.4	Antares	112 39.3	S26 25.8
17	217 40.3	67 43.7	21.9	351 58.6	19 00.0	184 40.0	49.5	172 27.5	35.4			
18	232 42.8	82 47.6	N 4 22.0	6 59.6	S19 00.4	199 42.4	N11 49.5	187 29.9	N14 35.4	Arcturus	146 05.6	N19 11.4
19	247 45.3	97 51.5	22.1	22 00.7	00.8	214 44.8	49.5	202 32.3	35.5	Atria	107 50.6	S69 01.7
20	262 47.7	112 55.4	22.2	37 01.7	01.2	229 47.2	49.5	217 34.7	35.5	Avior	234 23.0	S59 30.4
21	277 50.2	127 59.3	.. 22.3	52 02.8	.. 01.6	244 49.5	.. 49.5	232 37.1	.. 35.5	Bellatrix	278 43.7	N 6 20.9
22	292 52.7	143 03.2	22.4	67 03.8	02.0	259 51.9	49.6	247 39.5	35.5	Betelgeuse	271 13.1	N 7 24.4
23	307 55.1	158 07.0	22.5	82 04.9	02.4	274 54.3	49.6	262 41.8	35.5			
15 00	322 57.6	173 10.9	N 4 22.7	97 05.9	S19 02.8	289 56.7	N11 49.6	277 44.2	N14 35.5	Canopus	264 01.3	S52 41.6
01	338 00.1	188 14.8	22.8	112 07.0	03.2	304 59.1	49.6	292 46.6	35.5	Capella	280 50.5	N45 59.6
02	353 02.5	203 18.7	22.9	127 08.0	03.6	320 01.4	49.6	307 49.0	35.5	Deneb	49 38.3	N45 16.9
03	8 05.0	218 22.7	.. 23.0	142 09.0	.. 04.0	335 03.8	.. 49.7	322 51.4	.. 35.5	Denebola	182 44.9	N14 34.7
04	23 07.4	233 26.6	23.2	157 10.1	04.4	350 06.2	49.7	337 53.8	35.5	Diphda	349 06.4	S17 59.2
05	38 09.9	248 30.5	23.3	172 11.1	04.8	5 08.6	49.7	352 56.2	35.5			
06	53 12.4	263 34.4	N 4 23.4	187 12.2	S19 05.2	20 11.0	N11 49.7	7 58.6	N14 35.6	Dubhe	194 05.4	N61 45.4
07	68 14.8	278 38.3	23.5	202 13.2	05.6	35 13.4	49.7	23 01.0	35.6	Elnath	278 26.4	N28 36.3
08	83 17.3	293 42.2	23.7	217 14.2	06.1	50 15.7	49.7	38 03.4	35.6	Eltanin	90 50.8	N51 29.7
S 09	98 19.8	308 46.1	.. 23.8	232 15.3	.. 06.5	65 18.1	.. 49.8	53 05.8	.. 35.6	Enif	33 57.3	N 9 52.5
U 10	113 22.2	323 50.0	23.9	247 16.3	06.9	80 20.5	49.8	68 08.2	35.6	Fomalhaut	15 35.5	S29 37.3
N 11	128 24.7	338 53.9	24.1	262 17.3	07.3	95 22.9	49.8	83 10.6	35.6			
D 12	143 27.2	353 57.9	N 4 24.2	277 18.4	S19 07.7	110 25.3	N11 49.8	98 13.0	N14 35.6	Gacrux	172 13.3	S57 06.7
A 13	158 29.6	9 01.8	24.4	292 19.4	08.1	125 27.7	49.8	113 15.4	35.6	Gienah	176 03.6	S17 32.3
Y 14	173 32.1	24 05.7	24.5	307 20.4	08.5	140 30.0	49.8	128 17.8	35.6	Hadar	149 03.4	S60 22.4
15	188 34.6	39 09.6	.. 24.6	322 21.5	.. 08.9	155 32.4	.. 49.9	143 20.2	.. 35.6	Hamal	328 12.8	N23 27.5
16	203 37.0	54 13.5	24.8	337 22.5	09.3	170 34.8	49.9	158 22.6	35.6	Kaus Aust.	83 57.8	S34 23.0
17	218 39.5	69 17.5	24.9	352 23.5	09.7	185 37.2	49.9	173 25.0	35.6			
18	233 41.9	84 21.4	N 4 25.1	7 24.6	S19 10.1	200 39.6	N11 49.9	188 27.4	N14 35.7	Kochab	137 19.8	N74 09.9
19	248 44.4	99 25.3	25.2	22 25.6	10.5	215 42.0	49.9	203 29.8	35.7	Markab	13 48.7	N15 12.2
20	263 46.9	114 29.3	25.4	37 26.6	10.9	230 44.4	49.9	218 32.2	35.7	Menkar	314 26.3	N 4 05.3
21	278 49.3	129 33.2	.. 25.5	52 27.7	.. 11.3	245 46.8	.. 50.0	233 34.6	.. 35.7	Menkent	148 20.4	S36 22.1
22	293 51.8	144 37.1	25.7	67 28.7	11.7	260 49.1	50.0	248 37.0	35.7	Miaplacidus	221 42.8	S69 42.9
23	308 54.3	159 41.1	25.9	82 29.7	12.1	275 51.5	50.0	263 39.4	35.7			
16 00	323 56.7	174 45.0	N 4 26.0	97 30.8	S19 12.5	290 53.9	N11 50.0	278 41.8	N14 35.7	Mirfak	308 55.8	N49 51.3
01	338 59.2	189 48.9	26.2	112 31.8	12.9	305 56.3	50.0	293 44.2	35.7	Nunki	76 11.3	S26 17.7
02	354 01.7	204 52.9	26.3	127 32.8	13.3	320 58.7	50.0	308 46.6	35.7	Peacock	53 35.5	S56 44.2
03	9 04.1	219 56.8	.. 26.5	142 33.9	.. 13.8	336 01.1	.. 50.1	323 49.0	.. 35.7	Pollux	243 41.2	N28 01.6
04	24 06.6	235 00.7	26.7	157 34.9	14.2	351 03.5	50.1	338 51.4	35.7	Procyon	245 11.2	N 5 13.6
05	39 09.0	250 04.7	26.8	172 35.9	14.6	6 05.9	50.1	353 53.8	35.7			
06	54 11.5	265 08.6	N 4 27.0	187 36.9	S19 15.0	21 08.3	N11 50.1	8 56.2	N14 35.8	Rasalhague	96 16.2	N12 33.9
07	69 14.0	280 12.6	27.2	202 38.0	15.4	36 10.6	50.1	23 58.6	35.8	Regulus	207 55.2	N11 58.3
08	84 16.4	295 16.5	27.3	217 39.0	15.8	51 13.0	50.1	39 01.0	35.8	Rigel	281 22.5	S 8 12.1
M 09	99 18.9	310 20.5	.. 27.5	232 40.0	.. 16.2	66 15.4	.. 50.1	54 03.4	.. 35.8	Rigil Kent.	140 06.6	S60 50.1
O 10	114 21.4	325 24.4	27.7	247 41.0	16.6	81 17.8	50.2	69 05.8	35.8	Sabik	102 24.7	S15 43.3
N 11	129 23.8	340 28.4	27.9	262 42.1	17.0	96 20.2	50.2	84 08.2	35.8			
D 12	144 26.3	355 32.3	N 4 28.1	277 43.1	S19 17.4	111 22.6	N11 50.2	99 10.6	N14 35.8	Schedar	349 52.4	N56 31.9
A 13	159 28.8	10 36.3	28.2	292 44.1	17.8	126 25.0	50.2	114 13.0	35.8	Shaula	96 36.3	S37 06.2
Y 14	174 31.2	25 40.2	28.4	307 45.1	18.2	141 27.4	50.2	129 15.4	35.8	Sirius	258 43.4	S16 42.8
15	189 33.7	40 44.2	.. 28.6	322 46.1	.. 18.6	156 29.8	.. 50.2	144 17.8	.. 35.8	Spica	158 42.7	S11 09.4
16	204 36.2	55 48.1	28.8	337 47.2	19.0	171 32.2	50.2	159 20.2	35.8	Suhail	223 00.8	S43 25.8
17	219 38.6	70 52.1	29.0	352 48.2	19.4	186 34.6	50.3	174 22.6	35.8			
18	234 41.1	85 56.0	N 4 29.2	7 49.2	S19 19.8	201 37.0	N11 50.3	189 25.0	N14 35.8	Vega	80 45.9	N38 47.3
19	249 43.5	101 00.0	29.4	22 50.2	20.2	216 39.4	50.3	204 27.4	35.8	Zuben'ubi	137 17.4	S16 02.3
20	264 46.0	116 03.9	29.5	37 51.2	20.6	231 41.8	50.3	219 29.8	35.9		SHA	Mer. Pass
21	279 48.5	131 07.9	.. 29.7	52 52.3	.. 21.0	246 44.2	.. 50.3	234 32.2	.. 35.9		° ′	h m
22	294 50.9	146 11.9	29.9	67 53.3	21.4	261 46.5	50.3	249 34.6	35.9	Venus	210 13.4	12 24
23	309 53.4	161 15.8	30.1	82 54.3	21.8	276 48.9	50.3	264 37.0	35.9	Mars	134 08.3	17 30
	h m									Jupiter	326 59.1	4 39
Mer. Pass. 2 27.8		v 3.9	d 0.1	v 1.0	d 0.4	v 2.4	d 0.0	v 2.4	d 0.0	Saturn	314 46.7	5 28

UT	SUN GHA	SUN Dec	MOON GHA	v	MOON Dec	d	HP
d h	° ′	° ′	° ′	′	° ′	′	′
14 00	178 47.6	N14 33.8	147 18.8	12.3	N 5 59.6	10.9	57.0
01	193 47.8	33.1	161 50.1	12.4	5 48.7	10.9	56.9
02	208 47.9	32.3	176 21.5	12.4	5 37.8	10.9	56.9
03	223 48.0	31.5	190 52.9	12.5	5 26.9	10.9	56.9
04	238 48.1	30.8	205 24.4	12.5	5 16.0	10.9	56.8
05	253 48.2	30.0	219 55.9	12.6	5 05.0	10.9	56.8
06	268 48.3	N14 29.2	234 27.5	12.7	N 4 54.1	11.0	56.8
07	283 48.4	28.5	248 59.2	12.7	4 43.1	10.9	56.7
08	298 48.5	27.7	263 30.9	12.7	4 32.2	11.0	56.7
09	313 48.7	26.9	278 02.6	12.8	4 21.2	11.0	56.7
10	328 48.8	26.2	292 34.4	12.9	4 10.2	11.0	56.6
11	343 48.9	25.4	307 06.3	12.9	3 59.2	11.0	56.6
12	358 49.0	N14 24.6	321 38.2	12.9	N 3 48.2	11.0	56.6
13	13 49.1	23.9	336 10.1	13.0	3 37.2	11.0	56.6
14	28 49.2	23.1	350 42.1	13.1	3 26.2	11.0	56.5
15	43 49.4	22.3	5 14.2	13.1	3 15.2	11.0	56.5
16	58 49.5	21.5	19 46.3	13.1	3 04.2	11.0	56.5
17	73 49.6	20.8	34 18.4	13.2	2 53.2	11.0	56.4
18	88 49.7	N14 20.0	48 50.6	13.2	N 2 42.2	11.1	56.4
19	103 49.8	19.2	63 22.8	13.3	2 31.1	11.0	56.4
20	118 49.9	18.5	77 55.1	13.3	2 20.1	11.0	56.3
21	133 50.1	17.7	92 27.4	13.4	2 09.1	11.0	56.3
22	148 50.2	16.9	106 59.8	13.3	1 58.1	11.0	56.3
23	163 50.3	16.1	121 32.1	13.5	1 47.1	11.0	56.3
15 00	178 50.4	N14 15.4	136 04.6	13.5	N 1 36.1	11.0	56.2
01	193 50.5	14.6	150 37.1	13.5	1 25.1	11.0	56.2
02	208 50.6	13.8	165 09.6	13.5	1 14.1	11.0	56.2
03	223 50.8	13.0	179 42.1	13.6	1 03.1	11.0	56.1
04	238 50.9	12.3	194 14.7	13.6	0 52.1	10.9	56.1
05	253 51.0	11.5	208 47.3	13.7	0 41.2	11.0	56.1
06	268 51.1	N14 10.7	223 20.0	13.7	N 0 30.2	10.9	56.0
07	283 51.2	09.9	237 52.7	13.7	0 19.3	11.0	56.0
08	298 51.4	09.2	252 25.4	13.8	N 0 08.3	10.9	56.0
09	313 51.5	08.4	266 58.2	13.8	S 0 02.6	10.9	56.0
10	328 51.6	07.6	281 31.0	13.8	0 13.5	10.9	55.9
11	343 51.7	06.8	296 03.8	13.8	0 24.4	10.9	55.9
12	358 51.8	N14 06.1	310 36.6	13.9	S 0 35.3	10.9	55.9
13	13 52.0	05.3	325 09.5	13.9	0 46.2	10.8	55.8
14	28 52.1	04.5	339 42.4	14.0	0 57.0	10.9	55.8
15	43 52.2	03.7	354 15.4	13.9	1 07.9	10.8	55.8
16	58 52.3	02.9	8 48.3	14.0	1 18.7	10.8	55.7
17	73 52.5	02.2	23 21.3	14.1	1 29.5	10.8	55.7
18	88 52.6	N14 01.4	37 54.4	14.0	S 1 40.3	10.8	55.7
19	103 52.7	14 00.6	52 27.4	14.1	1 51.1	10.7	55.7
20	118 52.8	13 59.8	67 00.5	14.1	2 01.8	10.8	55.7
21	133 52.9	59.0	81 33.6	14.1	2 12.6	10.7	55.6
22	148 53.1	58.2	96 06.7	14.1	2 23.3	10.7	55.6
23	163 53.2	57.5	110 39.8	14.2	2 34.0	10.7	55.6
16 00	178 53.3	N13 56.7	125 13.0	14.2	S 2 44.7	10.6	55.6
01	193 53.4	55.9	139 46.2	14.2	2 55.3	10.6	55.5
02	208 53.6	55.1	154 19.4	14.2	3 05.9	10.6	55.5
03	223 53.7	54.3	168 52.6	14.3	3 16.5	10.6	55.5
04	238 53.8	53.5	183 25.9	14.2	3 27.1	10.6	55.5
05	253 53.9	52.8	197 59.1	14.3	3 37.7	10.5	55.4
06	268 54.1	N13 52.0	212 32.4	14.3	S 3 48.2	10.5	55.4
07	283 54.2	51.2	227 05.7	14.3	3 58.7	10.4	55.4
08	298 54.3	50.4	241 39.0	14.3	4 09.1	10.5	55.4
09	313 54.4	49.6	256 12.3	14.4	4 19.6	10.4	55.3
10	328 54.6	48.8	270 45.7	14.3	4 30.0	10.4	55.3
11	343 54.7	48.0	285 19.0	14.4	4 40.4	10.3	55.3
12	358 54.8	N13 47.3	299 52.4	14.4	S 4 50.7	10.4	55.3
13	13 54.9	46.5	314 25.8	14.4	5 01.1	10.3	55.2
14	28 55.1	45.7	328 59.2	14.4	5 11.4	10.2	55.2
15	43 55.2	44.9	343 32.6	14.4	5 21.6	10.3	55.2
16	58 55.3	44.1	358 06.0	14.4	5 31.9	10.2	55.2
17	73 55.5	43.3	12 39.4	14.4	5 42.1	10.1	55.1
18	88 55.6	N13 42.5	27 12.8	14.4	S 5 52.2	10.2	55.1
19	103 55.7	41.7	41 46.2	14.5	6 02.4	10.1	55.1
20	118 55.8	40.9	56 19.7	14.4	6 12.5	10.0	55.1
21	133 56.0	40.1	70 53.1	14.5	6 22.5	10.1	55.1
22	148 56.1	39.4	85 26.6	14.4	6 32.6	10.0	55.0
23	163 56.2	38.6	100 00.0	14.5	S 6 42.6	9.9	55.0
	SD 15.8	d 0.8	SD 15.4		15.2		15.1

Days labels: SATURDAY (14), SUNDAY (15), MONDAY (16)

Lat.	Twilight Naut.	Twilight Civil	Sunrise	Moonrise 14	15	16	17
°	h m	h m	h m	h m	h m	h m	h m
N 72	////	////	02 21	07 29	09 15	10 58	12 41
N 70	////	////	02 54	07 35	09 15	10 51	12 27
68	////	01 39	03 17	07 41	09 15	10 46	12 15
66	////	02 18	03 36	07 45	09 14	10 41	12 06
64	////	02 45	03 50	07 49	09 14	10 37	11 58
62	01 28	03 05	04 02	07 52	09 14	10 34	11 51
60	02 04	03 21	04 13	07 55	09 14	10 31	11 45
N 58	02 28	03 35	04 22	07 58	09 14	10 28	11 40
56	02 47	03 46	04 30	08 00	09 14	10 26	11 36
54	03 03	03 56	04 37	08 02	09 14	10 24	11 32
52	03 16	04 05	04 43	08 04	09 14	10 22	11 28
50	03 27	04 13	04 49	08 05	09 14	10 20	11 25
45	03 49	04 29	05 01	08 09	09 14	10 16	11 18
N 40	04 07	04 42	05 11	08 12	09 13	10 13	11 12
35	04 20	04 53	05 20	08 14	09 13	10 10	11 06
30	04 32	05 02	05 27	08 17	09 13	10 08	11 02
20	04 50	05 17	05 40	08 21	09 13	10 04	10 54
N 10	05 04	05 29	05 51	08 24	09 13	10 01	10 47
0	05 15	05 40	06 01	08 27	09 13	09 57	10 41
S 10	05 25	05 50	06 11	08 31	09 13	09 54	10 35
20	05 33	05 59	06 22	08 34	09 13	09 51	10 28
30	05 41	06 09	06 34	08 38	09 13	09 47	10 21
35	05 45	06 15	06 41	08 40	09 13	09 44	10 16
40	05 49	06 21	06 49	08 43	09 13	09 42	10 11
45	05 53	06 28	06 58	08 46	09 13	09 39	10 06
S 50	05 57	06 35	07 09	08 49	09 13	09 36	09 59
52	05 59	06 39	07 14	08 51	09 13	09 34	09 56
54	06 01	06 42	07 20	08 53	09 13	09 32	09 53
56	06 03	06 46	07 26	08 55	09 13	09 31	09 49
58	06 05	06 51	07 33	08 57	09 13	09 28	09 45
S 60	06 07	06 56	07 41	08 59	09 13	09 26	09 40

Lat.	Sunset	Twilight Civil	Twilight Naut.	Moonset 14	15	16	17
°	h m	h m	h m	h m	h m	h m	h m
N 72	21 43	////	////	21 15	21 05	20 55	20 43
N 70	21 11	23 47	////	21 12	21 08	21 04	20 59
68	20 49	22 23	////	21 10	21 11	21 11	21 12
66	20 31	21 46	////	21 08	21 13	21 17	21 23
64	20 17	21 21	23 49	21 07	21 15	21 23	21 32
62	20 05	21 01	22 35	21 05	21 16	21 27	21 39
60	19 54	20 46	22 01	21 04	21 18	21 31	21 46
N 58	19 46	20 33	21 38	21 03	21 19	21 35	21 52
56	19 38	20 21	21 20	21 02	21 20	21 38	21 57
54	19 31	20 12	21 05	21 01	21 21	21 41	22 02
52	19 25	20 03	20 52	21 00	21 23	21 44	22 06
50	19 19	19 55	20 41	21 00	21 23	21 46	22 10
45	19 07	19 39	20 19	20 58	21 25	21 51	22 18
N 40	18 57	19 26	20 02	20 57	21 26	21 56	22 25
35	18 49	19 16	19 48	20 56	21 28	21 59	22 32
30	18 42	19 07	19 37	20 54	21 29	22 03	22 37
20	18 29	18 52	19 19	20 53	21 31	22 08	22 46
N 10	18 18	18 40	19 05	20 51	21 33	22 14	22 54
0	18 08	18 29	18 54	20 49	21 34	22 18	23 02
S 10	17 58	18 19	18 44	20 48	21 36	22 23	23 10
20	17 47	18 10	18 36	20 46	21 38	22 28	23 18
30	17 35	18 00	18 28	20 44	21 40	22 34	23 28
35	17 28	17 55	18 24	20 43	21 41	22 38	23 33
40	17 21	17 49	18 21	20 42	21 42	22 41	23 39
45	17 12	17 42	18 17	20 40	21 44	22 46	23 47
S 50	17 01	17 35	18 13	20 38	21 46	22 51	23 55
52	16 56	17 31	18 11	20 37	21 46	22 54	23 59
54	16 50	17 28	18 09	20 36	21 47	22 56	24 04
56	16 44	17 24	18 07	20 35	21 48	22 59	24 09
58	16 37	17 19	18 06	20 34	21 50	23 03	24 14
S 60	16 29	17 14	18 04	20 33	21 51	23 07	24 20

Day	SUN Eqn. of Time 00h	SUN Eqn. of Time 12h	SUN Mer. Pass.	MOON Mer. Pass. Upper	MOON Mer. Pass. Lower	Age	Phase
d	m s	m s	h m	h m	h m	d	%
14	04 50	04 44	12 05	14 38	02 15	03	11
15	04 39	04 33	12 05	15 24	03 01	04	18
16	04 27	04 21	12 04	16 08	03 46	05	26

UT	ARIES GHA	VENUS −4.0 GHA	Dec	MARS +0.2 GHA	Dec	JUPITER −2.6 GHA	Dec	SATURN +0.2 GHA	Dec	STARS Name	SHA	Dec
17 00	324 55.9	176 19.8	N 4 30.3	97 55.3	S19 22.2	291 51.3	N11 50.4	279 39.4	N14 35.9	Acamar	315 26.4	S40 18.2
01	339 58.3	191 23.7	30.5	112 56.3	22.6	306 53.7	50.4	294 41.9	35.9	Achernar	335 34.5	S57 14.1
02	355 00.8	206 27.7	30.7	127 57.4	23.0	321 56.1	50.4	309 44.3	35.9	Acrux	173 21.8	S63 05.9
03	10 03.3	221 31.7 ..	30.9	142 58.4 ..	23.4	336 58.5 ..	50.4	324 46.7 ..	35.9	Adhara	255 21.2	S28 58.2
04	25 05.7	236 35.6	31.1	157 59.4	23.8	352 00.9	50.4	339 49.1	35.9	Aldebaran	291 01.8	N16 30.4
05	40 08.2	251 39.6	31.3	173 00.4	24.2	7 03.3	50.4	354 51.5	35.9			
06	55 10.6	266 43.6	N 4 31.6	188 01.4	S19 24.6	22 05.7	N11 50.4	9 53.9	N14 35.9	Alioth	166 30.5	N55 58.1
T 07	70 13.1	281 47.5	31.8	203 02.4	25.1	37 08.1	50.4	24 56.3	35.9	Alkaid	153 07.6	N49 19.3
U 08	85 15.6	296 51.5	32.0	218 03.4	25.5	52 10.5	50.5	39 58.7	35.9	Al Na'ir	27 56.7	S46 57.7
E 09	100 18.0	311 55.5 ..	32.2	233 04.5 ..	25.9	67 12.9 ..	50.5	55 01.1 ..	35.9	Alnilam	275 57.4	S 1 12.1
S 10	115 20.5	326 59.4	32.4	248 05.5	26.3	82 15.3	50.5	70 03.5	35.9	Alphard	218 06.9	S 8 39.3
D 11	130 23.0	342 03.4	32.6	263 06.5	26.7	97 17.7	50.5	85 05.9	36.0			
A 12	145 25.4	357 07.4	N 4 32.8	278 07.5	S19 27.1	112 20.1	N11 50.5	100 08.3	N14 36.0	Alphecca	126 20.1	N26 43.3
Y 13	160 27.9	12 11.4	33.1	293 08.5	27.5	127 22.5	50.5	115 10.7	36.0	Alpheratz	357 54.3	N29 05.2
14	175 30.4	27 15.3	33.3	308 09.5	27.9	142 24.9	50.5	130 13.1	36.0	Altair	62 18.4	N 8 52.2
15	190 32.8	42 19.3 ..	33.5	323 10.5 ..	28.3	157 27.3 ..	50.5	145 15.5 ..	36.0	Ankaa	353 26.0	S42 18.3
16	205 35.3	57 23.3	33.7	338 11.5	28.7	172 29.7	50.5	160 17.9	36.0	Antares	112 39.3	S26 25.8
17	220 37.8	72 27.3	33.9	353 12.5	29.1	187 32.1	50.6	175 20.3	36.0			
18	235 40.2	87 31.2	N 4 34.2	8 13.5	S19 29.5	202 34.5	N11 50.6	190 22.8	N14 36.0	Arcturus	146 05.6	N19 11.4
19	250 42.7	102 35.2	34.4	23 14.5	29.9	217 36.9	50.6	205 25.2	36.0	Atria	107 50.6	S69 01.7
20	265 45.1	117 39.2	34.6	38 15.6	30.3	232 39.3	50.6	220 27.6	36.0	Avior	234 23.0	S59 30.4
21	280 47.6	132 43.2 ..	34.9	53 16.6 ..	30.7	247 41.7 ..	50.6	235 30.0 ..	36.0	Bellatrix	278 43.7	N 6 20.9
22	295 50.1	147 47.2	35.1	68 17.6	31.1	262 44.1	50.6	250 32.4	36.0	Betelgeuse	271 13.1	N 7 24.4
23	310 52.5	162 51.1	35.3	83 18.6	31.5	277 46.5	50.6	265 34.8	36.0			
18 00	325 55.0	177 55.1	N 4 35.6	98 19.6	S19 31.9	292 49.0	N11 50.6	280 37.2	N14 36.0	Canopus	264 01.3	S52 41.6
01	340 57.5	192 59.1	35.8	113 20.6	32.3	307 51.4	50.6	295 39.6	36.0	Capella	280 50.5	N45 59.6
02	355 59.9	208 03.1	36.0	128 21.6	32.7	322 53.8	50.7	310 42.0	36.0	Deneb	49 38.3	N45 16.9
03	11 02.4	223 07.1 ..	36.3	143 22.6 ..	33.1	337 56.2 ..	50.7	325 44.4 ..	36.0	Denebola	182 44.9	N14 34.7
04	26 04.9	238 11.0	36.5	158 23.6	33.5	352 58.6	50.7	340 46.8	36.1	Diphda	349 06.4	S17 59.2
05	41 07.3	253 15.0	36.8	173 24.6	33.9	8 01.0	50.7	355 49.3	36.1			
06	56 09.8	268 19.0	N 4 37.0	188 25.6	S19 34.3	23 03.4	N11 50.7	10 51.7	N14 36.1	Dubhe	194 05.4	N61 45.4
W 07	71 12.3	283 23.0	37.3	203 26.6	34.7	38 05.8	50.7	25 54.1	36.1	Elnath	278 26.4	N28 36.3
E 08	86 14.7	298 27.0	37.5	218 27.6	35.1	53 08.2	50.7	40 56.5	36.1	Eltanin	90 50.8	N51 29.7
D 09	101 17.2	313 31.0 ..	37.8	233 28.6 ..	35.5	68 10.6 ..	50.7	55 58.9 ..	36.1	Enif	33 57.3	N 9 52.5
N 10	116 19.6	328 34.9	38.0	248 29.6	35.9	83 13.0	50.7	71 01.3	36.1	Fomalhaut	15 35.5	S29 37.4
E 11	131 22.1	343 38.9	38.3	263 30.6	36.3	98 15.4	50.7	86 03.7	36.1			
S 12	146 24.6	358 42.9	N 4 38.5	278 31.6	S19 36.7	113 17.8	N11 50.7	101 06.1	N14 36.1	Gacrux	172 13.3	S57 06.7
D 13	161 27.0	13 46.9	38.8	293 32.6	37.1	128 20.2	50.8	116 08.5	36.1	Gienah	176 03.6	S17 32.3
A 14	176 29.5	28 50.9	39.0	308 33.6	37.5	143 22.6	50.8	131 10.9	36.1	Hadar	149 03.4	S60 22.4
Y 15	191 32.0	43 54.9 ..	39.3	323 34.6 ..	37.9	158 25.1 ..	50.8	146 13.4 ..	36.1	Hamal	328 12.8	N23 27.5
16	206 34.4	58 58.9	39.5	338 35.6	38.3	173 27.5	50.8	161 15.8	36.1	Kaus Aust.	83 57.8	S34 23.0
17	221 36.9	74 02.9	39.8	353 36.6	38.7	188 29.9	50.8	176 18.2	36.1			
18	236 39.4	89 06.8	N 4 40.1	8 37.6	S19 39.1	203 32.3	N11 50.8	191 20.6	N14 36.1	Kochab	137 19.9	N74 09.9
19	251 41.8	104 10.8	40.3	23 38.6	39.5	218 34.7	50.8	206 23.0	36.1	Markab	13 48.7	N15 12.2
20	266 44.3	119 14.8	40.6	38 39.6	39.9	233 37.1	50.8	221 25.4	36.1	Menkar	314 26.2	N 4 05.3
21	281 46.7	134 18.8 ..	40.9	53 40.6 ..	40.3	248 39.5 ..	50.8	236 27.8 ..	36.1	Menkent	148 20.4	S36 22.1
22	296 49.2	149 22.8	41.1	68 41.5	40.7	263 41.9	50.8	251 30.2	36.1	Miaplacidus	221 42.8	S69 42.9
23	311 51.7	164 26.8	41.4	83 42.5	41.1	278 44.3	50.8	266 32.7	36.1			
19 00	326 54.1	179 30.8	N 4 41.7	98 43.5	S19 41.5	293 46.8	N11 50.8	281 35.1	N14 36.1	Mirfak	308 55.7	N49 51.3
01	341 56.6	194 34.8	41.9	113 44.5	41.9	308 49.2	50.9	296 37.5	36.2	Nunki	76 11.3	S26 17.7
02	356 59.1	209 38.8	42.2	128 45.5	42.3	323 51.6	50.9	311 39.9	36.2	Peacock	53 35.5	S56 44.2
03	12 01.5	224 42.7 ..	42.5	143 46.5 ..	42.7	338 54.0 ..	50.9	326 42.3 ..	36.2	Pollux	243 41.2	N28 01.6
04	27 04.0	239 46.7	42.8	158 47.5	43.1	353 56.4	50.9	341 44.7	36.2	Procyon	245 11.2	N 5 13.6
05	42 06.5	254 50.7	43.0	173 48.5	43.5	8 58.8	50.9	356 47.1	36.2			
06	57 08.9	269 54.7	N 4 43.3	188 49.5	S19 43.8	24 01.2	N11 50.9	11 49.5	N14 36.2	Rasalhague	96 16.2	N12 33.9
T 07	72 11.4	284 58.7	43.6	203 50.5	44.2	39 03.6	50.9	26 52.0	36.2	Regulus	207 55.2	N11 58.3
H 08	87 13.9	300 02.7	43.9	218 51.5	44.6	54 06.1	50.9	41 54.4	36.2	Rigel	281 22.5	S 8 12.1
U 09	102 16.3	315 06.7 ..	44.2	233 52.4 ..	45.0	69 08.5 ..	50.9	56 56.8 ..	36.2	Rigil Kent.	140 06.7	S60 50.1
R 10	117 18.8	330 10.7	44.5	248 53.4	45.4	84 10.9	50.9	71 59.2	36.2	Sabik	102 24.7	S15 43.3
S 11	132 21.2	345 14.7	44.7	263 54.4	45.8	99 13.3	50.9	87 01.6	36.2			
D 12	147 23.7	0 18.7	N 4 45.0	278 55.4	S19 46.2	114 15.7	N11 50.9	102 04.0	N14 36.2	Schedar	349 52.4	N56 31.9
A 13	162 26.2	15 22.7	45.3	293 56.4	46.6	129 18.1	50.9	117 06.4	36.2	Shaula	96 36.3	S37 06.2
Y 14	177 28.6	30 26.6	45.6	308 57.4	47.0	144 20.6	50.9	132 08.9	36.2	Sirius	258 43.4	S16 42.8
15	192 31.1	45 30.6 ..	45.9	323 58.4 ..	47.4	159 23.0 ..	50.9	147 11.3 ..	36.2	Spica	158 42.7	S11 09.4
16	207 33.6	60 34.6	46.2	338 59.3	47.8	174 25.4	51.0	162 13.7	36.2	Suhail	223 00.8	S43 25.8
17	222 36.0	75 38.6	46.5	354 00.3	48.2	189 27.8	51.0	177 16.1	36.2			
18	237 38.5	90 42.6	N 4 46.8	9 01.3	S19 48.6	204 30.2	N11 51.0	192 18.5	N14 36.2	Vega	80 45.9	N38 47.3
19	252 41.0	105 46.6	47.1	24 02.3	49.0	219 32.6	51.0	207 20.9	36.2	Zuben'ubi	137 17.4	S16 02.3
20	267 43.4	120 50.6	47.4	39 03.3	49.4	234 35.1	51.0	222 23.4	36.2		SHA	Mer.Pass.
21	282 45.9	135 54.6 ..	47.7	54 04.3 ..	49.8	249 37.5 ..	51.0	237 25.8 ..	36.2		° '	h m
22	297 48.4	150 58.6	48.0	69 05.2	50.2	264 39.9	51.0	252 28.2	36.2	Venus	212 00.1	12 05
23	312 50.8	166 02.6	48.3	84 06.2	50.6	279 42.3	51.0	267 30.6	36.2	Mars	132 24.6	17 26
Mer. Pass.	h m 2 16.0	v 4.0	d 0.3	v 1.0	d 0.4	v 2.4	d 0.0	v 2.4	d 0.0	Jupiter	326 53.9	4 28
										Saturn	314 42.2	5 17

SUN and MOON

UT	SUN GHA	SUN Dec	MOON GHA	v	MOON Dec	d	HP
d h	° ′	° ′	° ′	′	° ′	′	′
17 00	178 56.4	N13 37.8	114 33.5	14.5	S 6 52.5	9.9	55.0
01	193 56.5	37.0	129 06.9	14.5	7 02.4	9.9	55.0
02	208 56.6	36.2	143 40.4	14.5	7 12.3	9.9	55.0
03	223 56.7	.. 35.4	158 13.9	14.4	7 22.2	9.8	54.9
04	238 56.9	34.6	172 47.3	14.5	7 32.0	9.7	54.9
05	253 57.0	33.8	187 20.8	14.5	7 41.7	9.8	54.9
06	268 57.1	N13 33.0	201 54.3	14.4	S 7 51.5	9.6	54.9
07	283 57.3	32.2	216 27.7	14.5	8 01.1	9.7	54.9
08	298 57.4	31.4	231 01.2	14.5	8 10.8	9.6	54.8
09	313 57.5	.. 30.6	245 34.7	14.4	8 20.4	9.5	54.8
10	328 57.7	29.8	260 08.1	14.5	8 29.9	9.6	54.8
11	343 57.8	29.0	274 41.6	14.4	8 39.5	9.4	54.8
12	358 57.9	N13 28.2	289 15.0	14.5	S 8 48.9	9.5	54.8
13	13 58.1	27.4	303 48.5	14.4	8 58.4	9.4	54.7
14	28 58.2	26.6	318 21.9	14.4	9 07.8	9.3	54.7
15	43 58.3	.. 25.8	332 55.3	14.5	9 17.1	9.3	54.7
16	58 58.5	25.0	347 28.8	14.4	9 26.4	9.3	54.7
17	73 58.6	24.2	2 02.2	14.4	9 35.7	9.2	54.7
18	88 58.7	N13 23.4	16 35.6	14.4	S 9 44.9	9.1	54.7
19	103 58.9	22.6	31 09.0	14.4	9 54.0	9.1	54.7
20	118 59.0	21.8	45 42.4	14.4	10 03.1	9.1	54.6
21	133 59.1	.. 21.0	60 15.8	14.4	10 12.2	9.0	54.6
22	148 59.3	20.2	74 49.2	14.3	10 21.2	9.0	54.6
23	163 59.4	19.4	89 22.5	14.4	10 30.2	8.9	54.6
18 00	178 59.5	N13 18.6	103 55.9	14.3	S10 39.1	8.9	54.6
01	193 59.7	17.8	118 29.2	14.3	10 48.0	8.8	54.6
02	208 59.8	17.0	133 02.5	14.3	10 56.8	8.8	54.5
03	223 59.9	.. 16.2	147 35.8	14.3	11 05.6	8.7	54.5
04	239 00.1	15.4	162 09.1	14.3	11 14.3	8.7	54.5
05	254 00.2	14.6	176 42.4	14.3	11 23.0	8.6	54.5
06	269 00.3	N13 13.8	191 15.7	14.3	S11 31.6	8.5	54.5
07	284 00.5	13.0	205 49.0	14.2	11 40.1	8.5	54.5
08	299 00.6	12.2	220 22.2	14.2	11 48.6	8.5	54.5
09	314 00.8	.. 11.4	234 55.4	14.2	11 57.1	8.4	54.5
10	329 00.9	10.6	249 28.6	14.2	12 05.5	8.3	54.5
11	344 01.0	09.8	264 01.8	14.2	12 13.8	8.3	54.4
12	359 01.2	N13 09.0	278 35.0	14.1	S12 22.1	8.3	54.4
13	14 01.3	08.2	293 08.1	14.1	12 30.4	8.1	54.4
14	29 01.4	07.4	307 41.2	14.1	12 38.5	8.2	54.4
15	44 01.6	.. 06.6	322 14.3	14.1	12 46.7	8.0	54.4
16	59 01.7	05.8	336 47.4	14.1	12 54.7	8.0	54.4
17	74 01.9	05.0	351 20.5	14.0	13 02.7	8.0	54.4
18	89 02.0	N13 04.2	5 53.5	14.1	S13 10.7	7.9	54.4
19	104 02.1	03.4	20 26.6	14.0	13 18.6	7.8	54.4
20	119 02.3	02.5	34 59.6	13.9	13 26.4	7.8	54.4
21	134 02.4	.. 01.7	49 32.5	14.0	13 34.2	7.7	54.3
22	149 02.6	00.9	64 05.5	13.9	13 41.9	7.6	54.3
23	164 02.7	13 00.1	78 38.4	13.9	13 49.5	7.6	54.3
19 00	179 02.8	N12 59.3	93 11.3	13.9	S13 57.1	7.6	54.3
01	194 03.0	58.5	107 44.2	13.9	14 04.7	7.4	54.3
02	209 03.1	57.7	122 17.1	13.8	14 12.1	7.4	54.3
03	224 03.3	.. 56.9	136 49.9	13.8	14 19.5	7.4	54.3
04	239 03.4	56.1	151 22.7	13.8	14 26.9	7.3	54.3
05	254 03.5	55.3	165 55.5	13.7	14 34.2	7.2	54.3
06	269 03.7	N12 54.4	180 28.2	13.8	S14 41.4	7.1	54.3
07	284 03.8	53.6	195 01.0	13.7	14 48.5	7.1	54.3
08	299 04.0	52.8	209 33.7	13.6	14 55.6	7.0	54.3
09	314 04.1	.. 52.0	224 06.3	13.7	15 02.6	7.0	54.3
10	329 04.3	51.2	238 39.0	13.6	15 09.6	6.9	54.3
11	344 04.4	50.4	253 11.6	13.6	15 16.5	6.8	54.3
12	359 04.5	N12 49.6	267 44.2	13.5	S15 23.3	6.7	54.3
13	14 04.7	48.8	282 16.7	13.6	15 30.0	6.7	54.2
14	29 04.8	47.9	296 49.3	13.5	15 36.7	6.6	54.2
15	44 05.0	.. 47.1	311 21.8	13.4	15 43.3	6.6	54.3
16	59 05.1	46.3	325 54.2	13.5	15 49.9	6.5	54.2
17	74 05.3	45.5	340 26.7	13.4	15 56.4	6.4	54.2
18	89 05.4	N12 44.7	354 59.1	13.3	S16 02.8	6.3	54.2
19	104 05.6	43.9	9 31.4	13.4	16 09.1	6.3	54.2
20	119 05.7	43.0	24 03.8	13.3	16 15.4	6.2	54.2
21	134 05.8	.. 42.2	38 36.1	13.3	16 21.6	6.1	54.2
22	149 06.0	41.4	53 08.4	13.2	16 27.7	6.1	54.2
23	164 06.1	40.6	67 40.6	13.2	S16 33.8	5.9	54.2
	SD 15.8	d 0.8	SD 14.9		14.8		14.8

Day labels: 17 = TUESDAY, 18 = WEDNESDAY, 19 = THURSDAY

Twilight, Sunrise and Moonrise

Lat.	Twilight Naut.	Twilight Civil	Sunrise	Moonrise 17	18	19	20
°	h m	h m	h m	h m	h m	h m	h m
N 72	////	////	02 41	12 41	14 28	16 24	■■■
N 70	////	////	03 09	12 27	14 03	15 42	17 25
68	//// ·	02 02	03 30	12 15	13 44	15 13	16 41
66	////	02 34	03 46	12 06	13 30	14 52	16 12
64	00 58	02 57	03 59	11 58	13 18	14 35	15 50
62	01 48	03 15	04 11	11 51	13 07	14 22	15 32
60	02 17	03 30	04 20	11 45	12 59	14 10	15 18
N 58	02 39	03 42	04 28	11 40	12 51	14 00	15 06
56	02 56	03 53	04 36	11 36	12 44	13 51	14 55
54	03 10	04 02	04 42	11 32	12 38	13 43	14 46
52	03 22	04 10	04 48	11 28	12 33	13 36	14 37
50	03 33	04 18	04 53	11 25	12 28	13 30	14 30
45	03 54	04 33	05 05	11 18	12 18	13 16	14 14
N 40	04 10	04 45	05 14	11 12	12 09	13 05	14 01
35	04 23	04 55	05 22	11 06	12 02	12 56	13 50
30	04 34	05 04	05 29	11 02	11 55	12 48	13 40
20	04 51	05 18	05 41	10 54	11 44	12 34	13 24
N 10	05 04	05 29	05 51	10 47	11 34	12 21	13 09
0	05 15	05 39	06 01	10 41	11 25	12 10	12 56
S 10	05 24	05 48	06 10	10 35	11 16	11 58	12 42
20	05 31	05 57	06 20	10 28	11 06	11 46	12 28
30	05 39	06 07	06 31	10 21	10 55	11 32	12 12
35	05 42	06 12	06 38	10 16	10 49	11 24	12 02
40	05 45	06 17	06 45	10 11	10 42	11 15	11 51
45	05 49	06 23	06 53	10 06	10 34	11 04	11 39
S 50	05 52	06 30	07 03	09 59	10 24	10 52	11 24
52	05 53	06 33	07 08	09 56	10 19	10 46	11 16
54	05 55	06 36	07 13	09 53	10 14	10 39	11 09
56	05 56	06 40	07 19	09 49	10 09	10 32	11 00
58	05 58	06 44	07 25	09 45	10 03	10 24	10 50
S 60	05 59	06 48	07 32	09 40	09 56	10 15	10 38

Sunset, Twilight and Moonset

Lat.	Sunset	Twilight Civil	Twilight Naut.	Moonset 17	18	19	20
°	h m	h m	h m	h m	h m	h m	h m
N 72	21 22	////	////	20 43	20 28	20 06	■■■
N 70	20 55	22 50	////	20 59	20 54	20 49	20 42
68	20 35	22 00	////	21 12	21 14	21 18	21 26
66	20 19	21 30	////	21 23	21 30	21 40	21 56
64	20 06	21 08	22 59	21 32	21 43	21 57	22 18
62	19 55	20 50	22 15	21 39	21 54	22 12	22 36
60	19 46	20 36	21 47	21 46	22 03	22 24	22 51
N 58	19 38	20 24	21 26	21 52	22 11	22 34	23 03
56	19 31	20 13	21 10	21 57	22 18	22 44	23 14
54	19 24	20 04	20 56	22 02	22 25	22 52	23 24
52	19 19	19 56	20 44	22 06	22 31	22 59	23 32
50	19 14	19 49	20 34	22 10	22 36	23 06	23 40
45	19 02	19 34	20 13	22 18	22 48	23 20	23 57
N 40	18 53	19 22	19 57	22 25	22 57	23 32	24 10
35	18 45	19 12	19 44	22 32	23 05	23 42	24 22
30	18 39	19 04	19 33	22 37	23 13	23 51	24 32
20	18 27	18 50	19 16	22 46	23 25	24 06	00 06
N 10	18 17	18 38	19 04	22 54	23 36	24 19	00 19
0	18 07	18 29	18 53	23 02	23 46	24 32	00 32
S 10	17 58	18 19	18 44	23 10	23 57	24 44	00 44
20	17 48	18 11	18 37	23 18	24 08	00 08	00 58
30	17 37	18 02	18 30	23 28	24 21	00 21	01 13
35	17 31	17 57	18 26	23 33	24 28	00 28	01 22
40	17 23	17 51	18 23	23 39	24 36	00 36	01 32
45	17 15	17 45	18 20	23 47	24 46	00 46	01 44
S 50	17 05	17 39	18 17	23 55	24 58	00 58	01 59
52	17 00	17 36	18 15	23 59	25 03	01 03	02 06
54	16 55	17 32	18 14	24 04	00 04	01 10	02 13
56	16 50	17 29	18 12	24 09	00 09	01 16	02 22
58	16 43	17 25	18 11	24 14	00 14	01 24	02 31
S 60	16 36	17 21	18 10	24 20	00 20	01 33	02 43

SUN and MOON

Day	SUN Eqn. of Time 00h	12h	Mer. Pass.	MOON Mer. Pass. Upper	Lower	Age	Phase
d	m s	m s	h m	h m	h m	d %	
17	04 15	04 09	12 04	16 52	04 30	06 35	
18	04 02	03 56	12 04	17 36	05 14	07 45	◗
19	03 49	03 42	12 04	18 21	05 58	08 54	

UT	ARIES GHA	VENUS −4.0 GHA	Dec	MARS +0.2 GHA	Dec	JUPITER −2.6 GHA	Dec	SATURN +0.2 GHA	Dec	STARS Name	SHA	Dec
20 00	327 53.3	181 06.6 N 4	48.6	99 07.2 S19	51.0	294 44.7 N11	51.0	282 33.0 N14	36.2	Acamar	315 26.4	S40 18.2
01	342 55.7	196 10.5	48.9	114 08.2	51.4	309 47.2	51.0	297 35.4	36.2	Achernar	335 34.5	S57 14.1
02	357 58.2	211 14.5	49.2	129 09.2	51.8	324 49.6	51.0	312 37.9	36.2	Acrux	173 21.8	S63 05.9
03	13 00.7	226 18.5 ..	49.5	144 10.1 ..	52.2	339 52.0 ..	51.0	327 40.3 ..	36.2	Adhara	255 21.2	S28 58.2
04	28 03.1	241 22.5	49.8	159 11.1	52.6	354 54.4	51.0	342 42.7	36.2	Aldebaran	291 01.8	N16 30.4
05	43 05.6	256 26.5	50.1	174 12.1	53.0	9 56.8	51.0	357 45.1	36.3			
06	58 08.1	271 30.5 N 4	50.5	189 13.1 S19	53.4	24 59.3 N11	51.0	12 47.5 N14	36.3	Alioth	166 30.5	N55 58.1
07	73 10.5	286 34.5	50.8	204 14.0	53.8	40 01.7	51.0	27 50.0	36.3	Alkaid	153 07.6	N49 19.3
08	88 13.0	301 38.5	51.1	219 15.0	54.1	55 04.1	51.0	42 52.4	36.3	Al Na'ir	27 56.7	S46 57.7
F 09	103 15.5	316 42.5 ..	51.4	234 16.0 ..	54.5	70 06.5 ..	51.0	57 54.8 ..	36.3	Alnilam	275 57.4	S 1 12.1
R 10	118 17.9	331 46.4	51.7	249 17.0	54.9	85 09.0	51.0	72 57.2	36.3	Alphard	218 06.9	S 8 39.3
I 11	133 20.4	346 50.4	52.0	264 17.9	55.3	100 11.4	51.0	87 59.6	36.3			
D 12	148 22.8	1 54.4 N 4	52.4	279 18.9 S19	55.7	115 13.8 N11	51.0	103 02.0 N14	36.3	Alphecca	126 20.1	N26 43.3
A 13	163 25.3	16 58.4	52.7	294 19.9	56.1	130 16.2	51.0	118 04.5	36.3	Alpheratz	357 54.3	N29 05.2
Y 14	178 27.8	32 02.4	53.0	309 20.9	56.5	145 18.7	51.1	133 06.9	36.3	Altair	62 18.4	N 8 52.2
15	193 30.2	47 06.4 ..	53.3	324 21.8 ..	56.9	160 21.1 ..	51.1	148 09.3 ..	36.3	Ankaa	353 25.9	S42 18.4
16	208 32.7	62 10.4	53.6	339 22.8	57.3	175 23.5	51.1	163 11.7	36.3	Antares	112 39.4	S26 25.8
17	223 35.2	77 14.3	54.0	354 23.8	57.7	190 25.9	51.1	178 14.1	36.3			
18	238 37.6	92 18.3 N 4	54.3	9 24.8 S19	58.1	205 28.4 N11	51.1	193 16.6 N14	36.3	Arcturus	146 05.7	N19 11.4
19	253 40.1	107 22.3	54.6	24 25.7	58.5	220 30.8	51.1	208 19.0	36.3	Atria	107 50.7	S69 01.8
20	268 42.6	122 26.3	55.0	39 26.7	58.9	235 33.2	51.1	223 21.4	36.3	Avior	234 23.0	S59 30.4
21	283 45.0	137 30.3 ..	55.3	54 27.7 ..	59.3	250 35.6 ..	51.1	238 23.8 ..	36.3	Bellatrix	278 43.7	N 6 20.9
22	298 47.5	152 34.3	55.6	69 28.6 19	59.7	265 38.1	51.1	253 26.3	36.3	Betelgeuse	271 13.1	N 7 24.4
23	313 50.0	167 38.2	56.0	84 29.6 20	00.1	280 40.5	51.1	268 28.7	36.3			
21 00	328 52.4	182 42.2 N 4	56.3	99 30.6 S20	00.5	295 42.9 N11	51.1	283 31.1 N14	36.3	Canopus	264 01.2	S52 41.6
01	343 54.9	197 46.2	56.6	114 31.5	00.8	310 45.4	51.1	298 33.5	36.3	Capella	280 50.5	N45 59.6
02	358 57.3	212 50.2	57.0	129 32.5	01.2	325 47.8	51.1	313 35.9	36.3	Deneb	49 38.3	N45 16.9
03	13 59.8	227 54.2 ..	57.3	144 33.5 ..	01.6	340 50.2 ..	51.1	328 38.4 ..	36.3	Denebola	182 44.9	N14 34.7
04	29 02.3	242 58.1	57.6	159 34.4	02.0	355 52.6	51.1	343 40.8	36.3	Diphda	349 06.4	S17 59.2
05	44 04.7	258 02.1	58.0	174 35.4	02.4	10 55.1	51.1	358 43.2	36.3			
06	59 07.2	273 06.1 N 4	58.3	189 36.4 S20	02.8	25 57.5 N11	51.1	13 45.6 N14	36.3	Dubhe	194 05.4	N61 45.4
07	74 09.7	288 10.1	58.7	204 37.3	03.2	40 59.9	51.1	28 48.1	36.3	Elnath	278 26.3	N28 36.3
S 08	89 12.1	303 14.1	59.0	219 38.3	03.6	56 02.4	51.1	43 50.5	36.3	Eltanin	90 50.8	N51 29.7
A 09	104 14.6	318 18.0 ..	59.4	234 39.3 ..	04.0	71 04.8 ..	51.1	58 52.9 ..	36.3	Enif	33 57.3	N 9 52.5
T 10	119 17.1	333 22.0 4	59.7	249 40.2	04.4	86 07.2	51.1	73 55.3	36.3	Fomalhaut	15 35.4	S29 37.4
U 11	134 19.5	348 26.0 5	00.1	264 41.2	04.8	101 09.7	51.1	88 57.7	36.3			
R 12	149 22.0	3 30.0 N 5	00.4	279 42.1 S20	05.2	116 12.1 N11	51.1	104 00.2 N14	36.3	Gacrux	172 13.3	S57 06.7
D 13	164 24.5	18 33.9	00.8	294 43.1	05.5	131 14.5	51.1	119 02.6	36.3	Gienah	176 03.6	S17 32.3
A 14	179 26.9	33 37.9	01.1	309 44.1	05.9	146 16.9	51.1	134 05.0	36.3	Hadar	149 03.4	S60 22.3
Y 15	194 29.4	48 41.9 ..	01.5	324 45.0 ..	06.3	161 19.4 ..	51.1	149 07.4 ..	36.3	Hamal	328 12.7	N23 27.5
16	209 31.8	63 45.8	01.8	339 46.0	06.7	176 21.8	51.1	164 09.9	36.3	Kaus Aust.	83 57.8	S34 23.0
17	224 34.3	78 49.8	02.2	354 47.0	07.1	191 24.2	51.1	179 12.3	36.3			
18	239 36.8	93 53.8 N 5	02.5	9 47.9 S20	07.5	206 26.7 N11	51.1	194 14.7 N14	36.3	Kochab	137 19.9	N74 09.9
19	254 39.2	108 57.7	02.9	24 48.9	07.9	221 29.1	51.1	209 17.1	36.3	Markab	13 48.7	N15 12.2
20	269 41.7	124 01.7	03.2	39 49.8	08.3	236 31.6	51.1	224 19.6	36.3	Menkar	314 26.2	N 4 05.3
21	284 44.2	139 05.7 ..	03.6	54 50.8 ..	08.7	251 34.0 ..	51.1	239 22.0 ..	36.3	Menkent	148 20.4	S36 22.1
22	299 46.6	154 09.6	04.0	69 51.7	09.1	266 36.4	51.1	254 24.4	36.3	Miaplacidus	221 42.8	S69 42.9
23	314 49.1	169 13.6	04.3	84 52.7	09.5	281 38.9	51.1	269 26.8	36.3			
22 00	329 51.6	184 17.6 N 5	04.7	99 53.7 S20	09.8	296 41.3 N11	51.1	284 29.3 N14	36.3	Mirfak	308 55.7	N49 51.3
01	344 54.0	199 21.5	05.1	114 54.6	10.2	311 43.7	51.1	299 31.7	36.3	Nunki	76 11.3	S26 17.7
02	359 56.5	214 25.5	05.4	129 55.6	10.6	326 46.2	51.1	314 34.1	36.3	Peacock	53 35.5	S56 44.2
03	14 59.0	229 29.5 ..	05.8	144 56.5 ..	11.0	341 48.6 ..	51.1	329 36.5 ..	36.3	Pollux	243 41.2	N28 01.6
04	30 01.4	244 33.4	06.2	159 57.5	11.4	356 51.0	51.1	344 39.0	36.3	Procyon	245 11.2	N 5 13.6
05	45 03.9	259 37.4	06.5	174 58.4	11.8	11 53.5	51.1	359 41.4	36.3			
06	60 06.3	274 41.3 N 5	06.9	189 59.4 S20	12.2	26 55.9 N11	51.1	14 43.8 N14	36.3	Rasalhague	96 16.3	N12 33.9
07	75 08.8	289 45.3	07.3	205 00.3	12.6	41 58.4	51.1	29 46.3	36.3	Regulus	207 55.2	N11 58.3
08	90 11.3	304 49.2	07.6	220 01.3	13.0	57 00.8	51.1	44 48.7	36.3	Rigel	281 22.5	S 8 12.1
S 09	105 13.7	319 53.2 ..	08.0	235 02.2 ..	13.4	72 03.2 ..	51.1	59 51.1 ..	36.3	Rigil Kent.	140 06.7	S60 50.1
U 10	120 16.2	334 57.1	08.4	250 03.2	13.7	87 05.7	51.1	74 53.5	36.3	Sabik	102 24.7	S15 43.3
N 11	135 18.7	350 01.1	08.8	265 04.1	14.1	102 08.1	51.1	89 56.0	36.3			
D 12	150 21.1	5 05.0 N 5	09.1	280 05.1 S20	14.5	117 10.5 N11	51.1	104 58.4 N14	36.3	Schedar	349 52.3	N56 31.9
A 13	165 23.6	20 09.0	09.5	295 06.0	14.9	132 13.0	51.1	120 00.8	36.3	Shaula	96 36.3	S37 06.2
Y 14	180 26.1	35 12.9	09.9	310 07.0	15.3	147 15.4	51.1	135 03.2	36.3	Sirius	258 43.4	S16 42.8
15	195 28.5	50 16.9 ..	10.3	325 07.9 ..	15.7	162 17.9 ..	51.1	150 05.7 ..	36.3	Spica	158 42.7	S11 09.4
16	210 31.0	65 20.8	10.7	340 08.9	16.1	177 20.3	51.1	165 08.1	36.3	Suhail	223 00.8	S43 25.8
17	225 33.4	80 24.8	11.0	355 09.8	16.5	192 22.8	51.1	180 10.5	36.3			
18	240 35.9	95 28.7 N 5	11.4	10 10.8 S20	16.8	207 25.2 N11	51.1	195 13.0 N14	36.3	Vega	80 45.9	N38 47.3
19	255 38.4	110 32.7	11.8	25 11.7	17.2	222 27.6	51.1	210 15.4	36.3	Zuben'ubi	137 17.4	S16 02.3
20	270 40.8	125 36.6	12.2	40 12.7	17.6	237 30.1	51.1	225 17.8	36.3		SHA	Mer. Pass.
21	285 43.3	140 40.6 ..	12.6	55 13.6 ..	18.0	252 32.5 ..	51.1	240 20.3 ..	36.3			h m
22	300 45.8	155 44.5	13.0	70 14.6	18.4	267 35.0	51.1	255 22.7	36.3	Venus	213 49.8	11 46
23	315 48.2	170 48.4	13.3	85 15.5	18.8	282 37.4	51.1	270 25.1	36.3	Mars	130 38.2	17 21
	h m									Jupiter	326 50.5	4 16
Mer. Pass. 2 04.2	v 4.0 d 0.3	v 1.0	d 0.4	v 2.4	d 0.0	v 2.4	d 0.0			Saturn	314 38.7	5 05

UT	SUN GHA	SUN Dec	MOON GHA	MOON v	MOON Dec	MOON d	MOON HP
d h	° ′	° ′	° ′	′	° ′	′	′
20 00	179 06.3	N12 39.8	82 12.8 13.2		S16 39.7	6.0	54.2
01	194 06.4	39.0	96 45.0 13.2		16 45.7	5.8	54.2
02	209 06.6	38.1	111 17.2 13.1		16 51.5	5.8	54.2
03	224 06.7	.. 37.3	125 49.3 13.1		16 57.3	5.6	54.2
04	239 06.9	36.5	140 21.4 13.0		17 02.9	5.7	54.2
05	254 07.0	35.7	154 53.4 13.0		17 08.6	5.5	54.2
06	269 07.1	N12 34.9	169 25.4 13.0		S17 14.1	5.4	54.2
07	284 07.3	34.0	183 57.4 13.0		17 19.5	5.4	54.2
08	299 07.4	33.2	198 29.4 12.9		17 24.9	5.3	54.3
F 09	314 07.6	.. 32.4	213 01.3 12.9		17 30.2	5.3	54.3
R 10	329 07.7	31.6	227 33.2 12.8		17 35.5	5.1	54.3
I 11	344 07.9	30.7	242 05.0 12.8		17 40.6	5.1	54.3
D 12	359 08.0	N12 29.9	256 36.8 12.8		S17 45.7	5.0	54.3
A 13	14 08.2	29.1	271 08.6 12.8		17 50.7	4.9	54.3
Y 14	29 08.3	28.3	285 40.4 12.7		17 55.6	4.9	54.3
15	44 08.5	.. 27.5	300 12.1 12.7		18 00.5	4.7	54.3
16	59 08.6	26.6	314 43.8 12.6		18 05.2	4.7	54.3
17	74 08.8	25.8	329 15.4 12.6		18 09.9	4.6	54.3
18	89 08.9	N12 25.0	343 47.0 12.6		S18 14.5	4.5	54.3
19	104 09.1	24.2	358 18.6 12.5		18 19.0	4.4	54.3
20	119 09.2	23.3	12 50.1 12.5		18 23.4	4.4	54.2
21	134 09.4	.. 22.5	27 21.6 12.5		18 27.8	4.3	54.3
22	149 09.5	21.7	41 53.1 12.4		18 32.1	4.1	54.3
23	164 09.7	20.9	56 24.5 12.4		18 36.2	4.1	54.3
21 00	179 09.8	N12 20.0	70 55.9 12.4		S18 40.3	4.1	54.3
01	194 10.0	19.2	85 27.3 12.3		18 44.4	3.9	54.3
02	209 10.1	18.4	99 58.6 12.3		18 48.3	3.8	54.3
03	224 10.3	.. 17.6	114 29.9 12.3		18 52.1	3.8	54.4
04	239 10.4	16.7	129 01.2 12.2		18 55.9	3.7	54.4
05	254 10.6	15.9	143 32.4 12.2		18 59.6	3.6	54.4
06	269 10.7	N12 15.1	158 03.6 12.2		S19 03.2	3.5	54.4
S 07	284 10.9	14.2	172 34.8 12.1		19 06.7	3.4	54.4
A 08	299 11.0	13.4	187 05.9 12.1		19 10.1	3.3	54.4
T 09	314 11.2	.. 12.6	201 37.0 12.0		19 13.4	3.3	54.4
U 10	329 11.3	11.8	216 08.0 12.0		19 16.7	3.1	54.4
R 11	344 11.5	10.9	230 39.0 12.0		19 19.8	3.1	54.4
D 12	359 11.7	N12 10.1	245 10.0 12.0		S19 22.9	3.0	54.4
A 13	14 11.8	09.3	259 41.0 11.9		19 25.9	2.9	54.4
Y 14	29 12.0	08.4	274 11.9 11.9		19 28.8	2.8	54.5
15	44 12.1	.. 07.6	288 42.8 11.8		19 31.6	2.7	54.5
16	59 12.3	06.8	303 13.6 11.9		19 34.3	2.6	54.5
17	74 12.4	05.9	317 44.5 11.8		19 36.9	2.5	54.5
18	89 12.6	N12 05.1	332 15.3 11.7		S19 39.4	2.4	54.5
19	104 12.7	04.3	346 46.0 11.7		19 41.8	2.4	54.5
20	119 12.9	03.4	1 16.7 11.7		19 44.2	2.2	54.5
21	134 13.0	.. 02.6	15 47.4 11.7		19 46.4	2.2	54.5
22	149 13.2	01.8	30 18.1 11.6		19 48.6	2.1	54.5
23	164 13.4	00.9	44 48.7 11.6		19 50.7	1.9	54.6
22 00	179 13.5	N12 00.1	59 19.3 11.6		S19 52.6	1.9	54.6
01	194 13.7	11 59.3	73 49.9 11.5		19 54.5	1.8	54.6
02	209 13.8	58.4	88 20.4 11.5		19 56.3	1.7	54.6
03	224 14.0	.. 57.6	102 50.9 11.5		19 58.0	1.6	54.6
04	239 14.1	56.8	117 21.4 11.4		19 59.6	1.5	54.6
05	254 14.3	55.9	131 51.8 11.4		20 01.1	1.4	54.6
06	269 14.5	N11 55.1	146 22.2 11.4		S20 02.5	1.3	54.7
07	284 14.6	54.3	160 52.6 11.4		20 03.8	1.2	54.7
08	299 14.8	53.4	175 23.0 11.3		20 05.0	1.1	54.7
S 09	314 14.9	.. 52.6	189 53.3 11.3		20 06.1	1.1	54.7
U 10	329 15.1	51.7	204 23.6 11.3		20 07.2	0.9	54.7
N 11	344 15.2	50.9	218 53.9 11.2		20 08.1	0.8	54.7
D 12	359 15.4	N11 50.1	233 24.1 11.3		S20 08.9	0.7	54.8
A 13	14 15.6	49.2	247 54.4 11.2		20 09.6	0.7	54.8
Y 14	29 15.7	48.4	262 24.6 11.1		20 10.3	0.5	54.8
15	44 15.9	.. 47.5	276 54.7 11.2		20 10.8	0.4	54.8
16	59 16.0	46.7	291 24.9 11.1		20 11.2	0.4	54.8
17	74 16.2	45.9	305 55.0 11.1		20 11.6	0.2	54.8
18	89 16.4	N11 45.0	320 25.1 11.0		S20 11.8	0.2	54.9
19	104 16.5	44.2	334 55.1 11.1		20 12.0	0.0	54.9
20	119 16.7	43.3	349 25.2 11.0		20 12.0	0.2	54.9
21	134 16.8	.. 42.5	3 55.2 11.0		20 12.0	0.2	54.9
22	149 17.0	41.7	18 25.2 10.9		20 11.8	0.3	54.9
23	164 17.2	40.8	32 55.1 11.0		S20 11.5	0.3	54.9
	SD 15.8	d 0.8	SD 14.8	14.8			14.9

Lat.	Twilight Naut.	Twilight Civil	Sunrise	Moonrise 20	Moonrise 21	Moonrise 22	Moonrise 23
°	h m	h m	h m	h m	h m	h m	h m
N 72	////	////	02 59	■■	■■	■■	■■
N 70	////	01 40	03 24	17 25	19 20	■■	20 57
68	////	02 21	03 42	16 41	18 02	19 06	19 43
66	////	02 48	03 57	16 12	17 24	18 24	19 06
64	01 28	03 09	04 09	15 50	16 58	17 55	18 39
62	02 04	03 25	04 19	15 32	16 38	17 34	18 19
60	02 30	03 38	04 27	15 18	16 21	17 16	18 02
N 58	02 49	03 50	04 35	15 06	16 07	17 02	17 48
56	03 04	04 00	04 42	14 55	15 55	16 49	17 36
54	03 18	04 08	04 48	14 46	15 44	16 38	17 25
52	03 29	04 16	04 53	14 37	15 35	16 28	17 16
50	03 39	04 23	04 58	14 30	15 27	16 20	17 07
45	03 58	04 37	05 08	14 14	15 09	16 01	16 49
N 40	04 14	04 48	05 17	14 01	14 55	15 46	16 35
35	04 26	04 58	05 24	13 50	14 43	15 34	16 22
30	04 36	05 06	05 30	13 40	14 32	15 23	16 12
20	04 52	05 19	05 42	13 24	14 14	15 04	15 53
N 10	05 04	05 29	05 51	13 09	13 58	14 47	15 37
0	05 14	05 39	06 00	12 56	13 43	14 32	15 22
S 10	05 22	05 47	06 09	12 42	13 28	14 16	15 07
20	05 29	05 55	06 18	12 28	13 13	14 00	14 50
30	05 36	06 04	06 28	12 12	12 55	13 41	14 32
35	05 39	06 08	06 34	12 02	12 44	13 30	14 21
40	05 41	06 13	06 41	11 51	12 32	13 18	14 09
45	05 44	06 18	06 48	11 39	12 18	13 03	13 54
S 50	05 47	06 24	06 58	11 24	12 01	12 45	13 36
52	05 48	06 27	07 02	11 16	11 53	12 36	13 28
54	05 49	06 30	07 07	11 09	11 44	12 27	13 18
56	05 50	06 33	07 12	11 00	11 34	12 16	13 07
58	05 51	06 37	07 18	10 50	11 22	12 04	12 55
S 60	05 52	06 41	07 24	10 38	11 09	11 49	12 41

Lat.	Sunset	Twilight Civil	Twilight Naut.	Moonset 20	Moonset 21	Moonset 22	Moonset 23
°	h m	h m	h m	h m	h m	h m	h m
N 72	21 02	////	////	■■	■■	■■	■■
N 70	20 39	22 19	////	20 42	20 25	■■	22 15
68	20 22	21 41	////	21 26	21 44	22 22	23 29
66	20 07	21 15	////	21 56	22 22	23 04	24 06
64	19 56	20 55	22 32	22 18	22 48	23 32	24 32
62	19 46	20 39	21 58	22 36	23 09	23 54	24 52
60	19 37	20 26	21 34	22 51	23 26	24 11	00 11
N 58	19 30	20 15	21 15	23 03	23 40	24 26	00 26
56	19 24	20 05	21 00	23 14	23 52	24 39	00 39
54	19 18	19 57	20 47	23 24	24 03	00 03	00 50
52	19 12	19 49	20 36	23 32	24 12	00 12	00 59
50	19 08	19 43	20 26	23 40	24 21	00 21	01 08
45	18 57	19 29	20 07	23 57	24 38	00 38	01 26
N 40	18 49	19 18	19 52	24 10	00 10	00 53	01 41
35	18 42	19 08	19 40	24 22	00 22	01 06	01 54
30	18 36	19 00	19 30	24 32	00 32	01 16	02 05
20	18 25	18 47	19 14	00 06	00 49	01 35	02 24
N 10	18 15	18 37	19 02	00 19	01 04	01 51	02 40
0	18 07	18 28	18 52	00 32	01 18	02 06	02 56
S 10	17 58	18 19	18 44	00 44	01 33	02 22	03 11
20	17 49	18 11	18 37	00 58	01 48	02 38	03 28
30	17 39	18 03	18 31	01 13	02 05	02 56	03 46
35	17 33	17 59	18 28	01 22	02 15	03 07	03 57
40	17 26	17 54	18 26	01 32	02 27	03 20	04 10
45	17 19	17 49	18 23	01 44	02 41	03 34	04 25
S 50	17 09	17 43	18 21	01 59	02 57	03 52	04 43
52	17 05	17 40	18 20	02 06	03 05	04 01	04 51
54	17 01	17 37	18 19	02 13	03 14	04 10	05 01
56	16 55	17 34	18 18	02 22	03 24	04 21	05 11
58	16 50	17 31	18 17	02 31	03 35	04 33	05 24
S 60	16 43	17 27	18 16	02 43	03 48	04 48	05 38

Day	SUN Eqn. of Time 00h	SUN Eqn. of Time 12h	SUN Mer. Pass.	MOON Mer. Pass. Upper	MOON Mer. Pass. Lower	Age	Phase
d	m s	m s	h m	h m	h m	d	%
20	03 35	03 28	12 03	19 07	06 44	09	64
21	03 21	03 14	12 03	19 55	07 31	10	72
22	03 06	02 59	12 03	20 44	08 19	11	81

UT (d h)	ARIES GHA	VENUS −4.1 GHA	Dec	MARS +0.3 GHA	Dec	JUPITER −2.6 GHA	Dec	SATURN +0.2 GHA	Dec	STARS Name	SHA	Dec
23 00	330 50.7	185 52.4	N 5 13.7	100 16.5	S20 19.2	297 39.9	N11 51.1	285 27.5	N14 36.3	Acamar	315 26.4	S40 18.2
01	345 53.2	200 56.3	14.1	115 17.4	19.6	312 42.3	51.0	300 30.0	36.3	Achernar	335 34.4	S57 14.1
02	0 55.6	216 00.2	14.5	130 18.3	19.9	327 44.7	51.0	315 32.4	36.3	Acrux	173 21.8	S63 05.9
03	15 58.1	231 04.2 ..	14.9	145 19.3 ..	20.3	342 47.2 ..	51.0	330 34.8 ..	36.3	Adhara	255 21.2	S28 58.2
04	31 00.6	246 08.1	15.3	160 20.2	20.7	357 49.6	51.0	345 37.3	36.3	Aldebaran	291 01.7	N16 30.4
05	46 03.0	261 12.0	15.7	175 21.2	21.1	12 52.1	51.0	0 39.7	36.3			
06	61 05.5	276 15.9	N 5 16.1	190 22.1	S20 21.5	27 54.5	N11 51.0	15 42.1	N14 36.3	Alioth	166 30.5	N55 58.1
07	76 07.9	291 19.9	16.5	205 23.1	21.9	42 57.0	51.0	30 44.6	36.3	Alkaid	153 07.6	N49 19.3
08	91 10.4	306 23.8	16.9	220 24.0	22.3	57 59.4	51.0	45 47.0	36.3	Al Na'ir	27 56.7	S46 57.7
M 09	106 12.9	321 27.7 ..	17.3	235 24.9 ..	22.6	73 01.9 ..	51.0	60 49.4 ..	36.3	Alnilam	275 57.4	S 1 12.1
O 10	121 15.3	336 31.6	17.7	250 25.9	23.0	88 04.3	51.0	75 51.9	36.3	Alphard	218 06.9	S 8 39.3
N 11	136 17.8	351 35.6	18.1	265 26.8	23.4	103 06.8	51.0	90 54.3	36.3			
D 12	151 20.3	6 39.5	N 5 18.5	280 27.8	S20 23.8	118 09.2	N11 51.0	105 56.7	N14 36.3	Alphecca	126 20.1	N26 43.3
A 13	166 22.7	21 43.4	18.9	295 28.7	24.2	133 11.7	51.0	120 59.2	36.3	Alpheratz	357 54.3	N29 05.2
Y 14	181 25.2	36 47.3	19.3	310 29.6	24.6	148 14.1	51.0	136 01.6	36.3	Altair	62 18.4	N 8 52.2
15	196 27.7	51 51.2 ..	19.7	325 30.6 ..	25.0	163 16.6 ..	51.0	151 04.0 ..	36.3	Ankaa	353 25.9	S42 18.4
16	211 30.1	66 55.1	20.1	340 31.5	25.3	178 19.0	51.0	166 06.5	36.3	Antares	112 39.4	S26 25.8
17	226 32.6	81 59.1	20.5	355 32.4	25.7	193 21.4	51.0	181 08.9	36.3			
18	241 35.1	97 03.0	N 5 20.9	10 33.4	S20 26.1	208 23.9	N11 51.0	196 11.3	N14 36.3	Arcturus	146 05.7	N19 11.4
19	256 37.5	112 06.9	21.3	25 34.3	26.5	223 26.3	51.0	211 13.8	36.3	Atria	107 50.7	S69 01.8
20	271 40.0	127 10.8	21.7	40 35.2	26.9	238 28.8	51.0	226 16.2	36.3	Avior	234 22.9	S59 30.4
21	286 42.4	142 14.7 ..	22.1	55 36.2 ..	27.3	253 31.3 ..	51.0	241 18.6 ..	36.3	Bellatrix	278 43.6	N 6 20.9
22	301 44.9	157 18.6	22.5	70 37.1	27.6	268 33.7	51.0	256 21.1	36.3	Betelgeuse	271 13.1	N 7 24.4
23	316 47.4	172 22.5	22.9	85 38.0	28.0	283 36.2	50.9	271 23.5	36.3			
24 00	331 49.8	187 26.4	N 5 23.4	100 39.0	S20 28.4	298 38.6	N11 50.9	286 25.9	N14 36.3	Canopus	264 01.2	S52 41.5
01	346 52.3	202 30.3	23.8	115 39.9	28.8	313 41.1	50.9	301 28.4	36.3	Capella	280 50.5	N45 59.6
02	1 54.8	217 34.2	24.2	130 40.8	29.2	328 43.5	50.9	316 30.8	36.3	Deneb	49 38.3	N45 16.9
03	16 57.2	232 38.1 ..	24.6	145 41.8 ..	29.6	343 46.0 ..	50.9	331 33.2 ..	36.3	Denebola	182 44.9	N14 34.7
04	31 59.7	247 42.0	25.0	160 42.7	29.9	358 48.4	50.9	346 35.7	36.3	Diphda	349 06.4	S17 59.2
05	47 02.2	262 45.9	25.4	175 43.6	30.3	13 50.9	50.9	1 38.1	36.3			
06	62 04.6	277 49.7	N 5 25.9	190 44.6	S20 30.7	28 53.3	N11 50.9	16 40.5	N14 36.3	Dubhe	194 05.4	N61 45.4
07	77 07.1	292 53.6	26.3	205 45.5	31.1	43 55.8	50.9	31 43.0	36.3	Elnath	278 26.3	N28 36.3
T 08	92 09.5	307 57.5	26.7	220 46.4	31.5	58 58.2	50.9	46 45.4	36.3	Eltanin	90 50.9	N51 29.7
U 09	107 12.0	323 01.4 ..	27.1	235 47.4 ..	31.8	74 00.7 ..	50.9	61 47.8 ..	36.3	Enif	33 57.3	N 9 52.5
E 10	122 14.5	338 05.3	27.5	250 48.3	32.2	89 03.1	50.9	76 50.3	36.3	Fomalhaut	15 35.4	S29 37.4
S 11	137 16.9	353 09.2	28.0	265 49.2	32.6	104 05.6	50.9	91 52.7	36.3			
D 12	152 19.4	8 13.0	N 5 28.4	280 50.1	S20 33.0	119 08.1	N11 50.9	106 55.2	N14 36.3	Gacrux	172 13.3	S57 06.7
A 13	167 21.9	23 16.9	28.8	295 51.1	33.4	134 10.5	50.9	121 57.6	36.3	Gienah	176 03.6	S17 32.3
Y 14	182 24.3	38 20.8	29.2	310 52.0	33.8	149 13.0	50.8	137 00.0	36.3	Hadar	149 03.4	S60 22.3
15	197 26.8	53 24.7 ..	29.6	325 52.9 ..	34.2	164 15.4 ..	50.8	152 02.5 ..	36.3	Hamal	328 12.7	N23 27.5
16	212 29.3	68 28.5	30.1	340 53.8	34.5	179 17.9	50.8	167 04.9	36.3	Kaus Aust.	83 57.8	S34 23.0
17	227 31.7	83 32.4	30.5	355 54.8	34.9	194 20.3	50.8	182 07.3	36.3			
18	242 34.2	98 36.3	N 5 30.9	10 55.7	S20 35.3	209 22.8	N11 50.8	197 09.8	N14 36.3	Kochab	137 20.0	N74 09.9
19	257 36.7	113 40.1	31.4	25 56.6	35.7	224 25.3	50.8	212 12.2	36.3	Markab	13 48.7	N15 12.2
20	272 39.1	128 44.0	31.8	40 57.5	36.1	239 27.7	50.8	227 14.7	36.3	Menkar	314 26.2	N 4 05.3
21	287 41.6	143 47.9 ..	32.2	55 58.5 ..	36.4	254 30.2 ..	50.8	242 17.1 ..	36.2	Menkent	148 20.4	S36 22.0
22	302 44.0	158 51.7	32.6	70 59.4	36.8	269 32.6	50.8	257 19.5	36.2	Miaplacidus	221 42.8	S69 42.9
23	317 46.5	173 55.6	33.1	86 00.3	37.2	284 35.1	50.8	272 22.0	36.2			
25 00	332 49.0	188 59.4	N 5 33.5	101 01.2	S20 37.6	299 37.5	N11 50.8	287 24.4	N14 36.2	Mirfak	308 55.7	N49 51.3
01	347 51.4	204 03.3	33.9	116 02.1	38.0	314 40.0	50.8	302 26.8	36.2	Nunki	76 11.3	S26 17.7
02	2 53.9	219 07.1	34.4	131 03.1	38.3	329 42.5	50.7	317 29.3	36.2	Peacock	53 35.5	S56 44.2
03	17 56.4	234 11.0 ..	34.8	146 04.0 ..	38.7	344 44.9 ..	50.7	332 31.7 ..	36.2	Pollux	243 41.1	N28 01.6
04	32 58.8	249 14.8	35.2	161 04.9	39.1	359 47.4	50.7	347 34.2	36.2	Procyon	245 11.2	N 5 13.6
05	48 01.3	264 18.7	35.7	176 05.8	39.5	14 49.9	50.7	2 36.6	36.2			
06	63 03.8	279 22.5	N 5 36.1	191 06.7	S20 39.9	29 52.3	N11 50.7	17 39.0	N14 36.2	Rasalhague	96 16.3	N12 33.9
W 07	78 06.2	294 26.3	36.5	206 07.7	40.2	44 54.8	50.7	32 41.5	36.2	Regulus	207 55.2	N11 58.3
E 08	93 08.7	309 30.2	37.0	221 08.6	40.6	59 57.2	50.7	47 43.9	36.2	Rigel	281 22.5	S 8 12.1
D 09	108 11.2	324 34.0 ..	37.4	236 09.5 ..	41.0	74 59.7 ..	50.7	62 46.4 ..	36.2	Rigil Kent.	140 06.7	S60 50.1
N 10	123 13.6	339 37.9	37.9	251 10.4	41.4	90 02.2	50.7	77 48.8	36.2	Sabik	102 24.7	S15 43.3
E 11	138 16.1	354 41.7	38.3	266 11.3	41.8	105 04.6	50.7	92 51.3	36.2			
S 12	153 18.5	9 45.5	N 5 38.7	281 12.2	S20 42.1	120 07.1	N11 50.6	107 53.7	N14 36.2	Schedar	349 52.3	N56 31.9
D 13	168 21.0	24 49.3	39.2	296 13.2	42.5	135 09.6	50.6	122 56.1	36.2	Shaula	96 36.3	S37 06.2
A 14	183 23.5	39 53.2	39.6	311 14.1	42.9	150 12.0	50.6	137 58.6	36.2	Sirius	258 43.4	S16 42.8
Y 15	198 25.9	54 57.0 ..	40.1	326 15.0 ..	43.3	165 14.5 ..	50.6	153 01.0 ..	36.2	Spica	158 42.8	S11 09.4
16	213 28.4	70 00.8	40.5	341 15.9	43.6	180 17.0	50.6	168 03.5	36.2	Suhail	223 00.7	S43 25.7
17	228 30.9	85 04.6	41.0	356 16.8	44.0	195 19.4	50.6	183 05.9	36.2			
18	243 33.3	100 08.4	N 5 41.4	11 17.7	S20 44.4	210 21.9	N11 50.6	198 08.3	N14 36.2	Vega	80 45.9	N38 47.3
19	258 35.8	115 12.2	41.9	26 18.6	44.8	225 24.3	50.6	213 10.8	36.2	Zuben'ubi	137 17.4	S16 02.3
20	273 38.3	130 16.1	42.3	41 19.6	45.2	240 26.8	50.6	228 13.2	36.2			
21	288 40.7	145 19.9 ..	42.7	56 20.5 ..	45.5	255 29.3 ..	50.6	243 15.7 ..	36.2		SHA	Mer. Pass.
22	303 43.2	160 23.7	43.2	71 21.4	45.9	270 31.7	50.5	258 18.1	36.2	Venus	215 36.6	11 27
23	318 45.6	175 27.5	43.6	86 22.3	46.3	285 34.2	50.5	273 20.6	36.2	Mars	128 49.1	17 16
Mer. Pass.	1 52.4	v 3.9	d 0.4	v 0.9	d 0.4	v 2.5	d 0.0	v 2.4	d 0.0	Jupiter	326 48.8	4 05
										Saturn	314 36.1	4 53

UT	SUN GHA	Dec	MOON GHA	v	Dec	d	HP
d h	° '	° '	° '	'	° '	'	'
23 00	179 17.3	N11 40.0	47 25.1	10.9	S20 11.2	0.5	55.0
01	194 17.5	39.1	61 55.0	10.9	20 10.7	0.5	55.0
02	209 17.6	38.3	76 24.9	10.9	20 10.0	0.7	55.0
03	224 17.8	.. 37.4	90 54.8	10.9	20 09.5	0.7	55.0
04	239 18.0	36.6	105 24.7	10.8	20 08.8	0.9	55.0
05	254 18.1	35.8	119 54.5	10.8	20 07.9	0.9	55.1
06	269 18.3	N11 34.9	134 24.3	10.8	S20 07.0	1.1	55.1
07	284 18.4	34.1	148 54.1	10.8	20 05.9	1.2	55.1
M 08	299 18.6	33.2	163 23.9	10.8	20 04.7	1.2	55.1
O 09	314 18.8	.. 32.4	177 53.7	10.8	20 03.5	1.4	55.1
N 10	329 18.9	31.5	192 23.5	10.7	20 02.1	1.5	55.2
D 11	344 19.1	30.7	206 53.2	10.7	20 00.6	1.5	55.2
A 12	359 19.3	N11 29.8	221 22.9	10.7	S19 59.1	1.7	55.2
Y 13	14 19.4	29.0	235 52.6	10.7	19 57.4	1.8	55.2
14	29 19.6	28.2	250 22.3	10.7	19 55.6	1.8	55.2
15	44 19.7	.. 27.3	264 52.0	10.6	19 53.8	2.0	55.3
16	59 19.9	26.5	279 21.6	10.7	19 51.8	2.1	55.3
17	74 20.1	25.6	293 51.3	10.6	19 49.7	2.2	55.3
18	89 20.2	N11 24.8	308 20.9	10.6	S19 47.5	2.2	55.3
19	104 20.4	23.9	322 50.5	10.6	19 45.3	2.4	55.3
20	119 20.6	23.1	337 20.1	10.6	19 42.9	2.5	55.4
21	134 20.7	.. 22.2	351 49.7	10.6	19 40.4	2.6	55.4
22	149 20.9	21.4	6 19.3	10.5	19 37.8	2.7	55.4
23	164 21.1	20.5	20 48.8	10.6	19 35.1	2.8	55.4
24 00	179 21.2	N11 19.7	35 18.4	10.5	S19 32.3	2.9	55.5
01	194 21.4	18.8	49 47.9	10.6	19 29.4	2.9	55.5
02	209 21.6	18.0	64 17.5	10.5	19 26.5	3.1	55.5
03	224 21.7	.. 17.1	78 47.0	10.5	19 23.4	3.2	55.5
04	239 21.9	16.3	93 16.5	10.5	19 20.2	3.3	55.6
05	254 22.1	15.4	107 46.0	10.5	19 16.9	3.4	55.6
06	269 22.2	N11 14.6	122 15.5	10.5	S19 13.5	3.5	55.6
07	284 22.4	13.7	136 45.0	10.5	19 10.0	3.6	55.6
T 08	299 22.6	12.9	151 14.5	10.5	19 06.4	3.7	55.6
U 09	314 22.7	.. 12.0	165 44.0	10.5	19 02.7	3.9	55.7
E 10	329 22.9	11.2	180 13.5	10.5	18 58.8	3.9	55.7
S 11	344 23.1	10.3	194 43.0	10.4	18 54.9	4.0	55.7
D 12	359 23.2	N11 09.5	209 12.4	10.5	S18 50.9	4.1	55.7
A 13	14 23.4	08.6	223 41.9	10.5	18 46.8	4.2	55.8
Y 14	29 23.6	07.7	238 11.4	10.4	18 42.6	4.3	55.8
15	44 23.7	.. 06.9	252 40.8	10.5	18 38.3	4.4	55.8
16	59 23.9	06.0	267 10.3	10.4	18 33.9	4.5	55.8
17	74 24.1	05.2	281 39.7	10.5	18 29.4	4.6	55.9
18	89 24.2	N11 04.3	296 09.2	10.4	S18 24.8	4.7	55.9
19	104 24.4	03.5	310 38.6	10.5	18 20.1	4.8	55.9
20	119 24.6	02.6	325 08.1	10.4	18 15.3	4.9	55.9
21	134 24.7	.. 01.8	339 37.5	10.5	18 10.4	5.1	56.0
22	149 24.9	00.9	354 07.0	10.4	18 05.3	5.1	56.0
23	164 25.1	11 00.0	8 36.4	10.5	18 00.2	5.2	56.0
25 00	179 25.2	N10 59.2	23 05.9	10.4	S17 55.0	5.3	56.0
01	194 25.4	58.3	37 35.3	10.5	17 49.7	5.4	56.1
02	209 25.6	57.5	52 04.8	10.5	17 44.3	5.5	56.1
03	224 25.8	.. 56.6	66 34.3	10.4	17 38.8	5.5	56.1
04	239 25.9	55.8	81 03.7	10.5	17 33.3	5.7	56.1
05	254 26.1	54.9	95 33.2	10.4	17 27.6	5.8	56.2
06	269 26.3	N10 54.0	110 02.6	10.5	S17 21.8	5.9	56.2
07	284 26.4	53.2	124 32.1	10.5	17 15.9	6.0	56.2
W 08	299 26.6	52.3	139 01.6	10.5	17 09.9	6.0	56.2
E 09	314 26.8	.. 51.5	153 31.1	10.5	17 03.9	6.2	56.3
D 10	329 27.0	50.6	168 00.6	10.4	16 57.7	6.3	56.3
N 11	344 27.1	49.7	182 30.0	10.5	16 51.4	6.3	56.3
E 12	359 27.3	N10 48.9	196 59.5	10.5	S16 45.1	6.5	56.3
S 13	14 27.5	48.0	211 29.0	10.5	16 38.6	6.5	56.4
D 14	29 27.6	47.2	225 58.5	10.5	16 32.1	6.6	56.4
A 15	44 27.8	.. 46.3	240 28.1	10.5	16 25.5	6.8	56.4
Y 16	59 28.0	45.4	254 57.6	10.5	16 18.7	6.8	56.4
17	74 28.2	44.6	269 27.1	10.5	16 11.9	6.9	56.5
18	89 28.3	N10 43.7	283 56.6	10.6	S16 05.0	7.0	56.5
19	104 28.5	42.9	298 26.2	10.5	15 58.0	7.1	56.5
20	119 28.7	42.0	312 55.7	10.6	15 50.9	7.2	56.5
21	134 28.9	.. 41.1	327 25.3	10.6	15 43.7	7.2	56.6
22	149 29.0	40.3	341 54.9	10.6	15 36.5	7.4	56.6
23	164 29.2	39.4	356 24.4	10.6	S15 29.1	7.4	56.6
	SD 15.8	d 0.9	SD 15.0		15.2		15.3

Twilight / Moonrise

Lat.	Naut.	Civil	Sunrise	23	24	25	26
°	h m	h m	h m	h m	h m	h m	h m
N 72	////	01 07	03 17	■	■	21 14	20 52
N 70	////	02 05	03 38	20 57	20 42	20 36	20 30
68	////	02 38	03 54	19 43	20 01	20 09	20 13
66	00 58	03 02	04 07	19 06	19 32	19 48	19 59
64	01 49	03 20	04 18	18 39	19 10	19 32	19 47
62	02 19	03 34	04 27	18 19	18 53	19 18	19 37
60	02 41	03 47	04 35	18 02	18 38	19 06	19 29
N 58	02 59	03 57	04 41	17 48	18 26	18 56	19 21
56	03 13	04 06	04 47	17 36	18 15	18 47	19 14
54	03 25	04 14	04 53	17 25	18 06	18 40	19 08
52	03 35	04 21	04 58	17 16	17 57	18 32	19 03
50	03 44	04 27	05 02	17 07	17 49	18 26	18 58
45	04 03	04 41	05 12	16 49	17 33	18 12	18 48
N 40	04 17	04 51	05 20	16 35	17 20	18 01	18 39
35	04 29	05 00	05 26	16 22	17 08	17 51	18 31
30	04 38	05 07	05 32	16 12	16 58	17 43	18 24
20	04 53	05 20	05 42	15 53	16 41	17 28	18 13
N 10	05 05	05 30	05 51	15 37	16 26	17 15	18 03
0	05 14	05 38	05 59	15 22	16 12	17 03	17 53
S 10	05 21	05 46	06 07	15 07	15 58	16 51	17 43
20	05 27	05 53	06 15	14 50	15 43	16 38	17 33
30	05 33	06 01	06 25	14 32	15 26	16 23	17 21
35	05 35	06 05	06 30	14 21	15 16	16 14	17 15
40	05 37	06 09	06 36	14 09	15 04	16 04	17 07
45	05 39	06 14	06 43	13 54	14 51	15 52	16 58
S 50	05 41	06 19	06 52	13 36	14 34	15 38	16 47
52	05 42	06 21	06 56	13 28	14 26	15 32	16 42
54	05 43	06 24	07 00	13 18	14 18	15 24	16 36
56	05 43	06 26	07 05	13 07	14 08	15 16	16 30
58	05 44	06 29	07 10	12 55	13 57	15 07	16 23
S 60	05 44	06 33	07 16	12 41	13 44	14 56	16 15

Sunset / Twilight / Moonset

Lat.	Sunset	Civil	Naut.	23	24	25	26
°	h m	h m	h m	h m	h m	h m	h m
N 72	20 44	22 45	////	■	■	■	01 30
N 70	20 24	21 54	////	22 15	24 15	00 15	02 07
68	20 08	21 23	////	23 29	24 56	00 56	02 33
66	19 56	21 00	22 55	24 06	00 06	01 24	02 53
64	19 45	20 42	22 10	24 32	00 32	01 46	03 09
62	19 36	20 28	21 42	24 52	00 52	02 03	03 22
60	19 29	20 16	21 21	00 11	01 09	02 17	03 33
N 58	19 22	20 06	21 04	00 26	01 23	02 29	03 42
56	19 16	19 57	20 50	00 39	01 35	02 39	03 50
54	19 11	19 49	20 38	00 50	01 45	02 48	03 58
52	19 06	19 42	20 28	00 59	01 54	02 57	04 04
50	19 01	19 36	20 19	01 08	02 03	03 04	04 10
45	18 52	19 23	20 01	01 26	02 20	03 20	04 23
N 40	18 45	19 13	19 47	01 41	02 35	03 32	04 34
35	18 38	19 04	19 36	01 54	02 47	03 43	04 43
30	18 32	18 57	19 26	02 05	02 57	03 53	04 51
20	18 22	18 45	19 11	02 24	03 15	04 09	05 04
N 10	18 14	18 35	19 00	02 40	03 31	04 23	05 16
0	18 06	18 27	18 51	02 56	03 46	04 37	05 27
S 10	17 58	18 19	18 44	03 11	04 01	04 50	05 38
20	17 50	18 12	18 38	03 28	04 16	05 04	05 49
30	17 40	18 05	18 33	03 46	04 34	05 20	06 03
35	17 35	18 01	18 30	03 57	04 45	05 29	06 10
40	17 29	17 57	18 28	04 10	04 56	05 39	06 19
45	17 22	17 52	18 26	04 25	05 10	05 52	06 29
S 50	17 14	17 47	18 25	04 43	05 27	06 07	06 41
52	17 10	17 45	18 24	04 51	05 35	06 14	06 46
54	17 06	17 42	18 23	05 01	05 44	06 21	06 53
56	17 01	17 39	18 23	05 11	05 54	06 30	06 59
58	16 56	17 37	18 22	05 24	06 06	06 40	07 07
S 60	16 50	17 33	18 22	05 38	06 19	06 51	07 16

SUN / MOON

Day	Eqn. of Time 00h	12h	Mer. Pass.	Mer. Pass. Upper	Lower	Age	Phase
d	m s	m s	h m	h m	h m	d	%
23	02 51	02 43	12 03	21 34	09 09	12	88
24	02 35	02 27	12 02	22 24	09 59	13	93
25	02 19	02 11	12 02	23 15	10 50	14	98

UT	ARIES GHA	VENUS −4.1 GHA	Dec	MARS +0.3 GHA	Dec	JUPITER −2.7 GHA	Dec	SATURN +0.2 GHA	Dec	STARS Name	SHA	Dec
26 00	333 48.1	190 31.3	N 5 44.1	101 23.2	S20 46.7	300 36.7	N11 50.5	288 23.0	N14 36.2	Acamar	315 26.3	S40 18.2
01	348 50.6	205 35.1	44.5	116 24.1	47.0	315 39.2	50.5	303 25.4	36.1	Achernar	335 34.4	S57 14.1
02	3 53.0	220 38.9	45.0	131 25.0	47.4	330 41.6	50.5	318 27.9	36.1	Acrux	173 21.9	S63 05.8
03	18 55.5	235 42.7	.. 45.4	146 25.9	.. 47.8	345 44.1	.. 50.5	333 30.3	.. 36.1	Adhara	255 21.2	S28 58.1
04	33 58.0	250 46.5	45.9	161 26.8	48.2	0 46.6	50.5	348 32.8	36.1	Aldebaran	291 01.7	N16 30.4
05	49 00.4	265 50.2	46.3	176 27.7	48.5	15 49.0	50.5	3 35.2	36.1			
06	64 02.9	280 54.0	N 5 46.8	191 28.6	S20 48.9	30 51.5	N11 50.4	18 37.7	N14 36.1	Alioth	166 30.5	N55 58.0
07	79 05.4	295 57.8	47.3	206 29.5	49.3	45 54.0	50.4	33 40.1	36.1	Alkaid	153 07.6	N49 19.3
T 08	94 07.8	311 01.6	47.7	221 30.5	49.7	60 56.4	50.4	48 42.6	36.1	Al Na'ir	27 56.7	S46 57.7
H 09	109 10.3	326 05.4	.. 48.2	236 31.4	.. 50.0	75 58.9	.. 50.4	63 45.0	.. 36.1	Alnilam	275 57.4	S 1 12.1
U 10	124 12.8	341 09.1	48.6	251 32.3	50.4	91 01.4	50.4	78 47.4	36.1	Alphard	218 06.9	S 8 39.3
R 11	139 15.2	356 12.9	49.1	266 33.2	50.8	106 03.9	50.4	93 49.9	36.1			
S 12	154 17.7	11 16.7	N 5 49.5	281 34.1	S20 51.2	121 06.3	N11 50.4	108 52.3	N14 36.1	Alphecca	126 20.1	N26 43.3
D 13	169 20.1	26 20.5	50.0	296 35.0	51.5	136 08.8	50.4	123 54.8	36.1	Alpheratz	357 54.3	N29 05.3
A 14	184 22.6	41 24.2	50.4	311 35.9	51.9	151 11.3	50.3	138 57.2	36.1	Altair	62 18.4	N 8 52.2
Y 15	199 25.1	56 28.0	.. 50.9	326 36.8	.. 52.3	166 13.7	.. 50.3	153 59.7	.. 36.1	Ankaa	353 25.9	S42 18.4
16	214 27.5	71 31.7	51.4	341 37.7	52.7	181 16.2	50.3	169 02.1	36.1	Antares	112 39.4	S26 25.8
17	229 30.0	86 35.5	51.8	356 38.6	53.0	196 18.7	50.3	184 04.6	36.1			
18	244 32.5	101 39.3	N 5 52.3	11 39.5	S20 53.4	211 21.2	N11 50.3	199 07.0	N14 36.1	Arcturus	146 05.7	N19 11.4
19	259 34.9	116 43.0	52.7	26 40.4	53.8	226 23.6	50.3	214 09.5	36.1	Atria	107 50.7	S69 01.8
20	274 37.4	131 46.8	53.2	41 41.3	54.2	241 26.1	50.3	229 11.9	36.1	Avior	234 22.9	S59 30.4
21	289 39.9	146 50.5	.. 53.7	56 42.2	.. 54.5	256 28.6	.. 50.3	244 14.4	.. 36.1	Bellatrix	278 43.6	N 6 20.9
22	304 42.3	161 54.3	54.1	71 43.1	54.9	271 31.1	50.2	259 16.8	36.1	Betelgeuse	271 13.0	N 7 24.4
23	319 44.8	176 58.0	54.6	86 44.0	55.3	286 33.5	50.2	274 19.2	36.0			
27 00	334 47.3	192 01.7	N 5 55.0	101 44.9	S20 55.7	301 36.0	N11 50.2	289 21.7	N14 36.0	Canopus	264 01.2	S52 41.5
01	349 49.7	207 05.5	55.5	116 45.8	56.0	316 38.5	50.2	304 24.1	36.0	Capella	280 50.4	N45 59.6
02	4 52.2	222 09.2	56.0	131 46.7	56.4	331 41.0	50.2	319 26.6	36.0	Deneb	49 38.3	N45 16.9
03	19 54.6	237 12.9	.. 56.4	146 47.6	.. 56.8	346 43.4	.. 50.2	334 29.0	.. 36.0	Denebola	182 44.9	N14 34.7
04	34 57.1	252 16.7	56.9	161 48.5	57.1	1 45.9	50.2	349 31.5	36.0	Diphda	349 06.4	S17 59.2
05	49 59.6	267 20.4	57.4	176 49.4	57.5	16 48.4	50.1	4 33.9	36.0			
06	65 02.0	282 24.1	N 5 57.8	191 50.3	S20 57.9	31 50.9	N11 50.1	19 36.4	N14 36.0	Dubhe	194 05.4	N61 45.3
07	80 04.5	297 27.8	58.3	206 51.2	58.3	46 53.4	50.1	34 38.8	36.0	Elnath	278 26.3	N28 36.3
F 08	95 07.0	312 31.5	58.8	221 52.1	58.6	61 55.8	50.1	49 41.3	36.0	Eltanin	90 50.9	N51 29.7
R 09	110 09.4	327 35.3	.. 59.2	236 53.0	.. 59.0	76 58.3	.. 50.1	64 43.7	.. 36.0	Enif	33 57.3	N 9 52.5
I 10	125 11.9	342 39.0	5 59.7	251 53.8	59.4	92 00.8	50.1	79 46.2	36.0	Fomalhaut	15 35.4	S29 37.4
D 11	140 14.4	357 42.7	6 00.2	266 54.7	20 59.7	107 03.3	50.1	94 48.6	36.0			
A 12	155 16.8	12 46.4	N 6 00.6	281 55.6	S21 00.1	122 05.7	N11 50.0	109 51.1	N14 36.0	Gacrux	172 13.3	S57 06.7
Y 13	170 19.3	27 50.1	01.1	296 56.5	00.5	137 08.2	50.0	124 53.5	36.0	Gienah	176 03.6	S17 32.2
14	185 21.7	42 53.8	01.6	311 57.4	00.9	152 10.7	50.0	139 56.0	36.0	Hadar	149 03.5	S60 22.3
15	200 24.2	57 57.5	.. 02.0	326 58.3	.. 01.2	167 13.2	.. 50.0	154 58.4	.. 36.0	Hamal	328 12.7	N23 27.5
16	215 26.7	73 01.2	02.5	341 59.2	01.6	182 15.7	50.0	170 00.9	35.9	Kaus Aust.	83 57.8	S34 23.1
17	230 29.1	88 04.9	03.0	357 00.1	02.0	197 18.2	50.0	185 03.3	35.9			
18	245 31.6	103 08.6	N 6 03.5	12 01.0	S21 02.3	212 20.6	N11 49.9	200 05.8	N14 35.9	Kochab	137 20.0	N74 09.9
19	260 34.1	118 12.2	03.9	27 01.9	02.7	227 23.1	49.9	215 08.2	35.9	Markab	13 48.7	N15 12.2
20	275 36.5	133 15.9	04.4	42 02.8	03.1	242 25.6	49.9	230 10.7	35.9	Menkar	314 26.2	N 4 05.3
21	290 39.0	148 19.6	.. 04.9	57 03.6	.. 03.4	257 28.1	.. 49.9	245 13.1	.. 35.9	Menkent	148 20.4	S36 22.0
22	305 41.5	163 23.3	05.3	72 04.5	03.8	272 30.6	49.9	260 15.6	35.9	Miaplacidus	221 42.8	S69 42.8
23	320 43.9	178 27.0	05.8	87 05.4	04.2	287 33.0	49.9	275 18.0	35.9			
28 00	335 46.4	193 30.6	N 6 06.3	102 06.3	S21 04.6	302 35.5	N11 49.8	290 20.5	N14 35.9	Mirfak	308 55.6	N49 51.3
01	350 48.9	208 34.3	06.8	117 07.2	04.9	317 38.0	49.8	305 22.9	35.9	Nunki	76 11.3	S26 17.8
02	5 51.3	223 38.0	07.2	132 08.1	05.3	332 40.5	49.8	320 25.4	35.9	Peacock	53 35.5	S56 44.2
03	20 53.8	238 41.6	.. 07.7	147 09.0	.. 05.7	347 43.0	.. 49.8	335 27.9	.. 35.9	Pollux	243 41.1	N28 01.6
04	35 56.2	253 45.3	08.2	162 09.9	06.0	2 45.5	49.8	350 30.3	35.9	Procyon	245 11.2	N 5 13.6
05	50 58.7	268 48.9	08.7	177 10.7	06.4	17 48.0	49.8	5 32.8	35.9			
06	66 01.2	283 52.6	N 6 09.1	192 11.6	S21 06.8	32 50.4	N11 49.7	20 35.2	N14 35.9	Rasalhague	96 16.3	N12 33.9
07	81 03.6	298 56.2	09.6	207 12.5	07.1	47 52.9	49.7	35 37.7	35.8	Regulus	207 55.2	N11 58.3
S 08	96 06.1	313 59.9	10.1	222 13.4	07.5	62 55.4	49.7	50 40.1	35.8	Rigel	281 22.4	S 8 12.1
A 09	111 08.6	329 03.5	.. 10.6	237 14.3	.. 07.9	77 57.9	.. 49.7	65 42.6	.. 35.8	Rigil Kent.	140 06.7	S60 50.1
T 10	126 11.0	344 07.2	11.0	252 15.2	08.2	93 00.4	49.7	80 45.0	35.8	Sabik	102 24.7	S15 43.3
U 11	141 13.5	359 10.8	11.5	267 16.0	08.6	108 02.9	49.6	95 47.5	35.8			
R 12	156 16.0	14 14.4	N 6 12.0	282 16.9	S21 09.0	123 05.4	N11 49.6	110 49.9	N14 35.8	Schedar	349 52.3	N56 31.9
D 13	171 18.4	29 18.1	12.5	297 17.8	09.3	138 07.9	49.6	125 52.4	35.8	Shaula	96 36.3	S37 06.2
A 14	186 20.9	44 21.7	13.0	312 18.7	09.7	153 10.3	49.6	140 54.8	35.8	Sirius	258 43.4	S16 42.8
Y 15	201 23.3	59 25.3	.. 13.4	327 19.6	.. 10.1	168 12.8	.. 49.6	155 57.3	.. 35.8	Spica	158 42.8	S11 09.4
16	216 25.8	74 28.9	13.9	342 20.4	10.4	183 15.3	49.6	170 59.8	35.8	Suhail	223 00.7	S43 25.7
17	231 28.3	89 32.5	14.4	357 21.3	10.8	198 17.8	49.5	186 02.2	35.8			
18	246 30.7	104 36.2	N 6 14.9	12 22.2	S21 11.2	213 20.3	N11 49.5	201 04.7	N14 35.8	Vega	80 46.0	N38 47.3
19	261 33.2	119 39.8	15.3	27 23.1	11.5	228 22.8	49.5	216 07.1	35.8	Zuben'ubi	137 17.4	S16 02.3
20	276 35.7	134 43.4	15.8	42 24.0	11.9	243 25.3	49.5	231 09.6	35.7		SHA	Mer. Pass.
21	291 38.1	149 47.0	.. 16.3	57 24.8	.. 12.3	258 27.8	.. 49.5	246 12.0	.. 35.7			h m
22	306 40.6	164 50.6	16.8	72 25.7	12.6	273 30.3	49.4	261 14.5	35.7	Venus	217 14.5	11 09
23	321 43.1	179 54.2	17.3	87 26.6	13.0	288 32.8	49.4	276 16.9	35.7	Mars	126 57.6	17 12
Mer. Pass.	h m 1 40.6	*v* 3.7	*d* 0.5	*v* 0.9	*d* 0.4	*v* 2.5	*d* 0.0	*v* 2.5	*d* 0.0	Jupiter	326 48.8	3 53
										Saturn	314 34.4	4 42

UT	SUN GHA	Dec	MOON GHA	v	Dec	d	HP
d h	° ′	° ′	° ′	′	° ′	′	′
26 00	179 29.4	N10 38.5	10 54.0	10.6	S15 21.7	7.6	56.6
01	194 29.6	37.7	25 23.6	10.6	15 14.1	7.6	56.7
02	209 29.7	36.8	39 53.2	10.6	15 06.5	7.7	56.7
03	224 29.9	.. 35.9	54 22.8	10.6	14 58.8	7.8	56.7
04	239 30.1	35.1	68 52.4	10.6	14 51.0	7.9	56.7
05	254 30.3	34.2	83 22.0	10.7	14 43.1	7.9	56.8
06	269 30.4	N10 33.3	97 51.7	10.6	S14 35.2	8.1	56.8
07	284 30.6	32.5	112 21.3	10.7	14 27.1	8.1	56.8
T 08	299 30.8	31.6	126 51.0	10.6	14 19.0	8.2	56.8
H 09	314 31.0	.. 30.7	141 20.6	10.7	14 10.8	8.3	56.9
U 10	329 31.1	29.9	155 50.3	10.7	14 02.5	8.4	56.9
R 11	344 31.3	29.0	170 20.0	10.7	13 54.1	8.4	56.9
S 12	359 31.5	N10 28.1	184 49.7	10.7	S13 45.7	8.5	56.9
D 13	14 31.7	27.3	199 19.4	10.7	13 37.2	8.7	57.0
A 14	29 31.8	26.4	213 49.1	10.8	13 28.5	8.7	57.0
Y 15	44 32.0	.. 25.5	228 18.9	10.7	13 19.8	8.7	57.0
16	59 32.2	24.7	242 48.6	10.7	13 11.1	8.9	57.0
17	74 32.4	23.8	257 18.3	10.8	13 02.2	8.9	57.1
18	89 32.5	N10 22.9	271 48.1	10.8	S12 53.3	9.0	57.1
19	104 32.7	22.1	286 17.9	10.7	12 44.3	9.1	57.1
20	119 32.9	21.2	300 47.6	10.8	12 35.2	9.1	57.1
21	134 33.1	.. 20.3	315 17.4	10.8	12 26.1	9.2	57.2
22	149 33.3	19.5	329 47.2	10.8	12 16.9	9.3	57.2
23	164 33.4	18.6	344 17.0	10.9	12 07.6	9.4	57.2
27 00	179 33.6	N10 17.7	358 46.9	10.8	S11 58.2	9.4	57.2
01	194 33.8	16.8	13 16.7	10.8	11 48.8	9.5	57.3
02	209 34.0	16.0	27 46.5	10.8	11 39.3	9.6	57.3
03	224 34.1	.. 15.1	42 16.4	10.8	11 29.7	9.7	57.3
04	239 34.3	14.2	56 46.2	10.9	11 20.0	9.7	57.3
05	254 34.5	13.4	71 16.1	10.9	11 10.3	9.7	57.4
06	269 34.7	N10 12.5	85 46.0	10.9	S11 00.6	9.9	57.4
07	284 34.9	11.6	100 15.9	10.9	10 50.7	9.9	57.4
08	299 35.0	10.7	114 45.8	10.9	10 40.8	10.0	57.4
F 09	314 35.2	.. 09.9	129 15.7	10.9	10 30.8	10.0	57.5
R 10	329 35.4	09.0	143 45.6	10.9	10 20.8	10.1	57.5
I 11	344 35.6	08.1	158 15.5	11.0	10 10.7	10.2	57.5
D 12	359 35.8	N10 07.2	172 45.5	10.9	S10 00.5	10.2	57.5
A 13	14 35.9	06.4	187 15.4	11.0	9 50.3	10.3	57.6
Y 14	29 36.1	05.5	201 45.4	10.9	9 40.0	10.3	57.6
15	44 36.3	.. 04.6	216 15.3	11.0	9 29.7	10.4	57.6
16	59 36.5	03.7	230 45.3	10.9	9 19.3	10.5	57.6
17	74 36.7	02.9	245 15.2	11.0	9 08.8	10.5	57.6
18	89 36.9	N10 02.0	259 45.2	11.0	S 8 58.3	10.6	57.7
19	104 37.0	01.1	274 15.2	11.0	8 47.7	10.6	57.7
20	119 37.2	10 00.2	288 45.2	11.0	8 37.1	10.7	57.7
21	134 37.4	9 59.4	303 15.2	11.0	8 26.4	10.7	57.7
22	149 37.6	58.5	317 45.2	11.0	8 15.7	10.8	57.8
23	164 37.8	57.6	332 15.2	11.0	8 04.9	10.8	57.8
28 00	179 37.9	N 9 56.7	346 45.2	11.1	S 7 54.1	10.9	57.8
01	194 38.1	55.8	1 15.3	11.0	7 43.2	10.9	57.8
02	209 38.3	55.0	15 45.3	11.0	7 32.3	11.0	57.8
03	224 38.5	.. 54.1	30 15.3	11.0	7 21.3	11.0	57.9
04	239 38.7	53.2	44 45.3	11.1	7 10.3	11.1	57.9
05	254 38.9	52.3	59 15.4	11.0	6 59.2	11.1	57.9
06	269 39.0	N 9 51.5	73 45.4	11.1	S 6 48.1	11.2	57.9
07	284 39.2	50.6	88 15.5	11.0	6 36.9	11.2	57.9
S 08	299 39.4	49.7	102 45.5	11.1	6 25.7	11.2	58.0
A 09	314 39.6	.. 48.8	117 15.6	11.0	6 14.5	11.3	58.0
T 10	329 39.8	47.9	131 45.6	11.1	6 03.2	11.4	58.0
U 11	344 40.0	47.1	146 15.7	11.1	5 51.8	11.3	58.0
R 12	359 40.1	N 9 46.2	160 45.7	11.1	S 5 40.5	11.4	58.1
D 13	14 40.3	45.3	175 15.8	11.0	5 29.1	11.5	58.1
A 14	29 40.5	44.4	189 45.8	11.1	5 17.6	11.4	58.1
Y 15	44 40.7	.. 43.5	204 15.9	11.0	5 06.2	11.5	58.1
16	59 40.9	42.6	218 45.9	11.1	4 54.7	11.6	58.1
17	74 41.1	41.8	233 16.0	11.0	4 43.1	11.6	58.2
18	89 41.2	N 9 40.9	247 46.0	11.1	S 4 31.5	11.6	58.2
19	104 41.4	40.0	262 16.1	11.0	4 19.9	11.6	58.2
20	119 41.6	39.1	276 46.1	11.0	4 08.3	11.7	58.2
21	134 41.8	.. 38.2	291 16.1	11.1	3 56.6	11.7	58.2
22	149 42.0	37.3	305 46.2	11.0	3 44.9	11.7	58.3
23	164 42.2	36.5	320 16.2	11.0	S 3 33.2	11.7	58.3
	SD 15.9	d 0.9	SD 15.5		15.7		15.8

Lat.	Twilight Naut.	Twilight Civil	Sunrise	Moonrise 26	27	28	29
°	h m	h m	h m	h m	h m	h m	h m
N 72	////	01 44	03 33	20 52	20 38	20 26	20 15
N 70	////	02 26	03 51	20 30	20 25	20 20	20 16
68	////	02 54	04 05	20 13	20 15	20 16	20 16
66	01 30	03 14	04 17	19 59	20 06	20 12	20 17
64	02 07	03 31	04 26	19 47	19 59	20 08	20 17
62	02 33	03 44	04 35	19 37	19 52	20 05	20 18
60	02 52	03 55	04 42	19 29	19 47	20 03	20 18
N 58	03 08	04 05	04 48	19 21	19 42	20 01	20 18
56	03 21	04 13	04 53	19 14	19 38	19 59	20 19
54	03 32	04 20	04 58	19 08	19 34	19 57	20 19
52	03 41	04 27	05 03	19 03	19 30	19 55	20 19
50	03 49	04 32	05 07	18 58	19 27	19 53	20 19
45	04 07	04 44	05 15	18 48	19 20	19 50	20 20
N 40	04 21	04 54	05 22	18 39	19 14	19 47	20 20
35	04 31	05 02	05 29	18 31	19 09	19 45	20 20
30	04 40	05 09	05 34	18 24	19 04	19 43	20 21
20	04 54	05 21	05 43	18 13	18 56	19 39	20 21
N 10	05 05	05 30	05 51	18 03	18 49	19 36	20 22
0	05 13	05 37	05 58	17 53	18 43	19 33	20 22
S 10	05 20	05 44	06 06	17 43	18 36	19 29	20 23
20	05 25	05 51	06 13	17 33	18 29	19 26	20 23
30	05 30	05 57	06 22	17 21	18 22	19 22	20 24
35	05 31	06 01	06 26	17 15	18 17	19 20	20 25
40	05 33	06 05	06 32	17 07	18 12	19 18	20 25
45	05 34	06 09	06 38	16 58	18 06	19 15	20 25
S 50	05 36	06 13	06 46	16 47	17 58	19 12	20 26
52	05 36	06 15	06 49	16 42	17 55	19 10	20 26
54	05 36	06 17	06 53	16 36	17 51	19 08	20 27
56	05 36	06 19	06 57	16 30	17 47	19 06	20 27
58	05 36	06 22	07 02	16 23	17 43	19 04	20 28
S 60	05 36	06 24	07 07	16 15	17 37	19 02	20 28

Lat.	Sunset	Twilight Civil	Twilight Naut.	Moonset 26	27	28	29
°	h m	h m	h m	h m	h m	h m	h m
N 72	20 26	22 10	////	01 30	03 37	05 35	07 31
N 70	20 09	21 32	////	02 07	03 57	05 46	07 34
68	19 55	21 05	23 46	02 33	04 13	05 54	07 36
66	19 44	20 46	22 26	02 53	04 26	06 02	07 38
64	19 35	20 30	21 51	03 09	04 37	06 08	07 40
62	19 27	20 17	21 27	03 22	04 46	06 13	07 41
60	19 20	20 06	21 08	03 33	04 53	06 17	07 42
N 58	19 14	19 57	20 53	03 42	05 00	06 21	07 44
56	19 09	19 49	20 40	03 50	05 06	06 25	07 45
54	19 04	19 42	20 30	03 58	05 11	06 28	07 45
52	18 59	19 35	20 20	04 04	05 16	06 30	07 46
50	18 56	19 30	20 12	04 10	05 21	06 33	07 47
45	18 47	19 18	19 55	04 23	05 30	06 39	07 48
N 40	18 40	19 08	19 42	04 34	05 38	06 43	07 50
35	18 34	19 00	19 31	04 43	05 44	06 47	07 51
30	18 29	18 53	19 22	04 51	05 50	06 51	07 52
20	18 20	18 42	19 09	05 04	06 00	06 57	07 53
N 10	18 12	18 33	18 58	05 16	06 09	07 02	07 55
0	18 05	18 26	18 50	05 27	06 17	07 07	07 56
S 10	17 58	18 19	18 44	05 38	06 25	07 11	07 58
20	17 50	18 13	18 38	05 49	06 34	07 17	07 59
30	17 42	18 06	18 34	06 03	06 43	07 22	08 00
35	17 37	18 03	18 32	06 10	06 49	07 26	08 01
40	17 32	17 59	18 31	06 19	06 55	07 29	08 02
45	17 26	17 55	18 30	06 29	07 02	07 34	08 03
S 50	17 18	17 51	18 29	06 41	07 11	07 39	08 05
52	17 15	17 49	18 28	06 46	07 15	07 41	08 05
54	17 11	17 47	18 28	06 53	07 19	07 43	08 06
56	17 07	17 45	18 28	06 59	07 24	07 46	08 07
58	17 02	17 43	18 28	07 07	07 30	07 49	08 07
S 60	16 57	17 40	18 28	07 16	07 36	07 53	08 08

	SUN			MOON			
Day	Eqn. of Time 00h	12h	Mer. Pass.	Mer. Pass. Upper	Lower	Age	Phase
d	m s	m s	h m	h m	h m	d	%
26	02 03	01 54	12 02	24 05	11 40	15	100
27	01 46	01 37	12 02	00 05	12 30	16	100
28	01 29	01 20	12 01	00 55	13 20	17	97

UT (d h)	ARIES GHA	VENUS −4.2 GHA	Dec	MARS +0.3 GHA	Dec	JUPITER −2.7 GHA	Dec	SATURN +0.2 GHA	Dec	STARS Name	SHA	Dec
29 00	336 45.5	194 57.8	N 6 17.7	102 27.5	S21 13.4	303 35.2	N11 49.4	291 19.4	N14 35.7	Acamar	315 26.3	S40 18.2
01	351 48.0	210 01.4	· 18.2	117 28.3	13.7	318 37.7	49.4	306 21.9	35.7	Achernar	335 34.4	S57 14.2
02	6 50.5	225 05.0	18.7	132 29.2	14.1	333 40.2	49.4	321 24.3	35.7	Acrux	173 21.9	S63 05.8
03	21 52.9	240 08.5	.. 19.2	147 30.1	.. 14.5	348 42.7	.. 49.3	336 26.8	.. 35.7	Adhara	255 21.2	S28 58.1
04	36 55.4	255 12.1	19.7	162 31.0	14.8	3 45.2	49.3	351 29.2	35.7	Aldebaran	291 01.7	N16 30.4
05	51 57.8	270 15.7	20.2	177 31.8	15.2	18 47.7	49.3	6 31.7	35.7			
06	67 00.3	285 19.3	N 6 20.6	192 32.7	S21 15.5	33 50.2	N11 49.3	21 34.1	N14 35.7	Alioth	166 30.5	N55 58.0
07	82 02.8	300 22.9	21.1	207 33.6	15.9	48 52.7	49.3	36 36.6	35.7	Alkaid	153 07.6	N49 19.3
08	97 05.2	315 26.4	21.6	222 34.5	16.3	63 55.2	49.2	51 39.1	35.7	Al Na'ir	27 56.7	S46 57.7
S 09	112 07.7	330 30.0	.. 22.1	237 35.3	.. 16.6	78 57.7	.. 49.2	66 41.5	.. 35.6	Alnilam	275 57.3	S 1 12.1
U 10	127 10.2	345 33.5	22.6	252 36.2	17.0	94 00.2	49.2	81 44.0	35.6	Alphard	218 06.9	S 8 39.3
N 11	142 12.6	0 37.1	23.1	267 37.1	17.4	109 02.7	49.2	96 46.4	35.6			
D 12	157 15.1	15 40.7	N 6 23.5	282 37.9	S21 17.7	124 05.2	N11 49.2	111 48.9	N14 35.6	Alphecca	126 20.2	N26 43.3
A 13	172 17.6	30 44.2	24.0	297 38.8	18.1	139 07.7	49.1	126 51.4	35.6	Alpheratz	357 54.3	N29 05.3
Y 14	187 20.0	45 47.8	24.5	312 39.7	18.4	154 10.2	49.1	141 53.8	35.6	Altair	62 18.4	N 8 52.2
15	202 22.5	60 51.3	.. 25.0	327 40.6	.. 18.8	169 12.7	.. 49.1	156 56.3	.. 35.6	Ankaa	353 25.9	S42 18.4
16	217 25.0	75 54.9	25.5	342 41.4	19.2	184 15.2	49.1	171 58.7	35.6	Antares	112 39.4	S26 25.8
17	232 27.4	90 58.4	26.0	357 42.3	19.5	199 17.7	49.1	187 01.2	35.6			
18	247 29.9	106 01.9	N 6 26.4	12 43.2	S21 19.9	214 20.2	N11 49.0	202 03.7	N14 35.6	Arcturus	146 05.7	N19 11.4
19	262 32.3	121 05.5	26.9	27 44.0	20.3	229 22.7	49.0	217 06.1	35.6	Atria	107 50.8	S69 01.8
20	277 34.8	136 09.0	27.4	42 44.9	20.6	244 25.2	49.0	232 08.6	35.5	Avior	234 22.9	S59 30.3
21	292 37.3	151 12.5	.. 27.9	57 45.8	.. 21.0	259 27.7	.. 49.0	247 11.0	.. 35.5	Bellatrix	278 43.6	N 6 20.9
22	307 39.7	166 16.0	28.4	72 46.6	21.3	274 30.2	48.9	262 13.5	35.5	Betelgeuse	271 13.0	N 7 24.4
23	322 42.2	181 19.5	28.9	87 47.5	21.7	289 32.7	48.9	277 16.0	35.5			
30 00	337 44.7	196 23.1	N 6 29.4	102 48.4	S21 22.1	304 35.1	N11 48.9	292 18.4	N14 35.5	Canopus	264 01.2	S52 41.5
01	352 47.1	211 26.6	29.8	117 49.2	22.4	319 37.7	48.9	307 20.9	35.5	Capella	280 50.4	N45 59.6
02	7 49.6	226 30.1	30.3	132 50.1	22.8	334 40.2	48.9	322 23.3	35.5	Deneb	49 38.4	N45 16.9
03	22 52.1	241 33.6	.. 30.8	147 50.9	.. 23.1	349 42.7	.. 48.8	337 25.8	.. 35.5	Denebola	182 44.9	N14 34.7
04	37 54.5	256 37.1	31.3	162 51.8	23.5	4 45.2	48.8	352 28.3	35.5	Diphda	349 06.4	S17 59.2
05	52 57.0	271 40.6	31.8	177 52.7	23.9	19 47.7	48.8	7 30.7	35.5			
06	67 59.4	286 44.1	N 6 32.3	192 53.5	S21 24.2	34 50.2	N11 48.8	22 33.2	N14 35.5	Dubhe	194 05.4	N61 45.3
07	83 01.9	301 47.6	32.8	207 54.4	24.6	49 52.7	48.7	37 35.6	35.4	Elnath	278 26.3	N28 36.3
08	98 04.4	316 51.0	33.2	222 55.3	24.9	64 55.2	48.7	52 38.1	35.4	Eltanin	90 50.9	N51 29.7
M 09	113 06.8	331 54.5	.. 33.7	237 56.1	.. 25.3	79 57.7	.. 48.7	67 40.6	.. 35.4	Enif	33 57.3	N 9 52.5
O 10	128 09.3	346 58.0	34.2	252 57.0	25.7	95 00.2	48.7	82 43.0	35.4	Fomalhaut	15 35.4	S29 37.4
N 11	143 11.8	2 01.5	34.7	267 57.8	26.0	110 02.7	48.6	97 45.5	35.4			
D 12	158 14.2	17 05.0	N 6 35.2	282 58.7	S21 26.4	125 05.2	N11 48.6	112 48.0	N14 35.4	Gacrux	172 13.4	S57 06.7
A 13	173 16.7	32 08.4	35.7	297 59.6	26.7	140 07.7	48.6	127 50.4	35.4	Gienah	176 03.6	S17 32.2
Y 14	188 19.2	47 11.9	36.2	313 00.4	27.1	155 10.2	48.6	142 52.9	35.4	Hadar	149 03.5	S60 22.3
15	203 21.6	62 15.3	.. 36.6	328 01.3	.. 27.4	170 12.7	.. 48.6	157 55.4	.. 35.4	Hamal	328 12.7	N23 27.5
16	218 24.1	77 18.8	37.1	343 02.1	27.8	185 15.2	48.5	172 57.8	35.4	Kaus Aust.	83 57.8	S34 23.1
17	233 26.6	92 22.3	37.6	358 03.0	28.2	200 17.7	48.5	188 00.3	35.4			
18	248 29.0	107 25.7	N 6 38.1	13 03.8	S21 28.5	215 20.2	N11 48.5	203 02.7	N14 35.3	Kochab	137 20.1	N74 09.8
19	263 31.5	122 29.2	38.6	28 04.7	28.9	230 22.7	48.5	218 05.2	35.3	Markab	13 48.7	N15 12.3
20	278 33.9	137 32.6	39.1	43 05.6	29.2	245 25.2	48.4	233 07.7	35.3	Menkar	314 26.2	N 4 05.3
21	293 36.4	152 36.0	.. 39.6	58 06.4	.. 29.6	260 27.7	.. 48.4	248 10.1	.. 35.3	Menkent	148 20.4	S36 22.0
22	308 38.9	167 39.5	40.1	73 07.3	29.9	275 30.2	48.4	263 12.6	35.3	Miaplacidus	221 42.8	S69 42.8
23	323 41.3	182 42.9	40.5	88 08.1	30.3	290 32.7	48.4	278 15.1	35.3			
31 00	338 43.8	197 46.3	N 6 41.0	103 09.0	S21 30.7	305 35.2	N11 48.3	293 17.5	N14 35.3	Mirfak	308 55.6	N49 51.3
01	353 46.3	212 49.8	41.5	118 09.8	31.0	320 37.8	48.3	308 20.0	35.3	Nunki	76 11.4	S26 17.8
02	8 48.7	227 53.2	42.0	133 10.7	31.4	335 40.3	48.3	323 22.5	35.3	Peacock	53 35.6	S56 44.2
03	23 51.2	242 56.6	.. 42.5	148 11.5	.. 31.7	350 42.8	.. 48.3	338 24.9	.. 35.2	Pollux	243 41.1	N28 01.6
04	38 53.7	258 00.0	43.0	163 12.4	32.1	5 45.3	48.2	353 27.4	35.2	Procyon	245 11.2	N 5 13.6
05	53 56.1	273 03.4	43.5	178 13.2	32.4	20 47.8	48.2	8 29.9	35.2			
06	68 58.6	288 06.8	N 6 43.9	193 14.1	S21 32.8	35 50.3	N11 48.2	23 32.3	N14 35.2	Rasalhague	96 16.3	N12 33.9
07	84 01.0	303 10.2	44.4	208 14.9	33.1	50 52.8	48.2	38 34.8	35.2	Regulus	207 55.2	N11 58.3
08	99 03.5	318 13.6	44.9	223 15.8	33.5	65 55.3	48.1	53 37.3	35.2	Rigel	281 22.4	S 8 12.1
T 09	114 06.0	333 17.0	.. 45.4	238 16.6	.. 33.9	80 57.8	.. 48.1	68 39.7	.. 35.2	Rigil Kent.	140 06.8	S60 50.1
U 10	129 08.4	348 20.4	45.9	253 17.5	34.2	96 00.3	48.1	83 42.2	35.2	Sabik	102 24.8	S15 43.3
E 11	144 10.9	3 23.8	46.4	268 18.3	34.6	111 02.9	48.0	98 44.7	35.2			
S 12	159 13.4	18 27.2	N 6 46.9	283 19.2	S21 34.9	126 05.4	N11 48.0	113 47.1	N14 35.2	Schedar	349 52.3	N56 32.0
D 13	174 15.8	33 30.6	47.4	298 20.0	35.3	141 07.9	48.0	128 49.6	35.1	Shaula	96 36.3	S37 06.2
A 14	189 18.3	48 33.9	47.8	313 20.9	35.6	156 10.4	48.0	143 52.1	35.1	Sirius	258 43.4	S16 42.8
Y 15	204 20.8	63 37.3	.. 48.3	328 21.7	.. 36.0	171 12.9	.. 47.9	158 54.5	.. 35.1	Spica	158 42.8	S11 09.4
16	219 23.2	78 40.7	48.8	343 22.6	36.3	186 15.4	47.9	173 57.0	35.1	Suhail	223 00.7	S43 25.7
17	234 25.7	93 44.0	49.3	358 23.4	36.7	201 17.9	47.9	188 59.5	35.1			
18	249 28.2	108 47.4	N 6 49.8	13 24.3	S21 37.0	216 20.4	N11 47.9	204 01.9	N14 35.1	Vega	80 46.0	N38 47.3
19	264 30.6	123 50.8	50.3	28 25.1	37.4	231 23.0	47.8	219 04.4	35.1	Zuben'ubi	137 17.4	S16 02.3
20	279 33.1	138 54.1	50.8	43 26.0	37.7	246 25.5	47.8	234 06.9	35.1			
21	294 35.5	153 57.5	.. 51.2	58 26.8	.. 38.1	261 28.0	.. 47.8	249 09.3	.. 35.1		SHA	Mer. Pass.
22	309 38.0	169 00.8	51.7	73 27.7	38.4	276 30.5	47.8	264 11.8	35.0	Venus	218 38.4	10 52
23	324 40.5	184 04.1	52.2	88 28.5	38.8	291 33.0	47.7	279 14.3	35.0	Mars	125 03.7	17 08
Mer. Pass.	1 28.8	v 3.5	d 0.5	v 0.9	d 0.4	v 2.5	d 0.0	v 2.5	d 0.0	Jupiter	326 50.5	3 41
										Saturn	314 33.8	4 30

UT	SUN		MOON					Lat.	Twilight		Sunrise	Moonrise			
									Naut.	Civil		29	30	31	1
	GHA	Dec	GHA	v	Dec	d	HP	°	h m	h m	h m	h m	h m	h m	h m
d h	° ′	° ′	° ′	′	° ′	′	′	N 72	////	02 12	03 49	20 15	20 04	19 52	19 36
29 00	179 42.4	N 9 35.6	334 46.2	11.0	S 3 21.5	11.8	58.3	N 70	////	02 45	04 04	20 16	20 11	20 07	20 02
01	194 42.5	34.7	349 16.2	11.0	3 09.7	11.8	58.3	68	01 02	03 08	04 17	20 16	20 17	20 19	20 22
02	209 42.7	33.8	3 46.2	11.1	2 57.9	11.8	58.3	66	01 53	03 27	04 27	20 17	20 22	20 29	20 38
03	224 42.9	. . 32.9	18 16.3	11.0	2 46.1	11.8	58.3	64	02 23	03 41	04 35	20 17	20 27	20 37	20 51
04	239 43.1	32.0	32 46.3	10.9	2 34.3	11.9	58.4	62	02 45	03 53	04 43	20 18	20 30	20 45	21 03
05	254 43.3	31.2	47 16.2	11.0	2 22.4	11.9	58.4	60	03 03	04 03	04 49	20 18	20 34	20 51	21 12
06	269 43.5	N 9 30.3	61 46.2	11.0	S 2 10.5	11.9	58.4	N 58	03 17	04 12	04 54	20 18	20 37	20 57	21 21
07	284 43.7	29.4	76 16.2	11.0	1 58.6	11.9	58.4	56	03 29	04 19	04 59	20 19	20 39	21 02	21 28
08	299 43.9	28.5	90 46.2	10.9	1 46.7	11.9	58.4	54	03 39	04 26	05 04	20 19	20 42	21 06	21 35
S 09	314 44.0	. . 27.6	105 16.1	11.0	1 34.8	12.0	58.4	52	03 48	04 32	05 08	20 19	20 44	21 10	21 41
U 10	329 44.2	26.7	119 46.1	10.9	1 22.8	11.9	58.5	50	03 55	04 37	05 11	20 19	20 46	21 14	21 46
N 11	344 44.4	25.8	134 16.0	10.9	1 10.9	12.0	58.5	45	04 11	04 48	05 19	20 20	20 50	21 22	21 58
D 12	359 44.6	N 9 25.0	148 45.9	10.9	S 0 58.9	12.0	58.5	N 40	04 24	04 57	05 25	20 20	20 54	21 29	22 08
A 13	14 44.8	24.1	163 15.8	10.9	0 46.9	12.0	58.5	35	04 34	05 05	05 31	20 20	20 57	21 35	22 16
Y 14	29 45.0	23.2	177 45.7	10.9	0 34.9	12.0	58.5	30	04 42	05 11	05 36	20 21	21 00	21 40	22 23
15	44 45.2	. . 22.3	192 15.6	10.9	0 22.9	12.0	58.5	20	04 55	05 21	05 44	20 21	21 04	21 49	22 36
16	59 45.4	21.4	206 45.5	10.8	S 0 10.9	12.0	58.6	N 10	05 05	05 30	05 51	20 22	21 09	21 57	22 48
17	74 45.5	20.5	221 15.3	10.9	N 0 01.1	12.0	58.6	0	05 12	05 36	05 57	20 22	21 13	22 05	22 58
18	89 45.7	N 9 19.6	235 45.2	10.8	N 0 13.1	12.0	58.6	S 10	05 18	05 43	06 04	20 23	21 17	22 12	23 09
19	104 45.9	18.7	250 15.0	10.8	0 25.1	12.1	58.6	20	05 23	05 48	06 11	20 23	21 21	22 21	23 21
20	119 46.1	17.8	264 44.8	10.8	0 37.2	12.0	58.6	30	05 26	05 54	06 18	20 24	21 27	22 30	23 34
21	134 46.3	. . 17.0	279 14.6	10.8	0 49.2	12.0	58.6	35	05 28	05 57	06 23	20 25	21 30	22 35	23 42
22	149 46.5	16.1	293 44.4	10.7	1 01.2	12.1	58.6	40	05 29	06 00	06 27	20 25	21 33	22 42	23 51
23	164 46.7	15.2	308 14.1	10.8	1 13.3	12.0	58.7	45	05 29	06 03	06 33	20 25	21 37	22 49	24 01
30 00	179 46.9	N 9 14.3	322 43.9	10.7	N 1 25.3	12.0	58.7	S 50	05 30	06 07	06 40	20 26	21 42	22 58	24 14
01	194 47.1	13.4	337 13.6	10.7	1 37.3	12.0	58.7	52	05 30	06 09	06 43	20 26	21 44	23 02	24 19
02	209 47.3	12.5	351 43.3	10.7	1 49.3	12.1	58.7	54	05 29	06 10	06 46	20 27	21 46	23 06	24 26
03	224 47.4	. . 11.6	6 13.0	10.6	2 01.4	12.0	58.7	56	05 29	06 12	06 50	20 27	21 49	23 11	24 33
04	239 47.6	10.7	20 42.6	10.7	2 13.4	12.0	58.7	58	05 29	06 14	06 54	20 28	21 52	23 17	24 41
05	254 47.8	09.8	35 12.3	10.6	2 25.4	12.0	58.7	S 60	05 28	06 16	06 58	20 28	21 55	23 23	24 51
06	269 48.0	N 9 08.9	49 41.9	10.6	N 2 37.4	12.0	58.8								
07	284 48.2	08.0	64 11.5	10.5	2 49.4	11.9	58.8	Lat.	Sunset	Twilight		Moonset			
08	299 48.4	07.2	78 41.0	10.6	3 01.3	12.0	58.8			Civil	Naut.	29	30	31	1
M 09	314 48.6	. . 06.3	93 10.6	10.5	3 13.3	11.9	58.8	°	h m	h m	h m	h m	h m	h m	h m
O 10	329 48.8	05.4	107 40.1	10.5	3 25.2	12.0	58.8	N 72	20 09	21 43	////	07 31	09 27	11 27	13 34
N 11	344 49.0	04.5	122 09.6	10.5	3 37.2	11.9	58.8	N 70	19 54	21 12	////	07 34	09 23	11 14	13 09
D 12	359 49.2	N 9 03.6	136 39.1	10.4	N 3 49.1	11.9	58.8	68	19 42	20 49	22 47	07 36	09 19	11 04	12 50
A 13	14 49.3	02.7	151 08.5	10.4	4 01.0	11.9	58.8	66	19 32	20 32	22 02	07 38	09 16	10 55	12 36
Y 14	29 49.5	01.8	165 37.9	10.4	4 12.9	11.9	58.9	64	19 24	20 18	21 34	07 40	09 13	10 48	12 23
15	44 49.7	. . 00.9	180 07.3	10.3	4 24.8	11.8	58.9	62	19 17	20 06	21 13	07 41	09 11	10 42	12 13
16	59 49.9	9 00.0	194 36.6	10.4	4 36.6	11.8	58.9	60	19 11	19 56	20 56	07 42	09 09	10 37	12 04
17	74 50.1	8 59.1	209 06.0	10.3	4 48.4	11.8	58.9	N 58	19 06	19 48	20 42	07 44	09 07	10 32	11 57
18	89 50.3	N 8 58.2	223 35.3	10.2	N 5 00.2	11.8	58.9	56	19 01	19 41	20 31	07 45	09 06	10 28	11 50
19	104 50.5	57.3	238 04.5	10.3	5 12.0	11.8	58.9	54	18 57	19 34	20 21	07 45	09 04	10 24	11 44
20	119 50.7	56.4	252 33.8	10.2	5 23.8	11.7	58.9	52	18 53	19 28	20 12	07 46	09 03	10 21	11 38
21	134 50.9	. . 55.5	267 03.0	10.2	5 35.5	11.7	58.9	50	18 49	19 23	20 05	07 47	09 02	10 18	11 34
22	149 51.1	54.6	281 32.2	10.1	5 47.2	11.6	58.9	45	18 42	19 12	19 49	07 48	08 59	10 11	11 23
23	164 51.3	53.7	296 01.3	10.1	5 58.8	11.7	59.0	N 40	18 36	19 03	19 37	07 50	08 57	10 06	11 14
31 00	179 51.5	N 8 52.8	310 30.4	10.1	N 6 10.5	11.6	59.0	35	18 30	18 56	19 27	07 51	08 55	10 01	11 07
01	194 51.7	51.9	324 59.5	10.0	6 22.1	11.6	59.0	30	18 25	18 50	19 19	07 52	08 54	09 57	11 00
02	209 51.8	51.0	339 28.5	10.0	6 33.7	11.5	59.0	20	18 17	18 40	19 06	07 53	08 51	09 49	10 49
03	224 52.0	. . 50.1	353 57.5	10.0	6 45.2	11.5	59.0	N 10	18 10	18 32	18 57	07 55	08 49	09 43	10 39
04	239 52.2	49.2	8 26.5	10.0	6 56.7	11.5	59.0	0	18 04	18 25	18 49	07 56	08 46	09 37	10 30
05	254 52.4	48.4	22 55.5	9.9	7 08.2	11.4	59.0	S 10	17 58	18 19	18 44	07 58	08 44	09 31	10 21
06	269 52.6	N 8 47.5	37 24.4	9.8	N 7 19.6	11.4	59.0	20	17 51	18 13	18 39	07 59	08 41	09 25	10 11
07	284 52.8	46.6	51 53.2	9.8	7 31.0	11.4	59.0	30	17 44	18 08	18 36	08 00	08 39	09 18	10 00
08	299 53.0	45.7	66 22.0	9.8	7 42.4	11.3	59.0	35	17 39	18 05	18 34	08 01	08 37	09 14	09 53
T 09	314 53.2	. . 44.8	80 50.8	9.8	7 53.7	11.2	59.1	40	17 35	18 02	18 33	08 02	08 35	09 09	09 46
U 10	329 53.4	43.9	95 19.6	9.7	8 04.9	11.3	59.1	45	17 29	17 59	18 33	08 03	08 33	09 04	09 38
E 11	344 53.6	43.0	109 48.3	9.7	8 16.2	11.2	59.1	S 50	17 23	17 55	18 33	08 05	08 30	08 58	09 27
S 12	359 53.8	N 8 42.1	124 17.0	9.6	N 8 27.4	11.1	59.1	52	17 20	17 54	18 33	08 05	08 29	08 55	09 23
D 13	14 54.0	41.2	138 45.6	9.6	8 38.5	11.1	59.1	54	17 16	17 52	18 33	08 06	08 28	08 51	09 18
A 14	29 54.2	40.3	153 14.2	9.5	8 49.6	11.0	59.1	56	17 13	17 50	18 33	08 07	08 27	08 48	09 12
Y 15	44 54.4	. . 39.4	167 42.7	9.6	9 00.6	11.0	59.1	58	17 09	17 49	18 34	08 07	08 25	08 44	09 06
16	59 54.6	38.5	182 11.3	9.4	9 11.6	11.0	59.1	S 60	17 04	17 46	18 35	08 08	08 23	08 40	08 58
17	74 54.8	37.6	196 39.7	9.5	9 22.6	10.8	59.1								
18	89 55.0	N 8 36.7	211 08.2	9.3	N 9 33.4	10.9	59.1			SUN			MOON		
19	104 55.2	35.8	225 36.5	9.4	9 44.3	10.8	59.1								
20	119 55.3	34.9	240 04.9	9.3	9 55.1	10.7	59.1	Day	Eqn. of Time		Mer.	Mer. Pass.		Age	Phase
21	134 55.5	. . 34.0	254 33.2	9.2	10 05.8	10.7	59.1		00ʰ	12ʰ	Pass.	Upper	Lower		
22	149 55.7	33.1	269 01.4	9.3	10 16.5	10.6	59.2	d	m s	m s	h m	h m	h m	d %	
23	164 55.9	32.2	283 29.7	9.1	N10 27.1	10.5	59.2	29	01 11	01 02	12 01	01 44	14 09	18 92	
								30	00 53	00 44	12 01	02 34	14 59	19 85	
	SD 15.9	d 0.9	SD 15.9		16.0		16.1	31	00 35	00 25	12 00	03 25	15 51	20 77	

1999 SEPTEMBER 1, 2, 3 (WED., THURS., FRI.)

UT	ARIES	VENUS −4.3		MARS +0.3		JUPITER −2.7		SATURN +0.1		STARS		
	GHA	GHA	Dec	GHA	Dec	GHA	Dec	GHA	Dec	Name	SHA	Dec
d h	° ′	° ′	° ′	° ′	° ′	° ′	° ′	° ′	° ′		° ′	° ′
1 00	339 42.9	199 07.5 N 6 52.7		103 29.3 S21 39.1		306 35.5 N11 47.7		294 16.8 N14 35.0		Acamar	315 26.3	S40 18.2
01	354 45.4	214 10.8	53.2	118 30.2	39.5	321 38.1	47.7	309 19.2	35.0	Achernar	335 34.3	S57 14.2
02	9 47.9	229 14.1	53.7	133 31.0	39.9	336 40.6	47.6	324 21.7	35.0	Acrux	173 21.9	S63 05.8
03	24 50.3	244 17.5 . .	54.2	148 31.9 . .	40.2	351 43.1 . .	47.6	339 24.2 . .	35.0	Adhara	255 21.2	S28 58.1
04	39 52.8	259 20.8	54.6	163 32.7	40.6	6 45.6	47.6	354 26.6	35.0	Aldebaran	291 01.7	N16 30.4
05	54 55.3	274 24.1	55.1	178 33.5	40.9	21 48.1	47.6	9 29.1	35.0			
06	69 57.7	289 27.4 N 6 55.6		193 34.4 S21 41.3		36 50.6 N11 47.5		24 31.6 N14 34.9		Alioth	166 30.5	N55 58.0
W 07	85 00.2	304 30.7	56.1	208 35.2	41.6	51 53.2	47.5	39 34.0	34.9	Alkaid	153 07.7	N49 19.3
E 08	100 02.7	319 34.0	56.6	223 36.1	42.0	66 55.7	47.5	54 36.5	34.9	Al Na'ir	27 56.7	S46 57.7
D 09	115 05.1	334 37.3 . .	57.1	238 36.9 . .	42.3	81 58.2 . .	47.4	69 39.0 . .	34.9	Alnilam	275 57.3	S 1 12.1
N 10	130 07.6	349 40.6	57.6	253 37.7	42.7	97 00.7	47.4	84 41.5	34.9	Alphard	218 06.9	S 8 39.3
E 11	145 10.0	4 43.9	58.0	268 38.6	43.0	112 03.2	47.4	99 43.9	34.9			
S 12	160 12.5	19 47.2 N 6 58.5		283 39.4 S21 43.4		127 05.8 N11 47.4		114 46.4 N14 34.9		Alphecca	126 20.2	N26 43.3
D 13	175 15.0	34 50.5	59.0	298 40.3	43.7	142 08.3	47.3	129 48.9	34.9	Alpheratz	357 54.3	N29 05.3
A 14	190 17.4	49 53.8	6 59.5	313 41.1	44.0	157 10.8	47.3	144 51.4	34.9	Altair	62 18.4	N 8 52.2
Y 15	205 19.9	64 57.1	7 00.0	328 41.9 . .	44.4	172 13.3 . .	47.3	159 53.8 . .	34.8	Ankaa	353 25.9	S42 18.4
16	220 22.4	80 00.4	00.5	343 42.8	44.7	187 15.8	47.2	174 56.3	34.8	Antares	112 39.4	S26 25.8
17	235 24.8	95 03.6	00.9	358 43.6	45.1	202 18.4	47.2	189 58.8	34.8			
18	250 27.3	110 06.9 N 7 01.4		13 44.4 S21 45.4		217 20.9 N11 47.2		205 01.2 N14 34.8		Arcturus	146 05.7	N19 11.4
19	265 29.8	125 10.2	01.9	28 45.3	45.8	232 23.4	47.2	220 03.7	34.8	Atria	107 50.8	S69 01.8
20	280 32.2	140 13.4	02.4	43 46.1	46.1	247 25.9	47.1	235 06.2	34.8	Avior	234 22.9	S59 30.3
21	295 34.7	155 16.7 . .	02.9	58 46.9 . .	46.5	262 28.5 . .	47.1	250 08.7 . .	34.8	Bellatrix	278 43.6	N 6 20.9
22	310 37.1	170 19.9	03.4	73 47.8	46.8	277 31.0	47.1	265 11.1	34.8	Betelgeuse	271 13.0	N 7 24.4
23	325 39.6	185 23.2	03.8	88 48.6	47.2	292 33.5	47.0	280 13.6	34.7			
2 00	340 42.1	200 26.4 N 7 04.3		103 49.4 S21 47.5		307 36.0 N11 47.0		295 16.1 N14 34.7		Canopus	264 01.1	S52 41.5
01	355 44.5	215 29.7	04.8	118 50.3	47.9	322 38.5	47.0	310 18.6	34.7	Capella	280 50.4	N45 59.6
02	10 47.0	230 32.9	05.3	133 51.1	48.2	337 41.1	46.9	325 21.0	34.7	Deneb	49 38.4	N45 17.0
03	25 49.5	245 36.1 . .	05.8	148 51.9 . .	48.6	352 43.6 . .	46.9	340 23.5 . .	34.7	Denebola	182 44.9	N14 34.7
04	40 51.9	260 39.4	06.3	163 52.8	48.9	7 46.1	46.9	355 26.0	34.7	Diphda	349 06.3	S17 59.2
05	55 54.4	275 42.6	06.7	178 53.6	49.3	22 48.6	46.8	10 28.5	34.7			
06	70 56.9	290 45.8 N 7 07.2		193 54.4 S21 49.6		37 51.2 N11 46.8		25 30.9 N14 34.6		Dubhe	194 05.4	N61 45.3
T 07	85 59.3	305 49.0	07.7	208 55.2	49.9	52 53.7	46.8	40 33.4	34.6	Elnath	278 26.2	N28 36.3
H 08	101 01.8	320 52.2	08.2	223 56.1	50.3	67 56.2	46.8	55 35.9	34.6	Eltanin	90 50.9	N51 29.7
U 09	116 04.3	335 55.4 . .	08.7	238 56.9 . .	50.6	82 58.8 . .	46.7	70 38.4 . .	34.6	Enif	33 57.3	N 9 52.5
R 10	131 06.7	350 58.6	09.1	253 57.7	51.0	98 01.3	46.7	85 40.8	34.6	Fomalhaut	15 35.4	S29 37.4
S 11	146 09.2	6 01.8	09.6	268 58.6	51.3	113 03.8	46.7	100 43.3	34.6			
D 12	161 11.6	21 05.0 N 7 10.1		283 59.4 S21 51.7		128 06.3 N11 46.6		115 45.8 N14 34.6		Gacrux	172 13.4	S57 06.6
A 13	176 14.1	36 08.2	10.6	299 00.2	52.0	143 08.9	46.6	130 48.3	34.6	Gienah	176 03.6	S17 32.2
Y 14	191 16.6	51 11.4	11.1	314 01.0	52.4	158 11.4	46.6	145 50.7	34.5	Hadar	149 03.5	S60 22.3
15	206 19.0	66 14.6 . .	11.5	329 01.9 . .	52.7	173 13.9 . .	46.5	160 53.2 . .	34.5	Hamal	328 12.7	N23 27.5
16	221 21.5	81 17.8	12.0	344 02.7	53.0	188 16.5	46.5	175 55.7	34.5	Kaus Aust.	83 57.8	S34 23.1
17	236 24.0	96 21.0	12.5	359 03.5	53.4	203 19.0	46.5	190 58.2	34.5			
18	251 26.4	111 24.1 N 7 13.0		14 04.3 S21 53.7		218 21.5 N11 46.4		206 00.7 N14 34.5		Kochab	137 20.1	N74 09.8
19	266 28.9	126 27.3	13.4	29 05.2	54.1	233 24.0	46.4	221 03.1	34.5	Markab	13 48.7	N15 12.3
20	281 31.4	141 30.5	13.9	44 06.0	54.4	248 26.6	46.4	236 05.6	34.5	Menkar	314 26.1	N 4 05.3
21	296 33.8	156 33.6 . .	14.4	59 06.8 . .	54.8	263 29.1 . .	46.3	251 08.1 . .	34.4	Menkent	148 20.5	S36 22.0
22	311 36.3	171 36.8	14.9	74 07.6	55.1	278 31.6	46.3	266 10.6	34.4	Miaplacidus	221 42.8	S69 42.8
23	326 38.8	186 39.9	15.3	89 08.4	55.4	293 34.2	46.3	281 13.0	34.4			
3 00	341 41.2	201 43.1 N 7 15.8		104 09.3 S21 55.8		308 36.7 N11 46.2		296 15.5 N14 34.4		Mirfak	308 55.6	N49 51.3
01	356 43.7	216 46.2	16.3	119 10.1	56.1	323 39.2	46.2	311 18.0	34.4	Nunki	76 11.4	S26 17.8
02	11 46.1	231 49.4	16.8	134 10.9	56.5	338 41.8	46.2	326 20.5	34.4	Peacock	53 35.6	S56 44.2
03	26 48.6	246 52.5 . .	17.3	149 11.7 . .	56.8	353 44.3 . .	46.1	341 23.0 . .	34.4	Pollux	243 41.1	N28 01.6
04	41 51.1	261 55.6	17.7	164 12.5	57.2	8 46.8	46.1	356 25.4	34.4	Procyon	245 11.2	N 5 13.6
05	56 53.5	276 58.8	18.2	179 13.4	57.5	23 49.4	46.1	11 27.9	34.3			
06	71 56.0	292 01.9 N 7 18.7		194 14.2 S21 57.8		38 51.9 N11 46.0		26 30.4 N14 34.3		Rasalhague	96 16.3	N12 33.9
07	86 58.5	307 05.0	19.1	209 15.0	58.2	53 54.4	46.0	41 32.9	34.3	Regulus	207 55.2	N11 58.3
F 08	102 00.9	322 08.1	19.6	224 15.8	58.5	68 57.0	46.0	56 35.4	34.3	Rigel	281 22.4	S 8 12.1
R 09	117 03.4	337 11.2 . .	20.1	239 16.6 . .	58.9	83 59.5 . .	45.9	71 37.8 . .	34.3	Rigil Kent.	140 06.8	S60 50.0
I 10	132 05.9	352 14.3	20.6	254 17.5	59.2	99 02.0	45.9	86 40.3	34.3	Sabik	102 24.8	S15 43.3
11	147 08.3	7 17.4	21.0	269 18.3	59.5	114 04.6	45.9	101 42.8	34.3			
D 12	162 10.8	22 20.5 N 7 21.5		284 19.1 S21 59.9		129 07.1 N11 45.8		116 45.3 N14 34.2		Schedar	349 52.3	N56 32.0
A 13	177 13.2	37 23.6	22.0	299 19.9	22 00.2	144 09.6	45.8	131 47.8	34.2	Shaula	96 36.4	S37 06.2
Y 14	192 15.7	52 26.7	22.5	314 20.7	00.6	159 12.2	45.8	146 50.2	34.2	Sirius	258 43.3	S16 42.8
15	207 18.2	67 29.8 . .	22.9	329 21.5 . .	00.9	174 14.7 . .	45.7	161 52.7 . .	34.2	Spica	158 42.8	S11 09.4
16	222 20.6	82 32.9	23.4	344 22.3	01.2	189 17.3	45.7	176 55.2	34.2	Suhail	223 00 7	S43 25.7
17	237 23.1	97 36.0	23.9	359 23.2	01.6	204 19.8	45.7	191 57.7	34.2			
18	252 25.6	112 39.0 N 7 24.3		14 24.0 S22 01.9		219 22.3 N11 45.6		207 00.2 N14 34.1		Vega	80 46.0	N38 47.3
19	267 28.0	127 42.1	24.8	29 24.8	02.2	234 24.9	45.6	222 02.6	34.1	Zuben'ubi	137 17.4	S16 02.3
20	282 30.5	142 45.2	25.3	44 25.6	02.6	249 27.4	45.6	237 05.1	34.1			
21	297 33.0	157 48.2 . .	25.7	59 26.4 . .	02.9	264 29.9 . .	45.5	252 07.6 . .	34.1		SHA	Mer. Pass.
22	312 35.4	172 51.3	26.2	74 27.2	03.3	279 32.5	45.5	267 10.1	34.1	Venus	° ′ 219 44.3	h m 10 36
23	327 37.9	187 54.3	26.7	89 28.0	03.6	294 35.0	45.4	282 12.6	34.1	Mars	123 07.4	17 04
	h m									Jupiter	326 53.9	3 29
Mer. Pass. 1 17.0		v 3.2	d 0.5	v 0.8	d 0.3	v 2.5	d 0.0	v 2.5	d 0.0	Saturn	314 34.0	4 18

UT	SUN		MOON					Lat.	Twilight		Sunrise	Moonrise			
									Naut.	Civil		1	2	3	4
	GHA	Dec	GHA	v	Dec	d	HP								
d h	° ′	° ′	° ′	′	° ′	′	′	°	h m	h m	h m	h m	h m	h m	h m
1 00	179 56.1	N 8 31.2	297 57.8	9.1	N10 37.6	10.5	59.2	N 72	////	02 35	04 04	19 36	19 08	▭	▭
01	194 56.3	30.3	312 25.9	9.1	10 48.1	10.4	59.2	N 70	////	03 02	04 17	20 02	19 57	19 52	▭
02	209 56.5	29.4	326 54.0	9.1	10 58.5	10.4	59.2	68	01 35	03 22	04 28	20 22	20 29	20 45	21 20
03	224 56.7	.. 28.5	341 22.1	8.9	11 08.9	10.3	59.2	66	02 13	03 38	04 37	20 38	20 53	21 17	22 00
04	239 56.9	27.6	355 50.0	9.0	11 19.2	10.2	59.2	64	02 38	03 51	04 44	20 51	21 11	21 41	22 27
05	254 57.1	26.7	10 18.0	8.9	11 29.4	10.2	59.2	62	02 57	04 02	04 50	21 03	21 27	22 01	22 49
06	269 57.3	N 8 25.8	24 45.9	8.8	N11 39.6	10.1	59.2	60	03 13	04 11	04 56	21 12	21 40	22 16	23 06
W 07	284 57.5	24.9	39 13.7	8.8	11 49.7	10.0	59.2	N 58	03 25	04 19	05 01	21 21	21 51	22 30	23 20
E 08	299 57.7	24.0	53 41.5	8.8	11 59.7	10.0	59.2	56	03 36	04 26	05 05	21 28	22 00	22 41	23 33
D 09	314 57.9	.. 23.1	68 09.3	8.7	12 09.7	9.9	59.2	54	03 46	04 32	05 09	21 35	22 09	22 51	23 44
N 10	329 58.1	22.2	82 37.0	8.7	12 19.6	9.8	59.2	52	03 54	04 37	05 12	21 41	22 17	23 00	23 53
E 11	344 58.3	21.3	97 04.7	8.6	12 29.4	9.8	59.2	50	04 01	04 42	05 16	21 46	22 24	23 09	24 02
S 12	359 58.5	N 8 20.4	111 32.3	8.5	N12 39.2	9.6	59.2	45	04 16	04 52	05 22	21 58	22 39	23 26	24 20
D 13	14 58.7	19.5	125 59.8	8.6	12 48.8	9.6	59.2	N 40	04 27	05 00	05 28	22 08	22 51	23 40	24 35
A 14	29 58.9	18.6	140 27.4	8.4	12 58.4	9.6	59.2	35	04 36	05 07	05 33	22 16	23 01	23 52	24 48
Y 15	44 59.1	.. 17.7	154 54.8	8.4	13 08.0	9.4	59.2	30	04 44	05 13	05 37	22 23	23 11	24 03	00 03
16	59 59.3	16.8	169 22.2	8.4	13 17.4	9.4	59.2	20	04 56	05 22	05 44	22 36	23 27	24 21	00 21
17	74 59.5	15.9	183 49.6	8.3	13 26.8	9.3	59.2	N 10	05 05	05 29	05 51	22 48	23 41	24 37	00 37
								0	05 11	05 36	05 57	22 58	23 54	24 52	00 52
18	89 59.7	N 8 15.0	198 16.9	8.3	N13 36.1	9.2	59.3	S 10	05 16	05 41	06 02	23 09	24 07	00 07	01 07
19	104 59.9	14.1	212 44.2	8.2	13 45.3	9.1	59.3	20	05 20	05 46	06 08	23 21	24 22	00 22	01 23
20	120 00.1	13.2	227 11.4	8.2	13 54.4	9.0	59.3	30	05 23	05 51	06 15	23 34	24 38	00 38	01 41
21	135 00.3	.. 12.2	241 38.6	8.1	14 03.4	9.0	59.3	35	05 24	05 53	06 19	23 42	24 48	00 48	01 52
22	150 00.5	11.3	256 05.7	8.1	14 12.4	8.8	59.3	40	05 24	05 56	06 23	23 51	24 59	00 59	02 04
23	165 00.7	10.4	270 32.8	8.1	14 21.2	8.8	59.3	45	05 24	05 58	06 28	24 01	00 01	01 12	02 19
2 00	180 00.9	N 8 09.5	284 59.9	7.9	N14 30.0	8.7	59.3	S 50	05 24	06 01	06 33	24 14	00 14	01 27	02 37
01	195 01.1	08.6	299 26.8	8.0	14 38.7	8.6	59.3	52	05 23	06 02	06 36	24 19	00 19	01 35	02 45
02	210 01.3	07.7	313 53.8	7.9	14 47.3	8.5	59.3	54	05 23	06 03	06 39	24 26	00 26	01 43	02 55
03	225 01.5	.. 06.8	328 20.7	7.8	14 55.8	8.4	59.3	56	05 22	06 05	06 42	24 41	00 33	01 52	03 05
04	240 01.7	05.9	342 47.5	7.8	15 04.2	8.4	59.3	58	05 21	06 06	06 46	24 41	00 41	02 03	03 18
05	255 01.9	05.0	357 14.3	7.7	15 12.6	8.2	59.3	S 60	05 20	06 08	06 50	24 51	00 51	02 15	03 32
06	270 02.1	N 8 04.1	11 41.0	7.7	N15 20.8	8.1	59.3								

Lat.	Sunset	Twilight		Moonset			
		Civil	Naut.	1	2	3	4
°	h m	h m	h m	h m	h m	h m	h m
N 72	19 52	21 19	////	13 34	15 57	▭	▭
N 70	19 40	20 53	23 27	13 09	15 09	17 14	▭
68	19 29	20 34	22 16	12 50	14 38	16 22	17 48
66	19 21	20 18	21 42	12 36	14 15	15 49	17 08
64	19 14	20 06	21 18	12 23	13 57	15 26	16 41
62	19 07	19 56	20 59	12 13	13 43	15 07	16 20
60	19 02	19 47	20 44	12 04	13 30	14 51	16 02
N 58	18 57	19 39	20 32	11 57	13 20	14 38	15 48
56	18 53	19 32	20 21	11 50	13 11	14 27	15 36
54	18 49	19 26	20 12	11 44	13 03	14 17	15 25
52	18 46	19 21	20 04	11 38	12 55	14 08	15 15
50	18 43	19 16	19 57	11 34	12 49	14 01	15 07
45	18 36	19 07	19 43	11 23	12 35	13 44	14 48
N 40	18 31	18 58	19 31	11 14	12 23	13 30	14 34
35	18 26	18 52	19 22	11 07	12 13	13 18	14 21
30	18 22	18 46	19 15	11 00	12 05	13 08	14 10
20	18 15	18 37	19 03	10 49	11 50	12 51	13 51
N 10	18 09	18 30	18 55	10 39	11 37	12 36	13 35
0	18 03	18 24	18 48	10 30	11 25	12 21	13 19
S 10	17 58	18 19	18 43	10 21	11 13	12 07	13 04
20	17 52	18 14	18 40	10 11	11 00	11 52	12 48
30	17 45	18 09	18 37	10 00	10 45	11 35	12 29
35	17 42	18 07	18 36	09 53	10 37	11 24	12 18
40	17 37	18 05	18 36	09 46	10 27	11 13	12 05
45	17 33	18 02	18 36	09 38	10 16	10 59	11 50
S 50	17 27	18 00	18 37	09 27	10 02	10 43	11 32
52	17 24	17 58	18 37	09 23	09 56	10 35	11 23
54	17 22	17 57	18 38	09 18	09 49	10 26	11 14
56	17 18	17 56	18 39	09 12	09 41	10 17	11 03
58	17 15	17 55	18 40	09 06	09 32	10 06	10 50
S 60	17 11	17 53	18 41	08 58	09 22	09 53	10 36

UT	SUN		MOON				
	GHA	Dec	GHA	v	Dec	d	HP
07	285 02.3	03.2	26 07.7	7.7	15 28.9	8.1	59.3
T 08	300 02.5	02.3	40 34.4	7.6	15 37.0	7.9	59.3
H 09	315 02.7	.. 01.3	55 01.0	7.5	15 44.9	7.9	59.3
U 10	330 02.9	8 00.4	69 27.5	7.5	15 52.8	7.7	59.3
R 11	345 03.1	7 59.5	83 54.0	7.5	16 00.5	7.7	59.3
S 12	0 03.3	N 7 58.6	98 20.5	7.4	N16 08.2	7.5	59.3
D 13	15 03.5	57.7	112 46.9	7.4	16 15.7	7.5	59.3
A 14	30 03.7	56.8	127 13.3	7.3	16 23.2	7.3	59.3
Y 15	45 03.9	.. 55.9	141 39.6	7.3	16 30.5	7.3	59.3
16	60 04.1	55.0	156 05.9	7.2	16 37.8	7.1	59.3
17	75 04.3	54.1	170 32.1	7.2	16 44.9	7.0	59.3
18	90 04.5	N 7 53.1	184 58.3	7.1	N16 51.9	6.9	59.3
19	105 04.7	52.2	199 24.4	7.1	16 58.8	6.9	59.3
20	120 04.9	51.3	213 50.5	7.1	17 05.7	6.7	59.3
21	135 05.1	.. 50.4	228 16.6	7.0	17 12.4	6.6	59.3
22	150 05.3	49.5	242 42.6	6.9	17 19.0	6.5	59.3
23	165 05.5	48.6	257 08.5	7.0	17 25.5	6.3	59.3
3 00	180 05.7	N 7 47.7	271 34.5	6.8	N17 31.8	6.3	59.3
01	195 05.9	46.8	286 00.3	6.9	17 38.1	6.2	59.3
02	210 06.1	45.8	300 26.2	6.8	17 44.3	6.0	59.3
03	225 06.3	.. 44.9	314 52.0	6.7	17 50.3	5.9	59.3
04	240 06.5	44.0	329 17.7	6.8	17 56.2	5.8	59.3
05	255 06.7	43.1	343 43.5	6.6	18 02.0	5.7	59.3
06	270 06.9	N 7 42.2	358 09.1	6.7	N18 07.7	5.6	59.3
07	285 07.1	41.3	12 34.8	6.6	18 13.3	5.5	59.3
08	300 07.3	40.3	27 00.4	6.6	18 18.8	5.3	59.3
F 09	315 07.5	.. 39.4	41 26.0	6.5	18 24.1	5.2	59.3
R 10	330 07.7	38.5	55 51.5	6.5	18 29.3	5.2	59.3
I 11	345 07.9	37.6	70 17.0	6.5	18 34.5	4.9	59.3
D 12	0 08.1	N 7 36.7	84 42.5	6.4	N18 39.4	4.9	59.3
A 13	15 08.3	35.8	99 07.9	6.4	18 44.3	4.7	59.3
Y 14	30 08.5	34.9	113 33.3	6.4	18 49.0	4.7	59.3
15	45 08.7	.. 33.9	127 58.7	6.3	18 53.7	4.5	59.3
16	60 08.9	33.0	142 24.0	6.3	18 58.2	4.3	59.3
17	75 09.1	32.1	156 49.3	6.3	19 02.5	4.3	59.3
18	90 09.3	N 7 31.2	171 14.6	6.2	N19 06.8	4.1	59.3
19	105 09.5	30.3	185 39.8	6.3	19 10.9	4.0	59.2
20	120 09.7	29.4	200 05.1	6.2	19 14.9	3.9	59.2
21	135 09.9	.. 28.4	214 30.3	6.1	19 18.8	3.7	59.2
22	150 10.1	27.5	228 55.4	6.2	19 22.5	3.6	59.2
23	165 10.3	26.6	243 20.6	6.1	N19 26.1	3.5	59.2
	SD 15.9	d 0.9	SD 16.1		16.2		16.1

	SUN			MOON			
Day	Eqn. of Time		Mer.	Mer. Pass.		Age	Phase
	00ʰ	12ʰ	Pass.	Upper	Lower		
d	m s	m s	h m	h m	h m	d	%
1	00 16	00 06	12 00	04 17	16 44	21	66
2	00 03	00 13	12 00	05 11	17 39	22	55
3	00 22	00 32	11 59	06 08	18 36	23	44

UT	ARIES GHA	VENUS −4.4 GHA	Dec	MARS +0.4 GHA	Dec	JUPITER −2.7 GHA	Dec	SATURN +0.1 GHA	Dec	STAR Name	SHA	Dec
4 00	342 40.4	202 57.4	N 7 27.1	104 28.8	S22 03.9	309 37.6	N11 45.4	297 15.1	N14 34.1	Acamar	315 26.3	S40 18.2
01	357 42.8	218 00.4	.. 27.6	119 29.7	.. 04.3	324 40.1	.. 45.4	312 17.5	.. 34.0	Achernar	335 34.3	S57 14.2
02	12 45.3	233 03.5	28.1	134 30.5	04.6	339 42.6	45.3	327 20.0	34.0	Acrux	173 21.9	S63 05.8
03	27 47.7	248 06.5	.. 28.5	149 31.3	.. 04.9	354 45.2	.. 45.3	342 22.5	.. 34.0	Adhara	255 21.1	S28 58.1
04	42 50.2	263 09.6	29.0	164 32.1	05.3	9 47.7	45.3	357 25.0	34.0	Aldebaran	291 01.7	N16 30.4
05	57 52.7	278 12.6	29.5	179 32.9	05.6	24 50.3	45.2	12 27.5	34.0			
06	72 55.1	293 15.6	N 7 29.9	194 33.7	S22 06.0	39 52.8	N11 45.2	27 30.0	N14 34.0	Alioth	166 30.5	N55 58.0
07	87 57.6	308 18.6	30.4	209 34.5	06.3	54 55.4	45.2	42 32.4	34.0	Alkaid	153 07.7	N49 19.3
S 08	103 00.1	323 21.6	30.9	224 35.3	06.6	69 57.9	45.1	57 34.9	33.9	Al Na'ir	27 56.7	S46 57.7
A 09	118 02.5	338 24.7	.. 31.3	239 36.1	.. 07.0	85 00.4	.. 45.1	72 37.4	.. 33.9	Alnilam	275 57.3	S 1 12.1
T 10	133 05.0	353 27.7	31.8	254 36.9	07.3	100 03.0	45.0	87 39.9	33.9	Alphard	218 06.9	S 8 39.3
U 11	148 07.5	8 30.7	32.3	269 37.7	07.6	115 05.5	45.0	102 42.4	33.9			
R 12	163 09.9	23 33.7	N 7 32.7	284 38.5	S22 08.0	130 08.1	N11 45.0	117 44.9	N14 33.9	Alphecca	126 20.2	N26 43.3
D 13	178 12.4	38 36.7	33.2	299 39.3	08.3	145 10.6	44.9	132 47.4	33.9	Alpheratz	357 54.2	N29 05.3
A 14	193 14.9	53 39.7	33.7	314 40.1	08.6	160 13.2	44.9	147 49.8	33.8	Altair	62 18.4	N 8 52.3
Y 15	208 17.3	68 42.6	.. 34.1	329 40.9	.. 09.0	175 15.7	.. 44.9	162 52.3	.. 33.8	Ankaa	353 25.9	S42 18.4
16	223 19.8	83 45.6	34.6	344 41.7	09.3	190 18.3	44.8	177 54.8	33.8	Antares	112 39.4	S26 25.8
17	238 22.2	98 48.6	35.0	359 42.6	09.6	205 20.8	44.8	192 57.3	33.8			
18	253 24.7	113 51.6	N 7 35.5	14 43.4	S22 10.0	220 23.3	N11 44.8	207 59.8	N14 33.8	Arcturus	146 05.7	N19 11.4
19	268 27.2	128 54.5	36.0	29 44.2	10.3	235 25.9	44.7	223 02.3	33.8	Atria	107 50.9	S69 01.8
20	283 29.6	143 57.5	36.4	44 45.0	10.6	250 28.4	44.7	238 04.8	33.7	Avior	234 22.9	S59 30.3
21	298 32.1	159 00.5	.. 36.9	59 45.8	.. 11.0	265 31.0	.. 44.6	253 07.2	.. 33.7	Bellatrix	278 43.5	N 6 21.0
22	313 34.6	174 03.4	37.3	74 46.6	11.3	280 33.5	44.6	268 09.7	33.7	Betelgeuse	271 13.0	N 7 24.4
23	328 37.0	189 06.4	37.8	89 47.4	11.6	295 36.1	44.6	283 12.2	33.7			
5 00	343 39.5	204 09.3	N 7 38.2	104 48.2	S22 12.0	310 38.6	N11 44.5	298 14.7	N14 33.7	Canopus	264 01.1	S52 41.5
01	358 42.0	219 12.3	38.7	119 49.0	12.3	325 41.2	44.5	313 17.2	33.7	Capella	280 50.3	N45 59.6
02	13 44.4	234 15.2	39.2	134 49.8	12.6	340 43.7	44.4	328 19.7	33.7	Deneb	49 38.4	N45 17.0
03	28 46.9	249 18.2	.. 39.6	149 50.6	.. 12.9	355 46.3	.. 44.4	343 22.2	.. 33.6	Denebola	182 44.9	N14 34.7
04	43 49.4	264 21.1	40.1	164 51.4	13.3	10 48.8	44.4	358 24.7	33.6	Diphda	349 06.3	S17 59.2
05	58 51.8	279 24.0	40.5	179 52.2	13.6	25 51.4	44.3	13 27.1	33.6			
06	73 54.3	294 26.9	N 7 41.0	194 52.9	S22 13.9	40 53.9	N11 44.3	28 29.6	N14 33.6	Dubhe	194 05.4	N61 45.3
07	88 56.7	309 29.9	41.4	209 53.7	14.3	55 56.5	44.3	43 32.1	33.6	Elnath	278 26.2	N28 36.3
08	103 59.2	324 32.8	41.9	224 54.5	14.6	70 59.0	44.2	58 34.6	33.6	Eltanin	90 51.0	N51 29.7
S 09	119 01.7	339 35.7	.. 42.3	239 55.3	.. 14.9	86 01.6	.. 44.2	73 37.1	.. 33.5	Enif	33 57.3	N 9 52.5
U 10	134 04.1	354 38.6	42.8	254 56.1	15.3	101 04.1	44.1	88 39.6	33.5	Fomalhaut	15 35.4	S29 37.4
N 11	149 06.6	9 41.5	43.2	269 56.9	15.6	116 06.7	44.1	103 42.1	33.5			
D 12	164 09.1	24 44.4	N 7 43.7	284 57.7	S22 15.9	131 09.2	N11 44.1	118 44.6	N14 33.5	Gacrux	172 13.4	S57 06.6
A 13	179 11.5	39 47.3	44.1	299 58.5	16.2	146 11.8	44.0	133 47.1	33.5	Gienah	176 03.6	S17 32.2
Y 14	194 14.0	54 50.2	44.6	314 59.3	16.6	161 14.3	44.0	148 49.6	33.5	Hadar	149 03.5	S60 22.3
15	209 16.5	69 53.1	.. 45.0	330 00.1	.. 16.9	176 16.9	.. 43.9	163 52.0	.. 33.4	Hamal	328 12.6	N23 27.6
16	224 18.9	84 56.0	45.5	345 00.9	17.2	191 19.4	43.9	178 54.5	33.4	Kaus Aust.	83 57.8	S34 23.1
17	239 21.4	99 58.8	45.9	0 01.7	17.6	206 22.0	43.9	193 57.0	33.4			
18	254 23.8	115 01.7	N 7 46.4	15 02.5	S22 17.9	221 24.5	N11 43.8	208 59.5	N14 33.4	Kochab	137 20.2	N74 09.8
19	269 26.3	130 04.6	46.8	30 03.3	18.2	236 27.1	43.8	224 02.0	33.4	Markab	13 48.7	N15 12.3
20	284 28.8	145 07.4	47.3	45 04.1	18.5	251 29.7	43.7	239 04.5	33.3	Menkar	314 26.1	N 4 05.3
21	299 31.2	160 10.3	.. 47.7	60 04.8	.. 18.9	266 32.2	.. 43.7	254 07.0	.. 33.3	Menkent	148 20.5	S36 22.0
22	314 33.7	175 13.2	48.2	75 05.6	19.2	281 34.8	43.6	269 09.5	33.3	Miaplacidus	221 42.7	S69 42.8
23	329 36.2	190 16.0	48.6	90 06.4	19.5	296 37.3	43.6	284 12.0	33.3			
6 00	344 38.6	205 18.9	N 7 49.1	105 07.2	S22 19.9	311 39.9	N11 43.6	299 14.5	N14 33.3	Mirfak	308 55.5	N49 51.3
01	359 41.1	220 21.7	49.5	120 08.0	20.2	326 42.4	43.5	314 17.0	33.3	Nunki	76 11.4	S26 17.8
02	14 43.6	235 24.6	50.0	135 08.8	20.5	341 45.0	43.5	329 19.4	33.2	Peacock	53 35.6	S56 44.2
03	29 46.0	250 27.4	.. 50.4	150 09.6	.. 20.8	356 47.5	.. 43.4	344 21.9	.. 33.2	Pollux	243 41.1	N28 01.6
04	44 48.5	265 30.2	50.8	165 10.4	21.2	11 50.1	43.4	359 24.4	33.2	Procyon	245 11.1	N 5 13.6
05	59 51.0	280 33.0	51.3	180 11.2	21.5	26 52.7	43.4	14 26.9	33.2			
06	74 53.4	295 35.9	N 7 51.7	195 11.9	S22 21.8	41 55.2	N11 43.3	29 29.4	N14 33.2	Rasalhague	96 16.3	N12 33.9
07	89 55.9	310 38.7	52.2	210 12.7	22.1	56 57.8	43.3	44 31.9	33.2	Regulus	207 55.2	N11 58.3
M 08	104 58.3	325 41.5	52.6	225 13.5	22.5	72 00.3	43.2	59 34.4	33.1	Rigel	281 22.4	S 8 12.1
O 09	120 00.8	340 44.3	.. 53.0	240 14.3	.. 22.8	87 02.9	.. 43.2	74 36.9	.. 33.1	Rigil Kent.	140 05.8	S60 50.0
N 10	135 03.3	355 47.1	53.5	255 15.1	23.1	102 05.5	43.2	89 39.4	33.1	Sabik	102 24.8	S15 43.3
D 11	150 05.7	10 49.9	53.9	270 15.9	23.4	117 08.0	43.1	104 41.9	33.1			
A 12	165 08.2	25 52.7	N 7 54.4	285 16.7	S22 23.8	132 10.6	N11 43.1	119 44.4	N14 33.1	Schedar	349 52.2	N56 32.0
Y 13	180 10.7	40 55.5	54.8	300 17.4	24.1	147 13.1	43.0	134 46.9	33.0	Shaula	96 36.4	S37 06.2
14	195 13.1	55 58.3	55.2	315 18.2	24.4	162 15.7	43.0	149 49.4	33.0	Sirius	258 43.3	S16 42.8
15	210 15.6	71 01.1	.. 55.7	330 19.0	.. 24.7	177 18.3	.. 42.9	164 51.9	.. 33.0	Spica	158 42.8	S11 09.4
16	225 18.1	86 03.9	56.1	345 19.8	25.0	192 20.8	42.9	179 54.4	33.0	Suhail	223 00.7	S43 25.7
17	240 20.5	101 06.7	56.5	0 20.6	25.4	207 23.4	42.9	194 56.8	33.0			
18	255 23.0	116 09.4	N 7 57.0	15 21.3	S22 25.7	222 25.9	N11 42.8	209 59.3	N14 33.0	Vega	80 46.0	N38 47.4
19	270 25.5	131 12.2	57.4	30 22.1	26.0	237 28.5	42.8	225 01.8	32.9	Zuben'ubi	137 17.4	S16 02.3
20	285 27.9	146 15.0	57.8	45 22.9	26.3	252 31.1	42.7	240 04.3	32.9			
21	300 30.4	161 17.7	.. 58.3	60 23.7	.. 26.7	267 33.6	.. 42.7	255 06.8	.. 32.9			
22	315 32.8	176 20.5	58.7	75 24.5	27.0	282 36.2	42.6	270 09.3	32.9			
23	330 35.3	191 23.2	59.1	90 25.2	27.3	297 38.8	42.6	285 11.8	32.9			
Mer. Pass. 1 05.2		v 2.9	d 0.5	v 0.8	d 0.3	v 2.6	d 0.0	v 2.5	d 0.0			

	SHA	Mer. Pass.
Venus	220 29.8	10 21
Mars	121 08.7	17 00
Jupiter	326 59.1	3 17
Saturn	314 35.2	4 06

UT	SUN GHA	SUN Dec	MOON GHA	MOON v	MOON Dec	MOON d	MOON HP	Lat.	Twilight Naut.	Twilight Civil	Sunrise	Moonrise 4	Moonrise 5	Moonrise 6	Moonrise 7
d h	° ′	° ′	° ′	′	° ′	′	′	°	h m	h m	h m	h m	h m	h m	h m
4 00	180 10.6	N 7 25.7	257 45.7	6.1	N19 29.6	3.4	59.2	N 72	////	02 55	04 18	⬓	⬓	⬓	⬓
01	195 10.8	24.8	272 10.8	6.1	19 33.0	3.2	59.2	N 70	01 10	03 18	04 30	⬓	21 17	23 24	25 23
02	210 11.0	23.8	286 35.9	6.1	19 36.2	3.1	59.2	68	02 00	03 36	04 39	21 20	22 30	24 05	00 05
03	225 11.2	. . 22.9	301 01.0	6.0	19 39.3	3.0	59.2	66	02 30	03 50	04 46	22 00	23 06	24 32	00 32
04	240 11.4	22.0	315 26.0	6.0	19 42.3	2.8	59.2	64	02 51	04 01	04 53	22 27	23 33	24 54	00 54
05	255 11.6	21.1	329 51.0	6.0	19 45.1	2.7	59.2	62	03 08	04 11	04 58	22 49	23 53	25 10	01 10
06	270 11.8	N 7 20.2	344 16.0	6.0	N19 47.8	2.6	59.2	60	03 22	04 19	05 03	23 06	24 10	00 10	01 25
07	285 12.0	19.2	358 41.0	6.0	19 50.4	2.5	59.2	N 58	03 34	04 26	05 07	23 20	24 24	00 24	01 37
08	300 12.2	18.3	13 06.0	5.9	19 52.9	2.3	59.2	56	03 44	04 32	05 11	23 33	24 36	00 36	01 47
09	315 12.4	. . 17.4	27 30.9	6.0	19 55.2	2.2	59.2	54	03 52	04 37	05 14	23 44	24 46	00 46	01 56
10	330 12.6	16.5	41 55.9	5.9	19 57.4	2.0	59.2	52	04 00	04 42	05 17	23 53	24 55	00 55	02 04
11	345 12.8	15.6	56 20.8	6.0	19 59.4	2.0	59.2	50	04 06	04 47	05 20	24 02	00 02	01 04	02 12
12	0 13.0	N 7 14.6	70 45.8	5.9	N20 01.4	1.8	59.2	45	04 20	04 56	05 26	24 20	00 20	01 21	02 27
13	15 13.2	13.7	85 10.7	5.9	20 03.2	1.6	59.2	N 40	04 30	05 03	05 31	24 35	00 35	01 36	02 40
14	30 13.4	12.8	99 35.6	5.9	20 04.8	1.6	59.2	35	04 39	05 09	05 35	24 48	00 48	01 48	02 51
15	45 13.6	. . 11.9	114 00.5	5.9	20 06.4	1.4	59.2	30	04 48	05 15	05 39	00 03	00 59	01 59	03 00
16	60 13.8	11.0	128 25.4	5.9	20 07.8	1.2	59.1	20	04 57	05 23	05 45	00 21	01 18	02 17	03 17
17	75 14.0	10.0	142 50.3	5.9	20 09.0	1.1	59.1	N 10	05 05	05 29	05 51	00 37	01 34	02 33	03 31
18	90 14.2	N 7 09.1	157 15.2	5.9	N20 10.1	1.0	59.1	0	05 11	05 35	05 56	00 52	01 50	02 48	03 44
19	105 14.5	08.2	171 40.1	5.9	20 11.1	0.9	59.1	S 10	05 15	05 39	06 00	01 07	02 05	03 03	03 58
20	120 14.7	07.3	186 05.0	5.8	20 12.0	0.7	59.1	20	05 18	05 43	06 06	01 23	02 22	03 19	04 12
21	135 14.9	. . 06.3	200 29.8	5.9	20 12.7	0.6	59.1	30	05 19	05 47	06 11	01 41	02 41	03 37	04 28
22	150 15.1	05.4	214 54.7	5.9	20 13.3	0.5	59.1	35	05 20	05 49	06 14	01 52	02 52	03 48	04 38
23	165 15.3	04.5	229 19.6	5.9	20 13.8	0.3	59.1	40	05 20	05 51	06 18	02 04	03 05	04 00	04 48
5 00	180 15.5	N 7 03.6	243 44.5	5.9	N20 14.1	0.2	59.1	45	05 19	05 53	06 22	02 19	03 20	04 14	05 01
01	195 15.7	02.6	258 09.4	5.9	20 14.3	0.1	59.1	S 50	05 17	05 55	06 27	02 37	03 39	04 32	05 16
02	210 15.9	01.7	272 34.3	5.9	20 14.4	0.1	59.1	52	05 17	05 56	06 29	02 45	03 48	04 40	05 23
03	225 16.1	7 00.8	286 59.3	5.9	20 14.3	0.2	59.1	54	05 16	05 56	06 32	02 55	03 58	04 50	05 31
04	240 16.3	6 59.9	301 24.2	5.9	20 14.1	0.3	59.1	56	05 13	05 57	06 34	03 05	04 09	05 00	05 40
05	255 16.5	58.9	315 49.1	6.0	20 13.8	0.5	59.0	S 58	05 13	05 58	06 37	03 18	04 21	05 12	05 50
06	270 16.7	N 6 58.0	330 14.1	5.9	N20 13.3	0.6	59.0	S 60	05 11	05 59	06 41	03 32	04 36	05 25	06 02

UT	SUN GHA	SUN Dec	MOON GHA	MOON v	MOON Dec	MOON d	MOON HP	Lat.	Sunset	Twilight Civil	Twilight Naut.	Moonset 4	Moonset 5	Moonset 6	Moonset 7
07	285 16.9	57.1	344 39.0	6.0	20 12.7	0.7	59.0	°	h m	h m	h m	h m	h m	h m	h m
08	300 17.1	56.2	359 04.0	6.0	20 12.0	0.9	59.0	N 72	19 36	20 58	////	⬓	⬓	⬓	20 16
09	315 17.3	. . 55.2	13 29.0	6.0	20 11.1	1.0	59.0	N 70	19 25	20 36	22 36	⬓	19 53	19 45	19 40
10	330 17.6	54.3	27 54.0	6.1	20 10.1	1.1	59.0	68	19 16	20 19	21 52	17 48	18 40	19 04	19 14
11	345 17.8	53.4	42 19.0	6.1	20 09.0	1.3	59.0	66	19 09	20 05	21 24	17 08	18 03	18 35	18 54
12	0 18.0	N 6 52.5	56 44.1	6.0	N20 07.7	1.4	59.0	64	19 03	19 54	21 03	16 41	17 37	18 14	18 38
13	15 18.2	51.5	71 09.1	6.1	20 06.3	1.5	59.0	62	18 58	19 45	20 46	16 20	17 16	17 56	18 24
14	30 18.4	50.6	85 34.2	6.1	20 04.8	1.7	59.0	60	18 53	19 37	20 33	16 02	16 59	17 42	18 13
15	45 18.6	. . 49.7	99 59.3	6.2	20 03.1	1.7	59.0	N 58	18 49	19 30	20 22	15 48	16 45	17 29	18 03
16	60 18.8	48.8	114 24.5	6.1	20 01.4	2.0	58.9	56	18 45	19 24	20 12	15 36	16 33	17 19	17 54
17	75 19.0	47.8	128 49.6	6.2	19 59.4	2.0	58.9	54	18 42	19 19	20 04	15 25	16 22	17 09	17 47
18	90 19.2	N 6 46.9	143 14.8	6.2	N19 57.4	2.2	58.9	52	18 39	19 14	19 56	15 15	16 13	17 01	17 40
19	105 19.4	46.0	157 40.0	6.3	19 55.2	2.3	58.9	50	18 37	19 10	19 50	15 07	16 04	16 53	17 33
20	120 19.6	45.1	172 05.3	6.2	19 52.9	2.4	58.9	45	18 31	19 01	19 37	14 48	15 46	16 37	17 20
21	135 19.8	. . 44.1	186 30.5	6.3	19 50.5	2.6	58.9	N 40	18 26	18 54	19 26	14 34	15 32	16 23	17 08
22	150 20.1	43.2	200 55.8	6.4	19 47.9	2.7	58.9	35	18 22	18 48	19 18	14 21	15 19	16 12	16 59
23	165 20.3	42.3	215 21.2	6.5	19 45.2	2.8	58.9	30	18 18	18 43	19 11	14 10	15 08	16 02	16 50
6 00	180 20.5	N 6 41.3	229 46.5	6.4	N19 42.4	2.9	58.9	20	18 12	18 34	19 00	13 51	14 50	15 45	16 36
01	195 20.7	40.4	244 11.9	6.5	19 39.5	3.1	58.8	N 10	18 07	18 28	18 53	13 35	14 33	15 29	16 23
02	210 20.9	39.5	258 37.4	6.4	19 36.4	3.2	58.8	0	18 02	18 23	18 47	13 19	14 18	15 15	16 11
03	225 21.1	. . 38.6	273 02.8	6.5	19 33.2	3.3	58.8	S 10	17 57	18 18	18 43	13 04	14 02	15 01	15 58
04	240 21.3	37.6	287 28.3	6.6	19 29.9	3.4	58.8	20	17 52	18 14	18 40	12 48	13 46	14 46	15 45
05	255 21.5	36.7	301 53.9	6.6	19 26.5	3.6	58.8	30	17 47	18 11	18 39	12 29	13 27	14 28	15 30
06	270 21.7	N 6 35.8	316 19.5	6.6	N19 22.9	3.7	58.8	35	17 44	18 09	18 38	12 18	13 16	14 18	15 21
07	285 21.9	34.8	330 45.1	6.7	19 19.2	3.8	58.8	40	17 40	18 07	18 39	12 05	13 03	14 06	15 11
08	300 22.1	33.9	345 10.8	6.7	19 15.4	3.9	58.8	45	17 36	18 06	18 40	11 50	12 48	13 52	14 59
09	315 22.4	. . 33.0	359 36.5	6.7	19 11.5	4.0	58.7	S 50	17 31	18 04	18 41	11 32	12 30	13 35	14 45
10	330 22.6	32.1	14 02.2	6.8	19 07.5	4.2	58.7	52	17 29	18 03	18 42	11 23	12 21	13 27	14 38
11	345 22.8	31.1	28 28.0	6.9	19 03.3	4.3	58.7	54	17 27	18 02	18 43	11 14	12 11	13 18	14 31
12	0 23.0	N 6 30.2	42 53.9	6.8	N18 59.0	4.4	58.7	56	17 24	18 01	18 44	11 03	12 00	13 08	14 22
13	15 23.2	29.3	57 19.7	7.0	18 54.6	4.5	58.7	58	17 21	18 01	18 46	10 50	11 47	12 56	14 13
14	30 23.4	28.3	71 45.7	7.0	18 50.1	4.7	58.7	S 60	17 18	18 00	18 48	10 36	11 33	12 43	14 02
15	45 23.6	. . 27.4	86 11.7	7.0	18 45.4	4.7	58.7								
16	60 23.8	26.5	100 37.7	7.1	18 40.7	4.9	58.7			SUN			MOON		
17	75 24.0	25.5	115 03.8	7.1	18 35.8	5.0	58.6								
18	90 24.2	N 6 24.6	129 29.9	7.2	N18 30.8	5.1	58.6	Day	Eqn. of Time 00ʰ	Eqn. of Time 12ʰ	Mer. Pass.	Mer. Pass. Upper	Mer. Pass. Lower	Age	Phase
19	105 24.5	23.7	143 56.1	7.2	18 25.7	5.2	58.6	d	m s	m s	h m	h m	h m	d %	
20	120 24.7	22.7	158 22.3	7.3	18 20.5	5.3	58.6	4	00 42	00 52	11 59	07 05	19 35	24 32	
21	135 24.9	. . 21.8	172 48.6	7.3	18 15.2	5.4	58.6	5	01 02	01 11	11 59	08 04	20 33	25 22	
22	150 25.1	20.9	187 14.9	7.4	18 09.8	5.6	58.6	6	01 21	01 32	11 58	09 02	21 30	26 14	◑
23	165 25.3	19.9	201 41.3	7.5	N18 04.2	5.6	58.5								
	SD 15.9	d 0.9	SD 16.1	16.1		16.0										

1999 SEPTEMBER 7, 8, 9 (TUES., WED., THURS.)

UT	ARIES	VENUS −4.4		MARS +0.4		JUPITER −2.7		SATURN +0.1		STARS		
	GHA	GHA	Dec	GHA	Dec	GHA	Dec	GHA	Dec	Name	SHA	Dec
d h	° ′	° ′	° ′	° ′	° ′	° ′	° ′	° ′	° ′		° ′	° ′
7 00	345 37.8	206 26.0	N 7 59.6	105 26.0	S22 27.6	312 41.3	N11 42.5	300 14.3	N14 32.8	Acamar	315 26.2	S40 18.2
01	0 40.2	221 28.7	8 00.0	120 26.8	27.9	327 43.9	42.5	315 16.8	32.8	Achernar	335 34.3	S57 14.2
02	15 42.7	236 31.5	00.4	135 27.6	28.3	342 46.5	42.5	330 19.3	32.8	Acrux	173 21.9	S63 05.8
03	30 45.2	251 34.2 ..	00.9	150 28.4 ..	28.6	357 49.0 ..	42.4	345 21.8 ..	32.8	Adhara	255 21.1	S28 58.1
04	45 47.6	266 36.9	01.3	165 29.1	28.9	12 51.6	42.4	0 24.3	32.8	Aldebaran	291 01.6	N16 30.4
05	60 50.1	281 39.7	01.7	180 29.9	29.2	27 54.1	42.3	15 26.8	32.8			
06	75 52.6	296 42.4	N 8 02.1	195 30.7	S22 29.5	42 56.7	N11 42.3	30 29.3	N14 32.7	Alioth	166 30.6	N55 58.0
07	90 55.0	311 45.1	02.6	210 31.5	29.9	57 59.3	42.2	45 31.8	32.7	Alkaid	153 07.7	N49 19.3
T 08	105 57.5	326 47.8	03.0	225 32.2	30.2	73 01.8	42.2	60 34.3	32.7	Al Na'ir	27 56.7	S46 57.7
U 09	121 00.0	341 50.5 ..	03.4	240 33.0 ..	30.5	88 04.4 ..	42.2	75 36.8 ..	32.7	Alnilam	275 57.3	S 1 12.1
E 10	136 02.4	356 53.2	03.8	255 33.8	30.8	103 07.0	42.1	90 39.3	32.7	Alphard	218 06.9	S 8 39.3
S 11	151 04.9	11 55.9	04.3	270 34.6	31.1	118 09.5	42.1	105 41.8	32.6			
D 12	166 07.3	26 58.6	N 8 04.7	285 35.3	S22 31.5	133 12.1	N11 42.0	120 44.3	N14 32.6	Alphecca	126 20.2	N26 43.3
A 13	181 09.8	42 01.3	05.1	300 36.1	31.8	148 14.7	42.0	135 46.8	32.6	Alpheratz	357 54.2	N29 05.3
Y 14	196 12.3	57 04.0	05.5	315 36.9	32.1	163 17.3	41.9	150 49.3	32.6	Altair	62 18.4	N 8 52.3
15	211 14.7	72 06.7 ..	06.0	330 37.6 ..	32.4	178 19.8 ..	41.9	165 51.8 ..	32.6	Ankaa	353 25.8	S42 18.4
16	226 17.2	87 09.4	06.4	345 38.4	32.7	193 22.4	41.8	180 54.3	32.5	Antares	112 39.4	S26 25.8
17	241 19.7	102 12.1	06.8	0 39.2	33.0	208 25.0	41.8	195 56.8	32.5			
18	256 22.1	117 14.7	N 8 07.2	15 40.0	S22 33.4	223 27.5	N11 41.7	210 59.3	N14 32.5	Arcturus	146 05.7	N19 11.4
19	271 24.6	132 17.4	07.6	30 40.7	33.7	238 30.1	41.7	226 01.8	32.5	Atria	107 50.9	S69 01.8
20	286 27.1	147 20.1	08.1	45 41.5	34.0	253 32.7	41.7	241 04.3	32.5	Avior	234 22.8	S59 30.3
21	301 29.5	162 22.7 ..	08.5	60 42.3 ..	34.3	268 35.2 ..	41.6	256 06.8 ..	32.4	Bellatrix	278 43.5	N 6 21.0
22	316 32.0	177 25.4	08.9	75 43.0	34.6	283 37.8	41.6	271 09.3	32.4	Betelgeuse	271 13.0	N 7 24.4
23	331 34.4	192 28.0	09.3	90 43.8	34.9	298 40.4	41.5	286 11.8	32.4			
8 00	346 36.9	207 30.7	N 8 09.7	105 44.6	S22 35.3	313 43.0	N11 41.5	301 14.3	N14 32.4	Canopus	264 01.1	S52 41.5
01	1 39.4	222 33.3	10.1	120 45.3	35.6	328 45.5	41.4	316 16.8	32.4	Capella	280 50.3	N45 59.6
02	16 41.8	237 36.0	10.6	135 46.1	35.9	343 48.1	41.4	331 19.3	32.3	Deneb	49 38.4	N45 17.0
03	31 44.3	252 38.6 ..	11.0	150 46.9 ..	36.2	358 50.7 ..	41.3	346 21.8 ..	32.3	Denebola	182 44.9	N14 34.6
04	46 46.8	267 41.2	11.4	165 47.6	36.5	13 53.2	41.3	1 24.3	32.3	Diphda	349 06.3	S17 59.2
05	61 49.2	282 43.9	11.8	180 48.4	36.8	28 55.8	41.2	16 26.8	32.3			
06	76 51.7	297 46.5	N 8 12.2	195 49.2	S22 37.1	43 58.4	N11 41.2	31 29.3	N14 32.3	Dubhe	194 05.4	N61 45.3
W 07	91 54.2	312 49.1	12.6	210 49.9	37.5	59 01.0	41.1	46 31.8	32.2	Elnath	278 26.2	N28 36.3
E 08	106 56.6	327 51.7	13.0	225 50.7	37.8	74 03.5	41.1	61 34.3	32.2	Eltanin	90 51.0	N51 29.8
D 09	121 59.1	342 54.3 ..	13.4	240 51.5 ..	38.1	89 06.1 ..	41.0	76 36.8 ..	32.2	Enif	33 57.3	N 9 52.5
N 10	137 01.6	357 56.9	13.8	255 52.2	38.4	104 08.7	41.0	91 39.3	32.2	Fomalhaut	15 35.4	S29 37.4
E 11	152 04.0	12 59.5	14.2	270 53.0	38.7	119 11.3	41.0	106 41.8	32.2			
S 12	167 06.5	28 02.1	N 8 14.7	285 53.8	S22 39.0	134 13.8	N11 40.9	121 44.3	N14 32.1	Gacrux	172 13.4	S57 06.6
D 13	182 08.9	43 04.7	15.1	300 54.5	39.3	149 16.4	40.9	136 46.8	32.1	Gienah	176 03.6	S17 32.2
A 14	197 11.4	58 07.3	15.5	315 55.3	39.6	164 19.0	40.8	151 49.3	32.1	Hadar	149 03.6	S60 22.3
Y 15	212 13.9	73 09.9 ..	15.9	330 56.0 ..	40.0	179 21.6 ..	40.8	166 51.8 ..	32.1	Hamal	328 12.6	N23 27.6
16	227 16.3	88 12.5	16.3	345 56.8	40.3	194 24.1	40.7	181 54.3	32.1	Kaus Aust.	83 57.8	S34 23.1
17	242 18.8	103 15.1	16.7	0 57.6	40.6	209 26.7	40.7	196 56.8	32.0			
18	257 21.3	118 17.6	N 8 17.1	15 58.3	S22 40.9	224 29.3	N11 40.6	211 59.3	N14 32.0	Kochab	137 20.2	N74 09.8
19	272 23.7	133 20.2	17.5	30 59.0	41.2	239 31.9	40.6	227 01.8	32.0	Markab	13 48.7	N15 12.3
20	287 26.2	148 22.8	17.9	45 59.8	41.5	254 34.5	40.5	242 04.3	32.0	Menkar	314 26.1	N 4 05.3
21	302 28.7	163 25.3 ..	18.3	61 00.6 ..	41.8	269 37.0 ..	40.5	257 06.8 ..	32.0	Menkent	148 20.5	S36 22.0
22	317 31.1	178 27.9	18.7	76 01.4	42.1	284 39.6	40.4	272 09.3	31.9	Miaplacidus	221 42.7	S69 42.8
23	332 33.6	193 30.4	19.1	91 02.1	42.4	299 42.2	40.4	287 11.8	31.9			
9 00	347 36.0	208 33.0	N 8 19.5	106 02.9	S22 42.7	314 44.8	N11 40.3	302 14.4	N14 31.9	Mirfak	308 55.5	N49 51.3
01	2 38.5	223 35.5	19.9	121 03.6	43.1	329 47.4	40.3	317 16.9	31.9	Nunki	76 11.4	S26 17.8
02	17 41.0	238 38.1	20.3	136 04.4	43.4	344 49.9	40.2	332 19.4	31.9	Peacock	53 35.6	S56 44.2
03	32 43.4	253 40.6 ..	20.7	151 05.1 ..	43.7	359 52.5 ..	40.2	347 21.9 ..	31.8	Pollux	243 41.0	N28 01.6
04	47 45.9	268 43.1	21.1	166 05.9	44.0	14 55.1	40.1	2 24.4	31.8	Procyon	245 11.1	N 5 13.6
05	62 48.4	283 45.7	21.5	181 06.6	44.3	29 57.7	40.1	17 26.9	31.8			
06	77 50.8	298 48.2	N 8 21.9	196 07.4	S22 44.6	45 00.3	N11 40.0	32 29.4	N14 31.8	Rasalhague	96 16.3	N12 33.9
07	92 53.3	313 50.7	22.2	211 08.2	44.9	60 02.8	40.0	47 31.9	31.7	Regulus	207 55.2	N11 58.3
T 08	107 55.8	328 53.2	22.6	226 08.9	45.2	75 05.4	39.9	62 34.4	31.7	Rigel	281 22.4	S 8 12.1
H 09	122 58.2	343 55.7 ..	23.0	241 09.7 ..	45.5	90 08.0 ..	39.9	77 36.9 ..	31.7	Rigil Kent.	140 06.8	S60 50.0
U 10	138 00.7	358 58.2	23.4	256 10.4	45.8	105 10.6	39.8	92 39.4	31.7	Sabik	102 24.8	S15 43.3
R 11	153 03.2	14 00.7	23.8	271 11.2	46.1	120 13.2	39.8	107 41.9	31.7			
S 12	168 05.6	29 03.2	N 8 24.2	286 11.9	S22 46.4	135 15.8	N11 39.7	122 44.4	N14 31.6	Schedar	349 52.2	N56 32.0
D 13	183 08.1	44 05.7	24.6	301 12.7	46.8	150 18.3	39.7	137 46.9	31.6	Shaula	96 36.4	S37 06.2
A 14	198 10.5	59 08.2	25.0	316 13.4	47.1	165 20.9	39.6	152 49.4	31.6	Sirius	258 43.3	S16 42.8
Y 15	213 13.0	74 10.7 ..	25.4	331 14.2 ..	47.4	180 23.5 ..	39.6	167 52.0 ..	31.6	Spica	158 42.8	S11 09.4
16	228 15.5	89 13.2	25.8	346 14.9	47.7	195 26.1	39.5	182 54.5	31.6	Suhail	223 00.7	S43 25.7
17	243 17.9	104 15.7	26.1	1 15.7	48.0	210 28.7	39.5	197 57.0	31.5			
18	258 20.4	119 18.1	N 8 26.5	16 16.4	S22 48.3	225 31.3	N11 39.4	212 59.5	N14 31.5	Vega	80 46.0	N38 47.4
19	273 22.9	134 20.6	26.9	31 17.2	48.6	240 33.9	39.4	228 02.0	31.5	Zuben'ubi	137 17.4	S16 02.3
20	288 25.3	149 23.1	27.3	46 17.9	48.9	255 36.4	39.3	243 04.5	31.5		SHA	Mer. Pass.
21	303 27.8	164 25.5 ..	27.7	61 18.7 ..	49.2	270 39.0 ..	39.3	258 07.0 ..	31.5		° ′	h m
22	318 30.3	179 28.0	28.1	76 19.4	49.5	285 41.6	39.2	273 09.5	31.4	Venus	220 53.8	10 08
23	333 32.7	194 30.5	28.4	91 20.2	49.8	300 44.2	39.2	288 12.0	31.4	Mars	119 07.7	16 56
	h m									Jupiter	327 06.0	3 05
Mer. Pass.	0 53.4	v 2.6	d 0.4	v 0.8	d 0.3	v 2.6	d 0.0	v 2.5	d 0.0	Saturn	314 37.4	3 54

SUN / MOON

UT (d h)	SUN GHA	Dec	MOON GHA	v	Dec	d	HP
	° ′	° ′	° ′	′	° ′	′	′
7 00	180 25.5	N 6 19.0	216 07.8	7.5	N17 58.6	5.8	58.5
01	195 25.7	18.1	230 34.3	7.5	17 52.8	5.9	58.5
02	210 25.9	17.1	245 00.8	7.6	17 46.9	5.9	58.5
03	225 26.1	.. 16.2	259 27.4	7.7	17 41.0	6.1	58.5
04	240 26.4	15.3	273 54.1	7.7	17 34.9	6.2	58.5
05	255 26.6	14.3	288 20.8	7.8	17 28.7	6.3	58.5
06	270 26.8	N 6 13.4	302 47.6	7.9	N17 22.4	6.4	58.4
07	285 27.0	12.5	317 14.5	7.9	17 16.0	6.5	58.4
08	300 27.2	11.5	331 41.4	7.9	17 09.5	6.6	58.4
09	315 27.4	.. 10.6	346 08.3	8.1	17 02.9	6.7	58.4
10	330 27.6	09.7	0 35.4	8.1	16 56.2	6.7	58.4
11	345 27.8	08.7	15 02.5	8.1	16 49.5	6.9	58.4
12	0 28.0	N 6 07.8	29 29.6	8.2	N16 42.6	7.0	58.3
13	15 28.3	06.9	43 56.8	8.3	16 35.6	7.1	58.3
14	30 28.5	05.9	58 24.1	8.3	16 28.5	7.2	58.3
15	45 28.7	.. 05.0	72 51.4	8.4	16 21.3	7.2	58.3
16	60 28.9	04.1	87 18.8	8.5	16 14.1	7.4	58.3
17	75 29.1	03.1	101 46.3	8.5	16 06.7	7.4	58.2
18	90 29.3	N 6 02.2	116 13.8	8.6	N15 59.3	7.6	58.2
19	105 29.5	01.3	130 41.4	8.6	15 51.7	7.6	58.2
20	120 29.7	6 00.3	145 09.0	8.7	15 44.1	7.7	58.2
21	135 30.0	5 59.4	159 36.7	8.8	15 36.4	7.8	58.2
22	150 30.2	58.4	174 04.5	8.8	15 28.6	7.9	58.2
23	165 30.4	57.5	188 32.3	8.9	15 20.7	8.0	58.1
8 00	180 30.6	N 5 56.6	203 00.2	9.0	N15 12.7	8.0	58.1
01	195 30.8	55.6	217 28.2	9.0	15 04.7	8.2	58.1
02	210 31.0	54.7	231 56.2	9.1	14 56.5	8.2	58.1
03	225 31.2	.. 53.8	246 24.3	9.2	14 48.3	8.3	58.1
04	240 31.4	52.8	260 52.5	9.2	14 40.0	8.4	58.0
05	255 31.7	51.9	275 20.7	9.3	14 31.6	8.4	58.0
06	270 31.9	N 5 50.9	289 49.0	9.4	N14 23.2	8.6	58.0
07	285 32.1	50.0	304 17.4	9.4	14 14.6	8.6	58.0
08	300 32.3	49.1	318 45.8	9.5	14 06.0	8.6	58.0
09	315 32.5	.. 48.1	333 14.3	9.6	13 57.4	8.8	57.9
10	330 32.7	47.2	347 42.9	9.6	13 48.6	8.8	57.9
11	345 32.9	46.2	2 11.5	9.7	13 39.8	8.9	57.9
12	0 33.2	N 5 45.3	16 40.2	9.7	N13 30.9	9.0	57.9
13	15 33.4	44.4	31 08.9	9.8	13 21.9	9.0	57.9
14	30 33.6	43.4	45 37.7	9.9	13 12.9	9.1	57.8
15	45 33.8	.. 42.5	60 06.6	10.0	13 03.8	9.2	57.8
16	60 34.0	41.6	74 35.6	10.0	12 54.6	9.2	57.8
17	75 34.2	40.6	89 04.6	10.0	12 45.4	9.3	57.8
18	90 34.4	N 5 39.7	103 33.6	10.2	N12 36.1	9.4	57.7
19	105 34.7	38.7	118 02.8	10.2	12 26.7	9.4	57.7
20	120 34.9	37.8	132 32.0	10.3	12 17.3	9.5	57.7
21	135 35.1	.. 36.9	147 01.3	10.3	12 07.8	9.5	57.7
22	150 35.3	35.9	161 30.6	10.4	11 58.3	9.6	57.7
23	165 35.5	35.0	176 00.0	10.4	11 48.7	9.6	57.6
9 00	180 35.7	N 5 34.0	190 29.4	10.6	N11 39.1	9.7	57.6
01	195 35.9	33.1	204 59.0	10.5	11 29.4	9.8	57.6
02	210 36.2	32.1	219 28.5	10.7	11 19.6	9.8	57.6
03	225 36.4	.. 31.2	233 58.2	10.7	11 09.8	9.9	57.5
04	240 36.6	30.3	248 27.9	10.8	10 59.9	9.9	57.5
05	255 36.8	29.3	262 57.7	10.8	10 50.0	10.0	57.5
06	270 37.0	N 5 28.4	277 27.5	10.9	N10 40.0	10.0	57.5
07	285 37.2	27.4	291 57.4	10.9	10 30.0	10.1	57.5
08	300 37.4	26.5	306 27.3	11.1	10 19.9	10.1	57.4
09	315 37.7	.. 25.6	320 57.4	11.0	10 09.8	10.1	57.4
10	330 37.9	24.6	335 27.4	11.2	9 59.7	10.2	57.4
11	345 38.1	23.7	349 57.6	11.2	9 49.5	10.3	57.4
12	0 38.3	N 5 22.7	4 27.8	11.2	N 9 39.2	10.3	57.3
13	15 38.5	21.8	18 58.0	11.3	9 28.9	10.3	57.3
14	30 38.7	20.8	33 28.3	11.4	9 18.6	10.3	57.3
15	45 39.0	.. 19.9	47 58.7	11.4	9 08.3	10.5	57.3
16	60 39.2	18.9	62 29.1	11.5	8 57.8	10.4	57.2
17	75 39.4	18.0	76 59.6	11.5	8 47.4	10.5	57.2
18	90 39.6	N 5 17.1	91 30.1	11.6	N 8 36.9	10.5	57.2
19	105 39.8	16.1	106 00.7	11.7	8 26.4	10.5	57.2
20	120 40.0	15.2	120 31.4	11.7	8 15.9	10.6	57.1
21	135 40.3	.. 14.2	135 02.1	11.7	8 05.3	10.6	57.1
22	150 40.5	13.3	149 32.8	11.9	7 54.7	10.7	57.1
23	165 40.7	12.3	164 03.7	11.8	N 7 44.0	10.6	57.1
	SD 15.9	d 0.9	SD 15.9		15.8		15.6

(Left margin day labels: TUESDAY, WEDNESDAY, THURSDAY)

Twilight / Sunrise / Moonrise

Lat.	Twilight Naut.	Twilight Civil	Sunrise	Moonrise 7	Moonrise 8	Moonrise 9	Moonrise 10
°	h m	h m	h m	h m	h m	h m	h m
N 72	00 17	03 13	04 33	▭	00 48	02 56	04 52
N 70	01 43	03 33	04 42	25 23	01 23	03 16	05 02
68	02 20	03 48	04 50	00 05	01 48	03 31	05 10
66	02 45	04 01	04 56	00 32	02 07	03 43	05 17
64	03 04	04 11	05 01	00 54	02 22	03 53	05 22
62	03 19	04 19	05 06	01 10	02 35	04 02	05 27
60	03 31	04 27	05 10	01 25	02 46	04 09	05 31
N 58	03 42	04 33	05 14	01 37	02 55	04 16	05 35
56	03 51	04 38	05 17	01 47	03 03	04 21	05 38
54	03 59	04 43	05 20	01 56	03 11	04 26	05 41
52	04 05	04 48	05 22	02 04	03 17	04 31	05 44
50	04 11	04 51	05 25	02 12	03 23	04 35	05 48
45	04 24	05 00	05 30	02 27	03 36	04 44	05 52
N 40	04 34	05 06	05 34	02 40	03 46	04 52	05 56
35	04 42	05 12	05 37	02 51	03 55	04 58	06 00
30	04 48	05 16	05 40	03 00	04 03	05 04	06 03
20	04 58	05 24	05 46	03 17	04 16	05 13	06 09
N 10	05 05	05 29	05 50	03 31	04 28	05 22	06 14
0	05 10	05 34	05 55	03 44	04 38	05 30	06 18
S 10	05 13	05 38	05 59	03 58	04 49	05 38	06 23
20	05 15	05 41	06 03	04 12	05 01	05 46	06 28
30	05 16	05 44	06 08	04 28	05 14	05 56	06 34
35	05 16	05 45	06 10	04 38	05 22	06 01	06 37
40	05 15	05 46	06 13	04 48	05 30	06 07	06 41
45	05 13	05 47	06 17	05 01	05 41	06 15	06 45
S 50	05 11	05 48	06 21	05 16	05 53	06 23	06 50
52	05 10	05 49	06 23	05 23	05 58	06 27	06 52
54	05 08	05 49	06 25	05 31	06 05	06 32	06 55
56	05 07	05 50	06 27	05 40	06 11	06 37	06 58
58	05 05	05 50	06 29	05 50	06 19	06 42	07 01
S 60	05 02	05 50	06 32	06 02	06 28	06 48	07 04

Sunset / Twilight / Moonset

Lat.	Sunset	Twilight Civil	Twilight Naut.	Moonset 7	Moonset 8	Moonset 9	Moonset 10
°	h m	h m	h m	h m	h m	h m	h m
N 72	19 20	20 38	23 08	20 16	19 56	19 42	19 31
N 70	19 11	20 19	22 04	19 40	19 35	19 30	19 26
68	19 04	20 04	21 30	19 14	19 19	19 21	19 22
66	18 57	19 52	21 07	18 54	19 05	19 13	19 18
64	18 52	19 43	20 48	18 38	18 54	19 06	19 15
62	18 48	19 34	20 34	18 24	18 44	19 00	19 12
60	18 44	19 27	20 22	18 13	18 36	18 54	19 10
N 58	18 41	19 21	20 12	18 03	18 29	18 50	19 08
56	18 38	19 16	20 03	17 54	18 23	18 46	19 06
54	18 35	19 11	19 55	17 47	18 17	18 42	19 04
52	18 32	19 07	19 49	17 40	18 12	18 39	19 02
50	18 30	19 03	19 43	17 33	18 07	18 35	19 01
45	18 25	18 55	19 31	17 20	17 57	18 29	18 58
N 40	18 21	18 49	19 21	17 08	17 48	18 23	18 55
35	18 18	18 43	19 13	16 59	17 41	18 18	18 53
30	18 15	18 39	19 07	16 50	17 34	18 14	18 51
20	18 10	18 32	18 58	16 36	17 23	18 06	18 47
N 10	18 05	18 26	18 51	16 23	17 13	18 00	18 44
0	18 01	18 22	18 46	16 11	17 03	17 53	18 41
S 10	17 57	18 18	18 43	15 58	16 54	17 47	18 38
20	17 53	18 15	18 41	15 45	16 44	17 40	18 35
30	17 48	18 12	18 40	15 30	16 32	17 32	18 31
35	17 46	18 11	18 41	15 21	16 25	17 28	18 29
40	17 43	18 10	18 41	15 11	16 17	17 22	18 26
45	17 40	18 09	18 43	14 59	16 08	17 16	18 23
S 50	17 36	18 08	18 46	14 45	15 57	17 09	18 20
52	17 34	18 08	18 47	14 38	15 52	17 06	18 18
54	17 32	18 07	18 48	14 31	15 46	17 02	18 16
56	17 30	18 07	18 50	14 22	15 40	16 58	18 14
58	17 28	18 07	18 52	14 13	15 33	16 53	18 12
S 60	17 25	18 07	18 55	14 02	15 25	16 48	18 10

SUN / MOON

Day	SUN Eqn. of Time 00ʰ	SUN Eqn. of Time 12ʰ	SUN Mer. Pass.	MOON Mer. Pass. Upper	MOON Mer. Pass. Lower	Age	Phase
d	m s	m s	h m	h m	h m	d	%
7	01 42	01 52	11 58	09 58	22 25	27	7
8	02 02	02 12	11 58	10 51	23 17	28	2
9	02 22	02 33	11 57	11 42	24 06	29	0

UT	ARIES	VENUS −4.5		MARS +0.4		JUPITER −2.8		SATURN +0.1		STARS		
	GHA	GHA	Dec	GHA	Dec	GHA	Dec	GHA	Dec	Name	SHA	Dec
d h	° ′	° ′	° ′	° ′	° ′	° ′	° ′	° ′	° ′		° ′	° ′
10 00	348 35.2	209 32.9 N 8 28.8		106 20.9 S22 50.1		315 46.8 N11 39.1		303 14.5 N14 31.4		Acamar	315 26.2	S40 18.2
01	3 37.7	224 35.3	29.2	121 21.7	50.4	330 49.4	39.1	318 17.0	31.4	Achernar	335 34.3	S57 14.2
02	18 40.1	239 37.8	29.6	136 22.4	50.7	345 52.0	39.0	333 19.5	31.3	Acrux	173 21.9	S63 05.8
03	33 42.6	254 40.2 . .	30.0	151 23.2 . .	51.0	0 54.5 . .	39.0	348 22.1 . .	31.3	Adhara	255 21.1	S28 58.1
04	48 45.0	269 42.7	30.3	166 23.9	51.3	15 57.1	38.9	3 24.6	31.3	Aldebaran	291 01.6	N16 30.4
05	63 47.5	284 45.1	30.7	181 24.6	51.6	30 59.7	38.9	18 27.1	31.3			
06	78 50.0	299 47.5 N 8 31.1		196 25.4 S22 51.9		46 02.3 N11 38.8		33 29.6 N14 31.2		Alioth	166 30.6	N55 58.0
07	93 52.4	314 49.9	31.5	211 26.1	52.2	61 04.9	38.8	48 32.1	31.2	Alkaid	153 07.7	N49 19.2
08	108 54.9	329 52.4	31.8	226 26.9	52.5	76 07.5	38.7	63 34.6	31.2	Al Na'ir	27 56.7	S46 57.8
F 09	123 57.4	344 54.8 . .	32.2	241 27.6 . .	52.8	91 10.1 . .	38.6	78 37.1 . .	31.2	Alnilam	275 57.3	S 1 12.1
R 10	138 59.8	359 57.2	32.6	256 28.4	53.1	106 12.7	38.6	93 39.6	31.2	Alphard	218 06.9	S 8 39.3
I 11	154 02.3	14 59.6	32.9	271 29.1	53.4	121 15.3	38.5	108 42.1	31.1			
D 12	169 04.8	30 02.0 N 8 33.3		286 29.9 S22 53.7		136 17.9 N11 38.5		123 44.7 N14 31.1		Alphecca	126 20.2	N26 43.3
A 13	184 07.2	45 04.4	33.7	301 30.6	54.0	151 20.5	38.4	138 47.2	31.1	Alpheratz	357 54.2	N29 05.3
Y 14	199 09.7	60 06.8	34.1	316 31.3	54.3	166 23.0	38.4	153 49.7	31.1	Altair	62 18.5	N 8 52.3
15	214 12.1	75 09.2 . .	34.4	331 32.1 . .	54.6	181 25.6 . .	38.3	168 52.2 . .	31.0	Ankaa	353 25.8	S42 18.4
16	229 14.6	90 11.5	34.8	346 32.8	54.9	196 28.2	38.3	183 54.7	31.0	Antares	112 39.5	S26 25.8
17	244 17.1	105 13.9	35.2	1 33.6	55.2	211 30.8	38.2	198 57.2	31.0			
18	259 19.5	120 16.3 N 8 35.5		16 34.3 S22 55.5		226 33.4 N11 38.2		213 59.7 N14 31.0		Arcturus	146 05.7	N19 11.4
19	274 22.0	135 18.7	35.9	31 35.0	55.8	241 36.0	38.1	229 02.2	31.0	Atria	107 51.0	S69 01.8
20	289 24.5	150 21.0	36.3	46 35.8	56.1	256 38.6	38.1	244 04.8	30.9	Avior	234 22.8	S59 30.3
21	304 26.9	165 23.4 . .	36.6	61 36.5 . .	56.4	271 41.2 . .	38.0	259 07.3 . .	30.9	Bellatrix	278 43.5	N 6 21.0
22	319 29.4	180 25.8	37.0	76 37.2	56.7	286 43.8	38.0	274 09.8	30.9	Betelgeuse	271 12.9	N 7 24.4
23	334 31.9	195 28.1	37.3	91 38.0	57.0	301 46.4	37.9	289 12.3	30.9			
11 00	349 34.3	210 30.5 N 8 37.7		106 38.7 S22 57.3		316 49.0 N11 37.8		304 14.8 N14 30.8		Canopus	264 01.1	S52 41.5
01	4 36.8	225 32.8	38.1	121 39.5	57.6	331 51.6	37.8	319 17.3	30.8	Capella	280 50.3	N45 59.6
02	19 39.3	240 35.2	38.4	136 40.2	57.9	346 54.2	37.7	334 19.8	30.8	Deneb	49 38.4	N45 17.0
03	34 41.7	255 37.5 . .	38.8	151 40.9 . .	58.2	1 56.8 . .	37.7	349 22.4 . .	30.8	Denebola	182 44.9	N14 34.6
04	49 44.2	270 39.8	39.1	166 41.7	58.5	16 59.4	37.6	4 24.9	30.7	Diphda	349 06.3	S17 59.2
05	64 46.6	285 42.2	39.5	181 42.4	58.8	32 02.0	37.6	19 27.4	30.7			
06	79 49.1	300 44.5 N 8 39.9		196 43.1 S22 59.1		47 04.6 N11 37.5		34 29.9 N14 30.7		Dubhe	194 05.4	N61 45.3
07	94 51.6	315 46.8	40.2	211 43.9	59.4	62 07.2	37.5	49 32.4	30.7	Elnath	278 26.2	N28 36.3
S 08	109 54.0	330 49.1	40.6	226 44.6	22 59.7	77 09.8	37.4	64 34.9	30.6	Eltanin	90 51.0	N51 29.8
A 09	124 56.5	345 51.5 . .	40.9	241 45.3	23 00.0	92 12.3 . .	37.4	79 37.4 . .	30.6	Enif	33 57.3	N 9 52.5
T 10	139 59.0	0 53.8	41.3	256 46.1	00.3	107 14.9	37.3	94 40.0	30.6	Fomalhaut	15 35.4	S29 37.4
U 11	155 01.4	15 56.1	41.6	271 46.8	00.6	122 17.5	37.2	109 42.5	30.6			
R 12	170 03.9	30 58.4 N 8 42.0		286 47.5 S23 00.9		137 20.1 N11 37.2		124 45.0 N14 30.6		Gacrux	172 13.4	S57 06.6
D 13	185 06.4	46 00.7	42.3	301 48.3	01.2	152 22.7	37.1	139 47.5	30.5	Gienah	176 03.6	S17 32.2
A 14	200 08.8	61 03.0	42.7	316 49.0	01.5	167 25.3	37.1	154 50.0	30.5	Hadar	149 03.6	S60 22.3
Y 15	215 11.3	76 05.3 . .	43.0	331 49.7 . .	01.8	182 27.9 . .	37.0	169 52.5 . .	30.5	Hamal	328 12.6	N23 27.6
16	230 13.7	91 07.6	43.4	346 50.5	02.0	197 30.5	37.0	184 55.1	30.5	Kaus Aust.	83 57.9	S34 23.1
17	245 16.2	106 09.8	43.7	1 51.2	02.3	212 33.1	36.9	199 57.6	30.4			
18	260 18.7	121 12.1 N 8 44.1		16 51.9 S23 02.6		227 35.7 N11 36.9		215 00.1 N14 30.4		Kochab	137 20.3	N74 09.8
19	275 21.1	136 14.4	44.4	31 52.6	02.9	242 38.3	36.8	230 02.6	30.4	Markab	13 48.7	N15 12.3
20	290 23.6	151 16.7	44.7	46 53.4	03.2	257 40.9	36.7	245 05.1	30.4	Menkar	314 26.1	N 4 05.3
21	305 26.1	166 18.9 . .	45.1	61 54.1 . .	03.5	272 43.5 . .	36.7	260 07.6 . .	30.3	Menkent	148 20.5	S36 22.0
22	320 28.5	181 21.2	45.4	76 54.8	03.8	287 46.2	36.6	275 10.2	30.3	Miaplacidus	221 42.7	S69 42.8
23	335 31.0	196 23.5	45.8	91 55.6	04.1	302 48.8	36.6	290 12.7	30.3			
12 00	350 33.5	211 25.7 N 8 46.1		106 56.3 S23 04.4		317 51.4 N11 36.5		305 15.2 N14 30.3		Mirfak	308 55.5	N49 51.4
01	5 35.9	226 28.0	46.5	121 57.0	04.7	332 54.0	36.5	320 17.7	30.2	Nunki	76 11.4	S26 17.8
02	20 38.4	241 30.2	46.8	136 57.7	05.0	347 56.6	36.4	335 20.2	30.2	Peacock	53 35.6	S56 44.2
03	35 40.9	256 32.5 . .	47.1	151 58.5 . .	05.3	2 59.2 . .	36.3	350 22.7 . .	30.2	Pollux	243 41.0	N28 01.6
04	50 43.3	271 34.7	47.5	166 59.2	05.5	18 01.8	36.3	5 25.3	30.2	Procyon	245 11.1	N 5 13.6
05	65 45.8	286 36.9	47.8	181 59.9	05.8	33 04.4	36.2	20 27.8	30.1			
06	80 48.2	301 39.2 N 8 48.1		197 00.6 S23 06.1		48 07.0 N11 36.2		35 30.3 N14 30.1		Rasalhague	96 16.3	N12 33.9
07	95 50.7	316 41.4	48.5	212 01.4	06.4	63 09.6	36.1	50 32.8	30.1	Regulus	207 55.2	N11 58.3
08	110 53.2	331 43.6	48.8	227 02.1	06.7	78 12.2	36.1	65 35.3	30.1	Rigel	281 22.3	S 8 12.0
S 09	125 55.6	346 45.9 . .	49.1	242 02.8 . .	07.0	93 14.8 . .	36.0	80 37.9 . .	30.0	Rigil Kent.	140 06.9	S60 50.0
U 10	140 58.1	1 48.1	49.5	257 03.5	07.3	108 17.4	35.9	95 40.4	30.0	Sabik	102 24.8	S15 43.3
N 11	156 00.6	16 50.3	49.8	272 04.3	07.6	123 20.0	35.9	110 42.9	30.0			
D 12	171 03.0	31 52.5 N 8 50.1		287 05.0 S23 07.9		138 22.6 N11 35.8		125 45.4 N14 30.0		Schedar	349 52.2	N56 32.0
A 13	186 05.5	46 54.7	50.5	302 05.7	08.1	153 25.2	35.8	140 47.9	29.9	Shaula	96 36.4	S37 06.2
Y 14	201 08.0	61 56.9	50.8	317 06.4	08.4	168 27.8	35.7	155 50.5	29.9	Sirius	258 43.3	S16 42.8
15	216 10.4	76 59.1 . .	51.1	332 07.1 . .	08.7	183 30.4 . .	35.7	170 53.0 . .	29.9	Spica	158 42.8	S11 09.4
16	231 12.9	92 01.3	51.4	347 07.9	09.0	198 33.0	35.6	185 55.5	29.9	Suhail	223 00.7	S43 25.7
17	246 15.3	107 03.5	51.8	2 08.6	09.3	213 35.7	35.5	200 58.0	29.8			
18	261 17.8	122 05.7 N 8 52.1		17 09.3 S23 09.6		228 38.3 N11 35.5		216 00.5 N14 29.8		Vega	80 46.0	N38 47.4
19	276 20.3	137 07.9	52.4	32 10.0	09.9	243 40.9	35.4	231 03.1	29.8	Zuben'ubi	137 17.5	S16 02.3
20	291 22.7	152 10.0	52.7	47 10.7	10.2	258 43.5	35.4	246 05.6	29.8		SHA	Mer. Pass.
21	306 25.2	167 12.2 . .	53.1	62 11.5 . .	10.4	273 46.1 . .	35.3	261 08.1 . .	29.7		° ′	h m
22	321 27.7	182 14.4	53.4	77 12.2	10.7	288 48.7	35.2	276 10.6	29.7	Venus	220 56.1	9 56
23	336 30.1	197 16.5	53.7	92 12.9	11.0	303 51.3	35.2	291 13.2	29.7	Mars	117 04.4	16 53
	h m									Jupiter	327 14.7	2 52
Mer. Pass. 0 41.6		v 2.3	d 0.4	v 0.7	d 0.3	v 2.6	d 0.1	v 2.5	d 0.0	Saturn	314 40.5	3 42

SUN and MOON

UT	SUN GHA	SUN Dec	MOON GHA	v	MOON Dec	d	HP
d h	° ′	° ′	° ′	′	° ′	′	′
10 00	180 40.9	N 5 11.4	178 34.5	12.0	N 7 33.4	10.7	57.1
01	195 41.1	10.4	193 05.5	11.9	7 22.7	10.8	57.0
02	210 41.3	09.5	207 36.4	12.1	7 11.9	10.7	57.0
03	225 41.5	.. 08.6	222 07.5	12.0	7 01.2	10.8	57.0
04	240 41.8	07.6	236 38.5	12.2	6 50.4	10.8	57.0
05	255 42.0	06.7	251 09.7	12.1	6 39.6	10.9	56.9
06	270 42.2	N 5 05.7	265 40.8	12.3	N 6 28.7	10.8	56.9
07	285 42.4	04.8	280 12.1	12.3	6 17.9	10.9	56.9
08	300 42.6	03.8	294 43.4	12.3	6 07.0	10.9	56.9
F 09	315 42.8	.. 02.9	309 14.7	12.4	5 56.1	10.9	56.8
R 10	330 43.1	01.9	323 46.1	12.4	5 45.2	10.9	56.8
I 11	345 43.3	01.0	338 17.5	12.5	5 34.3	11.0	56.8
D 12	0 43.5	N 5 00.0	352 49.0	12.5	N 5 23.3	10.9	56.8
A 13	15 43.7	4 59.1	7 20.5	12.6	5 12.4	11.0	56.7
Y 14	30 43.9	58.2	21 52.1	12.6	5 01.4	11.0	56.7
15	45 44.2	.. 57.2	36 23.7	12.6	4 50.4	11.0	56.7
16	60 44.4	56.3	50 55.3	12.7	4 39.4	11.1	56.7
17	75 44.6	55.3	65 27.0	12.8	4 28.3	11.0	56.6
18	90 44.8	N 4 54.4	79 58.8	12.8	N 4 17.3	11.0	56.6
19	105 45.0	53.4	94 30.6	12.8	4 06.3	11.1	56.6
20	120 45.2	52.5	109 02.4	12.9	3 55.2	11.1	56.6
21	135 45.5	.. 51.5	123 34.3	12.9	3 44.1	11.0	56.5
22	150 45.7	50.6	138 06.2	12.9	3 33.1	11.1	56.5
23	165 45.9	49.6	152 38.1	13.0	3 22.0	11.1	56.5
11 00	180 46.1	N 4 48.7	167 10.1	13.0	N 3 10.9	11.1	56.5
01	195 46.3	47.7	181 42.1	13.1	2 59.8	11.1	56.4
02	210 46.5	46.8	196 14.2	13.1	2 48.7	11.1	56.4
03	225 46.8	.. 45.8	210 46.3	13.2	2 37.6	11.1	56.4
04	240 47.0	44.9	225 18.5	13.2	2 26.5	11.1	56.4
05	255 47.2	43.9	239 50.7	13.2	2 15.4	11.1	56.3
06	270 47.4	N 4 43.0	254 22.9	13.2	N 2 04.3	11.1	56.3
S 07	285 47.6	42.0	268 55.1	13.3	1 53.2	11.1	56.3
A 08	300 47.9	41.1	283 27.4	13.3	1 42.1	11.1	56.3
T 09	315 48.1	.. 40.1	297 59.7	13.4	1 31.0	11.1	56.2
U 10	330 48.3	39.2	312 32.1	13.4	1 19.9	11.0	56.2
R 11	345 48.5	38.2	327 04.5	13.4	1 08.9	11.1	56.2
D 12	0 48.7	N 4 37.3	341 36.9	13.5	N 0 57.8	11.1	56.2
A 13	15 48.9	36.3	356 09.4	13.4	0 46.7	11.1	56.1
Y 14	30 49.2	35.4	10 41.8	13.5	0 35.6	11.0	56.1
15	45 49.4	.. 34.4	25 14.3	13.6	0 24.6	11.1	56.1
16	60 49.6	33.5	39 46.9	13.6	0 13.5	11.1	56.1
17	75 49.8	32.5	54 19.5	13.6	N 0 02.4	11.0	56.0
18	90 50.0	N 4 31.6	68 52.1	13.6	S 0 08.6	11.0	56.0
19	105 50.3	30.6	83 24.7	13.6	0 19.6	11.0	56.0
20	120 50.5	29.7	97 57.3	13.7	0 30.6	11.0	56.0
21	135 50.7	.. 28.7	112 30.0	13.7	0 41.6	11.0	55.9
22	150 50.9	27.8	127 02.7	13.8	0 52.6	11.0	55.9
23	165 51.1	26.8	141 35.5	13.7	1 03.6	11.0	55.9
12 00	180 51.4	N 4 25.9	156 08.2	13.8	S 1 14.6	10.9	55.9
01	195 51.6	24.9	170 41.0	13.8	1 25.5	10.9	55.8
02	210 51.8	24.0	185 13.8	13.8	1 36.4	10.9	55.8
03	225 52.0	.. 23.0	199 46.6	13.9	1 47.3	10.9	55.8
04	240 52.2	22.1	214 19.5	13.8	1 58.2	10.9	55.8
05	255 52.4	21.1	228 52.3	13.9	2 09.1	10.9	55.7
06	270 52.7	N 4 20.2	243 25.2	13.9	S 2 20.0	10.8	55.7
07	285 52.9	19.2	257 58.1	14.0	2 30.8	10.8	55.7
08	300 53.1	18.2	272 31.1	13.9	2 41.6	10.8	55.7
S 09	315 53.3	.. 17.3	287 04.0	14.0	2 52.4	10.8	55.6
U 10	330 53.5	16.3	301 37.0	13.9	3 03.2	10.7	55.6
N 11	345 53.8	15.4	316 09.9	14.0	3 13.9	10.8	55.6
D 12	0 54.0	N 4 14.4	330 42.9	14.0	S 3 24.7	10.7	55.6
A 13	15 54.2	13.5	345 15.9	14.1	3 35.4	10.6	55.6
Y 14	30 54.4	12.5	359 49.0	14.0	3 46.0	10.7	55.5
15	45 54.6	.. 11.6	14 22.0	14.1	3 56.7	10.6	55.5
16	60 54.9	10.6	28 55.1	14.0	4 07.3	10.6	55.5
17	75 55.1	09.7	43 28.1	14.1	4 17.9	10.6	55.5
18	90 55.3	N 4 08.7	58 01.2	14.1	S 4 28.5	10.5	55.4
19	105 55.5	07.8	72 34.3	14.1	4 39.0	10.5	55.4
20	120 55.7	06.8	87 07.4	14.1	4 49.5	10.5	55.4
21	135 56.0	.. 05.9	101 40.5	14.1	5 00.0	10.4	55.4
22	150 56.2	04.9	116 13.6	14.2	5 10.4	10.5	55.3
23	165 56.4	03.9	130 46.8	14.1	S 5 20.9	10.3	55.3
	SD 15.9	d 1.0	SD 15.5		15.3		15.1

Twilight, Sunrise and Moonrise

Lat.	Naut.	Civil	Sunrise	Moonrise 10	11	12	13
°	h m	h m	h m	h m	h m	h m	h m
N 72	01 21	03 31	04 47	04 52	06 41	08 26	10 11
N 70	02 08	03 47	04 54	05 02	06 44	08 22	09 59
68	02 38	04 01	05 00	05 10	06 46	08 19	09 50
66	02 59	04 11	05 06	05 17	06 48	08 16	09 43
64	03 16	04 20	05 10	05 22	06 49	08 14	09 36
62	03 29	04 28	05 14	05 27	06 51	08 12	09 31
60	03 40	04 34	05 17	05 31	06 52	08 10	09 26
N 58	03 50	04 40	05 20	05 35	06 53	08 08	09 22
56	03 58	04 45	05 23	05 38	06 54	08 07	09 19
54	04 05	04 49	05 25	05 41	06 54	08 06	09 15
52	04 11	04 53	05 27	05 44	06 55	08 05	09 12
50	04 17	04 56	05 29	05 46	06 56	08 04	09 10
45	04 28	05 03	05 33	05 52	06 57	08 01	09 04
N 40	04 37	05 09	05 37	05 56	06 59	08 00	08 59
35	04 44	05 14	05 39	06 00	07 00	07 58	08 55
30	04 50	05 18	05 42	06 03	07 01	07 57	08 51
20	04 58	05 24	05 46	06 09	07 02	07 54	08 45
N 10	05 05	05 29	05 50	06 14	07 04	07 52	08 40
0	05 09	05 33	05 54	06 18	07 05	07 50	08 34
S 10	05 11	05 36	05 57	06 23	07 06	07 48	08 29
20	05 13	05 38	06 00	06 28	07 08	07 46	08 24
30	05 12	05 40	06 04	06 34	07 09	07 44	08 18
35	05 11	05 41	06 06	06 37	07 10	07 43	08 14
40	05 11	05 41	06 08	06 41	07 11	07 41	08 10
45	05 08	05 42	06 11	06 45	07 13	07 39	08 06
S 50	05 05	05 42	06 14	06 50	07 14	07 37	08 01
52	05 03	05 42	06 16	06 52	07 15	07 36	07 58
54	05 01	05 42	06 17	06 55	07 16	07 35	07 55
56	04 59	05 42	06 19	06 58	07 17	07 34	07 52
58	04 56	05 42	06 21	07 01	07 17	07 33	07 49
S 60	04 53	05 42	06 23	07 04	07 18	07 32	07 45

Sunset, Twilight and Moonset

Lat.	Sunset	Civil	Naut.	Moonset 10	11	12	13
°	h m	h m	h m	h m	h m	h m	h m
N 72	19 04	20 19	22 21	19 31	19 21	19 10	18 59
N 70	18 57	20 03	21 39	19 26	19 21	19 17	19 12
68	18 51	19 50	21 11	19 22	19 22	19 22	19 23
66	18 46	19 40	20 51	19 18	19 22	19 27	19 31
64	18 42	19 31	20 35	19 15	19 23	19 31	19 39
62	18 38	19 24	20 22	19 12	19 23	19 34	19 45
60	18 35	19 18	20 11	19 10	19 23	19 37	19 51
N 58	18 32	19 12	20 02	19 08	19 24	19 39	19 56
56	18 30	19 08	19 54	19 06	19 24	19 42	20 00
54	18 27	19 03	19 47	19 04	19 24	19 44	20 04
52	18 25	19 00	19 41	19 02	19 24	19 46	20 08
50	18 24	18 56	19 36	19 01	19 24	19 48	20 11
45	18 20	18 49	19 24	18 58	19 25	19 51	20 18
N 40	18 16	18 44	19 16	18 55	19 25	19 55	20 24
35	18 13	18 39	19 09	18 53	19 25	19 57	20 30
30	18 11	18 35	19 03	18 51	19 26	20 00	20 34
20	18 07	18 29	18 55	18 47	19 26	20 04	20 42
N 10	18 03	18 24	18 49	18 44	19 26	20 08	20 49
0	18 00	18 21	18 45	18 41	19 27	20 11	20 56
S 10	17 57	18 18	18 42	18 38	19 27	20 15	21 02
20	17 54	18 16	18 41	18 35	19 27	20 19	21 09
30	17 50	18 14	18 42	18 31	19 28	20 23	21 17
35	17 48	18 13	18 43	18 29	19 28	20 26	21 22
40	17 46	18 13	18 44	18 26	19 28	20 28	21 27
45	17 43	18 13	18 47	18 23	19 28	20 32	21 34
S 50	17 40	18 12	18 50	18 20	19 28	20 36	21 41
52	17 39	18 13	18 52	18 18	19 29	20 37	21 44
54	17 37	18 13	18 54	18 16	19 29	20 39	21 48
56	17 36	18 13	18 56	18 14	19 29	20 41	21 52
58	17 34	18 13	18 59	18 12	19 29	20 44	21 57
S 60	17 32	18 13	19 02	18 10	19 29	20 47	22 02

SUN and MOON

Day	Eqn. of Time 00h	12h	Mer. Pass.	Mer. Pass. Upper	Lower	Age	Phase
d	m s	m s	h m	h m	h m	d	%
10	02 43	02 54	11 57	12 30	00 06	01	0
11	03 04	03 14	11 57	13 16	00 53	02	3
12	03 25	03 35	11 56	14 01	01 38	03	7

UT	ARIES GHA	VENUS −4.5 GHA	Dec	MARS +0.4 GHA	Dec	JUPITER −2.8 GHA	Dec	SATURN +0.1 GHA	Dec
13 00	351 32.6	212 18.7	N 8 54.0	107 13.6	S23 11.3	318 53.9	N11 35.1	306 15.7	N14 29.7
01	6 35.1	227 20.9	54.3	122 14.3	11.6	333 56.5	35.1	321 18.2	29.6
02	21 37.5	242 23.0	54.7	137 15.0	11.9	348 59.1	35.0	336 20.7	29.6
03	36 40.0	257 25.2 ..	55.0	152 15.8 ..	12.1	4 01.7 ..	34.9	351 23.2 ..	29.6
04	51 42.5	272 27.3	55.3	167 16.5	12.4	19 04.4	34.9	6 25.8	29.6
05	66 44.9	287 29.5	55.6	182 17.2	12.7	34 07.0	34.8	21 28.3	29.5
M 06	81 47.4	302 31.6	N 8 55.9	197 17.9	S23 13.0	49 09.6	N11 34.8	36 30.8	N14 29.5
O 07	96 49.8	317 33.7	56.2	212 18.6	13.3	64 12.2	34.7	51 33.3	29.5
N 08	111 52.3	332 35.9	56.6	227 19.3	13.6	79 14.8	34.6	66 35.9	29.5
D 09	126 54.8	347 38.0 ..	56.9	242 20.0 ..	13.8	94 17.4 ..	34.6	81 38.4 ..	29.4
A 10	141 57.2	2 40.1	57.2	257 20.8	14.1	109 20.0	34.5	96 40.9	29.4
Y 11	156 59.7	17 42.2	57.5	272 21.5	14.4	124 22.6	34.5	111 43.4	29.4
12	172 02.2	32 44.4	N 8 57.8	287 22.2	S23 14.7	139 25.3	N11 34.4	126 46.0	N14 29.4
13	187 04.6	47 46.5	58.1	302 22.9	15.0	154 27.9	34.3	141 48.5	29.3
14	202 07.1	62 48.6	58.4	317 23.6	15.3	169 30.5	34.3	156 51.0	29.3
15	217 09.6	77 50.7 ..	58.7	332 24.3 ..	15.5	184 33.1 ..	34.2	171 53.5 ..	29.3
16	232 12.0	92 52.8	59.0	347 25.0	15.8	199 35.7	34.2	186 56.1	29.2
17	247 14.5	107 54.9	59.3	2 25.7	16.1	214 38.3	34.1	201 58.6	29.2
18	262 16.9	122 57.0	N 8 59.6	17 26.4	S23 16.4	229 41.0	N11 34.0	217 01.1	N14 29.2
19	277 19.4	137 59.1	8 59.9	32 27.2	16.7	244 43.6	34.0	232 03.6	29.2
20	292 21.9	153 01.2	9 00.2	47 27.9	16.9	259 46.2	33.9	247 06.2	29.1
21	307 24.3	168 03.2 ..	00.5	62 28.6 ..	17.2	274 48.8 ..	33.9	262 08.7 ..	29.1
22	322 26.8	183 05.3	00.8	77 29.3	17.5	289 51.4	33.8	277 11.2	29.1
23	337 29.3	198 07.4	01.1	92 30.0	17.8	304 54.0	33.7	292 13.7	29.1
14 00	352 31.7	213 09.5	N 9 01.4	107 30.7	S23 18.1	319 56.7	N11 33.7	307 16.3	N14 29.0
01	7 34.2	228 11.5	01.7	122 31.4	18.3	334 59.3	33.6	322 18.8	29.0
02	22 36.7	243 13.6	02.0	137 32.1	18.6	350 01.9	33.5	337 21.3	29.0
03	37 39.1	258 15.6 ..	02.3	152 32.8 ..	18.9	5 04.5 ..	33.5	352 23.8 ..	29.0
04	52 41.6	273 17.7	02.6	167 33.5	19.2	20 07.1	33.4	7 26.4	28.9
05	67 44.1	288 19.8	02.9	182 34.2	19.4	35 09.7	33.4	22 28.9	28.9
T 06	82 46.5	303 21.8	N 9 03.2	197 34.9	S23 19.7	50 12.4	N11 33.3	37 31.4	N14 28.9
U 07	97 49.0	318 23.8	03.5	212 35.6	20.0	65 15.0	33.2	52 34.0	28.8
E 08	112 51.4	333 25.9	03.8	227 36.3	20.3	80 17.6	33.2	67 36.5	28.8
S 09	127 53.9	348 27.9 ..	04.1	242 37.0 ..	20.5	95 20.2 ..	33.1	82 39.0 ..	28.8
D 10	142 56.4	3 30.0	04.3	257 37.7	20.8	110 22.8	33.0	97 41.5	28.8
A 11	157 58.8	18 32.0	04.6	272 38.5	21.1	125 25.5	33.0	112 44.1	28.7
Y 12	173 01.3	33 34.0	N 9 04.9	287 39.2	S23 21.4	140 28.1	N11 32.9	127 46.6	N14 28.7
13	188 03.8	48 36.0	05.2	302 39.9	21.6	155 30.7	32.9	142 49.1	28.7
14	203 06.2	63 38.1	05.5	317 40.6	21.9	170 33.3	32.8	157 51.7	28.7
15	218 08.7	78 40.1 ..	05.8	332 41.3 ..	22.2	185 36.0 ..	32.7	172 54.2 ..	28.6
16	233 11.2	93 42.1	06.1	347 42.0	22.5	200 38.6	32.7	187 56.7	28.6
17	248 13.6	108 44.1	06.3	2 42.7	22.7	215 41.2	32.6	202 59.2	28.6
18	263 16.1	123 46.1	N 9 06.6	17 43.4	S23 23.0	230 43.8	N11 32.5	218 01.8	N14 28.5
19	278 18.6	138 48.1	06.9	32 44.1	23.3	245 46.4	32.5	233 04.3	28.5
20	293 21.0	153 50.1	07.2	47 44.8	23.6	260 49.1	32.4	248 06.8	28.5
21	308 23.5	168 52.1 ..	07.5	62 45.5 ..	23.8	275 51.7 ..	32.4	263 09.4 ..	28.5
22	323 25.9	183 54.1	07.7	77 46.2	24.1	290 54.3	32.3	278 11.9	28.4
23	338 28.4	198 56.1	08.0	92 46.9	24.4	305 56.9	32.2	293 14.4	28.4
15 00	353 30.9	213 58.0	N 9 08.3	107 47.6	S23 24.6	320 59.6	N11 32.2	308 17.0	N14 28.4
01	8 33.3	229 00.0	08.6	122 48.3	24.9	336 02.2	32.1	323 19.5	28.4
02	23 35.8	244 02.0	08.8	137 48.9	25.2	351 04.8	32.0	338 22.0	28.3
03	38 38.3	259 04.0 ..	09.1	152 49.6 ..	25.5	6 07.4 ..	32.0	353 24.5 ..	28.3
04	53 40.7	274 05.9	09.4	167 50.3	25.7	21 10.1	31.9	8 27.1	28.3
05	68 43.2	289 07.9	09.6	182 51.0	26.0	36 12.7	31.8	23 29.6	28.2
W 06	83 45.7	304 09.8	N 9 09.9	197 51.7	S23 26.3	51 15.3	N11 31.8	38 32.1	N14 28.2
E 07	98 48.1	319 11.8	10.2	212 52.4	26.5	66 18.0	31.7	53 34.7	28.2
D 08	113 50.6	334 13.8	10.4	227 53.1	26.8	81 20.6	31.6	68 37.2	28.2
N 09	128 53.0	349 15.7 ..	10.7	242 53.8 ..	27.1	96 23.2 ..	31.6	83 39.7 ..	28.1
E 10	143 55.5	4 17.6	11.0	257 54.5	27.4	111 25.8	31.5	98 42.3	28.1
S 11	158 58.0	19 19.6	11.2	272 55.2	27.6	126 28.5	31.4	113 44.8	28.1
D 12	174 00.4	34 21.5	N 9 11.5	287 55.9	S23 27.9	141 31.1	N11 31.4	128 47.3	N14 28.0
A 13	189 02.9	49 23.5	11.8	302 56.6	28.2	156 33.7	31.3	143 49.9	28.0
Y 14	204 05.4	64 25.4	12.0	317 57.3	28.4	171 36.4	31.3	158 52.4	28.0
15	219 07.8	79 27.3 ..	12.3	332 58.0 ..	28.7	186 39.0 ..	31.2	173 54.9 ..	28.0
16	234 10.3	94 29.2	12.5	347 58.7	29.0	201 41.6	31.1	188 57.5	27.9
17	249 12.8	109 31.2	12.8	2 59.4	29.2	216 44.2	31.1	204 00.0	27.9
18	264 15.2	124 33.1	N 9 13.1	18 00.0	S23 29.5	231 46.9	N11 31.0	219 02.5	N14 27.8
19	279 17.7	139 35.0	13.3	33 00.7	29.8	246 49.5	30.9	234 05.1	27.8
20	294 20.2	154 36.9	13.6	48 01.4	30.0	261 52.1	30.9	249 07.6	27.8
21	309 22.6	169 38.8 ..	13.8	63 02.1 ..	30.3	276 54.8 ..	30.8	264 10.1 ..	27.8
22	324 25.1	184 40.7	14.1	78 02.8	30.6	291 57.4	30.7	279 12.7	27.8
23	339 27.5	199 42.6	14.3	93 03.5	30.8	307 00.0	30.7	294 15.2	27.7
Mer. Pass.	h m 0 29.8	v 2.0	d 0.3	v 0.7	d 0.3	v 2.6	d 0.1	v 2.5	d 0.0

STARS

Name	SHA	Dec
Acamar	315 26.2	S40 18.2
Achernar	335 34.2	S57 14.2
Acrux	173 21.9	S63 05.8
Adhara	255 21.1	S28 58.1
Aldebaran	291 01.6	N16 30.4
Alioth	166 30.6	N55 58.0
Alkaid	153 07.7	N49 19.2
Al Na'ir	27 56.7	S46 57.8
Alnilam	275 57.2	S 1 12.1
Alphard	218 06.9	S 8 39.3
Alphecca	126 20.2	N26 43.3
Alpheratz	357 54.2	N29 05.3
Altair	62 18.5	N 8 52.3
Ankaa	353 25.8	S42 18.4
Antares	112 39.5	S26 25.8
Arcturus	146 05.7	N19 11.4
Atria	107 51.0	S69 01.8
Avior	234 22.8	S59 30.3
Bellatrix	278 43.5	N 6 21.0
Betelgeuse	271 12.9	N 7 24.4
Canopus	264 01.0	S52 41.5
Capella	280 50.2	N45 59.6
Deneb	49 38.4	N45 17.0
Denebola	182 44.9	N14 34.6
Diphda	349 06.3	S17 59.2
Dubhe	194 05.4	N61 45.2
Elnath	278 26.1	N28 36.3
Eltanin	90 51.0	N51 29.8
Enif	33 57.3	N 9 52.5
Fomalhaut	15 35.4	S29 37.4
Gacrux	172 13.4	S57 06.6
Gienah	176 03.6	S17 32.2
Hadar	149 03.6	S60 22.3
Hamal	328 12.6	N23 27.6
Kaus Aust.	83 57.9	S34 23.1
Kochab	137 20.3	N74 09.8
Markab	13 48.7	N15 12.3
Menkar	314 26.1	N 4 05.3
Menkent	148 20.5	S36 22.0
Miaplacidus	221 42.7	S69 42.7
Mirfak	308 55.4	N49 51.4
Nunki	76 11.4	S26 17.8
Peacock	53 35.6	S56 44.3
Pollux	243 41.0	N28 01.6
Procyon	245 11.1	N 5 13.6
Rasalhague	96 16.4	N12 33.9
Regulus	207 55.2	N11 58.3
Rigel	281 22.3	S 8 12.0
Rigil Kent.	140 06.9	S60 50.0
Sabik	102 24.8	S15 43.3
Schedar	349 52.2	N56 32.0
Shaula	96 36.4	S37 06.2
Sirius	258 43.3	S16 42.8
Spica	158 42.8	S11 09.4
Suhail	223 00.7	S43 25.7
Vega	80 46.1	N38 47.4
Zuben'ubi	137 17.5	S16 02.2

	SHA	Mer. Pass.
Venus	220 37.7	h m 9 46
Mars	114 59.0	16 49
Jupiter	327 24.9	2 40
Saturn	314 44.5	3 30

UT	SUN GHA	SUN Dec	MOON GHA	v	MOON Dec	d	HP
d h	° ′	° ′	° ′	′	° ′	′	′
13 00	180 56.6	N 4 03.0	145 19.9	14.2	S 5 31.2	10.4	55.3
01	195 56.8	02.0	159 53.1	14.1	5 41.6	10.3	55.3
02	210 57.1	01.1	174 26.2	14.2	5 51.9	10.3	55.3
03	225 57.3	4 00.1	188 59.4	14.2	6 02.2	10.3	55.2
04	240 57.5	3 59.2	203 32.6	14.1	6 12.5	10.2	55.2
05	255 57.7	58.2	218 05.7	14.2	6 22.7	10.1	55.2
06	270 57.9	N 3 57.3	232 38.9	14.2	S 6 32.8	10.2	55.2
07	285 58.2	56.3	247 12.1	14.2	6 43.0	10.1	55.2
M 08	300 58.4	55.3	261 45.3	14.2	6 53.1	10.1	55.1
O 09	315 58.6	.. 54.4	276 18.5	14.2	7 03.2	10.0	55.1
N 10	330 58.8	53.4	290 51.7	14.2	7 13.2	10.0	55.1
D 11	345 59.0	52.5	305 24.9	14.2	7 23.2	9.9	55.1
A 12	0 59.3	N 3 51.5	319 58.1	14.2	S 7 33.1	10.0	55.1
Y 13	15 59.5	50.6	334 31.3	14.2	7 43.1	9.8	55.0
14	30 59.7	49.6	349 04.5	14.2	7 52.9	9.9	55.0
15	45 59.9	.. 48.7	3 37.7	14.2	8 02.8	9.7	55.0
16	61 00.2	47.7	18 10.9	14.2	8 12.5	9.8	55.0
17	76 00.4	46.7	32 44.1	14.2	8 22.3	9.7	55.0
18	91 00.6	N 3 45.8	47 17.3	14.2	S 8 32.0	9.6	54.9
19	106 00.8	44.8	61 50.5	14.2	8 41.6	9.7	54.9
20	121 01.0	43.9	76 23.7	14.2	8 51.3	9.5	54.9
21	136 01.3	.. 42.9	90 56.9	14.1	9 00.8	9.5	54.9
22	151 01.5	42.0	105 30.0	14.2	9 10.3	9.5	54.9
23	166 01.7	41.0	120 03.2	14.2	9 19.8	9.5	54.9
14 00	181 01.9	N 3 40.0	134 36.4	14.2	S 9 29.3	9.3	54.8
01	196 02.1	39.1	149 09.6	14.1	9 38.6	9.4	54.8
02	211 02.4	38.1	163 42.7	14.2	9 48.0	9.3	54.8
03	226 02.6	.. 37.2	178 15.9	14.1	9 57.3	9.2	54.8
04	241 02.8	36.2	192 49.0	14.2	10 06.5	9.2	54.8
05	256 03.0	35.2	207 22.2	14.1	10 15.7	9.1	54.8
06	271 03.2	N 3 34.3	221 55.3	14.1	S10 24.8	9.1	54.7
T 07	286 03.5	33.3	236 28.4	14.1	10 33.9	9.1	54.7
U 08	301 03.7	32.4	251 01.5	14.1	10 43.0	8.9	54.7
E 09	316 03.9	.. 31.4	265 34.6	14.1	10 51.9	9.0	54.7
S 10	331 04.1	30.5	280 07.7	14.1	11 00.9	8.9	54.7
D 11	346 04.4	29.5	294 40.8	14.1	11 09.8	8.8	54.7
A 12	1 04.6	N 3 28.5	309 13.9	14.1	S11 18.6	8.8	54.6
Y 13	16 04.8	27.6	323 47.0	14.0	11 27.4	8.7	54.6
14	31 05.0	26.6	338 20.0	14.0	11 36.1	8.7	54.6
15	46 05.2	.. 25.7	352 53.0	14.1	11 44.8	8.6	54.6
16	61 05.5	24.7	7 26.1	14.0	11 53.4	8.5	54.6
17	76 05.7	23.7	21 59.1	14.0	12 01.9	8.5	54.6
18	91 05.9	N 3 22.8	36 32.1	13.9	S12 10.4	8.5	54.6
19	106 06.1	21.8	51 05.0	14.0	12 18.9	8.3	54.5
20	121 06.3	20.9	65 38.0	14.0	12 27.2	8.4	54.5
21	136 06.6	.. 19.9	80 11.0	13.9	12 35.6	8.2	54.5
22	151 06.8	18.9	94 43.9	13.9	12 43.8	8.3	54.5
23	166 07.0	18.0	109 16.8	13.9	12 52.1	8.1	54.5
15 00	181 07.2	N 3 17.0	123 49.7	13.9	S13 00.2	8.1	54.5
01	196 07.5	16.1	138 22.6	13.9	13 08.3	8.0	54.5
02	211 07.7	15.1	152 55.5	13.8	13 16.3	8.0	54.5
03	226 07.9	.. 14.1	167 28.3	13.8	13 24.3	7.9	54.4
04	241 08.1	13.2	181 01.1	13.9	13 32.2	7.9	54.4
05	256 08.3	12.2	196 34.0	13.8	13 40.1	7.7	54.4
06	271 08.6	N 3 11.3	211 06.8	13.7	S13 47.8	7.8	54.4
W 07	286 08.8	10.3	225 39.5	13.8	13 55.6	7.6	54.4
E 08	301 09.0	09.3	240 12.3	13.7	14 03.2	7.6	54.4
D 09	316 09.2	.. 08.4	254 45.0	13.7	14 10.8	7.5	54.4
N 10	331 09.5	07.4	269 17.7	13.7	14 18.3	7.5	54.4
E 11	346 09.7	06.4	283 50.4	13.7	14 25.8	7.4	54.4
S 12	1 09.9	N 3 05.5	298 23.1	13.6	S14 33.2	7.3	54.4
D 13	16 10.1	04.5	312 55.7	13.7	14 40.5	7.3	54.4
A 14	31 10.3	03.6	327 28.4	13.6	14 47.8	7.2	54.3
Y 15	46 10.6	.. 02.6	342 01.0	13.6	14 55.0	7.2	54.3
16	61 10.8	01.6	356 33.6	13.5	15 02.2	7.0	54.3
17	76 11.0	3 00.7	11 06.1	13.6	15 09.2	7.0	54.3
18	91 11.2	N 2 59.7	25 38.7	13.5	S15 16.2	7.0	54.3
19	106 11.5	58.8	40 11.2	13.5	15 23.2	6.8	54.3
20	121 11.7	57.8	54 43.7	13.4	15 30.0	6.8	54.3
21	136 11.9	.. 56.8	69 16.1	13.5	15 36.8	6.7	54.3
22	151 12.1	55.9	83 48.6	13.4	15 43.5	6.7	54.3
23	166 12.3	54.9	98 21.0	13.4	S15 50.2	6.6	54.3
	SD 15.9	d 1.0	SD 15.0		14.9		14.8

Lat.	Twilight Naut.	Twilight Civil	Sunrise	Moonrise 13	14	15	16
°	h m	h m	h m	h m	h m	h m	h m
N 72	01 54	03 47	05 00	10 11	11 56	13 49	16 11
N 70	02 30	04 01	05 06	09 59	11 36	13 15	14 57
68	02 54	04 13	05 11	09 50	11 21	12 51	14 20
66	03 12	04 22	05 15	09 43	11 08	12 32	13 54
64	03 27	04 30	05 19	09 36	10 58	12 17	13 34
62	03 39	04 36	05 22	09 31	10 49	12 05	13 17
60	03 49	04 42	05 24	09 26	10 41	11 54	13 04
N 58	03 57	04 46	05 26	09 22	10 34	11 45	12 52
56	04 05	04 51	05 29	09 19	10 29	11 37	12 42
54	04 11	04 54	05 30	09 15	10 23	11 30	12 33
52	04 17	04 58	05 32	09 12	10 19	11 23	12 26
50	04 22	05 01	05 33	09 10	10 14	11 17	12 18
45	04 32	05 07	05 37	09 04	10 05	11 05	12 03
N 40	04 40	05 12	05 42	08 59	09 58	10 55	11 51
35	04 46	05 16	05 42	08 55	09 51	10 46	11 40
30	04 52	05 20	05 44	08 51	09 45	10 38	11 31
20	04 59	05 25	05 47	08 45	09 35	10 25	11 15
N 10	05 04	05 29	05 50	08 40	09 27	10 14	11 02
0	05 08	05 32	05 52	08 34	09 19	10 03	10 49
S 10	05 10	05 34	05 55	08 29	09 11	09 53	10 36
20	05 10	05 35	05 57	08 24	09 02	09 41	10 22
30	05 09	05 36	06 00	08 18	08 53	09 29	10 07
35	05 07	05 37	06 02	08 14	08 47	09 21	09 58
40	05 05	05 36	06 03	08 10	08 41	09 13	09 48
45	05 02	05 36	06 05	08 06	08 33	09 03	09 36
S 50	04 58	05 35	06 08	08 01	08 25	08 51	09 21
52	04 56	05 35	06 09	07 58	08 21	08 46	09 15
54	04 54	05 35	06 10	07 55	08 16	08 40	09 07
56	04 51	05 34	06 11	07 52	08 12	08 33	08 59
58	04 48	05 33	06 12	07 49	08 06	08 26	08 50
S 60	04 44	05 33	06 14	07 45	08 00	08 17	08 39

Lat.	Sunset	Twilight Civil	Twilight Naut.	Moonset 13	14	15	16
°	h m	h m	h m	h m	h m	h m	h m
N 72	18 48	20 01	21 49	18 59	18 45	18 26	17 39
N 70	18 43	19 47	21 16	19 12	19 07	19 01	18 54
68	18 38	19 36	20 53	19 23	19 24	19 26	19 32
66	18 34	19 27	20 36	19 31	19 37	19 46	19 58
64	18 31	19 20	20 22	19 39	19 49	20 01	20 19
62	18 28	19 14	20 10	19 45	19 58	20 15	20 36
60	18 26	19 08	20 00	19 51	20 07	20 26	20 50
N 58	18 24	19 03	19 52	19 56	20 14	20 35	21 02
56	18 22	18 59	19 45	20 00	20 21	20 44	21 12
54	18 20	18 56	19 39	20 04	20 26	20 52	21 21
52	18 18	18 52	19 33	20 08	20 32	20 58	21 29
50	18 17	18 49	19 28	20 11	20 36	21 05	21 37
45	18 14	18 43	19 18	20 18	20 47	21 18	21 53
N 40	18 11	18 39	19 11	20 24	20 55	21 29	22 06
35	18 09	18 35	19 04	20 30	21 03	21 38	22 17
30	18 07	18 31	18 59	20 34	21 09	21 47	22 26
20	18 04	18 26	18 52	20 42	21 21	22 01	22 43
N 10	18 01	18 22	18 47	20 49	21 31	22 13	22 58
0	17 59	18 20	18 44	20 56	21 40	22 25	23 11
S 10	17 57	18 18	18 42	21 02	21 49	22 37	23 25
20	17 54	18 16	18 42	21 09	22 00	22 50	23 40
30	17 52	18 16	18 43	21 17	22 11	23 04	23 56
35	17 50	18 15	18 45	21 22	22 18	23 12	24 06
40	17 49	18 16	18 47	21 27	22 25	23 22	24 17
45	17 47	18 16	18 50	21 34	22 34	23 33	24 31
S 50	17 45	18 17	18 54	21 41	22 45	23 47	24 47
52	17 44	18 17	18 57	21 44	22 50	23 53	24 54
54	17 43	18 18	18 59	21 48	22 55	24 00	00 00
56	17 41	18 19	19 02	21 52	23 01	24 08	00 08
58	17 40	18 19	19 05	21 57	23 08	24 17	00 17
S 60	17 39	18 20	19 09	22 02	23 16	24 27	00 27

Day	SUN Eqn. of Time 00h	SUN Eqn. of Time 12h	SUN Mer. Pass.	MOON Mer. Pass. Upper	MOON Mer. Pass. Lower	Age	Phase
d	m s	m s	h m	h m	h m	d	%
13	03 46	03 57	11 51	14 45	02 23	04	13
14	04 07	04 18	11 56	15 29	03 07	05	20
15	04 29	04 39	11 55	16 14	03 52	06	29

UT	ARIES GHA	VENUS −4.5 GHA	Dec	MARS +0.5 GHA	Dec	JUPITER −2.8 GHA	Dec	SATURN +0.1 GHA	Dec	Name	SHA	Dec
16 00	354 30.0	214 44.5 N 9	14.6	108 04.2 S23	31.1	322 02.7 N11	30.6	309 17.7 N14	27.7	Acamar	315 26.2	S40 18.2
01	9 32.5	229 46.4	14.8	123 04.9	31.3	337 05.3	30.5	324 20.3	27.7	Achernar	335 34.2	S57 14.2
02	24 34.9	244 48.3	15.1	138 05.6	31.6	352 07.9	30.5	339 22.8	27.6	Acrux	173 21.9	S63 05.8
03	39 37.4	259 50.1 ..	15.3	153 06.2 ..	31.9	7 10.6 ..	30.4	354 25.4 ..	27.6	Adhara	255 21.0	S28 58.1
04	54 39.9	274 52.0	15.6	168 06.9	32.1	22 13.2	30.3	9 27.9	27.6	Aldebaran	291 01.6	N16 30.4
05	69 42.3	289 53.9	15.8	183 07.6	32.4	37 15.8	30.3	24 30.4	27.6			
06	84 44.8	304 55.8 N 9	16.1	198 08.3 S23	32.7	52 18.5 N11	30.2	39 33.0 N14	27.5	Alioth	166 30.6	N55 58.0
07	99 47.3	319 57.6	16.3	213 09.0	32.9	67 21.1	30.1	54 35.5	27.5	Alkaid	153 07.7	N49 19.2
T 08	114 49.7	334 59.5	16.6	228 09.7	33.2	82 23.7	30.1	69 38.0	27.5	Al Na'ir	27 56.7	S46 57.8
H 09	129 52.2	350 01.4 ..	16.8	243 10.4 ..	33.5	97 26.4 ..	30.0	84 40.6 ..	27.4	Alnilam	275 57.2	S 1 12.1
U 10	144 54.7	5 03.2	17.1	258 11.0	33.7	112 29.0	29.9	99 43.1	27.4	Alphard	218 06.9	S 8 39.3
R 11	159 57.1	20 05.1	17.3	273 11.7	34.0	127 31.6	29.9	114 45.6	27.4			
S 12	174 59.6	35 06.9 N 9	17.5	288 12.4 S23	34.2	142 34.3 N11	29.8	129 48.2 N14	27.3	Alphecca	126 20.2	N26 43.3
D 13	190 02.0	50 08.8	17.8	303 13.1	34.5	157 36.9	29.7	144 50.7	27.3	Alpheratz	357 54.2	N29 05.3
A 14	205 04.5	65 10.6	18.0	318 13.8	34.8	172 39.5	29.6	159 53.3	27.3	Altair	62 18.5	N 8 52.3
Y 15	220 07.0	80 12.5 ..	18.2	333 14.5 ..	35.0	187 42.2 ..	29.6	174 55.8 ..	27.3	Ankaa	353 25.8	S42 18.4
16	235 09.4	95 14.3	18.5	348 15.1	35.3	202 44.8	29.5	189 58.3	27.2	Antares	112 39.5	S26 25.8
17	250 11.9	110 16.1	18.7	3 15.8	35.5	217 47.5	29.4	205 00.9	27.2			
18	265 14.4	125 18.0 N 9	19.0	18 16.5 S23	35.8	232 50.1 N11	29.4	220 03.4 N14	27.2	Arcturus	146 05.7	N19 11.4
19	280 16.8	140 19.8	19.2	33 17.2	36.1	247 52.7	29.3	235 05.9	27.1	Atria	107 51.0	S69 01.8
20	295 19.3	155 21.6	19.4	48 17.9	36.3	262 55.4	29.2	250 08.5	27.1	Avior	234 22.8	S59 30.3
21	310 21.8	170 23.4 ..	19.6	63 18.5 ..	36.6	277 58.0 ..	29.2	265 11.0 ..	27.1	Bellatrix	278 43.5	N 6 21.0
22	325 24.2	185 25.3	19.9	78 19.2	36.8	293 00.6	29.1	280 13.6	27.1	Betelgeuse	271 12.9	N 7 24.4
23	340 26.7	200 27.1	20.1	93 19.9	37.1	308 03.3	29.0	295 16.1	27.0			
17 00	355 29.1	215 28.9 N 9	20.3	108 20.6 S23	37.4	323 05.9 N11	29.0	310 18.6 N14	27.0	Canopus	264 01.0	S52 41.5
01	10 31.6	230 30.7	20.6	123 21.3	37.6	338 08.6	28.9	325 21.2	27.0	Capella	280 50.2	N45 59.6
02	25 34.1	245 32.5	20.8	138 21.9	37.9	353 11.2	28.8	340 23.7	26.9	Deneb	49 38.4	N45 17.0
03	40 36.5	260 34.3 ..	21.0	153 22.6 ..	38.1	8 13.8 ..	28.8	355 26.3 ..	26.9	Denebola	182 44.9	N14 34.6
04	55 39.0	275 36.1	21.2	168 23.3	38.4	23 16.5	28.7	10 28.8	26.9	Diphda	349 06.3	S17 59.2
05	70 41.5	290 37.9	21.5	183 24.0	38.6	38 19.1	28.6	25 31.3	26.8			
06	85 43.9	305 39.7 N 9	21.7	198 24.7 S23	38.9	53 21.8 N11	28.5	40 33.9 N14	26.8	Dubhe	194 05.4	N61 45.2
07	100 46.4	320 41.4	21.9	213 25.3	39.2	68 24.4	28.5	55 36.4	26.8	Elnath	278 26.1	N28 36.3
08	115 48.9	335 43.2	22.1	228 26.0	39.4	83 27.0	28.4	70 39.0	26.8	Eltanin	90 51.1	N51 29.8
F 09	130 51.3	350 45.0 ..	22.3	243 26.7 ..	39.7	98 29.7 ..	28.3	85 41.5 ..	26.7	Enif	33 57.3	N 9 52.6
R 10	145 53.8	5 46.8	22.6	258 27.4	39.9	113 32.3	28.3	100 44.0	26.7	Fomalhaut	15 35.4	S29 37.4
I 11	160 56.3	20 48.5	22.8	273 28.0	40.2	128 35.0	28.2	115 46.6	26.7			
D 12	175 58.7	35 50.3 N 9	23.0	288 28.7 S23	40.4	143 37.6 N11	28.1	130 49.1 N14	26.6	Gacrux	172 13.4	S57 06.6
A 13	191 01.2	50 52.1	23.2	303 29.4	40.7	158 40.3	28.1	145 51.7	26.6	Gienah	176 03.6	S17 32.2
Y 14	206 03.6	65 53.8	23.4	318 30.1	40.9	173 42.9	28.0	160 54.2	26.6	Hadar	149 03.6	S60 22.3
15	221 06.1	80 55.6 ..	23.6	333 30.7 ..	41.2	188 45.5 ..	27.9	175 56.7 ..	26.5	Hamal	328 12.6	N23 27.6
16	236 08.6	95 57.3	23.8	348 31.4	41.4	203 48.2	27.8	190 59.3	26.5	Kaus Aust.	83 57.9	S34 23.1
17	251 11.0	110 59.1	24.1	3 32.1	41.7	218 50.8	27.8	206 01.8	26.5			
18	266 13.5	126 00.8 N 9	24.3	18 32.7 S23	41.9	233 53.5 N11	27.7	221 04.4 N14	26.4	Kochab	137 20.4	N74 09.8
19	281 16.0	141 02.6	24.5	33 33.4	42.2	248 56.1	27.6	236 06.9	26.4	Markab	13 48.7	N15 12.3
20	296 18.4	156 04.3	24.7	48 34.1	42.4	263 58.8	27.6	251 09.5	26.4	Menkar	314 26.0	N 4 05.3
21	311 20.9	171 06.1 ..	24.9	63 34.8 ..	42.7	279 01.4 ..	27.5	266 12.0 ..	26.4	Menkent	148 20.5	S36 22.0
22	326 23.4	186 07.8	25.1	78 35.4	43.0	294 04.1	27.4	281 14.5	26.3	Miaplacidus	221 42.6	S69 42.7
23	341 25.8	201 09.5	25.3	93 36.1	43.2	309 06.7	27.4	296 17.1	26.3			
18 00	356 28.3	216 11.2 N 9	25.5	108 36.8 S23	43.5	324 09.4 N11	27.3	311 19.6 N14	26.3	Mirfak	308 55.4	N49 51.4
01	11 30.8	231 13.0	25.7	123 37.4	43.7	339 12.0	27.2	326 22.2	26.2	Nunki	76 11.4	S26 17.8
02	26 33.2	246 14.7	25.9	138 38.1	44.0	354 14.7	27.1	341 24.7	26.2	Peacock	53 35.6	S56 44.3
03	41 35.7	261 16.4 ..	26.1	153 38.8 ..	44.2	9 17.3 ..	27.1	356 27.3 ..	26.2	Pollux	243 41.0	N28 01.6
04	56 38.1	276 18.1	26.3	168 39.4	44.5	24 19.9	27.0	11 29.8	26.1	Procyon	245 11.1	N 5 13.6
05	71 40.6	291 19.8	26.5	183 40.1	44.7	39 22.6	26.9	26 32.3	26.1			
06	86 43.1	306 21.5 N 9	26.7	198 40.8 S23	45.0	54 25.2 N11	26.9	41 34.9 N14	26.1	Rasalhague	96 16.4	N12 33.9
07	101 45.5	321 23.2	26.9	213 41.4	45.2	69 27.9	26.8	56 37.4	26.0	Regulus	207 55.2	N11 58.3
S 08	116 48.0	336 24.9	27.1	228 42.1	45.4	84 30.5	26.7	71 40.0	26.0	Rigel	281 22.3	S 8 12.0
A 09	131 50.5	351 26.6 ..	27.3	243 42.8 ..	45.7	99 33.2 ..	26.6	86 42.5 ..	26.0	Rigil Kent.	140 06.9	S60 50.0
T 10	146 52.9	6 28.3	27.5	258 43.4	45.9	114 35.8	26.6	101 45.1	25.9	Sabik	102 24.8	S15 43.3
U 11	161 55.4	21 30.0	27.7	273 44.1	46.2	129 38.5	26.5	116 47.6	25.9			
R 12	176 57.9	36 31.7 N 9	27.9	288 44.8 S23	46.4	144 41.1 N11	26.4	131 50.2 N14	25.9	Schedar	349 52.2	N56 32.0
D 13	192 00.3	51 33.4	28.1	303 45.4	46.7	159 43.8	26.3	146 52.7	25.9	Shaula	96 36.4	S37 06.2
A 14	207 02.8	66 35.1	28.3	318 46.1	46.9	174 46.4	26.3	161 55.2	25.8	Sirius	258 43.2	S16 42.8
Y 15	222 05.2	81 36.7 ..	28.4	333 46.8 ..	47.2	189 49.1 ..	26.2	176 57.8 ..	25.8	Spica	158 42.8	S11 09.4
16	237 07.7	96 38.4	28.6	348 47.4	47.4	204 51.7	26.1	192 00.3	25.8	Suhail	223 00.6	S43 25.7
17	252 10.2	111 40.1	28.8	3 48.1	47.7	219 54.4	26.1	207 02.9	25.7			
18	267 12.6	126 41.7 N 9	29.0	18 48.8 S23	47.9	234 57.0 N11	26.0	222 05.4 N14	25.7	Vega	80 46.1	N38 47.4
19	282 15.1	141 43.4	29.2	33 49.4	48.2	249 59.7	25.9	237 08.0	25.7	Zuben'ubi	137 17.5	S16 02.2
20	297 17.6	156 45.1	29.4	48 50.1	48.4	265 02.3	25.8	252 10.5	25.6		SHA	Mer. Pass.
21	312 20.0	171 46.7 ..	29.6	63 50.7 ..	48.6	280 05.0 ..	25.8	267 13.1 ..	25.6			h m
22	327 22.5	186 48.4	29.7	78 51.4	48.9	295 07.7	25.7	282 15.6	25.6	Venus	219 59.7	9 37
23	342 25.0	201 50.0	29.9	93 52.1	49.1	310 10.3	25.6	297 18.2	25.5	Mars	112 51.4	16 46
Mer. Pass. 0 18.0		v 1.8	d 0.2	v 0.7	d 0.3	v 2.6	d 0.1	v 2.5	d 0.0	Jupiter	327 36.8	2 27
										Saturn	314 49.5	3 18

UT	SUN GHA	SUN Dec	MOON GHA	v	MOON Dec	d	HP
d h	° ′	° ′	° ′	′	° ′	′	′
16 00	181 12.6	N 2 53.9	112 53.4	13.3	S15 56.8	6.5	54.3
01	196 12.8	53.0	127 25.7	13.4	16 03.3	6.4	54.3
02	211 13.0	52.0	141 58.1	13.3	16 09.7	6.4	54.3
03	226 13.2 ..	51.1	156 30.4	13.3	16 16.1	6.3	54.3
04	241 13.5	50.1	171 02.7	13.3	16 22.4	6.2	54.3
05	256 13.7	49.1	185 35.0	13.2	16 28.6	6.2	54.3
06	271 13.9	N 2 48.2	200 07.2	13.2	S16 34.8	6.0	54.2
T 07	286 14.1	47.2	214 39.4	13.2	16 40.8	6.0	54.2
H 08	301 14.4	46.2	229 11.6	13.2	16 46.8	6.0	54.2
U 09	316 14.6 ..	45.3	243 43.8	13.1	16 52.8	5.8	54.2
R 10	331 14.8	44.3	258 15.9	13.1	16 58.6	5.8	54.2
S 11	346 15.0	43.3	272 48.0	13.1	17 04.4	5.7	54.2
D 12	1 15.2	N 2 42.4	287 20.1	13.0	S17 10.1	5.6	54.2
A 13	16 15.5	41.4	301 52.1	13.1	17 15.7	5.6	54.2
Y 14	31 15.7	40.5	316 24.2	12.9	17 21.3	5.4	54.2
15	46 15.9 ..	39.5	330 56.1	13.0	17 26.7	5.4	54.2
16	61 16.1	38.5	345 28.1	13.0	17 32.1	5.4	54.2
17	76 16.4	37.6	0 00.1	12.9	17 37.5	5.2	54.2
18	91 16.6	N 2 36.6	14 32.0	12.9	S17 42.7	5.1	54.2
19	106 16.8	35.6	29 03.9	12.8	17 47.8	5.1	54.2
20	121 17.0	34.7	43 35.7	12.8	17 52.9	5.0	54.2
21	136 17.2 ..	33.7	58 07.5	12.8	17 57.9	4.9	54.2
22	151 17.5	32.7	72 39.3	12.8	18 02.8	4.9	54.2
23	166 17.7	31.8	87 11.1	12.7	18 07.7	4.7	54.2
17 00	181 17.9	N 2 30.8	101 42.8	12.8	S18 12.4	4.7	54.3
01	196 18.1	29.8	116 14.6	12.6	18 17.1	4.6	54.3
02	211 18.4	28.9	130 46.2	12.7	18 21.7	4.5	54.3
03	226 18.6 ..	27.9	145 17.9	12.6	18 26.2	4.4	54.3
04	241 18.8	27.0	159 49.5	12.6	18 30.6	4.4	54.3
05	256 19.0	26.0	174 21.1	12.6	18 35.0	4.2	54.3
06	271 19.3	N 2 25.0	188 52.7	12.5	S18 39.2	4.2	54.2
F 07	286 19.5	24.1	203 24.2	12.5	18 43.4	4.1	54.2
R 08	301 19.7	23.1	217 55.7	12.5	18 47.5	4.0	54.2
I 09	316 19.9 ..	22.1	232 27.2	12.5	18 51.5	4.0	54.3
D 10	331 20.1	21.2	246 58.7	12.4	18 55.5	3.8	54.3
A 11	346 20.4	20.2	261 30.1	12.4	18 59.3	3.7	54.3
Y 12	1 20.6	N 2 19.2	276 01.5	12.4	S19 03.0	3.7	54.3
13	16 20.8	18.3	290 32.9	12.3	19 06.7	3.6	54.3
14	31 21.0	17.3	305 04.2	12.3	19 10.3	3.5	54.3
15	46 21.3 ..	16.3	319 35.5	12.3	19 13.8	3.4	54.3
16	61 21.5	15.4	334 06.8	12.2	19 17.2	3.3	54.3
17	76 21.7	14.4	348 38.0	12.3	19 20.5	3.3	54.3
18	91 21.9	N 2 13.4	3 09.3	12.2	S19 23.8	3.1	54.3
19	106 22.2	12.5	17 40.5	12.1	19 26.9	3.0	54.3
20	121 22.4	11.5	32 11.6	12.2	19 29.9	3.0	54.3
21	136 22.6 ..	10.5	46 42.8	12.1	19 32.9	2.9	54.3
22	151 22.8	09.6	61 13.9	12.0	19 35.8	2.8	54.3
23	166 23.0	08.6	75 44.9	12.1	19 38.6	2.7	54.3
18 00	181 23.3	N 2 07.6	90 16.0	12.0	S19 41.3	2.6	54.4
01	196 23.5	06.7	104 47.0	12.0	19 43.9	2.5	54.4
02	211 23.7	05.7	119 18.0	12.0	19 46.4	2.4	54.4
03	226 23.9 ..	04.7	133 49.0	11.9	19 48.8	2.4	54.4
04	241 24.2	03.8	148 19.9	12.0	19 51.2	2.2	54.4
05	256 24.4	02.8	162 50.9	11.8	19 53.4	2.2	54.4
06	271 24.6	N 2 01.8	177 21.7	11.9	S19 55.6	2.0	54.4
S 07	286 24.8	2 00.9	191 52.6	11.8	19 57.6	2.0	54.4
A 08	301 25.1	1 59.9	206 23.4	11.9	19 59.6	1.9	54.4
T 09	316 25.3 ..	58.9	220 54.3	11.7	20 01.5	1.7	54.5
U 10	331 25.5	58.0	235 25.0	11.8	20 03.2	1.7	54.5
R 11	346 25.7	57.0	249 55.8	11.7	20 04.9	1.6	54.5
D 12	1 25.9	N 1 56.0	264 26.5	11.7	S20 06.5	1.5	54.5
A 13	16 26.2	55.1	278 57.2	11.7	20 08.0	1.4	54.5
Y 14	31 26.4	54.1	293 27.9	11.7	20 09.4	1.3	54.5
15	46 26.6 ..	53.1	307 58.6	11.6	20 10.7	1.3	54.5
16	61 26.8	52.2	322 29.2	11.6	20 12.0	1.1	54.5
17	76 27.1	51.2	336 59.8	11.6	20 13.1	1.0	54.5
18	91 27.3	N 1 50.2	351 30.4	11.5	S20 14.1	0.9	54.6
19	106 27.5	49.3	6 00.9	11.6	20 15.0	0.9	54.6
20	121 27.7	48.3	20 31.5	11.5	20 15.9	0.7	54.6
21	136 28.0 ..	47.3	35 02.0	11.5	20 16.6	0.7	54.6
22	151 28.2	46.3	49 32.5	11.4	20 17.3	0.5	54.6
23	166 28.4	45.4	64 02.9	11.5	S20 17.8	0.4	54.6
	SD 15.9	d 1.0	SD 14.8		14.8		14.8

Lat.	Twilight Naut.	Civil	Sunrise	Moonrise 16	17	18	19
°	h m	h m	h m	h m	h m	h m	h m
N 72	02 20	04 03	05 14	16 11	▬▬	▬▬	▬▬
N 70	02 48	04 15	05 18	14 57	16 48	▬▬	▬▬
68	03 09	04 24	05 22	14 20	15 45	16 57	17 45
66	03 25	04 32	05 25	13 54	15 10	16 15	17 04
64	03 38	04 39	05 27	13 34	14 45	15 47	16 36
62	03 48	04 44	05 29	13 17	14 25	15 25	16 14
60	03 57	04 49	05 31	13 04	14 09	15 08	15 57
N 58	04 05	04 53	05 33	12 52	13 56	14 53	15 42
56	04 11	04 57	05 34	12 42	13 44	14 40	15 30
54	04 17	05 00	05 36	12 33	13 34	14 29	15 19
52	04 22	05 03	05 37	12 26	13 25	14 20	15 09
50	04 27	05 05	05 38	12 18	13 17	14 11	15 00
45	04 36	05 11	05 40	12 03	12 59	13 53	14 42
N 40	04 43	05 15	05 42	11 51	12 45	13 38	14 27
35	04 49	05 19	05 44	11 40	12 34	13 25	14 14
30	04 53	05 21	05 45	11 31	12 23	13 14	14 03
20	05 00	05 26	05 48	11 15	12 05	12 55	13 44
N 10	05 04	05 29	05 50	11 02	11 50	12 39	13 28
0	05 07	05 31	05 51	10 49	11 36	12 23	13 12
S 10	05 08	05 32	05 53	10 36	11 21	12 08	12 57
20	05 07	05 33	05 55	10 22	11 06	11 52	12 40
30	05 05	05 33	05 56	10 07	10 48	11 33	12 22
35	05 03	05 32	05 57	09 58	10 38	11 22	12 10
40	05 00	05 32	05 58	09 48	10 26	11 10	11 58
45	04 56	05 30	06 00	09 36	10 13	10 55	11 43
S 50	04 51	05 29	06 01	09 21	09 56	10 37	11 25
52	04 49	05 28	06 02	09 15	09 48	10 28	11 16
54	04 46	05 27	06 02	09 07	09 40	10 19	11 06
56	04 43	05 26	06 03	08 59	09 30	10 08	10 55
58	04 39	05 25	06 04	08 50	09 19	09 56	10 43
S 60	04 35	05 24	06 05	08 39	09 06	09 42	10 28

Lat.	Sunset	Twilight Civil	Naut.	Moonset 16	17	18	19
°	h m	h m	h m	h m	h m	h m	h m
N 72	18 33	19 43	21 23	17 39	▬▬	▬▬	▬▬
N 70	18 29	19 32	20 56	18 54	18 41	▬▬	▬▬
68	18 25	19 22	20 37	19 32	19 44	20 11	21 06
66	18 23	19 15	20 21	19 58	20 19	20 54	21 47
64	18 20	19 09	20 09	20 19	20 45	21 22	22 15
62	18 18	19 03	19 59	20 36	21 05	21 44	22 36
60	18 17	18 59	19 50	20 50	21 21	22 02	22 54
N 58	18 15	18 55	19 43	21 02	21 35	22 16	23 08
56	18 14	18 51	19 36	21 12	21 46	22 29	23 21
54	18 12	18 48	19 31	21 21	21 57	22 40	23 31
52	18 11	18 45	19 26	21 29	22 06	22 50	23 41
50	18 10	18 43	19 21	21 37	22 14	22 58	23 50
45	18 08	18 38	19 12	21 53	22 32	23 17	24 08
N 40	18 06	18 33	19 05	22 06	22 46	23 32	24 23
35	18 05	18 30	19 00	22 17	22 59	23 45	24 35
30	18 04	18 27	18 55	22 26	23 09	23 56	24 46
20	18 01	18 23	18 49	22 43	23 28	24 15	00 15
N 10	18 00	18 21	18 45	22 58	23 44	24 31	00 31
0	17 58	18 19	18 43	23 11	23 58	24 47	00 47
S 10	17 56	18 17	18 42	23 25	24 13	00 13	01 02
20	17 55	18 17	18 42	23 40	24 29	00 29	01 19
30	17 53	18 17	18 45	23 56	24 48	00 48	01 38
35	17 52	18 18	18 47	24 06	00 06	00 58	01 49
40	17 51	18 18	18 50	24 17	00 17	01 11	02 02
45	17 50	18 20	18 54	24 31	00 31	01 25	02 17
S 50	17 49	18 21	18 59	24 47	00 47	01 43	02 35
52	17 49	18 22	19 02	24 54	00 54	01 51	02 44
54	17 48	18 23	19 05	00 00	01 03	02 01	02 53
56	17 47	18 24	19 08	00 08	01 12	02 11	03 04
58	17 47	18 26	19 12	00 17	01 23	02 23	03 17
S 60	17 46	18 28	19 16	00 27	01 35	02 37	03 31

Day	SUN Eqn. of Time 00h	12h	Mer. Pass.	MOON Mer. Pass. Upper	Lower	Age	Phase
d	m s	m s	h m	h m	h m	d	%
16	04 50	05 01	11 55	17 00	04 37	07	38
17	05 11	05 22	11 55	17 47	05 23	08	47
18	05 33	05 43	11 54	18 35	06 11	09	56

UT	ARIES	VENUS −4.5		MARS +0.5		JUPITER −2.8		SATURN +0.0		STARS		
	GHA	GHA	Dec	GHA	Dec	GHA	Dec	GHA	Dec	Name	SHA	Dec
d h	° ′	° ′	° ′	° ′	° ′	° ′	° ′	° ′	° ′		° ′	° ′
19 00	357 27.4	216 51.7	N 9 30.1	108 52.7	S23 49.4	325 13.0	N11 25.5	312 20.7	N14 25.5	Acamar	315 26.2	S40 18.2
01	12 29.9	231 53.3	30.3	123 53.4	49.6	340 15.6	25.5	327 23.3	25.5	Achernar	335 34.2	S57 14.2
02	27 32.4	246 55.0	30.4	138 54.1	49.9	355 18.3	25.4	342 25.8	25.4	Acrux	173 21.9	S63 05.7
03	42 34.8	261 56.6 ..	30.6	153 54.7 ..	50.1	10 20.9 ..	25.3	357 28.4 ..	25.4	Adhara	255 21.0	S28 58.1
04	57 37.3	276 58.2	30.8	168 55.4	50.4	25 23.6	25.2	12 30.9	25.4	Aldebaran	291 01.5	N16 30.5
05	72 39.7	291 59.9	31.0	183 56.0	50.6	40 26.2	25.2	27 33.5	25.3			
06	87 42.2	307 01.5	N 9 31.1	198 56.7	S23 50.8	55 28.9	N11 25.1	42 36.0	N14 25.3	Alioth	166 30.6	N55 57.9
07	102 44.7	322 03.1	31.3	213 57.3	51.1	70 31.5	25.0	57 38.6	25.3	Alkaid	153 07.7	N49 19.2
08	117 47.1	337 04.7	31.5	228 58.0	51.3	85 34.2	25.0	72 41.1	25.2	Al Na'ir	27 56.7	S46 57.8
S 09	132 49.6	352 06.3 ..	31.7	243 58.7 ..	51.6	100 36.9 ..	24.9	87 43.6 ..	25.2	Alnilam	275 57.2	S 1 12.1
U 10	147 52.1	7 08.0	31.8	258 59.3	51.8	115 39.5	24.8	102 46.2	25.2	Alphard	218 06.8	S 8 39.3
N 11	162 54.5	22 09.6	32.0	274 00.0	52.0	130 42.2	24.7	117 48.7	25.1			
D 12	177 57.0	37 11.2	N 9 32.2	289 00.6	S23 52.3	145 44.8	N11 24.7	132 51.3	N14 25.1	Alphecca	126 20.3	N26 43.3
A 13	192 59.5	52 12.8	32.3	304 01.3	52.5	160 47.5	24.6	147 53.8	25.1	Alpheratz	357 54.2	N29 05.3
Y 14	208 01.9	67 14.4	32.5	319 01.9	52.8	175 50.1	24.5	162 56.4	25.1	Altair	62 18.5	N 8 52.3
15	223 04.5	82 16.0 ..	32.7	334 02.6 ..	53.0	190 52.8 ..	24.4	177 58.9 ..	25.0	Ankaa	353 25.8	S42 18.4
16	238 06.9	97 17.6	32.8	349 03.3	53.2	205 55.5	24.4	193 01.5	25.0	Antares	112 39.5	S26 25.8
17	253 09.3	112 19.2	33.0	4 03.9	53.5	220 58.1	24.3	208 04.0	25.0			
18	268 11.8	127 20.7	N 9 33.1	19 04.6	S23 53.7	236 00.8	N11 24.2	223 06.6	N14 24.9	Arcturus	146 05.8	N19 11.3
19	283 14.2	142 22.3	33.3	34 05.2	53.9	251 03.4	24.1	238 09.1	24.9	Atria	107 51.1	S69 01.8
20	298 16.7	157 23.9	33.5	49 05.9	54.2	266 06.1	24.1	253 11.7	24.9	Avior	234 22.7	S59 30.3
21	313 19.2	172 25.5 ..	33.6	64 06.5 ..	54.4	281 08.7 ..	24.0	268 14.2 ..	24.8	Bellatrix	278 43.4	N 6 21.0
22	328 21.6	187 27.1	33.8	79 07.2	54.7	296 11.4	23.9	283 16.8	24.8	Betelgeuse	271 12.9	N 7 24.4
23	343 24.1	202 28.6	33.9	94 07.8	54.9	311 14.1	23.8	298 19.3	24.8			
20 00	358 26.6	217 30.2	N 9 34.1	109 08.5	S23 55.1	326 16.7	N11 23.7	313 21.9	N14 24.7	Canopus	264 01.0	S52 41.5
01	13 29.0	232 31.8	34.2	124 09.1	55.4	341 19.4	23.7	328 24.5	24.7	Capella	280 50.2	N45 59.6
02	28 31.5	247 33.3	34.4	139 09.8	55.6	356 22.0	23.6	343 27.0	24.7	Deneb	49 38.4	N45 17.0
03	43 34.0	262 34.9 ..	34.5	154 10.4 ..	55.8	11 24.7 ..	23.5	358 29.6 ..	24.6	Denebola	182 44.9	N14 34.6
04	58 36.4	277 36.4	34.7	169 11.1	56.1	26 27.4	23.4	13 32.1	24.6	Diphda	349 06.3	S17 59.2
05	73 38.9	292 38.0	34.8	184 11.7	56.3	41 30.0	23.4	28 34.7	24.6			
06	88 41.3	307 39.5	N 9 35.0	199 12.4	S23 56.5	56 32.7	N11 23.3	43 37.2	N14 24.5	Dubhe	194 05.4	N61 45.2
07	103 43.8	322 41.1	35.1	214 13.0	56.8	71 35.4	23.2	58 39.8	24.5	Elnath	278 26.1	N28 36.3
08	118 46.3	337 42.6	35.3	229 13.7	57.0	86 38.0	23.1	73 42.3	24.5	Eltanin	90 51.1	N51 29.8
M 09	133 48.7	352 44.2 ..	35.4	244 14.3 ..	57.2	101 40.7 ..	23.1	88 44.9 ..	24.4	Enif	33 57.3	N 9 52.6
O 10	148 51.2	7 45.7	35.6	259 15.0	57.5	116 43.3	23.0	103 47.4	24.4	Fomalhaut	15 35.4	S29 37.4
N 11	163 53.7	22 47.2	35.7	274 15.6	57.7	131 46.0	22.9	118 50.0	24.4			
D 12	178 56.1	37 48.8	N 9 35.9	289 16.3	S23 57.9	146 48.7	N11 22.8	133 52.5	N14 24.3	Gacrux	172 13.4	S57 06.6
A 13	193 58.6	52 50.3	36.0	304 16.9	58.2	161 51.3	22.8	148 55.1	24.3	Gienah	176 03.6	S17 32.2
Y 14	209 01.1	67 51.8	36.1	319 17.6	58.4	176 54.0	22.7	163 57.6	24.3	Hadar	149 03.6	S60 22.3
15	224 03.5	82 53.4 ..	36.3	334 18.2 ..	58.6	191 56.7 ..	22.6	179 00.2 ..	24.2	Hamal	328 12.5	N23 27.6
16	239 06.0	97 54.9	36.4	349 18.9	58.9	206 59.3	22.5	194 02.7	24.2	Kaus Aust.	83 57.9	S34 23.1
17	254 08.5	112 56.4	36.6	4 19.5	59.1	222 02.0	22.4	209 05.3	24.2			
18	269 10.9	127 57.9	N 9 36.7	19 20.2	S23 59.3	237 04.7	N11 22.4	224 07.9	N14 24.1	Kochab	137 20.4	N74 09.8
19	284 13.4	142 59.4	36.8	34 20.8	59.6	252 07.3	22.3	239 10.4	24.1	Markab	13 48.7	N15 12.3
20	299 15.8	158 00.9	37.0	49 21.5	23 59.8	267 10.0	22.2	254 13.0	24.1	Menkar	314 26.0	N 4 05.3
21	314 18.3	173 02.4 ..	37.1	64 22.1	24 00.0	282 12.7 ..	22.1	269 15.5 ..	24.0	Menkent	148 20.5	S36 22.0
22	329 20.8	188 03.9	37.2	79 22.7	00.2	297 15.3	22.1	284 18.1	24.0	Miaplacidus	221 42.6	S69 42.7
23	344 23.2	203 05.4	37.4	94 23.4	00.5	312 18.0	22.0	299 20.6	23.9			
21 00	359 25.7	218 06.9	N 9 37.5	109 24.0	S24 00.7	327 20.7	N11 21.9	314 23.2	N14 23.9	Mirfak	308 55.4	N49 51.4
01	14 28.2	233 08.4	37.6	124 24.7	00.9	342 23.3	21.8	329 25.7	23.9	Nunki	76 11.4	S26 17.8
02	29 30.6	248 09.9	37.7	139 25.3	01.2	357 26.0	21.7	344 28.3	23.8	Peacock	53 35.7	S56 44.3
03	44 33.1	263 11.4 ..	37.9	154 26.0 ..	01.4	12 28.7 ..	21.7	359 30.8 ..	23.8	Pollux	243 41.0	N28 01.6
04	59 35.6	278 12.8	38.0	169 26.6	01.6	27 31.3	21.6	14 33.4	23.8	Procyon	245 11.0	N 5 13.6
05	74 38.0	293 14.3	38.1	184 27.2	01.8	42 34.0	21.5	29 36.0	23.7			
06	89 40.5	308 15.8	N 9 38.2	199 27.9	S24 02.1	57 36.7	N11 21.4	44 38.5	N14 23.7	Rasalhague	96 16.4	N12 33.9
07	104 43.0	323 17.3	38.4	214 28.5	02.3	72 39.3	21.4	59 41.1	23.7	Regulus	207 55.2	N11 58.3
08	119 45.4	338 18.7	38.5	229 29.2	02.5	87 42.0	21.3	74 43.6	23.6	Rigel	281 22.3	S 8 12.0
T 09	134 47.9	353 20.2 ..	38.6	244 29.8 ..	02.7	102 44.7 ..	21.2	89 46.2 ..	23.6	Rigil Kent.	140 06.9	S60 50.0
U 10	149 50.3	8 21.7	38.7	259 30.4	03.0	117 47.3	21.1	104 48.7	23.6	Sabik	102 24.8	S15 43.3
E 11	164 52.8	23 23.1	38.8	274 31.1	03.2	132 50.0	21.0	119 51.3	23.5			
S 12	179 55.3	38 24.6	N 9 38.9	289 31.7	S24 03.4	147 52.7	N11 21.0	134 53.9	N14 23.5	Schedar	349 52.2	N56 32.1
D 13	194 57.7	53 26.0	39.1	304 32.4	03.6	162 55.3	20.9	149 56.4	23.5	Shaula	96 36.4	S37 06.2
A 14	210 00.2	68 27.5	39.2	319 33.0	03.9	177 58.0	20.8	164 59.0	23.4	Sirius	258 43.2	S16 42.8
Y 15	225 02.7	83 28.9 ..	39.3	334 33.6 ..	04.1	193 00.7 ..	20.7	180 01.5 ..	23.4	Spica	158 42.8	S11 09.4
16	240 05.1	98 30.4	39.4	349 34.3	04.3	208 03.4	20.6	195 04.1	23.4	Suhail	223 00.6	S43 25.6
17	255 07.6	113 31.8	39.5	4 34.9	04.5	223 06.0	20.6	210 06.6	23.3			
18	270 10.1	128 33.3	N 9 39.6	19 35.6	S24 04.8	238 08.7	N11 20.5	225 09.2	N14 23.3	Vega	80 46.1	N38 47.4
19	285 12.5	143 34.7	39.7	34 36.2	05.0	253 11.4	20.4	240 11.8	23.3	Zuben'ubi	137 17.5	S16 02.2
20	300 15.0	158 36.1	39.8	49 36.8	05.2	268 14.0	20.3	255 14.3	23.2		SHA	Mer. Pass.
21	315 17.4	173 37.6 ..	40.0	64 37.5 ..	05.4	283 16.7 ..	20.2	270 16.9 ..	23.2		° ′	h m
22	330 19.9	188 39.0	40.1	79 38.1	05.6	298 19.4	20.2	285 19.4	23.2	Venus	219 03.6	9 29
23	345 22.4	203 40.4	40.2	94 38.7	05.9	313 22.1	20.1	300 22.0	23.1	Mars	110 41.9	16 43
Mer. Pass.	h m 0 06.2	v 1.5	d 0.1	v 0.6	d 0.2	v 2.7	d 0.1	v 2.6	d 0.0	Jupiter	327 50.2	2 14
										Saturn	314 55.3	3 06

UT	SUN GHA	SUN Dec	MOON GHA	v	MOON Dec	d	HP
d h	° ′	° ′	° ′	′	° ′	′	′
19 00	181 28.6	N 1 44.4	78 33.4	11.4	S20 18.2	0.4	54.7
01	196 28.8	43.4	93 03.8	11.4	20 18.6	0.3	54.7
02	211 29.1	42.5	107 34.2	11.4	20 18.9	0.1	54.7
03	226 29.3 ..	41.5	122 04.6	11.3	20 19.0	0.1	54.7
04	241 29.5	40.5	136 34.9	11.3	20 19.1	0.1	54.7
05	256 29.7	39.6	151 05.2	11.3	20 19.0	0.1	54.7
06	271 30.0	N 1 38.6	165 35.5	11.3	S20 18.9	0.2	54.8
07	286 30.2	37.6	180 05.8	11.3	20 18.7	0.4	54.8
S 08	301 30.4	36.7	194 36.1	11.2	20 18.3	0.4	54.8
U 09	316 30.6 ..	35.7	209 06.3	11.3	20 17.9	0.5	54.8
N 10	331 30.8	34.7	223 36.6	11.2	20 17.4	0.7	54.8
D 11	346 31.1	33.8	238 06.8	11.2	20 16.7	0.7	54.8
A 12	1 31.3	N 1 32.8	252 37.0	11.1	S20 16.0	0.8	54.9
Y 13	16 31.5	31.8	267 07.1	11.2	20 15.2	0.9	54.9
14	31 31.7	30.8	281 37.3	11.1	20 14.3	1.1	54.9
15	46 32.0 ..	29.9	296 07.4	11.1	20 13.2	1.1	54.9
16	61 32.2	28.9	310 37.5	11.1	20 12.1	1.2	54.9
17	76 32.4	27.9	325 07.6	11.1	20 10.9	1.3	55.0
18	91 32.6	N 1 27.0	339 37.7	11.1	S20 09.6	1.5	55.0
19	106 32.9	26.0	354 07.8	11.0	20 08.1	1.5	55.0
20	121 33.1	25.0	8 37.8	11.1	20 06.6	1.6	55.0
21	136 33.3 ..	24.1	23 07.9	11.0	20 05.0	1.7	55.0
22	151 33.5	23.1	37 37.9	11.0	20 03.3	1.9	55.1
23	166 33.7	22.1	52 07.9	11.0	20 01.4	1.9	55.1
20 00	181 34.0	N 1 21.2	66 37.9	10.9	S19 59.5	2.0	55.1
01	196 34.2	20.2	81 07.8	11.0	19 57.5	2.1	55.1
02	211 34.4	19.2	95 37.8	10.9	19 55.4	2.3	55.2
03	226 34.6 ..	18.2	110 07.7	11.0	19 53.1	2.3	55.2
04	241 34.9	17.3	124 37.7	10.9	19 50.8	2.4	55.2
05	256 35.1	16.3	139 07.6	10.9	19 48.4	2.6	55.2
06	271 35.3	N 1 15.3	153 37.5	10.9	S19 45.8	2.6	55.2
07	286 35.5	14.4	168 07.4	10.8	19 43.2	2.7	55.3
M 08	301 35.8	13.4	182 37.2	10.9	19 40.5	2.8	55.3
O 09	316 36.0 ..	12.4	197 07.1	10.9	19 37.7	3.0	55.3
N 10	331 36.2	11.5	211 37.0	10.8	19 34.7	3.0	55.3
D 11	346 36.4	10.5	226 06.8	10.8	19 31.7	3.1	55.4
A 12	1 36.6	N 1 09.5	240 36.6	10.9	S19 28.6	3.3	55.4
Y 13	16 36.9	08.5	255 06.5	10.8	19 25.3	3.3	55.4
14	31 37.1	07.6	269 36.3	10.8	19 22.0	3.5	55.4
15	46 37.3 ..	06.6	284 06.1	10.8	19 18.5	3.5	55.5
16	61 37.5	05.6	298 35.9	10.8	19 15.0	3.6	55.5
17	76 37.8	04.7	313 05.7	10.7	19 11.4	3.8	55.5
18	91 38.0	N 1 03.7	327 35.4	10.8	S19 07.6	3.8	55.5
19	106 38.2	02.7	342 05.2	10.8	19 03.8	3.9	55.6
20	121 38.4	01.7	356 35.0	10.7	18 59.9	4.1	55.6
21	136 38.6	1 00.8	11 04.7	10.8	18 55.8	4.1	55.6
22	151 38.9	0 59.8	25 34.5	10.7	18 51.7	4.3	55.7
23	166 39.1	58.8	40 04.2	10.7	18 47.4	4.3	55.7
21 00	181 39.3	N 0 57.9	54 33.9	10.7	S18 43.1	4.4	55.7
01	196 39.5	56.9	69 03.6	10.8	18 38.7	4.6	55.7
02	211 39.8	55.9	83 33.4	10.7	18 34.1	4.6	55.8
03	226 40.0 ..	54.9	98 03.1	10.7	18 29.5	4.7	55.8
04	241 40.2	54.0	112 32.8	10.7	18 24.8	4.9	55.8
05	256 40.4	53.0	127 02.5	10.7	18 19.9	4.9	55.8
06	271 40.6	N 0 52.0	141 32.2	10.7	S18 15.0	5.0	55.9
07	286 40.9	51.1	156 01.9	10.7	18 10.0	5.2	55.9
T 08	301 41.1	50.1	170 31.6	10.6	18 04.8	5.2	55.9
U 09	316 41.3 ..	49.1	185 01.2	10.7	17 59.6	5.3	56.0
E 10	331 41.5	48.2	199 30.9	10.7	17 54.3	5.4	56.0
S 11	346 41.8	47.2	214 00.6	10.7	17 48.9	5.6	56.0
D 12	1 42.0	N 0 46.2	228 30.3	10.6	S17 43.3	5.6	56.0
A 13	16 42.2	45.2	242 59.9	10.7	17 37.7	5.7	56.1
Y 14	31 42.4	44.3	257 29.6	10.7	17 32.0	5.8	56.1
15	46 42.6 ..	43.3	271 59.3	10.6	17 26.2	5.9	56.1
16	61 42.9	42.3	286 28.9	10.7	17 20.3	6.0	56.2
17	76 43.1	41.4	300 58.6	10.7	17 14.3	6.1	56.2
18	91 43.3	N 0 40.4	315 28.3	10.6	S17 08.2	6.2	56.2
19	106 43.5	39.4	329 57.9	10.7	17 02.0	6.3	56.3
20	121 43.8	38.4	344 27.6	10.6	16 55.7	6.4	56.3
21	136 44.0 ..	37.5	358 57.2	10.7	16 49.3	6.5	56.3
22	151 44.2	36.5	13 26.9	10.6	16 42.8	6.5	56.3
23	166 44.4	35.5	27 56.5	10.7	S16 36.3	6.7	56.4
	SD 16.0	d 1.0	SD 14.9		15.1		15.3

Lat.	Twilight Naut.	Twilight Civil	Sunrise	Moonrise 19	Moonrise 20	Moonrise 21	Moonrise 22
°	h m	h m	h m	h m	h m	h m	h m
N 72	02 42	04 18	05 27	■■	■■	19 45	19 14
N 70	03 05	04 28	05 30	■■	19 03	18 52	18 45
68	03 23	04 36	05 32	17 45	18 09	18 19	18 24
66	03 37	04 42	05 34	17 04	17 36	17 55	18 07
64	03 48	04 48	05 36	16 36	17 11	17 36	17 53
62	03 58	04 52	05 37	16 14	16 52	17 21	17 42
60	04 05	04 56	05 38	15 57	16 36	17 07	17 32
N 58	04 12	05 00	05 39	15 42	16 23	16 56	17 23
56	04 18	05 03	05 40	15 30	16 12	16 46	17 15
54	04 23	05 06	05 41	15 19	16 01	16 38	17 08
52	04 28	05 08	05 42	15 09	15 52	16 30	17 02
50	04 32	05 10	05 42	15 00	15 44	16 23	16 57
45	04 40	05 15	05 44	14 42	15 27	16 08	16 44
N 40	04 46	05 18	05 45	14 27	15 13	15 55	16 34
35	04 51	05 21	05 46	14 14	15 01	15 45	16 26
30	04 55	05 23	05 47	14 03	14 51	15 35	16 18
20	05 01	05 26	05 48	13 44	14 33	15 19	16 05
N 10	05 04	05 28	05 49	13 28	14 17	15 05	15 53
0	05 06	05 30	05 50	13 12	14 02	14 52	15 43
S 10	05 06	05 30	05 51	12 57	13 47	14 39	15 32
20	05 04	05 30	05 52	12 40	13 32	14 25	15 20
30	05 01	05 29	05 53	12 22	13 14	14 09	15 07
35	04 59	05 28	05 53	12 10	13 03	13 59	14 59
40	04 55	05 27	05 54	11 58	12 51	13 49	14 50
45	04 51	05 25	05 54	11 43	12 37	13 36	14 40
S 50	04 45	05 22	05 54	11 25	12 19	13 21	14 27
52	04 42	05 21	05 55	11 16	12 11	13 13	14 22
54	04 38	05 20	05 55	11 06	12 02	13 05	14 15
56	04 34	05 18	05 55	10 55	11 52	12 56	14 08
58	04 30	05 16	05 55	10 43	11 40	12 46	14 00
S 60	04 25	05 14	05 56	10 28	11 26	12 34	13 50

Lat.	Sunset	Twilight Civil	Twilight Naut.	Moonset 19	Moonset 20	Moonset 21	Moonset 22
°	h m	h m	h m	h m	h m	h m	h m
N 72	18 17	19 26	21 00	■■	■■	22 35	24 52
N 70	18 15	19 17	20 38	■■	21 32	23 28	25 19
68	18 13	19 09	20 21	21 06	22 26	24 00	00 00
66	18 11	19 03	20 07	21 47	22 59	24 23	00 23
64	18 10	18 58	19 56	22 15	23 22	24 42	00 42
62	18 09	18 53	19 47	22 36	23 41	24 57	00 57
60	18 07	18 49	19 40	22 54	23 57	25 09	01 09
N 58	18 07	18 46	19 33	23 08	24 10	00 10	01 20
56	18 06	18 43	19 27	23 21	24 21	00 21	01 29
54	18 05	18 40	19 22	23 31	24 31	00 31	01 38
52	18 04	18 38	19 18	23 41	24 40	00 40	01 45
50	18 04	18 36	19 14	23 50	24 48	00 48	01 52
45	18 02	18 32	19 06	24 08	00 08	01 04	02 06
N 40	18 01	18 28	19 00	24 23	00 23	01 18	02 18
35	18 01	18 26	18 55	24 35	00 35	01 30	02 28
30	18 00	18 24	18 52	24 46	00 46	01 40	02 36
20	17 59	18 21	18 46	00 15	01 05	01 57	02 51
N 10	17 58	18 19	18 43	00 31	01 21	02 12	03 04
0	17 57	18 17	18 41	00 47	01 36	02 26	03 16
S 10	17 56	18 17	18 41	01 02	01 51	02 40	03 28
20	17 55	18 17	18 43	01 19	02 08	02 55	03 41
30	17 55	18 19	18 47	01 38	02 26	03 12	03 56
35	17 55	18 20	18 49	01 49	02 37	03 22	04 04
40	17 54	18 21	18 53	02 02	02 49	03 33	04 14
45	17 54	18 23	18 58	02 17	03 04	03 47	04 25
S 50	17 54	18 25	19 04	02 35	03 22	04 03	04 39
52	17 54	18 27	19 07	02 44	03 30	04 10	04 45
54	17 53	18 29	19 10	02 53	03 39	04 18	04 52
56	17 53	18 30	19 14	03 04	03 50	04 28	04 59
58	17 53	18 32	19 19	03 17	04 02	04 38	05 08
S 60	17 53	18 34	19 24	03 31	04 16	04 51	05 18

	SUN			MOON			
Day	Eqn. of Time 00ʰ	Eqn. of Time 12ʰ	Mer. Pass.	Mer. Pass. Upper	Mer. Pass. Lower	Age	Phase
d	m s	m s	h m	h m	h m	d	%
19	05 54	06 05	11 54	19 24	07 00	10	66
20	06 15	06 26	11 54	20 14	07 49	11	75
21	06 37	06 47	11 53	21 04	08 39	12	83

UT	ARIES	VENUS −4.5		MARS +0.5		JUPITER −2.8		SATURN +0.0		STARS		
	GHA	GHA	Dec	GHA	Dec	GHA	Dec	GHA	Dec	Name	SHA	Dec
d h	° ′	° ′	° ′	° ′	° ′	° ′	° ′	° ′	° ′		° ′	° ′
22 00	0 24.8	218 41.8 N 9 40.3		109 39.4 S24 06.1		328 24.7 N11 20.0		315 24.6 N14 23.1		Acamar	315 26.1	S40 18.2
01	15 27.3	233 43.3	40.4	124 40.0	06.3	343 27.4	19.9	330 27.1	23.0	Achernar	335 34.2	S57 14.2
02	30 29.8	248 44.7	40.5	139 40.6	06.5	358 30.1	19.8	345 29.7	23.0	Acrux	173 21.9	S63 05.7
03	45 32.2	263 46.1 . .	40.6	154 41.3 . .	06.7	13 32.8 . .	19.8	0 32.2 . .	23.0	Adhara	255 21.0	S28 58.1
04	60 34.7	278 47.5	40.7	169 41.9	07.0	28 35.4	19.7	15 34.8	22.9	Aldebaran	291 01.5	N16 30.5
05	75 37.2	293 48.9	40.8	184 42.5	07.2	43 38.1	19.6	30 37.4	22.9			
06	90 39.6	308 50.3 N 9 40.9		199 43.2 S24 07.4		58 40.8 N11 19.5		45 39.9 N14 22.9		Alioth	166 30.6	N55 57.9
W 07	105 42.1	323 51.7	41.0	214 43.8	07.6	73 43.5	19.4	60 42.5	22.8	Alkaid	153 07.7	N49 19.2
E 08	120 44.6	338 53.1	41.1	229 44.4	07.8	88 46.1	19.4	75 45.0	22.8	Al Na'ir	27 56.7	S46 57.8
D 09	135 47.0	353 54.5 . .	41.2	244 45.1 . .	08.1	103 48.8 . .	19.3	90 47.6 . .	22.8	Alnilam	275 57.2	S 1 12.1
N 10	150 49.5	8 55.9	41.2	259 45.7	08.3	118 51.5	19.2	105 50.2	22.7	Alphard	218 06.8	S 8 39.3
E 11	165 51.9	23 57.3	41.3	274 46.3	08.5	133 54.2	19.1	120 52.7	22.7			
S 12	180 54.4	38 58.7 N 9 41.4		289 47.0 S24 08.7		148 56.8 N11 19.0		135 55.3 N14 22.7		Alphecca	126 20.3	N26 43.3
D 13	195 56.9	54 00.0	41.5	304 47.6	08.9	163 59.5	19.0	150 57.8	22.6	Alpheratz	357 54.2	N29 05.4
A 14	210 59.3	69 01.4	41.6	319 48.2	09.1	179 02.2	18.9	166 00.4	22.6	Altair	62 18.5	N 8 52.3
Y 15	226 01.8	84 02.8 . .	41.7	334 48.9 . .	09.4	194 04.9 . .	18.8	181 03.0 . .	22.6	Ankaa	353 25.8	S42 18.4
16	241 04.3	99 04.2	41.8	349 49.5	09.6	209 07.5	18.7	196 05.5	22.5	Antares	112 39.5	S26 25.8
17	256 06.7	114 05.5	41.9	4 50.1	09.8	224 10.2	18.6	211 08.1	22.5			
18	271 09.2	129 06.9 N 9 42.0		19 50.7 S24 10.0		239 12.9 N11 18.5		226 10.7 N14 22.4		Arcturus	146 05.8	N19 11.3
19	286 11.7	144 08.3	42.0	34 51.4	10.2	254 15.6	18.5	241 13.2	22.4	Atria	107 51.1	S69 01.8
20	301 14.1	159 09.6	42.1	49 52.0	10.4	269 18.3	18.4	256 15.8	22.4	Avior	234 22.7	S59 30.3
21	316 16.6	174 11.0 . .	42.2	64 52.6 . .	10.6	284 20.9 . .	18.3	271 18.3 . .	22.3	Bellatrix	278 43.4	N 6 21.0
22	331 19.1	189 12.4	42.3	79 53.3	10.9	299 23.6	18.2	286 20.9	22.3	Betelgeuse	271 12.8	N 7 24.4
23	346 21.5	204 13.7	42.4	94 53.9	11.1	314 26.3	18.1	301 23.5	22.3			
23 00	1 24.0	219 15.1 N 9 42.4		109 54.5 S24 11.3		329 29.0 N11 18.1		316 26.0 N14 22.2		Canopus	264 00.9	S52 41.5
01	16 26.4	234 16.4	42.5	124 55.1	11.5	344 31.7	18.0	331 28.6	22.2	Capella	280 50.1	N45 59.6
02	31 28.9	249 17.7	42.6	139 55.8	11.7	359 34.3	17.9	346 31.2	22.2	Deneb	49 38.5	N45 17.0
03	46 31.4	264 19.1 . .	42.7	154 56.4 . .	11.9	14 37.0 . .	17.8	1 33.7 . .	22.1	Denebola	182 44.9	N14 34.6
04	61 33.8	279 20.4	42.7	169 57.0	12.1	29 39.7	17.7	16 36.3	22.1	Diphda	349 06.3	S17 59.2
05	76 36.3	294 21.8	42.8	184 57.6	12.3	44 42.4	17.6	31 38.8	22.0			
06	91 38.8	309 23.1 N 9 42.9		199 58.3 S24 12.6		59 45.1 N11 17.6		46 41.4 N14 22.0		Dubhe	194 05.4	N61 45.2
07	106 41.2	324 24.4	43.0	214 58.9	12.8	74 47.7	17.5	61 44.0	22.0	Elnath	278 26.1	N28 36.3
T 08	121 43.7	339 25.8	43.0	229 59.5	13.0	89 50.4	17.4	76 46.5	21.9	Eltanin	90 51.1	N51 29.8
H 09	136 46.2	354 27.1 . .	43.1	245 00.1 . .	13.2	104 53.1 . .	17.3	91 49.1 . .	21.9	Enif	33 57.3	N 9 52.6
U 10	151 48.6	9 28.4	43.2	260 00.8	13.4	119 55.8	17.2	106 51.7	21.9	Fomalhaut	15 35.4	S29 37.4
R 11	166 51.1	24 29.7	43.2	275 01.4	13.6	134 58.5	17.1	121 54.2	21.8			
S 12	181 53.5	39 31.0 N 9 43.3		290 02.0 S24 13.8		150 01.2 N11 17.1		136 56.8 N14 21.8		Gacrux	172 13.4	S57 06.6
D 13	196 56.0	54 32.4	43.4	305 02.6	14.0	165 03.8	17.0	151 59.4	21.8	Gienah	176 03.6	S17 32.2
A 14	211 58.5	69 33.7	43.4	320 03.2	14.2	180 06.5	16.9	167 01.9	21.7	Hadar	149 03.6	S60 22.2
Y 15	227 00.9	84 35.0 . .	43.5	335 03.9 . .	14.4	195 09.2 . .	16.8	182 04.5 . .	21.7	Hamal	328 12.5	N23 27.6
16	242 03.4	99 36.3	43.6	350 04.5	14.6	210 11.9	16.7	197 07.1	21.6	Kaus Aust.	83 57.9	S34 23.1
17	257 05.9	114 37.6	43.6	5 05.1	14.8	225 14.6	16.6	212 09.6	21.6			
18	272 08.3	129 38.9 N 9 43.7		20 05.7 S24 15.1		240 17.3 N11 16.6		227 12.2 N14 21.6		Kochab	137 20.5	N74 09.8
19	287 10.8	144 40.2	43.7	35 06.3	15.3	255 19.9	16.5	242 14.8	21.5	Markab	13 48.7	N15 12.3
20	302 13.3	159 41.5	43.8	50 07.0	15.5	270 22.6	16.4	257 17.3	21.5	Menkar	314 26.0	N 4 05.3
21	317 15.7	174 42.8 . .	43.8	65 07.6 . .	15.7	285 25.3 . .	16.3	272 19.9 . .	21.5	Menkent	148 20.5	S36 22.0
22	332 18.2	189 44.1	43.9	80 08.2	15.9	300 28.0	16.2	287 22.5	21.4	Miaplacidus	221 42.6	S69 42.7
23	347 20.7	204 45.3	44.0	95 08.8	16.1	315 30.7	16.1	302 25.0	21.4			
24 00	2 23.1	219 46.6 N 9 44.0		110 09.4 S24 16.3		330 33.4 N11 16.1		317 27.6 N14 21.3		Mirfak	308 55.4	N49 51.4
01	17 25.6	234 47.9	44.1	125 10.1	16.5	345 36.1	16.0	332 30.2	21.3	Nunki	76 11.5	S26 17.8
02	32 28.0	249 49.2	44.1	140 10.7	16.7	0 38.7	15.9	347 32.7	21.3	Peacock	53 35.7	S56 44.3
03	47 30.5	264 50.5 . .	44.2	155 11.3 . .	16.9	15 41.4 . .	15.8	2 35.3 . .	21.2	Pollux	243 40.9	N28 01.6
04	62 33.0	279 51.7	44.2	170 11.9	17.1	30 44.1	15.7	17 37.9	21.2	Procyon	245 11.0	N 5 13.6
05	77 35.4	294 53.0	44.3	185 12.5	17.3	45 46.8	15.6	32 40.4	21.2			
06	92 37.9	309 54.3 N 9 44.3		200 13.1 S24 17.5		60 49.5 N11 15.5		47 43.0 N14 21.1		Rasalhague	96 16.4	N12 33.9
07	107 40.4	324 55.5	44.3	215 13.8	17.7	75 52.2	15.5	62 45.6	21.1	Regulus	207 55.1	N11 58.2
08	122 42.8	339 56.8	44.4	230 14.4	17.9	90 54.9	15.4	77 48.1	21.0	Rigel	281 22.3	S 8 12.0
F 09	137 45.3	354 58.1 . .	44.4	245 15.0 . .	18.1	105 57.6 . .	15.3	92 50.7 . .	21.0	Rigil Kent.	140 06.9	S60 50.0
R 10	152 47.8	9 59.3	44.5	260 15.6	18.3	121 00.2	15.2	107 53.3	21.0	Sabik	102 24.9	S15 43.3
I 11	167 50.2	25 00.6	44.5	275 16.2	18.5	136 02.9	15.1	122 55.8	20.9			
D 12	182 52.7	40 01.8 N 9 44.6		290 16.8 S24 18.7		151 05.6 N11 15.0		137 58.4 N14 20.9		Schedar	349 52.2	N56 32.1
A 13	197 55.1	55 03.1	44.6	305 17.5	18.9	166 08.3	14.9	153 01.0	20.9	Shaula	96 36.5	S37 06.2
Y 14	212 57.6	70 04.3	44.6	320 18.1	19.1	181 11.0	14.9	168 03.6	20.8	Sirius	258 43.2	S16 42.8
15	228 00.1	85 05.5 . .	44.7	335 18.7 . .	19.3	196 13.7 . .	14.8	183 06.1 . .	20.8	Spica	158 42.8	S11 09.4
16	243 02.5	100 06.8	44.7	350 19.3	19.5	211 16.4	14.7	198 08.7	20.7	Suhail	223 00.6	S43 25.6
17	258 05.0	115 08.0	44.7	5 19.9	19.7	226 19.1	14.6	213 11.3	20.7			
18	273 07.5	130 09.3 N 9 44.8		20 20.5 S24 19.9		241 21.8 N11 14.5		228 13.8 N14 20.7		Vega	80 46.1	N38 47.4
19	288 09.9	145 10.5	44.8	35 21.1	20.1	256 24.5	14.4	243 16.4	20.6	Zuben'ubi	137 17.5	S16 02.2
20	303 12.4	160 11.7	44.8	50 21.7	20.3	271 27.1	14.3	258 19.0	20.6		SHA	Mer. Pass
21	318 14.9	175 12.9 . .	44.9	65 22.4 . .	20.5	286 29.8 . .	14.3	273 21.5 . .	20.6		° ′	h m
22	333 17.3	190 14.2	44.9	80 23.0	20.7	301 32.5	14.2	288 24.1	20.5	Venus	217 51.1	9 22
23	348 19.8	205 15.4	44.9	95 23.6	20.9	316 35.2	14.1	303 26.7	20.5	Mars	108 30.5	16 40
	h m									Jupiter	328 05.0	2 02
Mer. Pass. 23 50.5		v 1.3	d 0.1	v 0.6	d 0.2	v 2.7	d 0.1	v 2.6	d 0.0	Saturn	315 02.1	2 54

UT	SUN GHA	SUN Dec	MOON GHA	v	MOON Dec	d	HP
d h	° ′	° ′	° ′	′	° ′	′	′
22 00	181 44.6	N 0 34.5	42 26.2	10.6	S16 29.6	6.8	56.4
01	196 44.9	33.6	56 55.8	10.7	16 22.8	6.8	56.4
02	211 45.1	32.6	71 25.5	10.6	16 16.0	7.0	56.5
03	226 45.3	.. 31.6	85 55.1	10.7	16 09.0	7.0	56.5
04	241 45.5	30.7	100 24.8	10.6	16 02.0	7.1	56.5
05	256 45.7	29.7	114 54.4	10.7	15 54.9	7.3	56.6
06	271 46.0	N 0 28.7	129 24.1	10.6	S15 47.6	7.3	56.6
W 07	286 46.2	27.7	143 53.7	10.7	15 40.3	7.4	56.6
E 08	301 46.4	26.8	158 23.4	10.7	15 32.9	7.5	56.7
D 09	316 46.6	.. 25.8	172 53.1	10.6	15 25.4	7.5	56.7
N 10	331 46.9	24.8	187 22.7	10.7	15 17.9	7.7	56.7
E 11	346 47.1	23.9	201 52.4	10.6	15 10.2	7.8	56.8
S 12	1 47.3	N 0 22.9	216 22.0	10.7	S15 02.4	7.8	56.8
D 13	16 47.5	21.9	230 51.7	10.6	14 54.6	8.0	56.8
A 14	31 47.7	20.9	245 21.3	10.7	14 46.6	8.0	56.8
Y 15	46 48.0	.. 20.0	259 51.0	10.7	14 38.6	8.1	56.9
16	61 48.2	19.0	274 20.7	10.6	14 30.5	8.2	56.9
17	76 48.4	18.0	288 50.3	10.7	14 22.3	8.3	56.9
18	91 48.6	N 0 17.0	303 20.0	10.6	S14 14.0	8.3	57.0
19	106 48.8	16.1	317 49.6	10.7	14 05.7	8.5	57.0
20	121 49.1	15.1	332 19.3	10.7	13 57.2	8.5	57.0
21	136 49.3	.. 14.1	346 49.0	10.6	13 48.7	8.6	57.1
22	151 49.5	13.2	1 18.6	10.7	13 40.1	8.7	57.1
23	166 49.7	12.2	15 48.3	10.7	13 31.4	8.8	57.1
23 00	181 49.9	N 0 11.2	30 18.0	10.6	S13 22.6	8.9	57.2
01	196 50.2	10.2	44 47.6	10.7	13 13.7	8.9	57.2
02	211 50.4	09.3	59 17.3	10.7	13 04.8	9.0	57.2
03	226 50.6	.. 08.3	73 47.0	10.7	12 55.8	9.1	57.3
04	241 50.8	07.3	88 16.7	10.6	12 46.7	9.2	57.3
05	256 51.0	06.4	102 46.3	10.7	12 37.5	9.3	57.3
06	271 51.3	N 0 05.4	117 16.0	10.7	S12 28.2	9.3	57.4
T 07	286 51.5	04.4	131 45.7	10.7	12 18.9	9.4	57.4
H 08	301 51.7	03.4	146 15.4	10.6	12 09.5	9.5	57.4
U 09	316 51.9	.. 02.5	160 45.0	10.7	12 00.0	9.6	57.5
R 10	331 52.2	01.5	175 14.7	10.7	11 50.4	9.6	57.5
S 11	346 52.4	N 00.5	189 44.4	10.7	11 40.8	9.7	57.5
D 12	1 52.6	S 0 00.5	204 14.1	10.7	S11 31.1	9.8	57.6
A 13	16 52.8	01.4	218 43.8	10.6	11 21.3	9.9	57.6
Y 14	31 53.0	02.4	233 13.4	10.7	11 11.4	9.9	57.6
15	46 53.3	.. 03.4	247 43.1	10.7	11 01.5	10.0	57.6
16	61 53.5	04.4	262 12.8	10.7	10 51.5	10.0	57.7
17	76 53.7	05.3	276 42.5	10.6	10 41.5	10.2	57.7
18	91 53.9	S 0 06.3	291 12.1	10.7	S10 31.3	10.2	57.7
19	106 54.1	07.3	305 41.8	10.7	10 21.1	10.3	57.8
20	121 54.4	08.2	320 11.5	10.7	10 10.8	10.3	57.8
21	136 54.6	.. 09.2	334 41.2	10.6	10 00.5	10.4	57.8
22	151 54.8	10.2	349 10.8	10.7	9 50.1	10.5	57.9
23	166 55.0	11.2	3 40.5	10.7	9 39.6	10.5	57.9
24 00	181 55.2	S 0 12.1	18 10.2	10.6	S 9 29.1	10.6	57.9
01	196 55.4	13.1	32 39.8	10.7	9 18.5	10.6	58.0
02	211 55.7	14.1	47 09.5	10.6	9 07.9	10.7	58.0
03	226 55.9	.. 15.1	61 39.1	10.7	8 57.2	10.8	58.0
04	241 56.1	16.0	76 08.8	10.6	8 46.4	10.9	58.0
05	256 56.3	17.0	90 38.4	10.7	8 35.5	10.9	58.1
06	271 56.5	S 0 18.0	105 08.1	10.6	S 8 24.6	10.9	58.1
07	286 56.8	18.9	119 37.7	10.7	8 13.7	11.0	58.1
08	301 57.0	19.9	134 07.4	10.6	8 02.7	11.1	58.2
F 09	316 57.2	.. 20.9	148 37.0	10.6	7 51.6	11.1	58.2
R 10	331 57.4	21.9	163 06.6	10.7	7 40.5	11.2	58.2
I 11	346 57.6	22.8	177 36.3	10.6	7 29.3	11.2	58.3
D 12	1 57.9	S 0 23.8	192 05.9	10.6	S 7 18.1	11.3	58.3
A 13	16 58.1	24.8	206 35.5	10.6	7 06.8	11.3	58.3
Y 14	31 58.3	25.8	221 05.1	10.6	6 55.5	11.4	58.3
15	46 58.5	.. 26.7	235 34.7	10.6	6 44.1	11.4	58.4
16	61 58.7	27.7	250 04.3	10.6	6 32.7	11.5	58.4
17	76 59.0	28.7	264 33.9	10.5	6 21.2	11.5	58.4
18	91 59.2	S 0 29.7	279 03.4	10.6	S 6 09.7	11.5	58.5
19	106 59.4	30.6	293 33.0	10.6	5 58.2	11.6	58.5
20	121 59.6	31.6	308 02.6	10.5	5 46.6	11.7	58.5
21	136 59.8	.. 32.6	322 32.1	10.5	5 34.9	11.7	58.5
22	152 00.0	33.5	337 01.6	10.6	5 23.2	11.7	58.6
23	167 00.3	34.5	351 31.2	10.5	S 5 11.5	11.8	58.6
	SD 16.0	d 1.0	SD 15.5		15.7		15.9

Lat.	Twilight Naut.	Twilight Civil	Sunrise	Moonrise 22	23	24	25
°	h m	h m	h m	h m	h m	h m	h m
N 72	03 01	04 32	05 41	19 14	18 56	18 43	18 31
N 70	03 21	04 40	05 42	18 45	18 40	18 34	18 29
68	03 36	04 47	05 43	18 24	18 26	18 27	18 28
66	03 48	04 52	05 44	18 07	18 15	18 21	18 27
64	03 58	04 57	05 44	17 53	18 06	18 16	18 25
62	04 06	05 00	05 45	17 42	17 58	18 12	18 25
60	04 13	05 04	05 45	17 32	17 51	18 08	18 24
N 58	04 19	05 06	05 46	17 23	17 45	18 05	18 23
56	04 25	05 09	05 46	17 15	17 40	18 02	18 22
54	04 29	05 11	05 46	17 08	17 35	17 59	18 22
52	04 33	05 13	05 47	17 02	17 31	17 56	18 21
50	04 37	05 15	05 47	16 57	17 27	17 54	18 21
45	04 44	05 18	05 48	16 44	17 18	17 49	18 19
N 40	04 49	05 21	05 48	16 34	17 11	17 45	18 19
35	04 53	05 23	05 48	16 26	17 04	17 41	18 18
30	04 57	05 25	05 49	16 18	16 59	17 38	18 17
20	05 01	05 27	05 49	16 05	16 49	17 33	18 16
N 10	05 04	05 28	05 49	15 53	16 41	17 28	18 15
0	05 05	05 29	05 49	15 43	16 33	17 23	18 14
S 10	05 04	05 28	05 49	15 32	16 25	17 18	18 13
20	05 02	05 27	05 49	15 20	16 16	17 14	18 12
30	04 57	05 25	05 49	15 07	16 07	17 08	18 11
35	04 54	05 24	05 49	14 59	16 01	17 05	18 10
40	04 50	05 22	05 49	14 50	15 55	17 01	18 09
45	04 45	05 19	05 48	14 40	15 47	16 57	18 08
S 50	04 38	05 16	05 48	14 27	15 38	16 52	18 07
52	04 34	05 14	05 48	14 22	15 34	16 49	18 07
54	04 30	05 12	05 47	14 15	15 29	16 47	18 06
56	04 26	05 10	05 47	14 08	15 24	16 44	18 06
58	04 21	05 08	05 47	14 00	15 18	16 41	18 05
S 60	04 15	05 05	05 47	13 50	15 12	16 37	18 05

Lat.	Sunset	Twilight Civil	Twilight Naut.	Moonset 22	23	24	25
°	h m	h m	h m	h m	h m	h m	h m
N 72	18 02	19 10	20 39	24 52	00 52	02 55	04 54
N 70	18 01	19 02	20 20	25 19	01 19	03 10	05 00
68	18 00	18 56	20 06	00 00	01 39	03 21	05 05
66	18 00	18 51	19 54	00 23	01 55	03 31	05 09
64	17 59	18 47	19 44	00 42	02 08	03 39	05 13
62	17 59	18 43	19 36	00 57	02 19	03 46	05 16
60	17 58	18 40	19 30	01 09	02 28	03 52	05 18
N 58	17 58	18 37	19 24	01 20	02 36	03 57	05 20
56	17 58	18 35	19 19	01 29	02 43	04 02	05 22
54	17 58	18 33	19 15	01 38	02 50	04 06	05 24
52	17 57	18 31	19 11	01 45	02 55	04 09	05 26
50	17 57	18 29	19 07	01 52	03 01	04 13	05 27
45	17 57	18 26	19 00	02 06	03 12	04 20	05 31
N 40	17 56	18 23	18 55	02 18	03 21	04 26	05 33
35	17 56	18 21	18 51	02 28	03 28	04 31	05 36
30	17 56	18 20	18 48	02 36	03 35	04 36	05 38
20	17 56	18 18	18 43	02 51	03 47	04 44	05 41
N 10	17 56	18 17	18 41	03 04	03 57	04 50	05 44
0	17 56	18 16	18 40	03 16	04 07	04 57	05 47
S 10	17 56	18 17	18 41	03 28	04 16	05 03	05 50
20	17 56	18 18	18 44	03 41	04 26	05 10	05 53
30	17 57	18 20	18 48	03 56	04 37	05 17	05 56
35	17 57	18 22	18 52	04 04	04 44	05 22	05 58
40	17 57	18 24	18 56	04 14	04 51	05 26	06 00
45	17 58	18 27	19 01	04 25	05 00	05 32	06 03
S 50	17 58	18 30	19 07	04 39	05 10	05 39	06 06
52	17 58	18 32	19 12	04 45	05 15	05 42	06 07
54	17 59	18 34	19 16	04 52	05 20	05 45	06 08
56	17 59	18 36	19 21	04 59	05 26	05 49	06 10
58	17 59	18 39	19 27	05 08	05 32	05 53	06 12
S 60	18 00	18 41	19 32	05 18	05 40	05 58	06 14

Day	SUN Eqn. of Time 00ʰ	SUN Eqn. of Time 12ʰ	Mer. Pass.	MOON Mer. Pass. Upper	MOON Mer. Pass. Lower	Age	Phase
d	m s	m s	h m	h m	h m	d	%
22	06 58	07 09	11 53	21 55	09 29	13	90
23	07 19	07 30	11 53	22 45	10 20	14	95
24	07 40	07 51	11 52	23 35	11 10	15	99

UT	ARIES GHA	VENUS −4.5 GHA	Dec	MARS +0.5 GHA	Dec	JUPITER −2.8 GHA	Dec	SATURN +0.0 GHA	Dec
25 00	3 22.3	220 16.6	N 9 45.0	110 24.2	S24 21.1	331 37.9	N11 14.0	318 29.3	N14 20.4
01	18 24.7	235 17.8	45.0	125 24.8	21.3	346 40.6	13.9	333 31.8	20.4
02	33 27.2	250 19.0	45.0	140 25.4	21.5	1 43.3	13.8	348 34.4	20.4
03	48 29.6	265 20.2 ..	45.0	155 26.0 ..	21.7	16 46.0 ..	13.7	3 37.0 ..	20.3
04	63 32.1	280 21.5	45.0	170 26.6	21.9	31 48.7	13.7	18 39.5	20.3
05	78 34.6	295 22.7	45.1	185 27.2	22.1	46 51.4	13.6	33 42.1	20.3
06	93 37.0	310 23.9	N 9 45.1	200 27.8	S24 22.3	61 54.1	N11 13.5	48 44.7	N14 20.2
07	108 39.5	325 25.1	45.1	215 28.5	22.5	76 56.8	13.4	63 47.3	20.2
S 08	123 42.0	340 26.3	45.1	230 29.1	22.7	91 59.5	13.3	78 49.8	20.1
A 09	138 44.4	355 27.5 ..	45.1	245 29.7 ..	22.9	107 02.2 ..	13.2	93 52.4 ..	20.1
T 10	153 46.9	10 28.6	45.2	260 30.3	23.0	122 04.9	13.1	108 55.0	20.1
U 11	168 49.4	25 29.8	45.2	275 30.9	23.2	137 07.5	13.0	123 57.5	20.0
R 12	183 51.8	40 31.0	N 9 45.2	290 31.5	S24 23.4	152 10.2	N11 13.0	139 00.1	N14 20.0
D 13	198 54.3	55 32.2	45.2	305 32.1	23.6	167 12.9	12.9	154 02.7	19.9
A 14	213 56.8	70 33.4	45.2	320 32.7	23.8	182 15.6	12.8	169 05.3	19.9
Y 15	228 59.2	85 34.6 ..	45.2	335 33.3 ..	24.0	197 18.3 ..	12.7	184 07.8 ..	19.9
16	244 01.7	100 35.7	45.2	350 33.9	24.2	212 21.0	12.6	199 10.4	19.8
17	259 04.1	115 36.9	45.2	5 34.5	24.4	227 23.7	12.5	214 13.0	19.8
18	274 06.6	130 38.1	N 9 45.3	20 35.1	S24 24.6	242 26.4	N11 12.4	229 15.6	N14 19.8
19	289 09.1	145 39.3	45.3	35 35.7	24.8	257 29.1	12.3	244 18.1	19.7
20	304 11.5	160 40.4	45.3	50 36.3	25.0	272 31.8	12.3	259 20.7	19.7
21	319 14.0	175 41.6 ..	45.3	65 36.9 ..	25.2	287 34.5 ..	12.2	274 23.3 ..	19.6
22	334 16.5	190 42.7	45.3	80 37.5	25.3	302 37.2	12.1	289 25.9	19.6
23	349 18.9	205 43.9	45.3	95 38.1	25.5	317 39.9	12.0	304 28.4	19.6
26 00	4 21.4	220 45.1	N 9 45.3	110 38.7	S24 25.7	332 42.6	N11 11.9	319 31.0	N14 19.5
01	19 23.9	235 46.2	45.3	125 39.3	25.9	347 45.3	11.8	334 33.6	19.5
02	34 26.3	250 47.4	45.3	140 40.0	26.1	2 48.0	11.7	349 36.1	19.4
03	49 28.8	265 48.5 ..	45.3	155 40.6 ..	26.3	17 50.7 ..	11.6	4 38.7 ..	19.4
04	64 31.2	280 49.7	45.3	170 41.2	26.5	32 53.4	11.5	19 41.3	19.4
05	79 33.7	295 50.8	45.3	185 41.8	26.7	47 56.1	11.5	34 43.9	19.3
06	94 36.2	310 51.9	N 9 45.3	200 42.4	S24 26.8	62 58.8	N11 11.3	49 46.5	N14 19.3
07	109 38.6	325 53.1	45.3	215 43.0	27.0	78 01.5	11.3	64 49.0	19.2
S 08	124 41.1	340 54.2	45.2	230 43.6	27.2	93 04.2	11.2	79 51.6	19.2
U 09	139 43.6	355 55.3 ..	45.2	245 44.2 ..	27.4	108 06.9 ..	11.1	94 54.2 ..	19.2
N 10	154 46.0	10 56.5	45.2	260 44.8	27.6	123 09.6	11.0	109 56.8	19.1
D 11	169 48.5	25 57.6	45.2	275 45.4	27.8	138 12.3	10.9	124 59.3	19.1
A 12	184 51.0	40 58.7	N 9 45.2	290 46.0	S24 27.9	153 15.0	N11 10.8	140 01.9	N14 19.0
Y 13	199 53.4	55 59.8	45.2	305 46.6	28.1	168 17.7	10.7	155 04.5	19.0
14	214 55.9	71 01.0	45.2	320 47.2	28.3	183 20.4	10.7	170 07.1	19.0
15	229 58.4	86 02.1 ..	45.2	335 47.7 ..	28.5	198 23.1 ..	10.6	185 09.6 ..	18.9
16	245 00.8	101 03.2	45.1	350 48.3	28.7	213 25.8	10.5	200 12.2	18.9
17	260 03.3	116 04.3	45.1	5 48.9	28.9	228 28.5	10.4	215 14.8	18.8
18	275 05.7	131 05.4	N 9 45.1	20 49.5	S24 29.0	243 31.2	N11 10.3	230 17.4	N14 18.8
19	290 08.2	146 06.5	45.1	35 50.1	29.2	258 33.9	10.2	245 19.9	18.8
20	305 10.7	161 07.6	45.1	50 50.7	29.4	273 36.6	10.1	260 22.5	18.7
21	320 13.1	176 08.7 ..	45.0	65 51.3 ..	29.6	288 39.3 ..	10.0	275 25.1 ..	18.7
22	335 15.6	191 09.8	45.0	80 51.9	29.8	303 42.0	09.9	290 27.7	18.6
23	350 18.1	206 10.9	45.0	95 52.5	30.0	318 44.7	09.8	305 30.3	18.6
27 00	5 20.5	221 12.0	N 9 45.0	110 53.1	S24 30.1	333 47.4	N11 09.8	320 32.8	N14 18.6
01	20 23.0	236 13.1	45.0	125 53.7	30.3	348 50.1	09.7	335 35.4	18.5
02	35 25.5	251 14.2	44.9	140 54.3	30.5	3 52.8	09.6	350 38.0	18.5
03	50 27.9	266 15.3 ..	44.9	155 54.9 ..	30.7	18 55.6 ..	09.5	5 40.6 ..	18.4
04	65 30.4	281 16.4	44.9	170 55.5	30.8	33 58.3	09.4	20 43.2	18.4
05	80 32.8	296 17.5	44.8	185 56.1	31.0	49 01.0	09.3	35 45.7	18.4
06	95 35.3	311 18.5	N 9 44.8	200 56.7	S24 31.2	64 03.7	N11 09.2	50 48.3	N14 18.3
07	110 37.8	326 19.6	44.8	215 57.3	31.4	79 06.4	09.1	65 50.9	18.3
08	125 40.2	341 20.7	44.7	230 57.9	31.6	94 09.1	09.0	80 53.5	18.2
M 09	140 42.7	356 21.8 ..	44.7	245 58.5 ..	31.7	109 11.8 ..	08.9	95 56.0 ..	18.2
O 10	155 45.2	11 22.8	44.7	260 59.0	31.9	124 14.5	08.8	110 58.6	18.2
N 11	170 47.6	26 23.9	44.6	275 59.6	32.1	139 17.2	08.7	126 01.2	18.1
D 12	185 50.1	41 25.0	N 9 44.6	291 00.2	S24 32.3	154 19.9	N11 08.7	141 03.8	N14 18.1
A 13	200 52.6	56 26.0	44.6	306 00.8	32.4	169 22.6	08.6	156 06.4	18.0
Y 14	215 55.0	71 27.1	44.5	321 01.4	32.6	184 25.3	08.5	171 09.0	18.0
15	230 57.5	86 28.2 ..	44.5	336 02.0 ..	32.8	199 28.0 ..	08.4	186 11.5 ..	18.0
16	246 00.0	101 29.2	44.4	351 02.6	33.0	214 30.7	08.3	201 14.1	17.9
17	261 02.4	116 30.3	44.4	6 03.2	33.1	229 33.4	08.2	216 16.7	17.9
18	276 04.9	131 31.3	N 9 44.4	21 03.8	S24 33.3	244 36.2	N11 08.1	231 19.3	N14 17.8
19	291 07.3	146 32.4	44.3	36 04.4	33.5	259 38.9	08.0	246 21.9	17.8
20	306 09.8	161 33.4	44.3	51 04.9	33.7	274 41.6	07.9	261 24.4	17.8
21	321 12.3	176 34.5 ..	44.2	66 05.5 ..	33.8	289 44.3 ..	07.8	276 27.0 ..	17.7
22	336 14.7	191 35.5	44.2	81 06.1	34.0	304 47.0	07.7	291 29.6	17.7
23	351 17.2	206 36.5	44.1	96 06.7	34.2	319 49.7	07.7	306 32.2	17.6
Mer. Pass.	h m 23 38.7	v 1.1	d 0.0	v 0.6	d 0.2	v 2.7	d 0.1	v 2.6	d 0.0

STARS

Name	SHA	Dec
Acamar	315 26.1	S40 18.2
Achernar	335 34.2	S57 14.2
Acrux	173 22.0	S63 05.7
Adhara	255 21.0	S28 58.1
Aldebaran	291 01.5	N16 30.5
Alioth	166 30.6	N55 57.9
Alkaid	153 07.7	N49 19.2
Al Na'ir	27 56.7	S46 57.8
Alnilam	275 57.2	S 1 12.1
Alphard	218 06.8	S 8 39.3
Alphecca	126 20.3	N26 43.3
Alpheratz	357 54.2	N29 05.4
Altair	62 18.5	N 8 52.3
Ankaa	353 25.8	S42 18.4
Antares	112 39.5	S26 25.8
Arcturus	146 05.8	N19 11.3
Atria	107 51.2	S69 01.7
Avior	234 22.7	S59 30.2
Bellatrix	278 43.4	N 6 21.0
Betelgeuse	271 12.8	N 7 24.4
Canopus	264 00.9	S52 41.5
Capella	280 50.1	N45 59.6
Deneb	49 38.5	N45 17.0
Denebola	182 44.9	N14 34.6
Diphda	349 06.3	S17 59.3
Dubhe	194 05.4	N61 45.2
Elnath	278 26.0	N28 36.3
Eltanin	90 51.1	N51 29.8
Enif	33 57.3	N 9 52.6
Fomalhaut	15 35.4	S29 37.4
Gacrux	172 13.4	S57 06.5
Gienah	176 03.6	S17 32.2
Hadar	149 03.7	S60 22.2
Hamal	328 12.5	N23 27.6
Kaus Aust.	83 58.0	S34 23.1
Kochab	137 20.5	N74 09.7
Markab	13 48.7	N15 12.3
Menkar	314 26.0	N 4 05.3
Menkent	148 20.5	S36 22.0
Miaplacidus	221 42.5	S69 42.7
Mirfak	308 55.3	N49 51.4
Nunki	76 11.5	S26 17.8
Peacock	53 35.7	S56 44.3
Pollux	243 40.9	N28 01.6
Procyon	245 11.0	N 5 13.6
Rasalhague	96 16.4	N12 33.9
Regulus	207 55.1	N11 58.2
Rigel	281 22.2	S 8 12.0
Rigil Kent.	140 07.0	S60 50.0
Sabik	102 24.9	S15 43.3
Schedar	349 52.2	N56 32.1
Shaula	96 36.5	S37 06.2
Sirius	258 43.2	S16 42.8
Spica	158 42.8	S11 09.4
Suhail	223 00.6	S43 25.6
Vega	80 46.1	N38 47.4
Zuben'ubi	137 17.5	S16 02.2

	SHA	Mer. Pass.
		h m
Venus	216 23.7	9 16
Mars	106 17.4	16 37
Jupiter	328 21.2	1 49
Saturn	315 09.6	2 41

UT	SUN GHA	SUN Dec	MOON GHA	v	MOON Dec	d	HP
d h	° ′	° ′	° ′	′	° ′	′	′
25 00	182 00.5	S 0 35.5	6 00.7	10.5	S 4 59.7	11.8	58.6
01	197 00.7	36.5	20 30.2	10.5	4 47.9	11.8	58.6
02	212 00.9	37.4	34 59.7	10.5	4 36.1	11.9	58.7
03	227 01.1	.. 38.4	49 29.2	10.5	4 24.2	11.9	58.7
04	242 01.4	39.4	63 58.7	10.4	4 12.3	12.0	58.7
05	257 01.6	40.4	78 28.1	10.5	4 00.3	12.0	58.8
06	272 01.8	S 0 41.3	92 57.6	10.4	S 3 48.3	12.0	58.8
07	287 02.0	42.3	107 27.0	10.4	3 36.3	12.0	58.8
08	302 02.2	43.3	121 56.4	10.4	3 24.3	12.1	58.8
09	317 02.4	.. 44.3	136 25.8	10.4	3 12.2	12.1	58.9
10	332 02.7	45.2	150 55.2	10.4	3 00.1	12.2	58.9
11	347 02.9	46.2	165 24.6	10.4	2 47.9	12.1	58.9
12	2 03.1	S 0 47.2	179 54.0	10.3	S 2 35.8	12.2	58.9
13	17 03.3	48.1	194 23.3	10.3	2 23.6	12.2	58.9
14	32 03.5	49.1	208 52.6	10.3	2 11.4	12.2	59.0
15	47 03.7	.. 50.1	223 22.0	10.2	1 59.2	12.3	59.0
16	62 04.0	51.1	237 51.2	10.3	1 46.9	12.3	59.0
17	77 04.2	52.0	252 20.5	10.3	1 34.6	12.3	59.0
18	92 04.4	S 0 53.0	266 49.8	10.2	S 1 22.3	12.3	59.1
19	107 04.6	54.0	281 19.0	10.2	1 10.0	12.3	59.1
20	122 04.8	55.0	295 48.2	10.2	0 57.7	12.3	59.1
21	137 05.0	.. 55.9	310 17.4	10.2	0 45.4	12.4	59.1
22	152 05.3	56.9	324 46.6	10.2	0 33.0	12.3	59.2
23	167 05.5	57.9	339 15.8	10.1	0 20.7	12.4	59.2
26 00	182 05.7	S 0 58.9	353 44.9	10.1	S 0 08.3	12.4	59.2
01	197 05.9	0 59.8	8 14.0	10.1	N 0 04.1	12.4	59.2
02	212 06.1	1 00.8	22 43.1	10.0	0 16.5	12.4	59.2
03	227 06.3	.. 01.8	37 12.2	10.0	0 28.9	12.4	59.3
04	242 06.6	02.7	51 41.2	10.0	0 41.3	12.4	59.3
05	257 06.8	03.7	66 10.2	10.0	0 53.7	12.4	59.3
06	272 07.0	S 1 04.7	80 39.2	10.0	N 1 06.1	12.4	59.3
07	287 07.2	05.7	95 08.2	10.0	1 18.5	12.4	59.3
08	302 07.4	06.6	109 37.2	9.9	1 30.9	12.4	59.4
09	317 07.6	.. 07.6	124 06.1	9.9	1 43.3	12.4	59.4
10	332 07.9	08.6	138 35.0	9.8	1 55.7	12.5	59.4
11	347 08.1	09.6	153 03.8	9.9	2 08.2	12.4	59.4
12	2 08.3	S 1 10.5	167 32.7	9.8	N 2 20.6	12.3	59.4
13	17 08.5	11.5	182 01.5	9.8	2 32.9	12.4	59.4
14	32 08.7	12.5	196 30.3	9.7	2 45.3	12.4	59.5
15	47 08.9	.. 13.5	210 59.0	9.7	2 57.7	12.4	59.5
16	62 09.1	14.4	225 27.7	9.7	3 10.1	12.3	59.5
17	77 09.4	15.4	239 56.4	9.7	3 22.4	12.4	59.5
18	92 09.6	S 1 16.4	254 25.1	9.6	N 3 34.8	12.3	59.5
19	107 09.8	17.3	268 53.7	9.6	3 47.1	12.3	59.5
20	122 10.0	18.3	283 22.3	9.6	3 59.4	12.3	59.5
21	137 10.2	.. 19.3	297 50.9	9.5	4 11.7	12.3	59.6
22	152 10.4	20.3	312 19.4	9.5	4 24.0	12.2	59.6
23	167 10.6	21.2	326 47.9	9.5	4 36.2	12.3	59.6
27 00	182 10.9	S 1 22.2	341 16.4	9.4	N 4 48.5	12.2	59.6
01	197 11.1	23.2	355 44.8	9.4	5 00.7	12.2	59.6
02	212 11.3	24.2	10 13.2	9.4	5 12.9	12.1	59.6
03	227 11.5	.. 25.1	24 41.6	9.3	5 25.0	12.2	59.6
04	242 11.7	26.1	39 09.9	9.3	5 37.2	12.1	59.7
05	257 11.9	27.1	53 38.2	9.3	5 49.3	12.0	59.7
06	272 12.1	S 1 28.1	68 06.5	9.2	N 6 01.3	12.1	59.7
07	287 12.4	29.0	82 34.7	9.2	6 13.4	12.0	59.7
08	302 12.6	30.0	97 02.9	9.2	6 25.4	12.0	59.7
09	317 12.8	.. 31.0	111 31.1	9.1	6 37.4	11.9	59.7
10	332 13.0	31.9	125 59.2	9.1	6 49.3	11.9	59.7
11	347 13.2	32.9	140 27.3	9.0	7 01.2	11.9	59.7
12	2 13.4	S 1 33.9	154 55.3	9.0	N 7 13.1	11.8	59.7
13	17 13.6	34.9	169 23.3	9.0	7 24.9	11.8	59.7
14	32 13.9	35.8	183 51.3	8.9	7 36.7	11.7	59.8
15	47 14.1	.. 36.8	198 19.2	8.9	7 48.4	11.7	59.8
16	62 14.3	37.8	212 47.1	8.8	8 00.1	11.7	59.8
17	77 14.5	38.8	227 14.9	8.8	8 11.8	11.6	59.8
18	92 14.7	S 1 39.7	241 42.7	8.8	N 8 23.4	11.6	59.8
19	107 14.9	40.7	256 10.5	8.7	8 35.0	11.5	59.8
20	122 15.1	41.7	270 38.2	8.7	8 46.5	11.4	59.8
21	137 15.3	.. 42.7	285 05.9	8.6	8 57.9	11.4	59.8
22	152 15.6	43.6	299 33.5	8.6	9 09.3	11.4	59.8
23	167 15.8	44.6	314 01.1	8.5	N 9 20.7	11.3	59.8
	SD 16.0	d 1.0	SD 16.1		16.2		16.3

Left margin day labels: SATURDAY (25), SUNDAY (26), MONDAY (27)

Lat.	Twilight Naut.	Twilight Civil	Sunrise	Moonrise 25	26	27	28
°	h m	h m	h m	h m	h m	h m	h m
N 72	03 19	04 46	05 54	18 31	18 20	18 07	17 52
N 70	03 36	04 53	05 54	18 29	18 25	18 20	18 14
68	03 49	04 58	05 53	18 28	18 28	18 29	18 32
66	03 59	05 02	05 53	18 27	18 32	18 38	18 46
64	04 08	05 05	05 53	18 25	18 35	18 45	18 57
62	04 15	05 08	05 53	18 25	18 37	18 51	19 07
60	04 21	05 11	05 52	18 24	18 39	18 56	19 16
N 58	04 26	05 13	05 52	18 23	18 41	19 01	19 23
56	04 31	05 15	05 52	18 22	18 43	19 05	19 30
54	04 35	05 17	05 52	18 22	18 44	19 09	19 36
52	04 38	05 18	05 52	18 21	18 46	19 12	19 42
50	04 41	05 19	05 51	18 21	18 47	19 15	19 46
45	04 48	05 22	05 51	18 19	18 50	19 22	19 57
N 40	04 52	05 24	05 51	18 19	18 52	19 28	20 06
35	04 56	05 25	05 50	18 18	18 54	19 33	20 14
30	04 59	05 26	05 50	18 17	18 56	19 37	20 21
20	05 02	05 28	05 50	18 16	19 00	19 45	20 32
N 10	05 04	05 28	05 49	18 15	19 02	19 52	20 43
0	05 04	05 28	05 48	18 14	19 05	19 58	20 53
S 10	05 02	05 26	05 47	18 13	19 08	20 05	21 02
20	04 59	05 24	05 46	18 12	19 11	20 11	21 13
30	04 53	05 21	05 45	18 11	19 15	20 19	21 25
35	04 50	05 19	05 44	18 10	19 17	20 24	21 32
40	04 45	05 17	05 44	18 09	19 19	20 29	21 40
45	04 39	05 13	05 43	18 08	19 22	20 36	21 50
S 50	04 31	05 09	05 41	18 07	19 25	20 43	22 02
52	04 27	05 07	05 41	18 07	19 26	20 47	22 07
54	04 22	05 05	05 40	18 06	19 28	20 50	22 13
56	04 17	05 02	05 39	18 06	19 30	20 55	22 19
58	04 12	04 59	05 38	18 05	19 32	20 59	22 27
S 60	04 05	04 56	05 37	18 05	19 34	21 05	22 35

Lat.	Sunset	Twilight Civil	Twilight Naut.	Moonset 25	26	27	28
°	h m	h m	h m	h m	h m	h m	h m
N 72	17 47	18 54	20 20	04 54	06 53	08 55	11 03
N 70	17 47	18 48	20 04	05 00	06 51	08 45	10 43
68	17 48	18 43	19 51	05 05	06 50	08 37	10 27
66	17 48	18 39	19 41	05 09	06 49	08 31	10 14
64	17 49	18 36	19 33	05 13	06 48	08 25	10 04
62	17 49	18 33	19 26	05 16	06 47	08 21	09 55
60	17 49	18 31	19 20	05 18	06 47	08 16	09 47
N 58	17 50	18 29	19 15	05 20	06 46	08 13	09 41
56	17 50	18 27	19 10	05 22	06 45	08 10	09 35
54	17 50	18 25	19 07	05 24	06 45	08 07	09 29
52	17 50	18 24	19 03	05 26	06 44	08 04	09 25
50	17 51	18 23	19 00	05 27	06 44	08 02	09 20
45	17 51	18 20	18 54	05 31	06 43	07 57	09 11
N 40	17 51	18 18	18 50	05 33	06 42	07 52	09 03
35	17 52	18 17	18 46	05 36	06 42	07 49	08 57
30	17 52	18 16	18 44	05 38	06 41	07 45	08 51
20	17 53	18 15	18 41	05 41	06 40	07 40	08 41
N 10	17 54	18 15	18 39	05 44	06 39	07 35	08 32
0	17 55	18 15	18 39	05 47	06 38	07 30	08 24
S 10	17 56	18 17	18 41	05 50	06 37	07 25	08 16
20	17 57	18 19	18 44	05 53	06 36	07 21	08 07
30	17 58	18 22	18 50	05 56	06 35	07 15	07 57
35	17 59	18 24	18 54	05 58	06 34	07 12	07 51
40	18 00	18 27	18 59	06 00	06 34	07 08	07 45
45	18 01	18 31	19 05	06 03	06 33	07 04	07 37
S 50	18 03	18 35	19 13	06 06	06 32	06 59	07 28
52	18 03	18 37	19 17	06 07	06 31	06 56	07 24
54	18 04	18 40	19 22	06 08	06 31	06 54	07 19
56	18 05	18 42	19 27	06 10	06 30	06 51	07 14
58	18 06	18 45	19 33	06 12	06 30	06 48	07 09
S 60	18 07	18 49	19 40	06 14	06 29	06 45	07 03

Day	SUN Eqn. of Time 00h	SUN Eqn. of Time 12h	SUN Mer. Pass.	MOON Mer. Pass. Upper	MOON Mer. Pass. Lower	Age	Phase
d	m s	m s	h m	h m	h m	d	%
25	08 01	08 12	11 52	24 26	12 00	16	100
26	08 22	08 33	11 51	00 26	12 52	17	98
27	08 43	08 53	11 51	01 18	13 44	18	94

1999 SEPTEMBER 28, 29, 30 (TUES., WED., THURS.)

UT	ARIES	VENUS −4.6		MARS +0.5		JUPITER −2.9		SATURN +0.0		STARS		
	GHA	GHA	Dec	GHA	Dec	GHA	Dec	GHA	Dec	Name	SHA	Dec
d h	° ′	° ′	° ′	° ′	° ′	° ′	° ′	° ′	° ′		° ′	° ′
28 00	6 19.7	221 37.6 N 9 44.1		111 07.3 S24 34.3		334 52.4 N11 07.6		321 34.8 N14 17.6		Acamar	315 26.1	S40 18.2
01	21 22.1	236 38.6	44.0	126 07.9	34.5	349 55.1	07.5	336 37.3	17.6	Achernar	335 34.2	S57 14.3
02	36 24.6	251 39.7	44.0	141 08.5	34.7	4 57.8	07.4	351 39.9	17.5	Acrux	173 22.0	S63 05.7
03	51 27.1	266 40.7 . .	43.9	156 09.1 . .	34.9	20 00.5 . .	07.3	6 42.5 . .	17.5	Adhara	255 21.0	S28 58.1
04	66 29.5	281 41.7	43.9	171 09.6	35.0	35 03.3	07.2	21 45.1	17.4	Aldebaran	291 01.5	N16 30.5
05	81 32.0	296 42.7	43.8	186 10.2	35.2	50 06.0	07.1	36 47.7	17.4			
06	96 34.4	311 43.8 N 9 43.7		201 10.8 S24 35.4		65 08.7 N11 07.0		51 50.3 N14 17.3		Alioth	166 30.6	N55 57.9
07	111 36.9	326 44.8	43.7	216 11.4	35.5	80 11.4	06.9	66 52.8	17.3	Alkaid	153 07.8	N49 19.2
08	126 39.4	341 45.8	43.6	231 12.0	35.7	95 14.1	06.8	81 55.4	17.3	Al Na'ir	27 56.7	S46 57.8
T 09	141 41.8	356 46.8 . .	43.6	246 12.6 . .	35.9	110 16.8 . .	06.7	96 58.0 . .	17.2	Alnilam	275 57.1	S 1 12.1
U 10	156 44.3	11 47.8	43.5	261 13.2	36.0	125 19.5	06.6	112 00.6	17.2	Alphard	218 06.8	S 8 39.3
E 11	171 46.8	26 48.8	43.4	276 13.7	36.2	140 22.2	06.5	127 03.2	17.1			
S 12	186 49.2	41 49.8 N 9 43.4		291 14.3 S24 36.4		155 24.9 N11 06.4		142 05.8 N14 17.1		Alphecca	126 20.3	N26 43.3
D 13	201 51.7	56 50.9	43.3	306 14.9	36.5	170 27.7	06.3	157 08.3	17.1	Alpheratz	357 54.2	N29 05.4
A 14	216 54.2	71 51.9	43.2	321 15.5	36.7	185 30.4	06.3	172 10.9	17.0	Altair	62 18.5	N 8 52.3
Y 15	231 56.6	86 52.9 . .	43.2	336 16.1 . .	36.9	200 33.1 . .	06.2	187 13.5 . .	17.0	Ankaa	353 25.8	S42 18.5
16	246 59.1	101 53.9	43.1	351 16.7	37.0	215 35.8	06.1	202 16.1	16.9	Antares	112 39.5	S26 25.8
17	262 01.6	116 54.9	43.0	6 17.2	37.2	230 38.5	06.0	217 18.7	16.9			
18	277 04.0	131 55.9 N 9 43.0		21 17.8 S24 37.4		245 41.2 N11 05.9		232 21.3 N14 16.9		Arcturus	146 05.8	N19 11.3
19	292 06.5	146 56.8	42.9	36 18.4	37.5	260 43.9	05.8	247 23.9	16.8	Atria	107 51.2	S69 01.7
20	307 08.9	161 57.8	42.8	51 19.0	37.7	275 46.7	05.7	262 26.4	16.8	Avior	234 22.7	S59 30.2
21	322 11.4	176 58.8 . .	42.8	66 19.6 . .	37.9	290 49.4 . .	05.6	277 29.0 . .	16.7	Bellatrix	278 43.4	N 6 21.0
22	337 13.9	191 59.8	42.7	81 20.1	38.0	305 52.1	05.5	292 31.6	16.7	Betelgeuse	271 12.8	N 7 24.4
23	352 16.3	207 00.8	42.6	96 20.7	38.2	320 54.8	05.4	307 34.2	16.6			
29 00	7 18.8	222 01.8 N 9 42.5		111 21.3 S24 38.3		335 57.5 N11 05.3		322 36.8 N14 16.6		Canopus	264 00.9	S52 41.5
01	22 21.3	237 02.8	42.5	126 21.9	38.5	351 00.2	05.2	337 39.4	16.6	Capella	280 50.1	N45 59.6
02	37 23.7	252 03.7	42.4	141 22.5	38.7	6 02.9	05.1	352 41.9	16.5	Deneb	49 38.5	N45 17.1
03	52 26.2	267 04.7 . .	42.3	156 23.0 . .	38.8	21 05.7 . .	05.0	7 44.5 . .	16.5	Denebola	182 44.9	N14 34.6
04	67 28.7	282 05.7	42.2	171 23.6	39.0	36 08.4	04.9	22 47.1	16.4	Diphda	349 06.3	S17 59.3
05	82 31.1	297 06.7	42.1	186 24.2	39.2	51 11.1	04.9	37 49.7	16.4			
06	97 33.6	312 07.6 N 9 42.0		201 24.8 S24 39.3		66 13.8 N11 04.8		52 52.3 N14 16.4		Dubhe	194 05.4	N61 45.2
W 07	112 36.1	327 08.6	42.0	216 25.4	39.5	81 16.5	04.7	67 54.9	16.3	Elnath	278 26.0	N28 36.3
E 08	127 38.5	342 09.5	41.9	231 25.9	39.6	96 19.2	04.6	82 57.5	16.3	Eltanin	90 51.2	N51 29.8
D 09	142 41.0	357 10.5 . .	41.8	246 26.5 . .	39.8	111 22.0 . .	04.5	98 00.1 . .	16.2	Enif	33 57.4	N 9 52.6
N 10	157 43.4	12 11.5	41.7	261 27.1	40.0	126 24.7	04.4	113 02.6	16.2	Fomalhaut	15 35.4	S29 37.4
E 11	172 45.9	27 12.4	41.6	276 27.7	40.1	141 27.4	04.3	128 05.2	16.1			
S 12	187 48.4	42 13.4 N 9 41.5		291 28.2 S24 40.3		156 30.1 N11 04.2		143 07.8 N14 16.1		Gacrux	172 13.4	S57 06.5
D 13	202 50.8	57 14.3	41.4	306 28.8	40.4	171 32.8	04.1	158 10.4	16.1	Gienah	176 03.6	S17 32.2
A 14	217 53.3	72 15.3	41.3	321 29.4	40.6	186 35.6	04.0	173 13.0	16.0	Hadar	149 03.7	S60 22.2
Y 15	232 55.8	87 16.2 . .	41.3	336 30.0 . .	40.7	201 38.3 . .	03.9	188 15.6 . .	16.0	Hamal	328 12.5	N23 27.6
16	247 58.2	102 17.2	41.2	351 30.5	40.9	216 41.0	03.8	203 18.2	15.9	Kaus Aust.	83 58.0	S34 23.1
17	263 00.7	117 18.1	41.1	6 31.1	41.1	231 43.7	03.7	218 20.8	15.9			
18	278 03.2	132 19.1 N 9 41.0		21 31.7 S24 41.2		246 46.4 N11 03.6		233 23.3 N14 15.8		Kochab	137 20.6	N74 09.7
19	293 05.6	147 20.0	40.9	36 32.3	41.4	261 49.2	03.5	248 25.9	15.8	Markab	13 48.7	N15 12.3
20	308 08.1	162 20.9	40.8	51 32.8	41.5	276 51.9	03.4	263 28.5	15.8	Menkar	314 26.0	N 4 05.3
21	323 10.5	177 21.9 . .	40.7	66 33.4 . .	41.7	291 54.6 . .	03.3	278 31.1 . .	15.7	Menkent	148 20.5	S36 22.0
22	338 13.0	192 22.8	40.6	81 34.0	41.8	306 57.3	03.2	293 33.7	15.7	Miaplacidus	221 42.5	S69 42.7
23	353 15.5	207 23.7	40.5	96 34.6	42.0	322 00.0	03.1	308 36.3	15.6			
30 00	8 17.9	222 24.7 N 9 40.4		111 35.1 S24 42.1		337 02.8 N11 03.0		323 38.9 N14 15.6		Mirfak	308 55.3	N49 51.4
01	23 20.4	237 25.6	40.3	126 35.7	42.3	352 05.5	02.9	338 41.5	15.5	Nunki	76 11.5	S26 17.8
02	38 22.9	252 26.5	40.2	141 36.3	42.4	7 08.2	02.8	353 44.1	15.5	Peacock	53 35.7	S56 44.3
03	53 25.3	267 27.4 . .	40.1	156 36.8 . .	42.6	22 10.9 . .	02.8	8 46.6 . .	15.5	Pollux	243 40.9	N28 01.5
04	68 27.8	282 28.4	40.0	171 37.4	42.8	37 13.6	02.7	23 49.2	15.4	Procyon	245 11.0	N 5 13.6
05	83 30.3	297 29.3	39.8	186 38.0	42.9	52 16.4	02.6	38 51.8	15.4			
06	98 32.7	312 30.2 N 9 39.7		201 38.6 S24 43.1		67 19.1 N11 02.5		53 54.4 N14 15.3		Rasalhague	96 16.4	N12 33.9
07	113 35.2	327 31.1	39.6	216 39.1	43.2	82 21.8	02.4	68 57.0	15.3	Regulus	207 55.1	N11 58.2
T 08	128 37.7	342 32.0	39.5	231 39.7	43.4	97 24.5	02.3	83 59.6	15.2	Rigel	281 22.2	S 8 12.0
H 09	143 40.1	357 32.9 . .	39.4	246 40.3 . .	43.5	112 27.3 . .	02.2	99 02.2 . .	15.2	Rigil Kent.	140 07.0	S60 50.0
U 10	158 42.6	12 33.8	39.3	261 40.8	43.7	127 30.0	02.1	114 04.8	15.2	Sabik	102 24.9	S15 43.3
R 11	173 45.0	27 34.7	39.2	276 41.4	43.8	142 32.7	02.0	129 07.4	15.1			
S 12	188 47.5	42 35.6 N 9 39.1		291 42.0 S24 44.0		157 35.4 N11 01.9		144 10.0 N14 15.1		Schedar	349 52.1	N56 32.1
D 13	203 50.0	57 36.5	38.9	306 42.5	44.1	172 38.1	01.8	159 12.6	15.0	Shaula	96 36.5	S37 06.2
A 14	218 52.4	72 37.4	38.8	321 43.1	44.3	187 40.9	01.7	174 15.1	15.0	Sirius	258 43.2	S16 42.8
Y 15	233 54.9	87 38.3 . .	38.7	336 43.7 . .	44.4	202 43.6 . .	01.6	189 17.7 . .	14.9	Spica	158 42.8	S11 09.4
16	248 57.4	102 39.2	38.6	351 44.3	44.6	217 46.3	01.5	204 20.3	14.9	Suhail	223 00.6	S43 25.6
17	263 59.8	117 40.1	38.5	6 44.8	44.7	232 49.0	01.4	219 22.9	14.9			
18	279 02.3	132 41.0 N 9 38.4		21 45.4 S24 44.8		247 51.8 N11 01.3		234 25.5 N14 14.8		Vega	80 46.2	N38 47.4
19	294 04.8	147 41.9	38.2	36 46.0	45.0	262 54.5	01.2	249 28.1	14.8	Zuben'ubi	137 17.5	S16 02.2
20	309 07.2	162 42.8	38.1	51 46.5	45.1	277 57.2	01.1	264 30.7	14.7		SHA	Mer. Pass.
21	324 09.7	177 43.7 . .	38.0	66 47.1 . .	45.3	292 59.9 . .	01.0	279 33.3 . .	14.7		° ′	h m
22	339 12.2	192 44.5	37.9	81 47.7	45.4	308 02.7	00.9	294 35.9	14.6	Venus	214 43.0	9 11
23	354 14.6	207 45.4	37.7	96 48.2	45.6	323 05.4	00.8	309 38.5	14.6	Mars	104 02.5	16 34
	h m									Jupiter	328 38.7	1 36
Mer. Pass. 23 26.9		v 1.0 d 0.1		v 0.6 d 0.2		v 2.7 d 0.1		v 2.6 d 0.0		Saturn	315 18.0	2 29

UT	SUN GHA	SUN Dec	MOON GHA	v	Dec	d	HP
d h	° ′	° ′	° ′	′	° ′	′	′
28 00	182 16.0	S 1 45.6	328 28.6	8.6	N 9 32.0	11.2	59.8
01	197 16.2	46.5	342 56.2	8.4	9 43.2	11.2	59.8
02	212 16.4	47.5	357 23.6	8.4	9 54.4	11.1	59.8
03	227 16.6	.. 48.5	11 51.0	8.4	10 05.5	11.1	59.8
04	242 16.8	49.5	26 18.4	8.4	10 16.6	11.0	59.8
05	257 17.0	50.4	40 45.8	8.3	10 27.6	10.9	59.8
06	272 17.3	S 1 51.4	55 13.1	8.2	N10 38.5	10.9	59.8
07	287 17.5	52.4	69 40.3	8.2	10 49.4	10.8	59.9
08	302 17.7	53.4	84 07.5	8.2	11 00.2	10.8	59.9
09	317 17.9	.. 54.3	98 34.7	8.1	11 11.0	10.6	59.9
10	332 18.1	55.3	113 01.8	8.1	11 21.6	10.6	59.9
11	347 18.3	56.3	127 28.9	8.0	11 32.2	10.6	59.9
12	2 18.5	S 1 57.2	141 55.9	8.0	N11 42.8	10.4	59.9
13	17 18.7	58.2	156 22.9	8.0	11 53.2	10.4	59.9
14	32 18.9	1 59.2	170 49.9	7.9	12 03.6	10.3	59.9
15	47 19.2	2 00.2	185 16.8	7.8	12 13.9	10.2	59.9
16	62 19.4	01.1	199 43.6	7.8	12 24.1	10.2	59.9
17	77 19.6	02.1	214 10.4	7.8	12 34.3	10.1	59.9
18	92 19.8	S 2 03.1	228 37.2	7.7	N12 44.4	10.0	59.9
19	107 20.0	04.0	243 03.9	7.7	12 54.4	9.9	59.9
20	122 20.2	05.0	257 30.6	7.7	13 04.3	9.8	59.9
21	137 20.4	.. 06.0	271 57.3	7.6	13 14.1	9.7	59.9
22	152 20.6	07.0	286 23.9	7.5	13 23.8	9.7	59.9
23	167 20.8	07.9	300 50.4	7.5	13 33.5	9.6	59.9
29 00	182 21.0	S 2 08.9	315 16.9	7.5	N13 43.1	9.5	59.9
01	197 21.3	09.9	329 43.4	7.4	13 52.6	9.4	59.9
02	212 21.5	10.9	344 09.8	7.4	14 02.0	9.3	59.9
03	227 21.7	.. 11.8	358 36.2	7.3	14 11.3	9.2	59.9
04	242 21.9	12.8	13 02.5	7.3	14 20.5	9.1	59.9
05	257 22.1	13.8	27 28.8	7.3	14 29.6	9.0	59.8
06	272 22.3	S 2 14.7	41 55.1	7.2	N14 38.6	9.0	59.8
07	287 22.5	15.7	56 21.3	7.1	14 47.6	8.8	59.8
08	302 22.7	16.7	70 47.4	7.2	14 56.4	8.7	59.8
09	317 22.9	.. 17.7	85 13.6	7.0	15 05.1	8.7	59.8
10	332 23.1	18.6	99 39.6	7.1	15 13.8	8.5	59.8
11	347 23.3	19.6	114 05.7	7.0	15 22.3	8.5	59.8
12	2 23.5	S 2 20.6	128 31.7	6.9	N15 30.8	8.3	59.8
13	17 23.8	21.5	142 57.6	7.0	15 39.1	8.2	59.8
14	32 24.0	22.5	157 23.6	6.8	15 47.3	8.2	59.8
15	47 24.2	.. 23.5	171 49.4	6.9	15 55.5	8.0	59.8
16	62 24.4	24.5	186 15.3	6.8	16 03.5	7.9	59.8
17	77 24.6	25.4	200 41.1	6.8	16 11.4	7.8	59.8
18	92 24.8	S 2 26.4	215 06.9	6.7	N16 19.2	7.7	59.8
19	107 25.0	27.4	229 32.6	6.7	16 26.9	7.6	59.8
20	122 25.2	28.4	243 58.3	6.6	16 34.5	7.5	59.8
21	137 25.4	.. 29.3	258 23.9	6.7	16 42.0	7.4	59.8
22	152 25.6	30.3	272 49.6	6.5	16 49.4	7.3	59.7
23	167 25.8	31.3	287 15.1	6.6	16 56.7	7.1	59.7
30 00	182 26.0	S 2 32.2	301 40.7	6.5	N17 03.8	7.1	59.7
01	197 26.2	33.2	316 06.2	6.5	17 10.9	6.9	59.7
02	212 26.5	34.2	330 31.7	6.4	17 17.8	6.8	59.7
03	227 26.7	.. 35.2	344 57.1	6.5	17 24.6	6.7	59.7
04	242 26.9	36.1	359 22.6	6.3	17 31.3	6.6	59.7
05	257 27.1	37.1	13 47.9	6.4	17 37.9	6.4	59.7
06	272 27.3	S 2 38.1	28 13.3	6.3	N17 44.3	6.4	59.7
07	287 27.5	39.0	42 38.6	6.3	17 50.7	6.2	59.7
08	302 27.7	40.0	57 03.9	6.3	17 56.9	6.1	59.7
09	317 27.9	.. 41.0	71 29.2	6.2	18 03.0	6.0	59.6
10	332 28.1	41.9	85 54.4	6.2	18 09.0	5.8	59.6
11	347 28.3	42.9	100 19.6	6.2	18 14.8	5.8	59.6
12	2 28.5	S 2 43.9	114 44.8	6.2	N18 20.6	5.6	59.6
13	17 28.7	44.9	129 10.0	6.1	18 26.2	5.5	59.6
14	32 28.9	45.8	143 35.1	6.1	18 31.7	5.3	59.6
15	47 29.1	.. 46.8	158 00.2	6.1	18 37.0	5.3	59.6
16	62 29.3	47.8	172 25.3	6.1	18 42.3	5.1	59.6
17	77 29.5	48.7	186 50.4	6.0	18 47.4	5.0	59.6
18	92 29.7	S 2 49.7	201 15.4	6.1	N18 52.4	4.8	59.5
19	107 30.0	50.7	215 40.5	6.0	18 57.2	4.8	59.5
20	122 30.2	51.7	230 05.5	6.0	19 02.0	4.6	59.5
21	137 30.4	.. 52.6	244 30.5	6.0	19 06.6	4.5	59.5
22	152 30.6	53.6	258 55.5	5.9	19 11.1	4.3	59.5
23	167 30.8	54.6	273 20.4	6.0	N19 15.4	4.2	59.5
	SD 16.0	d 1.0	SD 16.3		16.3		16.2

Days down left margin: TUESDAY (28), WEDNESDAY (29), THURSDAY (30)

Lat.	Twilight Naut.	Twilight Civil	Sunrise	Moonrise 28	Moonrise 29	Moonrise 30	Moonrise 1
°	h m	h m	h m	h m	h m	h m	h m
N 72	03 36	05 00	06 07	17 52	17 28	▭	▭
N 70	03 50	05 05	06 05	18 14	18 09	18 01	▭
68	04 01	05 08	06 04	18 32	18 36	18 48	19 14
66	04 10	05 11	06 03	18 46	18 58	19 18	19 54
64	04 17	05 14	06 01	18 57	19 15	19 41	20 22
62	04 24	05 16	06 00	19 07	19 29	20 00	20 43
60	04 29	05 18	05 59	19 16	19 41	20 15	21 01
N 58	04 33	05 20	05 59	19 23	19 52	20 28	21 15
56	04 37	05 21	05 58	19 30	20 01	20 39	21 28
54	04 41	05 22	05 57	19 36	20 09	20 49	21 38
52	04 44	05 23	05 57	19 42	20 16	20 58	21 48
50	04 46	05 24	05 56	19 46	20 23	21 06	21 57
45	04 51	05 26	05 55	19 57	20 37	21 23	22 15
N 40	04 55	05 27	05 54	20 06	20 49	21 36	22 30
35	04 58	05 27	05 53	20 14	20 59	21 48	22 43
30	05 00	05 28	05 52	20 21	21 08	21 59	22 54
20	05 03	05 28	05 50	20 32	21 23	22 17	23 13
N 10	05 03	05 28	05 49	20 43	21 36	22 32	23 30
0	05 02	05 27	05 47	20 53	21 49	22 47	23 45
S 10	05 00	05 25	05 46	21 02	22 02	23 01	24 01
20	04 56	05 22	05 44	21 13	22 15	23 17	24 18
30	04 50	05 18	05 41	21 25	22 31	23 35	24 37
35	04 45	05 15	05 40	21 32	22 40	23 46	24 48
40	04 40	05 12	05 39	21 40	22 51	23 58	25 01
45	04 33	05 07	05 37	21 50	23 03	24 13	00 13
S 50	04 24	05 02	05 35	22 02	23 18	24 30	00 30
52	04 19	05 00	05 34	22 07	23 25	24 39	00 39
54	04 14	04 57	05 33	22 13	23 33	24 48	00 48
56	04 09	04 54	05 31	22 19	23 42	24 58	00 58
58	04 02	04 50	05 30	22 27	23 52	25 10	01 10
S 60	03 55	04 46	05 28	22 35	24 04	00 04	01 24

Lat.	Sunset	Twilight Civil	Twilight Naut.	Moonset 28	Moonset 29	Moonset 30	Moonset 1
°	h m	h m	h m	h m	h m	h m	h m
N 72	17 31	18 38	20 01	11 03	13 25	▭	▭
N 70	17 33	18 34	19 48	10 43	12 45	14 53	▭
68	17 35	18 30	19 37	10 27	12 18	14 07	15 43
66	17 37	18 27	19 28	10 14	11 58	13 37	15 03
64	17 38	18 25	19 21	10 04	11 42	13 15	14 35
62	17 39	18 23	19 15	09 55	11 28	12 57	14 14
60	17 40	18 21	19 10	09 47	11 17	12 42	13 57
N 58	17 41	18 20	19 06	09 41	11 07	12 29	13 43
56	17 42	18 19	19 02	09 35	10 58	12 18	13 30
54	17 43	18 18	18 59	09 29	10 51	12 09	13 20
52	17 43	18 17	18 56	09 25	10 44	12 00	13 10
50	17 44	18 16	18 54	09 20	10 38	11 53	13 01
45	17 45	18 15	18 49	09 11	10 25	11 36	12 43
N 40	17 47	18 13	18 45	09 03	10 14	11 23	12 29
35	17 48	18 13	18 42	08 57	10 05	11 12	12 16
30	17 49	18 12	18 40	08 51	09 57	11 02	12 05
20	17 50	18 12	18 38	08 41	09 43	10 45	11 46
N 10	17 52	18 13	18 37	08 32	09 31	10 30	11 30
0	17 54	18 14	18 38	08 24	09 19	10 16	11 15
S 10	17 55	18 16	18 41	08 16	09 08	10 03	10 59
20	17 57	18 20	18 45	08 07	08 56	09 48	10 43
30	18 00	18 24	18 52	07 57	08 42	09 31	10 24
35	18 01	18 27	18 56	07 51	08 34	09 21	10 13
40	18 03	18 30	19 02	07 45	08 25	09 10	10 01
45	18 05	18 34	19 09	07 37	08 14	08 57	09 46
S 50	18 07	18 40	19 18	07 28	08 02	08 41	09 28
52	18 08	18 42	19 23	07 24	07 56	08 34	09 19
54	18 10	18 45	19 28	07 19	07 49	08 25	09 10
56	18 11	18 48	19 34	07 14	07 42	08 16	08 59
58	18 12	18 52	19 40	07 09	07 34	08 06	08 47
S 60	18 14	18 56	19 48	07 03	07 25	07 53	08 33

Day	SUN Eqn. of Time 00ʰ	SUN Eqn. of Time 12ʰ	Mer. Pass.	MOON Mer. Pass. Upper	MOON Mer. Pass. Lower	Age	Phase
d	m s	m s	h m	h m	h m	d	%
28	09 03	09 14	11 51	02 11	14 38	19	88
29	09 24	09 34	11 50	03 06	15 34	20	79
30	09 44	09 54	11 50	04 03	16 32	21	69

UT	ARIES GHA	VENUS −4.5 GHA	Dec	MARS +0.6 GHA	Dec	JUPITER −2.9 GHA	Dec	SATURN +0.0 GHA	Dec	STARS Name	SHA	Dec
1 00	9 17.1	222 46.3	N 9 37.6	111 48.8	S24 45.7	338 08.1	N11 00.7	324 41.1	N14 14.6	Acamar	315 26.1	S40 18.3
01	24 19.5	237 47.2	37.5	126 49.3	45.9	353 10.8	00.6	339 43.7	14.5	Achernar	335 34.1	S57 14.3
02	39 22.0	252 48.1	37.3	141 49.9	46.0	8 13.6	00.5	354 46.2	14.5	Acrux	173 21.9	S63 05.7
03	54 24.5	267 48.9 ..	37.2	156 50.5 ..	46.2	23 16.3 ..	00.4	9 48.8 ..	14.4	Adhara	255 20.9	S28 58.1
04	69 26.9	282 49.8	37.1	171 51.0	46.3	38 19.0	00.3	24 51.4	14.4	Aldebaran	291 01.5	N16 30.5
05	84 29.4	297 50.7	36.9	186 51.6	46.4	53 21.8	00.2	39 54.0	14.3			
06	99 31.9	312 51.5	N 9 36.8	201 52.2	S24 46.6	68 24.5	N11 00.1	54 56.6	N14 14.3	Alioth	166 30.6	N55 57.9
07	114 34.3	327 52.4	36.7	216 52.7	46.7	83 27.2	11 00.0	69 59.2	14.2	Alkaid	153 07.8	N49 19.2
F 08	129 36.8	342 53.2	36.5	231 53.3	46.9	98 29.9	10 59.9	85 01.8	14.2	Al Na'ir	27 56.7	S46 57.8
R 09	144 39.3	357 54.1 ..	36.4	246 53.9 ..	47.0	113 32.7 ..	59.8	100 04.4 ..	14.2	Alnilam	275 57.1	S 1 12.1
I 10	159 41.7	12 55.0	36.3	261 54.4	47.2	128 35.4	59.7	115 07.0	14.1	Alphard	218 06.8	S 8 39.3
D 11	174 44.2	27 55.8	36.1	276 55.0	47.3	143 38.1	59.6	130 09.6	14.1			
A 12	189 46.7	42 56.7	N 9 36.0	291 55.5	S24 47.4	158 40.9	N10 59.5	145 12.2	N14 14.0	Alphecca	126 20.3	N26 43.3
Y 13	204 49.1	57 57.5	35.8	306 56.1	47.6	173 43.6	59.4	160 14.8	14.0	Alpheratz	357 54.2	N29 05.4
14	219 51.6	72 58.4	35.7	321 56.7	47.7	188 46.3	59.3	175 17.4	13.9	Altair	62 18.5	N 8 52.3
15	234 54.0	87 59.2 ..	35.6	336 57.2 ..	47.9	203 49.0 ..	59.2	190 20.0 ..	13.9	Ankaa	353 25.8	S42 18.5
16	249 56.5	103 00.1	35.4	351 57.8	48.0	218 51.8	59.1	205 22.6	13.8	Antares	112 39.5	S26 25.8
17	264 59.0	118 00.9	35.3	6 58.3	48.1	233 54.5	59.0	220 25.2	13.8			
18	280 01.4	133 01.7	N 9 35.1	21 58.9	S24 48.3	248 57.2	N10 59.0	235 27.8	N14 13.8	Arcturus	146 05.8	N19 11.3
19	295 03.9	148 02.6	35.0	36 59.5	48.4	264 00.0	58.9	250 30.4	13.7	Atria	107 51.2	S69 01.7
20	310 06.4	163 03.4	34.8	52 00.0	48.5	279 02.7	58.8	265 32.9	13.7	Avior	234 22.6	S59 30.2
21	325 08.8	178 04.3 ..	34.7	67 00.6 ..	48.7	294 05.4 ..	58.7	280 35.5 ..	13.6	Bellatrix	278 43.4	N 6 21.0
22	340 11.3	193 05.1	34.5	82 01.1	48.8	309 08.1	58.6	295 38.1	13.6	Betelgeuse	271 12.8	N 7 24.4
23	355 13.8	208 05.9	34.4	97 01.7	49.0	324 10.9	58.5	310 40.7	13.5			
2 00	10 16.2	223 06.7	N 9 34.2	112 02.3	S24 49.1	339 13.6	N10 58.4	325 43.3	N14 13.5	Canopus	264 00.8	S52 41.5
01	25 18.7	238 07.6	34.1	127 02.8	49.2	354 16.3	58.3	340 45.9	13.5	Capella	280 50.1	N45 59.6
02	40 21.1	253 08.4	33.9	142 03.4	49.4	9 19.1	58.2	355 48.5	13.4	Deneb	49 38.5	N45 17.1
03	55 23.6	268 09.2 ..	33.8	157 03.9 ..	49.5	24 21.8 ..	58.1	10 51.1 ..	13.4	Denebola	182 44.8	N14 34.6
04	70 26.1	283 10.0	33.6	172 04.5	49.6	39 24.5	58.0	25 53.7	13.3	Diphda	349 06.2	S17 59.3
05	85 28.5	298 10.9	33.4	187 05.0	49.8	54 27.3	57.9	40 56.3	13.3			
06	100 31.0	313 11.7	N 9 33.3	202 05.6	S24 49.9	69 30.0	N10 57.8	55 58.9	N14 13.2	Dubhe	194 05.3	N61 45.1
07	115 33.5	328 12.5	33.1	217 06.2	50.0	84 32.7	57.7	71 01.5	13.2	Elnath	278 26.0	N28 36.3
S 08	130 35.9	343 13.3	33.0	232 06.7	50.2	99 35.5	57.6	86 04.1	13.1	Eltanin	90 51.2	N51 29.8
A 09	145 38.4	358 14.1 ..	32.8	247 07.3 ..	50.3	114 38.2 ..	57.5	101 06.7 ..	13.1	Enif	33 57.4	N 9 52.6
T 10	160 40.9	13 14.9	32.6	262 07.8	50.4	129 40.9	57.4	116 09.3	13.0	Fomalhaut	15 35.4	S29 37.4
U 11	175 43.3	28 15.7	32.5	277 08.4	50.6	144 43.7	57.3	131 11.9	13.0			
R 12	190 45.8	43 16.5	N 9 32.3	292 08.9	S24 50.7	159 46.4	N10 57.2	146 14.5	N14 13.0	Gacrux	172 13.4	S57 06.5
D 13	205 48.3	58 17.3	32.1	307 09.5	50.8	174 49.1	57.1	161 17.1	12.9	Gienah	176 03.6	S17 32.2
A 14	220 50.7	73 18.1	32.0	322 10.0	51.0	189 51.9	57.0	176 19.7	12.9	Hadar	149 03.7	S60 22.2
Y 15	235 53.2	88 18.9 ..	31.8	337 10.6 ..	51.1	204 54.6 ..	56.9	191 22.3 ..	12.8	Hamal	328 12.5	N23 27.6
16	250 55.6	103 19.7	31.6	352 11.2	51.2	219 57.3	56.8	206 24.9	12.8	Kaus Aust.	83 58.0	S34 23.1
17	265 58.1	118 20.5	31.5	7 11.7	51.4	235 00.1	56.7	221 27.5	12.7			
18	281 00.6	133 21.3	N 9 31.3	22 12.3	S24 51.5	250 02.8	N10 56.6	236 30.1	N14 12.7	Kochab	137 20.6	N74 09.7
19	296 03.0	148 22.1	31.1	37 12.8	51.6	265 05.5	56.5	251 32.7	12.6	Markab	13 48.7	N15 12.3
20	311 05.5	163 22.9	30.9	52 13.4	51.7	280 08.3	56.4	266 35.3	12.6	Menkar	314 26.0	N 4 05.3
21	326 08.0	178 23.7 ..	30.8	67 13.9 ..	51.9	295 11.0 ..	56.3	281 37.9 ..	12.6	Menkent	148 20.5	S36 22.0
22	341 10.4	193 24.5	30.6	82 14.5	52.0	310 13.8	56.2	296 40.5	12.5	Miaplacidus	221 42.5	S69 42.7
23	356 12.9	208 25.3	30.4	97 15.0	52.1	325 16.5	56.1	311 43.1	12.5			
3 00	11 15.4	223 26.0	N 9 30.2	112 15.6	S24 52.2	340 19.2	N10 56.0	326 45.7	N14 12.4	Mirfak	308 55.3	N49 51.4
01	26 17.8	238 26.8	30.0	127 16.1	52.4	355 22.0	55.9	341 48.3	12.4	Nunki	76 11.5	S26 17.8
02	41 20.3	253 27.6	29.9	142 16.7	52.5	10 24.7	55.8	356 50.9	12.3	Peacock	53 35.7	S56 44.3
03	56 22.8	268 28.4 ..	29.7	157 17.2 ..	52.6	25 27.4 ..	55.7	11 53.5 ..	12.3	Pollux	243 40.9	N28 01.5
04	71 25.2	283 29.1	29.5	172 17.8	52.8	40 30.2	55.6	26 56.1	12.2	Procyon	245 11.0	N 5 13.6
05	86 27.7	298 29.9	29.3	187 18.3	52.9	55 32.9	55.4	41 58.7	12.2			
06	101 30.1	313 30.7	N 9 29.1	202 18.9	S24 53.0	70 35.6	N10 55.3	57 01.3	N14 12.1	Rasalhague	96 16.4	N12 33.9
07	116 32.6	328 31.5	28.9	217 19.4	53.1	85 38.4	55.2	72 03.9	12.1	Regulus	207 55.1	N11 58.2
S 08	131 35.1	343 32.2	28.8	232 20.0	53.3	100 41.1	55.1	87 06.5	12.1	Rigel	281 22.2	S 8 12.0
U 09	146 37.5	358 33.0 ..	28.6	247 20.5 ..	53.4	115 43.9 ..	55.0	102 09.1 ..	12.0	Rigil Kent.	140 07.0	S60 50.0
N 10	161 40.0	13 33.8	28.4	262 21.1	53.5	130 46.6	54.9	117 11.7	12.0	Sabik	102 24.9	S15 43.3
D 11	176 42.5	28 34.5	28.2	277 21.6	53.6	145 49.3	54.8	132 14.3	11.9			
A 12	191 44.9	43 35.3	N 9 28.0	292 22.2	S24 53.7	160 52.1	N10 54.7	147 16.9	N14 11.9	Schedar	349 52.1	N56 32.1
Y 13	206 47.4	58 36.0	27.8	307 22.7	53.9	175 54.8	54.6	162 19.5	11.8	Shaula	96 36.5	S37 06.2
14	221 49.9	73 36.8	27.6	322 23.3	54.0	190 57.5	54.5	177 22.1	11.8	Sirius	258 43.1	S16 42.8
15	236 52.3	88 37.5 ..	27.4	337 23.8 ..	54.1	206 00.3 ..	54.4	192 24.7 ..	11.7	Spica	158 42.8	S11 09.4
16	251 54.8	103 38.3	27.2	352 24.4	54.2	221 03.0	54.3	207 27.3	11.7	Suhail	223 00.5	S43 25.6
17	266 57.3	118 39.0	27.0	7 24.9	54.4	236 05.8	54.2	222 29.9	11.6			
18	281 59.7	133 39.8	N 9 26.8	22 25.4	S24 54.5	251 08.5	N10 54.1	237 32.5	N14 11.6	Vega	80 46.2	N38 47.4
19	297 02.2	148 40.5	26.6	37 26.0	54.6	266 11.2	54.0	252 35.1	11.6	Zuben'ubi	137 17.5	S16 02.2
20	312 04.6	163 41.3	26.4	52 26.5	54.7	281 14.0	53.9	267 37.7	11.5			
21	327 07.1	178 42.0 ..	26.2	67 27.1 ..	54.8	296 16.7 ..	53.8	282 40.3 ..	11.5		SHA	Mer. Pass.
22	342 09.6	193 42.8	26.0	82 27.6	54.9	311 19.5	53.7	297 42.9	11.4	Venus	212 50.5	9 07
23	357 12.0	208 43.5	25.8	97 28.2	55.1	326 22.2	53.6	312 45.5	11.4	Mars	101 46.0	16 31
Mer. Pass. 23 15.1		v 0.8	d 0.2	v 0.6	d 0.1	v 2.7	d 0.1	v 2.6	d 0.0	Jupiter	328 57.4	1 23
										Saturn	315 27.1	2 17

UT	SUN GHA	SUN Dec	MOON GHA	v	MOON Dec	d	HP
d h	° ′	° ′	° ′	′	° ′	′	′
1 00	182 31.0	S 2 55.5	287 45.4	5.9	N19 19.6	4.1	59.5
01	197 31.2	56.5	302 10.3	5.9	19 23.7	4.0	59.5
02	212 31.4	57.5	316 35.2	5.9	19 27.7	3.8	59.4
03	227 31.6	.. 58.4	331 00.1	5.9	19 31.5	3.7	59.4
04	242 31.8	2 59.4	345 25.0	5.9	19 35.2	3.6	59.4
05	257 32.0	3 00.4	359 49.9	5.9	19 38.8	3.4	59.4
06	272 32.2	S 3 01.4	14 14.8	5.8	N19 42.2	3.3	59.4
07	287 32.4	02.3	28 39.6	5.9	19 45.5	3.2	59.4
08	302 32.6	03.3	43 04.5	5.9	19 48.7	3.0	59.4
09	317 32.8	.. 04.3	57 29.4	5.8	19 51.7	2.9	59.3
10	332 33.0	05.2	71 54.2	5.9	19 54.6	2.8	59.3
11	347 33.2	06.2	86 19.1	5.8	19 57.4	2.6	59.3
12	2 33.4	S 3 07.2	100 43.9	5.9	N20 00.0	2.5	59.3
13	17 33.6	08.1	115 08.8	5.8	20 02.5	2.4	59.3
14	32 33.8	09.1	129 33.6	5.9	20 04.9	2.2	59.3
15	47 34.0	.. 10.1	143 58.5	5.8	20 07.1	2.1	59.3
16	62 34.2	11.1	158 23.3	5.9	20 09.2	2.0	59.2
17	77 34.4	12.0	172 48.2	5.8	20 11.2	1.8	59.2
18	92 34.6	S 3 13.0	187 13.0	5.9	N20 13.0	1.7	59.2
19	107 34.8	14.0	201 37.9	5.9	20 14.7	1.6	59.2
20	122 35.0	14.9	216 02.8	5.9	20 16.3	1.4	59.2
21	137 35.2	.. 15.9	230 27.7	5.9	20 17.7	1.3	59.2
22	152 35.4	16.9	244 52.6	5.9	20 19.0	1.2	59.1
23	167 35.6	17.8	259 17.5	5.9	20 20.2	1.0	59.1
2 00	182 35.8	S 3 18.8	273 42.4	5.9	N20 21.2	0.9	59.1
01	197 36.0	19.8	288 07.3	6.0	20 22.1	0.8	59.1
02	212 36.2	20.7	302 32.3	5.9	20 22.9	0.6	59.1
03	227 36.4	.. 21.7	316 57.2	6.0	20 23.5	0.5	59.1
04	242 36.6	22.7	331 22.2	6.0	20 24.0	0.4	59.0
05	257 36.8	23.7	345 47.2	6.0	20 24.4	0.2	59.0
06	272 37.0	S 3 24.6	0 12.2	6.0	N20 24.6	0.1	59.0
07	287 37.2	25.6	14 37.2	6.1	20 24.7	0.1	59.0
08	302 37.4	26.6	29 02.3	6.1	20 24.6	0.1	59.0
09	317 37.6	.. 27.5	43 27.4	6.1	20 24.5	0.3	59.0
10	332 37.8	28.5	57 52.5	6.1	20 24.2	0.5	58.9
11	347 38.0	29.5	72 17.6	6.1	20 23.7	0.6	58.9
12	2 38.2	S 3 30.4	86 42.7	6.2	N20 23.1	0.7	58.9
13	17 38.4	31.4	101 07.9	6.2	20 22.4	0.8	58.9
14	32 38.6	32.4	115 33.1	6.2	20 21.6	1.0	58.9
15	47 38.8	.. 33.3	129 58.3	6.3	20 20.6	1.1	58.9
16	62 39.0	34.3	144 23.6	6.3	20 19.5	1.2	58.8
17	77 39.2	35.3	158 48.9	6.3	20 18.3	1.3	58.8
18	92 39.4	S 3 36.2	173 14.2	6.4	N20 17.0	1.5	58.8
19	107 39.6	37.2	187 39.6	6.4	20 15.5	1.6	58.8
20	122 39.8	38.2	202 05.0	6.4	20 13.9	1.8	58.8
21	137 40.0	.. 39.1	216 30.4	6.5	20 12.1	1.9	58.7
22	152 40.2	40.1	230 55.9	6.5	20 10.2	2.0	58.7
23	167 40.4	41.1	245 21.4	6.5	20 08.2	2.1	58.7
3 00	182 40.6	S 3 42.1	259 46.9	6.6	N20 06.1	2.2	58.7
01	197 40.8	43.0	274 12.5	6.6	20 03.9	2.4	58.7
02	212 41.0	44.0	288 38.1	6.7	20 01.5	2.5	58.6
03	227 41.2	.. 45.0	303 03.8	6.7	19 59.0	2.7	58.6
04	242 41.4	45.9	317 29.5	6.7	19 56.3	2.7	58.6
05	257 41.6	46.9	331 55.2	6.8	19 53.6	2.9	58.6
06	272 41.8	S 3 47.9	346 21.0	6.9	N19 50.7	3.0	58.6
07	287 42.0	48.8	0 46.9	6.8	19 47.7	3.1	58.6
08	302 42.2	49.8	15 12.7	7.0	19 44.6	3.3	58.6
09	317 42.4	.. 50.8	29 38.7	6.9	19 41.3	3.3	58.5
10	332 42.6	51.7	44 04.6	7.1	19 38.0	3.5	58.5
11	347 42.8	52.7	58 30.7	7.0	19 34.5	3.6	58.5
12	2 43.0	S 3 53.7	72 56.7	7.2	N19 30.9	3.8	58.5
13	17 43.2	54.6	87 22.9	7.1	19 27.1	3.8	58.5
14	32 43.4	55.6	101 49.0	7.2	19 23.3	4.0	58.4
15	47 43.6	.. 56.6	116 15.2	7.3	19 19.3	4.0	58.4
16	62 43.8	57.5	130 41.5	7.3	19 15.3	4.2	58.4
17	77 43.9	58.5	145 07.8	7.4	19 11.1	4.3	58.4
18	92 44.1	S 3 59.5	159 34.2	7.4	N19 06.8	4.5	58.4
19	107 44.3	4 00.4	174 00.6	7.5	19 02.3	4.5	58.3
20	122 44.5	01.4	188 27.1	7.6	18 57.8	4.7	58.3
21	137 44.7	.. 02.4	202 53.7	7.6	18 53.1	4.7	58.3
22	152 44.9	03.3	217 20.3	7.6	18 48.4	4.9	58.3
23	167 45.1	04.3	231 46.9	7.7	N18 43.5	5.0	58.3
	SD 16.0	d 1.0	SD 16.2		16.1		15.9

Left-margin labels: FRIDAY, SATURDAY, SUNDAY.

Lat.	Twilight Naut.	Twilight Civil	Sunrise	Moonrise 1	2	3	4
°	h m	h m	h m	h m	h m	h m	h m
N 72	03 52	05 14	06 21	□	□	□	22 09
N 70	04 03	05 17	06 17	□	□	20 53	22 54
68	04 13	05 19	06 15	19 14	20 13	21 43	23 24
66	04 20	05 21	06 12	19 54	20 53	22 14	23 46
64	04 27	05 23	06 10	20 22	21 21	22 37	24 03
62	04 32	05 24	06 08	20 43	21 43	22 56	24 18
60	04 36	05 25	06 07	21 01	22 00	23 11	24 30
N 58	04 40	05 26	06 05	21 15	22 14	23 24	24 40
56	04 43	05 27	06 04	21 28	22 27	23 35	24 49
54	04 46	05 27	06 03	21 38	22 38	23 45	24 57
52	04 49	05 28	06 02	21 48	22 47	23 54	25 04
50	04 51	05 28	06 01	21 57	22 56	24 01	00 01
45	04 55	05 29	05 58	22 15	23 14	24 18	00 18
N 40	04 58	05 30	05 57	22 30	23 29	24 31	00 31
35	05 00	05 30	05 55	22 43	23 42	24 43	00 43
30	05 02	05 30	05 54	22 54	23 53	24 53	00 53
20	05 03	05 29	05 51	23 13	24 11	00 11	01 10
N 10	05 03	05 28	05 49	23 30	24 28	00 28	01 25
0	05 01	05 26	05 46	23 45	24 43	00 43	01 39
S 10	04 58	05 23	05 44	24 01	00 01	00 59	01 53
20	04 53	05 19	05 41	24 18	00 18	01 15	02 08
30	04 46	05 14	05 38	24 37	00 37	01 34	02 26
35	04 41	05 11	05 36	24 48	00 48	01 45	02 35
40	04 35	05 07	05 34	25 01	01 01	01 57	02 47
45	04 27	05 02	05 31	00 13	01 16	02 12	03 00
S 50	04 17	04 56	05 28	00 30	01 35	02 31	03 16
52	04 12	04 53	05 27	00 39	01 44	02 39	03 24
54	04 06	04 49	05 25	00 48	01 54	02 49	03 33
56	04 00	04 46	05 23	00 58	02 05	03 00	03 42
58	03 53	04 42	05 21	01 10	02 18	03 12	03 53
S 60	03 45	04 37	05 19	01 24	02 33	03 26	04 05

Lat.	Sunset	Twilight Civil	Twilight Naut.	Moonset 1	2	3	4
°	h m	h m	h m	h m	h m	h m	h m
N 72	17 16	18 23	19 44	□	□	□	18 43
N 70	17 20	18 20	19 32	□	□	18 05	17 57
68	17 23	18 18	19 23	15 43	16 46	17 14	17 26
66	17 25	18 16	19 16	15 03	16 05	16 42	17 03
64	17 27	18 15	19 11	14 35	15 37	16 19	16 45
62	17 29	18 13	19 05	14 14	15 16	16 00	16 30
60	17 31	18 12	19 01	13 57	14 58	15 44	16 18
N 58	17 33	18 12	18 57	13 43	14 44	15 31	16 07
56	17 34	18 11	18 54	13 30	14 31	15 20	15 57
54	17 35	18 10	18 51	13 20	14 20	15 10	15 49
52	17 36	18 10	18 49	13 10	14 10	15 01	15 41
50	17 37	18 10	18 47	13 01	14 02	14 53	15 34
45	17 40	18 09	18 43	12 43	13 43	14 35	15 20
N 40	17 42	18 09	18 40	12 29	13 28	14 21	15 08
35	17 43	18 09	18 38	12 16	13 16	14 09	14 57
30	17 45	18 09	18 36	12 05	13 04	13 59	14 48
20	17 48	18 10	18 35	11 46	12 45	13 41	14 32
N 10	17 50	18 11	18 36	11 30	12 29	13 25	14 18
0	17 53	18 13	18 37	11 15	12 13	13 10	14 05
S 10	17 55	18 16	18 41	10 59	11 57	12 55	13 52
20	17 58	18 20	18 46	10 43	11 41	12 39	13 38
30	18 02	18 26	18 54	10 24	11 21	12 21	13 22
35	18 04	18 29	18 59	10 13	11 10	12 10	13 13
40	18 06	18 33	19 05	10 01	10 57	11 58	13 02
45	18 09	18 38	19 13	09 46	10 42	11 44	12 49
S 50	18 12	18 45	19 24	09 28	10 23	11 26	12 34
52	18 13	18 48	19 29	09 19	10 14	11 17	12 26
54	18 15	18 51	19 34	09 10	10 04	11 08	12 18
56	18 17	18 55	19 41	08 59	09 53	10 57	12 09
58	18 19	18 59	19 48	08 47	09 40	10 45	11 59
S 60	18 21	19 04	19 56	08 33	09 25	10 31	11 47

Day	SUN Eqn. of Time 00h	SUN Eqn. of Time 12h	SUN Mer. Pass.	MOON Mer. Pass. Upper	MOON Mer. Pass. Lower	Age	Phase
d	m s	m s	h m	h m	h m	d	%
1	10 03	10 13	11 50	05 01	17 30	22	58
2	10 23	10 33	11 49	05 59	18 28	23	46
3	10 42	10 51	11 49	06 57	19 25	24	35

UT	ARIES	VENUS −4.5		MARS +0.6		JUPITER −2.9		SATURN +0.0		STARS		
	GHA	GHA	Dec	GHA	Dec	GHA	Dec	GHA	Dec	Name	SHA	Dec
d h	° ′	° ′	° ′	° ′	° ′	° ′	° ′	° ′	° ′		° ′	° ′
4 00	12 14.5	223 44.2 N 9 25.6		112 28.7 S24 55.2		341 24.9 N10 53.5		327 48.1 N14 11.3		Acamar	315 26.1	S40 18.3
01	27 17.0	238 45.0	25.4	127 29.3	55.3	356 27.7	53.4	342 50.7	11.3	Achernar	335 34.1	S57 14.3
02	42 19.4	253 45.7	25.2	142 29.8	55.4	11 30.4	53.3	357 53.3	11.2	Acrux	173 21.9	S63 05.7
03	57 21.9	268 46.4 . .	25.0	157 30.3 . .	55.5	26 33.2 . .	53.2	12 55.9 . .	11.2	Adhara	255 20.9	S28 58.1
04	72 24.4	283 47.2	24.8	172 30.9	55.7	41 35.9	53.1	27 58.5	11.1	Aldebaran	291 01.4	N16 30.5
05	87 26.8	298 47.9	24.6	187 31.4	55.8	56 38.7	53.0	43 01.1	11.1			
06	102 29.3	313 48.6 N 9 24.4		202 32.0 S24 55.9		71 41.4 N10 52.9		58 03.7 N14 11.0		Alioth	166 30.6	N55 57.9
07	117 31.7	328 49.4	24.2	217 32.5	56.0	86 44.1	52.8	73 06.3	11.0	Alkaid	153 07.8	N49 19.1
08	132 34.2	343 50.1	24.0	232 33.1	56.1	101 46.9	52.7	88 08.9	11.0	Al Na'ir	27 56.7	S46 57.8
M 09	147 36.7	358 50.8 . .	23.7	247 33.6 . .	56.2	116 49.6 . .	52.6	103 11.6 . .	10.9	Alnilam	275 57.1	S 1 12.1
O 10	162 39.1	13 51.5	23.5	262 34.1	56.3	131 52.4	52.5	118 14.2	10.9	Alphard	218 06.8	S 8 39.3
N 11	177 41.6	28 52.2	23.3	277 34.7	56.5	146 55.1	52.4	133 16.8	10.8			
D 12	192 44.1	43 52.9 N 9 23.1		292 35.2 S24 56.6		161 57.9 N10 52.3		148 19.4 N14 10.8		Alphecca	126 20.3	N26 43.3
A 13	207 46.5	58 53.7	22.9	307 35.8	56.7	177 00.6	52.2	163 22.0	10.7	Alpheratz	357 54.2	N29 05.4
Y 14	222 49.0	73 54.4	22.7	322 36.3	56.8	192 03.3	52.1	178 24.6	10.7	Altair	62 18.5	N 8 52.3
15	237 51.5	88 55.1 . .	22.4	337 36.9 . .	56.9	207 06.1 . .	52.0	193 27.2 . .	10.6	Ankaa	353 25.8	S42 18.5
16	252 53.9	103 55.8	22.2	352 37.4	57.0	222 08.8	51.9	208 29.8	10.6	Antares	112 39.6	S26 25.8
17	267 56.4	118 56.5	22.0	7 37.9	57.1	237 11.6	51.8	223 32.4	10.5			
18	282 58.9	133 57.2 N 9 21.8		22 38.5 S24 57.2		252 14.3 N10 51.7		238 35.0 N14 10.5		Arcturus	146 05.8	N19 11.3
19	298 01.3	148 57.9	21.6	37 39.0	57.4	267 17.1	51.6	253 37.6	10.4	Atria	107 51.3	S69 01.7
20	313 03.8	163 58.6	21.3	52 39.5	57.5	282 19.8	51.5	268 40.2	10.4	Avior	234 22.6	S59 30.2
21	328 06.2	178 59.3 . .	21.1	67 40.1 . .	57.6	297 22.6 . .	51.3	283 42.8 . .	10.3	Bellatrix	278 43.3	N 6 21.0
22	343 08.7	194 00.0	20.9	82 40.6	57.7	312 25.3	51.2	298 45.4	10.3	Betelgeuse	271 12.8	N 7 24.4
23	358 11.2	209 00.7	20.7	97 41.2	57.8	327 28.0	51.1	313 48.0	10.3			
5 00	13 13.6	224 01.4 N 9 20.4		112 41.7 S24 57.9		342 30.8 N10 51.0		328 50.6 N14 10.2		Canopus	264 00.8	S52 41.5
01	28 16.1	239 02.1	20.2	127 42.2	58.0	357 33.5	50.9	343 53.2	10.2	Capella	280 50.0	N45 59.7
02	43 18.6	254 02.8	20.0	142 42.8	58.1	12 36.3	50.8	358 55.8	10.1	Deneb	49 38.5	N45 17.1
03	58 21.0	269 03.5 . .	19.7	157 43.3 . .	58.2	27 39.0 . .	50.7	13 58.4 . .	10.1	Denebola	182 44.8	N14 34.6
04	73 23.5	284 04.2	19.5	172 43.8	58.3	42 41.8	50.6	29 01.1	10.0	Diphda	349 06.2	S17 59.3
05	88 26.0	299 04.9	19.3	187 44.4	58.4	57 44.5	50.5	44 03.7	10.0			
06	103 28.4	314 05.5 N 9 19.0		202 44.9 S24 58.5		72 47.3 N10 50.4		59 06.3 N14 09.9		Dubhe	194 05.3	N61 45.1
07	118 30.9	329 06.2	18.8	217 45.5	58.6	87 50.0	50.3	74 08.9	09.9	Elnath	278 26.0	N28 36.3
T 08	133 33.4	344 06.9	18.6	232 46.0	58.8	102 52.8	50.2	89 11.5	09.8	Eltanin	90 51.2	N51 29.7
U 09	148 35.8	359 07.6 . .	18.3	247 46.5 . .	58.9	117 55.5 . .	50.1	104 14.1 . .	09.8	Enif	33 57.4	N 9 52.6
E 10	163 38.3	14 08.3	18.1	262 47.1	59.0	132 58.3	50.0	119 16.7	09.7	Fomalhaut	15 35.4	S29 37.4
S 11	178 40.7	29 08.9	17.8	277 47.6	59.1	148 01.0	49.9	134 19.3	09.7			
D 12	193 43.2	44 09.6 N 9 17.6		292 48.1 S24 59.2		163 03.7 N10 49.8		149 21.9 N14 09.6		Gacrux	172 13.4	S57 06.5
A 13	208 45.7	59 10.3	17.4	307 48.7	59.3	178 06.5	49.7	164 24.5	09.6	Gienah	176 03.6	S17 32.2
Y 14	223 48.1	74 11.0	17.1	322 49.2	59.4	193 09.2	49.6	179 27.1	09.5	Hadar	149 03.7	S60 22.2
15	238 50.6	89 11.6 . .	16.9	337 49.7 . .	59.5	208 12.0 . .	49.5	194 29.7 . .	09.5	Hamal	328 12.5	N23 27.6
16	253 53.1	104 12.3	16.6	352 50.3	59.6	223 14.7	49.4	209 32.3	09.5	Kaus Aust.	83 58.0	S34 23.1
17	268 55.5	119 13.0	16.4	7 50.8	59.7	238 17.5	49.3	224 35.0	09.4			
18	283 58.0	134 13.6 N 9 16.1		22 51.3 S24 59.8		253 20.2 N10 49.2		239 37.6 N14 09.4		Kochab	137 20.6	N74 09.7
19	299 00.5	149 14.3	15.9	37 51.9 24 59.9		268 23.0	49.1	254 40.2	09.3	Markab	13 48.7	N15 12.3
20	314 02.9	164 14.9	15.6	52 52.4 25 00.0		283 25.7	48.9	269 42.8	09.3	Menkar	314 25.9	N 4 05.3
21	329 05.4	179 15.6 . .	15.4	67 52.9 . . 00.1		298 28.5 . .	48.8	284 45.4 . .	09.2	Menkent	148 20.5	S36 22.0
22	344 07.8	194 16.3	15.1	82 53.5	00.2	313 31.2	48.7	299 48.0	09.2	Miaplacidus	221 42.4	S69 42.7
23	359 10.3	209 16.9	14.9	97 54.0	00.3	328 34.0	48.6	314 50.6	09.1			
6 00	14 12.8	224 17.6 N 9 14.6		112 54.5 S25 00.4		343 36.7 N10 48.5		329 53.2 N14 09.1		Mirfak	308 55.3	N49 51.4
01	29 15.2	239 18.2	14.4	127 55.1	00.5	358 39.5	48.4	344 55.8	09.0	Nunki	76 11.5	S26 17.8
02	44 17.7	254 18.9	14.1	142 55.6	00.6	13 42.2	48.3	359 58.4	09.0	Peacock	53 35.8	S56 44.3
03	59 20.2	269 19.5 . .	13.9	157 56.1 . .	00.7	28 45.0 . .	48.2	15 01.0 . .	08.9	Pollux	243 40.8	N28 01.5
04	74 22.6	284 20.2	13.6	172 56.6	00.8	43 47.7	48.1	30 03.7	08.9	Procyon	245 10.9	N 5 13.6
05	89 25.1	299 20.8	13.4	187 57.2	00.9	58 50.5	48.0	45 06.3	08.8			
06	104 27.6	314 21.5 N 9 13.1		202 57.7 S25 01.0		73 53.2 N10 47.9		60 08.9 N14 08.8		Rasalhague	96 16.5	N12 33.9
07	119 30.0	329 22.1	12.8	217 58.2	01.1	88 56.0	47.8	75 11.5	08.7	Regulus	207 55.1	N11 58.2
W 08	134 32.5	344 22.7	12.6	232 58.8	01.2	103 58.7	47.7	90 14.1	08.7	Rigel	281 22.2	S 8 12.0
E 09	149 35.0	359 23.4 . .	12.3	247 59.3 . .	01.3	119 01.5 . .	47.6	105 16.7 . .	08.6	Rigil Kent.	140 07.0	S60 49.9
D 10	164 37.4	14 24.0	12.1	262 59.8	01.4	134 04.2	47.5	120 19.3	08.6	Sabik	102 24.9	S15 43.3
N 11	179 39.9	29 24.7	11.8	278 00.4	01.5	149 07.0	47.4	135 21.9	08.5			
E 12	194 42.3	44 25.3 N 9 11.5		293 00.9 S25 01.5		164 09.7 N10 47.3		150 24.5 N14 08.5		Schedar	349 52.1	N56 32.1
S 13	209 44.8	59 25.9	11.3	308 01.4	01.6	179 12.5	47.2	165 27.2	08.4	Shaula	96 36.5	S37 06.2
D 14	224 47.3	74 26.6	11.0	323 01.9	01.7	194 15.2	47.0	180 29.8	08.4	Sirius	258 43.1	S16 42.8
A 15	239 49.7	89 27.2 . .	10.7	338 02.5 . .	01.8	209 18.0 . .	46.9	195 32.4 . .	08.4	Spica	158 42.8	S11 09.4
Y 16	254 52.2	104 27.8	10.5	353 03.0	01.9	224 20.7	46.8	210 35.0	08.3	Suhail	223 00.5	S43 25.6
17	269 54.7	119 28.4	10.2	8 03.5	02.0	239 23.5	46.7	225 37.6	08.3			
18	284 57.1	134 29.1 N 9 09.9		23 04.0 S25 02.1		254 26.3 N10 46.6		240 40.2 N14 08.2		Vega	80 46.2	N38 47.4
19	299 59.6	149 29.7	09.6	38 04.6	02.2	269 29.0	46.5	255 42.8	08.2	Zuben'ubi	137 17.5	S16 02.2
20	315 02.1	164 30.3	09.4	53 05.1	02.3	284 31.8	46.4	270 45.4	08.1			
21	330 04.5	179 30.9 . .	09.1	68 05.6 . .	02.4	299 34.5 . .	46.3	285 48.0 . .	08.1		SHA	Mer. Pass.
22	345 07.0	194 31.6	08.8	83 06.1	02.5	314 37.3	46.2	300 50.7	08.0		° ′	h m
23	0 09.4	209 32.2	08.5	98 06.7	02.6	329 40.0	46.1	315 53.3	08.0	Venus	210 47.8	9 03
	h m									Mars	99 28.1	16 29
Mer. Pass. 23 03.3		v 0.7 d 0.2		v 0.5 d 0.1		v 2.7 d 0.1		v 2.6 d 0.0		Jupiter	329 17.1	1 10
										Saturn	315 37.0	2 04

UT	SUN GHA	SUN Dec	MOON GHA	v	MOON Dec	d	HP
d h	° ′	° ′	° ′	′	° ′	′	′
4 00	182 45.3	S 4 05.2	246 13.6	7.8	N18 38.5	5.1	58.2
01	197 45.5	06.2	260 40.4	7.8	18 33.4	5.2	58.2
02	212 45.7	07.2	275 07.2	7.9	18 28.2	5.3	58.2
03	227 45.9	.. 08.1	289 34.1	7.9	18 22.9	5.4	58.2
04	242 46.1	09.1	304 01.0	8.0	18 17.5	5.5	58.2
05	257 46.3	10.1	318 28.0	8.1	18 12.0	5.7	58.1
06	272 46.5	S 4 11.0	332 55.1	8.1	N18 06.3	5.7	58.1
07	287 46.7	12.0	347 22.2	8.2	18 00.6	5.8	58.1
08	302 46.9	13.0	1 49.4	8.2	17 54.8	6.0	58.1
M 09	317 47.0	.. 13.9	16 16.6	8.3	17 48.8	6.0	58.1
O 10	332 47.2	14.9	30 43.9	8.4	17 42.8	6.2	58.0
N 11	347 47.4	15.9	45 11.3	8.4	17 36.6	6.2	58.0
D 12	2 47.6	S 4 16.8	59 38.7	8.5	N17 30.4	6.3	58.0
A 13	17 47.8	17.8	74 06.2	8.6	17 24.1	6.5	58.0
Y 14	32 48.0	18.8	88 33.8	8.6	17 17.6	6.5	58.0
15	47 48.2	.. 19.7	103 01.4	8.6	17 11.1	6.6	58.0
16	62 48.4	20.7	117 29.0	8.8	17 04.5	6.8	57.9
17	77 48.6	21.7	131 56.8	8.8	16 57.7	6.8	57.9
18	92 48.8	S 4 22.6	146 24.6	8.8	N16 50.9	6.9	57.9
19	107 49.0	23.6	160 52.4	9.0	16 44.0	7.0	57.9
20	122 49.2	24.5	175 20.4	9.0	16 37.0	7.1	57.9
21	137 49.3	.. 25.5	189 48.4	9.0	16 29.9	7.2	57.8
22	152 49.5	26.5	204 16.4	9.1	16 22.7	7.3	57.8
23	167 49.7	27.4	218 44.5	9.2	16 15.4	7.3	57.8
5 00	182 49.9	S 4 28.4	233 12.7	9.3	N16 08.1	7.5	57.8
01	197 50.1	29.4	247 41.0	9.3	16 00.6	7.5	57.8
02	212 50.3	30.3	262 09.3	9.4	15 53.1	7.6	57.7
03	227 50.5	.. 31.3	276 37.7	9.4	15 45.5	7.7	57.7
04	242 50.7	32.3	291 06.1	9.5	15 37.8	7.8	57.7
05	257 50.9	33.2	305 34.6	9.6	15 30.0	7.9	57.7
06	272 51.1	S 4 34.2	320 03.2	9.6	N15 22.1	7.9	57.6
07	287 51.2	35.1	334 31.8	9.7	15 14.2	8.0	57.6
T 08	302 51.4	36.1	349 00.5	9.7	15 06.2	8.1	57.6
U 09	317 51.6	.. 37.1	3 29.2	9.9	14 58.1	8.2	57.6
E 10	332 51.8	38.0	17 58.1	9.8	14 49.9	8.3	57.6
S 11	347 52.0	39.0	32 26.9	10.0	14 41.6	8.3	57.5
D 12	2 52.2	S 4 40.0	46 55.9	10.0	N14 33.3	8.4	57.5
A 13	17 52.4	40.9	61 24.9	10.1	14 24.9	8.5	57.5
Y 14	32 52.6	41.9	75 54.0	10.1	14 16.4	8.5	57.5
15	47 52.7	.. 42.8	90 23.1	10.2	14 07.9	8.7	57.5
16	62 52.9	43.8	104 52.3	10.3	13 59.2	8.7	57.4
17	77 53.1	44.8	119 21.6	10.3	13 50.5	8.7	57.4
18	92 53.3	S 4 45.7	133 50.9	10.4	N13 41.8	8.9	57.4
19	107 53.5	46.7	148 20.3	10.5	13 32.9	8.8	57.4
20	122 53.7	47.7	162 49.8	10.5	13 24.1	9.0	57.4
21	137 53.9	.. 48.6	177 19.3	10.6	13 15.1	9.0	57.3
22	152 54.1	49.6	191 48.9	10.6	13 06.1	9.1	57.3
23	167 54.2	50.5	206 18.5	10.7	12 57.0	9.2	57.3
6 00	182 54.4	S 4 51.5	220 48.2	10.7	N12 47.8	9.2	57.3
01	197 54.6	52.5	235 17.9	10.9	12 38.6	9.3	57.3
02	212 54.8	53.4	249 47.8	10.8	12 29.3	9.3	57.2
03	227 55.0	.. 54.4	264 17.6	11.0	12 20.0	9.4	57.2
04	242 55.2	55.3	278 47.6	11.0	12 10.6	9.5	57.2
05	257 55.4	56.3	293 17.6	11.0	12 01.1	9.5	57.2
06	272 55.5	S 4 57.3	307 47.6	11.1	N11 51.6	9.5	57.2
W 07	287 55.7	58.2	322 17.7	11.2	11 42.1	9.7	57.1
E 08	302 55.9	4 59.2	336 47.9	11.3	11 32.4	9.6	57.1
D 09	317 56.1	5 00.1	351 18.2	11.2	11 22.8	9.8	57.1
N 10	332 56.3	01.1	5 48.4	11.4	11 13.0	9.7	57.1
E 11	347 56.5	02.1	20 18.8	11.4	11 03.3	9.9	57.1
S 12	2 56.7	S 5 03.0	34 49.2	11.4	N10 53.4	9.9	57.0
D 13	17 56.8	04.0	49 19.6	11.6	10 43.5	9.9	57.0
A 14	32 57.0	04.9	63 50.2	11.5	10 33.6	10.0	57.0
Y 15	47 57.2	.. 05.9	78 20.7	11.7	10 23.6	10.0	57.0
16	62 57.4	06.9	92 51.4	11.6	10 13.6	10.0	57.0
17	77 57.6	07.8	107 22.0	11.8	10 03.6	10.1	56.9
18	92 57.8	S 5 08.8	121 52.8	11.8	N 9 53.5	10.2	56.9
19	107 57.9	09.7	136 23.6	11.8	9 43.3	10.2	56.9
20	122 58.1	10.7	150 54.4	11.9	9 33.1	10.2	56.9
21	137 58.3	.. 11.7	165 25.3	11.9	9 22.9	10.3	56.8
22	152 58.5	12.6	179 56.2	12.0	9 12.6	10.3	56.8
23	167 58.7	13.6	194 27.2	12.1	N 9 02.3	10.4	56.8
SD 16.0	d 1.0		SD 15.8		15.7		15.5

Twilight / Sunrise / Moonrise

Lat.	Naut.	Civil	Sunrise	4	5	6	7
°	h m	h m	h m	h m	h m	h m	h m
N 72	04 07	05 27	06 35	22 09	24 24	00 24	02 22
N 70	04 16	05 29	06 29	22 54	24 48	00 48	02 35
68	04 24	05 30	06 25	23 24	25 06	01 06	02 45
66	04 31	05 31	06 22	23 46	25 21	01 21	02 54
64	04 36	05 31	06 19	24 03	00 03	01 33	03 01
62	04 40	05 32	06 16	24 18	00 18	01 43	03 07
60	04 44	05 32	06 14	24 30	00 30	01 51	03 13
N 58	04 47	05 33	06 12	24 40	00 40	01 59	03 17
56	04 50	05 33	06 10	24 49	00 49	02 05	03 22
54	04 52	05 33	06 08	24 57	00 57	02 11	03 25
52	04 54	05 33	06 07	25 04	01 04	02 17	03 29
50	04 56	05 33	06 05	00 01	01 11	02 21	03 32
45	04 59	05 33	06 02	00 18	01 24	02 32	03 39
N 40	05 01	05 33	06 00	00 31	01 36	02 40	03 44
35	05 03	05 32	05 57	00 43	01 45	02 48	03 49
30	05 04	05 31	05 55	00 53	01 54	02 54	03 53
20	05 04	05 30	05 52	01 10	02 09	03 05	04 00
N 10	05 03	05 27	05 48	01 25	02 21	03 15	04 07
0	05 00	05 25	05 45	01 39	02 33	03 24	04 13
S 10	04 56	05 21	05 42	01 53	02 45	03 33	04 19
20	04 50	05 16	05 38	02 08	02 58	03 43	04 25
30	04 42	05 10	05 34	02 26	03 12	03 54	04 32
35	04 36	05 06	05 32	02 35	03 20	04 00	04 36
40	04 29	05 02	05 29	02 47	03 30	04 07	04 41
45	04 21	04 56	05 26	03 00	03 41	04 16	04 46
S 50	04 10	04 49	05 22	03 16	03 54	04 26	04 53
52	04 04	04 45	05 20	03 24	04 00	04 30	04 56
54	03 58	04 42	05 18	03 33	04 07	04 35	04 59
56	03 51	04 37	05 15	03 42	04 15	04 41	05 03
58	03 43	04 33	05 13	03 53	04 24	04 47	05 07
S 60	03 34	04 27	05 10	04 05	04 33	04 54	05 11

Sunset / Twilight / Moonset

Lat.	Sunset	Civil	Naut.	4	5	6	7
°	h m	h m	h m	h m	h m	h m	h m
N 72	17 00	18 07	19 27	18 43	18 16	18 00	17 48
N 70	17 06	18 06	19 18	17 57	17 51	17 45	17 40
68	17 10	18 05	19 10	17 26	17 31	17 33	17 34
66	17 14	18 05	19 04	17 03	17 16	17 23	17 29
64	17 17	18 04	18 59	16 45	17 03	17 15	17 24
62	17 20	18 04	18 55	16 30	16 52	17 07	17 20
60	17 22	18 03	18 52	16 18	16 42	17 01	17 17
N 58	17 24	18 03	18 49	16 07	16 34	16 55	17 13
56	17 26	18 03	18 46	15 57	16 27	16 50	17 11
54	17 28	18 03	18 44	15 49	16 20	16 46	17 08
52	17 29	18 03	18 42	15 41	16 14	16 42	17 06
50	17 31	18 03	18 40	15 34	16 09	16 38	17 04
45	17 34	18 03	18 37	15 20	15 57	16 30	16 59
N 40	17 37	18 04	18 35	15 08	15 48	16 23	16 55
35	17 39	18 04	18 34	14 57	15 39	16 17	16 52
30	17 41	18 05	18 33	14 48	15 32	16 12	16 49
20	17 45	18 07	18 33	14 32	15 20	16 03	16 44
N 10	17 48	18 10	18 34	14 18	15 08	15 55	16 40
0	17 52	18 13	18 37	14 05	14 58	15 48	16 35
S 10	17 55	18 16	18 41	13 52	14 47	15 40	16 31
20	17 59	18 21	18 47	13 38	14 36	15 32	16 26
30	18 03	18 27	18 56	13 22	14 23	15 23	16 21
35	18 06	18 31	19 01	13 13	14 15	15 17	16 18
40	18 09	18 36	19 09	13 02	14 07	15 11	16 14
45	18 12	18 42	19 17	12 49	13 57	15 04	16 10
S 50	18 15	18 49	19 29	12 34	13 44	14 55	16 05
52	18 18	18 53	19 34	12 26	13 38	14 51	16 03
54	18 21	18 57	19 41	12 18	13 32	14 47	16 00
56	18 23	19 01	19 48	12 09	13 25	14 42	15 58
58	18 26	19 06	19 56	11 59	13 17	14 36	15 54
S 60	18 28	19 12	20 05	11 47	13 08	14 30	15 51

SUN / MOON

Day	Eqn. of Time 00h	Eqn. of Time 12h	Mer. Pass.	Mer. Pass. Upper	Mer. Pass. Lower	Age	Phase
d	m s	m s	h m	h m	h m	d	%
4	11 01	11 10	11 49	07 52	20 19	25	25
5	11 19	11 28	11 49	08 46	21 11	26	16
6	11 37	11 46	11 48	09 36	22 00	27	9

UT	ARIES GHA	VENUS GHA	Dec	MARS GHA	Dec	JUPITER GHA	Dec	SATURN GHA	Dec	Name	SHA	Dec
7 00	15 11.9	224 32.8	N 9 08.3	113 07.2	S25 02.6	344 42.8	N10 46.0	330 55.9	N14 07.9	Acamar	315 26.1	S40 18.3
01	30 14.4	239 33.4	08.0	128 07.7	02.7	359 45.5	45.9	345 58.5	07.9	Achernar	335 34.1	S57 14.3
02	45 16.8	254 34.0	07.7	143 08.2	02.8	14 48.3	45.8	1 01.1	07.8	Acrux	173 21.9	S63 05.7
03	60 19.3	269 34.6 ..	07.4	158 08.8 ..	02.9	29 51.0 ..	45.7	16 03.7 ..	07.8	Adhara	255 20.9	S28 58.1
04	75 21.8	284 35.2	07.1	173 09.3	03.0	44 53.8	45.6	31 06.3	07.7	Aldebaran	291 01.4	N16 30.5
05	90 24.2	299 35.8	06.9	188 09.8	03.1	59 56.5	45.4	46 08.9	07.7			
06	105 26.7	314 36.5	N 9 06.6	203 10.3	S25 03.2	74 59.3	N10 45.3	61 11.6	N14 07.6	Alioth	166 30.6	N55 57.8
07	120 29.2	329 37.1	06.3	218 10.9	03.3	90 02.1	45.2	76 14.2	07.6	Alkaid	153 07.8	N49 19.1
T 08	135 31.6	344 37.7	06.0	233 11.4	03.4	105 04.8	45.1	91 16.8	07.5	Al Na'ir	27 56.7	S46 57.8
H 09	150 34.1	359 38.3 ..	05.7	248 11.9 ..	03.4	120 07.6 ..	45.0	106 19.4 ..	07.5	Alnilam	275 57.1	S 1 12.1
U 10	165 36.6	14 38.9	05.4	263 12.4	03.5	135 10.3	44.9	121 22.0	07.4	Alphard	218 06.7	S 8 39.3
R 11	180 39.0	29 39.5	05.1	278 13.0	03.6	150 13.1	44.8	136 24.6	07.4			
S 12	195 41.5	44 40.1	N 9 04.9	293 13.5	S25 03.7	165 15.8	N10 44.7	151 27.2	N14 07.3	Alphecca	126 20.3	N26 43.3
D 13	210 43.9	59 40.7	04.6	308 14.0	03.8	180 18.6	44.6	166 29.9	07.3	Alpheratz	357 54.2	N29 05.4
A 14	225 46.4	74 41.2	04.3	323 14.5	03.9	195 21.3	44.5	181 32.5	07.2	Altair	62 18.6	N 8 52.3
Y 15	240 48.9	89 41.8 ..	04.0	338 15.0 ..	03.9	210 24.1 ..	44.4	196 35.1 ..	07.2	Ankaa	353 25.8	S42 18.5
16	255 51.3	104 42.4	03.7	353 15.6	04.0	225 26.9	44.3	211 37.7	07.1	Antares	112 39.6	S26 25.8
17	270 53.8	119 43.0	03.4	8 16.1	04.1	240 29.6	44.2	226 40.3	07.1			
18	285 56.3	134 43.6	N 9 03.1	23 16.6	S25 04.2	255 32.4	N10 44.1	241 42.9	N14 07.0	Arcturus	146 05.8	N19 11.3
19	300 58.7	149 44.2	02.8	38 17.1	04.3	270 35.1	43.9	256 45.5	07.0	Atria	107 51.3	S69 01.7
20	316 01.2	164 44.8	02.5	53 17.6	04.4	285 37.9	43.8	271 48.2	06.9	Avior	234 22.6	S59 30.2
21	331 03.7	179 45.4 ..	02.2	68 18.2 ..	04.4	300 40.6 ..	43.7	286 50.8 ..	06.9	Bellatrix	278 43.3	N 6 21.0
22	346 06.1	194 45.9	01.9	83 18.7	04.5	315 43.4	43.6	301 53.4	06.8	Betelgeuse	271 12.7	N 7 24.4
23	1 08.6	209 46.5	01.6	98 19.2	04.6	330 46.2	43.5	316 56.0	06.8			
8 00	16 11.0	224 47.1	N 9 01.3	113 19.7	S25 04.7	345 48.9	N10 43.4	331 58.6	N14 06.7	Canopus	264 00.8	S52 41.5
01	31 13.5	239 47.7	01.0	128 20.2	04.8	0 51.7	43.3	347 01.2	06.7	Capella	280 50.0	N45 59.7
02	46 16.0	254 48.3	00.7	143 20.8	04.8	15 54.4	43.2	2 03.9	06.6	Deneb	49 38.5	N45 17.1
03	61 18.4	269 48.8 ..	00.4	158 21.3 ..	04.9	30 57.2 ..	43.1	17 06.5 ..	06.6	Denebola	182 44.8	N14 34.6
04	76 20.9	284 49.4	9 00.1	173 21.8	05.0	45 59.9	43.0	32 09.1	06.5	Diphda	349 06.2	S17 59.3
05	91 23.4	299 50.0	8 59.8	188 22.3	05.1	61 02.7	42.9	47 11.7	06.5			
06	106 25.8	314 50.5	N 8 59.5	203 22.8	S25 05.2	76 05.5	N10 42.8	62 14.3	N14 06.4	Dubhe	194 05.3	N61 45.1
07	121 28.3	329 51.1	59.2	218 23.3	05.2	91 08.2	42.7	77 16.9	06.4	Elnath	278 25.9	N28 36.3
08	136 30.8	344 51.7	58.9	233 23.9	05.3	106 11.0	42.5	92 19.6	06.3	Eltanin	90 51.2	N51 29.7
F 09	151 33.2	359 52.2 ..	58.5	248 24.4 ..	05.4	121 13.7 ..	42.4	107 22.2 ..	06.3	Enif	33 57.4	N 9 52.6
R 10	166 35.7	14 52.8	58.2	263 24.9	05.5	136 16.5	42.3	122 24.8	06.3	Fomalhaut	15 35.4	S29 37.4
I 11	181 38.2	29 53.4	57.9	278 25.4	05.5	151 19.3	42.2	137 27.4	06.2			
D 12	196 40.6	44 53.9	N 8 57.6	293 25.9	S25 05.6	166 22.0	N10 42.1	152 30.0	N14 06.2	Gacrux	172 13.4	S57 06.5
A 13	211 43.1	59 54.5	57.3	308 26.4	05.7	181 24.8	42.0	167 32.6	06.1	Gienah	176 03.6	S17 32.2
Y 14	226 45.5	74 55.1	57.0	323 27.0	05.8	196 27.5	41.9	182 35.3	06.1	Hadar	149 03.7	S60 22.2
15	241 48.0	89 55.6 ..	56.7	338 27.5 ..	05.8	211 30.3 ..	41.8	197 37.9 ..	06.0	Hamal	328 12.5	N23 27.6
16	256 50.5	104 56.2	56.3	353 28.0	05.9	226 33.1	41.7	212 40.5	06.0	Kaus Aust.	83 58.0	S34 23.1
17	271 52.9	119 56.7	56.0	8 28.5	06.0	241 35.8	41.6	227 43.1	05.9			
18	286 55.4	134 57.3	N 8 55.7	23 29.0	S25 06.1	256 38.6	N10 41.5	242 45.7	N14 05.9	Kochab	137 20.7	N74 09.7
19	301 57.9	149 57.8	55.4	38 29.5	06.1	271 41.3	41.3	257 48.3	05.8	Markab	13 48.7	N15 12.3
20	317 00.3	164 58.4	55.1	53 30.0	06.2	286 44.1	41.2	272 51.0	05.8	Menkar	314 25.9	N 4 05.3
21	332 02.8	179 58.9 ..	54.7	68 30.6 ..	06.3	301 46.9 ..	41.1	287 53.6 ..	05.7	Menkent	148 20.5	S36 21.9
22	347 05.3	194 59.5	54.4	83 31.1	06.3	316 49.6	41.0	302 56.2	05.7	Miaplacidus	221 42.4	S69 42.7
23	2 07.7	210 00.0	54.1	98 31.6	06.4	331 52.4	40.9	317 58.8	05.6			
9 00	17 10.2	225 00.6	N 8 53.8	113 32.1	S25 06.5	346 55.1	N10 40.8	333 01.4	N14 05.6	Mirfak	308 55.2	N49 51.4
01	32 12.7	240 01.1	53.4	128 32.6	06.6	1 57.9	40.7	348 04.1	05.5	Nunki	76 11.5	S26 17.8
02	47 15.1	255 01.6	53.1	143 33.1	06.6	17 00.7	40.6	3 06.7	05.5	Peacock	53 35.8	S56 44.3
03	62 17.6	270 02.2 ..	52.8	158 33.6 ..	06.7	32 03.4 ..	40.5	18 09.3 ..	05.4	Pollux	243 40.8	N28 01.5
04	77 20.0	285 02.7	52.5	173 34.1	06.8	47 06.2	40.4	33 11.9	05.4	Procyon	245 10.9	N 5 13.6
05	92 22.5	300 03.3	52.1	188 34.7	06.8	62 09.0	40.3	48 14.5	05.3			
06	107 25.0	315 03.8	N 8 51.8	203 35.2	S25 06.9	77 11.7	N10 40.1	63 17.2	N14 05.3	Rasalhague	96 16.5	N12 33.9
07	122 27.4	330 04.3	51.5	218 35.7	07.0	92 14.5	40.0	78 19.8	05.2	Regulus	207 55.1	N11 58.2
S 08	137 29.9	345 04.9	51.1	233 36.2	07.0	107 17.2	39.9	93 22.4	05.2	Rigel	281 22.2	S 8 12.1
A 09	152 32.4	0 05.4 ..	50.8	248 36.7 ..	07.1	122 20.0 ..	39.8	108 25.0 ..	05.1	Rigil Kent.	140 07.0	S60 49.9
T 10	167 34.8	15 05.9	50.5	263 37.2	07.2	137 22.8	39.7	123 27.6	05.1	Sabik	102 24.9	S15 43.3
U 11	182 37.3	30 06.4	50.1	278 37.7	07.2	152 25.5	39.6	138 30.2	05.0			
R 12	197 39.8	45 07.0	N 8 49.8	293 38.2	S25 07.3	167 28.3	N10 39.5	153 32.9	N14 05.0	Schedar	349 52.1	N56 32.2
D 13	212 42.2	60 07.5	49.4	308 38.7	07.4	182 31.1	39.4	168 35.5	04.9	Shaula	96 36.5	S37 06.2
A 14	227 44.7	75 08.0	49.1	323 39.2	07.4	197 33.8	39.3	183 38.1	04.9	Sirius	258 43.1	S16 42.8
Y 15	242 47.1	90 08.5 ..	48.8	338 39.8 ..	07.5	212 36.6 ..	39.2	198 40.7 ..	04.8	Spica	158 42.8	S11 09.4
16	257 49.6	105 09.1	48.4	353 40.3	07.6	227 39.3	39.1	213 43.4	04.8	Suhail	223 00.5	S43 25.6
17	272 52.1	120 09.6	48.1	8 40.8	07.6	242 42.1	38.9	228 46.0	04.7			
18	287 54.5	135 10.1	N 8 47.7	23 41.3	S25 07.7	257 44.9	N10 38.8	243 48.6	N14 04.7	Vega	80 46.2	N38 47.4
19	302 57.0	150 10.6	47.4	38 41.8	07.7	272 47.6	38.7	258 51.2	04.6	Zuben'ubi	137 17.5	S16 02.2
20	317 59.5	165 11.1	47.0	53 42.3	07.8	287 50.4	38.6	273 53.8	04.5			
21	333 01.9	180 11.7 ..	46.7	68 42.8 ..	07.9	302 53.2 ..	38.5	288 56.5 ..	04.5			
22	348 04.4	195 12.2	46.4	83 43.3	07.9	317 55.9	38.4	303 59.1	04.4			
23	3 06.9	210 12.7	46.0	98 43.8	08.0	332 58.7	38.3	319 01.7	04.4			

										Name	SHA	Mer. Pass.
												h m
										Venus	208 36.1	9 01
										Mars	97 08.7	16 26
										Jupiter	329 37.9	0 57
										Saturn	315 47.6	1 52

	h m	v	d	v	d	v	d	v	d
Mer. Pass.	22 51.5	0.6	0.3	0.5	0.1	2.8	0.1	2.6	0.0

UT	SUN GHA	Dec	MOON GHA	v	Dec	d	HP
d h	° ′	° ′	° ′	′	° ′	′	′
7 00	182 58.8	S 5 14.5	208 58.3	12.1	N 8 51.9	10.4	56.8
01	197 59.0	15.5	223 29.4	12.1	8 41.5	10.4	56.8
02	212 59.2	16.5	238 00.5	12.2	8 31.1	10.4	56.7
03	227 59.4	.. 17.4	252 31.7	12.3	8 20.7	10.5	56.7
04	242 59.6	18.4	267 03.0	12.2	8 10.2	10.6	56.7
05	257 59.8	19.3	281 34.2	12.4	7 59.6	10.5	56.7
06	272 59.9	S 5 20.3	296 05.6	12.4	N 7 49.1	10.6	56.7
T 07	288 00.1	21.3	310 37.0	12.4	7 38.5	10.6	56.6
H 08	303 00.3	22.2	325 08.4	12.5	7 27.9	10.7	56.6
U 09	318 00.5	.. 23.2	339 39.9	12.5	7 17.2	10.7	56.6
R 10	333 00.7	24.1	354 11.4	12.6	7 06.5	10.7	56.6
S 11	348 00.8	25.1	8 43.0	12.6	6 55.8	10.7	56.6
D 12	3 01.0	S 5 26.0	23 14.6	12.7	N 6 45.1	10.8	56.5
A 13	18 01.2	27.0	37 46.3	12.7	6 34.3	10.8	56.5
Y 14	33 01.4	28.0	52 18.0	12.7	6 23.5	10.8	56.5
15	48 01.6	.. 28.9	66 49.7	12.8	6 12.7	10.8	56.5
16	63 01.7	29.9	81 21.5	12.8	6 01.9	10.8	56.5
17	78 01.9	30.8	95 53.3	12.9	5 51.1	10.9	56.4
18	93 02.1	S 5 31.8	110 25.2	12.9	N 5 40.2	10.9	56.4
19	108 02.3	32.7	124 57.1	12.9	5 29.3	10.9	56.4
20	123 02.5	33.7	139 29.0	13.0	5 18.4	10.9	56.4
21	138 02.6	.. 34.6	154 01.0	13.1	5 07.5	11.0	56.4
22	153 02.8	35.6	168 33.1	13.0	4 56.5	10.9	56.3
23	168 03.0	36.6	183 05.1	13.1	4 45.6	11.0	56.3
8 00	183 03.2	S 5 37.5	197 37.2	13.2	N 4 34.6	11.0	56.3
01	198 03.3	38.5	212 09.4	13.1	4 23.6	11.0	56.3
02	213 03.5	39.4	226 41.5	13.2	4 12.6	11.0	56.2
03	228 03.7	.. 40.4	241 13.7	13.3	4 01.6	11.1	56.2
04	243 03.9	41.3	255 46.0	13.3	3 50.5	11.0	56.2
05	258 04.1	42.3	270 18.3	13.3	3 39.5	11.0	56.2
06	273 04.2	S 5 43.3	284 50.6	13.3	N 3 28.5	11.1	56.2
F 07	288 04.4	44.2	299 22.9	13.4	3 17.4	11.1	56.1
R 08	303 04.6	45.2	313 55.3	13.4	3 06.3	11.0	56.1
I 09	318 04.8	.. 46.1	328 27.7	13.4	2 55.3	11.1	56.1
D 10	333 04.9	47.1	343 00.1	13.5	2 44.2	11.1	56.1
A 11	348 05.1	48.0	357 32.6	13.5	2 33.1	11.1	56.1
Y 12	3 05.3	S 5 49.0	12 05.1	13.5	N 2 22.0	11.1	56.0
13	18 05.5	49.9	26 37.6	13.6	2 10.9	11.0	56.0
14	33 05.6	50.9	41 10.2	13.6	1 59.9	11.1	56.0
15	48 05.8	.. 51.8	55 42.8	13.6	1 48.8	11.1	56.0
16	63 06.0	52.8	70 15.4	13.6	1 37.7	11.1	56.0
17	78 06.2	53.7	84 48.0	13.7	1 26.6	11.1	55.9
18	93 06.3	S 5 54.7	99 20.7	13.7	N 1 15.5	11.1	55.9
19	108 06.5	55.7	113 53.4	13.7	1 04.4	11.1	55.9
20	123 06.7	56.6	128 26.1	13.7	0 53.3	11.1	55.9
21	138 06.9	.. 57.6	142 58.8	13.8	0 42.2	11.1	55.9
22	153 07.0	58.5	157 31.6	13.7	0 31.1	11.0	55.8
23	168 07.2	5 59.5	172 04.3	13.8	0 20.1	11.1	55.8
9 00	183 07.4	S 6 00.4	186 37.1	13.9	N 0 09.0	11.1	55.8
01	198 07.5	01.4	201 10.0	13.8	S 0 02.1	11.0	55.8
02	213 07.7	02.3	215 42.8	13.9	0 13.1	11.1	55.8
03	228 07.9	.. 03.3	230 15.7	13.9	0 24.2	11.0	55.7
04	243 08.1	04.2	244 48.6	13.9	0 35.2	11.1	55.7
05	258 08.2	05.2	259 21.5	13.9	0 46.3	11.0	55.7
06	273 08.4	S 6 06.1	273 54.4	13.9	S 0 57.3	11.0	55.7
S 07	288 08.6	07.1	288 27.3	14.0	1 08.3	11.0	55.7
A 08	303 08.8	08.0	303 00.3	14.0	1 19.3	11.0	55.6
T 09	318 08.9	.. 09.0	317 33.3	14.0	1 30.3	10.9	55.6
U 10	333 09.1	09.9	332 06.3	14.0	1 41.2	11.0	55.6
R 11	348 09.3	10.9	346 39.3	14.0	1 52.2	10.9	55.6
D 12	3 09.4	S 6 11.8	1 12.3	14.0	S 2 03.1	10.9	55.6
A 13	18 09.6	12.8	15 45.3	14.1	2 14.0	10.9	55.5
Y 14	33 09.8	13.7	30 18.4	14.0	2 24.9	10.9	55.5
15	48 10.0	.. 14.7	44 51.4	14.1	2 35.8	10.9	55.5
16	63 10.1	15.6	59 24.5	14.1	2 46.7	10.8	55.5
17	78 10.3	16.6	73 57.6	14.1	2 57.5	10.9	55.5
18	93 10.5	S 6 17.5	88 30.7	14.1	S 3 08.4	10.8	55.4
19	108 10.6	18.5	103 03.8	14.1	3 19.2	10.7	55.4
20	123 10.8	19.4	117 36.9	14.1	3 29.9	10.8	55.4
21	138 11.0	.. 20.4	132 10.0	14.2	3 40.7	10.7	55.4
22	153 11.1	21.3	146 43.2	14.1	3 51.4	10.8	55.4
23	168 11.3	22.3	161 16.3	14.2	S 4 02.2	10.7	55.4
	SD 16.0	d 1.0	SD 15.4		15.3		15.1

Lat.	Twilight Naut.	Civil	Sunrise	Moonrise 7	8	9	10
°	h m	h m	h m	h m	h m	h m	h m
N 72	04 21	05 40	06 48	02 22	04 12	05 57	07 42
N 70	04 29	05 40	06 42	02 35	04 17	05 56	07 33
68	04 35	05 40	06 36	02 45	04 21	05 55	07 27
66	04 40	05 40	06 31	02 54	04 25	05 54	07 21
64	04 45	05 40	06 27	03 01	04 28	05 53	07 16
62	04 48	05 40	06 24	03 07	04 31	05 52	07 12
60	04 51	05 39	06 21	03 13	04 33	05 51	07 09
N 58	04 53	05 39	06 18	03 17	04 35	05 51	07 05
56	04 56	05 39	06 16	03 22	04 37	05 50	07 03
54	04 57	05 38	06 14	03 25	04 38	05 50	07 00
52	04 59	05 38	06 12	03 29	04 40	05 49	06 58
50	05 00	05 38	06 10	03 32	04 41	05 49	06 56
45	05 03	05 37	06 06	03 39	04 44	05 48	06 51
N 40	05 04	05 36	06 03	03 44	04 47	05 48	06 48
35	05 05	05 34	06 00	03 49	04 49	05 47	06 44
30	05 05	05 33	05 57	03 53	04 50	05 47	06 42
20	05 05	05 30	05 53	04 00	04 54	05 46	06 37
N 10	05 03	05 27	05 48	04 07	04 57	05 45	06 33
0	04 59	05 24	05 44	04 13	04 59	05 44	06 29
S 10	04 55	05 19	05 40	04 19	05 02	05 44	06 25
20	04 48	05 14	05 36	04 25	05 05	05 43	06 21
30	04 38	05 06	05 31	04 32	05 08	05 42	06 16
35	04 32	05 02	05 28	04 36	05 10	05 42	06 13
40	04 24	04 57	05 24	04 41	05 12	05 41	06 10
45	04 15	04 50	05 20	04 46	05 14	05 41	06 07
S 50	04 02	04 42	05 15	04 53	05 17	05 40	06 03
52	03 56	04 38	05 13	04 56	05 19	05 40	06 01
54	03 50	04 34	05 10	04 59	05 20	05 40	05 59
56	03 42	04 29	05 08	05 03	05 22	05 39	05 57
58	03 33	04 24	05 05	05 07	05 23	05 39	05 54
S 60	03 23	04 18	05 01	05 11	05 25	05 38	05 51

Lat.	Sunset	Twilight Civil	Naut.	Moonset 7	8	9	10
°	h m	h m	h m	h m	h m	h m	h m
N 72	16 45	17 53	19 11	17 48	17 37	17 26	17 14
N 70	16 52	17 53	19 04	17 40	17 35	17 30	17 25
68	16 58	17 53	18 58	17 34	17 34	17 34	17 33
66	17 02	17 54	18 53	17 29	17 33	17 37	17 41
64	17 06	17 54	18 49	17 24	17 32	17 39	17 47
62	17 10	17 54	18 46	17 20	17 31	17 41	17 52
60	17 13	17 55	18 43	17 17	17 30	17 43	17 56
N 58	17 16	17 55	18 40	17 13	17 30	17 45	18 01
56	17 18	17 55	18 38	17 11	17 29	17 46	18 04
54	17 21	17 56	18 37	17 08	17 28	17 48	18 07
52	17 23	17 56	18 35	17 06	17 28	17 49	18 10
50	17 25	17 57	18 34	17 04	17 27	17 50	18 13
45	17 29	17 58	18 32	16 59	17 26	17 53	18 19
N 40	17 32	17 59	18 30	16 55	17 25	17 55	18 24
35	17 35	18 00	18 30	16 52	17 25	17 57	18 28
30	17 38	18 02	18 29	16 49	17 24	17 58	18 32
20	17 43	18 05	18 30	16 44	17 23	18 01	18 39
N 10	17 47	18 08	18 32	16 40	17 22	18 03	18 44
0	17 51	18 12	18 36	16 35	17 21	18 06	18 50
S 10	17 55	18 16	18 41	16 31	17 20	18 08	18 55
20	18 00	18 22	18 48	16 26	17 19	18 10	19 01
30	18 05	18 29	18 58	16 21	17 18	18 13	19 08
35	18 08	18 34	19 04	16 18	17 17	18 15	19 12
40	18 12	18 39	19 12	16 14	17 16	18 17	19 16
45	18 16	18 46	19 22	16 10	17 15	18 19	19 21
S 50	18 21	18 54	19 34	16 05	17 14	18 21	19 27
52	18 24	18 58	19 40	16 03	17 13	18 22	19 30
54	18 26	19 03	19 47	16 00	17 13	18 24	19 33
56	18 29	19 08	19 55	15 58	17 12	18 25	19 37
58	18 32	19 13	20 04	15 54	17 11	18 27	19 41
S 60	18 36	19 19	20 15	15 51	17 10	18 28	19 45

	SUN Eqn. of Time 00h	12h	Mer. Pass.	MOON Mer. Pass. Upper	Lower	Age	Phase
Day	m s	m s	h m	h m	h m	d	%
7	11 55	12 04	11 48	10 24	22 47	28	4
8	12 12	12 21	11 48	11 10	23 33	29	1
9	12 29	12 37	11 47	11 55	24 17	00	0

UT	ARIES GHA	VENUS −4.5 GHA	Dec	MARS +0.6 GHA	Dec	JUPITER −2.9 GHA	Dec	SATURN −0.1 GHA	Dec	STARS Name	SHA	Dec
10 00	18 09.3	225 13.2	N 8 45.7	113 44.3	S25 08.0	348 01.5	N10 38.2	334 04.3	N14 04.3	Acamar	315 26.0	S40 18.3
01	33 11.8	240 13.7	45.3	128 44.8	08.1	3 04.2	38.1	349 06.9	04.3	Achernar	335 34.1	S57 14.3
02	48 14.3	255 14.2	45.0	143 45.3	08.2	18 07.0	38.0	4 09.6	04.2	Acrux	173 21.9	S63 05.6
03	63 16.7	270 14.7 ..	44.6	158 45.8 ..	08.2	33 09.8 ..	37.8	19 12.2 ..	04.2	Adhara	255 20.9	S28 58.1
04	78 19.2	285 15.2	44.3	173 46.4	08.3	48 12.5	37.7	34 14.8	04.1	Aldebaran	291 01.4	N16 30.5
05	93 21.6	300 15.7	43.9	188 46.9	08.3	63 15.3	37.6	49 17.4	04.1			
06	108 24.1	315 16.2	N 8 43.5	203 47.4	S25 08.4	78 18.0	N10 37.5	64 20.1	N14 04.0	Alioth	166 30.6	N55 57.8
07	123 26.6	330 16.7	43.2	218 47.9	08.5	93 20.8	37.4	79 22.7	04.0	Alkaid	153 07.8	N49 19.1
08	138 29.0	345 17.2	42.8	233 48.4	08.5	108 23.6	37.3	94 25.3	03.9	Al Na'ir	27 56.8	S46 57.9
S 09	153 31.5	0 17.7 ..	42.5	248 48.9 ..	08.6	123 26.3 ..	37.2	109 27.9 ..	03.9	Alnilam	275 57.1	S 1 12.1
U 10	168 34.0	15 18.2	42.1	263 49.4	08.6	138 29.1	37.1	124 30.5	03.8	Alphard	218 06.7	S 8 39.3
N 11	183 36.4	30 18.7	41.8	278 49.9	08.7	153 31.9	37.0	139 33.2	03.8			
D 12	198 38.9	45 19.2	N 8 41.4	293 50.4	S25 08.7	168 34.6	N10 36.8	154 35.8	N14 03.7	Alphecca	126 20.3	N26 43.2
A 13	213 41.4	60 19.7	41.0	308 50.9	08.8	183 37.4	36.7	169 38.4	03.7	Alpheratz	357 54.2	N29 05.4
Y 14	228 43.8	75 20.2	40.7	323 51.4	08.9	198 40.2	36.6	184 41.0	03.6	Altair	62 18.6	N 8 52.3
15	243 46.3	90 20.7 ..	40.3	338 51.9 ..	08.9	213 42.9 ..	36.5	199 43.7 ..	03.6	Ankaa	353 25.8	S42 18.5
16	258 48.7	105 21.2	39.9	353 52.4	09.0	228 45.7	36.4	214 46.3	03.5	Antares	112 39.6	S26 25.8
17	273 51.2	120 21.7	39.6	8 52.9	09.0	243 48.5	36.3	229 48.9	03.5			
18	288 53.7	135 22.1	N 8 39.2	23 53.4	S25 09.1	258 51.2	N10 36.2	244 51.5	N14 03.4	Arcturus	146 05.8	N19 11.3
19	303 56.1	150 22.6	38.8	38 53.9	09.1	273 54.0	36.1	259 54.1	03.4	Atria	107 51.3	S69 01.7
20	318 58.6	165 23.1	38.5	53 54.4	09.2	288 56.8	36.0	274 56.8	03.3	Avior	234 22.5	S59 30.2
21	334 01.1	180 23.6 ..	38.1	68 54.9 ..	09.2	303 59.5 ..	35.8	289 59.4 ..	03.3	Bellatrix	278 43.3	N 6 21.0
22	349 03.5	195 24.1	37.7	83 55.4	09.3	319 02.3	35.7	305 02.0	03.2	Betelgeuse	271 12.7	N 7 24.4
23	4 06.0	210 24.6	37.4	98 55.9	09.3	334 05.1	35.6	320 04.6	03.2			
11 00	19 08.5	225 25.0	N 8 37.0	113 56.4	S25 09.4	349 07.9	N10 35.5	335 07.3	N14 03.1	Canopus	264 00.8	S52 41.5
01	34 10.9	240 25.5	36.6	128 56.9	09.4	4 10.6	35.4	350 09.9	03.1	Capella	280 50.0	N45 59.7
02	49 13.4	255 26.0	36.2	143 57.4	09.5	19 13.4	35.3	5 12.5	03.0	Deneb	49 38.6	N45 17.1
03	64 15.9	270 26.5 ..	35.9	158 57.9 ..	09.5	34 16.2 ..	35.2	20 15.1 ..	03.0	Denebola	182 44.8	N14 34.6
04	79 18.3	285 26.9	35.5	173 58.4	09.6	49 18.9	35.1	35 17.8	02.9	Diphda	349 06.2	S17 59.3
05	94 20.8	300 27.4	35.1	188 58.9	09.6	64 21.7	35.0	50 20.4	02.9			
06	109 23.2	315 27.9	N 8 34.7	203 59.4	S25 09.7	79 24.5	N10 34.8	65 23.0	N14 02.8	Dubhe	194 05.3	N61 45.1
07	124 25.7	330 28.4	34.4	218 59.9	09.7	94 27.2	34.7	80 25.6	02.8	Elnath	278 25.9	N28 36.3
08	139 28.2	345 28.8	34.0	234 00.4	09.8	109 30.0	34.6	95 28.3	02.7	Eltanin	90 51.3	N51 29.7
M 09	154 30.6	0 29.3 ..	33.6	249 00.9 ..	09.8	124 32.8 ..	34.5	110 30.9 ..	02.7	Enif	33 57.4	N 9 52.6
O 10	169 33.1	15 29.8	33.2	264 01.4	09.9	139 35.5	34.4	125 33.5	02.6	Fomalhaut	15 35.4	S29 37.5
N 11	184 35.6	30 30.2	32.8	279 01.9	09.9	154 38.3	34.3	140 36.1	02.6			
D 12	199 38.0	45 30.7	N 8 32.5	294 02.4	S25 10.0	169 41.1	N10 34.2	155 38.8	N14 02.5	Gacrux	172 13.4	S57 06.5
A 13	214 40.5	60 31.1	32.1	309 02.9	10.0	184 43.8	34.1	170 41.4	02.5	Gienah	176 03.6	S17 32.2
Y 14	229 43.0	75 31.6	31.7	324 03.4	10.0	199 46.6	34.0	185 44.0	02.4	Hadar	149 03.7	S60 22.2
15	244 45.4	90 32.1 ..	31.3	339 03.9 ..	10.1	214 49.4 ..	33.8	200 46.6 ..	02.4	Hamal	328 12.5	N23 27.6
16	259 47.9	105 32.5	30.9	354 04.4	10.1	229 52.2	33.7	215 49.3	02.3	Kaus Aust.	83 58.0	S34 23.1
17	274 50.3	120 33.0	30.5	9 04.9	10.2	244 54.9	33.6	230 51.9	02.2			
18	289 52.8	135 33.4	N 8 30.1	24 05.4	S25 10.2	259 57.7	N10 33.5	245 54.5	N14 02.2	Kochab	137 20.7	N74 09.7
19	304 55.3	150 33.9	29.7	39 05.9	10.3	275 00.5	33.4	260 57.2	02.1	Markab	13 48.7	N15 12.3
20	319 57.7	165 34.3	29.3	54 06.4	10.3	290 03.2	33.3	275 59.8	02.1	Menkar	314 25.9	N 4 05.3
21	335 00.2	180 34.8 ..	29.0	69 06.9 ..	10.3	305 06.0 ..	33.2	291 02.4 ..	02.0	Menkent	148 20.6	S36 21.9
22	350 02.7	195 35.2	28.6	84 07.4	10.4	320 08.8	33.1	306 05.0	02.0	Miaplacidus	221 42.3	S69 42.7
23	5 05.1	210 35.7	28.2	99 07.9	10.4	335 11.5	32.9	321 07.7	01.9			
12 00	20 07.6	225 36.1	N 8 27.8	114 08.4	S25 10.5	350 14.3	N10 32.8	336 10.3	N14 01.9	Mirfak	308 55.2	N49 51.5
01	35 10.1	240 36.6	27.4	129 08.9	10.5	5 17.1	32.7	351 12.9	01.8	Nunki	76 11.5	S26 17.8
02	50 12.5	255 37.0	27.0	144 09.4	10.6	20 19.9	32.6	6 15.5	01.8	Peacock	53 35.8	S56 44.3
03	65 15.0	270 37.5 ..	26.6	159 09.9 ..	10.6	35 22.6 ..	32.5	21 18.2 ..	01.7	Pollux	243 40.8	N28 01.5
04	80 17.5	285 37.9	26.2	174 10.4	10.6	50 25.4	32.4	36 20.8	01.7	Procyon	245 10.9	N 5 13.6
05	95 19.9	300 38.4	25.8	189 10.9	10.7	65 28.2	32.3	51 23.4	01.6			
06	110 22.4	315 38.8	N 8 25.4	204 11.4	S25 10.7	80 30.9	N10 32.2	66 26.0	N14 01.6	Rasalhague	96 16.5	N12 33.9
07	125 24.8	330 39.2	25.0	219 11.9	10.7	95 33.7	32.0	81 28.7	01.5	Regulus	207 55.1	N11 58.2
T 08	140 27.3	345 39.7	24.6	234 12.4	10.8	110 36.5	31.9	96 31.3	01.5	Rigel	281 22.1	S 8 12.1
U 09	155 29.8	0 40.1 ..	24.2	249 12.8 ..	10.8	125 39.3 ..	31.8	111 33.9 ..	01.4	Rigil Kent.	140 07.0	S60 49.9
E 10	170 32.2	15 40.6	23.8	264 13.3	10.9	140 42.0	31.7	126 36.6	01.4	Sabik	102 24.9	S15 43.3
S 11	185 34.7	30 41.0	23.4	279 13.8	10.9	155 44.8	31.6	141 39.2	01.3			
D 12	200 37.2	45 41.4	N 8 23.0	294 14.3	S25 10.9	170 47.6	N10 31.5	156 41.8	N14 01.3	Schedar	349 52.1	N56 32.2
A 13	215 39.6	60 41.9	22.6	309 14.8	11.0	185 50.4	31.4	171 44.4	01.2	Shaula	96 36.6	S37 06.2
Y 14	230 42.1	75 42.3	22.1	324 15.3	11.0	200 53.1	31.3	186 47.1	01.2	Sirius	258 43.1	S16 42.8
15	245 44.6	90 42.7 ..	21.7	339 15.8 ..	11.0	215 55.9 ..	31.1	201 49.7 ..	01.1	Spica	158 42.8	S11 09.4
16	260 47.0	105 43.1	21.3	354 16.3	11.1	230 58.7	31.0	216 52.3	01.1	Suhail	223 00.5	S43 25.6
17	275 49.5	120 43.6	20.9	9 16.8	11.1	246 01.4	30.9	231 55.0	01.0			
18	290 52.0	135 44.0	N 8 20.5	24 17.3	S25 11.1	261 04.2	N10 30.8	246 57.6	N14 00.9	Vega	80 46.2	N38 47.4
19	305 54.4	150 44.4	20.1	39 17.8	11.2	276 07.0	30.7	262 00.2	00.9	Zuben'ubi	137 17.5	S16 02.2
20	320 56.9	165 44.8	19.7	54 18.3	11.2	291 09.8	30.6	277 02.8	00.8		SHA	Mer. Pass.
21	335 59.3	180 45.3 ..	19.3	69 18.8 ..	11.2	306 12.5 ..	30.5	292 05.5 ..	00.8			
22	351 01.8	195 45.7	18.8	84 19.3	11.3	321 15.3	30.4	307 08.1	00.7	Venus	206 16.6	8 58
23	6 04.3	210 46.1	18.4	99 19.7	11.3	336 18.1	30.2	322 10.7	00.7	Mars	94 48.0	16 24
Mer. Pass. 22 39.7		v 0.5	d 0.4	v 0.5	d 0.0	v 2.8	d 0.1	v 2.6	d 0.1	Jupiter	329 59.4	0 43
										Saturn	315 58.8	1 39

UT	SUN		MOON				Lat.	Twilight		Sunrise	Moonrise			
	GHA	Dec	GHA	v	Dec	d	HP		Naut.	Civil		10	11	12	13
d h	° ′	° ′	° ′	′	° ′	′	′	°	h m	h m	h m	h m	h m	h m	h m
10 00	183 11.5	S 6 23.2	175 49.5	14.1	S 4 12.9	10.6	55.3	N 72	04 35	05 54	07 02	07 42	09 27	11 18	13 26
01	198 11.6	24.2	190 22.6	14.2	4 23.5	10.7	55.3	N 70	04 41	05 52	06 54	07 33	09 11	10 50	12 32
02	213 11.8	25.1	204 55.8	14.2	4 34.2	10.6	55.3	68	04 46	05 51	06 47	07 27	08 58	10 29	12 00
03	228 12.0 ..	26.1	219 29.0	14.1	4 44.8	10.6	55.3	66	04 50	05 49	06 41	07 21	08 47	10 13	11 37
04	243 12.2	27.0	234 02.1	14.2	4 55.4	10.5	55.3	64	04 53	05 48	06 36	07 16	08 38	09 59	11 18
05	258 12.3	28.0	248 35.3	14.2	5 05.9	10.5	55.2	62	04 56	05 47	06 32	07 12	08 31	09 48	11 03
06	273 12.5	S 6 28.9	263 08.5	14.2	S 5 16.4	10.5	55.2	60	04 58	05 46	06 28	07 09	08 24	09 39	10 50
07	288 12.7	29.9	277 41.7	14.2	5 26.9	10.5	55.2	N 58	05 00	05 45	06 25	07 05	08 19	09 30	10 40
08	303 12.8	30.8	292 14.9	14.2	5 37.4	10.4	55.2	56	05 02	05 45	06 22	07 03	08 14	09 23	10 30
S 09	318 13.0 ..	31.8	306 48.1	14.2	5 47.8	10.4	55.2	54	05 03	05 44	06 19	07 00	08 09	09 17	10 22
U 10	333 13.2	32.7	321 21.3	14.2	5 58.2	10.4	55.1	52	05 04	05 43	06 17	06 58	08 05	09 11	10 14
N 11	348 13.3	33.7	335 54.5	14.2	6 08.6	10.4	55.1	50	05 05	05 42	06 15	06 56	08 01	09 05	10 08
D 12	3 13.5	S 6 34.6	350 27.7	14.2	S 6 19.0	10.3	55.1	45	05 06	05 40	06 10	06 51	07 53	08 54	09 53
A 13	18 13.7	35.6	5 00.9	14.2	6 29.3	10.2	55.1	N 40	05 07	05 39	06 06	06 48	07 47	08 45	09 42
Y 14	33 13.8	36.5	19 34.1	14.2	6 39.5	10.3	55.1	35	05 07	05 37	06 02	06 44	07 41	08 37	09 32
15	48 14.0 ..	37.5	34 07.3	14.2	6 49.8	10.2	55.1	30	05 07	05 35	05 59	06 42	07 36	08 30	09 23
16	63 14.2	38.4	48 40.5	14.2	7 00.0	10.1	55.0	20	05 06	05 31	05 53	06 37	07 27	08 18	09 08
17	78 14.3	39.4	63 13.7	14.2	7 10.1	10.2	55.0	N 10	05 03	05 27	05 48	06 33	07 20	08 07	08 55
18	93 14.5	S 6 40.3	77 46.9	14.2	S 7 20.3	10.0	55.0	0	04 59	05 23	05 44	06 29	07 13	07 57	08 43
19	108 14.6	41.3	92 20.1	14.2	7 30.3	10.1	55.0	S 10	04 53	05 17	05 39	06 25	07 06	07 48	08 31
20	123 14.8	42.2	106 53.3	14.2	7 40.4	10.0	55.0	20	04 45	05 11	05 33	06 21	06 59	07 37	08 18
21	138 15.0 ..	43.2	121 26.5	14.1	7 50.4	10.0	55.0	30	04 34	05 03	05 27	06 16	06 50	07 26	08 03
22	153 15.1	44.1	135 59.6	14.2	8 00.4	9.9	54.9	35	04 28	04 58	05 23	06 13	06 45	07 19	07 55
23	168 15.3	45.0	150 32.8	14.2	8 10.3	9.9	54.9	40	04 09	04 52	05 19	06 10	06 40	07 11	07 45
								45	04 09	04 45	05 15	06 07	06 34	07 02	07 34
11 00	183 15.5	S 6 46.0	165 06.0	14.2	S 8 20.2	9.8	54.9	S 50	03 55	04 35	05 09	06 03	06 26	06 52	07 20
01	198 15.6	46.9	179 39.2	14.1	8 30.0	9.8	54.9	52	03 49	04 31	05 06	06 01	06 23	06 47	07 14
02	213 15.8	47.9	194 12.3	14.2	8 39.8	9.8	54.9	54	03 41	04 26	05 03	05 59	06 19	06 41	07 07
03	228 16.0 ..	48.8	208 45.5	14.1	8 49.6	9.7	54.9	56	03 33	04 21	05 00	05 57	06 15	06 35	06 59
04	243 16.1	49.8	223 18.6	14.2	8 59.3	9.7	54.8	58	03 23	04 15	04 56	05 54	06 10	06 29	06 50
05	258 16.3	50.7	237 51.8	14.1	9 09.0	9.6	54.8	S 60	03 12	04 08	04 52	05 51	06 05	06 21	06 40
06	273 16.4	S 6 51.7	252 24.9	14.1	S 9 18.6	9.6	54.8	Lat.	Sunset	Twilight		Moonset			
07	288 16.6	52.6	266 58.0	14.1	9 28.2	9.5	54.8			Civil	Naut.	10	11	12	13
08	303 16.8	53.6	281 31.1	14.2	9 37.7	9.5	54.8	°	h m	h m	h m	h m	h m	h m	h m
M 09	318 16.9 ..	54.5	296 04.3	14.1	9 47.2	9.5	54.8	N 72	16 29	17 38	18 56	17 14	17 01	16 43	16 11
O 10	333 17.1	55.4	310 37.4	14.0	9 56.7	9.4	54.7	N 70	16 38	17 40	18 50	17 25	17 19	17 13	17 05
N 11	348 17.3	56.4	325 10.4	14.1	10 06.1	9.3	54.7	68	16 45	17 41	18 45	17 33	17 34	17 35	17 38
D 12	3 17.4	S 6 57.3	339 43.5	14.1	S10 15.4	9.3	54.7	66	16 51	17 43	18 42	17 41	17 45	17 52	18 02
A 13	18 17.6	58.3	354 16.6	14.0	10 24.7	9.3	54.7	64	16 56	17 44	18 39	17 47	17 55	18 06	18 21
Y 14	33 17.7	6 59.2	8 49.6	14.1	10 34.0	9.1	54.7	62	17 00	17 45	18 36	17 52	18 04	18 18	18 37
15	48 17.9	7 00.2	23 22.7	14.0	10 43.1	9.2	54.7	60	17 04	17 46	18 34	17 56	18 11	18 28	18 50
16	63 18.1	01.1	37 55.7	14.0	10 52.3	9.1	54.7	N 58	17 08	17 47	18 32	18 01	18 18	18 37	19 01
17	78 18.2	02.0	52 28.7	14.0	11 01.4	9.0	54.6	56	17 11	17 48	18 31	18 04	18 23	18 45	19 11
18	93 18.4	S 7 03.0	67 01.7	14.0	S11 10.4	9.0	54.6	54	17 13	17 49	18 30	18 07	18 29	18 52	19 20
19	108 18.5	03.9	81 34.7	14.0	11 19.4	8.9	54.6	52	17 16	17 50	18 29	18 10	18 33	18 58	19 27
20	123 18.7	04.9	96 07.7	14.0	11 28.3	8.9	54.6	50	17 18	17 51	18 28	18 13	18 37	19 04	19 35
21	138 18.9 ..	05.8	110 40.7	13.9	11 37.2	8.8	54.6	45	17 23	17 53	18 27	18 19	18 47	19 16	19 50
22	153 19.0	06.8	125 13.6	14.0	11 46.0	8.8	54.6	N 40	17 27	17 55	18 26	18 24	18 54	19 27	20 02
23	168 19.2	07.7	139 46.6	13.9	11 54.8	8.7	54.6	35	17 31	17 56	18 26	18 28	19 01	19 35	20 13
12 00	183 19.3	S 7 08.6	154 19.5	13.9	S12 03.5	8.7	54.5	30	17 34	17 58	18 26	18 32	19 07	19 43	20 22
01	198 19.5	09.6	168 52.4	13.9	12 12.2	8.6	54.5	20	17 40	18 02	18 28	18 39	19 17	19 57	20 38
02	213 19.7	10.5	183 25.3	13.9	12 20.8	8.5	54.5	N 10	17 45	18 06	18 31	18 44	19 26	20 08	20 52
03	228 19.8 ..	11.5	197 58.2	13.8	12 29.3	8.5	54.5	0	17 50	18 11	18 35	18 50	19 34	20 19	21 05
04	243 20.0	12.4	212 31.0	13.9	12 37.8	8.4	54.5	S 10	17 55	18 16	18 41	18 55	19 43	20 30	21 18
05	258 20.1	13.3	227 03.9	13.8	12 46.2	8.4	54.5	20	18 01	18 23	18 49	19 01	19 52	20 42	21 32
06	273 20.3	S 7 14.3	241 36.7	13.8	S12 54.6	8.3	54.5	30	18 07	18 31	19 00	19 08	20 02	20 56	21 48
07	288 20.4	15.2	256 09.5	13.8	13 02.9	8.3	54.5	35	18 11	18 37	19 07	19 12	20 08	21 03	21 58
08	303 20.6	16.2	270 42.3	13.8	13 11.2	8.1	54.4	40	18 15	18 43	19 15	19 16	20 15	21 12	22 09
T 09	318 20.8 ..	17.1	285 15.1	13.8	13 19.3	8.2	54.4	45	18 20	18 50	19 26	19 21	20 23	21 23	22 21
U 10	333 20.9	18.1	299 47.9	13.7	13 27.5	8.0	54.4	S 50	18 26	18 59	19 40	19 27	20 32	21 36	22 37
E 11	348 21.1	19.0	314 20.6	13.7	13 35.5	8.0	54.4	52	18 29	19 04	19 47	19 30	20 37	21 41	22 44
S 12	3 21.2	S 7 19.9	328 53.3	13.7	S13 43.5	8.0	54.4	54	18 32	19 09	19 54	19 33	20 42	21 48	22 52
D 13	18 21.4	20.9	343 26.0	13.7	13 51.5	7.8	54.4	56	18 35	19 14	20 03	19 37	20 47	21 55	23 01
A 14	33 21.5	21.8	357 58.7	13.7	13 59.3	7.9	54.4	58	18 39	19 20	20 13	19 41	20 53	22 04	23 11
Y 15	48 21.7 ..	22.7	12 31.4	13.6	14 07.2	7.7	54.4	S 60	18 43	19 28	20 24	19 45	21 00	22 13	23 23
16	63 21.9	23.7	27 04.0	13.6	14 14.9	7.5	54.4								
17	78 22.0	24.6	41 36.6	13.6	14 22.6	7.6	54.3			SUN			MOON		
18	93 22.2	S 7 25.6	56 09.2	13.6	S14 30.2	7.5	54.3	Day	Eqn. of Time		Mer.	Mer. Pass.		Age	Phase
19	108 22.3	26.5	70 41.8	13.6	14 37.7	7.5	54.3		00ʰ	12ʰ	Pass.	Upper	Lower		
20	123 22.5	27.4	85 14.4	13.5	14 45.2	7.4	54.3	d	m s	m s	h m	h m	h m	d	%
21	138 22.6 ..	28.4	99 46.9	13.5	14 52.6	7.4	54.3	10	12 46	12 54	11 47	12 39	00 17	01	1
22	153 22.8	29.3	114 19.4	13.5	15 00.0	7.3	54.3	11	13 02	13 09	11 47	13 24	01 01	02	4
23	168 22.9	30.3	128 51.9	13.5	S15 07.3	7.2	54.3	12	13 17	13 25	11 47	14 08	01 46	03	9
	SD 16.0	d 0.9	SD 15.0		14.9		14.8									

UT	ARIES GHA	VENUS −4.5 GHA	Dec	MARS +0.6 GHA	Dec	JUPITER −2.9 GHA	Dec	SATURN −0.1 GHA	Dec	STARS Name	SHA	Dec
13 00	21 06.7	225 46.5	N 8 18.0	114 20.2	S25 11.3	351 20.9	N10 30.1	337 13.4	N14 00.6	Acamar	315 26.0	S40 18.3
01	36 09.2	240 46.9	17.6	129 20.7	11.4	6 23.6	30.0	352 16.0	00.6	Achernar	335 34.1	S57 14.3
02	51 11.7	255 47.4	17.2	144 21.2	11.4	21 26.4	29.9	7 18.6	00.5	Acrux	173 21.9	S63 05.6
03	66 14.1	270 47.8 ..	16.7	159 21.7 ..	11.4	36 29.2 ..	29.8	22 21.3 ..	00.5	Adhara	255 20.8	S28 58.1
04	81 16.6	285 48.2	16.3	174 22.2	11.4	51 31.9	29.7	37 23.9	00.4	Aldebaran	291 01.4	N16 30.5
05	96 19.1	300 48.6	15.9	189 22.7	11.5	66 34.7	29.6	52 26.5	00.4			
06	111 21.5	315 49.0	N 8 15.5	204 23.2	S25 11.5	81 37.5	N10 29.5	67 29.1	N14 00.3	Alioth	166 30.6	N55 57.8
07	126 24.0	330 49.4	15.1	219 23.7	11.5	96 40.3	29.3	82 31.8	00.3	Alkaid	153 07.8	N49 19.1
08	141 26.4	345 49.8	14.6	234 24.2	11.6	111 43.0	29.2	97 34.4	00.2	Al Na'ir	27 56.8	S46 57.9
09	156 28.9	0 50.3 ..	14.2	249 24.6 ..	11.6	126 45.8 ..	29.1	112 37.0 ..	00.2	Alnilam	275 57.0	S 1 12.1
10	171 31.4	15 50.7	13.8	264 25.1	11.6	141 48.6	29.0	127 39.7	00.1	Alphard	218 06.7	S 8 39.3
11	186 33.8	30 51.1	13.4	279 25.6	11.6	156 51.4	28.9	142 42.3	00.1			
12	201 36.3	45 51.5	N 8 12.9	294 26.1	S25 11.7	171 54.1	N10 28.8	157 44.9	N14 00.0	Alphecca	126 20.3	N26 43.2
13	216 38.8	60 51.9	12.5	309 26.6	11.7	186 56.9	28.7	172 47.6	13 59.9	Alpheratz	357 54.2	N29 05.4
14	231 41.2	75 52.3	12.1	324 27.1	11.7	201 59.7	28.6	187 50.2	59.9	Altair	62 18.6	N 8 52.3
15	246 43.7	90 52.7 ..	11.6	339 27.6 ..	11.7	217 02.5 ..	28.4	202 52.8 ..	59.8	Ankaa	353 25.8	S42 18.5
16	261 46.2	105 53.1	11.2	354 28.1	11.8	232 05.2	28.3	217 55.5	59.8	Antares	112 39.6	S26 25.8
17	276 48.6	120 53.5	10.8	9 28.5	11.8	247 08.0	28.2	232 58.1	59.7			
18	291 51.1	135 53.9	N 8 10.3	24 29.0	S25 11.8	262 10.8	N10 28.1	248 00.7	N13 59.7	Arcturus	146 05.8	N19 11.3
19	306 53.6	150 54.3	09.9	39 29.5	11.8	277 13.6	28.0	263 03.3	59.6	Atria	107 51.4	S69 01.7
20	321 56.0	165 54.7	09.5	54 30.0	11.9	292 16.3	27.9	278 06.0	59.6	Avior	234 22.5	S59 30.2
21	336 58.5	180 55.1 ..	09.0	69 30.5 ..	11.9	307 19.1 ..	27.8	293 08.6 ..	59.5	Bellatrix	278 43.3	N 6 21.0
22	352 00.9	195 55.5	08.6	84 31.0	11.9	322 21.9	27.6	308 11.2	59.5	Betelgeuse	271 12.7	N 7 24.4
23	7 03.4	210 55.8	08.1	99 31.5	11.9	337 24.7	27.5	323 13.9	59.4			
14 00	22 05.9	225 56.2	N 8 07.7	114 32.0	S25 11.9	352 27.4	N10 27.4	338 16.5	N13 59.4	Canopus	264 00.7	S52 41.5
01	37 08.3	240 56.6	07.3	129 32.4	12.0	7 30.2	27.3	353 19.1	59.3	Capella	280 49.9	N45 59.7
02	52 10.8	255 57.0	06.8	144 32.9	12.0	22 33.0	27.2	8 21.8	59.3	Deneb	49 38.6	N45 17.1
03	67 13.3	270 57.4 ..	06.4	159 33.4 ..	12.0	37 35.8 ..	27.1	23 24.4 ..	59.2	Denebola	182 44.8	N14 34.6
04	82 15.7	285 57.8	05.9	174 33.9	12.0	52 38.6	27.0	38 27.0	59.2	Diphda	349 06.2	S17 59.3
05	97 18.2	300 58.2	05.5	189 34.4	12.0	67 41.3	26.8	53 29.7	59.1			
06	112 20.7	315 58.6	N 8 05.0	204 34.9	S25 12.1	82 44.1	N10 26.7	68 32.3	N13 59.0	Dubhe	194 05.2	N61 45.1
07	127 23.1	330 58.9	04.6	219 35.4	12.1	97 46.9	26.6	83 34.9	59.0	Elnath	278 25.9	N28 36.3
08	142 25.6	345 59.3	04.2	234 35.8	12.1	112 49.7	26.5	98 37.6	58.9	Eltanin	90 51.3	N51 29.7
09	157 28.1	0 59.7 ..	03.7	249 36.3 ..	12.1	127 52.4 ..	26.4	113 40.2 ..	58.9	Enif	33 57.4	N 9 52.6
10	172 30.5	16 00.1	03.3	264 36.8	12.1	142 55.2	26.3	128 42.8	58.8	Fomalhaut	15 35.4	S29 37.5
11	187 33.0	31 00.5	02.8	279 37.3	12.1	157 58.0	26.2	143 45.5	58.8			
12	202 35.4	46 00.9	N 8 02.4	294 37.8	S25 12.2	173 00.8	N10 26.0	158 48.1	N13 58.7	Gacrux	172 13.4	S57 06.5
13	217 37.9	61 01.2	01.9	309 38.3	12.2	188 03.5	25.9	173 50.7	58.7	Gienah	176 03.6	S17 32.2
14	232 40.4	76 01.6	01.4	324 38.7	12.2	203 06.3	25.8	188 53.4	58.6	Hadar	149 03.7	S60 22.2
15	247 42.8	91 02.0 ..	01.0	339 39.2 ..	12.2	218 09.1 ..	25.7	203 56.0 ..	58.6	Hamal	328 12.5	N23 27.7
16	262 45.3	106 02.4	00.5	354 39.7	12.2	233 11.9	25.6	218 58.6	58.5	Kaus Aust.	83 58.0	S34 23.1
17	277 47.8	121 02.7	8 00.1	9 40.2	12.2	248 14.7	25.5	234 01.3	58.5			
18	292 50.2	136 03.1	N 7 59.6	24 40.7	S25 12.2	263 17.4	N10 25.4	249 03.9	N13 58.4	Kochab	137 20.7	N74 09.7
19	307 52.7	151 03.5	59.2	39 41.2	12.3	278 20.2	25.3	264 06.5	58.4	Markab	13 48.7	N15 12.3
20	322 55.2	166 03.8	58.7	54 41.6	12.3	293 23.0	25.1	279 09.2	58.3	Menkar	314 25.9	N 4 05.3
21	337 57.6	181 04.2 ..	58.3	69 42.1 ..	12.3	308 25.8 ..	25.0	294 11.8 ..	58.2	Menkent	148 20.6	S36 21.9
22	353 00.1	196 04.6	57.8	84 42.6	12.3	323 28.5	24.9	309 14.4	58.2	Miaplacidus	221 42.3	S69 42.7
23	8 02.5	211 04.9	57.3	99 43.1	12.3	338 31.3	24.8	324 17.1	58.1			
15 00	23 05.0	226 05.3	N 7 56.9	114 43.6	S25 12.3	353 34.1	N10 24.7	339 19.7	N13 58.1	Mirfak	308 55.2	N49 51.5
01	38 07.5	241 05.7	56.4	129 44.0	12.3	8 36.9	24.6	354 22.3	58.0	Nunki	76 11.6	S26 17.8
02	53 09.9	256 06.0	55.9	144 44.5	12.3	23 39.7	24.5	9 25.0	58.0	Peacock	53 35.8	S56 44.3
03	68 12.4	271 06.4 ..	55.5	159 45.0 ..	12.3	38 42.4 ..	24.3	24 27.6 ..	57.9	Pollux	243 40.8	N28 01.5
04	83 14.9	286 06.8	55.0	174 45.5	12.3	53 45.2	24.2	39 30.2	57.9	Procyon	245 10.9	N 5 13.6
05	98 17.3	301 07.1	54.5	189 46.0	12.4	68 48.0	24.1	54 32.9	57.8			
06	113 19.8	316 07.5	N 7 54.1	204 46.4	S25 12.4	83 50.8	N10 24.0	69 35.5	N13 57.8	Rasalhague	96 16.5	N12 33.9
07	128 22.3	331 07.8	53.6	219 46.9	12.4	98 53.6	23.9	84 38.2	57.7	Regulus	207 55.0	N11 58.2
08	143 24.7	346 08.2	53.1	234 47.4	12.4	113 56.3	23.8	99 40.3	57.7	Rigel	281 22.1	S 8 12.1
09	158 27.2	1 08.5 ..	52.7	249 47.9 ..	12.4	128 59.1 ..	23.6	114 43.4 ..	57.6	Rigil Kent.	140 07.0	S60 49.9
10	173 29.7	16 08.9	52.2	264 48.4	12.4	144 01.9	23.5	129 46.1	57.5	Sabik	102 25.0	S15 43.3
11	188 32.1	31 09.2	51.7	279 48.8	12.4	159 04.7	23.4	144 48.7	57.5			
12	203 34.6	46 09.6	N 7 51.3	294 49.3	S25 12.4	174 07.4	N10 23.3	159 51.3	N13 57.4	Schedar	349 52.1	N56 32.2
13	218 37.0	61 10.0	50.8	309 49.8	12.4	189 10.2	23.2	174 54.0	57.4	Shaula	96 36.6	S37 06.2
14	233 39.5	76 10.3	50.3	324 50.3	12.4	204 13.0	23.1	189 56.6	57.3	Sirius	258 43.1	S16 42.8
15	248 42.0	91 10.6 ..	49.8	339 50.8 ..	12.4	219 15.8 ..	23.0	204 59.2 ..	57.3	Spica	158 42.8	S11 09.4
16	263 44.4	106 11.0	49.4	354 51.2	12.4	234 18.6	22.8	220 01.9	57.2	Suhail	223 00.4	S43 25.6
17	278 46.9	121 11.3	48.9	9 51.7	12.4	249 21.3	22.7	235 04.5	57.2			
18	293 49.4	136 11.7	N 7 48.4	24 52.2	S25 12.4	264 24.1	N10 22.6	250 07.1	N13 57.1	Vega	80 46.3	N38 47.4
19	308 51.8	151 12.0	47.9	39 52.7	12.4	279 26.9	22.5	265 09.8	57.1	Zuben'ubi	137 17.5	S16 02.2
20	323 54.3	166 12.4	47.4	54 53.1	12.4	294 29.7	22.4	280 12.4	57.0		SHA	Mer. Pass.
21	338 56.8	181 12.7 ..	47.0	69 53.6 ..	12.4	309 32.5 ..	22.3	295 15.1 ..	57.0		° '	h m
22	353 59.2	196 13.1	46.5	84 54.1	12.4	324 35.2	22.2	310 17.7	56.9	Venus	203 50.4	8 56
23	9 01.7	211 13.4	46.0	99 54.6	12.4	339 38.0	22.0	325 20.3	56.8	Mars	92 26.1	16 21
	h m									Jupiter	330 21.6	0 30
Mer. Pass.	22 27.9	v 0.4	d 0.5	v 0.5	d 0.0	v 2.8	d 0.1	v 2.6	d 0.1	Saturn	316 10.6	1 27

Left day labels: 13 WEDNESDAY, 14 THURSDAY, 15 FRIDAY

UT	SUN		MOON					Lat.	Twilight		Sunrise	Moonrise			
	GHA	Dec	GHA	v	Dec	d	HP		Naut.	Civil		13	14	15	16
d h	° ′	° ′	° ′	′	° ′	′	′	N 72	h m 04 49	h m 06 07	h m 07 17	h m 13 26	h m ▬▬	h m ▬▬	h m ▬▬
13 00	183 23.1	S 7 31.2	143 24.4	13.5	S15 14.5	7.1	54.3	N 70	04 53	06 04	07 06	12 32	14 22	▬▬	▬▬
01	198 23.2	32.1	157 56.9	13.4	15 21.6	7.1	54.3	68	04 57	06 01	06 58	12 00	13 29	14 49	15 48
02	213 23.4	33.1	172 29.3	13.4	15 28.7	7.0	54.3	66	05 00	05 59	06 51	11 37	12 56	14 07	15 03
03	228 23.6	.. 34.0	187 01.7	13.4	15 35.7	6.9	54.3	64	05 02	05 57	06 45	11 18	12 33	13 39	14 33
04	243 23.7	34.9	201 34.1	13.4	15 42.6	6.9	54.2	62	05 04	05 55	06 40	11 03	12 14	13 17	14 11
05	258 23.9	35.9	216 06.5	13.3	15 49.5	6.8	54.2	60	05 05	05 53	06 36	10 50	11 58	13 00	13 53
06	273 24.0	S 7 36.8	230 38.8	13.3	S15 56.3	6.7	54.2	N 58	05 07	05 52	06 32	10 40	11 45	12 45	13 37
W 07	288 24.2	37.8	245 11.1	13.3	16 03.0	6.6	54.2	56	05 08	05 51	06 28	10 30	11 34	12 33	13 25
E 08	303 24.3	38.7	259 43.4	13.3	16 09.6	6.6	54.2	54	05 08	05 49	06 25	10 22	11 24	12 22	13 13
D 09	318 24.5	.. 39.6	274 15.7	13.2	16 16.2	6.5	54.2	52	05 09	05 48	06 22	10 14	11 15	12 12	13 03
N 10	333 24.6	40.6	288 47.9	13.3	16 22.7	6.4	54.2	50	05 09	05 47	06 19	10 08	11 07	12 03	12 55
E 11	348 24.8	41.5	303 20.2	13.2	16 29.1	6.4	54.2	45	05 10	05 44	06 14	09 53	10 51	11 45	12 36
S 12	3 24.9	S 7 42.4	317 52.4	13.2	S16 35.5	6.3	54.2	N 40	05 10	05 42	06 09	09 42	10 37	11 30	12 20
D 13	18 25.1	43.4	332 24.6	13.1	16 41.8	6.2	54.2	35	05 10	05 39	06 05	09 32	10 26	11 18	12 08
A 14	33 25.2	44.3	346 56.7	13.2	16 48.0	6.1	54.2	30	05 09	05 37	06 01	09 23	10 15	11 07	11 56
Y 15	48 25.4	.. 45.2	1 28.9	13.1	16 54.1	6.0	54.2	20	05 06	05 32	05 54	09 08	09 58	10 48	11 37
16	63 25.5	46.2	16 01.0	13.1	17 00.1	6.0	54.2	N 10	05 03	05 27	05 48	08 55	09 43	10 32	11 20
17	78 25.7	47.1	30 33.1	13.0	17 06.1	5.9	54.2	0	04 58	05 22	05 43	08 43	09 29	10 16	11 04
18	93 25.8	S 7 48.0	45 05.1	13.1	S17 12.0	5.8	54.2	S 10	04 51	05 16	05 37	08 31	09 15	10 01	10 49
19	108 26.0	49.0	59 37.2	13.0	17 17.8	5.8	54.2	20	04 42	05 09	05 31	08 18	09 00	09 45	10 32
20	123 26.1	49.9	74 09.2	13.0	17 23.6	5.6	54.1	30	04 31	04 59	05 24	08 03	08 43	09 26	10 13
21	138 26.3	.. 50.8	88 41.2	13.0	17 29.2	5.6	54.1	35	04 23	04 54	05 20	07 55	08 33	09 16	10 02
22	153 26.4	51.8	103 13.2	12.9	17 34.8	5.5	54.1	40	04 14	04 47	05 15	07 45	08 22	09 03	09 49
23	168 26.6	52.7	117 45.1	12.9	17 40.3	5.5	54.1	45	04 03	04 39	05 09	07 34	08 09	08 49	09 34
14 00	183 26.7	S 7 53.6	132 17.0	12.9	S17 45.8	5.3	54.1	S 50	03 48	04 29	05 02	07 20	07 53	08 31	09 15
01	198 26.9	54.6	146 48.9	12.9	17 51.1	5.3	54.1	52	03 41	04 24	04 59	07 14	07 45	08 22	09 06
02	213 27.0	55.5	161 20.8	12.8	17 56.4	5.2	54.1	54	03 33	04 19	04 56	07 07	07 37	08 13	08 57
03	228 27.2	.. 56.4	175 52.6	12.9	18 01.6	5.1	54.1	56	03 24	04 13	04 52	06 59	07 27	08 02	08 45
04	243 27.3	57.4	190 24.5	12.8	18 06.7	5.0	54.1	58	03 13	04 06	04 48	06 50	07 17	07 50	08 33
05	258 27.5	58.3	204 56.3	12.8	18 11.7	4.9	54.1	S 60	03 01	03 58	04 43	06 40	07 05	07 36	08 18
06	273 27.6	S 7 59.2	219 28.1	12.7	S18 16.6	4.9	54.1								

07	288 27.8	8 00.2	233 59.8	12.7	18 21.5	4.8	54.1	Lat.	Sunset	Twilight		Moonset			
T 08	303 27.9	01.1	248 31.5	12.7	18 26.3	4.7	54.1			Civil	Naut.	13	14	15	16
H 09	318 28.0	.. 02.0	263 03.2	12.7	18 31.0	4.6	54.1	°	h m	h m	h m	h m	h m	h m	h m
U 10	333 28.2	03.0	277 34.9	12.7	18 35.6	4.5	54.1	N 72	16 14	17 23	18 41	16 11	▬▬	▬▬	▬▬
R 11	348 28.3	03.9	292 06.6	12.6	18 40.1	4.4	54.1	N 70	16 24	17 26	18 37	17 05	16 51	▬▬	▬▬
S 12	3 28.5	S 8 04.8	306 38.2	12.6	S18 44.5	4.4	54.1	68	16 33	17 29	18 33	17 38	17 46	18 04	18 45
D 13	18 28.6	05.8	321 09.8	12.6	18 48.9	4.3	54.1	66	16 40	17 32	18 31	18 02	18 18	18 46	19 30
A 14	33 28.8	06.7	335 41.4	12.6	18 53.2	4.2	54.1	64	16 46	17 34	18 29	18 21	18 43	19 14	20 00
Y 15	48 28.9	.. 07.6	350 13.0	12.5	18 57.4	4.1	54.1	62	16 51	17 36	18 27	18 37	19 02	19 36	20 22
16	63 29.1	08.6	4 44.5	12.5	19 01.5	4.0	54.1	60	16 55	17 37	18 25	18 50	19 18	19 54	20 40
17	78 29.2	09.5	19 16.0	12.5	19 05.5	3.9	54.1								
18	93 29.4	S 8 10.4	33 47.5	12.5	S19 09.4	3.9	54.1	N 58	17 00	17 39	18 24	19 01	19 31	20 09	20 56
19	108 29.5	11.3	48 19.0	12.5	19 13.3	3.7	54.1	56	17 03	17 41	18 23	19 11	19 42	20 21	21 08
20	123 29.6	12.3	62 50.5	12.4	19 17.0	3.7	54.1	54	17 06	17 42	18 23	19 20	19 53	20 32	21 20
21	138 29.8	.. 13.2	77 21.9	12.4	19 20.7	3.6	54.1	52	17 09	17 43	18 22	19 27	20 02	20 42	21 30
22	153 29.9	14.1	91 53.3	12.4	19 24.3	3.5	54.1	50	17 12	17 44	18 22	19 35	20 10	20 51	21 38
23	168 30.1	15.1	106 24.7	12.3	19 27.8	3.4	54.1	45	17 18	17 47	18 21	19 50	20 27	21 09	21 57
15 00	183 30.2	S 8 16.0	120 56.0	12.4	S19 31.2	3.3	54.1	N 40	17 23	17 50	18 21	20 02	20 41	21 24	22 12
01	198 30.4	16.9	135 27.4	12.3	19 34.5	3.2	54.1	35	17 27	17 53	18 22	20 13	20 53	21 37	22 25
02	213 30.5	17.8	149 58.7	12.3	19 37.7	3.2	54.1	30	17 31	17 55	18 23	20 22	21 03	21 48	22 36
03	228 30.6	.. 18.8	164 30.0	12.2	19 40.9	3.0	54.1	20	17 38	18 00	18 25	20 38	21 21	22 07	22 56
04	243 30.8	19.7	179 01.2	12.3	19 43.9	3.0	54.1	N 10	17 44	18 05	18 29	20 52	21 37	22 24	23 12
05	258 30.9	20.6	193 32.5	12.2	19 46.9	2.8	54.1	0	17 49	18 10	18 35	21 05	21 52	22 40	23 28
06	273 31.1	S 8 21.6	208 03.7	12.2	S19 49.7	2.8	54.1	S 10	17 55	18 17	18 41	21 18	22 07	22 55	23 44
07	288 31.2	22.5	222 34.9	12.2	19 52.5	2.7	54.1	20	18 02	18 24	18 50	21 32	22 22	23 12	24 00
08	303 31.4	23.4	237 06.1	12.2	19 55.2	2.6	54.2	30	18 09	18 33	19 02	21 48	22 40	23 31	24 19
F 09	318 31.5	.. 24.3	251 37.3	12.1	19 57.8	2.5	54.2	35	18 13	18 39	19 10	21 58	22 51	23 42	24 30
R 10	333 31.6	25.3	266 08.4	12.1	20 00.3	2.5	54.2	40	18 18	18 46	19 19	22 09	23 03	23 55	24 43
I 11	348 31.8	26.2	280 39.5	12.1	20 02.8	2.3	54.2	45	18 24	18 54	19 31	22 21	23 17	24 10	00 10
D 12	3 31.9	S 8 27.1	295 10.6	12.1	S20 05.1	2.2	54.2	S 50	18 31	19 05	19 46	22 37	23 35	24 28	00 28
A 13	18 32.1	28.0	309 41.7	12.1	20 07.3	2.2	54.2	52	18 34	19 09	19 53	22 44	23 43	24 37	00 37
Y 14	33 32.2	29.0	324 12.8	12.0	20 09.5	2.0	54.2	54	18 38	19 15	20 01	22 52	23 52	24 47	00 47
15	48 32.3	.. 29.9	338 43.8	12.0	20 11.5	2.0	54.2	56	18 41	19 21	20 11	23 01	24 02	00 02	00 58
16	63 32.5	30.8	353 14.8	12.0	20 13.5	1.8	54.2	58	18 46	19 28	20 21	23 11	24 14	00 14	01 10
17	78 32.6	31.7	7 45.8	12.0	20 15.3	1.8	54.2	S 60	18 51	19 36	20 34	23 23	24 28	00 28	01 25

18	93 32.8	S 8 32.7	22 16.8	12.0	S20 17.1	1.7	54.2		SUN			MOON			
19	108 32.9	33.6	36 47.8	11.9	20 18.8	1.6	54.2	Day	Eqn. of Time		Mer.	Mer. Pass.		Age	Phase
20	123 33.0	34.5	51 18.7	11.9	20 20.4	1.5	54.2		00ʰ	12ʰ	Pass.	Upper	Lower		
21	138 33.2	.. 35.4	65 49.6	12.0	20 21.9	1.4	54.2	d	m s	m s	h m	h m	h m	d	%
22	153 33.3	36.4	80 20.6	11.8	20 23.3	1.3	54.2	13	13 32	13 39	11 46	14 54	02 31	04	15
23	168 33.4	S20 24.6	94 51.4	11.9	S20 24.6	1.2	54.3	14	13 47	13 54	11 46	15 40	03 17	05	22
	SD 16.1	d 0.9	SD 14.8		14.7		14.8	15	14 01	14 07	11 46	16 28	04 04	06	30

UT	ARIES GHA	VENUS −4.5 GHA	Dec	MARS +0.7 GHA	Dec	JUPITER −2.9 GHA	Dec	SATURN −0.1 GHA	Dec	STARS Name	SHA	Dec
d h 16 00	24 04.2	226 13.7	N 7 45.5	114 55.1	S25 12.4	354 40.8	N10 21.9	340 23.0	N13 56.8	Acamar	315 26.0	S40 18.3
01	39 06.6	241 14.1	45.0	129 55.5	12.4	9 43.6	21.8	355 25.6	56.7	Achernar	335 34.1	S57 14.3
02	54 09.1	256 14.4	44.5	144 56.0	12.4	24 46.4	21.7	10 28.2	56.7	Acrux	173 21.9	S63 05.6
03	69 11.5	271 14.8	.. 44.1	159 56.5	.. 12.4	39 49.1	.. 21.6	25 30.9	.. 56.6	Adhara	255 20.8	S28 58.1
04	84 14.0	286 15.1	43.6	174 57.0	12.4	54 51.9	21.5	40 33.5	56.6	Aldebaran	291 01.4	N16 30.5
05	99 16.5	301 15.4	43.1	189 57.4	12.4	69 54.7	21.4	55 36.2	56.5			
06	114 18.9	316 15.8	N 7 42.6	204 57.9	S25 12.4	84 57.5	N10 21.2	70 38.8	N13 56.5	Alioth	166 30.6	N55 57.8
07	129 21.4	331 16.1	42.1	219 58.4	12.4	100 00.3	21.1	85 41.4	56.4	Alkaid	153 07.8	N49 19.1
S 08	144 23.9	346 16.4	41.6	234 58.9	12.4	115 03.0	21.0	100 44.1	56.4	Al Na'ir	27 56.8	S46 57.9
A 09	159 26.3	1 16.8	.. 41.1	249 59.3	.. 12.4	130 05.8	.. 20.9	115 46.7	.. 56.3	Alnilam	275 57.0	S 1 12.1
T 10	174 28.8	16 17.1	40.6	264 59.8	12.4	145 08.6	20.8	130 49.3	56.3	Alphard	218 06.7	S 8 39.3
U 11	189 31.3	31 17.4	40.1	280 00.3	12.4	160 11.4	20.7	145 52.0	56.2			
R 12	204 33.7	46 17.7	N 7 39.6	295 00.8	S25 12.4	175 14.2	N10 20.5	160 54.6	N13 56.1	Alphecca	126 20.3	N26 43.2
D 13	219 36.2	61 18.1	39.1	310 01.2	12.4	190 17.0	20.4	175 57.3	56.1	Alpheratz	357 54.2	N29 05.4
A 14	234 38.7	76 18.4	38.6	325 01.7	12.4	205 19.7	20.3	190 59.9	56.0	Altair	62 18.6	N 8 52.3
Y 15	249 41.1	91 18.7	.. 38.2	340 02.2	.. 12.4	220 22.5	.. 20.2	206 02.5	.. 56.0	Ankaa	353 25.8	S42 18.5
16	264 43.6	106 19.0	37.7	355 02.7	12.4	235 25.3	20.1	221 05.2	55.9	Antares	112 39.6	S26 25.8
17	279 46.0	121 19.4	37.2	10 03.1	12.4	250 28.1	20.0	236 07.8	55.9			
18	294 48.5	136 19.7	N 7 36.7	25 03.6	S25 12.4	265 30.9	N10 19.9	251 10.4	N13 55.8	Arcturus	146 05.8	N19 11.3
19	309 51.0	151 20.0	36.2	40 04.1	12.4	280 33.6	19.7	266 13.1	55.8	Atria	107 51.4	S69 01.7
20	324 53.4	166 20.3	35.7	55 04.6	12.4	295 36.4	19.6	281 15.7	55.7	Avior	234 22.5	S59 30.2
21	339 55.9	181 20.6	.. 35.2	70 05.0	.. 12.3	310 39.2	.. 19.5	296 18.4	.. 55.7	Bellatrix	278 43.3	N 6 21.0
22	354 58.4	196 21.0	34.6	85 05.5	12.3	325 42.0	19.4	311 21.0	55.6	Betelgeuse	271 12.7	N 7 24.4
23	10 00.8	211 21.3	34.1	100 06.0	12.3	340 44.8	19.3	326 23.6	55.5			
17 00	25 03.3	226 21.6	N 7 33.6	115 06.5	S25 12.3	355 47.6	N10 19.2	341 26.3	N13 55.5	Canopus	264 00.7	S52 41.5
01	40 05.8	241 21.9	33.1	130 06.9	12.3	10 50.3	19.0	356 28.9	55.4	Capella	280 49.9	N45 59.7
02	55 08.2	256 22.2	32.6	145 07.4	12.3	25 53.1	18.9	11 31.6	55.4	Deneb	49 38.6	N45 17.1
03	70 10.7	271 22.5	.. 32.1	160 07.9	.. 12.3	40 55.9	.. 18.8	26 34.2	.. 55.3	Denebola	182 44.8	N14 34.6
04	85 13.1	286 22.8	31.6	175 08.3	12.3	55 58.7	18.7	41 36.8	55.3	Diphda	349 06.2	S17 59.3
05	100 15.6	301 23.2	31.1	190 08.8	12.3	71 01.5	18.6	56 39.5	55.2			
06	115 18.1	316 23.5	N 7 30.6	205 09.3	S25 12.2	86 04.2	N10 18.5	71 42.1	N13 55.2	Dubhe	194 05.2	N61 45.1
07	130 20.5	331 23.8	30.1	220 09.8	12.2	101 07.0	18.4	86 44.8	55.1	Elnath	278 25.9	N28 36.3
08	145 23.0	346 24.1	29.6	235 10.2	12.2	116 09.8	18.2	101 47.4	55.1	Eltanin	90 51.3	N51 29.7
S 09	160 25.5	1 24.4	.. 29.1	250 10.7	.. 12.2	131 12.6	.. 18.1	116 50.0	.. 55.0	Enif	33 57.4	N 9 52.6
U 10	175 27.9	16 24.7	28.5	265 11.2	12.2	146 15.4	18.0	131 52.7	54.9	Fomalhaut	15 35.4	S29 37.5
N 11	190 30.4	31 25.0	28.0	280 11.6	12.2	161 18.2	17.9	146 55.3	54.9			
D 12	205 32.9	46 25.3	N 7 27.5	295 12.1	S25 12.2	176 20.9	N10 17.8	161 58.0	N13 54.8	Gacrux	172 13.4	S57 06.5
A 13	220 35.3	61 25.6	27.0	310 12.6	12.1	191 23.7	17.7	177 00.6	54.8	Gienah	176 03.6	S17 32.2
Y 14	235 37.8	76 25.9	26.5	325 13.0	12.1	206 26.5	17.5	192 03.2	54.7	Hadar	149 03.7	S60 22.2
15	250 40.3	91 26.2	.. 26.0	340 13.5	.. 12.1	221 29.3	.. 17.4	207 05.9	.. 54.7	Hamal	328 12.4	N23 27.7
16	265 42.7	106 26.5	25.4	355 14.0	12.1	236 32.1	17.3	222 08.5	54.6	Kaus Aust.	83 58.1	S34 23.1
17	280 45.2	121 26.8	24.9	10 14.5	12.1	251 34.9	17.2	237 11.2	54.6			
18	295 47.6	136 27.1	N 7 24.4	25 14.9	S25 12.1	266 37.6	N10 17.1	252 13.8	N13 54.5	Kochab	137 20.8	N74 09.6
19	310 50.1	151 27.4	23.9	40 15.4	12.0	281 40.4	17.0	267 16.4	54.5	Markab	13 48.7	N15 12.3
20	325 52.6	166 27.7	23.4	55 15.9	12.0	296 43.2	16.9	282 19.1	54.4	Menkar	314 25.9	N 4 05.3
21	340 55.0	181 28.0	.. 22.8	70 16.3	.. 12.0	311 46.0	.. 16.7	297 21.7	.. 54.3	Menkent	148 20.5	S36 21.9
22	355 57.5	196 28.3	22.3	85 16.8	12.0	326 48.8	16.6	312 24.4	54.3	Miaplacidus	221 42.2	S69 42.6
23	11 00.0	211 28.6	21.8	100 17.3	12.0	341 51.6	16.5	327 27.0	54.2			
18 00	26 02.4	226 28.9	N 7 21.3	115 17.7	S25 11.9	356 54.3	N10 16.4	342 29.6	N13 54.2	Mirfak	308 55.2	N49 51.5
01	41 04.9	241 29.2	20.7	130 18.2	11.9	11 57.1	16.3	357 32.3	54.1	Nunki	76 11.6	S26 17.8
02	56 07.4	256 29.5	20.2	145 18.7	11.9	26 59.9	16.2	12 34.9	54.1	Peacock	53 35.9	S56 44.3
03	71 09.8	271 29.8	.. 19.7	160 19.1	.. 11.9	42 02.7	.. 16.0	27 37.6	.. 54.0	Pollux	243 40.7	N28 01.5
04	86 12.3	286 30.0	19.1	175 19.6	11.9	57 05.5	15.9	42 40.2	54.0	Procyon	245 10.9	N 5 13.6
05	101 14.8	301 30.3	18.6	190 20.1	11.8	72 08.3	15.8	57 42.9	53.9			
06	116 17.2	316 30.6	N 7 18.1	205 20.6	S25 11.8	87 11.0	N10 15.7	72 45.5	N13 53.8	Rasalhague	96 16.5	N12 33.9
07	131 19.7	331 30.9	17.6	220 21.0	11.8	102 13.8	15.6	87 48.1	53.8	Regulus	207 55.0	N11 58.2
08	146 22.1	346 31.2	17.0	235 21.5	11.8	117 16.6	15.5	102 50.8	53.7	Rigel	281 22.1	S 8 12.1
M 09	161 24.6	1 31.5	.. 16.5	250 22.0	.. 11.7	132 19.4	.. 15.3	117 53.4	.. 53.7	Rigil Kent.	140 07.0	S60 49.9
O 10	176 27.1	16 31.8	16.0	265 22.4	11.7	147 22.2	15.2	132 56.1	53.6	Sabik	102 25.0	S15 43.3
N 11	191 29.5	31 32.0	15.4	280 22.9	11.7	162 25.0	15.1	147 58.7	53.6			
D 12	206 32.0	46 32.3	N 7 14.9	295 23.4	S25 11.7	177 27.7	N10 15.0	163 01.3	N13 53.5	Schedar	349 52.1	N56 32.2
A 13	221 34.5	61 32.6	14.3	310 23.8	11.6	192 30.5	14.9	178 04.0	53.5	Shaula	96 36.6	S37 06.2
Y 14	236 36.9	76 32.9	13.8	325 24.3	11.6	207 33.3	14.8	193 06.6	53.4	Sirius	258 43.0	S16 42.8
15	251 39.4	91 33.2	.. 13.3	340 24.8	.. 11.6	222 36.1	.. 14.7	208 09.3	.. 53.3	Spica	158 42.8	S11 09.4
16	266 41.9	106 33.4	12.7	355 25.2	11.6	237 38.9	14.5	223 11.9	53.3	Suhail	223 00.4	S43 25.6
17	281 44.3	121 33.7	12.2	10 25.7	11.5	252 41.7	14.4	238 14.6	53.2			
18	296 46.8	136 34.0	N 7 11.7	25 26.2	S25 11.5	267 44.4	N10 14.3	253 17.2	N13 53.2	Vega	80 46.3	N38 47.4
19	311 49.2	151 34.3	11.1	40 26.6	11.5	282 47.2	14.2	268 19.8	53.1	Zuben'ubi	137 17.5	S16 02.2
20	326 51.7	166 34.5	10.6	55 27.1	11.4	297 50.0	14.1	283 22.5	53.1		SHA	Mer. Pass.
21	341 54.2	181 34.8	.. 10.0	70 27.5	.. 11.4	312 52.8	.. 14.0	298 25.1	.. 53.0		° ′	h m
22	356 56.6	196 35.1	09.5	85 28.0	11.4	327 55.6	13.8	313 27.8	53.0	Venus	201 18.3	8 54
23	11 59.1	211 35.4	08.9	100 28.5	11.4	342 58.4	13.7	328 30.4	52.9	Mars	90 03.2	16 19
	h m									Jupiter	330 44.3	0 17
Mer. Pass. 22 16.1	v 0.3	d 0.5	v 0.5	d 0.0	v 2.8	d 0.1	v 2.6	d 0.1	Saturn	316 23.0	1 14

UT	SUN GHA	SUN Dec	MOON GHA	v	Dec	d	HP
d h	° ′	° ′	° ′	′	° ′	′	′
16 00	183 33.6	S 8 38.2	109 22.3	11.9	S20 25.8	1.1	54.3
01	198 33.7	39.1	123 53.2	11.8	20 26.9	1.0	54.3
02	213 33.9	40.1	138 24.0	11.8	20 27.9	0.9	54.3
03	228 34.0	.. 41.0	152 54.8	11.8	20 28.8	0.9	54.3
04	243 34.1	41.9	167 25.6	11.8	20 29.7	0.7	54.3
05	258 34.3	42.8	181 56.4	11.8	20 30.4	0.7	54.3
06	273 34.4	S 8 43.7	196 27.2	11.8	S20 31.1	0.5	54.3
07	288 34.5	44.7	210 58.0	11.7	20 31.6	0.4	54.3
S 08	303 34.7	45.6	225 28.7	11.7	20 32.0	0.4	54.4
A 09	318 34.8	.. 46.5	239 59.4	11.7	20 32.4	0.3	54.4
T 10	333 34.9	47.4	254 30.1	11.7	20 32.7	0.1	54.4
U 11	348 35.1	48.4	269 00.8	11.7	20 32.8	0.1	54.4
R 12	3 35.2	S 8 49.3	283 31.5	11.7	S20 32.9	0.1	54.4
D 13	18 35.4	50.2	298 02.2	11.6	20 32.8	0.1	54.4
A 14	33 35.5	51.1	312 32.8	11.7	20 32.7	0.2	54.4
Y 15	48 35.6	.. 52.0	327 03.5	11.6	20 32.5	0.3	54.4
16	63 35.8	53.0	341 34.1	11.6	20 32.2	0.4	54.5
17	78 35.9	53.9	356 04.7	11.6	20 31.8	0.6	54.5
18	93 36.0	S 8 54.8	10 35.3	11.6	S20 31.2	0.6	54.5
19	108 36.2	55.7	25 05.9	11.6	20 30.6	0.7	54.5
20	123 36.3	56.6	39 36.5	11.5	20 29.9	0.8	54.5
21	138 36.4	.. 57.6	54 07.0	11.6	20 29.1	0.9	54.5
22	153 36.5	58.5	68 37.6	11.5	20 28.2	1.0	54.5
23	168 36.7	8 59.4	83 08.1	11.5	20 27.2	1.1	54.6
17 00	183 36.8	S 9 00.3	97 38.6	11.6	S20 26.1	1.2	54.6
01	198 36.9	01.2	112 09.2	11.5	20 24.9	1.3	54.6
02	213 37.1	02.1	126 39.7	11.5	20 23.6	1.4	54.6
03	228 37.2	.. 03.1	141 10.2	11.5	20 22.2	1.5	54.6
04	243 37.3	04.0	155 40.7	11.4	20 20.7	1.6	54.7
05	258 37.5	04.9	170 11.1	11.5	20 19.1	1.7	54.7
06	273 37.6	S 9 05.8	184 41.6	11.5	S20 17.4	1.8	54.7
07	288 37.7	06.7	199 12.1	11.4	20 15.6	1.8	54.7
S 08	303 37.9	07.6	213 42.5	11.4	20 13.8	2.0	54.7
U 09	318 38.0	.. 08.6	228 12.9	11.5	20 11.8	2.1	54.7
N 10	333 38.1	09.5	242 43.4	11.4	20 09.7	2.2	54.8
D 11	348 38.2	10.4	257 13.8	11.4	20 07.5	2.3	54.8
A 12	3 38.4	S 9 11.3	271 44.2	11.4	S20 05.2	2.3	54.8
Y 13	18 38.5	12.2	286 14.6	11.4	20 02.9	2.5	54.8
14	33 38.6	13.1	300 45.0	11.4	20 00.4	2.6	54.8
15	48 38.8	.. 14.1	315 15.4	11.4	19 57.8	2.6	54.9
16	63 38.9	15.0	329 45.8	11.4	19 55.2	2.8	54.9
17	78 39.0	15.9	344 16.2	11.4	19 52.4	2.9	54.9
18	93 39.1	S 9 16.8	358 46.6	11.3	S19 49.5	2.9	54.9
19	108 39.3	17.7	13 16.9	11.4	19 46.6	3.1	55.0
20	123 39.4	18.6	27 47.3	11.4	19 43.5	3.2	55.0
21	138 39.5	.. 19.5	42 17.7	11.3	19 40.3	3.2	55.0
22	153 39.6	20.5	56 48.0	11.3	19 37.1	3.4	55.0
23	168 39.8	21.4	71 18.3	11.4	19 33.7	3.4	55.0
18 00	183 39.9	S 9 22.3	85 48.7	11.3	S19 30.3	3.6	55.1
01	198 40.0	23.2	100 19.0	11.4	19 26.7	3.6	55.1
02	213 40.1	24.1	114 49.4	11.3	19 23.1	3.8	55.1
03	228 40.3	.. 24.9	129 19.7	11.3	19 19.3	3.8	55.1
04	243 40.4	25.9	143 50.0	11.3	19 15.5	3.9	55.2
05	258 40.5	26.8	158 20.3	11.3	19 11.6	4.1	55.2
06	273 40.6	S 9 27.8	172 50.6	11.4	S19 07.5	4.1	55.2
07	288 40.8	28.7	187 21.0	11.3	19 03.4	4.2	55.2
M 08	303 40.9	29.6	201 51.3	11.3	18 59.2	4.4	55.3
O 09	318 41.0	.. 30.5	216 21.6	11.3	18 54.8	4.4	55.3
N 10	333 41.1	31.4	230 51.9	11.3	18 50.4	4.5	55.3
D 11	348 41.2	32.3	245 22.2	11.3	18 45.9	4.6	55.3
A 12	3 41.4	S 9 33.2	259 52.5	11.3	S18 41.3	4.7	55.4
Y 13	18 41.5	34.1	274 22.8	11.2	18 36.6	4.9	55.4
14	33 41.6	35.0	288 53.0	11.3	18 31.7	4.9	55.4
15	48 41.8	.. 35.9	303 23.3	11.3	18 26.8	5.0	55.5
16	63 41.9	36.9	317 53.6	11.3	18 21.8	5.0	55.5
17	78 42.0	37.8	332 23.9	11.3	18 16.8	5.2	55.5
18	93 42.1	S 9 38.7	346 54.2	11.3	S18 11.6	5.3	55.5
19	108 42.2	39.6	1 24.5	11.2	18 06.3	5.4	55.6
20	123 42.4	40.5	15 54.7	11.3	18 00.9	5.5	55.6
21	138 42.5	.. 41.4	30 25.0	11.3	17 55.4	5.5	55.6
22	153 42.6	42.3	44 55.3	11.3	17 49.9	5.7	55.7
23	168 42.7	43.2	59 25.6	11.2	S17 44.2	5.8	55.7
	SD 16.1	d 0.9	SD 14.8		14.9		15.1

Lat.	Twilight Naut.	Twilight Civil	Sunrise	Moonrise 16	17	18	19
°	h m	h m	h m	h m	h m	h m	h m
N 72	05 02	06 20	07 32	■■	■■	■■	17 42
N 70	05 05	06 16	07 19	■■	17 45	17 14	17 04
68	05 07	06 12	07 09	15 48	16 19	16 32	16 37
66	05 09	06 08	07 00	15 03	15 40	16 03	16 17
64	05 10	06 05	06 54	14 33	15 13	15 41	16 00
62	05 12	06 03	06 48	14 11	14 52	15 24	15 47
60	05 12	06 01	06 43	13 53	14 35	15 09	15 35
N 58	05 13	05 58	06 38	13 37	14 21	14 56	15 25
56	05 13	05 57	06 34	13 25	14 09	14 46	15 16
54	05 14	05 55	06 31	13 13	13 58	14 36	15 08
52	05 14	05 53	06 27	13 03	13 49	14 28	15 01
50	05 14	05 51	06 24	12 55	13 40	14 20	14 55
45	05 14	05 48	06 18	12 36	13 22	14 04	14 41
N 40	05 13	05 45	06 12	12 20	13 07	13 50	14 30
35	05 12	05 42	06 07	12 08	12 55	13 39	14 20
30	05 11	05 39	06 03	11 56	12 44	13 29	14 11
20	05 07	05 33	05 55	11 37	12 25	13 11	13 57
N 10	05 03	05 27	05 49	11 20	12 09	12 56	13 44
0	04 57	05 21	05 42	11 04	11 53	12 42	13 32
S 10	04 49	05 14	05 36	10 49	11 38	12 28	13 19
20	04 40	05 06	05 29	10 32	11 22	12 13	13 06
30	04 27	04 56	05 20	10 13	11 03	11 56	12 52
35	04 19	04 50	05 16	10 02	10 52	11 46	12 43
40	04 09	04 42	05 10	09 49	10 39	11 34	12 33
45	03 57	04 33	05 04	09 34	10 24	11 21	12 21
S 50	03 41	04 22	04 56	09 15	10 06	11 04	12 07
52	03 33	04 17	04 53	09 06	09 58	10 56	12 01
54	03 24	04 11	04 49	08 57	09 48	10 47	11 53
56	03 14	04 05	04 44	08 45	09 37	10 38	11 45
58	03 03	03 57	04 40	08 33	09 25	10 26	11 36
S 60	02 49	03 49	04 34	08 18	09 10	10 13	11 25

Lat.	Sunset	Twilight Civil	Twilight Naut.	Moonset 16	17	18	19
°	h m	h m	h m	h m	h m	h m	h m
N 72	15 58	17 09	18 27	■■	■■	■■	21 59
N 70	16 10	17 14	18 24	■■	18 30	20 43	22 36
68	16 20	17 18	18 22	18 45	19 56	21 25	23 02
66	16 28	17 21	18 20	19 30	20 34	21 53	23 21
64	16 35	17 24	18 19	20 00	21 01	22 15	23 37
62	16 41	17 27	18 18	20 22	21 22	22 32	23 50
60	16 47	17 29	18 17	20 40	21 38	22 46	24 01
N 58	16 51	17 31	18 17	20 56	21 52	22 58	24 11
56	16 56	17 33	18 16	21 08	22 04	23 09	24 19
54	16 59	17 35	18 16	21 20	22 15	23 18	24 26
52	17 03	17 37	18 16	21 30	22 24	23 26	24 33
50	17 06	17 39	18 16	21 38	22 33	23 33	24 39
45	17 13	17 42	18 16	21 57	22 51	23 49	24 52
N 40	17 18	17 46	18 17	22 12	23 05	24 02	00 02
35	17 23	17 49	18 18	22 25	23 17	24 13	00 13
30	17 28	17 52	18 20	22 36	23 28	24 22	00 22
20	17 35	17 58	18 23	22 56	23 46	24 39	00 39
N 10	17 42	18 03	18 27	23 12	24 02	00 02	00 53
0	17 49	18 10	18 34	23 28	24 17	00 17	01 06
S 10	17 55	18 17	18 42	23 44	24 32	00 32	01 19
20	18 03	18 25	18 51	24 00	00 00	00 47	01 33
30	18 11	18 35	19 04	24 19	00 19	01 05	01 49
35	18 16	18 42	19 13	24 30	00 30	01 16	01 58
40	18 21	18 49	19 23	24 43	00 43	01 28	02 09
45	18 28	18 58	19 35	00 10	00 58	01 42	02 21
S 50	18 36	19 10	19 52	00 28	01 17	01 59	02 36
52	18 39	19 15	19 59	00 37	01 25	02 07	02 43
54	18 43	19 21	20 08	00 47	01 35	02 16	02 51
56	18 48	19 28	20 19	00 58	01 46	02 26	03 00
58	18 53	19 35	20 31	01 10	01 58	02 38	03 09
S 60	18 58	19 44	20 45	01 25	02 13	02 51	03 20

Day	SUN Eqn. of Time 00h	SUN Eqn. of Time 12h	Mer. Pass.	MOON Mer. Pass. Upper	MOON Mer. Pass. Lower	Age	Phase
d	m s	m s	h m	h m	h m	d	%
16	14 14	14 21	11 46	17 16	04 52	07	39
17	14 27	14 33	11 45	18 05	05 41	08	49
18	14 39	14 45	11 45	18 54	06 30	09	59

UT	ARIES GHA	VENUS −4.5 GHA	Dec	MARS +0.7 GHA	Dec	JUPITER −2.9 GHA	Dec	SATURN −0.1 GHA	Dec	STARS Name	SHA	Dec
19 00	27 01.6	226 35.6	N 7 08.4	115 28.9	S25 11.3	358 01.2	N10 13.6	343 33.1	N13 52.8	Acamar	315 26.0	S40 18.3
01	42 04.0	241 35.9	07.8	130 29.4	11.3	13 03.9	13.5	358 35.7	52.8	Achernar	335 34.1	S57 14.3
02	57 06.5	256 36.2	07.3	145 29.9	11.3	28 06.7	13.4	13 38.3	52.7	Acrux	173 21.9	S63 05.6
03	72 09.0	271 36.4 ..	06.7	160 30.3 ..	11.2	43 09.5 ..	13.3	28 41.0 ..	52.7	Adhara	255 20.8	S28 58.1
04	87 11.4	286 36.7	06.2	175 30.8	11.2	58 12.3	13.1	43 43.6	52.6	Aldebaran	291 01.3	N16 30.5
05	102 13.9	301 37.0	05.6	190 31.3	11.2	73 15.1	13.0	58 46.3	52.6			
06	117 16.4	316 37.2	N 7 05.1	205 31.7	S25 11.1	88 17.9	N10 12.9	73 48.9	N13 52.5	Alioth	166 30.6	N55 57.8
07	132 18.8	331 37.5	04.5	220 32.2	11.1	103 20.6	12.8	88 51.6	52.5	Alkaid	153 07.8	N49 19.1
T 08	147 21.3	346 37.8	04.0	235 32.7	11.1	118 23.4	12.7	103 54.2	52.4	Al Na'ir	27 56.8	S46 57.9
U 09	162 23.7	1 38.0 ..	03.4	250 33.1 ..	11.0	133 26.2 ..	12.6	118 56.9 ..	52.3	Alnilam	275 57.0	S 1 12.1
E 10	177 26.2	16 38.3	02.9	265 33.6	11.0	148 29.0	12.4	133 59.5	52.3	Alphard	218 06.7	S 8 39.3
S 11	192 28.7	31 38.5	02.3	280 34.0	11.0	163 31.8	12.3	149 02.1	52.2			
D 12	207 31.1	46 38.8	N 7 01.8	295 34.5	S25 10.9	178 34.6	N10 12.2	164 04.8	N13 52.2	Alphecca	126 20.3	N26 43.2
A 13	222 33.6	61 39.1	01.2	310 35.0	10.9	193 37.4	12.1	179 07.4	52.1	Alpheratz	357 54.2	N29 05.4
Y 14	237 36.1	76 39.3	00.7	325 35.4	10.8	208 40.1	12.0	194 10.1	52.1	Altair	62 18.6	N 8 52.3
15	252 38.5	91 39.6	7 00.1	340 35.9 ..	10.8	223 42.9 ..	11.9	209 12.7 ..	52.0	Ankaa	353 25.8	S42 18.5
16	267 41.0	106 39.8	6 59.5	355 36.4	10.8	238 45.7	11.8	224 15.4	52.0	Antares	112 39.6	S26 25.8
17	282 43.5	121 40.1	59.0	10 36.8	10.7	253 48.5	11.6	239 18.0	51.9			
18	297 45.9	136 40.3	N 6 58.4	25 37.3	S25 10.7	268 51.3	N10 11.5	254 20.7	N13 51.8	Arcturus	146 05.8	N19 11.3
19	312 48.4	151 40.6	57.8	40 37.7	10.7	283 54.1	11.4	269 23.3	51.8	Atria	107 51.4	S69 01.7
20	327 50.9	166 40.8	57.3	55 38.2	10.6	298 56.9	11.3	284 25.9	51.7	Avior	234 22.4	S59 30.2
21	342 53.3	181 41.1 ..	56.7	70 38.7 ..	10.6	313 59.6 ..	11.2	299 28.6 ..	51.7	Bellatrix	278 43.2	N 6 21.0
22	357 55.8	196 41.3	56.2	85 39.1	10.5	329 02.4	11.1	314 31.2	51.6	Betelgeuse	271 12.7	N 7 24.4
23	12 58.2	211 41.6	55.6	100 39.6	10.5	344 05.2	10.9	329 33.9	51.6			
20 00	28 00.7	226 41.8	N 6 55.0	115 40.1	S25 10.5	359 08.0	N10 10.8	344 36.5	N13 51.5	Canopus	264 00.7	S52 41.5
01	43 03.2	241 42.1	54.5	130 40.5	10.4	14 10.8	10.7	359 39.2	51.5	Capella	280 49.9	N45 59.7
02	58 05.6	256 42.3	53.9	145 41.0	10.4	29 13.6	10.6	14 41.8	51.4	Deneb	49 38.6	N45 17.1
03	73 08.1	271 42.6 ..	53.3	160 41.4 ..	10.3	44 16.4 ..	10.5	29 44.5 ..	51.3	Denebola	182 44.8	N14 34.6
04	88 10.6	286 42.8	52.8	175 41.9	10.3	59 19.1	10.4	44 47.1	51.3	Diphda	349 06.2	S17 59.3
05	103 13.0	301 43.1	52.2	190 42.4	10.2	74 21.9	10.2	59 49.8	51.2			
06	118 15.5	316 43.3	N 6 51.6	205 42.8	S25 10.2	89 24.7	N10 10.1	74 52.4	N13 51.2	Dubhe	194 05.2	N61 45.1
W 07	133 18.0	331 43.6	51.0	220 43.3	10.2	104 27.5	10.0	89 55.0	51.1	Elnath	278 25.9	N28 36.3
E 08	148 20.4	346 43.8	50.5	235 43.7	10.1	119 30.3	09.9	104 57.7	51.1	Eltanin	90 51.3	N51 29.7
D 09	163 22.9	1 44.1 ..	49.9	250 44.2 ..	10.1	134 33.1 ..	09.8	120 00.3 ..	51.0	Enif	33 57.4	N 9 52.6
N 10	178 25.3	16 44.3	49.3	265 44.7	10.0	149 35.9	09.7	135 03.0	50.9	Fomalhaut	15 35.4	S29 37.5
E 11	193 27.8	31 44.5	48.7	280 45.1	10.0	164 38.6	09.5	150 05.6	50.9			
S 12	208 30.3	46 44.8	N 6 48.2	295 45.6	S25 09.9	179 41.4	N10 09.4	165 08.3	N13 50.8	Gacrux	172 13.3	S57 06.5
D 13	223 32.7	61 45.0	47.6	310 46.0	09.9	194 44.2	09.3	180 10.9	50.8	Gienah	176 03.6	S17 32.2
A 14	238 35.2	76 45.2	47.0	325 46.5	09.8	209 47.0	09.2	195 13.6	50.7	Hadar	149 03.7	S60 22.1
Y 15	253 37.7	91 45.5 ..	46.4	340 47.0 ..	09.8	224 49.8 ..	09.1	210 16.2 ..	50.7	Hamal	328 12.4	N23 27.7
16	268 40.1	106 45.7	45.9	355 47.4	09.7	239 52.6	09.0	225 18.9	50.6	Kaus Aust.	83 58.1	S34 23.1
17	283 42.6	121 46.0	45.3	10 47.9	09.7	254 55.4	08.8	240 21.5	50.6			
18	298 45.1	136 46.2	N 6 44.7	25 48.3	S25 09.6	269 58.1	N10 08.7	255 24.2	N13 50.5	Kochab	137 20.8	N74 09.6
19	313 47.5	151 46.4	44.1	40 48.8	09.6	285 00.9	08.6	270 26.8	50.5	Markab	13 48.7	N15 12.4
20	328 50.0	166 46.7	43.5	55 49.3	09.5	300 03.7	08.5	285 29.4	50.4	Menkar	314 25.9	N 4 05.3
21	343 52.5	181 46.9 ..	42.9	70 49.7 ..	09.5	315 06.5 ..	08.4	300 32.1 ..	50.3	Menkent	148 20.5	S36 21.9
22	358 54.9	196 47.1	42.4	85 50.2	09.4	330 09.3	08.3	315 34.7	50.3	Miaplacidus	221 42.2	S69 42.6
23	13 57.4	211 47.3	41.8	100 50.6	09.4	345 12.1	08.1	330 37.4	50.2			
21 00	28 59.8	226 47.6	N 6 41.2	115 51.1	S25 09.3	0 14.9	N10 08.0	345 40.0	N13 50.2	Mirfak	308 55.2	N49 51.5
01	44 02.3	241 47.8	40.6	130 51.5	09.3	15 17.6	07.9	0 42.7	50.1	Nunki	76 11.6	S26 17.8
02	59 04.8	256 48.0	40.0	145 52.0	09.2	30 20.4	07.8	15 45.3	50.0	Peacock	53 35.9	S56 44.3
03	74 07.2	271 48.3 ..	39.4	160 52.5 ..	09.2	45 23.2 ..	07.7	30 48.0 ..	50.0	Pollux	243 40.7	N28 01.5
04	89 09.7	286 48.5	38.8	175 52.9	09.1	60 26.0	07.6	45 50.6	49.9	Procyon	245 10.8	N 5 13.6
05	104 12.2	301 48.7	38.2	190 53.4	09.1	75 28.8	07.4	60 53.3	49.9			
06	119 14.6	316 48.9	N 6 37.6	205 53.8	S25 09.0	90 31.6	N10 07.3	75 55.9	N13 49.8	Rasalhague	96 16.5	N12 33.9
07	134 17.1	331 49.2	37.1	220 54.3	09.0	105 34.4	07.2	90 58.6	49.8	Regulus	207 55.0	N11 58.2
T 08	149 19.6	346 49.4	36.5	235 54.7	08.9	120 37.2	07.1	106 01.2	49.7	Rigel	281 22.1	S 8 12.1
H 09	164 22.0	1 49.6 ..	35.9	250 55.2 ..	08.8	135 39.9 ..	07.0	121 03.9 ..	49.7	Rigil Kent.	140 07.0	S60 49.9
U 10	179 24.5	16 49.8	35.3	265 55.7	08.8	150 42.7	06.9	136 06.5	49.6	Sabik	102 25.0	S15 43.3
R 11	194 27.0	31 50.0	34.7	280 56.1	08.7	165 45.5	06.7	151 09.2	49.5			
S 12	209 29.4	46 50.3	N 6 34.1	295 56.6	S25 08.7	180 48.3	N10 06.6	166 11.8	N13 49.5	Schedar	349 52.1	N56 32.2
D 13	224 31.9	61 50.5	33.5	310 57.0	08.6	195 51.1	06.5	181 14.5	49.4	Shaula	96 36.6	S37 06.2
A 14	239 34.3	76 50.7	32.9	325 57.5	08.6	210 53.9	06.4	196 17.1	49.4	Sirius	258 43.0	S16 42.8
Y 15	254 36.8	91 50.9 ..	32.3	340 57.9 ..	08.5	225 56.7 ..	06.3	211 19.7 ..	49.3	Spica	158 42.8	S11 09.4
16	269 39.3	106 51.1	31.7	355 58.4	08.4	240 59.4	06.2	226 22.4	49.3	Suhail	223 00.4	S43 25.6
17	284 41.7	121 51.3	31.1	10 58.9	08.4	256 02.2	06.0	241 25.0	49.2			
18	299 44.2	136 51.6	N 6 30.5	25 59.3	S25 08.3	271 05.0	N10 05.9	256 27.7	N13 49.1	Vega	80 46.3	N38 47.4
19	314 46.7	151 51.8	29.9	40 59.8	08.3	286 07.8	05.8	271 30.3	49.1	Zuben'ubi	137 17.5	S16 02.2
20	329 49.1	166 52.0	29.3	56 00.2	08.2	301 10.6	05.7	286 33.0	49.0			
21	344 51.6	181 52.2 ..	28.7	71 00.7 ..	08.1	316 13.4 ..	05.6	301 35.6 ..	49.0			
22	359 54.1	196 52.4	28.1	86 01.1	08.1	331 16.2	05.5	316 38.3	48.9			
23	14 56.5	211 52.6	27.5	101 01.6	08.0	346 19.0	05.4	331 40.9	48.9			

										Name	SHA	Mer. Pass.
Mer. Pass. 22 04.3	v 0.2 d 0.6			v 0.5 d 0.0		v 2.8 d 0.1		v 2.6 d 0.1		Venus	198 41.1	8 53
										Mars	87 39.3	16 17
										Jupiter	331 07.3	0 03
										Saturn	316 35.8	1 01

SUN and MOON

UT	SUN GHA	SUN Dec	MOON GHA	v	Dec	d	HP
d h	° ′	° ′	° ′	′	° ′	′	′
19 00	183 42.8	S 9 44.1	73 55.8	11.3	S17 38.4	5.8	55.7
01	198 43.0	45.0	88 26.1	11.3	17 32.6	6.0	55.7
02	213 43.1	45.9	102 56.4	11.3	17 26.6	6.0	55.8
03	228 43.2 ..	46.8	117 26.7	11.2	17 20.6	6.1	55.8
04	243 43.3	47.7	131 56.9	11.3	17 14.5	6.2	55.8
05	258 43.4	48.6	146 27.2	11.3	17 08.3	6.4	55.9
T 06	273 43.6	S 9 49.6	160 57.5	11.2	S17 01.9	6.4	55.9
U 07	288 43.7	50.5	175 27.7	11.3	16 55.5	6.5	55.9
E 08	303 43.8	51.4	189 58.0	11.2	16 49.0	6.6	56.0
S 09	318 43.9 ..	52.3	204 28.2	11.3	16 42.4	6.6	56.0
D 10	333 44.0	53.2	218 58.5	11.3	16 35.8	6.8	56.0
A 11	348 44.1	54.1	233 28.8	11.2	16 29.0	6.9	56.1
Y 12	3 44.3	S 9 55.0	247 59.0	11.3	S16 22.1	6.9	56.1
13	18 44.4	55.9	262 29.3	11.2	16 15.2	7.1	56.1
14	33 44.5	56.8	276 59.5	11.3	16 08.1	7.1	56.2
15	48 44.6 ..	57.7	291 29.8	11.3	16 01.0	7.2	56.2
16	63 44.7	58.6	306 00.1	11.2	15 53.8	7.3	56.2
17	78 44.8	9 59.5	320 30.3	11.3	15 46.5	7.4	56.3
18	93 44.9	S10 00.4	335 00.6	11.2	S15 39.1	7.5	56.3
19	108 45.1	01.3	349 30.8	11.3	15 31.6	7.6	56.3
20	123 45.2	02.2	4 01.1	11.2	15 24.0	7.6	56.4
21	138 45.3 ..	03.1	18 31.3	11.2	15 16.4	7.8	56.4
22	153 45.4	04.0	33 01.5	11.3	15 08.6	7.8	56.4
23	168 45.5	04.9	47 31.8	11.2	15 00.8	7.9	56.5
20 00	183 45.6	S10 05.8	62 02.0	11.3	S14 52.9	8.0	56.5
01	198 45.7	06.7	76 32.3	11.2	14 44.9	8.1	56.5
02	213 45.9	07.6	91 02.5	11.2	14 36.8	8.2	56.6
03	228 46.0 ..	08.5	105 32.7	11.3	14 28.6	8.3	56.6
04	243 46.1	09.4	120 03.0	11.2	14 20.3	8.3	56.6
05	258 46.2	10.3	134 33.2	11.2	14 12.0	8.4	56.7
W 06	273 46.3	S10 11.2	149 03.4	11.3	S14 03.6	8.5	56.7
E 07	288 46.4	12.1	163 33.7	11.2	13 55.1	8.6	56.7
D 08	303 46.5	13.0	178 03.9	11.2	13 46.5	8.7	56.8
N 09	318 46.6 ..	13.9	192 34.1	11.2	13 37.8	8.8	56.8
E 10	333 46.7	14.8	207 04.3	11.2	13 29.0	8.8	56.8
S 11	348 46.9	15.7	221 34.5	11.2	13 20.2	8.9	56.9
D 12	3 47.0	S10 16.6	236 04.7	11.2	S13 11.3	9.0	56.9
A 13	18 47.1	17.5	250 34.9	11.2	13 02.3	9.1	57.0
Y 14	33 47.2	18.4	265 05.1	11.2	12 53.2	9.1	57.0
15	48 47.3 ..	19.3	279 35.3	11.2	12 44.1	9.3	57.0
16	63 47.4	20.2	294 05.5	11.2	12 34.8	9.3	57.1
17	78 47.5	21.1	308 35.7	11.1	12 25.5	9.4	57.1
18	93 47.6	S10 22.0	323 05.8	11.2	S12 16.1	9.4	57.1
19	108 47.7	22.9	337 36.0	11.2	12 06.7	9.5	57.2
20	123 47.8	23.8	352 06.2	11.1	11 57.2	9.7	57.2
21	138 47.9 ..	24.7	6 36.3	11.2	11 47.5	9.6	57.2
22	153 48.1	25.6	21 06.5	11.1	11 37.9	9.8	57.3
23	168 48.2	26.5	35 36.6	11.2	11 28.1	9.8	57.3
21 00	183 48.3	S10 27.3	50 06.8	11.1	S11 18.3	9.9	57.4
01	198 48.4	28.2	64 36.9	11.1	11 08.4	10.0	57.4
02	213 48.6 ..	29.1	79 07.0	11.1	10 58.4	10.1	57.4
03	228 48.6 ..	30.0	93 37.1	11.1	10 48.3	10.1	57.5
04	243 48.7	30.9	108 07.2	11.1	10 38.2	10.2	57.5
05	258 48.8	31.8	122 37.3	11.1	10 28.0	10.2	57.5
T 06	273 48.9	S10 32.7	137 07.4	11.1	S10 17.8	10.3	57.6
H 07	288 49.0	33.6	151 37.5	11.1	10 07.5	10.4	57.6
U 08	303 49.1	34.5	166 07.6	11.0	9 57.1	10.5	57.7
R 09	318 49.2 ..	35.4	180 37.6	11.1	9 46.6	10.5	57.7
S 10	333 49.3	36.3	195 07.7	11.0	9 36.1	10.6	57.7
D 11	348 49.4	37.2	209 37.7	11.0	9 25.5	10.7	57.8
A 12	3 49.5	S10 38.1	224 07.7	11.0	S 9 14.8	10.7	57.8
Y 13	18 49.6	39.0	238 37.7	11.0	9 04.1	10.8	57.9
14	33 49.7	39.8	253 07.7	11.0	8 53.3	10.8	57.9
15	48 49.8 ..	40.7	267 37.7	11.0	8 42.5	10.9	57.9
16	63 49.9	41.6	282 07.7	10.9	8 31.6	11.0	58.0
17	78 50.0	42.5	296 37.6	11.0	8 20.6	11.0	58.0
18	93 50.1	S10 43.4	311 07.6	10.9	S 8 09.6	11.1	58.0
19	108 50.2	44.3	325 37.5	10.9	7 58.5	11.1	58.1
20	123 50.3	45.2	340 07.4	10.9	7 47.4	11.2	58.1
21	138 50.4 ..	46.1	354 37.3	10.9	7 36.2	11.3	58.2
22	153 50.5	47.0	9 07.2	10.8	7 24.9	11.3	58.2
23	168 50.6	47.8	23 37.0	10.9	S 7 13.6	11.4	58.2
	SD 16.1	d 0.9	SD 15.3		15.5		15.8

Twilight / Sunrise / Moonrise

Lat.	Twilight Naut.	Twilight Civil	Sunrise	Moonrise 19	20	21	22
°	h m	h m	h m	h m	h m	h m	h m
N 72	05 15	06 33	07 47	17 42	17 18	17 03	16 50
N 70	05 16	06 27	07 32	17 04	16 57	16 50	16 45
68	05 17	06 22	07 21	16 37	16 39	16 40	16 40
66	05 18	06 18	07 11	16 17	16 26	16 32	16 37
64	05 19	06 14	07 03	16 00	16 14	16 25	16 34
62	05 19	06 11	06 56	15 47	16 04	16 18	16 31
60	05 19	06 08	06 50	15 35	15 56	16 13	16 28
N 58	05 19	06 05	06 45	15 25	15 48	16 08	16 26
56	05 19	06 02	06 41	15 16	15 42	16 04	16 24
54	05 19	06 00	06 36	15 08	15 36	16 00	16 23
52	05 19	05 58	06 33	15 01	15 30	15 57	16 21
50	05 19	05 56	06 29	14 55	15 25	15 53	16 20
45	05 18	05 52	06 21	14 41	15 15	15 46	16 17
N 40	05 16	05 48	06 15	14 30	15 06	15 41	16 14
35	05 15	05 44	06 10	14 20	14 59	15 36	16 12
30	05 13	05 41	06 05	14 11	14 52	15 31	16 10
20	05 08	05 34	05 56	13 57	14 40	15 24	16 06
N 10	05 03	05 27	05 49	13 44	14 30	15 17	16 03
0	04 56	05 21	05 42	13 32	14 21	15 10	16 00
S 10	04 48	05 13	05 34	13 19	14 11	15 04	15 58
20	04 37	05 04	05 26	13 06	14 01	14 57	15 55
30	04 24	04 53	05 17	12 52	13 49	14 49	15 51
35	04 15	04 46	05 12	12 43	13 43	14 45	15 49
40	04 04	04 38	05 06	12 33	13 35	14 40	15 47
45	03 51	04 28	04 59	12 21	13 26	14 34	15 44
S 50	03 34	04 16	04 50	12 07	13 15	14 27	15 41
52	03 25	04 10	04 46	12 01	13 10	14 23	15 40
54	03 16	04 04	04 42	11 53	13 04	14 20	15 38
56	03 05	03 57	04 37	11 45	12 58	14 16	15 36
58	02 52	03 48	04 32	11 36	12 51	14 11	15 35
S 60	02 37	03 39	04 25	11 25	12 43	14 06	15 32

Sunset / Twilight / Moonset

Lat.	Sunset	Twilight Civil	Twilight Naut.	Moonset 19	20	21	22
°	h m	h m	h m	h m	h m	h m	h m
N 72	15 41	16 54	18 13	21 59	24 06	00 06	02 06
N 70	15 56	17 01	18 11	22 36	24 26	00 26	02 16
68	16 08	17 06	18 10	23 02	24 42	00 42	02 24
66	16 17	17 11	18 10	23 21	24 55	00 55	02 31
64	16 25	17 14	18 09	23 37	25 05	01 05	02 37
62	16 32	17 18	18 09	23 50	25 14	01 14	02 42
60	16 38	17 21	18 09	24 01	00 01	01 22	02 46
N 58	16 44	17 24	18 09	24 11	00 11	01 29	02 50
56	16 48	17 26	18 09	24 19	00 19	01 34	02 54
54	16 53	17 29	18 10	24 26	00 26	01 40	02 57
52	16 56	17 31	18 10	24 33	00 33	01 44	02 59
50	17 00	17 33	18 10	24 39	00 39	01 49	03 02
45	17 08	17 37	18 11	24 52	00 52	01 58	03 07
N 40	17 14	17 41	18 13	00 02	01 02	02 06	03 12
35	17 20	17 45	18 15	00 13	01 11	02 12	03 15
30	17 25	17 49	18 17	00 22	01 19	02 18	03 19
20	17 33	17 55	18 21	00 39	01 33	02 28	03 24
N 10	17 41	18 02	18 27	00 53	01 44	02 36	03 29
0	17 48	18 09	18 34	01 06	01 55	02 44	03 34
S 10	17 56	18 17	18 42	01 19	02 06	02 52	03 39
20	18 04	18 26	18 53	01 33	02 18	03 01	03 44
30	18 13	18 38	19 07	01 49	02 31	03 10	03 49
35	18 18	18 45	19 16	01 58	02 38	03 16	03 52
40	18 25	18 53	19 27	02 09	02 47	03 22	03 56
45	18 32	19 03	19 40	02 21	02 57	03 29	04 00
S 50	18 41	19 15	19 58	02 36	03 09	03 38	04 05
52	18 45	19 21	20 06	02 43	03 14	03 42	04 07
54	18 49	19 27	20 16	02 51	03 21	03 46	04 10
56	18 54	19 35	20 27	03 00	03 28	03 51	04 12
58	19 00	19 43	20 40	03 09	03 35	03 56	04 15
S 60	19 06	19 53	20 56	03 20	03 44	04 02	04 18

SUN / MOON

Day	Eqn. of Time 00ʰ	Eqn. of Time 12ʰ	Mer. Pass.	Mer. Pass. Upper	Mer. Pass. Lower	Age	Phase
d	m s	m s	h m	h m	h m	d	%
19	14 51	14 57	11 45	19 43	07 19	10	68
20	15 02	15 08	11 45	20 33	08 08	11	77
21	15 13	15 18	11 45	21 22	08 57	12	86

UT (d h)	ARIES GHA	VENUS −4.4 GHA Dec	MARS +0.7 GHA Dec	JUPITER −2.9 GHA Dec	SATURN −0.2 GHA Dec	STARS Name SHA Dec
22 00	29 59.0	226 52.8 N 6 26.9	116 02.0 S25 08.0	1 21.7 N10 05.2	346 43.6 N13 48.8	Acamar 315 26.0 S40 18.3
01	45 01.4	241 53.0 26.3	131 02.5 07.9	16 24.5 05.1	1 46.2 48.7	Achernar 335 34.1 S57 14.4
02	60 03.9	256 53.2 25.7	146 03.0 07.8	31 27.3 05.0	16 48.9 48.7	Acrux 173 21.9 S63 05.6
03	75 06.4	271 53.5 .. 25.1	161 03.4 .. 07.8	46 30.1 .. 04.9	31 51.5 .. 48.6	Adhara 255 20.8 S28 58.1
04	90 08.8	286 53.7 24.4	176 03.9 07.7	61 32.9 04.8	46 54.2 48.6	Aldebaran 291 01.3 N16 30.5
05	105 11.3	301 53.9 23.8	191 04.3 07.6	76 35.7 04.7	61 56.8 48.5	
06	120 13.8	316 54.1 N 6 23.2	206 04.8 S25 07.6	91 38.5 N10 04.5	76 59.5 N13 48.5	Alioth 166 30.6 N55 57.7
07	135 16.2	331 54.3 22.6	221 05.2 07.5	106 41.2 04.4	92 02.1 48.4	Alkaid 153 07.8 N49 19.0
F 08	150 18.7	346 54.5 22.0	236 05.7 07.4	121 44.0 04.3	107 04.8 48.4	Al Na'ir 27 56.8 S46 57.9
R 09	165 21.2	1 54.7 .. 21.4	251 06.1 .. 07.4	136 46.8 .. 04.2	122 07.4 .. 48.3	Alnilam 275 57.0 S 1 12.1
I 10	180 23.6	16 54.9 20.8	266 06.6 07.3	151 49.6 04.1	137 10.1 48.2	Alphard 218 06.6 S 8 39.3
D 11	195 26.1	31 55.1 20.2	281 07.0 07.2	166 52.4 04.0	152 12.7 48.2	
A 12	210 28.6	46 55.3 N 6 19.5	296 07.5 S25 07.2	181 55.2 N10 03.8	167 15.4 N13 48.1	Alphecca 126 20.4 N26 43.2
Y 13	225 31.0	61 55.5 18.9	311 07.9 07.1	196 58.0 03.7	182 18.0 48.1	Alpheratz 357 54.2 N29 05.4
14	240 33.5	76 55.7 18.3	326 08.4 07.0	212 00.8 03.6	197 20.7 48.0	Altair 62 18.6 N 8 52.3
15	255 35.9	91 55.9 .. 17.7	341 08.9 .. 07.0	227 03.5 .. 03.5	212 23.3 .. 48.0	Ankaa 353 25.8 S42 18.5
16	270 38.4	106 56.1 17.1	356 09.3 06.9	242 06.3 03.4	227 26.0 47.9	Antares 112 39.6 S26 25.7
17	285 40.9	121 56.3 16.5	11 09.8 06.8	257 09.1 03.3	242 28.6 47.8	
18	300 43.3	136 56.5 N 6 15.8	26 10.2 S25 06.8	272 11.9 N10 03.1	257 31.3 N13 47.8	Arcturus 146 05.8 N19 11.2
19	315 45.8	151 56.7 15.2	41 10.7 06.7	287 14.7 03.0	272 33.9 47.7	Atria 107 51.4 S69 01.7
20	330 48.3	166 56.9 14.6	56 11.1 06.6	302 17.5 02.9	287 36.6 47.7	Avior 234 22.4 S59 30.2
21	345 50.7	181 57.1 .. 14.0	71 11.6 .. 06.5	317 20.3 .. 02.8	302 39.2 .. 47.6	Bellatrix 278 43.2 N 6 21.0
22	0 53.2	196 57.2 13.3	86 12.0 06.5	332 23.1 02.7	317 41.9 47.6	Betelgeuse 271 12.6 N 7 24.4
23	15 55.7	211 57.4 12.7	101 12.5 06.4	347 25.8 02.6	332 44.5 47.5	
23 00	30 58.1	226 57.6 N 6 12.1	116 12.9 S25 06.3	2 28.6 N10 02.4	347 47.2 N13 47.4	Canopus 264 00.6 S52 41.5
01	46 00.6	241 57.8 11.5	131 13.4 06.2	17 31.4 02.3	2 49.8 47.4	Capella 280 49.9 N45 59.7
02	61 03.0	256 58.0 10.8	146 13.8 06.2	32 34.2 02.2	17 52.5 47.3	Deneb 49 38.7 N45 17.1
03	76 05.5	271 58.2 .. 10.2	161 14.3 .. 06.1	47 37.0 .. 02.1	32 55.1 .. 47.3	Denebola 182 44.8 N14 34.5
04	91 08.0	286 58.4 09.6	176 14.7 06.0	62 39.8 02.0	47 57.8 47.2	Diphda 349 06.2 S17 59.3
05	106 10.4	301 58.6 09.0	191 15.2 05.9	77 42.6 01.9	63 00.4 47.2	
06	121 12.9	316 58.8 N 6 08.3	206 15.6 S25 05.9	92 45.3 N10 01.7	78 03.1 N13 47.1	Dubhe 194 05.2 N61 45.0
07	136 15.4	331 58.9 07.7	221 16.1 05.8	107 48.1 01.6	93 05.7 47.0	Elnath 278 25.8 N28 36.3
S 08	151 17.8	346 59.1 07.1	236 16.5 05.7	122 50.9 01.5	108 08.4 47.0	Eltanin 90 51.4 N51 29.7
A 09	166 20.3	1 59.3 .. 06.4	251 17.0 .. 05.6	137 53.7 .. 01.4	123 11.0 .. 46.9	Enif 33 57.4 N 9 52.6
T 10	181 22.8	16 59.5 05.8	266 17.4 05.5	152 56.5 01.3	138 13.7 46.9	Fomalhaut 15 35.4 S29 37.5
U 11	196 25.2	31 59.7 05.2	281 17.9 05.5	167 59.3 01.2	153 16.3 46.8	
R 12	211 27.7	46 59.9 N 6 04.5	296 18.3 S25 05.4	183 02.1 N10 01.0	168 19.0 N13 46.8	Gacrux 172 13.3 S57 06.4
D 13	226 30.2	62 00.0 03.9	311 18.8 05.3	198 04.9 00.9	183 21.6 46.7	Gienah 176 03.6 S17 32.2
A 14	241 32.6	77 00.2 03.3	326 19.2 05.2	213 07.6 00.8	198 24.3 46.6	Hadar 149 03.7 S60 22.1
Y 15	256 35.1	92 00.4 .. 02.6	341 19.7 .. 05.2	228 10.4 .. 00.7	213 26.9 .. 46.6	Hamal 328 12.4 N23 27.7
16	271 37.5	107 00.6 02.0	356 20.1 05.1	243 13.2 00.6	228 29.6 46.5	Kaus Aust. 83 58.1 S34 23.1
17	286 40.0	122 00.8 01.4	11 20.6 05.0	258 16.0 00.5	243 32.2 46.5	
18	301 42.5	137 00.9 N 6 00.7	26 21.0 S25 04.9	273 18.8 N10 00.3	258 34.9 N13 46.4	Kochab 137 20.8 N74 09.6
19	316 44.9	152 01.1 6 00.1	41 21.5 04.8	288 21.6 00.2	273 37.5 46.4	Markab 13 48.7 N15 12.4
20	331 47.4	167 01.3 5 59.4	56 21.9 04.8	303 24.4 00.1	288 40.2 46.3	Menkar 314 25.9 N 4 05.3
21	346 49.9	182 01.5 .. 58.8	71 22.4 .. 04.7	318 27.2 10 00.0	303 42.9 .. 46.2	Menkent 148 20.5 S36 21.9
22	1 52.3	197 01.6 58.2	86 22.8 04.6	333 29.9 9 59.9	318 45.5 46.2	Miaplacidus 221 42.2 S69 42.6
23	16 54.8	212 01.8 57.5	101 23.3 04.5	348 32.7 59.8	333 48.2 46.1	
24 00	31 57.3	227 02.0 N 5 56.9	116 23.7 S25 04.4	3 35.5 N 9 59.6	348 50.8 N13 46.1	Mirfak 308 55.1 N49 51.5
01	46 59.7	242 02.2 56.2	131 24.2 04.3	18 38.3 59.5	3 53.5 46.0	Nunki 76 11.6 S26 17.8
02	62 02.2	257 02.3 55.6	146 24.6 04.3	33 41.1 59.4	18 56.1 46.0	Peacock 53 35.9 S56 44.3
03	77 04.6	272 02.5 .. 54.9	161 25.1 .. 04.2	48 43.9 .. 59.3	33 58.8 .. 45.9	Pollux 243 40.7 N28 01.5
04	92 07.1	287 02.7 54.3	176 25.5 04.1	63 46.7 59.2	49 01.4 45.8	Procyon 245 10.8 N 5 13.6
05	107 09.6	302 02.8 53.6	191 26.0 04.0	78 49.4 59.1	64 04.1 45.8	
06	122 12.0	317 03.0 N 5 53.0	206 26.4 S25 03.9	93 52.2 N 9 59.0	79 06.7 N13 45.7	Rasalhague 96 16.5 N12 33.9
07	137 14.5	332 03.2 52.4	221 26.9 03.8	108 55.0 58.8	94 09.4 45.7	Regulus 207 55.0 N11 58.2
S 08	152 17.0	347 03.3 51.7	236 27.3 03.7	123 57.8 58.7	109 12.0 45.6	Rigel 281 22.1 S 8 12.1
U 09	167 19.4	2 03.5 .. 51.1	251 27.8 .. 03.7	139 00.6 .. 58.6	124 14.7 .. 45.6	Rigil Kent. 140 07.0 S60 49.9
N 10	182 21.9	17 03.7 50.4	266 28.2 03.6	154 03.4 58.5	139 17.3 45.5	Sabik 102 25.0 S15 43.3
D 11	197 24.4	32 03.8 49.7	281 28.7 03.5	169 06.2 58.4	154 20.0 45.4	
A 12	212 26.8	47 04.0 N 5 49.1	296 29.1 S25 03.4	184 09.0 N 9 58.3	169 22.6 N13 45.4	Schedar 349 52.1 N56 32.2
Y 13	227 29.3	62 04.2 48.4	311 29.6 03.3	199 11.7 58.1	184 25.3 45.3	Shaula 96 36.6 S37 06.2
14	242 31.8	77 04.3 47.8	326 30.0 03.2	214 14.5 58.0	199 27.9 45.3	Sirius 258 43.0 S16 42.8
15	257 34.2	92 04.5 .. 47.1	341 30.5 .. 03.1	229 17.3 .. 57.9	214 30.6 .. 45.2	Spica 158 42.8 S11 09.4
16	272 36.7	107 04.7 46.5	356 30.9 03.0	244 20.1 57.8	229 33.3 45.2	Suhail 223 00.4 S43 25.6
17	287 39.1	122 04.8 45.8	11 31.4 02.9	259 22.9 57.7	244 35.9 45.1	
18	302 41.6	137 05.0 N 5 45.2	26 31.8 S25 02.8	274 25.7 N 9 57.6	259 38.6 N13 45.0	Vega 80 46.3 N38 47.4
19	317 44.1	152 05.1 44.5	41 32.3 02.8	289 28.5 57.4	274 41.2 45.0	Zuben'ubi 137 17.5 S16 02.2
20	332 46.5	167 05.3 43.9	56 32.7 02.7	304 31.3 57.3	289 43.9 44.9	
21	347 49.0	182 05.5 .. 43.2	71 33.2 .. 02.6	319 34.0 .. 57.2	304 46.5 .. 44.9	
22	2 51.5	197 05.6 42.5	86 33.6 02.5	334 36.8 57.1	319 49.2 44.8	
23	17 53.9	212 05.8 41.9	101 34.1 02.4	349 39.6 57.0	334 51.8 44.8	

	SHA	Mer. Pass.
	° ′	h m
Venus	195 59.5	8 52
Mars	85 14.8	16 15
Jupiter	331 30.5	23 46
Saturn	316 49.1	0 49

| Mer. Pass. 21 52.5 | v 0.2 d 0.6 | v 0.5 d 0.1 | v 2.8 d 0.1 | v 2.7 d 0.1 |

UT	SUN GHA	SUN Dec	MOON GHA	v	Dec	d	HP
d h	° ′	° ′	° ′	′	° ′	′	′
22 00	183 50.7	S10 48.7	38 06.9	10.8	S 7 02.2	11.4	58.3
01	198 50.8	49.6	52 36.7	10.8	6 50.8	11.5	58.3
02	213 50.9	50.5	67 06.5	10.8	6 39.3	11.5	58.3
03	228 51.0	.. 51.4	81 36.3	10.8	6 27.8	11.5	58.4
04	243 51.1	52.3	96 06.1	10.7	6 16.3	11.7	58.4
05	258 51.2	53.2	110 35.8	10.8	6 04.6	11.6	58.5
06	273 51.3	S10 54.1	125 05.6	10.7	S 5 53.0	11.8	58.5
07	288 51.4	54.9	139 35.3	10.7	5 41.2	11.7	58.5
08	303 51.5	55.8	154 05.0	10.6	5 29.5	11.8	58.6
F 09	318 51.6	.. 56.7	168 34.6	10.7	5 17.7	11.9	58.6
R 10	333 51.7	57.6	183 04.3	10.6	5 05.8	11.9	58.6
I 11	348 51.8	58.5	197 33.9	10.6	4 53.9	11.9	58.7
D 12	3 51.9	S10 59.4	212 03.5	10.6	S 4 42.0	12.0	58.7
A 13	18 52.0	11 00.3	226 33.1	10.5	4 30.0	12.1	58.7
Y 14	33 52.1	01.1	241 02.6	10.6	4 17.9	12.0	58.8
15	48 52.2	.. 02.0	255 32.2	10.5	4 05.9	12.1	58.8
16	63 52.3	02.9	270 01.7	10.4	3 53.8	12.2	58.9
17	78 52.4	03.8	284 31.1	10.5	3 41.6	12.1	58.9
18	93 52.5	S11 04.7	299 00.6	10.4	S 3 29.5	12.2	58.9
19	108 52.6	05.6	313 30.0	10.4	3 17.3	12.3	59.0
20	123 52.7	06.4	327 59.4	10.4	3 05.0	12.3	59.0
21	138 52.8	.. 07.3	342 28.8	10.3	2 52.7	12.3	59.0
22	153 52.9	08.2	356 58.1	10.3	2 40.4	12.3	59.1
23	168 53.0	09.1	11 27.4	10.3	2 28.1	12.4	59.1
23 00	183 53.1	S11 10.0	25 56.7	10.2	S 2 15.7	12.4	59.1
01	198 53.2	10.8	40 25.9	10.2	2 03.3	12.4	59.2
02	213 53.2	11.7	54 55.1	10.2	1 50.9	12.5	59.2
03	228 53.3	.. 12.6	69 24.3	10.2	1 38.4	12.4	59.2
04	243 53.4	13.5	83 53.5	10.1	1 26.0	12.5	59.3
05	258 53.5	14.4	98 22.6	10.1	1 13.5	12.6	59.3
06	273 53.6	S11 15.2	112 51.7	10.0	S 1 00.9	12.5	59.3
S 07	288 53.7	16.1	127 20.7	10.0	0 48.4	12.6	59.4
A 08	303 53.8	17.0	141 49.7	10.0	0 35.8	12.5	59.4
T 09	318 53.9	.. 17.9	156 18.7	10.0	0 23.3	12.6	59.4
U 10	333 54.0	18.7	170 47.7	9.9	S 0 10.7	12.6	59.5
R 11	348 54.1	19.6	185 16.6	9.8	N 0 01.9	12.7	59.5
D 12	3 54.2	S11 20.5	199 45.4	9.9	N 0 14.6	12.6	59.5
A 13	18 54.2	21.4	214 14.3	9.8	0 27.2	12.6	59.6
Y 14	33 54.3	22.3	228 43.1	9.7	0 39.8	12.7	59.6
15	48 54.4	.. 23.1	243 11.8	9.7	0 52.5	12.7	59.6
16	63 54.5	24.0	257 40.5	9.7	1 05.2	12.6	59.6
17	78 54.6	24.9	272 09.2	9.7	1 17.8	12.7	59.7
18	93 54.7	S11 25.8	286 37.9	9.6	N 1 30.5	12.7	59.7
19	108 54.8	26.6	301 06.5	9.5	1 43.2	12.7	59.7
20	123 54.9	27.5	315 35.0	9.5	1 55.9	12.7	59.8
21	138 55.0	.. 28.4	330 03.5	9.5	2 08.6	12.7	59.8
22	153 55.1	29.3	344 32.0	9.4	2 21.3	12.7	59.8
23	168 55.1	30.1	359 00.4	9.4	2 34.0	12.7	59.9
24 00	183 55.2	S11 31.0	13 28.8	9.3	N 2 46.7	12.6	59.9
01	198 55.3	31.9	27 57.1	9.3	2 59.3	12.7	59.9
02	213 55.4	32.8	42 25.4	9.3	3 12.0	12.7	59.9
03	228 55.5	.. 33.6	56 53.7	9.2	3 24.7	12.6	60.0
04	243 55.6	34.5	71 21.9	9.2	3 37.3	12.7	60.0
05	258 55.6	35.4	85 50.1	9.1	3 50.0	12.6	60.0
06	273 55.7	S11 36.3	100 18.2	9.0	N 4 02.6	12.7	60.0
07	288 55.8	37.1	114 46.2	9.0	4 15.3	12.6	60.1
08	303 55.9	38.0	129 14.2	9.0	4 27.9	12.6	60.1
S 09	318 56.0	.. 38.9	143 42.2	8.9	4 40.5	12.6	60.1
U 10	333 56.1	39.7	158 10.1	8.9	4 53.1	12.5	60.1
N 11	348 56.1	40.6	172 38.0	8.8	5 05.6	12.6	60.2
D 12	3 56.2	S11 41.5	187 05.8	8.8	N 5 18.2	12.5	60.2
A 13	18 56.3	42.3	201 33.6	8.7	5 30.7	12.5	60.2
Y 14	33 56.4	43.2	216 01.3	8.7	5 43.2	12.4	60.2
15	48 56.5	.. 44.1	230 29.0	8.6	5 55.6	12.5	60.2
16	63 56.5	45.0	244 56.6	8.6	6 08.1	12.4	60.3
17	78 56.6	45.8	259 24.2	8.5	6 20.5	12.4	60.3
18	93 56.7	S11 46.7	273 51.7	8.5	N 6 32.9	12.3	60.3
19	108 56.8	47.6	288 19.2	8.4	6 45.2	12.3	60.3
20	123 56.9	48.4	302 46.6	8.3	6 57.5	12.3	60.3
21	138 56.9	.. 49.3	317 13.9	8.3	7 09.8	12.3	60.4
22	153 57.0	50.2	331 41.2	8.3	7 22.1	12.2	60.4
23	168 57.1	51.0	346 08.5	8.2	N 7 34.3	12.2	60.4
	SD 16.1	d 0.9	SD 16.0		16.2		16.4

Lat.	Twilight Naut.	Twilight Civil	Sunrise	Moonrise 22	23	24	25
°	h m	h m	h m	h m	h m	h m	h m
N 72	05 27	06 47	08 02	16 50	16 38	16 25	16 10
N 70	05 28	06 39	07 46	16 45	16 39	16 33	16 28
68	05 28	06 33	07 32	16 40	16 40	16 40	16 41
66	05 27	06 27	07 22	16 37	16 41	16 46	16 53
64	05 27	06 22	07 12	16 34	16 42	16 51	17 02
62	05 27	06 18	07 05	16 31	16 43	16 56	17 11
60	05 26	06 15	06 58	16 28	16 43	16 59	17 18
N 58	05 26	06 11	06 52	16 26	16 44	17 03	17 24
56	05 25	06 08	06 47	16 24	16 45	17 06	17 30
54	05 24	06 06	06 42	16 23	16 45	17 08	17 35
52	05 24	06 03	06 38	16 21	16 46	17 11	17 39
50	05 23	06 01	06 34	16 20	16 46	17 13	17 43
45	05 21	05 55	06 25	16 17	16 47	17 18	17 52
N 40	05 19	05 51	06 18	16 14	16 48	17 22	18 00
35	05 17	05 47	06 12	16 12	16 48	17 26	18 07
30	05 15	05 43	06 07	16 10	16 49	17 29	18 12
20	05 09	05 35	05 57	16 06	16 50	17 35	18 22
N 10	05 03	05 28	05 49	16 03	16 51	17 40	18 31
0	04 55	05 20	05 41	16 00	16 52	17 45	18 40
S 10	04 46	05 11	05 33	15 58	16 53	17 49	18 48
20	04 35	05 02	05 24	15 55	16 54	17 55	18 57
30	04 20	04 49	05 14	15 51	16 55	18 01	19 08
35	04 11	04 42	05 08	15 49	16 56	18 04	19 14
40	03 59	04 33	05 02	15 47	16 56	18 08	19 21
45	03 45	04 23	04 54	15 44	16 57	18 12	19 29
S 50	03 27	04 10	04 44	15 41	16 58	18 18	19 39
52	03 18	04 03	04 40	15 40	16 59	18 21	19 44
54	03 07	03 56	04 35	15 38	17 00	18 23	19 49
56	02 55	03 48	04 30	15 36	17 00	18 26	19 54
58	02 41	03 40	04 24	15 35	17 01	18 30	20 01
S 60	02 24	03 29	04 17	15 32	17 02	18 34	20 08

Lat.	Sunset	Twilight Civil	Twilight Naut.	Moonset 22	23	24	25
°	h m	h m	h m	h m	h m	h m	h m
N 72	15 25	16 40	17 59	02 06	04 05	06 08	08 16
N 70	15 42	16 48	17 59	02 16	04 07	06 02	08 01
68	15 55	16 55	17 59	02 24	04 09	05 57	07 49
66	16 06	17 00	18 00	02 31	04 11	05 53	07 39
64	16 15	17 05	18 00	02 37	04 12	05 50	07 31
62	16 23	17 09	18 01	02 42	04 13	05 47	07 24
60	16 30	17 13	18 01	02 46	04 14	05 45	07 18
N 58	16 36	17 16	18 02	02 50	04 15	05 43	07 12
56	16 41	17 19	18 03	02 54	04 16	05 41	07 08
54	16 46	17 22	18 03	02 57	04 16	05 39	07 03
52	16 50	17 25	18 04	02 59	04 17	05 37	07 00
50	16 54	17 27	18 05	03 02	04 18	05 36	06 56
45	17 03	17 33	18 07	03 07	04 19	05 33	06 49
N 40	17 10	17 37	18 09	03 12	04 20	05 30	06 42
35	17 16	17 42	18 11	03 15	04 21	05 28	06 37
30	17 22	17 46	18 14	03 19	04 21	05 26	06 32
20	17 31	17 54	18 19	03 24	04 23	05 22	06 24
N 10	17 40	18 01	18 26	03 29	04 24	05 19	06 17
0	17 48	18 09	18 33	03 34	04 25	05 17	06 11
S 10	17 56	18 17	18 43	03 39	04 26	05 14	06 04
20	18 05	18 27	18 54	03 44	04 27	05 11	05 57
30	18 15	18 40	19 09	03 49	04 28	05 07	05 49
35	18 21	18 47	19 19	03 52	04 28	05 05	05 44
40	18 28	18 56	19 31	03 56	04 29	05 03	05 39
45	18 36	19 07	19 45	04 00	04 30	05 00	05 33
S 50	18 46	19 20	20 04	04 05	04 31	04 57	05 26
52	18 50	19 27	20 13	04 07	04 31	04 56	05 22
54	18 55	19 34	20 24	04 10	04 32	04 54	05 19
56	19 01	19 42	20 36	04 12	04 32	04 53	05 15
58	19 07	19 51	20 50	04 15	04 33	04 51	05 10
S 60	19 14	20 02	21 08	04 18	04 33	04 49	05 05

	SUN			MOON			
Day	Eqn. of Time 00ʰ	12ʰ	Mer. Pass.	Mer. Pass. Upper	Lower	Age	Phase
d	m s	m s	h m	h m	h m	d	%
22	15 23	15 28	11 45	22 13	09 47	13	92
23	15 32	15 36	11 44	23 04	10 38	14	97
24	15 41	15 45	11 44	23 58	11 31	15	100

1999 OCTOBER 25, 26, 27 (MON., TUES., WED.)

UT	ARIES GHA	VENUS −4.4 GHA	Dec	MARS +0.7 GHA	Dec	JUPITER −2.9 GHA	Dec	SATURN −0.2 GHA	Dec	STARS Name	SHA	Dec
d h	° ′	° ′	° ′	° ′	° ′	° ′	° ′	° ′	° ′		° ′	° ′
25 00	32 56.4	227 05.9 N 5 41.2		116 34.5 S25 02.3		4 42.4 N 9 56.9		349 54.5 N13 44.7		Acamar	315 26.0	S40 18.3
01	47 58.9	242 06.1 40.5		131 34.9 02.2		19 45.2 56.7		4 57.1 44.6		Achernar	335 34.1	S57 14.4
02	63 01.3	257 06.2 39.9		146 35.4 02.1		34 48.0 56.6		19 59.8 44.6		Acrux	173 21.8	S63 05.6
03	78 03.8	272 06.4 .. 39.2		161 35.8 .. 02.0		49 50.8 .. 56.5		35 02.4 .. 44.5		Adhara	255 20.8	S28 58.1
04	93 06.3	287 06.5 38.6		176 36.3 01.9		64 53.5 56.4		50 05.1 44.5		Aldebaran	291 01.3	N16 30.5
05	108 08.7	302 06.7 37.9		191 36.7 01.8		79 56.3 56.3		65 07.7 44.4				
06	123 11.2	317 06.8 N 5 37.2		206 37.2 S25 01.7		94 59.1 N 9 56.2		80 10.4 N13 44.3		Alioth	166 30.5	N55 57.7
07	138 13.6	332 07.0 36.6		221 37.6 01.6		110 01.9 56.0		95 13.1 44.3		Alkaid	153 07.8	N49 19.0
08	153 16.1	347 07.1 35.9		236 38.1 01.5		125 04.7 55.9		110 15.7 44.2		Al Na'ir	27 56.8	S46 57.9
M 09	168 18.6	2 07.3 .. 35.2		251 38.5 .. 01.4		140 07.5 .. 55.8		125 18.4 .. 44.2		Alnilam	275 57.0	S 1 12.1
O 10	183 21.0	17 07.4 34.6		266 39.0 01.3		155 10.3 55.7		140 21.0 44.1		Alphard	218 06.6	S 8 39.3
N 11	198 23.5	32 07.6 33.9		281 39.4 01.2		170 13.1 55.6		155 23.7 44.1				
D 12	213 26.0	47 07.7 N 5 33.2		296 39.9 S25 01.1		185 15.8 N 9 55.5		170 26.3 N13 44.0		Alphecca	126 20.4	N26 43.2
A 13	228 28.4	62 07.9 32.5		311 40.3 01.0		200 18.6 55.4		185 29.0 43.9		Alpheratz	357 54.2	N29 05.4
Y 14	243 30.9	77 08.0 31.9		326 40.7 00.9		215 21.4 55.2		200 31.6 43.9		Altair	62 18.6	N 8 52.3
15	258 33.4	92 08.2 .. 31.2		341 41.2 .. 00.8		230 24.2 .. 55.1		215 34.3 .. 43.8		Ankaa	353 25.8	S42 18.6
16	273 35.8	107 08.3 30.5		356 41.6 00.7		245 27.0 55.0		230 36.9 43.8		Antares	112 39.6	S26 25.7
17	288 38.3	122 08.5 29.8		11 42.1 00.6		260 29.8 54.9		245 39.6 43.7				
18	303 40.7	137 08.6 N 5 29.2		26 42.5 S25 00.5		275 32.6 N 9 54.8		260 42.3 N13 43.7		Arcturus	146 05.8	N19 11.2
19	318 43.2	152 08.7 28.5		41 43.0 00.4		290 35.3 54.7		275 44.9 43.6		Atria	107 51.5	S69 01.7
20	333 45.7	167 08.9 27.8		56 43.4 00.3		305 38.1 54.5		290 47.6 43.5		Avior	234 22.3	S59 30.2
21	348 48.1	182 09.0 .. 27.1		71 43.9 .. 00.2		320 40.9 .. 54.4		305 50.2 .. 43.5		Bellatrix	278 43.2	N 6 21.0
22	3 50.6	197 09.2 26.5		86 44.3 00.1		335 43.7 54.3		320 52.9 43.4		Betelgeuse	271 12.6	N 7 24.4
23	18 53.1	212 09.3 25.8		101 44.8 25 00.0		350 46.5 54.2		335 55.5 43.4				
26 00	33 55.5	227 09.5 N 5 25.1		116 45.2 S24 59.9		5 49.3 N 9 54.1		350 58.2 N13 43.3		Canopus	264 00.6	S52 41.5
01	48 58.0	242 09.6 24.4		131 45.6 59.8		20 52.1 54.0		6 00.8 43.3		Capella	280 49.8	N45 59.7
02	64 00.5	257 09.7 23.7		146 46.1 59.7		35 54.9 53.8		21 03.5 43.2		Deneb	49 38.7	N45 17.1
03	79 02.9	272 09.9 .. 23.1		161 46.5 .. 59.6		50 57.6 .. 53.7		36 06.1 .. 43.1		Denebola	182 44.8	N14 34.5
04	94 05.4	287 10.0 22.4		176 47.0 59.5		66 00.4 53.6		51 08.8 43.1		Diphda	349 06.2	S17 59.3
05	109 07.9	302 10.1 21.7		191 47.4 59.4		81 03.2 53.5		66 11.5 43.0				
06	124 10.3	317 10.3 N 5 21.0		206 47.9 S24 59.2		96 06.0 N 9 53.4		81 14.1 N13 43.0		Dubhe	194 05.1	N61 45.0
07	139 12.8	332 10.4 20.3		221 48.3 59.1		111 08.8 53.3		96 16.8 42.9		Elnath	278 25.8	N28 36.3
08	154 15.2	347 10.5 19.6		236 48.7 59.0		126 11.6 53.2		111 19.4 42.8		Eltanin	90 51.4	N51 29.7
T 09	169 17.7	2 10.7 .. 19.0		251 49.2 .. 58.9		141 14.4 .. 53.0		126 22.1 .. 42.8		Enif	33 57.4	N 9 52.6
U 10	184 20.2	17 10.8 18.3		266 49.6 58.8		156 17.1 52.9		141 24.7 42.7		Fomalhaut	15 35.5	S29 37.5
E 11	199 22.6	32 10.9 17.6		281 50.1 58.7		171 19.9 52.8		156 27.4 42.7				
S 12	214 25.1	47 11.1 N 5 16.9		296 50.5 S24 58.6		186 22.7 N 9 52.7		171 30.0 N13 42.6		Gacrux	172 13.3	S57 06.4
D 13	229 27.6	62 11.2 16.2		311 51.0 58.5		201 25.5 52.6		186 32.7 42.6		Gienah	176 03.5	S17 32.2
A 14	244 30.0	77 11.3 15.5		326 51.4 58.4		216 28.3 52.5		201 35.4 42.5		Hadar	149 03.7	S60 22.1
Y 15	259 32.5	92 11.5 .. 14.8		341 51.9 .. 58.3		231 31.1 .. 52.3		216 38.0 .. 42.4		Hamal	328 12.4	N23 27.7
16	274 35.0	107 11.6 14.1		356 52.3 58.1		246 33.9 52.2		231 40.7 42.4		Kaus Aust.	83 58.1	S34 23.1
17	289 37.4	122 11.7 13.4		11 52.7 58.0		261 36.6 52.1		246 43.3 42.3				
18	304 39.9	137 11.8 N 5 12.8		26 53.2 S24 57.9		276 39.4 N 9 52.0		261 46.0 N13 42.3		Kochab	137 20.8	N74 09.6
19	319 42.4	152 12.0 12.1		41 53.6 57.8		291 42.2 51.9		276 48.6 42.2		Markab	13 48.7	N15 12.4
20	334 44.8	167 12.1 11.4		56 54.1 57.7		306 45.0 51.8		291 51.3 42.2		Menkar	314 25.9	N 4 05.3
21	349 47.3	182 12.2 .. 10.7		71 54.5 .. 57.6		321 47.8 .. 51.7		306 53.9 .. 42.1		Menkent	148 20.5	S36 21.9
22	4 49.7	197 12.3 10.0		86 55.0 57.5		336 50.6 51.5		321 56.6 42.0		Miaplacidus	221 42.1	S69 42.6
23	19 52.2	212 12.5 09.3		101 55.4 57.3		351 53.4 51.4		336 59.3 42.0				
27 00	34 54.7	227 12.6 N 5 08.6		116 55.8 S24 57.2		6 56.1 N 9 51.3		352 01.9 N13 41.9		Mirfak	308 55.1	N49 51.5
01	49 57.1	242 12.7 07.9		131 56.3 57.1		21 58.9 51.2		7 04.6 41.9		Nunki	76 11.6	S26 17.8
02	64 59.6	257 12.8 07.2		146 56.7 57.0		37 01.7 51.1		22 07.2 41.8		Peacock	53 35.9	S56 44.3
03	80 02.1	272 13.0 .. 06.5		161 57.2 .. 56.9		52 04.5 .. 51.0		37 09.9 .. 41.7		Pollux	243 40.7	N28 01.5
04	95 04.5	287 13.1 05.8		176 57.6 56.8		67 07.3 50.8		52 12.5 41.7		Procyon	245 10.8	N 5 13.6
05	110 07.0	302 13.2 05.1		191 58.1 56.6		82 10.1 50.7		67 15.2 41.6				
06	125 09.5	317 13.3 N 5 04.4		206 58.5 S24 56.5		97 12.9 N 9 50.6		82 17.8 N13 41.6		Rasalhague	96 16.5	N12 33.9
W 07	140 11.9	332 13.4 03.7		221 58.9 56.4		112 15.6 50.5		97 20.5 41.5		Regulus	207 55.0	N11 58.2
E 08	155 14.4	347 13.6 03.0		236 59.4 56.3		127 18.4 50.4		112 23.2 41.5		Rigel	281 22.0	S 8 12.1
D 09	170 16.8	2 13.7 .. 02.3		251 59.8 .. 56.2		142 21.2 .. 50.3		127 25.8 .. 41.4		Rigil Kent.	140 07.0	S60 49.9
N 10	185 19.3	17 13.8 01.6		267 00.3 56.0		157 24.0 50.2		142 28.5 41.3		Sabik	102 25.0	S15 43.3
E 11	200 21.8	32 13.9 00.9		282 00.7 55.9		172 26.8 50.0		157 31.1 41.3				
S 12	215 24.2	47 14.0 N 5 00.2		297 01.1 S24 55.8		187 29.6 N 9 49.9		172 33.8 N13 41.2		Schedar	349 52.1	N56 32.2
D 13	230 26.7	62 14.1 4 59.5		312 01.6 55.7		202 32.4 49.8		187 36.4 41.2		Shaula	96 36.6	S37 06.2
A 14	245 29.2	77 14.2 58.8		327 02.0 55.6		217 35.1 49.7		202 39.1 41.1		Sirius	258 43.0	S16 42.8
Y 15	260 31.6	92 14.4 .. 58.1		342 02.5 .. 55.4		232 37.9 .. 49.6		217 41.8 .. 41.1		Spica	158 42.8	S11 09.4
16	275 34.1	107 14.5 57.3		357 02.9 55.3		247 40.7 49.5		232 44.4 41.0		Suhail	223 00.3	S43 25.6
17	290 36.6	122 14.6 56.6		12 03.4 55.2		262 43.5 49.4		247 47.1 40.9				
18	305 39.0	137 14.7 N 4 55.9		27 03.8 S24 55.1		277 46.3 N 9 49.2		262 49.7 N13 40.9		Vega	80 46.3	N38 47.4
19	320 41.5	152 14.8 55.2		42 04.2 54.9		292 49.1 49.1		277 52.4 40.8		Zuben'ubi	137 17.5	S16 02.2
20	335 44.0	167 14.9 54.5		57 04.7 54.8		307 51.9 49.0		292 55.0 40.8			SHA	Mer. Pass.
21	350 46.4	182 15.0 .. 53.8		72 05.1 .. 54.7		322 54.6 .. 48.9		307 57.7 .. 40.7			° ′	h m
22	5 48.9	197 15.1 53.1		87 05.6 54.6		337 57.4 48.8		323 00.4 40.6		Venus	193 13.9	8 51
23	20 51.3	212 15.2 52.4		102 06.0 54.4		353 00.2 48.7		338 03.0 40.6		Mars	82 49.7	16 13
	h m									Jupiter	331 53.7	23 32
Mer. Pass. 21 40.7		v 0.1 d 0.7		v 0.4 d 0.1		v 2.8 d 0.1		v 2.7 d 0.1		Saturn	317 02.6	0 36

UT	SUN GHA	SUN Dec	MOON GHA	MOON v	MOON Dec	MOON d	MOON HP
d h	° ′	° ′	° ′	′	° ′	′	′
25 00	183 57.2	S11 51.9	0 35.7	8.1	N 7 46.5	12.1	60.4
01	198 57.3	52.8	15 02.8	8.1	7 58.6	12.1	60.4
02	213 57.3	53.6	29 29.9	8.0	8 10.7	12.0	60.5
03	228 57.4 ..	54.5	43 56.9	8.0	8 22.7	12.0	60.5
04	243 57.5	55.4	58 23.9	7.9	8 34.7	12.0	60.5
05	258 57.6	56.2	72 50.8	7.9	8 46.7	11.9	60.5
06	273 57.7	S11 57.1	87 17.7	7.8	N 8 58.6	11.8	60.5
07	288 57.7	58.0	101 44.5	7.8	9 10.4	11.8	60.5
08	303 57.8	58.8	116 11.3	7.7	9 22.2	11.7	60.5
M 09	318 57.9	11 59.7	130 38.0	7.6	9 33.9	11.7	60.6
O 10	333 58.0	12 00.5	145 04.6	7.6	9 45.6	11.7	60.6
N 11	348 58.0	01.4	159 31.2	7.5	9 57.3	11.5	60.6
D 12	3 58.1	S12 02.3	173 57.7	7.5	N10 08.8	11.5	60.6
A 13	18 58.2	03.1	188 24.2	7.4	10 20.3	11.5	60.6
Y 14	33 58.3	04.0	202 50.6	7.4	10 31.8	11.4	60.6
15	48 58.3 ..	04.9	217 17.0	7.3	10 43.2	11.3	60.6
16	63 58.4	05.7	231 43.3	7.2	10 54.5	11.2	60.6
17	78 58.5	06.6	246 09.5	7.2	11 05.7	11.2	60.7
18	93 58.5	S12 07.4	260 35.7	7.1	N11 16.9	11.1	60.7
19	108 58.6	08.3	275 01.8	7.1	11 28.0	11.1	60.7
20	123 58.7	09.2	289 27.9	7.0	11 39.1	11.0	60.7
21	138 58.8 ..	10.0	303 53.9	7.0	11 50.1	10.9	60.7
22	153 58.8	10.9	318 19.9	6.9	12 01.0	10.8	60.7
23	168 58.9	11.7	332 45.8	6.9	12 11.8	10.7	60.7
26 00	183 59.0	S12 12.6	347 11.7	6.8	N12 22.5	10.7	60.7
01	198 59.1	13.5	1 37.5	6.7	12 33.2	10.5	60.7
02	213 59.1	14.3	16 03.2	6.7	12 43.7	10.5	60.7
03	228 59.2 ..	15.2	30 28.9	6.6	12 54.2	10.5	60.7
04	243 59.3	16.0	44 54.5	6.6	13 04.7	10.3	60.7
05	258 59.3	16.9	59 20.1	6.5	13 15.0	10.2	60.7
06	273 59.4	S12 17.7	73 45.6	6.5	N13 25.2	10.2	60.7
07	288 59.5	18.6	88 11.1	6.4	13 35.4	10.0	60.7
T 08	303 59.5	19.5	102 36.5	6.3	13 45.4	10.0	60.7
U 09	318 59.6 ..	20.3	117 01.8	6.3	13 55.4	9.9	60.7
E 10	333 59.7	21.2	131 27.1	6.3	14 05.3	9.8	60.7
S 11	348 59.7	22.0	145 52.4	6.2	14 15.1	9.6	60.7
D 12	3 59.8	S12 22.9	160 17.6	6.1	N14 24.7	9.6	60.7
A 13	18 59.9	23.7	174 42.7	6.1	14 34.3	9.5	60.7
Y 14	33 59.9	24.6	189 07.8	6.0	14 43.8	9.4	60.7
15	49 00.0 ..	25.4	203 32.8	6.0	14 53.2	9.3	60.7
16	64 00.1	26.3	217 57.8	6.0	15 02.5	9.2	60.7
17	79 00.1	27.1	232 22.8	5.8	15 11.7	9.1	60.7
18	94 00.2	S12 28.0	246 47.6	5.9	N15 20.8	8.9	60.7
19	109 00.3	28.8	261 12.5	5.8	15 29.7	8.9	60.7
20	124 00.3	29.7	275 37.3	5.7	15 38.6	8.8	60.7
21	139 00.4 ..	30.6	290 02.0	5.7	15 47.4	8.6	60.7
22	154 00.5	31.4	304 26.7	5.7	15 56.0	8.5	60.7
23	169 00.5	32.3	318 51.4	5.6	16 04.5	8.5	60.7
27 00	184 00.6	S12 33.1	333 16.0	5.5	N16 13.0	8.3	60.7
01	199 00.7	34.0	347 40.5	5.5	16 21.3	8.2	60.7
02	214 00.7	34.8	2 05.0	5.5	16 29.5	8.1	60.7
03	229 00.8 ..	35.7	16 29.5	5.4	16 37.6	7.9	60.7
04	244 00.8	36.5	30 53.9	5.4	16 45.5	7.9	60.7
05	259 00.9	37.4	45 18.3	5.4	16 53.4	7.7	60.7
06	274 01.0	S12 38.2	59 42.7	5.3	N17 01.1	7.6	60.7
W 07	289 01.0	39.1	74 07.0	5.3	17 08.7	7.5	60.7
E 08	304 01.1	39.9	88 31.3	5.2	17 16.2	7.3	60.7
D 09	319 01.2 ..	40.7	102 55.5	5.2	17 23.5	7.3	60.7
N 10	334 01.2	41.6	117 19.7	5.1	17 30.8	7.1	60.6
E 11	349 01.3	42.4	131 43.8	5.2	17 37.9	7.0	60.6
S 12	4 01.3	S12 43.3	146 08.0	5.1	N17 44.9	6.8	60.6
D 13	19 01.4	44.1	160 32.1	5.0	17 51.7	6.8	60.6
A 14	34 01.5	45.0	174 56.1	5.0	17 58.5	6.6	60.6
Y 15	49 01.5 ..	45.8	189 20.1	5.0	18 05.1	6.5	60.6
16	64 01.6	46.7	203 44.1	5.0	18 11.6	6.5	60.6
17	79 01.6	47.5	218 08.1	4.9	18 17.9	6.2	60.6
18	94 01.7	S12 48.4	232 32.0	5.0	N18 24.1	6.1	60.6
19	109 01.7	49.2	246 56.0	4.8	18 30.2	5.9	60.5
20	124 01.8	50.1	261 19.8	4.9	18 36.1	5.9	60.5
21	139 01.9 ..	50.9	275 43.7	4.9	18 42.0	5.6	60.5
22	154 01.9	51.7	290 07.6	4.8	18 47.6	5.6	60.5
23	169 02.0	52.6	304 31.4	4.8	N18 53.2	5.4	60.5
	SD 16.1	d 0.9	SD 16.5		16.6		16.5

Lat.	Twilight Naut.	Twilight Civil	Sunrise	Moonrise 25	Moonrise 26	Moonrise 27	Moonrise 28
°	h m	h m	h m	h m	h m	h m	h m
N 72	05 40	07 00	08 19	16 10	15 49	14 48	▭
N 70	05 39	06 51	07 59	16 28	16 21	16 12	15 43
68	05 37	06 43	07 44	16 41	16 44	16 51	17 09
66	05 36	06 36	07 32	16 53	17 02	17 18	17 48
64	05 35	06 31	07 22	17 02	17 17	17 40	18 15
62	05 34	06 26	07 13	17 11	17 30	17 57	18 36
60	05 33	06 22	07 06	17 18	17 41	18 11	18 53
N 58	05 32	06 18	06 59	17 24	17 50	18 23	19 07
56	05 31	06 14	06 53	17 30	17 58	18 34	19 20
54	05 30	06 11	06 48	17 35	18 05	18 43	19 31
52	05 29	06 08	06 43	17 39	18 12	18 52	19 40
50	05 28	06 05	06 39	17 43	18 18	18 59	19 49
45	05 25	05 59	06 29	17 52	18 31	19 16	20 07
N 40	05 22	05 54	06 22	18 00	18 42	19 29	20 22
35	05 19	05 49	06 15	18 07	18 51	19 40	20 35
30	05 16	05 45	06 09	18 12	18 59	19 50	20 46
20	05 10	05 36	05 59	18 22	19 13	20 08	21 05
N 10	05 03	05 28	05 49	18 31	19 26	20 23	21 22
0	04 55	05 19	05 41	18 40	19 37	20 37	21 37
S 10	04 45	05 10	05 32	18 48	19 49	20 51	21 53
20	04 33	05 00	05 22	18 57	20 02	21 06	22 10
30	04 17	04 46	05 11	19 08	20 16	21 24	22 29
35	04 07	04 38	05 05	19 14	20 25	21 34	22 40
40	03 54	04 29	04 57	19 21	20 34	21 46	22 53
45	03 39	04 17	04 49	19 29	20 46	22 00	23 09
S 50	03 19	04 03	04 38	19 39	21 00	22 17	23 28
52	03 10	03 57	04 34	19 44	21 06	22 25	23 37
54	02 59	03 49	04 28	19 49	21 14	22 34	23 47
56	02 46	03 40	04 22	19 54	21 22	22 44	23 58
58	02 30	03 31	04 16	20 01	21 31	22 56	24 11
S 60	02 11	03 19	04 08	20 08	21 41	23 10	24 26

Lat.	Sunset	Twilight Civil	Twilight Naut.	Moonset 25	Moonset 26	Moonset 27	Moonset 28
°	h m	h m	h m	h m	h m	h m	h m
N 72	15 08	16 26	17 46	08 16	10 36	13 42	▭
N 70	15 27	16 36	17 47	08 01	10 06	12 19	14 54
68	15 42	16 44	17 49	07 49	09 44	11 41	13 29
66	15 55	16 50	17 50	07 39	09 27	11 14	12 51
64	16 05	16 56	17 51	07 31	09 13	10 53	12 24
62	16 14	17 01	17 53	07 24	09 01	10 37	12 03
60	16 21	17 05	17 54	07 18	08 52	10 23	11 46
N 58	16 28	17 09	17 55	07 12	08 43	10 11	11 32
56	16 34	17 13	17 56	07 08	08 35	10 01	11 20
54	16 39	17 16	17 57	07 03	08 29	09 52	11 09
52	16 44	17 19	17 58	07 00	08 23	09 44	10 59
50	16 48	17 22	18 00	06 56	08 17	09 37	10 51
45	16 58	17 28	18 02	06 49	08 06	09 21	10 33
N 40	17 06	17 34	18 05	06 42	07 56	09 09	10 19
35	17 13	17 38	18 08	06 37	07 48	08 58	10 06
30	17 19	17 43	18 11	06 32	07 40	08 49	09 55
20	17 29	17 52	18 18	06 24	07 28	08 33	09 37
N 10	17 39	18 00	18 25	06 17	07 17	08 19	09 21
0	17 47	18 09	18 33	06 11	07 07	08 05	09 06
S 10	17 56	18 18	18 43	06 04	06 57	07 52	08 51
20	18 06	18 29	18 56	05 57	06 46	07 38	08 34
30	18 17	18 42	19 12	05 49	06 34	07 22	08 16
35	18 24	18 50	19 22	05 44	06 26	07 13	08 05
40	18 31	19 00	19 35	05 39	06 18	07 03	07 53
45	18 40	19 12	19 50	05 33	06 09	06 50	07 38
S 50	18 51	19 26	20 10	05 26	05 58	06 35	07 21
52	18 56	19 33	20 20	05 22	05 52	06 28	07 12
54	19 01	19 41	20 31	05 19	05 47	06 21	07 03
56	19 07	19 49	20 45	05 15	05 40	06 12	06 53
58	19 14	19 59	21 01	05 10	05 33	06 02	06 41
S 60	19 22	20 11	21 21	05 05	05 25	05 51	06 27

	SUN			MOON			
Day	Eqn. of Time 00h	Eqn. of Time 12h	Mer. Pass.	Mer. Pass. Upper	Mer. Pass. Lower	Age	Phase
d	m s	m s	h m	h m	h m	d	%
25	15 49	15 52	11 44	24 53	12 25	16	99
26	15 56	15 59	11 44	00 53	13 22	17	96
27	16 02	16 05	11 44	01 51	14 21	18	90

UT	ARIES	VENUS −4.4		MARS +0.7		JUPITER −2.9		SATURN −0.2		STARS		
	GHA	GHA	Dec	GHA	Dec	GHA	Dec	GHA	Dec	Name	SHA	Dec
d h	° ′	° ′	° ′	° ′	° ′	° ′	° ′	° ′	° ′		° ′	° ′
28 00	35 53.8	227 15.4	N 4 51.7	117 06.4	S24 54.3	8 03.0	N 9 48.5	353 05.7	N13 40.5	Acamar	315 26.0	S40 18.4
01	50 56.3	242 15.5	50.9	132 06.9	54.2	23 05.8	48.4	8 08.3	40.5	Achernar	335 34.1	S57 14.4
02	65 58.7	257 15.6	50.2	147 07.3	54.0	38 08.6	48.3	23 11.0	40.4	Acrux	173 21.8	S63 05.6
03	81 01.2	272 15.7	.. 49.5	162 07.8	.. 53.9	53 11.3	.. 48.2	38 13.6	.. 40.4	Adhara	255 20.7	S28 58.1
04	96 03.7	287 15.8	48.8	177 08.2	53.8	68 14.1	48.1	53 16.3	40.3	Aldebaran	291 01.3	N16 30.5
05	111 06.1	302 15.9	48.1	192 08.6	53.7	83 16.9	48.0	68 19.0	40.2			
06	126 08.6	317 16.0	N 4 47.4	207 09.1	S24 53.5	98 19.7	N 9 47.9	83 21.6	N13 40.2	Alioth	166 30.5	N55 57.7
07	141 11.1	332 16.1	46.6	222 09.5	53.4	113 22.5	47.7	98 24.3	40.1	Alkaid	153 07.8	N49 19.0
T 08	156 13.5	347 16.2	45.9	237 10.0	53.3	128 25.3	47.6	113 26.9	40.1	Al Na'ir	27 56.8	S46 57.9
H 09	171 16.0	2 16.3	.. 45.2	252 10.4	.. 53.1	143 28.1	.. 47.5	128 29.6	.. 40.0	Alnilam	275 56.9	S 1 12.1
U 10	186 18.5	17 16.4	44.5	267 10.8	53.0	158 30.8	47.4	143 32.2	39.9	Alphard	218 06.6	S 8 39.3
R 11	201 20.9	32 16.5	43.8	282 11.3	52.9	173 33.6	47.3	158 34.9	39.9			
S 12	216 23.4	47 16.6	N 4 43.0	297 11.7	S24 52.7	188 36.4	N 9 47.2	173 37.6	N13 39.8	Alphecca	126 20.4	N26 43.2
D 13	231 25.8	62 16.7	42.3	312 12.2	52.6	203 39.2	47.1	188 40.2	39.8	Alpheratz	357 54.2	N29 05.5
A 14	246 28.3	77 16.8	41.6	327 12.6	52.5	218 42.0	46.9	203 42.9	39.7	Altair	62 18.7	N 8 52.3
Y 15	261 30.8	92 16.9	.. 40.9	342 13.0	.. 52.3	233 44.8	.. 46.8	218 45.5	.. 39.7	Ankaa	353 25.8	S42 18.6
16	276 33.2	107 17.0	40.1	357 13.5	52.2	248 47.5	46.7	233 48.2	39.6	Antares	112 39.6	S26 25.7
17	291 35.7	122 17.1	39.4	12 13.9	52.1	263 50.3	46.6	248 50.9	39.5			
18	306 38.2	137 17.2	N 4 38.7	27 14.4	S24 51.9	278 53.1	N 9 46.5	263 53.5	N13 39.5	Arcturus	146 05.8	N19 11.2
19	321 40.6	152 17.3	38.0	42 14.8	51.8	293 55.9	46.4	278 56.2	39.4	Atria	107 51.5	S69 01.7
20	336 43.1	167 17.4	37.2	57 15.2	51.7	308 58.7	46.3	293 58.8	39.4	Avior	234 22.3	S59 30.2
21	351 45.6	182 17.5	.. 36.5	72 15.7	.. 51.5	324 01.5	.. 46.1	309 01.5	.. 39.3	Bellatrix	278 43.2	N 6 20.9
22	6 48.0	197 17.6	35.8	87 16.1	51.4	339 04.2	46.0	324 04.1	39.2	Betelgeuse	271 12.6	N 7 24.4
23	21 50.5	212 17.7	35.0	102 16.5	51.3	354 07.0	45.9	339 06.8	39.2			
29 00	36 53.0	227 17.8	N 4 34.3	117 17.0	S24 51.1	9 09.8	N 9 45.8	354 09.5	N13 39.1	Canopus	264 00.6	S52 41.5
01	51 55.4	242 17.9	33.6	132 17.4	51.0	24 12.6	45.7	9 12.1	39.1	Capella	280 49.8	N45 59.7
02	66 57.9	257 17.9	32.9	147 17.9	50.9	39 15.4	45.6	24 14.8	39.0	Deneb	49 38.7	N45 17.1
03	82 00.3	272 18.0	.. 32.1	162 18.3	.. 50.7	54 18.2	.. 45.5	39 17.4	.. 39.0	Denebola	182 44.7	N14 34.5
04	97 02.8	287 18.1	31.4	177 18.7	50.6	69 20.9	45.3	54 20.1	38.9	Diphda	349 06.2	S17 59.3
05	112 05.3	302 18.2	30.7	192 19.2	50.4	84 23.7	45.2	69 22.8	38.8			
06	127 07.7	317 18.3	N 4 29.9	207 19.6	S24 50.3	99 26.5	N 9 45.1	84 25.4	N13 38.8	Dubhe	194 05.1	N61 45.0
07	142 10.2	332 18.4	29.2	222 20.1	50.2	114 29.3	45.0	99 28.1	38.7	Elnath	278 25.8	N28 36.3
08	157 12.7	347 18.5	28.4	237 20.5	50.0	129 32.1	44.9	114 30.7	38.7	Eltanin	90 51.4	N51 29.7
F 09	172 15.1	2 18.6	.. 27.7	252 20.9	.. 49.9	144 34.9	.. 44.8	129 33.4	.. 38.6	Enif	33 57.4	N 9 52.6
R 10	187 17.6	17 18.7	27.0	267 21.4	49.7	159 37.6	44.7	144 36.0	38.5	Fomalhaut	15 35.5	S29 37.5
I 11	202 20.1	32 18.7	26.2	282 21.8	49.6	174 40.4	44.5	159 38.7	38.5			
D 12	217 22.5	47 18.8	N 4 25.5	297 22.2	S24 49.4	189 43.2	N 9 44.4	174 41.4	N13 38.4	Gacrux	172 13.3	S57 06.4
A 13	232 25.0	62 18.9	24.8	312 22.7	49.3	204 46.0	44.3	189 44.0	38.4	Gienah	176 03.5	S17 32.2
Y 14	247 27.5	77 19.0	24.0	327 23.1	49.2	219 48.8	44.2	204 46.7	38.3	Hadar	149 03.7	S60 22.1
15	262 29.9	92 19.1	.. 23.3	342 23.6	.. 49.0	234 51.6	.. 44.1	219 49.3	.. 38.3	Hamal	328 12.4	N23 27.7
16	277 32.4	107 19.2	22.5	357 24.0	48.9	249 54.3	44.0	234 52.0	38.2	Kaus Aust.	83 58.1	S34 23.1
17	292 34.8	122 19.2	21.8	12 24.4	48.7	264 57.1	43.9	249 54.7	38.1			
18	307 37.3	137 19.3	N 4 21.1	27 24.9	S24 48.6	279 59.9	N 9 43.8	264 57.3	N13 38.1	Kochab	137 20.8	N74 09.6
19	322 39.8	152 19.4	20.3	42 25.3	48.4	295 02.7	43.6	280 00.0	38.0	Markab	13 48.7	N15 12.4
20	337 42.2	167 19.5	19.6	57 25.7	48.3	310 05.5	43.5	295 02.6	38.0	Menkar	314 25.9	N 4 05.3
21	352 44.7	182 19.6	.. 18.8	72 26.2	.. 48.1	325 08.3	.. 43.4	310 05.3	.. 37.9	Menkent	148 20.5	S36 21.9
22	7 47.2	197 19.7	18.1	87 26.6	48.0	340 11.0	43.3	325 08.0	37.8	Miaplacidus	221 42.1	S69 42.6
23	22 49.6	212 19.7	17.3	102 27.1	47.8	355 13.8	43.2	340 10.6	37.8			
30 00	37 52.1	227 19.8	N 4 16.6	117 27.5	S24 47.7	10 16.6	N 9 43.1	355 13.3	N13 37.7	Mirfak	308 55.1	N49 51.5
01	52 54.6	242 19.9	15.8	132 27.9	47.5	25 19.4	43.0	10 15.9	37.7	Nunki	76 11.6	S26 17.8
02	67 57.0	257 20.0	15.1	147 28.4	47.4	40 22.2	42.8	25 18.6	37.6	Peacock	53 36.0	S56 44.3
03	82 59.5	272 20.0	.. 14.3	162 28.8	.. 47.2	55 24.9	.. 42.7	40 21.3	.. 37.6	Pollux	243 40.6	N28 01.5
04	98 01.9	287 20.1	13.6	177 29.2	47.1	70 27.7	42.6	55 23.9	37.5	Procyon	245 10.8	N 5 13.6
05	113 04.4	302 20.2	12.8	192 29.7	46.9	85 30.5	42.5	70 26.6	37.4			
06	128 06.9	317 20.3	N 4 12.1	207 30.1	S24 46.8	100 33.3	N 9 42.4	85 29.2	N13 37.4	Rasalhague	96 16.5	N12 33.9
07	143 09.3	332 20.3	11.3	222 30.6	46.6	115 36.1	42.3	100 31.9	37.3	Regulus	207 54.9	N11 58.2
S 08	158 11.8	347 20.4	10.6	237 31.0	46.5	130 38.9	42.2	115 34.6	37.3	Rigel	281 22.0	S 8 12.1
A 09	173 14.3	2 20.5	.. 09.8	252 31.4	.. 46.3	145 41.6	.. 42.1	130 37.2	.. 37.2	Rigil Kent.	140 07.0	S60 49.8
T 10	188 16.7	17 20.6	09.1	267 31.9	46.2	160 44.4	41.9	145 39.9	37.1	Sabik	102 25.0	S15 43.3
U 11	203 19.2	32 20.6	08.3	282 32.3	46.0	175 47.2	41.8	160 42.5	37.1			
R 12	218 21.7	47 20.7	N 4 07.6	297 32.7	S24 45.9	190 50.0	N 9 41.7	175 45.2	N13 37.0	Schedar	349 52.1	N56 32.3
D 13	233 24.1	62 20.8	06.8	312 33.2	45.7	205 52.8	41.6	190 47.8	37.0	Shaula	96 36.6	S37 06.2
A 14	248 26.6	77 20.9	06.1	327 33.6	45.6	220 55.5	41.5	205 50.5	36.9	Sirius	258 42.9	S16 42.8
Y 15	263 29.1	92 20.9	.. 05.3	342 34.0	.. 45.4	235 58.3	.. 41.4	220 53.2	.. 36.9	Spica	158 42.8	S11 09.4
16	278 31.5	107 21.0	04.6	357 34.5	45.3	251 01.1	41.3	235 55.8	36.8	Suhail	223 00.3	S43 25.6
17	293 34.0	122 21.1	03.8	12 34.9	45.1	266 03.9	41.1	250 58.5	36.7			
18	308 36.4	137 21.1	N 4 03.0	27 35.4	S24 44.9	281 06.7	N 9 41.0	266 01.1	N13 36.7	Vega	80 46.4	N38 47.3
19	323 38.9	152 21.2	02.3	42 35.8	44.8	296 09.5	40.9	281 03.8	36.6	Zuben'ubi	137 17.5	S16 02.2
20	338 41.4	167 21.3	01.5	57 36.2	44.6	311 12.2	40.8	296 06.5	36.6		SHA	Mer. Pass.
21	353 43.8	182 21.3	.. 00.8	72 36.7	.. 44.5	326 15.0	.. 40.7	311 09.1	.. 36.5		° ′	h m
22	8 46.3	197 21.4	4 00.0	87 37.1	44.3	341 17.8	40.6	326 11.8	36.4	Venus	190 24.8	8 51
23	23 48.8	212 21.5	N 3 59.2	102 37.5	44.2	356 20.6	40.5	341 14.5	36.4	Mars	80 24.0	16 10
	h m									Jupiter	332 16.9	23 19
Mer. Pass. 21 28.9		v 0.1	d 0.7	v 0.4	d 0.1	v 2.8	d 0.1	v 2.7	d 0.1	Saturn	317 16.5	0 23

UT	SUN GHA	SUN Dec	MOON GHA	v	MOON Dec	d	HP
d h	° ′	° ′	° ′	′	° ′	′	′
28 00	184 02.0	S12 53.4	318 55.2	4.7	N18 58.6	5.3	60.5
01	199 02.1	54.3	333 18.9	4.8	19 03.9	5.1	60.5
02	214 02.1	55.1	347 42.7	4.8	19 09.0	5.0	60.4
03	229 02.2	.. 56.0	2 06.5	4.7	19 14.0	4.9	60.4
04	244 02.2	56.8	16 30.2	4.7	19 18.9	4.7	60.4
05	259 02.3	57.6	30 53.9	4.7	19 23.6	4.6	60.4
06	274 02.4	S12 58.5	45 17.6	4.7	N19 28.2	4.4	60.4
07	289 02.4	12 59.3	59 41.3	4.7	19 32.6	4.3	60.4
08	304 02.5	13 00.2	74 05.0	4.7	19 36.9	4.2	60.3
09	319 02.5	.. 01.0	88 28.7	4.6	19 41.1	4.0	60.3
10	334 02.6	01.8	102 52.3	4.7	19 45.1	3.9	60.3
11	349 02.6	02.7	117 16.0	4.6	19 49.0	3.7	60.3
12	4 02.7	S13 03.5	131 39.6	4.7	N19 52.7	3.6	60.3
13	19 02.7	04.3	146 03.3	4.7	19 56.3	3.4	60.2
14	34 02.8	05.2	160 27.0	4.6	19 59.7	3.3	60.2
15	49 02.8	.. 06.0	174 50.6	4.7	20 03.0	3.2	60.2
16	64 02.9	06.9	189 14.3	4.6	20 06.2	3.0	60.2
17	79 02.9	07.7	203 37.9	4.7	20 09.2	2.9	60.2
18	94 03.0	S13 08.5	218 01.6	4.7	N20 12.1	2.7	60.1
19	109 03.0	09.4	232 25.3	4.7	20 14.8	2.6	60.1
20	124 03.1	10.2	246 49.0	4.6	20 17.4	2.5	60.1
21	139 03.1	.. 11.0	261 12.6	4.7	20 19.9	2.3	60.1
22	154 03.2	11.9	275 36.3	4.8	20 22.2	2.1	60.1
23	169 03.2	12.7	290 00.1	4.7	20 24.3	2.0	60.0
29 00	184 03.3	S13 13.5	304 23.8	4.7	N20 26.3	1.9	60.0
01	199 03.3	14.4	318 47.5	4.8	20 28.2	1.7	60.0
02	214 03.4	15.2	333 11.3	4.8	20 29.9	1.6	60.0
03	229 03.4	.. 16.0	347 35.1	4.8	20 31.5	1.4	59.9
04	244 03.5	16.9	1 58.9	4.8	20 32.9	1.3	59.9
05	259 03.5	17.7	16 22.7	4.8	20 34.2	1.2	59.9
06	274 03.5	S13 18.5	30 46.5	4.9	N20 35.4	1.0	59.9
07	289 03.6	19.4	45 10.4	4.9	20 36.4	0.9	59.9
08	304 03.6	20.2	59 34.3	4.9	20 37.3	0.7	59.8
09	319 03.7	.. 21.0	73 58.2	5.0	20 38.0	0.6	59.8
10	334 03.7	21.9	88 22.2	4.9	20 38.6	0.4	59.8
11	349 03.8	22.7	102 46.1	5.0	20 39.0	0.3	59.8
12	4 03.8	S13 23.5	117 10.1	5.1	N20 39.3	0.1	59.7
13	19 03.9	24.4	131 34.2	5.1	20 39.4	0.0	59.7
14	34 03.9	25.2	145 58.3	5.1	20 39.4	0.1	59.7
15	49 03.9	.. 26.0	160 22.4	5.1	20 39.3	0.4	59.7
16	64 04.0	26.8	174 46.5	5.2	20 39.0	0.4	59.6
17	79 04.0	27.7	189 10.7	5.2	20 38.6	0.5	59.6
18	94 04.1	S13 28.5	203 34.9	5.3	N20 38.1	0.7	59.6
19	109 04.1	29.3	217 59.2	5.3	20 37.4	0.9	59.5
20	124 04.1	30.2	232 23.5	5.4	20 36.5	0.9	59.5
21	139 04.2	.. 31.0	246 47.9	5.4	20 35.6	1.1	59.5
22	154 04.2	31.8	261 12.3	5.4	20 34.5	1.3	59.5
23	169 04.3	32.6	275 36.7	5.5	20 33.2	1.4	59.4
30 00	184 04.3	S13 33.5	290 01.2	5.6	N20 31.8	1.5	59.4
01	199 04.3	34.3	304 25.8	5.5	20 30.3	1.6	59.4
02	214 04.4	35.1	318 50.3	5.7	20 28.7	1.8	59.4
03	229 04.4	.. 35.9	333 15.0	5.7	20 26.9	1.9	59.3
04	244 04.5	36.8	347 39.7	5.7	20 25.0	2.1	59.3
05	259 04.5	37.6	2 04.4	5.8	20 22.9	2.2	59.3
06	274 04.5	S13 38.4	16 29.2	5.9	N20 20.7	2.3	59.2
07	289 04.6	39.2	30 54.1	5.9	20 18.4	2.5	59.2
08	304 04.6	40.1	45 19.0	6.0	20 15.9	2.5	59.2
09	319 04.6	.. 40.9	59 44.0	6.0	20 13.4	2.7	59.2
10	334 04.7	41.7	74 09.0	6.1	20 10.7	2.9	59.1
11	349 04.7	42.5	88 34.1	6.1	20 07.8	3.0	59.1
12	4 04.8	S13 43.3	102 59.2	6.2	N20 04.8	3.3	59.1
13	19 04.8	44.2	117 24.4	6.3	20 01.8	3.3	59.1
14	34 04.8	45.0	131 49.7	6.3	19 58.5	3.3	59.0
15	49 04.9	.. 45.8	146 15.0	6.4	19 55.2	3.5	59.0
16	64 04.9	46.6	160 40.4	6.5	19 51.7	3.6	59.0
17	79 04.9	47.4	175 05.9	6.5	19 48.1	3.7	58.9
18	94 05.0	S13 48.3	189 31.4	6.6	N19 44.4	3.8	58.9
19	109 05.0	49.1	203 57.0	6.7	19 40.6	4.0	58.9
20	124 05.0	49.9	218 22.7	6.7	19 36.6	4.1	58.8
21	139 05.1	.. 50.7	232 48.4	6.8	19 32.5	4.3	58.8
22	154 05.1	51.5	247 14.2	6.9	19 28.3	4.3	58.8
23	169 05.1	52.3	261 40.1	6.9	N19 24.0	4.4	58.8
	SD 16.1	d 0.8	SD 16.4		16.3		16.1

Day 28 — THURSDAY; Day 29 — FRIDAY; Day 30 — SATURDAY.

Lat.	Twilight Naut.	Twilight Civil	Sunrise	Moonrise 28	29	30	31
°	h m	h m	h m	h m	h m	h m	h m
N 72	05 52	07 13	08 36	☐	☐	☐	19 20
N 70	05 50	07 02	08 13	15 43	☐	18 11	20 26
68	05 47	06 53	07 56	17 09	17 55	19 20	21 02
66	05 45	06 46	07 43	17 48	18 39	19 56	21 28
64	05 43	06 39	07 31	18 15	19 09	20 22	21 47
62	05 41	06 34	07 22	18 36	19 31	20 42	22 03
60	05 40	06 29	07 13	18 53	19 49	20 59	22 17
N 58	05 38	06 24	07 06	19 07	20 04	21 12	22 28
56	05 37	06 20	06 59	19 20	20 17	21 24	22 38
54	05 35	06 17	06 54	19 31	20 28	21 35	22 47
52	05 34	06 13	06 49	19 40	20 38	21 44	22 54
50	05 32	06 10	06 44	19 49	20 47	21 52	23 01
45	05 29	06 03	06 34	20 07	21 06	22 10	23 16
N 40	05 25	05 57	06 25	20 22	21 21	22 24	23 29
35	05 22	05 52	06 18	20 35	21 34	22 36	23 39
30	05 18	05 47	06 11	20 46	21 45	22 47	23 48
20	05 11	05 37	06 00	21 05	22 05	23 05	24 04
N 10	05 03	05 28	05 50	21 22	22 22	23 21	24 17
0	04 54	05 19	05 40	21 37	22 37	23 35	24 30
S 10	04 44	05 09	05 31	21 53	22 53	23 50	24 43
20	04 31	04 58	05 20	22 10	23 10	24 06	00 06
30	04 14	04 43	05 08	22 29	23 29	24 24	00 24
35	04 03	04 35	05 01	22 40	23 41	24 34	00 34
40	03 50	04 25	04 53	22 53	23 54	24 46	00 46
45	03 34	04 12	04 44	23 09	24 09	00 09	01 01
S 50	03 12	03 57	04 33	23 28	24 28	00 28	01 18
52	03 02	03 50	04 28	23 37	24 37	00 37	01 26
54	02 50	03 42	04 22	23 47	24 47	00 47	01 35
56	02 36	03 33	04 15	23 58	24 58	00 58	01 45
58	02 19	03 22	04 08	24 11	00 11	01 11	01 57
S 60	01 57	03 10	04 00	24 26	00 26	01 26	02 10

Lat.	Sunset	Twilight Civil	Twilight Naut.	Moonset 28	29	30	31
°	h m	h m	h m	h m	h m	h m	h m
N 72	14 50	16 12	17 33	☐	☐	☐	17 25
N 70	15 13	16 24	17 36	14 54	☐	16 36	16 17
68	15 30	16 33	17 39	13 29	14 49	15 27	15 41
66	15 44	16 40	17 41	12 51	14 05	14 50	15 15
64	15 55	16 47	17 43	12 24	13 35	14 24	14 54
62	16 05	16 53	17 45	12 03	13 13	14 03	14 38
60	16 13	16 58	17 47	11 46	12 55	13 47	14 24
N 58	16 21	17 02	17 48	11 32	12 40	13 33	14 12
56	16 27	17 06	17 50	11 20	12 27	13 21	14 02
54	16 33	17 10	17 52	11 09	12 16	13 10	13 52
52	16 38	17 13	17 53	10 59	12 06	13 00	13 44
50	16 43	17 17	17 55	10 51	11 57	12 52	13 37
45	16 53	17 24	17 58	10 33	11 38	12 34	13 21
N 40	17 02	17 30	18 02	10 19	11 23	12 19	13 08
35	17 09	17 35	18 05	10 06	11 10	12 07	12 57
30	17 16	17 40	18 09	09 55	10 58	11 56	12 47
20	17 27	17 50	18 16	09 37	10 39	11 37	12 31
N 10	17 38	17 59	18 24	09 21	10 22	11 21	12 16
0	17 47	18 08	18 33	09 06	10 06	11 05	12 02
S 10	17 57	18 19	18 44	08 51	09 50	10 50	11 48
20	18 07	18 30	18 57	08 34	09 33	10 33	11 33
30	18 20	18 45	19 14	08 16	09 14	10 14	11 16
35	18 27	18 53	19 25	08 05	09 02	10 03	11 06
40	18 35	19 04	19 39	07 53	08 49	09 50	10 54
45	18 44	19 16	19 55	07 38	08 34	09 35	10 41
S 50	18 56	19 32	20 17	07 21	08 15	09 17	10 24
52	19 01	19 39	20 27	07 12	08 06	09 08	10 16
54	19 07	19 47	20 40	07 03	07 55	08 58	10 08
56	19 14	19 57	20 54	06 53	07 44	08 47	09 58
58	19 21	20 08	21 12	06 41	07 31	08 34	09 47
S 60	19 30	20 20	21 34	06 27	07 16	08 19	09 34

Day	SUN Eqn. of Time 00h	SUN Eqn. of Time 12h	SUN Mer. Pass.	MOON Mer. Pass. Upper	MOON Mer. Pass. Lower	Age	Phase
d	m s	m s	h m	h m	h m	d	%
28	16 08	16 11	11 44	02 51	15 21	19	82
29	16 13	16 15	11 44	03 52	16 22	20	72
30	16 17	16 19	11 44	04 51	17 20	21	61

UT	ARIES	VENUS −4.4		MARS +0.7		JUPITER −2.9		SATURN −0.2		STARS		
	GHA	GHA	Dec	GHA	Dec	GHA	Dec	GHA	Dec	Name	SHA	Dec
d h	° ′	° ′	° ′	° ′	° ′	° ′	° ′	° ′	° ′		° ′	° ′
31 00	38 51.2	227 21.5 N 3 58.5		117 38.0 S24 44.0		11 23.4 N 9 40.4		356 17.1 N13 36.3		Acamar	315 26.0	S40 18.4
01	53 53.7	242 21.6	57.7	132 38.4	43.8	26 26.1	40.2	11 19.8	36.3	Achernar	335 34.1	S57 14.4
02	68 56.2	257 21.7	57.0	147 38.8	43.7	41 28.9	40.1	26 22.4	36.2	Acrux	173 21.8	S63 05.6
03	83 58.6	272 21.7 . .	56.2	162 39.3 . .	43.5	56 31.7 . .	40.0	41 25.1 . .	36.2	Adhara	255 20.7	S28 58.1
04	99 01.1	287 21.8	55.4	177 39.7	43.4	71 34.5	39.9	56 27.8	36.1	Aldebaran	291 01.3	N16 30.5
05	114 03.6	302 21.9	54.7	192 40.1	43.2	86 37.3	39.8	71 30.4	36.0			
06	129 06.0	317 21.9 N 3 53.9		207 40.6 S24 43.0		101 40.0 N 9 39.7		86 33.1 N13 36.0		Alioth	166 30.5	N55 57.7
07	144 08.5	332 22.0	53.1	222 41.0	42.9	116 42.8	39.6	101 35.7	35.9	Alkaid	153 07.7	N49 19.0
08	159 10.9	347 22.0	52.4	237 41.5	42.7	131 45.6	39.5	116 38.4	35.9	Al Na'ir	27 56.9	S46 57.9
S 09	174 13.4	2 22.1 . .	51.6	252 41.9 . .	42.5	146 48.4 . .	39.3	131 41.1 . .	35.8	Alnilam	275 56.9	S 1 12.1
U 10	189 15.9	17 22.2	50.8	267 42.3	42.4	161 51.2	39.2	146 43.7	35.7	Alphard	218 06.6	S 8 39.3
N 11	204 18.3	32 22.2	50.1	282 42.8	42.2	176 53.9	39.1	161 46.4	35.7			
D 12	219 20.8	47 22.3 N 3 49.3		297 43.2 S24 42.1		191 56.7 N 9 39.0		176 49.0 N13 35.6		Alphecca	126 20.4	N26 43.2
A 13	234 23.3	62 22.3	48.5	312 43.6	41.9	206 59.5	38.9	191 51.7	35.6	Alpheratz	357 54.2	N29 05.5
Y 14	249 25.7	77 22.4	47.7	327 44.1	41.7	222 02.3	38.8	206 54.4	35.5	Altair	62 18.7	N 8 52.3
15	264 28.2	92 22.4 . .	47.0	342 44.5 . .	41.6	237 05.1 . .	38.7	221 57.0 . .	35.5	Ankaa	353 25.8	S42 18.6
16	279 30.7	107 22.5	46.2	357 44.9	41.4	252 07.8	38.6	236 59.7	35.4	Antares	112 39.6	S26 25.7
17	294 33.1	122 22.6	45.4	12 45.4	41.2	267 10.6	38.4	252 02.3	35.3			
18	309 35.6	137 22.6 N 3 44.7		27 45.8 S24 41.1		282 13.4 N 9 38.3		267 05.0 N13 35.3		Arcturus	146 05.8	N19 11.2
19	324 38.1	152 22.7	43.9	42 46.2	40.9	297 16.2	38.2	282 07.7	35.2	Atria	107 51.5	S69 01.6
20	339 40.5	167 22.7	43.1	57 46.7	40.7	312 18.9	38.1	297 10.3	35.2	Avior	234 22.3	S59 30.2
21	354 43.0	182 22.8 . .	42.3	72 47.1 . .	40.6	327 21.7 . .	38.0	312 13.0 . .	35.1	Bellatrix	278 43.2	N 6 20.9
22	9 45.4	197 22.8	41.6	87 47.5	40.4	342 24.5	37.9	327 15.6	35.0	Betelgeuse	271 12.6	N 7 24.4
23	24 47.9	212 22.9	40.8	102 48.0	40.2	357 27.3	37.8	342 18.3	35.0			
1 00	39 50.4	227 22.9 N 3 40.0		117 48.4 S24 40.0		12 30.1 N 9 37.7		357 21.0 N13 34.9		Canopus	264 00.5	S52 41.5
01	54 52.8	242 23.0	39.2	132 48.8	39.9	27 32.8	37.6	12 23.6	34.9	Capella	280 49.8	N45 59.7
02	69 55.3	257 23.0	38.5	147 49.3	39.7	42 35.6	37.4	27 26.3	34.8	Deneb	49 38.7	N45 17.1
03	84 57.8	272 23.1 . .	37.7	162 49.7 . .	39.5	57 38.4 . .	37.3	42 28.9 . .	34.8	Denebola	182 44.7	N14 34.5
04	100 00.2	287 23.1	36.9	177 50.2	39.4	72 41.2	37.2	57 31.6	34.7	Diphda	349 06.2	S17 59.3
05	115 02.7	302 23.2	36.1	192 50.6	39.2	87 44.0	37.1	72 34.3	34.6			
06	130 05.2	317 23.2 N 3 35.3		207 51.0 S24 39.0		102 46.7 N 9 37.0		87 36.9 N13 34.6		Dubhe	194 05.1	N61 45.0
07	145 07.6	332 23.3	34.6	222 51.5	38.8	117 49.5	36.9	102 39.6	34.5	Elnath	278 25.8	N28 36.3
08	160 10.1	347 23.3	33.8	237 51.9	38.7	132 52.3	36.8	117 42.3	34.5	Eltanin	90 51.4	N51 29.7
M 09	175 12.5	2 23.4 . .	33.0	252 52.3 . .	38.5	147 55.1 . .	36.7	132 44.9 . .	34.4	Enif	33 57.5	N 9 52.6
O 10	190 15.0	17 23.4	32.2	267 52.8	38.3	162 57.8	36.5	147 47.6	34.3	Fomalhaut	15 35.5	S29 37.5
N 11	205 17.5	32 23.5	31.4	282 53.2	38.1	178 00.6	36.4	162 50.2	34.3			
D 12	220 19.9	47 23.5 N 3 30.6		297 53.6 S24 38.0		193 03.4 N 9 36.3		177 52.9 N13 34.2		Gacrux	172 13.3	S57 06.4
A 13	235 22.4	62 23.6	29.9	312 54.1	37.8	208 06.2	36.2	192 55.6	34.2	Gienah	176 03.5	S17 32.2
Y 14	250 24.9	77 23.6	29.1	327 54.5	37.6	223 09.0	36.1	207 58.2	34.1	Hadar	149 03.7	S60 22.1
15	265 27.3	92 23.7 . .	28.3	342 54.9 . .	37.4	238 11.7 . .	36.0	223 00.9 . .	34.1	Hamal	328 12.4	N23 27.7
16	280 29.8	107 23.7	27.5	357 55.4	37.3	253 14.5	35.9	238 03.5	34.0	Kaus Aust.	83 58.1	S34 23.1
17	295 32.3	122 23.7	26.7	12 55.8	37.1	268 17.3	35.8	253 06.2	33.9			
18	310 34.7	137 23.8 N 3 25.9		27 56.2 S24 36.9		283 20.1 N 9 35.7		268 08.9 N13 33.8		Kochab	137 20.8	N74 09.5
19	325 37.2	152 23.8	25.1	42 56.7	36.7	298 22.8	35.5	283 11.5	33.8	Markab	13 48.7	N15 12.4
20	340 39.7	167 23.9	24.3	57 57.1	36.5	313 25.6	35.4	298 14.2	33.8	Menkar	314 25.8	N 4 05.3
21	355 42.1	182 23.9 . .	23.6	72 57.5 . .	36.4	328 28.4 . .	35.3	313 16.9 . .	33.7	Menkent	148 20.5	S36 21.9
22	10 44.6	197 24.0	22.8	87 58.0	36.2	343 31.2	35.2	328 19.5	33.6	Miaplacidus	221 42.0	S69 42.6
23	25 47.0	212 24.0	22.0	102 58.4	36.0	358 33.9	35.1	343 22.2	33.6			
2 00	40 49.5	227 24.0 N 3 21.2		117 58.8 S24 35.8		13 36.7 N 9 35.0		358 24.8 N13 33.5		Mirfak	308 55.1	N49 51.5
01	55 52.0	242 24.1	20.4	132 59.3	35.6	28 39.5	34.9	13 27.5	33.5	Nunki	76 11.6	S26 17.8
02	70 54.4	257 24.1	19.6	147 59.7	35.5	43 42.3	34.8	28 30.2	33.4	Peacock	53 36.0	S56 44.3
03	85 56.9	272 24.1 . .	18.8	163 00.1 . .	35.3	58 45.1 . .	34.7	43 32.8 . .	33.4	Pollux	243 40.6	N28 01.5
04	100 59.4	287 24.2	18.0	178 00.6	35.1	73 47.8	34.5	58 35.5	33.3	Procyon	245 10.7	N 5 13.6
05	116 01.8	302 24.2	17.2	193 01.0	34.9	88 50.6	34.4	73 38.1	33.2			
06	131 04.3	317 24.3 N 3 16.4		208 01.4 S24 34.7		103 53.4 N 9 34.3		88 40.8 N13 33.2		Rasalhague	96 16.6	N12 33.9
07	146 06.8	332 24.3	15.6	223 01.9	34.5	118 56.2	34.2	103 43.5	33.1	Regulus	207 54.9	N11 58.2
08	161 09.2	347 24.3	14.8	238 02.3	34.4	133 58.9	34.1	118 46.1	33.1	Rigel	281 22.0	S 8 12.1
T 09	176 11.7	2 24.4 . .	14.0	253 02.7 . .	34.2	149 01.7 . .	34.0	133 48.8 . .	33.0	Rigil Kent.	140 07.0	S60 49.8
U 10	191 14.2	17 24.4	13.2	268 03.2	34.0	164 04.5	33.9	148 51.5	32.9	Sabik	102 25.0	S15 43.3
E 11	206 16.6	32 24.4	12.4	283 03.6	33.8	179 07.3	33.8	163 54.1	32.9			
S 12	221 19.1	47 24.5 N 3 11.6		298 04.0 S24 33.6		194 10.0 N 9 33.7		178 56.8 N13 32.8		Schedar	349 52.1	N56 32.3
D 13	236 21.5	62 24.5	10.8	313 04.5	33.4	209 12.8	33.6	193 59.4	32.8	Shaula	96 36.6	S37 06.2
A 14	251 24.0	77 24.5	10.0	328 04.9	33.2	224 15.6	33.4	209 02.1	32.7	Sirius	258 42.9	S16 42.8
Y 15	266 26.5	92 24.6 . .	09.2	343 05.3 . .	33.1	239 18.4 . .	33.3	224 04.8 . .	32.6	Spica	158 42.8	S11 09.4
16	281 28.9	107 24.6	08.4	358 05.8	32.9	254 21.1	33.2	239 07.4	32.6	Suhail	223 00.3	S43 25.6
17	296 31.4	122 24.6	07.6	13 06.2	32.7	269 23.9	33.1	254 10.1	32.5			
18	311 33.9	137 24.7 N 3 06.8		28 06.6 S24 32.5		284 26.7 N 9 33.0		269 12.7 N13 32.5		Vega	80 46.4	N38 47.3
19	326 36.3	152 24.7	06.0	43 07.1	32.3	299 29.5	32.9	284 15.4	32.4	Zuben'ubi	137 17.5	S16 02.2
20	341 38.8	167 24.7	05.2	58 07.5	32.1	314 32.2	32.8	299 18.1	32.4		SHA	Mer. Pass.
21	356 41.3	182 24.7 . .	04.4	73 07.9 . .	31.9	329 35.0 . .	32.7	314 20.7 . .	32.3		° ′	h m
22	11 43.7	197 24.8	03.6	88 08.3	31.7	344 37.8	32.6	329 23.4	32.2	Venus	187 32.6	8 50
23	26 46.2	212 24.8	02.8	103 08.8	31.5	359 40.6	32.4	344 26.1	32.2	Mars	77 58.0	16 08
	h m									Jupiter	332 39.7	23 06
Mer. Pass. 21 17.1		v 0.0 d 0.8		v 0.4 d 0.2		v 2.8 d 0.1		v 2.7 d 0.1		Saturn	317 30.6	0 11

SUN and MOON

UT (d h)	SUN GHA	SUN Dec	MOON GHA	v	Dec	d	HP
31 00	184 05.2	S13 53.2	276 06.0	7.0	N19 19.6	4.6	58.7
01	199 05.2	54.0	290 32.0	7.1	19 15.0	4.7	58.7
02	214 05.2	54.8	304 58.1	7.1	19 10.3	4.8	58.7
03	229 05.2	.. 55.6	319 24.2	7.3	19 05.5	4.9	58.6
04	244 05.3	56.4	333 50.5	7.2	19 00.6	5.0	58.6
05	259 05.3	57.2	348 16.7	7.4	18 55.6	5.1	58.6
06	274 05.3	S13 58.1	2 43.1	7.4	N18 50.5	5.2	58.6
07	289 05.4	58.9	17 09.5	7.6	18 45.3	5.4	58.5
08	304 05.4	13 59.7	31 36.1	7.5	18 39.9	5.4	58.5
09	319 05.4	14 00.5	46 02.6	7.7	18 34.5	5.6	58.5
10	334 05.4	01.3	60 29.3	7.7	18 28.9	5.6	58.4
11	349 05.5	02.1	74 56.0	7.9	18 23.3	5.8	58.4
12	4 05.5	S14 02.9	89 22.9	7.8	N18 17.5	5.9	58.4
13	19 05.5	03.7	103 49.7	8.0	18 11.6	5.9	58.4
14	34 05.6	04.6	118 16.7	8.0	18 05.7	6.1	58.3
15	49 05.6	.. 05.4	132 43.7	8.2	17 59.6	6.2	58.3
16	64 05.6	06.2	147 10.9	8.1	17 53.4	6.3	58.3
17	79 05.6	07.0	161 38.0	8.3	17 47.1	6.3	58.2
18	94 05.7	S14 07.8	176 05.3	8.4	N17 40.8	6.5	58.2
19	109 05.7	08.6	190 32.7	8.4	17 34.3	6.6	58.2
20	124 05.7	09.4	205 00.1	8.5	17 27.7	6.7	58.1
21	139 05.7	.. 10.2	219 27.6	8.6	17 21.0	6.8	58.1
22	154 05.8	11.0	233 55.2	8.6	17 14.3	6.9	58.1
23	169 05.8	11.8	248 22.8	8.7	17 07.4	6.9	58.1
1 00	184 05.8	S14 12.6	262 50.5	8.9	N17 00.5	7.1	58.0
01	199 05.8	13.5	277 18.4	8.8	16 53.4	7.1	58.0
02	214 05.8	14.3	291 46.2	9.0	16 46.3	7.2	58.0
03	229 05.9	.. 15.1	306 14.2	9.0	16 39.1	7.3	57.9
04	244 05.9	15.9	320 42.2	9.2	16 31.8	7.4	57.9
05	259 05.9	16.7	335 10.4	9.1	16 24.4	7.5	57.9
06	274 05.9	S14 17.5	349 38.5	9.3	N16 16.9	7.5	57.9
07	289 05.9	18.3	4 06.8	9.4	16 09.4	7.7	57.8
08	304 06.0	19.1	18 35.2	9.4	16 01.7	7.7	57.8
09	319 06.0	.. 19.9	33 03.6	9.5	15 54.0	7.8	57.8
10	334 06.0	20.7	47 32.1	9.6	15 46.2	7.9	57.7
11	349 06.0	21.5	62 00.7	9.6	15 38.3	8.0	57.7
12	4 06.0	S14 22.3	76 29.3	9.7	N15 30.3	8.0	57.7
13	19 06.1	23.1	90 58.0	9.8	15 22.3	8.1	57.7
14	34 06.1	23.9	105 26.8	9.9	15 14.2	8.2	57.6
15	49 06.1	.. 24.7	119 55.7	10.0	15 06.0	8.3	57.6
16	64 06.1	25.5	134 24.7	10.0	14 57.7	8.3	57.6
17	79 06.1	26.3	148 53.7	10.1	14 49.4	8.5	57.5
18	94 06.2	S14 27.1	163 22.8	10.2	N14 40.9	8.5	57.5
19	109 06.2	27.9	177 52.0	10.2	14 32.4	8.5	57.5
20	124 06.2	28.7	192 21.2	10.4	14 23.9	8.6	57.5
21	139 06.2	.. 29.5	206 50.6	10.4	14 15.3	8.7	57.4
22	154 06.2	30.3	221 20.0	10.4	14 06.6	8.8	57.4
23	169 06.2	31.1	235 49.4	10.6	13 57.8	8.8	57.4
2 00	184 06.2	S14 31.9	250 19.0	10.6	N13 49.0	8.9	57.4
01	199 06.3	32.7	264 48.6	10.7	13 40.1	9.0	57.3
02	214 06.3	33.5	279 18.3	10.7	13 31.1	9.0	57.3
03	229 06.3	.. 34.3	293 48.0	10.8	13 22.1	9.1	57.3
04	244 06.3	35.1	308 17.8	10.9	13 13.0	9.2	57.2
05	259 06.3	35.9	322 47.7	11.0	13 03.8	9.2	57.2
06	274 06.3	S14 36.7	337 17.7	11.0	N12 54.6	9.2	57.2
07	289 06.3	37.5	351 47.7	11.1	12 45.4	9.3	57.2
08	304 06.3	38.3	6 17.8	11.2	12 36.1	9.4	57.1
09	319 06.4	.. 39.1	20 48.0	11.2	12 26.7	9.5	57.1
10	334 06.4	39.9	35 18.2	11.3	12 17.2	9.4	57.1
11	349 06.4	40.7	49 48.5	11.4	12 07.8	9.6	57.1
12	4 06.4	S14 41.4	64 18.9	11.4	N11 58.2	9.6	57.0
13	19 06.4	42.2	78 49.3	11.5	11 48.6	9.6	57.0
14	34 06.4	43.0	93 19.8	11.6	11 39.0	9.7	57.0
15	49 06.4	.. 43.8	107 50.4	11.6	11 29.3	9.8	57.0
16	64 06.4	44.6	122 21.0	11.7	11 19.5	9.8	56.9
17	79 06.4	45.4	136 51.7	11.8	11 09.7	9.8	56.9
18	94 06.4	S14 46.2	151 22.5	11.8	N10 59.9	9.9	56.9
19	109 06.4	47.0	165 53.3	11.9	10 50.0	9.9	56.8
20	124 06.5	47.8	180 24.2	11.9	10 40.1	10.0	56.8
21	139 06.5	.. 48.6	194 55.1	12.0	10 30.1	10.0	56.8
22	154 06.5	49.4	209 26.1	12.1	10 20.1	10.1	56.8
23	169 06.5	50.1	223 57.2	12.1	N10 10.0	10.1	56.7
	SD 16.1	d 0.8	SD 15.9		15.7		15.5

Left margin day labels: **SUNDAY** (31), **MONDAY** (1), **TUESDAY** (2)

Moonrise

Lat.	Twilight Naut.	Twilight Civil	Sunrise	31	1	2	3
N 72	06 04	07 27	08 54	19 20	21 54	23 56	25 48
N 70	06 00	07 14	08 28	20 26	22 24	24 13	00 13
68	05 57	07 04	08 09	21 02	22 46	24 26	00 26
66	05 54	06 55	07 53	21 28	23 03	24 36	00 36
64	05 51	06 48	07 41	21 47	23 16	24 45	00 45
62	05 49	06 41	07 30	22 03	23 28	24 53	00 53
60	05 46	06 36	07 21	22 17	23 38	24 59	00 59
N 58	05 44	06 31	07 13	22 28	23 46	25 05	01 05
56	05 42	06 26	07 06	22 38	23 54	25 10	01 10
54	05 40	06 22	07 00	22 47	24 01	00 01	01 14
52	05 38	06 18	06 54	22 54	24 07	00 07	01 18
50	05 37	06 15	06 49	23 01	24 12	00 12	01 22
45	05 32	06 07	06 38	23 16	24 24	00 24	01 30
N 40	05 28	06 00	06 28	23 29	24 33	00 33	01 37
35	05 24	05 54	06 20	23 39	24 41	00 41	01 42
30	05 20	05 49	06 13	23 48	24 49	00 49	01 47
20	05 12	05 39	06 01	24 04	00 04	01 01	01 56
N 10	05 04	05 29	05 50	24 17	00 17	01 12	02 04
0	04 54	05 19	05 40	24 30	00 30	01 22	02 11
S 10	04 43	05 08	05 30	24 43	00 43	01 32	02 18
20	04 29	04 56	05 19	00 06	00 57	01 43	02 25
30	04 11	04 41	05 06	00 24	01 12	01 55	02 34
35	03 59	04 31	04 58	00 34	01 21	02 02	02 39
40	03 45	04 21	04 50	00 46	01 31	02 10	02 44
45	03 28	04 08	04 40	01 01	01 43	02 20	02 51
S 50	03 06	03 51	04 27	01 18	01 58	02 31	02 59
52	02 54	03 43	04 22	01 26	02 05	02 36	03 02
54	02 41	03 35	04 15	01 35	02 12	02 42	03 06
56	02 26	03 25	04 08	01 45	02 21	02 48	03 10
58	02 07	03 13	04 00	01 57	02 30	02 55	03 15
S 60	01 43	03 00	03 51	02 10	02 41	03 03	03 20

Moonset

Lat.	Sunset	Twilight Civil	Twilight Naut.	31	1	2	3
N 72	14 32	15 59	17 21	17 25	16 40	16 21	16 07
N 70	14 58	16 11	17 25	16 17	16 09	16 02	15 56
68	15 17	16 22	17 29	15 41	15 46	15 48	15 48
66	15 33	16 31	17 32	15 15	15 28	15 36	15 41
64	15 45	16 38	17 35	14 54	15 13	15 26	15 35
62	15 56	16 45	17 37	14 38	15 01	15 18	15 30
60	16 05	16 50	17 40	14 24	14 50	15 10	15 26
N 58	16 13	16 55	17 42	14 12	14 41	15 04	15 22
56	16 21	17 00	17 44	14 02	14 33	14 58	15 18
54	16 27	17 04	17 46	13 52	14 26	14 53	15 15
52	16 33	17 08	17 48	13 44	14 19	14 48	15 12
50	16 38	17 12	17 50	13 37	14 13	14 44	15 10
45	16 49	17 20	17 54	13 21	14 01	14 34	15 04
N 40	16 58	17 26	17 58	13 08	13 50	14 26	14 59
35	17 06	17 32	18 02	12 57	13 41	14 20	14 55
30	17 13	17 38	18 06	12 47	13 33	14 14	14 51
20	17 26	17 48	18 15	12 31	13 19	14 03	14 44
N 10	17 37	17 58	18 23	12 16	13 07	13 54	14 39
0	17 47	18 08	18 33	12 02	12 55	13 46	14 33
S 10	17 58	18 19	18 45	11 48	12 44	13 37	14 28
20	18 09	18 32	18 59	11 33	12 31	13 28	14 22
30	18 22	18 47	19 17	11 16	12 17	13 17	14 15
35	18 29	18 56	19 29	11 06	12 09	13 11	14 11
40	18 38	19 07	19 43	10 54	11 59	13 04	14 07
45	18 48	19 21	20 00	10 41	11 48	12 55	14 02
S 50	19 01	19 37	20 25	10 24	11 35	12 45	13 55
52	19 07	19 45	20 35	10 16	11 28	12 41	13 52
54	19 13	19 54	20 48	10 08	11 21	12 36	13 49
56	19 20	20 04	21 04	09 58	11 13	12 30	13 46
58	19 28	20 16	21 24	09 47	11 05	12 24	13 42
S 60	19 38	20 30	21 49	09 34	10 54	12 16	13 37

SUN and MOON

Day	Eqn. of Time 00h	Eqn. of Time 12h	Mer. Pass.	Mer. Pass. Upper	Mer. Pass. Lower	Age	Phase
d	m s	m s	h m	h m	h m	d	%
31	16 21	16 22	11 44	05 49	18 16	22	50
1	16 23	16 24	11 44	06 43	19 09	23	39
2	16 25	16 26	11 44	07 34	19 58	24	29

UT	ARIES GHA	VENUS −4.4 GHA	Dec	MARS +0.8 GHA	Dec	JUPITER −2.9 GHA	Dec	SATURN −0.2 GHA	Dec	STARS Name	SHA	Dec
d h	° ′	° ′	° ′	° ′	° ′	° ′	° ′	° ′	° ′		° ′	° ′
3 00	41 48.6	227 24.8	N 3 02.0	118 09.2	S24 31.4	14 43.3	N 9 32.3	359 28.7	N13 32.1	Acamar	315 26.0	S40 18.4
01	56 51.1	242 24.9	01.2	133 09.6	31.2	29 46.1	32.2	14 31.4	32.1	Achernar	335 34.1	S57 14.4
02	71 53.6	257 24.9	3 00.4	148 10.1	31.0	44 48.9	32.1	29 34.0	32.0	Acrux	173 21.8	S63 05.6
03	86 56.0	272 24.9	2 59.6	163 10.5	.. 30.8	59 51.7	.. 32.0	44 36.7	.. 31.9	Adhara	255 20.7	S28 58.1
04	101 58.5	287 24.9	58.8	178 10.9	30.6	74 54.4	31.9	59 39.4	31.9	Aldebaran	291 01.3	N16 30.5
05	117 01.0	302 25.0	58.0	193 11.4	30.4	89 57.2	31.8	74 42.0	31.8			
06	132 03.4	317 25.0	N 2 57.2	208 11.8	S24 30.2	105 00.0	N 9 31.7	89 44.7	N13 31.8	Alioth	166 30.5	N55 57.7
W 07	147 05.9	332 25.0	56.4	223 12.2	30.0	120 02.7	31.6	104 47.4	31.7	Alkaid	153 07.7	N49 19.0
E 08	162 08.4	347 25.0	55.5	238 12.7	29.8	135 05.5	31.5	119 50.0	31.7	Al Na'ir	27 56.9	S46 57.9
D 09	177 10.8	2 25.1	.. 54.7	253 13.1	.. 29.6	150 08.3	.. 31.4	134 52.7	.. 31.6	Alnilam	275 56.9	S 1 12.1
N 10	192 13.3	17 25.1	53.9	268 13.5	29.4	165 11.1	31.2	149 55.3	31.5	Alphard	218 06.6	S 8 39.3
E 11	207 15.8	32 25.1	53.1	283 14.0	29.2	180 13.8	31.1	164 58.0	31.5			
S 12	222 18.2	47 25.1	N 2 52.3	298 14.4	S24 29.0	195 16.6	N 9 31.0	180 00.7	N13 31.4	Alphecca	126 20.4	N26 43.2
D 13	237 20.7	62 25.1	51.5	313 14.8	28.8	210 19.4	30.9	195 03.3	31.4	Alpheratz	357 54.2	N29 05.5
A 14	252 23.1	77 25.2	50.7	328 15.3	28.6	225 22.2	30.8	210 06.0	31.3	Altair	62 18.7	N 8 52.3
Y 15	267 25.6	92 25.2	.. 49.9	343 15.7	.. 28.4	240 24.9	.. 30.7	225 08.7	.. 31.2	Ankaa	353 25.8	S42 18.6
16	282 28.1	107 25.2	49.0	358 16.1	28.2	255 27.7	30.6	240 11.3	31.2	Antares	112 39.6	S26 25.7
17	297 30.5	122 25.2	48.2	13 16.6	28.0	270 30.5	30.5	255 14.0	31.1			
18	312 33.0	137 25.2	N 2 47.4	28 17.0	S24 27.8	285 33.2	N 9 30.4	270 16.6	N13 31.1	Arcturus	146 05.8	N19 11.2
19	327 35.5	152 25.3	46.6	43 17.4	27.6	300 36.0	30.3	285 19.3	31.0	Atria	107 51.5	S69 01.6
20	342 37.9	167 25.3	45.8	58 17.9	27.4	315 38.8	30.2	300 22.0	31.0	Avior	234 22.2	S59 30.2
21	357 40.4	182 25.3	.. 45.0	73 18.3	.. 27.2	330 41.6	.. 30.0	315 24.6	.. 30.9	Bellatrix	278 43.1	N 6 20.9
22	12 42.9	197 25.3	44.1	88 18.7	27.0	345 44.3	29.9	330 27.3	30.8	Betelgeuse	271 12.6	N 7 24.4
23	27 45.3	212 25.3	43.3	103 19.1	26.8	0 47.1	29.8	345 30.0	30.8			
4 00	42 47.8	227 25.3	N 2 42.5	118 19.6	S24 26.6	15 49.9	N 9 29.7	0 32.6	N13 30.7	Canopus	264 00.5	S52 41.6
01	57 50.2	242 25.4	41.7	133 20.0	26.4	30 52.7	29.6	15 35.3	30.7	Capella	280 49.8	N45 59.7
02	72 52.7	257 25.4	40.9	148 20.4	26.2	45 55.4	29.5	30 37.9	30.6	Deneb	49 38.7	N45 17.1
03	87 55.2	272 25.4	.. 40.0	163 20.9	.. 26.0	60 58.2	.. 29.4	45 40.6	.. 30.5	Denebola	182 44.7	N14 34.5
04	102 57.6	287 25.4	39.2	178 21.3	25.8	76 01.0	29.3	60 43.3	30.5	Diphda	349 06.2	S17 59.3
05	118 00.1	302 25.4	38.4	193 21.7	25.6	91 03.7	29.2	75 45.9	30.4			
06	133 02.6	317 25.4	N 2 37.6	208 22.2	S24 25.4	106 06.5	N 9 29.1	90 48.6	N13 30.4	Dubhe	194 05.0	N61 45.0
07	148 05.0	332 25.4	36.8	223 22.6	25.2	121 09.3	29.0	105 51.3	30.3	Elnath	278 25.7	N28 36.3
T 08	163 07.5	347 25.4	35.9	238 23.0	25.0	136 12.0	28.8	120 53.9	30.3	Eltanin	90 51.4	N51 29.7
H 09	178 10.0	2 25.5	.. 35.1	253 23.5	.. 24.8	151 14.8	.. 28.7	135 56.6	.. 30.2	Enif	33 57.5	N 9 52.6
U 10	193 12.4	17 25.5	34.3	268 23.9	24.6	166 17.6	28.6	150 59.2	30.1	Fomalhaut	15 35.5	S29 37.5
R 11	208 14.9	32 25.5	33.5	283 24.3	24.4	181 20.4	28.5	166 01.9	30.1			
S 12	223 17.4	47 25.5	N 2 32.6	298 24.8	S24 24.2	196 23.1	N 9 28.4	181 04.6	N13 30.0	Gacrux	172 13.2	S57 06.4
D 13	238 19.8	62 25.5	31.8	313 25.2	24.0	211 25.9	28.3	196 07.2	30.0	Gienah	176 03.5	S17 32.2
A 14	253 22.3	77 25.5	31.0	328 25.6	23.7	226 28.7	28.2	211 09.9	29.9	Hadar	149 03.6	S60 22.1
Y 15	268 24.7	92 25.5	.. 30.1	343 26.1	.. 23.5	241 31.4	.. 28.1	226 12.6	.. 29.8	Hamal	328 12.4	N23 27.7
16	283 27.2	107 25.5	29.3	358 26.5	23.3	256 34.2	28.0	241 15.2	29.8	Kaus Aust.	83 58.1	S34 23.1
17	298 29.7	122 25.5	28.5	13 26.9	23.1	271 37.0	27.9	256 17.9	29.7			
18	313 32.1	137 25.5	N 2 27.7	28 27.3	S24 22.9	286 39.7	N 9 27.8	271 20.5	N13 29.7	Kochab	137 20.8	N74 09.5
19	328 34.6	152 25.5	26.8	43 27.8	22.7	301 42.5	27.7	286 23.2	29.6	Markab	13 48.7	N15 12.4
20	343 37.1	167 25.5	26.0	58 28.2	22.5	316 45.3	27.5	301 25.9	29.5	Menkar	314 25.8	N 4 05.3
21	358 39.5	182 25.6	.. 25.2	73 28.6	.. 22.3	331 48.1	.. 27.4	316 28.5	.. 29.5	Menkent	148 20.5	S36 21.9
22	13 42.0	197 25.6	24.3	88 29.1	22.1	346 50.8	27.3	331 31.2	29.4	Miaplacidus	221 42.0	S69 42.6
23	28 44.5	212 25.6	23.5	103 29.5	21.8	1 53.6	27.2	346 33.9	29.4			
5 00	43 46.9	227 25.6	N 2 22.7	118 29.9	S24 21.6	16 56.4	N 9 27.1	1 36.5	N13 29.3	Mirfak	308 55.1	N49 51.5
01	58 49.4	242 25.6	21.8	133 30.4	21.4	31 59.1	27.0	16 39.2	29.3	Nunki	76 11.6	S26 17.8
02	73 51.9	257 25.6	21.0	148 30.8	21.2	47 01.9	26.9	31 41.8	29.2	Peacock	53 36.0	S56 44.3
03	88 54.3	272 25.6	.. 20.2	163 31.2	.. 21.0	62 04.7	.. 26.8	46 44.5	.. 29.1	Pollux	243 40.6	N28 01.5
04	103 56.8	287 25.6	19.3	178 31.7	20.8	77 07.4	26.7	61 47.2	29.1	Procyon	245 10.7	N 5 13.6
05	118 59.2	302 25.6	18.5	193 32.1	20.6	92 10.2	26.6	76 49.8	29.0			
06	134 01.7	317 25.6	N 2 17.7	208 32.5	S24 20.3	107 13.0	N 9 26.5	91 52.5	N13 29.0	Rasalhague	96 16.6	N12 33.9
07	149 04.2	332 25.6	16.8	223 32.9	20.1	122 15.7	26.4	106 55.2	28.9	Regulus	207 54.9	N11 58.2
08	164 06.6	347 25.6	16.0	238 33.4	19.9	137 18.5	26.3	121 57.8	28.8	Rigel	281 22.0	S 8 12.1
F 09	179 09.1	2 25.6	.. 15.2	253 33.8	.. 19.7	152 21.3	.. 26.2	137 00.5	.. 28.8	Rigil Kent.	140 07.0	S60 49.8
R 10	194 11.6	17 25.6	14.3	268 34.2	19.5	167 24.0	26.0	152 03.1	28.7	Sabik	102 25.0	S15 43.3
I 11	209 14.0	32 25.6	13.5	283 34.7	19.3	182 26.8	25.9	167 05.8	28.7			
D 12	224 16.5	47 25.6	N 2 12.7	298 35.1	S24 19.0	197 29.6	N 9 25.8	182 08.5	N13 28.6	Schedar	349 52.2	N56 32.3
A 13	239 19.0	62 25.6	11.8	313 35.5	18.8	212 32.3	25.7	197 11.1	28.6	Shaula	96 36.6	S37 06.2
Y 14	254 21.4	77 25.6	11.0	328 36.0	18.6	227 35.1	25.6	212 13.8	28.5	Sirius	258 42.9	S16 42.8
15	269 23.9	92 25.6	.. 10.1	343 36.4	.. 18.4	242 37.9	.. 25.5	227 16.5	.. 28.4	Spica	158 42.8	S11 09.4
16	284 26.3	107 25.5	09.3	358 36.8	18.2	257 40.6	25.4	242 19.1	28.4	Suhail	223 00.3	S43 25.6
17	299 28.8	122 25.5	08.4	13 37.3	17.9	272 43.4	25.3	257 21.8	28.3			
18	314 31.3	137 25.6	N 2 07.6	28 37.7	S24 17.7	287 46.2	N 9 25.2	272 24.5	N13 28.3	Vega	80 46.4	N38 47.3
19	329 33.7	152 25.5	06.8	43 38.1	17.5	302 48.9	25.1	287 27.1	28.2	Zuben'ubi	137 17.5	S16 02.2
20	344 36.2	167 25.6	05.9	58 38.5	17.3	317 51.7	25.0	302 29.8	28.1			
21	359 38.7	182 25.5	.. 05.1	73 39.0	.. 17.0	332 54.5	.. 24.9	317 32.4	.. 28.1		SHA	Mer. Pass.
22	14 41.1	197 25.5	04.2	88 39.4	16.8	347 57.2	24.8	332 35.1	28.0	Venus	184 37.6	h m 8 50
23	29 43.6	212 25.5	03.4	103 39.8	16.6	3 00.0	24.7	347 37.8	28.0	Mars	75 31.8	16 06
	h m									Jupiter	333 02.1	22 52
Mer. Pass. 21 05.4	v 0.0	d 0.8		v 0.4	d 0.2	v 2.8	d 0.1	v 2.7	d 0.1	Saturn	317 44.8	23 54

UT	SUN GHA	SUN Dec	MOON GHA	v	MOON Dec	d	HP
d h	° ′	° ′	° ′	′	° ′	′	′
3 00	184 06.5	S14 50.9	238 28.3	12.1	N 9 59.9	10.2	56.7
01	199 06.5	51.7	252 59.4	12.3	9 49.7	10.2	56.7
02	214 06.5	52.5	267 30.7	12.3	9 39.5	10.2	56.7
03	229 06.5	.. 53.3	282 02.0	12.3	9 29.3	10.3	56.6
04	244 06.5	54.1	296 33.3	12.4	9 19.0	10.3	56.6
05	259 06.5	54.9	311 04.7	12.5	9 08.7	10.3	56.6
06	274 06.5	S14 55.6	325 36.2	12.5	N 8 58.4	10.4	56.6
W 07	289 06.5	56.4	340 07.7	12.5	8 48.0	10.4	56.5
E 08	304 06.5	57.2	354 39.2	12.6	8 37.6	10.4	56.5
D 09	319 06.5	.. 58.0	9 10.8	12.7	8 27.2	10.5	56.5
N 10	334 06.5	58.8	23 42.5	12.7	8 16.7	10.5	56.5
E 11	349 06.5	14 59.6	38 14.2	12.8	8 06.2	10.5	56.5
S 12	4 06.5	S15 00.4	52 46.0	12.8	N 7 55.7	10.6	56.4
D 13	19 06.5	01.1	67 17.8	12.9	7 45.1	10.6	56.4
A 14	34 06.5	01.9	81 49.7	12.9	7 34.5	10.6	56.4
Y 15	49 06.5	.. 02.7	96 21.6	12.9	7 23.9	10.7	56.4
16	64 06.5	03.5	110 53.5	13.1	7 13.2	10.6	56.3
17	79 06.5	04.3	125 25.6	13.0	7 02.6	10.7	56.3
18	94 06.5	S15 05.0	139 57.6	13.1	N 6 51.9	10.8	56.3
19	109 06.5	05.8	154 29.7	13.2	6 41.1	10.7	56.3
20	124 06.5	06.6	169 01.9	13.1	6 30.4	10.8	56.2
21	139 06.5	.. 07.4	183 34.0	13.3	6 19.6	10.8	56.2
22	154 06.5	08.2	198 06.3	13.3	6 08.8	10.8	56.2
23	169 06.5	08.9	212 38.6	13.3	5 58.0	10.8	56.2
4 00	184 06.5	S15 09.7	227 10.9	13.3	N 5 47.2	10.9	56.1
01	199 06.5	10.5	241 43.2	13.4	5 36.3	10.8	56.1
02	214 06.5	11.3	256 15.6	13.5	5 25.5	10.9	56.1
03	229 06.5	.. 12.0	270 48.1	13.4	5 14.6	10.9	56.1
04	244 06.5	12.8	285 20.5	13.6	5 03.7	10.9	56.1
05	259 06.5	13.6	299 53.1	13.5	4 52.8	11.0	56.0
06	274 06.5	S15 14.4	314 25.6	13.6	N 4 41.8	11.0	56.0
T 07	289 06.5	15.1	328 58.2	13.6	4 30.9	11.0	56.0
H 08	304 06.5	15.9	343 30.8	13.7	4 19.9	11.0	56.0
U 09	319 06.5	.. 16.7	358 03.5	13.7	4 08.9	10.9	55.9
R 10	334 06.5	17.5	12 36.2	13.7	3 58.0	11.0	55.9
S 11	349 06.5	18.2	27 08.9	13.8	3 47.0	11.0	55.9
D 12	4 06.4	S15 19.0	41 41.7	13.8	N 3 36.0	11.0	55.9
A 13	19 06.4	19.8	56 14.5	13.8	3 25.0	11.1	55.9
Y 14	34 06.4	20.6	70 47.3	13.8	3 13.9	11.0	55.8
15	49 06.4	.. 21.3	85 20.1	13.9	3 02.9	11.0	55.8
16	64 06.4	22.1	99 53.0	13.9	2 51.9	11.1	55.8
17	79 06.4	22.9	114 25.9	14.0	2 40.8	11.0	55.8
18	94 06.4	S15 23.6	128 58.9	13.9	N 2 29.8	11.1	55.8
19	109 06.4	24.4	143 31.8	14.0	2 18.7	11.0	55.7
20	124 06.4	25.2	158 04.8	14.1	2 07.7	11.0	55.7
21	139 06.4	.. 25.9	172 37.9	14.0	1 56.6	11.0	55.7
22	154 06.4	26.7	187 10.9	14.1	1 45.6	11.1	55.7
23	169 06.3	27.5	201 44.0	14.1	1 34.5	11.0	55.7
5 00	184 06.3	S15 28.3	216 17.1	14.1	N 1 23.5	11.1	55.6
01	199 06.3	29.0	230 50.2	14.2	1 12.4	11.1	55.6
02	214 06.3	29.8	245 23.4	14.1	1 01.3	11.0	55.6
03	229 06.3	.. 30.6	259 56.5	14.2	0 50.3	11.1	55.6
04	244 06.3	31.3	274 29.7	14.2	0 39.2	11.0	55.6
05	259 06.3	32.1	289 02.9	14.2	0 28.2	11.1	55.5
06	274 06.3	S15 32.8	303 36.1	14.3	N 0 17.1	11.0	55.5
07	289 06.2	33.6	318 09.4	14.2	N 0 06.1	11.0	55.5
08	304 06.2	34.4	332 42.6	14.3	S 0 04.9	11.1	55.5
F 09	319 06.2	.. 35.1	347 15.9	14.3	0 16.0	11.0	55.5
R 10	334 06.2	35.9	1 49.2	14.3	0 27.0	11.0	55.4
I 11	349 06.2	36.7	16 22.5	14.4	0 38.0	11.0	55.4
D 12	4 06.2	S15 37.4	30 55.9	14.3	S 0 49.0	11.0	55.4
A 13	19 06.2	38.2	45 29.2	14.4	1 00.0	11.0	55.4
Y 14	34 06.1	38.9	60 02.6	14.3	1 11.0	10.9	55.4
15	49 06.1	.. 39.7	74 35.9	14.4	1 21.9	11.0	55.4
16	64 06.1	40.5	89 09.3	14.4	1 32.9	10.9	55.3
17	79 06.1	41.2	103 42.7	14.4	1 43.8	11.0	55.3
18	94 06.1	S15 42.0	118 16.1	14.5	S 1 54.8	10.9	55.3
19	109 06.0	42.7	132 49.6	14.4	2 05.7	10.9	55.3
20	124 06.0	43.5	147 23.0	14.4	2 16.6	10.9	55.3
21	139 06.0	.. 44.3	161 56.4	14.5	2 27.5	10.8	55.2
22	154 06.0	45.0	176 29.9	14.4	2 38.3	10.9	55.2
23	169 06.0	45.8	191 03.3	14.5	S 2 49.2	10.8	55.2
SD 16.2	d 0.8		SD 15.4		15.2		15.1

Lat.	Twilight Naut.	Twilight Civil	Sunrise	Moonrise 3	Moonrise 4	Moonrise 5	Moonrise 6
°	h m	h m	h m	h m	h m	h m	h m
N 72	06 16	07 41	09 13	25 48	01 48	03 34	05 17
N 70	06 11	07 26	08 43	00 13	01 56	03 34	05 12
68	06 06	07 14	08 21	00 26	02 02	03 35	05 07
66	06 02	07 05	08 04	00 36	02 07	03 36	05 03
64	05 59	06 56	07 50	00 45	02 12	03 36	04 59
62	05 56	06 49	07 39	00 53	02 16	03 37	04 57
60	05 53	06 43	07 29	00 59	02 19	03 37	04 54
N 58	05 50	06 37	07 20	01 05	02 22	03 38	04 52
56	05 48	06 32	07 12	01 10	02 25	03 38	04 50
54	05 45	06 28	07 05	01 14	02 27	03 38	04 48
52	05 43	06 23	06 59	01 18	02 29	03 38	04 46
50	05 41	06 20	06 54	01 22	02 31	03 39	04 45
45	05 36	06 11	06 42	01 30	02 35	03 39	04 42
N 40	05 31	06 04	06 32	01 37	02 39	03 40	04 39
35	05 27	05 57	06 23	01 42	02 42	03 40	04 37
30	05 23	05 51	06 14	01 47	02 45	03 40	04 35
20	05 14	05 40	06 03	01 56	02 49	03 41	04 32
N 10	05 04	05 29	05 51	02 04	02 53	03 41	04 29
0	04 54	05 19	05 40	02 11	02 57	03 42	04 26
S 10	04 42	05 07	05 29	02 18	03 01	03 42	04 23
20	04 27	04 54	05 17	02 25	03 05	03 43	04 20
30	04 08	04 38	05 03	02 34	03 10	03 44	04 17
35	03 56	04 28	04 55	02 39	03 12	03 44	04 15
40	03 41	04 17	04 46	02 44	03 15	03 44	04 13
45	03 23	04 03	04 35	02 51	03 19	03 45	04 10
S 50	02 59	03 46	04 22	02 59	03 23	03 46	04 08
52	02 47	03 37	04 16	03 02	03 25	03 46	04 06
54	02 33	03 28	04 09	03 06	03 27	03 46	04 05
56	02 16	03 17	04 02	03 10	03 29	03 46	04 03
58	01 55	03 05	03 53	03 15	03 32	03 47	04 02
S 60	01 27	02 50	03 43	03 20	03 35	03 47	04 00

Lat.	Sunset	Twilight Civil	Twilight Naut.	Moonset 3	Moonset 4	Moonset 5	Moonset 6
°	h m	h m	h m	h m	h m	h m	h m
N 72	14 13	15 45	17 09	16 07	15 55	15 43	15 31
N 70	14 43	16 00	17 15	15 56	15 51	15 45	15 39
68	15 05	16 12	17 19	15 48	15 48	15 47	15 46
66	15 22	16 21	17 23	15 41	15 45	15 48	15 52
64	15 36	16 30	17 27	15 35	15 43	15 50	15 56
62	15 48	16 37	17 30	15 30	15 41	15 51	16 01
60	15 58	16 43	17 33	15 26	15 39	15 52	16 04
N 58	16 06	16 49	17 36	15 22	15 38	15 53	16 07
56	16 14	16 54	17 38	15 18	15 36	15 53	16 10
54	16 21	16 59	17 41	15 15	15 35	15 54	16 13
52	16 27	17 03	17 43	15 12	15 34	15 55	16 15
50	16 33	17 07	17 45	15 10	15 33	15 55	16 17
45	16 45	17 16	17 50	15 04	15 31	15 57	16 22
N 40	16 55	17 23	17 55	14 59	15 28	15 58	16 26
35	17 03	17 30	18 00	14 55	15 27	15 59	16 30
30	17 11	17 36	18 04	14 51	15 26	15 59	16 33
20	17 24	17 47	18 13	14 44	15 23	16 01	16 38
N 10	17 36	17 58	18 23	14 39	15 21	16 02	16 42
0	17 47	18 08	18 33	14 33	15 19	16 03	16 47
S 10	17 58	18 20	18 46	14 28	15 17	16 04	16 51
20	18 10	18 33	19 01	14 22	15 14	16 05	16 56
30	18 24	18 50	19 24	14 15	15 12	16 07	17 01
35	18 32	19 00	19 32	14 11	15 10	16 07	17 04
40	18 42	19 11	19 47	14 07	15 08	16 08	17 08
45	18 53	19 25	20 06	14 02	15 06	16 09	17 12
S 50	19 06	19 43	20 30	13 55	15 04	16 11	17 17
52	19 12	19 51	20 42	13 52	15 02	16 11	17 19
54	19 19	20 01	20 57	13 49	15 01	16 12	17 21
56	19 27	20 12	21 14	13 46	15 00	16 12	17 24
58	19 36	20 25	21 36	13 42	14 58	16 13	17 27
S 60	19 46	20 40	22 06	13 37	14 56	16 14	17 30

Day	SUN Eqn. of Time 00h	SUN Eqn. of Time 12h	SUN Mer. Pass.	MOON Mer. Pass. Upper	MOON Mer. Pass. Lower	Age	Phase
d	m s	m s	h m	h m	h m	d	%
3	16 26	16 26	11 44	08 22	20 45	25	20
4	16 26	16 26	11 44	09 08	21 30	26	13
5	16 25	16 25	11 44	09 52	22 14	27	7

UT	ARIES GHA	VENUS −4.3 GHA	Dec	MARS +0.8 GHA	Dec	JUPITER −2.9 GHA	Dec	SATURN −0.2 GHA	Dec	STARS Name	SHA	Dec
6 00	44 46.1	227 25.5	N 2 02.5	118 40.3	S24 16.4	18 02.8	N 9 24.6	2 40.4	N13 27.9	Acamar	315 26.0	S40 18.4
01	59 48.5	242 25.5	01.7	133 40.7	16.2	33 05.5	24.4	17 43.1	27.9	Achernar	335 34.1	S57 14.4
02	74 51.0	257 25.5	00.9	148 41.1	15.9	48 08.3	24.3	32 45.8	27.8	Acrux	173 21.7	S63 05.6
03	89 53.5	272 25.5	2 00.0	163 41.6 ..	15.7	63 11.1 ..	24.2	47 48.4 ..	27.7	Adhara	255 20.7	S28 58.2
04	104 55.9	287 25.5	1 59.2	178 42.0	15.5	78 13.8	24.1	62 51.1	27.7	Aldebaran	291 01.3	N16 30.5
05	119 58.4	302 25.5	58.3	193 42.4	15.3	93 16.6	24.0	77 53.7	27.6			
S 06	135 00.8	317 25.5	N 1 57.5	208 42.9	S24 15.0	108 19.4	N 9 23.9	92 56.4	N13 27.6	Alioth	166 30.5	N55 57.7
A 07	150 03.3	332 25.5	56.6	223 43.3	14.8	123 22.1	23.8	107 59.1	27.5	Alkaid	153 07.7	N49 18.9
T 08	165 05.8	347 25.5	55.8	238 43.7	14.6	138 24.9	23.7	123 01.7	27.5	Al Na'ir	27 56.9	S46 57.9
U 09	180 08.2	2 25.4 ..	54.9	253 44.1 ..	14.3	153 27.7 ..	23.6	138 04.4 ..	27.4	Alnilam	275 56.9	S 1 12.1
R 10	195 10.7	17 25.4	54.1	268 44.6	14.1	168 30.4	23.5	153 07.1	27.3	Alphard	218 06.5	S 8 39.3
D 11	210 13.2	32 25.4	53.2	283 45.0	13.9	183 33.2	23.4	168 09.7	27.3			
A 12	225 15.6	47 25.4	N 1 52.4	298 45.4	S24 13.7	198 35.9	N 9 23.3	183 12.4	N13 27.2	Alphecca	126 20.4	N26 43.1
Y 13	240 18.1	62 25.4	51.5	313 45.9	13.4	213 38.7	23.2	198 15.0	27.2	Alpheratz	357 54.2	N29 05.5
14	255 20.6	77 25.4	50.7	328 46.3	13.2	228 41.5	23.1	213 17.7	27.1	Altair	62 18.7	N 8 52.3
15	270 23.0	92 25.4 ..	49.8	343 46.7 ..	13.0	243 44.2 ..	23.0	228 20.4 ..	27.0	Ankaa	353 25.8	S42 18.6
16	285 25.5	107 25.4	49.0	358 47.2	12.7	258 47.0	22.9	243 23.0	27.0	Antares	112 39.6	S26 25.7
17	300 27.9	122 25.3	48.1	13 47.6	12.5	273 49.8	22.8	258 25.7	26.9			
18	315 30.4	137 25.3	N 1 47.3	28 48.0	S24 12.3	288 52.5	N 9 22.7	273 28.4	N13 26.9	Arcturus	146 05.8	N19 11.2
19	330 32.9	152 25.3	46.4	43 48.5	12.0	303 55.3	22.5	288 31.0	26.8	Atria	107 51.5	S69 01.6
20	345 35.3	167 25.3	45.5	58 48.9	11.8	318 58.1	22.4	303 33.7	26.8	Avior	234 22.2	S59 30.2
21	0 37.8	182 25.3 ..	44.7	73 49.3 ..	11.6	334 00.8 ..	22.3	318 36.4 ..	26.7	Bellatrix	278 43.1	N 6 20.9
22	15 40.3	197 25.3	43.8	88 49.7	11.3	349 03.6	22.2	333 39.0	26.6	Betelgeuse	271 12.5	N 7 24.4
23	30 42.7	212 25.2	43.0	103 50.2	11.1	4 06.3	22.1	348 41.7	26.6			
7 00	45 45.2	227 25.2	N 1 42.1	118 50.6	S24 10.9	19 09.1	N 9 22.0	3 44.3	N13 26.5	Canopus	264 00.5	S52 41.6
01	60 47.7	242 25.2	41.3	133 51.0	10.6	34 11.9	21.9	18 47.0	26.5	Capella	280 49.7	N45 59.7
02	75 50.1	257 25.2	40.4	148 51.5	10.4	49 14.6	21.8	33 49.7	26.4	Deneb	49 38.8	N45 17.1
03	90 52.6	272 25.2 ..	39.5	163 51.9 ..	10.2	64 17.4 ..	21.7	48 52.3 ..	26.3	Denebola	182 44.7	N14 34.5
04	105 55.1	287 25.2	38.7	178 52.3	09.9	79 20.1	21.6	63 55.0	26.3	Diphda	349 06.3	S17 59.3
05	120 57.5	302 25.1	37.8	193 52.8	09.7	94 22.9	21.5	78 57.7	26.2			
S 06	136 00.0	317 25.1	N 1 37.0	208 53.2	S24 09.5	109 25.7	N 9 21.4	94 00.3	N13 26.2	Dubhe	194 05.0	N61 45.0
U 07	151 02.4	332 25.1	36.1	223 53.6	09.3	124 28.4	21.3	109 03.0	26.1	Elnath	278 25.7	N28 36.3
N 08	166 04.9	347 25.1	35.2	238 54.0	09.0	139 31.2	21.2	124 05.6	26.1	Eltanin	90 51.5	N51 29.7
D 09	181 07.4	2 25.1 ..	34.4	253 54.5 ..	08.7	154 34.0 ..	21.1	139 08.3 ..	26.0	Enif	33 57.5	N 9 52.6
A 10	196 09.8	17 25.0	33.5	268 54.9	08.5	169 36.7	21.0	154 11.0	25.9	Fomalhaut	15 35.5	S29 37.5
Y 11	211 12.3	32 25.0	32.7	283 55.3	08.3	184 39.5	20.9	169 13.6	25.9			
12	226 14.8	47 25.0	N 1 31.8	298 55.8	S24 08.0	199 42.2	N 9 20.8	184 16.3	N13 25.8	Gacrux	172 13.2	S57 06.4
13	241 17.2	62 25.0	30.9	313 56.2	07.8	214 45.0	20.7	199 19.0	25.8	Gienah	176 03.5	S17 32.2
14	256 19.7	77 24.9	30.1	328 56.6	07.5	229 47.8	20.6	214 21.6	25.7	Hadar	149 03.6	S60 22.1
15	271 22.2	92 24.9 ..	29.2	343 57.1 ..	07.3	244 50.5 ..	20.5	229 24.3 ..	25.7	Hamal	328 12.4	N23 27.7
16	286 24.6	107 24.9	28.3	358 57.5	07.1	259 53.3	20.4	244 27.0	25.6	Kaus Aust.	83 58.1	S34 23.1
17	301 27.1	122 24.9	27.5	13 57.9	06.8	274 56.0	20.2	259 29.6	25.5			
18	316 29.6	137 24.8	N 1 26.6	28 58.4	S24 06.6	289 58.8	N 9 20.1	274 32.3	N13 25.5	Kochab	137 20.8	N74 09.5
19	331 32.0	152 24.8	25.7	43 58.8	06.3	305 01.6	20.0	289 34.9	25.4	Markab	13 48.7	N15 12.4
20	346 34.5	167 24.8	24.9	58 59.2	06.1	320 04.3	19.9	304 37.6	25.4	Menkar	314 25.8	N 4 05.3
21	1 36.9	182 24.8 ..	24.0	73 59.6 ..	05.8	335 07.1 ..	19.8	319 40.3 ..	25.3	Menkent	148 20.5	S36 21.9
22	16 39.4	197 24.7	23.1	89 00.1	05.6	350 09.8	19.7	334 42.9	25.2	Miaplacidus	221 41.9	S69 42.6
23	31 41.9	212 24.7	22.3	104 00.5	05.3	5 12.6	19.6	349 45.6	25.2			
8 00	46 44.3	227 24.7	N 1 21.4	119 00.9	S24 05.1	20 15.3	N 9 19.5	4 48.3	N13 25.1	Mirfak	308 55.1	N49 51.6
01	61 46.8	242 24.6	20.5	134 01.4	04.9	35 18.1	19.4	19 50.9	25.1	Nunki	76 11.7	S26 17.8
02	76 49.3	257 24.6	19.7	149 01.8	04.6	50 20.9	19.3	34 53.6	25.0	Peacock	53 36.0	S56 44.3
03	91 51.7	272 24.6 ..	18.8	164 02.2 ..	04.4	65 23.6 ..	19.2	49 56.2 ..	25.0	Pollux	243 40.6	N28 01.5
04	106 54.2	287 24.6	17.9	179 02.7	04.1	80 26.4	19.1	64 58.9	24.9	Procyon	245 10.7	N 5 13.5
05	121 56.7	302 24.5	17.1	194 03.1	03.9	95 29.1	19.0	80 01.6	24.8			
M 06	136 59.1	317 24.5	N 1 16.2	209 03.5	S24 03.6	110 31.9	N 9 18.9	95 04.2	N13 24.8	Rasalhague	96 16.6	N12 33.8
O 07	152 01.6	332 24.5	15.3	224 03.9	03.4	125 34.7	18.8	110 06.9	24.7	Regulus	207 54.9	N11 58.1
N 08	167 04.0	347 24.4	14.4	239 04.4	03.1	140 37.4	18.7	125 09.6	24.7	Rigel	281 22.0	S 8 12.1
D 09	182 06.5	2 24.4 ..	13.6	254 04.8 ..	02.9	155 40.2 ..	18.6	140 12.2 ..	24.6	Rigil Kent.	140 07.0	S60 49.8
A 10	197 09.0	17 24.4	12.7	269 05.2	02.6	170 42.9	18.5	155 14.9	24.6	Sabik	102 25.0	S15 43.3
Y 11	212 11.4	32 24.3	11.8	284 05.7	02.4	185 45.7	18.4	170 17.5	24.5			
12	227 13.9	47 24.3	N 1 11.0	299 06.1	S24 02.1	200 48.4	N 9 18.3	185 20.2	N13 24.4	Schedar	349 52.2	N56 32.3
13	242 16.4	62 24.3	10.1	314 06.5	01.9	215 51.2	18.2	200 22.9	24.4	Shaula	96 36.7	S37 06.2
14	257 18.8	77 24.2	09.2	329 07.0	01.6	230 53.9	18.1	215 25.5	24.3	Sirius	258 42.9	S16 42.8
15	272 21.3	92 24.2 ..	08.3	344 07.4 ..	01.4	245 56.7 ..	18.0	230 28.2 ..	24.3	Spica	158 42.7	S11 09.4
16	287 23.8	107 24.2	07.5	359 07.8	01.1	260 59.5	17.9	245 30.9	24.2	Suhail	223 00.2	S43 25.6
17	302 26.2	122 24.1	06.6	14 08.3	00.9	276 02.2	17.8	260 33.5	24.1			
18	317 28.7	137 24.1	N 1 05.7	29 08.7	S24 00.6	291 05.0	N 9 17.7	275 36.2	N13 24.1	Vega	80 46.4	N38 47.3
19	332 31.2	152 24.1	04.8	44 09.1	00.4	306 07.7	17.6	290 38.8	24.0	Zuben'ubi	137 17.5	S16 02.1
20	347 33.6	167 24.0	03.9	59 09.5	24 00.1	321 10.5	17.5	305 41.5	24.0		SHA	Mer. Pass.
21	2 36.1	182 24.0 ..	03.1	74 10.0	23 59.8	336 13.2 ..	17.4	320 44.2 ..	23.9			h m
22	17 38.5	197 24.0	02.2	89 10.4	59.6	351 16.0	17.3	335 46.8	23.9	Venus	181 40.0	8 50
23	32 41.0	212 23.9	01.3	104 10.8	59.3	6 18.7	17.2	350 49.5	23.8	Mars	73 05.4	16 04
	h m									Jupiter	333 23.9	22 39
Mer. Pass.	20 53.6	v 0.0	d 0.9	v 0.4	d 0.2	v 2.8	d 0.1	v 2.7	d 0.1	Saturn	317 59.1	23 41

UT	SUN GHA	SUN Dec	MOON GHA	v	MOON Dec	d	HP
d h	° ′	° ′	° ′	′	° ′	′	′
6 00	184 05.9	S15 46.5	205 36.8	14.5	S 3 00.0	10.9	55.2
01	199 05.9	47.3	220 10.3	14.4	3 10.9	10.8	55.2
02	214 05.9	48.0	234 43.7	14.5	3 21.7	10.7	55.2
03	229 05.9 ..	48.8	249 17.2	14.5	3 32.4	10.8	55.1
04	244 05.9	49.6	263 50.7	14.5	3 43.2	10.7	55.1
05	259 05.8	50.3	278 24.2	14.5	3 53.9	10.7	55.1
S 06	274 05.8	S15 51.1	292 57.7	14.5	S 4 04.6	10.7	55.1
A 07	289 05.8	51.8	307 31.2	14.5	4 15.3	10.7	55.1
T 08	304 05.8	52.6	322 04.7	14.5	4 26.0	10.6	55.1
U 09	319 05.7 ..	53.3	336 38.2	14.5	4 36.6	10.7	55.0
R 10	334 05.7	54.1	351 11.7	14.5	4 47.3	10.6	55.0
D 11	349 05.7	54.8	5 45.2	14.5	4 57.9	10.5	55.0
A 12	4 05.7	S15 55.6	20 18.7	14.5	S 5 08.4	10.6	55.0
Y 13	19 05.7	56.3	34 52.2	14.5	5 19.0	10.5	55.0
14	34 05.6	57.1	49 25.7	14.5	5 29.5	10.5	55.0
15	49 05.6 ..	57.8	63 59.2	14.5	5 40.0	10.4	54.9
16	64 05.6	58.6	78 32.7	14.5	5 50.4	10.4	54.9
17	79 05.5	15 59.3	93 06.2	14.5	6 00.8	10.4	54.9
18	94 05.5	S16 00.1	107 39.7	14.5	S 6 11.2	10.4	54.9
19	109 05.5	00.8	122 13.2	14.5	6 21.6	10.3	54.9
20	124 05.5	01.6	136 46.7	14.5	6 31.9	10.3	54.9
21	139 05.4 ..	02.3	151 20.2	14.5	6 42.2	10.3	54.9
22	154 05.4	03.1	165 53.7	14.4	6 52.5	10.2	54.8
23	169 05.4	03.8	180 27.1	14.5	7 02.7	10.2	54.8
7 00	184 05.4	S16 04.6	195 00.6	14.4	S 7 12.9	10.2	54.8
01	199 05.3	05.3	209 34.0	14.5	7 23.1	10.1	54.8
02	214 05.3	06.0	224 07.5	14.4	7 33.2	10.1	54.8
03	229 05.3 ..	06.8	238 40.9	14.5	7 43.3	10.1	54.8
04	244 05.2	07.5	253 14.4	14.4	7 53.4	10.0	54.7
05	259 05.2	08.3	267 47.8	14.4	8 03.4	10.0	54.7
S 06	274 05.2	S16 09.0	282 21.2	14.4	S 8 13.4	9.9	54.7
U 07	289 05.1	09.8	296 54.6	14.4	8 23.3	9.9	54.7
N 08	304 05.1	10.5	311 28.0	14.4	8 33.2	9.9	54.7
D 09	319 05.1 ..	11.2	326 01.4	14.3	8 43.1	9.8	54.7
A 10	334 05.0	12.0	340 34.7	14.4	8 52.9	9.8	54.7
Y 11	349 05.0	12.7	355 08.1	14.3	9 02.7	9.7	54.7
12	4 05.0	S16 13.5	9 41.4	14.3	S 9 12.4	9.7	54.6
13	19 04.9	14.2	24 14.8	14.3	9 22.1	9.6	54.6
14	34 04.9	15.0	38 48.1	14.3	9 31.7	9.6	54.6
15	49 04.9 ..	15.7	53 21.4	14.3	9 41.3	9.6	54.6
16	64 04.8	16.4	67 54.7	14.3	9 50.9	9.5	54.6
17	79 04.8	17.2	82 28.0	14.2	10 00.4	9.5	54.6
18	94 04.8	S16 17.9	97 01.2	14.3	S10 09.9	9.4	54.6
19	109 04.7	18.6	111 34.5	14.2	10 19.3	9.4	54.5
20	124 04.7	19.4	126 07.7	14.2	10 28.7	9.3	54.5
21	139 04.7 ..	20.1	140 40.9	14.2	10 38.0	9.3	54.5
22	154 04.6	20.8	155 14.1	14.2	10 47.3	9.2	54.5
23	169 04.6	21.6	169 47.3	14.1	10 56.5	9.2	54.5
8 00	184 04.5	S16 22.3	184 20.4	14.2	S11 05.7	9.1	54.5
01	199 04.5	23.0	198 53.6	14.1	11 14.8	9.1	54.5
02	214 04.5	23.8	213 26.7	14.1	11 23.9	9.0	54.5
03	229 04.4 ..	24.5	227 59.8	14.1	11 32.9	8.9	54.5
04	244 04.4	25.2	242 32.9	14.1	11 41.8	9.0	54.4
05	259 04.4	26.0	257 06.0	14.0	11 50.8	8.8	54.4
M 06	274 04.3	S16 26.7	271 39.0	14.1	S11 59.6	8.8	54.4
O 07	289 04.3	27.4	286 12.1	14.0	12 08.4	8.8	54.4
N 08	304 04.2	28.2	300 45.1	14.0	12 17.2	8.7	54.4
D 09	319 04.2 ..	28.9	315 18.1	13.9	12 25.9	8.6	54.4
A 10	334 04.2	29.6	329 51.0	14.0	12 34.5	8.6	54.4
Y 11	349 04.1	30.4	344 24.0	13.9	12 43.1	8.5	54.4
12	4 04.1	S16 31.1	358 56.9	13.9	S12 51.6	8.5	54.4
13	19 04.0	31.8	13 29.8	13.9	13 00.1	8.4	54.3
14	34 04.0	32.5	28 02.7	13.9	13 08.5	8.3	54.3
15	49 03.9 ..	33.3	42 35.6	13.8	13 16.8	8.3	54.3
16	64 03.9	34.0	57 08.4	13.8	13 25.1	8.3	54.3
17	79 03.9	34.7	71 41.2	13.8	13 33.4	8.1	54.3
18	94 03.8	S16 35.5	86 14.0	13.8	S13 41.5	8.1	54.3
19	109 03.8	36.2	100 46.8	13.7	13 49.6	8.1	54.3
20	124 03.7	36.9	115 19.5	13.8	13 57.7	8.0	54.3
21	139 03.7 ..	37.6	129 52.3	13.7	14 05.7	7.9	54.3
22	154 03.7	38.4	144 25.0	13.6	14 13.6	7.8	54.3
23	169 03.6	39.1	158 57.6	13.7	S14 21.4	7.8	54.2
SD	16.2	d 0.7	SD 15.0		14.9		14.8

Lat.	Naut. (Twilight)	Civil (Twilight)	Sunrise	Moonrise 6	7	8	9
°	h m	h m	h m	h m	h m	h m	h m
N 72	06 28	07 55	09 34	05 17	07 02	08 51	10 51
N 70	06 21	07 38	08 59	05 12	06 48	08 27	10 09
68	06 16	07 25	08 34	05 07	06 38	08 09	09 41
66	06 11	07 14	08 15	05 03	06 29	07 55	09 20
64	06 07	07 05	08 00	04 59	06 22	07 43	09 03
62	06 03	06 57	07 47	04 57	06 15	07 33	08 50
60	05 59	06 50	07 36	04 54	06 10	07 25	08 38
N 58	05 56	06 44	07 27	04 52	06 05	07 17	08 28
56	05 53	06 38	07 19	04 50	06 01	07 11	08 19
54	05 51	06 33	07 11	04 48	05 57	07 05	08 11
52	05 48	06 28	07 05	04 46	05 54	07 00	08 05
50	05 46	06 24	06 59	04 44	05 50	06 55	07 58
45	05 40	06 15	06 46	04 42	05 44	06 45	07 45
N 40	05 35	06 07	06 35	04 39	05 38	06 36	07 34
35	05 30	06 00	06 26	04 37	05 33	06 29	07 25
30	05 25	05 53	06 18	04 35	05 29	06 23	07 16
20	05 15	05 41	06 04	04 32	05 22	06 12	07 02
N 10	05 05	05 30	05 52	04 29	05 15	06 02	06 50
0	04 54	05 19	05 40	04 26	05 09	05 54	06 39
S 10	04 41	05 06	05 28	04 23	05 04	05 45	06 27
20	04 25	04 53	05 16	04 20	04 57	05 35	06 15
30	04 05	04 36	05 01	04 17	04 50	05 25	06 01
35	03 52	04 25	04 53	04 15	04 46	05 19	05 53
40	03 37	04 13	04 43	04 13	04 42	05 12	05 44
45	03 18	03 58	04 31	04 10	04 36	05 04	05 34
S 50	02 52	03 40	04 17	04 08	04 30	04 54	05 21
52	02 39	03 31	04 11	04 06	04 27	04 50	05 15
54	02 24	03 21	04 03	04 05	04 24	04 45	05 09
56	02 05	03 10	03 55	04 02	04 21	04 40	05 01
58	01 42	02 56	03 46	04 02	04 17	04 34	04 53
S 60	01 08	02 40	03 35	04 00	04 12	04 27	04 44

Lat.	Sunset	Civil (Twilight)	Naut. (Twilight)	Moonset 6	7	8	9
°	h m	h m	h m	h m	h m	h m	h m
N 72	13 52	15 31	16 58	15 31	15 18	15 01	14 35
N 70	14 27	15 48	17 05	15 39	15 33	15 26	15 18
68	14 52	16 01	17 10	15 46	15 45	15 45	15 47
66	15 11	16 12	17 15	15 52	15 56	16 01	16 09
64	15 26	16 22	17 20	15 56	16 04	16 13	16 26
62	15 39	16 30	17 23	16 01	16 11	16 24	16 40
60	15 50	16 37	17 27	16 04	16 18	16 33	16 53
N 58	16 00	16 43	17 30	16 07	16 23	16 41	17 03
56	16 08	16 49	17 33	16 10	16 28	16 49	17 12
54	16 15	16 54	17 36	16 13	16 33	16 55	17 21
52	16 22	16 58	17 39	16 15	16 37	17 01	17 28
50	16 28	17 02	17 41	16 17	16 41	17 06	17 35
45	16 41	17 12	17 47	16 22	16 49	17 17	17 49
N 40	16 52	17 20	17 52	16 26	16 55	17 27	18 01
35	17 01	17 27	17 57	16 30	17 01	17 35	18 11
30	17 09	17 34	18 02	16 33	17 06	17 42	18 19
20	17 23	17 46	18 12	16 38	17 15	17 54	18 35
N 10	17 35	17 57	18 22	16 42	17 23	18 05	18 48
0	17 47	18 09	18 34	16 47	17 31	18 15	19 01
S 10	17 59	18 21	18 47	16 51	17 38	18 25	19 13
20	18 12	18 35	19 02	16 56	17 46	18 36	19 27
30	18 27	18 52	19 23	17 01	17 55	18 49	19 42
35	18 35	19 03	19 36	17 04	18 00	18 56	19 51
40	18 45	19 15	19 51	17 08	18 06	19 04	20 01
45	18 57	19 30	20 11	17 12	18 13	19 14	20 13
S 50	19 11	19 49	20 37	17 17	18 22	19 26	20 28
52	19 18	19 58	20 50	17 19	18 25	19 31	20 35
54	19 25	20 08	21 06	17 21	18 30	19 37	20 42
56	19 34	20 20	21 25	17 24	18 34	19 44	20 51
58	19 43	20 33	21 49	17 27	18 40	19 51	21 01
S 60	19 54	20 50	22 25	17 30	18 46	20 00	21 12

Day	Eqn. of Time 00h	Eqn. of Time 12h	Mer. Pass.	Mer. Pass. Upper	Mer. Pass. Lower	Age	Phase
d	m s	m s	h m	h m	h m	d	%
6	16 24	16 23	11 44	10 36	22 58	28	3
7	16 21	16 20	11 44	11 20	23 42	29	1
8	16 18	16 16	11 44	12 04	24 27	00	0

UT	ARIES	VENUS −4.3		MARS +0.8		JUPITER −2.9		SATURN −0.2		STARS		
	GHA	GHA	Dec	GHA	Dec	GHA	Dec	GHA	Dec	Name	SHA	Dec
d h	° ′	° ′	° ′	° ′	° ′	° ′	° ′	° ′	° ′		° ′	° ′
9 00	47 43.5	227 23.9	N 1 00.4	119 11.3	S23 59.1	21 21.5	N 9 17.1	5 52.2	N13 23.7	Acamar	315 26.0	S40 18.4
01	62 45.9	242 23.8	0 59.6	134 11.7	58.8	36 24.3	17.0	20 54.8	23.7	Achernar	335 34.1	S57 14.5
02	77 48.4	257 23.8	58.7	149 12.1	58.6	51 27.0	16.9	35 57.5	23.6	Acrux	173 21.7	S63 05.5
03	92 50.9	272 23.8	.. 57.8	164 12.6	.. 58.3	66 29.8	.. 16.8	51 00.2	.. 23.6	Adhara	255 20.6	S28 58.2
04	107 53.3	287 23.7	56.9	179 13.0	58.1	81 32.5	16.7	66 02.8	23.5	Aldebaran	291 01.2	N16 30.5
05	122 55.8	302 23.7	56.0	194 13.4	57.8	96 35.3	16.6	81 05.5	23.5			
06	137 58.3	317 23.6	N 0 55.1	209 13.9	S23 57.5	111 38.0	N 9 16.5	96 08.1	N13 23.4	Alioth	166 30.5	N55 57.6
07	153 00.7	332 23.6	54.3	224 14.3	57.3	126 40.8	16.4	111 10.8	23.3	Alkaid	153 07.7	N49 18.9
T 08	168 03.2	347 23.6	53.4	239 14.7	57.0	141 43.5	16.3	126 13.5	23.3	Al Na'ir	27 56.9	S46 57.9
U 09	183 05.7	2 23.5	.. 52.5	254 15.1	.. 56.8	156 46.3	.. 16.1	141 16.1	.. 23.2	Alnilam	275 56.9	S 1 12.1
E 10	198 08.1	17 23.5	51.6	269 15.6	56.5	171 49.0	16.0	156 18.8	23.2	Alphard	218 06.5	S 8 39.3
S 11	213 10.6	32 23.4	50.7	284 16.0	56.2	186 51.8	15.9	171 21.5	23.1			
D 12	228 13.0	47 23.4	N 0 49.8	299 16.4	S23 56.0	201 54.5	N 9 15.8	186 24.1	N13 23.1	Alphecca	126 20.4	N26 43.1
A 13	243 15.5	62 23.3	49.0	314 16.9	55.7	216 57.3	15.7	201 26.8	23.0	Alpheratz	357 54.2	N29 05.5
Y 14	258 18.0	77 23.3	48.1	329 17.3	55.4	232 00.1	15.6	216 29.4	22.9	Altair	62 18.7	N 8 52.3
15	273 20.4	92 23.3	.. 47.2	344 17.7	.. 55.2	247 02.8	.. 15.5	231 32.1	.. 22.9	Ankaa	353 25.8	S42 18.6
16	288 22.9	107 23.2	46.3	359 18.2	54.9	262 05.6	15.4	246 34.8	22.8	Antares	112 39.6	S26 25.7
17	303 25.4	122 23.2	45.4	14 18.6	54.7	277 08.3	15.3	261 37.4	22.8			
18	318 27.8	137 23.1	N 0 44.5	29 19.0	S23 54.4	292 11.1	N 9 15.2	276 40.1	N13 22.7	Arcturus	146 05.8	N19 11.2
19	333 30.3	152 23.1	43.6	44 19.5	54.1	307 13.8	15.1	291 42.8	22.6	Atria	107 51.5	S69 01.6
20	348 32.8	167 23.0	42.8	59 19.9	53.9	322 16.6	15.0	306 45.4	22.6	Avior	234 22.2	S59 30.2
21	3 35.2	182 23.0	.. 41.9	74 20.3	.. 53.6	337 19.3	.. 14.9	321 48.1	.. 22.5	Bellatrix	278 43.1	N 6 20.9
22	18 37.7	197 22.9	41.0	89 20.7	53.3	352 22.1	14.8	336 50.7	22.5	Betelgeuse	271 12.5	N 7 24.4
23	33 40.1	212 22.9	40.1	104 21.2	53.1	7 24.8	14.7	351 53.4	22.4			
10 00	48 42.6	227 22.8	N 0 39.2	119 21.6	S23 52.8	22 27.6	N 9 14.6	6 56.1	N13 22.4	Canopus	264 00.5	S52 41.6
01	63 45.1	242 22.8	38.3	134 22.0	52.5	37 30.3	14.5	21 58.7	22.3	Capella	280 49.7	N45 59.7
02	78 47.5	257 22.7	37.4	149 22.5	52.3	52 33.1	14.4	37 01.4	22.2	Deneb	49 38.8	N45 17.1
03	93 50.0	272 22.7	.. 36.5	164 22.9	.. 52.0	67 35.8	.. 14.3	52 04.1	.. 22.2	Denebola	182 44.7	N14 34.5
04	108 52.5	287 22.6	35.6	179 23.3	51.7	82 38.6	14.2	67 06.7	22.1	Diphda	349 06.3	S17 59.3
05	123 54.9	302 22.6	34.7	194 23.8	51.5	97 41.3	14.1	82 09.4	22.1			
06	138 57.4	317 22.5	N 0 33.8	209 24.2	S23 51.2	112 44.1	N 9 14.0	97 12.0	N13 22.0	Dubhe	194 05.0	N61 45.0
W 07	153 59.9	332 22.5	33.0	224 24.6	50.9	127 46.8	13.9	112 14.7	22.0	Elnath	278 25.7	N28 36.3
E 08	169 02.3	347 22.4	32.1	239 25.1	50.6	142 49.6	13.8	127 17.4	21.9	Eltanin	90 51.5	N51 29.7
D 09	184 04.8	2 22.4	.. 31.2	254 25.5	.. 50.4	157 52.3	.. 13.7	142 20.0	.. 21.8	Enif	33 57.5	N 9 52.6
N 10	199 07.3	17 22.3	30.3	269 25.9	50.1	172 55.1	13.6	157 22.7	21.8	Fomalhaut	15 35.5	S29 37.5
E 11	214 09.7	32 22.3	29.4	284 26.4	49.8	187 57.8	13.5	172 25.4	21.7			
S 12	229 12.2	47 22.2	N 0 28.5	299 26.8	S23 49.6	203 00.6	N 9 13.4	187 28.0	N13 21.7	Gacrux	172 13.2	S57 06.4
D 13	244 14.6	62 22.2	27.6	314 27.2	49.3	218 03.3	13.3	202 30.7	21.6	Gienah	176 03.5	S17 32.2
A 14	259 17.1	77 22.1	26.7	329 27.6	49.0	233 06.1	13.2	217 33.3	21.6	Hadar	149 03.6	S60 22.1
Y 15	274 19.6	92 22.1	.. 25.8	344 28.1	.. 48.7	248 08.8	.. 13.1	232 36.0	.. 21.5	Hamal	328 12.4	N23 27.7
16	289 22.0	107 22.0	24.9	359 28.5	48.5	263 11.6	13.0	247 38.7	21.4	Kaus Aust.	83 58.2	S34 23.1
17	304 24.5	122 21.9	24.0	14 28.9	48.2	278 14.3	13.0	262 41.3	21.4			
18	319 27.0	137 21.9	N 0 23.1	29 29.4	S23 47.9	293 17.0	N 9 12.9	277 44.0	N13 21.3	Kochab	137 20.9	N74 09.5
19	334 29.4	152 21.8	22.2	44 29.8	47.6	308 19.8	12.8	292 46.7	21.3	Markab	13 48.7	N15 12.4
20	349 31.9	167 21.8	21.3	59 30.2	47.4	323 22.5	12.7	307 49.3	21.2	Menkar	314 25.8	N 4 05.3
21	4 34.4	182 21.7	.. 20.4	74 30.7	.. 47.1	338 25.3	.. 12.6	322 52.0	.. 21.2	Menkent	148 20.5	S36 21.9
22	19 36.8	197 21.7	19.5	89 31.1	46.8	353 28.0	12.5	337 54.6	21.1	Miaplacidus	221 41.8	S69 42.6
23	34 39.3	212 21.6	18.6	104 31.5	46.5	8 30.8	12.4	352 57.3	21.0			
11 00	49 41.8	227 21.5	N 0 17.7	119 32.0	S23 46.3	23 33.5	N 9 12.3	8 00.0	N13 21.0	Mirfak	308 55.1	N49 51.6
01	64 44.2	242 21.5	16.8	134 32.4	46.0	38 36.3	12.2	23 02.6	20.9	Nunki	76 11.7	S26 17.8
02	79 46.7	257 21.4	15.9	149 32.8	45.7	53 39.0	12.1	38 05.3	20.9	Peacock	53 36.1	S56 44.3
03	94 49.1	272 21.4	.. 15.0	164 33.3	.. 45.4	68 41.8	.. 12.0	53 07.9	.. 20.8	Pollux	243 40.5	N28 01.5
04	109 51.6	287 21.3	14.1	179 33.7	45.2	83 44.5	11.9	68 10.6	20.8	Procyon	245 10.7	N 5 13.5
05	124 54.1	302 21.3	13.2	194 34.1	44.9	98 47.3	11.8	83 13.3	20.7			
06	139 56.5	317 21.2	N 0 12.3	209 34.6	S23 44.6	113 50.0	N 9 11.7	98 15.9	N13 20.6	Rasalhague	96 16.6	N12 33.8
07	154 59.0	332 21.1	11.4	224 35.0	44.3	128 52.8	11.6	113 18.6	20.6	Regulus	207 54.9	N11 58.1
T 08	170 01.5	347 21.1	10.5	239 35.4	44.0	143 55.5	11.5	128 21.3	20.5	Rigel	281 22.0	S 8 12.1
H 09	185 03.9	2 21.0	.. 09.6	254 35.8	.. 43.7	158 58.2	.. 11.4	143 23.9	.. 20.5	Rigil Kent.	140 07.0	S60 49.8
U 10	200 06.4	17 20.9	08.7	269 36.3	43.5	174 01.0	11.3	158 26.6	20.4	Sabik	102 25.0	S15 43.3
R 11	215 08.9	32 20.9	07.8	284 36.7	43.2	189 03.7	11.2	173 29.2	20.4			
S 12	230 11.3	47 20.8	N 0 06.9	299 37.1	S23 42.9	204 06.5	N 9 11.1	188 31.9	N13 20.3	Schedar	349 52.2	N56 32.3
D 13	245 13.8	62 20.8	06.0	314 37.6	42.6	219 09.2	11.0	203 34.6	20.2	Shaula	96 36.7	S37 06.2
A 14	260 16.3	77 20.7	05.1	329 38.0	42.3	234 12.0	10.9	218 37.2	20.2	Sirius	258 42.9	S16 42.9
Y 15	275 18.7	92 20.6	.. 04.2	344 38.4	.. 42.1	249 14.7	.. 10.8	233 39.9	.. 20.1	Spica	158 42.7	S11 09.4
16	290 21.2	107 20.6	03.3	359 38.9	41.8	264 17.4	10.7	248 42.6	20.1	Suhail	223 00.2	S43 25.6
17	305 23.6	122 20.5	02.4	14 39.3	41.5	279 20.2	10.6	263 45.2	20.0			
18	320 26.1	137 20.4	N 0 01.4	29 39.7	S23 41.2	294 22.9	N 9 10.5	278 47.9	N13 20.0	Vega	80 46.4	N38 47.3
19	335 28.6	152 20.4	N 00.5	44 40.2	40.9	309 25.7	10.4	293 50.5	19.9	Zuben'ubi	137 17.5	S16 02.2
20	350 31.0	167 20.3	S 00.4	59 40.6	40.6	324 28.4	10.3	308 53.2	19.9			
21	5 33.5	182 20.2	.. 01.3	74 41.0	.. 40.3	339 31.2	.. 10.2	323 55.9	.. 19.8			
22	20 36.0	197 20.2	02.2	89 41.5	40.1	354 33.9	10.1	338 58.5	19.7			
23	35 38.4	212 20.1	03.1	104 41.9	39.8	9 36.6	10.0	354 01.2	19.7			

	h m										SHA	Mer. Pass.
Mer. Pass. 20 41.8		v −0.1	d 0.9	v 0.4	d 0.3	v 2.7	d 0.1	v 2.7	d 0.1		° ′	h m
										Venus	178 40.2	8 51
										Mars	70 39.0	16 02
										Jupiter	333 45.0	22 26
										Saturn	318 13.5	23 28

UT	SUN GHA	SUN Dec	MOON GHA	v	MOON Dec	d	HP
d h	° ′	° ′	° ′	′	° ′	′	′
9 00	184 03.5	S16 39.8	173 30.3 13.6		S14 29.2	7.7	54.2
01	199 03.5	40.5	188 02.9 13.6		14 36.9	7.7	54.2
02	214 03.4	41.2	202 35.5 13.6		14 44.6	7.6	54.2
03	229 03.4 ..	42.0	217 08.1 13.6		14 52.2	7.5	54.2
04	244 03.3	42.7	231 40.7 13.5		14 59.7	7.5	54.2
05	259 03.3	43.4	246 13.2 13.5		15 07.2	7.4	54.2
06	274 03.2	S16 44.1	260 45.7 13.5		S15 14.6	7.3	54.2
07	289 03.2	44.8	275 18.2 13.5		15 21.9	7.3	54.2
08	304 03.1	45.6	289 50.7 13.4		15 29.2	7.1	54.2
09	319 03.1 ..	46.3	304 23.1 13.4		15 36.3	7.2	54.2
10	334 03.0	47.0	318 55.5 13.4		15 43.5	7.0	54.2
11	349 03.0	47.7	333 27.9 13.4		15 50.5	7.0	54.1
12	4 02.9	S16 48.4	348 00.3 13.3		S15 57.5	6.9	54.1
13	19 02.9	49.2	2 32.6 13.3		16 04.4	6.8	54.1
14	34 02.8	49.9	17 04.9 13.3		16 11.2	6.8	54.1
15	49 02.8 ..	50.6	31 37.2 13.2		16 18.0	6.7	54.1
16	64 02.7	51.3	46 09.4 13.3		16 24.7	6.6	54.1
17	79 02.7	52.0	60 41.7 13.2		16 31.3	6.5	54.1
18	94 02.6	S16 52.7	75 13.9 13.2		S16 37.8	6.5	54.1
19	109 02.6	53.4	89 46.1 13.1		16 44.3	6.4	54.1
20	124 02.5	54.2	104 18.2 13.1		16 50.7	6.3	54.1
21	139 02.5 ..	54.9	118 50.3 13.2		16 57.0	6.2	54.1
22	154 02.4	55.6	133 22.5 13.0		17 03.2	6.2	54.1
23	169 02.4	56.3	147 54.5 13.1		17 09.4	6.0	54.1
10 00	184 02.3	S16 57.0	162 26.6 13.0		S17 15.4	6.1	54.1
01	199 02.3	57.7	176 58.6 13.0		17 21.5	5.9	54.1
02	214 02.2	58.4	191 30.6 13.0		17 27.4	5.8	54.1
03	229 02.1 ..	59.1	206 02.6 13.0		17 33.2	5.8	54.0
04	244 02.1	16 59.8	220 34.6 12.9		17 39.0	5.7	54.0
05	259 02.0	17 00.5	235 06.5 12.9		17 44.7	5.6	54.0
06	274 02.0	S17 01.3	249 38.4 12.9		S17 50.3	5.5	54.0
07	289 01.9	02.0	264 10.3 12.8		17 55.8	5.5	54.0
08	304 01.9	02.7	278 42.1 12.8		18 01.3	5.4	54.0
09	319 01.8 ..	03.4	293 13.9 12.8		18 06.7	5.2	54.0
10	334 01.7	04.1	307 45.7 12.8		18 11.9	5.3	54.0
11	349 01.7	04.8	322 17.5 12.8		18 17.2	5.1	54.0
12	4 01.6	S17 05.5	336 49.3 12.7		S18 22.3	5.0	54.0
13	19 01.6	06.2	351 21.0 12.7		18 27.3	5.0	54.0
14	34 01.5	06.9	5 52.7 12.7		18 32.3	4.9	54.0
15	49 01.4 ..	07.6	20 24.4 12.7		18 37.2	4.7	54.0
16	64 01.4	08.3	34 56.1 12.6		18 41.9	4.8	54.0
17	79 01.3	09.0	49 27.7 12.6		18 46.7	4.6	54.0
18	94 01.2	S17 09.7	63 59.3 12.6		S18 51.3	4.5	54.0
19	109 01.2	10.4	78 30.9 12.6		18 55.8	4.5	54.0
20	124 01.1	11.1	93 02.5 12.5		19 00.3	4.3	54.0
21	139 01.1 ..	11.8	107 34.0 12.5		19 04.6	4.3	54.0
22	154 01.0	12.5	122 05.5 12.5		19 08.9	4.2	54.0
23	169 00.9	13.2	136 37.0 12.5		19 13.1	4.1	54.0
11 00	184 00.9	S17 13.9	151 08.5 12.5		S19 17.2	4.0	54.0
01	199 00.8	14.6	165 40.0 12.4		19 21.2	4.0	54.0
02	214 00.7 ..	15.3	180 11.4 12.4		19 25.2	3.8	54.0
03	229 00.7 ..	16.0	194 42.8 12.4		19 29.0	3.8	54.0
04	244 00.6	16.7	209 14.2 12.4		19 32.8	3.6	54.0
05	259 00.5	17.4	223 45.6 12.3		19 36.4	3.6	54.0
06	274 00.5	S17 18.1	238 16.9 12.4		S19 40.0	3.5	54.0
07	289 00.4	18.8	252 48.3 12.3		19 43.5	3.4	54.0
08	304 00.3	19.5	267 19.6 12.3		19 46.9	3.3	54.0
09	319 00.3 ..	20.2	281 50.9 12.3		19 50.2	3.2	54.0
10	334 00.2	20.9	296 22.1 12.3		19 53.4	3.2	54.0
11	349 00.1	21.6	310 53.4 12.2		19 56.6	3.0	54.0
12	4 00.1	S17 22.3	325 24.6 12.2		S19 59.6	2.9	54.0
13	19 00.0	22.9	339 55.8 12.2		20 02.5	2.9	54.0
14	33 59.9	23.6	354 27.0 12.2		20 05.4	2.8	54.0
15	48 59.9 ..	24.3	8 58.2 12.2		20 08.2	2.6	54.0
16	63 59.8	25.0	23 29.4 12.1		20 10.8	2.6	54.0
17	78 59.7	25.7	38 00.5 12.2		20 13.4	2.5	54.0
18	93 59.7	S17 26.4	52 31.6 12.2		S20 15.9	2.4	54.0
19	108 59.6	27.1	67 02.8 12.0		20 18.3	2.3	54.0
20	123 59.5	27.8	81 33.8 12.1		20 20.6	2.2	54.0
21	138 59.4 ..	28.5	96 04.9 12.1		20 22.8	2.1	54.0
22	153 59.4	29.2	110 36.0 12.1		20 24.9	2.1	54.0
23	168 59.3	29.8	125 07.0 12.1		S20 27.0	1.9	54.0
	SD 16.2 d 0.7		SD 14.8		14.7		14.7

Left margin labels: TUESDAY, WEDNESDAY, THURSDAY

Twilight / Sunrise / Moonrise

Lat.	Naut.	Civil	Sunrise	Moonrise 9	10	11	12
°	h m	h m	h m	h m	h m	h m	h m
N 72	06 39	08 08	09 58	10 51	■	■	■
N 70	06 31	07 50	09 16	10 09	11 59	■	■
68	06 25	07 35	08 48	09 41	11 13	12 40	13 50
66	06 19	07 23	08 26	09 20	10 43	11 59	13 02
64	06 14	07 13	08 10	09 03	10 21	11 31	12 31
62	06 10	07 04	07 56	08 50	10 03	11 10	12 08
60	06 06	06 57	07 44	08 38	09 48	10 53	11 49
N 58	06 02	06 50	07 34	08 28	09 36	10 38	11 34
56	05 59	06 44	07 25	08 19	09 25	10 26	11 21
54	05 56	06 38	07 17	08 11	09 15	10 15	11 09
52	05 53	06 33	07 10	08 05	09 07	10 06	10 59
50	05 50	06 29	07 04	07 58	08 59	09 57	10 50
45	05 44	06 19	06 50	07 45	08 43	09 39	10 31
N 40	05 38	06 10	06 39	07 34	08 30	09 24	10 16
35	05 32	06 02	06 29	07 25	08 19	09 12	10 03
30	05 27	05 55	06 21	07 16	08 09	09 01	09 51
20	05 16	05 43	06 06	07 02	07 53	08 43	09 32
N 10	05 05	05 31	05 53	06 50	07 38	08 26	09 15
0	04 54	05 19	05 40	06 39	07 24	08 11	08 59
S 10	04 40	05 06	05 28	06 27	07 11	07 56	08 43
20	04 24	04 51	05 15	06 15	06 57	07 40	08 27
30	04 03	04 33	04 59	06 01	06 40	07 22	08 07
35	03 49	04 23	04 50	05 53	06 31	07 11	07 56
40	03 33	04 10	04 40	05 44	06 20	06 59	07 43
45	03 13	03 54	04 27	05 34	06 07	06 45	07 28
S 50	02 45	03 35	04 13	05 21	05 52	06 27	07 09
52	02 32	03 25	04 06	05 15	05 44	06 19	07 00
54	02 15	03 15	03 58	05 09	05 36	06 10	06 50
56	01 55	03 02	03 49	05 01	05 28	06 00	06 39
58	01 28	02 48	03 39	04 53	05 17	05 48	06 26
S 60	00 46	02 30	03 28	04 44	05 06	05 34	06 11

Sunset / Twilight / Moonset

Lat.	Sunset	Civil	Naut.	Moonset 9	10	11	12
°	h m	h m	h m	h m	h m	h m	h m
N 72	13 28	15 18	16 47	14 35	■	■	■
N 70	14 11	15 37	16 56	15 15	15 04	■	■
68	14 39	15 51	17 02	15 47	15 51	16 02	16 31
66	15 00	16 04	17 07	16 09	16 21	16 43	17 19
64	15 17	16 14	17 13	16 26	16 44	17 11	17 50
62	15 31	16 23	17 17	16 40	17 02	17 32	18 13
60	15 43	16 30	17 21	16 53	17 17	17 50	18 32
N 58	15 53	16 37	17 25	17 03	17 30	18 04	18 47
56	16 02	16 43	17 28	17 12	17 41	18 17	19 00
54	16 10	16 49	17 31	17 21	17 51	18 28	19 12
52	16 17	16 54	17 34	17 28	18 00	18 37	19 22
50	16 23	16 58	17 37	17 35	18 08	18 46	19 31
45	16 37	17 08	17 44	17 49	18 24	19 05	19 50
N 40	16 49	17 17	17 50	18 01	18 38	19 20	20 06
35	16 58	17 25	17 55	18 11	18 50	19 32	20 19
30	17 07	17 32	18 01	18 19	19 00	19 43	20 30
20	17 22	17 45	18 11	18 35	19 17	20 02	20 50
N 10	17 35	17 57	18 22	18 48	19 33	20 19	21 07
0	17 47	18 09	18 34	19 01	19 47	20 34	21 23
S 10	18 00	18 22	18 48	19 13	20 01	20 50	21 38
20	18 13	18 37	19 04	19 27	20 17	21 07	21 55
30	18 29	18 55	19 25	19 42	20 34	21 26	22 15
35	18 38	19 06	19 39	19 51	20 45	21 37	22 26
40	18 49	19 19	19 56	20 01	20 57	21 50	22 39
45	19 01	19 34	20 16	20 13	21 10	22 05	22 55
S 50	19 16	19 54	20 44	20 28	21 28	22 23	23 13
52	19 23	20 04	20 58	20 35	21 36	22 32	23 22
54	19 31	20 15	21 15	20 42	21 44	22 42	23 32
56	19 40	20 27	21 36	20 51	21 55	22 53	23 44
58	19 50	20 42	22 04	21 01	22 06	23 05	23 57
S 60	20 02	21 00	22 50	21 12	22 19	23 20	24 12

SUN / MOON

Day	Eqn. of Time 00h	Eqn. of Time 12h	Mer. Pass.	Mer. Pass. Upper	Mer. Pass. Lower	Age	Phase
d	m s	m s	h m	h m	h m	d	%
9	16 14	16 12	11 44	12 50	00 27	01	2
10	16 09	16 07	11 44	13 36	01 12	02	5
11	16 04	16 00	11 44	14 23	01 59	03	10

1999 NOVEMBER 12, 13, 14 (FRI., SAT., SUN.)

UT	ARIES	VENUS −4.3		MARS +0.8		JUPITER −2.9		SATURN −0.2		STARS		
	GHA	GHA	Dec	GHA	Dec	GHA	Dec	GHA	Dec	Name	SHA	Dec
d h	° ′	° ′	° ′	° ′	° ′	° ′	° ′	° ′	° ′		° ′	° ′
12 00	50 40.9	227 20.0	S 0 04.0	119 42.3	S23 39.5	24 39.4	N 9 09.9	9 03.8	N13 19.6	Acamar	315 26.0	S40 18.4
01	65 43.4	242 20.0	04.9	134 42.8	39.2	39 42.1	09.8	24 06.5	19.6	Achernar	335 34.1	S57 14.5
02	80 45.8	257 19.9	05.8	149 43.2	38.9	54 44.9	09.7	39 09.2	19.5	Acrux	173 21.7	S63 05.5
03	95 48.3	272 19.8	.. 06.7	164 43.6	.. 38.6	69 47.6	.. 09.6	54 11.8	.. 19.5	Adhara	255 20.6	S28 58.2
04	110 50.7	287 19.8	07.6	179 44.1	38.3	84 50.4	09.5	69 14.5	19.4	Aldebaran	291 01.2	N16 30.5
05	125 53.2	302 19.7	08.6	194 44.5	38.0	99 53.1	09.4	84 17.2	19.3			
06	140 55.7	317 19.6	S 0 09.5	209 44.9	S23 37.7	114 55.8	N 9 09.3	99 19.8	N13 19.3	Alioth	166 30.4	N55 57.6
07	155 58.1	332 19.5	10.4	224 45.4	37.4	129 58.6	09.3	114 22.5	19.2	Alkaid	153 07.7	N49 18.9
08	171 00.6	347 19.5	11.3	239 45.8	37.2	145 01.3	09.2	129 25.1	19.2	Al Na'ir	27 56.9	S46 57.9
F 09	186 03.1	2 19.4	.. 12.2	254 46.2	.. 36.9	160 04.1	.. 09.1	144 27.8	.. 19.1	Alnilam	275 56.8	S 1 12.1
R 10	201 05.5	17 19.3	13.1	269 46.7	36.6	175 06.8	09.0	159 30.5	19.1	Alphard	218 06.5	S 8 39.3
I 11	216 08.0	32 19.3	14.0	284 47.1	36.3	190 09.5	08.9	174 33.1	19.0			
D 12	231 10.5	47 19.2	S 0 14.9	299 47.5	S23 36.0	205 12.3	N 9 08.8	189 35.8	N13 18.9	Alphecca	126 20.4	N26 43.1
A 13	246 12.9	62 19.1	15.9	314 48.0	35.7	220 15.0	08.7	204 38.4	18.9	Alpheratz	357 54.2	N29 05.5
Y 14	261 15.4	77 19.0	16.8	329 48.4	35.4	235 17.8	08.6	219 41.1	18.8	Altair	62 18.7	N 8 52.2
15	276 17.9	92 19.0	.. 17.7	344 48.8	.. 35.1	250 20.5	.. 08.5	234 43.8	.. 18.8	Ankaa	353 25.8	S42 18.6
16	291 20.3	107 18.9	18.6	359 49.3	34.8	265 23.2	08.4	249 46.4	18.7	Antares	112 39.6	S26 25.7
17	306 22.8	122 18.8	19.5	14 49.7	34.5	280 26.0	08.3	264 49.1	18.7			
18	321 25.2	137 18.7	S 0 20.4	29 50.1	S23 34.2	295 28.7	N 9 08.2	279 51.7	N13 18.6	Arcturus	146 05.7	N19 11.2
19	336 27.7	152 18.7	21.4	44 50.6	33.9	310 31.4	08.1	294 54.4	18.5	Atria	107 51.5	S69 01.6
20	351 30.2	167 18.6	22.3	59 51.0	33.6	325 34.2	08.0	309 57.1	18.5	Avior	234 22.1	S59 30.3
21	6 32.6	182 18.5	.. 23.2	74 51.4	.. 33.3	340 36.9	.. 07.9	324 59.7	.. 18.4	Bellatrix	278 43.1	N 6 20.9
22	21 35.1	197 18.4	24.1	89 51.9	33.0	355 39.7	07.8	340 02.4	18.4	Betelgeuse	271 12.5	N 7 24.4
23	36 37.6	212 18.4	25.0	104 52.3	32.7	10 42.4	07.7	355 05.1	18.3			
13 00	51 40.0	227 18.3	S 0 25.9	119 52.7	S23 32.4	25 45.1	N 9 07.6	10 07.7	N13 18.3	Canopus	264 00.4	S52 41.6
01	66 42.5	242 18.2	26.9	134 53.2	32.1	40 47.9	07.5	25 10.4	18.2	Capella	280 49.7	N45 59.7
02	81 45.0	257 18.1	27.8	149 53.6	31.8	55 50.6	07.4	40 13.0	18.2	Deneb	49 38.8	N45 17.1
03	96 47.4	272 18.0	.. 28.7	164 54.0	.. 31.5	70 53.3	.. 07.3	55 15.7	.. 18.1	Denebola	182 44.7	N14 34.5
04	111 49.9	287 18.0	29.6	179 54.5	31.2	85 56.1	07.3	70 18.4	18.0	Diphda	349 06.3	S17 59.3
05	126 52.4	302 17.9	30.5	194 54.9	30.9	100 58.8	07.2	85 21.0	18.0			
06	141 54.8	317 17.8	S 0 31.5	209 55.3	S23 30.6	116 01.6	N 9 07.1	100 23.7	N13 17.9	Dubhe	194 04.9	N61 44.9
07	156 57.3	332 17.7	32.4	224 55.8	30.3	131 04.3	07.0	115 26.3	17.9	Elnath	278 25.7	N28 36.3
S 08	171 59.7	347 17.6	33.3	239 56.2	30.0	146 07.0	06.9	130 29.0	17.8	Eltanin	90 51.5	N51 29.6
A 09	187 02.2	2 17.6	.. 34.2	254 56.6	.. 29.7	161 09.8	.. 06.8	145 31.7	.. 17.8	Enif	33 57.5	N 9 52.6
T 10	202 04.7	17 17.5	35.1	269 57.1	29.4	176 12.5	06.7	160 34.3	17.7	Fomalhaut	15 35.5	S29 37.5
U 11	217 07.1	32 17.4	36.1	284 57.5	29.1	191 15.2	06.6	175 37.0	17.6			
R 12	232 09.6	47 17.3	S 0 37.0	299 57.9	S23 28.8	206 18.0	N 9 06.5	190 39.6	N13 17.6	Gacrux	172 13.2	S57 06.4
D 13	247 12.1	62 17.2	37.9	314 58.4	28.5	221 20.7	06.4	205 42.3	17.5	Gienah	176 03.4	S17 32.2
A 14	262 14.5	77 17.2	38.8	329 58.8	28.2	236 23.4	06.3	220 45.0	17.5	Hadar	149 03.6	S60 22.1
Y 15	277 17.0	92 17.1	.. 39.8	344 59.2	.. 27.9	251 26.2	.. 06.2	235 47.6	.. 17.4	Hamal	328 12.4	N23 27.7
16	292 19.5	107 17.0	40.7	359 59.7	27.6	266 28.9	06.1	250 50.3	17.4	Kaus Aust.	83 58.2	S34 23.1
17	307 21.9	122 16.9	41.6	15 00.1	27.3	281 31.6	06.0	265 52.9	17.3			
18	322 24.4	137 16.8	S 0 42.5	30 00.5	S23 27.0	296 34.4	N 9 05.9	280 55.6	N13 17.2	Kochab	137 20.9	N74 09.5
19	337 26.9	152 16.7	43.5	45 01.0	26.7	311 37.1	05.9	295 58.3	17.2	Markab	13 48.8	N15 12.4
20	352 29.3	167 16.7	44.4	60 01.4	26.4	326 39.8	05.8	311 00.9	17.1	Menkar	314 25.8	N 4 05.3
21	7 31.8	182 16.6	.. 45.3	75 01.8	.. 26.1	341 42.6	.. 05.7	326 03.6	.. 17.1	Menkent	148 20.5	S36 21.9
22	22 34.2	197 16.5	46.2	90 02.3	25.8	356 45.3	05.6	341 06.2	17.0	Miaplacidus	221 41.8	S69 42.6
23	37 36.7	212 16.4	47.2	105 02.7	25.4	11 48.0	05.5	356 08.9	17.0			
14 00	52 39.2	227 16.3	S 0 48.1	120 03.1	S23 25.1	26 50.8	N 9 05.4	11 11.6	N13 16.9	Mirfak	308 55.0	N49 51.6
01	67 41.6	242 16.2	49.0	135 03.6	24.8	41 53.5	05.3	26 14.2	16.9	Nunki	76 11.7	S26 17.8
02	82 44.1	257 16.1	49.9	150 04.0	24.5	56 56.2	05.2	41 16.9	16.8	Peacock	53 36.1	S56 44.3
03	97 46.6	272 16.0	.. 50.9	165 04.4	.. 24.2	71 59.0	.. 05.1	56 19.5	.. 16.8	Pollux	243 40.5	N28 01.5
04	112 49.0	287 16.0	51.8	180 04.9	23.9	87 01.7	05.0	71 22.2	16.7	Procyon	245 10.7	N 5 13.5
05	127 51.5	302 15.9	52.7	195 05.3	23.6	102 04.4	04.9	86 24.9	16.6			
06	142 54.0	317 15.8	S 0 53.7	210 05.7	S23 23.3	117 07.2	N 9 04.8	101 27.5	N13 16.6	Rasalhague	96 16.6	N12 33.8
07	157 56.4	332 15.7	54.6	225 06.2	23.0	132 09.9	04.7	116 30.2	16.5	Regulus	207 54.8	N11 58.1
08	172 58.9	347 15.6	55.5	240 06.6	22.7	147 12.6	04.6	131 32.8	16.5	Rigel	281 21.9	S 8 12.1
S 09	188 01.3	2 15.5	.. 56.4	255 07.0	.. 22.3	162 15.4	.. 04.6	146 35.5	.. 16.4	Rigil Kent.	140 07.0	S60 49.8
U 10	203 03.8	17 15.4	57.4	270 07.5	22.0	177 18.1	04.5	161 38.2	16.4	Sabik	102 25.0	S15 43.3
N 11	218 06.3	32 15.3	58.3	285 07.9	21.7	192 20.8	04.4	176 40.8	16.3			
D 12	233 08.7	47 15.2	S 0 59.2	300 08.4	S23 21.4	207 23.5	N 9 04.3	191 43.5	N13 16.2	Schedar	349 52.2	N56 32.3
A 13	248 11.2	62 15.1	1 00.2	315 08.8	21.1	222 26.3	04.2	206 46.1	16.2	Shaula	96 36.7	S37 06.1
Y 14	263 13.7	77 15.0	01.1	330 09.2	20.8	237 29.0	04.1	221 48.8	16.1	Sirius	258 42.8	S16 42.9
15	278 16.1	92 15.0	.. 02.0	345 09.7	.. 20.5	252 31.7	.. 04.0	236 51.5	.. 16.1	Spica	158 42.7	S11 09.4
16	293 18.6	107 14.9	03.0	0 10.1	20.1	267 34.5	03.9	251 54.1	16.0	Suhail	223 00.2	S43 25.6
17	308 21.1	122 14.8	03.9	15 10.5	19.8	282 37.2	03.8	266 56.8	16.0			
18	323 23.5	137 14.7	S 1 04.8	30 11.0	S23 19.5	297 39.9	N 9 03.7	281 59.4	N13 15.9	Vega	80 46.4	N38 47.3
19	338 26.0	152 14.6	05.8	45 11.4	19.2	312 42.6	03.6	297 02.1	15.9	Zuben'ubi	137 17.5	S16 02.2
20	353 28.5	167 14.5	06.7	60 11.8	18.9	327 45.4	03.6	312 04.8	15.8			
21	8 30.9	182 14.4	.. 07.6	75 12.3	.. 18.6	342 48.1	.. 03.5	327 07.4	.. 15.7		SHA	Mer. Pass.
22	23 33.4	197 14.3	08.6	90 12.7	18.2	357 50.8	03.4	342 10.1	15.7		° ′	h m
23	38 35.8	212 14.2	09.5	105 13.1	17.9	12 53.6	03.3	357 12.7	15.6	Venus	175 38.3	8 51
	h m									Mars	68 12.7	16 00
Mer. Pass. 20 30.0		v −0.1	d 0.9	v 0.4	d 0.3	v 2.7	d 0.1	v 2.7	d 0.1	Jupiter	334 05.1	22 13
										Saturn	318 27.7	23 15

UT	SUN GHA	SUN Dec	MOON GHA	v	MOON Dec	d	HP
d h	° ′	° ′	° ′	′	° ′	′	′
12 00	183 59.2	S17 30.5	139 38.1	12.0	S20 28.9	1.8	54.0
01	198 59.2	31.2	154 09.1	12.0	20 30.7	1.8	54.0
02	213 59.1	31.9	168 40.1	12.0	20 32.5	1.6	54.0
03	228 59.0	.. 32.6	183 11.1	12.0	20 34.1	1.6	54.0
04	243 58.9	33.3	197 42.1	11.9	20 35.7	1.4	54.0
05	258 58.9	34.0	212 13.0	12.0	20 37.1	1.4	54.0
06	273 58.8	S17 34.6	226 44.0	11.9	S20 38.5	1.3	54.0
07	288 58.7	35.3	241 14.9	11.9	20 39.8	1.1	54.0
08	303 58.6	36.0	255 45.8	11.9	20 40.9	1.1	54.1
F 09	318 58.6	.. 36.7	270 16.7	11.9	20 42.0	1.0	54.1
R 10	333 58.5	37.4	284 47.6	11.9	20 43.0	0.9	54.1
I 11	348 58.4	38.0	299 18.5	11.9	20 43.9	0.8	54.1
D 12	3 58.3	S17 38.7	313 49.4	11.9	S20 44.7	0.7	54.1
A 13	18 58.2	39.4	328 20.3	11.9	20 45.4	0.6	54.1
Y 14	33 58.2	40.1	342 51.2	11.8	20 46.0	0.5	54.1
15	48 58.1	.. 40.8	357 22.0	11.9	20 46.5	0.4	54.1
16	63 58.0	41.4	11 52.9	11.8	20 46.9	0.3	54.1
17	78 57.9	42.1	26 23.7	11.8	20 47.2	0.2	54.1
18	93 57.9	S17 42.8	40 54.5	11.8	S20 47.4	0.2	54.1
19	108 57.8	43.5	55 25.3	11.8	20 47.6	0.0	54.1
20	123 57.7	44.1	69 56.1	11.9	20 47.6	0.1	54.1
21	138 57.6	.. 44.8	84 27.0	11.7	20 47.5	0.1	54.1
22	153 57.5	45.5	98 57.7	11.8	20 47.4	0.3	54.2
23	168 57.5	46.2	113 28.5	11.8	20 47.1	0.4	54.2
13 00	183 57.4	S17 46.8	127 59.3	11.8	S20 46.7	0.4	54.2
01	198 57.3	47.5	142 30.1	11.8	20 46.3	0.6	54.2
02	213 57.2	48.2	157 00.9	11.8	20 45.7	0.6	54.2
03	228 57.1	.. 48.9	171 31.7	11.7	20 45.1	0.8	54.2
04	243 57.0	49.5	186 02.4	11.8	20 44.3	0.8	54.2
05	258 57.0	50.2	200 33.2	11.8	20 43.5	1.0	54.2
06	273 56.9	S17 50.9	215 03.9	11.8	S20 42.5	1.0	54.2
S 07	288 56.8	51.5	229 34.7	11.7	20 41.5	1.1	54.2
A 08	303 56.7	52.2	244 05.4	11.8	20 40.4	1.3	54.3
T 09	318 56.6	.. 52.9	258 36.2	11.7	20 39.1	1.3	54.3
U 10	333 56.5	53.6	273 06.9	11.8	20 37.8	1.4	54.3
R 11	348 56.4	54.2	287 37.7	11.7	20 36.4	1.6	54.3
D 12	3 56.4	S17 54.9	302 08.4	11.8	S20 34.8	1.6	54.3
A 13	18 56.3	55.6	316 39.2	11.7	20 33.2	1.7	54.3
Y 14	33 56.2	56.2	331 09.9	11.7	20 31.5	1.8	54.3
15	48 56.1	.. 56.9	345 40.6	11.8	20 29.7	1.9	54.3
16	63 56.0	57.5	0 11.4	11.7	20 27.8	2.0	54.4
17	78 55.9	58.2	14 42.1	11.8	20 25.8	2.1	54.4
18	93 55.8	S17 58.9	29 12.9	11.7	S20 23.7	2.2	54.4
19	108 55.8	17 59.5	43 43.6	11.7	20 21.5	2.3	54.4
20	123 55.7	18 00.2	58 14.3	11.8	20 19.2	2.4	54.4
21	138 55.6	.. 00.9	72 45.1	11.7	20 16.8	2.5	54.4
22	153 55.5	01.5	87 15.8	11.8	20 14.3	2.6	54.4
23	168 55.5	02.2	101 46.6	11.7	20 11.7	2.6	54.5
14 00	183 55.3	S18 02.8	116 17.3	11.8	S20 09.1	2.8	54.5
01	198 55.2	03.5	130 48.1	11.7	20 06.3	2.9	54.5
02	213 55.1	04.2	145 18.8	11.8	20 03.4	3.0	54.5
03	228 55.0	.. 04.8	159 49.6	11.7	20 00.4	3.0	54.5
04	243 54.9	05.5	174 20.3	11.8	19 57.4	3.2	54.5
05	258 54.8	06.1	188 51.1	11.8	19 54.2	3.2	54.6
06	273 54.8	S18 06.8	203 21.9	11.7	S19 51.0	3.4	54.6
07	288 54.7	07.5	217 52.6	11.8	19 47.6	3.4	54.6
08	303 54.6	08.1	232 23.4	11.8	19 44.2	3.5	54.6
S 09	318 54.5	.. 08.8	246 54.2	11.8	19 40.7	3.7	54.6
U 10	333 54.4	09.4	261 25.0	11.7	19 37.0	3.7	54.7
N 11	348 54.3	10.1	275 55.7	11.8	19 33.3	3.8	54.7
D 12	3 54.2	S18 10.7	290 26.5	11.8	S19 29.5	3.9	54.7
A 13	18 54.1	11.4	304 57.3	11.8	19 25.6	4.0	54.7
Y 14	33 54.0	12.0	319 28.1	11.8	19 21.6	4.1	54.7
15	48 53.9	.. 12.7	333 58.9	11.8	19 17.5	4.2	54.7
16	63 53.8	13.3	348 29.7	11.9	19 13.3	4.3	54.8
17	78 53.7	14.0	3 00.6	11.8	19 09.0	4.4	54.8
18	93 53.6	S18 14.6	17 31.4	11.8	S19 04.6	4.5	54.8
19	108 53.5	15.3	32 02.2	11.8	19 00.1	4.5	54.8
20	123 53.4	15.9	46 33.0	11.9	18 55.6	4.7	54.9
21	138 53.3	.. 16.6	61 03.9	11.8	18 50.9	4.8	54.9
22	153 53.2	17.2	75 34.7	11.9	18 46.1	4.8	54.9
23	168 53.1	17.9	90 05.6	11.8	S18 41.3	4.9	54.9
	SD 16.2	d 0.7	SD 14.7		14.8		14.9

Lat.	Twilight Naut.	Twilight Civil	Sunrise	Moonrise 12	13	14	15
°	h m	h m	h m	h m	h m	h m	h m
N 72	06 50	08 23	10 27	■■	■■	■■	16 20
N 70	06 41	08 02	09 34	■■	■■	15 44	15 26
68	06 34	07 45	09 01	13 50	14 30	14 46	14 52
66	06 27	07 32	08 38	13 02	13 46	14 12	14 28
64	06 22	07 21	08 19	12 31	13 16	13 48	14 09
62	06 16	07 12	08 04	12 08	12 54	13 28	13 53
60	06 12	07 03	07 52	11 49	12 36	13 12	13 40
N 58	06 08	06 56	07 41	11 34	12 21	12 59	13 29
56	06 04	06 50	07 31	11 21	12 08	12 47	13 19
54	06 01	06 44	07 23	11 09	11 57	12 37	13 10
52	05 57	06 38	07 15	10 59	11 47	12 27	13 02
50	05 54	06 33	07 09	10 50	11 38	12 19	12 55
45	05 47	06 23	06 54	10 31	11 19	12 02	12 40
N 40	05 41	06 13	06 42	10 16	11 04	11 48	12 28
35	05 35	06 05	06 32	10 03	10 51	11 35	12 17
30	05 29	05 58	06 23	09 51	10 39	11 25	12 08
20	05 18	05 44	06 07	09 32	10 20	11 07	11 51
N 10	05 06	05 32	05 54	09 15	10 03	10 51	11 37
0	04 54	05 19	05 41	08 59	09 48	10 36	11 24
S 10	04 40	05 05	05 28	08 43	09 32	10 21	11 11
20	04 22	04 50	05 14	08 27	09 15	10 05	10 57
30	04 00	04 31	04 57	08 07	08 56	09 47	10 40
35	03 46	04 20	04 48	07 56	08 44	09 36	10 31
40	03 29	04 07	04 37	07 43	08 31	09 24	10 20
45	03 08	03 50	04 24	07 28	08 16	09 10	10 07
S 50	02 39	03 30	04 08	07 09	07 57	08 52	09 52
52	02 24	03 20	04 01	07 00	07 48	08 44	09 45
54	02 06	03 08	03 52	06 50	07 39	08 34	09 37
56	01 44	02 55	03 43	06 39	07 27	08 24	09 27
58	01 13	02 39	03 33	06 26	07 14	08 12	09 17
S 60	00 13	02 21	03 20	06 11	06 59	07 58	09 05

Lat.	Sunset	Twilight Civil	Twilight Naut.	Moonset 12	13	14	15
°	h m	h m	h m	h m	h m	h m	h m
N 72	13 00	15 05	16 37	■■	■■	■■	19 03
N 70	13 54	15 26	16 46	■■	■■	17 58	19 57
68	14 26	15 42	16 54	16 31	17 31	18 56	20 29
66	14 50	15 55	17 00	17 19	18 16	19 29	20 53
64	15 08	16 06	17 06	17 50	18 45	19 53	21 12
62	15 23	16 16	17 11	18 13	19 07	20 13	21 27
60	15 36	16 24	17 16	18 32	19 25	20 28	21 39
N 58	15 47	16 32	17 20	18 47	19 40	20 42	21 50
56	15 56	16 38	17 24	19 00	19 53	20 53	22 00
54	16 05	16 44	17 27	19 12	20 04	21 03	22 08
52	16 12	16 50	17 30	19 22	20 14	21 12	22 15
50	16 19	16 54	17 34	19 31	20 22	21 20	22 22
45	16 34	17 05	17 41	19 50	20 41	21 37	22 36
N 40	16 46	17 15	17 47	20 06	20 56	21 50	22 48
35	16 56	17 23	17 53	20 19	21 09	22 02	22 58
30	17 05	17 30	17 59	20 30	21 20	22 12	23 07
20	17 21	17 44	18 11	20 50	21 39	22 30	23 22
N 10	17 35	17 57	18 22	21 07	21 55	22 45	23 35
0	17 48	18 10	18 35	21 23	22 11	22 59	23 47
S 10	18 01	18 23	18 49	21 38	22 26	23 13	23 59
20	18 15	18 39	19 06	21 55	22 43	23 28	24 12
30	18 32	18 58	19 29	22 15	23 02	23 45	24 24
35	18 41	19 09	19 43	22 26	23 12	23 55	24 35
40	18 52	19 23	20 00	22 39	23 25	24 07	00 07
45	19 05	19 39	20 22	22 55	23 40	24 20	00 20
S 50	19 21	20 00	20 51	23 13	23 58	24 36	00 36
52	19 29	20 10	21 06	23 22	24 06	00 06	00 44
54	19 37	20 22	21 25	23 32	24 16	00 16	00 52
56	19 47	20 35	21 48	23 44	24 27	00 27	01 02
58	19 57	20 51	22 20	23 57	24 39	00 39	01 13
S 60	20 10	21 10	////	24 12	00 12	00 53	01 25

Day	SUN Eqn. of Time 00h	SUN Eqn. of Time 12h	SUN Mer. Pass.	MOON Mer. Pass. Upper	MOON Mer. Pass. Lower	Age	Phase
d	m s	m s	h m	h m	h m	d	%
12	15 57	15 53	11 44	15 11	02 47	04	16
13	15 50	15 46	11 44	15 59	03 35	05	24
14	15 41	15 37	11 44	16 48	04 23	06	32

1999 NOVEMBER 15, 16, 17 (MON., TUES., WED.)

UT	ARIES GHA	VENUS −4.3 GHA	Dec	MARS +0.8 GHA	Dec	JUPITER −2.9 GHA	Dec	SATURN −0.2 GHA	Dec	STARS Name	SHA	Dec
d h	° ′	° ′	° ′	° ′	° ′	° ′	° ′	° ′	° ′		° ′	° ′
15 00	53 38.3	227 14.1	S 1 10.4	120 13.6	S23 17.6	27 56.3	N 9 03.2	12 15.4	N13 15.6	Acamar	315 25.9	S40 18.4
01	68 40.8	242 14.0	11.4	135 14.0	17.3	42 59.0	03.1	27 18.1	15.5	Achernar	335 34.1	S57 14.5
02	83 43.2	257 13.9	12.3	150 14.5	17.0	58 01.7	03.0	42 20.7	15.5	Acrux	173 21.6	S63 05.5
03	98 45.7	272 13.8	.. 13.2	165 14.9	.. 16.6	73 04.5	.. 02.9	57 23.4	.. 15.4	Adhara	255 20.6	S28 58.2
04	113 48.2	287 13.7	14.2	180 15.3	16.3	88 07.2	02.8	72 26.0	15.4	Aldebaran	291 01.2	N16 30.5
05	128 50.6	302 13.6	15.1	195 15.8	16.0	103 09.9	02.7	87 28.7	15.3			
M 06	143 53.1	317 13.5	S 1 16.0	210 16.2	S23 15.7	118 12.6	N 9 02.6	102 31.4	N13 15.2	Alioth	166 30.4	N55 57.6
O 07	158 55.6	332 13.4	17.0	225 16.6	15.3	133 15.4	02.6	117 34.0	15.2	Alkaid	153 07.7	N49 18.9
N 08	173 58.0	347 13.3	17.9	240 17.1	15.0	148 18.1	02.5	132 36.7	15.1	Al Na'ir	27 56.9	S46 57.9
D 09	189 00.5	2 13.2	.. 18.8	255 17.5	.. 14.7	163 20.8	.. 02.4	147 39.3	.. 15.1	Alnilam	275 56.8	S 1 12.1
A 10	204 03.0	17 13.1	19.8	270 17.9	14.4	178 23.5	02.3	162 42.0	15.0	Alphard	218 06.5	S 8 39.3
Y 11	219 05.4	32 13.0	20.7	285 18.4	14.1	193 26.3	02.2	177 44.6	15.0			
12	234 07.9	47 12.9	S 1 21.7	300 18.8	S23 13.7	208 29.0	N 9 02.1	192 47.3	N13 14.9	Alphecca	126 20.4	N26 43.1
13	249 10.3	62 12.8	22.6	315 19.3	13.4	223 31.7	02.0	207 50.0	14.9	Alpheratz	357 54.2	N29 05.5
14	264 12.8	77 12.7	23.5	330 19.7	13.1	238 34.4	01.9	222 52.6	14.8	Altair	62 18.7	N 8 52.2
15	279 15.3	92 12.6	.. 24.5	345 20.1	.. 12.8	253 37.2	.. 01.8	237 55.3	.. 14.8	Ankaa	353 25.9	S42 18.6
16	294 17.7	107 12.5	25.4	0 20.6	12.4	268 39.9	01.8	252 57.9	14.7	Antares	112 39.6	S26 25.7
17	309 20.2	122 12.4	26.4	15 21.0	12.1	283 42.6	01.7	268 00.6	14.6			
18	324 22.7	137 12.3	S 1 27.3	30 21.4	S23 11.8	298 45.3	N 9 01.6	283 03.3	N13 14.6	Arcturus	146 05.7	N19 11.2
19	339 25.1	152 12.2	28.2	45 21.9	11.4	313 48.1	01.5	298 05.9	14.5	Atria	107 51.5	S69 01.6
20	354 27.6	167 12.1	29.2	60 22.3	11.1	328 50.8	01.4	313 08.6	14.5	Avior	234 22.1	S59 30.3
21	9 30.1	182 12.0	.. 30.1	75 22.8	.. 10.8	343 53.5	.. 01.3	328 11.2	.. 14.4	Bellatrix	278 43.1	N 6 20.9
22	24 32.5	197 11.9	31.1	90 23.2	10.5	358 56.2	01.2	343 13.9	14.4	Betelgeuse	271 12.5	N 7 24.4
23	39 35.0	212 11.8	32.0	105 23.6	10.1	13 59.0	01.1	358 16.6	14.3			
16 00	54 37.4	227 11.7	S 1 32.9	120 24.1	S23 09.8	29 01.7	N 9 01.0	13 19.2	N13 14.3	Canopus	264 00.4	S52 41.6
01	69 39.9	242 11.6	33.9	135 24.5	09.5	44 04.4	01.0	28 21.9	14.2	Capella	280 49.7	N45 59.7
02	84 42.4	257 11.5	34.8	150 24.9	09.1	59 07.1	00.9	43 24.5	14.1	Deneb	49 38.8	N45 17.1
03	99 44.8	272 11.3	.. 35.8	165 25.4	.. 08.8	74 09.8	.. 00.8	58 27.2	.. 14.1	Denebola	182 44.6	N14 34.5
04	114 47.3	287 11.2	36.7	180 25.8	08.5	89 12.6	00.7	73 29.8	14.0	Diphda	349 06.3	S17 59.4
05	129 49.8	302 11.1	37.7	195 26.3	08.1	104 15.3	00.6	88 32.5	14.0			
T 06	144 52.2	317 11.0	S 1 38.6	210 26.7	S23 07.8	119 18.0	N 9 00.5	103 35.2	N13 13.9	Dubhe	194 04.9	N61 44.9
U 07	159 54.7	332 10.9	39.5	225 27.1	07.5	134 20.7	00.4	118 37.8	13.9	Elnath	278 25.7	N28 36.3
E 08	174 57.2	347 10.8	40.5	240 27.6	07.1	149 23.4	00.3	133 40.5	13.8	Eltanin	90 51.5	N51 29.6
S 09	189 59.6	2 10.7	.. 41.4	255 28.0	.. 06.8	164 26.2	.. 00.3	148 43.1	.. 13.8	Enif	33 57.5	N 9 52.6
D 10	205 02.1	17 10.6	42.4	270 28.4	06.5	179 28.9	00.2	163 45.8	13.7	Fomalhaut	15 35.5	S29 37.5
A 11	220 04.6	32 10.5	43.3	285 28.9	06.1	194 31.6	00.1	178 48.4	13.7			
Y 12	235 07.0	47 10.4	S 1 44.3	300 29.3	S23 05.8	209 34.3	N 9 00.0	193 51.1	N13 13.6	Gacrux	172 13.1	S57 06.4
13	250 09.5	62 10.3	45.2	315 29.8	05.5	224 37.0	8 59.9	208 53.8	13.5	Gienah	176 03.4	S17 32.2
14	265 11.9	77 10.1	46.2	330 30.2	05.1	239 39.8	59.8	223 56.4	13.5	Hadar	149 03.6	S60 22.0
15	280 14.4	92 10.0	.. 47.1	345 30.6	.. 04.8	254 42.5	.. 59.7	238 59.1	.. 13.4	Hamal	328 12.4	N23 27.7
16	295 16.9	107 09.9	48.1	0 31.1	04.5	269 45.2	59.6	254 01.7	13.4	Kaus Aust.	83 58.2	S34 23.1
17	310 19.3	122 09.8	49.0	15 31.5	04.1	284 47.9	59.6	269 04.4	13.3			
18	325 21.8	137 09.7	S 1 49.9	30 32.0	S23 03.8	299 50.6	N 8 59.5	284 07.1	N13 13.3	Kochab	137 20.8	N74 09.4
19	340 24.3	152 09.6	50.9	45 32.4	03.5	314 53.4	59.4	299 09.7	13.2	Markab	13 48.8	N15 12.4
20	355 26.7	167 09.5	51.8	60 32.8	03.1	329 56.1	59.3	314 12.4	13.2	Menkar	314 25.8	N 4 05.3
21	10 29.2	182 09.4	.. 52.8	75 33.3	.. 02.8	344 58.8	.. 59.2	329 15.0	.. 13.1	Menkent	148 20.5	S36 21.9
22	25 31.7	197 09.2	53.7	90 33.7	02.4	0 01.5	59.1	344 17.7	13.1	Miaplacidus	221 41.7	S69 42.7
23	40 34.1	212 09.1	54.7	105 34.1	02.1	15 04.2	59.0	359 20.3	13.0			
17 00	55 36.6	227 09.0	S 1 55.6	120 34.6	S23 01.8	30 06.9	N 8 59.0	14 23.0	N13 12.9	Mirfak	308 55.0	N49 51.6
01	70 39.1	242 08.9	56.6	135 35.0	01.4	45 09.7	58.9	29 25.7	12.9	Nunki	76 11.7	S26 17.8
02	85 41.5	257 08.8	57.5	150 35.5	01.1	60 12.4	58.8	44 28.3	12.8	Peacock	53 36.1	S56 44.3
03	100 44.0	272 08.7	.. 58.5	165 35.9	.. 00.7	75 15.1	.. 58.7	59 31.0	.. 12.8	Pollux	243 40.5	N28 01.5
04	115 46.4	287 08.5	1 59.4	180 36.3	00.4	90 17.8	58.6	74 33.6	12.7	Procyon	245 10.6	N 5 13.5
05	130 48.9	302 08.4	2 00.4	195 36.8	23 00.1	105 20.5	58.5	89 36.3	12.7			
W 06	145 51.4	317 08.3	S 2 01.3	210 37.2	S22 59.7	120 23.2	N 8 58.4	104 38.9	N13 12.6	Rasalhague	96 16.6	N12 33.8
E 07	160 53.8	332 08.2	02.3	225 37.7	59.4	135 25.9	58.3	119 41.6	12.6	Regulus	207 54.8	N11 58.1
D 08	175 56.3	347 08.1	03.2	240 38.1	59.0	150 28.7	58.3	134 44.3	12.5	Rigel	281 21.9	S 8 12.1
N 09	190 58.8	2 08.0	.. 04.2	255 38.5	.. 58.7	165 31.4	.. 58.2	149 46.9	.. 12.5	Rigil Kent.	140 07.0	S60 49.8
E 10	206 01.2	17 07.8	05.1	270 39.0	58.3	180 34.1	58.1	164 49.6	12.4	Sabik	102 25.0	S15 43.3
S 11	221 03.7	32 07.7	06.1	285 39.4	58.0	195 36.8	58.0	179 52.2	12.3			
D 12	236 06.2	47 07.6	S 2 07.0	300 39.9	S22 57.6	210 39.5	N 8 57.9	194 54.9	N13 12.3	Schedar	349 52.2	N56 32.3
A 13	251 08.6	62 07.5	08.0	315 40.3	57.3	225 42.2	57.8	209 57.5	12.2	Shaula	96 36.7	S37 06.1
Y 14	266 11.1	77 07.4	08.9	330 40.7	57.0	240 44.9	57.8	225 00.2	12.2	Sirius	258 42.8	S16 42.9
15	281 13.5	92 07.2	.. 09.9	345 41.2	.. 56.6	255 47.7	.. 57.7	240 02.8	.. 12.1	Spica	158 42.7	S11 09.4
16	296 16.0	107 07.1	10.9	0 41.6	56.3	270 50.4	57.6	255 05.5	12.1	Suhail	223 00.1	S43 25.6
17	311 18.5	122 07.0	11.8	15 42.1	55.9	285 53.1	57.5	270 08.2	12.0			
18	326 20.9	137 06.9	S 2 12.8	30 42.5	S22 55.6	300 55.8	N 8 57.4	285 10.8	N13 12.0	Vega	80 46.4	N38 47.3
19	341 23.4	152 06.7	13.7	45 42.9	55.2	315 58.5	57.3	300 13.5	11.9	Zuben'ubi	137 17.5	S16 02.2
20	356 25.9	167 06.6	14.7	60 43.4	54.9	331 01.2	57.2	315 16.1	11.9			
21	11 28.3	182 06.5	.. 15.6	75 43.8	.. 54.5	346 03.9	.. 57.2	330 18.8	.. 11.8			
22	26 30.8	197 06.4	16.6	90 44.3	54.2	1 06.6	57.1	345 21.4	11.7			
23	41 33.3	212 06.3	17.5	105 44.7	53.8	16 09.4	57.0	0 24.1	11.7			

											SHA	Mer. Pass.
											° ′	h m
										Venus	172 34.2	8 51
										Mars	65 46.6	15 58
										Jupiter	334 24.2	22 00
Mer. Pass. 20 18.2		v −0.1	d 0.9	v 0.4	d 0.3	v 2.7	d 0.1	v 2.7	d 0.1	Saturn	318 41.8	23 03

UT	SUN GHA	SUN Dec	MOON GHA	v	MOON Dec	d	HP
15 d h	° ′	° ′	° ′	′	° ′	′	′
00	183 53.0	S18 18.5	104 36.4	11.9	S18 36.4	5.1	54.9
01	198 52.9	19.2	119 07.3	11.9	18 31.3	5.1	55.0
02	213 52.8	19.8	133 38.2	11.9	18 26.2	5.2	55.0
03	228 52.7 ..	20.5	148 09.1	11.8	18 21.0	5.3	55.0
04	243 52.6	21.1	162 39.9	11.9	18 15.7	5.4	55.0
05	258 52.5	21.8	177 10.8	11.9	18 10.3	5.5	55.1
06	273 52.4	S18 22.4	191 41.7	11.9	S18 04.8	5.5	55.1
07	288 52.3	23.1	206 12.6	12.0	17 59.3	5.7	55.1
08	303 52.2	23.7	220 43.6	11.9	17 53.6	5.7	55.1
09	318 52.1 ..	24.3	235 14.5	11.9	17 47.9	5.9	55.2
10	333 52.0	25.0	249 45.4	11.9	17 42.0	5.9	55.2
11	348 51.9	25.6	264 16.3	12.0	17 36.1	6.0	55.2
12	3 51.8	S18 26.3	278 47.3	11.9	S17 30.1	6.1	55.2
13	18 51.7	26.9	293 18.2	12.0	17 24.0	6.2	55.3
14	33 51.6	27.5	307 49.2	11.9	17 17.8	6.3	55.3
15	48 51.5 ..	28.2	322 20.1	12.0	17 11.5	6.4	55.3
16	63 51.4	28.8	336 51.1	12.0	17 05.1	6.4	55.3
17	78 51.3	29.5	351 22.1	11.9	16 58.7	6.6	55.4
18	93 51.2	S18 30.1	5 53.0	12.0	S16 52.1	6.6	55.4
19	108 51.1	30.7	20 24.0	12.0	16 45.5	6.7	55.4
20	123 51.0	31.4	34 55.0	12.0	16 38.8	6.8	55.4
21	138 50.9 ..	32.0	49 26.0	12.0	16 32.0	6.9	55.5
22	153 50.8	32.6	63 57.0	12.0	16 25.1	7.0	55.5
23	168 50.7	33.3	78 28.0	12.0	16 18.1	7.0	55.5
16 00	183 50.6	S18 33.9	92 59.0	12.0	S16 11.1	7.2	55.6
01	198 50.4	34.5	107 30.0	12.1	16 03.9	7.2	55.6
02	213 50.3	35.2	122 01.1	12.0	15 56.7	7.3	55.6
03	228 50.2 ..	35.8	136 32.1	12.0	15 49.4	7.4	55.6
04	243 50.1	36.4	151 03.1	12.1	15 42.0	7.5	55.7
05	258 50.0	37.1	165 34.2	12.0	15 34.5	7.5	55.7
06	273 49.9	S18 37.7	180 05.2	12.0	S15 27.0	7.6	55.7
07	288 49.8	38.3	194 36.2	12.1	15 19.4	7.8	55.8
08	303 49.7	39.0	209 07.3	12.1	15 11.6	7.8	55.8
09	318 49.6 ..	39.6	223 38.4	12.0	15 03.8	7.8	55.8
10	333 49.5	40.2	238 09.4	12.1	14 56.0	8.0	55.9
11	348 49.4	40.8	252 40.5	12.0	14 48.0	8.0	55.9
12	3 49.2	S18 41.5	267 11.5	12.1	S14 40.0	8.2	55.9
13	18 49.1	42.1	281 42.6	12.1	14 31.8	8.2	56.0
14	33 49.0	42.7	296 13.7	12.0	14 23.6	8.2	56.0
15	48 48.9 ..	43.3	310 44.7	12.1	14 15.4	8.4	56.0
16	63 48.8	44.0	325 15.8	12.1	14 07.0	8.4	56.1
17	78 48.7	44.6	339 46.9	12.1	13 58.6	8.5	56.1
18	93 48.6	S18 45.2	354 18.0	12.0	S13 50.1	8.6	56.1
19	108 48.5	45.8	8 49.0	12.1	13 41.5	8.7	56.2
20	123 48.3	46.5	23 20.1	12.1	13 32.8	8.7	56.2
21	138 48.2 ..	47.1	37 51.2	12.1	13 24.1	8.9	56.2
22	153 48.1	47.7	52 22.3	12.1	13 15.2	8.8	56.3
23	168 48.0	48.3	66 53.3	12.1	13 06.4	9.0	56.3
17 00	183 47.9	S18 48.9	81 24.4	12.1	S12 57.4	9.1	56.3
01	198 47.8	49.6	95 55.5	12.0	12 48.3	9.1	56.4
02	213 47.6	50.2	110 26.5	12.1	12 39.2	9.1	56.4
03	228 47.5 ..	50.8	124 57.6	12.1	12 30.1	9.3	56.4
04	243 47.4	51.4	139 28.7	12.0	12 20.8	9.3	56.5
05	258 47.3	52.0	153 59.7	12.1	12 11.5	9.4	56.5
06	273 47.2	S18 52.7	168 30.8	12.1	S12 02.1	9.5	56.5
07	288 47.0	53.3	183 01.9	12.0	11 52.6	9.6	56.6
08	303 46.9	53.9	197 32.9	12.1	11 43.0	9.6	56.6
09	318 46.8 ..	54.5	212 03.9	12.1	11 33.4	9.6	56.6
10	333 46.7	55.1	226 35.0	12.0	11 23.8	9.8	56.7
11	348 46.5	55.7	241 06.0	12.0	11 14.0	9.8	56.7
12	3 46.4	S18 56.3	255 37.0	12.1	S11 04.2	9.9	56.8
13	18 46.3	57.0	270 08.1	12.0	10 54.3	10.0	56.8
14	33 46.2	57.6	284 39.1	12.0	10 44.3	10.0	56.8
15	48 46.1 ..	58.2	299 10.1	12.0	10 34.3	10.1	56.9
16	63 46.0	58.8	313 41.1	12.0	10 24.2	10.1	56.9
17	78 45.8	18 59.4	328 12.1	11.9	10 14.1	10.2	56.9
18	93 45.7	S19 00.0	342 43.0	12.0	S10 03.9	10.3	57.0
19	108 45.6	00.6	357 14.0	12.0	9 53.6	10.3	57.0
20	123 45.5	01.2	11 45.0	11.9	9 43.3	10.5	57.1
21	138 45.3 ..	01.8	26 15.9	11.9	9 32.8	10.4	57.1
22	153 45.2	02.4	40 46.8	12.0	9 22.4	10.5	57.1
23	168 45.1	03.0	55 17.8	11.9	S 9 11.9	10.6	57.2
	SD 16.2 d 0.6		SD 15.0		15.2		15.5

MONDAY · TUESDAY · WEDNESDAY

Lat.	Twilight Naut.	Twilight Civil	Sunrise	Moonrise 15	16	17	18
°	h m	h m	h m	h m	h m	h m	h m
N 72	07 01	08 37	11 14	16 20	15 44	15 25	15 11
N 70	06 51	08 14	09 53	15 26	15 16	15 08	15 02
68	06 42	07 56	09 15	14 52	14 54	14 55	14 55
66	06 35	07 41	08 49	14 28	14 37	14 44	14 48
64	06 29	07 29	08 29	14 09	14 24	14 34	14 43
62	06 23	07 19	08 13	13 53	14 12	14 26	14 39
60	06 18	07 10	07 59	13 40	14 02	14 19	14 35
N 58	06 14	07 02	07 48	13 29	13 53	14 13	14 31
56	06 09	06 55	07 38	13 19	13 45	14 08	14 28
54	06 05	06 49	07 29	13 10	13 38	14 03	14 25
52	06 02	06 43	07 21	13 02	13 32	13 58	14 23
50	05 59	06 38	07 14	12 55	13 26	13 54	14 20
45	05 51	06 26	06 58	12 40	13 14	13 46	14 15
N 40	05 44	06 17	06 46	12 28	13 04	13 38	14 11
35	05 37	06 08	06 35	12 17	12 55	13 32	14 07
30	05 31	06 00	06 25	12 08	12 48	13 26	14 04
20	05 19	05 46	06 09	11 51	12 35	13 17	13 58
N 10	05 07	05 33	05 55	11 37	12 23	13 08	13 53
0	04 54	05 19	05 41	11 24	12 12	13 00	13 48
S 10	04 39	05 05	05 27	11 11	12 01	12 52	13 43
20	04 21	04 49	05 13	10 57	11 49	12 43	13 38
30	03 58	04 30	04 56	10 40	11 36	12 33	13 33
35	03 44	04 18	04 46	10 31	11 28	12 28	13 29
40	03 26	04 04	04 34	10 20	11 19	12 21	13 25
45	03 03	03 47	04 21	10 07	11 09	12 14	13 21
S 50	02 33	03 25	04 04	09 52	10 56	12 05	13 16
52	02 17	03 14	03 56	09 45	10 51	12 00	13 13
54	01 58	03 02	03 47	09 37	10 44	11 56	13 11
56	01 33	02 48	03 38	09 27	10 37	11 51	13 08
58	00 56	02 32	03 26	09 17	10 29	11 45	13 04
S 60	////	02 11	03 13	09 05	10 19	11 38	13 01

Lat.	Sunset	Twilight Civil	Twilight Naut.	Moonset 15	16	17	18
°	h m	h m	h m	h m	h m	h m	h m
N 72	12 14	14 52	16 27	19 03	21 19	23 19	25 15
N 70	13 35	15 15	16 37	19 57	21 46	23 34	25 22
68	14 13	15 33	16 46	20 29	22 07	23 46	25 27
66	14 39	15 47	16 53	20 53	22 23	23 56	25 31
64	15 00	15 59	17 00	21 12	22 36	24 04	00 04
62	15 16	16 10	17 05	21 27	22 47	24 11	00 11
60	15 29	16 19	17 11	21 39	22 56	24 17	00 17
N 58	15 41	16 27	17 15	21 50	23 04	24 22	00 22
56	15 51	16 34	17 19	22 00	23 11	24 27	00 27
54	16 00	16 40	17 23	22 08	23 18	24 31	00 31
52	16 08	16 46	17 27	22 15	23 23	24 35	00 35
50	16 15	16 51	17 30	22 22	23 29	24 38	00 38
45	16 31	17 03	17 38	22 36	23 40	24 46	00 46
N 40	16 43	17 13	17 45	22 48	23 49	24 53	00 52
35	16 54	17 21	17 52	22 58	23 57	24 57	00 57
30	17 04	17 29	17 58	23 07	24 03	00 03	01 02
20	17 20	17 43	18 10	23 22	24 15	00 15	01 10
N 10	17 35	17 57	18 22	23 35	24 25	00 25	01 16
0	17 48	18 10	18 36	23 47	24 35	00 35	01 23
S 10	18 02	18 24	18 50	23 59	24 45	00 45	01 29
20	18 17	18 41	19 09	24 12	00 12	00 55	01 36
30	18 34	19 00	19 32	24 27	00 27	01 06	01 44
35	18 44	19 12	19 46	24 35	00 35	01 13	01 48
40	18 56	19 26	20 04	00 07	00 45	01 20	01 53
45	19 10	19 44	20 27	00 20	00 56	01 29	01 59
S 50	19 26	20 06	20 58	00 36	01 10	01 39	02 06
52	19 34	20 16	21 14	00 44	01 16	01 44	02 09
54	19 43	20 29	21 34	00 52	01 23	01 49	02 12
56	19 53	20 43	22 00	01 02	01 31	01 55	02 16
58	20 05	21 00	22 39	01 13	01 39	02 02	02 20
S 60	20 18	21 21	////	01 25	01 49	02 09	02 25

Day	SUN Eqn. of Time 00h	12h	Mer. Pass.	MOON Mer. Pass. Upper	Lower	Age	Phase
d	m s	m s	h m	h m	h m	d	%
15	15 32	15 27	11 45	17 36	05 12	07	41
16	15 22	15 17	11 45	18 24	06 00	08	51
17	15 12	15 06	11 45	19 11	06 47	09	61

1999 NOVEMBER 18, 19, 20 (THURS., FRI., SAT.)

UT	ARIES GHA	VENUS −4.3 GHA	VENUS Dec	MARS +0.8 GHA	MARS Dec	JUPITER −2.8 GHA	JUPITER Dec	SATURN −0.2 GHA	SATURN Dec
18 00	56 35.7	227 06.1	S 2 18.5	120 45.2	S22 53.5	31 12.1	N 8 56.9	15 26.8	N13 11.6
01	71 38.2	242 06.0	19.4	135 45.6	53.1	46 14.8	56.8	30 29.4	11.6
02	86 40.7	257 05.9	20.4	150 46.0	52.8	61 17.5	56.7	45 32.1	11.5
03	101 43.1	272 05.8	.. 21.4	165 46.5	.. 52.4	76 20.2	.. 56.7	60 34.7	.. 11.5
04	116 45.6	287 05.6	22.3	180 46.9	52.1	91 22.9	56.6	75 37.4	11.4
05	131 48.0	302 05.5	23.3	195 47.4	51.7	106 25.6	56.5	90 40.0	11.4
06	146 50.5	317 05.4	S 2 24.2	210 47.8	S22 51.4	121 28.3	N 8 56.4	105 42.7	N13 11.3
07	161 53.0	332 05.2	25.2	225 48.2	51.0	136 31.0	56.3	120 45.3	11.3
T 08	176 55.4	347 05.1	26.1	240 48.7	50.7	151 33.7	56.2	135 48.0	11.2
H 09	191 57.9	2 05.0	.. 27.1	255 49.1	.. 50.3	166 36.5	.. 56.2	150 50.7	.. 11.2
U 10	207 00.4	17 04.9	28.0	270 49.6	49.9	181 39.2	56.1	165 53.3	11.1
R 11	222 02.8	32 04.7	29.0	285 50.0	49.6	196 41.9	56.0	180 56.0	11.0
S 12	237 05.3	47 04.6	S 2 30.0	300 50.5	S22 49.2	211 44.6	N 8 55.9	195 58.6	N13 11.0
D 13	252 07.8	62 04.5	30.9	315 50.9	48.9	226 47.3	55.8	211 01.3	10.9
A 14	267 10.2	77 04.3	31.9	330 51.3	48.5	241 50.0	55.7	226 03.9	10.9
Y 15	282 12.7	92 04.2	.. 32.8	345 51.8	.. 48.2	256 52.7	.. 55.7	241 06.6	.. 10.8
16	297 15.2	107 04.1	33.8	0 52.2	47.8	271 55.4	55.6	256 09.2	10.8
17	312 17.6	122 03.9	34.8	15 52.7	47.4	286 58.1	55.5	271 11.9	10.7
18	327 20.1	137 03.8	S 2 35.7	30 53.1	S22 47.1	302 00.8	N 8 55.4	286 14.6	N13 10.7
19	342 22.5	152 03.7	36.7	45 53.5	46.7	317 03.5	55.3	301 17.2	10.6
20	357 25.0	167 03.6	37.6	60 54.0	46.4	332 06.2	55.3	316 19.9	10.6
21	12 27.5	182 03.4	.. 38.6	75 54.4	.. 46.0	347 08.9	.. 55.2	331 22.5	.. 10.5
22	27 29.9	197 03.3	39.6	90 54.9	45.7	2 11.6	55.1	346 25.2	10.5
23	42 32.4	212 03.2	40.5	105 55.3	45.3	17 14.4	55.0	1 27.8	10.4
19 00	57 34.9	227 03.0	S 2 41.5	120 55.8	S22 44.9	32 17.1	N 8 54.9	16 30.5	N13 10.4
01	72 37.3	242 02.9	42.4	135 56.2	44.6	47 19.8	54.8	31 33.1	10.3
02	87 39.8	257 02.7	43.4	150 56.7	44.2	62 22.5	54.8	46 35.8	10.2
03	102 42.3	272 02.6	.. 44.4	165 57.1	.. 43.9	77 25.2	.. 54.7	61 38.4	.. 10.2
04	117 44.7	287 02.5	45.3	180 57.5	43.5	92 27.9	54.6	76 41.1	10.1
05	132 47.2	302 02.3	46.3	195 58.0	43.1	107 30.6	54.5	91 43.8	10.1
06	147 49.6	317 02.2	S 2 47.2	210 58.4	S22 42.8	122 33.3	N 8 54.4	106 46.4	N13 10.0
07	162 52.1	332 02.1	48.2	225 58.9	42.4	137 36.0	54.4	121 49.1	10.0
F 08	177 54.6	347 01.9	49.2	240 59.3	42.0	152 38.7	54.3	136 51.7	09.9
R 09	192 57.0	2 01.8	.. 50.1	255 59.8	.. 41.7	167 41.4	.. 54.2	151 54.4	.. 09.9
I 10	207 59.5	17 01.7	51.1	271 00.2	41.3	182 44.1	54.1	166 57.0	09.8
11	223 02.0	32 01.5	52.1	286 00.6	40.9	197 46.8	54.0	181 59.7	09.8
D 12	238 04.4	47 01.4	S 2 53.0	301 01.1	S22 40.6	212 49.5	N 8 54.0	197 02.3	N13 09.7
A 13	253 06.9	62 01.2	54.0	316 01.5	40.2	227 52.2	53.9	212 05.0	09.7
Y 14	268 09.4	77 01.1	55.0	331 02.0	39.8	242 54.9	53.8	227 07.6	09.6
15	283 11.8	92 01.0	.. 55.9	346 02.4	.. 39.5	257 57.6	.. 53.7	242 10.3	.. 09.6
16	298 14.3	107 00.8	56.9	1 02.9	39.1	273 00.3	53.6	257 12.9	09.5
17	313 16.8	122 00.7	57.8	16 03.3	38.7	288 03.0	53.6	272 15.6	09.4
18	328 19.2	137 00.5	S 2 58.8	31 03.8	S22 38.4	303 05.7	N 8 53.5	287 18.3	N13 09.4
19	343 21.7	152 00.4	2 59.8	46 04.2	38.0	318 08.4	53.4	302 20.9	09.3
20	358 24.1	167 00.3	3 00.7	61 04.6	37.6	333 11.1	53.3	317 23.6	09.3
21	13 26.6	182 00.1	.. 01.7	76 05.1	.. 37.3	348 13.8	.. 53.2	332 26.2	.. 09.2
22	28 29.1	197 00.0	02.7	91 05.5	36.9	3 16.5	53.2	347 28.9	09.2
23	43 31.5	211 59.8	03.6	106 06.0	36.5	18 19.2	53.1	2 31.5	09.1
20 00	58 34.0	226 59.7	S 3 04.6	121 06.4	S22 36.2	33 21.9	N 8 53.0	17 34.2	N13 09.1
01	73 36.5	241 59.5	05.6	136 06.9	35.8	48 24.6	52.9	32 36.8	09.0
02	88 38.9	256 59.4	06.5	151 07.3	35.4	63 27.3	52.8	47 39.5	09.0
03	103 41.4	271 59.2	.. 07.5	166 07.8	.. 35.0	78 30.0	.. 52.8	62 42.1	.. 08.9
04	118 43.9	286 59.1	08.5	181 08.2	34.7	93 32.7	52.7	77 44.8	08.9
05	133 46.3	301 59.0	09.4	196 08.7	34.3	108 35.4	52.6	92 47.4	08.8
06	148 48.8	316 58.8	S 3 10.4	211 09.1	S22 33.9	123 38.1	N 8 52.5	107 50.1	N13 08.8
07	163 51.3	331 58.7	11.4	226 09.6	33.6	138 40.8	52.4	122 52.7	08.7
S 08	178 53.7	346 58.5	12.3	241 10.0	33.2	153 43.5	52.4	137 55.4	08.7
A 09	193 56.2	1 58.4	.. 13.3	256 10.4	.. 32.8	168 46.2	.. 52.3	152 58.1	.. 08.6
T 10	208 58.6	16 58.2	14.3	271 10.9	32.4	183 48.9	52.2	168 00.7	08.5
U 11	224 01.1	31 58.1	15.2	286 11.3	32.1	198 51.6	52.1	183 03.4	08.5
R 12	239 03.6	46 57.9	S 3 16.2	301 11.8	S22 31.7	213 54.3	N 8 52.1	198 06.0	N13 08.4
D 13	254 06.0	61 57.8	17.2	316 12.2	31.3	228 57.0	52.0	213 08.7	08.4
A 14	269 08.5	76 57.6	18.1	331 12.7	30.9	243 59.7	51.9	228 11.3	08.3
Y 15	284 11.0	91 57.5	.. 19.1	346 13.1	.. 30.5	259 02.4	.. 51.8	243 14.0	.. 08.3
16	299 13.4	106 57.3	20.1	1 13.6	30.2	274 05.1	51.7	258 16.6	08.2
17	314 15.9	121 57.2	21.1	16 14.0	29.8	289 07.8	51.7	273 19.3	08.2
18	329 18.4	136 57.0	S 3 22.0	31 14.5	S22 29.4	304 10.5	N 8 51.6	288 21.9	N13 08.1
19	344 20.8	151 56.9	23.0	46 14.9	29.0	319 13.1	51.5	303 24.6	08.1
20	359 23.3	166 56.7	24.0	61 15.4	28.7	334 15.8	51.4	318 27.2	08.0
21	14 25.7	181 56.6	.. 24.9	76 15.8	.. 28.3	349 18.5	.. 51.4	333 29.9	.. 08.0
22	29 28.2	196 56.4	25.9	91 16.3	27.9	4 21.2	51.3	348 32.5	07.9
23	44 30.7	211 56.3	26.9	106 16.7	27.5	19 23.9	51.2	3 35.2	07.9
Mer. Pass. 20 06.4		v −0.1 d 1.0		v 0.4 d 0.4		v 2.7 d 0.1		v 2.7 d 0.1	

STARS

Name	SHA	Dec
Acamar	315 25.9	S40 18.5
Achernar	335 34.1	S57 14.5
Acrux	173 21.6	S63 05.5
Adhara	255 20.6	S28 58.2
Aldebaran	291 01.2	N16 30.5
Alioth	166 30.4	N55 57.6
Alkaid	153 07.7	N49 18.9
Al Na'ir	27 57.0	S46 57.9
Alnilam	275 56.8	S 1 12.1
Alphard	218 06.4	S 8 39.3
Alphecca	126 20.4	N26 43.1
Alpheratz	357 54.3	N29 05.5
Altair	62 18.7	N 8 52.2
Ankaa	353 25.9	S42 18.6
Antares	112 39.6	S26 25.7
Arcturus	146 05.7	N19 11.1
Atria	107 51.6	S69 01.6
Avior	234 22.1	S59 30.3
Bellatrix	278 43.1	N 6 20.9
Betelgeuse	271 12.5	N 7 24.4
Canopus	264 00.4	S52 41.6
Capella	280 49.7	N45 59.7
Deneb	49 38.8	N45 17.1
Denebola	182 44.6	N14 34.5
Diphda	349 06.3	S17 59.4
Dubhe	194 04.8	N61 44.9
Elnath	278 25.7	N28 36.3
Eltanin	90 51.5	N51 29.6
Enif	33 57.5	N 9 52.6
Fomalhaut	15 35.5	S29 37.5
Gacrux	172 13.1	S57 06.4
Gienah	176 03.4	S17 32.2
Hadar	149 03.6	S60 22.0
Hamal	328 12.4	N23 27.7
Kaus Aust.	83 58.2	S34 23.1
Kochab	137 20.8	N74 09.4
Markab	13 48.8	N15 12.4
Menkar	314 25.8	N 4 05.3
Menkent	148 20.4	S36 21.9
Miaplacidus	221 41.7	S69 42.7
Mirfak	308 55.0	N49 51.6
Nunki	76 11.7	S26 17.8
Peacock	53 36.1	S56 44.3
Pollux	243 40.5	N28 01.5
Procyon	245 10.6	N 5 13.5
Rasalhague	96 16.6	N12 33.8
Regulus	207 54.8	N11 58.1
Rigel	281 21.9	S 8 12.1
Rigil Kent.	140 06.9	S60 49.8
Sabik	102 25.0	S15 43.3
Schedar	349 52.2	N56 32.3
Shaula	96 36.7	S37 06.1
Sirius	258 42.8	S16 42.9
Spica	158 42.7	S11 09.4
Suhail	223 00.1	S43 25.6
Vega	80 46.5	N38 47.3
Zuben'ubi	137 17.5	S16 02.2

	SHA	Mer. Pass.
Venus	169 28.2	h m 8 52
Mars	63 20.9	15 56
Jupiter	334 42.2	21 47
Saturn	318 55.6	22 50

UT	SUN GHA	SUN Dec	MOON GHA	MOON v	MOON Dec	MOON d	MOON HP
d h	° ′	° ′	° ′	′	° ′	′	′
18 00	183 45.0	S19 03.7	69 48.7	11.9	S 9 01.3	10.7	57.2
01	198 44.9	04.3	84 19.6	11.8	8 50.6	10.7	57.3
02	213 44.7	04.9	98 50.4	11.9	8 39.9	10.8	57.3
03	228 44.6	.. 05.5	113 21.3	11.9	8 29.1	10.8	57.3
04	243 44.5	06.1	127 52.2	11.8	8 18.3	10.9	57.4
05	258 44.3	06.7	142 23.0	11.8	8 07.4	10.9	57.4
T 06	273 44.2	S19 07.3	156 53.8	11.8	S 7 56.5	11.0	57.4
H 07	288 44.1	07.9	171 24.6	11.8	7 45.5	11.0	57.5
U 08	303 44.0	08.5	185 55.4	11.7	7 34.5	11.2	57.5
R 09	318 43.8	.. 09.1	200 26.1	11.8	7 23.3	11.1	57.6
S 10	333 43.7	09.7	214 56.9	11.7	7 12.2	11.2	57.6
D 11	348 43.6	10.3	229 27.6	11.7	7 01.0	11.3	57.6
A 12	3 43.5	S19 10.9	243 58.3	11.7	S 6 49.7	11.3	57.7
Y 13	18 43.3	11.5	258 29.0	11.6	6 38.4	11.4	57.7
14	33 43.2	12.1	272 59.6	11.7	6 27.0	11.4	57.8
15	48 43.1	.. 12.7	287 30.3	11.6	6 15.6	11.4	57.8
16	63 42.9	13.3	302 00.9	11.6	6 04.2	11.6	57.9
17	78 42.8	13.9	316 31.5	11.5	5 52.6	11.5	57.9
18	93 42.7	S19 14.5	331 02.0	11.6	S 5 41.1	11.6	57.9
19	108 42.5	15.0	345 32.6	11.5	5 29.5	11.7	58.0
20	123 42.4	15.6	0 03.1	11.5	5 17.8	11.7	58.0
21	138 42.3	.. 16.2	14 33.6	11.4	5 06.1	11.7	58.1
22	153 42.1	16.8	29 04.0	11.5	4 54.4	11.8	58.1
23	168 42.0	17.4	43 34.5	11.4	4 42.6	11.8	58.1
19 00	183 41.9	S19 18.0	58 04.9	11.3	S 4 30.8	11.9	58.2
01	198 41.8	18.6	72 35.2	11.4	4 18.9	11.9	58.2
02	213 41.6	19.2	87 05.6	11.3	4 07.0	11.9	58.3
03	228 41.5	.. 19.8	101 35.9	11.2	3 55.1	12.0	58.3
04	243 41.3	20.4	116 06.1	11.3	3 43.1	12.0	58.3
05	258 41.2	21.0	130 36.4	11.2	3 31.1	12.1	58.4
06	273 41.1	S19 21.5	145 06.6	11.2	S 3 19.0	12.1	58.4
07	288 40.9	22.1	159 36.8	11.1	3 06.9	12.1	58.5
08	303 40.8	22.7	174 06.9	11.1	2 54.8	12.2	58.5
F 09	318 40.7	.. 23.3	188 37.0	11.1	2 42.6	12.2	58.5
R 10	333 40.5	23.9	203 07.1	11.0	2 30.4	12.2	58.6
I 11	348 40.4	24.5	217 37.1	11.0	2 18.2	12.3	58.6
D 12	3 40.3	S19 25.1	232 07.1	10.9	S 2 05.9	12.2	58.7
A 13	18 40.1	25.6	246 37.0	10.9	1 53.7	12.4	58.7
Y 14	33 40.0	26.2	261 06.9	10.9	1 41.3	12.3	58.7
15	48 39.8	.. 26.8	275 36.8	10.8	1 29.0	12.4	58.8
16	63 39.7	27.4	290 06.6	10.8	1 16.6	12.4	58.8
17	78 39.6	28.0	304 36.4	10.8	1 04.2	12.4	58.9
18	93 39.4	S19 28.6	319 06.2	10.7	S 0 51.8	12.4	58.9
19	108 39.3	29.1	333 35.9	10.6	0 39.4	12.5	59.0
20	123 39.2	29.7	348 05.5	10.6	0 26.9	12.5	59.0
21	138 39.0	.. 30.3	2 35.1	10.6	0 14.4	12.5	59.0
22	153 38.9	30.9	17 04.7	10.5	S 0 01.9	12.5	59.1
23	168 38.7	31.5	31 34.2	10.5	N 0 10.6	12.5	59.1
20 00	183 38.6	S19 32.0	46 03.7	10.4	N 0 23.1	12.6	59.2
01	198 38.4	32.6	60 33.1	10.4	0 35.7	12.6	59.2
02	213 38.3	33.2	75 02.5	10.3	0 48.3	12.5	59.2
03	228 38.2	.. 33.8	89 31.8	10.3	1 00.8	12.6	59.3
04	243 38.0	34.3	104 01.1	10.2	1 13.4	12.6	59.3
05	258 37.9	34.9	118 30.3	10.2	1 26.0	12.7	59.3
06	273 37.7	S19 35.5	132 59.5	10.1	N 1 38.7	12.6	59.4
S 07	288 37.6	36.0	147 28.6	10.1	1 51.3	12.6	59.4
A 08	303 37.4	36.6	161 57.7	10.0	2 03.9	12.6	59.5
T 09	318 37.3	.. 37.2	176 26.7	9.9	2 16.5	12.7	59.5
U 10	333 37.2	37.8	190 55.6	9.9	2 29.2	12.6	59.5
R 11	348 37.0	38.3	205 24.5	9.8	2 41.8	12.7	59.6
D 12	3 36.9	S19 38.9	219 53.3	9.8	N 2 54.5	12.6	59.6
A 13	18 36.7	39.5	234 22.1	9.8	3 07.1	12.7	59.7
Y 14	33 36.6	40.0	248 50.9	9.6	3 19.8	12.6	59.7
15	48 36.4	.. 40.6	263 19.5	9.6	3 32.4	12.7	59.7
16	63 36.3	41.2	277 48.1	9.6	3 45.1	12.6	59.8
17	78 36.1	41.7	292 16.7	9.5	3 57.7	12.6	59.8
18	93 36.0	S19 42.3	306 45.2	9.4	N 4 10.3	12.6	59.8
19	108 35.8	42.9	321 13.6	9.3	4 22.9	12.7	59.9
20	123 35.7	43.4	335 41.9	9.3	4 35.6	12.6	59.9
21	138 35.5	.. 44.0	350 10.2	9.3	4 48.2	12.5	59.9
22	153 35.4	44.6	4 38.5	9.1	5 00.7	12.6	60.0
23	168 35.2	45.1	19 06.6	9.2	N 5 13.3	12.6	60.0
	SD 16.2	d 0.6	SD 15.7		16.0		16.2

Lat.	Twilight Naut.	Civil	Sunrise	Moonrise 18	19	20	21
°	h m	h m	h m	h m	h m	h m	h m
N 72	07 12	08 51	■	15 11	14 58	14 45	14 31
N 70	07 00	08 25	10 14	15 02	14 56	14 49	14 43
68	06 51	08 06	09 30	14 55	14 54	14 53	14 53
66	06 43	07 50	09 01	14 48	14 52	14 57	15 01
64	06 36	07 37	08 39	14 43	14 51	14 59	15 08
62	06 30	07 26	08 21	14 39	14 50	15 01	15 14
60	06 24	07 16	08 07	14 35	14 49	15 03	15 20
N 58	06 19	07 08	07 54	14 31	14 48	15 05	15 24
56	06 14	07 01	07 44	14 28	14 47	15 07	15 28
54	06 10	06 54	07 34	14 25	14 47	15 08	15 32
52	06 06	06 48	07 26	14 23	14 46	15 10	15 36
50	06 03	06 42	07 18	14 20	14 45	15 11	15 39
45	05 54	06 30	07 02	14 15	14 44	15 14	15 46
N 40	05 47	06 20	06 49	14 11	14 43	15 16	15 51
35	05 40	06 11	06 38	14 07	14 42	15 18	15 56
30	05 33	06 02	06 28	14 04	14 41	15 20	16 01
20	05 21	05 48	06 11	13 58	14 40	15 23	16 09
N 10	05 08	05 34	05 56	13 53	14 39	15 26	16 15
0	04 54	05 20	05 42	13 48	14 37	15 28	16 22
S 10	04 39	05 05	05 27	13 43	14 36	15 31	16 28
20	04 20	04 48	05 12	13 38	14 35	15 34	16 35
30	03 56	04 28	04 54	13 33	14 34	15 37	16 43
35	03 41	04 16	04 44	13 29	14 33	15 39	16 48
40	03 23	04 01	04 32	13 25	14 32	15 41	16 53
45	02 59	03 43	04 18	13 21	14 31	15 44	17 00
S 50	02 27	03 20	04 00	13 16	14 30	15 47	17 07
52	02 10	03 09	03 52	13 13	14 29	15 48	17 11
54	01 49	02 57	03 43	13 11	14 29	15 50	17 14
56	01 21	02 42	03 32	13 08	14 28	15 52	17 19
58	00 35	02 24	03 20	13 04	14 27	15 54	17 23
S 60	////	02 01	03 07	13 01	14 27	15 56	17 29

Lat.	Sunset	Twilight Civil	Naut.	Moonset 18	19	20	21
°	h m	h m	h m	h m	h m	h m	h m
N 72	■	14 39	16 18	25 15	01 15	03 13	05 17
N 70	13 15	15 04	16 29	25 22	01 22	03 12	05 08
68	14 00	15 24	16 39	25 27	01 27	03 11	05 00
66	14 29	15 40	16 47	25 31	01 31	03 10	04 53
64	14 51	15 53	16 54	00 04	01 35	03 09	04 48
62	15 09	16 04	17 00	00 11	01 38	03 09	04 43
60	15 23	16 13	17 06	00 17	01 41	03 08	04 39
N 58	15 36	16 22	17 11	00 22	01 43	03 08	04 36
56	15 46	16 29	17 16	00 27	01 45	03 07	04 32
54	15 56	16 36	17 20	00 31	01 47	03 07	04 30
52	16 04	16 42	17 24	00 35	01 49	03 06	04 27
50	16 12	16 48	17 27	00 38	01 51	03 06	04 25
45	16 28	17 00	17 36	00 46	01 54	03 05	04 19
N 40	16 41	17 10	17 43	00 52	01 57	03 05	04 15
35	16 52	17 20	17 50	00 57	01 59	03 04	04 12
30	17 02	17 28	17 57	01 02	02 02	03 04	04 08
20	17 20	17 43	18 10	01 10	02 05	03 03	04 03
N 10	17 35	17 57	18 23	01 16	02 08	03 02	03 58
0	17 49	18 11	18 36	01 23	02 11	03 01	03 53
S 10	18 03	18 26	18 52	01 29	02 14	03 01	03 49
20	18 19	18 43	19 11	01 36	02 18	03 00	03 44
30	18 37	19 03	19 35	01 44	02 21	02 59	03 38
35	18 47	19 15	19 50	01 48	02 23	02 58	03 35
40	18 59	19 30	20 09	01 53	02 25	02 58	03 31
45	19 14	19 48	20 32	01 59	02 28	02 57	03 27
S 50	19 31	20 11	21 05	02 06	02 31	02 56	03 22
52	19 40	20 23	21 22	02 09	02 32	02 56	03 20
54	19 49	20 36	21 44	02 12	02 34	02 55	03 18
56	20 00	20 51	22 13	02 16	02 36	02 55	03 15
58	20 12	21 09	23 04	02 20	02 37	02 54	03 12
S 60	20 26	21 32	////	02 25	02 40	02 54	03 08

Day	SUN Eqn. of Time 00h	12h	Mer. Pass.	MOON Mer. Pass. Upper	Lower	Age	Phase
d	m s	m s	h m	h m	h m	d	%
18	15 00	14 54	11 45	20 00	07 36	10	71
19	14 48	14 41	11 45	20 49	08 24	11	81
20	14 35	14 28	11 46	21 41	09 15	12	89

UT	ARIES GHA	VENUS −4.3 GHA	Dec	MARS +0.8 GHA	Dec	JUPITER −2.8 GHA	Dec	SATURN −0.1 GHA	Dec	STARS Name	SHA	Dec
d h												
21 00	59 33.1	226 56.1	S 3 27.8	121 17.2	S22 27.1	34 26.6	N 8 51.1	18 37.8	N13 07.8	Acamar	315 25.9	S40 18.5
01	74 35.6	241 56.0	28.8	136 17.6	26.8	49 29.3	51.0	33 40.5	07.8	Achernar	335 34.2	S57 14.5
02	89 38.1	256 55.8	29.8	151 18.0	26.4	64 32.0	51.0	48 43.1	07.7	Acrux	173 21.6	S63 05.5
03	104 40.5	271 55.7	.. 30.8	166 18.5	.. 26.0	79 34.7	.. 50.9	63 45.8	.. 07.7	Adhara	255 20.6	S28 58.2
04	119 43.0	286 55.5	31.7	181 18.9	25.6	94 37.4	50.8	78 48.4	07.6	Aldebaran	291 01.2	N16 30.5
05	134 45.5	301 55.3	32.7	196 19.4	25.2	109 40.1	50.7	93 51.1	07.6			
06	149 47.9	316 55.2	S 3 33.7	211 19.8	S22 24.8	124 42.8	N 8 50.7	108 53.7	N13 07.5	Alioth	166 30.4	N55 57.6
07	164 50.4	331 55.0	34.6	226 20.3	24.5	139 45.5	50.6	123 56.4	07.5	Alkaid	153 07.7	N49 18.9
08	179 52.9	346 54.9	35.6	241 20.7	24.1	154 48.2	50.5	138 59.0	07.4	Al Na'ir	27 57.0	S46 57.9
S 09	194 55.3	1 54.7	.. 36.6	256 21.2	.. 23.7	169 50.8	.. 50.4	154 01.7	.. 07.3	Alnilam	275 56.8	S 1 12.2
U 10	209 57.8	16 54.6	37.6	271 21.6	23.3	184 53.5	50.4	169 04.3	07.3	Alphard	218 06.4	S 8 39.4
N 11	225 00.2	31 54.4	38.5	286 22.1	22.9	199 56.2	50.3	184 07.0	07.2			
D 12	240 02.7	46 54.2	S 3 39.5	301 22.5	S22 22.5	214 58.9	N 8 50.2	199 09.7	N13 07.2	Alphecca	126 20.3	N26 43.1
A 13	255 05.2	61 54.1	40.5	316 23.0	22.2	230 01.6	50.1	214 12.3	07.1	Alpheratz	357 54.3	N29 05.5
Y 14	270 07.6	76 53.9	41.5	331 23.4	21.8	245 04.3	50.1	229 15.0	07.1	Altair	62 18.7	N 8 52.2
15	285 10.1	91 53.8	.. 42.4	346 23.9	.. 21.4	260 07.0	.. 50.0	244 17.6	.. 07.0	Ankaa	353 25.9	S42 18.7
16	300 12.6	106 53.6	43.4	1 24.3	21.0	275 09.7	49.9	259 20.3	07.0	Antares	112 39.6	S26 25.7
17	315 15.0	121 53.4	44.4	16 24.8	20.6	290 12.4	49.8	274 22.9	06.9			
18	330 17.5	136 53.3	S 3 45.4	31 25.2	S22 20.2	305 15.1	N 8 49.8	289 25.6	N13 06.9	Arcturus	146 05.7	N19 11.1
19	345 20.0	151 53.1	46.3	46 25.7	19.8	320 17.7	49.7	304 28.2	06.8	Atria	107 51.6	S69 01.6
20	0 22.4	166 53.0	47.3	61 26.1	19.4	335 20.4	49.6	319 30.9	06.8	Avior	234 22.0	S59 30.3
21	15 24.9	181 52.8	.. 48.3	76 26.6	.. 19.0	350 23.1	.. 49.5	334 33.5	.. 06.7	Bellatrix	278 43.0	N 6 20.9
22	30 27.3	196 52.6	49.3	91 27.0	18.7	5 25.8	49.5	349 36.2	06.7	Betelgeuse	271 12.5	N 7 24.4
23	45 29.8	211 52.5	50.2	106 27.5	18.3	20 28.5	49.4	4 38.8	06.6			
22 00	60 32.3	226 52.3	S 3 51.2	121 27.9	S22 17.9	35 31.2	N 8 49.3	19 41.5	N13 06.6	Canopus	264 00.4	S52 41.6
01	75 34.7	241 52.2	52.2	136 28.4	17.5	50 33.9	49.2	34 44.1	06.5	Capella	280 49.6	N45 59.7
02	90 37.2	256 52.0	53.2	151 28.8	17.1	65 36.5	49.2	49 46.8	06.5	Deneb	49 38.9	N45 17.1
03	105 39.7	271 51.8	.. 54.1	166 29.3	.. 16.7	80 39.2	.. 49.1	64 49.4	.. 06.4	Denebola	182 44.6	N14 34.4
04	120 42.1	286 51.7	55.1	181 29.7	16.3	95 41.9	49.0	79 52.1	06.4	Diphda	349 06.3	S17 59.4
05	135 44.6	301 51.5	56.1	196 30.2	15.9	110 44.6	48.9	94 54.7	06.3			
06	150 47.1	316 51.3	S 3 57.1	211 30.6	S22 15.5	125 47.3	N 8 48.9	109 57.4	N13 06.3	Dubhe	194 04.8	N61 44.9
07	165 49.5	331 51.2	58.0	226 31.1	15.1	140 50.0	48.8	125 00.0	06.2	Elnath	278 25.6	N28 36.3
08	180 52.0	346 51.0	3 59.0	241 31.5	14.7	155 52.7	48.7	140 02.7	06.2	Eltanin	90 51.5	N51 29.6
M 09	195 54.5	1 50.8	4 00.0	256 32.0	.. 14.3	170 55.3	.. 48.7	155 05.3	.. 06.1	Enif	33 57.5	N 9 52.6
O 10	210 56.9	16 50.7	01.0	271 32.4	14.0	185 58.0	48.6	170 08.0	06.1	Fomalhaut	15 35.6	S29 37.5
N 11	225 59.4	31 50.5	01.9	286 32.9	13.6	201 00.7	48.5	185 10.6	06.0			
D 12	241 01.8	46 50.3	S 4 02.9	301 33.3	S22 13.2	216 03.4	N 8 48.4	200 13.3	N13 06.0	Gacrux	172 13.1	S57 06.4
A 13	256 04.3	61 50.2	03.9	316 33.8	12.8	231 06.1	48.4	215 15.9	05.9	Gienah	176 03.4	S17 32.2
Y 14	271 06.8	76 50.0	04.9	331 34.2	12.4	246 08.8	48.3	230 18.6	05.9	Hadar	149 03.5	S60 22.0
15	286 09.2	91 49.8	.. 05.8	346 34.7	.. 12.0	261 11.5	.. 48.2	245 21.2	.. 05.8	Hamal	328 12.4	N23 27.7
16	301 11.7	106 49.7	06.8	1 35.2	11.6	276 14.1	48.1	260 23.9	05.8	Kaus Aust.	83 58.2	S34 23.0
17	316 14.2	121 49.5	07.8	16 35.6	11.2	291 16.8	48.1	275 26.5	05.7			
18	331 16.6	136 49.3	S 4 08.8	31 36.1	S22 10.8	306 19.5	N 8 48.0	290 29.1	N13 05.6	Kochab	137 20.8	N74 09.4
19	346 19.1	151 49.1	09.8	46 36.5	10.4	321 22.2	47.9	305 31.8	05.6	Markab	13 48.8	N15 12.4
20	1 21.6	166 49.0	10.7	61 37.0	10.0	336 24.9	47.9	320 34.4	05.5	Menkar	314 25.8	N 4 05.3
21	16 24.0	181 48.8	.. 11.7	76 37.4	.. 09.6	351 27.5	.. 47.8	335 37.1	.. 05.5	Menkent	148 20.4	S36 21.9
22	31 26.5	196 48.6	12.7	91 37.9	09.2	6 30.2	47.7	350 39.7	05.4	Miaplacidus	221 41.6	S69 42.7
23	46 29.0	211 48.5	13.7	106 38.3	08.8	21 32.9	47.6	5 42.4	05.4			
23 00	61 31.4	226 48.3	S 4 14.6	121 38.8	S22 08.4	36 35.6	N 8 47.6	20 45.0	N13 05.3	Mirfak	308 55.0	N49 51.6
01	76 33.9	241 48.1	15.6	136 39.2	08.0	51 38.3	47.5	35 47.7	05.3	Nunki	76 11.7	S26 17.8
02	91 36.3	256 47.9	16.6	151 39.7	07.6	66 40.9	47.4	50 50.3	05.2	Peacock	53 36.1	S56 44.3
03	106 38.8	271 47.8	.. 17.6	166 40.1	.. 07.2	81 43.6	.. 47.3	65 53.0	.. 05.2	Pollux	243 40.4	N28 01.5
04	121 41.3	286 47.6	18.6	181 40.6	06.8	96 46.3	47.3	80 55.6	05.1	Procyon	245 10.6	N 5 13.5
05	136 43.7	301 47.4	19.5	196 41.0	06.4	111 49.0	47.2	95 58.3	05.1			
06	151 46.2	316 47.2	S 4 20.5	211 41.5	S22 06.0	126 51.7	N 8 47.1	111 00.9	N13 05.0	Rasalhague	96 16.6	N12 33.8
07	166 48.7	331 47.1	21.5	226 41.9	05.6	141 54.3	47.1	126 03.6	05.0	Regulus	207 54.8	N11 58.1
08	181 51.1	346 46.9	22.5	241 42.4	05.2	156 57.0	47.0	141 06.2	04.9	Rigel	281 21.9	S 8 12.1
T 09	196 53.6	1 46.7	.. 23.5	256 42.9	.. 04.8	171 59.7	.. 46.9	156 08.9	.. 04.9	Rigil Kent.	140 06.9	S60 49.8
U 10	211 56.1	16 46.5	24.4	271 43.3	04.4	187 02.4	46.9	171 11.5	04.8	Sabik	102 25.0	S15 43.3
E 11	226 58.5	31 46.4	25.4	286 43.8	03.9	202 05.1	46.8	186 14.2	04.8			
S 12	242 01.0	46 46.2	S 4 26.4	301 44.2	S22 03.5	217 07.7	N 8 46.7	201 16.8	N13 04.7	Schedar	349 52.2	N56 32.3
D 13	257 03.5	61 46.0	27.4	316 44.7	03.1	232 10.4	46.6	216 19.5	04.7	Shaula	96 36.7	S37 06.1
A 14	272 05.9	76 45.8	28.4	331 45.1	02.7	247 13.1	46.6	231 22.1	04.6	Sirius	258 42.8	S16 42.9
Y 15	287 08.4	91 45.6	.. 29.3	346 45.6	.. 02.3	262 15.8	.. 46.5	246 24.8	.. 04.6	Spica	158 42.7	S11 09.4
16	302 10.8	106 45.5	30.3	1 46.0	01.9	277 18.4	46.4	261 27.4	04.5	Suhail	223 00.1	S43 25.6
17	317 13.3	121 45.3	31.3	16 46.5	01.5	292 21.1	46.4	276 30.1	04.5			
18	332 15.8	136 45.1	S 4 32.3	31 46.9	S22 01.1	307 23.8	N 8 46.3	291 32.7	N13 04.4	Vega	80 46.5	N38 47.3
19	347 18.2	151 44.9	33.3	46 47.4	00.7	322 26.5	46.2	306 35.3	04.4	Zuben'ubi	137 17.5	S16 02.2
20	2 20.7	166 44.7	34.3	61 47.9	22 00.3	337 29.1	46.2	321 38.0	04.3		SHA	Mer. Pass.
21	17 23.2	181 44.6	.. 35.2	76 48.3	21 59.9	352 31.8	.. 46.1	336 40.6	.. 04 3		° '	h m
22	32 25.6	196 44.4	36.2	91 48.8	59.5	7 34.5	46.0	351 43.3	04.2	Venus	166 20.0	8 53
23	47 28.1	211 44.2	37.2	106 49.2	59.1	22 37.2	45.9	6 45.9	04.2	Mars	60 55.7	15 54
	h m									Jupiter	334 58.9	21 34
Mer. Pass. 19 54.6		v −0.2	d 1.0	v 0.5	d 0.4	v 2.7	d 0.1	v 2.6	d 0.1	Saturn	319 09.2	22 37

SUN and MOON

UT	SUN GHA	SUN Dec	MOON GHA	v	MOON Dec	d	HP
d h	° ′	° ′	° ′	′	° ′	′	′
21 00	183 35.1	S19 45.7	33 34.8	9.0	N 5 25.9	12.5	60.0
01	198 34.9	46.2	48 02.8	9.0	5 38.4	12.5	60.1
02	213 34.8	46.8	62 30.8	8.9	5 50.9	12.5	60.1
03	228 34.6	.. 47.4	76 58.7	8.8	6 03.4	12.5	60.2
04	243 34.5	47.9	91 26.5	8.8	6 15.9	12.5	60.2
05	258 34.3	48.5	105 54.3	8.7	6 28.4	12.4	60.2
06	273 34.2	S19 49.0	120 22.0	8.6	N 6 40.8	12.4	60.3
S 07	288 34.0	49.6	134 49.6	8.6	6 53.2	12.4	60.3
U 08	303 33.9	50.2	149 17.2	8.5	7 05.6	12.4	60.3
N 09	318 33.7	.. 50.7	163 44.7	8.4	7 18.0	12.3	60.3
D 10	333 33.6	51.3	178 12.1	8.4	7 30.3	12.3	60.4
A 11	348 33.4	51.8	192 39.5	8.2	7 42.6	12.2	60.4
Y 12	3 33.3	S19 52.4	207 06.7	8.3	N 7 54.8	12.2	60.4
13	18 33.1	52.9	221 34.0	8.1	8 07.0	12.2	60.5
14	33 33.0	53.5	236 01.1	8.1	8 19.2	12.2	60.5
15	48 32.8	.. 54.0	250 28.2	7.9	8 31.4	12.1	60.5
16	63 32.7	54.6	264 55.1	8.0	8 43.5	12.0	60.6
17	78 32.5	55.1	279 22.1	7.8	8 55.5	12.0	60.6
18	93 32.3	S19 55.7	293 48.9	7.8	N 9 07.5	12.0	60.6
19	108 32.2	56.2	308 15.7	7.7	9 19.5	11.9	60.6
20	123 32.0	56.8	322 42.4	7.6	9 31.4	11.9	60.7
21	138 31.9	.. 57.3	337 09.0	7.5	9 43.3	11.8	60.7
22	153 31.7	57.9	351 35.5	7.5	9 55.1	11.8	60.7
23	168 31.6	58.4	6 02.0	7.4	10 06.9	11.7	60.7
22 00	183 31.4	S19 59.0	20 28.4	7.3	N10 18.6	11.7	60.8
01	198 31.2	19 59.5	34 54.7	7.2	10 30.3	11.6	60.8
02	213 31.1	20 00.1	49 20.9	7.2	10 41.9	11.5	60.8
03	228 30.9	.. 00.6	63 47.1	7.1	10 53.4	11.5	60.8
04	243 30.8	01.2	78 13.2	7.0	11 04.9	11.4	60.9
05	258 30.6	01.7	92 39.2	6.9	11 16.3	11.3	60.9
06	273 30.4	S20 02.3	107 05.1	6.9	N11 27.6	11.3	60.9
M 07	288 30.3	02.8	121 31.0	6.8	11 38.9	11.2	60.9
O 08	303 30.1	03.3	135 56.8	6.7	11 50.1	11.2	61.0
N 09	318 30.0	.. 03.9	150 22.5	6.6	12 01.3	11.0	61.0
D 10	333 29.8	04.4	164 48.1	6.6	12 12.3	11.0	61.0
A 11	348 29.6	05.0	179 13.7	6.4	12 23.3	11.0	61.0
Y 12	3 29.5	S20 05.5	193 39.1	6.4	N12 34.3	10.8	61.0
13	18 29.3	06.0	208 04.5	6.3	12 45.1	10.8	61.1
14	33 29.1	06.6	222 29.8	6.3	12 55.9	10.7	61.1
15	48 29.0	.. 07.1	236 55.1	6.2	13 06.6	10.6	61.1
16	63 28.8	07.6	251 20.3	6.0	13 17.2	10.5	61.1
17	78 28.7	08.2	265 45.3	6.1	13 27.7	10.4	61.1
18	93 28.5	S20 08.7	280 10.4	5.9	N13 38.1	10.4	61.1
19	108 28.3	09.3	294 35.3	5.9	13 48.5	10.2	61.2
20	123 28.2	09.8	309 00.2	5.8	13 58.7	10.2	61.2
21	138 28.0	.. 10.3	323 25.0	5.7	14 08.9	10.1	61.2
22	153 27.8	10.9	337 49.7	5.6	14 19.0	10.1	61.2
23	168 27.7	11.4	352 14.3	5.6	14 29.0	9.8	61.2
23 00	183 27.5	S20 11.9	6 38.9	5.5	N14 38.8	9.8	61.2
01	198 27.3	12.5	21 03.4	5.4	14 48.6	9.7	61.2
02	213 27.2	13.0	35 27.8	5.4	14 58.3	9.6	61.3
03	228 27.0	.. 13.5	49 52.2	5.2	15 07.9	9.5	61.3
04	243 26.8	14.0	64 16.4	5.3	15 17.4	9.4	61.3
05	258 26.7	14.6	78 40.7	5.1	15 26.8	9.2	61.3
06	273 26.5	S20 15.1	93 04.8	5.1	N15 36.0	9.2	61.3
T 07	288 26.3	15.6	107 28.9	5.0	15 45.2	9.1	61.3
U 08	303 26.2	16.1	121 52.9	4.9	15 54.3	8.9	61.3
E 09	318 26.0	.. 16.7	136 16.8	4.9	16 03.2	8.8	61.3
S 10	333 25.8	17.2	150 40.7	4.8	16 12.0	8.7	61.3
D 11	348 25.7	17.7	165 04.5	4.7	16 20.7	8.7	61.3
A 12	3 25.5	S20 18.2	179 28.2	4.7	N16 29.4	8.4	61.3
Y 13	18 25.3	18.8	193 51.9	4.6	16 37.8	8.4	61.4
14	33 25.1	19.3	208 15.5	4.6	16 46.2	8.3	61.4
15	48 25.0	.. 19.8	222 39.1	4.4	16 54.5	8.1	61.4
16	63 24.8	20.3	237 02.5	4.5	17 02.6	8.0	61.4
17	78 24.6	20.9	251 26.0	4.3	17 10.6	7.9	61.4
18	93 24.5	S20 21.4	265 49.3	4.4	N17 18.5	7.7	61.4
19	108 24.3	21.9	280 12.7	4.2	17 26.2	7.6	61.4
20	123 24.1	22.4	294 35.9	4.2	17 33.8	7.5	61.4
21	138 23.9	.. 22.9	308 59.1	4.2	17 41.3	7.4	61.4
22	153 23.8	23.4	323 22.3	4.1	17 48.7	7.3	61.4
23	168 23.6	24.0	337 45.4	4.0	N17 56.0	7.1	61.4
SD	16.2	d 0.5	SD 16.5		16.6		16.7

Twilight, Sunrise, Moonrise

Lat.	Twilight Naut.	Twilight Civil	Sunrise	Moonrise 21	22	23	24
°	h m	h m	h m	h m	h m	h m	h m
N 72	07 22	09 05	■■■	14 31	14 13	13 42	☐
N 70	07 09	08 37	10 40	14 43	14 36	14 27	14 10
68	06 59	08 15	09 45	14 53	14 54	14 57	15 07
66	06 50	07 58	09 12	15 01	15 08	15 20	15 41
64	06 42	07 45	08 48	15 08	15 20	15 38	16 06
62	06 36	07 33	08 29	15 14	15 31	15 53	16 26
60	06 30	07 23	08 14	15 20	15 39	16 05	16 42
N 58	06 24	07 14	08 01	15 24	15 47	16 16	16 55
56	06 19	07 06	07 50	15 28	15 54	16 26	17 07
54	06 15	06 59	07 40	15 32	16 00	16 34	17 18
52	06 11	06 53	07 31	15 36	16 06	16 42	17 27
50	06 07	06 47	07 23	15 39	16 11	16 49	17 35
45	05 58	06 34	07 06	15 46	16 22	17 03	17 53
N 40	05 50	06 23	06 52	15 51	16 31	17 16	18 07
35	05 43	06 13	06 41	15 56	16 39	17 26	18 20
30	05 36	06 05	06 30	16 01	16 46	17 35	18 30
20	05 22	05 49	06 13	16 09	16 58	17 51	18 49
N 10	05 09	05 35	05 57	16 15	17 08	18 05	19 05
0	04 55	05 20	05 42	16 22	17 18	18 18	19 20
S 10	04 39	05 05	05 28	16 28	17 29	18 31	19 36
20	04 20	04 48	05 12	16 35	17 39	18 46	19 52
30	03 55	04 27	04 53	16 43	17 52	19 02	20 11
35	03 39	04 14	04 42	16 48	17 59	19 11	20 22
40	03 20	03 59	04 30	16 53	18 08	19 22	20 35
45	02 55	03 40	04 15	17 00	18 17	19 35	20 50
S 50	02 22	03 16	03 57	17 07	18 29	19 51	21 08
52	02 03	03 05	03 48	17 11	18 35	19 58	21 17
54	01 41	02 51	03 39	17 14	18 41	20 07	21 27
56	01 09	02 35	03 28	17 19	18 48	20 16	21 38
58	////	02 16	03 15	17 23	18 55	20 26	21 51
S 60	////	01 52	03 00	17 29	19 04	20 39	22 05

Sunset, Twilight, Moonset

Lat.	Sunset	Twilight Civil	Naut.	Moonset 21	22	23	24
°	h m	h m	h m	h m	h m	h m	h m
N 72	■■■	14 26	16 09	05 17	07 31	10 06	☐
N 70	12 51	14 54	16 22	05 08	07 10	09 22	11 49
68	13 47	15 16	16 32	05 00	06 54	08 53	10 53
66	14 19	15 33	16 41	04 53	06 41	08 32	10 19
64	14 43	15 47	16 49	04 48	06 30	08 14	09 55
62	15 02	15 59	16 56	04 43	06 21	08 00	09 35
60	15 18	16 09	17 02	04 39	06 13	07 48	09 20
N 58	15 31	16 18	17 07	04 36	06 06	07 38	09 06
56	15 42	16 26	17 12	04 32	06 00	07 29	08 55
54	15 52	16 33	17 17	04 30	05 55	07 21	08 45
52	16 01	16 39	17 21	04 27	05 50	07 14	08 36
50	16 09	16 45	17 25	04 25	05 46	07 08	08 28
45	16 25	16 58	17 34	04 19	05 36	06 54	08 11
N 40	16 39	17 09	17 42	04 15	05 28	06 43	07 57
35	16 51	17 18	17 49	04 12	05 22	06 33	07 45
30	17 01	17 27	17 56	04 08	05 16	06 25	07 35
20	17 19	17 43	18 10	04 03	05 06	06 11	07 17
N 10	17 35	17 57	18 23	03 58	04 57	05 58	07 02
0	17 50	18 12	18 37	03 53	04 48	05 46	06 48
S 10	18 05	18 27	18 53	03 49	04 40	05 35	06 33
20	18 21	18 45	19 13	03 44	04 31	05 22	06 18
30	18 39	19 06	19 38	03 38	04 21	05 08	06 00
35	18 50	19 19	19 53	03 35	04 15	05 00	05 50
40	19 03	19 34	20 13	03 32	04 09	04 50	05 38
45	19 18	19 53	20 38	03 27	04 01	04 39	05 25
S 50	19 36	20 17	21 12	03 22	03 52	04 26	05 08
52	19 45	20 29	21 31	03 20	03 48	04 20	05 00
54	19 55	20 42	21 54	03 18	03 43	04 13	04 52
56	20 06	20 58	22 27	03 15	03 38	04 06	04 42
58	20 18	21 18	////	03 12	03 32	03 58	04 31
S 60	20 34	21 43	////	03 08	03 26	03 48	04 18

SUN and MOON

Day	Eqn. of Time 00h	Eqn. of Time 12h	Mer. Pass.	Mer. Pass. Upper	Mer. Pass. Lower	Age	Phase
d	m s	m s	h m	h m	h m	d	%
21	14 21	14 13	11 46	22 35	10 07	13	95
22	14 06	13 58	11 46	23 32	11 03	14	99
23	13 50	13 42	11 46	24 33	12 02	15	100

UT	ARIES GHA	VENUS −4.2 GHA	Dec	MARS +0.9 GHA	Dec	JUPITER −2.8 GHA	Dec	SATURN −0.1 GHA	Dec	STARS Name	SHA	Dec
24 00	62 30.6	226 44.0	S 4 38.2	121 49.7	S21 58.6	37 39.8	N 8 45.9	21 48.6	N13 04.1	Acamar	315 25.9	S40 18.5
01	77 33.0	241 43.8	39.2	136 50.1	58.2	52 42.5	45.8	36 51.2	04.1	Achernar	335 34.2	S57 14.5
02	92 35.5	256 43.6	40.1	151 50.6	57.8	67 45.2	45.7	51 53.9	04.0	Acrux	173 21.5	S63 05.5
03	107 38.0	271 43.5	.. 41.1	166 51.0	.. 57.4	82 47.9	.. 45.7	66 56.5	.. 04.0	Adhara	255 20.5	S28 58.2
04	122 40.4	286 43.3	42.1	181 51.5	57.0	97 50.5	45.6	81 59.2	03.9	Aldebaran	291 01.2	N16 30.5
05	137 42.9	301 43.1	43.1	196 52.0	56.6	112 53.2	45.5	97 01.8	03.9			
W 06	152 45.3	316 42.9	S 4 44.1	211 52.4	S21 56.2	127 55.9	N 8 45.5	112 04.5	N13 03.8	Alioth	166 30.3	N55 57.6
E 07	167 47.8	331 42.7	45.1	226 52.9	55.8	142 58.6	45.4	127 07.1	03.8	Alkaid	153 07.6	N49 18.8
D 08	182 50.3	346 42.5	46.0	241 53.3	55.4	158 01.2	45.3	142 09.8	03.7	Al Na'ir	27 57.0	S46 57.9
N 09	197 52.7	1 42.3	.. 47.0	256 53.8	.. 54.9	173 03.9	.. 45.3	157 12.4	.. 03.7	Alnilam	275 56.8	S 1 12.2
E 10	212 55.2	16 42.2	48.0	271 54.2	54.5	188 06.6	45.2	172 15.0	03.6	Alphard	218 06.4	S 8 39.4
S 11	227 57.7	31 42.0	49.0	286 54.7	54.1	203 09.2	45.1	187 17.7	03.6			
D 12	243 00.1	46 41.8	S 4 50.0	301 55.2	S21 53.7	218 11.9	N 8 45.0	202 20.3	N13 03.5	Alphecca	126 20.3	N26 43.1
A 13	258 02.6	61 41.6	51.0	316 55.6	53.3	233 14.6	45.0	217 23.0	03.5	Alpheratz	357 54.3	N29 05.5
Y 14	273 05.1	76 41.4	51.9	331 56.1	52.9	248 17.3	44.9	232 25.6	03.4	Altair	62 18.7	N 8 52.2
15	288 07.5	91 41.2	.. 52.9	346 56.5	.. 52.4	263 19.9	.. 44.9	247 28.3	.. 03.4	Ankaa	353 25.9	S42 18.7
16	303 10.0	106 41.0	53.9	1 57.0	52.0	278 22.6	44.8	262 30.9	03.3	Antares	112 39.6	S26 25.7
17	318 12.4	121 40.8	54.9	16 57.4	51.6	293 25.3	44.7	277 33.6	03.3			
18	333 14.9	136 40.7	S 4 55.9	31 57.9	S21 51.2	308 27.9	N 8 44.7	292 36.2	N13 03.2	Arcturus	146 05.7	N19 11.1
19	348 17.4	151 40.5	56.9	46 58.4	50.8	323 30.6	44.6	307 38.9	03.2	Atria	107 51.5	S69 01.5
20	3 19.8	166 40.3	57.8	61 58.8	50.4	338 33.3	44.5	322 41.5	03.1	Avior	234 22.0	S59 30.3
21	18 22.3	181 40.1	.. 58.8	76 59.3	.. 49.9	353 35.9	.. 44.5	337 44.1	.. 03.1	Bellatrix	278 43.0	N 6 20.9
22	33 24.8	196 39.9	4 59.8	91 59.7	49.5	8 38.6	44.4	352 46.8	03.0	Betelgeuse	271 12.4	N 7 24.4
23	48 27.2	211 39.7	5 00.8	107 00.2	49.1	23 41.3	44.3	7 49.4	03.0			
25 00	63 29.7	226 39.5	S 5 01.8	122 00.7	S21 48.7	38 43.9	N 8 44.3	22 52.1	N13 02.9	Canopus	264 00.4	S52 41.7
01	78 32.2	241 39.3	02.8	137 01.1	48.3	53 46.6	44.2	37 54.7	02.9	Capella	280 49.6	N45 59.7
02	93 34.6	256 39.1	03.7	152 01.6	47.8	68 49.3	44.1	52 57.4	02.8	Deneb	49 38.9	N45 17.1
03	108 37.1	271 38.9	.. 04.7	167 02.0	.. 47.4	83 51.9	.. 44.1	68 00.0	.. 02.8	Denebola	182 44.6	N14 34.4
04	123 39.6	286 38.7	05.7	182 02.5	47.0	98 54.6	44.0	83 02.7	02.7	Diphda	349 06.3	S17 59.4
05	138 42.0	301 38.5	06.7	197 03.0	46.6	113 57.3	43.9	98 05.3	02.7			
T 06	153 44.5	316 38.3	S 5 07.7	212 03.4	S21 46.2	128 59.9	N 8 43.9	113 07.9	N13 02.6	Dubhe	194 04.8	N61 44.9
H 07	168 46.9	331 38.1	08.7	227 03.9	45.7	144 02.6	43.8	128 10.6	02.6	Elnath	278 25.6	N28 36.3
U 08	183 49.4	346 37.9	09.7	242 04.3	45.3	159 05.3	43.7	143 13.2	02.5	Eltanin	90 51.6	N51 29.6
R 09	198 51.9	1 37.7	.. 10.6	257 04.8	.. 44.9	174 07.9	.. 43.7	158 15.9	.. 02.5	Enif	33 57.5	N 9 52.6
S 10	213 54.3	16 37.6	11.6	272 05.2	44.5	189 10.6	43.6	173 18.5	02.4	Fomalhaut	15 35.6	S29 37.6
D 11	228 56.8	31 37.4	12.6	287 05.7	44.0	204 13.3	43.5	188 21.2	02.4			
A 12	243 59.3	46 37.2	S 5 13.6	302 06.2	S21 43.6	219 15.9	N 8 43.5	203 23.8	N13 02.4	Gacrux	172 13.0	S57 06.4
Y 13	259 01.7	61 37.0	14.6	317 06.6	43.2	234 18.6	43.4	218 26.4	02.3	Gienah	176 03.4	S17 32.2
14	274 04.2	76 36.8	15.6	332 07.1	42.8	249 21.3	43.3	233 29.1	02.3	Hadar	149 03.5	S60 22.0
15	289 06.7	91 36.6	.. 16.6	347 07.5	.. 42.3	264 23.9	.. 43.3	248 31.7	.. 02.2	Hamal	328 12.4	N23 27.7
16	304 09.1	106 36.4	17.5	2 08.0	41.9	279 26.6	43.2	263 34.4	02.2	Kaus Aust.	83 58.2	S34 23.0
17	319 11.6	121 36.2	18.5	17 08.5	41.5	294 29.2	43.1	278 37.0	02.1			
18	334 14.1	136 36.0	S 5 19.5	32 08.9	S21 41.1	309 31.9	N 8 43.1	293 39.7	N13 02.1	Kochab	137 20.8	N74 09.4
19	349 16.5	151 35.8	20.5	47 09.4	40.6	324 34.6	43.0	308 42.3	02.0	Markab	13 48.8	N15 12.4
20	4 19.0	166 35.6	21.5	62 09.9	40.2	339 37.2	42.9	323 45.0	02.0	Menkar	314 25.8	N 4 05.3
21	19 21.4	181 35.4	.. 22.5	77 10.3	.. 39.8	354 39.9	.. 42.9	338 47.6	.. 01.9	Menkent	148 20.4	S36 21.9
22	34 23.9	196 35.2	23.5	92 10.8	39.3	9 42.6	42.8	353 50.2	01.9	Miaplacidus	221 41.6	S69 42.7
23	49 26.4	211 35.0	24.4	107 11.2	38.9	24 45.2	42.8	8 52.9	01.8			
26 00	64 28.8	226 34.8	S 5 25.4	122 11.7	S21 38.5	39 47.9	N 8 42.7	23 55.5	N13 01.8	Mirfak	308 55.0	N49 51.6
01	79 31.3	241 34.6	26.4	137 12.2	38.1	54 50.5	42.6	38 58.2	01.7	Nunki	76 11.7	S26 17.8
02	94 33.8	256 34.3	27.4	152 12.6	37.6	69 53.2	42.6	54 00.8	01.7	Peacock	53 36.1	S56 44.3
03	109 36.2	271 34.1	.. 28.4	167 13.1	.. 37.2	84 55.9	.. 42.5	69 03.5	.. 01.6	Pollux	243 40.4	N28 01.5
04	124 38.7	286 33.9	29.4	182 13.5	36.8	99 58.5	42.4	84 06.1	01.6	Procyon	245 10.6	N 5 13.5
05	139 41.2	301 33.7	30.4	197 14.0	36.3	115 01.2	42.4	99 08.7	01.5			
F 06	154 43.6	316 33.5	S 5 31.4	212 14.5	S21 35.9	130 03.8	N 8 42.3	114 11.4	N13 01.5	Rasalhague	96 16.6	N12 33.8
R 07	169 46.1	331 33.3	32.3	227 14.9	35.5	145 06.5	42.2	129 14.0	01.4	Regulus	207 54.7	N11 58.1
I 08	184 48.6	346 33.1	33.3	242 15.4	35.0	160 09.2	42.2	144 16.7	01.4	Rigel	281 21.9	S 8 12.2
D 09	199 51.0	1 32.9	.. 34.3	257 15.9	.. 34.6	175 11.8	.. 42.1	159 19.3	.. 01.3	Rigil Kent.	140 06.9	S60 49.8
A 10	214 53.5	16 32.7	35.3	272 16.3	34.2	190 14.5	42.1	174 21.9	01.3	Sabik	102 25.0	S15 43.3
Y 11	229 55.9	31 32.5	36.3	287 16.8	33.7	205 17.1	42.0	189 24.6	01.2			
12	244 58.4	46 32.3	S 5 37.3	302 17.2	S21 33.3	220 19.8	N 8 41.9	204 27.2	N13 01.2	Schedar	349 52.2	N56 32.4
13	260 00.9	61 32.1	38.3	317 17.7	32.9	235 22.4	41.9	219 29.9	01.1	Shaula	96 36.7	S37 06.1
14	275 03.3	76 31.9	39.3	332 18.2	32.4	250 25.1	41.8	234 32.5	01.1	Sirius	258 42.8	S16 42.9
15	290 05.8	91 31.7	.. 40.2	347 18.6	.. 32.0	265 27.8	.. 41.7	249 35.2	.. 01.0	Spica	158 42.7	S11 09.4
16	305 08.3	106 31.4	41.2	2 19.1	31.6	280 30.4	41.7	264 37.8	01.0	Suhail	223 00.1	S43 25.7
17	320 10.7	121 31.2	42.2	17 19.6	31.1	295 33.1	41.6	279 40.4	00.9			
18	335 13.2	136 31.0	S 5 43.2	32 20.0	S21 30.7	310 35.7	N 8 41.6	294 43.1	N13 00.9	Vega	80 46.5	N38 47.3
19	350 15.7	151 30.8	44.2	47 20.5	30.2	325 38.4	41.5	309 45.7	00.9	Zuben'ubi	137 17.5	S16 02.2
20	5 18.1	166 30.6	45.2	62 21.0	29.8	340 41.0	41.4	324 48.4	00.8			
21	20 20.6	181 30.4	.. 46.2	77 21.4	.. 29.4	355 43.7	.. 41.4	339 51.0	.. 00.8		SHA	Mer. Pass.
22	35 23.1	196 30.2	47.2	92 21.9	28.9	10 46.4	41.3	354 53.6	00.7	Venus	163 09.8	8 53
23	50 25.5	211 30.0	48.1	107 22.3	28.5	25 49.0	41.3	9 56.3	00.7	Mars	58 31.0	15 51
Mer. Pass.	19 42.8	v −0.2	d 1.0	v 0.5	d 0.4	v 2.7	d 0.1	v 2.6	d 0.0	Jupiter	335 14.2	21 21
										Saturn	319 22.4	22 25

UT	SUN GHA	SUN Dec	MOON GHA	v	MOON Dec	d	HP
d h	° ′	° ′	° ′	′	° ′	′	′
24 00	183 23.4	S20 24.5	352 08.4	4.0	N18 03.1	6.9	61.4
01	198 23.2	25.0	6 31.4	3.9	18 10.0	6.9	61.4
02	213 23.1	25.5	20 54.3	3.9	18 16.9	6.7	61.4
03	228 22.9	26.0	35 17.2	3.9	18 23.6	6.5	61.4
04	243 22.7	26.5	49 40.1	3.8	18 30.1	6.5	61.4
05	258 22.5	27.1	64 02.9	3.8	18 36.6	6.3	61.4
06	273 22.4	S20 27.6	78 25.7	3.7	N18 42.9	6.1	61.4
W 07	288 22.2	28.1	92 48.4	3.7	18 49.0	6.0	61.3
E 08	303 22.0	28.6	107 11.1	3.6	18 55.0	5.9	61.3
D 09	318 21.8	29.1	121 33.7	3.6	19 00.9	5.7	61.3
N 10	333 21.6	29.6	135 56.3	3.6	19 06.6	5.6	61.3
E 11	348 21.5	30.1	150 18.9	3.5	19 12.2	5.4	61.3
S 12	3 21.3	S20 30.6	164 41.4	3.5	N19 17.6	5.3	61.3
D 13	18 21.1	31.1	179 03.9	3.5	19 22.9	5.1	61.3
A 14	33 20.9	31.6	193 26.4	3.5	19 28.0	5.0	61.3
Y 15	48 20.8	32.1	207 48.9	3.4	19 33.0	4.9	61.3
16	63 20.6	32.6	222 11.3	3.4	19 37.9	4.7	61.3
17	78 20.4	33.2	236 33.7	3.4	19 42.6	4.5	61.3
18	93 20.2	S20 33.7	250 56.1	3.3	N19 47.1	4.4	61.3
19	108 20.0	34.2	265 18.4	3.4	19 51.5	4.2	61.2
20	123 19.9	34.7	279 40.8	3.3	19 55.7	4.1	61.2
21	138 19.7	35.2	294 03.1	3.3	19 59.8	4.0	61.2
22	153 19.5	35.7	308 25.4	3.3	20 03.8	3.8	61.2
23	168 19.3	36.2	322 47.7	3.3	20 07.6	3.6	61.2
25 00	183 19.1	S20 36.7	337 10.0	3.3	N20 11.2	3.5	61.2
01	198 18.9	37.2	351 32.3	3.2	20 14.7	3.3	61.2
02	213 18.8	37.7	5 54.5	3.3	20 18.0	3.2	61.1
03	228 18.6	38.2	20 16.8	3.3	20 21.2	3.0	61.1
04	243 18.4	38.7	34 39.1	3.2	20 24.2	2.8	61.1
05	258 18.2	39.2	49 01.3	3.3	20 27.0	2.7	61.1
06	273 18.0	S20 39.7	63 23.6	3.2	N20 29.7	2.6	61.1
T 07	288 17.8	40.2	77 45.8	3.3	20 32.3	2.4	61.1
H 08	303 17.7	40.6	92 08.1	3.3	20 34.7	2.2	61.0
U 09	318 17.5	41.1	106 30.4	3.3	20 36.9	2.1	61.0
R 10	333 17.3	41.6	120 52.7	3.3	20 39.0	1.9	61.0
S 11	348 17.1	42.1	135 15.0	3.3	20 40.9	1.8	61.0
D 12	3 16.9	S20 42.6	149 37.3	3.3	N20 42.7	1.6	61.0
A 13	18 16.7	43.1	163 59.6	3.3	20 44.3	1.5	60.9
Y 14	33 16.5	43.6	178 21.9	3.4	20 45.8	1.3	60.9
15	48 16.3	44.1	192 44.3	3.4	20 47.1	1.1	60.9
16	63 16.2	44.6	207 06.7	3.4	20 48.2	1.0	60.9
17	78 16.0	45.1	221 29.1	3.4	20 49.2	0.9	60.9
18	93 15.8	S20 45.6	235 51.5	3.4	N20 50.1	0.7	60.8
19	108 15.6	46.0	250 13.9	3.5	20 50.8	0.5	60.8
20	123 15.4	46.5	264 36.4	3.5	20 51.3	0.4	60.8
21	138 15.2	47.0	278 58.9	3.6	20 51.7	0.2	60.8
22	153 15.0	47.5	293 21.5	3.6	20 51.9	0.0	60.7
23	168 14.8	48.0	307 44.1	3.6	20 51.9	0.1	60.7
26 00	183 14.6	S20 48.5	322 06.7	3.6	N20 51.8	0.2	60.7
01	198 14.5	49.0	336 29.3	3.7	20 51.6	0.4	60.7
02	213 14.3	49.4	350 52.0	3.8	20 51.2	0.5	60.6
03	228 14.1	49.9	5 14.8	3.7	20 50.7	0.6	60.6
04	243 13.9	50.4	19 37.5	3.9	20 50.0	0.9	60.6
05	258 13.7	50.9	34 00.4	3.8	20 49.1	1.0	60.6
06	273 13.5	S20 51.4	48 23.2	4.0	N20 48.1	1.1	60.5
F 07	288 13.3	51.8	62 46.2	3.9	20 47.0	1.3	60.5
R 08	303 13.1	52.3	77 09.1	4.0	20 45.7	1.5	60.5
I 09	318 12.9	52.8	91 32.1	4.1	20 44.2	1.6	60.4
D 10	333 12.7	53.3	105 55.2	4.2	20 42.6	1.7	60.4
A 11	348 12.5	53.8	120 18.4	4.1	20 40.9	1.9	60.4
Y 12	3 12.3	S20 54.2	134 41.5	4.3	N20 39.0	2.1	60.4
13	18 12.1	54.7	149 04.8	4.3	20 36.9	2.1	60.3
14	33 11.9	55.2	163 28.1	4.4	20 34.8	2.4	60.3
15	48 11.7	55.6	177 51.5	4.4	20 32.4	2.4	60.3
16	63 11.6	56.1	192 14.9	4.5	20 30.0	2.6	60.2
17	78 11.4	56.6	206 38.4	4.6	20 27.4	2.8	60.2
18	93 11.2	S20 57.1	221 02.0	4.6	N20 24.6	2.9	60.2
19	108 11.0	57.5	235 25.6	4.7	20 21.7	3.0	60.1
20	123 10.8	58.0	249 49.3	4.8	20 18.7	3.2	60.1
21	138 10.6	58.5	264 13.1	4.8	20 15.5	3.3	60.1
22	153 10.4	59.0	278 36.9	4.9	20 12.2	3.4	60.0
23	168 10.2	59.4	293 00.8	5.0	N20 08.8	3.6	60.0
	SD 16.2	d 0.5	SD 16.7		16.6		16.4

Lat.	Twilight Naut.	Twilight Civil	Sunrise	Moonrise 24	Moonrise 25	Moonrise 26	Moonrise 27
°	h m	h m	h m	h m	h m	h m	h m
N 72	07 32	09 20	■■■	□	□	□	□
N 70	07 18	08 48	11 20	14 10	□	□	17 44
68	07 06	08 25	10 00	15 07	15 36	16 48	18 31
66	06 57	08 07	09 23	15 41	16 21	17 31	19 02
64	06 49	07 52	08 57	16 06	16 51	17 59	19 24
62	06 41	07 39	08 37	16 26	17 14	18 21	19 42
60	06 35	07 29	08 21	16 42	17 32	18 39	19 57
N 58	06 29	07 19	08 07	16 55	17 48	18 54	20 10
56	06 24	07 11	07 55	17 07	18 01	19 07	20 21
54	06 19	07 04	07 45	17 18	18 12	19 18	20 31
52	06 15	06 57	07 36	17 27	18 22	19 27	20 39
50	06 11	06 51	07 28	17 35	18 31	19 36	20 47
45	06 01	06 37	07 10	17 53	18 50	19 55	21 03
N 40	05 53	06 26	06 56	18 07	19 06	20 10	21 16
35	05 45	06 16	06 44	18 20	19 19	20 22	21 28
30	05 38	06 07	06 33	18 30	19 30	20 34	21 38
20	05 24	05 51	06 15	18 49	19 50	20 53	21 55
N 10	05 10	05 36	05 58	19 05	20 07	21 09	22 09
0	04 55	05 21	05 43	19 20	20 23	21 25	22 23
S 10	04 39	05 05	05 05	19 36	20 39	21 40	22 37
20	04 19	04 47	05 11	19 52	20 57	21 57	22 52
30	03 54	04 26	04 52	20 11	21 16	22 16	23 09
35	03 37	04 12	04 41	20 22	21 28	22 27	23 18
40	03 18	03 57	04 28	20 35	21 41	22 40	23 30
45	02 52	03 37	04 13	20 50	21 57	22 55	23 43
S 50	02 16	03 13	03 54	21 08	22 17	23 13	23 59
52	01 57	03 01	03 45	21 17	22 26	23 22	24 06
54	01 32	02 46	03 35	21 27	22 36	23 32	24 14
56	00 56	02 30	03 23	21 38	22 48	23 43	24 24
58	////	02 09	03 10	21 51	23 01	23 55	24 34
S 60	////	01 42	02 54	22 05	23 17	24 10	00 10

Lat.	Sunset	Twilight Civil	Twilight Naut.	Moonset 24	Moonset 25	Moonset 26	Moonset 27
°	h m	h m	h m	h m	h m	h m	h m
N 72	■■■	14 13	16 01	□	□	□	□
N 70	12 13	14 45	16 15	11 49	□	□	14 42
68	13 33	15 08	16 26	10 53	12 36	13 34	13 54
66	14 10	15 26	16 36	10 19	11 50	12 51	13 23
64	14 36	15 41	16 44	09 55	11 20	12 22	13 00
62	14 56	15 54	16 52	09 35	10 58	12 00	12 42
60	15 12	16 04	16 58	09 20	10 39	11 42	12 26
N 58	15 26	16 14	17 04	09 06	10 24	11 27	12 13
56	15 38	16 22	17 09	08 55	10 11	11 14	12 02
54	15 48	16 30	17 14	08 45	10 00	11 03	11 52
52	15 58	16 36	17 18	08 36	09 50	10 53	11 43
50	16 06	16 42	17 23	08 28	09 41	10 44	11 35
45	16 23	16 56	17 32	08 11	09 22	10 25	11 18
N 40	16 38	17 07	17 41	07 57	09 07	10 10	11 04
35	16 50	17 17	17 48	07 45	08 54	09 57	10 52
30	17 01	17 26	17 56	07 35	08 43	09 45	10 42
20	17 19	17 43	18 10	07 17	08 23	09 26	10 24
N 10	17 35	17 58	18 24	07 02	08 06	09 09	10 08
0	17 51	18 13	18 38	06 48	07 50	08 53	09 53
S 10	18 06	18 29	18 55	06 33	07 34	08 37	09 38
20	18 23	18 47	19 15	06 18	07 18	08 20	09 22
30	18 42	19 08	19 41	06 00	06 58	08 00	09 04
35	18 53	19 22	19 57	05 50	06 47	07 48	08 53
40	19 06	19 38	20 17	05 38	06 34	07 35	08 41
45	19 22	19 57	20 43	05 25	06 18	07 19	08 26
S 50	19 41	20 22	21 19	05 08	05 59	07 00	08 09
52	19 50	20 34	21 39	05 00	05 50	06 51	08 00
54	20 00	20 49	22 04	04 52	05 40	06 41	07 51
56	20 12	21 06	22 43	04 42	05 29	06 29	07 40
58	20 25	21 27	////	04 31	05 16	06 16	07 28
S 60	20 41	21 54	////	04 18	05 01	06 00	07 14

	SUN			MOON			
Day	Eqn. of Time 00ʰ	Eqn. of Time 12ʰ	Mer. Pass.	Mer. Pass. Upper	Mer. Pass. Lower	Age	Phase
d	m s	m s	h m	h m	h m	d	%
24	13 34	13 26	11 47	00 33	13 04	16	98
25	13 17	13 08	11 47	01 35	14 07	17	93
26	12 59	12 50	11 47	02 38	15 09	18	85

UT	ARIES GHA	VENUS −4.2 GHA	Dec	MARS +0.9 GHA	Dec	JUPITER −2.8 GHA	Dec	SATURN −0.1 GHA	Dec	STARS Name	SHA	Dec
27 00	65 28.0	226 29.8	S 5 49.1	122 22.8	S21 28.1	40 51.7	N 8 41.2	24 58.9	N13 00.6	Acamar	315 25.9	S40 18.5
01	80 30.4	241 29.5	50.1	137 23.3	27.6	55 54.3	41.1	40 01.6	00.6	Achernar	335 34.2	S57 14.5
02	95 32.9	256 29.3	51.1	152 23.7	27.2	70 57.0	41.1	55 04.2	00.5	Acrux	173 21.5	S63 05.5
03	110 35.4	271 29.1 ..	52.1	167 24.2 ..	26.7	85 59.6 ..	41.0	70 06.8 ..	00.5	Adhara	255 20.5	S28 58.2
04	125 37.8	286 28.9	53.1	182 24.7	26.3	101 02.3	41.0	85 09.5	00.4	Aldebaran	291 01.2	N16 30.5
05	140 40.3	301 28.7	54.1	197 25.1	25.9	116 04.9	40.9	100 12.1	00.4			
06	155 42.8	316 28.5	S 5 55.1	212 25.6	S21 25.4	131 07.6	N 8 40.8	115 14.8	N13 00.3	Alioth	166 30.3	N55 57.5
S 07	170 45.2	331 28.3	56.1	227 26.1	25.0	146 10.2	40.8	130 17.4	00.3	Alkaid	153 07.6	N49 18.8
A 08	185 47.7	346 28.0	57.0	242 26.5	24.5	161 12.9	40.7	145 20.0	00.2	Al Na'ir	27 57.0	S46 57.9
T 09	200 50.2	1 27.8 ..	58.0	257 27.0 ..	24.1	176 15.5 ..	40.7	160 22.7 ..	00.2	Alnilam	275 56.8	S 1 12.2
U 10	215 52.6	16 27.6	5 59.0	272 27.5	23.6	191 18.2	40.6	175 25.3	00.1	Alphard	218 06.4	S 8 39.4
R 11	230 55.1	31 27.4	6 00.0	287 27.9	23.2	206 20.8	40.5	190 28.0	00.1			
D 12	245 57.6	46 27.2	S 6 01.0	302 28.4	S21 22.8	221 23.5	N 8 40.5	205 30.6	N13 00.0	Alphecca	126 20.3	N26 43.0
A 13	261 00.0	61 26.9	02.0	317 28.9	22.3	236 26.1	40.4	220 33.2	13 00.0	Alpheratz	357 54.3	N29 05.5
Y 14	276 02.5	76 26.7	03.0	332 29.3	21.9	251 28.8	40.4	235 35.9	12 59.9	Altair	62 18.7	N 8 52.2
15	291 04.9	91 26.5 ..	04.0	347 29.8 ..	21.4	266 31.4 ..	40.3	250 38.5 ..	59.9	Ankaa	353 25.9	S42 18.7
16	306 07.4	106 26.3	04.9	2 30.3	21.0	281 34.1	40.2	265 41.2	59.9	Antares	112 39.6	S26 25.7
17	321 09.9	121 26.1	05.9	17 30.7	20.5	296 36.7	40.2	280 43.8	59.8			
18	336 12.3	136 25.8	S 6 06.9	32 31.2	S21 20.1	311 39.4	N 8 40.1	295 46.4	N12 59.8	Arcturus	146 05.7	N19 11.1
19	351 14.8	151 25.6	07.9	47 31.7	19.6	326 42.0	40.1	310 49.1	59.7	Atria	107 51.5	S69 01.5
20	6 17.3	166 25.4	08.9	62 32.1	19.2	341 44.7	40.0	325 51.7	59.7	Avior	234 22.0	S59 30.3
21	21 19.7	181 25.2 ..	09.9	77 32.6 ..	18.7	356 47.3 ..	39.9	340 54.4 ..	59.6	Bellatrix	278 43.0	N 6 20.9
22	36 22.2	196 25.0	10.9	92 33.1	18.3	11 50.0	39.9	355 57.0	59.6	Betelgeuse	271 12.4	N 7 24.4
23	51 24.7	211 24.7	11.9	107 33.5	17.9	26 52.6	39.8	10 59.6	59.5			
28 00	66 27.1	226 24.5	S 6 12.9	122 34.0	S21 17.4	41 55.3	N 8 39.8	26 02.3	N12 59.5	Canopus	264 00.3	S52 41.7
01	81 29.6	241 24.3	13.9	137 34.5	17.0	56 57.9	39.7	41 04.9	59.4	Capella	280 49.6	N45 59.8
02	96 32.0	256 24.1	14.8	152 34.9	16.5	72 00.6	39.7	56 07.6	59.4	Deneb	49 38.9	N45 17.1
03	111 34.5	271 23.8 ..	15.8	167 35.4 ..	16.1	87 03.2 ..	39.6	71 10.2 ..	59.3	Denebola	182 44.5	N14 34.4
04	126 37.0	286 23.6	16.8	182 35.9	15.6	102 05.9	39.5	86 12.8	59.3	Diphda	349 06.3	S17 59.4
05	141 39.4	301 23.4	17.8	197 36.3	15.2	117 08.5	39.5	101 15.5	59.2			
06	156 41.9	316 23.2	S 6 18.8	212 36.8	S21 14.7	132 11.1	N 8 39.4	116 18.1	N12 59.2	Dubhe	194 04.7	N61 44.9
S 07	171 44.4	331 22.9	19.8	227 37.3	14.3	147 13.8	39.4	131 20.7	59.2	Elnath	278 25.6	N28 36.3
U 08	186 46.8	346 22.7	20.8	242 37.7	13.8	162 16.4	39.3	146 23.4	59.1	Eltanin	90 51.6	N51 29.6
N 09	201 49.3	1 22.5 ..	21.8	257 38.2 ..	13.3	177 19.1 ..	39.2	161 26.0 ..	59.1	Enif	33 57.6	N 9 52.6
10	216 51.8	16 22.3	22.8	272 38.7	12.9	192 21.7	39.2	176 28.7	59.0	Fomalhaut	15 35.6	S29 37.6
11	231 54.2	31 22.0	23.7	287 39.2	12.4	207 24.4	39.1	191 31.3	59.0			
D 12	246 56.7	46 21.8	S 6 24.7	302 39.6	S21 12.0	222 27.0	N 8 39.1	206 33.9	N12 58.9	Gacrux	172 13.0	S57 06.4
A 13	261 59.2	61 21.6	25.7	317 40.1	11.5	237 29.7	39.0	221 36.6	58.9	Gienah	176 03.3	S17 32.2
Y 14	277 01.6	76 21.3	26.7	332 40.6	11.1	252 32.3	39.0	236 39.2	58.8	Hadar	149 03.5	S60 22.0
15	292 04.1	91 21.1 ..	27.7	347 41.0 ..	10.6	267 34.9 ..	38.9	251 41.8 ..	58.8	Hamal	328 12.4	N23 27.7
16	307 06.5	106 20.9	28.7	2 41.5	10.2	282 37.6	38.9	266 44.5	58.7	Kaus Aust.	83 58.2	S34 23.0
17	322 09.0	121 20.7	29.7	17 42.0	09.7	297 40.2	38.8	281 47.1	58.7			
18	337 11.5	136 20.4	S 6 30.7	32 42.4	S21 09.3	312 42.9	N 8 38.7	296 49.8	N12 58.6	Kochab	137 20.8	N74 09.4
19	352 13.9	151 20.2	31.7	47 42.9	08.8	327 45.5	38.7	311 52.4	58.6	Markab	13 48.8	N15 12.4
20	7 16.4	166 20.0	32.6	62 43.4	08.4	342 48.2	38.6	326 55.0	58.5	Menkar	314 25.8	N 4 05.3
21	22 18.9	181 19.7 ..	33.6	77 43.9 ..	07.9	357 50.8 ..	38.6	341 57.7 ..	58.5	Menkent	148 20.4	S36 21.9
22	37 21.3	196 19.5	34.6	92 44.3	07.4	12 53.4	38.5	357 00.3	58.5	Miaplacidus	221 41.5	S69 42.7
23	52 23.8	211 19.3	35.6	107 44.8	07.0	27 56.1	38.5	12 02.9	58.4			
29 00	67 26.3	226 19.0	S 6 36.6	122 45.3	S21 06.5	42 58.7	N 8 38.4	27 05.6	N12 58.4	Mirfak	308 55.0	N49 51.6
01	82 28.7	241 18.8	37.6	137 45.7	06.1	58 01.4	38.4	42 08.2	58.3	Nunki	76 11.7	S26 17.8
02	97 31.2	256 18.6	38.6	152 46.2	05.6	73 04.0	38.3	57 10.8	58.3	Peacock	53 36.2	S56 44.3
03	112 33.7	271 18.3 ..	39.6	167 46.7 ..	05.1	88 06.6 ..	38.2	72 13.5 ..	58.2	Pollux	243 40.4	N28 01.5
04	127 36.1	286 18.1	40.6	182 47.1	04.7	103 09.3	38.2	87 16.1	58.2	Procyon	245 10.5	N 5 13.5
05	142 38.6	301 17.8	41.6	197 47.6	04.2	118 11.9	38.1	102 18.8	58.1			
06	157 41.0	316 17.6	S 6 42.5	212 48.1	S21 03.8	133 14.5	N 8 38.1	117 21.4	N12 58.1	Rasalhague	96 16.6	N12 33.8
07	172 43.5	331 17.4	43.5	227 48.6	03.3	148 17.2	38.0	132 24.0	58.0	Regulus	207 54.7	N11 58.1
08	187 46.0	346 17.1	44.5	242 49.0	02.8	163 19.8	38.0	147 26.7	58.0	Rigel	281 21.9	S 8 12.2
M 09	202 48.4	1 16.9 ..	45.5	257 49.5 ..	02.4	178 22.5 ..	37.9	162 29.3 ..	58.0	Rigil Kent.	140 06.9	S60 49.7
O 10	217 50.9	16 16.7	46.5	272 50.0	01.9	193 25.1	37.9	177 31.9	57.9	Sabik	102 25.0	S15 43.3
N 11	232 53.4	31 16.4	47.5	287 50.5	01.5	208 27.7	37.8	192 34.6	57.9			
D 12	247 55.8	46 16.2	S 6 48.5	302 50.9	S21 01.0	223 30.4	N 8 37.8	207 37.2	N12 57.8	Schedar	349 52.2	N56 32.4
A 13	262 58.3	61 15.9	49.5	317 51.4	00.5	238 33.0	37.7	222 39.8	57.8	Shaula	96 36.7	S37 06.1
Y 14	278 00.8	76 15.7	50.5	332 51.9	21 00.1	253 35.6	37.6	237 42.5	57.7	Sirius	258 42.7	S16 42.9
15	293 03.2	91 15.5 ..	51.4	347 52.3	20 59.6	268 38.3 ..	37.6	252 45.1 ..	57.7	Spica	158 42.6	S11 09.4
16	308 05.7	106 15.2	52.4	2 52.8	59.1	283 40.9	37.5	267 47.7	57.6	Suhail	223 00.0	S43 25.7
17	323 08.2	121 15.0	53.4	17 53.3	58.7	298 43.6	37.5	282 50.4	57.6			
18	338 10.6	136 14.7	S 6 54.4	32 53.8	S20 58.2	313 46.2	N 8 37.4	297 53.0	N12 57.5	Vega	80 46.5	N38 47.2
19	353 13.1	151 14.5	55.4	47 54.2	57.8	328 48.8	37.4	312 55.6	57.5	Zuben'ubi	137 17.4	S16 02.3
20	8 15.6	166 14.3	56.4	62 54.7	57.3	343 51.5	37.3	327 58.3	57.5		SHA	Mer. Pass.
21	23 18.0	181 14.0 ..	57.4	77 55.2 ..	56.8	358 54.1 ..	37.3	343 00.9 ..	57.4			h m
22	38 20.5	196 13.8	58.4	92 55.7	56.4	13 56.7	37.2	358 03.5	57.4	Venus	159 57.4	8 54
23	53 22.9	211 13.5	59.4	107 56.1	55.9	28 59.4	37.2	13 06.2	57.3	Mars	56 06.9	15 49
	h m									Jupiter	335 28.1	21 09
Mer. Pass. 19 31.0	v −0.2	d 1.0	v 0.5	d 0.5	v 2.6	d 0.1	v 2.6	d 0.0	Saturn	319 35.2	22 12

UT	SUN GHA	SUN Dec	MOON GHA	v	MOON Dec	d	HP
d h	° ′	° ′	° ′	′	° ′	′	′
27 00	183 10.0	S20 59.9	307 24.8	5.1	N20 05.2	3.7	60.0
01	198 09.8	21 00.4	321 48.9	5.1	20 01.5	3.8	59.9
02	213 09.6	00.8	336 13.0	5.3	19 57.7	4.0	59.9
03	228 09.4	.. 01.3	350 37.3	5.2	19 53.7	4.1	59.9
04	243 09.2	01.8	5 01.5	5.4	19 49.6	4.2	59.8
05	258 09.0	02.2	19 25.9	5.5	19 45.4	4.4	59.8
06	273 08.8	S21 02.7	33 50.4	5.5	N19 41.0	4.5	59.8
07	288 08.6	03.1	48 14.9	5.6	19 36.5	4.6	59.7
S 08	303 08.4	03.6	62 39.5	5.8	19 31.9	4.8	59.7
A 09	318 08.2	.. 04.1	77 04.3	5.7	19 27.1	4.8	59.7
T 10	333 08.0	04.5	91 29.0	5.9	19 22.3	5.0	59.6
U 11	348 07.8	05.0	105 53.9	6.0	19 17.3	5.1	59.6
R 12	3 07.6	S21 05.5	120 18.9	6.0	N19 12.2	5.2	59.6
D 13	18 07.4	05.9	134 43.9	6.2	19 07.0	5.4	59.5
A 14	33 07.2	06.4	149 09.1	6.2	19 01.6	5.5	59.5
Y 15	48 07.0	.. 06.8	163 34.3	6.3	18 56.1	5.5	59.4
16	63 06.8	07.3	177 59.6	6.4	18 50.6	5.7	59.4
17	78 06.6	07.7	192 25.0	6.5	18 44.9	5.8	59.4
18	93 06.3	S21 08.2	206 50.5	6.6	N18 39.1	6.0	59.3
19	108 06.1	08.7	221 16.1	6.6	18 33.1	6.0	59.3
20	123 05.9	09.1	235 41.7	6.8	18 27.1	6.1	59.3
21	138 05.7	.. 09.6	250 07.5	6.8	18 21.0	6.3	59.2
22	153 05.5	10.0	264 33.3	7.0	18 14.7	6.3	59.2
23	168 05.3	10.5	278 59.3	7.0	18 08.4	6.5	59.2
28 00	183 05.1	S21 10.9	293 25.3	7.2	N18 01.9	6.6	59.1
01	198 04.9	11.4	307 51.5	7.2	17 55.3	6.7	59.1
02	213 04.7	11.8	322 17.7	7.3	17 48.6	6.7	59.0
03	228 04.5	.. 12.3	336 44.0	7.4	17 41.9	6.9	59.0
04	243 04.3	12.7	351 10.4	7.5	17 35.0	7.0	59.0
05	258 04.1	13.2	5 36.9	7.6	17 28.0	7.1	58.9
06	273 03.9	S21 13.6	20 03.5	7.7	N17 20.9	7.1	58.9
07	288 03.7	14.1	34 30.2	7.8	17 13.8	7.3	58.9
S 08	303 03.5	14.5	48 57.0	7.8	17 06.5	7.3	58.8
U 09	318 03.2	.. 14.9	63 23.8	8.0	16 59.2	7.5	58.8
N 10	333 03.0	15.4	77 50.8	8.1	16 51.7	7.5	58.7
D 11	348 02.8	15.8	92 17.9	8.1	16 44.2	7.7	58.7
A 12	3 02.6	S21 16.3	106 45.0	8.3	N16 36.5	7.7	58.7
Y 13	18 02.4	16.7	121 12.3	8.3	16 28.8	7.8	58.6
14	33 02.2	17.2	135 39.6	8.5	16 21.0	7.9	58.6
15	48 02.0	.. 17.6	150 07.1	8.5	16 13.1	8.0	58.6
16	63 01.8	18.0	164 34.6	8.6	16 05.1	8.0	58.5
17	78 01.6	18.5	179 02.2	8.7	15 57.1	8.2	58.5
18	93 01.4	S21 18.9	193 29.9	8.9	N15 48.9	8.2	58.4
19	108 01.1	19.4	207 57.8	8.9	15 40.7	8.3	58.4
20	123 00.9	19.8	222 25.7	9.0	15 32.4	8.4	58.4
21	138 00.7	.. 20.2	236 53.7	9.0	15 24.0	8.5	58.3
22	153 00.5	20.7	251 21.7	9.2	15 15.5	8.5	58.3
23	168 00.3	21.1	265 49.9	9.3	15 07.0	8.6	58.3
29 00	183 00.1	S21 21.5	280 18.2	9.4	N14 58.4	8.7	58.2
01	197 59.9	22.0	294 46.6	9.4	14 49.7	8.8	58.2
02	212 59.6	22.4	309 15.0	9.5	14 40.9	8.8	58.1
03	227 59.4	.. 22.8	323 43.5	9.7	14 32.1	8.9	58.1
04	242 59.2	23.3	338 12.2	9.7	14 23.2	8.9	58.1
05	257 59.0	23.7	352 40.9	9.8	14 14.3	9.1	58.0
06	272 58.8	S21 24.1	7 09.7	9.9	N14 05.2	9.1	58.0
07	287 58.6	24.6	21 38.6	10.0	13 56.1	9.1	58.0
M 08	302 58.4	25.0	36 07.6	10.1	13 47.0	9.3	57.9
O 09	317 58.1	.. 25.4	50 36.7	10.1	13 37.7	9.3	57.9
N 10	332 57.9	25.9	65 05.8	10.3	13 28.4	9.3	57.9
D 11	347 57.7	26.3	79 35.1	10.3	13 19.1	9.4	57.8
A 12	2 57.5	S21 26.7	94 04.4	10.4	N13 09.7	9.5	57.8
Y 13	17 57.3	27.1	108 33.8	10.5	13 00.2	9.5	57.7
14	32 57.1	27.6	123 03.3	10.6	12 50.7	9.6	57.7
15	47 56.8	.. 28.0	137 32.9	10.7	12 41.1	9.6	57.7
16	62 56.6	28.4	152 02.6	10.7	12 31.5	9.7	57.6
17	77 56.4	28.8	166 32.3	10.8	12 21.8	9.8	57.6
18	92 56.2	S21 29.3	181 02.1	10.9	N12 12.0	9.7	57.6
19	107 56.0	29.7	195 32.0	11.0	12 02.3	9.9	57.5
20	122 55.7	30.1	210 02.0	11.1	11 52.4	9.9	57.5
21	137 55.5	.. 30.5	224 32.1	11.1	11 42.5	9.9	57.5
22	152 55.3	30.9	239 02.2	11.3	11 32.6	10.0	57.4
23	167 55.1	31.4	253 32.5	11.3	N11 22.6	10.0	57.4
	SD 16.2	d 0.4	SD 16.2		16.0		15.7

Twilight — Sunrise — Moonrise

Lat.	Naut.	Civil	Sunrise	Moonrise 27	28	29	30
°	h m	h m	h m	h m	h m	h m	h m
N 72	07 41	09 34	■	□	19 14	21 28	23 24
N 70	07 26	08 59	■	17 44	19 53	21 48	23 35
68	07 14	08 34	10 16	18 31	20 20	22 04	23 43
66	07 03	08 15	09 34	19 02	20 40	22 17	23 50
64	06 55	07 59	09 06	19 24	20 56	22 28	23 56
62	06 47	07 46	08 45	19 42	21 10	22 37	24 02
60	06 40	07 34	08 28	19 57	21 21	22 45	24 06
N 58	06 34	07 25	08 13	20 10	21 31	22 51	24 10
56	06 29	07 16	08 01	20 21	21 39	22 57	24 13
54	06 23	07 08	07 50	20 31	21 47	23 03	24 17
52	06 19	07 01	07 40	20 39	21 53	23 07	24 19
50	06 14	06 55	07 32	20 47	22 00	23 12	24 22
45	06 04	06 41	07 14	21 03	22 13	23 21	24 28
N 40	05 56	06 29	06 59	21 16	22 23	23 29	24 32
35	05 48	06 19	06 46	21 28	22 33	23 36	24 36
30	05 40	06 09	06 35	21 38	22 41	23 41	24 40
20	05 26	05 53	06 16	21 55	22 55	23 52	24 46
N 10	05 11	05 37	06 00	22 09	23 07	24 00	00 00
0	04 56	05 22	05 44	22 23	23 18	24 09	00 09
S 10	04 39	05 06	05 28	22 37	23 29	24 17	00 17
20	04 19	04 47	05 11	22 52	23 41	24 26	00 26
30	03 53	04 25	04 52	23 09	23 55	24 36	00 36
35	03 36	04 11	04 40	23 18	24 03	00 03	00 41
40	03 15	03 55	04 27	23 30	24 12	00 12	00 48
45	02 49	03 35	04 11	23 43	24 22	00 22	00 55
S 50	02 12	03 09	03 51	23 59	24 35	00 35	01 04
52	01 51	02 57	03 42	24 06	00 06	00 41	01 09
54	01 24	02 42	03 31	24 14	00 14	00 47	01 13
56	00 41	02 24	03 19	24 24	00 24	00 54	01 18
58	////	02 02	03 05	24 34	00 34	01 02	01 24
S 60	////	01 33	02 49	00 10	00 46	01 12	01 30

Sunset — Twilight — Moonset

Lat.	Sunset	Civil	Naut.	Moonset 27	28	29	30
°	h m	h m	h m	h m	h m	h m	h m
N 72	■	14 01	15 54	□	15 09	14 43	14 27
N 70	■	14 36	16 09	14 42	14 29	14 21	14 14
68	13 19	15 01	16 21	13 54	14 01	14 03	14 04
66	14 01	15 20	16 31	13 23	13 40	13 49	13 55
64	14 29	15 36	16 40	13 00	13 23	13 38	13 48
62	14 50	15 49	16 48	12 42	13 09	13 28	13 41
60	15 08	16 01	16 55	12 26	12 57	13 19	13 36
N 58	15 22	16 10	17 01	12 13	12 47	13 12	13 31
56	15 34	16 19	17 07	12 02	12 38	13 05	13 27
54	15 45	16 27	17 12	11 52	12 29	12 59	13 23
52	15 55	16 34	17 16	11 43	12 22	12 53	13 19
50	16 03	16 40	17 21	11 35	12 16	12 49	13 16
45	16 22	16 54	17 31	11 18	12 02	12 38	13 09
N 40	16 36	17 06	17 40	11 04	11 50	12 29	13 03
35	16 49	17 17	17 48	10 52	11 40	12 21	12 58
30	17 00	17 26	17 55	10 42	11 31	12 15	12 53
20	17 19	17 43	18 10	10 24	11 16	12 03	12 45
N 10	17 36	17 58	18 24	10 08	11 02	11 52	12 38
0	17 51	18 14	18 39	09 53	10 50	11 43	12 32
S 10	18 07	18 30	18 57	09 38	10 37	11 33	12 25
20	18 24	18 49	19 17	09 22	10 24	11 22	12 18
30	18 44	19 11	19 43	09 04	10 08	11 10	12 10
35	18 56	19 25	20 00	08 53	09 59	11 03	12 05
40	19 09	19 41	20 21	08 41	09 48	10 55	11 59
45	19 25	20 01	20 48	08 26	09 36	10 45	11 53
S 50	19 45	20 27	21 25	08 09	09 21	10 34	11 45
52	19 55	20 40	21 46	08 00	09 14	10 29	11 42
54	20 05	20 55	22 14	07 51	09 06	10 23	11 38
56	20 17	21 13	23 01	07 40	08 57	10 16	11 34
58	20 31	21 35	////	07 28	08 47	10 09	11 29
S 60	20 48	22 05	////	07 14	08 36	10 00	11 23

	SUN		MOON			
Day	Eqn. of Time 00ʰ	12ʰ	Mer. Pass.	Mer. Pass. Upper	Lower	Age	Phase
d	m s	m s	h m	h m	h m	d	%
27	12 40	12 31	11 47	03 39	16 08	19	76
28	12 21	12 11	11 48	04 37	17 04	20	66
29	12 01	11 50	11 48	05 30	17 56	21	55

1999 NOV. 30, DEC. 1, 2 (TUES., WED., THURS.)

UT	ARIES GHA	VENUS −4.2 GHA	VENUS Dec	MARS +0.9 GHA	MARS Dec	JUPITER −2.8 GHA	JUPITER Dec	SATURN −0.1 GHA	SATURN Dec
30 00	68 25.4	226 13.3	S 7 00.4	122 56.6	S20 55.4	44 02.0	N 8 37.1	28 08.8	N12 57.3
01	83 27.9	241 13.0	01.3	137 57.1	55.0	59 04.6	37.1	43 11.4	57.2
02	98 30.3	256 12.8	02.3	152 57.6	54.5	74 07.3	37.0	58 14.1	57.2
03	113 32.8	271 12.5 ..	03.3	167 58.0 ..	54.0	89 09.9 ..	37.0	73 16.7 ..	57.1
04	128 35.3	286 12.3	04.3	182 58.5	53.5	104 12.5	36.9	88 19.3	57.1
05	143 37.7	301 12.1	05.3	197 59.0	53.1	119 15.1	36.9	103 22.0	57.0
06	158 40.2	316 11.8	S 7 06.3	212 59.5	S20 52.6	134 17.8	N 8 36.8	118 24.6	N12 57.0
07	173 42.6	331 11.6	07.3	227 59.9	52.1	149 20.4	36.7	133 27.2	57.0
08	188 45.1	346 11.3	08.3	243 00.4	51.7	164 23.0	36.7	148 29.9	56.9
09	203 47.6	1 11.1 ..	09.3	258 00.9 ..	51.2	179 25.7 ..	36.6	163 32.5 ..	56.9
10	218 50.0	16 10.8	10.2	273 01.4	50.7	194 28.3	36.6	178 35.1	56.8
11	233 52.5	31 10.6	11.2	288 01.8	50.3	209 30.9	36.5	193 37.8	56.8
12	248 55.0	46 10.3	S 7 12.2	303 02.3	S20 49.8	224 33.6	N 8 36.5	208 40.4	N12 56.7
13	263 57.4	61 10.1	13.2	318 02.8	49.3	239 36.2	36.4	223 43.0	56.7
14	278 59.9	76 09.8	14.2	333 03.3	48.8	254 38.8	36.4	238 45.7	56.6
15	294 02.4	91 09.6 ..	15.2	348 03.7 ..	48.4	269 41.4 ..	36.3	253 48.3 ..	56.6
16	309 04.8	106 09.3	16.2	3 04.2	47.9	284 44.1	36.3	268 50.9	56.6
17	324 07.3	121 09.1	17.2	18 04.7	47.4	299 46.7	36.2	283 53.6	56.5
18	339 09.8	136 08.8	S 7 18.2	33 05.2	S20 47.0	314 49.3	N 8 36.2	298 56.2	N12 56.5
19	354 12.2	151 08.6	19.1	48 05.6	46.5	329 52.0	36.1	313 58.8	56.4
20	9 14.7	166 08.3	20.1	63 06.1	46.0	344 54.6	36.1	329 01.5	56.4
21	24 17.1	181 08.1 ..	21.1	78 06.6 ..	45.5	359 57.2 ..	36.0	344 04.1 ..	56.3
22	39 19.6	196 07.8	22.1	93 07.1	45.1	14 59.8	36.0	359 06.7	56.3
23	54 22.1	211 07.5	23.1	108 07.5	44.6	30 02.5	35.9	14 09.4	56.2
1 00	69 24.5	226 07.3	S 7 24.1	123 08.0	S20 44.1	45 05.1	N 8 35.9	29 12.0	N12 56.2
01	84 27.0	241 07.0	25.1	138 08.5	43.6	60 07.7	35.8	44 14.6	56.2
02	99 29.5	256 06.8	26.1	153 09.0	43.1	75 10.3	35.8	59 17.3	56.1
03	114 31.9	271 06.5 ..	27.1	168 09.5 ..	42.7	90 13.0 ..	35.7	74 19.9 ..	56.1
04	129 34.4	286 06.3	28.0	183 09.9	42.2	105 15.6	35.7	89 22.5	56.0
05	144 36.9	301 06.0	29.0	198 10.4	41.7	120 18.2	35.6	104 25.1	56.0
06	159 39.3	316 05.7	S 7 30.0	213 10.9	S20 41.2	135 20.8	N 8 35.6	119 27.8	N12 55.9
07	174 41.8	331 05.5	31.0	228 11.4	40.8	150 23.5	35.5	134 30.4	55.9
08	189 44.2	346 05.2	32.0	243 11.8	40.3	165 26.1	35.5	149 33.0	55.8
09	204 46.7	1 05.0 ..	33.0	258 12.3 ..	39.8	180 28.7 ..	35.4	164 35.7 ..	55.8
10	219 49.2	16 04.7	34.0	273 12.8	39.3	195 31.3	35.4	179 38.3	55.8
11	234 51.6	31 04.5	35.0	288 13.3	38.8	210 33.9	35.3	194 40.9	55.7
12	249 54.1	46 04.2	S 7 35.9	303 13.8	S20 38.4	225 36.6	N 8 35.3	209 43.6	N12 55.7
13	264 56.6	61 03.9	36.9	318 14.2	37.9	240 39.2	35.3	224 46.2	55.6
14	279 59.0	76 03.7	37.9	333 14.7	37.4	255 41.8	35.2	239 48.8	55.6
15	295 01.5	91 03.4 ..	38.9	348 15.2 ..	36.9	270 44.4 ..	35.2	254 51.5 ..	55.5
16	310 04.0	106 03.1	39.9	3 15.7	36.4	285 47.1	35.1	269 54.1	55.5
17	325 06.4	121 02.9	40.9	18 16.2	35.9	300 49.7	35.1	284 56.7	55.5
18	340 08.9	136 02.6	S 7 41.9	33 16.6	S20 35.5	315 52.3	N 8 35.0	299 59.3	N12 55.4
19	355 11.4	151 02.4	42.9	48 17.1	35.0	330 54.9	35.0	315 02.0	55.4
20	10 13.8	166 02.1	43.8	63 17.6	34.5	345 57.5	34.9	330 04.6	55.3
21	25 16.3	181 01.8 ..	44.8	78 18.1 ..	34.0	1 00.2 ..	34.9	345 07.2 ..	55.3
22	40 18.7	196 01.6	45.8	93 18.6	33.5	16 02.8	34.8	0 09.9	55.2
23	55 21.2	211 01.3	46.8	108 19.0	33.0	31 05.4	34.8	15 12.5	55.2
2 00	70 23.7	226 01.0	S 7 47.8	123 19.5	S20 32.6	46 08.0	N 8 34.7	30 15.1	N12 55.1
01	85 26.1	241 00.8	48.8	138 20.0	32.1	61 10.6	34.7	45 17.7	55.1
02	100 28.6	256 00.5	49.8	153 20.5	31.6	76 13.2	34.6	60 20.4	55.1
03	115 31.1	271 00.3 ..	50.8	168 21.0 ..	31.1	91 15.9 ..	34.6	75 23.0 ..	55.0
04	130 33.5	286 00.0	51.7	183 21.4	30.6	106 18.5	34.5	90 25.6	55.0
05	145 36.0	300 59.7	52.7	198 21.9	30.1	121 21.1	34.5	105 28.3	54.9
06	160 38.5	315 59.4	S 7 53.7	213 22.4	S20 29.6	136 23.7	N 8 34.5	120 30.9	N12 54.9
07	175 40.9	330 59.2	54.7	228 22.9	29.2	151 26.3	34.4	135 33.5	54.8
08	190 43.4	345 58.9	55.7	243 23.4	28.7	166 28.9	34.4	150 36.1	54.8
09	205 45.9	0 58.6 ..	56.7	258 23.9 ..	28.2	181 31.6 ..	34.3	165 38.8 ..	54.8
10	220 48.3	15 58.4	57.7	273 24.3	27.7	196 34.2	34.3	180 41.4	54.7
11	235 50.8	30 58.1	58.7	288 24.8	27.2	211 36.8	34.2	195 44.0	54.7
12	250 53.2	45 57.8	S 7 59.6	303 25.3	S20 26.7	226 39.4	N 8 34.2	210 46.7	N12 54.6
13	265 55.7	60 57.5	8 00.6	318 25.8	26.2	241 42.0	34.1	225 49.3	54.6
14	280 58.2	75 57.3	01.6	333 26.3	25.7	256 44.6	34.1	240 51.9	54.5
15	296 00.6	90 57.0 ..	02.6	348 26.7 ..	25.2	271 47.2 ..	34.0	255 54.5 ..	54.5
16	311 03.1	105 56.7	03.6	3 27.2	24.7	286 49.9	34.0	270 57.2	54.5
17	326 05.6	120 56.5	04.6	18 27.7	24.3	301 52.5	34.0	285 59.8	54.4
18	341 08.0	135 56.2	S 8 05.6	33 28.2	S20 23.8	316 55.1	N 8 33.9	301 02.4	N12 54.4
19	356 10.5	150 55.9	06.5	48 28.7	23.3	331 57.7	33.9	316 05.0	54.3
20	11 13.0	165 55.6	07.5	63 29.2	22.8	347 00.3	33.8	331 07.7	54.3
21	26 15.4	180 55.4 ..	08.5	78 29.6 ..	22.3	2 02.9 ..	33.8	346 10.3 ..	54.2
22	41 17.9	195 55.1	09.5	93 30.1	21.8	17 05.5	33.7	1 12.9	54.2
23	56 20.3	210 54.8	10.5	108 30.6	21.3	32 08.1	33.7	16 15.5	54.2
Mer. Pass.	19 19.2	v −0.3	d 1.0	v 0.5	d 0.5	v 2.6	d 0.0	v 2.6	d 0.0

Day labels: TUESDAY (Nov 30), WEDNESDAY (Dec 1), THURSDAY (Dec 2).

STARS

Name	SHA	Dec
Acamar	315 25.9	S40 18.5
Achernar	335 34.2	S57 14.5
Acrux	173 21.4	S63 05.5
Adhara	255 20.5	S28 58.3
Aldebaran	291 01.2	N16 30.5
Alioth	166 30.3	N55 57.5
Alkaid	153 07.6	N49 18.8
Al Na'ir	27 57.0	S46 57.9
Alnilam	275 56.8	S 1 12.2
Alphard	218 06.3	S 8 39.4
Alphecca	126 20.3	N26 43.0
Alpheratz	357 54.3	N29 05.5
Altair	62 18.8	N 8 52.2
Ankaa	353 25.9	S42 18.7
Antares	112 39.6	S26 25.7
Arcturus	146 05.7	N19 11.1
Atria	107 51.5	S69 01.5
Avior	234 21.9	S59 30.3
Bellatrix	278 43.0	N 6 20.9
Betelgeuse	271 12.4	N 7 24.4
Canopus	264 00.3	S52 41.7
Capella	280 49.6	N45 59.8
Deneb	49 38.9	N45 17.1
Denebola	182 44.5	N14 34.4
Diphda	349 06.3	S17 59.4
Dubhe	194 04.7	N61 44.9
Elnath	278 25.6	N28 36.3
Eltanin	90 51.6	N51 29.5
Enif	33 57.6	N 9 52.6
Fomalhaut	15 35.6	S29 37.6
Gacrux	172 13.0	S57 06.4
Gienah	176 03.3	S17 32.2
Hadar	149 03.4	S60 22.0
Hamal	328 12.4	N23 27.7
Kaus Aust.	83 58.2	S34 23.0
Kochab	137 20.8	N74 09.3
Markab	13 48.8	N15 12.4
Menkar	314 25.8	N 4 05.3
Menkent	148 20.4	S36 21.9
Miaplacidus	221 41.5	S69 42.7
Mirfak	308 55.0	N49 51.6
Nunki	76 11.7	S26 17.8
Peacock	53 36.2	S56 44.3
Pollux	243 40.4	N28 01.5
Procyon	245 10.5	N 5 13.5
Rasalhague	96 16.6	N12 33.8
Regulus	207 54.7	N11 58.1
Rigel	281 21.9	S 8 12.2
Rigil Kent.	140 06.8	S60 49.7
Sabik	102 25.0	S15 43.3
Schedar	349 52.3	N56 32.4
Shaula	96 36.7	S37 06.1
Sirius	258 42.7	S16 42.9
Spica	158 42.6	S11 09.4
Suhail	223 00.0	S43 25.7
Vega	80 46.5	N38 47.2
Zuben'ubi	137 17.4	S16 02.3

	SHA	Mer. Pass.
Venus	156 42.8	8 56
Mars	53 43.5	15 47
Jupiter	335 40.5	20 56
Saturn	319 47.5	21 59

UT	SUN		MOON				Lat.	Twilight		Sunrise	Moonrise			
								Naut.	Civil		30	1	2	3
	GHA	Dec	GHA	v	Dec	d	HP							
d h	° ′	° ′	° ′	′	° ′	′	′	°	h m	h m	h m	h m	h m	h m	h m
30 00	182 54.9	S21 31.8	268 02.8	11.4	N11 12.6	10.1	57.3	N 72	07 50	09 48	■■■	23 24	25 12	01 12	02 56
01	197 54.6	32.2	282 33.2	11.4	11 02.5	10.2	57.3	N 70	07 34	09 09	■■■	23 35	25 15	01 15	02 53
02	212 54.4	32.6	297 03.6	11.5	10 52.3	10.1	57.3	68	07 21	08 42	10 33	23 43	25 18	01 18	02 50
03	227 54.2	.. 33.0	311 34.1	11.6	10 42.2	10.2	57.2	66	07 10	08 22	09 45	23 50	25 20	01 20	02 47
04	242 54.0	33.4	326 04.7	11.7	10 32.0	10.3	57.2	64	07 00	08 05	09 15	23 56	25 22	01 22	02 45
05	257 53.7	33.8	340 35.4	11.8	10 21.7	10.3	57.2	62	06 52	07 52	08 52	24 02	00 02	01 24	02 44
06	272 53.5	S21 34.3	355 06.2	11.8	N10 11.4	10.3	57.1	60	06 45	07 40	08 34	24 06	00 06	01 25	02 42
07	287 53.3	34.7	9 37.0	11.9	10 01.1	10.4	57.1	N 58	06 39	07 30	08 19	24 10	00 10	01 26	02 41
T 08	302 53.1	35.1	24 07.9	12.0	9 50.7	10.4	57.1	56	06 33	07 21	08 06	24 13	00 13	01 27	02 40
U 09	317 52.8	.. 35.5	38 38.9	12.0	9 40.3	10.4	57.0	54	06 27	07 13	07 55	24 17	00 17	01 28	02 38
E 10	332 52.6	35.9	53 09.9	12.1	9 29.9	10.5	57.0	52	06 23	07 05	07 45	24 19	00 19	01 29	02 38
S 11	347 52.4	36.3	67 41.0	12.2	9 19.4	10.5	57.0	50	06 18	06 59	07 36	24 22	00 22	01 30	02 37
D 12	2 52.2	S21 36.7	82 12.2	12.2	N 9 08.9	10.5	56.9	45	06 08	06 44	07 17	24 28	00 28	01 32	02 35
A 13	17 52.0	37.1	96 43.4	12.3	8 58.4	10.6	56.9	N 40	05 58	06 32	07 02	24 32	00 32	01 33	02 33
Y 14	32 51.7	37.5	111 14.7	12.4	8 47.8	10.6	56.9	35	05 50	06 21	06 49	24 36	00 36	01 35	02 32
15	47 51.5	.. 38.0	125 46.1	12.4	8 37.2	10.6	56.8	30	05 42	06 12	06 38	24 40	00 40	01 36	02 31
16	62 51.3	38.4	140 17.5	12.5	8 26.6	10.7	56.8	20	05 27	05 55	06 18	24 46	00 46	01 38	02 29
17	77 51.0	38.8	154 49.0	12.6	8 15.9	10.6	56.8	N 10	05 13	05 39	06 01	00 00	00 51	01 40	02 27
18	92 50.8	S21 39.2	169 20.6	12.6	N 8 05.3	10.8	56.7	0	04 57	05 23	05 45	00 09	00 56	01 41	02 25
19	107 50.6	39.6	183 52.2	12.7	7 54.5	10.7	56.7	S 10	04 40	05 06	05 29	00 17	01 01	01 43	02 23
20	122 50.4	40.0	198 23.9	12.7	7 43.8	10.8	56.7	20	04 19	04 47	05 12	00 26	01 06	01 45	02 22
21	137 50.1	.. 40.4	212 55.6	12.8	7 33.0	10.7	56.6	30	03 52	04 24	04 51	00 36	01 12	01 47	02 20
22	152 49.9	40.8	227 27.4	12.9	7 22.3	10.8	56.6	35	03 35	04 10	04 39	00 41	01 16	01 48	02 19
23	167 49.7	41.2	241 59.3	12.9	7 11.5	10.9	56.6	40	03 14	03 54	04 26	00 48	01 20	01 49	02 17
1 00	182 49.5	S21 41.6	256 31.2	13.0	N 7 00.6	10.8	56.5	45	02 46	03 33	04 09	00 55	01 24	01 51	02 16
01	197 49.2	42.0	271 03.2	13.0	6 49.8	10.9	56.5	S 50	02 07	03 07	03 49	01 04	01 30	01 53	02 14
02	212 49.0	42.4	285 35.2	13.1	6 38.9	10.9	56.5	52	01 46	02 53	03 39	01 09	01 32	01 54	02 14
03	227 48.8	.. 42.8	300 07.3	13.1	6 28.0	10.9	56.5	54	01 16	02 38	03 28	01 13	01 35	01 54	02 13
04	242 48.5	43.2	314 39.4	13.2	6 17.1	10.9	56.4	56	00 21	02 19	03 16	01 18	01 38	01 55	02 12
05	257 48.3	43.6	329 11.6	13.2	6 06.2	11.0	56.4	58	////	01 56	03 01	01 24	01 41	01 57	02 11
06	272 48.1	S21 44.0	343 43.8	13.3	N 5 55.2	10.9	56.4	S 60	////	01 24	02 44	01 30	01 45	01 58	02 10

UT	SUN		MOON				Lat.	Sunset	Twilight		Moonset			
									Civil	Naut.	30	1	2	3
d h	° ′	° ′	° ′	′	° ′	′	′	°	h m	h m	h m	h m	h m	h m	h m
W 07	287 47.8	44.4	358 16.1	13.4	5 44.3	11.0	56.3	N 72	■■■	13 49	15 47	14 27	14 14	14 02	13 50
E 08	302 47.6	44.8	12 48.5	13.4	5 33.3	11.0	56.3	N 70	■■■	14 28	16 03	14 14	14 08	14 02	13 56
D 09	317 47.4	.. 45.2	27 20.9	13.4	5 22.3	11.0	56.3	68	13 04	14 55	16 17	14 04	14 03	14 02	14 01
N 10	332 47.2	45.6	41 53.3	13.5	5 11.3	11.0	56.2	66	13 52	15 15	16 28	13 55	13 59	14 02	14 05
E 11	347 46.9	45.9	56 25.8	13.5	5 00.3	11.1	56.2	64	14 22	15 32	16 37	13 48	13 55	14 02	14 08
S 12	2 46.7	S21 46.3	70 58.3	13.6	N 4 49.2	11.0	56.2	62	14 45	15 46	16 45	13 41	13 52	14 02	14 11
D 13	17 46.5	46.7	85 30.9	13.6	4 38.2	11.1	56.2	60	15 03	15 57	16 52	13 36	13 50	14 02	14 14
A 14	32 46.2	47.1	100 03.5	13.7	4 27.1	11.0	56.1	N 58	15 18	16 08	16 59	13 31	13 47	14 02	14 16
Y 15	47 46.0	.. 47.5	114 36.2	13.7	4 16.1	11.1	56.1	56	15 31	16 17	17 05	13 27	13 45	14 02	14 19
16	62 45.8	47.9	129 08.9	13.8	4 05.0	11.1	56.1	54	15 43	16 25	17 10	13 23	13 43	14 02	14 21
17	77 45.5	48.3	143 41.7	13.8	3 53.9	11.1	56.0	52	15 53	16 32	17 15	13 19	13 42	14 02	14 22
18	92 45.3	S21 48.7	158 14.5	13.8	N 3 42.8	11.0	56.0	50	16 01	16 39	17 19	13 16	13 40	14 02	14 24
19	107 45.1	49.1	172 47.3	13.9	3 31.8	11.1	56.0	45	16 20	16 53	17 30	13 09	13 37	14 02	14 27
20	122 44.8	49.4	187 20.2	13.9	3 20.7	11.1	56.0	N 40	16 35	17 05	17 39	13 03	13 34	14 02	14 30
21	137 44.6	.. 49.8	201 53.1	13.9	3 09.6	11.1	55.9	35	16 48	17 16	17 47	12 58	13 31	14 02	14 33
22	152 44.4	50.2	216 26.0	14.0	2 58.5	11.2	55.9	30	17 00	17 26	17 55	12 53	13 29	14 02	14 35
23	167 44.1	50.6	230 59.0	14.1	2 47.3	11.1	55.9	20	17 19	17 43	18 10	12 45	13 25	14 02	14 39
2 00	182 43.9	S21 51.0	245 32.1	14.0	N 2 36.2	11.1	55.9	N 10	17 36	17 59	18 25	12 38	13 21	14 02	14 43
01	197 43.7	51.4	260 05.1	14.1	2 25.1	11.1	55.8	0	17 53	18 15	18 41	12 32	13 18	14 02	14 46
02	212 43.4	51.8	274 38.2	14.1	2 14.0	11.1	55.8	S 10	18 09	18 32	18 58	12 25	13 15	14 02	14 49
03	227 43.2	.. 52.1	289 11.3	14.2	2 02.9	11.1	55.8	20	18 26	18 51	19 19	12 18	13 11	14 02	14 53
04	242 42.9	52.5	303 44.5	14.2	1 51.8	11.1	55.7	30	18 47	19 14	19 46	12 10	13 07	14 02	14 57
05	257 42.7	52.9	318 17.7	14.2	1 40.7	11.1	55.7	35	18 59	19 28	20 04	12 05	13 05	14 02	14 59
06	272 42.5	S21 53.3	332 50.9	14.3	N 1 29.6	11.1	55.7	40	19 13	19 45	20 25	11 59	13 02	14 02	15 02
07	287 42.2	53.7	347 24.2	14.2	1 18.5	11.1	55.7	45	19 29	20 05	20 52	11 53	12 59	14 02	15 05
T 08	302 42.0	54.0	1 57.4	14.3	1 07.4	11.1	55.6	S 50	19 49	20 32	21 32	11 45	12 55	14 02	15 08
H 09	317 41.8	.. 54.4	16 30.7	14.4	0 56.3	11.1	55.6	52	19 59	20 45	21 54	11 42	12 53	14 02	15 10
U 10	332 41.5	54.8	31 04.1	14.3	0 45.2	11.1	55.6	54	20 10	21 01	22 24	11 38	12 51	14 02	15 12
R 11	347 41.3	55.2	45 37.4	14.4	0 34.1	11.1	55.6	56	20 23	21 20	23 26	11 34	12 49	14 02	15 14
S 12	2 41.0	S21 55.5	60 10.8	14.4	N 0 23.0	11.1	55.5	58	20 37	21 44	////	11 29	12 47	14 02	15 16
D 13	17 40.8	55.9	74 44.2	14.5	0 11.9	11.0	55.5	S 60	20 55	22 16	////	11 23	12 44	14 02	15 18
A 14	32 40.6	56.3	89 17.7	14.4	N 0 00.9	11.1	55.5							
Y 15	47 40.3	.. 56.7	103 51.1	14.5	S 0 10.2	11.1	55.5							
16	62 40.1	57.0	118 24.6	14.5	0 21.3	11.0	55.4							
17	77 39.8	57.4	132 58.1	14.5	0 32.3	11.0	55.4							

									SUN			MOON		
18	92 39.6	S21 57.8	147 31.6	14.6	S 0 43.3	11.0	55.4	Day	Eqn. of Time		Mer.	Mer. Pass.		Age Phase
19	107 39.4	58.1	162 05.2	14.5	0 54.3	11.0	55.4		00h	12h	Pass.	Upper	Lower	
20	122 39.1	58.5	176 38.7	14.6	1 05.3	11.0	55.3	d	m s	m s	h m	h m	h m	d %
21	137 38.9	.. 58.9	191 12.3	14.6	1 16.3	11.0	55.3	30	11 40	11 29	11 49	06 20	18 44	22 45
22	152 38.6	59.2	205 45.9	14.6	1 27.3	11.0	55.3	1	11 18	11 07	11 49	07 07	19 30	23 34
23	167 38.4	59.6	220 19.5	14.6	S 1 38.3	10.9	55.3	2	10 56	10 45	11 49	07 52	20 14	24 25
	SD 16.2	d 0.4	SD 15.5		15.3		15.1								

1999 DECEMBER 3, 4, 5 (FRI., SAT., SUN.)

UT	ARIES GHA	VENUS −4.2 GHA	Dec	MARS +0.9 GHA	Dec	JUPITER −2.7 GHA	Dec	SATURN −0.1 GHA	Dec	STARS Name	SHA	Dec
d h	° ′	° ′	° ′	° ′	° ′	° ′	° ′	° ′	° ′		° ′	° ′
3 00	71 22.8	225 54.5	S 8 11.5	123 31.1	S20 20.8	47 10.8	N 8 33.6	31 18.2	N12 54.1	Acamar	315 26.0	S40 18.5
01	86 25.3	240 54.3	12.5	138 31.6	20.3	62 13.4	33.6	46 20.8	54.1	Achernar	335 34.2	S57 14.6
02	101 27.7	255 54.0	13.4	153 32.1	19.8	77 16.0	33.6	61 23.4	54.0	Acrux	173 21.4	S63 05.5
03	116 30.2	270 53.7 ..	14.4	168 32.6 ..	19.3	92 18.6 ..	33.5	76 26.1 ..	54.0	Adhara	255 20.5	S28 58.3
04	131 32.7	285 53.4	15.4	183 33.0	18.8	107 21.2	33.5	91 28.7	54.0	Aldebaran	291 01.1	N16 30.5
05	146 35.1	300 53.1	16.4	198 33.5	18.3	122 23.8	33.4	106 31.3	53.9			
06	161 37.6	315 52.9	S 8 17.4	213 34.0	S20 17.8	137 26.4	N 8 33.4	121 33.9	N12 53.9	Alioth	166 30.3	N55 57.5
07	176 40.1	330 52.6	18.4	228 34.5	17.3	152 29.0	33.3	136 36.6	53.8	Alkaid	153 07.6	N49 18.8
08	191 42.5	345 52.3	19.3	243 35.0	16.8	167 31.6	33.3	151 39.2	53.8	Al Na'ir	27 57.0	S46 57.9
F 09	206 45.0	0 52.0 ..	20.3	258 35.5 ..	16.3	182 34.2 ..	33.3	166 41.8 ..	53.7	Alnilam	275 56.7	S 1 12.2
R 10	221 47.5	15 51.7	21.3	273 36.0	15.8	197 36.8	33.2	181 44.4	53.7	Alphard	218 06.3	S 8 39.4
I 11	236 49.9	30 51.5	22.3	288 36.4	15.3	212 39.4	33.2	196 47.1	53.7			
D 12	251 52.4	45 51.2	S 8 23.3	303 36.9	S20 14.8	227 42.1	N 8 33.1	211 49.7	N12 53.6	Alphecca	126 20.3	N26 43.0
A 13	266 54.8	60 50.9	24.3	318 37.4	14.3	242 44.7	33.1	226 52.3	53.6	Alpheratz	357 54.3	N29 05.5
Y 14	281 57.3	75 50.6	25.3	333 37.9	13.8	257 47.3	33.1	241 54.9	53.5	Altair	62 18.8	N 8 52.2
15	296 59.8	90 50.3 ..	26.2	348 38.4 ..	13.3	272 49.9 ..	33.0	256 57.6 ..	53.5	Ankaa	353 25.9	S42 18.7
16	312 02.2	105 50.0	27.2	3 38.9	12.8	287 52.5	33.0	272 00.2	53.5	Antares	112 39.6	S26 25.7
17	327 04.7	120 49.8	28.2	18 39.4	12.3	302 55.1	32.9	287 02.8	53.4			
18	342 07.2	135 49.5	S 8 29.2	33 39.8	S20 11.8	317 57.7	N 8 32.9	302 05.4	N12 53.4	Arcturus	146 05.7	N19 11.1
19	357 09.6	150 49.2	30.2	48 40.3	11.3	333 00.3	32.8	317 08.0	53.3	Atria	107 51.5	S69 01.5
20	12 12.1	165 48.9	31.2	63 40.8	10.8	348 02.9	32.8	332 10.7	53.3	Avior	234 21.9	S59 30.3
21	27 14.6	180 48.6 ..	32.1	78 41.3 ..	10.3	3 05.5 ..	32.8	347 13.3 ..	53.2	Bellatrix	278 43.0	N 6 20.9
22	42 17.0	195 48.3	33.1	93 41.8	09.8	18 08.1	32.7	2 15.9	53.2	Betelgeuse	271 12.4	N 7 24.4
23	57 19.5	210 48.1	34.1	108 42.3	09.3	33 10.7	32.7	17 18.5	53.2			
4 00	72 22.0	225 47.8	S 8 35.1	123 42.8	S20 08.8	48 13.3	N 8 32.6	32 21.2	N12 53.1	Canopus	264 00.3	S52 41.7
01	87 24.4	240 47.5	36.1	138 43.3	08.3	63 15.9	32.6	47 23.8	53.1	Capella	280 49.6	N45 59.8
02	102 26.9	255 47.2	37.1	153 43.7	07.8	78 18.5	32.6	62 26.4	53.0	Deneb	49 38.9	N45 17.0
03	117 29.3	270 46.9 ..	38.0	168 44.2 ..	07.3	93 21.1 ..	32.5	77 29.0 ..	53.0	Denebola	182 44.5	N14 34.4
04	132 31.8	285 46.6	39.0	183 44.7	06.8	108 23.7	32.5	92 31.7	53.0	Diphda	349 06.3	S17 59.4
05	147 34.3	300 46.3	40.0	198 45.2	06.3	123 26.3	32.4	107 34.3	52.9			
06	162 36.7	315 46.0	S 8 41.0	213 45.7	S20 05.8	138 28.9	N 8 32.4	122 36.9	N12 52.9	Dubhe	194 04.6	N61 44.9
07	177 39.2	330 45.7	42.0	228 46.2	05.3	153 31.5	32.4	137 39.5	52.8	Elnath	278 25.6	N28 36.3
S 08	192 41.7	345 45.5	42.9	243 46.7	04.8	168 34.1	32.3	152 42.1	52.8	Eltanin	90 51.6	N51 29.5
A 09	207 44.1	0 45.2 ..	43.9	258 47.2 ..	04.3	183 36.7 ..	32.3	167 44.8 ..	52.7	Enif	33 57.6	N 9 52.5
T 10	222 46.6	15 44.9	44.9	273 47.7	03.8	198 39.3	32.2	182 47.4	52.7	Fomalhaut	15 35.6	S29 37.6
U 11	237 49.1	30 44.6	45.9	288 48.1	03.3	213 41.9	32.2	197 50.0	52.7			
R 12	252 51.5	45 44.3	S 8 46.9	303 48.6	S20 02.8	228 44.5	N 8 32.2	212 52.6	N12 52.6	Gacrux	172 12.9	S57 06.4
D 13	267 54.0	60 44.0	47.9	318 49.1	02.3	243 47.1	32.1	227 55.3	52.6	Gienah	176 03.3	S17 32.2
A 14	282 56.4	75 43.7	48.8	333 49.6	01.8	258 49.7	32.1	242 57.9	52.5	Hadar	149 03.4	S60 22.0
Y 15	297 58.9	90 43.4 ..	49.8	348 50.1 ..	01.2	273 52.3 ..	32.0	258 00.5 ..	52.5	Hamal	328 12.4	N23 27.7
16	313 01.4	105 43.1	50.8	3 50.6	00.7	288 54.9	32.0	273 03.1	52.5	Kaus Aust.	83 58.2	S34 23.0
17	328 03.8	120 42.8	51.8	18 51.1	20 00.2	303 57.5	32.0	288 05.7	52.4			
18	343 06.3	135 42.5	S 8 52.8	33 51.6	S19 59.7	319 00.1	N 8 31.9	303 08.4	N12 52.4	Kochab	137 20.7	N74 09.3
19	358 08.8	150 42.2	53.7	48 52.1	59.2	334 02.7	31.9	318 11.0	52.3	Markab	13 48.8	N15 12.3
20	13 11.2	165 41.9	54.7	63 52.6	58.7	349 05.3	31.9	333 13.6	52.3	Menkar	314 25.8	N 4 05.3
21	28 13.7	180 41.6 ..	55.7	78 53.0 ..	58.2	4 07.9 ..	31.8	348 16.2 ..	52.3	Menkent	148 20.4	S36 21.9
22	43 16.2	195 41.3	56.7	93 53.5	57.7	19 10.5	31.8	3 18.9	52.2	Miaplacidus	221 41.4	S69 42.7
23	58 18.6	210 41.0	57.7	108 54.0	57.2	34 13.1	31.7	18 21.5	52.2			
5 00	73 21.1	225 40.7	S 8 58.6	123 54.5	S19 56.7	49 15.7	N 8 31.7	33 24.1	N12 52.1	Mirfak	308 55.0	N49 51.6
01	88 23.6	240 40.4	9 59.6	138 55.0	56.1	64 18.3	31.7	48 26.7	52.1	Nunki	76 11.7	S26 17.8
02	103 26.0	255 40.1	9 00.6	153 55.5	55.6	79 20.9	31.6	63 29.3	52.1	Peacock	53 36.2	S56 44.3
03	118 28.5	270 39.8 ..	01.6	168 56.0 ..	55.1	94 23.5 ..	31.6	78 32.0 ..	52.0	Pollux	243 40.3	N28 01.5
04	133 30.9	285 39.5	02.6	183 56.5	54.6	109 26.1	31.5	93 34.6	52.0	Procyon	245 10.5	N 5 13.5
05	148 33.4	300 39.2	03.5	198 57.0	54.1	124 28.7	31.5	108 37.2	51.9			
06	163 35.9	315 38.9	S 9 04.5	213 57.5	S19 53.6	139 31.3	N 8 31.5	123 39.8	N12 51.9	Rasalhague	96 16.6	N12 33.8
07	178 38.3	330 38.6	05.5	228 58.0	53.1	154 33.9	31.4	138 42.4	51.9	Regulus	207 54.7	N11 58.1
08	193 40.8	345 38.3	06.5	243 58.5	52.5	169 36.4	31.4	153 45.1	51.8	Rigel	281 21.9	S 8 12.2
S 09	208 43.3	0 38.0 ..	07.4	258 58.9 ..	52.0	184 39.0 ..	31.4	168 47.7 ..	51.8	Rigil Kent.	140 06.8	S60 49.7
U 10	223 45.7	15 37.7	08.4	273 59.4	51.5	199 41.6	31.3	183 50.3	51.7	Sabik	102 25.0	S15 43.3
N 11	238 48.2	30 37.4	09.4	288 59.9	51.0	214 44.2	31.3	198 52.9	51.7			
D 12	253 50.7	45 37.1	S 9 10.4	304 00.4	S19 50.5	229 46.8	N 8 31.3	213 55.5	N12 51.7	Schedar	349 52.3	N56 32.4
A 13	268 53.1	60 36.8	11.4	319 00.9	50.0	244 49.4	31.2	228 58.1	51.6	Shaula	96 36.7	S37 06.1
Y 14	283 55.6	75 36.5	12.3	334 01.4	49.5	259 52.0	31.2	244 00.8	51.6	Sirius	258 42.7	S16 42.9
15	298 58.1	90 36.2 ..	13.3	349 01.9 ..	48.9	274 54.6 ..	31.1	259 03.4 ..	51.5	Spica	158 42.6	S11 09.4
16	314 00.5	105 35.9	14.3	4 02.4	48.4	289 57.2	31.1	274 06.0	51.5	Suhail	223 00.0	S43 25.7
17	329 03.0	120 35.6	15.3	19 02.9	47.9	304 59.8	31.1	289 08.6	51.5			
18	344 05.4	135 35.3	S 9 16.2	34 03.4	S19 47.4	320 02.4	N 8 31.0	304 11.2	N12 51.4	Vega	80 46.5	N38 47.2
19	359 07.9	150 35.0	17.2	49 03.9	46.9	335 04.9	31.0	319 13.9	51.4	Zuben'ubi	137 17.4	S16 02.3
20	14 10.4	165 34.7	18.2	64 04.4	46.3	350 07.5	31.0	334 16.5	51.3		SHA	Mer. Pass.
21	29 12.8	180 34.4 ..	19.2	79 04.9 ..	45.8	5 10.1 ..	30.9	349 19.1 ..	51.3		° ′	h m
22	44 15.3	195 34.1	20.2	94 05.4	45.3	20 12.7	30.9	4 21.7	51.3	Venus	153 25.8	8 57
23	59 17.8	210 33.8	21.1	109 05.9	44.8	35 15.3	30.9	19 24.3	51.2	Mars	51 20.8	15 45
	h m									Jupiter	335 51.4	20 44
Mer. Pass. 19 07.4		v −0.3 d 1.0		v 0.5 d 0.5		v 2.6 d 0.0		v 2.6 d 0.0		Saturn	319 59.2	21 47

UT	SUN		MOON				Lat.	Twilight		Sunrise	Moonrise			
								Naut.	Civil		3	4	5	6
	GHA	Dec	GHA	v	Dec	d	HP							
d h	° ′	° ′	° ′	′	° ′	′	′	°	h m	h m	h m	h m	h m	h m	h m
3 00	182 38.2	S22 00.0	234 53.1	14.7	S 1 49.2	11.0	55.3	N 72	07 58	10 02	■■	02 56	04 39	06 26	08 21
01	197 37.9	00.3	249 26.8	14.6	2 00.2	10.9	55.2	N 70	07 41	09 19	■■	02 53	04 29	06 06	07 47
02	212 37.7	00.7	264 00.4	14.7	2 11.1	10.9	55.2	68	07 27	08 50	10 52	02 50	04 20	05 51	07 23
03	227 37.4	.. 01.1	278 34.1	14.6	2 22.0	10.9	55.2	66	07 15	08 29	09 56	02 47	04 13	05 39	07 04
04	242 37.2	01.4	293 07.8	14.6	2 32.9	10.9	55.2	64	07 06	08 11	09 23	02 45	04 07	05 29	06 49
05	257 36.9	01.8	307 41.4	14.7	2 43.8	10.8	55.2	62	06 57	07 57	08 59	02 44	04 02	05 20	06 37
06	272 36.7	S22 02.2	322 15.1	14.8	S 2 54.6	10.8	55.1	60	06 50	07 45	08 40	02 42	03 58	05 13	06 26
07	287 36.5	02.5	336 48.9	14.7	3 05.4	10.9	55.1	N 58	06 43	07 34	08 24	02 41	03 54	05 06	06 17
08	302 36.2	02.9	351 22.6	14.7	3 16.3	10.7	55.1	56	06 37	07 25	08 11	02 40	03 50	05 00	06 09
F 09	317 36.0	.. 03.2	5 56.3	14.7	3 27.0	10.8	55.1	54	06 31	07 17	07 59	02 38	03 47	04 55	06 02
R 10	332 35.7	03.6	20 30.0	14.8	3 37.8	10.8	55.1	52	06 26	07 09	07 49	02 38	03 45	04 51	05 56
I 11	347 35.5	03.9	35 03.8	14.7	3 48.6	10.7	55.0	50	06 21	07 02	07 40	02 37	03 42	04 46	05 50
D 12	2 35.2	S22 04.3	49 37.5	14.8	S 3 59.3	10.7	55.0	45	06 11	06 47	07 21	02 35	03 36	04 37	05 38
A 13	17 35.0	04.7	64 11.3	14.7	4 10.0	10.7	55.0	N 40	06 01	06 35	07 05	02 33	03 32	04 30	05 27
Y 14	32 34.7	05.0	78 45.0	14.8	4 20.7	10.6	55.0	35	05 53	06 24	06 52	02 32	03 28	04 23	05 19
15	47 34.5	.. 05.4	93 18.8	14.8	4 31.3	10.7	55.0	30	05 44	06 14	06 40	02 31	03 24	04 18	05 11
16	62 34.2	05.7	107 52.6	14.7	4 42.0	10.6	54.9	20	05 29	05 56	06 20	02 29	03 18	04 08	04 58
17	77 34.0	06.1	122 26.3	14.8	4 52.6	10.5	54.9	N 10	05 14	05 40	06 03	02 27	03 13	04 00	04 47
18	92 33.8	S22 06.4	137 00.1	14.8	S 5 03.1	10.6	54.9	0	04 58	05 24	05 46	02 25	03 08	03 52	04 36
19	107 33.5	06.8	151 33.9	14.8	5 13.7	10.5	54.9	S 10	04 40	05 07	05 29	02 23	03 04	03 44	04 25
20	122 33.3	07.1	166 07.7	14.7	5 24.2	10.5	54.9	20	04 19	04 48	05 12	02 22	02 58	03 36	04 14
21	137 33.0	.. 07.5	180 41.4	14.8	5 34.7	10.5	54.9	30	03 51	04 24	04 51	02 20	02 53	03 26	04 02
22	152 32.8	07.8	195 15.2	14.8	5 45.2	10.4	54.8	35	03 34	04 10	04 39	02 19	02 49	03 21	03 54
23	167 32.5	08.2	209 49.0	14.7	5 55.6	10.4	54.8	40	03 12	03 53	04 25	02 17	02 46	03 15	03 46
4 00	182 32.3	S22 08.5	224 22.7	14.8	S 6 06.0	10.4	54.8	45	02 44	03 32	04 08	02 16	02 41	03 08	03 36
01	197 32.0	08.9	238 56.5	14.7	6 16.4	10.4	54.8	S 50	02 04	03 04	03 47	02 14	02 36	02 59	03 24
02	212 31.8	09.2	253 30.2	14.8	6 26.8	10.3	54.8	52	01 41	02 51	03 37	02 14	02 34	02 55	03 19
03	227 31.5	.. 09.6	268 04.0	14.8	6 37.1	10.2	54.7	54	01 08	02 35	03 26	02 13	02 31	02 51	03 13
04	242 31.3	09.9	282 37.8	14.7	6 47.3	10.3	54.7	56	////	02 15	03 13	02 12	02 28	02 46	03 07
05	257 31.0	10.3	297 11.5	14.7	6 57.6	10.2	54.7	58	////	01 51	02 58	02 11	02 25	02 41	02 59
06	272 30.8	S22 10.6	311 45.2	14.8	S 7 07.8	10.2	54.7	S 60	////	01 16	02 40	02 10	02 22	02 35	02 51

UT	SUN		MOON				Lat.	Sunset	Twilight		Moonset			
									Civil	Naut.	3	4	5	6
d h	° ′	° ′	° ′	′	° ′	′	′	°	h m	h m	h m	h m	h m	h m	h m
07	287 30.5	11.0	326 19.0	14.7	7 18.0	10.1	54.7	N 72	■■	13 38	15 42	13 50	13 37	13 21	12 59
S 08	302 30.3	11.3	340 52.7	14.7	7 28.1	10.2	54.7	N 70	■■	14 20	15 59	13 56	13 49	13 42	13 34
A 09	317 30.0	.. 11.6	355 26.4	14.7	7 38.3	10.0	54.7	68	12 47	14 49	16 13	14 01	13 59	13 59	13 59
T 10	332 29.8	12.0	10 00.1	14.7	7 48.3	10.1	54.6	66	13 44	15 11	16 24	14 05	14 08	14 12	14 18
U 11	347 29.5	12.3	24 33.8	14.7	7 58.4	10.0	54.6	64	14 17	15 28	16 34	14 08	14 15	14 23	14 34
R 12	2 29.3	S22 12.7	39 07.5	14.7	S 8 08.4	9.9	54.6	62	14 41	15 43	16 43	14 11	14 21	14 33	14 47
D 13	17 29.0	13.0	53 41.2	14.6	8 18.3	9.9	54.6	60	15 00	15 55	16 50	14 14	14 27	14 41	14 58
A 14	32 28.8	13.3	68 14.8	14.7	8 28.2	9.9	54.6	N 58	15 16	16 05	16 57	14 16	14 31	14 48	15 08
Y 15	47 28.5	.. 13.7	82 48.5	14.6	8 38.1	9.7	54.5	56	15 29	16 15	17 03	14 19	14 36	14 55	15 17
16	62 28.3	14.0	97 22.1	14.7	8 48.0	9.8	54.5	54	15 40	16 23	17 08	14 21	14 40	15 00	15 24
17	77 28.0	14.3	111 55.8	14.6	8 57.8	9.7	54.5	52	15 51	16 31	17 14	14 22	14 43	15 06	15 31
18	92 27.8	S22 14.7	126 29.4	14.6	S 9 07.5	9.8	54.5	50	16 00	16 38	17 18	14 24	14 46	15 10	15 37
19	107 27.5	15.0	141 03.0	14.6	9 17.3	9.6	54.5	45	16 19	16 52	17 29	14 27	14 53	15 20	15 50
20	122 27.2	15.3	155 36.6	14.5	9 26.9	9.6	54.5	N 40	16 35	17 05	17 39	14 30	14 59	15 29	16 01
21	137 27.0	.. 15.7	170 10.1	14.6	9 36.6	9.6	54.5	35	16 48	17 16	17 47	14 33	15 04	15 36	16 11
22	152 26.7	16.0	184 43.7	14.5	9 46.2	9.5	54.5	30	17 00	17 26	17 55	14 35	15 08	15 43	16 19
23	167 26.5	16.3	199 17.2	14.5	9 55.7	9.5	54.5	20	17 20	17 44	18 11	14 39	15 16	15 54	16 33
5 00	182 26.2	S22 16.7	213 50.7	14.5	S10 05.2	9.5	54.4	N 10	17 37	18 00	18 26	14 43	15 23	16 04	16 46
01	197 26.0	17.0	228 24.2	14.5	10 14.7	9.4	54.4	0	17 54	18 16	18 42	14 46	15 29	16 13	16 58
02	212 25.7	17.3	242 57.7	14.5	10 24.1	9.4	54.4	S 10	18 10	18 33	19 00	14 49	15 36	16 22	17 10
03	227 25.5	.. 17.7	257 31.2	14.5	10 33.5	9.3	54.4	20	18 28	18 53	19 21	14 53	15 42	16 32	17 22
04	242 25.2	18.0	272 04.7	14.4	10 42.8	9.2	54.4	30	18 49	19 16	19 49	14 57	15 50	16 44	17 37
05	257 25.0	18.3	286 38.1	14.4	10 52.0	9.3	54.4	35	19 01	19 31	20 07	14 59	15 55	16 50	17 45
06	272 24.7	S22 18.6	301 11.5	14.4	S11 01.3	9.1	54.4	40	19 16	19 48	20 28	15 02	16 00	16 58	17 55
07	287 24.4	19.0	315 44.9	14.4	11 10.4	9.2	54.4	45	19 32	20 09	20 57	15 05	16 06	17 06	18 06
08	302 24.2	19.3	330 18.3	14.3	11 19.6	9.0	54.3	S 50	19 53	20 36	21 38	15 08	16 13	17 17	18 20
S 09	317 23.9	.. 19.6	344 51.6	14.3	11 28.6	9.0	54.3	52	20 03	20 50	22 01	15 10	16 16	17 22	18 26
U 10	332 23.7	19.9	359 24.9	14.3	11 37.6	9.0	54.3	54	20 15	21 06	22 34	15 12	16 20	17 27	18 33
N 11	347 23.4	20.3	13 58.2	14.3	11 46.6	8.9	54.3	56	20 28	21 26	////	15 14	16 24	17 33	18 41
D 12	2 23.2	S22 20.6	28 31.5	14.3	S11 55.5	8.9	54.3	58	20 43	21 51	////	15 16	16 29	17 40	18 50
A 13	17 22.9	20.9	43 04.8	14.2	12 04.4	8.8	54.3	S 60	21 01	22 27	////	15 18	16 34	17 48	19 01
Y 14	32 22.6	21.2	57 38.0	14.3	12 13.2	8.8	54.3								
15	47 22.4	.. 21.5	72 11.3	14.2	12 22.0	8.7	54.3								
16	62 22.1	21.9	86 44.5	14.1	12 30.7	8.6	54.3								
17	77 21.9	22.2	101 17.6	14.2	12 39.3	8.6	54.2								

18	92 21.6	S22 22.5	115 50.8	14.1	S12 47.9	8.6	54.2
19	107 21.3	22.8	130 23.9	14.1	12 56.5	8.4	54.2
20	122 21.1	23.1	144 57.0	14.1	13 04.9	8.5	54.2
21	137 20.8	.. 23.4	159 30.1	14.0	13 13.4	8.3	54.2
22	152 20.6	23.7	174 03.1	14.0	13 21.7	8.3	54.2
23	167 20.3	24.1	188 36.1	14.0	S13 30.0	8.3	54.2

	SUN			MOON		
Day	Eqn. of Time		Mer.	Mer. Pass.		Age	Phase
	00h	12h	Pass.	Upper	Lower	
d	m s	m s	h m	h m	h m	d %
3	10 33	10 21	11 50	08 36	20 57	25 17
4	10 10	09 58	11 50	09 19	21 41	26 11
5	09 45	09 33	11 50	10 02	22 25	27 5

SUN		MOON	
SD 16.3	d 0.3	SD 15.0	14.9	14.8

UT	ARIES GHA	VENUS −4.2 GHA	Dec	MARS +0.9 GHA	Dec	JUPITER −2.7 GHA	Dec	SATURN +0.0 GHA	Dec	STARS Name	SHA	Dec
MONDAY												
6 00	74 20.2	225 33.4	S 9 22.1	124 06.4	S19 44.3	50 17.9	N 8 30.8	34 26.9	N12 51.2	Acamar	315 26.0	S40 18.5
01	89 22.7	240 33.1	23.1	139 06.8	43.7	65 20.5	30.8	49 29.6	51.1	Achernar	335 34.2	S57 14.6
02	104 25.2	255 32.8	24.1	154 07.3	43.2	80 23.1	30.8	64 32.2	51.1	Acrux	173 21.4	S63 05.5
03	119 27.6	270 32.5 ..	25.0	169 07.8 ..	42.7	95 25.6 ..	30.7	79 34.8 ..	51.1	Adhara	255 20.5	S28 58.3
04	134 30.1	285 32.2	26.0	184 08.3	42.2	110 28.2	30.7	94 37.4	51.0	Aldebaran	291 01.1	N16 30.5
05	149 32.5	300 31.9	27.0	199 08.8	41.7	125 30.8	30.7	109 40.0	51.0			
06	164 35.0	315 31.6	S 9 28.0	214 09.3	S19 41.1	140 33.4	N 8 30.6	124 42.7	N12 51.0	Alioth	166 30.2	N55 57.5
07	179 37.5	330 31.3	28.9	229 09.8	40.6	155 36.0	30.6	139 45.3	50.9	Alkaid	153 07.6	N49 18.8
08	194 39.9	345 31.0	29.9	244 10.3	40.1	170 38.6	30.6	154 47.9	50.9	Al Na'ir	27 57.1	S46 57.9
09	209 42.4	0 30.6 ..	30.9	259 10.8 ..	39.6	185 41.2 ..	30.5	169 50.5 ..	50.8	Alnilam	275 56.7	S 1 12.2
10	224 44.9	15 30.3	31.9	274 11.3	39.0	200 43.7	30.5	184 53.1	50.8	Alphard	218 06.3	S 8 39.4
11	239 47.3	30 30.0	32.8	289 11.8	38.5	215 46.3	30.5	199 55.7	50.8			
12	254 49.8	45 29.7	S 9 33.8	304 12.3	S19 38.0	230 48.9	N 8 30.4	214 58.4	N12 50.7	Alphecca	126 20.3	N26 43.0
13	269 52.3	60 29.4	34.8	319 12.8	37.5	245 51.5	30.4	230 01.0	50.7	Alpheratz	357 54.3	N29 05.5
14	284 54.7	75 29.1	35.8	334 13.3	36.9	260 54.1	30.4	245 03.6	50.6	Altair	62 18.8	N 8 52.2
15	299 57.2	90 28.7 ..	36.7	349 13.8 ..	36.4	275 56.7 ..	30.3	260 06.2 ..	50.6	Ankaa	353 25.9	S42 18.7
16	314 59.7	105 28.4	37.7	4 14.3	35.9	290 59.2	30.3	275 08.8	50.6	Antares	112 39.6	S26 25.7
17	330 02.1	120 28.1	38.7	19 14.8	35.4	306 01.8	30.3	290 11.4	50.5			
18	345 04.6	135 27.8	S 9 39.6	34 15.3	S19 34.8	321 04.4	N 8 30.2	305 14.0	N12 50.5	Arcturus	146 05.6	N19 11.1
19	0 07.0	150 27.5	40.6	49 15.8	34.3	336 07.0	30.2	320 16.7	50.5	Atria	107 51.5	S69 01.5
20	15 09.5	165 27.2	41.6	64 16.3	33.8	351 09.6	30.2	335 19.3	50.4	Avior	234 21.9	S59 30.3
21	30 12.0	180 26.8 ..	42.6	79 16.8 ..	33.3	6 12.2 ..	30.1	350 21.9 ..	50.4	Bellatrix	278 43.0	N 6 20.9
22	45 14.4	195 26.5	43.5	94 17.3	32.7	21 14.7	30.1	5 24.5	50.3	Betelgeuse	271 12.4	N 7 24.3
23	60 16.9	210 26.2	44.5	109 17.8	32.2	36 17.3	30.1	20 27.1	50.3			
TUESDAY												
7 00	75 19.4	225 25.9	S 9 45.5	124 18.3	S19 31.7	51 19.9	N 8 30.0	35 29.7	N12 50.3	Canopus	264 00.3	S52 41.7
01	90 21.8	240 25.6	46.5	139 18.8	31.1	66 22.5	30.0	50 32.3	50.2	Capella	280 49.6	N45 59.8
02	105 24.3	255 25.2	47.4	154 19.3	30.6	81 25.1	30.0	65 35.0	50.2	Deneb	49 38.9	N45 17.0
03	120 26.8	270 24.9 ..	48.4	169 19.8 ..	30.1	96 27.6 ..	30.0	80 37.6 ..	50.1	Denebola	182 44.5	N14 34.4
04	135 29.2	285 24.6	49.4	184 20.3	29.6	111 30.2	29.9	95 40.2	50.1	Diphda	349 06.3	S17 59.4
05	150 31.7	300 24.3	50.3	199 20.8	29.1	126 32.8	29.9	110 42.8	50.1			
06	165 34.2	315 23.9	S 9 51.3	214 21.3	S19 28.5	141 35.4	N 8 29.9	125 45.4	N12 50.0	Dubhe	194 04.6	N61 44.9
07	180 36.6	330 23.6	52.3	229 21.8	28.0	156 37.9	29.8	140 48.0	50.0	Elnath	278 25.6	N28 36.3
08	195 39.1	345 23.3	53.2	244 22.3	27.4	171 40.5	29.8	155 50.6	50.0	Eltanin	90 51.6	N51 29.5
09	210 41.5	0 23.0 ..	54.2	259 22.8 ..	26.9	186 43.1 ..	29.8	170 53.3 ..	49.9	Enif	33 57.6	N 9 52.5
10	225 44.0	15 22.6	55.2	274 23.3	26.4	201 45.7	29.7	185 55.9	49.9	Fomalhaut	15 35.6	S29 37.6
11	240 46.5	30 22.3	56.2	289 23.8	25.8	216 48.2	29.7	200 58.5	49.8			
12	255 48.9	45 22.0	S 9 57.1	304 24.3	S19 25.3	231 50.8	N 8 29.7	216 01.1	N12 49.8	Gacrux	172 12.9	S57 06.4
13	270 51.4	60 21.7	58.1	319 24.8	24.8	246 53.4	29.6	231 03.7	49.8	Gienah	176 03.3	S17 32.3
14	285 53.9	75 21.3	9 59.1	334 25.3	24.2	261 56.0	29.6	246 06.3	49.7	Hadar	149 03.4	S60 22.0
15	300 56.3	90 21.0	10 00.0	349 25.8 ..	23.7	276 58.6 ..	29.6	261 08.9 ..	49.7	Hamal	328 12.4	N23 27.7
16	315 58.8	105 20.7	01.0	4 26.3	23.2	292 01.1	29.6	276 11.6	49.7	Kaus Aust.	83 58.2	S34 23.0
17	331 01.3	120 20.4	02.0	19 26.8	22.6	307 03.7	29.5	291 14.2	49.6			
18	346 03.7	135 20.0	S10 02.9	34 27.3	S19 22.1	322 06.3	N 8 29.5	306 16.8	N12 49.6	Kochab	137 20.7	N74 09.3
19	1 06.2	150 19.7	03.9	49 27.8	21.6	337 08.8	29.5	321 19.4	49.5	Markab	13 48.8	N15 12.3
20	16 08.7	165 19.4	04.9	64 28.3	21.0	352 11.4	29.4	336 22.0	49.5	Menkar	314 25.8	N 4 05.3
21	31 11.1	180 19.0 ..	05.8	79 28.8 ..	20.5	7 14.0 ..	29.4	351 24.6 ..	49.5	Menkent	148 20.3	S36 21.9
22	46 13.6	195 18.7	06.8	94 29.3	20.0	22 16.6	29.4	6 27.2	49.4	Miaplacidus	221 41.4	S69 42.7
23	61 16.0	210 18.4	07.8	109 29.8	19.4	37 19.1	29.4	21 29.8	49.4			
WEDNESDAY												
8 00	76 18.5	225 18.0	S10 08.7	124 30.3	S19 18.9	52 21.7	N 8 29.3	36 32.4	N12 49.4	Mirfak	308 55.0	N49 51.7
01	91 21.0	240 17.7	09.7	139 30.8	18.3	67 24.3	29.3	51 35.1	49.3	Nunki	76 11.7	S26 17.8
02	106 23.4	255 17.4	10.7	154 31.3	17.8	82 26.9	29.3	66 37.7	49.3	Peacock	53 36.2	S56 44.3
03	121 25.9	270 17.0 ..	11.6	169 31.8 ..	17.3	97 29.4 ..	29.2	81 40.3 ..	49.3	Pollux	243 40.3	N28 01.5
04	136 28.4	285 16.7	12.6	184 32.3	16.7	112 32.0	29.2	96 42.9	49.2	Procyon	245 10.5	N 5 13.5
05	151 30.8	300 16.4	13.6	199 32.8	16.2	127 34.6	29.2	111 45.5	49.2			
06	166 33.3	315 16.0	S10 14.5	214 33.3	S19 15.6	142 37.1	N 8 29.2	126 48.1	N12 49.1	Rasalhague	96 16.6	N12 33.8
07	181 35.8	330 15.7	15.5	229 33.8	15.1	157 39.7	29.1	141 50.7	49.1	Regulus	207 54.6	N11 58.1
08	196 38.2	345 15.4	16.5	244 34.3	14.6	172 42.3	29.1	156 53.3	49.1	Rigel	281 21.9	S 8 12.2
09	211 40.7	0 15.0 ..	17.4	259 34.8 ..	14.0	187 44.8 ..	29.1	171 55.9 ..	49.0	Rigil Kent.	140 06.8	S60 49.7
10	226 43.1	15 14.7	18.4	274 35.3	13.5	202 47.4	29.1	186 58.6	49.0	Sabik	102 25.0	S15 43.3
11	241 45.6	30 14.4	19.4	289 35.8	12.9	217 50.0	29.0	202 01.2	49.0			
12	256 48.1	45 14.0	S10 20.3	304 36.3	S19 12.4	232 52.5	N 8 29.0	217 03.8	N12 48.9	Schedar	349 52.3	N56 32.4
13	271 50.5	60 13.7	21.3	319 36.8	11.9	247 55.1	29.0	232 06.4	48.9	Shaula	96 36.7	S37 06.1
14	286 53.0	75 13.4	22.3	334 37.4	11.3	262 57.7	28.9	247 09.0	48.8	Sirius	258 42.7	S16 42.9
15	301 55.5	90 13.0 ..	23.2	349 37.9 ..	10.7	278 00.2 ..	28.9	262 11.6 ..	48.8	Spica	158 42.6	S11 09.4
16	316 57.9	105 12.7	24.2	4 38.4	10.2	293 02.8	28.9	277 14.2	48.8	Suhail	223 00.0	S43 25.7
17	332 00.4	120 12.3	25.2	19 38.9	09.7	308 05.4	28.9	292 16.8	48.7			
18	347 02.9	135 12.0	S10 26.1	34 39.4	S19 09.2	323 07.9	N 8 28.8	307 19.4	N12 48.7	Vega	80 46.5	N38 47.2
19	2 05.3	150 11.7	27.1	49 39.9	08.6	338 10.5	28.8	322 22.0	48.7	Zuben'ubi	137 17.4	S16 02.3
20	17 07.8	165 11.3	28.0	64 40.4	08.1	353 13.1	28.8	337 24.6	48.6			
21	32 10.3	180 11.0 ..	29.0	79 40.9 ..	07.5	8 15.6 ..	28.8	352 27.3 ..	48.6		SHA	Mer. Pass.
22	47 12.7	195 10.6	30.0	94 41.4	07.0	23 18.2	28.7	7 29.9	48.6	Venus	150 06.5	8 58
23	62 15.2	210 10.3	30.9	109 41.9	06.4	38 20.8	28.7	22 32.5	48.5	Mars	48 58.9	15 42
	h m									Jupiter	336 00.5	20 31
Mer. Pass. 18 55.6	v −0.3 d 1.0	v 0.5 d 0.5		v 2.6 d 0.0		v 2.6 d 0.0				Saturn	320 10.4	21 34

Day	UT	SUN GHA	SUN Dec	MOON GHA	*v*	MOON Dec	*d*	HP
	d h	° ′	° ′	° ′	′	° ′	′	′
MONDAY	6 00	182 20.0	S22 24.4	203 09.1	14.0	S13 38.3	8.2	54.2
	01	197 19.8	24.7	217 42.1	13.9	13 46.5	8.1	54.2
	02	212 19.5	25.0	232 15.0	14.0	13 54.6	8.1	54.2
	03	227 19.3	. . 25.3	246 48.0	13.8	14 02.7	8.0	54.2
	04	242 19.0	25.6	261 20.8	13.9	14 10.7	7.9	54.1
	05	257 18.7	25.9	275 53.7	13.8	14 18.6	7.9	54.1
	06	272 18.5	S22 26.2	290 26.5	13.8	S14 26.5	7.8	54.1
	07	287 18.2	26.5	304 59.3	13.8	14 34.3	7.8	54.1
	08	302 17.9	26.8	319 32.1	13.8	14 42.1	7.6	54.1
	09	317 17.7	. . 27.2	334 04.9	13.7	14 49.7	7.7	54.1
	10	332 17.4	27.5	348 37.6	13.7	14 57.4	7.5	54.1
	11	347 17.2	27.8	3 10.3	13.6	15 04.9	7.5	54.1
	12	2 16.9	S22 28.1	17 42.9	13.7	S15 12.4	7.4	54.1
	13	17 16.6	28.4	32 15.6	13.6	15 19.8	7.4	54.1
	14	32 16.4	28.7	46 48.2	13.6	15 27.2	7.3	54.1
	15	47 16.1	. . 29.0	61 20.8	13.5	15 34.5	7.2	54.1
	16	62 15.8	29.3	75 53.3	13.5	15 41.7	7.2	54.1
	17	77 15.6	29.6	90 25.8	13.5	15 48.9	7.1	54.1
	18	92 15.3	S22 29.9	104 58.3	13.5	S15 56.0	7.0	54.0
	19	107 15.0	30.2	119 30.8	13.4	16 03.0	6.9	54.0
	20	122 14.8	30.5	134 03.2	13.4	16 09.9	6.9	54.0
	21	137 14.5	. . 30.8	148 35.6	13.4	16 16.8	6.8	54.0
	22	152 14.2	31.1	163 08.0	13.3	16 23.6	6.7	54.0
	23	167 14.0	31.3	177 40.3	13.3	16 30.3	6.7	54.0
TUESDAY	7 00	182 13.7	S22 31.6	192 12.6	13.3	S16 37.0	6.5	54.0
	01	197 13.5	31.9	206 44.9	13.3	16 43.5	6.6	54.0
	02	212 13.2	32.2	221 17.2	13.2	16 50.1	6.4	54.0
	03	227 12.9	. . 32.5	235 49.4	13.2	16 56.5	6.3	54.0
	04	242 12.7	32.8	250 21.6	13.1	17 02.8	6.3	54.0
	05	257 12.4	33.1	264 53.7	13.2	17 09.1	6.2	54.0
	06	272 12.1	S22 33.4	279 25.9	13.1	S17 15.3	6.2	54.0
	07	287 11.8	33.7	293 58.0	13.0	17 21.5	6.0	54.0
	08	302 11.6	34.0	308 30.0	13.1	17 27.5	6.0	54.0
	09	317 11.3	. . 34.3	323 02.1	13.0	17 33.5	5.9	54.0
	10	332 11.0	34.5	337 34.1	13.0	17 39.4	5.8	54.0
	11	347 10.8	34.8	352 06.1	12.9	17 45.2	5.8	54.0
	12	2 10.5	S22 35.1	6 38.0	12.9	S17 51.0	5.6	54.0
	13	17 10.2	35.4	21 09.9	12.9	17 56.6	5.6	54.0
	14	32 10.0	35.7	35 41.8	12.9	18 02.2	5.5	54.0
	15	47 09.7	. . 36.0	50 13.7	12.8	18 07.7	5.4	54.0
	16	62 09.4	36.2	64 45.5	12.9	18 13.1	5.4	54.0
	17	77 09.2	36.5	79 17.4	12.7	18 18.5	5.2	53.9
	18	92 08.9	S22 36.8	93 49.1	12.8	S18 23.7	5.2	53.9
	19	107 08.6	37.1	108 20.9	12.7	18 28.9	5.1	53.9
	20	122 08.3	37.4	122 52.6	12.7	18 34.0	5.0	53.9
	21	137 08.1	. . 37.6	137 24.3	12.7	18 39.0	5.0	53.9
	22	152 07.8	37.9	151 56.0	12.6	18 44.0	4.8	53.9
	23	167 07.5	38.2	166 27.6	12.6	18 48.8	4.8	53.9
WEDNESDAY	8 00	182 07.3	S22 38.5	180 59.2	12.6	S18 53.6	4.6	53.9
	01	197 07.0	38.7	195 30.8	12.6	18 58.2	4.6	53.9
	02	212 06.7	39.0	210 02.4	12.5	19 02.8	4.5	53.9
	03	227 06.4	. . 39.3	224 33.9	12.5	19 07.3	4.5	53.9
	04	242 06.2	39.6	239 05.4	12.5	19 11.8	4.3	53.9
	05	257 05.9	39.8	253 36.9	12.5	19 16.1	4.2	53.9
	06	272 05.6	S22 40.1	268 08.4	12.4	S19 20.3	4.2	53.9
	07	287 05.4	40.4	282 39.8	12.4	19 24.5	4.1	53.9
	08	302 05.1	40.7	297 11.2	12.4	19 28.6	3.9	53.9
	09	317 04.8	. . 40.9	311 42.6	12.3	19 32.5	3.9	53.9
	10	332 04.5	41.2	326 13.9	12.4	19 36.4	3.8	53.9
	11	347 04.3	41.5	340 45.3	12.3	19 40.2	3.8	53.9
	12	2 04.0	S22 41.7	355 16.6	12.3	S19 44.0	3.6	53.9
	13	17 03.7	42.0	9 47.9	12.2	19 47.6	3.5	53.9
	14	32 03.4	42.3	24 19.1	12.3	19 51.1	3.5	53.9
	15	47 03.2	. . 42.5	38 50.4	12.2	19 54.6	3.3	53.9
	16	62 02.9	42.8	53 21.6	12.2	19 57.9	3.3	53.9
	17	77 02.6	43.0	67 52.8	12.1	20 01.2	3.2	53.9
	18	92 02.3	S22 43.3	82 23.9	12.2	S20 04.4	3.0	53.9
	19	107 02.1	43.6	96 55.1	12.1	20 07.4	3.0	53.9
	20	122 01.8	43.8	111 26.2	12.1	20 10.4	2.9	53.9
	21	137 01.5	. . 44.1	125 57.3	12.1	20 13.3	2.8	53.9
	22	152 01.2	44.3	140 28.4	12.1	20 16.1	2.7	53.9
	23	167 01.0	44.6	154 59.5	12.1	S20 18.8	2.7	53.9
		SD 16.3	*d* 0.3	SD 14.7		14.7		14.7

Lat.	Twilight Naut.	Twilight Civil	Sunrise	Moonrise 6	Moonrise 7	Moonrise 8	Moonrise 9
°	h m	h m	h m	h m	h m	h m	h m
N 72	08 05	10 15	■	08 21	11 00	■	■
N 70	07 47	09 28	■	07 47	09 34	11 45	■
68	07 32	08 58	11 15	07 23	08 55	10 26	11 47
66	07 20	08 35	10 05	07 04	08 29	09 49	10 58
64	07 10	08 17	09 30	06 49	08 08	09 22	10 27
62	07 01	08 02	09 05	06 37	07 52	09 02	10 04
60	06 54	07 49	08 45	06 26	07 38	08 45	09 45
N 58	06 47	07 39	08 29	06 17	07 26	08 31	09 30
56	06 40	07 29	08 15	06 09	07 16	08 19	09 17
54	06 35	07 20	08 03	06 02	07 07	08 09	09 06
52	06 29	07 13	07 53	05 56	06 59	08 00	08 55
50	06 24	07 06	07 44	05 50	06 52	07 51	08 47
45	06 13	06 50	07 24	05 38	06 37	07 34	08 28
N 40	06 04	06 38	07 08	05 27	06 24	07 19	08 12
35	05 55	06 26	06 54	05 19	06 13	07 07	07 59
30	05 47	06 16	06 42	05 11	06 04	06 57	07 48
20	05 31	05 58	06 22	04 58	05 48	06 38	07 28
N 10	05 15	05 42	06 04	04 47	05 34	06 23	07 11
0	04 59	05 25	05 48	04 36	05 21	06 08	06 56
S 10	04 41	05 08	05 31	04 25	05 09	05 53	06 40
20	04 19	04 48	05 13	04 14	04 55	05 38	06 23
30	03 51	04 24	04 51	04 02	04 39	05 20	06 04
35	03 33	04 10	04 39	03 54	04 30	05 10	05 53
40	03 11	03 52	04 25	03 46	04 20	04 58	05 40
45	02 42	03 31	04 07	03 36	04 08	04 44	05 25
S 50	02 01	03 03	03 46	03 24	03 53	04 27	05 06
52	01 36	02 49	03 36	03 19	03 47	04 19	04 58
54	01 01	02 32	03 24	03 13	03 39	04 10	04 48
56	////	02 12	03 11	03 07	03 31	04 00	04 37
58	////	01 46	02 55	02 59	03 21	03 49	04 24
S 60	////	01 08	02 37	02 51	03 10	03 36	04 09

Lat.	Sunset	Twilight Civil	Twilight Naut.	Moonset 6	Moonset 7	Moonset 8	Moonset 9
°	h m	h m	h m	h m	h m	h m	h m
N 72	■	13 27	15 37	12 59	11 54	■	■
N 70	■	14 14	15 55	13 34	13 21	12 48	■
68	12 27	14 44	16 10	13 59	14 01	14 07	14 26
66	13 37	15 07	16 22	14 18	14 28	14 45	15 15
64	14 12	15 25	16 32	14 34	14 49	15 12	15 46
62	14 37	15 40	16 41	14 47	15 06	15 33	16 09
60	14 57	15 53	16 49	14 58	15 20	15 49	16 28
N 58	15 13	16 04	16 55	15 08	15 32	16 04	16 43
56	15 27	16 13	17 02	15 17	15 43	16 16	16 56
54	15 39	16 22	17 08	15 24	15 52	16 26	17 08
52	15 49	16 30	17 13	15 31	16 01	16 36	17 18
50	15 59	16 37	17 18	15 37	16 08	16 44	17 27
45	16 19	16 52	17 29	15 50	16 24	17 03	17 46
N 40	16 35	17 05	17 39	16 01	16 37	17 17	18 02
35	16 48	17 16	17 48	16 11	16 48	17 30	18 15
30	17 00	17 26	17 56	16 19	16 58	17 41	18 26
20	17 20	17 44	18 12	16 33	17 15	17 59	18 46
N 10	17 38	18 01	18 27	16 46	17 30	18 16	19 03
0	17 55	18 17	18 43	16 58	17 44	18 31	19 19
S 10	18 12	18 35	19 02	17 10	17 58	18 46	19 35
20	18 30	18 55	19 24	17 22	18 13	19 03	19 52
30	18 51	19 19	19 52	17 37	18 30	19 21	20 12
35	19 04	19 33	20 10	17 45	18 40	19 32	20 23
40	19 18	19 51	20 32	17 55	18 51	19 45	20 36
45	19 36	20 12	21 01	18 06	19 04	20 00	20 52
S 50	19 57	20 41	21 43	18 20	19 21	20 18	21 11
52	20 07	20 55	22 08	18 26	19 28	20 27	21 20
54	20 19	21 12	22 44	18 33	19 37	20 36	21 30
56	20 32	21 32	////	18 41	19 47	20 47	21 41
58	20 48	21 58	////	18 50	19 58	21 00	21 54
S 60	21 07	22 38	////	19 01	20 10	21 14	22 10

Day	SUN Eqn. of Time 00^h	SUN Eqn. of Time 12^h	SUN Mer. Pass.	MOON Mer. Pass. Upper	MOON Mer. Pass. Lower	MOON Age	MOON Phase
d	m s	m s	h m	h m	h m	d	%
6	09 21	09 08	11 51	10 47	23 10	28	2
7	08 55	08 43	11 51	11 33	23 56	29	0 ●
8	08 30	08 17	11 52	12 20	24 43	01	0

UT (d h)	ARIES GHA	VENUS −4.2 GHA	Dec	MARS +0.9 GHA	Dec	JUPITER −2.7 GHA	Dec	SATURN +0.0 GHA	Dec
9 00	77 17.6	225 09.9	S10 31.9	124 42.4	S19 05.9	53 23.3	N 8 28.7	37 35.1	N12 48.5
01	92 20.1	240 09.6	32.9	139 42.9	05.3	68 25.9	28.7	52 37.7	48.5
02	107 22.6	255 09.3	33.8	154 43.4	04.8	83 28.5	28.6	67 40.3	48.4
03	122 25.0	270 08.9 ..	34.8	169 43.9 ..	04.2	98 31.0 ..	28.6	82 42.9 ..	48.4
04	137 27.5	285 08.6	35.7	184 44.4	03.7	113 33.6	28.6	97 45.5	48.3
05	152 30.0	300 08.2	36.7	199 44.9	03.2	128 36.2	28.6	112 48.1	48.3
06	167 32.4	315 07.9	S10 37.7	214 45.4	S19 02.6	143 38.7	N 8 28.5	127 50.7	N12 48.3
07	182 34.9	330 07.5	38.6	229 46.0	02.1	158 41.3	28.5	142 53.3	48.2
T 08	197 37.4	345 07.2	39.6	244 46.5	01.5	173 43.8	28.5	157 55.9	48.2
H 09	212 39.8	0 06.8 ..	40.5	259 47.0 ..	01.0	188 46.4 ..	28.5	172 58.6 ..	48.2
U 10	227 42.3	15 06.5	41.5	274 47.5	19 00.4	203 49.0	28.4	188 01.2	48.1
R 11	242 44.8	30 06.1	42.5	289 48.0	18 59.9	218 51.5	28.4	203 03.8	48.1
S 12	257 47.2	45 05.8	S10 43.4	304 48.5	S18 59.3	233 54.1	N 8 28.4	218 06.4	N12 48.1
D 13	272 49.7	60 05.4	44.4	319 49.0	58.8	248 56.6	28.4	233 09.0	48.0
A 14	287 52.1	75 05.1	45.3	334 49.5	58.2	263 59.2	28.3	248 11.6	48.0
Y 15	302 54.6	90 04.7 ..	46.3	349 50.0 ..	57.7	279 01.8 ..	28.3	263 14.2 ..	48.0
16	317 57.1	105 04.4	47.2	4 50.5	57.1	294 04.3	28.3	278 16.8	47.9
17	332 59.5	120 04.0	48.2	19 51.0	56.6	309 06.9	28.3	293 19.4	47.9
18	348 02.0	135 03.7	S10 49.2	34 51.6	S18 56.0	324 09.4	N 8 28.3	308 22.0	N12 47.9
19	3 04.5	150 03.3	50.1	49 52.1	55.5	339 12.0	28.2	323 24.6	47.8
20	18 06.9	165 03.0	51.1	64 52.6	54.9	354 14.5	28.2	338 27.2	47.8
21	33 09.4	180 02.6 ..	52.0	79 53.1 ..	54.4	9 17.1 ..	28.2	353 29.8 ..	47.7
22	48 11.9	195 02.3	53.0	94 53.6	53.8	24 19.7	28.2	8 32.4	47.7
23	63 14.3	210 01.9	53.9	109 54.1	53.2	39 22.2	28.1	23 35.0	47.7
10 00	78 16.8	225 01.6	S10 54.9	124 54.6	S18 52.7	54 24.8	N 8 28.1	38 37.6	N12 47.6
01	93 19.3	240 01.2	55.9	139 55.1	52.1	69 27.3	28.1	53 40.2	47.6
02	108 21.7	255 00.8	56.8	154 55.6	51.6	84 29.9	28.1	68 42.9	47.6
03	123 24.2	270 00.5 ..	57.8	169 56.1 ..	51.0	99 32.4 ..	28.1	83 45.5 ..	47.5
04	138 26.6	285 00.1	58.7	184 56.7	50.5	114 35.0	28.0	98 48.1	47.5
05	153 29.1	299 59.8	10 59.7	199 57.2	49.9	129 37.5	28.0	113 50.7	47.5
06	168 31.6	314 59.4	S11 00.6	214 57.7	S18 49.4	144 40.1	N 8 28.0	128 53.3	N12 47.4
07	183 34.0	329 59.1	01.6	229 58.2	48.8	159 42.7	28.0	143 55.9	47.4
08	198 36.5	344 58.7	02.5	244 58.7	48.3	174 45.2	28.0	158 58.5	47.4
F 09	213 39.0	359 58.3 ..	03.5	259 59.2 ..	47.7	189 47.8 ..	27.9	174 01.1 ..	47.3
R 10	228 41.4	14 58.0	04.4	274 59.7	47.1	204 50.3	27.9	189 03.7	47.3
I 11	243 43.9	29 57.6	05.4	290 00.2	46.6	219 52.9	27.9	204 06.3	47.3
D 12	258 46.4	44 57.3	S11 06.3	305 00.8	S18 46.0	234 55.4	N 8 27.9	219 08.9	N12 47.2
A 13	273 48.8	59 56.9	07.3	320 01.3	45.5	249 58.0	27.9	234 11.5	47.2
Y 14	288 51.3	74 56.5	08.2	335 01.8	44.9	265 00.5	27.8	249 14.1	47.2
15	303 53.8	89 56.2 ..	09.2	350 02.3 ..	44.4	280 03.1 ..	27.8	264 16.7 ..	47.1
16	318 56.2	104 55.8	10.2	5 02.8	43.8	295 05.6	27.8	279 19.3	47.1
17	333 58.7	119 55.5	11.1	20 03.3	43.2	310 08.2	27.8	294 21.9	47.1
18	349 01.1	134 55.1	S11 12.1	35 03.8	S18 42.7	325 10.7	N 8 27.8	309 24.5	N12 47.0
19	4 03.6	149 54.7	13.0	50 04.3	42.1	340 13.3	27.7	324 27.1	47.0
20	19 06.1	164 54.4	14.0	65 04.9	41.6	355 15.8	27.7	339 29.7	47.0
21	34 08.5	179 54.0 ..	14.9	80 05.4 ..	41.0	10 18.4 ..	27.7	354 32.3 ..	46.9
22	49 11.0	194 53.6	15.9	95 05.9	40.4	25 20.9	27.7	9 34.9	46.9
23	64 13.5	209 53.3	16.8	110 06.4	39.9	40 23.5	27.7	24 37.5	46.9
11 00	79 15.9	224 52.9	S11 17.8	125 06.9	S18 39.3	55 26.0	N 8 27.6	39 40.1	N12 46.8
01	94 18.4	239 52.5	18.7	140 07.4	38.7	70 28.6	27.6	54 42.7	46.8
02	109 20.9	254 52.2	19.7	155 07.9	38.2	85 31.1	27.6	69 45.3	46.8
03	124 23.3	269 51.8 ..	20.6	170 08.5 ..	37.6	100 33.7 ..	27.6	84 47.9 ..	46.7
04	139 25.8	284 51.4	21.5	185 09.0	37.1	115 36.2	27.6	99 50.5	46.7
05	154 28.3	299 51.1	22.5	200 09.5	36.5	130 38.7	27.5	114 53.1	46.7
06	169 30.7	314 50.7	S11 23.4	215 10.0	S18 35.9	145 41.3	N 8 27.5	129 55.7	N12 46.6
07	184 33.2	329 50.3	24.4	230 10.5	35.4	160 43.8	27.5	144 58.3	46.6
S 08	199 35.6	344 49.9	25.3	245 11.0	34.8	175 46.4	27.5	160 00.9	46.6
A 09	214 38.1	359 49.6 ..	26.3	260 11.6 ..	34.2	190 48.9 ..	27.5	175 03.5 ..	46.5
T 10	229 40.6	14 49.2	27.2	275 12.1	33.7	205 51.5	27.5	190 06.1	46.5
U 11	244 43.0	29 48.8	28.2	290 12.6	33.1	220 54.0	27.4	205 08.7	46.5
R 12	259 45.5	44 48.5	S11 29.1	305 13.1	S18 32.5	235 56.6	N 8 27.4	220 11.3	N12 46.4
D 13	274 48.0	59 48.1	30.1	320 13.6	32.0	250 59.1	27.4	235 13.9	46.4
A 14	289 50.4	74 47.7	31.0	335 14.1	31.4	266 01.6	27.4	250 16.5	46.4
Y 15	304 52.9	89 47.3 ..	32.0	350 14.7 ..	30.8	281 04.2 ..	27.4	265 19.1 ..	46.3
16	319 55.4	104 47.0	32.9	5 15.2	30.3	296 06.7	27.4	280 21.7	46.3
17	334 57.8	119 46.6	33.8	20 15.7	29.7	311 09.3	27.3	295 24.3	46.3
18	350 00.3	134 46.2	S11 34.8	35 16.2	S18 29.1	326 11.8	N 8 27.3	310 26.9	N12 46.2
19	5 02.7	149 45.8	35.7	50 16.7	28.6	341 14.4	27.3	325 29.5	46.2
20	20 05.2	164 45.5	36.7	65 17.2	28.0	356 16.9	27.3	340 32.1	46.2
21	35 07.7	179 45.1 ..	37.6	80 17.8 ..	27.4	11 19.4 ..	27.3	355 34.7 ..	46.1
22	50 10.1	194 44.7	38.6	95 18.3	26.9	26 22.0	27.3	10 37.3	46.1
23	65 12.6	209 44.3	39.5	110 18.8	26.3	41 24.5	27.2	25 39.9	46.1
Mer. Pass.	h m 18 43.8	v −0.4	d 1.0	v 0.5	d 0.6	v 2.6	d 0.0	v 2.6	d 0.0

STARS

Name	SHA	Dec
Acamar	315 26.0	S40 18.5
Achernar	335 34.3	S57 14.6
Acrux	173 21.3	S63 05.5
Adhara	255 20.4	S28 58.3
Aldebaran	291 01.1	N16 30.5
Alioth	166 30.2	N55 57.5
Alkaid	153 07.5	N49 18.8
Al Na'ir	27 57.1	S46 57.9
Alnilam	275 56.7	S 1 12.2
Alphard	218 06.3	S 8 39.4
Alphecca	126 20.3	N26 43.0
Alpheratz	357 54.3	N29 05.5
Altair	62 18.8	N 8 52.2
Ankaa	353 26.0	S42 18.7
Antares	112 39.6	S26 25.7
Arcturus	146 05.6	N19 11.0
Atria	107 51.5	S69 01.5
Avior	234 21.8	S59 30.4
Bellatrix	278 43.0	N 6 20.9
Betelgeuse	271 12.4	N 7 24.3
Canopus	264 00.3	S52 41.7
Capella	280 49.5	N45 59.8
Deneb	49 38.9	N45 17.0
Denebola	182 44.5	N14 34.4
Diphda	349 06.3	S17 59.4
Dubhe	194 04.5	N61 44.9
Elnath	278 25.6	N28 36.3
Eltanin	90 51.6	N51 29.5
Enif	33 57.6	N 9 52.5
Fomalhaut	15 35.6	S29 37.6
Gacrux	172 12.9	S57 06.4
Gienah	176 03.2	S17 32.3
Hadar	149 03.3	S60 22.0
Hamal	328 12.4	N23 27.7
Kaus Aust.	83 58.2	S34 23.0
Kochab	137 20.7	N74 09.3
Markab	13 48.8	N15 12.3
Menkar	314 25.8	N 4 05.3
Menkent	148 20.3	S36 21.9
Miaplacidus	221 41.4	S69 42.7
Mirfak	308 55.0	N49 51.7
Nunki	76 11.7	S26 17.8
Peacock	53 36.2	S56 44.3
Pollux	243 40.3	N28 01.5
Procyon	245 10.5	N 5 13.5
Rasalhague	96 16.6	N12 33.7
Regulus	207 54.6	N11 58.0
Rigel	281 21.8	S 8 12.2
Rigil Kent.	140 06.7	S60 49.7
Sabik	102 25.0	S15 43.3
Schedar	349 52.3	N56 32.4
Shaula	96 36.6	S37 06.1
Sirius	258 42.7	S16 43.0
Spica	158 42.5	S11 09.4
Suhail	222 59.9	S43 25.7
Vega	80 46.5	N38 47.2
Zuben'ubi	137 17.4	S16 02.3

	SHA	Mer. Pass.
	° ′	h m
Venus	146 44.8	9 00
Mars	46 37.8	15 40
Jupiter	336 08.0	20 19
Saturn	320 20.9	21 22

UT	SUN		MOON				Lat.	Twilight		Sunrise	Moonrise			
	GHA	Dec	GHA	v	Dec	d	HP		Naut.	Civil		9	10	11	12
d h	° ′	° ′	° ′	′	° ′	′	′	°	h m	h m	h m	h m	h m	h m	h m
9 00	182 00.7	S22 44.9	169 30.6	12.0	S20 21.5	2.5	53.9	N 72	08 11	10 28	■■	■■	■■	■■	■■
01	197 00.4	45.1	184 01.6	12.0	20 24.0	2.4	53.9	N 70	07 52	09 36	■■	■■	■■	14 38	13 49
02	212 00.1	45.4	198 32.6	12.0	20 26.4	2.4	53.9	68	07 37	09 04	■■	11 47	12 39	13 00	13 08
03	226 59.9 . .	45.6	213 03.6	12.0	20 28.8	2.2	53.9	66	07 25	08 40	10 14	10 58	11 49	12 21	12 39
04	241 59.6	45.9	227 34.6	12.0	20 31.0	2.2	53.9	64	07 15	08 22	09 37	10 27	11 18	11 54	12 18
05	256 59.3	46.1	242 05.6	11.9	20 33.2	2.0	53.9	62	07 05	08 07	09 10	10 04	10 54	11 33	12 00
06	271 59.0	S22 46.4	256 36.5	11.9	S20 35.2	2.0	54.0	60	06 57	07 54	08 50	09 45	10 36	11 16	11 46
T 07	286 58.7	46.6	271 07.4	12.0	20 37.2	1.9	54.0	N 58	06 50	07 42	08 33	09 30	10 20	11 01	11 34
H 08	301 58.5	46.9	285 38.4	11.9	20 39.1	1.7	54.0	56	06 44	07 33	08 19	09 17	10 07	10 49	11 23
U 09	316 58.2 . .	47.1	300 09.3	11.8	20 40.8	1.7	54.0	54	06 38	07 24	08 07	09 06	09 56	10 38	11 13
R 10	331 57.9	47.4	314 40.1	11.9	20 42.5	1.6	54.0	52	06 32	07 16	07 56	08 55	09 45	10 28	11 05
S 11	346 57.6	47.6	329 11.0	11.9	20 44.1	1.5	54.0	50	06 27	07 09	07 47	08 47	09 36	10 20	10 57
D 12	1 57.4	S22 47.9	343 41.9	11.8	S20 45.6	1.4	54.0	45	06 16	06 53	07 27	08 28	09 17	10 02	10 41
A 13	16 57.1	48.1	358 12.7	11.9	20 47.0	1.3	54.0	N 40	06 06	06 40	07 10	08 12	09 02	09 47	10 28
Y 14	31 56.8	48.4	12 43.6	11.8	20 48.3	1.2	54.0	35	05 57	06 29	06 57	07 59	08 48	09 34	10 17
15	46 56.5 . .	48.6	27 14.4	11.8	20 49.5	1.1	54.0	30	05 49	06 18	06 45	07 48	08 37	09 23	10 07
16	61 56.2	48.9	41 45.2	11.8	20 50.6	1.0	54.0	20	05 33	06 00	06 24	07 28	08 17	09 04	09 50
17	76 56.0	49.1	56 16.0	11.8	20 51.6	0.9	54.0	N 10	05 17	05 43	06 06	07 11	08 00	08 48	09 35
18	91 55.7	S22 49.4	70 46.8	11.8	S20 52.5	0.8	54.0	0	05 00	05 26	05 49	06 56	07 44	08 32	09 21
19	106 55.4	49.6	85 17.6	11.8	20 53.3	0.7	54.0	S 10	04 42	05 09	05 32	06 40	07 28	08 17	09 07
20	121 55.1	49.8	99 48.4	11.7	20 54.0	0.6	54.0	20	04 20	04 49	05 13	06 23	07 11	08 01	08 52
21	136 54.8 . .	50.1	114 19.1	11.8	20 54.6	0.5	54.0	30	03 51	04 25	04 52	06 04	06 51	07 42	08 34
22	151 54.6	50.3	128 49.9	11.7	20 55.1	0.5	54.0	35	03 33	04 10	04 39	05 53	06 40	07 31	08 24
23	166 54.3	50.6	143 20.6	11.8	20 55.6	0.3	54.0	40	03 11	03 52	04 25	05 40	06 27	07 18	08 13
10 00	181 54.0	S22 50.8	157 51.4	11.7	S20 55.9	0.2	54.0	45	02 41	03 30	04 07	05 25	06 11	07 03	07 59
01	196 53.7	51.0	172 22.1	11.7	20 56.1	0.1	54.0	S 50	01 58	03 01	03 45	05 06	05 52	06 45	07 43
02	211 53.4	51.3	186 52.8	11.7	20 56.2	0.1	54.0	52	01 33	02 47	03 35	04 58	05 43	06 36	07 35
03	226 53.2 . .	51.5	201 23.5	11.8	20 56.3	0.1	54.0	54	00 54	02 30	03 23	04 48	05 33	06 26	07 26
04	241 52.9	51.7	215 54.3	11.7	20 56.2	0.1	54.1	56	////	02 09	03 09	04 37	05 22	06 15	07 16
05	256 52.6	52.0	230 25.0	11.7	20 56.1	0.3	54.1	58	////	01 42	02 53	04 24	05 09	06 03	07 05
06	271 52.3	S22 52.2	244 55.7	11.7	S20 55.8	0.4	54.1	S 60	////	01 00	02 34	04 09	04 53	05 48	06 52

Lat.	Sunset	Twilight		Moonset			
		Civil	Naut.	9	10	11	12
	07	286 52.0	52.4	259 26.4	11.7	20 55.4	0.4	54.1

	08	301 51.7	52.7	273 57.1	11.7	20 55.0	0.6	54.1
F 09	316 51.5 . .	52.9	288 27.8	11.7	20 54.4	0.6	54.1
R 10	331 51.2	53.1	302 58.5	11.7	20 53.8	0.8	54.1
I 11	346 50.9	53.4	317 29.2	11.7	20 53.0	0.8	54.1

Lat.	Sunset	Civil	Naut.	9	10	11	12
°	h m	h m	h m	h m	h m	h m	h m
N 72	■■	13 17	15 34	■■	■■	■■	■■
N 70	■■	14 09	15 52	■■	■■	14 56	17 25
68	■■	14 41	16 07	14 26	15 14	16 34	18 06
66	13 31	15 04	16 20	15 15	16 04	17 12	18 33
64	14 08	15 23	16 30	15 46	16 35	17 39	18 54
62	14 34	15 38	16 39	16 09	16 58	18 00	19 11
60	14 55	15 51	16 48	16 28	17 17	18 17	19 25
N 58	15 12	16 03	16 55	16 43	17 33	18 31	19 37
56	15 26	16 12	17 01	16 56	17 46	18 43	19 47
54	15 38	16 21	17 07	17 08	17 57	18 54	19 56
52	15 49	16 29	17 13	17 18	18 07	19 03	20 05
50	15 58	16 36	17 18	17 27	18 16	19 12	20 12
45	16 18	16 52	17 29	17 46	18 35	19 29	20 27
N 40	16 35	17 05	17 39	18 02	18 51	19 44	20 40
35	16 48	17 16	17 48	18 15	19 04	19 56	20 51
30	17 01	17 27	17 57	18 26	19 15	20 07	21 00
20	17 21	17 45	18 13	18 46	19 35	20 25	21 16
N 10	17 39	18 02	18 28	19 03	19 52	20 41	21 30
0	17 56	18 19	18 45	19 19	20 07	20 56	21 44
S 10	18 14	18 37	19 03	19 35	20 23	21 11	21 57
20	18 32	18 57	19 26	19 52	20 40	21 26	22 10
30	18 54	19 21	19 54	20 12	20 59	21 44	22 26
35	19 06	19 36	20 12	20 23	21 11	21 55	22 35
40	19 21	19 54	20 35	20 36	21 24	22 07	22 46
45	19 39	20 16	21 04	20 52	21 39	22 21	22 58
S 50	20 00	20 44	21 48	21 11	21 57	22 38	23 13
52	20 11	20 59	22 14	21 20	22 06	22 46	23 20
54	20 23	21 16	22 53	21 30	22 16	22 55	23 27
56	20 37	21 37	////	21 41	22 27	23 05	23 36
58	20 53	22 05	////	21 54	22 40	23 17	23 45
S 60	21 12	22 48	////	22 10	22 55	23 30	23 56

	12	1 50.6	S22 53.6	331 59.9	11.7	S20 52.2	0.9	54.1
D 13	16 50.3	53.8	346 30.6	11.7	20 51.3	1.1	54.1
A 14	31 50.0	54.1	1 01.3	11.7	20 50.2	1.1	54.1
Y 15	46 49.8 . .	54.3	15 32.0	11.6	20 49.1	1.2	54.1
16	61 49.5	54.5	30 02.6	11.7	20 47.9	1.4	54.1
17	76 49.2	54.7	44 33.3	11.7	20 46.5	1.4	54.2
18	91 48.9	S22 55.0	59 04.0	11.7	S20 45.1	1.5	54.2
19	106 48.6	55.2	73 34.7	11.7	20 43.6	1.7	54.2
20	121 48.3	55.4	88 05.4	11.8	20 41.9	1.7	54.2
21	136 48.1 . .	55.6	102 36.2	11.7	20 40.2	1.8	54.2
22	151 47.8	55.8	117 06.9	11.7	20 38.4	1.9	54.2
23	166 47.5	56.1	131 37.6	11.7	20 36.5	2.0	54.2
11 00	181 47.2	S22 56.3	146 08.3	11.7	S20 34.5	2.1	54.2
01	196 46.9	56.5	160 39.0	11.8	20 32.4	2.2	54.2
02	211 46.6	56.7	175 09.8	11.7	20 30.2	2.3	54.2
03	226 46.3 . .	56.9	189 40.5	11.7	20 27.9	2.4	54.3
04	241 46.1	57.2	204 11.2	11.8	20 25.5	2.5	54.3
05	256 45.8	57.4	218 42.0	11.7	20 23.0	2.6	54.3
06	271 45.5	S22 57.6	233 12.7	11.8	S20 20.4	2.7	54.3
S 07	286 45.2	57.8	247 43.5	11.8	20 17.7	2.8	54.3
A 08	301 44.9	58.0	262 14.3	11.8	20 14.9	2.9	54.3
T 09	316 44.6 . .	58.2	276 45.1	11.8	20 12.0	2.9	54.3
U 10	331 44.3	58.4	291 15.9	11.8	20 09.1	3.1	54.3
R 11	346 44.0	58.7	305 46.7	11.8	20 06.0	3.2	54.3
D 12	1 43.8	S22 58.9	320 17.5	11.8	S20 02.8	3.2	54.4
A 13	16 43.5	59.1	334 48.3	11.8	19 59.6	3.4	54.4
Y 14	31 43.2	59.3	349 19.1	11.9	19 56.2	3.4	54.4
15	46 42.9 . .	59.5	3 50.0	11.8	19 52.8	3.5	54.4
16	61 42.6	59.7	18 20.8	11.9	19 49.3	3.7	54.4
17	76 42.3	22 59.9	32 51.7	11.9	19 45.6	3.7	54.4
18	91 42.0	S23 00.1	47 22.6	11.8	S19 41.9	3.8	54.4
19	106 41.7	00.3	61 53.4	11.9	19 38.1	3.9	54.4
20	121 41.5	00.5	76 24.3	12.0	19 34.2	4.0	54.5
21	136 41.2 . .	00.7	90 55.3	11.9	19 30.2	4.1	54.5
22	151 40.9	00.9	105 26.2	11.9	19 26.1	4.2	54.5
23	166 40.6	01.1	119 57.1	12.0	S19 21.9	4.3	54.5

	SUN			MOON			
Day	Eqn. of Time		Mer.	Mer. Pass.		Age	Phase
	00ʰ	12ʰ	Pass.	Upper	Lower		
d	m s	m s	h m	h m	h m	d	%
9	08 03	07 50	11 52	13 07	00 43	02	2
10	07 37	07 23	11 53	13 56	01 32	03	6
11	07 09	06 56	11 53	14 44	02 20	04	11

| SD 16.3 | d 0.2 | SD 14.7 | 14.7 | 14.8 |

UT	ARIES GHA	VENUS −4.2 GHA	Dec	MARS +0.9 GHA	Dec	JUPITER −2.7 GHA	Dec	SATURN +0.0 GHA	Dec	STARS Name	SHA	Dec
12 00	80 15.1	224 44.0	S11 40.4	125 19.3	S18 25.7	56 27.1	N 8 27.2	40 42.5	N12 46.0	Acamar	315 26.0	S40 18.6
01	95 17.5	239 43.6	41.4	140 19.8	25.2	71 29.6	27.2	55 45.1	46.0	Achernar	335 34.3	S57 14.6
02	110 20.0	254 43.2	42.3	155 20.4	24.6	86 32.1	27.2	70 47.7	46.0	Acrux	173 21.3	S63 05.5
03	125 22.5	269 42.8 ..	43.3	170 20.9 ..	24.0	101 34.7 ..	27.2	85 50.3 ..	45.9	Adhara	255 20.4	S28 58.3
04	140 24.9	284 42.4	44.2	185 21.4	23.5	116 37.2	27.2	100 52.9	45.9	Aldebaran	291 01.1	N16 30.5
05	155 27.4	299 42.1	45.1	200 21.9	22.9	131 39.8	27.1	115 55.5	45.9			
06	170 29.9	314 41.7	S11 46.1	215 22.4	S18 22.3	146 42.3	N 8 27.1	130 58.1	N12 45.8	Alioth	166 30.2	N55 57.5
07	185 32.3	329 41.3	47.0	230 22.9	21.7	161 44.8	27.1	146 00.7	45.8	Alkaid	153 07.5	N49 18.7
08	200 34.8	344 40.9	48.0	245 23.5	21.2	176 47.4	27.1	161 03.3	45.8	Al Na'ir	27 57.1	S46 57.9
S 09	215 37.2	359 40.5 ..	48.9	260 24.0 ..	20.6	191 49.9 ..	27.1	176 05.9 ..	45.8	Alnilam	275 56.7	S 1 12.2
U 10	230 39.7	14 40.1	49.8	275 24.5	20.0	206 52.4	27.1	191 08.5	45.7	Alphard	218 06.2	S 8 39.4
N 11	245 42.2	29 39.8	50.8	290 25.0	19.5	221 55.0	27.1	206 11.1	45.7			
D 12	260 44.6	44 39.4	S11 51.7	305 25.5	S18 18.9	236 57.5	N 8 27.0	221 13.7	N12 45.7	Alphecca	126 20.3	N26 43.0
A 13	275 47.1	59 39.0	52.7	320 26.1	18.3	252 00.0	27.0	236 16.3	45.6	Alpheratz	357 54.3	N29 05.5
Y 14	290 49.6	74 38.6	53.6	335 26.6	17.7	267 02.6	27.0	251 18.9	45.6	Altair	62 18.8	N 8 52.2
15	305 52.0	89 38.2 ..	54.5	350 27.1 ..	17.2	282 05.1 ..	27.0	266 21.5 ..	45.6	Ankaa	353 26.0	S42 18.7
16	320 54.5	104 37.8	55.5	5 27.6	16.6	297 07.7	27.0	281 24.1	45.5	Antares	112 39.6	S26 25.7
17	335 57.0	119 37.4	56.4	20 28.2	16.0	312 10.2	27.0	296 26.7	45.5			
18	350 59.4	134 37.1	S11 57.3	35 28.7	S18 15.4	327 12.7	N 8 27.0	311 29.3	N12 45.5	Arcturus	146 05.6	N19 11.0
19	6 01.9	149 36.7	58.3	50 29.2	14.9	342 15.3	27.0	326 31.9	45.4	Atria	107 51.4	S69 01.5
20	21 04.4	164 36.3	11 59.2	65 29.7	14.3	357 17.8	26.9	341 34.5	45.4	Avior	234 21.8	S59 30.4
21	36 06.8	179 35.9	12 00.2	80 30.2 ..	13.7	12 20.3 ..	26.9	356 37.0 ..	45.4	Bellatrix	278 43.0	N 6 20.9
22	51 09.3	194 35.5	01.1	95 30.8	13.1	27 22.8	26.9	11 39.6	45.3	Betelgeuse	271 12.4	N 7 24.3
23	66 11.7	209 35.1	02.0	110 31.3	12.6	42 25.4	26.9	26 42.2	45.3			
13 00	81 14.2	224 34.7	S12 03.0	125 31.8	S18 12.0	57 27.9	N 8 26.9	41 44.8	N12 45.3	Canopus	264 00.3	S52 41.8
01	96 16.7	239 34.3	03.9	140 32.3	11.4	72 30.4	26.9	56 47.4	45.3	Capella	280 49.5	N45 59.8
02	111 19.1	254 33.9	04.8	155 32.9	10.8	87 33.0	26.9	71 50.0	45.2	Deneb	49 39.0	N45 17.0
03	126 21.6	269 33.5 ..	05.8	170 33.4 ..	10.2	102 35.5 ..	26.9	86 52.6 ..	45.2	Denebola	182 44.4	N14 34.4
04	141 24.1	284 33.2	06.7	185 33.9	09.7	117 38.0	26.8	101 55.2	45.2	Diphda	349 06.3	S17 59.4
05	156 26.5	299 32.8	07.6	200 34.4	09.1	132 40.6	26.8	116 57.8	45.1			
06	171 29.0	314 32.4	S12 08.6	215 35.0	S18 08.5	147 43.1	N 8 26.8	132 00.4	N12 45.1	Dubhe	194 04.5	N61 44.8
07	186 31.5	329 32.0	09.5	230 35.5	07.9	162 45.6	26.8	147 03.0	45.1	Elnath	278 25.5	N28 36.3
08	201 33.9	344 31.6	10.4	245 36.0	07.4	177 48.2	26.8	162 05.6	45.0	Eltanin	90 51.6	N51 29.5
M 09	216 36.4	359 31.2 ..	11.4	260 36.5 ..	06.8	192 50.7 ..	26.8	177 08.2 ..	45.0	Enif	33 57.6	N 9 52.5
O 10	231 38.9	14 30.8	12.3	275 37.0	06.2	207 53.2	26.8	192 10.8	45.0	Fomalhaut	15 35.6	S29 37.6
N 11	246 41.3	29 30.4	13.2	290 37.6	05.6	222 55.7	26.8	207 13.4	44.9			
D 12	261 43.8	44 30.0	S12 14.1	305 38.1	S18 05.0	237 58.3	N 8 26.8	222 16.0	N12 44.9	Gacrux	172 12.8	S57 06.4
A 13	276 46.2	59 29.6	15.1	320 38.6	04.4	253 00.8	26.7	237 18.6	44.9	Gienah	176 03.2	S17 32.3
Y 14	291 48.7	74 29.2	16.0	335 39.1	03.9	268 03.3	26.7	252 21.1	44.9	Hadar	149 03.3	S60 22.0
15	306 51.2	89 28.8 ..	16.9	350 39.7 ..	03.3	283 05.8 ..	26.7	267 23.7 ..	44.8	Hamal	328 12.4	N23 27.7
16	321 53.6	104 28.4	17.9	5 40.2	02.7	298 08.4	26.7	282 26.3	44.8	Kaus Aust.	83 58.2	S34 23.0
17	336 56.1	119 28.0	18.8	20 40.7	02.1	313 10.9	26.7	297 28.9	44.8			
18	351 58.6	134 27.6	S12 19.7	35 41.3	S18 01.5	328 13.4	N 8 26.7	312 31.5	N12 44.7	Kochab	137 20.6	N74 09.3
19	7 01.0	149 27.2	20.6	50 41.8	01.0	343 15.9	26.7	327 34.1	44.7	Markab	13 48.9	N15 12.3
20	22 03.5	164 26.8	21.6	65 42.3	18 00.4	358 18.5	26.7	342 36.7	44.7	Menkar	314 25.8	N 4 05.3
21	37 06.0	179 26.4 ..	22.5	80 42.8	17 59.8	13 21.0 ..	26.7	357 39.3 ..	44.6	Menkent	148 20.3	S36 21.9
22	52 08.4	194 26.0	23.4	95 43.4	59.2	28 23.5	26.7	12 41.9	44.6	Miaplacidus	221 41.3	S69 42.7
23	67 10.9	209 25.6	24.4	110 43.9	58.6	43 26.0	26.6	27 44.5	44.6			
14 00	82 13.3	224 25.2	S12 25.3	125 44.4	S17 58.0	58 28.6	N 8 26.6	42 47.1	N12 44.6	Mirfak	308 55.0	N49 51.7
01	97 15.8	239 24.8	26.2	140 44.9	57.5	73 31.1	26.6	57 49.7	44.5	Nunki	76 11.7	S26 17.8
02	112 18.3	254 24.4	27.1	155 45.5	56.9	88 33.6	26.6	72 52.2	44.5	Peacock	53 36.2	S56 44.3
03	127 20.7	269 24.0 ..	28.1	170 46.0 ..	56.3	103 36.1 ..	26.6	87 54.8 ..	44.5	Pollux	243 40.3	N28 01.5
04	142 23.2	284 23.6	29.0	185 46.5	55.7	118 38.7	26.6	102 57.4	44.4	Procyon	245 10.4	N 5 13.5
05	157 25.7	299 23.2	29.9	200 47.0	55.1	133 41.2	26.6	118 00.0	44.4			
06	172 28.1	314 22.8	S12 30.8	215 47.6	S17 54.5	148 43.7	N 8 26.6	133 02.6	N12 44.4	Rasalhague	96 16.6	N12 33.7
07	187 30.6	329 22.4	31.8	230 48.1	53.9	163 46.2	26.6	148 05.2	44.3	Regulus	207 54.6	N11 58.0
08	202 33.1	344 22.0	32.7	245 48.6	53.3	178 48.7	26.6	163 07.8	44.3	Rigel	281 21.8	S 8 12.2
T 09	217 35.5	359 21.6 ..	33.6	260 49.2 ..	52.8	193 51.3 ..	26.6	178 10.4 ..	44.3	Rigil Kent.	140 06.7	S60 49.7
U 10	232 38.0	14 21.1	34.5	275 49.7	52.2	208 53.8	26.5	193 13.0	44.2	Sabik	102 25.0	S15 43.3
E 11	247 40.5	29 20.7	35.4	290 50.2	51.6	223 56.3	26.5	208 15.6	44.2			
S D 12	262 42.9	44 20.3	S12 36.4	305 50.7	S17 51.0	238 58.8	N 8 26.5	223 18.1	N12 44.2	Schedar	349 52.3	N56 32.4
A 13	277 45.4	59 19.9	37.3	320 51.3	50.4	254 01.3	26.5	238 20.7	44.2	Shaula	96 36.6	S37 06.1
Y 14	292 47.8	74 19.5	38.2	335 51.8	49.8	269 03.9	26.5	253 23.3	44.1	Sirius	258 42.7	S16 43.0
15	307 50.3	89 19.1 ..	39.1	350 52.3 ..	49.2	284 06.4 ..	26.5	268 25.9 ..	44.1	Spica	158 42.5	S11 09.5
16	322 52.8	104 18.7	40.0	5 52.9	48.6	299 08.9	26.5	283 28.5	44.1	Suhail	222 59.9	S43 25.7
17	337 55.2	119 18.3	41.0	20 53.4	48.0	314 11.4	26.5	298 31.1	44.1			
18	352 57.7	134 17.9	S12 41.9	35 53.9	S17 47.5	329 13.9	N 8 26.5	313 33.7	N12 44.0	Vega	80 46.5	N38 47.2
19	8 00.2	149 17.5	42.8	50 54.5	46.9	344 16.4	26.5	328 36.3	44.0	Zuben'ubi	137 17.4	S16 02.3
20	23 02.6	164 17.0	43.7	65 55.0	46.3	359 19.0	26.5	343 38.9	44.0			
21	38 05.1	179 16.6 ..	44.6	80 55.5 ..	45.7	14 21.5 ..	26.5	358 41.4 ..	43.9		SHA	Mer. Pass.
22	53 07.6	194 16.2	45.6	95 56.0	45.1	29 24.0	26.5	13 44.0	43.9	Venus	143 20.5	9 02
23	68 10.0	209 15.8	46.5	110 56.6	44.5	44 26.5	26.5	28 46.6	43.9	Mars	44 17.6	15 37
	h m									Jupiter	336 13.7	20 07
Mer. Pass. 18 32.0	v −0.4 d 0.9			v 0.5 d 0.6		v 2.5 d 0.0		v 2.6 d 0.0		Saturn	320 30.6	21 09

UT	SUN GHA	SUN Dec	MOON GHA	v	MOON Dec	d	HP
d h	° ′	° ′	° ′	′	° ′	′	′
12 00	181 40.3	S23 01.3	134 28.1	11.9	S19 17.6	4.4	54.5
01	196 40.0	01.5	148 59.0	12.0	19 13.2	4.5	54.5
02	211 39.7	01.7	163 30.0	12.0	19 08.7	4.5	54.5
03	226 39.4	.. 01.9	178 01.0	12.0	19 04.2	4.7	54.6
04	241 39.1	02.1	192 32.0	12.0	18 59.5	4.7	54.6
05	256 38.9	02.3	207 03.0	12.1	18 54.8	4.8	54.6
06	271 38.6	S23 02.5	221 34.1	12.0	S18 50.0	5.0	54.6
07	286 38.3	02.7	236 05.1	12.1	18 45.0	5.0	54.6
08	301 38.0	02.9	250 36.2	12.1	18 40.0	5.1	54.6
S 09	316 37.7	.. 03.1	265 07.3	12.1	18 34.9	5.1	54.7
U 10	331 37.4	03.3	279 38.4	12.1	18 29.8	5.3	54.7
N 11	346 37.1	03.5	294 09.5	12.1	18 24.5	5.4	54.7
D 12	1 36.8	S23 03.7	308 40.6	12.1	S18 19.1	5.4	54.7
A 13	16 36.5	03.9	323 11.7	12.2	18 13.7	5.4	54.7
Y 14	31 36.2	04.1	337 42.9	12.2	18 08.1	5.6	54.7
15	46 35.9	.. 04.2	352 14.1	12.2	18 02.5	5.7	54.8
16	61 35.7	04.4	6 45.3	12.2	17 56.8	5.8	54.8
17	76 35.4	04.6	21 16.5	12.2	17 51.0	5.9	54.8
18	91 35.1	S23 04.8	35 47.7	12.3	S17 45.1	6.0	54.8
19	106 34.8	05.0	50 18.9	12.3	17 39.1	6.0	54.8
20	121 34.5	05.2	64 50.2	12.2	17 33.1	6.2	54.9
21	136 34.2	.. 05.4	79 21.4	12.3	17 26.9	6.2	54.9
22	151 33.9	05.5	93 52.7	12.3	17 20.7	6.3	54.9
23	166 33.6	05.7	108 24.0	12.4	17 14.4	6.4	54.9
13 00	181 33.3	S23 05.9	122 55.4	12.3	S17 08.0	6.5	54.9
01	196 33.0	06.1	137 26.7	12.3	17 01.5	6.5	55.0
02	211 32.7	06.3	151 58.0	12.4	16 55.0	6.7	55.0
03	226 32.4	.. 06.4	166 29.4	12.4	16 48.3	6.7	55.0
04	241 32.1	06.6	181 00.8	12.4	16 41.6	6.8	55.0
05	256 31.8	06.8	195 32.2	12.4	16 34.8	6.9	55.0
06	271 31.6	S23 07.0	210 03.6	12.4	S16 27.9	7.0	55.1
07	286 31.3	07.2	224 35.0	12.5	16 20.9	7.0	55.1
08	301 31.0	07.3	239 06.5	12.4	16 13.9	7.1	55.1
M 09	316 30.7	.. 07.5	253 37.9	12.5	16 06.8	7.3	55.1
O 10	331 30.4	07.7	268 09.4	12.5	15 59.5	7.2	55.1
N 11	346 30.1	07.8	282 40.9	12.5	15 52.3	7.4	55.2
D 12	1 29.8	S23 08.0	297 12.4	12.5	S15 44.9	7.5	55.2
A 13	16 29.5	08.2	311 43.9	12.5	15 37.4	7.5	55.2
Y 14	31 29.2	08.4	326 15.4	12.6	15 29.9	7.6	55.2
15	46 28.9	.. 08.5	340 47.0	12.5	15 22.3	7.7	55.3
16	61 28.6	08.7	355 18.5	12.6	15 14.6	7.7	55.3
17	76 28.3	08.9	9 50.1	12.6	15 06.9	7.8	55.3
18	91 28.0	S23 09.0	24 21.7	12.6	S14 59.1	7.9	55.3
19	106 27.7	09.2	38 53.3	12.6	14 51.2	8.0	55.4
20	121 27.4	09.4	53 24.9	12.6	14 43.2	8.1	55.4
21	136 27.1	.. 09.5	67 56.5	12.7	14 35.1	8.1	55.4
22	151 26.8	09.7	82 28.2	12.6	14 27.0	8.2	55.4
23	166 26.5	09.9	96 59.8	12.7	14 18.8	8.3	55.5
14 00	181 26.2	S23 10.0	111 31.5	12.7	S14 10.5	8.3	55.5
01	196 25.9	10.2	126 03.2	12.6	14 02.2	8.4	55.5
02	211 25.7	10.3	140 34.8	12.7	13 53.8	8.5	55.5
03	226 25.4	.. 10.5	155 06.5	12.7	13 45.3	8.6	55.6
04	241 25.1	10.7	169 38.2	12.7	13 36.7	8.6	55.6
05	256 24.8	10.8	184 09.9	12.8	13 28.1	8.7	55.6
06	271 24.5	S23 11.0	198 41.7	12.7	S13 19.4	8.8	55.6
07	286 24.2	11.1	213 13.4	12.7	13 10.6	8.8	55.7
T 08	301 23.9	11.3	227 45.1	12.8	13 01.8	8.9	55.7
U 09	316 23.6	.. 11.5	242 16.9	12.8	12 52.9	9.0	55.7
E 10	331 23.3	11.6	256 48.7	12.7	12 43.9	9.0	55.7
S 11	346 23.0	11.8	271 20.4	12.8	12 34.9	9.1	55.8
D 12	1 22.7	S23 11.9	285 52.2	12.8	S12 25.8	9.2	55.8
A 13	16 22.4	12.1	300 24.0	12.8	12 16.6	9.3	55.8
Y 14	31 22.1	12.2	314 55.8	12.8	12 07.3	9.3	55.9
15	46 21.8	.. 12.4	329 27.6	12.8	11 58.0	9.3	55.9
16	61 21.5	12.5	343 59.4	12.8	11 48.7	9.5	55.9
17	76 21.2	12.7	358 31.2	12.8	11 39.2	9.5	55.9
18	91 20.9	S23 12.8	13 03.0	12.8	S11 29.7	9.5	56.0
19	106 20.6	13.0	27 34.8	12.8	11 20.2	9.7	56.0
20	121 20.3	13.1	42 06.6	12.8	11 10.5	9.8	56.0
21	136 20.0	.. 13.3	56 38.4	12.8	11 00.9	9.8	56.1
22	151 19.7	13.4	71 10.2	12.8	10 51.1	9.8	56.1
23	166 19.4	13.5	85 42.0	12.9	S10 41.3	9.9	56.1
	SD 16.3	d 0.2	SD 14.9		15.0		15.2

Lat.	Twilight Naut.	Twilight Civil	Sunrise	Moonrise 12	13	14	15
°	h m	h m	h m	h m	h m	h m	h m
N 72	08 16	10 39	■	■	14 12	13 48	13 32
N 70	07 57	09 43	■	13 49	13 36	13 27	13 19
68	07 42	09 10	■	13 08	13 10	13 10	13 10
66	07 29	08 45	10 22	12 39	12 50	12 57	13 01
64	07 18	08 26	09 42	12 18	12 34	12 45	12 54
62	07 09	08 10	09 15	12 00	12 21	12 36	12 48
60	07 01	07 57	08 54	11 46	12 09	12 28	12 43
N 58	06 53	07 46	08 37	11 34	11 59	12 20	12 38
56	06 47	07 36	08 23	11 23	11 51	12 14	12 34
54	06 41	07 27	08 10	11 13	11 43	12 08	12 30
52	06 35	07 19	07 59	11 05	11 36	12 03	12 27
50	06 30	07 11	07 50	10 57	11 30	11 58	12 24
45	06 19	06 56	07 29	10 41	11 16	11 48	12 17
N 40	06 08	06 42	07 13	10 28	11 05	11 39	12 11
35	05 59	06 31	06 59	10 17	10 56	11 32	12 06
30	05 51	06 20	06 47	10 07	10 47	11 25	12 02
20	05 34	06 02	06 26	09 50	10 33	11 14	11 54
N 10	05 18	05 45	06 07	09 35	10 20	11 04	11 48
0	05 02	05 28	05 50	09 21	10 08	10 55	11 42
S 10	04 43	05 10	05 33	09 07	09 56	10 46	11 35
20	04 21	04 50	05 14	08 52	09 43	10 36	11 29
30	03 52	04 25	04 52	08 34	09 29	10 24	11 21
35	03 34	04 10	04 40	08 24	09 20	10 18	11 17
40	03 11	03 52	04 25	08 13	09 10	10 10	11 12
45	02 41	03 30	04 07	07 59	08 59	10 01	11 06
S 50	01 57	03 01	03 45	07 43	08 45	09 51	10 59
52	01 30	02 46	03 34	07 35	08 38	09 46	10 55
54	00 48	02 29	03 22	07 26	08 31	09 40	10 52
56	////	02 07	03 08	07 16	08 23	09 34	10 48
58	////	01 39	02 52	07 05	08 14	09 27	10 43
S 60	////	00 54	02 32	06 52	08 04	09 20	10 38

Lat.	Sunset	Twilight Civil	Twilight Naut.	Moonset 12	13	14	15
°	h m	h m	h m	h m	h m	h m	h m
N 72	■	13 09	15 31	■	18 42	20 43	22 37
N 70	■	14 05	15 51	17 25	19 17	21 03	22 47
68	■	14 38	16 06	18 06	19 41	21 18	22 55
66	13 26	15 03	16 19	18 33	20 00	21 30	23 02
64	14 05	15 22	16 30	18 54	20 16	21 40	23 08
62	14 33	15 37	16 39	19 11	20 28	21 49	23 13
60	14 54	15 51	16 47	19 25	20 39	21 57	23 17
N 58	15 11	16 02	16 54	19 37	20 48	22 03	23 21
56	15 25	16 12	17 01	19 47	20 56	22 09	23 24
54	15 37	16 21	17 07	19 56	21 04	22 14	23 27
52	15 48	16 29	17 13	20 05	21 10	22 19	23 29
50	15 58	16 36	17 18	20 12	21 16	22 23	23 32
45	16 18	16 52	17 29	20 27	21 28	22 32	23 37
N 40	16 35	17 06	17 40	20 40	21 39	22 39	23 42
35	16 49	17 17	17 49	20 51	21 48	22 46	23 45
30	17 01	17 28	17 57	21 00	21 55	22 51	23 49
20	17 22	17 46	18 14	21 16	22 08	23 01	23 54
N 10	17 41	18 03	18 30	21 30	22 20	23 09	23 59
0	17 58	18 20	18 46	21 44	22 31	23 17	24 04
S 10	18 15	18 38	19 05	21 57	22 41	23 25	24 08
20	18 34	18 58	19 28	22 10	22 53	23 33	24 13
30	18 56	19 23	19 56	22 26	23 06	23 43	24 19
35	19 08	19 38	20 15	22 35	23 13	23 48	24 22
40	19 23	19 56	20 38	22 46	23 21	23 54	24 25
45	19 41	20 18	21 08	22 58	23 31	24 01	00 01
S 50	20 03	20 48	21 52	23 13	23 43	24 10	00 10
52	20 14	21 02	22 19	23 20	23 48	24 14	00 14
54	20 26	21 20	23 01	23 27	23 54	24 18	00 18
56	20 40	21 42	////	23 36	24 01	00 01	00 22
58	20 57	22 10	////	23 45	24 08	00 08	00 28
S 60	21 17	22 57	////	23 56	24 17	00 17	00 34

	SUN			MOON			
Day	Eqn. of Time 00h	12h	Mer. Pass.	Mer. Pass. Upper	Lower	Age	Phase
d	m s	m s	h m	h m	h m	d	%
12	06 42	06 28	11 54	15 32	03 08	05	18
13	06 14	06 00	11 54	16 19	03 56	06	26
14	05 46	05 31	11 54	17 06	04 43	07	35

UT	ARIES GHA	VENUS −4.1 GHA	Dec	MARS +1.0 GHA	Dec	JUPITER −2.7 GHA	Dec	SATURN +0.0 GHA	Dec	STARS Name	SHA	Dec
15 00	83 12.5	224 15.4	S12 47.4	125 57.1	S17 43.9	59 29.0	N 8 26.5	43 49.2	N12 43.9	Acamar	315 26.0	S40 18.6
01	98 15.0	239 15.0	48.3	140 57.6	43.3	74 31.5	26.4	58 51.8	43.8	Achernar	335 34.3	S57 14.6
02	113 17.4	254 14.6	49.2	155 58.2	42.7	89 34.1	26.4	73 54.4	43.8	Acrux	173 21.2	S63 05.5
03	128 19.9	269 14.1 ..	50.1	170 58.7 ..	42.1	104 36.6 ..	26.4	88 57.0 ..	43.8	Adhara	255 20.4	S28 58.3
04	143 22.3	284 13.7	51.1	185 59.2	41.5	119 39.1	26.4	103 59.6	43.7	Aldebaran	291 01.1	N16 30.5
05	158 24.8	299 13.3	52.0	200 59.8	40.9	134 41.6	26.4	119 02.1	43.7			
W 06	173 27.3	314 12.9	S12 52.9	216 00.3	S17 40.4	149 44.1	N 8 26.4	134 04.7	N12 43.7	Alioth	166 30.1	N55 57.5
E 07	188 29.7	329 12.5	53.8	231 00.8	39.8	164 46.6	26.4	149 07.3	43.7	Alkaid	153 07.5	N49 18.7
D 08	203 32.2	344 12.1	54.7	246 01.4	39.2	179 49.1	26.4	164 09.9	43.6	Al Na'ir	27 57.1	S46 57.9
N 09	218 34.7	359 11.6 ..	55.6	261 01.9 ..	38.6	194 51.7 ..	26.4	179 12.5 ..	43.6	Alnilam	275 56.7	S 1 12.2
E 10	233 37.1	14 11.2	56.5	276 02.4	38.0	209 54.2	26.4	194 15.1	43.6	Alphard	218 06.2	S 8 39.4
S 11	248 39.6	29 10.8	57.5	291 03.0	37.4	224 56.7	26.4	209 17.7	43.5			
D 12	263 42.1	44 10.4	S12 58.4	306 03.5	S17 36.8	239 59.2	N 8 26.4	224 20.2	N12 43.5	Alphecca	126 20.3	N26 43.0
A 13	278 44.5	59 10.0	12 59.3	321 04.0	36.2	255 01.7	26.4	239 22.8	43.5	Alpheratz	357 54.3	N29 05.5
Y 14	293 47.0	74 09.5	13 00.2	336 04.6	35.6	270 04.2	26.4	254 25.4	43.5	Altair	62 18.8	N 8 52.2
15	308 49.4	89 09.1 ..	01.1	351 05.1 ..	35.0	285 06.7 ..	26.4	269 28.0 ..	43.4	Ankaa	353 26.0	S42 18.7
16	323 51.9	104 08.7	02.0	6 05.6	34.4	300 09.2	26.4	284 30.6	43.4	Antares	112 39.5	S26 25.7
17	338 54.4	119 08.3	02.9	21 06.2	33.8	315 11.7	26.4	299 33.2	43.4			
18	353 56.8	134 07.8	S13 03.8	36 06.7	S17 33.2	330 14.2	N 8 26.4	314 35.8	N12 43.4	Arcturus	146 05.6	N19 11.0
19	8 59.3	149 07.4	04.7	51 07.2	32.6	345 16.8	26.4	329 38.3	43.3	Atria	107 51.4	S69 01.5
20	24 01.8	164 07.0	05.7	66 07.8	32.0	0 19.3	26.4	344 40.9	43.3	Avior	234 21.8	S59 30.4
21	39 04.2	179 06.6 ..	06.6	81 08.3 ..	31.4	15 21.8 ..	26.4	359 43.5 ..	43.3	Bellatrix	278 43.0	N 6 20.9
22	54 06.7	194 06.1	07.5	96 08.8	30.8	30 24.3	26.4	14 46.1	43.2	Betelgeuse	271 12.3	N 7 24.3
23	69 09.2	209 05.7	08.4	111 09.4	30.2	45 26.8	26.4	29 48.7	43.2			
16 00	84 11.6	224 05.3	S13 09.3	126 09.9	S17 29.6	60 29.3	N 8 26.4	44 51.3	N12 43.2	Canopus	264 00.3	S52 41.8
01	99 14.1	239 04.9	10.2	141 10.5	29.0	75 31.8	26.3	59 53.9	43.2	Capella	280 49.5	N45 59.8
02	114 16.6	254 04.4	11.1	156 11.0	28.4	90 34.3	26.3	74 56.4	43.1	Deneb	49 39.0	N45 17.0
03	129 19.0	269 04.0 ..	12.0	171 11.5 ..	27.8	105 36.8 ..	26.3	89 59.0 ..	43.1	Denebola	182 44.4	N14 34.4
04	144 21.5	284 03.6	12.9	186 12.1	27.2	120 39.3	26.3	105 01.6	43.1	Diphda	349 06.3	S17 59.4
05	159 23.9	299 03.1	13.8	201 12.6	26.6	135 41.8	26.3	120 04.2	43.1			
T 06	174 26.4	314 02.7	S13 14.7	216 13.1	S17 26.0	150 44.3	N 8 26.3	135 06.8	N12 43.0	Dubhe	194 04.5	N61 44.8
H 07	189 28.9	329 02.3	15.6	231 13.7	25.4	165 46.8	26.3	150 09.4	43.0	Elnath	278 25.5	N28 36.4
U 08	204 31.3	344 01.8	16.5	246 14.2	24.8	180 49.3	26.3	165 11.9	43.0	Eltanin	90 51.6	N51 29.5
R 09	219 33.8	359 01.4 ..	17.4	261 14.7 ..	24.2	195 51.8 ..	26.3	180 14.5 ..	42.9	Enif	33 57.6	N 9 52.5
S 10	234 36.3	14 01.0	18.3	276 15.3	23.6	210 54.3	26.3	195 17.1	42.9	Fomalhaut	15 35.6	S29 37.6
D 11	249 38.7	29 00.5	19.2	291 15.8	23.0	225 56.8	26.3	210 19.7	42.9			
A 12	264 41.2	44 00.1	S13 20.1	306 16.4	S17 22.4	240 59.4	N 8 26.3	225 22.3	N12 42.9	Gacrux	172 12.8	S57 06.4
Y 13	279 43.7	58 59.7	21.1	321 16.9	21.8	256 01.9	26.3	240 24.8	42.8	Gienah	176 03.2	S17 32.3
14	294 46.1	73 59.2	22.0	336 17.4	21.2	271 04.4	26.3	255 27.4	42.8	Hadar	149 03.3	S60 22.0
15	309 48.6	88 58.8 ..	22.9	351 18.0 ..	20.6	286 06.9 ..	26.3	270 30.0 ..	42.8	Hamal	328 12.4	N23 27.7
16	324 51.1	103 58.4	23.8	6 18.5	20.0	301 09.4	26.3	285 32.6	42.8	Kaus Aust.	83 58.2	S34 23.0
17	339 53.5	118 57.9	24.7	21 19.0	19.4	316 11.9	26.3	300 35.2	42.7			
18	354 56.0	133 57.5	S13 25.6	36 19.6	S17 18.8	331 14.4	N 8 26.3	315 37.8	N12 42.7	Kochab	137 20.6	N74 09.3
19	9 58.4	148 57.1	26.5	51 20.1	18.2	346 16.9	26.3	330 40.3	42.7	Markab	13 48.9	N15 12.3
20	25 00.9	163 56.6	27.4	66 20.7	17.6	1 19.4	26.3	345 42.9	42.7	Menkar	314 25.8	N 4 05.3
21	40 03.4	178 56.2 ..	28.3	81 21.2 ..	17.0	16 21.9 ..	26.3	0 45.5 ..	42.6	Menkent	148 20.3	S36 21.9
22	55 05.8	193 55.8	29.2	96 21.7	16.3	31 24.4	26.3	15 48.1	42.6	Miaplacidus	221 41.3	S69 42.7
23	70 08.3	208 55.3	30.1	111 22.3	15.7	46 26.9	26.3	30 50.7	42.6			
17 00	85 10.8	223 54.9	S13 30.9	126 22.8	S17 15.1	61 29.4	N 8 26.3	45 53.2	N12 42.6	Mirfak	308 55.0	N49 51.7
01	100 13.2	238 54.4	31.8	141 23.4	14.5	76 31.9	26.3	60 55.8	42.5	Nunki	76 11.7	S26 17.8
02	115 15.7	253 54.0	32.7	156 23.9	13.9	91 34.4	26.3	75 58.4	42.5	Peacock	53 36.2	S56 44.3
03	130 18.2	268 53.6 ..	33.6	171 24.4 ..	13.3	106 36.9 ..	26.3	91 01.0 ..	42.5	Pollux	243 40.3	N28 01.5
04	145 20.6	283 53.1	34.5	186 25.0	12.7	121 39.4	26.3	106 03.6	42.4	Procyon	245 10.4	N 5 13.5
05	160 23.1	298 52.7	35.4	201 25.5	12.1	136 41.8	26.3	121 06.1	42.4			
F 06	175 25.5	313 52.2	S13 36.3	216 26.1	S17 11.5	151 44.3	N 8 26.3	136 08.7	N12 42.4	Rasalhague	96 16.6	N12 33.7
R 07	190 28.0	328 51.8	37.2	231 26.6	10.9	166 46.8	26.3	151 11.3	42.4	Regulus	207 54.6	N11 58.0
I 08	205 30.5	343 51.3	38.1	246 27.2	10.3	181 49.3	26.3	166 13.9	42.3	Rigel	281 21.8	S 8 12.2
D 09	220 32.9	358 50.9 ..	39.0	261 27.7 ..	09.7	196 51.8 ..	26.3	181 16.4 ..	42.3	Rigil Kent.	140 06.7	S60 49.7
A 10	235 35.4	13 50.5	39.9	276 28.2	09.1	211 54.3	26.3	196 19.0	42.3	Sabik	102 25.0	S15 43.3
Y 11	250 37.9	28 50.0	40.8	291 28.8	08.4	226 56.8	26.3	211 21.6	42.3			
12	265 40.3	43 49.6	S13 41.7	306 29.3	S17 07.8	241 59.3	N 8 26.3	226 24.2	N12 42.2	Schedar	349 52.4	N56 32.4
13	280 42.8	58 49.1	42.6	321 29.9	07.2	257 01.8	26.3	241 26.8	42.2	Shaula	96 36.6	S37 06.1
14	295 45.3	73 48.7	43.5	336 30.4	06.6	272 04.3	26.3	256 29.3	42.2	Sirius	258 42.7	S16 43.0
15	310 47.7	88 48.2 ..	44.4	351 30.9 ..	06.0	287 06.8 ..	26.3	271 31.9 ..	42.2	Spica	158 42.5	S11 09.5
16	325 50.2	103 47.8	45.3	6 31.5	05.4	302 09.3	26.3	286 34.5	42.1	Suhail	222 59.9	S43 25.7
17	340 52.7	118 47.3	46.1	21 32.0	04.8	317 11.8	26.4	301 37.1	42.1			
18	355 55.1	133 46.9	S13 47.0	36 32.6	S17 04.2	332 14.3	N 8 26.4	316 39.7	N12 42.1	Vega	80 46.5	N38 47.2
19	10 57.6	148 46.4	47.9	51 33.1	03.6	347 16.8	26.4	331 42.2	42.1	Zuben'ubi	137 17.3	S16 02.3
20	26 00.0	163 46.0	48.8	66 33.7	02.9	2 19.3	26.4	346 44.8	42.0		SHA	Mer. Pass.
21	41 02.5	178 45.5 ..	49.7	81 34.2 ..	02.3	17 21.8 ..	26.4	1 47.4 ..	42.0			h m
22	56 05.0	193 45.1	50.6	96 34.8	01.7	32 24.2	26.4	16 50.0	42.0	Venus	139 53.7	9 04
23	71 07.4	208 44.6	51.5	111 35.3	01.1	47 26.7	26.4	31 52.5	42.0	Mars	41 58.3	15 35
Mer. Pass. 18 20.2		v −0.4	d 0.9	v 0.5	d 0.6	v 2.5	d 0.0	v 2.6	d 0.0	Jupiter	336 17.7	19 55
										Saturn	320 39.6	20 57

UT	SUN GHA	SUN Dec	MOON GHA	v	MOON Dec	d	HP
	° ′	° ′	° ′	′	° ′	′	′
15 00	181 19.1	S23 13.7	100 13.9	12.8	S10 31.4	9.9	56.2
01	196 18.8	13.8	114 45.7	12.8	10 21.5	10.0	56.2
02	211 18.5	14.0	129 17.5	12.8	10 11.5	10.0	56.2
03	226 18.2	.. 14.1	143 49.3	12.8	10 01.5	10.1	56.2
04	241 17.9	14.2	158 21.1	12.8	9 51.4	10.2	56.3
05	256 17.6	14.4	172 52.9	12.9	9 41.2	10.2	56.3
W 06	271 17.3	S23 14.5	187 24.8	12.8	S 9 31.0	10.3	56.3
E 07	286 17.0	14.7	201 56.6	12.8	9 20.7	10.3	56.4
D 08	301 16.7	14.8	216 28.4	12.8	9 10.4	10.4	56.4
N 09	316 16.4	.. 14.9	231 00.2	12.8	9 00.0	10.4	56.4
E 10	331 16.1	15.1	245 32.0	12.8	8 49.6	10.5	56.5
S 11	346 15.8	15.2	260 03.8	12.7	8 39.1	10.5	56.5
D 12	1 15.5	S23 15.3	274 35.5	12.8	S 8 28.6	10.6	56.5
A 13	16 15.2	15.5	289 07.3	12.8	8 18.0	10.7	56.6
Y 14	31 14.9	15.6	303 39.1	12.7	8 07.3	10.7	56.6
15	46 14.6	.. 15.7	318 10.8	12.8	7 56.6	10.7	56.6
16	61 14.3	15.9	332 42.6	12.7	7 45.9	10.8	56.7
17	76 14.0	16.0	347 14.3	12.8	7 35.1	10.8	56.7
18	91 13.7	S23 16.1	1 46.1	12.7	S 7 24.3	10.9	56.7
19	106 13.4	16.3	16 17.8	12.7	7 13.4	11.0	56.8
20	121 13.1	16.4	30 49.5	12.7	7 02.4	10.9	56.8
21	136 12.8	.. 16.5	45 21.2	12.6	6 51.5	11.1	56.8
22	151 12.5	16.6	59 52.8	12.7	6 40.4	11.1	56.9
23	166 12.2	16.8	74 24.5	12.7	6 29.3	11.1	56.9
16 00	181 11.9	S23 16.9	88 56.2	12.6	S 6 18.2	11.1	56.9
01	196 11.6	17.0	103 27.8	12.6	6 07.1	11.3	57.0
02	211 11.3	17.1	117 59.4	12.6	5 55.8	11.2	57.0
03	226 11.0	.. 17.2	132 31.0	12.6	5 44.6	11.3	57.1
04	241 10.7	17.4	147 02.6	12.5	5 33.3	11.3	57.1
05	256 10.4	17.5	161 34.1	12.6	5 22.0	11.4	57.1
T 06	271 10.1	S23 17.6	176 05.7	12.5	S 5 10.6	11.4	57.2
H 07	286 09.8	17.7	190 37.2	12.5	4 59.2	11.5	57.2
U 08	301 09.5	17.8	205 08.7	12.5	4 47.7	11.5	57.2
R 09	316 09.2	.. 18.0	219 40.2	12.4	4 36.2	11.5	57.3
S 10	331 08.9	18.1	234 11.6	12.4	4 24.7	11.6	57.3
D 11	346 08.6	18.2	248 43.0	12.4	4 13.1	11.6	57.3
A 12	1 08.3	S23 18.3	263 14.4	12.4	S 4 01.5	11.6	57.4
Y 13	16 08.0	18.4	277 45.8	12.3	3 49.9	11.7	57.4
14	31 07.7	18.5	292 17.1	12.4	3 38.2	11.7	57.5
15	46 07.4	.. 18.6	306 48.5	12.3	3 26.5	11.7	57.5
16	61 07.1	18.8	321 19.8	12.2	3 14.8	11.8	57.5
17	76 06.8	18.9	335 51.0	12.2	3 03.0	11.8	57.6
18	91 06.5	S23 19.0	350 22.2	12.2	S 2 51.2	11.8	57.6
19	106 06.1	19.1	4 53.4	12.2	2 39.4	11.9	57.6
20	121 05.8	19.2	19 24.6	12.1	2 27.5	11.8	57.7
21	136 05.5	.. 19.3	33 55.7	12.1	2 15.7	12.0	57.7
22	151 05.2	19.4	48 26.8	12.1	2 03.7	11.9	57.8
23	166 04.9	19.5	62 57.9	12.0	1 51.8	12.0	57.8
17 00	181 04.6	S23 19.6	77 28.9	12.0	S 1 39.8	12.0	57.8
01	196 04.3	19.7	91 59.9	12.0	1 27.8	12.0	57.9
02	211 04.0	19.8	106 30.9	11.9	1 15.8	12.0	57.9
03	226 03.7	.. 19.9	121 01.8	11.9	1 03.8	12.1	58.0
04	241 03.4	20.0	135 32.7	11.8	0 51.7	12.0	58.0
05	256 03.1	20.1	150 03.5	11.8	0 39.7	12.1	58.0
F 06	271 02.8	S23 20.2	164 34.3	11.8	S 0 27.6	12.2	58.1
R 07	286 02.5	20.3	179 05.1	11.7	0 15.4	12.1	58.1
I 08	301 02.2	20.4	193 35.8	11.7	S 0 03.3	12.2	58.1
D 09	316 01.9	.. 20.5	208 06.5	11.6	N 0 08.9	12.1	58.2
A 10	331 01.6	20.6	222 37.1	11.6	0 21.0	12.2	58.2
Y 11	346 01.3	20.7	237 07.7	11.5	0 33.2	12.2	58.3
12	1 01.0	S23 20.8	251 38.2	11.5	N 0 45.4	12.2	58.3
13	16 00.7	20.9	266 08.7	11.4	0 57.6	12.3	58.3
14	31 00.4	21.0	280 39.1	11.4	1 09.9	12.2	58.4
15	46 00.1	.. 21.1	295 09.5	11.3	1 22.1	12.2	58.4
16	60 59.8	21.2	309 39.8	11.3	1 34.3	12.3	58.5
17	75 59.5	21.3	324 10.1	11.2	1 46.6	12.3	58.5
18	90 59.2	S23 21.4	338 40.3	11.2	N 1 58.9	12.2	58.5
19	105 58.8	21.4	353 10.5	11.1	2 11.1	12.3	58.6
20	120 58.5	21.5	7 40.6	11.1	2 23.4	12.3	58.6
21	135 58.2	.. 21.6	22 10.7	11.0	2 35.7	12.3	58.7
22	150 57.9	21.7	36 40.7	11.0	2 48.0	12.3	58.7
23	165 57.6	21.8	51 10.7	10.9	N 3 00.3	12.2	58.7
	SD 16.3	d 0.1	SD 15.4		15.6		15.9

Twilight / Sunrise / Moonrise

Lat.	Twilight Naut.	Civil	Sunrise	Moonrise 15	16	17	18
°	h m	h m	h m	h m	h m	h m	h m
N 72	08 21	10 48	■	13 32	13 18	13 05	12 52
N 70	08 01	09 48	■	13 19	13 13	13 06	13 00
68	07 45	09 14	■	13 10	13 09	13 07	13 07
66	07 32	08 49	10 28	13 01	13 05	13 08	13 12
64	07 21	08 30	09 47	12 54	13 02	13 09	13 17
62	07 12	08 14	09 19	12 48	12 59	13 09	13 21
60	07 04	08 00	08 58	12 43	12 57	13 10	13 24
N 58	06 56	07 49	08 40	12 38	12 54	13 10	13 27
56	06 49	07 38	08 26	12 34	12 53	13 11	13 30
54	06 43	07 29	08 13	12 30	12 51	13 11	13 33
52	06 38	07 21	08 02	12 27	12 49	13 12	13 35
50	06 32	07 14	07 52	12 24	12 48	13 12	13 37
45	06 21	06 58	07 32	12 17	12 45	13 13	13 42
N 40	06 10	06 44	07 15	12 11	12 42	13 13	13 46
35	06 01	06 33	07 01	12 06	12 40	13 14	13 49
30	05 52	06 22	06 49	12 02	12 38	13 14	13 52
20	05 36	06 03	06 27	11 54	12 34	13 15	13 58
N 10	05 20	05 46	06 09	11 48	12 31	13 16	14 02
0	05 03	05 29	05 52	11 42	12 28	13 17	14 07
S 10	04 44	05 11	05 34	11 35	12 26	13 17	14 11
20	04 22	04 51	05 15	11 29	12 23	13 18	14 16
30	03 53	04 26	04 53	11 21	12 19	13 19	14 22
35	03 34	04 11	04 40	11 17	12 17	13 20	14 25
40	03 11	03 53	04 25	11 12	12 15	13 20	14 28
45	02 41	03 30	04 08	11 06	12 12	13 21	14 33
S 50	01 56	03 01	03 45	10 59	12 09	13 22	14 38
52	01 28	02 46	03 34	10 55	12 08	13 22	14 40
54	00 44	02 28	03 22	10 52	12 06	13 23	14 43
56	////	02 06	03 08	10 48	12 04	13 23	14 46
58	////	01 37	02 51	10 43	12 02	13 24	14 49
S 60	////	00 49	02 31	10 38	12 00	13 25	14 53

Sunset / Twilight / Moonset

Lat.	Sunset	Twilight Civil	Naut.	Moonset 15	16	17	18
°	h m	h m	h m	h m	h m	h m	h m
N 72	■	13 02	15 30	22 37	24 30	00 30	02 26
N 70	■	14 02	15 50	22 47	24 32	00 32	02 21
68	■	14 37	16 05	22 55	24 34	00 34	02 17
66	13 23	15 02	16 18	23 02	24 36	00 36	02 13
64	14 04	15 21	16 29	23 08	24 37	00 37	02 10
62	14 32	15 37	16 39	23 13	24 39	00 39	02 08
60	14 53	15 51	16 47	23 17	24 40	00 40	02 06
N 58	15 10	16 02	16 55	23 21	24 41	00 41	02 04
56	15 25	16 12	17 01	23 24	24 41	00 41	02 02
54	15 38	16 21	17 08	23 27	24 42	00 42	02 00
52	15 49	16 29	17 13	23 29	24 43	00 43	01 59
50	15 59	16 37	17 18	23 32	24 43	00 43	01 58
45	16 19	16 53	17 30	23 37	24 45	00 45	01 55
N 40	16 36	17 06	17 40	23 42	24 46	00 46	01 52
35	16 50	17 18	17 50	23 45	24 47	00 47	01 50
30	17 02	17 29	17 58	23 49	24 47	00 47	01 49
20	17 23	17 47	18 15	23 54	24 49	00 49	01 45
N 10	17 42	18 05	18 31	23 59	24 50	00 50	01 43
0	17 59	18 22	18 48	24 04	00 04	00 51	01 40
S 10	18 17	18 40	19 07	24 08	00 08	00 52	01 37
20	18 36	19 00	19 29	24 13	00 13	00 53	01 35
30	18 58	19 25	19 58	24 19	00 19	00 55	01 32
35	19 11	19 40	20 17	24 22	00 22	00 55	01 30
40	19 26	19 58	20 40	24 25	00 25	00 56	01 28
45	19 43	20 21	21 10	00 01	00 29	00 57	01 25
S 50	20 06	20 50	21 56	00 10	00 34	00 58	01 22
52	20 17	21 05	22 23	00 14	00 37	00 59	01 21
54	20 29	21 23	23 08	00 18	00 39	00 59	01 20
56	20 43	21 45	////	00 22	00 42	01 00	01 18
58	21 00	22 15	////	00 28	00 45	01 00	01 16
S 60	21 20	23 04	////	00 34	00 48	01 01	01 15

SUN / MOON

Day	Eqn. of Time 00h	12h	Mer. Pass.	Mer. Pass. Upper	Lower	Age	Phase
d	m s	m s	h m	h m	h m	d	%
15	05 17	05 03	11 55	17 53	05 29	08	45
16	04 48	04 34	11 55	18 40	06 16	09	55
17	04 19	04 05	11 56	19 28	07 04	10	66

UT	ARIES	VENUS −4.1		MARS +1.0		JUPITER −2.6		SATURN +0.1		STARS		
	GHA	GHA	Dec	GHA	Dec	GHA	Dec	GHA	Dec	Name	SHA	Dec
d h	° ′	° ′	° ′	° ′	° ′	° ′	° ′	° ′	° ′		° ′	° ′
18 00	86 09.9	223 44.2	S13 52.4	126 35.8	S17 00.5	62 29.2	N 8 26.4	46 55.1	N12 41.9	Acamar	315 26.0	S40 18.6
01	101 12.4	238 43.7	53.3	141 36.4	16 59.9	77 31.7	26.4	61 57.7	41.9	Achernar	335 34.3	S57 14.6
02	116 14.8	253 43.3	54.1	156 36.9	59.3	92 34.2	26.4	77 00.3	41.9	Acrux	173 21.2	S63 05.5
03	131 17.3	268 42.8	.. 55.0	171 37.5	.. 58.6	107 36.7	.. 26.4	92 02.8	.. 41.9	Adhara	255 20.4	S28 58.3
04	146 19.8	283 42.4	55.9	186 38.0	58.0	122 39.2	26.4	107 05.4	41.8	Aldebaran	291 01.1	N16 30.5
05	161 22.2	298 41.9	56.8	201 38.6	57.4	137 41.7	26.4	122 08.0	41.8			
06	176 24.7	313 41.4	S13 57.7	216 39.1	S16 56.8	152 44.2	N 8 26.4	137 10.6	N12 41.8	Alioth	166 30.1	N55 57.4
07	191 27.1	328 41.0	58.6	231 39.7	56.2	167 46.7	26.4	152 13.1	41.8	Alkaid	153 07.4	N49 18.7
S 08	206 29.6	343 40.5	13 59.4	246 40.2	55.6	182 49.1	26.4	167 15.7	41.8	Al Na'ir	27 57.1	S46 57.9
A 09	221 32.1	358 40.1	14 00.3	261 40.7	.. 55.0	197 51.6	.. 26.4	182 18.3	.. 41.7	Alnilam	275 56.7	S 1 12.2
T 10	236 34.5	13 39.6	01.2	276 41.3	54.3	212 54.1	26.4	197 20.9	41.7	Alphard	218 06.2	S 8 39.4
U 11	251 37.0	28 39.2	02.1	291 41.8	53.7	227 56.6	26.4	212 23.4	41.7			
R 12	266 39.5	43 38.7	S14 03.0	306 42.4	S16 53.1	242 59.1	N 8 26.4	227 26.0	N12 41.7	Alphecca	126 20.2	N26 42.9
D 13	281 41.9	58 38.2	03.9	321 42.9	52.5	258 01.6	26.4	242 28.6	41.6	Alpheratz	357 54.4	N29 05.5
A 14	296 44.4	73 37.8	04.7	336 43.5	51.9	273 04.1	26.4	257 31.2	41.6	Altair	62 18.8	N 8 52.2
Y 15	311 46.9	88 37.3	.. 05.6	351 44.0	.. 51.2	288 06.5	.. 26.4	272 33.7	.. 41.6	Ankaa	353 26.0	S42 18.7
16	326 49.3	103 36.9	06.5	6 44.6	50.6	303 09.0	26.5	287 36.3	41.6	Antares	112 39.5	S26 25.7
17	341 51.8	118 36.4	07.4	21 45.1	50.0	318 11.5	26.5	302 38.9	41.5			
18	356 54.3	133 35.9	S14 08.3	36 45.7	S16 49.4	333 14.0	N 8 26.5	317 41.5	N12 41.5	Arcturus	146 05.6	N19 11.0
19	11 56.7	148 35.5	09.1	51 46.2	48.8	348 16.5	26.5	332 44.0	41.5	Atria	107 51.4	S69 01.4
20	26 59.2	163 35.0	10.0	66 46.8	48.2	3 19.0	26.5	347 46.6	41.5	Avior	234 21.8	S59 30.4
21	42 01.6	178 34.6	.. 10.9	81 47.3	.. 47.5	18 21.5	.. 26.5	2 49.2	.. 41.4	Bellatrix	278 42.9	N 6 20.9
22	57 04.1	193 34.1	11.8	96 47.9	46.9	33 23.9	26.5	17 51.8	41.4	Betelgeuse	271 12.3	N 7 24.3
23	72 06.6	208 33.6	12.6	111 48.4	46.3	48 26.4	26.5	32 54.3	41.4			
19 00	87 09.0	223 33.2	S14 13.5	126 49.0	S16 45.7	63 28.9	N 8 26.5	47 56.9	N12 41.4	Canopus	264 00.2	S52 41.8
01	102 11.5	238 32.7	14.4	141 49.5	45.1	78 31.4	26.5	62 59.5	41.3	Capella	280 49.5	N45 59.8
02	117 14.0	253 32.2	15.3	156 50.1	44.4	93 33.9	26.5	78 02.0	41.3	Deneb	49 39.0	N45 17.0
03	132 16.4	268 31.8	.. 16.1	171 50.6	.. 43.8	108 36.3	.. 26.5	93 04.6	.. 41.3	Denebola	182 44.4	N14 34.3
04	147 18.9	283 31.3	17.0	186 51.2	43.2	123 38.8	26.5	108 07.2	41.3	Diphda	349 06.3	S17 59.4
05	162 21.4	298 30.8	17.9	201 51.7	42.6	138 41.3	26.5	123 09.8	41.3			
06	177 23.8	313 30.4	S14 18.8	216 52.3	S16 41.9	153 43.8	N 8 26.5	138 12.3	N12 41.2	Dubhe	194 04.4	N61 44.8
07	192 26.3	328 29.9	19.6	231 52.8	41.3	168 46.3	26.6	153 14.9	41.2	Elnath	278 25.5	N28 36.4
S 08	207 28.8	343 29.4	20.5	246 53.4	40.7	183 48.7	26.6	168 17.5	41.2	Eltanin	90 51.6	N51 29.4
U 09	222 31.2	358 29.0	.. 21.4	261 53.9	.. 40.1	198 51.2	.. 26.6	183 20.0	.. 41.2	Enif	33 57.6	N 9 52.5
N 10	237 33.7	13 28.5	22.3	276 54.5	39.5	213 53.7	26.6	198 22.6	41.1	Fomalhaut	15 35.7	S29 37.6
D 11	252 36.1	28 28.0	23.1	291 55.0	38.8	228 56.2	26.6	213 25.2	41.1			
A 12	267 38.6	43 27.5	S14 24.0	306 55.6	S16 38.2	243 58.7	N 8 26.6	228 27.8	N12 41.1	Gacrux	172 12.8	S57 06.4
Y 13	282 41.1	58 27.1	24.9	321 56.1	37.6	259 01.1	26.6	243 30.3	41.1	Gienah	176 03.2	S17 32.3
14	297 43.5	73 26.6	25.7	336 56.7	37.0	274 03.6	26.6	258 32.9	41.1	Hadar	149 03.2	S60 22.0
15	312 46.0	88 26.1	.. 26.6	351 57.2	.. 36.3	289 06.1	.. 26.6	273 35.5	.. 41.0	Hamal	328 12.4	N23 27.7
16	327 48.5	103 25.6	27.5	6 57.8	35.7	304 08.6	26.6	288 38.0	41.0	Kaus Aust.	83 58.2	S34 23.0
17	342 50.9	118 25.2	28.3	21 58.3	35.1	319 11.0	26.6	303 40.6	41.0			
18	357 53.4	133 24.7	S14 29.2	36 58.9	S16 34.5	334 13.5	N 8 26.6	318 43.2	N12 41.0	Kochab	137 20.6	N74 09.2
19	12 55.9	148 24.2	30.1	51 59.4	33.8	349 16.0	26.7	333 45.7	40.9	Markab	13 48.9	N15 12.3
20	27 58.3	163 23.7	30.9	67 00.0	33.2	4 18.5	26.7	348 48.3	40.9	Menkar	314 25.8	N 4 05.3
21	43 00.8	178 23.3	.. 31.8	82 00.5	.. 32.6	19 21.0	.. 26.7	3 50.9	.. 40.9	Menkent	148 20.2	S36 21.9
22	58 03.3	193 22.8	32.7	97 01.1	32.0	34 23.4	26.7	18 53.5	40.9	Miaplacidus	221 41.2	S69 42.8
23	73 05.7	208 22.3	33.5	112 01.6	31.3	49 25.9	26.7	33 56.0	40.9			
20 00	88 08.2	223 21.8	S14 34.4	127 02.2	S16 30.7	64 28.4	N 8 26.7	48 58.6	N12 40.8	Mirfak	308 55.0	N49 51.7
01	103 10.6	238 21.4	35.3	142 02.7	30.1	79 30.8	26.7	64 01.2	40.8	Nunki	76 11.7	S26 17.8
02	118 13.1	253 20.9	36.1	157 03.3	29.4	94 33.3	26.7	79 03.7	40.8	Peacock	53 36.3	S56 44.3
03	133 15.6	268 20.4	.. 37.0	172 03.9	.. 28.8	109 35.8	.. 26.7	94 06.3	.. 40.8	Pollux	243 40.2	N28 01.5
04	148 18.0	283 19.9	37.9	187 04.4	28.2	124 38.3	26.8	109 08.9	40.7	Procyon	245 10.4	N 5 13.4
05	163 20.5	298 19.4	38.7	202 05.0	27.6	139 40.7	26.8	124 11.4	40.7			
06	178 23.0	313 19.0	S14 39.6	217 05.5	S16 26.9	154 43.2	N 8 26.8	139 14.0	N12 40.7	Rasalhague	96 16.6	N12 33.7
07	193 25.4	328 18.5	40.4	232 06.1	26.3	169 45.7	26.8	154 16.6	40.7	Regulus	207 54.5	N11 58.0
08	208 27.9	343 18.0	41.3	247 06.6	25.7	184 48.2	26.8	169 19.1	40.7	Rigel	281 21.8	S 8 12.2
M 09	223 30.4	358 17.5	.. 42.2	262 07.2	.. 25.0	199 50.6	.. 26.8	184 21.7	.. 40.6	Rigil Kent.	140 06.7	S60 49.7
O 10	238 32.8	13 17.0	43.0	277 07.7	24.4	214 53.1	26.8	199 24.3	40.6	Sabik	102 25.0	S15 43.4
N 11	253 35.3	28 16.5	43.9	292 08.3	23.8	229 55.6	26.8	214 26.8	40.6			
D 12	268 37.7	43 16.1	S14 44.7	307 08.8	S16 23.1	244 58.0	N 8 26.8	229 29.4	N12 40.6	Schedar	349 52.4	N56 32.4
A 13	283 40.2	58 15.6	45.6	322 09.4	22.5	260 00.5	26.9	244 32.0	40.6	Shaula	96 36.6	S37 06.1
Y 14	298 42.7	73 15.1	46.4	337 10.0	21.9	275 03.0	26.9	259 34.5	40.5	Sirius	258 42.7	S16 43.0
15	313 45.1	88 14.6	.. 47.3	352 10.5	.. 21.3	290 05.4	.. 26.9	274 37.1	.. 40.5	Spica	158 42.5	S11 09.5
16	328 47.6	103 14.1	48.2	7 11.1	20.6	305 07.9	26.9	289 39.7	40.5	Suhail	222 59.9	S43 25.8
17	343 50.1	118 13.6	49.0	22 11.6	20.0	320 10.4	26.9	304 42.2	40.5			
18	358 52.5	133 13.1	S14 49.9	37 12.2	S16 19.4	335 12.9	N 8 26.9	319 44.8	N12 40.4	Vega	80 46.5	N38 47.1
19	13 55.0	148 12.7	50.7	52 12.7	18.7	350 15.3	26.9	334 47.4	40.4	Zuben'ubi	137 17.3	S16 02.3
20	28 57.5	163 12.2	51.6	67 13.3	18.1	5 17.8	26.9	349 49.9	40.4			
21	43 59.9	178 11.7	.. 52.4	82 13.9	.. 17.5	20 20.3	.. 27.0	4 52.5	.. 40.4		SHA	Mer. Pass.
22	59 02.4	193 11.2	53.3	97 14.4	16.8	35 22.7	27.0	19 55.1	40.4		° ′	h m
23	74 04.9	208 10.7	54.1	112 15.0	16.2	50 25.2	27.0	34 57.6	40.3	Venus	136 24.1	9 06
	h m									Mars	39 39.9	15 32
Mer. Pass. 18 08.4	v −0.5 d 0.9			v 0.6 d 0.6		v 2.5 d 0.0		v 2.6 d 0.0		Jupiter	336 19.9	19 43
										Saturn	320 47.9	20 45

UT	SUN GHA	SUN Dec	MOON GHA	v	MOON Dec	d	HP
d h	° ′	° ′	° ′	′	° ′	′	′
18 00	180 57.3	S23 21.9	65 40.6	10.8	N 3 12.5	12.3	58.8
01	195 57.0	22.0	80 10.4	10.8	3 24.8	12.3	58.8
02	210 56.7	22.0	94 40.2	10.7	3 37.1	12.3	58.9
03	225 56.4	.. 22.1	109 09.9	10.7	3 49.4	12.3	58.9
04	240 56.1	22.2	123 39.6	10.6	4 01.7	12.3	58.9
05	255 55.8	22.3	138 09.2	10.5	4 14.0	12.2	59.0
06	270 55.5	S23 22.4	152 38.7	10.5	N 4 26.2	12.3	59.0
07	285 55.2	22.4	167 08.2	10.4	4 38.5	12.3	59.1
S 08	300 54.9	22.5	181 37.6	10.3	4 50.8	12.2	59.1
A 09	315 54.6	.. 22.6	196 06.9	10.3	5 03.0	12.2	59.1
T 10	330 54.3	22.7	210 36.2	10.2	5 15.2	12.3	59.2
U 11	345 54.0	22.8	225 05.4	10.2	5 27.5	12.2	59.2
R 12	0 53.6	S23 22.8	239 34.6	10.0	N 5 39.7	12.2	59.2
D 13	15 53.3	22.9	254 03.6	10.0	5 51.9	12.1	59.3
A 14	30 53.0	23.0	268 32.6	9.9	6 04.0	12.2	59.3
Y 15	45 52.7	.. 23.1	283 01.5	9.9	6 16.2	12.1	59.4
16	60 52.4	23.1	297 30.4	9.8	6 28.3	12.2	59.4
17	75 52.1	23.2	311 59.2	9.7	6 40.5	12.1	59.4
18	90 51.8	S23 23.3	326 27.9	9.6	N 6 52.6	12.0	59.5
19	105 51.5	23.3	340 56.5	9.6	7 04.6	12.1	59.5
20	120 51.2	23.4	355 25.1	9.5	7 16.7	12.0	59.5
21	135 50.9	.. 23.5	9 53.6	9.4	7 28.7	12.0	59.6
22	150 50.6	23.5	24 22.0	9.3	7 40.7	12.0	59.6
23	165 50.3	23.6	38 50.3	9.3	7 52.7	11.9	59.7
19 00	180 50.0	S23 23.7	53 18.6	9.2	N 8 04.6	11.9	59.7
01	195 49.7	23.7	67 46.8	9.1	8 16.5	11.9	59.7
02	210 49.4	23.8	82 14.9	9.0	8 28.4	11.8	59.8
03	225 49.0	.. 23.9	96 42.9	8.9	8 40.2	11.8	59.8
04	240 48.7	23.9	111 10.8	8.9	8 52.0	11.8	59.8
05	255 48.4	24.0	125 38.7	8.7	9 03.8	11.7	59.9
06	270 48.1	S23 24.0	140 06.4		N 9 15.5	11.7	59.9
07	285 47.8	24.1	154 34.1	8.6	9 27.2	11.7	60.0
S 08	300 47.5	24.2	169 01.7	8.6	9 38.9	11.6	60.0
U 09	315 47.2	.. 24.2	183 29.3	8.4	9 50.5	11.5	60.0
N 10	330 46.9	24.3	197 56.7	8.4	10 02.0	11.5	60.1
D 11	345 46.6	24.3	212 24.1	8.2	10 13.5	11.5	60.1
A 12	0 46.3	S23 24.4	226 51.3	8.2	N10 25.0	11.4	60.1
Y 13	15 46.0	24.4	241 18.5	8.1	10 36.4	11.3	60.2
14	30 45.7	24.5	255 45.6	8.0	10 47.7	11.3	60.2
15	45 45.4	.. 24.6	270 12.6	8.0	10 59.0	11.3	60.2
16	60 45.1	24.6	284 39.6	7.8	11 10.3	11.2	60.3
17	75 44.7	24.7	299 06.4	7.8	11 21.5	11.1	60.3
18	90 44.4	S23 24.7	313 33.2	7.6	N11 32.6	11.1	60.3
19	105 44.1	24.8	327 59.8	7.6	11 43.7	11.0	60.4
20	120 43.8	24.8	342 26.4	7.5	11 54.7	10.9	60.4
21	135 43.5	.. 24.9	356 52.9	7.4	12 05.6	10.9	60.4
22	150 43.2	24.9	11 19.3	7.3	12 16.5	10.8	60.5
23	165 42.9	24.9	25 45.6	7.2	12 27.3	10.8	60.5
20 00	180 42.6	S23 25.0	40 11.8	7.1	N12 38.1	10.7	60.5
01	195 42.3	25.0	54 37.9	7.1	12 48.8	10.6	60.5
02	210 42.0	25.1	69 04.0	6.9	12 59.4	10.5	60.6
03	225 41.7	.. 25.1	83 29.9	6.9	13 09.9	10.5	60.6
04	240 41.3	25.2	97 55.8	6.7	13 20.4	10.4	60.6
05	255 41.0	25.2	112 21.5	6.7	13 30.8	10.3	60.7
06	270 40.7	S23 25.3	126 47.2	6.6	N13 41.1	10.2	60.7
07	285 40.4	25.3	141 12.8	6.5	13 51.3	10.1	60.7
M 08	300 40.1	25.3	155 38.3	6.4	14 01.4	10.1	60.7
O 09	315 39.8	.. 25.4	170 03.7	6.3	14 11.5	9.9	60.8
N 10	330 39.5	25.4	184 29.0	6.3	14 21.4	9.9	60.8
D 11	345 39.2	25.4	198 54.3	6.1	14 31.3	9.8	60.8
A 12	0 38.9	S23 25.5	213 19.4	6.1	N14 41.1	9.7	60.8
Y 13	15 38.6	25.5	227 44.5	5.9	14 50.8	9.6	60.9
14	30 38.3	25.6	242 09.4	5.9	15 00.4	9.6	60.9
15	45 38.0	.. 25.6	256 34.3	5.8	15 10.0	9.4	60.9
16	60 37.6	25.6	270 59.1	5.7	15 19.4	9.3	60.9
17	75 37.3	25.6	285 23.8	5.6	15 28.7	9.2	61.0
18	90 37.0	S23 25.7	299 48.4	5.5	N15 37.9	9.2	61.0
19	105 36.7	25.7	314 12.9	5.4	15 47.1	9.0	61.0
20	120 36.4	25.7	328 37.3	5.4	15 56.1	8.9	61.0
21	135 36.1	.. 25.8	343 01.7	5.2	16 05.0	8.8	61.1
22	150 35.8	25.8	357 25.9	5.2	16 13.8	8.7	61.1
23	165 35.5	25.8	11 50.1	5.1	N16 22.5	8.6	61.1
	SD 16.3	d 0.1	SD 16.1		16.4		16.6

Twilight / Sunrise / Moonrise

Lat.	Naut.	Civil	Sunrise	Moonrise 18	19	20	21
°	h m	h m	h m	h m	h m	h m	h m
N 72	08 24	10 55	■	12 52	12 37	12 15	11 16
N 70	08 04	09 52	■	13 00	12 53	12 45	12 33
68	07 48	09 17	■	13 07	13 06	13 08	13 12
66	07 35	08 52	10 33	13 12	13 17	13 25	13 39
64	07 24	08 32	09 50	13 17	13 26	13 40	14 00
62	07 14	08 16	09 22	13 21	13 34	13 52	14 17
60	07 06	08 03	09 00	13 24	13 41	14 02	14 32
N 58	06 58	07 51	08 43	13 27	13 47	14 11	14 44
56	06 52	07 41	08 28	13 30	13 52	14 19	14 55
54	06 45	07 32	08 15	13 33	13 57	14 27	15 04
52	06 40	07 23	08 04	13 35	14 02	14 33	15 12
50	06 34	07 16	07 54	13 37	14 06	14 39	15 20
45	06 23	07 00	07 34	13 42	14 14	14 52	15 36
N 40	06 12	06 46	07 17	13 46	14 22	15 02	15 49
35	06 03	06 35	07 03	13 49	14 28	15 11	16 01
30	05 54	06 24	06 50	13 52	14 33	15 19	16 11
20	05 38	06 05	06 29	13 58	14 43	15 33	16 28
N 10	05 21	05 48	06 11	14 02	14 52	15 45	16 43
0	05 04	05 31	05 53	14 07	15 00	15 57	16 57
S 10	04 45	05 12	05 36	14 11	15 08	16 08	17 11
20	04 23	04 52	05 17	14 16	15 17	16 21	17 27
30	03 54	04 27	04 55	14 22	15 27	16 35	17 44
35	03 35	04 12	04 42	14 25	15 33	16 43	17 55
40	03 12	03 54	04 26	14 28	15 39	16 53	18 07
45	02 41	03 31	04 08	14 33	15 47	17 04	18 21
S 50	01 56	03 01	03 46	14 38	15 57	17 18	18 38
52	01 28	02 46	03 35	14 40	16 01	17 24	18 46
54	00 42	02 28	03 23	14 43	16 06	17 31	18 55
56	////	02 06	03 09	14 46	16 11	17 39	19 05
58	////	01 36	02 52	14 49	16 17	17 48	19 17
S 60	////	00 46	02 31	14 53	16 24	17 58	19 30

Sunset / Twilight / Moonset

Lat.	Sunset	Civil	Naut.	Moonset 18	19	20	21
°	h m	h m	h m	h m	h m	h m	h m
N 72	■	12 59	15 30	02 26	04 30	06 48	09 53
N 70	■	14 01	15 50	02 21	04 16	06 20	08 36
68	13 21	14 36	16 06	02 17	04 05	05 59	07 58
66	13 21	15 02	16 19	02 13	03 55	05 42	07 32
64	14 03	15 21	16 30	02 10	03 48	05 29	07 11
62	14 32	15 38	16 40	02 08	03 41	05 18	06 55
60	14 53	15 51	16 48	02 06	03 35	05 08	06 41
N 58	15 11	16 03	16 55	02 04	03 30	05 00	06 30
56	15 26	16 13	17 02	02 02	03 26	04 52	06 19
54	15 38	16 22	17 08	02 00	03 22	04 46	06 11
52	15 49	16 30	17 14	01 59	03 18	04 40	06 03
50	15 59	16 38	17 19	01 58	03 15	04 35	05 55
45	16 20	16 54	17 31	01 55	03 08	04 23	05 40
N 40	16 37	17 07	17 42	01 52	03 02	04 14	05 28
35	16 51	17 19	17 51	01 50	02 57	04 06	05 17
30	17 03	17 30	18 00	01 49	02 52	03 59	05 08
20	17 25	17 49	18 16	01 45	02 45	03 47	04 52
N 10	17 43	18 06	18 32	01 43	02 38	03 36	04 38
0	18 01	18 23	18 49	01 40	02 31	03 26	04 25
S 10	18 18	18 41	19 08	01 37	02 25	03 16	04 12
20	18 37	19 02	19 31	01 35	02 18	03 06	03 58
30	18 59	19 27	20 00	01 32	02 11	02 54	03 42
35	19 12	19 42	20 19	01 30	02 06	02 47	03 33
40	19 27	20 00	20 42	01 28	02 01	02 39	03 23
45	19 45	20 23	21 13	01 25	01 56	02 30	03 11
S 50	20 08	20 53	21 58	01 22	01 49	02 19	02 56
52	20 19	21 08	22 26	01 21	01 46	02 14	02 49
54	20 31	21 26	23 13	01 20	01 42	02 09	02 41
56	20 45	21 48	////	01 18	01 38	02 02	02 33
58	21 02	22 18	////	01 16	01 34	01 56	02 23
S 60	21 23	23 09	////	01 15	01 30	01 48	02 12

SUN / MOON

Day	Eqn. of Time 00h	12h	Mer. Pass.	Mer. Pass. Upper	Lower	Age	Phase
d	m s	m s	h m	h m	h m	d	%
18	03 50	03 35	11 56	20 19	07 53	11	76
19	03 20	03 06	11 57	21 13	08 46	12	85
20	02 51	02 36	11 57	22 11	09 41	13	92

UT	ARIES	VENUS −4.1		MARS +1.0		JUPITER −2.6		SATURN +0.1		STARS		
d h	GHA	GHA	Dec	GHA	Dec	GHA	Dec	GHA	Dec	Name	SHA	Dec
21 00	89 07.3	223 10.2	S14 55.0	127 15.5	S16 15.6	65 27.7	N 8 27.0	50 00.2	N12 40.3	Acamar	315 26.0	S40 18.6
01	104 09.8	238 09.7	55.8	142 16.1	14.9	80 30.1	27.0	65 02.8	40.3	Achernar	335 34.3	S57 14.6
02	119 12.2	253 09.2	56.7	157 16.6	14.3	95 32.6	27.0	80 05.3	40.3	Acrux	173 21.1	S63 05.5
03	134 14.7	268 08.7 ..	57.5	172 17.2 ..	13.7	110 35.1 ..	27.0	95 07.9 ..	40.3	Adhara	255 20.4	S28 58.4
04	149 17.2	283 08.2	58.4	187 17.8	13.0	125 37.5	27.0	110 10.4	40.2	Aldebaran	291 01.1	N16 30.5
05	164 19.6	298 07.8	14 59.2	202 18.3	12.4	140 40.0	27.1	125 13.0	40.2			
06	179 22.1	313 07.3	S15 00.1	217 18.9	S16 11.7	155 42.4	N 8 27.1	140 15.6	N12 40.2	Alioth	166 30.1	N55 57.4
T 07	194 24.6	328 06.8	00.9	232 19.4	11.1	170 44.9	27.1	155 18.1	40.2	Alkaid	153 07.4	N49 18.7
U 08	209 27.0	343 06.3	01.8	247 20.0	10.5	185 47.4	27.1	170 20.7	40.2	Al Na'ir	27 57.1	S46 57.9
E 09	224 29.5	358 05.8 ..	02.6	262 20.6 ..	09.8	200 49.8 ..	27.1	185 23.3 ..	40.1	Alnilam	275 56.7	S 1 12.2
S 10	239 32.0	13 05.3	03.5	277 21.1	09.2	215 52.3	27.1	200 25.8	40.1	Alphard	218 06.2	S 8 39.5
D 11	254 34.4	28 04.8	04.3	292 21.7	08.6	230 54.8	27.1	215 28.4	40.1			
A 12	269 36.9	43 04.3	S15 05.2	307 22.2	S16 07.9	245 57.2	N 8 27.2	230 31.0	N12 40.1	Alphecca	126 20.2	N26 42.9
Y 13	284 39.4	58 03.8	06.0	322 22.8	07.3	260 59.7	27.2	245 33.5	40.1	Alpheratz	357 54.4	N29 05.5
14	299 41.8	73 03.3	06.9	337 23.4	06.7	276 02.1	27.2	260 36.1	40.0	Altair	62 18.8	N 8 52.2
15	314 44.3	88 02.8 ..	07.7	352 23.9 ..	06.0	291 04.6 ..	27.2	275 38.6 ..	40.0	Ankaa	353 26.0	S42 18.7
16	329 46.7	103 02.3	08.6	7 24.5	05.4	306 07.1	27.2	290 41.2	40.0	Antares	112 39.5	S26 25.7
17	344 49.2	118 01.8	09.4	22 25.0	04.7	321 09.5	27.2	305 43.8	40.0			
18	359 51.7	133 01.3	S15 10.2	37 25.6	S16 04.1	336 12.0	N 8 27.3	320 46.3	N12 40.0	Arcturus	146 05.5	N19 11.0
19	14 54.1	148 00.8	11.1	52 26.2	03.5	351 14.4	27.3	335 48.9	39.9	Atria	107 51.4	S69 01.4
20	29 56.6	163 00.3	11.9	67 26.7	02.8	6 16.9	27.3	350 51.4	39.9	Avior	234 21.7	S59 30.4
21	44 59.1	177 59.8 ..	12.8	82 27.3 ..	02.2	21 19.4 ..	27.3	5 54.0 ..	39.9	Bellatrix	278 42.9	N 6 20.9
22	60 01.5	192 59.3	13.6	97 27.8	01.5	36 21.8	27.3	20 56.6	39.9	Betelgeuse	271 12.3	N 7 24.3
23	75 04.0	207 58.8	14.4	112 28.4	00.9	51 24.3	27.3	35 59.1	39.9			
22 00	90 06.5	222 58.3	S15 15.3	127 29.0	S16 00.3	66 26.7	N 8 27.4	51 01.7	N12 39.8	Canopus	264 00.2	S52 41.8
01	105 08.9	237 57.8	16.1	142 29.5	15 59.6	81 29.2	27.4	66 04.3	39.8	Capella	280 49.5	N45 59.8
02	120 11.4	252 57.3	17.0	157 30.1	59.0	96 31.7	27.4	81 06.8	39.8	Deneb	49 39.0	N45 17.0
03	135 13.9	267 56.8 ..	17.8	172 30.7 ..	58.3	111 34.1 ..	27.4	96 09.4 ..	39.8	Denebola	182 44.4	N14 34.3
04	150 16.3	282 56.3	18.6	187 31.2	57.7	126 36.6	27.4	111 11.9	39.8	Diphda	349 06.4	S17 59.4
05	165 18.8	297 55.7	19.5	202 31.8	57.1	141 39.0	27.4	126 14.5	39.8			
06	180 21.2	312 55.2	S15 20.3	217 32.3	S15 56.4	156 41.5	N 8 27.5	141 17.1	N12 39.7	Dubhe	194 04.4	N61 44.8
W 07	195 23.7	327 54.7	21.1	232 32.9	55.8	171 43.9	27.5	156 19.6	39.7	Elnath	278 25.5	N28 36.4
E 08	210 26.2	342 54.2	22.0	247 33.5	55.1	186 46.4	27.5	171 22.2	39.7	Eltanin	90 51.6	N51 29.4
D 09	225 28.6	357 53.7 ..	22.8	262 34.0 ..	54.5	201 48.8 ..	27.5	186 24.7 ..	39.7	Enif	33 57.6	N 9 52.5
N 10	240 31.1	12 53.2	23.7	277 34.6	53.8	216 51.3	27.5	201 27.3	39.7	Fomalhaut	15 35.7	S29 37.6
E 11	255 33.6	27 52.7	24.5	292 35.2	53.2	231 53.8	27.5	216 29.8	39.6			
S 12	270 36.0	42 52.2	S15 25.3	307 35.7	S15 52.6	246 56.2	N 8 27.6	231 32.4	N12 39.6	Gacrux	172 12.7	S57 06.4
D 13	285 38.5	57 51.7	26.2	322 36.3	51.9	261 58.7	27.6	246 35.0	39.6	Gienah	176 03.1	S17 32.3
A 14	300 41.0	72 51.2	27.0	337 36.9	51.3	277 01.1	27.6	261 37.5	39.6	Hadar	149 03.2	S60 22.0
Y 15	315 43.4	87 50.6 ..	27.8	352 37.4 ..	50.6	292 03.6 ..	27.6	276 40.1 ..	39.6	Hamal	328 12.4	N23 27.7
16	330 45.9	102 50.1	28.6	7 38.0	50.0	307 06.0	27.6	291 42.6	39.5	Kaus Aust.	83 58.2	S34 23.0
17	345 48.4	117 49.6	29.5	22 38.6	49.3	322 08.5	27.7	306 45.2	39.5			
18	0 50.8	132 49.1	S15 30.3	37 39.1	S15 48.7	337 10.9	N 8 27.7	321 47.8	N12 39.5	Kochab	137 20.5	N74 09.2
19	15 53.3	147 48.6	31.1	52 39.7	48.0	352 13.4	27.7	336 50.3	39.5	Markab	13 48.9	N15 12.3
20	30 55.7	162 48.1	32.0	67 40.3	47.4	7 15.8	27.7	351 52.9	39.5	Menkar	314 25.8	N 4 05.3
21	45 58.2	177 47.6 ..	32.8	82 40.8 ..	46.7	22 18.3 ..	27.7	6 55.4 ..	39.5	Menkent	148 20.2	S36 21.9
22	61 00.7	192 47.0	33.6	97 41.4	46.1	37 20.7	27.7	21 58.0	39.4	Miaplacidus	221 41.2	S69 42.8
23	76 03.1	207 46.5	34.4	112 42.0	45.5	52 23.2	27.8	37 00.5	39.4			
23 00	91 05.6	222 46.0	S15 35.3	127 42.5	S15 44.8	67 25.6	N 8 27.8	52 03.1	N12 39.4	Mirfak	308 55.0	N49 51.7
01	106 08.1	237 45.5	36.1	142 43.1	44.2	82 28.1	27.8	67 05.7	39.4	Nunki	76 11.7	S26 17.8
02	121 10.5	252 45.0	36.9	157 43.7	43.5	97 30.5	27.8	82 08.2	39.4	Peacock	53 36.3	S56 44.3
03	136 13.0	267 44.5 ..	37.7	172 44.2 ..	42.9	112 33.0 ..	27.8	97 10.8 ..	39.3	Pollux	243 40.2	N28 01.5
04	151 15.5	282 43.9	38.6	187 44.8	42.2	127 35.4	27.9	112 13.3	39.3	Procyon	245 10.4	N 5 13.4
05	166 17.9	297 43.4	39.4	202 45.4	41.6	142 37.9	27.9	127 15.9	39.3			
06	181 20.4	312 42.9	S15 40.2	217 45.9	S15 40.9	157 40.3	N 8 27.9	142 18.4	N12 39.3	Rasalhague	96 16.6	N12 33.7
07	196 22.9	327 42.4	41.0	232 46.5	40.3	172 42.8	27.9	157 21.0	39.3	Regulus	207 54.5	N11 58.0
T 08	211 25.3	342 41.9	41.9	247 47.1	39.6	187 45.2	27.9	172 23.5	39.3	Rigel	281 21.8	S 8 12.2
H 09	226 27.8	357 41.3 ..	42.7	262 47.6 ..	39.0	202 47.7 ..	28.0	187 26.1 ..	39.2	Rigil Kent.	140 06.6	S60 49.7
U 10	241 30.2	12 40.8	43.5	277 48.2	38.3	217 50.1	28.0	202 28.7	39.2	Sabik	102 24.9	S15 43.4
R 11	256 32.7	27 40.3	44.3	292 48.8	37.7	232 52.5	28.0	217 31.2	39.2			
S 12	271 35.2	42 39.8	S15 45.1	307 49.3	S15 37.0	247 55.0	N 8 28.0	232 33.8	N12 39.2	Schedar	349 52.4	N56 32.4
D 13	286 37.6	57 39.2	46.0	322 49.9	36.4	262 57.4	28.1	247 36.3	39.2	Shaula	96 36.6	S37 06.1
A 14	301 40.1	72 38.7	46.8	337 50.5	35.7	277 59.9	28.1	262 38.9	39.2	Sirius	258 42.6	S16 43.0
Y 15	316 42.6	87 38.2 ..	47.6	352 51.0 ..	35.1	293 02.3 ..	28.1	277 41.4 ..	39.1	Spica	158 42.5	S11 09.5
16	331 45.0	102 37.7	48.4	7 51.6	34.4	308 04.8	28.1	292 44.0	39.1	Suhail	222 59.8	S43 25.8
17	346 47.5	117 37.1	49.2	22 52.2	33.8	323 07.2	28.1	307 46.5	39.1			
18	1 50.0	132 36.6	S15 50.0	37 52.8	S15 33.1	338 09.7	N 8 28.2	322 49.1	N12 39.1	Vega	80 46.5	N38 47.1
19	16 52.4	147 36.1	50.9	52 53.3	32.5	353 12.1	28.2	337 51.6	39.1	Zuben'ubi	137 17.3	S16 02.3
20	31 54.9	162 35.6	51.7	67 53.9	31.8	8 14.5	28.2	352 54.2	39.1			
21	46 57.4	177 35.0 ..	52.5	82 54.5 ..	31.2	23 17.0 ..	28.2	7 56.8 ..	39.0		SHA	Mer. Pass.
22	61 59.8	192 34.5	53.3	97 55.0	30.5	38 19.4	28.3	22 59.3	39.0	Venus	132 51.8	9 08
23	77 02.3	207 34.0	54.1	112 55.6	29.9	53 21.9	28.3	38 01.9	39.0	Mars	37 22.5	15 29
	h m									Jupiter	336 20.3	19 31
Mer. Pass. 17 56.6		v −0.5 d 0.8		v 0.6 d 0.6		v 2.5 d 0.0		v 2.6 d 0.0		Saturn	320 55.2	20 32

UT	SUN GHA	SUN Dec	MOON GHA	v	MOON Dec	d	HP
d h	° ′	° ′	° ′	′	° ′	′	′
21 00	180 35.2	S23 25.8	26 14.2	5.0	N16 31.1	8.5	61.1
01	195 34.9	25.9	40 38.2	4.9	16 39.6	8.4	61.1
02	210 34.6	25.9	55 02.1	4.9	16 48.0	8.2	61.2
03	225 34.2	.. 25.9	69 26.0	4.7	16 56.2	8.2	61.2
04	240 33.9	25.9	83 49.7	4.7	17 04.4	8.0	61.2
05	255 33.6	26.0	98 13.4	4.6	17 12.4	7.9	61.2
06	270 33.3	S23 26.0	112 37.0	4.5	N17 20.3	7.8	61.2
07	285 33.0	26.0	127 00.5	4.5	17 28.1	7.7	61.2
08	300 32.7	26.0	141 24.0	4.3	17 35.8	7.5	61.3
09	315 32.4	.. 26.0	155 47.3	4.3	17 43.3	7.4	61.3
10	330 32.1	26.1	170 10.6	4.3	17 50.7	7.3	61.3
11	345 31.8	26.1	184 33.9	4.1	17 58.0	7.2	61.3
12	0 31.5	S23 26.1	198 57.0	4.1	N18 05.2	7.0	61.3
13	15 31.2	26.1	213 20.1	4.0	18 12.2	6.9	61.3
14	30 30.8	26.1	227 43.1	3.9	18 19.1	6.8	61.4
15	45 30.5	.. 26.1	242 06.0	3.9	18 25.9	6.6	61.4
16	60 30.2	26.2	256 28.9	3.8	18 32.5	6.5	61.4
17	75 29.9	26.2	270 51.7	3.7	18 39.0	6.4	61.4
18	90 29.6	S23 26.2	285 14.4	3.7	N18 45.4	6.2	61.4
19	105 29.3	26.2	299 37.1	3.6	18 51.6	6.1	61.4
20	120 29.0	26.2	313 59.7	3.5	18 57.7	6.0	61.4
21	135 28.7	.. 26.2	328 22.2	3.5	19 03.7	5.8	61.4
22	150 28.4	26.2	342 44.7	3.4	19 09.5	5.7	61.4
23	165 28.1	26.2	357 07.1	3.4	19 15.2	5.5	61.4
22 00	180 27.7	S23 26.2	11 29.5	3.3	N19 20.7	5.4	61.4
01	195 27.4	26.2	25 51.8	3.3	19 26.1	5.2	61.5
02	210 27.1	26.2	40 14.1	3.2	19 31.3	5.1	61.5
03	225 26.8	.. 26.2	54 36.3	3.2	19 36.4	4.9	61.5
04	240 26.5	26.3	68 58.5	3.1	19 41.3	4.8	61.5
05	255 26.2	26.3	83 20.6	3.1	19 46.1	4.7	61.5
06	270 25.9	S23 26.3	97 42.7	3.0	N19 50.8	4.4	61.5
07	285 25.6	26.3	112 04.7	3.0	19 55.2	4.4	61.5
08	300 25.3	26.3	126 26.7	2.9	19 59.6	4.2	61.5
09	315 25.0	.. 26.3	140 48.6	2.9	20 03.8	4.0	61.5
10	330 24.6	26.3	155 10.5	2.9	20 07.8	3.9	61.5
11	345 24.3	26.3	169 32.4	2.8	20 11.7	3.7	61.5
12	0 24.0	S23 26.3	183 54.2	2.9	N20 15.4	3.6	61.5
13	15 23.7	26.2	198 16.1	2.7	20 19.0	3.4	61.5
14	30 23.4	26.2	212 37.8	2.8	20 22.4	3.2	61.5
15	45 23.1	.. 26.2	226 59.6	2.7	20 25.6	3.1	61.5
16	60 22.8	26.2	241 21.3	2.7	20 28.7	3.0	61.5
17	75 22.5	26.2	255 43.0	2.7	20 31.7	2.7	61.5
18	90 22.2	S23 26.2	270 04.7	2.7	N20 34.4	2.6	61.5
19	105 21.9	26.2	284 26.4	2.6	20 37.0	2.5	61.5
20	120 21.6	26.2	298 48.0	2.7	20 39.5	2.3	61.5
21	135 21.2	.. 26.2	313 09.7	2.6	20 41.8	2.1	61.5
22	150 20.9	26.2	327 31.3	2.6	20 43.9	2.0	61.4
23	165 20.6	26.2	341 52.9	2.6	20 45.9	1.8	61.4
23 00	180 20.3	S23 26.1	356 14.5	2.6	N20 47.7	1.7	61.4
01	195 20.0	26.1	10 36.1	2.6	20 49.4	1.5	61.4
02	210 19.7	26.1	24 57.7	2.6	20 50.9	1.3	61.4
03	225 19.4	.. 26.1	39 19.3	2.7	20 52.2	1.2	61.4
04	240 19.1	26.1	53 41.0	2.6	20 53.4	1.0	61.4
05	255 18.8	26.1	68 02.6	2.6	20 54.4	0.8	61.4
06	270 18.5	S23 26.1	82 24.2	2.6	N20 55.2	0.7	61.4
07	285 18.1	26.0	96 45.8	2.6	20 55.9	0.5	61.4
08	300 17.8	26.0	111 07.4	2.7	20 56.4	0.4	61.3
09	315 17.5	.. 26.0	125 29.1	2.7	20 56.8	0.2	61.3
10	330 17.2	26.0	139 50.8	2.6	20 57.0	0.0	61.3
11	345 16.9	26.0	154 12.4	2.8	20 57.0	0.1	61.3
12	0 16.6	S23 25.9	168 34.2	2.7	N20 56.9	0.3	61.3
13	15 16.3	25.9	182 55.9	2.7	20 56.6	0.4	61.3
14	30 16.0	25.9	197 17.6	2.8	20 56.2	0.6	61.3
15	45 15.7	.. 25.9	211 39.4	2.8	20 55.6	0.8	61.2
16	60 15.4	25.8	226 01.2	2.9	20 54.8	0.9	61.2
17	75 15.0	25.8	240 23.1	2.8	20 53.9	1.1	61.2
18	90 14.7	S23 25.8	254 44.9	3.0	N20 52.8	1.2	61.2
19	105 14.4	25.7	269 06.9	2.9	20 51.6	1.4	61.2
20	120 14.1	25.7	283 28.8	3.0	20 50.2	1.6	61.2
21	135 13.8	.. 25.7	297 50.8	3.0	20 48.6	1.7	61.1
22	150 13.5	25.7	312 12.8	3.1	20 46.9	1.9	61.1
23	165 13.2	25.6	326 34.9	3.1	N20 45.0	2.0	61.1
	SD 16.3	d 0.0	SD 16.7		16.8		16.7

Days noted: TUESDAY (21), WEDNESDAY (22), THURSDAY (23)

Lat.	Twilight Naut.	Twilight Civil	Sunrise	Moonrise 21	22	23	24
°	h m	h m	h m	h m	h m	h m	h m
N 72	08 26	10 58	■■	11 16	□	□	□
N 70	08 06	09 55	■■	12 33	□	□	14 28
68	07 50	09 19	■■	13 12	13 27	14 12	15 46
66	07 37	08 54	10 35	13 39	14 07	15 00	16 24
64	07 26	08 34	09 52	14 00	14 35	15 31	16 51
62	07 16	08 18	09 24	14 17	14 56	15 54	17 11
60	07 08	08 04	09 02	14 32	15 14	16 13	17 28
N 58	07 00	07 53	08 45	14 44	15 28	16 28	17 42
56	06 53	07 42	08 30	14 55	15 41	16 41	17 54
54	06 47	07 33	08 17	15 04	15 52	16 53	18 05
52	06 41	07 25	08 06	15 12	16 02	17 03	18 14
50	06 36	07 18	07 56	15 20	16 11	17 12	18 22
45	06 24	07 02	07 35	15 36	16 29	17 31	18 40
N 40	06 14	06 48	07 19	15 49	16 44	17 47	18 55
35	06 04	06 36	07 04	16 01	16 57	18 00	19 07
30	05 56	06 26	06 52	16 11	17 08	18 11	19 18
20	05 39	06 07	06 31	16 28	17 28	18 31	19 36
N 10	05 23	05 49	06 12	16 43	17 45	18 48	19 52
0	05 05	05 32	05 55	16 57	18 00	19 04	20 07
S 10	04 47	05 14	05 37	17 11	18 16	19 21	20 22
20	04 24	04 53	05 18	17 27	18 33	19 38	20 38
30	03 55	04 28	04 56	17 44	18 53	19 58	20 56
35	03 36	04 13	04 43	17 55	19 04	20 09	21 07
40	03 13	03 55	04 28	18 07	19 18	20 23	21 19
45	02 42	03 32	04 10	18 21	19 33	20 38	21 33
S 50	01 57	03 02	03 47	18 38	19 53	20 58	21 51
52	01 29	02 47	03 36	18 46	20 02	21 07	21 59
54	00 41	02 29	03 24	18 55	20 12	21 17	22 08
56	////	02 07	03 10	19 05	20 23	21 29	22 18
58	////	01 37	02 53	19 17	20 37	21 42	22 30
S 60	////	00 46	02 32	19 30	20 52	21 57	22 43

Lat.	Sunset	Twilight Civil	Twilight Naut.	Moonset 21	22	23	24
°	h m	h m	h m	h m	h m	h m	h m
N 72	■■	12 59	15 31	09 53	□	□	□
N 70	■■	14 02	15 51	08 36	□	□	13 21
68	■■	14 37	16 07	07 58	09 55	11 24	12 02
66	13 22	15 03	16 20	07 32	09 15	10 36	11 24
64	14 04	15 23	16 31	07 11	08 47	10 05	10 57
62	14 33	15 39	16 41	06 55	08 26	09 42	10 36
60	14 55	15 52	16 49	06 41	08 09	09 23	10 19
N 58	15 12	16 04	16 57	06 30	07 55	09 08	10 04
56	15 27	16 14	17 04	06 19	07 42	08 54	09 52
54	15 40	16 23	17 10	06 11	07 32	08 43	09 41
52	15 51	16 32	17 15	06 03	07 22	08 33	09 32
50	16 01	16 39	17 21	05 55	07 13	08 24	09 23
45	16 21	16 55	17 33	05 40	06 55	08 05	09 05
N 40	16 38	17 09	17 43	05 28	06 41	07 49	08 50
35	16 52	17 21	17 52	05 17	06 28	07 36	08 37
30	17 05	17 31	18 01	05 08	06 17	07 24	08 26
20	17 26	17 50	18 18	04 52	05 58	07 04	08 07
N 10	17 45	18 08	18 34	04 38	05 42	06 47	07 50
0	18 02	18 25	18 51	04 25	05 27	06 31	07 34
S 10	18 20	18 43	19 10	04 12	05 12	06 15	07 19
20	18 39	19 03	19 33	03 58	04 56	05 57	07 02
30	19 01	19 28	20 02	03 42	04 37	05 38	06 43
35	19 14	19 44	20 20	03 33	04 26	05 26	06 31
40	19 29	20 02	20 44	03 23	04 14	05 13	06 18
45	19 47	20 25	21 14	03 11	03 59	04 57	06 03
S 50	20 10	20 54	22 00	02 56	03 41	04 37	05 44
52	20 21	21 09	22 28	02 49	03 33	04 28	05 35
54	20 33	21 28	23 15	02 41	03 23	04 18	05 25
56	20 47	21 50	////	02 33	03 13	04 06	05 13
58	21 04	22 20	////	02 23	03 01	03 53	05 00
S 60	21 25	23 11	////	02 12	02 47	03 37	04 45

Day	SUN Eqn. of Time 00h	12h	SUN Mer. Pass.	MOON Mer. Pass. Upper	Lower	Age	Phase
d	m s	m s	h m	h m	h m	d	%
21	02 21	02 06	11 58	23 12	10 41	14	98
22	01 52	01 37	11 58	24 16	11 44	15	100
23	01 22	01 07	11 59	00 16	12 48	16	99

(Moon phase symbol: ○)

UT	ARIES GHA	VENUS −4.1 GHA	Dec	MARS +1.0 GHA	Dec	JUPITER −2.6 GHA	Dec	SATURN +0.1 GHA	Dec	STARS Name	SHA	Dec
d h	° ′	° ′	° ′	° ′	° ′	° ′	° ′	° ′	° ′		° ′	° ′
24 00	92 04.7	222 33.4	S15 54.9	127 56.2	S15 29.2	68 24.3	N 8 28.3	53 04.4	N12 39.0	Acamar	315 26.0	S40 18.6
01	107 07.2	237 32.9	55.7	142 56.7	28.6	83 26.8	28.3	68 07.0	39.0	Achernar	335 34.4	S57 14.6
02	122 09.7	252 32.4	56.5	157 57.3	27.9	98 29.2	28.3	83 09.5	39.0	Acrux	173 21.1	S63 05.5
03	137 12.1	267 31.9	. . 57.4	172 57.9	. . 27.2	113 31.6	. . 28.4	98 12.1	. . 38.9	Adhara	255 20.4	S28 58.4
04	152 14.6	282 31.3	58.2	187 58.5	26.6	128 34.1	28.4	113 14.6	38.9	Aldebaran	291 01.1	N16 30.5
05	167 17.1	297 30.8	59.0	202 59.0	25.9	143 36.5	28.4	128 17.2	38.9			
06	182 19.5	312 30.3	S15 59.8	217 59.6	S15 25.3	158 39.0	N 8 28.4	143 19.7	N12 38.9	Alioth	166 30.0	N55 57.4
07	197 22.0	327 29.7	16 00.6	233 00.2	24.6	173 41.4	28.5	158 22.3	38.9	Alkaid	153 07.4	N49 18.7
08	212 24.5	342 29.2	01.4	248 00.8	24.0	188 43.8	28.5	173 24.8	38.9	Al Na'ir	27 57.1	S46 57.9
F 09	227 26.9	357 28.6	. . 02.2	263 01.3	. . 23.3	203 46.3	. . 28.5	188 27.4	. . 38.8	Alnilam	275 56.7	S 1 12.2
R 10	242 29.4	12 28.1	03.0	278 01.9	22.7	218 48.7	28.5	203 29.9	38.8	Alphard	218 06.2	S 8 39.5
I 11	257 31.8	27 27.6	03.8	293 02.5	22.0	233 51.1	28.6	218 32.5	38.8			
D 12	272 34.3	42 27.0	S16 04.6	308 03.0	S15 21.3	248 53.6	N 8 28.6	233 35.0	N12 38.8	Alphecca	126 20.2	N26 42.9
A 13	287 36.8	57 26.5	05.4	323 03.6	20.7	263 56.0	28.6	248 37.6	38.8	Alpheratz	357 54.4	N29 05.5
Y 14	302 39.2	72 26.0	06.2	338 04.2	20.0	278 58.5	28.6	263 40.1	38.8	Altair	62 18.8	N 8 52.2
15	317 41.7	87 25.4	. . 07.0	353 04.8	. . 19.4	294 00.9	. . 28.7	278 42.7	. . 38.7	Ankaa	353 26.0	S42 18.7
16	332 44.2	102 24.9	07.8	8 05.3	18.7	309 03.3	28.7	293 45.2	38.7	Antares	112 39.5	S26 25.7
17	347 46.6	117 24.3	08.6	23 05.9	18.1	324 05.8	28.7	308 47.8	38.7			
18	2 49.1	132 23.8	S16 09.4	38 06.5	S15 17.4	339 08.2	N 8 28.7	323 50.3	N12 38.7	Arcturus	146 05.5	N19 11.0
19	17 51.6	147 23.3	10.2	53 07.1	16.7	354 10.6	28.8	338 52.9	38.7	Atria	107 51.3	S69 01.4
20	32 54.0	162 22.7	11.0	68 07.6	16.1	9 13.1	28.8	353 55.4	38.7	Avior	234 21.7	S59 30.4
21	47 56.5	177 22.2	. . 11.8	83 08.2	. . 15.4	24 15.5	. . 28.8	8 58.0	. . 38.7	Bellatrix	278 42.9	N 6 20.9
22	62 59.0	192 21.6	12.6	98 08.8	14.8	39 17.9	28.8	24 00.5	38.6	Betelgeuse	271 12.3	N 7 24.3
23	78 01.4	207 21.1	13.4	113 09.4	14.1	54 20.4	28.9	39 03.1	38.6			
25 00	93 03.9	222 20.6	S16 14.2	128 09.9	S15 13.5	69 22.8	N 8 28.9	54 05.6	N12 38.6	Canopus	264 00.2	S52 41.8
01	108 06.3	237 20.0	15.0	143 10.5	12.8	84 25.2	28.9	69 08.2	38.6	Capella	280 49.5	N45 59.8
02	123 08.8	252 19.5	15.8	158 11.1	12.1	99 27.7	28.9	84 10.7	38.6	Deneb	49 39.0	N45 17.0
03	138 11.3	267 18.9	. . 16.6	173 11.7	. . 11.5	114 30.1	. . 29.0	99 13.3	. . 38.6	Denebola	182 44.3	N14 34.3
04	153 13.7	282 18.4	17.4	188 12.2	10.8	129 32.5	29.0	114 15.8	38.6	Diphda	349 06.4	S17 59.4
05	168 16.2	297 17.8	18.2	203 12.8	10.2	144 35.0	29.0	129 18.4	38.5			
06	183 18.7	312 17.3	S16 19.0	218 13.4	S15 09.5	159 37.4	N 8 29.0	144 20.9	N12 38.5	Dubhe	194 04.3	N61 44.8
07	198 21.1	327 16.7	19.8	233 14.0	08.8	174 39.8	29.1	159 23.5	38.5	Elnath	278 25.5	N28 36.4
S 08	213 23.6	342 16.2	20.6	248 14.5	08.2	189 42.3	29.1	174 26.0	38.5	Eltanin	90 51.6	N51 29.4
A 09	228 26.1	357 15.6	. . 21.4	263 15.1	. . 07.5	204 44.7	. . 29.1	189 28.6	. . 38.5	Enif	33 57.6	N 9 52.5
T 10	243 28.5	12 15.1	22.2	278 15.7	06.9	219 47.1	29.2	204 31.1	38.5	Fomalhaut	15 35.7	S29 37.6
U 11	258 31.0	27 14.5	23.0	293 16.3	06.2	234 49.6	29.2	219 33.6	38.5			
R 12	273 33.5	42 14.0	S16 23.8	308 16.9	S15 05.5	249 52.0	N 8 29.2	234 36.2	N12 38.4	Gacrux	172 12.7	S57 06.4
D 13	288 35.9	57 13.4	24.6	323 17.4	04.9	264 54.4	29.2	249 38.7	38.4	Gienah	176 03.1	S17 32.3
A 14	303 38.4	72 12.9	25.3	338 18.0	04.2	279 56.8	29.3	264 41.3	38.4	Hadar	149 03.1	S60 22.0
Y 15	318 40.8	87 12.3	. . 26.1	353 18.6	. . 03.5	294 59.3	. . 29.3	279 43.8	. . 38.4	Hamal	328 12.4	N23 27.7
16	333 43.3	102 11.8	26.9	8 19.2	02.9	310 01.7	29.3	294 46.4	38.4	Kaus Aust.	83 58.1	S34 23.0
17	348 45.8	117 11.2	27.7	23 19.7	02.2	325 04.1	29.3	309 48.9	38.4			
18	3 48.2	132 10.7	S16 28.5	38 20.3	S15 01.5	340 06.6	N 8 29.4	324 51.5	N12 38.4	Kochab	137 20.5	N74 09.2
19	18 50.7	147 10.1	29.3	53 20.9	00.9	355 09.0	29.4	339 54.0	38.3	Markab	13 48.9	N15 12.3
20	33 53.2	162 09.6	30.1	68 21.5	15 00.2	10 11.4	29.4	354 56.6	38.3	Menkar	314 25.8	N 4 05.3
21	48 55.6	177 09.0	. . 30.9	83 22.1	14 59.6	25 13.8	. . 29.5	9 59.1	. . 38.3	Menkent	148 20.2	S36 21.9
22	63 58.1	192 08.5	31.6	98 22.6	58.9	40 16.3	29.5	25 01.6	38.3	Miaplacidus	221 41.2	S69 42.8
23	79 00.6	207 07.9	32.4	113 23.2	58.2	55 18.7	29.5	40 04.2	38.3			
26 00	94 03.0	222 07.3	S16 33.2	128 23.8	S14 57.6	70 21.1	N 8 29.5	55 06.7	N12 38.3	Mirfak	308 55.0	N49 51.7
01	109 05.5	237 06.8	34.0	143 24.4	56.9	85 23.5	29.6	70 09.3	38.3	Nunki	76 11.7	S26 17.8
02	124 08.0	252 06.2	34.8	158 25.0	56.2	100 26.0	29.6	85 11.8	38.2	Peacock	53 36.3	S56 44.2
03	139 10.4	267 05.7	. . 35.5	173 25.5	. . 55.6	115 28.4	. . 29.6	100 14.4	. . 38.2	Pollux	243 40.2	N28 01.5
04	154 12.9	282 05.1	36.3	188 26.1	54.9	130 30.8	29.7	115 16.9	38.2	Procyon	245 10.4	N 5 13.4
05	169 15.3	297 04.6	37.1	203 26.7	54.2	145 33.2	29.7	130 19.5	38.2			
06	184 17.8	312 04.0	S16 37.9	218 27.3	S14 53.6	160 35.7	N 8 29.7	145 22.0	N12 38.2	Rasalhague	96 16.5	N12 33.7
07	199 20.3	327 03.4	38.7	233 27.9	52.9	175 38.1	29.8	160 24.5	38.2	Regulus	207 54.5	N11 58.0
08	214 22.7	342 02.9	39.4	248 28.4	52.2	190 40.5	29.8	175 27.1	38.2	Rigel	281 21.8	S 8 12.2
S 09	229 25.2	357 02.3	. . 40.2	263 29.0	. . 51.6	205 42.9	. . 29.8	190 29.6	. . 38.2	Rigil Kent.	140 06.6	S60 49.7
U 10	244 27.7	12 01.8	41.0	278 29.6	50.9	220 45.3	29.8	205 32.2	38.1	Sabik	102 24.9	S15 43.4
N 11	259 30.1	27 01.2	41.8	293 30.2	50.2	235 47.8	29.9	220 34.7	38.1			
D 12	274 32.6	42 00.6	S16 42.5	308 30.8	S14 49.6	250 50.2	N 8 29.9	235 37.3	N12 38.1	Schedar	349 52.4	N56 32.4
A 13	289 35.1	57 00.1	43.3	323 31.4	48.9	265 52.6	29.9	250 39.8	38.1	Shaula	96 36.6	S37 06.1
Y 14	304 37.5	71 59.5	44.1	338 31.9	48.2	280 55.0	30.0	265 42.3	38.1	Sirius	258 42.6	S16 43.0
15	319 40.0	86 58.9	. . 44.9	353 32.5	. . 47.6	295 57.5	. . 30.0	280 44.9	. . 38.1	Spica	158 42.4	S11 09.5
16	334 42.5	101 58.4	45.6	8 33.1	46.9	310 59.9	30.0	295 47.4	38.1	Suhail	222 59.8	S43 25.8
17	349 44.9	116 57.8	46.4	23 33.7	46.2	326 02.3	30.1	310 50.0	38.1			
18	4 47.4	131 57.2	S16 47.2	38 34.3	S14 45.5	341 04.7	N 8 30.1	325 52.5	N12 38.0	Vega	80 46.5	N38 47.1
19	19 49.8	146 56.7	48.0	53 34.9	44.9	356 07.1	30.1	340 55.0	38.0	Zuben'ubi	137 17.3	S16 02.3
20	34 52.3	161 56.1	48.7	68 35.4	44.2	11 09.5	30.2	355 57.6	38.0		SHA	Mer. Pass.
21	49 54.8	176 55.5	. . 49.5	83 36.0	. . 43.5	26 12.0	. . 30.2	11 00.1	. . 38.0		° ′	h m
22	64 57.2	191 55.0	50.3	98 36.6	42.9	41 14.4	30.2	26 02.7	38.0	Venus	129 16.7	9 11
23	79 59.7	206 54.4	51.0	113 37.2	42.2	56 16.8	30.3	41 05.2	38.0	Mars	35 06.1	15 27
	h m									Jupiter	336 18.9	19 19
Mer. Pass. 17 44.8	v −0.6	d 0.8	v 0.6	d 0.7	v 2.4	d 0.0	v 2.5	d 0.0	Saturn	321 01.7	20 20

UT	SUN GHA	Dec	MOON GHA	v	Dec	d	HP
d h	° ′	° ′	° ′	′	° ′	′	′
24 00	180 12.9	S23 25.6	340 57.0	3.2	N20 43.0	2.2	61.1
01	195 12.6	25.6	355 19.2	3.2	20 40.8	2.3	61.1
02	210 12.3	25.5	9 41.4	3.3	20 38.5	2.5	61.0
03	225 11.9 ..	25.5	24 03.7	3.3	20 36.0	2.7	61.0
04	240 11.6	25.5	38 26.0	3.4	20 33.3	2.8	61.0
05	255 11.3	25.4	52 48.4	3.5	20 30.5	2.9	61.0
06	270 11.0	S23 25.4	67 10.9	3.5	N20 27.6	3.1	60.9
07	285 10.7	25.4	81 33.4	3.6	20 24.5	3.2	60.9
08	300 10.4	25.3	95 56.0	3.6	20 21.3	3.4	60.9
F 09	315 10.1 ..	25.3	110 18.6	3.7	20 17.9	3.5	60.9
R 10	330 09.8	25.2	124 41.3	3.7	20 14.4	3.7	60.8
I 11	345 09.5	25.2	139 04.0	3.9	20 10.7	3.8	60.8
D 12	0 09.2	S23 25.1	153 26.9	3.9	N20 06.9	4.0	60.8
A 13	15 08.8	25.1	167 49.8	4.0	20 02.9	4.1	60.8
Y 14	30 08.5	25.1	182 12.8	4.0	19 58.8	4.3	60.7
15	45 08.2 ..	25.0	196 35.8	4.1	19 54.5	4.4	60.7
16	60 07.9	25.0	210 58.9	4.2	19 50.1	4.5	60.7
17	75 07.6	24.9	225 22.1	4.3	19 45.6	4.7	60.6
18	90 07.3	S23 24.9	239 45.4	4.4	N19 40.9	4.8	60.6
19	105 07.0	24.8	254 08.8	4.4	19 36.1	4.9	60.6
20	120 06.7	24.8	268 32.2	4.5	19 31.2	5.1	60.5
21	135 06.4 ..	24.7	282 55.7	4.6	19 26.1	5.2	60.5
22	150 06.1	24.7	297 19.3	4.7	19 20.9	5.3	60.5
23	165 05.7	24.6	311 43.0	4.8	19 15.6	5.5	60.5
25 00	180 05.4	S23 24.6	326 06.8	4.9	N19 10.1	5.6	60.4
01	195 05.1	24.5	340 30.7	4.9	19 04.5	5.7	60.4
02	210 04.8	24.5	354 54.6	5.1	18 58.8	5.8	60.4
03	225 04.5 ..	24.4	9 18.7	5.1	18 53.0	6.0	60.3
04	240 04.2	24.3	23 42.8	5.2	18 47.0	6.1	60.3
05	255 03.9	24.3	38 07.0	5.3	18 40.9	6.2	60.3
06	270 03.6	S23 24.2	52 31.3	5.4	N18 34.7	6.3	60.2
S 07	285 03.3	24.2	66 55.7	5.5	18 28.4	6.5	60.2
A 08	300 03.0	24.1	81 20.2	5.6	18 21.9	6.5	60.2
T 09	315 02.6 ..	24.1	95 44.8	5.7	18 15.4	6.7	60.1
U 10	330 02.3	24.0	110 09.5	5.8	18 08.7	6.8	60.1
R 11	345 02.0	23.9	124 34.3	5.8	18 01.9	6.9	60.1
D 12	0 01.7	S23 23.9	138 59.1	6.0	N17 55.0	7.1	60.0
A 13	15 01.4	23.8	153 24.1	6.1	17 47.9	7.1	60.0
Y 14	30 01.1	23.8	167 49.2	6.1	17 40.8	7.2	59.9
15	45 00.8 ..	23.7	182 14.3	6.3	17 33.6	7.4	59.9
16	60 00.5	23.6	196 39.6	6.4	17 26.2	7.4	59.9
17	75 00.2	23.6	211 05.0	6.4	17 18.8	7.6	59.8
18	89 59.9	S23 23.5	225 30.4	6.6	N17 11.2	7.6	59.8
19	104 59.6	23.4	239 56.0	6.7	17 03.6	7.8	59.8
20	119 59.2	23.4	254 21.7	6.7	16 55.8	7.8	59.7
21	134 58.9 ..	23.3	268 47.4	6.9	16 48.0	8.0	59.7
22	149 58.6	23.2	283 13.3	7.0	16 40.0	8.0	59.6
23	164 58.3	23.1	297 39.3	7.0	16 32.0	8.2	59.6
26 00	179 58.0	S23 23.1	312 05.3	7.2	N16 23.8	8.2	59.6
01	194 57.7	23.0	326 31.5	7.3	16 15.6	8.3	59.5
02	209 57.4	22.9	340 57.8	7.3	16 07.3	8.4	59.5
03	224 57.1 ..	22.9	355 24.1	7.5	15 58.9	8.5	59.5
04	239 56.8	22.8	9 50.6	7.6	15 50.4	8.6	59.4
05	254 56.5	22.7	24 17.2	7.6	15 41.8	8.7	59.4
06	269 56.2	S23 22.6	38 43.8	7.8	N15 33.1	8.8	59.3
07	284 55.8	22.5	53 10.6	7.9	15 24.3	8.8	59.3
08	299 55.5	22.5	67 37.5	7.9	15 15.5	8.9	59.3
S 09	314 55.2 ..	22.4	82 04.4	8.1	15 06.6	9.0	59.2
U 10	329 54.9	22.3	96 31.5	8.2	14 57.6	9.1	59.2
N 11	344 54.6	22.2	110 58.7	8.3	14 48.5	9.2	59.1
D 12	359 54.3	S23 22.1	125 26.0	8.3	N14 39.3	9.2	59.1
A 13	14 54.0	22.1	139 53.3	8.5	14 30.1	9.3	59.1
Y 14	29 53.7	22.0	154 20.8	8.6	14 20.8	9.4	59.0
15	44 53.4 ..	21.9	168 48.4	8.7	14 11.4	9.4	59.0
16	59 53.1	21.8	183 16.1	8.7	14 02.0	9.5	58.9
17	74 52.8	21.7	197 43.8	8.9	13 52.5	9.6	58.9
18	89 52.5	S23 21.6	212 11.7	9.0	N13 42.9	9.6	58.9
19	104 52.1	21.6	226 39.7	9.0	13 33.3	9.7	58.8
20	119 51.8	21.5	241 07.7	9.2	13 23.6	9.8	58.8
21	134 51.5 ..	21.3	255 35.9	9.2	13 13.8	9.8	58.7
22	149 51.2	21.3	270 04.1	9.4	13 04.0	9.9	58.7
23	164 50.9	21.2	284 32.5	9.4	N12 54.1	10.0	58.6
	SD 16.3	d 0.1	SD 16.6		16.4		16.1

Twilight / Moonrise

Lat.	Naut.	Civil	Sunrise	Moonrise 24	25	26	27
°	h m	h m	h m	h m	h m	h m	h m
N 72	08 27	10 57	■■■	▭	16 01	18 43	20 50
N 70	08 07	09 55	■■■	14 28	17 04	19 11	21 05
68	07 51	09 20	■■■	15 46	17 39	19 31	21 16
66	07 38	08 55	10 35	16 24	18 04	19 47	21 26
64	07 27	08 35	09 53	16 51	18 24	20 00	21 34
62	07 17	08 19	09 25	17 11	18 40	20 11	21 40
60	07 09	08 06	09 03	17 28	18 53	20 21	21 46
N 58	07 01	07 54	08 46	17 42	19 04	20 29	21 51
56	06 54	07 44	08 31	17 54	19 14	20 36	21 56
54	06 48	07 35	08 18	18 05	19 23	20 42	22 00
52	06 43	07 26	08 07	18 14	19 30	20 48	22 04
50	06 37	07 19	07 57	18 22	19 37	20 53	22 07
45	06 26	07 03	07 37	18 40	19 52	21 04	22 14
N 40	06 15	06 49	07 20	18 55	20 04	21 13	22 20
35	06 06	06 38	07 06	19 07	20 15	21 21	22 25
30	05 57	06 27	06 53	19 18	20 24	21 28	22 30
20	05 41	06 08	06 32	19 36	20 39	21 40	22 38
N 10	05 24	05 51	06 14	19 52	20 53	21 51	22 44
0	05 07	05 34	05 56	20 07	21 06	22 00	22 51
S 10	04 48	05 15	05 39	20 22	21 18	22 10	22 57
20	04 26	04 55	05 20	20 38	21 32	22 20	23 04
30	03 57	04 30	04 58	20 56	21 47	22 32	23 12
35	03 38	04 15	04 44	21 07	21 56	22 39	23 16
40	03 15	03 57	04 29	21 19	22 06	22 47	23 21
45	02 44	03 34	04 11	21 33	22 18	22 56	23 27
S 50	01 59	03 04	03 49	21 51	22 33	23 06	23 34
52	01 31	02 49	03 38	21 59	22 39	23 11	23 37
54	00 44	02 31	03 26	22 08	22 47	23 17	23 41
56	////	02 09	03 13	22 18	22 55	23 23	23 45
58	////	01 39	02 55	22 30	23 04	23 30	23 49
S 60	////	00 48	02 34	22 43	23 15	23 37	23 54

Sunset / Twilight / Moonset

Lat.	Sunset	Civil	Naut.	Moonset 24	25	26	27
°	h m	h m	h m	h m	h m	h m	h m
N 72	■■■	13 02	15 33	▭	13 54	13 08	12 48
N 70	■■■	14 05	15 53	13 21	12 50	12 39	12 31
68	■■■	14 40	16 09	12 02	12 14	12 17	12 18
66	13 24	15 05	16 22	11 24	11 48	12 00	12 07
64	14 07	15 25	16 33	10 57	11 28	11 46	11 58
62	14 35	15 41	16 43	10 36	11 11	11 34	11 50
60	14 56	15 54	16 51	10 19	10 57	11 24	11 44
N 58	15 14	16 06	16 59	10 04	10 45	11 15	11 38
56	15 29	16 16	17 05	09 52	10 35	11 07	11 32
54	15 41	16 25	17 11	09 41	10 26	11 00	11 27
52	15 52	16 33	17 17	09 32	10 18	10 54	11 23
50	16 02	16 41	17 22	09 23	10 10	10 48	11 19
45	16 23	16 57	17 34	09 05	09 55	10 36	11 10
N 40	16 40	17 10	17 45	08 50	09 42	10 26	11 03
35	16 54	17 22	17 54	08 37	09 31	10 17	10 57
30	17 06	17 33	18 03	08 26	09 21	10 09	10 51
20	17 28	17 52	18 19	08 07	09 04	09 55	10 42
N 10	17 46	18 09	18 35	07 50	08 49	09 43	10 33
0	18 04	18 26	18 52	07 34	08 35	09 32	10 25
S 10	18 21	18 44	19 11	07 19	08 21	09 21	10 17
20	18 40	19 05	19 34	07 02	08 06	09 09	10 08
30	19 02	19 30	20 03	06 43	07 49	08 55	09 58
35	19 15	19 45	20 22	06 31	07 39	08 47	09 52
40	19 30	20 03	20 45	06 18	07 28	08 37	09 46
45	19 48	20 26	21 15	06 03	07 14	08 27	09 38
S 50	20 11	20 55	22 01	05 44	06 57	08 13	09 28
52	20 22	21 10	22 29	05 35	06 49	08 07	09 24
54	20 34	21 28	23 15	05 25	06 40	08 00	09 19
56	20 48	21 51	////	05 13	06 31	07 52	09 14
58	21 05	22 20	////	05 00	06 19	07 44	09 08
S 60	21 25	23 11	////	04 45	06 06	07 34	09 01

SUN / MOON

Day	Eqn. of Time 00ʰ	12ʰ	Mer. Pass.	Mer. Pass. Upper	Lower	Age	Phase
d	m s	m s	h m	h m	h m	d	%
24	00 52	00 37	11 59	01 20	13 51	17	95
25	00 22	00 08	12 00	02 21	14 51	18	89
26	00 07	00 22	12 00	03 19	15 46	19	81

UT	ARIES GHA	VENUS −4.1 GHA	Dec	MARS +1.0 GHA	Dec	JUPITER −2.6 GHA	Dec	SATURN +0.1 GHA	Dec
27 00	95 02.2	221 53.8	S16 51.8	128 37.8	S14 41.5	71 19.2	N 8 30.3	56 07.8	N12 38.0
01	110 04.6	236 53.3	52.6	143 38.4	40.9	86 21.6	30.3	71 10.3	38.0
02	125 07.1	251 52.7	53.3	158 38.9	40.2	101 24.1	30.3	86 12.8	37.9
03	140 09.6	266 52.1 ..	54.1	173 39.5 ..	39.5	116 26.5 ..	30.4	101 15.4 ..	37.9
04	155 12.0	281 51.5	54.9	188 40.1	38.8	131 28.9	30.4	116 17.9	37.9
05	170 14.5	296 51.0	55.6	203 40.7	38.2	146 31.3	30.4	131 20.4	37.9
M 06	185 16.9	311 50.4	S16 56.4	218 41.3	S14 37.5	161 33.7	N 8 30.5	146 23.0	N12 37.9
O 07	200 19.4	326 49.8	57.2	233 41.9	36.8	176 36.1	30.5	161 25.5	37.9
N 08	215 21.9	341 49.2	57.9	248 42.5	36.2	191 38.5	30.5	176 28.1	37.9
D 09	230 24.3	356 48.7 ..	58.7	263 43.0 ..	35.5	206 41.0 ..	30.6	191 30.6 ..	37.9
A 10	245 26.8	11 48.1	16 59.4	278 43.6	34.8	221 43.4	30.6	206 33.1	37.9
Y 11	260 29.3	26 47.5	17 00.2	293 44.2	34.1	236 45.8	30.6	221 35.7	37.8
12	275 31.7	41 46.9	S17 01.0	308 44.8	S14 33.5	251 48.2	N 8 30.7	236 38.2	N12 37.8
13	290 34.2	56 46.4	01.7	323 45.4	32.8	266 50.6	30.7	251 40.8	37.8
14	305 36.7	71 45.8	02.5	338 46.0	32.1	281 53.0	30.7	266 43.3	37.8
15	320 39.1	86 45.2 ..	03.2	353 46.6 ..	31.4	296 55.4 ..	30.8	281 45.8 ..	37.8
16	335 41.6	101 44.6	04.0	8 47.1	30.8	311 57.8	30.8	296 48.4	37.8
17	350 44.1	116 44.1	04.7	23 47.7	30.1	327 00.3	30.9	311 50.9	37.8
18	5 46.5	131 43.5	S17 05.5	38 48.3	S14 29.4	342 02.7	N 8 30.9	326 53.4	N12 37.8
19	20 49.0	146 42.9	06.3	53 48.9	28.7	357 05.1	30.9	341 56.0	37.7
20	35 51.4	161 42.3	07.0	68 49.5	28.1	12 07.5	31.0	356 58.5	37.7
21	50 53.9	176 41.7 ..	07.8	83 50.1 ..	27.4	27 09.9 ..	31.0	12 01.1 ..	37.7
22	65 56.4	191 41.1	08.5	98 50.7	26.7	42 12.3	31.0	27 03.6	37.7
23	80 58.8	206 40.6	09.3	113 51.3	26.0	57 14.7	31.1	42 06.1	37.7
28 00	96 01.3	221 40.0	S17 10.0	128 51.8	S14 25.4	72 17.1	N 8 31.1	57 08.7	N12 37.7
01	111 03.8	236 39.4	10.8	143 52.4	24.7	87 19.5	31.1	72 11.2	37.7
02	126 06.2	251 38.8	11.5	158 53.0	24.0	102 21.9	31.2	87 13.7	37.7
03	141 08.7	266 38.2 ..	12.3	173 53.6 ..	23.3	117 24.4 ..	31.2	102 16.3 ..	37.7
04	156 11.2	281 37.6	13.0	188 54.2	22.6	132 26.8	31.2	117 18.8	37.7
05	171 13.6	296 37.1	13.8	203 54.8	22.0	147 29.2	31.3	132 21.3	37.6
T 06	186 16.1	311 36.5	S17 14.5	218 55.4	S14 21.3	162 31.6	N 8 31.3	147 23.9	N12 37.6
U 07	201 18.6	326 35.9	15.3	233 56.0	20.6	177 34.0	31.3	162 26.4	37.6
E 08	216 21.0	341 35.3	16.0	248 56.6	19.9	192 36.4	31.4	177 28.9	37.6
S 09	231 23.5	356 34.7 ..	16.7	263 57.1 ..	19.3	207 38.8 ..	31.4	192 31.5 ..	37.6
D 10	246 25.9	11 34.1	17.5	278 57.7	18.6	222 41.2	31.5	207 34.0	37.6
A 11	261 28.4	26 33.5	18.2	293 58.3	17.9	237 43.6	31.5	222 36.5	37.6
Y 12	276 30.9	41 32.9	S17 19.0	308 58.9	S14 17.2	252 46.0	N 8 31.5	237 39.1	N12 37.6
13	291 33.3	56 32.4	19.7	323 59.5	16.5	267 48.4	31.6	252 41.6	37.6
14	306 35.8	71 31.8	20.5	339 00.1	15.9	282 50.8	31.6	267 44.1	37.6
15	321 38.3	86 31.2 ..	21.2	354 00.7 ..	15.2	297 53.2 ..	31.6	282 46.7 ..	37.5
16	336 40.7	101 30.6	21.9	9 01.3	14.5	312 55.6	31.7	297 49.2	37.5
17	351 43.2	116 30.0	22.7	24 01.9	13.8	327 58.0	31.7	312 51.7	37.5
18	6 45.7	131 29.4	S17 23.4	39 02.5	S14 13.1	343 00.4	N 8 31.8	327 54.3	N12 37.5
19	21 48.1	146 28.8	24.2	54 03.1	12.5	358 02.8	31.8	342 56.8	37.5
20	36 50.6	161 28.2	24.9	69 03.7	11.8	13 05.2	31.8	357 59.3	37.5
21	51 53.0	176 27.6 ..	25.6	84 04.2 ..	11.1	28 07.6 ..	31.9	13 01.9 ..	37.5
22	66 55.5	191 27.0	26.4	99 04.8	10.4	43 10.0	31.9	28 04.4	37.5
23	81 58.0	206 26.4	27.1	114 05.4	09.7	58 12.5	31.9	43 06.9	37.5
29 00	97 00.4	221 25.8	S17 27.8	129 06.0	S14 09.0	73 14.9	N 8 32.0	58 09.5	N12 37.5
01	112 02.9	236 25.2	28.6	144 06.6	08.4	88 17.3	32.0	73 12.0	37.4
02	127 05.4	251 24.6	29.3	159 07.2	07.7	103 19.7	32.1	88 14.5	37.4
03	142 07.8	266 24.0 ..	30.0	174 07.8 ..	07.0	118 22.1 ..	32.1	103 17.1 ..	37.4
04	157 10.3	281 23.4	30.8	189 08.4	06.3	133 24.5	32.1	118 19.6	37.4
05	172 12.8	296 22.8	31.5	204 09.0	05.6	148 26.9	32.2	133 22.1	37.4
W 06	187 15.2	311 22.2	S17 32.2	219 09.6	S14 04.9	163 29.3	N 8 32.2	148 24.7	N12 37.4
E 07	202 17.7	326 21.6	33.0	234 10.2	04.3	178 31.7	32.3	163 27.2	37.4
D 08	217 20.2	341 21.0	33.7	249 10.8	03.6	193 34.0	32.3	178 29.7	37.4
N 09	232 22.6	356 20.4 ..	34.4	264 11.4 ..	02.9	208 36.4 ..	32.3	193 32.3 ..	37.4
E 10	247 25.1	11 19.8	35.1	279 12.0	02.2	223 38.8	32.4	208 34.8	37.4
S 11	262 27.5	26 19.2	35.9	294 12.6	01.5	238 41.2	32.4	223 37.3	37.4
D 12	277 30.0	41 18.6	S17 36.6	309 13.1	S14 00.8	253 43.6	N 8 32.5	238 39.8	N12 37.3
A 13	292 32.5	56 18.0	37.3	324 13.7	14 00.2	268 46.0	32.5	253 42.4	37.3
Y 14	307 34.9	71 17.4	38.1	339 14.3	13 59.5	283 48.4	32.5	268 44.9	37.3
15	322 37.4	86 16.8 ..	38.8	354 14.9 ..	58.8	298 50.8 ..	32.6	283 47.4 ..	37.3
16	337 39.9	101 16.2	39.5	9 15.5	58.1	313 53.2	32.6	298 50.0	37.3
17	352 42.3	116 15.6	40.2	24 16.1	57.4	328 55.6	32.7	313 52.5	37.3
18	7 44.8	131 15.0	S17 40.9	39 16.7	S13 56.7	343 58.0	N 8 32.7	328 55.0	N12 37.3
19	22 47.3	146 14.4	41.7	54 17.3	56.0	359 00.4	32.7	343 57.5	37.3
20	37 49.7	161 13.8	42.4	69 17.9	55.4	14 02.8	32.8	359 00.1	37.3
21	52 52.2	176 13.2 ..	43.1	84 18.5 ..	54.7	29 05.2 ..	32.8	14 02.6 ..	37.3
22	67 54.7	191 12.6	43.8	99 19.1	54.0	44 07.6	32.9	29 05.1	37.3
23	82 57.1	206 12.0	44.5	114 19.7	53.3	59 10.0	32.9	44 07.7	37.3
Mer. Pass.	h m 17 33.0	v −0.6	d 0.7	v 0.6	d 0.7	v 2.4	d 0.0	v 2.5	d 0.0

STARS

Name	SHA	Dec
Acamar	315 26.0	S40 18.6
Achernar	335 34.4	S57 14.6
Acrux	173 21.0	S63 05.5
Adhara	255 20.4	S28 58.4
Aldebaran	291 01.1	N16 30.5
Alioth	166 30.0	N55 57.4
Alkaid	153 07.4	N49 18.7
Al Na'ir	27 57.1	S46 57.9
Alnilam	275 56.7	S 1 12.2
Alphard	218 06.1	S 8 39.5
Alphecca	126 20.2	N26 42.9
Alpheratz	357 54.4	N29 05.5
Altair	62 18.8	N 8 52.1
Ankaa	353 26.0	S42 18.7
Antares	112 39.5	S26 25.7
Arcturus	146 05.5	N19 11.0
Atria	107 51.3	S69 01.4
Avior	234 21.7	S59 30.5
Bellatrix	278 42.9	N 6 20.9
Betelgeuse	271 12.3	N 7 24.3
Canopus	264 00.2	S52 41.8
Capella	280 49.5	N45 59.8
Deneb	49 39.0	N45 17.0
Denebola	182 44.3	N14 34.3
Diphda	349 06.4	S17 59.4
Dubhe	194 04.3	N61 44.8
Elnath	278 25.5	N28 36.4
Eltanin	90 51.6	N51 29.4
Enif	33 57.6	N 9 52.5
Fomalhaut	15 35.7	S29 37.6
Gacrux	172 12.6	S57 06.4
Gienah	176 03.1	S17 32.3
Hadar	149 03.1	S60 22.0
Hamal	328 12.4	N23 27.7
Kaus Aust.	83 58.1	S34 23.0
Kochab	137 20.4	N74 09.2
Markab	13 48.9	N15 12.3
Menkar	314 25.8	N 4 05.3
Menkent	148 20.1	S36 21.9
Miaplacidus	221 41.1	S69 42.8
Mirfak	308 55.0	N49 51.7
Nunki	76 11.7	S26 17.8
Peacock	53 36.3	S56 44.2
Pollux	243 40.2	N28 01.5
Procyon	245 10.4	N 5 13.4
Rasalhague	96 16.5	N12 33.7
Regulus	207 54.5	N11 58.0
Rigel	281 21.8	S 8 12.2
Rigil Kent.	140 06.5	S60 49.7
Sabik	102 24.9	S15 43.4
Schedar	349 52.4	N56 32.4
Shaula	96 36.6	S37 06.1
Sirius	258 42.6	S16 43.0
Spica	158 42.4	S11 09.5
Suhail	222 59.8	S43 25.8
Vega	80 46.5	N38 47.1
Zuben'ubi	137 17.3	S16 02.3

	SHA	Mer. Pass.
		h m
Venus	125 38.7	9 14
Mars	32 50.5	15 24
Jupiter	336 15.8	19 08
Saturn	321 07.4	20 08

UT	SUN GHA	SUN Dec	MOON GHA	v	MOON Dec	d	HP
d h	° ′	° ′	° ′	′	° ′	′	′
27 00	179 50.6	S23 21.1	299 00.9	9.6	N12 44.1	10.0	58.6
01	194 50.3	21.0	313 29.5	9.6	12 34.1	10.1	58.6
02	209 50.0	20.9	327 58.1	9.7	12 24.0	10.1	58.5
03	224 49.7	.. 20.8	342 26.8	9.8	12 13.9	10.1	58.5
04	239 49.4	20.7	356 55.6	10.0	12 03.8	10.3	58.4
05	254 49.1	20.6	11 24.6	10.0	11 53.5	10.2	58.4
06	269 48.8	S23 20.5	25 53.6	10.1	N11 43.3	10.4	58.4
07	284 48.5	20.4	40 22.7	10.1	11 32.9	10.3	58.3
08	299 48.1	20.3	54 51.8	10.3	11 22.6	10.5	58.3
M 09	314 47.8	.. 20.2	69 21.1	10.4	11 12.1	10.4	58.2
O 10	329 47.5	20.1	83 50.5	10.4	11 01.7	10.5	58.2
N 11	344 47.2	20.0	98 19.9	10.6	10 51.2	10.6	58.2
D 12	359 46.9	S23 19.9	112 49.5	10.6	N10 40.6	10.6	58.1
A 13	14 46.6	19.8	127 19.1	10.7	10 30.0	10.6	58.1
Y 14	29 46.3	19.7	141 48.8	10.8	10 19.4	10.7	58.0
15	44 46.0	.. 19.6	156 18.6	10.9	10 08.7	10.7	58.0
16	59 45.7	19.5	170 48.5	10.9	9 58.0	10.7	57.9
17	74 45.4	19.4	185 18.4	11.1	9 47.3	10.8	57.9
18	89 45.1	S23 19.3	199 48.5	11.1	N 9 36.5	10.8	57.9
19	104 44.8	19.2	214 18.6	11.2	9 25.7	10.9	57.8
20	119 44.5	19.1	228 48.8	11.3	9 14.8	10.9	57.8
21	134 44.1	.. 19.0	243 19.1	11.4	9 03.9	10.9	57.7
22	149 43.8	18.9	257 49.5	11.4	8 53.0	10.9	57.7
23	164 43.5	18.8	272 19.9	11.5	8 42.1	11.0	57.7
28 00	179 43.2	S23 18.7	286 50.4	11.6	N 8 31.1	11.0	57.6
01	194 42.9	18.6	301 21.0	11.7	8 20.1	11.0	57.6
02	209 42.6	18.4	315 51.7	11.8	8 09.1	11.1	57.5
03	224 42.3	.. 18.3	330 22.5	11.8	7 58.0	11.1	57.5
04	239 42.0	18.2	344 53.3	11.9	7 47.0	11.1	57.5
05	254 41.7	18.1	359 24.2	11.9	7 35.9	11.2	57.4
06	269 41.4	S23 18.0	13 55.1	12.1	N 7 24.7	11.1	57.4
07	284 41.1	17.9	28 26.2	12.1	7 13.6	11.2	57.3
T 08	299 40.8	17.8	42 57.3	12.2	7 02.4	11.1	57.3
U 09	314 40.5	.. 17.6	57 28.5	12.2	6 51.3	11.2	57.3
E 10	329 40.2	17.5	71 59.7	12.3	6 40.1	11.3	57.2
S 11	344 39.9	17.4	86 31.0	12.4	6 28.8	11.2	57.2
D 12	359 39.6	S23 17.3	101 02.4	12.5	N 6 17.6	11.2	57.2
A 13	14 39.2	17.2	115 33.9	12.5	6 06.4	11.3	57.1
Y 14	29 38.9	17.0	130 05.4	12.5	5 55.1	11.3	57.1
15	44 38.6	.. 16.9	144 36.9	12.7	5 43.8	11.3	57.0
16	59 38.3	16.8	159 08.6	12.7	5 32.5	11.4	57.0
17	74 38.0	16.7	173 40.3	12.7	5 21.3	11.4	57.0
18	89 37.7	S23 16.5	188 12.0	12.8	N 5 09.9	11.3	56.9
19	104 37.4	16.4	202 43.8	12.9	4 58.6	11.3	56.9
20	119 37.1	16.3	217 15.7	13.0	4 47.3	11.3	56.9
21	134 36.8	.. 16.2	231 47.7	12.9	4 36.0	11.4	56.8
22	149 36.5	16.0	246 19.6	13.1	4 24.6	11.3	56.8
23	164 36.2	15.9	260 51.7	13.1	4 13.3	11.3	56.7
29 00	179 35.9	S23 15.8	275 23.8	13.1	N 4 02.0	11.4	56.7
01	194 35.6	15.6	289 55.9	13.3	3 50.6	11.4	56.7
02	209 35.3	15.5	304 28.2	13.2	3 39.2	11.3	56.6
03	224 35.0	.. 15.4	319 00.4	13.3	3 27.9	11.4	56.6
04	239 34.7	15.2	333 32.7	13.4	3 16.5	11.3	56.6
05	254 34.4	15.1	348 05.1	13.4	3 05.2	11.4	56.5
06	269 34.1	S23 15.0	2 37.5	13.4	N 2 53.8	11.3	56.5
W 07	284 33.7	14.8	17 09.9	13.5	2 42.5	11.4	56.5
E 08	299 33.4	14.7	31 42.4	13.6	2 31.1	11.4	56.4
D 09	314 33.1	.. 14.6	46 15.0	13.6	2 19.7	11.3	56.4
N 10	329 32.8	14.4	60 47.6	13.6	2 08.4	11.4	56.3
E 11	344 32.5	14.3	75 20.2	13.7	1 57.0	11.3	56.3
S 12	359 32.2	S23 14.1	89 52.9	13.7	N 1 45.7	11.3	56.2
D 13	14 31.9	14.0	104 25.6	13.8	1 34.4	11.4	56.2
A 14	29 31.6	13.9	118 58.4	13.8	1 23.0	11.3	56.2
Y 15	44 31.3	.. 13.7	133 31.2	13.8	1 11.7	11.3	56.2
16	59 31.0	13.6	148 04.0	13.9	1 00.4	11.3	56.1
17	74 30.7	13.4	162 36.9	13.9	0 49.1	11.3	56.1
18	89 30.4	S23 13.3	177 09.8	14.0	N 0 37.8	11.3	56.1
19	104 30.1	13.1	191 42.8	14.0	0 26.5	11.2	56.0
20	119 29.8	13.0	206 15.8	14.0	0 15.3	11.3	56.0
21	134 29.5	.. 12.8	220 48.8	14.1	N 0 04.0	11.3	56.0
22	149 29.2	12.7	235 21.9	14.1	S 0 07.3	11.2	56.0
23	164 28.9	12.5	249 55.0	14.1	S 0 18.5	11.2	55.9
	SD 16.3	d 0.1	SD 15.8		15.6		15.3

Lat.	Twilight Naut.	Twilight Civil	Sunrise	Moonrise 27	28	29	30
°	h m	h m	h m	h m	h m	h m	h m
N 72	08 27	10 54	■	20 50	22 45	24 32	00 32
N 70	08 07	09 54	■	21 05	22 51	24 31	00 31
68	07 51	09 20	■	21 16	22 55	24 30	00 30
66	07 38	08 55	10 34	21 26	23 00	24 29	00 29
64	07 27	08 35	09 53	21 34	23 03	24 29	00 29
62	07 18	08 20	09 25	21 40	23 06	24 28	00 28
60	07 09	08 06	09 04	21 46	23 09	24 28	00 28
N 58	07 02	07 55	08 46	21 51	23 11	24 28	00 28
56	06 55	07 44	08 32	21 56	23 13	24 27	00 27
54	06 49	07 35	08 19	22 00	23 15	24 27	00 27
52	06 44	07 27	08 08	22 04	23 16	24 27	00 27
50	06 38	07 20	07 58	22 07	23 18	24 26	00 26
45	06 27	07 04	07 38	22 14	23 21	24 26	00 26
N 40	06 16	06 50	07 21	22 20	23 24	24 25	00 25
35	06 07	06 39	07 07	22 25	23 26	24 25	00 25
30	05 58	06 28	06 55	22 30	23 28	24 25	00 25
20	05 42	06 09	06 33	22 38	23 32	24 24	00 24
N 10	05 26	05 52	06 15	22 44	23 35	24 24	00 24
0	05 09	05 35	05 58	22 51	23 38	24 23	00 23
S 10	04 50	05 17	05 40	22 57	23 41	24 23	00 23
20	04 27	04 57	05 21	23 04	23 44	24 22	00 22
30	03 59	04 32	04 59	23 12	23 48	24 22	00 22
35	03 40	04 17	04 46	23 16	23 50	24 22	00 22
40	03 17	03 59	04 31	23 21	23 52	24 21	00 21
45	02 46	03 36	04 13	23 27	23 55	24 21	00 21
S 50	02 01	03 07	03 51	23 34	23 58	24 21	00 21
52	01 34	02 52	03 40	23 37	24 00	00 00	00 21
54	00 49	02 34	03 28	23 41	24 02	00 02	00 20
56	////	02 12	03 14	23 45	24 03	00 03	00 20
58	////	01 42	02 57	23 49	24 05	00 05	00 20
S 60	////	00 54	02 37	23 54	24 08	00 08	00 20

Lat.	Sunset	Twilight Civil	Twilight Naut.	Moonset 27	28	29	30
°	h m	h m	h m	h m	h m	h m	h m
N 72	■	13 09	15 36	12 48	12 33	12 21	12 08
N 70	■	14 09	15 56	12 31	12 25	12 18	12 12
68	■	14 43	16 12	12 18	12 18	12 17	12 15
66	13 29	15 08	16 25	12 07	12 12	12 15	12 18
64	14 10	15 27	16 36	11 58	12 07	12 14	12 20
62	14 38	15 43	16 45	11 50	12 03	12 13	12 22
60	14 59	15 57	16 53	11 44	11 59	12 12	12 24
N 58	15 17	16 08	17 01	11 38	11 55	12 11	12 26
56	15 31	16 18	17 08	11 32	11 52	12 10	12 27
54	15 44	16 27	17 14	11 27	11 50	12 10	12 28
52	15 55	16 36	17 19	11 23	11 47	12 09	12 29
50	16 05	16 43	17 25	11 19	11 45	12 08	12 30
45	16 25	16 59	17 36	11 10	11 40	12 07	12 33
N 40	16 42	17 12	17 46	11 03	11 36	12 06	12 34
35	16 56	17 24	17 56	10 57	11 32	12 05	12 36
30	17 08	17 35	18 04	10 51	11 29	12 04	12 38
20	17 29	17 53	18 21	10 42	11 24	12 03	12 40
N 10	17 48	18 11	18 37	10 33	11 19	12 01	12 42
0	18 05	18 28	18 54	10 25	11 14	12 00	12 44
S 10	18 23	18 46	19 13	10 17	11 09	11 59	12 46
20	18 41	19 06	19 34	10 08	11 04	11 57	12 49
30	19 03	19 31	20 04	09 58	10 58	11 56	12 51
35	19 16	19 46	20 23	09 52	10 55	11 55	12 53
40	19 31	20 04	20 46	09 46	10 51	11 54	12 54
45	19 49	20 26	21 16	09 38	10 47	11 52	12 56
S 50	20 11	20 56	22 01	09 28	10 41	11 51	12 58
52	20 22	21 11	22 28	09 24	10 39	11 50	12 59
54	20 34	21 29	23 12	09 19	10 36	11 49	13 01
56	20 49	21 51	////	09 14	10 33	11 49	13 02
58	21 05	22 20	////	09 08	10 29	11 48	13 03
S 60	21 25	23 07	////	09 01	10 26	11 47	13 05

	SUN		MOON			
Day	Eqn. of Time 00h	Eqn. of Time 12h	Mer. Pass.	Mer. Pass. Upper	Lower	Age	Phase
d	m s	m s	h m	h m	h m	d	%
27	00 37	00 52	12 01	04 13	16 38	20	71	
28	01 06	01 21	12 01	05 02	17 26	21	61	
29	01 36	01 50	12 02	05 49	18 12	22	51	

UT	ARIES GHA	VENUS −4.1 GHA	Dec	MARS +1.0 GHA	Dec	JUPITER −2.5 GHA	Dec	SATURN +0.1 GHA	Dec	STARS Name	SHA	Dec
30 00	97 59.6	221 11.4	S17 45.3	129 20.3	S13 52.6	74 12.4	N 8 32.9	59 10.2	N12 37.2	Acamar	315 26.0	S40 18.6
01	113 02.0	236 10.7	46.0	144 20.9	51.9	89 14.8	33.0	74 12.7	37.2	Achernar	335 34.4	S57 14.6
02	128 04.5	251 10.1	46.7	159 21.5	51.2	104 17.2	33.0	89 15.2	37.2	Acrux	173 21.0	S63 05.6
03	143 07.0	266 09.5 ..	47.4	174 22.1 ..	50.5	119 19.6 ..	33.1	104 17.8 ..	37.2	Adhara	255 20.4	S28 58.4
04	158 09.4	281 08.9	48.1	189 22.7	49.9	134 21.9	33.1	119 20.3	37.2	Aldebaran	291 01.1	N16 30.5
05	173 11.9	296 08.3	48.8	204 23.3	49.2	149 24.3	33.1	134 22.8	37.2			
06	188 14.4	311 07.7	S17 49.5	219 23.9	S13 48.5	164 26.7	N 8 33.2	149 25.3	N12 37.2	Alioth	166 29.9	N55 57.4
T 07	203 16.8	326 07.1	50.3	234 24.5	47.8	179 29.1	33.2	164 27.9	37.2	Alkaid	153 07.3	N49 18.7
H 08	218 19.3	341 06.5	51.0	249 25.1	47.1	194 31.5	33.3	179 30.4	37.2	Al Na'ir	27 57.2	S46 57.9
U 09	233 21.8	356 05.8 ..	51.7	264 25.7 ..	46.4	209 33.9 ..	33.3	194 32.9 ..	37.2	Alnilam	275 56.7	S 1 12.2
R 10	248 24.2	11 05.2	52.4	279 26.3	45.7	224 36.3	33.4	209 35.4	37.2	Alphard	218 06.1	S 8 39.5
S 11	263 26.7	26 04.6	53.1	294 26.9	45.0	239 38.7	33.4	224 38.0	37.2			
D 12	278 29.1	41 04.0	S17 53.8	309 27.5	S13 44.3	254 41.1	N 8 33.4	239 40.5	N12 37.2	Alphecca	126 20.2	N26 42.9
A 13	293 31.6	56 03.4	54.5	324 28.1	43.6	269 43.5	33.5	254 43.0	37.2	Alpheratz	357 54.4	N29 05.5
Y 14	308 34.1	71 02.8	55.2	339 28.7	43.0	284 45.8	33.5	269 45.5	37.1	Altair	62 18.8	N 8 52.1
15	323 36.5	86 02.2 ..	55.9	354 29.3 ..	42.3	299 48.2 ..	33.6	284 48.1 ..	37.1	Ankaa	353 26.1	S42 18.7
16	338 39.0	101 01.5	56.6	9 29.9	41.6	314 50.6	33.6	299 50.6	37.1	Antares	112 39.5	S26 25.7
17	353 41.5	116 00.9	57.3	24 30.5	40.9	329 53.0	33.7	314 53.1	37.1			
18	8 43.9	131 00.3	S17 58.0	39 31.1	S13 40.2	344 55.4	N 8 33.7	329 55.6	N12 37.1	Arcturus	146 05.5	N19 11.0
19	23 46.4	145 59.7	58.8	54 31.7	39.5	359 57.8	33.8	344 58.2	37.1	Atria	107 51.3	S69 01.4
20	38 48.9	160 59.1	17 59.5	69 32.3	38.8	15 00.2	33.8	0 00.7	37.1	Avior	234 21.7	S59 30.5
21	53 51.3	175 58.4	18 00.2	84 32.9 ..	38.1	30 02.6 ..	33.8	15 03.2 ..	37.1	Bellatrix	278 42.9	N 6 20.9
22	68 53.8	190 57.8	00.9	99 33.5	37.4	45 04.9	33.9	30 05.7	37.1	Betelgeuse	271 12.3	N 7 24.3
23	83 56.3	205 57.2	01.6	114 34.1	36.7	60 07.3	33.9	45 08.3	37.1			
31 00	98 58.7	220 56.6	S18 02.3	129 34.7	S13 36.0	75 09.7	N 8 34.0	60 10.8	N12 37.1	Canopus	264 00.2	S52 41.9
01	114 01.2	235 56.0	03.0	144 35.3	35.3	90 12.1	34.0	75 13.3	37.1	Capella	280 49.5	N45 59.8
02	129 03.6	250 55.3	03.7	159 35.9	34.6	105 14.5	34.1	90 15.8	37.1	Deneb	49 39.0	N45 16.9
03	144 06.1	265 54.7 ..	04.4	174 36.5 ..	34.0	120 16.9 ..	34.1	105 18.4 ..	37.1	Denebola	182 44.3	N14 34.3
04	159 08.6	280 54.1	05.0	189 37.1	33.3	135 19.2	34.2	120 20.9	37.1	Diphda	349 06.4	S17 59.4
05	174 11.0	295 53.5	05.7	204 37.7	32.6	150 21.6	34.2	135 23.4	37.0			
06	189 13.5	310 52.8	S18 06.4	219 38.3	S13 31.9	165 24.0	N 8 34.2	150 25.9	N12 37.0	Dubhe	194 04.2	N61 44.8
07	204 16.0	325 52.2	07.1	234 38.9	31.2	180 26.4	34.3	165 28.4	37.0	Elnath	278 25.5	N28 36.4
08	219 18.4	340 51.6	07.8	249 39.5	30.5	195 28.8	34.3	180 31.0	37.0	Eltanin	90 51.6	N51 29.4
F 09	234 20.9	355 51.0 ..	08.5	264 40.1 ..	29.8	210 31.2 ..	34.4	195 33.5 ..	37.0	Enif	33 57.6	N 9 52.5
R 10	249 23.4	10 50.3	09.2	279 40.7	29.1	225 33.5	34.4	210 36.0	37.0	Fomalhaut	15 35.7	S29 37.6
I 11	264 25.8	25 49.7	09.9	294 41.3	28.4	240 35.9	34.5	225 38.5	37.0			
D 12	279 28.3	40 49.1	S18 10.6	309 41.9	S13 27.7	255 38.3	N 8 34.5	240 41.1	N12 37.0	Gacrux	172 12.6	S57 06.4
A 13	294 30.7	55 48.4	11.3	324 42.5	27.0	270 40.7	34.6	255 43.6	37.0	Gienah	176 03.1	S17 32.3
Y 14	309 33.2	70 47.8	12.0	339 43.1	26.3	285 43.1	34.6	270 46.1	37.0	Hadar	149 03.1	S60 22.0
15	324 35.7	85 47.2 ..	12.7	354 43.7 ..	25.6	300 45.4 ..	34.7	285 48.6 ..	37.0	Hamal	328 12.5	N23 27.7
16	339 38.1	100 46.6	13.3	9 44.3	24.9	315 47.8	34.7	300 51.1	37.0	Kaus Aust.	83 58.1	S34 23.0
17	354 40.6	115 45.9	14.0	24 44.9	24.2	330 50.2	34.7	315 53.7	37.0			
18	9 43.1	130 45.3	S18 14.7	39 45.5	S13 23.5	345 52.6	N 8 34.8	330 56.2	N12 37.0	Kochab	137 20.4	N74 09.2
19	24 45.5	145 44.7	15.4	54 46.1	22.8	0 55.0	34.8	345 58.7	37.0	Markab	13 48.9	N15 12.3
20	39 48.0	160 44.0	16.1	69 46.7	22.1	15 57.3	34.9	1 01.2	37.0	Menkar	314 25.8	N 4 05.2
21	54 50.5	175 43.4 ..	16.8	84 47.3 ..	21.4	30 59.7 ..	34.9	16 03.7 ..	37.0	Menkent	148 20.1	S36 21.9
22	69 52.9	190 42.8	17.5	99 47.9	20.7	46 02.1	35.0	31 06.2	37.0	Miaplacidus	221 41.1	S69 42.8
23	84 55.4	205 42.1	18.1	114 48.5	20.0	61 04.5	35.0	46 08.8	36.9			
1 00	99 57.9	220 41.5	S18 18.8	129 49.1	S13 19.3	76 06.9	N 8 35.1	61 11.3	N12 36.9	Mirfak	308 55.0	N49 51.7
01	115 00.3	235 40.9	19.5	144 49.7	18.6	91 09.2	35.1	76 13.8	36.9	Nunki	76 11.7	S26 17.8
02	130 02.8	250 40.2	20.2	159 50.4	17.9	106 11.6	35.2	91 16.3	36.9	Peacock	53 36.3	S56 44.2
03	145 05.2	265 39.6 ..	20.9	174 51.0 ..	17.2	121 14.0 ..	35.2	106 18.8 ..	36.9	Pollux	243 40.2	N28 01.5
04	160 07.7	280 38.9	21.5	189 51.6	16.5	136 16.4	35.3	121 21.4	36.9	Procyon	245 10.4	N 5 13.4
05	175 10.2	295 38.3	22.2	204 52.2	15.8	151 18.7	35.3	136 23.9	36.9			
06	190 12.6	310 37.7	S18 22.9	219 52.8	S13 15.1	166 21.1	N 8 35.4	151 26.4	N12 36.9	Rasalhague	96 16.5	N12 33.7
07	205 15.1	325 37.0	23.6	234 53.4	14.4	181 23.5	35.4	166 28.9	36.9	Regulus	207 54.5	N11 58.0
S 08	220 17.6	340 36.4	24.2	249 54.0	13.7	196 25.9	35.5	181 31.4	36.9	Rigel	281 21.8	S 8 12.3
A 09	235 20.0	355 35.8 ..	24.9	264 54.6 ..	13.0	211 28.2 ..	35.5	196 33.9 ..	36.9	Rigil Kent.	140 06.5	S60 49.7
T 10	250 22.5	10 35.1	25.6	279 55.2	12.3	226 30.6	35.6	211 36.5	36.9	Sabik	102 24.9	S15 43.4
U 11	265 25.0	25 34.5	26.3	294 55.8	11.6	241 33.0	35.6	226 39.0	36.9			
R 12	280 27.4	40 33.8	S18 26.9	309 56.4	S13 10.9	256 35.4	N 8 35.7	241 41.5	N12 36.9	Schedar	349 52.5	N56 32.4
D 13	295 29.9	55 33.2	27.6	324 57.0	10.2	271 37.7	35.7	256 44.0	36.9	Shaula	96 36.6	S37 06.1
A 14	310 32.4	70 32.5	28.3	339 57.6	09.5	286 40.1	35.8	271 46.5	36.9	Sirius	258 42.6	S16 43.0
Y 15	325 34.8	85 31.9 ..	29.0	354 58.2 ..	08.8	301 42.5 ..	35.8	286 49.0 ..	36.9	Spica	158 42.4	S11 09.5
16	340 37.3	100 31.3	29.6	9 58.8	08.1	316 44.8	35.9	301 51.6	36.9	Suhail	222 59.8	S43 25.8
17	355 39.7	115 30.6	30.3	24 59.5	07.4	331 47.2	35.9	316 54.1	36.9			
18	10 42.2	130 30.0	S18 31.0	40 00.1	S13 06.7	346 49.6	N 8 36.0	331 56.6	N12 36.9	Vega	80 46.5	N38 47.1
19	25 44.7	145 29.3	31.6	55 00.7	06.0	1 52.0	36.0	346 59.1	36.9	Zuben'ubi	137 17.2	S16 02.3
20	40 47.1	160 28.7	32.3	70 01.3	05.3	16 54.3	36.1	2 01.6	36.9		SHA	Mer. Pass.
21	55 49.6	175 28.0 ..	33.0	85 01.9 ..	04.6	31 56.7 ..	36.1	17 04.1 ..	36.9		° ′	h m
22	70 52.1	190 27.4	33.6	100 02.5	03.9	46 59.1	36.2	32 06.7	36.8	Venus	121 57.9	9 17
23	85 54.5	205 26.7	34.3	115 03.1	03.2	62 01.4	36.2	47 09.2	36.8	Mars	30 36.0	15 21
	h m									Jupiter	336 11.0	18 56
Mer. Pass. 17 21.2		v −0.6	d 0.7	v 0.6	d 0.7	v 2.4	d 0.0	v 2.5	d 0.0	Saturn	321 12.1	19 56

UT	SUN GHA	SUN Dec	MOON GHA	v	MOON Dec	d	HP	Lat.	Twilight Naut.	Twilight Civil	Sunrise	Moonrise 30	Moonrise 31	Moonrise 1	Moonrise 2
d h	° ′	° ′	° ′	′	° ′	′	′	°	h m	h m	h m	h m	h m	h m	h m
								N 72	08 25	10 47	■■		00 32	02 16	04 02	05 52
30 00	179 28.6	S23 12.4	264 28.1	14.1	S 0 29.7	11.2	55.9	N 70	08 06	09 51	■■	00 31	02 08	03 46	05 25
01	194 28.3	12.2	279 01.2	14.2	0 40.9	11.2	55.9	68	07 51	09 18	■■	00 30	02 02	03 33	05 04
02	209 28.0	12.1	293 34.4	14.2	0 52.1	11.2	55.8	66	07 38	08 54	10 30	00 29	01 57	03 23	04 48
03	224 27.7	.. 11.9	308 07.6	14.3	1 03.3	11.2	55.8	64	07 27	08 35	09 51	00 29	01 52	03 14	04 35
04	239 27.4	11.8	322 40.9	14.2	1 14.5	11.1	55.8	62	07 18	08 19	09 24	00 28	01 48	03 07	04 24
05	254 27.1	11.6	337 14.1	14.3	1 25.6	11.1	55.7	60	07 10	08 06	09 03	00 28	01 45	03 00	04 14
06	269 26.8	S23 11.5	351 47.4	14.3	S 1 36.7	11.1	55.7	N 58	07 02	07 55	08 46	00 28	01 42	02 55	04 06
07	284 26.5	11.3	6 20.7	14.4	1 47.8	11.1	55.7	56	06 56	07 45	08 32	00 27	01 39	02 50	03 59
T 08	299 26.2	11.2	20 54.1	14.3	1 58.9	11.1	55.6	54	06 50	07 36	08 19	00 27	01 37	02 45	03 52
H 09	314 25.9	.. 11.0	35 27.4	14.4	2 10.0	11.0	55.6	52	06 44	07 28	08 08	00 27	01 35	02 41	03 47
U 10	329 25.6	10.9	50 00.8	14.4	2 21.0	11.1	55.6	50	06 39	07 20	07 59	00 26	01 33	02 38	03 41
R 11	344 25.3	10.7	64 34.2	14.5	2 32.1	11.0	55.6	45	06 27	07 04	07 38	00 26	01 29	02 30	03 30
S 12	359 25.0	S23 10.5	79 07.7	14.4	S 2 43.1	10.9	55.5	N 40	06 17	06 51	07 22	00 25	01 25	02 23	03 21
D 13	14 24.6	10.4	93 41.1	14.5	2 54.0	11.0	55.5	35	06 08	06 40	07 08	00 25	01 22	02 18	03 13
A 14	29 24.3	10.2	108 14.6	14.4	3 05.0	10.9	55.5	30	05 59	06 29	06 55	00 25	01 19	02 13	03 06
Y 15	44 24.0	.. 10.1	122 48.0	14.6	3 15.9	11.0	55.5	20	05 43	06 11	06 35	00 24	01 15	02 05	02 54
16	59 23.7	09.9	137 21.6	14.5	3 26.9	10.8	55.4	N 10	05 27	05 53	06 16	00 24	01 11	01 57	02 44
17	74 23.4	09.7	151 55.1	14.5	3 37.7	10.9	55.4	0	05 10	05 37	05 59	00 23	01 07	01 50	02 34
18	89 23.1	S23 09.6	166 28.6	14.5	S 3 48.6	10.8	55.4	S 10	04 52	05 19	05 42	00 23	01 03	01 44	02 25
19	104 22.8	09.4	181 02.1	14.6	3 59.4	10.8	55.3	20	04 29	04 58	05 23	00 22	00 59	01 36	02 14
20	119 22.5	09.2	195 35.7	14.6	4 10.2	10.8	55.3	30	04 01	04 34	05 01	00 22	00 55	01 28	02 03
21	134 22.2	.. 09.1	210 09.3	14.6	4 21.0	10.8	55.3	35	03 42	04 19	04 48	00 22	00 53	01 24	01 56
22	149 21.9	08.9	224 42.9	14.6	4 31.8	10.7	55.3	40	03 19	04 01	04 34	00 21	00 50	01 18	01 49
23	164 21.6	08.7	239 16.5	14.6	4 42.5	10.7	55.2	45	02 49	03 39	04 16	00 21	00 46	01 12	01 40
31 00	179 21.3	S23 08.6	253 50.1	14.6	S 4 53.2	10.7	55.2	S 50	02 05	03 09	03 54	00 21	00 43	01 05	01 29
01	194 21.0	08.4	268 23.7	14.6	5 03.9	10.6	55.2	52	01 38	02 55	03 43	00 21	00 41	01 02	01 24
02	209 20.7	08.2	282 57.3	14.6	5 14.5	10.6	55.2	54	00 56	02 37	03 31	00 20	00 39	00 58	01 19
03	224 20.4	.. 08.1	297 30.9	14.7	5 25.1	10.6	55.1	56	////	02 15	03 17	00 20	00 37	00 54	01 13
04	239 20.1	07.9	312 04.6	14.6	5 35.7	10.5	55.1	58	////	01 47	03 01	00 20	00 34	00 49	01 06
05	254 19.8	07.7	326 38.2	14.7	5 46.2	10.5	55.1	S 60	////	01 01	02 41	00 20	00 32	00 44	00 59

UT	SUN GHA	SUN Dec	MOON GHA	v	MOON Dec	d	HP	Lat.	Sunset	Twilight Civil	Twilight Naut.	Moonset 30	Moonset 31	Moonset 1	Moonset 2
06	269 19.5	S23 07.5	341 11.9	14.6	S 5 56.7	10.5	55.1	°	h m	h m	h m	h m	h m	h m	h m
07	284 19.2	07.4	355 45.5	14.7	6 07.2	10.4	55.0	N 72	■■	13 19	15 41	12 08	11 56	11 41	11 22
08	299 18.9	07.2	10 19.2	14.7	6 17.6	10.5	55.0	N 70	■■	14 14	16 00	12 12	12 06	11 59	11 51
F 09	314 18.6	.. 07.0	24 52.9	14.6	6 28.1	10.3	55.0	68	■■	14 48	16 15	12 15	12 14	12 13	12 13
R 10	329 18.3	06.8	39 26.5	14.7	6 38.4	10.4	55.0	66	13 36	15 12	16 28	12 18	12 21	12 24	12 30
I 11	344 18.0	06.7	54 00.2	14.7	6 48.8	10.3	55.0	64	14 15	15 31	16 39	12 20	12 27	12 34	12 44
D 12	359 17.7	S23 06.5	68 33.9	14.6	S 6 59.1	10.2	54.9	62	14 42	15 47	16 48	12 22	12 32	12 43	12 56
A 13	14 17.4	06.3	83 07.5	14.7	7 09.3	10.3	54.9	60	15 03	16 00	16 56	12 24	12 36	12 50	13 06
Y 14	29 17.1	06.1	97 41.2	14.7	7 19.6	10.1	54.9	N 58	15 20	16 11	17 04	12 26	12 40	12 56	13 14
15	44 16.8	.. 05.9	112 14.9	14.6	7 29.7	10.2	54.9	56	15 34	16 21	17 10	12 27	12 44	13 02	13 22
16	59 16.5	05.8	126 48.5	14.7	7 39.9	10.1	54.8	54	15 47	16 30	17 16	12 28	12 47	13 07	13 29
17	74 16.2	05.6	141 22.2	14.6	7 50.0	10.1	54.8	52	15 58	16 38	17 22	12 29	12 50	13 11	13 35
18	89 15.9	S23 05.4	155 55.8	14.7	S 8 00.1	10.0	54.8	50	16 07	16 45	17 27	12 30	12 52	13 16	13 41
19	104 15.6	05.2	170 29.5	14.6	8 10.1	10.0	54.8	45	16 28	17 01	17 38	12 33	12 58	13 25	13 53
20	119 15.3	05.0	185 03.1	14.7	8 20.1	10.0	54.8	N 40	16 44	17 15	17 49	12 34	13 03	13 32	14 04
21	134 15.0	.. 04.8	199 36.8	14.6	8 30.1	9.9	54.7	35	16 58	17 26	17 58	12 36	13 07	13 39	14 12
22	149 14.7	04.6	214 10.4	14.7	8 40.0	9.8	54.7	30	17 10	17 37	18 06	12 38	13 11	13 44	14 20
23	164 14.4	04.5	228 44.1	14.6	8 49.8	9.9	54.7	20	17 31	17 55	18 23	12 40	13 17	13 54	14 33
1 00	179 14.1	S23 04.3	243 17.7	14.6	S 8 59.7	9.8	54.7	N 10	17 49	18 12	18 38	12 42	13 23	14 03	14 45
01	194 13.8	04.1	257 51.3	14.6	9 09.5	9.7	54.7	0	18 07	18 29	18 55	12 44	13 28	14 11	14 56
02	209 13.5	03.9	272 24.9	14.6	9 19.2	9.7	54.7	S 10	18 24	18 47	19 14	12 46	13 33	14 20	15 07
03	224 13.2	.. 03.7	286 58.5	14.6	9 28.9	9.6	54.6	20	18 43	19 07	19 36	12 49	13 39	14 29	15 18
04	239 13.0	03.5	301 32.1	14.5	9 38.5	9.6	54.6	30	19 04	19 32	20 05	12 51	13 45	14 39	15 32
05	254 12.7	03.3	316 05.6	14.6	9 48.1	9.6	54.6	35	19 17	19 47	20 23	12 53	13 49	14 45	15 40
06	269 12.4	S23 03.1	330 39.2	14.5	S 9 57.7	9.5	54.6	40	19 32	20 05	20 46	12 54	13 53	14 51	15 49
07	284 12.1	02.9	345 12.7	14.6	10 07.2	9.5	54.6	45	19 50	20 27	21 16	12 56	13 58	14 59	15 59
S 08	299 11.8	02.7	359 46.3	14.5	10 16.7	9.4	54.5	S 50	20 12	20 56	22 00	12 58	14 04	15 08	16 12
A 09	314 11.5	.. 02.5	14 19.8	14.5	10 26.1	9.4	54.5	52	20 22	21 11	22 26	12 59	14 07	15 13	16 18
T 10	329 11.2	02.3	28 53.3	14.5	10 35.5	9.3	54.5	54	20 34	21 28	23 08	13 01	14 10	15 18	16 24
U 11	344 10.9	02.1	43 26.8	14.5	10 44.8	9.2	54.5	56	20 48	21 49	////	13 02	14 13	15 23	16 31
R 12	359 10.6	S23 01.9	58 00.3	14.4	S10 54.0	9.3	54.5	58	21 05	22 18	////	13 03	14 17	15 29	16 40
D 13	14 10.3	01.7	72 33.7	14.5	11 03.3	9.1	54.5	S 60	21 24	23 02	////	13 05	14 21	15 36	16 49
A 14	29 10.0	01.5	87 07.2	14.4	11 12.4	9.2	54.5								
Y 15	44 09.7	.. 01.3	101 40.6	14.4	11 21.6	9.0	54.4								
16	59 09.4	01.1	116 14.0	14.4	11 30.6	9.0	54.4								
17	74 09.1	00.9	130 47.4	14.4	11 39.6	9.0	54.4								

18	89 08.8	S23 00.7	145 20.8	14.4	S11 48.6	8.9	54.4
19	104 08.5	00.5	159 54.2	14.3	11 57.5	8.9	54.4
20	119 08.2	00.3	174 27.5	14.3	12 06.4	8.8	54.4
21	134 07.9	23 00.1	189 00.8	14.3	12 15.2	8.7	54.4
22	149 07.6	22 59.9	203 34.1	14.3	12 23.9	8.7	54.3
23	164 07.3	S22 59.7	218 07.4	14.2	S12 32.6	8.6	54.3

	SUN			MOON			
Day	Eqn. of Time 00ʰ	Eqn. of Time 12ʰ	Mer. Pass.	Mer. Pass. Upper	Mer. Pass. Lower	Age	Phase
d	m s	m s	h m	h m	h m	d	%
30	02 05	02 20	12 02	06 34	18 56	23	41
31	02 34	02 48	12 03	07 17	19 39	24	32
1	03 03	03 17	12 03	08 01	20 23	25	23

SD 16.3   d 0.2 | SD 15.1   15.0   14.8

EXPLANATION

PRINCIPLE AND ARRANGEMENT

1. *Object.* The object of this Almanac is to provide, in a convenient form, the data required for the practice of astronomical navigation at sea.

2. *Principle.* The main contents of the Almanac consist of data from which the *Greenwich Hour Angle* (GHA) and the *Declination* (Dec) of all the bodies used for navigation can be obtained for any instant of *Universal Time* (UT), or *Greenwich Mean Time* (GMT). The *Local Hour Angle* (LHA) can then be obtained by means of the formula:

$$\text{LHA} = \text{GHA} \begin{array}{l} - \text{ west} \\ + \text{ east} \end{array} \text{longitude}$$

The remaining data consist of: times of rising and setting of the Sun and Moon, and times of twilight; miscellaneous calendarial and planning data and auxiliary tables, including a list of Standard Times; corrections to be applied to observed altitude.

For the Sun, Moon, and planets the GHA and Dec are tabulated directly for each hour of UT throughout the year. For the stars the *Sidereal Hour Angle* (SHA) is given, and the GHA is obtained from:

$$\text{GHA Star} = \text{GHA Aries} + \text{SHA Star}$$

The SHA and Dec of the stars change slowly and may be regarded as constant over periods of several days. GHA Aries, or the Greenwich Hour Angle of the first point of Aries (the Vernal Equinox), is tabulated for each hour. Permanent tables give the appropriate increments and corrections to the tabulated hourly values of GHA and Dec for the minutes and seconds of UT.

The six-volume series of *Sight Reduction Tables for Marine Navigation* (published in U.S.A. as Pub. No. 229 and in U.K. as N.P. 401) has been designed for the solution of the navigational triangle and is intended for use with *The Nautical Almanac*.

Two alternative procedures for sight reduction are described on pages 277–318. The first requires the use of programmable calculators or computers, while the second uses a set of concise tables that is given on pages 286–317.

The tabular accuracy is $0\!\!^.\!1$ throughout. The time argument on the daily pages of this Almanac is 12^{h} + the Greenwich Hour Angle of the mean sun and is here denoted by UT, although it is also known as GMT. This scale may differ from the broadcast time signals (UTC) by an amount which, if ignored, will introduce an error of up to $0\!\!^.\!2$ in longitude determined from astronomical observations. (The difference arises because the time argument depends on the variable rate of rotation of the Earth while the broadcast time signals are now based on an atomic time-scale.) Step adjustments of exactly one second are made to the time signals as required (normally at 24^{h} on December 31 and June 30) so that the difference between the time signals and UT, as used in this Almanac, may not exceed $0\!\!^{s}\!9$. Those who require to reduce observations to a precision of better than 1^{s} must therefore obtain the correction (DUT1) to the time signals from coding in the signal, or from other sources; the required time is given by UT1=UTC+DUT1 to a precision of $0\!\!^{s}\!1$. Alternatively, the longitude, when determined from astronomical observations, may be corrected by the corresponding amount shown in the following table:

Correction to time signals	Correction to longitude
$-0\!\!^{s}\!9$ to $-0\!\!^{s}\!7$	$0\!\!^.\!2$ to east
$-0\!\!^{s}\!6$ to $-0\!\!^{s}\!3$	$0\!\!^.\!1$ to east
$-0\!\!^{s}\!2$ to $+0\!\!^{s}\!2$	no correction
$+0\!\!^{s}\!3$ to $+0\!\!^{s}\!6$	$0\!\!^.\!1$ to west
$+0\!\!^{s}\!7$ to $+0\!\!^{s}\!9$	$0\!\!^.\!2$ to west

3. *Lay-out.*   The ephemeral data for three days are presented on an opening of two pages: the left-hand page contains the data for the planets and stars; the right-hand page contains the data for the Sun and Moon, together with times of twilight, sunrise, sunset, moonrise and moonset.

The remaining contents are arranged as follows: for ease of reference the altitude-correction tables are given on pages A2, A3, A4, xxxiv and xxxv; calendar, Moon's phases, eclipses, and planet notes (i.e. data of general interest) precede the main tabulations. The Explanation is followed by information on standard times, star charts and list of star positions, sight reduction procedures and concise sight reduction tables, tables of increments and corrections and other auxiliary tables that are frequently used.

MAIN DATA

4. *Daily pages.*   The daily pages give the GHA of Aries, the GHA and Dec of the Sun, Moon, and the four navigational planets, for each hour of UT. For the Moon, values of v and d are also tabulated for each hour to facilitate the correction of GHA and Dec to intermediate times; v and d for the Sun and planets change so slowly that they are given, at the foot of the appropriate columns, once only on the page; v is zero for Aries and negligible for the Sun, and is omitted. The SHA and Dec of the 57 selected stars, arranged in alphabetical order of proper name, are also given.

5. *Stars.*   The SHA and Dec of 173 stars, including the 57 selected stars, are tabulated for each month on pages 268–273; no interpolation is required and the data can be used in precisely the same way as those for the selected stars on the daily pages. The stars are arranged in order of SHA.

The list of 173 includes all stars down to magnitude 3·0, together with a few fainter ones to fill the larger gaps. The 57 selected stars have been chosen from amongst these on account of brightness and distribution in the sky; they will suffice for the majority of observations.

The 57 selected stars are known by their proper names, but they are also numbered in descending order of SHA. In the list of 173 stars, the constellation names are always given on the left-hand page; on the facing page proper names are given where well-known names exist. Numbers for the selected stars are given in both columns.

An index to the selected stars, containing lists in both alphabetical and numerical order, is given on page xxxiii and is also reprinted on the bookmark.

6. *Increments and corrections.*   The tables printed on tinted paper (pages ii–xxxi) at the back of the Almanac provide the increments and corrections for minutes and seconds to be applied to the hourly values of GHA and Dec. They consist of sixty tables, one for each minute, separated into two parts: increments to GHA for Sun and planets, Aries, and Moon for every minute and second; and, for each minute, corrections to be applied to GHA and Dec corresponding to the values of v and d given on the daily pages.

The increments are based on the following adopted hourly rates of increase of the GHA: Sun and planets, 15° precisely; Aries, 15° 02'·46; Moon, 14° 19'·0. The values of v on the daily pages are the excesses of the actual hourly motions over the adopted values; they are generally positive, except for Venus. The tabulated hourly values of the Sun's GHA have been adjusted to reduce to a minimum the error caused by treating v as negligible. The values of d on the daily pages are the hourly differences of the Dec. For the Moon, the true values of v and d are given for each hour; otherwise mean values are given for the three days on the page.

7. *Method of entry.*   The UT of an observation is expressed as a day and hour, followed by a number of minutes and seconds. The tabular values of GHA and Dec, and, where necessary, the corresponding values of v and d, are taken directly from the daily pages for the day and hour of UT; this hour is always *before* the time of observation. SHA and Dec of the selected stars are also taken from the daily pages.

The table of Increments and Corrections for the minute of UT is then selected. For the GHA, the increment for minutes and seconds is taken from the appropriate column opposite the seconds of UT; the v-correction is taken from the second part of the same table opposite the value of v as given on the daily pages. Both increment and v-correction are to be added to the GHA, except for Venus when v is prefixed by a minus sign and the v-correction is to be subtracted. For the Dec there is no increment, but a d-correction is applied in the same way as the v-correction; d is given without sign on the daily pages and the sign of the correction is to be supplied by inspection of the Dec column. In many cases the correction may be applied mentally.

8. *Examples.* (a) Sun and Moon. Required the GHA and Dec of the Sun and Moon on 1999 November 16 at 15^h 47^m 13^s UT.

		SUN			MOON			
		GHA	Dec	d	GHA	v	Dec	d
		° ′	° ′	′	° ′	′	° ′	′
Daily page, November 16^d 15^h		48 48·9	S 18 43·3	0·6	310 44·7	12·1	S 14 15·4	8·4
Increments for	47^m 13^s	11 48·3			11 16·0			
v or d corrections for	47^m		+0·5		+9·6		−6·7	
Sum for November 16^d 15^h 47^m 13^s		60 37·2	S 18 43·8		322 10·3		S 14 08·7	

(b) Planets. Required the LHA and Dec of (i) Venus on 1999 November 16 at 11^h 52^m 39^s UT in longitude W $100°$ $09′$; (ii) Mars on 1999 November 16 at 8^h 06^m 17^s UT in longitude E $159°$ $48′$.

		VENUS				MARS			
		GHA	v	Dec	d	GHA	v	Dec	d
		° ′	′	° ′	′	° ′	′	° ′	′
Daily page, Nov. 16^d	(11^h)	32 10·5	−0·1	S 1 43·3	0·9	(8^h) 240 27·6	0·4	S 23 07·1	0·3
Increments (planets)	$(52^m 39^s)$	13 09·8				$(06^m 17^s)$ 1 34·3			
v or d corrections	(52^m)	−0·1		+0·8		(06^m) +0·0		+0·0	
Sum = GHA and Dec.		45 20·2		S 1 44·1		242 01·9		S 23 07·1	
Longitude	(west)	−100 09·0				(east) +159 48·0			
Multiples of 360°		+360				−360			
LHA planet		305 11·2				41 49·9			

(c) Stars. Required the GHA and Dec of (i) *Regulus* on 1999 November 16 at 6^h 28^m 03^s UT; (ii) *Vega* on 1999 November 16 at 19^h 37^m 18^s UT.

		Regulus			*Vega*	
		GHA	Dec		GHA	Dec
		° ′	° ′		° ′	° ′
Daily page (SHA and Dec)		207 54·8	N 11 58.1		80 46·4	N 38 47.3
Daily page (GHA Aries)	(6^h)	144 52·2		(19^h)	340 24·3	
Increments (Aries)	$(28^m 03^s)$	7 01·9		$(37^m 18^s)$	9 21·0	
Sum = GHA star		359 48·9			430 31·7	
Multiples of 360°					−360	
GHA star		359 48·9			70 31·7	

9. *Polaris (Pole Star) tables.* The tables on pages 274–276 provide means by which the latitude can be deduced from an observed altitude of *Polaris*, and they also give its azimuth; their use is explained and illustrated on those pages. They are based on the following formula:

$$\text{Latitude} - H_O = -p \cos h + \tfrac{1}{2} p \sin p \sin^2 h \tan(\text{latitude})$$

where

H_O = Apparent altitude (corrected for refraction)

p = polar distance of *Polaris* = $90° -$ Dec

h = local hour angle of *Polaris* = LHA Aries + SHA

a_0, which is a function of LHA Aries only, is the value of both terms of the above formula calculated for mean values of the SHA ($322°$ $08′$) and Dec (N $89°$ $15′.6$) of *Polaris*, for a mean latitude of $50°$, and adjusted by the addition of a constant ($58′.8$).

a_1, which is a function of LHA Aries and latitude, is the excess of the value of the second term over its mean value for latitude 50°, increased by a constant (0.6) to make it always positive. a_2, which is a function of LHA Aries and date, is the correction to the first term for the variation of *Polaris* from its adopted mean position; it is increased by a constant (0.6) to make it positive. The sum of the added constants is 1°, so that:

$$\text{Latitude} = \text{Apparent altitude (corrected for refraction)} - 1° + a_0 + a_1 + a_2$$

RISING AND SETTING PHENOMENA

10. *General.* On the right-hand daily pages are given the times of sunrise and sunset, of the beginning and end of civil and nautical twilights, and of moonrise and moonset for a range of latitudes from N 72° to S 60°. These times, which are given to the nearest minute, are strictly the UT of the phenomena on the Greenwich meridian; they are given for every day for moonrise and moonset, but only for the middle day of the three on each page for the solar phenomena.

They are approximately the Local Mean Times (LMT) of the corresponding phenomena on other meridians; they can be formally interpolated if desired. The UT of a phenomenon is obtained from the LMT by:

$$\text{UT} = \text{LMT} \begin{array}{c} + \text{ west} \\ - \text{ east} \end{array} \text{longitude}$$

in which the longitude must first be converted to time by the table on page i or otherwise.

Interpolation for latitude can be done mentally or with the aid of Table I on page xxxii.

The following symbols are used to indicate the conditions under which, in high latitudes, some of the phenomena do not occur:

        ☐ Sun or Moon remains continuously above the horizon;

        ■ Sun or Moon remains continuously below the horizon;

        //// twilight lasts all night.

Basis of the tabulations. At sunrise and sunset 16′ is allowed for semi-diameter and 34′ for horizontal refraction, so that at the times given the Sun's upper limb is on the visible horizon; all times refer to phenomena as seen from sea level with a clear horizon.

At the times given for the beginning and end of twilight, the Sun's zenith distance is 96° for civil, and 102° for nautical twilight. The degree of illumination at the times given for civil twilight (in good conditions and in the absence of other illumination) is such that the brightest stars are visible and the horizon is clearly defined. At the times given for nautical twilight the horizon is in general not visible, and it is too dark for observation with a marine sextant.

Times corresponding to other depressions of the Sun may be obtained by interpolation or, for depressions of more than 12°, less reliably, by extrapolation; times so obtained will be subject to considerable uncertainty near extreme conditions.

At moonrise and moonset allowance is made for semi-diameter, parallax, and refraction (34′), so that at the times given the Moon's upper limb is on the visible horizon as seen from sea level.

11. *Sunrise, sunset, twilight.* The tabulated times may be regarded, without serious error, as the LMT of the phenomena on any of the three days on the page and in any longitude. Precise times may normally be obtained by interpolating the tabular values for latitude and to the correct day and longitude, the latter being expressed as a fraction of a day by dividing it by 360°, positive for west and negative for east longitudes. In the extreme conditions near ☐, ■ or //// interpolation may not be possible in one direction, but accurate times are of little value in these circumstances.

Examples. Required the UT of (a) the beginning of morning twilights and sunrise on 1999 January 22 for latitude S 48° 55′, longitude E 75° 18′; (b) sunset and the end of evening twilights on 1999 January 24 for latitude N 67° 10′, longitude W 168° 05′.

		Twilight		Sunrise			Sunset	Twilight	
(a)		Nautical	Civil		(b)			Civil	Nautical
		d h m	d h m	d h m			d h m	d h m	d h m
From p. 25									
LMT for Lat	S 45°	22 03 24	22 04 08	22 04 43	N 66°		24 14 56	24 16 06	24 17 14
Corr. to	S 48° 55′	−27	−20	−16	N 67° 10′		−17	−9	−6
(p. xxxii, Table I)									
Long (p. i)	E 75° 18′	−5 01	−5 01	−5 01	W 168° 05′		+11 12	+11 12	+11 12
UT		21 21 56	21 22 47	21 23 26			25 01 51	25 03 09	25 04 20

The LMT are strictly for January 23 (middle date on page) and 0° longitude; for more precise times it is necessary to interpolate, but rounding errors may accumulate to about 2^m.

(a) to January $22^d − 75°/360° =$ Jan. 21^d8, i.e. $\frac{1}{3}(1·2) = 0·4$ backwards towards the data for the same latitude interpolated similarly from page 23; the corrections are $−2^m$ to nautical twilight, $−2^m$ to civil twilight and $−2^m$ to sunrise.

(b) to January $24^d + 168°/360° =$ Jan. 24^d5, i.e. $\frac{1}{3}(1·5) = 0·5$ forwards towards the data for the same latitude interpolated similarly from page 27; the corrections are $+7^m$ to sunset, $+5^m$ to civil twilight, and $+4^m$ to nautical twilight.

12. *Moonrise, moonset.* Precise times of moonrise and moonset are rarely needed; a glance at the tables will generally give sufficient indication of whether the Moon is available for observation and of the hours of rising and setting. If needed, precise times may be obtained as follows. Interpolate for latitude, using Table I on page xxxii, on the day wanted and also on the preceding day in east longitudes or the following day in west longitudes; take the difference between these times and interpolate for longitude by applying to the time for the day wanted the correction from Table II on page xxxii, so that the resulting time is between the two times used. In extreme conditions near ☐ or ■ interpolation for latitude or longitude may be possible only in one direction; accurate times are of little value in these circumstances.

To facilitate this interpolation the times of moonrise and moonset are given for four days on each page; where no phenomenon occurs during a particular day (as happens once a month) the time of the phenomenon on the following day, increased by 24^h, is given; extra care must be taken when interpolating between two values, when one of those values exceeds 24^h. In practice it suffices to use the daily difference between the times for the nearest tabular latitude, and generally, to enter Table II with the nearest tabular arguments as in the examples below.

Examples. Required the UT of moonrise and moonset in latitude S 47° 10′, longitudes E 124° 00′ and W 78° 31′ on 1999 January 30.

	Longitude E 124° 00′		Longitude W 78° 31′	
	Moonrise	Moonset	Moonrise	Moonset
	d h m	d h m	d h m	d h m
LMT for Lat. S 45°	30 18 43	30 03 28	30 18 43	30 03 28
Lat correction (p. xxxii, Table I)	+07	−07	+07	−07
Long correction (p. xxxii, Table II)	−17	−20	+09	+13
Correct LMT	30 18 33	30 03 01	30 18 59	30 03 34
Longitude (p. i)	−8 16	−8 16	+5 14	+5 14
UT	30 10 17	29 18 45	31 00 13	30 08 48

ALTITUDE CORRECTION TABLES

13. *General.* In general two corrections are given for application to altitudes observed with a marine sextant; additional corrections are required for Venus and Mars and also for very low altitudes.

Tables of the correction for dip of the horizon, due to height of eye above sea level, are given on pages A2 and xxxiv. Strictly this correction should be applied first and subtracted from the sextant altitude to give apparent altitude, which is the correct argument for the other tables.

Separate tables are given of the second correction for the Sun, for stars and planets (on pages A2 and A3), and for the Moon (on pages xxxiv and xxxv). For the Sun, values are given for both lower and upper limbs, for two periods of the year. The star tables are used for the planets, but additional corrections for parallax (page A2) are required for Venus and Mars. The Moon tables are in two parts: the main correction is a function of apparent altitude only and is tabulated for the lower limb (30′ must be subtracted to obtain the correction for the upper limb); the other, which is given for both lower and upper limbs, depends also on the horizontal parallax, which has to be taken from the daily pages.

An additional correction, given on page A4, is required for the change in the refraction, due to variations of pressure and temperature from the adopted standard conditions; it may generally be ignored for altitudes greater than 10°, except possibly in extreme conditions. The correction tables for the Sun, stars, and planets are in two parts; only those for altitudes greater than 10° are reprinted on the bookmark.

14. *Critical tables.* Some of the altitude correction tables are arranged as critical tables. In these an interval of apparent altitude (or height of eye) corresponds to a single value of the correction; no interpolation is required. At a "critical" entry the upper of the two possible values of the correction is to be taken. For example, in the table of dip, a correction of −4′1 corresponds to all values of the height of eye from 5·3 to 5·5 metres (17·5 to 18·3 feet) inclusive.

15. *Examples.* The following examples illustrate the use of the altitude correction tables; the sextant altitudes given are assumed to be taken on 1999 November 16 with a marine sextant at height 5·4 metres (18 feet), temperature −3°C and pressure 982 mb, the Moon sights being taken at about 10^h UT.

	SUN lower limb	SUN upper limb	MOON lower limb	MOON upper limb	VENUS	*Polaris*
	° ′	° ′	° ′	° ′	° ′	° ′
Sextant altitude	21 19·7	3 20·2	33 27·6	26 06·7	4 32·6	49 36·5
Dip, height 5·4 metres (18 feet)	−4·1	−4·1	−4·1	−4·1	−4·1	−4·1
Main correction	+13·8	−29·6	+57·4	+60·5	−10·8	−0·8
−30′ for upper limb (Moon)	—	—	—	−30·0	—	—
L, U correction for Moon	—	—	+3·0	+2·5	—	—
Additional correction for Venus	—	—	—	—	+0·2	—
Additional refraction correction	−0·1	−0·3	0·0	−0·1	−0·3	0·0
Corrected sextant altitude	21 29·3	2 46·2	34 23·9	26 35·5	4 17·6	49 31·6

The main corrections have been taken out with apparent altitude (sextant altitude corrected for dip) as argument, interpolating where possible. These refinements are rarely necessary.

16. *Composition of the Corrections.* The table for the dip of the sea horizon is based on the formula:

Correction for dip $= -1'\!76\sqrt{(\text{height of eye in metres})} = -0'\!97\sqrt{(\text{height of eye in feet})}$

The correction table for the Sun includes the effects of semi-diameter, parallax and mean refraction.

The correction tables for the stars and planets allow for the effect of mean refraction.

The phase correction for Venus has been incorporated in the tabulations for GHA and Dec, and no correction for phase is required. The additional corrections for Venus and Mars allow for parallax. Alternatively, the correction for parallax may be calculated from $p\cos H$, where p is the parallax and H is the altitude. In 1999 the values for p are:

	Jan. 1	May 8	June 26	July 19	Aug. 4	Sept. 6	Sept. 23	Oct. 17	Dec. 8	Dec. 31
Venus	0′.1	0′.2	0′.3	0′.4	0′.5	0′.4	0′.3	0′.2	0′.1	

	Jan. 1	Feb. 21	Apr. 22	May 10	July 27	Dec. 31
Mars	0′.1	0′.2	0′.3	0′.2	0′.1	

The correction table for the Moon includes the effect of semi-diameter, parallax, augmentation and mean refraction.

Mean refraction is calculated for a temperature of 10°C (50°F) and a pressure of 1010 mb (29·83 inches).

17. *Bubble sextant observations.* When observing with a bubble sextant no correction is necessary for dip, semi-diameter, or augmentation. The altitude corrections for the stars and planets on page A2 and on the bookmark should be used for the Sun as well as for the stars and planets; for the Moon it is easiest to take the mean of the corrections for lower and upper limbs and subtract 15′ from the altitude; the correction for dip must not be applied.

AUXILIARY AND PLANNING DATA

18. *Sun and Moon.* On the daily pages are given: hourly values of the horizontal parallax of the Moon; the semi-diameters and the times of meridian passage of both Sun and Moon over the Greenwich meridian; the equation of time; the age of the Moon, the percent (%) illuminated and a symbol indicating the phase. The times of the phases of the Moon are given in UT on page 4. For the Moon, the semi-diameters for each of the three days are given at the foot of the column; for the Sun a single value is sufficient. Table II on page xxxii may be used for interpolating the time of the Moon's meridian passage for longitude. The equation of time is given daily at 00^h and 12^h UT. The sign is *positive* for unshaded values and *negative* for shaded values. To obtain apparent time add the equation of time to mean time when the sign is *positive*. Subtract the equation of time from mean time when the sign is *negative*. At 12^h UT, when the sign is *positive*, meridian passage of the Sun occurs *before* 12^h UT, otherwise it occurs *after* 12^h UT.

19. *Planets.* The magnitudes of the planets are given immediately following their names in the headings on the daily pages; also given, for the middle day of the three on the page, are their SHA at 00^h UT and their times of meridian passage.

The planet notes and diagram on pages 8 and 9 provide descriptive information as to the suitability of the planets for observation during the year, and of their positions and movements.

20. *Stars.* The time of meridian passage of the first point of Aries over the Greenwich meridian is given on the daily pages, for the middle day of the three on the page, to 0^m1. The interval between successive meridian passages is $23^h 56^m1$ (24^h less 3^m9) so that times for intermediate days and other meridians can readily be derived. If a precise time is required it may be obtained by finding the UT at which LHA Aries is zero.

The meridian passage of a star occurs when its LHA is zero, that is when LHA Aries + SHA = 360°. An approximate time can be obtained from the planet diagram on page 9.

The star charts on pages 266 and 267 are intended to assist identification. They show the relative positions of the stars in the sky as seen from the Earth and include all 173 stars used in the Almanac, together with a few others to complete the main constellation configurations. The local meridian at any time may be located on the chart by means of its SHA which is 360° − LHA Aries, or west longitude − GHA Aries.

21. *Star globe.* To set a star globe on which is printed a scale of LHA Aries, first set the globe for latitude and then rotate about the polar axis until the scale under the edge of the meridian circle reads LHA Aries.

To mark the positions of the Sun, Moon, and planets on the star globe, take the difference GHA Aries − GHA body and use this along the LHA Aries scale, in conjunction with the declination, to plot the position. GHA Aries − GHA body is most conveniently found by taking the difference when the GHA of the body is small (less than 15°), which happens once a day.

22. *Calendar.* On page 4 are given lists of ecclesiastical festivals, and of the principal anniversaries and holidays in the United Kingdom and the United States of America. The calendar on page 5 includes the day of the year as well as the day of the week.

Brief particulars are given, at the foot of page 5, of the solar and lunar eclipses occurring during the year; the times given are in UT. The principal features of the more important solar eclipses are shown on the maps on pages 6 and 7.

23. *Standard times.* The lists on pages 262–265 give the standard times used in most countries. In general no attempt is made to give details of the beginning and end of summer time, since they are liable to frequent changes at short notice. For the latest information consult Admiralty List of Radio Signals Volume 2 (NP 282) corrected by Section VI of the weekly edition of Admiralty Notices to Mariners.

The Date or Calendar Line is an arbitrary line, on either side of which the date differs by one day; when crossing this line on a westerly course, the date must be advanced one day; when crossing it on an easterly course, the date must be put back one day. The line is a modification of the line of the 180th meridian, and is drawn so as to include, as far as possible, islands of any one group, etc., on the same side of the line. It may be traced by starting at the South Pole and joining up to the following positions:

Lat	S 51·0	S 45·0	S 15·0	S 5·0	N 48·0	N 53·0	N 65·5
Long	180·0	W 172·5	W 172·5	180·0	180·0	E 170·0	W 169·0

thence through the middle of the Diomede Islands to Lat N 68°·0, Long W 169°·0, passing east of Ostrov Vrangelya (Wrangel Island) to Lat N 75°·0, Long 180°·0, and thence to the North Pole.

ACCURACY

24. *Main data.* The quantities tabulated in this Almanac are generally correct to the nearest 0'·1; the exception is the Sun's GHA which is deliberately adjusted by up to 0'·15 to reduce the error due to ignoring the v-correction. The GHA and Dec at intermediate times cannot be obtained to this precision, since at least two quantities must be added; moreover, the v- and d-corrections are based on mean values of v and d and are taken from tables for the whole minute only. The largest error that can occur in the GHA or Dec of any body other than the Sun or Moon is less than 0'·2; it may reach 0'·25 for the GHA of the Sun and 0'·3 for that of the Moon.

In practice it may be expected that only one third of the values of GHA and Dec taken out will have errors larger than 0'·05 and less than one tenth will have errors larger than 0'·1.

25. *Altitude corrections.* The errors in the altitude corrections are nominally of the same order as those in GHA and Dec, as they result from the addition of several quantities each correctly rounded off to 0'·1. But the actual values of the dip and of the refraction at low altitudes may, in extreme atmospheric conditions, differ considerably from the mean values used in the tables.

USE OF THIS ALMANAC IN 2000

This Almanac may be used for the Sun and stars in 2000 in the following manner.

For the Sun, take out the GHA and Dec for the same date but, for January and February (for February 29 use March 1), for a time 5^h 48^m 00^s *earlier* and, for March to December, for a time 18^h 12^m 00^s *later* than the UT of observation; in both cases *add* 87° 00' to the GHA so obtained. The error, mainly due to planetary perturbations of the Earth, is unlikely to exceed 0'·4.

For the stars, calculate the GHA and Dec for the same date and the same time, but for January and February (for February 29 use March 1) *subtract* 15'·1 and for March to December *add* 44'·0 to the GHA so found. The error, due to incomplete correction for precession and nutation, is unlikely to exceed 0'·4. If preferred, the same result can be obtained by using a time 5^h 48^m 00^s earlier for January and February (for February 29 use March 1) and 18^h 12^m 00^s later for March to December, than the UT of observation (as for the Sun) and adding 86° 59'·2 to the GHA (or adding 87° as for the Sun and subtracting 0'·8, for precession, from the SHA of the star).

The Almanac cannot be so used for the Moon or planets.

LIST I — PLACES FAST ON UTC (mainly those EAST OF GREENWICH)

The times given ⎱ *added* to UTC to give Standard Time
below should be ⎰ *subtracted* from Standard Time to give UTC.

	h	m		h	m
Admiralty Islands	10		Egypt, Arab Republic of*	02	
Afghanistan	04	30	Equatorial Guinea, Republic of	01	
Albania*	01		Eritrea	03	
Algeria	01		Estonia*	02	
Amirante Islands	04		Ethiopia	03	
Andaman Islands	05	30	Fiji	12	
Angola	01		Finland*†	02	
Armenia*	03		France*†	01	
Australia					
Australian Capital Territory*	10		Gabon	01	
New South Wales[1]*	10		Georgia	05	
Northern Territory	09	30	Germany*†	01	
Queensland	10		Gibraltar*	01	
South Australia*	09	30	Greece*†	02	
Tasmania*	10		Guam	10	
Victoria*	10		Hong Kong	08	
Western Australia	08		Hungary*	01	
Whitsunday Islands	10		India	05	30
Austria*†	01		Indonesia, Republic of		
Azerbaijan*	04		Bangka, Billiton, Java, West and		
			Central Kalimantan, Madura, Sumatra	07	
Bahrain	03		Bali, Flores, South and East		
Balearic Islands*	01		Kalimantan, Lombok, Sulawesi,		
Bangladesh	06		Sumba, Sumbawa, Timor	08	
Belarus*	02		Aru, Irian Jaya, Kai, Moluccas,		
Belgium*†	01		Tanimbar	09	
Benin	01		Iran*	03	30
Bosnia and Herzegovina*	01		Iraq*	03	
Botswana, Republic of	02		Israel*	02	
Brunei	08		Italy*†	01	
Bulgaria*	02		Jan Mayen Island*	01	
Burma (Myanmar)	06	30	Japan	09	
Burundi	02		Jordan*	02	
Cambodia	07		Kazakhstan*		
Cameroon Republic	01		Western, Aktau, Uralsk	04	
Caroline Islands[2]	10		Central, Aktyubinsk, Atyrau, Kzyl-Orda	05	
Central African Republic	01		Eastern	06	
Chad	01		Kenya	03	
Chagos Archipelago, ...	05		Kiribati Republic		
Diego Garcia	06		Gilbert Islands	12	
Chatham Islands*	12	45	Phoenix Islands	13	
China, People's Republic of	08		Line Islands[3]	14	
Christmas Island, Indian Ocean ...	07		Korea, North, ...	09	
Cocos (Keeling) Islands	06	30	Republic of (South)	09	
Comoro Islands (Comoros)	03		Kuril Islands	11	
Congo Republic	01		Kuwait	03	
Corsica*	01		Kyrgyzstan*	05	
Crete*	02		Laccadive Islands	05	30
Croatia*	01		Laos	07	
Cyprus: Ercan*, Larnaca*	02		Latvia*	02	
Czech Republic*	01		Lebanon*	02	
Denmark*†	01		Lesotho	02	
Djibouti	03				

* Summer time may be kept in these places.   † For Summer time dates see List II footnotes.
[1] Except Broken Hill Area which keeps 09^h 30^m.
[2] Except Pohnpei, Pingelap and Kosrae which keep 11^h.
[3] The Line Islands that are not part of the Kiribati Republic keep 10^h slow on UTC.

LIST I — (*continued*)

	h	m		h	m
Libya*	01		Russia (*continued*)		
Liechtenstein*	01		Zone 9 Vladivostok, Khabarovsk,		
Lithuania*	02		Okhotsk	10	
Lord Howe Island*	10	30	Zone 10 Magadan, Yuzhno	11	
Luxembourg*†	01		Zone 11 Petropavlovsk, Pevek	12	
			Rwanda	02	
Macau	08		Ryukyu Islands	09	
Macedonia*, former Yugoslav Republic	01				
Macias Nguema (Fernando Póo) ...	01		Sakhalin Island*	10	
Madagascar, Democratic Republic of	03		Santa Cruz Islands	11	
Malawi	02		Sardinia*	01	
Malaysia, Malaya, Sabah, Sarawak ...	08		Saudi Arabia	03	
Maldives, Republic of The	05		Schouten Islands	10	
Malta*	01		Serbia*	01	
Mariana Islands	10		Seychelles	04	
Marshall Islands[1]	12		Sicily*	01	
Mauritius	04		Singapore	08	
Moldova*	02		Slovakia*	01	
Monaco*	01		Slovenia*	01	
Mongolia*	08		Socotra	03	
Mozambique	02		Solomon Islands	11	
			Somalia Republic	03	
Namibia*	01		South Africa, Republic of	02	
Nauru	12		Spain*†	01	
Nepal	05	45	Spanish Possessions in North Africa*	01	
Netherlands, The*†	01		Spitsbergen (Svalbard)*	01	
New Caledonia	11		Sri Lanka	06	
New Zealand*	12		Sudan, Republic of	02	
Nicobar Islands	05	30	Swaziland	02	
Niger	01		Sweden*†	01	
Nigeria, Republic of	01		Switzerland*	01	
Norfolk Island	11	30	Syria (Syrian Arab Republic)*	02	
Norway*	01				
Novaya Zemlya	03		Taiwan	08	
			Tajikistan	05	
Okinawa	09		Tanzania	03	
Oman	04		Thailand	07	
			Tonga	13	
Pagalu (Annobon Islands)	01		Tunisia	01	
Pakistan	05		Turkey*	02	
Palau Islands	09		Turkmenistan	05	
Papua New Guinea	10		Tuvalu	12	
Pescadores Islands	08				
Philippine Republic	08		Uganda	03	
Poland*	01		Ukraine*	02	
			United Arab Emirates	04	
Qatar	03		Uzbekistan	05	
Reunion	04		Vanuatu, Republic of	11	
Romania*	02		Vietnam, Socialist Republic of	07	
Russia[2]*					
Zone 1 Kaliningrad	02		Yemen	03	
Zone 2 Moscow, St Petersburg,			Yugoslavia*, Federal Republic of ...	01	
Arkhangelsk, Astrakhan ...	03				
Zone 3 Samara, Izhevsk	04		Zaire		
Zone 4 Perm, Amderna, Novyy Port	05		Kinshasa, Mbandaka	01	
Zone 5 Omsk, Novosibirsk	06		Haut-Zaire, Kasai, Kivu, Shaba ...	02	
Zone 6 Norilsk, Kyzyl, Dikson ...	07		Zambia, Republic of	02	
Zone 7 Bratsk, Irkutsk, Ulan-Ude	08		Zimbabwe	02	
Zone 8 Yakutsk, Chita, Tiksi ...	09				

---

* Summer time may be kept in these places.   † For Summer time dates see List II footnotes.
[1] Except the Ebon Atol which keeps time 24^h slow on that of the rest of the islands.
[2] The boundaries between the zones are irregular; listed are chief towns in each zone.

LIST II — PLACES NORMALLY KEEPING UTC

Ascension Island	Ghana	Irish Republic*†	Morocco	Sierra Leone
Burkina-Faso	Great Britain†	Ivory Coast	Portugal*†	Togo Republic
Canary Islands*	Guinea-Bissau	Liberia	Principe	Tristan da Cunha
Channel Islands†	Guinea Republic	Madeira*	St. Helena	
Faeroes*, The	Iceland	Mali	São Tomé	
Gambia, The	Ireland, Northern†	Mauritania	Senegal	

* Summer time may be kept in these places.

† The European Union directive states that Summer time, one hour in advance of UTC, is kept from 1999 March 28ᵈ 01ʰ to October 31ᵈ 01ʰ UTC. For Great Britain, Northern Ireland and the Channel Islands, these dates are subject to confirmation.

LIST III — PLACES SLOW ON UTC (WEST OF GREENWICH)

The times given subtracted from UTC to give Standard Time
below should be added to Standard Time to give UTC.

	h	m		h	m
Argentina	03		Canada (continued)		
Austral (Tubuai) Islands[1]	10		Quebec, east of long. W. 63°[3]	04	
Azores*	01		west of long. W. 63°* ...	05	
			Saskatchewan[3]	06	
			Yukon*	08	
Bahamas*	05		Cape Verde Islands	01	
Barbados	04		Cayman Islands	05	
Belize	06		Chile*	04	
Bermuda*	04		Colombia	05	
Bolivia	04		Cook Islands	10	
Brazil			Costa Rica	06	
SE coastal states, Bahia, Goiás,			Cuba*	05	
Brasilia*	03		Curaçao Island	04	
NE coastal states, Eastern Para ...	03				
Mato Grosso, Mato Grosso do Sul*	04		Dominican Republic	04	
Amazones, NW States, Amapa,					
Western Para	04		Easter Island (I. de Pascua)*	06	
Territory of Acre	05		Ecuador	05	
British Antarctic Territory[2]	03		El Salvador	06	
			Falkland Islands*	04	
Canada			Fanning Island	10	
Alberta*	07		Fernando de Noronha Island	02	
British Columbia[3]*	08		French Guiana	03	
Labrador[3]*	04				
Manitoba*	06		Galápagos Islands	06	
New Brunswick*	04		Greenland[4]		
Newfoundland*	03	30	General*	03	
Northwest Territories[3]*			Scoresby Sound*	01	
east of long. W. 85°	05		Thule area*	04	
long. W. 85° to W. 102°	06		Grenada	04	
west of long. W. 102°	07		Guadeloupe	04	
Nova Scotia*	04		Guatemala	06	
Ontario, east of long. W. 90°*	05		Guyana, Republic of	04	
west of long. W. 90°* ...	06				
Prince Edward Island*	04		Haiti*	05	
			Honduras	06	

* Summer time may be kept in these places.
[1] This is the legal standard time, but local mean time is generally used.
[2] Most stations use UTC.
[3] Some areas may keep another time zone.
[4] Mesters Vig and Danmarkshavn keep UTC.

LIST III — (continued)

	h	m		h	m
Jamaica	05		United States of America[2] (continued)		
Johnston Island	10		Iowa	06	
Juan Fernandez Islands*	04		Kansas[4]	06	
			Kentucky, eastern part	05	
Leeward Islands	04		western part	06	
			Louisiana	06	
Marquesas Islands	09	30	Maine	05	
Martinique	04		Maryland	05	
Mexico*[1]	06		Massachusetts	05	
Midway Islands	11		Michigan[4]	05	
			Minnesota	06	
Nicaragua	06		Mississippi	06	
Niue	11		Missouri	06	
			Montana	07	
Panama, Republic of	05		Nebraska, eastern part	06	
Paraguay*	04		western part	07	
Peru	05		Nevada	08	
Puerto Rico	04		New Hampshire	05	
			New Jersey	05	
St. Pierre and Miquelon*	03		New Mexico	07	
Samoa	11		New York	05	
Society Islands	10		North Carolina	05	
South Georgia	02		North Dakota[4]	06	
Suriname	03		Ohio	05	
			Oklahoma	06	
Trindade Island, South Atlantic ...	02		Oregon[4]	08	
Trinidad and Tobago	04		Pennsylvania	05	
Tuamotu Archipelago	10		Rhode Island	05	
Tubuai (Austral) Islands	10		South Carolina	05	
Turks and Caicos Islands*	05		South Dakota, eastern part	06	
			western part	07	
United States of America[2]			Tennessee, eastern part	05	
Alabama	06		western part	06	
Alaska	09		Texas[4]	06	
Aleutian Islands, east of W. 169° 30′	09		Utah	07	
Aleutian Islands, west of W. 169° 30′	10		Vermont	05	
Arizona[3]	07		Virginia	05	
Arkansas	06		Washington D.C.	05	
California	08		Washington	08	
Colorado	07		West Virginia	05	
Connecticut	05		Wisconsin	06	
Delaware	05		Wyoming	07	
District of Columbia	05		Uruguay	03	
Florida[4]	05				
Georgia	05				
Hawaii[3]	10		Venezuela	04	
Idaho[4]	07		Virgin Islands	04	
Illinois	06				
Indiana[3,4]	05		Windward Islands	04	

* Summer time may be kept in these places.

[1] Except Quintana Roo* which keeps 05[h], the states of Sonora*, Sinaloa*, Nayarit* and the Southern District of Lower California* which keep 07[h], and the Northern District of Lower California* which keeps 08[h].

[2] Daylight-saving (Summer) time, one hour fast on the time given, is kept from the first Sunday in April to the last Sunday in October, changing at 02[h] 00[m] local clock time.

[3] Exempt from keeping daylight-saving time.

[4] A small portion of the state is in another time zone.

NORTHERN STARS

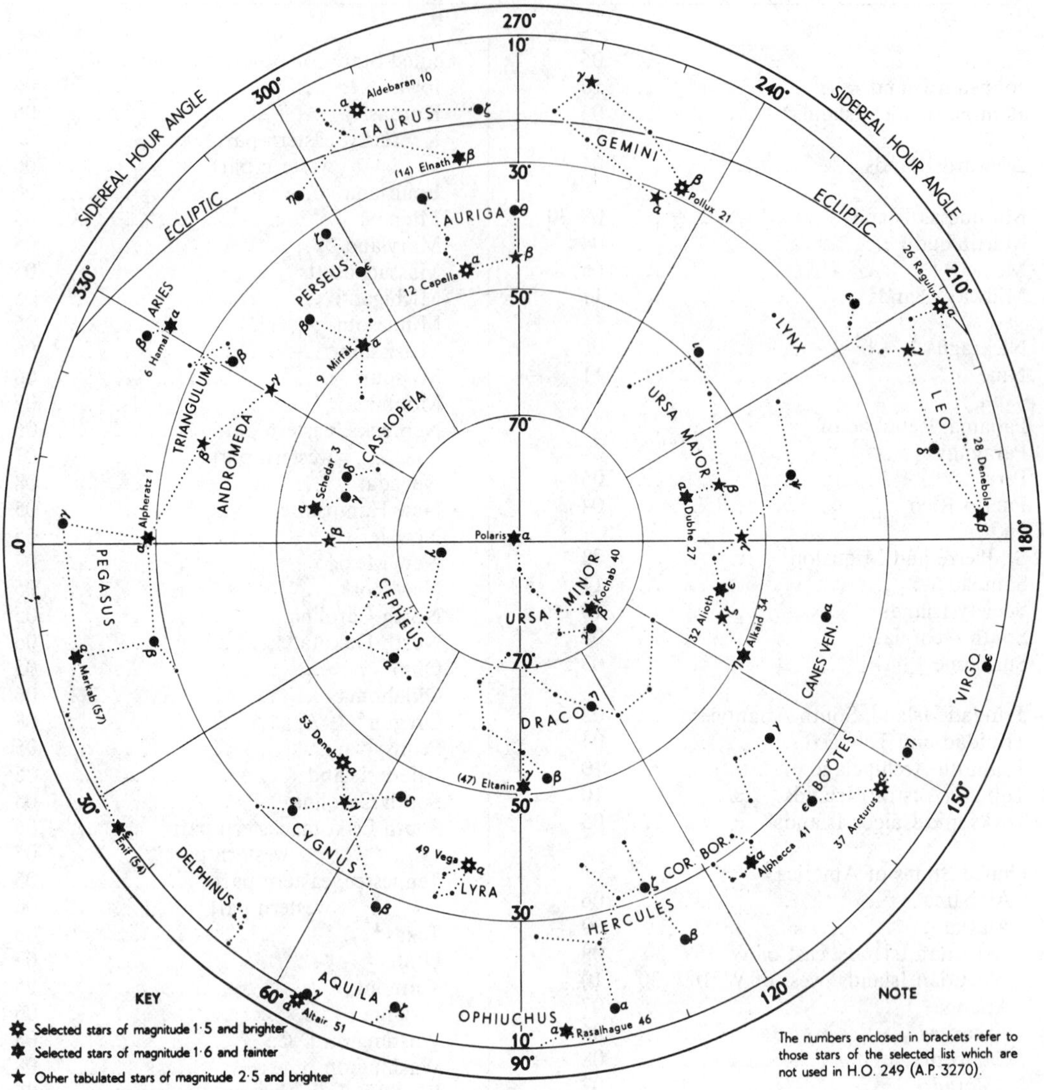

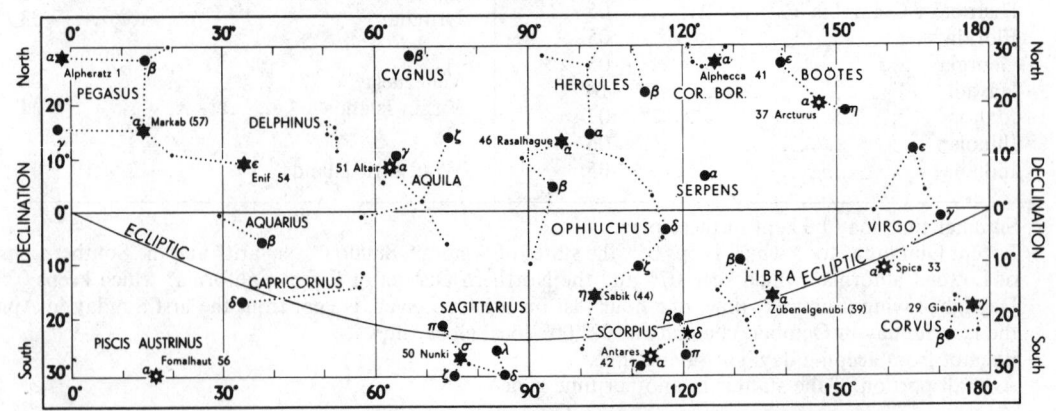

✷ Selected stars of magnitude 1·5 and brighter
★ Selected stars of magnitude 1·6 and fainter
★ Other tabulated stars of magnitude 2·5 and brighter
● Other tabulated stars of magnitude 2·6 and fainter
· Untabulated stars

NOTE

The numbers enclosed in brackets refer to those stars of the selected list which are not used in H.O. 249 (A.P. 3270).

EQUATORIAL STARS (S.H.A. 0° to 180°)

E.1663/2

SIDEREAL HOUR ANGLE

SOUTHERN STARS

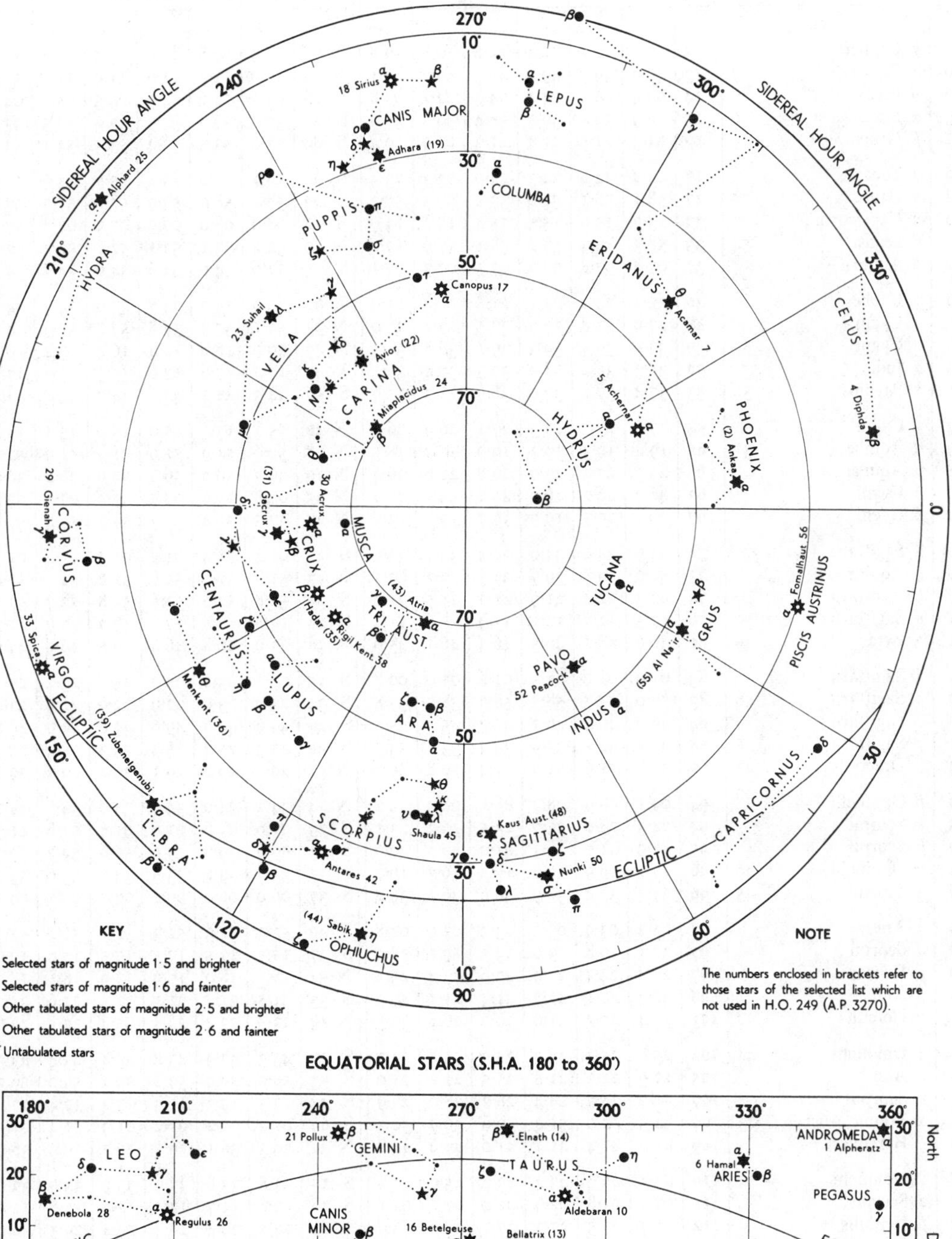

KEY

✳ Selected stars of magnitude 1·5 and brighter
★ Selected stars of magnitude 1·6 and fainter
★ Other tabulated stars of magnitude 2·5 and brighter
● Other tabulated stars of magnitude 2·6 and fainter
· Untabulated stars

NOTE

The numbers enclosed in brackets refer to those stars of the selected list which are not used in H.O. 249 (A.P. 3270).

EQUATORIAL STARS (S.H.A. 180° to 360°)

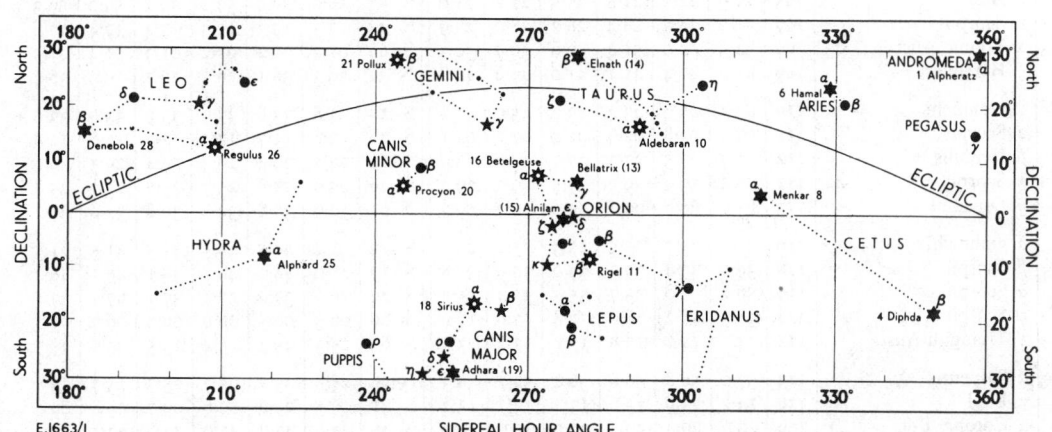

E.1663/1

Mag.	Name and Number		SHA							Declination						
			JAN.	FEB.	MAR.	APR.	MAY	JUNE			JAN.	FEB.	MAR.	APR.	MAY	JUNE
		°	′	′	′	′	′	′		°	′	′	′	′	′	′
3·4	γ Cephei	5	10·7	11·2	11·4	11·2	10·6	09·8	N 77		37·9	37·8	37·6	37·4	37·4	37·4
2·6	α Pegasi 57	13	49·6	49·7	49·6	49·5	49·3	49·1	N 15		12·0	11·9	11·9	11·9	11·9	12·0
2·6	β Pegasi	14	04·4	04·4	04·4	04·3	04·1	03·8	N 28		04·7	04·6	04·5	04·5	04·5	04·6
1·3	α Piscis Aust. 56	15	36·5	36·5	36·5	36·4	36·2	35·9	S 29		37·8	37·8	37·7	37·6	37·5	37·4
2·2	β Gruis	19	21·5	21·5	21·4	21·3	21·0	20·7	S 46		53·6	53·5	53·4	53·3	53·1	53·1
2·9	α Tucanæ	25	24·4	24·4	24·3	24·0	23·7	23·3	S 60		16·1	16·0	15·8	15·7	15·6	15·5
2·2	α Gruis 55	27	58·1	58·1	58·0	57·8	57·5	57·2	S 46		58·1	58·0	57·9	57·8	57·7	57·6
3·0	δ Capricorni	33	15·7	15·6	15·5	15·4	15·2	14·9	S 16		08·0	08·0	07·9	07·9	07·8	07·7
2·5	ε Pegasi 54	33	58·3	58·3	58·2	58·1	57·9	57·6	N 9		52·2	52·2	52·1	52·1	52·2	52·3
3·1	β Aquarii	37	07·8	07·8	07·7	07·5	07·3	07·1	S 5		34·6	34·6	34·6	34·6	34·5	34·4
2·6	α Cephei	40	22·2	22·2	22·1	21·8	21·4	21·0	N 62		35·0	34·9	34·7	34·6	34·7	34·8
2·6	ε Cygni	48	27·9	27·8	27·7	27·5	27·2	27·0	N 33		58·1	57·9	57·8	57·8	57·9	58·0
1·3	α Cygni 53	49	39·5	39·4	39·3	39·1	38·8	38·5	N 45		16·7	16·6	16·4	16·4	16·4	16·6
3·2	α Indi	50	38·3	38·2	38·0	37·7	37·4	37·1	S 47		17·7	17·6	17·6	17·5	17·4	17·4
2·1	α Pavonis 52	53	37·4	37·2	37·0	36·6	36·3	35·9	S 56		44·3	44·2	44·1	44·0	44·0	44·0
2·3	γ Cygni	54	27·6	27·5	27·3	27·1	26·9	26·6	N 40		15·3	15·1	15·0	15·0	15·1	15·2
0·9	α Aquilæ 51	62	19·4	19·3	19·2	19·0	18·7	18·5	N 8		52·0	51·9	51·9	51·9	51·9	52·0
2·8	γ Aquilæ	63	27·3	27·2	27·0	26·8	26·6	26·4	N 10		36·7	36·6	36·6	36·6	36·6	36·7
3·0	δ Cygni	63	46·3	46·2	46·0	45·8	45·5	45·3	N 45		07·8	07·6	07·5	07·5	07·6	07·7
3·2	β Cygni	67	20·2	20·1	19·9	19·7	19·5	19·3	N 27		57·5	57·4	57·3	57·3	57·4	57·5
3·0	π Sagittarii	72	34·9	34·8	34·6	34·4	34·1	33·9	S 21		01·4	01·4	01·4	01·4	01·4	01·3
3·0	ζ Aquilæ	73	40·0	39·8	39·7	39·5	39·2	39·1	N 13		51·8	51·7	51·6	51·6	51·7	51·8
2·7	ζ Sagittarii	74	22·3	22·2	21·9	21·7	21·5	21·2	S 29		52·8	52·8	52·8	52·8	52·7	52·7
2·1	σ Sagittarii 50	76	12·5	12·3	12·1	11·9	11·6	11·4	S 26		17·8	17·8	17·8	17·7	17·7	17·7
0·1	α Lyræ 49	80	46·9	46·7	46·5	46·3	46·1	45·9	N 38		47·0	46·8	46·8	46·8	46·9	47·0
2·9	λ Sagittarii	83	01·9	01·7	01·5	01·2	01·0	00·8	S 25		25·2	25·2	25·2	25·2	25·2	25·2
2·0	ε Sagittarii 48	83	59·0	58·8	58·5	58·3	58·0	57·8	S 34		23·0	23·0	22·9	22·9	22·9	23·0
2·8	δ Sagittarii	84	46·6	46·4	46·1	45·9	45·7	45·5	S 29		49·6	49·6	49·6	49·6	49·6	49·6
3·1	γ Sagittarii	88	34·4	34·1	33·9	33·7	33·4	33·3	S 30		25·3	25·3	25·3	25·3	25·3	25·3
2·4	γ Draconis 47	90	51·8	51·6	51·3	51·0	50·8	50·7	N 51		29·3	29·2	29·1	29·2	29·3	29·4
2·9	β Ophiuchi	94	09·1	08·9	08·7	08·5	08·3	08·2	N 4		34·1	34·0	34·0	34·0	34·1	34·2
2·5	κ Scorpii	94	24·3	24·0	23·7	23·5	23·2	23·1	S 39		01·6	01·6	01·6	01·6	01·6	01·7
2·0	θ Scorpii	95	41·9	41·6	41·3	41·0	40·8	40·6	S 42		59·6	59·6	59·6	59·6	59·7	59·7
2·1	α Ophiuchi 46	96	17·1	16·9	16·7	16·5	16·3	16·2	N 12		33·7	33·6	33·5	33·6	33·6	33·7
1·7	λ Scorpii 45	96	37·4	37·2	36·9	36·6	36·4	36·2	S 37		06·0	06·0	06·0	06·0	06·1	06·1
3·0	α Aræ	97	04·2	03·9	03·5	03·2	02·9	02·8	S 49		52·3	52·3	52·3	52·3	52·4	52·4
2·8	υ Scorpii	97	20·1	19·8	19·6	19·3	19·1	18·9	S 37		17·5	17·5	17·5	17·5	17·6	17·6
3·0	β Draconis	97	24·4	24·2	23·9	23·6	23·4	23·3	N 52		18·1	18·0	17·9	17·9	18·1	18·2
2·8	β Aræ	98	42·4	42·1	41·7	41·4	41·1	40·9	S 55		31·5	31·4	31·5	31·5	31·6	31·7
Var.‡	α Herculis	101	21·4	21·2	21·0	20·7	20·6	20·5	N 14		23·5	23·4	23·4	23·4	23·5	23·6
2·6	η Ophiuchi 44	102	25·6	25·4	25·2	24·9	24·8	24·7	S 15		43·3	43·3	43·4	43·4	43·4	43·3
3·1	ζ Aræ	105	22·6	22·2	21·8	21·5	21·2	21·0	S 55		59·0	59·0	59·0	59·1	59·2	59·3
2·4	ε Scorpii	107	29·0	28·7	28·4	28·2	28·0	27·9	S 34		17·3	17·3	17·3	17·4	17·4	17·4
1·9	α Triang. Aust. 43	107	52·5	52·0	51·4	50·9	50·5	50·3	S 69		01·2	01·2	01·2	01·3	01·4	01·5
3·0	ζ Herculis	109	41·7	41·4	41·2	41·0	40·9	40·8	N 31		36·3	36·1	36·1	36·2	36·3	36·4
2·7	ζ Ophiuchi	110	43·8	43·6	43·4	43·2	43·0	42·9	S 10		33·8	33·8	33·9	33·9	33·9	33·9
2·9	τ Scorpii	111	03·1	02·8	02·6	02·4	02·2	02·1	S 28		12·6	12·7	12·7	12·8	12·8	12·8
2·8	β Herculis	112	27·7	27·5	27·3	27·1	27·0	26·9	N 21		29·5	29·4	29·4	29·4	29·5	29·6
1·2	α Scorpii 42	112	40·2	39·9	39·7	39·5	39·3	39·2	S 26		25·6	25·6	25·7	25·7	25·7	25·8
2·9	η Draconis	113	61·0	60·6	60·2	59·9	59·7	59·7	N 61		30·9	30·8	30·8	30·8	31·0	31·2
3·0	δ Ophiuchi	116	25·9	25·7	25·5	25·3	25·2	25·1	S 3		41·4	41·5	41·5	41·5	41·5	41·5
2·8	β Scorpii	118	39·7	39·4	39·2	39·0	38·9	38·8	S 19		48·0	48·0	48·1	48·1	48·1	48·2
2·5	δ Scorpii	119	56·2	56·0	55·7	55·5	55·4	55·3	S 22		36·9	37·0	37·1	37·1	37·1	37·1
3·0	π Scorpii	120	18·5	18·2	18·0	17·8	17·6	17·6	S 26		06·5	06·5	06·6	06·6	06·7	06·7
3·0	β Trianguli Aust.	121	14·7	14·2	13·8	13·4	13·2	13·1	S 63		25·3	25·3	25·4	25·5	25·6	25·7
2·8	α Serpentis	123	57·0	56·8	56·6	56·4	56·3	56·3	N 6		25·8	25·7	25·7	25·7	25·7	25·8
3·0	γ Lupi	126	14·2	13·9	13·6	13·4	13·3	13·2	S 41		09·5	09·6	09·6	09·7	09·8	09·9
2·3	α Coronæ Bor. 41	126	20·6	20·4	20·2	20·0	19·9	19·9	N 26		43·0	42·9	42·9	43·0	43·1	43·2

‡ 3·0 — 3·7

Mag.	Name and Number			SHA						Declination						
				JULY	AUG.	SEPT.	OCT.	NOV.	DEC.		JULY	AUG.	SEPT.	OCT.	NOV.	DEC.
			°	′	′	′	′	′	′	°	′	′	′	′	′	′
3·4	γ Cephei		5	09·0	08·5	08·3	08·4	08·9	09·5	N 77	37·4	37·6	37·8	38·0	38·1	38·2
2·6	Markab	57	13	48·9	48·7	48·7	48·7	48·8	48·9	N 15	12·1	12·2	12·3	12·3	12·4	12·3
2·6	Scheat		14	03·6	03·5	03·4	03·4	03·5	03·6	N 28	04·7	04·8	04·9	05·0	05·1	05·1
1·3	Fomalhaut	56	15	35·6	35·5	35·4	35·4	35·5	35·6	S 29	37·3	37·3	37·4	37·5	37·5	37·6
2·2	β Gruis		19	20·4	20·2	20·1	20·2	20·3	20·5	S 46	53·0	53·1	53·2	53·3	53·4	53·4
2·9	α Tucanæ		25	22·9	22·6	22·6	22·7	23·0	23·2	S 60	15·5	15·6	15·7	15·8	15·9	15·9
2·2	Al Na'ir	55	27	56·9	56·7	56·7	56·8	56·9	57·1	S 46	57·6	57·7	57·8	57·9	57·9	57·9
3·0	δ Capricorni		33	14·7	14·6	14·6	14·6	14·8	14·9	S 16	07·7	07·6	07·7	07·7	07·7	07·7
2·5	Enif	54	33	57·4	57·3	57·3	57·4	57·5	57·6	N 9	52·4	52·5	52·5	52·6	52·6	52·5
3·1	β Aquarii		37	06·9	06·8	06·8	06·9	07·0	07·1	S 5	34·3	34·3	34·2	34·3	34·3	34·3
2·6	Alderamin		40	20·8	20·7	20·8	21·1	21·4	21·7	N 62	34·9	35·1	35·3	35·4	35·4	35·4
2·6	ε Cygni		48	26·8	26·8	26·8	27·0	27·1	27·3	N 33	58·1	58·3	58·4	58·4	58·4	58·4
1·3	Deneb	53	49	38·4	38·3	38·4	38·6	38·8	39·0	N 45	16·7	16·9	17·0	17·1	17·1	17·0
3·2	α Indi		50	36·8	36·7	36·8	37·0	37·1	37·3	S 47	17·4	17·5	17·6	17·7	17·7	17·7
2·1	Peacock	52	53	35·6	35·5	35·6	35·8	36·1	36·2	S 56	44·0	44·2	44·3	44·3	44·3	44·3
2·3	γ Cygni		54	26·5	26·4	26·5	26·7	26·9	27·0	N 40	15·3	15·5	15·6	15·7	15·7	15·6
0·9	Altair	51	62	18·4	18·4	18·5	18·6	18·7	18·8	N 8	52·1	52·2	52·3	52·3	52·2	52·2
2·8	γ Aquilæ		63	26·3	26·2	26·3	26·4	26·6	26·6	N 10	36·8	36·9	37·0	37·0	37·0	36·9
3·0	δ Cygni		63	45·2	45·2	45·3	45·5	45·8	45·9	N 45	07·9	08·0	08·1	08·2	08·1	08·0
3·2	Albireo		67	19·2	19·2	19·3	19·5	19·6	19·7	N 27	57·6	57·8	57·8	57·9	57·8	57·7
3·0	π Sagittarii		72	33·8	33·8	33·9	34·0	34·2	34·2	S 21	01·3	01·3	01·4	01·4	01·4	01·4
3·0	ζ Aquilæ		73	39·0	39·0	39·1	39·2	39·4	39·4	N 13	51·9	52·0	52·0	52·0	52·0	51·9
2·7	ζ Sagittarii		74	21·1	21·1	21·2	21·4	21·5	21·5	S 29	52·7	52·8	52·8	52·8	52·8	52·8
2·1	Nunki	50	76	11·3	11·3	11·4	11·6	11·7	11·7	S 26	17·7	17·7	17·8	17·8	17·8	17·8
0·1	Vega	49	80	45·8	45·9	46·1	46·3	46·4	46·5	N 38	47·2	47·3	47·4	47·4	47·3	47·2
2·9	λ Sagittarii		83	00·7	00·8	00·9	01·0	01·1	01·1	S 25	25·2	25·2	25·2	25·2	25·2	25·2
2·0	Kaus Australis	48	83	57·7	57·8	57·9	58·0	58·2	58·2	S 34	23·0	23·0	23·1	23·1	23·1	23·0
2·8	δ Sagittarii		84	45·4	45·4	45·5	45·7	45·8	45·8	S 29	49·6	49·6	49·7	49·7	49·6	49·6
3·1	γ Sagittarii		88	33·2	33·2	33·4	33·5	33·6	33·6	S 30	25·3	25·4	25·4	25·4	25·4	25·4
2·4	Eltanin	47	90	50·7	50·8	51·0	51·3	51·5	51·6	N 51	29·6	29·7	29·8	29·7	29·6	29·5
2·9	β Ophiuchi		94	08·1	08·2	08·3	08·4	08·5	08·5	N 4	34·2	34·3	34·3	34·3	34·2	34·2
2·5	κ Scorpii		94	23·0	23·1	23·2	23·4	23·5	23·5	S 39	01·7	01·8	01·8	01·8	01·7	01·7
2·0	θ Scorpii		95	40·5	40·6	40·8	41·0	41·1	41·0	S 42	59·8	59·9	59·9	59·9	59·8	59·8
2·1	Rasalhague	46	96	16·2	16·2	16·4	16·5	16·6	16·6	N 12	33·8	33·9	33·9	33·9	33·8	33·7
1·7	Shaula	45	96	36·2	36·3	36·4	36·6	36·7	36·6	S 37	06·1	06·2	06·2	06·2	06·1	06·1
3·0	α Aræ		97	02·7	02·8	03·0	03·2	03·3	03·3	S 49	52·5	52·6	52·6	52·6	52·5	52·4
2·8	υ Scorpii		97	18·9	18·9	19·1	19·3	19·3	19·3	S 37	17·7	17·7	17·7	17·7	17·7	17·6
3·0	β Draconis		97	23·3	23·5	23·7	24·0	24·2	24·2	N 52	18·4	18·5	18·5	18·5	18·4	18·2
2·8	β Aræ		98	40·8	41·0	41·2	41·4	41·5	41·5	S 55	31·8	31·8	31·9	31·8	31·8	31·7
Var.‡	α Herculis		101	20·5	20·5	20·7	20·8	20·9	20·9	N 14	23·7	23·7	23·8	23·7	23·7	23·5
2·6	Sabik	44	102	24·6	24·7	24·8	25·0	25·0	25·0	S 15	43·3	43·3	43·3	43·3	43·3	43·3
3·1	ζ Aræ		105	21·0	21·2	21·4	21·7	21·8	21·7	S 55	59·4	59·4	59·5	59·4	59·3	59·2
2·4	ε Scorpii		107	27·9	28·0	28·1	28·3	28·3	28·3	S 34	17·5	17·5	17·5	17·5	17·4	17·4
1·9	Atria	43	107	50·3	50·6	51·0	51·4	51·5	51·4	S 69	01·7	01·7	01·8	01·7	01·6	01·5
3·0	ζ Herculis		109	40·8	40·9	41·1	41·3	41·3	41·3	N 31	36·5	36·6	36·6	36·5	36·4	36·3
2·7	ζ Ophiuchi		110	42·9	43·0	43·1	43·3	43·3	43·2	S 10	33·8	33·8	33·8	33·8	33·8	33·9
2·9	τ Scorpii		111	02·1	02·2	02·3	02·5	02·5	02·4	S 28	12·8	12·8	12·8	12·8	12·8	12·8
2·8	β Herculis		112	26·9	27·0	27·2	27·3	27·3	27·3	N 21	29·7	29·8	29·8	29·7	29·6	29·5
1·2	Antares	42	112	39·2	39·3	39·5	39·6	39·6	39·6	S 26	25·8	25·8	25·8	25·8	25·7	25·7
2·9	η Draconis		113	59·9	60·1	60·5	60·8	61·0	61·0	N 61	31·3	31·3	31·3	31·3	31·1	30·9
3·0	δ Ophiuchi		116	25·1	25·2	25·4	25·5	25·5	25·4	S 3	41·4	41·4	41·4	41·4	41·4	41·5
2·8	β Scorpii		118	38·8	38·9	39·0	39·1	39·2	39·1	S 19	48·2	48·1	48·1	48·1	48·1	48·1
2·5	Dschubba		119	55·4	55·5	55·6	55·7	55·7	55·6	S 22	37·1	37·1	37·1	37·1	37·1	37·1
3·0	π Scorpii		120	17·6	17·7	17·8	17·9	18·0	17·9	S 26	06·7	06·7	06·7	06·7	06·6	06·6
3·0	β Trianguli Aust.		121	13·2	13·5	13·8	14·0	14·1	13·9	S 63	25·8	25·9	25·9	25·8	25·7	25·6
2·8	α Serpentis		123	56·3	56·4	56·5	56·6	56·6	56·5	N 6	25·8	25·9	25·9	25·9	25·8	25·7
3·0	γ Lupi		126	13·3	13·4	13·6	13·7	13·7	13·6	S 41	09·9	09·9	09·9	09·8	09·8	09·7
2·3	Alphecca	41	126	20·0	20·1	20·2	20·3	20·4	20·3	N 26	43·3	43·3	43·3	43·2	43·1	43·0

‡ 3·0 — 3·7

Mag.	Name and Number		No.	SHA °	JAN.	FEB.	MAR.	APR.	MAY	JUNE	Dec. °	JAN.	FEB.	MAR.	APR.	MAY	JUNE
3·1	γ	Ursæ Minoris		129	49·8	49·3	48·7	48·3	48·2	48·4	N 71	50·1	50·0	50·0	50·2	50·3	50·5
3·1	γ	Trianguli Aust.		130	18·2	17·6	17·1	16·8	16·5	16·5	S 68	40·2	40·2	40·3	40·4	40·6	40·7
2·7	β	Libræ		130	46·0	45·7	45·5	45·4	45·3	45·2	S 9	22·6	22·7	22·8	22·8	22·8	22·8
2·8	β	Lupi		135	23·2	22·9	22·7	22·5	22·4	22·4	S 43	07·5	07·6	07·7	07·8	07·8	07·9
2·9	α	Libræ	39	137	17·9	17·6	17·4	17·3	17·2	17·2	S 16	02·1	02·2	02·2	02·3	02·3	02·3
2·2	β	Ursæ Minoris	40	137	20·2	19·5	18·9	18·6	18·5	18·8	N 74	09·4	09·3	09·4	09·5	09·7	09·8
2·6	ε	Bootis		138	46·1	45·9	45·7	45·5	45·5	45·5	N 27	04·6	04·6	04·5	04·6	04·7	04·8
2·9	α	Lupi		139	32·3	31·9	31·7	31·5	31·4	31·4	S 47	22·7	22·8	22·9	23·0	23·1	23·2
0·1	α	Centauri	38	140	07·2	06·7	06·4	06·2	06·1	06·2	S 60	49·5	49·5	49·6	49·8	49·9	50·0
2·6	η	Centauri		141	08·5	08·2	08·0	07·8	07·7	07·7	S 42	08·9	09·0	09·1	09·2	09·3	09·4
3·0	γ	Bootis		141	59·7	59·4	59·2	59·1	59·0	59·1	N 38	18·6	18·6	18·6	18·7	18·8	18·9
0·2	α	Bootis	37	146	06·0	05·7	05·6	05·4	05·4	05·4	N 19	11·2	11·1	11·1	11·2	11·2	11·3
2·3	θ	Centauri	36	148	20·8	20·5	20·3	20·2	20·1	20·1	S 36	21·6	21·7	21·8	21·9	22·0	22·1
0·9	β	Centauri	35	149	03·8	03·4	03·1	02·9	02·8	02·9	S 60	21·7	21·8	21·9	22·1	22·2	22·3
3·1	ζ	Centauri		151	07·9	07·6	07·4	07·2	07·2	07·3	S 47	16·7	16·8	16·9	17·0	17·1	17·2
2·8	η	Bootis		151	20·6	20·4	20·2	20·1	20·1	20·1	N 18	24·1	24·0	24·0	24·1	24·2	24·2
1·9	η	Ursæ Majoris	34	153	07·7	07·4	07·2	07·1	07·1	07·2	N 49	18·9	18·9	18·9	19·0	19·2	19·3
2·6	ε	Centauri		155	02·7	02·3	02·1	01·9	01·9	02·0	S 53	27·3	27·4	27·6	27·7	27·8	27·9
1·2	α	Virginis	33	158	43·0	42·8	42·6	42·5	42·5	42·6	S 11	09·3	09·4	09·4	09·5	09·5	09·5
2·2	ζ	Ursæ Majoris		159	02·0	01·6	01·4	01·3	01·3	01·5	N 54	55·6	55·6	55·7	55·8	55·9	56·0
2·9	ι	Centauri		159	51·9	51·6	51·5	51·4	51·4	51·4	S 36	42·2	42·3	42·4	42·5	42·6	42·6
3·0	ε	Virginis		164	28·2	28·0	27·8	27·8	27·8	27·8	N 10	57·8	57·8	57·7	57·8	57·8	57·9
2·9	α	Canum Venat.		165	60·4	60·2	60·0	59·9	60·0	60·1	N 38	19·3	19·2	19·3	19·4	19·5	19·6
1·7	ε	Ursæ Majoris	32	166	30·4	30·1	29·9	29·8	29·9	30·1	N 55	57·7	57·7	57·8	57·9	58·0	58·1
1·5	β	Crucis		168	04·9	04·5	04·3	04·3	04·3	04·5	S 59	40·7	40·8	40·9	41·1	41·2	41·3
2·9	γ	Virginis		169	35·9	35·7	35·6	35·5	35·6	35·6	S 1	26·6	26·7	26·7	26·8	26·7	26·7
2·4	γ	Centauri		169	37·9	37·7	37·5	37·5	37·5	37·6	S 48	57·0	57·1	57·2	57·4	57·5	57·5
2·9	α	Muscæ		170	42·7	42·3	42·0	42·0	42·1	42·4	S 69	07·4	07·6	07·7	07·9	08·1	08·2
2·8	β	Corvi		171	25·0	24·7	24·6	24·6	24·6	24·7	S 23	23·3	23·4	23·5	23·6	23·7	23·7
1·6	γ	Crucis	31	172	13·1	12·8	12·6	12·6	12·7	12·8	S 57	06·1	06·3	06·4	06·6	06·7	06·8
1·1	α	Crucis	30	173	21·5	21·1	20·9	20·9	21·0	21·2	S 63	05·3	05·4	05·6	05·8	05·9	06·0
2·8	γ	Corvi	29	176	03·6	03·4	03·3	03·3	03·4	03·4	S 17	32·1	32·2	32·3	32·3	32·4	32·4
2·9	δ	Centauri		177	55·2	54·9	54·8	54·8	54·9	55·0	S 50	42·7	42·9	43·0	43·2	43·3	43·3
2·5	γ	Ursæ Majoris		181	33·4	33·1	33·0	33·0	33·1	33·3	N 53	41·8	41·8	41·9	42·0	42·2	42·2
2·2	β	Leonis	28	182	44·9	44·7	44·6	44·6	44·6	44·7	N 14	34·6	34·5	34·5	34·6	34·6	34·7
2·6	δ	Leonis		191	29·1	29·0	28·9	28·9	29·0	29·1	N 20	31·6	31·6	31·6	31·7	31·7	31·8
3·2	ψ	Ursæ Majoris		192	35·9	35·6	35·6	35·6	35·7	35·9	N 44	30·0	30·1	30·1	30·2	30·3	30·4
2·0	α	Ursæ Majoris	27	194	04·9	04·6	04·5	04·6	04·9	05·1	N 61	45·1	45·2	45·3	45·5	45·5	45·6
2·4	β	Ursæ Majoris		194	33·2	33·0	32·9	33·0	33·1	33·4	N 56	23·0	23·1	23·2	23·3	23·4	23·4
2·8	μ	Velorum		198	18·7	18·5	18·5	18·6	18·8	18·9	S 49	24·7	24·9	25·0	25·2	25·2	25·2
3·0	θ	Carinæ		199	15·5	15·3	15·3	15·4	15·7	16·0	S 64	23·1	23·3	23·5	23·7	23·7	23·8
2·3	γ	Leonis		205	01·1	01·0	01·0	01·0	01·1	01·2	N 19	50·7	50·6	50·7	50·7	50·8	50·8
1·3	α	Leonis	26	207	55·1	55·0	54·9	55·0	55·1	55·2	N 11	58·2	58·2	58·2	58·2	58·2	58·3
3·1	ε	Leonis		213	32·9	32·8	32·8	32·9	33·0	33·1	N 23	46·6	46·6	46·6	46·7	46·7	46·7
3·0	N	Velorum		217	11·5	11·4	11·5	11·7	12·0	12·2	S 57	01·7	01·9	02·1	02·2	02·2	02·2
2·2	α	Hydræ	25	218	06·7	06·6	06·6	06·7	06·9	06·9	S 8	39·3	39·4	39·5	39·5	39·5	39·4
2·6	κ	Velorum		219	28·2	28·1	28·2	28·4	28·6	28·9	S 55	00·3	00·5	00·7	00·8	00·8	00·8
2·2	ι	Carinæ		220	43·3	43·3	43·4	43·6	43·9	44·2	S 59	16·2	16·4	16·6	16·7	16·7	16·6
1·8	β	Carinæ	24	221	41·0	41·0	41·2	41·6	42·0	42·5	S 69	42·7	42·9	43·1	43·2	43·2	43·2
2·2	λ	Velorum	23	223	00·2	00·1	00·2	00·4	00·5	00·7	S 43	25·7	25·9	26·0	26·1	26·1	26·0
3·1	ι	Ursæ Majoris		225	12·7	12·6	12·6	12·8	13·0	13·1	N 48	02·5	02·6	02·7	02·8	02·8	02·8
2·0	δ	Velorum		228	49·2	49·2	49·3	49·6	49·8	50·0	S 54	42·3	42·5	42·6	42·7	42·7	42·6
1·7	ε	Carinæ	22	234	21·9	21·9	22·1	22·4	22·7	22·9	S 59	30·4	30·6	30·7	30·8	30·8	30·7
1·9	γ	Velorum		237	37·0	37·0	37·1	37·3	37·5	37·7	S 47	20·1	20·3	20·4	20·4	20·4	20·3
2·9	ρ	Puppis		238	07·2	07·2	07·2	07·4	07·5	07·6	S 24	18·2	18·3	18·4	18·4	18·4	18·3
2·3	ζ	Puppis		239	06·3	06·3	06·5	06·7	06·8	07·0	S 40	00·1	00·3	00·4	00·4	00·4	00·3
1·2	β	Geminorum	21	243	41·0	40·9	41·0	41·2	41·3	41·3	N 28	01·6	01·6	01·6	01·7	01·7	01·7
0·5	α	Canis Minoris	20	245	11·0	11·0	11·1	11·2	11·4	11·4	N 5	13·5	13·5	13·4	13·5	13·5	13·5

Mag.		Name and Number			SHA JULY	AUG.	SEPT.	OCT.	NOV.	DEC.	Declination	JULY	AUG.	SEPT.	OCT.	NOV.	DEC.
3·1	γ	Ursæ Minoris		129	48·8	49·3	49·8	50·2	50·3	50·2	N 71	50·6	50·6	50·5	50·4	50·2	50·0
3·1	γ	Trianguli Aust.		130	16·7	17·1	17·5	17·7	17·7	17·5	S 68	40·8	40·8	40·8	40·7	40·5	40·4
2·7	β	Libræ		130	45·3	45·4	45·5	45·6	45·6	45·4	S 9	22·7	22·7	22·7	22·7	22·7	22·8
2·8	β	Lupi		135	22·4	22·6	22·8	22·9	22·8	22·7	S 43	08·0	08·0	07·9	07·8	07·8	07·7
2·9		Zubenelgenubi	39	137	17·2	17·4	17·5	17·5	17·5	17·4	S 16	02·3	02·3	02·2	02·2	02·2	02·3
2·2		Kochab	40	137	19·2	19·8	20·4	20·7	20·8	20·6	N 74	09·9	09·9	09·8	09·6	09·5	09·3
2·6	ε	Bootis		138	45·6	45·7	45·8	45·9	45·9	45·7	N 27	04·9	04·9	04·9	04·8	04·7	04·5
2·9	α	Lupi		139	31·5	31·7	31·8	31·9	31·9	31·7	S 47	23·2	23·2	23·2	23·1	23·0	23·0
0·1		Rigil Kent.	38	140	06·3	06·6	06·9	07·0	07·0	06·7	S 60	50·1	50·1	50·0	49·9	49·8	49·7
2·6	η	Centauri		141	07·8	08·0	08·2	08·2	08·2	08·0	S 42	09·4	09·4	09·3	09·2	09·2	09·1
3·0	γ	Bootis		141	59·2	59·3	59·5	59·6	59·6	59·4	N 38	19·0	19·0	18·9	18·8	18·7	18·5
0·2		Arcturus	37	146	05·5	05·6	05·7	05·8	05·7	05·6	N 19	11·4	11·4	11·4	11·3	11·2	11·0
2·3		Menkent	36	148	20·2	20·4	20·5	20·5	20·5	20·3	S 36	22·1	22·1	22·0	21·9	21·9	21·9
0·9		Hadar	35	149	03·1	03·4	03·6	03·7	03·6	03·3	S 60	22·4	22·4	22·3	22·2	22·0	22·0
3·1	ζ	Centauri		151	07·4	07·6	07·7	07·8	07·7	07·4	S 47	17·3	17·2	17·1	17·0	17·0	16·9
2·8	η	Bootis		151	20·2	20·3	20·4	20·5	20·4	20·2	N 18	24·3	24·3	24·3	24·2	24·1	23·9
1·9		Alkaid	34	153	07·4	07·6	07·7	07·8	07·7	07·5	N 49	19·3	19·3	19·2	19·1	18·9	18·7
2·6	ε	Centauri		155	02·2	02·4	02·6	02·6	02·5	02·2	S 53	28·0	27·9	27·8	27·7	27·6	27·6
1·2		Spica	33	158	42·6	42·7	42·8	42·8	42·7	42·5	S 11	09·4	09·4	09·4	09·4	09·4	09·5
2·2		Mizar		159	01·7	01·9	02·0	02·1	02·0	01·7	N 54	56·1	56·0	55·9	55·8	55·6	55·4
2·9	ι	Centauri		159	51·6	51·7	51·8	51·8	51·7	51·5	S 36	42·6	42·6	42·5	42·4	42·4	42·4
3·0	ε	Virginis		164	27·9	28·0	28·1	28·1	28·0	27·8	N 10	57·9	57·9	57·9	57·9	57·8	57·6
2·9		Cor Caroli		166	00·2	00·3	00·4	00·4	00·3	00·0	N 38	19·6	19·6	19·5	19·4	19·2	19·0
1·7		Alioth	32	166	30·3	30·4	30·6	30·6	30·4	30·1	N 55	58·1	58·1	58·0	57·8	57·6	57·5
1·5		Mimosa		168	04·7	05·0	05·1	05·1	04·9	04·5	S 59	41·3	41·3	41·1	41·0	40·9	40·9
2·9	γ	Virginis		169	35·7	35·8	35·8	35·8	35·7	35·5	S 1	26·7	26·6	26·6	26·7	26·7	26·8
2·4		Muhlifain		169	37·8	38·0	38·1	38·0	37·9	37·9	S 48	57·5	57·5	57·4	57·3	57·2	57·2
2·9	α	Muscæ		170	42·8	43·1	43·4	43·4	43·1	42·6	S 69	08·2	08·1	08·0	07·8	07·7	07·7
2·8	β	Corvi		171	24·8	24·9	24·9	24·9	24·7	24·5	S 23	23·6	23·6	23·5	23·5	23·5	23·5
1·6		Gacrux	31	172	13·1	13·3	13·4	13·4	13·1	12·8	S 57	06·8	06·7	06·6	06·5	06·4	06·4
1·1		Acrux	30	173	21·5	21·8	21·9	21·9	21·6	21·2	S 63	06·0	05·9	05·8	05·6	05·5	05·5
2·8		Gienah	29	176	03·5	03·6	03·6	03·6	03·4	03·2	S 17	32·3	32·3	32·2	32·2	32·2	32·3
2·9	δ	Centauri		177	55·2	55·4	55·4	55·4	55·2	54·8	S 50	43·3	43·2	43·1	43·0	42·9	43·0
2·5		Phecda		181	33·4	33·6	33·6	33·5	33·3	33·0	N 53	42·2	42·1	42·0	41·8	41·6	41·5
2·2		Denebola	28	182	44·8	44·9	44·9	44·8	44·6	44·4	N 14	34·7	34·7	34·6	34·6	34·5	34·4
2·6	δ	Leonis		191	29·2	29·2	29·2	29·1	28·9	28·6	N 20	31·8	31·8	31·7	31·6	31·5	31·4
3·2	ψ	Ursæ Majoris		192	36·0	36·1	36·0	35·9	35·7	35·4	N 44	30·3	30·3	30·2	30·0	29·9	29·8
2·0		Dubhe	27	194	05·3	05·4	05·4	05·2	04·9	04·5	N 61	45·5	45·4	45·2	45·1	44·9	44·8
2·4		Merak		194	33·5	33·6	33·6	33·4	33·1	32·7	N 56	23·4	23·3	23·1	23·0	22·8	22·8
2·8	μ	Velorum		198	19·1	19·2	19·2	19·0	18·8	18·4	S 49	25·2	25·1	24·9	24·8	24·8	24·9
3·0	θ	Carinæ		199	16·3	16·5	16·5	16·3	15·9	15·5	S 64	23·7	23·6	23·4	23·3	23·2	23·3
2·3		Algeiba		205	01·3	01·3	01·2	01·1	00·9	00·6	N 19	50·8	50·8	50·7	50·7	50·6	50·5
1·3		Regulus	26	207	55·3	55·2	55·2	55·0	54·8	54·6	N 11	58·3	58·3	58·3	58·2	58·1	58·0
3·1	ε	Leonis		213	33·2	33·1	33·0	32·9	32·6	32·4	N 23	46·7	46·7	46·6	46·6	46·5	46·4
3·0	N	Velorum		217	12·4	12·4	12·3	12·1	11·7	11·4	S 57	02·1	01·9	01·8	01·7	01·7	01·8
2·2		Alphard	25	218	07·0	07·0	06·9	06·7	06·5	06·2	S 8	39·4	39·3	39·3	39·3	39·3	39·4
2·6	κ	Velorum		219	29·0	29·0	28·9	28·7	28·3	28·0	S 55	00·6	00·5	00·3	00·3	00·3	00·4
2·2	ι	Carinæ		220	44·4	44·4	44·3	44·0	43·6	43·3	S 59	16·5	16·4	16·2	16·1	16·1	16·2
1·8		Miaplacidus	24	221	42·7	42·8	42·7	42·3	41·8	41·3	S 69	43·1	42·9	42·7	42·7	42·6	42·7
2·2		Suhail	23	222	60·8	60·8	60·7	60·4	60·2	59·9	S 43	25·9	25·8	25·7	25·6	25·6	25·7
3·1	ι	Ursæ Majoris		225	13·1	13·1	12·9	12·6	12·3	12·0	N 48	02·7	02·6	02·5	02·4	02·3	02·3
2·0	δ	Velorum		228	50·2	50·1	50·0	49·7	49·4	49·1	S 54	42·5	42·3	42·2	42·1	42·2	42·3
1·7		Avior	22	234	23·0	23·0	22·8	22·5	22·1	21·8	S 59	30·6	30·4	30·3	30·2	30·3	30·4
1·9	γ	Velorum		237	37·7	37·7	37·5	37·3	37·0	36·7	S 47	20·2	20·0	19·9	19·9	19·9	20·1
2·9	ρ	Puppis		238	07·6	07·5	07·4	07·2	06·9	06·7	S 24	18·2	18·1	18·0	18·0	18·1	18·2
2·3	ζ	Puppis		239	07·0	06·9	06·7	06·5	06·2	06·0	S 39	60·2	60·0	59·9	59·9	59·9	60·1
1·2		Pollux	21	243	41·3	41·2	41·0	40·8	40·5	40·3	N 28	01·6	01·6	01·6	01·5	01·5	01·5
0·5		Procyon	20	245	11·4	11·2	11·1	10·9	10·6	10·4	N 5	13·6	13·6	13·6	13·6	13·5	13·5

Mag.	Name and Number		SHA						Declination						
			JAN.	FEB.	MAR.	APR.	MAY	JUNE		JAN.	FEB.	MAR.	APR.	MAY	JUNE
		°	′	′	′	′	′	′	°	′	′	′	′	′	′
1·6	α Geminorum	246	21·7	21·7	21·8	22·0	22·1	22·1	N 31	53·3	53·3	53·4	53·4	53·4	53·4
3·3	σ Puppis	247	41·6	41·6	41·8	42·0	42·2	42·3	S 43	18·1	18·3	18·4	18·4	18·3	18·2
3·1	β Canis Minoris	248	13·3	13·3	13·4	13·6	13·7	13·7	N 8	17·3	17·3	17·3	17·3	17·3	17·4
2·4	η Canis Majoris	248	58·8	58·9	59·0	59·2	59·3	59·4	S 29	18·2	18·4	18·4	18·4	18·4	18·3
2·7	π Puppis	250	43·0	43·1	43·2	43·4	43·6	43·6	S 37	05·9	06·0	06·1	06·1	06·1	06·0
2·0	δ Canis Majoris	252	54·4	54·5	54·6	54·8	54·9	54·9	S 26	23·7	23·8	23·8	23·9	23·8	23·7
3·1	o Canis Majoris	254	15·0	15·0	15·1	15·3	15·4	15·5	S 23	50·1	50·2	50·3	50·3	50·2	50·1
1·6	ε Canis Majoris 19	255	20·9	20·9	21·1	21·2	21·4	21·4	S 28	58·4	58·5	58·6	58·6	58·6	58·4
2·8	τ Puppis	257	30·8	30·9	31·1	31·4	31·6	31·7	S 50	37·0	37·1	37·2	37·2	37·2	37·0
−1·6	α Canis Majoris 18	258	43·2	43·2	43·4	43·5	43·6	43·6	S 16	43·1	43·1	43·2	43·2	43·1	43·0
1·9	γ Geminorum	260	35·0	35·0	35·1	35·3	35·3	35·4	N 16	23·9	23·9	23·9	23·9	23·9	23·9
−0·9	α Carinæ 17	264	00·5	00·7	00·9	01·2	01·4	01·5	S 52	41·9	42·1	42·1	42·1	42·0	41·9
2·0	β Canis Majoris	264	19·9	20·0	20·1	20·3	20·4	20·4	S 17	57·5	57·6	57·7	57·6	57·6	57·5
2·7	θ Aurigæ	270	05·0	05·0	05·2	05·3	05·4	05·4	N 37	12·6	12·7	12·7	12·7	12·7	12·6
2·1	β Aurigæ	270	07·9	08·0	08·1	08·3	08·4	08·4	N 44	56·8	56·8	56·9	56·9	56·8	56·7
Var.‡	α Orionis 16	271	13·0	13·1	13·2	13·3	13·4	13·4	N 7	24·2	24·2	24·2	24·2	24·2	24·3
2·2	κ Orionis	273	04·2	04·2	04·3	04·5	04·6	04·6	S 9	40·4	40·5	40·5	40·5	40·4	40·3
1·9	ζ Orionis	274	49·2	49·2	49·4	49·5	49·6	49·6	S 1	56·8	56·8	56·8	56·8	56·8	56·7
2·8	α Columbæ	275	05·5	05·6	05·8	06·0	06·1	06·1	S 34	04·8	04·8	04·9	04·8	04·7	04·6
3·0	ζ Tauri	275	36·0	36·1	36·2	36·4	36·4	36·4	N 21	08·4	08·4	08·4	08·4	08·4	08·4
1·8	ε Orionis 15	275	57·4	57·4	57·6	57·7	57·8	57·7	S 1	12·3	12·4	12·4	12·4	12·3	12·3
2·9	ι Orionis	276	09·1	09·1	09·2	09·4	09·5	09·4	S 5	54·8	54·9	54·9	54·9	54·8	54·8
2·7	α Leporis	276	49·5	49·6	49·7	49·9	50·0	49·9	S 17	49·6	49·7	49·7	49·7	49·6	49·5
2·5	δ Orionis	277	00·5	00·5	00·7	00·8	00·9	00·8	S 0	18·2	18·2	18·2	18·2	18·2	18·1
3·0	β Leporis	277	56·8	56·8	57·0	57·1	57·2	57·2	S 20	45·9	45·9	46·0	45·9	45·9	45·7
1·8	β Tauri 14	278	26·4	26·4	26·6	26·7	26·8	26·8	N 28	36·3	36·3	36·3	36·3	36·3	36·3
1·7	γ Orionis 13	278	43·7	43·7	43·9	44·0	44·1	44·0	N 6	20·8	20·7	20·7	20·7	20·8	20·8
0·2	α Aurigæ 12	280	50·5	50·6	50·8	51·0	51·1	51·0	N 45	59·8	59·8	59·8	59·8	59·8	59·7
0·3	β Orionis 11	281	22·5	22·6	22·7	22·8	22·9	22·8	S 8	12·4	12·4	12·5	12·4	12·4	12·3
2·9	β Eridani	283	02·8	02·9	03·0	03·2	03·2	03·2	S 5	05·5	05·5	05·5	05·5	05·5	05·4
2·9	ι Aurigæ	285	45·9	46·0	46·1	46·3	46·3	46·2	N 33	09·8	09·8	09·8	09·8	09·8	09·7
1·1	α Tauri 10	291	01·9	02·0	02·1	02·3	02·3	02·2	N 16	30·3	30·3	30·3	30·3	30·3	30·3
3·2	γ Eridani	300	30·2	30·3	30·4	30·5	30·5	30·4	S 13	30·9	31·0	31·0	30·9	30·8	30·7
3·0	ε Persei	300	33·0	33·2	33·3	33·5	33·5	33·3	N 40	00·4	00·5	00·4	00·4	00·3	00·3
2·9	ζ Persei	301	28·8	28·9	29·1	29·2	29·2	29·1	N 31	52·8	52·8	52·8	52·7	52·7	52·7
3·0	η Tauri	303	08·5	08·6	08·8	08·9	08·9	08·7	N 24	06·1	06·0	06·0	06·0	06·0	06·0
1·9	α Persei 9	308	56·0	56·2	56·4	56·6	56·5	56·4	N 49	51·5	51·5	51·5	51·4	51·3	51·3
Var.§	β Persei	312	58·3	58·5	58·6	58·7	58·7	58·5	N 40	57·1	57·1	57·1	57·0	57·0	56·9
2·8	α Ceti 8	314	26·6	26·7	26·8	26·9	26·8	26·7	N 4	05·0	05·0	05·0	05·0	05·0	05·1
3·1	θ Eridani 7	315	26·6	26·8	27·0	27·1	27·1	26·9	S 40	18·9	18·9	18·9	18·7	18·6	18·4
2·1	α Ursæ Minoris	322	07·8	19·8	30·0	35·5	33·7	26·0	N 89	15·8	15·8	15·7	15·6	15·4	15·3
3·1	β Trianguli	327	37·7	37·9	38·0	38·0	37·9	37·7	N 34	59·0	59·0	58·9	58·8	58·8	58·8
2·2	α Arietis 6	328	13·3	13·4	13·5	13·5	13·4	13·3	N 23	27·4	27·4	27·4	27·3	27·3	27·3
2·2	γ Andromedæ	329	02·4	02·6	02·7	02·7	02·7	02·4	N 42	19·6	19·5	19·5	19·4	19·3	19·3
3·0	α Hydri	330	19·1	19·4	19·6	19·7	19·7	19·4	S 61	34·9	34·9	34·8	34·6	34·4	34·2
2·7	β Arietis	331	21·3	21·4	21·5	21·5	21·4	21·2	N 20	48·1	48·1	48·1	48·0	48·0	48·1
0·6	α Eridani 5	335	35·1	35·3	35·5	35·6	35·5	35·2	S 57	14·9	14·9	14·8	14·6	14·4	14·3
2·8	δ Cassiopeiæ	338	33·7	34·0	34·1	34·2	34·0	33·7	N 60	14·0	13·9	13·8	13·7	13·6	13·6
2·4	β Andromedæ	342	34·9	35·1	35·1	35·1	35·0	34·8	N 35	37·0	36·9	36·8	36·8	36·7	36·8
Var.‖	γ Cassiopeiæ	345	50·3	50·5	50·7	50·7	50·5	50·1	N 60	42·9	42·8	42·7	42·5	42·5	42·4
2·2	β Ceti 4	349	07·1	07·2	07·3	07·2	07·1	06·9	S 17	59·8	59·8	59·7	59·6	59·5	59·4
2·5	α Cassiopeiæ 3	349	53·3	53·5	53·6	53·6	53·4	53·1	N 56	32·1	32·0	31·9	31·8	31·7	31·7
2·4	α Phœnicis 2	353	26·8	27·0	27·0	27·0	26·8	26·5	S 42	19·0	19·0	18·9	18·7	18·6	18·4
2·9	β Hydri	353	35·6	36·1	36·4	36·3	35·9	35·2	S 77	16·0	15·9	15·7	15·5	15·3	15·2
2·9	γ Pegasi	356	42·4	42·5	42·5	42·5	42·3	42·1	N 15	10·7	10·6	10·6	10·5	10·6	10·6
2·4	β Cassiopeiæ	357	43·3	43·5	43·6	43·5	43·2	42·9	N 59	08·8	08·8	08·6	08·5	08·4	08·4
2·2	α Andromedæ 1	357	55·1	55·2	55·3	55·2	55·0	54·8	N 29	05·1	05·1	05·0	04·9	04·9	05·0

‡ 0·1 — 1·2   § 2·3 — 3·5   ‖ Irregular variable; 1997 mag. 2·3

Mag.	Name and Number	SHA °	JULY	AUG.	SEPT.	OCT.	NOV.	DEC.	Declination °	JULY	AUG.	SEPT.	OCT.	NOV.	DEC.
1·6	*Castor*	246	22·1	22·0	21·8	21·5	21·2	21·0	N 31	53·4	53·3	53·3	53·2	53·2	53·2
3·3	σ Puppis	247	42·3	42·2	42·0	41·7	41·5	41·2	S 43	18·1	17·9	17·8	17·8	17·9	18·0
3·1	β Canis Minoris	248	13·6	13·5	13·4	13·1	12·9	12·7	N 8	17·4	17·4	17·4	17·4	17·4	17·3
2·4	η Canis Majoris	248	59·3	59·2	59·1	58·8	58·6	58·4	S 29	18·2	18·0	18·0	17·9	18·0	18·1
2·7	π Puppis	250	43·6	43·5	43·3	43·1	42·8	42·6	S 37	05·8	05·7	05·6	05·6	05·7	05·8
2·0	*Wezen*	252	54·9	54·8	54·6	54·4	54·1	54·0	S 26	23·6	23·5	23·4	23·4	23·5	23·6
3·1	o Canis Majoris	254	15·4	15·3	15·1	14·9	14·7	14·5	S 23	50·0	49·9	49·8	49·8	49·9	50·0
1·6	*Adhara* 19	255	21·4	21·3	21·1	20·8	20·6	20·4	S 28	58·3	58·2	58·1	58·1	58·2	58·3
2·8	τ Puppis	257	31·7	31·6	31·3	31·0	30·7	30·5	S 50	36·9	36·7	36·6	36·6	36·7	36·9
−1·6	*Sirius* 18	258	43·6	43·5	43·3	43·0	42·8	42·7	S 16	42·9	42·8	42·8	42·8	42·9	43·0
1·9	*Alhena*	260	35·3	35·1	34·9	34·7	34·4	34·3	N 16	23·9	23·9	23·9	23·9	23·9	23·9
−0·9	*Canopus* 17	264	01·5	01·3	01·0	00·7	00·4	00·3	S 52	41·7	41·6	41·5	41·5	41·6	41·8
2·0	*Mirzam*	264	20·3	20·2	20·0	19·7	19·5	19·4	S 17	57·4	57·3	57·2	57·2	57·3	57·4
2·7	θ Aurigæ	270	05·3	05·1	04·8	04·5	04·3	04·1	N 37	12·6	12·6	12·6	12·6	12·6	12·6
2·1	*Menkalinan*	270	08·3	08·0	07·7	07·4	07·2	07·0	N 44	56·7	56·6	56·6	56·6	56·7	56·7
Var.‡	*Betelgeuse* 16	271	13·3	13·1	12·9	12·7	12·5	12·3	N 7	24·3	24·4	24·4	24·4	24·4	24·3
2·2	κ Orionis	273	04·5	04·3	04·1	03·9	03·7	03·5	S 9	40·2	40·1	40·1	40·1	40·2	40·3
1·9	*Alnitak*	274	49·4	49·3	49·1	48·9	48·7	48·5	S 1	56·6	56·6	56·5	56·5	56·6	56·6
2·8	*Phact*	275	06·0	05·8	05·6	05·4	05·2	05·0	S 34	04·5	04·3	04·3	04·3	04·4	04·5
3·0	ζ Tauri	275	36·3	36·1	35·8	35·6	35·4	35·3	N 21	08·4	08·4	08·5	08·5	08·5	08·5
1·8	*Alnilam* 15	275	57·6	57·4	57·2	57·0	56·8	56·7	S 1	12·2	12·1	12·1	12·1	12·1	12·2
2·9	ι Orionis	276	09·3	09·1	08·9	08·7	08·5	08·4	S 5	54·7	54·6	54·5	54·5	54·6	54·7
2·7	α Leporis	276	49·8	49·6	49·4	49·2	49·0	48·9	S 17	49·4	49·3	49·2	49·2	49·3	49·4
2·5	δ Orionis	276	60·7	60·5	60·3	60·1	59·9	59·8	S 0	18·0	18·0	17·9	17·9	18·0	18·0
3·0	β Leporis	277	57·1	56·9	56·7	56·5	56·3	56·2	S 20	45·6	45·5	45·4	45·5	45·6	45·7
1·8	*Elnath* 14	278	26·6	26·4	26·1	25·9	25·7	25·5	N 28	36·3	36·3	36·3	36·3	36·3	36·4
1·7	*Bellatrix* 13	278	43·9	43·7	43·5	43·3	43·1	43·0	N 6	20·9	20·9	21·0	21·0	20·9	20·9
0·2	*Capella* 12	280	50·8	50·5	50·2	49·9	49·7	49·5	N 45	59·6	59·6	59·6	59·7	59·7	59·8
0·3	*Rigel* 11	281	22·7	22·5	22·3	22·1	21·9	21·8	S 8	12·2	12·1	12·0	12·1	12·1	12·2
2·9	β Eridani	283	03·0	02·9	02·6	02·4	02·3	02·2	S 5	05·3	05·2	05·2	05·2	05·2	05·3
2·9	ι Aurigæ	285	46·1	45·8	45·6	45·3	45·1	45·0	N 33	09·7	09·7	09·8	09·8	09·8	09·9
1·1	*Aldebaran* 10	291	02·0	01·8	01·6	01·4	01·2	01·1	N 16	30·4	30·4	30·4	30·5	30·5	30·5
3·2	γ Eridani	300	30·3	30·1	29·8	29·7	29·5	29·5	S 13	30·6	30·5	30·5	30·5	30·6	30·7
3·0	ε Persei	300	33·1	32·8	32·6	32·3	32·2	32·1	N 40	00·3	00·3	00·4	00·4	00·5	00·6
2·9	ζ Persei	301	28·9	28·6	28·4	28·2	28·0	27·9	N 31	52·7	52·7	52·8	52·9	52·9	53·0
3·0	*Alcyone*	303	08·5	08·3	08·1	07·9	07·7	07·7	N 24	06·0	06·1	06·1	06·2	06·2	06·2
1·9	*Mirfak* 9	308	56·1	55·8	55·4	55·2	55·0	55·0	N 49	51·3	51·3	51·4	51·5	51·6	51·7
Var.§	*Algol*	312	58·3	58·0	57·7	57·5	57·4	57·4	N 40	56·9	57·0	57·1	57·2	57·3	57·3
2·8	*Menkar* 8	314	26·5	26·3	26·1	25·9	25·8	25·8	N 4	05·2	05·3	05·3	05·3	05·3	05·3
3·1	*Acamar* 7	315	26·7	26·4	26·2	26·0	25·9	26·0	S 40	18·3	18·2	18·2	18·3	18·4	18·6
2·1	*Polaris*	321	74·4	61·4	50·0	42·3	40·0	44·6	N 89	15·3	15·3	15·4	15·6	15·8	15·9
3·1	β Trianguli	327	37·5	37·2	37·0	36·9	36·8	36·8	N 34	58·8	58·9	59·0	59·1	59·2	59·3
2·2	*Hamal* 6	328	13·0	12·8	12·6	12·5	12·4	12·4	N 23	27·4	27·5	27·6	27·7	27·7	27·7
2·2	*Almak*	329	02·1	01·9	01·6	01·5	01·4	01·5	N 42	19·3	19·4	19·5	19·7	19·8	19·8
3·0	α Hydri	330	19·1	18·7	18·3	18·2	18·2	18·3	S 61	34·1	34·1	34·2	34·3	34·5	34·6
2·7	*Sheratan*	331	21·0	20·8	20·6	20·5	20·4	20·4	N 20	48·2	48·2	48·3	48·4	48·4	48·5
0·6	*Achernar* 5	335	34·9	34·5	34·2	34·1	34·1	34·3	S 57	14·2	14·1	14·2	14·3	14·5	14·6
2·8	*Ruchbah*	338	33·3	32·9	32·6	32·5	32·5	32·6	N 60	13·6	13·7	13·8	14·0	14·2	14·3
2·4	*Mirach*	342	34·5	34·3	34·1	34·0	34·0	34·1	N 35	36·8	36·9	37·1	37·2	37·3	37·3
Var.‖	γ Cassiopeiæ	345	49·7	49·4	49·1	49·0	49·1	49·3	N 60	42·5	42·6	42·8	42·9	43·1	43·2
2·2	*Diphda* 4	349	06·7	06·4	06·3	06·2	06·3	06·3	S 17	59·3	59·2	59·2	59·3	59·4	59·4
2·5	*Schedar* 3	349	52·7	52·4	52·2	52·1	52·2	52·3	N 56	31·7	31·9	32·0	32·2	32·3	32·4
2·4	*Ankaa* 2	353	26·2	26·0	25·8	25·8	25·8	26·0	S 42	18·3	18·3	18·4	18·5	18·6	18·7
2·9	β Hydri	353	34·4	33·6	33·2	33·1	33·4	34·0	S 77	15·2	15·2	15·4	15·5	15·6	15·7
2·9	*Algenib*	356	41·9	41·7	41·6	41·5	41·6	41·6	N 15	10·7	10·8	10·9	11·0	11·0	11·0
2·4	*Caph*	357	42·5	42·2	42·0	42·0	42·1	42·3	N 59	08·5	08·6	08·8	09·0	09·1	09·2
2·2	*Alpheratz* 1	357	54·5	54·3	54·2	54·2	54·2	54·3	N 29	05·1	05·2	05·3	05·4	05·5	05·5

‡ 0·1 — 1·2   § 2·3 — 3·5   ‖ Irregular variable; 1997 mag. 2·3

POLARIS (POLE STAR) TABLES, 1999

FOR DETERMINING LATITUDE FROM SEXTANT ALTITUDE AND FOR AZIMUTH

LHA ARIES	0° – 9°	10° – 19°	20° – 29°	30° – 39°	40° – 49°	50° – 59°	60° – 69°	70° – 79°	80° – 89°	90° – 99°	100° – 109°	110° – 119°
	a_0	a_0	a_0	a_0	a_0	a_0	a_0	a_0	a_0	a_0	a_0	a_0
°	° ′	° ′	° ′	° ′	° ′	° ′	° ′	° ′	° ′	° ′	° ′	° ′
0	0 23·9	0 19·6	0 16·6	0 14·8	0 14·4	0 15·4	0 17·7	0 21·3	0 26·0	0 31·8	0 38·3	0 45·5
1	23·4	19·3	16·3	14·7	14·5	15·6	18·0	21·7	26·6	32·4	39·0	46·2
2	22·9	18·9	16·1	14·6	14·5	15·8	18·3	22·2	27·1	33·0	39·7	47·0
3	22·5	18·6	15·9	14·6	14·6	16·0	18·7	22·6	27·6	33·6	40·4	47·7
4	22·0	18·3	15·7	14·5	14·7	16·2	19·0	23·1	28·2	34·3	41·1	48·5
5	0 21·6	0 17·9	0 15·5	0 14·5	0 14·7	0 16·4	0 19·4	0 23·5	0 28·8	0 34·9	0 41·8	0 49·2
6	21·2	17·6	15·4	14·4	14·9	16·6	19·7	24·0	29·4	35·6	42·6	50·0
7	20·8	17·4	15·2	14·4	15·0	16·9	20·1	24·5	29·9	36·3	43·3	50·8
8	20·4	17·1	15·1	14·4	15·1	17·2	20·5	25·0	30·5	36·9	44·0	51·5
9	20·0	16·8	14·9	14·4	15·2	17·4	20·9	25·5	31·1	37·6	44·7	52·3
10	0 19·6	0 16·6	0 14·8	0 14·4	0 15·4	0 17·7	0 21·3	0 26·0	0 31·8	0 38·3	0 45·5	0 53·1

Lat.	a_1	a_1	a_1	a_1	a_1	a_1	a_1	a_1	a_1	a_1	a_1	a_1
°	′	′	′	′	′	′	′	′	′	′	′	′
0	0·5	0·5	0·6	0·6	0·6	0·6	0·5	0·5	0·4	0·4	0·3	0·3
10	·5	·6	·6	·6	·6	·6	·5	·5	·4	·4	·4	·3
20	·5	·6	·6	·6	·6	·6	·6	·5	·5	·4	·4	·4
30	·5	·6	·6	·6	·6	·6	·6	·5	·5	·5	·5	·4
40	0·6	0·6	0·6	0·6	0·6	0·6	0·6	0·6	0·5	0·5	0·5	0·5
45	·6	·6	·6	·6	·6	·6	·6	·6	·6	·6	·6	·5
50	·6	·6	·6	·6	·6	·6	·6	·6	·6	·6	·6	·6
55	·6	·6	·6	·6	·6	·6	·6	·6	·6	·6	·7	·7
60	·6	·6	·6	·6	·6	·6	·6	·6	·7	·7	·7	·7
62	0·7	0·6	0·6	0·6	0·6	0·6	0·6	0·7	0·7	0·7	0·8	0·8
64	·7	·6	·6	·6	·6	·6	·6	·7	·7	·8	·8	·8
66	·7	·6	·6	·6	·6	·6	·7	·7	·8	·8	·9	·9
68	0·7	0·7	0·6	0·6	0·6	0·6	0·7	0·7	0·8	0·9	0·9	0·9

Month	a_2	a_2	a_2	a_2	a_2	a_2	a_2	a_2	a_2	a_2	a_2	a_2
	′	′	′	′	′	′	′	′	′	′	′	′
Jan.	0·8	0·8	0·8	0·8	0·8	0·8	0·8	0·7	0·7	0·7	0·7	0·6
Feb.	·7	·7	·8	·8	·8	·8	·8	·8	·8	·8	·8	·8
Mar.	·5	·6	·7	·7	·8	·8	·8	·9	·9	·9	·9	·9
Apr.	0·4	0·4	0·5	0·6	0·6	0·7	0·7	0·8	0·8	0·9	0·9	0·9
May	·3	·3	·4	·4	·5	·5	·6	·7	·7	·8	·8	·9
June	·2	·3	·3	·3	·4	·4	·5	·5	·6	·6	·7	·8
July	0·3	0·3	0·3	0·3	0·3	0·3	0·4	0·4	0·4	0·5	0·6	0·6
Aug.	·4	·4	·3	·3	·3	·3	·3	·3	·3	·4	·4	·5
Sept.	·6	·5	·5	·4	·4	·4	·3	·3	·3	·3	·3	·3
Oct.	0·8	0·7	0·7	0·6	0·6	0·5	0·4	0·4	0·4	0·3	0·3	0·3
Nov.	0·9	0·9	0·9	0·8	·7	·7	·6	·5	·5	·4	·3	·3
Dec.	1·1	1·0	1·0	1·0	0·9	0·8	0·8	0·7	0·6	0·5	0·5	0·4

Lat.	AZIMUTH											
°	°	°	°	°	°	°	°	°	°	°	°	°
0	0·4	0·3	0·2	0·0	359·9	359·8	359·7	359·6	359·5	359·4	359·3	359·3
20	0·4	0·3	0·2	0·0	359·9	359·8	359·6	359·5	359·4	359·3	359·3	359·2
40	0·5	0·4	0·2	0·0	359·9	359·7	359·6	359·4	359·3	359·2	359·1	359·1
50	0·6	0·5	0·3	0·1	359·9	359·7	359·5	359·3	359·1	359·0	358·9	358·9
55	0·7	0·5	0·3	0·1	359·8	359·6	359·4	359·2	359·0	358·9	358·8	358·7
60	0·8	0·6	0·3	0·1	359·8	359·6	359·3	359·1	358·9	358·7	358·6	358·5
65	1·0	0·7	0·4	0·1	359·8	359·5	359·2	358·9	358·7	358·5	358·4	358·3

Latitude = Apparent altitude (corrected for refraction) $-1° + a_0 + a_1 + a_2$

The table is entered with LHA Aries to determine the column to be used; each column refers to a range of 10°. a_0 is taken, with mental interpolation, from the upper table with the units of LHA Aries in degrees as argument; a_1, a_2 are taken, without interpolation, from the second and third tables with arguments latitude and month respectively. a_0, a_1, a_2, are always positive. The final table gives the azimuth of *Polaris*.

LHA ARIES	120°– 129°	130°– 139°	140°– 149°	150°– 159°	160°– 169°	170°– 179°	180°– 189°	190°– 199°	200°– 209°	210°– 219°	220°– 229°	230°– 239°
°	a_0	a_0	a_0	a_0	a_0	a_0	a_0	a_0	a_0	a_0	a_0	a_0
0	0 53·1	I 00·8	I 08·5	I 15·8	I 22·7	I 28·8	I 34·0	I 38·1	I 41·1	I 42·8	I 43·2	I 42·2
1	53·8	01·6	09·2	16·5	23·3	29·3	34·4	38·5	41·3	42·9	43·1	42·1
2	54·6	02·3	10·0	17·2	23·9	29·9	34·9	38·8	41·5	43·0	43·1	41·9
3	55·4	03·1	10·7	17·9	24·6	30·4	35·3	39·1	41·7	43·0	43·0	41·7
4	56·1	03·9	11·5	18·6	25·2	31·0	35·8	39·5	41·9	43·1	42·9	41·5
5	0 56·9	I 04·6	I 12·2	I 19·3	I 25·8	I 31·5	I 36·2	I 39·8	I 42·1	I 43·1	I 42·9	I 41·3
6	57·7	05·4	12·9	20·0	26·4	32·0	36·6	40·1	42·3	43·2	42·8	41·0
7	58·5	06·2	13·7	20·7	27·0	32·5	37·0	40·3	42·4	43·2	42·6	40·8
8	0 59·2	06·9	14·4	21·3	27·6	33·0	37·4	40·6	42·6	43·2	42·5	40·5
9	I 00·0	07·7	15·1	22·0	28·2	33·5	37·8	40·9	42·7	43·2	42·4	40·3
10	I 00·8	I 08·5	I 15·8	I 22·7	I 28·8	I 34·0	I 38·1	I 41·1	I 42·8	I 43·2	I 42·2	I 40·0

Lat.	a_1	a_1	a_1	a_1	a_1	a_1	a_1	a_1	a_1	a_1	a_1	a_1
°	′	′	′	′	′	′	′	′	′	′	′	′
0	0·3	0·3	0·3	0·3	0·4	0·4	0·5	0·5	0·6	0·6	0·6	0·6
10	·3	·3	·3	·4	·4	·5	·5	·6	·6	·6	·6	·6
20	·4	·4	·4	·4	·4	·5	·5	·6	·6	·6	·6	·6
30	·4	·4	·4	·5	·5	·5	·5	·6	·6	·6	·6	·6
40	0·5	0·5	0·5	0·5	0·5	0·6	0·6	0·6	0·6	0·6	0·6	0·6
45	·5	·5	·5	·6	·6	·6	·6	·6	·6	·6	·6	·6
50	·6	·6	·6	·6	·6	·6	·6	·6	·6	·6	·6	·6
55	·7	·7	·7	·7	·6	·6	·6	·6	·6	·6	·6	·6
60	·8	·8	·7	·7	·7	·7	·6	·6	·6	·6	·6	·6
62	0·8	0·8	0·8	0·8	0·7	0·7	0·7	0·6	0·6	0·6	0·6	0·6
64	·8	·8	·8	·8	·8	·7	·7	·6	·6	·6	·6	·6
66	0·9	0·9	·9	·8	·8	·7	·7	·6	·6	·6	·6	·6
68	1·0	1·0	0·9	0·9	0·8	0·8	0·7	0·7	0·6	0·6	0·6	0·6

Month	a_2	a_2	a_2	a_2	a_2	a_2	a_2	a_2	a_2	a_2	a_2	a_2
	′	′	′	′	′	′	′	′	′	′	′	′
Jan.	0·6	0·6	0·5	0·5	0·5	0·5	0·4	0·4	0·4	0·4	0·4	0·4
Feb.	·8	·7	·7	·6	·6	·6	·5	·5	·4	·4	·4	·4
Mar.	0·9	0·9	·8	·8	·8	·7	·7	·6	·5	·5	·4	·4
Apr.	1·0	1·0	0·9	0·9	0·9	0·9	0·8	0·8	0·7	0·6	0·6	0·5
May	0·9	1·0	1·0	1·0	1·0	0·9	0·9	·9	·8	·8	·7	·7
June	·8	0·9	0·9	0·9	1·0	1·0	1·0	·9	·9	·9	·8	·8
July	0·7	0·7	0·8	0·8	0·9	0·9	0·9	0·9	0·9	0·9	0·9	0·9
Aug.	·5	·6	·6	·7	·7	·7	·8	·8	·9	·9	·9	·9
Sept.	·4	·4	·4	·5	·5	·6	·6	·7	·7	·8	·8	·8
Oct.	0·3	0·3	0·3	0·3	0·3	0·4	0·4	0·5	0·5	0·6	0·6	0·7
Nov.	·2	·2	·2	·2	·2	·2	·3	·3	·3	·4	·5	·5
Dec.	0·3	0·3	0·2	0·2	0·2	0·1	0·1	0·2	0·2	0·2	0·3	0·4

Lat.	AZIMUTH											
°	°	°	°	°	°	°	°	°	°	°	°	°
0	359·3	359·3	359·3	359·3	359·4	359·5	359·6	359·7	359·8	0·0	0·1	0·2
20	359·2	359·2	359·2	359·3	359·4	359·5	359·6	359·7	359·8	0·0	0·1	0·2
40	359·0	359·0	359·1	359·1	359·2	359·3	359·5	359·6	359·8	0·0	0·1	0·3
50	358·8	358·9	358·9	359·0	359·1	359·2	359·4	359·6	359·7	359·9	0·1	0·3
55	358·7	358·7	358·8	358·9	359·0	359·1	359·3	359·5	359·7	359·9	0·2	0·4
60	358·5	358·5	358·6	358·7	358·8	359·0	359·2	359·4	359·7	359·9	0·2	0·4
65	358·2	358·3	358·3	358·5	358·6	358·8	359·1	359·3	359·6	359·9	0·2	0·5

ILLUSTRATION

On 1999 April 21 at 23^h 18^m 56^s UT in longitude W 37° 14′ the apparent altitude (corrected for refraction), H_O, of *Polaris* was 49° 31′·6

From the daily pages:	° ′		H_O	° ′ 49 31·6
GHA Aries (23^h)	194 34·1		a_0 (argument 162° 05′)	I 24·0
Increment (18^m 56^s)	4 44·8		a_1 (Lat 50° approx.)	0·6
Longitude (west)	−37 14		a_2 (April)	0·9
LHA Aries	162 05		Sum − 1° = Lat =	49 57·1

POLARIS (POLE STAR) TABLES, 1999
FOR DETERMINING LATITUDE FROM SEXTANT ALTITUDE AND FOR AZIMUTH

LHA ARIES	240° – 249°	250° – 259°	260° – 269°	270° – 279°	280° – 289°	290° – 299°	300° – 309°	310° – 319°	320° – 329°	330° – 339°	340° – 349°	350° – 359°
°	a_0	a_0	a_0	a_0	a_0	a_0	a_0	a_0	a_0	a_0	a_0	a_0
0	1 40·0	1 36·5	1 31·9	1 26·3	1 19·8	1 12·7	1 05·2	0 57·5	0 49·8	0 42·4	0 35·4	0 29·2
1	39·7	36·1	31·4	25·7	19·1	12·0	04·4	56·7	49·0	41·6	34·8	28·6
2	39·4	35·7	30·8	25·0	18·4	11·3	03·7	55·9	48·3	40·9	34·1	28·1
3	39·1	35·2	30·3	24·4	17·8	10·5	02·9	55·2	47·5	40·2	33·5	27·5
4	38·7	34·8	29·7	23·8	17·1	09·8	02·1	54·4	46·8	39·5	32·8	27·0
5	1 38·4	1 34·3	1 29·2	1 23·1	1 16·3	1 09·0	1 01·4	0 53·6	0 46·0	0 38·8	0 32·2	0 26·4
6	38·0	33·9	28·6	22·5	15·6	08·3	1 00·6	52·9	45·3	38·1	31·6	25·9
7	37·7	33·4	28·0	21·8	14·9	07·5	0 59·8	52·1	44·6	37·4	31·0	25·4
8	37·3	32·9	27·5	21·2	14·2	06·7	59·0	51·3	43·8	36·8	30·4	24·9
9	36·9	32·4	26·9	20·5	13·5	06·0	58·3	50·6	43·1	36·1	29·8	24·4
10	1 36·5	1 31·9	1 26·3	1 19·8	1 12·7	1 05·2	0 57·5	0 49·8	0 42·4	0 35·4	0 29·2	0 23·9

Lat.	a_1	a_1	a_1	a_1	a_1	a_1	a_1	a_1	a_1	a_1	a_1	a_1
°	′	′	′	′	′	′	′	′	′	′	′	′
0	0·5	0·5	0·4	0·4	0·3	0·3	0·3	0·3	0·3	0·3	0·4	0·4
10	·5	·5	·4	·4	·4	·3	·3	·3	·3	·4	·4	·5
20	·6	·5	·5	·4	·4	·4	·4	·4	·4	·4	·4	·5
30	·6	·5	·5	·5	·5	·4	·4	·4	·4	·5	·5	·5
40	0·6	0·6	0·5	0·5	0·5	0·5	0·5	0·5	0·5	0·5	0·5	0·6
45	·6	·6	·6	·6	·6	·5	·5	·5	·5	·6	·6	·6
50	·6	·6	·6	·6	·6	·6	·6	·6	·6	·6	·6	·6
55	·6	·6	·6	·6	·7	·7	·7	·7	·7	·7	·6	·6
60	·6	·7	·7	·7	·7	·7	·8	·8	·7	·7	·7	·7
62	0·6	0·7	0·7	0·7	0·8	0·8	0·8	0·8	0·8	0·8	0·7	0·7
64	·7	·7	·7	·8	·8	·8	·8	·8	·8	·8	·8	·7
66	·7	·7	·8	·8	·9	·9	0·9	0·9	·9	·8	·8	·7
68	0·7	0·7	0·8	0·9	0·9	0·9	1·0	1·0	0·9	0·9	0·8	0·8

Month	a_2	a_2	a_2	a_2	a_2	a_2	a_2	a_2	a_2	a_2	a_2	a_2
	′	′	′	′	′	′	′	′	′	′	′	′
Jan.	0·4	0·5	0·5	0·5	0·5	0·6	0·6	0·6	0·7	0·7	0·7	0·7
Feb.	·4	·4	·4	·4	·4	·4	·4	·5	·5	·6	·6	·6
Mar.	·4	·3	·3	·3	·3	·3	·3	·3	·4	·4	·4	·5
Apr.	0·5	0·4	0·4	0·3	0·3	0·3	0·2	0·2	0·3	0·3	0·3	0·3
May	·6	·5	·5	·4	·4	·3	·3	·2	·2	·2	·2	·3
June	·7	·7	·6	·6	·5	·4	·4	·3	·3	·3	·2	·2
July	0·8	0·8	0·8	0·7	0·6	0·6	0·5	0·5	0·4	0·4	0·3	0·3
Aug.	·9	·9	·9	·8	·8	·7	·7	·6	·6	·5	·5	·5
Sept.	·9	·9	·9	·9	·9	·9	·8	·8	·8	·7	·7	·6
Oct.	0·8	0·8	0·8	0·9	0·9	0·9	0·9	0·9	0·9	0·9	0·9	0·8
Nov.	·6	·7	·7	·8	·9	·9	1·0	1·0	1·0	1·0	1·0	1·0
Dec.	0·4	0·5	0·6	0·7	0·7	0·8	0·9	0·9	1·0	1·0	1·0	1·1

Lat.	AZIMUTH											
°	°	°	°	°	°	°	°	°	°	°	°	°
0	0·3	0·4	0·5	0·6	0·7	0·7	0·7	0·7	0·7	0·7	0·6	0·5
20	0·4	0·5	0·6	0·7	0·7	0·8	0·8	0·8	0·8	0·7	0·6	0·5
40	0·4	0·6	0·7	0·8	0·9	0·9	1·0	1·0	0·9	0·9	0·8	0·7
50	0·5	0·7	0·8	1·0	1·1	1·1	1·1	1·1	1·1	1·0	0·9	0·8
55	0·6	0·8	0·9	1·1	1·2	1·3	1·3	1·3	1·2	1·2	1·0	0·9
60	0·7	0·9	1·1	1·2	1·4	1·4	1·5	1·5	1·4	1·3	1·2	1·0
65	0·8	1·0	1·3	1·4	1·6	1·7	1·7	1·7	1·7	1·6	1·4	1·2

Latitude = Apparent altitude (corrected for refraction) −1° + a_0 + a_1 + a_2

The table is entered with LHA Aries to determine the column to be used; each column refers to a range of 10°. a_0 is taken, with mental interpolation, from the upper table with the units of LHA Aries in degrees as argument; a_1, a_2 are taken, without interpolation, from the second and third tables with arguments latitude and month respectively. a_0, a_1, a_2, are always positive. The final table gives the azimuth of *Polaris*.

SIGHT REDUCTION PROCEDURES

METHODS AND FORMULAE FOR DIRECT COMPUTATION

1. *Introduction.* In this section formulae and methods are provided for *calculating* position at sea from observed altitudes taken with a marine sextant using a computer or programmable calculator.

The method uses analogous concepts and similar terminology as that used in *manual* methods of astro-navigation, where position is found by plotting position lines from their intercept and azimuth on a marine chart.

The algorithms are presented in standard algebra suitable for translating into the programming language of the user's computer. The basic ephemeris data may be taken directly from the main tabular pages of a current version of *The Nautical Almanac*. Formulae are given for calculating altitude and azimuth from the *GHA* and *Dec* of a body, and the estimated position of the observer. Formulae are also given for reducing sextant observations to observed altitudes by applying the corrections for dip, refraction, parallax and semi-diameter.

The intercept and azimuth obtained from each observation determines a position line, and the observer should lie on or close to each position line. The method of least squares is used to calculate the fix by finding the position where the sum of the squares of the distances from the position lines is a minimum. The use of least squares has other advantages. For example it is possible to improve the estimated position at the time of fix by repeating the calculation. It is also possible to include more observations in the solution and to reject doubtful ones.

2. *Notation.*

GHA = Greenwich hour angle. The range of GHA is from $0°$ to $360°$ starting at $0°$ on the Greenwich meridian increasing to the west, back to $360°$ on the Greenwich meridian.

SHA = sidereal hour angle. The range is $0°$ to $360°$.

Dec = declination. The sign convention for declination is north is positive, south is negative. The range is from $-90°$ at the south celestial pole to $+90°$ at the north celestial pole.

$Long$ = longitude. The sign convention is east is positive, west is negative. The range is $-180°$ to $+180°$.

Lat = latitude. The sign convention is north is positive, south is negative. The range is from $-90°$ to $+90°$.

LHA = $GHA + Long$ = local hour angle. The LHA increases to the west from $0°$ on the local meridian to $360°$.

H_C = calculated altitude. Above the horizon is positive, below the horizon is negative. The range is from $-90°$ in the nadir to $+90°$ in the zenith.

H_S = sextant altitude.

H = apparent altitude = sextant altitude corrected for instrumental error and dip.

H_O = observed altitude = apparent altitude corrected for refraction and, in appropriate cases, corrected for parallax and semi-diameter.

Z = Z_n = true azimuth. Z is measured from true north through east, south, west and back to north. The range is from $0°$ to $360°$.

I = sextant index error.

D = dip of horizon.

R = atmospheric refraction.

HP = horizontal parallax of the Sun, Moon, Venus or Mars.
PA = parallax in altitude of the Sun, Moon, Venus or Mars.
S = semi-diameter of the Sun or Moon.
p = intercept = $H_O - H_C$. Towards is positive, away is negative.
T = course or track, measured as for azimuth from the north.
V = speed in knots.

3. *Entering Basic Data.*   When quantities such as GHA are entered, which in *The Nautical Almanac* are given in degrees and minutes, convert them to degrees and decimals of a degree by dividing the minutes by 60 and adding to the degrees; for example, if $GHA = 123° 45'\!.6$, enter the two numbers 123 and 45·6 into the memory and set $GHA = 123 + 45·6/60 = 123°\!.7600$. Although four decimal places of a degree are shown in the examples, it is assumed that full precision is maintained in the calculations.

When using a computer or programmable calculator, write a subroutine to convert degrees and minutes to degrees and decimals. Scientific calculators usually have a special key for this purpose. For quantities like Dec which require a minus sign for southern declination, change the sign from plus to minus after the value has been converted to degrees and decimals, *e.g.* $Dec = S 0° 12'\!.3 = S 0°\!.2050 = -0°\!.2050$. Other quantities which require conversion are semi-diameter, horizontal parallax, longitude and latitude.

4. *Interpolation of GHA and Dec.*   The GHA and Dec of the Sun, Moon and planets are interpolated to the time of observation by direct calculation as follows: If the universal time is $a^h b^m c^s$, form the interpolation factor $x = b/60 + c/3600$. Enter the tabular value GHA_0 for the preceeding hour (a) and the tabular value GHA_1 for the following hour ($a + 1$) then the interpolated value GHA is given by

$$GHA = GHA_0 + x(GHA_1 - GHA_0)$$

If the GHA passes through 360° between tabular values add 360° to GHA_1 before interpolation. If the interpolated value exceeds 360°, subtract 360° from GHA.

Similarly for declination, enter the tabular value Dec_0 for the preceeding hour (a) and the tabular value Dec_1 for the following hour ($a + 1$), then the interpolated value Dec is given by

$$Dec = Dec_0 + x(Dec_1 - Dec_0)$$

5. *Example.*   (a) Find the GHA and Dec of the Sun on 1999 November 16 at $20^h 13^m 25^s$ UT.

The interpolation factor $x = 13/60 + 25/3600 = 0^h\!.2236$

page 223 $20^h\ GHA_0 = 123° 48'\!.3 = 123°\!.8050$

$21^h\ GHA_1 = 138° 48'\!.2 = 138°\!.8033$

$20^h\!.2236\ GHA = 123·8050 + 0·2236(138·8033 - 123·8050) = 127°\!.1588$

$20^h\ Dec_0 = S 18° 46'\!.5 = -18°\!.7750$

$21^h\ Dec_1 = S 18° 47'\!.1 = -18°\!.7850$

$20^h\!.2236\ Dec = -18·7750 + 0·2236(-18·7850 + 18·7750) = -18°\!.7772$

GHA Aries is interpolated in the same way as GHA of a body. For a star the SHA and Dec are taken from the tabular page and do not require interpolation, then

$$GHA = GHA\ \text{Aries} + SHA$$

where GHA Aries is interpolated to the time of observation.

(b) Find the *GHA* and *Dec* of *Vega* on 1999 November 16 at 20^h 13^m 25^s UT.
The interpolation factor $x = 0^h2236$ as in the previous example

page 222 20^h *GHA* $\text{Aries}_0 = 355°\ 26'\!7 = 355°\!4450$

21^h *GHA* $\text{Aries}_1 = 10°\ 29'\!2 = 370°\!4867$ (360° added)

$20^h\!2236$ *GHA* Aries $= 355·4450 + 0·2236(370·4867 - 355·4450) = 358°\!8085$

$SHA = 80°\ 46'\!4 = 80°\!7733$

$GHA = GHA$ Aries $+ SHA = 79°\!5818$ (multiple of 360° removed)

$Dec = \text{N}\,38°\ 47'\!3 = +38°\!7883$

6. *The calculated altitude and azimuth.* The calculated altitude H_C and true azimuth Z are determined from the *GHA* and *Dec* interpolated to the time of observation and from the *Long* and *Lat* estimated at the time of observation as follows:

Step 1.   Calculate the local hour angle

$$LHA = GHA + Long$$

Add or subtract multiples of 360° to set *LHA* in the range 0° to 360°.

Step 2.   Calculate S, C and the altitude H_C from

$$S = \sin Dec$$
$$C = \cos Dec \cos LHA$$
$$H_C = \sin^{-1}(S \sin Lat + C \cos Lat)$$

where $\sin^{-1}$ is the inverse function of sine.

Step 3.   Calculate X and A from

$$X = (S \cos Lat - C \sin Lat)/\cos H_C$$
$$\text{If}\ \ X > +1\ \ \text{set}\ \ X = +1$$
$$\text{If}\ \ X < -1\ \ \text{set}\ \ X = -1$$
$$A = \cos^{-1} X$$

where $\cos^{-1}$ is the inverse function of cosine.

Step 4.   Determine the azimuth Z

$$\text{If}\ \ LHA > 180°\ \ \text{then}\ \ Z = A$$
$$\text{Otherwise}\ \ Z = 360° - A$$

7. *Example.* Find the calculated altitude H_C and azimuth Z when

$$GHA = 53°\ \ \ Dec = \text{S}\,15°\ \ \ Lat = \text{N}\,32°\ \ \ Long = \text{W}\,16°$$

For the calculation

$$GHA = 53°\!0000\ \ \ Dec = -15°\!0000\ \ \ Lat = +32°\!0000\ \ \ Long = -16°\!0000$$

Step 1. $LHA = 53·0000 - 16·0000 = 37·0000$

Step 2. $S = -0·2588$

$C = +0·9659 \times 0·7986 = 0·7714$

$\sin H_C = -0·2588 \times 0·5299 + 0·7714 \times 0·8480 = 0·5171$

$H_C = 31°\!1346$

Step 3. $X = (-0\cdot2588 \times 0\cdot8480 - 0\cdot7714 \times 0\cdot5299)/0\cdot8560 = -0\cdot7340$

                        $A = 137\overset{\circ}{\cdot}2239$

Step 4.   Since $LHA \leq 180°$ then $Z = 360° - A = 222\overset{\circ}{\cdot}7761$

8. *Reduction from sextant altitude to observed altitude.*   The sextant altitude H_S is corrected for both dip and index error to produce the apparent altitude. The observed altitude H_O is calculated by applying a correction for refraction. For the Sun, Moon, Venus and Mars a correction for parallax is also applied to H, and for the Sun and Moon a further correction for semi-diameter is required. The corrections are calculated as follows:

Step 1.   Calculate dip

$$D = 0\overset{\circ}{\cdot}0293\sqrt{h}$$

where h is the height of eye above the horizon in metres.

Step 2.   Calculate apparent altitude

$$H = H_S + I - D$$

where I is the sextant index error.

Step 3.   Calculate refraction (R) at a standard temperature of $10°$ Celsius (C) and pressure of 1010 millibars (mb)

$$R_0 = 0\overset{\circ}{\cdot}0167/\tan(H + 7\cdot31/(H + 4\cdot4))$$

If the temperature $T°\,C$ and pressure P mb are known calculate the refraction from

$$R = fR_0 \quad \text{where} \quad f = 0\cdot28P/(T + 273)$$
otherwise set $R = R_0$

Step 4.   Calculate the parallax in altitude (PA) from the horizontal parallax (HP) and the apparent altitude (H) for the Sun, Moon, Venus and Mars as follows:

$$PA = HP\cos H$$

For the Sun $HP = 0\overset{\circ}{\cdot}0024$. This correction is very small and could be ignored.

For the Moon HP is taken for the nearest hour from the main tabular page and converted to degrees.

For Venus and Mars the HP is taken from the critical table at the bottom of page 259 and converted to degrees.

For the navigational stars and the remaining planets, Jupiter and Saturn set $PA = 0$.

If an error of $0\overset{!}{\cdot}2$ is significant the expression for the parallax in altitude for the Moon should include a small correction OB for the oblateness of the Earth as follows:

$$PA = HP\cos H + OB$$
where $OB = -0\overset{\circ}{\cdot}0032\sin^2 Lat \cos H + 0\overset{\circ}{\cdot}0032\sin(2Lat)\cos Z \sin H$

At mid-latitudes and for altitudes of the Moon below $60°$ a simple approximation to OB is

$$OB = -0\overset{\circ}{\cdot}0017\cos H$$

Step 5. Calculate the semi-diameter for the Sun and Moon as follows:

Sun: S is taken from the main tabular page and converted to degrees.

Moon: $S = 0°2724HP$ where HP is taken for the nearest hour from the main tabular page and converted to degrees.

Step 6. Calculate the observed altitude

$$H_O = H - R + PA \pm S$$

where the plus sign is used if the lower limb of the Sun or Moon was observed and the minus sign if the upper limb was observed.

9. *Example*. The following example illustrates how to use a calculator to reduce the sextant altitude (H_S) to observed altitude (H_O); the sextant altitudes given are assumed to be taken on 1999 November 16 with a marine sextant, zero index error, at height 5·4 m, temperature −3° C and pressure 982 mb, the Moon sights are assumed to be taken at 10^h UT.

Body limb	Sun lower	Sun upper	Moon lower	Moon upper	Venus −	*Polaris* −
Sextant altitude: H_S	21·3283	3·3367	33·4600	26·1117	4·5433	49·6083
Step 1. Dip: $D = 0·0293\sqrt{h}$	0·0681	0·0681	0·0681	0·0681	0·0681	0·0681
Step 2. Apparent altitude: $H = H_S + I - D$	21·2602	3·2686	33·3919	26·0436	4·4752	49·5402
Step 3. Refraction: R_0	0·0423	0·2262	0·0251	0·0338	0·1801	0·0142
f	1·0184	1·0184	1·0184	1·0184	1·0184	1·0184
$R = fR_0$	0·0431	0·2304	0·0256	0·0344	0·1834	0·0144
Step 4. Parallax:			(55ʹ9)	(55ʹ9)	(0ʹ2)	
HP	0·0024	0·0024	0·9317	0·9317	0·0033	−
Parallax in altitude: $PA = HP \cos H$	0·0022	0·0024	0·7779	0·8371	0·0033	−
Step 5. Semi-diameter: Sun : $S = 16·2/60$	0·2700	0·2700	−	−	−	−
Moon : $S = 0·2724HP$	−	−	0·2538	0·2538	−	−
Step 6. Observed altitude: $H_O = H - R + PA \pm S$	21·4894	2·7706	34·3980	26·5925	4·2952	49·5258

Note that for the Moon the correction for the oblateness of the Earth of about $-0°0017 \cos H$, which equals $-0°0014$ for the lower limb and $-0°0015$ for the upper limb, has been ignored in the above calculation.

10. *Position from intercept and azimuth using a chart.* An estimate is made of the position at the adopted time of fix. The position at the time of observation is then calculated by dead reckoning from the time of fix. For example if the course (track) T and the speed V (in knots) of the observer are constant then *Long* and *Lat* at the time of observation are calculated from

$$Long = L_F + t\,(V/60)\sin T / \cos B_F$$
$$Lat = B_F + t\,(V/60)\cos T$$

where L_F and B_F are the estimated longitude and latitude at the time of fix and t is the time interval in hours from the time of fix to the time of observation, t is positive if the time of observation is after the time of fix and negative if it was before.

The position line of an observation is plotted on a chart using the intercept

$$p = H_O - H_C$$

and azimuth Z with origin at the calculated position ($Long$, Lat) at the time of observation, where H_C and Z are calculated using the method in section 6, page 279. Starting from this calculated position a line is drawn on the chart along the direction of the azimuth to the body. Convert p to nautical miles by multiplying by 60. The position line is drawn at right angles to the azimuth line, distance p from ($Long$, Lat) towards the body if p is positive and distance p away from the body if p is negative. Provided there are no gross errors the navigator should be somewhere on or near the position line at the time of observation. Two or more position lines are required to determine a fix.

11. *Position from intercept and azimuth by calculation.* The position of the fix may be calculated from two or more sextant observations as follows.

If p_1, Z_1, are the intercept and azimuth of the first observation, p_2, Z_2, of the second observation and so on, form the summations

$$A = \cos^2 Z_1 + \cos^2 Z_2 + \cdots$$
$$B = \cos Z_1 \sin Z_1 + \cos Z_2 \sin Z_2 + \cdots$$
$$C = \sin^2 Z_1 + \sin^2 Z_2 + \cdots$$
$$D = p_1 \cos Z_1 + p_2 \cos Z_2 + \cdots$$
$$E = p_1 \sin Z_1 + p_2 \sin Z_2 + \cdots$$

where the number of terms in each summation is equal to the number of observations.

With $G = A C - B^2$, an improved estimate of the position at the time of fix (L_I, B_I) is given by

$$L_I = L_F + (A E - B D)/(G \cos B_F), \qquad B_I = B_F + (C D - B E)/G$$

Calculate the distance d between the initial estimated position (L_F, B_F) at the time of fix and the improved estimated position (L_I, B_I) in nautical miles from

$$d = 60 \sqrt{((L_I - L_F)^2 \cos^2 B_F + (B_I - B_F)^2)}$$

If d exceeds about 20 nautical miles set $L_F = L_I$, $B_F = B_I$ and repeat the calculation until d, the distance between the position at the previous estimate and the improved estimate, is less than about 20 nautical miles.

12. *Example of direct computation.* Using the method described above, calculate the position of a ship on 1999 July 4 at $21^h\ 00^m\ 00^s$ UT from the marine sextant observations of the three stars *Regulus* (No. 26) at $20^h\ 39^m\ 23^s$ UT, *Antares* (No. 42) at $20^h\ 45^m\ 47^s$ UT and *Kochab* (No. 40) at $21^h\ 10^m\ 34^s$ UT, where the observed altitudes of the three stars corrected for the effects of refraction, dip and instrumental error, are $27°.2333$, $25°.9536$ and $47°.4664$ respectively. The ship was travelling at a constant speed of 20 knots on a course of $325°$ during the period of observation, and the position of the ship at the time of fix $21^h\ 00^m\ 00^s$ UT is only known to the nearest whole degree W $15°$, N $32°$.

Intermediate values for the first iteration are shown in the table. GHA Aries was interpolated from the nearest tabular values on page 132. For the first iteration set $L_F = -15°0000$, $B_F = +32°0000$ at the time of fix at $21^h\ 00^m\ 00^s$ UT.

First Iteration

Body	Regulus	Antares	Kochab
No.	26	42	40
time of observation	$20^h\ 39^m\ 23^s$	$20^h\ 45^m\ 47^s$	$21^h\ 10^m\ 34^s$
H_O	27·2333	25·9536	47·4664
interpolation factor	0·6564	0·7631	0·1761
GHA Aries	232·2565	233·8610	240·0740
SHA (page 132)	207·9200	112·6533	137·3167
GHA	80·1765	346·5143	17·3907
Dec (page 132)	+11·9717	−26·4300	+74·1650
t	−0·3436	−0·2369	+0·1761
Long	−14·9225	−14·9466	−15·0397
Lat	+31·9062	+31·9353	+32·0481
Z	267·4002	151·7737	359·0440
H_C	27·2102	25·6478	47·8665
p	+0·0231	+0·3058	−0·4001

$$A = 1·7781 \quad B = -0·3881 \quad C = 1·2219 \quad D = -0·6705 \quad E = 0·1282 \quad G = 2·0221$$
$$(A\,E - B\,D)/(G\cos B_F) = -0·0188, \qquad (C\,D - B\,E)/G = -0·3806$$

An improved estimate of the position at the time of fix is

$$L_I = L_F - 0·0188 = -15·0188 \quad \text{and} \quad B_I = B_F - 0·3806 = +31·6194$$

Since the distance between the previous estimated position and the improved estimate $d = 22·9$ nautical miles set $L_F = -15·0188$, and $B_F = +31·6194$ and repeat the calculation. The table shows the intermediate values of the calculation for the second iteration. In each iteration the quantities H_O, GHA, Dec and t do not change.

Second Iteration

Body	Regulus	Antares	Kochab
No.	26	42	40
Long	−14·9416	−14·9656	−15·0583
Lat	+31·5256	+31·5547	+31·6675
Z	267·5854	151·6696	359·0584
H_C	27·2431	25·9753	47·4862
p	−0·0098	−0·0217	−0·0198

$$A = 1·7763 \quad B = -0·3921 \quad C = 1·2237 \quad D = -0·0003 \quad E = -0·0002 \quad G = 2·0200$$
$$(A\,E - B\,D)/(G\cos B_F) = -0·0003, \qquad (C\,D - B\,E)/G = -0·0002$$

An improved estimate of the position at the time of fix is

$$L_I = L_F - 0·0003 = -15·0191 \quad \text{and} \quad B_I = B_F - 0·0002 = +31·6192$$

The distance between the previous estimated position and the improved estimated position $d = 0·02$ nautical miles is so small that a third iteration would produce a negligible improvement to the estimate of the position.

USE OF CONCISE SIGHT REDUCTION TABLES

1. *Introduction.* The concise sight reduction tables given on pages 286 to 317 are intended for use when neither more extensive tables nor electronic computing aids are available. These "NAO sight reduction tables" provide for the reduction of the local hour angle and declination of a celestial object to azimuth and altitude, referred to an assumed position on the Earth, for use in the intercept method of celestial navigation which is now standard practice.

2. *Form of tables.* Entries in the reduction table are at a fixed interval of one degree for all latitudes and hour angles. A compact arrangement results from division of the navigational triangle into two right spherical triangles, so that the table has to be entered twice. Assumed latitude and local hour angle are the arguments for the first entry. The reduction table responds with the intermediate arguments A, B, and Z_1, where A is used as one of the arguments for the second entry to the table, B has to be incremented by the declination to produce the quantity F, and Z_1 is a component of the azimuth angle. The reduction table is then reentered with A and F and yields H, P, and Z_2 where H is the altitude, P is the complement of the parallactic angle, and Z_2 is the second component of the azimuth angle. It is usually necessary to adjust the tabular altitude for the fractional parts of the intermediate entering arguments to derive computed altitude, and an auxiliary table is provided for the purpose. Rules governing signs of the quantities which must be added or subtracted are given in the instructions and summarized on each tabular page. Azimuth angle is the sum of two components and is converted to true azimuth by familiar rules, repeated at the bottom of the tabular pages.

Tabular altitude and intermediate quantities are given to the nearest minute of arc, although errors of $2'$ in computed altitude may accrue during adjustment for the minutes parts of entering arguments. Components of azimuth angle are stated to $0°1$; for derived true azimuth, only whole degrees are warranted. Since objects near the zenith are difficult to observe with a marine sextant, they should be avoided; altitudes greater than about $80°$ are not suited to reduction by this method.

In many circumstances the accuracy provided by these tables is sufficient. However, to maintain the full accuracy ($0'1$) of the ephemeral data in the almanac throughout their reduction to altitude and azimuth, more extensive tables or a calculator should be used.

3. *Use of Tables.*

Step 1. Determine the Greenwich hour angle (*GHA*) and Declination (*Dec*) of the body from the almanac. Select an assumed latitude (*Lat*) of integral degrees nearest to the estimated latitude. Choose an assumed longitude nearest to the estimated longitude such that the local hour angle

$$LHA = GHA \; \genfrac{}{}{0pt}{}{- \text{ west}}{+ \text{ east}} \; \text{longitude}$$

has integral degrees.

Step 2. Enter the reduction table with *Lat* and *LHA* as arguments. Record the quantities A, B and Z_1. Apply the rules for the sign of B and Z_1: B is minus if $90° < LHA < 270°$: Z_1 has the same sign as B. Set $A° =$ nearest whole degree of A and $A' =$ minutes part of A. This step may be repeated for all reductions before leaving the latitude opening of the table.

Step 3. Record the declination *Dec*. Apply the rules for the sign of *Dec*: *Dec* is minus if the name of *Dec* (*i.e.* N or S) is contrary to latitude. Add B and *Dec* algebraically to produce F. If F is negative, the object is below the horizon (in sight reduction, this can occur when the objects are close to the horizon). Regard F as positive until step 7. Set $F° =$ nearest whole degree of F and $F' =$ minutes part of F.

Step 4. Enter the reduction table a second time with $A°$ and $F°$ as arguments and record H, P, and Z_2. Set $P° =$ nearest whole degree of P and $Z_2° =$ nearest whole degree of Z_2.

Step 5. Enter the auxiliary table with F' and $P°$ as arguments to obtain $corr_1$ to H for F'. Apply the rule for the sign of $corr_1$: $corr_1$ is minus if $F < 90°$ and $F' > 29'$ or if $F > 90°$ and $F' < 30'$, otherwise $corr_1$ is plus.

Step 6. Enter the auxiliary table with A' and $Z_2°$ as arguments to obtain $corr_2$ to H for A'. Apply the rule for the sign of $corr_2$: $corr_2$ is minus if $A' < 30'$, otherwise $corr_2$ is plus.

Step 7. Calculate the computed altitude H_C as the sum of H, $corr_1$ and $corr_2$. Apply the rule for the sign of H_C: H_C is minus if F is negative.

Step 8. Apply the rule for the sign of Z_2: Z_2 is minus if $F > 90°$. If F is negative, replace Z_2 by $180° - Z_2$. Set the azimuth angle Z equal to the algebraic sum of Z_1 and Z_2 and ignore the resulting sign. Obtain the true azimuth Z_n from the rules

$$\text{For N latitude, if } \quad LHA > 180° \quad Z_n = Z$$
$$\text{if } \quad LHA < 180° \quad Z_n = 360° - Z$$

$$\text{For S latitude, if } \quad LHA > 180° \quad Z_n = 180° - Z$$
$$\text{if } \quad LHA < 180° \quad Z_n = 180° + Z$$

Observed altitude H_O is compared with H_C to obtain the altitude difference, which, with Z_n, is used to plot the position line.

4. *Example.* (a) Required the altitude and azimuth of *Schedar* on 1999 February 5 at UT 06^h 29^m from the estimated position 5° east, 53° north.

1. Assumed latitude $Lat = $ 53° N
   From the almanac $GHA = $ 222° 07′
   Assumed longitude   4° 53′ E
   Local hour angle $LHA = $ 227

2. Reduction table, 1st entry
   $(Lat, LHA) = (53, 227)$ $A = $ 26   07 $A° = 26, A' = 7$
                                   $B = -27$ 12 $Z_1 = -49·4,$ $90° < LHA < 270°$
3. From the almanac $Dec = +56$ 32   *Lat* and *Dec* same
   Sum $= B + Dec$ $F = +29$ 20 $F° = 29, F' = 20$

4. Reduction table, 2nd entry
   $(A°, F°) = (26, 29)$ $H = $ 25   50 $P° = 61$
                                             $Z_2 = 76·3$
5. Auxiliary table, 1st entry
   $(F', P°) = (20, 61)$ $corr_1 = $ $+17$ $F < 90°, F' < 29'$
   Sum   26   07
6. Auxiliary table, 2nd entry
   $(A', Z_2°) = (7, 76)$ $corr_2 = $ -2 $A' < 30'$
7. Sum = computed altitude $H_C = +26°$ 05′ $F > 0°$

8. Azimuth, first component $Z_1 = -49·4$ same sign as B
       second component $Z_2 = +76·3$ $F < 90°, F > 0°$
   Sum = azimuth angle $Z = $ 26·9

   True azimuth $Z_n = $ 027°   N *Lat*, $LHA > 180°$

continued on page 318

SIGHT REDUCTION TABLE

B: (−) for 90° < LHA < 270°
Dec: (−) for Lat. contrary name

Z₁: same sign as B
Z₂: (−) for F > 90°

LHA/F	0° A/H	0° B/P	0° Z_1/Z_2	1° A/H	1° B/P	1° Z_1/Z_2	2° A/H	2° B/P	2° Z_1/Z_2	3° A/H	3° B/P	3° Z_1/Z_2	4° A/H	4° B/P	4° Z_1/Z_2	5° A/H	5° B/P	5° Z_1/Z_2	LHA
0 / 180	0 00	90 00	90.0	0 00	89 00	90.0	0 00	88 00	90.0	0 00	87 00	90.0	0 00	86 00	90.0	0 00	85 00	90.0	180 / 360
1 / 179	1 00	90 00	90.0	1 00	89 00	90.0	1 00	88 00	90.0	1 00	87 00	89.9	1 00	86 00	89.9	1 00	85 00	89.9	181 / 359
2 / 178	2 00	90 00	90.0	2 00	89 00	90.0	2 00	88 00	89.9	2 00	87 00	89.9	2 00	86 00	89.9	2 00	85 00	89.8	182 / 358
3 / 177	3 00	90 00	90.0	3 00	89 00	90.0	3 00	88 00	89.9	3 00	87 00	89.8	3 00	86 00	89.8	2 59	85 00	89.7	183 / 357
4 / 176	4 00	90 00	90.0	4 00	89 00	89.9	4 00	88 00	89.9	4 00	87 00	89.8	3 59	85 59	89.7	3 59	84 59	89.7	184 / 356
5 / 175	5 00	90 00	90.0	5 00	89 00	89.9	5 00	88 00	89.8	5 00	86 59	89.7	4 59	85 59	89.7	4 59	84 59	89.6	185 / 355
6 / 174	6 00	90 00	90.0	6 00	89 00	89.9	6 00	87 59	89.8	6 00	86 59	89.7	5 59	85 59	89.6	5 59	84 58	89.5	186 / 354
7 / 173	7 00	90 00	90.0	7 00	89 00	89.9	7 00	87 59	89.8	6 59	86 59	89.6	6 59	85 58	89.5	6 58	84 58	89.4	187 / 353
8 / 172	8 00	90 00	90.0	8 00	88 59	89.9	8 00	87 59	89.7	7 59	86 58	89.6	7 59	85 58	89.4	7 58	84 57	89.3	188 / 352
9 / 171	9 00	90 00	90.0	9 00	88 59	89.8	9 00	87 59	89.7	8 59	86 58	89.5	8 59	85 57	89.4	8 58	84 56	89.2	189 / 351
10 / 170	10 00	90 00	90.0	10 00	88 59	89.8	10 00	87 58	89.7	9 59	86 57	89.5	9 58	85 56	89.3	9 58	84 56	89.1	190 / 350
11 / 169	11 00	90 00	90.0	11 00	88 59	89.8	11 00	87 58	89.6	10 59	86 57	89.4	10 58	85 56	89.2	10 57	84 54	89.0	191 / 349
12 / 168	12 00	90 00	90.0	12 00	88 59	89.8	12 00	87 57	89.6	11 59	86 56	89.4	11 58	85 55	89.1	11 57	84 53	88.9	192 / 348
13 / 167	13 00	90 00	90.0	13 00	88 58	89.8	13 00	87 57	89.5	12 59	86 55	89.3	12 58	85 54	89.1	12 57	84 52	88.8	193 / 347
14 / 166	14 00	90 00	90.0	14 00	88 58	89.8	13 59	87 56	89.5	13 59	86 54	89.3	13 58	85 53	89.0	13 57	84 51	88.8	194 / 346
15 / 165	15 00	90 00	90.0	15 00	88 58	89.7	14 59	87 56	89.5	14 59	86 54	89.2	14 58	85 52	88.9	14 56	84 49	88.7	195 / 345
16 / 164	16 00	90 00	90.0	16 00	88 58	89.7	15 59	87 55	89.4	15 59	86 53	89.2	15 58	85 50	88.8	15 56	84 48	88.6	196 / 344
17 / 163	17 00	90 00	90.0	17 00	88 57	89.7	16 59	87 55	89.4	16 59	86 52	89.1	16 57	85 49	88.8	16 56	84 46	88.5	197 / 343
18 / 162	18 00	90 00	90.0	18 00	88 57	89.7	17 59	87 54	89.4	17 58	86 51	89.0	17 57	85 48	88.7	17 56	84 45	88.4	198 / 342
19 / 161	19 00	90 00	90.0	19 00	88 57	89.7	18 59	87 53	89.3	18 58	86 50	89.0	18 57	85 46	88.6	18 55	84 43	88.3	199 / 341
20 / 160	20 00	90 00	90.0	20 00	88 56	89.6	19 59	87 52	89.3	19 58	86 48	88.9	19 57	85 45	88.5	19 55	84 41	88.2	200 / 340
21 / 159	21 00	90 00	90.0	21 00	88 56	89.6	20 59	87 51	89.2	20 58	86 47	88.9	20 57	85 43	88.5	20 55	84 39	88.1	201 / 339
22 / 158	22 00	90 00	90.0	22 00	88 55	89.6	21 59	87 51	89.2	21 58	86 46	88.8	21 57	85 41	88.4	21 55	84 37	88.0	202 / 338
23 / 157	23 00	90 00	90.0	23 00	88 55	89.6	22 59	87 50	89.2	22 58	86 44	88.8	22 56	85 39	88.3	22 54	84 34	87.9	203 / 337
24 / 156	24 00	90 00	90.0	24 00	88 54	89.6	23 59	87 49	89.1	23 58	86 43	88.7	23 56	85 37	88.2	23 54	84 32	87.8	204 / 336
25 / 155	25 00	90 00	90.0	25 00	88 54	89.5	24 59	87 48	89.1	24 58	86 41	88.7	24 56	85 35	88.1	24 54	84 29	87.7	205 / 335
26 / 154	26 00	90 00	90.0	26 00	88 53	89.5	25 59	87 46	89.0	25 58	86 40	88.6	25 56	85 33	88.1	25 54	84 26	87.6	206 / 334
27 / 153	27 00	90 00	90.0	27 00	88 53	89.5	26 59	87 45	89.0	26 58	86 38	88.6	26 56	85 31	88.0	26 53	84 24	87.5	207 / 333
28 / 152	28 00	90 00	90.0	28 00	88 52	89.5	27 59	87 44	89.0	27 57	86 36	88.5	27 56	85 28	87.9	27 53	84 21	87.3	208 / 332
29 / 151	29 00	90 00	90.0	29 00	88 51	89.4	28 59	87 43	88.9	28 57	86 34	88.5	28 55	85 26	87.8	28 53	84 17	87.2	209 / 331
30 / 150	30 00	90 00	90.0	30 00	88 51	89.4	29 59	87 41	88.8	29 57	86 32	88.3	29 55	85 23	87.7	29 52	84 14	87.1	210 / 330
31 / 149	31 00	90 00	90.0	31 00	88 50	89.4	30 59	87 40	88.8	30 57	86 30	88.2	30 55	85 20	87.6	30 52	84 10	87.0	211 / 329
32 / 148	32 00	90 00	90.0	32 00	88 49	89.4	31 59	87 39	88.7	31 57	86 28	88.1	31 55	85 17	87.5	31 52	84 07	86.9	212 / 328
33 / 147	33 00	90 00	90.0	33 00	88 48	89.4	32 59	87 37	88.7	32 57	86 25	88.1	32 55	85 14	87.4	32 51	84 03	86.8	213 / 327
34 / 146	34 00	90 00	90.0	34 00	88 48	89.3	33 59	87 35	88.7	33 57	86 23	88.0	33 54	85 11	87.3	33 51	83 59	86.6	214 / 326
35 / 145	35 00	90 00	90.0	35 00	88 47	89.3	34 59	87 34	88.6	34 57	86 20	87.9	34 54	85 07	87.2	34 51	83 54	86.5	215 / 325
36 / 144	36 00	90 00	90.0	36 00	88 46	89.3	35 58	87 32	88.5	35 57	86 18	87.8	35 54	85 04	87.1	35 51	83 50	86.4	216 / 324
37 / 143	37 00	90 00	90.0	37 00	88 45	89.2	36 58	87 30	88.5	36 56	86 15	87.7	36 54	85 00	87.0	36 50	83 45	86.2	217 / 323
38 / 142	38 00	90 00	90.0	38 00	88 44	89.2	37 58	87 28	88.4	37 56	86 12	87.7	37 53	84 56	86.9	37 50	83 40	86.1	218 / 322
39 / 141	39 00	90 00	90.0	39 00	88 43	89.2	38 58	87 26	88.4	38 56	86 09	87.6	38 53	84 52	86.8	38 49	83 35	86.0	219 / 321
40 / 140	40 00	90 00	90.0	40 00	88 42	89.1	39 58	87 23	88.4	39 56	86 05	87.5	39 53	84 47	86.7	39 49	83 29	85.8	220 / 320
41 / 139	41 00	90 00	90.0	41 00	88 40	89.1	40 58	87 21	88.3	40 56	86 02	87.4	40 53	84 42	86.5	40 49	83 23	85.7	221 / 319
42 / 138	42 00	90 00	90.0	42 00	88 39	89.1	41 58	87 19	88.2	41 56	85 58	87.3	41 52	84 37	86.4	41 48	83 17	85.5	222 / 318
43 / 137	43 00	90 00	90.0	43 00	88 38	89.1	42 58	87 16	88.1	42 56	85 54	87.2	42 52	84 32	86.3	42 48	83 11	85.4	223 / 317
44 / 136	44 00	90 00	90.0	43 59	88 37	89.0	43 58	87 13	88.1	43 55	85 50	87.1	43 52	84 27	86.1	43 47	83 04	85.2	224 / 316
45 / 135	45 00	90 00	90.0	44 59	88 35	89.0	44 58	87 10	88.0	44 55	85 46	87.0	44 52	84 21	86.0	44 47	82 57	85.0	225 / 315

Lat./A	LHA/F	0° A/H	0° B/P	0° Z_1/Z_2	1° A/H	1° B/P	1° Z_1/Z_2	2° A/H	2° B/P	2° Z_1/Z_2	3° A/H	3° B/P	3° Z_1/Z_2	4° A/H	4° B/P	4° Z_1/Z_2	5° A/H	5° B/P	5° Z_1/Z_2	LHA	LHA
45	135	45 00	90 00	90.0	44 59	88 35	89.0	44 58	87 10	88.0	44 55	85 46	87.0	44 52	84 21	86.0	44 47	82 57	85.0	225	315
46	134	46 00	90 00	90.0	45 59	88 34	89.0	45 58	87 07	87.9	45 55	85 41	86.9	45 51	84 15	85.9	45 46	82 49	84.8	226	314
47	133	47 00	90 00	90.0	46 59	88 32	88.9	46 58	87 04	87.9	46 55	85 36	86.8	46 51	84 09	85.7	46 46	82 41	84.7	227	313
48	132	48 00	90 00	90.0	47 59	88 30	88.9	47 58	87 01	87.8	47 55	85 31	86.7	47 51	84 02	85.6	47 46	82 33	84.5	228	312
49	131	49 00	90 00	90.0	48 59	88 29	88.8	48 58	86 57	87.7	48 55	85 26	86.6	48 50	83 55	85.4	48 45	82 24	84.3	229	311
50	130	50 00	90 00	90.0	49 59	88 27	88.8	49 58	86 53	87.6	49 54	85 20	86.4	49 50	83 47	85.2	49 44	82 15	84.1	230	310
51	129	51 00	90 00	90.0	50 59	88 25	88.8	50 57	86 49	87.5	50 54	85 14	86.3	50 50	83 40	85.1	50 44	82 05	83.9	231	309
52	128	52 00	90 00	90.0	51 59	88 23	88.7	51 57	86 45	87.4	51 54	85 08	86.2	51 49	83 31	84.9	51 43	81 55	83.6	232	308
53	127	53 00	90 00	90.0	52 59	88 20	88.7	52 57	86 41	87.3	52 54	85 01	86.0	52 49	83 22	84.7	52 43	81 44	83.4	233	307
54	126	54 00	90 00	90.0	53 59	88 18	88.6	53 57	86 36	87.2	53 54	84 54	85.9	53 49	83 13	84.5	53 42	81 32	83.2	234	306
55	125	55 00	90 00	90.0	54 59	88 15	88.6	54 57	86 31	87.1	54 53	84 47	85.7	54 48	83 03	84.3	54 41	81 20	82.9	235	305
56	124	56 00	90 00	90.0	55 59	88 13	88.5	55 57	86 26	87.0	55 53	84 39	85.6	55 48	82 52	84.1	55 41	81 06	82.6	236	304
57	123	57 00	90 00	90.0	56 59	88 10	88.5	56 57	86 20	86.9	56 53	84 30	85.4	56 47	82 41	83.9	56 40	80 52	82.4	237	303
58	122	58 00	90 00	90.0	57 59	88 07	88.4	57 57	86 14	86.8	57 52	84 21	85.2	57 47	82 29	83.6	57 39	80 38	82.1	238	302
59	121	59 00	90 00	90.0	58 59	88 04	88.3	58 57	86 07	86.7	58 52	84 11	85.0	58 46	82 16	83.4	58 38	80 22	81.7	239	301
60	120	60 00	90 00	90.0	59 59	88 00	88.3	59 56	86 00	86.5	59 52	84 01	84.8	59 46	82 02	83.1	59 37	80 04	81.4	240	300
61	119	61 00	90 00	90.0	60 59	87 56	88.2	60 56	85 53	86.4	60 52	83 50	84.6	60 45	81 48	82.8	60 37	79 46	81.1	241	299
62	118	62 00	90 00	90.0	61 59	87 52	88.1	61 56	85 45	86.2	61 51	83 38	84.4	61 44	81 32	82.5	61 36	79 27	80.7	242	298
63	117	63 00	90 00	90.0	62 59	87 48	88.0	62 56	85 36	86.1	62 51	83 25	84.1	62 44	81 15	82.2	62 35	79 06	80.3	243	297
64	116	64 00	90 00	90.0	63 59	87 43	88.0	63 56	85 27	85.9	63 50	83 11	83.9	63 43	80 56	81.9	63 33	78 43	79.9	244	296
65	115	65 00	90 00	90.0	64 59	87 38	87.9	64 56	85 17	85.7	64 50	82 56	83.6	64 42	80 36	81.5	64 32	78 18	79.4	245	295
66	114	66 00	90 00	90.0	65 59	87 33	87.8	65 55	85 06	85.5	65 49	82 39	83.3	65 41	80 15	81.1	65 31	77 52	78.9	246	294
67	113	67 00	90 00	90.0	66 59	87 26	87.6	66 55	84 54	85.3	66 49	82 22	83.0	66 40	79 51	80.7	66 29	77 23	78.4	247	293
68	112	68 00	90 00	90.0	67 59	87 20	87.5	67 55	84 40	85.1	67 48	82 02	82.6	67 39	79 26	80.2	67 28	76 51	77.8	248	292
69	111	69 00	90 00	90.0	68 59	87 13	87.4	68 55	84 26	84.8	68 48	81 41	82.2	68 38	78 57	79.7	68 26	76 17	77.2	249	291
70	110	70 00	90 00	90.0	69 59	87 05	87.3	69 54	84 10	84.5	69 47	81 17	81.8	69 37	78 27	79.2	69 25	75 39	76.5	250	290
71	109	71 00	90 00	90.0	70 58	86 56	87.1	70 54	83 53	84.2	70 46	80 51	81.4	70 36	77 53	78.5	70 23	74 57	75.8	251	289
72	108	72 00	90 00	90.0	71 58	86 46	86.9	71 54	83 33	83.9	71 46	80 22	80.8	71 35	77 15	77.9	71 20	74 12	75.0	252	288
73	107	73 00	90 00	90.0	72 58	86 35	86.7	72 53	83 11	83.5	72 45	79 50	80.3	72 33	76 33	77.1	72 18	73 20	74.1	253	287
74	106	74 00	90 00	90.0	73 58	86 22	86.5	73 53	82 47	83.1	73 44	79 14	79.7	73 31	75 46	76.3	73 15	72 23	73.1	254	286
75	105	75 00	90 00	90.0	74 58	86 08	86.3	74 52	82 19	82.6	74 43	78 33	78.9	74 29	74 53	75.4	74 12	71 19	72.0	255	285
76	104	76 00	90 00	90.0	75 58	85 52	86.0	75 52	81 47	82.0	75 41	77 47	78.1	75 27	73 53	74.4	75 09	70 07	70.7	256	284
77	103	77 00	90 00	90.0	76 58	85 34	85.7	76 51	81 11	81.4	76 40	76 53	77.2	76 25	72 44	73.2	76 05	68 45	69.3	257	283
78	102	78 00	90 00	90.0	77 58	85 12	85.3	77 50	80 28	80.7	77 38	75 51	76.2	77 22	71 25	71.8	77 01	67 11	67.7	258	282
79	101	79 00	90 00	90.0	78 57	84 46	84.9	78 49	79 38	79.8	78 36	74 38	74.9	78 18	69 52	70.3	77 56	65 22	65.8	259	281
80	100	80 00	90 00	90.0	79 57	84 16	84.3	79 48	78 38	78.8	79 34	73 12	73.5	79 14	68 04	68.4	78 50	63 16	63.7	260	280
81	99	81 00	90 00	90.0	80 57	83 38	83.7	80 47	77 25	77.6	80 31	71 29	71.7	80 09	65 55	66.2	79 43	60 47	61.2	261	279
82	98	82 00	90 00	90.0	81 56	82 51	82.9	81 45	75 55	76.1	81 28	69 22	69.6	81 04	63 19	63.6	80 34	57 51	58.2	262	278
83	97	83 00	90 00	90.0	82 56	81 51	81.9	82 43	74 01	74.1	82 23	66 44	66.9	81 57	60 09	60.4	81 24	54 20	54.6	263	277
84	96	84 00	90 00	90.0	83 55	80 31	80.6	83 41	71 32	71.6	83 18	63 22	63.5	82 48	56 13	56.4	82 12	50 04	50.3	264	276
85	95	85 00	90 00	90.0	84 54	78 40	78.7	84 37	68 10	68.3	84 10	58 59	59.1	83 36	51 16	51.4	82 56	44 53	45.1	265	275
86	94	86 00	90 00	90.0	85 53	75 57	76.0	85 32	63 24	63.5	85 00	53 05	53.2	84 21	44 56	45.1	83 36	38 34	38.7	266	274
87	93	87 00	90 00	90.0	86 50	71 33	71.6	86 24	56 17	56.3	85 45	44 58	45.0	85 00	36 49	36.9	84 10	30 53	31.0	267	273
88	92	88 00	90 00	90.0	87 46	63 26	63.4	87 10	44 59	45.0	86 24	33 40	33.7	85 32	26 31	26.6	84 37	21 45	21.8	268	272
89	91	89 00	90 00	90.0	88 35	45 00	45.0	87 46	26 33	26.6	86 50	18 25	18.4	85 53	14 01	14.0	84 54	11 17	11.3	269	271
90	90	90 00	00 00	0.0	89 00	00 00	0.0	88 00	00 00	0.0	87 00	00 00	0.0	86 00	00 00	0.0	85 00	00 00	0.0	270	270

N. Lat.: for LHA > 180°.... $Z_n = Z$
for LHA < 180°.... $Z_n = 360° - Z$

S. Lat.: for LHA > 180°.... $Z_n = 180° - Z$
for LHA < 180°.... $Z_n = 180° + Z$

SIGHT REDUCTION TABLE

B: (−) for 90° < LHA < 270°
Dec: (−) for Lat. contrary name

Z₁: same sign as B
Z₂: (−) for F > 90°

Lat./A LHA/F		6° A/H	6° B/P	6° Z₁/Z₂	7° A/H	7° B/P	7° Z₁/Z₂	8° A/H	8° B/P	8° Z₁/Z₂	9° A/H	9° B/P	9° Z₁/Z₂	10° A/H	10° B/P	10° Z₁/Z₂	11° A/H	11° B/P	11° Z₁/Z₂	Lat./A LHA	
0	180	0 00	84 00	90.0	0 00	83 00	90.0	0 00	82 00	90.0	0 00	81 00	90.0	0 00	80 00	90.0	0 00	79 00	90.0	180	360
1	179	1 00	84 00	89.9	1 00	83 00	89.9	0 59	82 00	89.9	0 59	81 00	89.8	0 59	80 00	89.8	0 59	79 00	89.8	181	359
2	178	1 59	84 00	89.8	1 59	83 00	89.8	1 59	82 00	89.7	1 59	81 00	89.7	1 58	80 00	89.7	1 58	79 00	89.6	182	358
3	177	2 59	83 59	89.7	2 59	82 59	89.6	2 58	81 59	89.6	2 58	80 59	89.5	2 57	79 59	89.5	2 57	78 59	89.4	183	357
4	176	3 59	83 59	89.6	3 58	82 59	89.5	3 58	81 59	89.4	3 57	80 59	89.4	3 56	79 59	89.3	3 56	78 58	89.2	184	356
5	175	4 58	83 59	89.5	4 58	82 58	89.4	4 57	81 58	89.3	4 56	80 58	89.2	4 55	79 58	89.1	4 54	78 58	89.0	185	355
6	174	5 58	83 58	89.4	5 57	82 58	89.3	5 56	81 57	89.2	5 56	80 57	89.1	5 55	79 57	89.0	5 53	78 56	88.9	186	354
7	173	6 58	83 57	89.3	6 57	82 57	89.1	6 56	81 56	89.0	6 55	80 56	88.9	6 54	79 56	88.8	6 52	78 55	88.7	187	353
8	172	7 57	83 56	89.2	7 56	82 56	89.0	7 55	81 55	88.9	7 54	80 55	88.7	7 53	79 54	88.6	7 51	78 54	88.5	188	352
9	171	8 57	83 56	89.1	8 56	82 55	88.9	8 55	81 54	88.7	8 53	80 53	88.6	8 52	79 53	88.4	8 50	78 52	88.3	189	351
10	170	9 57	83 54	89.1	9 55	82 54	88.8	9 54	81 53	88.6	9 53	80 52	88.4	9 51	79 51	88.2	9 49	78 50	88.1	190	350
11	169	10 56	83 53	87.9	10 55	82 52	88.6	10 53	81 51	88.5	10 52	80 50	88.3	10 50	79 49	88.1	10 48	78 48	87.9	191	349
12	168	11 56	83 52	88.7	11 55	82 51	88.5	11 53	81 49	88.3	11 51	80 48	88.1	11 49	79 47	87.9	11 47	78 46	87.7	192	348
13	167	12 56	83 51	88.6	12 54	82 49	88.4	12 52	81 48	88.2	12 50	80 46	87.9	12 48	79 45	87.7	12 45	78 43	87.5	193	347
14	166	13 55	83 49	88.5	13 54	82 47	88.1	13 52	81 46	88.0	13 49	80 44	87.8	13 47	79 42	87.5	13 44	78 40	87.3	194	346
15	165	14 55	83 47	88.4	14 53	82 45	88.0	14 51	81 43	87.9	14 49	80 41	87.6	14 46	79 39	87.3	14 43	78 37	87.1	195	345
16	164	15 55	83 46	88.3	15 53	82 43	88.0	15 50	81 41	87.7	15 48	80 39	87.4	15 45	79 36	87.1	15 42	78 34	86.9	196	344
17	163	16 54	83 44	88.2	16 52	82 41	87.9	16 50	81 38	87.6	16 47	80 36	87.3	16 44	79 33	87.0	16 41	78 31	86.7	197	343
18	162	17 54	83 42	88.1	17 52	82 39	87.7	17 49	81 36	87.4	17 46	80 33	87.1	17 43	79 30	86.8	17 39	78 27	86.5	198	342
19	161	18 54	83 39	87.9	18 51	82 36	87.6	18 48	81 33	87.3	18 45	80 29	86.9	18 42	79 26	86.6	18 38	78 23	86.2	199	341
20	160	19 53	83 37	87.8	19 51	82 33	87.5	19 48	81 30	87.1	19 45	80 26	86.7	19 41	79 22	86.4	19 37	78 19	86.0	200	340
21	159	20 53	83 35	87.7	20 50	82 30	87.3	20 47	81 26	86.9	20 44	80 22	86.6	20 40	79 18	86.2	20 36	78 14	85.8	201	339
22	158	21 52	83 32	87.6	21 50	82 27	87.2	21 46	81 23	86.8	21 43	80 18	86.4	21 39	79 14	86.0	21 35	78 10	85.6	202	338
23	157	22 52	83 29	87.5	22 49	82 24	87.0	22 46	81 19	86.6	22 42	80 14	86.2	22 38	79 09	85.8	22 33	78 05	85.4	203	337
24	156	23 52	83 26	87.3	23 49	82 21	86.9	23 45	81 15	86.5	23 41	80 10	86.0	23 37	79 05	85.6	23 32	77 59	85.1	204	336
25	155	24 51	83 23	87.2	24 48	82 17	86.7	24 44	81 11	86.3	24 40	80 05	85.8	24 36	78 59	85.4	24 31	77 54	84.9	205	335
26	154	25 51	83 20	87.1	25 48	82 13	86.6	25 44	81 07	86.1	25 39	80 00	85.6	25 35	78 54	85.2	25 29	77 48	84.7	206	334
27	153	26 50	83 16	87.0	26 47	82 09	86.4	26 43	81 02	85.9	26 38	79 55	85.4	26 33	78 48	84.9	26 28	77 42	84.4	207	333
28	152	27 50	83 13	86.9	27 46	82 05	86.3	27 42	80 57	85.8	27 38	79 50	85.2	27 32	78 42	84.7	27 27	77 35	84.2	208	332
29	151	28 50	83 09	86.7	28 46	82 01	86.1	28 41	80 52	85.6	28 37	79 44	85.0	28 31	78 36	84.5	28 25	77 28	84.0	209	331
30	150	29 49	83 05	86.5	29 45	81 56	86.0	29 41	80 47	85.4	29 36	79 38	84.8	29 30	78 29	84.3	29 24	77 21	83.7	210	330
31	149	30 49	83 01	86.4	30 45	81 51	85.8	30 40	80 41	85.2	30 35	79 32	84.6	30 29	78 23	84.0	30 22	77 13	83.5	211	329
32	148	31 48	82 56	86.1	31 44	81 46	85.6	31 39	80 35	85.0	31 34	79 25	84.4	31 27	78 15	83.8	31 21	77 05	83.2	212	328
33	147	32 48	82 51	86.0	32 43	81 40	85.5	32 38	80 29	84.8	32 33	79 18	84.2	32 26	78 08	83.6	32 19	76 57	82.9	213	327
34	146	33 47	82 46	86.0	33 43	81 35	85.3	33 37	80 23	84.6	33 32	79 11	84.0	33 25	78 00	83.3	33 18	76 48	82.7	214	326
35	145	34 47	82 41	85.8	34 42	81 29	85.1	34 37	80 16	84.4	34 30	79 03	83.7	34 24	77 51	83.1	34 16	76 39	82.4	215	325
36	144	35 46	82 36	85.7	35 41	81 22	84.9	35 36	80 09	84.2	35 29	78 55	83.5	35 22	77 42	82.8	35 14	76 29	82.1	216	324
37	143	36 46	82 30	85.5	36 41	81 16	84.8	36 35	80 01	84.0	36 28	78 47	83.3	36 21	77 33	82.5	36 13	76 19	81.8	217	323
38	142	37 45	82 24	85.3	37 40	81 09	84.6	37 34	79 53	83.8	37 27	78 38	83.0	37 19	77 23	82.3	37 11	76 09	81.5	218	322
39	141	38 45	82 18	85.2	38 39	81 01	84.4	38 33	79 45	83.6	38 26	78 29	82.8	38 18	77 13	82.0	38 09	75 57	81.2	219	321
40	140	39 44	82 11	85.0	39 39	80 54	84.2	39 32	79 36	83.3	39 25	78 19	82.5	39 16	77 02	81.7	39 07	75 46	80.9	220	320
41	139	40 44	82 04	84.8	40 38	80 46	84.0	40 31	79 27	83.1	40 23	78 09	82.3	40 15	76 51	81.4	40 05	75 33	80.6	221	319
42	138	41 43	81 57	84.6	41 37	80 37	83.7	41 30	79 17	82.8	41 22	77 58	82.0	41 13	76 39	81.1	41 04	75 21	80.3	222	318
43	137	42 42	81 49	84.4	42 36	80 28	83.5	42 29	79 07	82.6	42 21	77 47	81.7	42 12	76 27	80.8	42 02	75 07	79.9	223	317
44	136	43 42	81 41	84.2	43 35	80 19	83.3	43 28	78 57	82.3	43 19	77 35	81.4	43 10	76 14	80.5	43 00	74 53	79.6	224	316
45	135	44 41	81 33	84.0	44 34	80 09	83.1	44 27	78 46	82.1	44 18	77 22	81.1	44 08	76 00	80.1	43 57	74 38	79.2	225	315

Lat./A LHA/F		6° A/H	6° B/P	6° Z1/Z2	7° A/H	7° B/P	7° Z1/Z2	8° A/H	8° B/P	8° Z1/Z2	9° A/H	9° B/P	9° Z1/Z2	10° A/H	10° B/P	10° Z1/Z2	11° A/H	11° B/P	11° Z1/Z2	Lat./A LHA	
45	135	44 41	81 33	84.0	44 34	80 09	83.1	44 27	78 46	82.1	44 18	77 22	81.1	44 08	76 00	80.1	43 57	74 38	79.2	225	315
46	134	45 41	81 24	83.8	45 34	79 59	82.8	45 26	78 34	81.8	45 16	77 09	80.8	45 06	75 45	79.8	44 55	74 22	78.8	226	314
47	133	46 40	81 14	83.6	46 33	79 48	82.6	46 24	78 21	81.5	46 15	76 56	80.5	46 04	75 30	79.5	45 53	74 05	78.4	227	313
48	132	47 39	81 04	83.4	47 32	79 36	82.3	47 23	78 08	81.2	47 13	76 41	80.1	47 03	75 14	79.1	46 51	73 48	78.0	228	312
49	131	48 38	80 54	83.1	48 31	79 24	82.0	48 22	77 55	80.9	48 12	76 26	79.8	48 01	74 57	78.7	47 48	73 30	77.6	229	311
50	130	49 38	80 43	82.9	49 30	79 11	81.7	49 20	77 40	80.6	49 10	76 09	79.4	48 58	74 40	78.3	48 46	73 10	77.2	230	310
51	129	50 37	80 31	82.6	50 29	78 58	81.4	50 19	77 25	80.2	50 08	75 52	79.1	49 56	74 21	77.9	49 43	72 50	76.7	231	309
52	128	51 36	80 19	82.4	51 27	78 43	81.1	51 18	77 08	79.9	51 06	75 34	78.7	50 54	74 01	77.5	50 40	72 29	76.3	232	308
53	127	52 35	80 06	82.1	52 26	78 28	80.8	52 16	76 51	79.5	52 04	75 15	78.3	51 52	73 40	77.0	51 37	72 06	75.8	233	307
54	126	53 34	79 52	81.8	53 25	78 12	80.5	53 14	76 33	79.2	53 02	74 55	77.8	52 49	73 18	76.6	52 35	71 42	75.3	234	306
55	125	54 33	79 37	81.5	54 24	77 55	80.1	54 13	76 14	78.8	54 00	74 34	77.4	53 47	72 55	76.1	53 31	71 17	74.8	235	305
56	124	55 32	79 21	81.2	55 22	77 37	79.8	55 11	75 54	78.3	54 58	74 11	76.9	54 44	72 30	75.6	54 28	70 50	74.2	236	304
57	123	56 31	79 05	80.9	56 21	77 18	79.4	56 09	75 32	77.9	55 56	73 47	76.5	55 41	72 04	75.0	55 25	70 22	73.6	237	303
58	122	57 30	78 47	80.5	57 19	76 57	79.0	57 07	75 09	77.4	56 53	73 22	75.9	56 38	71 36	74.5	56 21	69 51	73.0	238	302
59	121	58 29	78 28	80.1	58 18	76 35	78.5	58 05	74 44	77.0	57 51	72 54	75.4	57 35	71 06	73.9	57 17	69 19	72.4	239	301
60	120	59 28	78 08	79.7	59 16	76 12	78.1	59 03	74 18	76.4	58 48	72 25	74.8	58 32	70 34	73.3	58 13	68 45	71.7	240	300
61	119	60 26	77 46	79.3	60 14	75 47	77.6	60 01	73 50	75.9	59 45	71 54	74.2	59 28	70 01	72.6	59 09	68 09	71.0	241	299
62	118	61 25	77 23	78.9	61 12	75 21	77.1	60 58	73 20	75.3	60 42	71 21	73.6	60 24	69 25	71.9	60 05	67 30	70.3	242	298
63	117	62 23	76 58	78.4	62 10	74 52	76.5	61 56	72 48	74.7	61 39	70 46	72.9	61 20	68 46	71.2	61 00	66 49	69.5	243	297
64	116	63 22	76 31	77.9	63 08	74 21	76.0	62 53	72 13	74.1	62 35	70 08	72.2	62 16	68 05	70.4	61 55	66 05	68.6	244	296
65	115	64 20	76 02	77.4	64 06	73 48	75.4	63 50	71 36	73.4	63 32	69 27	71.5	63 12	67 21	69.6	62 50	65 18	67.7	245	295
66	114	65 18	75 31	76.8	65 03	73 12	74.7	64 47	70 56	72.6	64 28	68 43	70.6	64 07	66 34	68.7	63 44	64 27	66.8	246	294
67	113	66 16	74 57	76.2	66 01	72 33	74.0	65 43	70 13	71.8	65 23	67 56	69.8	65 02	65 43	67.8	64 38	63 33	65.8	247	293
68	112	67 14	74 20	75.5	66 58	71 51	73.2	66 40	69 26	71.0	66 19	67 05	68.8	65 56	64 48	66.7	65 32	62 35	64.7	248	292
69	111	68 12	73 39	74.8	67 55	71 05	72.4	67 36	68 35	70.1	67 14	66 09	67.8	66 50	63 48	65.7	66 25	61 31	63.6	249	291
70	110	69 09	72 55	74.0	68 51	70 15	71.5	68 31	67 40	69.1	68 09	65 09	66.7	67 44	62 44	64.5	67 17	60 23	62.3	250	290
71	109	70 07	72 06	73.1	69 48	69 20	70.5	69 27	66 39	68.0	69 03	64 03	65.6	68 37	61 34	63.2	68 09	59 10	61.0	251	289
72	108	71 03	71 13	72.2	70 44	68 20	69.4	70 21	65 33	66.8	69 57	62 52	64.3	69 29	60 17	61.9	69 00	57 50	59.6	252	288
73	107	72 00	70 14	71.1	71 39	67 13	68.3	71 16	64 20	65.5	70 50	61 33	62.9	70 21	58 54	60.4	69 50	56 23	58.0	253	287
74	106	72 56	69 08	70.0	72 34	65 59	67.0	72 09	62 59	64.1	71 42	60 07	61.4	71 12	57 24	58.8	70 40	54 48	56.4	254	286
75	105	73 52	67 54	68.7	73 29	64 37	65.5	73 03	61 30	62.6	72 34	58 32	59.7	72 02	55 44	57.1	71 28	53 06	54.5	255	285
76	104	74 48	66 31	67.3	74 23	63 05	64.0	73 55	59 51	60.8	73 24	56 47	57.9	72 51	53 55	55.1	72 16	51 13	52.6	256	284
77	103	75 42	64 57	65.6	75 16	61 22	62.2	74 46	58 00	58.9	74 14	54 51	55.9	73 39	51 55	53.1	73 02	49 10	50.4	257	283
78	102	76 36	63 11	63.8	76 08	59 26	60.2	75 37	55 57	56.8	75 02	52 42	53.6	74 26	49 42	50.8	73 47	46 56	48.1	258	282
79	101	77 29	61 09	61.7	76 59	57 14	57.9	76 26	53 38	54.4	75 49	50 18	51.2	75 11	47 16	48.2	74 30	44 28	45.5	259	281
80	100	78 21	58 49	59.3	77 49	54 44	55.3	77 13	51 01	51.7	76 35	47 38	48.4	75 54	44 34	45.4	75 11	41 47	42.7	260	280
81	99	79 12	56 06	56.6	78 37	51 52	52.4	77 59	48 04	48.7	77 18	44 39	45.4	76 35	41 35	42.4	75 49	38 50	39.7	261	279
82	98	80 01	52 56	53.4	79 23	48 35	49.1	78 42	44 43	45.3	77 59	41 18	41.9	77 13	38 17	39.0	76 26	35 36	36.4	262	278
83	97	80 47	49 13	49.6	80 07	44 47	45.2	79 23	40 56	41.4	78 37	37 35	38.1	77 49	34 39	35.3	76 59	32 05	32.8	263	277
84	96	81 31	44 51	45.2	80 47	40 24	40.8	80 01	36 38	37.1	79 12	33 29	33.9	78 21	30 40	31.2	77 29	28 16	28.8	264	276
85	95	82 12	39 40	39.9	81 24	35 22	35.7	80 34	31 48	32.2	79 43	28 49	29.2	78 50	26 18	26.7	77 56	24 09	24.6	265	275
86	94	82 48	33 34	33.8	81 57	29 36	29.8	81 04	26 24	26.7	80 09	23 46	24.1	79 14	21 35	21.9	78 18	19 44	20.1	266	274
87	93	83 18	26 28	26.6	82 23	23 05	23.3	81 28	20 25	20.6	80 31	18 17	18.5	79 34	16 32	16.8	78 36	15 04	15.4	267	273
88	92	83 41	18 22	18.5	82 43	15 52	16.0	81 45	13 57	14.1	80 47	12 26	12.6	79 48	11 12	11.4	78 49	10 11	10.4	268	272
89	91	83 55	9 26	9.5	82 56	8 05	8.2	81 56	7 05	7.1	80 57	6 17	6.4	79 57	5 39	5.7	78 57	5 08	5.2	269	271
90	90	84 00	0 00	0.0	83 00	0 00	0.0	82 00	0 00	0.0	81 00	0 00	0.0	80 00	0 00	0.0	79 00	0 00	0.0	270	270

N. Lat.: for LHA > 180°... $Z_n = Z$
for LHA < 180°... $Z_n = 360° - Z$

S. Lat.: for LHA > 180°... $Z_n = 180° - Z$
for LHA < 180°... $Z_n = 180° + Z$

LATITUDE / A: 12° – 17°

B: (−) for 90° < LHA < 270°
Dec: (−) for Lat. contrary name

Z_1: same sign as B
Z_2: (−) for F > 90°

SIGHT REDUCTION TABLE

LHA/F	12° A/H	12° B/P	12° Z_1/Z_2	13° A/H	13° B/P	13° Z_1/Z_2	14° A/H	14° B/P	14° Z_1/Z_2	15° A/H	15° B/P	15° Z_1/Z_2	16° A/H	16° B/P	16° Z_1/Z_2	17° A/H	17° B/P	17° Z_1/Z_2	LHA
0	0 00	78 00	90.0	0 00	77 00	90.0	0 00	76 00	90.0	0 00	75 00	90.0	0 00	74 00	90.0	0 00	73 00	90.0	180
1	0 59	78 00	89.8	0 58	77 00	89.8	0 58	76 00	89.8	0 58	75 00	89.7	0 58	74 00	89.7	0 57	73 00	89.7	181
2	1 57	78 00	89.6	1 57	77 00	89.5	1 56	76 00	89.5	1 56	74 59	89.5	1 55	73 59	89.4	1 55	72 59	89.4	182
3	2 56	77 59	89.4	2 55	76 59	89.3	2 55	75 59	89.3	2 54	74 59	89.2	2 53	73 59	89.2	2 52	72 59	89.1	183
4	3 55	77 58	89.2	3 54	76 58	89.1	3 53	75 58	89.1	3 52	74 58	89.0	3 51	73 58	89.0	3 49	72 58	88.8	184
5	4 53	77 57	89.0	4 52	76 57	88.9	4 51	75 57	88.8	4 50	74 57	88.7	4 48	73 57	88.6	4 47	72 56	88.5	185
6	5 52	77 56	88.7	5 51	76 56	88.6	5 49	75 56	88.5	5 48	74 55	88.4	5 46	73 55	88.3	5 44	72 55	88.2	186
7	6 51	77 55	88.5	6 49	76 54	88.4	6 47	75 54	88.3	6 46	74 54	88.2	6 44	73 53	88.1	6 42	72 53	87.9	187
8	7 49	77 53	88.3	7 48	76 53	88.2	7 46	75 52	88.1	7 44	74 52	87.9	7 41	73 51	87.8	7 39	72 51	87.6	188
9	8 48	77 51	88.1	8 46	76 51	88.0	8 44	75 50	87.8	8 41	74 49	87.7	8 39	73 49	87.5	8 36	72 48	87.3	189
10	9 47	77 49	87.9	9 44	76 48	87.7	9 42	75 48	87.6	9 39	74 47	87.4	9 37	73 46	87.2	9 34	72 45	87.0	190
11	10 45	77 47	87.7	10 43	76 46	87.5	10 40	75 45	87.3	10 37	74 44	87.1	10 34	73 43	86.9	10 31	72 42	86.7	191
12	11 44	77 44	87.5	11 41	76 43	87.3	11 38	75 42	87.1	11 35	74 41	86.9	11 32	73 40	86.6	11 28	72 39	86.4	192
13	12 43	77 42	87.3	12 40	76 40	87.0	12 36	75 39	86.8	12 33	74 37	86.6	12 29	73 36	86.4	12 25	72 36	86.1	193
14	13 41	77 39	87.0	13 38	76 37	86.8	13 35	75 35	86.6	13 31	74 34	86.3	13 27	73 32	86.1	13 23	72 31	85.8	194
15	14 40	77 37	86.8	14 36	76 33	86.6	14 33	75 32	86.3	14 29	74 30	86.0	14 24	73 28	85.8	14 20	72 26	85.5	195
16	15 38	77 35	86.6	15 35	76 30	86.3	15 31	75 28	86.0	15 26	74 25	85.8	15 22	73 23	85.5	15 17	72 21	85.2	196
17	16 37	77 32	86.4	16 33	76 26	86.1	16 29	75 23	85.8	16 24	74 21	85.5	16 19	73 19	85.2	16 14	72 16	84.9	197
18	17 36	77 28	86.1	17 31	76 21	85.8	17 27	75 19	85.5	17 22	74 16	85.2	17 17	73 13	84.9	17 11	72 11	84.6	198
19	18 34	77 24	85.9	18 30	76 17	85.6	18 25	75 14	85.2	18 20	74 11	84.9	18 14	73 08	84.6	18 08	72 05	84.3	199
20	19 33	77 20	85.7	19 28	76 12	85.3	19 23	75 08	85.0	19 17	74 05	84.6	19 12	73 02	84.3	19 05	71 59	83.9	200
21	20 31	77 15	85.4	20 26	76 07	85.1	20 21	75 03	84.7	20 15	73 59	84.3	20 09	72 56	84.0	20 03	71 52	83.6	201
22	21 30	77 10	85.2	21 24	76 01	84.8	21 19	74 57	84.4	21 13	73 53	84.0	21 06	72 49	83.6	21 00	71 45	83.3	202
23	22 28	77 05	85.0	22 23	75 55	84.5	22 17	74 51	84.1	22 10	73 46	83.7	22 04	72 42	83.3	21 56	71 38	82.9	203
24	23 27	77 00	84.7	23 21	75 49	84.3	23 15	74 44	83.9	23 08	73 39	83.4	23 01	72 34	83.0	22 53	71 30	82.6	204
25	24 25	76 54	84.5	24 19	75 43	84.0	24 13	74 37	83.6	24 06	73 32	83.1	23 58	72 27	82.7	23 50	71 22	82.2	205
26	25 23	76 48	84.2	25 17	75 36	83.7	25 10	74 30	83.3	25 03	73 24	82.8	24 55	72 18	82.3	24 47	71 13	81.9	206
27	26 22	76 42	84.0	26 15	75 28	83.5	26 08	74 22	83.0	26 01	73 16	82.5	25 52	72 10	82.0	25 44	71 04	81.5	207
28	27 20	76 35	83.7	27 13	75 21	83.2	27 06	74 14	82.7	26 58	73 07	82.2	26 50	72 00	81.7	26 41	70 54	81.2	208
29	28 18	76 28	83.4	28 11	75 13	82.9	28 04	74 05	82.4	27 55	72 58	81.8	27 47	71 51	81.3	27 37	70 44	80.8	209
30	29 17	76 20	83.2	29 09	75 04	82.6	29 01	73 56	82.0	28 53	72 48	81.5	28 44	71 41	81.0	28 34	70 33	80.4	210
31	30 15	76 13	82.9	30 07	74 56	82.3	29 59	73 47	81.7	29 50	72 38	81.2	29 41	71 30	80.6	29 30	70 22	80.0	211
32	31 13	76 04	82.6	31 05	74 46	82.0	30 57	73 37	81.4	30 47	72 28	80.8	30 37	71 19	80.2	30 27	70 11	79.6	212
33	32 11	75 56	82.3	32 03	74 37	81.7	31 54	73 27	81.1	31 44	72 17	80.5	31 34	71 07	79.9	31 23	69 58	79.2	213
34	33 10	75 47	82.0	33 01	74 26	81.4	32 52	73 16	80.7	32 42	72 05	80.1	32 31	70 55	79.5	32 20	69 45	78.8	214
35	34 08	75 37	81.7	33 59	74 16	81.0	33 49	73 04	80.4	33 39	71 53	79.7	33 28	70 42	79.1	33 16	69 32	78.4	215
36	35 06	75 27	81.4	34 56	74 04	80.7	34 46	72 52	80.0	34 36	71 40	79.4	34 24	70 29	78.7	34 12	69 18	78.0	216
37	36 04	75 17	81.1	35 54	73 53	80.4	35 44	72 40	79.7	35 33	71 27	79.0	35 21	70 15	78.3	35 08	69 03	77.6	217
38	37 02	75 06	80.8	36 52	73 40	80.0	36 41	72 27	79.3	36 29	71 13	78.6	36 17	70 00	77.8	36 04	68 48	77.1	218
39	38 00	74 54	80.4	37 49	73 27	79.7	37 38	72 13	78.9	37 26	70 59	78.2	37 13	69 45	77.4	37 00	68 32	76.7	219
40	38 57	74 42	80.1	38 47	73 14	79.3	38 35	71 58	78.5	38 23	70 43	77.7	38 10	69 29	77.0	37 56	68 15	76.2	220
41	39 55	74 30	79.8	39 44	72 59	78.9	39 32	71 43	78.1	39 19	70 27	77.3	39 06	69 12	76.5	38 51	67 57	75.7	221
42	40 53	74 16	79.4	40 41	72 45	78.5	40 29	71 27	77.7	40 16	70 10	76.9	40 02	68 54	76.1	39 47	67 38	75.3	222
43	41 51	74 02	79.0	41 39	72 29	78.2	41 26	71 11	77.3	41 12	69 53	76.4	40 58	68 35	75.6	40 42	67 19	74.7	223
44	42 48	73 48	78.6	42 36	72 12	77.7	42 23	70 53	76.9	42 09	69 34	76.0	41 54	68 16	75.1	41 38	66 58	74.2	224
45	43 46	73 32	78.3	43 33	71 55	77.3	43 19	70 35	76.4	43 05	69 15	75.5	42 49	67 56	74.6	42 33	66 37	73.7	225

Lat./A	LHA/F	12° A/H	B/P	Z1/Z2	13° A/H	B/P	Z1/Z2	14° A/H	B/P	Z1/Z2	15° A/H	B/P	Z1/Z2	16° A/H	B/P	Z1/Z2	17° A/H	B/P	Z1/Z2	Lat./A	LHA
45	135	43 46	73 16	78.3	43 33	71 55	77.3	43 19	70 35	76.4	43 05	69 15	75.5	42 49	67 56	74.6	42 33	66 37	73.7	225	315
46	134	44 43	72 59	78.0	44 30	71 37	76.9	44 16	70 15	75.9	44 01	68 54	75.0	43 45	67 34	74.1	43 28	66 15	73.2	226	314
47	133	45 40	72 41	77.4	45 27	71 18	76.4	45 12	69 55	75.5	44 57	68 33	74.5	44 40	67 12	73.5	44 23	65 51	72.6	227	313
48	132	46 38	72 23	77.0	46 24	70 58	76.0	46 09	69 34	75.0	45 53	68 11	74.0	45 35	66 48	73.0	45 17	65 27	72.0	228	312
49	131	47 35	72 03	76.5	47 20	70 37	75.5	47 05	69 11	74.4	46 48	67 47	73.4	46 30	66 23	72.4	46 12	65 01	71.4	229	311
50	130	48 32	71 42	76.1	48 17	70 15	75.0	48 01	68 48	73.9	47 44	67 22	72.9	47 25	65 58	71.8	47 06	64 34	70.8	230	310
51	129	49 29	71 20	75.6	49 13	69 51	74.5	48 57	68 23	73.4	48 39	66 56	72.3	48 20	65 30	71.2	48 00	64 05	70.1	231	309
52	128	50 25	70 57	75.1	50 09	69 27	73.9	49 52	67 57	72.8	49 34	66 29	71.7	49 15	65 02	70.6	48 54	63 35	69.5	232	308
53	127	51 22	70 33	74.6	51 06	69 01	73.4	50 48	67 30	72.2	50 29	66 00	71.0	50 09	64 31	69.9	49 48	63 04	68.8	233	307
54	126	52 19	70 07	74.0	52 02	68 33	72.8	51 43	67 01	71.6	51 24	65 30	70.4	51 03	64 00	69.2	50 41	62 31	68.1	234	306
55	125	53 15	69 40	73.5	52 57	68 04	72.2	52 38	66 30	70.9	52 18	64 58	69.7	51 57	63 26	68.5	51 34	61 56	67.3	235	305
56	124	54 11	69 11	72.9	53 53	67 34	71.6	53 33	65 58	70.3	53 12	64 24	69.0	52 50	62 51	67.8	52 27	61 20	66.6	236	304
57	123	55 07	68 41	72.2	54 48	67 02	70.9	54 28	65 24	69.6	54 06	63 48	68.3	53 43	62 14	67.0	53 19	60 42	65.8	237	303
58	122	56 03	68 09	71.6	55 43	66 28	70.2	55 22	64 48	68.9	55 00	63 11	67.5	54 36	61 35	66.2	54 12	60 01	64.9	238	302
59	121	56 59	67 34	70.9	56 38	65 51	69.5	56 16	64 10	68.1	55 53	62 31	66.7	55 28	60 54	65.4	55 04	59 18	64.1	239	301
60	120	57 54	66 58	70.2	57 33	65 13	68.7	57 10	63 30	67.3	56 46	61 49	65.9	56 21	60 10	64.5	55 55	58 33	63.1	240	300
61	119	58 49	66 20	69.4	58 27	64 32	67.9	58 04	62 47	66.4	57 39	61 04	65.0	57 13	59 24	63.6	56 46	57 46	62.2	241	299
62	118	59 44	65 38	68.6	59 21	63 49	67.1	58 57	62 02	65.5	58 31	60 17	64.0	58 05	58 35	62.6	57 36	56 56	61.2	242	298
63	117	60 38	64 55	67.8	60 15	63 03	66.2	59 50	61 13	64.6	59 23	59 27	63.1	58 55	57 43	61.6	58 26	56 03	60.2	243	297
64	116	61 32	64 08	66.9	61 08	62 14	65.3	60 42	60 22	63.6	60 15	58 34	62.0	59 46	56 49	60.5	59 16	55 08	59.1	244	296
65	115	62 26	63 18	66.0	62 01	61 21	64.2	61 34	59 28	62.6	61 06	57 37	61.0	60 36	55 51	59.4	60 05	54 07	57.9	245	295
66	114	63 20	62 25	65.0	62 53	60 25	63.2	62 26	58 30	61.5	61 56	56 37	59.8	61 25	54 49	58.2	60 53	53 04	56.7	246	294
67	113	64 13	61 27	63.9	63 45	59 25	62.1	63 16	57 27	60.3	62 46	55 34	58.6	62 14	53 44	57.0	61 41	51 57	55.4	247	293
68	112	65 05	60 26	62.8	64 37	58 21	60.9	64 07	56 21	59.1	63 35	54 25	57.4	63 02	52 34	55.7	62 27	50 47	54.1	248	292
69	111	65 57	59 20	61.6	65 27	57 13	59.6	64 56	55 10	57.8	64 23	53 13	56.0	63 49	51 20	54.3	63 14	49 32	52.7	249	291
70	110	66 48	58 08	60.3	66 18	55 59	58.3	65 45	53 55	56.4	65 11	51 55	54.6	64 36	50 01	52.9	63 59	48 12	51.2	250	290
71	109	67 39	56 52	58.9	67 07	54 40	56.8	66 33	52 33	54.9	65 58	50 33	53.1	65 21	48 38	51.3	64 43	46 48	49.7	251	289
72	108	68 29	55 29	57.4	67 55	53 14	55.3	67 20	51 06	53.3	66 44	49 04	51.5	66 06	47 08	49.7	65 26	45 18	48.0	252	288
73	107	69 18	53 59	55.8	68 43	51 42	53.7	68 07	49 33	51.6	67 29	47 30	49.8	66 49	45 33	48.0	66 08	43 43	46.3	253	287
74	106	70 06	52 22	54.1	69 30	50 03	51.9	68 52	47 52	49.8	68 12	45 49	47.9	67 31	43 52	46.1	66 49	42 02	44.4	254	286
75	105	70 53	50 36	52.2	70 15	48 16	50.0	69 36	46 04	47.9	68 55	44 00	46.0	68 12	42 04	44.2	67 29	40 15	42.5	255	285
76	104	71 38	48 42	50.2	70 59	46 20	47.9	70 18	44 08	45.9	69 36	42 05	43.9	68 52	40 09	42.1	68 07	38 21	40.5	256	284
77	103	72 23	46 37	48.0	71 42	44 15	45.7	70 59	42 03	43.7	70 15	40 01	41.7	69 30	38 07	39.9	68 43	36 21	38.3	257	283
78	102	73 06	44 22	45.6	72 23	42 00	43.4	71 38	39 49	41.3	70 53	37 49	39.4	70 06	35 57	37.6	69 18	34 13	36.0	258	282
79	101	73 47	41 55	43.1	73 02	39 34	40.8	72 16	37 26	38.8	71 28	35 27	36.9	70 40	33 38	35.2	69 50	31 58	33.6	259	281
80	100	74 26	39 15	40.3	73 39	36 57	38.1	72 51	34 51	36.1	72 02	32 57	34.3	71 12	31 12	32.6	70 21	29 36	31.1	260	280
81	99	75 02	36 21	37.3	74 14	34 07	35.1	73 24	32 06	33.2	72 34	30 17	31.5	71 42	28 37	29.9	70 50	27 06	28.4	261	279
82	98	75 37	33 13	34.1	74 46	31 05	32.0	73 55	29 10	30.2	73 03	27 27	28.5	72 09	25 53	27.0	71 16	24 29	25.7	262	278
83	97	76 08	29 50	30.6	75 16	27 50	28.6	74 23	26 03	26.9	73 29	24 27	25.4	72 34	23 02	24.0	71 39	21 44	22.8	263	277
84	96	76 36	26 11	26.8	75 42	24 22	25.0	74 48	22 45	23.5	73 52	21 19	22.1	72 56	20 02	20.9	72 00	18 53	19.8	264	276
85	95	77 01	22 18	22.8	76 05	20 41	21.3	75 09	19 16	19.9	74 12	18 01	18.7	73 15	16 54	17.6	72 18	15 55	16.7	265	275
86	94	77 22	18 10	18.6	76 25	16 49	17.3	75 27	15 38	16.1	74 29	14 36	15.1	73 31	13 40	14.2	72 33	12 51	13.5	266	274
87	93	77 38	13 50	14.1	76 40	12 46	13.1	75 41	11 51	12.2	74 43	11 03	11.4	73 44	10 21	10.8	72 45	9 43	10.2	267	273
88	92	77 50	9 19	9.5	76 51	8 36	8.8	75 52	7 58	8.2	74 52	7 25	7.7	73 53	6 56	7.2	72 53	6 31	6.8	268	272
89	91	77 58	4 42	4.8	76 58	4 19	4.4	75 58	4 00	4.1	74 58	3 44	3.9	73 58	3 29	3.6	72 58	3 16	3.4	269	271
90	90	78 00	0 00	0.0	77 00	0 00	0.0	76 00	0 00	0.0	75 00	0 00	0.0	74 00	0 00	0.0	73 00	0 00	0.0	270	270

N. Lat: for LHA > 180°.... Zn = Z
      for LHA < 180°.... Zn = 360° − Z

S. Lat.: for LHA > 180°... Zn = 180° − Z
      for LHA < 180°... Zn = 180° + Z

SIGHT REDUCTION TABLE

B: (–) for 90° < LHA < 270°
Dec: (–) for Lat. contrary name

Z_1: same sign as B
Z_2: (–) for F > 90°

Lat./A	LHA/F	18° A/H	18° B/P	18° Z_1/Z_2	19° A/H	19° B/P	19° Z_1/Z_2	20° A/H	20° B/P	20° Z_1/Z_2	21° A/H	21° B/P	21° Z_1/Z_2	22° A/H	22° B/P	22° Z_1/Z_2	23° A/H	23° B/P	23° Z_1/Z_2	Lat./A	LHA
0	180	0 00	72 00	90.0	0 00	71 00	90.0	0 00	70 00	90.0	0 00	69 00	90.0	0 00	68 00	90.0	0 00	67 00	90.0	0	180
1	179	0 57	72 00	89.7	0 57	71 00	89.7	0 56	70 00	89.7	0 56	69 00	89.6	0 56	68 00	89.6	0 55	67 00	89.6	1	181
2	178	1 54	71 59	89.4	1 53	70 59	89.3	1 53	69 59	89.3	1 52	68 59	89.3	1 51	67 59	89.3	1 50	66 59	89.2	2	182
3	177	2 51	71 59	89.1	2 50	70 59	89.0	2 49	69 59	89.0	2 48	68 58	88.9	2 47	67 58	88.9	2 46	66 58	88.8	3	183
4	176	3 48	71 58	88.8	3 46	70 57	88.7	3 46	69 58	88.6	3 44	68 57	88.6	3 42	67 57	88.5	3 41	66 58	88.5	4	184
5	175	4 45	71 56	88.5	4 44	70 56	88.4	4 42	69 56	88.3	4 40	68 56	88.2	4 38	67 55	88.1	4 36	66 55	88.0	5	185
6	174	5 42	71 54	88.1	5 40	70 54	88.0	5 38	69 54	87.9	5 36	68 54	87.8	5 34	67 53	87.7	5 31	66 53	87.6	6	186
7	173	6 39	71 52	87.8	6 37	70 52	87.7	6 35	69 52	87.6	6 32	68 51	87.5	6 29	67 51	87.4	6 26	66 51	87.3	7	187
8	172	7 36	71 50	87.5	7 34	70 50	87.4	7 31	69 49	87.2	7 28	68 49	87.1	7 25	67 48	87.0	7 22	66 49	86.9	8	188
9	171	8 33	71 47	87.2	8 30	70 47	87.0	8 27	69 46	86.9	8 24	68 46	86.8	8 20	67 45	86.6	8 17	66 45	86.5	9	189
10	170	9 30	71 44	86.9	9 27	70 44	86.7	9 23	69 43	86.6	9 20	68 42	86.4	9 16	67 42	86.2	9 12	66 41	86.1	10	190
11	169	10 27	71 41	86.6	10 24	70 40	86.4	10 20	69 39	86.2	10 16	68 39	86.0	10 11	67 38	85.8	10 07	66 37	85.7	11	191
12	168	11 24	71 37	86.2	11 20	70 36	86.0	11 16	69 35	85.8	11 12	68 34	85.6	11 07	67 33	85.4	11 02	66 32	85.3	12	192
13	167	12 21	71 33	85.9	12 17	70 32	85.7	12 12	69 31	85.5	12 07	68 30	85.3	12 02	67 29	85.1	11 57	66 28	84.8	13	193
14	166	13 18	71 29	85.6	13 13	70 28	85.4	13 08	69 26	85.1	13 03	68 25	84.9	12 58	67 24	84.7	12 52	66 22	84.4	14	194
15	165	14 15	71 24	85.3	14 10	70 23	85.0	14 05	69 21	84.8	13 59	68 20	84.5	13 53	67 18	84.3	13 47	66 17	84.0	15	195
16	164	15 12	71 19	84.9	15 06	70 18	84.7	15 01	69 16	84.4	14 55	68 14	84.1	14 48	67 12	83.9	14 42	66 10	83.6	16	196
17	163	16 09	71 14	84.6	16 03	70 12	84.3	15 57	69 10	84.0	15 50	68 08	83.7	15 44	67 06	83.5	15 37	66 04	83.2	17	197
18	162	17 05	71 08	84.3	16 59	70 06	84.0	16 53	69 03	83.7	16 46	68 01	83.4	16 39	66 59	83.1	16 32	65 57	82.8	18	198
19	161	18 02	71 02	83.9	17 56	70 00	83.6	17 49	68 57	83.3	17 42	67 54	83.0	17 34	66 52	82.7	17 26	65 49	82.3	19	199
20	160	18 59	70 56	83.6	18 52	69 53	83.2	18 45	68 50	82.9	18 37	67 47	82.6	18 29	66 44	82.2	18 21	65 41	81.9	20	200
21	159	19 56	70 49	83.2	19 48	69 45	82.9	19 41	68 42	82.5	19 33	67 39	82.2	19 24	66 36	81.8	19 16	65 33	81.5	21	201
22	158	20 52	70 41	82.9	20 45	69 38	82.5	20 37	68 34	82.1	20 28	67 31	81.8	20 19	66 27	81.4	20 10	65 24	81.0	22	202
23	157	21 49	70 33	82.5	21 41	69 29	82.1	21 32	68 26	81.7	21 24	67 22	81.4	21 14	66 18	81.0	21 05	65 15	80.6	23	203
24	156	22 45	70 25	82.2	22 37	69 21	81.8	22 28	68 17	81.3	22 19	67 12	80.9	22 09	66 09	80.5	21 59	65 05	80.1	24	204
25	155	23 42	70 17	81.8	23 33	69 12	81.4	23 24	68 07	80.9	23 14	67 03	80.5	23 04	65 58	80.1	22 54	64 54	79.7	25	205
26	154	24 38	70 07	81.4	24 29	69 02	81.0	24 20	67 57	80.5	24 09	66 53	80.1	23 59	65 48	79.6	23 48	64 43	79.2	26	206
27	153	25 35	69 58	81.1	25 25	68 52	80.6	25 15	67 47	80.1	25 05	66 42	79.7	24 54	65 36	79.2	24 42	64 32	78.7	27	207
28	152	26 31	69 48	80.7	26 21	68 42	80.2	26 11	67 36	79.7	26 00	66 30	79.2	25 48	65 25	78.7	25 36	64 19	78.3	28	208
29	151	27 27	69 37	80.3	27 17	68 31	79.8	27 06	67 24	79.3	26 55	66 18	78.8	26 43	65 12	78.3	26 30	64 07	77.8	29	209
30	150	28 24	69 26	79.9	28 13	68 19	79.4	28 01	67 12	78.8	27 50	66 06	78.3	27 37	64 59	77.8	27 24	63 53	77.3	30	210
31	149	29 20	69 14	79.5	29 09	68 07	78.9	28 57	67 00	78.4	28 44	65 53	77.9	28 31	64 46	77.3	28 18	63 39	76.8	31	211
32	148	30 16	69 02	79.1	30 04	67 54	78.5	29 52	66 46	77.9	29 39	65 39	77.4	29 26	64 32	76.8	29 12	63 25	76.3	32	212
33	147	31 12	68 49	78.7	31 00	67 41	78.1	30 47	66 32	77.5	30 34	65 24	76.9	30 20	64 17	76.3	30 05	63 09	75.8	33	213
34	146	32 08	68 36	78.2	31 55	67 27	77.6	31 42	66 18	77.0	31 28	65 09	76.4	31 14	64 01	75.8	30 59	62 53	75.2	34	214
35	145	33 04	68 22	77.8	32 51	67 12	77.2	32 37	66 03	76.5	32 23	64 54	75.9	32 08	63 45	75.3	31 52	62 36	74.7	35	215
36	144	33 59	68 07	77.3	33 46	66 57	76.7	33 32	65 47	76.0	33 17	64 37	75.4	33 01	63 28	74.8	32 45	62 19	74.2	36	216
37	143	34 55	67 52	76.9	34 41	66 41	76.2	34 26	65 30	75.5	34 11	64 20	74.9	33 55	63 10	74.2	33 38	62 01	73.6	37	217
38	142	35 50	67 36	76.4	35 36	66 24	75.7	35 21	65 13	75.0	35 05	64 02	74.4	34 48	62 51	73.7	34 31	61 41	73.0	38	218
39	141	36 46	67 19	76.0	36 31	66 06	75.2	36 15	64 54	74.5	35 59	63 43	73.8	35 42	62 32	73.1	35 24	61 21	72.4	39	219
40	140	37 41	67 01	75.5	37 26	65 48	74.7	37 10	64 35	74.0	36 53	63 23	73.3	36 35	62 12	72.6	36 17	61 01	71.8	40	220
41	139	38 36	66 42	75.0	38 20	65 29	74.2	38 04	64 15	73.4	37 46	63 02	72.7	37 28	61 50	72.0	37 09	60 39	71.2	41	221
42	138	39 31	66 23	74.5	39 15	65 08	73.7	38 58	63 54	72.9	38 40	62 41	72.1	38 21	61 28	71.4	38 01	60 16	70.6	42	222
43	137	40 26	66 03	73.9	40 09	64 47	73.1	39 51	63 33	72.3	39 33	62 18	71.5	39 13	61 05	70.7	38 53	59 52	70.0	43	223
44	136	41 21	65 42	73.4	41 03	64 25	72.5	40 45	63 10	71.7	40 26	61 55	70.9	40 06	60 41	70.1	39 45	59 27	69.3	44	224
45	135	42 16	65 19	72.8	41 57	64 02	72.0	41 38	62 46	71.1	41 19	61 30	70.3	40 58	60 15	69.5	40 37	59 01	68.7	45	225

Lat.	LHA/F	18° A/H	18° B/P	18° Z1/Z2	19° A/H	19° B/P	19° Z1/Z2	20° A/H	20° B/P	20° Z1/Z2	21° A/H	21° B/P	21° Z1/Z2	22° A/H	22° B/P	22° Z1/Z2	23° A/H	23° B/P	23° Z1/Z2	LHA
45	135	42 16	65 19	72.8	41 57	64 02	72.0	41 38	62 46	71.1	41 19	61 30	70.3	40 58	60 15	69.5	40 37	59 01	68.7	225
46	134	43 10	64 56	72.3	42 51	63 38	71.4	42 32	62 21	70.5	42 11	61 05	69.6	41 50	59 49	68.8	41 28	58 34	68.0	226
47	133	44 04	64 32	71.7	43 43	63 13	70.8	43 25	61 55	69.9	43 04	60 38	69.0	42 42	59 21	68.1	42 19	58 06	67.3	227
48	132	44 58	64 06	71.1	44 38	62 46	70.1	44 18	61 27	69.2	43 56	60 09	68.3	43 33	58 53	67.4	43 10	57 37	66.5	228
49	131	45 52	63 39	70.4	45 32	62 18	69.5	45 10	60 59	68.5	44 48	59 40	67.6	44 24	58 22	66.7	44 00	57 06	65.8	229
50	130	46 46	63 11	69.8	46 25	61 49	68.8	46 03	60 29	67.8	45 39	59 09	66.9	45 15	57 51	65.9	44 50	56 34	65.0	230
51	129	47 39	62 42	69.1	47 17	61 19	68.1	46 55	59 57	67.1	46 31	58 37	66.1	46 06	57 18	65.2	45 40	56 00	64.2	231
52	128	48 33	62 11	68.4	48 10	60 47	67.4	47 46	59 25	66.4	47 22	58 03	65.4	46 56	56 44	64.4	46 30	55 25	63.4	232
53	127	49 25	61 38	67.7	49 02	60 13	66.6	48 38	58 50	65.6	48 13	57 28	64.6	47 46	56 07	63.6	47 19	54 48	62.6	233
54	126	50 18	61 04	67.0	49 54	59 38	65.9	49 29	58 14	64.8	49 03	56 51	63.7	48 36	55 30	62.7	48 08	54 10	61.7	234
55	125	51 10	60 28	66.2	50 46	59 01	65.1	50 20	57 36	64.0	49 53	56 12	62.9	49 25	54 50	61.9	48 56	53 30	60.8	235
56	124	52 03	59 50	65.4	51 37	58 23	64.2	51 10	56 56	63.1	50 43	55 32	62.0	50 14	54 09	61.0	49 44	52 48	59.9	236
57	123	52 54	59 11	64.6	52 28	57 42	63.4	52 00	56 15	62.2	51 32	54 49	61.1	51 02	53 26	60.0	50 32	52 04	59.0	237
58	122	53 46	58 29	63.7	53 18	56 59	62.5	52 50	55 31	61.3	52 21	54 05	60.2	51 50	52 41	59.1	51 19	51 18	58.0	238
59	121	54 37	57 45	62.8	54 08	56 14	61.6	53 39	54 45	60.4	53 09	53 18	59.2	52 38	51 53	58.1	52 06	50 30	57.0	239
60	120	55 27	56 59	61.8	54 58	55 27	60.6	54 28	53 57	59.3	53 57	52 29	58.2	53 25	51 04	57.0	52 52	49 40	55.9	240
61	119	56 17	56 10	60.9	55 47	54 37	59.6	55 16	53 06	58.3	54 44	51 38	57.1	54 11	50 12	55.9	53 37	48 48	54.8	241
62	118	57 07	55 19	59.8	56 36	53 45	58.5	56 04	52 13	57.2	55 31	50 44	56.0	54 57	49 17	54.8	54 22	47 53	53.7	242
63	117	57 56	54 25	58.8	57 24	52 49	57.4	56 51	51 17	56.1	56 17	49 47	54.9	55 42	48 20	53.7	55 06	46 55	52.5	243
64	116	58 44	53 27	57.6	58 12	51 51	56.3	57 38	50 18	55.0	57 03	48 48	53.7	56 27	47 20	52.5	55 50	45 55	51.3	244
65	115	59 32	52 27	56.5	58 58	50 50	55.1	58 23	49 16	53.7	57 47	47 45	52.5	57 10	46 17	51.2	56 32	44 52	50.0	245
66	114	60 19	51 23	55.2	59 45	49 45	53.8	59 09	48 11	52.5	58 32	46 39	51.2	57 53	45 11	49.9	57 14	43 47	48.7	246
67	113	61 06	50 15	53.9	60 30	48 37	52.5	59 53	47 02	51.1	59 15	45 30	49.8	58 36	44 02	48.6	57 55	42 38	47.4	247
68	112	61 52	49 04	52.6	61 15	47 25	51.1	60 36	45 50	49.8	59 57	44 18	48.4	59 17	42 50	47.2	58 36	41 26	46.0	248
69	111	62 37	47 48	51.2	61 58	46 09	49.7	61 19	44 33	48.3	60 39	43 02	47.0	59 57	41 34	45.7	59 15	40 10	44.5	249
70	110	63 21	46 28	49.7	62 41	44 48	48.3	62 01	43 13	46.8	61 19	41 42	45.4	60 36	40 15	44.2	59 53	38 52	43.0	250
71	109	64 04	45 03	48.1	63 23	43 24	46.6	62 41	41 49	45.2	61 58	40 18	43.9	61 15	38 52	42.6	60 30	37 29	41.4	251
72	108	64 45	43 34	46.4	64 04	41 54	44.9	63 21	40 20	43.5	62 37	38 50	42.2	61 52	37 25	40.9	61 06	36 03	39.7	252
73	107	65 26	41 59	44.7	64 43	40 21	43.2	63 59	38 46	41.8	63 14	37 18	40.5	62 27	35 53	39.2	61 41	34 34	38.0	253
74	106	66 06	40 19	42.9	65 21	38 41	41.4	64 36	37 08	40.0	63 49	35 41	38.7	63 02	34 18	37.4	62 14	33 00	36.3	254
75	105	66 44	38 32	40.9	65 58	36 56	39.5	65 11	35 25	38.1	64 23	33 59	36.8	63 35	32 39	35.6	62 46	31 22	34.4	255
76	104	67 20	36 40	38.9	66 33	35 05	37.4	65 45	33 37	36.1	64 56	32 13	34.8	64 07	30 55	33.6	63 16	29 41	32.5	256
77	103	67 55	34 42	36.8	67 07	33 09	35.3	66 18	31 43	34.0	65 27	30 22	32.8	64 37	29 06	31.6	63 45	27 55	30.6	257
78	102	68 29	32 37	34.5	67 39	31 07	33.1	66 48	29 44	31.9	65 57	28 26	30.7	65 05	27 14	29.6	64 13	26 06	28.5	258
79	101	69 00	30 25	32.2	68 09	29 00	30.8	67 17	27 40	29.6	66 25	26 26	28.5	65 32	25 17	27.4	64 38	24 12	26.4	259
80	100	69 29	28 07	29.7	68 37	26 46	28.4	67 44	25 30	27.3	66 50	24 20	26.2	65 56	23 15	25.2	65 02	22 15	24.3	260
81	99	69 57	25 43	27.1	69 03	24 26	25.9	68 09	23 15	24.8	67 14	22 10	23.8	66 19	21 10	22.9	65 23	20 14	22.1	261
82	98	70 21	23 11	24.5	69 27	22 00	23.5	68 31	20 56	22.3	67 36	19 56	21.4	66 40	19 00	20.6	65 43	18 09	19.8	262
83	97	70 44	20 34	21.7	69 48	19 29	20.7	68 51	18 31	19.7	67 55	17 37	18.9	66 58	16 47	18.1	66 01	16 01	17.4	263
84	96	71 03	17 50	18.8	70 07	16 53	17.9	69 09	16 01	17.1	68 12	15 14	16.3	67 14	14 30	15.7	66 16	13 50	15.1	264
85	95	71 20	15 01	15.8	70 23	14 12	15.0	69 25	13 28	14.3	68 26	12 48	13.7	67 28	12 10	13.1	66 29	11 36	12.6	265
86	94	71 35	12 07	12.8	70 36	11 27	12.1	69 37	10 51	11.6	68 38	10 18	11.0	67 39	9 48	10.6	66 40	9 20	10.1	266
87	93	71 46	9 09	9.6	70 46	8 39	9.1	69 47	8 11	8.7	68 48	7 46	8.3	67 48	7 23	8.0	66 49	7 02	7.6	267
88	92	71 54	6 08	6.4	70 54	5 47	6.1	69 54	5 29	5.8	68 55	5 12	5.6	67 55	4 56	5.3	66 55	4 42	5.0	268
89	91	71 58	3 04	3.2	70 58	2 54	3.1	69 59	2 45	2.9	68 59	2 36	2.8	67 59	2 28	2.6	66 59	2 21	2.6	269
90	90	72 00	0 00	0.0	71 00	0 00	0.0	70 00	0 00	0.0	69 00	0 00	0.0	68 00	0 00	0.0	67 00	0 00	0.0	270

N. Lat.: for LHA > 180°... Zn = Z
for LHA < 180°... Zn = 360° − Z

S. Lat.: for LHA > 180°... Zn = 180° − Z
for LHA < 180°... Zn = 180° + Z

SIGHT REDUCTION TABLE

B: (−) for 90° < LHA < 270°
Dec: (−) for Lat. contrary name

Z₁: same sign as B
Z₂: (−) for F > 90°

Lat./A LHA/F	24° A/H	24° B/P	24° Z₁/Z₂	25° A/H	25° B/P	25° Z₁/Z₂	26° A/H	26° B/P	26° Z₁/Z₂	27° A/H	27° B/P	27° Z₁/Z₂	28° A/H	28° B/P	28° Z₁/Z₂	29° A/H	29° B/P	29° Z₁/Z₂	Lat./A LHA
0 180	0 00	66 00	90.0	0 00	65 00	90.0	0 00	64 00	90.0	0 00	63 00	90.0	0 00	62 00	90.0	0 00	61 00	90.0	180 360
1 179	0 55	66 00	89.6	0 54	65 00	89.6	0 54	64 00	89.6	0 53	63 00	89.6	0 53	62 00	89.5	0 52	61 00	89.5	181 359
2 178	1 50	65 59	89.2	1 49	64 59	89.2	1 48	63 59	89.1	1 47	62 59	89.1	1 46	61 59	89.1	1 45	60 59	89.0	182 358
3 177	2 44	65 58	88.8	2 43	64 58	88.7	2 42	63 58	88.7	2 40	62 58	88.6	2 39	61 58	88.6	2 37	60 58	88.5	183 357
4 176	3 39	65 57	88.4	3 37	64 57	88.3	3 36	63 57	88.2	3 34	62 57	88.2	3 32	61 57	88.1	3 30	60 56	88.1	184 356
5 175	4 34	65 55	88.0	4 32	64 55	87.9	4 30	63 55	87.8	4 27	62 55	87.7	4 25	61 55	87.6	4 22	60 54	87.6	185 355
6 174	5 29	65 53	87.6	5 26	64 53	87.5	5 23	63 53	87.4	5 21	62 52	87.3	5 18	61 52	87.2	5 15	60 52	87.1	186 354
7 173	6 24	65 50	87.1	6 20	64 50	87.0	6 17	63 50	86.9	6 14	62 50	86.8	6 11	61 49	86.7	6 07	60 49	86.6	187 353
8 172	7 18	65 47	86.7	7 15	64 47	86.6	7 11	63 47	86.5	7 07	62 46	86.3	7 04	61 46	86.2	6 59	60 46	86.1	188 352
9 171	8 13	65 44	86.3	8 09	64 44	86.2	8 05	63 43	86.0	8 01	62 43	85.9	7 56	61 42	85.7	7 52	60 42	85.6	189 351
10 170	9 08	65 40	85.9	9 03	64 40	85.7	8 59	63 39	85.6	8 54	62 39	85.4	8 49	61 38	85.3	8 44	60 38	85.1	190 350
11 169	10 02	65 36	85.5	9 57	64 35	85.3	9 52	63 35	85.1	9 47	62 34	85.0	9 42	61 33	84.8	9 36	60 33	84.6	191 349
12 168	10 57	65 32	85.1	10 52	64 31	84.9	10 46	63 30	84.7	10 41	62 29	84.5	10 35	61 28	84.3	10 29	60 28	84.1	192 348
13 167	11 52	65 27	84.6	11 46	64 26	84.4	11 40	63 25	84.2	11 34	62 24	84.0	11 27	61 23	83.8	11 21	60 22	83.6	193 347
14 166	12 46	65 21	84.2	12 40	64 20	84.0	12 34	63 19	83.8	12 27	62 18	83.5	12 20	61 17	83.3	12 13	60 16	83.1	194 346
15 165	13 41	65 15	83.8	13 34	64 14	83.5	13 27	63 13	83.3	13 20	62 11	83.1	13 13	61 10	82.8	13 05	60 09	82.6	195 345
16 164	14 35	65 09	83.3	14 28	64 07	83.1	14 21	63 06	82.8	14 13	62 04	82.6	14 05	61 03	82.3	13 57	60 02	82.1	196 344
17 163	15 29	65 02	82.9	15 22	64 00	82.6	15 14	62 59	82.4	15 06	61 57	82.1	14 58	60 56	81.8	14 49	59 54	81.6	197 343
18 162	16 24	64 55	82.5	16 16	63 53	82.2	16 08	62 51	81.9	15 59	61 49	81.6	15 50	60 47	81.3	15 41	59 46	81.0	198 342
19 161	17 18	64 47	82.0	17 10	63 45	81.7	17 01	62 43	81.4	16 52	61 41	81.1	16 42	60 39	80.8	16 33	59 37	80.5	199 341
20 160	18 12	64 39	81.6	18 03	63 36	81.3	17 54	62 34	80.9	17 45	61 32	80.6	17 35	60 30	80.3	17 24	59 28	80.0	200 340
21 159	19 07	64 30	81.1	18 57	63 28	80.8	18 47	62 25	80.4	18 37	61 23	80.1	18 27	60 20	79.8	18 16	59 18	79.5	201 339
22 158	20 01	64 21	80.7	19 51	63 18	80.3	19 41	62 15	79.9	19 30	61 13	79.6	19 19	60 10	79.3	19 08	59 08	78.9	202 338
23 157	20 55	64 11	80.2	20 44	63 08	79.8	20 34	62 05	79.5	20 22	61 02	79.1	20 11	59 59	78.7	19 59	58 57	78.4	203 337
24 156	21 49	64 01	79.7	21 38	62 58	79.3	21 27	61 54	79.0	21 15	60 51	78.6	21 03	59 48	78.2	20 50	58 45	77.8	204 336
25 155	22 43	63 50	79.3	22 31	62 46	78.9	22 19	61 43	78.4	22 07	60 39	78.0	21 55	59 36	77.7	21 42	58 33	77.3	205 335
26 154	23 36	63 39	78.8	23 25	62 35	78.4	23 12	61 31	77.9	22 59	60 27	77.5	22 46	59 24	77.1	22 33	58 20	76.7	206 334
27 153	24 30	63 27	78.3	24 18	62 22	77.8	24 05	61 18	77.4	23 52	60 14	77.0	23 38	59 10	76.5	23 24	58 07	76.1	207 333
28 152	25 24	63 14	77.8	25 11	62 10	77.3	24 57	61 05	76.9	24 44	60 01	76.4	24 29	58 57	76.0	24 15	57 53	75.5	208 332
29 151	26 17	63 01	77.3	26 04	61 56	76.8	25 50	60 51	76.3	25 36	59 47	75.9	25 21	58 42	75.4	25 05	57 38	75.0	209 331
30 150	27 11	62 48	76.8	26 57	61 42	76.3	26 42	60 37	75.8	26 27	59 32	75.3	26 12	58 27	74.8	25 56	57 23	74.4	210 330
31 149	28 04	62 33	76.3	27 50	61 27	75.8	27 35	60 22	75.2	27 19	59 16	74.7	27 03	58 11	74.2	26 46	57 07	73.8	211 329
32 148	28 57	62 18	75.7	28 42	61 12	75.2	28 27	60 06	74.7	28 10	59 00	74.2	27 54	57 55	73.7	27 37	56 50	73.1	212 328
33 147	29 50	62 02	75.2	29 35	60 56	74.7	29 19	59 49	74.1	29 02	58 43	73.6	28 45	57 38	73.0	28 27	56 32	72.5	213 327
34 146	30 43	61 46	74.7	30 27	60 39	74.1	30 10	59 32	73.5	29 53	58 26	73.0	29 35	57 20	72.4	29 17	56 14	71.9	214 326
35 145	31 36	61 28	74.1	31 19	60 21	73.5	31 02	59 14	72.9	30 44	58 07	72.4	30 26	57 01	71.8	30 07	55 55	71.2	215 325
36 144	32 29	61 10	73.5	32 11	60 02	72.9	31 53	58 55	72.3	31 35	57 48	71.7	31 16	56 41	71.2	30 56	55 35	70.6	216 324
37 143	33 21	60 52	73.0	33 03	59 43	72.3	32 45	58 35	71.7	32 26	57 28	71.1	32 06	56 21	70.5	31 46	55 14	69.9	217 323
38 142	34 13	60 32	72.4	33 55	59 23	71.7	33 36	58 15	71.1	33 16	57 07	70.5	32 56	55 59	69.8	32 35	54 53	69.3	218 322
39 141	35 06	60 11	71.8	34 47	59 02	71.1	34 27	57 53	70.5	34 06	56 45	69.8	33 45	55 37	69.2	33 24	54 30	68.6	219 321
40 140	35 58	59 50	71.2	35 38	58 40	70.5	35 17	57 31	69.8	34 56	56 22	69.1	34 35	55 14	68.5	34 12	54 07	67.9	220 320
41 139	36 49	59 28	70.5	36 29	58 17	69.8	36 08	57 08	69.1	35 46	55 59	68.5	35 24	54 50	67.8	35 01	53 42	67.1	221 319
42 138	37 41	59 04	69.9	37 20	57 54	69.2	36 58	56 43	68.5	36 36	55 34	67.8	36 13	54 25	67.1	35 49	53 17	66.4	222 318
43 137	38 32	58 40	69.2	38 11	57 29	68.5	37 48	56 18	67.8	37 25	55 08	67.1	37 02	53 59	66.4	36 37	52 50	65.7	223 317
44 136	39 23	58 15	68.6	39 01	57 03	67.8	38 38	55 52	67.1	38 14	54 41	66.3	37 50	53 32	65.6	37 25	52 23	64.9	224 316
45 135	40 14	57 48	67.9	39 51	56 36	67.1	39 28	55 24	66.3	39 03	54 13	65.6	38 38	53 04	64.9	38 12	51 54	64.1	225 315

LHA/F		24° A/H	24° B/P	24° Z_1/Z_2	25° A/H	25° B/P	25° Z_1/Z_2	26° A/H	26° B/P	26° Z_1/Z_2	27° A/H	27° B/P	27° Z_1/Z_2	28° A/H	28° B/P	28° Z_1/Z_2	29° A/H	29° B/P	29° Z_1/Z_2	LHA	
45	135	40 14	57 48	67.9	39 51	56 36	67.1	39 28	55 24	66.3	39 03	54 13	65.6	38 38	53 04	64.9	38 12	51 54	64.1	225	315
46	134	41 05	57 21	67.2	40 41	56 08	66.4	40 17	54 56	65.6	39 52	53 44	64.8	39 26	52 34	64.1	38 59	51 25	63.3	226	314
47	133	41 55	56 52	66.4	41 31	55 38	65.6	41 06	54 26	64.8	40 40	53 14	64.0	40 13	52 04	63.3	39 46	50 54	62.5	227	313
48	132	42 45	56 22	65.7	42 20	55 08	64.9	41 54	53 55	64.0	41 28	52 43	63.2	41 00	51 32	62.5	40 32	50 22	61.7	228	312
49	131	43 35	55 50	64.9	43 09	54 36	64.1	42 43	53 22	63.2	42 15	52 10	62.4	41 47	50 59	61.6	41 18	49 48	60.9	229	311
50	130	44 25	55 17	64.1	43 58	54 02	63.3	43 31	52 49	62.4	43 03	51 36	61.6	42 34	50 24	60.8	42 04	49 14	60.0	230	310
51	129	45 14	54 43	63.3	44 47	53 28	62.4	44 18	52 13	61.6	43 49	51 00	60.7	43 20	49 48	59.9	42 49	48 38	59.1	231	309
52	128	46 03	54 08	62.5	45 35	52 52	61.6	45 06	51 37	60.7	44 36	50 23	59.8	44 06	49 11	59.0	43 34	48 00	58.2	232	308
53	127	46 51	53 30	61.6	46 22	52 14	60.7	45 52	50 59	59.8	45 22	49 45	58.9	44 51	48 32	58.1	44 18	47 21	57.2	233	307
54	126	47 39	52 51	60.8	47 09	51 34	59.8	46 39	50 19	58.9	46 07	49 05	58.0	45 35	47 52	57.1	45 02	46 41	56.3	234	306
55	125	48 27	52 11	59.8	47 56	50 53	58.9	47 25	49 37	58.0	46 53	48 23	57.0	46 19	47 10	56.2	45 46	45 59	55.3	235	305
56	124	49 14	51 28	58.9	48 43	50 11	57.9	48 10	48 54	57.0	47 37	47 40	56.1	47 03	46 27	55.2	46 29	45 15	54.3	236	304
57	123	50 01	50 44	57.9	49 28	49 26	56.9	48 55	48 09	56.0	48 21	46 54	55.0	47 46	45 41	54.1	47 11	44 30	53.3	237	303
58	122	50 47	49 58	56.9	50 14	48 39	55.9	49 40	47 22	54.9	49 05	46 07	54.0	48 29	44 54	53.1	47 53	43 43	52.2	238	302
59	121	51 33	49 09	55.9	50 58	47 51	54.9	50 23	46 34	53.9	49 48	45 18	52.9	49 11	44 05	52.0	48 34	42 54	51.1	239	301
60	120	52 18	48 19	54.8	51 43	47 00	53.8	51 07	45 43	52.8	50 30	44 28	51.8	49 53	43 14	50.9	49 14	42 03	50.0	240	300
61	119	53 02	47 26	53.7	52 26	46 07	52.7	51 49	44 50	51.7	51 12	43 35	50.7	50 33	42 22	49.7	49 54	41 10	48.8	241	299
62	118	53 46	46 31	52.6	53 09	45 12	51.5	52 31	43 54	50.5	51 53	42 39	49.5	51 13	41 27	48.6	50 33	40 16	47.6	242	298
63	117	54 29	45 33	51.4	53 51	44 14	50.3	53 13	42 57	49.3	52 33	41 42	48.3	51 53	40 30	47.3	51 12	39 19	46.4	243	297
64	116	55 12	44 33	50.2	54 33	43 14	49.1	53 53	41 57	48.1	53 13	40 42	47.1	52 31	39 30	46.1	51 49	38 20	45.2	244	296
65	115	55 53	43 30	48.9	55 13	42 11	47.8	54 33	40 54	46.8	53 51	39 40	45.8	53 09	38 29	44.8	52 26	37 19	43.9	245	295
66	114	56 34	42 25	47.6	55 53	41 06	46.5	55 12	39 50	45.4	54 29	38 36	44.4	53 46	37 25	43.5	53 02	36 16	42.6	246	294
67	113	57 14	41 16	46.2	56 32	39 58	45.1	55 50	38 42	44.1	55 06	37 29	43.1	54 22	36 19	42.1	53 37	35 11	41.2	247	293
68	112	57 53	40 05	44.8	57 10	38 47	43.7	56 27	37 32	42.7	55 42	36 19	41.7	54 57	35 10	40.7	54 11	34 03	39.8	248	292
69	111	58 32	38 50	43.3	57 47	37 33	42.2	57 03	36 18	41.2	56 17	35 07	40.2	55 31	33 59	39.3	54 44	32 53	38.4	249	291
70	110	59 09	37 32	41.8	58 23	36 16	40.7	57 38	35 02	39.7	56 51	33 52	38.7	56 04	32 45	37.8	55 16	31 41	36.9	250	290
71	109	59 45	36 11	40.2	58 58	34 55	39.2	58 12	33 43	38.1	57 24	32 35	37.2	56 36	31 29	36.3	55 47	30 26	35.4	251	289
72	108	60 19	34 46	38.6	59 32	33 32	37.6	58 44	32 21	36.5	57 56	31 14	35.6	57 07	30 10	34.7	56 17	29 08	33.8	252	288
73	107	60 53	33 18	36.9	60 05	32 05	35.9	59 16	30 56	34.9	58 26	29 51	34.0	57 36	28 48	33.1	56 46	27 49	32.2	253	287
74	106	61 25	31 46	35.2	60 36	30 35	34.2	59 46	29 28	33.2	58 55	28 25	32.3	58 05	27 24	31.4	57 13	26 26	30.6	254	286
75	105	61 56	30 10	33.4	61 06	29 02	32.4	60 15	27 57	31.4	59 23	26 56	30.5	58 31	25 57	29.7	57 39	25 02	28.9	255	285
76	104	62 26	28 31	31.5	61 34	27 25	30.5	60 42	26 23	29.6	59 50	25 24	28.8	58 57	24 28	28.0	58 04	23 35	27.2	256	284
77	103	62 53	26 48	29.6	62 01	25 45	28.6	61 08	24 46	27.8	60 15	23 49	27.0	59 21	22 56	26.2	58 27	22 05	25.5	257	283
78	102	63 20	25 02	27.6	62 26	24 02	26.7	61 32	23 05	25.9	60 38	22 12	25.1	59 44	21 21	24.4	58 49	20 34	23.7	258	282
79	101	63 44	23 12	25.5	62 50	22 15	24.7	61 55	21 22	23.9	61 00	20 32	23.2	60 05	19 44	22.5	59 09	19 00	21.8	259	281
80	100	64 07	21 18	23.4	63 12	20 25	22.6	62 16	19 36	21.9	61 20	18 49	21.2	60 24	18 05	20.6	59 28	17 24	20.0	260	280
81	99	64 28	19 22	21.3	63 32	18 33	20.5	62 35	17 47	19.9	61 39	17 04	19.2	60 42	16 24	18.6	59 45	15 46	18.1	261	279
82	98	64 47	17 22	19.1	63 50	16 37	18.4	62 53	15 56	17.8	61 56	15 17	17.2	60 58	14 40	16.7	60 01	14 06	16.2	262	278
83	97	65 03	15 18	16.8	64 06	14 39	16.2	63 08	14 02	15.6	62 10	13 27	15.1	61 12	12 55	14.7	60 14	12 24	14.2	263	277
84	96	65 18	13 13	14.5	64 20	12 38	14.0	63 22	12 06	13.5	62 23	11 36	13.0	61 25	11 07	12.6	60 26	10 41	12.2	264	276
85	95	65 31	11 05	12.1	64 32	10 35	11.7	63 33	10 08	11.3	62 35	9 42	10.9	61 36	9 19	10.6	60 37	8 56	10.2	265	275
86	94	65 41	8 54	9.8	64 42	8 30	9.4	63 43	8 08	9.1	62 44	7 48	8.8	61 44	7 28	8.5	60 45	7 10	8.2	266	274
87	93	65 49	6 42	7.3	64 50	6 24	7.1	63 50	6 07	6.8	62 51	5 52	6.6	61 51	5 37	6.4	60 52	5 24	6.2	267	273
88	92	65 55	4 29	4.9	64 56	4 17	4.7	63 56	4 06	4.6	62 56	3 55	4.4	61 56	3 45	4.3	60 56	3 36	4.1	268	272
89	91	65 59	2 15	2.5	64 59	2 09	2.4	63 59	2 03	2.3	62 59	1 58	2.2	61 59	1 53	2.1	60 59	1 48	2.1	269	271
90	90	66 00	0 00	0.0	65 00	0 00	0.0	64 00	0 00	0.0	63 00	0 00	0.0	62 00	0 00	0.0	61 00	0 00	0.0	270	270

N. Lat.: for LHA > 180°... $Z_n = Z$
for LHA < 180°... $Z_n = 360° - Z$

S. Lat.: for LHA > 180°... $Z_n = 180° - Z$
for LHA < 180°... $Z_n = 180° + Z$

SIGHT REDUCTION TABLE

B: (–) for 90° < LHA < 270°
Dec: (–) for Lat. contrary name

Z₁: same sign as B
Z₂: (–) for F > 90°

Lat./A →	30°			31°			32°			33°			34°			35°			Lat./A
LHA/F	A/H	B/P	Z₁/Z₂	A/H	B/P	Z₁/Z₂	A/H	B/P	Z₁/Z₂	A/H	B/P	Z₁/Z₂	A/H	B/P	Z₁/Z₂	A/H	B/P	Z₁/Z₂	LHA
0 / 180	0 00	60 00	90.0	0 00	59 00	90.0	0 00	58 00	90.0	0 00	57 00	90.0	0 00	56 00	90.0	0 00	55 00	90.0	180 / 360
1 / 179	0 52	60 00	89.5	0 51	59 00	89.5	0 51	58 00	89.5	0 50	57 00	89.5	0 50	56 00	89.4	0 49	55 00	89.4	181 / 359
2 / 178	1 43	59 59	89.0	1 43	58 59	89.0	1 42	57 59	88.9	1 41	56 59	88.9	1 39	55 59	88.9	1 38	54 59	88.9	182 / 358
3 / 177	2 36	59 58	88.5	2 34	58 58	88.5	2 33	57 58	88.4	2 31	56 58	88.4	2 29	55 58	88.3	2 27	54 58	88.3	183 / 357
4 / 176	3 28	59 56	88.0	3 26	58 56	88.0	3 23	57 56	87.9	3 21	56 56	87.8	3 19	55 56	87.8	3 17	54 56	87.7	184 / 356
5 / 175	4 20	59 54	87.5	4 17	58 54	87.4	4 14	57 54	87.3	4 12	56 54	87.3	4 09	55 54	87.2	4 06	54 54	87.1	185 / 355
6 / 174	5 12	59 52	87.0	5 08	58 52	86.9	5 05	57 52	86.8	5 02	56 51	86.7	4 58	55 51	86.6	4 55	54 51	86.6	186 / 354
7 / 173	6 04	59 49	86.5	6 00	58 49	86.4	5 56	57 48	86.3	5 52	56 48	86.2	5 48	55 48	86.1	5 44	54 48	86.0	187 / 353
8 / 172	6 55	59 45	86.0	6 51	58 45	85.9	6 47	57 45	85.7	6 42	56 45	85.6	6 38	55 44	85.5	6 33	54 44	85.4	188 / 352
9 / 171	7 47	59 42	85.5	7 42	58 41	85.3	7 37	57 41	85.2	7 32	56 40	85.1	7 27	55 40	84.9	7 22	54 40	84.8	189 / 351
10 / 170	8 39	59 37	85.0	8 34	58 37	84.8	8 28	57 36	84.7	8 22	56 36	84.5	8 17	55 36	84.4	8 11	54 35	84.2	190 / 350
11 / 169	9 31	59 32	84.4	9 25	58 32	84.3	9 19	57 31	84.1	9 13	56 31	84.0	9 06	55 30	83.8	9 00	54 30	83.6	191 / 349
12 / 168	10 22	59 27	83.9	10 16	58 26	83.8	10 09	57 26	83.6	10 03	56 25	83.4	9 56	55 25	83.2	9 48	54 24	83.0	192 / 348
13 / 167	11 14	59 21	83.4	11 07	58 20	83.2	11 00	57 20	83.0	10 52	56 19	82.8	10 45	55 18	82.6	10 37	54 18	82.5	193 / 347
14 / 166	12 06	59 15	82.9	11 58	58 14	82.7	11 50	57 13	82.5	11 42	56 12	82.3	11 34	55 12	82.1	11 26	54 11	81.9	194 / 346
15 / 165	12 57	59 08	82.4	12 49	58 07	82.1	12 41	57 06	81.9	12 32	56 05	81.7	12 23	55 04	81.5	12 14	54 04	81.3	195 / 345
16 / 164	13 49	59 01	81.8	13 40	57 59	81.6	13 31	56 58	81.4	13 22	55 57	81.1	13 13	54 57	80.9	13 03	53 56	80.7	196 / 344
17 / 163	14 40	58 53	81.3	14 31	57 51	81.1	14 21	56 50	80.8	14 12	55 49	80.5	14 02	54 48	80.3	13 51	53 47	80.1	197 / 343
18 / 162	15 31	58 44	80.8	15 22	57 43	80.5	15 12	56 42	80.2	15 01	55 40	80.0	14 51	54 39	79.7	14 40	53 38	79.4	198 / 342
19 / 161	16 23	58 35	80.2	16 12	57 34	79.9	16 02	56 32	79.7	15 51	55 31	79.4	15 40	54 30	79.1	15 28	53 29	78.8	199 / 341
20 / 160	17 14	58 26	79.7	17 03	57 24	79.4	16 52	56 23	79.1	16 40	55 21	78.8	16 28	54 20	78.5	16 16	53 19	78.2	200 / 340
21 / 159	18 05	58 16	79.1	17 53	57 14	78.8	17 42	56 12	78.5	17 29	55 11	78.2	17 17	54 09	77.9	17 04	53 08	77.6	201 / 339
22 / 158	18 56	58 05	78.6	18 44	57 03	78.2	18 31	56 01	77.9	18 19	55 00	77.6	18 06	53 58	77.3	17 52	52 56	77.0	202 / 338
23 / 157	19 47	57 54	78.0	19 34	56 52	77.7	19 21	55 50	77.3	19 08	54 48	77.0	18 54	53 46	76.6	18 40	52 44	76.3	203 / 337
24 / 156	20 37	57 42	77.4	20 24	56 40	77.1	20 11	55 38	76.7	19 57	54 36	76.4	19 42	53 34	76.0	19 28	52 32	75.7	204 / 336
25 / 155	21 28	57 30	76.9	21 14	56 27	76.5	21 00	55 25	76.1	20 46	54 23	75.7	20 31	53 21	75.4	20 15	52 19	75.0	205 / 335
26 / 154	22 19	57 17	76.3	22 04	56 14	75.9	21 49	55 12	75.5	21 34	54 09	75.1	21 19	53 07	74.7	21 03	52 05	74.4	206 / 334
27 / 153	23 09	57 03	75.7	22 54	56 00	75.3	22 39	54 57	74.9	22 23	53 55	74.5	22 07	52 52	74.1	21 50	51 50	73.7	207 / 333
28 / 152	23 59	56 49	75.1	23 44	55 46	74.7	23 28	54 43	74.3	23 11	53 40	73.8	22 54	52 37	73.4	22 37	51 35	73.0	208 / 332
29 / 151	24 50	56 34	74.5	24 33	55 31	74.1	24 17	54 27	73.6	23 59	53 24	73.2	23 42	52 22	72.8	23 24	51 19	72.4	209 / 331
30 / 150	25 40	56 19	73.9	25 23	55 15	73.4	25 05	54 11	73.0	24 48	53 08	72.5	24 29	52 05	72.1	24 11	51 03	71.7	210 / 330
31 / 149	26 29	56 02	73.3	26 12	54 58	72.8	25 54	53 54	72.3	25 35	52 51	71.9	25 17	51 48	71.4	24 57	50 45	71.0	211 / 329
32 / 148	27 19	55 45	72.6	27 01	54 41	72.2	26 42	53 37	71.7	26 23	52 33	71.2	26 04	51 30	70.7	25 44	50 27	70.3	212 / 328
33 / 147	28 09	55 27	72.0	27 50	54 23	71.5	27 31	53 19	71.0	27 11	52 15	70.5	26 50	51 12	70.0	26 30	50 08	69.6	213 / 327
34 / 146	28 58	55 09	71.4	28 38	54 04	70.8	28 19	53 00	70.3	27 58	51 56	69.8	27 37	50 52	69.3	27 16	49 49	68.8	214 / 326
35 / 145	29 47	54 49	70.7	29 27	53 44	70.2	29 06	52 40	69.6	28 45	51 36	69.1	28 24	50 32	68.6	28 01	49 29	68.1	215 / 325
36 / 144	30 36	54 29	70.0	30 15	53 24	69.5	29 54	52 19	68.9	29 32	51 15	68.4	29 10	50 11	67.9	28 47	49 07	67.4	216 / 324
37 / 143	31 25	54 08	69.4	31 03	53 03	68.8	30 41	51 58	68.2	30 19	50 53	67.7	29 56	49 49	67.2	29 32	48 45	66.6	217 / 323
38 / 142	32 13	53 46	68.7	31 51	52 40	68.1	31 28	51 36	67.5	31 05	50 30	66.9	30 41	49 26	66.4	30 17	48 23	65.9	218 / 322
39 / 141	33 02	53 23	68.0	32 39	52 17	67.4	32 15	51 12	66.8	31 51	50 07	66.2	31 27	49 03	65.6	31 02	47 59	65.1	219 / 321
40 / 140	33 50	53 00	67.2	33 26	51 53	66.6	33 02	50 48	66.0	32 37	49 43	65.4	32 12	48 38	64.9	31 46	47 34	64.3	220 / 320
41 / 139	34 37	52 35	66.5	34 13	51 29	65.9	33 48	50 23	65.3	33 23	49 17	64.7	32 57	48 13	64.1	32 30	47 09	63.5	221 / 319
42 / 138	35 25	52 09	65.8	35 00	51 03	65.1	34 34	49 56	64.5	34 08	48 51	63.9	33 42	47 46	63.3	33 14	46 42	62.7	222 / 318
43 / 137	36 12	51 43	65.0	35 46	50 36	64.3	35 20	49 29	63.7	34 53	48 24	63.1	34 26	47 19	62.5	33 58	46 15	61.9	223 / 317
44 / 136	36 59	51 15	64.2	36 33	50 08	63.6	36 06	49 01	62.9	35 38	47 55	62.3	35 10	46 51	61.6	34 41	45 46	61.0	224 / 316
45 / 135	37 46	50 46	63.4	37 19	49 39	62.7	36 51	48 32	62.1	36 22	47 26	61.4	35 53	46 21	60.8	35 24	45 17	60.2	225 / 315

Lat./A		30°			31°			32°			33°			34°			35°			Lat./A	
LHA	F	A/H	B/P	Z1/Z2	A/H	B/P	Z1/Z2	A/H	B/P	Z1/Z2	A/H	B/P	Z1/Z2	A/H	B/P	Z1/Z2	A/H	B/P	Z1/Z2	LHA	
45	135	37 46	50 46	63.4	37 19	49 39	62.7	36 51	48 32	62.1	36 22	47 26	61.4	35 53	46 21	60.8	35 24	45 17	60.2	225	315
46	134	38 32	50 16	62.6	38 04	49 08	61.9	37 36	48 02	61.2	37 06	46 56	60.6	36 37	45 51	59.9	36 06	44 46	59.3	226	314
47	133	39 18	49 45	61.8	38 49	48 37	61.1	38 20	47 30	60.4	37 50	46 24	59.7	37 19	45 19	59.1	36 48	44 15	58.4	227	313
48	132	40 04	49 13	61.0	39 34	48 05	60.2	39 04	46 58	59.5	38 33	45 51	58.8	38 02	44 46	58.2	37 30	43 42	57.5	228	312
49	131	40 49	48 39	60.1	40 19	47 31	59.4	39 48	46 24	58.6	39 16	45 18	57.9	38 44	44 12	57.2	38 11	43 08	56.6	229	311
50	130	41 34	48 04	59.2	41 03	46 56	58.5	40 31	45 49	57.7	39 59	44 42	57.0	39 26	43 37	56.3	38 52	42 33	55.6	230	310
51	129	42 18	47 28	58.3	41 46	46 20	57.5	41 14	45 12	56.8	40 41	44 06	56.1	40 07	43 01	55.4	39 32	41 57	54.7	231	309
52	128	43 02	46 50	57.4	42 29	45 42	56.6	41 56	44 34	55.9	41 22	43 28	55.1	40 47	42 23	54.4	40 12	41 19	53.7	232	308
53	127	43 46	46 11	56.4	43 12	45 03	55.6	42 38	43 55	54.9	42 03	42 49	54.1	41 28	41 44	53.4	40 52	40 41	52.7	233	307
54	126	44 29	45 31	55.5	43 54	44 22	54.7	43 19	43 15	53.9	42 44	42 09	53.1	42 07	41 04	52.4	41 30	40 01	51.7	234	306
55	125	45 11	44 49	54.5	44 36	43 40	53.7	44 00	42 33	52.9	43 24	41 27	52.1	42 46	40 23	51.4	42 09	39 19	50.7	235	305
56	124	45 53	44 05	53.5	45 17	42 57	52.6	44 40	41 50	51.8	44 03	40 44	51.1	43 25	39 40	50.3	42 46	38 37	49.6	236	304
57	123	46 35	43 20	52.4	45 58	42 11	51.6	45 20	41 05	50.8	44 42	39 59	50.0	44 03	38 55	49.3	43 24	37 53	48.5	237	303
58	122	47 16	42 33	51.3	46 38	41 25	50.5	45 59	40 18	49.7	45 20	39 13	48.9	44 40	38 09	48.2	44 00	37 07	47.5	238	302
59	121	47 56	41 44	50.2	47 17	40 36	49.4	46 38	39 30	48.6	45 58	38 25	47.8	45 17	37 22	47.1	44 36	36 20	46.3	239	301
60	120	48 35	40 54	49.1	47 56	39 46	48.3	47 16	38 40	47.5	46 35	37 36	46.7	45 53	36 33	45.9	45 11	35 32	45.2	240	300
61	119	49 14	40 01	47.9	48 34	38 54	47.1	47 53	37 48	46.3	47 11	36 45	45.5	46 29	35 42	44.7	45 46	34 42	44.0	241	299
62	118	49 53	39 07	46.8	49 11	38 00	45.9	48 29	36 55	45.1	47 46	35 52	44.3	47 03	34 50	43.6	46 19	33 50	42.8	242	298
63	117	50 30	38 11	45.5	49 48	37 04	44.7	49 05	36 00	43.9	48 21	34 57	43.1	47 37	33 57	42.3	46 53	32 57	41.6	243	297
64	116	51 07	37 13	44.3	50 23	36 07	43.4	49 40	35 03	42.6	48 55	34 01	41.8	48 10	33 01	41.1	47 25	32 03	40.4	244	296
65	115	51 43	36 12	43.0	50 58	35 07	42.2	50 14	34 04	41.3	49 28	33 03	40.6	48 43	32 04	39.8	47 56	31 07	39.1	245	295
66	114	52 18	35 10	41.7	51 33	34 06	40.8	50 47	33 04	40.0	50 01	32 04	39.3	49 14	31 05	38.5	48 26	30 10	37.8	246	294
67	113	52 52	34 05	40.3	52 06	33 02	39.5	51 19	32 01	38.7	50 32	31 02	37.9	49 44	30 05	37.2	48 56	29 10	36.5	247	293
68	112	53 25	32 59	38.9	52 38	31 56	38.1	51 50	30 57	37.3	51 02	29 59	36.6	50 14	29 03	35.8	49 25	28 09	35.2	248	292
69	111	53 57	31 50	37.5	53 09	30 49	36.7	52 21	29 50	35.9	51 32	28 53	35.2	50 43	27 59	34.5	49 53	27 06	33.8	249	291
70	110	54 28	30 39	36.1	53 39	29 39	35.2	52 50	28 42	34.5	52 00	27 46	33.8	51 10	26 53	33.1	50 20	26 02	32.4	250	290
71	109	54 58	29 25	34.6	54 08	28 27	33.8	53 18	27 31	33.0	52 28	26 38	32.3	51 37	25 46	31.6	50 46	24 56	31.0	251	289
72	108	55 27	28 09	33.0	54 37	27 13	32.2	53 46	26 19	31.5	52 54	25 27	30.8	52 03	24 37	30.2	51 10	23 49	29.5	252	288
73	107	55 55	26 51	31.4	55 03	25 57	30.7	54 12	25 04	30.0	53 19	24 14	29.3	52 27	23 26	28.7	51 34	22 40	28.1	253	287
74	106	56 21	25 31	29.8	55 29	24 39	29.1	54 36	23 48	28.4	53 43	23 00	27.8	52 50	22 14	27.1	51 57	21 29	26.6	254	286
75	105	56 46	24 09	28.2	55 53	23 18	27.5	55 00	22 30	26.8	54 06	21 44	26.2	53 12	21 00	25.6	52 18	20 17	25.0	255	285
76	104	57 10	22 44	26.5	56 16	21 56	25.8	55 22	21 10	25.2	54 28	20 26	24.6	53 33	19 44	24.0	52 38	19 04	23.5	256	284
77	103	57 33	21 17	24.8	56 38	20 31	24.1	55 43	19 48	23.5	54 48	19 06	23.0	53 53	18 27	22.4	52 57	17 49	21.9	257	283
78	102	57 54	19 48	23.0	56 59	19 05	22.4	56 03	18 24	21.9	55 07	17 45	21.3	54 11	17 08	20.8	53 15	16 32	20.3	258	282
79	101	58 13	18 17	21.2	57 17	17 37	20.7	56 21	16 59	20.2	55 25	16 22	19.6	54 28	15 48	19.2	53 31	15 15	18.7	259	281
80	100	58 32	16 44	19.4	57 35	16 07	18.9	56 38	15 32	18.4	55 41	14 58	17.9	54 44	14 26	17.5	53 47	13 56	17.1	260	280
81	99	58 48	15 10	17.6	57 51	14 36	17.1	56 53	14 03	16.6	55 56	13 33	16.2	54 58	13 03	15.8	54 00	12 36	15.4	261	279
82	98	59 03	13 33	15.7	58 05	13 02	15.3	57 07	12 33	14.9	56 09	12 06	14.5	55 11	11 40	14.1	54 13	11 14	13.8	262	278
83	97	59 16	11 55	13.8	58 18	11 28	13.4	57 19	11 02	13.0	56 21	10 38	12.7	55 22	10 14	12.4	54 24	9 52	12.1	263	277
84	96	59 28	10 16	11.9	58 30	9 52	11.5	57 30	9 30	11.2	56 31	9 09	10.9	55 32	8 49	10.6	54 33	8 29	10.4	264	276
85	95	59 37	8 35	9.9	58 38	8 15	9.6	57 39	7 56	9.4	56 40	7 39	9.1	55 41	7 22	8.9	54 41	7 06	8.7	265	275
86	94	59 46	6 53	8.0	58 46	6 37	7.7	57 47	6 22	7.5	56 47	6 08	7.3	55 48	5 54	7.1	54 48	5 41	7.0	266	274
87	93	59 52	5 11	6.0	58 52	4 59	5.8	57 52	4 47	5.6	56 53	4 36	5.5	55 53	4 26	5.4	54 53	4 16	5.2	267	273
88	92	59 56	3 28	4.0	58 57	3 19	3.9	57 57	3 12	3.8	56 57	3 05	3.7	55 57	2 58	3.6	54 57	2 51	3.5	268	272
89	91	59 59	1 44	2.0	58 59	1 40	1.9	57 59	1 36	1.9	56 59	1 32	1.8	55 59	1 29	1.8	54 59	1 26	1.7	269	271
90	90	60 00	0 00	0.0	59 00	0 00	0.0	58 00	0 00	0.0	57 00	0 00	0.0	56 00	0 00	0.0	55 00	0 00	0.0	270	270

N. Lat.: for LHA > 180°.... $Z_n = Z$
for LHA < 180°.... $Z_n = 360° - Z$

S. Lat.: for LHA > 180°.... $Z_n = 180° - Z$
for LHA < 180°.... $Z_n = 180° + Z$

B: (–) for 90° < LHA < 270°
Dec: (–) for Lat. contrary name

Z1: same sign as B
Z2: (–) for F > 90°

SIGHT REDUCTION TABLE

Lat./A LHA/F	36° A/H	36° B/P	36° Z1/Z2	37° A/H	37° B/P	37° Z1/Z2	38° A/H	38° B/P	38° Z1/Z2	39° A/H	39° B/P	39° Z1/Z2	40° A/H	40° B/P	40° Z1/Z2	41° A/H	41° B/P	41° Z1/Z2	LHA Lat./A
0 / 180	0 00	54 00	90.0	0 00	53 00	90.0	0 00	52 00	90.0	0 00	51 00	90.0	0 00	50 00	90.0	0 00	49 00	90.0	180 / 360
1 / 179	0 49	54 00	89.4	0 48	53 00	89.4	0 47	52 00	89.4	0 47	51 00	89.4	0 46	50 00	89.4	0 45	49 00	89.3	181 / 359
2 / 178	1 37	53 59	88.8	1 36	52 59	88.8	1 35	51 59	88.8	1 33	50 59	88.8	1 32	49 59	88.7	1 31	48 59	88.7	182 / 358
3 / 177	2 26	53 58	88.2	2 24	52 58	88.2	2 22	51 58	88.2	2 20	50 58	88.1	2 18	49 58	88.1	2 16	48 58	88.0	183 / 357
4 / 176	3 14	53 56	87.6	3 12	52 56	87.6	3 09	51 56	87.5	3 06	50 56	87.5	3 04	49 56	87.4	3 01	48 56	87.4	184 / 356
5 / 175	4 03	53 54	87.1	3 59	52 54	87.0	3 56	51 54	86.9	3 53	50 54	86.9	3 50	49 54	86.8	3 46	48 54	86.7	185 / 355
6 / 174	4 51	53 51	86.5	4 47	52 51	86.4	4 43	51 51	86.3	4 40	50 51	86.2	4 36	49 51	86.1	4 31	48 51	86.1	186 / 354
7 / 173	5 39	53 48	85.9	5 35	52 48	85.8	5 31	51 48	85.7	5 26	50 47	85.6	5 21	49 47	85.5	5 17	48 47	85.4	187 / 353
8 / 172	6 28	53 44	85.3	6 23	52 44	85.2	6 18	51 44	85.1	6 13	50 44	84.9	6 07	49 43	84.8	6 02	48 43	84.7	188 / 352
9 / 171	7 16	53 40	84.7	7 11	52 39	84.6	7 05	51 39	84.4	6 59	50 39	84.3	6 53	49 39	84.2	6 47	48 39	84.1	189 / 351
10 / 170	8 05	53 35	84.1	7 58	52 35	83.9	7 52	51 34	83.8	7 45	50 34	83.7	7 39	49 34	83.5	7 32	48 34	83.4	190 / 350
11 / 169	8 53	53 30	83.5	8 46	52 29	83.3	8 39	51 29	83.2	8 32	50 29	83.0	8 24	49 29	82.9	8 17	48 28	82.7	191 / 349
12 / 168	9 41	53 24	82.9	9 33	52 23	82.7	9 26	51 23	82.5	9 18	50 23	82.4	9 10	49 23	82.2	9 02	48 22	82.1	192 / 348
13 / 167	10 29	53 17	82.3	10 21	52 17	82.1	10 13	51 17	81.9	10 04	50 16	81.7	9 55	49 16	81.6	9 46	48 16	81.4	193 / 347
14 / 166	11 17	53 10	81.7	11 08	52 10	81.5	10 59	51 10	81.3	10 50	50 09	81.1	10 41	49 09	80.9	10 31	48 09	80.7	194 / 346
15 / 165	12 05	53 03	81.1	11 56	52 02	80.8	11 46	51 02	80.6	11 36	50 02	80.4	11 26	49 01	80.2	11 16	48 01	80.0	195 / 345
16 / 164	12 53	52 55	80.4	12 43	51 54	80.2	12 33	50 54	80.0	12 22	49 53	79.8	12 11	48 53	79.6	12 00	47 53	79.3	196 / 344
17 / 163	13 41	52 46	79.8	13 30	51 46	79.6	13 19	50 45	79.3	13 08	49 45	79.1	12 57	48 44	78.9	12 45	47 44	78.7	197 / 343
18 / 162	14 29	52 37	79.2	14 17	51 37	78.9	14 06	50 36	78.7	13 54	49 35	78.4	13 42	48 35	78.2	13 29	47 34	78.0	198 / 342
19 / 161	15 16	52 28	78.6	15 04	51 27	78.3	14 52	50 26	78.0	14 39	49 25	77.8	14 27	48 25	77.5	14 13	47 24	77.3	199 / 341
20 / 160	16 04	52 18	78.0	15 51	51 16	77.6	15 38	50 16	77.4	15 25	49 15	77.1	15 11	48 14	76.8	14 58	47 14	76.6	200 / 340
21 / 159	16 51	52 07	77.3	16 38	51 05	77.0	16 24	50 05	76.7	16 10	49 04	76.4	15 56	48 03	76.1	15 42	47 03	75.9	201 / 339
22 / 158	17 39	51 55	76.6	17 24	50 54	76.3	17 10	49 53	76.0	16 56	48 52	75.7	16 41	47 51	75.4	16 25	46 51	75.2	202 / 338
23 / 157	18 26	51 43	76.0	18 11	50 42	75.7	17 56	49 41	75.4	17 41	48 40	75.0	17 25	47 39	74.7	17 09	46 38	74.4	203 / 337
24 / 156	19 13	51 30	75.3	18 57	50 29	75.0	18 42	49 28	74.7	18 26	48 27	74.3	18 09	47 26	74.0	17 53	46 25	73.7	204 / 336
25 / 155	20 00	51 17	74.7	19 44	50 15	74.3	19 27	49 14	74.0	19 10	48 13	73.6	18 53	47 12	73.3	18 36	46 12	73.0	205 / 335
26 / 154	20 46	51 03	74.0	20 30	50 01	73.6	20 13	49 00	73.3	19 55	47 59	72.9	19 37	46 58	72.6	19 19	45 57	72.3	206 / 334
27 / 153	21 33	50 48	73.3	21 15	49 47	73.0	20 58	48 45	72.6	20 40	47 44	72.2	20 21	46 43	71.9	20 02	45 42	71.5	207 / 333
28 / 152	22 19	50 33	72.6	22 01	49 31	72.3	21 43	48 30	71.9	21 24	47 28	71.5	21 05	46 28	71.1	20 45	45 27	70.8	208 / 332
29 / 151	23 06	50 17	72.0	22 47	49 15	71.6	22 28	48 14	71.2	22 08	47 12	70.8	21 48	46 11	70.4	21 28	45 11	70.0	209 / 331
30 / 150	23 52	50 00	71.3	23 32	48 58	70.8	23 12	47 57	70.4	22 52	46 55	70.0	22 31	45 54	69.6	22 10	44 54	69.3	210 / 330
31 / 149	24 37	49 43	70.5	24 17	48 41	70.1	23 57	47 39	69.7	23 36	46 38	69.3	23 14	45 37	68.9	22 52	44 36	68.5	211 / 329
32 / 148	25 23	49 25	69.8	25 02	48 23	69.4	24 41	47 21	69.0	24 19	46 19	68.5	23 57	45 18	68.1	23 34	44 17	67.7	212 / 328
33 / 147	26 08	49 06	69.1	25 47	48 04	68.7	25 25	47 02	68.2	25 02	46 00	67.8	24 40	44 59	67.3	24 16	43 58	66.9	213 / 327
34 / 146	26 54	48 46	68.4	26 32	47 44	67.9	26 09	46 42	67.4	25 45	45 40	67.0	25 22	44 39	66.6	24 58	43 39	66.1	214 / 326
35 / 145	27 39	48 26	67.6	27 16	47 23	67.1	26 52	46 21	66.7	26 28	45 20	66.2	26 04	44 19	65.8	25 39	43 18	65.3	215 / 325
36 / 144	28 24	48 04	66.9	28 00	47 02	66.4	27 36	46 00	65.9	27 11	44 58	65.4	26 46	43 57	65.0	26 20	42 57	64.5	216 / 324
37 / 143	29 08	47 42	66.1	28 44	46 40	65.6	28 19	45 38	65.1	27 53	44 36	64.6	27 27	43 35	64.2	27 01	42 34	63.7	217 / 323
38 / 142	29 52	47 19	65.3	29 27	46 17	64.8	29 01	45 15	64.3	28 35	44 13	63.8	28 08	43 12	63.3	27 41	42 12	62.9	218 / 322
39 / 141	30 36	46 56	64.5	30 10	45 53	64.0	29 44	44 51	63.5	29 17	43 49	63.0	28 49	42 48	62.5	28 21	41 48	62.0	219 / 321
40 / 140	31 20	46 31	63.7	30 53	45 28	63.2	30 26	44 26	62.7	29 58	43 25	62.2	29 30	42 24	61.7	29 01	41 23	61.2	220 / 320
41 / 139	32 03	46 05	62.9	31 36	45 03	62.4	31 08	44 01	61.8	30 39	42 59	61.3	30 10	41 58	60.8	29 41	40 58	60.3	221 / 319
42 / 138	32 46	45 39	62.1	32 18	44 36	61.5	31 49	43 34	61.0	31 20	42 33	60.5	30 50	41 32	59.9	30 20	40 32	59.4	222 / 318
43 / 137	33 29	45 11	61.3	33 00	44 09	60.7	32 30	43 07	60.1	32 00	42 05	59.6	31 30	41 05	59.1	30 59	40 04	58.5	223 / 317
44 / 136	34 12	44 43	60.4	33 42	43 40	59.8	33 11	42 38	59.3	32 40	41 37	58.7	32 09	40 36	58.2	31 37	39 36	57.6	224 / 316
45 / 135	34 54	44 13	59.6	34 23	43 11	59.0	33 52	42 09	58.4	33 20	41 08	57.8	32 48	40 07	57.3	32 15	39 08	56.7	225 / 315

B: (–) for 90° < LHA < 270° — Dec: (–) for Lat. contrary name

Lat./F	LHA/F	36° A/H	36° B/P	36° Z₁/Z₂	37° A/H	37° B/P	37° Z₁/Z₂	38° A/H	38° B/P	38° Z₁/Z₂	39° A/H	39° B/P	39° Z₁/Z₂	40° A/H	40° B/P	40° Z₁/Z₂	41° A/H	41° B/P	41° Z₁/Z₂	Lat./A	LHA
45	135	34 54	44 13	59.6	34 23	43 11	59.0	33 52	42 09	58.4	33 20	41 08	57.8	32 48	40 07	57.3	32 15	39 08	56.7	225	315
46	134	35 35	43 43	58.7	35 04	42 40	58.1	34 32	41 38	57.5	33 59	40 37	56.9	33 26	39 37	56.4	32 53	38 38	55.8	226	314
47	133	36 17	43 11	57.8	35 44	42 09	57.2	35 12	41 07	56.6	34 38	40 06	56.0	34 04	39 06	55.4	33 30	38 07	54.9	227	313
48	132	36 57	42 39	56.9	36 24	41 36	56.2	35 51	40 35	55.6	35 17	39 34	55.0	34 42	38 34	54.5	34 07	37 35	54.0	228	312
49	131	37 38	42 05	55.9	37 04	41 03	55.3	36 30	40 01	54.7	35 55	39 01	54.1	35 19	38 01	53.5	34 43	37 03	53.0	229	311
50	130	38 18	41 30	55.0	37 43	40 28	54.4	37 08	39 27	53.7	36 32	38 27	53.1	35 56	37 27	52.5	35 19	36 29	52.0	230	310
51	129	38 57	40 54	54.0	38 22	39 52	53.4	37 46	38 51	52.8	37 09	37 51	52.1	36 32	36 52	51.6	35 55	35 54	51.0	231	309
52	128	39 36	40 17	53.0	39 00	39 15	52.4	38 23	38 14	51.8	37 46	37 15	51.1	37 08	36 16	50.6	36 30	35 18	50.0	232	308
53	127	40 15	39 38	52.0	39 38	38 37	51.4	39 00	37 36	50.8	38 22	36 37	50.1	37 43	35 39	49.5	37 04	34 42	49.0	233	307
54	126	40 53	38 58	51.0	40 15	37 57	50.4	39 36	36 57	49.7	38 57	35 58	49.1	38 18	35 01	48.5	37 38	34 04	47.9	234	306
55	125	41 30	38 17	50.0	40 52	37 17	49.3	40 12	36 17	48.7	39 32	35 19	48.1	38 52	34 21	47.4	38 11	33 25	46.9	235	305
56	124	42 07	37 35	48.9	41 28	36 35	48.3	40 47	35 36	47.6	40 07	34 38	47.0	39 26	33 41	46.4	38 44	32 45	45.8	236	304
57	123	42 44	36 51	47.9	42 03	35 51	47.2	41 22	34 53	46.5	40 41	33 55	45.9	39 59	32 59	45.3	39 16	32 04	44.7	237	303
58	122	43 19	36 06	46.8	42 38	35 07	46.1	41 56	34 09	45.4	41 14	33 12	44.8	40 31	32 16	44.2	39 48	31 22	43.6	238	302
59	121	43 54	35 20	45.6	43 12	34 21	45.0	42 29	33 24	44.3	41 46	32 27	43.7	41 03	31 32	43.1	40 19	30 39	42.5	239	301
60	120	44 29	34 32	44.5	43 46	33 34	43.8	43 02	32 37	43.2	42 18	31 42	42.5	41 34	30 47	41.9	40 49	29 54	41.3	240	300
61	119	45 02	33 43	43.3	44 18	32 45	42.6	43 34	31 49	42.0	42 49	30 55	41.4	42 04	30 01	40.8	41 18	29 09	40.2	241	299
62	118	45 35	32 52	42.1	44 51	31 55	41.5	44 05	31 00	40.8	43 20	30 06	40.2	42 34	29 14	39.6	41 47	28 22	39.0	242	298
63	117	46 07	32 00	40.9	45 22	31 04	40.3	44 36	30 10	39.6	43 49	29 17	39.0	43 03	28 25	38.4	42 15	27 35	37.8	243	297
64	116	46 39	31 06	39.7	45 52	30 11	39.0	45 06	29 18	38.4	44 18	28 26	37.8	43 31	27 35	37.2	42 43	26 46	36.6	244	296
65	115	47 09	30 11	38.4	46 22	29 17	37.8	45 35	28 25	37.1	44 47	27 34	36.5	43 58	26 44	36.0	43 09	25 56	35.4	245	295
66	114	47 39	29 14	37.1	46 51	28 21	36.5	46 03	27 30	35.9	45 14	26 40	35.3	44 25	25 52	34.7	43 35	25 04	34.2	246	294
67	113	48 08	28 16	35.8	47 19	27 24	35.2	46 30	26 34	34.6	45 40	25 45	34.0	44 50	24 58	33.4	44 00	24 12	32.9	247	293
68	112	48 36	27 17	34.5	47 46	26 26	33.9	46 56	25 37	33.3	46 06	24 50	32.7	45 15	24 03	32.2	44 24	23 19	31.6	248	292
69	111	49 03	26 15	33.1	48 13	25 26	32.5	47 22	24 38	31.9	46 31	23 52	31.4	45 39	23 08	30.8	44 48	22 24	30.3	249	291
70	110	49 29	25 13	31.8	48 38	24 25	31.2	47 46	23 39	30.6	46 55	22 54	30.0	46 03	22 12	29.5	45 10	21 29	29.0	250	290
71	109	49 54	24 08	30.4	49 02	23 22	29.8	48 10	22 37	29.2	47 17	21 54	28.7	46 25	21 12	28.2	45 32	20 32	27.7	251	289
72	108	50 18	23 02	28.9	49 25	22 18	28.4	48 33	21 35	27.8	47 39	20 53	27.3	46 46	20 13	26.8	45 52	19 34	26.3	252	288
73	107	50 41	21 55	27.5	49 48	21 12	26.9	48 54	20 31	26.4	48 00	19 51	25.9	47 06	19 11	25.4	46 12	18 35	25.0	253	287
74	106	51 03	20 47	26.0	50 09	20 06	25.5	49 15	19 26	25.0	48 20	18 48	24.5	47 25	18 11	24.0	46 30	17 36	23.6	254	286
75	105	51 24	19 36	24.5	50 29	18 57	24.0	49 34	18 20	23.5	48 39	17 44	23.1	47 44	17 09	22.6	46 48	16 35	22.2	255	285
76	104	51 43	18 25	23.0	50 48	17 48	22.5	49 52	17 12	22.0	48 57	16 38	21.6	48 01	16 05	21.2	47 05	15 33	20.8	256	284
77	103	52 02	17 12	21.4	51 06	16 37	21.0	50 09	16 04	20.6	49 13	15 31	20.1	48 17	15 00	19.8	47 20	14 31	19.4	257	283
78	102	52 19	15 58	19.9	51 22	15 25	19.5	50 25	14 54	19.0	49 29	14 24	18.7	48 32	13 55	18.3	47 35	13 27	18.0	258	282
79	101	52 35	14 43	18.3	51 37	14 13	17.9	50 40	13 43	17.5	49 43	13 16	17.2	48 46	12 49	16.8	47 48	12 23	16.5	259	281
80	100	52 49	13 27	16.7	51 52	12 59	16.3	50 54	12 32	16.0	49 56	12 06	15.7	48 58	11 42	15.3	48 01	11 18	15.0	260	280
81	99	53 02	12 09	15.1	52 04	11 44	14.7	51 06	11 19	14.4	50 08	10 56	14.1	49 10	10 34	13.8	48 12	10 12	13.6	261	279
82	98	53 14	10 51	13.4	52 16	10 28	13.1	51 18	10 06	12.9	50 19	9 45	12.6	49 20	9 25	12.3	48 22	9 06	12.1	262	278
83	97	53 25	9 31	11.8	52 26	9 11	11.5	51 27	8 52	11.3	50 29	8 34	11.0	49 30	8 16	10.8	48 31	7 59	10.6	263	277
84	96	53 34	8 11	10.1	52 35	7 54	9.9	51 36	7 37	9.7	50 37	7 21	9.5	49 38	7 06	9.3	48 38	6 51	9.1	264	276
85	95	53 42	6 50	8.5	52 43	6 36	8.3	51 43	6 22	8.1	50 44	6 09	7.9	49 44	5 56	7.8	48 45	5 44	7.6	265	275
86	94	53 49	5 29	6.8	52 49	5 17	6.6	51 49	5 06	6.5	50 50	4 55	6.3	49 50	4 45	6.2	48 50	4 35	6.1	266	274
87	93	53 54	4 07	5.1	52 54	3 58	5.0	51 54	3 50	4.9	50 54	3 42	4.8	49 54	3 34	4.7	48 55	3 27	4.6	267	273
88	92	53 57	2 45	3.4	52 57	2 39	3.3	51 57	2 33	3.2	50 57	2 28	3.1	49 58	2 23	3.1	48 58	2 18	3.0	268	272
89	91	53 59	1 23	1.7	52 59	1 20	1.7	51 59	1 17	1.6	50 59	1 14	1.6	49 59	1 11	1.6	48 59	1 09	1.5	269	271
90	90	54 00	0 00	0.0	53 00	0 00	0.0	52 00	0 00	0.0	51 00	0 00	0.0	50 00	0 00	0.0	49 00	0 00	0.0	270	270

N. Lat.: for LHA > 180°.... Zn = Z
for LHA < 180°.... Zn = 360° − Z

S. Lat.: for LHA > 180°.... Zn = 180° − Z
for LHA < 180°.... Zn = 180° + Z

SIGHT REDUCTION TABLE

B: (−) for 90°< LHA < 270°
Dec: (−) for Lat. contrary name

Z₁: same sign as B
Z₂: (−) for F > 90°

LHA/F	42° A/H	42° B/P	42° Z_1/Z_2	43° A/H	43° B/P	43° Z_1/Z_2	44° A/H	44° B/P	44° Z_1/Z_2	45° A/H	45° B/P	45° Z_1/Z_2	46° A/H	46° B/P	46° Z_1/Z_2	47° A/H	47° B/P	47° Z_1/Z_2	LHA
0 / 180	0 00	48 00	90.0	0 00	47 00	90.0	0 00	46 00	90.0	0 00	45 00	90.0	0 00	44 00	90.0	0 00	43 00	90.0	180 / 360
1 / 179	0 45	48 00	89.3	0 44	47 00	89.3	0 43	46 00	89.3	0 42	45 00	89.3	0 42	44 00	89.3	0 41	43 00	89.3	181 / 359
2 / 178	1 29	47 59	88.7	1 28	46 59	88.6	1 26	45 59	88.6	1 25	44 59	88.6	1 23	43 59	88.6	1 22	43 00	88.5	182 / 358
3 / 177	2 14	47 58	88.0	2 12	46 58	88.0	2 09	45 58	87.9	2 07	44 58	87.9	2 05	43 58	87.8	2 03	42 58	87.8	183 / 357
4 / 176	2 58	47 56	87.3	2 55	46 56	87.3	2 53	45 56	87.2	2 50	44 56	87.2	2 47	43 56	87.1	2 44	42 56	87.1	184 / 356
5 / 175	3 43	47 53	86.6	3 39	46 53	86.6	3 36	45 53	86.5	3 32	44 53	86.5	3 28	43 53	86.4	3 24	42 53	86.3	185 / 355
6 / 174	4 27	47 51	86.0	4 23	46 51	85.9	4 19	45 51	85.8	4 14	44 51	85.7	4 10	43 51	85.7	4 05	42 51	85.6	186 / 354
7 / 173	5 12	47 47	85.3	5 07	46 47	85.2	5 02	45 47	85.1	4 57	44 47	85.0	4 51	43 47	85.0	4 46	42 47	84.9	187 / 353
8 / 172	5 56	47 43	84.6	5 51	46 43	84.5	5 45	45 43	84.4	5 39	44 43	84.3	5 33	43 43	84.2	5 27	42 43	84.1	188 / 352
9 / 171	6 41	47 39	84.0	6 34	46 39	83.8	6 28	45 39	83.7	6 21	44 39	83.6	6 14	43 39	83.5	6 07	42 39	83.4	189 / 351
10 / 170	7 25	47 34	83.3	7 18	46 34	83.1	7 11	45 34	83.0	7 03	44 34	82.9	6 56	43 34	82.8	6 48	42 34	82.7	190 / 350
11 / 169	8 09	47 28	82.6	8 01	46 28	82.4	7 53	45 28	82.3	7 45	44 28	82.2	7 37	43 28	82.0	7 29	42 28	81.9	191 / 349
12 / 168	8 53	47 22	81.9	8 45	46 22	81.8	8 36	45 22	81.6	8 27	44 22	81.5	8 18	43 22	81.3	8 09	42 22	81.2	192 / 348
13 / 167	9 37	47 16	81.2	9 28	46 15	81.1	9 19	45 15	80.9	9 09	44 15	80.7	8 59	43 15	80.6	8 49	42 16	80.4	193 / 347
14 / 166	10 21	47 08	80.5	10 11	46 08	80.3	10 01	45 08	80.2	9 51	44 08	80.0	9 40	43 08	79.8	9 30	42 08	79.7	194 / 346
15 / 165	11 05	47 01	79.8	10 55	46 00	79.6	10 44	45 00	79.5	10 33	44 00	79.3	10 21	43 00	79.1	10 10	42 01	78.9	195 / 345
16 / 164	11 49	46 52	79.1	11 38	45 52	78.9	11 26	44 52	78.7	11 14	43 52	78.5	11 02	42 52	78.3	10 50	41 52	78.2	196 / 344
17 / 163	12 33	46 43	78.4	12 21	45 43	78.2	12 08	44 43	78.0	11 56	43 43	77.8	11 43	42 43	77.6	11 30	41 44	77.4	197 / 343
18 / 162	13 17	46 34	77.7	13 04	45 34	77.5	12 51	44 34	77.3	12 37	43 34	77.1	12 24	42 34	76.8	12 10	41 34	76.6	198 / 342
19 / 161	14 00	46 24	77.0	13 46	45 24	76.8	13 33	44 24	76.5	13 19	43 24	76.3	13 04	42 24	76.1	12 50	41 24	75.9	199 / 341
20 / 160	14 43	46 13	76.3	14 29	45 13	76.1	14 15	44 13	75.8	14 00	43 13	75.6	13 45	42 13	75.3	13 29	41 14	75.1	200 / 340
21 / 159	15 27	46 02	75.6	15 12	45 02	75.3	14 56	44 02	75.1	14 41	43 02	74.8	14 25	42 02	74.6	14 09	41 03	74.3	201 / 339
22 / 158	16 10	45 50	74.9	15 54	44 50	74.6	15 38	43 50	74.3	15 22	42 50	74.1	15 05	41 50	73.8	14 48	40 51	73.5	202 / 338
23 / 157	16 53	45 38	74.1	16 36	44 38	73.9	16 19	43 38	73.6	16 02	42 38	73.3	15 45	41 38	73.0	15 27	40 39	72.8	203 / 337
24 / 156	17 36	45 25	73.4	17 18	44 25	73.1	17 01	43 25	72.8	16 43	42 25	72.5	16 25	41 25	72.2	16 06	40 26	72.0	204 / 336
25 / 155	18 18	45 11	72.7	18 00	44 11	72.4	17 42	43 11	72.1	17 23	42 11	71.8	17 04	41 12	71.5	16 45	40 12	71.2	205 / 335
26 / 154	19 01	44 57	71.9	18 42	43 57	71.6	18 23	42 57	71.3	18 03	41 57	71.0	17 44	40 57	70.7	17 24	39 58	70.4	206 / 334
27 / 153	19 43	44 42	71.2	19 24	43 42	70.8	19 04	42 42	70.5	18 43	41 42	70.2	18 23	40 42	69.9	18 02	39 43	69.6	207 / 333
28 / 152	20 25	44 26	70.4	20 05	43 26	70.1	19 44	42 26	69.7	19 23	41 27	69.4	19 02	40 27	69.1	18 40	39 28	68.8	208 / 332
29 / 151	21 07	44 10	69.6	20 46	43 10	69.3	20 25	42 10	68.9	20 03	41 10	68.6	19 41	40 11	68.3	19 18	39 12	67.9	209 / 331
30 / 150	21 49	43 53	68.9	21 27	42 53	68.5	21 05	41 53	68.1	20 42	40 54	67.8	20 19	39 54	67.4	19 56	38 55	67.1	210 / 330
31 / 149	22 30	43 35	68.1	22 08	42 35	67.7	21 45	41 36	67.3	21 21	40 36	67.0	20 58	39 37	66.6	20 34	38 38	66.3	211 / 329
32 / 148	23 11	43 17	67.3	22 48	42 17	66.9	22 24	41 17	66.5	22 00	40 18	66.2	21 36	39 19	65.8	21 11	38 20	65.4	212 / 328
33 / 147	23 53	42 58	66.5	23 28	41 58	66.1	23 04	40 58	65.7	22 39	39 59	65.3	22 14	39 00	65.0	21 48	38 02	64.6	213 / 327
34 / 146	24 33	42 38	65.7	24 08	41 38	65.3	23 43	40 39	64.9	23 17	39 40	64.5	22 51	38 41	64.1	22 25	37 42	63.7	214 / 326
35 / 145	25 14	42 18	64.9	24 48	41 18	64.5	24 22	40 18	64.1	23 56	39 19	63.7	23 29	38 21	63.3	23 02	37 23	62.9	215 / 325
36 / 144	25 54	41 56	64.1	25 28	40 57	63.6	25 01	39 57	63.2	24 34	38 58	62.8	24 06	38 00	62.4	23 38	37 02	62.0	216 / 324
37 / 143	26 34	41 34	63.2	26 07	40 35	62.8	25 39	39 35	62.4	25 11	38 37	61.9	24 43	37 38	61.5	24 14	36 41	61.1	217 / 323
38 / 142	27 14	41 11	62.4	26 46	40 12	61.9	26 17	39 13	61.5	25 48	38 14	61.1	25 19	37 16	60.7	24 50	36 19	60.3	218 / 322
39 / 141	27 53	40 48	61.5	27 24	39 48	61.1	26 55	38 50	60.6	26 25	37 51	60.2	25 55	36 53	59.8	25 25	35 56	59.4	219 / 321
40 / 140	28 32	40 23	60.7	28 02	39 24	60.2	27 32	38 25	59.8	27 02	37 27	59.3	26 31	36 30	58.9	26 00	35 32	58.5	220 / 320
41 / 139	29 11	39 58	59.8	28 40	38 59	59.3	28 10	38 01	58.9	27 38	37 03	58.4	27 07	36 05	58.0	26 35	35 08	57.6	221 / 319
42 / 138	29 49	39 32	58.9	29 18	38 33	58.4	28 46	37 35	58.0	28 14	36 37	57.5	27 42	35 40	57.1	27 09	34 43	56.6	222 / 318
43 / 137	30 27	39 05	58.0	29 55	38 06	57.5	29 23	37 08	57.1	28 50	36 11	56.6	28 17	35 14	56.3	27 43	34 18	55.7	223 / 317
44 / 136	31 05	38 37	57.1	30 32	37 39	56.6	29 59	36 41	56.1	29 25	35 44	55.7	28 51	34 47	55.2	28 17	33 51	54.8	224 / 316
45 / 135	31 42	38 09	56.2	31 08	37 10	55.7	30 34	36 13	55.2	30 00	35 16	54.7	29 25	34 20	54.3	28 50	33 24	53.8	225 / 315

B: (−) for 90°< LHA < 270° for Lat. contrary name

Lat./A		42°			43°			44°			45°			46°			47°			Lat./A	
LHA/F		A/H	B/P	Z_1/Z_2	A/H	B/P	Z_1/Z_2	A/H	B/P	Z_1/Z_2	A/H	B/P	Z_1/Z_2	A/H	B/P	Z_1/Z_2	A/H	B/P	Z_1/Z_2	LHA	
45	135	31 42	38 09	56.2	31 08	37 10	55.7	30 34	36 13	55.2	30 00	35 16	54.7	29 25	34 20	54.3	28 50	33 24	53.8	225	315
46	134	32 19	37 39	55.3	31 45	36 41	54.8	31 10	35 44	54.3	30 34	34 47	53.8	29 59	33 51	53.3	29 23	32 56	52.9	226	314
47	133	32 55	37 08	54.4	32 20	36 11	53.8	31 45	35 14	53.3	31 08	34 18	52.8	30 32	33 22	52.4	29 55	32 27	51.9	227	313
48	132	33 31	36 37	53.4	32 55	35 40	52.9	32 19	34 43	52.3	31 42	33 47	51.9	31 05	32 52	51.4	30 27	31 58	50.9	228	312
49	131	34 07	36 05	52.4	33 30	35 08	51.9	32 53	34 11	51.4	32 15	33 16	50.9	31 37	32 21	50.4	30 59	31 27	49.9	229	311
50	130	34 42	35 31	51.4	34 04	34 35	50.9	33 26	33 39	50.4	32 48	32 44	49.9	32 09	31 50	49.4	31 30	30 56	48.9	230	310
51	129	35 17	34 57	50.4	34 38	34 01	49.9	33 59	33 05	49.4	33 20	32 11	48.9	32 40	31 17	48.4	32 00	30 24	47.9	231	309
52	128	35 51	34 22	49.4	35 12	33 26	48.9	34 32	32 31	48.4	33 52	31 37	47.9	33 11	30 44	47.4	32 30	29 52	46.9	232	308
53	127	36 24	33 45	48.4	35 44	32 50	47.9	35 04	31 56	47.3	34 23	31 02	46.8	33 42	30 10	46.3	33 00	29 18	45.9	233	307
54	126	36 57	33 08	47.4	36 17	32 13	46.8	35 35	31 20	46.3	34 54	30 27	45.8	34 12	29 35	45.3	33 29	28 44	44.8	234	306
55	125	37 30	32 30	46.3	36 48	31 36	45.8	36 06	30 43	45.2	35 24	29 50	44.7	34 41	28 59	44.2	33 58	28 08	43.8	235	305
56	124	38 02	31 51	45.2	37 19	30 57	44.7	36 37	30 04	44.2	35 53	29 13	43.6	35 10	28 22	43.2	34 26	27 32	42.7	236	304
57	123	38 33	31 10	44.1	37 50	30 17	43.6	37 06	29 25	43.1	36 22	28 34	42.6	35 38	27 45	42.1	34 53	26 56	41.6	237	303
58	122	39 04	30 29	43.0	38 20	29 36	42.5	37 36	28 45	42.0	36 51	27 55	41.5	36 06	27 06	41.0	35 20	26 18	40.5	238	302
59	121	39 34	29 46	41.9	38 49	28 55	41.4	38 04	28 04	40.9	37 19	27 15	40.4	36 33	26 27	39.9	35 46	25 39	39.4	239	301
60	120	40 04	29 03	40.8	39 18	28 12	40.2	38 32	27 22	39.7	37 46	26 34	39.2	36 59	25 46	38.8	36 12	25 00	38.3	240	300
61	119	40 32	28 18	39.6	39 46	27 28	39.1	38 59	26 39	38.6	38 12	25 52	38.1	37 25	25 05	37.6	36 37	24 20	37.2	241	299
62	118	41 00	27 32	38.5	40 13	26 43	37.9	39 26	25 56	37.4	38 38	25 09	36.9	37 50	24 23	36.5	37 02	23 39	36.0	242	298
63	117	41 28	26 45	37.3	40 40	25 58	36.8	39 52	25 11	36.3	39 03	24 25	35.8	38 14	23 40	35.3	37 25	22 57	34.9	243	297
64	116	41 54	25 58	36.1	41 06	25 11	35.6	40 17	24 25	35.1	39 28	23 40	34.6	38 38	22 57	34.1	37 48	22 14	33.7	244	296
65	115	42 20	25 09	34.9	41 31	24 23	34.4	40 41	23 38	33.9	39 51	22 55	33.4	39 01	22 12	32.9	38 11	21 31	32.5	245	295
66	114	42 45	24 19	33.6	41 55	23 34	33.1	41 05	22 50	32.7	40 14	22 08	32.2	39 23	21 27	31.8	38 32	20 46	31.3	246	294
67	113	43 10	23 28	32.4	42 19	22 44	31.9	41 28	22 02	31.4	40 37	21 21	31.0	39 45	20 40	30.5	38 53	20 01	30.1	247	293
68	112	43 33	22 35	31.1	42 42	21 53	30.6	41 50	21 12	30.2	40 58	20 32	29.7	40 06	19 53	29.3	39 13	19 15	28.9	248	292
69	111	43 56	21 42	29.8	43 04	21 01	29.4	42 11	20 22	28.9	41 19	19 43	28.5	40 26	19 05	28.1	39 33	18 29	27.7	249	291
70	110	44 18	20 48	28.5	43 25	20 08	28.1	42 32	19 30	27.7	41 38	18 53	27.2	40 45	18 17	26.8	39 51	17 41	26.5	250	290
71	109	44 38	19 53	27.2	43 45	19 15	26.8	42 51	18 38	26.4	41 57	18 02	26.0	41 03	17 27	25.6	40 09	16 53	25.2	251	289
72	108	44 58	18 57	25.9	44 04	18 20	25.5	43 10	17 45	25.1	42 16	17 10	24.7	41 21	16 37	24.3	40 26	16 05	24.0	252	288
73	107	45 17	17 59	24.6	44 23	17 24	24.1	43 28	16 51	23.8	42 33	16 18	23.4	41 38	15 46	23.0	40 42	15 15	22.7	253	287
74	106	45 35	17 01	23.2	44 40	16 28	22.8	43 45	15 56	22.4	42 49	15 25	22.1	41 54	14 54	21.7	40 58	14 25	21.4	254	286
75	105	45 53	16 02	21.8	44 57	15 31	21.4	44 01	15 00	21.1	43 05	14 31	20.8	42 09	14 02	20.4	41 12	13 34	20.1	255	285
76	104	46 09	15 02	20.4	45 12	14 33	20.1	44 16	14 04	19.7	43 19	13 36	19.4	42 23	13 09	19.1	41 26	12 43	18.8	256	284
77	103	46 24	14 02	19.0	45 27	13 34	18.7	44 30	13 07	18.4	43 33	12 41	18.1	42 36	12 15	17.8	41 39	11 51	17.5	257	283
78	102	46 38	13 00	17.6	45 40	12 34	17.3	44 43	12 09	17.0	43 46	11 45	16.7	42 48	11 21	16.5	41 51	10 58	16.2	258	282
79	101	46 51	11 58	16.2	45 53	11 34	15.9	44 55	11 11	15.6	43 57	10 48	15.4	43 00	10 26	15.1	42 02	10 05	14.9	259	281
80	100	47 03	10 55	14.8	46 04	10 33	14.5	45 06	10 12	14.2	44 08	9 51	14.0	43 10	9 31	13.8	42 12	9 12	13.6	260	280
81	99	47 13	9 51	13.3	46 15	9 31	13.1	45 16	9 12	12.8	44 18	8 53	12.6	43 19	8 35	12.4	42 21	8 18	12.2	261	279
82	98	47 23	8 47	11.9	46 24	8 29	11.6	45 26	8 12	11.4	44 27	7 55	11.2	43 28	7 39	11.1	42 29	7 24	10.9	262	278
83	97	47 32	7 42	10.4	46 33	7 27	10.2	45 34	7 12	10.0	44 34	6 57	9.9	43 35	6 43	9.7	42 36	6 29	9.5	263	277
84	96	47 39	6 37	8.9	46 40	6 24	8.8	45 41	6 11	8.6	44 41	5 58	8.5	43 42	5 46	8.3	42 42	5 34	8.2	264	276
85	95	47 46	5 32	7.4	46 46	5 20	7.3	45 46	5 09	7.2	44 47	4 59	7.1	43 47	4 49	6.9	42 48	4 39	6.8	265	275
86	94	47 51	4 26	6.0	46 51	4 17	5.9	45 51	4 08	5.7	44 52	3 59	5.6	43 52	3 51	5.6	42 52	3 43	5.5	266	274
87	93	47 55	3 20	4.5	46 55	3 13	4.4	45 55	3 06	4.3	44 55	3 00	4.3	43 55	2 54	4.2	42 56	2 48	4.1	267	273
88	92	47 58	2 13	3.0	46 58	2 09	2.9	45 58	2 04	2.9	44 58	2 00	2.8	43 58	1 56	2.8	42 58	1 52	2.7	268	272
89	91	47 59	1 07	1.5	46 59	1 04	1.5	45 59	1 02	1.4	44 59	1 00	1.4	43 59	0 58	1.4	42 59	0 56	1.4	269	271
90	90	48 00	0 00	0.0	47 00	0 00	0.0	46 00	0 00	0.0	45 00	0 00	0.0	44 00	0 00	0.0	43 00	0 00	0.0	270	270

N. Lat.: for LHA > 180° ... $Z_n = Z$
for LHA < 180° ... $Z_n = 360° - Z$

S. Lat.: for LHA > 180° ... $Z_n = 180° - Z$
for LHA < 180° ... $Z_n = 180° + Z$

SIGHT REDUCTION TABLE

B: (−) for 90° < LHA < 270°
Dec: (−) for Lat. contrary name

Z₁: same sign as B
Z₂: (−) for F > 90°

Lat./A LHA/F	Lat./A	48° A/H	48° B/P	48° Z₁/Z₂	49° A/H	49° B/P	49° Z₁/Z₂	50° A/H	50° B/P	50° Z₁/Z₂	51° A/H	51° B/P	51° Z₁/Z₂	52° A/H	52° B/P	52° Z₁/Z₂	53° A/H	53° B/P	53° Z₁/Z₂	Lat./A	LHA
0	180	0 00	42 00	90.0	0 00	41 00	90.0	0 00	40 00	90.0	0 00	39 00	90.0	0 00	38 00	90.0	0 00	37 00	90.0	360	180
1	179	0 40	42 00	89.3	0 39	41 00	89.2	0 39	40 00	89.2	0 38	39 00	89.2	0 37	38 00	89.2	0 36	37 00	89.2	359	181
2	178	1 20	41 59	88.5	1 19	40 59	88.5	1 17	39 59	88.5	1 16	38 59	88.4	1 14	37 59	88.4	1 12	36 59	88.4	358	182
3	177	2 00	41 58	87.8	1 58	40 58	87.7	1 56	39 58	87.7	1 53	38 58	87.7	1 51	37 58	87.6	1 48	36 58	87.6	357	183
4	176	2 41	41 56	87.0	2 37	40 56	87.0	2 34	39 56	86.9	2 31	38 56	86.9	2 28	37 56	86.9	2 24	36 56	86.8	356	184
5	175	3 21	41 53	86.3	3 17	40 54	86.2	3 13	39 54	86.2	3 09	38 54	86.1	3 05	37 54	86.1	3 00	36 54	86.0	355	185
6	174	4 01	41 51	85.5	3 56	40 51	85.5	3 51	39 51	85.4	3 46	38 51	85.3	3 41	37 51	85.3	3 36	36 51	85.2	354	186
7	173	4 41	41 47	84.8	4 35	40 47	84.7	4 30	39 47	84.6	4 24	38 47	84.5	4 18	37 48	84.5	4 12	36 48	84.4	353	187
8	172	5 21	41 43	84.0	5 14	40 43	83.9	5 08	39 43	83.9	5 01	38 44	83.8	4 55	37 44	83.7	4 48	36 44	83.6	352	188
9	171	6 01	41 39	83.3	5 53	40 39	83.2	5 46	39 39	83.1	5 39	38 39	83.0	5 32	37 39	82.9	5 24	36 40	82.8	351	189
10	170	6 40	41 34	82.5	6 32	40 34	82.4	6 25	39 34	82.3	6 16	38 34	82.2	6 08	37 35	82.1	6 00	36 35	82.0	350	190
11	169	7 20	41 28	81.8	7 11	40 28	81.7	7 03	39 29	81.5	6 54	38 29	81.4	6 45	37 29	81.3	6 36	36 29	81.2	349	191
12	168	8 00	41 22	81.0	7 50	40 22	80.9	7 41	39 23	80.8	7 31	38 23	80.6	7 21	37 23	80.5	7 11	36 24	80.4	348	192
13	167	8 39	41 16	80.3	8 29	40 16	80.1	8 19	39 16	80.0	8 08	38 16	79.8	7 58	37 17	79.7	7 47	36 17	79.6	347	193
14	166	9 19	41 09	79.5	9 08	40 09	79.3	8 57	39 09	79.3	8 45	38 09	79.0	8 34	37 10	78.9	8 22	36 10	78.7	346	194
15	165	9 58	41 01	78.7	9 47	40 01	78.6	9 35	39 02	78.4	9 22	38 02	78.2	9 10	37 02	78.1	8 58	36 03	77.9	345	195
16	164	10 38	40 53	78.0	10 25	39 53	77.8	10 12	38 53	77.6	9 59	37 54	77.4	9 46	36 54	77.3	9 33	35 55	77.1	344	196
17	163	11 17	40 44	77.2	11 04	39 44	77.0	10 50	38 45	76.8	10 36	37 45	76.6	10 22	36 46	76.5	10 08	35 47	76.3	343	197
18	162	11 56	40 34	76.4	11 42	39 35	76.2	11 27	38 35	76.0	11 13	37 36	75.8	10 58	36 37	75.6	10 43	35 38	75.5	342	198
19	161	12 35	40 25	75.6	12 20	39 25	75.4	12 05	38 26	75.2	11 49	37 26	75.0	11 34	36 27	74.8	11 18	35 28	74.6	341	199
20	160	13 14	40 14	74.9	12 58	39 15	74.6	12 42	38 15	74.4	12 26	37 16	74.2	12 09	36 17	74.0	11 53	35 18	73.8	340	200
21	159	13 52	40 03	74.1	13 36	39 04	73.8	13 19	38 04	73.6	13 02	37 05	73.4	12 45	36 06	73.2	12 27	35 08	73.0	339	201
22	158	14 31	39 51	73.3	14 14	38 52	73.0	13 56	37 53	72.8	13 38	36 54	72.6	13 20	35 55	72.3	13 02	34 56	72.1	338	202
23	157	15 09	39 39	72.5	14 51	38 40	72.2	14 33	37 41	72.0	14 14	36 42	71.7	13 55	35 43	71.5	13 36	34 45	71.3	337	203
24	156	15 48	39 26	71.7	15 29	38 27	71.4	15 09	37 28	71.2	14 50	36 30	70.9	14 30	35 31	70.7	14 10	34 33	70.4	336	204
25	155	16 26	39 13	70.9	16 06	38 14	70.6	15 46	37 15	70.3	15 25	36 17	70.1	15 05	35 18	69.8	14 44	34 20	69.6	335	205
26	154	17 03	38 59	70.1	16 43	38 00	69.8	16 22	37 01	69.5	16 01	36 03	69.2	15 39	35 05	69.0	15 18	34 07	68.7	334	206
27	153	17 41	38 44	69.3	17 20	37 46	69.0	16 58	36 47	68.7	16 36	35 49	68.4	16 14	34 51	68.1	15 51	33 53	67.9	333	207
28	152	18 19	38 29	68.4	17 56	37 30	68.1	17 34	36 32	67.8	17 11	35 34	67.5	16 48	34 36	67.3	16 25	33 38	67.0	332	208
29	151	18 56	38 13	67.6	18 33	37 15	67.3	18 09	36 16	67.0	17 46	35 18	66.7	17 22	34 21	66.4	16 58	33 23	66.1	331	209
30	150	19 33	37 57	66.8	19 09	36 58	66.5	18 45	36 00	66.1	18 20	35 03	65.8	17 56	34 05	65.5	17 31	33 08	65.2	330	210
31	149	20 10	37 40	65.9	19 45	36 41	65.6	19 20	35 44	65.3	18 55	34 46	65.0	18 29	33 49	64.7	18 03	32 52	64.4	329	211
32	148	20 46	37 22	65.1	20 21	36 24	64.8	19 55	35 26	64.4	19 29	34 29	64.1	19 02	33 32	63.8	18 36	32 35	63.5	328	212
33	147	21 22	37 03	64.2	20 56	36 06	63.9	20 30	35 08	63.6	20 03	34 11	63.2	19 35	33 14	62.9	19 08	32 18	62.6	327	213
34	146	21 58	36 44	63.4	21 31	35 47	63.0	21 04	34 49	62.7	20 36	33 53	62.3	20 08	32 56	62.0	19 40	32 00	61.7	326	214
35	145	22 34	36 25	62.5	22 06	35 27	62.1	21 38	34 30	61.8	21 10	33 33	61.4	20 41	32 37	61.1	20 12	31 41	60.8	325	215
36	144	23 10	36 04	61.6	22 41	35 07	61.3	22 12	34 10	60.9	21 43	33 14	60.5	21 13	32 18	60.2	20 43	31 22	59.9	324	216
37	143	23 45	35 43	60.8	23 15	34 46	60.4	22 45	33 50	60.0	22 15	32 54	59.6	21 45	31 58	59.3	21 14	31 02	59.0	323	217
38	142	24 20	35 21	59.9	23 49	34 25	59.5	23 19	33 28	59.1	22 48	32 33	58.7	22 16	31 37	58.4	21 45	30 42	58.0	322	218
39	141	24 54	34 59	59.0	24 23	34 02	58.6	23 52	33 07	58.2	23 20	32 11	57.8	22 48	31 16	57.5	22 15	30 21	57.1	321	219
40	140	25 28	34 36	58.1	24 57	33 40	57.7	24 24	32 44	57.3	23 52	31 49	56.9	23 19	30 54	56.5	22 45	30 00	56.2	320	220
41	139	26 02	34 12	57.1	25 30	33 16	56.7	24 57	32 21	56.3	24 23	31 26	56.0	23 49	30 32	55.6	23 15	29 38	55.2	319	221
42	138	26 36	33 47	56.2	26 02	32 52	55.8	25 28	31 57	55.4	24 54	31 02	55.0	24 20	30 08	54.6	23 45	29 15	54.3	318	222
43	137	27 09	33 22	55.3	26 35	32 27	54.9	26 00	31 32	54.5	25 25	30 38	54.1	24 50	29 45	53.7	24 14	28 52	53.3	317	223
44	136	27 42	32 56	54.3	27 07	32 01	53.9	26 31	31 07	53.5	25 55	30 13	53.1	25 19	29 20	52.7	24 43	28 28	52.4	316	224
45	135	28 14	32 29	53.4	27 38	31 35	53.0	27 02	30 41	52.5	26 25	29 48	52.1	25 48	28 55	51.8	25 11	28 03	51.4	315	225

Lat./A	48°			49°			50°			51°			52°			53°			Lat./A
LHA/F	A/H	B/P	Z_1/Z_2	A/H	B/P	Z_1/Z_2	A/H	B/P	Z_1/Z_2	A/H	B/P	Z_1/Z_2	A/H	B/P	Z_1/Z_2	A/H	B/P	Z_1/Z_2	LHA
45	28 14	32 29	53.4	27 38	31 35	53.0	27 02	30 41	52.5	26 25	29 48	52.1	25 48	28 55	51.8	25 11	28 03	51.4	315
46	28 46	32 01	52.4	28 10	31 08	52.0	27 32	30 14	51.6	26 55	29 22	51.2	26 17	28 29	50.8	25 39	27 38	50.4	314
47	29 18	31 33	51.4	28 40	30 40	51.0	28 02	29 47	50.6	27 25	28 55	50.2	26 46	28 03	49.8	26 07	27 12	49.4	313
48	29 49	31 04	50.5	29 11	30 11	50.0	28 32	29 19	49.6	27 53	28 27	49.2	27 14	27 36	48.8	26 34	26 46	48.4	312
49	30 20	30 34	49.5	29 41	29 42	49.0	29 01	28 50	48.6	28 21	27 59	48.2	27 41	27 08	47.8	27 01	26 18	47.4	311
50	30 50	30 04	48.5	30 10	29 12	48.0	29 30	28 20	47.6	28 49	27 30	47.2	28 08	26 40	46.8	27 27	25 51	46.4	310
51	31 20	29 32	47.5	30 39	28 41	47.0	29 58	27 50	46.6	29 17	27 00	46.2	28 35	26 11	45.8	27 53	25 22	45.4	309
52	31 49	29 00	46.4	31 08	28 09	46.0	30 26	27 19	45.6	29 44	26 30	45.2	29 01	25 41	44.8	28 19	24 53	44.4	308
53	32 18	28 27	45.4	31 36	27 37	45.0	30 53	26 48	44.5	30 10	25 59	44.1	29 27	25 11	43.7	28 44	24 24	43.3	307
54	32 46	27 53	44.4	32 03	27 04	43.9	31 20	26 15	43.5	30 36	25 27	43.1	29 52	24 40	42.7	29 08	23 53	42.3	306
55	33 14	27 19	43.3	32 30	26 30	42.9	31 46	25 42	42.4	31 02	24 55	42.0	30 17	24 08	41.6	29 32	23 23	41.2	305
56	33 42	26 44	42.2	32 57	25 55	41.8	32 12	25 08	41.4	31 27	24 22	41.0	30 41	23 36	40.6	29 56	22 51	40.2	304
57	34 08	26 07	41.1	33 23	25 20	40.7	32 37	24 34	40.3	31 51	23 48	39.9	31 05	23 03	39.5	30 19	22 19	39.1	303
58	34 34	25 30	40.1	33 48	24 44	39.6	33 02	23 58	39.2	32 15	23 14	38.8	31 28	22 29	38.4	30 41	21 46	38.0	302
59	35 00	24 53	39.0	34 13	24 07	38.5	33 26	23 22	38.1	32 39	22 38	37.7	31 51	21 55	37.3	31 03	21 13	37.0	301
60	35 25	24 14	37.8	34 37	23 30	37.4	33 50	22 46	37.0	33 02	22 03	36.6	32 13	21 20	36.2	31 25	20 39	35.9	300
61	35 49	23 35	36.7	35 01	22 51	36.3	34 12	22 08	35.9	33 24	21 26	35.5	32 35	20 45	35.1	31 46	20 04	34.8	299
62	36 13	22 55	35.6	35 24	22 12	35.2	34 35	21 30	34.8	33 45	20 49	34.4	32 56	20 09	34.0	32 06	19 29	33.7	298
63	36 36	22 14	34.4	35 46	21 32	34.0	34 56	20 51	33.6	34 06	20 11	33.3	33 16	19 32	32.9	32 26	18 53	32.5	297
64	36 58	21 32	33.3	36 08	20 52	32.9	35 17	20 12	32.5	34 27	19 33	32.1	33 36	18 54	31.8	32 45	18 17	31.4	296
65	37 20	20 50	32.1	36 29	20 10	31.7	35 38	19 32	31.3	34 47	18 54	31.0	33 55	18 16	30.6	33 03	17 40	30.3	295
66	37 41	20 07	30.9	36 49	19 28	30.5	35 58	18 51	30.2	35 06	18 14	29.8	34 13	17 38	29.5	33 21	17 02	29.1	294
67	38 01	19 23	29.7	37 09	18 46	29.4	36 17	18 09	29.0	35 24	17 33	28.6	34 31	16 59	28.3	33 38	16 24	28.0	293
68	38 21	18 38	28.5	37 28	18 02	28.2	36 35	17 27	27.8	35 42	16 53	27.5	34 48	16 19	27.1	33 55	15 46	26.8	292
69	38 40	17 53	27.3	37 46	17 18	27.0	36 53	16 44	26.6	35 59	16 11	26.3	35 05	15 38	26.0	34 11	15 07	25.7	291
70	38 58	17 07	26.1	38 04	16 33	25.7	37 10	16 01	25.4	36 15	15 29	25.1	35 21	14 58	24.8	34 26	14 27	24.5	290
71	39 15	16 20	24.9	38 20	15 48	24.5	37 26	15 17	24.2	36 31	14 46	23.9	35 36	14 16	23.6	34 41	13 47	23.3	289
72	39 31	15 33	23.6	38 36	15 02	23.3	37 41	14 32	23.0	36 46	14 03	22.7	35 50	13 34	22.4	34 55	13 07	22.1	288
73	39 47	14 45	22.4	38 51	14 16	22.1	37 56	13 47	21.8	37 00	13 19	21.5	36 04	12 52	21.2	35 08	12 25	20.9	287
74	40 02	13 56	21.1	39 06	13 28	20.8	38 10	13 01	20.5	37 13	12 35	20.3	36 17	12 09	20.0	35 21	11 44	19.8	286
75	40 16	13 07	19.8	39 19	12 41	19.5	38 23	12 15	19.3	37 26	11 50	19.0	36 29	11 26	18.8	35 33	11 02	18.5	285
76	40 29	12 17	18.5	39 32	11 53	18.3	38 35	11 28	18.0	37 38	11 05	17.8	36 41	10 42	17.6	35 44	10 20	17.3	284
77	40 41	11 27	17.3	39 44	11 04	17.0	38 47	10 41	16.8	37 49	10 19	16.5	36 52	9 58	16.3	35 54	9 37	16.1	283
78	40 53	10 36	16.0	39 55	10 15	15.7	38 57	9 54	15.5	38 00	9 33	15.3	37 02	9 14	15.1	36 04	8 54	14.9	282
79	41 04	9 45	14.7	40 05	9 25	14.4	39 07	9 06	14.2	38 09	8 47	14.0	37 11	8 29	13.9	36 13	8 11	13.7	281
80	41 13	8 53	13.3	40 15	8 35	13.2	39 16	8 17	13.0	38 18	8 00	12.8	37 19	7 44	12.6	36 21	7 27	12.5	280
81	41 22	8 01	12.0	40 23	7 45	11.9	39 25	7 29	11.7	38 26	7 13	11.5	37 27	6 58	11.4	36 28	6 43	11.2	279
82	41 30	7 09	10.7	40 31	6 54	10.5	39 32	6 40	10.4	38 33	6 26	10.3	37 34	6 12	10.1	36 35	5 59	10.0	278
83	41 37	6 16	9.4	40 38	6 03	9.2	39 39	5 50	9.1	38 39	5 38	9.0	37 40	5 26	8.9	36 41	5 15	8.7	277
84	41 43	5 23	8.1	40 44	5 12	7.9	39 44	5 01	7.8	38 45	4 50	7.7	37 45	4 40	7.6	36 46	4 30	7.5	276
85	41 48	4 29	6.7	40 49	4 20	6.6	39 49	4 11	6.5	38 49	4 02	6.4	37 50	3 54	6.3	36 50	3 45	6.3	275
86	41 52	3 36	5.4	40 53	3 28	5.3	39 53	3 21	5.2	38 53	3 14	5.1	37 53	3 07	5.1	36 54	3 01	5.0	274
87	41 56	2 42	4.0	40 56	2 36	4.0	39 56	2 31	3.9	38 56	2 26	3.9	37 56	2 20	3.8	36 56	2 16	3.8	273
88	41 58	1 48	2.7	40 58	1 44	2.6	39 58	1 41	2.6	38 58	1 37	2.6	37 58	1 34	2.5	36 58	1 30	2.5	272
89	42 00	0 54	1.3	41 00	0 52	1.3	40 00	0 50	1.3	39 00	0 49	1.3	38 00	0 47	1.3	37 00	0 45	1.3	271
90	42 00	0 00	0.0	41 00	0 00	0.0	40 00	0 00	0.0	39 00	0 00	0.0	38 00	0 00	0.0	37 00	0 00	0.0	270

SIGHT REDUCTION TABLE

B: (−) for 90° < LHA < 270°
Dec: (−) for Lat. contrary name

Z₁: same sign as B
Z₂: (−) for F > 90°

LHA/F	54° A/H	54° B/P	54° Z₁/Z₂	55° A/H	55° B/P	55° Z₁/Z₂	56° A/H	56° B/P	56° Z₁/Z₂	57° A/H	57° B/P	57° Z₁/Z₂	58° A/H	58° B/P	58° Z₁/Z₂	59° A/H	59° B/P	59° Z₁/Z₂	LHA	LHA
0	0 00	36 00	90.0	0 00	35 00	90.0	0 00	34 00	90.0	0 00	33 00	90.0	0 00	32 00	90.0	0 00	31 00	90.0	180	360
1	0 35	36 00	89.2	0 34	35 00	89.2	0 34	34 00	89.2	0 33	33 00	89.2	0 32	32 00	89.2	0 31	31 00	89.1	181	359
2	1 11	35 59	88.4	1 09	34 59	88.4	1 07	33 59	88.3	1 05	32 59	88.3	1 04	31 59	88.3	1 02	30 59	88.3	182	358
3	1 46	35 58	87.6	1 43	34 58	87.5	1 41	33 58	87.5	1 38	32 58	87.5	1 35	31 58	87.5	1 33	30 58	87.4	183	357
4	2 21	35 56	86.8	2 18	34 56	86.7	2 14	33 56	86.6	2 11	32 56	86.6	2 07	31 56	86.6	2 04	30 56	86.6	184	356
5	2 56	35 54	86.0	2 52	34 54	85.9	2 48	33 54	85.9	2 43	32 54	85.8	2 39	31 54	85.8	2 34	30 54	85.7	185	355
6	3 31	35 51	85.1	3 26	34 51	85.1	3 21	33 51	85.0	3 16	32 51	85.0	3 11	31 52	84.9	3 05	30 52	84.9	186	354
7	4 06	35 48	84.3	4 00	34 48	84.3	3 54	33 48	84.2	3 48	32 48	84.1	3 42	31 48	84.1	3 36	30 49	84.0	187	353
8	4 42	35 44	83.5	4 35	34 44	83.4	4 28	33 44	83.4	4 21	32 45	83.3	4 14	31 45	83.2	4 07	30 45	83.1	188	352
9	5 17	35 40	82.7	5 09	34 40	82.6	5 01	33 40	82.5	4 53	32 41	82.4	4 45	31 41	82.3	4 37	30 41	82.3	189	351
10	5 51	35 35	81.9	5 43	34 35	81.8	5 34	33 36	81.7	5 26	32 36	81.6	5 17	31 36	81.5	5 08	30 37	81.4	190	350
11	6 26	35 30	81.1	6 17	34 30	81.0	6 08	33 31	80.8	5 58	32 31	80.7	5 48	31 31	80.6	5 38	30 32	80.5	191	349
12	7 01	35 24	80.2	6 51	34 24	80.1	6 41	33 25	80.0	6 30	32 25	79.9	6 20	31 26	79.8	6 09	30 27	79.7	192	348
13	7 36	35 18	79.4	7 25	34 18	79.3	7 14	33 19	79.2	7 02	32 19	79.0	6 51	31 20	78.9	6 39	30 21	78.8	193	347
14	8 11	35 11	78.6	7 59	34 12	78.5	7 46	33 12	78.3	7 34	32 13	78.2	7 22	31 14	78.1	7 09	30 15	77.9	194	346
15	8 45	35 04	77.8	8 32	34 04	77.6	8 19	33 05	77.5	8 06	32 06	77.3	7 53	31 07	77.2	7 40	30 08	77.1	195	345
16	9 19	34 56	76.9	9 06	33 57	76.8	8 52	32 58	76.6	8 38	31 58	76.5	8 24	31 00	76.3	8 10	30 01	76.2	196	344
17	9 54	34 47	76.1	9 39	33 48	76.0	9 25	32 49	75.8	9 10	31 50	75.6	8 55	30 52	75.5	8 40	29 53	75.3	197	343
18	10 28	34 39	75.3	10 13	33 40	75.1	9 57	32 41	74.9	9 41	31 42	74.8	9 25	30 43	74.6	9 09	29 45	74.4	198	342
19	11 02	34 29	74.4	10 46	33 30	74.2	10 29	32 32	74.1	10 13	31 33	73.9	9 56	30 35	73.7	9 39	29 36	73.6	199	341
20	11 36	34 19	73.6	11 19	33 21	73.4	11 02	32 22	73.2	10 44	31 24	73.0	10 27	30 25	72.8	10 09	29 27	72.7	200	340
21	12 10	34 09	72.7	11 52	33 10	72.5	11 34	32 12	72.3	11 15	31 14	72.2	10 57	30 15	72.0	10 38	29 17	71.8	201	339
22	12 43	33 58	71.9	12 24	33 00	71.7	12 06	32 01	71.5	11 46	31 03	71.3	11 27	30 05	71.1	11 07	29 07	70.9	202	338
23	13 17	33 46	71.0	12 57	32 48	70.8	12 37	31 50	70.6	12 17	30 52	70.4	11 57	29 54	70.2	11 37	28 57	70.0	203	337
24	13 50	33 34	70.2	13 29	32 36	70.0	13 09	31 38	69.7	12 48	30 41	69.5	12 27	29 43	69.3	12 06	28 46	69.1	204	336
25	14 23	33 22	69.3	14 02	32 24	69.1	13 40	31 26	68.9	13 18	30 29	68.6	12 56	29 31	68.4	12 34	28 34	68.2	205	335
26	14 56	33 09	68.5	14 34	32 11	68.2	14 11	31 14	68.0	13 49	30 16	67.8	13 26	29 19	67.5	13 03	28 22	67.3	206	334
27	15 29	32 55	67.6	15 06	31 58	67.3	14 42	31 00	67.1	14 19	30 03	66.8	13 55	29 06	66.6	13 31	28 10	66.4	207	333
28	16 01	32 41	66.7	15 37	31 44	66.5	15 13	30 47	66.2	14 49	29 50	66.0	14 24	28 53	65.7	14 00	27 57	65.5	208	332
29	16 33	32 26	65.8	16 09	31 29	65.6	15 44	30 32	65.3	15 19	29 36	65.1	14 53	28 39	64.8	14 28	27 43	64.6	209	331
30	17 05	32 11	65.0	16 40	31 14	64.7	16 14	30 17	64.4	15 48	29 21	64.2	15 22	28 25	63.9	14 55	27 29	63.7	210	330
31	17 37	31 55	64.1	17 11	30 58	63.8	16 44	30 02	63.6	16 17	29 06	63.3	15 50	28 10	63.0	15 23	27 15	62.7	211	329
32	18 09	31 38	63.2	17 42	30 42	62.9	17 14	29 46	62.6	16 47	28 51	62.3	16 19	27 55	62.1	15 50	27 00	61.8	212	328
33	18 40	31 21	62.3	18 12	30 25	62.0	17 44	29 30	61.7	17 15	28 34	61.4	16 47	27 39	61.2	16 17	26 45	60.9	213	327
34	19 11	31 04	61.4	18 42	30 08	61.1	18 13	29 13	60.8	17 44	28 18	60.5	17 14	27 23	60.2	16 44	26 29	60.0	214	326
35	19 42	30 46	60.5	19 12	29 50	60.2	18 42	28 55	59.9	18 12	28 01	59.6	17 42	27 06	59.3	17 11	26 12	59.0	215	325
36	20 13	30 27	59.6	19 42	29 32	59.2	19 11	28 37	58.9	18 40	27 43	58.6	18 09	26 49	58.4	17 37	25 55	58.1	216	324
37	20 43	30 07	58.6	20 12	29 13	58.3	19 40	28 19	58.0	19 08	27 25	57.7	18 36	26 31	57.4	18 03	25 38	57.1	217	323
38	21 13	29 48	57.7	20 41	28 53	57.4	20 08	27 59	57.1	19 35	27 06	56.8	19 02	26 13	56.5	18 29	25 20	56.2	218	322
39	21 43	29 27	56.8	21 10	28 33	56.4	20 36	27 40	56.1	20 03	26 47	55.8	19 29	25 54	55.5	18 55	25 02	55.2	219	321
40	22 12	29 06	55.8	21 38	28 13	55.5	21 04	27 20	55.2	20 30	26 27	54.9	19 55	25 35	54.6	19 20	24 43	54.3	220	320
41	22 41	28 44	54.9	22 06	27 51	54.5	21 31	26 59	54.2	20 56	26 07	53.9	20 21	25 15	53.6	19 45	24 24	53.3	221	319
42	23 10	28 22	53.9	22 34	27 29	53.6	21 58	26 37	53.3	21 22	25 46	52.9	20 46	24 55	52.6	20 10	24 04	52.3	222	318
43	23 38	27 59	53.0	23 02	27 07	52.6	22 25	26 15	52.3	21 48	25 24	52.0	21 11	24 34	51.7	20 34	23 43	51.4	223	317
44	24 06	27 36	52.0	23 29	26 44	51.7	22 51	25 53	51.3	22 14	25 02	51.0	21 36	24 12	50.7	20 58	23 23	50.4	224	316
45	24 34	27 11	51.0	23 56	26 20	50.7	23 17	25 30	50.3	22 39	24 40	50.0	22 00	23 50	49.7	21 21	23 01	49.4	225	315

Lat./A LHA/F	54° A/H	54° B/P	54° Z₁/Z₂	55° A/H	55° B/P	55° Z₁/Z₂	56° A/H	56° B/P	56° Z₁/Z₂	57° A/H	57° B/P	57° Z₁/Z₂	58° A/H	58° B/P	58° Z₁/Z₂	59° A/H	59° B/P	59° Z₁/Z₂	-Lat./A LHA
45 135	24 34	27 11	51.0	23 56	26 20	50.7	23 17	25 30	50.3	22 39	24 40	50.0	22 00	23 50	49.7	21 21	23 01	49.4	225 315
46 134	25 01	26 47	50.0	24 22	25 56	49.7	23 43	25 06	49.4	23 04	24 17	49.0	22 24	23 28	48.7	21 45	22 39	48.4	226 314
47 133	25 28	26 22	49.1	24 48	25 32	48.7	24 08	24 42	48.4	23 28	23 53	48.0	22 48	23 05	47.7	22 08	22 17	47.4	227 313
48 132	25 54	25 56	48.1	25 14	25 06	47.7	24 33	24 17	47.4	23 53	23 29	47.0	23 11	22 41	46.7	22 30	21 54	46.4	228 312
49 131	26 20	25 29	47.1	25 39	24 40	46.7	24 58	23 52	46.3	24 16	23 05	46.0	23 34	22 17	45.7	22 52	21 31	45.4	229 311
50 130	26 46	25 02	46.0	26 04	24 14	45.7	25 22	23 26	45.3	24 40	22 39	45.0	23 57	21 53	44.7	23 14	21 07	44.4	230 310
51 129	27 11	24 34	45.0	26 28	23 47	44.7	25 45	23 00	44.3	25 02	22 14	44.0	24 19	21 28	43.7	23 36	20 43	43.4	231 309
52 128	27 36	24 06	44.0	26 52	23 19	43.6	26 09	22 33	43.3	25 25	21 48	43.0	24 41	21 03	42.7	23 57	20 18	42.3	232 308
53 127	28 00	23 37	43.0	27 16	22 51	42.6	26 32	22 06	42.3	25 47	21 21	41.9	25 02	20 37	41.6	24 17	19 53	41.3	233 307
54 126	28 24	23 07	41.9	27 39	22 22	41.6	26 54	21 38	41.2	26 09	20 54	40.9	25 23	20 10	40.6	24 37	19 27	40.3	234 306
55 125	28 47	22 37	40.9	28 01	21 53	40.5	27 16	21 09	40.2	26 30	20 26	39.9	25 44	19 43	39.5	24 57	19 01	39.2	235 305
56 124	29 10	22 07	39.8	28 24	21 23	39.5	27 37	20 40	39.1	26 50	19 57	38.8	26 04	19 16	38.5	25 17	18 34	38.2	236 304
57 123	29 32	21 35	38.8	28 45	20 52	38.4	27 58	20 10	38.1	27 11	19 29	37.8	26 23	18 48	37.4	25 35	18 07	37.1	237 303
58 122	29 54	21 03	37.7	29 06	20 21	37.4	28 19	19 40	37.0	27 31	18 59	36.7	26 42	18 19	36.4	25 54	17 40	36.1	238 302
59 121	30 15	20 31	36.6	29 27	19 50	36.3	28 38	19 09	35.9	27 50	18 30	35.6	27 01	17 50	35.3	26 12	17 12	35.0	239 301
60 120	30 36	19 58	35.5	29 47	19 18	35.2	28 58	18 38	34.9	28 09	17 59	34.5	27 19	17 21	34.2	26 29	16 43	34.0	240 300
61 119	30 56	19 24	34.4	30 07	18 45	34.1	29 17	18 06	33.8	28 27	17 29	33.5	27 37	16 51	33.2	26 46	16 14	32.9	241 299
62 118	31 16	18 50	33.3	30 26	18 12	33.0	29 35	17 34	32.7	28 45	16 57	32.4	27 54	16 21	32.1	27 03	15 45	31.8	242 298
63 117	31 35	18 15	32.2	30 44	17 38	31.9	29 53	17 02	31.6	29 02	16 26	31.3	28 10	15 50	31.0	27 19	15 15	30.7	243 297
64 116	31 53	17 40	31.1	31 02	17 04	30.8	30 10	16 28	30.5	29 19	15 53	30.2	28 27	15 19	29.9	27 35	14 45	29.6	244 296
65 115	32 11	17 04	30.0	31 19	16 29	29.7	30 27	15 55	29.4	29 35	15 21	29.1	28 42	14 48	28.8	27 50	14 15	28.5	245 295
66 114	32 29	16 28	28.8	31 36	15 54	28.5	30 43	15 21	28.2	29 50	14 48	28.0	28 57	14 16	27.7	28 04	13 44	27.4	246 294
67 113	32 45	15 51	27.7	31 52	15 18	27.4	30 59	14 46	27.1	30 05	14 14	26.8	29 12	13 43	26.6	28 18	13 13	26.3	247 293
68 112	33 01	15 14	26.5	32 08	14 42	26.3	31 14	14 11	26.0	30 20	13 40	25.7	29 26	13 10	25.5	28 31	12 41	25.2	248 292
69 111	33 17	14 36	25.4	32 23	14 05	25.1	31 28	13 35	24.8	30 34	13 06	24.6	29 39	12 37	24.4	28 44	12 09	24.1	249 291
70 110	33 32	13 57	24.2	32 37	13 28	24.0	31 42	12 59	23.7	30 47	12 31	23.5	29 52	12 04	23.2	28 57	11 37	23.0	250 290
71 109	33 46	13 18	23.1	32 51	12 51	22.8	31 55	12 23	22.6	31 00	11 56	22.3	30 04	11 30	22.1	29 09	11 04	21.9	251 289
72 108	33 59	12 39	21.9	33 04	12 13	21.6	32 08	11 46	21.4	31 12	11 21	21.2	30 16	10 56	21.0	29 20	10 31	20.8	252 288
73 107	34 12	12 00	20.7	33 16	11 34	20.5	32 20	11 09	20.2	31 23	10 45	20.0	30 27	10 21	19.8	29 30	09 58	19.6	253 287
74 106	34 24	11 19	19.5	33 28	10 55	19.3	32 31	10 32	19.1	31 34	10 09	18.9	30 37	09 46	18.7	29 41	09 24	18.5	254 286
75 105	34 36	10 39	18.3	33 39	10 16	18.1	32 42	09 54	17.9	31 44	09 32	17.7	30 47	09 11	17.5	29 50	08 50	17.4	255 285
76 104	34 46	09 58	17.1	33 49	09 37	16.9	32 52	09 16	16.7	31 54	08 56	16.6	30 57	08 36	16.4	29 59	08 16	16.2	256 284
77 103	34 56	09 17	15.9	33 59	08 57	15.7	33 01	08 38	15.6	32 03	08 19	15.4	31 05	08 00	15.2	30 07	07 42	15.1	257 283
78 102	35 06	08 35	14.7	34 08	08 17	14.5	33 10	07 59	14.4	32 11	07 41	14.2	31 13	07 24	14.1	30 15	07 07	13.9	258 282
79 101	35 14	07 54	13.5	34 16	07 37	13.3	33 18	07 20	13.2	32 19	07 04	13.0	31 21	06 48	12.9	30 22	06 32	12.8	259 281
80 100	35 22	07 11	12.3	34 24	06 56	12.1	33 25	06 41	12.0	32 26	06 26	11.9	31 27	06 12	11.7	30 29	05 57	11.6	260 280
81 99	35 29	06 29	11.1	34 30	06 15	10.9	33 32	06 01	10.9	32 33	05 48	10.8	31 34	05 35	10.6	30 35	05 22	10.5	261 279
82 98	35 36	05 46	9.9	34 37	05 34	9.7	33 37	05 22	9.7	32 38	05 10	9.6	31 39	04 58	9.4	30 40	04 47	9.3	262 278
83 97	35 41	05 04	8.6	34 42	04 53	8.5	33 43	04 42	8.4	32 43	04 32	8.4	31 44	04 21	8.2	30 45	04 11	8.2	263 277
84 96	35 46	04 21	7.4	34 47	04 11	7.3	33 47	04 02	7.2	32 48	03 53	7.1	31 48	03 44	7.1	30 49	03 36	7.0	264 276
85 95	35 51	03 37	6.2	34 51	03 30	6.1	33 51	03 22	6.0	32 52	03 14	6.0	31 52	03 07	5.9	30 52	03 00	5.8	265 275
86 94	35 54	02 54	4.9	34 54	02 48	4.9	33 54	02 42	4.8	32 55	02 36	4.8	31 55	02 30	4.7	30 55	02 24	4.7	266 274
87 93	35 57	02 11	3.7	34 57	02 06	3.7	33 57	02 01	3.6	32 57	01 57	3.6	31 57	01 52	3.5	30 57	01 48	3.5	267 273
88 92	35 58	01 27	2.5	34 59	01 24	2.4	33 59	01 21	2.4	32 59	01 18	2.4	31 59	01 15	2.4	30 59	01 12	2.3	268 272
89 91	36 00	00 44	1.2	35 00	00 42	1.2	34 00	00 40	1.2	33 00	00 39	1.2	32 00	00 37	1.2	31 00	00 36	1.2	269 271
90 90	36 00	00 00	0.0	35 00	00 00	0.0	34 00	00 00	0.0	33 00	00 00	0.0	32 00	00 00	0.0	31 00	00 00	0.0	270 270

N. Lat.: for LHA > 180° ... Zn = Z
for LHA < 180° ... Zn = 360° − Z

S. Lat.: for LHA > 180° ... Zn = 180° − Z
for LHA < 180° ... Zn = 180° + Z

SIGHT REDUCTION TABLE

B: (−) for 90° < LHA < 270°
Dec: (−) for Lat. contrary name

Z_1: same sign as B
Z_2: (−) for F > 90°

Lat./A LHA/F	60° A/H	60° B/P	60° Z_1/Z_2	61° A/H	61° B/P	61° Z_1/Z_2	62° A/H	62° B/P	62° Z_1/Z_2	63° A/H	63° B/P	63° Z_1/Z_2	64° A/H	64° B/P	64° Z_1/Z_2	65° A/H	65° B/P	65° Z_1/Z_2	Lat./A LHA	LHA
0	0 00	30 00	90.0	0 00	29 00	90.0	0 00	28 00	90.0	0 00	27 00	90.0	0 00	26 00	90.0	0 00	25 00	90.0	180	360
1	0 30	30 00	89.1	0 29	29 00	89.1	0 28	28 00	89.1	0 27	27 00	89.1	0 26	26 00	89.1	0 25	25 00	89.1	181	359
2	1 00	29 59	88.3	0 58	28 59	88.3	0 56	27 58	88.2	0 54	26 58	88.2	0 53	25 59	88.2	0 51	25 00	88.2	182	358
3	1 30	29 58	87.4	1 27	28 58	87.4	1 24	27 58	87.4	1 22	26 58	87.3	1 19	25 58	87.3	1 16	24 58	87.3	183	357
4	2 00	29 56	86.5	1 56	28 56	86.5	1 53	27 57	86.5	1 49	26 57	86.4	1 45	25 57	86.4	1 41	24 57	86.4	184	356
5	2 30	29 54	85.7	2 25	28 54	85.6	2 21	27 55	85.6	2 16	26 55	85.5	2 11	25 55	85.5	2 07	24 55	85.5	185	355
6	3 00	29 52	84.8	2 54	28 52	84.7	2 49	27 52	84.7	2 43	26 52	84.6	2 38	25 53	84.6	2 32	24 53	84.6	186	354
7	3 30	29 49	83.9	3 23	28 49	83.9	3 17	27 49	83.8	3 10	26 50	83.8	3 04	25 50	83.7	2 57	24 50	83.7	187	353
8	3 59	29 45	83.1	3 52	28 46	83.0	3 45	27 46	82.9	3 37	26 46	82.9	3 30	25 47	82.8	3 22	24 47	82.7	188	352
9	4 29	29 41	82.2	4 21	28 42	82.1	4 13	27 42	82.0	4 04	26 43	82.0	3 56	25 43	81.9	3 47	24 44	81.8	189	351
10	4 59	29 37	81.3	4 50	28 38	81.2	4 41	27 38	81.2	4 31	26 39	81.1	4 22	25 39	81.0	4 13	24 40	80.9	190	350
11	5 28	29 33	80.4	5 18	28 33	80.4	5 08	27 34	80.3	4 58	26 34	80.2	4 48	25 35	80.1	4 38	24 36	80.0	191	349
12	5 58	29 27	79.6	5 47	28 28	79.5	5 36	27 29	79.4	5 25	26 29	79.3	5 14	25 30	79.2	5 02	24 31	79.1	192	348
13	6 27	29 22	78.7	6 16	28 22	78.6	6 04	27 23	78.5	5 52	26 24	78.4	5 40	25 25	78.3	5 27	24 26	78.2	193	347
14	6 57	29 15	77.9	6 44	28 16	77.7	6 31	27 17	77.6	6 18	26 18	77.5	6 05	25 20	77.4	5 52	24 21	77.3	194	346
15	7 26	29 09	76.9	7 13	28 10	76.8	6 59	27 11	76.7	6 45	26 12	76.6	6 31	25 14	76.5	6 17	24 15	76.4	195	345
16	7 55	29 02	76.1	7 41	28 03	75.9	7 26	27 04	75.8	7 11	26 06	75.7	6 56	25 07	75.5	6 41	24 09	75.4	196	344
17	8 24	28 54	75.2	8 09	27 56	75.0	7 53	26 57	74.9	7 38	25 59	74.8	7 22	25 00	74.6	7 06	24 02	74.5	197	343
18	8 53	28 46	74.3	8 37	27 48	74.1	8 20	26 50	74.0	8 04	25 51	73.9	7 47	24 53	73.7	7 30	23 55	73.6	198	342
19	9 22	28 38	73.4	9 05	27 40	73.2	8 48	26 41	73.1	8 30	25 43	72.9	8 12	24 45	72.8	7 55	23 48	72.7	199	341
20	9 51	28 29	72.5	9 33	27 31	72.3	9 14	26 33	72.2	8 56	25 35	72.0	8 37	24 37	71.9	8 19	23 40	71.7	200	340
21	10 19	28 19	71.6	10 00	27 22	71.4	9 41	26 24	71.3	9 22	25 26	71.1	9 02	24 29	71.0	8 43	23 32	70.8	201	339
22	10 48	28 10	70.7	10 28	27 12	70.5	10 08	26 15	70.4	9 48	25 17	70.2	9 27	24 20	70.0	9 07	23 23	69.9	202	338
23	11 16	27 59	69.8	10 55	27 02	69.6	10 34	26 05	69.5	10 13	25 08	69.3	9 52	24 11	69.1	9 30	23 14	69.0	203	337
24	11 44	27 49	68.9	11 22	26 51	68.7	11 00	25 54	68.5	10 38	24 58	68.4	10 16	24 01	68.2	9 54	23 04	68.0	204	336
25	12 12	27 37	68.0	11 49	26 40	67.8	11 27	25 44	67.6	11 04	24 47	67.4	10 41	23 51	67.3	10 17	22 55	67.1	205	335
26	12 40	27 26	67.1	12 16	26 29	66.9	11 53	25 33	66.7	11 29	24 36	66.5	11 05	23 40	66.3	10 41	22 44	66.2	206	334
27	13 07	27 13	66.1	12 43	26 17	65.9	12 18	25 21	65.8	11 54	24 25	65.6	11 29	23 29	65.4	11 04	22 34	65.2	207	333
28	13 35	27 01	65.2	13 09	26 05	65.0	12 44	25 09	64.9	12 18	24 13	64.7	11 53	23 18	64.5	11 27	22 23	64.3	208	332
29	14 02	26 48	64.4	13 36	25 52	64.1	13 09	24 56	63.9	12 43	24 01	63.7	12 16	23 06	63.5	11 49	22 11	63.3	209	331
30	14 29	26 34	63.4	14 02	25 39	63.2	13 35	24 43	63.0	13 07	23 49	62.8	12 40	22 54	62.6	12 12	21 59	62.4	210	330
31	14 55	26 20	62.5	14 28	25 25	62.3	14 00	24 30	62.1	13 31	23 36	61.8	13 03	22 41	61.6	12 34	21 47	61.4	211	329
32	15 22	26 05	61.6	14 53	25 11	61.3	14 24	24 16	61.1	13 55	23 22	60.9	13 26	22 28	60.7	12 56	21 35	60.5	212	328
33	15 48	25 50	60.6	15 19	24 56	60.4	14 49	24 02	60.2	14 19	23 08	59.9	13 49	22 15	59.7	13 18	21 22	59.5	213	327
34	16 14	25 35	59.7	15 44	24 41	59.5	15 13	23 47	59.2	14 42	22 54	59.0	14 11	22 01	58.8	13 40	21 08	58.6	214	326
35	16 40	25 19	58.8	16 09	24 25	58.5	15 37	23 32	58.3	15 06	22 39	58.0	14 34	21 47	57.8	14 02	20 54	57.6	215	325
36	17 05	25 02	57.8	16 33	24 09	57.6	16 01	23 17	57.3	15 29	22 24	57.1	14 56	21 32	56.9	14 23	20 40	56.6	216	324
37	17 31	24 45	56.9	16 58	23 53	56.6	16 25	23 00	56.4	15 51	22 09	56.1	15 18	21 17	55.9	14 44	20 26	55.7	217	323
38	17 56	24 28	55.9	17 22	23 36	55.7	16 48	22 44	55.4	16 14	21 53	55.2	15 39	21 01	54.9	15 05	20 11	54.7	218	322
39	18 20	24 10	55.0	17 46	23 18	54.7	17 11	22 27	54.4	16 36	21 36	54.2	16 01	20 46	54.0	15 25	19 55	53.7	219	321
40	18 45	23 52	54.0	18 09	23 00	53.7	17 34	22 10	53.5	16 58	21 19	53.2	16 22	20 29	53.0	15 46	19 39	52.7	220	320
41	19 09	23 33	53.0	18 33	22 42	52.8	17 56	21 52	52.5	17 20	21 02	52.2	16 43	20 13	52.0	16 06	19 23	51.8	221	319
42	19 33	23 13	52.1	18 56	22 23	51.8	18 19	21 34	51.5	17 41	20 44	51.3	17 03	19 55	51.0	16 26	19 07	50.8	222	318
43	19 56	22 54	51.1	19 18	22 04	50.8	18 40	21 15	50.5	18 02	20 26	50.3	17 24	19 38	50.0	16 45	18 50	49.8	223	317
44	20 19	22 33	50.1	19 41	21 44	49.8	19 02	20 56	49.5	18 23	20 08	49.3	17 44	19 20	49.0	17 04	18 33	48.8	224	316
45	20 42	22 12	49.1	20 03	21 24	48.8	19 23	20 36	48.6	18 43	19 49	48.3	18 03	19 02	48.1	17 23	18 15	47.8	225	315

Lat./A LHA/F	F	60° A/H	60° B/P	60° Z₁/Z₂	61° A/H	61° B/P	61° Z₁/Z₂	62° A/H	62° B/P	62° Z₁/Z₂	63° A/H	63° B/P	63° Z₁/Z₂	64° A/H	64° B/P	64° Z₁/Z₂	65° A/H	65° B/P	65° Z₁/Z₂	Lat./A LHA
45	135	20 42	22 12	49.1	20 03	21 24	48.8	19 23	20 36	48.8	18 43	19 49	48.3	18 03	19 02	48.1	17 23	18 15	47.8	225
46	134	21 05	21 51	48.1	20 25	21 04	47.8	19 44	20 16	47.8	19 04	19 29	47.3	18 23	18 43	47.1	17 42	17 57	46.8	226
47	133	21 27	21 30	47.1	20 46	20 43	46.8	20 05	19 56	46.6	19 24	19 10	46.3	18 42	18 24	46.1	18 00	17 39	45.8	227
48	132	21 49	21 07	46.1	21 07	20 21	45.8	20 25	19 35	45.6	19 43	18 50	45.3	19 01	18 04	45.1	18 18	17 20	44.8	228
49	131	22 10	20 45	45.1	21 28	19 59	44.8	20 45	19 14	44.6	20 02	18 29	44.3	19 19	17 45	44.0	18 36	17 01	43.8	229
50	130	22 31	20 22	44.1	21 48	19 37	43.8	21 05	18 52	43.8	20 21	18 08	43.3	19 37	17 24	43.0	18 53	16 41	42.8	230
51	129	22 52	19 58	43.1	22 08	19 14	42.8	21 24	18 30	42.8	20 40	17 47	42.3	19 55	17 04	42.0	19 10	16 21	41.8	231
52	128	23 12	19 34	42.1	22 28	18 51	41.8	21 43	18 08	41.5	20 58	17 25	41.2	20 13	16 43	41.0	19 27	16 01	40.8	232
53	127	23 32	19 10	41.0	22 47	18 27	40.7	22 01	17 45	40.5	21 15	17 03	40.2	20 30	16 21	40.0	19 44	15 41	39.7	233
54	126	23 52	18 45	40.0	23 06	18 03	39.7	22 19	17 21	39.4	21 33	16 40	39.2	20 46	16 00	39.0	20 00	15 20	38.7	234
55	125	24 11	18 19	39.0	23 24	17 38	38.7	22 37	16 58	38.4	21 50	16 17	38.2	21 03	15 38	37.9	20 15	14 58	37.7	235
56	124	24 29	17 54	37.9	23 42	17 13	37.6	22 54	16 34	37.4	22 07	15 54	37.1	21 19	15 15	36.9	20 31	14 37	36.7	236
57	123	24 48	17 27	36.9	23 59	16 48	36.6	23 11	16 09	36.3	22 23	15 31	36.1	21 34	14 53	35.8	20 46	14 15	35.6	237
58	122	25 05	17 01	35.8	24 17	16 22	35.5	23 28	15 44	35.3	22 39	15 07	35.0	21 49	14 29	34.8	21 00	13 53	34.6	238
59	121	25 23	16 34	34.8	24 33	15 56	34.5	23 44	15 19	34.2	22 54	14 42	34.0	22 04	14 06	33.8	21 14	13 30	33.5	239
60	120	25 40	16 06	33.7	24 50	15 29	33.4	23 59	14 53	33.2	23 09	14 18	32.9	22 19	13 42	32.7	21 28	13 07	32.5	240
61	119	25 56	15 38	32.6	25 05	15 03	32.4	24 15	14 27	32.1	23 24	13 53	31.9	22 33	13 18	31.7	21 42	12 44	31.5	241
62	118	26 12	15 10	31.5	25 21	14 35	31.3	24 29	14 01	31.1	23 38	13 27	30.8	22 46	12 54	30.6	21 55	12 21	30.4	242
63	117	26 27	14 41	30.5	25 36	14 08	30.2	24 44	13 34	30.0	23 52	13 01	29.8	22 59	12 29	29.5	22 07	11 57	29.3	243
64	116	26 42	14 12	29.4	25 50	13 39	29.1	24 57	13 07	28.9	24 05	12 35	28.7	23 12	12 04	28.5	22 19	11 33	28.3	244
65	115	26 57	13 43	28.3	26 04	13 11	28.1	25 11	12 40	27.8	24 18	12 09	27.6	23 25	11 39	27.4	22 31	11 09	27.2	245
66	114	27 11	13 13	27.2	26 18	12 42	27.0	25 24	12 12	26.8	24 30	11 43	26.6	23 36	11 13	26.4	22 43	10 44	26.2	246
67	113	27 24	12 43	26.1	26 30	12 13	25.9	25 36	11 44	25.7	24 42	11 16	25.5	23 48	10 47	25.3	22 54	10 20	25.1	247
68	112	27 37	12 12	25.0	26 43	11 44	24.8	25 48	11 16	24.6	24 54	10 48	24.4	23 59	10 21	24.2	23 04	9 55	24.0	248
69	111	27 50	11 41	23.9	26 55	11 14	23.7	26 00	10 47	23.5	25 05	10 21	23.3	24 09	9 55	23.1	23 14	9 29	23.0	249
70	110	28 01	11 10	22.8	27 06	10 44	22.6	26 11	10 18	22.4	25 15	9 53	22.2	24 20	9 28	22.0	23 24	9 04	21.9	250
71	109	28 13	10 39	21.7	27 17	10 14	21.5	26 21	9 49	21.3	25 25	9 25	21.1	24 29	9 01	21.0	23 33	8 38	20.8	251
72	108	28 24	10 07	20.6	27 27	9 43	20.4	26 31	9 20	20.2	25 35	8 57	20.0	24 38	8 34	19.9	23 42	8 12	19.7	252
73	107	28 34	9 35	19.4	27 37	9 12	19.3	26 41	8 50	19.1	25 44	8 28	18.9	24 47	8 07	18.8	23 50	7 46	18.6	253
74	106	28 44	9 03	18.3	27 47	8 41	18.2	26 50	8 20	18.0	25 52	8 00	17.8	24 55	7 39	17.7	23 58	7 19	17.6	254
75	105	28 53	8 30	17.2	27 55	8 10	17.0	26 58	7 50	16.9	26 01	7 31	16.7	25 03	7 12	16.6	24 06	6 53	16.5	255
76	104	29 01	7 57	16.1	28 04	7 38	15.9	27 06	7 20	15.8	26 08	7 02	15.6	25 10	6 44	15.5	24 13	6 26	15.4	256
77	103	29 09	7 24	14.9	28 11	7 06	14.8	27 13	6 49	14.7	26 15	6 32	14.5	25 17	6 16	14.4	24 19	5 59	14.3	257
78	102	29 17	6 51	13.8	28 18	6 34	13.7	27 20	6 19	13.5	26 22	6 03	13.4	25 23	5 47	13.3	24 25	5 32	13.2	258
79	101	29 24	6 17	12.7	28 25	6 02	12.5	27 27	5 48	12.4	26 28	5 33	12.3	25 29	5 19	12.1	24 31	5 05	12.1	259
80	100	29 30	5 44	11.5	28 31	5 30	11.4	27 32	5 17	11.3	26 33	5 03	11.2	25 35	4 50	11.1	24 36	4 38	11.0	260
81	99	29 36	5 10	10.4	28 37	4 57	10.3	27 38	4 45	10.2	26 38	4 33	10.1	25 39	4 22	10.0	24 40	4 10	9.9	261
82	98	29 41	4 36	9.2	28 41	4 25	9.1	27 42	4 14	9.0	26 43	4 03	8.9	25 44	3 53	8.9	24 44	3 43	8.8	262
83	97	29 45	4 01	8.1	28 46	3 52	8.0	27 46	3 42	7.9	26 47	3 33	7.8	25 48	3 24	7.8	24 48	3 15	7.7	263
84	96	29 49	3 27	6.9	28 50	3 19	6.9	27 50	3 11	6.8	26 50	3 03	6.7	25 51	2 55	6.7	24 51	2 47	6.6	264
85	95	29 52	2 53	5.8	28 53	2 46	5.7	27 53	2 39	5.7	26 53	2 33	5.6	25 54	2 26	5.6	24 54	2 20	5.5	265
86	94	29 55	2 18	4.6	28 55	2 13	4.6	27 56	2 07	4.5	26 56	2 02	4.5	25 56	1 57	4.4	24 56	1 52	4.4	266
87	93	29 57	1 44	3.5	28 57	1 40	3.4	27 57	1 36	3.4	26 58	1 32	3.4	25 58	1 28	3.3	24 58	1 24	3.3	267
88	92	29 59	1 09	2.3	28 59	1 06	2.3	27 59	1 04	2.3	26 59	1 01	2.2	25 59	0 59	2.2	24 59	0 56	2.2	268
89	91	30 00	0 35	1.2	29 00	0 33	1.2	28 00	0 32	1.1	27 00	0 31	1.1	26 00	0 29	1.1	25 00	0 28	1.1	269
90	90	30 00	0 00	0.0	29 00	0 00	0.0	28 00	0 00	0.0	27 00	0 00	0.0	26 00	0 00	0.0	25 00	0 00	0.0	270

N. Lat: for LHA > 180°... Zn = Z / for LHA < 180°... Zn = 360° − Z

S. Lat: for LHA > 180°... Zn = 180° − Z / for LHA < 180°... Zn = 180° + Z

SIGHT REDUCTION TABLE

B: (−) for 90°< LHA <270°
Dec: (−) for Lat. contrary name

Z₁: same sign as B
Z₂: (−) for F > 90°

Lat./A	LHA/F	66° A/H	66° B/P	66° Z₁/Z₂	67° A/H	67° B/P	67° Z₁/Z₂	68° A/H	68° B/P	68° Z₁/Z₂	69° A/H	69° B/P	69° Z₁/Z₂	70° A/H	70° B/P	70° Z₁/Z₂	71° A/H	71° B/P	71° Z₁/Z₂	Lat./A	LHA
0	180	0 00	24 00	90.0	0 00	23 00	90.0	0 00	22 00	90.0	0 00	21 00	90.0	0 00	20 00	90.0	0 00	19 00	90.0	180	360
1	179	0 24	24 00	89.1	0 23	23 00	89.1	0 22	22 00	89.1	0 22	21 00	89.1	0 21	20 00	89.1	0 20	19 00	89.1	181	359
2	178	0 49	23 59	88.2	0 47	22 59	88.2	0 45	21 59	88.1	0 43	20 59	88.1	0 41	19 59	88.1	0 39	18 59	88.2	182	358
3	177	1 13	23 58	87.3	1 10	22 58	87.2	1 07	21 58	87.2	1 04	20 58	87.2	1 02	19 58	87.2	0 59	18 59	87.2	183	357
4	176	1 38	23 57	86.4	1 34	22 57	86.3	1 30	21 57	86.3	1 26	20 57	86.3	1 22	19 57	86.2	1 18	18 57	86.2	184	356
5	175	2 02	23 55	85.4	1 57	22 55	85.4	1 52	21 55	85.4	1 47	20 56	85.3	1 42	19 56	85.3	1 38	18 56	85.3	185	355
6	174	2 26	23 53	84.5	2 20	22 53	84.5	2 15	21 53	84.4	2 09	20 54	84.4	2 03	19 54	84.4	1 57	18 54	84.3	186	354
7	173	2 50	23 50	83.6	2 44	22 51	83.6	2 37	21 51	83.5	2 30	20 51	83.5	2 23	19 52	83.4	2 16	18 52	83.4	187	353
8	172	3 15	23 48	82.7	3 07	22 48	82.6	2 59	21 48	82.6	2 52	20 49	82.5	2 44	19 49	82.5	2 36	18 50	82.4	188	352
9	171	3 39	23 44	81.8	3 30	22 45	81.7	3 22	21 45	81.6	3 13	20 46	81.6	3 04	19 46	81.5	2 55	18 47	81.5	189	351
10	170	4 03	23 41	80.8	3 53	22 41	80.8	3 44	21 42	80.7	3 34	20 42	80.7	3 24	19 43	80.6	3 14	18 44	80.5	190	350
11	169	4 27	23 36	79.9	4 17	22 37	79.9	4 06	21 38	79.8	3 55	20 39	79.7	3 45	19 40	79.6	3 34	18 41	79.6	191	349
12	168	4 51	23 32	79.0	4 40	22 33	78.9	4 28	21 34	78.8	4 16	20 35	78.8	4 05	19 36	78.7	3 53	18 37	78.6	192	348
13	167	5 15	23 27	78.1	5 03	22 28	78.0	4 50	21 29	77.9	4 37	20 30	77.8	4 25	19 32	77.8	4 12	18 33	77.7	193	347
14	166	5 39	23 22	77.2	5 25	22 23	77.1	5 12	21 24	77.0	4 58	20 26	76.9	4 45	19 27	76.8	4 31	18 28	76.7	194	346
15	165	6 03	23 16	76.2	5 48	22 18	76.1	5 34	21 18	76.0	5 19	20 21	76.0	5 05	19 22	75.9	4 50	18 24	75.8	195	345
16	164	6 26	23 10	75.3	6 11	22 12	75.2	5 56	21 13	75.1	5 40	20 15	75.1	5 25	19 17	74.9	5 09	18 19	74.8	196	344
17	163	6 50	23 04	74.4	6 34	22 06	74.3	6 17	21 08	74.2	6 01	20 09	74.1	5 44	19 11	74.0	5 28	18 14	73.9	197	343
18	162	7 13	22 57	73.5	6 56	21 59	73.3	6 39	21 01	73.2	6 21	20 03	73.1	6 04	19 06	73.0	5 46	18 08	72.9	198	342
19	161	7 37	22 50	72.5	7 19	21 52	72.4	7 00	20 54	72.3	6 42	19 57	72.2	6 24	18 59	72.1	6 05	18 02	72.0	199	341
20	160	8 00	22 42	71.6	7 41	21 45	71.5	7 22	20 47	71.4	7 02	19 50	71.2	6 43	18 53	71.1	6 24	17 56	71.0	200	340
21	159	8 23	22 34	70.7	8 03	21 37	70.5	7 43	20 40	70.4	7 23	19 43	70.3	7 02	18 46	70.2	6 42	17 49	70.1	201	339
22	158	8 46	22 26	69.7	8 25	21 29	69.6	8 04	20 32	69.5	7 43	19 35	69.3	7 22	18 39	69.2	7 00	17 42	69.1	202	338
23	157	9 09	22 17	68.8	8 47	21 21	68.7	8 25	20 24	68.5	8 03	19 28	68.4	7 41	18 31	68.3	7 19	17 35	68.1	203	337
24	156	9 31	22 08	67.9	9 09	21 12	67.7	8 46	20 16	67.6	8 23	19 19	67.4	8 00	18 24	67.3	7 37	17 28	67.2	204	336
25	155	9 54	21 58	66.9	9 30	21 03	66.8	9 07	20 07	66.6	8 43	19 11	66.5	8 19	18 15	66.3	7 55	17 20	66.2	205	335
26	154	10 16	21 49	66.0	9 52	20 53	65.8	9 27	19 57	65.7	9 02	19 02	65.5	8 37	18 07	65.4	8 12	17 12	65.2	206	334
27	153	10 38	21 38	65.0	10 13	20 43	64.9	9 48	19 48	64.7	9 22	18 53	64.6	8 56	17 58	64.4	8 30	17 03	64.3	207	333
28	152	11 00	21 28	64.1	10 34	20 33	63.9	10 08	19 38	63.8	9 41	18 43	63.6	9 14	17 49	63.5	8 48	16 55	63.4	208	332
29	151	11 22	21 17	63.1	10 55	20 22	63.0	10 28	19 28	62.8	10 00	18 34	62.6	9 33	17 39	62.5	9 05	16 46	62.3	209	331
30	150	11 44	21 05	62.2	11 16	20 11	62.0	10 48	19 17	61.8	10 19	18 23	61.7	9 51	17 30	61.5	9 22	16 36	61.4	210	330
31	149	12 06	20 53	61.2	11 37	20 00	61.1	11 07	19 06	60.9	10 38	18 13	60.7	10 09	17 20	60.5	9 39	16 27	60.4	211	329
32	148	12 27	20 41	60.3	11 57	19 48	60.1	11 27	18 55	59.9	10 57	18 02	59.7	10 27	17 09	59.6	9 56	16 17	59.4	212	328
33	147	12 48	20 29	59.3	12 17	19 36	59.1	11 46	18 43	58.9	11 15	17 51	58.8	10 44	16 58	58.6	10 13	16 06	58.4	213	327
34	146	13 09	20 16	58.4	12 37	19 23	58.2	12 06	18 31	58.0	11 34	17 39	57.8	11 02	16 47	57.6	10 29	15 56	57.5	214	326
35	145	13 29	20 02	57.4	12 57	19 10	57.2	12 24	18 19	57.0	11 52	17 27	56.8	11 19	16 36	56.7	10 46	15 45	56.5	215	325
36	144	13 50	19 49	56.4	13 17	18 57	56.2	12 43	18 06	56.0	12 10	17 15	55.9	11 36	16 24	55.7	11 02	15 34	55.5	216	324
37	143	14 10	19 34	55.5	13 36	18 44	55.3	13 02	17 53	55.1	12 27	17 03	54.9	11 53	16 12	54.7	11 18	15 23	54.5	217	323
38	142	14 30	19 20	54.5	13 55	18 30	54.3	13 20	17 40	54.1	12 45	16 50	53.9	12 09	16 00	53.7	11 34	15 11	53.5	218	322
39	141	14 50	19 05	53.5	14 14	18 15	53.3	13 38	17 26	53.1	13 02	16 37	52.9	12 26	15 48	52.7	11 49	14 59	52.6	219	321
40	140	15 09	18 50	52.5	14 33	18 01	52.3	13 56	17 12	52.1	13 19	16 23	51.9	12 42	15 35	51.7	12 05	14 47	51.6	220	320
41	139	15 29	18 34	51.5	14 51	17 46	51.3	14 14	16 57	51.1	13 36	16 09	50.9	12 58	15 22	50.8	12 20	14 34	50.6	221	319
42	138	15 48	18 18	50.6	15 09	17 30	50.3	14 31	16 43	50.1	13 52	15 55	49.9	13 14	15 08	49.8	12 35	14 21	49.6	222	318
43	137	16 06	18 02	49.6	15 27	17 15	49.4	14 48	16 28	49.2	14 09	15 41	49.0	13 29	14 54	48.8	12 50	14 08	48.6	223	317
44	136	16 25	17 46	48.6	15 45	16 59	48.4	15 05	16 12	48.2	14 25	15 26	48.0	13 45	14 40	47.8	13 04	13 55	47.6	224	316
45	135	16 43	17 29	47.6	16 02	16 42	47.4	15 22	15 57	47.2	14 41	15 11	47.0	14 00	14 26	46.8	13 19	13 41	46.6	225	315

Top-right angle conversions:

$Z_n = 180° - Z$
$Z_n = 180° + Z$

LHA	F	66° A/H	66° B/P	66° Z1/Z2	67° A/H	67° B/P	67° Z1/Z2	68° A/H	68° B/P	68° Z1/Z2	69° A/H	69° B/P	69° Z1/Z2	70° A/H	70° B/P	70° Z1/Z2	71° A/H	71° B/P	71° Z1/Z2	A	LHA
45	135	16 43	17 29	47.6	16 02	16 42	47.4	15 22	15 57	47.2	14 41	15 11	47.0	14 00	14 26	46.8	13 19	13 41	46.6	225	315
46	134	17 01	17 11	46.6	16 19	16 26	46.4	15 38	15 41	46.2	14 56	14 56	46.0	14 15	14 11	45.8	13 33	13 27	45.6	226	314
47	133	17 18	16 53	45.6	16 36	16 09	45.4	15 54	15 24	45.2	15 12	14 40	45.0	14 29	13 56	44.8	13 46	13 13	44.6	227	313
48	132	17 36	16 35	44.6	16 53	15 51	44.4	16 10	15 08	44.2	15 27	14 24	44.0	14 43	13 41	43.8	14 00	12 58	43.6	228	312
49	131	17 53	16 17	43.6	17 09	15 34	43.4	16 25	14 51	43.2	15 42	14 08	43.0	14 58	13 26	42.8	14 13	12 44	42.6	229	311
50	130	18 09	15 58	42.6	17 25	15 16	42.4	16 41	14 33	42.1	15 56	13 52	41.9	15 11	13 10	41.8	14 27	12 29	41.6	230	310
51	129	18 26	15 39	41.6	17 41	14 57	41.3	16 56	14 16	41.1	16 10	13 35	40.9	15 25	12 54	40.8	14 39	12 14	40.6	231	309
52	128	18 42	15 20	40.5	17 56	14 39	40.3	17 10	13 58	40.1	16 24	13 18	39.9	15 38	12 38	39.7	14 52	11 58	39.6	232	308
53	127	18 57	15 00	39.5	18 11	14 20	39.3	17 24	13 40	39.1	16 38	13 00	38.9	15 51	12 21	38.7	15 04	11 42	38.6	233	307
54	126	19 13	14 40	38.5	18 26	14 01	38.3	17 39	13 22	38.1	16 51	12 43	37.9	16 03	12 05	37.7	15 16	11 26	37.5	234	306
55	125	19 28	14 20	37.5	18 40	13 41	37.3	17 52	13 03	37.1	17 04	12 25	36.9	16 16	11 48	36.7	15 28	11 10	36.5	235	305
56	124	19 42	13 59	36.4	18 54	13 21	36.2	18 06	12 44	36.0	17 17	12 07	35.8	16 28	11 30	35.7	15 40	10 54	35.5	236	304
57	123	19 57	13 38	35.4	19 08	13 01	35.2	18 19	12 25	35.0	17 29	11 49	34.8	16 40	11 13	34.6	15 51	10 37	34.5	237	303
58	122	20 11	13 17	34.4	19 21	12 41	34.2	18 31	12 05	34.0	17 42	11 30	33.8	16 52	10 55	33.6	16 02	10 20	33.5	238	302
59	121	20 24	12 55	33.3	19 34	12 20	33.1	18 44	11 45	32.9	17 53	11 11	32.8	17 03	10 37	32.6	16 12	10 03	32.4	239	301
60	120	20 37	12 33	32.3	19 47	11 59	32.1	18 56	11 25	31.9	18 05	10 52	31.7	17 14	10 19	31.6	16 23	9 46	31.4	240	300
61	119	20 50	12 11	31.2	19 59	11 38	31.1	19 08	11 05	30.9	18 16	10 33	30.7	17 24	10 00	30.5	16 33	9 29	30.4	241	299
62	118	21 03	11 48	30.2	20 11	11 16	30.0	19 19	10 44	29.8	18 27	10 13	29.7	17 35	9 42	29.5	16 42	9 11	29.4	242	298
63	117	21 15	11 26	29.2	20 22	10 54	29.0	19 30	10 24	28.8	18 37	9 53	28.6	17 45	9 23	28.5	16 52	8 53	28.3	243	297
64	116	21 27	11 03	28.1	20 34	10 32	27.9	19 41	10 03	27.7	18 47	9 33	27.6	17 54	9 04	27.4	17 01	8 35	27.3	244	296
65	115	21 38	10 39	27.0	20 44	10 10	26.9	19 51	9 41	26.7	18 57	9 13	26.5	18 03	8 45	26.4	17 10	8 17	26.3	245	295
66	114	21 49	10 16	26.0	20 55	9 48	25.8	20 01	9 20	25.7	19 07	8 52	25.5	18 12	8 25	25.4	17 18	7 58	25.2	246	294
67	113	21 59	9 52	24.9	21 05	9 25	24.8	20 10	8 58	24.6	19 16	8 32	24.4	18 21	8 06	24.3	17 26	7 40	24.2	247	293
68	112	22 09	9 28	23.9	21 14	9 02	23.7	20 19	8 36	23.5	19 24	8 11	23.4	18 29	7 46	23.3	17 34	7 21	23.1	248	292
69	111	22 19	9 04	22.8	21 24	8 39	22.6	20 28	8 14	22.5	19 33	7 50	22.4	18 37	7 26	22.2	17 42	7 02	22.1	249	291
70	110	22 28	8 40	21.7	21 32	8 16	21.6	20 37	7 52	21.4	19 41	7 29	21.3	18 45	7 06	21.2	17 49	6 43	21.1	250	290
71	109	22 37	8 15	20.7	21 41	7 52	20.5	20 45	7 30	20.4	19 48	7 07	20.2	18 52	6 45	20.1	17 56	6 24	20.0	251	289
72	108	22 45	7 50	19.6	21 49	7 28	19.4	20 52	7 07	19.3	19 56	6 46	19.2	18 59	6 25	19.1	18 02	6 04	19.0	252	288
73	107	22 53	7 25	18.5	21 56	7 04	18.4	21 00	6 44	18.2	20 03	6 24	18.1	19 05	6 04	18.0	18 08	5 45	17.9	253	287
74	106	23 01	7 00	17.4	22 04	6 40	17.3	21 06	6 21	17.2	20 09	6 02	17.1	19 12	5 44	17.0	18 14	5 25	16.9	254	286
75	105	23 08	6 34	16.3	22 10	6 16	16.2	21 13	5 58	16.1	20 15	5 40	16.0	19 17	5 23	15.9	18 20	5 06	15.8	255	285
76	104	23 15	6 09	15.3	22 17	5 52	15.1	21 19	5 35	15.1	20 21	5 18	15.0	19 23	5 02	14.9	18 25	4 46	14.8	256	284
77	103	23 21	5 43	14.2	22 23	5 27	14.1	21 24	5 12	14.0	20 26	4 56	13.9	19 28	4 41	13.8	18 30	4 26	13.7	257	283
78	102	23 27	5 17	13.1	22 28	5 03	13.0	21 30	4 48	12.9	20 31	4 34	12.8	19 33	4 20	12.7	18 34	4 06	12.7	258	282
79	101	23 32	4 51	12.0	22 33	4 38	11.9	21 35	4 24	11.8	20 36	4 11	11.8	19 37	3 58	11.7	18 38	3 46	11.6	259	281
80	100	23 37	4 25	10.9	22 38	4 13	10.8	21 39	4 01	10.8	20 40	3 49	10.7	19 41	3 37	10.6	18 42	3 25	10.6	260	280
81	99	23 41	3 59	9.8	22 42	3 48	9.8	21 43	3 37	9.7	20 44	3 26	9.6	19 45	3 16	9.6	18 45	3 05	9.5	261	279
82	98	23 45	3 33	8.7	22 46	3 23	8.7	21 46	3 13	8.6	20 47	3 03	8.6	19 48	2 54	8.5	18 48	2 45	8.5	262	278
83	97	23 49	3 06	7.7	22 49	2 58	7.6	21 50	2 49	7.5	20 50	2 41	7.5	19 51	2 32	7.4	18 51	2 24	7.4	263	277
84	96	23 52	2 40	6.6	22 52	2 32	6.5	21 52	2 25	6.5	20 53	2 18	6.4	19 53	2 11	6.4	18 54	2 04	6.3	264	276
85	95	23 54	2 13	5.5	22 54	2 07	5.4	21 55	2 01	5.4	20 55	1 55	5.4	19 55	1 49	5.3	18 55	1 43	5.3	265	275
86	94	23 56	1 47	4.4	22 56	1 42	4.3	21 57	1 37	4.3	20 57	1 32	4.3	19 57	1 27	4.3	18 57	1 23	4.2	266	274
87	93	23 58	1 20	3.3	22 58	1 16	3.3	21 58	1 13	3.2	20 58	1 09	3.2	19 58	1 05	3.2	18 58	1 02	3.2	267	273
88	92	23 59	0 53	2.2	22 59	0 51	2.2	21 59	0 48	2.2	20 59	0 46	2.1	19 59	0 44	2.1	18 59	0 41	2.1	268	272
89	91	24 00	0 27	1.1	23 00	0 25	1.1	22 00	0 24	1.1	21 00	0 23	1.1	20 00	0 22	1.1	19 00	0 21	1.1	269	271
90	90	24 00	0 00	0.0	23 00	0 00	0.0	22 00	0 00	0.0	21 00	0 00	0.0	20 00	0 00	0.0	19 00	0 00	0.0	270	270

N. Lat.: for LHA > 180° .... $Z_n = Z$
for LHA < 180° .... $Z_n = 360° - Z$

S. Lat.: for LHA > 180° .... $Z_n = 180° - Z$
for LHA < 180° .... $Z_n = 180° + Z$

SIGHT REDUCTION TABLE

B: (−) for 90° < LHA < 270°
Dec: (−) for Lat. contrary name

Z₁: same sign as B
Z₂: (−) for F > 90°

Lat./A LHA/F		72° A/H	B/P	Z₁/Z₂	73° A/H	B/P	Z₁/Z₂	74° A/H	B/P	Z₁/Z₂	75° A/H	B/P	Z₁/Z₂	76° A/H	B/P	Z₁/Z₂	77° A/H	B/P	Z₁/Z₂	Lat./A LHA	
0	180	0 00	18 00	90.0	0 00	17 00	90.0	0 00	16 00	90.0	0 00	15 00	90.0	0 00	14 00	90.0	0 00	13 00	90.0	180	360
1	179	0 19	18 00	89.0	0 18	17 00	89.0	0 17	16 00	89.0	0 16	15 00	89.0	0 15	14 00	89.0	0 13	13 00	89.0	181	359
2	178	0 37	17 59	88.1	0 35	16 59	88.1	0 33	15 59	88.1	0 31	14 59	88.1	0 29	14 00	88.1	0 27	13 00	88.1	182	358
3	177	0 56	17 59	87.1	0 53	16 59	87.1	0 50	15 59	87.1	0 47	14 59	87.1	0 44	13 59	87.1	0 40	12 59	87.1	183	357
4	176	1 14	17 58	86.2	1 10	16 58	86.2	1 06	15 58	86.2	1 02	14 58	86.1	0 58	13 58	86.1	0 54	12 58	86.1	184	356
5	175	1 33	17 56	85.2	1 28	16 56	85.2	1 23	15 57	85.2	1 18	14 57	85.2	1 12	13 57	85.1	1 07	12 57	85.1	185	355
6	174	1 51	17 54	84.3	1 45	16 55	84.3	1 39	15 55	84.2	1 33	14 55	84.2	1 27	13 56	84.2	1 21	12 56	84.2	186	354
7	173	2 09	17 52	83.3	2 03	16 53	83.3	1 56	15 53	83.3	1 48	14 54	83.2	1 41	13 54	83.2	1 34	12 54	83.2	187	353
8	172	2 28	17 50	82.4	2 20	16 51	82.3	2 12	15 51	82.3	2 04	14 52	82.3	1 56	13 52	82.2	1 48	12 53	82.2	188	352
9	171	2 46	17 48	81.4	2 37	16 48	81.4	2 28	15 49	81.3	2 19	14 49	81.3	2 10	13 50	81.2	2 01	12 51	81.2	189	351
10	170	3 05	17 45	80.5	2 55	16 45	80.4	2 45	15 46	80.4	2 35	14 47	80.3	2 24	13 48	80.3	2 14	12 49	80.3	190	350
11	169	3 23	17 41	79.5	3 12	16 42	79.5	3 01	15 43	79.4	2 50	14 44	79.4	2 39	13 45	79.3	2 28	12 46	79.3	191	349
12	168	3 41	17 38	78.6	3 29	16 39	78.5	3 17	15 40	78.5	3 05	14 41	78.4	2 53	13 42	78.3	2 41	12 44	78.3	192	348
13	167	3 59	17 34	77.6	3 46	16 35	77.5	3 33	15 37	77.5	3 20	14 38	77.4	3 07	13 39	77.4	2 54	12 41	77.3	193	347
14	166	4 17	17 30	76.7	4 03	16 31	76.6	3 49	15 33	76.5	3 35	14 34	76.5	3 21	13 36	76.4	3 07	12 38	76.3	194	346
15	165	4 35	17 25	75.7	4 20	16 27	75.6	4 05	15 29	75.5	3 50	14 31	75.5	3 35	13 32	75.4	3 20	12 34	75.4	195	345
16	164	4 53	17 21	74.7	4 37	16 23	74.7	4 21	15 25	74.5	4 05	14 27	74.5	3 49	13 29	74.5	3 33	12 31	74.4	196	344
17	163	5 11	17 16	73.8	4 54	16 18	73.7	4 37	15 20	73.6	4 20	14 22	73.5	4 03	13 25	73.5	3 46	12 27	73.4	197	343
18	162	5 29	17 10	72.8	5 11	16 13	72.7	4 53	15 15	72.7	4 35	14 18	72.6	4 17	13 20	72.4	3 59	12 23	72.4	198	342
19	161	5 46	17 05	71.9	5 28	16 07	71.8	5 09	15 10	71.7	4 50	14 13	71.6	4 31	13 16	71.5	4 12	12 19	71.5	199	341
20	160	6 04	16 59	70.9	5 44	16 02	70.8	5 25	15 05	70.7	5 05	14 08	70.6	4 45	13 11	70.5	4 25	12 14	70.5	200	340
21	159	6 21	16 52	69.9	6 01	15 56	69.8	5 40	14 59	69.7	5 19	14 03	69.7	4 58	13 06	69.6	4 37	12 10	69.5	201	339
22	158	6 39	16 46	69.0	6 17	15 50	68.9	5 56	14 53	68.8	5 34	13 57	68.7	5 12	13 01	68.6	4 50	12 05	68.5	202	338
23	157	6 56	16 39	68.0	6 34	15 43	67.9	6 11	14 47	67.8	5 48	13 51	67.7	5 25	12 56	67.6	5 03	12 00	67.5	203	337
24	156	7 13	16 32	67.1	6 50	15 36	66.9	6 26	14 41	66.8	6 03	13 45	66.7	5 39	12 50	66.6	5 15	11 55	66.5	204	336
25	155	7 30	16 25	66.1	7 06	15 29	66.0	6 41	14 34	65.9	6 17	13 39	65.8	5 52	12 44	65.7	5 27	11 49	65.6	205	335
26	154	7 47	16 17	65.1	7 22	15 22	65.0	6 56	14 27	64.9	6 31	13 32	64.8	6 05	12 38	64.7	5 40	11 43	64.6	206	334
27	153	8 04	16 09	64.1	7 38	15 14	64.0	7 11	14 20	63.9	6 45	13 26	63.8	6 18	12 32	63.7	5 52	11 37	63.6	207	333
28	152	8 20	16 00	63.2	7 53	15 06	63.0	7 26	14 12	62.9	6 59	13 19	62.8	6 31	12 25	62.7	6 04	11 31	62.6	208	332
29	151	8 37	15 52	62.2	8 09	14 58	62.1	7 41	14 05	61.9	7 13	13 11	61.8	6 44	12 18	61.7	6 16	11 25	61.6	209	331
30	150	8 53	15 43	61.2	8 24	14 50	61.1	7 55	13 57	61.0	7 26	13 04	60.9	6 57	12 11	60.7	6 27	11 18	60.6	210	330
31	149	9 09	15 34	60.3	8 40	14 41	60.1	8 10	13 49	60.0	7 40	12 56	59.9	7 09	12 04	59.8	6 39	11 12	59.7	211	329
32	148	9 25	15 24	59.3	8 55	14 32	59.1	8 24	13 40	59.0	7 53	12 48	58.9	7 22	11 56	58.8	6 51	11 05	58.7	212	328
33	147	9 41	15 15	58.3	9 10	14 23	58.2	8 38	13 31	58.0	8 06	12 40	57.9	7 34	11 49	57.8	7 02	10 57	57.7	213	327
34	146	9 57	15 05	57.3	9 25	14 13	57.2	8 52	13 22	57.0	8 19	12 31	56.9	7 46	11 41	56.8	7 14	10 50	56.7	214	326
35	145	10 13	14 54	56.3	9 39	14 04	56.2	9 06	13 13	56.1	8 32	12 23	55.9	7 59	11 33	55.8	7 25	10 43	55.7	215	325
36	144	10 28	14 44	55.4	9 54	13 54	55.2	9 19	13 04	55.1	8 45	12 14	54.9	8 11	11 24	54.8	7 36	10 35	54.7	216	324
37	143	10 43	14 33	54.4	10 08	13 43	54.2	9 33	12 54	54.1	8 58	12 05	53.9	8 22	11 16	53.8	7 47	10 27	53.7	217	323
38	142	10 58	14 22	53.4	10 22	13 33	53.2	9 46	12 44	53.1	9 10	11 55	53.0	8 34	11 07	52.8	7 58	10 19	52.7	218	322
39	141	11 13	14 10	52.4	10 36	13 22	52.2	9 59	12 34	52.1	9 22	11 46	52.0	8 45	10 58	51.8	8 08	10 10	51.7	219	321
40	140	11 27	13 59	51.4	10 50	13 11	51.3	10 12	12 23	51.1	9 35	11 36	51.0	8 57	10 49	50.8	8 19	10 02	50.7	220	320
41	139	11 42	13 47	50.4	11 04	13 00	50.3	10 25	12 13	50.1	9 47	11 26	50.0	9 08	10 39	49.9	8 29	9 53	49.7	221	319
42	138	11 56	13 34	49.4	11 17	12 48	49.3	10 38	12 02	49.1	9 58	11 16	49.0	9 19	10 30	48.9	8 39	9 44	48.7	222	318
43	137	12 10	13 22	48.4	11 30	12 36	48.3	10 50	11 51	48.1	10 10	11 05	48.0	9 30	10 20	47.9	8 49	9 35	47.7	223	317
44	136	12 24	13 09	47.4	11 43	12 24	47.3	11 02	11 39	47.1	10 21	10 55	47.0	9 40	10 10	46.9	8 59	9 26	46.7	224	316
45	135	12 37	12 56	46.4	11 56	12 12	46.3	11 14	11 28	46.1	10 33	10 44	46.0	9 51	10 00	45.9	9 09	9 16	45.7	225	315

Lat.	LHA/F	72° A/H	72° B/P	72° Z1/Z2	73° A/H	73° B/P	73° Z1/Z2	74° A/H	74° B/P	74° Z1/Z2	75° A/H	75° B/P	75° Z1/Z2	76° A/H	76° B/P	76° Z1/Z2	77° A/H	77° B/P	77° Z1/Z2	LHA	A
45	135	12 37	12 56	46.4	11 56	12 12	46.3	11 14	11 28	46.1	10 33	10 44	46.0	9 51	10 00	45.9	9 09	9 16	45.7	225	315
46	134	12 51	12 43	45.4	12 08	11 59	45.3	11 26	11 16	45.1	10 44	10 33	45.0	10 01	9 50	44.9	9 19	9 07	44.7	226	314
47	133	13 04	12 30	44.4	12 21	11 47	44.3	11 38	11 04	44.1	10 55	10 21	44.0	10 11	9 39	43.9	9 28	8 57	43.7	227	313
48	132	13 17	12 16	43.4	12 33	11 34	43.3	11 49	10 52	43.1	11 05	10 10	43.0	10 21	9 28	42.9	9 37	8 47	42.7	228	312
49	131	13 29	12 02	42.4	12 45	11 21	42.3	12 00	10 39	42.1	11 16	9 58	42.0	10 31	9 17	41.9	9 46	8 37	41.7	229	311
50	130	13 42	11 48	41.4	12 57	11 07	41.3	12 11	10 27	41.1	11 26	9 46	41.0	10 41	9 06	40.9	9 55	8 26	40.7	230	310
51	129	13 54	11 33	40.4	13 08	10 53	40.3	12 22	10 14	40.1	11 36	9 34	40.0	10 50	8 55	39.8	10 04	8 16	39.7	231	309
52	128	14 06	11 19	39.4	13 19	10 40	39.2	12 33	10 01	39.1	11 46	9 22	39.0	10 59	8 44	38.8	10 13	8 05	38.7	232	308
53	127	14 17	11 04	38.4	13 30	10 26	38.2	12 43	9 47	38.1	11 56	9 10	38.0	11 08	8 32	37.8	10 21	7 55	37.7	233	307
54	126	14 29	10 49	37.4	13 41	10 11	37.2	12 53	9 34	37.1	12 05	8 57	36.9	11 17	8 20	36.8	10 29	7 44	36.7	234	306
55	125	14 40	10 33	36.4	13 51	9 57	36.2	13 03	9 20	36.1	12 14	8 44	35.9	11 26	8 08	35.8	10 37	7 33	35.7	235	305
56	124	14 51	10 18	35.3	14 02	9 42	35.2	13 13	9 07	35.1	12 23	8 31	34.9	11 34	7 56	34.8	10 45	7 21	34.7	236	304
57	123	15 01	10 02	34.3	14 12	9 27	34.2	13 22	8 53	34.0	12 32	8 18	33.9	11 42	7 44	33.8	10 52	7 10	33.7	237	303
58	122	15 12	9 46	33.3	14 21	9 12	33.2	13 31	8 38	33.0	12 41	8 05	32.9	11 50	7 32	32.8	11 00	6 59	32.7	238	302
59	121	15 22	9 30	32.3	14 31	8 57	32.1	13 40	8 24	32.0	12 49	7 51	31.9	11 58	7 19	31.8	11 07	6 47	31.7	239	301
60	120	15 31	9 14	31.3	14 40	8 41	31.1	13 49	8 10	31.0	12 57	7 38	30.9	12 06	7 06	30.8	11 14	6 35	30.6	240	300
61	119	15 41	8 57	30.2	14 49	8 26	30.1	13 57	7 55	30.0	13 05	7 24	29.8	12 13	6 54	29.7	11 21	6 23	29.6	241	299
62	118	15 50	8 40	29.2	14 58	8 10	29.1	14 05	7 40	28.9	13 13	7 10	28.8	12 20	6 41	28.7	11 27	6 11	28.6	242	298
63	117	15 59	8 23	28.2	15 06	7 54	28.0	14 13	7 25	27.9	13 20	6 56	27.8	12 27	6 27	27.7	11 34	5 59	27.6	243	297
64	116	16 08	8 06	27.2	15 14	7 38	27.0	14 21	7 10	26.9	13 28	6 42	26.8	12 34	6 14	26.7	11 40	5 47	26.6	244	296
65	115	16 16	7 49	26.1	15 22	7 22	26.0	14 28	6 55	25.9	13 34	6 28	25.8	12 40	6 01	25.7	11 46	5 34	25.6	245	295
66	114	16 24	7 32	25.1	15 29	7 05	25.0	14 35	6 39	24.9	13 41	6 13	24.7	12 46	5 47	24.6	11 52	5 22	24.6	246	294
67	113	16 32	7 14	24.1	15 37	6 49	23.9	14 42	6 24	23.8	13 47	5 59	23.7	12 52	5 34	23.6	11 57	5 09	23.5	247	293
68	112	16 39	6 56	23.0	15 44	6 32	22.9	14 48	6 08	22.8	13 53	5 44	22.7	12 58	5 20	22.6	12 02	4 57	22.5	248	292
69	111	16 46	6 39	22.0	15 50	6 15	21.9	14 55	5 52	21.8	13 59	5 29	21.7	13 03	5 06	21.6	12 07	4 44	21.5	249	291
70	110	16 53	6 20	20.9	15 57	5 58	20.8	15 01	5 36	20.7	14 05	5 14	20.6	13 08	4 52	20.6	12 12	4 31	20.5	250	290
71	109	16 59	6 02	19.9	16 03	5 41	19.8	15 06	5 20	19.7	14 10	4 59	19.6	13 13	4 38	19.5	12 17	4 18	19.5	251	289
72	108	17 05	5 44	18.9	16 09	5 24	18.8	15 12	5 04	18.7	14 15	4 44	18.6	13 18	4 24	18.5	12 21	4 05	18.4	252	288
73	107	17 11	5 26	17.8	16 14	5 06	17.7	15 17	4 48	17.6	14 20	4 29	17.6	13 23	4 10	17.5	12 25	3 52	17.4	253	287
74	106	17 17	5 07	16.8	16 19	4 49	16.7	15 22	4 31	16.6	14 24	4 13	16.5	13 27	3 56	16.5	12 29	3 38	16.4	254	286
75	105	17 22	4 48	15.7	16 24	4 31	15.7	15 26	4 15	15.6	14 29	3 58	15.5	13 31	3 42	15.4	12 33	3 25	15.4	255	285
76	104	17 27	4 30	14.7	16 29	4 14	14.6	15 31	3 58	14.5	14 33	3 43	14.5	13 35	3 27	14.4	12 36	3 12	14.4	256	284
77	103	17 31	4 11	13.6	16 33	3 56	13.6	15 35	3 41	13.5	14 36	3 27	13.4	13 38	3 13	13.4	12 40	2 58	13.3	257	283
78	102	17 36	3 52	12.6	16 37	3 38	12.5	15 38	3 25	12.5	14 40	3 11	12.4	13 41	2 58	12.4	12 43	2 45	12.3	258	282
79	101	17 39	3 33	11.6	16 41	3 20	11.5	15 42	3 08	11.4	14 43	2 56	11.4	13 44	2 43	11.3	12 45	2 31	11.3	259	281
80	100	17 43	3 14	10.5	16 44	3 02	10.4	15 45	2 51	10.4	14 46	2 40	10.3	13 47	2 29	10.3	12 48	2 18	10.3	260	280
81	99	17 46	2 55	9.5	16 47	2 44	9.4	15 48	2 34	9.4	14 49	2 24	9.3	13 49	2 14	9.3	12 50	2 04	9.2	261	279
82	98	17 49	2 35	8.4	16 50	2 26	8.4	15 50	2 17	8.3	14 51	2 08	8.3	13 52	1 59	8.2	12 52	1 50	8.2	262	278
83	97	17 52	2 16	7.4	16 52	2 08	7.3	15 53	2 00	7.3	14 53	1 52	7.2	13 54	1 44	7.2	12 54	1 37	7.2	263	277
84	96	17 54	1 57	6.3	16 54	1 50	6.3	15 55	1 43	6.2	14 55	1 36	6.2	13 55	1 30	6.2	12 56	1 23	6.2	264	276
85	95	17 56	1 37	5.3	16 56	1 32	5.2	15 56	1 26	5.2	14 56	1 20	5.2	13 57	1 15	5.1	12 57	1 09	5.1	265	275
86	94	17 57	1 18	4.2	16 57	1 13	4.2	15 58	1 09	4.2	14 58	1 04	4.1	13 58	1 00	4.1	12 58	0 55	4.1	266	274
87	93	17 58	0 58	3.2	16 59	0 55	3.1	15 59	0 52	3.1	14 59	0 48	3.1	13 59	0 45	3.1	12 59	0 42	3.1	267	273
88	92	17 59	0 39	2.1	16 59	0 37	2.1	15 59	0 34	2.1	14 59	0 32	2.1	13 59	0 30	2.1	13 00	0 28	2.1	268	272
89	91	18 00	0 19	1.1	17 00	0 18	1.0	16 00	0 17	1.0	15 00	0 16	1.0	14 00	0 15	1.0	13 00	0 14	1.0	269	271
90	90	18 00	0 00	0.0	17 00	0 00	0.0	16 00	0 00	0.0	15 00	0 00	0.0	14 00	0 00	0.0	13 00	0 00	0.0	270	270

N. Lat.: for LHA > 180°... $Z_n = Z$
for LHA < 180°... $Z_n = 360° - Z$

S. Lat.: for LHA > 180°... $Z_n = 180° - Z$
for LHA < 180°... $Z_n = 180° + Z$

SIGHT REDUCTION TABLE

B: (−) for 90° < LHA < 270°
Dec: (−) for Lat. contrary name

Z₁: same sign as B
Z₂: (−) for F > 90°

Lat./A		78°			79°			80°			81°			82°			83°			Lat./A	
LHA/F		A/H	B/P	Z_1/Z_2	A/H	B/P	Z_1/Z_2	A/H	B/P	Z_1/Z_2	A/H	B/P	Z_1/Z_2	A/H	B/P	Z_1/Z_2	A/H	B/P	Z_1/Z_2	LHA	
0	180	0 00	12 00	90.0	0 00	11 00	90.0	0 00	10 00	90.0	0 00	9 00	90.0	0 00	8 00	90.0	0 00	7 00	90.0	180	360
1	179	0 12	12 00	89.0	0 11	11 00	89.0	0 10	10 00	89.0	0 09	9 00	89.0	0 08	8 00	89.0	0 07	7 00	89.0	181	359
2	178	0 25	12 00	88.0	0 23	11 00	88.0	0 21	10 00	88.0	0 19	9 00	88.0	0 17	8 00	88.0	0 15	7 00	88.0	182	358
3	177	0 37	11 59	87.1	0 34	10 59	87.1	0 31	9 59	87.0	0 28	8 59	87.0	0 25	7 59	87.0	0 22	6 59	87.0	183	357
4	176	0 50	11 58	86.1	0 46	10 58	86.1	0 42	9 59	86.1	0 38	8 59	86.0	0 33	7 58	86.0	0 29	6 59	86.0	184	356
5	175	1 02	11 57	85.1	0 57	10 58	85.1	0 52	9 58	85.1	0 47	8 58	85.1	0 42	7 58	85.0	0 37	6 58	85.0	185	355
6	174	1 15	11 56	84.1	1 09	10 56	84.1	1 02	9 57	84.1	0 56	8 57	84.1	0 50	7 57	84.1	0 44	6 58	84.0	186	354
7	173	1 27	11 55	83.2	1 20	10 55	83.1	1 13	9 56	83.1	1 06	8 56	83.1	0 58	7 56	83.1	0 51	6 57	83.1	187	353
8	172	1 39	11 53	82.2	1 31	10 54	82.1	1 23	9 54	82.1	1 15	8 55	82.1	1 07	7 55	82.1	0 58	6 56	82.1	188	352
9	171	1 52	11 51	81.2	1 43	10 52	81.2	1 33	9 53	81.1	1 24	8 53	81.1	1 15	7 54	81.1	1 06	6 55	81.1	189	351
10	170	2 04	11 49	80.2	1 54	10 50	80.2	1 44	9 51	80.1	1 33	8 52	80.1	1 23	7 53	80.1	1 13	6 54	80.1	190	350
11	169	2 16	11 47	79.2	2 05	10 48	79.2	1 54	9 49	79.2	1 43	8 50	79.1	1 31	7 51	79.1	1 20	6 52	79.1	191	349
12	168	2 29	11 45	78.3	2 16	10 46	78.2	2 04	9 47	78.2	1 52	8 48	78.1	1 39	7 50	78.1	1 27	6 51	78.1	192	348
13	167	2 41	11 42	77.3	2 28	10 43	77.2	2 14	9 45	77.2	2 01	8 46	77.2	1 48	7 48	77.1	1 34	6 49	77.1	193	347
14	166	2 53	11 39	76.3	2 39	10 41	76.2	2 24	9 43	76.2	2 10	8 44	76.1	1 56	7 46	76.1	1 41	6 48	76.1	194	346
15	165	3 05	11 36	75.3	2 50	10 38	75.3	2 34	9 40	75.2	2 19	8 42	75.2	2 04	7 44	75.2	1 48	6 46	75.1	195	345
16	164	3 17	11 33	74.3	3 01	10 35	74.3	2 45	9 37	74.2	2 28	8 39	74.2	2 12	7 42	74.1	1 56	6 44	74.1	196	344
17	163	3 29	11 29	73.4	3 12	10 32	73.3	2 55	9 34	73.2	2 37	8 37	73.2	2 20	7 39	73.1	2 03	6 42	73.1	197	343
18	162	3 41	11 26	72.4	3 23	10 28	72.3	3 05	9 31	72.3	2 46	8 34	72.2	2 28	7 37	72.2	2 09	6 40	72.1	198	342
19	161	3 53	11 22	71.4	3 34	10 25	71.3	3 14	9 28	71.3	2 55	8 31	71.2	2 36	7 34	71.2	2 16	6 37	71.1	199	341
20	160	4 05	11 18	70.4	3 45	10 21	70.3	3 24	9 24	70.3	3 04	8 28	70.2	2 44	7 31	70.2	2 23	6 35	70.1	200	340
21	159	4 16	11 13	69.4	3 55	10 17	69.4	3 34	9 21	69.3	3 13	8 25	69.2	2 52	7 28	69.2	2 30	6 32	69.1	201	339
22	158	4 28	11 09	68.4	4 06	10 13	68.4	3 44	9 17	68.3	3 22	8 21	68.2	2 59	7 25	68.2	2 37	6 30	68.1	202	338
23	157	4 40	11 04	67.5	4 17	10 09	67.4	3 53	9 13	67.3	3 30	8 18	67.3	3 07	7 22	67.2	2 44	6 27	67.2	203	337
24	156	4 51	10 59	66.5	4 27	10 04	66.4	4 03	9 09	66.3	3 39	8 14	66.3	3 15	7 19	66.2	2 50	6 24	66.2	204	336
25	155	5 02	10 54	65.5	4 38	9 59	65.4	4 13	9 05	65.4	3 47	8 10	65.3	3 22	7 16	65.2	2 57	6 21	65.2	205	335
26	154	5 14	10 49	64.5	4 48	9 55	64.5	4 22	9 00	64.4	3 56	8 06	64.3	3 30	7 12	64.2	3 04	6 18	64.2	206	334
27	153	5 25	10 43	63.5	4 58	9 50	63.5	4 31	8 56	63.4	4 04	8 02	63.3	3 37	7 08	63.2	3 10	6 15	63.2	207	333
28	152	5 36	10 38	62.5	5 08	9 44	62.5	4 41	8 51	62.4	4 13	7 58	62.3	3 45	7 04	62.2	3 17	6 11	62.2	208	332
29	151	5 47	10 32	61.5	5 18	9 39	61.5	4 50	8 46	61.4	4 21	7 53	61.3	3 52	7 00	61.2	3 23	6 08	61.2	209	331
30	150	5 58	10 26	60.5	5 28	9 33	60.5	4 59	8 41	60.4	4 29	7 49	60.3	3 59	6 56	60.2	3 30	6 04	60.2	210	330
31	149	6 09	10 20	59.6	5 38	9 28	59.5	5 08	8 36	59.4	4 37	7 44	59.3	4 07	6 52	59.2	3 36	6 00	59.2	211	329
32	148	6 20	10 13	58.6	5 48	9 22	58.5	5 17	8 30	58.4	4 45	7 39	58.3	4 14	6 48	58.3	3 42	5 57	58.2	212	328
33	147	6 31	10 06	57.6	5 58	9 16	57.6	5 26	8 25	57.4	4 53	7 34	57.3	4 21	6 43	57.3	3 48	5 53	57.2	213	327
34	146	6 41	10 00	56.6	6 08	9 09	56.6	5 34	8 19	56.4	5 01	7 29	56.3	4 28	6 39	56.3	3 54	5 49	56.2	214	326
35	145	6 51	9 53	55.6	6 17	9 03	55.5	5 43	8 13	55.4	5 09	7 24	55.3	4 35	6 34	55.3	4 00	5 45	55.2	215	325
36	144	7 01	9 45	54.6	6 26	8 56	54.6	5 51	8 07	54.4	5 17	7 18	54.4	4 42	6 29	54.3	4 06	5 40	54.2	216	324
37	143	7 11	9 38	53.6	6 36	8 49	53.6	6 00	8 01	53.5	5 24	7 13	53.3	4 48	6 24	53.3	4 12	5 36	53.2	217	323
38	142	7 21	9 31	52.6	6 45	8 43	52.6	6 08	7 55	52.5	5 32	7 07	52.3	4 55	6 19	52.3	4 18	5 32	52.2	218	322
39	141	7 31	9 23	51.6	6 54	8 35	51.6	6 16	7 48	51.5	5 39	7 01	51.3	5 01	6 14	51.3	4 24	5 27	51.2	219	321
40	140	7 41	9 15	50.6	7 03	8 28	50.6	6 25	7 42	50.4	5 46	6 55	50.3	5 08	6 09	50.3	4 30	5 22	50.2	220	320
41	139	7 50	9 07	49.6	7 11	8 21	49.6	6 32	7 35	49.4	5 53	6 49	49.4	5 14	6 03	49.3	4 35	5 18	49.2	221	319
42	138	8 00	8 59	48.6	7 20	8 13	48.5	6 40	7 28	48.4	6 01	6 43	48.4	5 21	5 58	48.3	4 41	5 13	48.2	222	318
43	137	8 09	8 50	47.6	7 29	8 05	47.6	6 48	7 21	47.5	6 07	6 36	47.4	5 27	5 52	47.3	4 46	5 08	47.2	223	317
44	136	8 18	8 42	46.6	7 37	7 58	46.5	6 56	7 14	46.5	6 14	6 30	46.4	5 33	5 46	46.3	4 51	5 03	46.2	224	316
45	135	8 27	8 33	45.6	7 45	7 50	45.5	7 03	7 06	45.5	6 21	6 23	45.4	5 39	5 41	45.3	4 58	4 58	45.2	225	315

LHA	F	78° A/H	78° B/P	78° Z_1/Z_2	79° A/H	79° B/P	79° Z_1/Z_2	80° A/H	80° B/P	80° Z_1/Z_2	81° A/H	81° B/P	81° Z_1/Z_2	82° A/H	82° B/P	82° Z_1/Z_2	83° A/H	83° B/P	83° Z_1/Z_2	LHA	A
45	135	8 27	8 33	45.6	7 45	7 50	45.5	7 03	7 06	45.4	6 21	6 23	45.4	5 39	5 41	45.3	4 57	4 58	45.2	225	315
46	134	8 36	8 24	44.6	7 53	7 41	44.5	7 11	6 59	44.4	6 28	6 17	44.4	5 45	5 35	44.3	5 02	4 53	44.2	226	314
47	133	8 45	8 15	43.6	8 01	7 33	43.5	7 18	6 51	43.4	6 34	6 10	43.4	5 51	5 29	43.3	5 07	4 47	43.2	227	313
48	132	8 53	8 06	42.6	8 09	7 25	42.5	7 25	6 44	42.4	6 41	6 03	42.4	5 56	5 22	42.3	5 12	4 42	42.2	228	312
49	131	9 02	7 56	41.6	8 17	7 16	41.5	7 32	6 36	41.4	6 47	5 56	41.4	6 02	5 16	41.3	5 17	4 36	41.2	229	311
50	130	9 10	7 47	40.6	8 24	7 07	40.5	7 39	6 28	40.4	6 53	5 49	40.3	6 07	5 10	40.3	5 21	4 31	40.2	230	310
51	129	9 18	7 37	39.6	8 32	6 58	39.5	7 45	6 20	39.4	6 59	5 42	39.3	6 13	5 03	39.3	5 26	4 25	39.2	231	309
52	128	9 26	7 27	38.6	8 39	6 49	38.5	7 52	6 12	38.4	7 05	5 34	38.3	6 18	4 57	38.3	5 31	4 19	38.2	232	308
53	127	9 33	7 17	37.6	8 46	6 40	37.5	7 58	6 03	37.4	7 11	5 27	37.3	6 23	4 50	37.3	5 35	4 14	37.2	233	307
54	126	9 41	7 07	36.6	8 53	6 31	36.5	8 05	5 55	36.4	7 16	5 19	36.3	6 28	4 43	36.3	5 39	4 08	36.2	234	306
55	125	9 48	6 57	35.6	9 00	6 22	35.5	8 11	5 47	35.4	7 22	5 11	35.3	6 33	4 37	35.3	5 44	4 02	35.2	235	305
56	124	9 56	6 47	34.6	9 06	6 12	34.5	8 17	5 38	34.4	7 27	5 04	34.3	6 38	4 30	34.3	5 48	3 56	34.2	236	304
57	123	10 03	6 36	33.6	9 13	6 03	33.5	8 22	5 29	33.4	7 32	4 56	33.3	6 42	4 23	33.3	5 52	3 50	33.2	237	303
58	122	10 09	6 26	32.6	9 19	5 53	32.5	8 28	5 20	32.4	7 37	4 48	32.3	6 47	4 16	32.3	5 56	3 43	32.2	238	302
59	121	10 16	6 15	31.6	9 25	5 43	31.5	8 34	5 11	31.4	7 42	4 40	31.3	6 51	4 08	31.3	6 00	3 37	31.2	239	301
60	120	10 22	6 04	30.6	9 31	5 33	30.5	8 39	5 02	30.4	7 47	4 32	30.3	6 55	4 01	30.2	6 04	3 31	30.2	240	300
61	119	10 29	5 53	29.5	9 36	5 23	29.5	8 44	4 53	29.4	7 52	4 23	29.3	6 59	3 54	29.2	6 07	3 24	29.2	241	299
62	118	10 35	5 42	28.5	9 42	5 13	28.4	8 49	4 44	28.4	7 56	4 15	28.3	7 04	3 46	28.2	6 11	3 18	28.2	242	298
63	117	10 41	5 31	27.5	9 47	5 03	27.4	8 54	4 35	27.4	8 01	4 07	27.3	7 07	3 39	27.2	6 14	3 11	27.2	243	297
64	116	10 46	5 19	26.5	9 52	4 52	26.4	8 59	4 25	26.3	8 05	3 58	26.3	7 11	3 32	26.2	6 17	3 05	26.2	244	296
65	115	10 52	5 08	25.5	9 57	4 42	25.4	9 03	4 16	25.3	8 09	3 50	25.3	7 15	3 24	25.2	6 20	2 58	25.2	245	295
66	114	10 57	4 56	24.5	10 02	4 31	24.4	9 08	4 06	24.3	8 13	3 41	24.3	7 18	3 16	24.2	6 24	2 52	24.2	246	294
67	113	11 02	4 45	23.5	10 07	4 21	23.4	9 12	3 56	23.3	8 17	3 32	23.3	7 22	3 09	23.2	6 26	2 45	23.2	247	293
68	112	11 07	4 33	22.4	10 11	4 10	22.4	9 16	3 47	22.3	8 20	3 24	22.2	7 25	3 01	22.2	6 29	2 38	22.1	248	292
69	111	11 12	4 21	21.4	10 16	3 59	21.4	9 20	3 37	21.3	8 24	3 15	21.2	7 28	2 53	21.2	6 32	2 31	21.1	249	291
70	110	11 16	4 09	20.4	10 20	3 48	20.3	9 24	3 27	20.3	8 27	3 06	20.2	7 31	2 45	20.2	6 35	2 24	20.1	250	290
71	109	11 20	3 58	19.4	10 24	3 37	19.3	9 27	3 17	19.3	8 30	2 57	19.2	7 34	2 37	19.2	6 37	2 17	19.1	251	289
72	108	11 24	3 45	18.4	10 27	3 26	18.3	9 30	3 07	18.3	8 33	2 48	18.2	7 36	2 29	18.2	6 39	2 10	18.1	252	288
73	107	11 28	3 33	17.4	10 31	3 15	17.3	9 34	2 57	17.2	8 36	2 39	17.2	7 39	2 21	17.2	6 42	2 03	17.1	253	287
74	106	11 32	3 21	16.3	10 34	3 04	16.3	9 37	2 47	16.2	8 39	2 30	16.2	7 41	2 13	16.1	6 44	1 56	16.1	254	286
75	105	11 35	3 09	15.3	10 37	2 53	15.3	9 39	2 37	15.2	8 41	2 21	15.2	7 44	2 05	15.2	6 46	1 49	15.1	255	285
76	104	11 38	2 57	14.3	10 40	2 42	14.3	9 42	2 27	14.2	8 44	2 12	14.2	7 46	1 57	14.1	6 47	1 42	14.1	256	284
77	103	11 41	2 44	13.3	10 43	2 30	13.2	9 44	2 16	13.2	8 46	2 02	13.2	7 48	1 49	13.1	6 49	1 35	13.1	257	283
78	102	11 44	2 32	12.3	10 45	2 19	12.2	9 47	2 06	12.2	8 48	1 53	12.1	7 49	1 40	12.1	6 51	1 28	12.1	258	282
79	101	11 47	2 19	11.2	10 48	2 07	11.2	9 49	1 56	11.2	8 50	1 44	11.1	7 51	1 32	11.1	6 52	1 21	11.1	259	281
80	100	11 49	2 07	10.2	10 50	1 56	10.2	9 51	1 45	10.2	8 52	1 35	10.1	7 53	1 24	10.1	6 54	1 13	10.1	260	280
81	99	11 51	1 54	9.2	10 52	1 45	9.2	9 53	1 35	9.1	8 53	1 25	9.1	7 54	1 16	9.1	6 55	1 06	9.1	261	279
82	98	11 53	1 42	8.2	10 53	1 33	8.1	9 54	1 24	8.1	8 55	1 16	8.1	7 55	1 07	8.1	6 56	0 59	8.1	262	278
83	97	11 55	1 29	7.2	10 55	1 21	7.1	9 55	1 14	7.1	8 56	1 06	7.1	7 56	0 59	7.1	6 57	0 51	7.1	263	277
84	96	11 56	1 16	6.1	10 56	1 10	6.1	9 57	1 03	6.1	8 57	0 57	6.1	7 57	0 50	6.1	6 58	0 44	6.0	264	276
85	95	11 57	1 04	5.1	10 57	0 58	5.1	9 58	0 53	5.1	8 58	0 47	5.1	7 58	0 42	5.0	6 58	0 37	5.0	265	275
86	94	11 58	0 51	4.1	10 58	0 47	4.1	9 59	0 42	4.1	8 59	0 38	4.0	7 59	0 34	4.0	6 59	0 29	4.0	266	274
87	93	11 59	0 38	3.1	10 59	0 35	3.1	9 59	0 32	3.0	8 59	0 28	3.0	7 59	0 25	3.0	6 59	0 22	3.0	267	273
88	92	12 00	0 26	2.0	11 00	0 23	2.0	10 00	0 21	2.0	9 00	0 19	2.0	8 00	0 17	2.0	7 00	0 15	2.0	268	272
89	91	12 00	0 13	1.0	11 00	0 12	1.0	10 00	0 11	1.0	9 00	0 10	1.0	8 00	0 08	1.0	7 00	0 07	1.0	269	271
90	90	12 00	0 00	0.0	11 00	0 00	0.0	10 00	0 00	0.0	9 00	0 00	0.0	8 00	0 00	0.0	7 00	0 00	0.0	270	270

N. Lat.: for LHA > 180°..... $Z_n = Z$
for LHA < 180°..... $Z_n = 360° - Z$

S. Lat.: for LHA > 180°..... $Z_n = 180° - Z$
for LHA < 180°..... $Z_n = 180° + Z$

SIGHT REDUCTION TABLE

B: (–) for 90°< LHA < 270°
Dec: (–) for Lat. contrary name

Z₁: same sign as B
Z₂: (–) for F > 90°

Lat./A	LHA/F	84° A/H	84° B/P	84° Z₁/Z₂	85° A/H	85° B/P	85° Z₁/Z₂	86° A/H	86° B/P	86° Z₁/Z₂	87° A/H	87° B/P	87° Z₁/Z₂	88° A/H	88° B/P	88° Z₁/Z₂	89° A/H	89° B/P	89° Z₁/Z₂	Lat./A	LHA
0	180	0 00	6 00	90.0	0 00	5 00	90.0	0 00	4 00	90.0	0 00	3 00	90.0	0 00	2 00	90.0	0 00	1 00	90.0	180	360
1	179	0 06	6 00	89.0	0 05	5 00	89.0	0 04	4 00	89.0	0 03	3 00	89.0	0 02	2 00	89.0	0 01	1 00	89.0	181	359
2	178	0 13	6 00	88.0	0 10	5 00	88.0	0 08	4 00	88.0	0 06	3 00	88.0	0 04	2 00	88.0	0 02	1 00	88.0	182	358
3	177	0 19	6 00	87.0	0 16	5 00	87.0	0 13	4 00	87.0	0 09	3 00	87.0	0 06	2 00	87.0	0 03	1 00	87.0	183	357
4	176	0 25	5 59	86.0	0 21	4 59	86.0	0 17	3 59	86.0	0 13	3 00	86.0	0 08	2 00	86.0	0 04	1 00	86.0	184	356
5	175	0 31	5 59	85.0	0 26	4 59	85.0	0 21	3 59	85.0	0 16	2 59	85.0	0 10	2 00	85.0	0 05	1 00	85.0	185	355
6	174	0 38	5 58	84.0	0 31	4 58	84.0	0 25	3 59	84.0	0 19	2 59	84.0	0 13	1 59	84.0	0 06	1 00	84.0	186	354
7	173	0 44	5 57	83.0	0 37	4 58	83.0	0 29	3 58	83.0	0 22	2 59	83.0	0 15	1 59	83.0	0 07	1 00	83.0	187	353
8	172	0 50	5 57	82.0	0 42	4 57	82.0	0 33	3 58	82.0	0 25	2 58	82.0	0 17	1 59	82.0	0 08	0 59	82.0	188	352
9	171	0 56	5 56	81.0	0 47	4 56	81.0	0 38	3 57	81.0	0 28	2 58	81.0	0 19	1 58	81.0	0 09	0 59	81.0	189	351
10	170	1 02	5 55	80.1	0 52	4 55	80.0	0 42	3 56	80.0	0 31	2 57	80.0	0 21	1 58	80.0	0 10	0 59	80.0	190	350
11	169	1 09	5 53	79.1	0 57	4 55	79.1	0 46	3 56	79.0	0 34	2 57	79.0	0 23	1 58	79.0	0 11	0 59	79.0	191	349
12	168	1 15	5 52	78.1	1 02	4 53	78.0	0 50	3 55	78.0	0 37	2 56	78.0	0 25	1 57	78.0	0 12	0 59	78.0	192	348
13	167	1 21	5 51	77.1	1 07	4 52	77.0	0 54	3 54	77.0	0 40	2 55	77.0	0 27	1 57	77.0	0 13	0 58	77.0	193	347
14	166	1 27	5 49	76.1	1 12	4 51	76.1	0 58	3 53	76.1	0 44	2 55	76.0	0 29	1 56	76.0	0 15	0 58	76.0	194	346
15	165	1 33	5 48	75.1	1 18	4 50	75.1	1 02	3 52	75.1	0 47	2 54	75.0	0 31	1 56	75.0	0 16	0 58	75.0	195	345
16	164	1 39	5 46	74.1	1 23	4 48	74.1	1 06	3 51	74.1	0 50	2 53	74.0	0 33	1 55	74.0	0 16	0 58	74.0	196	344
17	163	1 45	5 44	73.1	1 28	4 47	73.1	1 10	3 50	73.1	0 53	2 52	73.0	0 35	1 55	73.0	0 17	0 57	73.0	197	343
18	162	1 51	5 43	72.1	1 33	4 45	72.1	1 14	3 48	72.0	0 56	2 51	72.0	0 37	1 54	72.0	0 19	0 57	72.0	198	342
19	161	1 57	5 41	71.1	1 38	4 44	71.1	1 18	3 47	71.1	0 59	2 50	71.0	0 39	1 53	71.0	0 20	0 57	71.0	199	341
20	160	2 03	5 38	70.1	1 42	4 42	70.1	1 22	3 46	70.1	1 02	2 49	70.0	0 41	1 53	70.0	0 21	0 56	70.0	200	340
21	159	2 09	5 36	69.1	1 47	4 40	69.1	1 26	3 44	69.1	1 04	2 48	69.0	0 43	1 52	69.0	0 22	0 56	69.0	201	339
22	158	2 15	5 34	68.1	1 52	4 38	68.1	1 30	3 43	68.1	1 07	2 47	68.0	0 45	1 51	68.0	0 23	0 56	68.0	202	338
23	157	2 20	5 32	67.1	1 57	4 36	67.1	1 34	3 41	67.1	1 10	2 46	67.0	0 47	1 50	67.0	0 23	0 55	67.0	203	337
24	156	2 26	5 29	66.1	2 02	4 34	66.1	1 38	3 39	66.1	1 13	2 44	66.0	0 49	1 50	66.0	0 24	0 55	66.0	204	336
25	155	2 32	5 26	65.1	2 07	4 32	65.1	1 41	3 38	65.1	1 16	2 43	65.0	0 51	1 49	65.0	0 25	0 54	65.0	205	335
26	154	2 38	5 24	64.1	2 11	4 30	64.1	1 45	3 36	64.1	1 19	2 42	64.0	0 53	1 48	64.0	0 26	0 54	64.0	206	334
27	153	2 43	5 21	63.1	2 16	4 27	63.1	1 49	3 34	63.1	1 22	2 40	63.0	0 54	1 47	63.0	0 27	0 53	63.0	207	333
28	152	2 49	5 18	62.1	2 21	4 25	62.1	1 53	3 32	62.1	1 24	2 39	62.0	0 56	1 46	62.0	0 28	0 53	62.0	208	332
29	151	2 54	5 15	61.1	2 25	4 23	61.1	1 56	3 30	61.1	1 27	2 37	61.0	0 58	1 45	61.0	0 29	0 52	61.0	209	331
30	150	3 00	5 12	60.1	2 30	4 20	60.1	2 00	3 28	60.1	1 30	2 36	60.1	1 00	1 44	60.0	0 30	0 52	60.0	210	330
31	149	3 05	5 09	59.1	2 34	4 17	59.1	2 04	3 26	59.1	1 33	2 34	59.1	1 02	1 43	59.0	0 31	0 51	59.0	211	329
32	148	3 11	5 06	58.1	2 39	4 15	58.1	2 07	3 24	58.1	1 35	2 33	58.1	1 04	1 42	58.0	0 32	0 51	58.0	212	328
33	147	3 16	5 02	57.1	2 43	4 12	57.1	2 11	3 21	57.1	1 38	2 31	57.1	1 05	1 41	57.0	0 33	0 50	57.0	213	327
34	146	3 21	4 59	56.1	2 48	4 09	56.1	2 14	3 19	56.1	1 41	2 29	56.1	1 07	1 39	56.0	0 34	0 50	56.0	214	326
35	145	3 26	4 55	55.1	2 52	4 06	55.1	2 18	3 17	55.1	1 43	2 27	55.1	1 09	1 38	55.0	0 35	0 49	55.0	215	325
36	144	3 31	4 52	54.1	2 56	4 03	54.1	2 21	3 14	54.1	1 46	2 26	54.1	1 11	1 37	54.0	0 36	0 48	54.0	216	324
37	143	3 36	4 48	53.1	3 00	4 00	53.1	2 24	3 12	53.1	1 48	2 24	53.1	1 12	1 36	53.0	0 37	0 48	53.0	217	323
38	142	3 41	4 44	52.2	3 05	3 57	52.1	2 28	3 09	52.1	1 51	2 22	52.1	1 14	1 35	52.0	0 38	0 47	52.0	218	322
39	141	3 46	4 40	51.2	3 09	3 53	51.1	2 31	3 07	51.1	1 53	2 20	51.1	1 16	1 33	51.0	0 39	0 47	51.0	219	321
40	140	3 51	4 36	50.2	3 13	3 50	50.1	2 34	3 04	50.1	1 56	2 18	50.1	1 17	1 32	50.0	0 39	0 45	50.0	220	320
41	139	3 56	4 32	49.2	3 17	3 47	49.1	2 37	3 01	49.1	1 58	2 16	49.1	1 19	1 31	49.0	0 40	0 45	49.0	221	319
42	138	4 01	4 28	48.2	3 21	3 43	48.1	2 41	2 58	48.1	2 00	2 14	48.1	1 20	1 29	48.0	0 40	0 45	48.0	222	318
43	137	4 05	4 24	47.2	3 24	3 40	47.1	2 44	2 56	47.1	2 03	2 12	47.1	1 22	1 28	47.0	0 41	0 44	47.0	223	317
44	136	4 10	4 19	46.2	3 28	3 36	46.1	2 47	2 53	46.1	2 05	2 10	46.1	1 23	1 26	46.0	0 42	0 43	46.0	224	316
45	135	4 14	4 15	45.2	3 32	3 32	45.1	2 50	2 50	45.1	2 07	2 07	45.1	1 25	1 25	45.0	0 42	0 42	45.0	225	315

LHA/F		84° A/H	84° B/P	84° Z₁/Z₂	85° A/H	85° B/P	85° Z₁/Z₂	86° A/H	86° B/P	86° Z₁/Z₂	87° A/H	87° B/P	87° Z₁/Z₂	88° A/H	88° B/P	88° Z₁/Z₂	89° A/H	89° B/P	89° Z₁/Z₂	LHA	
45	135	4 14	4 15	45.2	3 32	3 32	45.1	2 50	2 50	45.1	2 07	2 07	45.0	1 25	1 25	45.0	0 42	0 42	45.0	225	315
46	134	4 19	4 11	44.2	3 36	3 29	44.1	2 53	2 47	44.1	2 09	2 05	44.0	1 26	1 23	44.0	0 43	0 42	44.0	226	314
47	133	4 23	4 06	43.2	3 39	3 25	43.1	2 55	2 44	43.1	2 12	2 03	43.0	1 28	1 22	43.0	0 44	0 41	43.0	227	313
48	132	4 27	4 01	42.2	3 43	3 21	42.1	2 58	2 41	42.1	2 14	2 01	42.0	1 29	1 20	42.0	0 45	0 40	42.0	228	312
49	131	4 31	3 57	41.2	3 46	3 17	41.1	3 01	2 38	41.1	2 16	1 58	41.0	1 31	1 19	41.0	0 45	0 39	41.0	229	311
50	130	4 36	3 52	40.2	3 50	3 13	40.1	3 04	2 34	40.1	2 18	1 56	40.0	1 32	1 17	40.0	0 46	0 39	40.0	230	310
51	129	4 40	3 47	39.2	3 53	3 09	39.1	3 06	2 31	39.1	2 20	1 53	39.0	1 33	1 16	39.0	0 47	0 38	39.0	231	309
52	128	4 43	3 42	38.2	3 56	3 05	38.1	3 09	2 28	38.1	2 22	1 51	38.0	1 35	1 14	38.0	0 47	0 37	38.0	232	308
53	127	4 47	3 37	37.2	3 59	3 01	37.1	3 12	2 25	37.1	2 24	1 48	37.0	1 36	1 12	37.0	0 48	0 36	37.0	233	307
54	126	4 51	3 32	36.1	4 03	2 57	36.1	3 14	2 21	36.1	2 26	1 46	36.0	1 37	1 11	36.0	0 49	0 35	36.0	234	306
55	125	4 55	3 27	35.1	4 06	2 52	35.1	3 17	2 18	35.1	2 27	1 43	35.0	1 38	1 09	35.0	0 49	0 34	35.0	235	305
56	124	4 58	3 22	34.1	4 09	2 48	34.1	3 19	2 14	34.1	2 29	1 41	34.0	1 39	1 07	34.0	0 50	0 34	34.0	236	304
57	123	5 02	3 17	33.1	4 12	2 44	33.1	3 21	2 11	33.1	2 31	1 38	33.0	1 41	1 05	33.0	0 50	0 33	33.0	237	303
58	122	5 05	3 11	32.1	4 14	2 39	32.1	3 23	2 07	32.1	2 33	1 35	32.0	1 42	1 04	32.0	0 51	0 32	32.0	238	302
59	121	5 08	3 06	31.1	4 17	2 35	31.1	3 26	2 04	31.1	2 34	1 33	31.0	1 43	1 02	31.0	0 51	0 31	31.0	239	301
60	120	5 12	3 00	30.1	4 20	2 30	30.1	3 28	2 00	30.1	2 36	1 30	30.0	1 44	1 00	30.0	0 52	0 30	30.0	240	300
61	119	5 15	2 55	29.1	4 22	2 26	29.1	3 30	1 56	29.1	2 37	1 27	29.0	1 45	0 58	29.0	0 52	0 29	29.0	241	299
62	118	5 18	2 49	28.1	4 25	2 21	28.1	3 32	1 53	28.1	2 39	1 25	28.0	1 46	0 56	28.0	0 53	0 28	28.0	242	298
63	117	5 21	2 44	27.1	4 27	2 16	27.1	3 34	1 49	27.1	2 40	1 22	27.0	1 47	0 54	27.0	0 53	0 27	27.0	243	297
64	116	5 23	2 38	26.1	4 30	2 12	26.1	3 36	1 45	26.1	2 42	1 19	26.0	1 48	0 53	26.0	0 54	0 26	26.0	244	296
65	115	5 26	2 33	25.1	4 32	2 07	25.1	3 37	1 42	25.1	2 43	1 16	25.0	1 49	0 51	25.0	0 54	0 25	25.0	245	295
66	114	5 29	2 27	24.1	4 34	2 02	24.1	3 39	1 38	24.1	2 44	1 13	24.0	1 50	0 49	24.0	0 55	0 24	24.0	246	294
67	113	5 31	2 21	23.1	4 36	1 57	23.1	3 41	1 34	23.1	2 46	1 10	23.0	1 50	0 47	23.0	0 55	0 23	23.0	247	293
68	112	5 34	2 15	22.1	4 38	1 53	22.1	3 42	1 30	22.1	2 47	1 07	22.0	1 51	0 45	22.0	0 56	0 22	22.0	248	292
69	111	5 36	2 09	21.1	4 40	1 48	21.1	3 44	1 26	21.1	2 48	1 05	21.0	1 52	0 43	21.0	0 56	0 22	21.0	249	291
70	110	5 38	2 04	20.1	4 42	1 43	20.1	3 46	1 22	20.1	2 49	1 02	20.0	1 53	0 41	20.0	0 56	0 21	20.0	250	290
71	109	5 40	1 58	19.1	4 44	1 38	19.1	3 47	1 18	19.1	2 50	0 59	19.0	1 54	0 39	19.0	0 57	0 20	19.0	251	289
72	108	5 42	1 52	18.1	4 45	1 33	18.1	3 48	1 14	18.1	2 51	0 56	18.0	1 54	0 37	18.0	0 57	0 19	18.0	252	288
73	107	5 44	1 46	17.1	4 47	1 28	17.1	3 49	1 10	17.1	2 52	0 53	17.0	1 55	0 35	17.0	0 57	0 18	17.0	253	287
74	106	5 46	1 40	16.1	4 48	1 23	16.1	3 51	1 06	16.1	2 53	0 50	16.0	1 55	0 33	16.0	0 58	0 17	16.0	254	286
75	105	5 48	1 33	15.1	4 50	1 18	15.1	3 52	1 02	15.1	2 54	0 47	15.0	1 56	0 31	15.0	0 58	0 16	15.0	255	285
76	104	5 49	1 27	14.1	4 51	1 13	14.1	3 53	0 58	14.0	2 55	0 44	14.0	1 56	0 29	14.0	0 58	0 15	14.0	256	284
77	103	5 51	1 21	13.1	4 52	1 08	13.0	3 54	0 54	13.0	2 55	0 41	13.0	1 57	0 27	13.0	0 58	0 13	13.0	257	283
78	102	5 52	1 15	12.1	4 53	1 03	12.0	3 55	0 50	12.0	2 56	0 37	12.0	1 57	0 25	12.0	0 59	0 12	12.0	258	282
79	101	5 53	1 09	11.1	4 54	0 57	11.0	3 56	0 46	11.0	2 57	0 34	11.0	1 58	0 23	11.0	0 59	0 11	11.0	259	281
80	100	5 55	1 03	10.1	4 55	0 52	10.0	3 56	0 42	10.0	2 57	0 31	10.0	1 58	0 21	10.0	0 59	0 10	10.0	260	280
81	99	5 56	0 57	9.0	4 56	0 47	9.0	3 57	0 38	9.0	2 58	0 28	9.0	1 59	0 19	9.0	0 59	0 09	9.0	261	279
82	98	5 56	0 50	8.0	4 57	0 42	8.0	3 58	0 33	8.0	2 58	0 25	8.0	1 59	0 17	8.0	0 59	0 08	8.0	262	278
83	97	5 57	0 44	7.0	4 58	0 37	7.0	3 58	0 29	7.0	2 59	0 22	7.0	1 59	0 15	7.0	1 00	0 07	7.0	263	277
84	96	5 58	0 38	6.0	4 58	0 31	6.0	3 59	0 25	6.0	2 59	0 19	6.0	2 00	0 12	6.0	1 00	0 05	6.0	264	276
85	95	5 59	0 31	5.0	4 59	0 26	5.0	3 59	0 21	5.0	2 59	0 16	5.0	2 00	0 10	5.0	1 00	0 05	5.0	265	275
86	94	5 59	0 25	4.0	4 59	0 21	4.0	3 59	0 17	4.0	3 00	0 13	4.0	2 00	0 08	4.0	1 00	0 04	4.0	266	274
87	93	6 00	0 19	3.0	5 00	0 16	3.0	4 00	0 13	3.0	3 00	0 09	3.0	2 00	0 06	3.0	1 00	0 03	3.0	267	273
88	92	6 00	0 13	2.0	5 00	0 10	2.0	4 00	0 08	2.0	3 00	0 06	2.0	2 00	0 04	2.0	1 00	0 02	2.0	268	272
89	91	6 00	0 06	1.0	5 00	0 05	1.0	4 00	0 04	1.0	3 00	0 03	1.0	2 00	0 02	1.0	1 00	0 01	1.0	269	271
90	90	6 00	0 00	0.0	5 00	0 00	0.0	4 00	0 00	0.0	3 00	0 00	0.0	2 00	0 00	0.0	1 00	0 00	0.0	270	270

N. Lat.: for LHA > 180°... Zn = Z
for LHA < 180°... Zn = 360° − Z

S. Lat.: for LHA > 180°... Zn = 180° − Z
for LHA < 180°... Zn = 180° + Z

AUXILIARY TABLE

Top heading: **A' < 30' : (−) corr.** — **F' / A'**

Bottom heading: **F' < 90° and F' > 29' : (−) corr.** — **F' > 90° and F' < 30' : (−) corr.** — **F' / A'**

Z_2°	30'/30	29'/31	28'/32	27'/33	26'/34	25'/35	24'/36	23'/37	22'/38	21'/39	20'/40	19'/41	18'/42	17'/43	16'/44	15'/45	14'/46	13'/47	12'/48	11'/49	10'/50	9'/51	8'/52	7'/53	6'/54	5'/55	4'/56	3'/57	2'/58	1'/59	P°
89	·	·	·	·	·	·	·	·	·	·	·	·	·	·	·	·	·	·	·	·	·	·	·	·	·	·	·	·	·	·	1
88	1	1	0	0	0	0	0	0	0	0	0	0	0	0	0	0	0	0	0	0	0	0	0	0	0	0	0	0	0	0	2
87	1	1	1	1	1	1	1	1	1	1	1	1	1	1	1	1	0	0	0	0	0	0	0	0	0	0	0	0	0	0	3
86	2	2	1	1	1	1	1	1	1	1	1	1	1	1	1	1	1	1	1	1	1	1	0	0	0	0	0	0	0	0	4
85	2	2	2	2	2	2	2	2	2	2	2	2	1	1	1	1	1	1	1	1	1	1	1	1	1	0	0	0	0	0	5
84	3	3	2	2	2	2	2	2	2	2	2	2	2	2	2	2	1	1	1	1	1	1	1	1	1	1	1	1	0	0	6
83	3	3	3	3	3	3	2	2	3	3	2	2	2	2	2	2	2	2	2	2	1	1	1	1	1	1	1	1	1	0	7
82	4	4	3	3	3	3	3	3	3	3	2	2	3	2	2	2	2	2	2	2	2	2	2	1	1	1	1	1	1	0	8
81	4	4	4	4	4	4	3	3	3	3	3	3	3	3	3	3	2	2	2	2	2	2	2	2	2	1	1	1	1	0	9
80	5	5	4	4	4	4	4	4	4	4	3	3	3	3	3	3	2	2	3	3	2	2	2	2	2	2	1	1	1	0	10
79	5	5	5	5	5	5	4	4	4	4	4	4	4	4	4	4	3	3	2	2	3	3	2	2	2	1	1	1	1	0	11
78	6	6	5	5	5	5	5	5	5	5	4	4	4	4	4	4	3	3	3	3	3	3	2	2	2	1	1	1	1	0	12
77	6	6	6	6	5	5	5	5	5	5	5	5	4	4	4	4	3	3	3	3	3	3	2	2	2	2	1	1	1	0	13
76	7	7	6	6	6	6	6	6	6	6	5	5	5	4	4	4	4	4	4	4	3	3	3	3	2	2	1	1	1	0	14
75	7	7	7	7	6	6	6	6	6	6	5	5	5	5	5	5	4	4	4	4	4	4	3	3	2	2	2	1	1	0	15
74	8	8	7	7	7	7	7	7	7	7	6	6	5	5	5	5	4	4	4	4	4	4	4	3	2	2	2	1	1	0	16
73	8	8	8	8	7	7	7	7	7	7	6	6	6	6	6	6	5	5	5	5	4	4	4	3	3	2	2	1	1	0	17
72	9	9	8	8	8	8	7	7	7	7	7	7	6	6	6	6	5	5	5	5	4	4	4	3	3	2	2	1	1	0	18
71	9	9	9	8	8	8	8	8	8	8	7	7	7	7	7	7	6	6	5	5	5	5	4	3	3	2	2	1	1	0	19
70	10	10	9	9	9	9	8	8	8	8	8	8	7	7	7	7	6	6	6	6	5	5	4	3	3	2	2	1	1	0	20
69	10	10	10	9	9	9	9	9	8	8	8	8	8	8	8	8	6	6	6	6	5	5	4	4	3	3	2	1	1	1	21
68	11	10	10	10	10	10	9	9	9	9	9	9	8	8	8	8	7	7	6	6	5	5	4	4	3	3	2	1	1	1	22
67	11	11	10	10	10	10	10	10	9	9	9	9	9	9	9	8	7	7	7	7	6	6	4	4	3	3	2	1	1	1	23
66	12	11	11	11	11	11	10	10	10	10	9	9	9	9	9	9	8	8	7	7	6	6	5	4	3	3	2	1	1	1	24
65	12	12	11	11	11	11	11	10	11	10	10	10	10	10	9	9	8	8	7	7	6	6	5	4	3	3	2	1	1	1	25
64	13	12	12	12	12	12	11	11	11	11	10	10	10	10	9	9	8	8	8	8	6	6	5	4	3	3	2	2	1	1	26
63	13	13	13	12	12	12	12	12	12	12	11	11	10	10	10	9	9	8	8	8	7	6	5	4	3	3	2	2	1	1	27
62	14	13	13	13	13	13	12	12	12	12	11	11	11	11	10	9	9	8	8	8	7	6	5	4	3	3	2	2	1	1	28
61	14	14	13	13	13	13	13	13	13	13	12	12	11	11	10	10	9	8	8	8	7	7	5	4	3	3	2	2	1	1	29
60	15	14	14	14	14	14	14	14	13	13	13	13	11	11	10	10	9	8	8	8	7	7	5	4	3	3	2	2	1	1	30
59	15	15	14	14	14	15	14	14	13	13	12	12	11	11	10	10	9	8	7	6	6	5	5	4	4	3	2	2	1	1	31
58	16	15	15	15	15	15	14	14	14	14	13	13	11	11	10	10	9	8	7	6	6	5	5	4	4	3	2	2	1	1	32
57	16	16	16	16	16	16	15	15	14	14	13	13	11	11	10	10	9	8	7	6	6	5	5	4	4	3	2	2	1	1	33
56	17	16	16	16	16	16	15	15	14	14	13	13	12	11	10	10	9	8	7	6	6	5	5	4	4	3	2	2	1	1	34
55	17	17	17	17	17	16	15	15	14	14	13	13	12	11	10	9	9	8	8	7	6	6	5	4	4	3	2	2	1	1	35
54	18	17	16	16	15	15	14	14	13	13	12	12	11	11	9	9	8	8	7	7	6	5	5	4	4	3	2	2	1	1	36
53	18	18	17	17	16	16	15	15	14	14	13	13	11	11	10	9	8	8	7	7	6	5	5	4	4	3	2	2	1	1	37
52	18	18	17	17	16	16	15	15	14	14	13	13	12	11	10	9	8	8	8	7	6	6	5	4	3	3	3	2	1	1	38
51	19	19	18	17	16	16	15	15	14	14	13	12	12	11	10	9	9	8	8	7	6	6	5	4	4	3	3	2	1	1	39
50	19	19	18	17	17	16	15	15	14	13	13	12	12	11	10	10	9	8	8	7	6	6	5	4	4	3	3	2	1	1	40

For Z₂ <10°, use 10°.

Z₂°	P°	30' / 30	29' / 31	28' / 32	27' / 33	26' / 34	25' / 35	24' / 36	23' / 37	22' / 38	21' / 39	20' / 40	19' / 41	18' / 42	17' / 43	16' / 44	15' / 45	14' / 46	13' / 47	12' / 48	11' / 49	10' / 50	9' / 51	8' / 52	7' / 53	6' / 54	5' / 55	4' / 56	3' / 57	2' / 58	1' / 59
49	41	20	19	18	18	17	16	16	15	14	14	13	12	12	11	10	10	9	9	8	7	7	6	5	5	4	3	3	2	1	1
48	42	20	19	19	18	17	17	16	15	15	14	13	13	12	11	11	10	9	9	8	7	7	6	5	5	4	3	3	2	1	1
47	43	20	20	19	18	18	17	16	16	15	14	14	13	12	12	11	10	10	9	8	8	7	6	5	5	4	3	3	2	1	1
46	44	21	20	19	19	18	17	17	16	15	15	14	13	13	12	11	11	10	10	8	8	7	6	6	5	4	3	3	2	1	1
45	45	21	21	20	19	18	18	17	16	16	15	14	13	13	12	11	11	10	10	8	8	7	6	6	5	4	4	3	2	1	1
44	46	22	21	20	19	19	18	17	17	16	15	15	14	13	13	12	11	11	10	9	8	7	6	6	6	4	4	3	2	1	1
43	47	22	21	20	20	19	18	18	17	16	15	15	14	13	13	12	11	11	10	9	8	8	6	6	6	5	4	3	2	1	1
42	48	22	22	21	20	19	19	18	17	16	16	15	14	14	13	12	12	11	11	10	8	8	7	6	6	5	4	3	2	2	1
41	49	23	22	21	20	20	19	18	18	17	16	15	15	14	13	12	12	11	11	10	9	8	7	6	6	5	4	3	2	2	1
40	50	23	22	21	21	20	19	19	18	17	16	16	15	14	14	13	13	12	11	10	9	8	7	6	6	5	4	3	2	2	1
39	51	23	23	22	21	20	20	19	18	17	16	16	15	14	14	13	13	12	11	10	9	8	7	7	6	5	4	4	3	2	1
38	52	24	23	22	21	21	20	19	18	18	17	16	15	15	14	13	13	12	11	11	9	8	8	7	6	5	4	4	3	2	1
37	53	24	23	22	22	21	20	20	19	18	17	17	16	15	14	13	13	13	12	11	9	9	8	7	6	5	4	4	3	2	1
36	54	24	23	23	22	21	21	20	19	18	17	17	16	15	15	14	13	13	12	11	10	9	8	7	6	5	5	4	3	2	1
35	55	25	24	23	23	22	21	20	19	18	18	17	16	15	15	14	13	13	12	11	10	9	8	7	7	5	5	4	3	2	1
34	56	25	24	23	23	22	21	20	20	19	18	17	16	16	15	14	13	13	12	11	10	9	8	7	7	6	5	4	3	2	1
33	57	25	25	23	23	22	22	21	20	19	18	18	17	16	15	14	14	13	13	11	10	9	8	8	7	6	5	4	3	2	1
32	58	25	25	24	23	23	22	21	20	19	18	18	17	16	15	14	14	13	13	12	11	10	8	8	7	6	5	4	3	2	1
31	59	26	25	24	24	23	22	21	20	19	19	18	17	16	16	15	14	13	13	12	11	10	8	8	7	6	5	4	3	2	1
30	60	26	25	24	24	23	23	22	21	20	19	18	17	17	16	15	14	14	13	12	11	11	9	8	7	6	5	4	3	2	1
29	61	26	26	25	24	23	23	22	21	20	19	18	17	17	16	15	14	14	13	12	11	11	9	8	7	6	5	4	3	2	1
28	62	27	26	25	24	24	23	22	21	20	19	19	18	17	16	15	14	14	13	12	11	11	9	8	7	6	5	4	3	2	1
27	63	27	26	25	25	24	23	22	21	20	19	19	18	17	16	15	15	14	13	12	11	11	9	8	7	6	5	4	3	2	1
26	64	27	26	25	25	24	24	23	22	21	20	19	18	17	16	15	15	14	13	12	11	11	9	8	7	6	5	4	3	2	1
25	65	28	27	26	25	24	24	23	22	21	20	19	18	17	17	15	15	14	13	12	11	11	9	8	7	6	5	4	3	2	1
24	66	28	27	26	25	25	24	23	22	21	20	19	18	18	17	16	15	14	13	12	11	11	9	8	7	6	5	4	3	2	1
23	67	28	27	26	26	25	24	23	22	21	20	20	19	18	17	16	15	14	13	12	11	11	9	8	7	6	5	4	3	2	1
22	68	29	27	26	26	25	24	23	22	21	20	20	19	18	17	16	15	14	13	12	11	11	9	8	7	6	5	4	3	2	1
21	69	29	27	26	26	25	25	23	22	21	20	20	19	18	17	16	15	14	13	12	11	11	9	8	7	6	5	4	3	2	1
20	70	29	28	27	26	26	25	24	23	22	21	21	19	18	17	16	15	14	13	12	11	11	9	8	7	6	5	4	3	2	1
19	71	29	28	27	26	26	25	24	23	22	21	20	19	18	17	16	15	14	13	12	11	10	9	8	7	6	5	4	3	2	1
18	72	29	28	27	27	26	25	24	23	22	21	20	19	18	17	16	15	14	13	12	11	10	9	8	7	6	5	4	3	2	1
17	73	29	28	27	27	26	25	24	23	22	21	20	19	18	17	16	15	14	13	12	11	10	9	8	7	6	5	4	3	2	1
16	74	29	28	27	27	26	25	24	23	22	21	20	19	18	17	16	15	14	13	12	11	10	9	8	7	6	5	4	3	2	1
15	75	29	29	28	27	26	25	24	23	22	21	20	19	18	17	16	15	14	13	12	11	10	9	8	7	6	5	4	3	2	1
14	76	29	29	28	27	26	25	24	23	22	21	20	19	18	17	16	15	14	13	12	11	10	9	8	7	6	5	4	3	3	1
13	77	29	29	28	27	26	25	24	23	22	21	20	19	18	17	16	15	14	13	12	11	10	9	8	7	6	5	4	3	3	1
12	78	29	29	28	27	26	25	24	23	22	21	20	19	18	17	16	15	14	13	12	11	10	9	8	7	6	5	4	3	3	1
11	79	30	29	28	27	26	25	24	23	22	21	20	19	18	17	16	15	14	13	12	11	10	9	8	7	6	5	4	3	3	1
10	80	30	29	28	27	26	25	24	23	22	21	20	19	18	17	16	15	14	13	12	11	10	9	8	7	6	5	4	3	3	1

For P > 80°, use 80°.

USE OF CONCISE SIGHT REDUCTION TABLES (continued)

4. *Example.* (b) Required the altitude and azimuth of *Vega* on 1999 July 29 at UT 04^h 52^m from the estimated position 152° west, 15° south.

1. Assumed latitude $Lat = $ 15° S
   From the almanac $GHA = $ 100° 10′
   Assumed longitude   152° 10′ W
   Local hour angle $LHA = $ 308

2. Reduction table, 1st entry
   $(Lat, LHA) = (15, 308)$ $A = $ 49   34 $A° = 50$, $A' = 34$
                           $B = +66$ 29 $Z_1 = +71{\cdot}7$, $LHA > 270°$
3. From the almanac $Dec = -38$ 47   *Lat* and *Dec* contrary
   Sum $= B + Dec$ $F = +27$ 42 $F° = 28$, $F' = 42$

4. Reduction table, 2nd entry
   $(A°, F°) = (50, 28)$ $H = $ 17   34 $P° = 37$
                                      $Z_2 = 67{\cdot}8$
5. Auxiliary table, 1st entry
   $(F', P°) = (42, 37)$ $corr_1 = $ -11 $F < 90°$, $F' > 29'$
   Sum   17   23
6. Auxiliary table, 2nd entry
   $(A', Z_2°) = (34, 68)$ $corr_2 = $ $+10$ $A' > 30'$
7. Sum $=$ computed altitude $H_C = +17° \; 33'$ $F > 0°$

8. Azimuth, first component $Z_1 = +71{\cdot}7$ same sign as B
        second component $Z_2 = +67{\cdot}8$ $F < 90°$, $F > 0°$
   Sum $=$ azimuth angle $Z = $ 139{\cdot}5

   True azimuth $Z_n = $ 041°   S *Lat*, $LHA > 180°$

CONVERSION OF ARC TO TIME

°	h m	°	h m	°	h m	°	h m	°	h m	°	h m	′	0′·00 m s	0′·25 m s	0′·50 m s	0′·75 m s
0	0 00	60	4 00	120	8 00	180	12 00	240	16 00	300	20 00	0	0 00	0 01	0 02	0 03
1	0 04	61	4 04	121	8 04	181	12 04	241	16 04	301	20 04	1	0 04	0 05	0 06	0 07
2	0 08	62	4 08	122	8 08	182	12 08	242	16 08	302	20 08	2	0 08	0 09	0 10	0 11
3	0 12	63	4 12	123	8 12	183	12 12	243	16 12	303	20 12	3	0 12	0 13	0 14	0 15
4	0 16	64	4 16	124	8 16	184	12 16	244	16 16	304	20 16	4	0 16	0 17	0 18	0 19
5	0 20	65	4 20	125	8 20	185	12 20	245	16 20	305	20 20	5	0 20	0 21	0 22	0 23
6	0 24	66	4 24	126	8 24	186	12 24	246	16 24	306	20 24	6	0 24	0 25	0 26	0 27
7	0 28	67	4 28	127	8 28	187	12 28	247	16 28	307	20 28	7	0 28	0 29	0 30	0 31
8	0 32	68	4 32	128	8 32	188	12 32	248	16 32	308	20 32	8	0 32	0 33	0 34	0 35
9	0 36	69	4 36	129	8 36	189	12 36	249	16 36	309	20 36	9	0 36	0 37	0 38	0 39
10	0 40	70	4 40	130	8 40	190	12 40	250	16 40	310	20 40	10	0 40	0 41	0 42	0 43
11	0 44	71	4 44	131	8 44	191	12 44	251	16 44	311	20 44	11	0 44	0 45	0 46	0 47
12	0 48	72	4 48	132	8 48	192	12 48	252	16 48	312	20 48	12	0 48	0 49	0 50	0 51
13	0 52	73	4 52	133	8 52	193	12 52	253	16 52	313	20 52	13	0 52	0 53	0 54	0 55
14	0 56	74	4 56	134	8 56	194	12 56	254	16 56	314	20 56	14	0 56	0 57	0 58	0 59
15	1 00	75	5 00	135	9 00	195	13 00	255	17 00	315	21 00	15	1 00	1 01	1 02	1 03
16	1 04	76	5 04	136	9 04	196	13 04	256	17 04	316	21 04	16	1 04	1 05	1 06	1 07
17	1 08	77	5 08	137	9 08	197	13 08	257	17 08	317	21 08	17	1 08	1 09	1 10	1 11
18	1 12	78	5 12	138	9 12	198	13 12	258	17 12	318	21 12	18	1 12	1 13	1 14	1 15
19	1 16	79	5 16	139	9 16	199	13 16	259	17 16	319	21 16	19	1 16	1 17	1 18	1 19
20	1 20	80	5 20	140	9 20	200	13 20	260	17 20	320	21 20	20	1 20	1 21	1 22	1 23
21	1 24	81	5 24	141	9 24	201	13 24	261	17 24	321	21 24	21	1 24	1 25	1 26	1 27
22	1 28	82	5 28	142	9 28	202	13 28	262	17 28	322	21 28	22	1 28	1 29	1 30	1 31
23	1 32	83	5 32	143	9 32	203	13 32	263	17 32	323	21 32	23	1 32	1 33	1 34	1 35
24	1 36	84	5 36	144	9 36	204	13 36	264	17 36	324	21 36	24	1 36	1 37	1 38	1 39
25	1 40	85	5 40	145	9 40	205	13 40	265	17 40	325	21 40	25	1 40	1 41	1 42	1 43
26	1 44	86	5 44	146	9 44	206	13 44	266	17 44	326	21 44	26	1 44	1 45	1 46	1 47
27	1 48	87	5 48	147	9 48	207	13 48	267	17 48	327	21 48	27	1 48	1 49	1 50	1 51
28	1 52	88	5 52	148	9 52	208	13 52	268	17 52	328	21 52	28	1 52	1 53	1 54	1 55
29	1 56	89	5 56	149	9 56	209	13 56	269	17 56	329	21 56	29	1 56	1 57	1 58	1 59
30	2 00	90	6 00	150	10 00	210	14 00	270	18 00	330	22 00	30	2 00	2 01	2 02	2 03
31	2 04	91	6 04	151	10 04	211	14 04	271	18 04	331	22 04	31	2 04	2 05	2 06	2 07
32	2 08	92	6 08	152	10 08	212	14 08	272	18 08	332	22 08	32	2 08	2 09	2 10	2 11
33	2 12	93	6 12	153	10 12	213	14 12	273	18 12	333	22 12	33	2 12	2 13	2 14	2 15
34	2 16	94	6 16	154	10 16	214	14 16	274	18 16	334	22 16	34	2 16	2 17	2 18	2 19
35	2 20	95	6 20	155	10 20	215	14 20	275	18 20	335	22 20	35	2 20	2 21	2 22	2 23
36	2 24	96	6 24	156	10 24	216	14 24	276	18 24	336	22 24	36	2 24	2 25	2 26	2 27
37	2 28	97	6 28	157	10 28	217	14 28	277	18 28	337	22 28	37	2 28	2 29	2 30	2 31
38	2 32	98	6 32	158	10 32	218	14 32	278	18 32	338	22 32	38	2 32	2 33	2 34	2 35
39	2 36	99	6 36	159	10 36	219	14 36	279	18 36	339	22 36	39	2 36	2 37	2 38	2 39
40	2 40	100	6 40	160	10 40	220	14 40	280	18 40	340	22 40	40	2 40	2 41	2 42	2 43
41	2 44	101	6 44	161	10 44	221	14 44	281	18 44	341	22 44	41	2 44	2 45	2 46	2 47
42	2 48	102	6 48	162	10 48	222	14 48	282	18 48	342	22 48	42	2 48	2 49	2 50	2 51
43	2 52	103	6 52	163	10 52	223	14 52	283	18 52	343	22 52	43	2 52	2 53	2 54	2 55
44	2 56	104	6 56	164	10 56	224	14 56	284	18 56	344	22 56	44	2 56	2 57	2 58	2 59
45	3 00	105	7 00	165	11 00	225	15 00	285	19 00	345	23 00	45	3 00	3 01	3 02	3 03
46	3 04	106	7 04	166	11 04	226	15 04	286	19 04	346	23 04	46	3 04	3 05	3 06	3 07
47	3 08	107	7 08	167	11 08	227	15 08	287	19 08	347	23 08	47	3 08	3 09	3 10	3 11
48	3 12	108	7 12	168	11 12	228	15 12	288	19 12	348	23 12	48	3 12	3 13	3 14	3 15
49	3 16	109	7 16	169	11 16	229	15 16	289	19 16	349	23 16	49	3 16	3 17	3 18	3 19
50	3 20	110	7 20	170	11 20	230	15 20	290	19 20	350	23 20	50	3 20	3 21	3 22	3 23
51	3 24	111	7 24	171	11 24	231	15 24	291	19 24	351	23 24	51	3 24	3 25	3 26	3 27
52	3 28	112	7 28	172	11 28	232	15 28	292	19 28	352	23 28	52	3 28	3 29	3 30	3 31
53	3 32	113	7 32	173	11 32	233	15 32	293	19 32	353	23 32	53	3 32	3 33	3 34	3 35
54	3 36	114	7 36	174	11 36	234	15 36	294	19 36	354	23 36	54	3 36	3 37	3 38	3 39
55	3 40	115	7 40	175	11 40	235	15 40	295	19 40	355	23 40	55	3 40	3 41	3 42	3 43
56	3 44	116	7 44	176	11 44	236	15 44	296	19 44	356	23 44	56	3 44	3 45	3 46	3 47
57	3 48	117	7 48	177	11 48	237	15 48	297	19 48	357	23 48	57	3 48	3 49	3 50	3 51
58	3 52	118	7 52	178	11 52	238	15 52	298	19 52	358	23 52	58	3 52	3 53	3 54	3 55
59	3 56	119	7 56	179	11 56	239	15 56	299	19 56	359	23 56	59	3 56	3 57	3 58	3 59

The above table is for converting expressions in arc to their equivalent in time ; its main use in this Almanac is for the conversion of longitude for application to L.M.T. (*added if west, subtracted if east*) to give G.M.T. or vice versa, particularly in the case of sunrise, sunset, etc.

0ᵐ

s	SUN PLANETS	ARIES	MOON	v or d / Corrⁿ		v or d / Corrⁿ		v or d / Corrⁿ	
00	0 00.0	0 00.0	0 00.0	0.0	0.0	6.0	0.1	12.0	0.1
01	0 00.3	0 00.3	0 00.2	0.1	0.0	6.1	0.1	12.1	0.1
02	0 00.5	0 00.5	0 00.5	0.2	0.0	6.2	0.1	12.2	0.1
03	0 00.8	0 00.8	0 00.7	0.3	0.0	6.3	0.1	12.3	0.1
04	0 01.0	0 01.0	0 01.0	0.4	0.0	6.4	0.1	12.4	0.1
05	0 01.3	0 01.3	0 01.2	0.5	0.0	6.5	0.1	12.5	0.1
06	0 01.5	0 01.5	0 01.4	0.6	0.0	6.6	0.1	12.6	0.1
07	0 01.8	0 01.8	0 01.7	0.7	0.0	6.7	0.1	12.7	0.1
08	0 02.0	0 02.0	0 01.9	0.8	0.0	6.8	0.1	12.8	0.1
09	0 02.3	0 02.3	0 02.1	0.9	0.0	6.9	0.1	12.9	0.1
10	0 02.5	0 02.5	0 02.4	1.0	0.0	7.0	0.1	13.0	0.1
11	0 02.8	0 02.8	0 02.6	1.1	0.0	7.1	0.1	13.1	0.1
12	0 03.0	0 03.0	0 02.9	1.2	0.0	7.2	0.1	13.2	0.1
13	0 03.3	0 03.3	0 03.1	1.3	0.0	7.3	0.1	13.3	0.1
14	0 03.5	0 03.5	0 03.3	1.4	0.0	7.4	0.1	13.4	0.1
15	0 03.8	0 03.8	0 03.6	1.5	0.0	7.5	0.1	13.5	0.1
16	0 04.0	0 04.0	0 03.8	1.6	0.0	7.6	0.1	13.6	0.1
17	0 04.3	0 04.3	0 04.1	1.7	0.0	7.7	0.1	13.7	0.1
18	0 04.5	0 04.5	0 04.3	1.8	0.0	7.8	0.1	13.8	0.1
19	0 04.8	0 04.8	0 04.5	1.9	0.0	7.9	0.1	13.9	0.1
20	0 05.0	0 05.0	0 04.8	2.0	0.0	8.0	0.1	14.0	0.1
21	0 05.3	0 05.3	0 05.0	2.1	0.0	8.1	0.1	14.1	0.1
22	0 05.5	0 05.5	0 05.2	2.2	0.0	8.2	0.1	14.2	0.1
23	0 05.8	0 05.8	0 05.5	2.3	0.0	8.3	0.1	14.3	0.1
24	0 06.0	0 06.0	0 05.7	2.4	0.0	8.4	0.1	14.4	0.1
25	0 06.3	0 06.3	0 06.0	2.5	0.0	8.5	0.1	14.5	0.1
26	0 06.5	0 06.5	0 06.2	2.6	0.0	8.6	0.1	14.6	0.1
27	0 06.8	0 06.8	0 06.4	2.7	0.0	8.7	0.1	14.7	0.1
28	0 07.0	0 07.0	0 06.7	2.8	0.0	8.8	0.1	14.8	0.1
29	0 07.3	0 07.3	0 06.9	2.9	0.0	8.9	0.1	14.9	0.1
30	0 07.5	0 07.5	0 07.2	3.0	0.0	9.0	0.1	15.0	0.1
31	0 07.8	0 07.8	0 07.4	3.1	0.0	9.1	0.1	15.1	0.1
32	0 08.0	0 08.0	0 07.6	3.2	0.0	9.2	0.1	15.2	0.1
33	0 08.3	0 08.3	0 07.9	3.3	0.0	9.3	0.1	15.3	0.1
34	0 08.5	0 08.5	0 08.1	3.4	0.0	9.4	0.1	15.4	0.1
35	0 08.8	0 08.8	0 08.4	3.5	0.0	9.5	0.1	15.5	0.1
36	0 09.0	0 09.0	0 08.6	3.6	0.0	9.6	0.1	15.6	0.1
37	0 09.3	0 09.3	0 08.8	3.7	0.0	9.7	0.1	15.7	0.1
38	0 09.5	0 09.5	0 09.1	3.8	0.0	9.8	0.1	15.8	0.1
39	0 09.8	0 09.8	0 09.3	3.9	0.0	9.9	0.1	15.9	0.1
40	0 10.0	0 10.0	0 09.5	4.0	0.0	10.0	0.1	16.0	0.1
41	0 10.3	0 10.3	0 09.8	4.1	0.0	10.1	0.1	16.1	0.1
42	0 10.5	0 10.5	0 10.0	4.2	0.0	10.2	0.1	16.2	0.1
43	0 10.8	0 10.8	0 10.3	4.3	0.0	10.3	0.1	16.3	0.1
44	0 11.0	0 11.0	0 10.5	4.4	0.0	10.4	0.1	16.4	0.1
45	0 11.3	0 11.3	0 10.7	4.5	0.0	10.5	0.1	16.5	0.1
46	0 11.5	0 11.5	0 11.0	4.6	0.0	10.6	0.1	16.6	0.1
47	0 11.8	0 11.8	0 11.2	4.7	0.0	10.7	0.1	16.7	0.1
48	0 12.0	0 12.0	0 11.5	4.8	0.0	10.8	0.1	16.8	0.1
49	0 12.3	0 12.3	0 11.7	4.9	0.0	10.9	0.1	16.9	0.1
50	0 12.5	0 12.5	0 11.9	5.0	0.0	11.0	0.1	17.0	0.1
51	0 12.8	0 12.8	0 12.2	5.1	0.0	11.1	0.1	17.1	0.1
52	0 13.0	0 13.0	0 12.4	5.2	0.0	11.2	0.1	17.2	0.1
53	0 13.3	0 13.3	0 12.6	5.3	0.0	11.3	0.1	17.3	0.1
54	0 13.5	0 13.5	0 12.9	5.4	0.0	11.4	0.1	17.4	0.1
55	0 13.8	0 13.8	0 13.1	5.5	0.0	11.5	0.1	17.5	0.1
56	0 14.0	0 14.0	0 13.4	5.6	0.0	11.6	0.1	17.6	0.1
57	0 14.3	0 14.3	0 13.6	5.7	0.0	11.7	0.1	17.7	0.1
58	0 14.5	0 14.5	0 13.8	5.8	0.0	11.8	0.1	17.8	0.1
59	0 14.8	0 14.8	0 14.1	5.9	0.0	11.9	0.1	17.9	0.1
60	0 15.0	0 15.0	0 14.3	6.0	0.1	12.0	0.1	18.0	0.2

1ᵐ

s	SUN PLANETS	ARIES	MOON	v or d / Corrⁿ		v or d / Corrⁿ		v or d / Corrⁿ	
00	0 15.0	0 15.0	0 14.3	0.0	0.0	6.0	0.2	12.0	0.3
01	0 15.3	0 15.3	0 14.6	0.1	0.0	6.1	0.2	12.1	0.3
02	0 15.5	0 15.5	0 14.8	0.2	0.0	6.2	0.2	12.2	0.3
03	0 15.8	0 15.8	0 15.0	0.3	0.0	6.3	0.2	12.3	0.3
04	0 16.0	0 16.0	0 15.3	0.4	0.0	6.4	0.2	12.4	0.3
05	0 16.3	0 16.3	0 15.5	0.5	0.0	6.5	0.2	12.5	0.3
06	0 16.5	0 16.5	0 15.7	0.6	0.0	6.6	0.2	12.6	0.3
07	0 16.8	0 16.8	0 16.0	0.7	0.0	6.7	0.2	12.7	0.3
08	0 17.0	0 17.0	0 16.2	0.8	0.0	6.8	0.2	12.8	0.3
09	0 17.3	0 17.3	0 16.5	0.9	0.0	6.9	0.2	12.9	0.3
10	0 17.5	0 17.5	0 16.7	1.0	0.0	7.0	0.2	13.0	0.3
11	0 17.8	0 17.8	0 16.9	1.1	0.0	7.1	0.2	13.1	0.3
12	0 18.0	0 18.0	0 17.2	1.2	0.0	7.2	0.2	13.2	0.3
13	0 18.3	0 18.3	0 17.4	1.3	0.0	7.3	0.2	13.3	0.3
14	0 18.5	0 18.6	0 17.7	1.4	0.0	7.4	0.2	13.4	0.3
15	0 18.8	0 18.8	0 17.9	1.5	0.0	7.5	0.2	13.5	0.3
16	0 19.0	0 19.1	0 18.1	1.6	0.0	7.6	0.2	13.6	0.3
17	0 19.3	0 19.3	0 18.4	1.7	0.0	7.7	0.2	13.7	0.3
18	0 19.5	0 19.6	0 18.6	1.8	0.0	7.8	0.2	13.8	0.3
19	0 19.8	0 19.8	0 18.9	1.9	0.0	7.9	0.2	13.9	0.3
20	0 20.0	0 20.1	0 19.1	2.0	0.1	8.0	0.2	14.0	0.4
21	0 20.3	0 20.3	0 19.3	2.1	0.1	8.1	0.2	14.1	0.4
22	0 20.5	0 20.6	0 19.6	2.2	0.1	8.2	0.2	14.2	0.4
23	0 20.8	0 20.8	0 19.8	2.3	0.1	8.3	0.2	14.3	0.4
24	0 21.0	0 21.1	0 20.0	2.4	0.1	8.4	0.2	14.4	0.4
25	0 21.3	0 21.3	0 20.3	2.5	0.1	8.5	0.2	14.5	0.4
26	0 21.5	0 21.6	0 20.5	2.6	0.1	8.6	0.2	14.6	0.4
27	0 21.8	0 21.8	0 20.8	2.7	0.1	8.7	0.2	14.7	0.4
28	0 22.0	0 22.1	0 21.0	2.8	0.1	8.8	0.2	14.8	0.4
29	0 22.3	0 22.3	0 21.2	2.9	0.1	8.9	0.2	14.9	0.4
30	0 22.5	0 22.6	0 21.5	3.0	0.1	9.0	0.2	15.0	0.4
31	0 22.8	0 22.8	0 21.7	3.1	0.1	9.1	0.2	15.1	0.4
32	0 23.0	0 23.1	0 22.0	3.2	0.1	9.2	0.2	15.2	0.4
33	0 23.3	0 23.3	0 22.2	3.3	0.1	9.3	0.2	15.3	0.4
34	0 23.5	0 23.6	0 22.4	3.4	0.1	9.4	0.2	15.4	0.4
35	0 23.8	0 23.8	0 22.7	3.5	0.1	9.5	0.2	15.5	0.4
36	0 24.0	0 24.1	0 22.9	3.6	0.1	9.6	0.2	15.6	0.4
37	0 24.3	0 24.3	0 23.1	3.7	0.1	9.7	0.2	15.7	0.4
38	0 24.5	0 24.6	0 23.4	3.8	0.1	9.8	0.2	15.8	0.4
39	0 24.8	0 24.8	0 23.6	3.9	0.1	9.9	0.2	15.9	0.4
40	0 25.0	0 25.1	0 23.9	4.0	0.1	10.0	0.3	16.0	0.4
41	0 25.3	0 25.3	0 24.1	4.1	0.1	10.1	0.3	16.1	0.4
42	0 25.5	0 25.6	0 24.3	4.2	0.1	10.2	0.3	16.2	0.4
43	0 25.8	0 25.8	0 24.6	4.3	0.1	10.3	0.3	16.3	0.4
44	0 26.0	0 26.1	0 24.8	4.4	0.1	10.4	0.3	16.4	0.4
45	0 26.3	0 26.3	0 25.1	4.5	0.1	10.5	0.3	16.5	0.4
46	0 26.5	0 26.6	0 25.3	4.6	0.1	10.6	0.3	16.6	0.4
47	0 26.8	0 26.8	0 25.5	4.7	0.1	10.7	0.3	16.7	0.4
48	0 27.0	0 27.1	0 25.8	4.8	0.1	10.8	0.3	16.8	0.4
49	0 27.3	0 27.3	0 26.0	4.9	0.1	10.9	0.3	16.9	0.4
50	0 27.5	0 27.6	0 26.2	5.0	0.1	11.0	0.3	17.0	0.4
51	0 27.8	0 27.8	0 26.5	5.1	0.1	11.1	0.3	17.1	0.4
52	0 28.0	0 28.1	0 26.7	5.2	0.1	11.2	0.3	17.2	0.4
53	0 28.3	0 28.3	0 27.0	5.3	0.1	11.3	0.3	17.3	0.4
54	0 28.5	0 28.6	0 27.2	5.4	0.1	11.4	0.3	17.4	0.4
55	0 28.8	0 28.8	0 27.4	5.5	0.1	11.5	0.3	17.5	0.4
56	0 29.0	0 29.1	0 27.7	5.6	0.1	11.6	0.3	17.6	0.4
57	0 29.3	0 29.3	0 27.9	5.7	0.1	11.7	0.3	17.7	0.4
58	0 29.5	0 29.6	0 28.2	5.8	0.1	11.8	0.3	17.8	0.4
59	0 29.8	0 29.8	0 28.4	5.9	0.1	11.9	0.3	17.9	0.4
60	0 30.0	0 30.1	0 28.6	6.0	0.2	12.0	0.3	18.0	0.5

2^m

$\overset{m}{2}$	SUN PLANETS	ARIES	MOON	v or Corr^n d		v or Corr^n d		v or Corr^n d	
s	° ′	° ′	° ′	′	′	′	′	′	′
00	0 30·0	0 30·1	0 28·6	0·0	0·0	6·0	0·3	12·0	0·5
01	0 30·3	0 30·3	0 28·9	0·1	0·0	6·1	0·3	12·1	0·5
02	0 30·5	0 30·6	0 29·1	0·2	0·0	6·2	0·3	12·2	0·5
03	0 30·8	0 30·8	0 29·3	0·3	0·0	6·3	0·3	12·3	0·5
04	0 31·0	0 31·1	0 29·6	0·4	0·0	6·4	0·3	12·4	0·5
05	0 31·3	0 31·3	0 29·8	0·5	0·0	6·5	0·3	12·5	0·5
06	0 31·5	0 31·6	0 30·1	0·6	0·0	6·6	0·3	12·6	0·5
07	0 31·8	0 31·8	0 30·3	0·7	0·0	6·7	0·3	12·7	0·5
08	0 32·0	0 32·1	0 30·5	0·8	0·0	6·8	0·3	12·8	0·5
09	0 32·3	0 32·3	0 30·8	0·9	0·0	6·9	0·3	12·9	0·5
10	0 32·5	0 32·6	0 31·0	1·0	0·0	7·0	0·3	13·0	0·5
11	0 32·8	0 32·8	0 31·3	1·1	0·0	7·1	0·3	13·1	0·5
12	0 33·0	0 33·1	0 31·5	1·2	0·1	7·2	0·3	13·2	0·6
13	0 33·3	0 33·3	0 31·7	1·3	0·1	7·3	0·3	13·3	0·6
14	0 33·5	0 33·6	0 32·0	1·4	0·1	7·4	0·3	13·4	0·6
15	0 33·8	0 33·8	0 32·2	1·5	0·1	7·5	0·3	13·5	0·6
16	0 34·0	0 34·1	0 32·5	1·6	0·1	7·6	0·3	13·6	0·6
17	0 34·3	0 34·3	0 32·7	1·7	0·1	7·7	0·3	13·7	0·6
18	0 34·5	0 34·6	0 32·9	1·8	0·1	7·8	0·3	13·8	0·6
19	0 34·8	0 34·8	0 33·2	1·9	0·1	7·9	0·3	13·9	0·6
20	0 35·0	0 35·1	0 33·4	2·0	0·1	8·0	0·3	14·0	0·6
21	0 35·3	0 35·3	0 33·6	2·1	0·1	8·1	0·3	14·1	0·6
22	0 35·5	0 35·6	0 33·9	2·2	0·1	8·2	0·3	14·2	0·6
23	0 35·8	0 35·8	0 34·1	2·3	0·1	8·3	0·3	14·3	0·6
24	0 36·0	0 36·1	0 34·4	2·4	0·1	8·4	0·4	14·4	0·6
25	0 36·3	0 36·3	0 34·6	2·5	0·1	8·5	0·4	14·5	0·6
26	0 36·5	0 36·6	0 34·8	2·6	0·1	8·6	0·4	14·6	0·6
27	0 36·8	0 36·9	0 35·1	2·7	0·1	8·7	0·4	14·7	0·6
28	0 37·0	0 37·1	0 35·3	2·8	0·1	8·8	0·4	14·8	0·6
29	0 37·3	0 37·4	0 35·6	2·9	0·1	8·9	0·4	14·9	0·6
30	0 37·5	0 37·6	0 35·8	3·0	0·1	9·0	0·4	15·0	0·6
31	0 37·8	0 37·9	0 36·0	3·1	0·1	9·1	0·4	15·1	0·6
32	0 38·0	0 38·1	0 36·3	3·2	0·1	9·2	0·4	15·2	0·6
33	0 38·3	0 38·4	0 36·5	3·3	0·1	9·3	0·4	15·3	0·6
34	0 38·5	0 38·6	0 36·7	3·4	0·1	9·4	0·4	15·4	0·6
35	0 38·8	0 38·9	0 37·0	3·5	0·1	9·5	0·4	15·5	0·6
36	0 39·0	0 39·1	0 37·2	3·6	0·2	9·6	0·4	15·6	0·7
37	0 39·3	0 39·4	0 37·5	3·7	0·2	9·7	0·4	15·7	0·7
38	0 39·5	0 39·6	0 37·7	3·8	0·2	9·8	0·4	15·8	0·7
39	0 39·8	0 39·9	0 37·9	3·9	0·2	9·9	0·4	15·9	0·7
40	0 40·0	0 40·1	0 38·2	4·0	0·2	10·0	0·4	16·0	0·7
41	0 40·3	0 40·4	0 38·4	4·1	0·2	10·1	0·4	16·1	0·7
42	0 40·5	0 40·6	0 38·7	4·2	0·2	10·2	0·4	16·2	0·7
43	0 40·8	0 40·9	0 38·9	4·3	0·2	10·3	0·4	16·3	0·7
44	0 41·0	0 41·1	0 39·1	4·4	0·2	10·4	0·4	16·4	0·7
45	0 41·3	0 41·4	0 39·4	4·5	0·2	10·5	0·4	16·5	0·7
46	0 41·5	0 41·6	0 39·6	4·6	0·2	10·6	0·4	16·6	0·7
47	0 41·8	0 41·9	0 39·8	4·7	0·2	10·7	0·4	16·7	0·7
48	0 42·0	0 42·1	0 40·1	4·8	0·2	10·8	0·5	16·8	0·7
49	0 42·3	0 42·4	0 40·3	4·9	0·2	10·9	0·5	16·9	0·7
50	0 42·5	0 42·6	0 40·6	5·0	0·2	11·0	0·5	17·0	0·7
51	0 42·8	0 42·9	0 40·8	5·1	0·2	11·1	0·5	17·1	0·7
52	0 43·0	0 43·1	0 41·0	5·2	0·2	11·2	0·5	17·2	0·7
53	0 43·3	0 43·4	0 41·3	5·3	0·2	11·3	0·5	17·3	0·7
54	0 43·5	0 43·6	0 41·5	5·4	0·2	11·4	0·5	17·4	0·7
55	0 43·8	0 43·9	0 41·8	5·5	0·2	11·5	0·5	17·5	0·7
56	0 44·0	0 44·1	0 42·0	5·6	0·2	11·6	0·5	17·6	0·7
57	0 44·3	0 44·4	0 42·2	5·7	0·2	11·7	0·5	17·7	0·7
58	0 44·5	0 44·6	0 42·5	5·8	0·2	11·8	0·5	17·8	0·7
59	0 44·8	0 44·9	0 42·7	5·9	0·2	11·9	0·5	17·9	0·7
60	0 45·0	0 45·1	0 43·0	6·0	0·3	12·0	0·5	18·0	0·8

3^m

$\overset{m}{3}$	SUN PLANETS	ARIES	MOON	v or Corr^n d		v or Corr^n d		v or Corr^n d	
s	° ′	° ′	° ′	′	′	′	′	′	′
00	0 45·0	0 45·1	0 43·0	0·0	0·0	6·0	0·4	12·0	0·7
01	0 45·3	0 45·4	0 43·2	0·1	0·0	6·1	0·4	12·1	0·7
02	0 45·5	0 45·6	0 43·4	0·2	0·0	6·2	0·4	12·2	0·7
03	0 45·8	0 45·9	0 43·7	0·3	0·0	6·3	0·4	12·3	0·7
04	0 46·0	0 46·1	0 43·9	0·4	0·0	6·4	0·4	12·4	0·7
05	0 46·3	0 46·4	0 44·1	0·5	0·0	6·5	0·4	12·5	0·7
06	0 46·5	0 46·6	0 44·4	0·6	0·0	6·6	0·4	12·6	0·7
07	0 46·8	0 46·9	0 44·6	0·7	0·0	6·7	0·4	12·7	0·7
08	0 47·0	0 47·1	0 44·9	0·8	0·0	6·8	0·4	12·8	0·7
09	0 47·3	0 47·4	0 45·1	0·9	0·1	6·9	0·4	12·9	0·8
10	0 47·5	0 47·6	0 45·3	1·0	0·1	7·0	0·4	13·0	0·8
11	0 47·8	0 47·9	0 45·6	1·1	0·1	7·1	0·4	13·1	0·8
12	0 48·0	0 48·1	0 45·8	1·2	0·1	7·2	0·4	13·2	0·8
13	0 48·3	0 48·4	0 46·1	1·3	0·1	7·3	0·4	13·3	0·8
14	0 48·5	0 48·6	0 46·3	1·4	0·1	7·4	0·4	13·4	0·8
15	0 48·8	0 48·9	0 46·5	1·5	0·1	7·5	0·4	13·5	0·8
16	0 49·0	0 49·1	0 46·8	1·6	0·1	7·6	0·4	13·6	0·8
17	0 49·3	0 49·4	0 47·0	1·7	0·1	7·7	0·4	13·7	0·8
18	0 49·5	0 49·6	0 47·2	1·8	0·1	7·8	0·5	13·8	0·8
19	0 49·8	0 49·9	0 47·5	1·9	0·1	7·9	0·5	13·9	0·8
20	0 50·0	0 50·1	0 47·7	2·0	0·1	8·0	0·5	14·0	0·8
21	0 50·3	0 50·4	0 48·0	2·1	0·1	8·1	0·5	14·1	0·8
22	0 50·5	0 50·6	0 48·2	2·2	0·1	8·2	0·5	14·2	0·8
23	0 50·8	0 50·9	0 48·4	2·3	0·1	8·3	0·5	14·3	0·8
24	0 51·0	0 51·1	0 48·7	2·4	0·1	8·4	0·5	14·4	0·8
25	0 51·3	0 51·4	0 48·9	2·5	0·1	8·5	0·5	14·5	0·8
26	0 51·5	0 51·6	0 49·2	2·6	0·2	8·6	0·5	14·6	0·9
27	0 51·8	0 51·9	0 49·4	2·7	0·2	8·7	0·5	14·7	0·9
28	0 52·0	0 52·1	0 49·6	2·8	0·2	8·8	0·5	14·8	0·9
29	0 52·3	0 52·4	0 49·9	2·9	0·2	8·9	0·5	14·9	0·9
30	0 52·5	0 52·6	0 50·1	3·0	0·2	9·0	0·5	15·0	0·9
31	0 52·8	0 52·9	0 50·3	3·1	0·2	9·1	0·5	15·1	0·9
32	0 53·0	0 53·1	0 50·6	3·2	0·2	9·2	0·5	15·2	0·9
33	0 53·3	0 53·4	0 50·8	3·3	0·2	9·3	0·5	15·3	0·9
34	0 53·5	0 53·6	0 51·1	3·4	0·2	9·4	0·5	15·4	0·9
35	0 53·8	0 53·9	0 51·3	3·5	0·2	9·5	0·6	15·5	0·9
36	0 54·0	0 54·1	0 51·5	3·6	0·2	9·6	0·6	15·6	0·9
37	0 54·3	0 54·4	0 51·8	3·7	0·2	9·7	0·6	15·7	0·9
38	0 54·5	0 54·6	0 52·0	3·8	0·2	9·8	0·6	15·8	0·9
39	0 54·8	0 54·9	0 52·3	3·9	0·2	9·9	0·6	15·9	0·9
40	0 55·0	0 55·2	0 52·5	4·0	0·2	10·0	0·6	16·0	0·9
41	0 55·3	0 55·4	0 52·7	4·1	0·2	10·1	0·6	16·1	0·9
42	0 55·5	0 55·7	0 53·0	4·2	0·2	10·2	0·6	16·2	0·9
43	0 55·8	0 55·9	0 53·2	4·3	0·3	10·3	0·6	16·3	1·0
44	0 56·0	0 56·2	0 53·4	4·4	0·3	10·4	0·6	16·4	1·0
45	0 56·3	0 56·4	0 53·7	4·5	0·3	10·5	0·6	16·5	1·0
46	0 56·5	0 56·7	0 53·9	4·6	0·3	10·6	0·6	16·6	1·0
47	0 56·8	0 56·9	0 54·2	4·7	0·3	10·7	0·6	16·7	1·0
48	0 57·0	0 57·2	0 54·4	4·8	0·3	10·8	0·6	16·8	1·0
49	0 57·3	0 57·4	0 54·6	4·9	0·3	10·9	0·6	16·9	1·0
50	0 57·5	0 57·7	0 54·9	5·0	0·3	11·0	0·6	17·0	1·0
51	0 57·8	0 57·9	0 55·1	5·1	0·3	11·1	0·6	17·1	1·0
52	0 58·0	0 58·2	0 55·4	5·2	0·3	11·2	0·7	17·2	1·0
53	0 58·3	0 58·4	0 55·6	5·3	0·3	11·3	0·7	17·3	1·0
54	0 58·5	0 58·7	0 55·8	5·4	0·3	11·4	0·7	17·4	1·0
55	0 58·8	0 58·9	0 56·1	5·5	0·3	11·5	0·7	17·5	1·0
56	0 59·0	0 59·2	0 56·3	5·6	0·3	11·6	0·7	17·6	1·0
57	0 59·3	0 59·4	0 56·6	5·7	0·3	11·7	0·7	17·7	1·0
58	0 59·5	0 59·7	0 56·8	5·8	0·3	11·8	0·7	17·8	1·0
59	0 59·8	0 59·9	0 57·0	5·9	0·3	11·9	0·7	17·9	1·0
60	1 00·0	1 00·2	0 57·3	6·0	0·4	12·0	0·7	18·0	1·1

4ᵐ s	SUN PLANETS	ARIES	MOON	v or Corrn d	v or Corrn d	v or Corrn d
	° ′	° ′	° ′	′ ′	′ ′	′ ′
00	1 00·0	1 00·2	0 57·3	0·0 0·0	6·0 0·5	12·0 0·9
01	1 00·3	1 00·4	0 57·5	0·1 0·0	6·1 0·5	12·1 0·9
02	1 00·5	1 00·7	0 57·7	0·2 0·0	6·2 0·5	12·2 0·9
03	1 00·8	1 00·9	0 58·0	0·3 0·0	6·3 0·5	12·3 0·9
04	1 01·0	1 01·2	0 58·2	0·4 0·0	6·4 0·5	12·4 0·9
05	1 01·3	1 01·4	0 58·5	0·5 0·0	6·5 0·5	12·5 0·9
06	1 01·5	1 01·7	0 58·7	0·6 0·0	6·6 0·5	12·6 0·9
07	1 01·8	1 01·9	0 58·9	0·7 0·1	6·7 0·5	12·7 1·0
08	1 02·0	1 02·2	0 59·2	0·8 0·1	6·8 0·5	12·8 1·0
09	1 02·3	1 02·4	0 59·4	0·9 0·1	6·9 0·5	12·9 1·0
10	1 02·5	1 02·7	0 59·7	1·0 0·1	7·0 0·5	13·0 1·0
11	1 02·8	1 02·9	0 59·9	1·1 0·1	7·1 0·5	13·1 1·0
12	1 03·0	1 03·2	1 00·1	1·2 0·1	7·2 0·5	13·2 1·0
13	1 03·3	1 03·4	1 00·4	1·3 0·1	7·3 0·5	13·3 1·0
14	1 03·5	1 03·7	1 00·6	1·4 0·1	7·4 0·6	13·4 1·0
15	1 03·8	1 03·9	1 00·8	1·5 0·1	7·5 0·6	13·5 1·0
16	1 04·0	1 04·2	1 01·1	1·6 0·1	7·6 0·6	13·6 1·0
17	1 04·3	1 04·4	1 01·3	1·7 0·1	7·7 0·6	13·7 1·0
18	1 04·5	1 04·7	1 01·6	1·8 0·1	7·8 0·6	13·8 1·0
19	1 04·8	1 04·9	1 01·8	1·9 0·1	7·9 0·6	13·9 1·0
20	1 05·0	1 05·2	1 02·0	2·0 0·2	8·0 0·6	14·0 1·1
21	1 05·3	1 05·4	1 02·3	2·1 0·2	8·1 0·6	14·1 1·1
22	1 05·5	1 05·7	1 02·5	2·2 0·2	8·2 0·6	14·2 1·1
23	1 05·8	1 05·9	1 02·8	2·3 0·2	8·3 0·6	14·3 1·1
24	1 06·0	1 06·2	1 03·0	2·4 0·2	8·4 0·6	14·4 1·1
25	1 06·3	1 06·4	1 03·2	2·5 0·2	8·5 0·6	14·5 1·1
26	1 06·5	1 06·7	1 03·5	2·6 0·2	8·6 0·6	14·6 1·1
27	1 06·8	1 06·9	1 03·7	2·7 0·2	8·7 0·7	14·7 1·1
28	1 07·0	1 07·2	1 03·9	2·8 0·2	8·8 0·7	14·8 1·1
29	1 07·3	1 07·4	1 04·2	2·9 0·2	8·9 0·7	14·9 1·1
30	1 07·5	1 07·7	1 04·4	3·0 0·2	9·0 0·7	15·0 1·1
31	1 07·8	1 07·9	1 04·7	3·1 0·2	9·1 0·7	15·1 1·1
32	1 08·0	1 08·2	1 04·9	3·2 0·2	9·2 0·7	15·2 1·1
33	1 08·3	1 08·4	1 05·1	3·3 0·2	9·3 0·7	15·3 1·1
34	1 08·5	1 08·7	1 05·4	3·4 0·3	9·4 0·7	15·4 1·2
35	1 08·8	1 08·9	1 05·6	3·5 0·3	9·5 0·7	15·5 1·2
36	1 09·0	1 09·2	1 05·9	3·6 0·3	9·6 0·7	15·6 1·2
37	1 09·3	1 09·4	1 06·1	3·7 0·3	9·7 0·7	15·7 1·2
38	1 09·5	1 09·7	1 06·3	3·8 0·3	9·8 0·7	15·8 1·2
39	1 09·8	1 09·9	1 06·6	3·9 0·3	9·9 0·7	15·9 1·2
40	1 10·0	1 10·2	1 06·8	4·0 0·3	10·0 0·8	16·0 1·2
41	1 10·3	1 10·4	1 07·0	4·1 0·3	10·1 0·8	16·1 1·2
42	1 10·5	1 10·7	1 07·3	4·2 0·3	10·2 0·8	16·2 1·2
43	1 10·8	1 10·9	1 07·5	4·3 0·3	10·3 0·8	16·3 1·2
44	1 11·0	1 11·2	1 07·8	4·4 0·3	10·4 0·8	16·4 1·2
45	1 11·3	1 11·4	1 08·0	4·5 0·3	10·5 0·8	16·5 1·2
46	1 11·5	1 11·7	1 08·2	4·6 0·3	10·6 0·8	16·6 1·2
47	1 11·8	1 11·9	1 08·5	4·7 0·4	10·7 0·8	16·7 1·3
48	1 12·0	1 12·2	1 08·7	4·8 0·4	10·8 0·8	16·8 1·3
49	1 12·3	1 12·4	1 09·0	4·9 0·4	10·9 0·8	16·9 1·3
50	1 12·5	1 12·7	1 09·2	5·0 0·4	11·0 0·8	17·0 1·3
51	1 12·8	1 12·9	1 09·4	5·1 0·4	11·1 0·8	17·1 1·3
52	1 13·0	1 13·2	1 09·7	5·2 0·4	11·2 0·8	17·2 1·3
53	1 13·3	1 13·5	1 09·9	5·3 0·4	11·3 0·8	17·3 1·3
54	1 13·5	1 13·7	1 10·2	5·4 0·4	11·4 0·9	17·4 1·3
55	1 13·8	1 14·0	1 10·4	5·5 0·4	11·5 0·9	17·5 1·3
56	1 14·0	1 14·2	1 10·6	5·6 0·4	11·6 0·9	17·6 1·3
57	1 14·3	1 14·5	1 10·9	5·7 0·4	11·7 0·9	17·7 1·3
58	1 14·5	1 14·7	1 11·1	5·8 0·4	11·8 0·9	17·8 1·3
59	1 14·8	1 15·0	1 11·3	5·9 0·4	11·9 0·9	17·9 1·3
60	1 15·0	1 15·2	1 11·6	6·0 0·5	12·0 0·9	18·0 1·4

5ᵐ s	SUN PLANETS	ARIES	MOON	v or Corrn d	v or Corrn d	v or Corrn d
	° ′	° ′	° ′	′ ′	′ ′	′ ′
00	1 15·0	1 15·2	1 11·6	0·0 0·0	6·0 0·6	12·0 1·1
01	1 15·3	1 15·5	1 11·8	0·1 0·0	6·1 0·6	12·1 1·1
02	1 15·5	1 15·7	1 12·1	0·2 0·0	6·2 0·6	12·2 1·1
03	1 15·8	1 16·0	1 12·3	0·3 0·0	6·3 0·6	12·3 1·1
04	1 16·0	1 16·2	1 12·5	0·4 0·0	6·4 0·6	12·4 1·1
05	1 16·3	1 16·5	1 12·8	0·5 0·0	6·5 0·6	12·5 1·1
06	1 16·5	1 16·7	1 13·0	0·6 0·1	6·6 0·6	12·6 1·2
07	1 16·8	1 17·0	1 13·3	0·7 0·1	6·7 0·6	12·7 1·2
08	1 17·0	1 17·2	1 13·5	0·8 0·1	6·8 0·6	12·8 1·2
09	1 17·3	1 17·5	1 13·7	0·9 0·1	6·9 0·6	12·9 1·2
10	1 17·5	1 17·7	1 14·0	1·0 0·1	7·0 0·6	13·0 1·2
11	1 17·8	1 18·0	1 14·2	1·1 0·1	7·1 0·7	13·1 1·2
12	1 18·0	1 18·2	1 14·4	1·2 0·1	7·2 0·7	13·2 1·2
13	1 18·3	1 18·5	1 14·7	1·3 0·1	7·3 0·7	13·3 1·2
14	1 18·5	1 18·7	1 14·9	1·4 0·1	7·4 0·7	13·4 1·2
15	1 18·8	1 19·0	1 15·2	1·5 0·1	7·5 0·7	13·5 1·2
16	1 19·0	1 19·2	1 15·4	1·6 0·1	7·6 0·7	13·6 1·2
17	1 19·3	1 19·5	1 15·6	1·7 0·2	7·7 0·7	13·7 1·3
18	1 19·5	1 19·7	1 15·9	1·8 0·2	7·8 0·7	13·8 1·3
19	1 19·8	1 20·0	1 16·1	1·9 0·2	7·9 0·7	13·9 1·3
20	1 20·0	1 20·2	1 16·4	2·0 0·2	8·0 0·7	14·0 1·3
21	1 20·3	1 20·5	1 16·6	2·1 0·2	8·1 0·7	14·1 1·3
22	1 20·5	1 20·7	1 16·8	2·2 0·2	8·2 0·8	14·2 1·3
23	1 20·8	1 21·0	1 17·1	2·3 0·2	8·3 0·8	14·3 1·3
24	1 21·0	1 21·2	1 17·3	2·4 0·2	8·4 0·8	14·4 1·3
25	1 21·3	1 21·5	1 17·5	2·5 0·2	8·5 0·8	14·5 1·3
26	1 21·5	1 21·7	1 17·8	2·6 0·2	8·6 0·8	14·6 1·3
27	1 21·8	1 22·0	1 18·0	2·7 0·2	8·7 0·8	14·7 1·3
28	1 22·0	1 22·2	1 18·3	2·8 0·3	8·8 0·8	14·8 1·4
29	1 22·3	1 22·5	1 18·5	2·9 0·3	8·9 0·8	14·9 1·4
30	1 22·5	1 22·7	1 18·7	3·0 0·3	9·0 0·8	15·0 1·4
31	1 22·8	1 23·0	1 19·0	3·1 0·3	9·1 0·8	15·1 1·4
32	1 23·0	1 23·2	1 19·2	3·2 0·3	9·2 0·8	15·2 1·4
33	1 23·3	1 23·5	1 19·5	3·3 0·3	9·3 0·9	15·3 1·4
34	1 23·5	1 23·7	1 19·7	3·4 0·3	9·4 0·9	15·4 1·4
35	1 23·8	1 24·0	1 19·9	3·5 0·3	9·5 0·9	15·5 1·4
36	1 24·0	1 24·2	1 20·2	3·6 0·3	9·6 0·9	15·6 1·4
37	1 24·3	1 24·5	1 20·4	3·7 0·3	9·7 0·9	15·7 1·4
38	1 24·5	1 24·7	1 20·7	3·8 0·3	9·8 0·9	15·8 1·4
39	1 24·8	1 25·0	1 20·9	3·9 0·4	9·9 0·9	15·9 1·5
40	1 25·0	1 25·2	1 21·1	4·0 0·4	10·0 0·9	16·0 1·5
41	1 25·3	1 25·5	1 21·4	4·1 0·4	10·1 0·9	16·1 1·5
42	1 25·5	1 25·7	1 21·6	4·2 0·4	10·2 0·9	16·2 1·5
43	1 25·8	1 26·0	1 21·8	4·3 0·4	10·3 0·9	16·3 1·5
44	1 26·0	1 26·2	1 22·1	4·4 0·4	10·4 1·0	16·4 1·5
45	1 26·3	1 26·5	1 22·3	4·5 0·4	10·5 1·0	16·5 1·5
46	1 26·5	1 26·7	1 22·6	4·6 0·4	10·6 1·0	16·6 1·5
47	1 26·8	1 27·0	1 22·8	4·7 0·4	10·7 1·0	16·7 1·5
48	1 27·0	1 27·2	1 23·0	4·8 0·4	10·8 1·0	16·8 1·5
49	1 27·3	1 27·5	1 23·3	4·9 0·4	10·9 1·0	16·9 1·5
50	1 27·5	1 27·7	1 23·5	5·0 0·5	11·0 1·0	17·0 1·6
51	1 27·8	1 28·0	1 23·8	5·1 0·5	11·1 1·0	17·1 1·6
52	1 28·0	1 28·2	1 24·0	5·2 0·5	11·2 1·0	17·2 1·6
53	1 28·3	1 28·5	1 24·2	5·3 0·5	11·3 1·0	17·3 1·6
54	1 28·5	1 28·7	1 24·5	5·4 0·5	11·4 1·0	17·4 1·6
55	1 28·8	1 29·0	1 24·7	5·5 0·5	11·5 1·1	17·5 1·6
56	1 29·0	1 29·2	1 24·9	5·6 0·5	11·6 1·1	17·6 1·6
57	1 29·3	1 29·5	1 25·2	5·7 0·5	11·7 1·1	17·7 1·6
58	1 29·5	1 29·7	1 25·4	5·8 0·5	11·8 1·1	17·8 1·6
59	1 29·8	1 30·0	1 25·7	5·9 0·5	11·9 1·1	17·9 1·6
60	1 30·0	1 30·2	1 25·9	6·0 0·6	12·0 1·1	18·0 1·7

6ᵐ	SUN PLANETS	ARIES	MOON	v or Corrⁿ d	v or Corrⁿ d	v or Corrⁿ d
s	° ′	° ′	° ′	′ ′	′ ′	′ ′
00	1 30.0	1 30.2	1 25.9	0.0 0.0	6.0 0.7	12.0 1.3
01	1 30.3	1 30.5	1 26.1	0.1 0.0	6.1 0.7	12.1 1.3
02	1 30.5	1 30.7	1 26.4	0.2 0.0	6.2 0.7	12.2 1.3
03	1 30.8	1 31.0	1 26.6	0.3 0.0	6.3 0.7	12.3 1.3
04	1 31.0	1 31.2	1 26.9	0.4 0.0	6.4 0.7	12.4 1.3
05	1 31.3	1 31.5	1 27.1	0.5 0.1	6.5 0.7	12.5 1.4
06	1 31.5	1 31.8	1 27.3	0.6 0.1	6.6 0.7	12.6 1.4
07	1 31.8	1 32.0	1 27.6	0.7 0.1	6.7 0.7	12.7 1.4
08	1 32.0	1 32.3	1 27.8	0.8 0.1	6.8 0.7	12.8 1.4
09	1 32.3	1 32.5	1 28.0	0.9 0.1	6.9 0.7	12.9 1.4
10	1 32.5	1 32.8	1 28.3	1.0 0.1	7.0 0.8	13.0 1.4
11	1 32.8	1 33.0	1 28.5	1.1 0.1	7.1 0.8	13.1 1.4
12	1 33.0	1 33.3	1 28.8	1.2 0.1	7.2 0.8	13.2 1.4
13	1 33.3	1 33.5	1 29.0	1.3 0.1	7.3 0.8	13.3 1.4
14	1 33.5	1 33.8	1 29.2	1.4 0.2	7.4 0.8	13.4 1.5
15	1 33.8	1 34.0	1 29.5	1.5 0.2	7.5 0.8	13.5 1.5
16	1 34.0	1 34.3	1 29.7	1.6 0.2	7.6 0.8	13.6 1.5
17	1 34.3	1 34.5	1 30.0	1.7 0.2	7.7 0.8	13.7 1.5
18	1 34.5	1 34.8	1 30.2	1.8 0.2	7.8 0.8	13.8 1.5
19	1 34.8	1 35.0	1 30.4	1.9 0.2	7.9 0.9	13.9 1.5
20	1 35.0	1 35.3	1 30.7	2.0 0.2	8.0 0.9	14.0 1.5
21	1 35.3	1 35.5	1 30.9	2.1 0.2	8.1 0.9	14.1 1.5
22	1 35.5	1 35.8	1 31.1	2.2 0.2	8.2 0.9	14.2 1.5
23	1 35.8	1 36.0	1 31.4	2.3 0.2	8.3 0.9	14.3 1.5
24	1 36.0	1 36.3	1 31.6	2.4 0.3	8.4 0.9	14.4 1.6
25	1 36.3	1 36.5	1 31.9	2.5 0.3	8.5 0.9	14.5 1.6
26	1 36.5	1 36.8	1 32.1	2.6 0.3	8.6 0.9	14.6 1.6
27	1 36.8	1 37.0	1 32.3	2.7 0.3	8.7 0.9	14.7 1.6
28	1 37.0	1 37.3	1 32.6	2.8 0.3	8.8 1.0	14.8 1.6
29	1 37.3	1 37.5	1 32.8	2.9 0.3	8.9 1.0	14.9 1.6
30	1 37.5	1 37.8	1 33.1	3.0 0.3	9.0 1.0	15.0 1.6
31	1 37.8	1 38.0	1 33.3	3.1 0.3	9.1 1.0	15.1 1.6
32	1 38.0	1 38.3	1 33.5	3.2 0.3	9.2 1.0	15.2 1.6
33	1 38.3	1 38.5	1 33.8	3.3 0.4	9.3 1.0	15.3 1.7
34	1 38.5	1 38.8	1 34.0	3.4 0.4	9.4 1.0	15.4 1.7
35	1 38.8	1 39.0	1 34.3	3.5 0.4	9.5 1.0	15.5 1.7
36	1 39.0	1 39.3	1 34.5	3.6 0.4	9.6 1.0	15.6 1.7
37	1 39.3	1 39.5	1 34.7	3.7 0.4	9.7 1.1	15.7 1.7
38	1 39.5	1 39.8	1 35.0	3.8 0.4	9.8 1.1	15.8 1.7
39	1 39.8	1 40.0	1 35.2	3.9 0.4	9.9 1.1	15.9 1.7
40	1 40.0	1 40.3	1 35.4	4.0 0.4	10.0 1.1	16.0 1.7
41	1 40.3	1 40.5	1 35.7	4.1 0.4	10.1 1.1	16.1 1.7
42	1 40.5	1 40.8	1 35.9	4.2 0.5	10.2 1.1	16.2 1.8
43	1 40.8	1 41.0	1 36.2	4.3 0.5	10.3 1.1	16.3 1.8
44	1 41.0	1 41.3	1 36.4	4.4 0.5	10.4 1.1	16.4 1.8
45	1 41.3	1 41.5	1 36.6	4.5 0.5	10.5 1.1	16.5 1.8
46	1 41.5	1 41.8	1 36.9	4.6 0.5	10.6 1.1	16.6 1.8
47	1 41.8	1 42.0	1 37.1	4.7 0.5	10.7 1.2	16.7 1.8
48	1 42.0	1 42.3	1 37.4	4.8 0.5	10.8 1.2	16.8 1.8
49	1 42.3	1 42.5	1 37.6	4.9 0.5	10.9 1.2	16.9 1.8
50	1 42.5	1 42.8	1 37.8	5.0 0.5	11.0 1.2	17.0 1.8
51	1 42.8	1 43.0	1 38.1	5.1 0.6	11.1 1.2	17.1 1.9
52	1 43.0	1 43.3	1 38.3	5.2 0.6	11.2 1.2	17.2 1.9
53	1 43.3	1 43.5	1 38.5	5.3 0.6	11.3 1.2	17.3 1.9
54	1 43.5	1 43.8	1 38.8	5.4 0.6	11.4 1.2	17.4 1.9
55	1 43.8	1 44.0	1 39.0	5.5 0.6	11.5 1.2	17.5 1.9
56	1 44.0	1 44.3	1 39.3	5.6 0.6	11.6 1.3	17.6 1.9
57	1 44.3	1 44.5	1 39.5	5.7 0.6	11.7 1.3	17.7 1.9
58	1 44.5	1 44.8	1 39.7	5.8 0.6	11.8 1.3	17.8 1.9
59	1 44.8	1 45.0	1 40.0	5.9 0.6	11.9 1.3	17.9 1.9
60	1 45.0	1 45.3	1 40.2	6.0 0.7	12.0 1.3	18.0 2.0

7ᵐ	SUN PLANETS	ARIES	MOON	v or Corrⁿ d	v or Corrⁿ d	v or Corrⁿ d
s	° ′	° ′	° ′	′ ′	′ ′	′ ′
00	1 45.0	1 45.3	1 40.2	0.0 0.0	6.0 0.8	12.0 1.5
01	1 45.3	1 45.5	1 40.5	0.1 0.0	6.1 0.8	12.1 1.5
02	1 45.5	1 45.8	1 40.7	0.2 0.0	6.2 0.8	12.2 1.5
03	1 45.8	1 46.0	1 40.9	0.3 0.0	6.3 0.8	12.3 1.5
04	1 46.0	1 46.3	1 41.2	0.4 0.1	6.4 0.8	12.4 1.6
05	1 46.3	1 46.5	1 41.4	0.5 0.1	6.5 0.8	12.5 1.6
06	1 46.5	1 46.8	1 41.6	0.6 0.1	6.6 0.8	12.6 1.6
07	1 46.8	1 47.0	1 41.9	0.7 0.1	6.7 0.8	12.7 1.6
08	1 47.0	1 47.3	1 42.1	0.8 0.1	6.8 0.9	12.8 1.6
09	1 47.3	1 47.5	1 42.4	0.9 0.1	6.9 0.9	12.9 1.6
10	1 47.5	1 47.8	1 42.6	1.0 0.1	7.0 0.9	13.0 1.6
11	1 47.8	1 48.0	1 42.8	1.1 0.1	7.1 0.9	13.1 1.6
12	1 48.0	1 48.3	1 43.1	1.2 0.2	7.2 0.9	13.2 1.7
13	1 48.3	1 48.5	1 43.3	1.3 0.2	7.3 0.9	13.3 1.7
14	1 48.5	1 48.8	1 43.6	1.4 0.2	7.4 0.9	13.4 1.7
15	1 48.8	1 49.0	1 43.8	1.5 0.2	7.5 0.9	13.5 1.7
16	1 49.0	1 49.3	1 44.0	1.6 0.2	7.6 1.0	13.6 1.7
17	1 49.3	1 49.5	1 44.3	1.7 0.2	7.7 1.0	13.7 1.7
18	1 49.5	1 49.8	1 44.5	1.8 0.2	7.8 1.0	13.8 1.7
19	1 49.8	1 50.1	1 44.8	1.9 0.2	7.9 1.0	13.9 1.7
20	1 50.0	1 50.3	1 45.0	2.0 0.3	8.0 1.0	14.0 1.8
21	1 50.3	1 50.6	1 45.2	2.1 0.3	8.1 1.0	14.1 1.8
22	1 50.5	1 50.8	1 45.5	2.2 0.3	8.2 1.0	14.2 1.8
23	1 50.8	1 51.1	1 45.7	2.3 0.3	8.3 1.0	14.3 1.8
24	1 51.0	1 51.3	1 45.9	2.4 0.3	8.4 1.1	14.4 1.8
25	1 51.3	1 51.6	1 46.2	2.5 0.3	8.5 1.1	14.5 1.8
26	1 51.5	1 51.8	1 46.4	2.6 0.3	8.6 1.1	14.6 1.8
27	1 51.8	1 52.1	1 46.7	2.7 0.3	8.7 1.1	14.7 1.8
28	1 52.0	1 52.3	1 46.9	2.8 0.4	8.8 1.1	14.8 1.9
29	1 52.3	1 52.6	1 47.1	2.9 0.4	8.9 1.1	14.9 1.9
30	1 52.5	1 52.8	1 47.4	3.0 0.4	9.0 1.1	15.0 1.9
31	1 52.8	1 53.1	1 47.6	3.1 0.4	9.1 1.1	15.1 1.9
32	1 53.0	1 53.3	1 47.9	3.2 0.4	9.2 1.2	15.2 1.9
33	1 53.3	1 53.6	1 48.1	3.3 0.4	9.3 1.2	15.3 1.9
34	1 53.5	1 53.8	1 48.3	3.4 0.4	9.4 1.2	15.4 1.9
35	1 53.8	1 54.1	1 48.6	3.5 0.4	9.5 1.2	15.5 1.9
36	1 54.0	1 54.3	1 48.8	3.6 0.5	9.6 1.2	15.6 2.0
37	1 54.3	1 54.6	1 49.0	3.7 0.5	9.7 1.2	15.7 2.0
38	1 54.5	1 54.8	1 49.3	3.8 0.5	9.8 1.2	15.8 2.0
39	1 54.8	1 55.1	1 49.5	3.9 0.5	9.9 1.2	15.9 2.0
40	1 55.0	1 55.3	1 49.8	4.0 0.5	10.0 1.3	16.0 2.0
41	1 55.3	1 55.6	1 50.0	4.1 0.5	10.1 1.3	16.1 2.0
42	1 55.5	1 55.8	1 50.2	4.2 0.5	10.2 1.3	16.2 2.0
43	1 55.8	1 56.1	1 50.5	4.3 0.5	10.3 1.3	16.3 2.0
44	1 56.0	1 56.3	1 50.7	4.4 0.6	10.4 1.3	16.4 2.1
45	1 56.3	1 56.6	1 51.0	4.5 0.6	10.5 1.3	16.5 2.1
46	1 56.5	1 56.8	1 51.2	4.6 0.6	10.6 1.3	16.6 2.1
47	1 56.8	1 57.1	1 51.4	4.7 0.6	10.7 1.3	16.7 2.1
48	1 57.0	1 57.3	1 51.7	4.8 0.6	10.8 1.4	16.8 2.1
49	1 57.3	1 57.6	1 51.9	4.9 0.6	10.9 1.4	16.9 2.1
50	1 57.5	1 57.8	1 52.1	5.0 0.6	11.0 1.4	17.0 2.1
51	1 57.8	1 58.1	1 52.4	5.1 0.6	11.1 1.4	17.1 2.1
52	1 58.0	1 58.3	1 52.6	5.2 0.7	11.2 1.4	17.2 2.2
53	1 58.3	1 58.6	1 52.9	5.3 0.7	11.3 1.4	17.3 2.2
54	1 58.5	1 58.8	1 53.1	5.4 0.7	11.4 1.4	17.4 2.2
55	1 58.8	1 59.1	1 53.3	5.5 0.7	11.5 1.4	17.5 2.2
56	1 59.0	1 59.3	1 53.6	5.6 0.7	11.6 1.5	17.6 2.2
57	1 59.3	1 59.6	1 53.8	5.7 0.7	11.7 1.5	17.7 2.2
58	1 59.5	1 59.8	1 54.1	5.8 0.7	11.8 1.5	17.8 2.2
59	1 59.8	2 00.1	1 54.3	5.9 0.7	11.9 1.5	17.9 2.2
60	2 00.0	2 00.3	1 54.5	6.0 0.8	12.0 1.5	18.0 2.3

$\overset{m}{8}$	SUN PLANETS	ARIES	MOON	v or d	Corrⁿ	v or d	Corrⁿ	v or d	Corrⁿ
s	° ′	° ′	° ′	′	′	′	′	′	′
00	2 00·0	2 00·3	1 54·5	0·0	0·0	6·0	0·9	12·0	1·7
01	2 00·3	2 00·6	1 54·8	0·1	0·0	6·1	0·9	12·1	1·7
02	2 00·5	2 00·8	1 55·0	0·2	0·0	6·2	0·9	12·2	1·7
03	2 00·8	2 01·1	1 55·2	0·3	0·0	6·3	0·9	12·3	1·7
04	2 01·0	2 01·3	1 55·5	0·4	0·1	6·4	0·9	12·4	1·8
05	2 01·3	2 01·6	1 55·7	0·5	0·1	6·5	0·9	12·5	1·8
06	2 01·5	2 01·8	1 56·0	0·6	0·1	6·6	0·9	12·6	1·8
07	2 01·8	2 02·1	1 56·2	0·7	0·1	6·7	0·9	12·7	1·8
08	2 02·0	2 02·3	1 56·4	0·8	0·1	6·8	1·0	12·8	1·8
09	2 02·3	2 02·6	1 56·7	0·9	0·1	6·9	1·0	12·9	1·8
10	2 02·5	2 02·8	1 56·9	1·0	0·1	7·0	1·0	13·0	1·8
11	2 02·8	2 03·1	1 57·2	1·1	0·2	7·1	1·0	13·1	1·9
12	2 03·0	2 03·3	1 57·4	1·2	0·2	7·2	1·0	13·2	1·9
13	2 03·3	2 03·6	1 57·6	1·3	0·2	7·3	1·0	13·3	1·9
14	2 03·5	2 03·8	1 57·9	1·4	0·2	7·4	1·0	13·4	1·9
15	2 03·8	2 04·1	1 58·1	1·5	0·2	7·5	1·1	13·5	1·9
16	2 04·0	2 04·3	1 58·4	1·6	0·2	7·6	1·1	13·6	1·9
17	2 04·3	2 04·6	1 58·6	1·7	0·2	7·7	1·1	13·7	1·9
18	2 04·5	2 04·8	1 58·8	1·8	0·3	7·8	1·1	13·8	2·0
19	2 04·8	2 05·1	1 59·1	1·9	0·3	7·9	1·1	13·9	2·0
20	2 05·0	2 05·3	1 59·3	2·0	0·3	8·0	1·1	14·0	2·0
21	2 05·3	2 05·6	1 59·5	2·1	0·3	8·1	1·1	14·1	2·0
22	2 05·5	2 05·8	1 59·8	2·2	0·3	8·2	1·2	14·2	2·0
23	2 05·8	2 06·1	2 00·0	2·3	0·3	8·3	1·2	14·3	2·0
24	2 06·0	2 06·3	2 00·3	2·4	0·3	8·4	1·2	14·4	2·0
25	2 06·3	2 06·6	2 00·5	2·5	0·4	8·5	1·2	14·5	2·1
26	2 06·5	2 06·8	2 00·7	2·6	0·4	8·6	1·2	14·6	2·1
27	2 06·8	2 07·1	2 01·0	2·7	0·4	8·7	1·2	14·7	2·1
28	2 07·0	2 07·3	2 01·2	2·8	0·4	8·8	1·2	14·8	2·1
29	2 07·3	2 07·6	2 01·5	2·9	0·4	8·9	1·3	14·9	2·1
30	2 07·5	2 07·8	2 01·7	3·0	0·4	9·0	1·3	15·0	2·1
31	2 07·8	2 08·1	2 01·9	3·1	0·4	9·1	1·3	15·1	2·1
32	2 08·0	2 08·4	2 02·2	3·2	0·5	9·2	1·3	15·2	2·2
33	2 08·3	2 08·6	2 02·4	3·3	0·5	9·3	1·3	15·3	2·2
34	2 08·5	2 08·9	2 02·6	3·4	0·5	9·4	1·3	15·4	2·2
35	2 08·8	2 09·1	2 02·9	3·5	0·5	9·5	1·3	15·5	2·2
36	2 09·0	2 09·4	2 03·1	3·6	0·5	9·6	1·4	15·6	2·2
37	2 09·3	2 09·6	2 03·4	3·7	0·5	9·7	1·4	15·7	2·2
38	2 09·5	2 09·9	2 03·6	3·8	0·5	9·8	1·4	15·8	2·2
39	2 09·8	2 10·1	2 03·8	3·9	0·6	9·9	1·4	15·9	2·2
40	2 10·0	2 10·4	2 04·1	4·0	0·6	10·0	1·4	16·0	2·3
41	2 10·3	2 10·6	2 04·3	4·1	0·6	10·1	1·4	16·1	2·3
42	2 10·5	2 10·9	2 04·6	4·2	0·6	10·2	1·4	16·2	2·3
43	2 10·8	2 11·1	2 04·8	4·3	0·6	10·3	1·5	16·3	2·3
44	2 11·0	2 11·4	2 05·0	4·4	0·6	10·4	1·5	16·4	2·3
45	2 11·3	2 11·6	2 05·3	4·5	0·6	10·5	1·5	16·5	2·3
46	2 11·5	2 11·9	2 05·5	4·6	0·7	10·6	1·5	16·6	2·4
47	2 11·8	2 12·1	2 05·7	4·7	0·7	10·7	1·5	16·7	2·4
48	2 12·0	2 12·4	2 06·0	4·8	0·7	10·8	1·5	16·8	2·4
49	2 12·3	2 12·6	2 06·2	4·9	0·7	10·9	1·5	16·9	2·4
50	2 12·5	2 12·9	2 06·5	5·0	0·7	11·0	1·6	17·0	2·4
51	2 12·8	2 13·1	2 06·7	5·1	0·7	11·1	1·6	17·1	2·4
52	2 13·0	2 13·4	2 06·9	5·2	0·7	11·2	1·6	17·2	2·4
53	2 13·3	2 13·6	2 07·2	5·3	0·8	11·3	1·6	17·3	2·5
54	2 13·5	2 13·9	2 07·4	5·4	0·8	11·4	1·6	17·4	2·5
55	2 13·8	2 14·1	2 07·7	5·5	0·8	11·5	1·6	17·5	2·5
56	2 14·0	2 14·4	2 07·9	5·6	0·8	11·6	1·6	17·6	2·5
57	2 14·3	2 14·6	2 08·1	5·7	0·8	11·7	1·7	17·7	2·5
58	2 14·5	2 14·9	2 08·4	5·8	0·8	11·8	1·7	17·8	2·5
59	2 14·8	2 15·1	2 08·6	5·9	0·8	11·9	1·7	17·9	2·5
60	2 15·0	2 15·4	2 08·9	6·0	0·9	12·0	1·7	18·0	2·6

$\overset{m}{9}$	SUN PLANETS	ARIES	MOON	v or d	Corrⁿ	v or d	Corrⁿ	v or d	Corrⁿ
s	° ′	° ′	° ′	′	′	′	′	′	′
00	2 15·0	2 15·4	2 08·9	0·0	0·0	6·0	1·0	12·0	1·9
01	2 15·3	2 15·6	2 09·1	0·1	0·0	6·1	1·0	12·1	1·9
02	2 15·5	2 15·9	2 09·3	0·2	0·0	6·2	1·0	12·2	1·9
03	2 15·8	2 16·1	2 09·6	0·3	0·0	6·3	1·0	12·3	1·9
04	2 16·0	2 16·4	2 09·8	0·4	0·1	6·4	1·0	12·4	2·0
05	2 16·3	2 16·6	2 10·0	0·5	0·1	6·5	1·0	12·5	2·0
06	2 16·5	2 16·9	2 10·3	0·6	0·1	6·6	1·0	12·6	2·0
07	2 16·8	2 17·1	2 10·5	0·7	0·1	6·7	1·1	12·7	2·0
08	2 17·0	2 17·4	2 10·8	0·8	0·1	6·8	1·1	12·8	2·0
09	2 17·3	2 17·6	2 11·0	0·9	0·1	6·9	1·1	12·9	2·0
10	2 17·5	2 17·9	2 11·2	1·0	0·2	7·0	1·1	13·0	2·1
11	2 17·8	2 18·1	2 11·5	1·1	0·2	7·1	1·1	13·1	2·1
12	2 18·0	2 18·4	2 11·7	1·2	0·2	7·2	1·1	13·2	2·1
13	2 18·3	2 18·6	2 12·0	1·3	0·2	7·3	1·2	13·3	2·1
14	2 18·5	2 18·9	2 12·2	1·4	0·2	7·4	1·2	13·4	2·1
15	2 18·8	2 19·1	2 12·4	1·5	0·2	7·5	1·2	13·5	2·1
16	2 19·0	2 19·4	2 12·7	1·6	0·3	7·6	1·2	13·6	2·2
17	2 19·3	2 19·6	2 12·9	1·7	0·3	7·7	1·2	13·7	2·2
18	2 19·5	2 19·9	2 13·1	1·8	0·3	7·8	1·2	13·8	2·2
19	2 19·8	2 20·1	2 13·4	1·9	0·3	7·9	1·3	13·9	2·2
20	2 20·0	2 20·4	2 13·6	2·0	0·3	8·0	1·3	14·0	2·2
21	2 20·3	2 20·6	2 13·9	2·1	0·3	8·1	1·3	14·1	2·2
22	2 20·5	2 20·9	2 14·1	2·2	0·3	8·2	1·3	14·2	2·2
23	2 20·8	2 21·1	2 14·3	2·3	0·4	8·3	1·3	14·3	2·3
24	2 21·0	2 21·4	2 14·6	2·4	0·4	8·4	1·3	14·4	2·3
25	2 21·3	2 21·6	2 14·8	2·5	0·4	8·5	1·3	14·5	2·3
26	2 21·5	2 21·9	2 15·1	2·6	0·4	8·6	1·4	14·6	2·3
27	2 21·8	2 22·1	2 15·3	2·7	0·4	8·7	1·4	14·7	2·3
28	2 22·0	2 22·4	2 15·5	2·8	0·4	8·8	1·4	14·8	2·3
29	2 22·3	2 22·6	2 15·8	2·9	0·5	8·9	1·4	14·9	2·4
30	2 22·5	2 22·9	2 16·0	3·0	0·5	9·0	1·4	15·0	2·4
31	2 22·8	2 23·1	2 16·2	3·1	0·5	9·1	1·4	15·1	2·4
32	2 23·0	2 23·4	2 16·5	3·2	0·5	9·2	1·5	15·2	2·4
33	2 23·3	2 23·6	2 16·7	3·3	0·5	9·3	1·5	15·3	2·4
34	2 23·5	2 23·9	2 17·0	3·4	0·5	9·4	1·5	15·4	2·4
35	2 23·8	2 24·1	2 17·2	3·5	0·6	9·5	1·5	15·5	2·5
36	2 24·0	2 24·4	2 17·4	3·6	0·6	9·6	1·5	15·6	2·5
37	2 24·3	2 24·6	2 17·7	3·7	0·6	9·7	1·5	15·7	2·5
38	2 24·5	2 24·9	2 17·9	3·8	0·6	9·8	1·6	15·8	2·5
39	2 24·8	2 25·1	2 18·2	3·9	0·6	9·9	1·6	15·9	2·5
40	2 25·0	2 25·4	2 18·4	4·0	0·6	10·0	1·6	16·0	2·5
41	2 25·3	2 25·6	2 18·6	4·1	0·6	10·1	1·6	16·1	2·5
42	2 25·5	2 25·9	2 18·9	4·2	0·7	10·2	1·6	16·2	2·6
43	2 25·8	2 26·1	2 19·1	4·3	0·7	10·3	1·6	16·3	2·6
44	2 26·0	2 26·4	2 19·3	4·4	0·7	10·4	1·6	16·4	2·6
45	2 26·3	2 26·7	2 19·6	4·5	0·7	10·5	1·7	16·5	2·6
46	2 26·5	2 26·9	2 19·8	4·6	0·7	10·6	1·7	16·6	2·6
47	2 26·8	2 27·2	2 20·1	4·7	0·7	10·7	1·7	16·7	2·6
48	2 27·0	2 27·4	2 20·3	4·8	0·8	10·8	1·7	16·8	2·7
49	2 27·3	2 27·7	2 20·5	4·9	0·8	10·9	1·7	16·9	2·7
50	2 27·5	2 27·9	2 20·8	5·0	0·8	11·0	1·7	17·0	2·7
51	2 27·8	2 28·2	2 21·0	5·1	0·8	11·1	1·8	17·1	2·7
52	2 28·0	2 28·4	2 21·3	5·2	0·8	11·2	1·8	17·2	2·7
53	2 28·3	2 28·7	2 21·5	5·3	0·8	11·3	1·8	17·3	2·7
54	2 28·5	2 28·9	2 21·7	5·4	0·9	11·4	1·8	17·4	2·8
55	2 28·8	2 29·2	2 22·0	5·5	0·9	11·5	1·8	17·5	2·8
56	2 29·0	2 29·4	2 22·2	5·6	0·9	11·6	1·8	17·6	2·8
57	2 29·3	2 29·7	2 22·5	5·7	0·9	11·7	1·9	17·7	2·8
58	2 29·5	2 29·9	2 22·7	5·8	0·9	11·8	1·9	17·8	2·8
59	2 29·8	2 30·2	2 22·9	5·9	0·9	11·9	1·9	17·9	2·8
60	2 30·0	2 30·4	2 23·2	6·0	1·0	12·0	1·9	18·0	2·9

INCREMENTS AND CORRECTIONS

10ᵐ	SUN PLANETS	ARIES	MOON	v or Corrⁿ d	v or Corrⁿ d	v or Corrⁿ d
s	° ′	° ′	° ′	′ ′	′ ′	′ ′
00	2 30·0	2 30·4	2 23·2	0·0 0·0	6·0 1·1	12·0 2·1
01	2 30·3	2 30·7	2 23·4	0·1 0·0	6·1 1·1	12·1 2·1
02	2 30·5	2 30·9	2 23·6	0·2 0·0	6·2 1·1	12·2 2·1
03	2 30·8	2 31·2	2 23·9	0·3 0·1	6·3 1·1	12·3 2·2
04	2 31·0	2 31·4	2 24·1	0·4 0·1	6·4 1·1	12·4 2·2
05	2 31·3	2 31·7	2 24·4	0·5 0·1	6·5 1·1	12·5 2·2
06	2 31·5	2 31·9	2 24·6	0·6 0·1	6·6 1·2	12·6 2·2
07	2 31·8	2 32·2	2 24·8	0·7 0·1	6·7 1·2	12·7 2·2
08	2 32·0	2 32·4	2 25·1	0·8 0·1	6·8 1·2	12·8 2·2
09	2 32·3	2 32·7	2 25·3	0·9 0·2	6·9 1·2	12·9 2·3
10	2 32·5	2 32·9	2 25·6	1·0 0·2	7·0 1·2	13·0 2·3
11	2 32·8	2 33·2	2 25·8	1·1 0·2	7·1 1·2	13·1 2·3
12	2 33·0	2 33·4	2 26·0	1·2 0·2	7·2 1·3	13·2 2·3
13	2 33·3	2 33·7	2 26·3	1·3 0·2	7·3 1·3	13·3 2·3
14	2 33·5	2 33·9	2 26·5	1·4 0·2	7·4 1·3	13·4 2·3
15	2 33·8	2 34·2	2 26·7	1·5 0·3	7·5 1·3	13·5 2·4
16	2 34·0	2 34·4	2 27·0	1·6 0·3	7·6 1·3	13·6 2·4
17	2 34·3	2 34·7	2 27·2	1·7 0·3	7·7 1·3	13·7 2·4
18	2 34·5	2 34·9	2 27·5	1·8 0·3	7·8 1·4	13·8 2·4
19	2 34·8	2 35·2	2 27·7	1·9 0·3	7·9 1·4	13·9 2·4
20	2 35·0	2 35·4	2 27·9	2·0 0·4	8·0 1·4	14·0 2·5
21	2 35·3	2 35·7	2 28·2	2·1 0·4	8·1 1·4	14·1 2·5
22	2 35·5	2 35·9	2 28·4	2·2 0·4	8·2 1·4	14·2 2·5
23	2 35·8	2 36·2	2 28·7	2·3 0·4	8·3 1·5	14·3 2·5
24	2 36·0	2 36·4	2 28·9	2·4 0·4	8·4 1·5	14·4 2·5
25	2 36·3	2 36·7	2 29·1	2·5 0·4	8·5 1·5	14·5 2·5
26	2 36·5	2 36·9	2 29·4	2·6 0·5	8·6 1·5	14·6 2·6
27	2 36·8	2 37·2	2 29·6	2·7 0·5	8·7 1·5	14·7 2·6
28	2 37·0	2 37·4	2 29·8	2·8 0·5	8·8 1·5	14·8 2·6
29	2 37·3	2 37·7	2 30·1	2·9 0·5	8·9 1·6	14·9 2·6
30	2 37·5	2 37·9	2 30·3	3·0 0·5	9·0 1·6	15·0 2·6
31	2 37·8	2 38·2	2 30·6	3·1 0·5	9·1 1·6	15·1 2·6
32	2 38·0	2 38·4	2 30·8	3·2 0·6	9·2 1·6	15·2 2·7
33	2 38·3	2 38·7	2 31·0	3·3 0·6	9·3 1·6	15·3 2·7
34	2 38·5	2 38·9	2 31·3	3·4 0·6	9·4 1·6	15·4 2·7
35	2 38·8	2 39·2	2 31·5	3·5 0·6	9·5 1·7	15·5 2·7
36	2 39·0	2 39·4	2 31·8	3·6 0·6	9·6 1·7	15·6 2·7
37	2 39·3	2 39·7	2 32·0	3·7 0·6	9·7 1·7	15·7 2·7
38	2 39·5	2 39·9	2 32·2	3·8 0·7	9·8 1·7	15·8 2·8
39	2 39·8	2 40·2	2 32·5	3·9 0·7	9·9 1·7	15·9 2·8
40	2 40·0	2 40·4	2 32·7	4·0 0·7	10·0 1·8	16·0 2·8
41	2 40·3	2 40·7	2 32·9	4·1 0·7	10·1 1·8	16·1 2·8
42	2 40·5	2 40·9	2 33·2	4·2 0·7	10·2 1·8	16·2 2·8
43	2 40·8	2 41·2	2 33·4	4·3 0·8	10·3 1·8	16·3 2·9
44	2 41·0	2 41·4	2 33·7	4·4 0·8	10·4 1·8	16·4 2·9
45	2 41·3	2 41·7	2 33·9	4·5 0·8	10·5 1·8	16·5 2·9
46	2 41·5	2 41·9	2 34·1	4·6 0·8	10·6 1·9	16·6 2·9
47	2 41·8	2 42·2	2 34·4	4·7 0·8	10·7 1·9	16·7 2·9
48	2 42·0	2 42·4	2 34·6	4·8 0·8	10·8 1·9	16·8 2·9
49	2 42·3	2 42·7	2 34·9	4·9 0·9	10·9 1·9	16·9 3·0
50	2 42·5	2 42·9	2 35·1	5·0 0·9	11·0 1·9	17·0 3·0
51	2 42·8	2 43·2	2 35·3	5·1 0·9	11·1 1·9	17·1 3·0
52	2 43·0	2 43·4	2 35·6	5·2 0·9	11·2 2·0	17·2 3·0
53	2 43·3	2 43·7	2 35·8	5·3 0·9	11·3 2·0	17·3 3·0
54	2 43·5	2 43·9	2 36·1	5·4 0·9	11·4 2·0	17·4 3·0
55	2 43·8	2 44·2	2 36·3	5·5 1·0	11·5 2·0	17·5 3·1
56	2 44·0	2 44·4	2 36·5	5·6 1·0	11·6 2·0	17·6 3·1
57	2 44·3	2 44·7	2 36·8	5·7 1·0	11·7 2·0	17·7 3·1
58	2 44·5	2 45·0	2 37·0	5·8 1·0	11·8 2·1	17·8 3·1
59	2 44·8	2 45·2	2 37·2	5·9 1·0	11·9 2·1	17·9 3·1
60	2 45·0	2 45·5	2 37·5	6·0 1·1	12·0 2·1	18·0 3·2

11ᵐ	SUN PLANETS	ARIES	MOON	v or Corrⁿ d	v or Corrⁿ d	v or Corrⁿ d
s	° ′	° ′	° ′	′ ′	′ ′	′ ′
00	2 45·0	2 45·5	2 37·5	0·0 0·0	6·0 1·2	12·0 2·3
01	2 45·3	2 45·7	2 37·7	0·1 0·0	6·1 1·2	12·1 2·3
02	2 45·5	2 46·0	2 38·0	0·2 0·0	6·2 1·2	12·2 2·3
03	2 45·8	2 46·2	2 38·2	0·3 0·1	6·3 1·2	12·3 2·4
04	2 46·0	2 46·5	2 38·4	0·4 0·1	6·4 1·2	12·4 2·4
05	2 46·3	2 46·7	2 38·7	0·5 0·1	6·5 1·2	12·5 2·4
06	2 46·5	2 47·0	2 38·9	0·6 0·1	6·6 1·3	12·6 2·4
07	2 46·8	2 47·2	2 39·2	0·7 0·1	6·7 1·3	12·7 2·4
08	2 47·0	2 47·5	2 39·4	0·8 0·2	6·8 1·3	12·8 2·5
09	2 47·3	2 47·7	2 39·6	0·9 0·2	6·9 1·3	12·9 2·5
10	2 47·5	2 48·0	2 39·9	1·0 0·2	7·0 1·3	13·0 2·5
11	2 47·8	2 48·2	2 40·1	1·1 0·2	7·1 1·4	13·1 2·5
12	2 48·0	2 48·5	2 40·3	1·2 0·2	7·2 1·4	13·2 2·5
13	2 48·3	2 48·7	2 40·6	1·3 0·2	7·3 1·4	13·3 2·5
14	2 48·5	2 49·0	2 40·8	1·4 0·3	7·4 1·4	13·4 2·6
15	2 48·8	2 49·2	2 41·1	1·5 0·3	7·5 1·4	13·5 2·6
16	2 49·0	2 49·5	2 41·3	1·6 0·3	7·6 1·5	13·6 2·6
17	2 49·3	2 49·7	2 41·5	1·7 0·3	7·7 1·5	13·7 2·6
18	2 49·5	2 50·0	2 41·8	1·8 0·3	7·8 1·5	13·8 2·6
19	2 49·8	2 50·2	2 42·0	1·9 0·4	7·9 1·5	13·9 2·7
20	2 50·0	2 50·5	2 42·3	2·0 0·4	8·0 1·5	14·0 2·7
21	2 50·3	2 50·7	2 42·5	2·1 0·4	8·1 1·6	14·1 2·7
22	2 50·5	2 51·0	2 42·7	2·2 0·4	8·2 1·6	14·2 2·7
23	2 50·8	2 51·2	2 43·0	2·3 0·4	8·3 1·6	14·3 2·7
24	2 51·0	2 51·5	2 43·2	2·4 0·5	8·4 1·6	14·4 2·8
25	2 51·3	2 51·7	2 43·4	2·5 0·5	8·5 1·6	14·5 2·8
26	2 51·5	2 52·0	2 43·7	2·6 0·5	8·6 1·6	14·6 2·8
27	2 51·8	2 52·2	2 43·9	2·7 0·5	8·7 1·7	14·7 2·8
28	2 52·0	2 52·5	2 44·2	2·8 0·5	8·8 1·7	14·8 2·8
29	2 52·3	2 52·7	2 44·4	2·9 0·6	8·9 1·7	14·9 2·9
30	2 52·5	2 53·0	2 44·6	3·0 0·6	9·0 1·7	15·0 2·9
31	2 52·8	2 53·2	2 44·9	3·1 0·6	9·1 1·7	15·1 2·9
32	2 53·0	2 53·5	2 45·1	3·2 0·6	9·2 1·8	15·2 2·9
33	2 53·3	2 53·7	2 45·4	3·3 0·6	9·3 1·8	15·3 2·9
34	2 53·5	2 54·0	2 45·6	3·4 0·7	9·4 1·8	15·4 3·0
35	2 53·8	2 54·2	2 45·8	3·5 0·7	9·5 1·8	15·5 3·0
36	2 54·0	2 54·5	2 46·1	3·6 0·7	9·6 1·8	15·6 3·0
37	2 54·3	2 54·7	2 46·3	3·7 0·7	9·7 1·9	15·7 3·0
38	2 54·5	2 55·0	2 46·6	3·8 0·7	9·8 1·9	15·8 3·0
39	2 54·8	2 55·2	2 46·8	3·9 0·7	9·9 1·9	15·9 3·0
40	2 55·0	2 55·5	2 47·0	4·0 0·8	10·0 1·9	16·0 3·1
41	2 55·3	2 55·7	2 47·3	4·1 0·8	10·1 1·9	16·1 3·1
42	2 55·5	2 56·0	2 47·5	4·2 0·8	10·2 2·0	16·2 3·1
43	2 55·8	2 56·2	2 47·7	4·3 0·8	10·3 2·0	16·3 3·1
44	2 56·0	2 56·5	2 48·0	4·4 0·8	10·4 2·0	16·4 3·1
45	2 56·3	2 56·7	2 48·2	4·5 0·9	10·5 2·0	16·5 3·2
46	2 56·5	2 57·0	2 48·5	4·6 0·9	10·6 2·0	16·6 3·2
47	2 56·8	2 57·2	2 48·7	4·7 0·9	10·7 2·1	16·7 3·2
48	2 57·0	2 57·5	2 48·9	4·8 0·9	10·8 2·1	16·8 3·2
49	2 57·3	2 57·7	2 49·2	4·9 0·9	10·9 2·1	16·9 3·2
50	2 57·5	2 58·0	2 49·4	5·0 1·0	11·0 2·1	17·0 3·3
51	2 57·8	2 58·2	2 49·7	5·1 1·0	11·1 2·1	17·1 3·3
52	2 58·0	2 58·5	2 49·9	5·2 1·0	11·2 2·1	17·2 3·3
53	2 58·3	2 58·7	2 50·1	5·3 1·0	11·3 2·2	17·3 3·3
54	2 58·5	2 59·0	2 50·4	5·4 1·0	11·4 2·2	17·4 3·3
55	2 58·8	2 59·2	2 50·6	5·5 1·1	11·5 2·2	17·5 3·4
56	2 59·0	2 59·5	2 50·8	5·6 1·1	11·6 2·2	17·6 3·4
57	2 59·3	2 59·7	2 51·1	5·7 1·1	11·7 2·2	17·7 3·4
58	2 59·5	3 00·0	2 51·3	5·8 1·1	11·8 2·3	17·8 3·4
59	2 59·8	3 00·2	2 51·6	5·9 1·1	11·9 2·3	17·9 3·4
60	3 00·0	3 00·5	2 51·8	6·0 1·2	12·0 2·3	18·0 3·5

12^m s	SUN PLANETS	ARIES	MOON	v or d	Corrn	v or d	Corrn	v or d	Corrn
00	3 00·0	3 00·5	2 51·8	0·0	0·0	6·0	1·3	12·0	2·5
01	3 00·3	3 00·7	2 52·0	0·1	0·0	6·1	1·3	12·1	2·5
02	3 00·5	3 01·0	2 52·3	0·2	0·0	6·2	1·3	12·2	2·5
03	3 00·8	3 01·2	2 52·5	0·3	0·1	6·3	1·3	12·3	2·6
04	3 01·0	3 01·5	2 52·8	0·4	0·1	6·4	1·3	12·4	2·6
05	3 01·3	3 01·7	2 53·0	0·5	0·1	6·5	1·4	12·5	2·6
06	3 01·5	3 02·0	2 53·2	0·6	0·1	6·6	1·4	12·6	2·6
07	3 01·8	3 02·2	2 53·5	0·7	0·1	6·7	1·4	12·7	2·6
08	3 02·0	3 02·5	2 53·7	0·8	0·2	6·8	1·4	12·8	2·7
09	3 02·3	3 02·7	2 53·9	0·9	0·2	6·9	1·4	12·9	2·7
10	3 02·5	3 03·0	2 54·2	1·0	0·2	7·0	1·5	13·0	2·7
11	3 02·8	3 03·3	2 54·4	1·1	0·2	7·1	1·5	13·1	2·7
12	3 03·0	3 03·5	2 54·7	1·2	0·3	7·2	1·5	13·2	2·8
13	3 03·3	3 03·8	2 54·9	1·3	0·3	7·3	1·5	13·3	2·8
14	3 03·5	3 04·0	2 55·1	1·4	0·3	7·4	1·5	13·4	2·8
15	3 03·8	3 04·3	2 55·4	1·5	0·3	7·5	1·6	13·5	2·8
16	3 04·0	3 04·5	2 55·6	1·6	0·3	7·6	1·6	13·6	2·8
17	3 04·3	3 04·8	2 55·9	1·7	0·4	7·7	1·6	13·7	2·9
18	3 04·5	3 05·0	2 56·1	1·8	0·4	7·8	1·6	13·8	2·9
19	3 04·8	3 05·3	2 56·3	1·9	0·4	7·9	1·6	13·9	2·9
20	3 05·0	3 05·5	2 56·6	2·0	0·4	8·0	1·7	14·0	2·9
21	3 05·3	3 05·8	2 56·8	2·1	0·4	8·1	1·7	14·1	2·9
22	3 05·5	3 06·0	2 57·0	2·2	0·5	8·2	1·7	14·2	3·0
23	3 05·8	3 06·3	2 57·3	2·3	0·5	8·3	1·7	14·3	3·0
24	3 06·0	3 06·5	2 57·5	2·4	0·5	8·4	1·8	14·4	3·0
25	3 06·3	3 06·8	2 57·8	2·5	0·5	8·5	1·8	14·5	3·0
26	3 06·5	3 07·0	2 58·0	2·6	0·5	8·6	1·8	14·6	3·0
27	3 06·8	3 07·3	2 58·2	2·7	0·6	8·7	1·8	14·7	3·1
28	3 07·0	3 07·5	2 58·5	2·8	0·6	8·8	1·8	14·8	3·1
29	3 07·3	3 07·8	2 58·7	2·9	0·6	8·9	1·9	14·9	3·1
30	3 07·5	3 08·0	2 59·0	3·0	0·6	9·0	1·9	15·0	3·1
31	3 07·8	3 08·3	2 59·2	3·1	0·6	9·1	1·9	15·1	3·1
32	3 08·0	3 08·5	2 59·4	3·2	0·7	9·2	1·9	15·2	3·2
33	3 08·3	3 08·8	2 59·7	3·3	0·7	9·3	1·9	15·3	3·2
34	3 08·5	3 09·0	2 59·9	3·4	0·7	9·4	2·0	15·4	3·2
35	3 08·8	3 09·3	3 00·2	3·5	0·7	9·5	2·0	15·5	3·2
36	3 09·0	3 09·5	3 00·4	3·6	0·8	9·6	2·0	15·6	3·3
37	3 09·3	3 09·8	3 00·6	3·7	0·8	9·7	2·0	15·7	3·3
38	3 09·5	3 10·0	3 00·9	3·8	0·8	9·8	2·0	15·8	3·3
39	3 09·8	3 10·3	3 01·1	3·9	0·8	9·9	2·1	15·9	3·3
40	3 10·0	3 10·5	3 01·3	4·0	0·8	10·0	2·1	16·0	3·3
41	3 10·3	3 10·8	3 01·6	4·1	0·9	10·1	2·1	16·1	3·4
42	3 10·5	3 11·0	3 01·8	4·2	0·9	10·2	2·1	16·2	3·4
43	3 10·8	3 11·3	3 02·1	4·3	0·9	10·3	2·1	16·3	3·4
44	3 11·0	3 11·5	3 02·3	4·4	0·9	10·4	2·2	16·4	3·4
45	3 11·3	3 11·8	3 02·5	4·5	0·9	10·5	2·2	16·5	3·4
46	3 11·5	3 12·0	3 02·8	4·6	1·0	10·6	2·2	16·6	3·5
47	3 11·8	3 12·3	3 03·0	4·7	1·0	10·7	2·2	16·7	3·5
48	3 12·0	3 12·5	3 03·3	4·8	1·0	10·8	2·3	16·8	3·5
49	3 12·3	3 12·8	3 03·5	4·9	1·0	10·9	2·3	16·9	3·5
50	3 12·5	3 13·0	3 03·7	5·0	1·0	11·0	2·3	17·0	3·5
51	3 12·8	3 13·3	3 04·0	5·1	1·1	11·1	2·3	17·1	3·6
52	3 13·0	3 13·5	3 04·2	5·2	1·1	11·2	2·3	17·2	3·6
53	3 13·3	3 13·8	3 04·4	5·3	1·1	11·3	2·4	17·3	3·6
54	3 13·5	3 14·0	3 04·7	5·4	1·1	11·4	2·4	17·4	3·6
55	3 13·8	3 14·3	3 04·9	5·5	1·1	11·5	2·4	17·5	3·6
56	3 14·0	3 14·5	3 05·2	5·6	1·2	11·6	2·4	17·6	3·7
57	3 14·3	3 14·8	3 05·4	5·7	1·2	11·7	2·4	17·7	3·7
58	3 14·5	3 15·0	3 05·6	5·8	1·2	11·8	2·5	17·8	3·7
59	3 14·8	3 15·3	3 05·9	5·9	1·2	11·9	2·5	17·9	3·7
60	3 15·0	3 15·5	3 06·1	6·0	1·3	12·0	2·5	18·0	3·8

13^m s	SUN PLANETS	ARIES	MOON	v or d	Corrn	v or d	Corrn	v or d	Corrn
00	3 15·0	3 15·5	3 06·1	0·0	0·0	6·0	1·4	12·0	2·7
01	3 15·3	3 15·8	3 06·4	0·1	0·0	6·1	1·4	12·1	2·7
02	3 15·5	3 16·0	3 06·6	0·2	0·0	6·2	1·4	12·2	2·7
03	3 15·8	3 16·3	3 06·8	0·3	0·1	6·3	1·4	12·3	2·8
04	3 16·0	3 16·5	3 07·1	0·4	0·1	6·4	1·4	12·4	2·8
05	3 16·3	3 16·8	3 07·3	0·5	0·1	6·5	1·5	12·5	2·8
06	3 16·5	3 17·0	3 07·5	0·6	0·1	6·6	1·5	12·6	2·8
07	3 16·8	3 17·3	3 07·8	0·7	0·2	6·7	1·5	12·7	2·9
08	3 17·0	3 17·5	3 08·0	0·8	0·2	6·8	1·5	12·8	2·9
09	3 17·3	3 17·8	3 08·3	0·9	0·2	6·9	1·6	12·9	2·9
10	3 17·5	3 18·0	3 08·5	1·0	0·2	7·0	1·6	13·0	2·9
11	3 17·8	3 18·3	3 08·7	1·1	0·2	7·1	1·6	13·1	2·9
12	3 18·0	3 18·5	3 09·0	1·2	0·3	7·2	1·6	13·2	3·0
13	3 18·3	3 18·8	3 09·2	1·3	0·3	7·3	1·6	13·3	3·0
14	3 18·5	3 19·0	3 09·5	1·4	0·3	7·4	1·7	13·4	3·0
15	3 18·8	3 19·3	3 09·7	1·5	0·3	7·5	1·7	13·5	3·0
16	3 19·0	3 19·5	3 09·9	1·6	0·4	7·6	1·7	13·6	3·1
17	3 19·3	3 19·8	3 10·2	1·7	0·4	7·7	1·7	13·7	3·1
18	3 19·5	3 20·0	3 10·4	1·8	0·4	7·8	1·8	13·8	3·1
19	3 19·8	3 20·3	3 10·7	1·9	0·4	7·9	1·8	13·9	3·1
20	3 20·0	3 20·5	3 10·9	2·0	0·5	8·0	1·8	14·0	3·2
21	3 20·3	3 20·8	3 11·1	2·1	0·5	8·1	1·8	14·1	3·2
22	3 20·5	3 21·0	3 11·4	2·2	0·5	8·2	1·8	14·2	3·2
23	3 20·8	3 21·3	3 11·6	2·3	0·5	8·3	1·9	14·3	3·2
24	3 21·0	3 21·6	3 11·8	2·4	0·5	8·4	1·9	14·4	3·2
25	3 21·3	3 21·8	3 12·1	2·5	0·6	8·5	1·9	14·5	3·3
26	3 21·5	3 22·1	3 12·3	2·6	0·6	8·6	1·9	14·6	3·3
27	3 21·8	3 22·3	3 12·6	2·7	0·6	8·7	2·0	14·7	3·3
28	3 22·0	3 22·6	3 12·8	2·8	0·6	8·8	2·0	14·8	3·3
29	3 22·3	3 22·8	3 13·0	2·9	0·7	8·9	2·0	14·9	3·4
30	3 22·5	3 23·1	3 13·3	3·0	0·7	9·0	2·0	15·0	3·4
31	3 22·8	3 23·3	3 13·5	3·1	0·7	9·1	2·0	15·1	3·4
32	3 23·0	3 23·6	3 13·8	3·2	0·7	9·2	2·1	15·2	3·4
33	3 23·3	3 23·8	3 14·0	3·3	0·7	9·3	2·1	15·3	3·4
34	3 23·5	3 24·1	3 14·2	3·4	0·8	9·4	2·1	15·4	3·5
35	3 23·8	3 24·3	3 14·5	3·5	0·8	9·5	2·1	15·5	3·5
36	3 24·0	3 24·6	3 14·7	3·6	0·8	9·6	2·2	15·6	3·5
37	3 24·3	3 24·8	3 14·9	3·7	0·8	9·7	2·2	15·7	3·5
38	3 24·5	3 25·1	3 15·2	3·8	0·9	9·8	2·2	15·8	3·6
39	3 24·8	3 25·3	3 15·4	3·9	0·9	9·9	2·2	15·9	3·6
40	3 25·0	3 25·6	3 15·7	4·0	0·9	10·0	2·3	16·0	3·6
41	3 25·3	3 25·8	3 15·9	4·1	0·9	10·1	2·3	16·1	3·6
42	3 25·5	3 26·1	3 16·1	4·2	0·9	10·2	2·3	16·2	3·6
43	3 25·8	3 26·3	3 16·4	4·3	1·0	10·3	2·3	16·3	3·7
44	3 26·0	3 26·6	3 16·6	4·4	1·0	10·4	2·3	16·4	3·7
45	3 26·3	3 26·8	3 16·9	4·5	1·0	10·5	2·4	16·5	3·7
46	3 26·5	3 27·1	3 17·1	4·6	1·0	10·6	2·4	16·6	3·7
47	3 26·8	3 27·3	3 17·3	4·7	1·1	10·7	2·4	16·7	3·8
48	3 27·0	3 27·6	3 17·6	4·8	1·1	10·8	2·4	16·8	3·8
49	3 27·3	3 27·8	3 17·8	4·9	1·1	10·9	2·5	16·9	3·8
50	3 27·5	3 28·1	3 18·0	5·0	1·1	11·0	2·5	17·0	3·8
51	3 27·8	3 28·3	3 18·3	5·1	1·1	11·1	2·5	17·1	3·8
52	3 28·0	3 28·6	3 18·5	5·2	1·2	11·2	2·5	17·2	3·9
53	3 28·3	3 28·8	3 18·8	5·3	1·2	11·3	2·5	17·3	3·9
54	3 28·5	3 29·1	3 19·0	5·4	1·2	11·4	2·6	17·4	3·9
55	3 28·8	3 29·3	3 19·2	5·5	1·2	11·5	2·6	17·5	3·9
56	3 29·0	3 29·6	3 19·5	5·6	1·3	11·6	2·6	17·6	4·0
57	3 29·3	3 29·8	3 19·7	5·7	1·3	11·7	2·6	17·7	4·0
58	3 29·5	3 30·1	3 20·0	5·8	1·3	11·8	2·7	17·8	4·0
59	3 29·8	3 30·3	3 20·2	5·9	1·3	11·9	2·7	17·9	4·0
60	3 30·0	3 30·6	3 20·4	6·0	1·4	12·0	2·7	18·0	4·1

14ᵐ	SUN PLANETS	ARIES	MOON	v or Corrⁿ d	v or Corrⁿ d	v or Corrⁿ d
s	° ′	° ′	° ′	′ ′	′ ′	′ ′
00	3 30·0	3 30·6	3 20·4	0·0 0·0	6·0 1·5	12·0 2·9
01	3 30·3	3 30·8	3 20·7	0·1 0·0	6·1 1·5	12·1 2·9
02	3 30·5	3 31·1	3 20·9	0·2 0·0	6·2 1·5	12·2 2·9
03	3 30·8	3 31·3	3 21·1	0·3 0·1	6·3 1·5	12·3 3·0
04	3 31·0	3 31·6	3 21·4	0·4 0·1	6·4 1·5	12·4 3·0
05	3 31·3	3 31·8	3 21·6	0·5 0·1	6·5 1·6	12·5 3·0
06	3 31·5	3 32·1	3 21·9	0·6 0·1	6·6 1·6	12·6 3·0
07	3 31·8	3 32·3	3 22·1	0·7 0·2	6·7 1·6	12·7 3·1
08	3 32·0	3 32·6	3 22·3	0·8 0·2	6·8 1·6	12·8 3·1
09	3 32·3	3 32·8	3 22·6	0·9 0·2	6·9 1·7	12·9 3·1
10	3 32·5	3 33·1	3 22·8	1·0 0·2	7·0 1·7	13·0 3·1
11	3 32·8	3 33·3	3 23·1	1·1 0·3	7·1 1·7	13·1 3·2
12	3 33·0	3 33·6	3 23·3	1·2 0·3	7·2 1·7	13·2 3·2
13	3 33·3	3 33·8	3 23·5	1·3 0·3	7·3 1·8	13·3 3·2
14	3 33·5	3 34·1	3 23·8	1·4 0·3	7·4 1·8	13·4 3·2
15	3 33·8	3 34·3	3 24·0	1·5 0·4	7·5 1·8	13·5 3·3
16	3 34·0	3 34·6	3 24·3	1·6 0·4	7·6 1·8	13·6 3·3
17	3 34·3	3 34·8	3 24·5	1·7 0·4	7·7 1·9	13·7 3·3
18	3 34·5	3 35·1	3 24·7	1·8 0·4	7·8 1·9	13·8 3·3
19	3 34·8	3 35·3	3 25·0	1·9 0·5	7·9 1·9	13·9 3·4
20	3 35·0	3 35·6	3 25·2	2·0 0·5	8·0 1·9	14·0 3·4
21	3 35·3	3 35·8	3 25·4	2·1 0·5	8·1 2·0	14·1 3·4
22	3 35·5	3 36·1	3 25·7	2·2 0·5	8·2 2·0	14·2 3·4
23	3 35·8	3 36·3	3 25·9	2·3 0·6	8·3 2·0	14·3 3·5
24	3 36·0	3 36·6	3 26·2	2·4 0·6	8·4 2·0	14·4 3·5
25	3 36·3	3 36·8	3 26·4	2·5 0·6	8·5 2·1	14·5 3·5
26	3 36·5	3 37·1	3 26·6	2·6 0·6	8·6 2·1	14·6 3·5
27	3 36·8	3 37·3	3 26·9	2·7 0·7	8·7 2·1	14·7 3·6
28	3 37·0	3 37·6	3 27·1	2·8 0·7	8·8 2·1	14·8 3·6
29	3 37·3	3 37·8	3 27·4	2·9 0·7	8·9 2·2	14·9 3·6
30	3 37·5	3 38·1	3 27·6	3·0 0·7	9·0 2·2	15·0 3·6
31	3 37·8	3 38·3	3 27·8	3·1 0·7	9·1 2·2	15·1 3·7
32	3 38·0	3 38·6	3 28·1	3·2 0·8	9·2 2·2	15·2 3·7
33	3 38·3	3 38·8	3 28·3	3·3 0·8	9·3 2·2	15·3 3·7
34	3 38·5	3 39·1	3 28·5	3·4 0·8	9·4 2·3	15·4 3·7
35	3 38·8	3 39·3	3 28·8	3·5 0·8	9·5 2·3	15·5 3·7
36	3 39·0	3 39·6	3 29·0	3·6 0·9	9·6 2·3	15·6 3·8
37	3 39·3	3 39·9	3 29·3	3·7 0·9	9·7 2·3	15·7 3·8
38	3 39·5	3 40·1	3 29·5	3·8 0·9	9·8 2·4	15·8 3·8
39	3 39·8	3 40·4	3 29·7	3·9 0·9	9·9 2·4	15·9 3·8
40	3 40·0	3 40·6	3 30·0	4·0 1·0	10·0 2·4	16·0 3·9
41	3 40·3	3 40·9	3 30·2	4·1 1·0	10·1 2·4	16·1 3·9
42	3 40·5	3 41·1	3 30·5	4·2 1·0	10·2 2·5	16·2 3·9
43	3 40·8	3 41·4	3 30·7	4·3 1·0	10·3 2·5	16·3 3·9
44	3 41·0	3 41·6	3 30·9	4·4 1·1	10·4 2·5	16·4 4·0
45	3 41·3	3 41·9	3 31·2	4·5 1·1	10·5 2·5	16·5 4·0
46	3 41·5	3 42·1	3 31·4	4·6 1·1	10·6 2·6	16·6 4·0
47	3 41·8	3 42·4	3 31·6	4·7 1·1	10·7 2·6	16·7 4·0
48	3 42·0	3 42·6	3 31·9	4·8 1·2	10·8 2·6	16·8 4·1
49	3 42·3	3 42·9	3 32·1	4·9 1·2	10·9 2·6	16·9 4·1
50	3 42·5	3 43·1	3 32·4	5·0 1·2	11·0 2·7	17·0 4·1
51	3 42·8	3 43·4	3 32·6	5·1 1·2	11·1 2·7	17·1 4·1
52	3 43·0	3 43·6	3 32·8	5·2 1·3	11·2 2·7	17·2 4·2
53	3 43·3	3 43·9	3 33·1	5·3 1·3	11·3 2·7	17·3 4·2
54	3 43·5	3 44·1	3 33·3	5·4 1·3	11·4 2·8	17·4 4·2
55	3 43·8	3 44·4	3 33·6	5·5 1·3	11·5 2·8	17·5 4·2
56	3 44·0	3 44·6	3 33·8	5·6 1·4	11·6 2·8	17·6 4·3
57	3 44·3	3 44·9	3 34·0	5·7 1·4	11·7 2·8	17·7 4·3
58	3 44·5	3 45·1	3 34·3	5·8 1·4	11·8 2·9	17·8 4·3
59	3 44·8	3 45·4	3 34·5	5·9 1·4	11·9 2·9	17·9 4·3
60	3 45·0	3 45·6	3 34·8	6·0 1·5	12·0 2·9	18·0 4·4

15ᵐ	SUN PLANETS	ARIES	MOON	v or Corrⁿ d	v or Corrⁿ d	v or Corrⁿ d
s	° ′	° ′	° ′	′ ′	′ ′	′ ′
00	3 45·0	3 45·6	3 34·8	0·0 0·0	6·0 1·6	12·0 3·1
01	3 45·3	3 45·9	3 35·0	0·1 0·0	6·1 1·6	12·1 3·1
02	3 45·5	3 46·1	3 35·2	0·2 0·1	6·2 1·6	12·2 3·2
03	3 45·8	3 46·4	3 35·5	0·3 0·1	6·3 1·6	12·3 3·2
04	3 46·0	3 46·6	3 35·7	0·4 0·1	6·4 1·7	12·4 3·2
05	3 46·3	3 46·9	3 35·9	0·5 0·1	6·5 1·7	12·5 3·2
06	3 46·5	3 47·1	3 36·2	0·6 0·2	6·6 1·7	12·6 3·3
07	3 46·8	3 47·4	3 36·4	0·7 0·2	6·7 1·7	12·7 3·3
08	3 47·0	3 47·6	3 36·7	0·8 0·2	6·8 1·8	12·8 3·3
09	3 47·3	3 47·9	3 36·9	0·9 0·2	6·9 1·8	12·9 3·3
10	3 47·5	3 48·1	3 37·1	1·0 0·3	7·0 1·8	13·0 3·4
11	3 47·8	3 48·4	3 37·4	1·1 0·3	7·1 1·8	13·1 3·4
12	3 48·0	3 48·6	3 37·6	1·2 0·3	7·2 1·9	13·2 3·4
13	3 48·3	3 48·9	3 37·9	1·3 0·3	7·3 1·9	13·3 3·4
14	3 48·5	3 49·1	3 38·1	1·4 0·4	7·4 1·9	13·4 3·5
15	3 48·8	3 49·4	3 38·3	1·5 0·4	7·5 1·9	13·5 3·5
16	3 49·0	3 49·6	3 38·6	1·6 0·4	7·6 2·0	13·6 3·5
17	3 49·3	3 49·9	3 38·8	1·7 0·4	7·7 2·0	13·7 3·5
18	3 49·5	3 50·1	3 39·0	1·8 0·5	7·8 2·0	13·8 3·6
19	3 49·8	3 50·4	3 39·3	1·9 0·5	7·9 2·0	13·9 3·6
20	3 50·0	3 50·6	3 39·5	2·0 0·5	8·0 2·1	14·0 3·6
21	3 50·3	3 50·9	3 39·8	2·1 0·5	8·1 2·1	14·1 3·6
22	3 50·5	3 51·1	3 40·0	2·2 0·6	8·2 2·1	14·2 3·7
23	3 50·8	3 51·4	3 40·2	2·3 0·6	8·3 2·1	14·3 3·7
24	3 51·0	3 51·6	3 40·5	2·4 0·6	8·4 2·2	14·4 3·7
25	3 51·3	3 51·9	3 40·7	2·5 0·6	8·5 2·2	14·5 3·7
26	3 51·5	3 52·1	3 41·0	2·6 0·7	8·6 2·2	14·6 3·8
27	3 51·8	3 52·4	3 41·2	2·7 0·7	8·7 2·2	14·7 3·8
28	3 52·0	3 52·6	3 41·4	2·8 0·7	8·8 2·3	14·8 3·8
29	3 52·3	3 52·9	3 41·7	2·9 0·7	8·9 2·3	14·9 3·8
30	3 52·5	3 53·1	3 41·9	3·0 0·8	9·0 2·3	15·0 3·9
31	3 52·8	3 53·4	3 42·1	3·1 0·8	9·1 2·4	15·1 3·9
32	3 53·0	3 53·6	3 42·4	3·2 0·8	9·2 2·4	15·2 3·9
33	3 53·3	3 53·9	3 42·6	3·3 0·9	9·3 2·4	15·3 4·0
34	3 53·5	3 54·1	3 42·9	3·4 0·9	9·4 2·4	15·4 4·0
35	3 53·8	3 54·4	3 43·1	3·5 0·9	9·5 2·5	15·5 4·0
36	3 54·0	3 54·6	3 43·3	3·6 0·9	9·6 2·5	15·6 4·0
37	3 54·3	3 54·9	3 43·6	3·7 1·0	9·7 2·5	15·7 4·1
38	3 54·5	3 55·1	3 43·8	3·8 1·0	9·8 2·5	15·8 4·1
39	3 54·8	3 55·4	3 44·1	3·9 1·0	9·9 2·6	15·9 4·1
40	3 55·0	3 55·6	3 44·3	4·0 1·0	10·0 2·6	16·0 4·1
41	3 55·3	3 55·9	3 44·5	4·1 1·1	10·1 2·6	16·1 4·2
42	3 55·5	3 56·1	3 44·8	4·2 1·1	10·2 2·6	16·2 4·2
43	3 55·8	3 56·4	3 45·0	4·3 1·1	10·3 2·7	16·3 4·2
44	3 56·0	3 56·6	3 45·2	4·4 1·1	10·4 2·7	16·4 4·2
45	3 56·3	3 56·9	3 45·5	4·5 1·2	10·5 2·7	16·5 4·3
46	3 56·5	3 57·1	3 45·7	4·6 1·2	10·6 2·7	16·6 4·3
47	3 56·8	3 57·4	3 46·0	4·7 1·2	10·7 2·8	16·7 4·3
48	3 57·0	3 57·6	3 46·2	4·8 1·2	10·8 2·8	16·8 4·3
49	3 57·3	3 57·9	3 46·4	4·9 1·3	10·9 2·8	16·9 4·4
50	3 57·5	3 58·2	3 46·7	5·0 1·3	11·0 2·8	17·0 4·4
51	3 57·8	3 58·4	3 46·9	5·1 1·3	11·1 2·9	17·1 4·4
52	3 58·0	3 58·7	3 47·2	5·2 1·3	11·2 2·9	17·2 4·4
53	3 58·3	3 58·9	3 47·4	5·3 1·4	11·3 2·9	17·3 4·5
54	3 58·5	3 59·2	3 47·6	5·4 1·4	11·4 2·9	17·4 4·5
55	3 58·8	3 59·4	3 47·9	5·5 1·4	11·5 3·0	17·5 4·5
56	3 59·0	3 59·7	3 48·1	5·6 1·4	11·6 3·0	17·6 4·5
57	3 59·3	3 59·9	3 48·4	5·7 1·5	11·7 3·0	17·7 4·6
58	3 59·5	4 00·2	3 48·6	5·8 1·5	11·8 3·0	17·8 4·6
59	3 59·8	4 00·4	3 48·8	5·9 1·5	11·9 3·1	17·9 4·6
60	4 00·0	4 00·7	3 49·1	6·0 1·6	12·0 3·1	18·0 4·7

16ᵐ	SUN PLANETS	ARIES	MOON	v or Corrⁿ d		v or Corrⁿ d		v or Corrⁿ d	
s	° ′	° ′	° ′	′	′	′	′	′	′
00	4 00·0	4 00·7	3 49·1	0·0	0·0	6·0	1·7	12·0	3·3
01	4 00·3	4 00·9	3 49·3	0·1	0·0	6·1	1·7	12·1	3·3
02	4 00·5	4 01·2	3 49·5	0·2	0·1	6·2	1·7	12·2	3·4
03	4 00·8	4 01·4	3 49·8	0·3	0·1	6·3	1·7	12·3	3·4
04	4 01·0	4 01·7	3 50·0	0·4	0·1	6·4	1·8	12·4	3·4
05	4 01·3	4 01·9	3 50·3	0·5	0·1	6·5	1·8	12·5	3·4
06	4 01·5	4 02·2	3 50·5	0·6	0·2	6·6	1·8	12·6	3·5
07	4 01·8	4 02·4	3 50·7	0·7	0·2	6·7	1·8	12·7	3·5
08	4 02·0	4 02·7	3 51·0	0·8	0·2	6·8	1·9	12·8	3·5
09	4 02·3	4 02·9	3 51·2	0·9	0·2	6·9	1·9	12·9	3·5
10	4 02·5	4 03·2	3 51·5	1·0	0·3	7·0	1·9	13·0	3·6
11	4 02·8	4 03·4	3 51·7	1·1	0·3	7·1	2·0	13·1	3·6
12	4 03·0	4 03·7	3 51·9	1·2	0·3	7·2	2·0	13·2	3·6
13	4 03·3	4 03·9	3 52·2	1·3	0·4	7·3	2·0	13·3	3·7
14	4 03·5	4 04·2	3 52·4	1·4	0·4	7·4	2·0	13·4	3·7
15	4 03·8	4 04·4	3 52·6	1·5	0·4	7·5	2·1	13·5	3·7
16	4 04·0	4 04·7	3 52·9	1·6	0·4	7·6	2·1	13·6	3·7
17	4 04·3	4 04·9	3 53·1	1·7	0·5	7·7	2·1	13·7	3·8
18	4 04·5	4 05·2	3 53·4	1·8	0·5	7·8	2·1	13·8	3·8
19	4 04·8	4 05·4	3 53·6	1·9	0·5	7·9	2·2	13·9	3·8
20	4 05·0	4 05·7	3 53·8	2·0	0·6	8·0	2·2	14·0	3·9
21	4 05·3	4 05·9	3 54·1	2·1	0·6	8·1	2·2	14·1	3·9
22	4 05·5	4 06·2	3 54·3	2·2	0·6	8·2	2·3	14·2	3·9
23	4 05·8	4 06·4	3 54·6	2·3	0·6	8·3	2·3	14·3	3·9
24	4 06·0	4 06·7	3 54·8	2·4	0·7	8·4	2·3	14·4	4·0
25	4 06·3	4 06·9	3 55·0	2·5	0·7	8·5	2·3	14·5	4·0
26	4 06·5	4 07·2	3 55·3	2·6	0·7	8·6	2·4	14·6	4·0
27	4 06·8	4 07·4	3 55·5	2·7	0·7	8·7	2·4	14·7	4·0
28	4 07·0	4 07·7	3 55·7	2·8	0·8	8·8	2·4	14·8	4·1
29	4 07·3	4 07·9	3 56·0	2·9	0·8	8·9	2·4	14·9	4·1
30	4 07·5	4 08·2	3 56·2	3·0	0·8	9·0	2·5	15·0	4·1
31	4 07·8	4 08·4	3 56·5	3·1	0·9	9·1	2·5	15·1	4·2
32	4 08·0	4 08·7	3 56·7	3·2	0·9	9·2	2·5	15·2	4·2
33	4 08·3	4 08·9	3 56·9	3·3	0·9	9·3	2·6	15·3	4·2
34	4 08·5	4 09·2	3 57·2	3·4	0·9	9·4	2·6	15·4	4·2
35	4 08·8	4 09·4	3 57·4	3·5	1·0	9·5	2·6	15·5	4·3
36	4 09·0	4 09·7	3 57·7	3·6	1·0	9·6	2·6	15·6	4·3
37	4 09·3	4 09·9	3 57·9	3·7	1·0	9·7	2·7	15·7	4·3
38	4 09·5	4 10·2	3 58·1	3·8	1·0	9·8	2·7	15·8	4·3
39	4 09·8	4 10·4	3 58·4	3·9	1·1	9·9	2·7	15·9	4·4
40	4 10·0	4 10·7	3 58·6	4·0	1·1	10·0	2·8	16·0	4·4
41	4 10·3	4 10·9	3 58·8	4·1	1·1	10·1	2·8	16·1	4·4
42	4 10·5	4 11·2	3 59·1	4·2	1·2	10·2	2·8	16·2	4·5
43	4 10·8	4 11·4	3 59·3	4·3	1·2	10·3	2·8	16·3	4·5
44	4 11·0	4 11·7	3 59·6	4·4	1·2	10·4	2·9	16·4	4·5
45	4 11·3	4 11·9	3 59·8	4·5	1·2	10·5	2·9	16·5	4·5
46	4 11·5	4 12·2	4 00·0	4·6	1·3	10·6	2·9	16·6	4·6
47	4 11·8	4 12·4	4 00·3	4·7	1·3	10·7	2·9	16·7	4·6
48	4 12·0	4 12·7	4 00·5	4·8	1·3	10·8	3·0	16·8	4·6
49	4 12·3	4 12·9	4 00·8	4·9	1·3	10·9	3·0	16·9	4·6
50	4 12·5	4 13·2	4 01·0	5·0	1·4	11·0	3·0	17·0	4·7
51	4 12·8	4 13·4	4 01·2	5·1	1·4	11·1	3·1	17·1	4·7
52	4 13·0	4 13·7	4 01·5	5·2	1·4	11·2	3·1	17·2	4·7
53	4 13·3	4 13·9	4 01·7	5·3	1·5	11·3	3·1	17·3	4·8
54	4 13·5	4 14·2	4 02·0	5·4	1·5	11·4	3·1	17·4	4·8
55	4 13·8	4 14·4	4 02·2	5·5	1·5	11·5	3·2	17·5	4·8
56	4 14·0	4 14·7	4 02·4	5·6	1·5	11·6	3·2	17·6	4·8
57	4 14·3	4 14·9	4 02·7	5·7	1·6	11·7	3·2	17·7	4·9
58	4 14·5	4 15·2	4 02·9	5·8	1·6	11·8	3·2	17·8	4·9
59	4 14·8	4 15·4	4 03·1	5·9	1·6	11·9	3·3	17·9	4·9
60	4 15·0	4 15·7	4 03·4	6·0	1·7	12·0	3·3	18·0	5·0

17ᵐ	SUN PLANETS	ARIES	MOON	v or Corrⁿ d		v or Corrⁿ d		v or Corrⁿ d	
s	° ′	° ′	° ′	′	′	′	′	′	′
00	4 15·0	4 15·7	4 03·4	0·0	0·0	6·0	1·8	12·0	3·5
01	4 15·3	4 15·9	4 03·6	0·1	0·0	6·1	1·8	12·1	3·5
02	4 15·5	4 16·2	4 03·9	0·2	0·1	6·2	1·8	12·2	3·6
03	4 15·8	4 16·5	4 04·1	0·3	0·1	6·3	1·8	12·3	3·6
04	4 16·0	4 16·7	4 04·3	0·4	0·1	6·4	1·9	12·4	3·6
05	4 16·3	4 17·0	4 04·6	0·5	0·1	6·5	1·9	12·5	3·6
06	4 16·5	4 17·2	4 04·8	0·6	0·2	6·6	1·9	12·6	3·7
07	4 16·8	4 17·5	4 05·1	0·7	0·2	6·7	2·0	12·7	3·7
08	4 17·0	4 17·7	4 05·3	0·8	0·2	6·8	2·0	12·8	3·7
09	4 17·3	4 18·0	4 05·5	0·9	0·3	6·9	2·0	12·9	3·8
10	4 17·5	4 18·2	4 05·8	1·0	0·3	7·0	2·0	13·0	3·8
11	4 17·8	4 18·5	4 06·0	1·1	0·3	7·1	2·1	13·1	3·8
12	4 18·0	4 18·7	4 06·2	1·2	0·4	7·2	2·1	13·2	3·9
13	4 18·3	4 19·0	4 06·5	1·3	0·4	7·3	2·1	13·3	3·9
14	4 18·5	4 19·2	4 06·7	1·4	0·4	7·4	2·2	13·4	3·9
15	4 18·8	4 19·5	4 07·0	1·5	0·4	7·5	2·2	13·5	3·9
16	4 19·0	4 19·7	4 07·2	1·6	0·5	7·6	2·2	13·6	4·0
17	4 19·3	4 20·0	4 07·4	1·7	0·5	7·7	2·2	13·7	4·0
18	4 19·5	4 20·2	4 07·7	1·8	0·5	7·8	2·3	13·8	4·0
19	4 19·8	4 20·5	4 07·9	1·9	0·6	7·9	2·3	13·9	4·1
20	4 20·0	4 20·7	4 08·2	2·0	0·6	8·0	2·3	14·0	4·1
21	4 20·3	4 21·0	4 08·4	2·1	0·6	8·1	2·4	14·1	4·1
22	4 20·5	4 21·2	4 08·6	2·2	0·6	8·2	2·4	14·2	4·1
23	4 20·8	4 21·5	4 08·9	2·3	0·7	8·3	2·4	14·3	4·2
24	4 21·0	4 21·7	4 09·1	2·4	0·7	8·4	2·5	14·4	4·2
25	4 21·3	4 22·0	4 09·3	2·5	0·7	8·5	2·5	14·5	4·2
26	4 21·5	4 22·2	4 09·6	2·6	0·8	8·6	2·5	14·6	4·3
27	4 21·8	4 22·5	4 09·8	2·7	0·8	8·7	2·5	14·7	4·3
28	4 22·0	4 22·7	4 10·1	2·8	0·8	8·8	2·6	14·8	4·3
29	4 22·3	4 23·0	4 10·3	2·9	0·8	8·9	2·6	14·9	4·3
30	4 22·5	4 23·2	4 10·5	3·0	0·9	9·0	2·6	15·0	4·4
31	4 22·8	4 23·5	4 10·8	3·1	0·9	9·1	2·7	15·1	4·4
32	4 23·0	4 23·7	4 11·0	3·2	0·9	9·2	2·7	15·2	4·4
33	4 23·3	4 24·0	4 11·3	3·3	1·0	9·3	2·7	15·3	4·5
34	4 23·5	4 24·2	4 11·5	3·4	1·0	9·4	2·7	15·4	4·5
35	4 23·8	4 24·5	4 11·7	3·5	1·0	9·5	2·8	15·5	4·5
36	4 24·0	4 24·7	4 12·0	3·6	1·1	9·6	2·8	15·6	4·6
37	4 24·3	4 25·0	4 12·2	3·7	1·1	9·7	2·8	15·7	4·6
38	4 24·5	4 25·2	4 12·5	3·8	1·1	9·8	2·9	15·8	4·6
39	4 24·8	4 25·5	4 12·7	3·9	1·1	9·9	2·9	15·9	4·6
40	4 25·0	4 25·7	4 12·9	4·0	1·2	10·0	2·9	16·0	4·7
41	4 25·3	4 26·0	4 13·2	4·1	1·2	10·1	2·9	16·1	4·7
42	4 25·5	4 26·2	4 13·4	4·2	1·2	10·2	3·0	16·2	4·7
43	4 25·8	4 26·5	4 13·6	4·3	1·3	10·3	3·0	16·3	4·8
44	4 26·0	4 26·7	4 13·9	4·4	1·3	10·4	3·0	16·4	4·8
45	4 26·3	4 27·0	4 14·1	4·5	1·3	10·5	3·1	16·5	4·8
46	4 26·5	4 27·2	4 14·4	4·6	1·3	10·6	3·1	16·6	4·8
47	4 26·8	4 27·5	4 14·6	4·7	1·4	10·7	3·1	16·7	4·9
48	4 27·0	4 27·7	4 14·8	4·8	1·4	10·8	3·2	16·8	4·9
49	4 27·3	4 28·0	4 15·1	4·9	1·4	10·9	3·2	16·9	4·9
50	4 27·5	4 28·2	4 15·3	5·0	1·5	11·0	3·2	17·0	5·0
51	4 27·8	4 28·5	4 15·6	5·1	1·5	11·1	3·2	17·1	5·0
52	4 28·0	4 28·7	4 15·8	5·2	1·5	11·2	3·3	17·2	5·0
53	4 28·3	4 29·0	4 16·0	5·3	1·5	11·3	3·3	17·3	5·0
54	4 28·5	4 29·2	4 16·3	5·4	1·6	11·4	3·3	17·4	5·1
55	4 28·8	4 29·5	4 16·5	5·5	1·6	11·5	3·4	17·5	5·1
56	4 29·0	4 29·7	4 16·7	5·6	1·6	11·6	3·4	17·6	5·1
57	4 29·3	4 30·0	4 17·0	5·7	1·7	11·7	3·4	17·7	5·2
58	4 29·5	4 30·2	4 17·2	5·8	1·7	11·8	3·4	17·8	5·2
59	4 29·8	4 30·5	4 17·5	5·9	1·7	11·9	3·5	17·9	5·2
60	4 30·0	4 30·7	4 17·7	6·0	1·8	12·0	3·5	18·0	5·3

18ᵐ	SUN PLANETS	ARIES	MOON	v or Corrn d		v or Corrn d		v or Corrn d	
s	° ′	° ′	° ′	′	′	′	′	′	′
00	4 30·0	4 30·7	4 17·7	0·0	0·0	6·0	1·9	12·0	3·7
01	4 30·3	4 31·0	4 17·9	0·1	0·0	6·1	1·9	12·1	3·7
02	4 30·5	4 31·2	4 18·2	0·2	0·1	6·2	1·9	12·2	3·8
03	4 30·8	4 31·5	4 18·4	0·3	0·1	6·3	1·9	12·3	3·8
04	4 31·0	4 31·7	4 18·7	0·4	0·1	6·4	2·0	12·4	3·8
05	4 31·3	4 32·0	4 18·9	0·5	0·2	6·5	2·0	12·5	3·9
06	4 31·5	4 32·2	4 19·1	0·6	0·2	6·6	2·0	12·6	3·9
07	4 31·8	4 32·5	4 19·4	0·7	0·2	6·7	2·1	12·7	3·9
08	4 32·0	4 32·7	4 19·6	0·8	0·2	6·8	2·1	12·8	3·9
09	4 32·3	4 33·0	4 19·8	0·9	0·3	6·9	2·1	12·9	4·0
10	4 32·5	4 33·2	4 20·1	1·0	0·3	7·0	2·2	13·0	4·0
11	4 32·8	4 33·5	4 20·3	1·1	0·3	7·1	2·2	13·1	4·0
12	4 33·0	4 33·7	4 20·6	1·2	0·4	7·2	2·2	13·2	4·1
13	4 33·3	4 34·0	4 20·8	1·3	0·4	7·3	2·3	13·3	4·1
14	4 33·5	4 34·2	4 21·0	1·4	0·4	7·4	2·3	13·4	4·1
15	4 33·8	4 34·5	4 21·3	1·5	0·5	7·5	2·3	13·5	4·2
16	4 34·0	4 34·8	4 21·5	1·6	0·5	7·6	2·3	13·6	4·2
17	4 34·3	4 35·0	4 21·8	1·7	0·5	7·7	2·4	13·7	4·2
18	4 34·5	4 35·3	4 22·0	1·8	0·6	7·8	2·4	13·8	4·3
19	4 34·8	4 35·5	4 22·2	1·9	0·6	7·9	2·4	13·9	4·3
20	4 35·0	4 35·8	4 22·5	2·0	0·6	8·0	2·5	14·0	4·3
21	4 35·3	4 36·0	4 22·7	2·1	0·6	8·1	2·5	14·1	4·3
22	4 35·5	4 36·3	4 22·9	2·2	0·7	8·2	2·5	14·2	4·4
23	4 35·8	4 36·5	4 23·2	2·3	0·7	8·3	2·6	14·3	4·4
24	4 36·0	4 36·8	4 23·4	2·4	0·7	8·4	2·6	14·4	4·4
25	4 36·3	4 37·0	4 23·7	2·5	0·8	8·5	2·6	14·5	4·5
26	4 36·5	4 37·3	4 23·9	2·6	0·8	8·6	2·7	14·6	4·5
27	4 36·8	4 37·5	4 24·1	2·7	0·8	8·7	2·7	14·7	4·5
28	4 37·0	4 37·8	4 24·4	2·8	0·9	8·8	2·7	14·8	4·6
29	4 37·3	4 38·0	4 24·6	2·9	0·9	8·9	2·7	14·9	4·6
30	4 37·5	4 38·3	4 24·9	3·0	0·9	9·0	2·8	15·0	4·6
31	4 37·8	4 38·5	4 25·1	3·1	1·0	9·1	2·8	15·1	4·7
32	4 38·0	4 38·8	4 25·3	3·2	1·0	9·2	2·8	15·2	4·7
33	4 38·3	4 39·0	4 25·6	3·3	1·0	9·3	2·9	15·3	4·7
34	4 38·5	4 39·3	4 25·8	3·4	1·0	9·4	2·9	15·4	4·7
35	4 38·8	4 39·5	4 26·1	3·5	1·1	9·5	2·9	15·5	4·8
36	4 39·0	4 39·8	4 26·3	3·6	1·1	9·6	3·0	15·6	4·8
37	4 39·3	4 40·0	4 26·5	3·7	1·1	9·7	3·0	15·7	4·8
38	4 39·5	4 40·3	4 26·8	3·8	1·2	9·8	3·0	15·8	4·9
39	4 39·8	4 40·5	4 27·0	3·9	1·2	9·9	3·1	15·9	4·9
40	4 40·0	4 40·8	4 27·2	4·0	1·2	10·0	3·1	16·0	4·9
41	4 40·3	4 41·0	4 27·5	4·1	1·3	10·1	3·1	16·1	5·0
42	4 40·5	4 41·3	4 27·7	4·2	1·3	10·2	3·1	16·2	5·0
43	4 40·8	4 41·5	4 28·0	4·3	1·3	10·3	3·2	16·3	5·0
44	4 41·0	4 41·8	4 28·2	4·4	1·4	10·4	3·2	16·4	5·1
45	4 41·3	4 42·0	4 28·4	4·5	1·4	10·5	3·2	16·5	5·1
46	4 41·5	4 42·3	4 28·7	4·6	1·4	10·6	3·3	16·6	5·1
47	4 41·8	4 42·5	4 28·9	4·7	1·4	10·7	3·3	16·7	5·1
48	4 42·0	4 42·8	4 29·2	4·8	1·5	10·8	3·3	16·8	5·2
49	4 42·3	4 43·0	4 29·4	4·9	1·5	10·9	3·4	16·9	5·2
50	4 42·5	4 43·3	4 29·6	5·0	1·5	11·0	3·4	17·0	5·2
51	4 42·8	4 43·5	4 29·9	5·1	1·6	11·1	3·4	17·1	5·3
52	4 43·0	4 43·8	4 30·1	5·2	1·6	11·2	3·5	17·2	5·3
53	4 43·3	4 44·0	4 30·3	5·3	1·6	11·3	3·5	17·3	5·3
54	4 43·5	4 44·3	4 30·6	5·4	1·7	11·4	3·5	17·4	5·4
55	4 43·8	4 44·5	4 30·8	5·5	1·7	11·5	3·5	17·5	5·4
56	4 44·0	4 44·8	4 31·1	5·6	1·7	11·6	3·6	17·6	5·4
57	4 44·3	4 45·0	4 31·3	5·7	1·8	11·7	3·6	17·7	5·5
58	4 44·5	4 45·3	4 31·5	5·8	1·8	11·8	3·6	17·8	5·5
59	4 44·8	4 45·5	4 31·8	5·9	1·8	11·9	3·7	17·9	5·5
60	4 45·0	4 45·8	4 32·0	6·0	1·9	12·0	3·7	18·0	5·6

19ᵐ	SUN PLANETS	ARIES	MOON	v or Corrn d		v or Corrn d		v or Corrn d	
s	° ′	° ′	° ′	′	′	′	′	′	′
00	4 45·0	4 45·8	4 32·0	0·0	0·0	6·0	2·0	12·0	3·9
01	4 45·3	4 46·0	4 32·3	0·1	0·0	6·1	2·0	12·1	3·9
02	4 45·5	4 46·3	4 32·5	0·2	0·1	6·2	2·0	12·2	4·0
03	4 45·8	4 46·5	4 32·7	0·3	0·1	6·3	2·0	12·3	4·0
04	4 46·0	4 46·8	4 33·0	0·4	0·1	6·4	2·1	12·4	4·0
05	4 46·3	4 47·0	4 33·2	0·5	0·2	6·5	2·1	12·5	4·1
06	4 46·5	4 47·3	4 33·4	0·6	0·2	6·6	2·1	12·6	4·1
07	4 46·8	4 47·5	4 33·7	0·7	0·2	6·7	2·2	12·7	4·1
08	4 47·0	4 47·8	4 33·9	0·8	0·3	6·8	2·2	12·8	4·2
09	4 47·3	4 48·0	4 34·2	0·9	0·3	6·9	2·2	12·9	4·2
10	4 47·5	4 48·3	4 34·4	1·0	0·3	7·0	2·3	13·0	4·2
11	4 47·8	4 48·5	4 34·6	1·1	0·4	7·1	2·3	13·1	4·3
12	4 48·0	4 48·8	4 34·9	1·2	0·4	7·2	2·3	13·2	4·3
13	4 48·3	4 49·0	4 35·1	1·3	0·4	7·3	2·4	13·3	4·3
14	4 48·5	4 49·3	4 35·4	1·4	0·5	7·4	2·4	13·4	4·4
15	4 48·8	4 49·5	4 35·6	1·5	0·5	7·5	2·4	13·5	4·4
16	4 49·0	4 49·8	4 35·8	1·6	0·5	7·6	2·5	13·6	4·4
17	4 49·3	4 50·0	4 36·1	1·7	0·6	7·7	2·5	13·7	4·5
18	4 49·5	4 50·3	4 36·3	1·8	0·6	7·8	2·5	13·8	4·5
19	4 49·8	4 50·5	4 36·6	1·9	0·6	7·9	2·6	13·9	4·5
20	4 50·0	4 50·8	4 36·8	2·0	0·7	8·0	2·6	14·0	4·6
21	4 50·3	4 51·0	4 37·0	2·1	0·7	8·1	2·6	14·1	4·6
22	4 50·5	4 51·3	4 37·3	2·2	0·7	8·2	2·7	14·2	4·6
23	4 50·8	4 51·5	4 37·5	2·3	0·7	8·3	2·7	14·3	4·6
24	4 51·0	4 51·8	4 37·7	2·4	0·8	8·4	2·7	14·4	4·7
25	4 51·3	4 52·0	4 38·0	2·5	0·8	8·5	2·8	14·5	4·7
26	4 51·5	4 52·3	4 38·2	2·6	0·8	8·6	2·8	14·6	4·7
27	4 51·8	4 52·5	4 38·5	2·7	0·9	8·7	2·8	14·7	4·8
28	4 52·0	4 52·8	4 38·7	2·8	0·9	8·8	2·9	14·8	4·8
29	4 52·3	4 53·1	4 38·9	2·9	0·9	8·9	2·9	14·9	4·8
30	4 52·5	4 53·3	4 39·2	3·0	1·0	9·0	2·9	15·0	4·9
31	4 52·8	4 53·6	4 39·4	3·1	1·0	9·1	3·0	15·1	4·9
32	4 53·0	4 53·8	4 39·7	3·2	1·0	9·2	3·0	15·2	4·9
33	4 53·3	4 54·1	4 39·9	3·3	1·1	9·3	3·0	15·3	5·0
34	4 53·5	4 54·3	4 40·1	3·4	1·1	9·4	3·1	15·4	5·0
35	4 53·8	4 54·6	4 40·4	3·5	1·1	9·5	3·1	15·5	5·0
36	4 54·0	4 54·8	4 40·6	3·6	1·2	9·6	3·1	15·6	5·1
37	4 54·3	4 55·1	4 40·8	3·7	1·2	9·7	3·2	15·7	5·1
38	4 54·5	4 55·3	4 41·1	3·8	1·2	9·8	3·2	15·8	5·1
39	4 54·8	4 55·6	4 41·3	3·9	1·3	9·9	3·2	15·9	5·2
40	4 55·0	4 55·8	4 41·6	4·0	1·3	10·0	3·3	16·0	5·2
41	4 55·3	4 56·1	4 41·8	4·1	1·3	10·1	3·3	16·1	5·2
42	4 55·5	4 56·3	4 42·0	4·2	1·4	10·2	3·3	16·2	5·3
43	4 55·8	4 56·6	4 42·3	4·3	1·4	10·3	3·3	16·3	5·3
44	4 56·0	4 56·8	4 42·5	4·4	1·4	10·4	3·4	16·4	5·3
45	4 56·3	4 57·1	4 42·8	4·5	1·5	10·5	3·4	16·5	5·4
46	4 56·5	4 57·3	4 43·0	4·6	1·5	10·6	3·4	16·6	5·4
47	4 56·8	4 57·6	4 43·2	4·7	1·5	10·7	3·5	16·7	5·4
48	4 57·0	4 57·8	4 43·5	4·8	1·6	10·8	3·5	16·8	5·5
49	4 57·3	4 58·1	4 43·7	4·9	1·6	10·9	3·5	16·9	5·5
50	4 57·5	4 58·3	4 43·9	5·0	1·6	11·0	3·6	17·0	5·5
51	4 57·8	4 58·6	4 44·2	5·1	1·7	11·1	3·6	17·1	5·6
52	4 58·0	4 58·8	4 44·4	5·2	1·7	11·2	3·6	17·2	5·6
53	4 58·3	4 59·1	4 44·7	5·3	1·7	11·3	3·7	17·3	5·6
54	4 58·5	4 59·3	4 44·9	5·4	1·8	11·4	3·7	17·4	5·7
55	4 58·8	4 59·6	4 45·1	5·5	1·8	11·5	3·7	17·5	5·7
56	4 59·0	4 59·8	4 45·4	5·6	1·8	11·6	3·8	17·6	5·7
57	4 59·3	5 00·1	4 45·6	5·7	1·9	11·7	3·8	17·7	5·8
58	4 59·5	5 00·3	4 45·9	5·8	1·9	11·8	3·8	17·8	5·8
59	4 59·8	5 00·6	4 46·1	5·9	1·9	11·9	3·9	17·9	5·8
60	5 00·0	5 00·8	4 46·3	6·0	2·0	12·0	3·9	18·0	5·9

20ᵐ	SUN PLANETS	ARIES	MOON	v or Corrⁿ d		v or Corrⁿ d		v or Corrⁿ d	
s	° ′	° ′	° ′	′	′	′	′	′	′
00	5 00·0	5 00·8	4 46·3	0·0	0·0	6·0	2·1	12·0	4·1
01	5 00·3	5 01·1	4 46·6	0·1	0·0	6·1	2·1	12·1	4·1
02	5 00·5	5 01·3	4 46·8	0·2	0·1	6·2	2·1	12·2	4·2
03	5 00·8	5 01·6	4 47·0	0·3	0·1	6·3	2·2	12·3	4·2
04	5 01·0	5 01·8	4 47·3	0·4	0·1	6·4	2·2	12·4	4·2
05	5 01·3	5 02·1	4 47·5	0·5	0·2	6·5	2·2	12·5	4·3
06	5 01·5	5 02·3	4 47·8	0·6	0·2	6·6	2·3	12·6	4·3
07	5 01·8	5 02·6	4 48·0	0·7	0·2	6·7	2·3	12·7	4·3
08	5 02·0	5 02·8	4 48·2	0·8	0·3	6·8	2·3	12·8	4·4
09	5 02·3	5 03·1	4 48·5	0·9	0·3	6·9	2·4	12·9	4·4
10	5 02·5	5 03·3	4 48·7	1·0	0·3	7·0	2·4	13·0	4·4
11	5 02·8	5 03·6	4 49·0	1·1	0·4	7·1	2·4	13·1	4·5
12	5 03·0	5 03·8	4 49·2	1·2	0·4	7·2	2·5	13·2	4·5
13	5 03·3	5 04·1	4 49·4	1·3	0·4	7·3	2·5	13·3	4·5
14	5 03·5	5 04·3	4 49·7	1·4	0·5	7·4	2·5	13·4	4·6
15	5 03·8	5 04·6	4 49·9	1·5	0·5	7·5	2·6	13·5	4·6
16	5 04·0	5 04·8	4 50·2	1·6	0·5	7·6	2·6	13·6	4·6
17	5 04·3	5 05·1	4 50·4	1·7	0·6	7·7	2·6	13·7	4·7
18	5 04·5	5 05·3	4 50·6	1·8	0·6	7·8	2·7	13·8	4·7
19	5 04·8	5 05·6	4 50·9	1·9	0·7	7·9	2·7	13·9	4·7
20	5 05·0	5 05·8	4 51·1	2·0	0·7	8·0	2·7	14·0	4·8
21	5 05·3	5 06·1	4 51·3	2·1	0·7	8·1	2·8	14·1	4·8
22	5 05·5	5 06·3	4 51·6	2·2	0·8	8·2	2·8	14·2	4·9
23	5 05·8	5 06·6	4 51·8	2·3	0·8	8·3	2·8	14·3	4·9
24	5 06·0	5 06·8	4 52·1	2·4	0·8	8·4	2·9	14·4	4·9
25	5 06·3	5 07·1	4 52·3	2·5	0·9	8·5	2·9	14·5	5·0
26	5 06·5	5 07·3	4 52·5	2·6	0·9	8·6	2·9	14·6	5·0
27	5 06·8	5 07·6	4 52·8	2·7	0·9	8·7	3·0	14·7	5·0
28	5 07·0	5 07·8	4 53·0	2·8	1·0	8·8	3·0	14·8	5·1
29	5 07·3	5 08·1	4 53·3	2·9	1·0	8·9	3·0	14·9	5·1
30	5 07·5	5 08·3	4 53·5	3·0	1·0	9·0	3·1	15·0	5·1
31	5 07·8	5 08·6	4 53·7	3·1	1·1	9·1	3·1	15·1	5·2
32	5 08·0	5 08·8	4 54·0	3·2	1·1	9·2	3·1	15·2	5·2
33	5 08·3	5 09·1	4 54·2	3·3	1·1	9·3	3·2	15·3	5·2
34	5 08·5	5 09·3	4 54·4	3·4	1·2	9·4	3·2	15·4	5·3
35	5 08·8	5 09·6	4 54·7	3·5	1·2	9·5	3·2	15·5	5·3
36	5 09·0	5 09·8	4 54·9	3·6	1·2	9·6	3·3	15·6	5·3
37	5 09·3	5 10·1	4 55·2	3·7	1·3	9·7	3·3	15·7	5·4
38	5 09·5	5 10·3	4 55·4	3·8	1·3	9·8	3·3	15·8	5·4
39	5 09·8	5 10·6	4 55·6	3·9	1·3	9·9	3·4	15·9	5·4
40	5 10·0	5 10·8	4 55·9	4·0	1·4	10·0	3·4	16·0	5·5
41	5 10·3	5 11·1	4 56·1	4·1	1·4	10·1	3·5	16·1	5·5
42	5 10·5	5 11·4	4 56·4	4·2	1·4	10·2	3·5	16·2	5·5
43	5 10·8	5 11·6	4 56·6	4·3	1·5	10·3	3·5	16·3	5·6
44	5 11·0	5 11·9	4 56·8	4·4	1·5	10·4	3·6	16·4	5·6
45	5 11·3	5 12·1	4 57·1	4·5	1·5	10·5	3·6	16·5	5·6
46	5 11·5	5 12·4	4 57·3	4·6	1·6	10·6	3·6	16·6	5·7
47	5 11·8	5 12·6	4 57·5	4·7	1·6	10·7	3·7	16·7	5·7
48	5 12·0	5 12·9	4 57·8	4·8	1·6	10·8	3·7	16·8	5·7
49	5 12·3	5 13·1	4 58·0	4·9	1·7	10·9	3·7	16·9	5·8
50	5 12·5	5 13·4	4 58·3	5·0	1·7	11·0	3·8	17·0	5·8
51	5 12·8	5 13·6	4 58·5	5·1	1·7	11·1	3·8	17·1	5·8
52	5 13·0	5 13·9	4 58·7	5·2	1·8	11·2	3·8	17·2	5·9
53	5 13·3	5 14·1	4 59·0	5·3	1·8	11·3	3·9	17·3	5·9
54	5 13·5	5 14·4	4 59·2	5·4	1·8	11·4	3·9	17·4	5·9
55	5 13·8	5 14·6	4 59·5	5·5	1·9	11·5	3·9	17·5	6·0
56	5 14·0	5 14·9	4 59·7	5·6	1·9	11·6	4·0	17·6	6·0
57	5 14·3	5 15·1	4 59·9	5·7	1·9	11·7	4·0	17·7	6·0
58	5 14·5	5 15·4	5 00·2	5·8	2·0	11·8	4·0	17·8	6·1
59	5 14·8	5 15·6	5 00·4	5·9	2·0	11·9	4·1	17·9	6·1
60	5 15·0	5 15·9	5 00·7	6·0	2·1	12·0	4·1	18·0	6·2

21ᵐ	SUN PLANETS	ARIES	MOON	v or Corrⁿ d		v or Corrⁿ d		v or Corrⁿ d	
s	° ′	° ′	° ′	′	′	′	′	′	′
00	5 15·0	5 15·9	5 00·7	0·0	0·0	6·0	2·2	12·0	4·3
01	5 15·3	5 16·1	5 00·9	0·1	0·0	6·1	2·2	12·1	4·3
02	5 15·5	5 16·4	5 01·1	0·2	0·1	6·2	2·2	12·2	4·4
03	5 15·8	5 16·6	5 01·4	0·3	0·1	6·3	2·3	12·3	4·4
04	5 16·0	5 16·9	5 01·6	0·4	0·1	6·4	2·3	12·4	4·4
05	5 16·3	5 17·1	5 01·8	0·5	0·2	6·5	2·3	12·5	4·5
06	5 16·5	5 17·4	5 02·1	0·6	0·2	6·6	2·4	12·6	4·5
07	5 16·8	5 17·6	5 02·3	0·7	0·3	6·7	2·4	12·7	4·6
08	5 17·0	5 17·9	5 02·6	0·8	0·3	6·8	2·4	12·8	4·6
09	5 17·3	5 18·1	5 02·8	0·9	0·3	6·9	2·5	12·9	4·6
10	5 17·5	5 18·4	5 03·0	1·0	0·4	7·0	2·5	13·0	4·7
11	5 17·8	5 18·6	5 03·3	1·1	0·4	7·1	2·5	13·1	4·7
12	5 18·0	5 18·9	5 03·5	1·2	0·4	7·2	2·6	13·2	4·7
13	5 18·3	5 19·1	5 03·8	1·3	0·5	7·3	2·6	13·3	4·8
14	5 18·5	5 19·4	5 04·0	1·4	0·5	7·4	2·7	13·4	4·8
15	5 18·8	5 19·6	5 04·2	1·5	0·5	7·5	2·7	13·5	4·8
16	5 19·0	5 19·9	5 04·5	1·6	0·6	7·6	2·7	13·6	4·9
17	5 19·3	5 20·1	5 04·7	1·7	0·6	7·7	2·8	13·7	4·9
18	5 19·5	5 20·4	5 04·9	1·8	0·6	7·8	2·8	13·8	4·9
19	5 19·8	5 20·6	5 05·2	1·9	0·7	7·9	2·8	13·9	5·0
20	5 20·0	5 20·9	5 05·4	2·0	0·7	8·0	2·9	14·0	5·0
21	5 20·3	5 21·1	5 05·7	2·1	0·8	8·1	2·9	14·1	5·1
22	5 20·5	5 21·4	5 05·9	2·2	0·8	8·2	2·9	14·2	5·1
23	5 20·8	5 21·6	5 06·1	2·3	0·8	8·3	3·0	14·3	5·1
24	5 21·0	5 21·9	5 06·4	2·4	0·9	8·4	3·0	14·4	5·2
25	5 21·3	5 22·1	5 06·6	2·5	0·9	8·5	3·0	14·5	5·2
26	5 21·5	5 22·4	5 06·9	2·6	0·9	8·6	3·1	14·6	5·2
27	5 21·8	5 22·6	5 07·1	2·7	1·0	8·7	3·1	14·7	5·3
28	5 22·0	5 22·9	5 07·3	2·8	1·0	8·8	3·2	14·8	5·3
29	5 22·3	5 23·1	5 07·6	2·9	1·0	8·9	3·2	14·9	5·3
30	5 22·5	5 23·4	5 07·8	3·0	1·1	9·0	3·2	15·0	5·4
31	5 22·8	5 23·6	5 08·0	3·1	1·1	9·1	3·3	15·1	5·4
32	5 23·0	5 23·9	5 08·3	3·2	1·1	9·2	3·3	15·2	5·4
33	5 23·3	5 24·1	5 08·5	3·3	1·2	9·3	3·3	15·3	5·5
34	5 23·5	5 24·4	5 08·8	3·4	1·2	9·4	3·4	15·4	5·5
35	5 23·8	5 24·6	5 09·0	3·5	1·3	9·5	3·4	15·5	5·6
36	5 24·0	5 24·9	5 09·2	3·6	1·3	9·6	3·4	15·6	5·6
37	5 24·3	5 25·1	5 09·5	3·7	1·3	9·7	3·5	15·7	5·6
38	5 24·5	5 25·4	5 09·7	3·8	1·4	9·8	3·5	15·8	5·7
39	5 24·8	5 25·6	5 10·0	3·9	1·4	9·9	3·5	15·9	5·7
40	5 25·0	5 25·9	5 10·2	4·0	1·4	10·0	3·6	16·0	5·7
41	5 25·3	5 26·1	5 10·4	4·1	1·5	10·1	3·6	16·1	5·8
42	5 25·5	5 26·4	5 10·7	4·2	1·5	10·2	3·7	16·2	5·8
43	5 25·8	5 26·6	5 10·9	4·3	1·5	10·3	3·7	16·3	5·8
44	5 26·0	5 26·9	5 11·1	4·4	1·6	10·4	3·7	16·4	5·9
45	5 26·3	5 27·1	5 11·4	4·5	1·6	10·5	3·8	16·5	5·9
46	5 26·5	5 27·4	5 11·6	4·6	1·6	10·6	3·8	16·6	5·9
47	5 26·8	5 27·6	5 11·9	4·7	1·7	10·7	3·8	16·7	6·0
48	5 27·0	5 27·9	5 12·1	4·8	1·7	10·8	3·9	16·8	6·0
49	5 27·3	5 28·1	5 12·3	4·9	1·8	10·9	3·9	16·9	6·0
50	5 27·5	5 28·4	5 12·6	5·0	1·8	11·0	3·9	17·0	6·1
51	5 27·8	5 28·6	5 12·8	5·1	1·8	11·1	4·0	17·1	6·1
52	5 28·0	5 28·9	5 13·1	5·2	1·9	11·2	4·0	17·2	6·2
53	5 28·3	5 29·1	5 13·3	5·3	1·9	11·3	4·0	17·3	6·2
54	5 28·5	5 29·4	5 13·5	5·4	1·9	11·4	4·1	17·4	6·2
55	5 28·8	5 29·7	5 13·8	5·5	2·0	11·5	4·1	17·5	6·3
56	5 29·0	5 29·9	5 14·0	5·6	2·0	11·6	4·2	17·6	6·3
57	5 29·3	5 30·2	5 14·3	5·7	2·0	11·7	4·2	17·7	6·3
58	5 29·5	5 30·4	5 14·5	5·8	2·1	11·8	4·2	17·8	6·4
59	5 29·8	5 30·7	5 14·7	5·9	2·1	11·9	4·3	17·9	6·4
60	5 30·0	5 30·9	5 15·0	6·0	2·2	12·0	4·3	18·0	6·5

22ᵐ	SUN PLANETS	ARIES	MOON	v or d	Corrⁿ	v or d	Corrⁿ	v or d	Corrⁿ
s	° ′	° ′	° ′	′	′	′	′	′	′
00	5 30·0	5 30·9	5 15·0	0·0	0·0	6·0	2·3	12·0	4·5
01	5 30·3	5 31·2	5 15·2	0·1	0·0	6·1	2·3	12·1	4·5
02	5 30·5	5 31·4	5 15·4	0·2	0·1	6·2	2·3	12·2	4·6
03	5 30·8	5 31·7	5 15·7	0·3	0·1	6·3	2·4	12·3	4·6
04	5 31·0	5 31·9	5 15·9	0·4	0·2	6·4	2·4	12·4	4·7
05	5 31·3	5 32·2	5 16·2	0·5	0·2	6·5	2·4	12·5	4·7
06	5 31·5	5 32·4	5 16·4	0·6	0·2	6·6	2·5	12·6	4·7
07	5 31·8	5 32·7	5 16·6	0·7	0·3	6·7	2·5	12·7	4·8
08	5 32·0	5 32·9	5 16·9	0·8	0·3	6·8	2·6	12·8	4·8
09	5 32·3	5 33·2	5 17·1	0·9	0·3	6·9	2·6	12·9	4·8
10	5 32·5	5 33·4	5 17·4	1·0	0·4	7·0	2·6	13·0	4·9
11	5 32·8	5 33·7	5 17·6	1·1	0·4	7·1	2·7	13·1	4·9
12	5 33·0	5 33·9	5 17·8	1·2	0·5	7·2	2·7	13·2	5·0
13	5 33·3	5 34·2	5 18·1	1·3	0·5	7·3	2·7	13·3	5·0
14	5 33·5	5 34·4	5 18·3	1·4	0·5	7·4	2·8	13·4	5·0
15	5 33·8	5 34·7	5 18·5	1·5	0·6	7·5	2·8	13·5	5·1
16	5 34·0	5 34·9	5 18·8	1·6	0·6	7·6	2·9	13·6	5·1
17	5 34·3	5 35·2	5 19·0	1·7	0·6	7·7	2·9	13·7	5·1
18	5 34·5	5 35·4	5 19·3	1·8	0·7	7·8	2·9	13·8	5·2
19	5 34·8	5 35·7	5 19·5	1·9	0·7	7·9	3·0	13·9	5·2
20	5 35·0	5 35·9	5 19·7	2·0	0·8	8·0	3·0	14·0	5·3
21	5 35·3	5 36·2	5 20·0	2·1	0·8	8·1	3·0	14·1	5·3
22	5 35·5	5 36·4	5 20·2	2·2	0·8	8·2	3·1	14·2	5·3
23	5 35·8	5 36·7	5 20·5	2·3	0·9	8·3	3·1	14·3	5·4
24	5 36·0	5 36·9	5 20·7	2·4	0·9	8·4	3·2	14·4	5·4
25	5 36·3	5 37·2	5 20·9	2·5	0·9	8·5	3·2	14·5	5·4
26	5 36·5	5 37·4	5 21·2	2·6	1·0	8·6	3·2	14·6	5·5
27	5 36·8	5 37·7	5 21·4	2·7	1·0	8·7	3·3	14·7	5·5
28	5 37·0	5 37·9	5 21·6	2·8	1·1	8·8	3·3	14·8	5·6
29	5 37·3	5 38·2	5 21·9	2·9	1·1	8·9	3·3	14·9	5·6
30	5 37·5	5 38·4	5 22·1	3·0	1·1	9·0	3·4	15·0	5·6
31	5 37·8	5 38·7	5 22·4	3·1	1·2	9·1	3·4	15·1	5·7
32	5 38·0	5 38·9	5 22·6	3·2	1·2	9·2	3·5	15·2	5·7
33	5 38·3	5 39·2	5 22·8	3·3	1·2	9·3	3·5	15·3	5·7
34	5 38·5	5 39·4	5 23·1	3·4	1·3	9·4	3·5	15·4	5·8
35	5 38·8	5 39·7	5 23·3	3·5	1·3	9·5	3·6	15·5	5·8
36	5 39·0	5 39·9	5 23·6	3·6	1·4	9·6	3·6	15·6	5·9
37	5 39·3	5 40·2	5 23·8	3·7	1·4	9·7	3·6	15·7	5·9
38	5 39·5	5 40·4	5 24·0	3·8	1·4	9·8	3·7	15·8	5·9
39	5 39·8	5 40·7	5 24·3	3·9	1·5	9·9	3·7	15·9	6·0
40	5 40·0	5 40·9	5 24·5	4·0	1·5	10·0	3·8	16·0	6·0
41	5 40·3	5 41·2	5 24·7	4·1	1·5	10·1	3·8	16·1	6·0
42	5 40·5	5 41·4	5 25·0	4·2	1·6	10·2	3·8	16·2	6·1
43	5 40·8	5 41·7	5 25·2	4·3	1·6	10·3	3·9	16·3	6·1
44	5 41·0	5 41·9	5 25·5	4·4	1·7	10·4	3·9	16·4	6·2
45	5 41·3	5 42·2	5 25·7	4·5	1·7	10·5	3·9	16·5	6·2
46	5 41·5	5 42·4	5 25·9	4·6	1·7	10·6	4·0	16·6	6·2
47	5 41·8	5 42·7	5 26·2	4·7	1·8	10·7	4·0	16·7	6·3
48	5 42·0	5 42·9	5 26·4	4·8	1·8	10·8	4·1	16·8	6·3
49	5 42·3	5 43·2	5 26·7	4·9	1·8	10·9	4·1	16·9	6·3
50	5 42·5	5 43·4	5 26·9	5·0	1·9	11·0	4·1	17·0	6·4
51	5 42·8	5 43·7	5 27·1	5·1	1·9	11·1	4·2	17·1	6·4
52	5 43·0	5 43·9	5 27·4	5·2	2·0	11·2	4·2	17·2	6·5
53	5 43·3	5 44·2	5 27·6	5·3	2·0	11·3	4·2	17·3	6·5
54	5 43·5	5 44·4	5 27·9	5·4	2·0	11·4	4·3	17·4	6·5
55	5 43·8	5 44·7	5 28·1	5·5	2·1	11·5	4·3	17·5	6·6
56	5 44·0	5 44·9	5 28·3	5·6	2·1	11·6	4·4	17·6	6·6
57	5 44·3	5 45·2	5 28·6	5·7	2·1	11·7	4·4	17·7	6·6
58	5 44·5	5 45·4	5 28·8	5·8	2·2	11·8	4·4	17·8	6·7
59	5 44·8	5 45·7	5 29·0	5·9	2·2	11·9	4·5	17·9	6·7
60	5 45·0	5 45·9	5 29·3	6·0	2·3	12·0	4·5	18·0	6·8

23ᵐ	SUN PLANETS	ARIES	MOON	v or d	Corrⁿ	v or d	Corrⁿ	v or d	Corrⁿ
s	° ′	° ′	° ′	′	′	′	′	′	′
00	5 45·0	5 45·9	5 29·3	0·0	0·0	6·0	2·4	12·0	4·7
01	5 45·3	5 46·2	5 29·5	0·1	0·0	6·1	2·4	12·1	4·7
02	5 45·5	5 46·4	5 29·8	0·2	0·1	6·2	2·4	12·2	4·8
03	5 45·8	5 46·7	5 30·0	0·3	0·1	6·3	2·5	12·3	4·8
04	5 46·0	5 46·9	5 30·2	0·4	0·2	6·4	2·5	12·4	4·9
05	5 46·3	5 47·2	5 30·5	0·5	0·2	6·5	2·5	12·5	4·9
06	5 46·5	5 47·4	5 30·7	0·6	0·2	6·6	2·6	12·6	4·9
07	5 46·8	5 47·7	5 31·0	0·7	0·3	6·7	2·6	12·7	5·0
08	5 47·0	5 48·0	5 31·2	0·8	0·3	6·8	2·7	12·8	5·0
09	5 47·3	5 48·2	5 31·4	0·9	0·4	6·9	2·7	12·9	5·1
10	5 47·5	5 48·5	5 31·7	1·0	0·4	7·0	2·7	13·0	5·1
11	5 47·8	5 48·7	5 31·9	1·1	0·4	7·1	2·8	13·1	5·1
12	5 48·0	5 49·0	5 32·1	1·2	0·5	7·2	2·8	13·2	5·2
13	5 48·3	5 49·2	5 32·4	1·3	0·5	7·3	2·9	13·3	5·2
14	5 48·5	5 49·5	5 32·6	1·4	0·5	7·4	2·9	13·4	5·2
15	5 48·8	5 49·7	5 32·9	1·5	0·6	7·5	2·9	13·5	5·3
16	5 49·0	5 50·0	5 33·1	1·6	0·6	7·6	3·0	13·6	5·3
17	5 49·3	5 50·2	5 33·3	1·7	0·7	7·7	3·0	13·7	5·4
18	5 49·5	5 50·5	5 33·6	1·8	0·7	7·8	3·1	13·8	5·4
19	5 49·8	5 50·7	5 33·8	1·9	0·7	7·9	3·1	13·9	5·4
20	5 50·0	5 51·0	5 34·1	2·0	0·8	8·0	3·1	14·0	5·5
21	5 50·3	5 51·2	5 34·3	2·1	0·8	8·1	3·2	14·1	5·5
22	5 50·5	5 51·5	5 34·5	2·2	0·9	8·2	3·2	14·2	5·6
23	5 50·8	5 51·7	5 34·8	2·3	0·9	8·3	3·3	14·3	5·6
24	5 51·0	5 52·0	5 35·0	2·4	0·9	8·4	3·3	14·4	5·6
25	5 51·3	5 52·2	5 35·2	2·5	1·0	8·5	3·3	14·5	5·7
26	5 51·5	5 52·5	5 35·5	2·6	1·0	8·6	3·4	14·6	5·7
27	5 51·8	5 52·7	5 35·7	2·7	1·1	8·7	3·4	14·7	5·8
28	5 52·0	5 53·0	5 36·0	2·8	1·1	8·8	3·4	14·8	5·8
29	5 52·3	5 53·2	5 36·2	2·9	1·1	8·9	3·5	14·9	5·8
30	5 52·5	5 53·5	5 36·4	3·0	1·2	9·0	3·5	15·0	5·9
31	5 52·8	5 53·7	5 36·7	3·1	1·2	9·1	3·6	15·1	5·9
32	5 53·0	5 54·0	5 36·9	3·2	1·3	9·2	3·6	15·2	6·0
33	5 53·3	5 54·2	5 37·2	3·3	1·3	9·3	3·6	15·3	6·0
34	5 53·5	5 54·5	5 37·4	3·4	1·3	9·4	3·7	15·4	6·0
35	5 53·8	5 54·7	5 37·6	3·5	1·4	9·5	3·7	15·5	6·1
36	5 54·0	5 55·0	5 37·9	3·6	1·4	9·6	3·8	15·6	6·1
37	5 54·3	5 55·2	5 38·1	3·7	1·4	9·7	3·8	15·7	6·1
38	5 54·5	5 55·5	5 38·4	3·8	1·5	9·8	3·8	15·8	6·2
39	5 54·8	5 55·7	5 38·6	3·9	1·5	9·9	3·9	15·9	6·2
40	5 55·0	5 56·0	5 38·8	4·0	1·6	10·0	3·9	16·0	6·3
41	5 55·3	5 56·2	5 39·1	4·1	1·6	10·1	4·0	16·1	6·3
42	5 55·5	5 56·5	5 39·3	4·2	1·6	10·2	4·0	16·2	6·3
43	5 55·8	5 56·7	5 39·5	4·3	1·7	10·3	4·0	16·3	6·4
44	5 56·0	5 57·0	5 39·8	4·4	1·7	10·4	4·1	16·4	6·4
45	5 56·3	5 57·2	5 40·0	4·5	1·8	10·5	4·1	16·5	6·5
46	5 56·5	5 57·5	5 40·3	4·6	1·8	10·6	4·2	16·6	6·5
47	5 56·8	5 57·7	5 40·5	4·7	1·8	10·7	4·2	16·7	6·5
48	5 57·0	5 58·0	5 40·7	4·8	1·9	10·8	4·2	16·8	6·6
49	5 57·3	5 58·2	5 41·0	4·9	1·9	10·9	4·3	16·9	6·6
50	5 57·5	5 58·5	5 41·2	5·0	2·0	11·0	4·3	17·0	6·7
51	5 57·8	5 58·7	5 41·5	5·1	2·0	11·1	4·3	17·1	6·7
52	5 58·0	5 59·0	5 41·7	5·2	2·0	11·2	4·4	17·2	6·7
53	5 58·3	5 59·2	5 41·9	5·3	2·1	11·3	4·4	17·3	6·8
54	5 58·5	5 59·5	5 42·2	5·4	2·1	11·4	4·5	17·4	6·8
55	5 58·8	5 59·7	5 42·4	5·5	2·2	11·5	4·5	17·5	6·9
56	5 59·0	6 00·0	5 42·6	5·6	2·2	11·6	4·5	17·6	6·9
57	5 59·3	6 00·2	5 42·9	5·7	2·2	11·7	4·6	17·7	6·9
58	5 59·5	6 00·5	5 43·1	5·8	2·3	11·8	4·6	17·8	7·0
59	5 59·8	6 00·7	5 43·4	5·9	2·3	11·9	4·7	17·9	7·0
60	6 00·0	6 01·0	5 43·6	6·0	2·4	12·0	4·7	18·0	7·1

24ᵐ	SUN PLANETS	ARIES	MOON	v or d	Corrⁿ	v or d	Corrⁿ	v or d	Corrⁿ
s	° ′	° ′	° ′	′	′	′	′	′	′
00	6 00·0	6 01·0	5 43·6	0·0	0·0	6·0	2·5	12·0	4·9
01	6 00·3	6 01·2	5 43·8	0·1	0·0	6·1	2·5	12·1	4·9
02	6 00·5	6 01·5	5 44·1	0·2	0·1	6·2	2·5	12·2	5·0
03	6 00·8	6 01·7	5 44·3	0·3	0·1	6·3	2·6	12·3	5·0
04	6 01·0	6 02·0	5 44·6	0·4	0·2	6·4	2·6	12·4	5·1
05	6 01·3	6 02·2	5 44·8	0·5	0·2	6·5	2·7	12·5	5·1
06	6 01·5	6 02·5	5 45·0	0·6	0·2	6·6	2·7	12·6	5·1
07	6 01·8	6 02·7	5 45·3	0·7	0·3	6·7	2·7	12·7	5·2
08	6 02·0	6 03·0	5 45·5	0·8	0·3	6·8	2·8	12·8	5·2
09	6 02·3	6 03·2	5 45·7	0·9	0·4	6·9	2·8	12·9	5·3
10	6 02·5	6 03·5	5 46·0	1·0	0·4	7·0	2·9	13·0	5·3
11	6 02·8	6 03·7	5 46·2	1·1	0·4	7·1	2·9	13·1	5·3
12	6 03·0	6 04·0	5 46·5	1·2	0·5	7·2	2·9	13·2	5·4
13	6 03·3	6 04·2	5 46·7	1·3	0·5	7·3	3·0	13·3	5·4
14	6 03·5	6 04·5	5 46·9	1·4	0·6	7·4	3·0	13·4	5·5
15	6 03·8	6 04·7	5 47·2	1·5	0·6	7·5	3·1	13·5	5·5
16	6 04·0	6 05·0	5 47·4	1·6	0·7	7·6	3·1	13·6	5·6
17	6 04·3	6 05·2	5 47·7	1·7	0·7	7·7	3·1	13·7	5·6
18	6 04·5	6 05·5	5 47·9	1·8	0·7	7·8	3·2	13·8	5·6
19	6 04·8	6 05·7	5 48·1	1·9	0·8	7·9	3·2	13·9	5·7
20	6 05·0	6 06·0	5 48·4	2·0	0·8	8·0	3·3	14·0	5·7
21	6 05·3	6 06·3	5 48·6	2·1	0·9	8·1	3·3	14·1	5·8
22	6 05·5	6 06·5	5 48·8	2·2	0·9	8·2	3·3	14·2	5·8
23	6 05·8	6 06·8	5 49·1	2·3	0·9	8·3	3·4	14·3	5·8
24	6 06·0	6 07·0	5 49·3	2·4	1·0	8·4	3·4	14·4	5·9
25	6 06·3	6 07·3	5 49·6	2·5	1·0	8·5	3·5	14·5	5·9
26	6 06·5	6 07·5	5 49·8	2·6	1·1	8·6	3·5	14·6	6·0
27	6 06·8	6 07·8	5 50·0	2·7	1·1	8·7	3·6	14·7	6·0
28	6 07·0	6 08·0	5 50·3	2·8	1·1	8·8	3·6	14·8	6·0
29	6 07·3	6 08·3	5 50·5	2·9	1·2	8·9	3·6	14·9	6·1
30	6 07·5	6 08·5	5 50·8	3·0	1·2	9·0	3·7	15·0	6·1
31	6 07·8	6 08·8	5 51·0	3·1	1·3	9·1	3·7	15·1	6·2
32	6 08·0	6 09·0	5 51·2	3·2	1·3	9·2	3·8	15·2	6·2
33	6 08·3	6 09·3	5 51·5	3·3	1·3	9·3	3·8	15·3	6·2
34	6 08·5	6 09·5	5 51·7	3·4	1·4	9·4	3·8	15·4	6·3
35	6 08·8	6 09·8	5 52·0	3·5	1·4	9·5	3·9	15·5	6·3
36	6 09·0	6 10·0	5 52·2	3·6	1·5	9·6	3·9	15·6	6·4
37	6 09·3	6 10·3	5 52·4	3·7	1·5	9·7	4·0	15·7	6·4
38	6 09·5	6 10·5	5 52·7	3·8	1·6	9·8	4·0	15·8	6·5
39	6 09·8	6 10·8	5 52·9	3·9	1·6	9·9	4·0	15·9	6·5
40	6 10·0	6 11·0	5 53·1	4·0	1·6	10·0	4·1	16·0	6·5
41	6 10·3	6 11·3	5 53·4	4·1	1·7	10·1	4·1	16·1	6·6
42	6 10·5	6 11·5	5 53·6	4·2	1·7	10·2	4·2	16·2	6·6
43	6 10·8	6 11·8	5 53·9	4·3	1·8	10·3	4·2	16·3	6·7
44	6 11·0	6 12·0	5 54·1	4·4	1·8	10·4	4·2	16·4	6·7
45	6 11·3	6 12·3	5 54·3	4·5	1·8	10·5	4·3	16·5	6·7
46	6 11·5	6 12·5	5 54·6	4·6	1·9	10·6	4·3	16·6	6·8
47	6 11·8	6 12·8	5 54·8	4·7	1·9	10·7	4·4	16·7	6·8
48	6 12·0	6 13·0	5 55·1	4·8	2·0	10·8	4·4	16·8	6·9
49	6 12·3	6 13·3	5 55·3	4·9	2·0	10·9	4·5	16·9	6·9
50	6 12·5	6 13·5	5 55·5	5·0	2·0	11·0	4·5	17·0	6·9
51	6 12·8	6 13·8	5 55·8	5·1	2·1	11·1	4·5	17·1	7·0
52	6 13·0	6 14·0	5 56·0	5·2	2·1	11·2	4·6	17·2	7·0
53	6 13·3	6 14·3	5 56·2	5·3	2·2	11·3	4·6	17·3	7·1
54	6 13·5	6 14·5	5 56·5	5·4	2·2	11·4	4·7	17·4	7·1
55	6 13·8	6 14·8	5 56·7	5·5	2·2	11·5	4·7	17·5	7·1
56	6 14·0	6 15·0	5 57·0	5·6	2·3	11·6	4·7	17·6	7·2
57	6 14·3	6 15·3	5 57·2	5·7	2·3	11·7	4·8	17·7	7·2
58	6 14·5	6 15·5	5 57·4	5·8	2·4	11·8	4·8	17·8	7·3
59	6 14·8	6 15·8	5 57·7	5·9	2·4	11·9	4·9	17·9	7·3
60	6 15·0	6 16·0	5 57·9	6·0	2·5	12·0	4·9	18·0	7·4

25ᵐ	SUN PLANETS	ARIES	MOON	v or d	Corrⁿ	v or d	Corrⁿ	v or d	Corrⁿ
s	° ′	° ′	° ′	′	′	′	′	′	′
00	6 15·0	6 16·0	5 57·9	0·0	0·0	6·0	2·6	12·0	5·1
01	6 15·3	6 16·3	5 58·2	0·1	0·0	6·1	2·6	12·1	5·1
02	6 15·5	6 16·5	5 58·4	0·2	0·1	6·2	2·6	12·2	5·2
03	6 15·8	6 16·8	5 58·6	0·3	0·1	6·3	2·7	12·3	5·2
04	6 16·0	6 17·0	5 58·9	0·4	0·2	6·4	2·7	12·4	5·3
05	6 16·3	6 17·3	5 59·1	0·5	0·2	6·5	2·8	12·5	5·3
06	6 16·5	6 17·5	5 59·3	0·6	0·3	6·6	2·8	12·6	5·4
07	6 16·8	6 17·8	5 59·6	0·7	0·3	6·7	2·8	12·7	5·4
08	6 17·0	6 18·0	5 59·8	0·8	0·3	6·8	2·9	12·8	5·4
09	6 17·3	6 18·3	6 00·1	0·9	0·4	6·9	2·9	12·9	5·5
10	6 17·5	6 18·5	6 00·3	1·0	0·4	7·0	3·0	13·0	5·5
11	6 17·8	6 18·8	6 00·5	1·1	0·5	7·1	3·0	13·1	5·6
12	6 18·0	6 19·0	6 00·8	1·2	0·5	7·2	3·1	13·2	5·6
13	6 18·3	6 19·3	6 01·0	1·3	0·6	7·3	3·1	13·3	5·7
14	6 18·5	6 19·5	6 01·3	1·4	0·6	7·4	3·1	13·4	5·7
15	6 18·8	6 19·8	6 01·5	1·5	0·6	7·5	3·2	13·5	5·7
16	6 19·0	6 20·0	6 01·7	1·6	0·7	7·6	3·2	13·6	5·8
17	6 19·3	6 20·3	6 02·0	1·7	0·7	7·7	3·3	13·7	5·8
18	6 19·5	6 20·5	6 02·2	1·8	0·8	7·8	3·3	13·8	5·9
19	6 19·8	6 20·8	6 02·5	1·9	0·8	7·9	3·4	13·9	5·9
20	6 20·0	6 21·0	6 02·7	2·0	0·9	8·0	3·4	14·0	6·0
21	6 20·3	6 21·3	6 02·9	2·1	0·9	8·1	3·4	14·1	6·0
22	6 20·5	6 21·5	6 03·2	2·2	0·9	8·2	3·5	14·2	6·0
23	6 20·8	6 21·8	6 03·4	2·3	1·0	8·3	3·5	14·3	6·1
24	6 21·0	6 22·0	6 03·6	2·4	1·0	8·4	3·6	14·4	6·1
25	6 21·3	6 22·3	6 03·9	2·5	1·1	8·5	3·6	14·5	6·2
26	6 21·5	6 22·5	6 04·1	2·6	1·1	8·6	3·7	14·6	6·2
27	6 21·8	6 22·8	6 04·4	2·7	1·1	8·7	3·7	14·7	6·2
28	6 22·0	6 23·0	6 04·6	2·8	1·2	8·8	3·7	14·8	6·3
29	6 22·3	6 23·3	6 04·8	2·9	1·2	8·9	3·8	14·9	6·3
30	6 22·5	6 23·5	6 05·1	3·0	1·3	9·0	3·8	15·0	6·4
31	6 22·8	6 23·8	6 05·3	3·1	1·3	9·1	3·9	15·1	6·4
32	6 23·0	6 24·0	6 05·6	3·2	1·4	9·2	3·9	15·2	6·5
33	6 23·3	6 24·3	6 05·8	3·3	1·4	9·3	4·0	15·3	6·5
34	6 23·5	6 24·5	6 06·0	3·4	1·4	9·4	4·0	15·4	6·5
35	6 23·8	6 24·8	6 06·3	3·5	1·5	9·5	4·0	15·5	6·6
36	6 24·0	6 25·1	6 06·5	3·6	1·5	9·6	4·1	15·6	6·6
37	6 24·3	6 25·3	6 06·7	3·7	1·6	9·7	4·1	15·7	6·7
38	6 24·5	6 25·6	6 07·0	3·8	1·6	9·8	4·2	15·8	6·7
39	6 24·8	6 25·8	6 07·2	3·9	1·7	9·9	4·2	15·9	6·8
40	6 25·0	6 26·1	6 07·5	4·0	1·7	10·0	4·3	16·0	6·8
41	6 25·3	6 26·3	6 07·7	4·1	1·7	10·1	4·3	16·1	6·8
42	6 25·5	6 26·6	6 07·9	4·2	1·8	10·2	4·3	16·2	6·9
43	6 25·8	6 26·8	6 08·2	4·3	1·8	10·3	4·4	16·3	6·9
44	6 26·0	6 27·1	6 08·4	4·4	1·9	10·4	4·4	16·4	7·0
45	6 26·3	6 27·3	6 08·7	4·5	1·9	10·5	4·5	16·5	7·0
46	6 26·5	6 27·6	6 08·9	4·6	2·0	10·6	4·5	16·6	7·1
47	6 26·8	6 27·8	6 09·1	4·7	2·0	10·7	4·5	16·7	7·1
48	6 27·0	6 28·1	6 09·4	4·8	2·0	10·8	4·6	16·8	7·1
49	6 27·3	6 28·3	6 09·6	4·9	2·1	10·9	4·6	16·9	7·2
50	6 27·5	6 28·6	6 09·8	5·0	2·1	11·0	4·7	17·0	7·2
51	6 27·8	6 28·8	6 10·1	5·1	2·2	11·1	4·7	17·1	7·3
52	6 28·0	6 29·1	6 10·3	5·2	2·2	11·2	4·8	17·2	7·3
53	6 28·3	6 29·3	6 10·6	5·3	2·3	11·3	4·8	17·3	7·3
54	6 28·5	6 29·6	6 10·8	5·4	2·3	11·4	4·8	17·4	7·4
55	6 28·8	6 29·8	6 11·0	5·5	2·3	11·5	4·9	17·5	7·4
56	6 29·0	6 30·1	6 11·3	5·6	2·4	11·6	4·9	17·6	7·5
57	6 29·3	6 30·3	6 11·5	5·7	2·4	11·7	5·0	17·7	7·5
58	6 29·5	6 30·6	6 11·8	5·8	2·5	11·8	5·0	17·8	7·6
59	6 29·8	6 30·8	6 12·0	5·9	2·5	11·9	5·1	17·9	7·6
60	6 30·0	6 31·1	6 12·2	6·0	2·6	12·0	5·1	18·0	7·7

26^m	SUN PLANETS	ARIES	MOON	v or Corrⁿ d		v or Corrⁿ d		v or Corrⁿ d	
s	° ′	° ′	° ′	′	′	′	′	′	′
00	6 30·0	6 31·1	6 12·2	0·0	0·0	6·0	2·7	12·0	5·3
01	6 30·3	6 31·3	6 12·5	0·1	0·0	6·1	2·7	12·1	5·3
02	6 30·5	6 31·6	6 12·7	0·2	0·1	6·2	2·7	12·2	5·4
03	6 30·8	6 31·8	6 12·9	0·3	0·1	6·3	2·8	12·3	5·4
04	6 31·0	6 32·1	6 13·2	0·4	0·2	6·4	2·8	12·4	5·5
05	6 31·3	6 32·3	6 13·4	0·5	0·2	6·5	2·9	12·5	5·5
06	6 31·5	6 32·6	6 13·7	0·6	0·3	6·6	2·9	12·6	5·6
07	6 31·8	6 32·8	6 13·9	0·7	0·3	6·7	3·0	12·7	5·6
08	6 32·0	6 33·1	6 14·1	0·8	0·4	6·8	3·0	12·8	5·7
09	6 32·3	6 33·3	6 14·4	0·9	0·4	6·9	3·0	12·9	5·7
10	6 32·5	6 33·6	6 14·6	1·0	0·4	7·0	3·1	13·0	5·7
11	6 32·8	6 33·8	6 14·9	1·1	0·5	7·1	3·1	13·1	5·8
12	6 33·0	6 34·1	6 15·1	1·2	0·5	7·2	3·2	13·2	5·8
13	6 33·3	6 34·3	6 15·3	1·3	0·6	7·3	3·2	13·3	5·9
14	6 33·5	6 34·6	6 15·6	1·4	0·6	7·4	3·3	13·4	5·9
15	6 33·8	6 34·8	6 15·8	1·5	0·7	7·5	3·3	13·5	6·0
16	6 34·0	6 35·1	6 16·1	1·6	0·7	7·6	3·4	13·6	6·0
17	6 34·3	6 35·3	6 16·3	1·7	0·8	7·7	3·4	13·7	6·1
18	6 34·5	6 35·6	6 16·5	1·8	0·8	7·8	3·4	13·8	6·1
19	6 34·8	6 35·8	6 16·8	1·9	0·8	7·9	3·5	13·9	6·1
20	6 35·0	6 36·1	6 17·0	2·0	0·9	8·0	3·5	14·0	6·2
21	6 35·3	6 36·3	6 17·2	2·1	0·9	8·1	3·6	14·1	6·2
22	6 35·5	6 36·6	6 17·5	2·2	1·0	8·2	3·6	14·2	6·3
23	6 35·8	6 36·8	6 17·7	2·3	1·0	8·3	3·7	14·3	6·3
24	6 36·0	6 37·1	6 18·0	2·4	1·1	8·4	3·7	14·4	6·4
25	6 36·3	6 37·3	6 18·2	2·5	1·1	8·5	3·8	14·5	6·4
26	6 36·5	6 37·6	6 18·4	2·6	1·1	8·6	3·8	14·6	6·4
27	6 36·8	6 37·8	6 18·7	2·7	1·2	8·7	3·8	14·7	6·5
28	6 37·0	6 38·1	6 18·9	2·8	1·2	8·8	3·9	14·8	6·5
29	6 37·3	6 38·3	6 19·2	2·9	1·3	8·9	3·9	14·9	6·6
30	6 37·5	6 38·6	6 19·4	3·0	1·3	9·0	4·0	15·0	6·6
31	6 37·8	6 38·8	6 19·6	3·1	1·4	9·1	4·0	15·1	6·7
32	6 38·0	6 39·1	6 19·9	3·2	1·4	9·2	4·1	15·2	6·7
33	6 38·3	6 39·3	6 20·1	3·3	1·5	9·3	4·1	15·3	6·8
34	6 38·5	6 39·6	6 20·3	3·4	1·5	9·4	4·2	15·4	6·8
35	6 38·8	6 39·8	6 20·6	3·5	1·5	9·5	4·2	15·5	6·8
36	6 39·0	6 40·1	6 20·8	3·6	1·6	9·6	4·2	15·6	6·9
37	6 39·3	6 40·3	6 21·1	3·7	1·6	9·7	4·3	15·7	6·9
38	6 39·5	6 40·6	6 21·3	3·8	1·7	9·8	4·3	15·8	7·0
39	6 39·8	6 40·8	6 21·5	3·9	1·7	9·9	4·4	15·9	7·0
40	6 40·0	6 41·1	6 21·8	4·0	1·8	10·0	4·4	16·0	7·1
41	6 40·3	6 41·3	6 22·0	4·1	1·8	10·1	4·5	16·1	7·1
42	6 40·5	6 41·6	6 22·3	4·2	1·9	10·2	4·5	16·2	7·2
43	6 40·8	6 41·8	6 22·5	4·3	1·9	10·3	4·5	16·3	7·2
44	6 41·0	6 42·1	6 22·7	4·4	1·9	10·4	4·6	16·4	7·2
45	6 41·3	6 42·3	6 23·0	4·5	2·0	10·5	4·6	16·5	7·3
46	6 41·5	6 42·6	6 23·2	4·6	2·0	10·6	4·7	16·6	7·3
47	6 41·8	6 42·8	6 23·4	4·7	2·1	10·7	4·7	16·7	7·4
48	6 42·0	6 43·1	6 23·7	4·8	2·1	10·8	4·8	16·8	7·4
49	6 42·3	6 43·4	6 23·9	4·9	2·2	10·9	4·8	16·9	7·5
50	6 42·5	6 43·6	6 24·2	5·0	2·2	11·0	4·9	17·0	7·5
51	6 42·8	6 43·9	6 24·4	5·1	2·3	11·1	4·9	17·1	7·6
52	6 43·0	6 44·1	6 24·6	5·2	2·3	11·2	4·9	17·2	7·6
53	6 43·3	6 44·4	6 24·9	5·3	2·3	11·3	5·0	17·3	7·6
54	6 43·5	6 44·6	6 25·1	5·4	2·4	11·4	5·0	17·4	7·7
55	6 43·8	6 44·9	6 25·4	5·5	2·4	11·5	5·1	17·5	7·7
56	6 44·0	6 45·1	6 25·6	5·6	2·5	11·6	5·1	17·6	7·8
57	6 44·3	6 45·4	6 25·8	5·7	2·5	11·7	5·2	17·7	7·8
58	6 44·5	6 45·6	6 26·1	5·8	2·6	11·8	5·2	17·8	7·9
59	6 44·8	6 45·9	6 26·3	5·9	2·6	11·9	5·3	17·9	7·9
60	6 45·0	6 46·1	6 26·6	6·0	2·7	12·0	5·3	18·0	8·0

27^m	SUN PLANETS	ARIES	MOON	v or Corrⁿ d		v or Corrⁿ d		v or Corrⁿ d	
s	° ′	° ′	° ′	′	′	′	′	′	′
00	6 45·0	6 46·1	6 26·6	0·0	0·0	6·0	2·8	12·0	5·5
01	6 45·3	6 46·4	6 26·8	0·1	0·0	6·1	2·8	12·1	5·5
02	6 45·5	6 46·6	6 27·0	0·2	0·1	6·2	2·8	12·2	5·6
03	6 45·8	6 46·9	6 27·3	0·3	0·1	6·3	2·9	12·3	5·6
04	6 46·0	6 47·1	6 27·5	0·4	0·2	6·4	2·9	12·4	5·7
05	6 46·3	6 47·4	6 27·7	0·5	0·2	6·5	3·0	12·5	5·7
06	6 46·5	6 47·6	6 28·0	0·6	0·3	6·6	3·0	12·6	5·8
07	6 46·8	6 47·9	6 28·2	0·7	0·3	6·7	3·1	12·7	5·8
08	6 47·0	6 48·1	6 28·5	0·8	0·4	6·8	3·1	12·8	5·9
09	6 47·3	6 48·4	6 28·7	0·9	0·4	6·9	3·2	12·9	5·9
10	6 47·5	6 48·6	6 28·9	1·0	0·5	7·0	3·2	13·0	6·0
11	6 47·8	6 48·9	6 29·2	1·1	0·5	7·1	3·3	13·1	6·0
12	6 48·0	6 49·1	6 29·4	1·2	0·6	7·2	3·3	13·2	6·1
13	6 48·3	6 49·4	6 29·7	1·3	0·6	7·3	3·3	13·3	6·1
14	6 48·5	6 49·6	6 29·9	1·4	0·6	7·4	3·4	13·4	6·1
15	6 48·8	6 49·9	6 30·1	1·5	0·7	7·5	3·4	13·5	6·2
16	6 49·0	6 50·1	6 30·4	1·6	0·7	7·6	3·5	13·6	6·2
17	6 49·3	6 50·4	6 30·6	1·7	0·8	7·7	3·5	13·7	6·3
18	6 49·5	6 50·6	6 30·8	1·8	0·8	7·8	3·6	13·8	6·3
19	6 49·8	6 50·9	6 31·1	1·9	0·9	7·9	3·6	13·9	6·4
20	6 50·0	6 51·1	6 31·3	2·0	0·9	8·0	3·7	14·0	6·4
21	6 50·3	6 51·4	6 31·6	2·1	1·0	8·1	3·7	14·1	6·5
22	6 50·5	6 51·6	6 31·8	2·2	1·0	8·2	3·8	14·2	6·5
23	6 50·8	6 51·9	6 32·0	2·3	1·1	8·3	3·8	14·3	6·6
24	6 51·0	6 52·1	6 32·3	2·4	1·1	8·4	3·9	14·4	6·6
25	6 51·3	6 52·4	6 32·5	2·5	1·1	8·5	3·9	14·5	6·6
26	6 51·5	6 52·6	6 32·8	2·6	1·2	8·6	3·9	14·6	6·7
27	6 51·8	6 52·9	6 33·0	2·7	1·2	8·7	4·0	14·7	6·7
28	6 52·0	6 53·1	6 33·2	2·8	1·3	8·8	4·0	14·8	6·8
29	6 52·3	6 53·4	6 33·5	2·9	1·3	8·9	4·1	14·9	6·8
30	6 52·5	6 53·6	6 33·7	3·0	1·4	9·0	4·1	15·0	6·9
31	6 52·8	6 53·9	6 33·9	3·1	1·4	9·1	4·2	15·1	6·9
32	6 53·0	6 54·1	6 34·2	3·2	1·5	9·2	4·2	15·2	7·0
33	6 53·3	6 54·4	6 34·4	3·3	1·5	9·3	4·3	15·3	7·0
34	6 53·5	6 54·6	6 34·7	3·4	1·6	9·4	4·3	15·4	7·1
35	6 53·8	6 54·9	6 34·9	3·5	1·6	9·5	4·4	15·5	7·1
36	6 54·0	6 55·1	6 35·1	3·6	1·7	9·6	4·4	15·6	7·2
37	6 54·3	6 55·4	6 35·4	3·7	1·7	9·7	4·4	15·7	7·2
38	6 54·5	6 55·6	6 35·6	3·8	1·7	9·8	4·5	15·8	7·2
39	6 54·8	6 55·9	6 35·9	3·9	1·8	9·9	4·5	15·9	7·3
40	6 55·0	6 56·1	6 36·1	4·0	1·8	10·0	4·6	16·0	7·3
41	6 55·3	6 56·4	6 36·3	4·1	1·9	10·1	4·6	16·1	7·4
42	6 55·5	6 56·6	6 36·6	4·2	1·9	10·2	4·7	16·2	7·4
43	6 55·8	6 56·9	6 36·8	4·3	2·0	10·3	4·7	16·3	7·5
44	6 56·0	6 57·1	6 37·0	4·4	2·0	10·4	4·8	16·4	7·5
45	6 56·3	6 57·4	6 37·3	4·5	2·1	10·5	4·8	16·5	7·6
46	6 56·5	6 57·6	6 37·5	4·6	2·1	10·6	4·9	16·6	7·6
47	6 56·8	6 57·9	6 37·8	4·7	2·2	10·7	4·9	16·7	7·7
48	6 57·0	6 58·1	6 38·0	4·8	2·2	10·8	5·0	16·8	7·7
49	6 57·3	6 58·4	6 38·2	4·9	2·2	10·9	5·0	16·9	7·7
50	6 57·5	6 58·6	6 38·5	5·0	2·3	11·0	5·0	17·0	7·8
51	6 57·8	6 58·9	6 38·7	5·1	2·3	11·1	5·1	17·1	7·8
52	6 58·0	6 59·1	6 39·0	5·2	2·4	11·2	5·1	17·2	7·9
53	6 58·3	6 59·4	6 39·2	5·3	2·4	11·3	5·2	17·3	7·9
54	6 58·5	6 59·6	6 39·4	5·4	2·5	11·4	5·2	17·4	8·0
55	6 58·8	6 59·9	6 39·7	5·5	2·5	11·5	5·3	17·5	8·0
56	6 59·0	7 00·1	6 39·9	5·6	2·6	11·6	5·3	17·6	8·1
57	6 59·3	7 00·4	6 40·2	5·7	2·6	11·7	5·4	17·7	8·1
58	6 59·5	7 00·6	6 40·4	5·8	2·7	11·8	5·4	17·8	8·2
59	6 59·8	7 00·9	6 40·6	5·9	2·7	11·9	5·5	17·9	8·2
60	7 00·0	7 01·1	6 40·9	6·0	2·8	12·0	5·5	18·0	8·3

28ᵐ	SUN PLANETS	ARIES	MOON	v or Corrⁿ d	v or Corrⁿ d	v or Corrⁿ d
s	° ′	° ′	° ′	′ ′	′ ′	′ ′
00	7 00·0	7 01·1	6 40·9	0·0 0·0	6·0 2·9	12·0 5·7
01	7 00·3	7 01·4	6 41·1	0·1 0·0	6·1 2·9	12·1 5·7
02	7 00·5	7 01·7	6 41·3	0·2 0·1	6·2 2·9	12·2 5·8
03	7 00·8	7 01·9	6 41·6	0·3 0·1	6·3 3·0	12·3 5·8
04	7 01·0	7 02·2	6 41·8	0·4 0·2	6·4 3·0	12·4 5·9
05	7 01·3	7 02·4	6 42·1	0·5 0·2	6·5 3·1	12·5 5·9
06	7 01·5	7 02·7	6 42·3	0·6 0·3	6·6 3·1	12·6 6·0
07	7 01·8	7 02·9	6 42·5	0·7 0·3	6·7 3·2	12·7 6·0
08	7 02·0	7 03·2	6 42·8	0·8 0·4	6·8 3·2	12·8 6·1
09	7 02·3	7 03·4	6 43·0	0·9 0·4	6·9 3·3	12·9 6·1
10	7 02·5	7 03·7	6 43·3	1·0 0·5	7·0 3·3	13·0 6·2
11	7 02·8	7 03·9	6 43·5	1·1 0·5	7·1 3·4	13·1 6·2
12	7 03·0	7 04·2	6 43·7	1·2 0·6	7·2 3·4	13·2 6·3
13	7 03·3	7 04·4	6 44·0	1·3 0·6	7·3 3·5	13·3 6·3
14	7 03·5	7 04·7	6 44·2	1·4 0·7	7·4 3·5	13·4 6·4
15	7 03·8	7 04·9	6 44·4	1·5 0·7	7·5 3·6	13·5 6·4
16	7 04·0	7 05·2	6 44·7	1·6 0·8	7·6 3·6	13·6 6·5
17	7 04·3	7 05·4	6 44·9	1·7 0·8	7·7 3·7	13·7 6·5
18	7 04·5	7 05·7	6 45·2	1·8 0·9	7·8 3·7	13·8 6·6
19	7 04·8	7 05·9	6 45·4	1·9 0·9	7·9 3·8	13·9 6·6
20	7 05·0	7 06·2	6 45·6	2·0 1·0	8·0 3·8	14·0 6·7
21	7 05·3	7 06·4	6 45·9	2·1 1·0	8·1 3·8	14·1 6·7
22	7 05·5	7 06·7	6 46·1	2·2 1·0	8·2 3·9	14·2 6·7
23	7 05·8	7 06·9	6 46·4	2·3 1·1	8·3 3·9	14·3 6·8
24	7 06·0	7 07·2	6 46·6	2·4 1·1	8·4 4·0	14·4 6·8
25	7 06·3	7 07·4	6 46·8	2·5 1·2	8·5 4·0	14·5 6·9
26	7 06·5	7 07·7	6 47·1	2·6 1·2	8·6 4·1	14·6 6·9
27	7 06·8	7 07·9	6 47·3	2·7 1·3	8·7 4·1	14·7 7·0
28	7 07·0	7 08·2	6 47·5	2·8 1·3	8·8 4·2	14·8 7·0
29	7 07·3	7 08·4	6 47·8	2·9 1·4	8·9 4·2	14·9 7·1
30	7 07·5	7 08·7	6 48·0	3·0 1·4	9·0 4·3	15·0 7·1
31	7 07·8	7 08·9	6 48·3	3·1 1·5	9·1 4·3	15·1 7·2
32	7 08·0	7 09·2	6 48·5	3·2 1·5	9·2 4·4	15·2 7·2
33	7 08·3	7 09·4	6 48·7	3·3 1·6	9·3 4·4	15·3 7·3
34	7 08·5	7 09·7	6 49·0	3·4 1·6	9·4 4·5	15·4 7·3
35	7 08·8	7 09·9	6 49·2	3·5 1·7	9·5 4·5	15·5 7·4
36	7 09·0	7 10·2	6 49·5	3·6 1·7	9·6 4·6	15·6 7·4
37	7 09·3	7 10·4	6 49·7	3·7 1·8	9·7 4·6	15·7 7·5
38	7 09·5	7 10·7	6 49·9	3·8 1·8	9·8 4·7	15·8 7·5
39	7 09·8	7 10·9	6 50·2	3·9 1·9	9·9 4·7	15·9 7·6
40	7 10·0	7 11·2	6 50·4	4·0 1·9	10·0 4·8	16·0 7·6
41	7 10·3	7 11·4	6 50·6	4·1 1·9	10·1 4·8	16·1 7·6
42	7 10·5	7 11·7	6 50·9	4·2 2·0	10·2 4·8	16·2 7·7
43	7 10·8	7 11·9	6 51·1	4·3 2·0	10·3 4·9	16·3 7·7
44	7 11·0	7 12·2	6 51·4	4·4 2·1	10·4 4·9	16·4 7·8
45	7 11·3	7 12·4	6 51·6	4·5 2·1	10·5 5·0	16·5 7·8
46	7 11·5	7 12·7	6 51·8	4·6 2·2	10·6 5·0	16·6 7·9
47	7 11·8	7 12·9	6 52·1	4·7 2·2	10·7 5·1	16·7 7·9
48	7 12·0	7 13·2	6 52·3	4·8 2·3	10·8 5·1	16·8 8·0
49	7 12·3	7 13·4	6 52·6	4·9 2·3	10·9 5·2	16·9 8·0
50	7 12·5	7 13·7	6 52·8	5·0 2·4	11·0 5·2	17·0 8·1
51	7 12·8	7 13·9	6 53·0	5·1 2·4	11·1 5·3	17·1 8·1
52	7 13·0	7 14·2	6 53·3	5·2 2·5	11·2 5·3	17·2 8·2
53	7 13·3	7 14·4	6 53·5	5·3 2·5	11·3 5·4	17·3 8·2
54	7 13·5	7 14·7	6 53·8	5·4 2·6	11·4 5·4	17·4 8·3
55	7 13·8	7 14·9	6 54·0	5·5 2·6	11·5 5·5	17·5 8·3
56	7 14·0	7 15·2	6 54·2	5·6 2·7	11·6 5·5	17·6 8·4
57	7 14·3	7 15·4	6 54·5	5·7 2·7	11·7 5·6	17·7 8·4
58	7 14·5	7 15·7	6 54·7	5·8 2·8	11·8 5·6	17·8 8·5
59	7 14·8	7 15·9	6 54·9	5·9 2·8	11·9 5·7	17·9 8·5
60	7 15·0	7 16·2	6 55·2	6·0 2·9	12·0 5·7	18·0 8·6

29ᵐ	SUN PLANETS	ARIES	MOON	v or Corrⁿ d	v or Corrⁿ d	v or Corrⁿ d
s	° ′	° ′	° ′	′ ′	′ ′	′ ′
00	7 15·0	7 16·2	6 55·2	0·0 0·0	6·0 3·0	12·0 5·9
01	7 15·3	7 16·4	6 55·4	0·1 0·0	6·1 3·0	12·1 5·9
02	7 15·5	7 16·7	6 55·7	0·2 0·1	6·2 3·0	12·2 6·0
03	7 15·8	7 16·9	6 55·9	0·3 0·1	6·3 3·1	12·3 6·0
04	7 16·0	7 17·2	6 56·1	0·4 0·2	6·4 3·1	12·4 6·1
05	7 16·3	7 17·4	6 56·4	0·5 0·2	6·5 3·2	12·5 6·1
06	7 16·5	7 17·7	6 56·6	0·6 0·3	6·6 3·2	12·6 6·2
07	7 16·8	7 17·9	6 56·9	0·7 0·3	6·7 3·3	12·7 6·2
08	7 17·0	7 18·2	6 57·1	0·8 0·4	6·8 3·3	12·8 6·3
09	7 17·3	7 18·4	6 57·3	0·9 0·4	6·9 3·4	12·9 6·3
10	7 17·5	7 18·7	6 57·6	1·0 0·5	7·0 3·4	13·0 6·4
11	7 17·8	7 18·9	6 57·8	1·1 0·5	7·1 3·5	13·1 6·4
12	7 18·0	7 19·2	6 58·0	1·2 0·6	7·2 3·5	13·2 6·5
13	7 18·3	7 19·4	6 58·3	1·3 0·6	7·3 3·6	13·3 6·5
14	7 18·5	7 19·7	6 58·5	1·4 0·7	7·4 3·6	13·4 6·6
15	7 18·8	7 20·0	6 58·8	1·5 0·7	7·5 3·7	13·5 6·6
16	7 19·0	7 20·2	6 59·0	1·6 0·8	7·6 3·7	13·6 6·7
17	7 19·3	7 20·5	6 59·2	1·7 0·8	7·7 3·8	13·7 6·7
18	7 19·5	7 20·7	6 59·5	1·8 0·9	7·8 3·8	13·8 6·8
19	7 19·8	7 21·0	6 59·7	1·9 0·9	7·9 3·9	13·9 6·8
20	7 20·0	7 21·2	7 00·0	2·0 1·0	8·0 3·9	14·0 6·9
21	7 20·3	7 21·5	7 00·2	2·1 1·0	8·1 4·0	14·1 6·9
22	7 20·5	7 21·7	7 00·4	2·2 1·1	8·2 4·0	14·2 7·0
23	7 20·8	7 22·0	7 00·7	2·3 1·1	8·3 4·1	14·3 7·0
24	7 21·0	7 22·2	7 00·9	2·4 1·2	8·4 4·1	14·4 7·1
25	7 21·3	7 22·5	7 01·1	2·5 1·2	8·5 4·2	14·5 7·1
26	7 21·5	7 22·7	7 01·4	2·6 1·3	8·6 4·2	14·6 7·2
27	7 21·8	7 23·0	7 01·6	2·7 1·3	8·7 4·3	14·7 7·2
28	7 22·0	7 23·2	7 01·9	2·8 1·4	8·8 4·3	14·8 7·3
29	7 22·3	7 23·5	7 02·1	2·9 1·4	8·9 4·4	14·9 7·3
30	7 22·5	7 23·7	7 02·3	3·0 1·5	9·0 4·4	15·0 7·4
31	7 22·8	7 24·0	7 02·6	3·1 1·5	9·1 4·5	15·1 7·4
32	7 23·0	7 24·2	7 02·8	3·2 1·6	9·2 4·5	15·2 7·5
33	7 23·3	7 24·5	7 03·1	3·3 1·6	9·3 4·6	15·3 7·5
34	7 23·5	7 24·7	7 03·3	3·4 1·7	9·4 4·6	15·4 7·6
35	7 23·8	7 25·0	7 03·5	3·5 1·7	9·5 4·7	15·5 7·6
36	7 24·0	7 25·2	7 03·8	3·6 1·8	9·6 4·7	15·6 7·7
37	7 24·3	7 25·5	7 04·0	3·7 1·8	9·7 4·8	15·7 7·7
38	7 24·5	7 25·7	7 04·3	3·8 1·9	9·8 4·8	15·8 7·8
39	7 24·8	7 26·0	7 04·5	3·9 1·9	9·9 4·9	15·9 7·8
40	7 25·0	7 26·2	7 04·7	4·0 2·0	10·0 4·9	16·0 7·9
41	7 25·3	7 26·5	7 05·0	4·1 2·0	10·1 5·0	16·1 7·9
42	7 25·5	7 26·7	7 05·2	4·2 2·1	10·2 5·0	16·2 8·0
43	7 25·8	7 27·0	7 05·4	4·3 2·1	10·3 5·1	16·3 8·0
44	7 26·0	7 27·2	7 05·7	4·4 2·2	10·4 5·1	16·4 8·1
45	7 26·3	7 27·5	7 05·9	4·5 2·2	10·5 5·2	16·5 8·1
46	7 26·5	7 27·7	7 06·2	4·6 2·3	10·6 5·2	16·6 8·2
47	7 26·8	7 28·0	7 06·4	4·7 2·3	10·7 5·3	16·7 8·2
48	7 27·0	7 28·2	7 06·6	4·8 2·4	10·8 5·3	16·8 8·3
49	7 27·3	7 28·5	7 06·9	4·9 2·4	10·9 5·4	16·9 8·3
50	7 27·5	7 28·7	7 07·1	5·0 2·5	11·0 5·4	17·0 8·4
51	7 27·8	7 29·0	7 07·4	5·1 2·5	11·1 5·5	17·1 8·4
52	7 28·0	7 29·2	7 07·6	5·2 2·6	11·2 5·5	17·2 8·5
53	7 28·3	7 29·5	7 07·8	5·3 2·6	11·3 5·6	17·3 8·5
54	7 28·5	7 29·7	7 08·1	5·4 2·7	11·4 5·6	17·4 8·6
55	7 28·8	7 30·0	7 08·3	5·5 2·7	11·5 5·7	17·5 8·6
56	7 29·0	7 30·2	7 08·5	5·6 2·8	11·6 5·7	17·6 8·7
57	7 29·3	7 30·5	7 08·8	5·7 2·8	11·7 5·8	17·7 8·7
58	7 29·5	7 30·7	7 09·0	5·8 2·9	11·8 5·8	17·8 8·8
59	7 29·8	7 31·0	7 09·3	5·9 2·9	11·9 5·9	17·9 8·8
60	7 30·0	7 31·2	7 09·5	6·0 3·0	12·0 5·9	18·0 8·9

30ᵐ

30ᵐ s	SUN PLANETS ° ′	ARIES ° ′	MOON ° ′	v or d ′	Corrⁿ ′	v or d ′	Corrⁿ ′	v or d ′	Corrⁿ ′
00	7 30·0	7 31·2	7 09·5	0·0	0·0	6·0	3·1	12·0	6·1
01	7 30·3	7 31·5	7 09·7	0·1	0·1	6·1	3·1	12·1	6·2
02	7 30·5	7 31·7	7 10·0	0·2	0·1	6·2	3·2	12·2	6·2
03	7 30·8	7 32·0	7 10·2	0·3	0·2	6·3	3·2	12·3	6·3
04	7 31·0	7 32·2	7 10·5	0·4	0·2	6·4	3·3	12·4	6·3
05	7 31·3	7 32·5	7 10·7	0·5	0·3	6·5	3·3	12·5	6·4
06	7 31·5	7 32·7	7 10·9	0·6	0·3	6·6	3·4	12·6	6·4
07	7 31·8	7 33·0	7 11·2	0·7	0·4	6·7	3·4	12·7	6·5
08	7 32·0	7 33·2	7 11·4	0·8	0·4	6·8	3·5	12·8	6·5
09	7 32·3	7 33·5	7 11·6	0·9	0·5	6·9	3·5	12·9	6·6
10	7 32·5	7 33·7	7 11·9	1·0	0·5	7·0	3·6	13·0	6·6
11	7 32·8	7 34·0	7 12·1	1·1	0·6	7·1	3·6	13·1	6·7
12	7 33·0	7 34·2	7 12·4	1·2	0·6	7·2	3·7	13·2	6·7
13	7 33·3	7 34·5	7 12·6	1·3	0·7	7·3	3·7	13·3	6·8
14	7 33·5	7 34·7	7 12·8	1·4	0·7	7·4	3·8	13·4	6·8
15	7 33·8	7 35·0	7 13·1	1·5	0·8	7·5	3·8	13·5	6·9
16	7 34·0	7 35·2	7 13·3	1·6	0·8	7·6	3·9	13·6	6·9
17	7 34·3	7 35·5	7 13·6	1·7	0·9	7·7	3·9	13·7	7·0
18	7 34·5	7 35·7	7 13·8	1·8	0·9	7·8	4·0	13·8	7·0
19	7 34·8	7 36·0	7 14·0	1·9	1·0	7·9	4·0	13·9	7·1
20	7 35·0	7 36·2	7 14·3	2·0	1·0	8·0	4·1	14·0	7·1
21	7 35·3	7 36·5	7 14·5	2·1	1·1	8·1	4·1	14·1	7·2
22	7 35·5	7 36·7	7 14·7	2·2	1·1	8·2	4·2	14·2	7·2
23	7 35·8	7 37·0	7 15·0	2·3	1·2	8·3	4·2	14·3	7·3
24	7 36·0	7 37·2	7 15·2	2·4	1·2	8·4	4·3	14·4	7·3
25	7 36·3	7 37·5	7 15·5	2·5	1·3	8·5	4·3	14·5	7·4
26	7 36·5	7 37·7	7 15·7	2·6	1·3	8·6	4·4	14·6	7·4
27	7 36·8	7 38·0	7 15·9	2·7	1·4	8·7	4·4	14·7	7·5
28	7 37·0	7 38·3	7 16·2	2·8	1·4	8·8	4·5	14·8	7·5
29	7 37·3	7 38·5	7 16·4	2·9	1·5	8·9	4·5	14·9	7·6
30	7 37·5	7 38·8	7 16·7	3·0	1·5	9·0	4·6	15·0	7·6
31	7 37·8	7 39·0	7 16·9	3·1	1·6	9·1	4·6	15·1	7·7
32	7 38·0	7 39·3	7 17·1	3·2	1·6	9·2	4·7	15·2	7·7
33	7 38·3	7 39·5	7 17·4	3·3	1·7	9·3	4·7	15·3	7·8
34	7 38·5	7 39·8	7 17·6	3·4	1·7	9·4	4·8	15·4	7·8
35	7 38·8	7 40·0	7 17·9	3·5	1·8	9·5	4·8	15·5	7·9
36	7 39·0	7 40·3	7 18·1	3·6	1·8	9·6	4·9	15·6	7·9
37	7 39·3	7 40·5	7 18·3	3·7	1·9	9·7	4·9	15·7	8·0
38	7 39·5	7 40·8	7 18·6	3·8	1·9	9·8	5·0	15·8	8·0
39	7 39·8	7 41·0	7 18·8	3·9	2·0	9·9	5·0	15·9	8·1
40	7 40·0	7 41·3	7 19·0	4·0	2·0	10·0	5·1	16·0	8·1
41	7 40·3	7 41·5	7 19·3	4·1	2·1	10·1	5·1	16·1	8·2
42	7 40·5	7 41·8	7 19·5	4·2	2·1	10·2	5·2	16·2	8·2
43	7 40·8	7 42·0	7 19·8	4·3	2·2	10·3	5·2	16·3	8·3
44	7 41·0	7 42·3	7 20·0	4·4	2·2	10·4	5·3	16·4	8·3
45	7 41·3	7 42·5	7 20·2	4·5	2·3	10·5	5·3	16·5	8·4
46	7 41·5	7 42·8	7 20·5	4·6	2·3	10·6	5·4	16·6	8·4
47	7 41·8	7 43·0	7 20·7	4·7	2·4	10·7	5·4	16·7	8·5
48	7 42·0	7 43·3	7 21·0	4·8	2·4	10·8	5·5	16·8	8·5
49	7 42·3	7 43·5	7 21·2	4·9	2·5	10·9	5·5	16·9	8·6
50	7 42·5	7 43·8	7 21·4	5·0	2·5	11·0	5·6	17·0	8·6
51	7 42·8	7 44·0	7 21·7	5·1	2·6	11·1	5·6	17·1	8·7
52	7 43·0	7 44·3	7 21·9	5·2	2·6	11·2	5·7	17·2	8·7
53	7 43·3	7 44·5	7 22·1	5·3	2·7	11·3	5·7	17·3	8·8
54	7 43·5	7 44·8	7 22·4	5·4	2·7	11·4	5·8	17·4	8·8
55	7 43·8	7 45·0	7 22·6	5·5	2·8	11·5	5·8	17·5	8·9
56	7 44·0	7 45·3	7 22·9	5·6	2·8	11·6	5·9	17·6	8·9
57	7 44·3	7 45·5	7 23·1	5·7	2·9	11·7	5·9	17·7	9·0
58	7 44·5	7 45·8	7 23·3	5·8	2·9	11·8	6·0	17·8	9·0
59	7 44·8	7 46·0	7 23·6	5·9	3·0	11·9	6·0	17·9	9·1
60	7 45·0	7 46·3	7 23·8	6·0	3·1	12·0	6·1	18·0	9·2

31ᵐ

31ᵐ s	SUN PLANETS ° ′	ARIES ° ′	MOON ° ′	v or d ′	Corrⁿ ′	v or d ′	Corrⁿ ′	v or d ′	Corrⁿ ′
00	7 45·0	7 46·3	7 23·8	0·0	0·0	6·0	3·2	12·0	6·3
01	7 45·3	7 46·5	7 24·1	0·1	0·1	6·1	3·2	12·1	6·4
02	7 45·5	7 46·8	7 24·3	0·2	0·1	6·2	3·3	12·2	6·4
03	7 45·8	7 47·0	7 24·5	0·3	0·2	6·3	3·3	12·3	6·5
04	7 46·0	7 47·3	7 24·8	0·4	0·2	6·4	3·4	12·4	6·5
05	7 46·3	7 47·5	7 25·0	0·5	0·3	6·5	3·4	12·5	6·6
06	7 46·5	7 47·8	7 25·2	0·6	0·3	6·6	3·5	12·6	6·6
07	7 46·8	7 48·0	7 25·5	0·7	0·4	6·7	3·5	12·7	6·7
08	7 47·0	7 48·3	7 25·7	0·8	0·4	6·8	3·6	12·8	6·7
09	7 47·3	7 48·5	7 26·0	0·9	0·5	6·9	3·6	12·9	6·8
10	7 47·5	7 48·8	7 26·2	1·0	0·5	7·0	3·7	13·0	6·8
11	7 47·8	7 49·0	7 26·4	1·1	0·6	7·1	3·7	13·1	6·9
12	7 48·0	7 49·3	7 26·7	1·2	0·6	7·2	3·8	13·2	6·9
13	7 48·3	7 49·5	7 26·9	1·3	0·7	7·3	3·8	13·3	7·0
14	7 48·5	7 49·8	7 27·2	1·4	0·7	7·4	3·9	13·4	7·0
15	7 48·8	7 50·0	7 27·4	1·5	0·8	7·5	3·9	13·5	7·1
16	7 49·0	7 50·3	7 27·6	1·6	0·8	7·6	4·0	13·6	7·1
17	7 49·3	7 50·5	7 27·9	1·7	0·9	7·7	4·0	13·7	7·2
18	7 49·5	7 50·8	7 28·1	1·8	0·9	7·8	4·1	13·8	7·2
19	7 49·8	7 51·0	7 28·4	1·9	1·0	7·9	4·1	13·9	7·3
20	7 50·0	7 51·3	7 28·6	2·0	1·1	8·0	4·2	14·0	7·4
21	7 50·3	7 51·5	7 28·8	2·1	1·1	8·1	4·3	14·1	7·4
22	7 50·5	7 51·8	7 29·1	2·2	1·2	8·2	4·3	14·2	7·5
23	7 50·8	7 52·0	7 29·3	2·3	1·2	8·3	4·4	14·3	7·5
24	7 51·0	7 52·3	7 29·5	2·4	1·3	8·4	4·4	14·4	7·6
25	7 51·3	7 52·5	7 29·8	2·5	1·3	8·5	4·5	14·5	7·6
26	7 51·5	7 52·8	7 30·0	2·6	1·4	8·6	4·5	14·6	7·7
27	7 51·8	7 53·0	7 30·3	2·7	1·4	8·7	4·6	14·7	7·7
28	7 52·0	7 53·3	7 30·5	2·8	1·5	8·8	4·6	14·8	7·8
29	7 52·3	7 53·5	7 30·7	2·9	1·5	8·9	4·7	14·9	7·8
30	7 52·5	7 53·8	7 31·0	3·0	1·6	9·0	4·7	15·0	7·9
31	7 52·8	7 54·0	7 31·2	3·1	1·6	9·1	4·8	15·1	7·9
32	7 53·0	7 54·3	7 31·5	3·2	1·7	9·2	4·8	15·2	8·0
33	7 53·3	7 54·5	7 31·7	3·3	1·7	9·3	4·9	15·3	8·0
34	7 53·5	7 54·8	7 31·9	3·4	1·8	9·4	4·9	15·4	8·1
35	7 53·8	7 55·0	7 32·2	3·5	1·8	9·5	5·0	15·5	8·1
36	7 54·0	7 55·3	7 32·4	3·6	1·9	9·6	5·0	15·6	8·2
37	7 54·3	7 55·5	7 32·6	3·7	1·9	9·7	5·1	15·7	8·2
38	7 54·5	7 55·8	7 32·9	3·8	2·0	9·8	5·1	15·8	8·3
39	7 54·8	7 56·0	7 33·1	3·9	2·0	9·9	5·2	15·9	8·3
40	7 55·0	7 56·3	7 33·4	4·0	2·1	10·0	5·3	16·0	8·4
41	7 55·3	7 56·6	7 33·6	4·1	2·2	10·1	5·3	16·1	8·5
42	7 55·5	7 56·8	7 33·8	4·2	2·2	10·2	5·4	16·2	8·5
43	7 55·8	7 57·1	7 34·1	4·3	2·3	10·3	5·4	16·3	8·6
44	7 56·0	7 57·3	7 34·3	4·4	2·3	10·4	5·5	16·4	8·6
45	7 56·3	7 57·6	7 34·6	4·5	2·4	10·5	5·5	16·5	8·7
46	7 56·5	7 57·8	7 34·8	4·6	2·4	10·6	5·6	16·6	8·7
47	7 56·8	7 58·1	7 35·0	4·7	2·5	10·7	5·6	16·7	8·8
48	7 57·0	7 58·3	7 35·3	4·8	2·5	10·8	5·7	16·8	8·8
49	7 57·3	7 58·6	7 35·5	4·9	2·6	10·9	5·7	16·9	8·9
50	7 57·5	7 58·8	7 35·7	5·0	2·6	11·0	5·8	17·0	8·9
51	7 57·8	7 59·1	7 36·0	5·1	2·7	11·1	5·8	17·1	9·0
52	7 58·0	7 59·3	7 36·2	5·2	2·7	11·2	5·9	17·2	9·0
53	7 58·3	7 59·6	7 36·5	5·3	2·8	11·3	5·9	17·3	9·1
54	7 58·5	7 59·8	7 36·7	5·4	2·8	11·4	6·0	17·4	9·1
55	7 58·8	8 00·1	7 36·9	5·5	2·9	11·5	6·0	17·5	9·2
56	7 59·0	8 00·3	7 37·2	5·6	2·9	11·6	6·1	17·6	9·2
57	7 59·3	8 00·6	7 37·4	5·7	3·0	11·7	6·1	17·7	9·3
58	7 59·5	8 00·8	7 37·7	5·8	3·0	11·8	6·2	17·8	9·3
59	7 59·8	8 01·1	7 37·9	5·9	3·1	11·9	6·2	17·9	9·4
60	8 00·0	8 01·3	7 38·1	6·0	3·2	12·0	6·3	18·0	9·5

32ᵐ	SUN PLANETS	ARIES	MOON	v or Corrⁿ d	v or Corrⁿ d	v or Corrⁿ d
s	° ′	° ′	° ′	′ ′	′ ′	′ ′
00	8 00·0	8 01·3	7 38·1	0·0 0·0	6·0 3·3	12·0 6·5
01	8 00·3	8 01·6	7 38·4	0·1 0·1	6·1 3·3	12·1 6·6
02	8 00·5	8 01·8	7 38·6	0·2 0·1	6·2 3·4	12·2 6·6
03	8 00·8	8 02·1	7 38·8	0·3 0·2	6·3 3·4	12·3 6·7
04	8 01·0	8 02·3	7 39·1	0·4 0·2	6·4 3·5	12·4 6·7
05	8 01·3	8 02·6	7 39·3	0·5 0·3	6·5 3·5	12·5 6·8
06	8 01·5	8 02·8	7 39·6	0·6 0·3	6·6 3·6	12·6 6·8
07	8 01·8	8 03·1	7 39·8	0·7 0·4	6·7 3·6	12·7 6·9
08	8 02·0	8 03·3	7 40·0	0·8 0·4	6·8 3·7	12·8 6·9
09	8 02·3	8 03·6	7 40·3	0·9 0·5	6·9 3·7	12·9 7·0
10	8 02·5	8 03·8	7 40·5	1·0 0·5	7·0 3·8	13·0 7·0
11	8 02·8	8 04·1	7 40·8	1·1 0·6	7·1 3·8	13·1 7·1
12	8 03·0	8 04·3	7 41·0	1·2 0·7	7·2 3·9	13·2 7·2
13	8 03·3	8 04·6	7 41·2	1·3 0·7	7·3 4·0	13·3 7·2
14	8 03·5	8 04·8	7 41·5	1·4 0·8	7·4 4·0	13·4 7·3
15	8 03·8	8 05·1	7 41·7	1·5 0·8	7·5 4·1	13·5 7·3
16	8 04·0	8 05·3	7 42·0	1·6 0·9	7·6 4·1	13·6 7·4
17	8 04·3	8 05·6	7 42·2	1·7 0·9	7·7 4·2	13·7 7·4
18	8 04·5	8 05·8	7 42·4	1·8 1·0	7·8 4·2	13·8 7·5
19	8 04·8	8 06·1	7 42·7	1·9 1·0	7·9 4·3	13·9 7·5
20	8 05·0	8 06·3	7 42·9	2·0 1·1	8·0 4·3	14·0 7·6
21	8 05·3	8 06·6	7 43·1	2·1 1·1	8·1 4·4	14·1 7·6
22	8 05·5	8 06·8	7 43·4	2·2 1·2	8·2 4·4	14·2 7·7
23	8 05·8	8 07·1	7 43·6	2·3 1·2	8·3 4·5	14·3 7·7
24	8 06·0	8 07·3	7 43·9	2·4 1·3	8·4 4·6	14·4 7·8
25	8 06·3	8 07·6	7 44·1	2·5 1·4	8·5 4·6	14·5 7·9
26	8 06·5	8 07·8	7 44·3	2·6 1·4	8·6 4·7	14·6 7·9
27	8 06·8	8 08·1	7 44·6	2·7 1·5	8·7 4·7	14·7 8·0
28	8 07·0	8 08·3	7 44·8	2·8 1·5	8·8 4·8	14·8 8·0
29	8 07·3	8 08·6	7 45·1	2·9 1·6	8·9 4·8	14·9 8·1
30	8 07·5	8 08·8	7 45·3	3·0 1·6	9·0 4·9	15·0 8·1
31	8 07·8	8 09·1	7 45·5	3·1 1·7	9·1 4·9	15·1 8·2
32	8 08·0	8 09·3	7 45·8	3·2 1·7	9·2 5·0	15·2 8·2
33	8 08·3	8 09·6	7 46·0	3·3 1·8	9·3 5·0	15·3 8·3
34	8 08·5	8 09·8	7 46·2	3·4 1·8	9·4 5·1	15·4 8·3
35	8 08·8	8 10·1	7 46·5	3·5 1·9	9·5 5·1	15·5 8·4
36	8 09·0	8 10·3	7 46·7	3·6 2·0	9·6 5·2	15·6 8·5
37	8 09·3	8 10·6	7 47·0	3·7 2·0	9·7 5·3	15·7 8·5
38	8 09·5	8 10·8	7 47·2	3·8 2·1	9·8 5·3	15·8 8·6
39	8 09·8	8 11·1	7 47·4	3·9 2·1	9·9 5·4	15·9 8·6
40	8 10·0	8 11·3	7 47·7	4·0 2·2	10·0 5·4	16·0 8·7
41	8 10·3	8 11·6	7 47·9	4·1 2·2	10·1 5·5	16·1 8·7
42	8 10·5	8 11·8	7 48·2	4·2 2·3	10·2 5·5	16·2 8·8
43	8 10·8	8 12·1	7 48·4	4·3 2·3	10·3 5·6	16·3 8·8
44	8 11·0	8 12·3	7 48·6	4·4 2·4	10·4 5·6	16·4 8·9
45	8 11·3	8 12·6	7 48·9	4·5 2·4	10·5 5·7	16·5 8·9
46	8 11·5	8 12·8	7 49·1	4·6 2·5	10·6 5·7	16·6 9·0
47	8 11·8	8 13·1	7 49·3	4·7 2·5	10·7 5·8	16·7 9·0
48	8 12·0	8 13·3	7 49·6	4·8 2·6	10·8 5·9	16·8 9·1
49	8 12·3	8 13·6	7 49·8	4·9 2·7	10·9 5·9	16·9 9·2
50	8 12·5	8 13·8	7 50·1	5·0 2·7	11·0 6·0	17·0 9·2
51	8 12·8	8 14·1	7 50·3	5·1 2·8	11·1 6·0	17·1 9·3
52	8 13·0	8 14·3	7 50·5	5·2 2·8	11·2 6·1	17·2 9·3
53	8 13·3	8 14·6	7 50·8	5·3 2·9	11·3 6·1	17·3 9·4
54	8 13·5	8 14·9	7 51·0	5·4 2·9	11·4 6·2	17·4 9·4
55	8 13·8	8 15·1	7 51·3	5·5 3·0	11·5 6·2	17·5 9·5
56	8 14·0	8 15·4	7 51·5	5·6 3·0	11·6 6·3	17·6 9·5
57	8 14·3	8 15·6	7 51·7	5·7 3·1	11·7 6·3	17·7 9·6
58	8 14·5	8 15·9	7 52·0	5·8 3·1	11·8 6·4	17·8 9·6
59	8 14·8	8 16·1	7 52·2	5·9 3·2	11·9 6·4	17·9 9·7
60	8 15·0	8 16·4	7 52·5	6·0 3·3	12·0 6·5	18·0 9·8

33ᵐ	SUN PLANETS	ARIES	MOON	v or Corrⁿ d	v or Corrⁿ d	v or Corrⁿ d
s	° ′	° ′	° ′	′ ′	′ ′	′ ′
00	8 15·0	8 16·4	7 52·5	0·0 0·0	6·0 3·4	12·0 6·7
01	8 15·3	8 16·6	7 52·7	0·1 0·1	6·1 3·4	12·1 6·8
02	8 15·5	8 16·9	7 52·9	0·2 0·1	6·2 3·5	12·2 6·8
03	8 15·8	8 17·1	7 53·2	0·3 0·2	6·3 3·5	12·3 6·9
04	8 16·0	8 17·4	7 53·4	0·4 0·2	6·4 3·6	12·4 6·9
05	8 16·3	8 17·6	7 53·6	0·5 0·3	6·5 3·6	12·5 7·0
06	8 16·5	8 17·9	7 53·9	0·6 0·3	6·6 3·7	12·6 7·0
07	8 16·8	8 18·1	7 54·1	0·7 0·4	6·7 3·7	12·7 7·1
08	8 17·0	8 18·4	7 54·4	0·8 0·4	6·8 3·8	12·8 7·1
09	8 17·3	8 18·6	7 54·6	0·9 0·5	6·9 3·9	12·9 7·2
10	8 17·5	8 18·9	7 54·8	1·0 0·6	7·0 3·9	13·0 7·3
11	8 17·8	8 19·1	7 55·1	1·1 0·6	7·1 4·0	13·1 7·3
12	8 18·0	8 19·4	7 55·3	1·2 0·7	7·2 4·0	13·2 7·4
13	8 18·3	8 19·6	7 55·6	1·3 0·7	7·3 4·1	13·3 7·4
14	8 18·5	8 19·9	7 55·8	1·4 0·8	7·4 4·1	13·4 7·5
15	8 18·8	8 20·1	7 56·0	1·5 0·8	7·5 4·2	13·5 7·5
16	8 19·0	8 20·4	7 56·3	1·6 0·9	7·6 4·2	13·6 7·6
17	8 19·3	8 20·6	7 56·5	1·7 0·9	7·7 4·3	13·7 7·6
18	8 19·5	8 20·9	7 56·7	1·8 1·0	7·8 4·4	13·8 7·7
19	8 19·8	8 21·1	7 57·0	1·9 1·1	7·9 4·4	13·9 7·8
20	8 20·0	8 21·4	7 57·2	2·0 1·1	8·0 4·5	14·0 7·8
21	8 20·3	8 21·6	7 57·5	2·1 1·2	8·1 4·5	14·1 7·9
22	8 20·5	8 21·9	7 57·7	2·2 1·2	8·2 4·6	14·2 7·9
23	8 20·8	8 22·1	7 57·9	2·3 1·3	8·3 4·6	14·3 8·0
24	8 21·0	8 22·4	7 58·2	2·4 1·3	8·4 4·7	14·4 8·0
25	8 21·3	8 22·6	7 58·4	2·5 1·4	8·5 4·7	14·5 8·1
26	8 21·5	8 22·9	7 58·7	2·6 1·5	8·6 4·8	14·6 8·2
27	8 21·8	8 23·1	7 58·9	2·7 1·5	8·7 4·9	14·7 8·2
28	8 22·0	8 23·4	7 59·1	2·8 1·6	8·8 4·9	14·8 8·3
29	8 22·3	8 23·6	7 59·4	2·9 1·6	8·9 5·0	14·9 8·3
30	8 22·5	8 23·9	7 59·6	3·0 1·7	9·0 5·0	15·0 8·4
31	8 22·8	8 24·1	7 59·8	3·1 1·7	9·1 5·1	15·1 8·4
32	8 23·0	8 24·4	8 00·1	3·2 1·8	9·2 5·1	15·2 8·5
33	8 23·3	8 24·6	8 00·3	3·3 1·8	9·3 5·2	15·3 8·5
34	8 23·5	8 24·9	8 00·6	3·4 1·9	9·4 5·2	15·4 8·6
35	8 23·8	8 25·1	8 00·8	3·5 2·0	9·5 5·3	15·5 8·7
36	8 24·0	8 25·4	8 01·0	3·6 2·0	9·6 5·4	15·6 8·7
37	8 24·3	8 25·6	8 01·3	3·7 2·1	9·7 5·4	15·7 8·8
38	8 24·5	8 25·9	8 01·5	3·8 2·1	9·8 5·5	15·8 8·8
39	8 24·8	8 26·1	8 01·8	3·9 2·2	9·9 5·5	15·9 8·9
40	8 25·0	8 26·4	8 02·0	4·0 2·2	10·0 5·6	16·0 8·9
41	8 25·3	8 26·6	8 02·2	4·1 2·3	10·1 5·6	16·1 9·0
42	8 25·5	8 26·9	8 02·5	4·2 2·3	10·2 5·7	16·2 9·0
43	8 25·8	8 27·1	8 02·7	4·3 2·4	10·3 5·8	16·3 9·1
44	8 26·0	8 27·4	8 02·9	4·4 2·5	10·4 5·8	16·4 9·2
45	8 26·3	8 27·6	8 03·2	4·5 2·5	10·5 5·9	16·5 9·2
46	8 26·5	8 27·9	8 03·4	4·6 2·6	10·6 5·9	16·6 9·3
47	8 26·8	8 28·1	8 03·7	4·7 2·6	10·7 6·0	16·7 9·3
48	8 27·0	8 28·4	8 03·9	4·8 2·7	10·8 6·0	16·8 9·4
49	8 27·3	8 28·6	8 04·1	4·9 2·7	10·9 6·1	16·9 9·4
50	8 27·5	8 28·9	8 04·4	5·0 2·8	11·0 6·1	17·0 9·5
51	8 27·8	8 29·1	8 04·6	5·1 2·8	11·1 6·2	17·1 9·6
52	8 28·0	8 29·4	8 04·9	5·2 2·9	11·2 6·3	17·2 9·6
53	8 28·3	8 29·6	8 05·1	5·3 3·0	11·3 6·3	17·3 9·7
54	8 28·5	8 29·9	8 05·3	5·4 3·0	11·4 6·4	17·4 9·7
55	8 28·8	8 30·1	8 05·6	5·5 3·1	11·5 6·4	17·5 9·8
56	8 29·0	8 30·4	8 05·8	5·6 3·1	11·6 6·5	17·6 9·8
57	8 29·3	8 30·6	8 06·1	5·7 3·2	11·7 6·5	17·7 9·9
58	8 29·5	8 30·9	8 06·3	5·8 3·2	11·8 6·6	17·8 9·9
59	8 29·8	8 31·1	8 06·5	5·9 3·3	11·9 6·6	17·9 10·0
60	8 30·0	8 31·4	8 06·8	6·0 3·4	12·0 6·7	18·0 10·1

34ᵐ	SUN PLANETS	ARIES	MOON	v or Corrn d	v or Corrn d	v or Corrn d
s	° ′	° ′	° ′	′ ′	′ ′	′ ′
00	8 30·0	8 31·4	8 06·8	0·0 0·0	6·0 3·5	12·0 6·9
01	8 30·3	8 31·6	8 07·0	0·1 0·1	6·1 3·5	12·1 7·0
02	8 30·5	8 31·9	8 07·2	0·2 0·1	6·2 3·6	12·2 7·0
03	8 30·8	8 32·1	8 07·5	0·3 0·2	6·3 3·6	12·3 7·1
04	8 31·0	8 32·4	8 07·7	0·4 0·2	6·4 3·7	12·4 7·1
05	8 31·3	8 32·6	8 08·0	0·5 0·3	6·5 3·7	12·5 7·2
06	8 31·5	8 32·9	8 08·2	0·6 0·3	6·6 3·8	12·6 7·2
07	8 31·8	8 33·2	8 08·4	0·7 0·4	6·7 3·9	12·7 7·3
08	8 32·0	8 33·4	8 08·7	0·8 0·5	6·8 3·9	12·8 7·4
09	8 32·3	8 33·7	8 08·9	0·9 0·5	6·9 4·0	12·9 7·4
10	8 32·5	8 33·9	8 09·2	1·0 0·6	7·0 4·0	13·0 7·5
11	8 32·8	8 34·2	8 09·4	1·1 0·6	7·1 4·1	13·1 7·5
12	8 33·0	8 34·4	8 09·6	1·2 0·7	7·2 4·1	13·2 7·6
13	8 33·3	8 34·7	8 09·9	1·3 0·7	7·3 4·2	13·3 7·6
14	8 33·5	8 34·9	8 10·1	1·4 0·8	7·4 4·3	13·4 7·7
15	8 33·8	8 35·2	8 10·3	1·5 0·9	7·5 4·3	13·5 7·8
16	8 34·0	8 35·4	8 10·6	1·6 0·9	7·6 4·4	13·6 7·8
17	8 34·3	8 35·7	8 10·8	1·7 1·0	7·7 4·4	13·7 7·9
18	8 34·5	8 35·9	8 11·1	1·8 1·0	7·8 4·5	13·8 7·9
19	8 34·8	8 36·2	8 11·3	1·9 1·1	7·9 4·5	13·9 8·0
20	8 35·0	8 36·4	8 11·5	2·0 1·2	8·0 4·6	14·0 8·1
21	8 35·3	8 36·7	8 11·8	2·1 1·2	8·1 4·7	14·1 8·1
22	8 35·5	8 36·9	8 12·0	2·2 1·3	8·2 4·7	14·2 8·2
23	8 35·8	8 37·2	8 12·3	2·3 1·3	8·3 4·8	14·3 8·2
24	8 36·0	8 37·4	8 12·5	2·4 1·4	8·4 4·8	14·4 8·3
25	8 36·3	8 37·7	8 12·7	2·5 1·4	8·5 4·9	14·5 8·3
26	8 36·5	8 37·9	8 13·0	2·6 1·5	8·6 4·9	14·6 8·4
27	8 36·8	8 38·2	8 13·2	2·7 1·6	8·7 5·0	14·7 8·5
28	8 37·0	8 38·4	8 13·4	2·8 1·6	8·8 5·1	14·8 8·5
29	8 37·3	8 38·7	8 13·7	2·9 1·7	8·9 5·1	14·9 8·6
30	8 37·5	8 38·9	8 13·9	3·0 1·7	9·0 5·2	15·0 8·6
31	8 37·8	8 39·2	8 14·2	3·1 1·8	9·1 5·2	15·1 8·7
32	8 38·0	8 39·4	8 14·4	3·2 1·8	9·2 5·3	15·2 8·7
33	8 38·3	8 39·7	8 14·6	3·3 1·9	9·3 5·3	15·3 8·8
34	8 38·5	8 39·9	8 14·9	3·4 2·0	9·4 5·4	15·4 8·9
35	8 38·8	8 40·2	8 15·1	3·5 2·0	9·5 5·5	15·5 8·9
36	8 39·0	8 40·4	8 15·4	3·6 2·1	9·6 5·5	15·6 9·0
37	8 39·3	8 40·7	8 15·6	3·7 2·1	9·7 5·6	15·7 9·0
38	8 39·5	8 40·9	8 15·8	3·8 2·2	9·8 5·6	15·8 9·1
39	8 39·8	8 41·2	8 16·1	3·9 2·2	9·9 5·7	15·9 9·1
40	8 40·0	8 41·4	8 16·3	4·0 2·3	10·0 5·8	16·0 9·2
41	8 40·3	8 41·7	8 16·5	4·1 2·4	10·1 5·8	16·1 9·3
42	8 40·5	8 41·9	8 16·8	4·2 2·4	10·2 5·9	16·2 9·3
43	8 40·8	8 42·2	8 17·0	4·3 2·5	10·3 5·9	16·3 9·4
44	8 41·0	8 42·4	8 17·3	4·4 2·5	10·4 6·0	16·4 9·4
45	8 41·3	8 42·7	8 17·5	4·5 2·6	10·5 6·0	16·5 9·5
46	8 41·5	8 42·9	8 17·7	4·6 2·6	10·6 6·1	16·6 9·5
47	8 41·8	8 43·2	8 18·0	4·7 2·7	10·7 6·2	16·7 9·6
48	8 42·0	8 43·4	8 18·2	4·8 2·8	10·8 6·2	16·8 9·7
49	8 42·3	8 43·7	8 18·5	4·9 2·8	10·9 6·3	16·9 9·7
50	8 42·5	8 43·9	8 18·7	5·0 2·9	11·0 6·3	17·0 9·8
51	8 42·8	8 44·2	8 18·9	5·1 2·9	11·1 6·4	17·1 9·8
52	8 43·0	8 44·4	8 19·2	5·2 3·0	11·2 6·4	17·2 9·9
53	8 43·3	8 44·7	8 19·4	5·3 3·0	11·3 6·5	17·3 9·9
54	8 43·5	8 44·9	8 19·7	5·4 3·1	11·4 6·6	17·4 10·0
55	8 43·8	8 45·2	8 19·9	5·5 3·2	11·5 6·6	17·5 10·1
56	8 44·0	8 45·4	8 20·1	5·6 3·2	11·6 6·7	17·6 10·1
57	8 44·3	8 45·7	8 20·4	5·7 3·3	11·7 6·7	17·7 10·2
58	8 44·5	8 45·9	8 20·6	5·8 3·3	11·8 6·8	17·8 10·2
59	8 44·8	8 46·2	8 20·8	5·9 3·4	11·9 6·8	17·9 10·3
60	8 45·0	8 46·4	8 21·1	6·0 3·5	12·0 6·9	18·0 10·4

35ᵐ	SUN PLANETS	ARIES	MOON	v or Corrn d	v or Corrn d	v or Corrn d
s	° ′	° ′	° ′	′ ′	′ ′	′ ′
00	8 45·0	8 46·4	8 21·1	0·0 0·0	6·0 3·6	12·0 7·1
01	8 45·3	8 46·7	8 21·3	0·1 0·1	6·1 3·6	12·1 7·2
02	8 45·5	8 46·9	8 21·6	0·2 0·1	6·2 3·7	12·2 7·2
03	8 45·8	8 47·2	8 21·8	0·3 0·2	6·3 3·7	12·3 7·3
04	8 46·0	8 47·4	8 22·0	0·4 0·2	6·4 3·8	12·4 7·3
05	8 46·3	8 47·7	8 22·3	0·5 0·3	6·5 3·8	12·5 7·4
06	8 46·5	8 47·9	8 22·5	0·6 0·4	6·6 3·9	12·6 7·5
07	8 46·8	8 48·2	8 22·8	0·7 0·4	6·7 4·0	12·7 7·5
08	8 47·0	8 48·4	8 23·0	0·8 0·5	6·8 4·0	12·8 7·6
09	8 47·3	8 48·7	8 23·2	0·9 0·5	6·9 4·1	12·9 7·6
10	8 47·5	8 48·9	8 23·5	1·0 0·6	7·0 4·1	13·0 7·7
11	8 47·8	8 49·2	8 23·7	1·1 0·7	7·1 4·2	13·1 7·8
12	8 48·0	8 49·4	8 23·9	1·2 0·7	7·2 4·3	13·2 7·8
13	8 48·3	8 49·7	8 24·2	1·3 0·8	7·3 4·3	13·3 7·9
14	8 48·5	8 49·9	8 24·4	1·4 0·8	7·4 4·4	13·4 7·9
15	8 48·8	8 50·2	8 24·7	1·5 0·9	7·5 4·4	13·5 8·0
16	8 49·0	8 50·4	8 24·9	1·6 0·9	7·6 4·5	13·6 8·0
17	8 49·3	8 50·7	8 25·1	1·7 1·0	7·7 4·6	13·7 8·1
18	8 49·5	8 50·9	8 25·4	1·8 1·1	7·8 4·6	13·8 8·2
19	8 49·8	8 51·2	8 25·6	1·9 1·1	7·9 4·7	13·9 8·2
20	8 50·0	8 51·5	8 25·9	2·0 1·2	8·0 4·7	14·0 8·3
21	8 50·3	8 51·7	8 26·1	2·1 1·2	8·1 4·8	14·1 8·3
22	8 50·5	8 52·0	8 26·3	2·2 1·3	8·2 4·9	14·2 8·4
23	8 50·8	8 52·2	8 26·6	2·3 1·4	8·3 4·9	14·3 8·5
24	8 51·0	8 52·5	8 26·8	2·4 1·4	8·4 5·0	14·4 8·5
25	8 51·3	8 52·7	8 27·0	2·5 1·5	8·5 5·0	14·5 8·6
26	8 51·5	8 53·0	8 27·3	2·6 1·5	8·6 5·1	14·6 8·6
27	8 51·8	8 53·2	8 27·5	2·7 1·6	8·7 5·1	14·7 8·7
28	8 52·0	8 53·5	8 27·8	2·8 1·7	8·8 5·2	14·8 8·8
29	8 52·3	8 53·7	8 28·0	2·9 1·7	8·9 5·3	14·9 8·8
30	8 52·5	8 54·0	8 28·2	3·0 1·8	9·0 5·3	15·0 8·9
31	8 52·8	8 54·2	8 28·5	3·1 1·8	9·1 5·4	15·1 8·9
32	8 53·0	8 54·5	8 28·7	3·2 1·9	9·2 5·4	15·2 9·0
33	8 53·3	8 54·7	8 29·0	3·3 2·0	9·3 5·5	15·3 9·1
34	8 53·5	8 55·0	8 29·2	3·4 2·0	9·4 5·6	15·4 9·1
35	8 53·8	8 55·2	8 29·4	3·5 2·1	9·5 5·6	15·5 9·2
36	8 54·0	8 55·5	8 29·7	3·6 2·1	9·6 5·7	15·6 9·2
37	8 54·3	8 55·7	8 29·9	3·7 2·2	9·7 5·7	15·7 9·3
38	8 54·5	8 56·0	8 30·2	3·8 2·2	9·8 5·8	15·8 9·3
39	8 54·8	8 56·2	8 30·4	3·9 2·3	9·9 5·9	15·9 9·4
40	8 55·0	8 56·5	8 30·6	4·0 2·4	10·0 5·9	16·0 9·5
41	8 55·3	8 56·7	8 30·9	4·1 2·4	10·1 6·0	16·1 9·5
42	8 55·5	8 57·0	8 31·1	4·2 2·5	10·2 6·0	16·2 9·6
43	8 55·8	8 57·2	8 31·3	4·3 2·5	10·3 6·1	16·3 9·6
44	8 56·0	8 57·5	8 31·6	4·4 2·6	10·4 6·2	16·4 9·7
45	8 56·3	8 57·7	8 31·8	4·5 2·7	10·5 6·2	16·5 9·8
46	8 56·5	8 58·0	8 32·1	4·6 2·7	10·6 6·3	16·6 9·8
47	8 56·8	8 58·2	8 32·3	4·7 2·8	10·7 6·3	16·7 9·9
48	8 57·0	8 58·5	8 32·5	4·8 2·8	10·8 6·4	16·8 9·9
49	8 57·3	8 58·7	8 32·8	4·9 2·9	10·9 6·4	16·9 10·0
50	8 57·5	8 59·0	8 33·0	5·0 3·0	11·0 6·5	17·0 10·1
51	8 57·8	8 59·2	8 33·3	5·1 3·0	11·1 6·6	17·1 10·1
52	8 58·0	8 59·5	8 33·5	5·2 3·1	11·2 6·6	17·2 10·2
53	8 58·3	8 59·7	8 33·7	5·3 3·1	11·3 6·7	17·3 10·2
54	8 58·5	9 00·0	8 34·0	5·4 3·2	11·4 6·7	17·4 10·3
55	8 58·8	9 00·2	8 34·2	5·5 3·3	11·5 6·8	17·5 10·4
56	8 59·0	9 00·5	8 34·4	5·6 3·3	11·6 6·9	17·6 10·4
57	8 59·3	9 00·7	8 34·7	5·7 3·4	11·7 6·9	17·7 10·5
58	8 59·5	9 01·0	8 34·9	5·8 3·4	11·8 7·0	17·8 10·5
59	8 59·8	9 01·2	8 35·2	5·9 3·5	11·9 7·0	17·9 10·6
60	9 00·0	9 01·5	8 35·4	6·0 3·6	12·0 7·1	18·0 10·7

36ᵐ	SUN PLANETS	ARIES	MOON	v or d Corrⁿ		v or d Corrⁿ		v or d Corrⁿ	
s	° ′	° ′	° ′	′	′	′	′	′	′
00	9 00·0	9 01·5	8 35·4	0·0	0·0	6·0	3·7	12·0	7·3
01	9 00·3	9 01·7	8 35·6	0·1	0·1	6·1	3·7	12·1	7·4
02	9 00·5	9 02·0	8 35·9	0·2	0·1	6·2	3·8	12·2	7·4
03	9 00·8	9 02·2	8 36·1	0·3	0·2	6·3	3·8	12·3	7·5
04	9 01·0	9 02·5	8 36·4	0·4	0·2	6·4	3·9	12·4	7·5
05	9 01·3	9 02·7	8 36·6	0·5	0·3	6·5	4·0	12·5	7·6
06	9 01·5	9 03·0	8 36·8	0·6	0·4	6·6	4·0	12·6	7·7
07	9 01·8	9 03·2	8 37·1	0·7	0·4	6·7	4·1	12·7	7·7
08	9 02·0	9 03·5	8 37·3	0·8	0·5	6·8	4·1	12·8	7·8
09	9 02·3	9 03·7	8 37·5	0·9	0·5	6·9	4·2	12·9	7·8
10	9 02·5	9 04·0	8 37·8	1·0	0·6	7·0	4·3	13·0	7·9
11	9 02·8	9 04·2	8 38·0	1·1	0·7	7·1	4·3	13·1	8·0
12	9 03·0	9 04·5	8 38·3	1·2	0·7	7·2	4·4	13·2	8·0
13	9 03·3	9 04·7	8 38·5	1·3	0·8	7·3	4·4	13·3	8·1
14	9 03·5	9 05·0	8 38·7	1·4	0·9	7·4	4·5	13·4	8·2
15	9 03·8	9 05·2	8 39·0	1·5	0·9	7·5	4·6	13·5	8·2
16	9 04·0	9 05·5	8 39·2	1·6	1·0	7·6	4·6	13·6	8·3
17	9 04·3	9 05·7	8 39·5	1·7	1·0	7·7	4·7	13·7	8·3
18	9 04·5	9 06·0	8 39·7	1·8	1·1	7·8	4·7	13·8	8·4
19	9 04·8	9 06·2	8 39·9	1·9	1·2	7·9	4·8	13·9	8·5
20	9 05·0	9 06·5	8 40·2	2·0	1·2	8·0	4·9	14·0	8·5
21	9 05·3	9 06·7	8 40·4	2·1	1·3	8·1	4·9	14·1	8·6
22	9 05·5	9 07·0	8 40·6	2·2	1·3	8·2	5·0	14·2	8·6
23	9 05·8	9 07·2	8 40·9	2·3	1·4	8·3	5·0	14·3	8·7
24	9 06·0	9 07·5	8 41·1	2·4	1·5	8·4	5·1	14·4	8·8
25	9 06·3	9 07·7	8 41·4	2·5	1·5	8·5	5·2	14·5	8·8
26	9 06·5	9 08·0	8 41·6	2·6	1·6	8·6	5·2	14·6	8·9
27	9 06·8	9 08·2	8 41·8	2·7	1·6	8·7	5·3	14·7	8·9
28	9 07·0	9 08·5	8 42·1	2·8	1·7	8·8	5·4	14·8	9·0
29	9 07·3	9 08·7	8 42·3	2·9	1·8	8·9	5·4	14·9	9·1
30	9 07·5	9 09·0	8 42·6	3·0	1·8	9·0	5·5	15·0	9·1
31	9 07·8	9 09·2	8 42·8	3·1	1·9	9·1	5·5	15·1	9·2
32	9 08·0	9 09·5	8 43·0	3·2	1·9	9·2	5·6	15·2	9·2
33	9 08·3	9 09·8	8 43·3	3·3	2·0	9·3	5·7	15·3	9·3
34	9 08·5	9 10·0	8 43·5	3·4	2·1	9·4	5·7	15·4	9·4
35	9 08·8	9 10·3	8 43·8	3·5	2·1	9·5	5·8	15·5	9·4
36	9 09·0	9 10·5	8 44·0	3·6	2·2	9·6	5·8	15·6	9·5
37	9 09·3	9 10·8	8 44·2	3·7	2·3	9·7	5·9	15·7	9·6
38	9 09·5	9 11·0	8 44·5	3·8	2·3	9·8	6·0	15·8	9·6
39	9 09·8	9 11·3	8 44·7	3·9	2·4	9·9	6·0	15·9	9·7
40	9 10·0	9 11·5	8 44·9	4·0	2·4	10·0	6·1	16·0	9·7
41	9 10·3	9 11·8	8 45·2	4·1	2·5	10·1	6·1	16·1	9·8
42	9 10·5	9 12·0	8 45·4	4·2	2·6	10·2	6·2	16·2	9·9
43	9 10·8	9 12·3	8 45·7	4·3	2·6	10·3	6·3	16·3	9·9
44	9 11·0	9 12·5	8 45·9	4·4	2·7	10·4	6·3	16·4	10·0
45	9 11·3	9 12·8	8 46·1	4·5	2·7	10·5	6·4	16·5	10·0
46	9 11·5	9 13·0	8 46·4	4·6	2·8	10·6	6·4	16·6	10·1
47	9 11·8	9 13·3	8 46·6	4·7	2·9	10·7	6·5	16·7	10·2
48	9 12·0	9 13·5	8 46·9	4·8	2·9	10·8	6·6	16·8	10·2
49	9 12·3	9 13·8	8 47·1	4·9	3·0	10·9	6·6	16·9	10·3
50	9 12·5	9 14·0	8 47·3	5·0	3·0	11·0	6·7	17·0	10·3
51	9 12·8	9 14·3	8 47·6	5·1	3·1	11·1	6·8	17·1	10·4
52	9 13·0	9 14·5	8 47·8	5·2	3·2	11·2	6·8	17·2	10·5
53	9 13·3	9 14·8	8 48·0	5·3	3·2	11·3	6·9	17·3	10·5
54	9 13·5	9 15·0	8 48·3	5·4	3·3	11·4	6·9	17·4	10·6
55	9 13·8	9 15·3	8 48·5	5·5	3·3	11·5	7·0	17·5	10·6
56	9 14·0	9 15·5	8 48·8	5·6	3·4	11·6	7·0	17·6	10·7
57	9 14·3	9 15·8	8 49·0	5·7	3·5	11·7	7·1	17·7	10·8
58	9 14·5	9 16·0	8 49·2	5·8	3·5	11·8	7·2	17·8	10·8
59	9 14·8	9 16·3	8 49·5	5·9	3·6	11·9	7·2	17·9	10·9
60	9 15·0	9 16·5	8 49·7	6·0	3·7	12·0	7·3	18·0	11·0

37ᵐ	SUN PLANETS	ARIES	MOON	v or d Corrⁿ		v or d Corrⁿ		v or d Corrⁿ	
s	° ′	° ′	° ′	′	′	′	′	′	′
00	9 15·0	9 16·5	8 49·7	0·0	0·0	6·0	3·8	12·0	7·5
01	9 15·3	9 16·8	8 50·0	0·1	0·1	6·1	3·8	12·1	7·6
02	9 15·5	9 17·0	8 50·2	0·2	0·1	6·2	3·9	12·2	7·6
03	9 15·8	9 17·3	8 50·4	0·3	0·2	6·3	3·9	12·3	7·7
04	9 16·0	9 17·5	8 50·7	0·4	0·3	6·4	4·0	12·4	7·8
05	9 16·3	9 17·8	8 50·9	0·5	0·3	6·5	4·1	12·5	7·8
06	9 16·5	9 18·0	8 51·1	0·6	0·4	6·6	4·1	12·6	7·9
07	9 16·8	9 18·3	8 51·4	0·7	0·4	6·7	4·2	12·7	7·9
08	9 17·0	9 18·5	8 51·6	0·8	0·5	6·8	4·3	12·8	8·0
09	9 17·3	9 18·8	8 51·9	0·9	0·6	6·9	4·3	12·9	8·1
10	9 17·5	9 19·0	8 52·1	1·0	0·6	7·0	4·4	13·0	8·1
11	9 17·8	9 19·3	8 52·3	1·1	0·7	7·1	4·4	13·1	8·2
12	9 18·0	9 19·5	8 52·6	1·2	0·8	7·2	4·5	13·2	8·3
13	9 18·3	9 19·8	8 52·8	1·3	0·8	7·3	4·6	13·3	8·3
14	9 18·5	9 20·0	8 53·1	1·4	0·9	7·4	4·6	13·4	8·4
15	9 18·8	9 20·3	8 53·3	1·5	0·9	7·5	4·7	13·5	8·5
16	9 19·0	9 20·5	8 53·5	1·6	1·0	7·6	4·8	13·6	8·5
17	9 19·3	9 20·8	8 53·8	1·7	1·1	7·7	4·8	13·7	8·6
18	9 19·5	9 21·0	8 54·0	1·8	1·1	7·8	4·9	13·8	8·6
19	9 19·8	9 21·3	8 54·3	1·9	1·2	7·9	4·9	13·9	8·7
20	9 20·0	9 21·5	8 54·5	2·0	1·3	8·0	5·0	14·0	8·8
21	9 20·3	9 21·8	8 54·7	2·1	1·3	8·1	5·1	14·1	8·8
22	9 20·5	9 22·0	8 55·0	2·2	1·4	8·2	5·1	14·2	8·9
23	9 20·8	9 22·3	8 55·2	2·3	1·4	8·3	5·2	14·3	8·9
24	9 21·0	9 22·5	8 55·4	2·4	1·5	8·4	5·3	14·4	9·0
25	9 21·3	9 22·8	8 55·7	2·5	1·6	8·5	5·3	14·5	9·1
26	9 21·5	9 23·0	8 55·9	2·6	1·6	8·6	5·4	14·6	9·1
27	9 21·8	9 23·3	8 56·2	2·7	1·7	8·7	5·4	14·7	9·2
28	9 22·0	9 23·5	8 56·4	2·8	1·8	8·8	5·5	14·8	9·3
29	9 22·3	9 23·8	8 56·6	2·9	1·8	8·9	5·6	14·9	9·3
30	9 22·5	9 24·0	8 56·9	3·0	1·9	9·0	5·6	15·0	9·4
31	9 22·8	9 24·3	8 57·1	3·1	1·9	9·1	5·7	15·1	9·4
32	9 23·0	9 24·5	8 57·4	3·2	2·0	9·2	5·8	15·2	9·5
33	9 23·3	9 24·8	8 57·6	3·3	2·1	9·3	5·8	15·3	9·6
34	9 23·5	9 25·0	8 57·8	3·4	2·1	9·4	5·9	15·4	9·6
35	9 23·8	9 25·3	8 58·1	3·5	2·2	9·5	5·9	15·5	9·7
36	9 24·0	9 25·5	8 58·3	3·6	2·3	9·6	6·0	15·6	9·8
37	9 24·3	9 25·8	8 58·5	3·7	2·3	9·7	6·1	15·7	9·8
38	9 24·5	9 26·0	8 58·8	3·8	2·4	9·8	6·1	15·8	9·9
39	9 24·8	9 26·3	8 59·0	3·9	2·4	9·9	6·2	15·9	9·9
40	9 25·0	9 26·5	8 59·3	4·0	2·5	10·0	6·3	16·0	10·0
41	9 25·3	9 26·8	8 59·5	4·1	2·6	10·1	6·3	16·1	10·1
42	9 25·5	9 27·0	8 59·7	4·2	2·6	10·2	6·4	16·2	10·1
43	9 25·8	9 27·3	9 00·0	4·3	2·7	10·3	6·4	16·3	10·2
44	9 26·0	9 27·5	9 00·2	4·4	2·8	10·4	6·5	16·4	10·3
45	9 26·3	9 27·8	9 00·5	4·5	2·8	10·5	6·6	16·5	10·3
46	9 26·5	9 28·1	9 00·7	4·6	2·9	10·6	6·6	16·6	10·4
47	9 26·8	9 28·3	9 00·9	4·7	2·9	10·7	6·7	16·7	10·4
48	9 27·0	9 28·6	9 01·2	4·8	3·0	10·8	6·8	16·8	10·5
49	9 27·3	9 28·8	9 01·4	4·9	3·1	10·9	6·8	16·9	10·6
50	9 27·5	9 29·1	9 01·6	5·0	3·1	11·0	6·9	17·0	10·6
51	9 27·8	9 29·3	9 01·9	5·1	3·2	11·1	6·9	17·1	10·7
52	9 28·0	9 29·6	9 02·1	5·2	3·3	11·2	7·0	17·2	10·8
53	9 28·3	9 29·8	9 02·4	5·3	3·3	11·3	7·1	17·3	10·8
54	9 28·5	9 30·1	9 02·6	5·4	3·4	11·4	7·1	17·4	10·9
55	9 28·8	9 30·3	9 02·8	5·5	3·4	11·5	7·2	17·5	10·9
56	9 29·0	9 30·6	9 03·1	5·6	3·5	11·6	7·3	17·6	11·0
57	9 29·3	9 30·8	9 03·3	5·7	3·6	11·7	7·3	17·7	11·1
58	9 29·5	9 31·1	9 03·6	5·8	3·6	11·8	7·4	17·8	11·1
59	9 29·8	9 31·3	9 03·8	5·9	3·7	11·9	7·4	17·9	11·2
60	9 30·0	9 31·6	9 04·0	6·0	3·8	12·0	7·5	18·0	11·3

38	SUN PLANETS	ARIES	MOON	v or Corrn d		v or Corrn d		v or Corrn d	
s	° ′	° ′	° ′	′	′	′	′	′	′
00	9 30·0	9 31·6	9 04·0	0·0	0·0	6·0	3·9	12·0	7·7
01	9 30·3	9 31·8	9 04·3	0·1	0·1	6·1	3·9	12·1	7·8
02	9 30·5	9 32·1	9 04·5	0·2	0·1	6·2	4·0	12·2	7·8
03	9 30·8	9 32·3	9 04·7	0·3	0·2	6·3	4·0	12·3	7·9
04	9 31·0	9 32·6	9 05·0	0·4	0·3	6·4	4·1	12·4	8·0
05	9 31·3	9 32·8	9 05·2	0·5	0·3	6·5	4·2	12·5	8·0
06	9 31·5	9 33·1	9 05·5	0·6	0·4	6·6	4·2	12·6	8·1
07	9 31·8	9 33·3	9 05·7	0·7	0·4	6·7	4·3	12·7	8·1
08	9 32·0	9 33·6	9 05·9	0·8	0·5	6·8	4·4	12·8	8·2
09	9 32·3	9 33·8	9 06·2	0·9	0·6	6·9	4·4	12·9	8·3
10	9 32·5	9 34·1	9 06·4	1·0	0·6	7·0	4·5	13·0	8·3
11	9 32·8	9 34·3	9 06·7	1·1	0·7	7·1	4·6	13·1	8·4
12	9 33·0	9 34·6	9 06·9	1·2	0·8	7·2	4·6	13·2	8·5
13	9 33·3	9 34·8	9 07·1	1·3	0·8	7·3	4·7	13·3	8·5
14	9 33·5	9 35·1	9 07·4	1·4	0·9	7·4	4·7	13·4	8·6
15	9 33·8	9 35·3	9 07·6	1·5	1·0	7·5	4·8	13·5	8·7
16	9 34·0	9 35·6	9 07·9	1·6	1·0	7·6	4·9	13·6	8·7
17	9 34·3	9 35·8	9 08·1	1·7	1·1	7·7	4·9	13·7	8·8
18	9 34·5	9 36·1	9 08·3	1·8	1·2	7·8	5·0	13·8	8·9
19	9 34·8	9 36·3	9 08·6	1·9	1·2	7·9	5·1	13·9	8·9
20	9 35·0	9 36·6	9 08·8	2·0	1·3	8·0	5·1	14·0	9·0
21	9 35·3	9 36·8	9 09·1	2·1	1·3	8·1	5·2	14·1	9·0
22	9 35·5	9 37·1	9 09·3	2·2	1·4	8·2	5·3	14·2	9·1
23	9 35·8	9 37·3	9 09·5	2·3	1·5	8·3	5·3	14·3	9·2
24	9 36·0	9 37·6	9 09·8	2·4	1·5	8·4	5·4	14·4	9·2
25	9 36·3	9 37·8	9 10·0	2·5	1·6	8·5	5·5	14·5	9·3
26	9 36·5	9 38·1	9 10·2	2·6	1·7	8·6	5·5	14·6	9·4
27	9 36·8	9 38·3	9 10·5	2·7	1·7	8·7	5·6	14·7	9·4
28	9 37·0	9 38·6	9 10·7	2·8	1·8	8·8	5·6	14·8	9·5
29	9 37·3	9 38·8	9 11·0	2·9	1·9	8·9	5·7	14·9	9·6
30	9 37·5	9 39·1	9 11·2	3·0	1·9	9·0	5·8	15·0	9·6
31	9 37·8	9 39·3	9 11·4	3·1	2·0	9·1	5·8	15·1	9·7
32	9 38·0	9 39·6	9 11·7	3·2	2·1	9·2	5·9	15·2	9·8
33	9 38·3	9 39·8	9 11·9	3·3	2·1	9·3	6·0	15·3	9·8
34	9 38·5	9 40·1	9 12·1	3·4	2·2	9·4	6·0	15·4	9·9
35	9 38·8	9 40·3	9 12·4	3·5	2·2	9·5	6·1	15·5	9·9
36	9 39·0	9 40·6	9 12·6	3·6	2·3	9·6	6·2	15·6	10·0
37	9 39·3	9 40·8	9 12·9	3·7	2·4	9·7	6·2	15·7	10·1
38	9 39·5	9 41·1	9 13·1	3·8	2·4	9·8	6·3	15·8	10·1
39	9 39·8	9 41·3	9 13·3	3·9	2·5	9·9	6·4	15·9	10·2
40	9 40·0	9 41·6	9 13·6	4·0	2·6	10·0	6·4	16·0	10·3
41	9 40·3	9 41·8	9 13·8	4·1	2·6	10·1	6·5	16·1	10·3
42	9 40·5	9 42·1	9 14·1	4·2	2·7	10·2	6·5	16·2	10·4
43	9 40·8	9 42·3	9 14·3	4·3	2·8	10·3	6·6	16·3	10·5
44	9 41·0	9 42·6	9 14·5	4·4	2·8	10·4	6·7	16·4	10·5
45	9 41·3	9 42·8	9 14·8	4·5	2·9	10·5	6·7	16·5	10·6
46	9 41·5	9 43·1	9 15·0	4·6	3·0	10·6	6·8	16·6	10·7
47	9 41·8	9 43·3	9 15·2	4·7	3·0	10·7	6·9	16·7	10·7
48	9 42·0	9 43·6	9 15·5	4·8	3·1	10·8	6·9	16·8	10·8
49	9 42·3	9 43·8	9 15·7	4·9	3·1	10·9	7·0	16·9	10·8
50	9 42·5	9 44·1	9 16·0	5·0	3·2	11·0	7·1	17·0	10·9
51	9 42·8	9 44·3	9 16·2	5·1	3·3	11·1	7·1	17·1	11·0
52	9 43·0	9 44·6	9 16·4	5·2	3·3	11·2	7·2	17·2	11·0
53	9 43·3	9 44·8	9 16·7	5·3	3·4	11·3	7·3	17·3	11·1
54	9 43·5	9 45·1	9 16·9	5·4	3·5	11·4	7·3	17·4	11·2
55	9 43·8	9 45·3	9 17·2	5·5	3·5	11·5	7·4	17·5	11·2
56	9 44·0	9 45·6	9 17·4	5·6	3·6	11·6	7·4	17·6	11·3
57	9 44·3	9 45·8	9 17·6	5·7	3·7	11·7	7·5	17·7	11·4
58	9 44·5	9 46·1	9 17·9	5·8	3·7	11·8	7·6	17·8	11·4
59	9 44·8	9 46·4	9 18·1	5·9	3·8	11·9	7·6	17·9	11·5
60	9 45·0	9 46·6	9 18·4	6·0	3·9	12·0	7·7	18·0	11·6

39	SUN PLANETS	ARIES	MOON	v or Corrn d		v or Corrn d		v or Corrn d	
s	° ′	° ′	° ′	′	′	′	′	′	′
00	9 45·0	9 46·6	9 18·4	0·0	0·0	6·0	4·0	12·0	7·9
01	9 45·3	9 46·9	9 18·6	0·1	0·1	6·1	4·0	12·1	8·0
02	9 45·5	9 47·1	9 18·8	0·2	0·1	6·2	4·1	12·2	8·0
03	9 45·8	9 47·4	9 19·1	0·3	0·2	6·3	4·1	12·3	8·1
04	9 46·0	9 47·6	9 19·3	0·4	0·3	6·4	4·2	12·4	8·2
05	9 46·3	9 47·9	9 19·5	0·5	0·3	6·5	4·3	12·5	8·2
06	9 46·5	9 48·1	9 19·8	0·6	0·4	6·6	4·3	12·6	8·3
07	9 46·8	9 48·4	9 20·0	0·7	0·5	6·7	4·4	12·7	8·4
08	9 47·0	9 48·6	9 20·3	0·8	0·5	6·8	4·5	12·8	8·4
09	9 47·3	9 48·9	9 20·5	0·9	0·6	6·9	4·5	12·9	8·5
10	9 47·5	9 49·1	9 20·7	1·0	0·7	7·0	4·6	13·0	8·6
11	9 47·8	9 49·4	9 21·0	1·1	0·7	7·1	4·7	13·1	8·6
12	9 48·0	9 49·6	9 21·2	1·2	0·8	7·2	4·7	13·2	8·7
13	9 48·3	9 49·9	9 21·5	1·3	0·9	7·3	4·8	13·3	8·8
14	9 48·5	9 50·1	9 21·7	1·4	0·9	7·4	4·9	13·4	8·8
15	9 48·8	9 50·4	9 21·9	1·5	1·0	7·5	4·9	13·5	8·9
16	9 49·0	9 50·6	9 22·2	1·6	1·1	7·6	5·0	13·6	9·0
17	9 49·3	9 50·9	9 22·4	1·7	1·1	7·7	5·1	13·7	9·0
18	9 49·5	9 51·1	9 22·6	1·8	1·2	7·8	5·1	13·8	9·1
19	9 49·8	9 51·4	9 22·9	1·9	1·3	7·9	5·2	13·9	9·2
20	9 50·0	9 51·6	9 23·1	2·0	1·3	8·0	5·3	14·0	9·2
21	9 50·3	9 51·9	9 23·4	2·1	1·4	8·1	5·3	14·1	9·3
22	9 50·5	9 52·1	9 23·6	2·2	1·4	8·2	5·4	14·2	9·3
23	9 50·8	9 52·4	9 23·8	2·3	1·5	8·3	5·5	14·3	9·4
24	9 51·0	9 52·6	9 24·1	2·4	1·6	8·4	5·5	14·4	9·5
25	9 51·3	9 52·9	9 24·3	2·5	1·6	8·5	5·6	14·5	9·5
26	9 51·5	9 53·1	9 24·6	2·6	1·7	8·6	5·7	14·6	9·6
27	9 51·8	9 53·4	9 24·8	2·7	1·8	8·7	5·7	14·7	9·7
28	9 52·0	9 53·6	9 25·0	2·8	1·8	8·8	5·8	14·8	9·7
29	9 52·3	9 53·9	9 25·3	2·9	1·9	8·9	5·9	14·9	9·8
30	9 52·5	9 54·1	9 25·5	3·0	2·0	9·0	5·9	15·0	9·9
31	9 52·8	9 54·4	9 25·7	3·1	2·0	9·1	6·0	15·1	9·9
32	9 53·0	9 54·6	9 26·0	3·2	2·1	9·2	6·1	15·2	10·0
33	9 53·3	9 54·9	9 26·2	3·3	2·2	9·3	6·1	15·3	10·1
34	9 53·5	9 55·1	9 26·5	3·4	2·2	9·4	6·2	15·4	10·1
35	9 53·8	9 55·4	9 26·7	3·5	2·3	9·5	6·3	15·5	10·2
36	9 54·0	9 55·6	9 26·9	3·6	2·4	9·6	6·3	15·6	10·3
37	9 54·3	9 55·9	9 27·2	3·7	2·4	9·7	6·4	15·7	10·3
38	9 54·5	9 56·1	9 27·4	3·8	2·5	9·8	6·5	15·8	10·4
39	9 54·8	9 56·4	9 27·7	3·9	2·6	9·9	6·5	15·9	10·5
40	9 55·0	9 56·6	9 27·9	4·0	2·6	10·0	6·6	16·0	10·5
41	9 55·3	9 56·9	9 28·1	4·1	2·7	10·1	6·6	16·1	10·6
42	9 55·5	9 57·1	9 28·4	4·2	2·8	10·2	6·7	16·2	10·7
43	9 55·8	9 57·4	9 28·6	4·3	2·8	10·3	6·8	16·3	10·7
44	9 56·0	9 57·6	9 28·8	4·4	2·9	10·4	6·8	16·4	10·8
45	9 56·3	9 57·9	9 29·1	4·5	3·0	10·5	6·9	16·5	10·9
46	9 56·5	9 58·1	9 29·3	4·6	3·0	10·6	7·0	16·6	10·9
47	9 56·8	9 58·4	9 29·6	4·7	3·1	10·7	7·0	16·7	11·0
48	9 57·0	9 58·6	9 29·8	4·8	3·2	10·8	7·1	16·8	11·1
49	9 57·3	9 58·9	9 30·0	4·9	3·2	10·9	7·2	16·9	11·1
50	9 57·5	9 59·1	9 30·3	5·0	3·3	11·0	7·2	17·0	11·2
51	9 57·8	9 59·4	9 30·5	5·1	3·4	11·1	7·3	17·1	11·3
52	9 58·0	9 59·6	9 30·8	5·2	3·4	11·2	7·4	17·2	11·3
53	9 58·3	9 59·9	9 31·0	5·3	3·5	11·3	7·4	17·3	11·4
54	9 58·5	10 00·1	9 31·2	5·4	3·6	11·4	7·5	17·4	11·5
55	9 58·8	10 00·4	9 31·5	5·5	3·6	11·5	7·6	17·5	11·5
56	9 59·0	10 00·6	9 31·7	5·6	3·7	11·6	7·6	17·6	11·6
57	9 59·3	10 00·9	9 32·0	5·7	3·8	11·7	7·7	17·7	11·7
58	9 59·5	10 01·1	9 32·2	5·8	3·8	11·8	7·8	17·8	11·7
59	9 59·8	10 01·4	9 32·4	5·9	3·9	11·9	7·8	17·9	11·8
60	10 00·0	10 01·6	9 32·7	6·0	4·0	12·0	7·9	18·0	11·9

40^m s	SUN PLANETS	ARIES	MOON	v or Corrⁿ d	v or Corrⁿ d	v or Corrⁿ d
00	10 00·0	10 01·6	9 32·7	0·0 0·0	6·0 4·1	12·0 8·1
01	10 00·3	10 01·9	9 32·9	0·1 0·1	6·1 4·1	12·1 8·2
02	10 00·5	10 02·1	9 33·1	0·2 0·1	6·2 4·2	12·2 8·2
03	10 00·8	10 02·4	9 33·4	0·3 0·2	6·3 4·3	12·3 8·3
04	10 01·0	10 02·6	9 33·6	0·4 0·3	6·4 4·3	12·4 8·4
05	10 01·3	10 02·9	9 33·9	0·5 0·3	6·5 4·4	12·5 8·4
06	10 01·5	10 03·1	9 34·1	0·6 0·4	6·6 4·5	12·6 8·5
07	10 01·8	10 03·4	9 34·3	0·7 0·5	6·7 4·5	12·7 8·6
08	10 02·0	10 03·6	9 34·6	0·8 0·5	6·8 4·6	12·8 8·6
09	10 02·3	10 03·9	9 34·8	0·9 0·6	6·9 4·7	12·9 8·7
10	10 02·5	10 04·1	9 35·1	1·0 0·7	7·0 4·7	13·0 8·8
11	10 02·8	10 04·4	9 35·3	1·1 0·7	7·1 4·8	13·1 8·8
12	10 03·0	10 04·7	9 35·5	1·2 0·8	7·2 4·9	13·2 8·9
13	10 03·3	10 04·9	9 35·8	1·3 0·9	7·3 4·9	13·3 9·0
14	10 03·5	10 05·2	9 36·0	1·4 0·9	7·4 5·0	13·4 9·0
15	10 03·8	10 05·4	9 36·2	1·5 1·0	7·5 5·1	13·5 9·1
16	10 04·0	10 05·7	9 36·5	1·6 1·1	7·6 5·1	13·6 9·2
17	10 04·3	10 05·9	9 36·7	1·7 1·1	7·7 5·2	13·7 9·2
18	10 04·5	10 06·2	9 37·0	1·8 1·2	7·8 5·3	13·8 9·3
19	10 04·8	10 06·4	9 37·2	1·9 1·3	7·9 5·3	13·9 9·4
20	10 05·0	10 06·7	9 37·4	2·0 1·4	8·0 5·4	14·0 9·5
21	10 05·3	10 06·9	9 37·7	2·1 1·4	8·1 5·5	14·1 9·5
22	10 05·5	10 07·2	9 37·9	2·2 1·5	8·2 5·5	14·2 9·6
23	10 05·8	10 07·4	9 38·2	2·3 1·6	8·3 5·6	14·3 9·7
24	10 06·0	10 07·7	9 38·4	2·4 1·6	8·4 5·7	14·4 9·7
25	10 06·3	10 07·9	9 38·6	2·5 1·7	8·5 5·7	14·5 9·8
26	10 06·5	10 08·2	9 38·9	2·6 1·8	8·6 5·8	14·6 9·9
27	10 06·8	10 08·4	9 39·1	2·7 1·8	8·7 5·9	14·7 9·9
28	10 07·0	10 08·7	9 39·3	2·8 1·9	8·8 5·9	14·8 10·0
29	10 07·3	10 08·9	9 39·6	2·9 2·0	8·9 6·0	14·9 10·1
30	10 07·5	10 09·2	9 39·8	3·0 2·0	9·0 6·1	15·0 10·1
31	10 07·8	10 09·4	9 40·1	3·1 2·1	9·1 6·1	15·1 10·2
32	10 08·0	10 09·7	9 40·3	3·2 2·2	9·2 6·2	15·2 10·3
33	10 08·3	10 09·9	9 40·5	3·3 2·2	9·3 6·3	15·3 10·3
34	10 08·5	10 10·2	9 40·8	3·4 2·3	9·4 6·3	15·4 10·4
35	10 08·8	10 10·4	9 41·0	3·5 2·4	9·5 6·4	15·5 10·5
36	10 09·0	10 10·7	9 41·3	3·6 2·4	9·6 6·5	15·6 10·5
37	10 09·3	10 10·9	9 41·5	3·7 2·5	9·7 6·5	15·7 10·6
38	10 09·5	10 11·2	9 41·7	3·8 2·6	9·8 6·6	15·8 10·7
39	10 09·8	10 11·4	9 42·0	3·9 2·6	9·9 6·7	15·9 10·7
40	10 10·0	10 11·7	9 42·2	4·0 2·7	10·0 6·8	16·0 10·8
41	10 10·3	10 11·9	9 42·4	4·1 2·8	10·1 6·8	16·1 10·9
42	10 10·5	10 12·2	9 42·7	4·2 2·8	10·2 6·9	16·2 10·9
43	10 10·8	10 12·4	9 42·9	4·3 2·9	10·3 7·0	16·3 11·0
44	10 11·0	10 12·7	9 43·2	4·4 3·0	10·4 7·0	16·4 11·1
45	10 11·3	10 12·9	9 43·4	4·5 3·0	10·5 7·1	16·5 11·1
46	10 11·5	10 13·2	9 43·6	4·6 3·1	10·6 7·2	16·6 11·2
47	10 11·8	10 13·4	9 43·9	4·7 3·2	10·7 7·2	16·7 11·3
48	10 12·0	10 13·7	9 44·1	4·8 3·2	10·8 7·3	16·8 11·3
49	10 12·3	10 13·9	9 44·4	4·9 3·3	10·9 7·4	16·9 11·4
50	10 12·5	10 14·2	9 44·6	5·0 3·4	11·0 7·4	17·0 11·5
51	10 12·8	10 14·4	9 44·8	5·1 3·4	11·1 7·5	17·1 11·5
52	10 13·0	10 14·7	9 45·1	5·2 3·5	11·2 7·6	17·2 11·6
53	10 13·3	10 14·9	9 45·3	5·3 3·6	11·3 7·6	17·3 11·7
54	10 13·5	10 15·2	9 45·6	5·4 3·6	11·4 7·7	17·4 11·7
55	10 13·8	10 15·4	9 45·8	5·5 3·7	11·5 7·8	17·5 11·8
56	10 14·0	10 15·7	9 46·0	5·6 3·8	11·6 7·8	17·6 11·9
57	10 14·3	10 15·9	9 46·3	5·7 3·8	11·7 7·9	17·7 11·9
58	10 14·5	10 16·2	9 46·5	5·8 3·9	11·8 8·0	17·8 12·0
59	10 14·8	10 16·4	9 46·7	5·9 4·0	11·9 8·0	17·9 12·1
60	10 15·0	10 16·7	9 47·0	6·0 4·1	12·0 8·1	18·0 12·2

41^m s	SUN PLANETS	ARIES	MOON	v or Corrⁿ d	v or Corrⁿ d	v or Corrⁿ d
00	10 15·0	10 16·7	9 47·0	0·0 0·0	6·0 4·2	12·0 8·3
01	10 15·3	10 16·9	9 47·2	0·1 0·1	6·1 4·2	12·1 8·4
02	10 15·5	10 17·2	9 47·5	0·2 0·1	6·2 4·3	12·2 8·4
03	10 15·8	10 17·4	9 47·7	0·3 0·2	6·3 4·4	12·3 8·5
04	10 16·0	10 17·7	9 47·9	0·4 0·3	6·4 4·4	12·4 8·6
05	10 16·3	10 17·9	9 48·2	0·5 0·3	6·5 4·5	12·5 8·6
06	10 16·5	10 18·2	9 48·4	0·6 0·4	6·6 4·6	12·6 8·7
07	10 16·8	10 18·4	9 48·7	0·7 0·5	6·7 4·6	12·7 8·8
08	10 17·0	10 18·7	9 48·9	0·8 0·6	6·8 4·7	12·8 8·8
09	10 17·3	10 18·9	9 49·1	0·9 0·6	6·9 4·8	12·9 8·9
10	10 17·5	10 19·2	9 49·4	1·0 0·7	7·0 4·8	13·0 9·0
11	10 17·8	10 19·4	9 49·6	1·1 0·8	7·1 4·9	13·1 9·1
12	10 18·0	10 19·7	9 49·8	1·2 0·8	7·2 5·0	13·2 9·1
13	10 18·3	10 19·9	9 50·1	1·3 0·9	7·3 5·0	13·3 9·2
14	10 18·5	10 20·2	9 50·3	1·4 1·0	7·4 5·1	13·4 9·3
15	10 18·8	10 20·4	9 50·6	1·5 1·0	7·5 5·2	13·5 9·3
16	10 19·0	10 20·7	9 50·8	1·6 1·1	7·6 5·3	13·6 9·4
17	10 19·3	10 20·9	9 51·0	1·7 1·2	7·7 5·3	13·7 9·5
18	10 19·5	10 21·2	9 51·3	1·8 1·2	7·8 5·4	13·8 9·5
19	10 19·8	10 21·4	9 51·5	1·9 1·3	7·9 5·5	13·9 9·6
20	10 20·0	10 21·7	9 51·8	2·0 1·4	8·0 5·5	14·0 9·7
21	10 20·3	10 21·9	9 52·0	2·1 1·5	8·1 5·6	14·1 9·8
22	10 20·5	10 22·2	9 52·2	2·2 1·5	8·2 5·7	14·2 9·8
23	10 20·8	10 22·4	9 52·5	2·3 1·6	8·3 5·7	14·3 9·9
24	10 21·0	10 22·7	9 52·7	2·4 1·7	8·4 5·8	14·4 10·0
25	10 21·3	10 23·0	9 52·9	2·5 1·7	8·5 5·9	14·5 10·0
26	10 21·5	10 23·2	9 53·2	2·6 1·8	8·6 5·9	14·6 10·1
27	10 21·8	10 23·5	9 53·4	2·7 1·9	8·7 6·0	14·7 10·2
28	10 22·0	10 23·7	9 53·7	2·8 1·9	8·8 6·1	14·8 10·2
29	10 22·3	10 24·0	9 53·9	2·9 2·0	8·9 6·2	14·9 10·3
30	10 22·5	10 24·2	9 54·1	3·0 2·1	9·0 6·2	15·0 10·4
31	10 22·8	10 24·5	9 54·4	3·1 2·1	9·1 6·3	15·1 10·4
32	10 23·0	10 24·7	9 54·6	3·2 2·2	9·2 6·4	15·2 10·5
33	10 23·3	10 25·0	9 54·9	3·3 2·3	9·3 6·4	15·3 10·6
34	10 23·5	10 25·2	9 55·1	3·4 2·4	9·4 6·5	15·4 10·7
35	10 23·8	10 25·5	9 55·3	3·5 2·4	9·5 6·6	15·5 10·7
36	10 24·0	10 25·7	9 55·6	3·6 2·5	9·6 6·6	15·6 10·8
37	10 24·3	10 26·0	9 55·8	3·7 2·6	9·7 6·7	15·7 10·9
38	10 24·5	10 26·2	9 56·1	3·8 2·6	9·8 6·8	15·8 10·9
39	10 24·8	10 26·5	9 56·3	3·9 2·7	9·9 6·8	15·9 11·0
40	10 25·0	10 26·7	9 56·5	4·0 2·8	10·0 6·9	16·0 11·1
41	10 25·3	10 27·0	9 56·8	4·1 2·8	10·1 7·0	16·1 11·1
42	10 25·5	10 27·2	9 57·0	4·2 2·9	10·2 7·1	16·2 11·2
43	10 25·8	10 27·5	9 57·2	4·3 3·0	10·3 7·1	16·3 11·3
44	10 26·0	10 27·7	9 57·5	4·4 3·0	10·4 7·2	16·4 11·3
45	10 26·3	10 28·0	9 57·7	4·5 3·1	10·5 7·3	16·5 11·4
46	10 26·5	10 28·2	9 58·0	4·6 3·2	10·6 7·3	16·6 11·5
47	10 26·8	10 28·5	9 58·2	4·7 3·3	10·7 7·4	16·7 11·6
48	10 27·0	10 28·7	9 58·4	4·8 3·3	10·8 7·5	16·8 11·6
49	10 27·3	10 29·0	9 58·7	4·9 3·4	10·9 7·5	16·9 11·7
50	10 27·5	10 29·2	9 58·9	5·0 3·5	11·0 7·6	17·0 11·8
51	10 27·8	10 29·5	9 59·2	5·1 3·5	11·1 7·7	17·1 11·8
52	10 28·0	10 29·7	9 59·4	5·2 3·6	11·2 7·7	17·2 11·9
53	10 28·3	10 30·0	9 59·6	5·3 3·7	11·3 7·8	17·3 12·0
54	10 28·5	10 30·2	9 59·9	5·4 3·7	11·4 7·9	17·4 12·0
55	10 28·8	10 30·5	10 00·1	5·5 3·8	11·5 8·0	17·5 12·1
56	10 29·0	10 30·7	10 00·3	5·6 3·9	11·6 8·0	17·6 12·2
57	10 29·3	10 31·0	10 00·6	5·7 3·9	11·7 8·1	17·7 12·2
58	10 29·5	10 31·2	10 00·8	5·8 4·0	11·8 8·2	17·8 12·3
59	10 29·8	10 31·5	10 01·1	5·9 4·1	11·9 8·2	17·9 12·4
60	10 30·0	10 31·7	10 01·3	6·0 4·2	12·0 8·3	18·0 12·5

42ᵐ

42ᵐ	SUN PLANETS	ARIES	MOON	v or d Corrⁿ		v or d Corrⁿ		v or d Corrⁿ	
s	° ′	° ′	° ′	′	′	′	′	′	′
00	10 30·0	10 31·7	10 01·3	0·0	0·0	6·0	4·3	12·0	8·5
01	10 30·3	10 32·0	10 01·5	0·1	0·1	6·1	4·3	12·1	8·6
02	10 30·5	10 32·2	10 01·8	0·2	0·1	6·2	4·4	12·2	8·6
03	10 30·8	10 32·5	10 02·0	0·3	0·2	6·3	4·5	12·3	8·7
04	10 31·0	10 32·7	10 02·3	0·4	0·3	6·4	4·5	12·4	8·8
05	10 31·3	10 33·0	10 02·5	0·5	0·4	6·5	4·6	12·5	8·9
06	10 31·5	10 33·2	10 02·7	0·6	0·4	6·6	4·7	12·6	8·9
07	10 31·8	10 33·5	10 03·0	0·7	0·5	6·7	4·7	12·7	9·0
08	10 32·0	10 33·7	10 03·2	0·8	0·6	6·8	4·8	12·8	9·1
09	10 32·3	10 34·0	10 03·4	0·9	0·6	6·9	4·9	12·9	9·1
10	10 32·5	10 34·2	10 03·7	1·0	0·7	7·0	5·0	13·0	9·2
11	10 32·8	10 34·5	10 03·9	1·1	0·8	7·1	5·0	13·1	9·3
12	10 33·0	10 34·7	10 04·2	1·2	0·9	7·2	5·1	13·2	9·4
13	10 33·3	10 35·0	10 04·4	1·3	0·9	7·3	5·2	13·3	9·4
14	10 33·5	10 35·2	10 04·6	1·4	1·0	7·4	5·2	13·4	9·5
15	10 33·8	10 35·5	10 04·9	1·5	1·1	7·5	5·3	13·5	9·6
16	10 34·0	10 35·7	10 05·1	1·6	1·1	7·6	5·4	13·6	9·6
17	10 34·3	10 36·0	10 05·4	1·7	1·2	7·7	5·5	13·7	9·7
18	10 34·5	10 36·2	10 05·6	1·8	1·3	7·8	5·5	13·8	9·8
19	10 34·8	10 36·5	10 05·8	1·9	1·3	7·9	5·6	13·9	9·8
20	10 35·0	10 36·7	10 06·1	2·0	1·4	8·0	5·7	14·0	9·9
21	10 35·3	10 37·0	10 06·3	2·1	1·5	8·1	5·7	14·1	10·0
22	10 35·5	10 37·2	10 06·5	2·2	1·6	8·2	5·8	14·2	10·1
23	10 35·8	10 37·5	10 06·8	2·3	1·6	8·3	5·9	14·3	10·1
24	10 36·0	10 37·7	10 07·0	2·4	1·7	8·4	6·0	14·4	10·2
25	10 36·3	10 38·0	10 07·3	2·5	1·8	8·5	6·0	14·5	10·3
26	10 36·5	10 38·2	10 07·5	2·6	1·8	8·6	6·1	14·6	10·3
27	10 36·8	10 38·5	10 07·7	2·7	1·9	8·7	6·2	14·7	10·4
28	10 37·0	10 38·7	10 08·0	2·8	2·0	8·8	6·2	14·8	10·5
29	10 37·3	10 39·0	10 08·2	2·9	2·1	8·9	6·3	14·9	10·6
30	10 37·5	10 39·2	10 08·5	3·0	2·1	9·0	6·4	15·0	10·6
31	10 37·8	10 39·5	10 08·7	3·1	2·2	9·1	6·4	15·1	10·7
32	10 38·0	10 39·7	10 08·9	3·2	2·3	9·2	6·5	15·2	10·8
33	10 38·3	10 40·0	10 09·2	3·3	2·3	9·3	6·6	15·3	10·8
34	10 38·5	10 40·2	10 09·4	3·4	2·4	9·4	6·7	15·4	10·9
35	10 38·8	10 40·5	10 09·7	3·5	2·5	9·5	6·7	15·5	11·0
36	10 39·0	10 40·7	10 09·9	3·6	2·6	9·6	6·8	15·6	11·1
37	10 39·3	10 41·0	10 10·1	3·7	2·6	9·7	6·9	15·7	11·1
38	10 39·5	10 41·3	10 10·4	3·8	2·7	9·8	6·9	15·8	11·2
39	10 39·8	10 41·5	10 10·6	3·9	2·8	9·9	7·0	15·9	11·3
40	10 40·0	10 41·8	10 10·8	4·0	2·8	10·0	7·1	16·0	11·3
41	10 40·3	10 42·0	10 11·1	4·1	2·9	10·1	7·2	16·1	11·4
42	10 40·5	10 42·3	10 11·3	4·2	3·0	10·2	7·2	16·2	11·5
43	10 40·8	10 42·5	10 11·6	4·3	3·0	10·3	7·3	16·3	11·5
44	10 41·0	10 42·8	10 11·8	4·4	3·1	10·4	7·4	16·4	11·6
45	10 41·3	10 43·0	10 12·0	4·5	3·2	10·5	7·4	16·5	11·7
46	10 41·5	10 43·3	10 12·3	4·6	3·3	10·6	7·5	16·6	11·8
47	10 41·8	10 43·5	10 12·5	4·7	3·3	10·7	7·6	16·7	11·8
48	10 42·0	10 43·8	10 12·8	4·8	3·4	10·8	7·7	16·8	11·9
49	10 42·3	10 44·0	10 13·0	4·9	3·5	10·9	7·7	16·9	12·0
50	10 42·5	10 44·3	10 13·2	5·0	3·5	11·0	7·8	17·0	12·0
51	10 42·8	10 44·5	10 13·5	5·1	3·6	11·1	7·9	17·1	12·1
52	10 43·0	10 44·8	10 13·7	5·2	3·7	11·2	7·9	17·2	12·2
53	10 43·3	10 45·0	10 13·9	5·3	3·8	11·3	8·0	17·3	12·3
54	10 43·5	10 45·3	10 14·2	5·4	3·8	11·4	8·1	17·4	12·3
55	10 43·8	10 45·5	10 14·4	5·5	3·9	11·5	8·1	17·5	12·4
56	10 44·0	10 45·8	10 14·7	5·6	4·0	11·6	8·2	17·6	12·5
57	10 44·3	10 46·0	10 14·9	5·7	4·0	11·7	8·3	17·7	12·5
58	10 44·5	10 46·3	10 15·1	5·8	4·1	11·8	8·4	17·8	12·6
59	10 44·8	10 46·5	10 15·4	5·9	4·2	11·9	8·4	17·9	12·7
60	10 45·0	10 46·8	10 15·6	6·0	4·3	12·0	8·5	18·0	12·8

43ᵐ

43ᵐ	SUN PLANETS	ARIES	MOON	v or d Corrⁿ		v or d Corrⁿ		v or d Corrⁿ	
s	° ′	° ′	° ′	′	′	′	′	′	′
00	10 45·0	10 46·8	10 15·6	0·0	0·0	6·0	4·4	12·0	8·7
01	10 45·3	10 47·0	10 15·9	0·1	0·1	6·1	4·4	12·1	8·8
02	10 45·5	10 47·3	10 16·1	0·2	0·1	6·2	4·5	12·2	8·8
03	10 45·8	10 47·5	10 16·3	0·3	0·2	6·3	4·6	12·3	8·9
04	10 46·0	10 47·8	10 16·6	0·4	0·3	6·4	4·6	12·4	9·0
05	10 46·3	10 48·0	10 16·8	0·5	0·4	6·5	4·7	12·5	9·1
06	10 46·5	10 48·3	10 17·0	0·6	0·4	6·6	4·8	12·6	9·1
07	10 46·8	10 48·5	10 17·3	0·7	0·5	6·7	4·9	12·7	9·2
08	10 47·0	10 48·8	10 17·5	0·8	0·6	6·8	4·9	12·8	9·3
09	10 47·3	10 49·0	10 17·8	0·9	0·7	6·9	5·0	12·9	9·4
10	10 47·5	10 49·3	10 18·0	1·0	0·7	7·0	5·1	13·0	9·4
11	10 47·8	10 49·5	10 18·2	1·1	0·8	7·1	5·1	13·1	9·5
12	10 48·0	10 49·8	10 18·5	1·2	0·9	7·2	5·2	13·2	9·6
13	10 48·3	10 50·0	10 18·7	1·3	0·9	7·3	5·3	13·3	9·6
14	10 48·5	10 50·3	10 19·0	1·4	1·0	7·4	5·4	13·4	9·7
15	10 48·8	10 50·5	10 19·2	1·5	1·1	7·5	5·4	13·5	9·8
16	10 49·0	10 50·8	10 19·4	1·6	1·2	7·6	5·5	13·6	9·9
17	10 49·3	10 51·0	10 19·7	1·7	1·2	7·7	5·6	13·7	9·9
18	10 49·5	10 51·3	10 19·9	1·8	1·3	7·8	5·7	13·8	10·0
19	10 49·8	10 51·5	10 20·2	1·9	1·4	7·9	5·7	13·9	10·1
20	10 50·0	10 51·8	10 20·4	2·0	1·5	8·0	5·8	14·0	10·2
21	10 50·3	10 52·0	10 20·6	2·1	1·5	8·1	5·9	14·1	10·2
22	10 50·5	10 52·3	10 20·9	2·2	1·6	8·2	5·9	14·2	10·3
23	10 50·8	10 52·5	10 21·1	2·3	1·7	8·3	6·0	14·3	10·4
24	10 51·0	10 52·8	10 21·3	2·4	1·7	8·4	6·1	14·4	10·4
25	10 51·3	10 53·0	10 21·6	2·5	1·8	8·5	6·2	14·5	10·5
26	10 51·5	10 53·3	10 21·8	2·6	1·9	8·6	6·2	14·6	10·6
27	10 51·8	10 53·5	10 22·1	2·7	2·0	8·7	6·3	14·7	10·7
28	10 52·0	10 53·8	10 22·3	2·8	2·0	8·8	6·4	14·8	10·7
29	10 52·3	10 54·0	10 22·5	2·9	2·1	8·9	6·5	14·9	10·8
30	10 52·5	10 54·3	10 22·8	3·0	2·2	9·0	6·5	15·0	10·9
31	10 52·8	10 54·5	10 23·0	3·1	2·2	9·1	6·6	15·1	10·9
32	10 53·0	10 54·8	10 23·3	3·2	2·3	9·2	6·7	15·2	11·0
33	10 53·3	10 55·0	10 23·5	3·3	2·4	9·3	6·7	15·3	11·1
34	10 53·5	10 55·3	10 23·7	3·4	2·5	9·4	6·8	15·4	11·2
35	10 53·8	10 55·5	10 24·0	3·5	2·5	9·5	6·9	15·5	11·2
36	10 54·0	10 55·8	10 24·2	3·6	2·6	9·6	7·0	15·6	11·3
37	10 54·3	10 56·0	10 24·4	3·7	2·7	9·7	7·0	15·7	11·4
38	10 54·5	10 56·3	10 24·7	3·8	2·8	9·8	7·1	15·8	11·5
39	10 54·8	10 56·5	10 24·9	3·9	2·8	9·9	7·2	15·9	11·5
40	10 55·0	10 56·8	10 25·2	4·0	2·9	10·0	7·3	16·0	11·6
41	10 55·3	10 57·0	10 25·4	4·1	3·0	10·1	7·3	16·1	11·7
42	10 55·5	10 57·3	10 25·6	4·2	3·0	10·2	7·4	16·2	11·7
43	10 55·8	10 57·5	10 25·9	4·3	3·1	10·3	7·5	16·3	11·8
44	10 56·0	10 57·8	10 26·1	4·4	3·2	10·4	7·5	16·4	11·9
45	10 56·3	10 58·0	10 26·4	4·5	3·3	10·5	7·6	16·5	12·0
46	10 56·5	10 58·3	10 26·6	4·6	3·3	10·6	7·7	16·6	12·0
47	10 56·8	10 58·5	10 26·8	4·7	3·4	10·7	7·8	16·7	12·1
48	10 57·0	10 58·8	10 27·1	4·8	3·5	10·8	7·8	16·8	12·2
49	10 57·3	10 59·0	10 27·3	4·9	3·6	10·9	7·9	16·9	12·3
50	10 57·5	10 59·3	10 27·5	5·0	3·6	11·0	8·0	17·0	12·3
51	10 57·8	10 59·5	10 27·8	5·1	3·7	11·1	8·0	17·1	12·4
52	10 58·0	10 59·8	10 28·0	5·2	3·8	11·2	8·1	17·2	12·5
53	10 58·3	11 00·1	10 28·3	5·3	3·8	11·3	8·2	17·3	12·5
54	10 58·5	11 00·3	10 28·5	5·4	3·9	11·4	8·3	17·4	12·6
55	10 58·8	11 00·6	10 28·7	5·5	4·0	11·5	8·3	17·5	12·7
56	10 59·0	11 00·8	10 29·0	5·6	4·1	11·6	8·4	17·6	12·8
57	10 59·3	11 01·1	10 29·2	5·7	4·1	11·7	8·5	17·7	12·8
58	10 59·5	11 01·3	10 29·5	5·8	4·2	11·8	8·6	17·8	12·9
59	10 59·8	11 01·6	10 29·7	5·9	4·3	11·9	8·6	17·9	13·0
60	11 00·0	11 01·8	10 29·9	6·0	4·4	12·0	8·7	18·0	13·1

44m

s	SUN PLANETS	ARIES	MOON	v or Corrn d		v or Corrn d		v or Corrn d	
00	11 00·0	11 01·8	10 29·9	0·0	0·0	6·0	4·5	12·0	8·9
01	11 00·3	11 02·1	10 30·2	0·1	0·1	6·1	4·5	12·1	9·0
02	11 00·5	11 02·3	10 30·4	0·2	0·1	6·2	4·6	12·2	9·0
03	11 00·8	11 02·6	10 30·6	0·3	0·2	6·3	4·7	12·3	9·1
04	11 01·0	11 02·8	10 30·9	0·4	0·3	6·4	4·7	12·4	9·2
05	11 01·3	11 03·1	10 31·1	0·5	0·4	6·5	4·8	12·5	9·3
06	11 01·5	11 03·3	10 31·4	0·6	0·4	6·6	4·9	12·6	9·3
07	11 01·8	11 03·6	10 31·6	0·7	0·5	6·7	5·0	12·7	9·4
08	11 02·0	11 03·8	10 31·8	0·8	0·6	6·8	5·0	12·8	9·5
09	11 02·3	11 04·1	10 32·1	0·9	·0·7	6·9	5·1	12·9	9·6
10	11 02·5	11 04·3	10 32·3	1·0	0·7	7·0	5·2	13·0	9·6
11	11 02·8	11 04·6	10 32·6	1·1	0·8	7·1	5·3	13·1	9·7
12	11 03·0	11 04·8	10 32·8	1·2	0·9	7·2	5·3	13·2	9·8
13	11 03·3	11 05·1	10 33·0	1·3	1·0	7·3	5·4	13·3	9·9
14	11 03·5	11 05·3	10 33·3	1·4	1·0	7·4	5·5	13·4	9·9
15	11 03·8	11 05·6	10 33·5	1·5	1·1	7·5	5·6	13·5	10·0
16	11 04·0	11 05·8	10 33·8	1·6	1·2	7·6	5·6	13·6	10·1
17	11 04·3	11 06·1	10 34·0	1·7	1·3	7·7	5·7	13·7	10·2
18	11 04·5	11 06·3	10 34·2	1·8	1·3	7·8	5·8	13·8	10·2
19	11 04·8	11 06·6	10 34·5	1·9	1·4	7·9	5·9	13·9	10·3
20	11 05·0	11 06·8	10 34·7	2·0	1·5	8·0	5·9	14·0	10·4
21	11 05·3	11 07·1	10 34·9	2·1	1·6	8·1	6·0	14·1	10·5
22	11 05·5	11 07·3	10 35·2	2·2	1·6	8·2	6·1	14·2	10·5
23	11 05·8	11 07·6	10 35·4	2·3	1·7	8·3	6·2	14·3	10·6
24	11 06·0	11 07·8	10 35·7	2·4	1·8	8·4	6·2	14·4	10·7
25	11 06·3	11 08·1	10 35·9	2·5	1·9	8·5	6·3	14·5	10·8
26	11 06·5	11 08·3	10 36·1	2·6	1·9	8·6	6·4	14·6	10·8
27	11 06·8	11 08·6	10 36·4	2·7	2·0	8·7	6·5	14·7	10·9
28	11 07·0	11 08·8	10 36·6	2·8	2·1	8·8	6·5	14·8	11·0
29	11 07·3	11 09·1	10 36·9	2·9	2·2	8·9	6·6	14·9	11·1
30	11 07·5	11 09·3	10 37·1	3·0	2·2	9·0	6·7	15·0	11·1
31	11 07·8	11 09·6	10 37·3	3·1	2·3	9·1	6·7	15·1	11·2
32	11 08·0	11 09·8	10 37·6	3·2	2·4	9·2	6·8	15·2	11·3
33	11 08·3	11 10·1	10 37·8	3·3	2·4	9·3	6·9	15·3	11·3
34	11 08·5	11 10·3	10 38·0	3·4	2·5	9·4	7·0	15·4	11·4
35	11 08·8	11 10·6	10 38·3	3·5	2·6	9·5	7·0	15·5	11·5
36	11 09·0	11 10·8	10 38·5	3·6	2·7	9·6	7·1	15·6	11·6
37	11 09·3	11 11·1	10 38·8	3·7	2·7	9·7	7·2	15·7	11·6
38	11 09·5	11 11·3	10 39·0	3·8	2·8	9·8	7·3	15·8	11·7
39	11 09·8	11 11·6	10 39·2	3·9	2·9	9·9	7·3	15·9	11·8
40	11 10·0	11 11·8	10 39·5	4·0	3·0	10·0	7·4	16·0	11·9
41	11 10·3	11 12·1	10 39·7	4·1	3·0	10·1	7·5	16·1	11·9
42	11 10·5	11 12·3	10 40·0	4·2	3·1	10·2	7·6	16·2	12·0
43	11 10·8	11 12·6	10 40·2	4·3	3·2	10·3	7·6	16·3	12·1
44	11 11·0	11 12·8	10 40·4	4·4	3·3	10·4	7·7	16·4	12·2
45	11 11·3	11 13·1	10 40·7	4·5	3·3	10·5	7·8	16·5	12·2
46	11 11·5	11 13·3	10 40·9	4·6	3·4	10·6	7·9	16·6	12·3
47	11 11·8	11 13·6	10 41·1	4·7	3·5	10·7	7·9	16·7	12·4
48	11 12·0	11 13·8	10 41·4	4·8	3·6	10·8	8·0	16·8	12·5
49	11 12·3	11 14·1	10 41·6	4·9	3·6	10·9	8·1	16·9	12·5
50	11 12·5	11 14·3	10 41·9	5·0	3·7	11·0	8·2	17·0	12·6
51	11 12·8	11 14·6	10 42·1	5·1	3·8	11·1	8·2	17·1	12·7
52	11 13·0	11 14·8	10 42·3	5·2	3·9	11·2	8·3	17·2	12·8
53	11 13·3	11 15·1	10 42·6	5·3	3·9	11·3	8·4	17·3	12·8
54	11 13·5	11 15·3	10 42·8	5·4	4·0	11·4	8·5	17·4	12·9
55	11 13·8	11 15·6	10 43·1	5·5	4·1	11·5	8·5	17·5	13·0
56	11 14·0	11 15·8	10 43·3	5·6	4·2	11·6	8·6	17·6	13·1
57	11 14·3	11 16·1	10 43·5	5·7	4·2	11·7	8·7	17·7	13·1
58	11 14·5	11 16·3	10 43·8	5·8	4·3	11·8	8·8	17·8	13·2
59	11 14·8	11 16·6	10 44·0	5·9	4·4	11·9	8·8	17·9	13·3
60	11 15·0	11 16·8	10 44·3	6·0	4·5	12·0	8·9	18·0	13·4

45m

s	SUN PLANETS	ARIES	MOON	v or Corrn d		v or Corrn d		v or Corrn d	
00	11 15·0	11 16·8	10 44·3	0·0	0·0	6·0	4·6	12·0	9·1
01	11 15·3	11 17·1	10 44·5	0·1	0·1	6·1	4·6	12·1	9·2
02	11 15·5	11 17·3	10 44·7	0·2	0·2	6·2	4·7	12·2	9·3
03	11 15·8	11 17·6	10 45·0	0·3	0·2	6·3	4·8	12·3	9·3
04	11 16·0	11 17·9	10 45·2	0·4	0·3	6·4	4·9	12·4	9·4
05	11 16·3	11 18·1	10 45·4	0·5	0·4	6·5	4·9	12·5	9·5
06	11 16·5	11 18·4	10 45·7	0·6	0·5	6·6	5·0	12·6	9·6
07	11 16·8	11 18·6	10 45·9	0·7	0·5	6·7	5·1	12·7	9·6
08	11 17·0	11 18·9	10 46·2	0·8	0·6	6·8	5·2	12·8	9·7
09	11 17·3	11 19·1	10 46·4	0·9	0·7	6·9	5·2	12·9	9·8
10	11 17·5	11 19·4	10 46·6	1·0	0·8	7·0	5·3	13·0	9·9
11	11 17·8	11 19·6	10 46·9	1·1	0·8	7·1	5·4	13·1	9·9
12	11 18·0	11 19·9	10 47·1	1·2	0·9	7·2	5·5	13·2	10·0
13	11 18·3	11 20·1	10 47·4	1·3	1·0	7·3	5·5	13·3	10·1
14	11 18·5	11 20·4	10 47·6	1·4	1·1	7·4	5·6	13·4	10·2
15	11 18·8	11 20·6	10 47·8	1·5	1·1	7·5	5·7	13·5	10·2
16	11 19·0	11 20·9	10 48·1	1·6	1·2	7·6	5·8	13·6	10·3
17	11 19·3	11 21·1	10 48·3	1·7	1·3	7·7	5·8	13·7	10·4
18	11 19·5	11 21·4	10 48·5	1·8	1·4	7·8	5·9	13·8	10·5
19	11 19·8	11 21·6	10 48·8	1·9	1·4	7·9	6·0	13·9	10·5
20	11 20·0	11 21·9	10 49·0	2·0	1·5	8·0	6·1	14·0	10·6
21	11 20·3	11 22·1	10 49·3	2·1	1·6	8·1	6·1	14·1	10·7
22	11 20·5	11 22·4	10 49·5	2·2	1·7	8·2	6·2	14·2	10·8
23	11 20·8	11 22·6	10 49·7	2·3	1·7	8·3	6·3	14·3	10·8
24	11 21·0	11 22·9	10 50·0	2·4	1·8	8·4	6·4	14·4	10·9
25	11 21·3	11 23·1	10 50·2	2·5	1·9	8·5	6·4	14·5	11·0
26	11 21·5	11 23·4	10 50·5	2·6	2·0	8·6	6·5	14·6	11·1
27	11 21·8	11 23·6	10 50·7	2·7	2·0	8·7	6·6	14·7	11·1
28	11 22·0	11 23·9	10 50·9	2·8	2·1	8·8	6·7	14·8	11·2
29	11 22·3	11 24·1	10 51·2	2·9	2·2	8·9	6·7	14·9	11·3
30	11 22·5	11 24·4	10 51·4	3·0	2·3	9·0	6·8	15·0	11·4
31	11 22·8	11 24·6	10 51·6	3·1	2·4	9·1	6·9	15·1	11·5
32	11 23·0	11 24·9	10 51·9	3·2	2·4	9·2	7·0	15·2	11·5
33	11 23·3	11 25·1	10 52·1	3·3	2·5	9·3	7·1	15·3	11·6
34	11 23·5	11 25·4	10 52·4	3·4	2·6	9·4	7·1	15·4	11·7
35	11 23·8	11 25·6	10 52·6	3·5	2·7	9·5	7·2	15·5	11·8
36	11 24·0	11 25·9	10 52·8	3·6	2·7	9·6	7·3	15·6	11·8
37	11 24·3	11 26·1	10 53·1	3·7	2·8	9·7	7·4	15·7	11·9
38	11 24·5	11 26·4	10 53·3	3·8	2·9	9·8	7·4	15·8	12·0
39	11 24·8	11 26·6	10 53·6	3·9	3·0	9·9	7·5	15·9	12·1
40	11 25·0	11 26·9	10 53·8	4·0	3·0	10·0	7·6	16·0	12·1
41	11 25·3	11 27·1	10 54·0	4·1	3·1	10·1	7·7	16·1	12·2
42	11 25·5	11 27·4	10 54·3	4·2	3·2	10·2	7·7	16·2	12·3
43	11 25·8	11 27·6	10 54·5	4·3	3·3	10·3	7·8	16·3	12·4
44	11 26·0	11 27·9	10 54·7	4·4	3·3	10·4	7·9	16·4	12·4
45	11 26·3	11 28·1	10 55·0	4·5	3·4	10·5	8·0	16·5	12·5
46	11 26·5	11 28·4	10 55·2	4·6	3·5	10·6	8·0	16·6	12·6
47	11 26·8	11 28·6	10 55·5	4·7	3·6	10·7	8·1	16·7	12·7
48	11 27·0	11 28·9	10 55·7	4·8	3·6	10·8	8·2	16·8	12·7
49	11 27·3	11 29·1	10 55·9	4·9	3·7	10·9	8·3	16·9	12·8
50	11 27·5	11 29·4	10 56·2	5·0	3·8	11·0	8·3	17·0	12·9
51	11 27·8	11 29·6	10 56·4	5·1	3·9	11·1	8·4	17·1	13·0
52	11 28·0	11 29·9	10 56·7	5·2	3·9	11·2	8·5	17·2	13·0
53	11 28·3	11 30·1	10 56·9	5·3	4·0	11·3	8·6	17·3	13·1
54	11 28·5	11 30·4	10 57·1	5·4	4·1	11·4	8·6	17·4	13·2
55	11 28·8	11 30·6	10 57·4	5·5	4·2	11·5	8·7	17·5	13·3
56	11 29·0	11 30·9	10 57·6	5·6	4·2	11·6	8·8	17·6	13·3
57	11 29·3	11 31·1	10 57·9	5·7	4·3	11·7	8·9	17·7	13·4
58	11 29·5	11 31·4	10 58·1	5·8	4·4	11·8	8·9	17·8	13·5
59	11 29·8	11 31·6	10 58·3	5·9	4·5	11·9	9·0	17·9	13·6
60	11 30·0	11 31·9	10 58·6	6·0	4·6	12·0	9·1	18·0	13·7

46ᵐ

46ᵐ	SUN PLANETS	ARIES	MOON	v or Corrⁿ d		v or Corrⁿ d		v or Corrⁿ d	
s	° ′	° ′	° ′	′	′	′	′	′	′
00	11 30·0	11 31·9	10 58·6	0·0	0·0	6·0	4·7	12·0	9·3
01	11 30·3	11 32·1	10 58·8	0·1	0·1	6·1	4·7	12·1	9·4
02	11 30·5	11 32·4	10 59·0	0·2	0·2	6·2	4·8	12·2	9·5
03	11 30·8	11 32·6	10 59·3	0·3	0·2	6·3	4·9	12·3	9·5
04	11 31·0	11 32·9	10 59·5	0·4	0·3	6·4	5·0	12·4	9·6
05	11 31·3	11 33·1	10 59·8	0·5	0·4	6·5	5·0	12·5	9·7
06	11 31·5	11 33·4	11 00·0	0·6	0·5	6·6	5·1	12·6	9·8
07	11 31·8	11 33·6	11 00·2	0·7	0·5	6·7	5·2	12·7	9·8
08	11 32·0	11 33·9	11 00·5	0·8	0·6	6·8	5·3	12·8	9·9
09	11 32·3	11 34·1	11 00·7	0·9	0·7	6·9	5·3	12·9	10·0
10	11 32·5	11 34·4	11 01·0	1·0	0·8	7·0	5·4	13·0	10·1
11	11 32·8	11 34·6	11 01·2	1·1	0·9	7·1	5·5	13·1	10·2
12	11 33·0	11 34·9	11 01·4	1·2	0·9	7·2	5·6	13·2	10·2
13	11 33·3	11 35·1	11 01·7	1·3	1·0	7·3	5·7	13·3	10·3
14	11 33·5	11 35·4	11 01·9	1·4	1·1	7·4	5·7	13·4	10·4
15	11 33·8	11 35·6	11 02·1	1·5	1·2	7·5	5·8	13·5	10·5
16	11 34·0	11 35·9	11 02·4	1·6	1·2	7·6	5·9	13·6	10·5
17	11 34·3	11 36·2	11 02·6	1·7	1·3	7·7	6·0	13·7	10·6
18	11 34·5	11 36·4	11 02·9	1·8	1·4	7·8	6·0	13·8	10·7
19	11 34·8	11 36·7	11 03·1	1·9	1·5	7·9	6·1	13·9	10·8
20	11 35·0	11 36·9	11 03·3	2·0	1·6	8·0	6·2	14·0	10·9
21	11 35·3	11 37·2	11 03·6	2·1	1·6	8·1	6·3	14·1	10·9
22	11 35·5	11 37·4	11 03·8	2·2	1·7	8·2	6·4	14·2	11·0
23	11 35·8	11 37·7	11 04·1	2·3	1·8	8·3	6·4	14·3	11·1
24	11 36·0	11 37·9	11 04·3	2·4	1·9	8·4	6·5	14·4	11·2
25	11 36·3	11 38·2	11 04·5	2·5	1·9	8·5	6·6	14·5	11·2
26	11 36·5	11 38·4	11 04·8	2·6	2·0	8·6	6·7	14·6	11·3
27	11 36·8	11 38·7	11 05·0	2·7	2·1	8·7	6·7	14·7	11·4
28	11 37·0	11 38·9	11 05·2	2·8	2·2	8·8	6·8	14·8	11·5
29	11 37·3	11 39·2	11 05·5	2·9	2·2	8·9	6·9	14·9	11·5
30	11 37·5	11 39·4	11 05·7	3·0	2·3	9·0	7·0	15·0	11·6
31	11 37·8	11 39·7	11 06·0	3·1	2·4	9·1	7·1	15·1	11·7
32	11 38·0	11 39·9	11 06·2	3·2	2·5	9·2	7·1	15·2	11·8
33	11 38·3	11 40·2	11 06·4	3·3	2·6	9·3	7·2	15·3	11·9
34	11 38·5	11 40·4	11 06·7	3·4	2·6	9·4	7·3	15·4	11·9
35	11 38·8	11 40·7	11 06·9	3·5	2·7	9·5	7·4	15·5	12·0
36	11 39·0	11 40·9	11 07·2	3·6	2·8	9·6	7·4	15·6	12·1
37	11 39·3	11 41·2	11 07·4	3·7	2·9	9·7	7·5	15·7	12·2
38	11 39·5	11 41·4	11 07·6	3·8	2·9	9·8	7·6	15·8	12·2
39	11 39·8	11 41·7	11 07·9	3·9	3·0	9·9	7·7	15·9	12·3
40	11 40·0	11 41·9	11 08·1	4·0	3·1	10·0	7·8	16·0	12·4
41	11 40·3	11 42·2	11 08·3	4·1	3·2	10·1	7·8	16·1	12·5
42	11 40·5	11 42·4	11 08·6	4·2	3·3	10·2	7·9	16·2	12·6
43	11 40·8	11 42·7	11 08·8	4·3	3·3	10·3	8·0	16·3	12·6
44	11 41·0	11 42·9	11 09·1	4·4	3·4	10·4	8·1	16·4	12·7
45	11 41·3	11 43·2	11 09·3	4·5	3·5	10·5	8·1	16·5	12·8
46	11 41·5	11 43·4	11 09·5	4·6	3·6	10·6	8·2	16·6	12·9
47	11 41·8	11 43·7	11 09·8	4·7	3·6	10·7	8·3	16·7	12·9
48	11 42·0	11 43·9	11 10·0	4·8	3·7	10·8	8·4	16·8	13·0
49	11 42·3	11 44·2	11 10·3	4·9	3·8	10·9	8·4	16·9	13·1
50	11 42·5	11 44·4	11 10·5	5·0	3·9	11·0	8·5	17·0	13·2
51	11 42·8	11 44·7	11 10·7	5·1	4·0	11·1	8·6	17·1	13·3
52	11 43·0	11 44·9	11 11·0	5·2	4·0	11·2	8·7	17·2	13·3
53	11 43·3	11 45·2	11 11·2	5·3	4·1	11·3	8·8	17·3	13·4
54	11 43·5	11 45·4	11 11·5	5·4	4·2	11·4	8·8	17·4	13·5
55	11 43·8	11 45·7	11 11·7	5·5	4·3	11·5	8·9	17·5	13·6
56	11 44·0	11 45·9	11 11·9	5·6	4·3	11·6	9·0	17·6	13·6
57	11 44·3	11 46·2	11 12·2	5·7	4·4	11·7	9·1	17·7	13·7
58	11 44·5	11 46·4	11 12·4	5·8	4·5	11·8	9·1	17·8	13·8
59	11 44·8	11 46·7	11 12·6	5·9	4·6	11·9	9·2	17·9	13·9
60	11 45·0	11 46·9	11 12·9	6·0	4·7	12·0	9·3	18·0	14·0

47ᵐ

47ᵐ	SUN PLANETS	ARIES	MOON	v or Corrⁿ d		v or Corrⁿ d		v or Corrⁿ d	
s	° ′	° ′	° ′	′	′	′	′	′	′
00	11 45·0	11 46·9	11 12·9	0·0	0·0	6·0	4·8	12·0	9·5
01	11 45·3	11 47·2	11 13·1	0·1	0·1	6·1	4·8	12·1	9·6
02	11 45·5	11 47·4	11 13·4	0·2	0·2	6·2	4·9	12·2	9·7
03	11 45·8	11 47·7	11 13·6	0·3	0·2	6·3	5·0	12·3	9·7
04	11 46·0	11 47·9	11 13·8	0·4	0·3	6·4	5·1	12·4	9·8
05	11 46·3	11 48·2	11 14·1	0·5	0·4	6·5	5·1	12·5	9·9
06	11 46·5	11 48·4	11 14·3	0·6	0·5	6·6	5·2	12·6	10·0
07	11 46·8	11 48·7	11 14·6	0·7	0·6	6·7	5·3	12·7	10·1
08	11 47·0	11 48·9	11 14·8	0·8	0·6	6·8	5·4	12·8	10·1
09	11 47·3	11 49·2	11 15·0	0·9	0·7	6·9	5·5	12·9	10·2
10	11 47·5	11 49·4	11 15·3	1·0	0·8	7·0	5·5	13·0	10·3
11	11 47·8	11 49·7	11 15·5	1·1	0·9	7·1	5·6	13·1	10·4
12	11 48·0	11 49·9	11 15·7	1·2	1·0	7·2	5·7	13·2	10·5
13	11 48·3	11 50·2	11 16·0	1·3	1·0	7·3	5·8	13·3	10·5
14	11 48·5	11 50·4	11 16·2	1·4	1·1	7·4	5·9	13·4	10·6
15	11 48·8	11 50·7	11 16·5	1·5	1·2	7·5	5·9	13·5	10·7
16	11 49·0	11 50·9	11 16·7	1·6	1·3	7·6	6·0	13·6	10·8
17	11 49·3	11 51·2	11 16·9	1·7	1·3	7·7	6·1	13·7	10·8
18	11 49·5	11 51·4	11 17·2	1·8	1·4	7·8	6·2	13·8	10·9
19	11 49·8	11 51·7	11 17·4	1·9	1·5	7·9	6·3	13·9	11·0
20	11 50·0	11 51·9	11 17·7	2·0	1·6	8·0	6·3	14·0	11·1
21	11 50·3	11 52·2	11 17·9	2·1	1·7	8·1	6·4	14·1	11·2
22	11 50·5	11 52·4	11 18·1	2·2	1·7	8·2	6·5	14·2	11·2
23	11 50·8	11 52·7	11 18·4	2·3	1·8	8·3	6·6	14·3	11·3
24	11 51·0	11 52·9	11 18·6	2·4	1·9	8·4	6·7	14·4	11·4
25	11 51·3	11 53·2	11 18·8	2·5	2·0	8·5	6·7	14·5	11·5
26	11 51·5	11 53·4	11 19·1	2·6	2·1	8·6	6·8	14·6	11·6
27	11 51·8	11 53·7	11 19·3	2·7	2·1	8·7	6·9	14·7	11·6
28	11 52·0	11 53·9	11 19·6	2·8	2·2	8·8	7·0	14·8	11·7
29	11 52·3	11 54·2	11 19·8	2·9	2·3	8·9	7·0	14·9	11·8
30	11 52·5	11 54·5	11 20·0	3·0	2·4	9·0	7·1	15·0	11·9
31	11 52·8	11 54·7	11 20·3	3·1	2·5	9·1	7·2	15·1	12·0
32	11 53·0	11 55·0	11 20·5	3·2	2·5	9·2	7·3	15·2	12·0
33	11 53·3	11 55·2	11 20·8	3·3	2·6	9·3	7·4	15·3	12·1
34	11 53·5	11 55·5	11 21·0	3·4	2·7	9·4	7·4	15·4	12·2
35	11 53·8	11 55·7	11 21·2	3·5	2·8	9·5	7·5	15·5	12·3
36	11 54·0	11 56·0	11 21·5	3·6	2·9	9·6	7·6	15·6	12·4
37	11 54·3	11 56·2	11 21·7	3·7	2·9	9·7	7·7	15·7	12·4
38	11 54·5	11 56·5	11 22·0	3·8	3·0	9·8	7·8	15·8	12·5
39	11 54·8	11 56·7	11 22·2	3·9	3·1	9·9	7·8	15·9	12·6
40	11 55·0	11 57·0	11 22·4	4·0	3·2	10·0	7·9	16·0	12·7
41	11 55·3	11 57·2	11 22·7	4·1	3·2	10·1	8·0	16·1	12·7
42	11 55·5	11 57·5	11 22·9	4·2	3·3	10·2	8·1	16·2	12·8
43	11 55·8	11 57·7	11 23·1	4·3	3·4	10·3	8·2	16·3	12·9
44	11 56·0	11 58·0	11 23·4	4·4	3·5	10·4	8·2	16·4	13·0
45	11 56·3	11 58·2	11 23·6	4·5	3·6	10·5	8·3	16·5	13·1
46	11 56·5	11 58·5	11 23·9	4·6	3·6	10·6	8·4	16·6	13·1
47	11 56·8	11 58·7	11 24·1	4·7	3·7	10·7	8·5	16·7	13·2
48	11 57·0	11 59·0	11 24·3	4·8	3·8	10·8	8·5	16·8	13·3
49	11 57·3	11 59·2	11 24·6	4·9	3·9	10·9	8·6	16·9	13·4
50	11 57·5	11 59·5	11 24·8	5·0	4·0	11·0	8·7	17·0	13·5
51	11 57·8	11 59·7	11 25·1	5·1	4·0	11·1	8·8	17·1	13·5
52	11 58·0	12 00·0	11 25·3	5·2	4·1	11·2	8·9	17·2	13·6
53	11 58·3	12 00·2	11 25·5	5·3	4·2	11·3	8·9	17·3	13·7
54	11 58·5	12 00·5	11 25·8	5·4	4·3	11·4	9·0	17·4	13·8
55	11 58·8	12 00·7	11 26·0	5·5	4·4	11·5	9·1	17·5	13·9
56	11 59·0	12 01·0	11 26·2	5·6	4·4	11·6	9·2	17·6	13·9
57	11 59·3	12 01·2	11 26·5	5·7	4·5	11·7	9·3	17·7	14·0
58	11 59·5	12 01·5	11 26·7	5·8	4·6	11·8	9·3	17·8	14·1
59	11 59·8	12 01·7	11 27·0	5·9	4·7	11·9	9·4	17·9	14·2
60	12 00·0	12 02·0	11 27·2	6·0	4·8	12·0	9·5	18·0	14·3

48ᵐ	SUN PLANETS	ARIES	MOON	v or Corrⁿ d		v or Corrⁿ d		v or Corrⁿ d	
s	° ′	° ′	° ′	′	′	′	′	′	′
00	12 00·0	12 02·0	11 27·2	0·0	0·0	6·0	4·9	12·0	9·7
01	12 00·3	12 02·2	11 27·4	0·1	0·1	6·1	4·9	12·1	9·8
02	12 00·5	12 02·5	11 27·7	0·2	0·2	6·2	5·0	12·2	9·9
03	12 00·8	12 02·7	11 27·9	0·3	0·2	6·3	5·1	12·3	9·9
04	12 01·0	12 03·0	11 28·2	0·4	0·3	6·4	5·2	12·4	10·0
05	12 01·3	12 03·2	11 28·4	0·5	0·4	6·5	5·3	12·5	10·1
06	12 01·5	12 03·5	11 28·6	0·6	0·5	6·6	5·3	12·6	10·2
07	12 01·8	12 03·7	11 28·9	0·7	0·6	6·7	5·4	12·7	10·3
08	12 02·0	12 04·0	11 29·1	0·8	0·6	6·8	5·5	12·8	10·3
09	12 02·3	12 04·2	11 29·3	0·9	0·7	6·9	5·6	12·9	10·4
10	12 02·5	12 04·5	11 29·6	1·0	0·8	7·0	5·7	13·0	10·5
11	12 02·8	12 04·7	11 29·8	1·1	0·9	7·1	5·7	13·1	10·6
12	12 03·0	12 05·0	11 30·1	1·2	1·0	7·2	5·8	13·2	10·7
13	12 03·3	12 05·2	11 30·3	1·3	1·1	7·3	5·9	13·3	10·8
14	12 03·5	12 05·5	11 30·5	1·4	1·1	7·4	6·0	13·4	10·8
15	12 03·8	12 05·7	11 30·8	1·5	1·2	7·5	6·1	13·5	10·9
16	12 04·0	12 06·0	11 31·0	1·6	1·3	7·6	6·1	13·6	11·0
17	12 04·3	12 06·2	11 31·3	1·7	1·4	7·7	6·2	13·7	11·1
18	12 04·5	12 06·5	11 31·5	1·8	1·5	7·8	6·3	13·8	11·2
19	12 04·8	12 06·7	11 31·7	1·9	1·5	7·9	6·4	13·9	11·2
20	12 05·0	12 07·0	11 32·0	2·0	1·6	8·0	6·5	14·0	11·3
21	12 05·3	12 07·2	11 32·2	2·1	1·7	8·1	6·5	14·1	11·4
22	12 05·5	12 07·5	11 32·4	2·2	1·8	8·2	6·6	14·2	11·5
23	12 05·8	12 07·7	11 32·7	2·3	1·9	8·3	6·7	14·3	11·6
24	12 06·0	12 08·0	11 32·9	2·4	1·9	8·4	6·8	14·4	11·6
25	12 06·3	12 08·2	11 33·2	2·5	2·0	8·5	6·9	14·5	11·7
26	12 06·5	12 08·5	11 33·4	2·6	2·1	8·6	7·0	14·6	11·8
27	12 06·8	12 08·7	11 33·6	2·7	2·2	8·7	7·0	14·7	11·9
28	12 07·0	12 09·0	11 33·9	2·8	2·3	8·8	7·1	14·8	12·0
29	12 07·3	12 09·2	11 34·1	2·9	2·3	8·9	7·2	14·9	12·0
30	12 07·5	12 09·5	11 34·4	3·0	2·4	9·0	7·3	15·0	12·1
31	12 07·8	12 09·7	11 34·6	3·1	2·5	9·1	7·4	15·1	12·2
32	12 08·0	12 10·0	11 34·8	3·2	2·6	9·2	7·4	15·2	12·3
33	12 08·3	12 10·2	11 35·1	3·3	2·7	9·3	7·5	15·3	12·4
34	12 08·5	12 10·5	11 35·3	3·4	2·7	9·4	7·6	15·4	12·4
35	12 08·8	12 10·7	11 35·6	3·5	2·8	9·5	7·7	15·5	12·5
36	12 09·0	12 11·0	11 35·8	3·6	2·9	9·6	7·8	15·6	12·6
37	12 09·3	12 11·2	11 36·0	3·7	3·0	9·7	7·8	15·7	12·7
38	12 09·5	12 11·5	11 36·3	3·8	3·1	9·8	7·9	15·8	12·8
39	12 09·8	12 11·7	11 36·5	3·9	3·2	9·9	8·0	15·9	12·9
40	12 10·0	12 12·0	11 36·7	4·0	3·2	10·0	8·1	16·0	12·9
41	12 10·3	12 12·2	11 37·0	4·1	3·3	10·1	8·2	16·1	13·0
42	12 10·5	12 12·5	11 37·2	4·2	3·4	10·2	8·2	16·2	13·1
43	12 10·8	12 12·8	11 37·5	4·3	3·5	10·3	8·3	16·3	13·2
44	12 11·0	12 13·0	11 37·7	4·4	3·6	10·4	8·4	16·4	13·3
45	12 11·3	12 13·3	11 37·9	4·5	3·6	10·5	8·5	16·5	13·3
46	12 11·5	12 13·5	11 38·2	4·6	3·7	10·6	8·6	16·6	13·4
47	12 11·8	12 13·8	11 38·4	4·7	3·8	10·7	8·6	16·7	13·5
48	12 12·0	12 14·0	11 38·7	4·8	3·9	10·8	8·7	16·8	13·6
49	12 12·3	12 14·3	11 38·9	4·9	4·0	10·9	8·8	16·9	13·7
50	12 12·5	12 14·5	11 39·1	5·0	4·0	11·0	8·9	17·0	13·7
51	12 12·8	12 14·8	11 39·4	5·1	4·1	11·1	9·0	17·1	13·8
52	12 13·0	12 15·0	11 39·6	5·2	4·2	11·2	9·1	17·2	13·9
53	12 13·3	12 15·3	11 39·8	5·3	4·3	11·3	9·1	17·3	14·0
54	12 13·5	12 15·5	11 40·1	5·4	4·4	11·4	9·2	17·4	14·1
55	12 13·8	12 15·8	11 40·3	5·5	4·4	11·5	9·3	17·5	14·1
56	12 14·0	12 16·0	11 40·6	5·6	4·5	11·6	9·4	17·6	14·2
57	12 14·3	12 16·3	11 40·8	5·7	4·6	11·7	9·5	17·7	14·3
58	12 14·5	12 16·5	11 41·0	5·8	4·7	11·8	9·5	17·8	14·4
59	12 14·8	12 16·8	11 41·3	5·9	4·8	11·9	9·6	17·9	14·5
60	12 15·0	12 17·0	11 41·5	6·0	4·9	12·0	9·7	18·0	14·6

49ᵐ	SUN PLANETS	ARIES	MOON	v or Corrⁿ d		v or Corrⁿ d		v or Corrⁿ d	
s	° ′	° ′	° ′	′	′	′	′	′	′
00	12 15·0	12 17·0	11 41·5	0·0	0·0	6·0	5·0	12·0	9·9
01	12 15·3	12 17·3	11 41·8	0·1	0·1	6·1	5·0	12·1	10·0
02	12 15·5	12 17·5	11 42·0	0·2	0·2	6·2	5·1	12·2	10·1
03	12 15·8	12 17·8	11 42·2	0·3	0·2	6·3	5·2	12·3	10·1
04	12 16·0	12 18·0	11 42·5	0·4	0·3	6·4	5·3	12·4	10·2
05	12 16·3	12 18·3	11 42·7	0·5	0·4	6·5	5·4	12·5	10·3
06	12 16·5	12 18·5	11 42·9	0·6	0·5	6·6	5·4	12·6	10·4
07	12 16·8	12 18·8	11 43·2	0·7	0·6	6·7	5·5	12·7	10·5
08	12 17·0	12 19·0	11 43·4	0·8	0·7	6·8	5·6	12·8	10·6
09	12 17·3	12 19·3	11 43·7	0·9	0·7	6·9	5·7	12·9	10·6
10	12 17·5	12 19·5	11 43·9	1·0	0·8	7·0	5·8	13·0	10·7
11	12 17·8	12 19·8	11 44·1	1·1	0·9	7·1	5·9	13·1	10·8
12	12 18·0	12 20·0	11 44·4	1·2	1·0	7·2	5·9	13·2	10·9
13	12 18·3	12 20·3	11 44·6	1·3	1·1	7·3	6·0	13·3	11·0
14	12 18·5	12 20·5	11 44·9	1·4	1·2	7·4	6·1	13·4	11·1
15	12 18·8	12 20·8	11 45·1	1·5	1·2	7·5	6·2	13·5	11·1
16	12 19·0	12 21·0	11 45·3	1·6	1·3	7·6	6·3	13·6	11·2
17	12 19·3	12 21·3	11 45·6	1·7	1·4	7·7	6·4	13·7	11·3
18	12 19·5	12 21·5	11 45·8	1·8	1·5	7·8	6·4	13·8	11·4
19	12 19·8	12 21·8	11 46·1	1·9	1·6	7·9	6·5	13·9	11·5
20	12 20·0	12 22·0	11 46·3	2·0	1·7	8·0	6·6	14·0	11·6
21	12 20·3	12 22·3	11 46·5	2·1	1·7	8·1	6·7	14·1	11·6
22	12 20·5	12 22·5	11 46·8	2·2	1·8	8·2	6·8	14·2	11·7
23	12 20·8	12 22·8	11 47·0	2·3	1·9	8·3	6·8	14·3	11·8
24	12 21·0	12 23·0	11 47·2	2·4	2·0	8·4	6·9	14·4	11·9
25	12 21·3	12 23·3	11 47·5	2·5	2·1	8·5	7·0	14·5	12·0
26	12 21·5	12 23·5	11 47·7	2·6	2·1	8·6	7·1	14·6	12·0
27	12 21·8	12 23·8	11 48·0	2·7	2·2	8·7	7·2	14·7	12·1
28	12 22·0	12 24·0	11 48·2	2·8	2·3	8·8	7·3	14·8	12·2
29	12 22·3	12 24·3	11 48·4	2·9	2·4	8·9	7·3	14·9	12·3
30	12 22·5	12 24·5	11 48·7	3·0	2·5	9·0	7·4	15·0	12·4
31	12 22·8	12 24·8	11 48·9	3·1	2·6	9·1	7·5	15·1	12·5
32	12 23·0	12 25·0	11 49·2	3·2	2·6	9·2	7·6	15·2	12·5
33	12 23·3	12 25·3	11 49·4	3·3	2·7	9·3	7·7	15·3	12·6
34	12 23·5	12 25·5	11 49·6	3·4	2·8	9·4	7·8	15·4	12·7
35	12 23·8	12 25·8	11 49·9	3·5	2·9	9·5	7·8	15·5	12·8
36	12 24·0	12 26·0	11 50·1	3·6	3·0	9·6	7·9	15·6	12·9
37	12 24·3	12 26·3	11 50·3	3·7	3·1	9·7	8·0	15·7	13·0
38	12 24·5	12 26·5	11 50·6	3·8	3·1	9·8	8·1	15·8	13·0
39	12 24·8	12 26·8	11 50·8	3·9	3·2	9·9	8·2	15·9	13·1
40	12 25·0	12 27·0	11 51·1	4·0	3·3	10·0	8·3	16·0	13·2
41	12 25·3	12 27·3	11 51·3	4·1	3·4	10·1	8·3	16·1	13·3
42	12 25·5	12 27·5	11 51·5	4·2	3·5	10·2	8·4	16·2	13·4
43	12 25·8	12 27·8	11 51·8	4·3	3·5	10·3	8·5	16·3	13·4
44	12 26·0	12 28·0	11 52·0	4·4	3·6	10·4	8·6	16·4	13·5
45	12 26·3	12 28·3	11 52·3	4·5	3·7	10·5	8·7	16·5	13·6
46	12 26·5	12 28·5	11 52·5	4·6	3·8	10·6	8·7	16·6	13·7
47	12 26·8	12 28·8	11 52·7	4·7	3·9	10·7	8·8	16·7	13·8
48	12 27·0	12 29·0	11 53·0	4·8	4·0	10·8	8·9	16·8	13·9
49	12 27·3	12 29·3	11 53·2	4·9	4·0	10·9	9·0	16·9	13·9
50	12 27·5	12 29·5	11 53·4	5·0	4·1	11·0	9·1	17·0	14·0
51	12 27·8	12 29·8	11 53·7	5·1	4·2	11·1	9·2	17·1	14·1
52	12 28·0	12 30·0	11 53·9	5·2	4·3	11·2	9·2	17·2	14·2
53	12 28·3	12 30·3	11 54·2	5·3	4·4	11·3	9·3	17·3	14·3
54	12 28·5	12 30·5	11 54·4	5·4	4·5	11·4	9·4	17·4	14·4
55	12 28·8	12 30·8	11 54·6	5·5	4·5	11·5	9·5	17·5	14·4
56	12 29·0	12 31·1	11 54·9	5·6	4·6	11·6	9·6	17·6	14·5
57	12 29·3	12 31·3	11 55·1	5·7	4·7	11·7	9·7	17·7	14·6
58	12 29·5	12 31·6	11 55·4	5·8	4·8	11·8	9·7	17·8	14·7
59	12 29·8	12 31·8	11 55·6	5·9	4·9	11·9	9·8	17·9	14·8
60	12 30·0	12 32·1	11 55·8	6·0	5·0	12·0	9·9	18·0	14·9

50ᵐ	SUN PLANETS	ARIES	MOON	v or Corrⁿ d	v or Corrⁿ d	v or Corrⁿ d
s	° ′	° ′	° ′	′ ′	′ ′	′ ′
00	12 30·0	12 32·1	11 55·8	0·0 0·0	6·0 5·1	12·0 10·1
01	12 30·3	12 32·3	11 56·1	0·1 0·1	6·1 5·2	12·1 10·2
02	12 30·5	12 32·6	11 56·3	0·2 0·2	6·2 5·2	12·2 10·3
03	12 30·8	12 32·8	11 56·5	0·3 0·3	6·3 5·3	12·3 10·4
04	12 31·0	12 33·1	11 56·8	0·4 0·3	6·4 5·4	12·4 10·4
05	12 31·3	12 33·3	11 57·0	0·5 0·4	6·5 5·5	12·5 10·5
06	12 31·5	12 33·6	11 57·3	0·6 0·5	6·6 5·6	12·6 10·6
07	12 31·8	12 33·8	11 57·5	0·7 0·6	6·7 5·6	12·7 10·7
08	12 32·0	12 34·1	11 57·7	0·8 0·7	6·8 5·7	12·8 10·8
09	12 32·3	12 34·3	11 58·0	0·9 0·8	6·9 5·8	12·9 10·9
10	12 32·5	12 34·6	11 58·2	1·0 0·8	7·0 5·9	13·0 10·9
11	12 32·8	12 34·8	11 58·5	1·1 0·9	7·1 6·0	13·1 11·0
12	12 33·0	12 35·1	11 58·7	1·2 1·0	7·2 6·1	13·2 11·1
13	12 33·3	12 35·3	11 58·9	1·3 1·1	7·3 6·1	13·3 11·2
14	12 33·5	12 35·6	11 59·2	1·4 1·2	7·4 6·2	13·4 11·3
15	12 33·8	12 35·8	11 59·4	1·5 1·3	7·5 6·3	13·5 11·4
16	12 34·0	12 36·1	11 59·7	1·6 1·3	7·6 6·4	13·6 11·4
17	12 34·3	12 36·3	11 59·9	1·7 1·4	7·7 6·5	13·7 11·5
18	12 34·5	12 36·6	12 00·1	1·8 1·5	7·8 6·6	13·8 11·6
19	12 34·8	12 36·8	12 00·4	1·9 1·6	7·9 6·6	13·9 11·7
20	12 35·0	12 37·1	12 00·6	2·0 1·7	8·0 6·7	14·0 11·8
21	12 35·3	12 37·3	12 00·8	2·1 1·8	8·1 6·8	14·1 11·9
22	12 35·5	12 37·6	12 01·1	2·2 1·9	8·2 6·9	14·2 12·0
23	12 35·8	12 37·8	12 01·3	2·3 1·9	8·3 7·0	14·3 12·0
24	12 36·0	12 38·1	12 01·6	2·4 2·0	8·4 7·1	14·4 12·1
25	12 36·3	12 38·3	12 01·8	2·5 2·1	8·5 7·2	14·5 12·2
26	12 36·5	12 38·6	12 02·0	2·6 2·2	8·6 7·2	14·6 12·3
27	12 36·8	12 38·8	12 02·3	2·7 2·3	8·7 7·3	14·7 12·4
28	12 37·0	12 39·1	12 02·5	2·8 2·4	8·8 7·4	14·8 12·5
29	12 37·3	12 39·3	12 02·8	2·9 2·4	8·9 7·5	14·9 12·5
30	12 37·5	12 39·6	12 03·0	3·0 2·5	9·0 7·6	15·0 12·6
31	12 37·8	12 39·8	12 03·2	3·1 2·6	9·1 7·7	15·1 12·7
32	12 38·0	12 40·1	12 03·5	3·2 2·7	9·2 7·7	15·2 12·8
33	12 38·3	12 40·3	12 03·7	3·3 2·8	9·3 7·8	15·3 12·9
34	12 38·5	12 40·6	12 03·9	3·4 2·9	9·4 7·9	15·4 13·0
35	12 38·8	12 40·8	12 04·2	3·5 2·9	9·5 8·0	15·5 13·0
36	12 39·0	12 41·1	12 04·4	3·6 3·0	9·6 8·1	15·6 13·1
37	12 39·3	12 41·3	12 04·7	3·7 3·1	9·7 8·2	15·7 13·2
38	12 39·5	12 41·6	12 04·9	3·8 3·2	9·8 8·2	15·8 13·3
39	12 39·8	12 41·8	12 05·1	3·9 3·3	9·9 8·3	15·9 13·4
40	12 40·0	12 42·1	12 05·4	4·0 3·4	10·0 8·4	16·0 13·5
41	12 40·3	12 42·3	12 05·6	4·1 3·5	10·1 8·5	16·1 13·6
42	12 40·5	12 42·6	12 05·9	4·2 3·5	10·2 8·6	16·2 13·6
43	12 40·8	12 42·8	12 06·1	4·3 3·6	10·3 8·7	16·3 13·7
44	12 41·0	12 43·1	12 06·3	4·4 3·7	10·4 8·8	16·4 13·8
45	12 41·3	12 43·3	12 06·6	4·5 3·8	10·5 8·8	16·5 13·9
46	12 41·5	12 43·6	12 06·8	4·6 3·9	10·6 8·9	16·6 14·0
47	12 41·8	12 43·8	12 07·0	4·7 4·0	10·7 9·0	16·7 14·1
48	12 42·0	12 44·1	12 07·3	4·8 4·0	10·8 9·1	16·8 14·1
49	12 42·3	12 44·3	12 07·5	4·9 4·1	10·9 9·2	16·9 14·2
50	12 42·5	12 44·6	12 07·8	5·0 4·2	11·0 9·3	17·0 14·3
51	12 42·8	12 44·8	12 08·0	5·1 4·3	11·1 9·3	17·1 14·4
52	12 43·0	12 45·1	12 08·2	5·2 4·4	11·2 9·4	17·2 14·5
53	12 43·3	12 45·3	12 08·5	5·3 4·5	11·3 9·5	17·3 14·6
54	12 43·5	12 45·6	12 08·7	5·4 4·5	11·4 9·6	17·4 14·6
55	12 43·8	12 45·8	12 09·0	5·5 4·6	11·5 9·7	17·5 14·7
56	12 44·0	12 46·1	12 09·2	5·6 4·7	11·6 9·8	17·6 14·8
57	12 44·3	12 46·3	12 09·4	5·7 4·8	11·7 9·8	17·7 14·9
58	12 44·5	12 46·6	12 09·7	5·8 4·9	11·8 9·9	17·8 15·0
59	12 44·8	12 46·8	12 09·9	5·9 5·0	11·9 10·0	17·9 15·1
60	12 45·0	12 47·1	12 10·2	6·0 5·1	12·0 10·1	18·0 15·2

51ᵐ	SUN PLANETS	ARIES	MOON	v or Corrⁿ d	v or Corrⁿ d	v or Corrⁿ d
s	° ′	° ′	° ′	′ ′	′ ′	′ ′
00	12 45·0	12 47·1	12 10·2	0·0 0·0	6·0 5·2	12·0 10·3
01	12 45·3	12 47·3	12 10·4	0·1 0·1	6·1 5·2	12·1 10·4
02	12 45·5	12 47·6	12 10·6	0·2 0·2	6·2 5·3	12·2 10·5
03	12 45·8	12 47·8	12 10·9	0·3 0·3	6·3 5·4	12·3 10·6
04	12 46·0	12 48·1	12 11·1	0·4 0·3	6·4 5·5	12·4 10·6
05	12 46·3	12 48·3	12 11·3	0·5 0·4	6·5 5·6	12·5 10·7
06	12 46·5	12 48·6	12 11·6	0·6 0·5	6·6 5·7	12·6 10·8
07	12 46·8	12 48·8	12 11·8	0·7 0·6	6·7 5·8	12·7 10·9
08	12 47·0	12 49·1	12 12·1	0·8 0·7	6·8 5·8	12·8 11·0
09	12 47·3	12 49·4	12 12·3	0·9 0·8	6·9 5·9	12·9 11·1
10	12 47·5	12 49·6	12 12·5	1·0 0·9	7·0 6·0	13·0 11·2
11	12 47·8	12 49·9	12 12·8	1·1 0·9	7·1 6·1	13·1 11·2
12	12 48·0	12 50·1	12 13·0	1·2 1·0	7·2 6·2	13·2 11·3
13	12 48·3	12 50·4	12 13·3	1·3 1·1	7·3 6·3	13·3 11·4
14	12 48·5	12 50·6	12 13·5	1·4 1·2	7·4 6·4	13·4 11·5
15	12 48·8	12 50·9	12 13·7	1·5 1·3	7·5 6·4	13·5 11·6
16	12 49·0	12 51·1	12 14·0	1·6 1·4	7·6 6·5	13·6 11·7
17	12 49·3	12 51·4	12 14·2	1·7 1·5	7·7 6·6	13·7 11·8
18	12 49·5	12 51·6	12 14·4	1·8 1·5	7·8 6·7	13·8 11·8
19	12 49·8	12 51·9	12 14·7	1·9 1·6	7·9 6·8	13·9 11·9
20	12 50·0	12 52·1	12 14·9	2·0 1·7	8·0 6·9	14·0 12·0
21	12 50·3	12 52·4	12 15·2	2·1 1·8	8·1 7·0	14·1 12·1
22	12 50·5	12 52·6	12 15·4	2·2 1·9	8·2 7·0	14·2 12·2
23	12 50·8	12 52·9	12 15·6	2·3 2·0	8·3 7·1	14·3 12·3
24	12 51·0	12 53·1	12 15·9	2·4 2·1	8·4 7·2	14·4 12·4
25	12 51·3	12 53·4	12 16·1	2·5 2·1	8·5 7·3	14·5 12·4
26	12 51·5	12 53·6	12 16·4	2·6 2·2	8·6 7·4	14·6 12·5
27	12 51·8	12 53·9	12 16·6	2·7 2·3	8·7 7·5	14·7 12·6
28	12 52·0	12 54·1	12 16·8	2·8 2·4	8·8 7·6	14·8 12·7
29	12 52·3	12 54·4	12 17·1	2·9 2·5	8·9 7·6	14·9 12·8
30	12 52·5	12 54·6	12 17·3	3·0 2·6	9·0 7·7	15·0 12·9
31	12 52·8	12 54·9	12 17·5	3·1 2·7	9·1 7·8	15·1 13·0
32	12 53·0	12 55·1	12 17·8	3·2 2·7	9·2 7·9	15·2 13·0
33	12 53·3	12 55·4	12 18·0	3·3 2·8	9·3 8·0	15·3 13·1
34	12 53·5	12 55·6	12 18·3	3·4 2·9	9·4 8·1	15·4 13·2
35	12 53·8	12 55·9	12 18·5	3·5 3·0	9·5 8·2	15·5 13·3
36	12 54·0	12 56·1	12 18·7	3·6 3·1	9·6 8·2	15·6 13·4
37	12 54·3	12 56·4	12 19·0	3·7 3·2	9·7 8·3	15·7 13·5
38	12 54·5	12 56·6	12 19·2	3·8 3·3	9·8 8·4	15·8 13·6
39	12 54·8	12 56·9	12 19·5	3·9 3·3	9·9 8·5	15·9 13·6
40	12 55·0	12 57·1	12 19·7	4·0 3·4	10·0 8·6	16·0 13·7
41	12 55·3	12 57·4	12 19·9	4·1 3·5	10·1 8·7	16·1 13·8
42	12 55·5	12 57·6	12 20·2	4·2 3·6	10·2 8·8	16·2 13·9
43	12 55·8	12 57·9	12 20·4	4·3 3·7	10·3 8·8	16·3 14·0
44	12 56·0	12 58·1	12 20·6	4·4 3·8	10·4 8·9	16·4 14·1
45	12 56·3	12 58·4	12 20·9	4·5 3·9	10·5 9·0	16·5 14·2
46	12 56·5	12 58·6	12 21·1	4·6 3·9	10·6 9·1	16·6 14·2
47	12 56·8	12 58·9	12 21·4	4·7 4·0	10·7 9·2	16·7 14·3
48	12 57·0	12 59·1	12 21·6	4·8 4·1	10·8 9·3	16·8 14·4
49	12 57·3	12 59·4	12 21·8	4·9 4·2	10·9 9·4	16·9 14·5
50	12 57·5	12 59·6	12 22·1	5·0 4·3	11·0 9·4	17·0 14·6
51	12 57·8	12 59·9	12 22·3	5·1 4·4	11·1 9·5	17·1 14·7
52	12 58·0	13 00·1	12 22·6	5·2 4·5	11·2 9·6	17·2 14·8
53	12 58·3	13 00·4	12 22·8	5·3 4·5	11·3 9·7	17·3 14·8
54	12 58·5	13 00·6	12 23·0	5·4 4·6	11·4 9·8	17·4 14·9
55	12 58·8	13 00·9	12 23·3	5·5 4·7	11·5 9·9	17·5 15·0
56	12 59·0	13 01·1	12 23·5	5·6 4·8	11·6 10·0	17·6 15·1
57	12 59·3	13 01·4	12 23·8	5·7 4·9	11·7 10·0	17·7 15·2
58	12 59·5	13 01·6	12 24·0	5·8 5·0	11·8 10·1	17·8 15·3
59	12 59·8	13 01·9	12 24·2	5·9 5·1	11·9 10·2	17·9 15·4
60	13 00·0	13 02·1	12 24·5	6·0 5·2	12·0 10·3	18·0 15·5

52ᵐ	SUN PLANETS	ARIES	MOON	v or Corrⁿ d	v or Corrⁿ d	v or Corrⁿ d	53ᵐ	SUN PLANETS	ARIES	MOON	v or Corrⁿ d	v or Corrⁿ d	v or Corrⁿ d
s	° ′	° ′	° ′	′ ′	′ ′	′ ′	s	° ′	° ′	° ′	′ ′	′ ′	′ ′
00	13 00·0	13 02·1	12 24·5	0·0 0·0	6·0 5·3	12·0 10·5	00	13 15·0	13 17·2	12 38·8	0·0 0·0	6·0 5·4	12·0 10·7
01	13 00·3	13 02·4	12 24·7	0·1 0·1	6·1 5·3	12·1 10·6	01	13 15·3	13 17·4	12 39·0	0·1 0·1	6·1 5·4	12·1 10·8
02	13 00·5	13 02·6	12 24·9	0·2 0·2	6·2 5·4	12·2 10·7	02	13 15·5	13 17·7	12 39·3	0·2 0·2	6·2 5·5	12·2 10·9
03	13 00·8	13 02·9	12 25·2	0·3 0·3	6·3 5·5	12·3 10·8	03	13 15·8	13 17·9	12 39·5	0·3 0·3	6·3 5·6	12·3 11·0
04	13 01·0	13 03·1	12 25·4	0·4 0·4	6·4 5·6	12·4 10·9	04	13 16·0	13 18·2	12 39·7	0·4 0·4	6·4 5·7	12·4 11·1
05	13 01·3	13 03·4	12 25·7	0·5 0·4	6·5 5·7	12·5 10·9	05	13 16·3	13 18·4	12 40·0	0·5 0·4	6·5 5·8	12·5 11·1
06	13 01·5	13 03·6	12 25·9	0·6 0·5	6·6 5·8	12·6 11·0	06	13 16·5	13 18·7	12 40·2	0·6 0·5	6·6 5·9	12·6 11·2
07	13 01·8	13 03·9	12 26·1	0·7 0·6	6·7 5·9	12·7 11·1	07	13 16·8	13 18·9	12 40·5	0·7 0·6	6·7 6·0	12·7 11·3
08	13 02·0	13 04·1	12 26·4	0·8 0·7	6·8 6·0	12·8 11·2	08	13 17·0	13 19·2	12 40·7	0·8 0·7	6·8 6·1	12·8 11·4
09	13 02·3	13 04·4	12 26·6	0·9 0·8	6·9 6·0	12·9 11·3	09	13 17·3	13 19·4	12 40·9	0·9 0·8	6·9 6·2	12·9 11·5
10	13 02·5	13 04·6	12 26·9	1·0 0·9	7·0 6·1	13·0 11·4	10	13 17·5	13 19·7	12 41·2	1·0 0·9	7·0 6·2	13·0 11·6
11	13 02·8	13 04·9	12 27·1	1·1 1·0	7·1 6·2	13·1 11·5	11	13 17·8	13 19·9	12 41·4	1·1 1·0	7·1 6·3	13·1 11·7
12	13 03·0	13 05·1	12 27·3	1·2 1·1	7·2 6·3	13·2 11·6	12	13 18·0	13 20·2	12 41·6	1·2 1·1	7·2 6·4	13·2 11·8
13	13 03·3	13 05·4	12 27·6	1·3 1·1	7·3 6·4	13·3 11·6	13	13 18·3	13 20·4	12 41·9	1·3 1·2	7·3 6·5	13·3 11·9
14	13 03·5	13 05·6	12 27·8	1·4 1·2	7·4 6·5	13·4 11·7	14	13 18·5	13 20·7	12 42·1	1·4 1·2	7·4 6·6	13·4 11·9
15	13 03·8	13 05·9	12 28·0	1·5 1·3	7·5 6·6	13·5 11·8	15	13 18·8	13 20·9	12 42·4	1·5 1·3	7·5 6·7	13·5 12·0
16	13 04·0	13 06·1	12 28·3	1·6 1·4	7·6 6·7	13·6 11·9	16	13 19·0	13 21·2	12 42·6	1·6 1·4	7·6 6·8	13·6 12·1
17	13 04·3	13 06·4	12 28·5	1·7 1·5	7·7 6·7	13·7 12·0	17	13 19·3	13 21·4	12 42·8	1·7 1·5	7·7 6·9	13·7 12·2
18	13 04·5	13 06·6	12 28·8	1·8 1·6	7·8 6·8	13·8 12·1	18	13 19·5	13 21·7	12 43·1	1·8 1·6	7·8 7·0	13·8 12·3
19	13 04·8	13 06·9	12 29·0	1·9 1·7	7·9 6·9	13·9 12·2	19	13 19·8	13 21·9	12 43·3	1·9 1·7	7·9 7·0	13·9 12·4
20	13 05·0	13 07·1	12 29·2	2·0 1·8	8·0 7·0	14·0 12·3	20	13 20·0	13 22·2	12 43·6	2·0 1·8	8·0 7·1	14·0 12·5
21	13 05·3	13 07·4	12 29·5	2·1 1·8	8·1 7·1	14·1 12·3	21	13 20·3	13 22·4	12 43·8	2·1 1·9	8·1 7·2	14·1 12·6
22	13 05·5	13 07·7	12 29·7	2·2 1·9	8·2 7·2	14·2 12·4	22	13 20·5	13 22·7	12 44·0	2·2 2·0	8·2 7·3	14·2 12·7
23	13 05·8	13 07·9	12 30·0	2·3 2·0	8·3 7·3	14·3 12·5	23	13 20·8	13 22·9	12 44·3	2·3 2·1	8·3 7·4	14·3 12·8
24	13 06·0	13 08·2	12 30·2	2·4 2·1	8·4 7·4	14·4 12·6	24	13 21·0	13 23·2	12 44·5	2·4 2·1	8·4 7·5	14·4 12·8
25	13 06·3	13 08·4	12 30·4	2·5 2·2	8·5 7·4	14·5 12·7	25	13 21·3	13 23·4	12 44·7	2·5 2·2	8·5 7·6	14·5 12·9
26	13 06·5	13 08·7	12 30·7	2·6 2·3	8·6 7·5	14·6 12·8	26	13 21·5	13 23·7	12 45·0	2·6 2·3	8·6 7·7	14·6 13·0
27	13 06·8	13 08·9	12 30·9	2·7 2·4	8·7 7·6	14·7 12·9	27	13 21·8	13 23·9	12 45·2	2·7 2·4	8·7 7·8	14·7 13·1
28	13 07·0	13 09·2	12 31·1	2·8 2·5	8·8 7·7	14·8 13·0	28	13 22·0	13 24·2	12 45·5	2·8 2·5	8·8 7·8	14·8 13·2
29	13 07·3	13 09·4	12 31·4	2·9 2·5	8·9 7·8	14·9 13·0	29	13 22·3	13 24·4	12 45·7	2·9 2·6	8·9 7·9	14·9 13·3
30	13 07·5	13 09·7	12 31·6	3·0 2·6	9·0 7·9	15·0 13·1	30	13 22·5	13 24·7	12 45·9	3·0 2·7	9·0 8·0	15·0 13·4
31	13 07·8	13 09·9	12 31·9	3·1 2·7	9·1 8·0	15·1 13·2	31	13 22·8	13 24·9	12 46·2	3·1 2·8	9·1 8·1	15·1 13·5
32	13 08·0	13 10·2	12 32·1	3·2 2·8	9·2 8·1	15·2 13·3	32	13 23·0	13 25·2	12 46·4	3·2 2·9	9·2 8·2	15·2 13·6
33	13 08·3	13 10·4	12 32·3	3·3 2·9	9·3 8·1	15·3 13·4	33	13 23·3	13 25·4	12 46·7	3·3 2·9	9·3 8·3	15·3 13·6
34	13 08·5	13 10·7	12 32·6	3·4 3·0	9·4 8·2	15·4 13·5	34	13 23·5	13 25·7	12 46·9	3·4 3·0	9·4 8·4	15·4 13·7
35	13 08·8	13 10·9	12 32·8	3·5 3·1	9·5 8·3	15·5 13·6	35	13 23·8	13 26·0	12 47·1	3·5 3·1	9·5 8·5	15·5 13·8
36	13 09·0	13 11·2	12 33·1	3·6 3·2	9·6 8·4	15·6 13·7	36	13 24·0	13 26·2	12 47·4	3·6 3·2	9·6 8·6	15·6 13·9
37	13 09·3	13 11·4	12 33·3	3·7 3·2	9·7 8·5	15·7 13·7	37	13 24·3	13 26·5	12 47·6	3·7 3·3	9·7 8·6	15·7 14·0
38	13 09·5	13 11·7	12 33·5	3·8 3·3	9·8 8·6	15·8 13·8	38	13 24·5	13 26·7	12 47·9	3·8 3·4	9·8 8·7	15·8 14·1
39	13 09·8	13 11·9	12 33·8	3·9 3·4	9·9 8·7	15·9 13·9	39	13 24·8	13 27·0	12 48·1	3·9 3·5	9·9 8·8	15·9 14·2
40	13 10·0	13 12·2	12 34·0	4·0 3·5	10·0 8·8	16·0 14·0	40	13 25·0	13 27·2	12 48·3	4·0 3·6	10·0 8·9	16·0 14·3
41	13 10·3	13 12·4	12 34·2	4·1 3·6	10·1 8·8	16·1 14·1	41	13 25·3	13 27·5	12 48·6	4·1 3·7	10·1 9·0	16·1 14·4
42	13 10·5	13 12·7	12 34·5	4·2 3·7	10·2 8·9	16·2 14·2	42	13 25·5	13 27·7	12 48·8	4·2 3·7	10·2 9·1	16·2 14·4
43	13 10·8	13 12·9	12 34·7	4·3 3·8	10·3 9·0	16·3 14·3	43	13 25·8	13 28·0	12 49·0	4·3 3·8	10·3 9·2	16·3 14·5
44	13 11·0	13 13·2	12 35·0	4·4 3·9	10·4 9·1	16·4 14·4	44	13 26·0	13 28·2	12 49·3	4·4 3·9	10·4 9·3	16·4 14·6
45	13 11·3	13 13·4	12 35·2	4·5 3·9	10·5 9·2	16·5 14·4	45	13 26·3	13 28·5	12 49·5	4·5 4·0	10·5 9·4	16·5 14·7
46	13 11·5	13 13·7	12 35·4	4·6 4·0	10·6 9·3	16·6 14·5	46	13 26·5	13 28·7	12 49·8	4·6 4·1	10·6 9·5	16·6 14·8
47	13 11·8	13 13·9	12 35·7	4·7 4·1	10·7 9·4	16·7 14·6	47	13 26·8	13 29·0	12 50·0	4·7 4·2	10·7 9·5	16·7 14·9
48	13 12·0	13 14·2	12 35·9	4·8 4·2	10·8 9·5	16·8 14·7	48	13 27·0	13 29·2	12 50·2	4·8 4·3	10·8 9·6	16·8 15·0
49	13 12·3	13 14·4	12 36·2	4·9 4·3	10·9 9·5	16·9 14·8	49	13 27·3	13 29·5	12 50·5	4·9 4·4	10·9 9·7	16·9 15·1
50	13 12·5	13 14·7	12 36·4	5·0 4·4	11·0 9·6	17·0 14·9	50	13 27·5	13 29·7	12 50·7	5·0 4·5	11·0 9·8	17·0 15·2
51	13 12·8	13 14·9	12 36·6	5·1 4·5	11·1 9·7	17·1 15·0	51	13 27·8	13 30·0	12 51·0	5·1 4·5	11·1 9·9	17·1 15·2
52	13 13·0	13 15·2	12 36·9	5·2 4·6	11·2 9·8	17·2 15·1	52	13 28·0	13 30·2	12 51·2	5·2 4·6	11·2 10·0	17·2 15·3
53	13 13·3	13 15·4	12 37·1	5·3 4·6	11·3 9·9	17·3 15·1	53	13 28·3	13 30·5	12 51·4	5·3 4·7	11·3 10·1	17·3 15·4
54	13 13·5	13 15·7	12 37·4	5·4 4·7	11·4 10·0	17·4 15·2	54	13 28·5	13 30·7	12 51·7	5·4 4·8	11·4 10·2	17·4 15·5
55	13 13·8	13 15·9	12 37·6	5·5 4·8	11·5 10·1	17·5 15·3	55	13 28·8	13 31·0	12 51·9	5·5 4·9	11·5 10·3	17·5 15·6
56	13 14·0	13 16·2	12 37·8	5·6 4·9	11·6 10·2	17·6 15·4	56	13 29·0	13 31·2	12 52·1	5·6 5·0	11·6 10·3	17·6 15·7
57	13 14·3	13 16·4	12 38·1	5·7 5·0	11·7 10·2	17·7 15·5	57	13 29·3	13 31·5	12 52·4	5·7 5·1	11·7 10·4	17·7 15·8
58	13 14·5	13 16·7	12 38·3	5·8 5·1	11·8 10·3	17·8 15·6	58	13 29·5	13 31·7	12 52·6	5·8 5·2	11·8 10·5	17·8 15·9
59	13 14·8	13 16·9	12 38·5	5·9 5·2	11·9 10·4	17·9 15·7	59	13 29·8	13 32·0	12 52·9	5·9 5·3	11·9 10·6	17·9 16·0
60	13 15·0	13 17·2	12 38·8	6·0 5·3	12·0 10·5	18·0 15·8	60	13 30·0	13 32·2	12 53·1	6·0 5·4	12·0 10·7	18·0 16·1

54ᵐ	SUN PLANETS	ARIES	MOON	v or Corrn d	v or Corrn d	v or Corrn d
s	° ′	° ′	° ′	′ ′	′ ′	′ ′
00	13 30·0	13 32·2	12 53·1	0·0 0·0	6·0 5·5	12·0 10·9
01	13 30·3	13 32·5	12 53·3	0·1 0·1	6·1 5·5	12·1 11·0
02	13 30·5	13 32·7	12 53·6	0·2 0·2	6·2 5·6	12·2 11·1
03	13 30·8	13 33·0	12 53·8	0·3 0·3	6·3 5·7	12·3 11·2
04	13 31·0	13 33·2	12 54·1	0·4 0·4	6·4 5·8	12·4 11·3
05	13 31·3	13 33·5	12 54·3	0·5 0·5	6·5 5·9	12·5 11·4
06	13 31·5	13 33·7	12 54·5	0·6 0·5	6·6 6·0	12·6 11·4
07	13 31·8	13 34·0	12 54·8	0·7 0·6	6·7 6·1	12·7 11·5
08	13 32·0	13 34·2	12 55·0	0·8 0·7	6·8 6·2	12·8 11·6
09	13 32·3	13 34·5	12 55·2	0·9 0·8	6·9 6·3	12·9 11·7
10	13 32·5	13 34·7	12 55·5	1·0 0·9	7·0 6·4	13·0 11·8
11	13 32·8	13 35·0	12 55·7	1·1 1·0	7·1 6·4	13·1 11·9
12	13 33·0	13 35·2	12 56·0	1·2 1·1	7·2 6·5	13·2 12·0
13	13 33·3	13 35·5	12 56·2	1·3 1·2	7·3 6·6	13·3 12·1
14	13 33·5	13 35·7	12 56·4	1·4 1·3	7·4 6·7	13·4 12·2
15	13 33·8	13 36·0	12 56·7	1·5 1·4	7·5 6·8	13·5 12·3
16	13 34·0	13 36·2	12 56·9	1·6 1·5	7·6 6·9	13·6 12·4
17	13 34·3	13 36·5	12 57·2	1·7 1·5	7·7 7·0	13·7 12·4
18	13 34·5	13 36·7	12 57·4	1·8 1·6	7·8 7·1	13·8 12·5
19	13 34·8	13 37·0	12 57·6	1·9 1·7	7·9 7·2	13·9 12·6
20	13 35·0	13 37·2	12 57·9	2·0 1·8	8·0 7·3	14·0 12·7
21	13 35·3	13 37·5	12 58·1	2·1 1·9	8·1 7·4	14·1 12·8
22	13 35·5	13 37·7	12 58·3	2·2 2·0	8·2 7·4	14·2 12·9
23	13 35·8	13 38·0	12 58·6	2·3 2·1	8·3 7·5	14·3 13·0
24	13 36·0	13 38·2	12 58·8	2·4 2·2	8·4 7·6	14·4 13·1
25	13 36·3	13 38·5	12 59·1	2·5 2·3	8·5 7·7	14·5 13·2
26	13 36·5	13 38·7	12 59·3	2·6 2·4	8·6 7·8	14·6 13·3
27	13 36·8	13 39·0	12 59·5	2·7 2·5	8·7 7·9	14·7 13·4
28	13 37·0	13 39·2	12 59·8	2·8 2·5	8·8 8·0	14·8 13·4
29	13 37·3	13 39·5	13 00·0	2·9 2·6	8·9 8·1	14·9 13·5
30	13 37·5	13 39·7	13 00·3	3·0 2·7	9·0 8·2	15·0 13·6
31	13 37·8	13 40·0	13 00·5	3·1 2·8	9·1 8·3	15·1 13·7
32	13 38·0	13 40·2	13 00·7	3·2 2·9	9·2 8·4	15·2 13·8
33	13 38·3	13 40·5	13 01·0	3·3 3·0	9·3 8·4	15·3 13·9
34	13 38·5	13 40·7	13 01·2	3·4 3·1	9·4 8·5	15·4 14·0
35	13 38·8	13 41·0	13 01·5	3·5 3·2	9·5 8·6	15·5 14·1
36	13 39·0	13 41·2	13 01·7	3·6 3·3	9·6 8·7	15·6 14·2
37	13 39·3	13 41·5	13 01·9	3·7 3·4	9·7 8·8	15·7 14·3
38	13 39·5	13 41·7	13 02·2	3·8 3·5	9·8 8·9	15·8 14·4
39	13 39·8	13 42·0	13 02·4	3·9 3·5	9·9 9·0	15·9 14·4
40	13 40·0	13 42·2	13 02·6	4·0 3·6	10·0 9·1	16·0 14·5
41	13 40·3	13 42·5	13 02·9	4·1 3·7	10·1 9·2	16·1 14·6
42	13 40·5	13 42·7	13 03·1	4·2 3·8	10·2 9·3	16·2 14·7
43	13 40·8	13 43·0	13 03·4	4·3 3·9	10·3 9·4	16·3 14·8
44	13 41·0	13 43·2	13 03·6	4·4 4·0	10·4 9·4	16·4 14·9
45	13 41·3	13 43·5	13 03·8	4·5 4·1	10·5 9·5	16·5 15·0
46	13 41·5	13 43·7	13 04·1	4·6 4·2	10·6 9·6	16·6 15·1
47	13 41·8	13 44·0	13 04·3	4·7 4·3	10·7 9·7	16·7 15·2
48	13 42·0	13 44·3	13 04·6	4·8 4·4	10·8 9·8	16·8 15·3
49	13 42·3	13 44·5	13 04·8	4·9 4·5	10·9 9·9	16·9 15·4
50	13 42·5	13 44·8	13 05·0	5·0 4·5	11·0 10·0	17·0 15·4
51	13 42·8	13 45·0	13 05·3	5·1 4·6	11·1 10·1	17·1 15·5
52	13 43·0	13 45·3	13 05·5	5·2 4·7	11·2 10·2	17·2 15·6
53	13 43·3	13 45·5	13 05·7	5·3 4·8	11·3 10·3	17·3 15·7
54	13 43·5	13 45·8	13 06·0	5·4 4·9	11·4 10·4	17·4 15·8
55	13 43·8	13 46·0	13 06·2	5·5 5·0	11·5 10·4	17·5 15·9
56	13 44·0	13 46·3	13 06·5	5·6 5·1	11·6 10·5	17·6 16·0
57	13 44·3	13 46·5	13 06·7	5·7 5·2	11·7 10·6	17·7 16·1
58	13 44·5	13 46·8	13 06·9	5·8 5·3	11·8 10·7	17·8 16·2
59	13 44·8	13 47·0	13 07·2	5·9 5·4	11·9 10·8	17·9 16·3
60	13 45·0	13 47·3	13 07·4	6·0 5·5	12·0 10·9	18·0 16·4

55ᵐ	SUN PLANETS	ARIES	MOON	v or Corrn d	v or Corrn d	v or Corrn d
s	° ′	° ′	° ′	′ ′	′ ′	′ ′
00	13 45·0	13 47·3	13 07·4	0·0 0·0	6·0 5·6	12·0 11·1
01	13 45·3	13 47·5	13 07·7	0·1 0·1	6·1 5·6	12·1 11·2
02	13 45·5	13 47·8	13 07·9	0·2 0·2	6·2 5·7	12·2 11·3
03	13 45·8	13 48·0	13 08·1	0·3 0·3	6·3 5·8	12·3 11·4
04	13 46·0	13 48·3	13 08·4	0·4 0·4	6·4 5·9	12·4 11·5
05	13 46·3	13 48·5	13 08·6	0·5 0·5	6·5 6·0	12·5 11·6
06	13 46·5	13 48·8	13 08·8	0·6 0·6	6·6 6·1	12·6 11·7
07	13 46·8	13 49·0	13 09·1	0·7 0·6	6·7 6·2	12·7 11·7
08	13 47·0	13 49·3	13 09·3	0·8 0·7	6·8 6·3	12·8 11·8
09	13 47·3	13 49·5	13 09·6	0·9 0·8	6·9 6·4	12·9 11·9
10	13 47·5	13 49·8	13 09·8	1·0 0·9	7·0 6·5	13·0 12·0
11	13 47·8	13 50·0	13 10·0	1·1 1·0	7·1 6·6	13·1 12·1
12	13 48·0	13 50·3	13 10·3	1·2 1·1	7·2 6·7	13·2 12·2
13	13 48·3	13 50·5	13 10·5	1·3 1·2	7·3 6·8	13·3 12·3
14	13 48·5	13 50·8	13 10·8	1·4 1·3	7·4 6·8	13·4 12·4
15	13 48·8	13 51·0	13 11·0	1·5 1·4	7·5 6·9	13·5 12·5
16	13 49·0	13 51·3	13 11·2	1·6 1·5	7·6 7·0	13·6 12·6
17	13 49·3	13 51·5	13 11·5	1·7 1·6	7·7 7·1	13·7 12·7
18	13 49·5	13 51·8	13 11·7	1·8 1·7	7·8 7·2	13·8 12·8
19	13 49·8	13 52·0	13 12·0	1·9 1·8	7·9 7·3	13·9 12·9
20	13 50·0	13 52·3	13 12·2	2·0 1·9	8·0 7·4	14·0 13·0
21	13 50·3	13 52·5	13 12·4	2·1 1·9	8·1 7·5	14·1 13·0
22	13 50·5	13 52·8	13 12·7	2·2 2·0	8·2 7·6	14·2 13·1
23	13 50·8	13 53·0	13 12·9	2·3 2·1	8·3 7·7	14·3 13·2
24	13 51·0	13 53·3	13 13·1	2·4 2·2	8·4 7·8	14·4 13·3
25	13 51·3	13 53·5	13 13·4	2·5 2·3	8·5 7·9	14·5 13·4
26	13 51·5	13 53·8	13 13·6	2·6 2·4	8·6 8·0	14·6 13·5
27	13 51·8	13 54·0	13 13·9	2·7 2·5	8·7 8·0	14·7 13·6
28	13 52·0	13 54·3	13 14·1	2·8 2·6	8·8 8·1	14·8 13·7
29	13 52·3	13 54·5	13 14·3	2·9 2·7	8·9 8·2	14·9 13·8
30	13 52·5	13 54·8	13 14·6	3·0 2·8	9·0 8·3	15·0 13·9
31	13 52·8	13 55·0	13 14·8	3·1 2·9	9·1 8·4	15·1 14·0
32	13 53·0	13 55·3	13 15·1	3·2 3·0	9·2 8·5	15·2 14·1
33	13 53·3	13 55·5	13 15·3	3·3 3·1	9·3 8·6	15·3 14·2
34	13 53·5	13 55·8	13 15·5	3·4 3·1	9·4 8·7	15·4 14·2
35	13 53·8	13 56·0	13 15·8	3·5 3·2	9·5 8·8	15·5 14·3
36	13 54·0	13 56·3	13 16·0	3·6 3·3	9·6 8·9	15·6 14·4
37	13 54·3	13 56·5	13 16·2	3·7 3·4	9·7 9·0	15·7 14·5
38	13 54·5	13 56·8	13 16·5	3·8 3·5	9·8 9·1	15·8 14·6
39	13 54·8	13 57·0	13 16·7	3·9 3·6	9·9 9·2	15·9 14·7
40	13 55·0	13 57·3	13 17·0	4·0 3·7	10·0 9·3	16·0 14·8
41	13 55·3	13 57·5	13 17·2	4·1 3·8	10·1 9·3	16·1 14·9
42	13 55·5	13 57·8	13 17·4	4·2 3·9	10·2 9·4	16·2 15·0
43	13 55·8	13 58·0	13 17·7	4·3 4·0	10·3 9·5	16·3 15·1
44	13 56·0	13 58·3	13 17·9	4·4 4·1	10·4 9·6	16·4 15·2
45	13 56·3	13 58·5	13 18·2	4·5 4·2	10·5 9·7	16·5 15·3
46	13 56·5	13 58·8	13 18·4	4·6 4·3	10·6 9·8	16·6 15·4
47	13 56·8	13 59·0	13 18·6	4·7 4·3	10·7 9·9	16·7 15·4
48	13 57·0	13 59·3	13 18·9	4·8 4·4	10·8 10·0	16·8 15·5
49	13 57·3	13 59·5	13 19·1	4·9 4·5	10·9 10·1	16·9 15·6
50	13 57·5	13 59·8	13 19·3	5·0 4·6	11·0 10·2	17·0 15·7
51	13 57·8	14 00·0	13 19·6	5·1 4·7	11·1 10·3	17·1 15·8
52	13 58·0	14 00·3	13 19·8	5·2 4·8	11·2 10·4	17·2 15·9
53	13 58·3	14 00·5	13 20·1	5·3 4·9	11·3 10·5	17·3 16·0
54	13 58·5	14 00·8	13 20·3	5·4 5·0	11·4 10·5	17·4 16·1
55	13 58·8	14 01·0	13 20·5	5·5 5·1	11·5 10·6	17·5 16·2
56	13 59·0	14 01·3	13 20·8	5·6 5·2	11·6 10·7	17·6 16·3
57	13 59·3	14 01·5	13 21·0	5·7 5·3	11·7 10·8	17·7 16·4
58	13 59·5	14 01·8	13 21·3	5·8 5·4	11·8 10·9	17·8 16·5
59	13 59·8	14 02·0	13 21·5	5·9 5·5	11·9 11·0	17·9 16·6
60	14 00·0	14 02·3	13 21·7	6·0 5·6	12·0 11·1	18·0 16·7

56ᵐ

56ᵐ SUN PLANETS	ARIES	MOON	v or Corrⁿ d	v or Corrⁿ d	v or Corrⁿ d
s	° ′	° ′	° ′	′ ′	′ ′	′ ′
00	14 00·0	14 02·3	13 21·7	0·0 0·0	6·0 5·7	12·0 11·3
01	14 00·3	14 02·6	13 22·0	0·1 0·1	6·1 5·7	12·1 11·4
02	14 00·5	14 02·8	13 22·2	0·2 0·2	6·2 5·8	12·2 11·5
03	14 00·8	14 03·1	13 22·4	0·3 0·3	6·3 5·9	12·3 11·6
04	14 01·0	14 03·3	13 22·7	0·4 0·4	6·4 6·0	12·4 11·7
05	14 01·3	14 03·6	13 22·9	0·5 0·5	6·5 6·1	12·5 11·8
06	14 01·5	14 03·8	13 23·2	0·6 0·6	6·6 6·2	12·6 11·9
07	14 01·8	14 04·1	13 23·4	0·7 0·7	6·7 6·3	12·7 12·0
08	14 02·0	14 04·3	13 23·6	0·8 0·8	6·8 6·4	12·8 12·1
09	14 02·3	14 04·6	13 23·9	0·9 0·8	6·9 6·5	12·9 12·1
10	14 02·5	14 04·8	13 24·1	1·0 0·9	7·0 6·6	13·0 12·2
11	14 02·8	14 05·1	13 24·4	1·1 1·0	7·1 6·7	13·1 12·3
12	14 03·0	14 05·3	13 24·6	1·2 1·1	7·2 6·8	13·2 12·4
13	14 03·3	14 05·6	13 24·8	1·3 1·2	7·3 6·9	13·3 12·5
14	14 03·5	14 05·8	13 25·1	1·4 1·3	7·4 7·0	13·4 12·6
15	14 03·8	14 06·1	13 25·3	1·5 1·4	7·5 7·1	13·5 12·7
16	14 04·0	14 06·3	13 25·6	1·6 1·5	7·6 7·2	13·6 12·8
17	14 04·3	14 06·6	13 25·8	1·7 1·6	7·7 7·3	13·7 12·9
18	14 04·5	14 06·8	13 26·0	1·8 1·7	7·8 7·3	13·8 13·0
19	14 04·8	14 07·1	13 26·3	1·9 1·8	7·9 7·4	13·9 13·1
20	14 05·0	14 07·3	13 26·5	2·0 1·9	8·0 7·5	14·0 13·2
21	14 05·3	14 07·6	13 26·7	2·1 2·0	8·1 7·6	14·1 13·3
22	14 05·5	14 07·8	13 27·0	2·2 2·1	8·2 7·7	14·2 13·4
23	14 05·8	14 08·1	13 27·2	2·3 2·2	8·3 7·8	14·3 13·5
24	14 06·0	14 08·3	13 27·5	2·4 2·3	8·4 7·9	14·4 13·6
25	14 06·3	14 08·6	13 27·7	2·5 2·4	8·5 8·0	14·5 13·7
26	14 06·5	14 08·8	13 27·9	2·6 2·4	8·6 8·1	14·6 13·7
27	14 06·8	14 09·1	13 28·2	2·7 2·5	8·7 8·2	14·7 13·8
28	14 07·0	14 09·3	13 28·4	2·8 2·6	8·8 8·3	14·8 13·9
29	14 07·3	14 09·6	13 28·7	2·9 2·7	8·9 8·4	14·9 14·0
30	14 07·5	14 09·8	13 28·9	3·0 2·8	9·0 8·5	15·0 14·1
31	14 07·8	14 10·1	13 29·1	3·1 2·9	9·1 8·6	15·1 14·2
32	14 08·0	14 10·3	13 29·4	3·2 3·0	9·2 8·7	15·2 14·3
33	14 08·3	14 10·6	13 29·6	3·3 3·1	9·3 8·8	15·3 14·4
34	14 08·5	14 10·8	13 29·8	3·4 3·2	9·4 8·9	15·4 14·5
35	14 08·8	14 11·1	13 30·1	3·5 3·3	9·5 8·9	15·5 14·6
36	14 09·0	14 11·3	13 30·3	3·6 3·4	9·6 9·0	15·6 14·7
37	14 09·3	14 11·6	13 30·6	3·7 3·5	9·7 9·1	15·7 14·8
38	14 09·5	14 11·8	13 30·8	3·8 3·6	9·8 9·2	15·8 14·9
39	14 09·8	14 12·1	13 31·0	3·9 3·7	9·9 9·3	15·9 15·0
40	14 10·0	14 12·3	13 31·3	4·0 3·8	10·0 9·4	16·0 15·1
41	14 10·3	14 12·6	13 31·5	4·1 3·9	10·1 9·5	16·1 15·2
42	14 10·5	14 12·8	13 31·8	4·2 4·0	10·2 9·6	16·2 15·3
43	14 10·8	14 13·1	13 32·0	4·3 4·0	10·3 9·7	16·3 15·3
44	14 11·0	14 13·3	13 32·2	4·4 4·1	10·4 9·8	16·4 15·4
45	14 11·3	14 13·6	13 32·5	4·5 4·2	10·5 9·9	16·5 15·5
46	14 11·5	14 13·8	13 32·7	4·6 4·3	10·6 10·0	16·6 15·6
47	14 11·8	14 14·1	13 32·9	4·7 4·4	10·7 10·1	16·7 15·7
48	14 12·0	14 14·3	13 33·2	4·8 4·5	10·8 10·2	16·8 15·8
49	14 12·3	14 14·6	13 33·4	4·9 4·6	10·9 10·3	16·9 15·9
50	14 12·5	14 14·8	13 33·7	5·0 4·7	11·0 10·4	17·0 16·0
51	14 12·8	14 15·1	13 33·9	5·1 4·8	11·1 10·5	17·1 16·1
52	14 13·0	14 15·3	13 34·1	5·2 4·9	11·2 10·5	17·2 16·2
53	14 13·3	14 15·6	13 34·4	5·3 5·0	11·3 10·6	17·3 16·3
54	14 13·5	14 15·8	13 34·6	5·4 5·1	11·4 10·7	17·4 16·4
55	14 13·8	14 16·1	13 34·9	5·5 5·2	11·5 10·8	17·5 16·5
56	14 14·0	14 16·3	13 35·1	5·6 5·3	11·6 10·9	17·6 16·6
57	14 14·3	14 16·6	13 35·3	5·7 5·4	11·7 11·0	17·7 16·7
58	14 14·5	14 16·8	13 35·6	5·8 5·5	11·8 11·1	17·8 16·8
59	14 14·8	14 17·1	13 35·8	5·9 5·6	11·9 11·2	17·9 16·9
60	14 15·0	14 17·3	13 36·1	6·0 5·7	12·0 11·3	18·0 17·0

57ᵐ

57ᵐ SUN PLANETS	ARIES	MOON	v or Corrⁿ d	v or Corrⁿ d	v or Corrⁿ d
s	° ′	° ′	° ′	′ ′	′ ′	′ ′
00	14 15·0	14 17·3	13 36·1	0·0 0·0	6·0 5·8	12·0 11·5
01	14 15·3	14 17·6	13 36·3	0·1 0·1	6·1 5·8	12·1 11·6
02	14 15·5	14 17·8	13 36·5	0·2 0·2	6·2 5·9	12·2 11·7
03	14 15·8	14 18·1	13 36·8	0·3 0·3	6·3 6·0	12·3 11·8
04	14 16·0	14 18·3	13 37·0	0·4 0·4	6·4 6·1	12·4 11·9
05	14 16·3	14 18·6	13 37·2	0·5 0·5	6·5 6·2	12·5 12·0
06	14 16·5	14 18·8	13 37·5	0·6 0·6	6·6 6·3	12·6 12·1
07	14 16·8	14 19·1	13 37·7	0·7 0·7	6·7 6·4	12·7 12·2
08	14 17·0	14 19·3	13 38·0	0·8 0·8	6·8 6·5	12·8 12·3
09	14 17·3	14 19·6	13 38·2	0·9 0·9	6·9 6·6	12·9 12·4
10	14 17·5	14 19·8	13 38·4	1·0 1·0	7·0 6·7	13·0 12·5
11	14 17·8	14 20·1	13 38·7	1·1 1·1	7·1 6·8	13·1 12·6
12	14 18·0	14 20·3	13 38·9	1·2 1·2	7·2 6·9	13·2 12·7
13	14 18·3	14 20·6	13 39·2	1·3 1·2	7·3 7·0	13·3 12·7
14	14 18·5	14 20·9	13 39·4	1·4 1·3	7·4 7·1	13·4 12·8
15	14 18·8	14 21·1	13 39·6	1·5 1·4	7·5 7·2	13·5 12·9
16	14 19·0	14 21·4	13 39·9	1·6 1·5	7·6 7·3	13·6 13·0
17	14 19·3	14 21·6	13 40·1	1·7 1·6	7·7 7·4	13·7 13·1
18	14 19·5	14 21·9	13 40·3	1·8 1·7	7·8 7·5	13·8 13·2
19	14 19·8	14 22·1	13 40·6	1·9 1·8	7·9 7·6	13·9 13·3
20	14 20·0	14 22·4	13 40·8	2·0 1·9	8·0 7·7	14·0 13·4
21	14 20·3	14 22·6	13 41·1	2·1 2·0	8·1 7·8	14·1 13·5
22	14 20·5	14 22·9	13 41·3	2·2 2·1	8·2 7·9	14·2 13·6
23	14 20·8	14 23·1	13 41·5	2·3 2·2	8·3 8·0	14·3 13·7
24	14 21·0	14 23·4	13 41·8	2·4 2·3	8·4 8·1	14·4 13·8
25	14 21·3	14 23·6	13 42·0	2·5 2·4	8·5 8·1	14·5 13·9
26	14 21·5	14 23·9	13 42·3	2·6 2·5	8·6 8·2	14·6 14·0
27	14 21·8	14 24·1	13 42·5	2·7 2·6	8·7 8·3	14·7 14·1
28	14 22·0	14 24·4	13 42·7	2·8 2·7	8·8 8·4	14·8 14·2
29	14 22·3	14 24·6	13 43·0	2·9 2·8	8·9 8·5	14·9 14·3
30	14 22·5	14 24·9	13 43·2	3·0 2·9	9·0 8·6	15·0 14·4
31	14 22·8	14 25·1	13 43·4	3·1 3·0	9·1 8·7	15·1 14·5
32	14 23·0	14 25·4	13 43·7	3·2 3·1	9·2 8·8	15·2 14·6
33	14 23·3	14 25·6	13 43·9	3·3 3·2	9·3 8·9	15·3 14·7
34	14 23·5	14 25·9	13 44·2	3·4 3·3	9·4 9·0	15·4 14·8
35	14 23·8	14 26·1	13 44·4	3·5 3·4	9·5 9·1	15·5 14·9
36	14 24·0	14 26·4	13 44·6	3·6 3·5	9·6 9·2	15·6 15·0
37	14 24·3	14 26·6	13 44·9	3·7 3·5	9·7 9·3	15·7 15·0
38	14 24·5	14 26·9	13 45·1	3·8 3·6	9·8 9·4	15·8 15·1
39	14 24·8	14 27·1	13 45·4	3·9 3·7	9·9 9·5	15·9 15·2
40	14 25·0	14 27·4	13 45·6	4·0 3·8	10·0 9·6	16·0 15·3
41	14 25·3	14 27·6	13 45·8	4·1 3·9	10·1 9·7	16·1 15·4
42	14 25·5	14 27·9	13 46·1	4·2 4·0	10·2 9·8	16·2 15·5
43	14 25·8	14 28·1	13 46·3	4·3 4·1	10·3 9·9	16·3 15·6
44	14 26·0	14 28·4	13 46·5	4·4 4·2	10·4 10·0	16·4 15·7
45	14 26·3	14 28·6	13 46·8	4·5 4·3	10·5 10·1	16·5 15·8
46	14 26·5	14 28·9	13 47·0	4·6 4·4	10·6 10·2	16·6 15·9
47	14 26·8	14 29·1	13 47·3	4·7 4·5	10·7 10·3	16·7 16·0
48	14 27·0	14 29·4	13 47·5	4·8 4·6	10·8 10·4	16·8 16·1
49	14 27·3	14 29·6	13 47·7	4·9 4·7	10·9 10·4	16·9 16·2
50	14 27·5	14 29·9	13 48·0	5·0 4·8	11·0 10·5	17·0 16·3
51	14 27·8	14 30·1	13 48·2	5·1 4·9	11·1 10·6	17·1 16·4
52	14 28·0	14 30·4	13 48·5	5·2 5·0	11·2 10·7	17·2 16·5
53	14 28·3	14 30·6	13 48·7	5·3 5·1	11·3 10·8	17·3 16·6
54	14 28·5	14 30·9	13 48·9	5·4 5·2	11·4 10·9	17·4 16·7
55	14 28·8	14 31·1	13 49·2	5·5 5·3	11·5 11·0	17·5 16·8
56	14 29·0	14 31·4	13 49·4	5·6 5·4	11·6 11·1	17·6 16·9
57	14 29·3	14 31·6	13 49·7	5·7 5·5	11·7 11·2	17·7 17·0
58	14 29·5	14 31·9	13 49·9	5·8 5·6	11·8 11·3	17·8 17·1
59	14 29·8	14 32·1	13 50·1	5·9 5·7	11·9 11·4	17·9 17·2
60	14 30·0	14 32·4	13 50·4	6·0 5·8	12·0 11·5	18·0 17·3

58ᵐ	SUN PLANETS	ARIES	MOON	v or Corrⁿ d	v or Corrⁿ d	v or Corrⁿ d
s	° ′	° ′	° ′	′ ′	′ ′	′ ′
00	14 30·0	14 32·4	13 50·4	0·0 0·0	6·0 5·9	12·0 11·7
01	14 30·3	14 32·6	13 50·6	0·1 0·1	6·1 5·9	12·1 11·8
02	14 30·5	14 32·9	13 50·8	0·2 0·2	6·2 6·0	12·2 11·9
03	14 30·8	14 33·1	13 51·1	0·3 0·3	6·3 6·1	12·3 12·0
04	14 31·0	14 33·4	13 51·3	0·4 0·4	6·4 6·2	12·4 12·1
05	14 31·3	14 33·6	13 51·6	0·5 0·5	6·5 6·3	12·5 12·2
06	14 31·5	14 33·9	13 51·8	0·6 0·6	6·6 6·4	12·6 12·3
07	14 31·8	14 34·1	13 52·0	0·7 0·7	6·7 6·5	12·7 12·4
08	14 32·0	14 34·4	13 52·3	0·8 0·8	6·8 6·6	12·8 12·5
09	14 32·3	14 34·6	13 52·5	0·9 0·9	6·9 6·7	12·9 12·6
10	14 32·5	14 34·9	13 52·8	1·0 1·0	7·0 6·8	13·0 12·7
11	14 32·8	14 35·1	13 53·0	1·1 1·1	7·1 6·9	13·1 12·8
12	14 33·0	14 35·4	13 53·2	1·2 1·2	7·2 7·0	13·2 12·9
13	14 33·3	14 35·6	13 53·5	1·3 1·3	7·3 7·1	13·3 13·0
14	14 33·5	14 35·9	13 53·7	1·4 1·4	7·4 7·2	13·4 13·1
15	14 33·8	14 36·1	13 53·9	1·5 1·5	7·5 7·3	13·5 13·2
16	14 34·0	14 36·4	13 54·2	1·6 1·6	7·6 7·4	13·6 13·3
17	14 34·3	14 36·6	13 54·4	1·7 1·7	7·7 7·5	13·7 13·4
18	14 34·5	14 36·9	13 54·7	1·8 1·8	7·8 7·6	13·8 13·5
19	14 34·8	14 37·1	13 54·9	1·9 1·9	7·9 7·7	13·9 13·6
20	14 35·0	14 37·4	13 55·1	2·0 2·0	8·0 7·8	14·0 13·7
21	14 35·3	14 37·6	13 55·4	2·1 2·0	8·1 7·9	14·1 13·7
22	14 35·5	14 37·9	13 55·6	2·2 2·1	8·2 8·0	14·2 13·8
23	14 35·8	14 38·1	13 55·9	2·3 2·2	8·3 8·1	14·3 13·9
24	14 36·0	14 38·4	13 56·1	2·4 2·3	8·4 8·2	14·4 14·0
25	14 36·3	14 38·6	13 56·3	2·5 2·4	8·5 8·3	14·5 14·1
26	14 36·5	14 38·9	13 56·6	2·6 2·5	8·6 8·4	14·6 14·2
27	14 36·8	14 39·2	13 56·8	2·7 2·6	8·7 8·5	14·7 14·3
28	14 37·0	14 39·4	13 57·0	2·8 2·7	8·8 8·6	14·8 14·4
29	14 37·3	14 39·7	13 57·3	2·9 2·8	8·9 8·7	14·9 14·5
30	14 37·5	14 39·9	13 57·5	3·0 2·9	9·0 8·8	15·0 14·6
31	14 37·8	14 40·2	13 57·8	3·1 3·0	9·1 8·9	15·1 14·7
32	14 38·0	14 40·4	13 58·0	3·2 3·1	9·2 9·0	15·2 14·8
33	14 38·3	14 40·7	13 58·2	3·3 3·2	9·3 9·1	15·3 14·9
34	14 38·5	14 40·9	13 58·5	3·4 3·3	9·4 9·2	15·4 15·0
35	14 38·8	14 41·2	13 58·7	3·5 3·4	9·5 9·3	15·5 15·1
36	14 39·0	14 41·4	13 59·0	3·6 3·5	9·6 9·4	15·6 15·2
37	14 39·3	14 41·7	13 59·2	3·7 3·6	9·7 9·5	15·7 15·3
38	14 39·5	14 41·9	13 59·4	3·8 3·7	9·8 9·6	15·8 15·4
39	14 39·8	14 42·2	13 59·7	3·9 3·8	9·9 9·7	15·9 15·5
40	14 40·0	14 42·4	13 59·9	4·0 3·9	10·0 9·8	16·0 15·6
41	14 40·3	14 42·7	14 00·1	4·1 4·0	10·1 9·8	16·1 15·7
42	14 40·5	14 42·9	14 00·4	4·2 4·1	10·2 9·9	16·2 15·8
43	14 40·8	14 43·2	14 00·6	4·3 4·2	10·3 10·0	16·3 15·9
44	14 41·0	14 43·4	14 00·9	4·4 4·3	10·4 10·1	16·4 16·0
45	14 41·3	14 43·7	14 01·1	4·5 4·4	10·5 10·2	16·5 16·1
46	14 41·5	14 43·9	14 01·3	4·6 4·5	10·6 10·3	16·6 16·2
47	14 41·8	14 44·2	14 01·6	4·7 4·6	10·7 10·4	16·7 16·3
48	14 42·0	14 44·4	14 01·8	4·8 4·7	10·8 10·5	16·8 16·4
49	14 42·3	14 44·7	14 02·1	4·9 4·8	10·9 10·6	16·9 16·5
50	14 42·5	14 44·9	14 02·3	5·0 4·9	11·0 10·7	17·0 16·6
51	14 42·8	14 45·2	14 02·5	5·1 5·0	11·1 10·8	17·1 16·7
52	14 43·0	14 45·4	14 02·8	5·2 5·1	11·2 10·9	17·2 16·8
53	14 43·3	14 45·7	14 03·0	5·3 5·2	11·3 11·0	17·3 16·9
54	14 43·5	14 45·9	14 03·3	5·4 5·3	11·4 11·1	17·4 17·0
55	14 43·8	14 46·2	14 03·5	5·5 5·4	11·5 11·2	17·5 17·1
56	14 44·0	14 46·4	14 03·7	5·6 5·5	11·6 11·3	17·6 17·2
57	14 44·3	14 46·7	14 04·0	5·7 5·6	11·7 11·4	17·7 17·3
58	14 44·5	14 46·9	14 04·2	5·8 5·7	11·8 11·5	17·8 17·4
59	14 44·8	14 47·2	14 04·4	5·9 5·8	11·9 11·6	17·9 17·5
60	14 45·0	14 47·4	14 04·7	6·0 5·9	12·0 11·7	18·0 17·6

59ᵐ	SUN PLANETS	ARIES	MOON	v or Corrⁿ d	v or Corrⁿ d	v or Corrⁿ d
s	° ′	° ′	° ′	′ ′	′ ′	′ ′
00	14 45·0	14 47·4	14 04·7	0·0 0·0	6·0 6·0	12·0 11·9
01	14 45·3	14 47·7	14 04·9	0·1 0·1	6·1 6·0	12·1 12·0
02	14 45·5	14 47·9	14 05·2	0·2 0·2	6·2 6·1	12·2 12·1
03	14 45·8	14 48·2	14 05·4	0·3 0·3	6·3 6·2	12·3 12·2
04	14 46·0	14 48·4	14 05·6	0·4 0·4	6·4 6·3	12·4 12·3
05	14 46·3	14 48·7	14 05·9	0·5 0·5	6·5 6·4	12·5 12·4
06	14 46·5	14 48·9	14 06·1	0·6 0·6	6·6 6·5	12·6 12·5
07	14 46·8	14 49·2	14 06·4	0·7 0·7	6·7 6·6	12·7 12·6
08	14 47·0	14 49·4	14 06·6	0·8 0·8	6·8 6·7	12·8 12·7
09	14 47·3	14 49·7	14 06·8	0·9 0·9	6·9 6·8	12·9 12·8
10	14 47·5	14 49·9	14 07·1	1·0 1·0	7·0 6·9	13·0 12·9
11	14 47·8	14 50·2	14 07·3	1·1 1·1	7·1 7·0	13·1 13·0
12	14 48·0	14 50·4	14 07·5	1·2 1·2	7·2 7·1	13·2 13·1
13	14 48·3	14 50·7	14 07·8	1·3 1·3	7·3 7·2	13·3 13·2
14	14 48·5	14 50·9	14 08·0	1·4 1·4	7·4 7·3	13·4 13·3
15	14 48·8	14 51·2	14 08·3	1·5 1·5	7·5 7·4	13·5 13·4
16	14 49·0	14 51·4	14 08·5	1·6 1·6	7·6 7·5	13·6 13·5
17	14 49·3	14 51·7	14 08·7	1·7 1·7	7·7 7·6	13·7 13·6
18	14 49·5	14 51·9	14 09·0	1·8 1·8	7·8 7·7	13·8 13·7
19	14 49·8	14 52·2	14 09·2	1·9 1·9	7·9 7·8	13·9 13·8
20	14 50·0	14 52·4	14 09·5	2·0 2·0	8·0 7·9	14·0 13·9
21	14 50·3	14 52·7	14 09·7	2·1 2·1	8·1 8·0	14·1 14·0
22	14 50·5	14 52·9	14 09·9	2·2 2·2	8·2 8·1	14·2 14·1
23	14 50·8	14 53·2	14 10·2	2·3 2·3	8·3 8·2	14·3 14·2
24	14 51·0	14 53·4	14 10·4	2·4 2·4	8·4 8·3	14·4 14·3
25	14 51·3	14 53·7	14 10·6	2·5 2·5	8·5 8·4	14·5 14·4
26	14 51·5	14 53·9	14 10·9	2·6 2·6	8·6 8·5	14·6 14·5
27	14 51·8	14 54·2	14 11·1	2·7 2·7	8·7 8·6	14·7 14·6
28	14 52·0	14 54·4	14 11·4	2·8 2·8	8·8 8·7	14·8 14·7
29	14 52·3	14 54·7	14 11·6	2·9 2·9	8·9 8·8	14·9 14·8
30	14 52·5	14 54·9	14 11·8	3·0 3·0	9·0 8·9	15·0 14·9
31	14 52·8	14 55·2	14 12·1	3·1 3·1	9·1 9·0	15·1 15·0
32	14 53·0	14 55·4	14 12·3	3·2 3·2	9·2 9·1	15·2 15·1
33	14 53·3	14 55·7	14 12·6	3·3 3·3	9·3 9·2	15·3 15·2
34	14 53·5	14 55·9	14 12·8	3·4 3·4	9·4 9·3	15·4 15·3
35	14 53·8	14 56·2	14 13·0	3·5 3·5	9·5 9·4	15·5 15·4
36	14 54·0	14 56·4	14 13·3	3·6 3·6	9·6 9·5	15·6 15·5
37	14 54·3	14 56·7	14 13·5	3·7 3·7	9·7 9·6	15·7 15·6
38	14 54·5	14 56·9	14 13·8	3·8 3·8	9·8 9·7	15·8 15·7
39	14 54·8	14 57·2	14 14·0	3·9 3·9	9·9 9·8	15·9 15·8
40	14 55·0	14 57·5	14 14·2	4·0 4·0	10·0 9·9	16·0 15·9
41	14 55·3	14 57·7	14 14·5	4·1 4·1	10·1 10·0	16·1 16·0
42	14 55·5	14 58·0	14 14·7	4·2 4·2	10·2 10·1	16·2 16·1
43	14 55·8	14 58·2	14 14·9	4·3 4·3	10·3 10·2	16·3 16·2
44	14 56·0	14 58·5	14 15·2	4·4 4·4	10·4 10·3	16·4 16·3
45	14 56·3	14 58·7	14 15·4	4·5 4·5	10·5 10·4	16·5 16·4
46	14 56·5	14 59·0	14 15·7	4·6 4·6	10·6 10·5	16·6 16·5
47	14 56·8	14 59·2	14 15·9	4·7 4·7	10·7 10·6	16·7 16·6
48	14 57·0	14 59·5	14 16·1	4·8 4·8	10·8 10·7	16·8 16·7
49	14 57·3	14 59·7	14 16·4	4·9 4·9	10·9 10·8	16·9 16·8
50	14 57·5	15 00·0	14 16·6	5·0 5·0	11·0 10·9	17·0 16·9
51	14 57·8	15 00·2	14 16·9	5·1 5·1	11·1 11·0	17·1 17·0
52	14 58·0	15 00·5	14 17·1	5·2 5·2	11·2 11·1	17·2 17·1
53	14 58·3	15 00·7	14 17·3	5·3 5·3	11·3 11·2	17·3 17·2
54	14 58·5	15 01·0	14 17·6	5·4 5·4	11·4 11·3	17·4 17·3
55	14 58·8	15 01·2	14 17·8	5·5 5·5	11·5 11·4	17·5 17·4
56	14 59·0	15 01·5	14 18·0	5·6 5·6	11·6 11·5	17·6 17·5
57	14 59·3	15 01·7	14 18·3	5·7 5·7	11·7 11·6	17·7 17·6
58	14 59·5	15 02·0	14 18·5	5·8 5·8	11·8 11·7	17·8 17·7
59	14 59·8	15 02·2	14 18·8	5·9 5·9	11·9 11·8	17·9 17·8
60	15 00·0	15 02·5	14 19·0	6·0 6·0	12·0 11·9	18·0 17·9

TABLES FOR INTERPOLATING SUNRISE, MOONRISE, ETC.

TABLE I—FOR LATITUDE

10°	5°	2°	5m	10m	15m	20m	25m	30m	35m	40m	45m	50m	55m	60m	1h 05m	1h 10m	1h 15m	1h 20m
0 30	0 15	0 06	0	0	1	1	1	1	1	2	2	2	2	2	0 02	0 02	0 02	0 02
1 00	0 30	0 12	0	1	1	2	2	3	3	3	4	4	4	5	05	05	05	05
1 30	0 45	0 18	1	1	2	3	3	4	4	5	5	6	7	7	07	07	07	07
2 00	1 00	0 24	1	2	3	4	5	5	6	7	7	8	9	10	10	10	10	10
2 30	1 15	0 30	1	2	4	5	6	7	8	9	9	10	11	12	12	13	13	13
3 00	1 30	0 36	1	3	4	6	7	8	9	10	11	12	13	14	0 15	0 15	0 16	0 16
3 30	1 45	0 42	2	3	5	7	8	10	11	12	13	14	16	17	18	18	19	19
4 00	2 00	0 48	2	4	6	8	9	11	13	14	15	16	18	19	20	21	22	22
4 30	2 15	0 54	2	4	7	9	11	13	15	16	18	19	21	22	23	24	25	26
5 00	2 30	1 00	2	5	7	10	12	14	16	18	20	22	23	25	26	27	28	29
5 30	2 45	1 06	3	5	8	11	13	16	18	20	22	24	26	28	0 29	0 30	0 31	0 32
6 00	3 00	1 12	3	6	9	12	14	17	20	22	24	26	29	31	32	33	34	36
6 30	3 15	1 18	3	6	10	13	16	19	22	24	26	29	31	34	36	37	38	40
7 00	3 30	1 24	3	7	10	14	17	20	23	26	29	31	34	37	39	41	42	44
7 30	3 45	1 30	4	7	11	15	18	22	25	28	31	34	37	40	43	44	46	48
8 00	4 00	1 36	4	8	12	16	20	23	27	30	34	37	41	44	0 47	0 48	0 51	0 53
8 30	4 15	1 42	4	8	13	17	21	25	29	33	36	40	44	48	0 51	0 53	0 56	0 58
9 00	4 30	1 48	4	9	13	18	22	27	31	35	39	43	47	52	0 55	0 58	1 01	1 04
9 30	4 45	1 54	5	9	14	19	24	28	33	38	42	47	51	56	1 00	1 04	1 08	1 12
10 00	5 00	2 00	5	10	15	20	25	30	35	40	45	50	55	60	1 05	1 10	1 15	1 20

Table I is for interpolating the L.M.T. of sunrise, twilight, moonrise, etc., for latitude. It is to be entered, in the appropriate column on the left, with the difference between true latitude and the nearest tabular latitude which is *less* than the true latitude; and with the argument at the top which is the nearest value of the difference between the times for the tabular latitude and the next higher one; the correction so obtained is applied to the time for the tabular latitude; the sign of the correction can be seen by inspection. It is to be noted that the interpolation is not linear, so that when using this table it is essential to take out the tabular phenomenon for the latitude *less* than the true latitude.

TABLE II—FOR LONGITUDE

Long. East or West	10m	20m	30m	40m	50m	60m	1h+ 10m	1h+ 20m	1h+ 30m	1h+ 40m	1h+ 50m	1h+ 60m	2h 10m	2h 20m	2h 30m	2h 40m	2h 50m	3h 00m
0	0	0	0	0	0	0	0	0	0	0	0	0	0 00	0 00	0 00	0 00	0 00	0 00
10	0	1	1	1	1	2	2	2	2	3	3	3	04	04	04	04	05	05
20	1	1	2	2	3	3	4	4	5	6	6	7	07	08	08	09	09	10
30	1	2	2	3	4	5	6	7	7	8	9	10	11	12	12	13	14	15
40	1	2	3	4	6	7	8	9	10	11	12	13	14	16	17	18	19	20
50	1	3	4	6	7	8	10	11	12	14	15	17	0 18	0 19	0 21	0 22	0 24	0 25
60	2	3	5	7	8	10	12	13	15	17	18	20	22	23	25	27	28	30
70	2	4	6	8	10	12	14	16	17	19	21	23	25	27	29	31	33	35
80	2	4	7	9	11	13	16	18	20	22	24	27	29	31	33	36	38	40
90	2	5	7	10	12	15	17	20	22	25	27	30	32	35	37	40	42	45
100	3	6	8	11	14	17	19	22	25	28	31	33	0 36	0 39	0 42	0 44	0 47	0 50
110	3	6	9	12	15	18	21	24	27	31	34	37	40	43	46	49	0 52	0 55
120	3	7	10	13	17	20	23	27	30	33	37	40	43	47	50	53	0 57	1 00
130	4	7	11	14	18	22	25	29	32	36	40	43	47	51	54	0 58	1 01	1 05
140	4	8	12	16	19	23	27	31	35	39	43	47	51	54	0 58	1 02	1 06	1 10
150	4	8	13	17	21	25	29	33	38	42	46	50	0 54	0 58	1 03	1 07	1 11	1 15
160	4	9	13	18	22	27	31	36	40	44	49	53	0 58	1 02	1 07	1 11	1 16	1 20
170	5	9	14	19	24	28	33	38	42	47	52	57	1 01	1 06	1 11	1 16	1 20	1 25
180	5	10	15	20	25	30	35	40	45	50	55	60	1 05	1 10	1 15	1 20	1 25	1 30

Table II is for interpolating the L.M.T. of moonrise, moonset and the Moon's meridian passage for longitude. It is entered with longitude and with the difference between the times for the given date and for the preceding date (in east longitudes) or following date (in west longitudes). The correction is normally *added* for west longitudes and *subtracted* for east longitudes, but if, as occasionally happens, the times become earlier each day instead of later, the signs of the corrections must be reversed.

INDEX TO SELECTED STARS, 1999

Name	No	Mag	SHA	Dec
Acamar	7	3·1	315	S 40
Achernar	5	0·6	336	S 57
Acrux	30	1·1	173	S 63
Adhara	19	1·6	255	S 29
Aldebaran	10	1·1	291	N 17
Alioth	32	1·7	167	N 56
Alkaid	34	1·9	153	N 49
Al Na'ir	55	2·2	28	S 47
Alnilam	15	1·8	276	S 1
Alphard	25	2·2	218	S 9
Alphecca	41	2·3	126	N 27
Alpheratz	1	2·2	358	N 29
Altair	51	0·9	62	N 9
Ankaa	2	2·4	353	S 42
Antares	42	1·2	113	S 26
Arcturus	37	0·2	146	N 19
Atria	43	1·9	108	S 69
Avior	22	1·7	234	S 60
Bellatrix	13	1·7	279	N 6
Betelgeuse	16	Var.*	271	N 7
Canopus	17	−0·9	264	S 53
Capella	12	0·2	281	N 46
Deneb	53	1·3	50	N 45
Denebola	28	2·2	183	N 15
Diphda	4	2·2	349	S 18
Dubhe	27	2·0	194	N 62
Elnath	14	1·8	278	N 29
Eltanin	47	2·4	91	N 51
Enif	54	2·5	34	N 10
Fomalhaut	56	1·3	16	S 30
Gacrux	31	1·6	172	S 57
Gienah	29	2·8	176	S 18
Hadar	35	0·9	149	S 60
Hamal	6	2·2	328	N 23
Kaus Australis	48	2·0	84	S 34
Kochab	40	2·2	137	N 74
Markab	57	2·6	14	N 15
Menkar	8	2·8	314	N 4
Menkent	36	2·3	148	S 36
Miaplacidus	24	1·8	222	S 70
Mirfak	9	1·9	309	N 50
Nunki	50	2·1	76	S 26
Peacock	52	2·1	54	S 57
Pollux	21	1·2	244	N 28
Procyon	20	0·5	245	N 5
Rasalhague	46	2·1	96	N 13
Regulus	26	1·3	208	N 12
Rigel	11	0·3	281	S 8
Rigil Kentaurus	38	0·1	140	S 61
Sabik ·	44	2·6	102	S 16
Schedar	3	2·5	350	N 57
Shaula	45	1·7	97	S 37
Sirius	18	−1·6	259	S 17
Spica	33	1·2	159	S 11
Suhail	23	2·2	223	S 43
Vega	49	0·1	81	N 39
Zubenelgenubi	39	2·9	137	S 16

No	Name	Mag	SHA	Dec
1	Alpheratz	2·2	358	N 29
2	Ankaa	2·4	353	S 42
3	Schedar	2·5	350	N 57
4	Diphda	2·2	349	S 18
5	Achernar	0·6	336	S 57
6	Hamal	2·2	328	N 23
7	Acamar	3·1	315	S 40
8	Menkar	2·8	314	N 4
9	Mirfak	1·9	309	N 50
10	Aldebaran	1·1	291	N 17
11	Rigel	0·3	281	S 8
12	Capella	0·2	281	N 46
13	Bellatrix	1·7	279	N 6
14	Elnath	1·8	278	N 29
15	Alnilam	1·8	276	S 1
16	Betelgeuse	Var.*	271	N 7
17	Canopus	−0·9	264	S 53
18	Sirius	−1·6	259	S 17
19	Adhara	1·6	255	S 29
20	Procyon	0·5	245	N 5
21	Pollux	1·2	244	N 28
22	Avior	1·7	234	S 60
23	Suhail	2·2	223	S 43
24	Miaplacidus	1·8	222	S 70
25	Alphard	2·2	218	S 9
26	Regulus	1·3	208	N 12
27	Dubhe	2·0	194	N 62
28	Denebola	2·2	183	N 15
29	Gienah	2·8	176	S 18
30	Acrux	1·1	173	S 63
31	Gacrux	1·6	172	S 57
32	Alioth	1·7	167	N 56
33	Spica	1·2	159	S 11
34	Alkaid	1·9	153	N 49
35	Hadar	0·9	149	S 60
36	Menkent	2·3	148	S 36
37	Arcturus	0·2	146	N 19
38	Rigil Kentaurus	0·1	140	S 61
39	Zubenelgenubi	2·9	137	S 16
40	Kochab	2·2	137	N 74
41	Alphecca	2·3	126	N 27
42	Antares	1·2	113	S 26
43	Atria	1·9	108	S 69
44	Sabik	2·6	102	S 16
45	Shaula	1·7	97	S 37
46	Rasalhague	2·1	96	N 13
47	Eltanin	2·4	91	N 51
48	Kaus Australis	2·0	84	S 34
49	Vega	0·1	81	N 39
50	Nunki	2·1	76	S 26
51	Altair	0·9	62	N 9
52	Peacock	2·1	54	S 57
53	Deneb	1·3	50	N 45
54	Enif	2·5	34	N 10
55	Al Na'ir	2·2	28	S 47
56	Fomalhaut	1·3	16	S 30
57	Markab	2·6	14	N 15

*0·1 — 1·2

ALTITUDE CORRECTION TABLES 0°–35°—MOON

App. Alt.	0°–4° Corrn	5°–9° Corrn	10°–14° Corrn	15°–19° Corrn	20°–24° Corrn	25°–29° Corrn	30°–34° Corrn	App. Alt.
00	0 33.8	5 58.2	10 62.1	15 62.8	20 62.2	25 60.8	30 58.9	00
10	35.9	58.5	62.2	62.8	62.1	60.8	58.8	10
20	37.8	58.7	62.2	62.8	62.1	60.7	58.8	20
30	39.6	58.9	62.3	62.8	62.1	60.7	58.7	30
40	41.2	59.1	62.3	62.8	62.0	60.6	58.6	40
50	42.6	59.3	62.4	62.7	62.0	60.6	58.5	50
00	1 44.0	6 59.5	11 62.4	16 62.7	21 62.0	26 60.5	31 58.5	00
10	45.2	59.7	62.4	62.7	61.9	60.4	58.4	10
20	46.3	59.9	62.5	62.7	61.9	60.4	58.3	20
30	47.3	60.0	62.5	62.7	61.9	60.3	58.2	30
40	48.3	60.2	62.5	62.7	61.8	60.3	58.2	40
50	49.2	60.3	62.6	62.7	61.8	60.2	58.1	50
00	2 50.0	7 60.5	12 62.6	17 62.7	22 61.7	27 60.1	32 58.0	00
10	50.8	60.6	62.6	62.6	61.7	60.1	57.9	10
20	51.4	60.7	62.6	62.6	61.6	60.0	57.8	20
30	52.1	60.9	62.7	62.6	61.6	59.9	57.8	30
40	52.7	61.0	62.7	62.6	61.5	59.9	57.7	40
50	53.3	61.1	62.7	62.6	61.5	59.8	57.6	50
00	3 53.8	8 61.2	13 62.7	18 62.5	23 61.5	28 59.7	33 57.5	00
10	54.3	61.3	62.7	62.5	61.4	59.7	57.4	10
20	54.8	61.4	62.7	62.5	61.4	59.6	57.4	20
30	55.2	61.5	62.8	62.5	61.3	59.6	57.3	30
40	55.6	61.6	62.8	62.4	61.3	59.5	57.2	40
50	56.0	61.6	62.8	62.4	61.2	59.4	57.1	50
00	4 56.4	9 61.7	14 62.8	19 62.4	24 61.2	29 59.3	34 57.0	00
10	56.7	61.8	62.8	62.3	61.1	59.3	56.9	10
20	57.1	61.9	62.8	62.3	61.1	59.2	56.9	20
30	57.4	61.9	62.8	62.3	61.0	59.1	56.8	30
40	57.7	62.0	62.8	62.2	60.9	59.1	56.7	40
50	57.9	62.1	62.8	62.2	60.9	59.0	56.6	50

H.P.	L	U	L	U	L	U	L	U	L	U	L	U	L	U	H.P.
54.0	0.3	0.9	0.3	0.9	0.4	1.0	0.5	1.1	0.6	1.2	0.7	1.3	0.9	1.5	54.0
54.3	0.7	1.1	0.7	1.2	0.7	1.2	0.8	1.3	0.9	1.4	1.1	1.5	1.2	1.7	54.3
54.6	1.1	1.4	1.1	1.4	1.1	1.4	1.2	1.5	1.3	1.6	1.4	1.7	1.5	1.8	54.6
54.9	1.4	1.6	1.5	1.6	1.5	1.6	1.6	1.7	1.6	1.8	1.8	1.9	1.9	2.0	54.9
55.2	1.8	1.8	1.8	1.8	1.9	1.9	1.9	1.9	2.0	2.0	2.1	2.1	2.2	2.2	55.2
55.5	2.2	2.0	2.2	2.0	2.3	2.1	2.3	2.1	2.4	2.2	2.4	2.3	2.5	2.4	55.5
55.8	2.6	2.2	2.6	2.2	2.6	2.3	2.7	2.3	2.7	2.4	2.8	2.4	2.9	2.5	55.8
56.1	3.0	2.4	3.0	2.5	3.0	2.5	3.0	2.5	3.1	2.6	3.1	2.6	3.2	2.7	56.1
56.4	3.4	2.7	3.4	2.7	3.4	2.7	3.4	2.7	3.4	2.8	3.5	2.8	3.5	2.9	56.4
56.7	3.7	2.9	3.7	2.9	3.8	2.9	3.8	2.9	3.8	3.0	3.8	3.0	3.9	3.0	56.7
57.0	4.1	3.1	4.1	3.1	4.1	3.1	4.1	3.1	4.2	3.1	4.2	3.2	4.2	3.2	57.0
57.3	4.5	3.3	4.5	3.3	4.5	3.3	4.5	3.3	4.5	3.3	4.5	3.4	4.6	3.4	57.3
57.6	4.9	3.5	4.9	3.5	4.9	3.5	4.9	3.5	4.9	3.5	4.9	3.5	4.9	3.6	57.6
57.9	5.3	3.8	5.3	3.8	5.2	3.8	5.2	3.7	5.2	3.7	5.2	3.7	5.2	3.7	57.9
58.2	5.6	4.0	5.6	4.0	5.6	4.0	5.6	4.0	5.6	3.9	5.6	3.9	5.6	3.9	58.2
58.5	6.0	4.2	6.0	4.2	6.0	4.2	6.0	4.2	6.0	4.1	5.9	4.1	5.9	4.1	58.5
58.8	6.4	4.4	6.4	4.4	6.4	4.4	6.3	4.4	6.3	4.3	6.3	4.3	6.2	4.2	58.8
59.1	6.8	4.6	6.8	4.6	6.7	4.6	6.7	4.6	6.7	4.5	6.6	4.5	6.6	4.4	59.1
59.4	7.2	4.8	7.1	4.8	7.1	4.8	7.1	4.8	7.0	4.7	7.0	4.7	6.9	4.6	59.4
59.7	7.5	5.1	7.5	5.0	7.5	5.0	7.5	5.0	7.4	4.9	7.3	4.8	7.2	4.7	59.7
60.0	7.9	5.3	7.9	5.3	7.9	5.2	7.8	5.2	7.8	5.1	7.7	5.0	7.6	4.9	60.0
60.3	8.3	5.5	8.3	5.5	8.2	5.4	8.2	5.4	8.1	5.3	8.0	5.2	7.9	5.1	60.3
60.6	8.7	5.7	8.7	5.7	8.6	5.7	8.6	5.6	8.5	5.5	8.4	5.4	8.2	5.3	60.6
60.9	9.1	5.9	9.0	5.9	9.0	5.9	8.9	5.8	8.8	5.7	8.7	5.6	8.6	5.4	60.9
61.2	9.5	6.2	9.4	6.1	9.4	6.1	9.3	6.0	9.2	5.9	9.1	5.8	8.9	5.6	61.2
61.5	9.8	6.4	9.8	6.3	9.7	6.3	9.7	6.2	9.5	6.1	9.4	5.9	9.2	5.8	61.5

DIP

Ht. of Eye (m)	Ht. of Eye (ft.)	Corrn	Ht. of Eye (m)	Ht. of Eye (ft.)	Corrn
2.4	8.0	-2.8	9.5	31.5	-5.5
2.6	8.6	-2.9	9.9	32.7	-5.6
2.8	9.2	-3.0	10.3	33.9	-5.7
3.0	9.8	-3.1	10.6	35.1	-5.8
3.2	10.5	-3.2	11.0	36.3	-5.9
3.4	11.2	-3.3	11.4	37.6	-6.0
3.6	11.9	-3.4	11.8	38.9	-6.1
3.8	12.6	-3.5	12.2	40.1	-6.2
4.0	13.3	-3.6	12.6	41.5	-6.3
4.3	14.1	-3.7	13.0	42.8	-6.4
4.5	14.9	-3.8	13.4	44.2	-6.5
4.7	15.7	-3.9	13.8	45.5	-6.6
5.0	16.5	-4.0	14.2	46.9	-6.7
5.2	17.4	-4.1	14.7	48.4	-6.8
5.5	18.3	-4.2	15.1	49.8	-6.9
5.8	19.1	-4.3	15.5	51.3	-7.0
6.1	20.1	-4.4	16.0	52.8	-7.1
6.3	21.0	-4.5	16.5	54.3	-7.2
6.6	22.0	-4.6	16.9	55.8	-7.3
6.9	22.9	-4.7	17.4	57.4	-7.4
7.2	23.9	-4.8	17.9	58.9	-7.5
7.5	24.9	-4.9	18.4	60.5	-7.6
7.9	26.0	-5.0	18.8	62.1	-7.7
8.2	27.1	-5.1	19.3	63.8	-7.8
8.5	28.1	-5.2	19.8	65.4	-7.9
8.8	29.2	-5.3	20.4	67.1	-8.0
9.2	30.4	-5.4	20.9	68.8	-8.1
9.5	31.5		21.4	70.5	

MOON CORRECTION TABLE

The correction is in two parts; the first correction is taken from the upper part of the table with argument apparent altitude, and the second from the lower part, with argument H.P., in the same column as that from which the first correction was taken. Separate corrections are given in the lower part for lower (L) and upper (U) limbs. All corrections are to be **added** to apparent altitude, *but 30' is to be subtracted from the altitude of the upper limb.*

For corrections for pressure and temperature see page A4.

For bubble sextant observations ignore dip, take the mean of upper and lower limb corrections and subtract 15' from the altitude.

App. Alt. = Apparent altitude = Sextant altitude corrected for index error and dip.

OCT.—MAR. **SUN** APR.—SEPT.				**STARS AND PLANETS**		**DIP**		
App. Lower Upper Alt. Limb Limb		App. Lower Upper Alt. Limb Limb		App Alt. Corrⁿ	App. Additional Alt. Corrⁿ	Ht. of Corrⁿ Eye	Ht. of Eye	Ht. of Corrⁿ Eye

SUN Oct–Mar App. Alt	Lower Limb	Upper Limb	SUN Apr–Sept App. Alt	Lower Limb	Upper Limb	Stars App Alt	Corrⁿ	Additional Alt	Corrⁿ	Ht Eye m	Corrⁿ	Ht Eye ft	Ht Eye m	Corrⁿ
9 34	+10·8	−21·5	9 39	+10·6	−21·2	9 56	−5·3	**1999**		2·4	−2·8	8·0	1·0	−1·8
9 45	+10·9	−21·4	9 51	+10·7	−21·1	10 08	−5·2	**VENUS**		2·6	−2·9	8·6	1·5	−2·2
9 56	+11·0	−21·3	10 03	+10·8	−21·0	10 20	−5·1	Jan. 1–May 8		2·8	−3·0	9·2	2·0	−2·5
10 08	+11·1	−21·2	10 15	+10·9	−20·9	10 33	−5·0	Dec. 9–Dec. 31		3·0	−3·1	9·8	2·5	−2·8
10 21	+11·2	−21·1	10 27	+11·0	−20·8	10 46	−4·9	° ′		3·2	−3·2	10·5	3·0	−3·0
10 34	+11·3	−21·0	10 40	+11·1	−20·7	11 00	−4·8	60 +0·1		3·4	−3·3	11·2	See table	
10 47	+11·4	−20·9	10 54	+11·2	−20·6	11 14	−4·7			3·6	−3·4	11·9	←	
11 01	+11·5	−20·8	11 08	+11·3	−20·5	11 29	−4·6	May 9–June 26		3·8	−3·5	12·6		
11 15	+11·6	−20·7	11 23	+11·4	−20·4	11 45	−4·5	Oct. 18–Dec. 8		4·0	−3·6	13·3	m	′
11 30	+11·7	−20·6	11 38	+11·5	−20·3	12 01	−4·4	° ′		4·3	−3·7	14·1	20	−7·9
11 46	+11·8	−20·5	11 54	+11·6	−20·2	12 18	−4·3	41 +0·2		4·5	−3·8	14·9	22	−8·3
12 02	+11·9	−20·4	12 10	+11·7	−20·1	12 35	−4·2	76 +0·1		4·7	−3·9	15·7	24	−8·6
12 19	+12·0	−20·3	12 28	+11·8	−20·0	12 54	−4·1			5·0	−4·0	16·5	26	−9·0
12 37	+12·1	−20·2	12 46	+11·9	−19·9	13 13	−4·0	June 27–July 19		5·2	−4·1	17·4	28	−9·3
12 55	+12·2	−20·1	13 05	+12·0	−19·8	13 33	−3·9	Sept. 24–Oct. 17		5·5	−4·2	18·3		
13 14	+12·3	−20·0	13 24	+12·1	−19·7	13 54	−3·8	° ′		5·8	−4·3	19·1	30	−9·6
13 35	+12·4	−19·9	13 45	+12·2	−19·6	14 16	−3·7	34 +0·3		6·1	−4·4	20·1	32	−10·0
13 56	+12·5	−19·8	14 07	+12·3	−19·5	14 40	−3·6	60 +0·2		6·3	−4·5	21·0	34	−10·3
14 18	+12·6	−19·7	14 30	+12·4	−19·4	15 04	−3·5	80 +0·1		6·6	−4·6	22·0	36	−10·6
14 42	+12·7	−19·6	14 54	+12·5	−19·3	15 30	−3·4			6·9	−4·7	22·9	38	−10·8
15 06	+12·8	−19·5	15 19	+12·6	−19·2	15 57	−3·3	July 20–Aug. 4		7·2	−4·8	23·9		
15 32	+12·9	−19·4	15 46	+12·7	−19·1	16 26	−3·2	Sept. 7–Sept. 23		7·5	−4·9	24·9	40	−11·1
15 59	+13·0	−19·3	16 14	+12·8	−19·0	16 56	−3·1	° ′		7·9	−5·0	26·0	42	−11·4
16 28	+13·1	−19·2	16 44	+12·9	−18·9	17 28	−3·0	29 +0·4		8·2	−5·1	27·1	44	−11·7
16 59	+13·2	−19·1	17 15	+13·0	−18·8	18 02	−2·9	51 +0·3		8·5	−5·2	28·1	46	−11·9
17 32	+13·3	−19·0	17 48	+13·1	−18·7	18 38	−2·8	68 +0·2		8·8	−5·3	29·2	48	−12·2
18 06	+13·4	−18·9	18 24	+13·2	−18·6	19 17	−2·7	83 +0·1		9·2	−5·4	30·4		
18 42	+13·5	−18·8	19 01	+13·3	−18·5	19 58	−2·6	Aug. 5–Sept. 6		9·5	−5·5	31·5	ft.	′
19 21	+13·6	−18·7	19 42	+13·4	−18·4	20 42	−2·5	° ′		9·9	−5·6	32·7	2	−1·4
20 03	+13·7	−18·6	20 25	+13·5	−18·3	21 28	−2·4	26 +0·5		10·3	−5·7	33·9	4	−1·9
20 48	+13·8	−18·5	21 11	+13·6	−18·2	22 19	−2·3	46 +0·4		10·6	−5·8	35·1	6	−2·4
21 35	+13·9	−18·4	22 00	+13·7	−18·1	23 13	−2·2	60 +0·3		11·0	−5·9	36·3	8	−2·7
22 26	+14·0	−18·3	22 54	+13·8	−18·0	24 11	−2·1	73 +0·2		11·4	−6·0	37·6	10	−3·1
23 22	+14·1	−18·2	23 51	+13·9	−17·9	25 14	−2·0	84 +0·1		11·8	−6·1	38·9		
24 21	+14·2	−18·1	24 53	+14·0	−17·8	26 22	−1·9	**MARS**		12·2	−6·2	40·1	See table	
25 26	+14·3	−18·0	26 00	+14·1	−17·7	27 36	−1·8	Jan. 1–Feb. 21		12·6	−6·3	41·5	←	
26 36	+14·4	−17·9	27 13	+14·2	−17·6	28 56	−1·7	July 28–Dec. 31		13·0	−6·4	42·8	ft.	′
27 52	+14·5	−17·8	28 33	+14·3	−17·5	30 24	−1·6	° ′		13·4	−6·5	44·2	70	−8·1
29 15	+14·6	−17·7	30 00	+14·4	−17·4	32 00	−1·5	60 +0·1		13·8	−6·6	45·5	75	−8·4
30 46	+14·7	−17·6	31 35	+14·5	−17·3	33 45	−1·4			14·2	−6·7	46·9	80	−8·7
32 26	+14·8	−17·5	33 20	+14·6	−17·2	35 40	−1·3	Feb. 22–Apr. 22		14·7	−6·8	48·4	85	−8·9
34 17	+14·9	−17·4	35 17	+14·7	−17·1	37 48	−1·2	May 11–July 27		15·1	−6·9	49·8	90	−9·2
36 20	+15·0	−17·3	37 26	+14·8	−17·0	40 08	−1·1	° ′		15·5	−7·0	51·3	95	−9·5
38 36	+15·1	−17·2	39 50	+14·9	−16·9	42 44	−1·0	41 +0·2		16·0	−7·1	52·8		
41 08	+15·2	−17·1	42 31	+15·0	−16·8	45 36	−0·9	76 +0·1		16·5	−7·2	54·3	100	−9·7
43 59	+15·3	−17·0	45 31	+15·1	−16·7	48 47	−0·8	Apr. 23–May 10		16·9	−7·3	55·8	105	−9·9
47 10	+15·4	−16·9	48 55	+15·2	−16·6	52 18	−0·7	° ′		17·4	−7·4	57·4	110	−10·2
50 46	+15·5	−16·8	52 44	+15·3	−16·5	56 11	−0·6	34 +0·3		17·9	−7·5	58·9	115	−10·4
54 49	+15·6	−16·7	57 02	+15·4	−16·4	60 28	−0·5	60 +0·2		18·4	−7·6	60·5	120	−10·6
59 23	+15·7	−16·6	61 51	+15·5	−16·3	65 08	−0·4	80 +0·1		18·8	−7·7	62·1	125	−10·8
64 30	+15·8	−16·5	67 17	+15·6	−16·2	70 11	−0·3			19·3	−7·8	63·8	130	−11·1
70 12	+15·9	−16·4	73 16	+15·7	−16·1	75 34	−0·2			19·8	−7·9	65·4	135	−11·3
76 26	+16·0	−16·3	79 43	+15·8	−16·0	81 13	−0·1			20·4	−8·0	67·1	140	−11·5
83 05	+16·1	−16·2	86 32	+15·9	−15·9	87 03	0·0			20·9	−8·1	68·8	145	−11·7
90 00			90 00			90 00				21·4		70·5	150	−11·9
													155	−12·1

App. Alt. = Apparent altitude = Sextant altitude corrected for index error and dip.

INDEX TO SELECTED STARS, 1999

Name	No	Mag	SHA	Dec		No	Name	Mag	SHA	Dec
			°	°					°	°
Acamar	7	3·1	315	S 40		1	Alpheratz	2·2	358	N 29
Achernar	5	0·6	336	S 57		2	Ankaa	2·4	353	S 42
Acrux	30	1·1	173	S 63		3	Schedar	2·5	350	N 57
Adhara	19	1·6	255	S 29		4	Diphda	2·2	349	S 18
Aldebaran	10	1·1	291	N 17		5	Achernar	0·6	336	S 57
Alioth	32	1·7	167	N 56		6	Hamal	2·2	328	N 23
Alkaid	34	1·9	153	N 49		7	Acamar	3·1	315	S 40
Al Na'ir	55	2·2	28	S 47		8	Menkar	2·8	314	N 4
Alnilam	15	1·8	276	S 1		9	Mirfak	1·9	309	N 50
Alphard	25	2·2	218	S 9		10	Aldebaran	1·1	291	N 17
Alphecca	41	2·3	126	N 27		11	Rigel	0·3	281	S 8
Alpheratz	1	2·2	358	N 29		12	Capella	0·2	281	N 46
Altair	51	0·9	62	N 9		13	Bellatrix	1·7	279	N 6
Ankaa	2	2·4	353	S 42		14	Elnath	1·8	278	N 29
Antares	42	1·2	113	S 26		15	Alnilam	1·8	276	S 1
Arcturus	37	0·2	146	N 19		16	Betelgeuse	Var.*	271	N 7
Atria	43	1·9	108	S 69		17	Canopus	−0·9	264	S 53
Avior	22	1·7	234	S 60		18	Sirius	−1·6	259	S 17
Bellatrix	13	1·7	279	N 6		19	Adhara	1·6	255	S 29
Betelgeuse	16	Var.*	271	N 7		20	Procyon	0·5	245	N 5
Canopus	17	−0·9	264	S 53		21	Pollux	1·2	244	N 28
Capella	12	0·2	281	N 46		22	Avior	1·7	234	S 60
Deneb	53	1·3	50	N 45		23	Suhail	2·2	223	S 43
Denebola	28	2·2	183	N 15		24	Miaplacidus	1·8	222	S 70
Diphda	4	2·2	349	S 18		25	Alphard	2·2	218	S 9
Dubhe	27	2·0	194	N 62		26	Regulus	1·3	208	N 12
Elnath	14	1·8	278	N 29		27	Dubhe	2·0	194	N 62
Eltanin	47	2·4	91	N 51		28	Denebola	2·2	183	N 15
Enif	54	2·5	34	N 10		29	Gienah	2·8	176	S 18
Fomalhaut	56	1·3	16	S 30		30	Acrux	1·1	173	S 63
Gacrux	31	1·6	172	S 57		31	Gacrux	1·6	172	S 57
Gienah	29	2·8	176	S 18		32	Alioth	1·7	167	N 56
Hadar	35	0·9	149	S 60		33	Spica	1·2	159	S 11
Hamal	6	2·2	328	N 23		34	Alkaid	1·9	153	N 49
Kaus Australis	48	2·0	84	S 34		35	Hadar	0·9	149	S 60
Kochab	40	2·2	137	N 74		36	Menkent	2·3	148	S 36
Markab	57	2·6	14	N 15		37	Arcturus	0·2	146	N 19
Menkar	8	2·8	314	N 4		38	Rigil Kentaurus	0·1	140	S 61
Menkent	36	2·3	148	S 36		39	Zubenelgenubi	2·9	137	S 16
Miaplacidus	24	1·8	222	S 70		40	Kochab	2·2	137	N 74
Mirfak	9	1·9	309	N 50		41	Alphecca	2·3	126	N 27
Nunki	50	2·1	76	S 26		42	Antares	1·2	113	S 26
Peacock	52	2·1	54	S 57		43	Atria	1·9	108	S 69
Pollux	21	1·2	244	N 28		44	Sabik	2·6	102	S 16
Procyon	20	0·5	245	N 5		45	Shaula	1·7	97	S 37
Rasalhague	46	2·1	96	N 13		46	Rasalhague	2·1	96	N 13
Regulus	26	1·3	208	N 12		47	Eltanin	2·4	91	N 51
Rigel	11	0·3	281	S 8		48	Kaus Australis	2·0	84	S 34
Rigil Kentaurus	38	0·1	140	S 61		49	Vega	0·1	81	N 39
Sabik	44	2·6	102	S 16		50	Nunki	2·1	76	S 26
Schedar	3	2·5	350	N 57		51	Altair	0·9	62	N 9
Shaula	45	1·7	97	S 37		52	Peacock	2·1	54	S 57
Sirius	18	−1·6	259	S 17		53	Deneb	1·3	50	N 45
Spica	33	1·2	159	S 11		54	Enif	2·5	34	N 10
Suhail	23	2·2	223	S 43		55	Al Na'ir	2·2	28	S 47
Vega	49	0·1	81	N 39		56	Fomalhaut	1·3	16	S 30
Zubenelgenubi	39	2·9	137	S 16		57	Markab	2·6	14	N 15

*0·1 — 1·2